**Sports Collectors Digest**

# BASEBALL CARD POCKET PRICE GUIDE

## ALL NEW 1993 PRICES

**BY THE EDITORS OF SPORTS COLLECTORS DIGEST**

**WARNER BOOKS**

A Time Warner Company

The *SCD Baseball Card Pocket Price Guide* is compiled by the editors of *Sports Collectors Digest* and published by Krause Publications, Iola, Wis. For further baseball card news and pricing information, the reader is referred to *Baseball Card News* and *Sports Collectors Digest*. Subscription information and sample copies of either publication are available by writing to: Krause Publications, 700 E. State St., Iola, WI 54990.

WARNER BOOKS EDITION

Warner Books, Inc.
1271 Avenue of the Americas
New York, N.Y. 10020

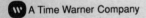 A Time Warner Company

Printed in the United States of America

First Printing: April , 1993

10 9 8 7 6 5 4 3 2 1

# TABLE OF CONTENTS

4

# BOWMAN

## 1948 Bowman

Bowman Gum Co.'s premiere set was produced in 1948, making it one of the first major issues of the post-war period. Forty-eight black and white cards comprise the set, with each card measuring 2-1/16" by 2-1/2" in size. The card backs, printed in black ink on grey stock, include the card number and the player's name, team, position, and a short biography. Twelve cards (#'s 7, 8, 13, 16, 20, 22, 24, 26, 29, 30 and 34) were printed in short supply when they were removed from the 36-card printing sheet to make room for the set's high numbers (#'s 37-48). These 24 cards command a higher price than the remaining cards in the set.

|  | NR MT | EX |
|---|---|---|
| Complete Set: | 3500.00 | 1750.00 |
| Common Player: 1-36 | 20.00 | 10.00 |
| Common Player: 37-48 | 25.00 | 12.50 |

|  |  | NR MT | EX |
|---|---|---|---|
| 1 | Bob Elliott | 100.00 | 35.00 |
| 2 | Ewell (The Whip) Blackwell | 25.00 | 12.50 |
| 3 | Ralph Kiner | 175.00 | 87.00 |
| 4 | Johnny Mize | 100.00 | 50.00 |
| 5 | Bob Feller | 200.00 | 100.00 |
| 6 | Larry (Yogi) Berra | 550.00 | 275.00 |
| 7 | Pete (Pistol Pete) Reiser | 60.00 | 30.00 |
| 8 | Phil (Scooter) Rizzuto | 225.00 | 112.00 |
| 9 | Walker Cooper | 20.00 | 10.00 |
| 10 | Buddy Rosar | 20.00 | 10.00 |
| 11 | Johnny Lindell | 20.00 | 10.00 |
| 12 | Johnny Sain | 25.00 | 12.50 |
| 13 | Willard Marshall | 30.00 | 15.00 |
| 14 | Allie Reynolds | 30.00 | 15.00 |
| 15 | Eddie Joost | 20.00 | 10.00 |
| 16 | Jack Lohrke | 30.00 | 15.00 |
| 17 | Enos (Country) Slaughter | 100.00 | 50.00 |
| 18 | Warren Spahn | 300.00 | 150.00 |
| 19 | Tommy (The Clutch) Henrich | 25.00 | 12.50 |
| 20 | Buddy Kerr | 30.00 | 15.00 |
| 21 | Ferris Fain | 20.00 | 10.00 |
| 22 | Floyd (Bill) Bevins (Bevens) | 40.00 | 20.00 |
| 23 | Larry Jansen | 20.00 | 10.00 |
| 24 | Emil (Dutch) Leonard | 40.00 | 20.00 |
| 25 | Barney McCoskey (McCosky) | 20.00 | 10.00 |
| 26 | Frank Shea | 40.00 | 20.00 |
| 27 | Sid Gordon | 20.00 | 10.00 |
| 28 | Emil (The Antelope) Verban | 30.00 | 15.00 |
| 29 | Joe Page | 55.00 | 33.00 |
| 30 | "Whitey" Lockman | 40.00 | 20.00 |
| 31 | Bill McCahan | 20.00 | 10.00 |
| 32 | Bill Rigney | 20.00 | 10.00 |
| 33 | Bill (The Bull) Johnson | 20.00 | 10.00 |
| 34 | Sheldon (Available) Jones | 30.00 | 15.00 |
| 35 | George (Snuffy) Stirnweiss | 20.00 | 10.00 |
| 36 | Stan Musial | 900.00 | 450.00 |
| 37 | Clint Hartung | 25.00 | 12.50 |
| 38 | Al "Red" Schoendienst | 150.00 | 75.00 |
| 39 | Augie Galan | 25.00 | 12.50 |
| 40 | Marty Marion | 80.00 | 40.00 |
| 41 | Rex Barney | 25.00 | 12.50 |
| 42 | Ray Poat | 25.00 | 12.50 |
| 43 | Bruce Edwards | 25.00 | 12.50 |
| 44 | Johnny Wyrostek | 25.00 | 12.50 |
| 45 | Hank Sauer | 25.00 | 12.50 |
| 46 | Herman Wehmeier | 25.00 | 12.50 |
| 47 | Bobby Thomson | 70.00 | 35.00 |
| 48 | George "Dave" Koslo | 70.00 | 20.00 |

## 1949 Bowman

In 1949, Bowman increased the size of its issue to

240 numbered cards. The cards, which measure 2-1/16" by 2-1/2", are black and white photos overprinted with various pastel colors. Beginning with card #109 in the set, Bowman inserted the player's names on the card fronts. Twelve cards (#'s 4, 78, 83, 85, 88, 98, 109, 124, 127, 132 and 143), which were produced in the first four series of printings, were reprinted in the seventh series with either a card front or back modification. These variations are noted in the checklist that follows. Card #'s 1-3 and 5-73 can be found with either white or grey backs. The complete set of value in the following checklist does not include the higher priced variation cards.

| | | NR MT | EX |
|---|---|---|---|
| Complete Set: | | 16000.00 | 8000.00 |
| Common Player: 1-36 | | 15.00 | 7.50 |
| Common Player: 37-73 | | 18.00 | 9.00 |
| | | 15.00 | 7.50 |
| Common Player: 74-144 | | | |
| | | 70.00 | 35.00 |
| Common Player: 145-240 | | | |
| 1 | Vernon Bickford | 100.00 | 30.00 |
| 2 | Carroll "Whitey" Lockman | 18.00 | 9.00 |
| 3 | Bob Porterfield | 18.00 | 9.00 |
| 4a | Jerry Priddy (no name on front) | 18.00 | 9.00 |
| 4b | Jerry Priddy (name on front) | 40.00 | 20.00 |
| 5 | Hank Sauer | 15.00 | 7.50 |
| 6 | Phil Cavarretta | 20.00 | 10.00 |
| 7 | Joe Dobson | 15.00 | 7.50 |
| 8 | Murry Dickson | 15.00 | 7.50 |
| 9 | Ferris Fain | 18.00 | 9.00 |
| 10 | Ted Gray | 15.00 | 7.50 |
| 11 | Lou Boudreau | 60.00 | 30.00 |
| 12 | Cass Michaels | 15.00 | 7.50 |
| 13 | Bob Chesnes | 15.00 | 7.50 |
| 14 | Curt Simmons | 30.00 | 15.00 |
| 15 | Ned Garver | 15.00 | 7.50 |
| 16 | Al Kozar | 15.00 | 7.50 |
| 17 | Earl Torgeson | 15.00 | 7.50 |
| 18 | Bobby Thomson | 30.00 | 15.00 |
| 19 | Bobby Brown | 50.00 | 25.00 |
| 20 | Gene Hermanski | 18.00 | 9.00 |
| 21 | Frank Baumholtz | 15.00 | 7.50 |
| 22 | Harry "P-Nuts" Lowrey | 15.00 | 7.50 |
| 23 | Bobby Doerr | 70.00 | 35.00 |
| 24 | Stan Musial | 550.00 | 275.00 |
| 25 | Carl Scheib | 15.00 | 7.50 |
| 26 | George Kell | 60.00 | 30.00 |
| 27 | Bob Feller | 150.00 | 75.00 |
| 28 | Don Kolloway | 15.00 | 7.50 |
| 29 | Ralph Kiner | 90.00 | 45.00 |
| 30 | Andy Seminick | 15.00 | 7.50 |
| 31 | Dick Kokos | 15.00 | 7.50 |
| 32 | Eddie Yost | 15.00 | 7.50 |
| 33 | Warren Spahn | 175.00 | 87.00 |
| 34 | Dave Koslo | 15.00 | 7.50 |
| 35 | Vic Raschi | 20.00 | 10.00 |
| 36 | Harold "Peewee" Reese | 200.00 | 100.00 |
| 37 | John Wyrostek | 18.00 | 9.00 |
| 38 | Emil "The Antelope" Verban | 18.00 | 9.00 |
| 39 | Bill Goodman | 18.00 | 9.00 |
| 40 | George "Red" Munger | 18.00 | 9.00 |
| 41 | Lou Brissie | 18.00 | 9.00 |
| 42 | Walter "Hoot" Evers | 18.00 | 9.00 |
| 43 | Dale Mitchell | 18.00 | 9.00 |
| 44 | Dave Philley | 18.00 | 9.00 |
| 45 | Wally Westlake | 18.00 | 9.00 |
| 46 | Robin Roberts | 250.00 | 125.00 |
| 47 | Johnny Sain | 18.00 | 9.00 |
| 48 | Willard Marshall | 18.00 | 9.00 |
| 49 | Frank Shea | 18.00 | 9.00 |
| 50 | Jackie Robinson | 800.00 | 400.00 |
| 51 | Herman Wehmeier | 18.00 | 9.00 |
| 52 | Johnny Schmitz | 18.00 | 9.00 |
| 53 | Jack Kramer | 18.00 | 9.00 |
| 54 | Marty "Slats" Marion | 20.00 | 10.00 |
| 55 | Eddie Joost | 18.00 | 9.00 |
| 56 | Pat Mullin | 18.00 | 9.00 |
| 57 | Gene Bearden | 18.00 | 9.00 |
| 58 | Bob Elliott | 18.00 | 9.00 |
| 59 | Jack "Lucky" Lohrke | 18.00 | 9.00 |
| 60 | Larry "Yogi" Berra | 300.00 | 150.00 |
| 61 | Rex Barney | 20.00 | 10.00 |
| 62 | Grady Hatton | 18.00 | 9.00 |
| 63 | Andy Pafko | 20.00 | 10.00 |
| 64 | Dom "The Little Professor" DiMaggio | 30.00 | 15.00 |
| 65 | Enos "Country" Slaughter | 75.00 | 37.00 |
| 66 | Elmer Valo | 18.00 | 9.00 |
| 67 | Alvin Dark | 30.00 | 15.00 |
| 68 | Sheldon "Available" Jones | 18.00 | 9.00 |
| 69 | Tommy "The Clutch" Henrich | 25.00 | 12.50 |
| 70 | Carl Furillo | 60.00 | 30.00 |
| 71 | Vern "Junior" Stephens | 18.00 | 9.00 |
| 72 | Tommy Holmes | 20.00 | 10.00 |
| 73 | Billy Cox | 20.00 | 10.00 |
| 74 | Tom McBride | 15.00 | 7.50 |
| 75 | Eddie Mayo | 15.00 | 7.50 |
| 76 | Bill Nicholson | 15.00 | 7.50 |
| 77 | Ernie (Jumbo and Tiny) Bonham | 15.00 | 7.50 |
| 78a | Sam Zoldak (no name on front) | 18.00 | 9.00 |
| 78b | Sam Zoldak (name on front) | 40.00 | 20.00 |

|  |  | NR MT | EX |
|---|---|---|---|
| 79 | Ron Northey | 15.00 | 7.50 |
| 80 | Bill McCahan | 15.00 | 7.50 |
| 81 | Virgil "Red" Stallcup | 15.00 | 7.50 |
| 82 | Joe Page | 20.00 | 10.00 |
| 83a | Bob Scheffing (no name on front) | 18.00 | 9.00 |
| 83b | Bob Scheffing (name on front) | 40.00 | 20.00 |
| 84 | *Roy Campanella* | 750.00 | 375.00 |
| 85a | Johnny "Big John" Mize (no name on front) | 75.00 | 37.00 |
| 85b | Johnny "Big John" Mize (name on front) | 125.00 | 62.00 |
| 86 | Johnny Pesky | 18.00 | 9.00 |
| 87 | Randy Gumpert | 15.00 | 7.50 |
| 88a | Bill Salkeld (no name on front) | 18.00 | 9.00 |
| 88b | Bill Salkeld (name on front) | 40.00 | 20.00 |
| 89 | Mizell "Whitey" Platt | 15.00 | 7.50 |
| 90 | Gil Coan | 15.00 | 7.50 |
| 91 | Dick Wakefield | 15.00 | 7.50 |
| 92 | Willie "Puddin-Head" Jones | 15.00 | 7.50 |
| 93 | Ed Stevens | 15.00 | 7.50 |
| 94 | James "Mickey" Vernon | 18.00 | 9.00 |
| 95 | Howie Pollett | 15.00 | 7.50 |
| 96 | Taft Wright | 15.00 | 7.50 |
| 97 | Danny Litwhiler | 15.00 | 7.50 |
| 98a | Phil Rizzuto (no name on front) | 100.00 | 50.00 |
| 98b | Phil Rizzuto (name on front) | 200.00 | 100.00 |
| 99 | Frank Gustine | 15.00 | 7.50 |
| 100 | Gil Hodges | 200.00 | 100.00 |
| 101 | Sid Gordon | 15.00 | 7.50 |
| 102 | Stan Spence | 15.00 | 7.50 |
| 103 | Joe Tipton | 15.00 | 7.50 |
| 104 | Ed Stanky | 18.00 | 9.00 |
| 105 | Bill Kennedy | 15.00 | 7.50 |
| 106 | Jake Early | 15.00 | 7.50 |
| 107 | Eddie Lake | 15.00 | 7.50 |
| 108 | Ken Heintzelman | 15.00 | 7.50 |
| 109a | Ed Fitzgerald (Fitz Gerald) (script name on back) | 18.00 | 9.00 |
| 109b | Ed Fitzgerald (Fitz Gerald) (printed name on back) | 40.00 | 20.00 |
| 110 | Early Wynn | 125.00 | 62.00 |
| 111 | Al "Red" Schoendienst | 80.00 | 40.00 |
| 112 | Sam Chapman | 15.00 | 7.50 |
| 113 | Ray Lamanno | 15.00 | 7.50 |
| 114 | Allie Reynolds | 30.00 | 15.00 |
| 115 | Emil "Dutch" Leonard | 15.00 | 7.50 |
| 116 | Joe Hatten | 18.00 | 9.00 |
| 117 | Walker Cooper | 15.00 | 7.50 |
| 118 | Sam Mele | 15.00 | 7.50 |
| 119 | Floyd Baker | 15.00 | 7.50 |
| 120 | Cliff Fannin | 15.00 | 7.50 |
| 121 | Mark Christman | 15.00 | 7.50 |
| 122 | George Vico | 15.00 | 7.50 |
| 123 | Johnny Blatnick | 15.00 | 7.50 |
| 124a | Danny Murtaugh (script name on back) | 18.00 | 9.00 |
| 124b | Danny Murtaugh (printed name on back) | 40.00 | 20.00 |
| 125 | Ken Keltner | 18.00 | 9.00 |
| 126a | Al Brazle (script name on back) | 18.00 | 9.00 |
| 126b | Al Brazle (printed name on back) | 40.00 | 20.00 |
| 127a | Henry "Heeney" Majeski (script name on back) | 18.00 | 9.00 |
| 127b | Henry "Heeney" Majeski (printed name on back) | 40.00 | 20.00 |
| 128 | Johnny Vander Meer | 20.00 | 10.00 |
| 129 | Bill "The Bull" Johnson | 20.00 | 10.00 |
| 130 | Harry "The Hat" Walker | 18.00 | 9.00 |
| 131 | Paul Lehner | 15.00 | 7.50 |
| 132a | Al Evans (script name on back) | 18.00 | 9.00 |
| 132b | Al Evans (printed name on back) | 40.00 | 20.00 |
| 133 | Aaron Robinson | 15.00 | 7.50 |
| 134 | Hank Borowy | 15.00 | 7.50 |
| 135 | Stan Rojek | 15.00 | 7.50 |
| 136 | Henry "Hank" Edwards | 15.00 | 7.50 |
| 137 | Ted Wilks | 15.00 | 7.50 |
| 138 | Warren "Buddy" Rosar | 15.00 | 7.50 |
| 139 | Hank "Bow-Wow" Arft | 15.00 | 7.50 |
| 140 | Rae Scarborough (Ray) | 15.00 | 7.50 |
| 141 | Ulysses "Tony" Lupien | 15.00 | 7.50 |
| 142 | Eddie Waitkus | 15.00 | 7.50 |
| 143a | Bob Dillinger (script name on back) | 18.00 | 9.00 |
| 143b | Bob Dillinger (printed name on back) | 40.00 | 20.00 |
| 144 | Milton "Mickey" Haefner | 15.00 | 7.50 |
| 145 | Sylvester "Blix" Donnelly | 70.00 | 35.00 |
| 146 | Myron "Mike" McCormick | 75.00 | 37.00 |
| 147 | Elmer "Bert" Singleton | 70.00 | 35.00 |
| 148 | Bob Swift | 70.00 | 35.00 |
| 149 | Roy Partee | 75.00 | 37.00 |
| 150 | Alfred "Allie" Clark | 70.00 | 35.00 |
| 151 | Maurice "Mickey" Harris | 70.00 | 35.00 |
| 152 | Clarence Maddern | 70.00 | 35.00 |
| 153 | Phil Masi | 70.00 | 35.00 |
| 154 | Clint Hartung | 70.00 | 35.00 |
| 155 | Fermin "Mickey" Guerra | 70.00 | 35.00 |

| | | NR MT | EX |
|---|---|---|---|
| 156 | Al "Zeke" Zarilla | 70.00 | 35.00 |
| 157 | Walt Masterson | 70.00 | 35.00 |
| 158 | Harry "The Cat" Brecheen | 70.00 | 35.00 |
| 159 | Glen Moulder | 70.00 | 35.00 |
| 160 | Jim Blackburn | 70.00 | 35.00 |
| 161 | John "Jocko" Thompson | 70.00 | 35.00 |
| 162 | Elwin "Preacher" Roe | 150.00 | 75.00 |
| 163 | Clyde McCullough | 70.00 | 35.00 |
| 164 | Vic Wertz | 110.00 | 55.00 |
| 165 | George "Snuffy" Stirnweiss | 70.00 | 35.00 |
| 166 | Mike Tresh | 70.00 | 35.00 |
| 167 | Boris "Babe" Martin | 70.00 | 35.00 |
| 168 | Doyle Lade | 70.00 | 35.00 |
| 169 | Jeff Heath | 70.00 | 35.00 |
| 170 | Bill Rigney | 75.00 | 37.00 |
| 171 | Dick Fowler | 70.00 | 35.00 |
| 172 | Eddie Pellagrini | 70.00 | 35.00 |
| 173 | Eddie Stewart | 70.00 | 35.00 |
| 174 | Terry Moore | 75.00 | 37.00 |
| 175 | Luke Appling | 125.00 | 62.00 |
| 176 | Ken Raffensberger | 70.00 | 35.00 |
| 177 | Stan Lopata | 70.00 | 35.00 |
| 178 | Tommy Brown | 75.00 | 37.00 |
| 179 | Hugh Casey | 75.00 | 37.00 |
| 180 | Connie Berry | 70.00 | 35.00 |
| 181 | Gus Niarhos | 70.00 | 35.00 |
| 182 | Hal Peck | 70.00 | 35.00 |
| 183 | Lou Stringer | 70.00 | 35.00 |
| 184 | Bob Chipman | 70.00 | 35.00 |
| 185 | Pete Reiser | 75.00 | 37.00 |
| 186 | John "Buddy" Kerr | 70.00 | 35.00 |
| 187 | Phil Marchildon | 70.00 | 35.00 |
| 188 | Karl Drews | 70.00 | 35.00 |
| 189 | Earl Wooten | 70.00 | 35.00 |
| 190 | Jim Hearn | 70.00 | 35.00 |
| 191 | Joe Haynes | 70.00 | 35.00 |
| 192 | Harry Gumbert | 70.00 | 35.00 |
| 193 | Ken Trinkle | 70.00 | 35.00 |
| 194 | Ralph Branca | 110.00 | 55.00 |
| 195 | Eddie Bockman | 70.00 | 35.00 |
| 196 | Fred Hutchinson | 75.00 | 37.00 |
| 197 | Johnny Lindell | 70.00 | 35.00 |
| 198 | Steve Gromek | 70.00 | 35.00 |
| 199 | Cecil "Tex" Hughson | 70.00 | 35.00 |
| 200 | Jess Dobernic | 70.00 | 35.00 |
| 201 | Sibby Sisti | 70.00 | 35.00 |
| 202 | Larry Jansen | 70.00 | 35.00 |
| 203 | Barney McCosky | 70.00 | 35.00 |
| 204 | Bob Savage | 70.00 | 35.00 |
| 205 | Dick Sisler | 70.00 | 35.00 |
| 206 | Bruce Edwards | 75.00 | 37.00 |
| 207 | Johnny "Hippity" Hopp | 70.00 | 35.00 |
| 208 | Paul "Dizzy" Trout | 75.00 | 37.00 |
| 209 | Charlie "King Kong" Keller | 100.00 | 50.00 |
| 210 | Joe "Flash" Gordon | | |

| | | NR MT | EX |
|---|---|---|---|
| | | 75.00 | 37.00 |
| 211 | Dave "Boo" Ferris | 70.00 | 35.00 |
| 212 | Ralph Hamner | 70.00 | 35.00 |
| 213 | Charles "Red" Barrett | 70.00 | 35.00 |
| 214 | *Richie Ashburn* | 550.00 | 275.00 |
| 215 | Kirby Higbe | 70.00 | 35.00 |
| 216 | Lynwood "Schoolboy" Rowe | 70.00 | 35.00 |
| 217 | Marino Pieretti | 70.00 | 35.00 |
| 218 | Dick Kryhoski | 70.00 | 35.00 |
| 219 | Virgil "Fire" Trucks | 75.00 | 37.00 |
| 220 | Johnny McCarthy | 70.00 | 35.00 |
| 221 | Bob Muncrief | 70.00 | 35.00 |
| 222 | Alex Kellner | 70.00 | 35.00 |
| 223 | Bob Hoffman (Hofman) | 70.00 | 35.00 |
| 224 | *Leroy "Satchel" Paige* | 1200.00 | 600.00 |
| 225 | *Gerry Coleman* | 100.00 | 50.00 |
| 226 | Edwin "Duke" Snider | 1200.00 | 600.00 |
| 227 | Fritz Ostermueller | 70.00 | 35.00 |
| 228 | Jackie Mayo | 70.00 | 35.00 |
| 229 | Ed Lopat | 125.00 | 60.00 |
| 230 | Augie Galan | 70.00 | 35.00 |
| 231 | Earl Johnson | 70.00 | 35.00 |
| 232 | George McQuinn | 70.00 | 35.00 |
| 233 | *Larry Doby* | 175.00 | 87.00 |
| 234 | Truett "Rip" Sewell | 75.00 | 37.00 |
| 235 | Jim Russell | 70.00 | 35.00 |
| 236 | Fred Sanford | 70.00 | 35.00 |
| 237 | Monte Kennedy | 70.00 | 35.00 |
| 238 | Bob Lemon | 225.00 | 112.00 |
| 239 | Frank McCormick | 70.00 | 35.00 |
| 240 | Norman "Babe" Young (photo actually Bobby Young) | 150.00 | 75.00 |

## 1950 Bowman

The quality of the 1950 Bowman issue showed a marked improvement over the company's previous efforts. The cards are beautiful color art reproductions of actual photographs and measure 2-1/16" by 2-1/2" in size. The card backs include the same type of information as found in the previous year's issue but are designed in a horizontal format. Cards found in the first two series of the set (#'s 1-72) are the scarcest in the issue. The backs of the final 72 cards in the set (#'s 181-252) can be found with or without the copyright line at the bottom of the card, the "without" version being the less common.

| | | NR MT | EX |
|---|---|---|---|
| | Complete Set: | 10000.00 | 5000.00 |
| | Common Player: 1-72 | 50.00 | 25.00 |
| | Common Player: 73-252 | | |
| | | 16.00 | 8.00 |
| 1 | Mel Parnell | 200.00 | 25.00 |
| 2 | Vern Stephens | 50.00 | 25.00 |
| 3 | Dom DiMaggio | 60.00 | 30.00 |
| 4 | Gus Zernial | 50.00 | 25.00 |
| 5 | Bob Kuzava | 50.00 | 25.00 |
| 6 | Bob Feller | 200.00 | 100.00 |
| 7 | Jim Hegan | 50.00 | 25.00 |
| 8 | George Kell | 90.00 | 45.00 |
| 9 | Vic Wertz | 50.00 | 25.00 |
| 10 | Tommy Henrich | 60.00 | 30.00 |
| 11 | Phil Rizzuto | 150.00 | 75.00 |
| 12 | Joe Page | 50.00 | 25.00 |
| 13 | Ferris Fain | 50.00 | 25.00 |
| 14 | Alex Kellner | 50.00 | 25.00 |
| 15 | Al Kozar | 50.00 | 25.00 |
| 16 | *Roy Sievers* | 50.00 | 25.00 |
| 17 | Sid Hudson | 50.00 | 25.00 |
| 18 | Eddie Robinson | 50.00 | 25.00 |
| 19 | Warren Spahn | 200.00 | 100.00 |
| 20 | Bob Elliott | 50.00 | 25.00 |
| 21 | Harold Reese | 200.00 | 100.00 |
| 22 | Jackie Robinson | 700.00 | 350.00 |
| 23 | *Don Newcombe* | 150.00 | 75.00 |
| 24 | Johnny Schmitz | 50.00 | 25.00 |
| 25 | Hank Sauer | 50.00 | 25.00 |
| 26 | Grady Hatton | 50.00 | 25.00 |
| 27 | Herman Wehmeier | | |
| | | 50.00 | 25.00 |
| 28 | Bobby Thomson | 70.00 | 35.00 |
| 29 | Ed Stanky | 50.00 | 25.00 |
| 30 | Eddie Waitkus | 50.00 | 25.00 |
| 31 | Del Ennis | 50.00 | 25.00 |
| 32 | Robin Roberts | 150.00 | 75.00 |
| 33 | Ralph Kiner | 125.00 | 62.00 |
| 34 | Murry Dickson | 50.00 | 25.00 |
| 35 | Enos Slaughter | 100.00 | 50.00 |
| 36 | Eddie Kazak | 50.00 | 25.00 |
| 37 | Luke Appling | 70.00 | 35.00 |
| 38 | Bill Wight | 50.00 | 25.00 |
| 39 | Larry Doby | 60.00 | 30.00 |
| 40 | Bob Lemon | 100.00 | 50.00 |
| 41 | Walter "Hoot" Evers | | |
| | | 50.00 | 25.00 |
| 42 | Art Houtteman | 50.00 | 25.00 |
| 43 | Bobby Doerr | 80.00 | 40.00 |
| 44 | Joe Dobson | 50.00 | 25.00 |
| 45 | Al "Zeke" Zarilla | 50.00 | 25.00 |
| 46 | Larry "Yogi" Berra | | |
| | | 400.00 | 200.00 |

| | | NR MT | EX |
|---|---|---|---|
| 47 | Jerry Coleman | 55.00 | 27.00 |
| 48 | Leland "Lou" Brissie | | |
| | | 50.00 | 25.00 |
| 49 | Elmer Valo | 50.00 | 25.00 |
| 50 | Dick Kokos | 50.00 | 25.00 |
| 51 | Ned Garver | 50.00 | 25.00 |
| 52 | Sam Mele | 50.00 | 25.00 |
| 53 | Clyde Vollmer | 50.00 | 25.00 |
| 54 | Gil Coan | 50.00 | 25.00 |
| 55 | John "Buddy" Kerr | | |
| | | 50.00 | 25.00 |
| 56 | *Del Crandell (Crandall)* | 60.00 | 30.00 |
| 57 | Vernon Bickford | 50.00 | 25.00 |
| 58 | Carl Furillo | 60.00 | 30.00 |
| 59 | Ralph Branca | 60.00 | 30.00 |
| 60 | Andy Pafko | 50.00 | 25.00 |
| 61 | Bob Rush | 50.00 | 25.00 |
| 62 | Ted Kluszewski | 70.00 | 35.00 |
| 63 | Ewell Blackwell | 50.00 | 25.00 |
| 64 | Alvin Dark | 50.00 | 25.00 |
| 65 | Dave Koslo | 50.00 | 25.00 |
| 66 | Larry Jansen | 50.00 | 25.00 |
| 67 | Willie Jones | 50.00 | 25.00 |
| 68 | Curt Simmons | 50.00 | 25.00 |
| 69 | Wally Westlake | 50.00 | 25.00 |
| 70 | Bob Chesnes | 50.00 | 25.00 |
| 71 | Al Schoendienst | 100.00 | 50.00 |
| 72 | Howie Pollet | 50.00 | 25.00 |
| 73 | Willard Marshall | 16.00 | 8.00 |
| 74 | *Johnny Antonelli* | 16.00 | 8.00 |
| 75 | Roy Campanella | 300.00 | 150.00 |
| 76 | Rex Barney | 16.00 | 8.00 |
| 77 | Edwin "Duke" Snider | | |
| | | 275.00 | 137.00 |
| 78 | Mickey Owen | 16.00 | 8.00 |
| 79 | Johnny Vander Meer | | |
| | | 16.00 | 8.00 |
| 80 | Howard Fox | 16.00 | 8.00 |
| 81 | Ron Northey | 16.00 | 8.00 |
| 82 | Carroll Lockman | 16.00 | 8.00 |
| 83 | Sheldon Jones | 16.00 | 8.00 |
| 84 | Richie Ashburn | 75.00 | 38.00 |
| 85 | Ken Heintzelman | 16.00 | 8.00 |
| 86 | Stan Rojek | 16.00 | 8.00 |
| 87 | Bill Werle | 16.00 | 8.00 |
| 88 | Marty Marion | 16.00 | 8.00 |
| 89 | George Munger | 16.00 | 8.00 |
| 90 | Harry Brecheen | 16.00 | 8.00 |
| 91 | Cass Michaels | 16.00 | 8.00 |
| 92 | Hank Majeski | 16.00 | 8.00 |
| 93 | Gene Bearden | 16.00 | 8.00 |
| 94 | Lou Boudreau | 50.00 | 25.00 |
| 95 | Aaron Robinson | 16.00 | 8.00 |
| 96 | Virgil "Fire" Trucks | | |
| | | 16.00 | 8.00 |
| 97 | Maurice McDermott | | |
| | | 16.00 | 8.00 |
| 98 | Ted Williams | 700.00 | 350.00 |
| 99 | Billy Goodman | 16.00 | 8.00 |
| 100 | Vic Raschi | 20.00 | 10.00 |
| 101 | Bobby Brown | 20.00 | 10.00 |
| 102 | Billy Johnson | 16.00 | 8.00 |
| 103 | Eddie Joost | 16.00 | 8.00 |
| 104 | Sam Chapman | 16.00 | 8.00 |
| 105 | Bob Dillinger | 16.00 | 8.00 |
| 106 | Cliff Fannin | 16.00 | 8.00 |

| | | NR MT | EX | | | | NR MT | EX |
|---|---|---|---|---|---|---|---|---|
| 107 | Sam Dente | 16.00 | 8.00 | 168 | Bob Scheffing | 16.00 | 8.00 |
| 108 | Rae Scarborough (Ray) | | | 169 | Hank Edwards | 16.00 | 8.00 |
| | | 16.00 | 8.00 | 170 | Emil Leonard | 16.00 | 8.00 |
| 109 | Sid Gordon | 16.00 | 8.00 | 171 | Harry Gumbert | 16.00 | 8.00 |
| 110 | Tommy Holmes | 16.00 | 8.00 | 172 | Harry Lowrey | 16.00 | 8.00 |
| 111 | Walker Cooper | 16.00 | 8.00 | 173 | Lloyd Merriman | 16.00 | 8.00 |
| 112 | Gil Hodges | 80.00 | 40.00 | 174 | Henry Thompson | 16.00 | 8.00 |
| 113 | Gene Hermanski | 16.00 | 8.00 | 175 | Monte Kennedy | 16.00 | 8.00 |
| 114 | Wayne Terwilliger | 16.00 | 8.00 | 176 | Sylvester Donnelly | | |
| 115 | Roy Smalley | 16.00 | 8.00 | | | 16.00 | 8.00 |
| 116 | Virgil "Red" Stallcup | | | 177 | Hank Borowy | 16.00 | 8.00 |
| | | 16.00 | 8.00 | 178 | Eddy Fitzgerald (Fitz | | |
| 117 | Bill Rigney | 16.00 | 8.00 | | Gerald) | 16.00 | 8.00 |
| 118 | Clint Hartung | 16.00 | 8.00 | 179 | Charles Diering | 16.00 | 8.00 |
| 119 | Dick Sisler | 16.00 | 8.00 | 180 | Harry Walker | 16.00 | 8.00 |
| 120 | John Thompson | 16.00 | 8.00 | 181 | Marino Pieretti | 16.00 | 8.00 |
| 121 | Andy Seminick | 16.00 | 8.00 | 182 | Sam Zoldak | 16.00 | 8.00 |
| 122 | Johnny Hopp | 16.00 | 8.00 | 183 | Mickey Haefner | 16.00 | 8.00 |
| 123 | Dino Restelli | 16.00 | 8.00 | 184 | Randy Gumpert | 16.00 | 8.00 |
| 124 | Clyde McCullough | | | 185 | Howie Judson | 16.00 | 8.00 |
| | | 16.00 | 8.00 | 186 | Ken Keltner | 16.00 | 8.00 |
| 125 | Del Rice | 16.00 | 8.00 | 187 | Lou Stringer | 16.00 | 8.00 |
| 126 | Al Brazle | 16.00 | 8.00 | 188 | Earl Johnson | 16.00 | 8.00 |
| 127 | Dave Philley | 16.00 | 8.00 | 189 | Owen Friend | 16.00 | 8.00 |
| 128 | Phil Masi | 16.00 | 8.00 | 190 | Ken Wood | 16.00 | 8.00 |
| 129 | Joe "Flash" Gordon | | | 191 | Dick Starr | 16.00 | 8.00 |
| | | 16.00 | 8.00 | 192 | Bob Chipman | 16.00 | 8.00 |
| 130 | Dale Mitchell | 16.00 | 8.00 | 193 | Harold "Pete" Reiser | | |
| 131 | Steve Gromek | 16.00 | 8.00 | | | 16.00 | 8.00 |
| 132 | James Vernon | 16.00 | 8.00 | 194 | Billy Cox | 16.00 | 8.00 |
| 133 | Don Kolloway | 16.00 | 8.00 | 195 | Phil Cavaretta | | |
| 134 | Paul "Dizzy" Trout | | | | (Cavarretta) | 16.00 | 8.00 |
| | | 16.00 | 8.00 | 196 | Doyle Lade | 16.00 | 8.00 |
| 135 | Pat Mullin | 16.00 | 8.00 | 197 | Johnny Wyrostek | 16.00 | 8.00 |
| 136 | Warren Rosar | 16.00 | 8.00 | 198 | Danny Litwhiler | 16.00 | 8.00 |
| 137 | Johnny Pesky | 16.00 | 8.00 | 199 | Jack Kramer | 16.00 | 8.00 |
| 138 | Allie Reynolds | 60.00 | 30.00 | 200 | Kirby Higbe | 16.00 | 8.00 |
| 139 | Johnny Mize | 60.00 | 30.00 | 201 | Pete Castiglione | 16.00 | 8.00 |
| 140 | Pete Suder | 16.00 | 8.00 | 202 | Cliff Chambers | 16.00 | 8.00 |
| 141 | Joe Coleman | 16.00 | 8.00 | 203 | Danny Murtaugh | 16.00 | 8.00 |
| 142 | *Sherman Lollar* | 16.00 | 8.00 | 204 | Granville Hamner | 16.00 | 8.00 |
| 143 | Eddie Stewart | 16.00 | 8.00 | 205 | Mike Goliat | 16.00 | 8.00 |
| 144 | Al Evans | 16.00 | 8.00 | 206 | Stan Lopata | 16.00 | 8.00 |
| 145 | Jack Graham | 16.00 | 8.00 | 207 | Max Lanier | 16.00 | 8.00 |
| 146 | Floyd Baker | 16.00 | 8.00 | 208 | Jim Hearn | 16.00 | 8.00 |
| 147 | *Mike Garcia* | 16.00 | 8.00 | 209 | Johnny Lindell | 16.00 | 8.00 |
| 148 | Early Wynn | 60.00 | 30.00 | 210 | Ted Gray | 16.00 | 8.00 |
| 149 | Bob Swift | 16.00 | 8.00 | 211 | Charlie Keller | 16.00 | 8.00 |
| 150 | George Vico | 16.00 | 8.00 | 212 | Gerry Priddy | 16.00 | 8.00 |
| 151 | Fred Hutchinson | 16.00 | 8.00 | 213 | Carl Scheib | 16.00 | 8.00 |
| 152 | Ellis Kinder | 16.00 | 8.00 | 214 | Dick Fowler | 16.00 | 8.00 |
| 153 | Walt Masterson | 16.00 | 8.00 | 215 | Ed Lopat | 20.00 | 10.00 |
| 154 | Gus Niarhos | 16.00 | 8.00 | 216 | Bob Porterfield | 16.00 | 8.00 |
| 155 | Frank "Spec" Shea | | | 217 | Casey Stengel | 150.00 | 75.00 |
| | | 16.00 | 8.00 | 218 | Cliff Mapes | 16.00 | 8.00 |
| 156 | Fred Sanford | 16.00 | 8.00 | 219 | *Hank Bauer* | 70.00 | 35.00 |
| 157 | Mike Guerra | 16.00 | 8.00 | 220 | Leo Durocher | 50.00 | 25.00 |
| 158 | Paul Lehner | 16.00 | 8.00 | 221 | Don Mueller | 16.00 | 8.00 |
| 159 | Joe Tipton | 16.00 | 8.00 | 222 | Bobby Morgan | 16.00 | 8.00 |
| 160 | Mickey Harris | 16.00 | 8.00 | 223 | Jimmy Russell | 16.00 | 8.00 |
| 161 | Sherry Robertson | 16.00 | 8.00 | 224 | Jack Banta | 16.00 | 8.00 |
| 162 | Eddie Yost | 16.00 | 8.00 | 225 | Eddie Sawyer | 16.00 | 8.00 |
| 163 | Earl Torgeson | 16.00 | 8.00 | 226 | Jim Konstanty | 16.00 | 8.00 |
| 164 | Sibby Sisti | 16.00 | 8.00 | 227 | Bob Miller | 16.00 | 8.00 |
| 165 | Bruce Edwards | 16.00 | 8.00 | 228 | Bill Nicholson | 16.00 | 8.00 |
| 166 | Joe Hatten | 16.00 | 8.00 | 229 | Frank Frisch | 60.00 | 30.00 |
| 167 | Elwin Roe | 60.00 | 30.00 | 230 | Bill Serena | 16.00 | 8.00 |

| | | NR MT | EX |
|---|---|---|---|
| 231 | Preston Ward | 16.00 | 8.00 |
| 232 | Al "Flip" Rosen | 60.00 | 30.00 |
| 233 | Allie Clark | 16.00 | 8.00 |
| 234 | Bobby Shantz | 25.00 | 12.50 |
| 235 | Harold Gilbert | 16.00 | 8.00 |
| 236 | Bob Cain | 16.00 | 8.00 |
| 237 | Bill Salkeld | 16.00 | 8.00 |
| 238 | Vernal Jones | 16.00 | 8.00 |
| 239 | Bill Howerton | 16.00 | 8.00 |
| 240 | Eddie Lake | 16.00 | 8.00 |
| 241 | Neil Berry | 16.00 | 8.00 |
| 242 | Dick Kryhoski | 16.00 | 8.00 |
| 243 | Johnny Groth | 16.00 | 8.00 |
| 244 | Dale Coogan | 16.00 | 8.00 |
| 245 | Al Papai | 16.00 | 8.00 |
| 246 | Walt Dropo | 25.00 | 12.50 |
| 247 | Irv Noren | 16.00 | 8.00 |
| 248 | Sam Jethroe | 16.00 | 8.00 |
| 249 | George Stirnweiss | 16.00 | 8.00 |
| 250 | Ray Coleman | 16.00 | 8.00 |
| 251 | John Lester Moss | 16.00 | 8.00 |
| 252 | Billy DeMars | 100.00 | 50.00 |

## 1951 Bowman

In 1951, Bowman increased the numbers of cards in its set for the third consecutive year when it issued 324 cards. The cards are, like 1950, color art reproductions of actual photographs but now measured 2-1/16" by 3-1/8" in size. The player's name is situated in a small, black box on the card front. Several of the card fronts are enlargements of the 1950 version. The high-numbered series of the set (#'s 253-324), which includes the rookie cards of Mantle and Mays, are the scarcest of the issue.

| | NR MT | EX |
|---|---|---|
| Complete Set: | 21500.00 | 15750.00 |
| Common Player: 1-36 | 20.00 | 10.00 |
| Common Player: 37-252 | 14.00 | 7.00 |
| Common Player: 253-324 | 60.00 | 30.00 |

| | | NR MT | EX |
|---|---|---|---|
| 1 | Ed Ford | 1300.00 | 575.00 |
| 2 | Larry "Yogi" Berra | 450.00 | 225.00 |
| 3 | Robin Roberts | 80.00 | 40.00 |
| 4 | Del Ennis | 20.00 | 10.00 |
| 5 | Dale Mitchell | 20.00 | 10.00 |
| 6 | Don Newcombe | 35.00 | 17.50 |
| 7 | Gil Hodges | 90.00 | 45.00 |
| 8 | Paul Lehner | 20.00 | 10.00 |
| 9 | Sam Chapman | 20.00 | 10.00 |
| 10 | Al "Red" Schoendienst | 75.00 | 38.00 |
| 11 | George "Red" Munger | 20.00 | 10.00 |
| 12 | Hank Majeski | 20.00 | 10.00 |
| 13 | Ed Stanky | 20.00 | 10.00 |
| 14 | Alvin Dark | 22.00 | 11.00 |
| 15 | Johnny Pesky | 20.00 | 10.00 |
| 16 | Maurice McDermott | 20.00 | 10.00 |
| 17 | Pete Castiglione | 20.00 | 10.00 |
| 18 | Gil Coan | 20.00 | 10.00 |
| 19 | Sid Gordon | 20.00 | 10.00 |
| 20 | Del Crandall | 20.00 | 10.00 |
| 21 | George "Snuffy" Stirnweiss | 20.00 | 10.00 |
| 22 | Hank Sauer | 20.00 | 10.00 |
| 23 | Walter "Hoot" Evers | 20.00 | 10.00 |
| 24 | Ewell Blackwell | 20.00 | 10.00 |
| 25 | Vic Raschi | 30.00 | 15.00 |
| 26 | Phil Rizzuto | 100.00 | 50.00 |
| 27 | Jim Konstanty | 20.00 | 10.00 |
| 28 | Eddie Waitkus | 20.00 | 10.00 |
| 29 | Allie Clark | 20.00 | 10.00 |
| 30 | Bob Feller | 125.00 | 62.00 |
| 31 | Roy Campanella | 260.00 | 130.00 |
| 32 | Duke Snider | 250.00 | 125.00 |
| 33 | Bob Hooper | 20.00 | 10.00 |
| 34 | Marty Marion | 20.00 | 10.00 |
| 35 | Al Zarilla | 20.00 | 10.00 |
| 36 | Joe Dobson | 20.00 | 10.00 |
| 37 | Whitey Lockman | 14.00 | 7.00 |
| 38 | Al Evans | 14.00 | 7.00 |
| 39 | Ray Scarborough | 14.00 | 7.00 |
| 40 | Dave "Gus" Bell | 20.00 | 10.00 |
| 41 | Eddie Yost | 20.00 | 10.00 |
| 42 | Vern Bickford | 14.00 | 7.00 |
| 43 | Billy DeMars | 14.00 | 7.00 |
| 44 | Roy Smalley | 14.00 | 7.00 |
| 45 | Art Houtteman | 14.00 | 7.00 |
| 46 | George Kell | 65.00 | 32.50 |
| 47 | Grady Hatton | 14.00 | 7.00 |
| 48 | Ken Raffensberger | 14.00 | 7.00 |
| 49 | Jerry Coleman | 20.00 | 10.00 |
| 50 | Johnny Mize | 60.00 | 30.00 |
| 51 | Andy Seminick | 14.00 | 7.00 |
| 52 | Dick Sisler | 14.00 | 7.00 |
| 53 | Bob Lemon | 40.00 | 20.00 |
| 54 | Ray Boone | 20.00 | 10.00 |
| 55 | Gene Hermanski | 20.00 | 10.00 |
| 56 | Ralph Branca | 30.00 | 15.00 |
| 57 | Alex Kellner | 14.00 | 7.00 |
| 58 | Enos Slaughter | 60.00 | 30.00 |

| | | NR MT | EX | | | | NR MT | EX |
|---|---|---|---|---|---|---|---|---|
| 59 | Randy Gumpert | 14.00 | 7.00 | | 118 | Preacher Roe | 40.00 | 20.00 |
| 60 | Alfonso Carrasquel | | | | 119 | Eddie Joost | 14.00 | 7.00 |
| | | 14.00 | 7.00 | | 120 | Joe Coleman | 14.00 | 7.00 |
| 61 | Jim Hearn | 14.00 | 7.00 | | 121 | Gerry Staley | 14.00 | 7.00 |
| 62 | Lou Boudreau | 55.00 | 27.50 | | 122 | Joe Garagiola | 150.00 | 75.00 |
| 63 | Bob Dillinger | 14.00 | 7.00 | | 123 | Howie Judson | 14.00 | 7.00 |
| 64 | Bill Werle | 14.00 | 7.00 | | 124 | Gus Niarhos | 14.00 | 7.00 |
| 65 | Mickey Vernon | 20.00 | 10.00 | | 125 | Bill Rigney | 20.00 | 10.00 |
| 66 | Bob Elliott | 14.00 | 7.00 | | 126 | Bobby Thomson | 30.00 | 15.00 |
| 67 | Roy Sievers | 20.00 | 10.00 | | 127 | Sal Maglie | 50.00 | 25.00 |
| 68 | Dick Kokos | 14.00 | 7.00 | | 128 | Ellis Kinder | 14.00 | 7.00 |
| 69 | Johnny Schmitz | 14.00 | 7.00 | | 129 | Matt Batts | 14.00 | 7.00 |
| 70 | Ron Northey | 14.00 | 7.00 | | 130 | Tom Saffell | 14.00 | 7.00 |
| 71 | Jerry Priddy | 14.00 | 7.00 | | 131 | Cliff Chambers | 14.00 | 7.00 |
| 72 | Lloyd Merriman | 14.00 | 7.00 | | 132 | Cass Michaels | 14.00 | 7.00 |
| 73 | Tommy Byrne | 20.00 | 10.00 | | 133 | Sam Dente | 14.00 | 7.00 |
| 74 | Billy Johnson | 20.00 | 10.00 | | 134 | Warren Spahn | 110.00 | 55.00 |
| 75 | Russ Meyer | 14.00 | 7.00 | | 135 | Walker Cooper | 14.00 | 7.00 |
| 76 | Stan Lopata | 14.00 | 7.00 | | 136 | Ray Coleman | 14.00 | 7.00 |
| 77 | Mike Goliat | 14.00 | 7.00 | | 137 | Dick Starr | 14.00 | 7.00 |
| 78 | Early Wynn | 60.00 | 30.00 | | 138 | Phil Cavarretta | 20.00 | 10.00 |
| 79 | Jim Hegan | 14.00 | 7.00 | | 139 | Doyle Lade | 14.00 | 7.00 |
| 80 | Harold "Peewee" Reese | | | | 140 | Eddie Lake | 14.00 | 7.00 |
| | | 150.00 | 75.00 | | 141 | Fred Hutchinson | 20.00 | 10.00 |
| 81 | Carl Furillo | 40.00 | 20.00 | | 142 | Aaron Robinson | 14.00 | 7.00 |
| 82 | Joe Tipton | 14.00 | 7.00 | | 143 | Ted Kluszewski | 40.00 | 20.00 |
| 83 | Carl Scheib | 14.00 | 7.00 | | 144 | Herman Wehmeier | | |
| 84 | Barney McCosky | 14.00 | 7.00 | | | | 14.00 | 7.00 |
| 85 | Eddie Kazak | 14.00 | 7.00 | | 145 | Fred Sanford | 20.00 | 10.00 |
| 86 | Harry Brecheen | 20.00 | 10.00 | | 146 | Johnny Hopp | 20.00 | 10.00 |
| 87 | Floyd Baker | 14.00 | 7.00 | | 147 | Ken Heintzelman | 14.00 | 7.00 |
| 88 | Eddie Robinson | 14.00 | 7.00 | | 148 | Granny Hamner | 14.00 | 7.00 |
| 89 | Henry Thompson | 14.00 | 7.00 | | 149 | Emory "Bubba" Church | | |
| 90 | Dave Koslo | 14.00 | 7.00 | | | | 14.00 | 7.00 |
| 91 | Clyde Vollmer | 14.00 | 7.00 | | 150 | Mike Garcia | 20.00 | 10.00 |
| 92 | Vern "Junior" Stephens | | | | 151 | Larry Doby | 25.00 | 12.50 |
| | | 20.00 | 10.00 | | 152 | Cal Abrams | 20.00 | 10.00 |
| 93 | Danny O'Connell | 14.00 | 7.00 | | 153 | Rex Barney | 20.00 | 10.00 |
| 94 | Clyde McCullough | | | | 154 | Pete Suder | 14.00 | 7.00 |
| | | 14.00 | 7.00 | | 155 | Lou Brissie | 14.00 | 7.00 |
| 95 | Sherry Robertson | 14.00 | 7.00 | | 156 | Del Rice | 14.00 | 7.00 |
| 96 | Sandalio Consuegra | | | | 157 | Al Brazle | 14.00 | 7.00 |
| | | 14.00 | 7.00 | | 158 | Chuck Diering | 14.00 | 7.00 |
| 97 | Bob Kuzava | 14.00 | 7.00 | | 159 | Eddie Stewart | 14.00 | 7.00 |
| 98 | Willard Marshall | 14.00 | 7.00 | | 160 | Phil Masi | 14.00 | 7.00 |
| 99 | Earl Torgeson | 14.00 | 7.00 | | 161 | Wes Westrum | 20.00 | 10.00 |
| 100 | Sherman Lollar | 20.00 | 10.00 | | 162 | Larry Jansen | 14.00 | 7.00 |
| 101 | Owen Friend | 14.00 | 7.00 | | 163 | Monte Kennedy | 14.00 | 7.00 |
| 102 | Emil "Dutch" Leonard | | | | 164 | Bill Wight | 14.00 | 7.00 |
| | | 14.00 | 7.00 | | 165 | Ted Williams | 600.00 | 300.00 |
| 103 | Andy Pafko | 20.00 | 10.00 | | 166 | Stan Rojek | 14.00 | 7.00 |
| 104 | Virgil "Fire" Trucks | | | | 167 | Murry Dickson | 14.00 | 7.00 |
| | | 20.00 | 10.00 | | 168 | Sam Mele | 14.00 | 7.00 |
| 105 | Don Kolloway | 14.00 | 7.00 | | 169 | Sid Hudson | 14.00 | 7.00 |
| 106 | Pat Mullin | 14.00 | 7.00 | | 170 | Sibby Sisti | 14.00 | 7.00 |
| 107 | Johnny Wyrostek | 14.00 | 7.00 | | 171 | Buddy Kerr | 14.00 | 7.00 |
| 108 | Virgil Stallcup | 14.00 | 7.00 | | 172 | Ned Garver | 14.00 | 7.00 |
| 109 | Allie Reynolds | 40.00 | 20.00 | | 173 | Hank Arft | 14.00 | 7.00 |
| 110 | Bobby Brown | 40.00 | 20.00 | | 174 | Mickey Owen | 14.00 | 7.00 |
| 111 | Curt Simmons | 20.00 | 10.00 | | 175 | Wayne Terwilliger | 14.00 | 7.00 |
| 112 | Willie Jones | 14.00 | 7.00 | | 176 | Vic Wertz | 20.00 | 10.00 |
| 113 | Bill "Swish" Nicholson | | | | 177 | Charlie Keller | 20.00 | 10.00 |
| | | 14.00 | 7.00 | | 178 | Ted Gray | 14.00 | 7.00 |
| 114 | Sam Zoldak | 14.00 | 7.00 | | 179 | Danny Litwhiler | 14.00 | 7.00 |
| 115 | Steve Gromek | 14.00 | 7.00 | | 180 | Howie Fox | 14.00 | 7.00 |
| 116 | Bruce Edwards | 20.00 | 10.00 | | 181 | Casey Stengel | 100.00 | 50.00 |
| 117 | Eddie Miksis | 20.00 | 10.00 | | 182 | Tom Ferrick | 20.00 | 10.00 |

| | | NR MT | EX |
|---|---|---|---|
| 183 | Hank Bauer | 40.00 | 20.00 |
| 184 | Eddie Sawyer | 14.00 | 7.00 |
| 185 | Jimmy Bloodworth | | |
| | | 14.00 | 7.00 |
| 186 | Richie Ashburn | 60.00 | 30.00 |
| 187 | Al "Flip" Rosen | 25.00 | 12.50 |
| 188 | *Roberto Avila* | 20.00 | 10.00 |
| 189 | Erv Palica | 20.00 | 10.00 |
| 190 | Joe Hatten | 20.00 | 10.00 |
| 191 | Billy Hitchcock | 14.00 | 7.00 |
| 192 | Hank Wyse | 14.00 | 7.00 |
| 193 | Ted Wilks | 14.00 | 7.00 |
| 194 | Harry "Peanuts" Lowrey | | |
| | | 14.00 | 7.00 |
| 195 | Paul Richards | 30.00 | 15.00 |
| 196 | Bill Pierce | 20.00 | 10.00 |
| 197 | Bob Cain | 14.00 | 7.00 |
| 198 | *Monte Irvin* | 100.00 | 50.00 |
| 199 | Sheldon Jones | 14.00 | 7.00 |
| 200 | Jack Kramer | 14.00 | 7.00 |
| 201 | Steve O'Neill | 14.00 | 7.00 |
| 202 | Mike Guerra | 14.00 | 7.00 |
| 203 | *Vernon Law* | 20.00 | 10.00 |
| 204 | Vic Lombardi | 14.00 | 7.00 |
| 205 | Mickey Grasso | 14.00 | 7.00 |
| 206 | Conrado Marrero | 14.00 | 7.00 |
| 207 | Billy Southworth | 14.00 | 7.00 |
| 208 | Blix Donnelly | 14.00 | 7.00 |
| 209 | Ken Wood | 14.00 | 7.00 |
| 210 | Les Moss | 14.00 | 7.00 |
| 211 | Hal Jeffcoat | 14.00 | 7.00 |
| 212 | Bob Rush | 14.00 | 7.00 |
| 213 | Neil Berry | 14.00 | 7.00 |
| 214 | Bob Swift | 14.00 | 7.00 |
| 215 | Kent Peterson | 14.00 | 7.00 |
| 216 | Connie Ryan | 14.00 | 7.00 |
| 217 | Joe Page | 20.00 | 10.00 |
| 218 | Ed Lopat | 20.00 | 10.00 |
| 219 | Gene Woodling | 40.00 | 20.00 |
| 220 | Bob Miller | 14.00 | 7.00 |
| 221 | Dick Whitman | 14.00 | 7.00 |
| 222 | Thurman Tucker | 14.00 | 7.00 |
| 223 | Johnny Vander Meer | | |
| | | 20.00 | 10.00 |
| 224 | Billy Cox | 20.00 | 10.00 |
| 225 | Dan Bankhead | 20.00 | 10.00 |
| 226 | Jimmy Dykes | 20.00 | 10.00 |
| 227 | Bobby Schantz (Shantz) | | |
| | | 20.00 | 10.00 |
| 228 | Cloyd Boyer | 14.00 | 7.00 |
| 229 | Bill Howerton | 14.00 | 7.00 |
| 230 | Max Lanier | 14.00 | 7.00 |
| 231 | Luis Aloma | 14.00 | 7.00 |
| 232 | Nelson Fox | 110.00 | 55.00 |
| 233 | Leo Durocher | 60.00 | 30.00 |
| 234 | Clint Hartung | 14.00 | 7.00 |
| 235 | Jack "Lucky" Lohrke | | |
| | | 14.00 | 7.00 |
| 236 | Warren "Buddy" Rosar | | |
| | | 14.00 | 7.00 |
| 237 | Billy Goodman | 14.00 | 7.00 |
| 238 | Pete Reiser | 20.00 | 10.00 |
| 239 | Bill MacDonald | 14.00 | 7.00 |
| 240 | Joe Haynes | 14.00 | 7.00 |
| 241 | Irv Noren | 14.00 | 7.00 |
| 242 | Sam Jethroe | 20.00 | 10.00 |
| 243 | John Antonelli | 20.00 | 10.00 |
| 244 | Cliff Fannin | 14.00 | 7.00 |
| 245 | John Berardino | 20.00 | 10.00 |
| 246 | Bill Serena | 14.00 | 7.00 |
| 247 | Bob Ramazotti | 14.00 | 7.00 |
| 248 | *Johnny Klippstein* | 20.00 | 10.00 |
| 249 | Johnny Groth | 14.00 | 7.00 |
| 250 | Hank Borowy | 14.00 | 7.00 |
| 251 | Willard Ramsdell | 14.00 | 7.00 |
| 252 | Homer "Dixie" Howell | | |
| | | 14.00 | 7.00 |
| 253 | *Mickey Mantle* | 8500.00 | 4250.00 |
| 254 | *Jackie Jensen* | 70.00 | 35.00 |
| 255 | Milo Candini | 60.00 | 30.00 |
| 256 | Ken Silvestri | 60.00 | 30.00 |
| 257 | Birdie Tebbetts | 60.00 | 30.00 |
| 258 | *Luke Easter* | 60.00 | 30.00 |
| 259 | Charlie Dressen | 60.00 | 30.00 |
| 260 | Carl Erskine | 90.00 | 45.00 |
| 261 | Wally Moses | 60.00 | 30.00 |
| 262 | Gus Zernial | 60.00 | 30.00 |
| 263 | Howie Pollett (Pollet) | | |
| | | 60.00 | 30.00 |
| 264 | Don Richmond | 60.00 | 30.00 |
| 265 | Steve Bilko | 60.00 | 30.00 |
| 266 | Harry Dorish | 60.00 | 30.00 |
| 267 | Ken Holcombe | 60.00 | 30.00 |
| 268 | Don Mueller | 60.00 | 30.00 |
| 269 | Ray Noble | 60.00 | 30.00 |
| 270 | Willard Nixon | 60.00 | 30.00 |
| 271 | Tommy Wright | 60.00 | 30.00 |
| 272 | Billy Meyer | 60.00 | 30.00 |
| 273 | Danny Murtaugh | 60.00 | 30.00 |
| 274 | George Metkovich | | |
| | | 60.00 | 30.00 |
| 275 | Bucky Harris | 60.00 | 30.00 |
| 276 | Frank Quinn | 60.00 | 30.00 |
| 277 | Roy Hartsfield | 60.00 | 30.00 |
| 278 | Norman Roy | 60.00 | 30.00 |
| 279 | Jim Delsing | 60.00 | 30.00 |
| 280 | Frank Overmire | 60.00 | 30.00 |
| 281 | Al Widmar | 60.00 | 30.00 |
| 282 | Frank Frisch | 80.00 | 40.00 |
| 283 | Walt Dubiel | 60.00 | 30.00 |
| 284 | Gene Bearden | 60.00 | 30.00 |
| 285 | Johnny Lipon | 60.00 | 30.00 |
| 286 | Bob Usher | 60.00 | 30.00 |
| 287 | Jim Blackburn | 60.00 | 30.00 |
| 288 | Bobby Adams | 60.00 | 30.00 |
| 289 | Cliff Mapes | 60.00 | 30.00 |
| 290 | Bill Dickey | 175.00 | 70.00 |
| 291 | Tommy Henrich | 70.00 | 35.00 |
| 292 | Eddie Pellagrini | 60.00 | 30.00 |
| 293 | Ken Johnson | 60.00 | 30.00 |
| 294 | Jocko Thompson | 60.00 | 30.00 |
| 295 | Al Lopez | 90.00 | 45.00 |
| 296 | Bob Kennedy | 60.00 | 30.00 |
| 297 | Dave Philley | 60.00 | 30.00 |
| 298 | Joe Astroth | 60.00 | 30.00 |
| 299 | Clyde King | 60.00 | 30.00 |
| 300 | Hal Rice | 60.00 | 30.00 |
| 301 | Tommy Glaviano | 60.00 | 30.00 |
| 302 | Jim Busby | 60.00 | 30.00 |
| 303 | Marv Rotblatt | 60.00 | 30.00 |
| 304 | Allen Gettel | 60.00 | 30.00 |
| 305 | *Willie Mays* | 3000.00 | 1500.00 |
| 306 | *Jim Piersall* | 110.00 | 55.00 |
| 307 | Walt Masterson | 60.00 | 30.00 |

|     |                      | NR MT  | EX    |
|-----|----------------------|--------|-------|
| 308 | Ted Beard            | 60.00  | 30.00 |
| 309 | Mel Queen            | 60.00  | 30.00 |
| 310 | Erv Dusak            | 60.00  | 30.00 |
| 311 | Mickey Harris        | 60.00  | 30.00 |
| 312 | Gene Mauch           | 60.00  | 30.00 |
| 313 | Ray Mueller          | 60.00  | 30.00 |
| 314 | Johnny Sain          | 60.00  | 30.00 |
| 315 | Zack Taylor          | 60.00  | 30.00 |
| 316 | Duane Pillette       | 60.00  | 30.00 |
| 317 | *Forrest Burgess*    | 70.00  | 35.00 |
| 318 | Warren Hacker        | 60.00  | 30.00 |
| 319 | Red Rolfe            | 60.00  | 30.00 |
| 320 | Hal White            | 60.00  | 30.00 |
| 321 | Earl Johnson         | 60.00  | 30.00 |
| 322 | Luke Sewell          | 60.00  | 30.00 |
| 323 | *Joe Adcock*         | 90.00  | 45.00 |
| 324 | Johnny Pramesa       | 110.00 | 40.00 |

## 1952 Bowman

Bowman reverted back to a 252-card set in 1952, but retained the card size (2-1/16" by 3-1/8") employed the preceding year. The cards, which are color art reproductions of actual photographs, feature a facsimile autograph on the fronts. Artwork for 15 cards that were never issued was uncovered several years ago and a set featuring those cards was subsequently made available to the collecting public.

|   |                         | NR MT   | EX      |
|---|-------------------------|---------|---------|
|   | Complete Set:           | 9000.00 | 4500.00 |
|   | Common Player: 1-36     | 18.00   | 9.00    |
|   | Common Player: 37-216   | 18.00   | 9.00    |
|   | Common Player: 217-252  | 30.00   | 15.00   |
| 1 | Larry "Yogi" Berra      | 600.00  | 250.00  |
| 2 | Bobby Thomson           | 30.00   | 10.00   |
| 3 | Fred Hutchinson         | 18.00   | 9.00    |
| 4 | Robin Roberts           | 60.00   | 30.00   |
| 5 | *Orestes Minoso*        | 100.00  | 50.00   |
| 6 | Virgil "Red" Stallcup   | 18.00   | 9.00    |
| 7 | Mike Garcia             | 18.00   | 9.00    |
| 8 | Harold "Pee Wee" Reese  | 100.00  | 50.00   |
| 9 | Vern Stephens           | 18.00   | 9.00    |
| 10 | Bob Hooper             | 18.00   | 9.00    |
| 11 | Ralph Kiner            | 60.00   | 30.00   |
| 12 | Max Surkont            | 18.00   | 9.00    |
| 13 | Cliff Mapes            | 18.00   | 9.00    |
| 14 | Cliff Chambers         | 18.00   | 9.00    |
| 15 | Sam Mele               | 18.00   | 9.00    |
| 16 | Omar Lown              | 18.00   | 9.00    |
| 17 | Ed Lopat               | 32.00   | 16.00   |
| 18 | Don Mueller            | 18.00   | 9.00    |
| 19 | Bob Cain               | 18.00   | 9.00    |
| 20 | Willie Jones           | 18.00   | 9.00    |
| 21 | Nelson Fox             | 50.00   | 25.00   |
| 22 | Willard Ramsdell       | 18.00   | 9.00    |
| 23 | Bob Lemon              | 40.00   | 20.00   |
| 24 | Carl Furillo           | 30.00   | 15.00   |
| 25 | Maurice McDermott      | 18.00   | 9.00    |
| 26 | Eddie Joost            | 18.00   | 9.00    |
| 27 | Joe Garagiola          | 80.00   | 40.00   |
| 28 | Roy Hartsfield         | 18.00   | 9.00    |
| 29 | Ned Garver             | 18.00   | 9.00    |
| 30 | Al "Red" Schoendienst  | 60.00   | 30.00   |
| 31 | Eddie Yost             | 18.00   | 9.00    |
| 32 | Eddie Miksis           | 18.00   | 9.00    |
| 33 | *Gil McDougald*        | 70.00   | 35.00   |
| 34 | Al Dark                | 20.00   | 10.00   |
| 35 | Gran Hamner            | 18.00   | 9.00    |
| 36 | Cass Michaels          | 18.00   | 9.00    |
| 37 | Vic Raschi             | 20.00   | 10.00   |
| 38 | Whitey Lockman         | 18.00   | 9.00    |
| 39 | Vic Wertz              | 18.00   | 9.00    |
| 40 | Emory Church           | 18.00   | 9.00    |
| 41 | Chico Carrasquel       | 18.00   | 9.00    |
| 42 | Johnny Wyrostek        | 18.00   | 9.00    |
| 43 | Bob Feller             | 125.00  | 67.00   |
| 44 | Roy Campanella         | 200.00  | 100.00  |
| 45 | Johnny Pesky           | 18.00   | 9.00    |
| 46 | Carl Scheib            | 18.00   | 9.00    |
| 47 | Pete Castiglione       | 18.00   | 9.00    |
| 48 | Vern Bickford          | 18.00   | 9.00    |
| 49 | Jim Hearn              | 18.00   | 9.00    |
| 50 | Gerry Staley           | 18.00   | 9.00    |
| 51 | Gil Coan               | 18.00   | 9.00    |
| 52 | Phil Rizzuto           | 80.00   | 40.00   |
| 53 | Richie Ashburn         | 50.00   | 25.00   |
| 54 | Billy Pierce           | 18.00   | 9.00    |
| 55 | Ken Raffensberger      | 18.00   | 9.00    |
| 56 | Clyde King             | 18.00   | 9.00    |
| 57 | Clyde Vollmer          | 18.00   | 9.00    |
| 58 | Hank Majeski           | 18.00   | 9.00    |
| 59 | Murray Dickson (Murry) | 18.00   | 9.00    |
| 60 | Sid Gordon             | 18.00   | 9.00    |
| 61 | Tommy Byrne            | 18.00   | 9.00    |
| 62 | Joe Presko             | 18.00   | 9.00    |
| 63 | Irv Noren              | 18.00   | 9.00    |
| 64 | Roy Smalley            | 18.00   | 9.00    |
| 65 | Hank Bauer             | 30.00   | 15.00   |
| 66 | Sal Maglie             | 30.00   | 15.00   |
| 67 | Johnny Groth           | 18.00   | 9.00    |

| | | NR MT | EX | | | NR MT | EX |
|---|---|---|---|---|---|---|---|
| 68 | Jim Busby | 18.00 | 9.00 | 131 | Bob Swift | 18.00 | 9.00 |
| 69 | Joe Adcock | 30.00 | 15.00 | 132 | Dave Cole | 18.00 | 9.00 |
| 70 | Carl Erskine | 30.00 | 15.00 | 133 | Dick Kryhoski | 18.00 | 9.00 |
| 71 | Vernon Law | 18.00 | 9.00 | 134 | Al Brazle | 18.00 | 9.00 |
| 72 | Earl Torgeson | 18.00 | 9.00 | 135 | Mickey Harris | 18.00 | 9.00 |
| 73 | Jerry Coleman | 18.00 | 9.00 | 136 | Gene Hermanski | 18.00 | 9.00 |
| 74 | Wes Westrum | 18.00 | 9.00 | 137 | Stan Rojek | 18.00 | 9.00 |
| 75 | George Kell | 40.00 | 20.00 | 138 | Ted Wilks | 18.00 | 9.00 |
| 76 | Del Ennis | 18.00 | 9.00 | 139 | Jerry Priddy | 18.00 | 9.00 |
| 77 | Eddie Robinson | 18.00 | 9.00 | 140 | Ray Scarborough | 18.00 | 9.00 |
| 78 | Lloyd Merriman | 18.00 | 9.00 | 141 | Hank Edwards | 18.00 | 9.00 |
| 79 | Lou Brissie | 18.00 | 9.00 | 142 | Early Wynn | 40.00 | 20.00 |
| 80 | Gil Hodges | 70.00 | 35.00 | 143 | Sandalio Consuegra | | |
| 81 | Billy Goodman | 18.00 | 9.00 | | | 18.00 | 9.00 |
| 82 | Gus Zernial | 18.00 | 9.00 | 144 | Joe Hatten | 18.00 | 9.00 |
| 83 | Howie Pollet | 18.00 | 9.00 | 145 | Johnny Mize | 50.00 | 30.00 |
| 84 | Sam Jethroe | 18.00 | 9.00 | 146 | Leo Durocher | 35.00 | 17.50 |
| 85 | Marty Marion | 18.00 | 9.00 | 147 | Marlin Stuart | 18.00 | 9.00 |
| 86 | Cal Abrams | 18.00 | 9.00 | 148 | Ken Heintzelman | 18.00 | 9.00 |
| 87 | Mickey Vernon | 18.00 | 9.00 | 149 | Howie Judson | 18.00 | 9.00 |
| 88 | Bruce Edwards | 18.00 | 9.00 | 150 | Herman Wehmeier | | |
| 89 | Billy Hitchcock | 18.00 | 9.00 | | | 18.00 | 9.00 |
| 90 | Larry Jansen | 18.00 | 9.00 | 151 | Al "Flip" Rosen | 30.00 | 15.00 |
| 91 | Don Kolloway | 18.00 | 9.00 | 152 | Billy Cox | 18.00 | 9.00 |
| 92 | Eddie Waitkus | 18.00 | 9.00 | 153 | Fred Hatfield | 18.00 | 9.00 |
| 93 | Paul Richards | 18.00 | 9.00 | 154 | Ferris Fain | 18.00 | 9.00 |
| 94 | Luke Sewell | 18.00 | 9.00 | 155 | Billy Meyer | 18.00 | 9.00 |
| 95 | Luke Easter | 18.00 | 9.00 | 156 | Warren Spahn | 100.00 | 50.00 |
| 96 | Ralph Branca | 18.00 | 9.00 | 157 | Jim Delsing | 18.00 | 9.00 |
| 97 | Willard Marshall | 18.00 | 9.00 | 158 | Bucky Harris | 30.00 | 15.00 |
| 98 | Jimmy Dykes | 18.00 | 9.00 | 159 | Dutch Leonard | 18.00 | 9.00 |
| 99 | Clyde McCullough | | | 160 | Eddie Stanky | 18.00 | 9.00 |
| | | 18.00 | 9.00 | 161 | Jackie Jensen | 32.00 | 16.00 |
| 100 | Sibby Sisti | 18.00 | 9.00 | 162 | Monte Irvin | 50.00 | 25.00 |
| 101 | Mickey Mantle | 2000.00 | 1000.00 | 163 | Johnny Lipon | 18.00 | 9.00 |
| 102 | Peanuts Lowrey | 18.00 | 9.00 | 164 | Connie Ryan | 18.00 | 9.00 |
| 103 | Joe Haynes | 18.00 | 9.00 | 165 | Saul Rogovin | 18.00 | 9.00 |
| 104 | Hal Jeffcoat | 18.00 | 9.00 | 166 | Bobby Adams | 18.00 | 9.00 |
| 105 | Bobby Brown | 20.00 | 10.00 | 167 | Bob Avila | 18.00 | 9.00 |
| 106 | Randy Gumpert | 18.00 | 9.00 | 168 | Preacher Roe | 32.00 | 16.00 |
| 107 | Del Rice | 18.00 | 9.00 | 169 | Walt Dropo | 18.00 | 9.00 |
| 108 | George Metkovich | | | 170 | Joe Astroth | 18.00 | 9.00 |
| | | 18.00 | 9.00 | 171 | Mel Queen | 18.00 | 9.00 |
| 109 | Tom Morgan | 15.00 | 7.50 | 172 | Ebba St. Claire | 18.00 | 9.00 |
| 110 | Max Lanier | 18.00 | 9.00 | 173 | Gene Bearden | 18.00 | 9.00 |
| 111 | Walter "Hoot" Evers | | | 174 | Mickey Grasso | 18.00 | 9.00 |
| | | 18.00 | 9.00 | 175 | Ransom Jackson | 18.00 | 9.00 |
| 112 | Forrest "Smokey" Burgess | 18.00 | 9.00 | 176 | Harry Brecheen | 18.00 | 9.00 |
| 113 | Al Zarilla | 18.00 | 9.00 | 177 | Gene Woodling | 30.00 | 15.00 |
| 114 | Frank Hiller | 18.00 | 9.00 | 178 | Dave Williams | 18.00 | 9.00 |
| 115 | Larry Doby | 30.00 | 15.00 | 179 | Pete Suder | 18.00 | 9.00 |
| 116 | Duke Snider | 200.00 | 100.00 | 180 | Eddie Fitzgerald (Fitz Gerald) | | |
| 117 | Bill Wight | 18.00 | 9.00 | | | 18.00 | 9.00 |
| 118 | Ray Murray | 18.00 | 9.00 | 181 | Joe Collins | 15.00 | 7.50 |
| 119 | Bill Howerton | 18.00 | 9.00 | 182 | Dave Koslo | 18.00 | 9.00 |
| 120 | Chet Nichols | 18.00 | 9.00 | 183 | Pat Mullin | 18.00 | 9.00 |
| 121 | Al Corwin | 18.00 | 9.00 | 184 | Curt Simmons | 18.00 | 9.00 |
| 122 | Billy Johnson | 18.00 | 9.00 | 185 | Eddie Stewart | 18.00 | 9.00 |
| 123 | Sid Hudson | 18.00 | 9.00 | 186 | Frank Smith | 18.00 | 9.00 |
| 124 | George Tebbetts | 18.00 | 9.00 | 187 | Jim Hegan | 18.00 | 9.00 |
| 125 | Howie Fox | 18.00 | 9.00 | 188 | Charlie Dressen | 15.00 | 7.50 |
| 126 | Phil Cavarretta | 18.00 | 9.00 | 189 | Jim Piersall | 18.00 | 9.00 |
| 127 | Dick Sisler | 18.00 | 9.00 | 190 | Dick Fowler | 18.00 | 9.00 |
| 128 | Don Newcombe | 30.00 | 15.00 | 191 | *Bob Friend* | 15.00 | 7.50 |
| 129 | Gus Niarhos | 18.00 | 9.00 | 192 | John Cusick | 18.00 | 9.00 |
| 130 | Allie Clark | 18.00 | 9.00 | 193 | Bobby Young | 18.00 | 9.00 |
| | | | | 194 | Bob Porterfield | 18.00 | 9.00 |

|  |  | NR MT | EX |
|---|---|---|---|
| 195 | Frank Baumholtz | 18.00 | 9.00 |
| 196 | Stan Musial | 500.00 | 250.00 |
| 197 | Charlie Silvera | 15.00 | 7.50 |
| 198 | Chuck Diering | 18.00 | 9.00 |
| 199 | Ted Gray | 18.00 | 9.00 |
| 200 | Ken Silvestri | 18.00 | 9.00 |
| 201 | Ray Coleman | 18.00 | 9.00 |
| 202 | Harry Perkowski | 18.00 | 9.00 |
| 203 | Steve Gromek | 18.00 | 9.00 |
| 204 | Andy Pafko | 18.00 | 9.00 |
| 205 | Walt Masterson | 18.00 | 9.00 |
| 206 | Elmer Valo | 18.00 | 9.00 |
| 207 | George Strickland | 18.00 | 9.00 |
| 208 | Walker Cooper | 18.00 | 9.00 |
| 209 | Dick Littlefield | 18.00 | 9.00 |
| 210 | Archie Wilson | 18.00 | 9.00 |
| 211 | Paul Minner | 18.00 | 9.00 |
| 212 | Solly Hemus | 18.00 | 9.00 |
| 213 | Monte Kennedy | 18.00 | 9.00 |
| 214 | Ray Boone | 18.00 | 9.00 |
| 215 | Sheldon Jones | 18.00 | 9.00 |
| 216 | Matt Batts | 18.00 | 9.00 |
| 217 | Casey Stengel | 125.00 | 67.00 |
| 218 | Willie Mays | 1000.00 | 500.00 |
| 219 | Neil Berry | 32.00 | 16.00 |
| 220 | Russ Meyer | 32.00 | 16.00 |
| 221 | Lou Kretlow | 32.00 | 16.00 |
| 222 | Homer "Dixie" Howell | 32.00 | 16.00 |
| 223 | Harry Simpson | 32.00 | 16.00 |
| 224 | Johnny Schmitz | 32.00 | 16.00 |
| 225 | Del Wilber | 32.00 | 16.00 |
| 226 | Alex Kellner | 32.00 | 16.00 |
| 227 | Clyde Sukeforth | 32.00 | 16.00 |
| 228 | Bob Chipman | 32.00 | 16.00 |
| 229 | Hank Arft | 32.00 | 16.00 |
| 230 | Frank Shea | 32.00 | 16.00 |
| 231 | Dee Fondy | 32.00 | 16.00 |
| 232 | Enos Slaughter | 90.00 | 45.00 |
| 233 | Bob Kuzava | 32.00 | 16.00 |
| 234 | Fred Fitzsimmons | 32.00 | 16.00 |
| 235 | Steve Souchock | 32.00 | 16.00 |
| 236 | Tommy Brown | 32.00 | 16.00 |
| 237 | Sherman Lollar | 32.00 | 16.00 |
| 238 | *Roy McMillan* | 32.00 | 16.00 |
| 239 | Dale Mitchell | 32.00 | 16.00 |
| 240 | *Billy Loes* | 40.00 | 20.00 |
| 241 | Mel Parnell | 32.00 | 16.00 |
| 242 | Everett Kell | 32.00 | 16.00 |
| 243 | George "Red" Munger | 32.00 | 16.00 |
| 244 | *Lew Burdette* | 70.00 | 35.00 |
| 245 | George Schmees | 32.00 | 16.00 |
| 246 | Jerry Snyder | 32.00 | 16.00 |
| 247 | John Pramesa | 32.00 | 16.00 |
| 248 | Bill Werle | 32.00 | 16.00 |
| 249 | Henry Thompson | 32.00 | 16.00 |
| 250 | Ivan Delock | 32.00 | 16.00 |
| 251 | Jack Lohrke | 32.00 | 12.50 |
| 252 | Frank Crosetti | 150.00 | 50.00 |

**The values quoted are intended to reflect the market price.**

## 1953 Bowman Color

The first set of current major league players featuring actual color photographs, the 160-card 1953 Bowman Color set remains one of the most popular issues of the post-war era. The set is greatly appreciated for its uncluttered look; card fronts that contain no names, teams or facsimile autographs. Bowman increased the size of their cards to a 2-1/2" by 3-3/4" size in order to better compete with Topps Chewing Gum. Bowman copied an idea from the 1952 Topps set and developed card backs that gave player career and previous year statistics. The high- numbered cards (#'s 113-160) are the scarcest of the set, with #'s 113-128 being exceptionally difficult to find.

|  |  | NR MT | EX |
|---|---|---|---|
| Complete Set: | | 12000.00 | 6000.00 |
| Common Player: 1-112 | | 30.00 | 15.00 |
| Common Player: 113-128 | | 40.00 | 20.00 |
| Common Player: 129-160 | | 40.00 | 20.00 |
| 1 | Davey Williams | 100.00 | 25.00 |
| 2 | Vic Wertz | 30.00 | 15.00 |
| 3 | Sam Jethroe | 30.00 | 15.00 |
| 4 | Art Houtteman | 30.00 | 15.00 |

**A player's name in *italic* type indicates a rookie card. An (FC) indicates a player's first card for that particular card company.**

| No. | Name | NR MT | EX |
|---|---|---|---|
| 5 | Sid Gordon | 30.00 | 15.00 |
| 6 | Joe Ginsberg | 30.00 | 15.00 |
| 7 | Harry Chiti | 30.00 | 15.00 |
| 8 | Al Rosen | 40.00 | 20.00 |
| 9 | Phil Rizzuto | 110.00 | 55.00 |
| 10 | Richie Ashburn | 85.00 | 42.00 |
| 11 | Bobby Shantz | 30.00 | 15.00 |
| 12 | Carl Erskine | 50.00 | 30.00 |
| 13 | Gus Zernial | 30.00 | 15.00 |
| 14 | Billy Loes | 30.00 | 15.00 |
| 15 | Jim Busby | 30.00 | 15.00 |
| 16 | Bob Friend | 30.00 | 15.00 |
| 17 | Gerry Staley | 30.00 | 15.00 |
| 18 | Nelson Fox | 75.00 | 38.00 |
| 19 | Al Dark | 30.00 | 15.00 |
| 20 | Don Lenhardt | 30.00 | 15.00 |
| 21 | Joe Garagiola | 80.00 | 40.00 |
| 22 | Bob Porterfield | 30.00 | 15.00 |
| 23 | Herman Wehmeier | 30.00 | 15.00 |
| 24 | Jackie Jensen | 40.00 | 20.00 |
| 25 | Walter "Hoot" Evers | 30.00 | 15.00 |
| 26 | Roy McMillan | 30.00 | 15.00 |
| 27 | Vic Raschi | 40.00 | 20.00 |
| 28 | Forrest "Smoky" Burgess | 30.00 | 15.00 |
| 29 | Roberto Avila | 30.00 | 15.00 |
| 30 | Phil Cavarretta | 30.00 | 15.00 |
| 31 | Jimmy Dykes | 30.00 | 15.00 |
| 32 | Stan Musial | 500.00 | 250.00 |
| 33 | Harold "Peewee" Reese | 450.00 | 225.00 |
| 34 | Gil Coan | 30.00 | 15.00 |
| 35 | Maury McDermott | 30.00 | 15.00 |
| 36 | Orestes Minoso | 50.00 | 30.00 |
| 37 | Jim Wilson | 30.00 | 15.00 |
| 38 | Harry Byrd | 30.00 | 15.00 |
| 39 | Paul Richards | 30.00 | 15.00 |
| 40 | Larry Doby | 40.00 | 20.00 |
| 41 | Sammy White | 30.00 | 15.00 |
| 42 | Tommy Brown | 30.00 | 15.00 |
| 43 | Mike Garcia | 30.00 | 15.00 |
| 44 | Hank Bauer, Yogi Berra, Mickey Mantle | 400.00 | 200.00 |
| 45 | Walt Dropo | 30.00 | 15.00 |
| 46 | Roy Campanella | 250.00 | 125.00 |
| 47 | Ned Garver | 30.00 | 15.00 |
| 48 | Hank Sauer | 30.00 | 15.00 |
| 49 | Eddie Stanky | 30.00 | 15.00 |
| 50 | Lou Kretlow | 30.00 | 15.00 |
| 51 | Monte Irvin | 50.00 | 25.00 |
| 52 | Marty Marion | 30.00 | 15.00 |
| 53 | Del Rice | 30.00 | 15.00 |
| 54 | Chico Carrasquel | 30.00 | 15.00 |
| 55 | Leo Durocher | 60.00 | 30.00 |
| 56 | Bob Cain | 30.00 | 15.00 |
| 57 | Lou Boudreau | 50.00 | 25.00 |
| 58 | Willard Marshall | 30.00 | 15.00 |
| 59 | Mickey Mantle | 2500.00 | 1250.00 |
| 60 | Granny Hamner | 30.00 | 15.00 |
| 61 | George Kell | 30.00 | 15.00 |
| 62 | Ted Kluszewski | 50.00 | 25.00 |
| 63 | Gil McDougald | 50.00 | 25.00 |
| 64 | Curt Simmons | 30.00 | 15.00 |
| 65 | Robin Roberts | 70.00 | 35.00 |
| 66 | Mel Parnell | 30.00 | 15.00 |
| 67 | Mel Clark | 30.00 | 15.00 |
| 68 | Allie Reynolds | 50.00 | 25.00 |
| 69 | Charlie Grimm | 30.00 | 15.00 |
| 70 | Clint Courtney | 30.00 | 15.00 |
| 71 | Paul Minner | 30.00 | 15.00 |
| 72 | Ted Gray | 30.00 | 15.00 |
| 73 | Billy Pierce | 30.00 | 15.00 |
| 74 | Don Mueller | 30.00 | 15.00 |
| 75 | Saul Rogovin | 30.00 | 15.00 |
| 76 | Jim Hearn | 30.00 | 15.00 |
| 77 | Mickey Grasso | 30.00 | 15.00 |
| 78 | Carl Furillo | 50.00 | 25.00 |
| 79 | Ray Boone | 30.00 | 15.00 |
| 80 | Ralph Kiner | 80.00 | 40.00 |
| 81 | Enos Slaughter | 70.00 | 35.00 |
| 82 | Joe Astroth | 30.00 | 15.00 |
| 83 | Jack Daniels | 30.00 | 15.00 |
| 84 | Hank Bauer | 50.00 | 25.00 |
| 85 | Solly Hemus | 30.00 | 15.00 |
| 86 | Harry Simpson | 30.00 | 15.00 |
| 87 | Harry Perkowski | 30.00 | 15.00 |
| 88 | Joe Dobson | 30.00 | 15.00 |
| 89 | Sandalio Consuegra | 30.00 | 15.00 |
| 90 | Joe Nuxhall | 30.00 | 15.00 |
| 91 | Steve Souchock | 30.00 | 15.00 |
| 92 | Gil Hodges | 100.00 | 45.00 |
| 93 | Billy Martin, Phil Rizzuto | 200.00 | 100.00 |
| 94 | Bob Addis | 30.00 | 15.00 |
| 95 | Wally Moses | 30.00 | 15.00 |
| 96 | Sal Maglie | 45.00 | 23.00 |
| 97 | Eddie Mathews | 200.00 | 100.00 |
| 98 | Hector Rodriguez | 30.00 | 15.00 |
| 99 | Warren Spahn | 175.00 | 87.00 |
| 100 | Bill Wight | 30.00 | 15.00 |
| 101 | Al "Red" Schoendienst | 80.00 | 40.00 |
| 102 | Jim Hegan | 30.00 | 15.00 |
| 103 | Del Ennis | 30.00 | 15.00 |
| 104 | Luke Easter | 30.00 | 15.00 |
| 105 | Eddie Joost | 30.00 | 15.00 |
| 106 | Ken Raffensberger | 30.00 | 15.00 |
| 107 | Alex Kellner | 30.00 | 15.00 |
| 108 | Bobby Adams | 30.00 | 15.00 |
| 109 | Ken Wood | 30.00 | 15.00 |
| 110 | Bob Rush | 30.00 | 15.00 |
| 111 | Jim Dyck | 30.00 | 15.00 |
| 112 | Toby Atwell | 30.00 | 15.00 |
| 113 | Karl Drews | 40.00 | 20.00 |
| 114 | Bob Feller | 250.00 | 125.00 |
| 115 | Cloyd Boyer | 40.00 | 20.00 |
| 116 | Eddie Yost | 40.00 | 20.00 |
| 117 | Duke Snider | 600.00 | 300.00 |
| 118 | Billy Martin | 300.00 | 150.00 |
| 119 | Dale Mitchell | 40.00 | 20.00 |
| 120 | Marlin Stuart | 40.00 | 20.00 |
| 121 | Yogi Berra | 500.00 | 250.00 |
| 122 | Bill Serena | 40.00 | 20.00 |
| 123 | Johnny Lipon | 40.00 | 20.00 |
| 124 | Charlie Dressen | 45.00 | 23.00 |
| 125 | Fred Hatfield | 40.00 | 20.00 |
| 126 | Al Corwin | 40.00 | 20.00 |
| 127 | Dick Kryhoski | 40.00 | 20.00 |
| 128 | Whitey Lockman | 40.00 | 20.00 |

| | | NR MT | EX |
|---|---|---|---|
| 129 | Russ Meyer | 50.00 | 25.00 |
| 130 | Cass Michaels | 40.00 | 20.00 |
| 131 | Connie Ryan | 40.00 | 20.00 |
| 132 | Fred Hutchinson | 50.00 | 25.00 |
| 133 | Willie Jones | 40.00 | 20.00 |
| 134 | Johnny Pesky | 50.00 | 25.00 |
| 135 | Bobby Morgan | 50.00 | 25.00 |
| 136 | Jim Brideweser | 40.00 | 20.00 |
| 137 | Sam Dente | 40.00 | 20.00 |
| 138 | Bubba Church | 40.00 | 20.00 |
| 139 | Pete Runnels | 50.00 | 25.00 |
| 140 | Alpha Brazle | 40.00 | 20.00 |
| 141 | Frank "Spec" Shea | 40.00 | 20.00 |
| 142 | Larry Miggins | 40.00 | 20.00 |
| 143 | Al Lopez | 60.00 | 30.00 |
| 144 | Warren Hacker | 40.00 | 20.00 |
| 145 | George Shuba | 50.00 | 25.00 |
| 146 | Early Wynn | 125.00 | 62.00 |
| 147 | Clem Koshorek | 40.00 | 20.00 |
| 148 | Billy Goodman | 40.00 | 20.00 |
| 149 | Al Corwin | 40.00 | 20.00 |
| 150 | Carl Scheib | 40.00 | 20.00 |
| 151 | Joe Adcock | 40.00 | 20.00 |
| 152 | Clyde Vollmer | 40.00 | 20.00 |
| 153 | Ed "Whitey" Ford | 450.00 | 225.00 |
| 154 | Omar "Turk" Lown | 40.00 | 20.00 |
| 155 | Allie Clark | 40.00 | 20.00 |
| 156 | Max Surkont | 40.00 | 20.00 |
| 157 | Sherman Lollar | 50.00 | 25.00 |
| 158 | Howard Fox | 40.00 | 20.00 |
| 159 | Mickey Vernon (Photo actually Floyd Baker) | 40.00 | 17.50 |
| 160 | Cal Abrams | 90.00 | 30.00 |

**Values for recent cards and sets are listed in Mint (MT), Near Mint (NM) and Excellent (EX), reflecting the fact that many cards from recent years have been preserved in top condition.**

## 1953 Bowman Black & White

The 1953 Bowman Black and White set is similar in all respects to the 1953 Bowman Color set, except that it lacks color. Purportedly, high costs in producing the color series forced Bowman to issue the set in black and white. Sixty-four cards, which measure 2-1/2" by 3-3/4", comprise the set.

| | | NR MT | EX |
|---|---|---|---|
| | Complete Set: | 2500.00 | 1250.00 |
| | Common Player: | 30.00 | 15.00 |
| 1 | Gus Bell | 125.00 | 55.00 |
| 2 | Willard Nixon | 32.00 | 11.00 |
| 3 | Bill Rigney | 32.00 | 16.00 |
| 4 | Pat Mullin | 30.00 | 15.00 |
| 5 | Dee Fondy | 30.00 | 15.00 |
| 6 | Ray Murray | 30.00 | 15.00 |
| 7 | Andy Seminick | 30.00 | 15.00 |
| 8 | Pete Suder | 30.00 | 15.00 |
| 9 | Walt Masterson | 30.00 | 15.00 |
| 10 | Dick Sisler | 30.00 | 15.00 |
| 11 | Dick Gernert | 30.00 | 15.00 |
| 12 | Randy Jackson | 30.00 | 15.00 |
| 13 | Joe Tipton | 30.00 | 15.00 |
| 14 | Bill Nicholson | 30.00 | 15.00 |
| 15 | Johnny Mize | 125.00 | 67.00 |
| 16 | Stu Miller | 30.00 | 15.00 |
| 17 | Virgil Trucks | 32.00 | 16.00 |
| 18 | Billy Hoeft | 30.00 | 15.00 |
| 19 | Paul LaPalme | 30.00 | 15.00 |
| 20 | Eddie Robinson | 30.00 | 15.00 |
| 21 | Clarence "Bud" Podbielan | 30.00 | 15.00 |
| 22 | Matt Batts | 30.00 | 15.00 |
| 23 | Wilmer Mizell | 30.00 | 15.00 |
| 24 | Del Wilber | 30.00 | 15.00 |
| 25 | John Sain | 60.00 | 30.00 |
| 26 | Preacher Roe | 60.00 | 30.00 |
| 27 | Bob Lemon | 125.00 | 67.00 |
| 28 | Hoyt Wilhelm | 125.00 | 67.00 |
| 29 | Sid Hudson | 30.00 | 15.00 |
| 30 | Walker Cooper | 30.00 | 15.00 |
| 31 | Gene Woodling | 50.00 | 25.00 |
| 32 | Rocky Bridges | 30.00 | 15.00 |
| 33 | Bob Kuzava | 32.00 | 16.00 |
| 34 | Ebba St. Clair (St. Claire) | 30.00 | 15.00 |
| 35 | Johnny Wyrostek | 30.00 | 15.00 |
| 36 | Jim Piersall | 50.00 | 25.00 |
| 37 | Hal Jeffcoat | 30.00 | 15.00 |
| 38 | Dave Cole | 30.00 | 15.00 |
| 39 | Casey Stengel | 300.00 | 150.00 |
| 40 | Larry Jansen | 30.00 | 15.00 |
| 41 | Bob Ramazotti | 30.00 | 15.00 |
| 42 | Howie Judson | 30.00 | 15.00 |
| 43 | Hal Bevan | 30.00 | 15.00 |
| 44 | Jim Delsing | 30.00 | 15.00 |
| 45 | Irv Noren | 32.00 | 16.00 |
| 46 | Bucky Harris | 50.00 | 25.00 |
| 47 | Jack Lohrke | 30.00 | 15.00 |
| 48 | Steve Ridzik | 30.00 | 15.00 |
| 49 | Floyd Baker | 30.00 | 15.00 |
| 50 | Emil "Dutch" Leonard | 30.00 | 15.00 |
| 51 | Lou Burdette | 50.00 | 25.00 |
| 52 | Ralph Branca | 40.00 | 20.00 |
| 53 | Morris Martin | 30.00 | 15.00 |
| 54 | Bill Miller | 32.00 | 16.00 |
| 55 | Don Johnson | 30.00 | 15.00 |
| 56 | Roy Smalley | 30.00 | 15.00 |
| 57 | Andy Pafko | 30.00 | 15.00 |
| 58 | Jim Konstanty | 30.00 | 15.00 |
| 59 | Duane Pillette | 30.00 | 15.00 |
| 60 | Billy Cox | 40.00 | 20.00 |
| 61 | Tom Gorman | 32.00 | 16.00 |

|    |                | NR MT | EX    |
|----|----------------|-------|-------|
| 62 | Keith Thomas   | 30.00 | 15.00 |
| 63 | Steve Gromek   | 32.00 | 16.00 |
| 64 | Andy Hansen    | 50.00 | 15.00 |
| 81 | Joe Black      | 50.00 | 25.00 |

# 1954 Bowman

Bowman's 1954 set consists of 224 full-color cards that measure 2-1/2" by 3-3/4". It is believed that contractual problems caused the pulling of card #66 (Ted Williams) from the set, creating one of the most sought-after scarcities of the post-war era. The Williams card was replaced by Jim Piersall (who is also #210) in subsequent print runs. The set contains over 40 variations, most involving statistical errors on the card backs that were corrected. Neither variation carries a premium value as both varieties appear to have been printed in equal amounts. The complete set price that follows does not include all variations or #66 Williams.

|                       | NR MT   | EX      |
|-----------------------|---------|---------|
| Complete Set:         | 4500.00 | 2250.00 |
| Common Player: 1-112  | 8.00    | 4.00    |
| Common Player: 113-224| 10.00   | 5.00    |

|     |                    | NR MT  | EX    |
|-----|--------------------|--------|-------|
| 1   | Phil Rizzuto       | 150.00 | 50.00 |
| 2   | Jack Jensen        | 15.00  | 7.50  |
| 3   | Marion Fricano     | 8.00   | 4.00  |
| 4   | Bob Hooper         | 8.00   | 4.00  |
| 5   | William Hunter     | 8.00   | 4.00  |
| 6   | Nelson Fox         | 25.00  | 12.50 |
| 7   | Walter Dropo       | 8.00   | 4.00  |
| 8   | James F. Busby     | 8.00   | 4.00  |
| 9   | Dave Williams      | 8.00   | 4.00  |
| 10  | Carl Daniel Erskine| 12.00  | 6.00  |
| 11  | Sid Gordon         | 8.00   | 4.00  |
| 12a | Roy McMillan (551 1290 At Bat) | 8.00 | 4.00 |

|     |                    | NR MT  | EX    |
|-----|--------------------|--------|-------|
| 12b | Roy McMillan (557 1296 At Bat) | 8.00 | 4.00 |
| 13  | Paul Minner        | 8.00   | 4.00  |
| 14  | Gerald Staley      | 8.00   | 4.00  |
| 15  | Richie Ashburn     | 35.00  | 17.50 |
| 16  | Jim Wilson         | 8.00   | 4.00  |
| 17  | Tom Gorman         | 8.00   | 4.00  |
| 18  | Walter "Hoot" Evers | 8.00  | 4.00  |
| 19  | Bobby Shantz       | 8.00   | 4.00  |
| 20  | Artie Houtteman    | 8.00   | 4.00  |
| 21  | Victor Wertz       | 8.00   | 4.00  |
| 22a | Sam Mele (213/1661 Putouts) | 8.00 | 4.00 |
| 22b | Sam Mele (217/1665 Putouts) | 8.00 | 4.00 |
| 23  | *Harvey Kuenn*     | 35.00  | 17.50 |
| 24  | Bob Porterfield    | 8.00   | 4.00  |
| 25a | Wes Westrum (1.000 .987 Field Avg.) | 8.00 | 4.00 |
| 25b | Wes Westrum (.982 .986 Field Avg.) | 8.00 | 4.00 |
| 26a | Billy Cox (1.000/.960 Field Avg.) | 8.00 | 4.00 |
| 26b | Billy Cox (.972/.960 Field Avg.) | 8.00 | 4.00 |
| 27  | Richard Roy Cole   | 8.00   | 4.00  |
| 28a | Jim Greengrass (Birthplace Addison, N.J.) | 8.00 | 4.00 |
| 28b | Jim Greengrass (Birthplace Addison, N.Y.) | 8.00 | 4.00 |
| 29  | Johnny Klippstein  | 8.00   | 4.00  |
| 30  | Delbert Rice Jr.   | 8.00   | 4.00  |
| 31  | "Smoky" Burgess    | 8.00   | 4.00  |
| 32  | Del Crandall       | 8.00   | 4.00  |
| 33a | Victor Raschi (no traded line) | 12.00 | 6.00 |
| 33b | Victor Raschi (with traded line) | 30.00 | 15.00 |
| 34  | Sammy White        | 8.00   | 4.00  |
| 35a | Eddie Joost (quiz answer is 8) | 8.00 | 4.00 |
| 35b | Eddie Joost (quiz answer is 33) | 8.00 | 4.00 |
| 36  | George Strickland  | 8.00   | 4.00  |
| 37  | Dick Kokos         | 8.00   | 4.00  |
| 38a | Orestes Minoso (.895 .961 Field Avg.) | 8.00 | 4.00 |
| 38b | Orestes Minoso (.963 .963 Field Avg.) | 8.00 | 4.00 |
| 39  | Ned Garver         | 8.00   | 4.00  |
| 40  | Gil Coan           | 8.00   | 4.00  |
| 41a | Alvin Dark (.986/.960 Field Avg.) | 8.00 | 4.00 |
| 41b | Alvin Dark (.968/.960 Field Avg.) | 8.00 | 4.00 |
| 42  | Billy Loes         | 8.00   | 4.00  |
| 43a | Robert B. Friend (20 shutouts in quiz question) | 8.00 | 4.00 |
| 43b | Robert B. Friend (16 shutouts in quiz question) | 8.00 | 4.00 |
| 44  | Harry Perkowski    | 8.00   | 4.00  |
| 45  | Ralph Kiner        | 40.00  | 20.00 |

| | | NR MT | EX | | | NR MT | EX |
|---|---|---|---|---|---|---|---|
| 46 | Eldon Repulski | 8.00 | 4.00 | | Field Avg.) | 8.00 | 4.00 |
| 47a | Granville Hamner (.970 | | | 85b | Jim Dyck (.947/.960 | | |
| | .953 Field Avg.) | 8.00 | 4.00 | | Field Avg.) | 8.00 | 4.00 |
| 47b | Granville Hamner (.953 | | | 86 | Harry Dorish | 8.00 | 4.00 |
| | .951 Field Avg.) | 8.00 | 4.00 | 87 | Don Lund | 8.00 | 4.00 |
| 48 | Jack Dittmer | 8.00 | 4.00 | 88 | Tommy Umphlett | 8.00 | 4.00 |
| 49 | Harry Byrd | 8.00 | 4.00 | 89 | Willie May (Mays) | | |
| 50 | George Kell | 25.00 | 12.50 | | | 350.00 | 175.00 |
| 51 | Alex Kellner | 8.00 | 4.00 | 90 | Roy Campanella | 150.00 | 60.00 |
| 52 | Myron N. Ginsberg | 8.00 | 4.00 | 91 | Cal Abrams | 8.00 | 4.00 |
| 53a | Don Lenhardt (.969 | | | 92 | Kenneth David | | |
| | .984 Field Avg.) | 8.00 | 4.00 | | Raffensberger | 8.00 | 4.00 |
| 53b | Don Lenhardt (.966 | | | 93a | Bill Serena (.983/.966 | | |
| | .983 Field Avg.) | 8.00 | 4.00 | | Field Avg.) | 8.00 | 4.00 |
| 54 | Alfonso Carrasquel | 8.00 | 4.00 | 93b | Bill Serena (.977/.966 | | |
| 55 | Jim Delsing | 8.00 | 4.00 | | Field Avg.) | 8.00 | 4.00 |
| 56 | Maurice M. McDermott | | | 94a | Solly Hemus (476/1343 | | |
| | | 8.00 | 4.00 | | Assists) | 8.00 | 4.00 |
| 57 | Hoyt Wilhelm | 30.00 | 15.00 | 94b | Solly Hemus (477/1343 | | |
| 58 | "Pee Wee" Reese | 70.00 | 35.00 | | Assists) | 8.00 | 4.00 |
| 59 | Robert D. Schultz | 8.00 | 4.00 | 95 | Robin Roberts | 40.00 | 20.00 |
| 60 | Fred Baczewski | 8.00 | 4.00 | 96 | Joe Adcock | 8.00 | 4.00 |
| 61a | Eddie Miksis (.954/.962 | | | 97 | Gil McDougald | 15.00 | 7.50 |
| | Field Avg.) | 8.00 | 4.00 | 98 | Ellis Kinder | 8.00 | 4.00 |
| 61b | Eddie Miksis (.954/.961 | | | 99a | Peter Suder (.985/.974 | | |
| | Field Avg.) | 8.00 | 4.00 | | Field Avg.) | 8.00 | 4.00 |
| 62 | Enos Slaughter | 40.00 | 20.00 | 99b | Peter Suder (.978/.974 | | |
| 63 | Earl Torgeson | 8.00 | 4.00 | | Field Avg.) | 8.00 | 4.00 |
| 64 | Ed Mathews | 60.00 | 30.00 | 100 | Mike Garcia | 8.00 | 4.00 |
| 65 | Mickey Mantle | 1000.00 | 500.00 | 101 | *Don James Larsen* | | |
| 66a | Ted Williams | 4250.00 | 2125.00 | | | 45.00 | 23.00 |
| 66b | Jimmy Piersall | 100.00 | 50.00 | 102 | Bill Pierce | 8.00 | 4.00 |
| 67a | Carl Scheib (.306 Pct. | | | 103a | Stephen Souchock (144 | | |
| | with two lines under bio) | | | | 1192 Putouts) | 8.00 | 4.00 |
| 67b | Carl Scheib (.306 Pct. | | | 103b | Stephen Souchock (147 | | |
| | with one line under bio) | | | | 1195 Putouts) | 8.00 | 4.00 |
| | | 8.00 | 4.00 | 104 | Frank Spec Shea | 8.00 | 4.00 |
| 67c | Carl Scheib (.300 Pct.) | | | 105a | Sal Maglie (quiz answer | | |
| | | 8.00 | 4.00 | | is 8) | 8.00 | 4.00 |
| 68 | Bob Avila | 8.00 | 4.00 | 105b | Sal Maglie (quiz answer | | |
| 69 | Clinton Courtney | 8.00 | 4.00 | | is 1904) | 8.00 | 4.00 |
| 70 | Willard Marshall | 8.00 | 4.00 | 106 | "Clem" Labine | 8.00 | 4.00 |
| 71 | Ted Gray | 8.00 | 4.00 | 107 | Paul E. LaPalme | 8.00 | 4.00 |
| 72 | Ed Yost | 8.00 | 4.00 | 108 | Bobby Adams | 8.00 | 4.00 |
| 73 | Don Mueller | 8.00 | 4.00 | 109 | Roy Smalley | 8.00 | 4.00 |
| 74 | James Gilliam | 15.00 | 7.50 | 110 | Al Schoendienst | 35.00 | 17.50 |
| 75 | Max Surkont | 8.00 | 4.00 | 111 | Murry Monroe Dickson | | |
| 76 | Joe Nuxhall | 8.00 | 4.00 | | | 8.00 | 4.00 |
| 77 | Bob Rush | 8.00 | 4.00 | 112 | Andy Pafko | 8.00 | 4.00 |
| 78 | Sal A. Yvars | 8.00 | 4.00 | 113 | Allie Reynolds | 12.00 | 6.00 |
| 79 | Curt Simmons | 8.00 | 4.00 | 114 | Willard Nixon | 12.00 | 6.00 |
| 80a | John Logan (106 Runs) | | | 115 | Don Bollweg | 12.00 | 6.00 |
| | | 8.00 | 4.00 | 116 | Luscious Luke Easter | | |
| 80b | John Logan (100 Runs) | | | | | 12.00 | 6.00 |
| | | 8.00 | 4.00 | 117 | Dick Kryhoski | 12.00 | 6.00 |
| 81a | Jerry Coleman (1.000 | | | 118 | Robert R. Boyd | 12.00 | 6.00 |
| | .975 Field Avg.) | 8.00 | 4.00 | 119 | Fred Hatfield | 12.00 | 6.00 |
| 81b | Jerry Coleman (.952 | | | 120 | Mel Hoderlein | 12.00 | 6.00 |
| | .975 Field Avg.) | 8.00 | 4.00 | 121 | Ray Katt | 12.00 | 6.00 |
| 82a | Bill Goodman (.965 | | | 122 | Carl Furillo | 15.00 | 7.50 |
| | .986 Field Avg.) | 8.00 | 4.00 | 123 | Toby Atwell | 12.00 | 6.00 |
| 82b | Bill Goodman (.972 | | | 124a | Gus Bell (15/27 Errors) | | |
| | .985 Field Avg.) | 8.00 | 4.00 | | | 12.00 | 6.00 |
| 83 | Ray Murray | 8.00 | 4.00 | 124b | Gus Bell (11/26 Errors) | | |
| 84 | Larry Doby | 12.00 | 6.00 | | | 12.00 | 6.00 |
| 85a | Jim Dyck (.926/.956 | | | 125 | Warren Hacker | 12.00 | 6.00 |
| | | | | 126 | Cliff Chambers | 12.00 | 6.00 |

|  |  | NR MT | EX |
|---|---|---|---|
| 127 | Del Ennis | 12.00 | 6.00 |
| 128 | Ebba St Claire | 12.00 | 6.00 |
| 129 | Hank Bauer | 20.00 | 10.00 |
| 130 | Milt Bolling | 12.00 | 6.00 |
| 131 | Joe Astroth | 12.00 | 6.00 |
| 132 | Bob Feller | 80.00 | 40.00 |
| 133 | Duane Pillette | 12.00 | 6.00 |
| 134 | Luis Aloma | 12.00 | 6.00 |
| 135 | Johnny Pesky | 12.00 | 6.00 |
| 136 | Clyde Vollmer | 12.00 | 6.00 |
| 137 | Elmer N. Corwin Jr. | 12.00 | 6.00 |
| 138a | Gil Hodges (.993/.991 Field Avg.) | 50.00 | 25.00 |
| 138b | Gil Hodges (.992/.991 Field Avg.) | 55.00 | 28.00 |
| 139a | Preston Ward (.961 .992 Field Avg.) | 12.00 | 6.00 |
| 139b | Preston Ward (.990 .992 Field Avg.) | 12.00 | 6.00 |
| 140a | Saul Rogovin (7-12 Won Lost with 2 Strikeouts) | 12.00 | 6.00 |
| 140b | Saul Rogovin (7-12 Won Lost with 62 Strikeouts) | 12.00 | 6.00 |
| 140c | Saul Rogovin (8-12 Won Lost) | 12.00 | 6.00 |
| 141 | Joe Garagiola | 45.00 | 23.00 |
| 142 | Al Brazle | 12.00 | 6.00 |
| 143 | Puddin Head Jones | 12.00 | 6.00 |
| 144 | Ernie Johnson | 12.00 | 6.00 |
| 145a | Billy Martin (.985/.983 Field Avg.) | 50.00 | 25.00 |
| 145b | Billy Martin (.983/.982 Field Avg.) | 60.00 | 30.00 |
| 146 | Dick Gernert | 12.00 | 6.00 |
| 147 | Joe DeMaestri | 12.00 | 6.00 |
| 148 | Dale Mitchell | 12.00 | 6.00 |
| 149 | Bob Young | 12.00 | 6.00 |
| 150 | Cass Michaels | 12.00 | 6.00 |
| 151 | Patrick J. Mullin | 12.00 | 6.00 |
| 152 | Mickey Vernon | 12.00 | 6.00 |
| 153a | Whitey Lockman (100 331 Assists) | 12.00 | 6.00 |
| 153b | Whitey Lockman (102 333 Assists) | 12.00 | 6.00 |
| 154 | Don Newcombe | 25.00 | 12.50 |
| 155 | Frank J. Thomas | 12.00 | 6.00 |
| 156a | Everett Lamar Bridges (320/467 Assists) | 12.00 | 6.00 |
| 156b | Everett Lamar Bridges (328/475 Assists) | 12.00 | 6.00 |
| 157 | Omar Lown | 12.00 | 6.00 |
| 158 | Stu Miller | 12.00 | 6.00 |
| 159 | John Lindell | 12.00 | 6.00 |
| 160 | Danny O'Connell | 12.00 | 6.00 |
| 161 | Yogi Berra | 175.00 | 87.00 |
| 162 | Ted Lepcio | 12.00 | 6.00 |
| 163a | Dave Philley (152 Games with no traded line) | 12.00 | 6.00 |
| 163b | Dave Philley (152 Games with traded line) | 25.00 | 12.50 |
| 163c | Dave Philley (157 Games with traded line) | 12.00 | 6.00 |
| 164 | Early "Gus" Wynn | 40.00 | 20.00 |
| 165 | Johnny Groth | 12.00 | 6.00 |
| 166 | Sandalio Consuegra | 12.00 | 6.00 |
| 167 | Bill Hoeft | 12.00 | 6.00 |
| 168 | Edward Fitzgerald (Fitz Gerald) | 12.00 | 6.00 |
| 169 | Larry Jansen | 12.00 | 6.00 |
| 170 | Edwin D. Snider | 150.00 | 75.00 |
| 171 | Carlos Bernier | 12.00 | 6.00 |
| 172 | Andy Seminick | 12.00 | 6.00 |
| 173 | Dee V. Fondy Jr. | 12.00 | 6.00 |
| 174a | Peter Paul Castiglione (.966/.959 Field Avg.) | 12.00 | 6.00 |
| 174b | Peter Paul Castiglione (.970/.959 Field Avg.) | 12.00 | 6.00 |
| 175 | Melvin E. Clark | 12.00 | 6.00 |
| 176 | Vernon Bickford | 12.00 | 6.00 |
| 177 | Edward Ford | 110.00 | 55.00 |
| 178 | Del Wilber | 12.00 | 6.00 |
| 179a | Morris Martin (44 ERA) | 12.00 | 6.00 |
| 179b | Morris Martin (4.44 ERA) | 12.00 | 6.00 |
| 180 | Joe Tipton | 12.00 | 6.00 |
| 181 | Lester Moss | 12.00 | 6.00 |
| 182 | Sherman Lollar | 12.00 | 6.00 |
| 183 | Matt Batts | 12.00 | 6.00 |
| 184 | Mickey Grasso | 12.00 | 6.00 |
| 185a | Daryl Spencer (.941 .944 Field Avg.) | 12.00 | 6.00 |
| 185b | Daryl Spencer (.933 .936 Field Avg.) | 12.00 | 6.00 |
| 186 | Russell Meyer | 12.00 | 6.00 |
| 187 | Verne Law (Vern) | 12.00 | 6.00 |
| 188 | Frank Smith | 12.00 | 6.00 |
| 189 | Ransom Jackson | 12.00 | 6.00 |
| 190 | Joe Presko | 12.00 | 6.00 |
| 191 | Karl A. Drews | 12.00 | 6.00 |
| 192 | Selva L. Burdette | 12.00 | 6.00 |
| 193 | Eddie Robinson | 12.00 | 6.00 |
| 194 | Sid Hudson | 12.00 | 6.00 |
| 195 | Bob Cain | 12.00 | 6.00 |
| 196 | Bob Lemon | 35.00 | 17.50 |
| 197 | Lou Kretlow | 12.00 | 6.00 |
| 198 | Virgil Trucks | 12.00 | 6.00 |
| 199 | Steve Gromek | 12.00 | 6.00 |
| 200 | C. Marrero | 12.00 | 6.00 |
| 201 | Bob Thomson | 12.00 | 6.00 |
| 202 | George Shuba | 12.00 | 6.00 |
| 203 | Vic Janowicz | 12.00 | 6.00 |
| 204 | Jack Collum | 12.00 | 6.00 |
| 205 | Hal Jeffcoat | 12.00 | 6.00 |
| 206 | Steve Bilko | 12.00 | 6.00 |
| 207 | Stan Lopata | 12.00 | 6.00 |
| 208 | Johnny Antonelli | 12.00 | 6.00 |
| 209 | Gene Woodling (photo reversed) | 12.00 | 6.00 |
| 210 | Jimmy Piersall | 20.00 | 10.00 |
| 211 | Alfred James Robertson Jr. | 12.00 | 6.00 |
| 212a | Owen L. Friend (.964 .957 Field Avg.) | 12.00 | 6.00 |

| | | NR MT | EX |
|---|---|---|---|
| 212b | Owen L. Friend (.967 | | |
| | .958 Field Avg.) | 12.00 | 6.00 |
| 213 | Dick Littlefield | 12.00 | 6.00 |
| 214 | Ferris Fain | 12.00 | 6.00 |
| 215 | Johnny Bucha | 12.00 | 6.00 |
| 216a | Jerry Snyder (.988 | | |
| | .988 Field Avg.) | 12.00 | 6.00 |
| 216b | Jerry Snyder (.968 | | |
| | .968 Field Avg.) | 12.00 | 6.00 |
| 217a | Henry Thompson (.956 | | |
| | .951 Field Avg.) | 12.00 | 6.00 |
| 217b | Henry Thompson (.958 | | |
| | .952 Field Avg.) | 12.00 | 6.00 |
| 218 | Preacher Roe | 12.00 | 6.00 |
| 219 | Hal Rice | 12.00 | 6.00 |
| 220 | Hobie Landrith | 12.00 | 6.00 |
| 221 | Frank Baumholtz | 12.00 | 6.00 |
| 222 | Memo Luna | 12.00 | 6.00 |
| 223 | Steve Ridzik | 12.00 | 6.00 |
| 224 | William Bruton | 30.00 | 9.00 |

## 1955 Bowman

Bowman produced its final baseball card set in 1955, a popular issue which has player photographs placed inside a television set design. The set consists of 320 cards that measure 2-1/2" by 3-3/4" in size. The high-numbered cards (#'s 225-320) are scarcest in the set and include 31 umpire cards.

| | | NR MT | EX |
|---|---|---|---|
| Complete Set: | | 5000.00 | 2500.00 |
| Common Player: 1-224 | | 9.00 | 4.50 |
| Common Player: 225-320 | | | |
| | | 25.00 | 12.50 |
| 1 | Hoyt Wilhelm | 100.00 | 20.00 |
| 2 | Al Dark | 10.00 | 5.00 |
| 3 | Joe Coleman | 9.00 | 4.50 |
| 4 | Eddie Waitkus | 9.00 | 4.50 |
| 5 | Jim Robertson | 9.00 | 4.50 |
| 6 | Pete Suder | 9.00 | 4.50 |
| 7 | Gene Baker | 9.00 | 4.50 |
| 8 | Warren Hacker | 9.00 | 4.50 |
| 9 | Gil McDougald | 12.00 | 6.00 |
| 10 | Phil Rizzuto | 50.00 | 25.00 |
| 11 | Billy Bruton | 9.00 | 4.50 |

| | | NR MT | EX |
|---|---|---|---|
| 12 | Andy Pafko | 10.00 | 5.00 |
| 13 | Clyde Vollmer | 9.00 | 4.50 |
| 14 | Gus Keriazakos | 9.00 | 4.50 |
| 15 | *Frank Sullivan* | 10.00 | 5.00 |
| 16 | Jim Piersall | 9.00 | 4.50 |
| 17 | Del Ennis | 10.00 | 5.00 |
| 18 | Stan Lopata | 9.00 | 4.50 |
| 19 | Bobby Avila | 9.00 | 4.50 |
| 20 | Al Smith | 9.00 | 4.50 |
| 21 | Don Hoak | 9.00 | 4.50 |
| 22 | Roy Campanella | 100.00 | 50.00 |
| 23 | Al Kaline | 150.00 | 75.00 |
| 24 | Al Aber | 9.00 | 4.50 |
| 25 | Orestes "Minnie" Minoso | | |
| | | 25.00 | 12.50 |
| 26 | Virgil Trucks | 10.00 | 5.00 |
| 27 | Preston Ward | 9.00 | 4.50 |
| 28 | Dick Cole | 9.00 | 4.50 |
| 29 | Al "Red" Schoendienst | | |
| | | 30.00 | 15.00 |
| 30 | Bill Sarni | 9.00 | 4.50 |
| 31 | Johnny Temple | 9.00 | 4.50 |
| 32 | Wally Post | 9.00 | 4.50 |
| 33 | Nelson Fox | 20.00 | 10.00 |
| 34 | Clint Courtney | 9.00 | 4.50 |
| 35 | Bill Tuttle | 9.00 | 4.50 |
| 36 | Wayne Belardi | 9.00 | 4.50 |
| 37 | Harold "Pee Wee" Reese | | |
| | | 70.00 | 35.00 |
| 38 | Early Wynn | 20.00 | 10.00 |
| 39 | Bob Darnell | 10.00 | 5.00 |
| 40 | Vic Wertz | 10.00 | 5.00 |
| 41 | Mel Clark | 9.00 | 4.50 |
| 42 | Bob Greenwood | 9.00 | 4.50 |
| 43 | Bob Buhl | 10.00 | 5.00 |
| 44 | Danny O'Connell | 9.00 | 4.50 |
| 45 | Tom Umphlett | 9.00 | 4.50 |
| 46 | Mickey Vernon | 10.00 | 5.00 |
| 47 | Sammy White | 9.00 | 4.50 |
| 48a | Milt Bolling (Frank Bolling back) | 10.00 | 5.00 |
| 48b | Milt Bolling (Milt Bolling back) | 25.00 | 12.50 |
| 49 | Jim Greengrass | 9.00 | 4.50 |
| 50 | Hobie Landrith | 9.00 | 4.50 |
| 51 | Elvin Tappe | 9.00 | 4.50 |
| 52 | Hal Rice | 9.00 | 4.50 |
| 53 | Alex Kellner | 9.00 | 4.50 |
| 54 | Don Bollweg | 9.00 | 4.50 |
| 55 | Cal Abrams | 9.00 | 4.50 |
| 56 | Billy Cox | 9.00 | 4.50 |
| 57 | Bob Friend | 10.00 | 5.00 |
| 58 | Frank Thomas | 9.00 | 4.50 |
| 59 | Ed "Whitey" Ford | 70.00 | 35.00 |
| 60 | Enos Slaughter | 30.00 | 15.00 |
| 61 | Paul LaPalme | 9.00 | 4.50 |
| 62 | Royce Lint | 9.00 | 4.50 |
| 63 | Irv Noren | 10.00 | 5.00 |
| 64 | Curt Simmons | 10.00 | 5.00 |
| 65 | *Don Zimmer* | 25.00 | 12.50 |
| 66 | George Shuba | 10.00 | 5.00 |
| 67 | Don Larsen | 20.00 | 10.00 |
| 68 | *Elston Howard* | 70.00 | 35.00 |
| 69 | Bill Hunter | 10.00 | 5.00 |
| 70 | Lou Burdette | 9.00 | 4.50 |
| 71 | Dave Jolly | 9.00 | 4.50 |
| 72 | Chet Nichols | 9.00 | 4.50 |

| | | NR MT | EX |
|---|---|---|---|
| 73 | Eddie Yost | 9.00 | 4.50 |
| 74 | Jerry Snyder | 9.00 | 4.50 |
| 75 | Brooks Lawrence | 9.00 | 4.50 |
| 76 | Tom Poholsky | 9.00 | 4.50 |
| 77 | Jim McDonald | 9.00 | 4.50 |
| 78 | Gil Coan | 9.00 | 4.50 |
| 79 | Willie Miranda | 9.00 | 4.50 |
| 80 | Lou Limmer | 9.00 | 4.50 |
| 81 | Bob Morgan | 9.00 | 4.50 |
| 82 | Lee Walls | 9.00 | 4.50 |
| 83 | Max Surkont | 9.00 | 4.50 |
| 84 | George Freese | 9.00 | 4.50 |
| 85 | Cass Michaels | 9.00 | 4.50 |
| 86 | Ted Gray | 9.00 | 4.50 |
| 87 | Randy Jackson | 9.00 | 4.50 |
| 88 | Steve Bilko | 9.00 | 4.50 |
| 89 | Lou Boudreau | 20.00 | 10.00 |
| 90 | Art Ditmar | 9.00 | 4.50 |
| 91 | Dick Marlowe | 9.00 | 4.50 |
| 92 | George Zuverink | 9.00 | 4.50 |
| 93 | Andy Seminick | 9.00 | 4.50 |
| 94 | Hank Thompson | 9.00 | 4.50 |
| 95 | Sal Maglie | 12.00 | 6.00 |
| 96 | Ray Narleski | 9.00 | 4.50 |
| 97 | John Podres | 20.00 | 10.00 |
| 98 | James "Junior" Gilliam | 12.00 | 6.00 |
| 99 | Jerry Coleman | 10.00 | 5.00 |
| 100 | Tom Morgan | 10.00 | 5.00 |
| 101a | Don Johnson (Ernie Johnson (Braves) on front) | 10.00 | 5.00 |
| 101b | Don Johnson (Don Johnson (Orioles) on front) | 25.00 | 12.50 |
| 102 | Bobby Thomson | 12.00 | 6.00 |
| 103 | Eddie Mathews | 60.00 | 30.00 |
| 104 | Bob Porterfield | 9.00 | 4.50 |
| 105 | Johnny Schmitz | 9.00 | 4.50 |
| 106 | Del Rice | 9.00 | 4.50 |
| 107 | Solly Hemus | 9.00 | 4.50 |
| 108 | Lou Kretlow | 9.00 | 4.50 |
| 109 | Vern Stephens | 9.00 | 4.50 |
| 110 | Bob Miller | 9.00 | 4.50 |
| 111 | Steve Ridzik | 9.00 | 4.50 |
| 112 | Gran Hamner | 9.00 | 4.50 |
| 113 | Bob Hall | 9.00 | 4.50 |
| 114 | Vic Janowicz | 9.00 | 4.50 |
| 115 | Roger Bowman | 9.00 | 4.50 |
| 116 | Sandalio Consuegra | 9.00 | 4.50 |
| 117 | Johnny Groth | 9.00 | 4.50 |
| 118 | Bobby Adams | 9.00 | 4.50 |
| 119 | Joe Astroth | 9.00 | 4.50 |
| 120 | Ed Burtschy | 9.00 | 4.50 |
| 121 | Rufus Crawford | 9.00 | 4.50 |
| 122 | Al Corwin | 9.00 | 4.50 |
| 123 | Marv Grissom | 9.00 | 4.50 |
| 124 | Johnny Antonelli | 10.00 | 5.00 |
| 125 | Paul Giel | 9.00 | 4.50 |
| 126 | Billy Goodman | 9.00 | 4.50 |
| 127 | Hank Majeski | 9.00 | 4.50 |
| 128 | Mike Garcia | 10.00 | 5.00 |
| 129 | Hal Naragon | 9.00 | 4.50 |
| 130 | Richie Ashburn | 25.00 | 12.50 |
| 131 | Willard Marshall | 9.00 | 4.50 |
| 132a | Harvey Kueen (incorrect spelling on back) | 10.00 | 5.00 |
| 132b | Harvey Kuenn (correct spelling on back) | 30.00 | 15.00 |
| 133 | Charles King | 9.00 | 4.50 |
| 134 | Bob Feller | 60.00 | 30.00 |
| 135 | Lloyd Merriman | 9.00 | 4.50 |
| 136 | Rocky Bridges | 9.00 | 4.50 |
| 137 | Bob Talbot | 9.00 | 4.50 |
| 138 | Davey Williams | 9.00 | 4.50 |
| 139 | Billy & Bobby Shantz | 9.00 | 4.50 |
| 140 | Bobby Shantz | 10.00 | 5.00 |
| 141 | Wes Westrum | 10.00 | 5.00 |
| 142 | Rudy Regalado | 9.00 | 4.50 |
| 143 | Don Newcombe | 25.00 | 12.50 |
| 144 | Art Houtteman | 9.00 | 4.50 |
| 145 | Bob Nieman | 9.00 | 4.50 |
| 146 | Don Liddle | 9.00 | 4.50 |
| 147 | Sam Mele | 9.00 | 4.50 |
| 148 | Bob Chakales | 9.00 | 4.50 |
| 149 | Cloyd Boyer | 9.00 | 4.50 |
| 150 | Bill Klaus | 9.00 | 4.50 |
| 151 | Jim Brideweser | 9.00 | 4.50 |
| 152 | Johnny Klippstein | 9.00 | 4.50 |
| 153 | Eddie Robinson | 10.00 | 5.00 |
| 154 | *Frank Lary* | 9.00 | 4.50 |
| 155 | Gerry Staley | 9.00 | 4.50 |
| 156 | Jim Hughes | 10.00 | 5.00 |
| 157a | Ernie Johnson (Don Johnson (Orioles) picture on front) | 10.00 | 5.00 |
| 157b | Ernie Johnson (Ernie Johnson (Braves) picture on front) | 18.00 | 9.00 |
| 158 | Gil Hodges | 40.00 | 20.00 |
| 159 | Harry Byrd | 9.00 | 4.50 |
| 160 | Bill Skowron | 25.00 | 12.50 |
| 161 | Matt Batts | 9.00 | 4.50 |
| 162 | Charlie Maxwell | 9.00 | 4.50 |
| 163 | Sid Gordon | 9.00 | 4.50 |
| 164 | Toby Atwell | 9.00 | 4.50 |
| 165 | Maurice McDermott | 9.00 | 4.50 |
| 166 | Jim Busby | 9.00 | 4.50 |
| 167 | Bob Grim | 10.00 | 5.00 |
| 168 | Larry "Yogi" Berra | 110.00 | 55.00 |
| 169 | Carl Furillo | 25.00 | 12.50 |
| 170 | Carl Erskine | 15.00 | 7.50 |
| 171 | Robin Roberts | 30.00 | 15.00 |
| 172 | Willie Jones | 9.00 | 4.50 |
| 173 | Al "Chico" Carrasquel | 9.00 | 4.50 |
| 174 | Sherman Lollar | 10.00 | 5.00 |
| 175 | Wilmer Shantz | 9.00 | 4.50 |
| 176 | Joe DeMaestri | 9.00 | 4.50 |
| 177 | Willard Nixon | 9.00 | 4.50 |
| 178 | Tom Brewer | 9.00 | 4.50 |
| 179 | Hank Aaron | 225.00 | 112.00 |
| 180 | Johnny Logan | 9.00 | 4.50 |
| 181 | Eddie Miksis | 9.00 | 4.50 |
| 182 | Bob Rush | 9.00 | 4.50 |
| 183 | Ray Katt | 9.00 | 4.50 |
| 184 | Willie Mays | 235.00 | 117.00 |
| 185 | Vic Raschi | 10.00 | 5.00 |
| 186 | Alex Grammas | 9.00 | 4.50 |
| 187 | Fred Hatfield | 9.00 | 4.50 |

| | | NR MT | EX | | | | NR MT | EX |
|---|---|---|---|---|---|---|---|---|
| 188 | Ned Garver | 9.00 | 4.50 | | 240 | Billy Loes | 16.00 | 8.00 |
| 189 | Jack Collum | 9.00 | 4.50 | | 241 | John Pesky | 16.00 | 8.00 |
| 190 | Fred Baczewski | 9.00 | 4.50 | | 242 | Ernie Banks | 400.00 | 200.00 |
| 191 | Bob Lemon | 25.00 | 12.50 | | 243 | Gus Bell | 16.00 | 8.00 |
| 192 | George Strickland | 9.00 | 4.50 | | 244 | Duane Pillette | 15.00 | 7.50 |
| 193 | Howie Judson | 9.00 | 4.50 | | 245 | Bill Miller | 15.00 | 7.50 |
| 194 | Joe Nuxhall | 10.00 | 5.00 | | 246 | Hank Bauer | 30.00 | 15.00 |
| 195a | Erv Palica (no traded line on back) | | | | 247 | Dutch Leonard | 15.00 | 7.50 |
| | | 9.00 | 4.50 | | 248 | Harry Dorish | 15.00 | 7.50 |
| 195b | Erv Palica (traded line on back) | | | | 249 | Billy Gardner | 15.00 | 7.50 |
| | | 25.00 | 12.50 | | 250 | Larry Napp (umpire) | | |
| 196 | Russ Meyer | 10.00 | 5.00 | | | | 25.00 | 12.50 |
| 197 | Ralph Kiner | 35.00 | 17.50 | | 251 | Stan Jok | 15.00 | 7.50 |
| 198 | Dave Pope | 9.00 | 4.50 | | 252 | Roy Smalley | 15.00 | 7.50 |
| 199 | Vernon Law | 10.00 | 5.00 | | 253 | Jim Wilson | 15.00 | 7.50 |
| 200 | Dick Littlefield | 9.00 | 4.50 | | 254 | Bennett Flowers | 15.00 | 7.50 |
| 201 | Allie Reynolds | 25.00 | 12.50 | | 255 | Pete Runnels | 16.00 | 8.00 |
| 202 | Mickey Mantle | 500.00 | 250.00 | | 256 | Owen Friend | 15.00 | 7.50 |
| 203 | Steve Gromek | 9.00 | 4.50 | | 257 | Tom Alston | 15.00 | 7.50 |
| 204a | Frank Bolling (Milt Bolling back) | | | | 258 | John W. Stevens (umpire) | | |
| | | 10.00 | 5.00 | | | | 25.00 | 12.50 |
| 204b | Frank Bolling (Frank Bolling back) | | | | 259 | Don Mossi | 25.00 | 12.50 |
| | | 20.00 | 10.00 | | 260 | Edwin H. Hurley (umpire) | | |
| 205 | Eldon "Rip" Repulski | | | | | | 25.00 | 12.50 |
| | | 9.00 | 4.50 | | 261 | Walt Moryn | 16.00 | 8.00 |
| 206 | Ralph Beard | 9.00 | 4.50 | | 262 | Jim Lemon | 16.00 | 8.00 |
| 207 | Frank Shea | 9.00 | 4.50 | | 263 | Eddie Joost | 15.00 | 7.50 |
| 208 | Eddy Fitzgerald (Fitz Gerald) | | | | 264 | Bill Henry | 15.00 | 7.50 |
| | | 9.00 | 4.50 | | 265 | Albert J. Barlick (umpire) | | |
| 209 | Forrest "Smoky" Burgess | | | | | | 80.00 | 40.00 |
| | | 10.00 | 5.00 | | 266 | Mike Fornieles | 15.00 | 7.50 |
| 210 | Earl Torgeson | 9.00 | 4.50 | | 267 | George (Jim) Honochick (umpire) | | |
| 211 | John "Sonny" Dixon | | | | | | 70.00 | 35.00 |
| | | 9.00 | 4.50 | | 268 | Roy Lee Hawes | 15.00 | 7.50 |
| 212 | Jack Dittmer | 9.00 | 4.50 | | 269 | Joe Amalfitano | 15.00 | 7.50 |
| 213 | George Kell | 25.00 | 12.50 | | 270 | Chico Fernandez | 16.00 | 8.00 |
| 214 | Billy Pierce | 10.00 | 5.00 | | 271 | Bob Hooper | 15.00 | 7.50 |
| 215 | Bob Kuzava | 9.00 | 4.50 | | 272 | John Flaherty (umpire) | | |
| 216 | Preacher Roe | 10.00 | 5.00 | | | | 25.00 | 12.50 |
| 217 | Del Crandall | 10.00 | 5.00 | | 273 | Emory "Bubba" Church | | |
| 218 | Joe Adcock | 10.00 | 5.00 | | | | 15.00 | 7.50 |
| 219 | Whitey Lockman | 9.00 | 4.50 | | 274 | Jim Delsing | 15.00 | 7.50 |
| 220 | Jim Hearn | 9.00 | 4.50 | | 275 | William T. Grieve (umpire) | | |
| 221 | Hector "Skinny" Brown | | | | | | 25.00 | 12.50 |
| | | 9.00 | 4.50 | | 276 | Ivan Delock | 15.00 | 7.50 |
| 222 | Russ Kemmerer | 9.00 | 4.50 | | 277 | Ed Runge (umpire) | | |
| 223 | Hal Jeffcoat | 9.00 | 4.50 | | | | 25.00 | 12.50 |
| 224 | Dee Fondy | 9.00 | 4.50 | | 278 | Charles Neal | 25.00 | 12.50 |
| 225 | Paul Richards | 16.00 | 8.00 | | 279 | Hank Soar (umpire) | | |
| 226 | W.F. McKinley (umpire) | | | | | | 25.00 | 12.50 |
| | | 25.00 | 12.50 | | 280 | Clyde McCullough | | |
| 227 | Frank Baumholtz | 15.00 | 7.50 | | | | 15.00 | 7.50 |
| 228 | John M. Phillips | 15.00 | 7.50 | | 281 | Charles Berry (umpire) | | |
| 229 | Jim Brosnan | 16.00 | 8.00 | | | | 25.00 | 12.50 |
| 230 | Al Brazle | 15.00 | 7.50 | | 282 | Phil Cavarretta | 16.00 | 8.00 |
| 231 | Jim Konstanty | 25.00 | 12.50 | | 283 | Nestor Chylak (umpire) | | |
| 232 | Birdie Tebbetts | 15.00 | 7.50 | | | | 25.00 | 12.50 |
| 233 | Bill Serena | 15.00 | 7.50 | | 284 | William A. Jackowski (umpire) | 25.00 | 12.50 |
| 234 | Dick Bartell | 15.00 | 7.50 | | 285 | Walt Dropo | 16.00 | 8.00 |
| 235 | J.A. Paparella (umpire) | | | | 286 | Frank E. Secory (umpire) | | |
| | | 25.00 | 12.50 | | | | 25.00 | 12.50 |
| 236 | Murray Dickson (Murry) | | | | 287 | Ron Mrozinski | 15.00 | 7.50 |
| | | 15.00 | 7.50 | | 288 | Dick Smith | 15.00 | 7.50 |
| 237 | Johnny Wyrostek | 15.00 | 7.50 | | 289 | Arthur J. Gore (umpire) | | |
| 238 | Eddie Stanky | 16.00 | 8.00 | | | | 25.00 | 12.50 |
| 239 | Edwin A. Rommel (umpire) | 25.00 | 12.50 | | 290 | Hershell Freeman | 15.00 | 7.50 |

|  |  | NR MT | EX |
|---|---|---|---|
| 291 | Frank Dascoli (umpire) | | |
| | | 25.00 | 12.50 |
| 292 | Marv Blaylock | 15.00 | 7.50 |
| 293 | Thomas D. Gorman | | |
| | (umpire) | 25.00 | 12.50 |
| 294 | Wally Moses | 15.00 | 7.50 |
| 295 | E. Lee Ballanfant | | |
| | (umpire) | 25.00 | 12.50 |
| 296 | *Bill Virdon* | 40.00 | 20.00 |
| 297 | L.R. "Dusty" Boggess | | |
| | (umpire) | 25.00 | 12.50 |
| 298 | Charlie Grimm | 25.00 | 12.50 |
| 299 | Lonnie Warneke | | |
| | (umpire) | 25.00 | 12.50 |
| 300 | Tommy Byrne | 16.00 | 8.00 |
| 301 | William R. Engeln | | |
| | (umpire) | 25.00 | 12.50 |
| 302 | *Frank Malzone* | 30.00 | 15.00 |
| 303 | J.B. "Jocko" Conlan | | |
| | (umpire) | 100.00 | 50.00 |
| 304 | Harry Chiti | 15.00 | 7.50 |
| 305 | Frank Umont (umpire) | | |
| | | 25.00 | 12.50 |
| 306 | Bob Cerv | 25.00 | 12.50 |
| 307 | R.A. "Babe" Pinelli | | |
| | (umpire) | 25.00 | 12.50 |
| 308 | Al Lopez | 40.00 | 20.00 |
| 309 | Hal H. Dixon (umpire) | | |
| | | 25.00 | 12.50 |
| 310 | Ken Lehman | 16.00 | 8.00 |
| 311 | Lawrence J. Goetz | | |
| | (umpire) | 25.00 | 12.50 |
| 312 | Bill Wight | 15.00 | 7.50 |
| 313 | A.J. Donatelli (umpire) | | |
| | | 25.00 | 12.50 |
| 314 | Dale Mitchell | 15.00 | 7.50 |
| 315 | Cal Hubbard (umpire) | | |
| | | 100.00 | 50.00 |
| 316 | Marion Fricano | 15.00 | 7.50 |
| 317 | Wm. R. Summers | | |
| | (umpire) | 25.00 | 12.50 |
| 318 | Sid Hudson | 15.00 | 7.50 |
| 319 | Albert B. Schroll | 25.00 | 12.50 |
| 320 | George D. Susce, Jr. | | |
| | | 60.00 | 30.00 |

## 1989 Bowman

Topps, which purchased the Bowman Co. back in 1955, revived the Bowman name in 1989, issuing a 484-card set modeled after the 1953 Bowman cards.

The cards are 2-1/2" by 3-3/4", slightly larger than a current standard-sized card. The fronts contain a full-color player photo, with facsimile autograph on the bottom and the Bowman logo in an upper corner. The unique card backs include a breakdown of the player's stats against each team in his league. A series of "Hot Rookie Stars" highlight the set. The cards were distributed in both wax packs and rack packs. Each pack included a special reproduction of a classic Bowman card with a sweepstakes on the back. The special cards said "reprint" on the front.

|  |  | MT | NR MT |
|---|---|---|---|
| Complete Set: | | 8.00 | 6.00 |
| Common Player: | | .03 | .02 |
| 1 | Oswald Peraza | .05 | .04 |
| 2 | Brian Holton | .05 | .04 |
| 3 | Jose Bautista | .05 | .04 |
| 4 | Pete Harnisch | .10 | .08 |
| 5 | Dave Schmidt | .03 | .02 |
| 6 | Gregg Olson | .30 | .25 |
| 7 | Jeff Ballard | .10 | .08 |
| 8 | Bob Melvin | .03 | .02 |
| 9 | Cal Ripken | .20 | .15 |
| 10 | Randy Milligan | .08 | .06 |
| 11 | Juan Bell | .15 | .11 |
| 12 | Billy Ripken | .05 | .04 |
| 13 | Jim Trabor | .03 | .02 |
| 14 | Pete Stanicek | .03 | .02 |
| 15 | Steve Finley | .20 | .15 |
| 16 | Larry Sheets | .03 | .02 |
| 17 | Phil Bradley | .05 | .04 |
| 18 | Brady Anderson | .10 | .08 |
| 19 | Lee Smith | .03 | .02 |
| 20 | Tom Fischer | .15 | .11 |
| 21 | Mike Boddicker | .03 | .02 |
| 22 | Rob Murphy | .03 | .02 |
| 23 | Wes Gardner | .03 | .02 |
| 24 | John Dopson | .10 | .08 |
| 25 | Bob Stanley | .03 | .02 |
| 26 | Roger Clemens | .20 | .15 |
| 27 | Rich Gedman | .03 | .02 |
| 28 | Marty Barrett | .03 | .02 |
| 29 | Luis Rivera | .03 | .02 |
| 30 | Jody Reed | .05 | .04 |
| 31 | Nick Esasky | .05 | .04 |
| 32 | Wade Boggs | .40 | .30 |
| 33 | Jim Rice | .10 | .08 |
| 34 | Mike Greenwell | .15 | .11 |
| 35 | Dwight Evans | .15 | .11 |
| 36 | Ellis Burks | .25 | .20 |
| 37 | Chuck Finley | .05 | .04 |
| 38 | Kirk McCaskill | .05 | .04 |
| 39 | Jim Abbott | .60 | .45 |
| 40 | Bryan Harvey | .05 | .04 |
| 41 | Bert Blyleven | .08 | .06 |

| | | MT | NR MT | | | | MT | NR MT |
|---|---|---|---|---|---|---|---|---|
| 42 | Mike Witt | .03 | .02 | | 109 | Keith Moreland | .03 | .02 |
| 43 | Bob McClure | .03 | .02 | | 110 | Mel Stottlemyre, Jr. | .15 | .11 |
| 44 | Bill Schroeder | .03 | .02 | | 111 | Bret Saberhagen | .10 | .08 |
| 45 | Lance Parrish | .05 | .04 | | 112 | Floyd Bannister | .03 | .02 |
| 46 | Dick Schofield | .03 | .02 | | 113 | Jeff Montgomery | .05 | .04 |
| 47 | Wally Joyner | .10 | .08 | | 114 | Steve Farr | .05 | .04 |
| 48 | Jack Howell | .03 | .02 | | 115 | Tom Gordon | .40 | .30 |
| 49 | Johnny Ray | .03 | .02 | | 116 | Charlie Leibrandt | .03 | .02 |
| 50 | Chili Davis | .05 | .04 | | 117 | Mark Gubicza | .08 | .06 |
| 51 | Tony Armas | .03 | .02 | | 118 | Mike MacFarlane | .03 | .02 |
| 52 | Claudell Washington | .03 | .02 | | 119 | Bob Boone | .05 | .04 |
| 53 | Brian Downing | .03 | .02 | | 120 | Kurt Stillwell | .05 | .04 |
| 54 | Devon White | .10 | .08 | | 121 | George Brett | .15 | .11 |
| 55 | Bobby Thigpen | .08 | .06 | | 122 | Frank White | .05 | .04 |
| 56 | Bill Long | .03 | .02 | | 123 | Kevin Seitzer | .08 | .06 |
| 57 | Jerry Reuss | .03 | .02 | | 124 | Willie Wilson | .03 | .02 |
| 58 | Shawn Hillegas | .03 | .02 | | 125 | Pat Tabler | .03 | .02 |
| 59 | Melido Perez | .05 | .04 | | 126 | Bo Jackson | .30 | .25 |
| 60 | Jeff Bittiger | .05 | .04 | | 127 | Hugh Walker | .20 | .15 |
| 61 | Jack McDowell | .03 | .02 | | 128 | Danny Tartabull | .05 | .04 |
| 62 | Carlton Fisk | .10 | .08 | | 129 | Teddy Higuera | .08 | .06 |
| 63 | Steve Lyons | .03 | .02 | | 130 | Don August | .03 | .02 |
| 64 | Ozzie Guillen | .05 | .04 | | 131 | Juan Nieves | .03 | .02 |
| 65 | Robin Ventura | 1.25 | .90 | | 132 | Mike Birkbeck | .03 | .02 |
| 66 | Fred Manrique | .03 | .02 | | 133 | Dan Plesac | .05 | .04 |
| 67 | Dan Pasqua | .03 | .02 | | 134 | Chris Bosio | .05 | .04 |
| 68 | Ivan Calderon | .03 | .02 | | 135 | Bill Wegman | .03 | .02 |
| 69 | Ron Kittle | .03 | .02 | | 136 | Chuck Crim | .03 | .02 |
| 70 | Daryl Boston | .03 | .02 | | 137 | B.J. Surhoff | .05 | .04 |
| 71 | Dave Gallagher | .05 | .04 | | 138 | Joey Meyer | .03 | .02 |
| 72 | Harold Baines | .08 | .06 | | 139 | Dale Sveum | .03 | .02 |
| 73 | Charles Nagy | .20 | .15 | | 140 | Paul Molitor | .08 | .06 |
| 74 | John Farrell | .03 | .02 | | 141 | Jim Gantner | .03 | .02 |
| 75 | Kevin Wickander | .25 | .20 | | 142 | Gary Sheffield | .80 | .60 |
| 76 | Greg Swindell | .15 | .11 | | 143 | Greg Brock | .03 | .02 |
| 77 | Mike Walker | .15 | .11 | | 144 | Robin Yount | .25 | .20 |
| 78 | Doug Jones | .05 | .04 | | 145 | Glenn Braggs | .03 | .02 |
| 79 | Rich Yett | .03 | .02 | | 146 | Rob Deer | .03 | .02 |
| 80 | Tom Candiotti | .03 | .02 | | 147 | Fred Toliver | .03 | .02 |
| 81 | Jesse Orosco | .03 | .02 | | 148 | Jeff Reardon | .03 | .02 |
| 82 | Bud Black | .03 | .02 | | 149 | Allan Anderson | .05 | .04 |
| 83 | Andy Allanson | .03 | .02 | | 150 | Frank Viola | .15 | .11 |
| 84 | Pete O'Brien | .05 | .04 | | 151 | Shane Rawley | .03 | .02 |
| 85 | Jerry Browne | .05 | .04 | | 152 | Juan Berenguer | .03 | .02 |
| 86 | Brook Jacoby | .03 | .02 | | 153 | Johnny Ard | .20 | .15 |
| 87 | Mark Lewis | .40 | .30 | | 154 | Tim Laudner | .03 | .02 |
| 88 | Luis Aguayo | .03 | .02 | | 155 | Brian Harper | .03 | .02 |
| 89 | Cory Snyder | .05 | .04 | | 156 | Al Newman | .03 | .02 |
| 90 | Oddibe McDowell | .05 | .04 | | 157 | Kent Hrbek | .08 | .06 |
| 91 | Joe Carter | .15 | .11 | | 158 | Gary Gaetti | .08 | .06 |
| 92 | Frank Tanana | .03 | .02 | | 159 | Wally Backman | .03 | .02 |
| 93 | Jack Morris | .03 | .02 | | 160 | Gene Larkin | .03 | .02 |
| 94 | Doyle Alexander | .03 | .02 | | 161 | Greg Gagne | .03 | .02 |
| 95 | Steve Searcy | .08 | .06 | | 162 | Kirby Puckett | .35 | .25 |
| 96 | Randy Bockus | .05 | .04 | | 163 | Danny Gladden | .03 | .02 |
| 97 | Jeff Robinson | .05 | .04 | | 164 | Randy Bush | .03 | .02 |
| 98 | Mike Henneman | .05 | .04 | | 165 | Dave LaPoint | .03 | .02 |
| 99 | Paul Gibson | .03 | .02 | | 166 | Andy Hawkins | .03 | .02 |
| 100 | Frank Williams | .03 | .02 | | 167 | Dave Righetti | .05 | .04 |
| 101 | Matt Nokes | .05 | .04 | | 168 | Lance McCullers | .03 | .02 |
| 102 | Rico Brogna | .15 | .11 | | 169 | Jimmy Jones | .03 | .02 |
| 103 | Lou Whitaker | .08 | .06 | | 170 | Al Leiter | .03 | .02 |
| 104 | Al Pedrique | .03 | .02 | | 171 | John Candelaria | .03 | .02 |
| 105 | Alan Trammell | .05 | .04 | | 172 | Don Slaught | .03 | .02 |
| 106 | Chris Brown | .03 | .02 | | 173 | Jamie Quirk | .03 | .02 |
| 107 | Pat Sheridan | .03 | .02 | | 174 | Rafael Santana | .03 | .02 |
| 108 | Gary Pettis | .03 | .02 | | 175 | Mike Pagliarulo | .03 | .02 |

| | | MT | NR MT | | | | MT | NR MT |
|---|---|---|---|---|---|---|---|---|
| 176 | Don Mattingly | .40 | .30 | | 243 | Jimmy Key | .05 | .04 |
| 177 | Ken Phelps | .03 | .02 | | 244 | Tony Castillo | .10 | .08 |
| 178 | Steve Sax | .08 | .06 | | 245 | Alex Sanchez | .05 | .04 |
| 179 | Dave Winfield | .20 | .15 | | 246 | Tom Henke | .03 | .02 |
| 180 | Stan Jefferson | .03 | .02 | | 247 | John Cerutti | .03 | .02 |
| 181 | Rickey Henderson | .40 | .30 | | 248 | Ernie Whitt | .03 | .02 |
| 182 | Bob Brower | .03 | .02 | | 249 | Bob Brenly | .03 | .02 |
| 183 | Roberto Kelly | .10 | .08 | | 250 | Rance Mulliniks | .03 | .02 |
| 184 | Curt Young | .03 | .02 | | 251 | Kelly Gruber | .10 | .08 |
| 185 | Gene Nelson | .03 | .02 | | 252 | Ed Sprague | .20 | .15 |
| 186 | Bob Welch | .03 | .02 | | 253 | Fred McGriff | .50 | .40 |
| 187 | Rick Honeycutt | .03 | .02 | | 254 | Tony Fernandez | .08 | .06 |
| 188 | Dave Stewart | .08 | .06 | | 255 | Tom Lawless | .03 | .02 |
| 189 | Mike Moore | .08 | .06 | | 256 | George Bell | .10 | .08 |
| 190 | Dennis Eckersley | .08 | .06 | | 257 | Jesse Barfield | .05 | .04 |
| 191 | Eric Plunk | .03 | .02 | | 258 | Sandy Alomar | .20 | .15 |
| 192 | Storm Davis | .03 | .02 | | 259 | Ken Griffey | 1.00 | .70 |
| 193 | Terry Steinbach | .10 | .08 | | 260 | Cal Ripken, Sr. | .15 | .11 |
| 194 | Ron Hassey | .03 | .02 | | 261 | Mel Stottlemyre | .15 | .11 |
| 195 | Stan Royer | .15 | .11 | | 262 | Zane Smith | .03 | .02 |
| 196 | Walt Weiss | .15 | .11 | | 263 | Charlie Puleo | .03 | .02 |
| 197 | Mark McGwire | .40 | .30 | | 264 | Derek Lilliquist | .15 | .11 |
| 198 | Carney Lansford | .08 | .06 | | 265 | Paul Assenmacher | .03 | .02 |
| 199 | Glenn Hubbard | .03 | .02 | | 266 | John Smoltz | .60 | .45 |
| 200 | Dave Henderson | .05 | .04 | | 267 | Tom Glavine | .10 | .08 |
| 201 | Jose Canseco | .40 | .30 | | 268 | Steve Avery | 1.00 | .70 |
| 202 | Dave Parker | .05 | .04 | | 269 | Pete Smith | .05 | .04 |
| 203 | Scott Bankhead | .05 | .04 | | 270 | Jody Davis | .03 | .02 |
| 204 | Tom Niedenfuer | .03 | .02 | | 271 | Bruce Benedict | .03 | .02 |
| 205 | Mark Langston | .15 | .11 | | 272 | Andres Thomas | .03 | .02 |
| 206 | Erik Hanson | .50 | .40 | | 273 | Gerald Perry | .05 | .04 |
| 207 | Mike Jackson | .03 | .02 | | 274 | Ron Gant | .05 | .04 |
| 208 | Dave Valle | .03 | .02 | | 275 | Darrell Evans | .03 | .02 |
| 209 | Scott Bradley | .03 | .02 | | 276 | Dale Murphy | .08 | .06 |
| 210 | Harold Reynolds | .08 | .06 | | 277 | Dion James | .03 | .02 |
| 211 | Tino Martinez | .50 | .40 | | 278 | Lonnie Smith | .08 | .06 |
| 212 | Rich Renteria | .03 | .02 | | 279 | Geronimo Berroa | .05 | .04 |
| 213 | Rey Quinones | .03 | .02 | | 280 | Steve Wilson | .20 | .15 |
| 214 | Jim Presley | .03 | .02 | | 281 | Rick Suctcliffe | .05 | .04 |
| 215 | Alvin Davis | .10 | .08 | | 282 | Kevin Coffman | .03 | .02 |
| 216 | Edgar Martinez | .03 | .02 | | 283 | Mitch Williams | .10 | .08 |
| 217 | Darnell Coles | .03 | .02 | | 284 | Greg Maddux | .05 | .04 |
| 218 | Jeffrey Leonard | .08 | .06 | | 285 | Paul Kilgus | .03 | .02 |
| 219 | Jay Buhner | .03 | .02 | | 286 | Mike Harkey | .10 | .08 |
| 220 | Ken Griffey, Jr. | 3.00 | 2.25 | | 287 | Lloyd McClendon | .05 | .04 |
| 221 | Drew Hall | .03 | .02 | | 288 | Damon Berryhill | .05 | .04 |
| 222 | Bobby Witt | .03 | .02 | | 289 | Ty Griffin | .10 | :08 |
| 223 | Jamie Moyer | .03 | .02 | | 290 | Ryne Sandberg | .15 | .11 |
| 224 | Charlie Hough | .03 | .02 | | 291 | Mark Grace | .30 | .25 |
| 225 | Nolan Ryan | .70 | .50 | | 292 | Curt Wilkerson | .03 | .02 |
| 226 | Jeff Russell | .05 | .04 | | 293 | Vance Law | .03 | .02 |
| 227 | Jim Sundberg | .03 | .02 | | 294 | Shawon Dunston | .08 | .06 |
| 228 | Julio Franco | .15 | .11 | | 295 | Jerome Walton | .15 | .11 |
| 229 | Buddy Bell | .03 | .02 | | 296 | Mitch Webster | .03 | .02 |
| 230 | Scott Fletcher | .03 | .02 | | 297 | Dwight Smith | .15 | .11 |
| 231 | Jeff Kunkel | .03 | .02 | | 298 | Andre Dawson | .15 | .11 |
| 232 | Steve Buechele | .03 | .02 | | 299 | Jeff Sellers | .03 | .02 |
| 233 | Monty Fariss | .25 | .20 | | 300 | Jose Rijo | .05 | .04 |
| 234 | Rick Leach | .03 | .02 | | 301 | John Franco | .05 | .04 |
| 235 | Ruben Sierra | .40 | .30 | | 302 | Rick Mahler | .03 | .02 |
| 236 | Cecil Espy | .05 | .04 | | 303 | Ron Robinson | .03 | .02 |
| 237 | Rafael Palmeiro | .10 | .08 | | 304 | Danny Jackson | .03 | .02 |
| 238 | Pete Incaviglia | .03 | .02 | | 305 | Rob Dibble | .08 | .06 |
| 239 | Dave Steib | .05 | .04 | | 306 | Tom Browning | .03 | .02 |
| 240 | Jeff Musselman | .03 | .02 | | 307 | Bo Diaz | .03 | .02 |
| 241 | Mike Flanagan | .03 | .02 | | 308 | Manny Trillo | .03 | .02 |
| 242 | Todd Stottlemyre | .05 | .04 | | 309 | Chris Sabo | .15 | .11 |

| | MT | NR MT | | | MT | NR MT |
|---|---|---|---|---|---|---|
| 310 | Ron Oester | .03 | .02 | 376 | Doc Gooden | .25 | .20 |
| 311 | Barry Larkin | .15 | .11 | 377 | Sid Fernandez | .05 | .04 |
| 312 | Todd Benzinger | .05 | .04 | 378 | Dave Proctor | .20 | .15 |
| 313 | Paul O'Neil | .05 | .04 | 379 | Gary Carter | .03 | .02 |
| 314 | Kal Daniels | .05 | .04 | 380 | Keith Miller | .05 | .04 |
| 315 | Joel Youngblood | .03 | .02 | 381 | Gregg Jefferies | .20 | .15 |
| 316 | Eric Davis | .25 | .20 | 382 | Tim Teufel | .03 | .02 |
| 317 | Dave Smith | .05 | .04 | 383 | Kevin Elster | .03 | .02 |
| 318 | Mark Portugal | .03 | .02 | 384 | Dave Magadan | .03 | .02 |
| 319 | Brian Meyer | .03 | .02 | 385 | Keith Hernandez | .05 | .04 |
| 320 | Jim Deshaies | .05 | .04 | 386 | Mookie Wilson | .05 | .04 |
| 321 | Juan Agosto | .03 | .02 | 387 | Darryl Strawberry | .40 | .30 |
| 322 | Mike Scott | .10 | .08 | 388 | Kevin McReynolds | .10 | .08 |
| 323 | Rick Rhoden | .03 | .02 | 389 | Mark Carreon | .05 | .04 |
| 324 | Jim Clancy | .03 | .02 | 390 | Jeff Parrett | .05 | .04 |
| 325 | Larry Andersen | .03 | .02 | 391 | Mike Maddux | .03 | .02 |
| 326 | Alex Trevino | .03 | .02 | 392 | Don Carman | .03 | .02 |
| 327 | Alan Ashby | .03 | .02 | 393 | Bruce Ruffin | .03 | .02 |
| 328 | Craig Reynolds | .03 | .02 | 394 | Ken Howell | .03 | .02 |
| 329 | Bill Doran | .03 | .02 | 395 | Steve Bedrosian | .05 | .04 |
| 330 | Rafael Ramirez | .03 | .02 | 396 | Floyd Youmans | .03 | .02 |
| 331 | Glenn Davis | .10 | .08 | 397 | Larry McWilliams | .03 | .02 |
| 332 | Willie Ansley | .25 | .20 | 398 | Pat Combs | .25 | .20 |
| 333 | Gerald Young | .03 | .02 | 399 | Steve Lake | .03 | .02 |
| 334 | Cameron Drew | .10 | .08 | 400 | Dickie Thon | .03 | .02 |
| 335 | Jay Howell | .05 | .04 | 401 | Ricky Jordan | .35 | .25 |
| 336 | Tim Belcher | .05 | .04 | 402 | Mike Schmidt | .40 | .30 |
| 337 | Fernando Valenzuela | | | 403 | Tom Herr | .03 | .02 |
| | | .05 | .04 | 404 | Chris James | .03 | .02 |
| 338 | Ricky Horton | .03 | .02 | 405 | Juan Samuel | .08 | .06 |
| 339 | Tim Leary | .03 | .02 | 406 | Von Hayes | .08 | .06 |
| 340 | Bill Bene | .15 | .11 | 407 | Ron Jones | .15 | .11 |
| 341 | Orel Hershiser | .20 | .15 | 408 | Curt Ford | .03 | .02 |
| 342 | Mike Scioscia | .05 | .04 | 409 | Bob Walk | .03 | .02 |
| 343 | Rick Dempsey | .03 | .02 | 410 | Jeff Robinson | .03 | .02 |
| 344 | Willie Randolph | .03 | .02 | 411 | Jim Gott | .03 | .02 |
| 345 | Alfredo Griffin | .03 | .02 | 412 | Scott Medvin | .03 | .02 |
| 346 | Eddie Murray | .08 | .06 | 413 | John Smiley | .03 | .02 |
| 347 | Mickey Hatcher | .03 | .02 | 414 | Bob Kipper | .03 | .02 |
| 348 | Mike Sharperson | .03 | .02 | 415 | Brian Fisher | .03 | .02 |
| 349 | John Shelby | .03 | .02 | 416 | Doug Drabek | .03 | .02 |
| 350 | Mike Marshall | .03 | .02 | 417 | Mike Lavalliere | .03 | .02 |
| 351 | Kirk Gibson | .05 | .04 | 418 | Ken Oberkfell | .03 | .02 |
| 352 | Mike Davis | .03 | .02 | 419 | Sid Bream | .03 | .02 |
| 353 | Bryn Smith | .03 | .02 | 420 | Austin Manahan | .20 | .15 |
| 354 | Pascual Perez | .03 | .02 | 421 | Jose Lind | .03 | .02 |
| 355 | Kevin Gross | .03 | .02 | 422 | Bobby Bonilla | .30 | .25 |
| 356 | Andy McGaffigan | .03 | .02 | 423 | Glenn Wilson | .03 | .02 |
| 357 | Brian Holman | .05 | .04 | 424 | Andy Van Slyke | .10 | .08 |
| 358 | Dave Wainhouse | .20 | .15 | 425 | Gary Redus | .03 | .02 |
| 359 | Denny Martinez | .03 | .02 | 426 | Barry Bonds | .30 | .25 |
| 360 | Tim Burke | .03 | .02 | 427 | Don Heinkel | .03 | .02 |
| 361 | Nelson Santovenia | .08 | .06 | 428 | Ken Dayley | .03 | .02 |
| 362 | Tim Wallach | .05 | .04 | 429 | Todd Worrell | .05 | .04 |
| 363 | Spike Owen | .03 | .02 | 430 | Brad DuVall | .20 | .15 |
| 364 | Rex Hudler | .03 | .02 | 431 | Jose DeLeon | .03 | .02 |
| 365 | Andres Galarraga | .08 | .06 | 432 | Joe Magrane | .10 | .08 |
| 366 | Otis Nixon | .03 | .02 | 433 | John Ericks | .20 | .15 |
| 367 | Hubie Brooks | .03 | .02 | 434 | Frank DiPino | .03 | .02 |
| 368 | Mike Aldrete | .03 | .02 | 435 | Tony Pena | .05 | .04 |
| 369 | Rock Raines | .08 | .06 | 436 | Ozzie Smith | .08 | .06 |
| 370 | Dave Martinez | .03 | .02 | 437 | Terry Pendleton | .03 | .02 |
| 371 | Bob Ojeda | .03 | .02 | 438 | Jose Oquendo | .03 | .02 |
| 372 | Ron Darling | .05 | .04 | 439 | Tim Jones | .05 | .04 |
| 373 | Wally Whitehurst | .20 | .15 | 440 | Pedro Guerrero | .10 | .08 |
| 374 | Randy Myers | .05 | .04 | 441 | Milt Thompson | .03 | .02 |
| 375 | David Cone | .05 | .04 | 442 | Willie McGee | .05 | .04 |

|     |                  | MT  | NR MT |
|-----|------------------|-----|-------|
| 443 | Vince Coleman    | .05 | .04   |
| 444 | Tom Brunansky    | .05 | .04   |
| 445 | Walt Terrell     | .03 | .02   |
| 446 | Eric Show        | .03 | .02   |
| 447 | Mark Davis       | .10 | .08   |
| 448 | Andy Benes       | .60 | .45   |
| 449 | Eddie Whitson    | .03 | .02   |
| 450 | Dennis Rasmussen | .03 | .02   |
| 451 | Bruce Hurst      | .03 | .02   |
| 452 | Pat Clements     | .03 | .02   |
| 453 | Benito Santiago  | .10 | .08   |
| 454 | Sandy Alomar, Jr.| .50 | .40   |
| 455 | Garry Templeton  | .03 | .02   |
| 456 | Jack Clark       | .05 | .04   |
| 457 | Tim Flannery     | .03 | .02   |
| 458 | Roberto Alomar   | .80 | .60   |
| 459 | Camelo Martinez  | .03 | .02   |
| 460 | John Kruk        | .03 | .02   |
| 461 | Tony Gwynn       | .20 | .15   |
| 462 | Jerald Clark     | .05 | .04   |
| 463 | Don Robinson     | .03 | .02   |
| 464 | Craig Lefferts   | .03 | .02   |
| 465 | Kelly Downs      | .03 | .02   |
| 466 | Rick Rueschel    | .05 | .04   |
| 467 | Scott Garrelts   | .03 | .02   |
| 468 | Wil Tejada       | .03 | .02   |
| 469 | Kirt Manwaring   | .10 | .08   |
| 470 | Terry Kennedy    | .03 | .02   |
| 471 | Jose Uribe       | .03 | .02   |
| 472 | Royce Clayton    | .50 | .40   |
| 473 | Robby Thompson   | .05 | .04   |
| 474 | Kevin Mitchell   | .25 | .20   |
| 475 | Ernie Riles      | .03 | .02   |
| 476 | Will Clark       | .40 | .30   |
| 477 | Donnell Nixon    | .03 | .02   |
| 478 | Candy Maldonado  | .03 | .02   |
| 479 | Tracy Jones      | .03 | .02   |
| 480 | Brett Butler     | .05 | .04   |
| 481 | Checklist        | .05 | .04   |
| 482 | Checklist        | .05 | .04   |
| 483 | Checklist        | .05 | .04   |
| 484 | Checklist        | .05 | .04   |

## 1990 Bowman

Bowman followed up its 1989 release with 528-card set in 1990. The 1990 cards follow the classic Bowman style featuring a full color photo bordered in white. The Bowman logo appears in the upper left corner. The player's team nickname and name appear on the bottom

border of the card photo. Unlike the 1989 set, the 1990 cards measure 2-1/2" by 3-1/2" in size. The card backs are horizontal and display the player's statistics against the teams in his respective league. Included in the set are special insert cards that feature a reproduction of a painting of a modern-day superstar done in the style of the 1951 Bowman cards. The paintings were produced for Bowman by artist Craig Pursley. The card backs contain a sweepstakes offer with a chance to win a complete set of 11 lithographs made from these paintings.

|     |                   | MT    | NR MT |
|-----|-------------------|-------|-------|
|     | Complete Set:     | 10.00 | 7.50  |
|     | Common Player:    | .05   | .04   |

| 1  | Tommy Greene      | .25 | .20 |
| 2  | Tom Glavine       | .06 | .05 |
| 3  | Andy Nezelek      | .08 | .06 |
| 4  | Mike Stanton      | .20 | .15 |
| 5  | Rick Lueken       | .08 | .06 |
| 6  | Kent Mercker      | .25 | .20 |
| 7  | Derek Lilliquist  | .06 | .05 |
| 8  | Charlie Liebrandt | .05 | .04 |
| 9  | Steve Avery       | .60 | .45 |
| 10 | John Smoltz       | .15 | .11 |
| 11 | Mark Lemke        | .08 | .06 |
| 12 | Lonnie Smith      | .06 | .05 |
| 13 | Oddibe McDowell   | .05 | .04 |
| 14 | Tyler Houston     | .10 | .08 |
| 15 | Jeff Blauser      | .05 | .04 |
| 16 | Ernie Whitt       | .05 | .04 |
| 17 | Alexis Infante    | .10 | .08 |
| 18 | Jim Presley       | .06 | .05 |
| 19 | Dale Murphy       | .10 | .08 |
| 20 | Nick Esasky       | .06 | .05 |
| 21 | Rick Sutcliffe    | .06 | .05 |
| 22 | Mike Bielecki     | .06 | .05 |
| 23 | Steve Wilson      | .10 | .08 |
| 24 | Kevin Blankenship | .10 | .08 |
| 25 | Mitch Williams    | .10 | .08 |
| 26 | Dean Wilkins      | .10 | .08 |
| 27 | Greg Maddux       | .12 | .09 |
| 28 | Mike Harkey       | .20 | .15 |
| 29 | Mark Grace        | .20 | .15 |
| 30 | Ryne Sandberg     | .40 | .30 |
| 31 | Greg Smith        | .20 | .15 |
| 32 | Dwight Smith      | .15 | .11 |
| 33 | Damon Berryhill   | .05 | .04 |
| 34 | Earl Cunningham   | .15 | .11 |
| 35 | Jerome Walton     | .25 | .20 |
| 36 | Lloyd McClendon   | .05 | .04 |
| 37 | Ty Griffin        | .20 | .15 |
| 38 | Shawon Dunston    | .10 | .08 |
| 39 | Andre Dawson      | .10 | .08 |
| 40 | Luis Salazar      | .05 | .04 |
| 41 | Tim Layana        | .20 | .15 |
| 42 | Rob Dibble        | .10 | .08 |
| 43 | Tom Browning      | .05 | .04 |

| | | MT | NR MT | | | MT | NR MT |
|---|---|---|---|---|---|---|---|
| 44 | Danny Jackson | .05 | .04 | 111 | Denny Martinez | .06 | .05 |
| 45 | Jose Rijo | .06 | .05 | 112 | Jerry Goff | .10 | .08 |
| 46 | Scott Scudder | .20 | .15 | 113 | Andres Galarraga | .08 | .06 |
| 47 | Randy Myers | .06 | .05 | 114 | Tim Welch | .12 | .09 |
| 48 | Brian Lane | .15 | .11 | 115 | Marquis Grissom | .50 | .40 |
| 49 | Paul O'Neill | .05 | .04 | 116 | Spike Owen | .05 | .04 |
| 50 | Barry Larkin | .10 | .08 | 117 | Larry Walker | .60 | .45 |
| 51 | Reggie Jefferson | .40 | .30 | 118 | Rock Raines | .08 | .06 |
| 52 | Jeff Branson | .20 | .15 | 119 | Delino DeShields | .40 | .30 |
| 53 | Chris Sabo | .08 | .06 | 120 | Tom Foley | .05 | .04 |
| 54 | Joe Oliver | .10 | .08 | 121 | Dave Martinez | .05 | .04 |
| 55 | Todd Benzinger | .05 | .04 | 122 | Frank Viola | .10 | .08 |
| 56 | Rolando Roomes | .05 | .04 | 123 | Julio Valera | .15 | .11 |
| 57 | Hal Morris | .30 | .25 | 124 | Alejandro Pena | .05 | .04 |
| 58 | Eric Davis | .15 | .11 | 125 | David Cone | .08 | .06 |
| 59 | Scott Bryant | .20 | .15 | 126 | Doc Gooden | .20 | .15 |
| 60 | Ken Griffey | .06 | .05 | 127 | Kevin Brown | .20 | .15 |
| 61 | Darryl Kile | .15 | .11 | 128 | John Franco | .08 | .06 |
| 62 | Dave Smith | .05 | .04 | 129 | Terry Bross | .25 | .20 |
| 63 | Mark Portugal | .05 | .04 | 130 | Blaine Beatty | .20 | .15 |
| 64 | Jeff Juden | .35 | .25 | 131 | Sid Fernandez | .08 | .06 |
| 65 | Bill Gullickson | .05 | .04 | 132 | Mike Marshall | .05 | .04 |
| 66 | Danny Darwin | .05 | .04 | 133 | Howard Johnson | .10 | .08 |
| 67 | Larry Andersen | .05 | .04 | 134 | Jaime Roseboro | .20 | .15 |
| 68 | Jose Cano | .10 | .08 | 135 | Alan Zinter | .20 | .15 |
| 69 | Dan Schatzeder | .05 | .04 | 136 | Keith Miller | .06 | .05 |
| 70 | Jim Deshaies | .05 | .04 | 137 | Kevin Elster | .05 | .04 |
| 71 | Mike Scott | .06 | .05 | 138 | Kevin McReynolds | .06 | .05 |
| 72 | Gerald Young | .05 | .04 | 139 | Barry Lyons | .05 | .04 |
| 73 | Ken Caminiti | .05 | .04 | 140 | Gregg Jefferies | .25 | .20 |
| 74 | Ken Oberkfell | .05 | .04 | 141 | Darryl Strawberry | .25 | .20 |
| 75 | Dave Rhode | .20 | .15 | 142 | Todd Hundley | .25 | .20 |
| 76 | Bill Doran | .06 | .05 | 143 | Scott Service | .15 | .11 |
| 77 | Andujar Cedeno | .20 | .15 | 144 | Chuck Malone | .15 | .11 |
| 78 | Craig Biggio | .08 | .06 | 145 | Steve Ontiveros | .05 | .04 |
| 79 | Karl Rhodes | .15 | .11 | 146 | Roger McDowell | .06 | .05 |
| 80 | Glenn Davis | .10 | .08 | 147 | Ken Howell | .05 | .04 |
| 81 | Eric Anthony | .30 | .25 | 148 | Pat Combs | .15 | .11 |
| 82 | John Wetteland | .20 | .15 | 149 | Jeff Parrett | .05 | .04 |
| 83 | Jay Howell | .06 | .05 | 150 | Chuck McElroy | .15 | .11 |
| 84 | Orel Hershiser | .10 | .08 | 151 | Jason Grimsley | .15 | .11 |
| 85 | Tim Belcher | .08 | .06 | 152 | Len Dykstra | .08 | .06 |
| 86 | Kiki Jones | .25 | .20 | 153 | Mickey Morandini | .15 | .11 |
| 87 | Mike Hartley | .20 | .15 | 154 | John Kruk | .05 | .04 |
| 88 | Ramon Martinez | .30 | .25 | 155 | Dickie Thon | .05 | .04 |
| 89 | Mike Scioscia | .06 | .05 | 156 | Ricky Jordan | .10 | .08 |
| 90 | Willie Randolph | .06 | .05 | 157 | Jeff Jackson | .10 | .08 |
| 91 | Juan Samuel | .06 | .05 | 158 | Darren Daulton | .05 | .04 |
| 92 | Jose Offerman | .30 | .25 | 159 | Tom Herr | .05 | .04 |
| 93 | Dave Hansen | .30 | .25 | 160 | Von Hayes | .06 | .05 |
| 94 | Jeff Hamilton | .05 | .04 | 161 | Dave Hollins | .50 | .40 |
| 95 | Alfredo Griffin | .05 | .04 | 162 | Carmelo Martinez | .05 | .04 |
| 96 | Tom Goodwin | .35 | .25 | 163 | Bob Walk | .05 | .04 |
| 97 | Kirk Gibson | .06 | .05 | 164 | Doug Drabek | .08 | .06 |
| 98 | Jose Vizcaino | .20 | .15 | 165 | Walt Terrell | .05 | .04 |
| 99 | Kal Daniels | .06 | .05 | 166 | Bill Landrum | .05 | .04 |
| 100 | Hubie Brooks | .06 | .05 | 167 | Scott Ruskin | .08 | .06 |
| 101 | Eddie Murray | .08 | .06 | 168 | Bob Patterson | .05 | .04 |
| 102 | Dennis Boyd | .05 | .04 | 169 | Bobby Bonilla | .10 | .08 |
| 103 | Tim Burke | .06 | .05 | 170 | Jose Lind | .05 | .04 |
| 104 | Bill Sampen | .20 | .15 | 171 | Andy Van Slyke | .08 | .06 |
| 105 | Brett Gideon | .06 | .05 | 172 | Mike LaValliere | .05 | .04 |
| 106 | Mark Gardner | .20 | .15 | 173 | Willie Greene | .20 | .15 |
| 107 | Howard Farmer | .15 | .11 | 174 | Jay Bell | .06 | .05 |
| 108 | Mel Rojas | .15 | .11 | 175 | Sid Bream | .05 | .04 |
| 109 | Kevin Gross | .05 | .04 | 176 | Tom Prince | .05 | .04 |
| 110 | Dave Schmidt | .05 | .04 | 177 | Wally Backman | .05 | .04 |

| | MT | NR MT | | | MT | NR MT |
|---|---|---|---|---|---|---|
| 178 Moises Alou | .25 | .20 | 245 Joe Price | .05 | .04 |
| 179 Steve Carter | .08 | .06 | 246 Curt Schilling | .05 | .04 |
| 180 Gary Redus | .05 | .04 | 247 Pete Harnisch | .06 | .05 |
| 181 Barry Bonds | .10 | .08 | 248 Mark Williamson | .05 | .04 |
| 182 Don Slaught | .05 | .04 | 249 Gregg Olson | .15 | .11 |
| 183 Joe Magrane | .06 | .05 | 250 Chris Myers | .15 | .11 |
| 184 Bryn Smith | .05 | .04 | 251 David Segui | .40 | .30 |
| 185 Todd Worrell | .06 | .05 | 252 Joe Orsulak | .05 | .04 |
| 186 Jose Deleon | .05 | .04 | 253 Craig Worthington | .05 | .04 |
| 187 Frank DiPino | .05 | .04 | 254 Mickey Tettleton | .06 | .05 |
| 188 John Tudor | .05 | .04 | 255 Cal Ripken | .20 | .15 |
| 189 Howard Hilton | .10 | .08 | 256 Billy Ripken | .05 | .04 |
| 190 John Ericks | .10 | .08 | 257 Randy Milligan | .06 | .05 |
| 191 Ken Dayley | .05 | .04 | 258 Brady Anderson | .05 | .04 |
| 192 Ray Lankford | .80 | .60 | 259 Chris Hoiles | .30 | .25 |
| 193 Todd Zeile | .80 | .60 | 260 Mike Devereaux | .05 | .04 |
| 194 Willie McGee | .06 | .05 | 261 Phil Bradley | .05 | .04 |
| 195 Ozzie Smith | .10 | .08 | 262 Leo Gomez | .30 | .25 |
| 196 Milt Thompson | .05 | .04 | 263 Lee Smith | .06 | .05 |
| 197 Terry Pendleton | .05 | .04 | 264 Mike Rochford | .06 | .05 |
| 198 Vince Coleman | .06 | .05 | 265 Jeff Reardon | .06 | .05 |
| 199 Paul Coleman | .25 | .20 | 266 Wes Gardner | .05 | .04 |
| 200 Jose Oquendo | .05 | .04 | 267 Mike Boddicker | .05 | .04 |
| 201 Pedro Guerrero | .06 | .05 | 268 Roger Clemens | .25 | .20 |
| 202 Tom Brunansky | .06 | .05 | 269 Rob Murphy | .05 | .04 |
| 203 Roger Smithberg | .10 | .08 | 270 Mickey Pina | .25 | .20 |
| 204 Eddie Whitson | .05 | .04 | 271 Tony Pena | .06 | .05 |
| 205 Dennis Rasmussen | .05 | .04 | 272 Jody Reed | .06 | .05 |
| 206 Craig Lefferts | .05 | .04 | 273 Kevin Romine | .05 | .04 |
| 207 Andy Benes | .15 | .11 | 274 Mike Greenwell | .08 | .06 |
| 208 Bruce Hurst | .06 | .05 | 275 Maurice Vaughn | .80 | .60 |
| 209 Eric Show | .05 | .04 | 276 Danny Heep | .05 | .04 |
| 210 Rafael Valdez | .10 | .08 | 277 Scott Cooper | .25 | .20 |
| 211 Joey Cora | .05 | .04 | 278 Greg Blosser | .25 | .20 |
| 212 Thomas Howard | .20 | .15 | 279 Dwight Evans | .06 | .05 |
| 213 Rob Nelson | .05 | .04 | 280 Ellis Burks | .08 | .06 |
| 214 Jack Clark | .06 | .05 | 281 Wade Boggs | .10 | .08 |
| 215 Garry Templeton | .05 | .04 | 282 Marty Barrett | .05 | .04 |
| 216 Fred Lynn | .05 | .04 | 283 Kirk McCaskill | .06 | .05 |
| 217 Tony Gwynn | .08 | .06 | 284 Mark Langston | .06 | .05 |
| 218 Benny Santiago | .08 | .06 | 285 Bert Blyleven | .06 | .05 |
| 219 Mike Pagliarulo | .05 | .04 | 286 Mike Fetters | .08 | .06 |
| 220 Joe Carter | .08 | .06 | 287 Kyle Abbott | .20 | .15 |
| 221 Roberto Alomar | .08 | .06 | 288 Jim Abbott | .10 | .08 |
| 222 Bip Roberts | .05 | .04 | 289 Chuck Finley | .06 | .05 |
| 223 Rick Reuschel | .05 | .04 | 290 Gary DiSarcina | .15 | .11 |
| 224 Russ Swan | .20 | .15 | 291 Dick Schofield | .05 | .04 |
| 225 Eric Gunderson | .20 | .15 | 292 Devon White | .06 | .05 |
| 226 Steve Bedrosian | .05 | .04 | 293 Bobby Rose | .15 | .11 |
| 227 Mike Remlinger | .40 | .30 | 294 Brian Downing | .05 | .04 |
| 228 Scott Garrelts | .05 | .04 | 295 Lance Parrish | .06 | .05 |
| 229 Ernie Camacho | .05 | .04 | 296 Jack Howell | .05 | .04 |
| 230 Andres Santana | .25 | .20 | 297 Claudell Washington | .05 | .04 |
| 231 Will Clark | .35 | .25 | 298 John Orton | .06 | .05 |
| 232 Kevin Mitchell | .25 | .20 | 299 Wally Joyner | .08 | .06 |
| 233 Robby Thompson | .05 | .04 | 300 Lee Stevens | .30 | .25 |
| 234 Bill Bathe | .06 | .05 | 301 Chili Davis | .05 | .04 |
| 235 Tony Perezchica | .08 | .06 | 302 Johnny Ray | .05 | .04 |
| 236 Gary Carter | .05 | .04 | 303 Greg Hibbard | .15 | .11 |
| 237 Brett Butler | .05 | .04 | 304 Eric King | .06 | .05 |
| 238 Matt Williams | .15 | .11 | 305 Jack McDowell | .08 | .06 |
| 239 Ernie Riles | .05 | .04 | 306 Bobby Thigpen | .08 | .06 |
| 240 Kevin Bass | .05 | .04 | 307 Adam Peterson | .05 | .04 |
| 241 Terry Kennedy | .05 | .04 | 308 Scott Radinsky | .20 | .15 |
| 242 Steve Hosey | .30 | .25 | 309 Wayne Edwards | .06 | .05 |
| 243 Ben McDonald | .40 | .30 | 310 Melido Perez | .06 | .05 |
| 244 Jeff Ballard | .05 | .04 | 311 Robin Ventura | .50 | .40 |

| | | MT | NR MT | | | | MT | NR MT |
|---|---|---|---|---|---|---|---|---|
| 312 | Sammy Sosa | .30 | .25 | | 379 | Bob Hamelin | .20 | .15 |
| 313 | Dan Pasqua | .05 | .04 | | 380 | Kevin Seitzer | .08 | .06 |
| 314 | Carlton Fisk | .08 | .06 | | 381 | Rey Palacios | .05 | .04 |
| 315 | Ozzie Guillen | .08 | .06 | | 382 | George Brett | .12 | .09 |
| 316 | Ivan Calderon | .08 | .06 | | 383 | Gerald Perry | .05 | .04 |
| 317 | Daryl Boston | .05 | .04 | | 384 | Teddy Higuera | .08 | .06 |
| 318 | Craig Grebeck | .15 | .11 | | 385 | Tom Filer | .05 | .04 |
| 319 | Scott Fletcher | .05 | .04 | | 386 | Dan Plesac | .06 | .05 |
| 320 | Frank Thomas | 3.00 | 2.25 | | 387 | Cal Eldred | .60 | .45 |
| 321 | Steve Lyons | .05 | .04 | | 388 | Jaime Navarro | .06 | .05 |
| 322 | Carlos Martinez | .10 | .08 | | 389 | Chris Bosio | .05 | .04 |
| 323 | Joe Skalski | .08 | .06 | | 390 | Randy Veres | .05 | .04 |
| 324 | Tom Candiotti | .05 | .04 | | 391 | Gary Sheffield | .20 | .15 |
| 325 | Greg Swindell | .06 | .05 | | 392 | George Canale | .10 | .08 |
| 326 | Steve Olin | .15 | .11 | | 393 | B.J. Surhoff | .06 | .05 |
| 327 | Kevin Wickander | .08 | .06 | | 394 | Tim McIntosh | .15 | .11 |
| 328 | Doug Jones | .06 | .05 | | 395 | Greg Brock | .05 | .04 |
| 329 | Jeff Shaw | .10 | .08 | | 396 | Greg Vaughn | .50 | .40 |
| 330 | Kevin Bearse | .10 | .08 | | 397 | Darryl Hamilton | .10 | .08 |
| 331 | Dion James | .05 | .04 | | 398 | Dave Parker | .10 | .08 |
| 332 | Jerry Browne | .06 | .05 | | 399 | Paul Molitor | .08 | .06 |
| 333 | Joey Belle | .40 | .30 | | 400 | Jim Gantner | .05 | .04 |
| 334 | Felix Fermin | .05 | .04 | | 401 | Rob Deer | .05 | .04 |
| 335 | Candy Maldonado | .06 | .05 | | 402 | Billy Spiers | .15 | .11 |
| 336 | Cory Snyder | .06 | .05 | | 403 | Glenn Braggs | .06 | .05 |
| 337 | Sandy Alomar | .30 | .25 | | 404 | Robin Yount | .15 | .11 |
| 338 | Mark Lewis | .12 | .09 | | 405 | Rick Aguilera | .05 | .04 |
| 339 | Carlos Baerga | .40 | .30 | | 406 | Johnny Ard | .15 | .11 |
| 340 | Chris James | .05 | .04 | | 407 | Kevin Tapani | .25 | .20 |
| 341 | Brook Jacoby | .06 | .05 | | 408 | Park Pittman | .20 | .15 |
| 342 | Keith Hernandez | .06 | .05 | | 409 | Allan Anderson | .05 | .04 |
| 343 | Frank Tanana | .05 | .04 | | 410 | Juan Berenguer | .05 | .04 |
| 344 | Scott Aldred | .15 | .11 | | 411 | Willie Banks | .40 | .30 |
| 345 | Mike Henneman | .06 | .05 | | 412 | Rich Yett | .05 | .04 |
| 346 | Steve Wapnick | .15 | .11 | | 413 | Dave West | .08 | .06 |
| 347 | Greg Gohr | .15 | .11 | | 414 | Greg Gagne | .05 | .04 |
| 348 | Eric Stone | .15 | .11 | | 415 | Chuck Knoblauch | 1.00 | .70 |
| 349 | Brian DuBois | .10 | .08 | | 416 | Randy Bush | .05 | .04 |
| 350 | Kevin Ritz | .10 | .08 | | 417 | Gary Gaetti | .08 | .06 |
| 351 | Rico Brogna | .10 | .08 | | 418 | Kent Hrbek | .08 | .06 |
| 352 | Mike Heath | .05 | .04 | | 419 | Al Newman | .05 | .04 |
| 353 | Alan Trammell | .08 | .06 | | 420 | Danny Gladden | .05 | .04 |
| 354 | Chet Lemon | .06 | .05 | | 421 | Paul Sorrento | .15 | .11 |
| 355 | Dave Bergman | .05 | .04 | | 422 | Derek Parks | .25 | .20 |
| 356 | Lou Whitaker | .08 | .06 | | 423 | Scott Leius | .20 | .15 |
| 357 | Cecil Fielder | .40 | .30 | | 424 | Kirby Puckett | .20 | .15 |
| 358 | Milt Cuyler | .20 | .15 | | 425 | Willie Smith | .20 | .15 |
| 359 | Tony Phillips | .06 | .05 | | 426 | Dave Righetti | .08 | .06 |
| 360 | Travis Fryman | 1.25 | .90 | | 427 | Jeff Robinson | .05 | .04 |
| 361 | Ed Romero | .05 | .04 | | 428 | Alan Mills | .20 | .15 |
| 362 | Lloyd Moseby | .06 | .05 | | 429 | Tim Leary | .05 | .04 |
| 363 | Mark Gubicza | .08 | .06 | | 430 | Pascual Perez | .05 | .04 |
| 364 | Bret Saberhagen | .10 | .08 | | 431 | Alvaro Espinoza | .05 | .04 |
| 365 | Tom Gordon | .15 | .11 | | 432 | Dave Winfield | .12 | .09 |
| 366 | Steve Farr | .05 | .04 | | 433 | Jesse Barfield | .06 | .05 |
| 367 | Kevin Appier | .30 | .25 | | 434 | Randy Velarde | .05 | .04 |
| 368 | Storm Davis | .05 | .04 | | 435 | Rick Cerone | .05 | .04 |
| 369 | Mark Davis | .05 | .04 | | 436 | Steve Balboni | .05 | .04 |
| 370 | Jeff Montgomery | .06 | .05 | | 437 | Mel Hall | .05 | .04 |
| 371 | Frank White | .06 | .05 | | 438 | Bob Geren | .06 | .05 |
| 372 | Brent Mayne | .20 | .15 | | 439 | Bernie Williams | .40 | .30 |
| 373 | Bob Boone | .06 | .05 | | 440 | Kevin Maas | .40 | .30 |
| 374 | Jim Eisenreich | .05 | .04 | | 441 | Mike Blowers | .15 | .11 |
| 375 | Danny Tartabull | .08 | .06 | | 442 | Steve Sax | .08 | .06 |
| 376 | Kurt Stillwell | .05 | .04 | | 443 | Don Mattingly | .35 | .25 |
| 377 | Bill Pecota | .05 | .04 | | 444 | Roberto Kelly | .08 | .06 |
| 378 | Bo Jackson | .40 | .30 | | 445 | Mike Moore | .06 | .05 |

| | | MT | NR MT |
|---|---|---|---|
| 446 | Reggie Harris | .15 | .11 |
| 447 | Scott Sanderson | .05 | .04 |
| 448 | Dave Otto | .05 | .04 |
| 449 | Dave Stewart | .08 | .06 |
| 450 | Rick Honeycutt | .05 | .04 |
| 451 | Dennis Eckersley | .08 | .06 |
| 452 | Carney Lansford | .06 | .05 |
| 453 | Scott Hemond | .15 | .11 |
| 454 | Mark McGwire | .20 | .15 |
| 455 | Felix Jose | .15 | .11 |
| 456 | Terry Steinbach | .06 | .05 |
| 457 | Rickey Henderson | .25 | .20 |
| 458 | Dave Henderson | .06 | .05 |
| 459 | Mike Gallego | .05 | .04 |
| 460 | Jose Canseco | .50 | .40 |
| 461 | Walt Weiss | .06 | .05 |
| 462 | Ken Phelps | .05 | .04 |
| 463 | Darren Lewis | .40 | .30 |
| 464 | Ron Hassey | .05 | .04 |
| 465 | Roger Salkeld | .30 | .25 |
| 466 | Scott Bankhead | .06 | .05 |
| 467 | Keith Comstock | .05 | .04 |
| 468 | Randy Johnson | .10 | .08 |
| 469 | Erik Hanson | .10 | .08 |
| 470 | Mike Schooler | .06 | .05 |
| 471 | Gary Eave | .15 | .11 |
| 472 | Jeffrey Leonard | .06 | .05 |
| 473 | Dave Valle | .05 | .04 |
| 474 | Omar Vizquel | .05 | .04 |
| 475 | Pete O'Brien | .05 | .04 |
| 476 | Henry Cotto | .05 | .04 |
| 477 | Jay Buhner | .06 | .05 |
| 478 | Harold Reynolds | .06 | .05 |
| 479 | Alvin Davis | .08 | .06 |
| 480 | Darnell Coles | .05 | .04 |
| 481 | Ken Griffey, Jr. | 2.00 | 1.50 |
| 482 | Greg Briley | .12 | .09 |
| 483 | Scott Bradley | .05 | .04 |
| 484 | Tino Martinez | .40 | .30 |
| 485 | Jeff Russell | .06 | .05 |
| 486 | Nolan Ryan | .40 | .30 |
| 487 | Robb Nen | .20 | .15 |
| 488 | Kevin Brown | .06 | .05 |
| 489 | Brian Bohanon | .20 | .15 |
| 490 | Ruben Sierra | .15 | .11 |
| 491 | Pete Incaviglia | .06 | .05 |
| 492 | Juan Gonzalez | 2.00 | 1.50 |
| 493 | Steve Buechele | .05 | .04 |
| 494 | Scott Coolbaugh | .15 | .11 |
| 495 | Geno Petralli | .05 | .04 |
| 496 | Rafael Palmeiro | .08 | .06 |
| 497 | Julio Franco | .08 | .06 |
| 498 | Gary Pettis | .05 | .04 |
| 499 | Donald Harris | .20 | .15 |
| 500 | Monty Fariss | .20 | .15 |
| 501 | Harold Baines | .08 | .06 |
| 502 | Cecil Espy | .05 | .04 |
| 503 | Jack Daugherty | .08 | .06 |
| 504 | Willie Blair | .15 | .11 |
| 505 | Dave Steib | .06 | .05 |
| 506 | Tom Henke | .06 | .05 |
| 507 | John Cerutti | .05 | .04 |
| 508 | Paul Kilgus | .05 | .04 |
| 509 | Jimmy Key | .06 | .05 |
| 510 | John Olerud | .40 | .30 |
| 511 | Ed Sprague | .25 | .20 |
| 512 | Manny Lee | .05 | .04 |

| | | MT | NR MT |
|---|---|---|---|
| 513 | Fred McGriff | .08 | .06 |
| 514 | Glenallen Hill | .10 | .08 |
| 515 | George Bell | .08 | .06 |
| 516 | Mookie Wilson | .06 | .05 |
| 517 | Luis Sojo | .15 | .11 |
| 518 | Nelson Liriano | .05 | .04 |
| 519 | Kelly Gruber | .08 | .06 |
| 520 | Greg Myers | .06 | .05 |
| 521 | Pat Borders | .06 | .05 |
| 522 | Junior Felix | .25 | .20 |
| 523 | Eddie Zosky | .25 | .20 |
| 524 | Tony Fernandez | .06 | .05 |
| 525 | Checklist | .05 | .04 |
| 526 | Checklist | .05 | .04 |
| 527 | Checklist | .05 | .04 |
| 528 | Checklist | .05 | .04 |

## 1991 Bowman

The 1991 Bowman set features 704 cards compared to 528 cards in the 1990 issue. The cards feature the 1953 Bowman style. Special Rod Carew cards, slugger cards and foil cards are included. The set is numbered by teams. Like the 1989 and 1990 issues, the card backs feature a breakdown of performance against each other team in the league.

| | | MT | NR MT |
|---|---|---|---|
| Complete Set: | | 15.00 | 11.00 |
| Common Player: | | .05 | .04 |
| 1 | Rod Carew-I | .15 | .11 |
| 2 | Rod Carew-II | .15 | .11 |
| 3 | Rod Carew-III | .15 | .11 |
| 4 | Rod Carew-IV | .15 | .11 |
| 5 | Rod Carew-V | .15 | .11 |
| 6 | Willie Fraser | .05 | .04 |
| 7 | John Olerud | .10 | .08 |
| 8 | William Suero | .15 | .11 |
| 9 | Roberto Alomar | .10 | .08 |
| 10 | Todd Stottlemyre | .06 | .05 |
| 11 | Joe Carter | .10 | .08 |
| 12 | Steve Karsay | .20 | .15 |
| 13 | Mark Whiten | .20 | .15 |
| 14 | Pat Borders | .05 | .04 |
| 15 | Mike Timlin | .15 | .11 |

| | | MT | NR MT | | | | MT | NR MT |
|---|---|---|---|---|---|---|---|---|
| 16 | Tom Henke | .06 | .05 | | 83 | Glenn Davis | .08 | .06 |
| 17 | Eddie Zosky | .08 | .06 | | 84 | Joe Orsulak | .05 | .04 |
| 18 | Kelly Gruber | .08 | .06 | | 85 | Mark Williamson | .05 | .04 |
| 19 | Jimmy Key | .06 | .05 | | 86 | Ben McDonald | .15 | .11 |
| 20 | Jerry Schunk | .12 | .09 | | 87 | Billy Ripken | .05 | .04 |
| 21 | Manny Lee | .05 | .04 | | 88 | Leo Gomez | .08 | .06 |
| 22 | Dave Steib | .08 | .06 | | 89 | Bob Melvin | .05 | .04 |
| 23 | Pat Hentgen | .12 | .09 | | 90 | Jeff Robinson | .05 | .04 |
| 24 | Glenallen Hill | .08 | .06 | | 91 | Jose Mesa | .05 | .04 |
| 25 | Rene Gonzales | .05 | .04 | | 92 | Gregg Olson | .08 | .06 |
| 26 | Ed Sprague | .10 | .08 | | 93 | Mike Devereaux | .06 | .05 |
| 27 | Ken Dayley | .05 | .04 | | 94 | Luis Mercedes | .20 | .15 |
| 28 | Pat Tabler | .05 | .04 | | 95 | Arthur Rhodes | .20 | .15 |
| 29 | Denis Boucher | .12 | .09 | | 96 | Juan Bell | .05 | .04 |
| 30 | Devon White | .08 | .06 | | 97 | Mike Mussina | .60 | .45 |
| 31 | Dante Bichette | .05 | .04 | | 98 | Jeff Ballard | .05 | .04 |
| 32 | Paul Molitor | .08 | .06 | | 99 | Chris Hoiles | .08 | .06 |
| 33 | Greg Vaughn | .08 | .06 | | 100 | Brady Anderson | .05 | .04 |
| 34 | Dan Plesac | .05 | .04 | | 101 | Bob Milacki | .05 | .04 |
| 35 | Chris George | .12 | .09 | | 102 | David Segui | .06 | .05 |
| 36 | Tim McIntosh | .08 | .06 | | 103 | Dwight Evans | .06 | .05 |
| 37 | Franklin Stubbs | .05 | .04 | | 104 | Cal Ripken | .12 | .09 |
| 38 | Bo Dodson | .15 | .11 | | 105 | Mike Linskey | .12 | .09 |
| 39 | Ron Robinson | .05 | .04 | | 106 | Jeff Tackett | .12 | .09 |
| 40 | Ed Nunez | .05 | .04 | | 107 | Jeff Reardon | .08 | .06 |
| 41 | Greg Brock | .05 | .04 | | 108 | Dana Kiecker | .05 | .04 |
| 42 | Jaime Navarro | .06 | .05 | | 109 | Ellis Burks | .08 | .06 |
| 43 | Chris Bosio | .05 | .05 | | 110 | Dave Owen | .12 | .09 |
| 44 | B.J. Surhoff | .06 | .05 | | 111 | Danny Darwin | .05 | .04 |
| 45 | Chris Johnson | .12 | .09 | | 112 | Mo Vaughn | .20 | .15 |
| 46 | Willie Randolph | .06 | .05 | | 113 | Jeff McNeely | .25 | .20 |
| 47 | Narciso Elvira | .10 | .08 | | 114 | Tom Bolton | .05 | .04 |
| 48 | Jim Gantner | .05 | .04 | | 115 | Greg Blosser | .12 | .09 |
| 49 | Kevin Brown | .05 | .04 | | 116 | Mike Greenwell | .10 | .08 |
| 50 | Julio Machado | .05 | .04 | | 117 | Phil Plantier | .80 | .60 |
| 51 | Chuck Crim | .05 | .04 | | 118 | Roger Clemens | .15 | .11 |
| 52 | Gary Sheffield | .08 | .06 | | 119 | John Marzano | .05 | .04 |
| 53 | Angel Miranda | .12 | .09 | | 120 | Jody Reed | .05 | .04 |
| 54 | Teddy Higuera | .06 | .05 | | 121 | Scott Taylor | .12 | .09 |
| 55 | Robin Yount | .10 | .08 | | 122 | Jack Clark | .06 | .05 |
| 56 | Cal Eldred | .12 | .09 | | 123 | Derek Livernois | .12 | .09 |
| 57 | Sandy Alomar | .08 | .06 | | 124 | Tony Pena | .05 | .04 |
| 58 | Greg Swindell | .06 | .05 | | 125 | Tom Brunansky | .05 | .04 |
| 59 | Brook Jacoby | .06 | .05 | | 126 | Carlos Quintana | .05 | .04 |
| 60 | Efrain Valdez | .08 | .06 | | 127 | Tim Naehring | .10 | .08 |
| 61 | Ever Magallanes | .12 | .09 | | 128 | Matt Young | .05 | .04 |
| 62 | Tom Candiotti | .05 | .04 | | 129 | Wade Boggs | .15 | .11 |
| 63 | Eric King | .05 | .04 | | 130 | Kevin Morton | .15 | .11 |
| 64 | Alex Cole | .05 | .04 | | 131 | Pete Incaviglia | .05 | .04 |
| 65 | Charles Nagy | .08 | .06 | | 132 | Rob Deer | .05 | .04 |
| 66 | Mitch Webster | .05 | .04 | | 133 | Bill Gullickson | .05 | .04 |
| 67 | Chris James | .05 | .04 | | 134 | Rico Brogna | .12 | .09 |
| 68 | Jim Thome | .60 | .45 | | 135 | Lloyd Moseby | .05 | .04 |
| 69 | Carlos Baerga | .06 | .05 | | 136 | Cecil Fielder | .15 | .11 |
| 70 | Mark Lewis | .08 | .06 | | 137 | Tony Phillips | .05 | .04 |
| 71 | Jerry Browne | .05 | .04 | | 138 | Mark Leiter | .05 | .04 |
| 72 | Jesse Orosco | .05 | .04 | | 139 | John Cerutti | .05 | .04 |
| 73 | Mike Huff | .06 | .05 | | 140 | Mickey Tettleton | .06 | .05 |
| 74 | Jose Escobar | .12 | .09 | | 141 | Milt Cuyler | .10 | .08 |
| 75 | Jeff Manto | .06 | .05 | | 142 | Greg Gohr | .10 | .08 |
| 76 | Turner Ward | .10 | .08 | | 143 | Tony Bernazard | .05 | .04 |
| 77 | Doug Jones | .05 | .04 | | 144 | Dan Gakeler | .12 | .09 |
| 78 | Bruce Egloff | .12 | .09 | | 145 | Travis Fryman | .30 | .25 |
| 79 | Tim Costo | .20 | .15 | | 146 | Dan Petry | .05 | .04 |
| 80 | Beau Allred | .06 | .05 | | 147 | Scott Aldred | .08 | .06 |
| 81 | Albert Belle | .20 | .15 | | 148 | John DeSilva | .12 | .09 |
| 82 | John Farrell | .05 | .04 | | 149 | Rusty Meacham | .12 | .09 |

| | | MT | NR MT | | | | MT | NR MT |
|---|---|---|---|---|---|---|---|---|
| 150 | Lou Whitaker | .06 | .05 | | 216 | Terry Steinbach | .06 | .05 |
| 151 | Dave Haas | .06 | .05 | | 217 | Ernie Riles | .05 | .04 |
| 152 | Luis de los Santos | .05 | .04 | | 218 | Todd Van Poppel | 1.25 | .90 |
| 153 | Ivan Cruz | .12 | .09 | | 219 | Mike Gallego | .05 | .04 |
| 154 | Alan Trammell | .08 | .06 | | 220 | Curt Young | .05 | .04 |
| 155 | Pat Kelly | .35 | .25 | | 221 | Todd Burns | .05 | .04 |
| 156 | Carl Everett | .35 | .25 | | 222 | Vance Law | .05 | .04 |
| 157 | Greg Cadaret | .05 | .04 | | 223 | Eric Show | .05 | .04 |
| 158 | Kevin Maas | .15 | .11 | | 224 | Don Peters | .15 | .11 |
| 159 | Jeff Johnson | .15 | .11 | | 225 | Dave Stewart | .10 | .08 |
| 160 | Willie Smith | .15 | .11 | | 226 | Dave Henderson | .06 | .05 |
| 161 | Gerald Williams | .20 | .15 | | 227 | Jose Canseco | .20 | .15 |
| 162 | Mike Humphreys | .15 | .11 | | 228 | Walt Weiss | .06 | .05 |
| 163 | Alvaro Espinoza | .05 | .04 | | 229 | Dann Howitt | .06 | .05 |
| 164 | Matt Nokes | .05 | .04 | | 230 | Willie Wilson | .05 | .04 |
| 165 | Wade Taylor | .12 | .09 | | 231 | Harold Baines | .06 | .05 |
| 166 | Roberto Kelly | .08 | .06 | | 232 | Scott Hemond | .06 | .05 |
| 167 | John Habyan | .05 | .04 | | 233 | Joe Slusarski | .12 | .09 |
| 168 | Steve Farr | .05 | .04 | | 234 | Mark McGwire | .10 | .08 |
| 169 | Jesse Barfield | .05 | .04 | | 235 | Kirk Dressendorfer | .30 | .25 |
| 170 | Steve Sax | .06 | .05 | | 236 | Craig Paquette | .15 | .11 |
| 171 | Jim Leyritz | .05 | .04 | | 237 | Dennis Eckersley | .10 | .08 |
| 172 | Robert Eenhoorn | .15 | .11 | | 238 | Dana Allison | .12 | .09 |
| 173 | Bernie Williams | .15 | .11 | | 239 | Scott Bradley | .05 | .04 |
| 174 | Scott Lusader | .05 | .04 | | 240 | Brian Holman | .06 | .05 |
| 175 | Torey Lovullo | .08 | .06 | | 241 | Mike Schooler | .06 | .05 |
| 176 | Chuck Cary | .05 | .04 | | 242 | Rich Delucia | .12 | .09 |
| 177 | Scott Sanderson | .05 | .04 | | 243 | Edgar Martinez | .08 | .06 |
| 178 | Don Mattingly | .15 | .11 | | 244 | Henry Cotto | .05 | .04 |
| 179 | Mel Hall | .06 | .05 | | 245 | Omar Vizquel | .05 | .04 |
| 180 | Juan Gonzalez | .30 | .25 | | 246 | Ken Griffey, Jr. | 1.50 | 1.25 |
| 181 | Hensley Meulens | .08 | .06 | | 247 | Jay Buhner | .06 | .05 |
| 182 | Jose Offerman | .15 | .11 | | 248 | Bill Krueger | .05 | .04 |
| 183 | Jeff Bagwell (Foil) | 1.50 | 1.25 | | 249 | Dave Fleming | .50 | .40 |
| 184 | Jeff Conine | .20 | .15 | | 250 | Patrick Lennon | .15 | .11 |
| 185 | Henry Rodriguez (Foil) | | | | 251 | Dave Valle | .05 | .04 |
| | | .25 | .20 | | 252 | Harold Reynolds | .06 | .05 |
| 186 | Jimmie Reese (Foil) | .15 | .11 | | 253 | Randy Johnson | .08 | .06 |
| 187 | Kyle Abbott | .10 | .08 | | 254 | Scott Bankhead | .06 | .05 |
| 188 | Lance Parrish | .06 | .05 | | 255 | Ken Griffey | .08 | .06 |
| 189 | Rafael Montalvo | .12 | .09 | | 256 | Greg Briley | .05 | .04 |
| 190 | Floyd Bannister | .05 | .04 | | 257 | Tino Martinez | .12 | .09 |
| 191 | Dick Schofield | .05 | .04 | | 258 | Alvin Davis | .06 | .05 |
| 192 | Scott Lewis | .12 | .09 | | 259 | Pete O'Brien | .05 | .04 |
| 193 | Jeff Robinson | .05 | .04 | | 260 | Erik Hanson | .08 | .06 |
| 194 | Kent Anderson | .05 | .04 | | 261 | Bret Boone | .15 | .11 |
| 195 | Wally Joyner | .10 | .08 | | 262 | Roger Salkeld | .15 | .11 |
| 196 | Chuck Finley | .08 | .06 | | 263 | Dave Burba | .08 | .06 |
| 197 | Luis Sojo | .05 | .04 | | 264 | Kerry Woodson | .12 | .09 |
| 198 | Jeff Richardson | .08 | .06 | | 265 | Julio Franco | .08 | .06 |
| 199 | Dave Parker | .08 | .06 | | 266 | Dan Peltier | .20 | .15 |
| 200 | Jim Abbott | .08 | .06 | | 267 | Jeff Russell | .05 | .04 |
| 201 | Junior Felix | .06 | .05 | | 268 | Steve Buechele | .06 | .05 |
| 202 | Mark Langston | .08 | .06 | | 269 | Donald Harris | .12 | .09 |
| 203 | Tim Salmon | .20 | .15 | | 270 | Robb Nen | .10 | .08 |
| 204 | Cliff Young | .08 | .06 | | 271 | Rich Gossage | .06 | .05 |
| 205 | Scott Bailes | .05 | .04 | | 272 | Ivan Rodriguez | 1.50 | 1.25 |
| 206 | Bobby Rose | .06 | .05 | | 273 | Jeff Huson | .06 | .05 |
| 207 | Gary Gaetti | .06 | .05 | | 274 | Kevin Brown | .06 | .05 |
| 208 | Ruben Amaro | .12 | .09 | | 275 | Dan Smith | .15 | .11 |
| 209 | Luis Polonia | .06 | .05 | | 276 | Gary Pettis | .05 | .04 |
| 210 | Dave Winfield | .10 | .08 | | 277 | Jack Daugherty | .05 | .04 |
| 211 | Bryan Harvey | .06 | .05 | | 278 | Mike Jeffcoat | .05 | .04 |
| 212 | Mike Moore | .05 | .04 | | 279 | Brad Arnsbarg | .06 | .05 |
| 213 | Rickey Henderson | .15 | .11 | | 280 | Nolan Ryan | .25 | .20 |
| 214 | Steve Chitren | .15 | .11 | | 281 | Eric McCray | .12 | .09 |
| 215 | Bob Welch | .06 | .05 | | 282 | Scott Chiamparino | .08 | .06 |

| | | MT | NR MT | | | MT | NR MT |
|---|---|---|---|---|---|---|---|
| 283 | Ruben Sierra | .15 | .11 | 350 | Sammy Sosa | .10 | .08 |
| 284 | Geno Petralli | .05 | .04 | 351 | Alex Fernandez | .20 | .15 |
| 285 | Monty Fariss | .08 | .06 | 352 | Jack McDowell | .10 | .08 |
| 286 | Rafael Palmeiro | .08 | .06 | 353 | Bob Wickman | .35 | .25 |
| 287 | Bobb Witt | .06 | .05 | 354 | Wilson Alvarez | .15 | .11 |
| 288 | Dean Palmer | .25 | .20 | 355 | Charlie Hough | .05 | .04 |
| 289 | Tony Scruggs | .12 | .09 | 356 | Ozzie Guillen | .06 | .05 |
| 290 | Kenny Rogers | .05 | .04 | 357 | Cory Snyder | .05 | .04 |
| 291 | Bret Saberhagen | .08 | .06 | 358 | Robin Ventura | .15 | .11 |
| 292 | Brian McRae | .40 | .30 | 359 | Scott Fletcher | .05 | .04 |
| 293 | Storm Davis | .05 | .04 | 360 | Cesar Bernhardt | .12 | .09 |
| 294 | Danny Tartabull | .08 | .06 | 361 | Dan Pasqua | .05 | .04 |
| 295 | David Howard | .12 | .09 | 362 | Rock Raines | .08 | .06 |
| 296 | Mike Boddicker | .06 | .05 | 363 | Brian Drahman | .12 | .09 |
| 297 | Joel Johnston | .12 | .09 | 364 | Wayne Edwards | .05 | .04 |
| 298 | Tim Spehr | .15 | .11 | 365 | Scott Radinsky | .06 | .05 |
| 299 | Hector Wagner | .12 | .09 | 366 | Frank Thomas | 1.50 | 1.25 |
| 300 | George Brett | .12 | .09 | 367 | Cecil Fielder (AL Slugger) | .10 | .08 |
| 301 | Mike Macfarlane | .06 | .05 | 368 | Julio Franco (AL Slugger) | .10 | .08 |
| 302 | Kirk Gibson | .06 | .05 | | | | |
| 303 | Harvey Pulliam | .15 | .11 | 369 | Kelly Gruber (AL Slugger) | .08 | .06 |
| 304 | Jim Eisenreich | .05 | .04 | | | | |
| 305 | Kevin Seitzer | .06 | .05 | 370 | Alan Trammell (AL Slugger) | .08 | .06 |
| 306 | Mark Davis | .05 | .04 | | | | |
| 307 | Kurt Stillwell | .05 | .04 | 371 | Rickey Henderson (AL Slugger) | .10 | .08 |
| 308 | Jeff Montgomery | .06 | .05 | | | | |
| 309 | Kevin Appier | .06 | .05 | 372 | Jose Canseco (AL Slugger) | .15 | .11 |
| 310 | Bob Hamelin | .10 | .08 | | | | |
| 311 | Tom Gordon | .06 | .05 | 373 | Ellis Burks (AL Slugger) | .08 | .06 |
| 312 | Kerwin Moore | .12 | .09 | | | | |
| 313 | Hugh Walker | .12 | .09 | 374 | Lance Parrish (AL Slugger) | .06 | .05 |
| 314 | Terry Shumpert | .05 | .04 | | | | |
| 315 | Warren Cromartie | .05 | .04 | 375 | Dave Parker (AL Slugger) | .08 | .06 |
| 316 | Gary Thurman | .05 | .04 | | | | |
| 317 | Steve Bedrosian | .05 | .04 | 376 | Eddie Murray (NL Slugger) | .08 | .06 |
| 318 | Danny Gladden | .05 | .04 | | | | |
| 319 | Jack Morris | .08 | .06 | 377 | Ryne Sandberg (NL Slugger) | .12 | .09 |
| 320 | Kirby Puckett | .15 | .11 | | | | |
| 321 | Kent Hrbek | .08 | .06 | 378 | Matt Williams (NL Slugger) | .08 | .06 |
| 322 | Kevin Tapani | .08 | .06 | | | | |
| 323 | Denny Neagle | .25 | .20 | 379 | Barry Larkin (NL Slugger) | .08 | .06 |
| 324 | Rich Garces | .12 | .09 | | | | |
| 325 | Larry Casian | .10 | .08 | 380 | Barry Bonds (NL Slugger) | .10 | .08 |
| 326 | Shane Mack | .08 | .06 | | | | |
| 327 | Allan Anderson | .05 | .04 | 381 | Bobby Bonilla (NL Slugger) | .10 | .08 |
| 328 | Junior Ortiz | .05 | .04 | | | | |
| 329 | Paul Abbott | .10 | .08 | 382 | Darryl Strawberry (NL Slugger) | .10 | .08 |
| 330 | Chuck Knoblauch | .30 | .25 | | | | |
| 331 | Chili Davis | .08 | .06 | 383 | Benny Santiago (NL Slugger) | .06 | .05 |
| 332 | Todd Ritchie | .12 | .09 | | | | |
| 333 | Brian Harper | .06 | .05 | 384 | Don Robinson (NL Slugger) | .05 | .04 |
| 334 | Rick Aguilera | .06 | .05 | | | | |
| 335 | Scott Erickson | .60 | .45 | 385 | Paul Coleman | .10 | .08 |
| 336 | Pedro Munoz | .30 | .25 | 386 | Milt Thompson | .05 | .04 |
| 337 | Scott Leuis | .10 | .08 | 387 | Lee Smith | .06 | .05 |
| 338 | Greg Gagne | .05 | .04 | 388 | Ray Lankford | .15 | .11 |
| 339 | Mike Pagliarulo | .05 | .04 | 389 | Tom Pagnozzi | .06 | .05 |
| 340 | Terry Leach | .05 | .04 | 390 | Ken Hill | .06 | .05 |
| 341 | Willie Banks | .10 | .08 | 391 | Jamie Moyer | .05 | .04 |
| 342 | Bobby Thigpen | .06 | .05 | 392 | Greg Carmona | .12 | .09 |
| 343 | Roberto Hernandez | .15 | .11 | 393 | John Ericks | .10 | .08 |
| 344 | Melido Perez | .05 | .04 | 394 | Bob Tewksbury | .05 | .04 |
| 345 | Carlton Fisk | .10 | .08 | 395 | Jose Oquendo | .05 | .04 |
| 346 | Norberto Martin | .12 | .09 | 396 | Rheal Cormier | .30 | .25 |
| 347 | Johnny Ruffin | .12 | .09 | 397 | Mike Milchin | .12 | .09 |
| 348 | Jeff Carter | .12 | .09 | 398 | Ozzie Smith | .10 | .08 |
| 349 | Lance Johnson | .05 | .04 | | | | |

| | MT | NR MT | | | MT | NR MT |
|---|---|---|---|---|---|---|
| 399 | Aaron Holbert | .15 | .11 | 465 | Chris Donnels | .15 | .11 |
| 400 | Jose DeLeon | .05 | .04 | 466 | Anthony Young | .15 | .11 |
| 401 | Felix Jose | .30 | .25 | 467 | Todd Hundley | .12 | .09 |
| 402 | Juan Agosto | .05 | .04 | 468 | Rick Cerone | .05 | .04 |
| 403 | Pedro Guerrero | .08 | .06 | 469 | Kevin Elster | .05 | .04 |
| 404 | Todd Zeile | .08 | .06 | 470 | Wally Whitehurst | .06 | .05 |
| 405 | Gerald Perry | .05 | .04 | 471 | Vince Coleman | .08 | .06 |
| 406 | Donovan Osborne | .12 | .09 | 472 | Doc Gooden | .08 | .06 |
| 407 | Bryn Smith | .05 | .04 | 473 | Charlie O'Brien | .05 | .04 |
| 408 | Bernard Gilkey | .15 | .11 | 474 | Jeromy Burnitz | .40 | .30 |
| 409 | Rex Hudler | .05 | .04 | 475 | John Franco | .08 | .06 |
| 410 | Thomson/Branca (Foil) | | | 476 | Daryl Boston | .05 | .04 |
| | | .10 | .08 | 477 | Frank Viola | .08 | .06 |
| 411 | Lance Dickson | .15 | .11 | 478 | D.J. Dozier | .10 | .08 |
| 412 | Danny Jackson | .05 | .04 | 479 | Kevin McReynolds | .06 | .05 |
| 413 | Jerome Walton | .06 | .05 | 480 | Tom Herr | .05 | .04 |
| 414 | Sean Cheetham | .12 | .09 | 481 | Gregg Jefferies | .08 | .06 |
| 415 | Joe Girardi | .05 | .04 | 482 | Pete Schourek | .12 | .09 |
| 416 | Ryne Sandberg | .15 | .11 | 483 | Ron Darling | .06 | .05 |
| 417 | Mike Harkey | .06 | .05 | 484 | Dave Magadan | .06 | .05 |
| 418 | George Bell | .08 | .06 | 485 | Andy Ashby | .10 | .08 |
| 419 | Rick Wilkins | .20 | .15 | 486 | Dale Murphy | .08 | .06 |
| 420 | Earl Cunningham | .06 | .05 | 487 | Von Hayes | .06 | .05 |
| 421 | Heathcliff Slocumb | .12 | .09 | 488 | Kim Batiste | .08 | .06 |
| 422 | Mike Bielecki | .05 | .04 | 489 | Tony Longmire | .15 | .11 |
| 423 | Jessie Hollins | .12 | .09 | 490 | Wally Backman | .05 | .04 |
| 424 | Shawon Dunston | .06 | .05 | 491 | Jeff Jackson | .08 | .06 |
| 425 | Dave Smith | .05 | .04 | 492 | Mickey Morandini | .08 | .06 |
| 426 | Greg Maddux | .08 | .06 | 493 | Darrel Akerfelds | .05 | .04 |
| 427 | Jose Vizcaino | .05 | .04 | 494 | Ricky Jordan | .06 | .05 |
| 428 | Luis Salazar | .05 | .04 | 495 | Randy Ready | .05 | .04 |
| 429 | Andre Dawson | .10 | .08 | 496 | Darrin Fletcher | .06 | .05 |
| 430 | Rick Sutcliffe | .05 | .04 | 497 | Chuck Malone | .05 | .04 |
| 431 | Paul Assenmacher | .05 | .04 | 498 | Pat Combs | .06 | .05 |
| 432 | Erik Pappas | .12 | .09 | 499 | Dickie Thon | .05 | .04 |
| 433 | Mark Grace | .08 | .06 | 500 | Roger McDowell | .06 | .05 |
| 434 | Denny Martinez | .06 | .05 | 501 | Len Dykstra | .06 | .05 |
| 435 | Marquis Grissom | .10 | .08 | 502 | Joe Boever | .05 | .04 |
| 436 | Wilfredo Cordero | .30 | .25 | 503 | John Kruk | .06 | .05 |
| 437 | Tim Wallach | .06 | .05 | 504 | Terry Mulholland | .06 | .05 |
| 438 | Brian Barnes | .15 | .11 | 505 | Wes Chamberlain | .35 | .25 |
| 439 | Barry Jones | .05 | .04 | 506 | Mike Lieberthal | .15 | .11 |
| 440 | Ivan Calderon | .08 | .06 | 507 | Darren Daulton | .06 | .05 |
| 441 | Stan Spencer | .12 | .09 | 508 | Charlie Hayes | .06 | .05 |
| 442 | Larry Walker | .08 | .06 | 509 | John Smiley | .06 | .05 |
| 443 | Chris Haney | .12 | .09 | 510 | Gary Varsho | .05 | .04 |
| 444 | Hector Rivera | .12 | .09 | 511 | Curt Wilkerson | .05 | .04 |
| 445 | Delino DeShields | .12 | .09 | 512 | Orlando Merced | .25 | .20 |
| 446 | Andres Galarraga | .06 | .05 | 513 | Barry Bonds | .12 | .09 |
| 447 | Gilberto Reyes | .06 | .05 | 514 | Mike Lavalliere | .05 | .04 |
| 448 | Willie Greene | .10 | .08 | 515 | Doug Drabek | .06 | .05 |
| 449 | Greg Colbrunn | .12 | .09 | 516 | Gary Redus | .05 | .04 |
| 450 | Rondell White | .30 | .25 | 517 | William Pennyfeather | | |
| 451 | Steve Frey | .06 | .05 | | | .15 | .11 |
| 452 | Shane Andrews | .15 | .11 | 518 | Randy Tomlin | .06 | .05 |
| 453 | Mike Fitzgerald | .05 | .04 | 519 | Mike Zimmerman | .12 | .09 |
| 454 | Spike Owen | .05 | .04 | 520 | Jeff King | .06 | .05 |
| 455 | Dave Martinez | .05 | .04 | 521 | Kurt Miller | .15 | .11 |
| 456 | Dennis Boyd | .05 | .04 | 522 | Jay Bell | .06 | .05 |
| 457 | Eric Bullock | .06 | .05 | 523 | Bill Landrum | .05 | .04 |
| 458 | Reid Cornelius | .15 | .11 | 524 | Zane Smith | .05 | .04 |
| 459 | Chris Nabholz | .15 | .11 | 525 | Bobby Bonilla | .10 | .08 |
| 460 | David Cone | .08 | .06 | 526 | Bob Walk | .05 | .04 |
| 461 | Hubie Brooks | .06 | .05 | 527 | Austin Manahan | .08 | .06 |
| 462 | Sid Fernandez | .06 | .05 | 528 | Joe Ausanio | .12 | .09 |
| 463 | Doug Simons | .10 | .08 | 529 | Andy Van Slyke | .08 | .06 |
| 464 | Howard Johnson | .10 | .08 | 530 | Jose Lind | .05 | .04 |

| | | MT | NR MT | | | MT | NR MT |
|---|---|---|---|---|---|---|---|
| 531 | Carlos Garcia | .12 | .09 | 598 | Gary Carter | .06 | .05 |
| 532 | Don Slaught | .05 | .04 | 599 | Stan Javier | .05 | .04 |
| 533 | Colin Powell (Foil) | .25 | .20 | 600 | Kal Daniels | .08 | .06 |
| 534 | Frank Bolick (Foil) | .25 | .20 | 601 | Jamie McAndrew | .15 | .11 |
| 535 | Gary Scott (Foil) | .30 | .25 | 602 | Mike Sharperson | .05 | .04 |
| 536 | Nikco Riesgo (Foil) | .30 | .25 | 603 | Jay Howell | .05 | .04 |
| 537 | Reggie Sanders | .60 | .45 | 604 | Eric Karros | .70 | .50 |
| 538 | Tim Howard (Foil) | .25 | .20 | 605 | Tim Belcher | .06 | .05 |
| 539 | Ryan Bowen | .15 | .11 | 606 | Dan Opperman | .12 | .09 |
| 540 | Eric Anthony | .08 | .06 | 607 | Lenny Harris | .05 | .04 |
| 541 | Jim Deshaies | .05 | .04 | 608 | Tom Goodwin | .10 | .08 |
| 542 | Tom Nevers | .12 | .09 | 609 | Darryl Strawberry | .15 | .11 |
| 543 | Ken Caminiti | .05 | .04 | 610 | Ramon Martinez | .12 | .09 |
| 544 | Karl Rhodes | .12 | .09 | 611 | Kevin Gross | .05 | .04 |
| 545 | Xavier Hernandez | .08 | .06 | 612 | Zakary Shinall | .12 | .09 |
| 546 | Mike Scott | .06 | .05 | 613 | Mike Scioscia | .05 | .04 |
| 547 | Jeff Juden | .15 | .11 | 614 | Eddie Murray | .08 | .06 |
| 548 | Darryl Kile | .08 | .06 | 615 | Ronnie Walden | .15 | .11 |
| 549 | Willie Ansley | .10 | .08 | 616 | Will Clark | .20 | .15 |
| 550 | Luis Gonzalez | .35 | .25 | 617 | Adam Hyzdu | .15 | .11 |
| 551 | Mike Simms | .15 | .11 | 618 | Matt Williams | .08 | .06 |
| 552 | Mark Portugal | .05 | .04 | 619 | Don Robinson | .05 | .04 |
| 553 | Jimmy Jones | .05 | .04 | 620 | Jeff Brantley | .05 | .04 |
| 554 | Jim Clancy | .05 | .04 | 621 | Greg Litton | .05 | .04 |
| 555 | Pete Harnisch | .06 | .05 | 622 | Steve Decker | .25 | .20 |
| 556 | Craig Biggio | .08 | .06 | 623 | Robby Thompson | .06 | .05 |
| 557 | Eric Yelding | .05 | .04 | 624 | Mark Leonard | .12 | .09 |
| 558 | Dave Rohde | .06 | .05 | 625 | Kevin Bass | .05 | .04 |
| 559 | Casey Candaele | .05 | .04 | 626 | Scott Garrelts | .05 | .04 |
| 560 | Curt Schilling | .05 | .04 | 627 | Jose Uribe | .05 | .04 |
| 561 | Steve Finley | .06 | .05 | 628 | Eric Gunderson | .08 | .06 |
| 562 | Javier Ortiz | .08 | .06 | 629 | Steve Hosey | .08 | .06 |
| 563 | Andujar Cedeno | .20 | .15 | 630 | Trevor Wilson | .06 | .05 |
| 564 | Rafael Ramirez | .05 | .04 | 631 | Terry Kennedy | .05 | .04 |
| 565 | Kenny Lofton | .50 | .40 | 632 | Dave Righetti | .06 | .05 |
| 566 | Steve Avery | .15 | .11 | 633 | Kelly Downs | .05 | .04 |
| 567 | Lonnie Smith | .05 | .04 | 634 | Johnny Ard | .08 | .06 |
| 568 | Kent Mercker | .06 | .05 | 635 | Eric Christopherson | .12 | .09 |
| 569 | Chipper Jones | .40 | .30 | 636 | Kevin Mitchell | .10 | .08 |
| 570 | Terry Pendleton | .06 | .05 | 637 | John Burkett | .05 | .04 |
| 571 | Otis Nixon | .05 | .04 | 638 | Kevin Rogers | .12 | .09 |
| 572 | Juan Berenguer | .05 | .04 | 639 | Bud Black | .05 | .04 |
| 573 | Charlie Leibrandt | .05 | .04 | 640 | Willie McGee | .06 | .05 |
| 574 | David Justice | .30 | .25 | 641 | Royce Clayton | .15 | .11 |
| 575 | Keith Mitchell | .25 | .20 | 642 | Tony Fernandez | .06 | .05 |
| 576 | Tom Glavine | .08 | .06 | 643 | Ricky Bones | .12 | .09 |
| 577 | Greg Olson | .05 | .04 | 644 | Thomas Howard | .06 | .05 |
| 578 | Rafael Belliard | .05 | .04 | 645 | Dave Staton | .15 | .11 |
| 579 | Ben Rivera | .10 | .08 | 646 | Jim Presley | .05 | .04 |
| 580 | John Smoltz | .06 | .05 | 647 | Tony Gwynn | .10 | .08 |
| 581 | Tyler Houston | .05 | .04 | 648 | Marty Barrett | .05 | .04 |
| 582 | Mark Wohlers | .40 | .30 | 649 | Scott Coolbaugh | .06 | .05 |
| 583 | Ron Gant | .30 | .25 | 650 | Craig Lefferts | .05 | .04 |
| 584 | Ramon Caraballo | .10 | .08 | 651 | Eddie Whitson | .05 | .04 |
| 585 | Sid Bream | .05 | .04 | 652 | Oscar Azocar | .05 | .04 |
| 586 | Jeff Treadway | .05 | .04 | 653 | Wes Gardner | .05 | .04 |
| 587 | Javier Lopez | .12 | .09 | 654 | Bip Roberts | .06 | .05 |
| 588 | Deion Sanders | .08 | .06 | 655 | Robbie Beckett | .15 | .11 |
| 589 | Mike Heath | .05 | .04 | 656 | Benny Santiago | .06 | .05 |
| 590 | Ryan Klesko | 1.25 | .90 | 657 | Greg W. Harris | .05 | .04 |
| 591 | Bob Ojeda | .05 | .04 | 658 | Jerald Clark | .06 | .05 |
| 592 | Alfredo Griffin | .05 | .04 | 659 | Fred McGriff | .10 | .08 |
| 593 | Raul Mondesi | .20 | .15 | 660 | Larry Andersen | .05 | .04 |
| 594 | Greg Smith | .05 | .04 | 661 | Bruce Hurst | .06 | .05 |
| 595 | Orel Hershiser | .08 | .06 | 662 | Steve Martin | .12 | .09 |
| 596 | Juan Samuel | .06 | .05 | 663 | Rafael Valdez | .06 | .05 |
| 597 | Brett Butler | .06 | .05 | 664 | Paul Faries | .06 | .05 |

| | | MT | NR MT |
|---|---|---|---|
| 665 | Andy Benes | .08 | .06 |
| 666 | Randy Myers | .06 | .05 |
| 667 | Rob Dibble | .08 | .06 |
| 668 | Glenn Sutko | .12 | .09 |
| 669 | Glenn Braggs | .05 | .04 |
| 670 | Billy Hatcher | .05 | .04 |
| 671 | Joe Oliver | .05 | .04 |
| 672 | Freddie Benavides | .12 | .09 |
| 673 | Barry Larkin | .08 | .06 |
| 674 | Chris Sabo | .08 | .06 |
| 675 | Mariano Duncan | .05 | .04 |
| 676 | Chris Jones | .15 | .11 |
| 677 | Gino Minutelli | .12 | .09 |
| 678 | Reggie Jefferson | .12 | .09 |
| 679 | Jack Armstrong | .06 | .05 |
| 680 | Chris Hammond | .06 | .05 |
| 681 | Jose Rijo | .08 | .06 |
| 682 | Bill Doran | .05 | .04 |
| 683 | Terry Lee | .06 | .05 |
| 684 | Tom Browning | .06 | .05 |
| 685 | Paul O'Neill | .08 | .06 |
| 686 | Eric Davis | .10 | .08 |
| 687 | Dan Wilson | .15 | .11 |
| 688 | Ted Power | .05 | .04 |
| 689 | Tim Layana | .05 | .04 |
| 690 | Norm Charlton | .06 | .05 |
| 691 | Hal Morris | .10 | .08 |
| 692 | Rickey Henderson (Foil) | .20 | .15 |
| 693 | Sam Militello (Foil) | .30 | .25 |
| 694 | Matt Mieske (Foil) | .60 | .45 |
| 695 | Paul Russo (Foil) | .25 | .20 |
| 696 | Domingo Mota (Foil) | .25 | .20 |
| 697 | Todd Guggiana (Foil) | .20 | .15 |
| 698 | Marc Newfield | .40 | .30 |
| 699 | Checklist | .05 | .04 |
| 700 | Checklist | .05 | .04 |
| 701 | Checklist | .05 | .04 |
| 702 | Checklist | .05 | .04 |
| 703 | Checklist | .05 | .04 |
| 704 | Checklist | .05 | .04 |

## 1992 Bowman

Topps introduced several changes with the release of its 1992 Bowman set. The 705-card set features 45 special insert cards stamped with gold foil. The cards are printed with a premium UV coated glossy card stock. Several players without major league experience are featured in the set. Included in this group are 1991 MVP's of the minor leagues and first round draft choices.

| | | MT | NR MT |
|---|---|---|---|
| Complete Set: | | 60.00 | 45.00 |
| Common Player: | | .07 | .05 |
| 1 | Ivan Rodriguez | .20 | .15 |
| 2 | Kirk McCaskill | .07 | .05 |
| 3 | Scott Livingstone | .10 | .08 |
| 4 | Salomon Torres | .20 | .15 |
| 5 | Carlos Hernandez | .20 | .15 |
| 6 | Dave Hollins | .12 | .09 |
| 7 | Scott Fletcher | .07 | .05 |
| 8 | Jorge Fabregas | .20 | .15 |
| 9 | Andujar Cedeno | .12 | .09 |
| 10 | Howard Johnson | .12 | .09 |
| 11 | Trevor Hoffman | .20 | .15 |
| 12 | Roberto Kelly | .10 | .08 |
| 13 | Gregg Jefferies | .12 | .09 |
| 14 | Marquis Grissom | .12 | .09 |
| 15 | Mike Ignasiak | .07 | .05 |
| 16 | Jack Morris | .10 | .08 |
| 17 | William Pennyfeather | .20 | .15 |
| 18 | Todd Stottlemyre | .07 | .05 |
| 19 | Chito Martinez | .12 | .09 |
| 20 | Roberto Alomar | .15 | .11 |
| 21 | Sam Militello | .20 | .15 |
| 22 | Hector Fajardo | .20 | .15 |
| 23 | Paul Quantrill | .20 | .15 |
| 24 | Chuck Knoblauch | .12 | .09 |
| 25 | Reggie Jefferson | .12 | .09 |
| 26 | Jeremy McGarity | .20 | .15 |
| 27 | Jerome Walton | .08 | .06 |
| 28 | Chipper Jones | .50 | .40 |
| 29 | Brian Barber | .20 | .15 |
| 30 | Ron Darling | .07 | .05 |
| 31 | Robert Petrone | .20 | .15 |
| 32 | Chuck Finley | .08 | .06 |
| 33 | Edgar Martinez | .10 | .08 |
| 34 | Napolean Robinson | .20 | .15 |
| 35 | Andy Van Slyke | .10 | .08 |
| 36 | Bobby Thigpen | .08 | .06 |
| 37 | Travis Fryman | .50 | .40 |
| 38 | Eric Christopherson | .10 | .08 |
| 39 | Terry Mulholland | .08 | .06 |
| 40 | Darryl Strawberry | .15 | .11 |
| 41 | Manny Alexander | .15 | .11 |
| 42 | Tracey Sanders | .20 | .15 |
| 43 | Pete Incaviglia | .08 | .06 |
| 44 | Kim Batiste | .10 | .08 |
| 45 | Frank Rodriguez | .40 | .30 |
| 46 | Greg Swindell | .10 | .08 |
| 47 | Delino DeShields | .12 | .09 |
| 48 | John Ericks | .20 | .15 |
| 49 | Franklin Stubbs | .07 | .05 |
| 50 | Tony Gwynn | .12 | .09 |
| 51 | Clifton Garrett | .20 | .15 |
| 52 | Mike Gardella | .20 | .15 |
| 53 | Scott Erickson | .10 | .08 |
| 54 | Gary Caballo | .20 | .15 |
| 55 | Jose Oliva | .20 | .15 |
| 56 | Brook Fordyce | .15 | .11 |

| | MT | NR MT | | | MT | NR MT |
|---|---|---|---|---|---|---|
| 57 | Mark Whiten | .10 | .08 | 124 | Brien Taylor | 3.00 | 2.25 |
| 58 | Joe Slusarski | .08 | .06 | 125 | Brian Williams | .15 | .11 |
| 59 | J.R. Phillips | .20 | .15 | 126 | Kevin Seitzer | .07 | .05 |
| 60 | Barry Bonds | .15 | .11 | 127 | Carlos Baerga | 1.50 | 1.25 |
| 61 | Bob Milacki | .07 | .05 | 128 | Gary Scott | .10 | .08 |
| 62 | Keith Mitchell | .10 | .08 | 129 | Scott Cooper | .10 | .08 |
| 63 | Angel Miranda | .20 | .15 | 130 | Domingo Jean | .25 | .20 |
| 64 | Raul Mondesi | .50 | .40 | 131 | Pat Mahomes | .25 | .20 |
| 65 | Brian Koelling | .20 | .15 | 132 | Mike Boddicker | .07 | .05 |
| 66 | Brian McRae | .10 | .08 | 133 | Roberto Hernandez | .20 | .15 |
| 67 | John Patterson | .12 | .09 | 134 | Dave Valle | .07 | .05 |
| 68 | John Wetteland | .12 | .09 | 135 | Kurt Stillwell | .07 | .05 |
| 69 | Wilson Alvarez | .08 | .06 | 136 | Brad Pennington | .20 | .15 |
| 70 | Wade Boggs | .10 | .08 | 137 | Jermaine Swifton | .20 | .15 |
| 71 | Darryl Ratliff | .20 | .15 | 138 | Ryan Hawblitzel | .25 | .20 |
| 72 | Jeff Jackson | .10 | .08 | 139 | Tito Navarro | .20 | .15 |
| 73 | Jeremy Hernandez | .20 | .15 | 140 | Sandy Alomar | .10 | .08 |
| 74 | Darryl Hamilton | .10 | .08 | 141 | Todd Benzinger | .07 | .05 |
| 75 | Rafael Belliard | .07 | .05 | 142 | Danny Jackson | .07 | .05 |
| 76 | Ricky Talicek | .20 | .15 | 143 | Melvin Nieves | .50 | .40 |
| 77 | Felipe Crespo | .20 | .15 | 144 | Jim Campanis | .20 | .15 |
| 78 | Carney Lansford | .08 | .06 | 145 | Luis Gonzalez | .10 | .08 |
| 79 | Ryan Long | .15 | .11 | 146 | Dave Doorneweerd | .20 | .15 |
| 80 | Kirby Puckett | .25 | .20 | 147 | Charlie Hayes | .08 | .06 |
| 81 | Earl Cunningham | .10 | .08 | 148 | Greg Maddux | .15 | .11 |
| 82 | Pedro Martinez | .20 | .15 | 149 | Brian Harper | .08 | .06 |
| 83 | Scott Hatteberg | .20 | .15 | 150 | Brent Miller | .20 | .15 |
| 84 | Juan Gonzalez | .30 | .25 | 151 | Shawn Estes | .20 | .15 |
| 85 | Robert Nutting | .15 | .11 | 152 | Mike Williams | .20 | .15 |
| 86 | Calvin Reese | .12 | .09 | 153 | Charlie Hough | .07 | .05 |
| 87 | Dave Silvestri | .10 | .08 | 154 | Randy Myers | .07 | .05 |
| 88 | Scott Ruffcorn | .07 | .05 | 155 | Kevin Young | .30 | .25 |
| 89 | Rick Aguilera | .08 | .06 | 156 | Rick Wilkins | .07 | .05 |
| 90 | Cecil Fielder | .20 | .15 | 157 | Terry Schumpert | .07 | .05 |
| 91 | Kirk Dressendorfer | .10 | .08 | 158 | Steve Karsay | .15 | .11 |
| 92 | Jerry Dipoto | .15 | .11 | 159 | Gary DiSarcina | .07 | .05 |
| 93 | Mike Felder | .07 | .05 | 160 | Deion Sanders | .20 | .15 |
| 94 | Craig Paquette | .15 | .11 | 161 | Tom Browning | .07 | .05 |
| 95 | Elvin Paulino | .20 | .15 | 162 | Dickie Thon | .07 | .05 |
| 96 | Donovan Osborne | .30 | .25 | 163 | Luis Mercedes | .10 | .08 |
| 97 | Hubie Brooks | .07 | .05 | 164 | Ricardo Ingram | .20 | .15 |
| 98 | Derek Lowe | .20 | .15 | 165 | Tavo Alavarez | .20 | .15 |
| 99 | David Zancanaro | .10 | .08 | 166 | Rickey Henderson | .20 | .15 |
| 100 | Ken Griffey, Jr. | 1.00 | .70 | 167 | Jaime Navarro | .10 | .08 |
| 101 | Todd Hundley | .10 | .08 | 168 | Billy Ashley | .30 | .25 |
| 102 | Mike Trombley | .20 | .15 | 169 | Phil Dauphin | .20 | .15 |
| 103 | Ricky Gutierrez | .20 | .15 | 170 | Ivan Cruz | .20 | .15 |
| 104 | Braulio Castillo | .20 | .15 | 171 | Harold Baines | .08 | .06 |
| 105 | Craig Lefferts | .07 | .05 | 172 | Bryan Harvey | .08 | .06 |
| 106 | Rick Sutcliffe | .10 | .08 | 173 | Alex Cole | .07 | .05 |
| 107 | Dean Palmer | .10 | .08 | 174 | Curtis Shaw | .20 | .15 |
| 108 | Henry Rodriguez | .15 | .11 | 175 | Matt Williams | .10 | .08 |
| 109 | Mark Clark | .20 | .15 | 176 | Felix Jose | .15 | .11 |
| 110 | Kenny Lofton | .30 | .25 | 177 | Sam Horn | .07 | .05 |
| 111 | Mark Carreon | .07 | .05 | 178 | Randy Johnson | .08 | .06 |
| 112 | J.T. Bruett | .20 | .15 | 179 | Ivan Calderon | .08 | .06 |
| 113 | Gerald Williams | .20 | .15 | 180 | Steve Avery | .15 | .11 |
| 114 | Frank Thomas | 1.50 | 1.25 | 181 | William Suero | .10 | .08 |
| 115 | Kevin Reimer | .08 | .06 | 182 | Bill Swift | .10 | .08 |
| 116 | Sammy Sosa | .08 | .06 | 183 | Howard Battle | .20 | .15 |
| 117 | Mickey Tettleton | .10 | .08 | 184 | Ruben Amaro | .10 | .08 |
| 118 | Reggie Sanders | .20 | .15 | 185 | Jim Abbott | .10 | .08 |
| 119 | Trevor Wilson | .07 | .05 | 186 | Mike Fitzgerald | .07 | .05 |
| 120 | Cliff Brantley | .20 | .15 | 187 | Bruce Hurst | .08 | .06 |
| 121 | Spike Owen | .07 | .05 | 188 | Jeff Juden | .10 | .08 |
| 122 | Jeff Montgomery | .07 | .05 | 189 | Jeromy Burnitz | .20 | .15 |
| 123 | Alex Sutherland | .20 | .15 | 190 | Dave Burba | .07 | .05 |

| | | MT | NR MT | | | MT | NR MT |
|---|---|---|---|---|---|---|---|
| 191 | Kevin Brown | .08 | .06 | 258 | Carl Everett | .30 | .25 |
| 192 | Patrick Lennon | .20 | .15 | 259 | Tim Salmon | .50 | .40 |
| 193 | Jeffrey McNeely | .20 | .15 | 260 | Will Clark | .20 | .15 |
| 194 | Wil Cordero | .30 | .25 | 261 | Ugueth Urbina | .20 | .15 |
| 195 | Chili Davis | .08 | .06 | 262 | Jason Wood | .20 | .15 |
| 196 | Milt Cuyler | .07 | .05 | 263 | Dave Magadan | .07 | .05 |
| 197 | Von Hayes | .07 | .05 | 264 | Dante Bichette | .07 | .05 |
| 198 | Todd Revening | .20 | .15 | 265 | Jose DeLeon | .07 | .05 |
| 199 | Joel Johnson | .15 | .11 | 266 | Mike Neill | .20 | .15 |
| 200 | Jeff Bagwell | .20 | .15 | 267 | Paul O'Neill | .08 | .06 |
| 201 | Alex Fernandez | .10 | .08 | 268 | Anthony Young | .08 | .06 |
| 202 | Todd Jones | .20 | .15 | 269 | Greg Harris | .07 | .05 |
| 203 | Charles Nagy | .10 | .08 | 270 | Todd Van Poppel | .30 | .25 |
| 204 | Tim Raines | .08 | .06 | 271 | Pete Castellano | .20 | .15 |
| 205 | Kevin Maas | .08 | .06 | 272 | Tony Phillips | .10 | .08 |
| 206 | Julio Franco | .10 | .08 | 273 | Mike Gallego | .07 | .05 |
| 207 | Randy Velarde | .07 | .05 | 274 | Steve Cooke | .25 | .20 |
| 208 | Lance Johnson | .08 | .06 | 275 | Robin Ventura | .15 | .11 |
| 209 | Scott Leius | .08 | .06 | 276 | Kevin Mitchell | .10 | .08 |
| 210 | Derek Lee | .20 | .15 | 277 | Doug Linton | .15 | .11 |
| 211 | Joe Sondrini | .20 | .15 | 278 | Robert Eenhorne | .20 | .15 |
| 212 | Royce Clayton | .20 | .15 | 279 | Gabe White | .25 | .20 |
| 213 | Chris George | .20 | .15 | 280 | Dave Stewart | .10 | .08 |
| 214 | Gary Sheffield | .20 | .15 | 281 | Mo Sanford | .20 | .15 |
| 215 | Mark Gubicza | .08 | .06 | 282 | Greg Perschke | .20 | .15 |
| 216 | Mike Moore | .07 | .05 | 283 | Kevin Flora | .20 | .15 |
| 217 | Rick Huisman | .10 | .08 | 284 | Jeff Williams | .20 | .15 |
| 218 | Jeff Russell | .08 | .06 | 285 | Keith Miller | .08 | .06 |
| 219 | D.J. Dozier | .15 | .11 | 286 | Andy Ashby | .12 | .09 |
| 220 | Dave Martinez | .07 | .05 | 287 | Doug Dascenzo | .07 | .05 |
| 221 | Al Newman | .07 | .05 | 288 | Eric Karros | 1.50 | 1.25 |
| 222 | Nolan Ryan | .30 | .25 | 289 | Glenn Murray | .25 | .20 |
| 223 | Teddy Higuera | .08 | .06 | 290 | Troy Percival | .20 | .15 |
| 224 | Damon Buford | .20 | .15 | 291 | Orlando Merced | .10 | .08 |
| 225 | Ruben Sierra | .20 | .15 | 292 | Peter Hoy | .20 | .15 |
| 226 | Tom Nevers | .20 | .15 | 293 | Tony Fernandez | .08 | .06 |
| 227 | Tommy Greene | .10 | .08 | 294 | Juan Guzman | .40 | .30 |
| 228 | Nigel Wilson | 2.00 | 1.50 | 295 | Jesse Barfield | .07 | .05 |
| 229 | John DeSilva | .20 | .15 | 296 | Sid Fernandez | .08 | .06 |
| 230 | Bobby Witt | .08 | .06 | 297 | Scott Cepicky | .20 | .15 |
| 231 | Greg Cadaret | .07 | .05 | 298 | Garret Anderson | .20 | .15 |
| 232 | John VanderWal | .25 | .20 | 299 | Cal Eldred | .50 | .40 |
| 233 | Jack Clark | .10 | .08 | 300 | Ryne Sandberg | .15 | .11 |
| 234 | Bill Doran | .07 | .05 | 301 | Jim Gantner | .07 | .05 |
| 235 | Bobby Bonilla | .20 | .15 | 302 | Mariano Rivera | .20 | .15 |
| 236 | Steve Olin | .10 | .08 | 303 | Ron Lockett | .20 | .15 |
| 237 | Derek Bell | .30 | .25 | 304 | David Nied, Jose | | |
| 238 | David Cone | .15 | .11 | | Offerman | .08 | .06 |
| 239 | Victor Cole | .15 | .11 | 305 | Denny Martinez | .08 | .06 |
| 240 | Rod Bolton | .20 | .15 | 306 | Luis Ortiz | .20 | .15 |
| 241 | Tom Pagnozzi | .08 | .06 | 307 | David Howard | .08 | .06 |
| 242 | Rob Dibble | .08 | .06 | 308 | Russ Springer | .10 | .08 |
| 243 | Michael Carter | .20 | .15 | 309 | Chris Howard | .15 | .11 |
| 244 | Don Peters | .15 | .11 | 310 | Kyle Abbott | .12 | .09 |
| 245 | Mike LaValliere | .07 | .05 | 311 | Aaron Sele | .20 | .15 |
| 246 | Joe Perona | .20 | .15 | 312 | David Justice | .15 | .11 |
| 247 | Mitch Williams | .08 | .06 | 313 | Pete O'Brien | .07 | .05 |
| 248 | Jay Buhner | .08 | .06 | 314 | Greg Hansell | .20 | .15 |
| 249 | Andy Benes | .10 | .08 | 315 | Dave Winfield | .20 | .15 |
| 250 | Alex Ochoa | .20 | .15 | 316 | Lance Dickson | .12 | .09 |
| 251 | Greg Blosser | .08 | .06 | 317 | Eric King | .07 | .05 |
| 252 | Jack Armstrong | .07 | .05 | 318 | Vaughn Eshelman | .20 | .15 |
| 253 | Juan Samuel | .07 | .05 | 319 | Tim Belcher | .08 | .06 |
| 254 | Terry Pendleton | .10 | .08 | 320 | Andres Galarraga | .08 | .06 |
| 255 | Ramon Martinez | .10 | .08 | 321 | Scott Bullett | .25 | .20 |
| 256 | Rico Brogna | .15 | .11 | 322 | Doug Strange | .08 | .06 |
| 257 | John Smiley | .08 | .06 | 323 | Jerald Clark | .08 | .06 |

| | | MT | NR MT | | | | MT | NR MT |
|---|---|---|---|---|---|---|---|---|
| 324 | Dave Righetti | .08 | .06 | | 391 | Dan Smith | .15 | .11 |
| 325 | Greg Hibbard | .08 | .06 | | 392 | Terry Steinbach | .08 | .06 |
| 326 | Eric Dillman | .20 | .15 | | 393 | Jon Farrell | .07 | .05 |
| 327 | Shane Reynolds | .20 | .15 | | 394 | Dave Anderson | .07 | .05 |
| 328 | Chris Hammond | .08 | .06 | | 395 | Benito Santiago | .10 | .08 |
| 329 | Albert Belle | .15 | .11 | | 396 | Mark Wohlers | .10 | .08 |
| 330 | Rich Becker | .15 | .11 | | 397 | Mo Vaughn | .10 | .08 |
| 331 | Eddie Williams | .08 | .06 | | 398 | Randy Kramer | .10 | .08 |
| 332 | Donald Harris | .08 | .06 | | 399 | John Jaha | .25 | .20 |
| 333 | Dave Smith | .08 | .06 | | 400 | Cal Ripken, Jr. | .50 | .40 |
| 334 | Steve Fireovoid | .20 | .15 | | 401 | Ryan Bowen | .15 | .11 |
| 335 | Steve Buechele | .07 | .05 | | 402 | Tim McIntosh | .07 | .05 |
| 336 | Mike Schooler | .07 | .05 | | 403 | Bernard Gilkey | .08 | .06 |
| 337 | Kevin McReynolds | .08 | .06 | | 404 | Junior Felix | .08 | .06 |
| 338 | Hensley Meulens | .08 | .06 | | 405 | Cris Colon | .20 | .15 |
| 339 | Benji Gil | .20 | .15 | | 406 | Marc Newfield | .10 | .08 |
| 340 | Don Mattingly | .15 | .11 | | 407 | Bernie Williams | .10 | .08 |
| 341 | Alvin Davis | .07 | .05 | | 408 | Jay Howell | .07 | .05 |
| 342 | Alan Mills | .07 | .05 | | 409 | Zane Smith | .07 | .05 |
| 343 | Kelly Downs | .07 | .05 | | 410 | Jeff Shaw | .07 | .05 |
| 344 | Leo Gomez | .10 | .08 | | 411 | Kerry Woodson | .08 | .06 |
| 345 | Tarrik Brock | .20 | .15 | | 412 | Wes Chamberlain | .10 | .08 |
| 346 | Ryan Turner | .50 | .40 | | 413 | Dave Mulicki | .20 | .15 |
| 347 | John Smoltz | .10 | .08 | | 414 | Benny Distefano | .08 | .06 |
| 348 | Bill Sampen | .07 | .05 | | 415 | Kevin Rogers | .20 | .15 |
| 349 | Paul Byrd | .20 | .15 | | 416 | Tim Naehring | .10 | .08 |
| 350 | Mike Bordick | .10 | .08 | | 417 | Clemente Nunez | .20 | .15 |
| 351 | Jose Lind | .08 | .06 | | 418 | Luis Sojo | .07 | .05 |
| 352 | David Wells | .07 | .05 | | 419 | Kevin Ritz | .07 | .05 |
| 353 | Barry Larkin | .15 | .11 | | 420 | Omar Oliveras | .07 | .05 |
| 354 | Bruce Ruffin | .07 | .05 | | 421 | Manuel Lee | .07 | .05 |
| 355 | Luis Rivera | .07 | .05 | | 422 | Julio Valera | .10 | .08 |
| 356 | Sid Bream | .07 | .05 | | 423 | Omar Vizquel | .07 | .05 |
| 357 | Julian Vasquez | .20 | .15 | | 424 | Darren Burton | .15 | .11 |
| 358 | Jason Bere | .20 | .15 | | 425 | Mel Hall | .08 | .06 |
| 359 | Ben McDonald | .10 | .08 | | 426 | Dennis Powell | .07 | .05 |
| 360 | Scott Stahoviak | .20 | .15 | | 427 | Lee Stevens | .08 | .06 |
| 361 | Kirt Manwaring | .08 | .06 | | 428 | Glenn Davis | .08 | .06 |
| 362 | Jeff Johnson | .10 | .08 | | 429 | Willie Greene | .12 | .09 |
| 363 | Rob Deer | .07 | .05 | | 430 | Kevin Wickander | .08 | .06 |
| 364 | Tony Pena | .07 | .05 | | 431 | Dennis Eckersley | .10 | .08 |
| 365 | Melido Perez | .07 | .05 | | 432 | Joe Orsulak | .07 | .05 |
| 366 | Clay Parker | .07 | .05 | | 433 | Eddie Murray | .08 | .06 |
| 367 | Dale Sveum | .07 | .05 | | 434 | Matt Stairs | .10 | .08 |
| 368 | Mike Scioscia | .07 | .05 | | 435 | Wally Joyner | .10 | .08 |
| 369 | Roger Salkeld | .12 | .09 | | 436 | Rondell White | .15 | .11 |
| 370 | Mike Stanley | .07 | .05 | | 437 | Rob Mauer | .10 | .08 |
| 371 | Jack McDowell | .15 | .11 | | 438 | Joe Redfield | .15 | .11 |
| 372 | Tim Wallach | .07 | .05 | | 439 | Mark Lewis | .08 | .06 |
| 373 | Billy Ripken | .07 | .05 | | 440 | Darren Daulton | .10 | .08 |
| 374 | Mike Christopher | .20 | .15 | | 441 | Mike Henneman | .08 | .06 |
| 375 | Paul Molitor | .10 | .08 | | 442 | John Cangelosi | .07 | .05 |
| 376 | Dave Stieb | .08 | .06 | | 443 | Vince Moore | .20 | .15 |
| 377 | Pedro Guerrero | .10 | .08 | | 444 | John Wehner | .08 | .06 |
| 378 | Russ Swan | .07 | .05 | | 445 | Kent Hrbek | .08 | .06 |
| 379 | Bob Ojeda | .07 | .05 | | 446 | Mark McLemore | .07 | .05 |
| 380 | Donn Pall | .07 | .05 | | 447 | Bill Wegman | .07 | .05 |
| 381 | Eddie Zosky | .10 | .08 | | 448 | Robby Thompson | .07 | .05 |
| 382 | Darnell Coles | .07 | .05 | | 449 | Mark Anthony | .15 | .11 |
| 383 | Tom Smith | .15 | .11 | | 450 | Archi Cianfrocco | .20 | .15 |
| 384 | Mark McGwire | .15 | .11 | | 451 | Johnny Ruffin | .12 | .09 |
| 385 | Gary Carter | .10 | .08 | | 452 | Javier Lopez | .35 | .25 |
| 386 | Rich Amarel | .10 | .08 | | 453 | Greg Gohr | .15 | .11 |
| 387 | Alan Embree | .15 | .11 | | 454 | Tim Scott | .15 | .11 |
| 388 | Jonathan Hurst | .15 | .11 | | 455 | Stan Belinda | .08 | .06 |
| 389 | Bobby Jones | .10 | .08 | | 456 | Darrin Jackson | .08 | .06 |
| 390 | Rico Rossy | .15 | .11 | | 457 | Chris Gardner | .12 | .09 |

| | MT | NR MT | | | MT | NR MT |
|---|---|---|---|---|---|---|
| 458 | Esteban Beltre | .10 | .08 | 526 | Pat Listach | 2.00 | 1.50 |
| 459 | Phil Plantier | .15 | .11 | 527 | Scott Brosius | .08 | .06 |
| 460 | Jim Thome | .10 | .08 | 528 | John Roper | .15 | .11 |
| 461 | Mike Piazza | .30 | .25 | 529 | Phil Pratt | .15 | .11 |
| 462 | Matt Sinatro | .07 | .05 | 530 | Denny Walling | .07 | .05 |
| 463 | Scott Servais | .10 | .08 | 531 | Carlos Baerga | .15 | .11 |
| 464 | Brian Jordan | .50 | .40 | 532 | Manny Ramirez | .80 | .60 |
| 465 | Doug Drabek | .10 | .08 | 533 | Pat Clements | .07 | .05 |
| 466 | Carl Willis | .07 | .05 | 534 | Ron Gant | .10 | .08 |
| 467 | Bret Barbarie | .08 | .06 | 535 | Pat Kelly | .07 | .05 |
| 468 | Hal Morris | .08 | .06 | 536 | Billy Spiers | .07 | .05 |
| 469 | Steve Sax | .08 | .06 | 537 | Darren Reed | .10 | .08 |
| 470 | Jerry Willard | .07 | .05 | 538 | Ken Caminiti | .08 | .06 |
| 471 | Dan Wilson | .20 | .15 | 539 | Butch Hosky | .15 | .11 |
| 472 | Chris Hoiles | .15 | .11 | 540 | Matt Nokes | .07 | .05 |
| 473 | Rheal Cormier | .08 | .06 | 541 | John Kruk | .08 | .06 |
| 474 | John Morris | .07 | .05 | 542 | John Jaha (Foil) | .35 | .25 |
| 475 | Jeff Reardon | .08 | .06 | 543 | Justin Thompson | .20 | .15 |
| 476 | Mark Leiter | .07 | .05 | 544 | Steve Hosey | .08 | .06 |
| 477 | Tom Gordon | .07 | .05 | 545 | Joe Kmak | .10 | .08 |
| 478 | Kent Bottenfield | .15 | .11 | 546 | John Franco | .08 | .06 |
| 479 | Gene Larkin | .07 | .05 | 547 | Devon White | .08 | .06 |
| 480 | Dwight Gooden | .15 | .11 | 548 | Elston Hansen (Foil) | .30 | .25 |
| 481 | B.J. Surhoff | .10 | .08 | 549 | Ryan Klesko | .30 | .25 |
| 482 | Andy Stankiewicz | .10 | .08 | 550 | Danny Tartabull | .08 | .06 |
| 483 | Tino Martinez | .10 | .08 | 551 | Frank Thomas (Foil) | | |
| 484 | Craig Biggio | .10 | .08 | | | 2.00 | 1.50 |
| 485 | Denny Neagle | .10 | .08 | 552 | Kevin Tapani | .08 | .06 |
| 486 | Rusty Meacham | .10 | .08 | 553 | Willie Banks | .08 | .06 |
| 487 | Kal Daniels | .08 | .06 | 554 | B.J. Wallace (Foil) | .50 | .40 |
| 488 | Dave Henderson | .08 | .06 | 555 | Orlando Miller | .20 | .15 |
| 489 | Tim Costo | .10 | .08 | 556 | Mark Smith | .20 | .15 |
| 490 | Doug Davis | .15 | .11 | 557 | Tim Wallach (Foil) | .20 | .15 |
| 491 | Frank Viola | .10 | .08 | 558 | Bill Gullickson | .08 | .06 |
| 492 | Cory Snyder | .08 | .06 | 559 | Derek Bell (Foil) | .35 | .25 |
| 493 | Chris Martin | .15 | .11 | 560 | Joe Randa (Foil) | .25 | .20 |
| 494 | Dion James | .07 | .05 | 561 | Frank Seminara | .10 | .08 |
| 495 | Randy Tomlin | .08 | .06 | 562 | Mark Gardner | .08 | .06 |
| 496 | Greg Vaughn | .10 | .08 | 563 | Rick Greene (Foil) | .25 | .20 |
| 497 | Dennis Cook | .07 | .05 | 564 | Gary Gaetti | .08 | .06 |
| 498 | Rosario Rodriguez | .07 | .05 | 565 | Ozzie Guillen | .08 | .06 |
| 499 | Dave Staton | .07 | .05 | 566 | Charles Nagy (Foil) | .35 | .25 |
| 500 | George Brett | .15 | .11 | 567 | Mike Milchin | .15 | .11 |
| 501 | Brian Barnes | .08 | .06 | 568 | Ben Shelton (Foil) | .25 | .20 |
| 502 | Butch Henry | .08 | .06 | 569 | Chris Roberts (Foil) | .25 | .20 |
| 503 | Harold Reynolds | .08 | .06 | 570 | Ellis Burks | .08 | .06 |
| 505 | Lee Smith | .08 | .06 | 571 | Scott Scudder | .07 | .05 |
| 506 | Steve Chitren | .07 | .05 | 572 | Jim Abbott (Foil) | .35 | .25 |
| 507 | Ken Hill | .10 | .08 | 573 | Joe Carter | .10 | .08 |
| 508 | Robbie Beckett | .15 | .11 | 574 | Steve Finley | .10 | .08 |
| 509 | Troy Afenir | .07 | .05 | 575 | Jim Olander (Foil) | .15 | .11 |
| 510 | Kelly Gruber | .08 | .06 | 576 | Carlos Garcia | .20 | .15 |
| 511 | Bret Boone | .50 | .40 | 577 | Greg Olson | .08 | .06 |
| 512 | Jeff Branson | .20 | .15 | 578 | Greg Swindell (Foil) | .25 | .20 |
| 513 | Mike Jackson | .07 | .05 | 579 | Matt Williams (Foil) | .25 | .20 |
| 514 | Pete Harnisch | .08 | .06 | 580 | Mark Grace | .10 | .08 |
| 515 | Chad Kreuter | .07 | .05 | 581 | Howard House (Foil) | .30 | .25 |
| 516 | Joe Vitko | .15 | .11 | 582 | Luis Polonia | .07 | .05 |
| 517 | Orel Hershiser | .10 | .08 | 583 | Erik Hanson | .08 | .06 |
| 518 | John Doherty | .10 | .08 | 584 | Salomon Torres (Foil) | | |
| 519 | Jay Bell | .10 | .08 | | | .25 | .20 |
| 520 | Mark Langston | .10 | .08 | 585 | Carlton Fisk | .10 | .08 |
| 521 | Dann Howitt | .07 | .05 | 586 | Bret Saberhagen | .10 | .08 |
| 522 | Bobby Reed | .10 | .08 | 587 | Chad McDonnell (Foil) | | |
| 523 | Roberto Munoz | .15 | .11 | | | .25 | .20 |
| 524 | Todd Ritchie | .07 | .05 | 588 | Jimmy Key | .08 | .06 |
| 525 | Bip Roberts | .08 | .06 | 589 | Mike MacFarlane | .08 | .06 |

| | | MT | NR MT |
|---|---|---|---|
| 590 | Barry Bonds (Foil) | .30 | .25 |
| 591 | Jamie McAndrew | .20 | .15 |
| 592 | Shane Mack | .10 | .08 |
| 593 | Kerwin Moore | .15 | .11 |
| 594 | Joe Oliver | .07 | .05 |
| 595 | Chris Sabo | .08 | .06 |
| 596 | Alex Gonzalez | .15 | .11 |
| 597 | Brett Butler | .08 | .06 |
| 598 | Mark Hutton | .15 | .11 |
| 599 | Andy Benes (Foil) | .20 | .15 |
| 600 | Jose Canseco | .15 | .11 |
| 601 | Darryl Kile | .08 | .06 |
| 602 | Matt Stairs (Foil) | .25 | .20 |
| 603 | Robert Butler (Foil) | .25 | .20 |
| 604 | Willie McGee | .08 | .06 |
| 605 | Jack McDowell | .10 | .08 |
| 606 | Tom Candiotti | .08 | .06 |
| 607 | Ed Martel | .15 | .11 |
| 608 | Matt Mieske (Foil) | .25 | .20 |
| 609 | Darrin Fletcher | .08 | .06 |
| 610 | Rafael Palmeiro | .08 | .06 |
| 611 | Bill Swift (Foil) | .20 | .15 |
| 612 | Mike Mussina | .30 | .25 |
| 613 | Vince Coleman | .08 | .06 |
| 614 | Scott Cepicky (Foil) | .20 | .15 |
| 615 | Mike Greenwell | .08 | .06 |
| 616 | Kevin McGehee | .15 | .11 |
| 617 | Jeffrey Hammonds (Foil) | 2.00 | 1.50 |
| 618 | Scott Taylor | .15 | .11 |
| 619 | Dave Otto | .07 | .05 |
| 620 | Mark McGwire (Foil) | .50 | .40 |
| 621 | Kevin Tatar | .20 | .15 |
| 622 | Steve Farr | .07 | .05 |
| 623 | Ryan Klesko (Foil) | .30 | .25 |
| 625 | Andre Dawson | .15 | .11 |
| 626 | Tino Martinez (Foil) | .20 | .15 |
| 627 | Chad Curtis | .20 | .15 |
| 628 | Mickey Morandini | .10 | .08 |
| 629 | Gregg Olson (Foil) | .20 | .15 |
| 630 | Lou Whitaker | .08 | .06 |
| 631 | Arthur Rhodes | .15 | .11 |
| 632 | Brandon Wilson | .20 | .15 |
| 633 | Lance Jennings | .20 | .15 |
| 634 | Allen Watson | .30 | .25 |
| 635 | Len Dykstra | .08 | .06 |
| 636 | Joe Girardi | .07 | .05 |
| 637 | Kiki Hernandez (Foil) | .25 | .20 |
| 638 | Mike Hampton | .20 | .15 |
| 639 | Al Osuna | .10 | .08 |
| 640 | Kevin Appier | .10 | .08 |
| 641 | Rick Helling (Foil) | .40 | .30 |
| 642 | Jody Reed | .07 | .05 |
| 643 | Ray Lankford | .15 | .11 |
| 644 | John Olerud | .10 | .08 |
| 645 | Paul Molitor (Foil) | .20 | .15 |
| 646 | Pat Borders | .08 | .06 |
| 647 | Mike Morgan | .07 | .05 |
| 648 | Larry Walker | .15 | .11 |
| 649 | Pete Castellano | .20 | .15 |
| 650 | Fred McGriff | .15 | .11 |
| 651 | Walt Weiss | .07 | .05 |
| 652 | Calvin Murray | .60 | .45 |
| 653 | Dave Nilsson | .30 | .25 |
| 654 | Greg Pirkl | .20 | .15 |
| 655 | Robin Ventura | .15 | .11 |

| | | MT | NR MT |
|---|---|---|---|
| 656 | Mark Portugal | .07 | .05 |
| 657 | Roger McDowell | .07 | .05 |
| 658 | Rick Hirtensteiner (Foil) | .20 | .15 |
| 659 | Glenallen Hill | .08 | .06 |
| 660 | Greg Gagne | .07 | .05 |
| 661 | Charles Johnson (Foil) | 2.00 | 1.50 |
| 662 | Brian Hunter | .10 | .08 |
| 663 | Mark Lemke | .07 | .05 |
| 664 | Tim Belcher (Foil) | .20 | .15 |
| 665 | Rich DeLucia | .07 | .05 |
| 666 | Bob Walk | .07 | .05 |
| 667 | Joe Carter (Foil) | .30 | .25 |
| 668 | Jose Guzman | .10 | .08 |
| 669 | Otis Nixon | .08 | .06 |
| 670 | Phil Nevin (Foil) | 2.00 | 1.50 |
| 671 | Eric Davis | .10 | .08 |
| 672 | Damion Easley | .20 | .15 |
| 673 | Will Clark (Foil) | .50 | .40 |
| 674 | Mark Kiefer | .20 | .15 |
| 675 | Ozzie Smith | .20 | .15 |
| 676 | Manny Ramirez (Foil) | 1.00 | .70 |
| 677 | Gregg Olson | .10 | .08 |
| 678 | Cliff Floyd | 1.00 | .70 |
| 679 | Duane Singleton | .20 | .15 |
| 680 | Jose Rijo | .08 | .06 |
| 681 | Willie Randolph | .08 | .06 |
| 682 | Michael Tucker (Foil) | 1.00 | .70 |
| 683 | Darren Lewis | .08 | .06 |
| 684 | Dale Murphy | .10 | .08 |
| 685 | Mike Pagliarulo | .07 | .05 |
| 686 | Paul Miller | .20 | .15 |
| 687 | Mike Robertson | .20 | .15 |
| 688 | Mike Devereaux | .10 | .08 |
| 689 | Pedro Astacio | .35 | .25 |
| 690 | Alan Trammell | .10 | .08 |
| 691 | Roger Clemens | .20 | .15 |
| 692 | Bud Black | .07 | .05 |
| 693 | Turuk Wendell | .25 | .20 |
| 694 | Barry Larkin (Foil) | .20 | .15 |
| 695 | Todd Zeile | .08 | .06 |
| 696 | Pat Hentgen | .15 | .11 |
| 697 | Eddie Taubensee | .15 | .11 |
| 698 | Guillermo Vasquez | .20 | .15 |
| 699 | Tom Glavine | .15 | .11 |
| 700 | Robin Yount | .15 | .11 |
| 701 | Checklist | .07 | .05 |
| 702 | Checklist | .07 | .05 |
| 703 | Checklist | .07 | .05 |
| 704 | Checklist | .07 | .05 |
| 705 | Checklist | .07 | .05 |

A player's name in italic type indicates a rookie card. An (FC) indicates a player's first card for that particular card company.

# DONRUSS

## 1981 Donruss

The Donruss Co. of Memphis, Tenn., produced its premiere baseball card issue in 1981 with a set that consisted of 600 numbered cards and five unnumbered checklists. The cards, which measure 2-1/2" by 3-1/2", are printed on thin stock. The card fronts contain the Donruss logo plus the year of issue. The card backs are designed on a vertical format and have black print on red and white. The set, entitled "First Edition Collector Series," contains nearly 40 variations, those being first-printing errors that were corrected in a subsequent print run. The cards were issued in gum wax packs, with hobby dealer sales being coordinated by TCMA of Amawalk, N.Y. The complete set price does not include the higher priced variations.

|  | MT | NR MT |
|---|---|---|
| Complete Set: | 60.00 | 45.00 |
| Common Player: | .06 | .05 |
| | | |
| 1 Ozzie Smith | 3.00 | 2.25 |
| 2 Rollie Fingers | 1.00 | .70 |
| 3 Rick Wise | .08 | .06 |
| 4 Gene Richards | .06 | .05 |
| 5 Alan Trammell | .40 | .30 |
| 6 Tom Brookens | .08 | .06 |

**Regional interest may affect the value of a card.**

| | MT | NR MT |
|---|---|---|
| 7a Duffy Dyer (1980 Avg. .185) | 1.00 | .70 |
| 7b Duffy Dyer (1980 Avg. 185) | .10 | .08 |
| 8 Mark Fidrych | .08 | .06 |
| 9 Dave Rozema | .06 | .05 |
| 10 Ricky Peters | .06 | .05 |
| 11 Mike Schmidt | 2.50 | 2.00 |
| 12 Willie Stargell | .80 | .60 |
| 13 Tim Foli | .06 | .05 |
| 14 Manny Sanguillen | .06 | .05 |
| 15 Grant Jackson | .06 | .05 |
| 16 Eddie Solomon | .06 | .05 |
| 17 Omar Moreno | .06 | .05 |
| 18 Joe Morgan | .60 | .45 |
| 19 Rafael Landestoy | .06 | .05 |
| 20 Bruce Bochy | .06 | .05 |
| 21 Joe Sambito | .06 | .05 |
| 22 Manny Trillo | .08 | .06 |
| 23a *Dave Smith* (incomplete box around stats) | 1.00 | .70 |
| 23b *Dave Smith* (complete box around stats) | .30 | .25 |
| 24 Terry Puhl | .06 | .05 |
| 25 Bump Wills | .06 | .05 |
| 26a John Ellis (Danny Walton photo - with bat) | 1.25 | .90 |
| 26b John Ellis (John Ellis photo - with glove) | .10 | .08 |
| 27 Jim Kern | .06 | .05 |
| 28 Richie Zisk | .08 | .06 |
| 29 John Mayberry | .08 | .06 |
| 30 Bob Davis | .06 | .05 |
| 31 Jackson Todd | .06 | .05 |
| 32 Al Woods | .06 | .05 |
| 33 Steve Carlton | 1.00 | .70 |
| 34 Lee Mazzilli | .08 | .06 |
| 35 John Stearns | .06 | .05 |
| 36 Roy Jackson | .06 | .05 |
| 37 Mike Scott | .70 | .50 |
| 38 Lamar Johnson | .06 | .05 |
| 39 Kevin Bell | .06 | .05 |
| 40 Ed Farmer | .06 | .05 |
| 41 Ross Baumgarten | .06 | .05 |
| 42 Leo Sutherland | .06 | .05 |
| 43 Dan Meyer | .06 | .05 |
| 44 Ron Reed | .06 | .05 |
| 45 Mario Mendoza | .06 | .05 |
| 46 Rick Honeycutt | .06 | .05 |
| 47 Glenn Abbott | .06 | .05 |
| 48 Leon Roberts | .06 | .05 |
| 49 Rod Carew | 1.50 | 1.25 |
| 50 Bert Campaneris | .10 | .08 |
| 51a Tom Donahue (incorrect spelling) | 1.00 | .70 |
| 51b Tom Donohue (Donohue on front) | .10 | .08 |
| 52 Dave Frost | .06 | .05 |
| 53 Ed Halicki | .06 | .05 |
| 54 Dan Ford | .06 | .05 |
| 55 Garry Maddox | .10 | .08 |
| 56a Steve Garvey ("Surpassed 25 HR..." on back) | 1.75 | 1.25 |
| 56b Steve Garvey ("Surpassed 21 HR..." on back) | .60 | .45 |

| | | MT | NR MT |
|---|---|---|---|
| 57 | Bill Russell | .08 | .06 |
| 58 | Don Sutton | .30 | .25 |
| 59 | Reggie Smith | .10 | .08 |
| 60 | Rick Monday | .10 | .08 |
| 61 | Ray Knight | .10 | .08 |
| 62 | Johnny Bench | 1.25 | .90 |
| 63 | Mario Soto | .08 | .06 |
| 64 | Doug Bair | .06 | .05 |
| 65 | George Foster | .20 | .15 |
| 66 | Jeff Burroughs | .08 | .06 |
| 67 | Keith Hernandez | .40 | .30 |
| 68 | Tom Herr | .10 | .08 |
| 69 | Bob Forsch | .08 | .06 |
| 70 | John Fulgham | .06 | .05 |
| 71a | Bobby Bonds (lifetime HR 986) | 1.00 | .70 |
| 71b | Bobby Bonds (lifetime HR 326) | .15 | .11 |
| 72a | Rennie Stennett ("...breaking broke leg..." on back) | 1.00 | .70 |
| 72b | Rennie Stennett ("...breaking leg..." on back) | .10 | .08 |
| 73 | Joe Strain | .06 | .05 |
| 74 | Ed Whitson | .06 | .05 |
| 75 | Tom Griffin | .06 | .05 |
| 76 | Bill North | .06 | .05 |
| 77 | Gene Garber | .06 | .05 |
| 78 | Mike Hargrove | .06 | .05 |
| 79 | Dave Rosello | .06 | .05 |
| 80 | Ron Hassey | .06 | .05 |
| 81 | Sid Monge | .06 | .05 |
| 82a | Joe Charboneau ("For some reason, Phillies..." on back) | 1.00 | .70 |
| 82b | Joe Charboneau ("Phillies..." on back) | .12 | .09 |
| 83 | Cecil Cooper | .15 | .11 |
| 84 | Sal Bando | .10 | .08 |
| 85 | Moose Haas | .06 | .05 |
| 86 | Mike Caldwell | .06 | .05 |
| 87a | Larry Hisle ("...Twins with 28 RBI." on back) | 1.00 | .70 |
| 87b | Larry Hisle ("...Twins with 28 HR" on back) | .10 | .08 |
| 88 | Luis Gomez | .06 | .05 |
| 89 | Larry Parrish | .10 | .08 |
| 90 | Gary Carter | .50 | .40 |
| 91 | Bill Gullickson | .15 | .11 |
| 92 | Fred Norman | .06 | .05 |
| 93 | Tommy Hutton | .06 | .05 |
| 94 | Carl Yastrzemski | 1.00 | .70 |
| 95 | Glenn Hoffman | .06 | .05 |
| 96 | Dennis Eckersley | 2.00 | 1.50 |
| 97a | Tom Burgmeier (Throws: Right) | 1.00 | .70 |
| 97b | Tom Burgmeier (Throws: Left) | .10 | .08 |
| 98 | Win Remmerswaal | .06 | .05 |
| 99 | Bob Horner | .12 | .09 |
| 100 | George Brett | 3.00 | 2.25 |
| 101 | Dave Chalk | .06 | .05 |
| 102 | Dennis Leonard | .08 | .06 |
| 103 | Renie Martin | .06 | .05 |
| 104 | Amos Otis | .08 | .06 |
| 105 | Graig Nettles | .15 | .11 |

| | | MT | NR MT |
|---|---|---|---|
| 106 | Eric Soderholm | .06 | .05 |
| 107 | Tommy John | .20 | .15 |
| 108 | Tom Underwood | .06 | .05 |
| 109 | Lou Piniella | .12 | .09 |
| 110 | Mickey Klutts | .06 | .05 |
| 111 | Bobby Murcer | .10 | .08 |
| 112 | Eddie Murray | 3.00 | 2.25 |
| 113 | Rick Dempsey | .08 | .06 |
| 114 | Scott McGregor | .08 | .06 |
| 115 | Ken Singleton | .10 | .08 |
| 116 | Gary Roenicke | .06 | .05 |
| 117 | Dave Revering | .06 | .05 |
| 118 | Mike Norris | .06 | .05 |
| 119 | Rickey Henderson | 18.00 | 13.50 |
| 120 | Mike Heath | .06 | .05 |
| 121 | Dave Cash | .06 | .05 |
| 122 | Randy Jones | .08 | .06 |
| 123 | Eric Rasmussen | .06 | .05 |
| 124 | Jerry Mumphrey | .06 | .05 |
| 125 | Richie Hebner | .06 | .05 |
| 126 | Mark Wagner | .06 | .05 |
| 127 | Jack Morris | 1.50 | 1.25 |
| 128 | Dan Petry | .08 | .06 |
| 129 | Bruce Robbins | .06 | .05 |
| 130 | Champ Summers | .06 | .05 |
| 131a | Pete Rose ("...see card 251." on back) | 2.25 | 1.75 |
| 131b | Pete Rose ("...see card 371." on back) | 1.25 | .90 |
| 132 | Willie Stargell | .40 | .30 |
| 133 | Ed Ott | .06 | .05 |
| 134 | Jim Bibby | .06 | .05 |
| 135 | Bert Blyleven | .12 | .09 |
| 136 | Dave Parker | .30 | .25 |
| 137 | Bill Robinson | .06 | .05 |
| 138 | Enos Cabell | .06 | .05 |
| 139 | Dave Bergman | .06 | .05 |
| 140 | J R Richard | .10 | .08 |
| 141 | Ken Forsch | .06 | .05 |
| 142 | Larry Bowa | .15 | .11 |
| 143 | Frank LaCorte (photo actually Randy Niemann) | .06 | .05 |
| 144 | Dennis Walling | .06 | .05 |
| 145 | Buddy Bell | .12 | .09 |
| 146 | Ferguson Jenkins | .50 | .40 |
| 147 | Danny Darwin | .06 | .05 |
| 148 | John Grubb | .06 | .05 |
| 149 | Alfredo Griffin | .08 | .06 |
| 150 | Jerry Garvin | .06 | .05 |
| 151 | Paul Mirabella(FC) | .10 | .08 |
| 152 | Rick Bosetti | .06 | .05 |
| 153 | Dick Ruthven | .06 | .05 |
| 154 | Frank Taveras | .06 | .05 |
| 155 | Craig Swan | .06 | .05 |
| 156 | Jeff Reardon | 5.00 | 3.75 |
| 157 | Steve Henderson | .06 | .05 |
| 158 | Jim Morrison | .06 | .05 |
| 159 | Glenn Borgmann | .06 | .05 |
| 160 | Lamarr Hoyt (LaMarr) | .10 | .08 |
| 161 | Rich Wortham | .06 | .05 |
| 162 | Thad Bosley | .06 | .05 |
| 163 | Julio Cruz | .06 | .05 |
| 164a | Del Unser (no 3B in stat | | |

| | | MT | NR MT | | | | MT | NR MT |
|---|---|---|---|---|---|---|---|---|
| | heads) | 1.00 | .70 | 229 | Oscar Gamble | | .08 | .06 |
| 164b | Del Unser (3B in stat | | | 230 | Jeff Cox | | .06 | .05 |
| | heads) | .10 | .08 | 231 | Luis Tiant | | .12 | .09 |
| 165 | Jim Anderson | .06 | .05 | 232 | Rich Dauer | | .06 | .05 |
| 166 | Jim Beattie | .06 | .05 | 233 | Dan Graham | | .06 | .05 |
| 167 | Shane Rawley | .10 | .08 | 234 | Mike Flanagan | | .10 | .08 |
| 168 | Joe Simpson | .06 | .05 | 235 | John Lowenstein | | .06 | .05 |
| 169 | Rod Carew | 1.50 | 1.25 | 236 | Benny Ayala | | .06 | .05 |
| 170 | Fred Patek | .06 | .05 | 237 | Wayne Gross | | .06 | .05 |
| 171 | Frank Tanana | .10 | .08 | 238 | Rick Langford | | .06 | .05 |
| 172 | Alfredo Martinez | .06 | .05 | 239 | Tony Armas | | .10 | .08 |
| 173 | Chris Knapp | .06 | .05 | 240a | Bob Lacy (incorrect | | |
| 174 | Joe Rudi | .10 | .08 | | spelling) | | 1.00 | .70 |
| 175 | Greg Luzinski | .15 | .11 | 240b | Bob Lacey (correct | | |
| 176 | Steve Garvey | .50 | .40 | | spelling) | | .10 | .08 |
| 177 | Joe Ferguson | .06 | .05 | 241 | Gene Tenace | | .08 | .06 |
| 178 | Bob Welch | .60 | .45 | 242 | Bob Shirley | | .06 | .05 |
| 179 | Dusty Baker | .10 | .08 | 243 | Gary Lucas | | .08 | .06 |
| 180 | Rudy Law | .06 | .05 | 244 | Jerry Turner | | .06 | .05 |
| 181 | Dave Concepcion | .15 | .11 | 245 | John Wockenfuss | | .06 | .05 |
| 182 | Johnny Bench | 1.00 | .70 | 246 | Stan Papi | | .06 | .05 |
| 183 | Mike LaCoss | .06 | .05 | 247 | Milt Wilcox | | .06 | .05 |
| 184 | Ken Griffey | .12 | .09 | 248 | Dan Schatzeder | | .06 | .05 |
| 185 | Dave Collins | .08 | .06 | 249 | Steve Kemp | | .08 | .06 |
| 186 | Brian Asselstine | .06 | .05 | 250 | Jim Lentine | | .06 | .05 |
| 187 | Garry Templeton | .10 | .08 | 251 | Pete Rose | | 1.00 | .70 |
| 188 | Mike Phillips | .06 | .05 | 252 | Bill Madlock | | .12 | .09 |
| 189 | Pete Vukovich | .08 | .06 | 253 | Dale Berra | | .06 | .05 |
| 190 | John Urrea | .06 | .05 | 254 | Kent Tekulve | | .08 | .06 |
| 191 | Tony Scott | .06 | .05 | 255 | Enrique Romo | | .06 | .05 |
| 192 | Darrell Evans | .12 | .09 | 256 | Mike Easler | | .08 | .06 |
| 193 | Milt May | .06 | .05 | 257 | Chuck Tanner | | .06 | .05 |
| 194 | Bob Knepper | .08 | .06 | 258 | Art Howe | | .06 | .05 |
| 195 | Randy Moffitt | .06 | .05 | 259 | Alan Ashby | | .06 | .05 |
| 196 | Larry Herndon | .08 | .06 | 260 | Nolan Ryan | | 7.00 | 5.25 |
| 197 | Rick Camp | .06 | .05 | 261a | Vern Ruhle (Ken Forsch | | |
| 198 | Andre Thornton | .10 | .08 | | photo - head shot) | | 1.25 | .90 |
| 199 | Tom Veryzer | .06 | .05 | 261b | Vern Ruhle (Vern Ruhle | | |
| 200 | Gary Alexander | .06 | .05 | | photo - waist to head shot) | | |
| 201 | Rick Waits | .06 | .05 | | | | .10 | .08 |
| 202 | Rick Manning | .06 | .05 | 262 | Bob Boone | | .10 | .08 |
| 203 | Paul Molitor | 1.25 | .90 | 263 | Cesar Cedeno | | .12 | .09 |
| 204 | Jim Gantner | .08 | .06 | 264 | Jeff Leonard | | .12 | .09 |
| 205 | Paul Mitchell | .06 | .05 | 265 | Pat Putnam | | .06 | .05 |
| 206 | Reggie Cleveland | .06 | .05 | 266 | Jon Matlack | | .08 | .06 |
| 207 | Sixto Lezcano | .06 | .05 | 267 | Dave Rajsich | | .06 | .05 |
| 208 | Bruce Benedict | .06 | .05 | 268 | Billy Sample | | .06 | .05 |
| 209 | Rodney Scott | .06 | .05 | 269 | Damaso Garcia | | .10 | .08 |
| 210 | John Tamargo | .06 | .05 | 270 | Tom Buskey | | .06 | .05 |
| 211 | Bill Lee | .08 | .06 | 271 | Joey McLaughlin | | .06 | .05 |
| 212 | Andre Dawson | 1.75 | 1.25 | 272 | Barry Bonnell | | .06 | .05 |
| 213 | Rowland Office | .06 | .05 | 273 | Tug McGraw | | .10 | .08 |
| 214 | Carl Yastrzemski | 1.25 | .90 | 274 | Mike Jorgensen | | .06 | .05 |
| 215 | Jerry Remy | .06 | .05 | 275 | Pat Zachry | | .06 | .05 |
| 216 | Mike Torrez | .08 | .06 | 276 | Neil Allen | | .08 | .06 |
| 217 | Skip Lockwood | .06 | .05 | 277 | Joel Youngblood | | .06 | .05 |
| 218 | Fred Lynn | .20 | .15 | 278 | Greg Pryor | | .06 | .05 |
| 219 | Chris Chambliss | .08 | .06 | 279 | Britt Burns | | .10 | .08 |
| 220 | Willie Aikens | .06 | .05 | 280 | Rich Dotson | | .25 | .20 |
| 221 | John Wathan | .08 | .06 | 281 | Chet Lemon | | .08 | .06 |
| 222 | Dan Quisenberry | .15 | .11 | 282 | Rusty Kuntz | | .06 | .05 |
| 223 | Willie Wilson | .15 | .11 | 283 | Ted Cox | | .06 | .05 |
| 224 | Clint Hurdle | .06 | .05 | 284 | Sparky Lyle | | .10 | .08 |
| 225 | Bob Watson | .08 | .06 | 285 | Larry Cox | | .06 | .05 |
| 226 | Jim Spencer | .06 | .05 | 286 | Floyd Bannister | | .10 | .08 |
| 227 | Ron Guidry | .25 | .20 | 287 | Byron McLaughlin | | .06 | .05 |
| 228 | Reggie Jackson | 4.00 | 3.00 | 288 | Rodney Craig | | .06 | .05 |

| | | MT | NR MT |
|---|---|---|---|
| 289 | Bobby Grich | .10 | .08 |
| 290 | Dickie Thon | .08 | .06 |
| 291 | Mark Clear | .06 | .05 |
| 292 | Dave Lemanczyk | .06 | .05 |
| 293 | Jason Thompson | .06 | .05 |
| 294 | Rick Miller | .06 | .05 |
| 295 | Lonnie Smith | .08 | .06 |
| 296 | Ron Cey | .12 | .09 |
| 297 | Steve Yeager | .06 | .05 |
| 298 | Bobby Castillo | .06 | .05 |
| 299 | Manny Mota | .08 | .06 |
| 300 | Jay Johnstone | .08 | .06 |
| 301 | Dan Driessen | .08 | .06 |
| 302 | Joe Nolan | .06 | .05 |
| 303 | Paul Householder | .06 | .05 |
| 304 | Harry Spilman | .06 | .05 |
| 305 | Cesar Geronimo | .06 | .05 |
| 306a | Gary Mathews (Mathews on front) | 1.25 | .90 |
| 306b | Gary Matthews (Matthews on front) | .10 | .08 |
| 307 | Ken Reitz | .06 | .05 |
| 308 | Ted Simmons | .12 | .09 |
| 309 | John Littlefield | .06 | .05 |
| 310 | George Frazier | .06 | .05 |
| 311 | Dane Iorg | .06 | .05 |
| 312 | Mike Ivie | .06 | .05 |
| 313 | Dennis Littlejohn | .06 | .05 |
| 314 | Gary LaVelle (Lavelle) | .06 | .05 |
| 315 | Jack Clark | .25 | .20 |
| 316 | Jim Wohlford | .06 | .05 |
| 317 | Rick Matula | .06 | .05 |
| 318 | Toby Harrah | .08 | .06 |
| 319a | Dwane Kuiper (Dwane on front) | 1.00 | .70 |
| 319b | Duane Kuiper (Duane on front) | .10 | .08 |
| 320 | Len Barker | .08 | .06 |
| 321 | Victor Cruz | .06 | .05 |
| 322 | Dell Alston | .06 | .05 |
| 323 | Robin Yount | 3.50 | 2.75 |
| 324 | Charlie Moore | .06 | .05 |
| 325 | Lary Sorensen | .06 | .05 |
| 326a | Gorman Thomas ("...30 HR mark 4th..." on back) | 1.25 | .90 |
| 326b | Gorman Thomas ("...30 HR mark 3rd..." on back) | .10 | .08 |
| 327 | Bob Rodgers | .08 | .06 |
| 328 | Phil Niekro | .30 | .25 |
| 329 | Chris Speier | .06 | .05 |
| 330a | Steve Rodgers (Rodgers on front) | 1.00 | .70 |
| 330b | Steve Rogers (Rogers on front) | .10 | .08 |
| 331 | Woodie Fryman | .08 | .06 |
| 332 | Warren Cromartie | .06 | .05 |
| 333 | Jerry White | .06 | .05 |
| 334 | Tony Perez | .20 | .15 |
| 335 | Carlton Fisk | 1.75 | 1.25 |
| 336 | Dick Drago | .06 | .05 |
| 337 | Steve Renko | .06 | .05 |
| 338 | Jim Rice | .50 | .40 |
| 339 | Jerry Royster | .06 | .05 |
| 340 | Frank White | .10 | .08 |

| | | MT | NR MT |
|---|---|---|---|
| 341 | Jamie Quirk | .06 | .05 |
| 342a | Paul Spittorff (Spittorff on front) | 1.00 | .70 |
| 342b | Paul Splittorff (Splittorff on front) | .08 | .06 |
| 343 | Marty Pattin | .06 | .05 |
| 344 | Pete LaCock | .06 | .05 |
| 345 | Willie Randolph | .10 | .08 |
| 346 | Rick Cerone | .06 | .05 |
| 347 | Rich Gossage | .20 | .15 |
| 348 | Reggie Jackson | 1.75 | 1.25 |
| 349 | Ruppert Jones | .06 | .05 |
| 350 | Dave McKay | .06 | .05 |
| 351 | Yogi Berra | .15 | .11 |
| 352 | Doug Decinces (DeCinces) | .10 | .08 |
| 353 | Jim Palmer | 1.00 | .70 |
| 354 | Tippy Martinez | .06 | .05 |
| 355 | Al Bumbry | .08 | .06 |
| 356 | Earl Weaver | .10 | .08 |
| 357a | Bob Picciolo (Bob on front) | 1.00 | .70 |
| 357b | Rob Picciolo (Rob on front) | .10 | .08 |
| 358 | Matt Keough | .06 | .05 |
| 359 | Dwayne Murphy | .08 | .06 |
| 360 | Brian Kingman | .06 | .05 |
| 361 | Bill Fahey | .06 | .05 |
| 362 | Steve Mura | .06 | .05 |
| 363 | Dennis Kinney | .06 | .05 |
| 364 | Dave Winfield | 2.50 | 2.00 |
| 365 | Lou Whitaker | .40 | .30 |
| 366 | Lance Parrish | .35 | .25 |
| 367 | Tim Corcoran | .06 | .05 |
| 368 | Pat Underwood | .06 | .05 |
| 369 | Al Cowens | .06 | .05 |
| 370 | Sparky Anderson | .10 | .08 |
| 371 | Pete Rose | 1.00 | .70 |
| 372 | Phil Garner | .08 | .06 |
| 373 | Steve Nicosia | .06 | .05 |
| 374 | John Candelaria | .10 | .08 |
| 375 | Don Robinson | .08 | .06 |
| 376 | Lee Lacy | .06 | .05 |
| 377 | John Milner | .06 | .05 |
| 378 | Craig Reynolds | .06 | .05 |
| 379a | Luis Pujois (Pujois on front) | 1.00 | .70 |
| 379b | Luis Pujols (Pujols on front) | .10 | .08 |
| 380 | Joe Niekro | .12 | .09 |
| 381 | Joaquin Andujar | .10 | .08 |
| 382 | *Keith Moreland* | .35 | .25 |
| 383 | Jose Cruz | .12 | .09 |
| 384 | Bill Virdon | .06 | .05 |
| 385 | Jim Sundberg | .08 | .06 |
| 386 | Doc Medich | .06 | .05 |
| 387 | Al Oliver | .15 | .11 |
| 388 | Jim Norris | .06 | .05 |
| 389 | Bob Bailor | .06 | .05 |
| 390 | Ernie Whitt | .08 | .06 |
| 391 | Otto Velez | .06 | .05 |
| 392 | Roy Howell | .06 | .05 |
| 393 | *Bob Walk* | .35 | .25 |
| 394 | Doug Flynn | .06 | .05 |
| 395 | Pete Falcone | .06 | .05 |
| 396 | Tom Hausman | .06 | .05 |
| 397 | Elliott Maddox | .06 | .05 |

| | | MT | NR MT |
|---|---|---|---|
| 398 | Mike Squires | .06 | .05 |
| 399 | Marvis Foley | .06 | .05 |
| 400 | Steve Trout | .06 | .05 |
| 401 | Wayne Nordhagen | .06 | .05 |
| 402 | Tony Larussa (LaRussa) | | |
| | | .08 | .06 |
| 403 | Bruce Bochte | .06 | .05 |
| 404 | Bake McBride | .06 | .05 |
| 405 | Jerry Narron | .06 | .05 |
| 406 | Rob Dressler | .06 | .05 |
| 407 | Dave Heaverlo | .06 | .05 |
| 408 | Tom Paciorek | .06 | .05 |
| 409 | Carney Lansford | .10 | .08 |
| 410 | Brian Downing | .10 | .08 |
| 411 | Don Aase | .06 | .05 |
| 412 | Jim Barr | .06 | .05 |
| 413 | Don Baylor | .12 | .09 |
| 414 | Jim Fregosi | .08 | .06 |
| 415 | Dallas Green | .08 | .06 |
| 416 | Dave Lopes | .10 | .08 |
| 417 | Jerry Reuss | .10 | .08 |
| 418 | Rick Sutcliffe | .20 | .15 |
| 419 | Derrel Thomas | .06 | .05 |
| 420 | Tommy LaSorda | | |
| | (Lasorda) | .10 | .08 |
| 421 | *Charlie Leibrandt* | .40 | .30 |
| 422 | Tom Seaver | 2.00 | 1.50 |
| 423 | Ron Oester | .06 | .05 |
| 424 | Junior Kennedy | .06 | .05 |
| 425 | Tom Seaver | 2.00 | 1.50 |
| 426 | Bobby Cox | .06 | .05 |
| 427 | *Leon Durham* | .20 | .15 |
| 428 | Terry Kennedy | .08 | .06 |
| 429 | Silvio Martinez | .06 | .05 |
| 430 | George Hendrick | .08 | .06 |
| 431 | Red Schoendienst | .08 | .06 |
| 432 | John LeMaster | .06 | .05 |
| 433 | Vida Blue | .12 | .09 |
| 434 | John Montefusco | .08 | .06 |
| 435 | Terry Whitfield | .06 | .05 |
| 436 | Dave Bristol | .06 | .05 |
| 437 | Dale Murphy | .90 | .70 |
| 438 | Jerry Dybzinski | .06 | .05 |
| 439 | Jorge Orta | .06 | .05 |
| 440 | Wayne Garland | .06 | .05 |
| 441 | Miguel Dilone | .06 | .05 |
| 442 | Dave Garcia | .06 | .05 |
| 443 | Don Money | .06 | .05 |
| 444a | Buck Martinez (photo | | |
| | reversed) | 1.00 | .70 |
| 444b | Buck Martinez (photo | | |
| | correct) | .10 | .08 |
| 445 | Jerry Augustine | .06 | .05 |
| 446 | Ben Oglivie | .08 | .06 |
| 447 | Jim Slaton | .06 | .05 |
| 448 | Doyle Alexander | .10 | .08 |
| 449 | Tony Bernazard | .06 | .05 |
| 450 | Scott Sanderson | .06 | .05 |
| 451 | Dave Palmer | .06 | .05 |
| 452 | Stan Bahnsen | .06 | .05 |
| 453 | Dick Williams | .06 | .05 |
| 454 | Rick Burleson | .08 | .06 |
| 455 | Gary Allenson | .06 | .05 |
| 456 | Bob Stanley | .06 | .05 |
| 457a | *John Tudor* (lifetime W | | |
| | L 9-7) | 1.50 | 1.25 |
| 457b | *John Tudor* (lifetime W | | |

| | | MT | NR MT |
|---|---|---|---|
| | L 9-7) | 1.00 | .70 |
| 458 | Dwight Evans | .15 | .11 |
| 459 | Glenn Hubbard | .08 | .06 |
| 460 | U L Washington | .06 | .05 |
| 461 | Larry Gura | .06 | .05 |
| 462 | Rich Gale | .06 | .05 |
| 463 | Hal McRae | .10 | .08 |
| 464 | Jim Frey | .06 | .05 |
| 465 | Bucky Dent | .10 | .08 |
| 466 | Dennis Werth | .06 | .05 |
| 467 | Ron Davis | .08 | .06 |
| 468 | Reggie Jackson | 3.50 | 2.75 |
| 469 | Bobby Brown | .06 | .05 |
| 470 | *Mike Davis* | .20 | .15 |
| 471 | Gaylord Perry | .50 | .40 |
| 472 | Mark Belanger | .08 | .06 |
| 473 | Jim Palmer | .80 | .60 |
| 474 | Sammy Stewart | .06 | .05 |
| 475 | Tim Stoddard | .06 | .05 |
| 476 | Steve Stone | .08 | .06 |
| 477 | Jeff Newman | .06 | .05 |
| 478 | Steve McCatty | .06 | .05 |
| 479 | Billy Martin | .12 | .09 |
| 480 | Mitchell Page | .06 | .05 |
| 481 | Cy Young 1980 (Steve | | |
| | Carlton) | .40 | .30 |
| 482 | Bill Buckner | .12 | .09 |
| 483a | Ivan DeJesus (lifetime | | |
| | hits 702) | 1.00 | .70 |
| 483b | Ivan DeJesus (lifetime | | |
| | hits 642) | .10 | .08 |
| 484 | Cliff Johnson | .06 | .05 |
| 485 | Lenny Randle | .06 | .05 |
| 486 | Larry Milbourne | .06 | .05 |
| 487 | Roy Smalley | .06 | .05 |
| 488 | John Castino | .06 | .05 |
| 489 | Ron Jackson | .06 | .05 |
| 490a | Dave Roberts (1980 | | |
| | highlights begins "Showed | | |
| | pop...") | 1.00 | .70 |
| 490b | Dave Roberts (1980 | | |
| | highlights begins "Declared | | |
| | himself...") | .10 | .08 |
| 491 | MVP (George Brett) | | |
| | | 1.00 | .70 |
| 492 | Mike Cubbage | .06 | .05 |
| 493 | Rob Wilfong | .06 | .05 |
| 494 | Danny Goodwin | .06 | .05 |
| 495 | Jose Morales | .06 | .05 |
| 496 | Mickey Rivers | .08 | .06 |
| 497 | Mike Edwards | .06 | .05 |
| 498 | Mike Sadek | .06 | .05 |
| 499 | Lenn Sakata | .06 | .05 |
| 500 | Gene Michael | .06 | .05 |
| 501 | Dave Roberts | .06 | .05 |
| 502 | Steve Dillard | .06 | .05 |
| 503 | Jim Essian | .06 | .05 |
| 504 | Rance Mulliniks | .06 | .05 |
| 505 | Darrell Porter | .08 | .06 |
| 506 | Joe Torre | .08 | .06 |
| 507 | Terry Crowley | .06 | .05 |
| 508 | Bill Travers | .06 | .05 |
| 509 | Nelson Norman | .06 | .05 |
| 510 | Bob McClure | .06 | .05 |
| 511 | *Steve Howe* | .10 | .08 |
| 512 | Dave Rader | .06 | .05 |
| 513 | Mick Kelleher | .06 | .05 |

| | | MT | NR MT |
|---|---|---|---|
| 514 | Kiko Garcia | .06 | .05 |
| 515 | Larry Biittner | .06 | .05 |
| 516a | Willie Norwood (1980 highlights begins "Spent most...") | 1.00 | .70 |
| 516b | Willie Norwood (1980 highlights begins "Traded to...") | .10 | .08 |
| 517 | Bo Diaz | .08 | .06 |
| 518 | Juan Beniquez | .06 | .05 |
| 519 | Scot Thompson | .06 | .05 |
| 520 | Jim Tracy | .06 | .05 |
| 521 | Carlos Lezcano | .06 | .05 |
| 522 | Joe Amalfitano | .06 | .05 |
| 523 | Preston Hanna | .06 | .05 |
| 524a | Ray Burris (1980 highlights begins "Went on...") | 1.00 | .70 |
| 524b | Ray Burris (1980 highlights begins "Drafted by...") | .10 | .08 |
| 525 | Broderick Perkins | .06 | .05 |
| 526 | Mickey Hatcher | .08 | .06 |
| 527 | John Goryl | .06 | .05 |
| 528 | Dick Davis | .06 | .05 |
| 529 | Butch Wynegar | .06 | .05 |
| 530 | Sal Butera | .06 | .05 |
| 531 | Jerry Koosman | .10 | .08 |
| 532a | Jeff Zahn (Geoff) (1980 highlights begins "Was 2nd in...") | 1.00 | .70 |
| 532b | Jeff Zahn (Geoff) (1980 highlights begins "Signed a 3 year...") | .10 | .08 |
| 533 | Dennis Martinez | .08 | .06 |
| 534 | Gary Thomasson | .06 | .05 |
| 535 | Steve Macko | .06 | .05 |
| 536 | Jim Kaat | .15 | .11 |
| 537 | Best Hitters (George Brett, Rod Carew) | 1.50 | 1.25 |
| 538 | *Tim Raines* | 5.00 | 3.75 |
| 539 | Keith Smith | .06 | .05 |
| 540 | Ken Macha | .06 | .05 |
| 541 | Burt Hooton | .08 | .06 |
| 542 | Butch Hobson | .06 | .05 |
| 543 | Bill Stein | .06 | .05 |
| 544 | Dave Stapleton | .06 | .05 |
| 545 | Bob Pate | .06 | .05 |
| 546 | Doug Corbett | .06 | .05 |
| 547 | Darrell Jackson | .06 | .05 |
| 548 | Pete Redfern | .06 | .05 |
| 549 | Roger Erickson | .06 | .05 |
| 550 | Al Hrabosky | .08 | .06 |
| 551 | Dick Tidrow | .06 | .05 |
| 552 | Dave Ford | .06 | .05 |
| 553 | Dave Kingman | .15 | .11 |
| 554a | Mike Vail (1980 highlights begins "After...") | 1.00 | .70 |
| 554b | Mike Vail (1980 highlights begins "Traded...") | .10 | .08 |
| 555a | Jerry Martin (1980 highlights begins "Overcame...") | 1.00 | .70 |
| 555b | Jerry Martin (1980 highlights begins "Traded...") | .10 | .08 |
| 556a | Jesus Figueroa (1980 highlights begins "Had...") | 1.00 | .70 |
| 556b | Jesus Figueroa (1980 highlights begins "Traded...") | .10 | .08 |
| 557 | Don Stanhouse | .06 | .05 |
| 558 | Barry Foote | .06 | .05 |
| 559 | Tim Blackwell | .06 | .05 |
| 560 | Bruce Sutter | .15 | .11 |
| 561 | Rick Reuschel | .10 | .08 |
| 562 | Lynn McGlothen | .06 | .05 |
| 563a | Bob Owchinko (1980 highlights begins "Traded...") | 1.00 | .70 |
| 563b | Bob Owchinko (1980 highlights begins "Involved...") | .10 | .08 |
| 564 | John Verhoeven | .06 | .05 |
| 565 | Ken Landreaux | .06 | .05 |
| 566a | Glen Adams (Glen on front) | 1.00 | .70 |
| 566b | Glenn Adams (Glenn on front) | .10 | .08 |
| 567 | Hosken Powell | .06 | .05 |
| 568 | Dick Noles | .06 | .05 |
| 569 | *Danny Ainge* | 1.50 | 1.25 |
| 570 | Bobby Mattick | .06 | .05 |
| 571 | Joe LeFebvre (Lefebvre) | .06 | .05 |
| 572 | Bobby Clark | .06 | .05 |
| 573 | Dennis Lamp | .06 | .05 |
| 574 | Randy Lerch | .06 | .05 |
| 575 | *Mookie Wilson* | .60 | .45 |
| 576 | Ron LeFlore | .08 | .06 |
| 577 | Jim Dwyer | .06 | .05 |
| 578 | Bill Castro | .06 | .05 |
| 579 | Greg Minton | .06 | .05 |
| 580 | Mark Littell | .06 | .05 |
| 581 | Andy Hassler | .06 | .05 |
| 582 | Dave Stieb | .60 | .45 |
| 583 | Ken Oberkfell | .06 | .05 |
| 584 | Larry Bradford | .06 | .05 |
| 585 | Fred Stanley | .06 | .05 |
| 586 | Bill Caudill | .06 | .05 |
| 587 | Doug Capilla | .06 | .05 |
| 588 | George Riley | .06 | .05 |
| 589 | Willie Hernandez | .10 | .08 |
| 590 | MVP (Mike Schmidt) | 1.00 | .70 |
| 591 | Cy Young 1980 (Steve Stone) | .08 | .06 |
| 592 | Rick Sofield | .06 | .05 |
| 593 | Bombo Rivera | .06 | .05 |
| 594 | Gary Ward | .08 | .06 |
| 595a | Dave Edwards (1980 highlights begins "Sidelined...") | 1.00 | .70 |
| 595b | Dave Edwards (1980 highlights begins "Traded...") | .10 | .08 |
| 596 | Mike Proly | .06 | .05 |
| 597 | Tommy Boggs | .06 | .05 |
| 598 | Greg Gross | .06 | .05 |
| 599 | Elias Sosa | .06 | .05 |
| 600 | Pat Kelly | .06 | .05 |

| | | MT | NR MT |
|---|---|---|---|
| ---a | Checklist 1-120 (51 Tom Donohue) | 2.00 | 1.50 |
| ---b | Checklist 1-120 (51 Tom Donohue) | .10 | .08 |
| ---- | Checklist 121-240 | .06 | .05 |
| ---a | Checklist 241-360 (306 Gary Mathews) | .70 | .50 |
| ---b | Checklist 241-360 (306 Gary Matthews) | .10 | .08 |
| ---a | Checklist 361-480 (379 Luis Pujois) | .70 | .50 |
| ---b | Checklist 361-480 (379 Luis Pujols) | .10 | .08 |
| ---a | Checklist 481-600 (566 Glen Adams) | .70 | .50 |
| ---b | Checklist 481-600 (566 Glenn Adams) | .10 | .08 |

# 1982 Donruss

Using card stock thicker than the previous year, Donruss issued a 660-card set which includes 653 numbered cards and seven un-numbered checklists. The cards, which measure 2-1/2" by 3-1/2", were sold with puzzle pieces rather than gum as a result of a lawsuit by Topps. The puzzle pieces (three pieces on one card per pack) feature Babe Ruth. The first 26 cards of the set, entitled Diamond Kings, showcase the artwork of Dick Perez of Perez-Steele Galleries. The card fronts display the Donruss logo and the year of issue. The card backs have black and blue ink on white stock and include the player's career highlights. The complete set price does not include the higher priced variations.

| | MT | NR MT |
|---|---|---|
| Complete Set: | 100.00 | 75.00 |
| Common Player: | .06 | .05 |

| | | MT | NR MT |
|---|---|---|---|
| 1 | Pete Rose (DK) | 1.50 | 1.25 |
| 2 | Gary Carter (DK) | .50 | .40 |
| 3 | Steve Garvey (DK) | .50 | .40 |
| 4 | Vida Blue (DK) | .12 | .09 |
| 5a | Alan Trammel (DK) (name incorrect) | 1.50 | 1.25 |
| 5b | Alan Trammell (DK) (name correct) | .40 | .30 |
| 6 | Len Barker (DK) | .08 | .06 |
| 7 | Dwight Evans (DK) | .15 | .11 |
| 8 | Rod Carew (DK) | .60 | .45 |
| 9 | George Hendrick (DK) | .08 | .06 |
| 10 | Phil Niekro (DK) | .30 | .25 |
| 11 | Richie Zisk (DK) | .08 | .06 |
| 12 | Dave Parker (DK) | .30 | .25 |
| 13 | Nolan Ryan (DK) | 3.00 | 2.25 |
| 14 | Ivan DeJesus (DK) | .08 | .06 |
| 15 | George Brett (DK) | 1.50 | 1.25 |
| 16 | Tom Seaver (DK) | .80 | .60 |
| 17 | Dave Kingman (DK) | .15 | .11 |
| 18 | Dave Winfield (DK) | .80 | .60 |
| 19 | Mike Norris (DK) | .08 | .06 |
| 20 | Carlton Fisk (DK) | .50 | .40 |
| 21 | Ozzie Smith (DK) | .20 | .15 |
| 22 | Roy Smalley (DK) | .08 | .06 |
| 23 | Buddy Bell (DK) | .12 | .09 |
| 24 | Ken Singleton (DK) | .10 | .08 |
| 25 | John Mayberry (DK) | .08 | .06 |
| 26 | Gorman Thomas (DK) | .10 | .08 |
| 27 | Earl Weaver | .10 | .08 |
| 28 | Rollie Fingers | .80 | .60 |
| 29 | Sparky Anderson | .10 | .08 |
| 30 | Dennis Eckersley | 1.25 | .90 |
| 31 | Dave Winfield | 2.50 | 2.00 |
| 32 | Burt Hooton | .08 | .06 |
| 33 | Rick Waits | .06 | .05 |
| 34 | George Brett | 2.00 | 1.50 |
| 35 | Steve McCatty | .06 | .05 |
| 36 | Steve Rogers | .08 | .06 |
| 37 | Bill Stein | .06 | .05 |
| 38 | Steve Renko | .06 | .05 |
| 39 | Mike Squires | .06 | .05 |
| 40 | George Hendrick | .08 | .06 |
| 41 | Bob Knepper | .08 | .06 |
| 42 | Steve Carlton | 1.00 | .70 |
| 43 | Larry Biittner | .06 | .05 |
| 44 | Chris Welsh | .06 | .05 |
| 45 | Steve Nicosia | .06 | .05 |
| 46 | Jack Clark | .25 | .20 |
| 47 | Chris Chambliss | .08 | .06 |
| 48 | Ivan DeJesus | .06 | .05 |
| 49 | Lee Mazzilli | .08 | .06 |
| 50 | Julio Cruz | .06 | .05 |
| 51 | Pete Redfern | .06 | .05 |
| 52 | Dave Stieb | .12 | .09 |
| 53 | Doug Corbett | .06 | .05 |
| 54 | *Jorge Bell* (FC) | 7.50 | 5.65 |
| 55 | Joe Simpson | .06 | .05 |
| 56 | Rusty Staub | .10 | .08 |
| 57 | Hector Cruz | .06 | .05 |
| 58 | Claudell Washington (FC) | .10 | .08 |
| 59 | Enrique Romo | .06 | .05 |
| 60 | Gary Lavelle | .06 | .05 |
| 61 | Tim Flannery | .06 | .05 |
| 62 | Joe Nolan | .06 | .05 |

| | | MT | NR MT | | | | MT | NR MT |
|---|---|---|---|---|---|---|---|---|
| 63 | Larry Bowa | .15 | .11 | | 126 | Randy Martz | .06 | .05 |
| 64 | Sixto Lezcano | .06 | .05 | | 127 | Richie Zisk | .08 | .06 |
| 65 | Joe Sambito | .06 | .05 | | 128 | Mike Scott | .15 | .11 |
| 66 | Bruce Kison | .06 | .05 | | 129 | Lloyd Moseby(FC) | .20 | .15 |
| 67 | Wayne Nordhagen | .06 | .05 | | 130 | Rob Wilfong | .06 | .05 |
| 68 | Woodie Fryman | .08 | .06 | | 131 | Tim Stoddard | .06 | .05 |
| 69 | Billy Sample | .06 | .05 | | 132 | Gorman Thomas | .10 | .08 |
| 70 | Amos Otis | .08 | .06 | | 133 | Dan Petry | .08 | .06 |
| 71 | Matt Keough | .06 | .05 | | 134 | Bob Stanley | .06 | .05 |
| 72 | Toby Harrah | .08 | .06 | | 135 | Lou Piniella | .12 | .09 |
| 73 | *Dave Righetti*(FC) | | | | 136 | Pedro Guerrero(FC) | .70 | .50 |
| | | 1.00 | .70 | | 137 | Len Barker | .08 | .06 |
| 74 | Carl Yastrzemski | 1.00 | .70 | | 138 | Richard Gale | .06 | .05 |
| 75 | Bob Welch | .12 | .09 | | 139 | Wayne Gross | .06 | .05 |
| 76a | Alan Trammel (name | | | | 140 | *Tim Wallach*(FC) | | |
| | incorrect) | 2.00 | 1.50 | | | | 2.00 | 1.50 |
| 76b | Alan Trammell (name | | | | 141 | Gene Mauch | .08 | .06 |
| | correct) | .60 | .45 | | 142 | Doc Medich | .06 | .05 |
| 77 | Rick Dempsey | .08 | .06 | | 143 | Tony Bernazard | .06 | .05 |
| 78 | Paul Molitor | .20 | .15 | | 144 | Bill Virdon | .06 | .05 |
| 79 | Dennis Martinez | .08 | .06 | | 145 | John Littlefield | .06 | .05 |
| 80 | Jim Slaton | .06 | .05 | | 146 | Dave Bergman | .06 | .05 |
| 81 | Champ Summers | .06 | .05 | | 147 | Dick Davis | .06 | .05 |
| 82 | Carney Lansford | .08 | .06 | | 148 | Tom Seaver | 1.50 | 1.25 |
| 83 | Barry Foote | .06 | .05 | | 149 | Matt Sinatro | .06 | .05 |
| 84 | Steve Garvey | .50 | .40 | | 150 | Chuck Tanner | .06 | .05 |
| 85 | Rick Manning | .06 | .05 | | 151 | Leon Durham | .08 | .06 |
| 86 | John Wathan | .08 | .06 | | 152 | Gene Tenace | .08 | .06 |
| 87 | Brian Kingman | .06 | .05 | | 153 | Al Bumbry | .08 | .06 |
| 88 | Andre Dawson | 1.50 | 1.25 | | 154 | Mark Brouhard | .06 | .05 |
| 89 | Jim Kern | .06 | .05 | | 155 | Rick Peters | .06 | .05 |
| 90 | Bobby Grich | .10 | .08 | | 156 | Jerry Remy | .06 | .05 |
| 91 | Bob Forsch | .08 | .06 | | 157 | Rick Reuschel | .10 | .08 |
| 92 | Art Howe | .06 | .05 | | 158 | Steve Howe | .08 | .06 |
| 93 | Marty Bystrom | .06 | .05 | | 159 | Alan Bannister | .06 | .05 |
| 94 | Ozzie Smith | 2.00 | 1.50 | | 160 | U L Washington | .06 | .05 |
| 95 | Dave Parker | .30 | .25 | | 161 | Rick Langford | .06 | .05 |
| 96 | Doyle Alexander | .10 | .08 | | 162 | Bill Gullickson | .08 | .06 |
| 97 | Al Hrabosky | .08 | .06 | | 163 | Mark Wagner | .06 | .05 |
| 98 | Frank Taveras | .06 | .05 | | 164 | Geoff Zahn | .06 | .05 |
| 99 | Tim Blackwell | .06 | .05 | | 165 | Ron LeFlore | .08 | .06 |
| 100 | Floyd Bannister | .10 | .08 | | 166 | Dane Iorg | .06 | .05 |
| 101 | Alfredo Griffin | .08 | .06 | | 167 | Joe Niekro | .12 | .09 |
| 102 | Dave Engle | .06 | .05 | | 168 | Pete Rose | 1.00 | .70 |
| 103 | Mario Soto | .08 | .06 | | 169 | Dave Collins | .08 | .06 |
| 104 | Ross Baumgarten | .06 | .05 | | 170 | Rick Wise | .08 | .06 |
| 105 | Ken Singleton | .10 | .08 | | 171 | Jim Bibby | .06 | .05 |
| 106 | Ted Simmons | .12 | .09 | | 172 | Larry Herndon | .08 | .06 |
| 107 | Jack Morris | .60 | .45 | | 173 | Bob Horner | .12 | .09 |
| 108 | Bob Watson | .08 | .06 | | 174 | Steve Dillard | .06 | .05 |
| 109 | Dwight Evans | .15 | .11 | | 175 | Mookie Wilson | .12 | .09 |
| 110 | Tom Lasorda | .10 | .08 | | 176 | Dan Meyer | .06 | .05 |
| 111 | Bert Blyleven | .12 | .09 | | 177 | Fernando Arroyo | .06 | .05 |
| 112 | Dan Quisenberry | .15 | .11 | | 178 | Jackson Todd | .06 | .05 |
| 113 | Rickey Henderson | 5.00 | 3.75 | | 179 | Darrell Jackson | .06 | .05 |
| 114 | Gary Carter | .35 | .25 | | 180 | Al Woods | .06 | .05 |
| 115 | Brian Downing | .10 | .08 | | 181 | Jim Anderson | .06 | .05 |
| 116 | Al Oliver | .15 | .11 | | 182 | Dave Kingman | .15 | .11 |
| 117 | LaMarr Hoyt | .06 | .05 | | 183 | Steve Henderson | .06 | .05 |
| 118 | Cesar Cedeno | .12 | .09 | | 184 | Brian Asselstine | .06 | .05 |
| 119 | Keith Moreland | .10 | .08 | | 185 | Rod Scurry | .06 | .05 |
| 120 | Bob Shirley | .06 | .05 | | 186 | Fred Breining | .06 | .05 |
| 121 | Terry Kennedy | .08 | .06 | | 187 | Danny Boone | .06 | .05 |
| 122 | Frank Pastore | .06 | .05 | | 188 | Junior Kennedy | .06 | .05 |
| 123 | Gene Garber | .06 | .05 | | 189 | Sparky Lyle | .10 | .08 |
| 124 | Tony Pena(FC) | .25 | .20 | | 190 | Whitey Herzog | .08 | .06 |
| 125 | Allen Ripley | .06 | .05 | | 191 | Dave Smith | .10 | .08 |

| | | MT | NR MT | | | | MT | NR MT |
|---|---|---|---|---|---|---|---|---|
| 192 | Ed Ott | .06 | .05 | | 259 | Dave Rozema | .06 | .05 |
| 193 | Greg Luzinski | .15 | .11 | | 260 | John Tudor | .15 | .11 |
| 194 | Bill Lee | .08 | .06 | | 261 | Jerry Mumphrey | .06 | .05 |
| 195 | Don Zimmer | .06 | .05 | | 262 | Jay Johnstone | .08 | .06 |
| 196 | Hal McRae | .12 | .09 | | 263 | Bo Diaz | .08 | .06 |
| 197 | Mike Norris | .06 | .05 | | 264 | Dennis Leonard | .08 | .06 |
| 198 | Duane Kuiper | .06 | .05 | | 265 | Jim Spencer | .06 | .05 |
| 199 | Rick Cerone | .06 | .05 | | 266 | John Milner | .06 | .05 |
| 200 | Jim Rice | .40 | .30 | | 267 | Don Aase | .06 | .05 |
| 201 | Steve Yeager | .06 | .05 | | 268 | Jim Sundberg | .08 | .06 |
| 202 | Tom Brookens | .06 | .05 | | 269 | Lamar Johnson | .06 | .05 |
| 203 | Jose Morales | .06 | .05 | | 270 | Frank LaCorte | .06 | .05 |
| 204 | Roy Howell | .06 | .05 | | 271 | Barry Evans | .06 | .05 |
| 205 | Tippy Martinez | .06 | .05 | | 272 | Enos Cabell | .06 | .05 |
| 206 | Moose Haas | .06 | .05 | | 273 | Del Unser | .06 | .05 |
| 207 | Al Cowens | .06 | .05 | | 274 | George Foster | .20 | .15 |
| 208 | Dave Stapleton | .06 | .05 | | 275 | Brett Butler (FC) | | |
| 209 | Bucky Dent | .10 | .08 | | | | 2.50 | 2.00 |
| 210 | Ron Cey | .12 | .09 | | 276 | Lee Lacy | .06 | .05 |
| 211 | Jorge Orta | .06 | .05 | | 277 | Ken Reitz | .06 | .05 |
| 212 | Jamie Quirk | .06 | .05 | | 278 | Keith Hernandez | .40 | .30 |
| 213 | Jeff Jones | .06 | .05 | | 279 | Doug DeCinces | .10 | .08 |
| 214 | Tim Raines | 1.00 | .70 | | 280 | Charlie Moore | .06 | .05 |
| 215 | Jon Matlack | .08 | .06 | | 281 | Lance Parrish | .35 | .25 |
| 216 | Rod Carew | 1.00 | .70 | | 282 | Ralph Houk | .08 | .06 |
| 217 | Jim Kaat | .15 | .11 | | 283 | Rich Gossage | .20 | .15 |
| 218 | Joe Pittman | .06 | .05 | | 284 | Jerry Reuss | .10 | .08 |
| 219 | Larry Christenson | .06 | .05 | | 285 | Mike Stanton | .06 | .05 |
| 220 | Juan Bonilla | .06 | .05 | | 286 | Frank White | .10 | .08 |
| 221 | Mike Easler | .08 | .06 | | 287 | Bob Owchinko | .06 | .05 |
| 222 | Vida Blue | .12 | .09 | | 288 | Scott Sanderson | .06 | .05 |
| 223 | Rick Camp | .06 | .05 | | 289 | Bump Wills | .06 | .05 |
| 224 | Mike Jorgensen | .06 | .05 | | 290 | Dave Frost | .06 | .05 |
| 225 | Jody Davis (FC) | .30 | .25 | | 291 | Chet Lemon | .08 | .06 |
| 226 | Mike Parrott | .06 | .05 | | 292 | Tito Landrum | .06 | .05 |
| 227 | Jim Clancy | .08 | .06 | | 293 | Vern Ruhle | .06 | .05 |
| 228 | Hosken Powell | .06 | .05 | | 294 | Mike Schmidt | 2.50 | 2.00 |
| 229 | Tom Hume | .06 | .05 | | 295 | Sam Mejias | .06 | .05 |
| 230 | Britt Burns | .06 | .05 | | 296 | Gary Lucas | .06 | .05 |
| 231 | Jim Palmer | .70 | .50 | | 297 | John Candelaria | .10 | .08 |
| 232 | Bob Rodgers | .08 | .06 | | 298 | Jerry Martin | .06 | .05 |
| 233 | Milt Wilcox | .06 | .05 | | 299 | Dale Murphy | .90 | .70 |
| 234 | Dave Revering | .06 | .05 | | 300 | Mike Lum | .06 | .05 |
| 235 | Mike Torrez | .08 | .06 | | 301 | Tom Hausman | .06 | .05 |
| 236 | Robert Castillo | .06 | .05 | | 302 | Glenn Abbott | .06 | .05 |
| 237 | Von Hayes (FC) | 1.00 | .70 | | 303 | Roger Erickson | .06 | .05 |
| 238 | Renie Martin | .06 | .05 | | 304 | Otto Velez | .06 | .05 |
| 239 | Dwayne Murphy | .08 | .06 | | 305 | Danny Goodwin | .06 | .05 |
| 240 | Rodney Scott | .06 | .05 | | 306 | John Mayberry | .08 | .06 |
| 241 | Fred Patek | .06 | .05 | | 307 | Lenny Randle | .06 | .05 |
| 242 | Mickey Rivers | .08 | .06 | | 308 | Bob Bailor | .06 | .05 |
| 243 | Steve Trout | .06 | .05 | | 309 | Jerry Morales | .06 | .05 |
| 244 | Jose Cruz | .12 | .09 | | 310 | Rufino Linares | .06 | .05 |
| 245 | Manny Trillo | .08 | .06 | | 311 | Kent Tekulve | .08 | .06 |
| 246 | Lary Sorensen | .06 | .05 | | 312 | Joe Morgan | .50 | .40 |
| 247 | Dave Edwards | .06 | .05 | | 313 | John Urrea | .06 | .05 |
| 248 | Dan Driessen | .08 | .06 | | 314 | Paul Householder | .06 | .05 |
| 249 | Tommy Boggs | .06 | .05 | | 315 | Garry Maddox | .10 | .08 |
| 250 | Dale Berra | .06 | .05 | | 316 | Mike Ramsey | .06 | .05 |
| 251 | Ed Whitson | .06 | .05 | | 317 | Alan Ashby | .06 | .05 |
| 252 | Lee Smith (FC) | 8.00 | 6.00 | | 318 | Bob Clark | .06 | .05 |
| 253 | Tom Paciorek | .06 | .05 | | 319 | Tony LaRussa | .08 | .06 |
| 254 | Pat Zachry | .06 | .05 | | 320 | Charlie Lea | .08 | .06 |
| 255 | Luis Leal | .06 | .05 | | 321 | Danny Darwin | .06 | .05 |
| 256 | John Castino | .06 | .05 | | 322 | Cesar Geronimo | .06 | .05 |
| 257 | Rich Dauer | .06 | .05 | | 323 | Tom Underwood | .06 | .05 |
| 258 | Cecil Cooper | .15 | .11 | | 324 | Andre Thornton | .10 | .08 |

| | MT | NR MT |
|---|---|---|
| 325 Rudy May | .06 | .05 |
| 326 Frank Tanana | .10 | .08 |
| 327 Davey Lopes | .10 | .08 |
| 328 Richie Hebner | .06 | .05 |
| 329 Mike Flanagan | .10 | .08 |
| 330 Mike Caldwell | .06 | .05 |
| 331 Scott McGregor | .08 | .06 |
| 332 Jerry Augustine | .06 | .05 |
| 333 Stan Papi | .06 | .05 |
| 334 Rick Miller | .06 | .05 |
| 335 Graig Nettles | .15 | .11 |
| 336 Dusty Baker | .10 | .08 |
| 337 Dave Garcia | .06 | .05 |
| 338 Larry Gura | .06 | .05 |
| 339 Cliff Johnson | .06 | .05 |
| 340 Warren Cromartie | .06 | .05 |
| 341 Steve Comer | .06 | .05 |
| 342 Rick Burleson | .08 | .06 |
| 343 John Martin | .06 | .05 |
| 344 Craig Reynolds | .06 | .05 |
| 345 Mike Proly | .06 | .05 |
| 346 Ruppert Jones | .06 | .05 |
| 347 Omar Moreno | .06 | .05 |
| 348 Greg Minton | .06 | .05 |
| 349 *Rick Mahler*(FC) | .25 | .20 |
| 350 Alex Trevino | .06 | .05 |
| 351 Mike Krukow | .08 | .06 |
| 352a Shane Rawley (Jim Anderson photo - shaking hands) | 1.25 | .90 |
| 352b Shane Rawley (correct photo - kneeling) | .15 | .11 |
| 353 Garth Iorg | .06 | .05 |
| 354 Pete Mackanin | .06 | .05 |
| 355 Paul Moskau | .06 | .05 |
| 356 Richard Dotson | .10 | .08 |
| 357 Steve Stone | .08 | .06 |
| 358 Larry Hisle | .08 | .06 |
| 359 Aurelio Lopez | .06 | .05 |
| 360 Oscar Gamble | .08 | .06 |
| 361 Tom Burgmeier | .06 | .05 |
| 362 Terry Forster | .08 | .06 |
| 363 Joe Charboneau | .08 | .06 |
| 364 Ken Brett | .08 | .06 |
| 365 Tony Armas | .10 | .08 |
| 366 Chris Speier | .06 | .05 |
| 367 Fred Lynn | .20 | .15 |
| 368 Buddy Bell | .12 | .09 |
| 369 Jim Essian | .06 | .05 |
| 370 Terry Puhl | .06 | .05 |
| 371 Greg Gross | .06 | .05 |
| 372 Bruce Sutter | .15 | .11 |
| 373 Joe Lefebvre | .06 | .05 |
| 374 Ray Knight | .10 | .08 |
| 375 Bruce Benedict | .06 | .05 |
| 376 Tim Foli | .06 | .05 |
| 377 Al Holland | .06 | .05 |
| 378 Ken Kravec | .06 | .05 |
| 379 Jeff Burroughs | .08 | .06 |
| 380 Pete Falcone | .06 | .05 |
| 381 Ernie Whitt | .08 | .06 |
| 382 Brad Havens | .06 | .05 |
| 383 Terry Crowley | .06 | .05 |
| 384 Don Money | .06 | .05 |
| 385 Dan Schatzeder | .06 | .05 |
| 386 Gary Allenson | .06 | .05 |
| 387 Yogi Berra | .15 | .11 |

| | MT | NR MT |
|---|---|---|
| 388 Ken Landreaux | .06 | .05 |
| 389 Mike Hargrove | .06 | .05 |
| 390 Darryl Motley | .06 | .05 |
| 391 Dave McKay | .06 | .05 |
| 392 Stan Bahnsen | .06 | .05 |
| 393 Ken Forsch | .06 | .05 |
| 394 Mario Mendoza | .06 | .05 |
| 395 Jim Morrison | .06 | .05 |
| 396 Mike Ivie | .06 | .05 |
| 397 Broderick Perkins | .06 | .05 |
| 398 Darrell Evans | .15 | .11 |
| 399 Ron Reed | .06 | .05 |
| 400 Johnny Bench | .60 | .45 |
| 401 *Steve Bedrosian*(FC) | .80 | .60 |
| 402 Bill Robinson | .06 | .05 |
| 403 Bill Buckner | .12 | .09 |
| 404 Ken Oberkfell | .06 | .05 |
| 405 *Cal Ripken, Jr.*(FC) | 50.00 | 37.00 |
| 406 Jim Gantner | .08 | .06 |
| 407 Kirk Gibson(FC) | .90 | .70 |
| 408 Tony Perez | .20 | .15 |
| 409 Tommy John | .20 | .15 |
| 410 *Dave Stewart*(FC) | 2.50 | 2.00 |
| 411 Dan Spillner | .06 | .05 |
| 412 Willie Aikens | .06 | .05 |
| 413 Mike Heath | .06 | .05 |
| 414 Ray Burris | .06 | .05 |
| 415 Leon Roberts | .06 | .05 |
| 416 *Mike Witt*(FC) | .35 | .25 |
| 417 Bobby Molinaro | .06 | .05 |
| 418 Steve Braun | .06 | .05 |
| 419 Nolan Ryan | 8.00 | 6.00 |
| 420 Tug McGraw | .12 | .09 |
| 421 Dave Concepcion | .12 | .09 |
| 422a Juan Eichelberger (Gary Lucas photo - white player) | 1.25 | .90 |
| 422b Juan Eichelberger (correct photo - black player) | .08 | .06 |
| 423 Rick Rhoden | .10 | .08 |
| 424 Frank Robinson | .12 | .09 |
| 425 Eddie Miller | .06 | .05 |
| 426 Bill Caudill | .06 | .05 |
| 427 Doug Flynn | .06 | .05 |
| 428 Larry Anderson (Andersen) | .06 | .05 |
| 429 Al Williams | .06 | .05 |
| 430 Jerry Garvin | .06 | .05 |
| 431 Glenn Adams | .06 | .05 |
| 432 Barry Bonnell | .06 | .05 |
| 433 Jerry Narron | .06 | .05 |
| 434 John Stearns | .06 | .05 |
| 435 Mike Tyson | .06 | .05 |
| 436 Glenn Hubbard | .08 | .06 |
| 437 Eddie Solomon | .06 | .05 |
| 438 Jeff Leonard | .10 | .08 |
| 439 Randy Bass | .06 | .05 |
| 440 Mike LaCoss | .06 | .05 |
| 441 Gary Matthews | .10 | .08 |
| 442 Mark Littell | .06 | .05 |
| 443 Don Sutton | .30 | .25 |
| 444 John Harris | .06 | .05 |
| 445 Vada Pinson | .08 | .06 |

| | | MT | NR MT |
|---|---|---|---|
| 446 | Elias Sosa | .06 | .05 |
| 447 | Charlie Hough | .10 | .08 |
| 448 | Willie Wilson | .15 | .11 |
| 449 | Fred Stanley | .06 | .05 |
| 450 | Tom Veryzer | .06 | .05 |
| 451 | Ron Davis | .06 | .05 |
| 452 | Mark Clear | .06 | .05 |
| 453 | Bill Russell | .08 | .06 |
| 454 | Lou Whitaker | .40 | .30 |
| 455 | Dan Graham | .06 | .05 |
| 456 | Reggie Cleveland | .06 | .05 |
| 457 | Sammy Stewart | .06 | .05 |
| 458 | Pete Vuckovich | .08 | .06 |
| 459 | John Wockenfuss | .06 | .05 |
| 460 | Glenn Hoffman | .06 | .05 |
| 461 | Willie Randolph | .10 | .08 |
| 462 | Fernando Valenzuela(FC) | .80 | .60 |
| 463 | Ron Hassey | .06 | .05 |
| 464 | Paul Splittorff | .06 | .05 |
| 465 | Rob Picciolo | .06 | .05 |
| 466 | Larry Parrish | .10 | .08 |
| 467 | Johnny Grubb | .06 | .05 |
| 468 | Dan Ford | .06 | .05 |
| 469 | Silvio Martinez | .06 | .05 |
| 470 | Kiko Garcia | .06 | .05 |
| 471 | Bob Boone | .10 | .08 |
| 472 | Luis Salazar | .08 | .06 |
| 473 | Randy Niemann | .06 | .05 |
| 474 | Tom Griffin | .06 | .05 |
| 475 | Phil Niekro | .30 | .25 |
| 476 | Hubie Brooks(FC) | .25 | .20 |
| 477 | Dick Tidrow | .06 | .05 |
| 478 | Jim Beattie | .06 | .05 |
| 479 | Damaso Garcia | .06 | .05 |
| 480 | Mickey Hatcher | .08 | .06 |
| 481 | Joe Price | .06 | .05 |
| 482 | Ed Farmer | .06 | .05 |
| 483 | Eddie Murray | 2.00 | 1.50 |
| 484 | Ben Oglivie | .08 | .06 |
| 485 | Kevin Saucier | .06 | .06 |
| 486 | Bobby Murcer | .10 | .08 |
| 487 | Bill Campbell | .06 | .05 |
| 488 | Reggie Smith | .10 | .08 |
| 489 | Wayne Garland | .06 | .05 |
| 490 | Jim Wright | .06 | .05 |
| 491 | Billy Martin | .12 | .09 |
| 492 | Jim Fanning | .06 | .05 |
| 493 | Don Baylor | .12 | .09 |
| 494 | Rick Honeycutt | .06 | .05 |
| 495 | Carlton Fisk | 1.50 | 1.25 |
| 496 | Denny Walling | .06 | .05 |
| 497 | Bake McBride | .06 | .05 |
| 498 | Darrell Porter | .08 | .06 |
| 499 | Gene Richards | .06 | .05 |
| 500 | Ron Oester | .06 | .05 |
| 501 | Ken Dayley(FC) | .20 | .15 |
| 502 | Jason Thompson | .06 | .05 |
| 503 | Milt May | .06 | .05 |
| 504 | Doug Bird | .06 | .05 |
| 505 | Bruce Bochte | .06 | .05 |
| 506 | Neil Allen | .06 | .05 |
| 507 | Joey McLaughlin | .06 | .05 |
| 508 | Butch Wynegar | .06 | .05 |
| 509 | Gary Roenicke | .06 | .05 |
| 510 | Robin Yount | 2.00 | 1.50 |
| 511 | Dave Tobik | .06 | .05 |
| 512 | Rich Gedman(FC) | .25 | .20 |
| 513 | Gene Nelson(FC) | .12 | .09 |
| 514 | Rick Monday | .10 | .08 |
| 515 | Miguel Dilone | .06 | .05 |
| 516 | Clint Hurdle | .06 | .05 |
| 517 | Jeff Newman | .06 | .05 |
| 518 | Grant Jackson | .06 | .05 |
| 519 | Andy Hassler | .06 | .05 |
| 520 | Pat Putnam | .06 | .05 |
| 521 | Greg Pryor | .06 | .05 |
| 522 | Tony Scott | .06 | .05 |
| 523 | Steve Mura | .06 | .05 |
| 524 | Johnnie LeMaster | .06 | .05 |
| 525 | Dick Ruthven | .06 | .05 |
| 526 | John McNamara | .06 | .05 |
| 527 | Larry McWilliams | .06 | .05 |
| 528 | Johnny Ray(FC) | .30 | .25 |
| 529 | Pat Tabler(FC) | .40 | .30 |
| 530 | Tom Herr | .10 | .08 |
| 531a | San Diego Chicken (trademark symbol on front) | 1.25 | .90 |
| 531b | San Diego Chicken (no trademark symbol) | .80 | .60 |
| 532 | Sal Butera | .06 | .05 |
| 533 | Mike Griffin | .06 | .05 |
| 534 | Kelvin Moore | .06 | .05 |
| 535 | Reggie Jackson | 2.00 | 1.50 |
| 536 | Ed Romero | .06 | .05 |
| 537 | Derrel Thomas | .06 | .05 |
| 538 | Mike O'Berry | .06 | .05 |
| 539 | Jack O'Connor | .06 | .05 |
| 540 | Bob Ojeda(FC) | .50 | .40 |
| 541 | Roy Lee Jackson | .06 | .05 |
| 542 | Lynn Jones | .06 | .05 |
| 543 | Gaylord Perry | .40 | .30 |
| 544a | Phil Garner (photo reversed) | 1.25 | .90 |
| 544b | Phil Garner (photo correct) | .10 | .08 |
| 545 | Garry Templeton | .10 | .08 |
| 546 | Rafael Ramirez(FC) | .10 | .08 |
| 547 | Jeff Reardon | .20 | .15 |
| 548 | Ron Guidry | .25 | .20 |
| 549 | Tim Laudner(FC) | .25 | .20 |
| 550 | John Henry Johnson | .06 | .05 |
| 551 | Chris Bando | .06 | .05 |
| 552 | Bobby Brown | .06 | .05 |
| 553 | Larry Bradford | .06 | .05 |
| 554 | Scott Fletcher(FC) | .30 | .25 |
| 555 | Jerry Royster | .06 | .05 |
| 556 | Shooty Babbitt | .06 | .05 |
| 557 | Kent Hrbek(FC) | 3.00 | 2.25 |
| 558 | Yankee Winners (Ron Guidry, Tommy John) | .15 | .11 |
| 559 | Mark Bomback | .06 | .05 |
| 560 | Julio Valdez | .06 | .05 |
| 561 | Buck Martinez | .06 | .05 |
| 562 | Mike Marshall(FC) | .25 | .20 |
| 563 | Rennie Stennett | .06 | .05 |

| | | MT | NR MT |
|---|---|---|---|
| 564 | Steve Crawford | .06 | .05 |
| 565 | Bob Babcock | .06 | .05 |
| 566 | Johnny Podres | .08 | .06 |
| 567 | Paul Serna | .06 | .05 |
| 568 | Harold Baines(FC) | 1.25 | .90 |
| 569 | Dave LaRoche | .06 | .05 |
| 570 | Lee May | .08 | .06 |
| 571 | Gary Ward(FC) | .10 | .08 |
| 572 | John Denny | .06 | .05 |
| 573 | Roy Smalley | .06 | .05 |
| 574 | *Bob Brenly*(FC) | .20 | .15 |
| 575 | Bronx Bombers (Reggie Jackson, Dave Winfield) | 1.00 | .70 |
| 576 | Luis Pujols | .06 | .05 |
| 577 | Butch Hobson | .06 | .05 |
| 578 | Harvey Kuenn | .08 | .06 |
| 579 | Cal Ripken, Sr. | .08 | .06 |
| 580 | Juan Berenguer | .08 | .06 |
| 581 | Benny Ayala | .06 | .05 |
| 582 | Vance Law(FC) | .15 | .11 |
| 583 | *Rick Leach*(FC) | .12 | .09 |
| 584 | George Frazier | .06 | .05 |
| 585 | Phillies Finest (Pete Rose, Mike Schmidt) | .70 | .50 |
| 586 | Joe Rudi | .10 | .08 |
| 587 | Juan Beniquez | .06 | .05 |
| 588 | *Luis DeLeon*(FC) | .08 | .06 |
| 589 | Craig Swan | .06 | .05 |
| 590 | Dave Chalk | .06 | .05 |
| 591 | Billy Gardner | .06 | .05 |
| 592 | Sal Bando | .08 | .06 |
| 593 | Bert Campaneris | .10 | .08 |
| 594 | Steve Kemp | .08 | .06 |
| 595a | Randy Lerch (Braves) | 1.25 | .90 |
| 595b | Randy Lerch (Brewers) | .08 | .06 |
| 596 | Bryan Clark | .06 | .05 |
| 597 | Dave Ford | .06 | .05 |
| 598 | Mike Scioscia(FC) | .20 | .15 |
| 599 | John Lowenstein | .06 | .05 |
| 600 | Rene Lachmann (Lachemann) | .06 | .05 |
| 601 | Mick Kelleher | .06 | .05 |
| 602 | Ron Jackson | .06 | .05 |
| 603 | Jerry Koosman | .10 | .08 |
| 604 | Dave Goltz | .08 | .06 |
| 605 | Ellis Valentine | .06 | .05 |
| 606 | Lonnie Smith | .08 | .06 |
| 607 | Joaquin Andujar | .08 | .06 |
| 608 | Garry Hancock | .06 | .05 |
| 609 | Jerry Turner | .06 | .05 |
| 610 | Bob Bonner | .06 | .05 |
| 611 | Jim Dwyer | .06 | .05 |
| 612 | Terry Bulling | .06 | .05 |
| 613 | Joel Youngblood | .06 | .05 |
| 614 | Larry Milbourne | .06 | .05 |
| 615 | Phil Roof (Gene) | .06 | .05 |
| 616 | Keith Drumright | .06 | .05 |
| 617 | Dave Rosello | .06 | .05 |
| 618 | Rickey Keeton | .06 | .05 |
| 619 | Dennis Lamp | .06 | .05 |
| 620 | Sid Monge | .06 | .05 |
| 621 | Jerry White | .06 | .05 |
| 622 | *Luis Aguayo*(FC) | .10 | .08 |
| 623 | Jamie Easterly | .06 | .05 |

| | | MT | NR MT |
|---|---|---|---|
| 624 | *Steve Sax*(FC) | 4.00 | 3.00 |
| 625 | Dave Roberts | .06 | .05 |
| 626 | Rick Bosetti | .06 | .05 |
| 627 | *Terry Francona*(FC) | .10 | .08 |
| 628 | Pride of the Reds (Johnny Bench, Tom Seaver) | .80 | .60 |
| 629 | Paul Mirabella | .06 | .05 |
| 630 | Rance Mulliniks | .06 | .05 |
| 631 | Kevin Hickey | .06 | .05 |
| 632 | Reid Nichols | .06 | .05 |
| 633 | Dave Geisel | .06 | .05 |
| 634 | Ken Griffey | .12 | .09 |
| 635 | Bob Lemon | .10 | .08 |
| 636 | Orlando Sanchez | .06 | .05 |
| 637 | Bill Almon | .06 | .05 |
| 638 | Danny Ainge | .12 | .09 |
| 639 | Willie Stargell | .40 | .30 |
| 640 | Bob Sykes | .06 | .05 |
| 641 | Ed Lynch | .06 | .05 |
| 642 | John Ellis | .06 | .05 |
| 643 | Fergie Jenkins | .15 | .11 |
| 644 | Lenn Sakata | .06 | .05 |
| 645 | Julio Gonzales | .06 | .05 |
| 646 | Jesse Orosco(FC) | .15 | .11 |
| 647 | Jerry Dybzinski | .06 | .05 |
| 648 | Tommy Davis | .08 | .06 |
| 649 | Ron Gardenhire | .06 | .05 |
| 650 | Felipe Alou | .08 | .06 |
| 651 | Harvey Haddix | .08 | .06 |
| 652 | Willie Upshaw(FC) | .15 | .11 |
| 653 | Bill Madlock | .12 | .09 |
| ---a | Checklist 1-26 DK (5 Trammel) | .70 | .50 |
| ---b | Checklist 1-26 DK (5 Trammell) | .08 | .06 |
| ---- | Checklist 27-130 | .06 | .05 |
| ---- | Checklist 131-234 | .06 | .05 |
| ---- | Checklist 235-338 | .06 | .05 |
| ---- | Checklist 339-442 | .06 | .05 |
| ---- | Checklist 443-544 | .06 | .05 |
| ---- | Checklist 545-653 | .06 | .05 |

## 1983 Donruss

The 1983 Donruss set consists of 653 numbered cards plus seven unnumbered checklists. The cards, which measure 2-1/2" by 3-1/2", were issued with puzzle pieces (three pieces on one card per pack) that feature Ty Cobb. The first 26 cards in the set were once again the Diamond Kings series. The card fronts display the Donruss logo and the year of issue. The card backs have black print on yellow and white and include statistics, career highlights, and the player's contract status. (DK) in the checklist that follows indicates cards which belong to the Diamond Kings series.

|  |  | MT | NR MT |
|---|---|---|---|
| Complete Set: | | 125.00 | 90.00 |
| Common Player: | | .06 | .05 |
| 1 | Fernando Valenzuela (DK) | .40 | .30 |
| 2 | Rollie Fingers (DK) | .20 | .15 |
| 3 | Reggie Jackson (DK) | .60 | .45 |
| 4 | Jim Palmer (DK) | .40 | .30 |
| 5 | Jack Morris (DK) | .30 | .25 |
| 6 | George Foster (DK) | .20 | .15 |
| 7 | Jim Sundberg (DK) | .08 | .06 |
| 8 | Willie Stargell (DK) | .40 | .30 |
| 9 | Dave Stieb (DK) | .12 | .09 |
| 10 | Joe Niekro (DK) | .12 | .09 |
| 11 | Rickey Henderson (DK) | 2.00 | 1.50 |
| 12 | Dale Murphy (DK) | .50 | .40 |
| 13 | Toby Harrah (DK) | .08 | .06 |
| 14 | Bill Buckner (DK) | .12 | .09 |
| 15 | Willie Wilson (DK) | .15 | .11 |
| 16 | Steve Carlton (DK) | .40 | .30 |
| 17 | Ron Guidry (DK) | .25 | .20 |
| 18 | Steve Rogers (DK) | .08 | .06 |
| 19 | Kent Hrbek (DK) | .40 | .30 |
| 20 | Keith Hernandez (DK) | .40 | .30 |
| 21 | Floyd Bannister (DK) | .10 | .08 |
| 22 | Johnny Bench (DK) | .40 | .30 |
| 23 | Britt Burns (DK) | .08 | .06 |
| 24 | Joe Morgan (DK) | .30 | .25 |
| 25 | Carl Yastrzemski (DK) | .80 | .60 |
| 26 | Terry Kennedy (DK) | .08 | .06 |
| 27 | Gary Roenicke | .06 | .05 |
| 28 | Dwight Bernard | .06 | .05 |
| 29 | Pat Underwood | .06 | .05 |
| 30 | Gary Allenson | .06 | .05 |
| 31 | Ron Guidry | .25 | .20 |
| 32 | Burt Hooton | .08 | .06 |
| 33 | Chris Bando | .06 | .05 |
| 34 | Vida Blue | .12 | .09 |
| 35 | Rickey Henderson | 4.00 | 3.00 |
| 36 | Ray Burris | .06 | .05 |
| 37 | John Butcher | .06 | .05 |
| 38 | Don Aase | .06 | .05 |
| 39 | Jerry Koosman | .10 | .08 |
| 40 | Bruce Sutter | .15 | .11 |
| 41 | Jose Cruz | .12 | .09 |
| 42 | Pete Rose | 1.00 | .70 |
| 43 | Cesar Cedeno | .12 | .09 |
| 44 | Floyd Chiffer | .06 | .05 |
| 45 | Larry McWilliams | .06 | .05 |
| 46 | Alan Fowlkes | .06 | .05 |
| 47 | Dale Murphy | .70 | .50 |
| 48 | Doug Bird | .06 | .05 |
| 49 | Hubie Brooks | .12 | .09 |
| 50 | Floyd Bannister | .10 | .08 |
| 51 | Jack O'Connor | .06 | .05 |
| 52 | Steve Senteney | .06 | .05 |
| 53 | *Gary Gaetti*(FC) | .80 | .60 |
| 54 | Damaso Garcia | .06 | .05 |
| 55 | Gene Nelson | .06 | .05 |
| 56 | Mookie Wilson | .10 | .08 |
| 57 | Allen Ripley | .06 | .05 |
| 58 | Bob Horner | .12 | .09 |
| 59 | Tony Pena | .10 | .08 |
| 60 | Gary Lavelle | .06 | .05 |
| 61 | Tim Lollar | .06 | .05 |
| 62 | Frank Pastore | .06 | .05 |
| 63 | Garry Maddox | .10 | .08 |
| 64 | Bob Forsch | .08 | .06 |
| 65 | Harry Spilman | .06 | .05 |
| 66 | Geoff Zahn | .06 | .05 |
| 67 | Salome Barojas | .06 | .05 |
| 68 | David Palmer | .06 | .05 |
| 69 | Charlie Hough | .10 | .08 |
| 70 | Dan Quisenberry | .15 | .11 |
| 71 | Tony Armas | .10 | .08 |
| 72 | Rick Sutcliffe | .12 | .09 |
| 73 | Steve Balboni(FC) | .15 | .11 |
| 74 | Jerry Remy | .06 | .05 |
| 75 | Mike Scioscia | .08 | .06 |
| 76 | John Wockenfuss | .06 | .05 |
| 77 | Jim Palmer | .80 | .60 |
| 78 | Rollie Fingers | .60 | .45 |
| 79 | Joe Nolan | .06 | .05 |
| 80 | Pete Vuckovich | .08 | .06 |
| 81 | Rick Leach | .06 | .05 |
| 82 | Rick Miller | .06 | .05 |
| 83 | Graig Nettles | .15 | .11 |
| 84 | Ron Cey | .12 | .09 |
| 85 | Miguel Dilone | .06 | .05 |
| 86 | John Wathan | .08 | .06 |
| 87 | Kelvin Moore | .06 | .05 |
| 88a | Byrn Smith (first name incorrect) | .70 | .50 |
| 88b | Bryn Smith (first name correct) | .08 | .06 |
| 89 | Dave Hostetler | .06 | .05 |
| 90 | Rod Carew | 1.00 | .70 |
| 91 | Lonnie Smith | .08 | .06 |
| 92 | Bob Knepper | .08 | .06 |
| 93 | Marty Bystrom | .06 | .05 |
| 94 | Chris Welsh | .06 | .05 |
| 95 | Jason Thompson | .06 | .05 |
| 96 | Tom O'Malley | .06 | .05 |
| 97 | Phil Niekro | .30 | .25 |
| 98 | Neil Allen | .06 | .05 |
| 99 | Bill Buckner | .12 | .09 |
| 100 | *Ed VandeBerg (Vande Berg)*(FC) | .10 | .08 |
| 101 | Jim Clancy | .08 | .06 |
| 102 | Robert Castillo | .06 | .05 |
| 103 | Bruce Berenyi | .06 | .05 |
| 104 | Carlton Fisk | 1.25 | .90 |
| 105 | Mike Flanagan | .10 | .08 |
| 106 | Cecil Cooper | .15 | .11 |

| | | MT | NR MT | | | | MT | NR MT |
|---|---|---|---|---|---|---|---|---|
| 107 | Jack Morris | .80 | .60 | 171 | Don Robinson | .08 | .06 |
| 108 | Mike Morgan(FC) | .12 | .09 | 172 | Richard Gale | .06 | .05 |
| 109 | Luis Aponte | .06 | .05 | 173 | Steve Bedrosian | .12 | .09 |
| 110 | Pedro Guerrero | .25 | .20 | 174 | Willie Hernandez | .08 | .06 |
| 111 | Len Barker | .08 | .06 | 175 | Ron Gardenhire | .06 | .05 |
| 112 | Willie Wilson | .15 | .11 | 176 | Jim Beattie | .06 | .05 |
| 113 | Dave Beard | .06 | .05 | 177 | Tim Laudner | .08 | .06 |
| 114 | Mike Gates | .06 | .05 | 178 | Buck Martinez | .06 | .05 |
| 115 | Reggie Jackson | .70 | .50 | 179 | Kent Hrbek | .80 | .60 |
| 116 | George Wright | .06 | .05 | 180 | Alfredo Griffin | .08 | .06 |
| 117 | Vance Law | .08 | .06 | 181 | Larry Andersen | .06 | .05 |
| 118 | Nolan Ryan | 7.00 | 5.25 | 182 | Pete Falcone | .06 | .05 |
| 119 | Mike Krukow | .08 | .06 | 183 | Jody Davis | .10 | .08 |
| 120 | Ozzie Smith | 1.25 | .90 | 184 | Glenn Hubbard | .06 | .05 |
| 121 | Broderick Perkins | .06 | .05 | 185 | Dale Berra | .06 | .05 |
| 122 | Tom Seaver | 1.50 | 1.25 | 186 | Greg Minton | .06 | .05 |
| 123 | Chris Chambliss | .08 | .06 | 187 | Gary Lucas | .06 | .05 |
| 124 | Chuck Tanner | .06 | .05 | 188 | Dave Van Gorder | .06 | .05 |
| 125 | Johnnie LeMaster | .06 | .05 | 189 | Bob Dernier(FC) | .10 | .08 |
| 126 | *Mel Hall*(FC) | 1.50 | 1.25 | 190 | *Willie McGee*(FC) | | |
| 127 | Bruce Bochte | .06 | .05 | | | 3.00 | 2.25 |
| 128 | *Charlie Puleo*(FC) | | | 191 | Dickie Thon | .08 | .06 |
| | | .12 | .09 | 192 | Bob Boone | .10 | .08 |
| 129 | Luis Leal | .06 | .05 | 193 | Britt Burns | .06 | .05 |
| 130 | John Pacella | .06 | .05 | 194 | Jeff Reardon | .80 | .60 |
| 131 | Glenn Gulliver | .06 | .05 | 195 | Jon Matlack | .08 | .06 |
| 132 | Don Money | .06 | .05 | 196 | *Don Slaught*(FC) | .20 | .15 |
| 133 | Dave Rozema | .06 | .05 | 197 | Fred Stanley | .06 | .05 |
| 134 | Bruce Hurst(FC) | .25 | .20 | 198 | Rick Manning | .06 | .05 |
| 135 | Rudy May | .06 | .05 | 199 | Dave Righetti | .25 | .20 |
| 136 | Tom LaSorda (Lasorda) | | | 200 | Dave Stapleton | .06 | .05 |
| | | .10 | .08 | 201 | Steve Yeager | .06 | .05 |
| 137 | Dan Spillner (photo | | | 202 | Enos Cabell | .06 | .05 |
| | actually Ed Whitson) | .06 | .05 | 203 | Sammy Stewart | .06 | .05 |
| 138 | Jerry Martin | .06 | .05 | 204 | Moose Haas | .06 | .05 |
| 139 | Mike Norris | .06 | .05 | 205 | Lenn Sakata | .06 | .05 |
| 140 | Al Oliver | .15 | .11 | 206 | Charlie Moore | .06 | .05 |
| 141 | Daryl Sconiers | .06 | .05 | 207 | Alan Trammell | .40 | .30 |
| 142 | Lamar Johnson | .06 | .05 | 208 | Jim Rice | .40 | .30 |
| 143 | Harold Baines | .15 | .11 | 209 | Roy Smalley | .06 | .05 |
| 144 | Alan Ashby | .06 | .05 | 210 | Bill Russell | .08 | .06 |
| 145 | Garry Templeton | .10 | .08 | 211 | Andre Thornton | .10 | .08 |
| 146 | Al Holland | .06 | .05 | 212 | Willie Aikens | .08 | .06 |
| 147 | Bo Diaz | .08 | .06 | 213 | Dave McKay | .06 | .05 |
| 148 | Dave Concepcion | .12 | .09 | 214 | Tim Blackwell | .06 | .05 |
| 149 | Rick Camp | .06 | .05 | 215 | Buddy Bell | .12 | .09 |
| 150 | Jim Morrison | .06 | .05 | 216 | Doug DeCinces | .10 | .08 |
| 151 | Randy Martz | .06 | .05 | 217 | Tom Herr | .10 | .08 |
| 152 | Keith Hernandez | .40 | .30 | 218 | Frank LaCorte | .06 | .05 |
| 153 | John Lowenstein | .06 | .05 | 219 | Steve Carlton | 1.00 | .70 |
| 154 | Mike Caldwell | .06 | .05 | 220 | Terry Kennedy | .08 | .06 |
| 155 | Milt Wilcox | .06 | .05 | 221 | Mike Easler | .08 | .06 |
| 156 | Rich Gedman | .08 | .06 | 222 | Jack Clark | .25 | .20 |
| 157 | Rich Gossage | .20 | .15 | 223 | Gene Garber | .06 | .05 |
| 158 | Jerry Reuss | .10 | .08 | 224 | Scott Holman | .06 | .05 |
| 159 | Ron Hassey | .06 | .05 | 225 | Mike Proly | .06 | .05 |
| 160 | Larry Gura | .06 | .05 | 226 | Terry Bulling | .06 | .05 |
| 161 | Dwayne Murphy | .08 | .06 | 227 | Jerry Garvin | .06 | .05 |
| 162 | Woodie Fryman | .08 | .06 | 228 | Ron Davis | .06 | .05 |
| 163 | Steve Comer | .06 | .05 | 229 | Tom Hume | .06 | .05 |
| 164 | Ken Forsch | .06 | .05 | 230 | Marc Hill | .06 | .05 |
| 165 | Dennis Lamp | .06 | .05 | 231 | Dennis Martinez | .08 | .06 |
| 166 | David Green | .06 | .05 | 232 | Jim Gantner | .08 | .06 |
| 167 | Terry Puhl | .06 | .05 | 233 | Larry Pashnick | .06 | .05 |
| 168 | *Mike Schmidt* | 2.00 | 1.50 | 234 | Dave Collins | .08 | .06 |
| 169 | Eddie Milner(FC) | .10 | .08 | 235 | Tom Burgmeier | .06 | .05 |
| 170 | John Curtis | .06 | .05 | 236 | Ken Landreaux | .06 | .05 |

| | | MT | NR MT |
|---|---|---|---|
| 237 | John Denny | .06 | .05 |
| 238 | Hal McRae | .12 | .09 |
| 239 | Matt Keough | .06 | .05 |
| 240 | Doug Flynn | .06 | .05 |
| 241 | Fred Lynn | .20 | .15 |
| 242 | Billy Sample | .06 | .05 |
| 243 | Tom Paciorek | .06 | .05 |
| 244 | Joe Sambito | .06 | .05 |
| 245 | Sid Monge | .06 | .05 |
| 246 | Ken Oberkfell | .06 | .05 |
| 247 | Joe Pittman (photo actually Juan Eichelberger) | | |
| | | .06 | .05 |
| 248 | Mario Soto | .08 | .06 |
| 249 | Claudell Washington | .08 | .06 |
| 250 | Rick Rhoden | .10 | .08 |
| 251 | Darrell Evans | .15 | .11 |
| 252 | Steve Henderson | .06 | .05 |
| 253 | Manny Castillo | .06 | .05 |
| 254 | Craig Swan | .06 | .05 |
| 255 | Joey McLaughlin | .06 | .05 |
| 256 | Pete Redfern | .06 | .05 |
| 257 | Ken Singleton | .10 | .08 |
| 258 | Robin Yount | 3.00 | 2.25 |
| 259 | Elias Sosa | .06 | .05 |
| 260 | Bob Ojeda | .12 | .09 |
| 261 | Bobby Murcer | .10 | .08 |
| 262 | *Candy Maldonado*(FC) | .60 | .45 |
| 263 | Rick Waits | .06 | .05 |
| 264 | Greg Pryor | .06 | .05 |
| 265 | Bob Owchinko | .06 | .05 |
| 266 | Chris Speier | .06 | .05 |
| 267 | Bruce Kison | .06 | .05 |
| 268 | Mark Wagner | .06 | .05 |
| 269 | Steve Kemp | .10 | .08 |
| 270 | Phil Garner | .08 | .06 |
| 271 | Gene Richards | .06 | .05 |
| 272 | Renie Martin | .06 | .05 |
| 273 | Dave Roberts | .06 | .05 |
| 274 | Dan Driessen | .08 | .06 |
| 275 | Rufino Linares | .06 | .05 |
| 276 | Lee Lacy | .06 | .05 |
| 277 | *Ryne Sandberg*(FC) | | |
| | | 40.00 | 30.00 |
| 278 | Darrell Porter | .08 | .06 |
| 279 | Cal Ripken | 15.00 | 11.00 |
| 280 | Jamie Easterly | .06 | .05 |
| 281 | Bill Fahey | .06 | .05 |
| 282 | Glenn Hoffman | .06 | .05 |
| 283 | Willie Randolph | .10 | .08 |
| 284 | Fernando Valenzuela | | |
| | | .30 | .25 |
| 285 | Alan Bannister | .06 | .05 |
| 286 | Paul Splittorff | .06 | .05 |
| 287 | Joe Rudi | .10 | .08 |
| 288 | Bill Gullickson | .06 | .05 |
| 289 | Danny Darwin | .06 | .05 |
| 290 | Andy Hassler | .06 | .05 |
| 291 | Ernesto Escarrega | .06 | .05 |
| 292 | Steve Mura | .06 | .05 |
| 293 | Tony Scott | .06 | .05 |
| 294 | Manny Trillo | .08 | .06 |
| 295 | Greg Harris(FC) | .08 | .06 |
| 296 | Luis DeLeon | .06 | .05 |
| 297 | Kent Tekulve | .08 | .06 |
| 298 | Atlee Hammaker(FC) | | |

| | | MT | NR MT |
|---|---|---|---|
| | | .12 | .09 |
| 299 | Bruce Benedict | .06 | .05 |
| 300 | Fergie Jenkins | .15 | .11 |
| 301 | Dave Kingman | .15 | .11 |
| 302 | Bill Caudill | .06 | .05 |
| 303 | John Castino | .06 | .05 |
| 304 | Ernie Whitt | .08 | .06 |
| 305 | Randy Johnson | .06 | .05 |
| 306 | Garth Iorg | .06 | .05 |
| 307 | Gaylord Perry | .40 | .30 |
| 308 | Ed Lynch | .06 | .05 |
| 309 | Keith Moreland | .08 | .06 |
| 310 | Rafael Ramirez | .06 | .05 |
| 311 | Bill Madlock | .12 | .09 |
| 312 | Milt May | .06 | .05 |
| 313 | John Montefusco | .06 | .05 |
| 314 | Wayne Krenchicki | .06 | .05 |
| 315 | George Vukovich | .06 | .05 |
| 316 | Joaquin Andujar | .08 | .06 |
| 317 | Craig Reynolds | .06 | .05 |
| 318 | Rick Burleson | .08 | .06 |
| 319 | Richard Dotson | .10 | .08 |
| 320 | Steve Rogers | .08 | .06 |
| 321 | Dave Schmidt(FC) | .10 | .08 |
| 322 | *Bud Black*(FC) | .20 | .15 |
| 323 | Jeff Burroughs | .08 | .06 |
| 324 | Von Hayes | .15 | .11 |
| 325 | Butch Wynegar | .06 | .05 |
| 326 | Carl Yastrzemski | .80 | .60 |
| 327 | Ron Roenicke | .06 | .05 |
| 328 | *Howard Johnson*(FC) | | |
| | | 6.00 | 4.50 |
| 329 | Rick Dempsey | .08 | .06 |
| 330a | Jim Slaton (one yellow box on back) | | |
| | | .70 | .50 |
| 330b | Jim Slaton (two yellow boxes on back) | | |
| | | .08 | .06 |
| 331 | Benny Ayala | .06 | .05 |
| 332 | Ted Simmons | .12 | .09 |
| 333 | Lou Whitaker | .40 | .30 |
| 334 | Chuck Rainey | .06 | .05 |
| 335 | Lou Piniella | .12 | .09 |
| 336 | Steve Sax | .30 | .25 |
| 337 | Toby Harrah | .08 | .06 |
| 338 | George Brett | 3.00 | 2.25 |
| 339 | Davey Lopes | .10 | .08 |
| 340 | Gary Carter | .40 | .30 |
| 341 | John Grubb | .06 | .05 |
| 342 | Tim Foli | .06 | .05 |
| 343 | Jim Kaat | .15 | .11 |
| 344 | Mike LaCoss | .06 | .05 |
| 345 | Larry Christenson | .06 | .05 |
| 346 | Juan Bonilla | .06 | .05 |
| 347 | Omar Moreno | .06 | .05 |
| 348 | Charles Davis(FC) | .20 | .15 |
| 349 | Tommy Boggs | .06 | .05 |
| 350 | Rusty Staub | .10 | .08 |
| 351 | Bump Wills | .06 | .05 |
| 352 | Rick Sweet | .06 | .05 |
| 353 | *Jim Gott*(FC) | .20 | .15 |
| 354 | Terry Felton | .06 | .05 |
| 355 | Jim Kern | .06 | .05 |
| 356 | Bill Almon | .06 | .05 |
| 357 | Tippy Martinez | .06 | .05 |
| 358 | Roy Howell | .06 | .05 |
| 359 | Dan Petry | .08 | .06 |
| 360 | Jerry Mumphrey | .06 | .05 |

| | MT | NR MT | | | MT | NR MT |
|---|---|---|---|---|---|---|
| 361 | Mark Clear | .06 | .05 | 425 | Jerry Royster | .06 | .05 |
| 362 | Mike Marshall | .20 | .15 | 426 | Dickie Noles | .06 | .05 |
| 363 | Lary Sorensen | .06 | .05 | 427 | George Foster | .15 | .11 |
| 364 | Amos Otis | .08 | .06 | 428 | *Mike Moore*(FC) | | |
| 365 | Rick Langford | .06 | .05 | | | 1.00 | .70 |
| 366 | Brad Mills | .06 | .05 | 429 | Gary Ward | .08 | .06 |
| 367 | Brian Downing | .10 | .08 | 430 | Barry Bonnell | .06 | .05 |
| 368 | Mike Richardt | .06 | .05 | 431 | Ron Washington | .06 | .05 |
| 369 | Aurelio Rodriguez | .08 | .06 | 432 | Rance Mulliniks | .06 | .05 |
| 370 | Dave Smith | .08 | .06 | 433 | Mike Stanton | .06 | .05 |
| 371 | Tug McGraw | .12 | .09 | 434 | Jesse Orosco | .10 | .08 |
| 372 | Doug Bair | .06 | .05 | 435 | Larry Bowa | .12 | .09 |
| 373 | Ruppert Jones | .06 | .05 | 436 | Biff Pocoroba | .06 | .05 |
| 374 | Alex Trevino | .06 | .05 | 437 | Johnny Ray | .12 | .09 |
| 375 | Ken Dayley | .06 | .05 | 438 | Joe Morgan | .40 | .30 |
| 376 | Rod Scurry | .06 | .05 | 439 | *Eric Show*(FC) | .30 | .25 |
| 377 | Bob Brenly(FC) | .08 | .06 | 440 | Larry Biittner | .06 | .05 |
| 378 | Scot Thompson | .06 | .05 | 441 | Greg Gross | .06 | .05 |
| 379 | Julio Cruz | .06 | .05 | 442 | Gene Tenace | .08 | .06 |
| 380 | John Stearns | .06 | .05 | 443 | Danny Heep | .06 | .05 |
| 381 | Dale Murray | .06 | .05 | 444 | Bobby Clark | .06 | .05 |
| 382 | *Frank Viola*(FC) | 4.00 | 3.00 | 445 | Kevin Hickey | .06 | .05 |
| 383 | Al Bumbry | .08 | .06 | 446 | Scott Sanderson | .06 | .05 |
| 384 | Ben Oglivie | .08 | .06 | 447 | Frank Tanana | .10 | .08 |
| 385 | Dave Tobik | .06 | .05 | 448 | Cesar Geronimo | .06 | .05 |
| 386 | Bob Stanley | .06 | .05 | 449 | Jimmy Sexton | .06 | .05 |
| 387 | Andre Robertson | .06 | .05 | 450 | Mike Hargrove | .06 | .05 |
| 388 | Jorge Orta | .06 | .05 | 451 | Doyle Alexander | .10 | .08 |
| 389 | Ed Whitson | .06 | .05 | 452 | Dwight Evans | .15 | .11 |
| 390 | Don Hood | .06 | .05 | 453 | Terry Forster | .08 | .06 |
| 391 | Tom Underwood | .06 | .05 | 454 | Tom Brookens | .06 | .05 |
| 392 | Tim Wallach | .20 | .15 | 455 | Rich Dauer | .06 | .05 |
| 393 | Steve Renko | .06 | .05 | 456 | Rob Picciolo | .06 | .05 |
| 394 | Mickey Rivers | .08 | .06 | 457 | Terry Crowley | .06 | .05 |
| 395 | Greg Luzinski | .12 | .09 | 458 | Ned Yost | .06 | .05 |
| 396 | Art Howe | .06 | .05 | 459 | Kirk Gibson | .40 | .30 |
| 397 | Alan Wiggins | .06 | .05 | 460 | Reid Nichols | .06 | .05 |
| 398 | Jim Barr | .06 | .05 | 461 | Oscar Gamble | .08 | .06 |
| 399 | Ivan DeJesus | .06 | .05 | 462 | Dusty Baker | .10 | .08 |
| 400 | *Tom Lawless*(FC) | | | 463 | Jack Perconte | .06 | .05 |
| | | .08 | .06 | 464 | Frank White | .10 | .08 |
| 401 | Bob Walk | .08 | .06 | 465 | Mickey Klutts | .06 | .05 |
| 402 | Jimmy Smith | .06 | .05 | 466 | Warren Cromartie | .06 | .05 |
| 403 | Lee Smith | 2.00 | 1.50 | 467 | Larry Parrish | .10 | .08 |
| 404 | George Hendrick | .08 | .06 | 468 | Bobby Grich | .10 | .08 |
| 405 | Eddie Murray | .80 | .60 | 469 | Dane Iorg | .06 | .05 |
| 406 | Marshall Edwards | .06 | .05 | 470 | Joe Niekro | .12 | .09 |
| 407 | Lance Parrish | .35 | .25 | 471 | Ed Farmer | .06 | .05 |
| 408 | Carney Lansford | .08 | .06 | 472 | Tim Flannery | .06 | .05 |
| 409 | Dave Winfield | 2.00 | 1.50 | 473 | Dave Parker | .30 | .25 |
| 410 | Bob Welch | .12 | .09 | 474 | Jeff Leonard | .10 | .08 |
| 411 | Larry Milbourne | .06 | .05 | 475 | Al Hrabosky | .08 | .06 |
| 412 | Dennis Leonard | .08 | .06 | 476 | Ron Hodges | .06 | .05 |
| 413 | Dan Meyer | .06 | .05 | 477 | Leon Durham | .08 | .06 |
| 414 | Charlie Lea | .06 | .05 | 478 | Jim Essian | .06 | .05 |
| 415 | Rick Honeycutt | .06 | .05 | 479 | Roy Lee Jackson | .06 | .05 |
| 416 | Mike Witt | .15 | .11 | 480 | Brad Havens | .06 | .05 |
| 417 | Steve Trout | .06 | .05 | 481 | Joe Price | .06 | .05 |
| 418 | Glenn Brummer | .06 | .05 | 482 | Tony Bernazard | .06 | .05 |
| 419 | Denny Walling | .06 | .05 | 483 | Scott McGregor | .08 | .06 |
| 420 | Gary Matthews | .10 | .08 | 484 | Paul Molitor | .20 | .15 |
| 421 | Charlie Liebrandt (Leibrandt) | .08 | .06 | 485 | Mike Ivie | .06 | .05 |
| 422 | Juan Eichelberger | .06 | .05 | 486 | Ken Griffey | .12 | .09 |
| 423 | *Matt Guante (Cecilio)*(FC) | .15 | .11 | 487 | Dennis Eckersley | 1.00 | .70 |
| | | | | 488 | Steve Garvey | .40 | .30 |
| 424 | Bill Laskey | .06 | .05 | 489 | Mike Fischlin | .06 | .05 |
| | | | | 490 | U.L. Washington | .06 | .05 |

| | | MT | NR MT | | | | MT | NR MT |
|---|---|---|---|---|---|---|---|---|
| 491 | Steve McCatty | .06 | .05 | 547 | Brad Lesley | | .06 | .05 |
| 492 | Roy Johnson | .06 | .05 | 548 | Luis Salazar | | .06 | .05 |
| 493 | Don Baylor | .12 | .09 | 549 | John Candelaria | | .10 | .08 |
| 494 | Bobby Johnson | .06 | .05 | 550 | Dave Bergman | | .06 | .05 |
| 495 | Mike Squires | .06 | .05 | 551 | Bob Watson | | .08 | .06 |
| 496 | Bert Roberge | .06 | .05 | 552 | Pat Tabler | | .10 | .08 |
| 497 | Dick Ruthven | .06 | .05 | 553 | Brent Gaff | | .06 | .05 |
| 498 | Tito Landrum | .06 | .05 | 554 | Al Cowens | | .06 | .05 |
| 499 | Sixto Lezcano | .06 | .05 | 555 | Tom Brunansky(FC) | | .25 | .20 |
| 500 | Johnny Bench | 1.00 | .70 | 556 | Lloyd Moseby | | .12 | .09 |
| 501 | Larry Whisenton | .06 | .05 | 557a | Pascual Perez | | | |
| 502 | Manny Sarmiento | .06 | .05 | | (Twins)(FC) | | .90 | .70 |
| 503 | Fred Breining | .06 | .05 | 557b | Pascual Perez | | | |
| 504 | Bill Campbell | .06 | .05 | | (Braves)(FC) | | .15 | .11 |
| 505 | Todd Cruz | .06 | .05 | 558 | Willie Upshaw | | .08 | .06 |
| 506 | Bob Bailor | .06 | .05 | 559 | Richie Zisk | | .08 | .06 |
| 507 | Dave Stieb | .12 | .09 | 560 | Pat Zachry | | .06 | .05 |
| 508 | Al Williams | .06 | .05 | 561 | Jay Johnstone | | .08 | .06 |
| 509 | Dan Ford | .06 | .05 | 562 | Carlos Diaz | | .06 | .05 |
| 510 | Gorman Thomas | .10 | .08 | 563 | John Tudor | | .10 | .08 |
| 511 | Chet Lemon | .08 | .06 | 564 | Frank Robinson | | .12 | .09 |
| 512 | Mike Torrez | .08 | .06 | 565 | Dave Edwards | | .06 | .05 |
| 513 | Shane Rawley | .10 | .08 | 566 | Paul Householder | | .06 | .05 |
| 514 | Mark Belanger | .08 | .06 | 567 | Ron Reed | | .06 | .05 |
| 515 | Rodney Craig | .06 | .05 | 568 | Mike Ramsey | | .06 | .05 |
| 516 | Onix Concepcion | .06 | .05 | 569 | Kiko Garcia | | .06 | .05 |
| 517 | Mike Heath | .06 | .05 | 570 | Tommy John | | .20 | .15 |
| 518 | Andre Dawson | 1.25 | .90 | 571 | Tony LaRussa | | .08 | .06 |
| 519 | Luis Sanchez | .06 | .05 | 572 | Joel Youngblood | | .06 | .05 |
| 520 | Terry Bogener | .06 | .05 | 573 | Wayne Tolleson(FC) | | | |
| 521 | Rudy Law | .06 | .05 | | | | .12 | .09 |
| 522 | Ray Knight | .10 | .08 | 574 | Keith Creel | | .06 | .05 |
| 523 | Joe Lefebvre | .06 | .05 | 575 | Billy Martin | | .12 | .09 |
| 524 | Jim Wohlford | .06 | .05 | 576 | Jerry Dybzinski | | .06 | .05 |
| 525 | Julio Franco(FC) | | | 577 | Rick Cerone | | .06 | .05 |
| | | 8.00 | 6.00 | 578 | Tony Perez | | .20 | .15 |
| 526 | Ron Oester | .06 | .05 | 579 | Greg Brock(FC) | | .35 | .25 |
| 527 | Rick Mahler | .08 | .06 | 580 | Glen Wilson | | | |
| 528 | Steve Nicosia | .06 | .05 | | (Glenn)(FC) | | .35 | .25 |
| 529 | Junior Kennedy | .06 | .05 | 581 | Tim Stoddard | | .06 | .05 |
| 530a | Whitey Herzog (one | | | 582 | Bob McClure | | .06 | .05 |
| | yellow box on back) | .70 | .50 | 583 | Jim Dwyer | | .06 | .05 |
| 530b | Whitey Herzog (two | | | 584 | Ed Romero | | .06 | .05 |
| | yellow boxes on back) | .10 | .08 | 585 | Larry Herndon | | .08 | .06 |
| 531a | Don Sutton (blue frame | | | 586 | Wade Boggs(FC) | | | |
| | around photo) | 1.00 | .70 | | | | 20.00 | 15.00 |
| 531b | Don Sutton (green | | | 587 | Jay Howell(FC) | | .15 | .11 |
| | frame around photo) | .30 | .25 | 588 | Dave Stewart | | 1.00 | .70 |
| 532 | Mark Brouhard | .06 | .05 | 589 | Bert Blyleven | | .12 | .09 |
| 533a | Sparky Anderson (one | | | 590 | Dick Howser | | .06 | .05 |
| | yellow box on back) | .70 | .50 | 591 | Wayne Gross | | .06 | .05 |
| 533b | Sparky Anderson (two | | | 592 | Terry Francona | | .06 | .05 |
| | yellow boxes on back) | .10 | .08 | 593 | Don Werner | | .06 | .05 |
| 534 | Roger LaFrancois | .06 | .05 | 594 | Bill Stein | | .06 | .05 |
| 535 | George Frazier | .06 | .05 | 595 | Jesse Barfield(FC) | | .70 | .50 |
| 536 | Tom Niedenfuer | .08 | .06 | 596 | Bobby Molinaro | | .06 | .05 |
| 537 | Ed Glynn | .06 | .05 | 597 | Mike Vail | | .06 | .05 |
| 538 | Lee May | .08 | .06 | 598 | Tony Gwynn(FC) | | | |
| 539 | Bob Kearney | .06 | .05 | | | | 25.00 | 18.00 |
| 540 | Tim Raines | .35 | .25 | 599 | Gary Rajsich | | .06 | .05 |
| 541 | Paul Mirabella | .06 | .05 | 600 | Jerry Ujdur | | .06 | .05 |
| 542 | Luis Tiant | .12 | .09 | 601 | Cliff Johnson | | .06 | .05 |
| 543 | Ron LeFlore | .08 | .06 | 602 | Jerry White | | .06 | .05 |
| 544 | Dave LaPoint(FC) | | | 603 | Bryan Clark | | .06 | .05 |
| | | .30 | .25 | 604 | Joe Ferguson | | .06 | .05 |
| 545 | Randy Moffitt | .06 | .05 | 605 | Guy Sularz | | .06 | .05 |
| 546 | Luis Aguayo | .06 | .05 | 606a | Ozzie Virgil (green frame | | | |

|  | | MT | NR MT |
|---|---|---|---|
| | around photo)(FC) | .90 | .70 |
| 606b | Ozzie Virgil (orange frame around photo)(FC) | | |
| | | .08 | .06 |
| 607 | Terry Harper(FC) | .06 | .05 |
| 608 | Harvey Kuenn | .08 | .06 |
| 609 | Jim Sundberg | .08 | .06 |
| 610 | Willie Stargell | .40 | .30 |
| 611 | Reggie Smith | .10 | .08 |
| 612 | Rob Wilfong | .06 | .05 |
| 613 | Niekro Brothers (Joe Niekro, Phil Niekro) | | |
| | | .15 | .11 |
| 614 | Lee Elia | .06 | .05 |
| 615 | Mickey Hatcher | .08 | .06 |
| 616 | Jerry Hairston | .06 | .05 |
| 617 | John Martin | .06 | .05 |
| 618 | Wally Backman(FC) | .15 | .11 |
| 619 | *Storm Davis*(FC) | .30 | .25 |
| 620 | Alan Knicely | .06 | .05 |
| 621 | John Stuper | .06 | .05 |
| 622 | Matt Sinatro | .06 | .05 |
| 623 | *Gene Petralli*(FC) | | |
| | | .15 | .11 |
| 624 | Duane Walker | .06 | .05 |
| 625 | Dick Williams | .06 | .05 |
| 626 | Pat Corrales | .06 | .05 |
| 627 | Vern Ruhle | .06 | .05 |
| 628 | Joe Torre | .08 | .06 |
| 629 | Anthony Johnson | .06 | .05 |
| 630 | Steve Howe | .08 | .06 |
| 631 | Gary Woods | .06 | .05 |
| 632 | Lamarr Hoyt (LaMarr) | | |
| | | .06 | .05 |
| 633 | Steve Swisher | .06 | .05 |
| 634 | Terry Leach(FC) | .12 | .09 |
| 635 | Jeff Newman | .06 | .05 |
| 636 | Brett Butler | .10 | .08 |
| 637 | Gary Gray | .06 | .05 |
| 638 | Lee Mazzilli | .08 | .06 |
| 639a | Ron Jackson (A's) | 10.00 | 7.50 |
| 639b | Ron Jackson (Angels — green frame around photo) | | |
| | | .90 | .70 |
| 639c | Ron Jackson (Angels — red frame around photo) | | |
| | | .20 | .15 |
| 640 | Juan Beniquez | .06 | .05 |
| 641 | Dave Rucker | .06 | .05 |
| 642 | Luis Pujols | .06 | .05 |
| 643 | Rick Monday | .10 | .08 |
| 644 | Hosken Powell | .06 | .05 |
| 645 | San Diego Chicken | .20 | .15 |
| 646 | Dave Engle | .06 | .05 |
| 647 | Dick Davis | .06 | .05 |
| 648 | MVP's (Vida Blue, Joe Morgan, Frank Robinson) | | |
| | | .15 | .11 |
| 649 | Al Chambers | .06 | .05 |
| 650 | Jesus Vega | .06 | .05 |
| 651 | Jeff Jones | .06 | .05 |
| 652 | Marvis Foley | .06 | .05 |
| 653 | Ty Cobb Puzzle | .06 | .05 |
| ---a | Dick Perez/DK Checklist (no word "Checklist" on back) | .70 | .50 |
| ---b | Dick Perez/DK Checklist (word "Checklist" | | |

|  | | MT | NR MT |
|---|---|---|---|
| | on back) | .08 | .06 |
| ---- | Checklist 27-130 | .06 | .05 |
| ---- | Checklist 131-234 | .06 | .05 |
| ---- | Checklist 235-338 | .06 | .05 |
| ---- | Checklist 339-442 | .06 | .05 |
| ---- | Checklist 443-546 | .06 | .05 |
| ---- | Checklist 547-653 | .06 | .05 |

## 1984 Donruss

The 1984 Donruss set consists of 651 numbered cards, seven unnumbered checklists and two "Living Legends" cards (designated A and B). The A and B cards were issued only in wax packs and not available to hobby dealers purchasing vending sets. The card fronts differ in style from the previous years, however the Donruss logo and year of issue are still included. The card backs have black print on green and white and are identical in format to the preceding year. The standard-size cards (2-1/2" by 3-1/2") were issued with a 63-piece puzzle of Duke Snider. A limited print run of the issue by Donruss has caused the set to escalate in price in recent years. The complete set price in the checklist that follows does not include the higher priced variations. Cards marked with (DK) or (RR) in the checklist refer to the Diamond Kings and Rated Rookies subsets.

|  | MT | NR MT |
|---|---|---|
| Complete Set: | 375.00 | 275.00 |
| Common Player: | .12 | .09 |

| | | MT | NR MT |
|---|---|---|---|
| 1a | Robin Yount (DK) (Perez Steel on back) | 1.50 | 1.25 |
| 1b | Robin Yount (DK) (Perez Steele on back) | 4.00 | 3.00 |
| 2a | Dave Concepcion (DK) | | |

| | MT | NR MT |
|---|---|---|
| (Perez-Steel on back) | .30 | .25 |
| 2b Dave Concepcion (DK) (Perez-Steele on back) | .60 | .45 |
| 3a Dwayne Murphy (DK) (Perez-Steel on back) | .25 | .20 |
| 3b Dwayne Murphy (DK) (Perez-Steele on back) | .60 | .45 |
| 4a John Castino (DK) (Perez-Steel on back) | .20 | .15 |
| 4b John Castino (DK) (Perez-Steele on back) | .60 | .45 |
| 5a Leon Durham (DK) (Perez-Steel on back) | .25 | .20 |
| 5b Leon Durham (DK) (Perez-Steele on back) | .60 | .45 |
| 6a Rusty Staub (DK) (Perez Steel on back) | .30 | .25 |
| 6b Rusty Staub (DK) (Perez Steele on back) | .60 | .45 |
| 7a Jack Clark (DK) (Perez Steel on back) | .40 | .30 |
| 7b Jack Clark (DK) (Perez Steele on back) | .80 | .60 |
| 8a Dave Dravecky (DK) (Perez-Steel on back) | .25 | .20 |
| 8b Dave Dravecky (DK) (Perez-Steele on back) | .60 | .45 |
| 9a Al Oliver (DK) (Perez Steel on back) | .35 | .25 |
| 9b Al Oliver (DK) (Perez Steele on back) | .70 | .50 |
| 10a Dave Righetti (DK) (Perez-Steel on back) | .40 | .30 |
| 10b Dave Righetti (DK) (Perez-Steele on back) | .80 | .60 |
| 11a Hal McRae (DK) (Perez Steel on back) | .30 | .25 |
| 11b Hal McRae (DK) (Perez Steele on back) | .60 | .45 |
| 12a Ray Knight (DK) (Perez Steel on back) | .25 | .20 |
| 12b Ray Knight (DK) (Perez Steele on back) | .60 | .45 |
| 13a Bruce Sutter (DK) (Perez-Steel on back) | .35 | .25 |
| 13b Bruce Sutter (DK) (Perez-Steele on back) | .70 | .50 |
| 14a Bob Horner (DK) (Perez Steel on back) | .40 | .30 |
| 14b Bob Horner (DK) (Perez Steele on back) | .80 | .60 |
| 15a Lance Parrish (DK) (Perez-Steel on back) | .60 | .45 |
| 15b Lance Parrish (DK) (Perez-Steele on back) | 1.25 | .90 |
| 16a Matt Young (DK) (Perez Steel on back) | .25 | .20 |
| 16b Matt Young (DK) (Perez Steele on back) | .60 | .45 |
| 17a Fred Lynn (DK) (Perez Steel on back) | .35 | .25 |
| 17b Fred Lynn (DK) (Perez Steele on back) | .70 | .50 |
| 18a Ron Kittle (DK) (Perez Steel on back)(FC) | .35 | .25 |
| 18b Ron Kittle (DK) (Perez | | |

| | MT | NR MT |
|---|---|---|
| Steele on back)(FC) | .70 | .50 |
| 19a Jim Clancy (DK) (Perez Steel on back) | .25 | .20 |
| 19b Jim Clancy (DK) (Perez Steele on back) | .60 | .45 |
| 20a Bill Madlock (DK) (Perez Steele on back) | .30 | .25 |
| 20b Bill Madlock (DK) (Perez Steele on back) | .60 | .45 |
| 21a Larry Parrish (DK) (Perez-Steel on back) | .30 | .25 |
| 21b Larry Parrish (DK) (Perez-Steele on back) | .60 | .45 |
| 22a Eddie Murray (DK) (Perez-Steel on back) | 1.25 | .90 |
| 22b Eddie Murray (DK) (Perez-Steele on back) | 2.50 | 2.00 |
| 23a Mike Schmidt (DK) (Perez-Steel on back) | 1.25 | .90 |
| 23b Mike Schmidt (DK) (Perez-Steele on back) | 2.50 | 2.00 |
| 24a Pedro Guerrero (DK) (Perez-Steel on back) | .50 | .40 |
| 24b Pedro Guerrero (DK) (Perez-Steele on back) | 1.00 | .70 |
| 25a Andre Thornton (DK) (Perez-Steel on back) | .30 | .25 |
| 25b Andre Thornton (DK) (Perez-Steele on back) | .60 | .45 |
| 26a Wade Boggs (DK) (Perez Steel on back) | 3.00 | 2.25 |
| 26b Wade Boggs (DK) (Perez Steele on back) | 4.00 | 3.00 |
| 27 *Joel Skinner (RR)(FC)* | .20 | .15 |
| 28 Tom Dunbar (RR) | .12 | .09 |
| 29a Mike Stenhouse (RR) (no number on back) | .15 | .11 |
| 29b Mike Stenhouse (RR) (29 on back) | 4.00 | 3.00 |
| 30a *Ron Darling (no number on back)(FC)* | 5.00 | 3.75 |
| 30b *Ron Darling (30 on back)(FC)* | 10.00 | 7.50 |
| 31 *Dion James (RR)(FC)* | .15 | .11 |
| 32 *Tony Fernandez (RR)(FC)* | 7.00 | 5.25 |
| 33 Angel Salazar (RR) | .12 | .09 |
| 34 *Kevin McReynolds (RR)(FC)* | 6.00 | 4.50 |
| 35 *Dick Schofield (RR)(FC)* | .40 | .30 |
| 36 *Brad Komminsk (RR)(FC)* | .15 | .11 |
| 37 *Tim Teufel (RR)(FC)* | .30 | .25 |
| 38 Doug Frobel (RR) | .12 | .09 |
| 39 *Greg Gagne (RR)(FC)* | .60 | .45 |
| 40 Mike Fuentes (RR) | .12 | .09 |
| 41 *Joe Carter (RR)(FC)* | 45.00 | 33.00 |
| 42 Mike Brown (RR) | .12 | .09 |

| | | MT | NR MT |
|---|---|---|---|
| 43 | Mike Jeffcoat (RR) | .12 | .09 |
| 44 | Sid Fernandez (RR)(FC) | 4.00 | 3.00 |
| 45 | Brian Dayett (RR) | .12 | .09 |
| 46 | Chris Smith (RR) | .12 | .09 |
| 47 | Eddie Murray | 5.00 | 3.75 |
| 48 | Robin Yount | 10.00 | 7.50 |
| 49 | Lance Parrish | .50 | .40 |
| 50 | Jim Rice | .90 | .70 |
| 51 | Dave Winfield | 8.00 | 6.00 |
| 52 | Fernando Valenzuela | .50 | .40 |
| 53 | George Brett | 10.00 | 7.50 |
| 54 | Rickey Henderson | 15.00 | 11.00 |
| 55 | Gary Carter | 1.00 | .70 |
| 56 | Buddy Bell | .20 | .15 |
| 57 | Reggie Jackson | 5.00 | 3.75 |
| 58 | Harold Baines | .25 | .20 |
| 59 | Ozzie Smith | 5.00 | 3.75 |
| 60 | Nolan Ryan | 20.00 | 15.00 |
| 61 | Pete Rose | 3.00 | 2.25 |
| 62 | Ron Oester | .12 | .09 |
| 63 | Steve Garvey | .90 | .70 |
| 64 | Jason Thompson | .12 | .09 |
| 65 | Jack Clark | .35 | .25 |
| 66 | Dale Murphy | 2.00 | 1.50 |
| 67 | Leon Durham | .12 | .09 |
| 68 | Darryl Strawberry(FC) | 40.00 | 30.00 |
| 69 | Richie Zisk | .12 | .09 |
| 70 | Kent Hrbek | .60 | .45 |
| 71 | Dave Stieb | .25 | .20 |
| 72 | Ken Schrom | .12 | .09 |
| 73 | George Bell | 2.00 | 1.50 |
| 74 | John Moses | .15 | .11 |
| 75 | Ed Lynch | .12 | .09 |
| 76 | Chuck Rainey | .12 | .09 |
| 77 | Biff Pocoroba | .12 | .09 |
| 78 | Cecilio Guante | .12 | .09 |
| 79 | Jim Barr | .12 | .09 |
| 80 | Kurt Bevacqua | .12 | .09 |
| 81 | Tom Foley | .12 | .09 |
| 82 | Joe Lefebvre | .12 | .09 |
| 83 | Andy Van Slyke(FC) | 12.00 | 9.00 |
| 84 | Bob Lillis | .12 | .09 |
| 85 | Rick Adams | .12 | .09 |
| 86 | Jerry Hairston | .12 | .09 |
| 87 | Bob James | .12 | .09 |
| 88 | Joe Altobelli | .12 | .09 |
| 89 | Ed Romero | .12 | .09 |
| 90 | John Grubb | .12 | .09 |
| 91 | John Henry Johnson | .12 | .09 |
| 92 | Juan Espino | .12 | .09 |
| 93 | Candy Maldonado | .20 | .15 |
| 94 | Andre Thornton | .20 | .15 |
| 95 | Onix Concepcion | .12 | .09 |
| 96 | Don Hill(FC) | .20 | .15 |
| 97 | Andre Dawson | 5.00 | 3.75 |
| 98 | Frank Tanana | .15 | .11 |
| 99 | Curt Wilkerson(FC) | .15 | .11 |
| 100 | Larry Gura | .12 | .09 |
| 101 | Dwayne Murphy | .12 | .09 |
| 102 | Tom Brennan | .12 | .09 |

| | | MT | NR MT |
|---|---|---|---|
| 103 | Dave Righetti | .40 | .30 |
| 104 | Steve Sax | .30 | .25 |
| 105 | Dan Petry | .12 | .09 |
| 106 | Cal Ripken | 25.00 | 18.00 |
| 107 | Paul Molitor | 1.25 | .90 |
| 108 | Fred Lynn | .35 | .25 |
| 109 | Neil Allen | .12 | .09 |
| 110 | Joe Niekro | .20 | .15 |
| 111 | Steve Carlton | 3.00 | 2.25 |
| 112 | Terry Kennedy | .15 | .11 |
| 113 | Bill Madlock | .20 | .15 |
| 114 | Chili Davis | .15 | .11 |
| 115 | Jim Gantner | .12 | .09 |
| 116 | Tom Seaver | 5.00 | 3.75 |
| 117 | Bill Buckner | .20 | .15 |
| 118 | Bill Caudill | .12 | .09 |
| 119 | Jim Clancy | .15 | .11 |
| 120 | John Castino | .12 | .09 |
| 121 | Dave Concepcion | .20 | .15 |
| 122 | Greg Luzinski | .20 | .15 |
| 123 | Mike Boddicker(FC) | .20 | .15 |
| 124 | Pete Ladd | .12 | .09 |
| 125 | Juan Berenguer | .12 | .09 |
| 126 | John Montefusco | .12 | .09 |
| 127 | Ed Jurak | .12 | .09 |
| 128 | Tom Niedenfuer | .12 | .09 |
| 129 | Bert Blyleven | .30 | .25 |
| 130 | Bud Black | .12 | .09 |
| 131 | Gorman Heimueller | .12 | .09 |
| 132 | Dan Schatzeder | .12 | .09 |
| 133 | Ron Jackson | .12 | .09 |
| 134 | Tom Henke(FC) | 2.00 | 1.50 |
| 135 | Kevin Hickey | .12 | .09 |
| 136 | Mike Scott | .30 | .25 |
| 137 | Bo Diaz | .12 | .09 |
| 138 | Glenn Brummer | .12 | .09 |
| 139 | Sid Monge | .12 | .09 |
| 140 | Rich Gale | .12 | .09 |
| 141 | Brett Butler | .15 | .11 |
| 142 | Brian Harper | .80 | .60 |
| 143 | John Rabb | .12 | .09 |
| 144 | Gary Woods | .12 | .09 |
| 145 | Pat Putnam | .12 | .09 |
| 146 | Jim Acker(FC) | .15 | .11 |
| 147 | Mickey Hatcher | .12 | .09 |
| 148 | Todd Cruz | .12 | .09 |
| 149 | Tom Tellmann | .12 | .09 |
| 150 | John Wockenfuss | .12 | .09 |
| 151 | Wade Boggs | 18.00 | 13.50 |
| 152 | Don Baylor | .20 | .15 |
| 153 | Bob Welch | .20 | .15 |
| 154 | Alan Bannister | .12 | .09 |
| 155 | Willie Aikens | .12 | .09 |
| 156 | Jeff Burroughs | .12 | .09 |
| 157 | Bryan Little | .12 | .09 |
| 158 | Bob Boone | .15 | .11 |
| 159 | Dave Hostetler | .12 | .09 |
| 160 | Jerry Dybzinski | .12 | .09 |
| 161 | Mike Madden | .12 | .09 |
| 162 | Luis DeLeon | .12 | .09 |
| 163 | Willie Hernandez | .15 | .11 |
| 164 | Frank Pastore | .12 | .09 |
| 165 | Rick Camp | .12 | .09 |
| 166 | Lee Mazzilli | .12 | .09 |
| 167 | Scot Thompson | .12 | .09 |
| 168 | Bob Forsch | .12 | .09 |

| | | MT | NR MT |
|---|---|---|---|
| 169 | Mike Flanagan | .15 | .11 |
| 170 | Rick Manning | .12 | .09 |
| 171 | Chet Lemon | .12 | .09 |
| 172 | Jerry Remy | .12 | .09 |
| 173 | Ron Guidry | .35 | .25 |
| 174 | Pedro Guerrero | .50 | .40 |
| 175 | Willie Wilson | .25 | .20 |
| 176 | Carney Lansford | .20 | .15 |
| 177 | Al Oliver | .30 | .25 |
| 178 | Jim Sundberg | .12 | .09 |
| 179 | Bobby Grich | .20 | .15 |
| 180 | Richard Dotson | .20 | .15 |
| 181 | Joaquin Andujar | .12 | .09 |
| 182 | Jose Cruz | .20 | .15 |
| 183 | Mike Schmidt | 12.00 | 9.00 |
| 184 | *Gary Redus*(FC) | .30 | .25 |
| 185 | Garry Templeton | .15 | .11 |
| 186 | Tony Pena | .20 | .15 |
| 187 | Greg Minton | .12 | .09 |
| 188 | Phil Niekro | .50 | .40 |
| 189 | Ferguson Jenkins | .30 | .25 |
| 190 | Mookie Wilson | .15 | .11 |
| 191 | Jim Beattie | .12 | .09 |
| 192 | Gary Ward | .12 | .09 |
| 193 | Jesse Barfield | .40 | .30 |
| 194 | Pete Filson | .12 | .09 |
| 195 | Roy Lee Jackson | .12 | .09 |
| 196 | Rick Sweet | .12 | .09 |
| 197 | Jesse Orosco | .15 | .11 |
| 198 | *Steve Lake*(FC) | .12 | .09 |
| 199 | Ken Dayley | .12 | .09 |
| 200 | Manny Sarmiento | .12 | .09 |
| 201 | Mark Davis(FC) | .25 | .20 |
| 202 | Tim Flannery | .12 | .09 |
| 203 | Bill Scherrer | .12 | .09 |
| 204 | Al Holland | .12 | .09 |
| 205 | David Von Ohlen | .12 | .09 |
| 206 | Mike LaCoss | .12 | .09 |
| 207 | Juan Beniquez | .12 | .09 |
| 208 | *Juan Agosto*(FC) | .20 | .15 |
| 209 | Bobby Ramos | .12 | .09 |
| 210 | Al Bumbry | .12 | .09 |
| 211 | Mark Brouhard | .12 | .09 |
| 212 | Howard Bailey | .12 | .09 |
| 213 | Bruce Hurst | .20 | .15 |
| 214 | Bob Shirley | .12 | .09 |
| 215 | Pat Zachry | .12 | .09 |
| 216 | Julio Franco | 4.50 | 3.35 |
| 217 | Mike Armstrong | .12 | .09 |
| 218 | Dave Beard | .12 | .09 |
| 219 | Steve Rogers | .12 | .09 |
| 220 | John Butcher | .12 | .09 |
| 221 | *Mike Smithson*(FC) | .20 | .15 |
| 222 | Frank White | .20 | .15 |
| 223 | Mike Heath | .12 | .09 |
| 224 | Chris Bando | .12 | .09 |
| 225 | Roy Smalley | .12 | .09 |
| 226 | Dusty Baker | .20 | .15 |
| 227 | Lou Whitaker | .60 | .45 |
| 228 | John Lowenstein | .12 | .09 |
| 229 | Ben Oglivie | .12 | .09 |
| 230 | Doug DeCinces | .15 | .11 |
| 231 | Lonnie Smith | .12 | .09 |
| 232 | Ray Knight | .15 | .11 |
| 233 | Gary Matthews | .20 | .15 |
| 234 | Juan Bonilla | .12 | .09 |

| | | MT | NR MT |
|---|---|---|---|
| 235 | Rod Scurry | .12 | .09 |
| 236 | Atlee Hammaker | .12 | .09 |
| 237 | Mike Caldwell | .12 | .09 |
| 238 | Keith Hernandez | .80 | .60 |
| 239 | Larry Bowa | .25 | .20 |
| 240 | Tony Bernazard | .12 | .09 |
| 241 | Damaso Garcia | .12 | .09 |
| 242 | Tom Brunansky | .35 | .25 |
| 243 | Dan Driessen | .12 | .09 |
| 244 | Ron Kittle(FC) | .30 | .25 |
| 245 | Tim Stoddard | .12 | .09 |
| 246 | Bob Gibson | .12 | .09 |
| 247 | Marty Castillo | .12 | .09 |
| 248 | *Don Mattingly*(FC) | 40.00 | 30.00 |
| 249 | Jeff Newman | .12 | .09 |
| 250 | *Alejandro Pena*(FC) | .70 | .50 |
| 251 | Toby Harrah | .12 | .09 |
| 252 | Cesar Geronimo | .12 | .09 |
| 253 | Tom Underwood | .12 | .09 |
| 254 | Doug Flynn | .12 | .09 |
| 255 | Andy Hassler | .12 | .09 |
| 256 | Odell Jones | .12 | .09 |
| 257 | Rudy Law | .12 | .09 |
| 258 | Harry Spilman | .12 | .09 |
| 259 | Marty Bystrom | .12 | .09 |
| 260 | Dave Rucker | .12 | .09 |
| 261 | Ruppert Jones | .12 | .09 |
| 262 | Jeff Jones | .12 | .09 |
| 263 | *Gerald Perry*(FC) | .50 | .40 |
| 264 | Gene Tenace | .12 | .09 |
| 265 | Brad Wellman | .12 | .09 |
| 266 | Dickie Noles | .12 | .09 |
| 267 | Jamie Allen | .12 | .09 |
| 268 | Jim Gott | .15 | .11 |
| 269 | Ron Davis | .12 | .09 |
| 270 | Benny Ayala | .12 | .09 |
| 271 | Ned Yost | .12 | .09 |
| 272 | Dave Rozema | .12 | .09 |
| 273 | Dave Stapleton | .12 | .09 |
| 274 | Lou Piniella | .20 | .15 |
| 275 | Jose Morales | .12 | .09 |
| 276 | Brod Perkins | .12 | .09 |
| 277 | Butch Davis | .12 | .09 |
| 278 | *Tony Phillips*(FC) | .20 | .15 |
| 279 | Jeff Reardon | .25 | .20 |
| 280 | Ken Forsch | .12 | .09 |
| 281 | *Pete O'Brien*(FC) | 1.00 | .70 |
| 282 | Tom Paciorek | .12 | .09 |
| 283 | Frank LaCorte | .12 | .09 |
| 284 | Tim Lollar | .12 | .09 |
| 285 | Greg Gross | .12 | .09 |
| 286 | Alex Trevino | .12 | .09 |
| 287 | Gene Garber | .12 | .09 |
| 288 | Dave Parker | .50 | .40 |
| 289 | Lee Smith | .20 | .15 |
| 290 | Dave LaPoint | .15 | .11 |
| 291 | *John Shelby*(FC) | .25 | .20 |
| 292 | Charlie Moore | .12 | .09 |
| 293 | Alan Trammell | .60 | .45 |
| 294 | Tony Armas | .20 | .15 |
| 295 | Shane Rawley | .20 | .15 |
| 296 | Greg Brock | .15 | .11 |

| | MT | NR MT | | | MT | NR MT |
|---|---|---|---|---|---|---|
| 297 Hal McRae | .20 | .15 | 361 Ron Cey | | .20 | .15 |
| 298 Mike Davis | .12 | .09 | 362 Matt Young(FC) | | .20 | .15 |
| 299 Tim Raines | .80 | .60 | 363 Lloyd Moseby | | .20 | .15 |
| 300 Bucky Dent | .15 | .11 | 364 Frank Viola | | 2.00 | 1.50 |
| 301 Tommy John | .35 | .25 | 365 Eddie Milner | | .12 | .09 |
| 302 Carlton Fisk | 4.00 | 3.00 | 366 Floyd Bannister | | .20 | .15 |
| 303 Darrell Porter | .12 | .09 | 367 Dan Ford | | .12 | .09 |
| 304 Dickie Thon | .12 | .09 | 368 Moose Haas | | .12 | .09 |
| 305 Garry Maddox | .12 | .09 | 369 Doug Bair | | .12 | .09 |
| 306 Cesar Cedeno | .20 | .15 | 370 Ray Fontenot(FC) | | | |
| 307 Gary Lucas | .12 | .09 | | | .12 | .09 |
| 308 Johnny Ray | .20 | .15 | 371 Luis Aponte | | .12 | .09 |
| 309 Andy McGaffigan | .12 | .09 | 372 Jack Fimple | | .12 | .09 |
| 310 Claudell Washington | .12 | .09 | 373 Neal Heaton(FC) | | .20 | .15 |
| 311 Ryne Sandberg | 25.00 | 20.00 | 374 Greg Pryor | | .12 | .09 |
| 312 George Foster | .30 | .25 | 375 Wayne Gross | | .12 | .09 |
| 313 Spike Owen(FC) | .70 | .50 | 376 Charlie Lea | | .12 | .09 |
| 314 Gary Gaetti | .40 | .30 | 377 Steve Lubratich | | .12 | .09 |
| 315 Willie Upshaw | .12 | .09 | 378 Jon Matlack | | .12 | .09 |
| 316 Al Williams | .12 | .09 | 379 Julio Cruz | | .12 | .09 |
| 317 Jorge Orta | .12 | .09 | 380 John Mizerock | | .12 | .09 |
| 318 Orlando Mercado | .12 | .09 | 381 Kevin Gross(FC) | | .50 | .40 |
| 319 Junior Ortiz(FC) | .12 | .09 | 382 Mike Ramsey | | .12 | .09 |
| 320 Mike Proly | .12 | .09 | 383 Doug Gwosdz | | .12 | .09 |
| 321 Randy Johnson | .12 | .09 | 384 Kelly Paris | | .12 | .09 |
| 322 Jim Morrison | .12 | .09 | 385 Pete Falcone | | .12 | .09 |
| 323 Max Venable | .12 | .09 | 386 Milt May | | .12 | .09 |
| 324 Tony Gwynn | 18.00 | 13.50 | 387 Fred Breining | | .12 | .09 |
| 325 Duane Walker | .12 | .09 | 388 Craig Lefferts(FC) | | | |
| 326 Ozzie Virgil | .12 | .09 | | | .25 | .20 |
| 327 Jeff Lahti | .12 | .09 | 389 Steve Henderson | | .12 | .09 |
| 328 Bill Dawley(FC) | .12 | .09 | 390 Randy Moffitt | | .12 | .09 |
| 329 Rob Wilfong | .12 | .09 | 391 Ron Washington | | .12 | .09 |
| 330 Marc Hill | .12 | .09 | 392 Gary Roenicke | | .12 | .09 |
| 331 Ray Burris | .12 | .09 | 393 Tom Candiotti(FC) | | | |
| 332 Allan Ramirez | .12 | .09 | | | 1.00 | .70 |
| 333 Chuck Porter | .12 | .09 | 394 Larry Pashnick | | .12 | .09 |
| 334 Wayne Krenchicki | .12 | .09 | 395 Dwight Evans | | .30 | .25 |
| 335 Gary Allenson | .12 | .09 | 396 Goose Gossage | | .40 | .30 |
| 336 Bob Meacham(FC) | | | 397 Derrel Thomas | | .12 | .09 |
| | .20 | .15 | 398 Juan Eichelberger | | .12 | .09 |
| 337 Joe Beckwith | .12 | .09 | 399 Leon Roberts | | .12 | .09 |
| 338 Rick Sutcliffe | .25 | .20 | 400 Davey Lopes | | .15 | .11 |
| 339 Mark Huismann(FC) | | | 401 Bill Gullickson | | .12 | .09 |
| | .15 | .11 | 402 Geoff Zahn | | .12 | .09 |
| 340 Tim Conroy(FC) | .15 | .11 | 403 Billy Sample | | .12 | .09 |
| 341 Scott Sanderson | .12 | .09 | 404 Mike Squires | | .12 | .09 |
| 342 Larry Biittner | .12 | .09 | 405 Craig Reynolds | | .12 | .09 |
| 343 Dave Stewart | 2.00 | 1.50 | 406 Eric Show | | .15 | .11 |
| 344 Darryl Motley | .12 | .09 | 407 John Denny | | .12 | .09 |
| 345 Chris Codiroli(FC) | | | 408 Dann Bilardello | | .12 | .09 |
| | .12 | .09 | 409 Bruce Benedict | | .12 | .09 |
| 346 Rick Behenna | .12 | .09 | 410 Kent Tekulve | | .12 | .09 |
| 347 Andre Robertson | .12 | .09 | 411 Mel Hall | | .20 | .15 |
| 348 Mike Marshall | .25 | .20 | 412 John Stuper | | .12 | .09 |
| 349 Larry Herndon | .12 | .09 | 413 Rick Dempsey | | .12 | .09 |
| 350 Rich Dauer | .12 | .09 | 414 Don Sutton | | 1.00 | .70 |
| 351 Cecil Cooper | .25 | .20 | 415 Jack Morris | | 4.00 | 3.00 |
| 352 Rod Carew | 4.00 | 3.00 | 416 John Tudor | | .20 | .15 |
| 353 Willie McGee | .40 | .30 | 417 Willie Randolph | | .20 | .15 |
| 354 Phil Garner | .12 | .09 | 418 Jerry Reuss | | .15 | .11 |
| 355 Joe Morgan | .60 | .45 | 419 Don Slaught | | .12 | .09 |
| 356 Luis Salazar | .12 | .09 | 420 Steve McCatty | | .12 | .09 |
| 357 John Candelaria | .20 | .15 | 421 Tim Wallach | | .25 | .20 |
| 358 Bill Laskey | .12 | .09 | 422 Larry Parrish | | .20 | .15 |
| 359 Bob McClure | .12 | .09 | 423 Brian Downing | | .20 | .15 |
| 360 Dave Kingman | .30 | .25 | 424 Britt Burns | | .12 | .09 |

| | | MT | NR MT | | | | MT | NR MT |
|---|---|---|---|---|---|---|---|---|
| 425 | David Green | .12 | .09 | | 487 | Bruce Berenyi | .12 | .09 |
| 426 | Jerry Mumphrey | .12 | .09 | | 488 | LaMarr Hoyt | .12 | .09 |
| 427 | Ivan DeJesus | .12 | .09 | | 489 | Joe Nolan | .12 | .09 |
| 428 | Mario Soto | .12 | .09 | | 490 | Marshall Edwards | .12 | .09 |
| 429 | Gene Richards | .12 | .09 | | 491 | Mike Laga(FC) | .12 | .09 |
| 430 | Dale Berra | .12 | .09 | | 492 | Rick Cerone | .12 | .09 |
| 431 | Darrell Evans | .25 | .20 | | 493 | Mike Miller (Rick) | .12 | .09 |
| 432 | Glenn Hubbard | .12 | .09 | | 494 | Rick Honeycutt | .12 | .09 |
| 433 | Jody Davis | .15 | .11 | | 495 | Mike Hargrove | .12 | .09 |
| 434 | Danny Heep | .12 | .09 | | 496 | Joe Simpson | .12 | .09 |
| 435 | Ed Nunez(FC) | .20 | .15 | | 497 | Keith Atherton(FC) | | |
| 436 | Bobby Castillo | .12 | .09 | | | | .25 | .20 |
| 437 | Ernie Whitt | .12 | .09 | | 498 | Chris Welsh | .12 | .09 |
| 438 | Scott Ullger | .12 | .09 | | 499 | Bruce Kison | .12 | .09 |
| 439 | Doyle Alexander | .15 | .11 | | 500 | Bob Johnson | .12 | .09 |
| 440 | Domingo Ramos | .12 | .09 | | 501 | Jerry Koosman | .15 | .11 |
| 441 | Craig Swan | .12 | .09 | | 502 | Frank DiPino | .12 | .09 |
| 442 | Warren Brusstar | .12 | .09 | | 503 | Tony Perez | .40 | .30 |
| 443 | Len Barker | .12 | .09 | | 504 | Ken Oberkfell | .12 | .09 |
| 444 | Mike Easler | .12 | .09 | | 505 | Mark Thurmond(FC) | | |
| 445 | Renie Martin | .12 | .09 | | | | .12 | .09 |
| 446 | Dennis | | | | 506 | Joe Price | .12 | .09 |
| | Rasmussen(FC) | .70 | .50 | | 507 | Pascual Perez | .15 | .11 |
| 447 | Ted Power(FC) | .15 | .11 | | 508 | Marvell Wynne(FC) | | |
| 448 | Charlie Hudson(FC) | | | | | | .25 | .20 |
| | | .25 | .20 | | 509 | Mike Krukow | .12 | .09 |
| 449 | Danny Cox(FC) | .70 | .50 | | 510 | Dick Ruthven | .12 | .09 |
| 450 | Kevin Bass(FC) | .30 | .25 | | 511 | Al Cowens | .12 | .09 |
| 451 | Daryl Sconiers | .12 | .09 | | 512 | Cliff Johnson | .12 | .09 |
| 452 | Scott Fletcher | .12 | .09 | | 513 | Randy Bush(FC) | .20 | .15 |
| 453 | Bryn Smith | .12 | .09 | | 514 | Sammy Stewart | .12 | .09 |
| 454 | Jim Dwyer | .12 | .09 | | 515 | Bill Schroeder(FC) | | |
| 455 | Rob Picciolo | .12 | .09 | | | | .25 | .20 |
| 456 | Enos Cabell | .12 | .09 | | 516 | Aurelio Lopez | .12 | .09 |
| 457 | Dennis "Oil Can" | | | | 517 | Mike Brown | .12 | .09 |
| | Boyd(FC) | .70 | .50 | | 518 | Graig Nettles | .35 | .25 |
| 458 | Butch Wynegar | .12 | .09 | | 519 | Dave Sax | .12 | .09 |
| 459 | Burt Hooton | .12 | .09 | | 520 | Gerry Willard | .12 | .09 |
| 460 | Ron Hassey | .12 | .09 | | 521 | Paul Splittorff | .12 | .09 |
| 461 | Danny Jackson(FC) | | | | 522 | Tom Burgmeier | .12 | .09 |
| | | 1.00 | .70 | | 523 | Chris Speier | .12 | .09 |
| 462 | Bob Kearney | .12 | .09 | | 524 | Bobby Clark | .12 | .09 |
| 463 | Terry Francona | .12 | .09 | | 525 | George Wright | .12 | .09 |
| 464 | Wayne Tolleson | .12 | .09 | | 526 | Dennis Lamp | .12 | .09 |
| 465 | Mickey Rivers | .12 | .09 | | 527 | Tony Scott | .12 | .09 |
| 466 | John Wathan | .12 | .09 | | 528 | Ed Whitson | .12 | .09 |
| 467 | Bill Almon | .12 | .09 | | 529 | Ron Reed | .12 | .09 |
| 468 | George Vukovich | .12 | .09 | | 530 | Charlie Puleo | .12 | .09 |
| 469 | Steve Kemp | .15 | .11 | | 531 | Jerry Royster | .12 | .09 |
| 470 | Ken Landreaux | .12 | .09 | | 532 | Don Robinson | .12 | .09 |
| 471 | Milt Wilcox | .12 | .09 | | 533 | Steve Trout | .12 | .09 |
| 472 | Tippy Martinez | .12 | .09 | | 534 | Bruce Sutter | .30 | .25 |
| 473 | Ted Simmons | .20 | .15 | | 535 | Bob Horner | .20 | .15 |
| 474 | Tim Foli | .12 | .09 | | 536 | Pat Tabler | .15 | .11 |
| 475 | George Hendrick | .12 | .09 | | 537 | Chris Chambliss | .12 | .09 |
| 476 | Terry Puhl | .12 | .09 | | 538 | Bob Ojeda | .15 | .11 |
| 477 | Von Hayes | .25 | .20 | | 539 | Alan Ashby | .12 | .09 |
| 478 | Bobby Brown | .12 | .09 | | 540 | Jay Johnstone | .12 | .09 |
| 479 | Lee Lacy | .12 | .09 | | 541 | Bob Dernier | .12 | .09 |
| 480 | Joel Youngblood | .12 | .09 | | 542 | Brook Jacoby(FC) | | |
| 481 | Jim Slaton | .12 | .09 | | | | 1.50 | 1.25 |
| 482 | Mike Fitzgerald(FC) | | | | 543 | U.L. Washington | .12 | .09 |
| | | .20 | .15 | | 544 | Danny Darwin | .12 | .09 |
| 483 | Keith Moreland | .12 | .09 | | 545 | Kiko Garcia | .12 | .09 |
| 484 | Ron Roenicke | .12 | .09 | | 546 | Vance Law | .12 | .09 |
| 485 | Luis Leal | .12 | .09 | | 547 | Tug McGraw | .20 | .15 |
| 486 | Bryan Oelkers | .12 | .09 | | 548 | Dave Smith | .12 | .09 |

| | | MT | NR MT |
|---|---|---|---|
| 549 | Len Matuszek | .12 | .09 |
| 550 | Tom Hume | .12 | .09 |
| 551 | Dave Dravecky | .15 | .11 |
| 552 | Rick Rhoden | .15 | .11 |
| 553 | Duane Kuiper | .12 | .09 |
| 554 | Rusty Staub | .20 | .15 |
| 555 | Bill Campbell | .12 | .09 |
| 556 | Mike Torrez | .12 | .09 |
| 557 | Dave Henderson(FC) | .25 | .20 |
| 558 | Len Whitehouse | .12 | .09 |
| 559 | Barry Bonnell | .12 | .09 |
| 560 | Rick Lysander | .12 | .09 |
| 561 | Garth Iorg | .12 | .09 |
| 562 | Bryan Clark | .12 | .09 |
| 563 | Brian Giles | .12 | .09 |
| 564 | Vern Ruhle | .12 | .09 |
| 565 | Steve Bedrosian | .20 | .15 |
| 566 | Larry McWilliams | .12 | .09 |
| 567 | Jeff Leonard | .15 | .11 |
| 568 | Alan Wiggins | .12 | .09 |
| 569 | *Jeff Russell*(FC) | .25 | .20 |
| 570 | Salome Barojas | .12 | .09 |
| 571 | Dane Iorg | .12 | .09 |
| 572 | Bob Knepper | .15 | .11 |
| 573 | Gary Lavelle | .12 | .09 |
| 574 | Gorman Thomas | .15 | .11 |
| 575 | Manny Trillo | .12 | .09 |
| 576 | Jim Palmer | 4.00 | 3.00 |
| 577 | Dale Murray | .12 | .09 |
| 578 | Tom Brookens | .12 | .09 |
| 579 | Rich Gedman | .15 | .11 |
| 580 | *Bill Doran*(FC) | 1.00 | .70 |
| 581 | Steve Yeager | .12 | .09 |
| 582 | Dan Spillner | .12 | .09 |
| 583 | Dan Quisenberry | .15 | .11 |
| 584 | Rance Mulliniks | .12 | .09 |
| 585 | Storm Davis | .15 | .11 |
| 586 | Dave Schmidt | .12 | .09 |
| 587 | Bill Russell | .12 | .09 |
| 588 | *Pat Sheridan*(FC) | .20 | .15 |
| 589 | Rafael Ramirez | .12 | .09 |
| 590 | Bud Anderson | .12 | .09 |
| 591 | George Frazier | .12 | .09 |
| 592 | *Lee Tunnell*(FC) | .12 | .09 |
| 593 | Kirk Gibson | .60 | .45 |
| 594 | Scott McGregor | .12 | .09 |
| 595 | Bob Bailor | .12 | .09 |
| 596 | Tom Herr | .20 | .15 |
| 597 | Luis Sanchez | .12 | .09 |
| 598 | Dave Engle | .12 | .09 |
| 599 | Craig McMurtry(FC) | .15 | .11 |
| 600 | Carlos Diaz | .12 | .09 |
| 601 | Tom O'Malley | .12 | .09 |
| 602 | *Nick Esasky*(FC) | .70 | .50 |
| 603 | Ron Hodges | .12 | .09 |
| 604 | Ed Vande Berg | .12 | .09 |
| 605 | Alfredo Griffin | .12 | .09 |
| 606 | Glenn Hoffman | .12 | .09 |
| 607 | Hubie Brooks | .20 | .15 |
| 608 | Richard Barnes (photo actually Neal Heaton) | .12 | .09 |
| 609 | *Greg Walker*(FC) | .40 | .30 |
| 610 | Ken Singleton | .20 | .15 |
| 611 | Mark Clear | .12 | .09 |

| | | MT | NR MT |
|---|---|---|---|
| 612 | Buck Martinez | .12 | .09 |
| 613 | Ken Griffey | .15 | .11 |
| 614 | Reid Nichols | .12 | .09 |
| 615 | *Doug Sisk*(FC) | .12 | .09 |
| 616 | Bob Brenly | .12 | .09 |
| 617 | Joey McLaughlin | .12 | .09 |
| 618 | Glenn Wilson | .12 | .09 |
| 619 | Bob Stoddard | .12 | .09 |
| 620 | Len Sakata (Lenn) | .12 | .09 |
| 621 | *Mike Young*(FC) | .25 | .20 |
| 622 | John Stefero | .12 | .09 |
| 623 | *Carmelo Martinez*(FC) | .30 | .25 |
| 624 | Dave Bergman | .12 | .09 |
| 625 | Runnin' Reds (David Green, Willie McGee, Lonnie Smith, Ozzie Smith) | .30 | .25 |
| 626 | Rudy May | .12 | .09 |
| 627 | Matt Keough | .12 | .09 |
| 628 | *Jose DeLeon*(FC) | .50 | .40 |
| 629 | Jim Essian | .12 | .09 |
| 630 | *Darnell Coles*(FC) | .15 | .11 |
| 631 | Mike Warren | .12 | .09 |
| 632 | Del Crandall | .12 | .09 |
| 633 | Dennis Martinez | .12 | .09 |
| 634 | Mike Moore | .12 | .09 |
| 635 | Lary Sorensen | .12 | .09 |
| 636 | Ricky Nelson | .12 | .09 |
| 637 | Omar Moreno | .12 | .09 |
| 638 | Charlie Hough | .15 | .11 |
| 639 | Dennis Eckersley | 4.00 | 3.00 |
| 640 | *Walt Terrell*(FC) | .20 | .15 |
| 641 | Denny Walling | .12 | .09 |
| 642 | *Dave Anderson*(FC) | .20 | .15 |
| 643 | *Jose Oquendo*(FC) | .25 | .20 |
| 644 | Bob Stanley | .12 | .09 |
| 645 | Dave Geisel | .12 | .09 |
| 646 | *Scott Garrelts*(FC) | .40 | .30 |
| 647 | *Gary Pettis*(FC) | .40 | .30 |
| 648 | Duke Snider Puzzle Card | .12 | .09 |
| 649 | Johnnie LeMaster | .12 | .09 |
| 650 | Dave Collins | .12 | .09 |
| 651 | San Diego Chicken | .25 | .20 |
| ---a | Checklist 1-26 DK (Perez-Steel on back) | .12 | .09 |
| ---b | Checklist 1-26 DK (Perez-Steele on back) | .40 | .30 |
| ---- | Checklist 27-130 | .12 | .09 |
| ---- | Checklist 131-234 | .12 | .09 |
| ---- | Checklist 235-338 | .12 | .09 |
| ---- | Checklist 339-442 | .12 | .09 |
| ---- | Checklist 443-546 | .12 | .09 |
| ---- | Checklist 547-651 | .12 | .09 |
| ---A | Living Legends (Rollie Fingers, Gaylord Perry) | 5.00 | 3.75 |
| ---B | Living Legends (Johnny Bench, Carl Yastrzemski) | 7.00 | 5.25 |

# 1985 Donruss

The black-bordered 1985 Don-russ set includes 653 numbered cards and seven unnumbered checklists. Displaying the artwork of Dick Perez for the fourth consecutive year, card #'s 1-26 feature the Diamond Kings series. Donruss, realizing the hobby craze over rookie cards, included a Rated Rookies subset (card #'s 27-46). The cards, which are the standard size of 2-1/2" by 3-1/2", were issued with a Lou Gehrig puzzle. The backs of the cards have black print on yellow and white. The complete set price does not include the higher priced variations. (DK) and (RR) refer to the Diamond Kings and Rated Rookies subsets.

|  |  | MT | NR MT |
|---|---|---|---|
| Complete Set: | | 200.00 | 150.00 |
| Common Player: | | .08 | .06 |
| 1 | Ryne Sandberg (DK) | | |
| | | 4.00 | 3.00 |
| 2 | Doug DeCinces (DK) | .10 | .08 |
| 3 | Rich Dotson (DK) | .12 | .09 |
| 4 | Bert Blyleven (DK) | .15 | .11 |
| 5 | Lou Whitaker (DK) | .30 | .25 |
| 6 | Dan Quisenberry (DK) | | |
| | | .15 | .11 |
| 7 | Don Mattingly (DK) | 2.50 | 2.00 |
| 8 | Carney Lansford (DK) | | |

A player's name in italic type indicates a rookie card. An (FC) indicates a player's first card for that particular card company.

|  |  | MT | NR MT |
|---|---|---|---|
| | | .10 | .08 |
| 9 | Frank Tanana (DK) | .12 | .09 |
| 10 | Willie Upshaw (DK) | .10 | .08 |
| 11 | Claudell Washington (DK) | | |
| | | .10 | .08 |
| 12 | Mike Marshall (DK) | .20 | .15 |
| 13 | Joaquin Andujar (DK) | | |
| | | .10 | .08 |
| 14 | Cal Ripken, Jr. (DK) | | |
| | | 4.00 | 3.00 |
| 15 | Jim Rice (DK) | .50 | .40 |
| 16 | Don Sutton (DK) | .30 | .25 |
| 17 | Frank Viola (DK) | .15 | .11 |
| 18 | Alvin Davis (DK)(FC) | .60 | .45 |
| 19 | Mario Soto (DK) | .10 | .08 |
| 20 | Jose Cruz (DK) | .12 | .09 |
| 21 | Charlie Lea (DK) | .10 | .08 |
| 22 | Jesse Orosco (DK) | .10 | .08 |
| 23 | Juan Samuel (DK)(FC) | | |
| | | .25 | .20 |
| 24 | Tony Pena (DK) | .12 | .09 |
| 25 | Tony Gwynn (DK) | 1.00 | .70 |
| 26 | Bob Brenly (DK) | .10 | .08 |
| 27 | *Danny Tartabull (RR)(FC)* | 10.00 | 7.50 |
| 28 | *Mike Bielecki (RR)(FC)* | .15 | .11 |
| 29 | *Steve Lyons (RR)(FC)* | .20 | .15 |
| 30 | *Jeff Reed (RR)(FC)* | .15 | .11 |
| 31 | Tony Brewer (RR) | .08 | .06 |
| 32 | *John Morris (RR)(FC)* | .15 | .11 |
| 33 | *Daryl Boston (RR)(FC)* | .25 | .20 |
| 34 | Alfonso Pulido (RR) | .08 | .06 |
| 35 | *Steve Kiefer (RR)(FC)* | .10 | .08 |
| 36 | *Larry Sheets (RR)(FC)* | .50 | .40 |
| 37 | *Scott Bradley (RR)(FC)* | .25 | .20 |
| 38 | *Calvin Schiraldi (RR)(FC)* | .20 | .15 |
| 39 | *Shawon Dunston (RR)(FC)* | 4.00 | 3.00 |
| 40 | Charlie Mitchell (RR) | | |
| | | .08 | .06 |
| 41 | *Billy Hatcher (RR)(FC)* | .60 | .45 |
| 42 | Russ Stephans (RR) | .08 | .06 |
| 43 | Alejandro Sanchez (RR) | | |
| | | .08 | .06 |
| 44 | *Steve Jeltz (RR)(FC)* | | |
| | | .15 | .11 |
| 45 | *Jim Traber (RR)(FC)* | | |
| | | .30 | .25 |
| 46 | Doug Loman (RR) | .08 | .06 |
| 47 | Eddie Murray | 1.50 | 1.25 |
| 48 | Robin Yount | 4.00 | 3.00 |
| 49 | Lance Parrish | .30 | .25 |
| 50 | Jim Rice | .50 | .40 |
| 51 | Dave Winfield | 3.00 | 2.25 |
| 52 | Fernando Valenzuela | | |
| | | .35 | .25 |
| 53 | George Brett | 4.00 | 3.00 |

| | | MT | NR MT | | | | MT | NR MT |
|---|---|---|---|---|---|---|---|---|
| 54 | Dave Kingman | .15 | .11 | | 115 | Chuck Porter | .08 | .06 |
| 55 | Gary Carter | .40 | .30 | | 116 | John Gibbons | .08 | .06 |
| 56 | Buddy Bell | .12 | .09 | | 117 | Keith Moreland | .10 | .08 |
| 57 | Reggie Jackson | .60 | .45 | | 118 | Darnell Coles | .12 | .09 |
| 58 | Harold Baines | .20 | .15 | | 119 | Dennis Lamp | .08 | .06 |
| 59 | Ozzie Smith | 1.50 | 1.25 | | 120 | Ron Davis | .08 | .06 |
| 60 | Nolan Ryan | 8.00 | 6.00 | | 121 | Nick Esasky | .10 | .08 |
| 61 | Mike Schmidt | 4.00 | 3.00 | | 122 | Vance Law | .10 | .08 |
| 62 | Dave Parker | .35 | .25 | | 123 | Gary Roenicke | .08 | .06 |
| 63 | Tony Gwynn | 5.00 | 3.75 | | 124 | Bill Schroeder | .08 | .06 |
| 64 | Tony Pena | .12 | .09 | | 125 | Dave Rozema | .08 | .06 |
| 65 | Jack Clark | .25 | .20 | | 126 | Bobby Meacham | .08 | .06 |
| 66 | Dale Murphy | .80 | .60 | | 127 | Marty Barrett(FC) | .25 | .20 |
| 67 | Ryne Sandberg | 10.00 | 7.50 | | 128 | *R.J. Reynolds*(FC) | | |
| 68 | Keith Hernandez | .40 | .30 | | | | .30 | .25 |
| 69 | *Alvin Davis*(FC) | 1.25 | .90 | | 129 | Ernie Camacho | .08 | .06 |
| 70 | Kent Hrbek | .30 | .25 | | 130 | Jorge Orta | .08 | .06 |
| 71 | Willie Upshaw | .10 | .08 | | 131 | Lary Sorensen | .08 | .06 |
| 72 | Dave Engle | .08 | .06 | | 132 | Terry Francona | .08 | .06 |
| 73 | Alfredo Griffin | .10 | .08 | | 133 | Fred Lynn | .25 | .20 |
| 74a | Jack Perconte (last line | | | | 134 | Bobby Jones | .08 | .06 |
| | of highlights begins "Batted | | | | 135 | Jerry Hairston | .08 | .06 |
| | .346...") | .10 | .08 | | 136 | Kevin Bass | .12 | .09 |
| 74b | Jack Perconte (last line | | | | 137 | Garry Maddox | .08 | .06 |
| | of highlights begins "Led | | | | 138 | Dave LaPoint | .10 | .08 |
| | the...") | 1.25 | .90 | | 139 | Kevin McReynolds | 1.00 | .70 |
| 75 | Jesse Orosco | .10 | .08 | | 140 | Wayne Krenchicki | .08 | .06 |
| 76 | Jody Davis | .12 | .09 | | 141 | Rafael Ramirez | .08 | .06 |
| 77 | Bob Horner | .12 | .09 | | 142 | Rod Scurry | .08 | .06 |
| 78 | Larry McWilliams | .08 | .06 | | 143 | Greg Minton | .08 | .06 |
| 79 | Joel Youngblood | .08 | .06 | | 144 | Tim Stoddard | .08 | .06 |
| 80 | Alan Wiggins | .08 | .06 | | 145 | Steve Henderson | .08 | .06 |
| 81 | Ron Oester | .08 | .06 | | 146 | George Bell | .70 | .50 |
| 82 | Ozzie Virgil | .08 | .06 | | 147 | Dave Meier | .08 | .06 |
| 83 | *Ricky Horton*(FC) | | | | 148 | Sammy Stewart | .08 | .06 |
| | | .35 | .25 | | 149 | Mark Brouhard | .08 | .06 |
| 84 | Bill Doran | .12 | .09 | | 150 | Larry Herndon | .10 | .08 |
| 85 | Rod Carew | 1.00 | .70 | | 151 | Oil Can Boyd | .10 | .08 |
| 86 | LaMarr Hoyt | .08 | .06 | | 152 | Brian Dayett | .08 | .06 |
| 87 | Tim Wallach | .15 | .11 | | 153 | Tom Niedenfuer | .10 | .08 |
| 88 | Mike Flanagan | .12 | .09 | | 154 | Brook Jacoby | .15 | .11 |
| 89 | Jim Sundberg | .10 | .08 | | 155 | Onix Concepcion | .08 | .06 |
| 90 | Chet Lemon | .10 | .08 | | 156 | Tim Conroy | .08 | .06 |
| 91 | Bob Stanley | .08 | .06 | | 157 | *Joe Hesketh*(FC) | .15 | .11 |
| 92 | Willie Randolph | .12 | .09 | | 158 | Brian Downing | .12 | .09 |
| 93 | Bill Russell | .10 | .08 | | 159 | Tommy Dunbar | .08 | .06 |
| 94 | Julio Franco | 1.50 | 1.25 | | 160 | Marc Hill | .08 | .06 |
| 95 | Dan Quisenberry | .12 | .09 | | 161 | Phil Garner | .10 | .08 |
| 96 | Bill Caudill | .08 | .06 | | 162 | Jerry Davis | .08 | .06 |
| 97 | Bill Gullickson | .08 | .06 | | 163 | Bill Campbell | .08 | .06 |
| 98 | Danny Darwin | .08 | .06 | | 164 | *John Franco*(FC) | | |
| 99 | Curtis Wilkerson | .08 | .06 | | | | 2.00 | 1.50 |
| 100 | Bud Black | .08 | .06 | | 165 | Len Barker | .10 | .08 |
| 101 | Tony Phillips | .08 | .06 | | 166 | *Benny Distefano*(FC) | | |
| 102 | Tony Bernazard | .08 | .06 | | | | .10 | .08 |
| 103 | Jay Howell | .10 | .08 | | 167 | George Frazier | .08 | .06 |
| 104 | Burt Hooton | .10 | .08 | | 168 | Tito Landrum | .08 | .06 |
| 105 | Milt Wilcox | .08 | .06 | | 169 | Cal Ripken | 10.00 | 7.50 |
| 106 | Rich Dauer | .08 | .06 | | 170 | Cecil Cooper | .15 | .11 |
| 107 | Don Sutton | .35 | .25 | | 171 | Alan Trammell | .40 | .30 |
| 108 | Mike Witt | .15 | .11 | | 172 | Wade Boggs | 5.00 | 3.75 |
| 109 | Bruce Sutter | .15 | .11 | | 173 | Don Baylor | .15 | .11 |
| 110 | Enos Cabell | .08 | .06 | | 174 | Pedro Guerrero | .30 | .25 |
| 111 | John Denny | .08 | .06 | | 175 | Frank White | .12 | .09 |
| 112 | Dave Dravecky | .10 | .08 | | 176 | Rickey Henderson | 5.00 | 3.75 |
| 113 | Marvell Wynne | .08 | .06 | | 177 | Charlie Lea | .08 | .06 |
| 114 | Johnnie LeMaster | .08 | .06 | | 178 | Pete O'Brien | .20 | .15 |

| | MT | NR MT | | | MT | NR MT |
|---|---|---|---|---|---|---|
| 179 Doug DeCinces | .12 | .09 | 244 Rudy Law | | .08 | .06 |
| 180 Ron Kittle | .12 | .09 | 245 John Lowenstein | | .08 | .06 |
| 181 George Hendrick | .10 | .08 | 246 Tom Tellmann | | .08 | .06 |
| 182 Joe Niekro | .12 | .09 | 247 Howard Johnson | | 1.75 | 1.25 |
| 183 Juan Samuel(FC) | .60 | .45 | 248 Ray Fontenot | | .08 | .06 |
| 184 Mario Soto | .10 | .08 | 249 Tony Armas | | .12 | .09 |
| 185 Goose Gossage | .25 | .20 | 250 Candy Maldonado | | .12 | .09 |
| 186 Johnny Ray | .15 | .11 | 251 *Mike Jeffcoat*(FC) | | | |
| 187 Bob Brenly | .08 | .06 | | | .10 | .08 |
| 188 Craig McMurtry | .08 | .06 | 252 Dane Iorg | | .08 | .06 |
| 189 Leon Durham | .10 | .08 | 253 Bruce Bochte | | .08 | .06 |
| 190 *Dwight Gooden*(FC) | | | 254 Pete Rose | | 1.25 | .90 |
| | 9.00 | 6.75 | 255 Don Aase | | .08 | .06 |
| 191 Barry Bonnell | .08 | .06 | 256 George Wright | | .08 | .06 |
| 192 Tim Teufel | .12 | .09 | 257 Britt Burns | | .08 | .06 |
| 193 Dave Stieb | .15 | .11 | 258 Mike Scott | | .20 | .15 |
| 194 Mickey Hatcher | .08 | .06 | 259 Len Matuszek | | .08 | .06 |
| 195 Jesse Barfield | .25 | .20 | 260 Dave Rucker | | .08 | .06 |
| 196 Al Cowens | .08 | .06 | 261 Craig Lefferts | | .10 | .08 |
| 197 Hubie Brooks | .12 | .09 | 262 *Jay Tibbs*(FC) | | .20 | .15 |
| 198 Steve Trout | .08 | .06 | 263 Bruce Benedict | | .08 | .06 |
| 199 Glenn Hubbard | .08 | .06 | 264 Don Robinson | | .10 | .08 |
| 200 Bill Madlock | .15 | .11 | 265 Gary Lavelle | | .08 | .06 |
| 201 *Jeff Robinson*(FC) | | | 266 Scott Sanderson | | .08 | .06 |
| | .35 | .25 | 267 Matt Young | | .08 | .06 |
| 202 Eric Show | .10 | .08 | 268 Ernie Whitt | | .10 | .08 |
| 203 Dave Concepcion | .15 | .11 | 269 Houston Jimenez | | .08 | .06 |
| 204 Ivan DeJesus | .08 | .06 | 270 *Ken Dixon*(FC) | | .12 | .09 |
| 205 Neil Allen | .08 | .06 | 271 Peter Ladd | | .08 | .06 |
| 206 Jerry Mumphrey | .08 | .06 | 272 Juan Berenguer | | .08 | .06 |
| 207 Mike Brown | .08 | .06 | 273 *Roger Clemens*(FC) | | | |
| 208 Carlton Fisk | .40 | .30 | | | 60.00 | 45.00 |
| 209 Bryn Smith | .08 | .06 | 274 Rick Cerone | | .08 | .06 |
| 210 Tippy Martinez | .08 | .06 | 275 Dave Anderson | | .08 | .06 |
| 211 Dion James | .10 | .08 | 276 George Vukovich | | .08 | .06 |
| 212 Willie Hernandez | .10 | .08 | 277 Greg Pryor | | .08 | .06 |
| 213 Mike Easler | .10 | .08 | 278 Mike Warren | | .08 | .06 |
| 214 Ron Guidry | .30 | .25 | 279 Bob James | | .08 | .06 |
| 215 Rick Honeycutt | .08 | .06 | 280 Bobby Grich | | .12 | .09 |
| 216 Brett Butler | .12 | .09 | 281 *Mike Mason*(FC) | | .12 | .09 |
| 217 Larry Gura | .08 | .06 | 282 Ron Reed | | .08 | .06 |
| 218 Ray Burris | .08 | .06 | 283 Alan Ashby | | .08 | .06 |
| 219 Steve Rogers | .10 | .08 | 284 Mark Thurmond | | .08 | .06 |
| 220 Frank Tanana | .12 | .09 | 285 Joe Lefebvre | | .08 | .06 |
| 221 Ned Yost | .08 | .06 | 286 Ted Power | | .08 | .06 |
| 222 *Bret Saberhagen* | 8.00 | 6.00 | 287 Chris Chambliss | | .10 | .08 |
| 223 Mike Davis | .10 | .08 | 288 Lee Tunnell | | .08 | .06 |
| 224 Bert Blyleven | .15 | .11 | 289 Rich Bordi | | .08 | .06 |
| 225 Steve Kemp | .10 | .08 | 290 Glenn Brummer | | .08 | .06 |
| 226 Jerry Reuss | .10 | .08 | 291 Mike Boddicker | | .12 | .09 |
| 227 Darrell Evans | .15 | .11 | 292 Rollie Fingers | | .25 | .20 |
| 228 Wayne Gross | .08 | .06 | 293 Lou Whitaker | | .40 | .30 |
| 229 Jim Gantner | .10 | .08 | 294 Dwight Evans | | .15 | .11 |
| 230 Bob Boone | .10 | .08 | 295 Don Mattingly | | 6.00 | 4.50 |
| 231 Lonnie Smith | .10 | .08 | 296 Mike Marshall | | .15 | .11 |
| 232 Frank DiPino | .08 | .06 | 297 Willie Wilson | | .15 | .11 |
| 233 Jerry Koosman | .12 | .09 | 298 Mike Heath | | .08 | .06 |
| 234 Graig Nettles | .20 | .15 | 299 Tim Raines | | .50 | .40 |
| 235 John Tudor | .12 | .09 | 300 Larry Parrish | | .12 | .09 |
| 236 John Rabb | .08 | .06 | 301 Geoff Zahn | | .08 | .06 |
| 237 Rick Manning | .08 | .06 | 302 Rich Dotson | | .12 | .09 |
| 238 Mike Fitzgerald | .08 | .06 | 303 David Green | | .08 | .06 |
| 239 Gary Matthews | .12 | .09 | 304 Jose Cruz | | .12 | .09 |
| 240 *Jim Presley*(FC) | .50 | .40 | 305 Steve Carlton | | .80 | .60 |
| 241 Dave Collins | .10 | .08 | 306 Gary Redus | | .10 | .08 |
| 242 Gary Gaetti | .30 | .25 | 307 Steve Garvey | | .50 | .40 |
| 243 Dann Bilardello | .08 | .06 | 308 Jose DeLeon | | .10 | .08 |

| | | MT | NR MT |
|---|---|---|---|
| 309 | Randy Lerch | .08 | .06 |
| 310 | Claudell Washington | .10 | .08 |
| 311 | Lee Smith | .12 | .09 |
| 312 | Darryl Strawberry | 8.00 | 6.00 |
| 313 | Jim Beattie | .08 | .06 |
| 314 | John Butcher | .08 | .06 |
| 315 | Damaso Garcia | .10 | .08 |
| 316 | Mike Smithson | .08 | .06 |
| 317 | Luis Leal | .08 | .06 |
| 318 | Ken Phelps(FC) | .25 | .20 |
| 319 | Wally Backman | .10 | .08 |
| 320 | Ron Cey | .12 | .09 |
| 321 | Brad Komminsk | .08 | .06 |
| 322 | Jason Thompson | .08 | .06 |
| 323 | Frank Williams(FC) | .20 | .15 |
| 324 | Tim Lollar | .08 | .06 |
| 325 | Eric Davis(FC) | 6.00 | 4.50 |
| 326 | Von Hayes | .12 | .09 |
| 327 | Andy Van Slyke | .40 | .30 |
| 328 | Craig Reynolds | .08 | .06 |
| 329 | Dick Schofield | .10 | .08 |
| 330 | Scott Fletcher | .10 | .08 |
| 331 | Jeff Reardon | .15 | .11 |
| 332 | Rick Dempsey | .10 | .08 |
| 333 | Ben Oglivie | .10 | .08 |
| 334 | Dan Petry | .10 | .08 |
| 335 | Jackie Gutierrez | .08 | .06 |
| 336 | Dave Righetti | .25 | .20 |
| 337 | Alejandro Pena | .10 | .08 |
| 338 | Mel Hall | .10 | .08 |
| 339 | Pat Sheridan | .08 | .06 |
| 340 | Keith Atherton | .08 | .06 |
| 341 | David Palmer | .08 | .06 |
| 342 | Gary Ward | .10 | .08 |
| 343 | Dave Stewart | .15 | .11 |
| 344 | Mark Gubicza(FC) | 1.25 | .90 |
| 345 | Carney Lansford | .12 | .09 |
| 346 | Jerry Willard | .08 | .06 |
| 347 | Ken Griffey | .12 | .09 |
| 348 | Franklin Stubbs(FC) | .60 | .45 |
| 349 | Aurelio Lopez | .08 | .06 |
| 350 | Al Bumbry | .10 | .08 |
| 351 | Charlie Moore | .08 | .06 |
| 352 | Luis Sanchez | .08 | .06 |
| 353 | Darrell Porter | .10 | .08 |
| 354 | Bill Dawley | .08 | .06 |
| 355 | Charlie Hudson | .10 | .08 |
| 356 | Garry Templeton | .10 | .08 |
| 357 | Cecilio Guante | .08 | .06 |
| 358 | Jeff Leonard | .12 | .09 |
| 359 | Paul Molitor | .20 | .15 |
| 360 | Ron Gardenhire | .08 | .06 |
| 361 | Larry Bowa | .12 | .09 |
| 362 | Bob Kearney | .08 | .06 |
| 363 | Garth Iorg | .08 | .06 |
| 364 | Tom Brunansky | .15 | .11 |
| 365 | Brad Gulden | .08 | .06 |
| 366 | Greg Walker | .12 | .09 |
| 367 | Mike Young | .10 | .08 |
| 368 | Rick Waits | .08 | .06 |
| 369 | Doug Bair | .08 | .06 |
| 370 | Bob Shirley | .08 | .06 |
| 371 | Bob Ojeda | .12 | .09 |
| 372 | Bob Welch | .15 | .11 |

| | | MT | NR MT |
|---|---|---|---|
| 373 | Neal Heaton | .08 | .06 |
| 374 | Danny Jackson (photo actually Steve Farr) | .80 | .60 |
| 375 | Donnie Hill | .08 | .06 |
| 376 | Mike Stenhouse | .08 | .06 |
| 377 | Bruce Kison | .08 | .06 |
| 378 | Wayne Tolleson | .08 | .06 |
| 379 | Floyd Bannister | .12 | .09 |
| 380 | Vern Ruhle | .08 | .06 |
| 381 | Tim Corcoran | .08 | .06 |
| 382 | Kurt Kepshire | .08 | .06 |
| 383 | Bobby Brown | .08 | .06 |
| 384 | Dave Van Gorder | .08 | .06 |
| 385 | Rick Mahler | .08 | .06 |
| 386 | Lee Mazzilli | .10 | .08 |
| 387 | Bill Laskey | .08 | .06 |
| 388 | Thad Bosley | .08 | .06 |
| 389 | Al Chambers | .08 | .06 |
| 390 | Tony Fernandez | .70 | .50 |
| 391 | Ron Washington | .08 | .06 |
| 392 | Bill Swaggerty | .08 | .06 |
| 393 | Bob Gibson | .08 | .06 |
| 394 | Marty Castillo | .08 | .06 |
| 395 | Steve Crawford | .08 | .06 |
| 396 | Clay Christiansen | .08 | .06 |
| 397 | Bob Bailor | .08 | .06 |
| 398 | Mike Hargrove | .08 | .06 |
| 399 | Charlie Leibrandt | .10 | .08 |
| 400 | Tom Burgmeier | .08 | .06 |
| 401 | Razor Shines | .08 | .06 |
| 402 | Rob Wilfong | .08 | .06 |
| 403 | Tom Henke | .12 | .09 |
| 404 | Al Jones | .08 | .06 |
| 405 | Mike LaCoss | .08 | .06 |
| 406 | Luis DeLeon | .08 | .06 |
| 407 | Greg Gross | .08 | .06 |
| 408 | Tom Hume | .08 | .06 |
| 409 | Rick Camp | .08 | .06 |
| 410 | Milt May | .08 | .06 |
| 411 | Henry Cotto(FC) | .20 | .15 |
| 412 | Dave Von Ohlen | .08 | .06 |
| 413 | Scott McGregor | .10 | .08 |
| 414 | Ted Simmons | .15 | .11 |
| 415 | Jack Morris | .30 | .25 |
| 416 | Bill Buckner | .15 | .11 |
| 417 | Butch Wynegar | .08 | .06 |
| 418 | Steve Sax | .25 | .20 |
| 419 | Steve Balboni | .10 | .08 |
| 420 | Dwayne Murphy | .10 | .08 |
| 421 | Andre Dawson | 1.25 | .90 |
| 422 | Charlie Hough | .10 | .08 |
| 423 | Tommy John | .25 | .20 |
| 424a | Tom Seaver (Floyd Bannister photo - throwing left) | 3.00 | 2.25 |
| 424b | Tom Seaver (correct photo - throwing right) | 30.00 | 22.00 |
| 425 | Tom Herr | .12 | .09 |
| 426 | Terry Puhl | .08 | .06 |
| 427 | Al Holland | .08 | .06 |
| 428 | Eddie Milner | .08 | .06 |
| 429 | Terry Kennedy | .10 | .08 |
| 430 | John Candelaria | .12 | .09 |
| 431 | Manny Trillo | .10 | .08 |
| 432 | Ken Oberkfell | .08 | .06 |
| 433 | Rick Sutcliffe | .15 | .11 |

| | MT | NR MT | | | MT | NR MT |
|---|---|---|---|---|---|---|
| 434 | Ron Darling | .70 | .50 | 498 | Gary Lucas | .08 | .06 |
| 435 | Spike Owen | .10 | .08 | 499 | Gary Pettis | .10 | .08 |
| 436 | Frank Viola | .25 | .20 | 500 | Marvis Foley | .08 | .06 |
| 437 | Lloyd Moseby | .12 | .09 | 501 | Mike Squires | .08 | .06 |
| 438 | *Kirby Puckett*(FC) | | | 502 | *Jim Pankovitz*(FC) | | |
| | | 50.00 | 37.00 | | | .15 | .11 |
| 439 | Jim Clancy | .10 | .08 | 503 | Luis Aguayo | .08 | .06 |
| 440 | Mike Moore | .08 | .06 | 504 | Ralph Citarella | .08 | .06 |
| 441 | Doug Sisk | .08 | .06 | 505 | Bruce Bochy | .08 | .06 |
| 442 | Dennis Eckersley | .15 | .11 | 506 | Bob Owchinko | .08 | .06 |
| 443 | Gerald Perry | .25 | .20 | 507 | Pascual Perez | .10 | .08 |
| 444 | Dale Berra | .08 | .06 | 508 | Lee Lacy | .08 | .06 |
| 445 | Dusty Baker | .10 | .08 | 509 | Atlee Hammaker | .08 | .06 |
| 446 | Ed Whitson | .08 | .06 | 510 | Bob Dernier | .08 | .06 |
| 447 | Cesar Cedeno | .12 | .09 | 511 | Ed Vande Berg | .08 | .06 |
| 448 | *Rick Schu*(FC) | .20 | .15 | 512 | Cliff Johnson | .08 | .06 |
| 449 | Joaquin Andujar | .10 | .08 | 513 | Len Whitehouse | .08 | .06 |
| 450 | *Mark Bailey*(FC) | .12 | .09 | 514 | Dennis Martinez | .10 | .08 |
| 451 | *Ron Romanick*(FC) | | | 515 | Ed Romero | .08 | .06 |
| | | .12 | .09 | 516 | Rusty Kuntz | .08 | .06 |
| 452 | Julio Cruz | .08 | .06 | 517 | Rick Miller | .08 | .06 |
| 453 | Miguel Dilone | .08 | .06 | 518 | Dennis Rasmussen | .15 | .11 |
| 454 | Storm Davis | .12 | .09 | 519 | Steve Yeager | .08 | .06 |
| 455 | Jaime Cocanower | .08 | .06 | 520 | Chris Bando | .08 | .06 |
| 456 | Barbaro Garbey | .12 | .09 | 521 | U.L. Washington | .08 | .06 |
| 457 | Rich Gedman | .12 | .09 | 522 | *Curt Young*(FC) | .40 | .30 |
| 458 | Phil Niekro | .30 | .25 | 523 | Angel Salazar | .08 | .06 |
| 459 | Mike Scioscia | .10 | .08 | 524 | Curt Kaufman | .08 | .06 |
| 460 | Pat Tabler | .10 | .08 | 525 | Odell Jones | .08 | .06 |
| 461 | Darryl Motley | .08 | .06 | 526 | Juan Agosto | .08 | .06 |
| 462 | Chris Codoroli (Codiroli) | | | 527 | Denny Walling | .08 | .06 |
| | | .08 | .06 | 528 | Andy Hawkins(FC) | .20 | .15 |
| 463 | Doug Flynn | .08 | .06 | 529 | Sixto Lezcano | .08 | .06 |
| 464 | Billy Sample | .08 | .06 | 530 | Skeeter Barnes | .08 | .06 |
| 465 | Mickey Rivers | .10 | .08 | 531 | Randy Johnson | .08 | .06 |
| 466 | John Wathan | .10 | .08 | 532 | Jim Morrison | .08 | .06 |
| 467 | Bill Krueger | .08 | .06 | 533 | Warren Brusstar | .08 | .06 |
| 468 | Andre Thornton | .12 | .09 | 534a | *Jeff Pendleton* (first | | |
| 469 | Rex Hudler | .12 | .09 | | name incorrect)(FC) | 8.00 | 6.00 |
| 470 | *Sid Bream*(FC) | .80 | .60 | 534b | *Terry Pendleton* (first | | |
| 471 | Kirk Gibson | .40 | .30 | | name correct)(FC) | 20.00 | 15.00 |
| 472 | John Shelby | .10 | .08 | 535 | Vic Rodriguez | .08 | .06 |
| 473 | Moose Haas | .08 | .06 | 536 | Bob McClure | .08 | .06 |
| 474 | Doug Corbett | .08 | .06 | 537 | Dave Bergman | .08 | .06 |
| 475 | Willie McGee | .35 | .25 | 538 | Mark Clear | .08 | .06 |
| 476 | Bob Knepper | .10 | .08 | 539 | *Mike Pagliarulo*(FC) | | |
| 477 | Kevin Gross | .12 | .09 | | | 1.00 | .70 |
| 478 | Carmelo Martinez | .10 | .08 | 540 | Terry Whitfield | .08 | .06 |
| 479 | Kent Tekulve | .10 | .08 | 541 | Joe Beckwith | .08 | .06 |
| 480 | Chili Davis | .12 | .09 | 542 | Jeff Burroughs | .10 | .08 |
| 481 | Bobby Clark | .08 | .06 | 543 | Dan Schatzeder | .08 | .06 |
| 482 | Mookie Wilson | .12 | .09 | 544 | Donnie Scott | .08 | .06 |
| 483 | Dave Owen | .08 | .06 | 545 | Jim Slaton | .08 | .06 |
| 484 | Ed Nunez | .08 | .06 | 546 | Greg Luzinski | .12 | .09 |
| 485 | Rance Mulliniks | .08 | .06 | 547 | *Mark Salas*(FC) | .15 | .11 |
| 486 | Ken Schrom | .08 | .06 | 548 | Dave Smith | .10 | .08 |
| 487 | Jeff Russell | .08 | .06 | 549 | John Wockenfuss | .08 | .06 |
| 488 | Tom Paciorek | .08 | .06 | 550 | Frank Pastore | .08 | .06 |
| 489 | Dan Ford | .08 | .06 | 551 | Tim Flannery | .08 | .06 |
| 490 | Mike Caldwell | .08 | .06 | 552 | Rick Rhoden | .12 | .09 |
| 491 | Scottie Earl | .08 | .06 | 553 | Mark Davis | .08 | .06 |
| 492 | *Jose Rijo*(FC) | 2.00 | 1.50 | 554 | *Jeff Dedmon*(FC) | | |
| 493 | Bruce Hurst | .15 | .11 | | | .15 | .11 |
| 494 | Ken Landreaux | .08 | .06 | 555 | Gary Woods | .08 | .06 |
| 495 | Mike Fischlin | .08 | .06 | 556 | Danny Heep | .08 | .06 |
| 496 | Don Slaught | .08 | .06 | 557 | *Mark Langston*(FC) | | |
| 497 | Steve McCatty | .08 | .06 | | | 5.00 | 3.75 |

| # | Player | MT | NR MT |
|---|--------|-----|-------|
| 558 | Darrell Brown | .08 | .06 |
| 559 | Jimmy Key(FC) | 2.00 | 1.50 |
| 560 | Rick Lysander | .08 | .06 |
| 561 | Doyle Alexander | .12 | .09 |
| 562 | Mike Stanton | .08 | .06 |
| 563 | Sid Fernandez | .50 | .40 |
| 564 | Richie Hebner | .08 | .06 |
| 565 | Alex Trevino | .08 | .06 |
| 566 | Brian Harper | .08 | .06 |
| 567 | Dan Gladden(FC) | .60 | .45 |
| 568 | Luis Salazar | .08 | .06 |
| 569 | Tom Foley | .08 | .06 |
| 570 | Larry Andersen | .08 | .06 |
| 571 | Danny Cox | .12 | .09 |
| 572 | Joe Sambito | .08 | .06 |
| 573 | Juan Beniquez | .08 | .06 |
| 574 | Joel Skinner | .08 | .06 |
| 575 | Randy St. Claire(FC) | .15 | .11 |
| 576 | Floyd Rayford | .08 | .06 |
| 577 | Roy Howell | .08 | .06 |
| 578 | John Grubb | .08 | .06 |
| 579 | Ed Jurak | .08 | .06 |
| 580 | John Montefusco | .08 | .06 |
| 581 | Orel Hershiser(FC) | 3.00 | 2.25 |
| 582 | Tom Waddell(FC) | .08 | .06 |
| 583 | Mark Huismann | .08 | .06 |
| 584 | Joe Morgan | .30 | .25 |
| 585 | Jim Wohlford | .08 | .06 |
| 586 | Dave Schmidt | .08 | .06 |
| 587 | Jeff Kunkel(FC) | .12 | .09 |
| 588 | Hal McRae | .12 | .09 |
| 589 | Bill Almon | .08 | .06 |
| 590 | Carmen Castillo(FC) | .10 | .08 |
| 591 | Omar Moreno | .08 | .06 |
| 592 | Ken Howell(FC) | .20 | .15 |
| 593 | Tom Brookens | .08 | .06 |
| 594 | Joe Nolan | .08 | .06 |
| 595 | Willie Lozado | .08 | .06 |
| 596 | Tom Nieto(FC) | .12 | .09 |
| 597 | Walt Terrell | .10 | .08 |
| 598 | Al Oliver | .15 | .11 |
| 599 | Shane Rawley | .12 | .09 |
| 600 | Denny Gonzalez(FC) | .10 | .08 |
| 601 | Mark Grant(FC) | .15 | .11 |
| 602 | Mike Armstrong | .08 | .06 |
| 603 | George Foster | .15 | .11 |
| 604 | Davey Lopes | .10 | .08 |
| 605 | Salome Barojas | .08 | .06 |
| 606 | Roy Lee Jackson | .08 | .06 |
| 607 | Pete Filson | .08 | .06 |
| 608 | Duane Walker | .08 | .06 |
| 609 | Glenn Wilson | .10 | .08 |
| 610 | Rafael Santana(FC) | .20 | .15 |
| 611 | Roy Smith | .08 | .06 |
| 612 | Ruppert Jones | .08 | .06 |
| 613 | Joe Cowley(FC) | .08 | .06 |
| 614 | Al Nipper (photo actually Mike Brown)(FC) | .20 | .15 |
| 615 | Gene Nelson | .08 | .06 |
| 616 | Joe Carter | 8.00 | 6.00 |
| 617 | Ray Knight | .12 | .09 |

| # | Player | MT | NR MT |
|---|--------|-----|-------|
| 618 | Chuck Rainey | .08 | .06 |
| 619 | Dan Driessen | .10 | .08 |
| 620 | Daryl Sconiers | .08 | .06 |
| 621 | Bill Stein | .08 | .06 |
| 622 | Roy Smalley | .08 | .06 |
| 623 | Ed Lynch | .08 | .06 |
| 624 | Jeff Stone(FC) | .15 | .11 |
| 625 | Bruce Berenyi | .08 | .06 |
| 626 | Kelvin Chapman | .08 | .06 |
| 627 | Joe Price | .08 | .06 |
| 628 | Steve Bedrosian | .12 | .09 |
| 629 | Vic Mata | .08 | .06 |
| 630 | Mike Krukow | .10 | .08 |
| 631 | Phil Bradley(FC) | .90 | .70 |
| 632 | Jim Gott | .08 | .06 |
| 633 | Randy Bush | .08 | .06 |
| 634 | Tom Browning(FC) | 1.50 | 1.25 |
| 635 | Lou Gehrig Puzzle Card | .08 | .06 |
| 636 | Reid Nichols | .08 | .06 |
| 637 | Dan Pasqua(FC) | .60 | .45 |
| 638 | German Rivera | .08 | .06 |
| 639 | Don Schulze(FC) | .10 | .08 |
| 640a | Mike Jones (last line of highlights begins "Was 11 7...") | .10 | .08 |
| 640b | Mike Jones (last line of highlights begins "Spent some ...") | 1.25 | .90 |
| 641 | Pete Rose | 1.25 | .90 |
| 642 | Wade Rowdon(FC) | .10 | .08 |
| 643 | Jerry Narron | .08 | .06 |
| 644 | Darrell Miller(FC) | .15 | .11 |
| 645 | Tim Hulett(FC) | .15 | .11 |
| 646 | Andy McGaffigan | .08 | .06 |
| 647 | Kurt Bevacqua | .08 | .06 |
| 648 | John Russell(FC) | .20 | .15 |
| 649 | Ron Robinson(FC) | .25 | .20 |
| 650 | Donnie Moore(FC) | .08 | .06 |
| 651a | Two for the Title (Don Mattingly, Dave Winfield) (player names in yellow) | 8.00 | 6.00 |
| 651b | Two for the Title (Don Mattingly, Dave Winfield) (player names in white) | 6.00 | 4.50 |
| 652 | Tim Laudner | .08 | .06 |
| 653 | Steve Farr(FC) | .40 | .30 |
| ---- | Checklist 1-26 DK | .08 | .06 |
| ---- | Checklist 27-130 | .08 | .06 |
| ---- | Checklist 131-234 | .08 | .06 |
| ---- | Checklist 235-338 | .08 | .06 |
| ---- | Checklist 339-442 | .08 | .06 |
| ---- | Checklist 443-546 | .08 | .06 |
| ---- | Checklist 547-653 | .08 | .06 |

**NOTE: A card number in parentheses ( ) indicates the set is unnumbered.**

# 1986 Donruss

In 1986, Donruss issued a 660-card set which included 653 numbered cards and seven unnum- bered checklists. The cards, which measure 2-1/2" by 3-1/2", have fronts that feature blue borders and backs that have black print on blue and white. For the fifth year in a row, the first 26 cards in the set are Diamond Kings. The Rated Rookies subset (card #'s 27-46) appears once again. The cards were distributed with a Hank Aaron puzzle. The complete set price does not include the higher priced varia- tions. In the checklist that follows, (DK) and (RR) refer to the Diamond Kings and Rated Rookies series.

|  | MT | NR MT |
|---|---|---|
| Complete Set: | 175.00 | 125.00 |
| Common Player: | .06 | .05 |
| 1 Kirk Gibson (DK) | .30 | .25 |
| 2 Goose Gossage (DK) | .20 | .15 |
| 3 Willie McGee (DK) | .15 | .11 |
| 4 George Bell (DK) | .30 | .25 |
| 5 Tony Armas (DK) | .10 | .08 |
| 6 Chili Davis (DK) | .10 | .08 |
| 7 Cecil Cooper (DK) | .12 | .09 |
| 8 Mike Boddicker (DK) | | |
| | .10 | .08 |
| 9 Davey Lopes (DK) | .10 | .08 |
| 10 Bill Doran (DK) | .12 | .09 |
| 11 Bret Saberhagen (DK) | | |
| | .25 | .20 |

A player's name in *italic* type indicates a rookie card. An (FC) indicates a player's first card for that particular card company.

|  | MT | NR MT |
|---|---|---|
| 12 Brett Butler (DK) | .10 | .08 |
| 13 Harold Baines (DK) | .15 | .11 |
| 14 Mike Davis (DK) | .10 | .08 |
| 15 Tony Perez (DK) | .15 | .11 |
| 16 Willie Randolph (DK) | | |
| | .12 | .09 |
| 17 Bob Boone (DK) | .10 | .08 |
| 18 Orel Hershiser (DK) | .40 | .30 |
| 19 Johnny Ray (DK) | .12 | .09 |
| 20 Gary Ward (DK) | .10 | .08 |
| 21 Rick Mahler (DK) | .08 | .06 |
| 22 Phil Bradley (DK) | .20 | .15 |
| 23 Jerry Koosman (DK) | .12 | .09 |
| 24 Tom Brunansky (DK) | | |
| | .15 | .11 |
| 25 Andre Dawson (DK) | .30 | .25 |
| 26 Dwight Gooden (DK) | | |
| | 1.00 | .70 |
| 27 *Kal Daniels (RR)(FC)* | | |
| | 1.00 | .70 |
| 28 *Fred McGriff (RR)(FC)* | 26.00 | 18.70 |
| 29 *Cory Snyder (RR)(FC)* | 1.00 | .70 |
| 30 *Jose Guzman (RR)(FC)* | .40 | .30 |
| 31 *Ty Gainey (RR)(FC)* | | |
| | .10 | .08 |
| 32 *Johnny Abrego (RR)(FC)* | .08 | .06 |
| 33a *Andres Galarraga (RR)* (no accent mark above "e" in Andres on back)(FC) | | |
| | 1.00 | .70 |
| 33b *Andres Galarraga (RR)* (accent mark above "e" in Andres on back)(FC) | 1.50 | 1.25 |
| 34 *Dave Shipanoff (RR)(FC)* | .08 | .06 |
| 35 *Mark McLemore (RR)(FC)* | .20 | .15 |
| 36 *Marty Clary (RR)(FC)* | .08 | .06 |
| 37 *Paul O'Neill (RR)(FC)* | 2.50 | 2.00 |
| 38 Danny Tartabull (RR) | 2.00 | 1.50 |
| 39 *Jose Canseco (RR)(FC)* | 60.00 | 45.00 |
| 40 *Juan Nieves (RR)(FC)* | .10 | .08 |
| 41 *Lance McCullers (RR)(FC)* | .35 | .25 |
| 42 *Rick Surhoff (RR)(FC)* | .08 | .06 |
| 43 *Todd Worrell (RR)(FC)* | .40 | .30 |
| 44 *Bob Kipper (RR)(FC)* | .20 | .15 |
| 45 *John Habyan (RR)(FC)* | .15 | .11 |
| 46 *Mike Woodard (RR)(FC)* | .10 | .08 |
| 47 Mike Boddicker | .10 | .08 |
| 48 Robin Yount | 2.00 | 1.50 |
| 49 Lou Whitaker | .30 | .25 |
| 50 "Oil Can" Boyd | .08 | .06 |

| # | Player | MT | NR MT |
|---|--------|----|----|
| 51 | Rickey Henderson | 2.00 | 1.50 |
| 52 | Mike Marshall | .15 | .11 |
| 53 | George Brett | 2.00 | 1.50 |
| 54 | Dave Kingman | .15 | .11 |
| 55 | Hubie Brooks | .10 | .08 |
| 56 | *Oddibe McDowell*(FC) | .20 | .15 |
| 57 | Doug DeCinces | .10 | .08 |
| 58 | Britt Burns | .06 | .05 |
| 59 | Ozzie Smith | 1.00 | .70 |
| 60 | Jose Cruz | .10 | .08 |
| 61 | Mike Schmidt | 2.00 | 1.50 |
| 62 | Pete Rose | .80 | .60 |
| 63 | Steve Garvey | .40 | .30 |
| 64 | Tony Pena | .10 | .08 |
| 65 | Chili Davis | .10 | .08 |
| 66 | Dale Murphy | .60 | .45 |
| 67 | Ryne Sandberg | 4.00 | 3.00 |
| 68 | Gary Carter | .35 | .25 |
| 69 | Alvin Davis | .30 | .25 |
| 70 | Kent Hrbek | .25 | .20 |
| 71 | George Bell | .30 | .25 |
| 72 | Kirby Puckett | 9.00 | 6.75 |
| 73 | Lloyd Moseby | .10 | .08 |
| 74 | Bob Kearney | .06 | .05 |
| 75 | Dwight Gooden | 2.00 | 1.50 |
| 76 | Gary Matthews | .10 | .08 |
| 77 | Rick Mahler | .06 | .05 |
| 78 | Benny Distefano | .06 | .05 |
| 79 | Jeff Leonard | .08 | .06 |
| 80 | Kevin McReynolds | .30 | .25 |
| 81 | Ron Oester | .06 | .05 |
| 82 | John Russell | .06 | .05 |
| 83 | Tommy Herr | .10 | .08 |
| 84 | Jerry Mumphrey | .06 | .05 |
| 85 | Ron Romanick | .06 | .05 |
| 86 | Daryl Boston | .08 | .06 |
| 87 | Andre Dawson | .50 | .40 |
| 88 | Eddie Murray | .50 | .40 |
| 89 | Dion James | .08 | .06 |
| 90 | Chet Lemon | .08 | .06 |
| 91 | Bob Stanley | .06 | .05 |
| 92 | Willie Randolph | .10 | .08 |
| 93 | Mike Scioscia | .08 | .06 |
| 94 | Tom Waddell | .06 | .05 |
| 95 | Danny Jackson | .30 | .25 |
| 96 | Mike Davis | .08 | .06 |
| 97 | Mike Fitzgerald | .06 | .05 |
| 98 | Gary Ward | .08 | .06 |
| 99 | Pete O'Brien | .10 | .08 |
| 100 | Bret Saberhagen | .60 | .45 |
| 101 | Alfredo Griffin | .08 | .06 |
| 102 | Brett Butler | .08 | .06 |
| 103 | Ron Guidry | .20 | .15 |
| 104 | Jerry Reuss | .08 | .06 |
| 105 | Jack Morris | .30 | .25 |
| 106 | Rick Dempsey | .08 | .06 |
| 107 | Ray Burris | .06 | .05 |
| 108 | Brian Downing | .10 | .08 |
| 109 | Willie McGee | .15 | .11 |
| 110 | Bill Doran | .10 | .08 |
| 111 | Kent Tekulve | .08 | .06 |
| 112 | Tony Gwynn | 2.00 | 1.50 |
| 113 | Marvell Wynne | .06 | .05 |
| 114 | David Green | .06 | .05 |
| 115 | Jim Gantner | .08 | .06 |
| 116 | George Foster | .15 | .11 |

| # | Player | MT | NR MT |
|---|--------|----|----|
| 117 | Steve Trout | .06 | .05 |
| 118 | Mark Langston | .30 | .25 |
| 119 | Tony Fernandez | .20 | .15 |
| 120 | John Butcher | .06 | .05 |
| 121 | Ron Robinson | .08 | .06 |
| 122 | Dan Spillner | .06 | .05 |
| 123 | Mike Young | .06 | .05 |
| 124 | Paul Molitor | .15 | .11 |
| 125 | Kirk Gibson | .35 | .25 |
| 126 | Ken Griffey | .12 | .09 |
| 127 | Tony Armas | .08 | .06 |
| 128 | *Mariano Duncan*(FC) | .15 | .11 |
| 129 | Mr. Clutch (Pat Tabler) | .08 | .06 |
| 130 | Frank White | .10 | .08 |
| 131 | Carney Lansford | .10 | .08 |
| 132 | Vance Law | .08 | .06 |
| 133 | Dick Schofield | .06 | .05 |
| 134 | Wayne Tolleson | .06 | .05 |
| 135 | Greg Walker | .10 | .08 |
| 136 | Denny Walling | .06 | .05 |
| 137 | Ozzie Virgil | .06 | .05 |
| 138 | Ricky Horton | .06 | .05 |
| 139 | LaMarr Hoyt | .06 | .05 |
| 140 | Wayne Krenchicki | .06 | .05 |
| 141 | Glenn Hubbard | .06 | .05 |
| 142 | Cecilio Guante | .06 | .05 |
| 143 | Mike Krukow | .08 | .06 |
| 144 | Lee Smith | .10 | .08 |
| 145 | Edwin Nunez | .06 | .05 |
| 146 | Dave Stieb | .12 | .09 |
| 147 | Mike Smithson | .06 | .05 |
| 148 | Ken Dixon | .06 | .05 |
| 149 | Danny Darwin | .06 | .05 |
| 150 | Chris Pittaro | .06 | .05 |
| 151 | Bill Buckner | .12 | .09 |
| 152 | Mike Pagliarulo | .20 | .15 |
| 153 | Bill Russell | .08 | .06 |
| 154 | Brook Jacoby | .06 | .05 |
| 155 | Pat Sheridan | .06 | .05 |
| 156 | *Mike Gallego*(FC) | .15 | .11 |
| 157 | Jim Wohlford | .06 | .05 |
| 158 | Gary Pettis | .06 | .05 |
| 159 | Toby Harrah | .08 | .06 |
| 160 | Richard Dotson | .10 | .08 |
| 161 | Bob Knepper | .08 | .06 |
| 162 | Dave Dravecky | .08 | .06 |
| 163 | Greg Gross | .06 | .05 |
| 164 | Eric Davis | 1.50 | 1.25 |
| 165 | Gerald Perry | .15 | .1 |
| 166 | Rick Rhoden | .10 | .08 |
| 167 | Keith Moreland | .08 | .06 |
| 168 | Jack Clark | .20 | .1 |
| 169 | Storm Davis | .10 | .0 |
| 170 | Cecil Cooper | .12 | .0 |
| 171 | Alan Trammell | .35 | .0 |
| 172 | Roger Clemens | 10.00 | 7.50 |
| 173 | Don Mattingly | 4.00 | 3.00 |
| 174 | Pedro Guerrero | .20 | .1 |
| 175 | Willie Wilson | .12 | .0 |
| 176 | Dwayne Murphy | .08 | .0 |
| 177 | Tim Raines | .40 | .3 |
| 178 | Larry Parrish | .10 | .0 |
| 179 | Mike Witt | .10 | .0 |
| 180 | Harold Baines | .15 | .1 |

| | | MT | NR MT |
|---|---|---|---|
| 181 | *Vince Coleman*(FC) | | |
| | | 1.50 | 1.25 |
| 182 | *Jeff Heathcock*(FC) | | |
| | | .10 | .08 |
| 183 | Steve Carlton | .50 | .40 |
| 184 | Mario Soto | .08 | .06 |
| 185 | Goose Gossage | .20 | .15 |
| 186 | Johnny Ray | .12 | .09 |
| 187 | Dan Gladden | .08 | .06 |
| 188 | Bob Horner | .12 | .09 |
| 189 | Rick Sutcliffe | .12 | .09 |
| 190 | Keith Hernandez | .25 | .20 |
| 191 | Phil Bradley | .20 | .15 |
| 192 | Tom Brunansky | .12 | .09 |
| 193 | Jesse Barfield | .20 | .15 |
| 194 | Frank Viola | .20 | .15 |
| 195 | Willie Upshaw | .08 | .06 |
| 196 | Jim Beattie | .06 | .05 |
| 197 | Darryl Strawberry | 5.00 | 3.75 |
| 198 | Ron Cey | .10 | .08 |
| 199 | Steve Bedrosian | .12 | .09 |
| 200 | Steve Kemp | .08 | .06 |
| 201 | Manny Trillo | .08 | .06 |
| 202 | Garry Templeton | .08 | .06 |
| 203 | Dave Parker | .25 | .20 |
| 204 | John Denny | .06 | .05 |
| 205 | Terry Pendleton | .15 | .11 |
| 206 | Terry Puhl | .06 | .05 |
| 207 | Bobby Grich | .10 | .08 |
| 208 | *Ozzie Guillen*(FC) | | |
| | | .90 | .70 |
| 209 | Jeff Reardon | .12 | .09 |
| 210 | Cal Ripken Jr. | 5.00 | 3.75 |
| 211 | Bill Schroeder | .06 | .05 |
| 212 | Dan Petry | .08 | .06 |
| 213 | Jim Rice | .40 | .30 |
| 214 | Dave Righetti | .20 | .15 |
| 215 | Fernando Valenzuela | | |
| | | .35 | .25 |
| 216 | Julio Franco | .50 | .40 |
| 217 | Darryl Motley | .06 | .05 |
| 218 | Dave Collins | .08 | .06 |
| 219 | Tim Wallach | .12 | .09 |
| 220 | George Wright | .06 | .05 |
| 221 | Tommy Dunbar | .06 | .05 |
| 222 | Steve Balboni | .08 | .06 |
| 223 | Jay Howell | .08 | .06 |
| 224 | Joe Carter | 1.25 | .90 |
| 225 | Ed Whitson | .06 | .05 |
| 226 | Orel Hershiser | .80 | .60 |
| 227 | Willie Hernandez | .08 | .06 |
| 228 | Lee Lacy | .06 | .05 |
| 229 | Rollie Fingers | .20 | .15 |
| 230 | Bob Boone | .08 | .06 |
| 231 | Joaquin Andujar | .08 | .06 |
| 232 | Craig Reynolds | .06 | .05 |
| 233 | Shane Rawley | .10 | .08 |
| 234 | Eric Show | .08 | .06 |
| 235 | Jose DeLeon | .08 | .06 |
| 236 | *Jose Uribe*(FC) | .25 | .20 |
| 237 | Moose Haas | .06 | .05 |
| 238 | Wally Backman | .08 | .06 |
| 239 | Dennis Eckersley | .12 | .09 |
| 240 | Mike Moore | .06 | .05 |
| 241 | Damaso Garcia | .06 | .05 |
| 242 | Tim Teufel | .06 | .05 |
| 243 | Dave Concepcion | .12 | .09 |

| | | MT | NR MT |
|---|---|---|---|
| 244 | Floyd Bannister | .10 | .08 |
| 245 | Fred Lynn | .20 | .15 |
| 246 | Charlie Moore | .06 | .05 |
| 247 | Walt Terrell | .08 | .06 |
| 248 | Dave Winfield | 1.25 | .90 |
| 249 | Dwight Evans | .12 | .09 |
| 250 | *Dennis Powell*(FC) | | |
| | | .10 | .08 |
| 251 | Andre Thornton | .10 | .08 |
| 252 | Onix Concepcion | .06 | .05 |
| 253 | Mike Heath | .06 | .05 |
| 254a | David Palmer (2B on front) | .06 | .05 |
| 254b | David Palmer (P on front) | 1.00 | .70 |
| 255 | Donnie Moore | .06 | .05 |
| 256 | Curtis Wilkerson | .06 | .05 |
| 257 | Julio Cruz | .06 | .05 |
| 258 | Nolan Ryan | 5.00 | 3.75 |
| 259 | Jeff Stone | .06 | .05 |
| 260a | John Tudor (1981 Games is .18) | .10 | .08 |
| 260b | John Tudor (1981 Games is 18) | 1.00 | .70 |
| 261 | Mark Thurmond | .06 | .05 |
| 262 | Jay Tibbs | .06 | .05 |
| 263 | Rafael Ramirez | .06 | .05 |
| 264 | Larry McWilliams | .06 | .05 |
| 265 | Mark Davis | .06 | .05 |
| 266 | Bob Dernier | .06 | .05 |
| 267 | Matt Young | .06 | .05 |
| 268 | Jim Clancy | .08 | .06 |
| 269 | Mickey Hatcher | .06 | .05 |
| 270 | Sammy Stewart | .06 | .05 |
| 271 | Bob Gibson | .06 | .05 |
| 272 | Nelson Simmons | .06 | .05 |
| 273 | Rich Gedman | .10 | .08 |
| 274 | Butch Wynegar | .06 | .05 |
| 275 | Ken Howell | .06 | .05 |
| 276 | Mel Hall | .08 | .06 |
| 277 | Jim Sundberg | .08 | .06 |
| 278 | Chris Codiroli | .06 | .05 |
| 279 | *Herman Winningham*(FC) | .15 | .11 |
| 280 | Rod Carew | .70 | .50 |
| 281 | Don Slaught | .06 | .05 |
| 282 | Scott Fletcher | .08 | .06 |
| 283 | Bill Dawley | .06 | .05 |
| 284 | Andy Hawkins | .06 | .05 |
| 285 | Glenn Wilson | .08 | .06 |
| 286 | Nick Esasky | .08 | .06 |
| 287 | Claudell Washington | .08 | .06 |
| 288 | Lee Mazzilli | .08 | .06 |
| 289 | Jody Davis | .10 | .08 |
| 290 | Darrell Porter | .08 | .06 |
| 291 | Scott McGregor | .08 | .06 |
| 292 | Ted Simmons | .12 | .09 |
| 293 | Aurelio Lopez | .06 | .05 |
| 294 | Marty Barrett | .10 | .08 |
| 295 | Dale Berra | .06 | .05 |
| 296 | Greg Brock | .08 | .06 |
| 297 | Charlie Leibrandt | .08 | .06 |
| 298 | Bill Krueger | .06 | .05 |
| 299 | Bryn Smith | .06 | .05 |
| 300 | Burt Hooton | .08 | .06 |
| 301 | *Stu Cliburn*(FC) | .12 | .09 |
| 302 | Luis Salazar | .06 | .05 |

| | | MT | NR MT |
|---|---|---|---|
| 303 | Ken Dayley | .06 | .05 |
| 304 | Frank DiPino | .06 | .05 |
| 305 | Von Hayes | .10 | .08 |
| 306a | Gary Redus (1983 2B is .20) | .08 | .06 |
| 306b | Gary Redus (1983 2B is 20) | 1.00 | .70 |
| 307 | Craig Lefferts | .06 | .05 |
| 308 | Sam Khalifa | .06 | .05 |
| 309 | Scott Garrelts | .06 | .05 |
| 310 | Rick Cerone | .06 | .05 |
| 311 | Shawon Dunston | .20 | .15 |
| 312 | Howard Johnson | .12 | .09 |
| 313 | Jim Presley | .15 | .11 |
| 314 | Gary Gaetti | .25 | .20 |
| 315 | Luis Leal | .06 | .05 |
| 316 | Mark Salas | .06 | .05 |
| 317 | Bill Caudill | .06 | .05 |
| 318 | Dave Henderson | .10 | .08 |
| 319 | Rafael Santana | .06 | .05 |
| 320 | Leon Durham | .08 | .06 |
| 321 | Bruce Sutter | .15 | .11 |
| 322 | Jason Thompson | .06 | .05 |
| 323 | Bob Brenly | .06 | .05 |
| 324 | Carmelo Martinez | .08 | .06 |
| 325 | Eddie Milner | .06 | .05 |
| 326 | Juan Samuel | .15 | .11 |
| 327 | Tom Nieto | .06 | .05 |
| 328 | Dave Smith | .08 | .06 |
| 329 | Urbano Lugo(FC) | .08 | .06 |
| 330 | Joel Skinner | .06 | .05 |
| 331 | Bill Gullickson | .06 | .05 |
| 332 | Floyd Rayford | .06 | .05 |
| 333 | Ben Oglivie | .08 | .06 |
| 334 | Lance Parrish | .30 | .25 |
| 335 | Jackie Gutierrez | .06 | .05 |
| 336 | Dennis Rasmussen | .12 | .09 |
| 337 | Terry Whitfield | .06 | .05 |
| 338 | Neal Heaton | .06 | .05 |
| 339 | Jorge Orta | .06 | .05 |
| 340 | Donnie Hill | .06 | .05 |
| 341 | Joe Hesketh | .06 | .05 |
| 342 | Charlie Hough | .10 | .08 |
| 343 | Dave Rozema | .06 | .05 |
| 344 | Greg Pryor | .06 | .05 |
| 345 | Mickey Tettleton(FC) | 2.00 | 1.50 |
| 346 | George Vukovich | .06 | .05 |
| 347 | Don Baylor | .12 | .09 |
| 348 | Carlos Diaz | .06 | .05 |
| 349 | Barbaro Garbey | .06 | .05 |
| 350 | Larry Sheets | .12 | .09 |
| 351 | Ted Higuera(FC) | 1.00 | .70 |
| 352 | Juan Beniquez | .06 | .05 |
| 353 | Bob Forsch | .08 | .06 |
| 354 | Mark Bailey | .06 | .05 |
| 355 | Larry Andersen | .06 | .05 |
| 356 | Terry Kennedy | .08 | .06 |
| 357 | Don Robinson | .08 | .06 |
| 358 | Jim Gott | .06 | .05 |
| 359 | Earnest Riles(FC) | .30 | .25 |
| 360 | John Christensen(FC) | .10 | .08 |
| 361 | Ray Fontenot | .06 | .05 |
| 362 | Spike Owen | .06 | .05 |
| 363 | Jim Acker | .06 | .05 |
| 364a | Ron Davis (last line in highlights ends with "...in May.") | .08 | .06 |
| 364b | Ron Davis (last line in highlights ends with "...relievers (9).") | 1.00 | .70 |
| 365 | Tom Hume | .06 | .05 |
| 366 | Carlton Fisk | .60 | .45 |
| 367 | Nate Snell | .06 | .05 |
| 368 | Rick Manning | .06 | .05 |
| 369 | Darrell Evans | .15 | .11 |
| 370 | Ron Hassey | .06 | .05 |
| 371 | Wade Boggs | 2.00 | 1.50 |
| 372 | Rick Honeycutt | .06 | .05 |
| 373 | Chris Bando | .06 | .05 |
| 374 | Bud Black | .06 | .05 |
| 375 | Steve Henderson | .06 | .05 |
| 376 | Charlie Lea | .06 | .05 |
| 377 | Reggie Jackson | .40 | .30 |
| 378 | Dave Schmidt | .06 | .05 |
| 379 | Bob James | .06 | .05 |
| 380 | Glenn Davis(FC) | 1.25 | .90 |
| 381 | Tim Corcoran | .06 | .05 |
| 382 | Danny Cox | .10 | .08 |
| 383 | Tim Flannery | .06 | .05 |
| 384 | Tom Browning | .20 | .15 |
| 385 | Rick Camp | .06 | .05 |
| 386 | Jim Morrison | .06 | .05 |
| 387 | Dave LaPoint | .08 | .06 |
| 388 | Davey Lopes | .08 | .06 |
| 389 | Al Cowens | .06 | .05 |
| 390 | Doyle Alexander | .10 | .08 |
| 391 | Tim Laudner | .06 | .05 |
| 392 | Don Aase | .06 | .05 |
| 393 | Jaime Cocanower | .06 | .05 |
| 394 | Randy O'Neal(FC) | .08 | .06 |
| 395 | Mike Easler | .08 | .06 |
| 396 | Scott Bradley | .06 | .05 |
| 397 | Tom Niedenfuer | .08 | .06 |
| 398 | Jerry Willard | .06 | .05 |
| 399 | Lonnie Smith | .08 | .06 |
| 400 | Bruce Bochte | .06 | .05 |
| 401 | Terry Francona | .06 | .05 |
| 402 | Jim Slaton | .06 | .05 |
| 403 | Bill Stein | .06 | .05 |
| 404 | Tim Hulett | .06 | .05 |
| 405 | Alan Ashby | .06 | .05 |
| 406 | Tim Stoddard | .06 | .05 |
| 407 | Garry Maddox | .08 | .06 |
| 408 | Ted Power | .06 | .05 |
| 409 | Len Barker | .08 | .06 |
| 410 | Denny Gonzalez | .06 | .05 |
| 411 | George Frazier | .06 | .05 |
| 412 | Andy Van Slyke | .15 | .11 |
| 413 | Jim Dwyer | .06 | .05 |
| 414 | Paul Householder | .06 | .05 |
| 415 | Alejandro Sanchez | .06 | .05 |
| 416 | Steve Crawford | .06 | .05 |
| 417 | Dan Pasqua | .15 | .11 |
| 418 | Enos Cabell | .06 | .05 |
| 419 | Mike Jones | .06 | .05 |
| 420 | Steve Kiefer | .06 | .05 |
| 421 | Tim Burke(FC) | .30 | .25 |
| 422 | Mike Mason | .06 | .05 |
| 423 | Ruppert Jones | .06 | .05 |

| # | Player | MT | NR MT |
|---|--------|-----|-----|
| 424 | Jerry Hairston | .06 | .05 |
| 425 | Tito Landrum | .06 | .05 |
| 426 | Jeff Calhoun | .06 | .05 |
| 427 | *Don Carman*(FC) | .20 | .15 |
| 428 | Tony Perez | .15 | .11 |
| 429 | Jerry Davis | .06 | .05 |
| 430 | Bob Walk | .06 | .05 |
| 431 | Brad Wellman | .06 | .05 |
| 432 | Terry Forster | .08 | .06 |
| 433 | Billy Hatcher | .10 | .08 |
| 434 | Clint Hurdle | .06 | .05 |
| 435 | *Ivan Calderon*(FC) | 2.00 | 1.50 |
| 436 | Pete Filson | .06 | .05 |
| 437 | Tom Henke | .08 | .06 |
| 438 | Dave Engle | .06 | .05 |
| 439 | Tom Filer | .06 | .05 |
| 440 | Gorman Thomas | .10 | .08 |
| 441 | *Rick Aguilera*(FC) | .90 | .70 |
| 442 | Scott Sanderson | .06 | .05 |
| 443 | Jeff Dedmon | .06 | .05 |
| 444 | *Joe Orsulak*(FC) | .15 | .11 |
| 445 | Atlee Hammaker | .06 | .05 |
| 446 | Jerry Royster | .06 | .05 |
| 447 | Buddy Bell | .10 | .08 |
| 448 | Dave Rucker | .06 | .05 |
| 449 | Ivan DeJesus | .06 | .05 |
| 450 | Jim Pankovits | .06 | .05 |
| 451 | Jerry Narron | .06 | .05 |
| 452 | Bryan Little | .06 | .05 |
| 453 | Gary Lucas | .06 | .05 |
| 454 | Dennis Martinez | .08 | .06 |
| 455 | Ed Romero | .06 | .05 |
| 456 | *Bob Melvin*(FC) | .12 | .09 |
| 457 | Glenn Hoffman | .06 | .05 |
| 458 | Bob Shirley | .06 | .05 |
| 459 | Bob Welch | .12 | .09 |
| 460 | Carmen Castillo | .06 | .05 |
| 461 | Dave Leeper | .06 | .05 |
| 462 | *Tim Birtsas*(FC) | .12 | .09 |
| 463 | Randy St. Claire | .06 | .05 |
| 464 | Chris Welsh | .06 | .05 |
| 465 | Greg Harris | .06 | .05 |
| 466 | Lynn Jones | .06 | .05 |
| 467 | Dusty Baker | .08 | .06 |
| 468 | Roy Smith | .06 | .05 |
| 469 | Andre Robertson | .06 | .05 |
| 470 | Ken Landreaux | .06 | .05 |
| 471 | Dave Bergman | .06 | .05 |
| 472 | Gary Roenicke | .06 | .05 |
| 473 | Pete Vuckovich | .08 | .06 |
| 474 | *Kirk McCaskill*(FC) | .40 | .30 |
| 475 | Jeff Lahti | .06 | .05 |
| 476 | Mike Scott | .20 | .15 |
| 477 | *Darren Daulton*(FC) | 2.25 | 1.75 |
| 478 | Graig Nettles | .15 | .11 |
| 479 | Bill Almon | .06 | .05 |
| 480 | Greg Minton | .06 | .05 |
| 481 | Randy Ready(FC) | .10 | .08 |
| 482 | *Lenny Dykstra*(FC) | 1.50 | 1.25 |
| 483 | Thad Bosley | .06 | .05 |
| 484 | *Harold Reynolds*(FC) | .70 | .50 |
| 485 | Al Oliver | 1.00 | .70 |
| 486 | Roy Smalley | .06 | .05 |
| 487 | John Franco | .15 | .11 |
| 488 | Juan Agosto | .06 | .05 |
| 489 | Al Pardo | .06 | .05 |
| 490 | *Bill Wegman*(FC) | .25 | .20 |
| 491 | Frank Tanana | .10 | .08 |
| 492 | *Brian Fisher*(FC) | .20 | .15 |
| 493 | Mark Clear | .06 | .05 |
| 494 | Len Matuszek | .06 | .05 |
| 495 | Ramon Romero | .06 | .05 |
| 496 | John Wathan | .08 | .06 |
| 497 | Rob Picciolo | .06 | .05 |
| 498 | U.L. Washington | .06 | .05 |
| 499 | John Candelaria | .10 | .08 |
| 500 | Duane Walker | .06 | .05 |
| 501 | Gene Nelson | .06 | .05 |
| 502 | John Mizerock | .06 | .05 |
| 503 | Luis Aguayo | .06 | .05 |
| 504 | Kurt Kepshire | .06 | .05 |
| 505 | Ed Wojna | .06 | .05 |
| 506 | Joe Price | .06 | .05 |
| 507 | *Milt Thompson*(FC) | .30 | .25 |
| 508 | Junior Ortiz | .06 | .05 |
| 509 | Vida Blue | .10 | .08 |
| 510 | Steve Engel | .06 | .05 |
| 511 | Karl Best | .06 | .05 |
| 512 | *Cecil Fielder*(FC) | 25.00 | 18.00 |
| 513 | Frank Eufemia | .06 | .05 |
| 514 | Tippy Martinez | .06 | .05 |
| 515 | *Billy Robidoux*(FC) | .10 | .08 |
| 516 | Bill Scherrer | .06 | .05 |
| 517 | Bruce Hurst | .12 | .09 |
| 518 | Rich Bordi | .06 | .05 |
| 519 | Steve Yeager | .06 | .05 |
| 520 | Tony Bernazard | .06 | .05 |
| 521 | Hal McRae | .10 | .08 |
| 522 | Jose Rijo | .10 | .08 |
| 523 | *Mitch Webster*(FC) | .25 | .20 |
| 524 | *Jack Howell*(FC) | .35 | .25 |
| 525 | Alan Bannister | .06 | .05 |
| 526 | Ron Kittle | .10 | .08 |
| 527 | Phil Garner | .08 | .06 |
| 528 | Kurt Bevacqua | .06 | .05 |
| 529 | Kevin Gross | .08 | .06 |
| 530 | Bo Diaz | .08 | .06 |
| 531 | Ken Oberkfell | .06 | .05 |
| 532 | Rick Reuschel | .10 | .08 |
| 533 | Ron Meridith | .06 | .05 |
| 534 | Steve Braun | .06 | .05 |
| 535 | Wayne Gross | .06 | .05 |
| 536 | Ray Searage | .06 | .05 |
| 537 | Tom Brookens | .06 | .05 |
| 538 | Al Nipper | .06 | .05 |
| 539 | Billy Sample | .06 | .05 |
| 540 | Steve Sax | .20 | .15 |
| 541 | Dan Quisenberry | .10 | .08 |
| 542 | Tony Phillips | .06 | .05 |
| 543 | *Floyd Youmans*(FC) | .20 | .15 |
| 544 | *Steve Buechele*(FC) | .70 | .50 |

| | | MT | NR MT |
|---|---|---|---|
| 545 | Craig Gerber | .06 | .05 |
| 546 | Joe DeSa | .06 | .05 |
| 547 | Brian Harper | .06 | .05 |
| 548 | Kevin Bass | .10 | .08 |
| 549 | Tom Foley | .06 | .05 |
| 550 | Dave Van Gorder | .06 | .05 |
| 551 | Bruce Bochy | .06 | .05 |
| 552 | R.J. Reynolds | .08 | .06 |
| 553 | Chris Brown(FC) | .20 | .15 |
| 554 | Bruce Benedict | .06 | .05 |
| 555 | Warren Brusstar | .06 | .05 |
| 556 | Danny Heep | .06 | .05 |
| 557 | Darnell Coles | .08 | .06 |
| 558 | Greg Gagne | .08 | .06 |
| 559 | Ernie Whitt | .08 | .06 |
| 560 | Ron Washington | .06 | .05 |
| 561 | Jimmy Key | .15 | .11 |
| 562 | Billy Swift(FC) | .15 | .11 |
| 563 | Ron Darling | .15 | .11 |
| 564 | Dick Ruthven | .06 | .05 |
| 565 | Zane Smith(FC) | .15 | .11 |
| 566 | Sid Bream | .10 | .08 |
| 567a | Joel Youngblood (P on front) | .08 | .06 |
| 567b | Joel Youngblood (IF on front) | 1.00 | .70 |
| 568 | Mario Ramirez | .06 | .05 |
| 569 | Tom Runnells | .06 | .05 |
| 570 | Rick Schu | .06 | .05 |
| 571 | Bill Campbell | .06 | .05 |
| 572 | Dickie Thon | .08 | .06 |
| 573 | Al Holland | .06 | .05 |
| 574 | Reid Nichols | .06 | .05 |
| 575 | Bert Roberge | .06 | .05 |
| 576 | Mike Flanagan | .10 | .08 |
| 577 | Tim Leary(FC) | .35 | .25 |
| 578 | Mike Laga | .06 | .05 |
| 579 | Steve Lyons | .06 | .05 |
| 580 | Phil Niekro | .30 | .25 |
| 581 | Gilberto Reyes | .06 | .05 |
| 582 | Jamie Easterly | .06 | .05 |
| 583 | Mark Gubicza | .12 | .09 |
| 584 | Stan Javier(FC) | .15 | .11 |
| 585 | Bill Laskey | .06 | .05 |
| 586 | Jeff Russell | .06 | .05 |
| 587 | Dickie Noles | .06 | .05 |
| 588 | Steve Farr | .08 | .06 |
| 589 | Steve Ontiveros(FC) | .15 | .11 |
| 590 | Mike Hargrove | .06 | .05 |
| 591 | Marty Bystrom | .06 | .05 |
| 592 | Franklin Stubbs | .08 | .06 |
| 593 | Larry Herndon | .08 | .06 |
| 594 | Bill Swaggerty | .06 | .05 |
| 595 | Carlos Ponce | .06 | .05 |
| 596 | Pat Perry(FC) | .12 | .09 |
| 597 | Ray Knight | .08 | .06 |
| 598 | Steve Lombardozzi(FC) | .15 | .11 |
| 599 | Brad Havens | .06 | .05 |
| 600 | Pat Clements(FC) | .12 | .09 |
| 601 | Joe Niekro | .12 | .09 |
| 602 | Hank Aaron Puzzle Card | .06 | .05 |
| 603 | Dwayne Henry(FC) | .10 | .08 |

| | | MT | NR MT |
|---|---|---|---|
| 604 | Mookie Wilson | .10 | .08 |
| 605 | Buddy Biancalana | .06 | .05 |
| 606 | Rance Mulliniks | .06 | .05 |
| 607 | Alan Wiggins | .06 | .05 |
| 608 | Joe Cowley | .06 | .05 |
| 609a | Tom Seaver (green stripes around name) | 1.00 | .70 |
| 609b | Tom Seaver (yellow stripes around name) | 3.00 | 2.25 |
| 610 | Neil Allen | .06 | .05 |
| 611 | Don Sutton | .30 | .25 |
| 612 | Fred Toliver(FC) | .15 | .11 |
| 613 | Jay Baller | .06 | .05 |
| 614 | Marc Sullivan | .06 | .05 |
| 615 | John Grubb | .06 | .05 |
| 616 | Bruce Kison | .06 | .05 |
| 617 | Bill Madlock | .12 | .09 |
| 618 | Chris Chambliss | .08 | .06 |
| 619 | Dave Stewart | .12 | .09 |
| 620 | Tim Lollar | .06 | .05 |
| 621 | Gary Lavelle | .06 | .05 |
| 622 | Charles Hudson | .06 | .05 |
| 623 | Joel Davis(FC) | .08 | .06 |
| 624 | Joe Johnson(FC) | .08 | .06 |
| 625 | Sid Fernandez | .12 | .09 |
| 626 | Dennis Lamp | .06 | .05 |
| 627 | Terry Harper | .06 | .05 |
| 628 | Jack Lazorko | .06 | .05 |
| 629 | Roger McDowell(FC) | .60 | .45 |
| 630 | Mark Funderburk | .06 | .05 |
| 631 | Ed Lynch | .06 | .05 |
| 632 | Rudy Law | .06 | .05 |
| 633 | Roger Mason(FC) | .08 | .06 |
| 634 | Mike Felder(FC) | .15 | .11 |
| 635 | Ken Schrom | .06 | .05 |
| 636 | Bob Ojeda | .08 | .06 |
| 637 | Ed Vande Berg | .06 | .05 |
| 638 | Bobby Meacham | .06 | .05 |
| 639 | Cliff Johnson | .06 | .05 |
| 640 | Garth Iorg | .06 | .05 |
| 641 | Dan Driessen | .08 | .06 |
| 642 | Mike Brown | .06 | .05 |
| 643 | John Shelby | .06 | .05 |
| 644 | Ty-Breaking Hit (Pete Rose) | .50 | .40 |
| 645 | Knuckle Brothers (Joe Niekro, Phil Niekro) | .15 | .11 |
| 646 | Jesse Orosco | .08 | .06 |
| 647 | Billy Beane(FC) | .06 | .05 |
| 648 | César Cedeno | .10 | .08 |
| 649 | Bert Blyleven | .15 | .11 |
| 650 | Max Venable | .06 | .05 |
| 651 | Fleet Feet (Vince Coleman, Willie McGee) | .35 | .25 |
| 652 | Calvin Schiraldi | .08 | .06 |
| 653 | King of Kings (Pete Rose) | .70 | .50 |
| ——— | Checklist 1-26 DK | .06 | .05 |
| ——a | Checklist 27-130 (45 is Beane) | .08 | .06 |
| ——b | Checklist 27-130 (45 is Habyan) | .60 | .45 |
| ——— | Checklist 131-234 | .06 | .05 |
| ——— | Checklist 235-338 | .06 | .05 |

|  |  | MT | NR MT |
|---|---|---|---|
| ---- | Checklist 339-442 | .06 | .05 |
| ---- | Checklist 443-546 | .06 | .05 |
| ---- | Checklist 547-653 | .06 | .05 |

## 1986 Donruss Rookies

Entitled "The Rookies," this 56-card set includes the top 55 rookies of 1986 plus an unnumbered checklist. The cards, which measure 2-1/2" by 3-1/2", are similar to the format used for the 1986 Donruss regular issue, except that the borders are green rather than blue. Several of the rookies who had cards in the regular 1986 Donruss set appear again in "The Rookies" set. The sets, which were only available through hobby dealers, came in a specially designed box.

|  |  | MT | NR MT |
|---|---|---|---|
| Complete Set: | | 60.00 | 45.00 |
| Common Player: | | .15 | .11 |
| 1 | Wally Joyner(FC) | 3.00 | 2.25 |
| 2 | Tracy Jones(FC) | .20 | .15 |
| 3 | Allan Anderson(FC) | .20 | .15 |
| 4 | Ed Correa(FC) | .25 | .20 |
| 5 | Reggie Williams | .20 | .15 |
| 6 | Charlie Kerfeld(FC) | .15 | .11 |
| 7 | Andres Galarraga | .40 | .30 |
| 8 | Bob Tewksbury(FC) | .80 | .60 |
| 9 | Al Newman | .15 | .11 |
| 10 | Andres Thomas(FC) | .20 | .15 |
| 11 | Barry Bonds(FC) | 12.00 | 9.00 |
| 12 | Juan Nieves | .15 | .11 |
| 13 | Mark Eichhorn(FC) | .25 | .20 |
| 14 | Dan Plesac(FC) | .25 | .20 |
| 15 | Cory Snyder | .40 | .30 |
| 16 | Kelly Gruber | 2.00 | 1.50 |
| 17 | Kevin Mitchell(FC) | 6.00 | 4.50 |
| 18 | Steve Lombardozzi(FC) | .15 | .11 |
| 19 | Mitch Williams | .50 | .40 |
| 20 | John Cerutti(FC) | .25 | .20 |
| 21 | Todd Worrell | .35 | .25 |
| 22 | Jose Canseco | 10.00 | 7.50 |
| 23 | Pete Incaviglia(FC) | .70 | .50 |
| 24 | Jose Guzman | .25 | .20 |
| 25 | Scott Bailes(FC) | .25 | .20 |
| 26 | Greg Mathews(FC) | .25 | .20 |
| 27 | Eric King(FC) | .20 | .15 |
| 28 | Paul Assenmacher(FC) | .20 | .15 |
| 29 | Jeff Sellers | .25 | .20 |
| 30 | Bobby Bonilla(FC) | 7.00 | 5.25 |
| 31 | Doug Drabek(FC) | 1.50 | 1.25 |
| 32 | Will Clark(FC) | 12.00 | 9.00 |
| 33 | Bip Roberts | .90 | .70 |
| 34 | Jim Deshaies(FC) | .25 | .20 |
| 35 | Mike Lavalliere (LaValliere)(FC) | .40 | .30 |
| 36 | Scott Bankhead(FC) | .20 | .15 |
| 37 | Dale Sveum(FC) | .25 | .20 |
| 38 | Bo Jackson(FC) | 6.00 | 4.50 |
| 39 | Rob Thompson(FC) | .50 | .40 |
| 40 | Eric Plunk(FC) | .20 | .15 |
| 41 | Bill Bathe | .15 | .11 |
| 42 | John Kruk(FC) | 2.00 | 1.50 |
| 43 | Andy Allanson(FC) | .20 | .15 |
| 44 | Mark Portugal | .15 | .11 |
| 45 | Danny Tartabull | 2.00 | 1.50 |
| 46 | Bob Kipper | .15 | .11 |
| 47 | Gene Walter | .15 | .11 |
| 48 | Rey Quinonez | .15 | .11 |
| 49 | Bobby Witt(FC) | .80 | .60 |
| 50 | Bill Mooneyham | .15 | .11 |
| 51 | John Cangelosi(FC) | .20 | .15 |
| 52 | Ruben Sierra(FC) | 12.00 | 9.00 |
| 53 | Rob Woodward | .15 | .11 |
| 54 | Ed Hearn | .15 | .11 |
| 55 | Joel McKeon | .15 | .11 |
| 56 | Checklist 1-56 | .05 | .04 |

## 1987 Donruss

 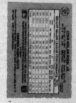

The 1987 Donruss set consists of 660 numbered cards, each measuring 2-1/2" by 3-1/2" in size. Full color photos are surrounded by a bold black border separated by two narrow bands of yellow which enclose a brown area filled with baseballs. The player's name, team and team logo appear on the card fronts along with the words "Donruss '87." The card backs are designed on a horizontal format and contain black print on a yellow and white background.

The backs are very similar to those in previous years' sets. Backs of cards issued in wax and rack packs face to the left when turned over, while those issued in vending sets face to the right.

| | | MT | NR MT |
|---|---|---|---|
| | Complete Set: | 60.00 | 45.00 |
| | Common Player: | .05 | .04 |
| 1 | Wally Joyner (DK) | .50 | .40 |
| 2 | Roger Clemens (DK) | .70 | .50 |
| 3 | Dale-Murphy (DK) | .30 | .25 |
| 4 | Darryl Strawberry (DK) | .40 | .30 |
| 5 | Ozzie Smith (DK) | .12 | .09 |
| 6 | Jose Canseco (DK) | .80 | .60 |
| 7 | Charlie Hough (DK) | .07 | .05 |
| 8 | Brook Jacoby (DK) | .10 | .08 |
| 9 | Fred Lynn (DK) | .12 | .09 |
| 10 | Rick Rhoden (DK) | .10 | .08 |
| 11 | Chris Brown (DK) | .10 | .08 |
| 12 | Von Hayes (DK) | .10 | .08 |
| 13 | Jack Morris (DK) | .20 | .15 |
| 14a | Kevin McReynolds (DK) ("Donruss Diamond Kings" in white band on back) | 1.25 | .90 |
| 14b | Kevin McReynolds (DK) ("Donruss Diamond Kings" in yellow band on back) | .20 | .15 |
| 15 | George Brett (DK) | .40 | .30 |
| 16 | Ted Higuera (DK) | .20 | .15 |
| 17 | Hubie Brooks (DK) | .10 | .08 |
| 18 | Mike Scott (DK) | .12 | .09 |
| 19 | Kirby Puckett (DK) | .40 | .30 |
| 20 | Dave Winfield (DK) | .25 | .20 |
| 21 | Lloyd Moseby (DK) | .10 | .08 |
| 22a | Eric Davis (DK) ("Donruss Diamond Kings" in white band on back) | 1.00 | .70 |
| 22b | Eric Davis (DK) ("Donruss Diamond Kings" in yellow band on back) | .40 | .30 |
| 23 | Jim Presley (DK) | .12 | .09 |
| 24 | Keith Moreland (DK) | .07 | .05 |
| 25a | Greg Walker (DK) ("Donruss Diamond Kings" in white band on back) | .50 | .40 |
| 25b | Greg Walker (DK) ("Donruss Diamond Kings" in yellow band on back) | .10 | .08 |
| 26 | Steve Sax (DK) | .12 | .09 |
| 27 | Checklist 1-27 | .05 | .04 |
| 28 | B.J. Surhoff (RR)(FC) | .50 | .40 |
| 29 | Randy Myers (RR)(FC) | .30 | .25 |
| 30 | Ken Gerhart (RR)(FC) | .15 | .11 |
| 31 | Benito Santiago (RR)(FC) | .60 | .45 |
| 32 | Greg Swindell (RR)(FC) | 1.00 | .70 |
| 33 | Mike Birkbeck (RR)(FC) | .20 | .15 |

| | | MT | NR MT |
|---|---|---|---|
| 34 | Terry Steinbach (RR)(FC) | .50 | .40 |
| 35 | Bo Jackson (RR) | 3.00 | 2.25 |
| 36 | Greg Maddux (RR)(FC) | 6.00 | 4.50 |
| 37 | Jim Lindeman (RR)(FC) | .15 | .11 |
| 38 | Devon White (RR)(FC) | .80 | .60 |
| 39 | Eric Bell (RR)(FC) | .12 | .09 |
| 40 | Will Fraser (RR)(FC) | .20 | .15 |
| 41 | Jerry Browne (RR)(FC) | .25 | .20 |
| 42 | Chris James (RR)(FC) | .40 | .30 |
| 43 | Rafael Palmeiro (RR)(FC) | 6.00 | 4.50 |
| 44 | Pat Dodson (RR)(FC) | .12 | .09 |
| 45 | Duane Ward (RR)(FC) | .30 | .25 |
| 46 | Mark McGwire (RR)(FC) | 8.00 | 6.00 |
| 47 | Bruce Fields (RR) (photo actually Darnell Coles)(FC) | .10 | .08 |
| 48 | Eddie Murray | .50 | .40 |
| 49 | Ted Higuera | .20 | .15 |
| 50 | Kirk Gibson | .25 | .20 |
| 51 | Oil Can Boyd | .07 | .05 |
| 52 | Don Mattingly | 1.00 | .70 |
| 53 | Pedro Guerrero | .15 | .11 |
| 54 | George Brett | .40 | .30 |
| 55 | Jose Rijo | .07 | .05 |
| 56 | Tim Raines | .30 | .25 |
| 57 | Ed Correa | .15 | .11 |
| 58 | Mike Witt | .10 | .08 |
| 59 | Greg Walker | .10 | .08 |
| 60 | Ozzie Smith | .15 | .11 |
| 61 | Glenn Davis | .35 | .25 |
| 62 | Glenn Wilson | .07 | .05 |
| 63 | Tom Browning | .10 | .08 |
| 64 | Tony Gwynn | .35 | .25 |
| 65 | R.J. Reynolds | .07 | .05 |
| 66 | Will Clark | 10.00 | 7.50 |
| 67 | Ozzie Virgil | .05 | .04 |
| 68 | Rick Sutcliffe | .12 | .09 |
| 69 | Gary Carter | .30 | .25 |
| 70 | Mike Moore | .05 | .04 |
| 71 | Bert Blyleven | .12 | .09 |
| 72 | Tony Fernandez | .12 | .09 |
| 73 | Kent Hrbek | .15 | .11 |
| 74 | Lloyd Moseby | .10 | .08 |
| 75 | Alvin Davis | .12 | .09 |
| 76 | Keith Hernandez | .25 | .20 |
| 77 | Ryne Sandberg | 1.00 | .70 |
| 78 | Dale Murphy | .40 | .30 |
| 79 | Sid Bream | .07 | .05 |
| 80 | Chris Brown | .07 | .05 |
| 81 | Steve Garvey | .25 | .20 |
| 82 | Mario Soto | .07 | .05 |
| 83 | Shane Rawley | .07 | .05 |
| 84 | Willie McGee | .12 | .09 |
| 85 | Jose Cruz | .10 | .08 |
| 86 | Brian Downing | .07 | .05 |

| | MT | NR MT | | | MT | NR MT |
|---|---|---|---|---|---|---|
| 87 | Ozzie Guillen | .10 | .08 | 153 | Rich Gedman | .10 | .08 |
| 88 | Hubie Brooks | .10 | .08 | 154 | Willie Randolph | .10 | .08 |
| 89 | Cal Ripken | 2.00 | 1.50 | 155a | Bill Madlock (name in brown band) | .12 | .09 |
| 90 | Juan Nieves | .07 | .05 | | | | |
| 91 | Lance Parrish | .20 | .15 | 155b | Bill Madlock (name in red band) | .70 | .50 |
| 92 | Jim Rice | .30 | .25 | | | | |
| 93 | Ron Guidry | .15 | .11 | 156a | Joe Carter (name in brown band) | .15 | .11 |
| 94 | Fernando Valenzuela | .25 | .20 | | | | |
| 95 | *Andy Allanson* | .15 | .11 | 156b | Joe Carter (name in red band) | .70 | .50 |
| 96 | Willie Wilson | .12 | .09 | 157 | Danny Jackson | .15 | .11 |
| 97 | Jose Canseco | 6.00 | 4.50 | 158 | Carney Lansford | .10 | .08 |
| 98 | Jeff Reardon | .10 | .08 | 159 | Bryn Smith | .05 | .04 |
| 99 | *Bobby Witt* | .50 | .40 | 160 | Gary Pettis | .05 | .04 |
| 100 | Checklist 28-133 | .05 | .04 | 161 | Oddibe McDowell | .10 | .08 |
| 101 | Jose Guzman | .10 | .08 | 162 | *John Cangelosi* | .12 | .09 |
| 102 | Steve Balboni | .07 | .05 | 163 | Mike Scott | .15 | .11 |
| 103 | Tony Phillips | .05 | .04 | 164 | Eric Show | .07 | .05 |
| 104 | Brook Jacoby | .10 | .08 | 165 | Juan Samuel | .12 | .09 |
| 105 | Dave Winfield | .30 | .25 | 166 | Nick Esasky | .07 | .05 |
| 106 | Orel Hershiser | .40 | .30 | 167 | Zane Smith | .07 | .05 |
| 107 | Lou Whitaker | .25 | .20 | 168 | Mike Brown | .05 | .04 |
| 108 | Fred Lynn | .15 | .11 | 169 | Keith Moreland | .07 | .05 |
| 109 | Bill Wegman | .07 | .05 | 170 | John Tudor | .10 | .08 |
| 110 | Donnie Moore | .05 | .04 | 171 | Ken Dixon | .05 | .04 |
| 111 | Jack Clark | .15 | .11 | 172 | Jim Gantner | .07 | .05 |
| 112 | Bob Knepper | .07 | .05 | 173 | Jack Morris | .20 | .15 |
| 113 | Von Hayes | .10 | .08 | 174 | Bruce Hurst | .10 | .08 |
| 114 | *Leon "Bip" Roberts* | .50 | .40 | 175 | Dennis Rasmussen | .10 | .08 |
| 115 | Tony Pena | .08 | .06 | 176 | Mike Marshall | .12 | .09 |
| 116 | Scott Garrelts | .05 | .04 | 177 | Dan Quisenberry | .07 | .05 |
| 117 | Paul Molitor | .15 | .11 | 178 | Eric Plunk(FC) | .10 | .08 |
| 118 | Darryl Strawberry | 1.00 | .70 | 179 | Tim Wallach | .12 | .09 |
| 119 | Shawon Dunston | .10 | .08 | 180 | Steve Buechele | .07 | .05 |
| 120 | Jim Presley | .10 | .08 | 181 | Don Sutton | .20 | .15 |
| 121 | Jesse Barfield | .20 | .15 | 182 | Dave Schmidt | .05 | .04 |
| 122 | Gary Gaetti | .15 | .11 | 183 | Terry Pendleton | .10 | .08 |
| 123 | *Kurt Stillwell* | .40 | .30 | 184 | *Jim Deshaies* | .35 | .25 |
| 124 | Joel Davis | .05 | .04 | 185 | Steve Bedrosian | .12 | .09 |
| 125 | Mike Boddicker | .07 | .05 | 186 | Pete Rose | .60 | .45 |
| 126 | Robin Yount | .50 | .40 | 187 | Dave Dravecky | .07 | .05 |
| 127 | Alan Trammell | .25 | .20 | 188 | Rick Reuschel | .10 | .08 |
| 128 | Dave Righetti | .15 | .11 | 189 | Dan Gladden | .05 | .04 |
| 129 | Dwight Evans | .12 | .09 | 190 | Rick Mahler | .05 | .04 |
| 130 | Mike Scioscia | .07 | .05 | 191 | Thad Bosley | .05 | .04 |
| 131 | Julio Franco | .10 | .08 | 192 | Ron Darling | .15 | .11 |
| 132 | Bret Saberhagen | .25 | .20 | 193 | Matt Young | .05 | .04 |
| 133 | Mike Davis | .07 | .05 | 194 | Tom Brunansky | .10 | .08 |
| 134 | Joe Hesketh | .05 | .04 | 195 | Dave Stieb | .12 | .09 |
| 135 | *Wally Joyner* | 1.00 | .70 | 196 | Frank Viola | .15 | .11 |
| 136 | Don Slaught | .05 | .04 | 197 | Tom Henke | .07 | .05 |
| 137 | Daryl Boston | .05 | .04 | 198 | Karl Best | .05 | .04 |
| 138 | Nolan Ryan | 2.00 | 1.50 | 199 | Dwight Gooden | .60 | .45 |
| 139 | Mike Schmidt | 1.00 | .70 | 200 | Checklist 134-239 | .05 | .04 |
| 140 | Tommy Herr | .10 | .08 | 201 | Steve Trout | .05 | .04 |
| 141 | Garry Templeton | .07 | .05 | 202 | Rafael Ramirez | .05 | .04 |
| 142 | Kal Daniels | .80 | .60 | 203 | Bob Walk | .05 | .04 |
| 143 | Billy Sample | .05 | .04 | 204 | Roger Mason | .05 | .04 |
| 144 | Johnny Ray | .10 | .08 | 205 | Terry Kennedy | .07 | .05 |
| 145 | *Rob Thompson* | .30 | .25 | 206 | Ron Oester | .05 | .04 |
| 146 | Bob Dernier | .05 | .04 | 207 | John Russell | .05 | .04 |
| 147 | Danny Tartabull | .25 | .20 | 208 | *Greg Mathews* | .20 | .15 |
| 148 | Ernie Whitt | .07 | .05 | 209 | Charlie Kerfeld | .10 | .08 |
| 149 | Kirby Puckett | 2.00 | 1.50 | 210 | Reggie Jackson | .35 | .25 |
| 150 | Mike Young | .05 | .04 | 211 | Floyd Bannister | .10 | .08 |
| 151 | Ernest Riles | .05 | .04 | 212 | Vance Law | .07 | .05 |
| 152 | Frank Tanana | .07 | .05 | 213 | Rich Bordi | .05 | .04 |

| | MT | NR MT | | | MT | NR MT |
|---|---|---|---|---|---|---|
| 214 | *Dan Plesac* | .35 | .25 | 280 | Jim Sundberg | .07 | .05 |
| 215 | Dave Collins | .07 | .05 | 281 | Bill Bathe | .05 | .04 |
| 216 | Bob Stanley | .05 | .04 | 282 | Jay Tibbs | .05 | .04 |
| 217 | Joe Niekro | .10 | .08 | 283 | Dick Schofield | .05 | .04 |
| 218 | Tom Niedenfuer | .07 | .05 | 284 | Mike Mason | .05 | .04 |
| 219 | Brett Butler | .07 | .05 | 285 | Jerry Hairston | .05 | .04 |
| 220 | Charlie Leibrandt | .07 | .05 | 286 | Bill Doran | .10 | .08 |
| 221 | Steve Ontiveros | .05 | .04 | 287 | Tim Flannery | .05 | .04 |
| 222 | Tim Burke | .05 | .04 | 288 | Gary Redus | .05 | .04 |
| 223 | Curtis Wilkerson | .05 | .04 | 289 | John Franco | .10 | .08 |
| 224 | Pete Incaviglia | .40 | .20 | 290 | *Paul Assenmacher* | .15 | .11 |
| 225 | Lonnie Smith | .07 | .05 | 291 | Joe Orsulak | .05 | .04 |
| 226 | Chris Codiroli | .05 | .04 | 292 | Lee Smith | .10 | .08 |
| 227 | *Scott Bailes* | .20 | .15 | 293 | Mike Laga | .05 | .04 |
| 228 | Rickey Henderson | 1.00 | .70 | 294 | Rick Dempsey | .07 | .05 |
| 229 | Ken Howell | .05 | .04 | 295 | Mike Felder | .05 | .04 |
| 230 | Darnell Coles | .07 | .05 | 296 | Tom Brookens | .05 | .04 |
| 231 | Don Aase | .05 | .04 | 297 | Al Nipper | .05 | .04 |
| 232 | Tim Leary | .07 | .05 | 298 | Mike Pagliarulo | .10 | .08 |
| 233 | Bob Boone | .07 | .05 | 299 | Franklin Stubbs | .07 | .05 |
| 234 | Ricky Horton | .07 | .05 | 300 | Checklist 240-345 | .05 | .04 |
| 235 | Mark Bailey | .05 | .04 | 301 | Steve Farr | .05 | .04 |
| 236 | Kevin Gross | .07 | .05 | 302 | *Bill Mooneyham* | .10 | .08 |
| 237 | Lance McCullers | .07 | .05 | 303 | Andres Galarraga | .25 | .20 |
| 238 | Cecilio Guante | .05 | .04 | 304 | Scott Fletcher | .07 | .05 |
| 239 | Bob Melvin | .05 | .04 | 305 | Jack Howell | .07 | .05 |
| 240 | Billy Jo Robidoux | .05 | .04 | 306 | *Russ Morman*(FC) | | |
| 241 | Roger McDowell | .12 | .09 | | | .10 | .08 |
| 242 | Leon Durham | .07 | .05 | 307 | Todd Worrell | .20 | .15 |
| 243 | Ed Nunez | .05 | .04 | 308 | Dave Smith | .07 | .05 |
| 244 | Jimmy Key | .12 | .09 | 309 | Jeff Stone | .05 | .04 |
| 245 | Mike Smithson | .05 | .04 | 310 | Ron Robinson | .05 | .04 |
| 246 | Bo Diaz | .07 | .05 | 311 | Bruce Bochy | .05 | .04 |
| 247 | Carlton Fisk | .20 | .15 | 312 | Jim Winn | .05 | .04 |
| 248 | Larry Sheets | .08 | .06 | 313 | Mark Davis | .05 | .04 |
| 249 | *Juan Castillo*(FC) | | | 314 | Jeff Dedmon | .05 | .04 |
| | | .10 | .08 | 315 | *Jamie Moyer*(FC) | | |
| 250 | *Eric King* | .25 | .20 | | | .20 | .15 |
| 251 | Doug Drabek | 1.50 | 1.25 | 316 | Wally Backman | .07 | .05 |
| 252 | Wade Boggs | .80 | .60 | 317 | Ken Phelps | .07 | .05 |
| 253 | Mariano Duncan | .05 | .04 | 318 | Steve Lombardozzi | .05 | .04 |
| 254 | Pat Tabler | .07 | .05 | 319 | Rance Mulliniks | .05 | .04 |
| 255 | Frank White | .10 | .08 | 320 | Tim Laudner | .05 | .04 |
| 256 | Alfredo Griffin | .07 | .05 | 321 | *Mark Eichhorn* | .15 | .11 |
| 257 | Floyd Youmans | .07 | .05 | 322 | *Lee Guetterman* | .15 | .11 |
| 258 | Rob Wilfong | .05 | .04 | 323 | Sid Fernandez | .12 | .09 |
| 259 | Pete O'Brien | .10 | .08 | 324 | Jerry Mumphrey | .05 | .04 |
| 260 | Tim Hulett | .05 | .04 | 325 | David Palmer | .05 | .04 |
| 261 | Dickie Thon | .07 | .05 | 326 | Bill Almon | .05 | .04 |
| 262 | Darren Daulton | .05 | .04 | 327 | Candy Maldonado | .07 | .05 |
| 263 | Vince Coleman | .50 | .40 | 328 | *John Kruk* | .60 | .45 |
| 264 | Andy Hawkins | .05 | .04 | 329 | John Denny | .05 | .04 |
| 265 | Eric Davis | 1.25 | .90 | 330 | Milt Thompson | .07 | .05 |
| 266 | *Andres Thomas* | .15 | .11 | 331 | *Mike LaValliere* | .25 | .20 |
| 267 | *Mike Diaz*(FC) | .15 | .11 | 332 | Alan Ashby | .05 | .04 |
| 268 | Chili Davis | .07 | .05 | 333 | Doug Corbett | .05 | .04 |
| 269 | Jody Davis | .07 | .05 | 334 | *Ron Karkovice*(FC) | | |
| 270 | Phil Bradley | .12 | .09 | | | .10 | .08 |
| 271 | George Bell | .25 | .20 | 335 | Mitch Webster | .07 | .05 |
| 272 | Keith Atherton | .05 | .04 | 336 | Lee Lacy | .05 | .04 |
| 273 | Storm Davis | .10 | .08 | 337 | *Glenn Braggs*(FC) | | |
| 274 | Rob Deer(FC) | .20 | .15 | | | .30 | .25 |
| 275 | Walt Terrell | .07 | .05 | 338 | Dwight Lowry | .05 | .04 |
| 276 | Roger Clemens | 2.00 | 1.50 | 339 | Don Baylor | .12 | .09 |
| 277 | Mike Easler | .07 | .05 | 340 | Brian Fisher | .07 | .05 |
| 278 | Steve Sax | .15 | .11 | 341 | *Reggie Williams* | .10 | .08 |
| 279 | Andre Thornton | .07 | .05 | 342 | Tom Candiotti | .05 | .04 |

| | | MT | NR MT |
|---|---|---|---|
| 343 | Rudy Law | .05 | .04 |
| 344 | Curt Young | .07 | .05 |
| 345 | Mike Fitzgerald | .05 | .04 |
| 346 | *Ruben Sierra* | 10.00 | 7.50 |
| 347 | Mitch Williams | .40 | .30 |
| 348 | Jorge Orta | .05 | .04 |
| 349 | Mickey Tettleton | .10 | .08 |
| 350 | Ernie Camacho | .05 | .04 |
| 351 | Ron Kittle | .10 | .08 |
| 352 | Ken Landreaux | .05 | .04 |
| 353 | Chet Lemon | .07 | .05 |
| 354 | John Shelby | .05 | .04 |
| 355 | Mark Clear | .05 | .04 |
| 356 | Doug DeCinces | .07 | .05 |
| 357 | Ken Dayley | .05 | .04 |
| 358 | Phil Garner | .05 | .04 |
| 359 | Steve Jeltz | .05 | .04 |
| 360 | Ed Whitson | .05 | .04 |
| 361 | Barry Bonds | 8.00 | 6.00 |
| 362 | Vida Blue | .10 | .08 |
| 363 | Cecil Cooper | .12 | .09 |
| 364 | Bob Ojeda | .07 | .05 |
| 365 | Dennis Eckersley | .12 | .09 |
| 366 | Mike Morgan | .05 | .04 |
| 367 | Willie Upshaw | .07 | .05 |
| 368 | *Allan Anderson*(FC) | .25 | .20 |
| 369 | Bill Gullickson | .07 | .05 |
| 370 | *Bobby Thigpen*(FC) | 1.00 | .70 |
| 371 | Juan Beniquez | .05 | .04 |
| 372 | Charlie Moore | .05 | .04 |
| 373 | Dan Petry | .07 | .05 |
| 374 | Rod Scurry | .05 | .04 |
| 375 | Tom Seaver | .40 | .30 |
| 376 | Ed Vande Berg | .05 | .04 |
| 377 | Tony Bernazard | .05 | .04 |
| 378 | Greg Pryor | .05 | .04 |
| 379 | Dwayne Murphy | .07 | .05 |
| 380 | Andy McGaffigan | .05 | .04 |
| 381 | Kirk McCaskill | .07 | .05 |
| 382 | Greg Harris | .05 | .04 |
| 383 | Rich Dotson | .07 | .05 |
| 384 | Craig Reynolds | .05 | .04 |
| 385 | Greg Gross | .05 | .04 |
| 386 | Tito Landrum | .05 | .04 |
| 387 | Craig Lefferts | .05 | .04 |
| 388 | Dave Parker | .20 | .15 |
| 389 | Bob Horner | .10 | .08 |
| 390 | Pat Clements | .05 | .04 |
| 391 | Jeff Leonard | .07 | .05 |
| 392 | Chris Speier | .05 | .04 |
| 393 | John Moses | .05 | .04 |
| 394 | Garth Iorg | .05 | .04 |
| 395 | Greg Gagne | .05 | .04 |
| 396 | Nate Snell | .05 | .04 |
| 397 | *Bryan Clutterbuck*(FC) | .10 | .08 |
| 398 | Darrell Evans | .12 | .09 |
| 399 | Steve Crawford | .05 | .04 |
| 400 | Checklist 346-451 | .05 | .04 |
| 401 | *Phil Lombardi*(FC) | .10 | .08 |
| 402 | Rick Honeycutt | .05 | .04 |
| 403 | Ken Schrom | .05 | .04 |
| 404 | Bud Black | .05 | .04 |
| 405 | Donnie Hill | .05 | .04 |

| | | MT | NR MT |
|---|---|---|---|
| 406 | Wayne Krenchicki | .05 | .04 |
| 407 | *Chuck Finley*(FC) | 1.00 | .70 |
| 408 | Toby Harrah | .07 | .05 |
| 409 | Steve Lyons | .05 | .04 |
| 410 | Kevin Bass | .10 | .08 |
| 411 | Marvell Wynne | .05 | .04 |
| 412 | Ron Roenicke | .05 | .04 |
| 413 | *Tracy Jones* | .25 | .20 |
| 414 | Gene Garber | .05 | .04 |
| 415 | Mike Bielecki | .05 | .04 |
| 416 | Frank DiPino | .05 | .04 |
| 417 | Andy Van Slyke | .12 | .09 |
| 418 | Jim Dwyer | .05 | .04 |
| 419 | Ben Oglivie | .07 | .05 |
| 420 | Dave Bergman | .05 | .04 |
| 421 | Joe Sambito | .05 | .04 |
| 422 | *Bob Tewksbury* | .12 | .09 |
| 423 | Len Matuszek | .05 | .04 |
| 424 | *Mike Kingery*(FC) | .15 | .11 |
| 425 | Dave Kingman | .12 | .09 |
| 426 | *Al Newman* | .07 | .05 |
| 427 | Gary Ward | .07 | .05 |
| 428 | Ruppert Jones | .05 | .04 |
| 429 | Harold Baines | .15 | .11 |
| 430 | Pat Perry | .05 | .04 |
| 431 | Terry Puhl | .05 | .04 |
| 432 | Don Carman | .07 | .05 |
| 433 | Eddie Milner | .05 | .04 |
| 434 | LaMarr Hoyt | .05 | .04 |
| 435 | Rick Rhoden | .10 | .08 |
| 436 | Jose Uribe | .07 | .05 |
| 437 | Ken Oberkfell | .05 | .04 |
| 438 | Ron Davis | .05 | .04 |
| 439 | Jesse Orosco | .07 | .05 |
| 440 | Scott Bradley | .05 | .04 |
| 441 | Randy Bush | .05 | .04 |
| 442 | *John Cerutti* | .20 | .15 |
| 443 | Roy Smalley | .05 | .04 |
| 444 | Kelly Gruber | 2.00 | 1.50 |
| 445 | Bob Kearney | .05 | .04 |
| 446 | *Ed Hearn* | .10 | .08 |
| 447 | Scott Sanderson | .05 | .04 |
| 448 | Bruce Benedict | .05 | .04 |
| 449 | Junior Ortiz | .05 | .04 |
| 450 | *Mike Aldrete* | .15 | .11 |
| 451 | Kevin McReynolds | .15 | .11 |
| 452 | *Rob Murphy*(FC) | .20 | .15 |
| 453 | Kent Tekulve | .07 | .05 |
| 454 | Curt Ford(FC) | .07 | .05 |
| 455 | Davey Lopes | .07 | .05 |
| 456 | Bobby Grich | .10 | .08 |
| 457 | Jose DeLeon | .07 | .05 |
| 458 | Andre Dawson | .20 | .15 |
| 459 | Mike Flanagan | .07 | .05 |
| 460 | *Joey Meyer*(FC) | .20 | .15 |
| 461 | *Chuck Cary*(FC) | .10 | .08 |
| 462 | Bill Buckner | .10 | .08 |
| 463 | Bob Shirley | .05 | .04 |
| 464 | *Jeff Hamilton*(FC) | .20 | .15 |
| 465 | Phil Niekro | .20 | .15 |
| 466 | Mark Gubicza | .12 | .09 |
| 467 | Jerry Willard | .05 | .04 |
| 468 | *Bob Sebra*(FC) | .10 | .08 |
| 469 | Larry Parrish | .10 | .08 |

| # | Player | MT | NR MT |
|---|--------|----|----|
| 470 | Charlie Hough | .07 | .05 |
| 471 | Hal McRae | .10 | .08 |
| 472 | Dave Leiper(FC) | .10 | .08 |
| 473 | Mel Hall | .07 | .05 |
| 474 | Dan Pasqua | .10 | .08 |
| 475 | Bob Welch | .10 | .08 |
| 476 | Johnny Grubb | .05 | .04 |
| 477 | Jim Traber | .07 | .05 |
| 478 | Chris Bosio(FC) | .40 | .30 |
| 479 | Mark McLemore | .07 | .05 |
| 480 | John Morris | .05 | .04 |
| 481 | Billy Hatcher | .07 | .05 |
| 482 | Dan Schatzeder | .05 | .04 |
| 483 | Rich Gossage | .15 | .11 |
| 484 | Jim Morrison | .05 | .04 |
| 485 | Bob Brenly | .05 | .04 |
| 486 | Bill Schroeder | .05 | .04 |
| 487 | Mookie Wilson | .10 | .08 |
| 488 | Dave Martinez(FC) | .25 | .20 |
| 489 | Harold Reynolds | .10 | .08 |
| 490 | Jeff Hearron | .05 | .04 |
| 491 | Mickey Hatcher | .05 | .04 |
| 492 | Barry Larkin(FC) | 4.00 | 3.00 |
| 493 | Bob James | .05 | .04 |
| 494 | John Habyan | .05 | .04 |
| 495 | Jim Adduci(FC) | .07 | .05 |
| 496 | Mike Heath | .05 | .04 |
| 497 | Tim Stoddard | .05 | .04 |
| 498 | Tony Armas | .07 | .05 |
| 499 | Dennis Powell | .05 | .04 |
| 500 | Checklist 452-557 | .05 | .04 |
| 501 | Chris Bando | .05 | .04 |
| 502 | David Cone(FC) | 5.00 | 3.75 |
| 503 | Jay Howell | .07 | .05 |
| 504 | Tom Foley | .05 | .04 |
| 505 | Ray Chadwick(FC) | .10 | .08 |
| 506 | Mike Loynd(FC) | .15 | .11 |
| 507 | Neil Allen | .05 | .04 |
| 508 | Danny Darwin | .05 | .04 |
| 509 | Rick Schu | .05 | .04 |
| 510 | Jose Oquendo | .05 | .04 |
| 511 | Gene Walter | .07 | .05 |
| 512 | Terry McGriff(FC) | .12 | .09 |
| 513 | Ken Griffey | .10 | .08 |
| 514 | Benny Distefano | .05 | .04 |
| 515 | Terry Mulholland(FC) | .12 | .09 |
| 516 | Ed Lynch | .05 | .04 |
| 517 | Bill Swift | .05 | .04 |
| 518 | Manny Lee(FC) | .07 | .05 |
| 519 | Andre David | .05 | .04 |
| 520 | Scott McGregor | .07 | .05 |
| 521 | Rick Manning | .05 | .04 |
| 522 | Willie Hernandez | .07 | .05 |
| 523 | Marty Barrett | .10 | .08 |
| 524 | Wayne Tolleson | .05 | .04 |
| 525 | Jose Gonzalez(FC) | .15 | .11 |
| 526 | Cory Snyder | .35 | .25 |
| 527 | Buddy Biancalana | .05 | .04 |
| 528 | Moose Haas | .05 | .04 |
| 529 | Wilfredo Tejada(FC) | .10 | .08 |
| 530 | Stu Cliburn | .05 | .04 |
| 531 | Dale Mohorcic(FC) | .20 | .15 |
| 532 | Ron Hassey | .05 | .04 |
| 533 | Ty Gainey | .05 | .04 |
| 534 | Jerry Royster | .05 | .04 |
| 535 | Mike Maddux(FC) | .20 | .15 |
| 536 | Ted Power | .05 | .04 |
| 537 | Ted Simmons | .12 | .09 |
| 538 | Rafael Belliard(FC) | .12 | .09 |
| 539 | Chico Walker | .05 | .04 |
| 540 | Bob Forsch | .07 | .05 |
| 541 | John Stefero | .05 | .04 |
| 542 | Dale Sveum | .20 | .15 |
| 543 | Mark Thurmond | .05 | .04 |
| 544 | Jeff Sellers | .20 | .15 |
| 545 | Joel Skinner | .05 | .04 |
| 546 | Alex Trevino | .05 | .04 |
| 547 | Randy Kutcher(FC) | .10 | .08 |
| 548 | Joaquin Andujar | .07 | .05 |
| 549 | Casey Candaele(FC) | .15 | .11 |
| 550 | Jeff Russell | .05 | .04 |
| 551 | John Candelaria | .10 | .08 |
| 552 | Joe Cowley | .05 | .04 |
| 553 | Danny Cox | .07 | .05 |
| 554 | Denny Walling | .05 | .04 |
| 555 | Bruce Ruffin(FC) | .20 | .15 |
| 556 | Buddy Bell | .10 | .08 |
| 557 | Jimmy Jones(FC) | .20 | .15 |
| 558 | Bobby Bonilla | 3.00 | 2.25 |
| 559 | Jeff Robinson | .07 | .05 |
| 560 | Ed Olwine | .05 | .04 |
| 561 | Glenallen Hill(FC) | .50 | .40 |
| 562 | Lee Mazzilli | .07 | .05 |
| 563 | Mike Brown | .05 | .04 |
| 564 | George Frazier | .05 | .04 |
| 565 | Mike Sharperson(FC) | .10 | .08 |
| 566 | Mark Portugal | .10 | .08 |
| 567 | Rick Leach | .05 | .04 |
| 568 | Mark Langston | .12 | .09 |
| 569 | Rafael Santana | .05 | .04 |
| 570 | Manny Trillo | .07 | .05 |
| 571 | Cliff Speck | .05 | .04 |
| 572 | Bob Kipper | .05 | .04 |
| 573 | Kelly Downs(FC) | .30 | .25 |
| 574 | Randy Asadoor(FC) | .10 | .08 |
| 575 | Dave Magadan(FC) | .40 | .30 |
| 576 | Marvin Freeman(FC) | .12 | .09 |
| 577 | Jeff Lahti | .05 | .04 |
| 578 | Jeff Calhoun | .05 | .04 |
| 579 | Gus Polidor(FC) | .07 | .05 |
| 580 | Gene Nelson | .05 | .04 |
| 581 | Tim Teufel | .05 | .04 |
| 582 | Odell Jones | .05 | .04 |
| 583 | Mark Ryal | .05 | .04 |
| 584 | Randy O'Neal | .05 | .04 |

| | | MT | NR MT |
|---|---|---|---|
| 585 | *Mike Greenwell*(FC) | | |
| | | 1.00 | .70 |
| 586 | Ray Knight | .07 | .05 |
| 587 | *Ralph Bryant*(FC) | | |
| | | .12 | .09 |
| 588 | Carmen Castillo | .05 | .04 |
| 589 | Ed Wojna | .05 | .04 |
| 590 | Stan Javier | .05 | .04 |
| 591 | *Jeff Musselman*(FC) | | |
| | | .20 | .15 |
| 592 | *Mike Stanley*(FC) | | |
| | | .20 | .15 |
| 593 | Darrell Porter | .07 | .05 |
| 594 | *Drew Hall*(FC) | .20 | .15 |
| 595 | Rob Nelson(FC) | .10 | .08 |
| 596 | Bryan Oelkers | .05 | .04 |
| 597 | *Scott Nielsen*(FC) | | |
| | | .10 | .08 |
| 598 | *Brian Holton*(FC) | | |
| | | .20 | .15 |
| 599 | *Kevin Mitchell* | 2.00 | 1.50 |
| 600 | Checklist 558-660 | .05 | .04 |
| 601 | Jackie Gutierrez | .05 | .04 |
| 602 | *Barry Jones*(FC) | .12 | .09 |
| 603 | Jerry Narron | .05 | .04 |
| 604 | Steve Lake | .05 | .04 |
| 605 | Jim Pankovits | .05 | .04 |
| 606 | Ed Romero | .05 | .04 |
| 607 | Dave LaPoint | .07 | .05 |
| 608 | Don Robinson | .07 | .05 |
| 609 | Mike Krukow | .07 | .05 |
| 610 | *Dave Valle*(FC) | .12 | .09 |
| 611 | Len Dykstra | .80 | .60 |
| 612 | Roberto Clemente Puzzle Card | .05 | .04 |
| 613 | Mike Trujillo(FC) | .05 | .04 |
| 614 | Damaso Garcia | .05 | .04 |
| 615 | Neal Heaton | .05 | .04 |
| 616 | Juan Berenguer | .05 | .04 |
| 617 | Steve Carlton | .25 | .20 |
| 618 | Gary Lucas | .05 | .04 |
| 619 | Geno Petralli | .05 | .04 |
| 620 | Rick Aguilera | .07 | .05 |
| 621 | Fred McGriff | 4.00 | 3.00 |
| 622 | Dave Henderson | .10 | .08 |
| 623 | *Dave Clark*(FC) | .20 | .15 |
| 624 | Angel Salazar | .05 | .04 |
| 625 | Randy Hunt | .05 | .04 |
| 626 | John Gibbons | .05 | .04 |
| 627 | *Kevin Brown*(FC) | | |
| | | 2.00 | 1.50 |
| 628 | Bill Dawley | .05 | .04 |
| 629 | Aurelio Lopez | .05 | .04 |
| 630 | Charlie Hudson | .05 | .04 |
| 631 | Ray Soff | .05 | .04 |
| 632 | *Ray Hayward*(FC) | | |
| | | .12 | .09 |
| 633 | Spike Owen | .05 | .04 |
| 634 | Glenn Hubbard | .05 | .04 |
| 635 | *Kevin Elster*(FC) | .40 | .30 |
| 636 | Mike LaCoss | .05 | .04 |
| 637 | Dwayne Henry | .05 | .04 |
| 638 | *Rey Quinones* | .15 | .11 |
| 639 | Jim Clancy | .07 | .05 |
| 640 | Larry Andersen | .05 | .04 |
| 641 | Calvin Schiraldi | .05 | .04 |
| 642 | *Stan Jefferson*(FC) | | |

| | | MT | NR MT |
|---|---|---|---|
| | | .15 | .11 |
| 643 | Marc Sullivan | .05 | .04 |
| 644 | Mark Grant | .05 | .04 |
| 645 | Cliff Johnson | .05 | .04 |
| 646 | Howard Johnson | .25 | .20 |
| 647 | Dave Sax | .05 | .04 |
| 648 | Dave Stewart | .25 | .20 |
| 649 | Danny Heep | .05 | .04 |
| 650 | Joe Johnson | .05 | .04 |
| 651 | *Bob Brower*(FC) | .15 | .11 |
| 652 | Rob Woodward | .07 | .05 |
| 653 | John Mizerock | .05 | .04 |
| 654 | *Tim Pyznarski*(FC) | | |
| | | .10 | .08 |
| 655 | *Luis Aquino*(FC) | .10 | .08 |
| 656 | Mickey Brantley(FC) | .10 | .08 |
| 657 | Doyle Alexander | .07 | .05 |
| 658 | Sammy Stewart | .05 | .04 |
| 659 | Jim Acker | .05 | .04 |
| 660 | Pete Ladd | .05 | .04 |

# 1987 Donruss Rookies

As they did in 1986, Donruss issued a 56-card set highlighting the major league's most promising rookies. The cards are the standard 2-1/2" by 3-1/2" size and are identical in design to the regular Donruss issue. The card fronts have green borders as opposed to the black found in the regular issue and carry the words "The Rookies" in the lower left portion of the card. The set came housed in a specially designed box and was available only through hobby dealers.

| | | MT | NR MT |
|---|---|---|---|
| Complete Set: | | 20.00 | 15.00 |
| Common Player: | | .10 | .08 |
| 1 | Mark McGwire | 6.00 | 4.50 |
| 2 | Eric Bell | .10 | .08 |
| 3 | Mark Williamson(FC) | | |
| | | .15 | .11 |
| 4 | Mike Greenwell | 1.00 | .70 |
| 5 | Ellis Burks(FC) | 1.00 | .70 |
| 6 | DeWayne Buice(FC) | .20 | .15 |

| | | MT | NR MT |
|---|---|---|---|
| 7 | Mark Mclemore (McLemore) | .10 | .08 |
| 8 | Devon White | .40 | .30 |
| 9 | Willie Fraser | .15 | .11 |
| 10 | Lester Lancaster(FC) | .15 | .11 |
| 11 | Ken Williams(FC) | .20 | .15 |
| 12 | Matt Nokes(FC) | .50 | .40 |
| 13 | Jeff Robinson(FC) | .30 | .25 |
| 14 | Bo Jackson | 2.50 | 2.00 |
| 15 | Kevin Seitzer(FC) | .50 | .40 |
| 16 | Billy Ripken(FC) | .25 | .20 |
| 17 | B.J. Surhoff | .20 | .15 |
| 18 | Chuck Crim(FC) | .15 | .11 |
| 19 | Mike Birbeck | .10 | .08 |
| 20 | Chris Bosio | .10 | .08 |
| 21 | Les Straker(FC) | .20 | .15 |
| 22 | Mark Davidson(FC) | .15 | .11 |
| 23 | Gene Larkin(FC) | .35 | .25 |
| 24 | Ken Gerhart | .15 | .11 |
| 25 | Luis Polonia(FC) | .50 | .40 |
| 26 | Terry Steinbach | .25 | .20 |
| 27 | Mickey Brantley | .10 | .08 |
| 28 | Mike Stanley | .20 | .15 |
| 29 | Jerry Browne | .10 | .08 |
| 30 | Todd Benzinger(FC) | .30 | .25 |
| 31 | Fred McGriff | 4.00 | 3.00 |
| 32 | Mike Henneman(FC) | .35 | .25 |
| 33 | Casey Candaele | .10 | .08 |
| 34 | Dave Magadan | .50 | .40 |
| 35 | David Cone | 3.00 | 2.25 |
| 36 | Mike Jackson(FC) | .20 | .15 |
| 37 | John Mitchell(FC) | .20 | .15 |
| 38 | Mike Dunne(FC) | .15 | .11 |
| 39 | John Smiley(FC) | 1.00 | .70 |
| 40 | Joe Magrane(FC) | .60 | .45 |
| 41 | Jim Lindeman | .10 | .08 |
| 42 | Shane Mack(FC) | 1.00 | .70 |
| 43 | Stan Jefferson | .10 | .08 |
| 44 | Benito Santiago | .80 | .60 |
| 45 | Matt Williams(FC) | 3.00 | 2.25 |
| 46 | Dave Meads(FC) | .20 | .15 |
| 47 | Rafael Palmeiro | 3.00 | 2.25 |
| 48 | Bill Long(FC) | .20 | .15 |
| 49 | Bob Brower | .10 | .08 |
| 50 | James Steels(FC) | .15 | .11 |
| 51 | Paul Noce(FC) | .15 | .11 |
| 52 | Greg Maddux | 4.00 | 3.00 |
| 53 | Jeff Musselman | .15 | .11 |
| 54 | Brian Holton | .15 | .11 |
| 55 | Chuck Jackson(FC) | .20 | .15 |
| 56 | Checklist 1-56 | .10 | .08 |

## 1988 Donruss

The 1988 Donruss set consists of 660 cards, each measuring 2-1/2" by 3-1/2" in size. The card fronts feature a full-color photo surrounded by a colorful border - alternating stripes of black, red, black, blue, black, blue, black, red and black (in that order), separated by soft-focus edges and air-brushed fades. The player's name and position appear in a red band at the bottom of the card. The Donruss logo is situated in the upper left corner of the card, while the team logo is located in the lower right corner. For the seventh consecutive season, Donruss included a subset of "Diamond Kings" cards (#'s 1-27) in the issue. And for the fifth straight year, Donruss incorporated their highly popular "Rated Rookies" (card #'s 28-47) with the set.

| | | MT | NR MT |
|---|---|---|---|
| | Complete Set: | 15.00 | 11.00 |
| | Common Player | .05 | .04 |
| 1 | Mark McGwire (DK) | .25 | .20 |
| 2 | Tim Raines (DK) | .25 | .20 |
| 3 | Benito Santiago (DK) | .30 | .25 |
| 4 | Alan Trammell (DK) | .25 | .20 |
| 5 | Danny Tartabull (DK) | .20 | .15 |
| 6 | Ron Darling (DK) | .12 | .09 |
| 7 | Paul Molitor (DK) | .12 | .09 |
| 8 | Devon White (DK) | .10 | .08 |
| 9 | Andre Dawson (DK) | .20 | .15 |
| 10 | Julio Franco (DK) | .10 | .08 |
| 11 | Scott Fletcher (DK) | .07 | .05 |
| 12 | Tony Fernandez (DK) | .12 | .09 |
| 13 | Shane Rawley (DK) | .07 | .05 |
| 14 | Kal Daniels (DK) | .20 | .15 |
| 15 | Jack Clark (DK) | .15 | .11 |
| 16 | Dwight Evans (DK) | .12 | .09 |
| 17 | Tommy John (DK) | .15 | .11 |
| 18 | Andy Van Slyke (DK) | .15 | .11 |
| 19 | Gary Gaetti (DK) | .12 | .09 |
| 20 | Mark Langston (DK) | .10 | .08 |
| 21 | Will Clark (DK) | .60 | .45 |
| 22 | Glenn Hubbard (DK) | .07 | .05 |
| 23 | Billy Hatcher (DK) | .07 | .05 |
| 24 | Bob Welch (DK) | .10 | .08 |
| 25 | Ivan Calderon (DK) | .10 | .08 |
| 26 | Cal Ripken, Jr. (DK) | .35 | .25 |
| 27 | Checklist 1-27 | .05 | .04 |
| 28 | *Mackey Sasser* (RR)(FC) | .20 | .15 |
| 29 | *Jeff Treadway* (RR)(FC) | .25 | .20 |

| | | MT | NR MT |
|---|---|---|---|
| 30 | Mike Campbell (RR)(FC) | .12 | .09 |
| 31 | Lance Johnson (RR)(FC) | .50 | .40 |
| 32 | Nelson Liriano (RR)(FC) | .15 | .11 |
| 33 | Shawn Abner (RR)(FC) | .20 | .15 |
| 34 | Roberto Alomar (RR)(FC) | 4.00 | 3.00 |
| 35 | Shawn Hillegas (RR)(FC) | .25 | .20 |
| 36 | Joey Meyer (RR) | .20 | .15 |
| 37 | Kevin Elster (RR) | .30 | .25 |
| 38 | Jose Lind (RR)(FC) | .30 | .25 |
| 39 | Kirt Manwaring (RR)(FC) | .20 | .15 |
| 40 | Mark Grace (RR)(FC) | 1.25 | .90 |
| 41 | Jody Reed (RR)(FC) | .40 | .30 |
| 42 | John Farrell (RR)(FC) | .15 | .11 |
| 43 | Al Leiter (RR)(FC) | .12 | .09 |
| 44 | Gary Thurman (RR)(FC) | .20 | .15 |
| 45 | Vicente Palacios (RR)(FC) | .15 | .11 |
| 46 | Eddie Williams (RR)(FC) | .15 | .11 |
| 47 | Jack McDowell (RR)(FC) | 1.25 | .90 |
| 48 | Ken Dixon | .05 | .04 |
| 49 | Mike Birkbeck | .07 | .05 |
| 50 | Eric King | .07 | .05 |
| 51 | Roger Clemens | .60 | .45 |
| 52 | Pat Clements | .05 | .04 |
| 53 | Fernando Valenzuela | .15 | .11 |
| 54 | Mark Gubicza | .12 | .09 |
| 55 | Jay Howell | .07 | .05 |
| 56 | Floyd Youmans | .05 | .04 |
| 57 | Ed Correa | .05 | .04 |
| 58 | DeWayne Buice | .15 | .11 |
| 59 | Jose DeLeon | .07 | .05 |
| 60 | Danny Cox | .07 | .05 |
| 61 | Nolan Ryan | .50 | .40 |
| 62 | Steve Bedrosian | .12 | .09 |
| 63 | Tom Browning | .10 | .08 |
| 64 | Mark Davis | .05 | .04 |
| 65 | R.J. Reynolds | .05 | .04 |
| 66 | Kevin Mitchell | .60 | .45 |
| 67 | Ken Oberkfell | .05 | .04 |
| 68 | Rick Sutcliffe | .10 | .08 |
| 69 | Dwight Gooden | .60 | .45 |
| 70 | Scott Bankhead | .07 | .05 |
| 71 | Bert Blyleven | .12 | .09 |
| 72 | Jimmy Key | .10 | .08 |
| 73 | Les Straker | .15 | .11 |
| 74 | Jim Clancy | .07 | .05 |
| 75 | Mike Moore | .05 | .04 |
| 76 | Ron Darling | .12 | .09 |
| 77 | Ed Lynch | .05 | .04 |
| 78 | Dale Murphy | .40 | .30 |
| 79 | Doug Drabek | .07 | .05 |
| 80 | Scott Garrelts | .05 | .04 |
| 81 | Ed Whitson | .05 | .04 |
| 82 | Rob Murphy | .07 | .05 |

| | | MT | NR MT |
|---|---|---|---|
| 83 | Shane Rawley | .07 | .05 |
| 84 | Greg Mathews | .07 | .05 |
| 85 | Jim Deshaies | .07 | .05 |
| 86 | Mike Witt | .07 | .05 |
| 87 | Donnie Hill | .05 | .04 |
| 88 | Jeff Reed | .05 | .04 |
| 89 | Mike Boddicker | .07 | .05 |
| 90 | Ted Higuera | .10 | .08 |
| 91 | Walt Terrell | .07 | .05 |
| 92 | Bob Stanley | .05 | .04 |
| 93 | Dave Righetti | .15 | .11 |
| 94 | Orel Hershiser | .25 | .20 |
| 95 | Chris Bando | .05 | .04 |
| 96 | Bret Saberhagen | .15 | .11 |
| 97 | Curt Young | .07 | .05 |
| 98 | Tim Burke | .05 | .04 |
| 99 | Charlie Hough | .07 | .05 |
| 100a | Checklist 28-137 | .05 | .04 |
| 100b | Checklist 28-133 | .10 | .08 |
| 101 | Bobby Witt | .10 | .08 |
| 102 | George Brett | .40 | .30 |
| 103 | Mickey Tettleton | .25 | .20 |
| 104 | Scott Bailes | .07 | .05 |
| 105 | Mike Pagliarulo | .10 | .08 |
| 106 | Mike Scioscia | .07 | .05 |
| 107 | Tom Brookens | .05 | .04 |
| 108 | Ray Knight | .07 | .05 |
| 109 | Dan Plesac | .10 | .08 |
| 110 | Wally Joyner | .30 | .25 |
| 111 | Bob Forsch | .07 | .05 |
| 112 | Mike Scott | .12 | .09 |
| 113 | Kevin Gross | .07 | .05 |
| 114 | Benito Santiago | .35 | .25 |
| 115 | Bob Kipper | .05 | .04 |
| 116 | Mike Krukow | .07 | .05 |
| 117 | Chris Bosio | .07 | .05 |
| 118 | Sid Fernandez | .10 | .08 |
| 119 | Jody Davis | .07 | .05 |
| 120 | Mike Morgan | .05 | .04 |
| 121 | Mark Eichhorn | .07 | .05 |
| 122 | Jeff Reardon | .10 | .08 |
| 123 | John Franco | .10 | .08 |
| 124 | Richard Dotson | .07 | .05 |
| 125 | Eric Bell | .05 | .04 |
| 126 | Juan Nieves | .07 | .05 |
| 127 | Jack Morris | .20 | .15 |
| 128 | Rick Rhoden | .07 | .05 |
| 129 | Rich Gedman | .07 | .05 |
| 130 | Ken Howell | .05 | .04 |
| 131 | Brook Jacoby | .10 | .08 |
| 132 | Danny Jackson | .12 | .09 |
| 133 | Gene Nelson | .05 | .04 |
| 134 | Neal Heaton | .05 | .04 |
| 135 | Willie Fraser | .05 | .04 |
| 136 | Jose Guzman | .07 | .05 |
| 137 | Ozzie Guillen | .07 | .05 |
| 138 | Bob Knepper | .07 | .05 |
| 139 | Mike Jackson | .20 | .15 |
| 140 | Joe Magrane | .30 | .25 |
| 141 | Jimmy Jones | .07 | .05 |
| 142 | Ted Power | .05 | .04 |
| 143 | Ozzie Virgil | .05 | .04 |
| 144 | Felix Fermin(FC) | .15 | .11 |
| 145 | Kelly Downs | .10 | .08 |
| 146 | Shawon Dunston | .10 | .08 |
| 147 | Scott Bradley | .05 | .04 |
| 148 | Dave Stieb | .10 | .08 |

| | | MT | NR MT | | | | MT | NR MT |
|---|---|---|---|---|---|---|---|---|
| 149 | Frank Viola | .15 | .11 | | 214 | Jim Gantner | .05 | .04 |
| 150 | Terry Kennedy | .07 | .05 | | 215 | Chet Lemon | .07 | .05 |
| 151 | Bill Wegman | .05 | .04 | | 216 | Dwight Evans | .12 | .09 |
| 152 | *Matt Nokes* | .50 | .40 | | 217 | Don Mattingly | .80 | .60 |
| 153 | Wade Boggs | .60 | .45 | | 218 | Franklin Stubbs | .07 | .05 |
| 154 | Wayne Tolleson | .05 | .04 | | 219 | Pat Tabler | .07 | .05 |
| 155 | Mariano Duncan | .05 | .04 | | 220 | Bo Jackson | .50 | .40 |
| 156 | Julio Franco | .10 | .08 | | 221 | Tony Phillips | .05 | .04 |
| 157 | Charlie Leibrandt | .07 | .05 | | 222 | Tim Wallach | .10 | .08 |
| 158 | Terry Steinbach | .10 | .08 | | 223 | Ruben Sierra | .60 | .45 |
| 159 | Mike Fitzgerald | .05 | .04 | | 224 | Steve Buechele | .05 | .04 |
| 160 | Jack Lazorko | .05 | .04 | | 225 | Frank White | .07 | .05 |
| 161 | Mitch Williams | .07 | .05 | | 226 | Alfredo Griffin | .05 | .05 |
| 162 | Greg Walker | .07 | .05 | | 227 | Greg Swindell | .20 | .15 |
| 163 | Alan Ashby | .05 | .04 | | 228 | Willie Randolph | .07 | .05 |
| 164 | Tony Gwynn | .35 | .25 | | 229 | Mike Marshall | .12 | .09 |
| 165 | Bruce Ruffin | .07 | .05 | | 230 | Alan Trammell | .25 | .20 |
| 166 | Ron Robinson | .05 | .04 | | 231 | Eddie Murray | .35 | .25 |
| 167 | Zane Smith | .07 | .05 | | 232 | Dale Sveum | .07 | .05 |
| 168 | Junior Ortiz | .05 | .04 | | 233 | Dick Schofield | .05 | .04 |
| 169 | Jamie Moyer | .07 | .05 | | 234 | Jose Oquendo | .05 | .04 |
| 170 | Tony Pena | .07 | .05 | | 235 | Bill Doran | .07 | .05 |
| 171 | Cal Ripken | .35 | .25 | | 236 | Milt Thompson | .05 | .04 |
| 172 | B.J. Surhoff | .12 | .09 | | 237 | Marvell Wynne | .05 | .04 |
| 173 | Lou Whitaker | .25 | .20 | | 238 | Bobby Bonilla | .40 | .30 |
| 174 | *Ellis Burks* | .70 | .50 | | 239 | Chris Speier | .05 | .04 |
| 175 | Ron Guidry | .15 | .11 | | 240 | Glenn Braggs | .10 | .08 |
| 176 | Steve Sax | .15 | .11 | | 241 | Wally Backman | .07 | .05 |
| 177 | Danny Tartabull | .20 | .15 | | 242 | Ryne Sandberg | .50 | .40 |
| 178 | Carney Lansford | .10 | .08 | | 243 | Phil Bradley | .10 | .08 |
| 179 | Casey Candaele | .05 | .04 | | 244 | Kelly Gruber | .05 | .04 |
| 180 | Scott Fletcher | .07 | .05 | | 245 | Tom Brunansky | .10 | .08 |
| 181 | Mark McLemore | .05 | .04 | | 246 | Ron Oester | .05 | .04 |
| 182 | Ivan Calderon | .10 | .08 | | 247 | Bobby Thigpen | .10 | .08 |
| 183 | Jack Clark | .15 | .11 | | 248 | Fred Lynn | .15 | .11 |
| 184 | Glenn Davis | .15 | .11 | | 249 | Paul Molitor | .12 | .09 |
| 185 | Luis Aguayo | .05 | .04 | | 250 | Darrell Evans | .10 | .08 |
| 186 | Bo Diaz | .07 | .05 | | 251 | Gary Ward | .07 | .05 |
| 187 | Stan Jefferson | .07 | .05 | | 252 | Bruce Hurst | .10 | .08 |
| 188 | Sid Bream | .07 | .05 | | 253 | Bob Welch | .10 | .08 |
| 189 | Bob Brenly | .05 | .04 | | 254 | Joe Carter | .12 | .09 |
| 190 | Dion James | .07 | .05 | | 255 | Willie Wilson | .10 | .08 |
| 191 | Leon Durham | .07 | .05 | | 256 | Mark McGwire | .50 | .40 |
| 192 | Jesse Orosco | .07 | .05 | | 257 | Mitch Webster | .07 | .05 |
| 193 | Alvin Davis | .12 | .09 | | 258 | Brian Downing | .07 | .05 |
| 194 | Gary Gaetti | .12 | .09 | | 259 | Mike Stanley | .10 | .08 |
| 195 | Fred McGriff | .40 | .30 | | 260 | Carlton Fisk | .20 | .15 |
| 196 | Steve Lombardozzi | .05 | .04 | | 261 | Billy Hatcher | .07 | .05 |
| 197 | Rance Mulliniks | .05 | .04 | | 262 | Glenn Wilson | .05 | .05 |
| 198 | Rey Quinones | .05 | .04 | | 263 | Ozzie Smith | .15 | .11 |
| 199 | Gary Carter | .25 | .20 | | 264 | Randy Ready | .05 | .04 |
| 200a | Checklist 138-247 | .05 | .04 | | 265 | Kurt Stillwell | .10 | .08 |
| 200b | Checklist 134-239 | .10 | .08 | | 266 | David Palmer | .05 | .04 |
| 201 | Keith Moreland | .07 | .05 | | 267 | Mike Diaz | .05 | .05 |
| 202 | Ken Griffey | .07 | .05 | | 268 | Rob Thompson | .07 | .05 |
| 203 | *Tommy Gregg*(FC) | | | | 269 | Andre Dawson | .20 | .15 |
| | | .20 | .15 | | 270 | Lee Guetterman | .05 | .04 |
| 204 | Will Clark | 1.00 | .70 | | 271 | Willie Upshaw | .07 | .05 |
| 205 | John Kruk | .10 | .08 | | 272 | Randy Bush | .05 | .04 |
| 206 | Buddy Bell | .07 | .05 | | 273 | Larry Sheets | .05 | .05 |
| 207 | Von Hayes | .07 | .05 | | 274 | Rob Deer | .07 | .05 |
| 208 | Tommy Herr | .07 | .05 | | 275 | Kirk Gibson | .20 | .15 |
| 209 | Craig Reynolds | .05 | .04 | | 276 | Marty Barrett | .07 | .05 |
| 210 | Gary Pettis | .05 | .04 | | 277 | Rickey Henderson | .40 | .30 |
| 211 | Harold Baines | .12 | .09 | | 278 | Pedro Guerrero | .15 | .11 |
| 212 | Vance Law | .07 | .05 | | 279 | Brett Butler | .07 | .05 |
| 213 | Ken Gerhart | .07 | .05 | | 280 | Kevin Seitzer | .40 | .30 |

| | MT | NR MT |
|---|---|---|
| 281 Mike Davis | .07 | .05 |
| 282 Andres Galarraga | .15 | .11 |
| 283 Devon White | .30 | .25 |
| 284 Pete O'Brien | .07 | .05 |
| 285 Jerry Hairston | .05 | .04 |
| 286 Kevin Bass | .07 | .05 |
| 287 Carmelo Martinez | .07 | .05 |
| 288 Juan Samuel | .12 | .09 |
| 289 Kal Daniels | .20 | .15 |
| 290 Albert Hall | .05 | .04 |
| 291 Andy Van Slyke | .12 | .09 |
| 292 Lee Smith | .10 | .08 |
| 293 Vince Coleman | .20 | .15 |
| 294 Tom Niedenfuer | .07 | .05 |
| 295 Robin Yount | .30 | .25 |
| 296 *Jeff Robinson* | .15 | .11 |
| 297 *Todd Benzinger* | .30 | .25 |
| 298 Dave Winfield | .30 | .25 |
| 299 Mickey Hatcher | .05 | .04 |
| 300a Checklist 248-357 | .05 | .04 |
| 300b Checklist 240-345 | .10 | .08 |
| 301 Bud Black | .05 | .04 |
| 302 Jose Canseco | .80 | .60 |
| 303 Tom Foley | .05 | .04 |
| 304 Pete Incaviglia | .15 | .11 |
| 305 Bob Boone | .07 | .05 |
| 306 *Bill Long* | .20 | .15 |
| 307 Willie McGee | .12 | .09 |
| 308 *Ken Caminiti*(FC) | | |
| | .30 | .25 |
| 309 Darren Daulton | .05 | .04 |
| 310 Tracy Jones | .12 | .09 |
| 311 Greg Booker | .07 | .05 |
| 312 Mike LaValliere | .07 | .05 |
| 313 Chili Davis | .07 | .05 |
| 314 Glenn Hubbard | .05 | .04 |
| 315 *Paul Noce* | .10 | .08 |
| 316 Keith Hernandez | .20 | .15 |
| 317 Mark Langston | .12 | .09 |
| 318 Keith Atherton | .05 | .04 |
| 319 Tony Fernandez | .12 | .09 |
| 320 Kent Hrbek | .15 | .11 |
| 321 John Cerutti | .07 | .05 |
| 322 Mike Kingery | .05 | .04 |
| 323 Dave Magadan | .12 | .09 |
| 324 Rafael Palmeiro | .40 | .30 |
| 325 Jeff Dedmon | .05 | .04 |
| 326 Barry Bonds | .40 | .30 |
| 327 Jeffrey Leonard | .07 | .05 |
| 328 Tim Flannery | .05 | .04 |
| 329 Dave Concepcion | .07 | .05 |
| 330 Mike Schmidt | .50 | .40 |
| 331 Bill Dawley | .05 | .04 |
| 332 Larry Andersen | .05 | .04 |
| 333 Jack Howell | .07 | .05 |
| 334 *Ken Williams* | .20 | .15 |
| 335 Bryn Smith | .05 | .04 |
| 336 *Billy Ripken* | .25 | .20 |
| 337 Greg Brock | .07 | .05 |
| 338 Mike Heath | .05 | .04 |
| 339 Mike Greenwell | .25 | .20 |
| 340 Claudell Washington | .07 | .05 |
| 341 Jose Gonzalez | .05 | .04 |
| 342 Mel Hall | .07 | .05 |
| 343 Jim Eisenreich | .07 | .05 |
| 344 Tony Bernazard | .05 | .04 |
| 345 Tim Raines | .25 | .20 |

| | MT | NR MT |
|---|---|---|
| 346 Bob Brower | .07 | .05 |
| 347 Larry Parrish | .07 | .05 |
| 348 Thad Bosley | .05 | .04 |
| 349 Dennis Eckersley | .12 | .09 |
| 350 Cory Snyder | .20 | .15 |
| 351 Rick Cerone | .05 | .04 |
| 352 John Shelby | .05 | .04 |
| 353 Larry Herndon | .05 | .04 |
| 354 John Habyan | .05 | .04 |
| 355 *Chuck Crim* | .12 | .09 |
| 356 Gus Polidor | .05 | .04 |
| 357 Ken Dayley | .05 | .04 |
| 358 Danny Darwin | .05 | .04 |
| 359 Lance Parrish | .15 | .11 |
| 360 *James Steels* | .12 | .09 |
| 361 *Al Pedrique*(FC) | .15 | .11 |
| 362 Mike Aldrete | .07 | .05 |
| 363 Juan Castillo | .05 | .04 |
| 364 Len Dykstra | .10 | .08 |
| 365 Luis Quinones | .05 | .04 |
| 366 Jim Presley | .10 | .08 |
| 367 Lloyd Moseby | .07 | .05 |
| 368 Kirby Puckett | .50 | .40 |
| 369 Eric Davis | .60 | .45 |
| 370 Gary Redus | .05 | .04 |
| 371 Dave Schmidt | .05 | .04 |
| 372 Mark Clear | .05 | .04 |
| 373 Dave Bergman | .05 | .04 |
| 374 Charles Hudson | .05 | .04 |
| 375 Calvin Schiraldi | .05 | .04 |
| 376 Alex Trevino | .05 | .04 |
| 377 Tom Candiotti | .05 | .04 |
| 378 Steve Farr | .05 | .04 |
| 379 Mike Gallego | .05 | .04 |
| 380 Andy McGaffigan | .05 | .04 |
| 381 Kirk McCaskill | .07 | .05 |
| 382 Oddibe McDowell | .07 | .05 |
| 383 Floyd Bannister | .07 | .05 |
| 384 Denny Walling | .05 | .04 |
| 385 Don Carman | .07 | .05 |
| 386 Todd Worrell | .10 | .08 |
| 387 Eric Show | .07 | .05 |
| 388 Dave Parker | .20 | .15 |
| 389 Rick Mahler | .05 | .04 |
| 390 *Mike Dunne* | .15 | .11 |
| 391 Candy Maldonado | .07 | .05 |
| 392 Bob Dernier | .05 | .04 |
| 393 Dave Valle | .05 | .04 |
| 394 Ernie Whitt | .07 | .05 |
| 395 Juan Berenguer | .05 | .04 |
| 396 Mike Young | .05 | .04 |
| 397 Mike Felder | .05 | .04 |
| 398 Willie Hernandez | .07 | .05 |
| 399 Jim Rice | .30 | .25 |
| 400a Checklist 358-467 | .05 | .04 |
| 400b Checklist 346-451 | .10 | .08 |
| 401 Tommy John | .15 | .11 |
| 402 Brian Holton | .07 | .05 |
| 403 Carmen Castillo | .05 | .04 |
| 404 Jamie Quirk | .05 | .04 |
| 405 Dwayne Murphy | .07 | .05 |
| 406 *Jeff Parrett*(FC) | .25 | .20 |
| 407 Don Sutton | .20 | .15 |
| 408 Jerry Browne | .07 | .05 |
| 409 Jim Winn | .05 | .04 |
| 410 Dave Smith | .07 | .05 |
| 411 *Shane Mack* | .15 | .11 |

| | MT | NR MT | | | MT | NR MT |
|---|---|---|---|---|---|---|
| 412 | Greg Gross | .05 | .04 | 476 | Dan Petry | .07 | .05 |
| 413 | Nick Esasky | .07 | .05 | 477 | *Carl Nichols*(FC) | .12 | .09 |
| 414 | Damaso Garcia | .05 | .04 | 478 | Ernest Riles | .05 | .04 |
| 415 | Brian Fisher | .07 | .05 | 479 | George Hendrick | .07 | .05 |
| 416 | Brian Dayett | .05 | .04 | 480 | John Morris | .05 | .04 |
| 417 | Curt Ford | .05 | .04 | 481 | *Manny* | | |
| 418 | *Mark Williamson* | .12 | .09 | | *Hernandez*(FC) | .10 | .08 |
| 419 | Bill Schroeder | .05 | .04 | 482 | Jeff Stone | .05 | .04 |
| 420 | *Mike Henneman* | .25 | .20 | 483 | Chris Brown | .07 | .05 |
| 421 | *John Marzano*(FC) | | | 484 | Mike Bielecki | .05 | .04 |
| | | .20 | .15 | 485 | Dave Dravecky | .07 | .05 |
| 422 | Ron Kittle | .07 | .05 | 486 | Rick Manning | .05 | .04 |
| 423 | Matt Young | .05 | .04 | 487 | Bill Almon | .05 | .04 |
| 424 | Steve Balboni | .07 | .05 | 488 | Jim Sundberg | .07 | .05 |
| 425 | *Luis Polonia* | .30 | .25 | 489 | Ken Phelps | .07 | .05 |
| 426 | Randy St. Claire | .05 | .04 | 490 | Tom Henke | .07 | .05 |
| 427 | Greg Harris | .05 | .04 | 491 | Dan Gladden | .05 | .04 |
| 428 | Johnny Ray | .07 | .05 | 492 | Barry Larkin | .40 | .30 |
| 429 | Ray Searage | .05 | .04 | 493 | *Fred Manrique*(FC) | | |
| 430 | Ricky Horton | .07 | .05 | | | .15 | .11 |
| 431 | *Gerald Young*(FC) | | | 494 | Mike Griffin | .05 | .04 |
| | | .20 | .15 | 495 | *Mark Knudson*(FC) | | |
| 432 | Rick Schu | .05 | .04 | | | .10 | .08 |
| 433 | Paul O'Neill | .07 | .05 | 496 | Bill Madlock | .10 | .08 |
| 434 | Rich Gossage | .15 | .11 | 497 | Tim Stoddard | .05 | .04 |
| 435 | John Cangelosi | .05 | .04 | 498 | *Sam Horn*(FC) | .30 | .25 |
| 436 | Mike LaCoss | .05 | .04 | 499 | *Tracy Woodson*(FC) | | |
| 437 | Gerald Perry | .10 | .08 | | | .15 | .11 |
| 438 | Dave Martinez | .07 | .05 | 500a | Checklist 468-577 | .05 | .04 |
| 439 | Darryl Strawberry | .35 | .25 | 500b | Checklist 452-557 | .10 | .04 |
| 440 | John Moses | .05 | .04 | 501 | Ken Schrom | .05 | .04 |
| 441 | Greg Gagne | .05 | .04 | 502 | Angel Salazar | .05 | .04 |
| 442 | Jesse Barfield | .12 | .09 | 503 | Eric Plunk | .05 | .04 |
| 443 | George Frazier | .05 | .04 | 504 | Joe Hesketh | .05 | .04 |
| 444 | Garth Iorg | .05 | .04 | 505 | Greg Minton | .05 | .04 |
| 445 | Ed Nunez | .05 | .04 | 506 | Geno Petralli | .05 | .04 |
| 446 | Rick Aguilera | .05 | .04 | 507 | Bob James | .05 | .04 |
| 447 | Jerry Mumphrey | .05 | .04 | 508 | *Robbie Wine*(FC) | .12 | .09 |
| 448 | Rafael Ramirez | .05 | .04 | 509 | Jeff Calhoun | .05 | .04 |
| 449 | *John Smiley* | .40 | .30 | 510 | Steve Lake | .05 | .04 |
| 450 | Atlee Hammaker | .05 | .04 | 511 | Mark Grant | .05 | .04 |
| 451 | Lance McCullers | .07 | .05 | 512 | Frank Williams | .05 | .04 |
| 452 | Guy Hoffman(FC) | .07 | .05 | 513 | *Jeff Blauser*(FC) | .30 | .25 |
| 453 | Chris James | .12 | .09 | 514 | Bob Walk | .05 | .04 |
| 454 | Terry Pendleton | .07 | .05 | 515 | Craig Lefferts | .05 | .04 |
| 455 | *Dave Meads* | .15 | .11 | 516 | Manny Trillo | .07 | .05 |
| 456 | Bill Buckner | .10 | .08 | 517 | Jerry Reed | .05 | .04 |
| 457 | *John Pawlowski*(FC) | | | 518 | Rick Leach | .05 | .04 |
| | | .10 | .08 | 519 | *Mark Davidson* | .12 | .09 |
| 458 | Bob Sebra | .05 | .04 | 520 | *Jeff Ballard*(FC) | .15 | .11 |
| 459 | Jim Dwyer | .05 | .04 | 521 | *Dave Stapleton*(FC) | | |
| 460 | *Jay Aldrich*(FC) | .12 | .09 | | | .10 | .08 |
| 461 | Frank Tanana | .07 | .05 | 522 | Pat Sheridan | .05 | .04 |
| 462 | Oil Can Boyd | .07 | .05 | 523 | Al Nipper | .05 | .04 |
| 463 | Dan Pasqua | .10 | .08 | 524 | Steve Trout | .05 | .04 |
| 464 | *Tim Crews*(FC) | .15 | .11 | 525 | Jeff Hamilton | .07 | .05 |
| 465 | Andy Allanson | .07 | .05 | 526 | *Tommy Hinzo*(FC) | | |
| 466 | *Bill Pecota*(FC) | .15 | .11 | | | .15 | .11 |
| 467 | Steve Ontiveros | .05 | .04 | 527 | Lonnie Smith | .07 | .05 |
| 468 | Hubie Brooks | .10 | .08 | 528 | *Greg Cadaret*(FC) | | |
| 469 | *Paul Kilgus*(FC) | .15 | .11 | | | .20 | .15 |
| 470 | Dale Mohorcic | .05 | .04 | 529 | Rob McClure (Bob) | .05 | .04 |
| 471 | Dan Quisenberry | .07 | .05 | 530 | Chuck Finley | .10 | .08 |
| 472 | Dave Stewart | .10 | .08 | 531 | Jeff Russell | .05 | .04 |
| 473 | Dave Clark | .07 | .05 | 532 | Steve Lyons | .05 | .04 |
| 474 | Joel Skinner | .05 | .04 | 533 | Terry Puhl | .05 | .04 |
| 475 | Dave Anderson | .05 | .04 | 534 | *Eric Nolte*(FC) | .15 | .11 |

| | | MT | NR MT |
|---|---|---|---|
| 535 | Kent Tekulve | .07 | .05 |
| 536 | Pat Pacillo(FC) | .15 | .11 |
| 537 | Charlie Puleo | .05 | .04 |
| 538 | Tom Prince(FC) | .15 | .11 |
| 539 | Greg Maddux | .15 | .11 |
| 540 | Jim Lindeman | .07 | .05 |
| 541 | Pete Stanicek(FC) | | |
| | | .15 | .11 |
| 542 | Steve Kiefer | .05 | .04 |
| 543 | Jim Morrison | .05 | .04 |
| 544 | Spike Owen | .05 | .04 |
| 545 | Jay Buhner(FC) | .50 | .40 |
| 546 | Mike Devereaux(FC) | | |
| | | .70 | .50 |
| 547 | Jerry Don Gleaton | .05 | .04 |
| 548 | Jose Rijo | .07 | .05 |
| 549 | Dennis Martinez | .05 | .04 |
| 550 | Mike Loynd | .05 | .04 |
| 551 | Darrell Miller | .05 | .04 |
| 552 | Dave LaPoint | .07 | .05 |
| 553 | John Tudor | .10 | .08 |
| 554 | Rocky Childress(FC) | | |
| | | .12 | .09 |
| 555 | Wally Ritchie(FC) | | |
| | | .15 | .11 |
| 556 | Terry McGriff | .05 | .04 |
| 557 | Dave Leiper | .05 | .04 |
| 558 | Jeff Robinson | .07 | .05 |
| 559 | Jose Uribe | .05 | .04 |
| 560 | Ted Simmons | .10 | .08 |
| 561 | Lester Lancaster | .15 | .11 |
| 562 | Keith Miller(FC) | .25 | .20 |
| 563 | Harold Reynolds | .07 | .05 |
| 564 | Gene Larkin | .20 | .15 |
| 565 | Cecil Fielder | .70 | .50 |
| 566 | Roy Smalley | .05 | .04 |
| 567 | Duane Ward | .07 | .05 |
| 568 | Bill Wilkinson(FC) | | |
| | | .15 | .11 |
| 569 | Howard Johnson | .10 | .08 |
| 570 | Frank DiPino | .05 | .04 |
| 571 | Pete Smith(FC) | .20 | .15 |
| 572 | Darnell Coles | .07 | .05 |
| 573 | Don Robinson | .07 | .05 |
| 574 | Rob Nelson | .05 | .04 |
| 575 | Dennis Rasmussen | .10 | .08 |
| 576 | Steve Jeltz (photo actually Juan Samuel) | .05 | .04 |
| 577 | Tom Pagnozzi(FC) | | |
| | | .30 | .25 |
| 578 | Ty Gainey | .05 | .04 |
| 579 | Gary Lucas | .05 | .04 |
| 580 | Ron Hassey | .05 | .04 |
| 581 | Herm Winningham | .05 | .04 |
| 582 | Rene Gonzales(FC) | | |
| | | .15 | .11 |
| 583 | Brad Komminsk | .05 | .04 |
| 584 | Doyle Alexander | .07 | .05 |
| 585 | Jeff Sellers | .07 | .05 |
| 586 | Bill Gullickson | .05 | .04 |
| 587 | Tim Belcher(FC) | .35 | .25 |
| 588 | Doug Jones(FC) | .25 | .20 |
| 589 | Melido Perez(FC) | | |
| | | .30 | .25 |
| 590 | Rick Honeycutt | .05 | .04 |
| 591 | Pascual Perez | .07 | .05 |
| 592 | Curt Wilkerson | .05 | .04 |

| | | MT | NR MT |
|---|---|---|---|
| 593 | Steve Howe | .07 | .05 |
| 594 | John Davis(FC) | .15 | .11 |
| 595 | Storm Davis | .10 | .08 |
| 596 | Sammy Stewart | .05 | .04 |
| 597 | Neil Allen | .05 | .04 |
| 598 | Alejandro Pena | .07 | .05 |
| 599 | Mark Thurmond | .05 | .04 |
| 600a | Checklist 578-BC26 | .25 | .04 |
| 600b | Checklist 558-660 | .10 | .08 |
| 601 | Jose Mesa(FC) | .20 | .15 |
| 602 | Don August(FC) | .15 | .11 |
| 603 | Terry Leach | .10 | .08 |
| 604 | Tom Newell(FC) | .15 | .11 |
| 605 | Randall Byers(FC) | | |
| | | .15 | .11 |
| 606 | Jim Gott | .05 | .04 |
| 607 | Harry Spilman | .05 | .04 |
| 608 | John Candelaria | .07 | .05 |
| 609 | Mike Brumley(FC) | | |
| | | .15 | .11 |
| 610 | Mickey Brantley | .07 | .05 |
| 611 | Jose Nunez(FC) | .15 | .11 |
| 612 | Tom Nieto | .05 | .04 |
| 613 | Rick Reuschel | .10 | .08 |
| 614 | Lee Mazzilli | .12 | .09 |
| 615 | Scott Lusader(FC) | | |
| | | .15 | .11 |
| 616 | Bobby Meacham | .05 | .04 |
| 617 | Kevin McReynolds | .15 | .11 |
| 618 | Gene Garber | .05 | .04 |
| 619 | Barry Lyons(FC) | .15 | .11 |
| 620 | Randy Myers | .10 | .08 |
| 621 | Donnie Moore | .05 | .04 |
| 622 | Domingo Ramos | .05 | .04 |
| 623 | Ed Romero | .05 | .04 |
| 624 | Greg Myers(FC) | .25 | .20 |
| 625 | Ripken Baseball Family (Billy Ripken, Cal Ripken, Jr., Cal Ripken, Sr.) | .15 | .11 |
| 626 | Pat Perry | .05 | .04 |
| 627 | Andres Thomas | .10 | .08 |
| 628 | Matt Williams | 2.00 | 1.50 |
| 629 | Dave Hengel(FC) | .15 | .11 |
| 630 | Jeff Musselman | .07 | .05 |
| 631 | Tim Laudner | .05 | .04 |
| 632 | Bob Ojeda | .07 | .05 |
| 633 | Rafael Santana | .05 | .04 |
| 634 | Wes Gardner(FC) | | |
| | | .15 | .11 |
| 635 | Roberto Kelly(FC) | | |
| | | 1.25 | .90 |
| 636 | Mike Flanagan | .12 | .09 |
| 637 | Jay Bell(FC) | .50 | .40 |
| 638 | Bob Melvin | .05 | .04 |
| 639 | Damon Berryhill(FC) | | |
| | | .20 | .15 |
| 640 | David Wells(FC) | .25 | .20 |
| 641 | Stan Musial Puzzle Card | | |
| | | .05 | .04 |
| 642 | Doug Sisk | .05 | .04 |
| 643 | Keith Hughes(FC) | | |
| | | .20 | .15 |
| 644 | Tom Glavine(FC) | | |
| | | 2.00 | 1.50 |
| 645 | Al Newman | .05 | .04 |
| 646 | Scott Sanderson | .05 | .04 |
| 647 | Scott Terry | .10 | .08 |

| | | MT | NR MT |
|---|---|---|---|
| 648 | Tim Teufel | .12 | .09 |
| 649 | Garry Templeton | .12 | .09 |
| 650 | Manny Lee | .05 | .04 |
| 651 | Roger McDowell | .10 | .08 |
| 652 | Mookie Wilson | .15 | .11 |
| 653 | David Cone | .60 | .45 |
| 654 | *Ron Gant*(FC) | 2.50 | 2.00 |
| 655 | Joe Price | .12 | .09 |
| 656 | George Bell | .25 | .20 |
| 657 | *Gregg Jefferies*(FC) | | |
| | | 1.00 | .70 |
| 658 | *Todd Stottlemyre*(FC) | .50 | .40 |
| 659 | *Geronimo Berroa*(FC) | .25 | .20 |
| 660 | Jerry Royster | .12 | .09 |

# 1988 Donruss Rookies

For the third consecutive year, Donruss issued this 56-card boxed set highlighting current rookies. The complete set includes a checklist and a 15-piece Stan Musial Diamond Kings puzzle. As in previous years, the set is similar to the company's basic issue, with the exception of the logo and border color. Card fronts feature red, green and black-striped borders, with a red-and-white player name printed in the lower left corner beneath the full-color photo. "The Rookies" logo is printed in red, white and black in the lower right corner. The card backs are printed in black on bright aqua and include personal data, recent performance stats and major league totals, as well as 1984-88 year-by-year minor league stats. The cards are the standard 2-1/2" by 3-1/2" size.

| | MT | NR MT |
|---|---|---|
| Complete Set: | 20.00 | 15.00 |
| Common Player: | .10 | .08 |

| | | MT | NR MT |
|---|---|---|---|
| 1 | Mark Grace | 2.00 | 1.50 |
| 2 | Mike Campbell | .10 | .08 |
| 3 | Todd Frowirth(FC) | .20 | .15 |
| 4 | Dave Stapleton | .10 | .08 |
| 5 | Shawn Abner | .15 | .11 |
| 6 | Jose Cecena(FC) | .25 | .20 |
| 7 | Dave Gallagher(FC) | .20 | .15 |
| 8 | Mark Parent(FC) | .20 | .15 |
| 9 | Cecil Espy(FC) | .15 | .11 |
| 10 | Pete Smith | .10 | .08 |
| 11 | Jay Buhner | .20 | .15 |
| 12 | Pat Borders(FC) | .40 | .30 |
| 13 | Doug Jennings(FC) | .15 | .11 |
| 14 | Brady Anderson(FC) | .75 | .55 |
| 15 | Pete Stanicek | .15 | .11 |
| 16 | Roberto Kelly | 1.00 | .70 |
| 17 | Jeff Treadway | .15 | .11 |
| 18 | Walt Weiss(FC) | .30 | .25 |
| 19 | Paul Gibson(FC) | .20 | .15 |
| 20 | Tim Crews | .10 | .08 |
| 21 | Melido Perez | .25 | .20 |
| 22 | Steve Peters(FC) | .20 | .15 |
| 23 | Craig Worthington(FC) | | |
| | | .20 | .15 |
| 24 | John Trautwein(FC) | .15 | .11 |
| 25 | DeWayne Vaughn(FC) | | |
| | | .15 | .11 |
| 26 | David Wells | .10 | .08 |
| 27 | Al Leiter | .10 | .08 |
| 28 | Tim Belcher | .20 | .15 |
| 29 | Johnny Paredes(FC) | .20 | .15 |
| 30 | Chris Sabo(FC) | 2.00 | 1.50 |
| 31 | Damon Berryhill | .25 | .20 |
| 32 | Randy Milligan(FC) | .50 | .40 |
| 33 | Gary Thurman | .20 | .15 |
| 34 | Kevin Elster | .15 | .11 |
| 35 | Roberto Alomar | 12.00 | 9.00 |
| 36 | Edgar Martinez(FC) | | |
| | | 2.00 | 1.50 |
| 37 | Todd Stottlemyre | .25 | .20 |
| 38 | Joey Meyer | .15 | .11 |
| 39 | Carl Nichols | .10 | .08 |
| 40 | Jack McDowell | 1.00 | .70 |
| 41 | Jose Bautista(FC) | .20 | .15 |
| 42 | Sil Campusano(FC) | .15 | .11 |
| 43 | John Dopson(FC) | .20 | .15 |
| 44 | Jody Reed | .35 | .25 |
| 45 | Darrin Jackson(FC) | .20 | .15 |
| 46 | Mike Capel(FC) | .20 | .15 |
| 47 | Ron Gant | 3.00 | 2.25 |
| 48 | John Davis | .10 | .08 |
| 49 | Kevin Coffman(FC) | .15 | .11 |
| 50 | Cris Carpenter(FC) | .20 | .15 |
| 51 | Mackey Sasser | .10 | .08 |
| 52 | Luis Alicea(FC) | .25 | .20 |
| 53 | Bryan Harvey(FC) | .50 | .40 |
| 54 | Steve Ellsworth(FC) | .15 | .11 |
| 55 | Mike Macfarlane(FC) | | |
| | | .25 | .20 |
| 56 | Checklist 1-56 | .10 | .08 |

**Regional interest may affect the value of a card.**

# 1989 Donruss

This basic annual issue consists of 660 standard- size (2-1/2" by 3-1/2") cards, including 26 Diamond Kings portrait cards and 20 Rated Rookies cards. Top and bottom borders of the cards are printed in a variety of colors that fade from dark to light (i.e. dark blue to light purple, bright red to pale yellow). A white-lettered player name is printed across the top margin. The team logo appears upper right and the Donruss logo lower left. A black stripe and thin white line make up the vertical side borders. The black outer stripe has a special varnish that gives a faintly visible filmstrip texture to the border. The backs (horizontal format) are printed in orange and black, similar to the 1988 design, with personal info, recent stats and major league totals. Team logo sticker cards (22 total) and Warren Spahn puzzle cards (63 total) are included in individual wax packs of cards.

|  | MT | NR MT |
|---|---|---|
| Complete Set: | 15.00 | 11.00 |
| Common Player: | .04 | .03 |

| | | MT | NR MT |
|---|---|---|---|
| 1 | Mike Greenwell (DK) | .20 | .15 |
| 2 | Bobby Bonilla (DK) | .12 | .09 |

A player's name in italic indicates a rookie card. An (FC) indicates a player's first card for that particular card company.

| | | MT | NR MT |
|---|---|---|---|
| 3 | Pete Incaviglia (DK) | .12 | .09 |
| 4 | Chris Sabo (DK) | .25 | .20 |
| 5 | Robin Yount (DK) | .25 | .20 |
| 6 | Tony Gwynn (DK) | .35 | .25 |
| 7 | Carlton Fisk (DK) | .12 | .09 |
| 8 | Cory Snyder (DK) | .15 | .11 |
| 9 | David Cone (DK) | .20 | .15 |
| 10 | Kevin Seitzer (DK) | .25 | .20 |
| 11 | Rick Reuschel (DK) | .10 | .08 |
| 12 | Johnny Ray (DK) | .10 | .08 |
| 13 | Dave Schmidt (DK) | .08 | .06 |
| 14 | Andres Galarraga (DK) | .15 | .11 |
| 15 | Kirk Gibson (DK) | .20 | .15 |
| 16 | Fred McGriff (DK) | .25 | .20 |
| 17 | Mark Grace (DK) | .20 | .15 |
| 18 | Jeff Robinson (DK) | .12 | .09 |
| 19 | Vince Coleman (DK) | .20 | .15 |
| 20 | Dave Henderson (DK) | .10 | .08 |
| 21 | Harold Reynolds (DK) | .08 | .06 |
| 22 | Gerald Perry (DK) | .10 | .08 |
| 23 | Frank Viola (DK) | .15 | .11 |
| 24 | Steve Bedrosian (DK) | .10 | .08 |
| 25 | Glenn Davis (DK) | .15 | .11 |
| 26 | Don Mattingly (DK) | .50 | .40 |
| 27 | Checklist 1-27 | .04 | .03 |
| 28 | *Sandy Alomar, Jr.* (RR)(FC) | .40 | .30 |
| 29 | *Steve Searcy* (RR)(FC) | .15 | .11 |
| 30 | *Cameron Drew* (RR)(FC) | .15 | .11 |
| 31 | *Gary Sheffield* (RR)(FC) | 1.00 | .70 |
| 32 | *Erik Hanson* (RR)(FC) | .50 | .40 |
| 33 | *Ken Griffey, Jr.* (RR)(FC) | 6.00 | 4.50 |
| 34 | *Greg Harris* (RR)(FC) | .25 | .20 |
| 35 | *Gregg Jefferies* (RR) | .40 | .30 |
| 36 | *Luis Medina* (RR)(FC) | .20 | .15 |
| 37 | *Carlos Quintana* (RR) | .20 | .15 |
| 38 | *Felix Jose* (RR)(FC) | 1.00 | .70 |
| 39 | *Cris Carpenter* (RR)(FC) | .20 | .15 |
| 40 | *Ron Jones* (RR)(FC) | .10 | .08 |
| 41 | *Dave West* (RR)(FC) | .20 | .15 |
| 42 | *Randy Johnson* (RR)(FC) | .40 | .30 |
| 43 | *Mike Harkey* (RR)(FC) | .15 | .11 |
| 44 | *Pete Harnisch* (RR)(FC) | .25 | .20 |
| 45 | *Tom Gordon* (RR)(FC) | .20 | .15 |
| 46 | *Gregg Olson* (RR)(FC) | .35 | .25 |
| 47 | *Alex Sanchez* (RR)(FC) | .15 | .11 |
| 48 | Ruben Sierra | .35 | .25 |

| | | MT | NR MT | | | MT | NR MT |
|---|---|---|---|---|---|---|---|
| 49 | Rafael Palmeiro | .25 | .20 | 115 | *Keith Brown*(FC) | .15 | .11 |
| 50 | Ron Gant | .50 | .40 | 116 | Matt Nokes | .15 | .11 |
| 51 | Cal Ripken, Jr. | .50 | .40 | 117 | Keith Hernandez | .20 | .15 |
| 52 | Wally Joyner | .20 | .15 | 118 | Bob Forsch | .06 | .05 |
| 53 | Gary Carter | .20 | .15 | 119 | Bert Blyleven | .10 | .08 |
| 54 | Andy Van Slyke | .12 | .09 | 120 | Willie Wilson | .08 | .06 |
| 55 | Robin Yount | .25 | .20 | 121 | Tommy Gregg | .08 | .06 |
| 56 | Pete Incaviglia | .10 | .08 | 122 | Jim Rice | .25 | .20 |
| 57 | Greg Brock | .06 | .05 | 123 | Bob Knepper | .06 | .05 |
| 58 | Melido Perez | .08 | .06 | 124 | Danny Jackson | .12 | .09 |
| 59 | Craig Lefferts | .04 | .03 | 125 | Eric Plunk | .04 | .03 |
| 60 | Gary Pettis | .04 | .03 | 126 | Brian Fisher | .06 | .05 |
| 61 | Danny Tartabull | .15 | .11 | 127 | Mike Pagliarulo | .08 | .06 |
| 62 | Guillermo Hernandez | | | 128 | Tony Gwynn | .30 | .25 |
| | | .06 | .05 | 129 | Lance McCullers | .06 | .05 |
| 63 | Ozzie Smith | .12 | .09 | 130 | Andres Galarraga | .15 | .11 |
| 64 | Gary Gaetti | .12 | .09 | 131 | Jose Uribe | .04 | .03 |
| 65 | Mark Davis | .04 | .03 | 132 | Kirk Gibson | .20 | .15 |
| 66 | Lee Smith | .08 | .06 | 133 | David Palmer | .04 | .03 |
| 67 | Dennis Eckersley | .10 | .08 | 134 | R.J. Reynolds | .04 | .03 |
| 68 | Wade Boggs | .90 | .70 | 135 | Greg Walker | .06 | .05 |
| 69 | Mike Scott | .10 | .08 | 136 | Kirk McCaskill | .06 | .05 |
| 70 | Fred McGriff | .50 | .40 | 137 | Shawon Dunston | .08 | .06 |
| 71 | Tom Browning | .08 | .06 | 138 | Andy Allanson | .04 | .03 |
| 72 | Claudell Washington | .06 | .05 | 139 | Rob Murphy | .04 | .03 |
| 73 | Mel Hall | .06 | .05 | 140 | Mike Aldrete | .06 | .05 |
| 74 | Don Mattingly | .50 | .40 | 141 | Terry Kennedy | .06 | .05 |
| 75 | Steve Bedrosian | .08 | .06 | 142 | Scott Fletcher | .06 | .05 |
| 76 | Juan Samuel | .10 | .08 | 143 | Steve Balboni | .06 | .05 |
| 77 | Mike Scioscia | .06 | .05 | 144 | Bret Saberhagen | .12 | .09 |
| 78 | Dave Righetti | .12 | .09 | 145 | Ozzie Virgil | .04 | .03 |
| 79 | Alfredo Griffin | .06 | .05 | 146 | Dale Sveum | .06 | .05 |
| 80 | Eric Davis | .40 | .30 | 147 | Darryl Strawberry | .40 | .30 |
| 81 | Juan Berenguer | .04 | .03 | 148 | Harold Baines | .10 | .08 |
| 82 | Todd Worrell | .08 | .06 | 149 | George Bell | .25 | .20 |
| 83 | Joe Carter | .12 | .09 | 150 | Dave Parker | .12 | .09 |
| 84 | Steve Sax | .12 | .09 | 151 | Bobby Bonilla | .25 | .20 |
| 85 | Frank White | .06 | .05 | 152 | Mookie Wilson | .06 | .05 |
| 86 | John Kruk | .06 | .05 | 153 | Ted Power | .04 | .03 |
| 87 | Rance Mulliniks | .04 | .03 | 154 | Nolan Ryan | .60 | .45 |
| 88 | Alan Ashby | .04 | .03 | 155 | Jeff Reardon | .08 | .06 |
| 89 | Charlie Leibrandt | .06 | .05 | 156 | Tim Wallach | .08 | .06 |
| 90 | Frank Tanana | .06 | .05 | 157 | Jamie Moyer | .04 | .03 |
| 91 | Jose Canseco | .50 | .40 | 158 | Rich Gossage | .10 | .08 |
| 92 | Barry Bonds | .30 | .25 | 159 | Dave Winfield | .25 | .20 |
| 93 | Harold Reynolds | .06 | .05 | 160 | Von Hayes | .08 | .06 |
| 94 | Mark McLemore | .04 | .03 | 161 | Willie McGee | .10 | .08 |
| 95 | Mark McGwire | .30 | .25 | 162 | Rich Gedman | .06 | .05 |
| 96 | Eddie Murray | .25 | .20 | 163 | Tony Pena | .06 | .05 |
| 97 | Tim Raines | .25 | .20 | 164 | Mike Morgan | .04 | .03 |
| 98 | Rob Thompson | .06 | .05 | 165 | Charlie Hough | .06 | .05 |
| 99 | Kevin McReynolds | .12 | .09 | 166 | Mike Stanley | .04 | .03 |
| 100 | Checklist 28-137 | .04 | .03 | 167 | Andre Dawson | .20 | .15 |
| 101 | Carlton Fisk | .20 | .15 | 168 | Joe Boever(FC) | .04 | .03 |
| 102 | Dave Martinez | .06 | .05 | 169 | Pete Stanicek | .08 | .06 |
| 103 | Glenn Braggs | .06 | .05 | 170 | Bob Boone | .06 | .05 |
| 104 | Dale Murphy | .30 | .25 | 171 | Ron Darling | .10 | .08 |
| 105 | Ryne Sandberg | .40 | .30 | 172 | Bob Walk | .04 | .03 |
| 106 | Dennis Martinez | .06 | .05 | 173 | Rob Deer | .06 | .05 |
| 107 | Pete O'Brien | .06 | .05 | 174 | Steve Buechele | .04 | .03 |
| 108 | Dick Schofield | .04 | .03 | 175 | Ted Higuera | .08 | .06 |
| 109 | Henry Cotto | .04 | .03 | 176 | Ozzie Guillen | .06 | .05 |
| 110 | Mike Marshall | .12 | .09 | 177 | Candy Maldonado | .06 | .05 |
| 111 | Keith Moreland | .06 | .05 | 178 | Doyle Alexander | .06 | .05 |
| 112 | Tom Brunansky | .10 | .08 | 179 | Mark Gubicza | .10 | .08 |
| 113 | Kelly Gruber | .04 | .03 | 180 | Alan Trammell | .15 | .11 |
| 114 | Brook Jacoby | .08 | .06 | 181 | Vince Coleman | .15 | .11 |

| | | MT | NR MT | | | MT | NR MT |
|---|---|---|---|---|---|---|---|
| 182 | Kirby Puckett | .30 | .25 | 246 | Roberto Alomar | .25 | .20 |
| 183 | Chris Brown | .06 | .05 | 247 | Jimmy Jones | .04 | .03 |
| 184 | Marty Barrett | .06 | .05 | 248 | Pascual Perez | .06 | .05 |
| 185 | Stan Javier | .04 | .03 | 249 | Will Clark | .40 | .30 |
| 186 | Mike Greenwell | .30 | .25 | 250 | Fernando Valenzuela | | |
| 187 | Billy Hatcher | .06 | .05 | | | .15 | .11 |
| 188 | Jimmy Key | .08 | .06 | 251 | Shane Rawley | .06 | .05 |
| 189 | Nick Esasky | .06 | .05 | 252 | Sid Bream | .06 | .05 |
| 190 | Don Slaught | .04 | .03 | 253 | Steve Lyons | .04 | .03 |
| 191 | Cory Snyder | .15 | .11 | 254 | Brian Downing | .06 | .05 |
| 192 | John Candelaria | .06 | .05 | 255 | Mark Grace | .60 | .45 |
| 193 | Mike Schmidt | .40 | .30 | 256 | Tom Candiotti | .04 | .03 |
| 194 | Kevin Gross | .06 | .05 | 257 | Barry Larkin | .30 | .25 |
| 195 | John Tudor | .08 | .06 | 258 | Mike Krukow | .06 | .05 |
| 196 | Neil Allen | .04 | .03 | 259 | Billy Ripken | .06 | .05 |
| 197 | Orel Hershiser | .25 | .20 | 260 | Cecilio Guante | .04 | .03 |
| 198 | Kal Daniels | .15 | .11 | 261 | Scott Bradley | .04 | .03 |
| 199 | Kent Hrbek | .15 | .11 | 262 | Floyd Bannister | .06 | .05 |
| 200 | Checklist 138-247 | .04 | .03 | 263 | Pete Smith | .08 | .06 |
| 201 | Joe Magrane | .08 | .06 | 264 | Jim Gantner | .04 | .03 |
| 202 | Scott Bailes | .04 | .03 | 265 | Roger McDowell | .08 | .06 |
| 203 | Tim Belcher | .10 | .08 | 266 | Bobby Thigpen | .08 | .06 |
| 204 | George Brett | .30 | .25 | 267 | Jim Clancy | .06 | .05 |
| 205 | Benito Santiago | .12 | .09 | 268 | Terry Steinbach | .08 | .06 |
| 206 | Tony Fernandez | .10 | .08 | 269 | Mike Dunne | .06 | .05 |
| 207 | Gerald Young | .10 | .08 | 270 | Dwight Gooden | .50 | .40 |
| 208 | Bo Jackson | .30 | .25 | 271 | Mike Heath | .04 | .03 |
| 209 | Chet Lemon | .06 | .05 | 272 | Dave Smith | .06 | .05 |
| 210 | Storm Davis | .08 | .06 | 273 | Keith Atherton | .04 | .03 |
| 211 | Doug Drabek | .06 | .05 | 274 | Tim Burke | .04 | .03 |
| 212 | Mickey Brantley (photo | | | 275 | Damon Berryhill | .12 | .09 |
| | actually Nelson Simmons) | | | 276 | Vance Law | .06 | .05 |
| | | .04 | .03 | 277 | Rich Dotson | .06 | .05 |
| 213 | Devon White | .10 | .08 | 278 | Lance Parrish | .15 | .11 |
| 214 | Dave Stewart | .08 | .06 | 279 | Denny Walling | .04 | .03 |
| 215 | Dave Schmidt | .04 | .03 | 280 | Roger Clemens | .40 | .30 |
| 216 | Bryn Smith | .04 | .03 | 281 | Greg Mathews | .06 | .05 |
| 217 | Brett Butler | .06 | .05 | 282 | Tom Niedenfuer | .06 | .05 |
| 218 | Bob Ojeda | .06 | .05 | 283 | Paul Kilgus | .10 | .08 |
| 219 | *Steve* | | | 284 | Jose Guzman | .08 | .06 |
| | *Rosenberg* (FC) | .15 | .11 | 285 | Calvin Schiraldi | .04 | .03 |
| 220 | Hubie Brooks | .08 | .06 | 286 | Charlie Puleo | .04 | .03 |
| 221 | B.J. Surhoff | .08 | .06 | 287 | Joe Orsulak | .04 | .03 |
| 222 | Rick Mahler | .04 | .03 | 288 | Jack Howell | .06 | .05 |
| 223 | Rick Sutcliffe | .08 | .06 | 289 | Kevin Elster | .08 | .06 |
| 224 | Neal Heaton | .04 | .03 | 290 | Jose Lind | .10 | .08 |
| 225 | Mitch Williams | .06 | .05 | 291 | Paul Molitor | .12 | .09 |
| 226 | Chuck Finley | .08 | .06 | 292 | Cecil Espy | .08 | .06 |
| 227 | Mark Langston | .10 | .08 | 293 | Bill Wegman | .04 | .03 |
| 228 | Jesse Orosco | .06 | .05 | 294 | Dan Pasqua | .08 | .06 |
| 229 | Ed Whitson | .04 | .03 | 295 | Scott Garrelts | .04 | .03 |
| 230 | Terry Pendleton | .08 | .06 | 296 | Walt Terrell | .06 | .05 |
| 231 | Lloyd Moseby | .06 | .05 | 297 | Ed Hearn | .04 | .03 |
| 232 | Greg Swindell | .10 | .08 | 298 | Lou Whitaker | .20 | .15 |
| 233 | John Franco | .08 | .06 | 299 | Ken Dayley | .04 | .03 |
| 234 | Jack Morris | .15 | .11 | 300 | Checklist 248-357 | .04 | .03 |
| 235 | Howard Johnson | .08 | .06 | 301 | Tommy Herr | .06 | .05 |
| 236 | Glenn Davis | .12 | .09 | 302 | Mike Brumley | .06 | .05 |
| 237 | Frank Viola | .12 | .09 | 303 | Ellis Burks | .60 | .45 |
| 238 | Kevin Seitzer | .25 | .20 | 304 | Curt Young | .06 | .05 |
| 239 | Gerald Perry | .08 | .06 | 305 | Jody Reed | .10 | .08 |
| 240 | Dwight Evans | .10 | .08 | 306 | Bill Doran | .06 | .05 |
| 241 | Jim Deshaies | .04 | .03 | 307 | David Wells | .06 | .05 |
| 242 | Bo Diaz | .06 | .05 | 308 | Ron Robinson | .04 | .03 |
| 243 | Carney Lansford | .06 | .05 | 309 | Rafael Santana | .04 | .03 |
| 244 | Mike LaValliere | .06 | .05 | 310 | Julio Franco | .10 | .08 |
| 245 | Rickey Henderson | .40 | .30 | 311 | Jack Clark | .15 | .11 |

| | | MT | NR MT |
|---|---|---|---|
| 312 | Chris James | .08 | .06 |
| 313 | Milt Thompson | .04 | .03 |
| 314 | John Shelby | .04 | .03 |
| 315 | Al Leiter | .15 | .11 |
| 316 | Mike Davis | .06 | .05 |
| 317 | *Chris Sabo* | .60 | .45 |
| 318 | Greg Gagne | .04 | .03 |
| 319 | Jose Oquendo | .04 | .03 |
| 320 | John Farrell | .10 | .08 |
| 321 | Franklin Stubbs | .04 | .03 |
| 322 | Kurt Stillwell | .06 | .05 |
| 323 | Shawn Abner | .10 | .08 |
| 324 | Mike Flanagan | .06 | .05 |
| 325 | Kevin Bass | .06 | .05 |
| 326 | Pat Tabler | .06 | .05 |
| 327 | Mike Henneman | .08 | .06 |
| 328 | Rick Honeycutt | .04 | .03 |
| 329 | John Smiley | .10 | .08 |
| 330 | Rey Quinones | .04 | .03 |
| 331 | Johnny Ray | .06 | .05 |
| 332 | Bob Welch | .08 | .06 |
| 333 | Larry Sheets | .06 | .05 |
| 334 | Jeff Parrett | .08 | .06 |
| 335 | Rick Reuschel | .08 | .06 |
| 336 | Randy Myers | .10 | .08 |
| 337 | Ken Williams | .06 | .05 |
| 338 | Andy McGaffigan | .04 | .03 |
| 339 | Joey Meyer | .08 | .06 |
| 340 | Dion James | .04 | .03 |
| 341 | Les Lancaster | .06 | .05 |
| 342 | Tom Foley | .04 | .03 |
| 343 | Geno Petralli | .04 | .03 |
| 344 | Dan Petry | .06 | .05 |
| 345 | Alvin Davis | .12 | .09 |
| 346 | Mickey Hatcher | .04 | .03 |
| 347 | Marvell Wynne | .04 | .03 |
| 348 | Danny Cox | .06 | .05 |
| 349 | Dave Stieb | .08 | .06 |
| 350 | Jay Bell | .06 | .05 |
| 351 | Jeff Treadway | .10 | .08 |
| 352 | Luis Salazar | .04 | .03 |
| 353 | Lenny Dykstra | .08 | .06 |
| 354 | Juan Agosto | .04 | .03 |
| 355 | Gene Larkin | .10 | .08 |
| 356 | Steve Farr | .04 | .03 |
| 357 | Paul Assenmacher | .04 | .03 |
| 358 | Todd Benzinger | .12 | .09 |
| 359 | Larry Andersen | .04 | .03 |
| 360 | Paul O'Neill | .04 | .03 |
| 361 | Ron Hassey | .04 | .03 |
| 362 | Jim Gott | .04 | .03 |
| 363 | Ken Phelps | .06 | .05 |
| 364 | Tim Flannery | .04 | .03 |
| 365 | Randy Ready | .04 | .03 |
| 366 | *Nelson Santovenia*(FC) | .15 | .11 |
| 367 | Kelly Downs | .08 | .06 |
| 368 | Danny Heep | .04 | .03 |
| 369 | Phil Bradley | .08 | .06 |
| 370 | Jeff Robinson | .06 | .05 |
| 371 | Ivan Calderon | .06 | .05 |
| 372 | Mike Witt | .06 | .05 |
| 373 | Greg Maddux | .10 | .08 |
| 374 | Carmen Castillo | .04 | .03 |
| 375 | Jose Rijo | .06 | .05 |
| 376 | Joe Price | .04 | .03 |
| 377 | R.C. Gonzalez | .04 | .03 |

| | | MT | NR MT |
|---|---|---|---|
| 378 | Oddibe McDowell | .06 | .05 |
| 379 | Jim Presley | .06 | .05 |
| 380 | Brad Wellman | .04 | .03 |
| 381 | Tom Glavine | .10 | |
| 382 | Dan Plesac | .08 | .06 |
| 383 | Wally Backman | .06 | .05 |
| 384 | *Dave Gallagher* | .25 | .20 |
| 385 | Tom Henke | .06 | .05 |
| 386 | Luis Polonia | .06 | .05 |
| 387 | Junior Ortiz | .04 | .03 |
| 388 | David Cone | .35 | .25 |
| 389 | Dave Bergman | .04 | .03 |
| 390 | Danny Darwin | .04 | .03 |
| 391 | Dan Gladden | .04 | .03 |
| 392 | *John Dopson* | .25 | .20 |
| 393 | Frank DiPino | .04 | .03 |
| 394 | Al Nipper | .04 | .03 |
| 395 | Willie Randolph | .06 | .05 |
| 396 | Don Carman | .06 | .05 |
| 397 | Scott Terry | .06 | .05 |
| 398 | Rick Cerone | .04 | .03 |
| 399 | Tom Pagnozzi | .06 | .05 |
| 400 | Checklist 358-467 | .04 | .03 |
| 401 | Mickey Tettleton | .08 | .06 |
| 402 | Curtis Wilkerson | .04 | .03 |
| 403 | Jeff Russell | .04 | .03 |
| 404 | Pat Perry | .04 | .03 |
| 405 | *Jose Alvarez*(FC) | .15 | .11 |
| 406 | Rick Schu | .04 | .03 |
| 407 | *Sherman Corbett*(FC) | .15 | .11 |
| 408 | Dave Magadan | .10 | .08 |
| 409 | Bob Kipper | .04 | .03 |
| 410 | Don August | .08 | .06 |
| 411 | Bob Brower | .04 | .03 |
| 412 | Chris Bosio | .04 | .03 |
| 413 | Jerry Reuss | .06 | .05 |
| 414 | Atlee Hammaker | .04 | .03 |
| 415 | Jim Walewander(FC) | .06 | .05 |
| 416 | *Mike Macfarlane* | .25 | .20 |
| 417 | Pat Sheridan | .04 | .03 |
| 418 | Pedro Guerrero | .15 | .11 |
| 419 | Allan Anderson | .06 | .05 |
| 420 | *Mark Parent* | .20 | .15 |
| 421 | Bob Stanley | .04 | .03 |
| 422 | Mike Gallego | .04 | .03 |
| 423 | Bruce Hurst | .08 | .06 |
| 424 | Dave Meads | .04 | .03 |
| 425 | Jesse Barfield | .10 | .08 |
| 426 | *Rob Dibble*(FC) | .50 | .40 |
| 427 | Joel Skinner | .04 | .03 |
| 428 | Ron Kittle | .06 | .05 |
| 429 | Rick Rhoden | .08 | .06 |
| 430 | Bob Dernier | .04 | .03 |
| 431 | Steve Jeltz | .04 | .03 |
| 432 | Rick Dempsey | .06 | .05 |
| 433 | Roberto Kelly | .10 | .08 |
| 434 | Dave Anderson | .04 | .03 |
| 435 | Herm Winningham | .04 | .03 |
| 436 | Al Newman | .04 | .03 |
| 437 | Jose DeLeon | .06 | .05 |
| 438 | Doug Jones | .10 | .08 |
| 439 | Brian Holton | .06 | .05 |
| 440 | Jeff Montgomery(FC) | .06 | .05 |
| 441 | Dickie Thon | .04 | .03 |

| | | MT | NR MT | | | MT | NR MT |
|---|---|---|---|---|---|---|---|
| 442 | Cecil Fielder | .35 | .25 | 503 | Shawn Hillegas | .06 | .05 |
| 443 | *John Fishel*(FC) | .15 | .11 | 504 | Manny Lee | .04 | .03 |
| 444 | Jerry Don Gleaton | .04 | .03 | 505 | *Doug Jennings* | .15 | .11 |
| 445 | *Paul Gibson* | .15 | .11 | 506 | Ken Oberkfell | .04 | .03 |
| 446 | Walt Weiss | .40 | .30 | 507 | Tim Teufel | .04 | .03 |
| 447 | Glenn Wilson | .06 | .05 | 508 | Tom Brookens | .04 | .03 |
| 448 | Mike Moore | .04 | .03 | 509 | Rafael Ramirez | .04 | .03 |
| 449 | Chili Davis | .06 | .05 | 510 | Fred Toliver | .04 | .03 |
| 450 | Dave Henderson | .08 | .06 | 511 | *Brian Holman*(FC) | | |
| 451 | *Jose Bautista* | .20 | .15 | | | .30 | .25 |
| 452 | Rex Hudler | .04 | .03 | 512 | Mike Bielecki | .04 | .03 |
| 453 | Bob Brenly | .04 | .03 | 513 | *Jeff Pico*(FC) | .15 | .11 |
| 454 | Mackey Sasser | .06 | .05 | 514 | Charles Hudson | .04 | .03 |
| 455 | Daryl Boston | .04 | .03 | 515 | Bruce Ruffin | .04 | .03 |
| 456 | Mike Fitzgerald | .04 | .03 | 516 | Larry McWilliams | .04 | .03 |
| 457 | Jeffery Leonard | .06 | .05 | 517 | Jeff Sellers | .04 | .03 |
| 458 | Bruce Sutter | .08 | .06 | 518 | *John Costello*(FC) | | |
| 459 | Mitch Webster | .06 | .05 | | | .15 | .11 |
| 460 | Joe Hesketh | .04 | .03 | 519 | *Brady Anderson* | .40 | .30 |
| 461 | Bobby Witt | .08 | .06 | 520 | Craig McMurtry | .04 | .03 |
| 462 | Stew Cliburn | .04 | .03 | 521 | Ray Hayward | .08 | .06 |
| 463 | Scott Bankhead | .04 | .03 | 522 | Drew Hall | .08 | .06 |
| 464 | *Ramon Martinez*(FC) | | | 523 | *Mark Lemke*(FC) | .20 | .15 |
| | | .50 | .40 | 524 | *Oswald Peraza*(FC) | | |
| 465 | Dave Leiper | .04 | .03 | | | .15 | .11 |
| 466 | *Luis Alicea* | .20 | .15 | 525 | *Bryan Harvey* | .30 | .25 |
| 467 | John Cerutti | .06 | .05 | 526 | Rick Aguilera | .04 | .03 |
| 468 | Ron Washington | .04 | .03 | 527 | Tom Prince | .06 | .05 |
| 469 | Jeff Reed | .04 | .03 | 528 | Mark Clear | .04 | .03 |
| 470 | Jeff Robinson | .12 | .09 | 529 | Jerry Browne | .04 | .03 |
| 471 | Sid Fernandez | .08 | .06 | 530 | Juan Castillo | .04 | .03 |
| 472 | Terry Puhl | .04 | .03 | 531 | Jack McDowell | .08 | .06 |
| 473 | Charlie Lea | .04 | .03 | 532 | Chris Speier | .04 | .03 |
| 474 | *Israel Sanchez*(FC) | | | 533 | Darrell Evans | .08 | .06 |
| | | .15 | .11 | 534 | Luis Aquino | .04 | .03 |
| 475 | Bruce Benedict | .04 | .03 | 535 | Eric King | .04 | .03 |
| 476 | Oil Can Boyd | .06 | .05 | 536 | *Ken Hill*(FC) | .25 | .20 |
| 477 | Craig Reynolds | .04 | .03 | 537 | Randy Bush | .04 | .03 |
| 478 | Frank Williams | .04 | .03 | 538 | Shane Mack | .06 | .05 |
| 479 | Greg Cadaret | .10 | .08 | 539 | Tom Bolton(FC) | .06 | .05 |
| 480 | *Randy Kramer*(FC) | | | 540 | Gene Nelson | .04 | .03 |
| | | .15 | .11 | 541 | Wes Gardner | .06 | .05 |
| 481 | *Dave Eiland*(FC) | .20 | .15 | 542 | Ken Caminiti | .06 | .05 |
| 482 | Eric Show | .06 | .05 | 543 | Duane Ward | .04 | .03 |
| 483 | Garry Templeton | .06 | .05 | 544 | *Norm Charlton*(FC) | | |
| 484 | Wallace Johnson(FC) | | | | | .30 | .25 |
| | | .04 | .03 | 545 | *Hal Morris*(FC) | .50 | .40 |
| 485 | Kevin Mitchell | .25 | .20 | 546 | *Rich Yett*(FC) | .04 | .03 |
| 486 | Tim Crews | .06 | .05 | 547 | *Hensley Meulens*(FC) | | |
| 487 | Mike Maddux | .04 | .03 | | | .25 | .20 |
| 488 | Dave LaPoint | .06 | .05 | 548 | Greg Harris | .04 | .03 |
| 489 | Fred Manrique | .06 | .05 | 549 | Darren Daulton | .04 | .03 |
| 490 | Greg Minton | .04 | .03 | 550 | Jeff Hamilton | .06 | .05 |
| 491 | *Doug Dascenzo*(FC) | | | 551 | Luis Aguayo | .04 | .03 |
| | | .25 | .20 | 552 | Tim Leary | .06 | .05 |
| 492 | Willie Upshaw | .06 | .05 | 553 | Ron Oester | .04 | .03 |
| 493 | *Jack Armstrong*(FC) | | | 554 | Steve Lombardozzi | .04 | .03 |
| | | .15 | .11 | 555 | *Tim Jones*(FC) | .15 | .11 |
| 494 | Kirt Manwaring | .10 | .08 | 556 | Bud Black | .04 | .03 |
| 495 | Jeff Ballard | .06 | .05 | 557 | Alejandro Pena | .04 | .03 |
| 496 | Jeff Kunkel | .04 | .03 | 558 | *Jose DeJesus*(FC) | | |
| 497 | Mike Campbell | .08 | .06 | | | .15 | .11 |
| 498 | Gary Thurman | .10 | .08 | 559 | Dennis Rasmussen | .08 | .06 |
| 499 | Zane Smith | .06 | .05 | 560 | *Pat Borders* | .30 | .25 |
| 500 | Checklist 468-577 | .04 | .03 | 561 | *Craig Biggio*(FC) | .60 | .45 |
| 501 | Mike Birkbeck | .04 | .03 | 562 | *Luis de los* | | |
| 502 | Terry Leach | .04 | .03 | | *Santos*(FC) | .15 | .11 |

| | | MT | NR MT |
|---|---|---|---|
| 563 | Fred Lynn | .10 | .08 |
| 564 | *Todd Burns*(FC) | .20 | .15 |
| 565 | Felix Fermin | .06 | .05 |
| 566 | Darnell Coles | .06 | .05 |
| 567 | Willie Fraser | .04 | .03 |
| 568 | Glenn Hubbard | .04 | .03 |
| 569 | *Craig Worthington* | .15 | .11 |
| 570 | *Johnny Paredes* | .15 | .11 |
| 571 | Don Robinson | .04 | .03 |
| 572 | Barry Lyons | .04 | .03 |
| 573 | Bill Long | .06 | .05 |
| 574 | Tracy Jones | .10 | .08 |
| 575 | Juan Nieves | .06 | .05 |
| 576 | Andres Thomas | .06 | .05 |
| 577 | Rolando Roomes(FC) | .15 | .11 |
| 578 | Luis Rivera(FC) | .04 | .03 |
| 579 | *Chad Kreuter*(FC) | .15 | .11 |
| 580 | Tony Armas | .06 | .05 |
| 581 | Jay Buhner | .10 | .08 |
| 582 | Ricky Horton | .06 | .05 |
| 583 | Andy Hawkins | .04 | .03 |
| 584 | Sil Campusano | .15 | .11 |
| 585 | Dave Clark | .06 | .05 |
| 586 | *Van Snider*(FC) | .15 | .11 |
| 587 | Todd Frohwirth(FC) | .06 | .05 |
| 588 | Warren Spahn Puzzle Card | .04 | .03 |
| 589 | *William Brennan*(FC) | .15 | .11 |
| 590 | *German Gonzalez*(FC) | .15 | .11 |
| 591 | Ernie Whitt | .06 | .05 |
| 592 | Jeff Blauser | .08 | .06 |
| 593 | Spike Owen | .04 | .03 |
| 594 | Matt Williams | .40 | .30 |
| 595 | Lloyd McClendon(FC) | .04 | .03 |
| 596 | Steve Ontiveros | .04 | .03 |
| 597 | *Scott Medvin*(FC) | .15 | .11 |
| 598 | *Hipolito Pena*(FC) | .15 | .11 |
| 599 | *Jerald Clark*(FC) | .30 | .25 |
| 600a | Checklist 578-BC26 (#635 is Kurt Schilling) | .15 | .11 |
| 600b | Checklist 578-BC26 (#635 is Curt Schilling) | .06 | .05 |
| 601 | Carmelo Martinez | .04 | .03 |
| 602 | Mike LaCoss | .04 | .03 |
| 603 | Mike Devereaux | .15 | .11 |
| 604 | Alex Madrid(FC) | .15 | .11 |
| 605 | Gary Redus | .04 | .03 |
| 606 | Lance Johnson | .06 | .05 |
| 607 | *Terry Clark*(FC) | .15 | .11 |
| 608 | Manny Trillo | .04 | .03 |
| 609 | *Scott Jordan*(FC) | .15 | .11 |
| 610 | Jay Howell | .06 | .05 |
| 611 | *Francisco Melendez*(FC) | .15 | .11 |
| 612 | Mike Boddicker | .06 | .05 |
| 613 | Kevin Brown | .20 | .15 |
| 614 | Dave Valle | .04 | .03 |
| 615 | Tim Laudner | .04 | .03 |
| 616 | *Andy Nezelek*(FC) | .15 | .11 |
| 617 | Chuck Crim | .04 | .03 |
| 618 | Jack Savage(FC) | .10 | .08 |
| 619 | Adam Peterson(FC) | .10 | .08 |
| 620 | Todd Stottlemyre | .10 | .08 |
| 621 | Lance Blankenship(FC) | .25 | .20 |
| 622 | *Miguel Garcia*(FC) | .15 | .11 |
| 623 | Keith Miller | .06 | .05 |
| 624 | *Ricky Jordan*(FC) | .20 | .15 |
| 625 | Ernest Riles | .04 | .03 |
| 626 | John Moses | .04 | .03 |
| 627 | Nelson Liriano | .06 | .05 |
| 628 | Mike Smithson | .04 | .03 |
| 629 | Scott Sanderson | .04 | .03 |
| 630 | Dale Mohorcic | .04 | .03 |
| 631 | Marvin Freeman | .04 | .03 |
| 632 | Mike Young | .04 | .03 |
| 633 | Dennis Lamp | .04 | .03 |
| 634 | *Dante Bichette*(FC) | .25 | .20 |
| 635 | *Curt Schilling*(FC) | .25 | .20 |
| 636 | *Scott May*(FC) | .15 | .11 |
| 637 | *Mike Schooler*(FC) | .25 | .20 |
| 638 | Rick Leach | .04 | .03 |
| 639 | *Tom Lampkin*(FC) | .15 | .11 |
| 640 | *Brian Meyer*(FC) | .15 | .11 |
| 641 | Brian Harper | .04 | .03 |
| 642 | *John Smoltz*(FC) | .80 | .60 |
| 643 | 40/40 Club (Jose Canseco) | .35 | .25 |
| 644 | Bill Schroeder | .04 | .03 |
| 645 | *Edgar Martinez* | .60 | .45 |
| 646 | *Dennis Cook*(FC) | .15 | .11 |
| 647 | Barry Jones | .04 | .03 |
| 648 | 59 and Counting (Orel Hershiser) | .15 | .11 |
| 649 | *Rod Nichols*(FC) | .15 | .11 |
| 650 | Jody Davis | .06 | .05 |
| 651 | *Bob Milacki*(FC) | .25 | .20 |
| 652 | Mike Jackson | .06 | .05 |
| 653 | *Derek Lilliquist*(FC) | .15 | .11 |
| 654 | Paul Mirabella | .04 | .03 |
| 655 | Mike Diaz | .06 | .05 |
| 656 | Jeff Musselman | .06 | .05 |
| 657 | Jerry Reed | .04 | .03 |
| 658 | Kevin Blankenship(FC) | .15 | .11 |
| 659 | Wayne Tolleson | .04 | .03 |
| 660 | Eric Hetzel(FC) | .15 | .11 |

# 1989 Donruss Rookies

For the fourth straight year, Donruss issued a 56-card "Rookies" set in 1989. As in previous years, the set is similar in design to the

|  |  | MT | NR MT |
|---|---|---|---|
| 44 | Kevin Brown | .10 | .08 |
| 45 | Ramon Martinez | .50 | .40 |
| 46 | Greg Harris | .10 | .08 |
| 47 | Steve Finley(FC) | .40 | .30 |
| 48 | Randy Kramer | .10 | .08 |
| 49 | Erik Hanson | .70 | .50 |
| 50 | Matt Merullo(FC) | .15 | .11 |
| 51 | Mike Devereaux | .10 | .08 |
| 52 | Clay Parker(FC) | .15 | .11 |
| 53 | Omar Vizquel(FC) | .20 | .15 |
| 54 | Derek Lilliquist | .10 | .08 |
| 55 | Junior Felix(FC) | .30 | .25 |
| 56 | Checklist | .10 | .08 |

regular Donruss set, except for a new "The Rookies" logo and a green and black border.

| | | MT | NR MT |
|---|---|---|---|
| Complete Set: | | 12.00 | 9.00 |
| Common Player: | | .10 | .08 |
| 1 | Gary Sheffield | 2.00 | 1.50 |
| 2 | Gregg Jefferies | .30 | .25 |
| 3 | Ken Griffey, Jr. | 6.00 | 4.50 |
| 4 | Tom Gordon | .40 | .30 |
| 5 | Billy Spiers(FC) | .25 | .20 |
| 6 | Deion Sanders(FC) | 1.50 | 1.25 |
| 7 | Donn Pall(FC) | .20 | .15 |
| 8 | Steve Carter(FC) | .20 | .15 |
| 9 | Francisco Oliveras(FC) | .15 | .11 |
| 10 | Steve Wilson(FC) | .20 | .15 |
| 11 | Bob Geren(FC) | .20 | .15 |
| 12 | Tony Castillo(FC) | .15 | .11 |
| 13 | Kenny Rogers(FC) | .20 | .15 |
| 14 | Carlos Martinez(FC) | .30 | .25 |
| 15 | Edgar Martinez | .50 | .35 |
| 16 | Jim Abbott(FC) | 1.00 | .70 |
| 17 | Torey Lovullo(FC) | .20 | .15 |
| 18 | Mark Carreon(FC) | .15 | .11 |
| 19 | Geronimo Berroa | .10 | .08 |
| 20 | Luis Medina | .10 | .08 |
| 21 | Sandy Alomar, Jr. | .30 | .25 |
| 22 | Bob Milacki | .10 | .08 |
| 23 | Joe Girardi(FC) | .30 | .25 |
| 24 | German Gonzalez | .10 | .08 |
| 25 | Craig Worthington | .15 | .11 |
| 26 | Jerome Walton(FC) | .30 | .25 |
| 27 | Gary Wayne(FC) | .20 | .15 |
| 28 | Tim Jones | .10 | .08 |
| 29 | Dante Bichette | .10 | .08 |
| 30 | Alexis Infante(FC) | .15 | .11 |
| 31 | Ken Hill | .10 | .08 |
| 32 | Dwight Smith(FC) | .30 | .25 |
| 33 | Luis de los Santos | .10 | .08 |
| 34 | Eric Yelding(FC) | .40 | .30 |
| 35 | Gregg Olson | .40 | .30 |
| 36 | Phil Stephenson(FC) | .15 | .11 |
| 37 | Ken Patterson(FC) | .15 | .11 |
| 38 | Rick Wrona(FC) | .15 | .11 |
| 39 | Mike Brumley | .10 | .08 |
| 40 | Cris Carpenter | .10 | .08 |
| 41 | Jeff Brantley(FC) | .20 | .15 |
| 42 | Ron Jones | .10 | .08 |
| 43 | Randy Johnson | .10 | .08 |

## 1990 Donruss

Donruss celebrated its 10th anniversary in the baseball card hobby with a 715-card set in 1990, up from the 660-card sets of previous years. The standard-size cards feature bright red borders with the player's name in script along the top. The 1990 set included 26 "Diamond Kings" and 20 "Rated Rookies," along with a Carl Yastrzemski puzzle.

| | | MT | NR MT |
|---|---|---|---|
| Complete Set: | | 18.00 | 13.50 |
| Common Player: | | .04 | .03 |
| 1 | Bo Jackson (DK) | .20 | .15 |
| 2 | Steve Sax (DK) | .12 | .09 |
| 3a | Ruben Sierra (DK — missing line on top border) | 1.00 | .70 |
| 3b | Ruben Sierra (DK) | .30 | .25 |
| 4 | Ken Griffey, Jr. (DK) | .80 | .60 |
| 5 | Mickey Tettleton (DK) | .12 | .09 |
| 6 | Dave Stewart (DK) | .12 | .09 |
| 7 | Jim Deshaies (DK) | .07 | .05 |
| 8 | John Smoltz (DK) | .25 | .20 |
| 9 | Mike Bielecki (DK) | .07 | .05 |
| 10a | Brian Downing DK (Reverse Negative) | 1.00 | .70 |
| 10b | Brian Downing DK (Corrected) | .25 | .20 |
| 11 | Kevin Mitchell (DK) | .35 | .25 |

| # | Player | MT | NR MT | # | Player | MT | NR MT |
|---|--------|----|----|---|--------|----|----|
| 12 | Kelly Gruber (DK) | .08 | .06 | 59 | Kirt Manwaring | .10 | .08 |
| 13 | Joe Magrane (DK) | .08 | .06 | 60 | Chet Lemon | .06 | .05 |
| 14 | John Franco (DK) | .08 | .06 | 61 | Bo Jackson | .30 | .25 |
| 15 | Ozzie Guillen (DK) | .08 | .06 | 62 | Doyle Alexander | .05 | .04 |
| 16 | Lou Whitaker (DK) | .08 | .06 | 63 | Pedro Guerrero | .12 | .09 |
| 17 | John Smiley (DK) | .08 | .06 | 64 | Allan Anderson | .07 | .05 |
| 18 | Howard Johnson (DK) | .30 | .25 | 65 | Greg Harris | .07 | .05 |
| 19 | Willie Randolph (DK) | .08 | .06 | 66 | Mike Greenwell | .25 | .20 |
| 20 | Chris Bosio (DK) | .07 | .05 | 67 | Walt Weiss | .08 | .06 |
| 21 | Tommy Herr (DK) | .07 | .05 | 68 | Wade Boggs | .30 | .25 |
| 22 | Dan Gladden (DK) | .07 | .05 | 69 | Jim Clancy | .04 | .03 |
| 23 | Ellis Burks (DK) | .20 | .15 | 70 | Junior Felix | .20 | .15 |
| 24 | Pete O'Brien (DK) | .08 | .06 | 71 | Barry Larkin | .12 | .09 |
| 25 | Bryn Smith (DK) | .07 | .05 | 72 | Dave LaPoint | .05 | .04 |
| 26 | Ed Whitson (DK) | .07 | .05 | 73 | Joel Skinner | .04 | .03 |
| 27 | Checklist 1-27 | .04 | .03 | 74 | Jesse Barfield | .08 | .06 |
| 28 | Robin Ventura (RR)(FC) | .80 | .60 | 75 | Tommy Herr | .08 | .06 |
| 29 | Todd Zeile (RR)(FC) | .50 | .40 | 76 | Ricky Jordan | .20 | .15 |
| 30 | Sandy Alomar, Jr. (RR) | .35 | .25 | 77 | Eddie Murray | .15 | .11 |
| 31 | Kent Mercker (RR)(FC) | .30 | .25 | 78 | Steve Sax | .10 | .08 |
| 32 | Ben McDonald (RR)(FC) | 1.50 | 1.25 | 79 | Tim Belcher | .10 | .08 |
| 33a | Juan Gonzalez RR (Reverse Negative)(FC) | 4.00 | 3.00 | 80 | Danny Jackson | .06 | .05 |
| 33b | Juan Gonzalez RR (Corrected)(FC) | 2.00 | 1.50 | 81 | Kent Hrbek | .10 | .08 |
| 34 | Eric Anthony (RR)(FC) | .50 | .40 | 82 | Milt Thompson | .05 | .04 |
| 35 | Mike Fetters (RR)(FC) | .20 | .15 | 83 | Brook Jacoby | .07 | .05 |
| 36 | Marquis Grissom (RR)(FC) | .60 | .45 | 84 | Mike Marshall | .08 | .06 |
| 37 | Greg Vaughn (RR)(FC) | .50 | .40 | 85 | Kevin Seitzer | .12 | .09 |
| 38 | Brian Dubois (RR)(FC) | .15 | .11 | 86 | Tony Gwynn | .15 | .11 |
| 39 | Steve Avery (RR)(FC) | .60 | .45 | 87 | Dave Steib | .08 | .06 |
| 40 | Mark Gardner (RR)(FC) | .20 | .15 | 88 | Dave Smith | .06 | .05 |
| 41 | Andy Benes (RR)(FC) | .40 | .30 | 89 | Bret Saberhagen | .15 | .11 |
| 42 | Delino Deshields (RR)(FC) | .80 | .60 | 90 | Alan Trammell | .10 | .08 |
| 43 | Scott Coolbaugh (RR)(FC) | .15 | .11 | 91 | Tony Phillips | .05 | .04 |
| 44 | Pat Combs (RR)(FC) | .25 | .20 | 92 | Doug Drabek | .05 | .04 |
| 45 | Alex Sanchez (RR) | .15 | .11 | 93 | Jeffrey Leonard | .09 | .07 |
| 46 | Kelly Mann (RR)(FC) | .20 | .15 | 94 | Wally Joyner | .15 | .11 |
| 47 | Julio Machado (RR)(FC) | .20 | .15 | 95 | Carney Lansford | .09 | .07 |
| 48 | Pete Incaviglia | .05 | .04 | 96 | Cal Ripken | .15 | .11 |
| 49 | Shawon Dunston | .07 | .05 | 97 | Andres Galarraga | .15 | .11 |
| 50 | Jeff Treadway | .05 | .04 | 98 | Kevin Mitchell | .30 | .25 |
| 51 | Jeff Ballard | .10 | .08 | 99 | Howard Johnson | .15 | .11 |
| 52 | Claudell Washington | .08 | .06 | 100 | Checklist | .04 | .03 |
| 53 | Juan Samuel | .10 | .08 | 101 | Melido Perez | .07 | .05 |
| 54 | John Smiley | .08 | .06 | 102 | Spike Owen | .05 | .04 |
| 55 | Rob Deer | .06 | .05 | 103 | Paul Molitor | .10 | .08 |
| 56 | Geno Petralli | .04 | .03 | 104 | Geronimo Berroa | .06 | .05 |
| 57 | Chris Bosio | .10 | .08 | 105 | Ryne Sandberg | .25 | .20 |
| 58 | Carlton Fisk | .12 | .09 | 106 | Bryn Smith | .06 | .05 |
|  |  |  |  | 107 | Steve Buechele | .04 | .03 |
|  |  |  |  | 108 | Jim Abbott | .30 | .25 |
|  |  |  |  | 109 | Alvin Davis | .10 | .08 |
|  |  |  |  | 110 | Lee Smith | .05 | .04 |
|  |  |  |  | 111 | Roberto Alomar | .15 | .11 |
|  |  |  |  | 112 | Rick Reuschel | .09 | .07 |
|  |  |  |  | 113 | Kelly Gruber | .09 | .07 |
|  |  |  |  | 114 | Joe Carter | .09 | .07 |
|  |  |  |  | 115 | Jose Rijo | .06 | .05 |
|  |  |  |  | 116 | Greg Minton | .04 | .03 |
|  |  |  |  | 117 | Bob Ojeda | .04 | .03 |
|  |  |  |  | 118 | Glenn Davis | .08 | .06 |
|  |  |  |  | 119 | Jeff Reardon | .05 | .04 |
|  |  |  |  | 120 | Kurt Stillwell | .05 | .04 |
|  |  |  |  | 121 | John Smoltz | .15 | .11 |
|  |  |  |  | 122 | Dwight Evans | .08 | .06 |
|  |  |  |  | 123 | Eric Yelding | .08 | .06 |
|  |  |  |  | 124 | John Franco | .05 | .04 |
|  |  |  |  | 125 | Jose Canseco | .50 | .40 |

| | | MT | NR MT |
|---|---|---|---|
| 126 | Barry Bonds | .25 | .20 |
| 127 | Lee Guetterman | .04 | .03 |
| 128 | Jack Clark | .10 | .08 |
| 129 | Dave Valle | .04 | .03 |
| 130 | Hubie Brooks | .05 | .04 |
| 131 | Ernest Riles | .04 | .03 |
| 132 | Mike Morgan | .04 | .03 |
| 133 | Steve Jeltz | .04 | .03 |
| 134 | Jeff Robinson | .05 | .04 |
| 135 | Ozzie Guillen | .05 | .04 |
| 136 | Chili Davis | .06 | .05 |
| 137 | Mitch Webster | .04 | .03 |
| 138 | Jerry Browne | .06 | .05 |
| 139 | Bo Diaz | .04 | .03 |
| 140 | Robby Thompson | .07 | .05 |
| 141 | Craig Worthington | .09 | .07 |
| 142 | Julio Franco | .09 | .07 |
| 143 | Brian Holman | .05 | .04 |
| 144 | George Brett | .10 | .08 |
| 145 | Tom Glavine | .10 | .08 |
| 146 | Robin Yount | .20 | .15 |
| 147 | Gary Carter | .06 | .05 |
| 148 | Ron Kittle | .06 | .05 |
| 149 | Tony Fernandez | .07 | .05 |
| 150 | Dave Stewart | .07 | .05 |
| 151 | Gary Gaetti | .07 | .05 |
| 152 | Kevin Elster | .04 | .03 |
| 153 | Gerald Perry | .05 | .04 |
| 154 | Jesse Orosco | .05 | .04 |
| 155 | Wally Backman | .05 | .04 |
| 156 | Dennis Martinez | .05 | .04 |
| 157 | Rick Sutcliffe | .08 | .06 |
| 158 | Greg Maddux | .12 | .09 |
| 159 | Andy Hawkins | .05 | .04 |
| 160 | John Kruk | .05 | .04 |
| 161 | Jose Oquendo | .05 | .04 |
| 162 | John Dopson | .08 | .06 |
| 163 | Joe Magrane | .08 | .06 |
| 164 | Billy Ripken | .04 | .03 |
| 165 | Fred Manrique | .04 | .03 |
| 166 | Nolan Ryan | .40 | .30 |
| 167 | Damon Berryhill | .06 | .05 |
| 168 | Dale Murphy | .09 | .07 |
| 169 | Mickey Tettleton | .08 | .06 |
| 170 | Kirk McCaskill | .05 | .04 |
| 171 | Dwight Gooden | .15 | .11 |
| 172 | Jose Lind | .04 | .03 |
| 173 | B.J. Surhoff | .07 | .05 |
| 174 | Ruben Sierra | .15 | .11 |
| 175 | Dan Plesac | .08 | .06 |
| 176 | Dan Pasqua | .05 | .04 |
| 177 | Kelly Downs | .05 | .04 |
| 178 | Matt Nokes | .08 | .06 |
| 179 | Luis Aquino | .04 | .03 |
| 180 | Frank Tanana | .04 | .03 |
| 181 | Tony Pena | .07 | .05 |
| 182 | Dan Gladden | .05 | .04 |
| 183 | Bruce Hurst | .05 | .04 |
| 184 | Roger Clemens | .20 | .15 |
| 185 | Mark McGwire | .30 | .25 |
| 186 | Rob Murphy | .04 | .03 |
| 187 | Jim Deshaies | .06 | .05 |
| 188 | Fred McGriff | .20 | .15 |
| 189 | Rob Dibble | .06 | .05 |
| 190 | Don Mattingly | .40 | .30 |
| 191 | Felix Fermin | .04 | .03 |
| 192 | Roberto Kelly | .08 | .06 |

| | | MT | NR MT |
|---|---|---|---|
| 193 | Dennis Cook | .08 | .06 |
| 194 | Darren Daulton | .04 | .03 |
| 195 | Alfredo Griffin | .05 | .04 |
| 196 | Eric Plunk | .05 | .04 |
| 197 | Orel Hershiser | .20 | .15 |
| 198 | Paul O'Neil | .07 | .05 |
| 199 | Randy Bush | .04 | .03 |
| 200 | Checklist | .04 | .03 |
| 201 | Ozzie Smith | .10 | .08 |
| 202 | Pete O'Brien | .06 | .05 |
| 203 | Jay Howell | .06 | .05 |
| 204 | Mark Gibicza | .08 | .06 |
| 205 | Ed Whitson | .04 | .03 |
| 206 | George Bell | .09 | .07 |
| 207 | Mike Scott | .09 | .07 |
| 208 | Charlie Leibrandt | .04 | .03 |
| 209 | Mike Heath | .04 | .03 |
| 210 | Dennis Eckersley | .09 | .07 |
| 211 | Mike LaValliere | .04 | .03 |
| 212 | Darnell Coles | .04 | .03 |
| 213 | Lance Parrish | .07 | .05 |
| 214 | Mike Moore | .07 | .05 |
| 215 | *Steve Finley* | .20 | .15 |
| 216 | Tim Raines | .09 | .07 |
| 217 | Scott Garrelts | .06 | .05 |
| 218 | Kevin McReynolds | .09 | .07 |
| 219 | Dave Gallagher | .08 | .06 |
| 220 | Tim Wallach | .08 | .06 |
| 221 | Chuck Crim | .04 | .03 |
| 222 | Lonnie Smith | .08 | .06 |
| 223 | Andre Dawson | .10 | .08 |
| 224 | Nelson Santovenia | .07 | .05 |
| 225 | Rafael Palmeiro | .07 | .05 |
| 226 | Devon White | .07 | .05 |
| 227 | Harold Reynolds | .07 | .05 |
| 228 | Ellis Burks | .15 | .11 |
| 229 | Mark Parent | .04 | .03 |
| 230 | Will Clark | .40 | .30 |
| 231 | Jimmy Key | .08 | .06 |
| 232 | John Farrell | .04 | .03 |
| 233 | Eric Davis | .30 | .25 |
| 234 | Johnny Ray | .05 | .04 |
| 235 | Darryl Strawberry | .30 | .25 |
| 236 | Bill Doran | .05 | .04 |
| 237 | Greg Gagne | .05 | .04 |
| 238 | Jim Eisenreich | .04 | .03 |
| 239 | Tommy Gregg | .06 | .05 |
| 240 | Marty Barrett | .05 | .04 |
| 241 | Rafael Ramirez | .05 | .04 |
| 242 | Chris Sabo | .10 | .08 |
| 243 | Dave Henderson | .07 | .05 |
| 244 | Andy Van Slyke | .07 | .05 |
| 245 | Alvaro Espinoza | .10 | .07 |
| 246 | Garry Templeton | .06 | .05 |
| 247 | Gene Harris | .04 | .03 |
| 248 | Kevin Gross | .05 | .04 |
| 249 | Brett Butler | .09 | .07 |
| 250 | Willie Randolph | .07 | .05 |
| 251 | Roger McDowell | .05 | .04 |
| 252 | Rafael Belliard | .04 | .03 |
| 253 | Steve Rosenberg | .04 | .03 |
| 254 | Jack Howell | .04 | .03 |
| 255 | Marvell Wynne | .04 | .03 |
| 256 | Tom Candiotti | .05 | .04 |
| 257 | Todd Benzinger | .05 | .04 |
| 258 | Don Robinson | .04 | .03 |
| 259 | Phil Bradley | .08 | .06 |

| #   | Player | MT | NR MT | | #   | Player | MT | NR MT |
| --- | --- | --- | --- | --- | --- | --- | --- | --- |
| 260 | Cecil Espy | .05 | .04 | | 327 | Frank Williams | .04 | .03 |
| 261 | Scott Bankhead | .05 | .04 | | 328 | Dave Parker | .09 | .07 |
| 262 | Frank White | .07 | .05 | | 329 | Sid Bream | .04 | .03 |
| 263 | Andres Thomas | .05 | .04 | | 330 | Mike Schooler | .06 | .05 |
| 264 | Glenn Braggs | .05 | .04 | | 331 | Bert Blyleven | .08 | .06 |
| 265 | David Cone | .10 | .08 | | 332 | Bob Welch | .07 | .05 |
| 266 | Bobby Thigpen | .07 | .05 | | 333 | Bob Milacki | .06 | .05 |
| 267 | Nelson Liriano | .04 | .03 | | 334 | Tim Burke | .05 | .04 |
| 268 | Terry Steinbach | .09 | .07 | | 335 | Jose Uribe | .05 | .04 |
| 269 | Kirby Puckett | .30 | .25 | | 336 | Randy Myers | .05 | .04 |
| 270 | Gregg Jefferies | .25 | .20 | | 337 | Eric King | .04 | .03 |
| 271 | Jeff Blauser | .05 | .04 | | 338 | Mark Langston | .12 | .09 |
| 272 | Cory Snyder | .07 | .05 | | 339 | Ted Higuera | .08 | .06 |
| 273 | Roy Smith | .05 | .04 | | 340 | Oddibe McDowell | .06 | .05 |
| 274 | Tom Foley | .04 | .03 | | 341 | Lloyd McClendon | .07 | .05 |
| 275 | Mitch Williams | .09 | .07 | | 342 | Pascual Perez | .05 | .04 |
| 276 | Paul Kilgus | .04 | .03 | | 343 | Kevin Brown | .08 | .06 |
| 277 | Don Slaught | .04 | .03 | | 344 | Chuck Finley | .05 | .04 |
| 278 | Von Hayes | .08 | .06 | | 345 | Erik Hanson | .09 | .07 |
| 279 | Vince Coleman | .10 | .08 | | 346 | Rich Gedman | .05 | .04 |
| 280 | Mike Boddicker | .05 | .04 | | 347 | Bip Roberts | .10 | .08 |
| 281 | Ken Dayley | .04 | .03 | | 348 | Matt Williams | .20 | .15 |
| 282 | Mike Devereaux | .07 | .05 | | 349 | Tom Henke | .05 | .04 |
| 283 | *Kenny Rogers* | .09 | .07 | | 350 | Brad Komminsk | .05 | .04 |
| 284 | *Jerome Walton* | .15 | .11 | | 351 | Jeff Reed | .04 | .03 |
| 285 | Jerome Walton | .15 | .11 | | 352 | Brian Downing | .05 | .04 |
| 286 | Derek Lilliquist | .08 | .06 | | 353 | Frank Viola | .09 | .07 |
| 287 | Joe Orsulak | .04 | .03 | | 354 | Terry Puhl | .05 | .04 |
| 288 | Dick Schofield | .04 | .03 | | 355 | Brian Harper | .05 | .04 |
| 289 | Ron Darling | .09 | .07 | | 356 | Steve Farr | .05 | .04 |
| 290 | Bobby Bonilla | .10 | .07 | | 357 | Joe Boever | .05 | .04 |
| 291 | Jim Gantner | .05 | .04 | | 358 | Danny Heep | .04 | .03 |
| 292 | Bobby Witt | .05 | .04 | | 359 | Larry Andersen | .04 | .03 |
| 293 | Greg Brock | .05 | .04 | | 360 | Rolando Roomes | .10 | .08 |
| 294 | Ivan Calderon | .05 | .04 | | 361 | Mike Gallego | .05 | .04 |
| 295 | Steve Bedrosian | .06 | .05 | | 362 | Bob Kipper | .04 | .03 |
| 296 | Mike Henneman | .06 | .05 | | 363 | Clay Parker | .07 | .05 |
| 297 | Tom Gordon | .25 | .20 | | 364 | Mike Pagliarulo | .05 | .04 |
| 298 | Lou Whitaker | .08 | .06 | | 365 | Ken Griffey, Jr. | 1.00 | .70 |
| 299 | Terry Pendleton | .07 | .05 | | 366 | Rex Hudler | .04 | .03 |
| 300 | Checklist | .04 | .03 | | 367 | Pat Sheridan | .04 | .03 |
| 301 | Juan Berenguer | .04 | .03 | | 368 | Kirk Gibson | .09 | .07 |
| 302 | Mark Davis | .09 | .07 | | 369 | Jeff Parrett | .05 | .04 |
| 303 | Nick Esasky | .09 | .07 | | 370 | Bob Walk | .05 | .04 |
| 304 | Rickey Henderson | .15 | .11 | | 371 | Ken Patterson | .04 | .03 |
| 305 | Rick Cerone | .04 | .03 | | 372 | Bryan Harvey | .05 | .04 |
| 306 | Craig Biggio | .15 | .11 | | 373 | Mike Bielecki | .07 | .05 |
| 307 | Duane Ward | .04 | .03 | | 374 | *Tom Magrann*(FC) | | |
| 308 | Tom Browning | .07 | .05 | | | | .12 | .09 |
| 309 | Walt Terrell | .05 | .04 | | 375 | Rick Mahler | .05 | .04 |
| 310 | Greg Swindell | .10 | .08 | | 376 | Craig Lefferts | .05 | .04 |
| 311 | Dave Righetti | .07 | .05 | | 377 | Gregg Olson | .20 | .15 |
| 312 | Mike Maddux | .04 | .03 | | 378 | Jamie Moyer | .04 | .03 |
| 313 | Lenny Dykstra | .07 | .05 | | 379 | Randy Johnson | .09 | .07 |
| 314 | Jose Gonzalez | .08 | .06 | | 380 | Jeff Montgomery | .06 | .05 |
| 315 | Steve Balboni | .04 | .03 | | 381 | Marty Clary | .06 | .05 |
| 316 | Mike Scioscia | .07 | .05 | | 382 | *Bill Spiers* | .15 | .11 |
| 317 | Ron Oester | .04 | .03 | | 383 | Dave Magadan | .06 | .05 |
| 318 | *Gary Wayne* | .09 | .07 | | 384 | *Greg Hibbard*(FC) | | |
| 319 | Todd Worrell | .06 | .05 | | | | .20 | .11 |
| 320 | Doug Jones | .05 | .04 | | 385 | Ernie Whitt | .05 | .0 |
| 321 | Jeff Hamilton | .05 | .04 | | 386 | Rick Honeycutt | .04 | .0 |
| 322 | Danny Tartabull | .09 | .07 | | 387 | Dave West | .08 | .06 |
| 323 | Chris James | .05 | .04 | | 388 | Keith Hernandez | .07 | .05 |
| 324 | Mike Flanagan | .05 | .04 | | 389 | Jose Alvarez | .04 | .0 |
| 325 | Gerald Young | .05 | .04 | | 390 | *Joey Belle*(FC) | .70 | .50 |
| 326 | Bob Boone | .09 | .07 | | 391 | Rick Aguilera | .05 | .0 |

| | MT | NR MT | | | MT | NR MT |
|---|---|---|---|---|---|---|
| 392 | Mike Fitzgerald | .04 | .03 | 457 | Tony Fossas(FC) | .10 | .08 |
| 393 | Dwight Smith | .15 | .11 | 458 | John Russell | .04 | .03 |
| 394 | Steve Wilson | .09 | .07 | 459 | Paul Assenmacher | .04 | .03 |
| 395 | Bob Geren | .20 | .15 | 460 | Zane Smith | .04 | .03 |
| 396 | Randy Ready | .04 | .03 | 461 | Jack Daugherty | .25 | .20 |
| 397 | Ken Hill | .07 | .05 | 462 | Rich | | |
| 398 | Jody Reed | .05 | .04 | | Monteleone(FC) | .15 | .11 |
| 399 | Tom Brunansky | .07 | .05 | 463 | Greg Briley(FC) | .25 | .20 |
| 400 | Checklist | .04 | .03 | 464 | Mike Smithson | .04 | .03 |
| 401 | Rene Gonzales | .04 | .03 | 465 | Benito Santiago | .09 | .07 |
| 402 | Harold Baines | .09 | .07 | 466 | Jeff Brantley | .10 | .08 |
| 403 | Cecilio Guante | .04 | .03 | 467 | Jose Nunez | .07 | .05 |
| 404 | Joe Girardi | .15 | .11 | 468 | Scott Bailes | .04 | .03 |
| 405 | Sergio Valdez(FC) | | | 469 | Ken Griffey | .06 | .05 |
| | | .30 | .25 | 470 | Bob McClure | .04 | .03 |
| 406 | Mark Williamson | .04 | .03 | 471 | Mackey Sasser | .04 | .03 |
| 407 | Glenn Hoffman | .04 | .03 | 472 | Glenn Wilson | .04 | .03 |
| 408 | Jeff Innis(FC) | .10 | .08 | 473 | Kevin Tapani(FC) | | |
| 409 | Randy Kramer | .04 | .03 | | | .30 | .25 |
| 410 | Charlie O'Brien(FC) | .04 | .03 | 474 | Bill Buckner | .05 | .04 |
| 411 | Charlie Hough | .06 | .05 | 475 | Ron Gant | .05 | .04 |
| 412 | Gus Polidor | .04 | .03 | 476 | Kevin Romine(FC) | .05 | .04 |
| 413 | Ron Karkovice | .04 | .03 | 477 | Juan Agosto | .04 | .03 |
| 414 | Trevor Wilson(FC) | .07 | .05 | 478 | Herm Winningham | .04 | .03 |
| 415 | Kevin Ritz(FC) | .20 | .15 | 479 | Storm Davis | .04 | .03 |
| 416 | Gary Thurman | .04 | .03 | 480 | Jeff King(FC) | .09 | .07 |
| 417 | Jeff Robinson | .04 | .03 | 481 | Kevin Mmahat(FC) | | |
| 418 | Scott Terry | .05 | .04 | | | .25 | .20 |
| 419 | Tim Laudner | .04 | .03 | 482 | Carmelo Martinez | .05 | .04 |
| 420 | Dennis Rasmussen | .04 | .03 | 483 | Omar Vizquel | .10 | .08 |
| 421 | Luis Rivera | .04 | .03 | 484 | Jim Dwyer | .04 | .03 |
| 422 | Jim Corsi(FC) | .07 | .05 | 485 | Bob Knepper | .04 | .03 |
| 423 | Dennis Lamp | .04 | .03 | 486 | Dave Anderson | .04 | .03 |
| 424 | Ken Caminiti | .06 | .05 | 487 | Ron Jones | .09 | .07 |
| 425 | David Wells | .06 | .05 | 488 | Jay Bell | .05 | .04 |
| 426 | Norm Charlton | .09 | .07 | 489 | Sammy Sosa(FC) | | |
| 427 | Deion Sanders | .50 | .40 | | | .35 | .25 |
| 428 | Dion James | .05 | .04 | 490 | Kent Anderson(FC) | | |
| 429 | Chuck Cary | .05 | .04 | | | .15 | .11 |
| 430 | Ken Howell | .04 | .03 | 491 | Domingo Ramos | .04 | .03 |
| 431 | Steve Lake | .04 | .03 | 492 | Dave Clark | .05 | .04 |
| 432 | Kal Daniels | .09 | .07 | 493 | Tim Birtsas | .04 | .03 |
| 433 | Lance McCullers | .05 | .04 | 494 | Ken Oberkfell | .04 | .03 |
| 434 | Lenny Harris(FC) | .10 | .08 | 495 | Larry Sheets | .04 | .03 |
| 435 | Scott Scudder(FC) | | | 496 | Jeff Kunkel | .04 | .03 |
| | | .20 | .15 | 497 | Jim Presley | .04 | .03 |
| 436 | Gene Larkin | .04 | .03 | 498 | Mike Macfarlane | .04 | .03 |
| 437 | Dan Quisenberry | .05 | .04 | 499 | Pete Smith | .05 | .04 |
| 438 | Steve Olin(FC) | .15 | .11 | 500 | Checklist | .04 | .03 |
| 439 | Mickey Hatcher | .05 | .04 | 501 | Gary Sheffield | .35 | .25 |
| 440 | Willie Wilson | .05 | .04 | 502 | Terry Bross(FC) | .15 | .11 |
| 441 | Mark Grant | .05 | .04 | 503 | Jerry Kutzler(FC) | | |
| 442 | Mookie Wilson | .07 | .05 | | | .20 | .15 |
| 443 | Alex Trevino | .04 | .03 | 504 | Lloyd Moseby | .05 | .04 |
| 444 | Pat Tabler | .05 | .04 | 505 | Curt Young | .04 | .03 |
| 445 | Dave Bergman | .04 | .03 | 506 | Al Newman | .04 | .03 |
| 446 | Todd Burns | .05 | .04 | 507 | Keith Miller | .04 | .03 |
| 447 | R.J. Reynolds | .04 | .03 | 508 | Mike Stanton(FC) | | |
| 448 | Jay Buhner | .08 | .06 | | | .20 | .15 |
| 449 | Lee Stevens(FC) | .20 | .15 | 509 | Rich Yett | .04 | .03 |
| 450 | Ron Hassey | .04 | .03 | 510 | Tim Drummond(FC) | | |
| 451 | Bob Melvin | .04 | .03 | | | .20 | .15 |
| 452 | Dave Martinez | .05 | .04 | 511 | Joe Hesketh | .04 | .03 |
| 453 | Greg Litton(FC) | .15 | .11 | 512 | Rick Wrona | .10 | .08 |
| 454 | Mark Carreon | .10 | .07 | 513 | Luis Salazar | .04 | .03 |
| 455 | Scott Fletcher | .05 | .04 | 514 | Hal Morris | .06 | .05 |
| 456 | Otis Nixon | .04 | .03 | 515 | Terry Mullholland | .07 | .05 |

| | | MT | NR MT | | | | MT | NR MT |
|---|---|---|---|---|---|---|---|---|
| 516 | John Morris | .05 | .04 | | 579 | Mike Stanley | .04 | .03 |
| 517 | Carlos Quintana | .08 | .06 | | 580 | Mike Witt | .05 | .04 |
| 518 | Frank DiPino | .04 | .03 | | 581 | Scott Bradley | .04 | .03 |
| 519 | Randy Milligan | .06 | .05 | | 582 | Greg Harris | .07 | .05 |
| 520 | Chad Kreuter | .07 | .05 | | 583 | Kevin Hickey | .04 | .03 |
| 521 | Mike Jeffcoat | .04 | .03 | | 584 | Lee Mazzilli | .04 | .03 |
| 522 | Mike Harkey | .10 | .08 | | 585 | Jeff Pico | .04 | .03 |
| 523 | Andy Nezelek | .07 | .05 | | 586 | *Joe Oliver*(FC) | .20 | .15 |
| 524 | Dave Schmidt | .04 | .03 | | 587 | Willie Fraser | .04 | .03 |
| 525 | Tony Armas | .04 | .03 | | 588 | Puzzle Card | .04 | .03 |
| 526 | Barry Lyons | .04 | .03 | | 589 | Kevin Bass | .06 | .05 |
| 527 | *Rick Reed*(FC) | .20 | .15 | | 590 | John Moses | .04 | .03 |
| 528 | Jerry Reuss | .06 | .05 | | 591 | Tom Pagnozzi | .04 | .03 |
| 529 | *Dean Palmer*(FC) | | | | 592 | *Tony Castillo* | .10 | .08 |
| | | 1.00 | .70 | | 593 | Jerald Clark | .06 | .05 |
| 530 | *Jeff Peterek*(FC) | .20 | .15 | | 594 | Dan Schatzeder | .04 | .03 |
| 531 | *Carlos Martinez* | .20 | .15 | | 595 | Luis Quinones | .04 | .03 |
| 532 | Atlee Hammaker | .05 | .04 | | 596 | Pete Harnisch | .08 | .06 |
| 533 | Mike Brumley | .04 | .03 | | 597 | Gary Redus | .04 | .03 |
| 534 | Terry Leach | .04 | .03 | | 598 | Mel Hall | .05 | .04 |
| 535 | *Doug Strange*(FC) | | | | 599 | Rick Schu | .04 | .03 |
| | | .20 | .15 | | 600 | Checklist | .04 | .03 |
| 536 | Jose DeLeon | .05 | .04 | | 601 | Mike Kingery | .04 | .03 |
| 537 | Shane Rawley | .05 | .04 | | 602 | Terry Kennedy | .04 | .03 |
| 538 | Joey Cora(FC) | .10 | .08 | | 603 | Mike Sharperson | .06 | .05 |
| 539 | Eric Hetzel | .08 | .06 | | 604 | Don Carman | .04 | .03 |
| 540 | Gene Nelson | .04 | .03 | | 605 | Jim Gott | .05 | .04 |
| 541 | Wes Gardner | .04 | .03 | | 606 | Donn Pall | .05 | .04 |
| 542 | Mark Portugal | .04 | .03 | | 607 | Rance Mulliniks | .04 | .03 |
| 543 | Al Leiter | .05 | .04 | | 608 | Curt Wilkerson | .04 | .03 |
| 544 | Jack Armstrong | .04 | .03 | | 609 | Mike Felder | .04 | .03 |
| 545 | Greg Cadaret | .04 | .03 | | 610 | Guillermo Hernandez | | |
| 546 | Rod Nichols | .04 | .03 | | | | .04 | .03 |
| 547 | Luis Polonia | .05 | .04 | | 611 | Candy Maldonado | .05 | .04 |
| 548 | Charlie Hayes(FC) | .20 | .15 | | 612 | Mark Thurmond | .04 | .03 |
| 549 | Dickie Thon | .04 | .03 | | 613 | Rick Leach | .04 | .03 |
| 550 | Tim Crews | .04 | .03 | | 614 | Jerry Reed | .04 | .03 |
| 551 | Dave Winfield | .20 | .15 | | 615 | Franklin Stubbs | .05 | .04 |
| 552 | Mike Davis | .04 | .03 | | 616 | Billy Hatcher | .05 | .04 |
| 553 | Ron Robinson | .04 | .03 | | 617 | Don August | .05 | .04 |
| 554 | Carmen Castillo | .04 | .03 | | 618 | Tim Teufel | .04 | .03 |
| 555 | John Costello | .04 | .03 | | 619 | Shawn Hillegas | .04 | .03 |
| 556 | Bud Black | .04 | .03 | | 620 | Manny Lee | .04 | .03 |
| 557 | Rick Dempsey | .04 | .03 | | 621 | Gary Ward | .05 | .04 |
| 558 | Jim Acker | .04 | .03 | | 622 | *Mark Guthrie*(FC) | | |
| 559 | Eric Show | .06 | .05 | | | | .20 | .15 |
| 560 | Pat Borders | .06 | .05 | | 623 | Jeff Musselman | .05 | .04 |
| 561 | Danny Darwin | .04 | .03 | | 624 | Mark Lemke | .07 | .05 |
| 562 | *Rick Luecken*(FC) | | | | 625 | Fernando Valenzuela | | |
| | | .20 | .15 | | | | .07 | .05 |
| 563 | Edwin Nunez | .05 | .04 | | 626 | *Paul Sorrento*(FC) | | |
| 564 | Felix Jose | .09 | .07 | | | | .25 | .20 |
| 565 | John Cangelosi | .04 | .03 | | 627 | Glenallen Hill | .20 | .15 |
| 566 | Billy Swift | .04 | .03 | | 628 | Les Lancaster | .05 | .04 |
| 567 | Bill Schroeder | .04 | .03 | | 629 | Vance Law | .04 | .03 |
| 568 | Stan Javier | .04 | .03 | | 630 | Randy Velarde(FC) | .10 | .08 |
| 569 | Jim Traber | .04 | .03 | | 631 | Todd Frohwirth | .04 | .03 |
| 570 | Wallace Johnson | .04 | .03 | | 632 | Willie McGee | .06 | .05 |
| 571 | Donell Nixon | .04 | .03 | | 633 | Oil Can Boyd | .06 | .05 |
| 572 | Sid Fernandez | .08 | .06 | | 634 | Cris Carpenter | .09 | .07 |
| 573 | Lance Johnson | .09 | .07 | | 635 | Brian Holton | .04 | .03 |
| 574 | Andy McGaffigan | .04 | .03 | | 636 | Tracy Jones | .05 | .04 |
| 575 | Mark Knudson | .04 | .03 | | 637 | Terry Steinbach (AS) | | |
| 576 | *Tommy Greene*(FC) | | | | | | .09 | .07 |
| | | .30 | .25 | | 638 | Brady Anderson | .09 | .07 |
| 577 | Mark Grace | .25 | .20 | | 639 | Jack Morris | .06 | .05 |
| 578 | *Larry Walker*(FC) | .50 | .40 | | | | | |

| | | MT | NR MT |
|---|---|---|---|
| 640 | *Jaime Navarro*(FC) | .30 | .25 |
| 641 | Darrin Jackson | .05 | .04 |
| 642 | *Mike Dyer*(FC) | .20 | .15 |
| 643 | Mike Schmidt | .40 | .30 |
| 644 | Henry Cotto | .04 | .03 |
| 645 | John Cerutti | .05 | .04 |
| 646 | *Francisco Cabrera*(FC) | .40 | .30 |
| 647 | Scott Sanderson | .05 | .04 |
| 648 | Brian Meyer | .05 | .04 |
| 649 | Ray Searage | .05 | .04 |
| 650a | Bo Jackson AS (Recent Major League Performance on back) | 1.50 | 1.25 |
| 650b | Bo Jackson AS (Corrected) | .50 | .40 |
| 651 | Steve Lyons | .04 | .03 |
| 652 | Mike LaCoss | .04 | .03 |
| 653 | Ted Power | .04 | .03 |
| 654 | Howard Johnson (AS) | .20 | .15 |
| 655 | *Mauro Gozzo*(FC) | .15 | .11 |
| 656 | *Mike Blowers*(FC) | .25 | .20 |
| 657 | Paul Gibson | .05 | .04 |
| 658 | Neal Heaton | .05 | .04 |
| 659a | 5000 K (Nolan Ryan) (King card number 665 back) | 9.00 | 6.75 |
| 659b | 5000 K (Nolan Ryan) (Corrected) | 1.00 | .70 |
| 660a | Harold Baines (AS — recent major league performance on back) | 5.00 | 3.75 |
| 660b | Harold Baines (AS - line through star on front incorrect back) | 7.00 | 5.25 |
| 660c | Harold Baines (AS — Incorrect front and back) | 7.00 | 5.25 |
| 660d | Harold Baines (AS — Corrected) | .10 | .08 |
| 661 | Gary Pettis | .05 | .04 |
| 662 | *Clint Zavaras*(FC) | .20 | .15 |
| 663 | Rick Reuschel | .08 | .06 |
| 664 | Alejandro Pena | .05 | .04 |
| 665a | King of Kings (Nolan Ryan) (5000 K card number 659 back) | 10.00 | 7.50 |
| 665b | King of Kings (Nolan Ryan) (Corrected) | 1.00 | .70 |
| 665c | King of Kings (Nolan Ryan) (No card #) | 5.00 | 3.75 |
| 666 | Ricky Horton | .04 | .03 |
| 667 | Curt Schilling | .06 | .05 |
| 668 | Bill Landrum(FC) | .05 | .04 |
| 669 | Todd Stottlemyre | .05 | .04 |
| 670 | Tim Leary | .05 | .04 |
| 671 | *John Wetteland*(FC) | .30 | .25 |
| 672 | Calvin Schiraldi | .04 | .03 |
| 673 | Ruben Sierra (AS) | .09 | .07 |
| 674 | Pedro Guerrero (AS) | .09 | .07 |

| | | MT | NR MT |
|---|---|---|---|
| 675 | Ken Phelps | .04 | .03 |
| 676 | Cal Ripken (AS) | .09 | .07 |
| 677 | Denny Walling | .04 | .03 |
| 678 | Goose Gossage | .04 | .03 |
| 679 | *Gary Mielke*(FC) | .20 | .15 |
| 680 | Bill Bathe | .04 | .03 |
| 681 | Tom Lawless | .04 | .03 |
| 682 | *Xavier Hernandez*(FC) | .20 | .15 |
| 683 | Kirby Puckett (AS) | .09 | .07 |
| 684 | Mariano Duncan | .05 | .04 |
| 685 | Ramon Martinez | .10 | .08 |
| 686 | Tim Jones | .05 | .04 |
| 687 | Tom Filer | .04 | .03 |
| 688 | Steve Lombardozzi | .04 | .03 |
| 689 | *Bernie Williams*(FC) | .50 | .40 |
| 690 | *Chip Hale*(FC) | .15 | .11 |
| 691 | *Beau Allred*(FC) | .15 | .11 |
| 692 | Ryne Sandberg (AS) | .09 | .07 |
| 693 | *Jeff Huson*(FC) | .25 | .20 |
| 694 | Curt Ford | .04 | .03 |
| 695 | Eric Davis (AS) | .09 | .07 |
| 696 | Scott Lusader | .05 | .04 |
| 697 | Mark McGwire (AS) | .09 | .07 |
| 698 | *Steve Cummings*(FC) | .15 | .11 |
| 699 | *George Canale*(FC) | .15 | .11 |
| 700 | Checklist | .04 | .03 |
| 701 | Julio Franco (AS) | .09 | .07 |
| 702 | *Dave Johnson*(FC) | .10 | .08 |
| 703 | Dave Stewart (AS) | .08 | .06 |
| 704 | *Dave Justice*(FC) | 2.50 | 2.00 |
| 705 | Tony Gwynn (AS) | .09 | .07 |
| 706 | Greg Myers | .06 | .05 |
| 707 | Will Clark (AS) | .15 | .11 |
| 708 | Benito Santiago (AS) | .08 | .06 |
| 709 | Larry McWilliams | .04 | .03 |
| 710 | Ozzie Smith (AS) | .08 | .06 |
| 711 | *John Olerud*(FC) | .70 | .50 |
| 712 | Wade Boggs (AS) | .09 | .07 |
| 713 | *Gary Eave*(FC) | .15 | .11 |
| 714 | Bob Tewksbury | .05 | .04 |
| 715 | Kevin Mitchell (AS) | .09 | .07 |
| 716 | A. Bartlett Giamatti | .35 | .25 |

## 1990 Donruss Rookies

For the fifth straight year, Donruss issued a 56-card

"Rookies" set in 1990. As in previous years, the set is similar in design to the regular Donruss set, except for a new "The Rookies" logo and green borders instead of red. The set is packaged in a special box and includes a special Carl Yastrzemski puzzle card.

|  | | MT | NR MT |
|---|---|---|---|
| Complete Set: | | 8.00 | 6.00 |
| Common Player: | | .10 | .08 |
| 1 | Sandy Alomar | .15 | .11 |
| 2 | John Olerud | .50 | .40 |
| 3 | Pat Combs | .20 | .15 |
| 4 | Brian Dubois | .10 | .08 |
| 5 | Felix Jose | .12 | .09 |
| 6 | Delino DeShields | .50 | .40 |
| 7 | Mike Stanton | .10 | .08 |
| 8 | Mike Munoz(FC) | .10 | .08 |
| 9 | Craig Grebeck(FC) | .15 | .11 |
| 10 | Joe Kraemer(FC) | .10 | .08 |
| 11 | Jeff Huson | .10 | .08 |
| 12 | Bill Sampen(FC) | .30 | .25 |
| 13 | Brian Bohanon(FC) | .12 | .09 |
| 14 | Dave Justice | 2.00 | 1.50 |
| 15 | Robin Ventura | .80 | .60 |
| 16 | Greg Vaughn | .60 | .45 |
| 17 | Wayne Edwards(FC) | .15 | .11 |
| 18 | Shawn Boskie | .25 | .20 |
| 19 | Carlos Baerga(FC) | 1.00 | .70 |
| 20 | Mark Gardner | .20 | .15 |
| 21 | Kevin Appier(FC) | .30 | .25 |
| 22 | Mike Harkey | .20 | .15 |
| 23 | Tim Layana(FC) | .20 | .15 |
| 24 | Glenallen Hill | .20 | .15 |
| 25 | Jerry Kutzler | .10 | .08 |
| 26 | Mike Blowers | .15 | .11 |
| 27 | Scott Ruskin(FC) | .25 | .20 |
| 28 | Dana Kiecker(FC) | .15 | .11 |
| 29 | Willie Blair(FC) | .10 | .08 |
| 30 | Ben McDonald | .60 | .45 |
| 31 | Todd Zeile | .40 | .30 |
| 32 | Scott Coolbaugh | .12 | .09 |
| 33 | Xavier Hernandez | .10 | .08 |
| 34 | Mike Hartley(FC) | .15 | .11 |
| 35 | Kevin Tapani | .30 | .25 |
| 36 | Kevin Wickander(FC) | | |
|  | | .10 | .08 |
| 37 | Carlos Hernandez(FC) | | |
|  | | .15 | .11 |
| 38 | Brian Traxler(FC) | .20 | .15 |
| 39 | Marty Brown(FC) | .10 | .08 |
| 40 | Scott Radinsky(FC) | .25 | .20 |
| 41 | Julio Machado | .15 | .11 |
| 42 | Steve Avery | .80 | .60 |
| 43 | Mark Lemke | .12 | .09 |
| 44 | Alan Mills(FC) | .25 | .20 |
| 45 | Marquis Grissom | .50 | .40 |
| 46 | Greg Olson(FC) | .15 | .11 |
| 47 | Dave Hollins(FC) | .30 | .25 |
| 48 | Jerald Clark | .10 | .08 |
| 49 | Eric Anthony | .20 | .15 |
| 50 | Tim Drummond | .10 | .08 |
| 51 | John Burkett(FC) | .20 | .15 |

|  | | MT | NR MT |
|---|---|---|---|
| 52 | Brent Knackert(FC) | .12 | .09 |
| 53 | Jeff Shaw(FC) | .12 | .09 |
| 54 | John Orton(FC) | .10 | .08 |
| 55 | Terry Shumpert(FC) | .15 | .11 |
| 56 | Checklist | .10 | .08 |

## 1991 Donruss

Donruss decided to use a two series format in 1991. The first series was released in December and the second in February. The 1991 design is somewhat reminiscent of the 1986 set. Blue borders are used. Limited edition cards including an autographed Ryne Sandberg card (5,000) were randomly inserted in wax packs. Other features of the set include 40 Rated Rookies, a "Legends Series," Elite Series, and another Diamond King subset. Collectors could also take part in Donruss' Instant Win promotion.

|  | | MT | NR MT |
|---|---|---|---|
| Complete Set: | | 18.00 | 13.50 |
| Common Player: | | .04 | .03 |
| 1 | Dave Steib (DK) | .04 | .03 |
| 2 | Craig Biggio (DK) | .05 | .04 |
| 3 | Cecil Fielder (DK) | .15 | .11 |
| 4 | Barry Bonds (DK) | .10 | .08 |
| 5 | Barry Larkin (DK) | .06 | .05 |
| 6 | Dave Parker (DK) | .05 | .04 |
| 7 | Len Dykstra (DK) | .06 | .05 |
| 8 | Bobby Thigpen (DK) | .05 | .04 |
| 9 | Roger Clemens (DK) | .10 | .08 |
| 10 | Ron Gant (DK) | .08 | .06 |
| 11 | Delino DeShields (DK) | | |
|  | | .08 | .06 |
| 12 | Roberto Alomar (DK) | | |
|  | | .08 | .06 |
| 13 | Sandy Alomar (DK) | .12 | .09 |
| 14 | Ryne Sandberg (DK) | .15 | .11 |
| 15 | Ramon Martinez (DK) | | |
|  | | .06 | .05 |
| 16 | Edgar Martinez (DK) | .08 | .06 |
| 17 | Dave Magadan (DK) | .04 | .03 |

| | | MT | NR MT | | | MT | NR MT |
|---|---|---|---|---|---|---|---|
| 18 | Matt Williams (DK) | .12 | .09 | 64 | Mark Guthrie | .05 | .04 |
| 19 | Rafael Palmeiro (DK) | | | 65 | Mark Salas | .04 | .03 |
| | | .05 | .04 | 66 | Tim Jones | .04 | .03 |
| 20 | Bob Welch (DK) | .06 | .05 | 67 | Tim Leary | .05 | .04 |
| 21 | Dave Righetti (DK) | .04 | .03 | 68 | Andres Galarraga | .08 | .06 |
| 22 | Brian Harper (DK) | .04 | .03 | 69 | Bob Milacki | .05 | .04 |
| 23 | Gregg Olson (DK) | .05 | .04 | 70 | Tim Belcher | .08 | .06 |
| 24 | Kurt Stillwell (DK) | .04 | .03 | 71 | Todd Zeile | .20 | .15 |
| 25 | Pedro Guerrero (DK) | | | 72 | Jerome Walton | .08 | .06 |
| | | .05 | .04 | 73 | Kevin Seitzer | .06 | .05 |
| 26 | Chuck Finley (DK) | .05 | .04 | 74 | Jerald Clark | .06 | .05 |
| 27 | DK Checklist | .04 | .03 | 75 | John Smoltz | .08 | .06 |
| 28 | Tino Martinez (RR)(FC) | | | 76 | Mike Henneman | .05 | .04 |
| | | .20 | .15 | 77 | Ken Griffey,Jr. | .80 | .60 |
| 29 | Mark Lewis (RR)(FC) | | | 78 | Jim Abbott | .06 | .05 |
| | | .35 | .25 | 79 | Gregg Jefferies | .15 | .11 |
| 30 | *Bernard Gilkey* (RR)(FC) | | | 80 | Kevin Reimer(FC) | .20 | .15 |
| | | .20 | .15 | 81 | Roger Clemens | .15 | .11 |
| 31 | Hensley Meulens (RR) | | | 82 | Mike Fitzgerald | .04 | .03 |
| | | .08 | .06 | 83 | Bruce Hurst | .06 | .05 |
| 32 | *Derek Bell* (RR)(FC) | .40 | .30 | 84 | Eric Davis | .15 | .11 |
| 33 | Jose Offerman (RR)(FC) | | | 85 | Paul Molitor | .08 | .06 |
| | | .25 | .20 | 86 | Will Clark | .25 | .20 |
| 34 | Terry Bross (RR) | .10 | .08 | 87 | Mike Bielecki | .04 | .03 |
| 35 | *Leo Gomez* (RR)(FC) | | | 88 | Bret Saberhagen | .10 | .08 |
| | | .40 | .30 | 89 | Nolan Ryan | .25 | .20 |
| 36 | Derrick May (RR)(FC) | | | 90 | Bobby Thigpen | .08 | .06 |
| | | .25 | .20 | 91 | Dickie Thon | .04 | .03 |
| 37 | *Kevin Morton* (RR)(FC) | | | 92 | Duane Ward | .04 | .03 |
| | | .25 | .20 | 93 | Luis Polonia | .04 | .03 |
| 38 | Moises Alou (RR)(FC) | | | 94 | Terry Kennedy | .04 | .03 |
| | | .10 | .08 | 95 | Kent Hrbek | .08 | .06 |
| 39 | *Julio Valera* (RR)(FC) | | | 96 | Danny Jackson | .06 | .05 |
| | | .15 | .11 | 97 | Sid Fernandez | .08 | .06 |
| 40 | Milt Cuyler (RR)(FC) | .10 | .08 | 98 | Jimmy Key | .06 | .05 |
| 41 | *Phil Plantier* (RR)(FC) | | | 99 | Franklin Stubbs | .05 | .04 |
| | | .80 | .60 | 100 | Checklist | .04 | .03 |
| 42 | *Scott Chiamparino* (RR)(FC) | | | 101 | R.J. Reynolds | .04 | .03 |
| | | .30 | .25 | 102 | Dave Stewart | .08 | .06 |
| 43 | *Ray Lankford* (RR)(FC) | | | 103 | Dan Pasqua | .05 | .04 |
| | | .40 | .30 | 104 | Dan Plesac | .06 | .05 |
| 44 | *Mickey Morandini* (RR)(FC) | | | 105 | Mark McGwire | .20 | .15 |
| | | .20 | .15 | 106 | John Farrell | .04 | .03 |
| 45 | Dave Hansen (RR)(FC) | | | 107 | Don Mattingly | .20 | .15 |
| | | .10 | .08 | 108 | Carlton Fisk | .10 | .08 |
| 46 | *Kevin Belcher* (RR)(FC) | | | 109 | Ken Oberkfell | .04 | .03 |
| | | .15 | .11 | 110 | Darrel Akerfelds | .04 | .03 |
| 47 | Darrin Fletcher (RR)(FC) | | | 111 | Gregg Olson | .08 | .06 |
| | | .10 | .08 | 112 | Mike Scioscia | .06 | .05 |
| 48 | Steve Sax (AS) | .05 | .04 | 113 | Bryn Smith | .04 | .03 |
| 49 | Ken Griffey,Jr. (AS) | .40 | .30 | 114 | Bob Geren | .05 | .04 |
| 50 | Jose Canseco (AS) | .25 | .20 | 115 | Tom Candiotti | .04 | .03 |
| 51 | Sandy Alomar (AS) | .10 | .08 | 116 | Kevin Tapani | .15 | .11 |
| 52 | Cal Ripken (AS) | .05 | .04 | 117 | Jeff Treadway | .05 | .04 |
| 53 | Rickey Henderson (AS) | | | 118 | Alan Trammell | .08 | .06 |
| | | .15 | .11 | 119 | Pete O'Brien | .04 | .03 |
| 54 | Bob Welch (AS) | .05 | .04 | 120 | Joel Skinner | .04 | .03 |
| 55 | Wade Boggs (AS) | .10 | .08 | 121 | Mike LaValliere | .05 | .04 |
| 56 | Mark McGwire (AS) | .10 | .08 | 122 | Dwight Evans | .08 | .06 |
| 57 | Jack McDowell | .06 | .05 | 123 | Jody Reed | .08 | .06 |
| 58 | Jose Lind | .05 | .04 | 124 | Lee Guetterman | .04 | .03 |
| 59 | *Alex Fernandez*(FC) | | | 125 | Tim Burke | .05 | .04 |
| | | .50 | .40 | 126 | Dave Johnson | .04 | .03 |
| 60 | Pat Combs | .08 | .06 | 127 | Fernando Valenzuela | | |
| 61 | *Mike Walker*(FC) | .15 | .11 | | | .08 | .06 |
| 62 | Juan Samuel | .05 | .04 | 128 | Jose DeLeon | .06 | .05 |
| 63 | Mike Blowers | .05 | .04 | 129 | Andre Dawson | .10 | .08 |

| | | MT | NR MT | | | | MT | NR MT |
|---|---|---|---|---|---|---|---|---|
| 130 | Gerald Perry | .05 | .04 | 197 | Edgar Diaz(FC) | | .08 | .06 |
| 131 | Greg Harris | .04 | .03 | 198 | Greg Litton | | .05 | .04 |
| 132 | Tom Glavine | .08 | .06 | 199 | Mark Grace | | .10 | .08 |
| 133 | Lance McCullers | .04 | .03 | 200 | Checklist | | .04 | .03 |
| 134 | Randy Johnson | .08 | .06 | 201 | George Brett | | .10 | .08 |
| 135 | Lance Parrish | .08 | .06 | 202 | Jeff Russell | | .06 | .05 |
| 136 | Mackey Sasser | .08 | .06 | 203 | Ivan Calderon | | .08 | .06 |
| 137 | Geno Petralli | .04 | .03 | 204 | Ken Howell | | .04 | .03 |
| 138 | Dennis Lamp | .04 | .03 | 205 | Tom Henke | | .08 | .06 |
| 139 | Dennis Martinez | .06 | .05 | 206 | Bryan Harvey | | .06 | .05 |
| 140 | Mike Pagliarulo | .05 | .04 | 207 | Steve Bedrosian | | .08 | .06 |
| 141 | Hal Morris | .10 | .08 | 208 | Al Newman | | .04 | .03 |
| 142 | Dave Parker | .10 | .08 | 209 | Randy Myers | | .08 | .06 |
| 143 | Brett Butler | .06 | .05 | 210 | Daryl Boston | | .04 | .03 |
| 144 | Paul Assenmacher | .04 | .03 | 211 | Manny Lee | | .06 | .05 |
| 145 | Mark Gubicza | .06 | .05 | 212 | Dave Smith | | .06 | .05 |
| 146 | Charlie Hough | .05 | .04 | 213 | Don Slaught | | .04 | .03 |
| 147 | Sammy Sosa | .15 | .11 | 214 | Walt Weiss | | .06 | .05 |
| 148 | Randy Ready | .04 | .03 | 215 | Donn Pall | | .04 | .03 |
| 149 | Kelly Gruber | .08 | .06 | 216 | Jamie Navarro | | .06 | .05 |
| 150 | Devon White | .06 | .05 | 217 | Willie Randolph | | .06 | .05 |
| 151 | Gary Carter | .08 | .06 | 218 | Rudy Seanez(FC) | | .08 | .06 |
| 152 | Gene Larkin | .05 | .04 | 219 | Jim Leyritz(FC) | | .08 | .06 |
| 153 | Chris Sabo | .08 | .06 | 220 | Ron Karkovice | | .05 | .04 |
| 154 | David Cone | .08 | .06 | 221 | Ken Caminiti | | .05 | .04 |
| 155 | Todd Stottlemyre | .06 | .05 | 222 | Von Hayes | | .08 | .06 |
| 156 | Glenn Wilson | .05 | .04 | 223 | Cal Ripken | | .10 | .08 |
| 157 | Bob Walk | .05 | .04 | 224 | Lenny Harris | | .06 | .05 |
| 158 | Mike Gallego | .04 | .03 | 225 | Milt Thompson | | .05 | .04 |
| 159 | Greg Hibbard | .06 | .05 | 226 | Alvaro Espinoza | | .05 | .04 |
| 160 | Chris Bosio | .05 | .04 | 227 | Chris James | | .05 | .04 |
| 161 | Mike Moore | .06 | .05 | 228 | Dan Gladden | | .06 | .05 |
| 162 | Jerry Browne | .06 | .05 | 229 | Jeff Blauser | | .05 | .04 |
| 163 | Steve Sax | .08 | .06 | 230 | Mike Heath | | .04 | .03 |
| 164 | Melido Perez | .06 | .05 | 231 | Omar Vizquel | | .05 | .04 |
| 165 | Danny Darwin | .05 | .04 | 232 | Doug Jones | | .08 | .06 |
| 166 | Roger McDowell | .06 | .05 | 233 | Jeff King | | .06 | .05 |
| 167 | Bill Ripken | .04 | .03 | 234 | Luis Rivera | | .04 | .03 |
| 168 | Mike Sharperson | .05 | .04 | 235 | Ellis Burks | | .10 | .08 |
| 169 | Lee Smith | .08 | .06 | 236 | Greg Cadaret | | .04 | .03 |
| 170 | Matt Nokes | .06 | .05 | 237 | Dave Martinez | | .05 | .04 |
| 171 | Jesse Orosco | .05 | .04 | 238 | Mark Williamson | | .04 | .03 |
| 172 | Rick Aguilera | .06 | .05 | 239 | Stan Javier | | .05 | .04 |
| 173 | Jim Presley | .06 | .05 | 240 | Ozzie Smith | | .10 | .08 |
| 174 | Lou Whitaker | .08 | .06 | 241 | Shawn Boskie | | .15 | .11 |
| 175 | Harold Reynolds | .08 | .06 | 242 | Tom Gordon | | .10 | .08 |
| 176 | Brook Jacoby | .06 | .05 | 243 | Tony Gwynn | | .10 | .08 |
| 177 | Wally Backman | .05 | .04 | 244 | Tommy Gregg | | .04 | .03 |
| 178 | Wade Boggs | .20 | .15 | 245 | Jeff Robinson | | .05 | .04 |
| 179 | Chuck Cary | .04 | .03 | 246 | Keith Comstock | | .04 | .03 |
| 180 | Tom Foley | .04 | .03 | 247 | Jack Howell | | .05 | .04 |
| 181 | Pete Harnisch | .05 | .04 | 248 | Keith Miller | | .05 | .04 |
| 182 | Mike Morgan | .05 | .04 | 249 | Bobby Witt | | .08 | .06 |
| 183 | Bob Tewksbury | .05 | .04 | 250 | Rob Murphy | | .04 | .03 |
| 184 | Joe Girardi | .06 | .05 | 251 | Spike Owen | | .06 | .05 |
| 185 | Storm Davis | .05 | .04 | 252 | Garry Templeton | | .06 | .05 |
| 186 | Ed Whitson | .06 | .05 | 253 | Glenn Braggs | | .06 | .05 |
| 187 | Steve Avery | .25 | .20 | 254 | Ron Robinson | | .06 | .05 |
| 188 | Lloyd Moseby | .06 | .05 | 255 | Kevin Mitchell | | .20 | .15 |
| 189 | Scott Bankhead | .06 | .05 | 256 | Les Lancaster | | .04 | .03 |
| 190 | Mark Langston | .08 | .06 | 257 | Mel Stottlemyre(FC) | | | |
| 191 | Kevin McReynolds | .06 | .05 | | | | .10 | .08 |
| 192 | Julio Franco | .08 | .06 | 258 | Kenny Rogers | | .06 | .05 |
| 193 | John Dopson | .05 | .04 | 259 | Lance Johnson | | .06 | .05 |
| 194 | Oil Can Boyd | .05 | .04 | 260 | John Kruk | | .06 | .05 |
| 195 | Bip Roberts | .06 | .05 | 261 | Fred McGriff | | .15 | .11 |
| 196 | Billy Hatcher | .06 | .05 | 262 | Dick Schofield | | .04 | .03 |

| | | MT | NR MT | | | | MT | NR MT |
|---|---|---|---|---|---|---|---|---|
| 263 | Trevor Wilson | .05 | .04 | | 329 | Terry Steinbach | .06 | .05 |
| 264 | Scott Scudder, David West | .05 | .04 | | 330 | Colby Ward(FC) | .20 | .15 |
| 266 | Dwight Gooden | .20 | .15 | | 331 | Oscar Azocar(FC) | .15 | .11 |
| 267 | Willie Blair(FC) | .15 | .11 | | 332 | Scott Radinsky | .15 | .11 |
| 268 | Mark Portugal | .04 | .03 | | 333 | Eric Anthony | .10 | .08 |
| 269 | Doug Drabek | .10 | .08 | | 334 | Steve Lake | .04 | .03 |
| 270 | Dennis Eckersley | .10 | .08 | | 335 | Bob Melvin | .04 | .03 |
| 271 | Eric King | .05 | .04 | | 336 | Kal Daniels | .08 | .06 |
| 272 | Robin Yount | .10 | .08 | | 337 | Tom Pagnozzi | .05 | .04 |
| 273 | Carney Lansford | .08 | .06 | | 338 | Alan Mills | .15 | .11 |
| 274 | Carlos Baerga | .25 | .20 | | 339 | Steve Olin | .06 | .05 |
| 275 | Dave Righetti | .08 | .06 | | 340 | Juan Berenguer | .04 | .03 |
| 276 | Scott Fletcher | .04 | .03 | | 341 | Francisco Cabrera | .06 | .05 |
| 277 | Eric Yelding | .08 | .06 | | 342 | Dave Bergman | .04 | .03 |
| 278 | Charlie Hayes | .08 | .06 | | 343 | Henry Cotto | .04 | .03 |
| 279 | Jeff Ballard | .05 | .04 | | 344 | Sergio Valdez | .08 | .06 |
| 280 | Orel Hershiser | .10 | .08 | | 345 | Bob Patterson | .04 | .03 |
| 281 | Jose Oquendo | .04 | .03 | | 346 | John Marzano | .05 | .04 |
| 282 | Mike Witt | .05 | .04 | | 347 | Dana Kiecker | .08 | .06 |
| 283 | Mitch Webster | .04 | .03 | | 348 | Dion James | .04 | .03 |
| 284 | Greg Gagne | .05 | .04 | | 349 | Hubie Brooks | .08 | .06 |
| 285 | Greg Olson | .10 | .08 | | 350 | Bill Landrum | .05 | .04 |
| 286 | Tony Phillips | .05 | .04 | | 351 | Bill Sampen | .20 | .15 |
| 287 | Scott Bradley | .04 | .03 | | 352 | Greg Briley | .05 | .04 |
| 288 | Cory Snyder | .08 | .06 | | 353 | Paul Gibson | .04 | .03 |
| 289 | Jay Bell | .06 | .05 | | 354 | Dave Eiland | .04 | .03 |
| 290 | Kevin Romine | .04 | .03 | | 355 | Steve Finley | .06 | .05 |
| 291 | Jeff Robinson | .05 | .04 | | 356 | Bob Boone | .06 | .05 |
| 292 | Steve Frey(FC) | .06 | .05 | | 357 | Steve Buechele | .06 | .05 |
| 293 | Craig Worthington | .05 | .04 | | 358 | Chris Hoiles(FC) | .30 | .25 |
| 294 | Tim Crews | .04 | .03 | | 359 | Larry Walker | .10 | .08 |
| 295 | Joe Magrane | .08 | .06 | | 360 | Frank DiPino | .04 | .03 |
| 296 | Hector Villanueva(FC) | .20 | .15 | | 361 | Mark Grant | .04 | .03 |
| 297 | Terry Shumpert | .10 | .08 | | 362 | Dave Magadan | .08 | .06 |
| 298 | Joe Carter | .10 | .08 | | 363 | Robby Thompson | .06 | .05 |
| 299 | Kent Mercker | .10 | .08 | | 364 | Lonnie Smith | .05 | .04 |
| 300 | Checklist | .04 | .03 | | 365 | Steve Farr | .05 | .04 |
| 301 | Chet Lemon | .05 | .04 | | 366 | Dave Valle | .05 | .04 |
| 302 | Mike Schooler | .08 | .06 | | 367 | Tim Naehring(FC) | .25 | .20 |
| 303 | Dante Bichette | .06 | .05 | | 368 | Jim Acker | .04 | .03 |
| 304 | Kevin Elster | .05 | .04 | | 369 | Jeff Reardon | .08 | .06 |
| 305 | Jeff Huson | .06 | .05 | | 370 | Tim Teufel | .04 | .03 |
| 306 | Greg Harris | .05 | .04 | | 371 | Juan Gonzalez | .35 | .25 |
| 307 | Marquis Grissom | .10 | .08 | | 372 | Luis Salazar | .04 | .03 |
| 308 | Calvin Schiraldi | .04 | .03 | | 373 | Rick Honeycutt | .04 | .03 |
| 309 | Mariano Duncan | .06 | .05 | | 374 | Greg Maddux | .08 | .06 |
| 310 | Bill Spiers | .06 | .05 | | 375 | Jose Uribe | .05 | .04 |
| 311 | Scott Garrelts | .06 | .05 | | 376 | Donnie Hill | .04 | .03 |
| 312 | Mitch Williams | .08 | .06 | | 377 | Don Carman | .04 | .03 |
| 313 | Mike Macfarlane | .05 | .04 | | 378 | Craig Grebeck | .06 | .05 |
| 314 | Kevin Brown | .06 | .05 | | 379 | Willie Fraser | .05 | .04 |
| 315 | Robin Ventura | .10 | .08 | | 380 | Glenallen Hill | .08 | .06 |
| 316 | Darren Daulton | .06 | .05 | | 381 | Joe Oliver | .06 | .05 |
| 317 | PUuat Borders | .06 | .05 | | 382 | Randy Bush | .04 | .03 |
| 318 | Mark Eichhorn | .04 | .03 | | 383 | Alex Cole(FC) | .30 | .25 |
| 319 | Jeff Brantley | .08 | .06 | | 384 | Norm Charlton | .08 | .06 |
| 320 | Shane Mack | .05 | .04 | | 385 | Gene Nelson | .04 | .03 |
| 321 | Rob Dibble | .10 | .08 | | 386 | Checklist | .04 | .03 |
| 322 | John Franco | .10 | .08 | | 387 | Rickey Henderson (MVP) | .15 | .11 |
| 323 | Junior Felix | .08 | .06 | | 388 | Lance Parrish (MVP) | .05 | .04 |
| 324 | Casey Candaele | .04 | .03 | | 389 | Fred McGriff (MVP) | .10 | .08 |
| 325 | Bobby Bonilla | .10 | .08 | | 390 | Dave Parker (MVP) | .10 | .08 |
| 326 | Dave Henderson | .06 | .05 | | 391 | Candy Maldonado | .05 | .04 |
| 327 | Wayne Edwards | .06 | .05 | | | | | |
| 328 | Mark Knudson | .04 | .03 | | | | | |

|  |  | MT | NR MT |
|---|---|---|---|
| 392 | Ken Griffey,Jr. (MVP) | | |
|  |  | .40 | .30 |
| 393 | Gregg Olson (MVP) | .10 | .08 |
| 394 | Rafael Palmeiro (MVP) | | |
|  |  | .10 | .08 |
| 395 | Roger Clemens (MVP) | | |
|  |  | .15 | .11 |
| 396 | George Brett (MVP) | .10 | .08 |
| 397 | Cecil Fielder (MVP) | .15 | .11 |
| 398 | Brian Harper (MVP) | .05 | .04 |
| 399 | Bobby Thigpen (MVP) | | |
|  |  | .06 | .05 |
| 400 | Roberto Kelly (MVP) | .08 | .06 |
| 401 | Danny Darwin (MVP) | | |
|  |  | .05 | .04 |
| 402 | Dave Justice (MVP) | .25 | .20 |
| 403 | Lee Smith (MVP) | .05 | .04 |
| 404 | Ryne Sanberg (MVP) | | |
|  |  | .15 | .11 |
| 405 | Eddie Murray (MVP) | .10 | .08 |
| 406 | Tim Wallach (MVP) | .06 | .05 |
| 407 | Kevin Mitchell (MVP) | | |
|  |  | .10 | .08 |
| 408 | Darryl Strawberry (MVP) | | |
|  |  | .15 | .11 |
| 409 | Joe Carter (MVP) | .06 | .05 |
| 410 | Len Dykstra (MVP) | .06 | .05 |
| 411 | Doug Drabek (MVP) | .05 | .04 |
| 412 | Chris Sabo (MVP) | .08 | .06 |
| 413 | *Paul Marak (RR)(FC)* | | |
|  |  | .15 | .11 |
| 414 | *Tim McIntosh (RR)(FC)* | | |
|  |  | .10 | .08 |
| 415 | *Brian Barnes (RR)(FC)* | | |
|  |  | .20 | .15 |
| 416 | *Eric Gunderson (RR)(FC)* | | |
|  |  | .15 | .11 |
| 417 | *Mike Gardiner (RR)(FC)* | | |
|  |  | .20 | .15 |
| 418 | Steve Carter (RR) | .08 | .06 |
| 419 | *Gerald Alexander (RR)(FC)* | | |
|  |  | .15 | .11 |
| 420 | *Rich Garces (RR)(FC)* | | |
|  |  | .20 | .15 |
| 421 | Chuck Knoblauch (RR)(FC) | | |
|  |  | .60 | .45 |
| 422 | *Scott Aldred (RR)(FC)* | | |
|  |  | .15 | .11 |
| 423 | *Wes Chamberlain (RR)(FC)* | | |
|  |  | .40 | .30 |
| 424 | *Lance Dickson (RR)(FC)* | | |
|  |  | .25 | .20 |
| 425 | *Greg Colbrunn (RR)(FC)* | | |
|  |  | .20 | .15 |
| 426 | *Rich Delucia (RR)(FC)* | | |
|  |  | .20 | .15 |
| 427 | *Jeff Conine (RR)(FC)* | | |
|  |  | .20 | .15 |
| 428 | *Steve Decker (RR)(FC)* | | |
|  |  | .25 | .20 |
| 429 | *Turner Ward (RR)(FC)* | | |
|  |  | .20 | .15 |
| 430 | Mo Vaughn (RR)(FC) | | |
|  |  | .35 | .25 |
| 431 | *Steve Chitren (RR)(FC)* | | |
|  |  | .20 | .15 |
| 432 | Mike Benjamin (RR)(FC) | | |

|  |  | MT | NR MT |
|---|---|---|---|
|  |  | .10 | .08 |
| 433 | Ryne Sandberg (All-Star) | | |
|  |  | .10 | .08 |
| 434 | Len Dykstra (All-Star) | | |
|  |  | .06 | .05 |
| 435 | Andre Dawson (All-Star) | | |
|  |  | .10 | .08 |
| 436 | Mike Scioscia (All-Star) | | |
|  |  | .06 | .05 |
| 437 | Ozzie Smith (All-Star) | | |
|  |  | .10 | .08 |
| 438 | Kevin Mitchell (All-Star) | | |
|  |  | .10 | .08 |
| 439 | Jack Armstrong (All Star) | .06 | .05 |
| 440 | Chris Sabo (All-Star) | .08 | .06 |
| 441 | Will Clark (All-Star) | .15 | .11 |
| 442 | Mel Hall | .05 | .04 |
| 443 | Mark Gardner | .06 | .05 |
| 444 | Mike Devereaux | .06 | .05 |
| 445 | Kirk Gibson | .06 | .05 |
| 446 | Terry Pendleton | .08 | .06 |
| 447 | Mike Harkey | .08 | .06 |
| 448 | Jim Eisenreich | .04 | .03 |
| 449 | Benito Santiago | .08 | .06 |
| 450 | Oddibe McDowell | .04 | .03 |
| 451 | Cecil Fielder | .20 | .15 |
| 452 | Ken Griffey,Sr. | .08 | .06 |
| 453 | Bert Blyleven | .06 | .05 |
| 454 | Howard Johnson | .10 | .08 |
| 455 | Monty Farris(FC) | .15 | .11 |
| 456 | Tony Pena | .05 | .04 |
| 457 | Tim Raines | .08 | .06 |
| 458 | Dennis Rasmussen | .04 | .03 |
| 459 | Luis Quinones | .04 | .03 |
| 460 | B.J. Surhoff | .06 | .05 |
| 461 | Ernest Riles | .04 | .03 |
| 462 | Rick Sutcliffe | .06 | .05 |
| 463 | Danny Tartabull | .10 | .08 |
| 464 | Pete Incaviglia | .06 | .05 |
| 465 | Carlos Martinez | .05 | .04 |
| 466 | Ricky Jordan | .06 | .05 |
| 467 | John Cerutti | .04 | .03 |
| 468 | Dave Winfield | .12 | .09 |
| 469 | Francisco Oliveras | .04 | .03 |
| 470 | Roy Smith | .04 | .03 |
| 471 | Barry Larkin | .12 | .09 |
| 472 | Ron Darling | .06 | .05 |
| 473 | David Wells | .06 | .05 |
| 474 | Glenn Davis | .10 | .08 |
| 475 | Neal Heaton | .04 | .03 |
| 476 | Ron Hassey | .04 | .03 |
| 477 | Frank Thomas(FC) | 1.25 | .90 |
| 478 | Greg Vaughn | .15 | .11 |
| 479 | Todd Burns | .04 | .03 |
| 480 | Candy Maldonado | .05 | .04 |
| 481 | Dave LaPoint | .04 | .03 |
| 482 | Alvin Davis | .08 | .06 |
| 483 | Mike Scott | .06 | .05 |
| 484 | Dale Murphy | .12 | .09 |
| 485 | Ben McDonald | .35 | .25 |
| 486 | Jay Howell | .06 | .05 |
| 487 | Vince Coleman | .08 | .06 |
| 488 | Alfredo Griffin | .05 | .04 |
| 489 | Sandy Alomar | .15 | .11 |
| 490 | Kirby Puckett | .15 | .11 |
| 491 | Andres Thomas | .04 | .03 |

| | MT | NR MT | | | MT | NR MT |
|---|---|---|---|---|---|---|
| 492 Jack Morris | .08 | .06 | | 556 Curt Schilling | .05 | .04 |
| 493 Matt Young | .04 | .03 | | 557 Ramon Martinez | .20 | .15 |
| 494 Greg Myers | .04 | .03 | | 558 Pedro Guerrero | .08 | .06 |
| 495 Barry Bonds | .15 | .11 | | 559 Dwight Smith | .05 | .04 |
| 496 Scott Cooper(FC) | .20 | .15 | | 560 Mark Davis | .04 | .03 |
| 497 Dan Schatzeder | .04 | .03 | | 561 Shawn Abner | .05 | .04 |
| 498 Jesse Barfield | .06 | .05 | | 562 Charlie Leibrandt | .05 | .04 |
| 499 Jerry Goff(FC) | .05 | .04 | | 563 John Shelby | .04 | .03 |
| 500 Checklist | .04 | .03 | | 564 Bill Swift | .05 | .04 |
| 501 *Anthony Telford*(FC) | | | | 565 Mike Fetters | .06 | .05 |
| | .15 | .11 | | 566 Alejandro Pena | .05 | .04 |
| 502 Eddie Murray | .12 | .09 | | 567 Ruben Sierra | .15 | .11 |
| 503 *Omar Olivares*(FC) | | | | 568 Calos Quintana | .08 | .06 |
| | .12 | .09 | | 569 Kevin Gross | .05 | .04 |
| 504 Ryne Sandberg | .15 | .11 | | 570 Derek Lilliquist | .04 | .03 |
| 505 Jeff Montgomery | .06 | .05 | | 571 Jack Armstrong | .06 | .05 |
| 506 Mark Parent | .04 | .03 | | 572 Greg Brock | .04 | .03 |
| 507 Ron Gant | .15 | .11 | | 573 Mike Kingery | .04 | .03 |
| 508 Frank Tanana | .05 | .04 | | 574 Greg Smith(FC) | .06 | .05 |
| 509 Jay Buhner | .06 | .05 | | 575 *Brian McRae*(FC) | | |
| 510 Max Venable | .04 | .03 | | | .40 | .30 |
| 511 Wally Whitehurst | .06 | .05 | | 576 Jack Daugherty | .05 | .04 |
| 512 Gary Pettis | .04 | .03 | | 577 Ozzie Guillen | .06 | .05 |
| 513 Tom Brunansky | .06 | .05 | | 578 Joe Boever | .04 | .03 |
| 514 Tim Wallach | .08 | .06 | | 579 Luis Sojo | .06 | .05 |
| 515 Craig Lefferts | .05 | .04 | | 580 Chili Davis | .05 | .04 |
| 516 *Tim Layana* | .10 | .08 | | 581 Don Robinson | .04 | .03 |
| 517 Darryl Hamilton | .08 | .06 | | 582 Brian Harper | .06 | .05 |
| 518 Rick Reuschel | .05 | .04 | | 583 Paul O'Neill | .06 | .05 |
| 519 Steve Wilson | .06 | .05 | | 584 Bob Ojeda | .05 | .04 |
| 520 Kurt Stillwell | .05 | .04 | | 585 Mookie Wilson | .05 | .04 |
| 521 Rafael Palmeiro | .12 | .09 | | 586 Rafael Ramirez | .04 | .03 |
| 522 Ken Patterson | .04 | .03 | | 587 Gary Redus | .04 | .03 |
| 523 Len Dykstra | .12 | .09 | | 588 Jamie Quirk | .04 | .03 |
| 524 Tony Fernandez | .06 | .05 | | 589 Shawn Hilligas | .04 | .03 |
| 525 Kent Anderson | .04 | .03 | | 590 *Tom Edens*(FC) | .08 | .06 |
| 526 *Mark Leonard*(FC) | | | | 591 Joe Klink(FC) | .05 | .04 |
| | .20 | .15 | | 592 Charles Nagy(FC) | .20 | .15 |
| 527 Allan Anderson | .04 | .03 | | 593 Eric Plunk | .04 | .03 |
| 528 Tom Browning | .06 | .05 | | 594 Tracy Jones | .04 | .03 |
| 529 Frank Viola | .12 | .09 | | 595 Craig Biggio | .08 | .06 |
| 530 John Olerud | .30 | .25 | | 596 Jose DeJesus | .06 | .05 |
| 531 Juan Agosto | .04 | .03 | | 597 Mickey Tettleton | .08 | .06 |
| 532 Zane Smith | .06 | .05 | | 598 Chris Gwynn | .05 | .04 |
| 533 Scott Sanderson | .06 | .05 | | 599 Rex Hudler | .06 | .05 |
| 534 Barry Jones | .05 | .04 | | 600 Checklist | .04 | .03 |
| 535 Mike Felder | .04 | .03 | | 601 Jim Gott | .04 | .03 |
| 536 Jose Canseco | .30 | .25 | | 602 Jeff Manto(FC) | .12 | .09 |
| 537 Felix Fermin | .04 | .03 | | 603 Nelson Liriano | .04 | .03 |
| 538 Roberto Kelly | .08 | .06 | | 604 Mark Lemke | .06 | .05 |
| 539 Brian Holman | .05 | .04 | | 605 Clay Parker | .04 | .03 |
| 540 Mark Davidson | .04 | .03 | | 606 Edgar Martinez | .08 | .06 |
| 541 Terry Mulholland | .06 | .05 | | 607 *Mark Whiten*(FC) | | |
| 542 Randy Milligan | .06 | .05 | | | .35 | .25 |
| 543 Jose Gonzalez | .04 | .03 | | 608 Ted Power | .04 | .03 |
| 544 *Craig Wilson*(FC) | .10 | .08 | | 609 Tom Bolton | .05 | .04 |
| 545 Mike Hartley | .04 | .03 | | 610 Tom Herr | .05 | .04 |
| 546 Greg Swindell | .06 | .05 | | 611 Andy Hawkins | .04 | .03 |
| 547 Gary Gaetti | .08 | .06 | | 612 Scott Ruskin | -.04 | .03 |
| 548 Dave Justice | .50 | .40 | | 613 Ron Kittle | .05 | .04 |
| 549 Steve Searcy | .04 | .03 | | 614 John Wetteland | .06 | .05 |
| 550 Erik Hanson | .12 | .09 | | 615 *Mike Perez*(FC) | .12 | .09 |
| 551 Dave Stieb | .08 | .06 | | 616 Dave Clark | .04 | .03 |
| 552 Andy Van Slyke | .08 | .06 | | 617 Brent Mayne(FC) | .12 | .09 |
| 553 Mike Greenwell | .12 | .09 | | 618 Jack Clark | .08 | .06 |
| 554 Kevin Maas | .30 | .25 | | 619 Marvin Freeman | .04 | .03 |
| 555 Delino Deshields | .20 | .15 | | 620 Edwin Nunez | .04 | .03 |

| | MT | NR MT |
|---|---|---|
| 621 Russ Swan(FC) | .08 | .06 |
| 622 Johnny Ray | .04 | .03 |
| 623 Charlie O'Brien | .04 | .03 |
| 624 Joe Bitker(FC) | .12 | .09 |
| 625 Mike Marshall | .04 | .03 |
| 626 Otis Nixon | .05 | .04 |
| 627 Andy Benes | .15 | .11 |
| 628 Ron Oester | .04 | .03 |
| 629 Ted Higuera | .06 | .05 |
| 630 Kevin Bass | .05 | .04 |
| 631 Damon Berryhill | .05 | .04 |
| 632 Bo Jackson | .30 | .25 |
| 633 Brad Arnsberg | .05 | .04 |
| 634 Jerry Willard | .04 | .03 |
| 635 Tommy Greene | .06 | .05 |
| 636 Bob MacDonald(FC) | .15 | .11 |
| 637 Kirk McCaskill | .05 | .04 |
| 638 John Burkett | .04 | .03 |
| 639 Paul Abbott(FC) | .15 | .11 |
| 640 Todd Benzinger | .05 | .04 |
| 641 Todd Hundley(FC) | .10 | .08 |
| 642 George Bell | .10 | .08 |
| 643 Javier Ortiz(FC) | .12 | .09 |
| 644 Sid Bream | .05 | .04 |
| 645 Bob Welch | .06 | .05 |
| 646 Phil Bradley | .05 | .04 |
| 647 Bill Krueger | .04 | .03 |
| 648 Rickey Henderson | .20 | .15 |
| 649 Kevin Wickander | .05 | .04 |
| 650 Steve Balboni | .04 | .03 |
| 651 Gene Harris | .05 | .04 |
| 652 Jim Deshaies | .04 | .03 |
| 653 Jason Grimsley(FC) | .12 | .09 |
| 654 Joe Orsulak | .05 | .04 |
| 655 Jimmy Poole(FC) | .12 | .09 |
| 656 Felix Jose | .10 | .08 |
| 657 Dennis Cook | .05 | .04 |
| 658 Tom Brookens | .04 | .03 |
| 659 Junior Ortiz | .04 | .03 |
| 660 Jeff Parrett | .04 | .03 |
| 661 Jerry Don Gleaton | .04 | .03 |
| 662 Brent Knackert | .04 | .03 |
| 663 Rance Mulliniks | .04 | .03 |
| 664 John Smiley | .06 | .05 |
| 665 Larry Andersen | .04 | .03 |
| 666 Willie McGee | .08 | .06 |
| 667 Chris Nabholz(FC) | .20 | .15 |
| 668 Brady Anderson | .04 | .03 |
| 669 Darren Holmes(FC) | .12 | .09 |
| 670 Ken Hill | .06 | .05 |
| 671 Gary Varsho | .04 | .03 |
| 672 Bill Pecota | .05 | .04 |
| 673 Fred Lynn | .05 | .04 |
| 674 Kevin D. Brown(FC) | .10 | .08 |
| 675 Dan Petry | .04 | .03 |
| 676 Mike Jackson | .05 | .04 |
| 677 Wally Joyner | .12 | .09 |
| 678 Danny Jackson | .05 | .04 |
| 679 Bill Haselman(FC) | .12 | .09 |
| 680 Mike Boddicker | .06 | .05 |
| 681 Mel Rojas(FC) | .12 | .09 |
| 682 Roberto Alomar | .12 | .09 |

| | MT | NR MT |
|---|---|---|
| 683 Dave Justice (R.O.Y.) | .25 | .20 |
| 684 Chuck Crim | .04 | .03 |
| 685 Matt Williams | .12 | .09 |
| 686 Shawon Dunston | .06 | .05 |
| 687 Jeff Schulz(FC) | .08 | .06 |
| 688 John Barfield(FC) | .08 | .06 |
| 689 Gerald Young | .04 | .03 |
| 690 Luis Gonzalez(FC) | .50 | .40 |
| 691 Frank Wills | .05 | .04 |
| 692 Chuck Finley | .08 | .06 |
| 693 Sandy Alomar (R.O.Y.) | .15 | .11 |
| 694 Tim Drummond | .05 | .04 |
| 695 Herm Winningham | .04 | .03 |
| 696 Darryl Strawberry | .25 | .20 |
| 697 Al Leiter | .04 | .03 |
| 698 Karl Rhodes(FC) | .25 | .20 |
| 699 Stan Belinda(FC) | .08 | .06 |
| 700 Checklist | .04 | .03 |
| 701 Lance Blankenship | .04 | .03 |
| 702 Willie Stargell (Puzzle Card) | .10 | .08 |
| 703 Jim Gantner | .05 | .04 |
| 704 Reggie Harris(FC) | .15 | .11 |
| 705 Rob Ducey | .04 | .03 |
| 706 Tim Hulett | .04 | .03 |
| 707 Atlee Hammaker | .04 | .03 |
| 708 Xavier Hernandez | .04 | .03 |
| 709 Chuck McElroy(FC) | .08 | .06 |
| 710 John Mitchell | .04 | .03 |
| 711 Carlos Hernandez | .05 | .04 |
| 712 Geronimo Pena(FC) | .10 | .08 |
| 713 Jim Neidlinger(FC) | .15 | .11 |
| 714 John Orton | .04 | .03 |
| 715 Terry Leach | .04 | .03 |
| 716 Mike Stanton | .06 | .05 |
| 717 Walt Terrell | .04 | .03 |
| 718 Luis Aquino | .05 | .04 |
| 719 Bud Black | .05 | .04 |
| 720 Bob Kipper | .04 | .03 |
| 721 Jeff Gray(FC) | .15 | .11 |
| 722 Jose Rijo | .08 | .06 |
| 723 Curt Young | .04 | .03 |
| 724 Jose Vizcaino(FC) | .08 | .06 |
| 725 Randy Tomlin(FC) | .15 | .11 |
| 726 Junior Noboa | .05 | .04 |
| 727 Bob Welch (Award Winner) | .08 | .06 |
| 728 Gary Ward | .04 | .03 |
| 729 Rob Deer | .05 | .04 |
| 730 David Segui(FC) | .25 | .20 |
| 731 Mark Carreon | .04 | .03 |
| 732 Vicente Palacios | .04 | .03 |
| 733 Sam Horn | .05 | .04 |
| 734 Howard Farmer(FC) | .15 | .11 |
| 735 Ken Dayley | .04 | .03 |
| 736 Kelly Mann | .08 | .06 |
| 737 Joe Grahe(FC) | .12 | .09 |
| 738 Kelly Downs | .04 | .03 |
| 739 Jimmy Kremers(FC) | | |

| | | MT | NR MT |
|---|---|---|---|
| 740 | Kevin Appier | .15 | .11 |
| 741 | Jeff Reed | .12 | .09 |
| 742 | Jose Rijo (World Series) | .04 | .03 |
| | | .08 | .06 |
| 743 | *Dave Rohde*(FC) | .12 | .09 |
| 744 | Dr. Dirt/ Mr. Clean (Len Dykstra, Dale Murphy) | .25 | .20 |
| 745 | Paul Sorrento | .06 | .05 |
| 746 | Thomas Howard(FC) | | |
| | | .10 | .08 |
| 747 | *Matt Stark*(FC) | .20 | .15 |
| 748 | Harold Baines | .08 | .06 |
| 749 | Doug Dascenzo | .05 | .04 |
| 750 | Doug Drabek (Award Winner) | | |
| | | .08 | .06 |
| 751 | Gary Sheffield | .15 | .11 |
| 752 | Terry Lee(FC) | .20 | .15 |
| 753 | *Jim Vatcher*(FC) | .08 | .06 |
| 754 | Lee Stevens | .12 | .09 |
| 755 | Randy Veres(FC) | .08 | .06 |
| 756 | Bill Doran | .06 | .05 |
| 757 | Gary Wayne | .04 | .03 |
| 758 | *Pedro Munoz*(FC) | | |
| | | .35 | .25 |
| 759 | Chris Hammond(FC) | | |
| | | .08 | .06 |
| 760 | Checklist | .04 | .03 |
| 761 | Rickey Henderson (MVP) | | |
| | | .12 | .09 |
| 762 | Barry Bonds (MVP) | .12 | .09 |
| 763 | Billy Hatcher (World Series) | | |
| | | .05 | .04 |
| 764 | Julio Machado | .05 | .04 |
| 765 | Jose Mesa | .05 | .04 |
| 766 | Willie Randolph (World Series) | | |
| | | .05 | .04 |
| 767 | *Scott Erickson*(FC) | | |
| | | .40 | .30 |
| 768 | *Travis Fryman*(FC) | | |
| | | .60 | .45 |
| 769 | *Rich Rodriguez*(FC) | | |
| | | .12 | .09 |
| 770 | Checklist, Checklist | .04 | .03 |

## 1991 Donruss Rookies

Red borders highlight the 1991 Donruss Rookies cards. This set marks the sixth year that Donruss has produced such an issue. Like in past years, "The Rookies" logo appears on the card fronts. The set is

packaged in a special box and includes a Willie Stargell puzzle card.

| | | MT | NR MT |
|---|---|---|---|
| Complete Set: | | 6.00 | 4.50 |
| Common Player: | | .10 | .08 |
| 1 | Pat Kelly(FC) | .20 | .15 |
| 2 | Rich DeLucia | .10 | .08 |
| 3 | Wes Chamberlain | .40 | .30 |
| 4 | Scott Leius(FC) | .10 | .08 |
| 5 | Darryl Kile(FC) | .15 | .11 |
| 6 | Milt Cuyler | .15 | .11 |
| 7 | Todd Van Poppel(FC) | | |
| | | .60 | .45 |
| 8 | Ray Lankford | .20 | .15 |
| 9 | Brian Hunter(FC) | .40 | .30 |
| 10 | Tony Perezchica | .10 | .08 |
| 11 | Ced Landrum(FC) | .10 | .08 |
| 12 | Dave Burba(FC) | .10 | .08 |
| 13 | Ramon Garcia(FC) | .20 | .15 |
| 14 | Ed Sprague(FC) | .15 | .11 |
| 15 | Warren Newson(FC) | .15 | .11 |
| 16 | Paul Faries(FC) | .10 | .08 |
| 17 | Luis Gonzalez | .35 | .25 |
| 18 | Charles Nagy | .15 | .11 |
| 19 | Chris Hammond | .10 | .08 |
| 20 | Frank Castillo(FC) | .25 | .20 |
| 21 | Pedro Munoz | .20 | .15 |
| 22 | Orlando Merced(FC) | .40 | .30 |
| 23 | Jose Melendez(FC) | .10 | .08 |
| 24 | Kirk Dressendorfer(FC) | | |
| | | .30 | .25 |
| 25 | Heathcliff Slocumb(FC) | | |
| | | .10 | .08 |
| 26 | Doug Simons(FC) | .10 | .08 |
| 27 | Mike Timlin(FC) | .20 | .15 |
| 28 | Jeff Fassero(FC) | .10 | .08 |
| 29 | Mark Leiter(FC) | .10 | .08 |
| 30 | Jeff Bagwell(FC) | 1.25 | .90 |
| 31 | Brian McRae | .35 | .25 |
| 32 | Mark Whiten | .20 | .15 |
| 33 | Ivan Rodriguez(FC) | 1.25 | .90 |
| 34 | Wade Taylor(FC) | .10 | .08 |
| 35 | Darren Lewis(FC) | .35 | .25 |
| 36 | Mo Vaughn | .40 | .30 |
| 37 | Mike Remlinger(FC) | .10 | .08 |
| 38 | Rick Wilkins(FC) | .20 | .15 |
| 39 | Chuck Knoblauch | .40 | .30 |
| 40 | Kevin Morton | .15 | .11 |
| 41 | Carlos Rodriguez(FC) | | |
| | | .10 | .08 |
| 42 | Mark Lewis | .20 | .15 |
| 43 | Brent Mayne | .10 | .08 |
| 44 | Chris Haney(FC) | .15 | .11 |
| 45 | Denis Boucher(FC) | .15 | .11 |
| 46 | Mike Gardiner | .10 | .08 |
| 47 | Jeff Johnson(FC) | .15 | .11 |
| 48 | Dean Palmer | .30 | .25 |
| 49 | Chuck McElroy | .10 | .08 |
| 50 | Chris Jones(FC) | .10 | .08 |
| 51 | Scott Kamieniecki(FC) | | |
| | | .10 | .08 |
| 52 | Al Osuna(FC) | .10 | .08 |
| 53 | Rusty Meacham(FC) | .15 | .11 |

| | | MT | NR MT |
|---|---|---|---|
| 54 | Chito Martinez(FC) | .25 | .20 |
| 55 | Reggie Jefferson(FC) | | |
| | | .25 | .20 |
| 56 | Checklist | .05 | .04 |

## GRADING GUIDE

**Mint (MT):** A perfect card. Well-centered with all corners sharp and square. No creases, stains, edge nicks, surface marks, yellowing or fading.

**Near Mint (NM):** A nearly perfect card. At first glance, a NM card appears to be perfect. May be slightly off-center. No surface marks, creases or loss of gloss.

**Excellent (EX):** Corners are still fairly sharp with only moderate wear. Borders may be off-center. No creases or stains on fronts or backs, but may show slight loss of surface luster.

**Very Good (VG):** Shows obvious handling. May have rounded corners, minor creases, major gum or wax stains. No major creases, tape marks, writing, etc.

**Good (G):** A well-worn card, but exhibits no intentional damage. May have major or multiple creases. Corners may be rounded well beyond card border.

---

## 1992 Donruss

For the second consecutive year, Donruss chose to release its card set in two series. The 1992 cards feature improved stock, an anti-couterfeit feature and include both front and back photos. Once again Rated Rookies and All-Stars are included in the set. Special highlight cards also can be found in the 1992 Donruss set. Production was reduced in 1992 compared to other years.

| | | MT | NR MT |
|---|---|---|---|
| | Complete Set: | 35.00 | 26.00 |
| | Common Player: | .05 | .04 |
| 1 | *Mark Wohlers (RR)(FC)* | | |
| | | .15 | .11 |
| 2 | Will Cordero (RR)(FC) | | |
| | | .30 | .25 |
| 3 | Kyle Abbott (RR)(FC) | | |
| | | .30 | .25 |
| 4 | *Dave Nilsson (RR)(FC)* | | |
| | | .50 | .40 |
| 5 | *Kenny Lofton (RR)(FC)* | | |
| | | .60 | .45 |
| 6 | *Luis Mercedes (RR)(FC)* | | |
| | | .20 | .15 |
| 7 | Roger Salkeld (RR)(FC) | | |
| | | .30 | .25 |
| 8 | Eddie Zosky (RR)(FC) | | |
| | | .25 | .20 |
| 9 | Todd Van Poppel (RR) | | |
| | | .30 | .25 |
| 10 | *Frank Seminara* (RR)(FC) | .25 | .20 |
| 11 | Andy Ashby (RR)(FC) | | |
| | | .20 | .15 |
| 12 | Reggie Jefferson (RR)(FC) | .35 | .25 |
| 13 | *Ryan Klesko (RR)(FC)* | | |
| | | .50 | .40 |
| 14 | *Carlos Garcia (RR)(FC)* | | |
| | | .25 | .20 |
| 15 | *John Ramos (RR)(FC)* | | |
| | | .25 | .20 |
| 16 | Eric Karros (RR)(FC) | | |
| | | .70 | .50 |
| 17 | *Pat Lennon (RR)(FC)* | | |
| | | .35 | .25 |
| 18 | *Eddie Taubensee* (RR)(FC) | .40 | .30 |
| 19 | *Roberto Hernandez* (RR)(FC) | .20 | .15 |
| 20 | D.J. Dozier (RR)(FC) | .20 | .15 |
| 21 | Dave Henderson (AS) | | |
| | | .10 | .08 |
| 22 | Cal Ripken (AS) | .20 | .15 |
| 23 | Wade Boggs (AS) | .20 | .15 |
| 24 | Ken Griffey,Jr. (AS) | .60 | .45 |
| 25 | Jack Morris (AS) | .10 | .08 |
| 26 | Danny Tartabull (AS) | | |
| | | .10 | .08 |
| 27 | Cecil Fielder (AS) | .20 | .15 |
| 28 | Roberto Alomar (AS) | | |
| | | .20 | .15 |
| 29 | Sandy Alomar (AS) | .10 | .08 |
| 30 | Rickey Henderson (AS) | | |
| | | .20 | .15 |
| 31 | Ken Hill | .06 | .05 |
| 32 | John Habyan | .05 | .04 |
| 33 | Otis Nixon (Highlight) | | |
| | | .10 | .08 |
| 34 | Tim Wallach | .08 | .06 |
| 35 | Cal Ripken | .25 | .20 |
| 36 | Gary Carter | .08 | .06 |
| 37 | Juan Agosto | .05 | .04 |
| 38 | Doug Dascenzo | .05 | .04 |
| 39 | Kirk Gibson | .08 | .06 |
| 40 | Benito Santiago | .08 | .06 |

| | | MT | NR MT | | | MT | NR MT |
|---|---|---|---|---|---|---|---|
| 41 | Otis Nixon | .06 | .05 | 107 | Rafael Belliard | .05 | .04 |
| 42 | Andy Allanson | .05 | .04 | 108 | Joey Cora | .05 | .04 |
| 43 | Brian Holman | .06 | .05 | 109 | Tommy Greene | .08 | .06 |
| 44 | Dick Schofield | .05 | .04 | 110 | Gregg Olson | .08 | .06 |
| 45 | Dave Magadan | .08 | .06 | 111 | Frank Tanana | .06 | .05 |
| 46 | Rafael Palmeiro | .10 | .08 | 112 | Lee Smith | .08 | .06 |
| 47 | Jody Reed | .06 | .03 | 113 | Greg Harris | .05 | .04 |
| 48 | Ivan Calderon | .08 | .06 | 114 | Dwayne Henry | .05 | .04 |
| 49 | Greg Harris | .05 | .04 | 115 | Chili Davis | .08 | .06 |
| 50 | Chris Sabo | .08 | .06 | 116 | Kent Mercker | .08 | .06 |
| 51 | Paul Molitor | .10 | .08 | 117 | Brian Barnes | .08 | .06 |
| 52 | Robby Thompson | .06 | .05 | 118 | Rich DeLucia | .06 | .05 |
| 53 | Dave Smith | .05 | .04 | 119 | Andre Dawson | .15 | .11 |
| 54 | Mark Davis | .05 | .04 | 120 | Carlos Baerga | .08 | .06 |
| 55 | Kevin Brown | .06 | .05 | 121 | Mike LaValliere | .06 | .05 |
| 56 | Donn Pall | .05 | .04 | 122 | Jeff Gray | .06 | .05 |
| 57 | Lenny Dykstra | .08 | .06 | 123 | Bruce Hurst | .08 | .06 |
| 58 | Roberto Alomar | .15 | .11 | 124 | Alvin Davis | .08 | .06 |
| 59 | Jeff Robinson | .05 | .04 | 125 | John Candelaria | .06 | .05 |
| 60 | Willie McGee | .08 | .06 | 126 | Matt Nokes | .08 | .06 |
| 61 | Jay Buhner | .08 | .06 | 127 | George Bell | .10 | .08 |
| 62 | Mike Pagliarulo | .05 | .04 | 128 | Bret Saberhagen | .10 | .08 |
| 63 | Paul O'Neill | .08 | .06 | 129 | Jeff Russell | .08 | .06 |
| 64 | Hubie Brooks | .06 | .05 | 130 | Jim Abbott | .15 | .11 |
| 65 | Kelly Gruber | .08 | .06 | 131 | Bill Gullickson | .06 | .05 |
| 66 | Ken Caminiti | .06 | .05 | 132 | Todd Zeile | .15 | .11 |
| 67 | Gary Redus | .05 | .04 | 133 | Dave Winfield | .10 | .08 |
| 68 | Harold Baines | .08 | .06 | 134 | Wally Whitehurst | .06 | .05 |
| 69 | Charlie Hough | .06 | .05 | 135 | Matt Williams | .15 | .11 |
| 70 | B.J. Surhoff | .06 | .05 | 136 | Tom Browning | .08 | .06 |
| 71 | Walt Weiss | .06 | .05 | 137 | Marquis Grissom | .15 | .11 |
| 72 | Shawn Hillegas | .05 | .04 | 138 | Erik Hanson | .10 | .08 |
| 73 | Roberto Kelly | .08 | .06 | 139 | Rob Dibble | .08 | .06 |
| 74 | Jeff Ballard | .05 | .04 | 140 | Don August | .05 | .04 |
| 75 | Craig Biggio | .08 | .06 | 141 | Tom Henke | .08 | .06 |
| 76 | Pat Combs | .06 | .05 | 142 | Dan Pasqua | .06 | .05 |
| 77 | Jeff Robinson | .05 | .04 | 143 | George Brett | .15 | .11 |
| 78 | Tim Belcher | .06 | .05 | 144 | Jerald Clark | .06 | .05 |
| 79 | Cris Carpenter | .06 | .05 | 145 | Robin Ventura | .25 | .20 |
| 80 | Checklist | .05 | .04 | 146 | Dale Murphy | .10 | .08 |
| 81 | Steve Avery | .30 | .25 | 147 | Dennis Eckersley | .10 | .08 |
| 82 | Chris James | .05 | .04 | 148 | Eric Yelding | .05 | .04 |
| 83 | Brian Harper | .06 | .05 | 149 | Mario Diaz | .05 | .04 |
| 84 | Charlie Leibrandt | .06 | .05 | 150 | Casey Candaele | .05 | .04 |
| 85 | Mickey Tettleton | .08 | .06 | 151 | Steve Olin | .06 | .05 |
| 86 | Pete O'Brien | .06 | .05 | 152 | Luis Salazar | .05 | .04 |
| 87 | Danny Darwin | .05 | .04 | 153 | Kevin Maas | .15 | .11 |
| 88 | Bob Walk | .05 | .04 | 154 | Nolan Ryan (Highlight) | | |
| 89 | Jeff Reardon | .08 | .06 | | | .40 | .30 |
| 90 | Bobby Rose | .08 | .06 | 155 | Barry Jones | .05 | .04 |
| 91 | Danny Jackson | .06 | .05 | 156 | Chris Hoiles | .15 | .11 |
| 92 | John Morris | .05 | .04 | 157 | Bobby Ojeda | .06 | .05 |
| 93 | Bud Black | .06 | .05 | 158 | Pedro Guerrero | .08 | .06 |
| 94 | Tommy Greene | | | 159 | Paul Assenmacher | .05 | .04 |
| | (Highlight) | .10 | .08 | 160 | Checklist | .05 | .04 |
| 95 | Rick Aguilera | .08 | .06 | 161 | Mike Macfarlane | .06 | .05 |
| 96 | Gary Gaetti | .08 | .06 | 162 | Craig Lefferts | .06 | .05 |
| 97 | David Cone | .08 | .06 | 163 | *Brian Hunter* | .20 | .15 |
| 98 | John Olerud | .20 | .15 | 164 | Alan Trammell | .10 | .08 |
| 99 | Joel Skinner | .05 | .04 | 165 | Ken Griffey,Jr. | .50 | .40 |
| 100 | Jay Bell | .08 | .06 | 166 | Lance Parrish | .08 | .06 |
| 101 | Bob Milacki | .05 | .04 | 167 | Brian Downing | .05 | .04 |
| 102 | Norm Charlton | .06 | .05 | 168 | John Barfield | .06 | .05 |
| 103 | Chuck Crim | .05 | .04 | 169 | Jack Clark | .08 | .06 |
| 104 | Terry Steinbach | .06 | .05 | 170 | Chris Nabholz | .06 | .05 |
| 105 | Juan Samuel | .08 | .06 | 171 | Tim Teufel | .05 | .04 |
| 106 | Steve Howe | .06 | .05 | 172 | Chris Hammond | .08 | .06 |

| | | MT | NR MT | | | MT | NR MT |
|---|---|---|---|---|---|---|---|
| 173 | Robin Yount | .20 | .15 | 238 | Mark Gardner | .08 | .06 |
| 174 | Dave Righetti | .08 | .04 | 239 | Harold Reynolds | .06 | .05 |
| 175 | Joe Girardi | .06 | .05 | 240 | Checklist | .05 | .04 |
| 176 | Mike Boddicker | .06 | .05 | 241 | Mike Harkey | .06 | .05 |
| 177 | Dean Palmer | .25 | .20 | 242 | Felix Fermin | .05 | .04 |
| 178 | Greg Hibbard | .06 | .05 | 243 | Barry Bonds | .20 | .15 |
| 179 | Randy Ready | .05 | .04 | 244 | Roger Clemens | .25 | .20 |
| 180 | Devon White | .08 | .06 | 245 | Dennis Rasmussen | .05 | .04 |
| 181 | Mark Eichhorn | .05 | .04 | 246 | Jose DeLeon | .06 | .05 |
| 182 | Mike Felder | .05 | .04 | 247 | Orel Hershiser | .10 | .08 |
| 183 | Joe Klink | .05 | .04 | 248 | Mel Hall | .06 | .05 |
| 184 | Steve Bedrosian | .06 | .05 | 249 | *Rick Wilkins* | .25 | .20 |
| 185 | Barry Larkin | .15 | .11 | 250 | Tom Gordon | .08 | .06 |
| 186 | John Franco | .08 | .06 | 251 | Kevin Reimer | .06 | .05 |
| 187 | *Ed Sprague* | .15 | .11 | 252 | Luis Polonia | .06 | .05 |
| 188 | Mark Portugal | .05 | .04 | 253 | Mike Henneman | .06 | .05 |
| 189 | Jose Lind | .05 | .04 | 254 | Tom Pagnozzi | .06 | .05 |
| 190 | Bob Welch | .08 | .06 | 255 | Chuck Finley | .10 | .08 |
| 191 | Alex Fernandez | .25 | .20 | 256 | Mackey Sasser | .05 | .04 |
| 192 | Gary Sheffield | .25 | .20 | 257 | John Burkett | .06 | .05 |
| 193 | Rickey Henderson | .20 | .15 | 258 | Hal Morris | .15 | .11 |
| 194 | Rod Nichols | .05 | .04 | 259 | Larry Walker | .10 | .08 |
| 195 | *Scott Kamieniecki* | .15 | .11 | 260 | Billy Swift | .06 | .05 |
| 196 | Mike Flanagan | .05 | .04 | 261 | Joe Oliver | .06 | .05 |
| 197 | Steve Finley | .08 | .06 | 262 | Julio Machado | .05 | .04 |
| 198 | Darren Daulton | .06 | .05 | 263 | Todd Stottlemyre | .08 | .06 |
| 199 | Leo Gomez | .15 | .11 | 264 | Matt Merullo | .05 | .04 |
| 200 | Mike Morgan | .06 | .05 | 265 | Brent Mayne | .08 | .06 |
| 201 | Bob Tewksbury | .05 | .04 | 266 | Thomas Howard | .06 | .05 |
| 202 | Sid Bream | .08 | .06 | 267 | Lance Johnson | .06 | .05 |
| 203 | Sandy Alomar | .15 | .11 | 268 | Terry Mulholland | .08 | .06 |
| 204 | Greg Gagne | .05 | .04 | 269 | Rick Honeycutt | .05 | .04 |
| 205 | Juan Berenguer | .05 | .04 | 270 | Luis Gonzalez | .25 | .20 |
| 206 | Cecil Fielder | .25 | .20 | 271 | Jose Guzman | .06 | .05 |
| 207 | Randy Johnson | .08 | .06 | 272 | Jimmy Jones | .05 | .04 |
| 208 | Tony Pena | .06 | .05 | 273 | Mark Lewis | .20 | .15 |
| 209 | Doug Drabek | .10 | .08 | 274 | Rene Gonzales | .05 | .04 |
| 210 | Wade Boggs | .20 | .15 | 275 | *Jeff Johnson* | .25 | .20 |
| 211 | Bryan Harvey | .08 | .06 | 276 | Dennis Martinez | | |
| 212 | Jose Vizcaino | .06 | .05 | | (Highlight) | .10 | .08 |
| 213 | *Alonzo Powell*(FC) | | | 277 | Delino DeShields | .08 | .06 |
| | | .15 | .11 | 278 | Sam Horn | .05 | .04 |
| 214 | Will Clark | .30 | .25 | 279 | Kevin Gross | .06 | .05 |
| 215 | Rickey Henderson | | | 280 | Jose Oquendo | .05 | .04 |
| | (Highlight) | | | 281 | Mark Grace | .15 | .11 |
| | | .20 | .15 | 282 | Mark Gubicza | .08 | .06 |
| 216 | Jack Morris | .08 | .06 | 283 | Fred McGriff | .10 | .08 |
| 217 | Junior Felix | .06 | .05 | 284 | Ron Gant | .15 | .11 |
| 218 | Vince Coleman | .08 | .06 | 285 | Lou Whitaker | .08 | .06 |
| 219 | Jimmy Key | .08 | .06 | 286 | Edgar Martinez | .08 | .06 |
| 220 | Alex Cole | .08 | .06 | 287 | Ron Tingley | .05 | .04 |
| 221 | Bill Landrum | .06 | .05 | 288 | Kevin McReynolds | .08 | .06 |
| 222 | Randy Milligan | .08 | .06 | 289 | *Ivan Rodriguez* | .50 | .40 |
| 223 | Jose Rijo | .08 | .06 | 290 | Mike Gardiner | .08 | .06 |
| 224 | Greg Vaughn | .10 | .08 | 291 | *Chris Haney* | .20 | .15 |
| 225 | Dave Stewart | .08 | .06 | 292 | Darrin Jackson | .06 | .05 |
| 226 | Lenny Harris | .06 | .05 | 293 | Bill Doran | .08 | .06 |
| 227 | Scott Sanderson | .06 | .05 | 294 | Ted Higuera | .08 | .06 |
| 228 | Jeff Blauser | .06 | .05 | 295 | Jeff Brantley | .06 | .05 |
| 229 | Ozzie Guillen | .08 | .06 | 296 | Les Lancaster | .05 | .04 |
| 230 | John Kruk | .08 | .06 | 297 | Jim Eisenreich | .05 | .04 |
| 231 | Bob Melvin | .05 | .04 | 298 | Ruben Sierra | .20 | .15 |
| 232 | Milt Cuyler | .15 | .11 | 299 | Scott Radinsky | .08 | .06 |
| 233 | Felix Jose | .15 | .11 | 300 | Jose DeJesus | .08 | .06 |
| 234 | Ellis Burks | .10 | .08 | 301 | *Mike Timlin* | .20 | .15 |
| 235 | Pete Harnisch | .06 | .05 | 302 | Luis Sojo | .08 | .06 |
| 236 | Kevin Tapani | .08 | .06 | 303 | Kelly Downs | .05 | .04 |
| 237 | Terry Pendleton | .08 | .06 | | | | |

| | | MT | NR MT |
|---|---|---|---|
| 304 | Scott Bankhead | .06 | .05 |
| 305 | Pedro Munoz | .20 | .15 |
| 306 | Scott Scudder | .06 | .05 |
| 307 | Kevin Elster | .06 | .05 |
| 308 | Duane Ward | .06 | .05 |
| 309 | *Darryl Kile* | .15 | .11 |
| 310 | Orlando Merced | .35 | .25 |
| 311 | Dave Henderson | .10 | .08 |
| 312 | Tim Raines | .10 | .08 |
| 313 | Mark Lee(FC) | .06 | .05 |
| 314 | Mike Gallego | .06 | .05 |
| 315 | Charles Nagy | .10 | .08 |
| 316 | Jesse Barfield | .08 | .06 |
| 317 | Todd Frohwirth | .05 | .04 |
| 318 | Al Osuna | .06 | .05 |
| 319 | Darrin Fletcher | .06 | .05 |
| 320 | Checklist | .05 | .04 |
| 321 | David Segui | .10 | .08 |
| 322 | Stan Javier | .05 | .04 |
| 323 | Bryn Smith | .05 | .04 |
| 324 | Jeff Treadway | .06 | .05 |
| 325 | Mark Whiten | .15 | .11 |
| 326 | Kent Hrbek | .08 | .06 |
| 327 | David Justice | .35 | .25 |
| 328 | Tony Phillips | .06 | .05 |
| 329 | Rob Murphy | .05 | .04 |
| 330 | Kevin Morton | .10 | .08 |
| 331 | John Smiley | .08 | .06 |
| 332 | Luis Rivera | .05 | .04 |
| 333 | Wally Joyner | .15 | .11 |
| 334 | *Heathcliff Slocumb* | .15 | .11 |
| 335 | Rick Cerone | .05 | .04 |
| 336 | *Mike Remlinger*(FC) | .15 | .11 |
| 337 | Mike Moore | .06 | .05 |
| 338 | Lloyd McClendon | .05 | .04 |
| 339 | Al Newman | .05 | .04 |
| 340 | Kirk McCaskill | .08 | .06 |
| 341 | Howard Johnson | .15 | .11 |
| 342 | Greg Myers | .05 | .04 |
| 343 | Kal Daniels | .08 | .06 |
| 344 | Bernie Williams | .30 | .25 |
| 345 | Shane Mack | .10 | .08 |
| 346 | Gary Thurman | .05 | .04 |
| 347 | Dante Bichette | .06 | .05 |
| 348 | Mark McGwire | .15 | .11 |
| 349 | Travis Fryman | .25 | .20 |
| 350 | Ray Lankford | .20 | .15 |
| 351 | Mike Jeffcoat | .05 | .04 |
| 352 | Jack McDowell | .10 | .08 |
| 353 | Mitch Williams | .08 | .06 |
| 354 | Mike Devereaux | .06 | .05 |
| 355 | Andre Galarraga | .06 | .05 |
| 356 | Henry Cotto | .05 | .04 |
| 357 | Scott Bailes | .05 | .04 |
| 358 | *Jeff Bagwell* | .60 | .45 |
| 359 | Scott Leius | .08 | .06 |
| 360 | Zane Smith | .06 | .05 |
| 361 | Bill Pecota | .06 | .05 |
| 362 | Tony Fernandez | .08 | .06 |
| 363 | Glenn Braggs | .06 | .05 |
| 364 | Bill Spiers | .06 | .05 |
| 365 | Vicente Palacios | .05 | .04 |
| 366 | Tim Burke | .06 | .05 |
| 367 | Randy Tomlin | .06 | .05 |
| 368 | Kenny Rogers | .06 | .05 |
| 369 | Brett Butler | .08 | .06 |

| | | MT | NR MT |
|---|---|---|---|
| 370 | Pat Kelly | .20 | .15 |
| 371 | Bip Roberts | .06 | .05 |
| 372 | Gregg Jefferies | .15 | .11 |
| 373 | Kevin Bass | .06 | .05 |
| 374 | Ron Karkovice | .05 | .04 |
| 375 | Paul Gibson | .05 | .04 |
| 376 | Bernard Gilkey | .10 | .08 |
| 377 | Dave Gallagher | .06 | .05 |
| 378 | Bill Wegman | .06 | .05 |
| 379 | Pat Borders | .06 | .05 |
| 380 | Ed Whitson | .06 | .05 |
| 381 | Gilberto Reyes | .08 | .06 |
| 382 | Russ Swan | .08 | .06 |
| 383 | Andy Van Slyke | .10 | .08 |
| 384 | Wes Chamberlain | .20 | .15 |
| 385 | Steve Chitren | .08 | .06 |
| 386 | Greg Olson | .06 | .05 |
| 387 | Brian McRae | .20 | .15 |
| 388 | Rich Rodriguez | .06 | .05 |
| 389 | Steve Decker | .15 | .11 |
| 390 | Chuck Knoblauch | .20 | .15 |
| 391 | Bobby Witt | .06 | .05 |
| 392 | Eddie Murray | .10 | .08 |
| 393 | Juan Gonzalez | .25 | .20 |
| 394 | Scott Ruskin | .05 | .04 |
| 395 | Jay Howell | .06 | .05 |
| 396 | Checklist | .05 | .04 |
| 397 | Royce Clayton | .30 | .25 |
| 398 | *John Jaha*(FC) | .40 | .30 |
| 399 | Dan Wilson (RR)(FC) | .15 | .11 |
| 400 | *Archie Corbin*(FC) | .20 | .15 |
| 401 | *Barry Manuel*(FC) | .20 | .15 |
| 402 | Kim Batiste (RR)(FC) | .10 | .08 |
| 403 | *Pat Mahomes*(FC) | .70 | .50 |
| 404 | Dave Fleming | .40 | .30 |
| 405 | Jeff Juden | .15 | .11 |
| 406 | *Jim Thome*(FC) | .50 | .40 |
| 407 | Sam Militello (RR)(FC) | .10 | .08 |
| 408 | Jeff Nelson (RR)(FC) | .10 | .08 |
| 409 | Anthony Young (RR) | .15 | .11 |
| 410 | Tino Martinez (RR) | .15 | .11 |
| 411 | *Jeff Mutis* (RR)(FC) | .15 | .11 |
| 412 | *Rey Sanchez* (RR)(FC) | .15 | .11 |
| 413 | *Chris Gardner*(FC) | .25 | .20 |
| 414 | *John Vander Wal*(FC) | .30 | .25 |
| 415 | Reggie Sanders(FC) | .40 | .30 |
| 416 | *Brian Williams*(FC) | .20 | .15 |
| 417 | Mo Sanford (RR)(FC) | .15 | .11 |
| 418 | *David Weathers*(FC) | .15 | .11 |
| 419 | *Hector Fajardo*(FC) | .30 | .25 |
| 420 | *Steve Foster*(FC) | .30 | .25 |
| 421 | Lance Dickson (RR) | .10 | .08 |
| 422 | Andre Dawson (AS) | .08 | .06 |

| | | MT | NR MT | | | | MT | NR MT |
|---|---|---|---|---|---|---|---|---|
| 423 | Ozzie Smith (AS) | .08 | .06 | | 488 | Phil Plantier | .30 | .25 |
| 424 | Chris Sabo (AS) | .08 | .06 | | 489 | Curtis Wilkerson | .05 | .04 |
| 425 | Tony Gwynn (AS) | .10 | .08 | | 490 | Tom Brunansky | .06 | .05 |
| 426 | Tom Glavine (AS) | .08 | .06 | | 491 | Mike Fetters | .05 | .04 |
| 427 | Bobby Bonilla (AS) | .10 | .08 | | 492 | Frank Castillo | .08 | .06 |
| 428 | Will Clark (AS) | .15 | .11 | | 493 | Joe Boever | .05 | .04 |
| 429 | Ryne Sandberg (AS) | .15 | .11 | | 494 | Kirt Manwaring | .05 | .04 |
| 430 | Benito Santiago (AS) | | | | 495 | Wilson Alvarez (HL) | .06 | .05 |
| | | .08 | .06 | | 496 | Gene Larkin | .05 | .04 |
| 431 | Ivan Calderon (AS) | .08 | .06 | | 497 | Gary DiSarcina | .06 | .05 |
| 432 | Ozzie Smith | .08 | .06 | | 498 | Frank Viola | .08 | .06 |
| 433 | Tim Leary | .05 | .04 | | 499 | Manuel Lee | .05 | .04 |
| 434 | Bret Saberhagen (HL) | | | | 500 | Albert Belle | .15 | .11 |
| | | .08 | .06 | | 501 | Stan Belinda | .05 | .04 |
| 435 | Mel Rojas | .06 | .05 | | 502 | Dwight Evans | .06 | .05 |
| 436 | Ben McDonald | .10 | .08 | | 503 | Eric Davis | .10 | .08 |
| 437 | Tim Crews | .05 | .04 | | 504 | Darren Holmes | .05 | .04 |
| 438 | Rex Hudler | .05 | .04 | | 505 | Mike Bordick | .12 | .09 |
| 439 | Chico Walker | .05 | .04 | | 506 | Dave Hansen | .06 | .05 |
| 440 | Kurt Stillwell | .05 | .04 | | 507 | Lee Guetterman | .05 | .04 |
| 441 | Tony Gwynn | .15 | .11 | | 508 | *Keith Mitchell*(FC) | | |
| 442 | John Smoltz | .08 | .06 | | | | .15 | .11 |
| 443 | Lloyd Moseby | .05 | .04 | | 509 | Melido Perez | .05 | .04 |
| 444 | Mike Schooler | .06 | .05 | | 510 | Dickie Thon | .05 | .04 |
| 445 | Joe Grahe | .06 | .05 | | 511 | Mark Williamson | .05 | .04 |
| 446 | Dwight Gooden | .10 | .08 | | 512 | Mark Salas | .05 | .04 |
| 447 | Oil Can Boyd | .05 | .04 | | 513 | Milt Thompson | .05 | .04 |
| 448 | John Marzano | .05 | .04 | | 514 | Mo Vaughn | .20 | .15 |
| 449 | Bret Barberie | .10 | .08 | | 515 | Jim Deshaies | .05 | .04 |
| 450 | Mike Maddux | .05 | .04 | | 516 | Rich Garces | .05 | .04 |
| 451 | Jeff Reed | .05 | .04 | | 517 | Lonnie Smith | .05 | .04 |
| 452 | Dale Sveum | .05 | .04 | | 518 | Spike Owen | .06 | .05 |
| 453 | Jose Uribe | .05 | .04 | | 519 | Tracy Jones | .05 | .04 |
| 454 | Bob Scanlan | .05 | .04 | | 520 | Greg Maddux | .08 | .06 |
| 455 | Kevin Appier | .08 | .06 | | 521 | Carlos Martinez | .05 | .04 |
| 456 | Jeff Huson | .05 | .04 | | 522 | Neal Heaton | .05 | .04 |
| 457 | Ken Patterson | .05 | .04 | | 523 | Mike Greenwell | .08 | .06 |
| 458 | Ricky Jordan | .08 | .06 | | 524 | Andy Benes | .08 | .06 |
| 459 | Tom Candiotti | .06 | .05 | | 525 | Jeff Schaefer | .05 | .04 |
| 460 | Lee Stevens | .08 | .06 | | 526 | Mike Sharperson | .05 | .04 |
| 461 | *Rod Beck*(FC) | .15 | .11 | | 527 | Wade Taylor | .06 | .05 |
| 462 | Dave Valle | .05 | .04 | | 528 | Jerome Walton | .06 | .05 |
| 463 | Scott Erickson | .25 | .20 | | 529 | Storm Davis | .05 | .04 |
| 464 | Chris Jones | .06 | .05 | | 530 | *Jose Hernandez*(FC) | | |
| 465 | Mark Carreon | .05 | .04 | | | | .20 | .15 |
| 466 | Rob Ducey | .05 | .04 | | 531 | Mark Langston | .08 | .06 |
| 467 | Jim Corsi | .05 | .04 | | 532 | Rob Deer | .06 | .05 |
| 468 | Jeff King | .05 | .04 | | 533 | Geronimo Pena | .06 | .05 |
| 469 | Curt Young | .05 | .04 | | 534 | *Juan Guzman*(FC) | | |
| 470 | Bo Jackson | .15 | .11 | | | | .80 | .60 |
| 471 | Chris Bosio | .06 | .05 | | 535 | Pete Schourek | .08 | .06 |
| 472 | Jamie Quirk | .05 | .04 | | 536 | Todd Benzinger | .05 | .04 |
| 473 | Jesse Orosco | .05 | .04 | | 537 | Billy Hatcher | .05 | .04 |
| 474 | Alvaro Espinoza | .05 | .04 | | 538 | Tom Foley | .05 | .04 |
| 475 | Joe Orsulak | .05 | .04 | | 539 | Dave Cochrane | .05 | .04 |
| 476 | Checklist | .05 | .04 | | 540 | Mariano Duncan | .05 | .04 |
| 477 | Gerald Young | .05 | .04 | | 541 | Edwin Nunez | .05 | .04 |
| 478 | Wally Backman | .05 | .04 | | 542 | Rance Mulliniks | .05 | .04 |
| 479 | Juan Bell | .05 | .04 | | 543 | Carlton Fisk | .10 | .08 |
| 480 | Mike Scioscia | .06 | .05 | | 544 | Luis Aquino | .05 | .04 |
| 481 | Omar Olivares | .06 | .05 | | 545 | Ricky Bones | .08 | .06 |
| 482 | Francisco Cabrera | .05 | .04 | | 546 | Craig Grebeck | .05 | .04 |
| 483 | Greg Swindell | .08 | .06 | | 547 | Charlie Hayes | .06 | .05 |
| 484 | Terry Leach | .05 | .04 | | 548 | Jose Canseco | .20 | .15 |
| 485 | Tommy Gregg | .05 | .04 | | 549 | Andujar Cedeno | .10 | .08 |
| 486 | Scott Aldred | .05 | .04 | | 550 | Geno Petralli | .05 | .04 |
| 487 | Greg Briley | .05 | .04 | | 551 | Javier Ortiz | .05 | .04 |

| | | MT | NR MT |
|---|---|---|---|
| 552 | Rudy Seanez | .06 | .05 |
| 553 | Rich Gedman | .05 | .04 |
| 554 | Eric Plunk | .05 | .04 |
| 555 | Nolan Ryan, Rich Gossage (HL) | .20 | .15 |
| 556 | Checklist | .05 | .04 |
| 557 | Greg Colbrunn | .06 | .05 |
| 558 | *Chito Martinez*(FC) | .20 | .15 |
| 559 | Darryl Strawberry | .20 | .15 |
| 560 | Luis Alicea | .05 | .04 |
| 561 | Dwight Smith | .06 | .05 |
| 562 | Terry Shumpert | .05 | .04 |
| 563 | Jim Vatcher | .05 | .04 |
| 564 | Deion Sanders | .08 | .06 |
| 565 | Walt Terrell | .05 | .04 |
| 566 | Dave Burba | .05 | .04 |
| 567 | Dave Howard | .05 | .04 |
| 568 | Todd Hundley | .08 | .06 |
| 569 | Jack Daugherty | .05 | .04 |
| 570 | Scott Cooper | .10 | .08 |
| 571 | Bill Sampen | .05 | .04 |
| 572 | Jose Melendez | .10 | .08 |
| 573 | Freddie Benavides | .05 | .04 |
| 574 | Jim Gantner | .05 | .04 |
| 575 | Trevor Wilson | .05 | .04 |
| 576 | Ryne Sandberg | .20 | .15 |
| 577 | Kevin Seitzer | .05 | .04 |
| 578 | Gerald Alexander | .05 | .04 |
| 579 | Mike Huff | .05 | .04 |
| 580 | Von Hayes | .06 | .05 |
| 581 | Derek Bell | .30 | .25 |
| 582 | Mike Stanley | .05 | .04 |
| 583 | Kevin Mitchell | .08 | .06 |
| 584 | Mike Jackson | .05 | .04 |
| 585 | Dan Gladden | .05 | .04 |
| 586 | Ted Power | .05 | .04 |
| 587 | Jeff Innis | .05 | .04 |
| 588 | Bob MacDonald | .08 | .06 |
| 589 | *Jose Tolentino*(FC) | .08 | .06 |
| 590 | Bob Patterson | .05 | .04 |
| 591 | *Scott Brosius*(FC) | .10 | .08 |
| 592 | Frank Thomas | .80 | .60 |
| 593 | Darryl Hamilton | .08 | .06 |
| 594 | Kirk Dressendorfer | .08 | .06 |
| 595 | Jeff Shaw | .08 | .06 |
| 596 | Don Mattingly | .12 | .09 |
| 597 | Glenn Davis | .06 | .05 |
| 598 | Andy Mota | .10 | .08 |
| 599 | Jason Grimsley | .05 | .04 |
| 600 | Jimmy Poole | .06 | .05 |
| 601 | Jim Gott | .05 | .04 |
| 602 | Stan Royer | .08 | .06 |
| 603 | Marvin Freeman | .05 | .04 |
| 604 | Denis Boucher | .08 | .06 |
| 605 | Denny Neagle | .10 | .08 |
| 606 | Mark Lemke | .06 | .05 |
| 607 | Jerry Don Gleaton | .05 | .04 |
| 608 | Brent Knackert | .05 | .04 |
| 609 | Carlos Quintana | .05 | .04 |
| 610 | Bobby Bonilla | .12 | .09 |
| 611 | Joe Hesketh | .05 | .04 |
| 612 | Daryl Boston | .05 | .04 |
| 613 | Shawon Dunston | .08 | .06 |
| 614 | Danny Cox | .05 | .04 |

| | | MT | NR MT |
|---|---|---|---|
| 615 | Darren Lewis | .12 | .09 |
| 616 | Alejandro Pena, Kent Mercker, Mark Wohlers (HL) | .10 | .08 |
| 617 | Kirby Puckett | .15 | .11 |
| 618 | Franklin Stubbs | .05 | .04 |
| 619 | Chris Donnels | .10 | .08 |
| 620 | David Wells | .05 | .04 |
| 621 | Mike Aldrete | .05 | .04 |
| 622 | Bob Kipper | .05 | .04 |
| 623 | Anthony Telford | .05 | .04 |
| 624 | Randy Myers | .05 | .04 |
| 625 | Willie Randolph | .05 | .04 |
| 626 | Joe Slusarski | .08 | .06 |
| 627 | John Wetteland | .06 | .05 |
| 628 | Greg Cadaret | .05 | .04 |
| 629 | Tom Glavine | .10 | .08 |
| 630 | Wilson Alvarez | .10 | .08 |
| 631 | Wally Ritchie | .05 | .04 |
| 632 | *Mike Mussina*(FC) | .50 | .40 |
| 633 | Mark Leiter | .05 | .04 |
| 634 | Gerald Perry | .05 | .04 |
| 635 | Matt Young | .05 | .04 |
| 636 | Checklist | .05 | .04 |
| 637 | Scott Hemond | .05 | .04 |
| 638 | David West | .05 | .04 |
| 639 | Jim Clancy | .05 | .04 |
| 640 | *Doug Piatt*(FC) | .10 | .08 |
| 641 | Omar Vizquel | .05 | .04 |
| 642 | Rick Sutcliffe | .08 | .06 |
| 643 | Glenallen Hill | .08 | .06 |
| 644 | Gary Varsho | .05 | .04 |
| 645 | Tony Fossas | .05 | .04 |
| 646 | Jack Howell | .05 | .04 |
| 647 | *Jim Campanis*(FC) | .15 | .11 |
| 648 | Chris Gwynn | .05 | .04 |
| 649 | Jim Leyritz | .05 | .04 |
| 650 | Chuck McElroy | .05 | .04 |
| 651 | *Sean Berry*(FC) | .08 | .06 |
| 652 | *Donald Harris*(FC) | .10 | .08 |
| 653 | Don Slaught | .05 | .04 |
| 654 | *Rusty Meacham* | .10 | .08 |
| 655 | Scott Terry | .05 | .04 |
| 656 | Ramon Martinez | .12 | .09 |
| 657 | Keith Miller | .05 | .04 |
| 658 | *Ramon Garcia*(FC) | .08 | .06 |
| 659 | *Milt Hill*(FC) | .10 | .08 |
| 660 | Steve Frey | .05 | .04 |
| 661 | Bob McClure | .05 | .04 |
| 662 | *Ced Landrum* | .08 | .06 |
| 663 | *Doug Henry*(FC) | .20 | .15 |
| 664 | Candy Maldonado | .05 | .04 |
| 665 | Carl Willis | .05 | .04 |
| 666 | Jeff Montgomery | .08 | .06 |
| 667 | *Craig Shipley*(FC) | .10 | .08 |
| 668 | *Warren Newson* | .08 | .06 |
| 669 | Mickey Morandini | .08 | .06 |
| 670 | Brook Jacoby | .05 | .04 |
| 671 | *Ryan Bowen* | .10 | .08 |
| 672 | Bill Krueger | .05 | .04 |
| 673 | Rob Mallicoat | .05 | .04 |
| 674 | Doug Jones | .05 | .04 |
| 675 | Scott Livingstone | .10 | .08 |
| 676 | Danny Tartabull | .10 | .08 |
| 677 | Joe Carter (HL) | .08 | .06 |

| | | MT | NR MT | | | | MT | NR MT |
|---|---|---|---|---|---|---|---|---|
| 678 | Cecil Espy | .05 | .04 | 741 | Julio Franco | | .08 | .06 |
| 679 | Randy Velarde | .05 | .04 | 742 | Tim Naehring | | .08 | .06 |
| 680 | Bruce Ruffin | .05 | .04 | 743 | Steve Wapnick(FC) | | | |
| 681 | Ted Wood(FC) | .25 | .20 | | | | .10 | .08 |
| 682 | Dan Plesac | .05 | .04 | 744 | Craig Wilson | | .08 | .06 |
| 683 | Eric Bullock | .05 | .04 | 745 | Darrin Chapin(FC) | | | |
| 684 | Junior Ortiz | .05 | .04 | | | | .15 | .11 |
| 685 | Dave Hollins | .06 | .05 | 746 | Chris George(FC) | | | |
| 686 | Dennis Martinez | .08 | .06 | | | | .08 | .06 |
| 687 | Larry Andersen | .05 | .04 | 747 | Mike Simms | | .08 | .06 |
| 688 | Doug Simons | .05 | .04 | 748 | Rosario Rodriguez | | .08 | .06 |
| 689 | Tim Spehr | .08 | .06 | 749 | Skeeter Barnes | | .05 | .04 |
| 690 | Calvin Jones(FC) | .12 | .09 | 750 | Roger McDowell | | .05 | .04 |
| 691 | Mark Guthrie | .05 | .04 | 751 | Dann Howitt | | .05 | .04 |
| 692 | Alfredo Griffin | .05 | .04 | 752 | Paul Sorrento | | .05 | .04 |
| 693 | Joe Carter | .12 | .09 | 753 | Braulio Castillo(FC) | | | |
| 694 | Terry Mathews(FC) | | | | | | .15 | .11 |
| | | .08 | .06 | 754 | Yorkis Perez(FC) | | .15 | .11 |
| 695 | Pascual Perez | .05 | .04 | 755 | Willie Fraser | | .05 | .04 |
| 696 | Gene Nelson | .05 | .04 | 756 | Jeremy | | | |
| 697 | Gerald Williams | .15 | .11 | | Hernandez(FC) | | .10 | .08 |
| 698 | Chris Cron(FC) | .15 | .11 | 757 | Curt Schilling | | .05 | .04 |
| 699 | Steve Buechele | .06 | .05 | 758 | Steve Lyons | | .05 | .04 |
| 700 | Paul McClellan(FC) | .08 | .06 | 759 | Dave Anderson | | .05 | .04 |
| 701 | Jim Lindeman | .05 | .04 | 760 | Willie Banks | | .12 | .09 |
| 702 | Francisco Oliveras | .05 | .04 | 761 | Mark Leonard | | .05 | .04 |
| 703 | Rob Maurer(FC) | .25 | .20 | 762 | Jack Armstrong | | .06 | .05 |
| 704 | Pat Hentgen(FC) | .15 | .11 | 763 | Scott Servais | | .08 | .06 |
| 705 | Jaime Navarro | .06 | .05 | 764 | Ray Stephens | | .08 | .06 |
| 706 | Mike Magnante(FC) | | | 765 | Junior Noboa | | .05 | .04 |
| | | .10 | .08 | 766 | Jim Olander(FC) | | .10 | .08 |
| 707 | Nolan Ryan | .30 | .25 | 767 | Joe Magrane | | .06 | .05 |
| 708 | Bobby Thigpen | .08 | .06 | 768 | Lance Blankenship | | .05 | .04 |
| 709 | John Cerutti | .05 | .04 | 769 | Mike | | | |
| 710 | Steve Wilson | .05 | .04 | | Humphreys(FC) | | .10 | .08 |
| 711 | Hensley Meulens | .08 | .06 | 770 | Jarvis Brown(FC) | | | |
| 712 | Rheal Cormier(FC) | | | | | | .12 | .09 |
| | | .20 | .15 | 771 | Damon Berryhill | | .05 | .04 |
| 713 | Scott Bradley | .05 | .04 | 772 | Alejandro Pena | | .06 | .05 |
| 714 | Mitch Webster | .05 | .04 | 773 | Jose Mesa | | .05 | .04 |
| 715 | Roger Mason | .05 | .04 | 774 | Gary Cooper(FC) | | | |
| 716 | Checklist | .05 | .04 | | | | .10 | .08 |
| 717 | Jeff Fassero | .08 | .06 | 775 | Carney Lansford | | .06 | .05 |
| 718 | Cal Eldred(FC) | .35 | .25 | 776 | Mike Bielecki | | .05 | .04 |
| 719 | Sid Fernandez | .08 | .06 | 777 | Charlie O'Brien | | .05 | .04 |
| 720 | Bob Zupcic(FC) | .30 | .25 | 778 | Carlos Hernandez | | .05 | .04 |
| 721 | Jose Offerman | .08 | .06 | 779 | Howard Farmer | | .05 | .04 |
| 722 | Cliff Brantley(FC) | | | 780 | Mike Stanton | | .05 | .04 |
| | | .20 | .15 | 781 | Reggie Harris | | .05 | .04 |
| 723 | Ron Darling | .06 | .05 | 782 | Xavier Hernandez | | .05 | .04 |
| 724 | Dave Stieb | .06 | .05 | 783 | Bryan Hickerson(FC) | | | |
| 725 | Hector Villanueva | .06 | .05 | | | | .10 | .08 |
| 726 | Mike Hartley | .05 | .04 | 784 | Checklist | | .05 | .04 |
| 727 | Arthur Rhodes | .15 | .11 | ---- | Cal Ripken (MVP) | | .20 | .15 |
| 728 | Randy Bush | .05 | .04 | ---- | Terry Pendleton (MVP) | | | |
| 729 | Steve Sax | .08 | .06 | | | | .08 | .06 |
| 730 | Dave Otto | .05 | .04 | ---- | Roger Clemens (CY | | | |
| 731 | John Wehner | .10 | .08 | | Young) | | .10 | .08 |
| 732 | Dave Martinez | .05 | .04 | ---- | Tom Glavine (CY Young) | | | |
| 733 | Ruben Amaro | .10 | .08 | | | | .08 | .06 |
| 734 | Billy Ripken | .05 | .04 | ---- | Chuck Knoblauch (ROY) | | | |
| 735 | Steve Farr | .05 | .04 | | | | .20 | .15 |
| 736 | Shawn Abner | .05 | .04 | ---- | Jeff Bagwell (ROY) | | .50 | .40 |
| 737 | Gil Heredia(FC) | .10 | .08 | ---- | Colorado Rockies | | .50 | .40 |
| 738 | Ron Jones | .05 | .04 | ---- | Florida Marlins | | .50 | .40 |
| 739 | Tony Castillo | .05 | .04 | | | | | |
| 740 | Sammy Sosa | .08 | .06 | | | | | |

## Card Grading Guide

**Mint (MT):** A perfect card. Well-centered with all corners sharp and square. No creases, stains, edge nicks, surface marks, yellowing or fading.

**Near Mint (NM):** A nearly perfect card. At first glance may appear to be perfect. May have one corner not perfectly sharp. May be slightly off-center. No surface marks, creases or loss of gloss.

**Excellent (EX):** Corners are still fairly sharp with only moderate wear. Borders may be off-center. No creases or stains on front or back, but may show slight loss of surface luster.

**Very Good (VG):** Shows obvious handling. May have rounded corners, minor creases, major gum or wax stains. No major creases, tape marks, writing, etc.

**Good (G):** A well-worn card but exhibits no intentional damage. Corners may be rounded beyond card border. May have major or multiple creases.

## 1992 Donruss Rookies

Donruss increased the size of its Rookies set in 1992 to include 132 cards. In the past the cards were released only in boxed set form, but the 1992 cards were available in packs. Special phenoms insert cards were randomly inserted into Rookies packs. The phenoms cards feature black borders, while the Rookies cards are styled after the regular 1992 Donruss issue. The cards are numbered alphabetically.

|  |  | MT | NR MT |
|---|---|---|---|
| Complete Set: |  | 13.00 | 9.75 |
| Common Player: |  | .08 | .06 |
| 1 | Kyle Abbott | .08 | .06 |
| 2 | Troy Afenir | .08 | .06 |
| 3 | Rich Amaral(FC) | .12 | .09 |
| 4 | Ruben Amaro(FC) | .12 | .09 |
| 5 | Billy Ashley(FC) | .30 | .25 |
| 6 | Pedro Astacio(FC) | .25 | .20 |
| 7 | Jim Austin(FC) | .08 | .06 |
| 8 | Robert Ayrault(FC) | .10 | .08 |
| 9 | Kevin Baez(FC) | .10 | .08 |
| 10 | Estaban Beltre | .08 | .06 |
| 11 | Brian Bohanon(FC) | .08 | .06 |
| 12 | Kent Bottenfield(FC) | .12 | .09 |
| 13 | Jeff Branson(FC) | .20 | .15 |
| 14 | Brad Brink | .08 | .06 |
| 15 | John Briscoe(FC) | .10 | .08 |
| 16 | Doug Brocail(FC) | .10 | .08 |
| 17 | Rico Brogna(FC) | .15 | .11 |
| 18 | J.T. Bruett(FC) | .15 | .11 |
| 19 | Jacob Brumfield | .12 | .09 |
| 20 | Jim Bullinger(FC) | .12 | .09 |
| 21 | Kevin Campbell(FC) | .08 | .06 |
| 22 | Pedro Castellano(FC) | .20 | .15 |
| 23 | Mike Christopher(FC) | .08 | .06 |
| 24 | Archi Cianfrocco(FC) | .40 | .30 |
| 25 | Mark Clark(FC) | .12 | .09 |
| 26 | Craig Colbert(FC) | .08 | .06 |
| 27 | Victor Cole(FC) | .12 | .09 |
| 28 | Steve Cooke(FC) | .12 | .09 |
| 29 | Tim Costo(FC) | .15 | .11 |
| 30 | Chad Curtis(FC) | .25 | .20 |
| 31 | Doug Davis(FC) | .10 | .08 |
| 32 | Gary DiSarcina | .08 | .06 |
| 33 | John Doherty(FC) | .10 | .08 |
| 34 | Mike Draper(FC) | .20 | .15 |
| 35 | Monty Fariss | .08 | .06 |
| 36 | Bien Figueroa(FC) | .10 | .08 |
| 37 | John Flaherty(FC) | .08 | .06 |
| 38 | Tim Fortugno(FC) | .10 | .08 |
| 39 | Eric Fox(FC) | .10 | .08 |
| 40 | Jeff Frye(FC) | .10 | .08 |
| 41 | Ramon Garcia(FC) | .12 | .09 |
| 42 | Brent Gates(FC) | .25 | .20 |
| 43 | Tom Goodwin(FC) | .10 | .08 |
| 44 | Buddy Groom(FC) | .12 | .09 |
| 45 | Jeff Grotewold(FC) | .20 | .15 |
| 46 | Juan Guerrero(FC) | .20 | .15 |
| 47 | Johnny Guzman(FC) | .10 | .08 |
| 48 | Shawn Hare(FC) | .12 | .09 |
| 49 | Ryan Hawblitzel(FC) | .20 | .15 |
| 50 | Bert Heffernan(FC) | .08 | .06 |
| 51 | Butch Henry(FC) | .10 | .08 |
| 52 | Cesar Hernandez(FC) | .10 | .08 |
| 53 | Vince Horsman(FC) | .10 | .08 |
| 54 | Steve Hosey(FC) | .10 | .08 |
| 55 | Pat Howell(FC) | .10 | .08 |
| 56 | Peter Hoy(FC) | .10 | .08 |
| 57 | Jon Hurst(FC) | .10 | .08 |

|    |                      | MT  | NR MT |
|----|----------------------|-----|-------|
| 58 | Mark Hutton(FC)      | .30 | .25   |
| 59 | Shawn Jeter(FC)      | .12 | .09   |
| 60 | Joel Johnston(FC)    | .08 | .06   |
| 61 | Jeff Kent(FC)        | .30 | .25   |
| 62 | Kurt Knudsen(FC)     | .08 | .06   |
| 63 | Kevin Koslofski(FC)  | .20 | .15   |
| 64 | Danny Leon(FC)       | .10 | .08   |
| 65 | Jesse Levis(FC)      | .20 | .15   |
| 66 | Tom Marsh(FC)        | .10 | .08   |
| 67 | Ed Martel(FC)        | .10 | .08   |
| 68 | Al Martin(FC)        | .20 | .15   |
| 69 | Pedro Martinez(FC)   | .25 | .20   |
| 70 | Derrick May          | .10 | .08   |
| 71 | Matt Maysey          | .12 | .09   |
| 72 | Russ McGinnis        | .08 | .06   |
| 73 | Tim McIntosh         | .08 | .06   |
| 74 | Jim McNamara(FC)     | .08 | .06   |
| 75 | Jeff McNeely(FC)     | .30 | .25   |
| 76 | Rusty Meacham        | .08 | .06   |
| 77 | Tony Melendez(FC)    | .10 | .08   |
| 78 | Henry Mercedes(FC)   |     |       |
|    |                      | .10 | .08   |
| 79 | Paul Miller(FC)      | .10 | .08   |
| 80 | Joe Millette(FC)     | .10 | .08   |
| 81 | Blas Minor(FC)       | .10 | .08   |
| 82 | Dennis Moeller(FC)   | .10 | .08   |
| 83 | Raul Mondesi(FC)     | .25 | .20   |
| 84 | Rob Natal(FC)        | .20 | .15   |
| 85 | Troy Neel(FC)        | .25 | .20   |
| 86 | David Nied(FC)       | .30 | .25   |
| 87 | Jerry Nielsen(FC)    | .20 | .15   |
| 88 | Donovan Osborne(FC)  |     |       |
|    |                      | .25 | .20   |
| 89 | John Patterson(FC)   | .12 | .09   |
| 90 | Roger Pavlik(FC)     | .10 | .08   |
| 91 | Dan Peltier(FC)      | .20 | .15   |
| 92 | Jim Pena(FC)         | .10 | .08   |
| 93 | William Pennyfeather(FC) | .30 | .25 |
| 94 | Mike Perez           | .08 | .06   |
| 95 | Hipolito Pichardo(FC)|     |       |
|    |                      | .20 | .15   |
| 96 | Greg Pirkl(FC)       | .08 | .06   |
| 97 | Harvey Pulliam(FC)   | .08 | .06   |
| 98 | Manny Ramirez(FC)    | .50 | .40   |
| 99 | Pat Rapp(FC)         | .12 | .09   |
| 100 | Jeff Reboulet(FC)   | .10 | .08   |
| 101 | Darren Reed(FC)     | .10 | .08   |
| 102 | Shane Reynolds(FC)  | .10 | .08   |
| 103 | Bill Risley(FC)     | .10 | .08   |
| 104 | Ben Rivera(FC)      | .10 | .08   |
| 105 | Henry Rodriguez(FC) |     |       |
|    |                      | .10 | .08   |
| 106 | Rico Rossy(FC)      | .10 | .08   |
| 107 | Johnny Ruffin(FC)   | .10 | .08   |
| 108 | Steve Scarsone(FC)  | .20 | .15   |
| 109 | Tim Scott(FC)       | .08 | .06   |
| 110 | Steve Shifflett(FC) | .10 | .08   |
| 111 | Dave Silvestri(FC)  | .20 | .15   |
| 112 | Matt Stairs(FC)     | .08 | .06   |
| 113 | William Suero(FC)   | .08 | .06   |
| 114 | Jeff Tackett(FC)    | .10 | .08   |
| 115 | Eddie Taubensee(FC) |     |       |
|    |                      | .12 | .09   |
| 116 | Rick Trlicek(FC)    | .10 | .08   |
| 117 | Scooter Tucker(FC)  | .10 | .08   |
| 118 | Shane Turner(FC)    | .10 | .08   |

|     |                       | MT  | NR MT |
|-----|-----------------------|-----|-------|
| 119 | Julio Valera(FC)      | .10 | .08   |
| 120 | Paul Wagner(FC)       | .10 | .08   |
| 121 | Tim Wakefield(FC)     | .50 | .40   |
| 122 | Mike Walker(FC)       | .08 | .06   |
| 123 | Bruce Walton(FC)      | .08 | .06   |
| 124 | Lenny Webster         | .08 | .06   |
| 125 | Bob Wickman(FC)       | .40 | .30   |
| 126 | Mike Williams(FC)     | .10 | .08   |
| 127 | Kerry Woodson(FC)     | .10 | .08   |
| 128 | Eric Young(FC)        | .12 | .09   |
| 129 | Kevin Young(FC)       | .30 | .25   |
| 130 | Pete Young(FC)        | .10 | .08   |
| 131 | Checklist             | .08 | .06   |
| 132 | Checklist             | .08 | .06   |

## 1993 Donruss Series I

Rated Rookies and a randomly inserted Diamond Kings subset once again are featured in the 1993 Donruss set. Series I of the set was released first and includes 396 cards. The card fronts feature white borders surrounding a full-color player photo. the player's name and position appear at the bottom of the photo along with a diamond featuring the team logo. The flip sides feature and additional photo, biographical information and career statistics. The cards are numbered on the back and the series the card appears in is given with the number. The cards are UV coated.

|    |                    | MT    | NR MT |
|----|--------------------|-------|-------|
| Complete Set:       |        | 15.00 | 11.00 |
| Common Player:      |        | .05   | .04   |
| 1  | Craig Lefferts     | .05   | .04   |
| 2  | Kent Mercker       | .06   | .05   |
| 3  | Phil Plantier      | .10   | .08   |
| 4  | *Alex Arias*(FC)   | .15   | .11   |
| 5  | Julio Valera       | .08   | .06   |
| 6  | Dan Wilson(FC)     | .12   | .09   |
| 7  | Frank Thomas       | .30   | .25   |
| 8  | Eric Anthony       | .08   | .06   |
| 9  | Derek Lilliquist   | .05   | .04   |
| 10 | *Rafael Bournigal*(FC) |   |       |
|    |                    | .15   | .11   |

| | | MT | NR MT | | | | MT | NR MT |
|---|---|---|---|---|---|---|---|---|
| 11 | *Manny Alexander*(FC) | .15 | .11 | | 75 | Paul Molitor | .08 | .06 |
| 12 | Bret Barberie | .08 | .06 | | 76 | *Larry Carter*(FC) | .15 | .11 |
| 13 | Mickey Tettleton | .08 | .06 | | 77 | Rich Rowland(FC) | .10 | .08 |
| 14 | Anthony Young | .08 | .06 | | 78 | Damon Berryhill | .06 | .05 |
| 15 | Tim Spehr | .08 | .06 | | 79 | Willie Banks | .08 | .06 |
| 16 | *Bob Ayrault* | .10 | .08 | | 80 | Hector Villanueva | .06 | .05 |
| 17 | Bill Wegman | .06 | .05 | | 81 | Mike Gallego | .06 | .05 |
| 18 | Jay Bell | .08 | .06 | | 82 | Tim Belcher | .06 | .05 |
| 19 | Rick Aguilera | .08 | .06 | | 83 | Mike Bordick | .08 | .06 |
| 20 | Todd Zeile | .08 | .06 | | 84 | Criag Biggio | .08 | .06 |
| 21 | Steve Farr | .06 | .05 | | 85 | Lance Parrish | .06 | .05 |
| 22 | Andy Benes | .08 | .06 | | 86 | Brett Butler | .06 | .05 |
| 23 | Lance Blankenship | .05 | .04 | | 87 | Mike Timlin | .06 | .05 |
| 24 | Ted Wood | .08 | .06 | | 88 | Brian Barnes | .06 | .05 |
| 25 | Omar Vizquel | .05 | .04 | | 89 | Brady Anderson | .08 | .06 |
| 26 | Steve Avery | .08 | .06 | | 90 | D.J. Dozier | .08 | .06 |
| 27 | Brian Bohanon | .08 | .06 | | 91 | Frank Viola | .08 | .06 |
| 28 | Rick Wilkins | .08 | .06 | | 92 | Darren Daulton | .08 | .06 |
| 29 | Devon White | .08 | .06 | | 93 | Chad Curtis | .10 | .08 |
| 30 | *Bobby Ayala*(FC) | .12 | .09 | | 94 | Zane Smith | .05 | .04 |
| 31 | Leo Gomez | .08 | .06 | | 95 | George Bell | .08 | .06 |
| 32 | Mike Simms | .08 | .06 | | 96 | Rex Hudler | .05 | .04 |
| 33 | Ellis Burks | .03 | .06 | | 97 | Mark Whiten | .08 | .06 |
| 34 | Steve Wilson | .05 | .04 | | 98 | Tim Teufel | .05 | .04 |
| 35 | Jim Abbott | .08 | .06 | | 99 | Kevin Ritz | .05 | .04 |
| 36 | Tim Wallach | .06 | .05 | | 100 | Jeff Brantley | .05 | .04 |
| 37 | Wilson Alvarez | .06 | .05 | | 101 | Jeff Conine | .08 | .06 |
| 38 | Daryl Boston | .05 | .04 | | 102 | *Vinny Castilla*(FC) | .15 | .11 |
| 39 | Sandy Alomar Jr. | .10 | .08 | | | | | |
| 40 | Mitch Williams | .08 | .06 | | 103 | Greg Vaughn | .08 | .06 |
| 41 | Rico Brogna | .10 | .08 | | 104 | Steve Buechele | .06 | .05 |
| 42 | Gary Varsho | .05 | .04 | | 106 | Darren Reed, Bip Roberts | .08 | .06 |
| 43 | Kevin Appier | .08 | .06 | | 107 | John Habyan | .05 | .04 |
| 44 | Eric Wedge | .12 | .09 | | 108 | Scott Servais | .05 | .04 |
| 45 | Dante Bichette | .05 | .04 | | 109 | Walt Weiss | .05 | .04 |
| 46 | Jose Oquendo | .05 | .04 | | 110 | *J.T. Snow*(FC) | .15 | .11 |
| 47 | *Mike Trombley*(FC) | .12 | .09 | | 111 | Jay Buhner | .08 | .06 |
| 48 | Dan Walters | .08 | .06 | | 112 | Darryl Strawberry | .08 | .06 |
| 49 | Gerald Williams | .08 | .06 | | 113 | *Roger Pavlik* | .12 | .09 |
| 50 | Bud Black | .05 | .04 | | 114 | Chris Nabholz | .06 | .05 |
| 51 | Bobby Witt | .06 | .05 | | 115 | Pat Borders | .06 | .05 |
| 52 | Mark Davis | .05 | .04 | | 116 | *Pat Howell* | .12 | .09 |
| 53 | *Shawn Barton*(FC) | .15 | .11 | | 117 | Gregg Olson | .08 | .06 |
| 54 | Paul Assenmacher | .05 | .04 | | 118 | Curt Schilling | .08 | .06 |
| 55 | Kevin Reimer | .06 | .05 | | 119 | Roger Clemens | .12 | .09 |
| 56 | *Billy Ashley*(FC) | .20 | .15 | | 120 | *Victor Cole* | .12 | .09 |
| 57 | Eddie Zosky | .08 | .06 | | 121 | Gary DiSarcina | .05 | .04 |
| 58 | Chris Sabo | .08 | .06 | | 122 | Checklist | .05 | .04 |
| 59 | Billy Ripken | .05 | .04 | | 123 | Steve Sax | .08 | .06 |
| 60 | *Scooter Tucker* | .12 | .09 | | 124 | Chuck Carr(FC) | .08 | .06 |
| 61 | *Tim Wakefield* | .30 | .25 | | 125 | Mark Lewis | .08 | .06 |
| 62 | Mitch Webster | .05 | .04 | | 126 | Tony Gwynn | .08 | .06 |
| 63 | Jack Clark | .06 | .05 | | 127 | Travis Fryman | .12 | .09 |
| 64 | Mark Gardner | .06 | .05 | | 129 | Dave Burba | .06 | .05 |
| 65 | Lee Stevens | .06 | .05 | | 130 | John Smoltz | .08 | .06 |
| 66 | Todd Hundley | .08 | .06 | | 131 | Cal Eldred | .15 | .11 |
| 67 | Bobby Thigpen | .08 | .06 | | 132 | Checklist | .05 | .04 |
| 68 | Dave Hollins | .10 | .08 | | 133 | Arthur Rhodes | .10 | .08 |
| 69 | Jack Armstrong | .06 | .05 | | 134 | Jeff Blauser | .06 | .05 |
| 70 | Alex Cole | .06 | .05 | | 135 | Scott Cooper | .06 | .05 |
| 71 | Mark Carreon | .05 | .04 | | 136 | Doug Strange | .06 | .05 |
| 72 | Todd Worrell | .06 | .05 | | 137 | Luis Sojo | .06 | .05 |
| 73 | *Steve Shifflett* | .12 | .09 | | 138 | *Jeff Branson* | .15 | .11 |
| 74 | Jerald Clark | .06 | .05 | | 139 | Alex Fernandez | .08 | .06 |
| | | | | | 140 | Ken Caminiti | .06 | .05 |
| | | | | | 141 | Charles Nagy | .08 | .06 |

| | | MT | NR MT |
|---|---|---|---|
| 142 | Tom Candiotti | .06 | .05 |
| 143 | Willie Green | .10 | .08 |
| 144 | Kurt Knudsen | .10 | .08 |
| 146 | John Franco | .06 | .05 |
| 147 | *Eddie Pierce*(FC) | .15 | .11 |
| 148 | Kim Batiste | .08 | .06 |
| 149 | Darren Holmes | .05 | .04 |
| 150 | Steve Cooke | .15 | .11 |
| 151 | Terry Jorgensen | .08 | .06 |
| 152 | *Mark Clark* | .12 | .09 |
| 153 | Randy Velarde | .05 | .04 |
| 154 | Greg Harris | .05 | .04 |
| 155 | *Kevin Campbell* | .10 | .08 |
| 156 | John Burkett | .06 | .05 |
| 157 | Kevin Mitchell | .08 | .06 |
| 158 | Deion Sanders | .10 | .08 |
| 159 | Jose Canseco | .10 | .08 |
| 160 | *Jeff Hartsock*(FC) | | |
| | | .15 | .11 |
| 161 | *Tom Quinlan*(FC) | | |
| | | .15 | .11 |
| 162 | *Tim Pugh*(FC) | .15 | .11 |
| 163 | Glenn Davis | .08 | .06 |
| 164 | *Shane Reynolds* | .12 | .09 |
| 165 | Jody Reed | .06 | .05 |
| 166 | Mike Sharperson | .06 | .05 |
| 167 | Scott Lewis | .06 | .05 |
| 168 | Dennis Martinez | .06 | .05 |
| 169 | Scott Radinsky | .06 | .05 |
| 170 | Dave Gallagher | .05 | .04 |
| 171 | Jime Thome | .08 | .06 |
| 172 | Terry Mulholland | .06 | .05 |
| 173 | Milt Cuyler | .06 | .05 |
| 174 | Bob Patterson | .05 | .04 |
| 175 | Jeff Montgomery | .06 | .05 |
| 177 | Franklin Stubbs | .05 | .04 |
| 178 | Donovan Osborne | .10 | .08 |
| 179 | *Jeff Reboulet* | .10 | .08 |
| 180 | *Jeremy Hernandez*(FC) | .15 | .11 |
| 181 | Charlie Hayes | .06 | .05 |
| 182 | Matt Williams | .08 | .06 |
| 183 | Mike Raczka | .15 | .11 |
| 184 | Francisco Cabrera | .05 | .04 |
| 185 | Rich DeLucia | .05 | .04 |
| 186 | Sammy Sosa | .06 | .05 |
| 187 | Ivan Rodriguez | .10 | .08 |
| 188 | *Bret Boone*(FC) | .20 | .15 |
| 189 | Juan Guzman | .10 | .08 |
| 190 | Randy Milligan | .06 | .05 |
| 191 | Ivan Calderon | .08 | .06 |
| 197 | Junior Felix | .06 | .05 |
| 198 | Pete Schourek | .06 | .05 |
| 199 | Craig Grebeck | .06 | .05 |
| 200 | Juan Bell | .06 | .05 |
| 201 | Glenallen Hill | .06 | .05 |
| 202 | Danny Jackson | .06 | .05 |
| 203 | John Kiely | | |
| 204 | Bob Tewksbury | .08 | .06 |
| 205 | *Kevin Koslofski*(FC) | | |
| | | .15 | .11 |
| 206 | Craig Shipley | .08 | .06 |
| 207 | John Jaha(FC) | .20 | .15 |
| 208 | Royce Clayton | .10 | .08 |
| 209 | *Mike Piazza*(FC) | .25 | .20 |
| 210 | Ron Gant | .08 | .06 |
| 211 | Scott Erickson | .08 | .06 |

| | | MT | NR MT |
|---|---|---|---|
| 212 | Doug Dascenzo | .05 | .04 |
| 213 | Andy Stankiewicz(FC) | | |
| | | .12 | .09 |
| 214 | Geronimo Berroa | .05 | .04 |
| 215 | Dennis Eckersley | .08 | .06 |
| 216 | Al Osuna | .05 | .04 |
| 217 | Tino Martinez | .08 | .06 |
| 218 | *Henry Rodriguez* | .12 | .09 |
| 219 | Ed Sprague | .08 | .06 |
| 220 | Ken Hill | .08 | .06 |
| 221 | Chito Martinez | .08 | .06 |
| 222 | Bret Saberhagen | .08 | .06 |
| 223 | Mike Greenwell | .08 | .06 |
| 224 | Mickey Morandini | .08 | .06 |
| 225 | Chuck Finley | .08 | .06 |
| 226 | Denny Neagle | .08 | .06 |
| 227 | Kirk McCaskill | .06 | .05 |
| 228 | Rheal Cormier | .08 | .06 |
| 229 | Paul Sorrento | .08 | .06 |
| 230 | Darrin Jackson | .06 | .05 |
| 231 | Rob Deer | .06 | .05 |
| 232 | Bill Swift | .06 | .05 |
| 233 | Kevin McReynolds | .08 | .06 |
| 234 | Terry Pendleton | .08 | .06 |
| 235 | Dave Nilsson | .12 | .09 |
| 236 | Chuck McElroy | .05 | .04 |
| 237 | Derek Parks | .06 | .05 |
| 238 | Norm Charlton | .08 | .06 |
| 239 | Matt Nokes | .06 | .05 |
| 240 | *Juan Guerrero* | .15 | .11 |
| 241 | Jeff Parrett | .05 | .04 |
| 242 | *Ryan Thompson*(FC) | | |
| | | .20 | .15 |
| 243 | Dave Fleming | .10 | .08 |
| 244 | Dave Hansen | .05 | .04 |
| 245 | Monty Fariss | .05 | .04 |
| 246 | *Archi Cianfrocco* | .15 | .11 |
| 247 | *Pat Hentgen*(FC) | .15 | .11 |
| 248 | Bill Pecota | .05 | .04 |
| 249 | Ben McDonald | .08 | .06 |
| 250 | Cliff Brantley | .08 | .06 |
| 251 | *John Valentin*(FC) | | |
| | | .15 | .11 |
| 252 | Jeff King | .06 | .05 |
| 253 | *Reggie Williams*(FC) | | |
| | | .15 | .11 |
| 254 | Checklist | .05 | .04 |
| 255 | Ozzie Guillen | .08 | .06 |
| 256 | Mike Perez | .06 | .05 |
| 257 | Thomas Howard | .06 | .05 |
| 258 | Kurt Stillwell | .06 | .05 |
| 259 | Mike Henneman | .06 | .05 |
| 260 | Steve Decker | .06 | .05 |
| 261 | Brent Mayne | .06 | .05 |
| 262 | Otis Nixon | .08 | .06 |
| 263 | *Mark Keifer*(FC) | .15 | .11 |
| 264 | Checklist | .05 | .04 |
| 265 | *Richie Lewis*(FC) | .15 | .11 |
| 266 | *Pat Gomez*(FC) | .15 | .11 |
| 267 | *Scott Taylor*(FC) | .15 | .11 |
| 268 | Shawon Dunston | .06 | .05 |
| 269 | Greg Myers | .05 | .04 |
| 270 | Tim Costo | .10 | .08 |
| 271 | Greg Hibbard | .06 | .05 |
| 272 | Pete Harnisch | .06 | .05 |
| 273 | *Dave Mlicki*(FC) | .12 | .09 |
| 274 | Orel Hershiser | .08 | .06 |

| | MT | NR MT | | | MT | NR MT |
|---|---|---|---|---|---|---|
| 275 | Sean Berry | .08 | .06 | 336 | Ozzie Canseco | .10 | .08 |
| 276 | Doug Simons | .08 | .06 | 337 | Bill Sampen | .05 | .04 |
| 277 | John Doherty | .10 | .08 | 338 | Rich Rodriguez | .05 | .04 |
| 278 | Eddie Murray | .08 | .06 | 339 | Dean Palmer | .08 | .06 |
| 279 | Chris Haney | .08 | .06 | 340 | Greg Litton | .05 | .04 |
| 280 | Stan Javier | .05 | .04 | 341 | Jim Tatum(FC) | .20 | .15 |
| 281 | Jaime Navarro | .08 | .06 | 342 | Todd Haney(FC) | .20 | .15 |
| 282 | Orlando Merced | .08 | .06 | 343 | Larry Casian | .06 | .05 |
| 283 | Kent Hrbek | .08 | .06 | 344 | Ryne Sandberg | .12 | .09 |
| 284 | Bernard Gilkey | .08 | .06 | 345 | Sterling | | |
| 285 | Russ Springer | .06 | .05 | | Hitchcock(FC) | .15 | .11 |
| 286 | Mike Maddux | .05 | .04 | 346 | Chris Hammond | .06 | .05 |
| 287 | Eric Fox | .12 | .09 | 347 | Vince Horseman | .12 | .09 |
| 288 | Mark Leonard | .05 | .04 | 348 | Butch Henry | .12 | .09 |
| 289 | Tim Leary | .05 | .04 | 349 | Dann Howitt | .05 | .04 |
| 290 | Brian Hunter | .08 | .06 | 350 | Roger McDowell | .05 | .04 |
| 291 | Donald Harris | .08 | .06 | 351 | Jack Morris | .08 | .06 |
| 292 | Bob Scanlan | .05 | .04 | 352 | Bill Krueger | .05 | .04 |
| 293 | Turner Ward | .08 | .06 | 353 | Cris Colon(FC) | .15 | .11 |
| 294 | Hal Morris | .08 | .06 | 354 | Joe Vitko(FC) | .15 | .11 |
| 295 | Jimmy Poole | .08 | .06 | 355 | Willie McGee | .08 | .06 |
| 296 | Doug Jones | .06 | .05 | 356 | Jay Baller | .06 | .05 |
| 297 | Tony Pena | .06 | .05 | 357 | Pat Mahomes | .20 | .15 |
| 298 | Ramon Martinez | .08 | .06 | 358 | Roger Mason | .05 | .04 |
| 299 | Tim Fortugno | .12 | .09 | 359 | Jerry Nielsen | .15 | .11 |
| 300 | Marquis Grissom | .10 | .08 | 360 | Tom Pagnozzi | .06 | .05 |
| 301 | Lance Johnson | .06 | .05 | 361 | Kevin Baez | .15 | .11 |
| 302 | Jeff Kent | .15 | .11 | 362 | Tim Scott | .15 | .11 |
| 303 | Reggie Jefferson | .08 | .06 | 363 | Domingo | | |
| 304 | Wes Chamberlain | .08 | .06 | | Martinez(FC) | .20 | .15 |
| 305 | Shawn Hare | .12 | .09 | 364 | Kirt Manwaring | .05 | .04 |
| 306 | Mike LaValliere | .05 | .04 | 365 | Rafael Palmeiro | .08 | .06 |
| 307 | Gregg Jefferies | .08 | .06 | 366 | Ray Lankford | .12 | .09 |
| 308 | Troy Neel | .20 | .15 | 367 | Tim McIntosh | .08 | .06 |
| 309 | Pat Listach(FC) | .30 | .25 | 368 | Jessie Hollins(FC) | | |
| 310 | Geronimo Pena | .06 | .05 | | | .15 | .11 |
| 311 | Pedro Munoz | .08 | .06 | 369 | Scott Leius | .06 | .05 |
| 312 | Guillermo Pena(FC) | | | 370 | Bill Doran | .05 | .04 |
| | | .15 | .11 | 371 | Sam Militello(FC) | | |
| 313 | Roberto Kelly | .08 | .06 | | | .20 | .15 |
| 314 | Mike Jackson | .05 | .04 | 372 | Ryan Bowen | .08 | .06 |
| 315 | Rickey Henderson | .12 | .09 | 373 | Dave Henderson | .08 | .06 |
| 316 | Mark Lemke | .06 | .05 | 374 | Dan Smith(FC) | .12 | .09 |
| 317 | Erik Hanson | .08 | .06 | 375 | Steve Reed(FC) | .12 | .09 |
| 318 | Derrick May | .08 | .06 | 376 | Jose Offerman | .08 | .06 |
| 319 | Geno Petralli | .05 | .04 | 377 | Kevin Brown | .08 | .06 |
| 320 | Melvin Nieves(FC) | | | 378 | Darrin Fletcher | .05 | .04 |
| | | .20 | .15 | 379 | Duane Ward | .06 | .05 |
| 321 | Doug Linton(FC) | .15 | .11 | 380 | Wayne Kirby(FC) | .12 | .09 |
| 322 | Rob Dibble | .08 | .06 | 381 | Steve Scarsone | .15 | .11 |
| 323 | Chris Hoiles | .10 | .08 | 382 | Mariano Duncan | .06 | .05 |
| 324 | Jimmy Jones | .05 | .04 | 383 | Ken Ryan(FC) | .15 | .11 |
| 325 | Dave Staton | .06 | .05 | 384 | Lloyd McClendon | .05 | .04 |
| 326 | Pedro Martinez | .15 | .11 | 385 | Brian Holman | .05 | .04 |
| 327 | Paul Quantrill(FC) | | | 386 | Braulio Castillo | .08 | .06 |
| | | .15 | .11 | 387 | Danny Leon | .12 | .09 |
| 328 | Greg Colbrunn | .05 | .04 | 388 | Omar Olivares | .05 | .04 |
| 329 | Hilly Hathaway(FC) | | | 389 | Kevin Wickander | .05 | .04 |
| | | .20 | .15 | 390 | Fred McGriff | .10 | .08 |
| 330 | Jeff Innis | .06 | .05 | 391 | Phil Clark(FC) | .12 | .09 |
| 331 | Ron Karkovice | .06 | .05 | 392 | Darren Lewis | .06 | .05 |
| 332 | Keith Shepherd(FC) | | | 393 | Phil Hiatt(FC) | .15 | .11 |
| | | .15 | .11 | 394 | Mike Morgan | .06 | .05 |
| 333 | Alan Embree(FC) | | | 395 | Shane Mack | .08 | .06 |
| | | .15 | .11 | 396 | Checklist | .05 | .04 |
| 334 | Paul Wagner | .15 | .11 | | | | |
| 335 | Dave Haas(FC) | .15 | .11 | | | | |

# FLEER

## 1963 Fleer

A lawsuit by Topps stopped Fleer's 1963 set at one series of 66 cards. Issued with a cookie rather than gum, the set features color photos of current players. The card backs include statistical information for 1962 and career plus a brief player biography. The cards, which measure 2-1/2" by 3-1/2", are numbered 1-66. An unnumbered checklist was issued with the set and is included in the complete set price in the checklist that follows. The checklist and #46 Adcock are scarce.

|  |  | NR MT | EX |
|---|---|---|---|
| | Complete Set: | 1100.00 | 550.00 |
| | Common Player: | 6.00 | 3.00 |
| 1 | Steve Barber | 10.00 | 2.00 |
| 2 | Ron Hansen | 6.00 | 3.00 |
| 3 | Milt Pappas | 2.25 | 1.25 |
| 4 | Brooks Robinson | 40.00 | 20.00 |
| 5 | Willie Mays | 110.00 | 55.00 |
| 6 | Lou Clinton | 6.00 | 3.00 |
| 7 | Bill Monbouquette | 6.00 | 3.00 |
| 8 | Carl Yastrzemski | 90.00 | 45.00 |
| 9 | Ray Herbert | 6.00 | 3.00 |
| 10 | Jim Landis | 6.00 | 3.00 |
| 11 | Dick Donovan | 6.00 | 3.00 |
| 12 | Tito Francona | 6.00 | 3.00 |
| 13 | Jerry Kindall | 6.00 | 3.00 |
| 14 | Frank Lary | 2.25 | 1.25 |
| 15 | Dick Howser | 8.00 | 4.00 |
| 16 | Jerry Lumpe | 6.00 | 3.00 |
| 17 | Norm Siebern | 6.00 | 3.00 |
| 18 | Don Lee | 6.00 | 3.00 |
| 19 | Albie Pearson | 6.00 | 3.00 |
| 20 | Bob Rodgers | 2.25 | 1.25 |
| 21 | Leon Wagner | 6.00 | 3.00 |
| 22 | Jim Kaat | 7.00 | 3.50 |
| 23 | Vic Power | 6.00 | 3.00 |
| 24 | Rich Rollins | 6.00 | 3.00 |
| 25 | Bobby Richardson | 7.00 | 3.50 |
| 26 | Ralph Terry | 10.00 | 5.00 |
| 27 | Tom Cheney | 2.25 | 1.25 |
| 28 | Chuck Cottier | 6.00 | 3.00 |
| 29 | Jimmy Piersall | 10.00 | 5.00 |
| 30 | Dave Stenhouse | 6.00 | 3.00 |
| 31 | Glen Hobbie | 6.00 | 3.00 |
| 32 | Ron Santo | 12.00 | 6.00 |
| 33 | Gene Freese | 6.00 | 3.00 |
| 34 | Vada Pinson | 10.00 | 5.00 |
| 35 | Bob Purkey | 6.00 | 3.00 |
| 36 | Joe Amalfitano | 6.00 | 3.00 |
| 37 | Bob Aspromonte | 6.00 | 3.00 |
| 38 | Dick Farrell | 6.00 | 3.00 |
| 39 | Al Spangler | 6.00 | 3.00 |
| 40 | Tommy Davis | 10.00 | 5.00 |
| 41 | Don Drysdale | 30.00 | 15.00 |
| 42 | Sandy Koufax | 130.00 | 65.00 |
| 43 | Maury Wills | 50.00 | 25.00 |
| 44 | Frank Bolling | 6.00 | 3.00 |
| 45 | Warren Spahn | 40.00 | 20.00 |
| 46 | Joe Adcock | 150.00 | 75.00 |
| 47 | Roger Craig | 12.00 | 6.00 |
| 48 | Al Jackson | 2.25 | 1.25 |
| 49 | Rod Kanehl | 2.25 | 1.25 |
| 50 | Ruben Amaro | 6.00 | 3.00 |
| 51 | John Callison | 2.25 | 1.25 |
| 52 | Clay Dalrymple | 6.00 | 3.00 |
| 53 | Don Demeter | 6.00 | 3.00 |
| 54 | Art Mahaffey | 6.00 | 3.00 |
| 55 | "Smoky" Burgess | 2.25 | 1.25 |
| 56 | Roberto Clemente | 125.00 | 67.00 |
| 57 | Elroy Face | 2.25 | 1.25 |
| 58 | Vernon Law | 2.25 | 1.25 |
| 59 | Bill Mazeroski | 10.00 | 5.00 |
| 60 | Ken Boyer | 10.00 | 5.00 |
| 61 | Bob Gibson | 40.00 | 20.00 |
| 62 | Gene Oliver | 6.00 | 3.00 |
| 63 | Bill White | 12.00 | 6.00 |
| 64 | Orlando Cepeda | 15.00 | 7.50 |
| 65 | Jimmy Davenport | 6.00 | 3.00 |
| 66 | Billy O'Dell | 8.00 | 4.00 |
| ---- | Checklist 1-66 | 375.00 | 150.00 |

## 1981 Fleer

For the first time in 18 years, Fleer issued a baseball card set featuring current players. Fleer's

660-card effort included numerous errors in the first printing run which were subsequently corrected in additional runs. The cards, which measure 2-1/2" by 3-1/2", are numbered alphabetically by team. The card fronts feature a full-color photo inside a border which is color-coded by team. The card backs have black, grey and yellow ink on white stock and carry player statistical information. The player's batting average or earned run average is located in a circle in the upper right corner of the card. The complete set price in the checklist that follows does not include the higher priced variations.

| | | MT | NR MT |
|---|---|---|---|
| | Complete Set: | 60.00 | 45.00 |
| | Common Player: | .06 | .05 |
| 1 | Pete Rose | 1.75 | 1.25 |
| 2 | Larry Bowa | .15 | .11 |
| 3 | Manny Trillo | .08 | .06 |
| 4 | Bob Boone | .10 | .08 |
| 5a | Mike Schmidt (portrait) | 2.00 | 1.50 |
| 5b | Mike Schmidt (batting) | 2.00 | 1.50 |
| 6a | Steve Carlton ("Lefty" on front) | 1.00 | .70 |
| 6b | Steve Carlton (Pitcher of the Year on front, date 1066 on back) | 2.00 | 1.50 |
| 6c | Steve Carlton (Pitcher of the Year on front, date 1966 on back) | 3.00 | 2.25 |
| 7a | Tug McGraw (Game Saver on front) | .50 | .40 |
| 7b | Tug McGraw (Pitcher on front) | .12 | .09 |
| 8 | Larry Christenson | .06 | .05 |
| 9 | Bake McBride | .06 | .05 |
| 10 | Greg Luzinski | .15 | .11 |
| 11 | Ron Reed | .06 | .05 |
| 12 | Dickie Noles | .06 | .05 |
| 13 | Keith Moreland | .20 | .15 |
| 14 | Bob Walk | .25 | .20 |
| 15 | Lonnie Smith | .08 | .06 |
| 16 | Dick Ruthven | .06 | .05 |
| 17 | Sparky Lyle | .10 | .08 |
| 18 | Greg Gross | .06 | .05 |
| 19 | Garry Maddox | .10 | .08 |
| 20 | Nino Espinosa | .06 | .05 |
| 21 | George Vukovich | .06 | .05 |
| 22 | John Vukovich | .06 | .05 |
| 23 | Ramon Aviles | .06 | .05 |
| 24a | Kevin Saucier (Ken Saucier on back) | .15 | .11 |
| 24b | Kevin Saucier (Kevin Saucier on back) | .70 | .50 |

| | | MT | NR MT |
|---|---|---|---|
| 25 | Randy Lerch | .06 | .05 |
| 26 | Del Unser | .06 | .05 |
| 27 | Tim McCarver | .15 | .11 |
| 28a | George Brett (batting) | 3.00 | 2.25 |
| 28b | George Brett (portrait) | 1.00 | .70 |
| 29a | Willie Wilson (portrait) | .60 | .45 |
| 29b | Willie Wilson (batting) | .15 | .11 |
| 30 | Paul Splittorff | .06 | .05 |
| 31 | Dan Quisenberry | .15 | .11 |
| 32a | Amos Otis (batting) | .50 | .40 |
| 32b | Amos Otis (portrait) | .10 | .08 |
| 33 | Steve Busby | .08 | .06 |
| 34 | U.L. Washington | .06 | .05 |
| 35 | Dave Chalk | .06 | .05 |
| 36 | Darrell Porter | .08 | .06 |
| 37 | Marty Pattin | .06 | .05 |
| 38 | Larry Gura | .06 | .05 |
| 39 | Renie Martin | .06 | .05 |
| 40 | Rich Gale | .06 | .05 |
| 41a | Hal McRae (dark blue "Royals" on front) | .40 | .30 |
| 41b | Hal McRae (light blue "Royals" on front) | .10 | .08 |
| 42 | Dennis Leonard | .08 | .06 |
| 43 | Willie Aikens | .06 | .05 |
| 44 | Frank White | .10 | .08 |
| 45 | Clint Hurdle | .06 | .05 |
| 46 | John Wathan | .08 | .06 |
| 47 | Pete LaCock | .06 | .05 |
| 48 | Rance Mulliniks | .06 | .05 |
| 49 | Jeff Twitty | .06 | .05 |
| 50 | Jamie Quirk | .06 | .05 |
| 51 | Art Howe | .06 | .05 |
| 52 | Ken Forsch | .06 | .05 |
| 53 | Vern Ruhle | .06 | .05 |
| 54 | Joe Niekro | .12 | .09 |
| 55 | Frank LaCorte | .06 | .05 |
| 56 | J.R. Richard | .10 | .08 |
| 57 | Nolan Ryan | 7.00 | 5.25 |
| 58 | Enos Cabell | .06 | .05 |
| 59 | Cesar Cedeno | .12 | .09 |
| 60 | Jose Cruz | .12 | .09 |
| 61 | Bill Virdon | .06 | .05 |
| 62 | Terry Puhl | .06 | .05 |
| 63 | Joaquin Andujar | .10 | .08 |
| 64 | Alan Ashby | .06 | .05 |
| 65 | Joe Sambito | .06 | .05 |
| 66 | Denny Walling | .06 | .05 |
| 67 | Jeff Leonard | .12 | .09 |
| 68 | Luis Pujols | .06 | .05 |
| 69 | Bruce Bochy | .06 | .05 |
| 70 | Rafael Landestoy | .06 | .05 |
| 71 | Dave Smith | .30 | .25 |
| 72 | Danny Heep | .10 | .08 |
| 73 | Julio Gonzalez | .06 | .05 |
| 74 | Craig Reynolds | .06 | .05 |
| 75 | Gary Woods | .06 | .05 |
| 76 | Dave Bergman | .06 | .05 |
| 77 | Randy Niemann | .06 | .05 |
| 78 | Joe Morgan | .70 | .50 |
| 79a | Reggie Jackson (portrait) | 4.00 | 3.00 |

| | | MT | NR MT |
|---|---|---|---|
| 79b | Reggie Jackson (batting) | 2.00 | 1.50 |
| 80 | Bucky Dent | .10 | .08 |
| 81 | Tommy John | .20 | .15 |
| 82 | Luis Tiant | .12 | .09 |
| 83 | Rick Cerone | .06 | .05 |
| 84 | Dick Howser | .06 | .05 |
| 85 | Lou Piniella | .12 | .09 |
| 86 | Ron Davis | .08 | .06 |
| 87a | Graig Nettles (Craig on back) | 12.00 | 9.00 |
| 87b | Graig Nettles (Graig on back) | .30 | .25 |
| 88 | Ron Guidry | .25 | .20 |
| 89 | Rich Gossage | .20 | .15 |
| 90 | Rudy May | .06 | .05 |
| 91 | Gaylord Perry | .60 | .45 |
| 92 | Eric Soderholm | .06 | .05 |
| 93 | Bob Watson | .08 | .06 |
| 94 | Bobby Murcer | .10 | .08 |
| 95 | Bobby Brown | .06 | .05 |
| 96 | Jim Spencer | .06 | .05 |
| 97 | Tom Underwood | .06 | .05 |
| 98 | Oscar Gamble | .08 | .06 |
| 99 | Johnny Oates | .06 | .05 |
| 100 | Fred Stanley | .06 | .05 |
| 101 | Ruppert Jones | .06 | .05 |
| 102 | Dennis Werth | .06 | .05 |
| 103 | Joe Lefebvre | .06 | .05 |
| 104 | Brian Doyle | .06 | .05 |
| 105 | Aurelio Rodriguez | .08 | .06 |
| 106 | Doug Bird | .06 | .05 |
| 107 | Mike Griffin | .06 | .05 |
| 108 | Tim Lollar | .06 | .05 |
| 109 | Willie Randolph | .10 | .08 |
| 110 | Steve Garvey | .70 | .50 |
| 111 | Reggie Smith | .10 | .08 |
| 112 | Don Sutton | .30 | .25 |
| 113 | Burt Hooton | .08 | .06 |
| 114a | Davy Lopes (Davey) (no finger on back) | .10 | .08 |
| 114b | Davy Lopes (Davey) (small finger on back) | 1.00 | .70 |
| 115 | Dusty Baker | .10 | .08 |
| 116 | Tom Lasorda | .10 | .08 |
| 117 | Bill Russell | .08 | .06 |
| 118 | Jerry Reuss | .10 | .08 |
| 119 | Terry Forster | .08 | .06 |
| 120a | Robert Welch (Bob Welch on back) | .60 | .45 |
| 120b | Robert Welch (Robert Welch on back) | 1.00 | .70 |
| 121 | Don Stanhouse | .06 | .05 |
| 122 | Rick Monday | .10 | .08 |
| 123 | Derrel Thomas | .06 | .05 |
| 124 | Joe Ferguson | .06 | .05 |
| 125 | Rick Sutcliffe | .20 | .15 |
| 126a | Ron Cey (no finger on back) | .12 | .09 |
| 126b | Ron Cey (small finger on back) | 1.00 | .70 |
| 127 | Dave Goltz | .08 | .06 |
| 128 | Jay Johnstone | .08 | .06 |
| 129 | Steve Yeager | .06 | .05 |
| 130 | Gary Weiss | .06 | .05 |
| 131 | *Mike Scioscia* | 1.00 | .70 |
| 132 | Vic Davalillo | .08 | .06 |

| | | MT | NR MT |
|---|---|---|---|
| 133 | Doug Rau | .06 | .05 |
| 134 | Pepe Frias | .06 | .05 |
| 135 | Mickey Hatcher | .08 | .06 |
| 136 | *Steve Howe* | .10 | .08 |
| 137 | Robert Castillo | .06 | .05 |
| 138 | Gary Thomasson | .06 | .05 |
| 139 | Rudy Law | .06 | .05 |
| 140 | Fernand Valenzuela (Fernando) | 3.00 | 2.25 |
| 141 | Manny Mota | .08 | .06 |
| 142 | Gary Carter | .70 | .50 |
| 143 | Steve Rogers | .08 | .06 |
| 144 | Warren Cromartie | .06 | .05 |
| 145 | Andre Dawson | 2.00 | 1.50 |
| 146 | Larry Parrish | .10 | .08 |
| 147 | Rowland Office | .06 | .05 |
| 148 | Ellis Valentine | .06 | .05 |
| 149 | Dick Williams | .06 | .05 |
| 150 | *Bill Gullickson* | .15 | .11 |
| 151 | Elias Sosa | .06 | .05 |
| 152 | John Tamargo | .06 | .05 |
| 153 | Chris Speier | .06 | .05 |
| 154 | Ron LeFlore | .08 | .06 |
| 155 | Rodney Scott | .06 | .05 |
| 156 | Stan Bahnsen | .06 | .05 |
| 157 | Bill Lee | .08 | .06 |
| 158 | Fred Norman | .06 | .05 |
| 159 | Woodie Fryman | .06 | .05 |
| 160 | Dave Palmer | .06 | .05 |
| 161 | Jerry White | .06 | .05 |
| 162 | Roberto Ramos | .06 | .05 |
| 163 | John D'Acquisto | .06 | .05 |
| 164 | Tommy Hutton | .06 | .05 |
| 165 | *Charlie Lea* | .12 | .09 |
| 166 | Scott Sanderson | .06 | .05 |
| 167 | Ken Macha | .06 | .05 |
| 168 | Tony Bernazard | .06 | .05 |
| 169 | Jim Palmer | 1.00 | .70 |
| 170 | Steve Stone | .08 | .06 |
| 171 | Mike Flanagan | .10 | .08 |
| 172 | Al Bumbry | .08 | .06 |
| 173 | Doug DeCinces | .10 | .08 |
| 174 | Scott McGregor | .08 | .06 |
| 175 | Mark Belanger | .08 | .06 |
| 176 | Tim Stoddard | .06 | .05 |
| 177a | Rick Dempsey (no finger on front) | .10 | .08 |
| 177b | Rick Dempsey (small finger on front) | 1.00 | .70 |
| 178 | Earl Weaver | .10 | .08 |
| 179 | Tippy Martinez | .06 | .05 |
| 180 | Dennis Martinez | .08 | .06 |
| 181 | Sammy Stewart | .06 | .05 |
| 182 | Rich Dauer | .06 | .05 |
| 183 | Lee May | .08 | .06 |
| 184 | Eddie Murray | 3.00 | 2.25 |
| 185 | Benny Ayala | .06 | .05 |
| 186 | John Lowenstein | .06 | .05 |
| 187 | Gary Roenicke | .06 | .05 |
| 188 | Ken Singleton | .10 | .08 |
| 189 | Dan Graham | .06 | .05 |
| 190 | Terry Crowley | .06 | .05 |
| 191 | Kiko Garcia | .06 | .05 |
| 192 | Dave Ford | .06 | .05 |
| 193 | Mark Corey | .06 | .05 |
| 194 | Lenn Sakata | .06 | .05 |
| 195 | Doug DeCinces | .10 | .08 |

| | | MT | NR MT | | | | MT | NR MT |
|---|---|---|---|---|---|---|---|---|
| 196 | Johnny Bench | 1.00 | .70 | | 254 | Bill Nahorodny | .06 | .05 |
| 197 | Dave Concepcion | .15 | .11 | | 255 | Doyle Alexander | .10 | .08 |
| 198 | Ray Knight | .10 | .08 | | 256 | Brian Asselstine | .06 | .05 |
| 199 | Ken Griffey | .12 | .09 | | 257 | Biff Pocoroba | .06 | .05 |
| 200 | Tom Seaver | 2.00 | 1.50 | | 258 | Mike Lum | .06 | .05 |
| 201 | Dave Collins | .08 | .06 | | 259 | Charlie Spikes | .06 | .05 |
| 202 | George Foster | .20 | .15 | | 260 | Glenn Hubbard | .08 | .06 |
| 203 | Junior Kennedy | .06 | .05 | | 261 | Tommy Boggs | .06 | .05 |
| 204 | Frank Pastore | .06 | .05 | | 262 | Al Hrabosky | .08 | .06 |
| 205 | Dan Driessen | .08 | .06 | | 263 | Rick Matula | .06 | .05 |
| 206 | Hector Cruz | .06 | .05 | | 264 | Preston Hanna | .06 | .05 |
| 207 | Paul Moskau | .06 | .05 | | 265 | Larry Bradford | .06 | .05 |
| 208 | *Charlie Leibrandt* | .40 | .30 | | 266 | *Rafael Ramirez* | .20 | .15 |
| 209 | Harry Spilman | .06 | .05 | | 267 | Larry McWilliams | .06 | .05 |
| 210 | *Joe Price* | .12 | .09 | | 268 | Rod Carew | 1.50 | 1.25 |
| 211 | Tom Hume | .06 | .05 | | 269 | Bobby Grich | .10 | .08 |
| 212 | Joe Nolan | .06 | .05 | | 270 | Carney Lansford | .10 | .08 |
| 213 | Doug Bair | .06 | .05 | | 271 | Don Baylor | .12 | .09 |
| 214 | Mario Soto | .08 | .06 | | 272 | Joe Rudi | .10 | .08 |
| 215a | Bill Bonham (no finger on back) | .08 | .06 | | 273 | Dan Ford | .06 | .05 |
| 215b | Bill Bonham (small finger on back) | 1.00 | .70 | | 274 | Jim Fregosi | .08 | .06 |
| | | | | | 275 | Dave Frost | .06 | .05 |
| 216a | George Foster (Slugger on front) | .25 | .20 | | 276 | Frank Tanana | .10 | .08 |
| | | | | | 277 | Dickie Thon | .08 | .06 |
| 216b | George Foster (Outfield on front) | .20 | .15 | | 278 | Jason Thompson | .06 | .05 |
| | | | | | 279 | Rick Miller | .06 | .05 |
| 217 | Paul Householder | .06 | .05 | | 280 | Bert Campaneris | .10 | .08 |
| 218 | Ron Oester | .06 | .05 | | 281 | Tom Donohue | .06 | .05 |
| 219 | Sam Mejias | .06 | .05 | | 282 | Brian Downing | .10 | .08 |
| 220 | Sheldon Burnside | .06 | .05 | | 283 | Fred Patek | .06 | .05 |
| 221 | Carl Yastrzemski | 1.25 | .90 | | 284 | Bruce Kison | .06 | .05 |
| 222 | Jim Rice | .50 | .40 | | 285 | Dave LaRoche | .06 | .05 |
| 223 | Fred Lynn | .20 | .15 | | 286 | Don Aase | .06 | .05 |
| 224 | Carlton Fisk | 2.00 | 1.50 | | 287 | Jim Barr | .06 | .05 |
| 225 | Rick Burleson | .08 | .06 | | 288 | Alfredo Martinez | .06 | .05 |
| 226 | Dennis Eckersley | 1.50 | 1.25 | | 289 | Larry Harlow | .06 | .05 |
| 227 | Butch Hobson | .06 | .05 | | 290 | Andy Hassler | .06 | .05 |
| 228 | Tom Burgmeier | .06 | .05 | | 291 | Dave Kingman | .15 | .11 |
| 229 | Garry Hancock | .06 | .05 | | 292 | Bill Buckner | .12 | .09 |
| 230 | Don Zimmer | .06 | .05 | | 293 | Rick Reuschel | .10 | .08 |
| 231 | Steve Renko | .06 | .05 | | 294 | Bruce Sutter | .15 | .11 |
| 232 | Dwight Evans | .15 | .11 | | 295 | Jerry Martin | .06 | .05 |
| 233 | Mike Torrez | .08 | .06 | | 296 | Scot Thompson | .06 | .05 |
| 234 | Bob Stanley | .06 | .05 | | 297 | Ivan DeJesus | .06 | .05 |
| 235 | Jim Dwyer | .06 | .05 | | 298 | Steve Dillard | .06 | .05 |
| 236 | Dave Stapleton | .06 | .05 | | 299 | Dick Tidrow | .06 | .05 |
| 237 | Glenn Hoffman | .06 | .05 | | 300 | Randy Martz | .06 | .05 |
| 238 | Jerry Remy | .06 | .05 | | 301 | Lenny Randle | .06 | .05 |
| 239 | Dick Drago | .06 | .05 | | 302 | Lynn McGlothen | .06 | .05 |
| 240 | Bill Campbell | .06 | .05 | | 303 | Cliff Johnson | .06 | .05 |
| 241 | Tony Perez | .20 | .15 | | 304 | Tim Blackwell | .06 | .05 |
| 242 | Phil Niekro | .30 | .25 | | 305 | Dennis Lamp | .06 | .05 |
| 243 | Dale Murphy | .90 | .70 | | 306 | Bill Caudill | .06 | .05 |
| 244 | Bob Horner | .12 | .09 | | 307 | Carlos Lezcano | .06 | .05 |
| 245 | Jeff Burroughs | .08 | .06 | | 308 | Jim Tracy | .06 | .05 |
| 246 | Rick Camp | .06 | .05 | | 309 | Doug Capilla | .06 | .05 |
| 247 | Bob Cox | .06 | .05 | | 310 | Willie Hernandez | .10 | .08 |
| 248 | Bruce Benedict | .06 | .05 | | 311 | Mike Vail | .06 | .05 |
| 249 | Gene Garber | .06 | .05 | | 312 | Mike Krukow | .08 | .06 |
| 250 | Jerry Royster | .06 | .05 | | 313 | Barry Foote | .06 | .05 |
| 251a | Gary Matthews (no finger on back) | .12 | .09 | | 314 | Larry Biittner | .06 | .05 |
| | | | | | 315 | Mike Tyson | .06 | .05 |
| 251b | Gary Matthews (small finger on back) | 1.00 | .70 | | 316 | Lee Mazzilli | .08 | .06 |
| | | | | | 317 | John Stearns | .06 | .05 |
| 252 | Chris Chambliss | .08 | .06 | | 318 | Alex Trevino | .06 | .05 |
| 253 | Luis Gomez | .06 | .05 | | 319 | Craig Swan | .06 | .05 |
| | | | | | 320 | Frank Taveras | .06 | .05 |

| | | MT | NR MT |
|---|---|---|---|
| 321 | Steve Henderson | .06 | .05 |
| 322 | Neil Allen | .08 | .06 |
| 323 | Mark Bomback | .06 | .05 |
| 324 | Mike Jorgensen | .06 | .05 |
| 325 | Joe Torre | .08 | .06 |
| 326 | Elliott Maddox | .06 | .05 |
| 327 | Pete Falcone | .06 | .05 |
| 328 | Ray Burris | .06 | .05 |
| 329 | Claudell Washington | .08 | .06 |
| 330 | Doug Flynn | .06 | .05 |
| 331 | Joel Youngblood | .06 | .05 |
| 332 | Bill Almon | .06 | .05 |
| 333 | Tom Hausman | .06 | .05 |
| 334 | Pat Zachry | .06 | .05 |
| 335 | *Jeff Reardon* | 5.00 | 3.75 |
| 336 | *Wally Backman* | .35 | .25 |
| 337 | Dan Norman | .06 | .05 |
| 338 | Jerry Morales | .06 | .05 |
| 339 | Ed Farmer | .06 | .05 |
| 340 | Bob Molinaro | .06 | .05 |
| 341 | Todd Cruz | .06 | .05 |
| 342a | Britt Burns (no finger on front) | .20 | .15 |
| 342b | Britt Burns (small finger on front) | 1.00 | .70 |
| 343 | Kevin Bell | .06 | .05 |
| 344 | Tony LaRussa | .08 | .06 |
| 345 | Steve Trout | .06 | .05 |
| 346 | *Harold Baines* | 5.00 | 3.75 |
| 347 | Richard Wortham | .06 | .05 |
| 348 | Wayne Nordhagen | .06 | .05 |
| 349 | Mike Squires | .06 | .05 |
| 350 | Lamar Johnson | .06 | .05 |
| 351 | Rickey Henderson | 8.00 | 6.00 |
| 352 | Francisco Barrios | .06 | .05 |
| 353 | Thad Bosley | .06 | .05 |
| 354 | Chet Lemon | .08 | .06 |
| 355 | Bruce Kimm | .06 | .05 |
| 356 | *Richard Dotson* | .25 | .20 |
| 357 | Jim Morrison | .06 | .05 |
| 358 | Mike Proly | .06 | .05 |
| 359 | Greg Pryor | .06 | .05 |
| 360 | Dave Parker | .30 | .25 |
| 361 | Omar Moreno | .06 | .05 |
| 362a | Kent Tekulve (1071 Waterbury on back) | .15 | .11 |
| 362b | Kent Tekulve (1971 Waterbury on back) | .70 | .50 |
| 363 | Willie Stargell | .40 | .30 |
| 364 | Phil Garner | .08 | .06 |
| 365 | Ed Ott | .06 | .05 |
| 366 | Don Robinson | .08 | .06 |
| 367 | Chuck Tanner | .06 | .05 |
| 368 | Jim Rooker | .06 | .05 |
| 369 | Dale Berra | .06 | .05 |
| 370 | Jim Bibby | .06 | .05 |
| 371 | Steve Nicosia | .06 | .05 |
| 372 | Mike Easler | .08 | .06 |
| 373 | Bill Robinson | .06 | .05 |
| 374 | Lee Lacy | .06 | .05 |
| 375 | John Candelaria | .10 | .08 |
| 376 | Manny Sanguillen | .06 | .05 |
| 377 | Rick Rhoden | .10 | .08 |
| 378 | Grant Jackson | .06 | .05 |
| 379 | Tim Foli | .06 | .05 |
| 380 | *Rod Scurry* | .08 | .06 |
| 381 | Bill Madlock | .12 | .09 |
| 382a | Kurt Bevacqua (photo reversed, backwards "P" on cap) | .15 | .11 |
| 382b | Kurt Bevacqua (correct photo) | .70 | .50 |
| 383 | Bert Blyleven | .12 | .09 |
| 384 | Eddie Solomon | .06 | .05 |
| 385 | Enrique Romo | .06 | .05 |
| 386 | John Milner | .06 | .05 |
| 387 | Mike Hargrove | .06 | .05 |
| 388 | Jorge Orta | .06 | .05 |
| 389 | Toby Harrah | .08 | .06 |
| 390 | Tom Veryzer | .06 | .05 |
| 391 | Miguel Dilone | .06 | .05 |
| 392 | Dan Spillner | .06 | .05 |
| 393 | Jack Brohamer | .06 | .05 |
| 394 | Wayne Garland | .06 | .05 |
| 395 | Sid Monge | .06 | .05 |
| 396 | Rick Waits | .06 | .05 |
| 397 | *Joe Charboneau* | .10 | .08 |
| 398 | Gary Alexander | .06 | .05 |
| 399 | Jerry Dybzinski | .06 | .05 |
| 400 | Mike Stanton | .06 | .05 |
| 401 | Mike Paxton | .06 | .05 |
| 402 | Gary Gray | .06 | .05 |
| 403 | Rick Manning | .06 | .05 |
| 404 | Bo Diaz | .08 | .06 |
| 405 | Ron Hassey | .06 | .05 |
| 406 | Ross Grimsley | .06 | .05 |
| 407 | Victor Cruz | .06 | .05 |
| 408 | Len Barker | .08 | .06 |
| 409 | Bob Bailor | .06 | .05 |
| 410 | Otto Velez | .06 | .05 |
| 411 | Ernie Whitt | .08 | .06 |
| 412 | Jim Clancy | .08 | .06 |
| 413 | Barry Bonnell | .06 | .05 |
| 414 | Dave Stieb | .60 | .45 |
| 415 | *Damaso Garcia* | .10 | .08 |
| 416 | John Mayberry | .08 | .06 |
| 417 | Roy Howell | .06 | .05 |
| 418 | Dan Ainge | 1.50 | 1.25 |
| 419a | Jesse Jefferson (Pirates on back) | .10 | .08 |
| 419b | Jesse Jefferson (Blue Jays on back) | .50 | .40 |
| 420 | Joey McLaughlin | .06 | .05 |
| 421 | *Lloyd Moseby* | .40 | .30 |
| 422 | Al Woods | .06 | .05 |
| 423 | Garth Iorg | .06 | .05 |
| 424 | Doug Ault | .06 | .05 |
| 425 | *Ken Schrom* | .06 | .05 |
| 426 | Mike Willis | .06 | .05 |
| 427 | Steve Braun | .06 | .05 |
| 428 | Bob Davis | .06 | .05 |
| 429 | Jerry Garvin | .06 | .05 |
| 430 | Alfredo Griffin | .08 | .06 |
| 431 | Bob Mattick | .06 | .05 |
| 432 | Vida Blue | .12 | .09 |
| 433 | Jack Clark | .25 | .20 |
| 434 | Willie McCovey | .40 | .30 |
| 435 | Mike Ivie | .06 | .05 |
| 436a | Darrel Evans (Darrel on front) | .15 | .11 |
| 436b | Darrell Evans (Darrell on front) | .70 | .50 |
| 437 | Terry Whitfield | .06 | .05 |
| 438 | Rennie Stennett | .06 | .05 |

| | | MT | NR MT |
|---|---|---|---|
| 439 | John Montefusco | .08 | .06 |
| 440 | Jim Wohlford | .06 | .05 |
| 441 | Bill North | .06 | .05 |
| 442 | Milt May | .06 | .05 |
| 443 | Max Venable | .06 | .05 |
| 444 | Ed Whitson | .06 | .05 |
| 445 | *Al Holland* | .08 | .06 |
| 446 | Randy Moffitt | .06 | .05 |
| 447 | Bob Knepper | .08 | .06 |
| 448 | Gary Lavelle | .06 | .05 |
| 449 | Greg Minton | .06 | .05 |
| 450 | Johnnie LeMaster | .06 | .05 |
| 451 | Larry Herndon | .08 | .06 |
| 452 | Rich Murray | .06 | .05 |
| 453 | Joe Pettini | .06 | .05 |
| 454 | Allen Ripley | .06 | .05 |
| 455 | Dennis Littlejohn | .06 | .05 |
| 456 | Tom Griffin | .06 | .05 |
| 457 | Alan Hargesheimer | .06 | .05 |
| 458 | Joe Strain | .06 | .05 |
| 459 | Steve Kemp | .08 | .06 |
| 460 | Sparky Anderson | .10 | .08 |
| 461 | Alan Trammell | .40 | .30 |
| 462 | Mark Fidrych | .08 | .06 |
| 463 | Lou Whitaker | .40 | .30 |
| 464 | Dave Rozema | .06 | .05 |
| 465 | Milt Wilcox | .06 | .05 |
| 466 | Champ Summers | .06 | .05 |
| 467 | Lance Parrish | .35 | .25 |
| 468 | Dan Petry | .08 | .06 |
| 469 | Pat Underwood | .06 | .05 |
| 470 | Rick Peters | .06 | .05 |
| 471 | Al Cowens | .06 | .05 |
| 472 | John Wockenfuss | .06 | .05 |
| 473 | Tom Brookens | .08 | .06 |
| 474 | Richie Hebner | .06 | .05 |
| 475 | Jack Morris | 2.00 | 1.50 |
| 476 | Jim Lentine | .06 | .05 |
| 477 | Bruce Robbins | .06 | .05 |
| 478 | Mark Wagner | .06 | .05 |
| 479 | Tim Corcoran | .06 | .05 |
| 480a | Stan Papi (Pitcher on front) | .15 | .11 |
| 480b | Stan Papi (Shortstop on front) | .70 | .50 |
| 481 | *Kirk Gibson* | 2.50 | 2.00 |
| 482 | Dan Schatzeder | .06 | .05 |
| 483 | Amos Otis | .70 | .50 |
| 484 | Dave Winfield | 1.50 | 1.25 |
| 485 | Rollie Fingers | 1.00 | .70 |
| 486 | Gene Richards | .06 | .05 |
| 487 | Randy Jones | .08 | .06 |
| 488 | Ozzie Smith | 2.00 | 1.50 |
| 489 | Gene Tenace | .08 | .06 |
| 490 | Bill Fahey | .06 | .05 |
| 491 | John Curtis | .06 | .05 |
| 492 | Dave Cash | .06 | .05 |
| 493a | Tim Flannery (photo reversed, batting righty) | .15 | .11 |
| 493b | Tim Flannery (photo correct, batting lefty) | .70 | .50 |
| 494 | Jerry Mumphrey | .06 | .05 |
| 495 | Bob Shirley | .06 | .05 |
| 496 | Steve Mura | .06 | .05 |
| 497 | Eric Rasmussen | .06 | .05 |
| 498 | Broderick Perkins | .06 | .05 |
| 499 | Barry Evans | .06 | .05 |
| 500 | Chuck Baker | .06 | .05 |
| 501 | *Luis Salazar* | .15 | .11 |
| 502 | Gary Lucas | .08 | .06 |
| 503 | Mike Armstrong | .06 | .05 |
| 504 | Jerry Turner | .06 | .05 |
| 505 | Dennis Kinney | .06 | .05 |
| 506 | Willy Montanez (Willie) | .06 | .05 |
| 507 | Gorman Thomas | .10 | .08 |
| 508 | Ben Oglivie | .08 | .06 |
| 509 | Larry Hisle | .08 | .06 |
| 510 | Sal Bando | .10 | .08 |
| 511 | Robin Yount | 3.00 | 2.25 |
| 512 | Mike Caldwell | .06 | .05 |
| 513 | Sixto Lezcano | .06 | .05 |
| 514a | Jerry Augustine (Billy Travers photo) | .15 | .11 |
| 514b | Billy Travers (correct name with photo) | .70 | .50 |
| 515 | Paul Molitor | .20 | .15 |
| 516 | Moose Haas | .06 | .05 |
| 517 | Bill Castro | .06 | .05 |
| 518 | Jim Slaton | .06 | .05 |
| 519 | Lary Sorensen | .06 | .05 |
| 520 | Bob McClure | .06 | .05 |
| 521 | Charlie Moore | .06 | .05 |
| 522 | Jim Gantner | .08 | .06 |
| 523 | Reggie Cleveland | .06 | .05 |
| 524 | Don Money | .06 | .05 |
| 525 | Billy Travers | .06 | .05 |
| 526 | Buck Martinez | .06 | .05 |
| 527 | Dick Davis | .06 | .05 |
| 528 | Ted Simmons | .12 | .09 |
| 529 | Garry Templeton | .10 | .08 |
| 530 | Ken Reitz | .06 | .05 |
| 531 | Tony Scott | .06 | .05 |
| 532 | Ken Oberkfell | .06 | .05 |
| 533 | Bob Sykes | .06 | .05 |
| 534 | Keith Smith | .06 | .05 |
| 535 | John Littlefield | .06 | .05 |
| 536 | Jim Kaat | .15 | .11 |
| 537 | Bob Forsch | .08 | .06 |
| 538 | Mike Phillips | .06 | .05 |
| 539 | *Terry Landrum* | .10 | .08 |
| 540 | *Leon Durham* | .20 | .15 |
| 541 | Terry Kennedy | .08 | .06 |
| 542 | George Hendrick | .08 | .06 |
| 543 | Dane Iorg | .06 | .05 |
| 544 | Mark Littell (photo actually Jeff Little) | .06 | .05 |
| 545 | Keith Hernandez | .40 | .30 |
| 546 | Silvio Martinez | .06 | .05 |
| 547a | Pete Vuckovich (photo actually Don Hood) | .15 | .11 |
| 547b | Don Hood (correct name with photo) | .70 | .50 |
| 548 | Bobby Bonds | .10 | .08 |
| 549 | Mike Ramsey | .06 | .05 |
| 550 | Tom Herr | .10 | .08 |
| 551 | Roy Smalley | .06 | .05 |
| 552 | Jerry Koosman | .10 | .08 |
| 553 | Ken Landreaux | .06 | .05 |
| 554 | John Castino | .06 | .05 |
| 555 | Doug Corbett | .06 | .05 |
| 556 | Bombo Rivera | .06 | .05 |
| 557 | Ron Jackson | .06 | .05 |

| | MT | NR MT |
|---|---|---|
| 558 Butch Wynegar | .06 | .05 |
| 559 Hosken Powell | .06 | .05 |
| 560 Pete Redfern | .06 | .05 |
| 561 Roger Erickson | .06 | .05 |
| 562 Glenn Adams | .06 | .05 |
| 563 Rick Sofield | .06 | .05 |
| 564 Geoff Zahn | .06 | .05 |
| 565 Pete Mackanin | .06 | .05 |
| 566 Mike Cubbage | .06 | .05 |
| 567 Darrell Jackson | .06 | .05 |
| 568 Dave Edwards | .06 | .05 |
| 569 Rob Wilfong | .06 | .05 |
| 570 Sal Butera | .06 | .05 |
| 571 Jose Morales | .06 | .05 |
| 572 Rick Langford | .06 | .05 |
| 573 Mike Norris | .06 | .05 |
| 574 Rickey Henderson | 12.00 | 9.00 |
| 575 Tony Armas | .10 | .08 |
| 576 Dave Revering | .06 | .05 |
| 577 Jeff Newman | .06 | .05 |
| 578 Bob Lacey | .06 | .05 |
| 579 Brian Kingman (photo actually Alan Wirth) | .06 | .05 |
| 580 Mitchell Page | .06 | .05 |
| 581 Billy Martin | .12 | .09 |
| 582 Rob Picciolo | .06 | .05 |
| 583 Mike Heath | .06 | .05 |
| 584 Mickey Klutts | .06 | .05 |
| 585 Orlando Gonzalez | .06 | .05 |
| 586 *Mike Davis* | .25 | .20 |
| 587 Wayne Gross | .06 | .05 |
| 588 Matt Keough | .06 | .05 |
| 589 Steve McCatty | .06 | .05 |
| 590 Dwayne Murphy | .08 | .06 |
| 591 Mario Guerrero | .06 | .05 |
| 592 Dave McKay | .06 | .05 |
| 593 Jim Essian | .06 | .05 |
| 594 Dave Heaverlo | .06 | .05 |
| 595 Maury Wills | .10 | .08 |
| 596 Juan Beniquez | .06 | .05 |
| 597 Rodney Craig | .06 | .05 |
| 598 Jim Anderson | .06 | .05 |
| 599 Floyd Bannister | .10 | .08 |
| 600 Bruce Bochte | .06 | .05 |
| 601 Julio Cruz | .06 | .05 |
| 602 Ted Cox | .06 | .05 |
| 603 Dan Meyer | .06 | .05 |
| 604 Larry Cox | .06 | .05 |
| 605 Bill Stein | .06 | .05 |
| 606 Steve Garvey | .50 | .40 |
| 607 Dave Roberts | .06 | .05 |
| 608 Leon Roberts | .06 | .05 |
| 609 Reggie Walton | .06 | .05 |
| 610 Dave Edler | .06 | .05 |
| 611 Larry Milbourne | .06 | .05 |
| 612 Kim Allen | .06 | .05 |
| 613 Mario Mendoza | .06 | .05 |
| 614 Tom Paciorek | .06 | .05 |
| 615 Glenn Abbott | .06 | .05 |
| 616 Joe Simpson | .06 | .05 |
| 617 Mickey Rivers | .08 | .06 |
| 618 Jim Kern | .06 | .05 |
| 619 Jim Sundberg | .08 | .06 |
| 620 Richie Zisk | .08 | .06 |
| 621 Jon Matlack | .08 | .06 |
| 622 Ferguson Jenkins | .50 | .40 |

| | MT | NR MT |
|---|---|---|
| 623 Pat Corrales | .06 | .05 |
| 624 Ed Figueroa | .06 | .05 |
| 625 Buddy Bell | .12 | .09 |
| 626 Al Oliver | .15 | .11 |
| 627 Doc Medich | .06 | .05 |
| 628 Bump Wills | .06 | .05 |
| 629 Rusty Staub | .10 | .08 |
| 630 Pat Putnam | .06 | .05 |
| 631 John Grubb | .06 | .05 |
| 632 Danny Darwin | .06 | .05 |
| 633 Ken Clay | .06 | .05 |
| 634 Jim Norris | .06 | .05 |
| 635 John Butcher | .06 | .05 |
| 636 Dave Roberts | .06 | .05 |
| 637 Billy Sample | .06 | .05 |
| 638 Carl Yastrzemski | 1.00 | .70 |
| 639 Cecil Cooper | .15 | .11 |
| 640 Mike Schmidt | 2.00 | 1.50 |
| 641a Checklist 1-50 (41 Hal McRae) | .10 | .08 |
| 641b Checklist 1-50 (41 Hal McRae Double Threat) | .40 | .30 |
| 642 Checklist 51-109 | .06 | .05 |
| 643 Checklist 110-168 | .06 | .05 |
| 644a Checklist 169-220 (202 George Foster) | .10 | .08 |
| 644b Checklist 169-220 (202 George Foster "Slugger") | .40 | .30 |
| 645a Triple Threat (Larry Bowa, Pete Rose, Mike Schmidt) (no number on back) | 1.00 | .70 |
| 645b Triple Threat (Larry Bowa, Pete Rose, Mike Schmidt) (645 on back) | 2.00 | 1.50 |
| 646 Checklist 221-267 | .06 | .05 |
| 647 Checklist 268-315 | .06 | .05 |
| 648 Checklist 316-359 | .06 | .05 |
| 649 Checklist 360-408 | .06 | .05 |
| 650 Reggie Jackson | 3.25 | 2.50 |
| 651 Checklist 409-458 | .06 | .05 |
| 652a Checklist 459-509 (483 Aurelio Lopez) | .10 | .08 |
| 652b Checklist 459-506 (no 483) | .40 | .30 |
| 653 Willie Wilson | 1.00 | .70 |
| 654a Checklist 507-550 (514 Jerry Augustine) | .10 | .08 |
| 654b Checklist 507-550 (514 Billy Travers) | .40 | .30 |
| 655 George Brett | 2.00 | 1.50 |
| 656 Checklist 551-593 | .06 | .05 |
| 657 Tug McGraw | 1.00 | .70 |
| 658 Checklist 594-637 | .06 | .05 |
| 659a Checklist 640-660 (last number on front is 551) | .10 | .08 |
| 659b Checklist 640-660 (last number on front is 483) | .40 | .30 |
| 660a Steve Carlton (date 1066 on back) | 1.00 | .70 |
| 660b Steve Carlton (date 1966 on back) | 2.00 | 1.50 |

# 1982 Fleer

Fleer's 1982 set did not match the quality of the previous year's effort. Many of the photos in the set are blurred and have muddied backgrounds. The cards, which measure 2-1/2" by 3-1/2", feature color photos surrounded by a border frame which is color-coded by team. The card backs are blue, white, and yellow and contain the player's team logo plus the logos of Major League Baseball and the Major League Baseball Players Association. Due to a lawsuit by Topps, Fleer was forced to issue the set with team logo stickers rather than gum. The complete set price does not include the higher priced variations.

|  |  | MT | NR MT |
|---|---|---|---|
| | Complete Set: | 100.00 | 75.00 |
| | Common Player: | .06 | .05 |
| 1 | Dusty Baker | .10 | .08 |
| 2 | Robert Castillo | .06 | .05 |
| 3 | Ron Cey | .12 | .09 |
| 4 | Terry Forster | .08 | .06 |
| 5 | Steve Garvey | .50 | .40 |
| 6 | Dave Goltz | .08 | .06 |
| 7 | Pedro Guerrero(FC) | .35 | .25 |
| 8 | Burt Hooton | .08 | .06 |
| 9 | Steve Howe | .08 | .06 |
| 10 | Jay Johnstone | .08 | .06 |
| 11 | Ken Landreaux | .06 | .05 |
| 12 | Davey Lopes | .10 | .08 |

A player's name in *italic* type indicates a rookie card. An (FC) indicates a player's first card for that particular card company.

|  |  | MT | NR MT |
|---|---|---|---|
| 13 | *Mike Marshall*(FC) | .25 | .20 |
| 14 | Bobby Mitchell | .06 | .05 |
| 15 | Rick Monday | .10 | .08 |
| 16 | *Tom Niedenfuer*(FC) | .20 | .15 |
| 17 | *Ted Power*(FC) | .20 | .15 |
| 18 | Jerry Reuss | .10 | .08 |
| 19 | Ron Roenicke | .06 | .05 |
| 20 | Bill Russell | .08 | .06 |
| 21 | *Steve Sax*(FC) | 4.00 | 3.00 |
| 22 | Mike Scioscia | .08 | .06 |
| 23 | Reggie Smith | .10 | .08 |
| 24 | *Dave Stewart*(FC) | 3.00 | 2.25 |
| 25 | Rick Sutcliffe | .15 | .11 |
| 26 | Derrel Thomas | .06 | .05 |
| 27 | Fernando Valenzuela | .60 | .45 |
| 28 | Bob Welch | .12 | .09 |
| 29 | Steve Yeager | .06 | .05 |
| 30 | Bobby Brown | .06 | .05 |
| 31 | Rick Cerone | .06 | .05 |
| 32 | Ron Davis | .06 | .05 |
| 33 | Bucky Dent | .10 | .08 |
| 34 | Barry Foote | .06 | .05 |
| 35 | George Frazier | .06 | .05 |
| 36 | Oscar Gamble | .08 | .06 |
| 37 | Rich Gossage | .20 | .15 |
| 38 | Ron Guidry | .25 | .20 |
| 39 | Reggie Jackson | 2.00 | 1.50 |
| 40 | Tommy John | .20 | .15 |
| 41 | Rudy May | .06 | .05 |
| 42 | Larry Milbourne | .06 | .05 |
| 43 | Jerry Mumphrey | .06 | .05 |
| 44 | Bobby Murcer | .10 | .08 |
| 45 | *Gene Nelson* | .12 | .09 |
| 46 | Graig Nettles | .15 | .11 |
| 47 | Johnny Oates | .06 | .05 |
| 48 | Lou Piniella | .12 | .09 |
| 49 | Willie Randolph | .10 | .08 |
| 50 | Rick Reuschel | .10 | .08 |
| 51 | Dave Revering | .06 | .05 |
| 52 | *Dave Righetti*(FC) | 1.00 | .70 |
| 53 | Aurelio Rodriguez | .08 | .06 |
| 54 | Bob Watson | .08 | .06 |
| 55 | Dennis Werth | .06 | .05 |
| 56 | Dave Winfield | 2.50 | 2.00 |
| 57 | Johnny Bench | .80 | .60 |
| 58 | Bruce Berenyi | .06 | .05 |
| 59 | Larry Biittner | .06 | .05 |
| 60 | Scott Brown | .06 | .05 |
| 61 | Dave Collins | .08 | .06 |
| 62 | Geoff Combe | .06 | .05 |
| 63 | Dave Concepcion | .12 | .09 |
| 64 | Dan Driessen | .08 | .06 |
| 65 | Joe Edelen | .06 | .05 |
| 66 | George Foster | .20 | .15 |
| 67 | Ken Griffey | .12 | .09 |
| 68 | Paul Householder | .06 | .05 |
| 69 | Tom Hume | .06 | .05 |
| 70 | Junior Kennedy | .06 | .05 |
| 71 | Ray Knight | .10 | .08 |
| 72 | Mike LaCoss | .06 | .05 |
| 73 | Rafael Landestoy | .06 | .05 |
| 74 | Charlie Leibrandt | .10 | .08 |

| | | MT | NR MT |
|---|---|---|---|
| 75 | Sam Mejias | .06 | .05 |
| 76 | Paul Moskau | .06 | .05 |
| 77 | Joe Nolan | .06 | .05 |
| 78 | Mike O'Berry | .06 | .05 |
| 79 | Ron Oester | .06 | .05 |
| 80 | Frank Pastore | .06 | .05 |
| 81 | Joe Price | .06 | .05 |
| 82 | Tom Seaver | 1.50 | 1.25 |
| 83 | Mario Soto | .08 | .06 |
| 84 | Mike Vail | .06 | .05 |
| 85 | Tony Armas | .10 | .08 |
| 86 | Shooty Babitt | .06 | .05 |
| 87 | Dave Beard | .06 | .05 |
| 88 | Rick Bosetti | .06 | .05 |
| 89 | Keith Drumright | .06 | .05 |
| 90 | Wayne Gross | .06 | .05 |
| 91 | Mike Heath | .06 | .05 |
| 92 | Rickey Henderson | 6.00 | 4.50 |
| 93 | Cliff Johnson | .06 | .05 |
| 94 | Jeff Jones | .06 | .05 |
| 95 | Matt Keough | .06 | .05 |
| 96 | Brian Kingman | .06 | .05 |
| 97 | Mickey Klutts | .06 | .05 |
| 98 | Rick Langford | .06 | .05 |
| 99 | Steve McCatty | .06 | .05 |
| 100 | Dave McKay | .06 | .05 |
| 101 | Dwayne Murphy | .08 | .06 |
| 102 | Jeff Newman | .06 | .05 |
| 103 | Mike Norris | .06 | .05 |
| 104 | Bob Owchinko | .06 | .05 |
| 105 | Mitchell Page | .06 | .05 |
| 106 | Rob Picciolo | .06 | .05 |
| 107 | Jim Spencer | .06 | .05 |
| 108 | Fred Stanley | .06 | .05 |
| 109 | Tom Underwood | .06 | .05 |
| 110 | Joaquin Andujar | .08 | .06 |
| 111 | Steve Braun | .06 | .05 |
| 112 | Bob Forsch | .08 | .06 |
| 113 | George Hendrick | .08 | .06 |
| 114 | Keith Hernandez | .40 | .30 |
| 115 | Tom Herr | .10 | .08 |
| 116 | Dane Iorg | .06 | .05 |
| 117 | Jim Kaat | .15 | .11 |
| 118 | Tito Landrum | .06 | .05 |
| 119 | Sixto Lezcano | .06 | .05 |
| 120 | Mark Littell | .06 | .05 |
| 121 | John Martin | .06 | .05 |
| 122 | Silvio Martinez | .06 | .05 |
| 123 | Ken Oberkfell | .06 | .05 |
| 124 | Darrell Porter | .08 | .06 |
| 125 | Mike Ramsey | .06 | .05 |
| 126 | Orlando Sanchez | .06 | .05 |
| 127 | Bob Shirley | .06 | .05 |
| 128 | Lary Sorensen | .06 | .05 |
| 129 | Bruce Sutter | .15 | .11 |
| 130 | Bob Sykes | .06 | .05 |
| 131 | Garry Templeton | .10 | .08 |
| 132 | Gene Tenace | .08 | .06 |
| 133 | Jerry Augustine | .06 | .05 |
| 134 | Sal Bando | .08 | .06 |
| 135 | Mark Brouhard | .06 | .05 |
| 136 | Mike Caldwell | .06 | .05 |
| 137 | Reggie Cleveland | .06 | .05 |
| 138 | Cecil Cooper | .15 | .11 |
| 139 | Jamie Easterly | .06 | .05 |
| 140 | Marshall Edwards | .06 | .05 |
| 141 | Rollie Fingers | .50 | .40 |

| | | MT | NR MT |
|---|---|---|---|
| 142 | Jim Gantner | .08 | .06 |
| 143 | Moose Haas | .06 | .05 |
| 144 | Larry Hisle | .08 | .06 |
| 145 | Roy Howell | .06 | .05 |
| 146 | Rickey Keeton | .06 | .05 |
| 147 | Randy Lerch | .06 | .05 |
| 148 | Paul Molitor | .20 | .15 |
| 149 | Don Money | .06 | .05 |
| 150 | Charlie Moore | .06 | .05 |
| 151 | Ben Oglivie | .08 | .06 |
| 152 | Ted Simmons | .12 | .09 |
| 153 | Jim Slaton | .06 | .05 |
| 154 | Gorman Thomas | .10 | .08 |
| 155 | Robin Yount | 2.00 | 1.50 |
| 156 | Pete Vukovich | .08 | .06 |
| 157 | Benny Ayala | .06 | .05 |
| 158 | Mark Belanger | .08 | .06 |
| 159 | Al Bumbry | .08 | .06 |
| 160 | Terry Crowley | .06 | .05 |
| 161 | Rich Dauer | .06 | .05 |
| 162 | Doug DeCinces | .10 | .08 |
| 163 | Rick Dempsey | .08 | .06 |
| 164 | Jim Dwyer | .06 | .05 |
| 165 | Mike Flanagan | .10 | .08 |
| 166 | Dave Ford | .06 | .05 |
| 167 | Dan Graham | .06 | .05 |
| 168 | Wayne Krenchicki | .06 | .05 |
| 169 | John Lowenstein | .06 | .05 |
| 170 | Dennis Martinez | .08 | .06 |
| 171 | Tippy Martinez | .06 | .05 |
| 172 | Scott McGregor | .08 | .06 |
| 173 | Jose Morales | .06 | .05 |
| 174 | Eddie Murray | .80 | .60 |
| 175 | Jim Palmer | .60 | .45 |
| 176 | Cal Ripken, Jr.(FC) | 50.00 | 37.00 |
| 177 | Gary Roenicke | .06 | .05 |
| 178 | Lenn Sakata | .06 | .05 |
| 179 | Ken Singleton | .10 | .08 |
| 180 | Sammy Stewart | .06 | .05 |
| 181 | Tim Stoddard | .06 | .05 |
| 182 | Steve Stone | .08 | .06 |
| 183 | Stan Bahnsen | .06 | .05 |
| 184 | Ray Burris | .06 | .05 |
| 185 | Gary Carter | .35 | .25 |
| 186 | Warren Cromartie | .06 | .05 |
| 187 | Andre Dawson | 2.00 | 1.50 |
| 188 | Terry Francona(FC) | .10 | .08 |
| 189 | Woodie Fryman | .08 | .06 |
| 190 | Bill Gullickson | .08 | .06 |
| 191 | Grant Jackson | .06 | .05 |
| 192 | Wallace Johnson | .06 | .05 |
| 193 | Charlie Lea | .06 | .05 |
| 194 | Bill Lee | .08 | .06 |
| 195 | Jerry Manuel | .06 | .05 |
| 196 | Brad Mills | .06 | .05 |
| 197 | John Milner | .06 | .05 |
| 198 | Rowland Office | .06 | .05 |
| 199 | David Palmer | .06 | .05 |
| 200 | Larry Parrish | .10 | .08 |
| 201 | Mike Phillips | .06 | .05 |
| 202 | Tim Raines | 1.50 | 1.25 |
| 203 | Bobby Ramos | .06 | .05 |
| 204 | Jeff Reardon | 1.00 | .70 |
| 205 | Steve Rogers | .08 | .06 |
| 206 | Scott Sanderson | .06 | .05 |

| | MT | NR MT | | | MT | NR MT |
|---|---|---|---|---|---|---|
| 207 | Rodney Scott (photo actually Tim Raines) | .10 | .08 | 272 | *Rick Leach*(FC) | .12 | .09 |
| 208 | Elias Sosa | .06 | .05 | 273 | Aurelio Lopez | .06 | .05 |
| 209 | Chris Speier | .06 | .05 | 274 | Jack Morris | .30 | .25 |
| 210 | *Tim Wallach*(FC) | | | 275 | Kevin Saucier | .06 | .05 |
| | | 2.00 | 1.50 | 276 | Lance Parrish | .35 | .25 |
| 211 | Jerry White | .06 | .05 | 277 | Rick Peters | .06 | .05 |
| 212 | Alan Ashby | .06 | .05 | 278 | Dan Petry | .08 | .06 |
| 213 | Cesar Cedeno | .12 | .09 | 279 | David Rozema | .06 | .05 |
| 214 | Jose Cruz | .12 | .09 | 280 | Stan Papi | .06 | .05 |
| 215 | Kiko Garcia | .06 | .05 | 281 | Dan Schatzeder | .06 | .05 |
| 216 | Phil Garner | .08 | .06 | 282 | Champ Summers | .06 | .05 |
| 217 | Danny Heep | .06 | .05 | 283 | Alan Trammell | .40 | .30 |
| 218 | Art Howe | .06 | .05 | 284 | Lou Whitaker | .40 | .30 |
| 219 | Bob Knepper | .08 | .06 | 285 | Milt Wilcox | .06 | .05 |
| 220 | Frank LaCorte | .06 | .05 | 286 | John Wockenfuss | .06 | .05 |
| 221 | Joe Niekro | .12 | .09 | 287 | Gary Allenson | .06 | .05 |
| 222 | Joe Pittman | .06 | .05 | 288 | Tom Burgmeier | .06 | .05 |
| 223 | Terry Puhl | .06 | .05 | 289 | Bill Campbell | .06 | .05 |
| 224 | Luis Pujols | .06 | .05 | 290 | Mark Clear | .06 | .05 |
| 225 | Craig Reynolds | .06 | .05 | 291 | Steve Crawford | .06 | .05 |
| 226 | J.R. Richard | .10 | .08 | 292 | Dennis Eckersley | 1.50 | 1.25 |
| 227 | Dave Roberts | .06 | .05 | 293 | Dwight Evans | .15 | .11 |
| 228 | Vern Ruhle | .06 | .05 | 294 | *Rich Gedman*(FC) | | |
| 229 | Nolan Ryan | 8.00 | 6.00 | | | .25 | .20 |
| 230 | Joe Sambito | .06 | .05 | 295 | Garry Hancock | .06 | .05 |
| 231 | Tony Scott | .06 | .05 | 296 | Glenn Hoffman | .06 | .05 |
| 232 | Dave Smith | .10 | .08 | 297 | Bruce Hurst(FC) | .30 | .25 |
| 233 | Harry Spilman | .06 | .05 | 298 | Carney Lansford | .08 | .06 |
| 234 | Don Sutton | .30 | .25 | 299 | Rick Miller | .06 | .05 |
| 235 | Dickie Thon | .08 | .06 | 300 | Reid Nichols | .06 | .05 |
| 236 | Denny Walling | .06 | .05 | 301 | *Bob Ojeda*(FC) | .50 | .40 |
| 237 | Gary Woods | .06 | .05 | 302 | Tony Perez | .20 | .15 |
| 238 | *Luis Aguayo*(FC) | .10 | .08 | 303 | Chuck Rainey | .06 | .05 |
| 239 | Ramon Aviles | .06 | .05 | 304 | Jerry Remy | .06 | .05 |
| 240 | Bob Boone | .10 | .08 | 305 | Jim Rice | .40 | .30 |
| 241 | Larry Bowa | .15 | .11 | 306 | Joe Rudi | .10 | .08 |
| 242 | Warren Brusstar | .06 | .05 | 307 | Bob Stanley | .06 | .05 |
| 243 | Steve Carlton | 1.00 | .70 | 308 | Dave Stapleton | .06 | .05 |
| 244 | Larry Christenson | .06 | .05 | 309 | Frank Tanana | .10 | .08 |
| 245 | Dick Davis | .06 | .05 | 310 | Mike Torrez | .08 | .06 |
| 246 | Greg Gross | .06 | .05 | 311 | John Tudor(FC) | .25 | .20 |
| 247 | Sparky Lyle | .10 | .08 | 312 | Carl Yastrzemski | 1.00 | .70 |
| 248 | Garry Maddox | .10 | .08 | 313 | Buddy Bell | .12 | .09 |
| 249 | Gary Matthews | .10 | .08 | 314 | Steve Comer | .06 | .05 |
| 250 | Bake McBride | .06 | .05 | 315 | Danny Darwin | .06 | .05 |
| 251 | Tug McGraw | .12 | .09 | 316 | John Ellis | .06 | .05 |
| 252 | Keith Moreland | .10 | .08 | 317 | John Grubb | .06 | .05 |
| 253 | Dickie Noles | .06 | .05 | 318 | Rick Honeycutt | .06 | .05 |
| 254 | Mike Proly | .06 | .05 | 319 | Charlie Hough | .10 | .08 |
| 255 | Ron Reed | .06 | .05 | 320 | Ferguson Jenkins | .15 | .11 |
| 256 | Pete Rose | 1.00 | .70 | 321 | John Henry Johnson | | |
| 257 | Dick Ruthven | .06 | .05 | | | .06 | .05 |
| 258 | Mike Schmidt | 2.00 | 1.50 | 322 | Jim Kern | .06 | .05 |
| 259 | Lonnie Smith | .08 | .06 | 323 | Jon Matlack | .08 | .06 |
| 260 | Manny Trillo | .08 | .06 | 324 | Doc Medich | .06 | .05 |
| 261 | Del Unser | .06 | .05 | 325 | Mario Mendoza | .06 | .05 |
| 262 | George Vukovich | .06 | .05 | 326 | Al Oliver | .15 | .11 |
| 263 | Tom Brookens | .06 | .05 | 327 | Pat Putnam | .06 | .05 |
| 264 | George Cappuzzello | .06 | .05 | 328 | Mickey Rivers | .08 | .06 |
| 265 | Marty Castillo | .06 | .05 | 329 | Leon Roberts | .06 | .05 |
| 266 | Al Cowens | .06 | .05 | 330 | Billy Sample | .06 | .05 |
| 267 | Kirk Gibson | .70 | .50 | 331 | Bill Stein | .06 | .05 |
| 268 | Richie Hebner | .06 | .05 | 332 | Jim Sundberg | .08 | .06 |
| 269 | Ron Jackson | .06 | .05 | 333 | Mark Wagner | .06 | .05 |
| 270 | Lynn Jones | .06 | .05 | 334 | Bump Wills | .06 | .05 |
| 271 | Steve Kemp | .08 | .06 | 335 | Bill Almon | .06 | .05 |
| | | | | 336 | Harold Baines | .30 | .25 |

| | | MT | NR MT |
|---|---|---|---|
| 337 | Ross Baumgarten | .06 | .05 |
| 338 | Tony Bernazard | .06 | .05 |
| 339 | Britt Burns | .06 | .05 |
| 340 | Richard Dotson | .10 | .08 |
| 341 | Jim Essian | .06 | .05 |
| 342 | Ed Farmer | .06 | .05 |
| 343 | Carlton Fisk | 1.50 | 1.25 |
| 344 | Kevin Hickey | .06 | .05 |
| 345 | Lamarr Hoyt (LaMarr) | | |
| | | .06 | .05 |
| 346 | Lamar Johnson | .06 | .05 |
| 347 | Jerry Koosman | .10 | .08 |
| 348 | Rusty Kuntz | .06 | .05 |
| 349 | Dennis Lamp | .06 | .05 |
| 350 | Ron LeFlore | .08 | .06 |
| 351 | Chet Lemon | .08 | .06 |
| 352 | Greg Luzinski | .15 | .11 |
| 353 | Bob Molinaro | .06 | .05 |
| 354 | Jim Morrison | .06 | .05 |
| 355 | Wayne Nordhagen | .06 | .05 |
| 356 | Greg Pryor | .06 | .05 |
| 357 | Mike Squires | .06 | .05 |
| 358 | Steve Trout | .06 | .05 |
| 359 | Alan Bannister | .06 | .05 |
| 360 | Len Barker | .08 | .06 |
| 361 | Bert Blyleven | .12 | .09 |
| 362 | Joe Charboneau | .08 | .06 |
| 363 | John Denny | .06 | .05 |
| 364 | Bo Diaz | .08 | .06 |
| 365 | Miguel Dilone | .06 | .05 |
| 366 | Jerry Dybzinski | .06 | .05 |
| 367 | Wayne Garland | .06 | .05 |
| 368 | Mike Hargrove | .06 | .05 |
| 369 | Toby Harrah | .08 | .06 |
| 370 | Ron Hassey | .06 | .05 |
| 371 | Von Hayes(FC) | 1.00 | .70 |
| 372 | Pat Kelly | .06 | .05 |
| 373 | Duane Kuiper | .06 | .05 |
| 374 | Rick Manning | .06 | .05 |
| 375 | Sid Monge | .06 | .05 |
| 376 | Jorge Orta | .06 | .05 |
| 377 | Dave Rosello | .06 | .05 |
| 378 | Dan Spillner | .06 | .05 |
| 379 | Mike Stanton | .06 | .05 |
| 380 | Andre Thornton | .10 | .08 |
| 381 | Tom Veryzer | .06 | .05 |
| 382 | Rick Waits | .06 | .05 |
| 383 | Doyle Alexander | .10 | .08 |
| 384 | Vida Blue | .12 | .09 |
| 385 | Fred Breining | .06 | .05 |
| 386 | Enos Cabell | .06 | .05 |
| 387 | Jack Clark | .25 | .20 |
| 388 | Darrell Evans | .15 | .11 |
| 389 | Tom Griffin | .06 | .05 |
| 390 | Larry Herndon | .08 | .06 |
| 391 | Al Holland | .06 | .05 |
| 392 | Gary Lavelle | .06 | .05 |
| 393 | Johnnie LeMaster | .06 | .05 |
| 394 | Jerry Martin | .06 | .05 |
| 395 | Milt May | .06 | .05 |
| 396 | Greg Minton | .06 | .05 |
| 397 | Joe Morgan | .50 | .40 |
| 398 | Joe Pettini | .06 | .05 |
| 399 | Alan Ripley | .06 | .05 |
| 400 | Billy Smith | .06 | .05 |
| 401 | Rennie Stennett | .06 | .05 |
| 402 | Ed Whitson | .06 | .05 |

| | | MT | NR MT |
|---|---|---|---|
| 403 | Jim Wohlford | .06 | .05 |
| 404 | Willie Aikens | .06 | .05 |
| 405 | George Brett | 2.00 | 1.50 |
| 406 | Ken Brett | .08 | .06 |
| 407 | Dave Chalk | .06 | .05 |
| 408 | Rich Gale | .06 | .05 |
| 409 | Cesar Geronimo | .06 | .05 |
| 410 | Larry Gura | .06 | .05 |
| 411 | Clint Hurdle | .06 | .05 |
| 412 | Mike Jones | .06 | .05 |
| 413 | Dennis Leonard | .08 | .06 |
| 414 | Renie Martin | .06 | .05 |
| 415 | Lee May | .08 | .06 |
| 416 | Hal McRae | .12 | .09 |
| 417 | Darryl Motley | .06 | .05 |
| 418 | Rance Mulliniks | .06 | .05 |
| 419 | Amos Otis | .08 | .06 |
| 420 | Ken Phelps(FC) | .10 | .08 |
| 421 | Jamie Quirk | .06 | .05 |
| 422 | Dan Quisenberry | .15 | .11 |
| 423 | Paul Splittorff | .06 | .05 |
| 424 | U.L. Washington | .06 | .05 |
| 425 | John Wathan | .08 | .06 |
| 426 | Frank White | .10 | .08 |
| 427 | Willie Wilson | .15 | .11 |
| 428 | Brian Asselstine | .06 | .05 |
| 429 | Bruce Benedict | .06 | .05 |
| 430 | Tom Boggs | .06 | .05 |
| 431 | Larry Bradford | .06 | .05 |
| 432 | Rick Camp | .06 | .05 |
| 433 | Chris Chambliss | .08 | .06 |
| 434 | Gene Garber | .06 | .05 |
| 435 | Preston Hanna | .06 | .05 |
| 436 | Bob Horner | .12 | .09 |
| 437 | Glenn Hubbard | .08 | .06 |
| 438a | Al Hrabosky (All Hrabosky, 5'1" on back) | | |
| | | 20.00 | 15.00 |
| 438b | Al Hrabosky (Al Hrabosky, 5'1" on back) | | |
| | | 1.25 | .90 |
| 438c | Al Hrabosky (Al Hrabosky, 5'10" on back) | | |
| | | .35 | .25 |
| 439 | Rufino Linares | .06 | .05 |
| 440 | Rick Mahler(FC) | .25 | .20 |
| 441 | Ed Miller | .06 | .05 |
| 442 | John Montefusco | .08 | .06 |
| 443 | Dale Murphy | .90 | .70 |
| 444 | Phil Niekro | .30 | .25 |
| 445 | Gaylord Perry | .40 | .30 |
| 446 | Biff Pocoroba | .06 | .05 |
| 447 | Rafael Ramirez | .08 | .06 |
| 448 | Jerry Royster | .06 | .05 |
| 449 | Claudell Washington | .08 | .06 |
| 450 | Don Aase | .06 | .05 |
| 451 | Don Baylor | .12 | .09 |
| 452 | Juan Beniquez | .06 | .05 |
| 453 | Rick Burleson | .08 | .06 |
| 454 | Bert Campaneris | .10 | .08 |
| 455 | Rod Carew | 1.00 | .70 |
| 456 | Bob Clark | .06 | .05 |
| 457 | Brian Downing | .10 | .08 |
| 458 | Dan Ford | .06 | .05 |
| 459 | Ken Forsch | .06 | .05 |
| 460 | Dave Frost | .06 | .05 |
| 461 | Bobby Grich | .10 | .08 |

| | | MT | NR MT | | | MT | NR MT |
|---|---|---|---|---|---|---|---|
| 462 | Larry Harlow | .06 | .05 | 529 | Mike Jorgensen | .06 | .05 |
| 463 | John Harris | .06 | .05 | 530 | Dave Kingman | .15 | .11 |
| 464 | Andy Hassler | .06 | .05 | 531 | Ed Lynch | .06 | .05 |
| 465 | Butch Hobson | .06 | .05 | 532 | Mike Marshall | .10 | .08 |
| 466 | Jesse Jefferson | .06 | .05 | 533 | Lee Mazzilli | .08 | .06 |
| 467 | Bruce Kison | .06 | .05 | 534 | Dyar Miller | .06 | .05 |
| 468 | Fred Lynn | .20 | .15 | 535 | Mike Scott(FC) | .20 | .15 |
| 469 | Angel Moreno | .06 | .05 | 536 | Rusty Staub | .10 | .08 |
| 470 | Ed Ott | .06 | .05 | 537 | John Stearns | .06 | .05 |
| 471 | Fred Patek | .06 | .05 | 538 | Craig Swan | .06 | .05 |
| 472 | Steve Renko | .06 | .05 | 539 | Frank Taveras | .06 | .05 |
| 473 | *Mike Witt*(FC) | .35 | .25 | 540 | Alex Trevino | .06 | .05 |
| 474 | Geoff Zahn | .06 | .05 | 541 | Ellis Valentine | .06 | .05 |
| 475 | Gary Alexander | .06 | .05 | 542 | Mookie Wilson(FC) | .15 | .11 |
| 476 | Dale Berra | .06 | .05 | 543 | Joel Youngblood | .06 | .05 |
| 477 | Kurt Bevacqua | .06 | .05 | 544 | Pat Zachry | .06 | .05 |
| 478 | Jim Bibby | .06 | .05 | 545 | Glenn Adams | .06 | .05 |
| 479 | John Candelaria | .10 | .08 | 546 | Fernando Arroyo | .06 | .05 |
| 480 | Victor Cruz | .06 | .05 | 547 | John Verhoeven | .06 | .05 |
| 481 | Mike Easler | .08 | .06 | 548 | Sal Butera | .06 | .05 |
| 482 | Tim Foli | .06 | .05 | 549 | John Castino | .06 | .05 |
| 483 | Lee Lacy | .06 | .05 | 550 | Don Cooper | .06 | .05 |
| 484 | Vance Law(FC) | .12 | .09 | 551 | Doug Corbett | .06 | .05 |
| 485 | Bill Madlock | .12 | .09 | 552 | Dave Engle | .06 | .05 |
| 486 | Willie Montanez | .06 | .05 | 553 | Roger Erickson | .06 | .05 |
| 487 | Omar Moreno | .06 | .05 | 554 | Danny Goodwin | .06 | .05 |
| 488 | Steve Nicosia | .06 | .05 | 555a | Darrell Jackson (black cap) | 1.00 | .70 |
| 489 | Dave Parker | .30 | .25 | | | | |
| 490 | Tony Pena(FC) | .25 | .20 | 555b | Darrell Jackson (red cap with emblem) | .10 | .08 |
| 491 | Pascual Perez(FC) | .15 | .11 | | | | |
| 492 | *Johnny Ray*(FC) | .30 | .25 | 555c | Darrell Jackson (red cap, no emblem) | .25 | .20 |
| 493 | Rick Rhoden | .10 | .08 | | | | |
| 494 | Bill Robinson | .06 | .05 | 556 | Pete Mackanin | .06 | .05 |
| 495 | Don Robinson | .08 | .06 | 557 | Jack O'Connor | .06 | .05 |
| 496 | Enrique Romo | .06 | .05 | 558 | Hosken Powell | .06 | .05 |
| 497 | Rod Scurry | .06 | .05 | 559 | Pete Redfern | .06 | .05 |
| 498 | Eddie Solomon | .06 | .05 | 560 | Roy Smalley | .06 | .05 |
| 499 | Willie Stargell | .40 | .30 | 561 | Chuck Baker | .06 | .05 |
| 500 | Kent Tekulve | .08 | .06 | 562 | Gary Ward | .08 | .06 |
| 501 | Jason Thompson | .06 | .05 | 563 | Rob Wilfong | .06 | .05 |
| 502 | Glenn Abbott | .06 | .05 | 564 | Al Williams | .06 | .05 |
| 503 | Jim Anderson | .06 | .05 | 565 | Butch Wynegar | .06 | .05 |
| 504 | Floyd Bannister | .10 | .08 | 566 | Randy Bass | .06 | .05 |
| 505 | Bruce Bochte | .06 | .05 | 567 | Juan Bonilla | .06 | .05 |
| 506 | Jeff Burroughs | .08 | .06 | 568 | Danny Boone | .06 | .05 |
| 507 | Bryan Clark | .06 | .05 | 569 | John Curtis | .06 | .05 |
| 508 | Ken Clay | .06 | .05 | 570 | Juan Eichelberger | .06 | .05 |
| 509 | Julio Cruz | .06 | .05 | 571 | Barry Evans | .06 | .05 |
| 510 | Dick Drago | .06 | .05 | 572 | Tim Flannery | .06 | .05 |
| 511 | Gary Gray | .06 | .05 | 573 | Ruppert Jones | .06 | .05 |
| 512 | Dan Meyer | .06 | .05 | 574 | Terry Kennedy | .08 | .06 |
| 513 | Jerry Narron | .06 | .05 | 575 | Joe Lefebvre | .06 | .05 |
| 514 | Tom Paciorek | .06 | .05 | 576a | John Littlefield (pitching lefty) | 200.00 | 150.00 |
| 515 | Casey Parsons | .06 | .05 | | | | |
| 516 | Lenny Randle | .06 | .05 | 576b | John Littlefield (pitching righty) | .08 | .06 |
| 517 | Shane Rawley | .10 | .08 | | | | |
| 518 | Joe Simpson | .06 | .05 | 577 | Gary Lucas | .06 | .05 |
| 519 | Richie Zisk | .08 | .06 | 578 | Steve Mura | .06 | .05 |
| 520 | Neil Allen | .06 | .05 | 579 | Broderick Perkins | .06 | .05 |
| 521 | Bob Bailor | .06 | .05 | 580 | Gene Richards | .06 | .05 |
| 522 | Hubie Brooks(FC) | .50 | .40 | 581 | Luis Salazar | .06 | .05 |
| 523 | Mike Cubbage | .06 | .05 | 582 | Ozzie Smith | 1.00 | .70 |
| 524 | Pete Falcone | .06 | .05 | 583 | John Urrea | .06 | .05 |
| 525 | Doug Flynn | .06 | .05 | 584 | Chris Welsh | .06 | .05 |
| 526 | Tom Hausman | .06 | .05 | 585 | Rick Wise | .08 | .06 |
| 527 | Ron Hodges | .06 | .05 | 586 | Doug Bird | .06 | .05 |
| 528 | Randy Jones | .08 | .06 | 587 | Tim Blackwell | .06 | .05 |

|  |  | MT | NR MT |
|---|---|---|---|
| 588 | Bobby Bonds | .10 | .08 |
| 589 | Bill Buckner | .12 | .09 |
| 590 | Bill Caudill | .06 | .05 |
| 591 | Hector Cruz | .06 | .05 |
| 592 | *Jody Davis*(FC) | .10 | .08 |
| 593 | Ivan DeJesus | .06 | .05 |
| 594 | Steve Dillard | .06 | .05 |
| 595 | Leon Durham | .08 | .06 |
| 596 | Rawly Eastwick | .06 | .05 |
| 597 | Steve Henderson | .06 | .05 |
| 598 | Mike Krukow | .08 | .06 |
| 599 | Mike Lum | .06 | .05 |
| 600 | Randy Martz | .06 | .05 |
| 601 | Jerry Morales | .06 | .05 |
| 602 | Ken Reitz | .06 | .05 |
| 603a | *Lee Smith* (Cubs logo reversed on back)(FC) | 8.00 | 6.00 |
| 603b | *Lee Smith* (Cubs logo correct)(FC) | 5.00 | 3.75 |
| 604 | Dick Tidrow | .06 | .05 |
| 605 | Jim Tracy | .06 | .05 |
| 606 | Mike Tyson | .06 | .05 |
| 607 | Ty Waller | .06 | .05 |
| 608 | Danny Ainge | .25 | .20 |
| 609 | *Jorge Bell*(FC) | 7.50 | 5.65 |
| 610 | Mark Bomback | .06 | .05 |
| 611 | Barry Bonnell | .06 | .05 |
| 612 | Jim Clancy | .08 | .06 |
| 613 | Damaso Garcia | .06 | .05 |
| 614 | Jerry Garvin | .06 | .05 |
| 615 | Alfredo Griffin | .08 | .06 |
| 616 | Garth Iorg | .06 | .05 |
| 617 | Luis Leal | .06 | .05 |
| 618 | Ken Macha | .06 | .05 |
| 619 | John Mayberry | .08 | .06 |
| 620 | Joey McLaughlin | .06 | .05 |
| 621 | Lloyd Moseby | .12 | .09 |
| 622 | Dave Stieb | .12 | .09 |
| 623 | Jackson Todd | .06 | .05 |
| 624 | Willie Upshaw(FC) | .15 | .11 |
| 625 | Otto Velez | .06 | .05 |
| 626 | Ernie Whitt | .08 | .06 |
| 627 | Al Woods | .06 | .05 |
| 628 | 1981 All-Star Game | .08 | .06 |
| 629 | All-Star Infielders (Bucky Dent, Frank White) | .10 | .08 |
| 630 | Big Red Machine (Dave Concepcion, Dan Driessen, George Foster) | .15 | .11 |
| 631 | Top N.L. Relief Pitcher (Bruce Sutter) | .15 | .11 |
| 632 | Steve & Carlton (Steve Carlton, Carlton Fisk) | .25 | .20 |
| 633 | 3000th Game, May 25, 1981 (Carl Yastrzemski) | .35 | .25 |
| 634 | Dynamic Duo (Johnny Bench, Tom Seaver) | .30 | .25 |
| 635 | West Meets East (Gary Carter, Fernando Valenzuela) | .30 | .25 |
| 636a | N.L. Strikeout King (Fernando Valenzuela) ("...led he National League...") | 1.00 | .70 |
| 636b | N.L. Strikeout King (Fernando Valenzuela) |  |  |

|  |  | MT | NR MT |
|---|---|---|---|
|  | ("...led the National League...") | .50 | .40 |
| 637 | 1981 Home Run King (Mike Schmidt) | .40 | .30 |
| 638 | N.L. All-Stars (Gary Carter, Dave Parker) | .25 | .20 |
| 639 | Perfect Game! (Len Barker, Bo Diaz) | .08 | .06 |
| 640 | Pete & Re-Pete (Pete Rose, Pete Rose, Jr.) | 2.50 | 2.00 |
| 641 | Phillies' Finest (Steve Carlton, Mike Schmidt, Lonnie Smith) | .50 | .40 |
| 642 | Red Sox Reunion (Dwight Evans, Fred Lynn) | .15 | .11 |
| 643 | 1981 Most Hits, Most Runs (Rickey Henderson) | 3.00 | 2.25 |
| 644 | Most Saves 1981 A.L. (Rollie Fingers) | .15 | .11 |
| 645 | Most 1981 Wins (Tom Seaver) | .25 | .20 |
| 646a | Yankee Powerhouse (Reggie Jackson, Dave Winfield) (comma after "outfielder" on back) | 2.00 | 1.50 |
| 646b | Yankee Powerhouse (Reggie Jackson, Dave Winfield) (no comma after "oufielder") | 1.00 | .70 |
| 647 | Checklist 1-56 | .06 | .05 |
| 648 | Checklist 57-109 | .06 | .05 |
| 649 | Checklist 110-156 | .06 | .05 |
| 650 | Checklist 157-211 | .06 | .05 |
| 651 | Checklist 212-262 | .06 | .05 |
| 652 | Checklist 263-312 | .06 | .05 |
| 653 | Checklist 313-358 | .06 | .05 |
| 654 | Checklist 359-403 | .06 | .05 |
| 655 | Checklist 404-449 | .06 | .05 |
| 656 | Checklist 450-501 | .06 | .05 |
| 657 | Checklist 502-544 | .06 | .05 |
| 658 | Checklist 545-585 | .06 | .05 |
| 659 | Checklist 586-627 | .06 | .05 |
| 660 | Checklist 628-646 | .06 | .05 |

## 1983 Fleer

The 1983 Fleer set features color photos set inside a light brown border. The cards are the standard size of 2-1/2" by 3-1/2". A team logo is located at the card bottom and the word "Fleer" is found at the top. The card backs are designed on a vertical format and include a small black and white photo of the player along with biographical and statistical information. The reverses are done in two shades of brown on white stock. The set was issued with team logo stickers.

|  |  | MT | NR MT |
|---|---|---|---|
| Complete Set: | | 125.00 | 90.00 |
| Common Player: | | .06 | .05 |
| 1 | Joaquin Andujar | .08 | .06 |
| 2 | Doug Bair | .06 | .05 |
| 3 | Steve Braun | .06 | .05 |
| 4 | Glenn Brummer | .06 | .05 |
| 5 | Bob Forsch | .08 | .06 |
| 6 | David Green | .06 | .05 |
| 7 | George Hendrick | .08 | .06 |
| 8 | Keith Hernandez | .40 | .30 |
| 9 | Tom Herr | .10 | .08 |
| 10 | Dane Iorg | .06 | .05 |
| 11 | Jim Kaat | .15 | .11 |
| 12 | Jeff Lahti | .06 | .05 |
| 13 | Tito Landrum | .06 | .05 |
| 14 | *Dave LaPoint*(FC) | | |
| | | .30 | .25 |
| 15 | *Willie McGee*(FC) | | |
| | | 3.00 | 2.25 |
| 16 | Steve Mura | .06 | .05 |
| 17 | Ken Oberkfell | .06 | .05 |
| 18 | Darrell Porter | .08 | .06 |
| 19 | Mike Ramsey | .06 | .05 |
| 20 | Gene Roof | .06 | .05 |
| 21 | Lonnie Smith | .08 | .06 |
| 22 | Ozzie Smith | 1.25 | .90 |
| 23 | John Stuper | .06 | .05 |
| 24 | Bruce Sutter | .15 | .11 |
| 25 | Gene Tenace | .08 | .06 |
| 26 | Jerry Augustine | .06 | .05 |
| 27 | Dwight Bernard | .06 | .05 |
| 28 | Mark Brouhard | .06 | .05 |
| 29 | Mike Caldwell | .06 | .05 |
| 30 | Cecil Cooper | .15 | .11 |
| 31 | Jamie Easterly | .06 | .05 |
| 32 | Marshall Edwards | .06 | .05 |
| 33 | Rollie Fingers | .60 | .45 |
| 34 | Jim Gantner | .08 | .06 |
| 35 | Moose Haas | .06 | .05 |
| 36 | Roy Howell | .06 | .05 |
| 37 | Peter Ladd | .06 | .05 |
| 38 | Bob McClure | .06 | .05 |
| 39 | Doc Medich | .06 | .05 |
| 40 | Paul Molitor | .20 | .15 |
| 41 | Don Money | .06 | .05 |
| 42 | Charlie Moore | .06 | .05 |
| 43 | Ben Oglivie | .08 | .06 |
| 44 | Ed Romero | .06 | .05 |
| 45 | Ted Simmons | .12 | .09 |
| 46 | Jim Slaton | .06 | .05 |
| 47 | Don Sutton | .30 | .25 |
| 48 | Gorman Thomas | .10 | .08 |
| 49 | Pete Vuckovich | .08 | .06 |
| 50 | Ned Yost | .06 | .05 |
| 51 | Robin Yount | 3.00 | 2.25 |
| 52 | Benny Ayala | .06 | .05 |
| 53 | Bob Bonner | .06 | .05 |
| 54 | Al Bumbry | .08 | .06 |
| 55 | Terry Crowley | .06 | .05 |
| 56 | *Storm Davis*(FC) | .30 | .25 |
| 57 | Rich Dauer | .06 | .05 |
| 58 | Rick Dempsey | .08 | .06 |
| 59 | Jim Dwyer | .06 | .05 |
| 60 | Mike Flanagan | .10 | .08 |
| 61 | Dan Ford | .06 | .05 |
| 62 | Glenn Gulliver | .06 | .05 |
| 63 | John Lowenstein | .06 | .05 |
| 64 | Dennis Martinez | .08 | .06 |
| 65 | Tippy Martinez | .06 | .05 |
| 66 | Scott McGregor | .08 | .06 |
| 67 | Eddie Murray | 1.00 | .70 |
| 68 | Joe Nolan | .06 | .05 |
| 69 | Jim Palmer | .50 | .40 |
| 70 | Cal Ripken, Jr. | 18.00 | 13.50 |
| 71 | Gary Roenicke | .06 | .05 |
| 72 | Lenn Sakata | .06 | .05 |
| 73 | Ken Singleton | .10 | .08 |
| 74 | Sammy Stewart | .06 | .05 |
| 75 | Tim Stoddard | .06 | .05 |
| 76 | Don Aase | .06 | .05 |
| 77 | Don Baylor | .12 | .09 |
| 78 | Juan Beniquez | .06 | .05 |
| 79 | Bob Boone | .10 | .08 |
| 80 | Rick Burleson | .08 | .06 |
| 81 | Rod Carew | 1.00 | .70 |
| 82 | Bobby Clark | .06 | .05 |
| 83 | Doug Corbett | .06 | .05 |
| 84 | John Curtis | .06 | .05 |
| 85 | Doug DeCinces | .10 | .08 |
| 86 | Brian Downing | .10 | .08 |
| 87 | Joe Ferguson | .06 | .05 |
| 88 | Tim Foli | .06 | .05 |
| 89 | Ken Forsch | .06 | .05 |
| 90 | Dave Goltz | .08 | .06 |
| 91 | Bobby Grich | .10 | .08 |
| 92 | Andy Hassler | .06 | .05 |
| 93 | Reggie Jackson | .50 | .40 |
| 94 | Ron Jackson | .06 | .05 |
| 95 | Tommy John | .20 | .15 |
| 96 | Bruce Kison | .06 | .05 |
| 97 | Fred Lynn | .20 | .15 |
| 98 | Ed Ott | .06 | .05 |
| 99 | Steve Renko | .06 | .05 |
| 100 | Luis Sanchez | .06 | .05 |
| 101 | Rob Wilfong | .06 | .05 |
| 102 | Mike Witt | .15 | .11 |
| 103 | Geoff Zahn | .06 | .05 |
| 104 | Willie Aikens | .06 | .05 |
| 105 | Mike Armstrong | .06 | .05 |
| 106 | Vida Blue | .12 | .09 |
| 107 | *Bud Black*(FC) | .50 | .40 |
| 108 | George Brett | 3.00 | 2.25 |
| 109 | Bill Castro | .06 | .05 |
| 110 | Onix Concepcion | .06 | .05 |
| 111 | Dave Frost | .06 | .05 |
| 112 | Cesar Geronimo | .06 | .05 |
| 113 | Larry Gura | .06 | .05 |
| 114 | Steve Hammond | .06 | .05 |

| | MT | NR MT | | | MT | NR MT |
|---|---|---|---|---|---|---|
| 115 Don Hood | .06 | .05 | 180 Tom Burgmeier | | .06 | .05 |
| 116 Dennis Leonard | .08 | .06 | 181 Mark Clear | | .06 | .05 |
| 117 Jerry Martin | .06 | .05 | 182 Dennis Eckersley | | .12 | .09 |
| 118 Lee May | .08 | .06 | 183 Dwight Evans | | .15 | .11 |
| 119 Hal McRae | .12 | .09 | 184 Rich Gedman | | .08 | .06 |
| 120 Amos Otis | .08 | .06 | 185 Glenn Hoffman | | .06 | .05 |
| 121 Greg Pryor | .06 | .05 | 186 Bruce Hurst | | .10 | .08 |
| 122 Dan Quisenberry | .15 | .11 | 187 Carney Lansford | | .08 | .06 |
| 123 *Don Slaught*(FC) | .20 | .15 | 188 Rick Miller | | .06 | .05 |
| 124 Paul Splittorff | .06 | .05 | 189 Reid Nichols | | .06 | .05 |
| 125 U.L. Washington | .06 | .05 | 190 Bob Ojeda | | .12 | .09 |
| 126 John Wathan | .08 | .06 | 191 Tony Perez | | .20 | .15 |
| 127 Frank White | .10 | .08 | 192 Chuck Rainey | | .06 | .05 |
| 128 Willie Wilson | .15 | .11 | 193 Jerry Remy | | .06 | .05 |
| 129 Steve Bedrosian(FC) | | | 194 Jim Rice | | .40 | .30 |
| | .25 | .20 | 195 Bob Stanley | | .06 | .05 |
| 130 Bruce Benedict | .06 | .05 | 196 Dave Stapleton | | .06 | .05 |
| 131 Tommy Boggs | .06 | .05 | 197 Mike Torrez | | .08 | .06 |
| 132 Brett Butler(FC) | .15 | .11 | 198 John Tudor | | .10 | .08 |
| 133 Rick Camp | .06 | .05 | 199 Julio Valdez | | .06 | .05 |
| 134 Chris Chambliss | .08 | .06 | 200 Carl Yastrzemski | 1.00 | .70 |
| 135 Ken Dayley(FC) | .10 | .08 | 201 Dusty Baker | | .10 | .08 |
| 136 Gene Garber | .06 | .05 | 202 Joe Beckwith | | .06 | .05 |
| 137 Terry Harper | .06 | .05 | 203 *Greg Brock*(FC) | | .35 | .25 |
| 138 Bob Horner | .12 | .09 | 204 Ron Cey | | .12 | .09 |
| 139 Glenn Hubbard | .08 | .06 | 205 Terry Forster | | .08 | .06 |
| 140 Rufino Linares | .06 | .05 | 206 Steve Garvey | | .40 | .30 |
| 141 Rick Mahler | .08 | .06 | 207 Pedro Guerrero | | .25 | .20 |
| 142 Dale Murphy | .90 | .70 | 208 Burt Hooton | | .08 | .06 |
| 143 Phil Niekro | .30 | .25 | 209 Steve Howe | | .08 | .06 |
| 144 Pascual Perez | .08 | .06 | 210 Ken Landreaux | | .06 | .05 |
| 145 Biff Pocoroba | .06 | .05 | 211 Mike Marshall | | .20 | .15 |
| 146 Rafael Ramirez | .06 | .05 | 212 *Candy* | | | |
| 147 Jerry Royster | .06 | .05 | *Maldonado*(FC) | | .80 | .60 |
| 148 Ken Smith | .06 | .05 | 213 Rick Monday | | .10 | .08 |
| 149 Bob Walk | .08 | .06 | 214 Tom Niedenfuer | | .10 | .08 |
| 150 Claudell Washington | .08 | .06 | 215 Jorge Orta | | .06 | .05 |
| 151 Bob Watson | .08 | .06 | 216 Jerry Reuss | | .10 | .08 |
| 152 Larry Whisenton | .06 | .05 | 217 Ron Roenicke | | .06 | .05 |
| 153 Porfirio Altamirano | .06 | .05 | 218 Vicente Romo | | .06 | .05 |
| 154 Marty Bystrom | .06 | .05 | 219 Bill Russell | | .08 | .06 |
| 155 Steve Carlton | .50 | .40 | 220 Steve Sax | | .30 | .25 |
| 156 Larry Christenson | .06 | .05 | 221 Mike Scioscia | | .08 | .06 |
| 157 Ivan DeJesus | .06 | .05 | 222 Dave Stewart | | .70 | .50 |
| 158 John Denny | .06 | .05 | 223 Derrel Thomas | | .06 | .05 |
| 159 Bob Dernier(FC) | .10 | .08 | 224 Fernando Valenzuela | | | |
| 160 Bo Diaz | .08 | .06 | | | .30 | .25 |
| 161 Ed Farmer | .06 | .05 | 225 Bob Welch | | .12 | .09 |
| 162 Greg Gross | .06 | .05 | 226 Ricky Wright | | .06 | .05 |
| 163 Mike Krukow | .08 | .06 | 227 Steve Yeager | | .06 | .05 |
| 164 Garry Maddox | .10 | .08 | 228 Bill Almon | | .06 | .05 |
| 165 Gary Matthews | .10 | .08 | 229 Harold Baines | | .15 | .11 |
| 166 Tug McGraw | .12 | .09 | 230 Salome Barojas | | .06 | .05 |
| 167 Bob Molinaro | .06 | .05 | 231 Tony Bernazard | | .06 | .05 |
| 168 Sid Monge | .06 | .05 | 232 Britt Burns | | .06 | .05 |
| 169 Ron Reed | .06 | .05 | 233 Richard Dotson | | .10 | .08 |
| 170 Bill Robinson | .06 | .05 | 234 Ernesto Escarrega | | .06 | .05 |
| 171 Pete Rose | 1.00 | .70 | 235 Carlton Fisk | 1.00 | .70 |
| 172 Dick Ruthven | .06 | .05 | 236 Jerry Hairston | | .06 | .05 |
| 173 Mike Schmidt | 1.50 | 1.25 | 237 Kevin Hickey | | .06 | .05 |
| 174 Manny Trillo | .08 | .06 | 238 LaMarr Hoyt | | .06 | .05 |
| 175 Ozzie Virgil(FC) | .10 | .08 | 239 Steve Kemp | | .10 | .08 |
| 176 George Vukovich | .06 | .05 | 240 Jim Kern | | .06 | .05 |
| 177 Gary Allenson | .06 | .05 | 241 *Ron Kittle*(FC) | | .30 | .25 |
| 178 Luis Aponte | .06 | .05 | 242 Jerry Koosman | | .10 | .08 |
| 179 *Wade Boggs*(FC) | | | 243 Dennis Lamp | | .06 | .05 |
| | 20.00 | 15.00 | 244 Rudy Law | | .06 | .05 |

| | | MT | NR MT | | | | MT | NR MT |
|---|---|---|---|---|---|---|---|---|
| 245 | Vance Law | .08 | .06 | 311 | John Milner | | .06 | .05 |
| 246 | Ron LeFlore | .08 | .06 | 312 | Omar Moreno | | .06 | .05 |
| 247 | Greg Luzinski | .12 | .09 | 313 | Jim Morrison | | .06 | .05 |
| 248 | Tom Paciorek | .06 | .05 | 314 | Steve Nicosia | | .06 | .05 |
| 249 | Aurelio Rodriguez | .08 | .06 | 315 | Dave Parker | | .30 | .25 |
| 250 | Mike Squires | .06 | .05 | 316 | Tony Pena | | .10 | .08 |
| 251 | Steve Trout | .06 | .05 | 317 | Johnny Ray | | .12 | .09 |
| 252 | Jim Barr | .06 | .05 | 318 | Rick Rhoden | | .10 | .08 |
| 253 | Dave Bergman | .06 | .05 | 319 | Don Robinson | | .08 | .06 |
| 254 | Fred Breining | .06 | .05 | 320 | Enrique Romo | | .06 | .05 |
| 255 | Bob Brenly(FC) | .08 | .06 | 321 | Manny Sarmiento | | .06 | .05 |
| 256 | Jack Clark | .25 | .20 | 322 | Rod Scurry | | .06 | .05 |
| 257 | Chili Davis(FC) | .20 | .15 | 323 | Jim Smith | | .06 | .05 |
| 258 | Darrell Evans | .15 | .11 | 324 | Willie Stargell | | .40 | .30 |
| 259 | Alan Fowlkes | .06 | .05 | 325 | Jason Thompson | | .06 | .05 |
| 260 | Rich Gale | .06 | .05 | 326 | Kent Tekulve | | .08 | .06 |
| 261 | Atlee Hammaker(FC) | | | 327a | Tom Brookens (narrow (1/4") brown box at bottom on back) | | .30 | .25 |
| | | .12 | .09 | 327b | Tom Brookens (wide (1 1/4") brown box at bottom on back) | | .08 | .06 |
| 262 | Al Holland | .06 | .05 | | | | | |
| 263 | Duane Kuiper | .06 | .05 | 328 | Enos Cabell | | .06 | .05 |
| 264 | Bill Laskey | .06 | .05 | 329 | Kirk Gibson | | .40 | .30 |
| 265 | Gary Lavelle | .06 | .05 | 330 | Larry Herndon | | .08 | .06 |
| 266 | Johnnie LeMaster | .06 | .05 | 331 | Mike Ivie | | .06 | .05 |
| 267 | Renie Martin | .06 | .05 | 332 | *Howard Johnson*(FC) | | 6.00 | 4.50 |
| 268 | Milt May | .06 | .05 | 333 | Lynn Jones | | .06 | .05 |
| 269 | Greg Minton | .06 | .05 | 334 | Rick Leach | | .06 | .05 |
| 270 | Joe Morgan | .50 | .40 | 335 | Chet Lemon | | .08 | .06 |
| 271 | Tom O'Malley | .06 | .05 | 336 | Jack Morris | | .80 | .60 |
| 272 | Reggie Smith | .10 | .08 | 337 | Lance Parrish | | .35 | .25 |
| 273 | Guy Sularz | .06 | .05 | 338 | Larry Pashnick | | .06 | .05 |
| 274 | Champ Summers | .06 | .05 | 339 | Dan Petry | | .08 | .06 |
| 275 | Max Venable | .06 | .05 | 340 | Dave Rozema | | .06 | .05 |
| 276 | Jim Wohlford | .06 | .05 | 341 | Dave Rucker | | .06 | .05 |
| 277 | Ray Burris | .06 | .05 | 342 | Elias Sosa | | .06 | .05 |
| 278 | Gary Carter | .35 | .25 | 343 | Dave Tobik | | .06 | .05 |
| 279 | Warren Cromartie | .06 | .05 | 344 | Alan Trammell | | .40 | .30 |
| 280 | Andre Dawson | 1.25 | .90 | 345 | Jerry Turner | | .06 | .05 |
| 281 | Terry Francona | .06 | .05 | 346 | Jerry Ujdur | | .06 | .05 |
| 282 | Doug Flynn | .06 | .05 | 347 | Pat Underwood | | .06 | .05 |
| 283 | Woody Fryman | .08 | .06 | 348 | Lou Whitaker | | .40 | .30 |
| 284 | Bill Gullickson | .06 | .05 | 349 | Milt Wilcox | | .06 | .05 |
| 285 | Wallace Johnson | .06 | .05 | 350 | *Glenn Wilson*(FC) | | .35 | .25 |
| 286 | Charlie Lea | .06 | .05 | | | | | |
| 287 | Randy Lerch | .06 | .05 | 351 | John Wockenfuss | | .06 | .05 |
| 288 | Brad Mills | .06 | .05 | 352 | Kurt Bevacqua | | .06 | .05 |
| 289 | Dan Norman | .06 | .05 | 353 | Juan Bonilla | | .06 | .05 |
| 290 | Al Oliver | .15 | .11 | 354 | Floyd Chiffer | | .06 | .05 |
| 291 | David Palmer | .06 | .05 | 355 | Luis DeLeon | | .06 | .05 |
| 292 | Tim Raines | .35 | .25 | 356 | *Dave Dravecky*(FC) | | .60 | .45 |
| 293 | Jeff Reardon | .80 | .60 | | | | | |
| 294 | Steve Rogers | .08 | .06 | 357 | Dave Edwards | | .06 | .05 |
| 295 | Scott Sanderson | .06 | .05 | 358 | Juan Eichelberger | | .06 | .05 |
| 296 | Dan Schatzeder | .06 | .05 | 359 | Tim Flannery | | .06 | .05 |
| 297 | Bryn Smith | .08 | .06 | 360 | *Tony Gwynn*(FC) | | 25.00 | 18.00 |
| 298 | Chris Speier | .06 | .05 | | | | | |
| 299 | Tim Wallach | .20 | .15 | 361 | Ruppert Jones | | .06 | .05 |
| 300 | Jerry White | .06 | .05 | 362 | Terry Kennedy | | .08 | .06 |
| 301 | Joel Youngblood | .06 | .05 | 363 | Joe Lefebvre | | .06 | .05 |
| 302 | Ross Baumgarten | .06 | .05 | 364 | Sixto Lezcano | | .06 | .05 |
| 303 | Dale Berra | .06 | .05 | 365 | Tim Lollar | | .06 | .05 |
| 304 | John Candelaria | .10 | .08 | 366 | Gary Lucas | | .06 | .05 |
| 305 | Dick Davis | .06 | .05 | 367 | John Montefusco | | .06 | .05 |
| 306 | Mike Easler | .08 | .06 | 368 | Broderick Perkins | | .06 | .05 |
| 307 | Richie Hebner | .06 | .05 | | | | | |
| 308 | Lee Lacy | .06 | .05 | | | | | |
| 309 | Bill Madlock | .12 | .09 | | | | | |
| 310 | Larry McWilliams | .06 | .05 | | | | | |

| | MT | NR MT | | | MT | NR MT |
|---|---|---|---|---|---|---|
| 369 | Joe Pittman | .06 | .05 | 434 | Joey McLaughlin | .06 | .05 |
| 370 | Gene Richards | .06 | .05 | 435 | Lloyd Moseby | .12 | .09 |
| 371 | Luis Salazar | .06 | .05 | 436 | Rance Mulliniks | .06 | .05 |
| 372 | Eric Show(FC) | .30 | .25 | 437 | Dale Murray | .06 | .05 |
| 373 | Garry Templeton | .10 | .08 | 438 | Wayne Nordhagen | .06 | .05 |
| 374 | Chris Welsh | .06 | .05 | 439 | Gene Petralli(FC) | | |
| 375 | Alan Wiggins | .06 | .05 | | | .15 | .11 |
| 376 | Rick Cerone | .06 | .05 | 440 | Hosken Powell | .06 | .05 |
| 377 | Dave Collins | .08 | .06 | 441 | Dave Stieb | .12 | .09 |
| 378 | Roger Erickson | .06 | .05 | 442 | Willie Upshaw | .08 | .06 |
| 379 | George Frazier | .06 | .05 | 443 | Ernie Whitt | .08 | .06 |
| 380 | Oscar Gamble | .08 | .06 | 444 | Al Woods | .06 | .05 |
| 381 | Goose Gossage | .20 | .15 | 445 | Alan Ashby | .06 | .05 |
| 382 | Ken Griffey | .12 | .09 | 446 | Jose Cruz | .12 | .09 |
| 383 | Ron Guidry | .25 | .20 | 447 | Kiko Garcia | .06 | .05 |
| 384 | Dave LaRoche | .06 | .05 | 448 | Phil Garner | .08 | .06 |
| 385 | Rudy May | .06 | .05 | 449 | Danny Heep | .06 | .05 |
| 386 | John Mayberry | .08 | .06 | 450 | Art Howe | .06 | .05 |
| 387 | Lee Mazzilli | .08 | .06 | 451 | Bob Knepper | .08 | .06 |
| 388 | Mike Morgan(FC) | .12 | .09 | 452 | Alan Knicely | .06 | .05 |
| 389 | Jerry Mumphrey | .06 | .05 | 453 | Ray Knight | .10 | .08 |
| 390 | Bobby Murcer | .10 | .08 | 454 | Frank LaCorte | .06 | .05 |
| 391 | Graig Nettles | .15 | .11 | 455 | Mike LaCoss | .06 | .05 |
| 392 | Lou Piniella | .12 | .09 | 456 | Randy Moffitt | .06 | .05 |
| 393 | Willie Randolph | .10 | .08 | 457 | Joe Niekro | .12 | .09 |
| 394 | Shane Rawley | .10 | .08 | 458 | Terry Puhl | .06 | .05 |
| 395 | Dave Righetti | .25 | .20 | 459 | Luis Pujols | .06 | .05 |
| 396 | Andre Robertson | .06 | .05 | 460 | Craig Reynolds | .06 | .05 |
| 397 | Roy Smalley | .06 | .05 | 461 | Bert Roberge | .06 | .05 |
| 398 | Dave Winfield | 2.00 | 1.50 | 462 | Vern Ruhle | .06 | .05 |
| 399 | Butch Wynegar | .06 | .05 | 463 | Nolan Ryan | 7.00 | 5.25 |
| 400 | Chris Bando | .06 | .05 | 464 | Joe Sambito | .06 | .05 |
| 401 | Alan Bannister | .06 | .05 | 465 | Tony Scott | .06 | .05 |
| 402 | Len Barker | .08 | .06 | 466 | Dave Smith | .08 | .06 |
| 403 | Tom Brennan | .06 | .05 | 467 | Harry Spilman | .06 | .05 |
| 404 | Carmelo Castillo(FC) | | | 468 | Dickie Thon | .08 | .06 |
| | | .12 | .09 | 469 | Denny Walling | .06 | .05 |
| 405 | Miguel Dilone | .06 | .05 | 470 | Larry Andersen | .06 | .05 |
| 406 | Jerry Dybzinski | .06 | .05 | 471 | Floyd Bannister | .10 | .08 |
| 407 | Mike Fischlin | .06 | .05 | 472 | Jim Beattie | .06 | .05 |
| 408 | Ed Glynn (photo actually | | | 473 | Bruce Bochte | .06 | .05 |
| | Bud Anderson) | .06 | .05 | 474 | Manny Castillo | .06 | .05 |
| 409 | Mike Hargrove | .06 | .05 | 475 | Bill Caudill | .06 | .05 |
| 410 | Toby Harrah | .08 | .06 | 476 | Bryan Clark | .06 | .05 |
| 411 | Ron Hassey | .06 | .05 | 477 | Al Cowens | .06 | .05 |
| 412 | Von Hayes | .15 | .11 | 478 | Julio Cruz | .06 | .05 |
| 413 | Rick Manning | .06 | .05 | 479 | Todd Cruz | .06 | .05 |
| 414 | Bake McBride | .06 | .05 | 480 | Gary Gray | .06 | .05 |
| 415 | Larry Milbourne | .06 | .05 | 481 | Dave Henderson(FC) | | |
| 416 | Bill Nahorodny | .06 | .05 | | | .20 | .15 |
| 417 | Jack Perconte | .06 | .05 | 482 | Mike Moore(FC) | | |
| 418 | Lary Sorensen | .06 | .05 | | | 1.00 | .70 |
| 419 | Dan Spillner | .06 | .05 | 483 | Gaylord Perry | .40 | .30 |
| 420 | Rick Sutcliffe | .12 | .09 | 484 | Dave Revering | .06 | .05 |
| 421 | Andre Thornton | .10 | .08 | 485 | Joe Simpson | .06 | .05 |
| 422 | Rick Waits | .06 | .05 | 486 | Mike Stanton | .06 | .05 |
| 423 | Eddie Whitson | .06 | .05 | 487 | Rick Sweet | .06 | .05 |
| 424 | Jesse Barfield(FC) | .60 | .45 | 488 | Ed Vande Berg(FC) | | |
| 425 | Barry Bonnell | .06 | .05 | | | .10 | .08 |
| 426 | Jim Clancy | .08 | .06 | 489 | Richie Zisk | .08 | .06 |
| 427 | Damaso Garcia | .06 | .05 | 490 | Doug Bird | .06 | .05 |
| 428 | Jerry Garvin | .06 | .05 | 491 | Larry Bowa | .12 | .09 |
| 429 | Alfredo Griffin | .08 | .06 | 492 | Bill Buckner | .12 | .09 |
| 430 | Garth Iorg | .06 | .05 | 493 | Bill Campbell | .06 | .05 |
| 431 | Roy Lee Jackson | .06 | .05 | 494 | Jody Davis | .10 | .08 |
| 432 | Luis Leal | .06 | .05 | 495 | Leon Durham | .08 | .06 |
| 433 | Buck Martinez | .06 | .05 | 496 | Steve Henderson | .06 | .05 |

| | MT | NR MT |
|---|---|---|
| 497 Willie Hernandez | .08 | .06 |
| 498 Ferguson Jenkins | .15 | .11 |
| 499 Jay Johnstone | .08 | .06 |
| 500 Junior Kennedy | .06 | .05 |
| 501 Randy Martz | .06 | .05 |
| 502 Jerry Morales | .06 | .05 |
| 503 Keith Moreland | .08 | .06 |
| 504 Dickie Noles | .06 | .05 |
| 505 Mike Proly | .06 | .05 |
| 506 Allen Ripley | .06 | .05 |
| 507 Ryne Sandberg(FC) | | |
| | 35.00 | 27.00 |
| 508 Lee Smith | 2.00 | 1.50 |
| 509 Pat Tabler(FC) | .15 | .11 |
| 510 Dick Tidrow | .06 | .05 |
| 511 Bump Wills | .06 | .05 |
| 512 Gary Woods | .06 | .05 |
| 513 Tony Armas | .10 | .08 |
| 514 Dave Beard | .06 | .05 |
| 515 Jeff Burroughs | .08 | .06 |
| 516 John D'Acquisto | .06 | .05 |
| 517 Wayne Gross | .06 | .05 |
| 518 Mike Heath | .06 | .05 |
| 519 Rickey Henderson | 4.00 | 3.00 |
| 520 Cliff Johnson | .06 | .05 |
| 521 Matt Keough | .06 | .05 |
| 522 Brian Kingman | .06 | .05 |
| 523 Rick Langford | .06 | .05 |
| 524 Davey Lopes | .10 | .08 |
| 525 Steve McCatty | .06 | .05 |
| 526 Dave McKay | .06 | .05 |
| 527 Dan Meyer | .06 | .05 |
| 528 Dwayne Murphy | .08 | .06 |
| 529 Jeff Newman | .06 | .05 |
| 530 Mike Norris | .06 | .05 |
| 531 Bob Owchinko | .06 | .05 |
| 532 Joe Rudi | .10 | .08 |
| 533 Jimmy Sexton | .06 | .05 |
| 534 Fred Stanley | .06 | .05 |
| 535 Tom Underwood | .06 | .05 |
| 536 Neil Allen | .06 | .05 |
| 537 Wally Backman | .08 | .06 |
| 538 Bob Bailor | .06 | .05 |
| 539 Hubie Brooks | .12 | .09 |
| 540 Carlos Diaz | .06 | .05 |
| 541 Pete Falcone | .06 | .05 |
| 542 George Foster | .15 | .11 |
| 543 Ron Gardenhire | .06 | .05 |
| 544 Brian Giles | .06 | .05 |
| 545 Ron Hodges | .06 | .05 |
| 546 Randy Jones | .08 | .06 |
| 547 Mike Jorgensen | .06 | .05 |
| 548 Dave Kingman | .15 | .11 |
| 549 Ed Lynch | .06 | .05 |
| 550 Jesse Orosco(FC) | .15 | .11 |
| 551 Rick Ownbey | .06 | .05 |
| 552 Charlie Puleo(FC) | | |
| | .12 | .09 |
| 553 Gary Rajsich | .06 | .05 |
| 554 Mike Scott | .15 | .11 |
| 555 Rusty Staub | .10 | .08 |
| 556 John Stearns | .06 | .05 |
| 557 Craig Swan | .06 | .05 |
| 558 Ellis Valentine | .06 | .05 |
| 559 Tom Veryzer | .06 | .05 |
| 560 Mookie Wilson | .10 | .08 |
| 561 Pat Zachry | .06 | .05 |

| | MT | NR MT |
|---|---|---|
| 562 Buddy Bell | .12 | .09 |
| 563 John Butcher | .06 | .05 |
| 564 Steve Comer | .06 | .05 |
| 565 Danny Darwin | .06 | .05 |
| 566 Bucky Dent | .10 | .08 |
| 567 John Grubb | .06 | .05 |
| 568 Rick Honeycutt | .06 | .05 |
| 569 Dave Hostetler | .06 | .05 |
| 570 Charlie Hough | .10 | .08 |
| 571 Lamar Johnson | .06 | .05 |
| 572 Jon Matlack | .08 | .06 |
| 573 Paul Mirabella | .06 | .05 |
| 574 Larry Parrish | .10 | .08 |
| 575 Mike Richardt | .06 | .05 |
| 576 Mickey Rivers | .08 | .06 |
| 577 Billy Sample | .06 | .05 |
| 578 Dave Schmidt(FC) | | |
| | .10 | .08 |
| 579 Bill Stein | .06 | .05 |
| 580 Jim Sundberg | .08 | .06 |
| 581 Frank Tanana | .10 | .08 |
| 582 Mark Wagner | .06 | .05 |
| 583 George Wright | .06 | .05 |
| 584 Johnny Bench | 1.00 | .70 |
| 585 Bruce Berenyi | .06 | .05 |
| 586 Larry Biittner | .06 | .05 |
| 587 Cesar Cedeno | .12 | .09 |
| 588 Dave Concepcion | .12 | .09 |
| 589 Dan Driessen | .08 | .06 |
| 590 Greg Harris(FC) | .08 | .06 |
| 591 Ben Hayes | .06 | .05 |
| 592 Paul Householder | .06 | .05 |
| 593 Tom Hume | .06 | .05 |
| 594 Wayne Krenchicki | .06 | .05 |
| 595 Rafael Landestoy | .06 | .05 |
| 596 Charlie Leibrandt | .08 | .06 |
| 597 Eddie Milner(FC) | .10 | .08 |
| 598 Ron Oester | .06 | .05 |
| 599 Frank Pastore | .06 | .05 |
| 600 Joe Price | .06 | .05 |
| 601 Tom Seaver | 1.00 | .70 |
| 602 Bob Shirley | .06 | .05 |
| 603 Mario Soto | .08 | .06 |
| 604 Alex Trevino | .06 | .05 |
| 605 Mike Vail | .06 | .05 |
| 606 Duane Walker | .06 | .05 |
| 607 Tom Brunansky(FC) | .25 | .20 |
| 608 Bobby Castillo | .06 | .05 |
| 609 John Castino | .06 | .05 |
| 610 Ron Davis | .06 | .05 |
| 611 Lenny Faedo | .06 | .05 |
| 612 Terry Felton | .06 | .05 |
| 613 Gary Gaetti(FC) | .80 | .60 |
| 614 Mickey Hatcher | .08 | .06 |
| 615 Brad Havens | .06 | .05 |
| 616 Kent Hrbek(FC) | 1.00 | .70 |
| 617 Randy Johnson | .06 | .05 |
| 618 Tim Laudner(FC) | .12 | .09 |
| 619 Jeff Little | .06 | .05 |
| 620 Bob Mitchell | .06 | .05 |
| 621 Jack O'Connor | .06 | .05 |
| 622 John Pacella | .06 | .05 |
| 623 Pete Redfern | .06 | .05 |
| 624 Jesus Vega | .06 | .05 |
| 625 Frank Viola(FC) | 4.00 | 3.00 |
| 626 Ron Washington | .06 | .05 |
| 627 Gary Ward | .08 | .06 |

| | | MT | NR MT |
|---|---|---|---|
| 628 | Al Williams | .06 | .05 |
| 629 | Red Sox All-Stars (Mark Clear, Dennis Eckersley, Carl Yastrzemski) | .25 | .20 |
| 630 | 300 Career Wins (Terry Bulling, Gaylord Perry) | .15 | .11 |
| 631 | Pride of Venezuela (Dave Concepcion, Manny Trillo) | .10 | .08 |
| 632 | All-Star Infielders (Buddy Bell, Robin Yount) | .15 | .11 |
| 633 | Mr. Vet & Mr. Rookie (Kent Hrbek, Dave Winfield) | .25 | .20 |
| 634 | Fountain of Youth (Pete Rose, Willie Stargell) | .40 | .30 |
| 635 | Big Chiefs (Toby Harrah, Andre Thornton) | .08 | .06 |
| 636 | "Smith Bros." (Lonnie Smith, Ozzie Smith) | .10 | .08 |
| 637 | Base Stealers' Threat (Gary Carter, Bo Diaz) | .15 | .11 |
| 638 | All-Star Catchers (Gary Carter, Carlton Fisk) | .20 | .15 |
| 639 | The Silver Shoe (Rickey Henderson) | 2.00 | 1.50 |
| 640 | Home Run Threats (Reggie Jackson, Ben Oglivie) | .25 | .20 |
| 641 | Two Teams - Same Day (Joel Youngblood) | .08 | |
| 642 | Last Perfect Game (Len Barker, Ron Hassey) | .08 | .06 |
| 643 | Blue (Vida Blue) | .10 | .08 |
| 644 | Black & (Bud Black) | .10 | .08 |
| 645 | Power (Reggie Jackson) | .30 | .25 |
| 646 | Speed & (Rickey Henderson) | .30 | .25 |
| 647 | Checklist 1-51 | .06 | .05 |
| 648 | Checklist 52-103 | .06 | .05 |
| 649 | Checklist 104-152 | .06 | .05 |
| 650 | Checklist 153-200 | .06 | .05 |
| 651 | Checklist 201-251 | .06 | .05 |
| 652 | Checklist 252-301 | .06 | .05 |
| 653 | Checklist 302-351 | .06 | .05 |
| 654 | Checklist 352-399 | .06 | .05 |
| 655 | Checklist 400-444 | .06 | .05 |
| 656 | Checklist 445-489 | .06 | .05 |
| 657 | Checklist 490-535 | .06 | .05 |
| 658 | Checklist 536-583 | .06 | .05 |
| 659 | Checklist 584-628 | .06 | .05 |
| 660 | Checklist 629-646 | .06 | .05 |

## 1984 Fleer

The 1984 Fleer set contained 660 cards for the fourth consecutive year. The cards, which measure 2-1/2" by 3-1/2", feature a color photo surrounded by four white borders and two blue stripes. The top stripe contains the word "Fleer" with the lower carrying the player's name. The card backs contain a small black and white photo of the player and are done in blue ink on white stock. The set was issued with team logo stickers.

| | | MT | NR MT |
|---|---|---|---|
| Complete Set: | | 200.00 | 150.00 |
| Common Player: | | .08 | .06 |
| 1 | Mike Boddicker(FC) | .20 | .15 |
| 2 | Al Bumbry | .10 | .08 |
| 3 | Todd Cruz | .08 | .06 |
| 4 | Rich Dauer | .08 | .06 |
| 5 | Storm Davis | .12 | .09 |
| 6 | Rick Dempsey | .10 | .08 |
| 7 | Jim Dwyer | .08 | .06 |
| 8 | Mike Flanagan | .12 | .09 |
| 9 | Dan Ford | .08 | .06 |
| 10 | John Lowenstein | .08 | .06 |
| 11 | Dennis Martinez | .10 | .08 |
| 12 | Tippy Martinez | .08 | .06 |
| 13 | Scott McGregor | .10 | .08 |
| 14 | Eddie Murray | 2.00 | 1.50 |
| 15 | Joe Nolan | .08 | .06 |
| 16 | Jim Palmer | 1.25 | .90 |
| 17 | Cal Ripken, Jr. | 18.00 | 13.50 |
| 18 | Gary Roenicke | .08 | .06 |
| 19 | Lenn Sakata | .08 | .06 |
| 20 | *John Shelby*(FC) | .25 | .20 |
| 21 | Ken Singleton | .12 | .09 |
| 22 | Sammy Stewart | .08 | .06 |
| 23 | Tim Stoddard | .08 | .06 |
| 24 | Marty Bystrom | .08 | .06 |
| 25 | Steve Carlton | 2.00 | 1.50 |
| 26 | Ivan DeJesus | .08 | .06 |
| 27 | John Denny | .08 | .06 |
| 28 | Bob Dernier | .08 | .06 |
| 29 | Bo Diaz | .10 | .08 |
| 30 | Kiko Garcia | .08 | .06 |
| 31 | Greg Gross | .08 | .06 |
| 32 | *Kevin Gross*(FC) | .35 | .25 |
| 33 | Von Hayes | .15 | .11 |
| 34 | Willie Hernandez | .12 | .09 |
| 35 | Al Holland | .08 | .06 |
| 36 | *Charles Hudson*(FC) | .20 | .15 |
| 37 | Joe Lefebvre | .08 | .06 |
| 38 | Sixto Lezcano | .08 | .06 |
| 39 | Garry Maddox | .10 | .08 |
| 40 | Gary Matthews | .12 | .09 |
| 41 | Len Matuszek | .08 | .06 |
| 42 | Tug McGraw | .12 | .09 |
| 43 | Joe Morgan | .40 | .30 |
| 44 | Tony Perez | .20 | .15 |

| | | MT | NR MT |
|---|---|---|---|
| 45 | Ron Reed | .08 | .06 |
| 46 | Pete Rose | 2.00 | 1.50 |
| 47 | Juan Samuel(FC) | | |
| | | 2.50 | 2.00 |
| 48 | Mike Schmidt | 8.00 | 6.00 |
| 49 | Ozzie Virgil | .08 | .06 |
| 50 | Juan Agosto(FC) | .15 | .11 |
| 51 | Harold Baines | .25 | .20 |
| 52 | Floyd Bannister | .12 | .09 |
| 53 | Salome Barojas | .08 | .06 |
| 54 | Britt Burns | .08 | .06 |
| 55 | Julio Cruz | .08 | .06 |
| 56 | Richard Dotson | .12 | .09 |
| 57 | Jerry Dybzinski | .08 | .06 |
| 58 | Carlton Fisk | 2.50 | 2.00 |
| 59 | Scott Fletcher(FC) | .15 | .11 |
| 60 | Jerry Hairston | .08 | .06 |
| 61 | Kevin Hickey | .08 | .06 |
| 62 | Marc Hill | .08 | .06 |
| 63 | LaMarr Hoyt | .08 | .06 |
| 64 | Ron Kittle | .15 | .11 |
| 65 | Jerry Koosman | .12 | .09 |
| 66 | Dennis Lamp | .08 | .06 |
| 67 | Rudy Law | .08 | .06 |
| 68 | Vance Law | .10 | .08 |
| 69 | Greg Luzinski | .12 | .09 |
| 70 | Tom Paciorek | .08 | .06 |
| 71 | Mike Squires | .08 | .06 |
| 72 | Dick Tidrow | .08 | .06 |
| 73 | Greg Walker(FC) | .45 | .35 |
| 74 | Glenn Abbott | .08 | .06 |
| 75 | Howard Bailey | .08 | .06 |
| 76 | Doug Bair | .08 | .06 |
| 77 | Juan Berenguer | .08 | .06 |
| 78 | Tom Brookens | .08 | .06 |
| 79 | Enos Cabell | .08 | .06 |
| 80 | Kirk Gibson | .40 | .30 |
| 81 | John Grubb | .08 | .06 |
| 82 | Larry Herndon | .10 | .08 |
| 83 | Wayne Krenchicki | .08 | .06 |
| 84 | Rick Leach | .08 | .06 |
| 85 | Chet Lemon | .10 | .08 |
| 86 | Aurelio Lopez | .08 | .06 |
| 87 | Jack Morris | 2.00 | 1.50 |
| 88 | Lance Parrish | .35 | .25 |
| 89 | Dan Petry | .10 | .08 |
| 90 | Dave Rozema | .08 | .06 |
| 91 | Alan Trammell | .40 | .30 |
| 92 | Lou Whitaker | .40 | .30 |
| 93 | Milt Wilcox | .08 | .06 |
| 94 | Glenn Wilson | .10 | .08 |
| 95 | John Wockenfuss | .08 | .06 |
| 96 | Dusty Baker | .12 | .09 |
| 97 | Joe Beckwith | .08 | .06 |
| 98 | Greg Brock | .12 | .09 |
| 99 | Jack Fimple | .08 | .06 |
| 100 | Pedro Guerrero | .35 | .25 |
| 101 | Rick Honeycutt | .08 | .06 |
| 102 | Burt Hooton | .10 | .08 |
| 103 | Steve Howe | .12 | .09 |
| 104 | Ken Landreaux | .08 | .06 |
| 105 | Mike Marshall | .15 | .11 |
| 106 | Rick Monday | .10 | .08 |
| 107 | Jose Morales | .08 | .06 |
| 108 | Tom Niedenfuer | .10 | .08 |
| 109 | Alejandro Pena(FC) | | |
| | | .30 | .25 |

| | | MT | NR MT |
|---|---|---|---|
| 110 | Jerry Reuss | .12 | .09 |
| 111 | Bill Russell | .10 | .08 |
| 112 | Steve Sax | .20 | .15 |
| 113 | Mike Scioscia | .10 | .08 |
| 114 | Derrel Thomas | .08 | .06 |
| 115 | Fernando Valenzuela | | |
| | | .40 | .30 |
| 116 | Bob Welch | .15 | .11 |
| 117 | Steve Yeager | .08 | .06 |
| 118 | Pat Zachry | .08 | .06 |
| 119 | Don Baylor | .15 | .11 |
| 120 | Bert Campaneris | .12 | .09 |
| 121 | Rick Cerone | .08 | .06 |
| 122 | Ray Fontenot(FC) | | |
| | | .10 | .08 |
| 123 | George Frazier | .08 | .06 |
| 124 | Oscar Gamble | .10 | .08 |
| 125 | Goose Gossage | .25 | .20 |
| 126 | Ken Griffey | .12 | .09 |
| 127 | Ron Guidry | .30 | .25 |
| 128 | Jay Howell(FC) | .15 | .11 |
| 129 | Steve Kemp | .10 | .08 |
| 130 | Matt Keough | .08 | .06 |
| 131 | Don Mattingly(FC) | | |
| | | 20.00 | 15.00 |
| 132 | John Montefusco | .08 | .06 |
| 133 | Omar Moreno | .08 | .06 |
| 134 | Dale Murray | .08 | .06 |
| 135 | Graig Nettles | .20 | .15 |
| 136 | Lou Piniella | .15 | .11 |
| 137 | Willie Randolph | .12 | .09 |
| 138 | Shane Rawley | .12 | .09 |
| 139 | Dave Righetti | .25 | .20 |
| 140 | Andre Robertson | .08 | .06 |
| 141 | Bob Shirley | .08 | .06 |
| 142 | Roy Smalley | .08 | .06 |
| 143 | Dave Winfield | 4.00 | 3.00 |
| 144 | Butch Wynegar | .08 | .06 |
| 145 | Jim Acker(FC) | .12 | .09 |
| 146 | Doyle Alexander | .12 | .09 |
| 147 | Jesse Barfield | .25 | .20 |
| 148 | Jorge Bell | 2.00 | 1.50 |
| 149 | Barry Bonnell | .08 | .06 |
| 150 | Jim Clancy | .10 | .08 |
| 151 | Dave Collins | .10 | .08 |
| 152 | Tony Fernandez(FC) | | |
| | | 4.00 | 3.00 |
| 153 | Damaso Garcia | .08 | .06 |
| 154 | Dave Geisel | .08 | .06 |
| 155 | Jim Gott(FC) | .10 | .08 |
| 156 | Alfredo Griffin | .10 | .08 |
| 157 | Garth Iorg | .08 | .06 |
| 158 | Roy Lee Jackson | .08 | .06 |
| 159 | Cliff Johnson | .08 | .06 |
| 160 | Luis Leal | .08 | .06 |
| 161 | Buck Martinez | .08 | .06 |
| 162 | Joey McLaughlin | .08 | .06 |
| 163 | Randy Moffitt | .08 | .06 |
| 164 | Lloyd Moseby | .12 | .09 |
| 165 | Rance Mulliniks | .08 | .06 |
| 166 | Jorge Orta | .08 | .06 |
| 167 | Dave Stieb | .15 | .11 |
| 168 | Willie Upshaw | .10 | .08 |
| 169 | Ernie Whitt | .10 | .08 |
| 170 | Len Barker | .10 | .08 |
| 171 | Steve Bedrosian | .12 | .09 |
| 172 | Bruce Benedict | .08 | .06 |

| # | Player | MT | NR MT |
|---|--------|----|-------|
| 173 | Brett Butler | .10 | .08 |
| 174 | Rick Camp | .08 | .06 |
| 175 | Chris Chambliss | .10 | .08 |
| 176 | Ken Dayley | .08 | .06 |
| 177 | Pete Falcone | .08 | .06 |
| 178 | Terry Forster | .10 | .08 |
| 179 | Gene Garber | .08 | .06 |
| 180 | Terry Harper | .08 | .06 |
| 181 | Bob Horner | .12 | .09 |
| 182 | Glenn Hubbard | .10 | .08 |
| 183 | Randy Johnson | .08 | .06 |
| 184 | *Craig McMurtry*(FC) | .12 | .09 |
| 185 | Donnie Moore(FC) | .10 | .08 |
| 186 | Dale Murphy | 1.00 | .70 |
| 187 | Phil Niekro | .30 | .25 |
| 188 | Pascual Perez | .10 | .08 |
| 189 | Biff Pocoroba | .08 | .06 |
| 190 | Rafael Ramirez | .08 | .06 |
| 191 | Jerry Royster | .08 | .06 |
| 192 | Claudell Washington | .10 | .08 |
| 193 | Bob Watson | .10 | .08 |
| 194 | Jerry Augustine | .08 | .06 |
| 195 | Mark Brouhard | .08 | .06 |
| 196 | Mike Caldwell | .08 | .06 |
| 197 | *Tom Candiotti*(FC) | 1.00 | .70 |
| 198 | Cecil Cooper | .15 | .11 |
| 199 | Rollie Fingers | .25 | .20 |
| 200 | Jim Gantner | .10 | .08 |
| 201 | Bob Gibson | .08 | .06 |
| 202 | Moose Haas | .08 | .06 |
| 203 | Roy Howell | .08 | .06 |
| 204 | Pete Ladd | .08 | .06 |
| 205 | Rick Manning | .08 | .06 |
| 206 | Bob McClure | .08 | .06 |
| 207 | Paul Molitor | .20 | .15 |
| 208 | Don Money | .08 | .06 |
| 209 | Charlie Moore | .08 | .06 |
| 210 | Ben Oglivie | .10 | .08 |
| 211 | Chuck Porter | .08 | .06 |
| 212 | Ed Romero | .08 | .06 |
| 213 | Ted Simmons | .15 | .11 |
| 214 | Jim Slaton | .08 | .06 |
| 215 | Don Sutton | .30 | .25 |
| 216 | Tom Tellmann | .08 | .06 |
| 217 | Pete Vuckovich | .10 | .08 |
| 218 | Ned Yost | .08 | .06 |
| 219 | Robin Yount | 5.00 | 3.75 |
| 220 | Alan Ashby | .08 | .06 |
| 221 | Kevin Bass(FC) | .20 | .15 |
| 222 | Jose Cruz | .12 | .09 |
| 223 | *Bill Dawley*(FC) | .10 | .08 |
| 224 | Frank DiPino | .08 | .06 |
| 225 | *Bill Doran*(FC) | 1.00 | .70 |
| 226 | Phil Garner | .10 | .08 |
| 227 | Art Howe | .08 | .06 |
| 228 | Bob Knepper | .10 | .08 |
| 229 | Ray Knight | .12 | .09 |
| 230 | Frank LaCorte | .08 | .06 |
| 231 | Mike LaCoss | .08 | .06 |
| 232 | Mike Madden | .08 | .06 |
| 233 | Jerry Mumphrey | .08 | .06 |
| 235 | Terry Puhl | .08 | .06 |
| 236 | Luis Pujols | .08 | .06 |
| 237 | Craig Reynolds | .08 | .06 |
| 238 | Vern Ruhle | .08 | .06 |
| 239 | Nolan Ryan | 15.00 | 11.00 |
| 240 | Mike Scott | .20 | .15 |
| 241 | Tony Scott | .08 | .06 |
| 242 | Dave Smith | .10 | .08 |
| 243 | Dickie Thon | .10 | .08 |
| 244 | Denny Walling | .08 | .06 |
| 245 | Dale Berra | .08 | .06 |
| 246 | Jim Bibby | .08 | .06 |
| 247 | John Candelaria | .12 | .09 |
| 248 | *Jose DeLeon*(FC) | .50 | .40 |
| 249 | Mike Easler | .10 | .08 |
| 250 | Cecilio Guante(FC) | .10 | .08 |
| 251 | Richie Hebner | .08 | .06 |
| 252 | Lee Lacy | .08 | .06 |
| 253 | Bill Madlock | .12 | .09 |
| 254 | Milt May | .08 | .06 |
| 255 | Lee Mazzilli | .10 | .08 |
| 256 | Larry McWilliams | .08 | .06 |
| 257 | Jim Morrison | .08 | .06 |
| 258 | Dave Parker | .30 | .25 |
| 259 | Tony Pena | .12 | .09 |
| 260 | Johnny Ray | .12 | .09 |
| 261 | Rick Rhoden | .12 | .09 |
| 262 | Don Robinson | .10 | .08 |
| 263 | Manny Sarmiento | .08 | .06 |
| 264 | Rod Scurry | .08 | .06 |
| 265 | Kent Tekulve | .10 | .08 |
| 266 | Gene Tenace | .10 | .08 |
| 267 | Jason Thompson | .08 | .06 |
| 268 | *Lee Tunnell*(FC) | .10 | .08 |
| 269 | *Marvell Wynne*(FC) | .20 | .15 |
| 270 | Ray Burris | .08 | .06 |
| 271 | Gary Carter | .40 | .30 |
| 272 | Warren Cromartie | .08 | .06 |
| 273 | Andre Dawson | 3.00 | 2.25 |
| 274 | Doug Flynn | .08 | .06 |
| 275 | Terry Francona | .08 | .06 |
| 276 | Bill Gullickson | .08 | .06 |
| 277 | Bob James | .08 | .06 |
| 278 | Charlie Lea | .08 | .06 |
| 279 | Bryan Little | .08 | .06 |
| 280 | Al Oliver | .20 | .15 |
| 281 | Tim Raines | .70 | .50 |
| 282 | Bobby Ramos | .08 | .06 |
| 283 | Jeff Reardon | .15 | .11 |
| 284 | Steve Rogers | .10 | .08 |
| 285 | Scott Sanderson | .08 | .06 |
| 286 | Dan Schatzeder | .08 | .06 |
| 287 | Bryn Smith | .08 | .06 |
| 288 | Chris Speier | .08 | .06 |
| 289 | Manny Trillo | .10 | .08 |
| 290 | Mike Vail | .08 | .06 |
| 291 | Tim Wallach | .15 | .11 |
| 292 | Chris Welsh | .08 | .06 |
| 293 | Jim Wohlford | .08 | .06 |
| 294 | Kurt Bevacqua | .08 | .06 |
| 295 | Juan Bonilla | .08 | .06 |
| 296 | Bobby Brown | .08 | .06 |
| 297 | Luis DeLeon | .08 | .06 |
| 298 | Dave Dravecky | .10 | .08 |
| 299 | Tim Flannery | .08 | .06 |
| 300 | Steve Garvey | .50 | .40 |
| 301 | Tony Gwynn | 12.00 | 9.00 |
| 302 | *Andy Hawkins*(FC) | .20 | .15 |

| | MT | NR MT | | | MT | NR MT |
|---|---|---|---|---|---|---|
| 303 Ruppert Jones | .08 | .06 | 366 Dave Bergman | | .08 | .06 |
| 304 Terry Kennedy | .10 | .08 | 367 Fred Breining | | .08 | .06 |
| 305 Tim Lollar | .08 | .06 | 368 Bob Brenly | | .08 | .06 |
| 306 Gary Lucas | .08 | .06 | 369 Jack Clark | | .25 | .20 |
| 307 Kevin | | | 370 Chili Davis | | .12 | .09 |
| McReynolds(FC) | 3.00 | 2.25 | 371 Mark Davis(FC) | | .20 | .15 |
| 308 Sid Monge | .08 | .06 | 372 Darrell Evans | | .15 | .11 |
| 309 Mario Ramirez | .08 | .06 | 373 Atlee Hammaker | | .08 | .06 |
| 310 Gene Richards | .08 | .06 | 374 Mike Krukow | | .10 | .08 |
| 311 Luis Salazar | .08 | .06 | 375 Duane Kuiper | | .08 | .06 |
| 312 Eric Show | .12 | .09 | 376 Bill Laskey | | .08 | .06 |
| 313 Elias Sosa | .08 | .06 | 377 Gary Lavelle | | .08 | .06 |
| 314 Garry Templeton | .12 | .09 | 378 Johnnie LeMaster | | .08 | .06 |
| 315 Mark Thurmond(FC) | | | 379 Jeff Leonard | | .12 | .09 |
| | .10 | .08 | 380 Randy Lerch | | .08 | .06 |
| 316 Ed Whitson | .08 | .06 | 381 Renie Martin | | .08 | .06 |
| 317 Alan Wiggins | .08 | .06 | 382 Andy McGaffigan | | .08 | .06 |
| 318 Neil Allen | .08 | .06 | 383 Greg Minton | | .08 | .06 |
| 319 Joaquin Andujar | .10 | .08 | 384 Tom O'Malley | | .08 | .06 |
| 320 Steve Braun | .08 | .06 | 385 Max Venable | | .08 | .06 |
| 321 Glenn Brummer | .08 | .06 | 386 Brad Wellman | | .08 | .06 |
| 322 Bob Forsch | .10 | .08 | 387 Joel Youngblood | | .08 | .06 |
| 323 David Green | .08 | .06 | 388 Gary Allenson | | .08 | .06 |
| 324 George Hendrick | .10 | .08 | 389 Luis Aponte | | .08 | .06 |
| 325 Tom Herr | .12 | .09 | 390 Tony Armas | | .12 | .09 |
| 326 Dane Iorg | .08 | .06 | 391 Doug Bird | | .08 | .06 |
| 327 Jeff Lahti | .08 | .06 | 392 Wade Boggs | | 12.00 | 9.00 |
| 328 Dave LaPoint | .10 | .08 | 393 Dennis Boyd(FC) | | .70 | .50 |
| 329 Willie McGee | .35 | .25 | 394 Mike Brown | | .08 | .06 |
| 330 Ken Oberkfell | .08 | .06 | 395 Mark Clear | | .08 | .06 |
| 331 Darrell Porter | .10 | .08 | 396 Dennis Eckersley | | .15 | .11 |
| 332 Jamie Quirk | .08 | .06 | 397 Dwight Evans | | .20 | .15 |
| 333 Mike Ramsey | .08 | .06 | 398 Rich Gedman | | .10 | .08 |
| 334 Floyd Rayford | .08 | .06 | 399 Glenn Hoffman | | .08 | .06 |
| 335 Lonnie Smith | .10 | .08 | 400 Bruce Hurst | | .15 | .11 |
| 336 Ozzie Smith | 1.50 | 1.25 | 401 John Henry Johnson | | | |
| 337 John Stuper | .08 | .06 | | | .08 | .06 |
| 338 Bruce Sutter | .20 | .15 | 402 Ed Jurak | | .08 | .06 |
| 339 Andy Van Slyke(FC) | | | 403 Rick Miller | | .08 | .06 |
| | 6.00 | 4.50 | 404 Jeff Newman | | .08 | .06 |
| 340 Dave Von Ohlen | .08 | .06 | 405 Reid Nichols | | .08 | .06 |
| 341 Willie Aikens | .08 | .06 | 406 Bob Ojeda | | .12 | .09 |
| 342 Mike Armstrong | .08 | .06 | 407 Jerry Remy | | .08 | .06 |
| 343 Bud Black | .10 | .08 | 408 Jim Rice | | .40 | .30 |
| 344 George Brett | 5.00 | 3.75 | 409 Bob Stanley | | .08 | .06 |
| 345 Onix Concepcion | .08 | .06 | 410 Dave Stapleton | | .08 | .06 |
| 346 Keith Creel | .08 | .06 | 411 John Tudor | | .12 | .09 |
| 347 Larry Gura | .08 | .06 | 412 Carl Yastrzemski | | .80 | .60 |
| 348 Don Hood | .08 | .06 | 413 Buddy Bell | | .12 | .09 |
| 349 Dennis Leonard | .10 | .08 | 414 Larry Biittner | | .08 | .06 |
| 350 Hal McRae | .12 | .09 | 415 John Butcher | | .08 | .06 |
| 351 Amos Otis | .12 | .09 | 416 Danny Darwin | | .08 | .06 |
| 352 Gaylord Perry | .60 | .45 | 417 Bucky Dent | | .12 | .09 |
| 353 Greg Pryor | .08 | .06 | 418 Dave Hostetler | | .08 | .06 |
| 354 Dan Quisenberry | .12 | .09 | 419 Charlie Hough | | .12 | .09 |
| 355 Steve Renko | .08 | .06 | 420 Bobby Johnson | | .08 | .06 |
| 356 Leon Roberts | .08 | .06 | 421 Odell Jones | | .08 | .06 |
| 357 Pat Sheridan(FC) | | | 422 Jon Matlack | | .10 | .08 |
| | .15 | .11 | 423 Pete O'Brien(FC) | | | |
| 358 Joe Simpson | .08 | .06 | | | .80 | .60 |
| 359 Don Slaught | .08 | .06 | 424 Larry Parrish | | .12 | .09 |
| 360 Paul Splittorff | .08 | .06 | 425 Mickey Rivers | | .10 | .08 |
| 361 U.L. Washington | .08 | .06 | 426 Billy Sample | | .08 | .06 |
| 362 John Wathan | .10 | .08 | 427 Dave Schmidt | | .08 | .06 |
| 363 Frank White | .12 | .09 | 428 Mike Smithson(FC) | | | |
| 364 Willie Wilson | .15 | .11 | | | .15 | .11 |
| 365 Jim Barr | .08 | .06 | 429 Bill Stein | | .08 | .06 |

| | MT | NR MT | | | MT | NR MT |
|---|---|---|---|---|---|---|
| 430 | Dave Stewart | .15 | .11 | 493 | Mel Hall(FC) | .20 | .15 |
| 431 | Jim Sundberg | .10 | .08 | 494 | Ferguson Jenkins | .20 | .15 |
| 432 | Frank Tanana | .12 | .09 | 495 | Jay Johnstone | .10 | .08 |
| 433 | Dave Tobik | .08 | .06 | 496 | Craig Lefferts(FC) | | |
| 434 | Wayne Tolleson(FC) | .10 | .08 | | | .20 | .15 |
| 435 | George Wright | .08 | .06 | 497 | Carmelo | | |
| 436 | Bill Almon | .08 | .06 | | Martinez(FC) | .15 | .11 |
| 437 | Keith Atherton(FC) | | | 498 | Jerry Morales | .08 | .06 |
| | | .20 | .15 | 499 | Keith Moreland | .10 | .08 |
| 438 | Dave Beard | .08 | .06 | 500 | Dickie Noles | .08 | .06 |
| 439 | Tom Burgmeier | .08 | .06 | 501 | Mike Proly | .08 | .06 |
| 440 | Jeff Burroughs | .10 | .08 | 502 | Chuck Rainey | .08 | .06 |
| 441 | Chris Codiroli(FC) | | | 503 | Dick Ruthven | .08 | .06 |
| | | .10 | .08 | 504 | Ryne Sandberg | 18.00 | 13.50 |
| 442 | Tim Conroy(FC) | .12 | .09 | 505 | Lee Smith | .15 | .11 |
| 443 | Mike Davis | .10 | .08 | 506 | Steve Trout | .08 | .06 |
| 444 | Wayne Gross | .08 | .06 | 507 | Gary Woods | .08 | .06 |
| 445 | Garry Hancock | .08 | .06 | 508 | Juan Beniquez | .08 | .06 |
| 446 | Mike Heath | .08 | .06 | 509 | Bob Boone | .10 | .08 |
| 447 | Rickey Henderson | | | 510 | Rick Burleson | .10 | .08 |
| | | 10.00 | 7.50 | 511 | Rod Carew | 1.25 | .90 |
| 448 | Don Hill(FC) | .15 | .11 | 512 | Bobby Clark | .08 | .06 |
| 449 | Bob Kearney | .08 | .06 | 513 | John Curtis | .08 | .06 |
| 450 | Bill Krueger | .08 | .06 | 514 | Doug DeCinces | .12 | .09 |
| 451 | Rick Langford | .08 | .06 | 515 | Brian Downing | .12 | .09 |
| 452 | Carney Lansford | .12 | .09 | 516 | Tim Foli | .08 | .06 |
| 453 | Davey Lopes | .10 | .08 | 517 | Ken Forsch | .08 | .06 |
| 454 | Steve McCatty | .08 | .06 | 518 | Bobby Grich | .12 | .09 |
| 455 | Dan Meyer | .08 | .06 | 519 | Andy Hassler | .08 | .06 |
| 456 | Dwayne Murphy | .10 | .08 | 520 | Reggie Jackson | 1.50 | 1.25 |
| 457 | Mike Norris | .08 | .06 | 521 | Ron Jackson | .08 | .06 |
| 458 | Ricky Peters | .08 | .06 | 522 | Tommy John | .25 | .20 |
| 459 | Tony Phillips(FC) | | | 523 | Bruce Kison | .08 | .06 |
| | | .15 | .11 | 524 | Steve Lubratich | .08 | .06 |
| 460 | Tom Underwood | .08 | .06 | 525 | Fred Lynn | .25 | .20 |
| 461 | Mike Warren | .08 | .06 | 526 | Gary Pettis(FC) | .25 | .20 |
| 462 | Johnny Bench | .80 | .60 | 527 | Luis Sanchez | .08 | .06 |
| 463 | Bruce Berenyi | .08 | .06 | 528 | Daryl Sconiers | .08 | .06 |
| 464 | Dann Bilardello | .08 | .06 | 529 | Ellis Valentine | .08 | .06 |
| 465 | Cesar Cedeno | .12 | .09 | 530 | Rob Wilfong | .08 | .06 |
| 466 | Dave Concepcion | .15 | .11 | 531 | Mike Witt | .15 | .11 |
| 467 | Dan Driessen | .10 | .08 | 532 | Geoff Zahn | .08 | .06 |
| 468 | Nick Esasky(FC) | .70 | .50 | 533 | Bud Anderson | .08 | .06 |
| 469 | Rich Gale | .08 | .06 | 534 | Chris Bando | .08 | .06 |
| 470 | Ben Hayes | .08 | .06 | 535 | Alan Bannister | .08 | .06 |
| 471 | Paul Householder | .08 | .06 | 536 | Bert Blyleven | .20 | .15 |
| 472 | Tom Hume | .08 | .06 | 537 | Tom Brennan | .08 | .06 |
| 473 | Alan Knicely | .08 | .06 | 538 | Jamie Easterly | .08 | .06 |
| 474 | Eddie Milner | .08 | .06 | 539 | Juan Eichelberger | .08 | .06 |
| 475 | Ron Oester | .08 | .06 | 540 | Jim Essian | .08 | .06 |
| 476 | Kelly Paris | .08 | .06 | 541 | Mike Fischlin | .08 | .06 |
| 477 | Frank Pastore | .08 | .06 | 542 | Julio Franco(FC) | 4.50 | 3.50 |
| 478 | Ted Power | .10 | .08 | 543 | Mike Hargrove | .10 | .08 |
| 479 | Joe Price | .08 | .06 | 544 | Toby Harrah | .10 | .08 |
| 480 | Charlie Puleo | .08 | .06 | 545 | Ron Hassey | .08 | .06 |
| 481 | Gary Redus(FC) | .25 | .20 | 546 | Neal Heaton(FC) | .15 | .11 |
| 482 | Bill Scherrer | .08 | .06 | 547 | Bake McBride | .08 | .06 |
| 483 | Mario Soto | .10 | .08 | 548 | Broderick Perkins | .08 | .06 |
| 484 | Alex Trevino | .08 | .06 | 549 | Lary Sorensen | .08 | .06 |
| 485 | Duane Walker | .08 | .06 | 550 | Dan Spillner | .08 | .06 |
| 486 | Larry Bowa | .15 | .11 | 551 | Rick Sutcliffe | .15 | .11 |
| 487 | Warren Brusstar | .08 | .06 | 552 | Pat Tabler | .10 | .08 |
| 488 | Bill Buckner | .15 | .11 | 553 | Gorman Thomas | .10 | .08 |
| 489 | Bill Campbell | .08 | .06 | 554 | Andre Thornton | .12 | .09 |
| 490 | Ron Cey | .12 | .09 | 555 | George Vukovich | .08 | .06 |
| 491 | Jody Davis | .10 | .08 | 556 | Darrell Brown | .08 | .06 |
| 492 | Leon Durham | .10 | .08 | 557 | Tom Brunansky | .20 | .15 |

| | MT | NR MT |
|---|---|---|
| 558 *Randy Bush*(FC) | .15 | .11 |
| 559 Bobby Castillo | .08 | .06 |
| 560 John Castino | .08 | .06 |
| 561 Ron Davis | .08 | .06 |
| 562 Dave Engle | .08 | .06 |
| 563 Lenny Faedo | .08 | .06 |
| 564 Pete Filson | .08 | .06 |
| 565 Gary Gaetti | .60 | .45 |
| 566 Mickey Hatcher | .10 | .08 |
| 567 Kent Hrbek | .40 | .30 |
| 568 Rusty Kuntz | .08 | .06 |
| 569 Tim Laudner | .08 | .06 |
| 570 Rick Lysander | .08 | .06 |
| 571 Bobby Mitchell | .08 | .06 |
| 572 Ken Schrom | .08 | .06 |
| 573 Ray Smith | .08 | .06 |
| 574 *Tim Teufel*(FC) | .30 | .25 |
| 575 Frank Viola | 1.50 | 1.25 |
| 576 Gary Ward | .10 | .08 |
| 577 Ron Washington | .08 | .06 |
| 578 Len Whitehouse | .08 | .06 |
| 579 Al Williams | .08 | .06 |
| 580 Bob Bailor | .08 | .06 |
| 581 Mark Bradley | .08 | .06 |
| 582 Hubie Brooks | .15 | .11 |
| 583 Carlos Diaz | .08 | .06 |
| 584 George Foster | .20 | .15 |
| 585 Brian Giles | .08 | .06 |
| 586 Danny Heep | .08 | .06 |
| 587 Keith Hernandez | .40 | .30 |
| 588 Ron Hodges | .08 | .06 |
| 589 Scott Holman | .08 | .06 |
| 590 Dave Kingman | .15 | .11 |
| 591 Ed Lynch | .08 | .06 |
| 592 *Jose Oquendo*(FC) | .15 | .11 |
| 593 Jesse Orosco | .10 | .08 |
| 594 *Junior Ortiz*(FC) | .10 | .08 |
| 595 Tom Seaver | 4.00 | 3.00 |
| 596 *Doug Sisk*(FC) | .10 | .08 |
| 597 Rusty Staub | .12 | .09 |
| 598 John Stearns | .08 | .06 |
| 599 *Darryl Strawberry*(FC) | 25.00 | 20.00 |
| 600 Craig Swan | .08 | .06 |
| 601 *Walt Terrell*(FC) | .25 | .20 |
| 602 Mike Torrez | .10 | .08 |
| 603 Mookie Wilson | .12 | .09 |
| 604 Jamie Allen | .08 | .06 |
| 605 Jim Beattie | .08 | .06 |
| 606 Tony Bernazard | .08 | .06 |
| 607 Manny Castillo | .08 | .06 |
| 608 Bill Caudill | .08 | .06 |
| 609 Bryan Clark | .08 | .06 |
| 610 Al Cowens | .08 | .06 |
| 611 Dave Henderson | .12 | .09 |
| 612 Steve Henderson | .08 | .06 |
| 613 Orlando Mercado | .08 | .06 |
| 614 Mike Moore | .10 | .08 |
| 615 Ricky Nelson | .08 | .06 |
| 616 *Spike Owen*(FC) | .20 | .15 |
| 617 Pat Putnam | .08 | .06 |
| 618 Ron Roenicke | .08 | .06 |
| 619 Mike Stanton | .08 | .06 |
| 620 Bob Stoddard | .08 | .06 |
| 621 Rick Sweet | .08 | .06 |
| 622 Roy Thomas | .08 | .06 |

| | MT | NR MT |
|---|---|---|
| 623 Ed Vande Berg | .08 | .06 |
| 624 *Matt Young*(FC) | .15 | .11 |
| 625 Richie Zisk | .10 | .08 |
| 626 '83 All-Star Game Record Breaker (Fred Lynn) | .12 | .09 |
| 627 '83 All-Star Game Record Breaker (Manny Trillo) | .10 | .08 |
| 628 N.L. Iron Man (Steve Garvey) | .20 | .15 |
| 629 A.L. Batting Runner-Up (Rod Carew) | .25 | .20 |
| 630 A.L. Batting Champion (Wade Boggs) | 1.00 | .70 |
| 631 Letting Go Of The Raines (Tim Raines) | .20 | .15 |
| 632 Double Trouble (Al Oliver) | .10 | .08 |
| 633 All-Star Second Base (Steve Sax) | .15 | .11 |
| 634 All-Star Shortstop (Dickie Thon) | .10 | .08 |
| 635 Ace Firemen (Tippy Martinez, Dan Quisenberry) | .10 | .08 |
| 636 Reds Reunited (Joe Morgan, Tony Perez, Pete Rose) | .50 | .40 |
| 637 Backstop Stars (Bob Boone, Lance Parrish) | .15 | .11 |
| 638 The Pine Tar Incident, 7 24/83 (George Brett, Gaylord Perry) | .30 | .25 |
| 639 1983 No-Hitters (Bob Forsch, Dave Righetti, Mike Warren) | .10 | .08 |
| 640 Retiring Superstars (Johnny Bench, Carl Yastrzemski) | 2.00 | 1.50 |
| 641 Going Out In Style (Gaylord Perry) | .15 | .11 |
| 642 300 Club & Strikeout Record (Steve Carlton) | .20 | .15 |
| 643 The Managers (Joe Altobelli, Paul Owens) | .10 | .08 |
| 644 The MVP (Rick Dempsey) | .10 | .08 |
| 645 The Rookie Winner (Mike Boddicker)(FC) | .12 | .09 |
| 646 The Clincher (Scott McGregor) | .10 | .08 |
| 647 Checklist: Orioles Royals (Joe Altobelli) | .08 | .06 |
| 648 Checklist: Phillies Giants (Paul Owens) | .08 | .06 |
| 649 Checklist: White Sox Red Sox (Tony LaRussa) | .08 | .06 |
| 650 Checklist: Tigers Rangers (Sparky Anderson) | .08 | .06 |
| 651 Checklist: Dodgers/A's (Tom Lasorda) | .08 | .06 |
| 652 Checklist: Yankees Reds (Billy Martin) | .08 | .06 |
| 653 Checklist: Blue Jays | | |

|  |  | MT | NR MT |
|---|---|---|---|
|  | Cubs (Bobby Cox) | .08 | .06 |
| 654 | Checklist: Braves Angels (Joe Torre) | .08 | .06 |
| 655 | Checklist: Brewers Indians (Rene Lachemann) | .08 | .06 |
| 656 | Checklist: Astros/Twins (Bob Lillis) | .08 | .06 |
| 657 | Checklist: Pirates/Mets (Chuck Tanner) | .08 | .06 |
| 658 | Checklist: Expos Mariners (Bill Virdon) | .08 | .06 |
| 659 | Checklist: Padres Specials (Dick Williams) | .08 | .06 |
| 660 | Checklist: Cardinals Specials (Whitey Herzog) | .08 | .06 |

## 1984 Fleer Update

Following the lead of Topps, Fleer issued near the end of the baseball season a 132-card set to update player trades and include rookies not depicted in the regular issue. The cards, which measure 2-1/2" by 3-1/2", are identical in design to the regular issue but are numbered U-1 through U-132. Available to the collecting public only through hobby dealers, the set was printed in limited quantities and has escalated in price quite rapidly the past several years. The set was issued with team logo stickers in a specially designed box.

|  |  | MT | NR MT |
|---|---|---|---|
| Complete Set: |  | 900.00 | 675.00 |
| Common Player: |  | .15 | .11 |
| 1 | Willie Aikens | .15 | .11 |
| 2 | Luis Aponte | .15 | .11 |
| 3 | Mark Bailey(FC) | .20 | .15 |
| 4 | Bob Bailor | .15 | .11 |
| 5 | Dusty Baker | .30 | .25 |
| 6 | Steve Balboni(FC) | .40 | .30 |

|  |  | MT | NR MT |
|---|---|---|---|
| 7 | Alan Bannister | .15 | .11 |
| 8 | Marty Barrett(FC) | .50 | .40 |
| 9 | Dave Beard | .15 | .11 |
| 10 | Joe Beckwith | .15 | .11 |
| 11 | Dave Bergman | .15 | .11 |
| 12 | Tony Bernazard | .15 | .11 |
| 13 | Bruce Bochte | .15 | .11 |
| 14 | Barry Bonnell | .15 | .11 |
| 15 | Phil Bradley(FC) | .80 | .60 |
| 16 | Fred Breining | .15 | .11 |
| 17 | Mike Brown | .15 | .11 |
| 18 | Bill Buckner | .50 | .40 |
| 19 | Ray Burris | .15 | .11 |
| 20 | John Butcher | .15 | .11 |
| 21 | Brett Butler | 2.00 | 1.50 |
| 22 | Enos Cabell | .15 | .11 |
| 23 | Bill Campbell | .15 | .11 |
| 24 | Bill Caudill | .15 | .11 |
| 25 | Bobby Clark | .15 | .11 |
| 26 | Bryan Clark | .15 | .11 |
| 27 | Roger Clemens(FC) | 400.00 | 300.00 |
| 28 | Jaime Cocanower | .15 | .11 |
| 29 | Ron Darling(FC) | 7.00 | 5.25 |
| 30 | Alvin Davis(FC) | 5.00 | 3.75 |
| 31 | Bob Dernier | .15 | .11 |
| 32 | Carlos Diaz | .15 | .11 |
| 33 | Mike Easler | .20 | .15 |
| 34 | Dennis Eckersley | 15.00 | 11.00 |
| 35 | Jim Essian | .15 | .11 |
| 36 | Darrell Evans | .60 | .45 |
| 37 | Mike Fitzgerald(FC) | .20 | .15 |
| 38 | Tim Foli | .15 | .11 |
| 39 | John Franco(FC) | 10.00 | 7.50 |
| 40 | George Frazier | .15 | .11 |
| 41 | Rich Gale | .15 | .11 |
| 42 | Barbaro Garbey | .20 | .15 |
| 43 | Dwight Gooden(FC) | 100.00 | 75.00 |
| 44 | Goose Gossage | 1.00 | .70 |
| 45 | Wayne Gross | .15 | .11 |
| 46 | Mark Gubicza(FC) | 4.00 | 3.00 |
| 47 | Jackie Gutierrez | .15 | .11 |
| 48 | Toby Harrah | .20 | .15 |
| 49 | Ron Hassey | .15 | .11 |
| 50 | Richie Hebner | .15 | .11 |
| 51 | Willie Hernandez | .40 | .30 |
| 52 | Ed Hodge | .15 | .11 |
| 53 | Ricky Horton(FC) | .50 | .40 |
| 54 | Art Howe | .15 | .11 |
| 55 | Dane Iorg | .15 | .11 |
| 56 | Brook Jacoby(FC) | 4.00 | 3.00 |
| 57 | Dion James(FC) | .30 | .25 |
| 58 | Mike Jeffcoat(FC) | .20 | .15 |
| 59 | Ruppert Jones | .15 | .11 |
| 60 | Bob Kearney | .15 | .11 |
| 61 | Jimmy Key(FC) | 10.00 | 7.50 |
| 62 | Dave Kingman | .70 | .50 |
| 63 | Brad Komminsk(FC) | .20 | .15 |
| 64 | Jerry Koosman | .50 | .40 |
| 65 | Wayne Krenchicki | .15 | .11 |
| 66 | Rusty Kuntz | .15 | .11 |
| 67 | Frank LaCorte | .15 | .11 |
| 68 | Dennis Lamp | .15 | .11 |
| 69 | Tito Landrum | .15 | .11 |
| 70 | Mark Langston(FC) | 20.00 | 15.00 |

| | | MT | NR MT |
|---|---|---|---|
| 71 | Rick Leach | .15 | .11 |
| 72 | Craig Lefferts(FC) | .30 | .25 |
| 73 | Gary Lucas | .15 | .11 |
| 74 | Jerry Martin | .15 | .11 |
| 75 | Carmelo Martinez | .30 | .25 |
| 76 | Mike Mason(FC) | .20 | .15 |
| 77 | Gary Matthews | .30 | .25 |
| 78 | Andy McGaffigan | .15 | .11 |
| 79 | Joey McLaughlin | .15 | .11 |
| 80 | Joe Morgan | 6.00 | 4.50 |
| 81 | Darryl Motley | .15 | .11 |
| 82 | Graig Nettles | 1.00 | .70 |
| 83 | Phil Niekro | 4.00 | 3.00 |
| 84 | Ken Oberkfell | .15 | .11 |
| 85 | Al Oliver | .80 | .60 |
| 86 | Jorge Orta | .15 | .11 |
| 87 | Amos Otis | .30 | .25 |
| 88 | Bob Owchinko | .15 | .11 |
| 89 | Dave Parker | 4.00 | 3.00 |
| 90 | Jack Perconte | .15 | .11 |
| 91 | Tony Perez | 6.00 | 4.50 |
| 92 | Gerald Perry(FC) | 1.00 | .70 |
| 93 | Kirby Puckett(FC) | 350.00 | 250.00 |
| 94 | Shane Rawley | .35 | .30 |
| 95 | Floyd Rayford | .15 | .11 |
| 96 | Ron Reed | .20 | .15 |
| 97 | R.J. Reynolds(FC) | .90 | .70 |
| 98 | Gene Richards | .15 | .11 |
| 99 | Jose Rijo(FC) | 18.00 | 13.50 |
| 100 | Jeff Robinson(FC) | .50 | .40 |
| 101 | Ron Romanick(FC) | .20 | .15 |
| 102 | Pete Rose | 15.00 | 11.00 |
| 103 | Bret Saberhagen(FC) | 38.00 | 28.50 |
| 104 | Scott Sanderson | .15 | .11 |
| 105 | Dick Schofield(FC) | .40 | .30 |
| 106 | Tom Seaver | 25.00 | 18.00 |
| 107 | Jim Slaton | .15 | .11 |
| 108 | Mike Smithson | .20 | .15 |
| 109 | Lary Sorensen | .15 | .11 |
| 110 | Tim Stoddard | .15 | .11 |
| 111 | Jeff Stone(FC) | .30 | .25 |
| 112 | Champ Summers | .15 | .11 |
| 113 | Jim Sundberg | .20 | .15 |
| 114 | Rick Sutcliffe | .80 | .60 |
| 115 | Craig Swan | .15 | .11 |
| 116 | Derrel Thomas | .15 | .11 |
| 117 | Gorman Thomas | .35 | .30 |
| 118 | Alex Trevino | .15 | .11 |
| 119 | Manny Trillo | .20 | .15 |
| 120 | John Tudor | .60 | .45 |
| 121 | Tom Underwood | .15 | .11 |
| 122 | Mike Vail | .15 | .11 |
| 123 | Tom Waddell(FC) | .15 | .11 |
| 124 | Gary Ward | .20 | .15 |
| 125 | Terry Whitfield | .15 | .11 |
| 126 | Curtis Wilkerson | .15 | .11 |
| 127 | Frank Williams(FC) | .35 | .25 |
| 128 | Glenn Wilson | .25 | .20 |
| 129 | John Wockenfuss | .15 | .11 |
| 130 | Ned Yost | .15 | .11 |
| 131 | Mike Young(FC) | .35 | .25 |
| 132 | Checklist 1-132 | .15 | .11 |

# 1985 Fleer

The 1985 Fleer set consists of 660 cards, each measuring 2-1/2 by 3-1/2" in size. The card fronts feature a color photo plus the player's team logo and the word "Fleer." The photos have a color-coded frame which corresponds to the player's team. A grey border surrounds the color-coded frame. The card backs are similar in design to the previous two years, but have two shades of red and black ink on white stock. For the fourth consecutive year, Fleer included special cards and team checklists in the set. Also incorporated in a set for the first time were ten "Major League Prospect" cards, each featuring two rookie hopefuls. The set was issued with team logo stickers.

| | | MT | NR MT |
|---|---|---|---|
| Complete Set: | | 200.00 | 150.00 |
| Common Player: | | .06 | .05 |
| 1 | Doug Bair | .06 | .05 |
| 2 | Juan Berenguer | .06 | .05 |
| 3 | Dave Bergman | .06 | .05 |
| 4 | Tom Brookens | .06 | .05 |
| 5 | Marty Castillo | .06 | .05 |
| 6 | Darrell Evans | .12 | .09 |
| 7 | Barbaro Garbey | .12 | .09 |
| 8 | Kirk Gibson | .35 | .25 |

A player's name in *italic* type indicates a rookie card. An (FC) indicates a player's first card for that particular card company.

| | | MT | NR MT | | | MT | NR MT |
|---|---|---|---|---|---|---|---|
| 9 | John Grubb | .06 | .05 | 75 | Kelvin Chapman | .06 | .05 |
| 10 | Willie Hernandez | .08 | .06 | 76 | Ron Darling | .80 | .60 |
| 11 | Larry Herndon | .08 | .06 | 77 | Sid Fernandez(FC) | 1.00 | .70 |
| 12 | Howard Johnson | 3.00 | 2.25 | 78 | Mike Fitzgerald | .08 | .06 |
| 13 | Ruppert Jones | .06 | .05 | 79 | George Foster | .15 | .11 |
| 14 | Rusty Kuntz | .06 | .05 | 80 | Brent Gaff | .06 | .05 |
| 15 | Chet Lemon | .08 | .06 | 81 | Ron Gardenhire | .06 | .05 |
| 16 | Aurelio Lopez | .06 | .05 | 82 | *Dwight Gooden* | 9.00 | 6.75 |
| 17 | Sid Monge | .06 | .05 | 83 | Tom Gorman | .06 | .05 |
| 18 | Jack Morris | .25 | .20 | 84 | Danny Heep | .06 | .05 |
| 19 | Lance Parrish | .30 | .25 | 85 | Keith Hernandez | .30 | .25 |
| 20 | Dan Petry | .08 | .06 | 86 | Ray Knight | .10 | .08 |
| 21 | Dave Rozema | .06 | .05 | 87 | Ed Lynch | .06 | .05 |
| 22 | Bill Scherrer | .06 | .05 | 88 | Jose Oquendo | .08 | .06 |
| 23 | Alan Trammell | .35 | .25 | 89 | Jesse Orosco | .08 | .06 |
| 24 | Lou Whitaker | .35 | .25 | 90 | *Rafael Santana*(FC) | | |
| 25 | Milt Wilcox | .06 | .05 | | | .20 | .15 |
| 26 | Kurt Bevacqua | .06 | .05 | 91 | Doug Sisk | .06 | .05 |
| 27 | *Greg Booker*(FC) | | | 92 | Rusty Staub | .12 | .09 |
| | | .15 | .11 | 93 | Darryl Strawberry | 8.00 | 6.00 |
| 28 | Bobby Brown | .06 | .05 | 94 | Walt Terrell | .08 | .06 |
| 29 | Luis DeLeon | .06 | .05 | 95 | Mookie Wilson | .10 | .08 |
| 30 | Dave Dravecky | .08 | .06 | 96 | Jim Acker | .06 | .05 |
| 31 | Tim Flannery | .06 | .05 | 97 | Willie Aikens | .06 | .05 |
| 32 | Steve Garvey | .40 | .30 | 98 | Doyle Alexander | .10 | .08 |
| 33 | Goose Gossage | .20 | .15 | 99 | Jesse Barfield | .25 | .20 |
| 34 | Tony Gwynn | 5.00 | 3.75 | 100 | George Bell | .50 | .40 |
| 35 | Greg Harris | .06 | .05 | 101 | Jim Clancy | .08 | .06 |
| 36 | Andy Hawkins | .08 | .06 | 102 | Dave Collins | .08 | .06 |
| 37 | Terry Kennedy | .08 | .06 | 103 | Tony Fernandez | .35 | .25 |
| 38 | Craig Lefferts | .08 | .06 | 104 | Damaso Garcia | .06 | .05 |
| 39 | Tim Lollar | .06 | .05 | 105 | Jim Gott | .06 | .05 |
| 40 | Carmelo Martinez | .08 | .06 | 106 | Alfredo Griffin | .08 | .06 |
| 41 | Kevin McReynolds | 1.00 | .70 | 107 | Garth Iorg | .06 | .05 |
| 42 | Graig Nettles | .15 | .11 | 108 | Roy Lee Jackson | .06 | .05 |
| 43 | Luis Salazar | .06 | .05 | 109 | Cliff Johnson | .06 | .05 |
| 44 | Eric Show | .08 | .06 | 110 | *Jimmy Key* | 2.00 | 1.50 |
| 45 | Garry Templeton | .08 | .06 | 111 | Dennis Lamp | .06 | .05 |
| 46 | Mark Thurmond | .06 | .05 | 112 | Rick Leach | .06 | .05 |
| 47 | Ed Whitson | .06 | .05 | 113 | Luis Leal | .06 | .05 |
| 48 | Alan Wiggins | .06 | .05 | 114 | Buck Martinez | .06 | .05 |
| 49 | Rich Bordi | .06 | .05 | 115 | Lloyd Moseby | .10 | .08 |
| 50 | Larry Bowa | .12 | .09 | 116 | Rance Mulliniks | .06 | .05 |
| 51 | Warren Brusstar | .06 | .05 | 117 | Dave Stieb | .12 | .09 |
| 52 | Ron Cey | .10 | .08 | 118 | Willie Upshaw | .08 | .06 |
| 53 | *Henry Cotto*(FC) | .15 | .11 | 119 | Ernie Whitt | .08 | .06 |
| 54 | Jody Davis | .10 | .08 | 120 | Mike Armstrong | .06 | .05 |
| 55 | Bob Dernier | .06 | .05 | 121 | Don Baylor | .12 | .09 |
| 56 | Leon Durham | .08 | .06 | 122 | Marty Bystrom | .06 | .05 |
| 57 | Dennis Eckersley | 1.25 | .90 | 123 | Rick Cerone | .06 | .05 |
| 58 | George Frazier | .06 | .05 | 124 | Joe Cowley(FC) | .06 | .05 |
| 59 | Richie Hebner | .06 | .05 | 125 | Brian Dayett(FC) | .06 | .05 |
| 60 | Dave Lopes | .08 | .06 | 126 | Tim Foli | .06 | .05 |
| 61 | Gary Matthews | .10 | .08 | 127 | Ray Fontenot | .06 | .05 |
| 62 | Keith Moreland | .08 | .06 | 128 | Ken Griffey | .10 | .08 |
| 63 | Rick Reuschel | .10 | .08 | 129 | Ron Guidry | .25 | .20 |
| 64 | Dick Ruthven | .06 | .05 | 130 | Toby Harrah | .08 | .06 |
| 65 | Ryne Sandberg | 8.00 | 6.00 | 131 | Jay Howell | .08 | .06 |
| 66 | Scott Sanderson | .06 | .05 | 132 | Steve Kemp | .06 | .05 |
| 67 | Lee Smith | .10 | .08 | 133 | Don Mattingly | 6.00 | 4.50 |
| 68 | Tim Stoddard | .06 | .05 | 134 | Bobby Meacham | .06 | .05 |
| 69 | Rick Sutcliffe | .12 | .09 | 135 | John Montefusco | .06 | .05 |
| 70 | Steve Trout | .06 | .05 | 136 | Omar Moreno | .06 | .05 |
| 71 | Gary Woods | .06 | .05 | 137 | Dale Murray | .06 | .05 |
| 72 | Wally Backman | .08 | .06 | 138 | Phil Niekro | .25 | .20 |
| 73 | Bruce Berenyi | .06 | .05 | 139 | *Mike Pagliarulo*(FC) | | |
| 74 | Hubie Brooks | .10 | .08 | | | .70 | .50 |

| | | MT | NR MT | | | | MT | NR MT |
|---|---|---|---|---|---|---|---|---|
| 140 | Willie Randolph | .10 | .08 | 205 | Danny Jackson(FC) | | | |
| 141 | Dennis Rasmussen(FC) | | | | | | 1.00 | .70 |
| | | .30 | .25 | 206 | Charlie Leibrandt | | .08 | .06 |
| 142 | Dave Righetti | .20 | .15 | 207 | Hal McRae | | .10 | .08 |
| 143 | *Jose Rijo* | 3.00 | 2.25 | 208 | Darryl Motley | | .06 | .05 |
| 144 | Andre Robertson | .06 | .05 | 209 | Jorge Orta | | .06 | .05 |
| 145 | Bob Shirley | .06 | .05 | 210 | Greg Pryor | | .06 | .05 |
| 146 | Dave Winfield | 3.00 | 2.25 | 211 | Dan Quisenberry | | .10 | .08 |
| 147 | Butch Wynegar | .06 | .05 | 212 | *Bret Saberhagen* | | 6.00 | 4.50 |
| 148 | Gary Allenson | .06 | .05 | 213 | Pat Sheridan | | .06 | .05 |
| 149 | Tony Armas | .10 | .08 | 214 | Don Slaught | | .06 | .05 |
| 150 | Marty Barrett | .20 | .15 | 215 | U.L. Washington | | .06 | .05 |
| 151 | Wade Boggs | 4.00 | 3.00 | 216 | John Wathan | | .08 | .06 |
| 152 | Dennis Boyd | .10 | .08 | 217 | Frank White | | .10 | .08 |
| 153 | Bill Buckner | .12 | .09 | 218 | Willie Wilson | | .12 | .09 |
| 154 | Mark Clear | .06 | .05 | 219 | Neil Allen | | .06 | .05 |
| 155 | *Roger Clemens* | 60.00 | 45.00 | 220 | Joaquin Andujar | | .08 | .06 |
| 156 | Steve Crawford | .06 | .05 | 221 | Steve Braun | | .06 | .05 |
| 157 | Mike Easler | .08 | .06 | 222 | Danny Cox(FC) | | .20 | .20 |
| 158 | Dwight Evans | .12 | .09 | 223 | Bob Forsch | | .08 | .06 |
| 159 | Rich Gedman | .10 | .08 | 224 | David Green | | .06 | .05 |
| 160 | Jackie Gutierrez | .06 | .05 | 225 | George Hendrick | | .08 | .06 |
| 161 | Bruce Hurst | .12 | .09 | 226 | Tom Herr | | .10 | .08 |
| 162 | John Henry Johnson | | | 227 | *Ricky Horton* | | .30 | .25 |
| | | .06 | .05 | 228 | Art Howe | | .06 | .05 |
| 163 | Rick Miller | .06 | .05 | 229 | Mike Jorgensen | | .06 | .05 |
| 164 | Reid Nichols | .06 | .05 | 230 | Kurt Kepshire | | .06 | .05 |
| 165 | *Al Nipper*(FC) | .15 | .11 | 231 | Jeff Lahti | | .06 | .05 |
| 166 | Bob Ojeda | .10 | .08 | 232 | Tito Landrum | | .06 | .05 |
| 167 | Jerry Remy | .06 | .05 | 233 | Dave LaPoint | | .08 | .06 |
| 168 | Jim Rice | .35 | .25 | 234 | Willie McGee | | .30 | .25 |
| 169 | Bob Stanley | .06 | .05 | 235 | *Tom Nieto*(FC) | | .10 | .08 |
| 170 | Mike Boddicker | .10 | .08 | 236 | *Terry Pendleton*(FC) | | | |
| 171 | Al Bumbry | .08 | .06 | | | | 8.00 | 6.00 |
| 172 | Todd Cruz | .06 | .05 | 237 | Darrell Porter | | .08 | .06 |
| 173 | Rich Dauer | .06 | .05 | 238 | Dave Rucker | | .06 | .05 |
| 174 | Storm Davis | .10 | .08 | 239 | Lonnie Smith | | .08 | .06 |
| 175 | Rick Dempsey | .08 | .06 | 240 | Ozzie Smith | | .15 | .11 |
| 176 | Jim Dwyer | .06 | .05 | 241 | Bruce Sutter | | .12 | .09 |
| 177 | Mike Flanagan | .10 | .08 | 242 | Andy Van Slyke | | .35 | .25 |
| 178 | Dan Ford | .06 | .05 | 243 | Dave Von Ohlen | | .06 | .05 |
| 179 | Wayne Gross | .06 | .05 | 244 | Larry Andersen | | .06 | .05 |
| 180 | John Lowenstein | .06 | .05 | 245 | Bill Campbell | | .06 | .05 |
| 181 | Dennis Martinez | .08 | .06 | 246 | Steve Carlton | | .40 | .30 |
| 182 | Tippy Martinez | .06 | .05 | 247 | Tim Corcoran | | .06 | .05 |
| 183 | Scott McGregor | .08 | .06 | 248 | Ivan DeJesus | | .06 | .05 |
| 184 | Eddie Murray | .50 | .40 | 249 | John Denny | | .06 | .05 |
| 185 | Joe Nolan | .06 | .05 | 250 | Bo Diaz | | .08 | .06 |
| 186 | Floyd Rayford | .06 | .05 | 251 | Greg Gross | | .06 | .05 |
| 187 | Cal Ripken, Jr. | 10.00 | 7.50 | 252 | Kevin Gross | | .10 | .08 |
| 188 | Gary Roenicke | .06 | .05 | 253 | Von Hayes | | .12 | .09 |
| 189 | Lenn Sakata | .06 | .05 | 254 | Al Holland | | .06 | .05 |
| 190 | John Shelby | .08 | .06 | 255 | Charles Hudson | | .08 | .06 |
| 191 | Ken Singleton | .08 | .06 | 256 | Jerry Koosman | | .10 | .08 |
| 192 | Sammy Stewart | .06 | .05 | 257 | Joe Lefebvre | | .06 | .05 |
| 193 | Bill Swaggerty | .06 | .05 | 258 | Sixto Lezcano | | .06 | .05 |
| 194 | Tom Underwood | .06 | .05 | 259 | Garry Maddox | | .10 | .08 |
| 195 | Mike Young | .12 | .09 | 260 | Len Matuszek | | .06 | .05 |
| 196 | Steve Balboni | .08 | .06 | 261 | Tug McGraw | | .10 | .08 |
| 197 | Joe Beckwith | .06 | .05 | 262 | Al Oliver | | .12 | .09 |
| 198 | Bud Black | .06 | .05 | 263 | Shane Rawley | | .10 | .08 |
| 199 | George Brett | 4.00 | 3.00 | 264 | Juan Samuel | | .20 | .15 |
| 200 | Onix Concepcion | .06 | .05 | 265 | Mike Schmidt | | 2.00 | 1.50 |
| 201 | *Mark Gubicza* | 1.25 | .90 | 266 | *Jeff Stone* | | .12 | .09 |
| 202 | Larry Gura | .06 | .05 | 267 | Ozzie Virgil | | .06 | .05 |
| 203 | Mark Huismann(FC) | .06 | .05 | 268 | Glenn Wilson | | .08 | .06 |
| 204 | Dane Iorg | .06 | .05 | 269 | John Wockenfuss | | .06 | .05 |

| | MT | NR MT | | | MT | NR MT |
|---|---|---|---|---|---|---|
| 270 | Darrell Brown | .06 | .05 | 336 | Ken Oberkfell | .06 | .05 |
| 271 | Tom Brunansky | .12 | .09 | 337 | Pascual Perez | .08 | .06 |
| 272 | Randy Bush | .06 | .05 | 338 | Gerald Perry | .35 | .25 |
| 273 | John Butcher | .06 | .05 | 339 | Rafael Ramirez | .06 | .05 |
| 274 | Bobby Castillo | .06 | .05 | 340 | Jerry Royster | .06 | .05 |
| 275 | Ron Davis | .06 | .05 | 341 | Alex Trevino | .06 | .05 |
| 276 | Dave Engle | .06 | .05 | 342 | Claudell Washington | .08 | .06 |
| 277 | Pete Filson | .06 | .05 | 343 | Alan Ashby | .06 | .05 |
| 278 | Gary Gaetti | .25 | .20 | 344 | *Mark Bailey* | .10 | .08 |
| 279 | Mickey Hatcher | .06 | .05 | 345 | Kevin Bass | .10 | .08 |
| 280 | Ed Hodge | .06 | .05 | 346 | Enos Cabell | .06 | .05 |
| 281 | Kent Hrbek | .25 | .20 | 347 | Jose Cruz | .10 | .08 |
| 282 | Houston Jimenez | .06 | .05 | 348 | Bill Dawley | .06 | .05 |
| 283 | Tim Laudner | .06 | .05 | 349 | Frank DiPino | .06 | .05 |
| 284 | Rick Lysander | .06 | .05 | 350 | Bill Doran | .12 | .09 |
| 285 | Dave Meier | .06 | .05 | 351 | Phil Garner | .08 | .06 |
| 286 | *Kirby Puckett* | 50.00 | 37.00 | 352 | Bob Knepper | .08 | .06 |
| 287 | Pat Putnam | .06 | .05 | 353 | Mike LaCoss | .06 | .05 |
| 288 | Ken Schrom | .06 | .05 | 354 | Jerry Mumphrey | .06 | .05 |
| 289 | Mike Smithson | .06 | .05 | 355 | Joe Niekro | .10 | .08 |
| 290 | Tim Teufel | .08 | .06 | 356 | Terry Puhl | .06 | .05 |
| 291 | Frank Viola | .20 | .15 | 357 | Craig Reynolds | .06 | .05 |
| 292 | Ron Washington | .06 | .05 | 358 | Vern Ruhle | .06 | .05 |
| 293 | Don Aase | .06 | .05 | 359 | Nolan Ryan | 8.00 | 6.00 |
| 294 | Juan Beniquez | .06 | .05 | 360 | Joe Sambito | .06 | .05 |
| 295 | Bob Boone | .08 | .06 | 361 | Mike Scott | .15 | .11 |
| 296 | Mike Brown | .06 | .05 | 362 | Dave Smith | .08 | .06 |
| 297 | Rod Carew | .40 | .30 | 363 | *Julio Solano*(FC) | .08 | .06 |
| 298 | Doug Corbett | .06 | .05 | 364 | Dickie Thon | .08 | .06 |
| 299 | Doug DeCinces | .10 | .08 | 365 | Denny Walling | .06 | .05 |
| 300 | Brian Downing | .10 | .08 | 366 | Dave Anderson | .06 | .05 |
| 301 | Ken Forsch | .06 | .05 | 367 | Bob Bailor | .06 | .05 |
| 302 | Bobby Grich | .10 | .08 | 368 | Greg Brock | .08 | .06 |
| 303 | Reggie Jackson | .40 | .30 | 369 | Carlos Diaz | .06 | .05 |
| 304 | Tommy John | .20 | .15 | 370 | Pedro Guerrero | .25 | .20 |
| 305 | Curt Kaufman | .06 | .05 | 371 | *Orel Hershiser*(FC) | | |
| 306 | Bruce Kison | .06 | .05 | | | 4.00 | 3.00 |
| 307 | Fred Lynn | .20 | .15 | 372 | Rick Honeycutt | .06 | .05 |
| 308 | Gary Pettis | .08 | .06 | 373 | Burt Hooton | .08 | .06 |
| 309 | *Ron Romanick* | .10 | .08 | 374 | *Ken Howell*(FC) | .15 | .11 |
| 310 | Luis Sanchez | .06 | .05 | 375 | Ken Landreaux | .08 | .06 |
| 311 | Dick Schofield | .12 | .09 | 376 | Candy Maldonado | .10 | .08 |
| 312 | Daryl Sconiers | .06 | .05 | 377 | Mike Marshall | .15 | .11 |
| 313 | Jim Slaton | .06 | .05 | 378 | Tom Niedenfuer | .08 | .06 |
| 314 | Derrel Thomas | .06 | .05 | 379 | Alejandro Pena | .08 | .06 |
| 315 | Rob Wilfong | .06 | .05 | 380 | Jerry Reuss | .08 | .06 |
| 316 | Mike Witt | .12 | .09 | 381 | *R.J. Reynolds* | .25 | .20 |
| 317 | Geoff Zahn | .06 | .05 | 382 | German Rivera | .06 | .05 |
| 318 | Len Barker | .08 | .06 | 383 | Bill Russell | .08 | .06 |
| 319 | Steve Bedrosian | .12 | .09 | 384 | Steve Sax | .20 | .15 |
| 320 | Bruce Benedict | .06 | .05 | 385 | Mike Scioscia | .08 | .06 |
| 321 | Rick Camp | .06 | .05 | 386 | *Franklin Stubbs*(FC) | | |
| 322 | Chris Chambliss | .08 | .06 | | | .60 | .45 |
| 323 | *Jeff Dedmon*(FC) | | | 387 | Fernando Valenzuela | | |
| | | .12 | .09 | | | .35 | .25 |
| 324 | Terry Forster | .08 | .06 | 388 | Bob Welch | .12 | .09 |
| 325 | Gene Garber | .06 | .05 | 389 | Terry Whitfield | .06 | .05 |
| 326 | *Albert Hall*(FC) | .15 | .11 | 390 | Steve Yeager | .06 | .05 |
| 327 | Terry Harper | .06 | .05 | 391 | Pat Zachry | .06 | .05 |
| 328 | Bob Horner | .12 | .09 | 392 | Fred Breining | .06 | .05 |
| 329 | Glenn Hubbard | .06 | .05 | 393 | Gary Carter | .35 | .25 |
| 330 | Randy Johnson | .06 | .05 | 394 | Andre Dawson | .60 | .45 |
| 331 | Brad Komminsk | .06 | .05 | 395 | Miguel Dilone | .06 | .05 |
| 332 | Rick Mahler | .06 | .05 | 396 | Dan Driessen | .08 | .06 |
| 333 | Craig McMurtry | .06 | .05 | 397 | Doug Flynn | .06 | .05 |
| 334 | Donnie Moore | .06 | .05 | 398 | Terry Francona | .06 | .05 |
| 335 | Dale Murphy | .60 | .45 | 399 | Bill Gullickson | .06 | .05 |

| | | MT | NR MT | | | | MT | NR MT |
|---|---|---|---|---|---|---|---|---|
| 400 | Bob James | .06 | .05 | | 467 | Lee Lacy | .06 | .05 |
| 401 | Charlie Lea | .06 | .05 | | 468 | Bill Madlock | .12 | .09 |
| 402 | Bryan Little | .06 | .05 | | 469 | Lee Mazzilli | .08 | .06 |
| 403 | Gary Lucas | .06 | .05 | | 470 | Larry McWilliams | .06 | .05 |
| 404 | David Palmer | .06 | .05 | | 471 | Jim Morrison | .06 | .05 |
| 405 | Tim Raines | .35 | .25 | | 472 | Tony Pena | .10 | .08 |
| 406 | Mike Ramsey | .06 | .05 | | 473 | Johnny Ray | .12 | .09 |
| 407 | Jeff Reardon | .12 | .09 | | 474 | Rick Rhoden | .10 | .08 |
| 408 | Steve Rogers | .08 | .06 | | 475 | Don Robinson | .08 | .06 |
| 409 | Dan Schatzeder | .06 | .05 | | 476 | Rod Scurry | .06 | .05 |
| 410 | Bryn Smith | .06 | .05 | | 477 | Kent Tekulve | .08 | .06 |
| 411 | Mike Stenhouse | .06 | .05 | | 478 | Jason Thompson | .06 | .05 |
| 412 | Tim Wallach | .12 | .09 | | 479 | John Tudor | .10 | .08 |
| 413 | Jim Wohlford | .06 | .05 | | 480 | Lee Tunnell | .06 | .05 |
| 414 | Bill Almon | .06 | .05 | | 481 | Marvell Wynne | .06 | .05 |
| 415 | Keith Atherton | .06 | .05 | | 482 | Salome Barojas | .06 | .05 |
| 416 | Bruce Bochte | .06 | .05 | | 483 | Dave Beard | .06 | .05 |
| 417 | Tom Burgmeier | .06 | .05 | | 484 | Jim Beattie | .06 | .05 |
| 418 | Ray Burris | .06 | .05 | | 485 | Barry Bonnell | .06 | .05 |
| 419 | Bill Caudill | .06 | .05 | | 486 | Phil Bradley | .90 | .70 |
| 420 | Chris Codiroli | .06 | .05 | | 487 | Al Cowens | .06 | .05 |
| 421 | Tim Conroy | .06 | .05 | | 488 | Alvin Davis | 1.00 | .70 |
| 422 | Mike Davis | .08 | .06 | | 489 | Dave Henderson | .10 | .08 |
| 423 | Jim Essian | .06 | .05 | | 490 | Steve Henderson | .06 | .05 |
| 424 | Mike Heath | .06 | .05 | | 491 | Bob Kearney | .06 | .05 |
| 425 | Rickey Henderson | 4.00 | 3.00 | | 492 | Mark Langston | 5.00 | 3.75 |
| 426 | Donnie Hill | .06 | .05 | | 493 | Larry Milbourne | .06 | .05 |
| 427 | Dave Kingman | .15 | .11 | | 494 | Paul Mirabella | .06 | .05 |
| 428 | Bill Krueger | .06 | .05 | | 495 | Mike Moore | .06 | .05 |
| 429 | Carney Lansford | .10 | .08 | | 496 | Edwin Nunez(FC) | .08 | .06 |
| 430 | Steve McCatty | .06 | .05 | | 497 | Spike Owen | .08 | .06 |
| 431 | Joe Morgan | .30 | .25 | | 498 | Jack Perconte | .06 | .05 |
| 432 | Dwayne Murphy | .08 | .06 | | 499 | Ken Phelps | .10 | .08 |
| 433 | Tony Phillips | .06 | .05 | | 500 | Jim Presley(FC) | .50 | .40 |
| 434 | Lary Sorensen | .06 | .05 | | 501 | Mike Stanton | .06 | .05 |
| 435 | Mike Warren | .06 | .05 | | 502 | Bob Stoddard | .06 | .05 |
| 436 | Curt Young(FC) | .35 | .25 | | 503 | Gorman Thomas | .10 | .08 |
| 437 | Luis Aponte | .06 | .05 | | 504 | Ed Vande Berg | .06 | .05 |
| 438 | Chris Bando | .06 | .05 | | 505 | Matt Young | .06 | .05 |
| 439 | Tony Bernazard | .06 | .05 | | 506 | Juan Agosto | .06 | .05 |
| 440 | Bert Blyleven | .15 | .11 | | 507 | Harold Baines | .15 | .11 |
| 441 | Brett Butler | .10 | .08 | | 508 | Floyd Bannister | .10 | .08 |
| 442 | Ernie Camacho | .06 | .05 | | 509 | Britt Burns | .06 | .05 |
| 443 | Joe Carter(FC) | 9.00 | 6.75 | | 510 | Julio Cruz | .06 | .05 |
| 444 | Carmelo Castillo | .06 | .05 | | 511 | Richard Dotson | .10 | .08 |
| 445 | Jamie Easterly | .06 | .05 | | 512 | Jerry Dybzinski | .06 | .05 |
| 446 | Steve Farr(FC) | .40 | .30 | | 513 | Carlton Fisk | .40 | .30 |
| 447 | Mike Fischlin | .06 | .05 | | 514 | Scott Fletcher | .08 | .06 |
| 448 | Julio Franco | .12 | .09 | | 515 | Jerry Hairston | .06 | .05 |
| 449 | Mel Hall | .08 | .06 | | 516 | Marc Hill | .06 | .05 |
| 450 | Mike Hargrove | .06 | .05 | | 517 | LaMarr Hoyt | .06 | .05 |
| 451 | Neal Heaton | .06 | .05 | | 518 | Ron Kittle | .10 | .08 |
| 452 | Brook Jacoby | .30 | .25 | | 519 | Rudy Law | .06 | .05 |
| 453 | Mike Jeffcoat | .08 | .06 | | 520 | Vance Law | .08 | .06 |
| 454 | Don Schulze(FC) | .08 | .06 | | 521 | Greg Luzinski | .10 | .08 |
| 455 | Roy Smith | .06 | .05 | | 522 | Gene Nelson | .06 | .05 |
| 456 | Pat Tabler | .08 | .06 | | 523 | Tom Paciorek | .06 | .05 |
| 457 | Andre Thornton | .10 | .08 | | 524 | Ron Reed | .06 | .05 |
| 458 | George Vukovich | .06 | .05 | | 525 | Bert Roberge | .06 | .05 |
| 459 | Tom Waddell | .06 | .05 | | 526 | Tom Seaver | .40 | .30 |
| 460 | Jerry Willard | .06 | .05 | | 527 | Roy Smalley | .06 | .05 |
| 461 | Dale Berra | .06 | .05 | | 528 | Dan Spillner | .06 | .05 |
| 462 | John Candelaria | .10 | .08 | | 529 | Mike Squires | .06 | .05 |
| 463 | Jose DeLeon | .08 | .06 | | 530 | Greg Walker | .12 | .09 |
| 464 | Doug Frobel | .06 | .05 | | 531 | Cesar Cedeno | .10 | .08 |
| 465 | Cecilio Guante | .06 | .05 | | 532 | Dave Concepcion | .12 | .09 |
| 466 | Brian Harper | .06 | .05 | | 533 | Eric Davis(FC) | 6.00 | 4.50 |

| | MT | NR MT |
|---|---|---|
| 534 Nick Esasky | .08 | .06 |
| 535 Tom Foley | .06 | .05 |
| 536 *John Franco* | 2.00 | 1.50 |
| 537 Brad Gulden | .06 | .05 |
| 538 Tom Hume | .06 | .05 |
| 539 Wayne Krenchicki | .06 | .05 |
| 540 Andy McGaffigan | .06 | .05 |
| 541 Eddie Milner | .06 | .05 |
| 542 Ron Oester | .06 | .05 |
| 543 Bob Owchinko | .06 | .05 |
| 544 Dave Parker | .25 | .20 |
| 545 Frank Pastore | .06 | .05 |
| 546 Tony Perez | .15 | .11 |
| 547 Ted Power | .06 | .05 |
| 548 Joe Price | .06 | .05 |
| 549 Gary Redus | .08 | .06 |
| 550 Pete Rose | 1.00 | .70 |
| 551 Jeff Russell(FC) | .10 | .08 |
| 552 Mario Soto | .08 | .06 |
| 553 *Jay Tibbs*(FC) | .15 | .11 |
| 554 Duane Walker | .06 | .05 |
| 555 Alan Bannister | .06 | .05 |
| 556 Buddy Bell | .12 | .09 |
| 557 Danny Darwin | .06 | .05 |
| 558 Charlie Hough | .08 | .06 |
| 559 Bobby Jones | .06 | .05 |
| 560 Odell Jones | .06 | .05 |
| 561 *Jeff Kunkel*(FC) | .10 | .08 |
| 562 *Mike Mason* | .10 | .08 |
| 563 Pete O'Brien | .12 | .09 |
| 564 Larry Parrish | .10 | .08 |
| 565 Mickey Rivers | .08 | .06 |
| 566 Billy Sample | .06 | .05 |
| 567 Dave Schmidt | .06 | .05 |
| 568 Donnie Scott | .06 | .05 |
| 569 Dave Stewart | .12 | .09 |
| 570 Frank Tanana | .10 | .08 |
| 571 Wayne Tolleson | .06 | .05 |
| 572 Gary Ward | .08 | .06 |
| 573 Curtis Wilkerson | .08 | .06 |
| 574 George Wright | .06 | .05 |
| 575 Ned Yost | .06 | .05 |
| 576 Mark Brouhard | .06 | .05 |
| 577 Mike Caldwell | .06 | .05 |
| 578 Bobby Clark | .06 | .05 |
| 579 Jaime Cocanower | .06 | .05 |
| 580 Cecil Cooper | .15 | .11 |
| 581 Rollie Fingers | .20 | .15 |
| 582 Jim Gantner | .08 | .06 |
| 583 Moose Haas | .06 | .05 |
| 584 Dion James | .12 | .09 |
| 585 Pete Ladd | .06 | .05 |
| 586 Rick Manning | .06 | .05 |
| 587 Bob McClure | .06 | .05 |
| 588 Paul Molitor | .15 | .11 |
| 589 Charlie Moore | .06 | .05 |
| 590 Ben Oglivie | .08 | .06 |
| 591 Chuck Porter | .06 | .05 |
| 592 *Randy Ready*(FC) | .20 | .15 |
| 593 Ed Romero | .06 | .05 |
| 594 Bill Schroeder(FC) | .10 | .08 |
| 595 Ray Searage | .06 | .05 |
| 596 Ted Simmons | .12 | .09 |
| 597 Jim Sundberg | .08 | .06 |
| 598 Don Sutton | .30 | .25 |
| 599 Tom Tellmann | .06 | .05 |

| | MT | NR MT |
|---|---|---|
| 600 Rick Waits | .06 | .05 |
| 601 Robin Yount | 4.00 | 3.00 |
| 602 Dusty Baker | .08 | .06 |
| 603 Bob Brenly | .06 | .05 |
| 604 Jack Clark | .20 | .15 |
| 605 Chili Davis | .10 | .08 |
| 606 Mark Davis | .06 | .05 |
| 607 *Dan Gladden*(FC) | .50 | .40 |
| 608 Atlee Hammaker | .06 | .05 |
| 609 Mike Krukow | .08 | .06 |
| 610 Duane Kuiper | .06 | .05 |
| 611 Bob Lacey | .06 | .05 |
| 612 Bill Laskey | .06 | .05 |
| 613 Gary Lavelle | .06 | .05 |
| 614 Johnnie LeMaster | .06 | .05 |
| 615 Jeff Leonard | .10 | .08 |
| 616 Randy Lerch | .06 | .05 |
| 617 Greg Minton | .06 | .05 |
| 618 Steve Nicosia | .06 | .05 |
| 619 Gene Richards | .06 | .05 |
| 620 *Jeff Robinson* | .30 | .25 |
| 621 Scot Thompson | .06 | .05 |
| 622 Manny Trillo | .08 | .06 |
| 623 Brad Wellman | .06 | .05 |
| 624 *Frank Williams* | .15 | .11 |
| 625 Joel Youngblood | .06 | .05 |
| 626 Ripken-In-Action (Cal Ripken) | 2.50 | 2.00 |
| 627 Schmidt-In-Action (Mike Schmidt) | 1.00 | .70 |
| 628 Giving the Signs (Sparky Anderson) | .08 | .06 |
| 629 A.L. Pitcher's Nightmare (Rickey Henderson, Dave Winfield) | .30 | .25 |
| 630 N.L. Pitcher's Nightmare (Ryne Sandberg, Mike Schmidt) | .30 | .25 |
| 631 N.L. All-Stars (Gary Carter, Steve Garvey, Ozzie Smith, Darryl Strawberry) | .30 | .25 |
| 632 All-Star Game Winning Battery (Gary Carter, Charlie Lea) | .15 | .11 |
| 633 N.L. Pennant Clinchers (Steve Garvey, Goose Gossage) | .20 | .15 |
| 634 N.L. Rookie Phenoms (Dwight Gooden, Juan Samuel) | 1.00 | .70 |
| 635 Toronto's Big Guns (Willie Upshaw) | .08 | .06 |
| 636 Toronto's Big Guns (Lloyd Moseby) | .08 | .06 |
| 637 Holland (Al Holland) | .08 | .06 |
| 638 Tunnell (Lee Tunnell) | .08 | .06 |
| 639 500th Homer (Reggie Jackson) | .30 | .25 |
| 640 4,000th Hit (Pete Rose) | .50 | .40 |
| 641 Father & Son (Cal Ripken, Jr., Cal Ripken, Sr.) | .30 | .25 |
| 642 Cubs Team | .08 | .06 |

| | | MT | NR MT |
|---|---|---|---|
| 643 | 1984's Two Perfect Games & One No-Hitter (Jack Morris, David Palmer, Mike Witt) | .15 | .11 |
| 644 | Major League Prospect (Willie Lozado, Vic Mata) | .06 | .05 |
| 645 | Major League Prospect (Kelly Gruber, Randy O'Neal)(FC) | 6.00 | 4.50 |
| 646 | Major League Prospect (Jose Roman, Joel Skinner)(FC) | .12 | .09 |
| 647 | Major League Prospect (Steve Kiefer, Danny Tartabull)(FC) | 8.00 | 6.00 |
| 648 | Major League Prospect (Rob Deer, Alejandro Sanchez)(FC) | 1.75 | 1.25 |
| 649 | Major League Prospect (Shawon Dunston, Bill Hatcher)(FC) | 2.00 | 1.50 |
| 650 | Major League Prospect (Mike Bielecki, Ron Robinson)(FC) | .30 | .25 |
| 651 | Major League Prospect (Zane Smith, Paul Zuvella)(FC) | 1.25 | .90 |
| 652 | Major League Prospect (Glenn Davis, Joe Hesketh)(FC) | 4.00 | 3.00 |
| 653 | Major League Prospect (Steve Jeltz, John Russell)(FC) | .20 | .15 |
| 654 | Checklist 1-95 | .06 | .05 |
| 655 | Checklist 96-195 | .06 | .05 |
| 656 | Checklist 196-292 | .06 | .05 |
| 657 | Checklist 293-391 | .06 | .05 |
| 658 | Checklist 392-481 | .06 | .05 |
| 659 | Checklist 482-575 | .06 | .05 |
| 660 | Checklist 576-660 | .06 | .05 |

# 1985 Fleer Update

For the second straight year, Fleer issued a 132- card update set. The cards, which measure 2-1/2" by 3-1/2", portray players on their new teams and also includes rookies not depicted in the regular issue. The cards are identical in design to the 1985 Fleer set but are numbered U-1 through U-132. The set was issued with team logo stickers in a specially designed box and was available only through hobby dealers.

| | | MT | NR MT |
|---|---|---|---|
| Complete Set: | | 30.00 | 22.00 |
| Common Player: | | .10 | .08 |
| 1 | Don Aase | .15 | .11 |
| 2 | Bill Almon | .10 | .08 |
| 3 | Dusty Baker | .15 | .11 |
| 4 | Dale Berra | .10 | .08 |
| 5 | Karl Best(FC) | .10 | .08 |
| 6 | Tim Birtsas(FC) | .20 | .15 |
| 7 | Vida Blue | .20 | .15 |
| 8 | Rich Bordi | .10 | .08 |
| 9 | Daryl Boston(FC) | .20 | .15 |
| 10 | Hubie Brooks | .20 | .15 |
| 11 | Chris Brown(FC) | .25 | .20 |
| 12 | Tom Browning(FC) | 1.50 | 1.25 |
| 13 | Al Bumbry | .10 | .08 |
| 14 | Tim Burke(FC) | .40 | .30 |
| 15 | Ray Burris | .10 | .08 |
| 16 | Jeff Burroughs | .15 | .11 |
| 17 | Ivan Calderon(FC) | 1.50 | 1.25 |
| 18 | Jeff Calhoun | .10 | .08 |
| 19 | Bill Campbell | .10 | .08 |
| 20 | Don Carman(FC) | .15 | .11 |
| 21 | Gary Carter | 1.00 | .70 |
| 22 | Bobby Castillo | .10 | .08 |
| 23 | Bill Caudill | .10 | .08 |
| 24 | Rick Cerone | .10 | .08 |
| 25 | Jack Clark | .35 | .25 |
| 26 | Pat Clements(FC) | .20 | .15 |
| 27 | Stewart Cliburn(FC) | .15 | .11 |
| 28 | Vince Coleman | 4.00 | 3.00 |
| 29 | Dave Collins | .15 | .11 |
| 30 | Fritz Connally | .10 | .08 |
| 31 | Henry Cotto(FC) | .20 | .15 |
| 32 | Danny Darwin | .15 | .11 |
| 33 | Darren Daulton(FC) | 4.00 | 3.00 |
| 34 | Jerry Davis | .10 | .08 |
| 35 | Brian Dayett | .10 | .08 |
| 36 | Ken Dixon(FC) | .10 | .08 |
| 37 | Tommy Dunbar | .10 | .08 |
| 38 | Mariano Duncan(FC) | .80 | .60 |
| 39 | Bob Fallon | .10 | .08 |
| 40 | Brian Fisher(FC) | .15 | .11 |
| 41 | Mike Fitzgerald | .10 | .08 |
| 42 | Ray Fontenot | .10 | .08 |
| 43 | Greg Gagne(FC) | .35 | .25 |
| 44 | Oscar Gamble | .15 | .11 |
| 45 | Jim Gott | .10 | .08 |
| 46 | David Green | .10 | .08 |
| 47 | Alfredo Griffin | .15 | .11 |
| 48 | Ozzie Guillen(FC) | 1.25 | .90 |
| 49 | Toby Harrah | .15 | .11 |
| 50 | Ron Hassey | .10 | .08 |
| 51 | Rickey Henderson | 5.00 | 3.75 |
| 52 | Steve Henderson | .10 | .08 |
| 53 | George Hendrick | .15 | .11 |
| 54 | Teddy Higuera(FC) | .50 | .40 |
| 55 | Al Holland | .10 | .08 |

| | | MT | NR MT |
|---|---|---|---|
| 56 | Burt Hooton | .15 | .11 |
| 57 | Jay Howell | .15 | .11 |
| 58 | LaMarr Hoyt | .10 | .08 |
| 59 | Tim Hulett(FC) | .20 | .15 |
| 60 | Bob James | .10 | .08 |
| 61 | Cliff Johnson | .10 | .08 |
| 62 | Howard Johnson | 3.00 | 2.25 |
| 63 | Ruppert Jones | .10 | .08 |
| 64 | Steve Kemp | .15 | .11 |
| 65 | Bruce Kison | .10 | .08 |
| 66 | Mike LaCoss | .15 | .11 |
| 67 | Lee Lacy | .15 | .11 |
| 68 | Dave LaPoint | .20 | .15 |
| 69 | Gary Lavelle | .10 | .08 |
| 70 | Vance Law | .15 | .11 |
| 71 | Manny Lee(FC) | .20 | .15 |
| 72 | Sixto Lezcano | .10 | .08 |
| 73 | Tim Lollar | .10 | .08 |
| 74 | Urbano Lugo(FC) | .15 | .11 |
| 75 | Fred Lynn | .30 | .25 |
| 76 | Steve Lyons(FC) | .15 | .11 |
| 77 | Mickey Mahler | .10 | .08 |
| 78 | Ron Mathis(FC) | .10 | .08 |
| 79 | Len Matuszek | .10 | .08 |
| 80 | Oddibe McDowell(FC) | .15 | .11 |
| 81 | Roger McDowell(FC) | .50 | .40 |
| 82 | Donnie Moore | .10 | .08 |
| 83 | Ron Musselman | .10 | .08 |
| 84 | Al Oliver | .25 | .20 |
| 85 | Joe Orsulak(FC) | .20 | .15 |
| 86 | Dan Pasqua(FC) | .60 | .45 |
| 87 | Chris Pittaro(FC) | .10 | .08 |
| 88 | Rick Reuschel | .20 | .15 |
| 89 | Earnie Riles(FC) | .20 | .15 |
| 90 | Jerry Royster | .10 | .08 |
| 91 | Dave Rozema | .10 | .08 |
| 92 | Dave Rucker | .10 | .08 |
| 93 | Vern Ruhle | .10 | .08 |
| 94 | Mark Salas(FC) | .20 | .15 |
| 95 | Luis Salazar | .10 | .08 |
| 96 | Joe Sambito | .10 | .08 |
| 97 | Billy Sample | .10 | .08 |
| 98 | Alex Sanchez | .10 | .08 |
| 99 | Calvin Schiraldi(FC) | .25 | .20 |
| 100 | Rick Schu(FC) | .20 | .15 |
| 101 | Larry Sheets(FC) | .50 | .40 |
| 102 | Ron Shepherd | .10 | .08 |
| 103 | Nelson Simmons(FC) | .10 | .08 |
| 104 | Don Slaught | .10 | .08 |
| 105 | Roy Smalley | .15 | .11 |
| 106 | Lonnie Smith | .15 | .11 |
| 107 | Nate Snell(FC) | .10 | .08 |
| 108 | Lary Sorensen | .10 | .08 |
| 109 | Chris Speier | .10 | .08 |
| 110 | Mike Stenhouse | .10 | .08 |
| 111 | Tim Stoddard | .10 | .08 |
| 112 | John Stuper | .10 | .08 |
| 113 | Jim Sundberg | .15 | .11 |
| 114 | Bruce Sutter | .25 | .20 |
| 115 | Don Sutton | .60 | .45 |
| 116 | Bruce Tanner(FC) | .10 | .08 |
| 117 | Kent Tekulve | .15 | .11 |
| 118 | Walt Terrell | .15 | .11 |
| 119 | Mickey Tettleton(FC) | 5.00 | 3.75 |
| 120 | Rich Thompson | .10 | .08 |
| 121 | Louis Thornton(FC) | .10 | .08 |
| 122 | Alex Trevino | .10 | .08 |
| 123 | John Tudor | .30 | .25 |
| 124 | Jose Uribe(FC) | .25 | .20 |
| 125 | Dave Valle(FC) | .20 | .15 |
| 126 | Dave Von Ohlen | .10 | .08 |
| 127 | Curt Wardle | .10 | .08 |
| 128 | U.L. Washington | .10 | .08 |
| 129 | Ed Whitson | .10 | .08 |
| 130 | Herm Winningham(FC) | .20 | .15 |
| 131 | Rich Yett(FC) | .15 | .11 |
| 132 | Checklist | .10 | .08 |

# 1986 Fleer

The 1986 Fleer set contains 660 color photos, with each card measuring 2-1/2" by 3-1/2" in size. The card fronts include the word "Fleer," the player's team logo, and a player picture enclosed by a dark blue border. The card reverses are minus the black and white photo that was included in past Fleer efforts. Player biographical and statistical information appear in black and yellow ink on white stock. As in 1985, Fleer devoted ten cards, entitled "Major League Prospects," to twenty promising rookie players. The 1986 set, as in the previous four years, was issued with team logo stickers.

| | | MT | NR MT |
|---|---|---|---|
| Complete Set: | | 125.00 | 90.00 |
| Common Player: | | .06 | .05 |
| 1 | Steve Balboni | .08 | .06 |
| 2 | Joe Beckwith | .06 | .05 |
| 3 | Buddy Biancalana | .06 | .05 |
| 4 | Bud Black | .06 | .05 |
| 5 | George Brett | 2.00 | 1.50 |
| 6 | Onix Concepcion | .06 | .05 |
| 7 | Steve Farr | .08 | .06 |

| | | MT | NR MT | | | | MT | NR MT |
|---|---|---|---|---|---|---|---|---|
| 8 | Mark Gubicza | .12 | .09 | | 74 | *Rick Aguilera*(FC) | | |
| 9 | Dane Iorg | .06 | .05 | | | | 1.00 | .70 |
| 10 | Danny Jackson | .20 | .15 | | 75 | Wally Backman | .08 | .06 |
| 11 | Lynn Jones | .06 | .05 | | 76 | Gary Carter | .25 | .20 |
| 12 | Mike Jones | .06 | .05 | | 77 | Ron Darling | .15 | .11 |
| 13 | Charlie Leibrandt | .08 | .06 | | 78 | *Len Dykstra*(FC) | | |
| 14 | Hal McRae | .10 | .08 | | | | 2.00 | 1.50 |
| 15 | Omar Moreno | .06 | .05 | | 79 | Sid Fernandez | .12 | .09 |
| 16 | Darryl Motley | .06 | .05 | | 80 | George Foster | .15 | .11 |
| 17 | Jorge Orta | .06 | .05 | | 81 | Dwight Gooden | 2.00 | 1.50 |
| 18 | Dan Quisenberry | .08 | .06 | | 82 | Tom Gorman | .06 | .05 |
| 19 | Bret Saberhagen | 1.00 | .70 | | 83 | Danny Heep | .06 | .05 |
| 20 | Pat Sheridan | .06 | .05 | | 84 | Keith Hernandez | .30 | .25 |
| 21 | Lonnie Smith | .08 | .06 | | 85 | Howard Johnson | .50 | .40 |
| 22 | Jim Sundberg | .08 | .06 | | 86 | Ray Knight | .08 | .06 |
| 23 | John Wathan | .08 | .06 | | 87 | Terry Leach | .08 | .06 |
| 24 | Frank White | .10 | .08 | | 88 | Ed Lynch | .06 | .05 |
| 25 | Willie Wilson | .12 | .09 | | 89 | *Roger McDowell*(FC) | | |
| 26 | Joaquin Andujar | .08 | .06 | | | | .40 | .30 |
| 27 | Steve Braun | .06 | .05 | | 90 | Jesse Orosco | .08 | .06 |
| 28 | Bill Campbell | .06 | .05 | | 91 | Tom Paciorek | .06 | .05 |
| 29 | Cesar Cedeno | .10 | .08 | | 92 | Ronn Reynolds | .06 | .05 |
| 30 | Jack Clark | .20 | .15 | | 93 | Rafael Santana | .06 | .05 |
| 31 | *Vince Coleman* | 1.50 | 1.25 | | 94 | Doug Sisk | .06 | .05 |
| 32 | Danny Cox | .10 | .08 | | 95 | Rusty Staub | .10 | .08 |
| 33 | Ken Dayley | .06 | .05 | | 96 | Darryl Strawberry | 3.00 | 2.25 |
| 34 | Ivan DeJesus | .06 | .05 | | 97 | Mookie Wilson | .10 | .08 |
| 35 | Bob Forsch | .08 | .06 | | 98 | Neil Allen | .06 | .05 |
| 36 | Brian Harper | .06 | .05 | | 99 | Don Baylor | .12 | .09 |
| 37 | Tom Herr | .10 | .08 | | 100 | Dale Berra | .06 | .05 |
| 38 | Ricky Horton | .08 | .06 | | 101 | Rich Bordi | .06 | .05 |
| 39 | Kurt Kepshire | .06 | .05 | | 102 | Marty Bystrom | .06 | .05 |
| 40 | Jeff Lahti | .06 | .05 | | 103 | Joe Cowley | .06 | .05 |
| 41 | Tito Landrum | .06 | .05 | | 104 | *Brian Fisher* | .15 | .11 |
| 42 | Willie McGee | .15 | .11 | | 105 | Ken Griffey | .10 | .08 |
| 43 | Tom Nieto | .06 | .05 | | 106 | Ron Guidry | .20 | .15 |
| 44 | Terry Pendleton | .80 | .60 | | 107 | Ron Hassey | .06 | .05 |
| 45 | Darrell Porter | .08 | .06 | | 108 | Rickey Henderson | 2.00 | 1.50 |
| 46 | Ozzie Smith | 1.00 | .70 | | 109 | Don Mattingly | 2.50 | 2.00 |
| 47 | John Tudor | .10 | .08 | | 110 | Bobby Meacham | .06 | .05 |
| 48 | Andy Van Slyke | .15 | .11 | | 111 | John Montefusco | .06 | .05 |
| 49 | *Todd Worrell*(FC) | | | | 112 | Phil Niekro | .25 | .20 |
| | | .40 | .30 | | 113 | Mike Pagliarulo | .20 | .15 |
| 50 | Jim Acker | .06 | .05 | | 114 | Dan Pasqua | .20 | .15 |
| 51 | Doyle Alexander | .10 | .08 | | 115 | Willie Randolph | .10 | .08 |
| 52 | Jesse Barfield | .20 | .15 | | 116 | Dave Righetti | .20 | .15 |
| 53 | George Bell | .30 | .25 | | 117 | Andre Robertson | .06 | .05 |
| 54 | Jeff Burroughs | .08 | .06 | | 118 | Billy Sample | .06 | .05 |
| 55 | Bill Caudill | .06 | .05 | | 119 | Bob Shirley | .06 | .05 |
| 56 | Jim Clancy | .08 | .06 | | 120 | Ed Whitson | .06 | .05 |
| 57 | Tony Fernandez | .20 | .15 | | 121 | Dave Winfield | 1.00 | .70 |
| 58 | Tom Filer | .06 | .05 | | 122 | Butch Wynegar | .06 | .05 |
| 59 | Damaso Garcia | .06 | .05 | | 123 | Dave Anderson | .06 | .05 |
| 60 | Tom Henke(FC) | .15 | .11 | | 124 | Bob Bailor | .06 | .05 |
| 61 | Garth Iorg | .06 | .05 | | 125 | Greg Brock | .08 | .06 |
| 62 | Cliff Johnson | .06 | .05 | | 126 | Enos Cabell | .06 | .05 |
| 63 | Jimmy Key | .15 | .11 | | 127 | Bobby Castillo | .06 | .05 |
| 64 | Dennis Lamp | .06 | .05 | | 128 | Carlos Diaz | .06 | .05 |
| 65 | Gary Lavelle | .06 | .05 | | 129 | *Mariano Duncan* | .15 | .11 |
| 66 | Buck Martinez | .06 | .05 | | 130 | Pedro Guerrero | .20 | .15 |
| 67 | Lloyd Moseby | .10 | .08 | | 131 | Orel Hershiser | .70 | .50 |
| 68 | Rance Mulliniks | .06 | .05 | | 132 | Rick Honeycutt | .06 | .05 |
| 69 | Al Oliver | .10 | .08 | | 133 | Ken Howell | .06 | .05 |
| 70 | Dave Stieb | .12 | .09 | | 134 | Ken Landreaux | .06 | .05 |
| 71 | Louis Thornton | .06 | .05 | | 135 | Bill Madlock | .12 | .09 |
| 72 | Willie Upshaw | .08 | .06 | | 136 | Candy Maldonado | .10 | .08 |
| 73 | Ernie Whitt | .08 | .06 | | 137 | Mike Marshall | .15 | .11 |

| # | Player | MT | NR MT |
|---|--------|-----|------|
| 138 | Len Matuszek | .06 | .05 |
| 139 | Tom Niedenfuer | .08 | .06 |
| 140 | Alejandro Pena | .08 | .06 |
| 141 | Jerry Reuss | .08 | .06 |
| 142 | Bill Russell | .08 | .06 |
| 143 | Steve Sax | .20 | .15 |
| 144 | Mike Scioscia | .08 | .06 |
| 145 | Fernando Valenzuela | .30 | .25 |
| 146 | Bob Welch | .12 | .09 |
| 147 | Terry Whitfield | .06 | .05 |
| 148 | Juan Beniquez | .06 | .05 |
| 149 | Bob Boone | .08 | .06 |
| 150 | John Candelaria | .10 | .08 |
| 151 | Rod Carew | .70 | .50 |
| 152 | *Stewart Cliburn*(FC) | .12 | .09 |
| 153 | Doug DeCinces | .10 | .08 |
| 154 | Brian Downing | .08 | .06 |
| 155 | Ken Forsch | .06 | .05 |
| 156 | Craig Gerber | .06 | .05 |
| 157 | Bobby Grich | .10 | .08 |
| 158 | George Hendrick | .08 | .06 |
| 159 | Al Holland | .06 | .05 |
| 160 | Reggie Jackson | .50 | .40 |
| 161 | Ruppert Jones | .06 | .05 |
| 162 | *Urbano Lugo* | .08 | .06 |
| 163 | *Kirk McCaskill*(FC) | .35 | .25 |
| 164 | Donnie Moore | .06 | .05 |
| 165 | Gary Pettis | .06 | .05 |
| 166 | Ron Romanick | .06 | .05 |
| 167 | Dick Schofield | .06 | .05 |
| 168 | Daryl Sconiers | .06 | .05 |
| 169 | Jim Slaton | .06 | .05 |
| 170 | Don Sutton | .25 | .20 |
| 171 | Mike Witt | .10 | .08 |
| 172 | Buddy Bell | .10 | .08 |
| 173 | Tom Browning | .30 | .25 |
| 174 | Dave Concepcion | .12 | .09 |
| 175 | Eric Davis | 1.00 | .70 |
| 176 | Bo Diaz | .08 | .06 |
| 177 | Nick Esasky | .08 | .06 |
| 178 | John Franco | .12 | .09 |
| 179 | Tom Hume | .06 | .05 |
| 180 | Wayne Krenchicki | .06 | .05 |
| 181 | Andy McGaffigan | .06 | .05 |
| 182 | Eddie Milner | .06 | .05 |
| 183 | Ron Oester | .06 | .05 |
| 184 | Dave Parker | .20 | .15 |
| 185 | Frank Pastore | .06 | .05 |
| 186 | Tony Perez | .15 | .11 |
| 187 | Ted Power | .08 | .06 |
| 188 | Joe Price | .06 | .05 |
| 189 | Gary Redus | .06 | .05 |
| 190 | Ron Robinson | .08 | .06 |
| 191 | Pete Rose | .70 | .50 |
| 192 | Mario Soto | .08 | .06 |
| 193 | John Stuper | .06 | .05 |
| 194 | Jay Tibbs | .06 | .05 |
| 195 | Dave Van Gorder | .06 | .05 |
| 196 | Max Venable | .06 | .05 |
| 197 | Juan Agosto | .06 | .05 |
| 198 | Harold Baines | .15 | .11 |
| 199 | Floyd Bannister | .10 | .08 |
| 200 | Britt Burns | .06 | .05 |
| 201 | Julio Cruz | .06 | .05 |
| 202 | *Joel Davis*(FC) | .08 | .06 |
| 203 | Richard Dotson | .10 | .08 |
| 204 | Carlton Fisk | .50 | .40 |
| 205 | Scott Fletcher | .08 | .06 |
| 206 | *Ozzie Guillen* | .80 | .60 |
| 207 | Jerry Hairston | .06 | .05 |
| 208 | Tim Hulett | .08 | .06 |
| 209 | Bob James | .06 | .05 |
| 210 | Ron Kittle | .10 | .08 |
| 211 | Rudy Law | .06 | .05 |
| 212 | Bryan Little | .06 | .05 |
| 213 | Gene Nelson | .06 | .05 |
| 214 | Reid Nichols | .06 | .05 |
| 215 | Luis Salazar | .06 | .05 |
| 216 | Tom Seaver | 1.00 | .70 |
| 217 | Dan Spillner | .06 | .05 |
| 218 | Bruce Tanner | .06 | .05 |
| 219 | Greg Walker | .10 | .08 |
| 220 | Dave Wehrmeister | .06 | .05 |
| 221 | Juan Berenguer | .06 | .05 |
| 222 | Dave Bergman | .06 | .05 |
| 223 | Tom Brookens | .06 | .05 |
| 224 | Darrell Evans | .12 | .09 |
| 225 | Barbaro Garbey | .06 | .05 |
| 226 | Kirk Gibson | .30 | .25 |
| 227 | John Grubb | .06 | .05 |
| 228 | Willie Hernandez | .08 | .06 |
| 229 | Larry Herndon | .08 | .06 |
| 230 | Chet Lemon | .08 | .06 |
| 231 | Aurelio Lopez | .06 | .05 |
| 232 | Jack Morris | .20 | .15 |
| 233 | Randy O'Neal | .06 | .05 |
| 234 | Lance Parrish | .20 | .15 |
| 235 | Dan Petry | .08 | .06 |
| 236 | Alex Sanchez | .06 | .05 |
| 237 | Bill Scherrer | .06 | .05 |
| 238 | Nelson Simmons | .06 | .05 |
| 239 | Frank Tanana | .10 | .08 |
| 240 | Walt Terrell | .08 | .06 |
| 241 | Alan Trammell | .30 | .25 |
| 242 | Lou Whitaker | .30 | .25 |
| 243 | Milt Wilcox | .06 | .05 |
| 244 | Hubie Brooks | .10 | .08 |
| 245 | *Tim Burke*(FC) | .30 | .25 |
| 246 | Andre Dawson | .30 | .25 |
| 247 | Mike Fitzgerald | .06 | .05 |
| 248 | Terry Francona | .06 | .05 |
| 249 | Bill Gullickson | .06 | .05 |
| 250 | Joe Hesketh | .06 | .05 |
| 251 | Bill Laskey | .06 | .05 |
| 252 | Vance Law | .08 | .06 |
| 253 | Charlie Lea | .06 | .05 |
| 254 | Gary Lucas | .06 | .05 |
| 255 | David Palmer | .06 | .05 |
| 256 | Tim Raines | .30 | .25 |
| 257 | Jeff Reardon | .12 | .09 |
| 258 | Bert Roberge | .06 | .05 |
| 259 | Dan Schatzeder | .06 | .05 |
| 260 | Bryn Smith | .06 | .05 |
| 261 | Randy St. Claire(FC) | .08 | .06 |
| 262 | Scot Thompson | .06 | .05 |
| 263 | Tim Wallach | .12 | .09 |
| 264 | U.L. Washington | .06 | .05 |
| 265 | *Mitch Webster*(FC) | .25 | .20 |
| 266 | *Herm Winningham* | .15 | .11 |
| 267 | *Floyd Youmans*(FC) | | |

| | | MT | NR MT | | | | MT | NR MT |
|---|---|---|---|---|---|---|---|---|
| | | .15 | .11 | 331 | Kevin McReynolds | | .30 | .25 |
| 268 | Don Aase | .06 | .05 | 332 | Graig Nettles | | .15 | .11 |
| 269 | Mike Boddicker | .08 | .06 | 333 | Jerry Royster | | .06 | .05 |
| 270 | Rich Dauer | .06 | .05 | 334 | Eric Show | | .08 | .06 |
| 271 | Storm Davis | .10 | .08 | 335 | Tim Stoddard | | .06 | .05 |
| 272 | Rick Dempsey | .08 | .06 | 336 | Garry Templeton | | .08 | .06 |
| 273 | Ken Dixon | .06 | .05 | 337 | Mark Thurmond | | .06 | .05 |
| 274 | Jim Dwyer | .06 | .05 | 338 | Ed Wojna | | .06 | .05 |
| 275 | Mike Flanagan | .10 | .08 | 339 | Tony Armas | | .08 | .06 |
| 276 | Wayne Gross | .06 | .05 | 340 | Marty Barrett | | .10 | .08 |
| 277 | Lee Lacy | .06 | .05 | 341 | Wade Boggs | | 2.25 | 1.75 |
| 278 | Fred Lynn | .20 | .15 | 342 | Dennis Boyd | | .08 | .06 |
| 279 | Tippy Martinez | .06 | .05 | 343 | Bill Buckner | | .12 | .09 |
| 280 | Dennis Martinez | .08 | .06 | 344 | Mark Clear | | .06 | .05 |
| 281 | Scott McGregor | .08 | .06 | 345 | Roger Clemens | | 10.00 | 7.50 |
| 282 | Eddie Murray | .40 | .30 | 346 | Steve Crawford | | .06 | .05 |
| 283 | Floyd Rayford | .06 | .05 | 347 | Mike Easler | | .08 | .06 |
| 284 | Cal Ripken, Jr. | 5.00 | 3.75 | 348 | Dwight Evans | | .12 | .09 |
| 285 | Gary Roenicke | .06 | .05 | 349 | Rich Gedman | | .10 | .08 |
| 286 | Larry Sheets | .20 | .15 | 350 | Jackie Gutierrez | | .06 | .05 |
| 287 | John Shelby | .06 | .05 | 351 | Glenn Hoffman | | .06 | .05 |
| 288 | Nate Snell | .06 | .05 | 352 | Bruce Hurst | | .12 | .09 |
| 289 | Sammy Stewart | .06 | .05 | 353 | Bruce Kison | | .06 | .05 |
| 290 | Alan Wiggins | .06 | .05 | 354 | Tim Lollar | | .06 | .05 |
| 291 | Mike Young | .06 | .05 | 355 | Steve Lyons | | .08 | .06 |
| 292 | Alan Ashby | .06 | .05 | 356 | Al Nipper | | .08 | .06 |
| 293 | Mark Bailey | .06 | .05 | 357 | Bob Ojeda | | .08 | .06 |
| 294 | Kevin Bass | .10 | .08 | 358 | Jim Rice | | .30 | .25 |
| 295 | Jeff Calhoun | .06 | .05 | 359 | Bob Stanley | | .06 | .05 |
| 296 | Jose Cruz | .10 | .08 | 360 | Mike Trujillo | | .06 | .05 |
| 297 | Glenn Davis | 1.50 | 1.25 | 361 | Thad Bosley | | .06 | .05 |
| 298 | Bill Dawley | .06 | .05 | 362 | Warren Brusstar | | .06 | .05 |
| 299 | Frank DiPino | .06 | .05 | 363 | Ron Cey | | .10 | .08 |
| 300 | Bill Doran | .10 | .08 | 364 | Jody Davis | | .10 | .08 |
| 301 | Phil Garner | .08 | .06 | 365 | Bob Dernier | | .06 | .05 |
| 302 | *Jeff Heathcock*(FC) | | | 366 | Shawon Dunston | | .70 | .50 |
| | | .10 | .08 | 367 | Leon Durham | | .08 | .06 |
| 303 | *Charlie Kerfeld*(FC) | | | 368 | Dennis Eckersley | | .12 | .09 |
| | | .15 | .11 | 369 | Ray Fontenot | | .06 | .05 |
| 304 | Bob Knepper | .08 | .06 | 370 | George Frazier | | .06 | .05 |
| 305 | Ron Mathis | .06 | .05 | 371 | Bill Hatcher | | .10 | .08 |
| 306 | Jerry Mumphrey | .06 | .05 | 372 | Dave Lopes | | .08 | .06 |
| 307 | Jim Pankovits | .06 | .05 | 373 | Gary Matthews | | .10 | .08 |
| 308 | Terry Puhl | .06 | .05 | 374 | Ron Meredith | | .06 | .05 |
| 309 | Craig Reynolds | .06 | .05 | 375 | Keith Moreland | | .08 | .06 |
| 310 | Nolan Ryan | 6.00 | 4.50 | 376 | Reggie Patterson | | .06 | .05 |
| 311 | Mike Scott | .15 | .11 | 377 | Dick Ruthven | | .06 | .05 |
| 312 | Dave Smith | .08 | .06 | 378 | Ryne Sandberg | | 4.00 | 3.00 |
| 313 | Dickie Thon | .08 | .06 | 379 | Scott Sanderson | | .06 | .05 |
| 314 | Denny Walling | .06 | .05 | 380 | Lee Smith | | .10 | .08 |
| 315 | Kurt Bevacqua | .06 | .05 | 381 | Lary Sorensen | | .06 | .05 |
| 316 | Al Bumbry | .06 | .05 | 382 | Chris Speier | | .06 | .05 |
| 317 | Jerry Davis | .06 | .05 | 383 | Rick Sutcliffe | | .12 | .09 |
| 318 | Luis DeLeon | .06 | .05 | 384 | Steve Trout | | .06 | .05 |
| 319 | Dave Dravecky | .08 | .06 | 385 | Gary Woods | | .06 | .05 |
| 320 | Tim Flannery | .06 | .05 | 386 | Bert Blyleven | | .15 | .11 |
| 321 | Steve Garvey | .30 | .25 | 387 | Tom Brunansky | | .12 | .09 |
| 322 | Goose Gossage | .20 | .15 | 388 | Randy Bush | | .06 | .05 |
| 323 | Tony Gwynn | .70 | .50 | 389 | John Butcher | | .06 | .05 |
| 324 | Andy Hawkins | .06 | .05 | 390 | Ron Davis | | .06 | .05 |
| 325 | LaMarr Hoyt | .06 | .05 | 391 | Dave Engle | | .06 | .05 |
| 326 | Roy Lee Jackson | .06 | .05 | 392 | Frank Eufemia | | .06 | .05 |
| 327 | Terry Kennedy | .08 | .06 | 393 | Pete Filson | | .06 | .05 |
| 328 | Craig Lefferts | .06 | .05 | 394 | Gary Gaetti | | .20 | .15 |
| 329 | Carmelo Martinez | .08 | .06 | 395 | Greg Gagne | | .10 | .08 |
| 330 | *Lance McCullers*(FC) | | | 396 | Mickey Hatcher | | .06 | .05 |
| | | .25 | .20 | 397 | Kent Hrbek | | .20 | .15 |

| # | Player | MT | NR MT |
|---|---|---|---|
| 398 | Tim Laudner | .06 | .05 |
| 399 | Rick Lysander | .06 | .05 |
| 400 | Dave Meier | .06 | .05 |
| 401 | Kirby Puckett | 8.00 | 6.00 |
| 402 | Mark Salas | .08 | .06 |
| 403 | Ken Schrom | .06 | .05 |
| 404 | Roy Smalley | .06 | .05 |
| 405 | Mike Smithson | .06 | .05 |
| 406 | Mike Stenhouse | .06 | .05 |
| 407 | Tim Teufel | .06 | .05 |
| 408 | Frank Viola | .15 | .11 |
| 409 | Ron Washington | .06 | .05 |
| 410 | Keith Atherton | .06 | .05 |
| 411 | Dusty Baker | .08 | .06 |
| 412 | *Tim Birtsas* | .12 | .09 |
| 413 | Bruce Bochte | .06 | .05 |
| 414 | Chris Codiroli | .06 | .05 |
| 415 | Dave Collins | .08 | .06 |
| 416 | Mike Davis | .08 | .06 |
| 417 | Alfredo Griffin | .08 | .06 |
| 418 | Mike Heath | .06 | .05 |
| 419 | Steve Henderson | .06 | .05 |
| 420 | Donnie Hill | .06 | .05 |
| 421 | Jay Howell | .08 | .06 |
| 422 | Tommy John | .20 | .15 |
| 423 | Dave Kingman | .15 | .11 |
| 424 | Bill Krueger | .06 | .05 |
| 425 | Rick Langford | .06 | .05 |
| 426 | Carney Lansford | .10 | .08 |
| 427 | Steve McCatty | .06 | .05 |
| 428 | Dwayne Murphy | .08 | .06 |
| 429 | *Steve Ontiveros*(FC) | .12 | .09 |
| 430 | Tony Phillips | .06 | .05 |
| 431 | Jose Rijo | .10 | .08 |
| 432 | *Mickey Tettleton* | 2.00 | 1.50 |
| 433 | Luis Aguayo | .06 | .05 |
| 434 | Larry Andersen | .06 | .05 |
| 435 | Steve Carlton | .30 | .25 |
| 436 | *Don Carman* | .30 | .25 |
| 437 | Tim Corcoran | .06 | .05 |
| 438 | *Darren Daulton* | 2.25 | 1.75 |
| 439 | John Denny | .06 | .05 |
| 440 | Tom Foley | .06 | .05 |
| 441 | Greg Gross | .06 | .05 |
| 442 | Kevin Gross | .08 | .06 |
| 443 | Von Hayes | .10 | .08 |
| 444 | Charles Hudson | .06 | .05 |
| 445 | Garry Maddox | .08 | .06 |
| 446 | Shane Rawley | .10 | .08 |
| 447 | Dave Rucker | .06 | .05 |
| 448 | John Russell | .06 | .05 |
| 449 | Juan Samuel | .12 | .09 |
| 450 | Mike Schmidt | 2.00 | 1.50 |
| 451 | Rick Schu | .08 | .06 |
| 452 | Dave Shipanoff | .06 | .05 |
| 453 | Dave Stewart | .12 | .09 |
| 454 | Jeff Stone | .06 | .05 |
| 455 | Kent Tekulve | .08 | .06 |
| 456 | Ozzie Virgil | .06 | .05 |
| 457 | Glenn Wilson | .08 | .06 |
| 458 | Jim Beattie | .06 | .05 |
| 459 | Karl Best | .06 | .05 |
| 460 | Barry Bonnell | .06 | .05 |
| 461 | Phil Bradley | .20 | .15 |
| 462 | *Ivan Calderon* | 2.00 | 1.50 |
| 463 | Al Cowens | .06 | .05 |
| 464 | Alvin Davis | .30 | .25 |
| 465 | Dave Henderson | .10 | .08 |
| 466 | Bob Kearney | .06 | .05 |
| 467 | Mark Langston | .30 | .25 |
| 468 | Bob Long | .06 | .05 |
| 469 | Mike Moore | .06 | .05 |
| 470 | Edwin Nunez | .06 | .05 |
| 471 | Spike Owen | .06 | .05 |
| 472 | Jack Perconte | .06 | .05 |
| 473 | Jim Presley | .15 | .11 |
| 474 | Donnie Scott | .06 | .05 |
| 475 | Bill Swift(FC) | .12 | .09 |
| 476 | Danny Tartabull | 2.00 | 1.50 |
| 477 | Gorman Thomas | .10 | .08 |
| 478 | Roy Thomas | .06 | .05 |
| 479 | Ed Vande Berg | .06 | .05 |
| 480 | Frank Wills | .06 | .05 |
| 481 | Matt Young | .06 | .05 |
| 482 | Ray Burris | .06 | .05 |
| 483 | Jaime Cocanower | .06 | .05 |
| 484 | Cecil Cooper | .12 | .09 |
| 485 | Danny Darwin | .06 | .05 |
| 486 | Rollie Fingers | .20 | .15 |
| 487 | Jim Gantner | .08 | .06 |
| 488 | Bob Gibson | .06 | .05 |
| 489 | Moose Haas | .06 | .05 |
| 490 | *Teddy Higuera* | .60 | .45 |
| 491 | Paul Householder | .06 | .05 |
| 492 | Pete Ladd | .06 | .05 |
| 493 | Rick Manning | .06 | .05 |
| 494 | Bob McClure | .06 | .05 |
| 495 | Paul Molitor | .15 | .11 |
| 496 | Charlie Moore | .06 | .05 |
| 497 | Ben Oglivie | .08 | .06 |
| 498 | Randy Ready | .06 | .05 |
| 499 | *Earnie Riles* | .20 | .15 |
| 500 | Ed Romero | .06 | .05 |
| 501 | Bill Schroeder | .06 | .05 |
| 502 | Ray Searage | .06 | .05 |
| 503 | Ted Simmons | .12 | .09 |
| 504 | Pete Vuckovich | .08 | .06 |
| 505 | Rick Waits | .06 | .05 |
| 506 | Robin Yount | 2.00 | 1.50 |
| 507 | Len Barker | .08 | .06 |
| 508 | Steve Bedrosian | .12 | .09 |
| 509 | Bruce Benedict | .06 | .05 |
| 510 | Rick Camp | .06 | .05 |
| 511 | Rick Cerone | .06 | .05 |
| 512 | Chris Chambliss | .08 | .06 |
| 513 | Jeff Dedmon | .06 | .05 |
| 514 | Terry Forster | .08 | .06 |
| 515 | Gene Garber | .06 | .05 |
| 516 | Terry Harper | .06 | .05 |
| 517 | Bob Horner | .12 | .09 |
| 518 | Glenn Hubbard | .06 | .05 |
| 519 | *Joe Johnson*(FC) | .08 | .06 |
| 520 | Brad Komminsk | .06 | .05 |
| 521 | Rick Mahler | .06 | .05 |
| 522 | Dale Murphy | .50 | .40 |
| 523 | Ken Oberkfell | .06 | .05 |
| 524 | Pascual Perez | .08 | .06 |
| 525 | Gerald Perry | .12 | .09 |
| 526 | Rafael Ramirez | .06 | .05 |
| 527 | *Steve Shields*(FC) | .12 | .09 |
| 528 | Zane Smith | .10 | .08 |

| | | MT | NR MT |
|---|---|---|---|
| 529 | Bruce Sutter | .12 | .09 |
| 530 | *Milt Thompson*(FC) | | |
| | | .15 | .11 |
| 531 | Claudell Washington | .08 | .06 |
| 532 | Paul Zuvella | .06 | .05 |
| 533 | Vida Blue | .10 | .08 |
| 534 | Bob Brenly | .06 | .05 |
| 535 | *Chris Brown* | .20 | .15 |
| 536 | Chili Davis | .10 | .08 |
| 537 | Mark Davis | .06 | .05 |
| 538 | Rob Deer | .12 | .09 |
| 539 | Dan Driessen | .08 | .06 |
| 540 | Scott Garrelts | .08 | .06 |
| 541 | Dan Gladden | .08 | .06 |
| 542 | Jim Gott | .06 | .05 |
| 543 | David Green | .06 | .05 |
| 544 | Atlee Hammaker | .06 | .05 |
| 545 | Mike Jeffcoat | .06 | .05 |
| 546 | Mike Krukow | .08 | .06 |
| 547 | Dave LaPoint | .08 | .06 |
| 548 | Jeff Leonard | .08 | .06 |
| 549 | Greg Minton | .06 | .05 |
| 550 | Alex Trevino | .06 | .05 |
| 551 | Manny Trillo | .08 | .06 |
| 552 | *Jose Uribe* | .20 | .15 |
| 553 | Brad Wellman | .06 | .05 |
| 554 | Frank Williams | .06 | .05 |
| 555 | Joel Youngblood | .06 | .05 |
| 556 | Alan Bannister | .06 | .05 |
| 557 | Glenn Brummer | .06 | .05 |
| 558 | *Steve Buechele*(FC) | | |
| | | .20 | .15 |
| 559 | *Jose Guzman*(FC) | | |
| | | .20 | .15 |
| 560 | Toby Harrah | .08 | .06 |
| 561 | Greg Harris | .06 | .05 |
| 562 | *Dwayne Henry*(FC) | | |
| | | .10 | .08 |
| 563 | Burt Hooton | .08 | .06 |
| 564 | Charlie Hough | .08 | .06 |
| 565 | Mike Mason | .06 | .05 |
| 566 | *Oddibe McDowell* | .20 | .15 |
| 567 | Dickie Noles | .06 | .05 |
| 568 | Pete O'Brien | .10 | .08 |
| 569 | Larry Parrish | .10 | .08 |
| 570 | Dave Rozema | .06 | .05 |
| 571 | Dave Schmidt | .06 | .05 |
| 572 | Don Slaught | .06 | .05 |
| 573 | Wayne Tolleson | .06 | .05 |
| 574 | Duane Walker | .06 | .05 |
| 575 | Gary Ward | .08 | .06 |
| 576 | Chris Welsh | .06 | .05 |
| 577 | Curtis Wilkerson | .06 | .05 |
| 578 | George Wright | .06 | .05 |
| 579 | Chris Bando | .06 | .05 |
| 580 | Tony Bernazard | .06 | .05 |
| 581 | Brett Butler | .08 | .06 |
| 582 | Ernie Camacho | .06 | .05 |
| 583 | Joe Carter | .20 | .15 |
| 584 | Carmello Castillo (Carmelo) | .06 | .05 |
| 585 | Jamie Easterly | .06 | .05 |
| 586 | Julio Franco | .10 | .08 |
| 587 | Mel Hall | .08 | .06 |
| 588 | Mike Hargrove | .06 | .05 |
| 589 | Neal Heaton | .06 | .05 |
| 590 | Brook Jacoby | .10 | .08 |

| | | MT | NR MT |
|---|---|---|---|
| 591 | *Otis Nixon*(FC) | .12 | .09 |
| 592 | Jerry Reed | .06 | .05 |
| 593 | Vern Ruhle | .06 | .05 |
| 594 | Pat Tabler | .08 | .06 |
| 595 | Rich Thompson | .06 | .05 |
| 596 | Andre Thornton | .08 | .06 |
| 597 | Dave Von Ohlen | .06 | .05 |
| 598 | George Vukovich | .06 | .05 |
| 599 | Tom Waddell | .06 | .05 |
| 600 | Curt Wardle | .06 | .05 |
| 601 | Jerry Willard | .06 | .05 |
| 602 | Bill Almon | .06 | .05 |
| 603 | Mike Bielecki | .08 | .06 |
| 604 | Sid Bream | .10 | .08 |
| 605 | Mike Brown | .06 | .05 |
| 606 | *Pat Clements* | .12 | .09 |
| 607 | Jose DeLeon | .08 | .06 |
| 608 | Denny Gonzalez | .06 | .05 |
| 609 | Cecilio Guante | .06 | .05 |
| 610 | Steve Kemp | .08 | .06 |
| 611 | Sam Khalifa | .06 | .05 |
| 612 | Lee Mazzilli | .08 | .06 |
| 613 | Larry McWilliams | .06 | .05 |
| 614 | Jim Morrison | .06 | .05 |
| 615 | *Joe Orsulak* | .15 | .11 |
| 616 | Tony Pena | .10 | .08 |
| 617 | Johnny Ray | .10 | .08 |
| 618 | Rick Reuschel | .10 | .08 |
| 619 | R.J. Reynolds | .08 | .06 |
| 620 | Rick Rhoden | .10 | .08 |
| 621 | Don Robinson | .08 | .06 |
| 622 | Jason Thompson | .06 | .05 |
| 623 | Lee Tunnell | .06 | .05 |
| 624 | Jim Winn | .06 | .05 |
| 625 | Marvell Wynne | .06 | .05 |
| 626 | Gooden In Action (Dwight Gooden) | .50 | .40 |
| 627 | Mattingly In Action (Don Mattingly) | 1.25 | .90 |
| 628 | 4,192! (Pete Rose) | .50 | .40 |
| 629 | 3,000 Career Hits (Rod Carew) | .50 | .40 |
| 630 | 300 Career Wins (Phil Niekro, Tom Seaver) | .20 | .15 |
| 631 | Ouch! (Don Baylor) | .08 | .06 |
| 632 | Instant Offense (Tim Raines, Darryl Strawberry) | .30 | .25 |
| 633 | Shortstops Supreme (Cal Ripken, Jr., Alan Trammell) | .30 | .25 |
| 634 | Boggs & "Hero" (Wade Boggs, George Brett) | .60 | .45 |
| 635 | Braves Dynamic Duo (Bob Horner, Dale Murphy) | .30 | .25 |
| 636 | Cardinal Ignitors (Vince Coleman, Willie McGee) | .35 | .25 |
| 637 | Terror on the Basepaths (Vince Coleman) | .50 | .40 |
| 638 | Charlie Hustle & Dr. K (Dwight Gooden, Pete Rose) | .70 | .50 |
| 639 | 1984 and 1985 A.L. Batting Champs (Wade Boggs, Don Mattingly) | 1.00 | .70 |
| 640 | N.L. West Sluggers | | |

| | MT | NR MT |
|---|---|---|
| (Steve Garvey, Dale Murphy, Dave Parker) | .30 | .25 |
| 641 Staff Aces (Dwight Gooden, Fernando Valenzuela) | .40 | .30 |
| 642 Blue Jay Stoppers (Jimmy Key, Dave Stieb) | .10 | .08 |
| 643 A.L. All-Star Backstops (Carlton Fisk, Rich Gedman) | .10 | .08 |
| 644 Major League Prospect (Benito Santiago, Gene Walter)(FC) | 3.00 | 2.25 |
| 645 Major League Prospect (Colin Ward, Mike Woodard)(FC) | .10 | .08 |
| 646 Major League Prospect (Kal Daniels, Paul O'Neill)(FC) | 4.00 | 3.00 |
| 647 Major League Prospect (Andres Galarraga, Fred Toliver)(FC) | .80 | .60 |
| 648 Major League Prospect (Curt Ford, Bob Kipper)(FC) | .25 | .20 |
| 649 Major League Prospect (Jose Canseco, Eric Plunk)(FC) | 40.00 | 30.00 |
| 650 Major League Prospect (Mark McLemore, Gus Polidor)(FC) | .15 | .11 |
| 651 Major League Prospect (Mickey Brantley, Rob Woodward)(FC) | .15 | .11 |
| 652 Major League Prospect (Mark Funderburk, Billy Joe Robidoux)(FC) | .10 | .08 |
| 653 Major League Prospect (Cecil Fielder, Cory Snyder)(FC) | 20.00 | 15.00 |
| 654 Checklist 1-97 | .06 | .05 |
| 655 Checklist 98-196 | .06 | .05 |
| 656 Checklist 197-291 | .06 | .05 |
| 657 Checklist 292-385 | .06 | .05 |
| 658 Checklist 386-482 | .06 | .05 |
| 659 Checklist 483-578 | .06 | .05 |
| 660 Checklist 579-660 | .06 | .05 |

## 1986 Fleer Update

Issued near the end of the baseball season, the 1986 Fleer Update set consists of 132 cards numbered U-1 through U-132. The cards, which measure 2-1/2" by 3-1/2" in size, are identical in design to the regular 1986 Fleer set. The purpose of the set is to update player trades and include new players not depicted in the regular issue. The set was issued with team logo stickers in a specially designed box and was available only through hobby dealers.

| | | MT | NR MT |
|---|---|---|---|
| | Complete Set: | 30.00 | 22.00 |
| | Common Player: | .08 | .06 |
| 1 | Mike Aldrete(FC) | .15 | .11 |
| 2 | Andy Allanson(FC) | .20 | .15 |
| 3 | Neil Allen | .08 | .06 |
| 4 | Joaquin Andujar | .10 | .08 |
| 5 | Paul Assenmacher(FC) | .20 | .15 |
| 6 | Scott Bailes(FC) | .15 | .11 |
| 7 | Jay Baller(FC) | .15 | .11 |
| 8 | Scott Bankhead(FC) | .20 | .15 |
| 9 | Bill Bathe(FC) | .08 | .06 |
| 10 | Don Baylor | .15 | .11 |
| 11 | Billy Beane(FC) | .08 | .06 |
| 12 | Steve Bedrosian | .15 | .11 |
| 13 | Juan Beniquez | .08 | .06 |
| 14 | Barry Bonds(FC) | 9.00 | 6.75 |
| 15 | Bobby Bonilla(FC) | 7.00 | 5.25 |
| 16 | Rich Bordi | .08 | .06 |
| 17 | Bill Campbell | .08 | .06 |
| 18 | Tom Candiotti | .08 | .06 |
| 19 | John Cangelosi(FC) | .20 | .15 |
| 20 | Jose Canseco | 10.00 | 7.50 |
| 21 | Chuck Cary(FC) | .15 | .11 |
| 22 | Juan Castillo(FC) | .10 | .08 |
| 23 | Rick Cerone | .08 | .06 |
| 24 | John Cerutti(FC) | .15 | .11 |
| 25 | Will Clark(FC) | 10.00 | 7.50 |
| 26 | Mark Clear | .08 | .06 |
| 27 | Darnell Coles(FC) | .15 | .11 |
| 28 | Dave Collins | .10 | .08 |
| 29 | Tim Conroy | .08 | .06 |
| 30 | Ed Correa(FC) | .20 | .15 |
| 31 | Joe Cowley | .08 | .06 |
| 32 | Bill Dawley | .08 | .06 |
| 33 | Rob Deer | .15 | .11 |
| 34 | John Denny | .08 | .06 |
| 35 | Jim DeShaies (Deshaies)(FC) | .25 | .20 |
| 36 | Doug Drabek(FC) | 1.25 | .90 |
| 37 | Mike Easler | .12 | .09 |
| 38 | Mark Eichhorn(FC) | .20 | .15 |
| 39 | Dave Engle | .08 | .06 |
| 40 | Mike Fischlin | .08 | .06 |
| 41 | Scott Fletcher | .15 | .11 |
| 42 | Terry Forster | .12 | .09 |
| 43 | Terry Francona | .08 | .06 |
| 44 | Andres Galarraga | .40 | .30 |
| 45 | Lee Guetterman(FC) | .20 | .15 |
| 46 | Bill Gullickson | .08 | .06 |

| | | MT | NR MT |
|---|---|---|---|
| 47 | Jackie Gutierrez | .08 | .06 |
| 48 | Moose Haas | .08 | .06 |
| 49 | Billy Hatcher | .15 | .11 |
| 50 | Mike Heath | .08 | .06 |
| 51 | Guy Hoffman(FC) | .10 | .08 |
| 52 | Tom Hume | .08 | .06 |
| 53 | Pete Incaviglia(FC) | .40 | .30 |
| 54 | Dane Iorg | .08 | .06 |
| 55 | Chris James(FC) | .50 | .40 |
| 56 | Stan Javier(FC) | .25 | .20 |
| 57 | Tommy John | .20 | .15 |
| 58 | Tracy Jones(FC) | .20 | .15 |
| 59 | Wally Joyner(FC) | 1.50 | 1.25 |
| 60 | Wayne Krenchicki | .08 | .06 |
| 61 | John Kruk(FC) | 1.00 | .70 |
| 62 | Mike LaCoss | .08 | .06 |
| 63 | Pete Ladd | .08 | .06 |
| 64 | Dave LaPoint | .15 | .11 |
| 65 | Mike LaValliere(FC) | .40 | .30 |
| 66 | Rudy Law | .08 | .06 |
| 67 | Dennis Leonard | .10 | .08 |
| 68 | Steve Lombardozzi(FC) | .20 | .15 |
| 69 | Aurelio Lopez | .08 | .06 |
| 70 | Mickey Mahler | .08 | .06 |
| 71 | Candy Maldonado | .15 | .11 |
| 72 | Roger Mason(FC) | .10 | .08 |
| 73 | Greg Mathews(FC) | .25 | .20 |
| 74 | Andy McGaffigan | .08 | .06 |
| 75 | Joel McKeon(FC) | .12 | .09 |
| 76 | Kevin Mitchell(FC) | 2.00 | 1.50 |
| 77 | Bill Mooneyham(FC) | .12 | .09 |
| 78 | Omar Moreno | .08 | .06 |
| 79 | Jerry Mumphrey | .08 | .06 |
| 80 | Al Newman(FC) | .12 | .09 |
| 81 | Phil Niekro | .40 | .30 |
| 82 | Randy Niemann | .08 | .06 |
| 83 | Juan Nieves(FC) | .20 | .15 |
| 84 | Bob Ojeda | .12 | .09 |
| 85 | Rick Ownbey | .08 | .06 |
| 86 | Tom Paciorek | .08 | .06 |
| 87 | David Palmer | .08 | .06 |
| 88 | Jeff Parrett(FC) | .25 | .20 |
| 89 | Pat Perry(FC) | .15 | .11 |
| 90 | Dan Plesac(FC) | .25 | .20 |
| 91 | Darrell Porter | .12 | .09 |
| 92 | Luis Quinones(FC) | .12 | .09 |
| 93 | Rey Quinonez(FC) | .20 | .15 |
| 94 | Gary Redus | .10 | .08 |
| 95 | Jeff Reed(FC) | .12 | .09 |
| 96 | Bip Roberts(FC) | .08 | .06 |
| 97 | Billy Joe Robidoux(FC) | .12 | .09 |
| 98 | Gary Roenicke | .08 | .06 |
| 99 | Ron Roenicke | .08 | .06 |
| 100 | Angel Salazar | .08 | .06 |
| 101 | Joe Sambito | .08 | .06 |
| 102 | Billy Sample | .08 | .06 |
| 103 | Dave Schmidt | .08 | .06 |
| 104 | Ken Schrom | .08 | .06 |
| 105 | Ruben Sierra(FC) | 7.00 | 5.25 |
| 106 | Ted Simmons | .20 | .15 |
| 107 | Sammy Stewart | .08 | .06 |
| 108 | Kurt Stillwell(FC) | .30 | .25 |
| 109 | Dale Sveum(FC) | .25 | .20 |
| 110 | Tim Teufel | .08 | .06 |
| 111 | Bob Tewksbury(FC) | .12 | .09 |
| 112 | Andres Thomas(FC) | .15 | .11 |

| | | MT | NR MT |
|---|---|---|---|
| 113 | Jason Thompson | .08 | .06 |
| 114 | Milt Thompson | .12 | .09 |
| 115 | Rob Thompson(FC) | .40 | .30 |
| 116 | Jay Tibbs | .08 | .06 |
| 117 | Fred Toliver | .12 | .09 |
| 118 | Wayne Tolleson | .08 | .06 |
| 119 | Alex Trevino | .08 | .06 |
| 120 | Manny Trillo | .10 | .08 |
| 121 | Ed Vande Berg | .08 | .06 |
| 122 | Ozzie Virgil | .08 | .06 |
| 123 | Tony Walker(FC) | .08 | .06 |
| 124 | Gene Walter | .12 | .09 |
| 125 | Duane Ward(FC) | .30 | .25 |
| 126 | Jerry Willard | .08 | .06 |
| 127 | Mitch Williams(FC) | .40 | .30 |
| 128 | Reggie Williams(FC) | .20 | .15 |
| 129 | Bobby Witt(FC) | .50 | .40 |
| 130 | Marvell Wynne | .08 | .06 |
| 131 | Steve Yeager | .08 | .06 |
| 132 | Checklist | .08 | .06 |

## 1987 Fleer

The 1987 Fleer set consists of 660 cards, each measuring 2-1/2" by 3-1/2". The card fronts feature an attractive blue and white border. The player's name and position appears in the upper left corner of the card. The player's team logo is located in the lower right corner. The card backs are done in blue, red and white and contain an innovative "Pro Scouts Report" feature which lists the hitter's or pitcher's batting and pitching strengths. For the third year in a row, Fleer included its "Major League Prospects" subset. Fleer produced a glossy-finish Collectors Edition set which came housed in a specially-designed tin box. It was speculated that 100,000 of the glossy sets were produced. After experiencing a dramatic drop in price during 1987, the glossy set now sells for only a few dollars more than the regular issue.

|  | | MT | NR MT |
|---|---|---|---|
| | Complete Set: | 90.00 | 67.00 |
| | Common Player: | .06 | .05 |
| 1 | Rick Aguilera | .08 | .06 |
| 2 | Richard Anderson | .06 | .05 |
| 3 | Wally Backman | .08 | .06 |
| 4 | Gary Carter | .25 | .20 |
| 5 | Ron Darling | .15 | .11 |
| 6 | Len Dykstra | .70 | .50 |
| 7 | Kevin Elster(FC) | .50 | .40 |
| 8 | Sid Fernandez | .12 | .09 |
| 9 | Dwight Gooden | 1.00 | .70 |
| 10 | Ed Hearn(FC) | .10 | .08 |
| 11 | Danny Heep | .06 | .05 |
| 12 | Keith Hernandez | .25 | .20 |
| 13 | Howard Johnson | .10 | .08 |
| 14 | Ray Knight | .08 | .06 |
| 15 | Lee Mazzilli | .08 | .06 |
| 16 | Roger McDowell | .12 | .09 |
| 17 | Kevin Mitchell | 4.00 | 3.00 |
| 18 | Randy Niemann | .06 | .05 |
| 19 | Bob Ojeda | .08 | .06 |
| 20 | Jesse Orosco | .08 | .06 |
| 21 | Rafael Santana | .06 | .05 |
| 22 | Doug Sisk | .06 | .05 |
| 23 | Darryl Strawberry | 3.00 | 2.25 |
| 24 | Tim Teufel | .06 | .05 |
| 25 | Mookie Wilson | .10 | .08 |
| 26 | Tony Armas | .08 | .06 |
| 27 | Marty Barrett | .10 | .08 |
| 28 | Don Baylor | .12 | .09 |
| 29 | Wade Boggs | 1.50 | 1.25 |
| 30 | Oil Can Boyd | .08 | .06 |
| 31 | Bill Buckner | .10 | .08 |
| 32 | Roger Clemens | 4.00 | 3.00 |
| 33 | Steve Crawford | .06 | .05 |
| 34 | Dwight Evans | .12 | .09 |
| 35 | Rich Gedman | .10 | .08 |
| 36 | Dave Henderson | .10 | .08 |
| 37 | Bruce Hurst | .10 | .08 |
| 38 | Tim Lollar | .06 | .05 |
| 39 | Al Nipper | .06 | .05 |
| 40 | Spike Owen | .06 | .05 |
| 41 | Jim Rice | .20 | .15 |
| 42 | Ed Romero | .06 | .05 |
| 43 | Joe Sambito | .06 | .05 |
| 44 | Calvin Schiraldi | .10 | .08 |
| 45 | Tom Seaver | 1.00 | .70 |
| 46 | Jeff Sellers(FC) | .20 | .15 |
| 47 | Bob Stanley | .06 | .05 |
| 48 | Sammy Stewart | .06 | .05 |
| 49 | Larry Andersen | .06 | .05 |
| 50 | Alan Ashby | .06 | .05 |
| 51 | Kevin Bass | .10 | .08 |
| 52 | Jeff Calhoun | .06 | .05 |
| 53 | Jose Cruz | .10 | .08 |
| 54 | Danny Darwin | .06 | .05 |
| 55 | Glenn Davis | .40 | .30 |
| 56 | Jim Deshaies | .25 | .20 |
| 57 | Bill Doran | .10 | .08 |
| 58 | Phil Garner | .06 | .05 |
| 59 | Billy Hatcher | .08 | .06 |
| 60 | Charlie Kerfeld | .06 | .05 |
| 61 | Bob Knepper | .08 | .06 |
| 62 | Dave Lopes | .08 | .06 |
| 63 | Aurelio Lopez | .06 | .05 |
| 64 | Jim Pankovits | .06 | .05 |
| 65 | Terry Puhl | .06 | .05 |

|  | | MT | NR MT |
|---|---|---|---|
| 66 | Craig Reynolds | .06 | .05 |
| 67 | Nolan Ryan | 4.00 | 3.00 |
| 68 | Mike Scott | .15 | .11 |
| 69 | Dave Smith | .08 | .06 |
| 70 | Dickie Thon | .08 | .06 |
| 71 | Tony Walker | .06 | .05 |
| 72 | Denny Walling | .06 | .05 |
| 73 | Bob Boone | .08 | .06 |
| 74 | Rick Burleson | .08 | .06 |
| 75 | John Candelaria | .10 | .08 |
| 76 | Doug Corbett | .06 | .05 |
| 77 | Doug DeCinces | .08 | .06 |
| 78 | Brian Downing | .08 | .06 |
| 79 | Chuck Finley(FC) | 3.00 | 2.25 |
| 80 | Terry Forster | .08 | .06 |
| 81 | Bobby Grich | .10 | .08 |
| 82 | George Hendrick | .08 | .06 |
| 83 | Jack Howell(FC) | .10 | .08 |
| 84 | Reggie Jackson | .35 | .25 |
| 85 | Ruppert Jones | .06 | .05 |
| 86 | Wally Joyner | 2.00 | 1.50 |
| 87 | Gary Lucas | .06 | .05 |
| 88 | Kirk McCaskill | .06 | .05 |
| 89 | Donnie Moore | .06 | .05 |
| 90 | Gary Pettis | .06 | .05 |
| 91 | Vern Ruhle | .06 | .05 |
| 92 | Dick Schofield | .06 | .05 |
| 93 | Don Sutton | .20 | .15 |
| 94 | Rob Wilfong | .06 | .05 |
| 95 | Mike Witt | .10 | .08 |
| 96 | Doug Drabek | 3.00 | 2.25 |
| 97 | Mike Easler | .08 | .06 |
| 98 | Mike Fischlin | .06 | .05 |
| 99 | Brian Fisher | .08 | .06 |
| 100 | Ron Guidry | .15 | .11 |
| 101 | Rickey Henderson | 2.00 | 1.50 |
| 102 | Tommy John | .20 | .15 |
| 103 | Ron Kittle | .10 | .08 |
| 104 | Don Mattingly | 2.00 | 1.50 |
| 105 | Bobby Meacham | .06 | .05 |
| 106 | Joe Niekro | .10 | .08 |
| 107 | Mike Pagliarulo | .10 | .08 |
| 108 | Dan Pasqua | .10 | .08 |
| 109 | Willie Randolph | .10 | .08 |
| 110 | Dennis Rasmussen | .10 | .08 |
| 111 | Dave Righetti | .15 | .11 |
| 112 | Gary Roenicke | .06 | .05 |
| 113 | Rod Scurry | .06 | .05 |
| 114 | Bob Shirley | .06 | .05 |
| 115 | Joel Skinner | .06 | .05 |
| 116 | Tim Stoddard | .06 | .05 |
| 117 | Bob Tewksbury | .80 | .60 |
| 118 | Wayne Tolleson | .06 | .05 |
| 119 | Claudell Washington | .08 | .06 |
| 120 | Dave Winfield | .30 | .25 |
| 121 | Steve Buechele | .08 | .06 |
| 122 | Ed Correa | .15 | .11 |
| 123 | Scott Fletcher | .08 | .06 |
| 124 | Jose Guzman | .10 | .08 |
| 125 | Toby Harrah | .08 | .06 |
| 126 | Greg Harris | .06 | .05 |
| 127 | Charlie Hough | .08 | .06 |
| 128 | Pete Incaviglia | .60 | .45 |
| 129 | Mike Mason | .06 | .05 |
| 130 | Oddibe McDowell | .10 | .08 |
| 131 | Dale Mohorcic(FC) | | |

| | | MT | NR MT | | | | MT | NR MT |
|---|---|---|---|---|---|---|---|---|
| | | .20 | .15 | 197 | Kal Daniels | | .80 | .60 |
| 132 | Pete O'Brien | .10 | .08 | 198 | Eric Davis | | 1.50 | 1.25 |
| 133 | Tom Paciorek | .06 | .05 | 199 | John Denny | | .06 | .05 |
| 134 | Larry Parrish | .08 | .06 | 200 | Bo Diaz | | .08 | .06 |
| 135 | Geno Petralli | .06 | .05 | 201 | Nick Esasky | | .08 | .06 |
| 136 | Darrell Porter | .08 | .06 | 202 | John Franco | | .10 | .08 |
| 137 | Jeff Russell | .06 | .05 | 203 | Bill Gullickson | | .06 | .05 |
| 138 | *Ruben Sierra* | 10.00 | 7.50 | 204 | *Barry Larkin*(FC) | | | |
| 139 | Don Slaught | .06 | .05 | | | | 7.00 | 5.25 |
| 140 | Gary Ward | .08 | .06 | 205 | Eddie Milner | | .06 | .05 |
| 141 | Curtis Wilkerson | .06 | .05 | 206 | *Rob Murphy*(FC) | | .20 | .15 |
| 142 | Mitch Williams | .60 | .45 | 207 | Ron Oester | | .06 | .05 |
| 143 | *Bobby Witt* | 1.00 | .70 | 208 | Dave Parker | | .20 | .15 |
| 144 | Dave Bergman | .06 | .05 | 209 | Tony Perez | | .15 | .11 |
| 145 | Tom Brookens | .06 | .05 | 210 | Ted Power | | .06 | .05 |
| 146 | Bill Campbell | .06 | .05 | 211 | Joe Price | | .06 | .05 |
| 147 | *Chuck Cary* | .10 | .08 | 212 | Ron Robinson | | .06 | .05 |
| 148 | Darnell Coles | .08 | .06 | 213 | Pete Rose | | .60 | .45 |
| 149 | Dave Collins | .08 | .06 | 214 | Mario Soto | | .08 | .06 |
| 150 | Darrell Evans | .12 | .09 | 215 | *Kurt Stillwell* | | .60 | .45 |
| 151 | Kirk Gibson | .25 | .20 | 216 | Max Venable | | .06 | .05 |
| 152 | John Grubb | .06 | .05 | 217 | Chris Welsh | | .06 | .05 |
| 153 | Willie Hernandez | .08 | .06 | 218 | *Carl Willis*(FC) | | .10 | .08 |
| 154 | Larry Herndon | .08 | .06 | 219 | Jesse Barfield | | .15 | .11 |
| 155 | *Eric King* | .25 | .20 | 220 | George Bell | | .25 | .20 |
| 156 | Chet Lemon | .08 | .06 | 221 | Bill Caudill | | .06 | .05 |
| 157 | Dwight Lowry | .06 | .05 | 222 | *John Cerutti* | | .20 | .15 |
| 158 | Jack Morris | .20 | .15 | 223 | Jim Clancy | | .08 | .06 |
| 159 | Randy O'Neal | .06 | .05 | 224 | *Mark Eichhorn* | | .15 | .11 |
| 160 | Lance Parrish | .20 | .15 | 225 | Tony Fernandez | | .12 | .09 |
| 161 | Dan Petry | .08 | .06 | 226 | Damaso Garcia | | .06 | .05 |
| 162 | Pat Sheridan | .06 | .05 | 227 | Kelly Gruber | | 1.00 | .70 |
| 163 | Jim Slaton | .06 | .05 | 228 | Tom Henke | | .08 | .06 |
| 164 | Frank Tanana | .08 | .06 | 229 | Garth Iorg | | .06 | .05 |
| 165 | Walt Terrell | .08 | .06 | 230 | Cliff Johnson | | .06 | .05 |
| 166 | Mark Thurmond | .06 | .05 | 231 | Joe Johnson | | .06 | .05 |
| 167 | Alan Trammell | .25 | .20 | 232 | Jimmy Key | | .12 | .09 |
| 168 | Lou Whitaker | .25 | .20 | 233 | Dennis Lamp | | .06 | .05 |
| 169 | Luis Aguayo | .06 | .05 | 234 | Rick Leach | | .06 | .05 |
| 170 | Steve Bedrosian | .12 | .09 | 235 | Buck Martinez | | .06 | .05 |
| 171 | Don Carman | .10 | .08 | 236 | Lloyd Moseby | | .10 | .08 |
| 172 | Darren Daulton | .06 | .05 | 237 | Rance Mulliniks | | .06 | .05 |
| 173 | Greg Gross | .06 | .05 | 238 | Dave Stieb | | .12 | .09 |
| 174 | Kevin Gross | .08 | .06 | 239 | Willie Upshaw | | .08 | .06 |
| 175 | Von Hayes | .10 | .08 | 240 | Ernie Whitt | | .08 | .06 |
| 176 | Charles Hudson | .06 | .05 | 241 | *Andy Allanson* | | .15 | .11 |
| 177 | Tom Hume | .06 | .05 | 242 | *Scott Bailes* | | .20 | .15 |
| 178 | Steve Jeltz | .06 | .05 | 243 | Chris Bando | | .06 | .05 |
| 179 | *Mike Maddux*(FC) | | | 244 | Tony Bernazard | | .06 | .05 |
| | | .20 | .15 | 245 | John Butcher | | .06 | .05 |
| 180 | Shane Rawley | .08 | .06 | 246 | Brett Butler | | .08 | .06 |
| 181 | Gary Redus | .06 | .05 | 247 | Ernie Camacho | | .06 | .05 |
| 182 | Ron Roenicke | .06 | .05 | 248 | Tom Candiotti | | .06 | .05 |
| 183 | *Bruce Ruffin*(FC) | .20 | .15 | 249 | Joe Carter | | .80 | .60 |
| 184 | John Russell | .06 | .05 | 250 | Carmen Castillo | | .06 | .05 |
| 185 | Juan Samuel | .12 | .09 | 251 | Julio Franco | | .10 | .08 |
| 186 | Dan Schatzeder | .06 | .05 | 252 | Mel Hall | | .08 | .06 |
| 187 | Mike Schmidt | 1.50 | 1.25 | 253 | Brook Jacoby | | .10 | .08 |
| 188 | Rick Schu | .06 | .05 | 254 | Phil Niekro | | .20 | .15 |
| 189 | Jeff Stone | .06 | .05 | 255 | Otis Nixon | | .06 | .05 |
| 190 | Kent Tekulve | .08 | .06 | 256 | Dickie Noles | | .06 | .05 |
| 191 | Milt Thompson | .08 | .06 | 257 | Bryan Oelkers | | .06 | .05 |
| 192 | Glenn Wilson | .08 | .06 | 258 | Ken Schrom | | .06 | .05 |
| 193 | Buddy Bell | .10 | .08 | 259 | Don Schulze | | .06 | .05 |
| 194 | Tom Browning | .10 | .08 | 260 | Cory Snyder | | .50 | .40 |
| 195 | Sal Butera | .06 | .05 | 261 | Pat Tabler | | .08 | .06 |
| 196 | Dave Concepcion | .12 | .09 | 262 | Andre Thornton | | .08 | .06 |

| | | MT | NR MT |
|---|---|---|---|
| 263 | *Rich Yett*(FC) | .12 | .09 |
| 264 | *Mike Aldrete* | .25 | .20 |
| 265 | Juan Berenguer | .06 | .05 |
| 266 | Vida Blue | .10 | .08 |
| 267 | Bob Brenly | .06 | .05 |
| 268 | Chris Brown | .08 | .06 |
| 269 | *Will Clark* | 25.00 | 18.00 |
| 270 | Chili Davis | .08 | .06 |
| 271 | Mark Davis | .06 | .05 |
| 272 | *Kelly Downs*(FC) | .30 | .25 |
| 273 | Scott Garrelts | .06 | .05 |
| 274 | Dan Gladden | .06 | .05 |
| 275 | Mike Krukow | .08 | .06 |
| 276 | *Randy Kutcher*(FC) | | |
| | | .10 | .08 |
| 277 | Mike LaCoss | .06 | .05 |
| 278 | Jeff Leonard | .08 | .06 |
| 279 | Candy Maldonado | .08 | .06 |
| 280 | Roger Mason | .06 | .05 |
| 281 | Bob Melvin(FC) | .08 | .06 |
| 282 | Greg Minton | .06 | .05 |
| 283 | Jeff Robinson | .08 | .06 |
| 284 | Harry Spilman | .06 | .05 |
| 285 | *Rob Thompson* | .35 | .25 |
| 286 | Jose Uribe | .08 | .06 |
| 287 | Frank Williams | .06 | .05 |
| 288 | Joel Youngblood | .06 | .05 |
| 289 | Jack Clark | .15 | .11 |
| 290 | Vince Coleman | .70 | .50 |
| 291 | Tim Conroy | .06 | .05 |
| 292 | Danny Cox | .08 | .06 |
| 293 | Ken Dayley | .06 | .05 |
| 294 | Curt Ford | .06 | .05 |
| 295 | Bob Forsch | .08 | .06 |
| 296 | Tom Herr | .10 | .08 |
| 297 | Ricky Horton | .08 | .06 |
| 298 | Clint Hurdle | .06 | .05 |
| 299 | Jeff Lahti | .06 | .05 |
| 300 | Steve Lake | .06 | .05 |
| 301 | Tito Landrum | .06 | .05 |
| 302 | *Mike LaValliere* | .25 | .20 |
| 303 | *Greg Mathews*(FC) | | |
| | | .20 | .15 |
| 304 | Willie McGee | .12 | .09 |
| 305 | Jose Oquendo | .06 | .05 |
| 306 | Terry Pendleton | .10 | .08 |
| 307 | Pat Perry | .08 | .06 |
| 308 | Ozzie Smith | .80 | .60 |
| 309 | Ray Soff | .06 | .05 |
| 310 | John Tudor | .10 | .08 |
| 311 | Andy Van Slyke | .12 | .09 |
| 312 | Todd Worrell | .20 | .15 |
| 313 | Dann Bilardello | .06 | .05 |
| 314 | Hubie Brooks | .10 | .08 |
| 315 | Tim Burke | .06 | .05 |
| 316 | Andre Dawson | .20 | .15 |
| 317 | Mike Fitzgerald | .06 | .05 |
| 318 | Tom Foley | .06 | .05 |
| 319 | Andres Galarraga | .40 | .30 |
| 320 | Joe Hesketh | .06 | .05 |
| 321 | Wallace Johnson | .06 | .05 |
| 322 | Wayne Krenchicki | .06 | .05 |
| 323 | Vance Law | .08 | .06 |
| 324 | Dennis Martinez | .08 | .06 |
| 325 | Bob McClure | .06 | .05 |
| 326 | Andy McGaffigan | .06 | .05 |
| 327 | *Al Newman* | .08 | .06 |

| | | MT | NR MT |
|---|---|---|---|
| 328 | Tim Raines | .30 | .25 |
| 329 | Jeff Reardon | .10 | .08 |
| 330 | *Luis Rivera*(FC) | .10 | .08 |
| 331 | *Bob Sebra*(FC) | .10 | .08 |
| 332 | Bryn Smith | .06 | .05 |
| 333 | Jay Tibbs | .06 | .05 |
| 334 | Tim Wallach | .12 | .09 |
| 335 | Mitch Webster | .08 | .06 |
| 336 | Jim Wohlford | .06 | .05 |
| 337 | Floyd Youmans | .08 | .06 |
| 338 | *Chris Bosio*(FC) | .40 | .30 |
| 339 | *Glenn Braggs*(FC) | | |
| | | .40 | .30 |
| 340 | Rick Cerone | .06 | .05 |
| 341 | Mark Clear | .06 | .05 |
| 342 | *Bryan Clutterbuck*(FC) | .10 | .08 |
| 343 | Cecil Cooper | .12 | .09 |
| 344 | Rob Deer | .10 | .08 |
| 345 | Jim Gantner | .08 | .06 |
| 346 | Ted Higuera | .20 | .15 |
| 347 | John Henry Johnson | | |
| | | .06 | .05 |
| 348 | Tim Leary(FC) | .30 | .25 |
| 349 | Rick Manning | .06 | .05 |
| 350 | Paul Molitor | .15 | .11 |
| 351 | Charlie Moore | .06 | .05 |
| 352 | Juan Nieves | .10 | .08 |
| 353 | Ben Oglivie | .08 | .06 |
| 354 | *Dan Plesac* | .35 | .25 |
| 355 | Ernest Riles | .06 | .05 |
| 356 | Billy Joe Robidoux | .06 | .05 |
| 357 | Bill Schroeder | .06 | .05 |
| 358 | *Dale Sveum* | .20 | .15 |
| 359 | Gorman Thomas | .10 | .08 |
| 360 | Bill Wegman(FC) | .10 | .08 |
| 361 | Robin Yount | .50 | .40 |
| 362 | Steve Balboni | .08 | .06 |
| 363 | *Scott Bankhead* | .30 | .25 |
| 364 | Buddy Biancalana | .06 | .05 |
| 365 | Bud Black | .06 | .05 |
| 366 | George Brett | .50 | .40 |
| 367 | Steve Farr | .06 | .05 |
| 368 | Mark Gubicza | .12 | .09 |
| 369 | *Bo Jackson* | 5.00 | 3.75 |
| 370 | Danny Jackson | .15 | .11 |
| 371 | *Mike Kingery* | .15 | .11 |
| 372 | Rudy Law | .06 | .05 |
| 373 | Charlie Leibrandt | .08 | .06 |
| 374 | Dennis Leonard | .08 | .06 |
| 375 | Hal McRae | .10 | .08 |
| 376 | Jorge Orta | .06 | .05 |
| 377 | Jamie Quirk | .06 | .05 |
| 378 | Dan Quisenberry | .08 | .06 |
| 379 | Bret Saberhagen | .30 | .25 |
| 380 | Angel Salazar | .06 | .05 |
| 381 | Lonnie Smith | .08 | .06 |
| 382 | Jim Sundberg | .08 | .06 |
| 383 | Frank White | .10 | .08 |
| 384 | Willie Wilson | .12 | .09 |
| 385 | Joaquin Andujar | .08 | .06 |
| 386 | Doug Bair | .06 | .05 |
| 387 | Dusty Baker | .08 | .06 |
| 388 | Bruce Bochte | .06 | .05 |
| 389 | Jose Canseco | 10.00 | 7.50 |
| 390 | Chris Codiroli | .06 | .05 |
| 391 | Mike Davis | .08 | .06 |

| | MT | NR MT | | | MT | NR MT |
|---|---|---|---|---|---|---|
| 392 | Alfredo Griffin | .08 | .06 | | | .25 | .20 |
| 393 | Moose Haas | .06 | .05 | 458 | Ed Vande Berg | .06 | .05 |
| 394 | Donnie Hill | .06 | .05 | 459 | Bob Welch | .10 | .08 |
| 395 | Jay Howell | .08 | .06 | 460 | *Reggie Williams* | .10 | .08 |
| 396 | Dave Kingman | .12 | .09 | 461 | Don Aase | .06 | .05 |
| 397 | Carney Lansford | .10 | .08 | 462 | Juan Beniquez | .06 | .05 |
| 398 | *David Leiper*(FC) | .12 | .09 | 463 | Mike Boddicker | .08 | .06 |
| 399 | *Bill Mooneyham* | .10 | .08 | 464 | Juan Bonilla | .06 | .05 |
| 400 | Dwayne Murphy | .08 | .06 | 465 | Rich Bordi | .06 | .05 |
| 401 | Steve Ontiveros | .06 | .05 | 466 | Storm Davis | .10 | .08 |
| 402 | Tony Phillips | .06 | .05 | 467 | Rick Dempsey | .08 | .06 |
| 403 | Eric Plunk | .08 | .06 | 468 | Ken Dixon | .06 | .05 |
| 404 | Jose Rijo | .08 | .06 | 469 | Jim Dwyer | .06 | .05 |
| 405 | *Terry Steinbach*(FC) | | | 470 | Mike Flanagan | .08 | .06 |
| | | .90 | .70 | 471 | Jackie Gutierrez | .06 | .05 |
| 406 | Dave Stewart | .12 | .09 | 472 | Brad Havens | .06 | .05 |
| 407 | Mickey Tettleton | .06 | .05 | 473 | Lee Lacy | .06 | .05 |
| 408 | Dave Von Ohlen | .06 | .05 | 474 | Fred Lynn | .15 | .11 |
| 409 | Jerry Willard | .06 | .05 | 475 | Scott McGregor | .08 | .06 |
| 410 | Curt Young | .08 | .06 | 476 | Eddie Murray | .35 | .25 |
| 411 | Bruce Bochy | .06 | .05 | 477 | Tom O'Malley | .06 | .05 |
| 412 | Dave Dravecky | .08 | .06 | 478 | Cal Ripken, Jr. | 3.00 | 2.25 |
| 413 | Tim Flannery | .06 | .05 | 479 | Larry Sheets | .08 | .06 |
| 414 | Steve Garvey | .25 | .20 | 480 | John Shelby | .06 | .05 |
| 415 | Goose Gossage | .15 | .11 | 481 | Nate Snell | .06 | .05 |
| 416 | Tony Gwynn | 1.00 | .70 | 482 | Jim Traber(FC) | .10 | .08 |
| 417 | Andy Hawkins | .06 | .05 | 483 | Mike Young | .06 | .05 |
| 418 | LaMarr Hoyt | .06 | .05 | 484 | Neil Allen | .06 | .05 |
| 419 | Terry Kennedy | .08 | .06 | 485 | Harold Baines | .15 | .11 |
| 420 | *John Kruk* | 1.50 | 1.25 | 486 | Floyd Bannister | .10 | .08 |
| 421 | Dave LaPoint | .08 | .06 | 487 | Daryl Boston | .03 | .06 |
| 422 | Craig Lefferts | .06 | .05 | 488 | Ivan Calderon | .50 | .40 |
| 423 | Carmelo Martinez | .08 | .06 | 489 | *John Cangelosi* | .12 | .09 |
| 424 | Lance McCullers | .08 | .06 | 490 | Steve Carlton | .25 | .20 |
| 425 | Kevin McReynolds | .15 | .11 | 491 | Joe Cowley | .06 | .05 |
| 426 | Graig Nettles | .12 | .09 | 492 | Julio Cruz | .06 | .05 |
| 427 | *Bip Roberts* | .80 | .60 | 493 | Bill Dawley | .06 | .05 |
| 428 | Jerry Royster | .06 | .05 | 494 | Jose DeLeon | .08 | .06 |
| 429 | Benito Santiago | .70 | .50 | 495 | Richard Dotson | .08 | .06 |
| 430 | Eric Show | .08 | .06 | 496 | Carlton Fisk | .30 | .25 |
| 431 | Bob Stoddard | .06 | .05 | 497 | Ozzie Guillen | .10 | .08 |
| 432 | Garry Templeton | .08 | .06 | 498 | Jerry Hairston | .06 | .05 |
| 433 | Gene Walter | .06 | .05 | 499 | Ron Hassey | .06 | .05 |
| 434 | Ed Whitson | .06 | .05 | 500 | Tim Hulett | .06 | .05 |
| 435 | Marvell Wynne | .06 | .05 | 501 | Bob James | .06 | .05 |
| 436 | Dave Anderson | .06 | .05 | 502 | Steve Lyons | .06 | .05 |
| 437 | Greg Brock | .08 | .06 | 503 | *Joel McKeon* | .10 | .08 |
| 438 | Enos Cabell | .06 | .05 | 504 | Gene Nelson | .06 | .05 |
| 439 | Mariano Duncan | .06 | .05 | 505 | Dave Schmidt | .06 | .05 |
| 440 | Pedro Guerrero | .15 | .11 | 506 | Ray Searage | .06 | .05 |
| 441 | Orel Hershiser | .40 | .30 | 507 | *Bobby Thigpen*(FC) | | |
| 442 | Rick Honeycutt | .06 | .05 | | | 1.50 | 1.25 |
| 443 | Ken Howell | .06 | .05 | 508 | Greg Walker | .10 | .08 |
| 444 | Ken Landreaux | .06 | .05 | 509 | Jim Acker | .06 | .05 |
| 445 | Bill Madlock | .12 | .09 | 510 | Doyle Alexander | .08 | .06 |
| 446 | Mike Marshall | .12 | .09 | 511 | *Paul Assenmacher* | .15 | .11 |
| 447 | Len Matuszek | .06 | .05 | 512 | Bruce Benedict | .06 | .05 |
| 448 | Tom Niedenfuer | .08 | .06 | 513 | Chris Chambliss | .08 | .06 |
| 449 | Alejandro Pena | .06 | .05 | 514 | Jeff Dedmon | .06 | .05 |
| 450 | Dennis Powell(FC) | .08 | .06 | 515 | Gene Garber | .06 | .05 |
| 451 | Jerry Reuss | .08 | .06 | 516 | Ken Griffey | .10 | .08 |
| 452 | Bill Russell | .08 | .06 | 517 | Terry Harper | .06 | .05 |
| 453 | Steve Sax | .15 | .11 | 518 | Bob Horner | .10 | .08 |
| 454 | Mike Scioscia | .08 | .06 | 519 | Glenn Hubbard | .06 | .05 |
| 455 | Franklin Stubbs | .08 | .06 | 520 | Rick Mahler | .06 | .05 |
| 456 | Alex Trevino | .06 | .05 | 521 | Omar Moreno | .06 | .05 |
| 457 | Fernando Valenzuela | | | 522 | Dale Murphy | .40 | .30 |

| | | MT | NR MT |
|---|---|---|---|
| 523 | Ken Oberkfell | .06 | .05 |
| 524 | Ed Olwine | .06 | .05 |
| 525 | David Palmer | .06 | .05 |
| 526 | Rafael Ramirez | .06 | .05 |
| 527 | Billy Sample | .06 | .05 |
| 528 | Ted Simmons | .12 | .09 |
| 529 | Zane Smith | .08 | .06 |
| 530 | Bruce Sutter | .12 | .09 |
| 531 | *Andres Thomas* | .15 | .11 |
| 532 | Ozzie Virgil | .06 | .05 |
| 533 | *Allan Anderson*(FC) | | |
| | | .25 | .20 |
| 534 | Keith Atherton | .06 | .05 |
| 535 | Billy Beane | .06 | .05 |
| 536 | Bert Blyleven | .12 | .09 |
| 537 | Tom Brunansky | .10 | .08 |
| 538 | Randy Bush | .06 | .05 |
| 539 | George Frazier | .06 | .05 |
| 540 | Gary Gaetti | .15 | .11 |
| 541 | Greg Gagne | .06 | .05 |
| 542 | Mickey Hatcher | .06 | .05 |
| 543 | Neal Heaton | .06 | .05 |
| 544 | Kent Hrbek | .15 | .11 |
| 545 | Roy Lee Jackson | .06 | .05 |
| 546 | Tim Laudner | .06 | .05 |
| 547 | Steve Lombardozzi | .10 | .08 |
| 548 | *Mark Portugal*(FC) | | |
| | | .10 | .08 |
| 549 | Kirby Puckett | 3.00 | 2.25 |
| 550 | Jeff Reed | .08 | .06 |
| 551 | Mark Salas | .06 | .05 |
| 552 | Roy Smalley | .06 | .05 |
| 553 | Mike Smithson | .06 | .05 |
| 554 | Frank Viola | .15 | .11 |
| 555 | Thad Bosley | .06 | .05 |
| 556 | Ron Cey | .10 | .08 |
| 557 | Jody Davis | .08 | .06 |
| 558 | Ron Davis | .06 | .05 |
| 559 | Bob Dernier | .06 | .05 |
| 560 | Frank DiPino | .06 | .05 |
| 561 | Shawon Dunston | .35 | .25 |
| 562 | Leon Durham | .08 | .06 |
| 563 | Dennis Eckersley | .12 | .09 |
| 564 | Terry Francona | .06 | .05 |
| 565 | Dave Gumpert | .06 | .05 |
| 566 | Guy Hoffman | .08 | .06 |
| 567 | Ed Lynch | .06 | .05 |
| 568 | Gary Matthews | .10 | .08 |
| 569 | Keith Moreland | .08 | .06 |
| 570 | *Jamie Moyer*(FC) | | |
| | | .20 | .15 |
| 571 | Jerry Mumphrey | .06 | .05 |
| 572 | Ryne Sandberg | 2.50 | 2.00 |
| 573 | Scott Sanderson | .06 | .05 |
| 574 | Lee Smith | .10 | .08 |
| 575 | Chris Speier | .06 | .05 |
| 576 | Rick Sutcliffe | .12 | .09 |
| 577 | Manny Trillo | .08 | .06 |
| 578 | Steve Trout | .06 | .05 |
| 579 | Karl Best | .06 | .05 |
| 580 | Scott Bradley(FC) | .08 | .06 |
| 581 | Phil Bradley | .12 | .09 |
| 582 | Mickey Brantley | .08 | .06 |
| 583 | Mike Brown | .06 | .05 |
| 584 | Alvin Davis | .12 | .09 |
| 585 | *Lee Guetterman*(FC) | | |
| | | .15 | .11 |

| | | MT | NR MT |
|---|---|---|---|
| 586 | Mark Huismann | .06 | .05 |
| 587 | Bob Kearney | .06 | .05 |
| 588 | Pete Ladd | .06 | .05 |
| 589 | Mark Langston | .12 | .09 |
| 590 | Mike Moore | .06 | .05 |
| 591 | Mike Morgan | .06 | .05 |
| 592 | John Moses | .06 | .05 |
| 593 | Ken Phelps | .08 | .06 |
| 594 | Jim Presley | .10 | .08 |
| 595 | *Rey Quinonez* | | |
| | (Quinones) | .15 | .11 |
| 596 | Harold Reynolds | .15 | .11 |
| 597 | Billy Swift | .06 | .05 |
| 598 | Danny Tartabull | .50 | .40 |
| 599 | Steve Yeager | .06 | .05 |
| 600 | Matt Young | .06 | .05 |
| 601 | Bill Almon | .06 | .05 |
| 602 | *Rafael Belliard*(FC) | | |
| | | .12 | .09 |
| 603 | Mike Bielecki | .06 | .05 |
| 604 | *Barry Bonds* | 18.00 | 13.50 |
| 605 | *Bobby Bonilla* | 8.00 | 6.00 |
| 606 | Sid Bream | .08 | .06 |
| 607 | Mike Brown | .06 | .05 |
| 608 | Pat Clements | .06 | .05 |
| 609 | *Mike Diaz*(FC) | .15 | .11 |
| 610 | Cecilio Guante | .06 | .05 |
| 611 | *Barry Jones*(FC) | .12 | .09 |
| 612 | Bob Kipper | .06 | .05 |
| 613 | Larry McWilliams | .06 | .05 |
| 614 | Jim Morrison | .06 | .05 |
| 615 | Joe Orsulak | .06 | .05 |
| 616 | Junior Ortiz | .06 | .05 |
| 617 | Tony Pena | .08 | .06 |
| 618 | Johnny Ray | .10 | .08 |
| 619 | Rick Reuschel | .10 | .08 |
| 620 | R.J. Reynolds | .06 | .05 |
| 621 | Rick Rhoden | .10 | .08 |
| 622 | Don Robinson | .08 | .06 |
| 623 | Bob Walk | .06 | .05 |
| 624 | Jim Winn | .06 | .05 |
| 625 | Youthful Power (Jose Canseco, Pete Incaviglia) | .70 | .50 |
| 626 | 300 Game Winners (Phil Niekro, Don Sutton) | .12 | .09 |
| 627 | A.L. Firemen (Don Aase, Dave Righetti) | .08 | .06 |
| 628 | Rookie All-Stars (Jose Canseco, Wally Joyner) | 1.50 | 1.25 |
| 629 | Magic Mets (Gary Carter, Sid Fernandez, Dwight Gooden, Keith Hernandez, Darryl Strawberry) | .60 | .45 |
| 630 | N.L. Best Righties (Mike Krukow, Mike Scott) | .08 | .06 |
| 631 | Sensational Southpaws (John Franco, Fernando Valenzuela) | .10 | .08 |
| 632 | Count 'Em (Bob Horner) | .08 | .06 |
| 633 | A.L. Pitcher's Nightmare (Jose Canseco, Kirby Puckett, Jim Rice) | .70 | .50 |
| 634 | All Star Battery (Gary | | |

| | MT | NR MT |
|---|---|---|
| Carter, Roger Clemens) | .25 | .20 |
| 635 4,000 Strikeouts (Steve Carlton) | .12 | .09 |
| 636 Big Bats At First Sack (Glenn Davis, Eddie Murray) | .20 | .15 |
| 637 On Base (Wade Boggs, Keith Hernandez) | .35 | .25 |
| 638 Sluggers From Left Side (Don Mattingly, Darryl Strawberry) | .90 | .70 |
| 639 Former MVP's (Dave Parker, Ryne Sandberg) | .12 | .09 |
| 640 Dr. K. & Super K (Roger Clemens, Dwight Gooden) | .50 | .40 |
| 641 A.L. West Stoppers (Charlie Hough, Mike Witt) | .08 | .06 |
| 642 Doubles & Triples (Tim Raines, Juan Samuel) | .12 | .09 |
| 643 Outfielders With Punch (Harold Baines, Jesse Barfield) | .10 | .08 |
| 644 Major League Prospects (Dave Clark, Greg Swindell)(FC) | 2.00 | 1.50 |
| 645 Major League Prospects (Ron Karkovice, Russ Morman)(FC) | .12 | .09 |
| 646 Major League Prospects (Willie Fraser, Devon White)(FC) | 1.50 | 1.25 |
| 647 Major League Prospects (Jerry Browne, Mike Stanley)(FC) | .40 | .30 |
| 648 Major League Prospects (Phil Lombardi, Dave Magadan)(FC) | .50 | .40 |
| 649 Major League Prospects (Ralph Bryant, Jose Gonzalez)(FC) | .20 | .15 |
| 650 Major League Prospects (Randy Asadoor, Jimmy Jones)(FC) | .20 | .15 |
| 651 Major League Prospects (Marvin Freeman, Tracy Jones) | .25 | .20 |
| 652 Major League Prospects (Kevin Seitzer, John Stefero)(FC) | .90 | .70 |
| 653 Major League Prospects (Steve Fireovid, Rob Nelson)(FC) | .10 | .08 |
| 654 Checklist 1-95 | .06 | .05 |
| 655 Checklist 96-192 | .06 | .05 |
| 656 Checklist 193-288 | .06 | .05 |
| 657 Checklist 289-384 | .06 | .05 |
| 658 Checklist 385-483 | .06 | .05 |
| 659 Checklist 484-578 | .06 | .05 |
| 660 Checklist 579-660 | .06 | .05 |

**Regional interest may affect the value of a card.**

# 1987 Fleer Update

Fleer followed suit on a Topps idea in 1984 and began producing "Update" sets. The 1987 edition brings the regular Fleer set to date by including traded players and hot rookies. The cards measure 2-1/2" by 3-1/2" and are housed in a specially designed box with 25 team logo stickers. As a companion to the glossy-coated Fleer Collectors Edition set, Fleer produced a special edition Update set in its own tin box. Values of the glossy-coated cards are only a few dollars more than the regular Update cards.

| | | MT | NR MT |
|---|---|---|---|
| Complete Set: | | 15.00 | 11.00 |
| Common Player: | | .06 | .05 |
| 1 | Scott Bankhead | .08 | .06 |
| 2 | Eric Bell(FC) | .15 | .11 |
| 3 | Juan Beniquez | .06 | .05 |
| 4 | Juan Berenguer | .06 | .05 |
| 5 | Mike Birkbeck(FC) | .20 | .15 |
| 6 | Randy Bockus(FC) | .15 | .11 |
| 7 | Rod Booker(FC) | .15 | .11 |
| 8 | Thad Bosley | .06 | .05 |
| 9 | Greg Brock | .10 | .08 |
| 10 | Bob Brower(FC) | .15 | .11 |
| 11 | Chris Brown | .12 | .09 |
| 12 | Jerry Browne | .15 | .11 |
| 13 | Ralph Bryant | .10 | .08 |
| 14 | DeWayne Buice(FC) | .20 | .15 |
| 15 | Ellis Burks(FC) | 1.00 | .70 |
| 16 | Casey Candaele(FC) | .15 | .11 |
| 17 | Steve Carlton | .40 | .30 |

**A player's name in italic type indicates a rookie card. An (FC) indicates a player's first card for that particular card company.**

| | | MT | NR MT |
|---|---|---|---|
| 18 | Juan Castillo | .08 | .06 |
| 19 | Chuck Crim(FC) | .15 | .11 |
| 20 | Mark Davidson(FC) | .20 | .15 |
| 21 | Mark Davis | .06 | .05 |
| 22 | Storm Davis | .12 | .09 |
| 23 | Bill Dawley | .06 | .05 |
| 24 | Andre Dawson | .40 | .30 |
| 25 | Brian Dayett | .06 | .05 |
| 26 | Rick Dempsey | .08 | .06 |
| 27 | Ken Dowell(FC) | .15 | .11 |
| 28 | Dave Dravecky | .10 | .08 |
| 29 | Mike Dunne(FC) | .20 | .15 |
| 30 | Dennis Eckersley | .30 | .25 |
| 31 | Cecil Fielder | 2.00 | 1.50 |
| 32 | Brian Fisher | .10 | .08 |
| 33 | Willie Fraser | .10 | .08 |
| 34 | Ken Gerhart(FC) | .15 | .11 |
| 35 | Jim Gott | .06 | .05 |
| 36 | Dan Gladden | .06 | .05 |
| 37 | Mike Greenwell(FC) | | |
| | | 1.00 | .70 |
| 38 | Cecilio Guante | .06 | .05 |
| 39 | Albert Hall | .06 | .05 |
| 40 | Atlee Hammaker | .06 | .05 |
| 41 | Mickey Hatcher | .06 | .05 |
| 42 | Mike Heath | .06 | .05 |
| 43 | Neal Heaton | .06 | .05 |
| 44 | Mike Henneman(FC) | .30 | .25 |
| 45 | Guy Hoffman | .06 | .05 |
| 46 | Charles Hudson | .06 | .05 |
| 47 | Chuck Jackson(FC) | .20 | .15 |
| 48 | Mike Jackson(FC) | .20 | .15 |
| 49 | Reggie Jackson | .60 | .45 |
| 50 | Chris James | .35 | .25 |
| 51 | Dion James | .12 | .09 |
| 52 | Stan Javier | .06 | .05 |
| 53 | Stan Jefferson(FC) | .20 | .15 |
| 54 | Jimmy Jones | .10 | .08 |
| 55 | Tracy Jones | .20 | .15 |
| 56 | Terry Kennedy | .08 | .06 |
| 57 | Mike Kingery | .08 | .06 |
| 58 | Ray Knight | .10 | .08 |
| 59 | Gene Larkin(FC) | .30 | .25 |
| 60 | Mike LaValliere | .12 | .09 |
| 61 | Jack Lazorko(FC) | .06 | .05 |
| 62 | Terry Leach | .06 | .05 |
| 63 | Rick Leach | .06 | .05 |
| 64 | Craig Lefferts | .06 | .05 |
| 65 | Jim Lindeman(FC) | .15 | .11 |
| 66 | Bill Long(FC) | .20 | .15 |
| 67 | Mike Loynd(FC) | .15 | .11 |
| 68 | Greg Maddux(FC) | 4.00 | 3.00 |
| 69 | Bill Madlock | .15 | .11 |
| 70 | Dave Magadan | .80 | .60 |
| 71 | Joe Magrane(FC) | .60 | .45 |
| 72 | Fred Manrique(FC) | .20 | .15 |
| 73 | Mike Mason | .06 | .05 |
| 74 | Lloyd McClendon(FC) | | |
| | | .15 | .11 |
| 75 | Fred McGriff(FC) | 4.00 | 3.00 |
| 76 | Mark McGwire(FC) | 6.00 | 4.50 |
| 77 | Mark McLemore | .06 | .05 |
| 78 | Kevin McReynolds | .30 | .25 |
| 79 | Dave Meads(FC) | .15 | .11 |
| 80 | Greg Minton | .06 | .05 |
| 81 | John Mitchell(FC) | .15 | .11 |
| 82 | Kevin Mitchell | 1.00 | .70 |

| | | MT | NR MT |
|---|---|---|---|
| 83 | John Morris | .06 | .05 |
| 84 | Jeff Musselman(FC) | .15 | .11 |
| 85 | Randy Myers(FC) | .25 | .20 |
| 86 | Gene Nelson | .06 | .05 |
| 87 | Joe Niekro | .10 | .08 |
| 88 | Tom Nieto | .06 | .05 |
| 89 | Reid Nichols | .06 | .05 |
| 90 | Matt Nokes(FC) | .40 | .30 |
| 91 | Dickie Noles | .06 | .05 |
| 92 | Edwin Nunez | .06 | .05 |
| 93 | Jose Nunez(FC) | .12 | .09 |
| 94 | Paul O'Neill | .50 | .40 |
| 95 | Jim Paciorek(FC) | .06 | .05 |
| 96 | Lance Parrish | .20 | .15 |
| 97 | Bill Pecota(FC) | .20 | .15 |
| 98 | Tony Pena | .12 | .09 |
| 99 | Luis Polonia | .40 | .30 |
| 100 | Randy Ready | .06 | .05 |
| 101 | Jeff Reardon | .15 | .11 |
| 102 | Gary Redus | .08 | .06 |
| 103 | Rick Rhoden | .10 | .08 |
| 104 | Wally Ritchie(FC) | .15 | .11 |
| 105 | Jeff Robinson(FC) | .30 | .25 |
| 106 | Mark Salas | .06 | .05 |
| 107 | Dave Schmidt | .06 | .05 |
| 108 | Kevin Seitzer | .40 | .30 |
| 109 | John Shelby | .06 | .05 |
| 110 | John Smiley(FC) | .90 | .70 |
| 111 | Lary Sorenson | .06 | .05 |
| 112 | Chris Speier | .06 | .05 |
| 113 | Randy St. Claire | .06 | .05 |
| 114 | Jim Sundberg | .08 | .06 |
| 115 | B.J. Surhoff(FC) | .35 | .25 |
| 116 | Greg Swindell | .50 | .40 |
| 117 | Danny Tartabull | .40 | .30 |
| 118 | Dorn Taylor(FC) | .12 | .09 |
| 119 | Lee Tunnell | .06 | .05 |
| 120 | Ed Vande Berg | .06 | .05 |
| 121 | Andy Van Slyke | .20 | .15 |
| 122 | Gary Ward | .06 | .05 |
| 123 | Devon White | .40 | .30 |
| 124 | Alan Wiggins | .06 | .05 |
| 125 | Bill Wilkinson(FC) | .15 | .11 |
| 126 | Jim Winn | .06 | .05 |
| 127 | Frank Williams | .06 | .05 |
| 128 | Ken Williams(FC) | .15 | .11 |
| 129 | Matt Williams(FC) | 2.00 | 1.50 |
| 130 | Herm Winningham | .06 | .05 |
| 131 | Matt Young | .06 | .05 |
| 132 | Checklist 1-132 | .06 | .05 |

## 1988 Fleer

A clean, uncluttered look was the trademark of the 660-card 1988 Fleer set. The cards, which are the standard 2-1/2" by 3-1/2", feature blue and red diagonal lines set inside a white border. The player name and position are located on a slant in the upper left corner of the card. The player's team logo appears in the upper right corner. Below the player photo a blue and red band with the word "Fleer" appears. The backs of the cards include the card number, player personal information, and career statistics, plus a new feature called "At Their Best." This feature graphically shows a player's pitching or hitting statistics for home and road games and how he fared during day games as opposed to night contests. The set includes 19 special cards (#'s 622-640) and 12 "Major League Prospects" cards (#'s 641-653).

|  |  | MT | NR MT |
|---|---|---|---|
| Complete Set: |  | 35.00 | 27.00 |
| Common Player: |  | .06 | .05 |
| 1 | Keith Atherton | .06 | .05 |
| 2 | Don Baylor | .10 | .08 |
| 3 | Juan Berenguer | .06 | .05 |
| 4 | Bert Blyleven | .12 | .09 |
| 5 | Tom Brunansky | .10 | .08 |
| 6 | Randy Bush | .06 | .05 |
| 7 | Steve Carlton | .30 | .25 |
| 8 | *Mark Davidson*(FC) | | |
|  |  | .12 | .09 |
| 9 | George Frazier | .06 | .05 |
| 10 | Gary Gaetti | .15 | .11 |
| 11 | Greg Gagne | .06 | .05 |
| 12 | Dan Gladden | .06 | .05 |
| 13 | Kent Hrbek | .15 | .11 |
| 14 | *Gene Larkin* | .20 | .15 |
| 15 | Tim Laudner | .06 | .05 |
| 16 | Steve Lombardozzi | .06 | .05 |
| 17 | Al Newman | .06 | .05 |
| 18 | Joe Niekro | .08 | .06 |
| 19 | Kirby Puckett | .60 | .45 |
| 20 | Jeff Reardon | .10 | .08 |
| 21a | Dan Schatzader (incorrect spelling) | .20 | .15 |
| 21b | Dan Schatzeder (correct spelling) | .06 | .05 |
| 22 | Roy Smalley | .06 | .05 |
| 23 | Mike Smithson | .06 | .05 |
| 24 | *Les Straker*(FC) | .15 | .11 |
| 25 | Frank Viola | .15 | .11 |
| 26 | Jack Clark | .15 | .11 |

|  |  | MT | NR MT |
|---|---|---|---|
| 27 | Vince Coleman | .20 | .15 |
| 28 | Danny Cox | .08 | .06 |
| 29 | Bill Dawley | .06 | .05 |
| 30 | Ken Dayley | .06 | .05 |
| 31 | Doug DeCinces | .08 | .06 |
| 32 | Curt Ford | .06 | .05 |
| 33 | Bob Forsch | .08 | .06 |
| 34 | David Green | .06 | .05 |
| 35 | Tom Herr | .08 | .06 |
| 36 | Ricky Horton | .08 | .06 |
| 37 | *Lance Johnson*(FC) | .75 | .55 |
| 38 | Steve Lake | .06 | .05 |
| 39 | Jim Lindeman | .10 | .08 |
| 40 | *Joe Magrane* | .30 | .25 |
| 41 | Greg Mathews | .08 | .06 |
| 42 | Willie McGee | .12 | .09 |
| 43 | John Morris | .06 | .05 |
| 44 | Jose Oquendo | .06 | .05 |
| 45 | Tony Pena | .08 | .06 |
| 46 | Terry Pendleton | .08 | .06 |
| 47 | Ozzie Smith | .15 | .11 |
| 48 | John Tudor | .10 | .08 |
| 49 | Lee Tunnell | .06 | .05 |
| 50 | Todd Worrell | .10 | .08 |
| 51 | Doyle Alexander | .08 | .06 |
| 52 | Dave Bergman | .06 | .05 |
| 53 | Tom Brookens | .06 | .05 |
| 54 | Darrell Evans | .10 | .08 |
| 55 | Kirk Gibson | .20 | .15 |
| 56 | Mike Heath | .06 | .05 |
| 57 | *Mike Henneman* | .25 | .20 |
| 58 | Willie Hernandez | .08 | .06 |
| 59 | Larry Herndon | .06 | .05 |
| 60 | Eric King | .08 | .06 |
| 61 | Chet Lemon | .08 | .06 |
| 62 | *Scott Lusader*(FC) | .15 | .11 |
| 63 | Bill Madlock | .10 | .08 |
| 64 | Jack Morris | .20 | .15 |
| 65 | Jim Morrison | .06 | .05 |
| 66 | *Matt Nokes* | .50 | .40 |
| 67 | Dan Petry | .08 | .06 |
| 68a | *Jeff Robinson* (Born 12 13-60 on back) | .30 | .25 |
| 68b | *Jeff Robinson* (Born 12 14/61 on back) | .15 | .11 |
| 69 | Pat Sheridan | .06 | .05 |
| 70 | Nate Snell | .06 | .05 |
| 71 | Frank Tanana | .08 | .06 |
| 72 | Walt Terrell | .08 | .06 |
| 73 | Mark Thurmond | .06 | .05 |
| 74 | Alan Trammell | .25 | .20 |
| 75 | Lou Whitaker | .25 | .20 |
| 76 | Mike Aldrete | .08 | .06 |
| 77 | Bob Brenly | .06 | .05 |
| 78 | Will Clark | 2.00 | 1.50 |
| 79 | Chili Davis | .08 | .06 |
| 80 | Kelly Downs | .10 | .08 |
| 81 | Dave Dravecky | .08 | .06 |
| 82 | Scott Garrelts | .06 | .05 |
| 83 | Atlee Hammaker | .06 | .05 |
| 84 | Dave Henderson | .10 | .08 |
| 85 | Mike Krukow | .08 | .06 |
| 86 | Mike LaCoss | .06 | .05 |
| 87 | Craig Lefferts | .06 | .05 |
| 88 | Jeff Leonard | .08 | .06 |

| | MT | NR MT |
|---|---|---|
| 89 Candy Maldonado | .08 | .06 |
| 90 Ed Milner | .06 | .05 |
| 91 Bob Melvin | .06 | .05 |
| 92 Kevin Mitchell | .70 | .50 |
| 93 *Jon Perlman*(FC) | | |
| | .12 | .09 |
| 94 Rick Reuschel | .10 | .08 |
| 95 Don Robinson | .08 | .06 |
| 96 Chris Speier | .06 | .05 |
| 97 Harry Spilman | .06 | .05 |
| 98 Robbie Thompson | .08 | .06 |
| 99 Jose Uribe | .06 | .05 |
| 100 *Mark Wasinger*(FC) | | |
| | .15 | .11 |
| 101 *Matt Williams* | 4.00 | 3.00 |
| 102 Jesse Barfield | .15 | .11 |
| 103 George Bell | .25 | .20 |
| 104 Juan Beniquez | .06 | .05 |
| 105 John Cerutti | .08 | .06 |
| 106 Jim Clancy | .08 | .06 |
| 107 *Rob Ducey*(FC) | .15 | .11 |
| 108 Mark Eichhorn | .08 | .06 |
| 109 Tony Fernandez | .12 | .09 |
| 110 Cecil Fielder | 1.50 | 1.25 |
| 111 Kelly Gruber | .50 | .40 |
| 112 Tom Henke | .08 | .06 |
| 113 Garth Iorg (Iorg) | .06 | .05 |
| 114 Jimmy Key | .10 | .08 |
| 115 Rick Leach | .06 | .05 |
| 116 Manny Lee | .08 | .06 |
| 117 *Nelson Liriano*(FC) | | |
| | .15 | .11 |
| 118 *Fred McGriff* | 1.75 | 1.25 |
| 119 Lloyd Moseby | .08 | .06 |
| 120 Rance Mulliniks | .06 | .05 |
| 121 Jeff Musselman | .10 | .08 |
| 122 *Jose Nunez* | .15 | .11 |
| 123 Dave Stieb | .10 | .08 |
| 124 Willie Upshaw | .08 | .06 |
| 125 Duane Ward(FC) | .08 | .06 |
| 126 Ernie Whitt | .08 | .06 |
| 127 Rick Aguilera | .06 | .05 |
| 128 Wally Backman | .08 | .06 |
| 129 *Mark Carreon*(FC) | | |
| | .12 | .09 |
| 130 Gary Carter | .25 | .20 |
| 131 David Cone(FC) | 1.00 | .70 |
| 132 Ron Darling | .12 | .09 |
| 133 Len Dykstra | .10 | .08 |
| 134 Sid Fernandez | .10 | .08 |
| 135 Dwight Gooden | .60 | .45 |
| 136 Keith Hernandez | .20 | .15 |
| 137 *Gregg Jefferies*(FC) | | |
| | 1.25 | .90 |
| 138 Howard Johnson | .10 | .08 |
| 139 Terry Leach | .06 | .05 |
| 140 *Barry Lyons*(FC) | .15 | .11 |
| 141 Dave Magadan | .30 | .25 |
| 142 Roger McDowell | .10 | .08 |
| 143 Kevin McReynolds | .15 | .11 |
| 144 *Keith Miller*(FC) | .15 | .11 |
| 145 *John Mitchell*(FC) | | |
| | .20 | .15 |
| 146 Randy Myers | .15 | .11 |
| 147 Bob Ojeda | .08 | .06 |
| 148 Jesse Orosco | .08 | .06 |
| 149 Rafael Santana | .06 | .05 |

| | MT | NR MT |
|---|---|---|
| 150 Doug Sisk | .06 | .05 |
| 151 Darryl Strawberry | .60 | .45 |
| 152 Tim Teufel | .06 | .05 |
| 153 Gene Walter | .06 | .05 |
| 154 Mookie Wilson | .08 | .06 |
| 155 *Jay Aldrich*(FC) | .12 | .09 |
| 156 Chris Bosio | .08 | .06 |
| 157 Glenn Braggs | .10 | .08 |
| 158 Greg Brock | .08 | .06 |
| 159 Juan Castillo | .06 | .05 |
| 160 Mark Clear | .06 | .05 |
| 161 Cecil Cooper | .10 | .08 |
| 162 *Chuck Crim* | .12 | .09 |
| 163 Rob Deer | .08 | .06 |
| 164 Mike Felder | .06 | .05 |
| 165 Jim Gantner | .06 | .05 |
| 166 Ted Higuera | .10 | .08 |
| 167 Steve Kiefer | .06 | .05 |
| 168 Rick Manning | .06 | .05 |
| 169 Paul Molitor | .12 | .09 |
| 170 Juan Nieves | .08 | .06 |
| 171 Dan Plesac | .10 | .08 |
| 172 Earnest Riles | .06 | .05 |
| 173 Bill Schroeder | .06 | .05 |
| 174 *Steve Stanicek*(FC) | | |
| | .15 | .11 |
| 175 B.J. Surhoff | .15 | .11 |
| 176 Dale Sveum | .08 | .06 |
| 177 Bill Wegman | .06 | .05 |
| 178 Robin Yount | .30 | .25 |
| 179 Hubie Brooks | .10 | .08 |
| 180 Tim Burke | .06 | .05 |
| 181 Casey Candaele | .06 | .05 |
| 182 Mike Fitzgerald | .06 | .05 |
| 183 Tom Foley | .06 | .05 |
| 184 Andres Galarraga | .15 | .11 |
| 185 Neal Heaton | .06 | .05 |
| 186 Wallace Johnson | .06 | .05 |
| 187 Vance Law | .08 | .06 |
| 188 Dennis Martinez | .08 | .06 |
| 189 Bob McClure | .06 | .05 |
| 190 Andy McGaffigan | .06 | .05 |
| 191 Reid Nichols | .06 | .05 |
| 192 Pascual Perez | .08 | .06 |
| 193 Tim Raines | .25 | .20 |
| 194 Jeff Reed | .06 | .05 |
| 195 Bob Sebra | .06 | .05 |
| 196 Bryn Smith | .06 | .05 |
| 197 Randy St. Claire | .06 | .05 |
| 198 Tim Wallach | .10 | .08 |
| 199 Mitch Webster | .08 | .06 |
| 200 Herm Winningham | .06 | .05 |
| 201 Floyd Youmans | .06 | .05 |
| 202 *Brad Arnsberg*(FC) | | |
| | .20 | .15 |
| 203 Rick Cerone | .06 | .05 |
| 204 Pat Clements | .06 | .05 |
| 205 Henry Cotto | .06 | .05 |
| 206 Mike Easler | .08 | .06 |
| 207 Ron Guidry | .15 | .11 |
| 208 Bill Gullickson | .06 | .05 |
| 209 Rickey Henderson | .60 | .45 |
| 210 Charles Hudson | .06 | .05 |
| 211 Tommy John | .15 | .11 |
| 212 *Roberto Kelly*(FC) | | |
| | 2.00 | 1.50 |
| 213 Ron Kittle | .08 | .06 |

| | | MT | NR MT |
|---|---|---|---|
| 214 | Don Mattingly | .60 | .45 |
| 215 | Bobby Meacham | .06 | .05 |
| 216 | Mike Pagliarulo | .10 | .08 |
| 217 | Dan Pasqua | .10 | .08 |
| 218 | Willie Randolph | .08 | .06 |
| 219 | Rick Rhoden | .08 | .06 |
| 220 | Dave Righetti | .15 | .11 |
| 221 | Jerry Royster | .06 | .05 |
| 222 | Tim Stoddard | .06 | .05 |
| 223 | Wayne Tolleson | .06 | .05 |
| 224 | Gary Ward | .08 | .06 |
| 225 | Claudell Washington | .08 | .06 |
| 226 | Dave Winfield | .30 | .25 |
| 227 | Buddy Bell | .08 | .06 |
| 228 | Tom Browning | .10 | .08 |
| 229 | Dave Concepcion | .08 | .06 |
| 230 | Kal Daniels | .20 | .15 |
| 231 | Eric Davis | .80 | .60 |
| 232 | Bo Diaz | .08 | .06 |
| 233 | Nick Esasky | .08 | .06 |
| 234 | John Franco | .10 | .08 |
| 235 | Guy Hoffman | .06 | .05 |
| 236 | Tom Hume | .06 | .05 |
| 237 | Tracy Jones | .12 | .09 |
| 238 | *Bill Landrum*(FC) | | |
| | | .10 | .08 |
| 239 | Barry Larkin | 1.00 | .70 |
| 240 | Terry McGriff(FC) | .06 | .05 |
| 241 | Rob Murphy | .08 | .06 |
| 242 | Ron Oester | .06 | .05 |
| 243 | Dave Parker | .20 | .15 |
| 244 | Pat Perry | .06 | .05 |
| 245 | Ted Power | .06 | .05 |
| 246 | Dennis Rasmussen | .10 | .08 |
| 247 | Ron Robinson | .06 | .05 |
| 248 | Kurt Stillwell | .10 | .08 |
| 249 | *Jeff Treadway*(FC) | | |
| | | .40 | .30 |
| 250 | Frank Williams | .06 | .05 |
| 251 | Steve Balboni | .08 | .06 |
| 252 | Bud Black | .06 | .05 |
| 253 | Thad Bosley | .06 | .05 |
| 254 | George Brett | .40 | .30 |
| 255 | *John Davis*(FC) | .15 | .11 |
| 256 | Steve Farr | .06 | .05 |
| 257 | Gene Garber | .06 | .05 |
| 258 | Jerry Gleaton | .06 | .05 |
| 259 | Mark Gubicza | .12 | .09 |
| 260 | Bo Jackson | 2.00 | 1.50 |
| 261 | Danny Jackson | .12 | .09 |
| 262 | *Ross Jones*(FC) | .12 | .09 |
| 263 | Charlie Leibrandt | .08 | .06 |
| 264 | *Bill Pecota* | .15 | .11 |
| 265 | *Melido Perez*(FC) | | |
| | | .30 | .25 |
| 266 | Jamie Quirk | .06 | .05 |
| 267 | Dan Quisenberry | .08 | .06 |
| 268 | Bret Saberhagen | .15 | .11 |
| 269 | Angel Salazar | .06 | .05 |
| 270 | Kevin Seitzer | .50 | .40 |
| 271 | Danny Tartabull | .30 | .25 |
| 272 | *Gary Thurman*(FC) | | |
| | | .20 | .15 |
| 273 | Frank White | .08 | .06 |
| 274 | Willie Wilson | .10 | .08 |
| 275 | Tony Bernazard | .06 | .05 |
| 276 | Jose Canseco | 2.00 | 1.50 |

| | | MT | NR MT |
|---|---|---|---|
| 277 | Mike Davis | .08 | .06 |
| 278 | Storm Davis | .10 | .08 |
| 279 | Dennis Eckersley | .12 | .09 |
| 280 | Alfredo Griffin | .08 | .06 |
| 281 | Rick Honeycutt | .06 | .05 |
| 282 | Jay Howell | .08 | .06 |
| 283 | Reggie Jackson | .50 | .40 |
| 284 | Dennis Lamp | .06 | .05 |
| 285 | Carney Lansford | .10 | .08 |
| 286 | Mark McGwire | 2.00 | 1.50 |
| 287 | Dwayne Murphy | .08 | .06 |
| 288 | Gene Nelson | .06 | .05 |
| 289 | Steve Ontiveros | .06 | .05 |
| 290 | Tony Phillips | .06 | .05 |
| 291 | Eric Plunk | .06 | .05 |
| 292 | *Luis Polonia* | .40 | .30 |
| 293 | *Rick Rodriguez*(FC) | | |
| | | .12 | .09 |
| 294 | Terry Steinbach | .10 | .08 |
| 295 | Dave Stewart | .10 | .08 |
| 296 | Curt Young | .08 | .06 |
| 297 | Luis Aguayo | .06 | .05 |
| 298 | Steve Bedrosian | .12 | .09 |
| 299 | Jeff Calhoun | .06 | .05 |
| 300 | Don Carman | .08 | .06 |
| 301 | *Todd Frohwirth*(FC) | | |
| | | .20 | .15 |
| 302 | Greg Gross | .06 | .05 |
| 303 | Kevin Gross | .08 | .06 |
| 304 | Von Hayes | .08 | .06 |
| 305 | *Keith Hughes*(FC) | | |
| | | .15 | .11 |
| 306 | *Mike Jackson* | .20 | .15 |
| 307 | Chris James | .20 | .15 |
| 308 | Steve Jeltz | .06 | .05 |
| 309 | Mike Maddux | .07 | .05 |
| 310 | Lance Parrish | .15 | .11 |
| 311 | Shane Rawley | .08 | .06 |
| 312 | *Wally Ritchie* | .15 | .11 |
| 313 | Bruce Ruffin | .08 | .06 |
| 314 | Juan Samuel | .12 | .09 |
| 315 | Mike Schmidt | .50 | .40 |
| 316 | Rick Schu | .06 | .05 |
| 317 | Jeff Stone | .06 | .05 |
| 318 | Kent Tekulve | .08 | .06 |
| 319 | Milt Thompson | .06 | .05 |
| 320 | Glenn Wilson | .08 | .06 |
| 321 | Rafael Belliard | .06 | .05 |
| 322 | Barry Bonds | 1.75 | 1.25 |
| 323 | Bobby Bonilla | 1.25 | .90 |
| 324 | Sid Bream | .08 | .06 |
| 325 | John Cangelosi | .06 | .05 |
| 326 | Mike Diaz | .08 | .06 |
| 327 | Doug Drabek | .08 | .06 |
| 328 | *Mike Dunne* | .15 | .11 |
| 329 | Brian Fisher | .08 | .06 |
| 330 | *Brett Gideon*(FC) | | |
| | | .12 | .09 |
| 331 | Terry Harper | .06 | .05 |
| 332 | Bob Kipper | .06 | .05 |
| 333 | Mike LaValliere | .08 | .06 |
| 334 | *Jose Lind*(FC) | .30 | .25 |
| 335 | Junior Ortiz | .06 | .05 |
| 336 | *Vicente Palacios*(FC) | | |
| | | .30 | .25 |
| 337 | *Bob Patterson*(FC) | | |
| | | .12 | .09 |

| | | MT | NR MT |
|---|---|---|---|
| 338 | *Al Pedrique*(FC) | .15 | .11 |
| 339 | R.J. Reynolds | .06 | .05 |
| 340 | *John Smiley* | 1.00 | .70 |
| 341 | Andy Van Slyke | .12 | .09 |
| 342 | Bob Walk | .06 | .05 |
| 343 | Marty Barrett | .08 | .06 |
| 344 | Todd Benzinger(FC) | | |
| | | .30 | .25 |
| 345 | Wade Boggs | .70 | .50 |
| 346 | Tom Bolton(FC) | .15 | .11 |
| 347 | Oil Can Boyd | .08 | .06 |
| 348 | *Ellis Burks* | 1.50 | 1.25 |
| 349 | Roger Clemens | 1.00 | .70 |
| 350 | Steve Crawford | .06 | .05 |
| 351 | Dwight Evans | .12 | .09 |
| 352 | *Wes Gardner*(FC) | | |
| | | .25 | .20 |
| 353 | Rich Gedman | .08 | .06 |
| 354 | Mike Greenwell | .70 | .50 |
| 355 | *Sam Horn*(FC) | .30 | .25 |
| 356 | Bruce Hurst | .10 | .08 |
| 357 | *John Marzano*(FC) | | |
| | | .20 | .15 |
| 358 | Al Nipper | .06 | .05 |
| 359 | Spike Owen | .06 | .05 |
| 360 | *Jody Reed*(FC) | .60 | .45 |
| 361 | Jim Rice | .30 | .25 |
| 362 | Ed Romero | .06 | .05 |
| 363 | Kevin Romine(FC) | .08 | .06 |
| 364 | Joe Sambito | .06 | .05 |
| 365 | Calvin Schiraldi | .06 | .05 |
| 366 | Jeff Sellers | .08 | .06 |
| 367 | Bob Stanley | .06 | .05 |
| 368 | Scott Bankhead | .06 | .05 |
| 369 | Phil Bradley | .10 | .08 |
| 370 | Scott Bradley | .06 | .05 |
| 371 | Mickey Brantley | .06 | .05 |
| 372 | *Mike Campbell*(FC) | | |
| | | .15 | .11 |
| 373 | Alvin Davis | .12 | .09 |
| 374 | Lee Guetterman | .06 | .05 |
| 375 | *Dave Hengel*(FC) | .20 | .15 |
| 376 | Mike Kingery | .06 | .05 |
| 377 | Mark Langston | .12 | .09 |
| 378 | *Edgar Martinez*(FC) | | |
| | | 1.50 | 1.25 |
| 379 | Mike Moore | .06 | .05 |
| 380 | Mike Morgan | .06 | .05 |
| 381 | John Moses | .06 | .05 |
| 382 | *Donnell Nixon*(FC) | | |
| | | .20 | .15 |
| 383 | Edwin Nunez | .06 | .05 |
| 384 | Ken Phelps | .08 | .06 |
| 385 | Jim Presley | .10 | .08 |
| 386 | Rey Quinones | .06 | .05 |
| 387 | Jerry Reed | .06 | .05 |
| 388 | Harold Reynolds | .08 | .06 |
| 389 | Dave Valle | .08 | .06 |
| 390 | *Bill Wilkinson* | .15 | .11 |
| 391 | Harold Baines | .12 | .09 |
| 392 | Floyd Bannister | .08 | .06 |
| 393 | Daryl Boston | .06 | .05 |
| 394 | Ivan Calderon | .30 | .25 |
| 395 | Jose DeLeon | .08 | .06 |
| 396 | Richard Dotson | .08 | .06 |
| 397 | Carlton Fisk | .20 | .15 |
| 398 | Ozzie Guillen | .08 | .06 |

| | | MT | NR MT |
|---|---|---|---|
| 399 | Ron Hassey | .06 | .05 |
| 400 | Donnie Hill | .06 | .05 |
| 401 | Bob James | .06 | .05 |
| 402 | Dave LaPoint | .08 | .06 |
| 403 | *Bill Lindsey*(FC) | .12 | .09 |
| 404 | Bill Long(FC) | .15 | .11 |
| 405 | Steve Lyons | .06 | .05 |
| 406 | *Fred Manrique* | .15 | .11 |
| 407 | Jack McDowell(FC) | | |
| | | 2.00 | 1.50 |
| 408 | Gary Redus | .06 | .05 |
| 409 | Ray Searage | .06 | .05 |
| 410 | Bobby Thigpen | .20 | .15 |
| 411 | Greg Walker | .08 | .06 |
| 412 | *Kenny Williams* | .20 | .15 |
| 413 | Jim Winn | .06 | .05 |
| 414 | Jody Davis | .08 | .06 |
| 415 | Andre Dawson | .20 | .15 |
| 416 | Brian Dayett | .06 | .05 |
| 417 | Bob Dernier | .06 | .05 |
| 418 | Frank DiPino | .06 | .05 |
| 419 | Shawon Dunston | .10 | .08 |
| 420 | Leon Durham | .08 | .06 |
| 421 | *Les Lancaster*(FC) | | |
| | | .20 | .15 |
| 422 | Ed Lynch | .06 | .05 |
| 423 | Greg Maddux | 1.50 | 1.25 |
| 424 | Dave Martinez(FC) | .07 | .05 |
| 425a | Keith Moreland (bunting, photo actually Jody Davis) | | |
| | | 3.00 | 2.25 |
| 425b | Keith Moreland (standing upright, correct photo) | .08 | .06 |
| 426 | Jamie Moyer | .08 | .06 |
| 427 | Jerry Mumphrey | .06 | .05 |
| 428 | *Paul Noce*(FC) | .10 | .08 |
| 429 | Rafael Palmeiro(FC) | | |
| | | 1.75 | 1.25 |
| 430 | Wade Rowdon(FC) | .08 | .06 |
| 431 | Ryne Sandberg | 1.00 | .70 |
| 432 | Scott Sanderson | .06 | .05 |
| 433 | Lee Smith | .10 | .08 |
| 434 | Jim Sundberg | .08 | .06 |
| 435 | Rick Sutcliffe | .10 | .08 |
| 436 | Manny Trillo | .08 | .06 |
| 437 | Juan Agosto | .06 | .05 |
| 438 | Larry Andersen | .06 | .05 |
| 439 | Alan Ashby | .06 | .05 |
| 440 | Kevin Bass | .08 | .06 |
| 441 | *Ken Caminiti*(FC) | | |
| | | .35 | .25 |
| 442 | *Rocky Childress*(FC) | | |
| | | .12 | .09 |
| 443 | Jose Cruz | .08 | .06 |
| 444 | Danny Darwin | .06 | .05 |
| 445 | Glenn Davis | .15 | .11 |
| 446 | Jim Deshaies | .08 | .06 |
| 447 | Bill Doran | .08 | .06 |
| 448 | Ty Gainey | .06 | .05 |
| 449 | Billy Hatcher | .08 | .06 |
| 450 | Jeff Heathcock | .06 | .05 |
| 451 | Bob Knepper | .08 | .06 |
| 452 | *Rob Mallicoat*(FC) | | |
| | | .12 | .09 |
| 453 | *Dave Meads* | .15 | .11 |
| 454 | Craig Reynolds | .06 | .05 |

| # | Player | MT | NR MT |
|---|--------|----|-------|
| 455 | Nolan Ryan | 1.25 | .90 |
| 456 | Mike Scott | .12 | .09 |
| 457 | Dave Smith | .08 | .06 |
| 458 | Denny Walling | .06 | .05 |
| 459 | Robbie Wine(FC) | .12 | .09 |
| 460 | Gerald Young(FC) | .15 | .11 |
| 461 | Bob Brower | .08 | .06 |
| 462a | Jerry Browne (white player, photo actually Bob Brower) | 3.50 | 2.75 |
| 462b | Jerry Browne (black player, correct photo) | .08 | .06 |
| 463 | Steve Buechele | .06 | .05 |
| 464 | Edwin Correa | .06 | .05 |
| 465 | Cecil Espy(FC) | .15 | .11 |
| 466 | Scott Fletcher | .08 | .06 |
| 467 | Jose Guzman | .08 | .06 |
| 468 | Greg Harris | .06 | .05 |
| 469 | Charlie Hough | .08 | .06 |
| 470 | Pete Incaviglia | .15 | .11 |
| 471 | Paul Kilgus(FC) | .15 | .11 |
| 472 | Mike Loynd | .08 | .06 |
| 473 | Oddibe McDowell | .08 | .06 |
| 474 | Dale Mohorcic | .08 | .06 |
| 475 | Pete O'Brien | .08 | .06 |
| 476 | Larry Parrish | .08 | .06 |
| 477 | Geno Petralli | .06 | .05 |
| 478 | Jeff Russell | .06 | .05 |
| 479 | Ruben Sierra | 2.00 | 1.50 |
| 480 | Mike Stanley | .08 | .06 |
| 481 | Curtis Wilkerson | .06 | .05 |
| 482 | Mitch Williams | .08 | .06 |
| 483 | Bobby Witt | .10 | .08 |
| 484 | Tony Armas | .08 | .06 |
| 485 | Bob Boone | .08 | .06 |
| 486 | Bill Buckner | .10 | .08 |
| 487 | DeWayne Buice | .15 | .11 |
| 488 | Brian Downing | .08 | .06 |
| 489 | Chuck Finley | .06 | .05 |
| 490 | Willie Fraser | .06 | .05 |
| 491 | Jack Howell | .08 | .06 |
| 492 | Ruppert Jones | .06 | .05 |
| 493 | Wally Joyner | .40 | .30 |
| 494 | Jack Lazorko | .06 | .05 |
| 495 | Gary Lucas | .06 | .05 |
| 496 | Kirk McCaskill | .08 | .06 |
| 497 | Mark McLemore | .06 | .05 |
| 498 | Darrell Miller | .06 | .05 |
| 499 | Greg Minton | .06 | .05 |
| 500 | Donnie Moore | .06 | .05 |
| 501 | Gus Polidor | .06 | .05 |
| 502 | Johnny Ray | .08 | .06 |
| 503 | Mark Ryal(FC) | .06 | .05 |
| 504 | Dick Schofield | .06 | .05 |
| 505 | Don Sutton | .20 | .15 |
| 506 | Devon White | .25 | .20 |
| 507 | Mike Witt | .08 | .06 |
| 508 | Dave Anderson | .06 | .05 |
| 509 | Tim Belcher(FC) | .60 | .45 |
| 510 | Ralph Bryant | .06 | .05 |
| 511 | Tim Crews(FC) | .15 | .11 |
| 512 | Mike Devereaux(FC) | 2.00 | 1.50 |
| 513 | Mariano Duncan | .06 | .05 |
| 514 | Pedro Guerrero | .15 | .11 |
| 515 | Jeff Hamilton(FC) | .12 | .09 |
| 516 | Mickey Hatcher | .06 | .05 |
| 517 | Brad Havens | .06 | .05 |
| 518 | Orel Hershiser | .25 | .20 |
| 519 | Shawn Hillegas(FC) | .20 | .15 |
| 520 | Ken Howell | .06 | .05 |
| 521 | Tim Leary | .08 | .06 |
| 522 | Mike Marshall | .12 | .09 |
| 523 | Steve Sax | .15 | .11 |
| 524 | Mike Scioscia | .08 | .06 |
| 525 | Mike Sharperson(FC) | .06 | .05 |
| 526 | John Shelby | .06 | .05 |
| 527 | Franklin Stubbs | .08 | .06 |
| 528 | Fernando Valenzuela | .20 | .15 |
| 529 | Bob Welch | .10 | .08 |
| 530 | Matt Young | .06 | .05 |
| 531 | Jim Acker | .06 | .05 |
| 532 | Paul Assenmacher | .06 | .05 |
| 533 | Jeff Blauser(FC) | .25 | .20 |
| 534 | Joe Boever(FC) | .25 | .20 |
| 535 | Martin Clary(FC) | .06 | .05 |
| 536 | Kevin Coffman(FC) | .12 | .09 |
| 537 | Jeff Dedmon | .06 | .05 |
| 538 | Ron Gant(FC) | 6.00 | 4.50 |
| 539 | Tom Glavine(FC) | 8.00 | 6.00 |
| 540 | Ken Griffey | .08 | .06 |
| 541 | Al Hall | .06 | .05 |
| 542 | Glenn Hubbard | .06 | .05 |
| 543 | Dion James | .08 | .06 |
| 544 | Dale Murphy | .40 | .30 |
| 545 | Ken Oberkfell | .06 | .05 |
| 546 | David Palmer | .06 | .05 |
| 547 | Gerald Perry | .10 | .08 |
| 548 | Charlie Puleo | .06 | .05 |
| 549 | Ted Simmons | .10 | .08 |
| 550 | Zane Smith | .08 | .06 |
| 551 | Andres Thomas | .08 | .06 |
| 552 | Ozzie Virgil | .06 | .05 |
| 553 | Don Aase | .06 | .05 |
| 554 | Jeff Ballard(FC) | .35 | .25 |
| 555 | Eric Bell | .06 | .05 |
| 556 | Mike Boddicker | .08 | .06 |
| 557 | Ken Dixon | .06 | .05 |
| 558 | Jim Dwyer | .06 | .05 |
| 559 | Ken Gerhart | .08 | .06 |
| 560 | Rene Gonzales(FC) | .15 | .11 |
| 561 | Mike Griffin | .06 | .05 |
| 562 | John Hayban (Habyan) | .06 | .05 |
| 563 | Terry Kennedy | .08 | .06 |
| 564 | Ray Knight | .08 | .06 |
| 565 | Lee Lacy | .06 | .05 |
| 566 | Fred Lynn | .15 | .11 |
| 567 | Eddie Murray | .35 | .25 |
| 568 | Tom Niedenfuer | .08 | .06 |
| 569 | Bill Ripken(FC) | .25 | .20 |
| 570 | Cal Ripken, Jr. | .60 | .45 |
| 571 | Dave Schmidt | .06 | .05 |
| 572 | Larry Sheets | .08 | .06 |
| 573 | Pete Stanicek(FC) | .15 | .11 |
| 574 | Mark Williamson(FC) | | |

| | | MT | NR MT |
|---|---|---|---|
| | | .12 | .09 |
| 575 | Mike Young | .06 | .05 |
| 576 | Shawn Abner(FC) | .20 | .15 |
| 577 | Greg Booker | .06 | .05 |
| 578 | Chris Brown | .08 | .06 |
| 579 | *Keith Comstock*(FC) | | |
| | | .12 | .09 |
| 580 | *Joey Cora*(FC) | .12 | .09 |
| 581 | Mark Davis | .06 | .05 |
| 582 | Tim Flannery | .06 | .05 |
| 583 | Goose Gossage | .15 | .11 |
| 584 | Mark Grant | .06 | .05 |
| 585 | Tony Gwynn | .35 | .25 |
| 586 | Andy Hawkins | .06 | .05 |
| 587 | Stan Jefferson | .10 | .08 |
| 588 | Jimmy Jones | .08 | .06 |
| 589 | John Kruk | .10 | .08 |
| 590 | *Shane Mack*(FC) | .50 | .40 |
| 591 | Carmelo Martinez | .08 | .06 |
| 592 | Lance McCullers | .08 | .06 |
| 593 | *Eric Nolte*(FC) | .15 | .11 |
| 594 | Randy Ready | .06 | .05 |
| 595 | Luis Salazar | .06 | .05 |
| 596 | Benito Santiago | .35 | .25 |
| 597 | Eric Show | .08 | .06 |
| 598 | Garry Templeton | .08 | .06 |
| 599 | Ed Whitson | .06 | .05 |
| 600 | Scott Bailes | .08 | .06 |
| 601 | Chris Bando | .06 | .05 |
| 602 | *Jay Bell*(FC) | .60 | .45 |
| 603 | Brett Butler | .08 | .06 |
| 604 | Tom Candiotti | .06 | .05 |
| 605 | Joe Carter | .12 | .09 |
| 606 | Carmen Castillo | .06 | .05 |
| 607 | *Brian Dorsett*(FC) | | |
| | | .15 | .11 |
| 608 | *John Farrell*(FC) | .20 | .15 |
| 609 | Julio Franco | .10 | .08 |
| 610 | Mel Hall | .08 | .06 |
| 611 | *Tommy Hinzo*(FC) | | |
| | | .15 | .11 |
| 612 | Brook Jacoby | .10 | .08 |
| 613 | *Doug Jones*(FC) | .40 | .30 |
| 614 | Ken Schrom | .06 | .05 |
| 615 | Cory Snyder | .20 | .15 |
| 616 | Sammy Stewart | .06 | .05 |
| 617 | Greg Swindell | .25 | .20 |
| 618 | Pat Tabler | .08 | .06 |
| 619 | Ed Vande Berg | .06 | .05 |
| 620 | *Eddie Williams*(FC) | | |
| | | .15 | .11 |
| 621 | Rich Yett | .06 | .05 |
| 622 | Slugging Sophomores (Wally Joyner, Cory Snyder) | | |
| | | .35 | .25 |
| 623 | Dominican Dynamite (George Bell, Pedro Guerrero) | | |
| | | .12 | .09 |
| 624 | Oakland's Power Team (Jose Canseco, Mark McGwire) | | |
| | | .50 | .40 |
| 625 | Classic Relief (Dan Plesac, Dave Righetti) | .08 | .06 |
| 626 | All Star Righties (Jack Morris, Bret Saberhagen, Mike Witt) | | |
| | | .10 | .08 |
| 627 | Game Closers (Steve | | |

| | | MT | NR MT |
|---|---|---|---|
| | Bedrosian, John Franco) | | |
| | | .08 | .06 |
| 628 | Masters of the Double Play (Ryne Sandberg, Ozzie Smith) | .12 | .09 |
| 629 | Rookie Record Setter (Mark McGwire) | 1.00 | .70 |
| 630 | Changing the Guard in Boston (Todd Benzinger, Ellis Burks, Mike Greenwell) | | |
| | | 1.00 | .70 |
| 631 | N.L. Batting Champs (Tony Gwynn, Tim Raines) | | |
| | | .15 | .11 |
| 632 | Pitching Magic (Orel Hershiser, Mike Scott) | .12 | .09 |
| 633 | Big Bats At First (Mark McGwire, Pat Tabler) | .60 | .45 |
| 634 | Hitting King and the Thief (Vince Coleman, Tony Gwynn) | .12 | .09 |
| 635 | A.L. Slugging Shortstops (Tony Fernandez, Cal Ripken, Jr., Alan Trammell) | | |
| | | .15 | .11 |
| 636 | Tried and True Sluggers (Gary Carter, Mike Schmidt) | .20 | .15 |
| 637 | Crunch Time (Eric Davis, Darryl Strawberry) | .70 | .50 |
| 638 | A.L. All Stars (Matt Nokes, Kirby Puckett) | .20 | .15 |
| 639 | N.L. All Stars (Keith Hernandez, Dale Murphy) | | |
| | | .20 | .15 |
| 640 | The "O's" Brothers (Bill Ripken, Cal Ripken, Jr.) | .12 | .09 |
| 641 | Major League Prospects (Mark Grace, Darrin Jackson)(FC) | 4.00 | 3.00 |
| 642 | Major League Prospects (Damon Berryhill, Jeff Montgomery)(FC) | .80 | .60 |
| 643 | Major League Prospects (Felix Fermin, Jessie Reid)(FC) | .20 | .15 |
| 644 | Major League Prospects (Greg Myers, Greg Tabor)(FC) | .20 | .15 |
| 645 | Major League Prospects (Jim Eppard, Joey Meyer)(FC) | .20 | .15 |
| 646 | Major League Prospects (Adam Peterson, Randy Velarde)(FC) | .20 | .15 |
| 647 | Major League Prospects (Chris Gwynn, Peter Smith)(FC) | .25 | .20 |
| 648 | Major League Prospects (Greg Jelks, Tom Newell)(FC) | .25 | .20 |
| 649 | Major League Prospects (Mario Diaz, Clay Parker)(FC) | .25 | .20 |
| 650 | Major League Prospects (Jack Savage, Todd Simmons)(FC) | .25 | .20 |

| | | MT | NR MT |
|---|---|---|---|
| 651 | Major League Prospects *(John Burkett, Kirt Manwaring)*(FC) | .35 | .25 |
| 652 | Major League Prospects *(Dave Otto, Walt Weiss)*(FC) | .40 | .30 |
| 653 | Major League Prospects *(Randell Byers (Randall), Jeff King)*(FC) | .40 | .30 |
| 654a | Checklist 1-101 (21 is Schatzader) | .10 | .08 |
| 654b | Checklist 1-101 (21 is Schatzeder) | .06 | .05 |
| 655 | Checklist 102-201 | .06 | .05 |
| 656 | Checklist 202-296 | .06 | .05 |
| 657 | Checklist 297-390 | .06 | .05 |
| 658 | Checklist 391-483 | .06 | .05 |
| 659 | Checklist 484-575 | .06 | .05 |
| 660 | Checklist 576-660 | .06 | .05 |

## 1988 Fleer Update

This 132-card update set (numbered U-1 through U-132 and 2-1/2" by 3-1/2") features traded veterans and rookies in a mixture of full-color action shots and close-ups, framed by white borders with red and blue stripes. Player name and position appear upper left, printed on an upward slant leading into the team logo, upper right. A bright stripe in a variety of colors (blue, red, green, yellow) edges the bottom of the photo and leads into the Fleer logo at lower right. The backs are red, white and blue-grey and include personal info, along with yearly and "At Their Best" (day, night, home, road) stats charts. The set was packaged in white cardboard boxes with red and blue stripes. A glossy-coated edition of the update set was issued in its own tin box and is valued at two times greater than the regular issue.

| | | MT | NR MT |
|---|---|---|---|
| | Complete Set: | 15.00 | 11.00 |
| | Common Player: | .06 | .05 |
| 1 | Jose Bautista(FC) | .20 | .15 |
| 2 | Joe Orsulak | .06 | .05 |
| 3 | Doug Sisk | .06 | .05 |
| 4 | Craig Worthington(FC) | .20 | .15 |
| 5 | Mike Boddicker | .08 | .06 |
| 6 | Rick Cerone | .06 | .05 |
| 7 | Larry Parrish | .08 | .06 |
| 8 | Lee Smith | .10 | .08 |
| 9 | Mike Smithson | .06 | .05 |
| 10 | John Trautwein(FC) | .15 | .11 |
| 11 | Sherman Corbett(FC) | .15 | .11 |
| 12 | Chili Davis | .10 | .08 |
| 13 | Jim Eppard | .08 | .06 |
| 14 | Bryan Harvey(FC) | .50 | .40 |
| 15 | John Davis | .08 | .06 |
| 16 | Dave Gallagher(FC) | .20 | .15 |
| 17 | Ricky Horton | .08 | .06 |
| 18 | Dan Pasqua | .10 | .08 |
| 19 | Melido Perez | .12 | .09 |
| 20 | Jose Segura(FC) | .15 | .11 |
| 21 | Andy Allanson | .08 | .06 |
| 22 | Jon Perlman | .06 | .05 |
| 23 | Domingo Ramos | .06 | .05 |
| 24 | Rick Rodriguez | .08 | .06 |
| 25 | Willie Upshaw | .10 | .08 |
| 26 | Paul Gibson(FC) | .15 | .11 |
| 27 | Don Heinkel(FC) | .15 | .11 |
| 28 | Ray Knight | .08 | .06 |
| 29 | Gary Pettis | .08 | .06 |
| 30 | Luis Salazar | .06 | .05 |
| 31 | Mike MacFarlane (Macfarlane)(FC) | .25 | .20 |
| 32 | Jeff Montgomery | .08 | .06 |
| 33 | Ted Power | .06 | .05 |
| 34 | Israel Sanchez(FC) | .15 | .11 |
| 35 | Kurt Stillwell | .10 | .08 |
| 36 | Pat Tabler | .08 | .06 |
| 37 | Don August(FC) | .15 | .11 |
| 38 | Darryl Hamilton(FC) | .40 | .30 |
| 39 | Jeff Leonard | .08 | .06 |
| 40 | Joey Meyer | .15 | .11 |
| 41 | Allan Anderson | .10 | .08 |
| 42 | Brian Harper | .06 | .05 |
| 43 | Tom Herr | .10 | .08 |
| 44 | Charlie Lea | .06 | .05 |
| 45 | John Moses | .06 | .05 |
| 46 | John Candelaria | .10 | .08 |
| 47 | Jack Clark | .15 | .11 |
| 48 | Richard Dotson | .10 | .08 |
| 49 | Al Leiter(FC) | .15 | .11 |
| 50 | Rafael Santana | .06 | .05 |
| 51 | Don Slaught | .06 | .05 |
| 52 | Todd Burns(FC) | .25 | .20 |
| 53 | Dave Henderson | .10 | .08 |
| 54 | Doug Jennings(FC) | .20 | .15 |
| 55 | Dave Parker | .12 | .09 |
| 56 | Walt Weiss | .20 | .15 |
| 57 | Bob Welch | .10 | .08 |
| 58 | Henry Cotto | .06 | .05 |
| 59 | Marion Diaz (Mario) | .08 | .06 |
| 60 | Mike Jackson | .06 | .05 |
| 61 | Bill Swift | .06 | .05 |

| | | MT | NR MT |
|---|---|---|---|
| 62 | Jose Cecena(FC) | .15 | .11 |
| 63 | Ray Hayward(FC) | .08 | .06 |
| 64 | Jim Steels(FC) | .08 | .06 |
| 65 | Pat Borders(FC) | .60 | .45 |
| 66 | Sil Campusano(FC) | .20 | .15 |
| 67 | Mike Flanagan | .10 | .08 |
| 68 | Todd Stottlemyre(FC) | | |
| | | .70 | .50 |
| 69 | David Wells(FC) | .08 | .06 |
| 70 | Jose Alvarez(FC) | .15 | .11 |
| 71 | Paul Runge | .06 | .05 |
| 72 | Cesar Jimenez | | |
| | (German)(FC) | .15 | .11 |
| 73 | Pete Smith | .08 | .06 |
| 74 | John Smoltz(FC) | 5.00 | 3.75 |
| 75 | Damon Berryhill | .10 | .08 |
| 76 | Goose Gossage | .15 | .11 |
| 77 | Mark Grace | 2.00 | 1.50 |
| 78 | Darrin Jackson | .08 | .06 |
| 79 | Vance Law | .08 | .06 |
| 80 | Jeff Pico(FC) | .20 | .15 |
| 81 | Gary Varsho(FC) | .20 | .15 |
| 82 | Tim Birtsas | .06 | .05 |
| 83 | Rob Dibble(FC) | .80 | .60 |
| 84 | Danny Jackson | .15 | .11 |
| 85 | Paul O'Neill | .15 | .11 |
| 86 | Jose Rijo | .08 | .06 |
| 87 | Chris Sabo(FC) | 1.00 | .70 |
| 88 | John Fishel(FC) | .15 | .11 |
| 89 | Craig Biggio(FC) | 1.50 | 1.25 |
| 90 | Terry Puhl | .06 | .05 |
| 91 | Rafael Ramirez | .06 | .05 |
| 92 | Louie Meadows(FC) | .15 | .11 |
| 93 | Kirk Gibson(FC) | .20 | .15 |
| 94 | Alfredo Griffin | .08 | .06 |
| 95 | Jay Howell | .08 | .06 |
| 96 | Jesse Orosco | .08 | .06 |
| 97 | Alejandro Pena | .08 | .06 |
| 98 | Tracy Woodson(FC) | .10 | .08 |
| 99 | John Dopson(FC) | .25 | .20 |
| 100 | Brian Holman(FC) | .40 | .30 |
| 101 | Rex Hudler(FC) | .08 | .06 |
| 102 | Jeff Parrett(FC) | .10 | .08 |
| 103 | Nelson Santovenia(FC) | | |
| | | .15 | .11 |
| 104 | Kevin Elster | .12 | .09 |
| 105 | Jeff Innis(FC) | .20 | .15 |
| 106 | Mackey Sasser(FC) | .10 | .08 |
| 107 | Phil Bradley | .10 | .08 |
| 108 | Danny Clay(FC) | .15 | .11 |
| 109 | Greg Harris | .06 | .05 |
| 110 | Ricky Jordan(FC) | .30 | .25 |
| 111 | David Palmer | .06 | .05 |
| 112 | Jim Gott | .06 | .05 |
| 113 | Tommy Gregg (photo actually Randy Milligan)(FC) | | |
| | | .10 | .08 |
| 114 | Barry Jones | .06 | .05 |
| 115 | Randy Milligan(FC) | .60 | .45 |
| 116 | Luis Alicea(FC) | .15 | .11 |
| 117 | Tom Brunansky | .12 | .09 |
| 118 | John Costello(FC) | .15 | .11 |
| 119 | Jose DeLeon | .08 | .06 |
| 120 | Bob Horner | .10 | .08 |
| 121 | Scott Terry(FC) | .10 | .08 |
| 122 | Roberto Alomar(FC) | | |
| | | 10.00 | 7.50 |

| | | MT | NR MT |
|---|---|---|---|
| 123 | Dave Leiper | .06 | .05 |
| 124 | Keith Moreland | .08 | .06 |
| 125 | Mark Parent(FC) | .20 | .15 |
| 126 | Dennis Rasmussen | .10 | .08 |
| 127 | Randy Bockus | .06 | .05 |
| 128 | Brett Butler | .08 | .06 |
| 129 | Donell Nixon | .06 | .05 |
| 130 | Earnest Riles | .06 | .05 |
| 131 | Roger Samuels(FC) | .15 | .11 |
| 132 | Checklist | .06 | .05 |

## 1989 Fleer

This set includes 660 standard-size cards and was issued with 45 team logo stickers. Individual card fronts feature a grey and white striped background with full-color player photos framed by a bright line of color that slants upward to the right. The set also includes two subsets: 15 Major League Prospects and 12 SuperStar Specials. A special bonus set of 12 All-Star Team cards was randomly inserted in individual wax packs of 15 cards. The last seven cards in the set are checklists, with players listed alphabetically by teams.

| | | MT | NR MT |
|---|---|---|---|
| Complete Set: | | 15.00 | 11.00 |
| Common Player: | | .05 | .04 |
| 1 | Don Baylor | .10 | .08 |
| 2 | Lance Blankenship(FC) | .15 | .11 |
| 3 | Todd Burns | .15 | .11 |
| 4 | Greg Cadaret(FC) | .07 | .05 |
| 5 | Jose Canseco | .80 | .60 |
| 6 | Storm Davis | .10 | .08 |
| 7 | Dennis Eckersley | .12 | .09 |
| 8 | Mike Gallego(FC) | .05 | .04 |
| 9 | Ron Hassey | .05 | .04 |
| 10 | Dave Henderson | .10 | .08 |
| 11 | Rick Honeycutt | .05 | .04 |
| 12 | Glenn Hubbard | .05 | .04 |

| | | MT | NR MT |
|---|---|---|---|
| 13 | Stan Javier | .05 | .04 |
| 14 | *Doug Jennings* | .15 | .11 |
| 15 | *Felix Jose*(FC) | 1.00 | .70 |
| 16 | Carney Lansford | .07 | .05 |
| 17 | Mark McGwire | .40 | .30 |
| 18 | Gene Nelson | .05 | .04 |
| 19 | Dave Parker | .12 | .09 |
| 20 | Eric Plunk | .05 | .04 |
| 21 | Luis Polonia | .07 | .05 |
| 22 | Terry Steinbach | .10 | .08 |
| 23 | Dave Stewart | .10 | .08 |
| 24 | Walt Weiss | .20 | .15 |
| 25 | Bob Welch | .10 | .08 |
| 26 | Curt Young | .07 | .05 |
| 27 | Rick Aguilera | .05 | .04 |
| 28 | Wally Backman | .07 | .05 |
| 29 | Mark Carreon | .07 | .05 |
| 30 | Gary Carter | .20 | .15 |
| 31 | David Cone | .25 | .20 |
| 32 | Ron Darling | .12 | .09 |
| 33 | Len Dykstra | .10 | .08 |
| 34 | Kevin Elster | .10 | .08 |
| 35 | Sid Fernandez | .10 | .08 |
| 36 | Dwight Gooden | .20 | .15 |
| 37 | Keith Hernandez | .25 | .20 |
| 38 | Gregg Jefferies | .30 | .25 |
| 39 | Howard Johnson | .10 | .08 |
| 40 | Terry Leach | .05 | .04 |
| 41 | Dave Magadan | .10 | .08 |
| 42 | Bob McClure | .05 | .04 |
| 43 | Roger McDowell | .10 | .08 |
| 44 | Kevin McReynolds | .15 | .11 |
| 45 | Keith Miller | .10 | .08 |
| 46 | Randy Myers | .10 | .08 |
| 47 | Bob Ojeda | .07 | .05 |
| 48 | Mackey Sasser | .07 | .05 |
| 49 | Darryl Strawberry | .40 | .30 |
| 50 | Tim Teufel | .05 | .04 |
| 51 | *Dave West*(FC) | .20 | .15 |
| 52 | Mookie Wilson | .07 | .05 |
| 53 | Dave Anderson | .05 | .04 |
| 54 | Tim Belcher | .10 | .08 |
| 55 | Mike Davis | .07 | .05 |
| 56 | Mike Devereaux | .15 | .11 |
| 57 | Kirk Gibson | .20 | .15 |
| 58 | Alfredo Griffin | .07 | .05 |
| 59 | Chris Gwynn | .12 | .09 |
| 60 | Jeff Hamilton | .07 | .05 |
| 61a | Danny Heep (Home: San Antonio, TX) | .70 | .50 |
| 61b | Danny Heep (Home: Lake Hills, TX) | .05 | .04 |
| 62 | Orel Hershiser | .25 | .20 |
| 63 | Brian Holton(FC) | .07 | .05 |
| 64 | Jay Howell | .07 | .05 |
| 65 | Tim Leary | .07 | .05 |
| 66 | Mike Marshall | .12 | .09 |
| 67 | *Ramon Martinez*(FC) | 1.00 | .70 |
| 68 | Jesse Orosco | .07 | .05 |
| 69 | Alejandro Pena | .07 | .05 |
| 70 | Steve Sax | .15 | .11 |
| 71 | Mike Scioscia | .07 | .05 |
| 72 | Mike Sharperson | .05 | .04 |
| 73 | John Shelby | .05 | .04 |
| 74 | Franklin Stubbs | .05 | .04 |
| 75 | John Tudor | .10 | .08 |

| | | MT | NR MT |
|---|---|---|---|
| 76 | Fernando Valenzuela | .20 | .15 |
| 77 | Tracy Woodson | .10 | .08 |
| 78 | Marty Barrett | .07 | .05 |
| 79 | Todd Benzinger | .12 | .09 |
| 80 | Mike Boddicker | .07 | .05 |
| 81 | Wade Boggs | .50 | .40 |
| 82 | "Oil Can" Boyd | .07 | .05 |
| 83 | Ellis Burks | .40 | .30 |
| 84 | Rick Cerone | .05 | .04 |
| 85 | Roger Clemens | .50 | .40 |
| 86 | *Steve Curry*(FC) | .20 | .15 |
| 87 | Dwight Evans | .10 | .08 |
| 88 | Wes Gardner | .07 | .05 |
| 89 | Rich Gedman | .07 | .05 |
| 90 | Mike Greenwell | .40 | .30 |
| 91 | Bruce Hurst | .10 | .08 |
| 92 | Dennis Lamp | .05 | .04 |
| 93 | Spike Owen | .05 | .04 |
| 94 | Larry Parrish | .07 | .05 |
| 95 | *Carlos Quintana*(FC) | .20 | .15 |
| 96 | Jody Reed | .12 | .09 |
| 97 | Jim Rice | .25 | .20 |
| 98a | Kevin Romine (batting follow-thru, photo actually Randy Kutcher) | .50 | .40 |
| 98b | Kevin Romine (arms crossed on chest, correct photo) | .60 | .45 |
| 99 | Lee Smith | .10 | .08 |
| 100 | Mike Smithson | .05 | .04 |
| 101 | Bob Stanley | .05 | .04 |
| 102 | Allan Anderson | .07 | .05 |
| 103 | Keith Atherton | .05 | .04 |
| 104 | Juan Berenguer | .05 | .04 |
| 105 | Bert Blyleven | .12 | .09 |
| 106 | *Eric Bullock*(FC) | .15 | .11 |
| 107 | Randy Bush | .05 | .04 |
| 108 | John Christensen(FC) | .05 | .04 |
| 109 | Mark Davidson | .07 | .05 |
| 110 | Gary Gaetti | .15 | .11 |
| 111 | Greg Gagne | .05 | .04 |
| 112 | Dan Gladden | .05 | .04 |
| 113 | *German Gonzalez*(FC) | .20 | .15 |
| 114 | Brian Harper | .05 | .04 |
| 115 | Tom Herr | .07 | .05 |
| 116 | Kent Hrbek | .20 | .15 |
| 117 | Gene Larkin | .10 | .08 |
| 118 | Tim Laudner | .05 | .04 |
| 119 | Charlie Lea | .05 | .04 |
| 120 | Steve Lombardozzi | .05 | .04 |
| 121a | John Moses (Home: Phoenix, AZ) | 1.00 | .70 |
| 121b | John Moses (Home: Tempe, AZ) | .05 | .04 |
| 122 | Al Newman | .05 | .04 |
| 123 | Mark Portugal | .05 | .04 |
| 124 | Kirby Puckett | .35 | .25 |
| 125 | Jeff Reardon | .10 | .08 |
| 126 | Fred Toliver | .05 | .04 |
| 127 | Frank Viola | .15 | .11 |
| 128 | Doyle Alexander | .07 | .05 |
| 129 | Dave Bergman | .05 | .04 |
| 130a | Tom Brookens (Mike | | |

| | | MT | NR MT |
|---|---|---|---|
| | Heath stats on back) | 2.25 | 1.75 |
| 130b | Tom Brookens (correct | | |
| | stats on back) | .30 | .25 |
| 131 | *Paul Gibson* | .15 | .11 |
| 132a | Mike Heath (Tom | | |
| | Brookens stats on back) | | |
| | | 2.25 | 1.75 |
| 132b | Mike Heath (correct | | |
| | stats on back) | .30 | .25 |
| 133 | *Don Heinkel* | .15 | .11 |
| 134 | Mike Henneman | .10 | .08 |
| 135 | Guillermo Hernandez | | |
| | | .07 | .05 |
| 136 | Eric King | .05 | .04 |
| 137 | Chet Lemon | .07 | .05 |
| 138 | Fred Lynn | .10 | .08 |
| 139 | Jack Morris | .15 | .11 |
| 140 | Matt Nokes | .20 | .15 |
| 141 | Gary Pettis | .05 | .04 |
| 142 | Ted Power | .05 | .04 |
| 143 | Jeff Robinson | .12 | .09 |
| 144 | Luis Salazar | .05 | .04 |
| 145 | *Steve Searcy*(FC) | | |
| | | .20 | .15 |
| 146 | Pat Sheridan | .05 | .04 |
| 147 | Frank Tanana | .07 | .05 |
| 148 | Alan Trammell | .20 | .15 |
| 149 | Walt Terrell | .07 | .05 |
| 150 | Jim Walewander(FC) | | |
| | | .07 | .05 |
| 151 | Lou Whitaker | .20 | .15 |
| 152 | Tim Birtsas | .05 | .04 |
| 153 | Tom Browning | .10 | .08 |
| 154 | *Keith Brown*(FC) | .15 | .11 |
| 155 | *Norm Charlton*(FC) | | |
| | | .30 | .25 |
| 156 | Dave Concepcion | .10 | .08 |
| 157 | Kal Daniels | .15 | .11 |
| 158 | Eric Davis | .30 | .25 |
| 159 | Bo Diaz | .07 | .05 |
| 160 | *Rob Dibble* | .30 | .25 |
| 161 | Nick Esasky | .07 | .05 |
| 162 | John Franco | .10 | .08 |
| 163 | Danny Jackson | .15 | .11 |
| 164 | Barry Larkin | .25 | .20 |
| 165 | Rob Murphy | .05 | .04 |
| 166 | Paul O'Neill | .05 | .04 |
| 167 | Jeff Reed | .05 | .04 |
| 168 | Jose Rijo | .07 | .05 |
| 169 | Ron Robinson | .05 | .04 |
| 170 | *Chris Sabo* | .40 | .30 |
| 171 | *Candy Sierra*(FC) | | |
| | | .15 | .11 |
| 172 | *Van Snider*(FC) | .15 | .11 |
| 173 | Jeff Treadway | .12 | .09 |
| 174 | Frank Williams | .05 | .04 |
| 175 | Herm Winningham | .05 | .04 |
| 176 | Jim Adduci(FC) | .05 | .04 |
| 177 | Don August | .10 | .08 |
| 178 | Mike Birkbeck | .05 | .04 |
| 179 | Chris Bosio | .05 | .04 |
| 180 | Glenn Braggs | .07 | .05 |
| 181 | Greg Brock | .07 | .05 |
| 182 | Mark Clear | .05 | .04 |
| 183 | Chuck Crim | .05 | .04 |
| 184 | Rob Deer | .07 | .05 |
| 185 | Tom Filer | .05 | .04 |

| | | MT | NR MT |
|---|---|---|---|
| 186 | Jim Gantner | .05 | .04 |
| 187 | *Darryl Hamilton* | .30 | .25 |
| 188 | Ted Higuera | .10 | .08 |
| 189 | Odell Jones | .05 | .04 |
| 190 | Jeffrey Leonard | .07 | .05 |
| 191 | Joey Meyer | .10 | .08 |
| 192 | Paul Mirabella | .05 | .04 |
| 193 | Paul Molitor | .15 | .11 |
| 194 | Charlie O'Brien(FC) | .07 | .05 |
| 195 | Dan Plesac | .10 | .08 |
| 196 | *Gary Sheffield*(FC) | | |
| | | 1.00 | .70 |
| 197 | B.J. Surhoff | .10 | .08 |
| 198 | Dale Sveum | .07 | .05 |
| 199 | Bill Wegman | .05 | .04 |
| 200 | Robin Yount | .25 | .20 |
| 201 | Rafael Belliard | .05 | .04 |
| 202 | Barry Bonds | .40 | .30 |
| 203 | Bobby Bonilla | .30 | .25 |
| 204 | Sid Bream | .07 | .05 |
| 205 | Benny Distefano(FC) | | |
| | | .05 | .04 |
| 206 | Doug Drabek | .07 | .05 |
| 207 | Mike Dunne | .10 | .08 |
| 208 | Felix Fermin | .07 | .05 |
| 209 | Brian Fisher | .07 | .05 |
| 210 | Jim Gott | .05 | .04 |
| 211 | Bob Kipper | .05 | .04 |
| 212 | Dave LaPoint | .07 | .05 |
| 213 | Mike LaValliere | .07 | .05 |
| 214 | Jose Lind | .10 | .08 |
| 215 | Junior Ortiz | .05 | .04 |
| 216 | Vicente Palacios | .07 | .05 |
| 217 | Tom Prince(FC) | .10 | .08 |
| 218 | Gary Redus | .05 | .04 |
| 219 | R.J. Reynolds | .05 | .04 |
| 220 | Jeff Robinson | .07 | .05 |
| 221 | John Smiley | .12 | .09 |
| 222 | Andy Van Slyke | .12 | .09 |
| 223 | Bob Walk | .05 | .04 |
| 224 | Glenn Wilson | .07 | .05 |
| 225 | Jesse Barfield | .10 | .08 |
| 226 | George Bell | .25 | .20 |
| 227 | *Pat Borders* | .30 | .25 |
| 228 | John Cerutti | .07 | .05 |
| 229 | Jim Clancy | .07 | .05 |
| 230 | Mark Eichhorn | .07 | .05 |
| 231 | Tony Fernandez | .12 | .09 |
| 232 | Cecil Fielder | .25 | .20 |
| 233 | Mike Flanagan | .07 | .05 |
| 234 | Kelly Gruber | .05 | .04 |
| 235 | Tom Henke | .07 | .05 |
| 236 | Jimmy Key | .10 | .08 |
| 237 | Rick Leach | .05 | .04 |
| 238 | Manny Lee | .05 | .04 |
| 239 | Nelson Liriano | .07 | .05 |
| 240 | Fred McGriff | .50 | .40 |
| 241 | Lloyd Moseby | .07 | .05 |
| 242 | Rance Mulliniks | .05 | .04 |
| 243 | Jeff Musselman | .07 | .05 |
| 244 | Dave Stieb | .10 | .08 |
| 245 | Todd Stottlemyre | .10 | .08 |
| 246 | Duane Ward | .05 | .04 |
| 247 | David Wells | .10 | .08 |
| 248 | Ernie Whitt | .07 | .05 |
| 249 | Luis Aguayo | .05 | .04 |
| 250a | Neil Allen (Home: | | |

| | MT | NR MT |
|---|---|---|
| Sarasota, FL) | 1.50 | 1.25 |
| 250b Neil Allen (Home: Syosset, NY) | .05 | .04 |
| 251 John Candelaria | .07 | .05 |
| 252 Jack Clark | .15 | .11 |
| 253 Richard Dotson | .07 | .05 |
| 254 Rickey Henderson | .35 | .25 |
| 255 Tommy John | .12 | .09 |
| 256 Roberto Kelly | .20 | .15 |
| 257 Al Leiter | .15 | .11 |
| 258 Don Mattingly | .80 | .60 |
| 259 Dale Mohorcic | .05 | .04 |
| 260 *Hal Morris*(FC) | 1.25 | .90 |
| 261 Scott Nielsen(FC) | .10 | .08 |
| 262 Mike Pagliarulo | .10 | .08 |
| 263 *Hipolito Pena*(FC) | .15 | .11 |
| 264 Ken Phelps | .07 | .05 |
| 265 Willie Randolph | .07 | .05 |
| 266 Rick Rhoden | .07 | .05 |
| 267 Dave Righetti | .12 | .09 |
| 268 Rafael Santana | .05 | .04 |
| 269 Steve Shields(FC) | .07 | .05 |
| 270 Joel Skinner | .05 | .04 |
| 271 Don Slaught | .05 | .04 |
| 272 Claudell Washington | .07 | .05 |
| 273 Gary Ward | .07 | .05 |
| 274 Dave Winfield | .30 | .25 |
| 275 Luis Aquino(FC) | .05 | .04 |
| 276 Floyd Bannister | .07 | .05 |
| 277 George Brett | .35 | .25 |
| 278 Bill Buckner | .10 | .08 |
| 279 *Nick Capra*(FC) | .15 | .11 |
| 280 *Jose DeJesus*(FC) | .15 | .11 |
| 281 Steve Farr | .05 | .04 |
| 282 Jerry Gleaton | .05 | .04 |
| 283 Mark Gubicza | .10 | .08 |
| 284 Tom Gordon(FC) | .40 | .30 |
| 285 Bo Jackson | .80 | .60 |
| 286 Charlie Leibrandt | .07 | .05 |
| 287 *Mike Macfarlane* | .20 | .15 |
| 288 Jeff Montgomery | .07 | .05 |
| 289 Bill Pecota | .05 | .04 |
| 290 Jamie Quirk | .05 | .04 |
| 291 Bret Saberhagen | .15 | .11 |
| 292 Kevin Seitzer | .30 | .25 |
| 293 Kurt Stillwell | .07 | .05 |
| 294 Pat Tabler | .07 | .05 |
| 295 Danny Tartabull | .20 | .15 |
| 296 Gary Thurman | .12 | .09 |
| 297 Frank White | .07 | .05 |
| 298 Willie Wilson | .10 | .08 |
| 299 Roberto Alomar | 1.00 | .70 |
| 300 *Sandy Alomar, Jr.*(FC) | .60 | .45 |
| 301 Chris Brown | .07 | .05 |
| 302 Mike Brumley(FC) | .07 | .05 |
| 303 Mark Davis | .05 | .04 |
| 304 Mark Grant | .05 | .04 |
| 305 Tony Gwynn | .35 | .25 |
| 306 *Greg Harris*(FC) | .20 | .15 |
| 307 Andy Hawkins | .05 | .04 |
| 308 Jimmy Jones | .05 | .04 |
| 309 John Kruk | .07 | .05 |
| 310 Dave Leiper | .05 | .04 |

| | MT | NR MT |
|---|---|---|
| 311 Carmelo Martinez | .05 | .04 |
| 312 Lance McCullers | .07 | .05 |
| 313 Keith Moreland | .07 | .05 |
| 314 Dennis Rasmussen | .10 | .08 |
| 315 Randy Ready | .05 | .04 |
| 316 Benito Santiago | .15 | .11 |
| 317 Eric Show | .07 | .05 |
| 318 Todd Simmons | .10 | .08 |
| 319 Garry Templeton | .07 | .05 |
| 320 Dickie Thon | .05 | .04 |
| 321 Ed Whitson | .05 | .04 |
| 322 Marvell Wynne | .05 | .04 |
| 323 Mike Aldrete | .07 | .05 |
| 324 Brett Butler | .07 | .05 |
| 325 Will Clark | .80 | .60 |
| 326 Kelly Downs | .10 | .08 |
| 327 Dave Dravecky | .07 | .05 |
| 328 Scott Garrelts | .05 | .04 |
| 329 Atlee Hammaker | .05 | .04 |
| 330 *Charlie Hayes*(FC) | .30 | .25 |
| 331 Mike Krukow | .07 | .05 |
| 332 Craig Lefferts | .05 | .04 |
| 333 Candy Maldonado | .07 | .05 |
| 334 Kirt Manwaring | .10 | .08 |
| 335 Bob Melvin | .05 | .04 |
| 336 Kevin Mitchell | .60 | .45 |
| 337 Donell Nixon | .05 | .04 |
| 338 *Tony Perezchica*(FC) | .15 | .11 |
| 339 Joe Price | .05 | .04 |
| 340 Rick Reuschel | .10 | .08 |
| 341 Earnest Riles | .05 | .04 |
| 342 Don Robinson | .05 | .04 |
| 343 Chris Speier | .05 | .04 |
| 344 Robby Thompson | .07 | .05 |
| 345 Jose Uribe | .05 | .04 |
| 346 Matt Williams | .12 | .09 |
| 347 *Trevor Wilson*(FC) | .15 | .11 |
| 348 Juan Agosto | .05 | .04 |
| 349 Larry Andersen | .05 | .04 |
| 350 Alan Ashby | .05 | .04 |
| 351 Kevin Bass | .07 | .05 |
| 352 Buddy Bell | .07 | .05 |
| 353 *Craig Biggio* | .60 | .45 |
| 354 Danny Darwin | .05 | .04 |
| 355 Glenn Davis | .25 | .20 |
| 356 Jim Deshaies | .05 | .04 |
| 357 Bill Doran | .07 | .05 |
| 358 *John Fishel* | .20 | .15 |
| 359 Billy Hatcher | .07 | .05 |
| 360 Bob Knepper | .07 | .05 |
| 361 *Louie Meadows* | .15 | .11 |
| 362 Dave Meads | .05 | .04 |
| 363 Jim Pankovits | .05 | .04 |
| 364 Terry Puhl | .05 | .04 |
| 365 Rafael Ramirez | .05 | .04 |
| 366 Craig Reynolds | .05 | .04 |
| 367 Mike Scott | .12 | .09 |
| 368 Nolan Ryan | .50 | .40 |
| 369 Dave Smith | .07 | .05 |
| 370 Gerald Young | .12 | .09 |
| 371 Hubie Brooks | .10 | .08 |
| 372 Tim Burke | .05 | .04 |
| 373 *John Dopson* | .25 | .20 |
| 374 Mike Fitzgerald | .05 | .04 |

| | MT | NR MT |
|---|---|---|
| 375 Tom Foley | .05 | .04 |
| 376 Andres Galarraga | .15 | .11 |
| 377 Neal Heaton | .05 | .04 |
| 378 Joe Hesketh | .05 | .04 |
| 379 *Brian Holman* | .35 | .25 |
| 380 Rex Hudler | .05 | .04 |
| 381 *Randy Johnson*(FC) | | |
| | .50 | .40 |
| 382 Wallace Johnson | .05 | .04 |
| 383 Tracy Jones | .10 | .08 |
| 384 Dave Martinez | .07 | .05 |
| 385 Dennis Martinez | .07 | .05 |
| 386 Andy McGaffigan | .05 | .04 |
| 387 Otis Nixon | .05 | .04 |
| 388 *Johnny Paredes*(FC) | | |
| | .12 | .09 |
| 389 Jeff Parrett | .10 | .08 |
| 390 Pascual Perez | .07 | .05 |
| 391 Tim Raines | .25 | .20 |
| 392 Luis Rivera | .05 | .04 |
| 393 *Nelson Santovenia* | .15 | .11 |
| 394 Bryn Smith | .05 | .04 |
| 395 Tim Wallach | .10 | .08 |
| 396 Andy Allanson | .05 | .04 |
| 397 *Rod Allen* | .15 | .11 |
| 398 Scott Bailes | .05 | .04 |
| 399 Tom Candiotti | .05 | .04 |
| 400 Joe Carter | .12 | .09 |
| 401 Carmen Castillo | .05 | .04 |
| 402 Dave Clark | .07 | .05 |
| 403 John Farrell | .10 | .08 |
| 404 Julio Franco | .10 | .08 |
| 405 Don Gordon | .05 | .04 |
| 406 Mel Hall | .07 | .05 |
| 407 Brad Havens | .05 | .04 |
| 408 Brook Jacoby | .10 | .08 |
| 409 Doug Jones | .12 | .09 |
| 410 *Jeff Kaiser*(FC) | .15 | .11 |
| 411 *Luis Medina*(FC) | .20 | .15 |
| 412 Cory Snyder | .15 | .11 |
| 413 Greg Swindell | .12 | .09 |
| 414 *Ron Tingley*(FC) | .15 | .11 |
| 415 Willie Upshaw | .07 | .05 |
| 416 Ron Washington | .05 | .04 |
| 417 Rich Yett | .05 | .04 |
| 418 Damon Berryhill | .12 | .09 |
| 419 Mike Bielecki | .05 | .04 |
| 420 *Doug Dascenzo*(FC) | | |
| | .20 | .15 |
| 421 Jody Davis | .07 | .05 |
| 422 Andre Dawson | .20 | .15 |
| 423 Frank DiPino | .05 | .04 |
| 424 Shawon Dunston | .10 | .08 |
| 425 "Goose" Gossage | .12 | .09 |
| 426 Mark Grace | .40 | .30 |
| 427 *Mike Harkey*(FC) | .35 | .25 |
| 428 Darrin Jackson | .07 | .05 |
| 429 Les Lancaster | .07 | .05 |
| 430 Vance Law | .07 | .05 |
| 431 Greg Maddux | .12 | .09 |
| 432 Jamie Moyer | .05 | .04 |
| 433 Al Nipper | .05 | .04 |
| 434 Rafael Palmeiro | .20 | .15 |
| 435 Pat Perry | .05 | .04 |
| 436 *Jeff Pico* | .12 | .09 |
| 437 Ryne Sandberg | .40 | .30 |
| 438 Calvin Schiraldi | .05 | .04 |

| | MT | NR MT |
|---|---|---|
| 439 Rick Sutcliffe | .10 | .08 |
| 440 Manny Trillo | .05 | .04 |
| 441 *Gary Varsho* | .20 | .15 |
| 442 Mitch Webster | .07 | .05 |
| 443 *Luis Alicea* | .15 | .11 |
| 444 Tom Brunansky | .12 | .09 |
| 445 Vince Coleman | .15 | .11 |
| 446 *John Costello* | .15 | .11 |
| 447 Danny Cox | .07 | .05 |
| 448 Ken Dayley | .05 | .04 |
| 449 Jose DeLeon | .07 | .05 |
| 450 Curt Ford | .05 | .04 |
| 451 Pedro Guerrero | .15 | .11 |
| 452 Bob Horner | .10 | .08 |
| 453 *Tim Jones*(FC) | .15 | .11 |
| 454 Steve Lake | .05 | .04 |
| 455 Joe Magrane | .10 | .08 |
| 456 Greg Mathews | .07 | .05 |
| 457 Willie McGee | .12 | .09 |
| 458 Larry McWilliams | .05 | .04 |
| 459 Jose Oquendo | .05 | .04 |
| 460 Tony Pena | .07 | .05 |
| 461 Terry Pendleton | .10 | .08 |
| 462 *Steve Peters*(FC) | | |
| | .15 | .11 |
| 463 Ozzie Smith | .15 | .11 |
| 464 Scott Terry | .08 | .06 |
| 465 Denny Walling | .05 | .04 |
| 466 Todd Worrell | .10 | .08 |
| 467 Tony Armas | .07 | .05 |
| 468 *Dante Bichette*(FC) | | |
| | .30 | .25 |
| 469 Bob Boone | .07 | .05 |
| 470 *Terry Clark*(FC) | .15 | .11 |
| 471 Stew Cliburn(FC) | .05 | .04 |
| 472 *Mike Cook*(FC) | .15 | .11 |
| 473 *Sherman Corbett* | .15 | .11 |
| 474 Chili Davis | .07 | .05 |
| 475 Brian Downing | .07 | .05 |
| 476 Jim Eppard | .05 | .04 |
| 477 Chuck Finley | .05 | .04 |
| 478 Willie Fraser | .05 | .04 |
| 479 *Bryan Harvey* | .30 | .25 |
| 480 Jack Howell | .07 | .05 |
| 481 Wally Joyner | .25 | .20 |
| 482 Jack Lazorko | .05 | .04 |
| 483 Kirk McCaskill | .07 | .05 |
| 484 Mark McLemore | .05 | .04 |
| 485 Greg Minton | .05 | .04 |
| 486 Dan Petry | .07 | .05 |
| 487 Johnny Ray | .07 | .05 |
| 488 Dick Schofield | .05 | .04 |
| 489 Devon White | .12 | .09 |
| 490 Mike Witt | .07 | .05 |
| 491 Harold Baines | .12 | .09 |
| 492 Daryl Boston | .05 | .04 |
| 493 Ivan Calderon | .07 | .05 |
| 494 Mike Diaz | .07 | .05 |
| 495 Carlton Fisk | .20 | .15 |
| 496 *Dave Gallagher* | .15 | .11 |
| 497 Ozzie Guillen | .07 | .05 |
| 498 Shawn Hillegas | .07 | .05 |
| 499 Lance Johnson | .07 | .05 |
| 500 Barry Jones | .05 | .04 |
| 501 Bill Long | .07 | .05 |
| 502 Steve Lyons | .05 | .04 |
| 503 Fred Manrique | .07 | .05 |

| | | MT | NR MT |
|---|---|---|---|
| 504 | Jack McDowell | .10 | .08 |
| 505 | *Donn Pall* | .15 | .11 |
| 506 | Kelly Paris | .05 | .04 |
| 507 | Dan Pasqua | .10 | .08 |
| 508 | *Ken Patterson* | .15 | .11 |
| 509 | Melido Perez | .10 | .08 |
| 510 | Jerry Reuss | .07 | .05 |
| 511 | Mark Salas | .05 | .04 |
| 512 | Bobby Thigpen | .10 | .08 |
| 513 | Mike Woodard | .05 | .04 |
| 514 | Bob Brower | .05 | .04 |
| 515 | Steve Buechele | .05 | .04 |
| 516 | *Jose Cecena* | .15 | .11 |
| 517 | Cecil Espy | .07 | .05 |
| 518 | Scott Fletcher | .07 | .05 |
| 519 | Cecilio Guante | .05 | .04 |
| 520 | Jose Guzman | .10 | .08 |
| 521 | Ray Hayward | .05 | .04 |
| 522 | Charlie Hough | .07 | .05 |
| 523 | Pete Incaviglia | .12 | .09 |
| 524 | Mike Jeffcoat | .05 | .04 |
| 525 | Paul Kilgus | .10 | .08 |
| 526 | *Chad Kreuter*(FC) | .15 | .11 |
| 527 | Jeff Kunkel | .05 | .04 |
| 528 | Oddibe McDowell | .07 | .05 |
| 529 | Pete O'Brien | .07 | .05 |
| 530 | Geno Petralli | .05 | .04 |
| 531 | Jeff Russell | .05 | .04 |
| 532 | Ruben Sierra | .35 | .25 |
| 533 | Mike Stanley | .05 | .04 |
| 534 | Ed Vande Berg | .05 | .04 |
| 535 | Curtis Wilkerson | .05 | .04 |
| 536 | Mitch Williams | .07 | .05 |
| 537 | Bobby Witt | .10 | .08 |
| 538 | Steve Balboni | .07 | .05 |
| 539 | Scott Bankhead | .05 | .04 |
| 540 | Scott Bradley | .05 | .04 |
| 541 | Mickey Brantley | .05 | .04 |
| 542 | Jay Buhner(FC) | .10 | .08 |
| 543 | Mike Campbell | .10 | .08 |
| 544 | Darnell Coles | .07 | .05 |
| 545 | Henry Cotto | .05 | .04 |
| 546 | Alvin Davis | .12 | .09 |
| 547 | Mario Diaz | .07 | .05 |
| 548 | *Ken Griffey, Jr.*(FC) | 6.00 | 4.50 |
| 549 | *Erik Hanson*(FC) | .50 | .40 |
| 550 | Mike Jackson | .07 | .05 |
| 551 | Mark Langston | .10 | .08 |
| 552 | Edgar Martinez | .40 | .30 |
| 553 | *Bill McGuire*(FC) | .15 | .11 |
| 554 | Mike Moore | .05 | .04 |
| 555 | Jim Presley | .07 | .05 |
| 556 | Rey Quinones | .05 | .04 |
| 557 | Jerry Reed | .05 | .04 |
| 558 | Harold Reynolds | .07 | .05 |
| 559 | *Mike Schooler*(FC) | .35 | .25 |
| 560 | Bill Swift | .05 | .04 |
| 561 | Dave Valle | .05 | .04 |
| 562 | Steve Bedrosian | .10 | .08 |
| 563 | Phil Bradley | .10 | .08 |
| 564 | Don Carman | .07 | .05 |
| 565 | Bob Dernier | .05 | .04 |
| 566 | Marvin Freeman | .05 | .04 |
| 567 | Todd Frohwirth | .07 | .05 |
| 568 | Greg Gross | .05 | .04 |
| 569 | Kevin Gross | .07 | .05 |
| 570 | Greg Harris | .05 | .04 |
| 571 | Von Hayes | .10 | .08 |
| 572 | Chris James | .10 | .08 |
| 573 | Steve Jeltz | .05 | .04 |
| 574 | *Ron Jones*(FC) | .15 | .11 |
| 575 | *Ricky Jordan* | .50 | .40 |
| 576 | Mike Maddux | .05 | .04 |
| 577 | David Palmer | .05 | .04 |
| 578 | Lance Parrish | .15 | .11 |
| 579 | Shane Rawley | .07 | .05 |
| 580 | Bruce Ruffin | .05 | .04 |
| 581 | Juan Samuel | .12 | .09 |
| 582 | Mike Schmidt | .50 | .40 |
| 583 | Kent Tekulve | .07 | .05 |
| 584 | Milt Thompson | .05 | .04 |
| 585 | *Jose Alvarez* | .15 | .11 |
| 586 | Paul Assenmacher | .05 | .04 |
| 587 | Bruce Benedict | .05 | .04 |
| 588 | Jeff Blauser | .10 | .08 |
| 589 | *Terry Blocker*(FC) | .15 | .11 |
| 590 | Ron Gant | .12 | .09 |
| 591 | Tom Glavine | .10 | .08 |
| 592 | Tommy Gregg | .10 | .08 |
| 593 | Albert Hall | .05 | .04 |
| 594 | Dion James | .05 | .04 |
| 595 | Rick Mahler | .05 | .04 |
| 596 | Dale Murphy | .40 | .30 |
| 597 | Gerald Perry | .10 | .08 |
| 598 | Charlie Puleo | .05 | .04 |
| 599 | Ted Simmons | .10 | .08 |
| 600 | Pete Smith | .10 | .08 |
| 601 | Zane Smith | .07 | .05 |
| 602 | *John Smoltz* | .80 | .60 |
| 603 | Bruce Sutter | .10 | .08 |
| 604 | Andres Thomas | .07 | .05 |
| 605 | Ozzie Virgil | .05 | .04 |
| 606 | *Brady Anderson*(FC) | .70 | .50 |
| 607 | Jeff Ballard | .07 | .05 |
| 608 | *Jose Bautista* | .20 | .15 |
| 609 | Ken Gerhart | .07 | .05 |
| 610 | Terry Kennedy | .07 | .05 |
| 611 | Eddie Murray | .30 | .25 |
| 612 | Carl Nichols(FC) | .10 | .08 |
| 613 | Tom Niedenfuer | .07 | .05 |
| 614 | Joe Orsulak | .05 | .04 |
| 615 | *Oswaldo Peraza (Oswald)*(FC) | .15 | .11 |
| 616a | Bill Ripken (obscenity on bat) | 15.00 | 11.00 |
| 616b | Bill Ripken (obscenity on bat scrawled out in black) | 15.00 | 11.00 |
| 616c | Bill Ripken (obscenity on bat blocked out in black) | .60 | .45 |
| 616d | Bill Ripken (obscenity on bat whiteout) | 30.00 | 22.00 |
| 617 | Cal Ripken, Jr. | .40 | .30 |
| 618 | Dave Schmidt | .05 | .04 |
| 619 | Rick Schu | .05 | .04 |
| 620 | Larry Sheets | .07 | .05 |
| 621 | Doug Sisk | .05 | .04 |
| 622 | Pete Stanicek | .10 | .08 |

|     |                                                             | MT   | NR MT |
|-----|-------------------------------------------------------------|------|-------|
| 623 | Mickey Tettleton                                            | .05  | .04   |
| 624 | Jay Tibbs                                                    | .05  | .04   |
| 625 | Jim Traber                                                   | .07  | .05   |
| 626 | Mark Williamson                                             | .07  | .05   |
| 627 | Craig Worthington                                           | .20  | .15   |
| 628 | Speed and Power (Jose Canseco)                              | .60  | .45   |
| 629 | Pitcher Perfect (Tom Browning)                              | .10  | .08   |
| 630 | Like Father - Like Sons (Roberto Alomar, Sandy Alomar, Jr.) | .50  | .40   |
| 631 | N.L. All-Stars (Will Clark, Rafael Palmeiro)                | .40  | .30   |
| 632 | Homeruns Coast to Coast (Will Clark, Darryl Strawberry)     | .30  | .25   |
| 633 | Hot Corner's - Hot Hitters (Wade Boggs, Carney Lansford)    | .40  | .30   |
| 634 | Triple A's (Jose Canseco, Mark McGwire, Terry Steinbach)    | .30  | .25   |
| 635 | Dual Heat (Mark Davis, Dwight Gooden)                       | .20  | .15   |
| 636 | N.L. Pitching Power (David Cone, Danny Jackson)             | .15  | .11   |
| 637 | Cannon Arms (Bobby Bonilla, Chris Sabo)                     | .20  | .15   |
| 638 | Double Trouble (Andres Galarraga, Gerald Perry)             | .10  | .08   |
| 639 | Power Center (Eric Davis, Kirby Puckett)                    | .15  | .11   |
| 640 | Major League Prospects (Cameron Drew, Steve Wilson)(FC)     | .15  | .11   |
| 641 | Major League Prospects (Kevin Brown, Kevin Reimer)(FC)      | .80  | .60   |
| 642 | Major League Prospects (Jerald Clark, Brad Pounders)(FC)    | .40  | .30   |
| 643 | Major League Prospects (Mike Capel, Drew Hall)(FC)          | .15  | .11   |
| 644 | Major League Prospects (Joe Girardi, Rolando Roomes)(FC)    | .30  | .25   |
| 645 | Major League Prospects (Marty Brown, Lenny Harris)(FC)      | .40  | .30   |
| 646 | Major League Prospects (Luis de los Santos, Jim Campbell)(FC) | .20 | .15   |
| 647 | Major League Prospects (Miguel Garcia, Randy Kramer)(FC)    | .15  | .11   |
| 648 | Major League Prospects (Torey Lovullo, Robert Palacios)(FC) | .15  | .11   |
| 649 | Major League Prospects (Jim Corsi, Bob Milacki)(FC)         | .25  | .20   |
| 650 | Major League Prospects (Grady Hall, Mike                    |      |       |

|     |                                                              | MT   | NR MT |
|-----|--------------------------------------------------------------|------|-------|
|     | Rochford)(FC)                                                | .15  | .11   |
| 651 | Major League Prospects (Vance Lovelace, Terry Taylor)(FC)    | .15  | .11   |
| 652 | Major League Prospects (Dennis Cook, Ken Hill)(FC)           | .35  | .25   |
| 653 | Major League Prospects (Scott Service, Shane Turner)(FC)     | .15  | .11   |
| 654 | Checklist 1-101                                              | .05  | .04   |
| 655 | Checklist 102-200                                            | .05  | .04   |
| 656 | Checklist 201-298                                            | .05  | .04   |
| 657 | Checklist 299-395                                            | .05  | .04   |
| 658 | Checklist 396-490                                            | .05  | .04   |
| 659 | Checklist 491-584                                            | .05  | .04   |
| 660 | Checklist 585-660                                            | .05  | .04   |

## 1989 Fleer Update

Fleer produced its sixth consecutive "Update" set in 1989 to supplement the company's regular set. As in the past, the set consisted of 132 cards (numbered U-1 through U-132) that were sold by hobby dealers in special collector's boxes.

|                |                   | MT    | NR MT |
|----------------|-------------------|-------|-------|
| Complete Set:  |                   | 12.00 | 9.00  |
| Common Player: |                   | .06   | .05   |
| 1              | Phil Bradley      | .06   | .05   |
| 2              | Mike Devereaux    | .10   | .08   |
| 3              | Steve Finley(FC)  | .40   | .30   |
| 4              | Kevin Hickey      | .06   | .05   |
| 5              | Brian Holton      | .06   | .05   |
| 6              | Bob Milacki       | .20   | .15   |
| 7              | Randy Milligan    | .10   | .08   |
| 8              | John Dopson       | .15   | .11   |
| 9              | Nick Esasky       | .10   | .08   |
| 10             | Rob Murphy        | .06   | .05   |
| 11             | Jim Abbott(FC)    | 1.00  | .70   |
| 12             | Bert Blyleven     | .06   | .05   |
| 13             | Jeff Manto(FC)    | .30   | .25   |
| 14             | Bob McClure       | .06   | .05   |
| 15             | Lance Parrish     | .06   | .05   |
| 16             | Lee Stevens(FC)   | .60   | .45   |
| 17             | Claudell Washington | .06 | .05   |
| 18             | Mark Davis        | .06   | .05   |

| | | MT | NR MT | | | | MT | NR MT |
|---|---|---|---|---|---|---|---|---|
| 19 | Eric King | .06 | .05 | 82 | Steve Wilson | | .25 | .20 |
| 20 | Ron Kittle | .06 | .05 | 83 | Todd Benzinger | | .06 | .05 |
| 21 | Matt Merullo(FC) | .15 | .11 | 84 | Ken Griffey | | .20 | .15 |
| 22 | Steve Rosenberg(FC) | | | 85 | Rick Mahler | | .06 | .05 |
| | | .08 | .06 | 86 | Rolando Roomes | | .15 | .11 |
| 23 | Robin Ventura(FC) | 3.00 | 2.25 | 87 | Scott Scudder(FC) | | .20 | .15 |
| 24 | Keith Atherton | .06 | .05 | 88 | Jim Clancy | | .06 | .05 |
| 25 | Joey Belle(FC) | 2.00 | 1.50 | 89 | Rick Rhoden | | .06 | .05 |
| 26 | Jerry Browne | .06 | .05 | 90 | Dan Schatzeder | | .06 | .05 |
| 27 | Felix Fermin | .06 | .05 | 91 | Mike Morgan | | .06 | .05 |
| 28 | Brad Komminsk | .06 | .05 | 92 | Eddie Murray | | .20 | .15 |
| 29 | Pete O'Brien | .06 | .05 | 93 | Willie Randolph | | .06 | .05 |
| 30 | Mike Brumley | .06 | .05 | 94 | Ray Searage | | .06 | .05 |
| 31 | Tracy Jones | .06 | .05 | 95 | Mike Aldrete | | .06 | .05 |
| 32 | Mike Schwabe(FC) | .30 | .25 | 96 | Kevin Gross | | .06 | .05 |
| 33 | Gary Ward | .06 | .05 | 97 | Mark Langston | | .15 | .11 |
| 34 | Frank Williams | .06 | .05 | 98 | Spike Owen | | .06 | .05 |
| 35 | Kevin Appier(FC) | .50 | .40 | 99 | Zane Smith | | .06 | .05 |
| 36 | Bob Boone | .06 | .05 | 100 | Don Aase | | .06 | .05 |
| 37 | Luis de los Santos | .10 | .08 | 101 | Barry Lyons | | .06 | .05 |
| 38 | Jim Eisenreich(FC) | .06 | .05 | 102 | Juan Samuel | | .06 | .05 |
| 39 | Jaime Navarro(FC) | .50 | .40 | 103 | Wally Whitehurst(FC) | | | |
| 40 | Bill Spiers(FC) | .40 | .30 | | | | .20 | .15 |
| 41 | Greg Vaughn(FC) | 1.25 | .90 | 104 | Dennis Cook | | .15 | .11 |
| 42 | Randy Veres(FC) | .15 | .11 | 105 | Lenny Dykstra | | .06 | .05 |
| 43 | Wally Backman | .06 | .05 | 106 | Charlie Hayes(FC) | | .10 | .08 |
| 44 | Shane Rawley | .06 | .05 | 107 | Tommy Herr | | .06 | .05 |
| 45 | Steve Balboni | .06 | .05 | 108 | Ken Howell | | .06 | .05 |
| 46 | Jesse Barfield | .06 | .05 | 109 | John Kruk | | .06 | .05 |
| 47 | Alvaro Espinoza(FC) | .25 | .20 | 110 | Roger McDowell | | .06 | .05 |
| 48 | Bob Geren(FC) | .40 | .30 | 111 | Terry Mulholland(FC) | | | |
| 49 | Mel Hall | .06 | .05 | | | | .06 | .05 |
| 50 | Andy Hawkins | .06 | .05 | 112 | Jeff Parrett | | .06 | .05 |
| 51 | Hensley Meulens(FC) | | | 113 | Neal Heaton | | .06 | .05 |
| | | .50 | .40 | 114 | Jeff King | | .10 | .08 |
| 52 | Steve Sax | .15 | .11 | 115 | Randy Kramer | | .06 | .05 |
| 53 | Deion Sanders(FC) | 2.00 | 1.50 | 116 | Bill Landrum | | .06 | .05 |
| 54 | Rickey Henderson | .50 | .40 | 117 | Cris Carpenter(FC) | | .15 | .11 |
| 55 | Mike Moore | .10 | .08 | 118 | Frank DiPino | | .06 | .05 |
| 56 | Tony Phillips | .06 | .05 | 119 | Ken Hill | | .15 | .11 |
| 57 | Greg Briley(FC) | .35 | .25 | 120 | Dan Quisenberry | | .06 | .05 |
| 58 | Gene Harris | .10 | .08 | 121 | Milt Thompson | | .06 | .05 |
| 59 | Randy Johnson | .08 | .06 | 122 | Todd Zeile(FC) | | .80 | .60 |
| 60 | Jeffrey Leonard | .06 | .05 | 123 | Jack Clark | | .10 | .08 |
| 61 | Dennis Powell | .06 | .05 | 124 | Bruce Hurst | | .06 | .05 |
| 62 | Omar Vizquel(FC) | .20 | .15 | 125 | Mark Parent | | .06 | .05 |
| 63 | Kevin Brown | .08 | .06 | 126 | Bip Roberts | | .06 | .05 |
| 64 | Julio Franco | .25 | .20 | 127 | Jeff Brantley(FC) | | .25 | .20 |
| 65 | Jamie Moyer | .06 | .05 | 128 | Terry Kennedy | | .06 | .05 |
| 66 | Rafael Palmeiro | .15 | .11 | 129 | Mike LaCoss | | .06 | .05 |
| 67 | Nolan Ryan | 1.75 | 1.25 | 130 | Greg Litton(FC) | | .25 | .20 |
| 68 | Francisco Cabrera(FC) | | | 131 | Mike Schmidt | | .60 | .45 |
| | | .20 | .15 | 132 | Checklist | | .06 | .05 |
| 69 | Junior Felix(FC) | .40 | .30 | | | | | |
| 70 | Al Leiter | .06 | .05 | | | | | |
| 71 | Alex Sanchez(FC) | .12 | .09 | | | | | |
| 72 | Geronimo Berroa(FC) | | | | | | | |
| | | .08 | .06 | | | | | |
| 73 | Derek Lilliquist(FC) | .15 | .11 | | | | | |
| 74 | Lonnie Smith | .10 | .08 | | | | | |
| 75 | Jeff Treadway | .06 | .05 | | | | | |
| 76 | Paul Kilgus | .06 | .05 | | | | | |
| 77 | Lloyd McClendon | .15 | .11 | | | | | |
| 78 | Scott Sanderson | .06 | .05 | | | | | |
| 79 | Dwight Smith(FC) | .15 | .11 | | | | | |
| 80 | Jerome Walton(FC) | .15 | .11 | | | | | |
| 81 | Mitch Williams | .15 | .11 | | | | | |

## 1990 Fleer

Fleer's 1990 set, its 10th consecutive baseball card offering, again consisted of 660 cards numbered by team. The front of the cards feature mostly action photos surrounded by one of several different color bands and a white border. The "Fleer '90" logo appears in the upper left corner, while the team logo is the upper right. The player's name and position are printed in a flowing banner below the photo. The set includes various special cards, including a series of "Major League Prospects," Players of the Decade, team checklist cards and a series of multi-player cards. The backs include complete career stats, player data, and a special "Vital Signs" section showing on-base percentage, slugging percentage, etc. for batters; and strikeout and walk ratios, opposing batting averages, etc. for pitchers.

|  |  | MT | NR MT |
|---|---|---|---|
| Complete Set: |  | 18.00 | 13.50 |
| Common Player: |  | .05 | .04 |

|  |  | MT | NR MT |
|---|---|---|---|
| 1 | Lance Blankenship | .07 | .05 |
| 2 | Todd Burns | .06 | .05 |
| 3 | Jose Canseco | .50 | .40 |
| 4 | Jim Corsi | .09 | .07 |
| 5 | Storm Davis | .06 | .05 |
| 6 | Dennis Eckersley | .12 | .09 |
| 7 | Mike Gallego | .06 | .05 |
| 8 | Ron Hassey | .05 | .04 |
| 9 | Dave Henderson | .10 | .08 |
| 10 | Rickey Henderson | .30 | .25 |
| 11 | Rick Honeycutt | .05 | .04 |
| 12 | Stan Javier | .05 | .04 |
| 13 | Felix Jose | .20 | .15 |
| 14 | Carney Lansford | .07 | .05 |
| 15 | Mark McGwire | .25 | .20 |
| 16 | Mike Moore | .10 | .08 |
| 17 | Gene Nelson | .05 | .04 |
| 18 | Dave Parker | .12 | .09 |
| 19 | Tony Phillips | .05 | .04 |
| 20 | Terry Steinbach | .10 | .08 |
| 21 | Dave Stewart | .10 | .08 |
| 22 | Walt Weiss | .10 | .08 |
| 23 | Bob Welch | .06 | .05 |
| 24 | Curt Young | .05 | .04 |
| 25 | Paul Assenmacher | .05 | .04 |
| 26 | Damon Berryhill | .10 | .08 |
| 27 | Mike Bielecki | .10 | .08 |
| 28 | Kevin Blankenship | .07 | .05 |
| 29 | Andre Dawson | .12 | .09 |
| 30 | Shawon Dunston | .09 | .07 |
| 31 | Joe Girardi | .12 | .09 |
| 32 | Mark Grace | .25 | .20 |
| 33 | Mike Harkey | .12 | .09 |
| 34 | Paul Kilgus | .05 | .04 |
| 35 | Les Lancaster | .06 | .05 |
| 36 | Vance Law | .05 | .04 |
| 37 | Greg Maddux | .10 | .08 |
| 38 | Lloyd McClendon | .10 | .08 |
| 39 | Jeff Pico | .05 | .04 |
| 40 | Ryne Sandberg | .35 | .25 |
| 41 | Scott Sanderson | .05 | .04 |
| 42 | Dwight Smith | .25 | .20 |
| 43 | Rick Sutcliffe | .08 | .06 |
| 44 | *Jerome Walton* | .30 | .25 |
| 45 | Mitch Webster | .05 | .04 |
| 46 | Curt Wilkerson | .05 | .04 |
| 47 | *Dean Wilkins*(FC) | .15 | .11 |
| 48 | Mitch Williams | .08 | .06 |
| 49 | Steve Wilson | .15 | .11 |
| 50 | Steve Bedrosian | .06 | .05 |
| 51 | *Mike Benjamin*(FC) | | |
| | | .25 | .20 |
| 52 | *Jeff Brantley* | .25 | .20 |
| 53 | Brett Butler | .07 | .05 |
| 54 | Will Clark | .40 | .30 |
| 55 | Kelly Downs | .05 | .04 |
| 56 | Scott Garrelts | .09 | .07 |
| 57 | Atlee Hammaker | .05 | .04 |
| 58 | Terry Kennedy | .05 | .04 |
| 59 | Mike LaCoss | .05 | .04 |
| 60 | Craig Lefferts | .06 | .05 |
| 61 | *Greg Litton* | .25 | .20 |
| 62 | Candy Maldonado | .06 | .05 |
| 63 | Kirt Manwaring | .09 | .07 |
| 64 | *Randy McCament*(FC) | | |
| | | .20 | .15 |
| 65 | Kevin Mitchell | .30 | .25 |
| 66 | Donell Nixon | .05 | .04 |
| 67 | Ken Oberkfell | .05 | .04 |
| 68 | Rick Reuschel | .09 | .07 |
| 69 | Ernest Riles | .05 | .04 |
| 70 | Don Robinson | .05 | .04 |
| 71 | Pat Sheridan | .05 | .04 |
| 72 | Chris Speier | .05 | .04 |
| 73 | Robby Thompson | .07 | .05 |
| 74 | Jose Uribe | .06 | .05 |
| 75 | Matt Williams | .20 | .15 |
| 76 | George Bell | .10 | .08 |
| 77 | Pat Borders | .07 | .05 |
| 78 | John Cerutti | .05 | .04 |
| 79 | *Junior Felix* | .20 | .15 |
| 80 | Tony Fernandez | .09 | .07 |
| 81 | Mike Flanagan | .05 | .04 |
| 82 | *Mauro Gozzo*(FC) | | |
| | | .15 | .11 |
| 83 | Kelly Gruber | .07 | .05 |
| 84 | Tom Henke | .05 | .04 |
| 85 | Jimmy Key | .07 | .05 |
| 86 | Manny Lee | .05 | .04 |
| 87 | Nelson Liriano | .05 | .04 |
| 88 | Lee Mazzilli | .05 | .04 |
| 89 | Fred McGriff | .25 | .20 |
| 90 | Lloyd Moseby | .06 | .05 |
| 91 | Rance Mulliniks | .05 | .04 |
| 92 | Alex Sanchez | .15 | .11 |
| 93 | Dave Steib | .09 | .07 |
| 94 | Todd Stottlemyre | .09 | .07 |

| | MT | NR MT | | | MT | NR MT |
|---|---|---|---|---|---|---|
| 95 Duane Ward | .05 | .04 | 160 Darrin Jackson | | .05 | .04 |
| 96 David Wells | .05 | .04 | 161 Chris James | | .06 | .05 |
| 97 Ernie Whitt | .06 | .05 | 162 Carmelo Martinez | | .06 | .05 |
| 98 Frank Wills | .05 | .04 | 163 Mike Pagliarulo | | .06 | .05 |
| 99 Mookie Wilson | .09 | .07 | 164 Mark Parent | | .05 | .04 |
| 100 *Kevin Appier*(FC) | | | 165 Dennis Rasmussen | | .05 | .04 |
| | .25 | .20 | 166 Bip Roberts | | .08 | .06 |
| 101 Luis Aquino | .05 | .04 | 167 Benito Santiago | | .12 | .09 |
| 102 Bob Boone | .07 | .05 | 168 Calvin Schiraldi | | .05 | .04 |
| 103 George Brett | .15 | .11 | 169 Eric Show | | .06 | .05 |
| 104 Jose DeJesus | .08 | .06 | 170 Garry Templeton | | .06 | .05 |
| 105 Luis de los Santos | .08 | .06 | 171 Ed Whitson | | .06 | .05 |
| 106 Jim Eisenreich | .05 | .04 | 172 Brady Anderson | | .07 | .05 |
| 107 Steve Farr | .05 | .04 | 173 Jeff Ballard | | .07 | .05 |
| 108 Tom Gordon | .25 | .20 | 174 Phil Bradley | | .07 | .05 |
| 109 Mark Gubicza | .09 | .07 | 175 Mike Devereaux | | .07 | .05 |
| 110 Bo Jackson | .35 | .25 | 176 *Steve Finley* | | .20 | .15 |
| 111 Terry Leach | .05 | .04 | 177 Pete Harnisch(FC) | | .10 | .08 |
| 112 Charlie Leibrandt | .05 | .04 | 178 Kevin Hickey | | .10 | .08 |
| 113 *Rick Luecken*(FC) | | | 179 Brian Holton | | .05 | .04 |
| | .20 | .15 | 180 *Ben McDonald*(FC) | | | |
| 114 Mike Macfarlane | .05 | .04 | | | .80 | .60 |
| 115 Jeff Montgomery | .06 | .05 | 181 Bob Melvin | | .05 | .04 |
| 116 Bret Saberhagen | .10 | .08 | 182 Bob Milacki | | .07 | .05 |
| 117 Kevin Seitzer | .10 | .08 | 183 Randy Milligan | | .06 | .05 |
| 118 Kurt Stillwell | .06 | .05 | 184 Gregg Olson(FC) | | .30 | .25 |
| 119 Pat Tabler | .05 | .04 | 185 Joe Orsulak | | .05 | .04 |
| 121 Gary Thurman | .05 | .04 | 186 Bill Ripken | | .05 | .04 |
| 122 Frank White | .07 | .05 | 187 Cal Ripken, Jr. | | .30 | .25 |
| 123 Willie Wilson | .06 | .05 | 188 Dave Schmidt | | .05 | .04 |
| 124 *Matt Winters*(FC) | | | 189 Larry Sheets | | .05 | .04 |
| | .20 | .15 | 190 Mickey Tettleton | | .08 | .06 |
| 125 Jim Abbott | .35 | .25 | 191 Mark Thurmond | | .05 | .04 |
| 126 Tony Armas | .05 | .04 | 192 Jay Tibbs | | .05 | .04 |
| 127 Dante Bichette | .09 | .07 | 193 Jim Traber | | .05 | .04 |
| 128 Bert Blyleven | .09 | .07 | 194 Mark Williamson | | .05 | .04 |
| 129 Chili Davis | .06 | .05 | 195 Craig Worthington | | .15 | .11 |
| 130 Brian Downing | .06 | .05 | 196 Don Aase | | .05 | .04 |
| 131 *Mike Fetters*(FC) | .20 | .15 | 197 *Blaine Beatty*(FC) | | | |
| 132 Chuck Finley | .06 | .05 | | | .25 | .20 |
| 133 Willie Fraser | .05 | .04 | 198 Mark Carreon | | .10 | .08 |
| 134 Bryan Harvey | .05 | .04 | 199 Gary Carter | | .06 | .05 |
| 135 Jack Howell | .05 | .04 | 200 David Cone | | .10 | .08 |
| 136 Wally Joyner | .10 | .08 | 201 Ron Darling | | .07 | .05 |
| 137 *Jeff Manto* | .20 | .15 | 202 Kevin Elster | | .05 | .04 |
| 138 Kirk McCaskill | .06 | .05 | 203 Sid Fernandez | | .09 | .07 |
| 139 Bob McClure | .05 | .04 | 204 Dwight Gooden | | .20 | .15 |
| 140 Greg Minton | .05 | .04 | 205 Keith Hernandez | | .06 | .05 |
| 141 Lance Parrish | .07 | .05 | 206 *Jeff Innis* | | .15 | .11 |
| 142 Dan Petry | .05 | .04 | 207 Gregg Jefferies | | .20 | .15 |
| 143 Johnny Ray | .05 | .04 | 208 Howard Johnson | | .15 | .11 |
| 144 Dick Schofield | .06 | .05 | 209 Barry Lyons | | .05 | .04 |
| 145 *Lee Stevens* | .20 | .15 | 210 Dave Magadan | | .06 | .05 |
| 146 Claudell Washington | .06 | .05 | 211 Kevin McReynolds | | .07 | .05 |
| 147 Devon White | .08 | .06 | 212 Jeff Musselman | | .05 | .04 |
| 148 Mike Witt | .06 | .05 | 213 Randy Myers | | .06 | .05 |
| 149 Roberto Alomar | .30 | .25 | 214 Bob Ojeda | | .06 | .05 |
| 150 Sandy Alomar, Jr. | .25 | .20 | 215 Juan Samuel | | .06 | .05 |
| 151 Andy Benes(FC) | .30 | .25 | 216 Mackey Sasser | | .05 | .04 |
| 152 Jack Clark | .06 | .05 | 217 Darryl Strawberry | | .25 | .20 |
| 153 Pat Clements | .05 | .04 | 218 Tim Teufel | | .05 | .04 |
| 154 Joey Cora | .15 | .11 | 219 Frank Viola | | .10 | .08 |
| 155 Mark Davis | .09 | .07 | 220 Juan Agosto | | .05 | .04 |
| 156 Mark Grant | .05 | .04 | 221 Larry Anderson | | .05 | .04 |
| 157 Tony Gwynn | .25 | .20 | 222 *Eric Anthony*(FC) | | | |
| 158 Greg Harris | .10 | .08 | | | .50 | .40 |
| 159 Bruce Hurst | .06 | .05 | 223 Kevin Bass | | .08 | .06 |

| No. | Player | MT | NR MT | No. | Player | MT | NR MT |
|---|---|---|---|---|---|---|---|
| 224 | Craig Biggio | .10 | .08 | 292 | Steve Buechele | .05 | .04 |
| 225 | Ken Caminiti | .06 | .05 | 293 | Scott Coolbaugh(FC) | .25 | .20 |
| 226 | Jim Clancy | .05 | .04 | 294 | Jack Daugherty(FC) | .25 | .20 |
| 227 | Danny Darwin | .05 | .04 | 295 | Cecil Espy | .06 | .05 |
| 228 | Glenn Davis | .09 | .07 | 296 | Julio Franco | .07 | .05 |
| 229 | Jim Deshaies | .07 | .05 | 297 | Juan Gonzalez(FC) | 2.00 | 1.50 |
| 230 | Bill Doran | .06 | .05 | 298 | Cecilio Guante | .05 | .04 |
| 231 | Bob Forsch | .05 | .04 | 299 | Drew Hall | .05 | .04 |
| 233 | Terry Puhl | .05 | .04 | 300 | Charlie Hough | .06 | .05 |
| 234 | Rafael Ramirez | .05 | .04 | 301 | Pete Incaviglia | .08 | .06 |
| 235 | Rick Rhoden | .05 | .04 | 302 | Mike Jeffcoat | .05 | .04 |
| 236 | Dan Schatzeder | .05 | .04 | 303 | Chad Kreuter | .08 | .06 |
| 237 | Mike Scott | .08 | .06 | 304 | Jeff Kunkel | .05 | .04 |
| 238 | Dave Smith | .06 | .05 | 305 | Rick Leach | .05 | .04 |
| 239 | Alex Trevino | .05 | .04 | 306 | Fred Manrique | .05 | .04 |
| 240 | Glenn Wilson | .05 | .04 | 307 | Jamie Moyer | .06 | .05 |
| 241 | Gerald Young | .05 | .04 | 308 | Rafael Palmeiro | .07 | .05 |
| 242 | Tom Brunansky | .07 | .05 | 309 | Geno Petralli | .05 | .04 |
| 243 | Cris Carpenter | .10 | .08 | 310 | Kevin Reimer | .10 | .08 |
| 244 | Alex Cole(FC) | .20 | .15 | 311 | Kenny Rogers(FC) | .20 | .15 |
| 245 | Vince Coleman | .10 | .08 | 312 | Jeff Russell | .06 | .05 |
| 246 | John Costello | .05 | .04 | 313 | Nolan Ryan | .50 | .40 |
| 247 | Ken Dayley | .05 | .04 | 314 | Ruben Sierra | .15 | .11 |
| 248 | Jose DeLeon | .06 | .05 | 315 | Bobby Witt | .05 | .04 |
| 249 | Frank DiPino | .05 | .04 | 316 | Chris Bosio | .07 | .05 |
| 250 | Pedro Guerrero | .09 | .07 | 317 | Glenn Braggs | .07 | .05 |
| 251 | Ken Hill | .09 | .07 | 318 | Greg Brock | .05 | .04 |
| 252 | Joe Magrane | .09 | .07 | 319 | Chuck Crim | .05 | .04 |
| 253 | Willie McGee | .06 | .05 | 320 | Rob Deer | .06 | .05 |
| 254 | John Morris | .05 | .04 | 321 | Mike Felder | .05 | .04 |
| 255 | Jose Oquendo | .06 | .05 | 322 | Tom Filer | .05 | .04 |
| 256 | Tony Pena | .06 | .05 | 323 | Tony Fossas(FC) | .10 | .08 |
| 257 | Terry Pendleton | .06 | .05 | 324 | Jim Gantner | .06 | .05 |
| 258 | Ted Power | .05 | .04 | 325 | Darryl Hamilton | .08 | .06 |
| 259 | Dan Quisenberry | .05 | .04 | 326 | Ted Higuera | .08 | .06 |
| 260 | Ozzie Smith | .09 | .07 | 327 | Mark Knudson(FC) | .10 | .08 |
| 261 | Scott Terry | .06 | .05 | 328 | Bill Krueger | .05 | .04 |
| 262 | Milt Thompson | .05 | .04 | 329 | Tim McIntosh(FC) | .20 | .15 |
| 263 | Denny Walling | .05 | .04 | 330 | Paul Molitor | .08 | .06 |
| 264 | Todd Worrell | .06 | .05 | 331 | Jaime Navarro | .25 | .20 |
| 265 | Todd Zeile | .50 | .40 | 332 | Charlie O'Brien | .05 | .04 |
| 266 | Marty Barrett | .05 | .04 | 333 | Jeff Peterek(FC) | .15 | .11 |
| 267 | Mike Boddicker | .05 | .04 | 334 | Dan Plesac | .07 | .05 |
| 268 | Wade Boggs | .40 | .30 | 335 | Jerry Reuss | .06 | .05 |
| 269 | Ellis Burks | .35 | .25 | 336 | Gary Sheffield | .30 | .25 |
| 270 | Rick Cerone | .05 | .04 | 337 | Bill Spiers | .35 | .25 |
| 271 | Roger Clemens | .25 | .20 | 338 | B.J. Surhoff | .07 | .05 |
| 272 | John Dopson | .06 | .05 | 339 | Greg Vaughn | .60 | .45 |
| 273 | Nick Esasky | .07 | .05 | 340 | Robin Yount | .20 | .15 |
| 274 | Dwight Evans | .09 | .07 | 341 | Hubie Brooks | .06 | .05 |
| 275 | Wes Gardner | .05 | .04 | 342 | Tim Burke | .06 | .05 |
| 276 | Rich Gedman | .05 | .04 | 343 | Mike Fitzgerald | .05 | .04 |
| 277 | Mike Greenwell | .50 | .40 | 344 | Tom Foley | .05 | .04 |
| 278 | Danny Heep | .05 | .04 | 345 | Andres Galarraga | .15 | .11 |
| 279 | Eric Hetzel | .10 | .08 | 346 | Damaso Garcia | .05 | .04 |
| 280 | Dennis Lamp | .05 | .04 | 347 | Marquis Grissom(FC) | .50 | .40 |
| 281 | Rob Murphy | .05 | .04 | 348 | Kevin Gross | .06 | .05 |
| 282 | Joe Price | .05 | .04 | 349 | Joe Hesketh | .05 | .04 |
| 283 | Carlos Quintana | .10 | .07 | 350 | Jeff Huson(FC) | .25 | .20 |
| 284 | Jody Reed | .06 | .05 | 351 | Wallace Johnson | .05 | .04 |
| 285 | Luis Rivera | .05 | .04 | 352 | Mark Langston | .15 | .11 |
| 286 | Kevin Romine | .05 | .04 | | | | |
| 287 | Lee Smith | .05 | .04 | | | | |
| 288 | Mike Smithson | .05 | .04 | | | | |
| 289 | Bob Stanley | .05 | .04 | | | | |
| 290 | Harold Baines | .09 | .07 | | | | |
| 291 | Kevin Brown | .09 | .07 | | | | |

| | MT | NR MT | | | MT | NR MT |
|---|---|---|---|---|---|---|
| 353 | Dave Martinez | .06 | .05 | 416 | Norm Charlton | .08 | .06 |
| 354 | Dennis Martinez | .06 | .05 | 417 | Eric Davis | .20 | .15 |
| 355 | Andy McGaffigan | .05 | .04 | 418 | Rob Dibble | .15 | .11 |
| 356 | Otis Nixon | .05 | .04 | 419 | John Franco | .07 | .05 |
| 357 | Spike Owen | .05 | .04 | 420 | Ken Griffey, Sr. | .07 | .05 |
| 358 | Pascual Perez | .06 | .05 | 421 | *Chris Hammond*(FC) | | |
| 359 | Tim Raines | .10 | .08 | | | .25 | .20 |
| 360 | Nelson Santovenia | .10 | .08 | 422 | Danny Jackson | .06 | .05 |
| 361 | Bryn Smith | .06 | .05 | 423 | Barry Larkin | .15 | .11 |
| 362 | Zane Smith | .05 | .04 | 424 | Tim Leary | .06 | .05 |
| 363 | *Larry Walker*(FC) | | | 425 | Rick Mahler | .05 | .04 |
| | | .60 | .45 | 426 | *Joe Oliver*(FC) | .30 | .25 |
| 364 | Tim Wallach | .06 | .05 | 427 | Paul O'Neill | .07 | .05 |
| 365 | Rick Aguilera | .05 | .04 | 428 | Luis Quinones | .05 | .04 |
| 366 | Allan Anderson | .06 | .05 | 429 | Jeff Reed | .05 | .04 |
| 367 | Wally Backman | .06 | .05 | 430 | Jose Rijo | .07 | .05 |
| 368 | Doug Baker(FC) | .08 | .06 | 431 | Ron Robinson | .05 | .04 |
| 369 | Juan Berenguer | .05 | .04 | 432 | Rolando Roomes | .10 | .08 |
| 370 | Randy Bush | .05 | .04 | 433 | Chris Sabo | .15 | .11 |
| 371 | Carmen Castillo | .05 | .04 | 434 | *Scott Scudder* | .30 | .25 |
| 372 | *Mike Dyer*(FC) | .15 | .11 | 435 | Herm Winningham | .05 | .04 |
| 373 | Gary Gaetti | .07 | .05 | 436 | Steve Balboni | .05 | .04 |
| 374 | Greg Gagne | .05 | .04 | 437 | Jesse Barfield | .08 | .06 |
| 375 | Dan Gladden | .05 | .04 | 438 | *Mike Blowers*(FC) | | |
| 376 | German Gonzalez | .05 | .04 | | | .20 | .15 |
| 377 | Brian Harper | .06 | .05 | 439 | Tom Brookens | .05 | .04 |
| 378 | Kent Hrbek | .10 | .08 | 440 | Greg Cadaret | .05 | .04 |
| 379 | Gene Larkin | .05 | .04 | 441 | Alvaro Espinoza | .25 | .20 |
| 380 | Tim Laudner | .05 | .04 | 442 | *Bob Geren* | .15 | .11 |
| 381 | John Moses | .05 | .04 | 443 | Lee Guetterman | .05 | .04 |
| 382 | Al Newman | .05 | .04 | 444 | Mel Hall | .06 | .05 |
| 383 | Kirby Puckett | .40 | .30 | 445 | Andy Hawkins | .06 | .05 |
| 384 | Shane Rawley | .06 | .05 | 446 | Roberto Kelly | .15 | .11 |
| 385 | Jeff Reardon | .06 | .05 | 447 | Don Mattingly | .35 | .25 |
| 386 | Roy Smith | .05 | .04 | 448 | Lance McCullers | .05 | .04 |
| 387 | *Gary Wayne*(FC) | .15 | .11 | 449 | Hensley Meulens | .35 | .25 |
| 388 | Dave West | .25 | .20 | 450 | Dale Mohorcic | .05 | .04 |
| 389 | Tim Belcher | .12 | .09 | 451 | Clay Parker | .10 | .07 |
| 390 | Tim Crews | .05 | .04 | 452 | Eric Plunk | .05 | .04 |
| 391 | Mike Davis | .05 | .04 | 453 | Dave Righetti | .07 | .05 |
| 392 | Rick Dempsey | .05 | .04 | 454 | *Deion Sanders* | .30 | .25 |
| 393 | Kirk Gibson | .09 | .07 | 455 | Steve Sax | .07 | .05 |
| 394 | Jose Gonzalez | .05 | .04 | 456 | Don Slaught | .05 | .04 |
| 395 | Alfredo Griffin | .06 | .05 | 457 | Walt Terrell | .05 | .04 |
| 396 | Jeff Hamilton | .06 | .05 | 458 | Dave Winfield | .15 | .11 |
| 397 | Lenny Harris | .10 | .08 | 459 | Jay Bell | .05 | .04 |
| 398 | Mickey Hatcher | .05 | .04 | 460 | Rafael Belliard | .05 | .04 |
| 399 | Orel Hershiser | .12 | .09 | 461 | Barry Bonds | .10 | .08 |
| 400 | Jay Howell | .06 | .05 | 462 | Bobby Bonilla | .10 | .08 |
| 401 | Mike Marshall | .06 | .05 | 463 | Sid Bream | .05 | .04 |
| 402 | Ramon Martinez | .25 | .20 | 464 | Benny Distefano | .06 | .05 |
| 403 | Mike Morgan | .05 | .04 | 465 | Doug Drabek | .06 | .05 |
| 404 | Eddie Murray | .10 | .08 | 466 | Jim Gott | .06 | .05 |
| 405 | Alejandro Pena | .05 | .04 | 467 | Billy Hatcher | .06 | .05 |
| 406 | Willie Randolph | .08 | .06 | 468 | Neal Heaton | .06 | .05 |
| 407 | Mike Scioscia | .06 | .05 | 469 | Jeff King | .20 | .15 |
| 408 | Ray Searage | .05 | .04 | 470 | Bob Kipper | .05 | .04 |
| 409 | Fernando Valenzuela | | | 471 | Randy Kramer | .05 | .04 |
| | | .07 | .05 | 472 | Bill Landrum | .06 | .05 |
| 410 | *Jose Vizcaino*(FC) | | | 473 | Mike LaValliere | .06 | .05 |
| | | .20 | .15 | 474 | Jose Lind | .06 | .05 |
| 411 | *John Wetteland*(FC) | | | 475 | Junior Ortiz | .05 | .04 |
| | | .15 | .11 | 476 | Gary Redus | .05 | .04 |
| 412 | Jack Armstrong | .05 | .04 | 477 | *Rick Reed*(FC) | .15 | .11 |
| 413 | Todd Benzinger | .07 | .05 | 478 | R.J. Reynolds | .05 | .04 |
| 414 | Tim Birtsas | .05 | .04 | 479 | Jeff Robinson | .05 | .04 |
| 415 | Tom Browning | .07 | .05 | 480 | John Smiley | .07 | .05 |

| | MT | NR MT | | | MT | NR MT |
|---|---|---|---|---|---|---|
| 481 | Andy Van Slyke | .09 | .07 | 546 | Melido Perez | .07 | .05 |
| 482 | Bob Walk | .06 | .05 | 547 | Steve Rosenberg | .07 | .05 |
| 483 | Andy Allanson | .05 | .04 | 548 | *Sammy Sosa*(FC) | | |
| 484 | Scott Bailes | .05 | .04 | | | .40 | .30 |
| 485 | *Joey Belle* | .80 | .60 | 549 | Bobby Thigpen | .07 | .05 |
| 486 | Bud Black | .05 | .04 | 550 | Robin Ventura | .60 | .45 |
| 487 | Jerry Browne | .07 | .05 | 551 | Greg Walker | .06 | .05 |
| 488 | Tom Candiotti | .05 | .04 | 552 | Don Carman | .05 | .04 |
| 489 | Joe Carter | .08 | .06 | 553 | *Pat Combs*(FC) | .25 | .20 |
| 490 | David Clark | .06 | .05 | 554 | Dennis Cook | .20 | .15 |
| 491 | John Farrell | .06 | .05 | 555 | Darren Daulton | .05 | .04 |
| 492 | Felix Fermin | .05 | .04 | 556 | Lenny Dykstra | .07 | .05 |
| 493 | Brook Jacoby | .06 | .05 | 557 | Curt Ford | .05 | .04 |
| 494 | Dion James | .06 | .05 | 558 | Charlie Hayes | .10 | .08 |
| 495 | Doug Jones | .06 | .05 | 559 | Von Hayes | .07 | .05 |
| 496 | Brad Komminsk | .05 | .04 | 560 | Tom Herr | .06 | .05 |
| 497 | Rod Nichols | .05 | .04 | 561 | Ken Howell | .05 | .04 |
| 498 | Pete O'Brien | .07 | .05 | 562 | Steve Jeltz | .05 | .04 |
| 499 | *Steve Olin*(FC) | .35 | .25 | 563 | Ron Jones | .15 | .11 |
| 500 | Jesse Orosco | .05 | .04 | 564 | Ricky Jordan | .35 | .25 |
| 501 | Joel Skinner | .05 | .04 | 565 | John Kruk | .07 | .05 |
| 502 | Cory Snyder | .09 | .07 | 566 | Steve Lake | .05 | .04 |
| 503 | Greg Swindell | .10 | .08 | 567 | Roger McDowell | .06 | .05 |
| 504 | Rich Yett | .05 | .04 | 568 | Terry Mulholland | .05 | .04 |
| 505 | Scott Bankhead | .07 | .05 | 569 | Dwayne Murphy | .05 | .04 |
| 506 | Scott Bradley | .05 | .04 | 570 | Jeff Parrett | .06 | .05 |
| 507 | Greg Briley | .15 | .11 | 571 | Randy Ready | .05 | .04 |
| 508 | Jay Buhner | .07 | .05 | 572 | Bruce Ruffin | .05 | .04 |
| 509 | Darnell Coles | .05 | .04 | 573 | Dickie Thon | .05 | .04 |
| 510 | Keith Comstock | .05 | .04 | 574 | Jose Alvarez | .05 | .04 |
| 511 | Henry Cotto | .05 | .04 | 575 | Geronimo Berroa | .06 | .05 |
| 512 | Alvin Davis | .12 | .09 | 576 | Jeff Blauser | .05 | .04 |
| 513 | Ken Griffey, Jr. | 1.00 | .70 | 577 | Joe Boever | .07 | .05 |
| 514 | Erik Hanson | .20 | .15 | 578 | Marty Clary | .05 | .04 |
| 515 | Gene Harris | .15 | .11 | 579 | Jody Davis | .05 | .04 |
| 516 | Brian Holman | .07 | .05 | 580 | Mark Eichhorn | .05 | .04 |
| 517 | Mike Jackson | .05 | .04 | 581 | Darrell Evans | .06 | .05 |
| 518 | Randy Johnson | .15 | .11 | 582 | Ron Gant | .06 | .05 |
| 519 | Jeffrey Leonard | .08 | .06 | 583 | Tom Glavine | .09 | .07 |
| 520 | Edgar Martinez | .10 | .08 | 584 | *Tommy Greene*(FC) | | |
| 521 | Dennis Powell | .05 | .04 | | | .35 | .25 |
| 522 | Jim Presley | .06 | .05 | 585 | Tommy Gregg | .10 | .07 |
| 523 | Jerry Reed | .05 | .04 | 586 | *David Justice*(FC) | | |
| 524 | Harold Reynolds | .07 | .05 | | | 2.00 | 1.50 |
| 525 | Mike Schooler | .06 | .05 | 587 | Mark Lemke(FC) | .10 | .08 |
| 526 | Bill Swift | .05 | .04 | 588 | Derek Lilliquist | .10 | .08 |
| 527 | David Valle | .05 | .04 | 589 | Oddibe McDowell | .07 | .05 |
| 528 | *Omar Vizquel* | .20 | .15 | 590 | *Kent Mercker*(FC) | | |
| 529 | Ivan Calderon | .06 | .05 | | | .30 | .25 |
| 530 | Carlton Fisk | .10 | .08 | 591 | Dale Murphy | .15 | .11 |
| 531 | Scott Fletcher | .06 | .05 | 592 | Gerald Perry | .06 | .05 |
| 532 | Dave Gallagher | .09 | .07 | 593 | Lonnie Smith | .06 | .05 |
| 533 | Ozzie Guillen | .07 | .05 | 594 | Pete Smith | .07 | .05 |
| 534 | *Greg Hibbard*(FC) | | | 595 | John Smoltz | .15 | .11 |
| | | .20 | .15 | 596 | *Mike Stanton*(FC) | | |
| 535 | Shawn Hillegas | .05 | .04 | | | .25 | .20 |
| 536 | Lance Johnson | .07 | .05 | 597 | Andres Thomas | .06 | .05 |
| 537 | Eric King | .05 | .04 | 598 | Jeff Treadway | .06 | .05 |
| 538 | Ron Kittle | .07 | .05 | 599 | Doyle Alexander | .06 | .05 |
| 539 | Steve Lyons | .05 | .04 | 600 | Dave Bergman | .05 | .04 |
| 540 | Carlos Martinez | .15 | .11 | 601 | *Brian Dubois*(FC) | | |
| 541 | *Tom McCarthy*(FC) | | | | | .15 | .11 |
| | | .10 | .07 | 602 | Paul Gibson | .06 | .05 |
| 542 | Matt Merullo | .25 | .20 | 603 | Mike Heath | .05 | .04 |
| 543 | Donn Pall | .05 | .04 | 604 | Mike Henneman | .07 | .05 |
| 544 | Dan Pasqua | .06 | .05 | 605 | Guillermo Hernandez | | |
| 545 | Ken Patterson | .06 | .05 | | | .05 | .04 |

| | | MT | NR MT |
|---|---|---|---|
| 606 | Shawn Holman(FC) | .20 | .15 |
| 607 | Tracy Jones | .09 | .07 |
| 608 | Chet Lemon | .06 | .05 |
| 609 | Fred Lynn | .06 | .05 |
| 610 | Jack Morris | .07 | .05 |
| 611 | Matt Nokes | .10 | .08 |
| 612 | Gary Pettis | .05 | .04 |
| 613 | Kevin Ritz(FC) | .15 | .11 |
| 614 | Jeff Robinson | .07 | .05 |
| 615 | Steve Searcy | .10 | .08 |
| 616 | Frank Tanana | .06 | .05 |
| 617 | Alan Trammell | .09 | .07 |
| 618 | Gary Ward | .05 | .04 |
| 619 | Lou Whitaker | .09 | .07 |
| 620 | Frank Williams | .05 | .04 |
| 621a | Players Of The Decade — 1980 (George Brett) (10 .390 hitting seasons) | 2.25 | 1.75 |
| 621b | Players Of The Decade — 1980 (George Brett) (10 .300 hitting seasons) | .50 | .40 |
| 622 | Players Of The Decade — 1981 (Fernando Valenzuela) | .20 | .15 |
| 623 | Players Of The Decade — 1982 (Dale Murphy) | .25 | .20 |
| 624a | Players Of The Decade — 1983 (Cal Ripkin, Jr.) | 3.00 | 2.25 |
| 624b | Players Of The Decade — 1983 (Cal Ripken, Jr.) | .25 | .20 |
| 625 | Players Of The Decade — 1984 (Ryne Sandberg) | .25 | .20 |
| 626 | Players Of The Decade — 1985 (Don Mattingly) | .50 | .40 |
| 627 | Players Of The Decade — 1986 (Roger Clemens) | .25 | .20 |
| 628 | Players Of The Decade — 1987 (George Bell) | .20 | .15 |
| 629 | Players Of The Decade — (Jose Canseco) | .60 | .45 |
| 630a | Players Of The Decade — 1989 (Will Clark) (total bases (32)) | 1.50 | 1.25 |
| 630b | Players Of The Decade — 1989 (Will Clark) (total bases (321)) | .60 | .45 |
| 631 | Game Savers | .10 | .08 |
| 632 | Boston Igniters | .10 | .08 |
| 633 | The Starter & Stopper | .10 | .08 |
| 634 | League's Best Shortstops | .10 | .08 |
| 635 | Human Dynamos | .10 | .08 |
| 636 | 300 Strikeout Club | .10 | .08 |
| 637 | The Dynamic Duo | .10 | .08 |
| 638 | A.L. All Stars | .10 | .08 |
| 639 | N.L. East Rivals | .10 | .08 |
| 640 | Rudy Seanez, Colin Charland(FC) | .15 | .11 |
| 641 | George Canale, Kevin Maas(FC) | .50 | .40 |
| 642 | Kelly Mann, Dave Hansen(FC) | .30 | .25 |
| 643 | Greg Smith, Stu Tate(FC) | .15 | .11 |
| 644 | Tom Drees, Dan Howitt(FC) | .15 | .11 |
| 645 | Mike Roesler, Derrick May(FC) | .50 | .40 |
| 646 | Scott Hemond, Mark Gardner(FC) | .35 | .25 |
| 647 | John Orton, Scott Leuis(FC) | .25 | .20 |
| 648 | Rich Monteleone, Dana Williams(FC) | .15 | .11 |
| 649 | Mike Huff, Steve Frey(FC) | .25 | .20 |
| 650 | Chuck McElroy, Moises Alou(FC) | .25 | .20 |
| 651 | Bobby Rose, Mike Hartley(FC) | .15 | .11 |
| 652 | Matt Kinzer, Wayne Edwards(FC) | .20 | .15 |
| 653 | Delino DeShields, Jason Grimsley(FC) | .80 | .60 |
| 654 | Athletics, Cubs, Giants & Blue Jays (Checklist) | .05 | .04 |
| 655 | Royals, Angels, Padres & Orioles (Checklist) | .05 | .04 |
| 656 | Mets, Astros, Cardinals & Red Sox (Checklist) | .05 | .04 |
| 657 | Rangers, Brewers, Expos & Twins (Checklist) | .05 | .04 |
| 658 | Dodgers, Reds, Yankees & Pirates (Checklist) | .05 | .04 |
| 659 | Indians, Mariners, White Sox & Phillies (Checklist) | .05 | .04 |
| 660 | Braves, Tigers & Special Cards (Checklist) | .05 | .04 |

## 1990 Fleer Update

 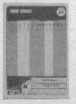

Fleer produced its seventh consecutive "Update" set in 1990 to supplement the company's regular set. As in the past, the set consists of 132 cards (numbered U-1 through U-132) that were sold by hobby dealers in special collectors boxes. The cards are designed in the exact same style as the regular issue. A special Nolan Ryan commemorative card is included in the 1990 Fleer Update set.

|  | MT | NR MT |
|---|---|---|
| Complete Set: | 10.00 | 7.50 |
| Common Player: | .06 | .05 |

| | | | MT | NR MT |
|---|---|---|---|---|
| 1 | Steve Avery(FC) | | 1.00 | .70 |
| 2 | Francisco Cabrera | | .20 | .15 |
| 3 | Nick Esasky | | .06 | .05 |
| 4 | Jim Kremers(FC) | | .15 | .11 |
| 5 | Greg Olson(FC) | | .12 | .09 |
| 6 | Jim Presley | | .06 | .05 |
| 7 | Shawn Boskie(FC) | | .25 | .20 |
| 8 | Joe Kraemer(FC) | | .08 | .06 |
| 9 | Luis Salazar | | .06 | .05 |
| 10 | Hector Villanueva(FC) | | .30 | .25 |
| 11 | Glenn Braggs | | .06 | .05 |
| 12 | Mariano Duncan | | .06 | .05 |
| 13 | Billy Hatcher | | .06 | .05 |
| 14 | Tim Layana(FC) | | .20 | .15 |
| 15 | Hal Morris | | .40 | .30 |
| 16 | Javier Ortiz(FC) | | .20 | .15 |
| 17 | Dave Rohde(FC) | | .15 | .11 |
| 18 | Eric Yelding(FC) | | .20 | .15 |
| 19 | Hubie Brooks | | .08 | .06 |
| 20 | Kal Daniels | | .08 | .06 |
| 21 | Dave Hansen | | .15 | .11 |
| 22 | Mike Hartley | | .15 | .11 |
| 23 | Stan Javier | | .06 | .05 |
| 24 | Jose Offerman(FC) | | .30 | .25 |
| 25 | Juan Samuel | | .06 | .05 |
| 26 | Dennis Boyd | | .06 | .05 |
| 27 | Delino DeShields | | .70 | .50 |
| 28 | Steve Frey | | .12 | .09 |
| 29 | Mark Gardner | | .15 | .11 |
| 30 | Chris Nabholz(FC) | | .40 | .30 |
| 31 | Bill Sampen(FC) | | .25 | .20 |
| 32 | Dave Schmidt | | .06 | .05 |
| 33 | Daryl Boston | | .06 | .05 |
| 34 | Chuck Carr(FC) | | .20 | .15 |
| 35 | John Franco | | .08 | .06 |
| 36 | Todd Hundley(FC) | | .25 | .20 |
| 37 | Julio Machado(FC) | | .15 | .11 |
| 38 | Alejandro Pena | | .06 | .05 |
| 39 | Darren Reed(FC) | | .25 | .20 |
| 40 | Kelvin Torve(FC) | | .12 | .09 |
| 41 | Darrel Akerfelds(FC) | | .12 | .09 |
| 42 | Jose DeJesus | | .20 | .15 |
| 43 | Dave Hollins(FC) | | .40 | .30 |
| 44 | Carmelo Martinez | | .06 | .05 |
| 45 | Brad Moore(FC) | | .15 | .11 |
| 46 | Dale Murphy | | .10 | .08 |
| 47 | Wally Backman | | .06 | .05 |
| 48 | Stan Belinda(FC) | | .20 | .15 |
| 49 | Bob Patterson | | .06 | .05 |
| 50 | Ted Power | | .06 | .05 |
| 51 | Don Slaught | | .06 | .05 |
| 52 | Geronimo Pena(FC) | | .25 | .20 |
| 53 | Lee Smith | | .08 | .06 |
| 54 | John Tudor | | .06 | .05 |
| 55 | Joe Carter | | .10 | .08 |
| 56 | Tom Howard(FC) | | .20 | .15 |
| 57 | Craig Lefferts | | .06 | .05 |
| 58 | Rafael Valdez(FC) | | .20 | .15 |
| 59 | Dave Anderson | | .06 | .05 |
| 60 | Kevin Bass | | .06 | .05 |
| 61 | John Burkett | | .25 | .20 |
| 62 | Gary Carter | | .10 | .08 |
| 63 | Rick Parker(FC) | | .10 | .08 |
| 64 | Trevor Wilson | | .10 | .08 |
| 65 | Chris Hoiles(FC) | | .25 | .20 |
| 66 | Tim Hulett | | .06 | .05 |
| 67 | Dave Johnson(FC) | | .10 | .08 |
| 68 | Curt Schilling(FC) | | .10 | .08 |
| 69 | David Segui(FC) | | .35 | .25 |
| 70 | Tom Brunansky | | .08 | .06 |
| 71 | Greg Harris | | .06 | .05 |
| 72 | Dana Kiecker(FC) | | .12 | .09 |
| 73 | Tim Naehring(FC) | | .40 | .30 |
| 74 | Tony Pena | | .06 | .05 |
| 75 | Jeff Reardon | | .08 | .06 |
| 76 | Jerry Reed | | .06 | .05 |
| 77 | Mark Eichhorn | | .06 | .05 |
| 78 | Mark Langston | | .08 | .06 |
| 79 | John Orton | | .12 | .09 |
| 80 | Luis Polonia | | .06 | .05 |
| 81 | Dave Winfield | | .12 | .09 |
| 82 | Cliff Young(FC) | | .20 | .15 |
| 83 | Wayne Edwards | | .10 | .08 |
| 84 | Alex Fernandez(FC) | | .50 | .40 |
| 85 | Craig Grebeck(FC) | | .15 | .11 |
| 86 | Scott Radinsky(FC) | | .25 | .20 |
| 87 | Frank Thomas(FC) | | 5.00 | 3.75 |
| 88 | Beau Allred(FC) | | .20 | .15 |
| 89 | Sandy Alomar,Jr. | | .35 | .25 |
| 90 | Carlos Baerga(FC) | | 1.00 | .70 |
| 91 | Kevin Bearse(FC) | | .25 | .20 |
| 92 | Chris James | | .06 | .05 |
| 93 | Candy Maldonado | | .06 | .05 |
| 94 | Jeff Manto | | .12 | .09 |
| 95 | Cecil Fielder | | .40 | .30 |
| 96 | Travis Fryman(FC) | | 1.50 | 1.25 |
| 97 | Lloyd Moseby | | .06 | .05 |
| 98 | Edwin Nunez | | .06 | .05 |
| 99 | Tony Phillips | | .06 | .05 |
| 100 | Larry Sheets | | .06 | .05 |
| 101 | Mark Davis | | .06 | .05 |
| 102 | Storm Davis | | .06 | .05 |
| 103 | Gerald Perry | | .06 | .05 |
| 104 | Terry Shumpert(FC) | | .15 | .11 |
| 105 | Edgar Diaz(FC) | | .15 | .11 |
| 106 | Dave Parker | | .10 | .08 |
| 107 | Tim Drummond(FC) | | .15 | .11 |
| 108 | Junior Ortiz | | .06 | .05 |
| 109 | Park Pittman(FC) | | .15 | .11 |
| 110 | Kevin Tapani(FC) | | .25 | .20 |
| 111 | Oscar Azocar(FC) | | .15 | .11 |
| 112 | Jim Leyritz(FC) | | .15 | .11 |
| 113 | Kevin Maas | | .30 | .25 |
| 114 | Alan Mills(FC) | | .25 | .20 |
| 115 | Matt Nokes | | .06 | .05 |
| 116 | Pascual Perez | | .06 | .05 |
| 117 | Ozzie Canseco(FC) | | .20 | .15 |
| 118 | Scott Sanderson | | .06 | .05 |
| 119 | Tino Martinez(FC) | | .60 | .45 |
| 120 | Jeff Schaefer(FC) | | .15 | .11 |
| 121 | Matt Young | | .06 | .05 |
| 122 | Brian Bohanon(FC) | | .20 | .15 |
| 123 | Jeff Huson | | .15 | .11 |
| 124 | Ramon Manon(FC) | | .20 | .15 |
| 125 | Gary Mielke(FC) | | .15 | .11 |
| 126 | Willie Blair(FC) | | .15 | .11 |
| 127 | Glenallen Hill(FC) | | .15 | .11 |
| 128 | John Olerud(FC) | | .50 | .40 |
| 129 | Luis Sojo(FC) | | .15 | .11 |
| 130 | Mark Whiten(FC) | | .70 | .50 |

|  | | MT | NR MT |
|---|---|---|---|
| 131 | Three Decades Of No Hitters (Nolan Ryan) | .70 | .50 |
| 132 | Checklist | .06 | .05 |

## 1991 Fleer

Fleer expanded its 1991 set to include 720 cards. The cards feature yellow boders surrounding full- color action photos. The player's name appears above the photo, while the team and position in displayed below. The "Fleer 91" logo appears in the lower right corner of the photo. The card backs feature a player photo in a circle design, biographical information, complete statistics, and career highlights. Five special Super Star cards are among the cards in the regular set. Once again the cards are numbered according to team.

|  | | MT | NR MT |
|---|---|---|---|
| Complete Set: | | 20.00 | 15.00 |
| Common Player: | | .05 | .04 |
| 1 | *Troy Afenir*(FC) | .10 | .08 |
| 2 | Harold Baines | .08 | .06 |
| 3 | Lance Blankenship | .06 | .05 |
| 4 | Todd Burns | .05 | .04 |
| 5 | Jose Canseco | .30 | .25 |
| 6 | Dennis Eckersley | .10 | .08 |
| 7 | Mike Gallego | .05 | .04 |
| 8 | Ron Hassey | .05 | .04 |
| 9 | Dave Henderson | .08 | .06 |
| 10 | Rickey Henderson | .20 | .15 |
| 11 | Rick Honeycutt | .05 | .04 |
| 12 | Doug Jennings | .06 | .05 |
| 13 | *Joe Klink*(FC) | .10 | .08 |
| 14 | Carney Lansford | .08 | .06 |
| 15 | *Darren Lewis*(FC) | .20 | .15 |
| 16 | Willie McGee | .08 | .06 |
| 17 | Mark McGwire | .20 | .15 |
| 18 | Mike Moore | .06 | .05 |
| 19 | Gene Nelson | .05 | .04 |
| 20 | Dave Otto | .05 | .04 |
| 21 | Jamie Quirk | .05 | .04 |

|  | | MT | NR MT |
|---|---|---|---|
| 22 | Willie Randolph | .06 | .05 |
| 23 | Scott Sanderson | .06 | .05 |
| 24 | Terry Steinbach | .06 | .05 |
| 25 | Dave Stewart | .10 | .08 |
| 26 | Walt Weiss | .06 | .05 |
| 27 | Bob Welch | .08 | .06 |
| 28 | Curt Young | .05 | .04 |
| 29 | Wally Backman | .05 | .04 |
| 30 | *Stan Belinda* | .10 | .08 |
| 31 | Jay Bell | .06 | .05 |
| 32 | Rafael Belliard | .05 | .04 |
| 33 | Barry Bonds | .20 | .15 |
| 34 | Bobby Bonilla | .15 | .11 |
| 35 | Sid Bream | .06 | .05 |
| 36 | Doug Drabek | .10 | .08 |
| 37 | *Carlos Garcia*(FC) | .15 | .11 |
| 38 | Neal Heaton | .06 | .05 |
| 39 | Jeff King | .08 | .06 |
| 40 | Bob Kipper | .05 | .04 |
| 41 | Bill Landrum | .06 | .05 |
| 42 | Mike LaValliere | .06 | .05 |
| 43 | Jose Lind | .06 | .05 |
| 44 | Carmelo Martinez | .05 | .04 |
| 45 | Bob Patterson | .05 | .04 |
| 46 | Ted Power | .05 | .04 |
| 47 | Gary Redus | .05 | .04 |
| 48 | R.J. Reynolds | .05 | .04 |
| 49 | Don Slaught | .05 | .04 |
| 50 | John Smiley | .05 | .04 |
| 51 | Zane Smith | .06 | .05 |
| 52 | *Randy Tomlin*(FC) | .20 | .15 |
| 53 | Andy Van Slyke | .08 | .06 |
| 54 | Bob Walk | .05 | .04 |
| 55 | Jack Armstrong | .08 | .06 |
| 56 | Todd Benzinger | .06 | .05 |
| 57 | Glenn Braggs | .06 | .05 |
| 58 | Keith Brown | .06 | .05 |
| 59 | Tom Browning | .06 | .05 |
| 60 | Norm Charlton | .08 | .06 |
| 61 | Eric Davis | .20 | .15 |
| 62 | Rob Dibble | .10 | .08 |
| 63 | Bill Doran | .08 | .06 |
| 64 | Mariano Duncan | .06 | .05 |
| 65 | Chris Hammond | .06 | .05 |
| 66 | Billy Hatcher | .06 | .05 |
| 67 | Danny Jackson | .06 | .05 |
| 68 | Barry Larkin | .15 | .11 |
| 69 | *Tim Layana* | .10 | .08 |
| 70 | *Terry Lee*(FC) | .15 | .11 |
| 71 | Rick Mahler | .05 | .04 |
| 72 | Hal Morris | .15 | .11 |
| 73 | Randy Myers | .08 | .06 |
| 74 | Ron Oester | .05 | .04 |
| 75 | Joe Oliver | .08 | .06 |
| 76 | Paul O'Neill | .06 | .05 |
| 77 | Luis Quinones | .05 | .04 |
| 78 | Jeff Reed | .05 | .04 |
| 79 | Jose Rijo | .08 | .06 |
| 80 | Chris Sabo | .08 | .06 |
| 81 | Scott Scudder | .06 | .05 |
| 82 | Herm Winningham | .05 | .04 |
| 83 | Larry Andersen | .05 | .04 |
| 84 | Marty Barrett | .05 | .04 |
| 85 | Mike Boddicker | .06 | .05 |
| 86 | Wade Boggs | .20 | .15 |

| | | MT | NR MT |
|---|---|---|---|
| 87 | Tom Bolton | .05 | .04 |
| 88 | Tom Brunansky | .06 | .05 |
| 89 | Ellis Burks | .15 | .11 |
| 90 | Roger Clemens | .20 | .15 |
| 91 | Scott Cooper(FC) | .15 | .11 |
| 92 | John Dopson | .05 | .04 |
| 93 | Dwight Evans | .06 | .05 |
| 94 | Wes Gardner | .05 | .04 |
| 95 | Jeff Gray(FC) | .15 | .11 |
| 96 | Mike Greenwell | .10 | .08 |
| 97 | Greg Harris | .05 | .04 |
| 98 | Daryl Irvine(FC) | .20 | .15 |
| 99 | Dana Kiecker | .10 | .08 |
| 100 | Randy Kutcher | .05 | .04 |
| 101 | Dennis Lamp | .05 | .04 |
| 102 | Mike Marshall | .05 | .04 |
| 103 | John Marzano | .05 | .04 |
| 104 | Rob Murphy | .05 | .04 |
| 105 | Tim Naehring | .20 | .15 |
| 106 | Tony Pena | .06 | .05 |
| 107 | Phil Plantier(FC) | | |
| | | 1.00 | .70 |
| 108 | Carlos Quintana | .06 | .05 |
| 109 | Jeff Reardon | .06 | .05 |
| 110 | Jerry Reed | .05 | .04 |
| 111 | Jody Reed | .06 | .05 |
| 112 | Luis Rivera | .05 | .04 |
| 113 | Kevin Romine | .05 | .04 |
| 114 | Phil Bradley | .06 | .05 |
| 115 | Ivan Calderon | .06 | .05 |
| 116 | Wayne Edwards | .05 | .04 |
| 117 | Alex Fernandez | .25 | .20 |
| 118 | Carlton Fisk | .10 | .08 |
| 119 | Scott Fletcher | .05 | .04 |
| 120 | Craig Grebeck | .15 | .11 |
| 121 | Ozzie Guillen | .08 | .06 |
| 122 | Greg Hibbard | .06 | .05 |
| 123 | Lance Johnson | .06 | .05 |
| 124 | Barry Jones | .05 | .04 |
| 125 | Ron Karkovice | .05 | .04 |
| 126 | Eric King | .05 | .04 |
| 127 | Steve Lyons | .05 | .04 |
| 128 | Carlos Martinez | .06 | .05 |
| 129 | Jack McDowell | .06 | .05 |
| 130 | Donn Pall | .05 | .04 |
| 131 | Dan Pasqua | .05 | .04 |
| 132 | Ken Patterson | .05 | .04 |
| 133 | Melido Perez | .06 | .05 |
| 134 | Adam Peterson | .05 | .04 |
| 135 | Scott Radinsky | .15 | .11 |
| 136 | Sammy Sosa | .15 | .11 |
| 137 | Bobby Thigpen | .08 | .06 |
| 138 | Frank Thomas | 1.25 | .90 |
| 139 | Robin Ventura | .25 | .20 |
| 140 | Daryl Boston | .05 | .04 |
| 141 | Chuck Carr | .10 | .08 |
| 142 | Mark Carreon | .05 | .04 |
| 143 | David Cone | .06 | .05 |
| 144 | Ron Darling | .06 | .05 |
| 145 | Kevin Elster | .05 | .04 |
| 146 | Sid Fernandez | .06 | .05 |
| 147 | John Franco | .08 | .06 |
| 148 | Dwight Gooden | .20 | .15 |
| 149 | Tom Herr | .06 | .05 |
| 150 | Todd Hundley | .20 | .15 |
| 151 | Gregg Jefferies | .15 | .11 |
| 152 | Howard Johnson | .08 | .06 |

| | | MT | NR MT |
|---|---|---|---|
| 153 | Dave Magadan | .08 | .06 |
| 154 | Kevin McReynolds | .08 | .06 |
| 155 | Keith Miller | .06 | .05 |
| 156 | Bob Ojeda | .05 | .04 |
| 157 | Tom O'Malley | .05 | .04 |
| 158 | Alejandro Pena | .05 | .04 |
| 159 | Darren Reed | .20 | .15 |
| 160 | Mackey Sasser | .06 | .05 |
| 161 | Darryl Strawberry | .25 | .20 |
| 162 | Tim Teufel | .05 | .04 |
| 163 | Kelvin Torve | .08 | .06 |
| 164 | Julio Valera | .25 | .20 |
| 165 | Frank Viola | .12 | .09 |
| 166 | Wally Whitehurst | .05 | .04 |
| 167 | Jim Acker | .05 | .04 |
| 168 | Derek Bell(FC) | .35 | .25 |
| 169 | George Bell | .08 | .06 |
| 170 | Willie Blair | .15 | .11 |
| 171 | Pat Borders | .06 | .05 |
| 172 | John Cerutti | .05 | .04 |
| 173 | Juunior Felix | .12 | .09 |
| 174 | Tony Fernandez | .08 | .06 |
| 175 | Kelly Gruber | .12 | .09 |
| 176 | Tom Henke | .06 | .05 |
| 177 | Glenallen Hill | .08 | .06 |
| 178 | Jimmy Key | .06 | .05 |
| 179 | Manny Lee | .05 | .04 |
| 180 | Fred McGriff | .15 | .11 |
| 181 | Rance Mulliniks | .05 | .04 |
| 182 | Greg Myers | .05 | .04 |
| 183 | John Olerud | .50 | .40 |
| 184 | Luis Sojo | .15 | .11 |
| 185 | Dave Steib | .08 | .06 |
| 186 | Todd Stottlemyre | .06 | .05 |
| 187 | Duane Ward | .05 | .04 |
| 188 | David Wells | .05 | .04 |
| 189 | Mark Whiten | .40 | .30 |
| 190 | Ken Williams | .05 | .04 |
| 191 | Frank Wills | .05 | .04 |
| 192 | Mookie Wilson | .05 | .04 |
| 193 | Don Aase | .05 | .04 |
| 194 | Tim Belcher | .08 | .06 |
| 195 | Hubie Brooks | .08 | .06 |
| 196 | Dennis Cook | .06 | .05 |
| 197 | Tim Crews | .05 | .04 |
| 198 | Kal Daniels | .06 | .05 |
| 199 | Kirk Gibson | .08 | .06 |
| 200 | Jim Gott | .05 | .04 |
| 201 | Alfredo Griffin | .05 | .04 |
| 202 | Chris Gwynn | .06 | .05 |
| 203 | Dave Hansen | .20 | .15 |
| 204 | Lenny Harris | .06 | .05 |
| 205 | Mike Hartley | .10 | .08 |
| 206 | Mickey Hatcher | .05 | .04 |
| 207 | Carlos Hernandez(FC) | .20 | .15 |
| 208 | Orel Hershiser | .10 | .08 |
| 209 | Jay Howell | .06 | .05 |
| 210 | Mike Huff | .10 | .08 |
| 211 | Stan Javier | .05 | .04 |
| 212 | Ramon Martinez | .20 | .15 |
| 213 | Mike Morgan | .05 | .04 |
| 214 | Eddie Murray | .08 | .06 |
| 215 | Jim Neidlinger(FC) | .20 | .15 |
| 216 | Jose Offerman | .30 | .25 |
| 217 | Jim Poole(FC) | .20 | .15 |

| | | MT | NR MT | | | | MT | NR MT |
|---|---|---|---|---|---|---|---|---|
| | | | | | *Alexander*(FC) | | .15 | .11 |
| 218 | Juan Samuel | .06 | .05 | 279 | Brad Arnsberg | | .06 | .05 |
| 219 | Mike Scioscia | .06 | .05 | 280 | *Kevin Belcher*(FC) | | | |
| 220 | Ray Searage | .05 | .04 | | | | .15 | .11 |
| 221 | Mike Sharperson | .06 | .05 | 281 | *Joe Bitker*(FC) | | .15 | .11 |
| 222 | Fernando Valenzuela | | | 282 | Kevin Brown | | .06 | .05 |
| | | .06 | .05 | 283 | Steve Buechele | | .05 | .04 |
| 223 | Jose Vizcaino | .10 | .08 | 284 | Jack Daugherty | | .06 | .05 |
| 224 | Mike Aldrete | .05 | .04 | 285 | Julio Franco | | .10 | .08 |
| 225 | *Scott Anderson*(FC) | | | 286 | Juan Gonzalez | | .30 | .25 |
| | | .20 | .15 | 287 | *Bill Haselman*(FC) | | | |
| 226 | Dennis Boyd | .06 | .05 | | | | .15 | .11 |
| 227 | Tim Burke | .06 | .05 | 288 | Charlie Hough | | .05 | .04 |
| 228 | Delino DeShields | .30 | .25 | 289 | Jeff Huson | | .06 | .05 |
| 229 | Mike Fitzgerald | .05 | .04 | 290 | Pete Incaviglia | | .06 | .05 |
| 230 | Tom Foley | .05 | .04 | 291 | Mike Jeffcoat | | .05 | .04 |
| 231 | Steve Frey | .05 | .04 | 292 | Jeff Kunkel | | .05 | .04 |
| 232 | Andres Galarraga | .08 | .06 | 293 | Gary Mielke | | .08 | .06 |
| 233 | Mark Gardner | .10 | .08 | 294 | Jamie Moyer | | .05 | .04 |
| 234 | Marquis Grissom(FC) | | | 295 | Rafael Palmeiro | | .08 | .06 |
| | | .20 | .15 | 296 | Geno Petralli | | .05 | .04 |
| 235 | Kevin Gross | .06 | .05 | 297 | Gary Pettis | | .06 | .05 |
| 236 | Drew Hall | .05 | .04 | 298 | Kevin Reimer | | .10 | .08 |
| 237 | Dave Martinez | .06 | .05 | 299 | Kenny Rogers | | .06 | .05 |
| 238 | Dennis Martinez | .06 | .05 | 300 | Jeff Russell | | .06 | .05 |
| 239 | Dale Mohorcic | .05 | .04 | 301 | John Russell | | .05 | .04 |
| 240 | *Chris Nabholz* | .25 | .20 | 302 | Nolan Ryan | | .25 | .20 |
| 241 | Otis Nixon | .05 | .04 | 303 | Ruben Sierra | | .12 | .09 |
| 242 | Junior Noboa(FC) | .08 | .06 | 304 | Bobby Witt | | .08 | .06 |
| 243 | Spike Owen | .06 | .05 | 305 | Jim Abbott | | .08 | .06 |
| 244 | Tim Raines | .08 | .06 | 306 | Kent Anderson(FC) | | .06 | .05 |
| 245 | *Mel Rojas*(FC) | .12 | .09 | 307 | Dante Bichette | | .06 | .05 |
| 246 | *Scott Ruskin*(FC) | | | 308 | Bert Blyleven | | .08 | .06 |
| | | .15 | .11 | 309 | Chili Davis | | .06 | .05 |
| 247 | *Bill Sampen* | .25 | .20 | 310 | Brian Downing | | .05 | .04 |
| 248 | Nelson Santovenia | .05 | .04 | 311 | Mark Eichhorn | | .05 | .04 |
| 249 | Dave Schmidt | .05 | .04 | 312 | Mike Fetters | | .08 | .06 |
| 250 | Larry Walker | .15 | .11 | 313 | Chuck Finley | | .08 | .06 |
| 251 | Tim Wallach | .08 | .06 | 314 | Willie Fraser | | .05 | .04 |
| 252 | Dave Anderson | .05 | .04 | 315 | Bryan Harvey | | .06 | .05 |
| 253 | Kevin Bass | .06 | .05 | 316 | Donnie Hill | | .05 | .04 |
| 254 | Steve Bedrosian | .06 | .05 | 317 | Wally Joyner | | .10 | .08 |
| 255 | Jeff Brantley | .08 | .06 | 318 | Mark Langston | | .10 | .08 |
| 256 | John Burkett | .12 | .09 | 319 | Kirk McCaskill | | .06 | .05 |
| 257 | Brett Butler | .06 | .05 | 320 | John Orton | | .06 | .05 |
| 258 | Gary Carter | .08 | .06 | 321 | Lance Parrish | | .08 | .06 |
| 259 | Will Clark | .25 | .20 | 322 | Luis Polonia | | .05 | .04 |
| 260 | *Steve Decker*(FC) | | | 323 | Johnny Ray | | .05 | .04 |
| | | .20 | .15 | 324 | Bobby Rose | | .06 | .05 |
| 261 | Kelly Downs | .05 | .04 | 325 | Dick Schofield | | .05 | .04 |
| 262 | Scott Garrelts | .06 | .05 | 326 | Rick Schu | | .05 | .04 |
| 263 | Terry Kennedy | .05 | .04 | 327 | Lee Stevens | | .10 | .08 |
| 264 | Mike LaCoss | .05 | .04 | 328 | Devon White | | .06 | .05 |
| 265 | *Mark Leonard*(FC) | | | 329 | Dave Winfield | | .12 | .09 |
| | | .20 | .15 | 330 | *Cliff Young* | | .15 | .11 |
| 266 | Greg Litton | .06 | .05 | 331 | Dave Bergman | | .05 | .04 |
| 267 | Kevin Mitchell | .20 | .15 | 332 | *Phil Clark*(FC) | | .25 | .20 |
| 268 | Randy O'Neal(FC) | .05 | .04 | 333 | Darnell Coles | | .05 | .04 |
| 269 | *Rick Parker* | .15 | .11 | 334 | Milt Cuyler(FC) | | .20 | .15 |
| 270 | Rick Reuschel | .06 | .05 | 335 | Cecil Fielder | | .30 | .25 |
| 271 | Ernest Riles | .05 | .04 | 336 | *Travis Fryman* | | .60 | .45 |
| 272 | Don Robinson | .05 | .04 | 337 | Paul Gibson | | .05 | .04 |
| 273 | Robby Thompson | .06 | .05 | 338 | Jerry Don Gleaton | | .05 | .04 |
| 274 | Mark Thurmond | .05 | .04 | 339 | Mike Heath | | .05 | .04 |
| 275 | Jose Uribe | .05 | .04 | 340 | Mike Henneman | | .06 | .05 |
| 276 | Matt Williams | .15 | .11 | 341 | Chet Lemon | | .06 | .05 |
| 277 | Trevor Wilson | .06 | .05 | 342 | Lance McCullers | | .05 | .04 |
| 278 | *Gerald* | | | | | | | |

| | | MT | NR MT | | | | MT | NR MT |
|---|---|---|---|---|---|---|---|---|
| 343 | Jack Morris | .08 | .06 | 407 | *Mickey* | | | |
| 344 | lloyd Moseby | .06 | .05 | | *Morandini*(FC) | | .15 | .11 |
| 345 | Edwin Nunez | .05 | .04 | 408 | Terry Mulholland | .06 | .05 |
| 346 | Clay Parker | .05 | .04 | 409 | Dale Murphy | .10 | .08 |
| 347 | Dan Petry | .05 | .04 | 410 | Randy Ready | .05 | .04 |
| 348 | Tony Phillips | .06 | .05 | 411 | Bruce Ruffin | .05 | .04 |
| 349 | Jeff Robinson | .06 | .05 | 412 | Dickie Thon | .05 | .04 |
| 350 | Mark Salas | .05 | .04 | 413 | Paul Assenmacher | .05 | .04 |
| 351 | *Mike Schwabe* | .15 | .11 | 414 | Damon Berryhill | .06 | .05 |
| 352 | Larry Sheets | .05 | .04 | 415 | Mike Bielecki | .05 | .04 |
| 353 | John Shelby | .05 | .04 | 416 | *Shawn Boskie* | .15 | .11 |
| 354 | Frank Tanana | .06 | .05 | 417 | Dave Clark | .05 | .04 |
| 355 | Alan Trammell | .08 | .06 | 418 | Doug Dascenzo | .05 | .04 |
| 356 | Gary Ward | .05 | .04 | 419 | Andre Dawson | .10 | .08 |
| 357 | Lou Whitaker | .08 | .06 | 420 | Shawon Dunston | .10 | .08 |
| 358 | Beau Allred | .15 | .11 | 421 | Joe Girardi | .06 | .05 |
| 359 | Sandy Alomar,Jr. | .20 | .15 | 422 | Mark Grace | .15 | .11 |
| 360 | *Carlos Baerga* | .25 | .20 | 423 | Mike Harkey | .08 | .06 |
| 361 | *Kevin Bearse* | .12 | .09 | 424 | Les Lancaster | .05 | .04 |
| 362 | Tom Brookens | .05 | .04 | 425 | Bill Long | .05 | .04 |
| 363 | Jerry Browne | .06 | .05 | 426 | Greg Maddux | .08 | .06 |
| 364 | Tom Candiotti | .05 | .04 | 427 | Derrick May | .25 | .20 |
| 365 | Alex Cole | .25 | .20 | 428 | Jeff Pico | .05 | .04 |
| 366 | John Farrell | .05 | .04 | 429 | Domingo Ramos | .05 | .04 |
| 367 | Felix Fermin | .05 | .04 | 430 | Luis Salazar | .05 | .04 |
| 368 | Keith Hernandez | .08 | .06 | 431 | Ryne Sandberg | .20 | .15 |
| 369 | Brook Jacoby | .08 | .06 | 432 | Dwight Smith | .06 | .05 |
| 370 | Chris James | .06 | .05 | 433 | Greg Smith | .08 | .06 |
| 371 | Dion James | .05 | .04 | 434 | Rick Sutcliffe | .08 | .06 |
| 372 | Doug Jones | .08 | .06 | 435 | Gary Varsho | .05 | .04 |
| 373 | Candy Maldonado | .08 | .06 | 436 | *Hector Villanueva* | .15 | .11 |
| 374 | Steve Olin | .06 | .05 | 437 | Jerome Walton | .08 | .06 |
| 375 | Jesse Orosco | .05 | .04 | 438 | Curtis Wilkerson | .05 | .04 |
| 376 | Rudy Seanez | .06 | .05 | 439 | Mitch Williams | .08 | .06 |
| 377 | Joel Skinner | .05 | .04 | 440 | Steve Wilson | .06 | .05 |
| 378 | Cory Snyder | .08 | .06 | 441 | Marvell Wynne | .05 | .04 |
| 379 | Greg Swindell | .06 | .05 | 442 | Scott Bankhead | .06 | .05 |
| 380 | Sergio Valdez(FC) | .08 | .06 | 443 | Scott Bradley | .05 | .04 |
| 381 | *Mike Walker*(FC) | .15 | .11 | 444 | Greg Briley | .06 | .05 |
| 382 | *Colby Ward*(FC) | .20 | .15 | 445 | Mike Brumley | .05 | .04 |
| 383 | *Turner Ward*(FC) | .20 | .15 | 446 | Jay Buhner | .05 | .04 |
| 384 | Mitch Webster | .05 | .04 | 447 | *Dave Burba*(FC) | .15 | .11 |
| 385 | Kevin Wickander(FC) | | | 448 | Henry Cotto | .05 | .04 |
| | | .15 | .11 | 449 | Alvin Davis | .06 | .05 |
| 386 | Darrel Akerfelds | .06 | .05 | 450 | Ken Griffey,Jr. | 1.00 | .70 |
| 387 | Joe Boever | .05 | .04 | 451 | Erik Hanson | .12 | .09 |
| 388 | Rod Booker | .05 | .04 | 452 | Gene Harris | .05 | .04 |
| 389 | Sil Campusano | .05 | .04 | 453 | Brian Holman | .06 | .05 |
| 390 | Don Carman | .05 | .04 | 454 | Mike Jackson | .06 | .05 |
| 391 | *Wes* | | | 455 | Randy Johnson | .10 | .08 |
| | *Chamberlain*(FC) | .50 | .40 | 456 | Jeffrey Leonard | .05 | .04 |
| 392 | Pat Combs | .06 | .05 | 457 | Edgar Martinez | .06 | .05 |
| 393 | Darren Daulton | .06 | .05 | 458 | Tino Martinez | .35 | .25 |
| 394 | Jose DeJesus | .06 | .05 | 459 | Pete O'Brien | .05 | .04 |
| 395 | Len Dykstra | .08 | .06 | 460 | Harold Reynolds | .08 | .06 |
| 396 | Jason Grimsley | .06 | .05 | 461 | Mike Schooler | .06 | .05 |
| 397 | Charlie Hayes | .08 | .06 | 462 | Bill Swift | .06 | .05 |
| 398 | Von Hayes | .08 | .06 | 463 | David Valle | .05 | .04 |
| 399 | *David Hollins* | .30 | .25 | 464 | Omar Vizquel | .06 | .05 |
| 400 | Ken Howell | .06 | .05 | 465 | Matt Young | .06 | .05 |
| 401 | Ricky Jordan | .10 | .08 | 466 | Brady Anderson | .06 | .05 |
| 402 | John Kruk | .06 | .05 | 467 | Jeff Ballard | .06 | .05 |
| 403 | Steve Lake | .05 | .04 | 468 | Juan Bell(FC) | .20 | .15 |
| 404 | *Chuck Malone*(FC) | | | 469 | Mike Devereaux | .06 | .05 |
| | | .15 | .11 | 470 | Steve Finley | .06 | .05 |
| 405 | Roger McDowell | .08 | .06 | 471 | Dave Gallagher | .05 | .04 |
| 406 | Chuck McElroy | .15 | .11 | 472 | *Leo Gomez*(FC) | .30 | .25 |

| | MT | NR MT | | | MT | NR MT |
|---|---|---|---|---|---|---|
| 473 | Rene Gonzales | .05 | .04 | 535 | Derek Lilliquist | .06 | .05 |
| 474 | Pete Harnisch | .06 | .05 | 536 | Fred Lynn | .06 | .05 |
| 475 | Kevin Hickey | .05 | .04 | 537 | Mike Pagliarulo | .06 | .05 |
| 476 | *Chris Hoiles* | .20 | .15 | 538 | Mark Parent | .05 | .04 |
| 477 | Sam Horn | .06 | .05 | 539 | Dennis Rasmussen | .05 | .04 |
| 478 | Tim Hulett | .05 | .04 | 540 | *Bip Roberts* | .08 | .06 |
| 479 | Dave Johnson | .05 | .04 | 541 | *Richard* | | |
| 480 | Ron Kittle | .08 | .06 | | *Rodriguez*(FC) | .20 | .15 |
| 481 | Ben McDonald | .40 | .30 | 542 | Benito Santiago | .10 | .08 |
| 482 | Bob Melvin | .05 | .04 | 543 | Calvin Schiraldi | .05 | .04 |
| 483 | Bob Milacki | .06 | .05 | 544 | Eric Show | .06 | .05 |
| 484 | Randy Milligan | .06 | .05 | 545 | Phil Stephenson | .05 | .04 |
| 485 | *John Mitchell*(FC) | | | 546 | Garry Templeton | .06 | .05 |
| | | .15 | .11 | 547 | Ed Whitson | .06 | .05 |
| 486 | Gregg Olson | .08 | .06 | 548 | Eddie Williams | .05 | .04 |
| 487 | Joe Orsulak | .05 | .04 | 549 | Kevin Appier | .10 | .08 |
| 488 | Joe Price | .05 | .04 | 550 | Luis Aquino | .05 | .04 |
| 489 | Bill Ripken | .05 | .04 | 551 | Bob Boone | .08 | .06 |
| 490 | Cal Ripken,Jr. | .20 | .15 | 552 | George Brett | .12 | .09 |
| 491 | Curt Schilling | .06 | .05 | 553 | *Jeff Conine*(FC) | .20 | .15 |
| 492 | *David Segui* | .30 | .25 | 554 | Steve Crawford | .05 | .04 |
| 493 | *Anthony Telford*(FC) | | | 555 | Mark Davis | .06 | .05 |
| | | .20 | .15 | 556 | Storm Davis | .06 | .05 |
| 494 | Mickey Tettleton | .06 | .05 | 557 | Jim Eisenreich | .06 | .05 |
| 495 | Mark Williamson | .05 | .04 | 558 | Steve Farr | .05 | .04 |
| 496 | Craig Worthington | .06 | .05 | 559 | Tom Gordon | .10 | .08 |
| 497 | Juan Agosto | .05 | .04 | 560 | Mark Gubicza | .08 | .06 |
| 498 | Eric Anthony | .15 | .11 | 561 | Bo Jackson | .30 | .25 |
| 499 | Craig Biggio | .08 | .06 | 562 | Mike Macfarlane | .05 | .04 |
| 500 | Ken Caminiti | .06 | .05 | 563 | *Brian McRae*(FC) | | |
| 501 | Casey Candaele | .05 | .04 | | | .40 | .30 |
| 502 | *Andujar Cedeno*(FC) | | | 564 | Jeff Montgomery | .06 | .05 |
| | | .25 | .20 | 565 | Bill Pecota | .05 | .04 |
| 503 | Danny Darwin | .06 | .05 | 566 | Gerald Perry | .06 | .05 |
| 504 | Mark Davidson | .05 | .04 | 567 | Bret Saberhagen | .10 | .08 |
| 505 | Glenn Davis | .15 | .11 | 568 | *Jeff Schulz*(FC) | .15 | .11 |
| 506 | Jim Deshaies | .06 | .05 | 569 | Kevin Seitzer | .08 | .06 |
| 507 | *Luis Gonzalez*(FC) | | | 570 | *Terry Shumpert* | .15 | .11 |
| | | .50 | .40 | 571 | Kurt Stillwell | .06 | .05 |
| 508 | Bill Gullickson | .05 | .04 | 572 | Danny Tartabull | .08 | .06 |
| 509 | Xavier Hernandez(FC) | | | 573 | Gary Thurman | .05 | .04 |
| | | .08 | .06 | 574 | Frank White | .06 | .05 |
| 510 | Brian Meyer | .06 | .05 | 575 | Willie Wilson | .06 | .05 |
| 511 | Ken Oberkfell | .05 | .04 | 576 | Chris Bosio | .06 | .05 |
| 512 | Mark Portugal | .05 | .04 | 577 | Greg Brock | .06 | .05 |
| 513 | Rafael Ramirez | .05 | .04 | 578 | George Canale | .06 | .05 |
| 514 | *Karl Rhodes*(FC) | .25 | .20 | 579 | Chuck Crim | .05 | .04 |
| 515 | Mike Scott | .08 | .06 | 580 | Rob Deer | .06 | .05 |
| 516 | *Mike Simms*(FC) | .25 | .20 | 581 | *Edgar Diaz* | .06 | .05 |
| 517 | Dave Smith | .06 | .05 | 582 | *Tom Edens*(FC) | .08 | .06 |
| 518 | Franklin Stubbs | .06 | .05 | 583 | Mike Felder | .05 | .04 |
| 519 | Glenn Wilson | .06 | .05 | 584 | Jim Gantner | .06 | .05 |
| 520 | Eric Yelding | .10 | .08 | 585 | Darryl Hamilton | .06 | .05 |
| 521 | Gerald Young | .05 | .04 | 586 | Ted Higuera | .08 | .06 |
| 522 | Shawn Abner | .05 | .04 | 587 | Mark Knudson | .05 | .04 |
| 523 | Roberto Alomar | .10 | .08 | 588 | Bill Krueger | .05 | .04 |
| 524 | Andy Benes | .15 | .11 | 589 | Tim McIntosh | .08 | .06 |
| 525 | Joe Carter | .10 | .08 | 590 | Paul Mirabella | .05 | .04 |
| 526 | Jack Clark | .08 | .06 | 591 | Paul Molitor | .10 | .08 |
| 527 | Joey Cora | .06 | .05 | 592 | Jaime Navarro | .08 | .06 |
| 528 | *Paul Faries*(FC) | .20 | .15 | 593 | Dave Parker | .12 | .09 |
| 529 | Tony Gwynn | .15 | .11 | 594 | Dan Plesac | .06 | .05 |
| 530 | Atlee Hammaker | .05 | .04 | 595 | Ron Robinson | .06 | .05 |
| 531 | Greg Harris | .06 | .05 | 596 | Gary Sheffield | .15 | .11 |
| 532 | *Thomas Howard* | .20 | .15 | 597 | Bill Spiers | .06 | .05 |
| 533 | Bruce Hurst | .06 | .05 | 598 | B.J. Surhoff | .06 | .05 |
| 534 | Craig Lefferts | .06 | .05 | 599 | Greg Vaughn | .15 | .11 |

| | | MT | NR MT |
|---|---|---|---|
| 600 | Randy Veres | .05 | .04 |
| 601 | Robin Yount | .15 | .11 |
| 602 | Rick Aguilera | .06 | .05 |
| 603 | Allan Anderson | .05 | .04 |
| 604 | Juan Berenguer | .05 | .04 |
| 605 | Randy Bush | .05 | .04 |
| 606 | Carmen Castillo | .05 | .04 |
| 607 | Tim Drummond | .06 | .05 |
| 608 | *Scott Erickson*(FC) | | |
| | | .30 | .25 |
| 609 | Gary Gaetti | .08 | .06 |
| 610 | Greg Gagne | .06 | .05 |
| 611 | Dan Gladden | .06 | .05 |
| 612 | Mark Guthrie(FC) | .06 | .05 |
| 613 | Brian Harper | .06 | .05 |
| 614 | Kent Hrbek | .08 | .06 |
| 615 | Gene Larkin | .06 | .05 |
| 616 | Terry Leach | .05 | .04 |
| 617 | Nelson Liriano | .05 | .04 |
| 618 | Shane Mack | .06 | .05 |
| 619 | John Moses | .05 | .04 |
| 620 | *Pedro Munoz*(FC) | | |
| | | .35 | .25 |
| 621 | Al Newman | .05 | .04 |
| 622 | Junior Ortiz | .05 | .04 |
| 623 | Kirby Puckett | .15 | .11 |
| 624 | Roy Smith | .05 | .04 |
| 625 | Kevin Tapani | .10 | .08 |
| 626 | Gary Wayne | .05 | .04 |
| 627 | David West | .06 | .05 |
| 628 | Cris Carpenter | .06 | .05 |
| 629 | Vince Coleman | .08 | .06 |
| 630 | Ken Dayley | .06 | .05 |
| 631 | Jose DeLeon | .06 | .05 |
| 632 | Frank DiPino | .05 | .04 |
| 633 | *Bernard Gilkey*(FC) | | |
| | | .25 | .20 |
| 634 | Pedro Guerrero | .08 | .06 |
| 635 | Ken Hill | .06 | .05 |
| 636 | Felix Jose | .08 | .06 |
| 637 | *Ray Lankford*(FC) | | |
| | | .50 | .40 |
| 638 | Joe Magrane | .08 | .06 |
| 639 | Tom Niedenfuer | .05 | .04 |
| 640 | Jose Oquendo | .05 | .04 |
| 641 | Tom Pagnozzi | .05 | .04 |
| 642 | Terry Pendleton | .06 | .05 |
| 643 | *Mike Perez*(FC) | .20 | .15 |
| 644 | Bryn Smith | .05 | .04 |
| 645 | Lee Smith | .08 | .06 |
| 646 | Ozzie Smith | .10 | .08 |
| 647 | Scott Terry | .05 | .04 |
| 648 | Bob Tewksbury | .05 | .04 |
| 649 | Milt Thompson | .05 | .04 |
| 650 | John Tudor | .06 | .05 |
| 651 | Denny Walling | .05 | .04 |
| 652 | Craig Wilson(FC) | .15 | .11 |
| 653 | Todd Worrell | .06 | .05 |
| 654 | Todd Zeile | .20 | .15 |
| 655 | *Oscar Azocar* | .20 | .15 |
| 656 | Steve Balboni | .05 | .04 |
| 657 | Jesse Barfield | .08 | .06 |
| 658 | Greg Cadaret | .05 | .04 |
| 659 | Chuck Cary | .05 | .04 |
| 660 | Rick Cerone | .05 | .04 |
| 661 | Dave Eiland(FC) | .06 | .05 |
| 662 | Alvaro Espinoza | .06 | .05 |

| | | MT | NR MT |
|---|---|---|---|
| 663 | Bob Geren | .06 | .05 |
| 664 | Lee Guettuerman | .05 | .04 |
| 665 | Mel Hall | .06 | .05 |
| 666 | Andy Hawkins | .06 | .05 |
| 667 | Jimmy Jones | .05 | .04 |
| 668 | Roberto Kelly | .10 | .08 |
| 669 | Dave LaPoint | .05 | .04 |
| 670 | Tim Leary | .06 | .05 |
| 671 | *Jim Leyritz* | .15 | .11 |
| 672 | Kevin Maas | .20 | .15 |
| 673 | Don Mattingly | .20 | .15 |
| 674 | Matt Nokes | .06 | .05 |
| 675 | Pascual Perez | .06 | .05 |
| 676 | Eric Plunk | .05 | .04 |
| 677 | Dave Righetti | .08 | .06 |
| 678 | Jeff Robinson | .05 | .04 |
| 679 | Steve Sax | .10 | .08 |
| 680 | Mike Witt | .06 | .05 |
| 681 | Steve Avery | .30 | .25 |
| 682 | Mike Bell | .15 | .11 |
| 683 | Jeff Blauser | .06 | .05 |
| 684 | Francisco Cabrera | .10 | .08 |
| 685 | Tony Castillo(FC) | .08 | .06 |
| 686 | Marty Clary | .05 | .04 |
| 687 | Nick Esasky | .08 | .06 |
| 688 | Ron Gant | .10 | .08 |
| 689 | Tom Glavine | .06 | .05 |
| 690 | Mark Grant | .05 | .04 |
| 691 | Tommy Gregg | .06 | .05 |
| 692 | Dwayne Henry | .05 | .04 |
| 693 | Dave Justice | .50 | .40 |
| 694 | *Jimmy Kremers* | .15 | .11 |
| 695 | Charlie Leibrandt | .06 | .05 |
| 696 | Mark Lemke | .06 | .05 |
| 697 | Oddibe McDowell | .06 | .05 |
| 698 | *Greg Olson* | .08 | .06 |
| 699 | Jeff Parrett | .06 | .05 |
| 700 | Jim Presley | .06 | .05 |
| 701 | *Victor Rosario*(FC) | | |
| | | .20 | .15 |
| 702 | Lonnie Smith | .06 | .05 |
| 703 | Pete Smith | .06 | .05 |
| 704 | John Smoltz | .06 | .05 |
| 705 | Mike Stanton | .08 | .06 |
| 706 | Andres Thomas | .05 | .04 |
| 707 | Jeff Treadway | .06 | .05 |
| 708 | *Jim Vatcher*(FC) | .15 | .11 |
| 709 | Home Run Kings (Ryne Sandberg, Cecil Fielder) | .25 | .20 |
| 710 | Second Generation Stars (Barry Bonds, Ken Griffey,Jr.) | .30 | .25 |
| 711 | NLCS Team Leaders (Bobby Bonilla, Barry Larkin) | .15 | .11 |
| 712 | Top Game Savers (Bobby Thigpen, John Franco) | .10 | .08 |
| 713 | Chicago's 100 Club (Andre Dawson, Ryne Sandberg) | .15 | .11 |
| 714 | Checklists (Athletics, Pirates, Reds, Red Sox) | .05 | .04 |
| 715 | Checklists (White Sox, Mets Blue Jays, Dodgers) | .05 | .04 |
| 716 | Checklists (Expos, | | |

|  | | MT | NR MT |
|--|--|----|-------|
| | Giants, Rangers, Angels) | .05 | .04 |
| 717 | Checklists (Tigers, Indians, Phillies, Cubs) | .05 | .04 |
| 718 | Checklists (Mariners, Orioles, Astros, Padres) | .05 | .04 |
| 719 | Checklists (Royals, Brewers, Twins, Cardinals) | .05 | .04 |
| 720 | Checklists (Yankees, Braves, Super Stars) | .05 | .04 |

## 1991 Fleer Ultra

BOBBY THIGPEN

This 400-card set was originally going to be called the Elite set, but Fleer chose to use the Ultra label. The card fronts feature gray borders surrounding full-color action photos. The backs feature three player photos and statistics. Hot Prospects and Great Performers are among the special cards featured within the set. This set is the premier release for Fleer Ultra.

|  | | MT | NR MT |
|--|--|----|-------|
| | Complete Set: | 30.00 | 22.00 |
| | Common Player: | .06 | .05 |
| 1 | Steve Avery | 1.00 | .70 |
| 2 | Jeff Blauser | .06 | .05 |
| 3 | Francisco Cabrera | .08 | .06 |
| 4 | Ron Gant | .35 | .25 |
| 5 | Tom Glavine | .15 | .11 |
| 6 | Tommy Gregg | .06 | .05 |
| 7 | Dave Justice | 1.25 | .90 |
| 8 | Oddibe McDowell | .06 | .05 |
| 9 | Greg Olson | .08 | .06 |
| 10 | Terry Pendleton | .15 | .11 |
| 11 | Lonnie Smith | .06 | .05 |
| 12 | John Smoltz | .15 | .11 |
| 13 | Jeff Treadway | .06 | .05 |
| 14 | Glenn Davis | .10 | .08 |
| 15 | Mike Devereaux | .08 | .06 |
| 16 | Leo Gomez | .40 | .30 |
| 17 | Chris Hoiles | .50 | .40 |
| 18 | Dave Johnson | .06 | .05 |
| 19 | Ben McDonald | .20 | .15 |
| 20 | Randy Milligan | .08 | .06 |

|  | | MT | NR MT |
|--|--|----|-------|
| 21 | Gregg Olson | .10 | .08 |
| 22 | Joe Orsulak | .06 | .05 |
| 23 | Bill Ripken | .06 | .05 |
| 24 | Cal Ripken,Jr. | .50 | .40 |
| 25 | David Segui | .15 | .11 |
| 26 | Craig Worthington | .08 | .06 |
| 27 | Wade Boggs | .25 | .20 |
| 28 | Tom Bolton | .06 | .05 |
| 29 | Tom Brunansky | .08 | .06 |
| 30 | Ellis Burks | .12 | .09 |
| 31 | Roger Clemens | .50 | .40 |
| 32 | Mike Greenwell | .15 | .11 |
| 33 | Greg Harris | .06 | .05 |
| 34 | Daryl Irvine | .15 | .11 |
| 35 | Mike Marshall | .06 | .05 |
| 36 | Tim Naehring | .15 | .11 |
| 37 | Tony Pena | .06 | .05 |
| 38 | Phil Plantier | 2.00 | 1.50 |
| 39 | Carlos Quintana | .08 | .06 |
| 40 | Jeff Reardon | .08 | .06 |
| 41 | Jody Reed | .06 | .05 |
| 42 | Luis Rivera | .06 | .05 |
| 43 | Jim Abbott | .20 | .15 |
| 44 | Chuck Finley | .15 | .11 |
| 45 | Bryan Harvey | .08 | .06 |
| 46 | Donnie Hill | .06 | .05 |
| 47 | Jack Howell | .06 | .05 |
| 48 | Wally Joyner | .15 | .11 |
| 49 | Mark Langston | .12 | .09 |
| 50 | Kirk McCaskill | .06 | .05 |
| 51 | Lance Parrish | .08 | .06 |
| 52 | Dick Schofield | .06 | .05 |
| 53 | Lee Stevens | .15 | .11 |
| 54 | Dave Winfield | .15 | .11 |
| 55 | George Bell | .12 | .09 |
| 56 | Damon Berryhill | .06 | .05 |
| 57 | Mike Bielecki | .06 | .05 |
| 58 | Andre Dawson | .20 | .15 |
| 59 | Shawon Dunston | .10 | .08 |
| 60 | Joe Girardi | .06 | .05 |
| 61 | Mark Grace | .15 | .11 |
| 62 | Mike Harkey | .08 | .06 |
| 63 | Les Lancaster | .06 | .05 |
| 64 | Greg Maddux | .08 | .06 |
| 65 | Derrick May | .20 | .15 |
| 66 | Ryne Sandberg | .50 | .40 |
| 67 | Luis Salazar | .06 | .05 |
| 68 | Dwight Smith | .06 | .05 |
| 69 | Hector Villanueva | .08 | .06 |
| 70 | Jerome Walton | .12 | .09 |
| 71 | Mitch Williams | .08 | .06 |
| 72 | Carlton Fisk | .20 | .15 |
| 73 | Scott Fletcher | .06 | .05 |
| 74 | Ozzie Guillen | .10 | .08 |
| 75 | Greg Hibbard | .08 | .06 |
| 76 | Lance Johnson | .06 | .05 |
| 77 | Steve Lyons | .06 | .05 |
| 78 | Jack McDowell | .12 | .09 |
| 79 | Dan Pasqua | .06 | .05 |
| 80 | Melido Perez | .06 | .05 |
| 81 | Tim Raines | .10 | .08 |
| 82 | Sammy Sosa | .10 | .08 |
| 83 | Cory Snyder | .06 | .05 |
| 84 | Bobby Thigpen | .08 | .06 |
| 85 | Frank Thomas | 6.00 | 4.50 |
| 86 | Robin Ventura | 1.00 | .70 |
| 87 | Todd Benzinger | .06 | .05 |

| | | MT | NR MT |
|---|---|---|---|
| 88 | Glenn Braggs | .06 | .05 |
| 89 | Tom Browning | .08 | .06 |
| 90 | Norm Charlton | .08 | .06 |
| 91 | Eric Davis | .15 | .11 |
| 92 | Rob Dibble | .10 | .08 |
| 93 | Bill Doran | .08 | .06 |
| 94 | Mariano Duncan | .06 | .05 |
| 95 | Billy Hatcher | .06 | .05 |
| 96 | Barry Larkin | .15 | .11 |
| 97 | Randy Myers | .08 | .06 |
| 98 | Hal Morris | .20 | .15 |
| 99 | Joe Oliver | .06 | .05 |
| 100 | Paul O'Neill | .08 | .06 |
| 101 | Jeff Reed | .06 | .05 |
| 102 | Jose Rijo | .08 | .06 |
| 103 | Chris Sabo | .10 | .08 |
| 104 | Beau Allred | .06 | .05 |
| 105 | Sandy Alomar, Jr. | .10 | .08 |
| 106 | Carlos Baerga | .15 | .11 |
| 107 | Albert Belle | .50 | .40 |
| 108 | Jerry Browne | .06 | .05 |
| 109 | Tom Candiotti | .06 | .05 |
| 110 | Alex Cole | .06 | .05 |
| 111 | John Farrell | .06 | .05 |
| 112 | Felix Fermin | .06 | .05 |
| 113 | Brook Jacoby | .06 | .05 |
| 114 | Chris James | .06 | .05 |
| 115 | Doug Jones | .06 | .05 |
| 116 | Steve Olin | .06 | .05 |
| 117 | Greg Swindell | .08 | .06 |
| 118 | Turner Ward | .20 | .15 |
| 119 | Mitch Webster | .06 | .05 |
| 120 | Dave Bergman | .06 | .05 |
| 121 | Cecil Fielder | .40 | .30 |
| 122 | Travis Fryman | 2.00 | 1.50 |
| 123 | Mike Henneman | .08 | .06 |
| 124 | Lloyd Moseby | .06 | .05 |
| 125 | Dan Petry | .06 | .05 |
| 126 | Tony Phillips | .06 | .05 |
| 127 | Mark Salas | .06 | .05 |
| 128 | Frank Tanana | .06 | .05 |
| 129 | Alan Trammell | .15 | .11 |
| 130 | Lou Whitaker | .08 | .06 |
| 131 | Eric Anthony | .10 | .08 |
| 132 | Craig Biggio | .15 | .11 |
| 133 | Ken Caminiti | .08 | .06 |
| 134 | Casey Candaele | .06 | .05 |
| 135 | Andujar Cedeno | .60 | .45 |
| 136 | Mark Davidson | .06 | .05 |
| 137 | Jim Deshaies | .06 | .05 |
| 138 | Mark Portugal | .06 | .05 |
| 139 | Rafael Ramirez | .06 | .05 |
| 140 | Mike Scott | .08 | .06 |
| 141 | Eric Yelding | .06 | .05 |
| 142 | Gerald Young | .06 | .05 |
| 143 | Kevin Appier | .10 | .08 |
| 144 | George Brett | .25 | .20 |
| 145 | Jeff Conine | .20 | .15 |
| 146 | Jim Eisenreich | .06 | .05 |
| 147 | Tom Gordon | .10 | .08 |
| 148 | Mark Gubicza | .08 | .06 |
| 149 | Bo Jackson | .60 | .45 |
| 150 | Brent Mayne | .15 | .11 |
| 151 | Mike Macfarlane | .06 | .05 |
| 152 | Brian McRae | .60 | .45 |
| 153 | Jeff Montgomery | .08 | .06 |
| 154 | Bret Saberhagen | .10 | .08 |

| | | MT | NR MT |
|---|---|---|---|
| 155 | Kevin Seitzer | .06 | .05 |
| 156 | Terry Shumpert | .06 | .05 |
| 157 | Kurt Stillwell | .06 | .05 |
| 158 | Danny Tartabull | .15 | .11 |
| 159 | Tim Belcher | .08 | .06 |
| 160 | Kal Daniels | .10 | .08 |
| 161 | Alfredo Griffin | .06 | .05 |
| 162 | Lenny Harris | .06 | .05 |
| 163 | Jay Howell | .06 | .05 |
| 164 | Ramon Martinez | .40 | .30 |
| 165 | Mike Morgan | .06 | .05 |
| 166 | Eddie Murray | .20 | .15 |
| 167 | Jose Offerman | .15 | .11 |
| 168 | Juan Samuel | .08 | .06 |
| 169 | Mike Scioscia | .08 | .06 |
| 170 | Mike Sharperson | .06 | .05 |
| 171 | Darryl Strawberry | .40 | .30 |
| 172 | Greg Brock | .06 | .05 |
| 173 | Chuck Crim | .06 | .05 |
| 174 | Jim Gantner | .08 | .06 |
| 175 | Ted Higuera | .08 | .06 |
| 176 | Mark Knudson | .06 | .05 |
| 177 | Tim McIntosh | .08 | .06 |
| 178 | Paul Molitor | .15 | .11 |
| 179 | Dan Plesac | .06 | .05 |
| 180 | Gary Sheffield | .12 | .09 |
| 181 | Bill Spiers | .06 | .05 |
| 182 | B.J. Surhoff | .06 | .05 |
| 183 | Greg Vaughn | .20 | .15 |
| 184 | Robin Yount | .20 | .15 |
| 185 | Rick Aguilera | .08 | .06 |
| 186 | Greg Gagne | .06 | .05 |
| 187 | Dan Gladden | .06 | .05 |
| 188 | Brian Harper | .06 | .05 |
| 189 | Kent Hrbek | .08 | .06 |
| 190 | Gene Larkin | .06 | .05 |
| 191 | Shane Mack | .08 | .06 |
| 192 | Pedro Munoz | .80 | .60 |
| 193 | Al Newman | .06 | .05 |
| 194 | Junior Ortiz | .06 | .05 |
| 195 | Kirby Puckett | .25 | .20 |
| 196 | Kevin Tapani | .08 | .06 |
| 197 | Dennis Boyd | .06 | .05 |
| 198 | Tim Burke | .06 | .05 |
| 199 | Ivan Calderon | .08 | .06 |
| 200 | Delino DeShields | .10 | .08 |
| 201 | Mike Fitzgerald | .06 | .05 |
| 202 | Steve Frey | .06 | .05 |
| 203 | Andres Galarraga | .08 | .06 |
| 204 | Marquis Grissom | .20 | .15 |
| 205 | Dave Martinez | .06 | .05 |
| 206 | Dennis Martinez | .08 | .06 |
| 207 | Junior Noboa | .06 | .05 |
| 208 | Spike Owen | .06 | .05 |
| 209 | Scott Ruskin | .06 | .05 |
| 210 | Tim Wallach | .08 | .06 |
| 211 | Daryl Boston | .06 | .05 |
| 212 | Vince Coleman | .10 | .08 |
| 213 | David Cone | .10 | .08 |
| 214 | Ron Darling | .08 | .06 |
| 215 | Kevin Elster | .06 | .05 |
| 216 | Sid Fernandez | .08 | .06 |
| 217 | John Franco | .08 | .06 |
| 218 | Dwight Gooden | .20 | .15 |
| 219 | Tom Herr | .06 | .05 |
| 220 | Todd Hundley | .15 | .11 |
| 221 | Gregg Jefferies | .15 | .11 |

| | | MT | NR MT | | | MT | NR MT |
|---|---|---|---|---|---|---|---|
| 222 | Howard Johnson | .15 | .11 | 289 | Pedro Guerrero | .10 | .08 |
| 223 | Dave Magadan | .10 | .08 | 290 | Ray Lankford | 1.00 | .70 |
| 224 | Kevin McReynolds | .10 | .08 | 291 | Joe Magrane | .08 | .06 |
| 225 | Keith Miller | .06 | .05 | 292 | Jose Oquendo | .06 | .05 |
| 226 | Mackey Sasser | .06 | .05 | 293 | Tom Pagnozzi | .06 | .05 |
| 227 | Frank Viola | .10 | .08 | 294 | Bryn Smith | .06 | .05 |
| 228 | Jesse Barfield | .08 | .06 | 295 | Lee Smith | .08 | .06 |
| 229 | Greg Cadaret | .06 | .05 | 296 | Ozzie Smith | .20 | .15 |
| 230 | Alvaro Espinoza | .06 | .05 | 297 | Milt Thompson | .06 | .05 |
| 231 | Bob Geren | .06 | .05 | 298 | Craig Wilson | .12 | .09 |
| 232 | Lee Guetterman | .06 | .05 | 299 | Todd Zeile | .20 | .15 |
| 233 | Mel Hall | .08 | .06 | 300 | Shawn Abner | .06 | .05 |
| 234 | Andy Hawkins | .06 | .05 | 301 | Andy Benes | .15 | .11 |
| 235 | Roberto Kelly | .10 | .08 | 302 | Paul Faries | .15 | .11 |
| 236 | Tim Leary | .06 | .05 | 303 | Tony Gwynn | .20 | .15 |
| 237 | Jim Leyritz | .06 | .05 | 304 | Greg Harris | .06 | .05 |
| 238 | Kevin Maas | .25 | .20 | 305 | Thomas Howard | .10 | .08 |
| 239 | Don Mattingly | .30 | .25 | 306 | Bruce Hurst | .08 | .06 |
| 240 | Hensley Meulens | .10 | .08 | 307 | Craig Lefferts | .06 | .05 |
| 241 | Eric Plunk | .06 | .05 | 308 | Fred McGriff | .15 | .11 |
| 242 | Steve Sax | .08 | .06 | 309 | Dennis Rasmussen | .06 | .05 |
| 243 | Todd Burns | .06 | .05 | 310 | Bip Roberts | .08 | .06 |
| 244 | Jose Canseco | .60 | .45 | 311 | Benito Santiago | .10 | .08 |
| 245 | Dennis Eckersley | .10 | .08 | 312 | Garry Templeton | .06 | .05 |
| 246 | Mike Gallego | .06 | .05 | 313 | Ed Whitson | .06 | .05 |
| 247 | Dave Henderson | .10 | .08 | 314 | Dave Anderson | .06 | .05 |
| 248 | Rickey Henderson | .50 | .40 | 315 | Kevin Bass | .06 | .05 |
| 249 | Rick Honeycutt | .06 | .05 | 316 | Jeff Brantley | .06 | .05 |
| 250 | Carney Lansford | .08 | .06 | 317 | John Burkett | .08 | .06 |
| 251 | Mark McGwire | .15 | .11 | 318 | Will Clark | .50 | .40 |
| 252 | Mike Moore | .06 | .05 | 319 | Steve Decker | .30 | .25 |
| 253 | Terry Steinbach | .06 | .05 | 320 | Scott Garrelts | .06 | .05 |
| 254 | Dave Stewart | .10 | .08 | 321 | Terry Kennedy | .06 | .05 |
| 255 | Walt Weiss | .06 | .05 | 322 | Mark Leonard | .20 | .15 |
| 256 | Bob Welch | .08 | .06 | 323 | Darren Lewis | .50 | .40 |
| 257 | Curt Young | .06 | .05 | 324 | Greg Litton | .06 | .05 |
| 258 | Wes Chamberlain | .60 | .45 | 325 | Willie McGee | .10 | .08 |
| 259 | Pat Combs | .08 | .06 | 326 | Kevin Mitchell | .15 | .11 |
| 260 | Darren Daulton | .06 | .05 | 327 | Don Robinson | .06 | .05 |
| 261 | Jose DeJesus | .06 | .05 | 328 | Andres Santana | .25 | .20 |
| 262 | Len Dykstra | .10 | .08 | 329 | Robby Thompson | .06 | .05 |
| 263 | Charlie Hayes | .08 | .06 | 330 | Jose Uribe | .06 | .05 |
| 264 | Von Hayes | .08 | .06 | 331 | Matt Williams | .15 | .11 |
| 265 | Ken Howell | .06 | .05 | 332 | Scott Bradley | .06 | .05 |
| 266 | John Kruk | .08 | .06 | 334 | Alvin Davis | .08 | .06 |
| 267 | Roger McDowell | .06 | .05 | 335 | Ken Griffey,Sr. | .08 | .06 |
| 268 | Mickey Morandini | .15 | .11 | 336 | Ken Griffey,Jr. | 2.00 | 1.50 |
| 269 | Terry Mulholland | .08 | .06 | 337 | Erik Hanson | .10 | .08 |
| 270 | Dale Murphy | .10 | .08 | 338 | Brian Holman | .06 | .05 |
| 271 | Randy Ready | .06 | .05 | 339 | Randy Johnson | .08 | .06 |
| 272 | Dickie Thon | .06 | .05 | 340 | Edgar Martinez | .08 | .06 |
| 273 | Stan Belinda | .06 | .05 | 341 | Tino Martinez | .20 | .15 |
| 274 | Jay Bell | .08 | .06 | 342 | Pete O'Brien | .06 | .05 |
| 275 | Barry Bonds | .25 | .20 | 343 | Harold Reynolds | .08 | .06 |
| 276 | Bobby Bonilla | .25 | .20 | 344 | David Valle | .06 | .05 |
| 277 | Doug Drabek | .10 | .08 | 345 | Omar Vizquel | .06 | .05 |
| 278 | Carlos Garcia | .20 | .15 | 346 | Brad Arnsberg | .06 | .05 |
| 279 | Neal Heaton | .06 | .05 | 347 | Kevin Brown | .06 | .05 |
| 280 | Jeff King | .08 | .06 | 348 | Julio Franco | .10 | .08 |
| 281 | Bill Landrum | .06 | .05 | 349 | Jeff Huson | .06 | .05 |
| 282 | Mike LaValliere | .06 | .05 | 350 | Rafael Palmeiro | .20 | .15 |
| 283 | Jose Lind | .06 | .05 | 351 | Geno Petralli | .06 | .05 |
| 284 | Orlando Merced | .70 | .50 | 352 | Gary Pettis | .06 | .05 |
| 285 | Gary Redus | .06 | .05 | 353 | Kenny Rogers | .06 | .05 |
| 286 | Don Slaught | .06 | .05 | 354 | Jeff Russell | .06 | .05 |
| 287 | Andy Van Slyke | .10 | .08 | 355 | Nolan Ryan | 1.00 | .70 |
| 288 | Jose DeLeon | .06 | .05 | 356 | Ruben Sierra | .25 | .20 |

| | | MT | NR MT |
|---|---|---|---|
| 357 | Bobby Witt | .08 | .06 |
| 358 | Roberto Alomar | .70 | .50 |
| 359 | Pat Borders | .06 | .05 |
| 360 | Joe Carter | .15 | .11 |
| 361 | Kelly Gruber | .08 | .06 |
| 362 | Tom Henke | .08 | .06 |
| 363 | Glenallen Hill | .08 | .06 |
| 364 | Jimmy Key | .08 | .06 |
| 365 | Manny Lee | .06 | .05 |
| 366 | Rance Mulliniks | .06 | .05 |
| 367 | John Olerud | .20 | .15 |
| 368 | Dave Stieb | .08 | .06 |
| 369 | Duane Ward | .06 | .05 |
| 370 | David Wells | .06 | .05 |
| 371 | Mark Whiten | .30 | .25 |
| 372 | Mookie Wilson | .06 | .05 |
| 373 | Willie Banks | .30 | .25 |
| 374 | Steve Carter | .06 | .05 |
| 375 | Scott Chiamparino | .10 | .08 |
| 376 | Steve Chitren | .10 | .08 |
| 377 | Darrin Fletcher | .10 | .08 |
| 378 | Rich Garces | .10 | .08 |
| 379 | Reggie Jefferson | .60 | .45 |
| 380 | Eric Karros | .70 | .50 |
| 381 | Pat Kelly | .70 | .50 |
| 382 | Chuck Knoblauch | 2.00 | 1.50 |
| 383 | Denny Neagle | .50 | .40 |
| 384 | Dan Opperman | .20 | .15 |
| 385 | John Ramos | .20 | .15 |
| 386 | Henry Rodriguez | .30 | .25 |
| 387 | Maurice Vaughn | .40 | .30 |
| 388 | Gerald Williams | .40 | .30 |
| 389 | Mike York | .20 | .15 |
| 390 | Eddie Zosky | .20 | .15 |
| 391 | Barry Bonds (Great Performer) | .20 | .15 |
| 392 | Cecil Fielder (Great Performer) | .20 | .15 |
| 393 | Rickey Henderson (Great Performer) | .20 | .15 |
| 394 | Dave Justice (Great Performer) | .60 | .45 |
| 395 | Nolan Ryan (Great Performer) | .40 | .30 |
| 396 | Bobby Thigpen (Great Performer) | .10 | .08 |
| 397 | Checklist | .06 | .05 |
| 398 | Checklist | .06 | .05 |
| 399 | Checklist | .06 | .05 |
| 400 | Checklist | .06 | .05 |

# 1991 Fleer Ultra Update

This 120-card set was produced as a supplement to the premier Fleer Ultra set. The cards feature the same style as the regular Fleer Ultra cards. The 4-photo Ultra look is featured on each card. The cards were sold in full color, overwrapped boxes.

| | | MT | NR MT |
|---|---|---|---|
| | Complete Set: | 30.00 | 22.00 |
| | Common Player: | .06 | .05 |
| 1 | Dwight Evans | .08 | .06 |
| 2 | Chito Martinez | 1.25 | .90 |
| 3 | Bob Melvin | .06 | .05 |
| 4 | Mike Mussina | 5.00 | 3.75 |
| 5 | Jack Clark | .08 | .06 |
| 6 | Dana Kiecker | .06 | .05 |
| 7 | Steve Lyons | .06 | .05 |
| 8 | Gary Gaetti | .08 | .06 |
| 9 | Dave Gallagher | .06 | .05 |
| 10 | Dave Parker | .08 | .06 |
| 11 | Luis Polonia | .06 | .05 |
| 12 | Luis Sojo | .08 | .06 |
| 13 | Wilson Alvarez | .20 | .15 |
| 14 | Alex Fernandez | .40 | .30 |
| 15 | Craig Grebeck | .06 | .05 |
| 16 | Ron Karkovice | .06 | .05 |
| 17 | Warren Newson | .40 | .30 |
| 18 | Scott Radinsky | .08 | .06 |
| 19 | Glenallen Hill | .12 | .09 |
| 20 | Charles Nagy | .15 | .11 |
| 21 | Mark Whiten | .30 | .25 |
| 22 | Milt Cuyler | .35 | .25 |
| 23 | Paul Gibson | .06 | .05 |
| 24 | Mickey Tettleton | .08 | .06 |
| 25 | Todd Benzinger | .08 | .06 |
| 26 | Storm Davis | .06 | .05 |
| 27 | Kirk Gibson | .08 | .06 |
| 28 | Bill Pecota | .06 | .05 |
| 29 | Gary Thurman | .06 | .05 |
| 30 | Darryl Hamilton | .08 | .06 |
| 31 | Jaime Navarro | .08 | .06 |
| 32 | Willie Randolph | .08 | .06 |
| 33 | Bill Wegman | .06 | .05 |
| 34 | Randy Bush | .06 | .05 |
| 35 | Chili Davis | .08 | .06 |
| 36 | Scott Erickson | 1.25 | 1.25 |
| 37 | Chuck Knoblauch | 2.00 | 1.50 |
| 38 | Scott Leius | .15 | .11 |
| 39 | Jack Morris | .12 | .09 |
| 40 | John Habyan | .08 | .06 |
| 41 | Pat Kelly | .60 | .45 |
| 42 | Matt Nokes | .08 | .06 |
| 43 | Scott Sanderson | .08 | .06 |
| 44 | Bernie Williams | .70 | .50 |
| 45 | Harold Baines | .10 | .08 |
| 46 | Brook Jacoby | .08 | .06 |
| 47 | Ernest Riles | .06 | .05 |
| 48 | Willie Wilson | .06 | .05 |
| 49 | Jay Buhner | .08 | .06 |
| 50 | Rich DeLucia | .20 | .15 |
| 51 | Mike Jackson | .06 | .05 |
| 52 | Bill Krueger | .06 | .05 |
| 53 | Bill Swift | .06 | .05 |
| 54 | Brian Downing | .06 | .05 |
| 55 | Juan Gonzalez | 3.00 | 2.25 |
| 56 | Dean Palmer | 2.00 | 1.50 |
| 57 | Kevin Reimer | .20 | .15 |
| 58 | Ivan Rodriguez | 4.00 | 3.00 |
| 59 | Tom Candiotti | .06 | .05 |
| 60 | Juan Guzman | 5.00 | 3.75 |
| 61 | Bob MacDonald | .20 | .15 |
| 62 | Greg Myers | .06 | .05 |
| 63 | Ed Sprague | .20 | .15 |
| 64 | Devon White | .08 | .06 |

| | | MT | NR MT |
|---|---|---|---|
| 65 | Rafael Belliard | .06 | .05 |
| 66 | Juan Berenguer | .06 | .05 |
| 67 | Brian Hunter | 1.00 | .70 |
| 68 | Kent Mercker | .08 | .06 |
| 69 | Otis Nixon | .06 | .05 |
| 70 | Danny Jackson | .06 | .05 |
| 71 | Chuck McElroy | .06 | .05 |
| 72 | Gary Scott | .35 | .25 |
| 73 | Heathcliff Slocumb | .15 | .11 |
| 74 | Chico Walker | .10 | .08 |
| 75 | Rick Wilkins | .35 | .25 |
| 76 | Chris Hammond | .15 | .11 |
| 77 | Luis Quinones | .06 | .05 |
| 78 | Herm Winningham | .06 | .05 |
| 79 | Jeff Bagwell | 5.00 | 3.75 |
| 80 | Jim Corsi | .06 | .05 |
| 81 | Steve Finley | .08 | .06 |
| 82 | Luis Gonzalez | 1.25 | .90 |
| 83 | Pete Harnisch | .08 | .06 |
| 84 | Darryl Kile | .25 | .20 |
| 85 | Brett Butler | .08 | .06 |
| 86 | Gary Carter | .15 | .11 |
| 87 | Tim Crews | .06 | .05 |
| 88 | Orel Hershiser | .15 | .11 |
| 89 | Bob Ojeda | .06 | .05 |
| 90 | Bret Barberie | .40 | .30 |
| 91 | Barry Jones | .06 | .05 |
| 92 | Gilberto Reyes | .08 | .06 |
| 93 | Larry Walker | .15 | .11 |
| 94 | Hubie Brooks | .08 | .06 |
| 95 | Tim Burke | .06 | .05 |
| 96 | Rick Cerone | .06 | .05 |
| 97 | Jeff Innis | .08 | .06 |
| 98 | Wally Backman | .06 | .05 |
| 99 | Tommy Greene | .15 | .11 |
| 100 | Ricky Jordan | .10 | .08 |
| 101 | Mitch Williams | .08 | .06 |
| 102 | John Smiley | .08 | .06 |
| 103 | Randy Tomlin | .40 | .30 |
| 104 | Gary Varsho | .06 | .05 |
| 105 | Cris Carpenter | .06 | .05 |
| 106 | Ken Hill | .08 | .06 |
| 107 | Felix Jose | .25 | .20 |
| 108 | Omar Oliveras | .25 | .20 |
| 109 | Gerald Perry | .06 | .05 |
| 110 | Jerald Clark | .08 | .06 |
| 111 | Tony Fernandez | .08 | .06 |
| 112 | Darrin Jackson | .08 | .06 |
| 113 | Mike Maddux | .06 | .05 |
| 114 | Tim Teufel | .06 | .05 |
| 115 | Bud Black | .06 | .05 |
| 116 | Kelly Downs | .06 | .05 |
| 117 | Mike Felder | .06 | .05 |
| 118 | Willie McGee | .12 | .09 |
| 119 | Trevor Wilson | .12 | .09 |
| 120 | Checklist | .06 | .05 |

## 1992 Fleer

For the second consecutive year, Fleer produced a 720-card set. The standard card fronts feature full-color action photos bordered in blue with the player's name,

position and team logo on the right border. The backs feature another full-color action photo, biographical information and statistics. A special twelve card Roger Clemens subset is also included in the 1992 Fleer set. Three more Clemens cards are available through a mail-in offer, and 2,000 Roger Clemens autographed cards were inserted in 1992 packs. Once again the cards are numbered according to team.

| | | MT | NR MT |
|---|---|---|---|
| Complete Set: | | 25.00 | 18.00 |
| Common Player: | | .04 | .03 |
| 1 | Brady Anderson | .04 | .03 |
| 2 | Jose Bautista | .04 | .03 |
| 3 | Juan Bell | .06 | .05 |
| 4 | Glenn Davis | .08 | .06 |
| 5 | Mike Devereaux | .05 | .04 |
| 6 | Dwight Evans | .08 | .06 |
| 7 | Mike Flanagan | .04 | .03 |
| 8 | Leo Gomez | .15 | .11 |
| 9 | Chris Hoiles | .10 | .08 |
| 10 | Sam Horn | .05 | .04 |
| 11 | Tim Hulett | .04 | .03 |
| 12 | Dave Johnson | .04 | .03 |
| 13 | *Chito Martinez*(FC) | .20 | .15 |
| 14 | Ben McDonald | .10 | .08 |
| 15 | Bob Melvin | .04 | .03 |
| 16 | *Luis Mercedes*(FC) | .15 | .11 |
| 17 | Jose Mesa | .05 | .04 |
| 18 | Bob Milacki | .05 | .04 |
| 19 | Randy Milligan | .06 | .05 |
| 20 | Mike Mussina | .50 | .40 |
| 21 | Gregg Olson | .08 | .06 |
| 22 | Joe Orsulak | .04 | .03 |
| 23 | Jim Poole | .05 | .04 |
| 24 | *Arthur Rhodes*(FC) | .40 | .30 |
| 25 | Billy Ripken | .04 | .03 |
| 26 | Cal Ripken, Jr. | .20 | .15 |
| 27 | David Segui | .08 | .06 |
| 28 | Roy Smith | .04 | .03 |
| 29 | Anthony Telford | .04 | .03 |
| 30 | Mark Williamson | .04 | .03 |
| 31 | Craig Worthington | .06 | .05 |
| 32 | Wade Boggs | .15 | .11 |
| 33 | Tom Bolton | .04 | .03 |

| | | MT | NR MT | | | | MT | NR MT |
|---|---|---|---|---|---|---|---|---|
| 34 | Tom Brunansky | .05 | .04 | | 97 | Tim Raines | .10 | .08 |
| 35 | Ellis Burks | .08 | .06 | | 98 | Sammy Sosa | .08 | .06 |
| 36 | Jack Clark | .08 | .06 | | 99 | Bobby Thigpen | .08 | .06 |
| 37 | Roger Clemens | .15 | .11 | | 100 | Frank Thomas | 1.00 | .70 |
| 38 | Danny Darwin | .04 | .03 | | 101 | Robin Ventura | .20 | .15 |
| 39 | Mike Greenwell | .08 | .06 | | 102 | Mike Aldrete | .04 | .03 |
| 40 | Joe Hesketh | .04 | .03 | | 103 | Sandy Alomar, Jr. | .10 | .08 |
| 41 | Daryl Irvine | .05 | .04 | | 104 | Carlos Baerga | .10 | .08 |
| 42 | Dennis Lamp | .04 | .03 | | 105 | Albert Belle | .15 | .11 |
| 43 | Tony Pena | .05 | .04 | | 106 | Willie Blair | .05 | .04 |
| 44 | Phil Plantier | .25 | .20 | | 107 | Jerry Browne | .04 | .03 |
| 45 | Carlos Quintana | .06 | .05 | | 108 | Alex Cole | .06 | .05 |
| 46 | Jeff Reardon | .08 | .06 | | 109 | Felix Fermin | .04 | .03 |
| 47 | Jody Reed | .05 | .04 | | 110 | Glenallen Hill | .06 | .05 |
| 48 | Luis Rivera | .04 | .03 | | 111 | Shawn Hillegas | .04 | .03 |
| 49 | Mo Vaughn | .30 | .25 | | 112 | Chris James | .05 | .04 |
| 50 | Jim Abbott | .10 | .08 | | 113 | Reggie Jefferson(FC) | | |
| 51 | Kyle Abbott | .08 | .06 | | | | .20 | .15 |
| 52 | Ruben Amaro, | | | | 114 | Doug Jones | .05 | .04 |
| | Jr.(FC) | .15 | .11 | | 115 | Eric King | .04 | .03 |
| 53 | Scott Bailes | .04 | .03 | | 116 | Mark Lewis | .15 | .11 |
| 54 | Chris Beasley(FC) | | | | 117 | Carlos Martinez | .05 | .04 |
| | | .12 | .09 | | 118 | Charles Nagy | .08 | .06 |
| 55 | Mark Eichhorn | .04 | .03 | | 119 | Rod Nichols | .04 | .03 |
| 56 | Mike Fetters | .04 | .03 | | 120 | Steve Olin | .04 | .03 |
| 57 | Chuck Finley | .08 | .06 | | 121 | Jesse Orosco | .04 | .03 |
| 58 | Gary Gaetti | .08 | .06 | | 122 | Rudy Seanez | .04 | .03 |
| 59 | Dave Gallagher | .05 | .04 | | 123 | Joel Skinner | .04 | .03 |
| 60 | Donnie Hill | .04 | .03 | | 124 | Greg Swindell | .08 | .06 |
| 61 | Bryan Harvey | .06 | .05 | | 125 | Jim Thome(FC) | .50 | .40 |
| 62 | Wally Joyner | .10 | .08 | | 126 | Mark Whiten | .10 | .08 |
| 63 | Mark Langston | .10 | .08 | | 127 | Scott Aldred | .10 | .08 |
| 64 | Kirk McCaskill | .05 | .04 | | 128 | Andy Allanson | .04 | .03 |
| 65 | John Orton | .04 | .03 | | 129 | John Cerutti | .04 | .03 |
| 66 | Lance Parrish | .06 | .05 | | 130 | Milt Cuyler | .10 | .08 |
| 67 | Luis Polonia | .05 | .04 | | 131 | Mike Dalton(FC) | .15 | .11 |
| 68 | Bobby Rose | .05 | .04 | | 132 | Rob Deer | .05 | .04 |
| 69 | Dick Schofield | .04 | .03 | | 133 | Cecil Fielder | .15 | .11 |
| 70 | Luis Sojo | .05 | .04 | | 134 | Travis Fryman | .25 | .20 |
| 71 | Lee Stevens | .08 | .06 | | 135 | Dan Gakeler(FC) | .15 | .11 |
| 72 | Dave Winfield | .12 | .09 | | 136 | Paul Gibson | .04 | .03 |
| 73 | Cliff Young | .06 | .05 | | 137 | Bill Gullickson | .05 | .04 |
| 74 | Wilson Alvarez | .08 | .06 | | 138 | Mike Henneman | .05 | .04 |
| 75 | Esteban Beltre(FC) | | | | 139 | Pete Incaviglia | .05 | .04 |
| | | .20 | .15 | | 140 | Mark Leiter(FC) | .12 | .09 |
| 76 | Joey Cora | .04 | .03 | | 141 | Scott | | |
| 77 | Brian Drahman(FC) | | | | | Livingstone(FC) | .20 | .15 |
| | | .15 | .11 | | 142 | Lloyd Moseby | .04 | .03 |
| 78 | Alex Fernandez | .15 | .11 | | 143 | Tony Phillips | .05 | .04 |
| 79 | Carlton Fisk | .10 | .08 | | 144 | Mark Salas | .04 | .03 |
| 80 | Scott Fletcher | .04 | .03 | | 145 | Frank Tanana | .05 | .04 |
| 81 | Craig Grebeck | .04 | .03 | | 146 | Walt Terrell | .04 | .03 |
| 82 | Ozzie Guillen | .06 | .05 | | 147 | Mickey Tettleton | .06 | .05 |
| 83 | Greg Hibbard | .06 | .05 | | 148 | Alan Trammell | .10 | .08 |
| 84 | Charlie Hough | .05 | .04 | | 149 | Lou Whitaker | .08 | .06 |
| 85 | Mike Huff | .05 | .04 | | 150 | Kevin Appier | .06 | .05 |
| 86 | Bo Jackson | .40 | .30 | | 151 | Luis Aquino | .04 | .03 |
| 87 | Lance Johnson | .04 | .03 | | 152 | Todd Benzinger | .05 | .04 |
| 88 | Ron Karkovice | .04 | .03 | | 153 | Mike Boddicker | .05 | .04 |
| 89 | Jack McDowell | .08 | .06 | | 154 | George Brett | .15 | .11 |
| 90 | Matt Merullo | .04 | .03 | | 155 | Storm Davis | .05 | .04 |
| 91 | Warren Newson | .15 | .11 | | 156 | Jim Eisenreich | .04 | .03 |
| 92 | Donn Pall | .04 | .03 | | 157 | Kirk Gibson | .08 | .06 |
| 93 | Dan Pasqua | .05 | .04 | | 158 | Tom Gordon | .06 | .05 |
| 94 | Ken Patterson | .04 | .03 | | 159 | Mark Gubicza | .05 | .04 |
| 95 | Melido Perez | .05 | .04 | | 160 | David Howard(FC) | | |
| 96 | Scott Radinsky | .04 | .03 | | | | .20 | .15 |

| | MT | NR MT | | | MT | NR MT |
|---|---|---|---|---|---|---|
| 161 Mike Macfarlane | .05 | .04 | 226 | Bob Geren | .04 | .03 |
| 162 Brent Mayne | .05 | .04 | 227 | Lee Guetterman | .04 | .03 |
| 163 Brian McRae | .25 | .20 | 228 | John Habyan | .04 | .03 |
| 164 Jeff Montgomery | .05 | .04 | 229 | Mel Hall | .06 | .05 |
| 165 Bill Pecota | .04 | .03 | 230 | Steve Howe | .06 | .05 |
| 166 *Harvey Pulliam*(FC) | | | 231 | *Mike* | | |
| | .15 | .11 | | *Humphreys*(FC) | .20 | .15 |
| 167 Bret Saberhagen | .08 | .06 | 232 | *Scott Kamieniecki* | .15 | .11 |
| 168 Kevin Seitzer | .05 | .04 | 233 | Pat Kelly | .15 | .11 |
| 169 Terry Shumpert | .05 | .04 | 234 | Roberto Kelly | .08 | .06 |
| 170 Kurt Stillwell | .05 | .04 | 235 | Tim Leary | .04 | .03 |
| 171 Danny Tartabull | .08 | .06 | 236 | Kevin Maas | .15 | .11 |
| 172 Gary Thurman | .04 | .03 | 237 | Don Mattingly | .25 | .20 |
| 173 Dante Bichette | .05 | .04 | 238 | Hensley Meulens | .08 | .06 |
| 174 Kevin Brown | .04 | .03 | 239 | Matt Nokes | .06 | .05 |
| 175 Chuck Crim | .04 | .03 | 240 | Pascual Perez | .05 | .04 |
| 176 Jim Gantner | .05 | .04 | 241 | Eric Plunk | .04 | .03 |
| 177 Darryl Hamilton | .05 | .04 | 242 | *John Ramos*(FC) | .15 | .11 |
| 178 Ted Higuera | .06 | .05 | 243 | Scott Sanderson | .05 | .04 |
| 179 Darren Holmes | .04 | .03 | 244 | Steve Sax | .06 | .05 |
| 180 Mark Lee | .04 | .03 | 245 | *Wade Taylor* | .15 | .11 |
| 181 Julio Machado | .04 | .03 | 246 | Randy Velarde | .04 | .03 |
| 182 Paul Molitor | .10 | .08 | 247 | Bernie Williams | .20 | .15 |
| 183 Jaime Navarro | .06 | .04 | 248 | Troy Afenir | .05 | .04 |
| 184 Edwin Nunez | .04 | .03 | 249 | Harold Baines | .08 | .06 |
| 185 Dan Plesac | .05 | .04 | 250 | Lance Blankenship | .04 | .03 |
| 186 Willie Randolph | .05 | .04 | 251 | *Mike Bordick*(FC) | | |
| 187 Ron Robinson | .04 | .03 | | | .10 | .08 |
| 188 Gary Sheffield | .25 | .20 | 252 | Jose Canseco | .25 | .20 |
| 189 Bill Spiers | .05 | .04 | 253 | Steve Chitren | .06 | .05 |
| 190 B.J. Surhoff | .05 | .04 | 254 | Ron Darling | .06 | .05 |
| 191 Dale Sveum | .04 | .03 | 255 | Dennis Eckersley | .08 | .06 |
| 192 Greg Vaughn | .10 | .08 | 256 | Mike Gallego | .04 | .03 |
| 193 Bill Wegman | .05 | .04 | 257 | Dave Henderson | .08 | .06 |
| 194 Robin Yount | .15 | .11 | 258 | Rickey Henderson | .20 | .15 |
| 195 Rick Aguilera | .05 | .04 | 259 | Rick Honeycutt | .04 | .03 |
| 196 Allan Anderson | .04 | .03 | 260 | Brook Jacoby | .06 | .05 |
| 197 Steve Bedrosian | .04 | .03 | 261 | Carney Lansford | .06 | .05 |
| 198 Randy Bush | .04 | .03 | 262 | Mark McGwire | .15 | .11 |
| 199 Larry Casian(FC) | .05 | .04 | 263 | Mike Moore | .05 | .04 |
| 200 Chili Davis | .06 | .05 | 264 | Gene Nelson | .04 | .03 |
| 201 Scott Erickson | .20 | .15 | 265 | Jamie Quirk | .04 | .03 |
| 202 Greg Gagne | .04 | .03 | 266 | *Joe Slusarski*(FC) | | |
| 203 Dan Gladden | .04 | .03 | | | .15 | .11 |
| 204 Brian Harper | .05 | .04 | 267 | Terry Steinbach | .06 | .05 |
| 205 Kent Hrbek | .06 | .05 | 268 | Dave Stewart | .08 | .06 |
| 206 Chuck Knoblauch | .20 | .15 | 269 | Todd Van Poppel(FC) | | |
| 207 Gene Larkin | .04 | .03 | | | .70 | .50 |
| 208 Terry Leach | .04 | .03 | 270 | Walt Weiss | .06 | .05 |
| 209 Scott Leius | .10 | .08 | 271 | Bob Welch | .06 | .05 |
| 210 Shane Mack | .08 | .06 | 272 | Curt Young | .04 | .03 |
| 211 Jack Morris | .08 | .06 | 273 | Scott Bradley | .04 | .03 |
| 212 Pedro Munoz(FC) | .20 | .15 | 274 | Greg Briley | .04 | .03 |
| 213 *Denny Neagle*(FC) | | | 275 | Jay Buhner | .06 | .05 |
| | .20 | .15 | 276 | Henry Cotto | .04 | .03 |
| 214 Al Newman | .04 | .03 | 277 | Alvin Davis | .06 | .05 |
| 215 Junior Ortiz | .04 | .03 | 278 | Rich DeLucia | .06 | .05 |
| 216 Mike Pagliarulo | .04 | .03 | 279 | Ken Griffey, Jr. | .70 | .50 |
| 217 Kirby Puckett | .15 | .11 | 280 | Erik Hanson | .08 | .06 |
| 218 Paul Sorrento | .06 | .05 | 281 | Brian Holman | .05 | .04 |
| 219 Kevin Tapani | .08 | .06 | 282 | Mike Jackson | .04 | .03 |
| 220 Lenny Webster | .06 | .05 | 283 | Randy Johnson | .08 | .06 |
| 221 Jesse Barfield | .06 | .05 | 284 | Tracy Jones | .04 | .03 |
| 222 Greg Cadaret | .04 | .03 | 285 | Bill Krueger | .04 | .03 |
| 223 Dave Eiland | .04 | .03 | 286 | Edgar Martinez | .06 | .05 |
| 224 Alvaro Espinoza | .04 | .03 | 287 | Tino Martinez | .10 | .08 |
| 225 Steve Farr | .05 | .04 | 288 | Rob Murphy | .04 | .03 |

| | | MT | NR MT | | | | MT | NR MT |
|---|---|---|---|---|---|---|---|---|
| 289 | Pete O'Brien | .04 | .03 | | 351 | Rafael Belliard | .04 | .03 |
| 290 | Alonzo Powell | .06 | .05 | | 352 | Juan Berenguer | .04 | .03 |
| 291 | Harold Reynolds | .06 | .05 | | 353 | Jeff Blauser | .05 | .04 |
| 292 | Mike Schooler | .05 | .04 | | 354 | Sid Bream | .05 | .04 |
| 293 | Russ Swan | .04 | .03 | | 355 | Francisco Cabrera | .05 | .04 |
| 294 | Bill Swift | .04 | .03 | | 356 | Marvin Freeman | .04 | .03 |
| 295 | Dave Valle | .04 | .03 | | 357 | Ron Gant | .15 | .11 |
| 296 | Omar Vizquel | .04 | .03 | | 358 | Tom Glavine | .10 | .08 |
| 297 | Gerald Alexander | .05 | .04 | | 359 | *Brian Hunter*(FC) | | |
| 298 | Brad Arnsberg | .05 | .04 | | | | .25 | .20 |
| 299 | Kevin Brown | .05 | .04 | | 360 | Dave Justice | .20 | .15 |
| 300 | Jack Daugherty | .04 | .03 | | 361 | Charlie Leibrandt | .04 | .03 |
| 301 | Mario Diaz | .04 | .03 | | 362 | Mark Lemke | .05 | .04 |
| 302 | Brian Downing | .05 | .04 | | 363 | Kent Mercker | .05 | .04 |
| 303 | Julio Franco | .08 | .06 | | 364 | *Keith Mitchell*(FC) | | |
| 304 | Juan Gonzalez | .25 | .20 | | | | .20 | .15 |
| 305 | Rich Gossage | .05 | .04 | | 365 | Greg Olson | .05 | .04 |
| 306 | Jose Guzman | .05 | .04 | | 366 | Terry Pendleton | .08 | .06 |
| 307 | *Jose Hernandez*(FC) | | | | 367 | *Armando* | | |
| | | .20 | .15 | | | *Reynoso*(FC) | .15 | .11 |
| 308 | Jeff Huson | .05 | .04 | | 368 | Deion Sanders | .15 | .11 |
| 309 | Mike Jeffcoat | .04 | .03 | | 369 | Lonnie Smith | .04 | .03 |
| 310 | *Terry Mathews*(FC) | | | | 370 | Pete Smith | .04 | .03 |
| | | .20 | .15 | | 371 | John Smoltz | .10 | .08 |
| 311 | Rafael Palmeiro | .10 | .08 | | 372 | Mike Stanton | .05 | .04 |
| 312 | Dean Palmer | .20 | .15 | | 373 | Jeff Treadway | .05 | .04 |
| 313 | Geno Petralli | .04 | .03 | | 374 | *Mark Wohlers*(FC) | | |
| 314 | Gary Pettis | .04 | .03 | | | | .25 | .20 |
| 315 | Kevin Reimer | .05 | .04 | | 375 | Paul Assenmacher | .04 | .03 |
| 316 | *Ivan Rodriguez* | .80 | .60 | | 376 | George Bell | .08 | .06 |
| 317 | Kenny Rogers | .05 | .04 | | 377 | Shawn Boskie | .06 | .05 |
| 318 | *Wayne* | | | | 378 | *Frank Castillo*(FC) | | |
| | *Rosenthal*(FC) | .10 | .08 | | | | .25 | .20 |
| 319 | Jeff Russell | .05 | .04 | | 379 | Andre Dawson | .12 | .09 |
| 320 | Nolan Ryan | .25 | .20 | | 380 | Shawon Dunston | .08 | .06 |
| 321 | Ruben Sierra | .15 | .11 | | 381 | Mark Grace | .08 | .06 |
| 322 | Jim Acker | .04 | .03 | | 382 | Mike Harkey | .05 | .04 |
| 323 | Roberto Alomar | .10 | .08 | | 383 | Danny Jackson | .05 | .04 |
| 324 | Derek Bell | .35 | .25 | | 384 | Les Lancaster | .04 | .03 |
| 325 | Pat Borders | .05 | .04 | | 385 | *Cedric Landrum*(FC) | | |
| 326 | Tom Candiotti | .05 | .04 | | | | .15 | .11 |
| 327 | Joe Carter | .08 | .06 | | 386 | Greg Maddux | .06 | .05 |
| 328 | Rob Ducey | .05 | .04 | | 387 | Derrick May | .15 | .11 |
| 329 | Kelly Gruber | .08 | .06 | | 388 | Chuck McElroy | .04 | .03 |
| 330 | *Juan Guzman*(FC) | | | | 389 | Ryne Sandberg | .20 | .15 |
| | | .80 | .60 | | 390 | *Heathcliff Slocumb* | .10 | .08 |
| 331 | Tom Henke | .06 | .05 | | 391 | Dave Smith | .05 | .04 |
| 332 | Jimmy Key | .06 | .05 | | 392 | Dwight Smith | .05 | .04 |
| 333 | Manny Lee | .05 | .04 | | 393 | Rick Sutcliffe | .05 | .04 |
| 334 | Al Leiter | .04 | .03 | | 394 | Hector Villanueva | .06 | .05 |
| 335 | *Bob MacDonald*(FC) | | | | 395 | *Chico Walker*(FC) | | |
| | | .10 | .08 | | | | .10 | .08 |
| 336 | Candy Maldonado | .05 | .04 | | 396 | Jerome Walton | .06 | .05 |
| 337 | Rance Mulliniks | .04 | .03 | | 397 | *Rick Wilkins* | .15 | .11 |
| 338 | Greg Myers | .05 | .04 | | 398 | Jack Armstrong | .06 | .05 |
| 339 | John Olerud | .15 | .11 | | 399 | *Freddie Benavides* | .10 | .08 |
| 340 | *Ed Sprague* | .10 | .08 | | 400 | Glenn Braggs | .05 | .04 |
| 341 | Dave Stieb | .08 | .06 | | 401 | Tom Browning | .06 | .05 |
| 342 | Todd Stottlemyre | .05 | .04 | | 402 | Norm Charlton | .06 | .05 |
| 343 | *Mike Timlin* | .15 | .11 | | 403 | Eric Davis | .12 | .09 |
| 344 | Duane Ward | .05 | .04 | | 404 | Rob Dibble | .08 | .06 |
| 345 | David Wells | .05 | .04 | | 405 | Bill Doran | .05 | .04 |
| 346 | Devon White | .08 | .06 | | 406 | Mariano Duncan | .05 | .04 |
| 347 | Mookie Wilson | .04 | .03 | | 407 | *Kip Gross*(FC) | .10 | .08 |
| 348 | Eddie Zosky | .08 | .06 | | 408 | Chris Hammond | .06 | .05 |
| 349 | Steve Avery | .20 | .15 | | 409 | Billy Hatcher | .04 | .03 |
| 350 | *Mike Bell*(FC) | .08 | .06 | | 410 | *Chris Jones*(FC) | .15 | .11 |

| | | MT | NR MT | | | MT | NR MT |
|---|---|---|---|---|---|---|---|
| 411 | Barry Larkin | .10 | .08 | 475 | Ivan Calderon | .08 | .06 |
| 412 | Hal Morris | .10 | .08 | 476 | Delino DeShields | .08 | .06 |
| 413 | Randy Myers | .05 | .04 | 477 | *Jeff Fassero*(FC) | .10 | .08 |
| 414 | Joe Oliver | .05 | .04 | 478 | Mike Fitzgerald | .04 | .03 |
| 415 | Paul O'Neill | .06 | .05 | 479 | Steve Frey | .04 | .03 |
| 416 | Ted Power | .04 | .03 | 480 | Andres Galarraga | .06 | .05 |
| 417 | Luis Quinones | .04 | .03 | 481 | Mark Gardner | .06 | .05 |
| 418 | Jeff Reed | .04 | .03 | 482 | Marquis Grissom | .12 | .09 |
| 419 | Jose Rijo | .08 | .06 | 483 | *Chris Haney*(FC) | .20 | .15 |
| 420 | Chris Sabo | .08 | .06 | 484 | Barry Jones | .04 | .03 |
| 421 | Reggie Sanders(FC) | .40 | .30 | 485 | Dave Martinez | .05 | .04 |
| 422 | Scott Scudder | .05 | .04 | 486 | Dennis Martinez | .08 | .06 |
| 423 | Glenn Sutko | .05 | .04 | 487 | Chris Nabholz | .06 | .05 |
| 424 | Eric Anthony | .08 | .06 | 488 | Spike Owen | .04 | .03 |
| 425 | *Jeff Bagwell* | .80 | .60 | 489 | Gilberto Reyes | .05 | .04 |
| 426 | Craig Biggio | .08 | .06 | 490 | Mel Rojas | .05 | .04 |
| 427 | Ken Caminiti | .05 | .04 | 491 | Scott Ruskin | .05 | .04 |
| 428 | Casey Candaele | .04 | .03 | 492 | Bill Sampen | .05 | .04 |
| 429 | Mike Capel | .04 | .03 | 493 | Larry Walker | .10 | .08 |
| 430 | Andujar Cedeno | .15 | .11 | 494 | Tim Wallach | .08 | .06 |
| 431 | Jim Corsi | .04 | .03 | 495 | Daryl Boston | .04 | .03 |
| 432 | Mark Davidson | .04 | .03 | 496 | Hubie Brooks | .06 | .05 |
| 433 | Steve Finley | .06 | .05 | 497 | Tim Burke | .05 | .04 |
| 434 | Luis Gonzalez | .20 | .15 | 498 | Mark Carreon | .04 | .03 |
| 435 | Pete Harnisch | .06 | .05 | 499 | Tony Castillo | .04 | .03 |
| 436 | Dwayne Henry | .04 | .03 | 500 | Vince Coleman | .08 | .06 |
| 437 | Xavier Hernandez | .04 | .03 | 501 | David Cone | .08 | .06 |
| 438 | Jimmy Jones | .04 | .03 | 502 | Kevin Elster | .04 | .03 |
| 439 | *Darryl Kile* | .10 | .08 | 503 | Sid Fernandez | .06 | .05 |
| 440 | *Rob Mallicoat*(FC) | | | 504 | John Franco | .06 | .05 |
| | | .15 | .11 | 505 | Dwight Gooden | .12 | .09 |
| 441 | *Andy Mota*(FC) | .15 | .11 | 506 | Todd Hundley | .12 | .09 |
| 442 | Al Osuna | .05 | .04 | 507 | Jeff Innis | .04 | .03 |
| 443 | Mark Portugal | .04 | .03 | 508 | Gregg Jefferies | .12 | .09 |
| 444 | *Scott Servais*(FC) | | | 509 | Howard Johnson | .12 | .09 |
| | | .10 | .08 | 510 | Dave Magadan | .06 | .05 |
| 445 | Mike Simms | .10 | .08 | 511 | *Terry McDaniel*(FC) | | |
| 446 | Gerald Young | .04 | .03 | | | .20 | .15 |
| 447 | Tim Belcher | .06 | .05 | 512 | Kevin McReynolds | .08 | .06 |
| 448 | Brett Butler | .08 | .06 | 513 | Keith Miller | .04 | .03 |
| 449 | John Candelaria | .04 | .03 | 514 | Charlie O'Brien | .04 | .03 |
| 450 | Gary Carter | .08 | .06 | 515 | Mackey Sasser | .04 | .03 |
| 451 | Dennis Cook | .04 | .03 | 516 | *Pete Schourek* | .10 | .08 |
| 452 | Tim Crews | .04 | .03 | 517 | Julio Valera | .06 | .05 |
| 453 | Kal Daniels | .08 | .06 | 518 | Frank Viola | .10 | .08 |
| 454 | Jim Gott | .04 | .03 | 519 | Wally Whitehurst | .05 | .04 |
| 455 | Alfredo Griffin | .04 | .03 | 520 | *Anthony Young*(FC) | | |
| 456 | Kevin Gross | .04 | .03 | | | .20 | .15 |
| 457 | Chris Gwynn | .04 | .03 | 521 | *Andy Ashby* | .10 | .08 |
| 458 | Lenny Harris | .05 | .04 | 522 | *Kim Batiste*(FC) | .10 | .08 |
| 459 | Orel Hershiser | .08 | .06 | 523 | Joe Boever | .04 | .03 |
| 460 | Jay Howell | .05 | .04 | 524 | Wes Chamberlain | .20 | .15 |
| 461 | Stan Javier | .04 | .03 | 525 | Pat Combs | .05 | .04 |
| 462 | Eric Karros(FC) | .50 | .40 | 526 | Danny Cox | .04 | .03 |
| 463 | Ramon Martinez | .12 | .09 | 527 | Darren Daulton | .05 | .04 |
| 464 | Roger McDowell | .05 | .04 | 528 | Jose DeJesus | .05 | .04 |
| 465 | Mike Morgan | .05 | .04 | 529 | Lenny Dykstra | .08 | .06 |
| 466 | Eddie Murray | .12 | .09 | 530 | Darrin Fletcher | .05 | .04 |
| 467 | Jose Offerman | .12 | .09 | 531 | Tommy Greene | .06 | .05 |
| 468 | Bob Ojeda | .05 | .04 | 532 | Jason Grimsley | .05 | .04 |
| 469 | Juan Samuel | .06 | .05 | 533 | Charlie Hayes | .05 | .04 |
| 470 | Mike Scioscia | .06 | .05 | 534 | Von Hayes | .06 | .05 |
| 471 | Darryl Strawberry | .15 | .11 | 535 | Dave Hollins | .08 | .06 |
| 472 | *Bret Barberie*(FC) | | | 536 | Ricky Jordan | .08 | .06 |
| | | .15 | .11 | 537 | John Kruk | .06 | .05 |
| 473 | Brian Barnes | .06 | .05 | 538 | Jim Lindeman | .04 | .03 |
| 474 | Eric Bullock | .04 | .03 | 539 | Mickey Morandini | .08 | .06 |

| | | MT | NR MT |
|---|---|---|---|
| 540 | Terry Mulholland | .06 | .05 |
| 541 | Dale Murphy | .12 | .09 |
| 542 | Randy Ready | .04 | .03 |
| 543 | Wally Ritchie | .04 | .03 |
| 544 | Bruce Ruffin | .04 | .03 |
| 545 | Steve Searcy | .04 | .03 |
| 546 | Dickie Thon | .04 | .03 |
| 547 | Mitch Williams | .08 | .06 |
| 548 | Stan Belinda | .04 | .03 |
| 549 | Jay Bell | .06 | .05 |
| 550 | Barry Bonds | .15 | .11 |
| 551 | Bobby Bonilla | .12 | .09 |
| 552 | Steve Buechele | .05 | .04 |
| 553 | Doug Drabek | .08 | .06 |
| 554 | Neal Heaton | .04 | .03 |
| 555 | Jeff King | .05 | .04 |
| 556 | Bob Kipper | .04 | .03 |
| 557 | Bill Landrum | .04 | .03 |
| 558 | Mike LaValliere | .05 | .04 |
| 559 | Jose Lind | .04 | .03 |
| 560 | Lloyd McClendon | .04 | .03 |
| 561 | Orlando Merced | .25 | .20 |
| 562 | Bob Patterson | .04 | .03 |
| 563 | Joe Redfield(FC) | .10 | .08 |
| 564 | Gary Redus | .04 | .03 |
| 565 | Rosario Rodriguez | .04 | .03 |
| 566 | Don Slaught | .04 | .03 |
| 567 | John Smiley | .06 | .05 |
| 568 | Zane Smith | .05 | .04 |
| 569 | Randy Tomlin | .08 | .06 |
| 570 | Andy Van Slyke | .08 | .06 |
| 571 | Gary Varsho | .04 | .03 |
| 572 | Bob Walk | .04 | .03 |
| 573 | John Wehner(FC) | .25 | .20 |
| 574 | Juan Agosto | .04 | .03 |
| 575 | Cris Carpenter | .05 | .04 |
| 576 | Jose DeLeon | .05 | .04 |
| 577 | Rich Gedman | .04 | .03 |
| 578 | Bernard Gilkey | .10 | .08 |
| 579 | Pedro Guerrero | .08 | .06 |
| 580 | Ken Hill | .05 | .04 |
| 581 | Rex Hudler | .04 | .03 |
| 582 | Felix Jose | .10 | .08 |
| 583 | Ray Lankford | .15 | .11 |
| 584 | Omar Olivares | .06 | .05 |
| 585 | Jose Oquendo | .04 | .03 |
| 586 | Tom Pagnozzi | .05 | .04 |
| 587 | Geronimo Pena | .05 | .04 |
| 588 | Mike Perez | .05 | .04 |
| 589 | Gerald Perry | .04 | .03 |
| 590 | Bryn Smith | .04 | .03 |
| 591 | Lee Smith | .06 | .05 |
| 592 | Ozzie Smith | .12 | .09 |
| 593 | Scott Terry | .04 | .03 |
| 594 | Bob Teksbury | .04 | .03 |
| 595 | Milt Thompson | .04 | .03 |
| 596 | Todd Zeile | .12 | .09 |
| 597 | Larry Andersen | .04 | .03 |
| 598 | Oscar Azocar | .04 | .03 |
| 599 | Andy Benes | .10 | .08 |
| 600 | Ricky Bones(FC) | .10 | .08 |
| 601 | Jerald Clark | .05 | .04 |
| 602 | Pat Clements | .04 | .03 |
| 603 | Paul Faries | .06 | .05 |
| 604 | Tony Fernandez | .06 | .05 |
| 605 | Tony Gwynn | .12 | .09 |

| | | MT | NR MT |
|---|---|---|---|
| 606 | Greg Harris | .05 | .04 |
| 607 | Thomas Howard | .05 | .04 |
| 608 | Bruce Hurst | .06 | .05 |
| 609 | Darrin Jackson | .04 | .03 |
| 610 | Tom Lampkin | .04 | .03 |
| 611 | Craig Lefferts | .04 | .03 |
| 612 | Jim Lewis(FC) | .20 | .15 |
| 613 | Mike Maddux | .04 | .03 |
| 614 | Fred McGriff | .10 | .08 |
| 615 | Jose Melendez(FC) | .20 | .15 |
| 616 | Jose Mota | .15 | .11 |
| 617 | Dennis Rasmussen | .04 | .03 |
| 618 | Bip Roberts | .06 | .05 |
| 619 | Rich Rodriguez | .04 | .03 |
| 620 | Benito Santiago | .08 | .06 |
| 621 | Craig Shipley(FC) | .10 | .08 |
| 622 | Tim Teufel | .04 | .03 |
| 623 | Kevin Ward(FC) | .15 | .11 |
| 624 | Ed Whitson | .05 | .04 |
| 625 | Dave Anderson | .04 | .03 |
| 626 | Kevin Bass | .05 | .04 |
| 627 | Rod Beck(FC) | .10 | .08 |
| 628 | Bud Black | .05 | .04 |
| 629 | Jeff Brantley | .05 | .04 |
| 630 | John Burkett | .05 | .04 |
| 631 | Will Clark | .25 | .20 |
| 632 | Royce Clayton(FC) | .20 | .15 |
| 633 | Steve Decker | .10 | .08 |
| 634 | Kelly Downs | .04 | .03 |
| 635 | Mike Felder | .04 | .03 |
| 636 | Scott Garrelts | .04 | .03 |
| 637 | Eric Gunderson | .08 | .06 |
| 638 | Bryan Hickerson(FC) | .20 | .15 |
| 639 | Darren Lewis | .15 | .11 |
| 640 | Greg Litton | .04 | .03 |
| 641 | Kirt Manwaring | .06 | .05 |
| 642 | Paul McClellan(FC) | .10 | .08 |
| 643 | Willie McGee | .08 | .06 |
| 644 | Kevin Mitchell | .12 | .09 |
| 645 | Francisco Olivares | .04 | .03 |
| 646 | Mike Remlinger(FC) | .10 | .08 |
| 647 | Dave Righetti | .06 | .05 |
| 648 | Robby Thompson | .05 | .04 |
| 649 | Jose Uribe | .04 | .03 |
| 650 | Matt Williams | .12 | .09 |
| 651 | Trevor Wilson | .06 | .05 |
| 652 | Tom Goodwin(FC) | .25 | .20 |
| 653 | Terry Bross(FC) | .08 | .06 |
| 654 | Mike Christopher(FC) | .20 | .15 |
| 655 | Kenny Lofton(FC) | .50 | .40 |
| 656 | Chris Cron(FC) | .20 | .15 |
| 657 | Willie Banks(FC) | .25 | .20 |
| 658 | Pat Rice(FC) | .25 | .20 |
| 659a | Rob Mauer(FC) | 1.25 | .90 |
| 659b | Rob Mauer(FC) | .25 | .20 |
| 660 | Don Harris(FC) | .20 | .15 |
| 661 | Henry Rodriguez(FC) | .10 | .08 |
| 662 | Cliff Brantley(FC) | .20 | .15 |

| | | MT | NR MT |
|---|---|---|---|
| 663 | *Mike Linskey*(FC) | .20 | .15 |
| 664 | Gary Disarcina(FC) | .08 | .06 |
| 665 | Gil Heredia(FC) | .20 | .15 |
| 666 | Vinny Castilla(FC) | .25 | .20 |
| 667 | Paul Abbott(FC) | .08 | .06 |
| 668 | Monty Fariss(FC) | .08 | .06 |
| 669 | *Jarvis Brown*(FC) | .10 | .08 |
| 670 | Wayne Kirby(FC) | .20 | .15 |
| 671 | *Scott Brosius*(FC) | .15 | .11 |
| 672 | Bob Hamelin(FC) | .10 | .08 |
| 673 | *Joel Johnston*(FC) | .20 | .15 |
| 674 | Tim Spehr(FC) | .15 | .11 |
| 675 | *Jeff Gardner*(FC) | .15 | .11 |
| 676 | Rico Rossy(FC) | .20 | .15 |
| 677 | *Roberto Hernandez*(FC) | .20 | .15 |
| 678 | *Ted Wood*(FC) | .25 | .20 |
| 679 | Cal Eldred(FC) | .40 | .30 |
| 680 | Sean Berry(FC) | .08 | .06 |
| 681 | Rickey Henderson (RS) | .15 | .11 |
| 682 | Nolan Ryan (RS) | .20 | .15 |
| 683 | Dennis Martinez (RS) | .05 | .04 |
| 684 | Wilson Alvarez (RS) | .05 | .04 |
| 685 | Joe Carter (RS) | .06 | .05 |
| 686 | Dave Winfield (RS) | .10 | .08 |
| 687 | David Cone (RS) | .06 | .05 |
| 688 | Jose Canseco (LL) | .15 | .11 |
| 689 | Howard Johnson (LL) | .08 | .06 |
| 690 | Julio Franco (LL) | .08 | .06 |
| 691 | Terry Pendleton (LL) | .08 | .06 |
| 692 | Cecil Fielder (LL) | .10 | .08 |
| 693 | Scott Erickson (LL) | .10 | .08 |
| 694 | Tom Glavine (LL) | .08 | .06 |
| 695 | Dennis Martinez (LL) | .05 | .04 |
| 696 | Bryan Harvey (LL) | .05 | .04 |
| 697 | Lee Smith (LL) | .05 | .04 |
| 698 | Super Siblings (Roberto & Sandy Alomar) | .08 | .06 |
| 699 | The Indispensables (Bonilla & Clark) | .10 | .08 |
| 700 | Teamwork (Wohlers, Mercker & Pena) | .06 | .05 |
| 701 | Tiger Tandems (Jones, Jackson, Olson & Thomas) | .20 | .15 |
| 702 | The Ignitors (Molitor & Butler) | .06 | .05 |
| 703 | The Indespensables II (Ripken, Jr. & Carter) | .15 | .11 |
| 704 | Power Packs (Larkin & Puckett) | .10 | .08 |
| 705 | Today & Tomorrow (Vaughn & Fielder) | .15 | .11 |
| 706 | Teenage Sensations (Martinez & Guillen) | .08 | .06 |
| 707 | Designated Hitters (Baines & Boggs) | .08 | .06 |
| 708 | Robin Yount (PV) | .40 | .30 |
| 709 | Ken Griffey, Jr. (PV) | .80 | .60 |
| 710 | Nolan Ryan (PV) | .80 | .60 |
| 711 | Cal Ripken, Jr. (PV) | .70 | .50 |

| | | MT | NR MT |
|---|---|---|---|
| 712 | Frank Thomas (PV) | 1.00 | .70 |
| 713 | Dave Justice (PV) | .70 | .50 |
| 714 | Checklist | .04 | .03 |
| 715 | Checklist | .04 | .03 |
| 716 | Checklist | .04 | .03 |
| 717 | Checklist | .04 | .03 |
| 718 | Checklist | .04 | .03 |
| 719 | Checklist | .04 | .03 |
| 720 | Checklist | .04 | .03 |

## 1992 Fleer Ultra

Fleer released its second consecutive Ultra set in 1992. The card fronts feature full-color action photos with a marble accent at the card bottom. The flip sides are horizontal with two additional player photos. Many subsets including rookies, award winners and others were inserted in the set. A two-card Tony Gwynn send-away set was also available through an offer from Fleer. For $1 and 10 Ultra wrappers, collectors could receive the Gwynn cards. The cards are numbered in order by team.

| | | MT | NR MT |
|---|---|---|---|
| | Complete Set: | 70.00 | 52.00 |
| | Common Player: | .12 | .09 |
| | | | |
| 1 | Glenn Davis | .12 | .09 |
| 2 | Mike Devereaux | .15 | .11 |
| 3 | Dwight Evans | .12 | .09 |
| 4 | Leo Gomez | .30 | .25 |
| 5 | Chris Hoiles | .30 | .25 |
| 6 | Sam Horn | .12 | .09 |
| 7 | Chito Martinez | .15 | .11 |
| 8 | Randy Milligan | .12 | .09 |
| 9 | Mike Mussina | 3.50 | 2.75 |
| 10 | Billy Ripken | .12 | .09 |
| 11 | Cal Ripken | 2.50 | 2.00 |
| 12 | Tom Brunansky | .12 | .09 |
| 13 | Ellis Burks | .15 | .11 |
| 14 | Jack Clark | .12 | .09 |
| 15 | Roger Clemens | 1.50 | 1.25 |
| 16 | Mike Greenwell | .12 | .09 |

| | | MT | NR MT | | | | MT | NR MT |
|---|---|---|---|---|---|---|---|---|
| 17 | Joe Hesketh | .12 | .09 | | 84 | Bill Spiers | .12 | .09 |
| 18 | Tony Pena | .12 | .09 | | 85 | B.J. Surhoff | .12 | .09 |
| 19 | Carlos Quintana | .12 | .09 | | 86 | Greg Vaughn | .30 | .25 |
| 20 | Jeff Reardon | .12 | .09 | | 87 | Robin Yount | .40 | .30 |
| 21 | Jody Reed | .12 | .09 | | 88 | Rick Aguilera | .12 | .09 |
| 22 | Luis Rivera | .12 | .09 | | 89 | Chili Davis | .12 | .09 |
| 23 | Mo Vaughn | .40 | .30 | | 90 | Scott Erickson | .40 | .30 |
| 24 | Gary DiSarcina | .12 | .09 | | 91 | Brian Harper | .12 | .09 |
| 25 | Chuck Finley | .15 | .11 | | 92 | Kent Hrbek | .12 | .09 |
| 26 | Gary Gaetti | .12 | .09 | | 93 | Chuck Knoblauch | 1.00 | .70 |
| 27 | Bryan Harvey | .15 | .11 | | 94 | Scott Leius | .12 | .09 |
| 28 | Lance Parrish | .12 | .09 | | 95 | Shane Mack | .15 | .11 |
| 29 | Luis Polonia | .12 | .09 | | 96 | Mike Pagliarulo | .12 | .09 |
| 30 | Dick Schofield | .12 | .09 | | 97 | Kirby Puckett | 1.50 | 1.25 |
| 31 | Luis Polonia | .12 | .09 | | 98 | Kevin Tapani | .12 | .09 |
| 32 | Wilson Alvarez | .12 | .09 | | 99 | Jesse Barfield | .12 | .09 |
| 33 | Carlton Fisk | .30 | .25 | | 100 | Alvaro Espinoza | .12 | .09 |
| 34 | Craig Grebeck | .12 | .09 | | 101 | Mel Hall | .12 | .09 |
| 35 | Ozzie Guillen | .12 | .09 | | 102 | Pat Kelly | .12 | .09 |
| 36 | Greg Hibbard | .12 | .09 | | 103 | Roberto Kelly | .30 | .25 |
| 37 | Charlie Hough | .12 | .09 | | 104 | Kevin Maas | .12 | .09 |
| 38 | Lance Johnson | .12 | .09 | | 105 | Don Mattingly | .50 | .40 |
| 39 | Ron Karkovice | .12 | .09 | | 106 | Hensley Meulens | .12 | .09 |
| 40 | Jack McDowell | .15 | .11 | | 107 | Matt Nokes | .12 | .09 |
| 41 | Donn Pall | .12 | .09 | | 108 | Steve Sax | .15 | .11 |
| 42 | Melido Perez | .12 | .09 | | 109 | Harold Baines | .15 | .11 |
| 43 | Tim Raines | .15 | .11 | | 110 | Jose Canseco | 2.00 | 1.50 |
| 44 | Frank Thomas | 5.00 | 3.75 | | 111 | Ron Darling | .12 | .09 |
| 45 | Sandy Alomar, Jr. | .15 | .11 | | 112 | Mike Gallego | .12 | .09 |
| 46 | Carlos Baerga | .15 | .11 | | 113 | Dave Henderson | .12 | .09 |
| 47 | Albert Belle | .60 | .45 | | 114 | Rickey Henderson | 1.00 | .70 |
| 48 | Jerry Browne | .12 | .09 | | 115 | Mark McGwire | 1.00 | .70 |
| 49 | Felix Fermin | .12 | .09 | | 116 | Terry Steinbach | .12 | .09 |
| 50 | Reggie Jefferson | .15 | .11 | | 117 | Dave Stewart | .15 | .11 |
| 51 | Mark Lewis | .40 | .30 | | 118 | Todd Van Poppel | 1.00 | .70 |
| 52 | Carlos Martinez | .12 | .09 | | 119 | Bob Welch | .12 | .09 |
| 53 | Steve Olin | .12 | .09 | | 120 | Greg Briley | .12 | .09 |
| 54 | Jim Thome | 1.50 | 1.25 | | 121 | Jay Buhner | .12 | .09 |
| 55 | Mark Whiten | .15 | .11 | | 122 | Rich DeLucia | .12 | .09 |
| 56 | Dave Bergman | .12 | .09 | | 123 | Ken Griffey, Jr. | 4.00 | 3.00 |
| 57 | Milt Cuyler | .12 | .09 | | 124 | Erik Hanson | .12 | .09 |
| 58 | Rob Deer | .12 | .09 | | 125 | Randy Johnson | .12 | .09 |
| 59 | Cecil Fielder | 1.50 | 1.25 | | 126 | Edgar Martinez | .15 | .11 |
| 60 | Travis Fryman | 1.75 | 1.25 | | 127 | Tino Martinez | .15 | .11 |
| 61 | Scott Livingstone | .15 | .11 | | 128 | Pete O'Brien | .12 | .09 |
| 62 | Tony Phillips | .15 | .11 | | 129 | Harold Reynolds | .12 | .09 |
| 63 | Mickey Tettleton | .15 | .11 | | 130 | Dave Valle | .12 | .09 |
| 64 | Alan Trammell | .15 | .11 | | 131 | Julio Franco | .15 | .11 |
| 65 | Lou Whitaker | .15 | .11 | | 132 | Juan Gonzalez | 2.00 | 1.50 |
| 66 | Kevin Appier | .15 | .11 | | 133 | Jeff Huson | .12 | .09 |
| 67 | Mike Boddicker | .12 | .09 | | 134 | Mike Jeffcoat | .12 | .09 |
| 68 | George Brett | .40 | .30 | | 135 | Terry Mathews | .12 | .09 |
| 69 | Jim Eisenreich | .12 | .09 | | 136 | Rafael Palmeiro | .30 | .25 |
| 70 | Mark Gubicza | .12 | .09 | | 137 | Dean Palmer | 1.00 | .70 |
| 71 | David Howard | .12 | .09 | | 138 | Geno Petralli | .12 | .09 |
| 72 | Joel Johnston | .12 | .09 | | 139 | Ivan Rodriguez | 2.00 | 1.50 |
| 73 | Mike Macfarlane | .12 | .09 | | 140 | Jeff Russell | .12 | .09 |
| 74 | Brent Mayne | .12 | .09 | | 141 | Nolan Ryan | 3.00 | 2.25 |
| 75 | Brian McRae | .30 | .25 | | 142 | Ruben Sierra | 1.00 | .70 |
| 76 | Jeff Montgomery | .12 | .09 | | 143 | Roberto Alomar | 1.00 | .70 |
| 77 | Danny Tartabull | .15 | .11 | | 144 | Pat Borders | .12 | .09 |
| 78 | Danny Tartabull | .30 | .25 | | 145 | Joe Carter | .30 | .25 |
| 79 | Dante Bichette | .12 | .09 | | 146 | Kelly Gruber | .12 | .09 |
| 80 | Ted Higuera | .12 | .09 | | 147 | Jimmy Key | .12 | .09 |
| 81 | Paul Molitor | .15 | .11 | | 148 | Manny Lee | .12 | .09 |
| 82 | Jamie Navarro | .15 | .11 | | 149 | Rance Mulliniks | .12 | .09 |
| 83 | Gary Sheffield | 1.50 | 1.25 | | 150 | Greg Myers | .12 | .09 |

| | MT | NR MT | | | MT | NR MT |
|---|---|---|---|---|---|---|
| 151 | John Olerud | .30 | .25 | 219 | Darryl Strawberry | 1.00 | .70 |
| 152 | Dave Stieb | .12 | .09 | 220 | Delino DeShields | .15 | .11 |
| 153 | Todd Stottlemyre | .12 | .09 | 221 | Tom Foley | .12 | .09 |
| 154 | Duane Ward | .12 | .09 | 222 | Steve Frey | .12 | .09 |
| 155 | Devon White | .12 | .09 | 223 | Dennis Martinez | .12 | .09 |
| 156 | Eddie Zosky | .15 | .11 | 224 | Spike Owen | .12 | .09 |
| 157 | Steve Avery | 1.00 | .70 | 225 | Gilberto Reyes | .12 | .09 |
| 158 | Rafael Belliard | .12 | .09 | 226 | Tim Wallach | .12 | .09 |
| 159 | Jeff Blauser | .12 | .09 | 227 | Daryl Boston | .12 | .09 |
| 160 | Mark Lemke | .12 | .09 | 228 | Tim Burke | .12 | .09 |
| 161 | Ron Gant | .60 | .45 | 229 | Vince Coleman | .12 | .09 |
| 162 | Tom Glavine | .50 | .40 | 230 | David Cone | .15 | .11 |
| 163 | Brian Hunter | .30 | .25 | 231 | Kevin Elster | .12 | .09 |
| 164 | Dave Justice | 2.00 | 1.50 | 232 | Dwight Gooden | .40 | .30 |
| 166 | Greg Olson | .12 | .09 | 233 | Todd Hundley | .15 | .11 |
| 167 | Terry Pendleton | .15 | .11 | 234 | Jeff Innis | .12 | .09 |
| 168 | Lonnie Smith | .12 | .09 | 235 | Howard Johnson | .15 | .11 |
| 169 | John Smoltz | .15 | .11 | 236 | Dave Magadan | .12 | .09 |
| 170 | Mike Stanton | .12 | .09 | 237 | Mackey Sasser | .12 | .09 |
| 171 | Jeff Treadway | .12 | .09 | 238 | Anthony Young | .40 | .30 |
| 172 | Paul Assenmacher | .12 | .09 | 239 | Wes Chamberlain, Wes | | |
| 173 | George Bell | .15 | .11 | | Chamberlain | .15 | .11 |
| 174 | Shawon Dunston | .12 | .09 | 240 | Darren Daulton | .15 | .11 |
| 175 | Mark Grace | .30 | .25 | 241 | Lenny Dykstra | .15 | .11 |
| 176 | Danny Jackson | .12 | .09 | 242 | Tommy Greene | .12 | .09 |
| 177 | Les Lancaster | .12 | .09 | 243 | Charlie Hayes | .12 | .09 |
| 178 | Greg Maddux | .15 | .11 | 244 | Dave Hollins | .15 | .11 |
| 179 | Luis Salazar | .12 | .09 | 245 | Ricky Jordan | .15 | .11 |
| 180 | Rey Sanchez | .15 | .11 | 246 | John Kruk | .15 | .11 |
| 181 | Ryne Sandberg | 1.50 | 1.25 | 247 | Mickey Morandini | .15 | .11 |
| 182 | Jose Vizcaino | .12 | .09 | 248 | Terry Mulholland | .12 | .09 |
| 183 | Chico Walker | .12 | .09 | 249 | Dale Murphy | .15 | .11 |
| 184 | Jerome Walton | .12 | .09 | 250 | Jay Bell | .15 | .11 |
| 185 | Glenn Braggs | .12 | .09 | 251 | Barry Bonds | 1.00 | .70 |
| 186 | Tom Browning | .12 | .09 | 252 | Steve Buechele | .12 | .09 |
| 187 | Rob Dibble | .15 | .11 | 253 | Doug Drabek | .15 | .11 |
| 188 | Bill Doran | .12 | .09 | 254 | Mike LaValliere | .12 | .09 |
| 189 | Chris Hammond | .15 | .11 | 255 | Jose Lind | .12 | .09 |
| 190 | Billy Hatcher | .12 | .09 | 256 | Lloyd McClendon | .12 | .09 |
| 191 | Barry Larkin | .40 | .30 | 257 | Orlando Merced | .30 | .25 |
| 192 | Hal Morris | .15 | .11 | 258 | Don Slaught | .12 | .09 |
| 193 | Joe Oliver | .12 | .09 | 259 | John Smiley | .12 | .09 |
| 194 | Paul O'Neill | .12 | .09 | 260 | Zane Smith | .12 | .09 |
| 195 | Jeff Reed | .12 | .09 | 261 | Randy Tomlin | .30 | .25 |
| 196 | Jose Rijo | .12 | .09 | 262 | Andy Van Slyke | .15 | .11 |
| 197 | Chris Sabo | .15 | .11 | 263 | Pedro Guererro | .15 | .11 |
| 198 | Jeff Bagwell | 2.00 | 1.50 | 264 | Felix Jose | .30 | .25 |
| 199 | Craig Biggio | .15 | .11 | 265 | Ray Lankford | .80 | .60 |
| 200 | Ken Caminiti | .12 | .09 | 266 | Omar Olivares | .12 | .09 |
| 201 | Andujar Cedeno | .15 | .11 | 267 | Jose Oquendo | .12 | .09 |
| 202 | Steve Finley | .15 | .11 | 268 | Tom Pagnozzi | .12 | .09 |
| 203 | Luis Gonzalez | .15 | .11 | 269 | Bryn Smith | .12 | .09 |
| 204 | Pete Harnisch | .15 | .11 | 270 | Lee Smith | .12 | .09 |
| 205 | Xavier Hernandez | .12 | .09 | 271 | Ozzie Smith | .50 | .40 |
| 206 | Darryl Kile | .12 | .09 | 272 | Milt Thompson | .12 | .09 |
| 207 | Al Osuna | .12 | .09 | 273 | Todd Zeile | .12 | .09 |
| 208 | Curt Schilling | .12 | .09 | 274 | Andy Benes | .40 | .30 |
| 209 | Brett Butler | .12 | .09 | 275 | Jerald Clark | .12 | .09 |
| 210 | Kal Daniels | .12 | .09 | 276 | Tony Fernandez | .12 | .09 |
| 211 | Lenny Harris | .12 | .09 | 277 | Tony Gwynn | 1.00 | .70 |
| 212 | Stan Javier | .12 | .09 | 278 | Greg Harris | .12 | .09 |
| 213 | Ramon Martinez | .15 | .11 | 279 | Thomas Howard | .12 | .09 |
| 214 | Roger McDowell | .12 | .09 | 280 | Bruce Hurst | .12 | .09 |
| 215 | Jose Offerman | .12 | .09 | 281 | Mike Maddux | .12 | .09 |
| 216 | Juan Samuel | .12 | .09 | 282 | Fred McGriff | .35 | .25 |
| 217 | Mike Scioscia | .12 | .09 | 283 | Benito Santiago | .15 | .11 |
| 218 | Mike Sharperson | .12 | .09 | 284 | Kevin Bass | .12 | .09 |

| | | MT | NR MT | | | | MT | NR MT |
|---|---|---|---|---|---|---|---|---|
| 285 | Jeff Brantley | .12 | .09 | | 352 | Rod Nichols | .12 | .09 |
| 286 | John Burkett | .12 | .09 | | 353 | Junior Ortiz | .12 | .09 |
| 287 | Will Clark | 2.00 | 1.50 | | 354 | Dave Otto | .12 | .09 |
| 288 | Royce Clayton | .60 | .45 | | 355 | Tony Perezchica | .12 | .09 |
| 289 | Steve Decker | .12 | .09 | | 356 | Scott Scudder | .12 | .09 |
| 290 | Kelly Downs | .12 | .09 | | 357 | Paul Sorrento | .12 | .09 |
| 291 | Mike Felder | .12 | .09 | | 358 | Skeeter Barnes | .12 | .09 |
| 292 | Darren Lewis | .40 | .30 | | 359 | Mark Carreon | .12 | .09 |
| 293 | Kirt Manwaring | .12 | .09 | | 360 | John Doherty | .12 | .09 |
| 294 | Willie McGee | .12 | .09 | | 361 | Dan Gladden | .12 | .09 |
| 295 | Robby Thompson | .12 | .09 | | 362 | Bill Gullickson | .20 | .15 |
| 296 | Matt Williams | .40 | .30 | | 363 | Shawn Hare | .15 | .11 |
| 297 | Trevor Wilson | .12 | .09 | | 364 | Mike Henneman | .20 | .15 |
| 298 | Checklist | .10 | .08 | | 365 | Chad Kreuter | .12 | .09 |
| 299 | Checklist | .10 | .08 | | 366 | Mark Leiter | .12 | .09 |
| 300 | Checklist | .10 | .08 | | 367 | Mike Munoz | .12 | .09 |
| 301 | Brady Anderson | .20 | .15 | | 368 | Kevin Ritz | .12 | .09 |
| 302 | Todd Frohwirth | .12 | .09 | | 369 | Mark Davis | .12 | .09 |
| 303 | Ben McDonald | .30 | .25 | | 370 | Tom Gordon | .12 | .09 |
| 304 | Mark McLemore | .12 | .09 | | 371 | Tony Gwynn | .12 | .09 |
| 305 | Jose Mesa | .12 | .09 | | 372 | Gregg Jefferies | .25 | .20 |
| 306 | Bob Milacki | .12 | .09 | | 373 | Wally Joyner | .40 | .30 |
| 307 | Gregg Olson | .20 | .15 | | 374 | Kevin McReynolds | .20 | .15 |
| 308 | David Segui | .12 | .09 | | 375 | Keith Miller | .12 | .09 |
| 309 | Rick Sutcliffe | .20 | .15 | | 376 | Rico Rossy | .25 | .20 |
| 310 | Jeff Tackett | .20 | .15 | | 377 | Curtis Wilkerson | .12 | .09 |
| 311 | Wade Boggs | .50 | .40 | | 378 | Ricky Bones | .12 | .09 |
| 312 | Scott Cooper | .20 | .15 | | 379 | Chris Bosio | .12 | .09 |
| 313 | John Flaherty | .25 | .20 | | 380 | Cal Eldred | 2.00 | 1.50 |
| 314 | Wayne Housie | .20 | .15 | | 381 | Scott Fletcher | .12 | .09 |
| 315 | Peter Hoy | .20 | .15 | | 382 | Jim Gantner | .12 | .09 |
| 316 | John Marzano | .12 | .09 | | 383 | Darryl Hamilton | .12 | .09 |
| 317 | Tim Naehring | .20 | .15 | | 384 | Doug Henry | .25 | .20 |
| 318 | Phil Plantier | .60 | .45 | | 385 | Pat Listach | 4.00 | 3.00 |
| 319 | Frank Viola | .40 | .30 | | 386 | Tim McIntosh | .12 | .09 |
| 320 | Matt Young | .12 | .09 | | 387 | Edwin Nunez | .12 | .09 |
| 321 | Jim Abbott | .40 | .30 | | 388 | Dan Plesac | .12 | .09 |
| 322 | Hubie Brooks | .12 | .09 | | 389 | Kevin Seitzer | .12 | .09 |
| 323 | Chad Curtis | .35 | .25 | | 390 | Franklin Stubbs | .12 | .09 |
| 324 | Alvin Davis | .12 | .09 | | 391 | William Suero | .25 | .20 |
| 325 | Junior Felix | .20 | .15 | | 392 | Bill Wegman | .12 | .09 |
| 326 | Von Hayes | .12 | .09 | | 393 | Willie Banks | .12 | .09 |
| 327 | Mark Langston | .30 | .25 | | 394 | Jarvis Brown | .20 | .15 |
| 328 | Scott Lewis | .12 | .09 | | 395 | Greg Gagne | .12 | .09 |
| 329 | Don Robinson | .12 | .09 | | 396 | Mark Guthrie | .12 | .09 |
| 330 | Bobby Rose | .12 | .09 | | 397 | Bill Krueger | .12 | .09 |
| 331 | Lee Stevens | .12 | .09 | | 398 | Pat Mahomes | .50 | .40 |
| 332 | George Bell | .30 | .25 | | 399 | Pedro Munoz | .50 | .40 |
| 333 | Esteban Beltre | .12 | .09 | | 400 | John Smiley | .12 | .09 |
| 334 | Joey Cora | .12 | .09 | | 401 | Gary Wayne | .12 | .09 |
| 335 | Alex Fernandez | .40 | .30 | | 402 | Lenny Webster | .12 | .09 |
| 336 | Roberto Hernandez | .15 | .11 | | 403 | Carl Willis | .12 | .09 |
| 337 | Mike Huff | .12 | .09 | | 404 | Greg Cadaret | .12 | .09 |
| 338 | Kirk McCaskill | .12 | .09 | | 405 | Steve Farr | .12 | .09 |
| 339 | Dan Pasqua | .12 | .09 | | 406 | Mike Gallego | .12 | .09 |
| 340 | Scott Radinsky | .12 | .09 | | 407 | Charlie Hayes | .12 | .09 |
| 341 | Steve Sax | .20 | .15 | | 408 | Steve Howe | .12 | .09 |
| 342 | Bobby Thigpen | .30 | .25 | | 409 | Dion James | .12 | .09 |
| 343 | Robin Ventura | 1.00 | .70 | | 410 | Jeff Johnson | .12 | .09 |
| 344 | Jack Armstrong | .12 | .09 | | 411 | Tim Leary | .12 | .09 |
| 345 | Alex Cole | .12 | .09 | | 412 | Jim Leyritz | .12 | .09 |
| 346 | Dennis Cook | .12 | .09 | | 413 | Melido Perez | .12 | .09 |
| 347 | Glenallen Hill | .12 | .09 | | 414 | Scott Sanderson | .12 | .09 |
| 348 | Thomas Howard | .12 | .09 | | 415 | Andy Stankiewicz | .35 | .25 |
| 349 | Brook Jacoby | .12 | .09 | | 416 | Mike Stanley | .12 | .09 |
| 350 | Kenny Lofton | 2.00 | 1.50 | | 417 | Danny Tartabull | .40 | .30 |
| 351 | Charles Nagy | .50 | .40 | | 418 | Lance Blankenship | .12 | .09 |

| | MT | NR MT | | | MT | NR MT |
|---|---|---|---|---|---|---|
| 419 | Mike Bordick | .20 | .15 | 487 | Greg Swindell | .15 | .11 |
| 420 | Scott Brosius | .12 | .09 | 488 | Ryan Bowen | .25 | .20 |
| 421 | Dennis Eckersley | .35 | .25 | 489 | Casey Candaele | .12 | .09 |
| 422 | Scott Hemond | .12 | .09 | 490 | Juan Guerrero | .25 | .20 |
| 423 | Carney Lansford | .12 | .09 | 491 | Pete Incaviglia | .12 | .09 |
| 424 | Henry Mercedes | .25 | .20 | 492 | Jeff Juden | .20 | .15 |
| 425 | Mike Moore | .12 | .09 | 493 | Rob Murphy | .12 | .09 |
| 426 | Gene Nelson | .12 | .09 | 494 | Mark Portugal | .12 | .09 |
| 427 | Randy Ready | .12 | .09 | 495 | Rafael Ramirez | .12 | .09 |
| 428 | Bruce Wilson | .20 | .15 | 496 | Scott Servais | .12 | .09 |
| 429 | Willie Wilson | .12 | .09 | 497 | Ed Taubensee | .35 | .25 |
| 430 | Rich Amaral | .20 | .15 | 498 | Brian Williams | .30 | .25 |
| 431 | Dave Cochrane | .12 | .09 | 499 | Todd Benzinger | .12 | .09 |
| 432 | Henry Cotto | .12 | .09 | 500 | John Candelaria | .12 | .09 |
| 433 | Calvin Jones | .20 | .15 | 501 | Tom Candiotti | .12 | .09 |
| 434 | Kevin Mitchell | .25 | .20 | 502 | Tim Crews | .12 | .09 |
| 435 | Clay Parker | .12 | .09 | 503 | Eric Davis | .50 | .40 |
| 436 | Omar Vizquel | .12 | .09 | 504 | Jim Gott | .12 | .09 |
| 437 | Floyd Bannister | .12 | .09 | 505 | Dave Hansen | .12 | .09 |
| 438 | Kevin Brown | .12 | .09 | 506 | Carlos Hernandez | .12 | .09 |
| 439 | John Cangelosi | .12 | .09 | 507 | Orel Hershiser | .30 | .25 |
| 440 | Brian Downing | .12 | .09 | 508 | Eric Karros | 3.00 | 1.50 |
| 441 | Monty Fariss | .12 | .09 | 509 | Bob Ojeda | .12 | .09 |
| 443 | Donald Harris | .25 | .20 | 510 | Steve Wilson | .12 | .09 |
| 444 | Kevin Reimer | .12 | .09 | 511 | Moises Alou | .15 | .11 |
| 445 | Kenny Rogers | .12 | .09 | 512 | Bret Barberie | .20 | .15 |
| 446 | Wayne Rosenthal | .12 | .09 | 513 | Ivan Calderon | .25 | .20 |
| 447 | Dickie Thon | .12 | .09 | 514 | Gary Carter | .25 | .20 |
| 448 | Derek Bell | .50 | .40 | 515 | Archi Cianfrocco | .60 | .45 |
| 449 | Juan Guzman | 4.00 | 3.00 | 516 | Jeff Fassero | .12 | .09 |
| 450 | Tom Henke | .12 | .09 | 517 | Darrin Fletcher | .12 | .09 |
| 451 | Candy Maldonado | .12 | .09 | 518 | Marquis Grissom | .30 | .25 |
| 452 | Jack Morris | .30 | .25 | 519 | Chris Haney | .20 | .15 |
| 453 | David Wells | .12 | .09 | 520 | Ken Hill | .15 | .11 |
| 454 | Dave Winfield | .50 | .40 | 521 | Chris Nabholz | .12 | .09 |
| 455 | Juan Berenguer | .12 | .09 | 522 | Bill Sampen | .12 | .09 |
| 456 | Damon Berryhill | .12 | .09 | 523 | John VanderWal | .30 | .25 |
| 457 | Mike Bielecki | .12 | .09 | 524 | David Wainhouse | .25 | .20 |
| 458 | Marvin Freeman | .12 | .09 | 525 | Larry Walker | .25 | .20 |
| 459 | Charlie Leibrandt | .12 | .09 | 526 | John Wetteland | .15 | .11 |
| 460 | Kent Mercker | .12 | .09 | 527 | Bobby Bonilla | .80 | .60 |
| 461 | Otis Nixon | .15 | .11 | 528 | Sid Fernandez | .15 | .11 |
| 462 | Alejandro Pena | .12 | .09 | 529 | John Franco | .12 | .09 |
| 463 | Ben Rivera | .15 | .11 | 530 | Dave Gallagher | .12 | .09 |
| 464 | Deion Sanders | .50 | .40 | 531 | Paul Gibson | .12 | .09 |
| 465 | Mark Wohlers | .30 | .25 | 532 | Eddie Murray | .50 | .40 |
| 466 | Shawn Boskie | .12 | .09 | 533 | Junior Noboa | .12 | .09 |
| 467 | Frank Castillo | .12 | .09 | 534 | Charlie O'Brien | .12 | .09 |
| 468 | Andre Dawson | .40 | .30 | 535 | Bill Pecota | .12 | .09 |
| 469 | Joe Girardi | .12 | .09 | 536 | Willie Randolph | .12 | .09 |
| 470 | Chuck McElroy | .12 | .09 | 537 | Bret Saberhagen | .25 | .20 |
| 471 | Mike Morgan | .12 | .09 | 538 | Dick Schofield | .12 | .09 |
| 472 | Ken Patterson | .12 | .09 | 539 | Pete Schourek | .12 | .09 |
| 473 | Bob Scanlan | .12 | .09 | 540 | Ruben Amaro | .20 | .15 |
| 474 | Gary Scott | .25 | .20 | 541 | Andy Ashby | .12 | .09 |
| 475 | Dave Smith | .12 | .09 | 542 | Kim Batiste | .25 | .20 |
| 476 | Sammy Sosa | .20 | .15 | 543 | Cliff Brantley | .20 | .15 |
| 477 | Hector Villanueva | .12 | .09 | 544 | Mariano Duncan | .12 | .09 |
| 478 | Scott Bankhead | .12 | .09 | 545 | Jeff Grotewold | .20 | .15 |
| 479 | Tim Belcher | .12 | .09 | 546 | Barry Jones | .12 | .09 |
| 480 | Freddie Benavides | .15 | .11 | 547 | Julio Peguero | .20 | .15 |
| 481 | Jacob Brumfield | .25 | .20 | 548 | Curt Schilling | .12 | .09 |
| 482 | Norm Charlton | .15 | .11 | 549 | Mitch Williams | .20 | .15 |
| 483 | Dwayne Henry | .12 | .09 | 550 | Stan Belinda | .12 | .09 |
| 484 | Dave Martinez | .12 | .09 | 551 | Scott Bullett | .20 | .15 |
| 485 | Bip Roberts | .15 | .11 | 552 | Cecil Espy | .12 | .09 |
| 486 | Reggie Sanders | 1.50 | 1.25 | 553 | Jeff King | .12 | .09 |

| | MT | NR MT |
|---|---|---|
| 554 Roger Mason | .12 | .09 |
| 555 Paul Miller | .20 | .15 |
| 556 Denny Neagle | .20 | .15 |
| 557 Vocente Palacios | .12 | .09 |
| 558 Bob Patterson | .12 | .09 |
| 559 Tom Prince | .12 | .09 |
| 560 Gary Redus | .12 | .09 |
| 561 Gary Varsho | .12 | .09 |
| 562 Juan Agosto | .12 | .09 |
| 563 Cris Carpenter | .12 | .09 |
| 564 Mark Clark | .20 | .15 |
| 565 Jose DeLeon | .12 | .09 |
| 566 Rich Gedman | .12 | .09 |
| 567 Bernard Gilkey | .15 | .11 |
| 568 Rex Hudler | .12 | .09 |
| 569 Tim Jones | .12 | .09 |
| 570 Donovan Osborne | .60 | .45 |
| 571 Mike Perez | .12 | .09 |
| 572 Gerald Perry | .12 | .09 |
| 573 Bob Tewksbury | .15 | .11 |
| 574 Todd Worrell | .12 | .09 |
| 575 Dave Eiland | .12 | .09 |
| 576 Jeremy Hernandez | .20 | .15 |
| 577 Craig Lefferts | .12 | .09 |
| 578 Jose Melendez | .12 | .09 |
| 579 Randy Myers | .12 | .09 |
| 580 Gary Pettis | .12 | .09 |
| 581 Rich Rodriguez | .12 | .09 |
| 582 Gary Sheffield | 1.00 | .70 |
| 583 Craig Shipley | .12 | .09 |
| 584 Kurt Stillwell | .12 | .09 |
| 585 Tim Teufel | .12 | .09 |
| 586 Rod Beck | .20 | .15 |
| 587 Dave Burba | .12 | .09 |
| 588 Craig Colbert | .20 | .15 |
| 589 Bryan Hickerson | .12 | .09 |
| 590 Mike Jackson | .12 | .09 |
| 591 Mark Leonard | .12 | .09 |
| 592 Jim McNamara | .25 | .20 |
| 593 John Patterson | .20 | .15 |
| 594 Dave Righetti | .12 | .09 |
| 595 Cory Snyder | .12 | .09 |
| 596 Bill Swift | .20 | .15 |
| 597 Ted Wood | .15 | .11 |
| 598 Checklist | .10 | .08 |
| 599 Checklist | .10 | .08 |
| 600 Checklist | .10 | .08 |

## 1993 Fleer Series I

Fleer introduced a two series format in 1993. Series one featured cards 1-343. The card fronts feature silver borders with the player's name, team and position in a banner along the left side of the card. The Fleer logo appears in the lower right corner. The backs feature an action photo of the player with his name in bold behind him. A box featuring biographical information, statistics and player information is located to the right of the action photo. The cards are numbered alphabetically by team.

| | | MT | NR MT |
|---|---|---|---|
| Complete Set: | | 15.00 | 11.00 |
| Common Player: | | .04 | .03 |
| 1 | Steve Avery | .10 | .08 |
| 2 | Sid Bream | .04 | .03 |
| 3 | Ron Gant | .08 | .06 |
| 4 | Tom Glavine | .10 | .08 |
| 5 | Brian Hunter | .08 | .06 |
| 6 | Ryan Klesko(FC) | .15 | .11 |
| 7 | Charlie Leibrandt | .04 | .03 |
| 8 | Kent Mercker | .04 | .03 |
| 9 | *David Nied*(FC) | .25 | .20 |
| 10 | Otis Nixon | .06 | .05 |
| 11 | Greg Olson | .04 | .03 |
| 12 | Terry Pendleton | .08 | .06 |
| 13 | Deion Sanders | .15 | .11 |
| 14 | John Smoltz | .08 | .06 |
| 15 | Mike Stanton | .04 | .03 |
| 16 | Mark Wohlers | .08 | .06 |
| 17 | Paul Assenmacher | .04 | .03 |
| 18 | Steve Buechele | .04 | .03 |
| 19 | Shawon Dunston | .06 | .05 |
| 20 | Mark Grace | .08 | .06 |
| 21 | Derrick May | .10 | .08 |
| 22 | Chuck McElroy | .04 | .03 |
| 23 | Mike Morgan | .06 | .05 |
| 24 | Rey Sanchez | .10 | .08 |
| 25 | Ryne Sandberg | .12 | .09 |
| 26 | Bob Scanlan | .04 | .03 |
| 27 | Sammy Sosa | .06 | .05 |
| 28 | Rick Wilkins | .06 | .05 |
| 29 | *Bobby Ayala*(FC) | .15 | .11 |
| 30 | Tim Belcher | .06 | .05 |
| 31 | *Jeff Branson*(FC) | .12 | .09 |
| 32 | Norm Charlton | .08 | .06 |
| 33 | *Steve Foster*(FC) | .12 | .09 |
| 34 | Willie Greene(FC) | .12 | .09 |
| 35 | Chris Hammond | .06 | .05 |
| 36 | Milt Hill(FC) | .10 | .08 |
| 37 | Hal Morris | .06 | .05 |
| 38 | Joe Oliver | .06 | .05 |
| 39 | Paul O'Neill | .06 | .05 |
| 40 | *Tim Pugh*(FC) | .12 | .09 |
| 41 | Jose Rijo | .08 | .06 |
| 42 | Bip Roberts | .08 | .06 |
| 43 | Chris Sabo | .08 | .06 |
| 44 | Reggie Sanders | .15 | .11 |
| 45 | Eric Anthony | .08 | .06 |
| 46 | Jeff Bagwell | .12 | .09 |
| 47 | Craig Biggio | .08 | .06 |

| | | MT | NR MT | | | | MT | NR MT |
|---|---|---|---|---|---|---|---|---|
| 48 | Joe Boever | .04 | .03 | | 113 | Jeff King | .05 | .04 |
| 49 | Casey Candaele | .04 | .03 | | 114 | Mike LaValliere | .04 | .03 |
| 50 | Steve Finley | .06 | .05 | | 115 | Jose Lind | .04 | .03 |
| 51 | Luis Gonzalez | .08 | .06 | | 116 | Roger Mason | .04 | .03 |
| 52 | Pete Harnisch | .08 | .06 | | 117 | Orlando Merced | .06 | .05 |
| 53 | Xavier Hernandez | .04 | .03 | | 118 | Bob Patterson | .04 | .03 |
| 54 | Doug Jones | .05 | .04 | | 119 | Don Slaught | .04 | .03 |
| 55 | Eddie Taubensee | .08 | .06 | | 120 | Zane Smith | .05 | .04 |
| 56 | Brian Williams | .08 | .06 | | 121 | Randy Tomlin | .06 | .05 |
| 57 | *Pedro Astacio*(FC) | | | | 122 | Andy Van Slyke | .08 | .06 |
| | | .20 | .15 | | 123 | *Tim Wakefield* | .15 | .11 |
| 58 | Todd Benzinger | .04 | .03 | | 124 | Rheal Cormier | .08 | .06 |
| 59 | Brett Butler | .06 | .05 | | 125 | Bernard Gilkey | .08 | .06 |
| 60 | Tom Candiotti | .06 | .05 | | 126 | Felix Jose | .08 | .06 |
| 61 | Lenny Harris | .04 | .03 | | 127 | Ray Lankford | .12 | .09 |
| 62 | Carlos Hernandez | .08 | .06 | | 128 | Bob McClure | .04 | .03 |
| 63 | Orel Hershiser | .08 | .06 | | 129 | Donovan Osborne | .10 | .08 |
| 64 | Eric Karros | .15 | .11 | | 130 | Tom Pagnozzi | .06 | .05 |
| 65 | Ramon Martinez | .08 | .06 | | 131 | Geronimo Pena | .06 | .05 |
| 66 | Jose Offerman | .06 | .05 | | 132 | Mike Perez | .06 | .05 |
| 67 | Mike Scioscia | .04 | .03 | | 133 | Lee Smith | .06 | .05 |
| 68 | Mike Sharperson | .04 | .03 | | 134 | Bob Tewksbury | .06 | .05 |
| 69 | *Eric Young*(FC) | .15 | .11 | | 135 | Todd Worrell | .06 | .05 |
| 70 | Moises Alou | .08 | .06 | | 136 | Todd Zeile | .08 | .06 |
| 71 | Ivan Calderon | .08 | .06 | | 137 | Jerald Clark | .05 | .04 |
| 72 | *Archi Cianfrocco* | .15 | .11 | | 138 | Tony Gwynn | .12 | .09 |
| 73 | Wil Cordero | .10 | .08 | | 139 | Greg Harris | .04 | .03 |
| 74 | Delino DeShields | .08 | .06 | | 140 | Jeremy Hernandez | .05 | .04 |
| 75 | Mark Gardner | .05 | .04 | | 141 | Darrin Jackson | .05 | .04 |
| 76 | Ken Hill | .08 | .06 | | 142 | Mike Maddux | .04 | .03 |
| 77 | *Tim Laker*(FC) | .15 | .11 | | 143 | Fred McGriff | .10 | .08 |
| 78 | Chris Nabholz | .06 | .05 | | 144 | Jose Melendez | .08 | .06 |
| 79 | Mel Rojas | .04 | .03 | | 145 | Rich Rodriguez | .04 | .03 |
| 80 | *John Vander Wal* | .12 | .09 | | 146 | Frank Seminara | .08 | .06 |
| 81 | Larry Walker | .10 | .08 | | 147 | Gary Sheffield | .12 | .09 |
| 82 | Tim Wallach | .06 | .05 | | 148 | Kurt Stillwell | .05 | .04 |
| 83 | John Wetteland | .08 | .06 | | 149 | *Dan Walters* | .10 | .08 |
| 84 | Bobby Bonilla | .12 | .09 | | 150 | Rod Beck | .06 | .05 |
| 85 | Daryl Boston | .04 | .03 | | 151 | Bud Black | .04 | .03 |
| 86 | Sid Fernandez | .08 | .06 | | 152 | Jeff Brantley | .05 | .04 |
| 87 | *Eric Hillman*(FC) | .12 | .09 | | 153 | John Burkett | .05 | .04 |
| 88 | Todd Hundley | .08 | .06 | | 154 | Will Clark | .15 | .11 |
| 89 | Howard Johnson | .08 | .06 | | 155 | Royce Clayton | .08 | .06 |
| 90 | *Jeff Kent* | .15 | .11 | | 156 | Mike Jackson | .04 | .03 |
| 91 | Eddie Murray | .10 | .08 | | 157 | Darren Lewis | .08 | .06 |
| 92 | Bill Pecota | .04 | .03 | | 158 | Kirt Manwaring | .05 | .04 |
| 93 | Bret Saberhagen | .08 | .06 | | 159 | Willie McGee | .06 | .05 |
| 94 | Dick Schofield | .04 | .03 | | 160 | Cory Snyder | .06 | .05 |
| 95 | Pete Schourek | .04 | .03 | | 161 | Bill Swift | .06 | .05 |
| 96 | Anthony Young | .06 | .05 | | 162 | Trevor Wilson | .05 | .04 |
| 97 | Ruben Amaro Jr. | .06 | .05 | | 163 | Brady Anderson | .10 | .08 |
| 98 | Juan Bell | .06 | .05 | | 164 | Glenn Davis | .06 | .05 |
| 99 | Wes Chamberlain | .06 | .05 | | 165 | Mike Devereaux | .08 | .06 |
| 100 | Darren Daulton | .08 | .06 | | 166 | Todd Frohwirth | .04 | .03 |
| 101 | Mariano Duncan | .04 | .03 | | 167 | Leo Gomez | .06 | .05 |
| 102 | Mike Hartley | .04 | .03 | | 168 | Chris Hoiles | .08 | .06 |
| 103 | Ricky Jordan | .06 | .05 | | 169 | Ben McDonald | .08 | .06 |
| 104 | John Kruk | .08 | .06 | | 170 | Randy Milligan | .04 | .03 |
| 105 | Mickey Morandini | .08 | .06 | | 171 | Alan Mills | .04 | .03 |
| 106 | Terry Mulholland | .06 | .05 | | 172 | Mike Mussina | .12 | .09 |
| 107 | *Ben Rivera*(FC) | .12 | .09 | | 173 | Gregg Olson | .08 | .06 |
| 108 | Curt Schilling | .08 | .06 | | 174 | Arthur Rhodes | .10 | .08 |
| 109 | *Keith Shepherd*(FC) | | | | 175 | David Segui | .05 | .04 |
| | | .12 | .09 | | 176 | Ellis Burks | .08 | .06 |
| 110 | Stan Belinda | .05 | .04 | | 177 | Roger Clemens | .15 | .11 |
| 111 | Jay Bell | .06 | .05 | | 178 | Scott Cooper | .08 | .06 |
| 112 | Barry Bonds | .12 | .09 | | 179 | Danny Darwin | .04 | .03 |

| | | MT | NR MT | | | MT | NR MT |
|---|---|---|---|---|---|---|---|
| 180 | Tony Fossas | .04 | .03 | 246 | *Hipolito Pichardo* | .10 | .08 |
| 181 | *Paul Quantrill*(FC) | | | 247 | Ricky Bones | .08 | .06 |
| | | .12 | .09 | 248 | Cal Eldred | .15 | .11 |
| 182 | Jody Reed | .05 | .04 | 249 | Mike Fetters | .05 | .04 |
| 183 | *John Valentin* | .12 | .09 | 250 | Darryl Hamilton | .08 | .06 |
| 184 | Mo Vaughn | .08 | .06 | 251 | Doug Henry | .06 | .05 |
| 185 | Frank Viola | .08 | .06 | 252 | John Jaha(FC) | .15 | .11 |
| 186 | Bob Zupcic | .08 | .06 | 253 | *Pat Listach* | .20 | .15 |
| 187 | Jim Abbott | .08 | .06 | 254 | Paul Molitor | .12 | .09 |
| 188 | Gary DiSarcina | .04 | .03 | 255 | Jaime Navarro | .08 | .06 |
| 189 | *Damion Easley* | .15 | .11 | 256 | Kevin Seitzer | .06 | .05 |
| 190 | Junior Felix | .06 | .05 | 257 | B.J. Surhoff | .06 | .05 |
| 191 | Chuck Finley | .06 | .05 | 258 | Greg Vaughn | .06 | .05 |
| 192 | Joe Grahe | .06 | .05 | 259 | Bill Wegman | .06 | .05 |
| 193 | Bryan Harvey | .06 | .05 | 260 | Robin Yount | .15 | .11 |
| 194 | Mark Langston | .08 | .06 | 261 | Rick Aguilera | .08 | .06 |
| 195 | John Orton | .04 | .03 | 262 | Chili Davis | .06 | .05 |
| 196 | Luis Polonia | .05 | .04 | 263 | Scott Erickson | .06 | .05 |
| 197 | *Tim Salmon* | .20 | .15 | 264 | Greg Gagne | .05 | .04 |
| 198 | Luis Sojo | .05 | .04 | 265 | Mark Guthrie | .04 | .03 |
| 199 | Wilson Alvarez | .05 | .04 | 266 | Brian Harper | .08 | .06 |
| 200 | George Bell | .08 | .04 | 267 | Kent Hrbek | .08 | .06 |
| 201 | Alex Fernandez | .08 | .04 | 268 | Terry Jorgensen | .08 | .06 |
| 202 | Craig Grebeck | .04 | .03 | 269 | Gene Larkin | .04 | .03 |
| 203 | Ozzie Guillen | .06 | .05 | 270 | Scott Leius | .06 | .05 |
| 204 | Lance Johnson | .06 | .05 | 271 | Pat Mahomes | .15 | .11 |
| 205 | Ron Karkovice | .04 | .03 | 272 | Pedro Munoz | .10 | .08 |
| 206 | Kirk McCaskill | .05 | .04 | 273 | Kirby Puckett | .15 | .11 |
| 207 | Jack McDowell | .10 | .08 | 274 | Kevin Tapani | .08 | .06 |
| 208 | Scott Radinsky | .04 | .03 | 275 | Carl Willis | .04 | .03 |
| 209 | Tim Raines | .08 | .06 | 276 | Steve Farr | .05 | .04 |
| 210 | Frank Thomas | .40 | .30 | 277 | John Habyan | .04 | .03 |
| 211 | Robin Ventura | .12 | .09 | 278 | Mel Hall | .06 | .05 |
| 212 | Sandy Alomar Jr. | .10 | .08 | 279 | Charlie Hayes | .06 | .05 |
| 213 | Carlos Baerga | .12 | .09 | 280 | Pat Kelly | .06 | .05 |
| 214 | Dennis Cook | .04 | .03 | 281 | Don Mattingly | .12 | .09 |
| 215 | Thomas Howard | .06 | .05 | 282 | Sam Militello | .12 | .09 |
| 216 | Mark Lewis | .08 | .06 | 283 | Matt Nokes | .06 | .05 |
| 217 | Derek Lilliquist | .04 | .03 | 284 | Melido Perez | .06 | .05 |
| 218 | Kenny Lofton | .15 | .11 | 285 | Andy Stankiewicz | .10 | .08 |
| 219 | Charles Nagy | .15 | .11 | 286 | Danny Tartabull | .10 | .08 |
| 220 | Steve Olin | .06 | .05 | 287 | Randy Velarde | .04 | .03 |
| 221 | Paul Sorrento | .06 | .05 | 288 | Bob Wickman | .15 | .11 |
| 222 | Jim Thome | .10 | .08 | 289 | Bernie Williams | .10 | .08 |
| 223 | Mark Whiten | .10 | .08 | 290 | Lance Blankenship | .05 | .04 |
| 224 | Milt Cuyler | .06 | .05 | 291 | Mike Bordick | .08 | .06 |
| 225 | Rob Deer | .06 | .05 | 292 | Jerry Browne | .04 | .03 |
| 226 | *John Doherty* | .12 | .09 | 293 | Dennis Eckersley | .10 | .08 |
| 227 | Cecil Fielder | .12 | .09 | 294 | Rickey Henderson | .15 | .11 |
| 228 | Travis Fryman | .15 | .11 | 295 | *Vince Horsman* | .12 | .09 |
| 229 | Mike Henneman | .06 | .05 | 296 | Mark McGwire | .20 | .15 |
| 230 | *John Kiely* | .12 | .09 | 297 | Jeff Parrett | .04 | .03 |
| 231 | *Kurt Knudsen* | .12 | .09 | 298 | Ruben Sierra | .15 | .11 |
| 232 | Scott Livingstone | .10 | .08 | 299 | Terry Steinbach | .06 | .05 |
| 233 | Tony Phillips | .08 | .06 | 300 | Walt Weiss | .05 | .04 |
| 234 | Mickey Tettleton | .08 | .06 | 301 | Bob Welch | .06 | .05 |
| 235 | Kevin Appier | .08 | .06 | 302 | Willie Wilson | .06 | .05 |
| 236 | George Brett | .12 | .09 | 303 | Bobby Witt | .06 | .05 |
| 237 | Tom Gordon | .05 | .04 | 304 | *Bret Boone* | .20 | .15 |
| 238 | Gregg Jefferies | .10 | .08 | 305 | Jay Buhner | .06 | .05 |
| 239 | Wally Joyner | .10 | .08 | 306 | Dave Fleming | .12 | .09 |
| 240 | *Kevin Koslofski* | .12 | .09 | 307 | Ken Griffey Jr. | .40 | .30 |
| 241 | Mike Macfarlane | .05 | .04 | 308 | Erik Hanson | .06 | .05 |
| 242 | Brian McRae | .08 | .06 | 309 | Edgar Martinez | .12 | .09 |
| 243 | Rusty Meacham | .08 | .06 | 310 | Tino Martinez | .08 | .06 |
| 244 | Keith Miller | .06 | .05 | 311 | Jeff Nelson | .12 | .09 |
| 245 | Jeff Montgomery | .06 | .05 | 312 | Dennis Powell | .04 | .03 |

| | | MT | NR MT |
|---|---|---|---|
| 313 | Mike Schooler | .05 | .04 |
| 314 | Russ Swan | .04 | .03 |
| 315 | Dave Valle | .04 | .03 |
| 316 | Omar Vizquel | .04 | .03 |
| 317 | Kevin Brown | .08 | .06 |
| 318 | Todd Burns | .04 | .03 |
| 319 | Jose Canseco | .20 | .15 |
| 320 | Julio Franco | .08 | .06 |
| 321 | Jeff Frye(FC) | .12 | .09 |
| 322 | Juan Gonzalez | .25 | .20 |
| 323 | Jose Guzman | .06 | .05 |
| 324 | Jeff Huson | .05 | .04 |
| 325 | Dean Palmer | .08 | .06 |
| 326 | Kevin Reimer | .06 | .05 |
| 327 | Ivan Rodriguez | .15 | .11 |
| 328 | Kenny Rogers | .04 | .03 |
| 329 | Dan Smith(FC) | .08 | .06 |
| 330 | Roberto Alomar | .20 | .15 |
| 331 | Derek Bell | .12 | .09 |
| 332 | Pat Borders | .06 | .05 |
| 333 | Joe Carter | .12 | .09 |
| 334 | Kelly Gruber | .08 | .06 |
| 335 | Tom Henke | .08 | .06 |
| 336 | Jimmy Key | .08 | .06 |
| 337 | Manuel Lee | .05 | .04 |
| 338 | Candy Maldonado | .06 | .05 |
| 339 | John Olerud | .15 | .11 |
| 340 | Todd Stottlemyre | .05 | .04 |
| 341 | Duane Ward | .05 | .04 |
| 342 | Devon White | .08 | .06 |
| 343 | Dave Winfield | .15 | .11 |

## GRADING GUIDE

**Mint (MT):** A perfect card. Well-centered with all corners sharp and square. No creases, stains, edge nicks, surface marks, yellowing or fading.

**Near Mint (NM):** A nearly perfect card. At first glance, a NM card appears to be perfect. May be slightly off-center. No surface marks, creases or loss of gloss.

**Excellent (EX):** Corners are still fairly sharp with only moderate wear. Borders may be off-center. No creases or stains on fronts or backs, but may show slight loss of surface luster.

**Very Good (VG):** Shows obvious handling. May have rounded corners, minor creases, major gum or wax stains. No major creases, tape marks, writing, etc.

**Good (G):** A well-worn card, but exhibits no intentional damage. May have major or multiple creases. Corners may be rounded well beyond card border.

# SCORE

## 1988 Score

A fifth member joined the group of nationally distributed baseball cards in 1988. Titled "Score," the new cards are characterized by extremely sharp and excellent full-color photography and printing. Card backs are full-color also and carry a player head-shot, along with a brief biography and player personal and statistical information. The 660 cards in the set each measure 2-1/2" by 3-1/2" in size. The fronts come with one of six different border colors - blue, red, green, purple, orange and gold - which are equally divided at 110 cards per color. The Score set was produced by Major League Marketing, the same company that markets the "triple-action" Sportflics card sets.

| | MT | NR MT |
|---|---|---|
| Complete Set: | 20.00 | 15.00 |
| Common Player: | .04 | .03 |

Values for recent cards and sets are listed in Mint (MT), Near Mint (NM) and Excellent (EX), reflecting the fact that many cards from recent years have been preserved in top condition. Recent cards and sets in less than Excellent condition have little collector interest.

# HOW TO USE THIS CATALOG

This catalog has been uniquely designed to serve the needs of beginning and advanced collectors. It provides a comprehensive guide to more than 100 years of baseball card issues, arranged so that even the most novice collector can consult it with confidence and ease.

The following explanations summarize the general practices used in preparing this catalog's listings. However, because of specialized requirements which may vary from card set to card set, these must not be considered ironclad. Where these standards have been set aside, appropriate notations are incorporated.

# ARRANGEMENT

Because the most important feature in identifying, and pricing, a baseball card is its set of origin, this catalog has been alphabetically arranged according to the name by which the set is most popularly known to collectors.

Those sets that were issued for more than one year are then listed chronologically, from earliest to most recent.

Within each set, the cards are listed by their designated card number, or in the absence of card numbers, alphabetically according to the last name of the player pictured.

# IDENTIFICATION

While most modern baseball cards are well identified on front, back or both, as to date and issue, such has not always been the case. In general, the back of the card is more useful in identifying the set of origin than the front. The issuer or sponsor's name will usually appear on the back since, after all, baseball cards were first issued as a promotional item to stimulate sales of other products. As often as not, that issuer's name is the name by which the set is known to collectors and under which it will be found listed in this catalog.

Virtually every set listed in this catalog is accompanied by a photograph of a representative card. If all else fails, a comparison of an unknown card with the photos in this book will usually produce a match.

As a special feature, each set listed in this catalog has been cross-indexed by its date of issue. This will allow identification in some difficult cases because a baseball card's general age, if not specific year of issue, can usually be fixed by studying the biographical or statistical information on the back of the card. The last year mentioned in either the biography or stats is usually the year which preceded the year of issue.

# PHOTOGRAPHS

A photograph on the front and back of at least one representative card from virtually every set listed in this catalog has been incorporated into the listings to aid in identification.

Photographs have been printed in reduced size. The actual size of cards in each set is given in the introductory text preceding its listing.

| | | MT | NR MT | | | | MT | NR MT |
|---|---|---|---|---|---|---|---|---|
| 1 | Don Mattingly | .30 | .25 | | 68 | Vince Coleman | .15 | .11 |
| 2 | Wade Boggs | .40 | .30 | | 69 | Howard Johnson | .08 | .06 |
| 3 | Tim Raines | .20 | .15 | | 70 | Tim Wallach | .08 | .06 |
| 4 | Andre Dawson | .15 | .11 | | 71 | Keith Moreland | .06 | .05 |
| 5 | Mark McGwire | .70 | .50 | | 72 | Barry Larkin | .40 | .30 |
| 6 | Kevin Seitzer | .30 | .25 | | 73 | Alan Ashby | .04 | .03 |
| 7 | Wally Joyner | .35 | .25 | | 74 | Rick Rhoden | .06 | .05 |
| 8 | Jesse Barfield | .10 | .08 | | 75 | Darrell Evans | .08 | .06 |
| 9 | Pedro Guerrero | .15 | .11 | | 76 | Dave Stieb | .08 | .06 |
| 10 | Eric Davis | .30 | .25 | | 77 | Dan Plesac | .08 | .06 |
| 11 | George Brett | .30 | .25 | | 78 | Will Clark | .80 | .60 |
| 12 | Ozzie Smith | .12 | .09 | | 79 | Frank White | .06 | .05 |
| 13 | Rickey Henderson | .40 | .30 | | 80 | Joe Carter | .25 | .20 |
| 14 | Jim Rice | .20 | .15 | | 81 | Mike Witt | .06 | .05 |
| 15 | *Matt Nokes* | .30 | .25 | | 82 | Terry Steinbach | .10 | .08 |
| 16 | Mike Schmidt | .40 | .30 | | 83 | Alvin Davis | .10 | .08 |
| 17 | Dave Parker | .12 | .09 | | 84 | Tom Herr | .06 | .05 |
| 18 | Eddie Murray | .25 | .20 | | 85 | Vance Law | .06 | .05 |
| 19 | Andres Galarraga | .12 | .09 | | 86 | Kal Daniels | .15 | .11 |
| 20 | Tony Fernandez | .10 | .08 | | 87 | Rick Honeycutt | .04 | .03 |
| 21 | Kevin McReynolds | .12 | .09 | | 88 | Alfredo Griffin | .06 | .05 |
| 22 | B.J. Surhoff | .10 | .08 | | 89 | Bret Saberhagen | .20 | .15 |
| 23 | Pat Tabler | .06 | .05 | | 90 | Bert Blyleven | .10 | .08 |
| 24 | Kirby Puckett | .25 | .20 | | 91 | Jeff Reardon | .08 | .06 |
| 25 | Benny Santiago | .25 | .20 | | 92 | Cory Snyder | .15 | .11 |
| 26 | Ryne Sandberg | .40 | .30 | | 93 | Greg Walker | .06 | .05 |
| 27 | Kelly Downs | .08 | .06 | | 94 | *Joe Magrane* | .30 | .25 |
| 28 | Jose Cruz | .06 | .05 | | 95 | Rob Deer | .06 | .05 |
| 29 | Pete O'Brien | .06 | .05 | | 96 | Ray Knight | .06 | .05 |
| 30 | Mark Langston | .10 | .08 | | 97 | Casey Candaele | .04 | .03 |
| 31 | Lee Smith | .08 | .06 | | 98 | John Cerutti | .06 | .05 |
| 32 | Juan Samuel | .10 | .08 | | 99 | Buddy Bell | .08 | .06 |
| 33 | Kevin Bass | .06 | .05 | | 100 | Jack Clark | .12 | .09 |
| 34 | R.J. Reynolds | .04 | .03 | | 101 | Eric Bell | .06 | .05 |
| 35 | Steve Sax | .12 | .09 | | 102 | Willie Wilson | .08 | .06 |
| 36 | John Kruk | .08 | .06 | | 103 | Dave Schmidt | .04 | .03 |
| 37 | Alan Trammell | .15 | .11 | | 104 | Dennis Eckersley | .10 | .08 |
| 38 | Chris Bosio | .06 | .05 | | 105 | Don Sutton | .12 | .09 |
| 39 | Brook Jacoby | .08 | .06 | | 106 | Danny Tartabull | .15 | .11 |
| 40 | Willie McGee | .10 | .08 | | 107 | Fred McGriff | .80 | .60 |
| 41 | Dave Magadan | .10 | .08 | | 108 | *Les Straker* | .15 | .11 |
| 42 | Fred Lynn | .10 | .08 | | 109 | Lloyd Moseby | .06 | .05 |
| 43 | Kent Hrbek | .12 | .09 | | 110 | Roger Clemens | .50 | .40 |
| 44 | Brian Downing | .06 | .05 | | 111 | Glenn Hubbard | .04 | .03 |
| 45 | Jose Canseco | .80 | .60 | | 112 | *Ken Williams* | .20 | .15 |
| 46 | Jim Presley | .08 | .06 | | 113 | Ruben Sierra | .35 | .25 |
| 47 | Mike Stanley | .06 | .05 | | 114 | Stan Jefferson | .06 | .05 |
| 48 | Tony Pena | .06 | .05 | | 115 | Milt Thompson | .04 | .03 |
| 49 | David Cone | .40 | .30 | | 116 | Bobby Bonilla | .40 | .30 |
| 50 | Rick Sutcliffe | .08 | .06 | | 117 | Wayne Tolleson | .04 | .03 |
| 51 | Doug Drabek | .10 | .08 | | 118 | *Matt Williams* | 1.25 | .90 |
| 52 | Bill Doran | .06 | .05 | | 119 | Chet Lemon | .06 | .05 |
| 53 | Mike Scioscia | .06 | .05 | | 120 | Dale Sveum | .06 | .05 |
| 54 | Candy Maldonado | .06 | .05 | | 121 | Dennis Boyd | .06 | .05 |
| 55 | Dave Winfield | .20 | .15 | | 122 | Brett Butler | .06 | .05 |
| 56 | Lou Whitaker | .20 | .15 | | 123 | Terry Kennedy | .06 | .05 |
| 57 | Tom Henke | .06 | .05 | | 124 | Jack Howell | .06 | .05 |
| 58 | Ken Gerhart | .06 | .05 | | 125 | Curt Young | .06 | .05 |
| 59 | Glenn Braggs | .08 | .06 | | 126a | Dale Valle (first name incorrect) | .25 | .20 |
| 60 | Julio Franco | .08 | .06 | | 126b | Dave Valle (correct spelling) | .06 | .05 |
| 61 | Charlie Leibrandt | .06 | .05 | | 127 | Curt Wilkerson | .04 | .03 |
| 62 | Gary Gaetti | .10 | .08 | | 128 | Tim Teufel | .04 | .03 |
| 63 | Bob Boone | .06 | .05 | | 129 | Ozzie Virgil | .04 | .03 |
| 64 | *Luis Polonia* | .35 | .25 | | 130 | Brian Fisher | .06 | .05 |
| 65 | Dwight Evans | .10 | .08 | | 131 | Lance Parrish | .12 | .09 |
| 66 | Phil Bradley | .08 | .06 | | | | | |
| 67 | Mike Boddicker | .06 | .05 | | | | | |

| | MT | NR MT |
|---|---|---|
| 132 Tom Browning | .08 | .06 |
| 133a Larry Anderson (incorrect spelling) | .25 | .20 |
| 133b Larry Andersen (correct spelling) | .06 | .05 |
| 134a Bob Brenley (incorrect spelling) | .25 | .20 |
| 134b Bob Brenly (correct spelling) | .06 | .05 |
| 135 Mike Marshall | .10 | .08 |
| 136 Gerald Perry | .08 | .06 |
| 137 Bobby Meacham | .04 | .03 |
| 138 Larry Herndon | .04 | .03 |
| 139 *Fred Manrique* | .12 | .09 |
| 140 Charlie Hough | .06 | .05 |
| 141 Ron Darling | .10 | .08 |
| 142 Herm Winningham | .04 | .03 |
| 143 Mike Diaz | .06 | .05 |
| 144 *Mike Jackson* | .15 | .11 |
| 145 Denny Walling | .04 | .03 |
| 146 Rob Thompson | .06 | .05 |
| 147 Franklin Stubbs | .06 | .05 |
| 148 Albert Hall | .04 | .03 |
| 149 Bobby Witt | .08 | .06 |
| 150 Lance McCullers | .06 | .05 |
| 151 Scott Bradley | .04 | .03 |
| 152 Mark McLemore | .04 | .03 |
| 153 Tim Laudner | .04 | .03 |
| 154 Greg Swindell | .15 | .11 |
| 155 Marty Barrett | .06 | .05 |
| 156 Mike Heath | .04 | .03 |
| 157 Gary Ward | .06 | .05 |
| 158a Lee Mazilli (incorrect spelling) | .25 | .20 |
| 158b Lee Mazzilli (correct spelling) | .08 | .06 |
| 159 Tom Foley | .04 | .03 |
| 160 Robin Yount | .30 | .25 |
| 161 Steve Bedrosian | .10 | .08 |
| 162 Bob Walk | .04 | .03 |
| 163 Nick Esasky | .06 | .05 |
| 164 *Ken Caminiti* | .25 | .20 |
| 165 Jose Uribe | .04 | .03 |
| 166 Dave Anderson | .04 | .03 |
| 167 Ed Whitson | .04 | .03 |
| 168 Ernie Whitt | .06 | .05 |
| 169 Cecil Cooper | .08 | .06 |
| 170 Mike Pagliarulo | .08 | .06 |
| 171 Pat Sheridan | .04 | .03 |
| 172 Chris Bando | .04 | .03 |
| 173 Lee Lacy | .04 | .03 |
| 174 Steve Lombardozzi | .04 | .03 |
| 175 Mike Greenwell | .70 | .50 |
| 176 Greg Minton | .04 | .03 |
| 177 Moose Haas | .04 | .03 |
| 178 Mike Kingery | .04 | .03 |
| 179 Greg Harris | .04 | .03 |
| 180 Bo Jackson | .70 | .50 |
| 181 Carmelo Martinez | .06 | .05 |
| 182 Alex Trevino | .04 | .03 |
| 183 Ron Oester | .04 | .03 |
| 184 Danny Darwin | .04 | .03 |
| 185 Mike Krukow | .06 | .05 |
| 186 Rafael Palmeiro | .50 | .40 |
| 187 Tim Burke | .04 | .03 |
| 188 Roger McDowell | .08 | .06 |
| 189 Garry Templeton | .06 | .05 |

| | MT | NR MT |
|---|---|---|
| 190 Terry Pendleton | .06 | .05 |
| 191 Larry Parrish | .06 | .05 |
| 192 Rey Quinones | .04 | .03 |
| 193 Joaquin Andujar | .06 | .05 |
| 194 Tom Brunansky | .08 | .06 |
| 195 Donnie Moore | .04 | .03 |
| 196 Dan Pasqua | .08 | .06 |
| 197 Jim Gantner | .04 | .03 |
| 198 Mark Eichhorn | .06 | .05 |
| 199 John Grubb | .04 | .03 |
| 200 *Bill Ripken* | .20 | .15 |
| 201 *Sam Horn* | .30 | .25 |
| 202 Todd Worrell | .08 | .06 |
| 203 Terry Leach | .04 | .03 |
| 204 Garth Iorg | .04 | .03 |
| 205 Brian Dayett | .04 | .03 |
| 206 Bo Diaz | .06 | .05 |
| 207 Craig Reynolds | .04 | .03 |
| 208 Brian Holton | .08 | .06 |
| 209 Marvelle Wynne (Marvell) | .04 | .03 |
| 210 Dave Concepcion | .06 | .05 |
| 211 Mike Davis | .06 | .05 |
| 212 Devon White | .15 | .11 |
| 213 Mickey Brantley | .04 | .03 |
| 214 Greg Gagne | .04 | .03 |
| 215 Oddibe McDowell | .06 | .05 |
| 216 Jimmy Key | .08 | .06 |
| 217 Dave Bergman | .04 | .03 |
| 218 Calvin Schiraldi | .04 | .03 |
| 219 Larry Sheets | .06 | .05 |
| 220 Mike Easler | .06 | .05 |
| 221 Kurt Stillwell | .08 | .06 |
| 222 *Chuck Jackson* | .15 | .11 |
| 223 Dave Martinez | .08 | .06 |
| 224 Tim Leary | .06 | .05 |
| 225 Steve Garvey | .20 | .15 |
| 226 Greg Mathews | .06 | .05 |
| 227 Doug Sisk | .04 | .03 |
| 228 Dave Henderson | .08 | .06 |
| 229 Jimmy Dwyer | .04 | .03 |
| 230 Larry Owen | .04 | .03 |
| 231 Andre Thornton | .06 | .05 |
| 232 Mark Salas | .04 | .03 |
| 233 Tom Brookens | .04 | .03 |
| 234 Greg Brock | .06 | .05 |
| 235 Rance Mulliniks | .04 | .03 |
| 236 Bob Brower | .06 | .05 |
| 237 Joe Niekro | .06 | .05 |
| 238 Scott Bankhead | .04 | .03 |
| 239 Doug DeCinces | .06 | .05 |
| 240 Tommy John | .12 | .09 |
| 241 Rich Gedman | .06 | .05 |
| 242 Ted Power | .04 | .03 |
| 243 *Dave Meads* | .12 | .09 |
| 244 Jim Sundberg | .06 | .05 |
| 245 Ken Oberkfell | .04 | .03 |
| 246 Jimmy Jones | .06 | .05 |
| 247 Ken Landreaux | .04 | .03 |
| 248 Jose Oquendo | .04 | .03 |
| 249 *John Mitchell* | .15 | .11 |
| 250 Don Baylor | .08 | .06 |
| 251 Scott Fletcher | .06 | .05 |
| 252 Al Newman | .04 | .03 |
| 253 Carney Lansford | .08 | .06 |
| 254 Johnny Ray | .06 | .05 |
| 255 Gary Pettis | .04 | .03 |

| | | MT | NR MT | | | | MT | NR MT |
|---|---|---|---|---|---|---|---|---|
| 256 | Ken Phelps | .06 | .05 | | 317 | Frank Williams | .04 | .03 |
| 257 | Rick Leach | .04 | .03 | | 318 | Mike Fitzgerald | .04 | .03 |
| 258 | Tim Stoddard | .04 | .03 | | 319 | Rick Mahler | .04 | .03 |
| 259 | Ed Romero | .04 | .03 | | 320 | Jim Gott | .04 | .03 |
| 260 | Sid Bream | .06 | .05 | | 321 | Mariano Duncan | .04 | .03 |
| 261a | Tom Neidenfuer | | | | 322 | Jose Guzman | .06 | .05 |
| | (incorrect spelling) | .25 | .20 | | 323 | Lee Guetterman | .04 | .03 |
| 261b | Tom Neidenfuer | | | | 324 | Dan Gladden | .04 | .03 |
| | (correct spelling) | .06 | .05 | | 325 | Gary Carter | .15 | .11 |
| 262 | Rick Dempsey | .06 | .05 | | 326 | Tracy Jones | .10 | .08 |
| 263 | Lonnie Smith | .06 | .05 | | 327 | Floyd Youmans | .04 | .03 |
| 264 | Bob Forsch | .06 | .05 | | 328 | Bill Dawley | .04 | .03 |
| 265 | Barry Bonds | .40 | .30 | | 329 | *Paul Noce* | .10 | .08 |
| 266 | Willie Randolph | .06 | .05 | | 330 | Angel Salazar | .04 | .03 |
| 267 | Mike Ramsey | .04 | .03 | | 331 | Goose Gossage | .12 | .09 |
| 268 | Don Slaught | .04 | .03 | | 332 | George Frazier | .04 | .03 |
| 269 | Mickey Tettleton | .04 | .03 | | 333 | Ruppert Jones | .04 | .03 |
| 270 | Jerry Reuss | .06 | .05 | | 334 | Billy Jo Robidoux | .04 | .03 |
| 271 | Marc Sullivan | .04 | .03 | | 335 | Mike Scott | .10 | .08 |
| 272 | Jim Morrison | .04 | .03 | | 336 | Randy Myers | .10 | .08 |
| 273 | Steve Balboni | .06 | .05 | | 337 | Bob Sebra | .04 | .03 |
| 274 | Dick Schofield | .04 | .03 | | 338 | Eric Show | .06 | .05 |
| 275 | John Tudor | .08 | .06 | | 339 | Mitch Williams | .06 | .05 |
| 276 | *Gene Larkin* | .20 | .15 | | 340 | Paul Molitor | .10 | .08 |
| 277 | Harold Reynolds | .06 | .05 | | 341 | Gus Polidor | .04 | .03 |
| 278 | Jerry Browne | .06 | .05 | | 342 | Steve Trout | .04 | .03 |
| 279 | Willie Upshaw | .06 | .05 | | 343 | Jerry Don Gleaton | .04 | .03 |
| 280 | Ted Higuera | .08 | .06 | | 344 | Bob Knepper | .06 | .05 |
| 281 | Terry McGriff | .04 | .03 | | 345 | Mitch Webster | .06 | .05 |
| 282 | Terry Puhl | .04 | .03 | | 346 | John Morris | .04 | .03 |
| 283 | *Mark Wasinger* | .12 | .09 | | 347 | Andy Hawkins | .04 | .03 |
| 284 | Luis Salazar | .04 | .03 | | 348 | Dave Leiper | .04 | .03 |
| 285 | Ted Simmons | .08 | .06 | | 349 | Ernest Riles | .04 | .03 |
| 286 | John Shelby | .04 | .03 | | 350 | Dwight Gooden | .40 | .30 |
| 287 | *John Smiley* | .50 | .40 | | 351 | Dave Righetti | .12 | .09 |
| 288 | Curt Ford | .04 | .03 | | 352 | Pat Dodson | .04 | .03 |
| 289 | Steve Crawford | .04 | .03 | | 353 | John Habyan | .04 | .03 |
| 290 | Dan Quisenberry | .06 | .05 | | 354 | Jim Deshaies | .06 | .05 |
| 291 | Alan Wiggins | .04 | .03 | | 355 | Butch Wynegar | .04 | .03 |
| 292 | Randy Bush | .04 | .03 | | 356 | Bryn Smith | .04 | .03 |
| 293 | John Candelaria | .06 | .05 | | 357 | Matt Young | .04 | .03 |
| 294 | Tony Phillips | .04 | .03 | | 358 | *Tom Pagnozzi* | .25 | .20 |
| 295 | Mike Morgan | .04 | .03 | | 359 | Floyd Rayford | .04 | .03 |
| 296 | Bill Wegman | .04 | .03 | | 360 | Darryl Strawberry | .30 | .25 |
| 297a | Terry Franconia | | | | 361 | Sal Butera | .04 | .03 |
| | (incorrect spelling) | .25 | .20 | | 362 | Domingo Ramos | .04 | .03 |
| 297b | Terry Francona (correct | | | | 363 | Chris Brown | .06 | .05 |
| | spelling) | .06 | .05 | | 364 | Jose Gonzalez | .04 | .03 |
| 298 | Mickey Hatcher | .04 | .03 | | 365 | Dave Smith | .06 | .05 |
| 299 | Andres Thomas | .06 | .05 | | 366 | Andy McGaffigan | .04 | .03 |
| 300 | Bob Stanley | .04 | .03 | | 367 | Stan Javier | .04 | .03 |
| 301 | *Alfredo Pedrique* | .12 | .09 | | 368 | Henry Cotto | .04 | .03 |
| 302 | Jim Lindeman | .06 | .05 | | 369 | Mike Birkbeck | .06 | .05 |
| 303 | Wally Backman | .06 | .05 | | 370 | Len Dykstra | .08 | .06 |
| 304 | Paul O'Neill | .06 | .05 | | 371 | Dave Collins | .06 | .05 |
| 305 | Hubie Brooks | .08 | .06 | | 372 | Spike Owen | .04 | .03 |
| 306 | Steve Buechele | .04 | .03 | | 373 | Geno Petralli | .04 | .03 |
| 307 | Bobby Thigpen | .08 | .06 | | 374 | Ron Karkovice | .04 | .03 |
| 308 | George Hendrick | .06 | .05 | | 375 | Shane Rawley | .06 | .05 |
| 309 | John Moses | .04 | .03 | | 376 | *DeWayne Buice* | .15 | .11 |
| 310 | Ron Guidry | .12 | .09 | | 377 | *Bill Pecota* | .15 | .11 |
| 311 | Bill Schroeder | .04 | .03 | | 378 | Leon Durham | .06 | .05 |
| 312 | *Jose Nunez* | .08 | .06 | | 379 | Ed Olwine | .04 | .03 |
| 313 | Bud Black | .04 | .03 | | 380 | Bruce Hurst | .08 | .06 |
| 314 | Joe Sambito | .04 | .03 | | 381 | Bob McClure | .04 | .03 |
| 315 | Scott McGregor | .06 | .05 | | 382 | Mark Thurmond | .04 | .03 |
| 316 | Rafael Santana | .04 | .03 | | 383 | Buddy Biancalana | .04 | .03 |

| | | MT | NR MT |
|---|---|---|---|
| 384 | Tim Conroy | .04 | .03 |
| 385 | Tony Gwynn | .25 | .20 |
| 386 | Greg Gross | .04 | .03 |
| 387 | *Barry Lyons* | .12 | .09 |
| 388 | Mike Felder | .04 | .03 |
| 389 | Pat Clements | .04 | .03 |
| 390 | Ken Griffey | .06 | .05 |
| 391 | Mark Davis | .04 | .03 |
| 392 | Jose Rijo | .06 | .05 |
| 393 | Mike Young | .04 | .03 |
| 394 | Willie Fraser | .06 | .05 |
| 395 | Dion James | .06 | .05 |
| 396 | *Steve Shields* | .12 | .09 |
| 397 | Randy St. Claire | .04 | .03 |
| 398 | Danny Jackson | .12 | .09 |
| 399 | Cecil Fielder | .60 | .45 |
| 400 | Keith Hernandez | .15 | .11 |
| 401 | Don Carman | .06 | .05 |
| 402 | *Chuck Crim* | .12 | .09 |
| 403 | Rob Woodward | .04 | .03 |
| 404 | Junior Ortiz | .04 | .03 |
| 405 | Glenn Wilson | .06 | .05 |
| 406 | Ken Howell | .04 | .03 |
| 407 | Jeff Kunkel | .04 | .03 |
| 408 | Jeff Reed | .04 | .03 |
| 409 | Chris James | .10 | .08 |
| 410 | Zane Smith | .06 | .05 |
| 411 | Ken Dixon | .04 | .03 |
| 412 | Ricky Horton | .06 | .05 |
| 413 | Frank DiPino | .04 | .03 |
| 414 | *Shane Mack* | .25 | .20 |
| 415 | Danny Cox | .06 | .05 |
| 416 | Andy Van Slyke | .10 | .08 |
| 417 | Danny Heep | .04 | .03 |
| 418 | John Cangelosi | .04 | .03 |
| 419a | John Christiansen (incorrect spelling) | .25 | .20 |
| 419b | John Christensen (correct spelling) | .06 | .05 |
| 420 | *Joey Cora* | .12 | .09 |
| 421 | Mike LaValliere | .06 | .05 |
| 422 | Kelly Gruber | .35 | .25 |
| 423 | Bruce Benedict | .04 | .03 |
| 424 | Len Matuszek | .04 | .03 |
| 425 | Kent Tekulve | .06 | .05 |
| 426 | Rafael Ramirez | .04 | .03 |
| 427 | Mike Flanagan | .06 | .05 |
| 428 | Mike Gallego | .04 | .03 |
| 429 | Juan Castillo | .04 | .03 |
| 430 | Neal Heaton | .04 | .03 |
| 431 | Phil Garner | .04 | .03 |
| 432 | *Mike Dunne* | .12 | .09 |
| 433 | Wallace Johnson | .04 | .03 |
| 434 | Jack O'Connor | .04 | .03 |
| 435 | Steve Jeltz | .04 | .03 |
| 436 | *Donnell Nixon* | .15 | .11 |
| 437 | Jack Lazorko | .04 | .03 |
| 438 | *Keith Comstock* | .12 | .09 |
| 439 | Jeff Robinson | .04 | .03 |
| 440 | Graig Nettles | .08 | .06 |
| 441 | Mel Hall | .06 | .05 |
| 442 | *Gerald Young* | .15 | .11 |
| 443 | Gary Redus | .04 | .03 |
| 444 | Charlie Moore | .04 | .03 |
| 445 | Bill Madlock | .08 | .06 |
| 446 | Mark Clear | .04 | .03 |
| 447 | Greg Booker | .04 | .03 |

| | | MT | NR MT |
|---|---|---|---|
| 448 | Rick Schu | .04 | .03 |
| 449 | Ron Kittle | .06 | .05 |
| 450 | Dale Murphy | .30 | .25 |
| 451 | Bob Dernier | .04 | .03 |
| 452 | Dale Mohorcic | .06 | .05 |
| 453 | Rafael Belliard | .04 | .03 |
| 454 | Charlie Puleo | .04 | .03 |
| 455 | Dwayne Murphy | .06 | .05 |
| 456 | Jim Eisenreich | .04 | .03 |
| 457 | David Palmer | .04 | .03 |
| 458 | Dave Stewart | .08 | .06 |
| 459 | Pascual Perez | .06 | .05 |
| 460 | Glenn Davis | .12 | .09 |
| 461 | Dan Petry | .06 | .05 |
| 462 | Jim Winn | .04 | .03 |
| 463 | Darrell Miller | .04 | .03 |
| 464 | Mike Moore | .04 | .03 |
| 465 | Mike LaCoss | .04 | .03 |
| 466 | Steve Farr | .04 | .03 |
| 467 | Jerry Mumphrey | .04 | .03 |
| 468 | Kevin Gross | .06 | .05 |
| 469 | Bruce Bochy | .04 | .03 |
| 470 | Orel Hershiser | .20 | .15 |
| 471 | Eric King | .06 | .05 |
| 472 | *Ellis Burks* | .80 | .60 |
| 473 | Darren Daulton | .04 | .03 |
| 474 | Mookie Wilson | .06 | .05 |
| 475 | Frank Viola | .12 | .09 |
| 476 | Ron Robinson | .04 | .03 |
| 477 | Bob Melvin | .04 | .03 |
| 478 | Jeff Musselman | .06 | .05 |
| 479 | Charlie Kerfeld | .04 | .03 |
| 480 | Richard Dotson | .06 | .05 |
| 481 | Kevin Mitchell | .50 | .40 |
| 482 | Gary Roenicke | .04 | .03 |
| 483 | Tim Flannery | .04 | .03 |
| 484 | Rich Yett | .04 | .03 |
| 485 | Pete Incaviglia | .12 | .09 |
| 486 | Rick Cerone | .04 | .03 |
| 487 | Tony Armas | .06 | .05 |
| 488 | Jerry Reed | .04 | .03 |
| 489 | Davey Lopes | .06 | .05 |
| 490 | Frank Tanana | .06 | .05 |
| 491 | Mike Loynd | .04 | .03 |
| 492 | Bruce Ruffin | .06 | .05 |
| 493 | Chris Speier | .04 | .03 |
| 494 | Tom Hume | .04 | .03 |
| 495 | Jesse Orosco | .06 | .05 |
| 496 | *Robby Wine, Jr.* | .12 | .09 |
| 497 | *Jeff Montgomery* | .25 | .20 |
| 498 | Jeff Dedmon | .04 | .03 |
| 499 | Luis Aguayo | .04 | .03 |
| 500 | Reggie Jackson (1968 Oakland Athletics) | .20 | .15 |
| 501 | Reggie Jackson (1976 Baltimore Orioles) | .20 | .15 |
| 502 | Reggie Jackson (1977 New York Yankees) | .20 | .15 |
| 503 | Reggie Jackson (1982 California Angels) | .20 | .15 |
| 504 | Reggie Jackson (1987 Oakland Athletics) | .20 | .15 |
| 505 | Billy Hatcher | .06 | .05 |
| 506 | Ed Lynch | .04 | .03 |
| 507 | Willie Hernandez | .06 | .05 |
| 508 | Jose DeLeon | .06 | .05 |
| 509 | Joel Youngblood | .04 | .03 |

| | | MT | NR MT | | | | MT | NR MT |
|---|---|---|---|---|---|---|---|---|
| 510 | Bob Welch | .08 | .06 | | 577 | Jamie Quirk | .04 | .03 |
| 511 | Steve Ontiveros | .04 | .03 | | 578 | Jay Aldrich | .10 | .08 |
| 512 | Randy Ready | .04 | .03 | | 579 | Claudell Washington | .06 | .05 |
| 513 | Juan Nieves | .06 | .05 | | 580 | Jeff Leonard | .06 | .05 |
| 514 | Jeff Russell | .04 | .03 | | 581 | Carmen Castillo | .04 | .03 |
| 515 | Von Hayes | .06 | .05 | | 582 | Daryl Boston | .04 | .03 |
| 516 | Mark Gubicza | .10 | .08 | | 583 | Jeff DeWillis | .15 | .11 |
| 517 | Ken Dayley | .04 | .03 | | 584 | John Marzano | .20 | .15 |
| 518 | Don Aase | .04 | .03 | | 585 | Bill Gullickson | .06 | .05 |
| 519 | Rick Reuschel | .08 | .06 | | 586 | Andy Allanson | .08 | .06 |
| 520 | Mike Henneman | .25 | .20 | | 587 | Lee Tunnell | .04 | .03 |
| 521 | Rick Aguilera | .04 | .03 | | 588 | Gene Nelson | .04 | .03 |
| 522 | Jay Howell | .06 | .05 | | 589 | Dave LaPoint | .06 | .05 |
| 523 | Ed Correa | .04 | .03 | | 590 | Harold Baines | .10 | .08 |
| 524 | Manny Trillo | .06 | .05 | | 591 | Bill Buckner | .08 | .06 |
| 525 | Kirk Gibson | .15 | .11 | | 592 | Carlton Fisk | .20 | .15 |
| 526 | Wally Ritchie | .12 | .09 | | 593 | Rick Manning | .04 | .03 |
| 527 | Al Nipper | .04 | .03 | | 594 | Doug Jones | .20 | .15 |
| 528 | Atlee Hammaker | .04 | .03 | | 595 | Tom Candiotti | .04 | .03 |
| 529 | Shawon Dunston | .08 | .06 | | 596 | Steve Lake | .04 | .03 |
| 530 | Jim Clancy | .06 | .05 | | 597 | Jose Lind | .25 | .20 |
| 531 | Tom Paciorek | .04 | .03 | | 598 | Ross Jones | .12 | .09 |
| 532 | Joel Skinner | .04 | .03 | | 599 | Gary Matthews | .06 | .05 |
| 533 | Scott Garrelts | .04 | .03 | | 600 | Fernando Valezuela | .15 | .11 |
| 534 | Tom O'Malley | .04 | .03 | | 601 | Dennis Martinez | .06 | .05 |
| 535 | John Franco | .08 | .06 | | 602 | Les Lancaster | .15 | .11 |
| 536 | Paul Kilgus | .20 | .15 | | 603 | Ozzie Guillen | .06 | .05 |
| 537 | Darrell Porter | .06 | .05 | | 604 | Tony Bernazard | .04 | .03 |
| 538 | Walt Terrell | .06 | .05 | | 605 | Chili Davis | .06 | .05 |
| 539 | Bill Long | .15 | .11 | | 606 | Roy Smalley | .04 | .03 |
| 540 | George Bell | .20 | .15 | | 607 | Ivan Calderon | .08 | .06 |
| 541 | Jeff Sellers | .06 | .05 | | 608 | Jay Tibbs | .04 | .03 |
| 542 | Joe Boever | .12 | .09 | | 609 | Guy Hoffman | .04 | .03 |
| 543 | Steve Howe | .06 | .05 | | 610 | Doyle Alexander | .06 | .05 |
| 544 | Scott Sanderson | .04 | .03 | | 611 | Mike Bielecki | .04 | .03 |
| 545 | Jack Morris | .15 | .11 | | 612 | Shawn Hillegas | .20 | .15 |
| 546 | Todd Benzinger | .30 | .25 | | 613 | Keith Atherton | .04 | .03 |
| 547 | Steve Henderson | .04 | .03 | | 614 | Eric Plunk | .04 | .03 |
| 548 | Eddie Milner | .04 | .03 | | 615 | Sid Fernandez | .08 | .06 |
| 549 | Jeff Robinson | .25 | .20 | | 616 | Dennis Lamp | .04 | .03 |
| 550 | Cal Ripken, Jr. | .40 | .30 | | 617 | Dave Engle | .04 | .03 |
| 551 | Jody Davis | .06 | .05 | | 618 | Harry Spilman | .04 | .03 |
| 552 | Kirk McCaskill | .06 | .05 | | 619 | Don Robinson | .06 | .05 |
| 553 | Craig Lefferts | .04 | .03 | | 620 | John Farrell | .20 | .15 |
| 554 | Darnell Coles | .06 | .05 | | 621 | Nelson Liriano | .15 | .11 |
| 555 | Phil Niekro | .15 | .11 | | 622 | Floyd Bannister | .06 | .05 |
| 556 | Mike Aldrete | .06 | .05 | | 623 | Rookie Prospect (Randy Milligan) | .60 | .45 |
| 557 | Pat Perry | .04 | .03 | | | | | |
| 558 | Juan Agosto | .04 | .03 | | 624 | Rookie Prospect (Kevin Elster) | .25 | .20 |
| 559 | Rob Murphy | .06 | .05 | | | | | |
| 560 | Dennis Rasmussen | .08 | .06 | | 625 | Rookie Prospect (Jody Reed) | .40 | .30 |
| 561 | Manny Lee | .04 | .03 | | | | | |
| 562 | Jeff Blauser | .20 | .15 | | 626 | Rookie Prospect (Shawn Abner) | .20 | .15 |
| 563 | Bob Ojeda | .06 | .05 | | | | | |
| 564 | Dave Dravecky | .06 | .05 | | 627 | Rookie Prospect (Kirt Manwaring) | .20 | .15 |
| 565 | Gene Garber | .04 | .03 | | | | | |
| 566 | Ron Roenicke | .04 | .03 | | 628 | Rookie Prospect (Pete Stanicek) | .15 | .11 |
| 567 | Tommy Hinzo | .12 | .09 | | | | | |
| 568 | Eric Nolte | .12 | .09 | | 629 | Rookie Prospect (Rob Ducey) | .12 | .09 |
| 569 | Ed Hearn | .04 | .03 | | | | | |
| 570 | Mark Davidson | .12 | .09 | | 630 | Rookie Prospect (Steve Kiefer) | .04 | .03 |
| 571 | Jim Walewander | .12 | .09 | | | | | |
| 572 | Donnie Hill | .04 | .03 | | 631 | Rookie Prospect (Gary Thurman) | .20 | .15 |
| 573 | Jamie Moyer | .06 | .05 | | | | | |
| 574 | Ken Schrom | .04 | .03 | | 632 | Rookie Prospect (Darrel Akerfelds) | .12 | .09 |
| 575 | Nolan Ryan | .60 | .45 | | | | | |
| 576 | Jim Acker | .04 | .03 | | 633 | Rookie Prospect (Dave | | |

|   |   | MT | NR MT |
|---|---|---|---|
| | Clark) | .10 | .08 |
| 634 | Rookie Prospect (Roberto Kelly) | 1.00 | .70 |
| 635 | Rookie Prospect (Keith Hughes) | .15 | .11 |
| 636 | Rookie Prospect (John Davis) | .15 | .11 |
| 637 | Rookie Prospect (Mike Devereaux) | .80 | .60 |
| 638 | Rookie Prospect (Tom Glavine) | 2.00 | 1.50 |
| 639 | Rookie Prospect (Keith Miller) | .20 | .15 |
| 640 | Rookie Prospect (Chris Gwynn) | .20 | .15 |
| 641 | Rookie Prospect (Tim Crews) | .15 | .11 |
| 642 | Rookie Prospect (Mackey Sasser) | .20 | .15 |
| 643 | Rookie Prospect (Vicente Palacios) | .15 | .11 |
| 644 | Rookie Prospect (Kevin Romine) | .06 | .05 |
| 645 | Rookie Prospect (Gregg Jefferies) | 1.00 | .70 |
| 646 | Rookie Prospect (Jeff Treadway) | .25 | .20 |
| 647 | Rookie Prospect (Ronnie Gant) | 2.00 | 1.50 |
| 648 | Rookie Sluggers (Mark McGwire, Matt Nokes) | .30 | .25 |
| 649 | Speed and Power (Eric Davis, Tim Raines) | .25 | .20 |
| 650 | Game Breakers (Jack Clark, Don Mattingly) | .20 | .15 |
| 651 | Super Shortstops (Tony Fernandez, Cal Ripken, Jr., Alan Trammell) | .20 | .15 |
| 652 | 1987 Highlights (Vince Coleman) | .08 | .06 |
| 653 | 1987 Highlights (Kirby Puckett) | .12 | .09 |
| 654 | 1987 Highlights (Benito Santiago) | .10 | .08 |
| 655 | 1987 Highlights (Juan Nieves) | .06 | .05 |
| 656 | 1987 Highlights (Steve Bedrosian) | .06 | .05 |
| 657 | 1987 Highlights (Mike Schmidt) | .20 | .15 |
| 658 | 1987 Highlights (Don Mattingly) | .30 | .25 |
| 659 | 1987 Highlights (Mark McGwire) | .15 | .11 |
| 660 | 1987 Highlights (Paul Molitor) | .08 | .06 |

## 1988 Score Traded

This 110-card set featuring new rookies and traded veterans is similar in design to the 1988 Score set, except for a change in border color. Individual

standard-size player cards (2-1/2" by 3-1/2") feature a bright orange border framing full-figure action photos highlighted by a thin white outline. The player name (in white) is centered in the bottom margin, flanked by three yellow stars lower left and a yellow Score logo lower right. The backs carry full-color player close-ups on a cream-colored background, followed by card number, team name and logo, player personal information and a purple stats chart that lists year-by-year and major league totals. A brief player profile follows the stats chart and, on some cards, information is included about the player's trade or acquisition. The update set also includes 10 Magic Motion 3-D trivia cards.

|   |   | MT | NR MT |
|---|---|---|---|
| Complete Set: | | 100.00 | 75.00 |
| Common Player: | | .08 | .06 |
| 1T | Jack Clark | .20 | .15 |
| 2T | Danny Jackson | .20 | .15 |
| 3T | Brett Butler | .10 | .08 |
| 4T | Kurt Stillwell | .12 | .09 |
| 5T | Tom Brunansky | .15 | .11 |
| 6T | Dennis Lamp | .08 | .06 |
| 7T | Jose DeLeon | .10 | .08 |
| 8T | Tom Herr | .12 | .09 |
| 9T | Keith Moreland | .10 | .08 |
| 10T | Kirk Gibson | .20 | .15 |
| 11T | Bud Black | .08 | .06 |
| 12T | Rafael Ramirez | .08 | .06 |
| 13T | Luis Salazar | .08 | .06 |
| 14T | Goose Gossage | .15 | .11 |
| 15T | Bob Welch | .15 | .11 |
| 16T | Vance Law | .10 | .08 |
| 17T | Ray Knight | .10 | .08 |
| 18T | Dan Quisenberry | .10 | .08 |
| 19T | Don Slaught | .08 | .06 |
| 20T | Lee Smith | .25 | .20 |
| 21T | Rick Cerone | .08 | .06 |
| 22T | Pat Tabler | .10 | .08 |
| 23T | Larry McWilliams | .08 | .06 |

| | | MT | NR MT |
|---|---|---|---|
| 24T | Rick Horton | .10 | .08 |
| 25T | Graig Nettles | .12 | .09 |
| 26T | Dan Petry | .10 | .08 |
| 27T | Joe Rijo | .10 | .08 |
| 28T | Chili Davis | .10 | .08 |
| 29T | Dickie Thon | .10 | .08 |
| 30T | Mackey Sasser(FC) | .15 | .11 |
| 31T | Mickey Tettleton | .08 | .06 |
| 32T | Rick Dempsey | .08 | .06 |
| 33T | Ron Hassey | .08 | .06 |
| 34T | Phil Bradley | .12 | .09 |
| 35T | Jay Howell | .10 | .08 |
| 36T | Bill Buckner | .12 | .09 |
| 37T | Alfredo Griffin | .10 | .08 |
| 38T | Gary Pettis | .08 | .06 |
| 39T | Calvin Schiraldi | .08 | .06 |
| 40T | John Candelaria | .10 | .08 |
| 41T | Joe Orsulak | .08 | .06 |
| 42T | Willie Upshaw | .10 | .08 |
| 43T | Herm Winningham | .08 | .06 |
| 44T | Ron Kittle | .12 | .09 |
| 45T | Bob Dernier | .08 | .06 |
| 46T | Steve Balboni | .10 | .08 |
| 47T | Steve Shields | .08 | .06 |
| 48T | Henry Cotto | .08 | .06 |
| 49T | Dave Henderson | .10 | .08 |
| 50T | Dave Parker | .15 | .11 |
| 51T | Mike Young | .08 | .06 |
| 52T | Mark Salas | .08 | .06 |
| 53T | Mike Davis | .08 | .06 |
| 54T | Rafael Santana | .08 | .06 |
| 55T | Don Baylor | .15 | .11 |
| 56T | Dan Pasqua | .12 | .09 |
| 57T | Ernest Riles | .08 | .06 |
| 58T | Glenn Hubbard | .08 | .06 |
| 59T | Mike Smithson | .08 | .06 |
| 60T | Richard Dotson | .10 | .08 |
| 61T | Jerry Reuss | .10 | .08 |
| 62T | Mike Jackson | .10 | .08 |
| 63T | Floyd Bannister | .10 | .08 |
| 64T | Jesse Orosco | .10 | .08 |
| 65T | Larry Parrish | .10 | .08 |
| 66T | Jeff Bittiger(FC) | .20 | .15 |
| 67T | Ray Hayward(FC) | .10 | .08 |
| 68T | Ricky Jordan(FC) | .60 | .45 |
| 69T | Tommy Gregg(FC) | .12 | .09 |
| 70T | Brady Anderson(FC) | 8.00 | 6.00 |
| 71T | Jeff Montgomery | .08 | .06 |
| 72T | Darryl Hamilton(FC) | .75 | .55 |
| 73T | Cecil Espy(FC) | .10 | .08 |
| 74T | Greg Briley(FC) | .50 | .40 |
| 75T | Joey Meyer(FC) | .20 | .15 |
| 76T | Mike Macfarlane(FC) | .40 | .30 |
| 77T | Oswald Peraza(FC) | .20 | .15 |
| 78T | Jack Armstrong(FC) | .60 | .45 |
| 79T | Don Heinkel(FC) | .20 | .15 |
| 80T | Mark Grace(FC) | 15.00 | 11.00 |
| 81T | Steve Curry(FC) | .20 | .15 |
| 82T | Damon Berryhill(FC) | .40 | .30 |
| 83T | Steve Ellsworth(FC) | .20 | .15 |
| 84T | Pete Smith(FC) | .12 | .09 |
| 85T | Jack McDowell(FC) | 15.00 | 11.00 |
| 86T | Rob Dibble(FC) | 3.00 | 2.25 |
| 87T | Brian Harvey(FC) | 2.00 | 1.50 |
| 88T | John Dopson(FC) | .25 | .20 |

| | | MT | NR MT |
|---|---|---|---|
| 89T | Dave Gallagher(FC) | .25 | .20 |
| 90T | Todd Stottlemyre(FC) | 2.50 | 2.00 |
| 91T | Mike Schooler(FC) | 1.00 | .70 |
| 92T | Don Gordon(FC) | .08 | .06 |
| 93T | Sil Campusano(FC) | .25 | .20 |
| 94T | Jeff Pico(FC) | .25 | .20 |
| 95T | Jay Buhner(FC) | 2.00 | 1.50 |
| 96T | Nelson Santovenia(FC) | .25 | .20 |
| 97T | Al Leiter(FC) | .30 | .25 |
| 98T | Luis Alicea(FC) | .20 | .15 |
| 99T | Pat Borders(FC) | 3.00 | 2.25 |
| 100T | Chris Sabo(FC) | 4.00 | 3.00 |
| 101T | Tim Belcher(FC) | .70 | .50 |
| 102T | Walt Weiss(FC) | .80 | .60 |
| 103T | Craig Biggio(FC) | 5.00 | 3.75 |
| 104T | Don August(FC) | .25 | .20 |
| 105T | Roberto Alomar(FC) | 60.00 | 45.00 |
| 106T | Todd Burns(FC) | .30 | .25 |
| 107T | John Costello(FC) | .20 | .15 |
| 108T | Melido Perez(FC) | .60 | .45 |
| 109T | Darrin Jackson(FC) | .12 | .09 |
| 110T | Orestes Destrade(FC) | .15 | .11 |

**NOTE: A card number in parentheses ( ) indicates the set is unnumbered.**

## 1989 Score

This set of 660 cards plus 56 Magic Motion trivia cards is the second annual basic issue from Score. Full-color player photos highlight 651 individual players and 9 season highlights, including the first Wrigley Field night game. Action photos are framed by thin brightly colored borders (green, cyan blue, purple, orange, red, royal blue) with a baseball diamond logo/player name beneath the photo. Full-color player close-ups (1-5/16" by 1-5/8") are printed on the pastel-colored backs, along with the card number, personal information, stats and career highlights. The cards measure 2-1/2" by 3-1/2" in size.

|  | | MT | NR MT |
|---|---|---|---|
| Complete Set: | | 15.00 | 11.00 |
| Common Player: | | .03 | .02 |
| 1 | Jose Canseco | .35 | .25 |
| 2 | Andre Dawson | .15 | .11 |
| 3 | Mark McGwire | .30 | .25 |
| 4 | Benny Santiago | .12 | .09 |
| 5 | Rick Reuschel | .08 | .06 |
| 6 | Fred McGriff | .35 | .25 |
| 7 | Kal Daniels | .12 | .09 |
| 8 | Gary Gaetti | .12 | .09 |
| 9 | Ellis Burks | .35 | .25 |
| 10 | Darryl Strawberry | .35 | .25 |
| 11 | Julio Franco | .08 | .06 |
| 12 | Lloyd Moseby | .06 | .05 |
| 13 | *Jeff Pico* | .15 | .11 |
| 14 | Johnny Ray | .06 | .05 |
| 15 | Cal Ripken, Jr. | .40 | .30 |
| 16 | Dick Schofield | .03 | .02 |
| 17 | Mel Hall | .06 | .05 |
| 18 | Bill Ripken | .06 | .05 |
| 19 | Brook Jacoby | .08 | .06 |
| 20 | Kirby Puckett | .35 | .25 |
| 21 | Bill Doran | .06 | .05 |
| 22 | Pete O'Brien | .06 | .05 |
| 23 | Matt Nokes | .15 | .11 |
| 24 | Brian Fisher | .06 | .05 |
| 25 | Jack Clark | .12 | .09 |
| 26 | Gary Pettis | .03 | .02 |
| 27 | Dave Valle | .03 | .02 |
| 28 | Willie Wilson | .08 | .06 |
| 29 | Curt Young | .06 | .05 |
| 30 | Dale Murphy | .30 | .25 |
| 31 | Barry Larkin | .25 | .20 |
| 32 | Dave Stewart | .08 | .06 |
| 33 | Mike LaValliere | .06 | .05 |
| 34 | Glen Hubbard | .03 | .02 |
| 35 | Ryne Sandberg | .40 | .30 |
| 36 | Tony Pena | .06 | .05 |
| 37 | Greg Walker | .06 | .05 |
| 38 | Von Hayes | .08 | .06 |
| 39 | Kevin Mitchell | .30 | .25 |
| 40 | Tim Raines | .25 | .20 |
| 41 | Keith Hernandez | .20 | .15 |
| 42 | Keith Moreland | .06 | .05 |
| 43 | Ruben Sierra | .30 | .25 |
| 44 | Chet Lemon | .06 | .05 |
| 45 | Willie Randolph | .06 | .05 |
| 46 | Andy Allanson | .03 | .02 |
| 47 | Candy Maldonado | .06 | .05 |
| 48 | Sid Bream | .06 | .05 |
| 49 | Denny Walling | .03 | .02 |
| 50 | Dave Winfield | .25 | .20 |
| 51 | Alvin Davis | .10 | .08 |
| 52 | Cory Snyder | .15 | .11 |
| 53 | Hubie Brooks | .08 | .06 |
| 54 | Chili Davis | .06 | .05 |
| 55 | Kevin Seitzer | .12 | .09 |
| 56 | Jose Uribe | .03 | .02 |
| 57 | Tony Fernandez | .10 | .08 |
| 58 | Tim Teufel | .03 | .02 |
| 59 | Oddibe McDowell | .06 | .05 |
| 60 | Les Lancaster | .06 | .05 |
| 61 | Billy Hatcher | .06 | .05 |
| 62 | Dan Gladden | .03 | .02 |
| 63 | Marty Barrett | .06 | .05 |
| 64 | Nick Esasky | .06 | .05 |
| 65 | Wally Joyner | .20 | .15 |

|  | | MT | NR MT |
|---|---|---|---|
| 66 | Mike Greenwell | .35 | .25 |
| 67 | Ken Williams | .06 | .05 |
| 68 | Bob Horner | .08 | .06 |
| 69 | Steve Sax | .12 | .09 |
| 70 | Rickey Henderson | .30 | .25 |
| 71 | Mitch Webster | .06 | .05 |
| 72 | Rob Deer | .06 | .05 |
| 73 | Jim Presley | .06 | .05 |
| 74 | Albert Hall | .03 | .02 |
| 75a | George Brett ("...game's top hitters at 33..." on back) | 1.00 | .70 |
| 75b | George Brett ("...game's top hitters at 35..." on back) | .30 | .25 |
| 76 | Brian Downing | .06 | .05 |
| 77 | Dave Martinez | .06 | .05 |
| 78 | Scott Fletcher | .06 | .05 |
| 79 | Phil Bradley | .08 | .06 |
| 80 | Ozzie Smith | .12 | .09 |
| 81 | Larry Sheets | .06 | .05 |
| 82 | Mike Aldrete | .06 | .05 |
| 83 | Darnell Coles | .06 | .05 |
| 84 | Len Dykstra | .08 | .06 |
| 85 | Jim Rice | .20 | .15 |
| 86 | Jeff Treadway | .10 | .08 |
| 87 | Jose Lind | .08 | .06 |
| 88 | Willie McGee | .10 | .08 |
| 89 | Mickey Brantley | .03 | .02 |
| 90 | Tony Gwynn | .20 | .15 |
| 91 | R.J. Reynolds | .03 | .02 |
| 92 | Milt Thompson | .03 | .02 |
| 93 | Kevin McReynolds | .12 | .09 |
| 94 | Eddie Murray | .25 | .20 |
| 95 | Lance Parrish | .12 | .09 |
| 96 | Ron Kittle | .06 | .05 |
| 97 | Gerald Young | .10 | .08 |
| 98 | Ernie Whitt | .06 | .05 |
| 99 | Jeff Reed | .03 | .02 |
| 100 | Don Mattingly | .40 | .30 |
| 101 | Gerald Perry | .08 | .06 |
| 102 | Vance Law | .06 | .05 |
| 103 | John Shelby | .03 | .02 |
| 104 | *Chris Sabo* | .40 | .30 |
| 105 | Danny Tartabull | .15 | .11 |
| 106 | Glenn Wilson | .06 | .05 |
| 107 | Mark Davidson | .06 | .05 |
| 108 | Dave Parker | .10 | .08 |
| 109 | Eric Davis | .35 | .25 |
| 110 | Alan Trammell | .15 | .11 |
| 111 | Ozzie Virgil | .03 | .02 |
| 112 | Frank Tanana | .06 | .05 |
| 113 | Rafael Ramirez | .03 | .02 |
| 114 | Dennis Martinez | .06 | .05 |
| 115 | Jose DeLeon | .06 | .05 |
| 116 | Bob Ojeda | .06 | .05 |
| 117 | Doug Drabek | .06 | .05 |
| 118 | Andy Hawkins | .03 | .02 |
| 119 | Greg Maddux(FC) | .10 | .08 |
| 120 | Cecil Fielder (photo on back reversed) | .60 | .45 |
| 121 | Mike Scioscia | .06 | .05 |
| 122 | Dan Petry | .06 | .05 |
| 123 | Terry Kennedy | .06 | .05 |
| 124 | Kelly Downs | .08 | .06 |
| 125a | Greg Gross (first name incorrect on card back) | .20 | .15 |

| | | MT | NR MT |
|---|---|---|---|
| 125b | Greg Gross (first name correct on card back) | .08 | .06 |
| 126 | Fred Lynn | .10 | .08 |
| 127 | Barry Bonds | .25 | .20 |
| 128 | Harold Baines | .10 | .08 |
| 129 | Doyle Alexander | .06 | .05 |
| 130 | Kevin Elster | .08 | .06 |
| 131 | Mike Heath | .03 | .02 |
| 132 | Teddy Higuera | .08 | .06 |
| 133 | Charlie Leibrandt | .06 | .05 |
| 134 | Tim Laudner | .03 | .02 |
| 135a | Ray Knight (photo reversed) | .60 | .45 |
| 135b | Ray Knight (correct photo) | .08 | .06 |
| 136 | Howard Johnson | .08 | .06 |
| 137 | Terry Pendleton | .08 | .06 |
| 138 | Andy McGaffigan | .03 | .02 |
| 139 | Ken Oberkfell | .03 | .02 |
| 140 | Butch Wynegar | .03 | .02 |
| 141 | Rob Murphy | .03 | .02 |
| 142 | *Rich Renteria*(FC) | .12 | .09 |
| 143 | Jose Guzman | .08 | .06 |
| 144 | Andres Galarraga | .12 | .09 |
| 145 | Rick Horton | .06 | .05 |
| 146 | Frank DiPino | .03 | .02 |
| 147 | Glenn Braggs | .06 | .05 |
| 148 | John Kruk | .06 | .05 |
| 149 | Mike Schmidt | .35 | .25 |
| 150 | Lee Smith | .08 | .06 |
| 151 | Robin Yount | .25 | .20 |
| 152 | Mark Eichhorn | .06 | .05 |
| 153 | DeWayne Buice | .04 | .03 |
| 154 | B.J. Surhoff | .08 | .06 |
| 155 | Vince Coleman | .12 | .09 |
| 156 | Tony Phillips | .03 | .02 |
| 157 | Willie Fraser | .03 | .02 |
| 158 | Lance McCullers | .06 | .05 |
| 159 | Greg Gagne | .03 | .02 |
| 160 | Jesse Barfield | .08 | .06 |
| 161 | Mark Langston | .08 | .06 |
| 162 | Kurt Stillwell | .06 | .05 |
| 163 | Dion James | .03 | .02 |
| 164 | Glenn Davis | .12 | .09 |
| 165 | Walt Weiss | .25 | .20 |
| 166 | Dave Concepcion | .08 | .06 |
| 167 | Alfredo Griffin | .06 | .05 |
| 168 | *Don Heinkel* | .15 | .11 |
| 169 | Luis Rivera(FC) | .03 | .02 |
| 170 | Shane Rawley | .06 | .05 |
| 171 | Darrell Evans | .08 | .06 |
| 172 | Robby Thompson | .06 | .05 |
| 173 | Jody Davis | .06 | .05 |
| 174 | Andy Van Slyke | .12 | .09 |
| 175 | Wade Boggs ("And his .364 career BA..." on back) | .50 | .40 |
| 176 | Garry Templeton | .06 | .05 |
| 177 | Gary Redus | .03 | .02 |
| 178 | Craig Lefferts | .03 | .02 |
| 179 | Carney Lansford | .06 | .05 |
| 180 | Ron Darling | .10 | .08 |
| 181 | Kirk McCaskill | .06 | .05 |
| 182 | Tony Armas | .06 | .05 |
| 183 | Steve Farr | .03 | .02 |
| 184 | Tom Brunansky | .10 | .08 |

| | | MT | NR MT |
|---|---|---|---|
| 185 | *Bryan Harvey* | .25 | .20 |
| 186 | Mike Marshall | .10 | .08 |
| 187 | Bo Diaz | .06 | .05 |
| 188 | Willie Upshaw | .06 | .05 |
| 189 | Mike Pagliarulo | .08 | .06 |
| 190 | Mike Krukow | .06 | .05 |
| 191 | Tommy Herr | .06 | .05 |
| 192 | Jim Pankovits | .03 | .02 |
| 193 | Dwight Evans | .10 | .08 |
| 194 | Kelly Gruber | .03 | .02 |
| 195 | Bobby Bonilla | .25 | .20 |
| 196 | Wallace Johnson | .03 | .02 |
| 197 | Dave Stieb | .08 | .06 |
| 198 | *Pat Borders* | .20 | .15 |
| 199 | Rafael Palmeiro | .15 | .11 |
| 200 | Doc Gooden | .20 | .15 |
| 201 | Pete Incaviglia | .08 | .06 |
| 202 | Chris James | .08 | .06 |
| 203 | Marvell Wynne | .03 | .02 |
| 204 | Pat Sheridan | .03 | .02 |
| 205 | Don Baylor | .08 | .06 |
| 206 | Paul O'Neill | .03 | .02 |
| 207 | Pete Smith | .08 | .06 |
| 208 | Mark McLemore | .03 | .02 |
| 209 | Henry Cotto | .03 | .02 |
| 210 | Kirk Gibson | .15 | .11 |
| 211 | Claudell Washington | .06 | .05 |
| 212 | Randy Bush | .03 | .02 |
| 213 | Joe Carter | .10 | .08 |
| 214 | Bill Buckner | .08 | .06 |
| 215 | Bert Blyleven (year of birth is 1957) | .25 | .20 |
| 216 | Brett Butler | .06 | .05 |
| 217 | Lee Mazzilli | .06 | .05 |
| 218 | Spike Owen | .03 | .02 |
| 219 | Bill Swift | .03 | .02 |
| 220 | Tim Wallach | .08 | .06 |
| 221 | David Cone | .20 | .15 |
| 222 | Don Carman | .06 | .05 |
| 223 | Rich Gossage | .10 | .08 |
| 224 | Bob Walk | .03 | .02 |
| 225 | Dave Righetti | .10 | .08 |
| 226 | Kevin Bass | .06 | .05 |
| 227 | Kevin Gross | .06 | .05 |
| 228 | Tim Burke | .03 | .02 |
| 229 | Rick Mahler | .03 | .02 |
| 230 | Lou Whitaker | .15 | .11 |
| 231 | *Luis Alicea* | .15 | .11 |
| 232 | Roberto Alomar | 1.00 | .70 |
| 233 | Bob Boone | .06 | .05 |
| 234 | Dickie Thon | .03 | .02 |
| 235 | Shawon Dunston | .08 | .06 |
| 236 | Pete Stanicek | .08 | .06 |
| 237 | *Craig Biggio* | .50 | .40 |
| 238 | Dennis Boyd | .06 | .05 |
| 239 | Tom Candiotti | .03 | .02 |
| 240 | Gary Carter | .15 | .11 |
| 241 | Mike Stanley | .03 | .02 |
| 242 | Ken Phelps | .06 | .05 |
| 243 | Chris Bosio | .03 | .02 |
| 244 | Les Straker | .06 | .05 |
| 245 | Dave Smith | .06 | .05 |
| 246 | John Candelaria | .06 | .05 |
| 247 | Joe Orsulak | .03 | .02 |
| 248 | Storm Davis | .08 | .06 |
| 249 | Floyd Bannister | .06 | .05 |
| 250 | Jack Morris | .12 | .09 |

| | MT | NR MT | | | MT | NR MT |
|---|---|---|---|---|---|---|
| 251 | Bret Saberhagen | .12 | .09 | 317 | Rick Rhoden | .06 | .05 |
| 252 | Tom Niedenfuer | .06 | .05 | 318 | Tom Henke | .06 | .05 |
| 253 | Neal Heaton | .03 | .02 | 319 | *Mike Macfarlane* | .20 | .15 |
| 254 | Eric Show | .06 | .05 | 320 | Dan Plesac | .08 | .06 |
| 255 | Juan Samuel | .10 | .08 | 321 | Calvin Schiraldi | .03 | .02 |
| 256 | Dale Sveum | .06 | .05 | 322 | Stan Javier | .03 | .02 |
| 257 | Jim Gott | .03 | .02 | 323 | Devon White | .10 | .08 |
| 258 | Scott Garrelts | .03 | .02 | 324 | Scott Bradley | .03 | .02 |
| 259 | Larry McWilliams | .03 | .02 | 325 | Bruce Hurst | .08 | .06 |
| 260 | Steve Bedrosian | .08 | .06 | 326 | Manny Lee | .03 | .02 |
| 261 | Jack Howell | .06 | .05 | 327 | Rick Aguilera | .03 | .02 |
| 262 | Jay Tibbs | .03 | .02 | 328 | Bruce Ruffin | .03 | .02 |
| 263 | Jamie Moyer | .03 | .02 | 329 | Ed Whitson | .03 | .02 |
| 264 | Doug Sisk | .03 | .02 | 330 | Bo Jackson | .40 | .30 |
| 265 | Todd Worrell | .08 | .06 | 331 | Ivan Calderon | .06 | .05 |
| 266 | John Farrell | .08 | .06 | 332 | Mickey Hatcher | .03 | .02 |
| 267 | Dave Collins | .06 | .05 | 333 | Barry Jones(FC) | .03 | .02 |
| 268 | Sid Fernandez | .08 | .06 | 334 | Ron Hassey | .03 | .02 |
| 269 | Tom Brookens | .03 | .02 | 335 | Bill Wegman | .03 | .02 |
| 270 | Shane Mack | .06 | .05 | 336 | Damon Berryhill | .15 | .11 |
| 271 | Paul Kilgus | .08 | .06 | 337 | Steve Ontiveros | .03 | .02 |
| 272 | Chuck Crim | .03 | .02 | 338 | Dan Pasqua | .08 | .06 |
| 273 | Bob Knepper | .06 | .05 | 339 | Bill Pecota | .06 | .05 |
| 274 | Mike Moore | .03 | .02 | 340 | Greg Cadaret | .06 | .05 |
| 275 | Guillermo Hernandez | | | 341 | Scott Bankhead | .03 | .02 |
| | | .06 | .05 | 342 | Ron Guidry | .12 | .09 |
| 276 | Dennis Eckersley | .10 | .08 | 343 | Danny Heep | .03 | .02 |
| 277 | Graig Nettles | .10 | .08 | 344 | Bob Brower | .03 | .02 |
| 278 | Rich Dotson | .06 | .05 | 345 | Rich Gedman | .06 | .05 |
| 279 | Larry Herndon | .03 | .02 | 346 | *Nelson Santovenia* | .15 | .11 |
| 280 | Gene Larkin | .08 | .06 | 347 | George Bell | .20 | .15 |
| 281 | Roger McDowell | .08 | .06 | 348 | Ted Power | .03 | .02 |
| 282 | Greg Swindell | .10 | .08 | 349 | Mark Grant | .03 | .02 |
| 283 | Juan Agosto | .03 | .02 | 350a | Roger Clemens (778 | | |
| 284 | Jeff Robinson | .06 | .05 | | Wins) | 4.00 | 3.00 |
| 285 | Mike Dunne | .08 | .06 | 350b | Roger Clemens (78 | | |
| 286 | Greg Mathews | .06 | .05 | | Wins) | .40 | .30 |
| 287 | Kent Tekulve | .06 | .05 | 351 | Bill Long | .06 | .05 |
| 288 | Jerry Mumphrey | .03 | .02 | 352 | Jay Bell(FC) | .06 | .05 |
| 289 | Jack McDowell | .08 | .06 | 353 | Steve Balboni | .06 | .05 |
| 290 | Frank Viola | .12 | .09 | 354 | Bob Kipper | .03 | .02 |
| 291 | Mark Gubicza | .08 | .06 | 355 | Steve Jeltz | .03 | .02 |
| 292 | Dave Schmidt | .03 | .02 | 356 | Jesse Orosco | .06 | .05 |
| 293 | Mike Henneman | .08 | .06 | 357 | Bob Dernier | .03 | .02 |
| 294 | Jimmy Jones | .03 | .02 | 358 | Mickey Tettleton | .03 | .02 |
| 295 | Charlie Hough | .06 | .05 | 359 | Duane Ward(FC) | .03 | .02 |
| 296 | Rafael Santana | .03 | .02 | 360 | Darrin Jackson(FC) | .08 | .06 |
| 297 | Chris Speier | .03 | .02 | 361 | Rey Quinones | .03 | .02 |
| 298 | Mike Witt | .06 | .05 | 362 | Mark Grace | .80 | .60 |
| 299 | Pascual Perez | .06 | .05 | 363 | Steve Lake | .03 | .02 |
| 300 | Nolan Ryan | .50 | .40 | 364 | Pat Perry | .03 | .02 |
| 301 | Mitch Williams | .06 | .05 | 365 | Terry Steinbach | .08 | .06 |
| 302 | Mookie Wilson | .06 | .05 | 366 | Alan Ashby | .03 | .02 |
| 303 | Mackey Sasser | .06 | .05 | 367 | Jeff Montgomery | .06 | .05 |
| 304 | John Cerutti | .06 | .05 | 368 | Steve Buechele | .03 | .02 |
| 305 | Jeff Reardon | .08 | .06 | 369 | Chris Brown | .06 | .05 |
| 306 | Randy Myers | .08 | .06 | 370 | Orel Hershiser | .20 | .15 |
| 307 | Greg Brock | .06 | .05 | 371 | Todd Benzinger | .10 | .08 |
| 308 | Bob Welch | .08 | .06 | 372 | Ron Gant | .50 | .40 |
| 309 | Jeff Robinson | .12 | .09 | 373 | Paul Assenmacher(FC) | | |
| 310 | Harold Reynolds | .06 | .05 | | | .03 | .02 |
| 311 | Jim Walewander | .03 | .02 | 374 | Joey Meyer | .08 | .06 |
| 312 | Dave Magadan | .08 | .06 | 375 | Neil Allen | .03 | .02 |
| 313 | Jim Gantner | .03 | .02 | 376 | Mike Davis | .06 | .05 |
| 314 | Walt Terrell | .06 | .05 | 377 | Jeff Parrett(FC) | .08 | .06 |
| 315 | Wally Backman | .06 | .05 | 378 | Jay Howell | .06 | .05 |
| 316 | Luis Salazar | .03 | .02 | 379 | Rafael Belliard | .03 | .02 |

| | MT | NR MT | | | MT | NR MT |
|---|---|---|---|---|---|---|
| 380 | Luis Polonia | .06 | .05 | 446 | Manny Trillo | .03 | .02 |
| 381 | Keith Atherton | .03 | .02 | 447 | Joel Skinner | .03 | .02 |
| 382 | Kent Hrbek | .15 | .11 | 448 | Charlie Puleo | .03 | .02 |
| 383 | Bob Stanley | .03 | .02 | 449 | Carlton Fisk | .12 | .09 |
| 384 | Dave LaPoint | .06 | .05 | 450 | Will Clark | .50 | .40 |
| 385 | Rance Mulliniks | .03 | .02 | 451 | Otis Nixon | .03 | .02 |
| 386 | Melido Perez | .08 | .06 | 452 | Rick Schu | .03 | .02 |
| 387 | Doug Jones | .10 | .08 | 453 | Todd Stottlemyre | .15 | .11 |
| 388 | Steve Lyons | .03 | .02 | 454 | Tim Birtsas | .03 | .02 |
| 389 | Alejandro Pena | .06 | .05 | 455 | *Dave Gallagher* | .20 | .15 |
| 390 | Frank White | .06 | .05 | 456 | Barry Lyons | .03 | .02 |
| 391 | Pat Tabler | .06 | .05 | 457 | Fred Manrique | .06 | .05 |
| 392 | Eric Plunk(FC) | .03 | .02 | 458 | Ernest Riles | .03 | .02 |
| 393 | Mike Maddux(FC) | .03 | .02 | 459 | *Doug Jennings*(FC) | | |
| 394 | Allan Anderson(FC) | .06 | .05 | | | .15 | .11 |
| 395 | Bob Brenly | .03 | .02 | 460 | Joe Magrane | .08 | .06 |
| 396 | Rick Cerone | .03 | .02 | 461 | Jamie Quirk | .03 | .02 |
| 397 | Scott Terry(FC) | .08 | .06 | 462 | *Jack Armstrong* | .25 | .20 |
| 398 | Mike Jackson | .06 | .05 | 463 | Bobby Witt | .08 | .06 |
| 399 | Bobby Thigpen | .08 | .06 | 464 | Keith Miller | .06 | .05 |
| 400 | Don Sutton | .12 | .09 | 465 | *Todd Burns* | .15 | .11 |
| 401 | Cecil Espy | .06 | .05 | 466 | *John Dopson* | .15 | .11 |
| 402 | Junior Ortiz | .03 | .02 | 467 | Rich Yett | .03 | .02 |
| 403 | Mike Smithson | .03 | .02 | 468 | Craig Reynolds | .03 | .02 |
| 404 | Bud Black | .03 | .02 | 469 | Dave Bergman | .03 | .02 |
| 405 | Tom Foley | .03 | .02 | 470 | Rex Hudler | .03 | .02 |
| 406 | Andres Thomas | .06 | .05 | 471 | Eric King | .03 | .02 |
| 407 | Rick Sutcliffe | .08 | .06 | 472 | Joaquin Andujar | .06 | .05 |
| 408 | Brian Harper | .03 | .02 | 473 | *Sil Campusano* | .15 | .11 |
| 409 | John Smiley | .10 | .08 | 474 | Terry Mulholland(FC) | | |
| 410 | Juan Nieves | .06 | .05 | | | .03 | .02 |
| 411 | Shawn Abner | .08 | .06 | 475 | Mike Flanagan | .06 | .05 |
| 412 | Wes Gardner(FC) | .06 | .05 | 476 | Greg Harris | .03 | .02 |
| 413 | Darren Daulton | .03 | .02 | 477 | Tommy John | .10 | .08 |
| 414 | Juan Berenguer | .03 | .02 | 478 | Dave Anderson | .03 | .02 |
| 415 | Charles Hudson | .03 | .02 | 479 | Fred Toliver | .03 | .02 |
| 416 | Rick Honeycutt | .03 | .02 | 480 | Jimmy Key | .08 | .06 |
| 417 | Greg Booker | .03 | .02 | 481 | Donell Nixon | .03 | .02 |
| 418 | Tim Belcher | .08 | .06 | 482 | Mark Portugal(FC) | .03 | .02 |
| 419 | Don August | .08 | .06 | 483 | Tom Pagnozzi | .06 | .05 |
| 420 | Dale Mohorcic | .03 | .02 | 484 | Jeff Kunkel | .03 | .02 |
| 421 | Steve Lombardozzi | .03 | .02 | 485 | Frank Williams | .03 | .02 |
| 422 | Atlee Hammaker | .03 | .02 | 486 | Jody Reed | .10 | .08 |
| 423 | Jerry Don Gleaton | .03 | .02 | 487 | Roberto Kelly | .25 | .20 |
| 424 | Scott Bailes(FC) | .03 | .02 | 488 | Shawn Hillegas | .06 | .05 |
| 425 | Bruce Sutter | .08 | .06 | 489 | Jerry Reuss | .06 | .05 |
| 426 | Randy Ready | .03 | .02 | 490 | Mark Davis | .03 | .02 |
| 427 | Jerry Reed | .03 | .02 | 491 | Jeff Sellers | .03 | .02 |
| 428 | Bryn Smith | .03 | .02 | 492 | Zane Smith | .06 | .05 |
| 429 | Tim Leary | .06 | .05 | 493 | Al Newman(FC) | .03 | .02 |
| 430 | Mark Clear | .03 | .02 | 494 | Mike Young | .03 | .02 |
| 431 | Terry Leach | .03 | .02 | 495 | Larry Parrish | .06 | .05 |
| 432 | John Moses | .03 | .02 | 496 | Herm Winningham | .03 | .02 |
| 433 | Ozzie Guillen | .06 | .05 | 497 | Carmen Castillo | .03 | .02 |
| 434 | Gene Nelson | .03 | .02 | 498 | Joe Hesketh | .03 | .02 |
| 435 | Gary Ward | .06 | .05 | 499 | Darrell Miller | .03 | .02 |
| 436 | Luis Aguayo | .03 | .02 | 500 | Mike LaCoss | .03 | .02 |
| 437 | Fernando Valenzuela | | | 501 | Charlie Lea | .03 | .02 |
| | | .15 | .11 | 502 | Bruce Benedict | .03 | .02 |
| 438 | Jeff Russell | .03 | .02 | 503 | Chuck Finley(FC) | .03 | .02 |
| 439 | Cecilio Guante | .03 | .02 | 504 | Brad Wellman(FC) | .03 | .02 |
| 440 | Don Robinson | .03 | .02 | 505 | Tim Crews | .06 | .05 |
| 441 | Rick Anderson(FC) | .03 | .02 | 506 | Ken Gerhart | .06 | .05 |
| 442 | Tom Glavine | .08 | .06 | 507 | Brian Holton (Born: Jan. | | |
| 443 | Daryl Boston | .03 | .02 | | 25, 1965 Denver, CO) | .20 | .15 |
| 444 | Joe Price | .03 | .02 | 508 | Dennis Lamp | .03 | .02 |
| 445 | Stewart Cliburn | .03 | .02 | 509 | Bobby Meacham (1984 | | |

| | | MT | NR MT |
|---|---|---|---|
| | Games is 099) | .20 | .15 |
| 510 | Tracy Jones | .08 | .06 |
| 511 | Mike Fitzgerald | .03 | .02 |
| 512 | *Jeff Bittiger* | .12 | .09 |
| 513 | Tim Flannery | .03 | .02 |
| 514 | Ray Hayward(FC) | .03 | .02 |
| 515 | Dave Leiper | .03 | .02 |
| 516 | Rod Scurry | .03 | .02 |
| 517 | Carmelo Martinez | .03 | .02 |
| 518 | Curtis Wilkerson | .03 | .02 |
| 519 | Stan Jefferson | .03 | .02 |
| 520 | Dan Quisenberry | .06 | .05 |
| 521 | Lloyd McClendon(FC) | | |
| | | .03 | .02 |
| 522 | Steve Trout | .03 | .02 |
| 523 | Larry Andersen | .03 | .02 |
| 524 | Don Aase | .03 | .02 |
| 525 | Bob Forsch | .06 | .05 |
| 526 | Geno Petralli | .03 | .02 |
| 527 | Angel Salazar | .03 | .02 |
| 528 | *Mike Schooler* | .20 | .15 |
| 529 | Jose Oquendo | .03 | .02 |
| 530 | Jay Buhner | .10 | .08 |
| 531 | Tom Bolton(FC) | .06 | .05 |
| 532 | Al Nipper | .03 | .02 |
| 533 | Dave Henderson | .08 | .06 |
| 534 | *John Costello*(FC) | | |
| | | .15 | .11 |
| 535 | Donnie Moore | .03 | .02 |
| 536 | Mike Laga | .03 | .02 |
| 537 | Mike Gallego | .03 | .02 |
| 538 | Jim Clancy | .06 | .05 |
| 539 | Joel Youngblood | .03 | .02 |
| 540 | Rick Leach | .03 | .02 |
| 541 | Kevin Romine | .03 | .02 |
| 542 | Mark Salas | .03 | .02 |
| 543 | Greg Minton | .03 | .02 |
| 544 | Dave Palmer | .03 | .02 |
| 545 | Dwayne Murphy | .06 | .05 |
| 546 | Jim Deshaies | .03 | .02 |
| 547 | Don Gordon(FC) | .03 | .02 |
| 548 | *Ricky Jordan* | .30 | .25 |
| 549 | Mike Boddicker | .06 | .05 |
| 550 | Mike Scott | .10 | .08 |
| 551 | Jeff Ballard(FC) | .08 | .06 |
| 552a | Jose Rijo (uniform | | |
| | number #24 on card back) | | |
| | | .20 | .15 |
| 552b | Jose Rijo (uniform | | |
| | number #27 on card back) | | |
| | | .08 | .06 |
| 553 | Danny Darwin | .03 | .02 |
| 554 | Tom Browning | .08 | .06 |
| 555 | Danny Jackson | .12 | .09 |
| 556 | Rick Dempsey | .06 | .05 |
| 557 | Jeffrey Leonard | .06 | .05 |
| 558 | Jeff Musselman | .06 | .05 |
| 559 | Ron Robinson | .03 | .02 |
| 560 | John Tudor | .08 | .06 |
| 561 | Don Slaught | .03 | .02 |
| 562 | Dennis Rasmussen | .08 | .06 |
| 563 | *Brady Anderson* | .20 | .15 |
| 564 | Pedro Guerrero | .12 | .09 |
| 565 | Paul Molitor | .12 | .09 |
| 566 | *Terry Clark*(FC) | .15 | .11 |
| 567 | Terry Puhl | .03 | .02 |
| 568 | Mike Campbell(FC) | .08 | .06 |

| | | MT | NR MT |
|---|---|---|---|
| 569 | Paul Mirabella | .03 | .02 |
| 570 | Jeff Hamilton(FC) | .06 | .05 |
| 571 | *Oswald Peraza* | .15 | .11 |
| 572 | Bob McClure | .03 | .02 |
| 573 | *Jose Bautista*(FC) | | |
| | | .15 | .11 |
| 574 | Alex Trevino | .03 | .02 |
| 575 | John Franco | .08 | .06 |
| 576 | *Mark Parent*(FC) | .15 | .11 |
| 577 | Nelson Liriano | .06 | .05 |
| 578 | Steve Shields | .03 | .02 |
| 579 | Odell Jones | .03 | .02 |
| 580 | Al Leiter | .15 | .11 |
| 581 | Dave Stapleton(FC) | .06 | .05 |
| 582 | 1988 World Series (Jose | | |
| | Canseco, Kirk Gibson, Orel | | |
| | Hershiser, Dave Stewart) | | |
| | | .20 | .15 |
| 583 | Donnie Hill | .03 | .02 |
| 584 | Chuck Jackson | .06 | .05 |
| 585 | Rene Gonzales(FC) | .06 | .05 |
| 586 | Tracy Woodson(FC) | .08 | .06 |
| 587 | Jim Adduci(FC) | .03 | .02 |
| 588 | Mario Soto | .06 | .05 |
| 589 | Jeff Blauser | .08 | .06 |
| 590 | Jim Traber | .06 | .05 |
| 591 | Jon Perlman(FC) | .03 | .02 |
| 592 | Mark Williamson(FC) | | |
| | | .06 | .05 |
| 593 | Dave Meads | .03 | .02 |
| 594 | *Jim Eisenreich* | .03 | .02 |
| 595 | *Paul Gibson*(FC) | .15 | .11 |
| 596 | Mike Birkbeck | .03 | .02 |
| 597 | Terry Francona | .03 | .02 |
| 598 | Paul Zuvella(FC) | .03 | .02 |
| 599 | Franklin Stubbs | .03 | .02 |
| 600 | Gregg Jefferies | .30 | .25 |
| 601 | John Cangelosi | .03 | .02 |
| 602 | Mike Sharperson(FC) | | |
| | | .03 | .02 |
| 603 | Mike Diaz | .06 | .05 |
| 604 | *Gary Varsho*(FC) | .20 | .15 |
| 605 | *Terry Blocker*(FC) | | |
| | | .12 | .09 |
| 606 | Charlie O'Brien(FC) | .03 | .02 |
| 607 | Jim Eppard(FC) | .08 | .06 |
| 608 | John Davis | .03 | .02 |
| 609 | Ken Griffey, Sr. | .08 | .06 |
| 610 | Buddy Bell | .06 | .05 |
| 611 | Ted Simmons | .08 | .06 |
| 612 | Matt Williams | .10 | .08 |
| 613 | Danny Cox | .06 | .05 |
| 614 | Al Pedrique | .03 | .02 |
| 615 | Ron Oester | .03 | .02 |
| 616 | *John Smoltz*(FC) | .80 | .60 |
| 617 | Bob Melvin | .03 | .02 |
| 618 | *Rob Dibble* | .50 | .40 |
| 619 | Kirt Manwaring | .10 | .08 |
| 620 | 1989 Rookie (Felix | | |
| | Fermin)(FC) | .06 | .05 |
| 621 | 1989 Rookie (*Doug* | | |
| | *Dascenzo*)(FC) | .20 | .15 |
| 622 | 1989 Rookie (*Bill* | | |
| | *Brennan*)(FC) | .15 | .11 |
| 623 | 1989 Rookie (*Carlos* | | |
| | *Quintana*)(FC) | .40 | .30 |
| 624 | 1989 Rookie (*Mike* | | |

| | MT | NR MT |
|---|---|---|
| Harkey)(FC) | .25 | .20 |
| 625 1989 Rookie (Gary Sheffield)(FC) | .80 | .60 |
| 626 1989 Rookie (Tom Prince)(FC) | .08 | .06 |
| 627 1989 Rookie (Steve Searcy)(FC) | .15 | .11 |
| 628 1989 Rookie (Charlie Hayes)(FC) | .25 | .20 |
| 629 1989 Rookie (Felix Jose)(FC) | 1.00 | .70 |
| 630 1989 Rookie (Sandy Alomar)(FC) | .40 | .30 |
| 631 1989 Rookie (Derek Lilliquist)(FC) | .15 | .11 |
| 632 1989 Rookie (Geronimo Berroa)(FC) | .06 | .05 |
| 633 1989 Rookie (Luis Medina)(FC) | .15 | .11 |
| 634 1989 Rookie (Tom Gordon)(FC) | .40 | .30 |
| 635 1989 Rookie (Ramon Martinez)(FC) | .80 | .60 |
| 636 1989 Rookie (Craig Worthington)(FC) | .20 | .15 |
| 637 1989 Rookie (Edgar Martinez)(FC) | .70 | .50 |
| 638 1989 Rookie (Chad Krueter)(FC) | .15 | .11 |
| 639 1989 Rookie (Ron Jones)(FC) | .20 | .15 |
| 640 1989 Rookie (Van Snider)(FC) | .15 | .11 |
| 641 1989 Rookie (Lance Blankenship)(FC) | .15 | .11 |
| 642 1989 Rookie (Dwight Smith)(FC) | .20 | .15 |
| 643 1989 Rookie (Cameron Drew)(FC) | .15 | .11 |
| 644 1989 Rookie (Jerald Clark)(FC) | .30 | .25 |
| 645 1989 Rookie (Randy Johnson)(FC) | .30 | .25 |
| 646 1989 Rookie (Norm Charlton)(FC) | .30 | .25 |
| 647 1989 Rookie (Todd Frohwirth)(FC) | .08 | .06 |
| 648 1989 Rookie (Luis de los Santos)(FC) | .15 | .11 |
| 649 1989 Rookie (Tim Jones)(FC) | .15 | .11 |
| 650 1989 Rookie (Dave West)(FC) | .20 | .15 |
| 651 1989 Rookie (Bob Milacki)(FC) | .25 | .20 |
| 652 1988 Highlight (Wrigley Field) | .06 | .05 |
| 653 1988 Highlight (Orel Hershiser) | .10 | .08 |
| 654a 1988 Highlight (Wade Boggs) ("...sixth consecutive seaason..." on back) | 3.00 | 2.25 |
| 654b 1988 Highlight (Wade Boggs) ("...sixth consecutive season..." on back) | .30 | .25 |

| | MT | NR MT |
|---|---|---|
| 655 1988 Highlight (Jose Canseco) | .20 | .15 |
| 656 1988 Highlight (Doug Jones) | .06 | .05 |
| 657 1988 Highlight (Rickey Henderson) | .12 | .09 |
| 658 1988 Highlight (Tom Browning) | .06 | .05 |
| 659 1988 Highlight (Mike Greenwell) | .15 | .11 |
| 660 1988 Highlight (A.L. Win Streak) | .06 | .05 |

# 1989 Score Traded

Score issued its second consecutive traded set in 1989 to supplement and update its regular set. The 110-card traded set features the same basic card design as the regular 1989 Score set. The set consists of rookies and traded players pictured with correct teams. The set was sold by hobby dealers in a special box that included an assortment of "Magic Motion" trivia cards.

| | | MT | NR MT |
|---|---|---|---|
| Complete Set: | | 8.00 | 6.00 |
| Common Player: | | .06 | .05 |
| | | | |
| 1T | Rafael Palmeiro | .10 | .08 |
| 2T | Nolan Ryan | 1.50 | 1.25 |
| 3T | Jack Clark | .10 | .08 |
| 4T | Dave LaPoint | .06 | .05 |
| 5T | Mike Moore | .08 | .06 |
| 6T | Pete O'Brien | .06 | .05 |
| 7T | Jeffrey Leonard | .06 | .05 |
| 8T | Rob Murphy | .06 | .05 |
| 9T | Tom Herr | .06 | .05 |
| 10T | Claudell Washington | .06 | .05 |
| 11T | Mike Pagliarulo | .06 | .05 |
| 12T | Steve Lake | .06 | .05 |
| 13T | Spike Owen | .06 | .05 |
| 14T | Andy Hawkins | .06 | .05 |
| 15T | Todd Benzinger | .06 | .05 |
| 16T | Mookie Wilson | .06 | .05 |
| 17T | Bert Blyleven | .08 | .06 |

| | | MT | NR MT |
|---|---|---|---|
| 18T | Jeff Treadway | .06 | .05 |
| 19T | Bruce Hurst | .08 | .06 |
| 20T | Steve Sax | .12 | .09 |
| 21T | Juan Samuel | .06 | .05 |
| 22T | Jesse Barfield | .06 | .05 |
| 23T | Carmelo Castillo | .06 | .05 |
| 24T | Terry Leach | .06 | .05 |
| 25T | Mark Langston | .12 | .09 |
| 26T | Eric King | .06 | .05 |
| 27T | Steve Balboni | .06 | .05 |
| 28T | Len Dykstra | .06 | .05 |
| 29T | Keith Moreland | .06 | .05 |
| 30T | Terry Kennedy | .06 | .05 |
| 31T | Eddie Murray | .12 | .09 |
| 32T | Mitch Williams | .10 | .08 |
| 33T | Jeff Parrett | .06 | .05 |
| 34T | Wally Backman | .06 | .05 |
| 35T | Julio Franco | .10 | .08 |
| 36T | Lance Parrish | .06 | .05 |
| 37T | Nick Esasky | .06 | .05 |
| 38T | Luis Polonia | .06 | .05 |
| 39T | Kevin Gross | .06 | .05 |
| 40T | John Dopson | .06 | .05 |
| 41T | Willie Randolph | .08 | .06 |
| 42T | Jim Clancy | .06 | .05 |
| 43T | Tracy Jones | .06 | .05 |
| 44T | Phil Bradley | .06 | .05 |
| 45T | Milt Thompson | .06 | .05 |
| 46T | Chris James | .06 | .05 |
| 47T | Scott Fletcher | .06 | .05 |
| 48T | Kal Daniels | .08 | .06 |
| 49T | Steve Bedrosian | .06 | .05 |
| 50T | Rickey Henderson | .50 | .40 |
| 51T | Dion James | .06 | .05 |
| 52T | Tim Leary | .06 | .05 |
| 53T | Roger McDowell | .06 | .05 |
| 54T | Mel Hall | .06 | .05 |
| 55T | Dickie Thon | .06 | .05 |
| 56T | Zane Smith | .06 | .05 |
| 57T | Danny Heep | .06 | .05 |
| 58T | Bob McClure | .06 | .05 |
| 59T | Brian Holton | .06 | .05 |
| 60T | Randy Ready | .06 | .05 |
| 61T | Bob Melvin | .06 | .05 |
| 62T | Harold Baines | .08 | .06 |
| 63T | Lance McCullers | .06 | .05 |
| 64T | Jody Davis | .06 | .05 |
| 65T | Darrell Evans | .06 | .05 |
| 66T | Joel Youngblood | .08 | .06 |
| 67T | Frank Viola | .08 | .06 |
| 68T | Mike Aldrete | .06 | .05 |
| 69T | Greg Cadaret | .06 | .05 |
| 70T | John Kruk | .06 | .05 |
| 71T | Pat Sheridan | .06 | .05 |
| 72T | Oddibe McDowell | .06 | .05 |
| 73T | Tom Brookens | .06 | .05 |
| 74T | Bob Boone | .08 | .06 |
| 75T | Walt Terrell | .06 | .05 |
| 76T | Joel Skinner | .06 | .05 |
| 77T | Randy Johnson | .10 | .08 |
| 78T | Felix Fermin | .06 | .05 |
| 79T | Rick Mahler | .06 | .05 |
| 80T | Rich Dotson | .06 | .05 |
| 81T | Cris Carpenter(FC) | .20 | .15 |
| 82T | Bill Spiers(FC) | .25 | .20 |
| 83T | Junior Felix(FC) | .25 | .20 |
| 84T | Joe Girardi(FC) | .20 | .15 |

| | | MT | NR MT |
|---|---|---|---|
| 85T | Jerome Walton(FC) | .25 | .20 |
| 86T | Greg Litton(FC) | .25 | .20 |
| 87T | Greg Harris(FC) | .20 | .15 |
| 88T | Jim Abbott(FC) | 1.00 | .70 |
| 89T | Kevin Brown(FC) | .20 | .15 |
| 90T | John Wetteland(FC) | .20 | .15 |
| 91T | Gary Wayne(FC) | .15 | .11 |
| 92T | Rich Monteleone(FC) | .15 | .11 |
| 93T | Bob Geren(FC) | .20 | .15 |
| 94T | Clay Parker(FC) | .15 | .11 |
| 95T | Steve Finley(FC) | .40 | .30 |
| 96T | Gregg Olson(FC) | .35 | .25 |
| 97T | Ken Patterson(FC) | .15 | .11 |
| 98T | Ken Hill(FC) | .30 | .25 |
| 99T | Scott Scudder(FC) | .25 | .20 |
| 100T | Ken Griffey, Jr.(FC) | 5.00 | 3.75 |
| 101T | Jeff Brantley(FC) | .25 | .20 |
| 102T | Donn Pall(FC) | .15 | .11 |
| 103T | Carlos Martinez(FC) | .20 | .15 |
| 104T | Joe Oliver(FC) | .30 | .25 |
| 105T | Omar Vizquel(FC) | .15 | .11 |
| 106T | Joey Belle(FC) | 2.50 | 2.00 |
| 107T | Kenny Rogers(FC) | .20 | .15 |
| 108T | Mark Carreon(FC) | .15 | .11 |
| 109T | Rolando Roomes(FC) | .15 | .11 |
| 110T | Pete Harnisch(FC) | .35 | .25 |

## 1990 Score

The regular Score set increased to 704 cards in 1990. Included were a series of cards picturing first-round draft picks, an expanded subset of rookie cards, four World Series specials, five Highlight cards, and a 13-card "Dream Team" series featuring the game's top players pictured on old tobacco-style cards. For the first time in a Score set, team logos are displayed on the card fronts in the lower right corner. Card backs again include a full-color portrait photo with player data. A one-paragraph write-up of each player was again provided by former Sports Illustrated editor

Les Woodcock. The Score set was again distributed with "Magic Motion" triva cards, this year using "Baseball's Most Valuable Players" as its theme.

| | | MT | NR MT |
|---|---|---|---|
| | Complete Set: | 20.00 | 15.00 |
| | Common Player: | .04 | .03 |
| 1 | Don Mattingly | .35 | .25 |
| 2 | Cal Ripken, Jr. | .40 | .30 |
| 3 | Dwight Evans | .08 | .06 |
| 4 | Barry Bonds | .12 | .09 |
| 5 | Kevin McReynolds | .12 | .09 |
| 6 | Ozzie Guillen | .05 | .04 |
| 7 | Terry Kennedy | .04 | .03 |
| 8 | Bryan Harvey | .06 | .05 |
| 9 | Alan Trammell | .09 | .07 |
| 10 | Cory Snyder | .09 | .07 |
| 11 | Jody Reed | .05 | .04 |
| 12 | Roberto Alomar | .30 | .25 |
| 13 | Pedro Guerrero | .09 | .07 |
| 14 | Gary Redus | .04 | .03 |
| 15 | Marty Barrett | .05 | .04 |
| 16 | Ricky Jordan | .20 | .15 |
| 17 | Joe Magrane | .07 | .05 |
| 18 | Sid Fernandez | .07 | .05 |
| 19 | Rich Dotson | .04 | .03 |
| 20 | Jack Clark | .09 | .07 |
| 21 | Bob Walk | .05 | .04 |
| 22 | Ron Karkovice | .04 | .03 |
| 23 | Lenny Harris(FC) | .10 | .07 |
| 24 | Phil Bradley | .06 | .05 |
| 25 | Andres Galarraga | .15 | .11 |
| 26 | Brian Downing | .06 | .05 |
| 27 | Dave Martinez | .06 | .05 |
| 28 | Eric King | .04 | .03 |
| 29 | Barry Lyons | .04 | .03 |
| 30 | Dave Schmidt | .04 | .03 |
| 31 | Mike Boddicker | .06 | .05 |
| 32 | Tom Foley | .04 | .03 |
| 33 | Brady Anderson | .07 | .05 |
| 34 | Jim Presley | .05 | .04 |
| 35 | Lance Parrish | .06 | .05 |
| 36 | Von Hayes | .09 | .07 |
| 37 | Lee Smith | .06 | .05 |
| 38 | Herm Winningham | .04 | .03 |
| 39 | Alejandro Pena | .04 | .03 |
| 40 | Mike Scott | .09 | .07 |
| 41 | Joe Orsulak | .04 | .03 |
| 42 | Rafael Ramirez | .05 | .04 |
| 43 | Gerald Young | .05 | .04 |
| 44 | Dick Schofield | .05 | .04 |
| 45 | Dave Smith | .06 | .05 |
| 46 | Dave Magadan | .07 | .05 |
| 47 | Dennis Martinez | .06 | .05 |
| 48 | Greg Minton | .04 | .03 |
| 49 | Milt Thompson | .04 | .03 |
| 50 | Orel Hershiser | .12 | .09 |
| 51 | Bip Roberts(FC) | .09 | .07 |
| 52 | Jerry Browne | .09 | .07 |
| 53 | Bob Ojeda | .05 | .04 |
| 54 | Fernando Valenzuela | .09 | .07 |
| 55 | Matt Nokes | .09 | .07 |
| 56 | Brook Jacoby | .08 | .06 |
| 57 | Frank Tanana | .05 | .04 |
| 58 | Scott Fletcher | .05 | .04 |
| 59 | Ron Oester | .05 | .04 |
| 60 | Bob Boone | .08 | .06 |
| 61 | Dan Gladden | .08 | .06 |
| 62 | Darnell Coles | .04 | .03 |
| 63 | Gregg Olson | .25 | .20 |
| 64 | Todd Burns | .05 | .04 |
| 65 | Todd Benzinger | .07 | .05 |
| 66 | Dale Murphy | .12 | .09 |
| 67 | Mike Flanagan | .06 | .05 |
| 68 | Jose Oquendo | .06 | .05 |
| 69 | Cecil Espy | .08 | .06 |
| 70 | Chris Sabo | .10 | .07 |
| 71 | Shane Rawley | .05 | .04 |
| 72 | Tom Brunansky | .08 | .06 |
| 73 | Vance Law | .05 | .04 |
| 74 | B.J. Surhoff | .08 | .06 |
| 75 | Lou Whitaker | .09 | .07 |
| 76 | Ken Caminiti | .09 | .07 |
| 77 | Nelson Liriano | .04 | .03 |
| 78 | Tommy Gregg | .09 | .07 |
| 79 | Don Slaught | .05 | .04 |
| 80 | Eddie Murray | .12 | .09 |
| 81 | Joe Boever | .08 | .06 |
| 82 | Charlie Leibrandt | .06 | .05 |
| 83 | Jose Lind | .06 | .05 |
| 84 | Tony Phillips | .05 | .04 |
| 85 | Mitch Webster | .04 | .03 |
| 86 | Dan Plesac | .07 | .05 |
| 87 | Rick Mahler | .05 | .04 |
| 88 | Steve Lyons | .05 | .04 |
| 89 | Tony Fernandez | .09 | .07 |
| 90 | Ryne Sandberg | .30 | .25 |
| 91 | Nick Esasky | .09 | .07 |
| 92 | Luis Salazar | .04 | .03 |
| 93 | Pete Incaviglia | .08 | .06 |
| 94 | Ivan Calderon | .06 | .05 |
| 95 | Jeff Treadway | .06 | .05 |
| 96 | Kurt Stillwell | .06 | .05 |
| 97 | Gary Sheffield | .25 | .20 |
| 98 | Jeffrey Leonard | .07 | .05 |
| 99 | Andres Thomas | .05 | .04 |
| 100 | Roberto Kelly | .15 | .11 |
| 101 | Alvaro Espinoza(FC) | .15 | .11 |
| 102 | Greg Gagne | .05 | .04 |
| 103 | John Farrell | .05 | .04 |
| 104 | Willie Wilson | .05 | .04 |
| 105 | Glenn Braggs | .08 | .06 |
| 106 | Chet Lemon | .06 | .05 |
| 107 | Jamie Moyer | .06 | .05 |
| 108 | Chuck Crim | .04 | .03 |
| 109 | Dave Valle | .04 | .03 |
| 110 | Walt Weiss | .10 | .07 |
| 111 | Larry Sheets | .04 | .03 |
| 112 | Don Robinson | .05 | .04 |
| 113 | Danny Heep | .04 | .03 |
| 114 | Carmelo Martinez | .06 | .05 |
| 115 | Dave Gallagher | .08 | .06 |
| 116 | Mike LaValliere | .05 | .04 |
| 117 | Bob McClure | .04 | .03 |
| 118 | Rene Gonzales | .04 | .03 |
| 119 | Mark Parent | .05 | .04 |
| 120 | Wally Joyner | .15 | .11 |
| 121 | Mark Gubicza | .09 | .07 |
| 122 | Tony Pena | .08 | .06 |

| | | MT | NR MT | | | | MT | NR MT |
|---|---|---|---|---|---|---|---|---|
| 123 | Carmen Castillo | .04 | .03 | 185 | Eric Davis | | .20 | .15 |
| 124 | Howard Johnson | .20 | .15 | 186 | Lance McCullers | | .06 | .05 |
| 125 | Steve Sax | .10 | .08 | 187 | Steve Davis(FC) | | .15 | .11 |
| 126 | Tim Belcher | .10 | .08 | 188 | Bill Wegman | | .05 | .04 |
| 127 | Tim Burke | .06 | .05 | 189 | Brian Harper | | .06 | .05 |
| 128 | Al Newman | .04 | .03 | 190 | Mike Moore | | .09 | .07 |
| 129 | Dennis Rasmussen | .05 | .04 | 191 | Dale Mohorcic | | .04 | .03 |
| 130 | Doug Jones | .06 | .05 | 192 | Tim Wallach | | .09 | .07 |
| 131 | Fred Lynn | .09 | .07 | 193 | Keith Hernandez | | .09 | .07 |
| 132 | Jeff Hamilton | .06 | .05 | 194 | Dave Righetti | | .07 | .05 |
| 133 | German Gonzalez | .05 | .04 | 195a | Bret Saberhagen ("joke" | | | |
| 134 | John Morris | .05 | .04 | | on card back) | | .25 | .20 |
| 135 | Dave Parker | .10 | .08 | 195b | Bret Saberhagen | | | |
| 136 | Gary Pettis | .05 | .04 | | ("joker" on card back) | | .30 | .25 |
| 137 | Dennis Boyd | .07 | .05 | 196 | Paul Kilgus | | .04 | .03 |
| 138 | Candy Maldonado | .06 | .05 | 197 | Bud Black | | .05 | .04 |
| 139 | Rick Cerone | .04 | .03 | 198 | Juan Samuel | | .09 | .07 |
| 140 | George Brett | .15 | .11 | 199 | Kevin Seitzer | | .15 | .11 |
| 141 | Dave Clark | .05 | .04 | 200 | Darryl Strawberry | | .30 | .25 |
| 142 | Dickie Thon | .05 | .04 | 201 | Dave Steib | | .09 | .07 |
| 143 | Junior Ortiz | .04 | .03 | 202 | Charlie Hough | | .06 | .05 |
| 144 | Don August | .06 | .05 | 203 | Jack Morris | | .08 | .06 |
| 145 | Gary Gaetti | .10 | .08 | 204 | Rance Mulliniks | | .04 | .03 |
| 146 | Kirt Manwaring | .12 | .09 | 205 | Alvin Davis | | .10 | .08 |
| 147 | Jeff Reed | .04 | .03 | 206 | Jack Howell | | .06 | .05 |
| 148 | Jose Alvarez(FC) | .08 | .06 | 207 | Ken Patterson(FC) | | .06 | .05 |
| 149 | Mike Schooler | .08 | .06 | 208 | Terry Pendleton | | .09 | .07 |
| 150 | Mark Grace | .25 | .20 | 209 | Craig Lefferts | | .06 | .05 |
| 151 | Geronimo Berroa | .08 | .06 | 210 | Kevin Brown(FC) | | .10 | .08 |
| 152 | Barry Jones | .04 | .03 | 211 | Dan Petry | | .04 | .03 |
| 153 | Geno Petralli | .05 | .04 | 212 | Dave Leiper | | .06 | .05 |
| 154 | Jim Deshaies | .08 | .06 | 213 | Daryl Boston | | .04 | .03 |
| 155 | Barry Larkin | .15 | .11 | 214 | Kevin Hickey(FC) | | .08 | .06 |
| 156 | Alfredo Griffin | .05 | .04 | 215 | Mike Krukow | | .06 | .05 |
| 157 | Tom Henke | .06 | .05 | 216 | Terry Francona | | .04 | .03 |
| 158 | Mike Jeffcoat(FC) | .05 | .04 | 217 | Kirk McCaskill | | .08 | .06 |
| 159 | Bob Welch | .09 | .07 | 218 | Scott Bailes | | .05 | .04 |
| 160 | Julio Franco | .10 | .08 | 219 | Bob Forsch | | .04 | .03 |
| 161 | Henry Cotto | .04 | .03 | 220 | Mike Aldrete | | .05 | .04 |
| 162 | Terry Steinbach | .10 | .08 | 221 | Steve Buechele | | .06 | .05 |
| 163 | Damon Berryhill | .08 | .06 | 222 | Jesse Barfield | | .09 | .07 |
| 164 | Tim Crews | .04 | .03 | 223 | Juan Berenguer | | .06 | .05 |
| 165 | Tom Browning | .09 | .07 | 224 | Andy McGaffigan | | .06 | .05 |
| 166 | Frd Manrique | .04 | .03 | 225 | Pete Smith | | .09 | .07 |
| 167 | Harold Reynolds | .09 | .07 | 226 | Mike Witt | | .06 | .05 |
| 168 | Ron Hassey | .05 | .04 | 227 | Jay Howell | | .08 | .06 |
| 169 | Shawon Dunston | .08 | .06 | 228 | Scott Bradley | | .05 | .04 |
| 170 | Bobby Bonilla | .15 | .11 | 229 | Jerome Walton | | .15 | .11 |
| 171 | Tom Herr | .07 | .05 | 230 | Greg Swindell | | .15 | .11 |
| 172 | Mike Heath | .04 | .03 | 231 | Atlee Hammaker | | .04 | .03 |
| 173 | Rich Gedman | .05 | .04 | 232 | Mike Devereaux | | .09 | .07 |
| 174 | Bill Ripken | .05 | .04 | 233 | Ken Hill | | .09 | .07 |
| 175 | Pete O'Brien | .07 | .05 | 234 | Craig Worthington | | .15 | .11 |
| 176a | Lloyd McClendon | | | 235 | Scott Terry | | .08 | .06 |
| | (uniform number 1 on back) | | | 236 | Brett Butler | | .09 | .07 |
| | | 1.00 | .70 | 237 | Doyle Alexander | | .07 | .05 |
| 176b | Lloyd McClendon | | | 238 | Dave Anderson | | .04 | .03 |
| | (uniform number 10 on | | | 239 | Bob Milacki | | .10 | .08 |
| | back) | .20 | .15 | 240 | Dwight Smith | | .50 | .40 |
| 177 | Brian Holton | .05 | .04 | 241 | Otis Nixon | | .04 | .03 |
| 178 | Jeff Blauser | .05 | .04 | 242 | Pat Tabler | | .06 | .05 |
| 179 | Jim Eisenreich | .05 | .04 | 243 | Derek Lilliquist | | .12 | .09 |
| 180 | Bert Blyleven | .09 | .07 | 244 | Danny Tartabull | | .15 | .11 |
| 181 | Rob Murphy | .05 | .04 | 245 | Wade Boggs | | .30 | .25 |
| 182 | Bill Doran | .07 | .05 | 246 | Scott Garrelts | | .08 | .06 |
| 183 | Curt Ford | .04 | .03 | 247 | Spike Owen | | .04 | .03 |
| 184 | Mike Henneman | .06 | .05 | 248 | Norm Charlton | | .12 | .09 |

| | MT | NR MT |
|---|---|---|
| 249 Gerald Perry | .06 | .05 |
| 250 Nolan Ryan | .50 | .40 |
| 251 Kevin Gross | .07 | .05 |
| 252 Randy Milligan | .07 | .05 |
| 253 Mike LaCoss | .05 | .04 |
| 254 Dave Bergman | .04 | .03 |
| 255 Tony Gwynn | .35 | .25 |
| 256 Felix Fermin | .04 | .03 |
| 257 Greg Harris | .10 | .08 |
| 258 *Junior Felix* | .20 | .15 |
| 259 Mark Davis | .09 | .07 |
| 260 Vince Coleman | .15 | .11 |
| 261 Paul Gibson | .10 | .08 |
| 262 Mitch Williams | .10 | .08 |
| 263 Jeff Russell | .08 | .06 |
| 264 *Omar Vizquel* | .10 | .07 |
| 265 Andre Dawson | .12 | .09 |
| 266 Storm Davis | .08 | .06 |
| 267 Guillermo Hernandez | .04 | .03 |
| 268 Mike Felder | .05 | .04 |
| 269 Tom Candiotti | .05 | .04 |
| 270 Bruce Hurst | .09 | .07 |
| 271 Fred McGriff | .30 | .25 |
| 272 Glenn Davis | .15 | .11 |
| 273 John Franco | .09 | .07 |
| 274 Rich Yett | .04 | .03 |
| 275 Craig Biggio | .15 | .11 |
| 276 Gene Larkin | .05 | .04 |
| 277 Rob Dibble | .15 | .11 |
| 278 Randy Bush | .05 | .04 |
| 279 Kevin Bass | .08 | .06 |
| 280a Bo Jackson ("Watham" on card back) | .60 | .45 |
| 280b Bo Jackson ("Wathan" on card back) | 1.00 | .70 |
| 281 Wally Backman | .06 | .05 |
| 282 Larry Andersen | .04 | .03 |
| 283 Chris Bosio | .09 | .07 |
| 284 Juan Agosto | .04 | .03 |
| 285 Ozzie Smith | .10 | .08 |
| 286 George Bell | .10 | .08 |
| 287 Rex Hudler | .05 | .04 |
| 288 Pat Borders | .10 | .08 |
| 289 Danny Jackson | .07 | .05 |
| 290 Carlton Fisk | .09 | .07 |
| 291 Tracy Jones | .05 | .04 |
| 292 Allan Anderson | .07 | .05 |
| 293 Johnny Ray | .07 | .05 |
| 294 Lee Guetterman | .04 | .03 |
| 295 Paul O'Neill | .09 | .07 |
| 296 Carney Lansford | .08 | .06 |
| 297 Tom Brookens | .04 | .03 |
| 298 Claudell Washington | .08 | .06 |
| 299 Hubie Brooks | .08 | .06 |
| 300 Will Clark | .60 | .45 |
| 301 *Kenny Rogers* | .20 | .15 |
| 302 Darrell Evans | .07 | .05 |
| 303 Greg Briley | .25 | .20 |
| 304 Donn Pall | .09 | .07 |
| 305 Teddy Higuera | .09 | .07 |
| 306 Dan Pasqua | .07 | .05 |
| 307 Dave Winfield | .15 | .11 |
| 308 Dennis Powell | .04 | .03 |
| 309 Jose DeLeon | .08 | .06 |
| 310 Roger Clemens | .25 | .20 |
| 311 Melido Perez | .09 | .07 |

| | MT | NR MT |
|---|---|---|
| 312 Devon White | .09 | .07 |
| 313 Doc Gooden | .25 | .20 |
| 314 *Carlos Martinez* | .20 | .15 |
| 315 Dennis Eckersley | .10 | .08 |
| 316 Clay Parker | .12 | .09 |
| 317 Rick Honeycutt | .05 | .04 |
| 318 Tim Laudner | .05 | .04 |
| 319 Joe Carter | .10 | .08 |
| 320 Robin Yount | .20 | .15 |
| 321 Felix Jose | .30 | .25 |
| 322 Mickey Tettleton | .09 | .07 |
| 323 Mike Gallego | .04 | .03 |
| 324 Edgar Martinez | .09 | .07 |
| 325 Dave Henderson | .09 | .07 |
| 326 Chili Davis | .09 | .07 |
| 327 Steve Balboni | .05 | .04 |
| 328 Jody Davis | .04 | .03 |
| 329 Shawn Hillegas | .04 | .03 |
| 330 Jim Abbott | .35 | .25 |
| 331 John Dopson | .10 | .08 |
| 332 Mark Williamson | .04 | .03 |
| 333 Jeff Robinson | .08 | .06 |
| 334 John Smiley | .09 | .07 |
| 335 Bobby Thigpen | .07 | .05 |
| 336 Garry Templeton | .05 | .04 |
| 337 Marvell Wynne | .05 | .04 |
| 338a Ken Griffey, Sr. (uniform number 25 on card back) | .25 | .20 |
| 338b Ken Griffey, Sr. (uniform number 30 on card back) | 3.00 | 2.25 |
| 339 *Steve Finley* | .25 | .20 |
| 340 Ellis Burks | .25 | .20 |
| 341 Frank Williams | .04 | .03 |
| 342 Mike Morgan | .05 | .04 |
| 343 Kevin Mitchell | .35 | .25 |
| 344 Joel Youngblood | .04 | .03 |
| 345 Mike Greenwell | .25 | .20 |
| 346 Glenn Wilson | .05 | .04 |
| 347 John Costello | .05 | .04 |
| 348 Wes Gardner | .04 | .03 |
| 349 Jeff Ballard | .09 | .07 |
| 350 Mark Thurmond | .04 | .03 |
| 351 Randy Myers | .07 | .05 |
| 352 Shawn Abner | .07 | .05 |
| 353 Jesse Orosco | .04 | .03 |
| 354 Greg Walker | .05 | .04 |
| 355 Pete Harnisch | .15 | .11 |
| 356 Steve Farr | .05 | .04 |
| 357 Dave LaPoint | .05 | .04 |
| 358 Willie Fraser | .05 | .04 |
| 359 Mickey Hatcher | .04 | .03 |
| 360 Rickey Henderson | .30 | .25 |
| 361 Mike Fitzgerald | .04 | .03 |
| 362 Bill Schroeder | .04 | .03 |
| 363 Mark Carreon | .10 | .08 |
| 364 Ron Jones | .10 | .08 |
| 365 Jeff Montgomery | .06 | .05 |
| 366 Bill Krueger(FC) | .04 | .03 |
| 367 John Cangelosi | .04 | .03 |
| 368 Jose Gonzalez | .10 | .08 |
| 369 *Greg Hibbard*(FC) | .30 | .25 |
| 370 John Smoltz | .15 | .11 |
| 371 *Jeff Brantley* | .15 | .11 |
| 372 Frank White | .08 | .06 |

| | | MT | NR MT | | | | MT | NR MT |
|---|---|---|---|---|---|---|---|---|
| 373 | Ed Whitson | .06 | .05 | 439 | Duane Ward | | .04 | .03 |
| 374 | Willie McGee | .09 | .07 | 440 | Andy Van Slyke | | .10 | .08 |
| 375 | Jose Canseco | .70 | .50 | 441 | Gene Nelson | | .04 | .03 |
| 376 | Randy Ready | .04 | .03 | 442 | Luis Polonia | | .06 | .05 |
| 377 | Don Aase | .04 | .03 | 443 | Kevin Elster | | .06 | .05 |
| 378 | Tony Armas | .05 | .04 | 444 | Keith Moreland | | .06 | .05 |
| 379 | Steve Bedrosian | .07 | .05 | 445 | Roger McDowell | | .06 | .05 |
| 380 | Chuck Finley | .07 | .05 | 446 | Ron Darling | | .08 | .06 |
| 381 | Kent Hrbek | .12 | .09 | 447 | Ernest Riles | | .04 | .03 |
| 382 | Jim Gantner | .06 | .05 | 448 | Mookie Wilson | | .08 | .06 |
| 383 | Mel Hall | .06 | .05 | 449a | *Bill Spiers* (66 missing | | | |
| 384 | Mike Marshall | .07 | .05 | | for year of birth) | | 1.25 | .90 |
| 385 | Mark McGwire | .20 | .15 | 449b | *Bill Spiers* (1966 for | | | |
| 386 | Wayne Tolleson | .04 | .03 | | birth year) | | .30 | .25 |
| 387 | Brian Holton | .05 | .04 | 450 | Rick Sutcliffe | | .07 | .05 |
| 388 | *John Wetteland* | .20 | .15 | 451 | Nelson Santovenia | | .10 | .08 |
| 389 | Darren Daulton | .04 | .03 | 452 | Andy Allanson | | .04 | .03 |
| 390 | Rob Deer | .07 | .05 | 453 | Bob Melvin | | .04 | .03 |
| 391 | John Moses | .04 | .03 | 454 | Benny Santiago | | .12 | .09 |
| 392 | Todd Worrell | .07 | .05 | 455 | Jose Uribe | | .05 | .04 |
| 393 | Chuck Cary(FC) | .10 | .08 | 456 | Bill Landrum(FC) | | .08 | .05 |
| 394 | Stan Javier | .05 | .04 | 457 | Bobby Witt | | .07 | .05 |
| 395 | Willie Randolph | .09 | .07 | 458 | Kevin Romine | | .07 | .05 |
| 396 | Bill Buckner | .06 | .05 | 459 | Lee Mazzilli | | .04 | .03 |
| 397 | Robby Thompson | .07 | .05 | 460 | Paul Molitor | | .10 | .08 |
| 398 | Mike Scioscia | .07 | .05 | 461 | Ramon Martinez(FC) | | | |
| 399 | Lonnie Smith | .09 | .07 | | | | .60 | .45 |
| 400 | Kirby Puckett | .40 | .30 | 462 | Frank DiPino | | .04 | .03 |
| 401 | Mark Langston | .15 | .11 | 463 | Walt Terrell | | .06 | .05 |
| 402 | Danny Darwin | .04 | .03 | 464 | *Bob Geren* | | .30 | .25 |
| 403 | Greg Maddux | .15 | .11 | 465 | Rick Reuchel | | .09 | .07 |
| 404 | Lloyd Moseby | .07 | .05 | 466 | Mark Grant | | .06 | .05 |
| 405 | Rafael Palmeiro | .09 | .07 | 467 | John Kruk | | .07 | .05 |
| 406 | Chad Kreuter | .10 | .08 | 468 | Gregg Jefferies | | .60 | .45 |
| 407 | Jimmy Key | .09 | .07 | 469 | R.J. Reynolds | | .04 | .03 |
| 408 | Tim Birtsas | .04 | .03 | 470 | Harold Baines | | .09 | .07 |
| 409 | Tim Raines | .10 | .08 | 471 | Dennis Lamp | | .04 | .03 |
| 410 | Dave Stewart | .09 | .07 | 472 | Tom Gordon | | .20 | .15 |
| 411 | *Eric Yelding*(FC) | .15 | .11 | 473 | Terry Puhl | | .04 | .03 |
| 412 | *Kent Anderson*(FC) | | | 474 | Curtis Wilkerson | | .04 | .03 |
| | | .15 | .11 | 475 | Dan Quisenberry | | .05 | .04 |
| 413 | Les Lancaster | .05 | .04 | 476 | Oddibe McDowell | | .07 | .05 |
| 414 | Rick Dempsey | .04 | .03 | 477 | Zane Smith | | .04 | .03 |
| 415 | Randy Johnson | .10 | .08 | 478 | Franklin Stubbs | | .04 | .03 |
| 416 | Gary Carter | .07 | .05 | 479 | Wallace Johnson | | .04 | .03 |
| 417 | Rolando Roomes | .15 | .11 | 480 | Jay Tibbs | | .04 | .03 |
| 418 | Dan Schatzeder | .04 | .03 | 481 | Tom Glavine | | .09 | .07 |
| 419 | Bryn Smith | .07 | .05 | 482 | Manny Lee | | .05 | .04 |
| 420 | Ruben Sierra | .20 | .15 | 483 | Joe Hesketh | | .04 | .03 |
| 421 | Steve Jeltz | .04 | .03 | 484 | Mike Bielecki | | .07 | .05 |
| 422 | Ken Oberkfell | .04 | .03 | 485 | Greg Brock | | .06 | .05 |
| 423 | Sid Bream | .04 | .03 | 486 | Pascual Perez | | .06 | .05 |
| 424 | Jim Clancy | .04 | .03 | 487 | Kirk Gibson | | .09 | .07 |
| 425 | Kelly Gruber | .09 | .07 | 488 | Scott Sanderson | | .05 | .04 |
| 426 | Rick Leach | .04 | .03 | 489 | Domingo Ramos | | .04 | .03 |
| 427 | Lenny Dykstra | .07 | .05 | 490 | Kal Daniels | | .10 | .08 |
| 428 | Jeff Pico | .06 | .05 | 491a | David Wells (Reverse | | | |
| 429 | John Cerutti | .06 | .05 | | negative on back photo) | | | |
| 430 | David Cone | .15 | .11 | | | | 3.00 | 2.25 |
| 431 | Jeff Kunkel | .04 | .03 | 491b | David Wells (Corrected) | | | |
| 432 | Luis Aquino | .05 | .04 | | | | .05 | .04 |
| 433 | Ernie Whitt | .05 | .04 | 492 | Jerry Reed | | .04 | .03 |
| 434 | Bo Diaz | .05 | .04 | 493 | Eric Show | | .06 | .05 |
| 435 | Steve Lake | .04 | .03 | 494 | Mike Pagliarulo | | .06 | .05 |
| 436 | Pat Perry | .04 | .03 | 495 | Ron Robinson | | .05 | .04 |
| 437 | Mike Davis | .05 | .04 | 496 | Brad Komminsk | | .04 | .03 |
| 438 | Cecilio Guante | .04 | .03 | 497 | *Greg Litton* | | .15 | .11 |

| | MT | NR MT |
|---|---|---|
| 498 Chris James | .07 | .05 |
| 499 Luis Quinones(FC) | .05 | .04 |
| 500 Frank Viola | .10 | .08 |
| 501 Tim Teufel | .05 | .04 |
| 502 Terry Leach | .04 | .03 |
| 503 Matt Williams | .20 | .15 |
| 504 Tim Leary | .06 | .05 |
| 505 Doug Drabek | .06 | .05 |
| 506 Mariano Duncan | .06 | .05 |
| 507 Charlie Hayes | .10 | .08 |
| 508 *Joey Belle* | .70 | .50 |
| 509 Pat Sheridan | .05 | .04 |
| 510 Mackey Sasser | .05 | .04 |
| 511 Jose Rijo | .09 | .07 |
| 512 Mike Smithson | .04 | .03 |
| 513 Gary Ward | .04 | .03 |
| 514 Dion James | .06 | .05 |
| 515 Jim Gott | .06 | .05 |
| 516 Drew Hall(FC) | .07 | .05 |
| 517 Doug Bair | .04 | .03 |
| 518 *Scott Scudder* | .20 | .15 |
| 519 Rick Aguilera | .06 | .05 |
| 520 Rafael Belliard | .05 | .04 |
| 521 Jay Buhner | .10 | .08 |
| 522 Jeff Reardon | .06 | .05 |
| 523 Steve Rosenberg(FC) | .09 | .07 |
| 524 Randy Velarde(FC) | .09 | .07 |
| 525 Jeff Musselman | .09 | .07 |
| 526 Bill Long | .06 | .05 |
| 527 *Gary Wayne* | .10 | .08 |
| 528 *Dave Johnson*(FC) | .15 | .11 |
| 529 Ron Kittle | .08 | .06 |
| 530 Erik Hanson(FC) | .20 | .15 |
| 531 Steve Wilson(FC) | .20 | .15 |
| 532 Joey Meyer | .04 | .03 |
| 533 Curt Young | .04 | .03 |
| 534 Kelly Downs | .06 | .05 |
| 535 Joe Girardi | .20 | .15 |
| 536 Lance Blankenship | .09 | .07 |
| 537 Greg Mathews | .05 | .04 |
| 538 Donell Nixon | .04 | .03 |
| 539 Mark Knudson(FC) | .09 | .07 |
| 540 *Jeff Wetherby*(FC) | .15 | .11 |
| 541 Darrin Jackson | .04 | .03 |
| 542 Terry Mulholland | .09 | .07 |
| 543 Eric Hetzel(FC) | .15 | .11 |
| 544 *Rick Reed*(FC) | .15 | .11 |
| 545 Dennis Cook(FC) | .20 | .15 |
| 546 Mike Jackson | .05 | .04 |
| 547 Brian Fisher | .06 | .05 |
| 548 *Gene Harris*(FC) | .20 | .15 |
| 549 Jeff King(FC) | .20 | .15 |
| 550 Dave Dravecky (Salute) | .10 | .08 |
| 551 Randy Kutcher(FC) | .08 | .06 |
| 552 Mark Portugal | .06 | .05 |
| 553 *Jim Corsi*(FC) | .12 | .09 |
| 554 Todd Stottlemyre | .12 | .09 |
| 555 Scott Bankhead | .09 | .07 |
| 556 Ken Dayley | .05 | .04 |
| 557 *Rick Wrona*(FC) | .15 | .11 |
| 558 *Sammy Sosa*(FC) | .40 | .30 |
| 559 Keith Miller | .08 | .06 |

| | MT | NR MT |
|---|---|---|
| 560 Ken Griffey Jr. | 2.00 | 1.50 |
| 561a Ryne Sandberg (No Errors- 3B Position designation) | 10.00 | 7.50 |
| 561b Ryne Sandberg (No Errors- No position designation) | .50 | .40 |
| 562 Billy Hatcher | .06 | .05 |
| 563 Jay Bell(FC) | .09 | .07 |
| 564 *Jack Daugherty*(FC) | .15 | .11 |
| 565 *Rich Monteleone* | .20 | .15 |
| 566 Bo Jackson (All-Star MVP) | .30 | .25 |
| 567 *Tony Fossas*(FC) | .10 | .08 |
| 568 *Roy Smith*(FC) | .15 | .11 |
| 569 *Jaime Navarro*(FC) | .25 | .20 |
| 570 Lance Johnson(FC) | .15 | .11 |
| 571 *Mike Dyer*(FC) | .25 | .20 |
| 572 *Kevin Ritz*(FC) | .20 | .15 |
| 573 Dave West | .15 | .11 |
| 574 *Gary Mielke*(FC) | .25 | .20 |
| 575 Scott Lusader(FC) | .09 | .07 |
| 576 *Joe Oliver* | .30 | .25 |
| 577 Sandy Alomar, Jr. | .25 | .20 |
| 578 Andy Benes(FC) | .30 | .25 |
| 579 Tim Jones | .07 | .05 |
| 580 *Randy McCament*(FC) | .15 | .11 |
| 581 Curt Schilling(FC) | .15 | .11 |
| 582 *John Orton*(FC) | .15 | .11 |
| 583a Milt Cuyler (played in 998 games)(FC) | 2.00 | 1.50 |
| 583b Milt Cuyler (played in 98 games)(FC) | .40 | .30 |
| 584 *Eric Anthony*(FC) | .25 | .20 |
| 585 *Greg Vaughn*(FC) | .60 | .45 |
| 586 *Deion Sanders*(FC) | .50 | .40 |
| 587 Jose DeJesus(FC) | .15 | .11 |
| 588 *Chip Hale*(FC) | .15 | .11 |
| 589 John Olerud(FC) | .70 | .50 |
| 590 *Steve Olin*(FC) | .20 | .15 |
| 591 *Marquis Grissom*(FC) | .60 | .45 |
| 592 *Moises Alou*(FC) | .50 | .40 |
| 593 Mark Lemke(FC) | .10 | .08 |
| 594 *Dean Palmer*(FC) | .80 | .60 |
| 595 Robin Ventura(FC) | 1.00 | .70 |
| 596 *Tino Martinez*(FC) | .50 | .40 |
| 597 *Mike Huff*(FC) | .25 | .20 |
| 598 *Scott Hemond*(FC) | .25 | .20 |
| 599 *Wally Whitehurst*(FC) | .20 | .15 |
| 600 *Todd Zeile*(FC) | .50 | .40 |
| 601 Glenallen Hill(FC) | .35 | .25 |
| 602 Hal Morris(FC) | .15 | .11 |
| 603 Juan Bell(FC) | .15 | .11 |
| 604 Bobby Rose(FC) | .25 | .20 |
| 605 *Matt Merullo*(FC) | .20 | .15 |

| | MT | NR MT |
|---|---|---|
| 606 Kevin Maas(FC) | .50 | .40 |
| 607 Randy Nosek(FC) | .15 | .11 |
| 608 Billy Bates(FC) | .15 | .11 |
| 609 Mike Stanton(FC) | .25 | .20 |
| 610 Goose Gozzo(FC) | .20 | .15 |
| 611 Charles Nagy(FC) | .40 | .30 |
| 612 Scott Coolbaugh(FC) | .20 | .15 |
| 613 Jose Vizcaino(FC) | .25 | .20 |
| 614 Greg Smith(FC) | .20 | .15 |
| 615 Jeff Huson(FC) | .25 | .20 |
| 616 Mickey Weston(FC) | .15 | .11 |
| 617 John Pawlowski(FC) | .15 | .11 |
| 618a Joe Skalski (uniform #27)(FC) | .15 | .11 |
| 618b Joe Skalski (uniform #67)(FC) | 2.00 | 1.50 |
| 619 Bernie Williams(FC) | .60 | .45 |
| 620 Shawn Holman(FC) | .15 | .11 |
| 621 Gary Eave(FC) | .15 | .11 |
| 622 Darrin Fletcher(FC) | .25 | .20 |
| 623 Pat Combs(FC) | .20 | .15 |
| 624 Mike Blowers(FC) | .25 | .20 |
| 625 Kevin Appier(FC) | .30 | .25 |
| 626 Pat Austin(FC) | .15 | .11 |
| 627 Kelly Mann(FC) | .20 | .15 |
| 628 Matt Kinzer(FC) | .15 | .11 |
| 629 Chris Hammond(FC) | .25 | .20 |
| 630 Dean Wilkins(FC) | .15 | .11 |
| 631 Larry Walker(FC) | .60 | .45 |
| 632 Blaine Beatty(FC) | .20 | .15 |
| 633a Tom Barrett (uniform #29)(FC) | .15 | .11 |
| 633b Tom Barrett (uniform #14)(FC) | 4.00 | 3.00 |
| 634 Stan Belinda(FC) | .35 | .25 |
| 635 Tex Smith(FC) | .15 | .11 |
| 636 Hensley Meulens(FC) | .15 | .11 |
| 637 Juan Gonzalez(FC) | 3.00 | 2.25 |
| 638 Lenny Webster(FC) | .20 | .15 |
| 639 Mark Gardner(FC) | .25 | .20 |
| 640 Tommy Greene(FC) | .20 | .15 |
| 641 Mike Hartley(FC) | .20 | .15 |
| 642 Phil Stephenson(FC) | .15 | .11 |
| 643 Kevin Mmahat(FC) | .15 | .11 |
| 644 Ed Whited(FC) | .15 | .11 |
| 645 Delino DeShields(FC) | .40 | .30 |
| 646 Kevin Blankenship(FC) | .15 | .11 |
| 647 Paul Sorrento(FC) | .40 | .30 |
| 648 Mike Roesler(FC) | .15 | .11 |
| 649 Jason Grimsley(FC) | .25 | .20 |
| 650 Dave Justice(FC) | 2.00 | 1.50 |
| 651 Scott Cooper(FC) | .25 | .20 |
| 652 Dave Eiland(FC) | .15 | .11 |
| 653 Mike Munoz(FC) | .20 | .15 |
| 654 Jeff Fischer(FC) | .15 | .11 |
| 655 Terry Jorgenson(FC) | .20 | .15 |
| 656 George Canale(FC) | .20 | .15 |
| 657 Brian DuBois(FC) | .15 | .11 |
| 658 Carlos Quintana | .10 | .08 |
| 659 Luis De los santos | .10 | .08 |
| 660 Jerald Clark | .10 | .08 |
| 661 #1 Draft Pick (Donald Harris)(FC) | .20 | .15 |
| 662 #1 Draft Pick (Paul Coleman)(FC) | .20 | .15 |
| 663 #1 Draft Pick (Frank Thomas)(FC) | 7.00 | 5.25 |
| 664 #1 Draft Pick (Brent Mayne)(FC) | .30 | .25 |
| 665 #1 Draft Pick (Eddie Zosky)(FC) | .25 | .20 |
| 666 #1 Draft Pick (Steve Hosey)(FC) | .20 | .15 |
| 667 #1 Draft Pick (Scott Bryant)(FC) | .20 | .15 |
| 668 #1 Draft Pick (Tom Goodwin)(FC) | .40 | .30 |
| 669 #1 Draft Pick (Cal Eldred)(FC) | 1.50 | 1.25 |
| 670 #1 Draft Pick (Earl Cunningham)(FC) | .25 | .20 |
| 671 #1 Draft Pick (Alan Zinter)(FC) | .25 | .20 |
| 672 #1 Draft Pick (Chuck Knoblauch)(FC) | 2.00 | 1.50 |
| 673 #1 Draft Pick (Kyle Abbott)(FC) | .25 | .20 |
| 674 #1 Draft Pick (Roger Salkeld)(FC) | .60 | .45 |
| 675 #1 Draft Pick (Maurice Vaughn)(FC) | .60 | .45 |
| 676 #1 Draft Pick (Kiki Jones)(FC) | .20 | .15 |
| 677 #1 Draft Pick (Tyler Houston)(FC) | .25 | .20 |
| 678 #1 Draft Pick (Jeff Jackson)(FC) | .15 | .11 |
| 679 #1 Draft Pick (Greg Gohr) (#1 Draft Pick)(FC) | | |

|  | MT | NR MT |
|---|---|---|
|  | .25 | .20 |
| 680 #1 Draft Pick *(Ben McDonald)* (#1 Draft Pick)(FC) | .60 | .45 |
| 681 #1 Draft Pick *(Greg Blosser)* (#1 Draft Pick)(FC) | .50 | .40 |
| 682 #1 Draft Pick *(Willie Green)* (#1 Draft Pick)(FC) | .25 | .20 |
| 683 Dream Team (Wade Boggs) | .20 | .15 |
| 684 Dream Team (Will Clark) | .20 | .15 |
| 685 Dream Team (Tony Gwynn) | .20 | .15 |
| 686 Dream Team (Rickey Henderson) | .20 | .15 |
| 687 Dream Team (Bo Jackson) | .30 | .25 |
| 688 Dream Team (Mark Langston) | .20 | .15 |
| 689 Dream Team (Barry Larkin) | .20 | .15 |
| 690 Dream Team (Kirby Puckett) | .20 | .15 |
| 691 Dream Team (Ryne Sandberg) | .30 | .25 |
| 692 Dream Team (Mike Scott) | .20 | .15 |
| 693 Dream Team (Terry Steinbach) | .20 | .15 |
| 694 Dream Team (Bobby Thigpen) | .20 | .15 |
| 695 Dream Team (Mitch Williams) | .20 | .15 |
| 696 5000 K (Nolan Ryan) | .50 | .40 |
| 697 FB/BB NIKE (Bo Jackson) | 2.00 | 1.50 |
| 698 ALCS MVP (Rickey Henderson) | .25 | .20 |
| 699 NLCS MVP (Will Clark) | .25 | .20 |
| 700 World Series 1,2 | .30 | .25 |
| 701 Candlestick | .30 | .25 |
| 702 World Series Game 3 | .30 | .25 |
| 703 World Series Wrap-up | .30 | .25 |
| 704 200 Hit (Wade Boggs) | .25 | .20 |
| ----- A. Bartlett Giamatti (Bonus-Dream Team) | 2.00 | 1.50 |
| ----- Pat Combs (Bonus Dream Team) | .30 | .25 |
| ----- Todd Zeile (Bonus Dream Team) | 2.00 | 1.50 |
| ----- Luis de los Santos (Bonus-Dream Team) | .30 | .25 |
| ----- Mark Lemke (Bonus Dream Team) | .50 | .40 |
| ----- Robin Ventura (Bonus Dream Team) | 8.00 | 6.00 |
| ----- Jeff Huson (Bonus Dream Team) | .30 | .25 |
| ----- Greg Vaughn (Bonus Dream Team) | 3.00 | 2.25 |
| ----- Marquis Grissom (Bonus Dream Team) | 3.00 | 2.25 |
| ----- Eric Anthony (Bonus Dream Team) | .60 | .45 |

# 1990 Score Traded

This 110-card set features players with new teams as well as 1990 Major League rookies. The cards feature full-color action photos framed in yellow with an orange border. The player's name and position appear in green print below the photo. The team logo is displayed next to the player's name. The card backs feature posed player photos and follow the style of the regular 1990 Score issue. The cards are numbered 1T-110T. Young hockey phenom Eric Lindros is featured trying out for the Toronto Blue Jays.

|  | MT | NR MT |
|---|---|---|
| Complete Set: | 12.00 | 9.00 |
| Common Player: | .06 | .05 |
| 1T Dave Winfield | .15 | .11 |
| 2T Kevin Bass | .06 | .05 |
| 3T Nick Esasky | .06 | .05 |
| 4T Mitch Webster | .06 | .05 |
| 5T Pascual Perez | .06 | .05 |
| 6T Gary Pettis | .06 | .05 |
| 7T Tony Pena | .08 | .06 |
| 8T Candy Maldonado | .08 | .06 |
| 9T Cecil Fielder | .30 | .25 |
| 10T Carmelo Martinez | .06 | .05 |
| 11T Mark Langston | .08 | .06 |
| 12T Dave Parker | .15 | .11 |
| 13T Don Slaught | .06 | .05 |
| 14T Tony Phillips | .06 | .05 |
| 15T John Franco | .08 | .06 |
| 16T Randy Myers | .08 | .06 |
| 17T Jeff Reardon | .08 | .06 |
| 18T Sandy Alomar, Jr. | .20 | .15 |
| 19T Joe Carter | .10 | .08 |
| 20T Fred Lynn | .06 | .05 |

| | MT | NR MT |
|---|---|---|
| 21T Storm Davis | .06 | .05 |
| 22T Craig Lefferts | .06 | .05 |
| 23T Pete O'Brien | .06 | .05 |
| 24T Dennis Boyd | .06 | .05 |
| 25T Lloyd Moseby | .06 | .05 |
| 26T Mark Davis | .06 | .05 |
| 27T Tim Leary | .06 | .05 |
| 28T Gerald Perry | .06 | .05 |
| 29T Don Aase | .06 | .05 |
| 30T Ernie Whitt | .06 | .05 |
| 31T Dale Murphy | .10 | .08 |
| 32T Alejandro Pena | .06 | .05 |
| 33T Juan Samuel | .08 | .06 |
| 34T Hubie Brooks | .08 | .06 |
| 35T Gary Carter | .10 | .08 |
| 36T Jim Presley | .06 | .05 |
| 37T Wally Backman | .06 | .05 |
| 38T Matt Nokes | .06 | .05 |
| 39T Dan Petry | .06 | .05 |
| 40T Franklin Stubbs | .06 | .05 |
| 41T Jeff Huson | .15 | .11 |
| 42T Billy Hatcher | .06 | .05 |
| 43T Terry Leach | .06 | .05 |
| 44T Phil Bradley | .06 | .05 |
| 45T Claudell Washington | .06 | .05 |
| 46T Luis Polonia | .06 | .05 |
| 47T Daryl Boston | .06 | .05 |
| 48T Lee Smith | .08 | .06 |
| 49T Tom Brunansky | .08 | .06 |
| 50T Mike Witt | .06 | .05 |
| 51T Willie Randolph | .08 | .06 |
| 52T Stan Javier | .06 | .05 |
| 53T Brad Komminsk | .06 | .05 |
| 54T John Candelaria | .06 | .05 |
| 55T Bryn Smith | .06 | .05 |
| 56T Glenn Braggs | .06 | .05 |
| 57T Keith Hernandez | .08 | .06 |
| 58T Ken Oberkfell | .06 | .05 |
| 59T Steve Jeltz | .06 | .05 |
| 60T Chris James | .06 | .05 |
| 61T Scott Sanderson | .06 | .05 |
| 62T Bill Long | .06 | .05 |
| 63T Rick Cerone | .06 | .05 |
| 64T Scott Bailes | .06 | .05 |
| 65T Larry Sheets | .06 | .05 |
| 66T Junior Ortiz | .06 | .05 |
| 67T Francisco Cabrera(FC) | .20 | .15 |
| 68T Gary DiSarcina(FC) | .15 | .11 |
| 69T Greg Olson(FC) | .20 | .15 |
| 70T Beau Allred(FC) | .20 | .15 |
| 71T Oscar Azocar(FC) | .15 | .11 |
| 72T Kent Mercker(FC) | .25 | .20 |
| 73T John Burkett(FC) | .20 | .15 |
| 74T Carlos Baerga(FC) | 1.00 | .70 |
| 75T Dave Hollins(FC) | .30 | .25 |
| 76T Todd Hundley(FC) | .20 | .15 |
| 77T Rick Parker(FC) | .15 | .11 |
| 78T Steve Cummings(FC) | .15 | .11 |
| 79T Bill Sampen(FC) | .25 | .20 |
| 80T Jerry Kutzler(FC) | .15 | .11 |
| 81T Derek Bell(FC) | 1.00 | .70 |
| 82T Kevin Tapani(FC) | .35 | .25 |
| 83T Jim Leyritz(FC) | .20 | .15 |
| 84T Ray Lankford(FC) | 1.25 | .90 |
| 85T Wayne Edwards(FC) | .15 | .11 |

| | MT | NR MT |
|---|---|---|
| 86T Frank Thomas | 7.00 | 5.25 |
| 87T Tim Naehring(FC) | .20 | .15 |
| 88T Willie Blair(FC) | .15 | .11 |
| 89T Alan Mills(FC) | .25 | .20 |
| 90T Scott Radinsky(FC) | .25 | .20 |
| 91T Howard Farmer(FC) | .25 | .20 |
| 92T Julio Machado(FC) | .15 | .11 |
| 93T Rafael Valdez(FC) | .15 | .11 |
| 94T Shawn Boskie(FC) | .25 | .20 |
| 95T David Segui(FC) | .20 | .15 |
| 96T Chris Hoiles(FC) | .30 | .25 |
| 97T D.J. Dozier(FC) | .50 | .40 |
| 98T Hector Villanueva(FC) | .25 | .20 |
| 99T Eric Gunderson(FC) | .25 | .20 |
| 100T Eric Lindros(FC) | 6.00 | 4.50 |
| 101T Dave Otto(FC) | .12 | .09 |
| 102T Dana Kiecker(FC) | .20 | .15 |
| 103T Tim Drummond(FC) | .15 | .11 |
| 104T Mickey Pina(FC) | .25 | .20 |
| 105T Craig Grebeck(FC) | .20 | .15 |
| 106T Bernard Gilkey(FC) | .50 | .40 |
| 107T Tim Layana(FC) | .25 | .20 |
| 108T Scott Chiamparino(FC) | .30 | .25 |
| 109T Steve Avery(FC) | 2.00 | 1.50 |
| 110T Terry Shumpert(FC) | .20 | .15 |

# 1991 Score

Score introduced a two series format in 1991. The first series includes cards 1-441. Score cards once again feature multiple border colors within the set, several subsets (Master Blaster, K-Man, Highlights and Rifleman), full-color action photos on the front, posed photos on the flip side. Score eliminated providing the player's uniform number on the 1991 cards. Card number 441 of Series I features a Jose Canseco Vanity Fair photo. All of the 1991 Dream Team cards feature this style. The 1991 Score set when complete with Series II will mark its biggest issue. Rookie prospects and #1 Draft Picks highlight the 1991 Score set. The second series was due for release in February of

1991.

| | MT | NR MT |
|---|---|---|
| Complete Set: | 20.00 | 15.00 |
| Common Player: | .04 | .03 |

| # | Player | MT | NR MT |
|---|---|---|---|
| 1 | Jose Canseco | .35 | .25 |
| 2 | Ken Griffey, Jr. | .80 | .60 |
| 3 | Ryne Sandberg | .20 | .15 |
| 4 | Nolan Ryan | .30 | .25 |
| 5 | Bo Jackson | .30 | .25 |
| 6 | Bret Saberhagen | .12 | .09 |
| 7 | Will Clark | .20 | .15 |
| 8 | Ellis Burks | .15 | .11 |
| 9 | Joe Carter | .15 | .11 |
| 10 | Rickey Henderson | .25 | .20 |
| 11 | Ozzie Guillen | .10 | .08 |
| 12 | Wade Boggs | .20 | .15 |
| 13 | Jerome Walton | .15 | .11 |
| 14 | John Franco | .10 | .08 |
| 15 | Ricky Jordan | .08 | .06 |
| 16 | Wally Backman | .04 | .03 |
| 17 | Rob Dibble | .10 | .08 |
| 18 | Glenn Braggs | .05 | .04 |
| 19 | Cory Snyder | .10 | .08 |
| 20 | Kal Daniels | .10 | .08 |
| 21 | Mark Langston | .10 | .08 |
| 22 | Kevin Gross | .06 | .05 |
| 23 | Don Mattingly | .25 | .20 |
| 24 | Dave Righetti | .08 | .06 |
| 25 | Roberto Alomar | .25 | .20 |
| 26 | Robby Thompson | .06 | .05 |
| 27 | Jack McDowell | .08 | .06 |
| 28 | Bip Roberts | .08 | .06 |
| 29 | Jay Howell | .05 | .04 |
| 30 | Dave Steib | .08 | .06 |
| 31 | Johnny Ray | .04 | .03 |
| 32 | Steve Sax | .10 | .08 |
| 33 | Terry Mulholland | .08 | .06 |
| 34 | Lee Guetterman | .04 | .03 |
| 35 | Tim Raines | .12 | .09 |
| 36 | Scott Fletcher | .04 | .03 |
| 37 | Lance Parrish | .08 | .06 |
| 38 | Tony Phillips | .05 | .04 |
| 39 | Todd Stottlemyre | .06 | .05 |
| 40 | Alan Trammell | .12 | .09 |
| 41 | Todd Burns | .04 | .03 |
| 42 | Mookie Wilson | .06 | .05 |
| 43 | Chris Bosio | .05 | .04 |
| 44 | Jeffrey Leonard | .06 | .05 |
| 45 | Doug Jones | .08 | .06 |
| 46 | Mike Scott | .08 | .06 |
| 47 | Andy Hawkins | .05 | .04 |
| 48 | Harold Reynolds | .08 | .06 |
| 49 | Paul Molitor | .12 | .09 |
| 50 | John Farrell | .05 | .04 |
| 51 | Danny Darwin | .06 | .05 |
| 52 | Jeff Blauser | .04 | .03 |
| 53 | John Tudor | .05 | .04 |
| 54 | Milt Thompson | .04 | .03 |
| 55 | Dave Justice | .30 | .25 |
| 56 | *Greg Olson* | .12 | .09 |
| 57 | *Willie Blair* | .12 | .09 |
| 58 | *Rick Parker* | .10 | .08 |
| 59 | *Shawn Boskie* | .15 | .11 |
| 60 | Kevin Tapani | .10 | .08 |
| 61 | *Dave Hollins* | .20 | .15 |
| 62 | *Scott Radinsky* | .12 | .09 |
| 63 | Francisco Cabrera | .10 | .08 |
| 64 | *Tim Layana* | .12 | .09 |
| 65 | *Jim Leyritz* | .12 | .09 |
| 66 | Wayne Edwards | .08 | .06 |
| 67 | Lee Stevens(FC) | .15 | .11 |
| 68 | *Bill Sampen* | .15 | .11 |
| 69 | *Craig Grebeck* | .10 | .08 |
| 70 | John Burkett | .15 | .11 |
| 71 | *Hector Villanueva* | .15 | .11 |
| 72 | *Oscar Azocar* | .15 | .11 |
| 73 | *Alan Mills* | .15 | .11 |
| 74 | *Carlos Baerga* | .25 | .20 |
| 75 | Charles Nagy | .08 | .06 |
| 76 | Tim Drummond | .08 | .06 |
| 77 | *Dana Kiecker* | .15 | .11 |
| 78 | *Tom Edens*(FC) | .10 | .08 |
| 79 | Kent Mercker | .08 | .06 |
| 80 | Steve Avery | .20 | .15 |
| 81 | Lee Smith | .08 | .06 |
| 82 | Dave Martinez | .05 | .04 |
| 83 | Dave Winfield | .12 | .09 |
| 84 | Bill Spiers | .06 | .05 |
| 85 | Dan Pasqua | .05 | .04 |
| 86 | Randy Milligan | .06 | .05 |
| 87 | Tracy Jones | .04 | .03 |
| 88 | Greg Myers(FC) | .06 | .05 |
| 89 | Keith Hernandez | .06 | .05 |
| 90 | Todd Benzinger | .06 | .05 |
| 91 | Mike Jackson | .05 | .04 |
| 92 | Mike Stanley | .04 | .03 |
| 93 | Candy Maldonado | .06 | .05 |
| 94 | John Kruk | .05 | .04 |
| 95 | Cal Ripken, Jr. | .30 | .25 |
| 96 | Willie Fraser | .04 | .03 |
| 97 | Mike Felder | .04 | .03 |
| 98 | Bill Landrum | .05 | .04 |
| 99 | Chuck Crim | .04 | .03 |
| 100 | Chuck Finley | .08 | .06 |
| 101 | Kirt Manwaring | .06 | .05 |
| 102 | Jaime Navarro | .08 | .06 |
| 103 | Dickie Thon | .04 | .03 |
| 104 | Brian Downing | .05 | .04 |
| 105 | Jim Abbott | .12 | .09 |
| 106 | Tom Brookens | .04 | .03 |
| 107 | Darryl Hamilton | .06 | .05 |
| 108 | Bryan Harvey | .06 | .05 |
| 109 | Greg Harris | .04 | .03 |
| 110 | Greg Swindell | .08 | .06 |
| 111 | Juan Berenguer | .04 | .03 |
| 112 | Mike Heath | .04 | .03 |
| 113 | Scott Bradley | .04 | .03 |
| 114 | Jack Morris | .08 | .06 |
| 115 | Barry Jones | .05 | .04 |
| 116 | Kevin Romine | .04 | .03 |
| 117 | Garry Templeton | .05 | .04 |
| 118 | Scott Sanderson | .05 | .04 |
| 119 | Roberto Kelly | .08 | .06 |
| 120 | George Brett | .15 | .11 |
| 121 | Oddibe McDowell | .05 | .04 |
| 122 | Jim Acker | .04 | .03 |
| 123 | Bill Swift | .05 | .04 |
| 124 | Eric King | .05 | .04 |
| 125 | Jay Buhner | .06 | .05 |
| 126 | Matt Young | .04 | .03 |
| 127 | Alvaro Espinoza | .05 | .04 |

| | | MT | NR MT | | | | MT | NR MT |
|---|---|---|---|---|---|---|---|---|
| 128 | Greg Hibbard | .08 | .06 | | 195 | George Bell | .10 | .08 |
| 129 | Jeff Robinson | .05 | .04 | | 196 | Hubie Brooks | .10 | .08 |
| 130 | Mike Greenwell | .15 | .11 | | 197 | Tom Gordon | .10 | .08 |
| 131 | Dion James | .04 | .03 | | 198 | Mike Fitzgerald | .04 | .03 |
| 132 | Donn Pall | .04 | .03 | | 199 | Mike Pagliarulo | .05 | .04 |
| 133 | Lloyd Moseby | .06 | .05 | | 200 | Kirby Puckett | .15 | .11 |
| 134 | Randy Velarde | .04 | .03 | | 201 | Shawon Dunston | .08 | .06 |
| 135 | Allan Anderson | .05 | .04 | | 202 | Dennis Boyd | .05 | .04 |
| 136 | Mark Davis | .06 | .05 | | 203 | Junior Felix | .08 | .06 |
| 137 | Eric Davis | .15 | .11 | | 204 | Alejandro Pena | .04 | .03 |
| 138 | Phil Stephenson | .04 | .03 | | 205 | Pete Smith | .05 | .04 |
| 139 | Felix Fermin | .04 | .03 | | 206 | Tom Glavine | .06 | .05 |
| 140 | Pedro Guerrero | .08 | .06 | | 207 | Luis Salazar | .04 | .03 |
| 141 | Charlie Hough | .05 | .04 | | 208 | John Smoltz | .08 | .06 |
| 142 | Mike Henneman | .06 | .05 | | 209 | Doug Dascenzo | .05 | .04 |
| 143 | Jeff Montgomery | .06 | .05 | | 210 | Tim Wallach | .08 | .06 |
| 144 | Lenny Harris | .06 | .05 | | 211 | Greg Gagne | .05 | .04 |
| 145 | Bruce Hurst | .06 | .05 | | 212 | Mark Gubicza | .08 | .06 |
| 146 | Eric Anthony | .15 | .11 | | 213 | Mark Parent | .04 | .03 |
| 147 | Paul Assenmacher | .04 | .03 | | 214 | Ken Oberkfell | .04 | .03 |
| 148 | Jesse Barfield | .06 | .05 | | 215 | Gary Carter | .08 | .06 |
| 149 | Carlos Quintana | .08 | .06 | | 216 | Rafael Palmeiro | .10 | .08 |
| 150 | Dave Stewart | .12 | .09 | | 217 | Tom Niedenfuer | .04 | .03 |
| 151 | Roy Smith | .04 | .03 | | 218 | Dave LaPoint | .05 | .04 |
| 152 | Paul Gibson | .04 | .03 | | 219 | Jeff Treadway | .05 | .04 |
| 153 | Mickey Hatcher | .04 | .03 | | 220 | Mitch Williams | .06 | .05 |
| 154 | Jim Eisenreich | .04 | .03 | | 221 | Jose DeLeon | .05 | .04 |
| 155 | Kenny Rogers | .06 | .05 | | 222 | Mike LaValliere | .05 | .04 |
| 156 | Dave Schmidt | .04 | .03 | | 223 | Darrel Akerfelds | .04 | .03 |
| 157 | Lance Johnson | .06 | .05 | | 224 | Kent Anderson | .05 | .04 |
| 158 | Dave West | .05 | .04 | | 225 | Dwight Evans | .08 | .06 |
| 159 | Steve Balboni | .04 | .03 | | 226 | Gary Redus | .04 | .03 |
| 160 | Jeff Brantley | .08 | .06 | | 227 | Paul O'Neill | .06 | .05 |
| 161 | Craig Biggio | .06 | .05 | | 228 | Marty Barrett | .05 | .04 |
| 162 | Brook Jacoby | .06 | .05 | | 229 | Tom Browning | .06 | .05 |
| 163 | Dan Gladden | .05 | .04 | | 230 | Terry Pendleton | .06 | .05 |
| 164 | Jeff Reardon | .08 | .06 | | 231 | Jack Armstrong | .08 | .06 |
| 165 | Mark Carreon | .05 | .04 | | 232 | Mike Boddicker | .06 | .05 |
| 166 | Mel Hall | .05 | .04 | | 233 | Neal Heaton | .05 | .04 |
| 167 | Gary Mielke | .06 | .05 | | 234 | Marquis Grissom | .10 | .08 |
| 168 | Cecil Fielder | .25 | .20 | | 235 | Bert Blyleven | .08 | .06 |
| 169 | Darrin Jackson | .04 | .03 | | 236 | Curt Young | .05 | .04 |
| 170 | Rick Aguilera | .06 | .05 | | 237 | Don Carman | .05 | .04 |
| 171 | Walt Weiss | .06 | .05 | | 238 | Charlie Hayes | .06 | .05 |
| 172 | Steve Farr | .05 | .04 | | 239 | Mark Knudson | .04 | .03 |
| 173 | Jody Reed | .06 | .05 | | 240 | Todd Zeile | .20 | .15 |
| 174 | Mike Jeffcoat | .04 | .03 | | 241 | Larry Walker | .10 | .08 |
| 175 | Mark Grace | .15 | .11 | | 242 | Jerald Clark | .06 | .05 |
| 176 | Larry Sheets | .04 | .03 | | 243 | Jeff Ballard | .05 | .04 |
| 177 | Bill Gullickson | .05 | .04 | | 244 | Jeff King | .06 | .05 |
| 178 | Chris Gwynn | .06 | .05 | | 245 | Tom Brunansky | .08 | .06 |
| 179 | Melido Perez | .06 | .05 | | 246 | Darren Daulton | .06 | .05 |
| 180 | Sid Fernandez | .08 | .06 | | 247 | Scott Terry | .04 | .03 |
| 181 | Tim Burke | .06 | .05 | | 248 | Rob Deer | .06 | .05 |
| 182 | Gary Pettis | .05 | .04 | | 249 | Brady Anderson | .04 | .03 |
| 183 | Rob Murphy | .04 | .03 | | 250 | Lenny Dykstra | .08 | .06 |
| 184 | Craig Lefferts | .06 | .05 | | 251 | Greg Harris | .06 | .05 |
| 185 | Howard Johnson | .10 | .08 | | 252 | Mike Hartley | .08 | .06 |
| 186 | Ken Caminiti | .05 | .04 | | 253 | Joey Cora | .04 | .03 |
| 187 | Tim Belcher | .06 | .05 | | 254 | Ivan Calderon | .08 | .06 |
| 188 | Greg Cadaret | .04 | .03 | | 255 | Ted Power | .04 | .03 |
| 189 | Matt Williams | .15 | .11 | | 256 | Sammy Sosa | .15 | .11 |
| 190 | Dave Magadan | .08 | .06 | | 257 | Steve Buechele | .05 | .04 |
| 191 | Geno Petralli | .04 | .03 | | 258 | Mike Devereaux | .05 | .04 |
| 192 | Jeff Robinson | .05 | .04 | | 259 | Brad Komminsk | .04 | .03 |
| 193 | Jim Deshaies | .05 | .04 | | 260 | Teddy Higuera | .08 | .06 |
| 194 | Willie Randolph | .06 | .05 | | 261 | Shawn Abner | .05 | .04 |

| | | MT | NR MT | | | | MT | NR MT |
|---|---|---|---|---|---|---|---|---|
| 262 | Dave Valle | .05 | .04 | | 329 | Eric Yelding | .06 | .05 |
| 263 | Jeff Huson | .06 | .05 | | 330 | Barry Bonds | .20 | .15 |
| 264 | Edgar Martinez | .06 | .05 | | 331 | *Brian McRae*(FC) | | |
| 265 | Carlton Fisk | .10 | .08 | | | | .30 | .25 |
| 266 | Steve Finley | .06 | .05 | | 332 | *Pedro Munoz*(FC) | | |
| 267 | John Wetteland | .06 | .05 | | | | .40 | .30 |
| 268 | Kevin Appier | .08 | .06 | | 333 | *Daryl Irvine*(FC) | .15 | .11 |
| 269 | Steve Lyons | .04 | .03 | | 334 | Chris Hoiles | .25 | .20 |
| 270 | Mickey Tettleton | .05 | .04 | | 335 | *Thomas Howard*(FC) | | |
| 271 | Luis Rivera | .04 | .03 | | | | .20 | .15 |
| 272 | Steve Jeltz | .04 | .03 | | 336 | *Jeff Schulz*(FC) | .15 | .11 |
| 273 | R.J. Reynolds | .04 | .03 | | 337 | Jeff Manto(FC) | .15 | .11 |
| 274 | Carlos Martinez | .05 | .04 | | 338 | Beau Allred | .10 | .08 |
| 275 | Dan Plesac | .06 | .05 | | 339 | *Mike Bordick*(FC) | | |
| 276 | Mike Morgan | .04 | .03 | | | | .15 | .11 |
| 277 | Jeff Russell | .06 | .05 | | 340 | *Todd Hundley* | .15 | .11 |
| 278 | Pete Incaviglia | .06 | .05 | | 341 | *Jim Vatcher*(FC) | .15 | .11 |
| 279 | Kevin Seitzer | .08 | .06 | | 342 | Luis Sojo(FC) | .10 | .08 |
| 280 | Bobby Thigpen | .08 | .06 | | 343 | Jose Offerman(FC) | .30 | .25 |
| 281 | Stan Javier | .04 | .03 | | 344 | *Pete Coachman*(FC) | | |
| 282 | Henry Cotto | .04 | .03 | | | | .15 | .11 |
| 283 | Gary Wayne | .05 | .04 | | 345 | Mike Benjamin(FC) | .10 | .08 |
| 284 | Shane Mack | .05 | .04 | | 346 | *Ozzie Canseco*(FC) | | |
| 285 | Brian Holman | .06 | .05 | | | | .15 | .11 |
| 286 | Gerald Perry | .05 | .04 | | 347 | Tim McIntosh(FC) | .15 | .11 |
| 287 | Steve Crawford | .04 | .03 | | 348 | Phil Plantier(FC) | .80 | .60 |
| 288 | Nelson Liriano | .04 | .03 | | 349 | *Terry Shumpert* | .15 | .11 |
| 289 | Don Aase | .04 | .03 | | 350 | *Darren Lewis*(FC) | | |
| 290 | Randy Johnson | .06 | .05 | | | | .30 | .25 |
| 291 | Harold Baines | .08 | .06 | | 351 | *David Walsh*(FC) | .20 | .15 |
| 292 | Kent Hrbek | .08 | .06 | | 352 | *Scott Chiamparino* | .15 | .11 |
| 293 | Les Lancaster | .04 | .03 | | 353 | *Julio Valera*(FC) | .15 | .11 |
| 294 | Jeff Musselman | .04 | .03 | | 354 | *Anthony Telford*(FC) | | |
| 295 | Kurt Stillwell | .06 | .05 | | | | .20 | .15 |
| 296 | Stan Belinda | .06 | .05 | | 355 | Kevin Wickander(FC) | | |
| 297 | Lou Whitaker | .08 | .06 | | | | .10 | .08 |
| 298 | Glenn Wilson | .05 | .04 | | 356 | *Tim Naehring* | .20 | .15 |
| 299 | Omar Vizquel | .04 | .03 | | 357 | *Jim Poole*(FC) | .20 | .15 |
| 300 | Ramon Martinez | .20 | .15 | | 358 | *Mark Whiten*(FC) | | |
| 301 | Dwight Smith | .06 | .05 | | | | .40 | .30 |
| 302 | Tim Crews | .04 | .03 | | 359 | *Terry Wells*(FC) | .20 | .15 |
| 303 | Lance Blankenship | .05 | .04 | | 360 | *Rafael Valdez* | .10 | .08 |
| 304 | Sid Bream | .06 | .05 | | 361 | *Mel Stottlemyre*(FC) | | |
| 305 | Rafael Ramirez | .04 | .03 | | | | .15 | .11 |
| 306 | Steve Wilson | .06 | .05 | | 362 | *David Segui* | .20 | .15 |
| 307 | Mackey Sasser | .06 | .05 | | 363 | Paul Abbott | .15 | .11 |
| 308 | Franklin Stubbs | .06 | .05 | | 364 | *Steve Howard*(FC) | | |
| 309 | Jack Daugherty | .06 | .05 | | | | .15 | .11 |
| 310 | Eddie Murray | .10 | .08 | | 365 | *Karl Rhodes*(FC) | .25 | .20 |
| 311 | Bob Welch | .08 | .06 | | 366 | *Rafael Novoa*(FC) | | |
| 312 | Brian Harper | .06 | .05 | | | | .15 | .11 |
| 313 | Lance McCullers | .04 | .03 | | 367 | *Joe Grahe*(FC) | .15 | .11 |
| 314 | Dave Smith | .06 | .05 | | 368 | *Darren Reed*(FC) | | |
| 315 | Bobby Bonilla | .15 | .11 | | | | .15 | .11 |
| 316 | Jerry Don Gleaton | .04 | .03 | | 369 | Jeff McKnight(FC) | .10 | .08 |
| 317 | Greg Maddux | .08 | .06 | | 370 | Scott Leius(FC) | .10 | .08 |
| 318 | Keith Miller | .05 | .04 | | 371 | *Mark Dewey*(FC) | .15 | .11 |
| 319 | Mark Portugal | .04 | .03 | | 372 | *Mark Lee*(FC) | .15 | .11 |
| 320 | Robin Ventura | .25 | .20 | | 373 | *Rosario* | | |
| 321 | Bob Ojeda | .04 | .03 | | | *Rodriguez*(FC) | .15 | .11 |
| 322 | Mike Harkey | .08 | .06 | | 374 | Chuck McElroy(FC) | .10 | .08 |
| 323 | Jay Bell | .06 | .05 | | 375 | *Mike Bell*(FC) | .15 | .11 |
| 324 | Mark McGwire | .20 | .15 | | 376 | Mickey Morandini(FC) | | |
| 325 | Gary Gaetti | .10 | .08 | | | | .10 | .08 |
| 326 | Jeff Pico | .04 | .03 | | 377 | *Bill Haselman*(FC) | | |
| 327 | Kevin McReynolds | .08 | .06 | | | | .15 | .11 |
| 328 | Frank Tanana | .05 | .04 | | 378 | *Dave Pavlas*(FC) | .15 | .11 |

| | MT | NR MT |
|---|---|---|
| 379 Derrick May(FC) | .30 | .25 |
| 380 *Jeromy Burnitz* (#1 Draft Pick)(FC) | .80 | .60 |
| 381 *Donald Peters* (#1 Draft Pick)(FC) | .25 | .20 |
| 382 *Alex Fernandez* (#1 Draft Pick)(FC) | .30 | .25 |
| 383 *Michael Mussina* (#1 Draft Pick)(FC) | 1.50 | 1.25 |
| 384 *Daniel Smith* (#1 Draft Pick)(FC) | .25 | .20 |
| 385 *Lance Dickson* (#1 Draft Pick)(FC) | .40 | .30 |
| 386 *Carl Everett* (#1 Draft Pick)(FC) | .40 | .30 |
| 387 *Thomas Nevers* (#1 Draft Pick)(FC) | .30 | .25 |
| 388 *Adam Hyzdu* (#1 Draft Pick)(FC) | .40 | .30 |
| 389 *Todd Van Poppel* (#1 Draft Pick)(FC) | 1.00 | .70 |
| 390 *Rondell White* (#1 Draft Pick)(FC) | .60 | .45 |
| 391 *Marc Newfield* (#1 Draft Pick)(FC) | 1.25 | .90 |
| 392 Julio Franco (AS) | .10 | .08 |
| 393 Wade Boggs (AS) | .20 | .15 |
| 394 Ozzie Guillen (AS) | .10 | .08 |
| 395 Cecil Fielder (AS) | .20 | .15 |
| 396 Ken Griffey,Jr. (AS) | .40 | .30 |
| 397 Rickey Henderson (AS) | .20 | .15 |
| 398 Jose Canseco (AS) | .30 | .25 |
| 399 Roger Clemens (AS) | .15 | .11 |
| 400 Sandy Alomar,Jr. (AS) | .10 | .08 |
| 401 Bobby Thigpen (AS) | .10 | .08 |
| 402 Bobby Bonilla (Master Blaster) | .10 | .08 |
| 403 Eric Davis (Master Blaster) | .10 | .08 |
| 404 Fred McGriff (Master Blaster) | .10 | .08 |
| 405 Glenn Davis (Master Blaster) | .10 | .08 |
| 406 Kevin Mitchell (Master Blaster) | .10 | .08 |
| 407 Rob Dibble (K-Man) | .10 | .08 |
| 408 Ramon Martinez (K-Man) | .15 | .11 |
| 409 David Cone (K-Man) | .10 | .08 |
| 410 Bobby Witt (K-Man) | .10 | .08 |
| 411 Mark Langston (K-Man) | .10 | .08 |
| 412 Bo Jackson (Rifleman) | .30 | .25 |
| 413 Shawon Dunston (Rifleman) | .10 | .08 |
| 414 Jesse Barfield (Rifleman) | .08 | .06 |
| 415 Ken Caminiti (Rifleman) | .08 | .06 |
| 416 Benito Santiago (Rifleman) | .10 | .08 |
| 417 Nolan Ryan (Highlight) | .30 | .25 |
| 418 Bobby Thigpen (Highlight) | .10 | .08 |
| 419 Ramon Martinez (Highlight) | .15 | .11 |
| 420 Bo Jackson (Highlight) | .20 | .15 |
| 421 Carlton Fisk (Highlight) | .10 | .08 |
| 422 Jimmy Key | .06 | .05 |
| 423 Junior Noboa(FC) | .05 | .04 |
| 424 Al Newman | .04 | .03 |
| 425 Pat Borders | .05 | .04 |
| 426 Von Hayes | .08 | .06 |
| 427 Tim Teufel | .04 | .03 |
| 428 Eric Plunk | .04 | .03 |
| 429 John Moses | .04 | .03 |
| 430 Mike Witt | .05 | .04 |
| 431 Otis Nixon | .04 | .03 |
| 432 Tony Fernandez | .08 | .06 |
| 433 Rance Mulliniks | .04 | .03 |
| 434 Dan Petry | .04 | .03 |
| 435 Bob Geren | .05 | .04 |
| 436 Steve Frey(FC) | .06 | .05 |
| 437 Jamie Moyer | .05 | .04 |
| 438 Junior Ortiz | .04 | .03 |
| 439 Tom O'Malley | .04 | .03 |
| 440 Pat Combs | .06 | .05 |
| 441 Jose Canseco (Dream Team) | 2.00 | 1.50 |
| 442 Alfredo Griffin | .04 | .03 |
| 443 Andres Galarraga | .08 | .06 |
| 444 Bryn Smith | .04 | .03 |
| 445 Andre Dawson | .12 | .09 |
| 446 Juan Samuel | .06 | .05 |
| 447 Mike Aldrete | .04 | .03 |
| 448 Ron Gant | .12 | .09 |
| 449 Fernando Valenzuela | .08 | .06 |
| 450 Vince Coleman | .08 | .06 |
| 451 Kevin Mitchell | .15 | .11 |
| 452 Spike Owen | .04 | .03 |
| 453 Mike Bielecki | .04 | .03 |
| 454 Dennis Martinez | .08 | .06 |
| 455 Brett Butler | .08 | .06 |
| 456 Ron Darling | .06 | .05 |
| 457 Dennis Rasmussen | .04 | .03 |
| 458 Ken Howell | .04 | .03 |
| 459 Steve Bedrosian | .05 | .04 |
| 460 Frank Viola | .12 | .09 |
| 461 Jose Lind | .04 | .03 |
| 462 Chris Sabo | .08 | .06 |
| 463 Dante Bichette | .05 | .04 |
| 464 Rick Mahler | .04 | .03 |
| 465 John Smiley | .06 | .05 |
| 466 Devon White | .06 | .05 |
| 467 John Orton | .04 | .03 |
| 468 Mike Stanton | .08 | .06 |
| 469 Billy Hatcher | .04 | .03 |
| 470 Wally Joyner | .12 | .09 |
| 471 Gene Larkin | .05 | .04 |
| 472 Doug Drabek | .08 | .06 |
| 473 Gary Sheffield | .15 | .11 |
| 474 David Wells | .04 | .03 |
| 475 Andy Van Slyke | .08 | .06 |
| 476 Mike Gallego | .05 | .04 |
| 477 B.J. Surhoff | .08 | .06 |
| 478 Gene Nelson | .04 | .03 |
| 479 Mariano Duncan | .05 | .04 |

| | MT | NR MT | | | MT | NR MT |
|---|---|---|---|---|---|---|
| 480 | Fred McGriff | .12 | .09 | 547 | Mike Kingery | .04 | .03 |
| 481 | Jerry Browne | .04 | .03 | 548 | Terry Kennedy | .04 | .03 |
| 482 | Alvin Davis | .06 | .05 | 549 | David Cone | .08 | .06 |
| 483 | Bill Wegman | .05 | .04 | 550 | Orel Hershiser | .12 | .09 |
| 484 | Dave Parker | .08 | .06 | 551 | Matt Nokes | .06 | .05 |
| 485 | Dennis Eckersley | .12 | .09 | 552 | Eddie Williams | .04 | .03 |
| 486 | Erik Hanson | .12 | .09 | 553 | Frank DiPino | .04 | .03 |
| 487 | Bill Ripken | .04 | .03 | 554 | Fred Lynn | .05 | .04 |
| 488 | Tom Candiotti | .05 | .04 | 555 | Alex Cole(FC) | .25 | .20 |
| 489 | Mike Schooler | .06 | .05 | 556 | Terry Leach | .04 | .03 |
| 490 | Gregg Olson | .12 | .09 | 557 | Chet Lemon | .04 | .03 |
| 491 | Chris James | .05 | .04 | 558 | Paul Mirabella | .04 | .03 |
| 492 | Pete Harnisch | .06 | .05 | 559 | Bill Long | .04 | .03 |
| 493 | Julio Franco | .10 | .08 | 560 | Phil Bradley | .05 | .04 |
| 494 | Greg Briley | .05 | .04 | 561 | Duane Ward | .05 | .04 |
| 495 | Ruben Sierra | .15 | .11 | 562 | Dave Bergman | .04 | .03 |
| 496 | Steve Olin | .05 | .04 | 563 | Eric Show | .04 | .03 |
| 497 | Mike Fetters | .05 | .04 | 564 | Xavier Hernandez(FC) | | |
| 498 | Mark Williamson | .04 | .03 | | | .08 | .06 |
| 499 | Bob Tewksbury | .04 | .03 | 565 | Jeff Parrett | .04 | .03 |
| 500 | Tony Gwynn | .15 | .11 | 566 | Chuck Cary | .04 | .03 |
| 501 | Randy Myers | .08 | .06 | 567 | Ken Hill | .06 | .05 |
| 502 | Keith Comstock | .04 | .03 | 568 | Bob Welch | .08 | .06 |
| 503 | Craig Worthington | .08 | .06 | 569 | John Mitchell | .04 | .03 |
| 504 | Mark Eichhorn | .04 | .03 | 570 | *Travis Fryman*(FC) | | |
| 505 | Barry Larkin | .12 | .09 | | | .60 | .45 |
| 506 | Dave Johnson | .04 | .03 | 571 | Derek Lilliquist | .04 | .03 |
| 507 | Bobby Witt | .06 | .05 | 572 | Steve Lake | .04 | .03 |
| 508 | Joe Orsulak | .04 | .03 | 573 | *John Barfield*(FC) | | |
| 509 | Pete O'Brien | .04 | .03 | | | .10 | .08 |
| 510 | Brad Arnsberg | .05 | .04 | 574 | Randy Bush | .04 | .03 |
| 511 | Storm Davis | .05 | .04 | 575 | Joe Magrane | .06 | .05 |
| 512 | Bob Milacki | .05 | .04 | 576 | Edgar Diaz | .04 | .03 |
| 513 | Bill Pecota | .05 | .04 | 577 | Casy Candaele | .04 | .03 |
| 514 | Glenallen Hill | .08 | .06 | 578 | Jesse Orosco | .04 | .03 |
| 515 | Danny Tartabull | .10 | .08 | 579 | Tom Henke | .06 | .05 |
| 516 | Mike Moore | .05 | .04 | 580 | Rick Cerone | .04 | .03 |
| 517 | Ron Robinson | .04 | .03 | 581 | Drew Hall | .04 | .03 |
| 518 | Mark Gardner | .08 | .06 | 582 | Tony Castillo | .04 | .03 |
| 519 | Rick Wrona | .04 | .03 | 583 | Jimmy Jones | .04 | .03 |
| 520 | Mike Scioscia | .06 | .05 | 584 | Rick Reed | .04 | .03 |
| 521 | Frank Wills | .04 | .03 | 585 | Joe Girardi | .05 | .04 |
| 522 | Greg Brock | .04 | .03 | 586 | *Jeff Gray*(FC) | .15 | .11 |
| 523 | Jack Clark | .08 | .06 | 587 | Luis Polonia | .06 | .05 |
| 524 | Bruce Ruffin | .05 | .04 | 588 | Joe Klink(FC) | .08 | .06 |
| 525 | Robin Yount | .15 | .11 | 589 | Rex Hudler | .05 | .04 |
| 526 | Tom Foley | .04 | .03 | 590 | Kirk McCaskill | .06 | .05 |
| 527 | Pat Perry | .04 | .03 | 591 | Juan Agosto | .04 | .03 |
| 528 | Greg Vaughn | .15 | .11 | 592 | Wes Gardner | .04 | .03 |
| 529 | Wally Whitehurst | .06 | .05 | 593 | *Rich Rodriguez*(FC) | | |
| 530 | Norm Charlton | .06 | .05 | | | .12 | .09 |
| 531 | Marvell Wynne | .04 | .03 | 594 | Mitch Webster | .04 | .03 |
| 532 | Jim Gantner | .05 | .04 | 595 | Kelly Gruber | .12 | .09 |
| 533 | Greg Litton | .04 | .03 | 596 | Dale Mohorcic | .04 | .03 |
| 534 | Manny Lee | .05 | .04 | 597 | Willie McGee | .08 | .06 |
| 535 | Scott Bailes | .04 | .03 | 598 | Bill Krueger | .05 | .04 |
| 536 | Charlie Leibrandt | .04 | .03 | 599 | Bob Walk | .04 | .03 |
| 537 | Roger McDowell | .05 | .04 | 600 | Kevin Maas | .30 | .25 |
| 538 | Andy Benes | .15 | .11 | 601 | Danny Jackson | .06 | .05 |
| 539 | Rick Honeycutt | .04 | .03 | 602 | Craig McMurtry | .04 | .03 |
| 540 | Doc Gooden | .15 | .11 | 603 | Curtis Wilkerson | .04 | .03 |
| 541 | Scott Garrelts | .04 | .03 | 604 | Adam Peterson | .04 | .03 |
| 542 | Dave Clark | .04 | .03 | 605 | Sam Horn | .06 | .05 |
| 543 | Lonnie Smith | .04 | .03 | 606 | Tommy Gregg | .04 | .03 |
| 544 | Rick Rueschel | .05 | .04 | 607 | Ken Dayley | .04 | .03 |
| 545 | Delino DeShields | .20 | .15 | 608 | Carmelo Castillo | .04 | .03 |
| 546 | Mike Sharperson | .04 | .03 | 609 | John Shelby | .04 | .03 |

| | MT | NR MT | | MT | NR MT |
|---|---|---|---|---|---|
| 610 Don Slaught | .04 | .03 | 673 #1 Draft Pick (Robbie Beckett)(FC) | .15 | .11 |
| 611 Calvin Schiraldi | .04 | .03 | 674 #1 Draft Pick (Shane Andrews)(FC) | .20 | .15 |
| 612 Dennis Lamp | .04 | .03 | 675 #1 Draft Pick (Steve Karsay)(FC) | .40 | .30 |
| 613 Andres Thomas | .04 | .03 | | | |
| 614 Jose Gonzales | .04 | .03 | 676 #1 Draft Pick (Aaron Holbert)(FC) | .20 | .15 |
| 615 Randy Ready | .04 | .03 | | | |
| 616 Kevin Bass | .06 | .05 | 677 #1 Draft Pick (Donovan Osborne)(FC) | .60 | .45 |
| 617 Mike Marshall | .05 | .04 | | | |
| 618 Daryl Boston | .04 | .03 | 678 #1 Draft Pick (Todd Ritchie)(FC) | .15 | .11 |
| 619 Andy McGaffigan | .04 | .03 | | | |
| 620 Joe Oliver | .06 | .05 | 679 #1 Draft Pick (Ron Walden)(FC) | .20 | .15 |
| 621 Jim Gott | .04 | .03 | | | |
| 622 Jose Oquendo | .04 | .03 | 680 #1 Draft Pick (Tim Costo)(FC) | .40 | .30 |
| 623 Jose DeJesus | .06 | .05 | | | |
| 624 Mike Brumley | .04 | .03 | 681 #1 Draft Pick (Dan Wilson)(FC) | .40 | .30 |
| 625 John Olerud | .30 | .25 | | | |
| 626 Ernest Riles | .04 | .03 | 682 #1 Draft Pick (Kurt Miller)(FC) | .15 | .11 |
| 627 Gene Harris | .05 | .04 | | | |
| 628 Jose Uribe | .04 | .03 | 683 #1 Draft Pick (Mike Lieberthal)(FC) | .25 | .20 |
| 629 Darnell Coles | .04 | .03 | | | |
| 630 Carney Lansford | .06 | .05 | 684 Roger Clemens (K Man)(FC) | .15 | .11 |
| 631 Tim Leary | .05 | .04 | | | |
| 632 Tim Hulett | .04 | .03 | 685 Doc Gooden (K-Man) | .15 | .11 |
| 633 Kevin Elster | .06 | .05 | | | |
| 634 Tony Fossas | .04 | .03 | 686 Nolan Ryan (K-Man) | .20 | .15 |
| 635 Francisco Oliveras | .04 | .03 | 687 Frank Viola (K-Man) | .08 | .06 |
| 636 Bob Patterson | .04 | .03 | 688 Erik Hanson (K-Man) | .08 | .06 |
| 637 Gary Ward | .04 | .03 | | | |
| 638 Rene Gonzales | .04 | .03 | 689 Matt Williams (Master Blaster) | .10 | .08 |
| 639 Don Robinson | .04 | .03 | | | |
| 640 Darryl Strawberry | .20 | .15 | 690 Jose Canseco (Master Blaster) | .20 | .15 |
| 641 Dave Anderson | .04 | .03 | | | |
| 642 Scott Scudder | .06 | .05 | 691 Darryl Strawberry (Master Blaster) | .15 | .11 |
| 643 Reggie Harris(FC) | | | | | |
| | .20 | .15 | 692 Bo Jackson (Master Blaster) | .30 | .25 |
| 644 Dave Henderson | .08 | .06 | | | |
| 645 Ben McDonald | .35 | .25 | 693 Cecil Fielder (Master Blaster) | .20 | .15 |
| 646 Bob Kipper | .04 | .03 | | | |
| 647 Hal Morris | .15 | .11 | 694 Sandy Alomar, Jr. (Rifleman) | .08 | .06 |
| 648 Tim Birtsas | .04 | .03 | | | |
| 649 Steve Searcy | .04 | .03 | 695 Cory Snyder (Rifleman) | .05 | .04 |
| 650 Dale Murphy | .12 | .09 | | | |
| 651 Ron Oester | .04 | .03 | 696 Eric Davis, Eric Davis (Rifleman) | .08 | .06 |
| 652 Mike LaCoss | .04 | .03 | | | |
| 653 Ron Jones | .05 | .04 | 697 Ken Griffey, Jr. (Rifleman) | .30 | .25 |
| 654 Kelly Downs | .04 | .03 | | | |
| 655 Roger Clemens | .20 | .15 | 698 Andy Van Slyke (Rifleman) | .08 | .06 |
| 656 Herm Winningham | .04 | .03 | | | |
| 657 Trevor Wilson | .06 | .05 | 699 Langston/Witt (No-Hit Club) | .08 | .06 |
| 658 Jose Rijo | .08 | .06 | | | |
| 659 Dann Bilardello | .04 | .03 | 700 Randy Johnson (No-Hit Club) | .08 | .06 |
| 660 Gregg Jefferies | .15 | .11 | | | |
| 661 Doug Drabek (AS) | .08 | .06 | 701 Nolan Ryan (No-Hit Club) | .20 | .15 |
| 662 Randy Myers (AS) | .06 | .05 | | | |
| 663 Benito Santiago (AS) | | | 702 Dave Stewart (No-Hit Club) | .08 | .06 |
| | .08 | .06 | | | |
| 664 Will Clark (AS) | .15 | .11 | 703 Fernando Valenzuela (No-Hit Club) | .06 | .05 |
| 665 Ryne Sandberg (AS) | .15 | .11 | | | |
| 666 Barry Larkin (AS) | .08 | .06 | 704 Andy Hawkins (No-Hit Club) | .04 | .03 |
| 667 Matt Williams (AS) | .08 | .06 | | | |
| 668 Barry Bonds (AS) | .12 | .09 | 705 Melido Perez (No-Hit Club) | .04 | .03 |
| 669 Eric Davis | .12 | .09 | | | |
| 670 Bobby Bonilla (AS) | .08 | .06 | 706 Terry Mulholland (No-Hit Club) | .06 | .05 |
| 671 #1 Draft Pick (Chipper Jones)(FC) | .50 | .40 | | | |
| 672 #1 Draft Pick (Eric Christopherson)(FC) | .15 | .11 | 707 Dave Stieb (No-Hit Club) | | |

| | | MT | NR MT |
|---|---|---|---|
| 708 | Brian Barnes(FC) | .06 | .05 |
| | | .20 | .15 |
| 709 | Bernard Gilkey(FC) | .30 | .25 |
| 710 | Steve Decker(FC) | | |
| | | .25 | .20 |
| 711 | Paul Faries(FC) | .12 | .09 |
| 712 | Paul Marak(FC) | .10 | .08 |
| 713 | Wes Chamberlain(FC) | .40 | .30 |
| 714 | Kevin Belcher(FC) | | |
| | | .10 | .08 |
| 715 | Dan Boone(FC) | .05 | .04 |
| 716 | Steve Adkins(FC) | | |
| | | .10 | .08 |
| 717 | Geronimo Pena(FC) | | |
| | | .10 | .08 |
| 718 | Howard Farmer | .08 | .06 |
| 719 | Mark Leonard(FC) | | |
| | | .25 | .20 |
| 720 | Tom Lampkin | .04 | .03 |
| 721 | Mike Gardiner | | |
| | | .15 | .11 |
| 722 | Jeff Conine(FC) | .15 | .11 |
| 723 | Efrain Valdez(FC) | | |
| | | .10 | .08 |
| 724 | Chuck Malone(FC) | .08 | .06 |
| 725 | Leo Gomez(FC) | .30 | .25 |
| 726 | Paul McClellan(FC) | | |
| | | .15 | .11 |
| 727 | Mark Leiter(FC) | .10 | .08 |
| 728 | Rich DeLucia(FC) | | |
| | | .15 | .11 |
| 729 | Mel Rojas(FC) | .08 | .06 |
| 730 | Hector Wagner(FC) | | |
| | | .10 | .08 |
| 731 | Ray Lankford | .40 | .30 |
| 732 | Turner Ward(FC) | .25 | .20 |
| 733 | Gerald Alexander(FC) | .10 | .08 |
| 734 | Scott Anderson(FC) | | |
| | | .10 | .08 |
| 735 | Tony Perezchica(FC) | | |
| | | .05 | .04 |
| 736 | Jimmy Kremers(FC) | .08 | .06 |
| 737 | American Flag | .30 | .25 |
| 738 | Mike York(FC) | .10 | .08 |
| 739 | Mike Rochford(FC) | .06 | .05 |
| 740 | Scott Aldred(FC) | .08 | .06 |
| 741 | Rico Brogna(FC) | .25 | .20 |
| 742 | Dave Burba(FC) | .10 | .08 |
| 743 | Ray Stephens(FC) | | |
| | | .10 | .08 |
| 744 | Eric Gunderson | .08 | .06 |
| 745 | Troy Afenir(FC) | .08 | .06 |
| 746 | Jeff Shaw(FC) | .08 | .06 |
| 747 | Orlando Merced(FC) | | |
| | | .35 | .25 |
| 748 | Omar Oliveras(FC) | | |
| | | .10 | .08 |
| 749 | Jerry Kutzler(FC) | .06 | .05 |
| 750 | Maurice Vaughn(FC) | .35 | .25 |
| 751 | Matt Stark(FC) | .20 | .15 |
| 752 | Randy Hennis(FC) | | |
| | | .10 | .08 |
| 753 | Andujar Cedeno(FC) | | |
| | | .30 | .25 |
| 754 | Kelvin Torve(FC) | .08 | .06 |
| 755 | Joe Kraemer(FC) | .08 | .06 |
| 756 | Phil Clark(FC) | .15 | .11 |
| 757 | Ed Vosberg(FC) | .10 | .08 |
| 758 | Mike Perez(FC) | .10 | .08 |
| 759 | Scott Lewis(FC) | .10 | .08 |
| 760 | Steve Chitren(FC) | | |
| | | .10 | .08 |
| 761 | Ray Young(FC) | .10 | .08 |
| 762 | Andres Santana(FC) | | |
| | | .15 | .11 |
| 763 | Rodney McCray(FC) | | |
| | | .10 | .08 |
| 764 | Sean Berry(FC) | .10 | .08 |
| 765 | Brent Mayne | .08 | .06 |
| 766 | Mike Simms(FC) | .15 | .11 |
| 767 | Glenn Sutko(FC) | .10 | .08 |
| 768 | Gary Disarcina | .06 | .05 |
| 769 | George Brett (Highlight) | | |
| | | .08 | .06 |
| 770 | Cecil Fielder (Highlight) | | |
| | | .08 | .06 |
| 771 | Jim Presley | .05 | .04 |
| 772 | John Dopson | .05 | .04 |
| 773 | Bo Jackson (Bo Breaker) | .35 | .25 |
| 774 | Brent Knackert(FC) | .08 | .06 |
| 775 | Bill Doran | .06 | .05 |
| 776 | Dick Schofield | .04 | .03 |
| 777 | Nelson Santovenia | .04 | .03 |
| 778 | Mark Guthrie(FC) | .08 | .06 |
| 779 | Mark Lemke | .08 | .06 |
| 780 | Terry Steinbach | .06 | .05 |
| 781 | Tom Bolton | .05 | .04 |
| 782 | Randy Tomlin(FC) | | |
| | | .20 | .15 |
| 783 | Jeff Kunkel | .04 | .03 |
| 784 | Felix Jose | .10 | .08 |
| 785 | Rick Sutcliffe | .05 | .04 |
| 786 | John Cerutti | .04 | .03 |
| 787 | Jose Vizcaino | .05 | .04 |
| 788 | Curt Schilling | .06 | .05 |
| 789 | Ed Whitson | .05 | .04 |
| 790 | Tony Pena | .06 | .05 |
| 791 | John Candelaria | .04 | .03 |
| 792 | Carmelo Martinez | .04 | .03 |
| 793 | Sandy Alomar, Jr. | | |
| 794 | Jim Neidlinger(FC) | | |
| | | .08 | .06 |
| 795 | Red's October | .08 | .06 |
| 796 | Paul Sorrento | .05 | .04 |
| 797 | Tom Pagnozzi | .06 | .05 |
| 798 | Tino Martinez | .15 | .11 |
| 799 | Scott Ruskin(FC) | .08 | .06 |
| 800 | Kirk Gibson | .08 | .06 |
| 801 | Walt Terrell | .04 | .03 |
| 802 | John Russell | .04 | .03 |
| 803 | Chili Davis | .08 | .06 |
| 804 | Chris Nabholz(FC) | .08 | .06 |
| 805 | Juan Gonzalez | .30 | .25 |
| 806 | Ron Hassey | .04 | .03 |
| 807 | Todd Worrell | .06 | .05 |
| 808 | Tommy Greene | .06 | .05 |
| 809 | Joel Skinner | .04 | .03 |
| 810 | Benito Santiago | .08 | .06 |
| 811 | Pat Tabler | .04 | .03 |
| 812 | Scott Erickson(FC) | | |

| | | MT | NR MT |
|---|---|---|---|
| | | .50 | .40 |
| 813 | Moises Alou | .06 | .05 |
| 814 | Dale Sveum | .04 | .03 |
| 815 | Ryne Sandberg (Man of the Year) | .20 | .15 |
| 816 | Rick Dempsey | .04 | .03 |
| 817 | Scott Bankhead | .05 | .04 |
| 818 | Jason Grimsley | .05 | .04 |
| 819 | Doug Jennings | .04 | .03 |
| 820 | Tom Herr | .05 | .04 |
| 821 | Rob Ducey | .04 | .03 |
| 822 | Luis Quinones | .04 | .03 |
| 823 | Greg Minton | .04 | .03 |
| 824 | Mark Grant | .04 | .03 |
| 825 | Ozzie Smith | .10 | .08 |
| 826 | Dave Eiland | .04 | .03 |
| 827 | Danny Heep | .04 | .03 |
| 828 | Hensley Meulens | .08 | .06 |
| 829 | Charlie O'Brien | .04 | .03 |
| 830 | Glenn Davis | .08 | .06 |
| 831 | John Marzano | .04 | .03 |
| 832 | Steve Ontiveros | .04 | .03 |
| 833 | Ron Karkovice | .04 | .03 |
| 834 | Jerry Goff(FC) | .08 | .06 |
| 835 | Ken Griffey, Sr. | .08 | .06 |
| 836 | Kevin Reimer(FC) | .10 | .08 |
| 837 | Randy Kutcher | .04 | .03 |
| 838 | Mike Blowers | .05 | .04 |
| 839 | Mike Macfarlane | .05 | .04 |
| 840 | Frank Thomas | 1.25 | .90 |
| 841 | Ken Griffey, Jr. & Sr. (FS) | 1.25 | .90 |
| 842 | Jack Howell | .04 | .03 |
| 843 | Mauro Gozzo(FC) | .06 | .05 |
| 844 | Gerald Young | .04 | .03 |
| 845 | Zane Smith | .05 | .04 |
| 846 | Kevin Brown | .05 | .04 |
| 847 | Sil Campusano | .04 | .03 |
| 848 | Larry Andersen | .04 | .03 |
| 849 | Cal Ripken, Jr. (FR) | .12 | .09 |
| 850 | Roger Clemens (FR) | .12 | .09 |
| 851 | Sandy Alomar, Jr. (FR) | .08 | .06 |
| 852 | Alan Trammell (FR) | .08 | .06 |
| 853 | George Brett (FR) | .08 | .06 |
| 854 | Robin Yount (FR) | .08 | .06 |
| 855 | Kirby Puckett (FR) | .08 | .06 |
| 856 | Don Mattingly (FR) | .15 | .11 |
| 857 | Rickey Henderson (FR) | .15 | .11 |
| 858 | Ken Griffey,Jr. (FR) | 1.00 | .70 |
| 859 | Ruben Sierra (FR) | .10 | .08 |
| 860 | John Olerud (FR) | .10 | .08 |
| 861 | Dave Justice (FR) | .50 | .40 |
| 862 | Ryne Sandberg (FR) | .15 | .11 |
| 863 | Eric Davis (FR) | .08 | .06 |
| 864 | Darryl Strawberry (FR) | .10 | .08 |
| 865 | Tim Wallach (FR) | .05 | .04 |
| 866 | Doc Gooden (FR) | .08 | .06 |
| 867 | Lenny Dykstra (FR) | .06 | .05 |
| 868 | Barry Bonds (FR) | .10 | .08 |
| 869 | Todd Zeile (FR) | .10 | .08 |
| 870 | Benito Santiago (FR) | .08 | .06 |
| 871 | Will Clark (FR) | .20 | .15 |

| | | MT | NR MT |
|---|---|---|---|
| 872 | Craig Biggio (FR) | .08 | .06 |
| 873 | Wally Joyner (FR) | .08 | .06 |
| 874 | Frank Thomas (FR) | .60 | .45 |
| 875 | Rickey Henderson (MVP) | .10 | .08 |
| 876 | Barry Bonds (MVP) | .10 | .08 |
| 877 | Bob Welch (Cy Young) | .05 | .04 |
| 878 | Doug Drabek (Cy Young) | .06 | .05 |
| 879 | Sandy Alomar, Jr. (ROY) | .08 | .06 |
| 880 | Dave Justice (ROY) | .25 | .20 |
| 881 | Damon Berryhill | .05 | .04 |
| 882 | Frank Viola (Dream Team) | .10 | .08 |
| 883 | Dave Stewart (Dream Team) | .10 | .08 |
| 884 | Doug Jones (Dream Team) | .05 | .04 |
| 885 | Randy Myers (Dream Team) | .06 | .05 |
| 886 | Will Clark (Dream Team) | .30 | .25 |
| 887 | Roberto Alomar (Dream Team) | .08 | .06 |
| 888 | Barry Larkin (Dream Team) | .12 | .09 |
| 889 | Wade Boggs (Dream Team) | .20 | .15 |
| 890 | Rickey Henderson (Dream Team) | .80 | .60 |
| 891 | Kirby Puckett (Dream Team) | .20 | .15 |
| 892 | Ken Griffey,Jr. (Dream Team) | 1.50 | 1.25 |
| 893 | Benito Santiago (Dream Team) | .10 | .08 |

## 1991 Score Traded

This 110-card set features players with new teams as well as 1991 Major League rookies. The cards are designed in the same style as the regular 1991 Score issue. The cards once again feature a "T" designation along with the card number. The complete set was sold at hobby shops in a special box.

|  | MT | NR MT |
|---|---|---|
| Complete Set: | 6.00 | 4.50 |
| Common Player: | .06 | .05 |

| # | Player | MT | NR MT |
|---|---|---|---|
| 1 | Bo Jackson | .35 | .25 |
| 2 | Mike Flanagan | .06 | .05 |
| 3 | Pete Incaviglia | .08 | .06 |
| 4 | Jack Clark | .10 | .08 |
| 5 | Hubie Brooks | .08 | .06 |
| 6 | Ivan Calderon | .12 | .09 |
| 7 | Glenn Davis | .12 | .09 |
| 8 | Wally Backman | .06 | .05 |
| 9 | Dave Smith | .08 | .06 |
| 10 | Tim Raines | .15 | .11 |
| 11 | Joe Carter | .15 | .11 |
| 12 | Sid Bream | .08 | .06 |
| 13 | George Bell | .12 | .09 |
| 14 | Steve Bedrosian | .06 | .05 |
| 15 | Willie Wilson | .06 | .05 |
| 16 | Darryl Strawberry | .30 | .25 |
| 17 | Danny Jackson | .06 | .05 |
| 18 | Kirk Gibson | .08 | .06 |
| 19 | Willie McGee | .10 | .08 |
| 20 | Junior Felix | .08 | .06 |
| 21 | Steve Farr | .06 | .05 |
| 22 | Pat Tabler | .06 | .05 |
| 23 | Brett Butler | .10 | .08 |
| 24 | Danny Darwin | .06 | .05 |
| 25 | Mikey Tettleton | .08 | .06 |
| 26 | Gary Carter | .10 | .08 |
| 27 | Mitch Williams | .08 | .06 |
| 28 | Candy Maldonado | .08 | .06 |
| 29 | Otis Nixon | .08 | .06 |
| 30 | Brian Downing | .06 | .05 |
| 31 | Tom Candiotti | .06 | .05 |
| 32 | John Candelaria | .06 | .05 |
| 33 | Rob Murphy | .06 | .05 |
| 34 | Deion Sanders | .20 | .15 |
| 35 | Willie Randolph | .08 | .06 |
| 36 | Pete Harnisch | .08 | .06 |
| 37 | Dante Bichette | .06 | .05 |
| 38 | Garry Templeton | .08 | .06 |
| 39 | Gary Gaetti | .08 | .06 |
| 40 | John Cerutti | .06 | .05 |
| 41 | Rick Cerone | .06 | .05 |
| 42 | Mike Pagliarulo | .06 | .05 |
| 43 | Ron Hassey | .06 | .05 |
| 44 | Roberto Alomar | .30 | .25 |
| 45 | Mike Boddicker | .08 | .06 |
| 46 | Bud Black | .06 | .05 |
| 47 | Rob Deer | .06 | .05 |
| 48 | Devon White | .08 | .06 |
| 49 | Luis Sojo | .06 | .05 |
| 50 | Terry Pendleton | .08 | .06 |
| 51 | Kevin Gross | .06 | .05 |
| 52 | Mike Huff | .08 | .06 |
| 53 | Dave Righetti | .08 | .06 |
| 54 | Matt Young | .06 | .05 |
| 55 | Ernest Riles | .06 | .05 |
| 56 | Bill Gullickson | .08 | .06 |
| 57 | Vince Coleman | .10 | .08 |
| 58 | Fred McGriff | .12 | .09 |
| 59 | Franklin Stubbs | .06 | .05 |
| 60 | Eric King | .06 | .05 |
| 61 | Cory Snyder | .06 | .05 |
| 62 | Dwight Evans | .08 | .06 |
| 63 | Gerald Perry | .06 | .05 |
| 64 | Eric Show | .06 | .05 |
| 65 | Shawn Hillegas | .06 | .05 |
| 66 | Tony Fernandez | .08 | .06 |
| 67 | Tim Teufel | .06 | .05 |
| 68 | Mitch Webster | .06 | .05 |
| 69 | Mike Heath | .06 | .05 |
| 70 | Chili Davis | .08 | .06 |
| 71 | Larry Andersen | .06 | .05 |
| 72 | Gary Varsho | .06 | .05 |
| 73 | Juan Berenguer | .06 | .05 |
| 74 | Jack Morris | .08 | .06 |
| 75 | Barry Jones | .06 | .05 |
| 76 | Rafael Belliard | .06 | .05 |
| 77 | Steve Buechele | .06 | .05 |
| 78 | Scott Sanderson | .06 | .05 |
| 79 | Bob Ojeda | .06 | .05 |
| 80 | Curt Schilling | .06 | .05 |
| 81 | Brian Drahman(FC) | .15 | .11 |
| 82 | Ivan Rodriguez(FC) | 1.00 | .70 |
| 83 | David Howard(FC) | .20 | .15 |
| 84 | Heath Slocumb(FC) | .15 | .11 |
| 85 | Mike Timlin(FC) | .20 | .15 |
| 86 | Darruyl Kile(FC) | .20 | .15 |
| 87 | Pete Schourek(FC) | .20 | .15 |
| 88 | Bruce Walton(FC) | .12 | .09 |
| 89 | Al Osuna(FC) | .15 | .11 |
| 90 | Gary Scott(FC) | .35 | .25 |
| 91 | Doug Simons(FC) | .15 | .11 |
| 92 | Chris Jones(FC) | .25 | .20 |
| 93 | Chuck Knoblauch | .40 | .30 |
| 94 | Dana Allison(FC) | .15 | .11 |
| 95 | Erik Pappas(FC) | .20 | .15 |
| 96 | Jeff Bagwell(FC) | 1.25 | .90 |
| 97 | Kirk Dressendorfer(FC) | .35 | .25 |
| 98 | Freddie Benavides(FC) | .20 | .15 |
| 99 | Luis Gonzalez(FC) | .40 | .30 |
| 100 | Wade Taylor(FC) | .20 | .15 |
| 101 | Ed Sprague(FC) | .15 | .11 |
| 102 | Bob Scanlan(FC) | .15 | .11 |
| 103 | Rick Wilkins(FC) | .30 | .25 |
| 104 | Chris Donnels(FC) | .20 | .15 |
| 105 | Joe Slusarski(FC) | .20 | .15 |
| 106 | Mark Lewis(FC) | .30 | .25 |
| 107 | Pat Kelly(FC) | .25 | .20 |
| 108 | John Briscoe(FC) | .15 | .11 |
| 109 | Luis Lopez(FC) | .20 | .15 |
| 110 | Jeff Johnson(FC) | .25 | .20 |

## 1992 Score

Score used a two series format for the second consecutive year in 1992. Cards 1-442 are featured in the first series.

The card fronts feature full-color game action photos. The player's name, in white lettering, is across the top with the team logo on the upper-right corner. The player's position is across the bottom. Four-color borders are used. Card backs feature color head shots of the players, team logo and career stats on a vertical layout. Several subsets are included in 1992, including a five-card Joe DiMaggio set. DiMaggio autographed cards were also inserted into random packs. Cards 736-772 can be found with or without a "Rookie Prospects" banner on the card front.

|  |  | MT | NR MT |
|---|---|---|---|
| Complete Set: |  | 20.00 | 15.00 |
| Common Player: |  | .04 | .03 |
| 1 | Ken Griffey, Jr. | .50 | .40 |
| 2 | Nolan Ryan | .25 | .20 |
| 3 | Will Clark | .25 | .20 |
| 4 | Dave Justice | .30 | .25 |
| 5 | Dave Henderson | .08 | .06 |
| 6 | Bret Saberhagen | .08 | .06 |
| 7 | Fred McGriff | .08 | .06 |
| 8 | Erik Hanson | .08 | .06 |
| 9 | Darryl Strawberry | .20 | .15 |
| 10 | Doc Gooden | .12 | .09 |
| 11 | Juan Gonzalez | .20 | .15 |
| 12 | Mark Langston | .08 | .06 |
| 13 | Lonnie Smith | .04 | .03 |
| 14 | Jeff Montgomery | .05 | .04 |
| 15 | Roberto Alomar | .15 | .11 |
| 16 | Delino DeShields | .08 | .06 |
| 17 | Steve Bedrosian | .04 | .03 |
| 18 | Terry Pendleton | .08 | .06 |
| 19 | Mark Carreon | .04 | .03 |
| 20 | Mark McGwire | .15 | .11 |
| 21 | Roger Clemens | .15 | .11 |
| 22 | Chuck Crim | .04 | .03 |
| 23 | Don Mattingly | .25 | .20 |
| 24 | Dickie Thon | .04 | .03 |
| 25 | Ron Gant | .15 | .11 |
| 26 | Milt Cuyler | .10 | .08 |
| 27 | Mike Macfarlane | .05 | .04 |
| 28 | Dan Gladden | .04 | .03 |
| 29 | Melido Perez | .04 | .03 |
| 30 | Willie Randolph | .05 | .04 |
| 31 | Albert Belle | .20 | .15 |
| 32 | Dave Winfield | .08 | .06 |
| 33 | Jimmy Jones | .04 | .03 |
| 34 | Kevin Gross | .04 | .03 |
| 35 | Andres Galarraga | .06 | .05 |
| 36 | Mike Devereaux | .05 | .04 |
| 37 | Chris Bosio | .05 | .04 |
| 38 | Mike LaValliere | .05 | .04 |
| 39 | Gary Gaetti | .08 | .06 |
| 40 | Felix Jose | .10 | .08 |
| 41 | Alvaro Espinoza | .04 | .03 |
| 42 | Rick Aguilera | .06 | .05 |
| 43 | Mike Gallego | .04 | .03 |
| 44 | Eric Davis | .12 | .09 |
| 45 | George Bell | .08 | .06 |
| 46 | Tom Brunansky | .06 | .05 |
| 47 | Steve Farr | .04 | .03 |
| 48 | Duane Ward | .05 | .04 |
| 49 | David Wells | .04 | .03 |
| 50 | Cecil Fielder | .20 | .15 |
| 51 | Walt Weiss | .06 | .05 |
| 52 | Todd Zeile | .10 | .08 |
| 53 | Doug Jones | .04 | .03 |
| 54 | Bob Walk | .04 | .03 |
| 55 | Rafael Palmeiro | .08 | .06 |
| 56 | Rob Deer | .04 | .03 |
| 57 | Paul O'Neill | .08 | .06 |
| 58 | Jeff Reardon | .08 | .06 |
| 59 | Randy Ready | .04 | .03 |
| 60 | Scott Erickson | .20 | .15 |
| 61 | Paul Molitor | .08 | .06 |
| 62 | Jack McDowell | .08 | .06 |
| 63 | Jim Acker | .04 | .03 |
| 64 | Jay Buhner | .06 | .05 |
| 65 | Travis Fryman | .20 | .15 |
| 66 | Marquis Grissom | .10 | .08 |
| 67 | Mike Harkey | .05 | .04 |
| 68 | Luis Polonia | .05 | .04 |
| 69 | Ken Caminiti | .05 | .04 |
| 70 | Chris Sabo | .08 | .06 |
| 71 | Gregg Olson | .08 | .06 |
| 72 | Carlton Fisk | .12 | .09 |
| 73 | Juan Samuel | .06 | .05 |
| 74 | Todd Stottlemyre | .06 | .05 |
| 75 | Andre Dawson | .12 | .09 |
| 76 | Alvin Davis | .06 | .05 |
| 77 | Bill Doran | .06 | .05 |
| 78 | B.J. Surhoff | .06 | .05 |
| 79 | Kirk McCaskill | .06 | .05 |
| 80 | Dale Murphy | .12 | .09 |
| 81 | Jose DeLeon | .05 | .04 |
| 82 | Alex Fernandez | .20 | .15 |
| 83 | Ivan Calderon | .08 | .06 |
| 84 | Brent Mayne | .06 | .05 |
| 85 | Jody Reed | .06 | .05 |
| 86 | Randy Tomlin | .06 | .05 |
| 87 | Randy Milligan | .06 | .05 |
| 88 | Pascual Perez | .04 | .03 |
| 89 | Hensley Meulens | .08 | .06 |
| 90 | Joe Carter | .10 | .08 |
| 91 | Mike Moore | .05 | .04 |
| 92 | Ozzie Guillen | .08 | .06 |
| 93 | Shawn Hillegas | .04 | .03 |
| 94 | Chili Davis | .08 | .06 |
| 95 | Vince Coleman | .08 | .06 |
| 96 | Jimmy Key | .06 | .05 |
| 97 | Billy Ripken | .04 | .03 |
| 98 | Dave Smith | .06 | .05 |
| 99 | Tom Bolton | .04 | .03 |
| 100 | Barry Larkin | .12 | .09 |
| 101 | Kenny Rogers | .04 | .03 |
| 102 | Mike Boddicker | .06 | .05 |
| 103 | Kevin Elster | .04 | .03 |
| 104 | Ken Hill | .06 | .05 |
| 105 | Charlie Leibrandt | .04 | .03 |
| 106 | Pat Combs | .06 | .05 |
| 107 | Hubie Brooks | .06 | .05 |
| 108 | Julio Franco | .10 | .08 |
| 109 | Vicente Palacios | .04 | .03 |
| 110 | Kal Daniels | .08 | .06 |

| | MT | NR MT | | | MT | NR MT |
|---|---|---|---|---|---|---|
| 111 | Bruce Hurst | .06 | .05 | 178 | Kent Mercker | .06 | .05 |
| 112 | Willie McGee | .08 | .06 | 179 | John Cerutti | .04 | .03 |
| 113 | Ted Power | .04 | .03 | 180 | Jay Bell | .06 | .05 |
| 114 | Milt Thompson | .04 | .03 | 181 | Dale Sveum | .04 | .03 |
| 115 | Doug Drabek | .08 | .06 | 182 | Greg Gagne | .04 | .03 |
| 116 | Rafael Belliard | .04 | .03 | 183 | Donnie Hill | .04 | .03 |
| 117 | Scott Garrelts | .04 | .03 | 184 | Rex Hudler | .04 | .03 |
| 118 | Terry Mulholland | .06 | .05 | 185 | Pat Kelly | .25 | .20 |
| 119 | Jay Howell | .05 | .04 | 186 | Jeff Robinson | .04 | .03 |
| 120 | Danny Jackson | .05 | .04 | 187 | Jeff Gray | .08 | .06 |
| 121 | Scott Ruskin | .05 | .04 | 188 | Jerry Willard | .04 | .03 |
| 122 | Robin Ventura | .15 | .11 | 189 | Carlos Quintana | .08 | .06 |
| 123 | Bip Roberts | .06 | .05 | 190 | Dennis Eckersley | .08 | .06 |
| 124 | Jeff Russell | .05 | .04 | 191 | Kelly Downs | .04 | .03 |
| 125 | Hal Morris | .12 | .09 | 192 | Gregg Jefferies | .12 | .09 |
| 126 | Teddy Higuera | .06 | .05 | 193 | Darrin Fletcher | .05 | .04 |
| 127 | Luis Sojo | .05 | .04 | 194 | Mike Jackson | .05 | .04 |
| 128 | Carlos Baerga | .10 | .08 | 195 | Eddie Murray | .12 | .09 |
| 129 | Jeff Ballard | .04 | .03 | 196 | Billy Landrum | .04 | .03 |
| 130 | Tom Gordon | .08 | .06 | 197 | Eric Yelding | .04 | .03 |
| 131 | Sid Bream | .06 | .05 | 198 | Devon White | .06 | .05 |
| 132 | Rance Mulliniks | .04 | .03 | 199 | Larry Walker | .08 | .06 |
| 133 | Andy Benes | .10 | .08 | 200 | Ryne Sandberg | .20 | .15 |
| 134 | Mickey Tettleton | .08 | .06 | 201 | Dave Magadan | .08 | .06 |
| 135 | Rich DeLucia | .06 | .05 | 202 | Steve Chitren | .06 | .05 |
| 136 | Tom Pagnozzi | .06 | .05 | 203 | Scott Fletcher | .04 | .03 |
| 137 | Harold Baines | .08 | .06 | 204 | Dwayne Henry | .04 | .03 |
| 138 | Danny Darwin | .04 | .03 | 205 | Scott Coolbaugh | .05 | .04 |
| 139 | Kevin Bass | .06 | .05 | 206 | Tracy Jones | .04 | .03 |
| 140 | Chris Nabholz | .06 | .05 | 207 | Von Hayes | .06 | .05 |
| 141 | Pete O'Brien | .04 | .03 | 208 | Bob Melvin | .04 | .03 |
| 142 | Jeff Treadway | .05 | .04 | 209 | Scott Scudder | .05 | .04 |
| 143 | Mickey Morandini | .08 | .06 | 210 | Luis Gonzalez | .20 | .15 |
| 144 | Eric King | .04 | .03 | 211 | Scott Sanderson | .05 | .04 |
| 145 | Danny Tartabull | .08 | .06 | 212 | *Chris Donnels* | .05 | .04 |
| 146 | Lance Johnson | .04 | .03 | 213 | *Heath Slocumb* | .08 | .06 |
| 147 | Casey Candaele | .04 | .03 | 214 | Mike Timlin | .12 | .09 |
| 148 | Felix Fermin | .04 | .03 | 215 | Brian Harper | .06 | .05 |
| 149 | Rich Rodriguez | .06 | .05 | 216 | Juan Berenguer | .04 | .03 |
| 150 | Dwight Evans | .08 | .06 | 217 | Mike Henneman | .06 | .05 |
| 151 | Joe Klink | .04 | .03 | 218 | Bill Spiers | .04 | .03 |
| 152 | Kevin Reimer | .08 | .06 | 219 | Scott Terry | .04 | .03 |
| 153 | Orlando Merced | .20 | .15 | 220 | Frank Viola | .12 | .09 |
| 154 | Mel Hall | .05 | .04 | 221 | Mark Eichhorn | .04 | .03 |
| 155 | Randy Myers | .06 | .05 | 222 | Ernest Riles | .04 | .03 |
| 156 | Greg Harris | .04 | .03 | 223 | Ray Lankford | .20 | .15 |
| 157 | Jeff Brantley | .05 | .04 | 224 | Pete Harnisch | .06 | .05 |
| 158 | Jim Eisenreich | .05 | .04 | 225 | Bobby Bonilla | .12 | .09 |
| 159 | Luis Rivera | .04 | .03 | 226 | Mike Scioscia | .05 | .04 |
| 160 | Cris Carpenter | .05 | .04 | 227 | Joel Skinner | .04 | .03 |
| 161 | Bruce Ruffin | .04 | .03 | 228 | Brian Holman | .05 | .04 |
| 162 | Omar Vizquel | .04 | .03 | 229 | Gilberto Reyes(FC) | .06 | .05 |
| 163 | Gerald Alexander | .05 | .04 | 230 | Matt Williams | .15 | .11 |
| 164 | Mark Guthrie | .06 | .05 | 231 | Jaime Navarro | .06 | .05 |
| 165 | Scott Lewis | .06 | .05 | 232 | Jose Rijo | .08 | .06 |
| 166 | Bill Sampen | .06 | .05 | 233 | Atlee Hammaker | .04 | .03 |
| 167 | Dave Anderson | .04 | .03 | 234 | Tim Teufel | .04 | .03 |
| 168 | Kevin McReynolds | .08 | .06 | 235 | John Kruk | .08 | .06 |
| 169 | Jose Vizcaino | .04 | .03 | 236 | Kurt Stillwell | .05 | .04 |
| 170 | Bob Geren | .04 | .03 | 237 | Dan Pasqua | .05 | .04 |
| 171 | Mike Morgan | .05 | .04 | 238 | Tim Crews | .04 | .03 |
| 172 | Jim Gott | .04 | .03 | 239 | Dave Gallagher | .05 | .04 |
| 173 | Mike Pagliarulo | .05 | .04 | 240 | Leo Gomez | .15 | .11 |
| 174 | Mike Jeffcoat | .04 | .03 | 241 | Steve Avery | .25 | .20 |
| 175 | Craig Lefferts | .05 | .04 | 242 | Bill Gullickson | .06 | .05 |
| 176 | Steve Finley | .08 | .06 | 243 | Mark Portugal | .04 | .03 |
| 177 | Wally Backman | .04 | .03 | 244 | Lee Guetterman | .04 | .03 |

| | MT | NR MT | | | MT | NR MT |
|---|---|---|---|---|---|---|
| 245 | Benny Santiago | .08 | .06 | 312 | Pat Tabler | .04 | .03 |
| 246 | Jim Gantner | .04 | .03 | 313 | Mike Maddux | .04 | .03 |
| 247 | Robby Thompson | .05 | .04 | 314 | Bob Milacki | .04 | .03 |
| 248 | Terry Shumpert | .04 | .03 | 315 | Eric Anthony | .10 | .08 |
| 249 | Mike Bell(FC) | .15 | .11 | 316 | Dante Bichette | .05 | .04 |
| 250 | Harold Reynolds | .06 | .05 | 317 | Steve Decker | .15 | .11 |
| 251 | Mike Felder | .04 | .03 | 318 | Jack Clark | .08 | .06 |
| 252 | Bill Pecota | .04 | .03 | 319 | Doug Dascenzo | .04 | .03 |
| 253 | Bill Krueger | .04 | .03 | 320 | Scott Leius | .10 | .08 |
| 254 | Alfredo Griffin | .04 | .03 | 321 | Jim Lindeman | .04 | .03 |
| 255 | Lou Whitaker | .08 | .06 | 322 | Bryan Harvey | .08 | .06 |
| 256 | Roy Smith | .04 | .03 | 323 | Spike Owen | .04 | .03 |
| 257 | Jerald Clark | .05 | .04 | 324 | Roberto Kelly | .12 | .09 |
| 258 | Sammy Sosa | .08 | .06 | 325 | Stan Belinda | .05 | .04 |
| 259 | Tim Naehring | .15 | .11 | 326 | Joey Cora | .04 | .03 |
| 260 | Dave Righetti | .08 | .06 | 327 | Jeff Innis | .04 | .03 |
| 261 | Paul Gibson | .04 | .03 | 328 | Willie Wilson | .05 | .04 |
| 262 | Chris James | .05 | .04 | 329 | Juan Agosto | .04 | .03 |
| 263 | Larry Andersen | .04 | .03 | 330 | Charles Nagy | .10 | .08 |
| 264 | Storm Davis | .05 | .04 | 331 | Scott Bailes | .04 | .03 |
| 265 | Jose Lind | .04 | .03 | 332 | Pete Schourek | .12 | .09 |
| 266 | Greg Hibbard | .06 | .05 | 333 | Mike Flanagan | .04 | .03 |
| 267 | Norm Charlton | .06 | .05 | 334 | Omar Olivares | .10 | .08 |
| 268 | Paul Kilgus | .04 | .03 | 335 | Dennis Lamp | .04 | .03 |
| 269 | Greg Maddux | .06 | .05 | 336 | Tommy Greene | .06 | .05 |
| 270 | Ellis Burks | .12 | .09 | 337 | Randy Velarde | .04 | .03 |
| 271 | Frank Tanana | .05 | .04 | 338 | Tom Lampkin | .04 | .03 |
| 272 | Gene Larkin | .05 | .04 | 339 | John Russell | .04 | .03 |
| 273 | Ron Hassey | .04 | .03 | 340 | Bob Kipper | .04 | .03 |
| 274 | Jeff Robinson | .04 | .03 | 341 | Todd Burns | .04 | .03 |
| 275 | Steve Howe | .05 | .04 | 342 | Ron Jones | .05 | .04 |
| 276 | Daryl Boston | .04 | .03 | 343 | Dave Valle | .04 | .03 |
| 277 | Mark Lee | .04 | .03 | 344 | Mike Heath | .04 | .03 |
| 278 | Jose Segura(FC) | .12 | .09 | 345 | John Olerud | .15 | .11 |
| 279 | Lance Blankenship | .04 | .03 | 346 | Gerald Young | .04 | .03 |
| 280 | Don Slaught | .04 | .03 | 347 | Ken Patterson | .04 | .03 |
| 281 | Russ Swan | .08 | .06 | 348 | Les Lancaster | .04 | .03 |
| 282 | Bob Tewksbury | .04 | .03 | 349 | Steve Crawford | .04 | .03 |
| 283 | Geno Petralli | .04 | .03 | 350 | John Candelaria | .04 | .03 |
| 284 | Shane Mack | .08 | .06 | 351 | Mike Aldrete | .04 | .03 |
| 285 | Bob Scanlan | .25 | .20 | 352 | Mariano Duncan | .05 | .04 |
| 286 | Tim Leary | .05 | .04 | 353 | Julio Machado | .04 | .03 |
| 287 | John Smoltz | .15 | .11 | 354 | Ken Williams | .04 | .03 |
| 288 | Pat Borders | .05 | .04 | 355 | Walt Terrell | .04 | .03 |
| 289 | Mark Davidson | .04 | .03 | 356 | Mitch Williams | .08 | .06 |
| 290 | Sam Horn | .06 | .05 | 357 | Al Newman | .04 | .03 |
| 291 | Lenny Harris | .05 | .04 | 358 | Bud Black | .05 | .04 |
| 292 | Franklin Stubbs | .04 | .03 | 359 | Joe Hesketh | .04 | .03 |
| 293 | Thomas Howard | .05 | .04 | 360 | Paul Assenmacher | .05 | .04 |
| 294 | Steve Lyons | .04 | .03 | 361 | Bo Jackson | .25 | .20 |
| 295 | Francisco Oliveras | .04 | .03 | 362 | Jeff Blauser | .04 | .03 |
| 296 | Terry Leach | .04 | .03 | 363 | Mike Brumley | .04 | .03 |
| 297 | Barry Jones | .04 | .03 | 364 | Jim Deshaies | .04 | .03 |
| 298 | Lance Parrish | .08 | .06 | 365 | Brady Anderson | .04 | .03 |
| 299 | Wally Whitehurst | .06 | .05 | 366 | Chuck McElroy | .04 | .03 |
| 300 | Bob Welch | .06 | .05 | 367 | Matt Merullo | .04 | .03 |
| 301 | Charlie Hayes | .05 | .04 | 368 | Tim Belcher | .06 | .05 |
| 302 | Charlie Hough | .05 | .04 | 369 | Luis Aquino | .04 | .03 |
| 303 | Gary Redus | .04 | .03 | 370 | Joe Oliver | .05 | .04 |
| 304 | Scott Bradley | .04 | .03 | 371 | Greg Swindell | .08 | .06 |
| 305 | Jose Oquendo | .04 | .03 | 372 | Lee Stevens | .10 | .08 |
| 306 | Pete Incaviglia | .06 | .05 | 373 | Mark Knudson | .04 | .03 |
| 307 | Marvin Freeman | .04 | .03 | 374 | Bill Wegman | .05 | .04 |
| 308 | Gary Pettis | .04 | .03 | 375 | Jerry Don Gleaton | .04 | .03 |
| 309 | Joe Slusarski | .25 | .20 | 376 | Pedro Guerrero | .10 | .08 |
| 310 | Kevin Seitzer | .05 | .04 | 377 | Randy Bush | .04 | .03 |
| 311 | Jeff Reed | .04 | .03 | 378 | Greg Harris | .04 | .03 |

| | | MT | NR MT |
|---|---|---|---|
| 379 | Eric Plunk | .04 | .03 |
| 380 | Jose DeJesus | .08 | .06 |
| 381 | Bobby Witt | .06 | .05 |
| 382 | Curtis Wilkerson | .04 | .03 |
| 383 | Gene Nelson | .04 | .03 |
| 384 | Wes Chamberlain | .20 | .15 |
| 385 | Tom Henke | .06 | .05 |
| 386 | Mark Lemke | .06 | .05 |
| 387 | Greg Briley | .04 | .03 |
| 388 | Rafael Ramirez | .04 | .03 |
| 389 | Tony Fossas | .04 | .03 |
| 390 | Henry Cotto | .04 | .03 |
| 391 | Tim Hulett | .04 | .03 |
| 392 | Dean Palmer | .25 | .20 |
| 393 | Glenn Braggs | .05 | .04 |
| 394 | Mark Salas | .04 | .03 |
| 395 | Rusty Meacham(FC) | .20 | .15 |
| 396 | Andy Ashby(FC) | .15 | .11 |
| 397 | Jose Melendez(FC) | .20 | .15 |
| 398 | Warren Newson(FC) | .20 | .15 |
| 399 | Frank Castillo(FC) | .15 | .11 |
| 400 | Chito Martinez(FC) | .25 | .20 |
| 401 | Bernie Williams | .20 | .15 |
| 402 | Derek Bell(FC) | .20 | .15 |
| 403 | Javier Ortiz(FC) | .15 | .11 |
| 404 | Tim Sherrill(FC) | .12 | .09 |
| 405 | Rob MacDonald(FC) | .15 | .11 |
| 406 | Phil Plantier | .40 | .30 |
| 407 | Troy Afenir | .10 | .08 |
| 408 | Gino Minutelli(FC) | .10 | .08 |
| 409 | Reggie Jefferson(FC) | .20 | .15 |
| 410 | Mike Remlinger(FC) | .15 | .11 |
| 411 | Carlos Rodriguez(FC) | .15 | .11 |
| 412 | Joe Redfield(FC) | .20 | .15 |
| 413 | Alonzo Powell(FC) | .08 | .06 |
| 414 | Scott Livingstone(FC) | .30 | .25 |
| 415 | Scott Kamieniecki(FC) | .15 | .11 |
| 416 | Tim Spehr(FC) | .20 | .15 |
| 417 | Brian Hunter(FC) | .30 | .25 |
| 418 | Ced Landrum(FC) | .15 | .11 |
| 419 | Bret Barberie(FC) | .15 | .11 |
| 420 | Kevin Morton(FC) | .20 | .15 |
| 421 | Doug Henry(FC) | .20 | .15 |
| 422 | Doug Piatt(FC) | .15 | .11 |
| 423 | Pat Rice(FC) | .15 | .11 |
| 424 | Juan Guzman(FC) | .60 | .45 |
| 425 | Nolan Ryan (No-Hit Club) | .30 | .25 |
| 426 | Tommy Greene (No-Hit Club) | .10 | .08 |
| 427 | Milacki/Flanagan/ | | |

| | | MT | NR MT |
|---|---|---|---|
| | Williamson (No-Hit Club) | .10 | .08 |
| 428 | Wilson Alvarez (No-Hit Club) | .20 | .15 |
| 429 | Otis Nixon (Highlight) | .08 | .06 |
| 430 | Rickey Henderson (Highlight) | .20 | .15 |
| 431 | Cecil Fielder (AS) | .10 | .08 |
| 432 | Julio Franco (AS) | .08 | .06 |
| 433 | Cal Ripken, Jr. (AS) | .15 | .11 |
| 434 | Wade Boggs (AS) | .10 | .08 |
| 435 | Joe Carter (AS) | .10 | .08 |
| 436 | Ken Griffey, Jr. (AS) | .40 | .30 |
| 437 | Ruben Sierra (AS) | .10 | .08 |
| 438 | Scott Erickson (AS) | .15 | .11 |
| 439 | Tom Henke (AS) | .05 | .04 |
| 440 | Terry Steinbach (AS) | .05 | .04 |
| 441 | Rickey Henderson (Dream Team) | .25 | .20 |
| 442 | Ryne Sandberg (Dream Team) | .35 | .25 |
| 443 | Otis Nixon | .06 | .05 |
| 444 | Scott Radinsky | .04 | .03 |
| 445 | Mark Grace | .08 | .06 |
| 446 | Tony Pena | .06 | .05 |
| 447 | Billy Hatcher | .04 | .03 |
| 448 | Glenallen Hill | .06 | .05 |
| 449 | Chris Gwynn | .04 | .03 |
| 450 | Tom Glavine | .08 | .06 |
| 451 | John Habyan | .04 | .03 |
| 452 | Al Osuna | .04 | .03 |
| 453 | Tony Phillips | .06 | .05 |
| 454 | Greg Cadaret | .04 | .03 |
| 455 | Rob Dibble | .08 | .06 |
| 456 | Rick Honeycutt | .04 | .03 |
| 457 | Jerome Walton | .04 | .03 |
| 458 | Mookie Wilson | .04 | .03 |
| 459 | Mark Gubicza | .04 | .03 |
| 460 | Craig Biggio | .08 | .06 |
| 461 | Dave Cochrane | .04 | .03 |
| 462 | Keith Miller | .04 | .03 |
| 463 | Alex Cole | .06 | .05 |
| 464 | Pete Smith | .04 | .03 |
| 465 | Brett Butler | .06 | .05 |
| 466 | Jeff Huson | .04 | .03 |
| 467 | Steve Lake | .04 | .03 |
| 468 | Lloyd Moseby | .04 | .03 |
| 469 | Tim McIntosh | .04 | .03 |
| 470 | Dennis Martinez | .06 | .05 |
| 471 | Greg Myers | .04 | .03 |
| 472 | Mackey Sasser | .04 | .03 |
| 473 | Junior Ortiz | .04 | .03 |
| 474 | Greg Olson | .04 | .03 |
| 475 | Steve Sax | .06 | .05 |
| 476 | Ricky Jordan | .06 | .05 |
| 477 | Max Venable | .04 | .03 |
| 478 | Brian McRae | .10 | .08 |
| 479 | Doug Simons | .04 | .03 |
| 480 | Rickey Henderson | .15 | .11 |
| 481 | Gary Varsho | .04 | .03 |
| 482 | Carl Willis | .04 | .03 |
| 483 | Rick Wilkins | .10 | .08 |
| 484 | Donn Pall | .04 | .03 |
| 485 | Edgar Martinez | .08 | .06 |
| 486 | Tom Foley | .08 | .06 |

| | MT | NR MT | | | MT | NR MT |
|---|---|---|---|---|---|---|
| 487 | Mark Williamson | .08 | .06 | 554 | David Segui | .06 | .05 |
| 488 | Jack Armstrong | .08 | .06 | 555 | Barry Bonds | .20 | .15 |
| 489 | Gary Carter | .08 | .06 | 556 | Mo Vaughn | .20 | .15 |
| 490 | Ruben Sierra | .15 | .11 | 557 | Craig Wilson | .06 | .05 |
| 491 | Gerald Perry | .04 | .03 | 558 | Bobby Rose | .04 | .03 |
| 492 | Rob Murphy | .04 | .03 | 559 | Rod Nichols | .04 | .03 |
| 493 | Zane Smith | .04 | .03 | 560 | Len Dykstra | .08 | .06 |
| 494 | *Darryl Kile* | .10 | .08 | 561 | Craig Grebeck | .04 | .03 |
| 495 | Kelly Gruber | .06 | .05 | 562 | Darren Lewis | .10 | .08 |
| 496 | Jerry Browne | .04 | .03 | 563 | Todd Benzinger | .04 | .03 |
| 497 | Darryl Hamilton | .06 | .05 | 564 | Ed Whitson | .04 | .03 |
| 498 | Mike Stanton | .04 | .03 | 565 | Jesse Barfield | .04 | .03 |
| 499 | Mark Leonard | .04 | .03 | 566 | Lloyd McClendon | .04 | .03 |
| 500 | Jose Canseco | .20 | .15 | 567 | Dan Plesac | .04 | .03 |
| 501 | Dave Martinez | .04 | .03 | 568 | Danny Cox | .04 | .03 |
| 502 | Jose Guzman | .04 | .03 | 569 | Skeeter Barnes | .04 | .03 |
| 503 | Terry Kennedy | .04 | .03 | 570 | Bobby Thigpen | .08 | .06 |
| 504 | *Ed Sprague* | .08 | .06 | 571 | Deion Sanders | .10 | .08 |
| 505 | Frank Thomas | .60 | .45 | 572 | Chuck Knoblauch | .20 | .15 |
| 506 | Darren Daulton | .06 | .05 | 573 | Matt Nokes | .06 | .05 |
| 507 | Kevin Tapani | .06 | .05 | 574 | Herm Winningham | .04 | .03 |
| 508 | Luis Salazar | .04 | .03 | 575 | Tom Candiotti | .06 | .05 |
| 509 | Paul Faries | .04 | .03 | 576 | *Jeff Bagwell* | .50 | .40 |
| 510 | Sandy Alomar, Jr. | .08 | .06 | 577 | Brook Jacoby | .04 | .03 |
| 511 | Jeff King | .04 | .03 | 578 | Chico Walker | .04 | .03 |
| 512 | Gary Thurman | .04 | .03 | 579 | Brian Downing | .04 | .03 |
| 513 | Chris Hammond | .06 | .05 | 580 | Dave Stewart | .06 | .05 |
| 514 | Pedro Munoz | .15 | .11 | 581 | Francisco Cabrera | .04 | .03 |
| 515 | Alan Trammell | .08 | .06 | 582 | Rene Gonzales | .04 | .03 |
| 516 | Geronimo Pena | .06 | .05 | 583 | Stan Javier | .04 | .03 |
| 517 | Rodney McCray | .04 | .03 | 584 | Randy Johnson | .06 | .05 |
| 518 | Manny Lee | .04 | .03 | 585 | Chuck Finley | .06 | .05 |
| 519 | Junior Felix | .06 | .05 | 586 | Mark Gardner | .04 | .03 |
| 520 | Kirk Gibson | .06 | .05 | 587 | Mark Whiten | .10 | .08 |
| 521 | Darrin Jackson | .06 | .05 | 588 | Garry Templeton | .04 | .03 |
| 522 | John Burkett | .06 | .05 | 589 | Gary Sheffield | .20 | .15 |
| 523 | Jeff Johnson | .06 | .05 | 590 | Ozzie Smith | .08 | .06 |
| 524 | Jim Corsi | .04 | .03 | 591 | Candy Maldonado | .04 | .03 |
| 525 | Robin Yount | .12 | .09 | 592 | Mike Sharperson | .04 | .03 |
| 526 | Jamie Quirk | .04 | .03 | 593 | Carlos Martinez | .04 | .03 |
| 527 | Bob Ojeda | .04 | .03 | 594 | Scott Bankhead | .04 | .03 |
| 528 | Mark Lewis | .10 | .08 | 595 | Tim Wallach | .06 | .05 |
| 529 | Bryn Smith | .04 | .03 | 596 | Tino Martinez | .08 | .06 |
| 530 | Kent Hrbek | .06 | .05 | 597 | Roger McDowell | .04 | .03 |
| 531 | Dennis Boyd | .04 | .03 | 598 | Cory Snyder | .06 | .05 |
| 532 | Ron Karkovice | .04 | .03 | 599 | Andujar Cedeno | .10 | .08 |
| 533 | Don August | .04 | .03 | 600 | Kirby Puckett | .15 | .11 |
| 534 | Todd Frohwirth | .04 | .03 | 601 | Rick Parker | .04 | .03 |
| 535 | Wally Joyner | .08 | .06 | 602 | Todd Hundley | .08 | .06 |
| 536 | Dennis Rasmussen | .04 | .03 | 603 | Greg Litton | .04 | .03 |
| 537 | Andy Allanson | .04 | .03 | 604 | Dave Johnson | .04 | .03 |
| 538 | Rich Gossage | .04 | .03 | 605 | John Franco | .04 | .03 |
| 539 | John Marzano | .04 | .03 | 606 | Mike Fetters | .04 | .03 |
| 540 | Cal Ripken | .20 | .15 | 607 | Luis Alicea | .04 | .03 |
| 541 | Bill Swift | .06 | .05 | 608 | Trevor Wilson | .04 | .03 |
| 542 | Kevin Appier | .06 | .05 | 609 | Rob Ducey | .04 | .03 |
| 543 | Dave Bergman | .04 | .03 | 610 | Ramon Martinez | .08 | .06 |
| 544 | Bernard Gilkey | .10 | .08 | 611 | Dave Burba | .04 | .03 |
| 545 | Mike Greenwell | .08 | .06 | 612 | Dwight Smith | .04 | .03 |
| 546 | Jose Uribe | .04 | .03 | 613 | Kevin Maas | .08 | .06 |
| 547 | Jesse Orosco | .04 | .03 | 614 | John Costello | .04 | .03 |
| 548 | Bob Patterson | .04 | .03 | 615 | Glenn Davis | .06 | .05 |
| 549 | Mike Stanley | .04 | .03 | 616 | Shawn Abner | .04 | .03 |
| 550 | Howard Johnson | .08 | .06 | 617 | Scott Hemond | .04 | .03 |
| 551 | Joe Orsulak | .04 | .03 | 618 | Tom Prince | .04 | .03 |
| 552 | Dick Schofield | .04 | .03 | 619 | Wally Ritchie | .04 | .03 |
| 553 | Dave Hollins | .08 | .06 | 620 | Jim Abbott | .08 | .06 |

| | MT | NR MT | | | MT | NR MT |
|---|---|---|---|---|---|---|
| 621 | Charlie O'Brien | .04 | .03 | 688 | Scott Chiamparino | .04 | .03 |
| 622 | Jack Daugherty | .04 | .03 | 689 | Rich Gedman | .04 | .03 |
| 623 | Tommy Gregg | .04 | .03 | 690 | Rich Monteleone | .04 | .03 |
| 624 | Jeff Shaw | .04 | .03 | 691 | Alejandro Pena | .04 | .03 |
| 625 | Tony Gwynn | .15 | .11 | 692 | Oscar Azocar | .04 | .03 |
| 626 | Mark Leiter | .04 | .03 | 693 | Jim Poole | .04 | .03 |
| 627 | Jim Clancy | .04 | .03 | 694 | Mike Gardiner | .04 | .03 |
| 628 | Tim Layana | .04 | .03 | 695 | Steve Buechele | .04 | .03 |
| 629 | Jeff Schaefer | .04 | .03 | 696 | Rudy Seanez | .04 | .03 |
| 630 | Lee Smith | .06 | .05 | 697 | Paul Abbott | .04 | .03 |
| 631 | Wade Taylor | .06 | .05 | 698 | Steve Searcy | .04 | .03 |
| 632 | Mike Simms | .06 | .05 | 699 | Jose Offerman | .06 | .05 |
| 633 | Terry Steinbach | .04 | .03 | 700 | *Ivan Rodriguez* | .50 | .40 |
| 634 | Shawon Dunston | .06 | .05 | 701 | Joe Girardi | .04 | .03 |
| 635 | Tim Raines | .06 | .05 | 702 | Tony Perezchica | .04 | .03 |
| 636 | Kirt Manwaring | .04 | .03 | 703 | Paul McClellan | .05 | .04 |
| 637 | Warren Cromartie | .04 | .03 | 704 | *David Howard* | .06 | .05 |
| 638 | Luis Quinones | .04 | .03 | 705 | Dan Petry | .04 | .03 |
| 639 | Greg Vaughn | .08 | .06 | 706 | Jack Howell | .04 | .03 |
| 640 | Kevin Mitchell | .08 | .06 | 707 | Jose Mesa | .04 | .03 |
| 641 | Chris Hoiles | .10 | .08 | 708 | Randy St. Claire | .04 | .03 |
| 642 | Tom Browning | .04 | .03 | 709 | Kevin Brown | .06 | .05 |
| 643 | Mitch Webster | .04 | .03 | 710 | Ron Darling | .06 | .05 |
| 644 | Steve Olin | .06 | .05 | 711 | Jason Grimsley | .04 | .03 |
| 645 | Tony Fernandez | .06 | .05 | 712 | John Orton | .04 | .03 |
| 646 | Juan Bell | .04 | .03 | 713 | Shawn Boskie | .04 | .03 |
| 647 | Joe Boever | .04 | .03 | 714 | Pat Clements | .04 | .03 |
| 648 | Carney Lansford | .06 | .05 | 715 | Brian Barnes | .06 | .05 |
| 649 | Mike Benjamin | .04 | .03 | 716 | *Luis Lopez(FC)* | .08 | .06 |
| 650 | George Brett | .10 | .08 | 717 | Bob McClure | .04 | .03 |
| 651 | Tim Burke | .04 | .03 | 718 | Mark Davis | .04 | .03 |
| 652 | Jack Morris | .06 | .05 | 719 | Dann Billardello | .04 | .03 |
| 653 | Orel Hershiser | .06 | .05 | 720 | Tom Edens | .04 | .03 |
| 654 | Mike Schooler | .04 | .03 | 721 | Willie Fraser | .04 | .03 |
| 655 | Andy Van Slyke | .08 | .06 | 722 | Curt Young | .04 | .03 |
| 656 | Dave Stieb | .06 | .05 | 723 | Neal Heaton | .04 | .03 |
| 657 | Dave Clark | .04 | .03 | 724 | Craig Worthington | .04 | .03 |
| 658 | Ben McDonald | .10 | .08 | 725 | Mel Rojas | .04 | .03 |
| 659 | John Smiley | .06 | .05 | 726 | Daryl Irvine | .04 | .03 |
| 660 | Wade Boggs | .12 | .09 | 727 | Roger Mason | .04 | .03 |
| 661 | Eric Bullock | .04 | .03 | 728 | Kirk Dressendorfer | .08 | .06 |
| 662 | Eric Show | .04 | .03 | 729 | Scott Aldred | .04 | .03 |
| 663 | Lenny Webster | .06 | .05 | 730 | Willie Blair | .04 | .03 |
| 664 | Mike Huff | .04 | .03 | 731 | Allan Anderson | .04 | .03 |
| 665 | Rick Sutcliffe | .06 | .05 | 732 | Dana Kiecker | .04 | .03 |
| 666 | Jeff Manto | .04 | .03 | 733 | Jose Gonzalez | .04 | .03 |
| 667 | Mike Fitzgerald | .04 | .03 | 734 | Brian Drahman | .04 | .03 |
| 668 | Matt Young | .04 | .03 | 735 | Brad Komminsk | .04 | .03 |
| 669 | Dave West | .04 | .03 | 736 | *Arthur Rhodes(FC)* | | |
| 670 | Mike Hartley | .04 | .03 | | | .15 | .11 |
| 671 | Curt Schilling | .06 | .05 | 737 | *Terry Mathews(FC)* | | |
| 672 | Brian Bohanon | .04 | .03 | | | .10 | .08 |
| 673 | Cecil Espy | .04 | .03 | 738 | *Jeff Fassero(FC)* | .08 | .06 |
| 674 | Joe Grahe | .04 | .03 | 739 | *Mike Magnante(FC)* | | |
| 675 | Sid Fernandez | .06 | .05 | | | .08 | .06 |
| 676 | Edwin Nunez | .04 | .03 | 740 | *Kip Gross(FC)* | .08 | .06 |
| 677 | Hector Villanueva | .04 | .03 | 741 | *Jim Hunter(FC)* | .06 | .05 |
| 678 | Sean Berry | .06 | .05 | 742 | *Jose Mota(FC)* | .08 | .06 |
| 679 | Dave Eiland | .04 | .03 | 743 | Joe Bitker | .04 | .03 |
| 680 | David Cone | .08 | .06 | 744 | *Tim Mauser(FC)* | .08 | .06 |
| 681 | Mike Bordick | .06 | .05 | 745 | *Ramon Garcia(FC)* | | |
| 682 | Tony Castillo | .04 | .03 | | | .08 | .06 |
| 683 | John Barfield | .04 | .03 | 746 | *Rod Beck(FC)* | .08 | .06 |
| 684 | Jeff Hamilton | .04 | .03 | 747 | *Jim Austin(FC)* | .08 | .06 |
| 685 | Ken Dayley | .04 | .03 | 748 | *Keith Mitchell(FC)* | | |
| 686 | Carmelo Martinez | .04 | .03 | | | .10 | .08 |
| 687 | Mike Capel | .04 | .03 | 749 | *Wayne* | | |

| | | MT | NR MT |
|---|---|---|---|
| | *Rosenthal*(FC) | .06 | .05 |
| 750 | *Bryan Hickerson*(FC) | | |
| | | .08 | .06 |
| 751 | *Bruce Egloff*(FC) | .08 | .06 |
| 752 | *John Wehner*(FC) | | |
| | | .08 | .06 |
| 753 | Darren Holmes(FC) | .05 | .04 |
| 754 | Dave Hansen | .06 | .05 |
| 755 | Mike Mussina(FC) | .20 | .15 |
| 756 | *Anthony Young*(FC) | | |
| | | .10 | .08 |
| 757 | Ron Tingley | .04 | .03 |
| 758 | *Ricky Bones*(FC) | .10 | .08 |
| 759 | *Mark Wohlers*(FC) | | |
| | | .25 | .20 |
| 760 | Wilson Alvarez(FC) | .08 | .06 |
| 761 | *Harvey Pulliam*(FC) | | |
| | | .08 | .06 |
| 762 | Ryan Bowen(FC) | .10 | .08 |
| 763 | Terry Bross(FC) | .04 | .03 |
| 764 | Joel Johnston(FC) | | |
| | | .08 | .06 |
| 765 | *Terry McDaniel*(FC) | | |
| | | .10 | .08 |
| 766 | Esteban Beltre(FC) | | |
| | | .08 | .06 |
| 767 | *Rob Maurer*(FC) | .20 | .15 |
| 768 | Ted Wood | .20 | .15 |
| 769 | *Mo Sanford*(FC) | .10 | .08 |
| 770 | *Jeff Carter*(FC) | .08 | .06 |
| 771 | *Gil Heredia*(FC) | .08 | .06 |
| 772 | Monty Fariss(FC) | .08 | .06 |
| 773 | Will Clark (AS) | .10 | .08 |
| 774 | Ryne Sandberg (AS) | .10 | .08 |
| 775 | Barry Larkin (AS) | .08 | .06 |
| 776 | Howard Johnson (AS) | | |
| | | .08 | .06 |
| 777 | Barry Bonds (AS) | .10 | .08 |
| 778 | Brett Butler (AS) | .06 | .05 |
| 779 | Tony Gwynn (AS) | .10 | .08 |
| 780 | Ramon Martinez (AS) | | |
| | | .06 | .05 |
| 781 | Lee Smith (AS) | .06 | .05 |
| 782 | Mike Scioscia (AS) | .04 | .03 |
| 783 | Dennis Martinez (Highlight) | .04 | .03 |
| 784 | Dennis Martinez (No-Hit Club) | .04 | .03 |
| 785 | Mark Gardner (No-Hit Club) | .04 | .03 |
| 786 | Bret Saberhagen (No-Hit Club) | .06 | .05 |
| 787 | Kent Mercker, Mark Wohlers, Alejandro Pena (No-Hit Club) | .06 | .05 |
| 788 | Cal Ripken (MVP) | .10 | .08 |
| 789 | Terry Pendleton (MVP) | | |
| | | .08 | .06 |
| 790 | Roger Clemens (CY YOUNG) | .10 | .08 |
| 791 | Tom Glavine (CY YOUNG) | .08 | .06 |
| 792 | Chuck Knoblauch (ROY) | .20 | .15 |
| 793 | Jeff Bagwell (ROY) | .30 | .25 |
| 794 | Cal Ripken (Man of the Year) | .08 | .06 |

| | | MT | NR MT |
|---|---|---|---|
| 795 | David Cone (Highlight) | .06 | .05 |
| 796 | Kirby Puckett (Highlight) | .08 | .06 |
| 797 | Steve Avery (Highlight) | .10 | .08 |
| 798 | Jack Morris (Highlight) | .06 | .05 |
| 799 | *Allen Watson*(FC) | | |
| | | .20 | .15 |
| 800 | *Manny Ramirez*(FC) | | |
| | | .80 | .60 |
| 801 | Cliff Floyd | .35 | .25 |
| 802 | *Al Shirley*(FC) | .35 | .25 |
| 803 | *Brian Barber*(FC) | | |
| | | .20 | .15 |
| 804 | *John Farrell*(FC) | .20 | .15 |
| 805 | *Brent Gates*(FC) | .20 | .15 |
| 806 | *Scott Ruffcorn*(FC) | | |
| | | .20 | .15 |
| 807 | *Tyrone Hill*(FC) | .30 | .25 |
| 808 | *Benji Gill*(FC) | .30 | .25 |
| 809 | *Aaron Sele*(FC) | .30 | .25 |
| 810 | *Tyler Green*(FC) | .70 | .50 |
| 811 | Chris Jones | .04 | .03 |
| 812 | Steve Wilson | .04 | .03 |
| 813 | *Cliff Young* | .08 | .06 |
| 814 | *Don Wakamatsu* | .08 | .06 |
| 815 | *Mike Humphreys* | .08 | .06 |
| 816 | *Scott Servais* | .08 | .06 |
| 817 | *Rico Rossy* | .08 | .06 |
| 818 | John Ramos | .08 | .06 |
| 819 | Rob Mallicoat | .06 | .05 |
| 820 | Milt Hill | .06 | .05 |
| 821 | Carlos Carcia | .06 | .05 |
| 822 | Stan Royer | .06 | .05 |
| 823 | *Jeff Plympton*(FC) | | |
| | | .15 | .11 |
| 824 | *Braulio Castillo*(FC) | | |
| | | .20 | .15 |
| 825 | *David Haas*(FC) | .08 | .06 |
| 826 | *Luis Mercedes*(FC) | | |
| | | .10 | .08 |
| 827 | Eric Karros(FC) | .25 | .20 |
| 828 | *Shawn Hare*(FC) | .10 | .08 |
| 829 | *Reggie Sanders*(FC) | | |
| | | .30 | .25 |
| 830 | Tom Goodwin | .10 | .08 |
| 831 | *Dan Gakeler*(FC) | .08 | .06 |
| 832 | Stacy Jones(FC) | .08 | .06 |
| 833 | *Kim Batiste* | .08 | .06 |
| 834 | Cal Eldred | .08 | .06 |
| 835 | Chris George | | |
| | | .10 | .08 |
| 836 | *Wayne Housie*(FC) | | |
| | | .10 | .08 |
| 837 | *Mike Ignasiak*(FC) | | |
| | | .10 | .08 |
| 838 | *Josias Manzanillo*(FC) | .10 | .08 |
| 839 | *Jim Olander*(FC) | .10 | .08 |
| 840 | *Gary Cooper*(FC) | | |
| | | .10 | .08 |
| 841 | *Royce Clayton*(FC) | | |
| | | .20 | .15 |
| 842 | *Hector Fajardo*(FC) | | |
| | | .20 | .15 |

| | MT | NR MT |
|---|---|---|
| 843 Blaine Beatty | .04 | .03 |
| 844 Jorge Pedre(FC) | .10 | .08 |
| 845 Kenny Lofton(FC) | .40 | .30 |
| 846 Scott Brosius(FC) | .08 | .06 |
| 847 Chris Cron(FC) | .08 | .06 |
| 848 Denis Boucher | .06 | .05 |
| 849 Kyle Abbott | .10 | .08 |
| 850 Bob Zupcic(FC) | .30 | .25 |
| 851 Rheal Cormier(FC) | .15 | .11 |
| 852 Jim Lewis(FC) | .08 | .06 |
| 853 Anthony Telford | .04 | .03 |
| 854 Cliff Brantley(FC) | .10 | .08 |
| 855 Kevin Campbell(FC) | | |
| | .10 | .08 |
| 856 Craig Shipley(FC) | .08 | .06 |
| 857 Chuck Carr | .04 | .03 |
| 858 Tony Eusebio(FC) | | |
| | .10 | .08 |
| 859 Jim Thome(FC) | .40 | .30 |
| 860 Vinny Castilla(FC) | | |
| | .10 | .08 |
| 861 Dann Howitt | .04 | .03 |
| 862 Kevin Ward(FC) | .10 | .08 |
| 863 Steve Wapnick(FC) | | |
| | .08 | .06 |
| 864 Rod Brewer | .08 | .06 |
| 865 Todd Van Poppel | .35 | .25 |
| 866 Jose Hernandez(FC) | | |
| | .10 | .08 |
| 867 Amalio Carreno(FC) | | |
| | .10 | .08 |
| 868 Calvin Jones(FC) | .10 | .08 |
| 869 Jeff Gardner(FC) | .10 | .08 |
| 870 Jarvis Brown(FC) | .10 | .08 |
| 871 Eddie Taubensee(FC) | .20 | .15 |
| 872 Andy Mota(FC) | .08 | .06 |
| 873 Chris Haney | .06 | .05 |
| 874 Roberto Hernandez | .10 | .08 |
| 875 Laddie Renfroe(FC) | | |
| | .10 | .08 |
| 876 Scott Cooper | .08 | .06 |
| 877 Armando Reynoso(FC) | | |
| | .10 | .08 |
| 878 Ty Cobb (Memorabilia) | | |
| | .30 | .25 |
| 879 Babe Ruth (Memorabilia) | .40 | .30 |
| 880 Honus Wagner (Memorabilia) | .20 | .15 |
| 881 Lou Gehrig (Memorabilia) | .30 | .25 |
| 882 Satchel Paige (Memorabilia) | .20 | .15 |
| 883 Will Clark (Dream Team) | .20 | .15 |
| 884 Cal Ripken (Dream Team) | .30 | .25 |
| 885 Wade Boggs (Dream Team) | .20 | .15 |
| 886 Kirby Puckett (Dream Team) | .20 | .15 |
| 887 Tony Gwynn (Dream Team) | .20 | .15 |
| 889 Scott Erickson (Dream Team) | .25 | .20 |

| | MT | NR MT |
|---|---|---|
| 890 Tom Glavine (Dream Team) | .10 | .08 |
| 891 Rob Dibble (Dream Team) | .08 | .06 |
| 892 Mitch Williams (Dream Team) | .06 | .05 |
| 893 Frank Thomas (Dream Team) | .80 | .60 |

---

## Baseball
## AMERICAN LEAGUE

**Baltimore Orioles**, 333 W. Camden St., Baltimore, MD 21201.

**Boston Red Sox**, Fenway Park, 24 Yawkey Way, Boston, MA 02215.

**California Angels**, P.O. Box 2000, Anaheim, CA 92803.

**Chicago White Sox**, 333 W. 35th Street, Chicago, IL 60616.

**Cleveland Indians**, Cleveland Stadium, Cleveland, OH 44114.

**Detroit Tigers**, 2121 Trumbull Ave., Detroit, MI 48216.

**Kansas City Royals**, P.O. Box 419969, Kansas City, MO 64141.

**Milwaukee Brewers**, Milwaukee County Stadium, Milwaukee, WI 53214.

**Minnesota Twins**, 501 Chicago Ave. South, Minneapolis, MN 55415.

**New York Yankees**, Yankee Stadium, Bronx, NY 10451.

**Oakland Athletics**, Oakland Coliseum, Oakland, CA 94621.

**Seattle Mariners**, P.O. Box 4100, Seattle, WA 98104.

**Texas Rangers**, P.O. Box 1111, Arlington, TX 76010.

**Toronto Blue Jays**, The Sky-Dome, 300 Bremner Blvd., Suite 3200, Toronto Ontario, Canada M5V 3B3, (416) 341-1000.

---

**The values quoted are intended to reflect the market price.**

---

# DATING

The dating of baseball cards by year of issue on the front or back of the card itself is a relatively new phenomenon. In most cases, to accurately determine a date of issue for an unidentified card, it must be studied for clues. As mentioned, the biography, career summary or statistics on the back of the card are the best way to pinpoint a year of issue. In most cases, the year of issue will be the year after the last season mentioned on the card.

Luckily for today's collector, earlier generations have done much of the research in determining year of issue for those cards which bear no clues. The painstaking task of matching players' listed and/or pictured team against their career records often allowed an issue date to be determined.

In some cases, particular cards sets were issued over a period of more than one calendar year, but since they are collected together as a single set, their specific year of issue is not important. Such sets will be listed with their complete known range of issue years.

# NUMBERING

While many baseball card issues as far back as the 1880s have contained card numbers assigned by the issuer, to facilitate the collecting of a compete set, the practice has by no means been universal. Even today, not every set bears card numbers.

Logically, those baseball cards which were numbered by their manufacturer are presented in that numerical order within the listings of this catalog. The many unnumbered issues, however, have been assigned *Sports Collectors Digest Baseball Card Price Guide* numbers to facilitate their universal identification within the hobby, especially when buying and selling by mail. In all cases, numbers which have been assigned, or which otherwise do not appear on the card through error or by design, are shown in this catalog within parentheses. In virtually all cases, unless a more natural system suggested itself by the unique nature of a particular set, the assignment of *Sports Collectors Digest Baseball Card Price Guide* numbers by the cataloging staff has been done by alphabetical arrangement of the player's last names or the card's principal title.

Significant collectible variations of any particular card are noted within the listings by the application of a suffix letter within parentheses. In instances of variations, the suffix "a" is assigned to the variation which was created first.

# NAMES

The identification of a player by full name on the front of his baseball card has been a common practice only since the 1920s. Prior to that, the player's last name and team were the usual information found on the card front.

As a standard practice, the listings in the *Sports Collectors Digest Baseball Card Price Guide* present the player's name exactly as it appears on the front of the card, if his full name is given there. If the player's full name only appears on the back, rather than the front of the card, the listing corresponds to that designation.

In cases where only the player's last name is given on the card, the cataloging staff has included the first name by which he was most often known for ease of identification.

Cards which contain misspelled first or last names, or even wrong initials, will have included in their listings the incorrect information, with a correction accompanying in parentheses. This extends, also, to cases where the name on the card does not correspond to the player actually pictured.

## 1992 Score Rookie & Traded

This 110-card set features traded players, free agents and top rookies from 1992. The cards are styled after the regular 1992 Score cards. Cards 80-110 feature the rookies. The set was released as a boxed set and was available at hobby shops and through hobby dealers.

|  | | MT | NR MT |
|---|---|---|---|
| Complete Set: | | 9.00 | 6.75 |
| Common Player: | | .05 | .04 |
| 1 | Gary Sheffield | .20 | .15 |
| 2 | Kevin Seitzer | .05 | .04 |
| 3 | Danny Tartabull | .08 | .06 |
| 4 | Steve Sax | .06 | .05 |
| 5 | Bobby Bonilla | .10 | .08 |
| 6 | Frank Viola | .08 | .06 |
| 7 | Dave Winfield | .10 | .08 |
| 8 | Rick Sutcliffe | .08 | .04 |
| 9 | Jose Canseco | .25 | .20 |
| 10 | Greg Swindell | .08 | .04 |
| 11 | Eddie Murray | .08 | .04 |
| 12 | Randy Myers | .06 | .05 |
| 13 | Wally Joyner | .08 | .06 |
| 14 | Kenny Lofton | .30 | .25 |
| 15 | Jack Morris | .08 | .06 |
| 16 | Charlie Hayes | .06 | .05 |
| 17 | Pete Incaviglia | .06 | .05 |
| 18 | Kevin Mitchell | .08 | .06 |
| 19 | Kurt Stillwell | .05 | .04 |
| 20 | Bret Saberhagen | .08 | .06 |
| 21 | Steve Buechele | .05 | .04 |
| 22 | John Smiley | .06 | .05 |
| 23 | Sammy Sosa | .06 | .05 |
| 24 | George Bell | .08 | .06 |
| 25 | Curt Schilling | .08 | .06 |

**Values for recent cards and sets are listed in Mint (MT), Near Mint (NM) and Excellent (EX), reflecting the fact that many cards from recent years have been preserved in top condition. Recent cards and sets in less than Excellent condition have little collector interest.**

| | | MT | NR MT |
|---|---|---|---|
| 26 | Dick Schofield | .05 | .04 |
| 27 | David Cone | .08 | .06 |
| 28 | Dan Gladden | .05 | .04 |
| 29 | Kirk McCaskill | .05 | .04 |
| 30 | Mike Gallego | .05 | .04 |
| 31 | Kevin McReynolds | .06 | .05 |
| 32 | Bill Swift | .06 | .05 |
| 33 | Dave Martinez | .05 | .04 |
| 34 | Storm Davis | .05 | .04 |
| 35 | Willie Randolph | .06 | .05 |
| 36 | Melido Perez | .05 | .04 |
| 37 | Mark Carreon | .05 | .04 |
| 38 | Doug Jones | .05 | .04 |
| 39 | Gregg Jefferies | .08 | .06 |
| 40 | Mike Jackson | .05 | .04 |
| 41 | Dickie Thon | .05 | .04 |
| 42 | Eric King | .05 | .04 |
| 43 | Herm Winningham | .05 | .04 |
| 44 | Derek Lilliquist | .05 | .04 |
| 45 | Dave Anderson | .05 | .04 |
| 46 | Jeff Reardon | .08 | .06 |
| 47 | Scott Bankhead | .05 | .04 |
| 48 | Cory Snyder | .05 | .04 |
| 49 | Al Newman | .05 | .04 |
| 50 | Keith Miller | .05 | .04 |
| 51 | Dave Burba | .05 | .04 |
| 52 | Bill Pecota | .05 | .04 |
| 53. | Chuck Crim | .05 | .04 |
| 54 | Mariano Duncan | .05 | .04 |
| 55 | Dave Gallagher | .05 | .04 |
| 56 | Chris Gwynn | .05 | .04 |
| 57 | Scott Ruskin | .05 | .04 |
| 58 | Jack Armstrong | .05 | .04 |
| 59 | Gary Carter | .12 | .09 |
| 60 | Andres Galarraga | .06 | .05 |
| 61 | Ken Hill | .08 | .06 |
| 62 | Eric Davis | .08 | .06 |
| 63 | Ruben Sierra | .12 | .09 |
| 64 | Darrin Fletcher | .05 | .04 |
| 65 | Tim Belcher | .06 | .05 |
| 66 | Mike Morgan | .06 | .05 |
| 67 | Scott Scudder | .05 | .04 |
| 68 | Tom Candiotti | .05 | .04 |
| 69 | Hubie Brooks | .05 | .04 |
| 70 | Kal Daniels | .05 | .04 |
| 71 | Bruce Ruffin | .05 | .04 |
| 72 | Billy Hatcher | .05 | .04 |
| 73 | Bob Melvin | .05 | .04 |
| 74 | Lee Guetterman | .05 | .04 |
| 75 | Rene Gonzales | .05 | .04 |
| 76 | Kevin Bass | .05 | .04 |
| 77 | Tom Bolton | .05 | .04 |
| 78 | John Wetteland | .08 | .06 |
| 79 | Bip Roberts | .08 | .06 |
| 80 | Pat Listach(FC) | 1.00 | .70 |
| 81 | John Doherty(FC) | .12 | .09 |
| 82 | Sam Militello(FC) | .50 | .40 |
| 83 | Brian Jordan(FC) | .35 | .25 |
| 84 | Jeff Kent(FC) | .20 | .15 |
| 85 | Dave Fleming(FC) | .50 | .40 |
| 86 | Jeff Tackett(FC) | .12 | .09 |
| 87 | Chad Curtis(FC) | .15 | .11 |
| 88 | Eric Fox | .12 | .09 |
| 89 | Denny Neagle(FC) | .12 | .09 |
| 90 | Donovan Osborne(FC) | .25 | .20 |
| 91 | Carlos Hernandez(FC) | | |

| | | MT | NR MT |
|---|---|---|---|
| | | .12 | .09 |
| 92 | Tim Wakefield(FC) | .35 | .25 |
| 93 | Tim Salmon(FC) | .70 | .50 |
| 94 | Dave Nilsson(FC) | .20 | .15 |
| 95 | Mike Perez(FC) | .12 | .09 |
| 96 | Pat Hentgen(FC) | .12 | .09 |
| 97 | Frank Seminara(FC) | .12 | .09 |
| 98 | Ruben Amaro, Jr.(FC) | | |
| | | .12 | .09 |
| 99 | Archi Cianfrocco(FC) | | |
| | | .35 | .25 |
| 100 | Andy Stankiewicz(FC) | | |
| | | .35 | .25 |
| 101 | Jim Bullinger(FC) | .12 | .09 |
| 102 | Pat Mahomes(FC) | .50 | .40 |
| 103 | Hipolito Pichardo(FC) | | |
| | | .12 | .09 |
| 104 | Bret Boone(FC) | .60 | .45 |
| 105 | John Vander Wal(FC) | | |
| | | .12 | .09 |
| 106 | Vince Horsman(FC) | .10 | .08 |
| 107 | James Austin(FC) | .10 | .08 |
| 108 | Brian Williams(FC) | .12 | .09 |
| 109 | Dan Walters(FC) | .12 | .09 |
| 110 | Wil Cordero(FC) | .35 | .25 |

## 1993 Score Select

This 400-card set from Score is designed for the mid-priced card market. The card fronts feature green borders on two sides of the card with the photo filling the remaining portion of the card front. "Score Select" appears within the photo. The backs feature an additional photo, player information and statistics. Cards numbered 271-360 are devoted to rookies and draft picks. Several cards from this set are printed horizontally. The cards are UV coated on both sides.

| | | MT | NR MT |
|---|---|---|---|
| Complete Set: | | 30.00 | 22.00 |
| Common Player: | | .06 | .05 |
| | | | |
| 1 | Barry Bonds | .20 | .15 |
| 2 | Ken Griffey Jr. | .60 | .45 |
| 3 | Will Clark | .20 | .15 |
| 4 | Kirby Puckett | .25 | .20 |

| | | MT | NR MT |
|---|---|---|---|
| 5 | Tony Gwynn | .20 | .15 |
| 6 | Frank Thomas | 1.00 | .70 |
| 7 | Tom Glavine | .20 | .15 |
| 8 | Roberto Alomar | .25 | .20 |
| 9 | Andre Dawson | .15 | .11 |
| 10 | Ron Darling | .08 | .06 |
| 11 | Bobby Bonilla | .15 | .11 |
| 12 | Danny Tartabull | .15 | .11 |
| 13 | Darren Daulton | .12 | .09 |
| 14 | Roger Clemens | .25 | .20 |
| 15 | Ozzie Smith | .12 | .09 |
| 16 | Mark McGwire | .40 | .30 |
| 17 | Terry Pendleton | .15 | .11 |
| 18 | Cal Ripken Jr. | .50 | .40 |
| 19 | Fred McGriff | .20 | .15 |
| 20 | Cecil Fielder | .25 | .20 |
| 21 | Darryl Strawberry | .25 | .20 |
| 22 | Robin Yount | .25 | .20 |
| 23 | Barry Larkin | .20 | .15 |
| 24 | Don Mattingly | .20 | .15 |
| 25 | Craig Biggio | .10 | .08 |
| 26 | Sandy Alomar Jr. | .15 | .11 |
| 27 | Larry Walker | .15 | .11 |
| 28 | Junior Felix | .06 | .05 |
| 29 | Eddie Murray | .15 | .11 |
| 30 | Robin Ventura | .15 | .11 |
| 31 | Greg Maddux | .15 | .11 |
| 32 | Dave Winfield | .20 | .15 |
| 33 | John Kruk | .12 | .09 |
| 34 | Wally Joyner | .12 | .09 |
| 35 | Andy Van Slyke | .12 | .09 |
| 36 | Chuck Knoblauch | .15 | .11 |
| 37 | Tom Pagnozzi | .08 | .06 |
| 38 | Dennis Eckersley | .15 | .11 |
| 39 | Dave Justice | .20 | .15 |
| 40 | Juan Gonzalez | .35 | .25 |
| 41 | Gary Sheffield | .20 | .15 |
| 42 | Paul Molitor | .15 | .11 |
| 43 | Delino DeShields | .12 | .09 |
| 44 | Travis Fryman | .25 | .20 |
| 45 | Hal Morris | .10 | .08 |
| 46 | Gregg Olson | .10 | .08 |
| 47 | Ken Caminiti | .08 | .06 |
| 48 | Wade Boggs | .15 | .11 |
| 49 | Orel Hershiser | .12 | .09 |
| 50 | Albert Belle | .15 | .11 |
| 51 | Bill Swift | .08 | .06 |
| 52 | Mark Langston | .12 | .09 |
| 53 | Joe Girardi | .06 | .05 |
| 54 | Keith Miller | .06 | .05 |
| 55 | Gary Carter | .12 | .09 |
| 56 | Brady Anderson | .15 | .11 |
| 57 | Doc Gooden | .15 | .11 |
| 58 | Julio Franco | .10 | .08 |
| 59 | Lenny Dykstra | .10 | .08 |
| 60 | Mickey Tettleton | .10 | .08 |
| 61 | Randy Tomlin | .10 | .08 |
| 62 | B.J. Surhoff | .08 | .06 |
| 63 | Todd Zeile | .08 | .06 |
| 64 | Roberto Kelly | .10 | .08 |
| 65 | Rob Dibble | .10 | .08 |
| 66 | Leo Gomez | .10 | .08 |
| 67 | Doug Jones | .06 | .05 |
| 68 | Ellis Burks | .12 | .09 |
| 69 | Mike Scioscia | .06 | .05 |
| 70 | Charles Nagy | .12 | .09 |
| 71 | Cory Snyder | .06 | .05 |

| # | Player | MT | NR MT | # | Player | MT | NR MT |
|---|--------|-----|-------|---|--------|-----|-------|
| 72 | Devon White | .08 | .06 | 139 | Robby Thompson | .08 | .06 |
| 73 | Mark Grace | .12 | .09 | 140 | Scott Fletcher | .06 | .05 |
| 74 | Luis Polonia | .06 | .05 | 141 | Bruce Hurst | .08 | .06 |
| 75 | John Smiley | .08 | .06 | 142 | Kevin Maas | .08 | .06 |
| 76 | Carlton Fisk | .15 | .11 | 143 | Tom Candiotti | .08 | .06 |
| 77 | Luis Sojo | .06 | .05 | 144 | Chris Hoiles | .20 | .15 |
| 78 | George Brett | .20 | .15 | 145 | Mike Morgan | .08 | .06 |
| 79 | Mitch Williams | .10 | .08 | 146 | Mark Whiten | .15 | .11 |
| 80 | Kent Hrbek | .10 | .08 | 147 | Dennis Martinez | .10 | .08 |
| 81 | Jay Bell | .10 | .08 | 148 | Tony Pena | .08 | .06 |
| 82 | Edgar Martinez | .15 | .11 | 149 | Dave Magadan | .08 | .06 |
| 83 | Lee Smith | .10 | .08 | 150 | Mark Lewis | .10 | .08 |
| 84 | Deion Sanders | .20 | .15 | 151 | Mariano Duncan | .06 | .05 |
| 85 | Bill Gullickson | .08 | .06 | 152 | Gregg Jefferies | .15 | .11 |
| 86 | Paul O'Neill | .08 | .06 | 153 | Doug Drabek | .12 | .09 |
| 87 | Kevin Seitzer | .08 | .06 | 154 | Brian Harper | .12 | .09 |
| 88 | Steve Finley | .08 | .06 | 155 | Ray Lankford | .20 | .15 |
| 89 | Mel Hall | .08 | .06 | 156 | Carney Lansford | .08 | .06 |
| 90 | Nolan Ryan | .50 | .40 | 157 | Mike Sharperson | .08 | .06 |
| 91 | Eric Davis | .15 | .11 | 158 | Jack Morris | .15 | .11 |
| 92 | Mike Mussina | .50 | .40 | 159 | Otis Nixon | .10 | .08 |
| 93 | Tony Fernandez | .08 | .06 | 160 | Steve Sax | .10 | .08 |
| 94 | Frank Viola | .12 | .09 | 161 | Mark Lemke | .08 | .06 |
| 95 | Matt Williams | .12 | .09 | 162 | Rafael Palmeiro | .12 | .09 |
| 96 | Joe Carter | .15 | .11 | 163 | Jose Rijo | .12 | .09 |
| 97 | Ryne Sandberg | .35 | .25 | 164 | Omar Vizquel | .06 | .05 |
| 98 | Jim Abbott | .15 | .11 | 165 | Sammy Sosa | .08 | .06 |
| 99 | Marquis Grissom | .15 | .11 | 166 | Milt Cuyler | .08 | .06 |
| 100 | George Bell | .15 | .11 | 167 | John Franco | .08 | .06 |
| 101 | Howard Johnson | .10 | .08 | 168 | Darryl Hamilton | .08 | .06 |
| 102 | Kevin Appier | .12 | .09 | 169 | Ken Hill | .10 | .08 |
| 103 | Dale Murphy | .12 | .09 | 170 | Mike Devereaux | .10 | .08 |
| 104 | Shane Mack | .10 | .08 | 171 | Don Slaught | .06 | .05 |
| 105 | Jose Lind | .08 | .06 | 172 | Steve Farr | .06 | .05 |
| 106 | Rickey Henderson | .30 | .25 | 173 | Bernard Gilkey | .10 | .08 |
| 107 | Bob Tewksbury | .08 | .06 | 174 | Mike Fetters | .06 | .05 |
| 108 | Kevin Mitchell | .12 | .09 | 175 | Vince Coleman | .08 | .06 |
| 109 | Steve Avery | .15 | .11 | 176 | Kevin McReynolds | .10 | .08 |
| 110 | Candy Maldonado | .08 | .06 | 177 | John Smoltz | .15 | .11 |
| 111 | Bip Roberts | .10 | .08 | 178 | Greg Gagne | .08 | .06 |
| 112 | Lou Whitaker | .10 | .08 | 179 | Greg Swindell | .15 | .11 |
| 113 | Jeff Bagwell | .25 | .20 | 180 | Juan Guzman | .20 | .15 |
| 114 | Dante Bichette | .06 | .05 | 181 | Kal Daniels | .08 | .06 |
| 115 | Brett Butler | .10 | .08 | 182 | Rick Sutcliffe | .12 | .09 |
| 116 | Melido Perez | .06 | .05 | 183 | Orlando Merced | .12 | .09 |
| 117 | Andy Benes | .12 | .09 | 184 | Bill Wegman | .08 | .06 |
| 118 | Randy Johnson | .08 | .06 | 185 | Mark Gardner | .08 | .06 |
| 119 | Willie McGee | .08 | .06 | 186 | Rob Deer | .08 | .06 |
| 120 | Jody Reed | .08 | .06 | 187 | Dave Hollins | .15 | .11 |
| 121 | Shawon Dunston | .08 | .06 | 188 | Jack Clark | .08 | .06 |
| 122 | Carlos Baerga | .20 | .15 | 189 | Brian Hunter | .15 | .11 |
| 123 | Bret Saberhagen | .12 | .09 | 190 | Tim Wallach | .08 | .06 |
| 124 | John Olerud | .15 | .11 | 191 | Tim Belcher | .08 | .06 |
| 125 | Ivan Calderon | .08 | .06 | 192 | Walt Weiss | .08 | .06 |
| 126 | Bryan Harvey | .10 | .08 | 193 | Kurt Stillwell | .06 | .05 |
| 127 | Terry Mulholland | .08 | .06 | 194 | Charlie Hayes | .08 | .06 |
| 128 | Ozzie Guillen | .10 | .08 | 195 | Willie Randolph | .08 | .06 |
| 129 | Steve Buechele | .08 | .06 | 196 | Jack McDowell | .15 | .11 |
| 130 | Kevin Tapani | .08 | .06 | 197 | Jose Offerman | .10 | .08 |
| 131 | Felix Jose | .12 | .09 | 198 | Chuck Finley | .10 | .08 |
| 132 | Terry Steinbach | .08 | .06 | 199 | Darrin Jackson | .08 | .06 |
| 133 | Ron Gant | .12 | .09 | 200 | Kelly Gruber | .08 | .06 |
| 134 | Harold Reynolds | .08 | .06 | 201 | John Wetteland | .12 | .09 |
| 135 | Chris Sabo | .10 | .08 | 202 | Jay Buhner | .08 | .06 |
| 136 | Ivan Rodriguez | .20 | .15 | 203 | Mike LaValliere | .06 | .05 |
| 137 | Eric Anthony | .08 | .06 | 204 | Kevin Brown | .12 | .09 |
| 138 | Mike Henneman | .08 | .06 | 205 | Luis Gonzalez | .12 | .09 |

| | MT | NR MT | | | MT | NR MT |
|---|---|---|---|---|---|---|
| 206 | Rick Aguilera | .12 | .09 | 273 | Pat Listach | .40 | .30 |
| 207 | Norm Charlton | .12 | .09 | 274 | Reggie Sanders | .30 | .25 |
| 208 | Mike Bordick | .12 | .09 | 275 | Kenny Lofton | .30 | .25 |
| 209 | Charlie Leibrandt | .06 | .05 | 276 | Donovan Osborne | .20 | .15 |
| 210 | Tom Brunansky | .08 | .06 | 277 | Rusty Meacham | .20 | .15 |
| 211 | Tom Henke | .10 | .08 | 278 | Eric Karros | .40 | .30 |
| 212 | Randy Milligan | .06 | .05 | 279 | Andy Stankiewicz | .15 | .11 |
| 213 | Ramon Martinez | .15 | .11 | 280 | Brian Jordan | .25 | .20 |
| 214 | Mo Vaughn | .08 | .06 | 281 | Gary DiSarcina | .08 | .06 |
| 215 | Randy Myers | .08 | .06 | 282 | Mark Wohlers | .08 | .06 |
| 216 | Greg Hibbard | .08 | .06 | 283 | Dave Nilsson | .20 | .15 |
| 217 | Wes Chamberlain | .10 | .08 | 284 | Anthony Young | .10 | .08 |
| 218 | Tony Phillips | .10 | .08 | 285 | Jim Bullinger | .12 | .09 |
| 219 | Pete Harnisch | .10 | .08 | 286 | Derek Bell | .20 | .15 |
| 220 | Mike Gallego | .06 | .05 | 287 | Brian Williams | .15 | .11 |
| 221 | Bud Black | .06 | .05 | 288 | Julio Valera | .15 | .11 |
| 222 | Greg Vaughn | .10 | .08 | 289 | Dan Walters | .15 | .11 |
| 223 | Milt Thompson | .06 | .05 | 290 | Chad Curtis | .25 | .20 |
| 224 | Ben McDonald | .15 | .11 | 291 | Michael Tucker | .25 | .20 |
| 225 | Billy Hatcher | .06 | .05 | 292 | Bob Zupcic | .15 | .11 |
| 226 | Paul Sorrento | .08 | .06 | 293 | Todd Hundley | .15 | .11 |
| 227 | Mark Gubicza | .08 | .06 | 294 | Jeff Tackett | .15 | .11 |
| 228 | Mike Greenwell | .08 | .06 | 295 | Greg Colbrunn | .15 | .11 |
| 229 | Curt Schilling | .08 | .06 | 296 | Cal Eldred | .40 | .30 |
| 230 | Alan Trammell | .10 | .08 | 297 | Chris Roberts | .20 | .15 |
| 231 | Zane Smith | .08 | .06 | 298 | John Doherty | .20 | .15 |
| 232 | Bobby Thigpen | .10 | .08 | 299 | Denny Neagle | .12 | .09 |
| 233 | Greg Olson | .06 | .05 | 300 | Arthur Rhodes | .20 | .15 |
| 234 | Joe Orsulak | .06 | .05 | 301 | Mark Clark | .20 | .15 |
| 235 | Joe Oliver | .06 | .05 | 302 | Scott Cooper | .20 | .15 |
| 236 | Tim Raines | .12 | .09 | 303 | Jamie Arnold | .20 | .15 |
| 237 | Juan Samuel | .06 | .05 | 304 | Jim Thome | .15 | .11 |
| 238 | Chili Davis | .08 | .06 | 305 | Frank Seminara | .15 | .11 |
| 239 | Spike Owen | .06 | .05 | 306 | Kurt Knudsen | .15 | .11 |
| 240 | Dave Stewart | .12 | .09 | 307 | Tim Wakefield | .30 | .25 |
| 241 | Jim Eisenreich | .06 | .05 | 308 | John Jaha | .20 | .15 |
| 242 | Phil Plantier | .20 | .15 | 309 | Pat Hentgen | .15 | .11 |
| 243 | Sid Fernandez | .10 | .08 | 310 | B.J. Wallace | .20 | .15 |
| 244 | Dan Gladden | .06 | .03 | 311 | Roberto Hernandez | .20 | .15 |
| 245 | Mickey Morandini | .12 | .09 | 312 | Hipolito Pichardo | .20 | .15 |
| 246 | Tino Martinez | .12 | .09 | 313 | Eric Fox | .15 | .11 |
| 247 | Kirt Manwaring | .06 | .05 | 314 | Willie Banks | .15 | .11 |
| 248 | Dean Palmer | .12 | .09 | 315 | Sam Militello | .20 | .15 |
| 249 | Tom Browning | .08 | .06 | 316 | Vince Horsman | .15 | .11 |
| 250 | Brian McRae | .12 | .09 | 317 | Carlos Hernandez | .15 | .11 |
| 251 | Scott Leius | .08 | .06 | 318 | Jeff Kent | .20 | .15 |
| 252 | Bert Blyleven | .08 | .06 | 319 | Mike Perez | .12 | .09 |
| 253 | Scott Erickson | .10 | .08 | 320 | Scott Livingstone | .15 | .11 |
| 254 | Bob Welch | .10 | .08 | 321 | Jeff Conine | .15 | .11 |
| 255 | Pat Kelly | .10 | .08 | 322 | James Austin | .15 | .11 |
| 256 | Felix Fermin | .06 | .05 | 323 | John Vander Wal | .15 | .11 |
| 257 | Harold Baines | .12 | .09 | 324 | Pat Mahomes | .25 | .20 |
| 258 | Duane Ward | .08 | .06 | 325 | Pedro Astacio | .25 | .20 |
| 259 | Bill Spiers | .08 | .06 | 326 | Bret Boone | .25 | .20 |
| 260 | Jaime Navarro | .10 | .08 | 327 | Matt Stairs | .15 | .11 |
| 261 | Scott Sanderson | .08 | .06 | 328 | Damion Easley | .20 | .15 |
| 262 | Gary Gaetti | .08 | .06 | 329 | Ben Rivera | .20 | .15 |
| 263 | Bob Ojeda | .06 | .05 | 330 | Reggie Jefferson | .20 | .15 |
| 264 | Jeff Montgomery | .08 | .06 | 331 | Luis Mercedes | .20 | .15 |
| 265 | Scott Bankhead | .08 | .06 | 332 | Kyle Abbott | .20 | .15 |
| 266 | Lance Johnson | .08 | .06 | 333 | Eddie Taubensee | .20 | .15 |
| 267 | Rafael Belliard | .06 | .05 | 334 | Tim McIntosh | .10 | .08 |
| 268 | Kevin Reimer | .08 | .06 | 335 | Phil Clark | .10 | .08 |
| 269 | Benito Santiago | .12 | .09 | 336 | Will Cordero | .20 | .15 |
| 270 | Mike Moore | .08 | .06 | 337 | Russ Springer | .15 | .11 |
| 271 | Dave Fleming | .15 | .11 | 338 | Craig Colbert | .10 | .08 |
| 272 | Moises Alou | .15 | .11 | 339 | Tim Salmon | .20 | .15 |

| | | MT | NR MT |
|---|---|---|---|
| 340 | Braulio Castillo | .20 | .15 |
| 341 | Donald Harris | .12 | .09 |
| 342 | Eric Young | .20 | .15 |
| 343 | Bob Wickman | .25 | .20 |
| 344 | John Valentin | .15 | .11 |
| 345 | Dan Wilson | .15 | .11 |
| 346 | Steve Hosey | .15 | .11 |
| 347 | Mike Piazza | .30 | .25 |
| 348 | Willie Greene | .20 | .15 |
| 349 | Tom Goodwin | .10 | .08 |
| 350 | Eric Hillman | .15 | .11 |
| 351 | Steve Reed | .15 | .11 |
| 352 | Dan Serafini | .25 | .20 |
| 353 | Todd Steverson | .25 | .20 |
| 354 | Benji Grigsby | .25 | .20 |
| 355 | Shannon Stewart | .25 | .20 |
| 356 | Sean Lowe | .25 | .20 |
| 357 | Derek Wallace | .25 | .20 |
| 358 | Rick Helling | .25 | .20 |
| 359 | Jason Kendall | .25 | .20 |
| 360 | Derek Jeter | .25 | .20 |
| 361 | David Cone | .15 | .11 |
| 362 | Jeff Reardon | .15 | .11 |
| 363 | Bobby Witt | .08 | .06 |
| 364 | Jose Canseco | .40 | .30 |
| 365 | Jeff Russell | .08 | .06 |
| 366 | Ruben Sierra | .25 | .20 |
| 367 | Alan Mills | .06 | .05 |
| 368 | Matt Nokes | .08 | .06 |
| 369 | Pat Borders | .08 | .06 |
| 370 | Pedro Munoz | .12 | .09 |
| 371 | Danny Jackson | .06 | .05 |
| 372 | Geronimo Pena | .10 | .08 |
| 373 | Craig Lefferts | .08 | .06 |
| 374 | Joe Grahe | .08 | .06 |
| 375 | Roger McDowell | .06 | .05 |
| 376 | Jimmy Key | .10 | .08 |
| 377 | Steve Olin | .10 | .08 |
| 378 | Glenn Davis | .10 | .08 |
| 379 | Rene Gonzales | .06 | .05 |
| 380 | Manuel Lee | .06 | .05 |
| 381 | Ron Karkovice | .06 | .05 |
| 382 | Sid Bream | .06 | .05 |
| 383 | Gerald Williams | .12 | .09 |
| 384 | Lenny Harris | .06 | .05 |
| 385 | J.T. Snow | .20 | .15 |
| 386 | Dave Stieb | .08 | .06 |
| 387 | Kirk McCaskill | .08 | .06 |
| 388 | Lance Parrish | .08 | .06 |
| 389 | Craig Greback | .06 | .05 |
| 390 | Rick Wilkins | .12 | .09 |
| 391 | Manny Alexander | .25 | .20 |
| 392 | Mike Schooler | .06 | .05 |
| 393 | Bernie Williams | .12 | .09 |
| 394 | Kevin Koslofski | .20 | .15 |
| 395 | Willie Wilson | .08 | .06 |
| 396 | Jeff Parrett | .06 | .05 |
| 397 | Mike Harkey | .08 | .06 |
| 398 | Frank Tanana | .08 | .06 |
| 399 | Doug Henry | .08 | .06 |
| 400 | Royce Clayton | .15 | .11 |
| 401 | Eric Wedge | .12 | .09 |
| 402 | Derrick May | .12 | .09 |
| 403 | Carlos Garcia | .15 | .11 |
| 404 | Henry Rodriguez | .12 | .09 |
| 405 | Ryan Klesko | .20 | .15 |

# TOPPS

## 1952 Topps

At 407 cards, the 1952 Topps set was the largest set of its day, both in number of cards and physical dimensions of the cards. Cards are 2-5/8" by 3-3/4" with a hand-colored black and white photo on front. Major baseball card innovations presented in the set include the first-ever use of color team logos as part of the design, and the inclusion of stats for the previous season and overall career on the backs. A major variety in the set is that first 80 cards can be found with backs printed entirely in black or black and red. Backs entirely in black command a $10-15 premium. Card numbers 311-407 were printed in limited supplies and are extremely rare.

| | NR MT | EX |
|---|---|---|
| Complete Set: | 70000.00 | 35000.00 |
| Common Player: 1-80 | 50.00 | 25.00 |
| Common Player: 81-250 | | |
| | 25.00 | 12.50 |
| Common Player: 251-280 | | |
| | 40.00 | 20.00 |
| Common Player: 281-300 | | |
| | 50.00 | 25.00 |
| Common Player: 301-310 | | |
| | 40.00 | 20.00 |
| Common Player: 311-407 | | |
| | 175.00 | 87.00 |

| | | | |
|---|---|---|---|
| 1 | Andy Pafko | 1200.00 | 150.00 |
| 2 | *James E. Runnels* | 80.00 | 20.00 |
| 3 | Hank Thompson | 55.00 | 15.00 |
| 4 | Don Lenhardt | 55.00 | 15.00 |
| 5 | Larry Jansen | 55.00 | 15.00 |

| | | NR MT | EX |
|---|---|---|---|
| 6 | Grady Hatton | 55.00 | 15.00 |
| 7 | Wayne Terwilliger | 60.00 | 16.00 |
| 8 | Fred Marsh | 55.00 | 15.00 |
| 9 | Bobby Hogue | 65.00 | 18.00 |
| 10 | Al Rosen | 80.00 | 24.00 |
| 11 | Phil Rizzuto | 175.00 | 87.00 |
| 12 | Monty Basgall | 55.00 | 15.00 |
| 13 | Johnny Wyrostek | 55.00 | 15.00 |
| 14 | Bob Elliott | 55.00 | 15.00 |
| 15 | Johnny Pesky | 60.00 | 16.00 |
| 16 | Gene Hermanski | 55.00 | 15.00 |
| 17 | Jim Hegan | 55.00 | 15.00 |
| 18 | Merrill Combs | 55.00 | 15.00 |
| 19 | Johnny Bucha | 55.00 | 15.00 |
| 20 | *Billy Loes* | 110.00 | 55.00 |
| 21 | Ferris Fain | 60.00 | 16.00 |
| 22 | Dom DiMaggio | 100.00 | 50.00 |
| 23 | Billy Goodman | 55.00 | 15.00 |
| 24 | Luke Easter | 60.00 | 16.00 |
| 25 | Johnny Groth | 55.00 | 15.00 |
| 26 | Monty Irvin | 90.00 | 45.00 |
| 27 | Sam Jethroe | 55.00 | 15.00 |
| 28 | Jerry Priddy | 55.00 | 15.00 |
| 29 | Ted Kluszewski | 90.00 | 45.00 |
| 30 | Mel Parnell | 60.00 | 16.00 |
| 31 | Gus Zernial | 60.00 | 16.00 |
| 32 | Eddie Robinson | 55.00 | 15.00 |
| 33 | Warren Spahn | 225.00 | 112.00 |
| 34 | Elmer Valo | 55.00 | 15.00 |
| 35 | Hank Sauer | 60.00 | 16.00 |
| 36 | Gil Hodges | 150.00 | 75.00 |
| 37 | Duke Snider | 300.00 | 150.00 |
| 38 | Wally Westlake | 55.00 | 15.00 |
| 39 | "Dizzy" Trout | 60.00 | 16.00 |
| 40 | Irv Noren | 55.00 | 15.00 |
| 41 | Bob Wellman | 55.00 | 15.00 |
| 42 | Lou Kretlow | 55.00 | 15.00 |
| 43 | Ray Scarborough | 55.00 | 15.00 |
| 44 | Con Dempsey | 55.00 | 15.00 |
| 45 | Eddie Joost | 55.00 | 15.00 |
| 46 | Gordon Goldsberry | 55.00 | 15.00 |
| 47 | Willie Jones | 55.00 | 15.00 |
| 48a | Joe Page (Johnny Sain bio) | 225.00 | 68.00 |
| 48b | Joe Page (correct bio) | 80.00 | 24.00 |
| 49a | Johnny Sain (Joe Page bio) | 225.00 | 68.00 |
| 49b | Johnny Sain (correct bio) | 80.00 | 24.00 |
| 50 | Marv Rickert | 55.00 | 15.00 |
| 51 | Jim Russell | 60.00 | 16.00 |
| 52 | Don Mueller | 55.00 | 15.00 |
| 53 | Chris Van Cuyk | 60.00 | 16.00 |
| 54 | Leo Kiely | 55.00 | 15.00 |
| 55 | Ray Boone | 60.00 | 16.00 |
| 56 | Tommy Glaviano | 55.00 | 15.00 |
| 57 | Ed Lopat | 80.00 | 40.00 |
| 58 | Bob Mahoney | 55.00 | 15.00 |
| 59 | Robin Roberts | 125.00 | 62.00 |
| 60 | Sid Hudson | 55.00 | 15.00 |
| 61 | "Tookie" Gilbert | 55.00 | 15.00 |
| 62 | Chuck Stobbs | 55.00 | 15.00 |
| 63 | Howie Pollet | 55.00 | 15.00 |
| 64 | Roy Sievers | 65.00 | 18.00 |
| 65 | Enos Slaughter | 100.00 | 50.00 |

| | | NR MT | EX |
|---|---|---|---|
| 66 | "Preacher" Roe | 100.00 | 50.00 |
| 67 | Allie Reynolds | 90.00 | 45.00 |
| 68 | Cliff Chambers | 55.00 | 15.00 |
| 69 | Virgil Stallcup | 55.00 | 15.00 |
| 70 | Al Zarilla | 55.00 | 15.00 |
| 71 | Tom Upton | 55.00 | 15.00 |
| 72 | Karl Olson | 55.00 | 15.00 |
| 73 | William Werle | 55.00 | 15.00 |
| 74 | Andy Hansen | 55.00 | 15.00 |
| 75 | Wes Westrum | 60.00 | 16.00 |
| 76 | Eddie Stanky | 65.00 | 18.00 |
| 77 | Bob Kennedy | 55.00 | 15.00 |
| 78 | Ellis Kinder | 55.00 | 15.00 |
| 79 | Gerald Staley | 55.00 | 15.00 |
| 80 | Herman Wehmeier | 55.00 | 15.00 |
| 81 | Vernon Law | 25.00 | 11.00 |
| 82 | Duane Pillette | 25.00 | 12.50 |
| 83 | Billy Johnson | 25.00 | 12.50 |
| 84 | Vern Stephens | 25.00 | 12.50 |
| 85 | Bob Kuzava | 50.00 | 25.00 |
| 86 | Ted Gray | 25.00 | 12.50 |
| 87 | Dale Coogan | 25.00 | 12.50 |
| 88 | Bob Feller | 175.00 | 87.00 |
| 89 | Johnny Lipon | 25.00 | 12.50 |
| 90 | Mickey Grasso | 25.00 | 12.50 |
| 91 | Al Schoendienst | 80.00 | 20.00 |
| 92 | Dale Mitchell | 25.00 | 12.50 |
| 93 | Al Sima | 25.00 | 12.50 |
| 94 | Sam Mele | 25.00 | 12.50 |
| 95 | Ken Holcombe | 25.00 | 12.50 |
| 96 | Willard Marshall | 25.00 | 12.50 |
| 97 | Earl Torgeson | 25.00 | 12.50 |
| 98 | Bill Pierce | 25.00 | 11.00 |
| 99 | Gene Woodling | 50.00 | 25.00 |
| 100 | Del Rice | 25.00 | 12.50 |
| 101 | Max Lanier | 25.00 | 12.50 |
| 102 | Bill Kennedy | 25.00 | 12.50 |
| 103 | Cliff Mapes | 25.00 | 12.50 |
| 104 | Don Kolloway | 25.00 | 12.50 |
| 105 | John Pramesa | 25.00 | 12.50 |
| 106 | Mickey Vernon | 25.00 | 11.00 |
| 107 | Connie Ryan | 25.00 | 12.50 |
| 108 | Jim Konstanty | 25.00 | 11.00 |
| 109 | Ted Wilks | 25.00 | 12.50 |
| 110 | Dutch Leonard | 25.00 | 12.50 |
| 111 | Harry Lowrey | 25.00 | 12.50 |
| 112 | Henry Majeski | 25.00 | 12.50 |
| 113 | Dick Sisler | 25.00 | 12.50 |
| 114 | Willard Ramsdell | 25.00 | 12.50 |
| 115 | George Munger | 25.00 | 12.50 |
| 116 | Carl Scheib | 25.00 | 12.50 |
| 117 | Sherman Lollar | 25.00 | 11.00 |
| 118 | Ken Raffensberger | 25.00 | 12.50 |
| 119 | Maurice McDermott | 25.00 | 12.50 |
| 120 | Bob Chakales | 25.00 | 12.50 |
| 121 | Gus Niarhos | 25.00 | 12.50 |
| 122 | Jack Jensen | 70.00 | 35.00 |
| 123 | Eddie Yost | 25.00 | 11.00 |
| 124 | Monte Kennedy | 25.00 | 12.50 |
| 125 | Bill Rigney | 25.00 | 11.00 |
| 126 | Fred Hutchinson | 25.00 | 11.00 |
| 127 | Paul Minner | 25.00 | 12.50 |
| 128 | Don Bollweg | 50.00 | 25.00 |
| 129 | Johnny Mize | 70.00 | 35.00 |

| | | NR MT | EX | | | | NR MT | EX |
|---|---|---|---|---|---|---|---|---|
| 130 | Sheldon Jones | 25.00 | 12.50 | | 195 | *Orestes Minoso* | 125.00 | 62.00 |
| 131 | Morrie Martin | 25.00 | 12.50 | | 196 | Solly Hemus | 25.00 | 12.50 |
| 132 | Clyde Kluttz | 25.00 | 12.50 | | 197 | George Strickland | 25.00 | 12.50 |
| 133 | Al Widmar | 25.00 | 12.50 | | 198 | Phil Haugstad | 25.00 | 11.00 |
| 134 | Joe Tipton | 25.00 | 12.50 | | 199 | George Zuverink | 25.00 | 12.50 |
| 135 | Dixie Howell | 25.00 | 12.50 | | 200 | Ralph Houk | 60.00 | 30.00 |
| 136 | Johnny Schmitz | 25.00 | 11.00 | | 201 | Alex Kellner | 25.00 | 12.50 |
| 137 | *Roy McMillan* | 25.00 | 11.00 | | 202 | Joe Collins | 50.00 | 25.00 |
| 138 | Bill MacDonald | 25.00 | 12.50 | | 203 | Curt Simmons | 25.00 | 11.00 |
| 139 | Ken Wood | 25.00 | 12.50 | | 204 | Ron Northey | 25.00 | 12.50 |
| 140 | John Antonelli | 25.00 | 11.00 | | 205 | Clyde King | 25.00 | 11.00 |
| 141 | Clint Hartung | 25.00 | 12.50 | | 206 | Joe Ostrowski | 50.00 | 25.00 |
| 142 | Harry Perkowski | 25.00 | 12.50 | | 207 | Mickey Harris | 25.00 | 12.50 |
| 143 | Les Moss | 25.00 | 12.50 | | 208 | Marlin Stuart | 25.00 | 12.50 |
| 144 | Ed Blake | 25.00 | 12.50 | | 209 | Howie Fox | 25.00 | 12.50 |
| 145 | Joe Haynes | 25.00 | 12.50 | | 210 | Dick Fowler | 25.00 | 12.50 |
| 146 | Frank House | 25.00 | 12.50 | | 211 | Ray Coleman | 25.00 | 12.50 |
| 147 | Bob Young | 25.00 | 12.50 | | 212 | Ned Garver | 25.00 | 12.50 |
| 148 | Johnny Klippstein | 25.00 | 12.50 | | 213 | Nippy Jones | 25.00 | 12.50 |
| 149 | Dick Kryhoski | 25.00 | 12.50 | | 214 | Johnny Hopp | 50.00 | 25.00 |
| 150 | Ted Beard | 25.00 | 12.50 | | 215 | Hank Bauer | 40.00 | 18.00 |
| 151 | Wally Post | 25.00 | 12.50 | | 216 | Richie Ashburn | 80.00 | 40.00 |
| 152 | Al Evans | 25.00 | 12.50 | | 217 | George Stirnweiss | | |
| 153 | Bob Rush | 25.00 | 12.50 | | | | 25.00 | 12.50 |
| 154 | Joe Muir | 25.00 | 12.50 | | 218 | Clyde McCullough | | |
| 155 | Frank Overmire | 50.00 | 25.00 | | | | 25.00 | 12.50 |
| 156 | Frank Hiller | 25.00 | 12.50 | | 219 | Bobby Shantz | 25.00 | 11.00 |
| 157 | Bob Usher | 25.00 | 12.50 | | 220 | Joe Presko | 25.00 | 12.50 |
| 158 | Eddie Waitkus | 25.00 | 12.50 | | 221 | Granny Hamner | 25.00 | 12.50 |
| 159 | Saul Rogovin | 25.00 | 12.50 | | 222 | "Hoot" Evers | 25.00 | 12.50 |
| 160 | Owen Friend | 25.00 | 12.50 | | 223 | Del Ennis | 25.00 | 11.00 |
| 161 | Bud Byerly | 25.00 | 12.50 | | 224 | Bruce Edwards | 25.00 | 12.50 |
| 162 | Del Crandall | 25.00 | 11.00 | | 225 | Frank Baumholtz | 25.00 | 12.50 |
| 163 | Stan Rojek | 25.00 | 12.50 | | 226 | Dave Philley | 25.00 | 11.00 |
| 164 | Walt Dubiel | 25.00 | 12.50 | | 227 | Joe Garagiola | 100.00 | 50.00 |
| 165 | Eddie Kazak | 25.00 | 12.50 | | 228 | Al Brazle | 25.00 | 12.50 |
| 166 | Paul LaPalme | 25.00 | 12.50 | | 229 | Gene Bearden | 25.00 | 12.50 |
| 167 | Bill Howerton | 25.00 | 12.50 | | 230 | Matt Batts | 25.00 | 12.50 |
| 168 | Charlie Silvera | 50.00 | 25.00 | | 231 | Sam Zoldak | 25.00 | 12.50 |
| 169 | Howie Judson | 25.00 | 12.50 | | 232 | Billy Cox | 50.00 | 25.00 |
| 170 | Gus Bell | 25.00 | 11.00 | | 233 | *Bob Friend* | 25.00 | 11.00 |
| 171 | Ed Erautt | 25.00 | 12.50 | | 234 | Steve Souchock | 25.00 | 12.50 |
| 172 | Eddie Miksis | 25.00 | 12.50 | | 235 | Walt Dropo | 25.00 | 11.00 |
| 173 | Roy Smalley | 25.00 | 12.50 | | 236 | Ed Fitz Gerald | 25.00 | 12.50 |
| 174 | Clarence Marshall | | | | 237 | Jerry Coleman | 50.00 | 25.00 |
| | | 25.00 | 12.50 | | 238 | Art Houtteman | 25.00 | 12.50 |
| 175 | *Billy Martin* | 350.00 | 175.00 | | 239 | Rocky Bridges | 25.00 | 11.00 |
| 176 | Hank Edwards | 25.00 | 12.50 | | 240 | Jack Phillips | 25.00 | 12.50 |
| 177 | Bill Wight | 25.00 | 12.50 | | 241 | Tommy Byrne | 25.00 | 12.50 |
| 178 | Cass Michaels | 25.00 | 12.50 | | 242 | Tom Poholsky | 25.00 | 12.50 |
| 179 | Frank Smith | 25.00 | 12.50 | | 243 | Larry Doby | 40.00 | 18.00 |
| 180 | *Charley Maxwell* | 25.00 | 11.00 | | 244 | Vic Wertz | 25.00 | 11.00 |
| 181 | Bob Swift | 25.00 | 12.50 | | 245 | Sherry Robertson | 25.00 | 12.50 |
| 182 | Billy Hitchcock | 25.00 | 12.50 | | 246 | George Kell | 60.00 | 30.00 |
| 183 | Erv Dusak | 25.00 | 12.50 | | 247 | Randy Gumpert | 25.00 | 12.50 |
| 184 | Bob Ramazzotti | 25.00 | 12.50 | | 248 | Frank Shea | 25.00 | 12.50 |
| 185 | Bill Nicholson | 25.00 | 12.50 | | 249 | Bobby Adams | 25.00 | 12.50 |
| 186 | Walt Masterson | 25.00 | 12.50 | | 250 | Carl Erskine | 60.00 | 30.00 |
| 187 | Bob Miller | 25.00 | 12.50 | | 251 | Chico Carrasquel | 40.00 | 20.00 |
| 188 | Clarence Podbielan | | | | 252 | Vern Bickford | 40.00 | 20.00 |
| | | 25.00 | 11.00 | | 253 | Johnny Berardino | 50.00 | 25.00 |
| 189 | Pete Reiser | 25.00 | 11.00 | | 254 | Joe Dobson | 40.00 | 20.00 |
| 190 | Don Johnson | 25.00 | 12.50 | | 255 | Clyde Vollmer | 40.00 | 20.00 |
| 191 | Yogi Berra | 350.00 | 175.00 | | 256 | Pete Suder | 40.00 | 20.00 |
| 192 | Myron Ginsberg | 25.00 | 12.50 | | 257 | Bobby Avila | 40.00 | 20.00 |
| 193 | Harry Simpson | 25.00 | 12.50 | | 258 | Steve Gromek | 40.00 | 20.00 |
| 194 | Joe Hatten | 25.00 | 12.50 | | 259 | Bob Addis | 40.00 | 20.00 |

| | NR MT | EX | | | NR MT | EX |
|---|---|---|---|---|---|---|
| 260 | Pete Castiglione | 40.00 | 20.00 | 326 | George Shuba | 175.00 | 87.00 |
| 261 | Willie Mays | 2500.00 | 1250.00 | 327 | Archie Wilson | 175.00 | 87.00 |
| 262 | Virgil Trucks | 50.00 | 25.00 | 328 | Bob Borkowski | 175.00 | 87.00 |
| 263 | Harry Brecheen | 50.00 | 25.00 | 329 | Ivan Delock | 175.00 | 87.00 |
| 264 | Roy Hartsfield | 40.00 | 20.00 | 330 | Turk Lown | 175.00 | 87.00 |
| 265 | Chuck Diering | 40.00 | 20.00 | 331 | Tom Morgan | 160.00 | 80.00 |
| 266 | Murry Dickson | 40.00 | 20.00 | 332 | Tony Bartirome | 175.00 | 87.00 |
| 267 | Sid Gordon | 40.00 | 20.00 | 333 | Pee Wee Reese | 1200.00 | 600.00 |
| 268 | Bob Lemon | 200.00 | 100.00 | 334 | Wilmer Mizell | 175.00 | 87.00 |
| 269 | Willard Nixon | 40.00 | 20.00 | 335 | Ted Lepcio | 175.00 | 87.00 |
| 270 | Lou Brissie | 40.00 | 20.00 | 336 | Dave Koslo | 175.00 | 87.00 |
| 271 | Jim Delsing | 40.00 | 20.00 | 337 | Jim Hearn | 175.00 | 87.00 |
| 272 | Mike Garcia | 50.00 | 25.00 | 338 | Sal Yvars | 175.00 | 87.00 |
| 273 | Erv Palica | 50.00 | 25.00 | 339 | Russ Meyer | 175.00 | 87.00 |
| 274 | Ralph Branca | 70.00 | 35.00 | 340 | Bob Hooper | 175.00 | 87.00 |
| 275 | Pat Mullin | 40.00 | 20.00 | 341 | Hal Jeffcoat | 175.00 | 87.00 |
| 276 | Jim Wilson | 40.00 | 20.00 | 342 | *Clem Labine* | 200.00 | 90.00 |
| 277 | Early Wynn | 175.00 | 87.00 | 343 | Dick Gernert | 175.00 | 87.00 |
| 278 | Al Clark | 40.00 | 20.00 | 344 | Ewell Blackwell | 160.00 | 80.00 |
| 279 | Ed Stewart | 40.00 | 20.00 | 345 | Sam White | 175.00 | 87.00 |
| 280 | Cloyd Boyer | 40.00 | 20.00 | 346 | George Spencer | 175.00 | 87.00 |
| 281 | Tommy Brown | 50.00 | 25.00 | 347 | Joe Adcock | 200.00 | 100.00 |
| 282 | Birdie Tebbetts | 50.00 | 25.00 | 348 | Bob Kelly | 175.00 | 87.00 |
| 283 | Phil Masi | 50.00 | 25.00 | 349 | Bob Cain | 175.00 | 87.00 |
| 284 | Hank Arft | 50.00 | 25.00 | 350 | Cal Abrams | 175.00 | 87.00 |
| 285 | Cliff Fannin | 50.00 | 25.00 | 351 | Al Dark | 175.00 | 87.00 |
| 286 | Joe DeMaestri | 50.00 | 25.00 | 352 | Karl Drews | 175.00 | 87.00 |
| 287 | Steve Bilko | 50.00 | 25.00 | 353 | Bob Del Greco | 175.00 | 87.00 |
| 288 | Chet Nichols | 50.00 | 25.00 | 354 | Fred Hatfield | 175.00 | 87.00 |
| 289 | Tommy Holmes | 55.00 | 25.00 | 355 | Bobby Morgan | 175.00 | 87.00 |
| 290 | Joe Astroth | 50.00 | 25.00 | 356 | Toby Atwell | 175.00 | 87.00 |
| 291 | Gil Coan | 50.00 | 25.00 | 357 | Smoky Burgess | 250.00 | 125.00 |
| 292 | Floyd Baker | 50.00 | 25.00 | 358 | John Kucab | 175.00 | 87.00 |
| 293 | Sibby Sisti | 50.00 | 25.00 | 359 | Dee Fondy | 175.00 | 87.00 |
| 294 | Walker Cooper | 50.00 | 25.00 | 360 | George Crowe | 175.00 | 87.00 |
| 295 | Phil Cavarretta | 55.00 | 22.00 | 361 | Bill Posedel | 175.00 | 87.00 |
| 296 | "Red" Rolfe | 50.00 | 25.00 | 362 | Ken Heintzelman | | |
| 297 | Andy Seminick | 50.00 | 25.00 | | | 175.00 | 87.00 |
| 298 | Bob Ross | 50.00 | 25.00 | 363 | Dick Rozek | 175.00 | 87.00 |
| 299 | Ray Murray | 50.00 | 25.00 | 364 | Clyde Sukeforth | 175.00 | 87.00 |
| 300 | Barney McCosky | 50.00 | 25.00 | 365 | "Cookie" Lavagetto | | |
| 301 | Bob Porterfield | 40.00 | 20.00 | | | 175.00 | 87.00 |
| 302 | Max Surkont | 40.00 | 20.00 | 366 | Dave Madison | 175.00 | 87.00 |
| 303 | Harry Dorish | 40.00 | 20.00 | 367 | Bob Thorpe | 175.00 | 87.00 |
| 304 | Sam Dente | 40.00 | 20.00 | 368 | Ed Wright | 175.00 | 87.00 |
| 305 | Paul Richards | 50.00 | 25.00 | 369 | *Dick Groat* | 300.00 | 150.00 |
| 306 | Lou Sleator | 40.00 | 20.00 | 370 | Billy Hoeft | 175.00 | 87.00 |
| 307 | Frank Campos | 40.00 | 20.00 | 371 | Bob Hofman | 175.00 | 87.00 |
| 308 | Luis Aloma | 40.00 | 20.00 | 372 | *Gil McDougald* | 300.00 | 150.00 |
| 309 | Jim Busby | 40.00 | 20.00 | 373 | Jim Turner | 160.00 | 80.00 |
| 310 | George Metkovich | | | 374 | Al Benton | 175.00 | 87.00 |
| | | 40.00 | 20.00 | 375 | Jack Merson | 175.00 | 87.00 |
| 311 | Mickey Mantle | 30000.00 | 15000.00 | 376 | Faye Throneberry | | |
| 312 | Jackie Robinson | 1200.00 | 600.00 | | | 175.00 | 87.00 |
| 313 | Bobby Thomson | 175.00 | 87.00 | 377 | Chuck Dressen | 175.00 | 90.00 |
| 314 | Roy Campanella | 1500.00 | 750.00 | 378 | Les Fusselman | 175.00 | 87.00 |
| 315 | Leo Durocher | 250.00 | 100.00 | 379 | Joe Rossi | 175.00 | 87.00 |
| 316 | Davey Williams | 175.00 | 87.00 | 380 | Clem Koshorek | 175.00 | 87.00 |
| 317 | Connie Marrero | 175.00 | 87.00 | 381 | Milton Stock | 175.00 | 87.00 |
| 318 | Hal Gregg | 175.00 | 87.00 | 382 | Sam Jones | 175.00 | 87.00 |
| 319 | Al Walker | 175.00 | 87.00 | 383 | Del Wilber | 175.00 | 87.00 |
| 320 | John Rutherford | 175.00 | 87.00 | 384 | Frank Crosetti | 250.00 | 125.00 |
| 321 | *Joe Black* | 225.00 | 90.00 | 385 | Herman Franks | 175.00 | 87.00 |
| 322 | Randy Jackson | 175.00 | 87.00 | 386 | Eddie Yuhas | 175.00 | 87.00 |
| 323 | Bubba Church | 175.00 | 87.00 | 387 | Billy Meyer | 175.00 | 87.00 |
| 324 | Warren Hacker | 175.00 | 87.00 | 388 | Bob Chipman | 175.00 | 87.00 |
| 325 | Bill Serena | 175.00 | 87.00 | 389 | Ben Wade | 175.00 | 87.00 |

| | | NR MT | EX |
|---|---|---|---|
| 390 | Glenn Nelson | 175.00 | 87.00 |
| 391 | Ben Chapman (photo actually Sam Chapman) | 175.00 | 87.00 |
| 392 | *Hoyt Wilhelm* | 600.00 | 300.00 |
| 393 | Ebba St. Claire | 175.00 | 87.00 |
| 394 | Billy Herman | 250.00 | 125.00 |
| 395 | Jake Pitler | 175.00 | 87.00 |
| 396 | *Dick Williams* | 250.00 | 125.00 |
| 397 | Forrest Main | 175.00 | 87.00 |
| 398 | Hal Rice | 175.00 | 87.00 |
| 399 | Jim Fridley | 175.00 | 87.00 |
| 400 | Bill Dickey | 600.00 | 300.00 |
| 401 | Bob Schultz | 175.00 | 87.00 |
| 402 | Earl Harrist | 175.00 | 87.00 |
| 403 | Bill Miller | 160.00 | 80.00 |
| 404 | Dick Brodowski | 175.00 | 87.00 |
| 405 | Eddie Pellagrini | 175.00 | 87.00 |
| 406 | *Joe Nuxhall* | 200.00 | 100.00 |
| 407 | *Ed Mathews* | 3000.00 | 1500.00 |

## 1953 Topps

The 1953 Topps set reflects the company's continuing legal battles with Bowman. The set, originally intended to consist of 280 cards, is lacking six numbers (#'s 253, 261, 267, 268, 271 and 275) which probably represent players whose contracts were lost to the competition. The 2-5/8" by 3-3/4" cards feature painted player pictures. A color team logo appears at a bottom panel (red for American League and black for National.) Card backs contain the first baseball trivia questions along with brief statistics and player biographies. In the red panel at the top which lists the player's personal data, cards from the 2nd Series (#'s 86-165 plus 10, 44, 61, 72 and 81) can be found with that data printed in either black or white, black being the scarcer variety. Card numbers 221-280 are the scarce high numbers.

| | | NR MT | EX |
|---|---|---|---|
| Complete Set: | | 14000.00 | 7000.00 |
| Common Player Singleprint: 1-165 | | 25.00 | 12.50 |
| Common Player: 1-165 | | 16.00 | 8.00 |
| Common Player: 166-220 | | 16.00 | 8.00 |
| Common Player Singleprint: 221-280 | | 90.00 | 45.00 |
| Common Player: 221-280 | | 50.00 | 25.00 |
| | | | |
| 1 | Jackie Robinson | 650.00 | 275.00 |
| 2 | Luke Easter | 25.00 | 12.50 |
| 3 | George Crowe | 25.00 | 12.50 |
| 4 | Ben Wade | 25.00 | 12.50 |
| 5 | Joe Dobson | 25.00 | 12.50 |
| 6 | Sam Jones | 25.00 | 12.50 |
| 7 | Bob Borkowski | 16.00 | 8.00 |
| 8 | Clem Koshorek | 16.00 | 8.00 |
| 9 | Joe Collins | 30.00 | 15.00 |
| 10 | Smoky Burgess | 40.00 | 20.00 |
| 11 | Sal Yvars | 25.00 | 12.50 |
| 12 | Howie Judson | 16.00 | 8.00 |
| 13 | Connie Marrero | 16.00 | 8.00 |
| 14 | Clem Labine | 25.00 | 12.50 |
| 15 | Bobo Newsom | 25.00 | 12.50 |
| 16 | Harry Lowrey | 16.00 | 8.00 |
| 17 | Billy Hitchcock | 25.00 | 12.50 |
| 18 | Ted Lepcio | 16.00 | 8.00 |
| 19 | Mel Parnell | 16.00 | 8.00 |
| 20 | Hank Thompson | 25.00 | 12.50 |
| 21 | Billy Johnson | 25.00 | 12.50 |
| 22 | Howie Fox | 25.00 | 12.50 |
| 23 | Toby Atwell | 16.00 | 8.00 |
| 24 | Ferris Fain | 25.00 | 12.50 |
| 25 | Ray Boone | 25.00 | 12.50 |
| 26 | Dale Mitchell | 16.00 | 8.00 |
| 27 | Roy Campanella | 225.00 | 112.00 |
| 28 | Eddie Pellagrini | 25.00 | 12.50 |
| 29 | Hal Jeffcoat | 25.00 | 12.50 |
| 30 | Willard Nixon | 25.00 | 12.50 |
| 31 | Ewell Blackwell | 40.00 | 20.00 |
| 32 | Clyde Vollmer | 25.00 | 12.50 |
| 33 | Bob Kennedy | 16.00 | 8.00 |
| 34 | George Shuba | 25.00 | 12.50 |
| 35 | Irv Noren | 25.00 | 12.50 |
| 36 | Johnny Groth | 16.00 | 8.00 |
| 37 | Ed Mathews | 115.00 | 57.50 |
| 38 | Jim Hearn | 16.00 | 8.00 |
| 39 | Eddie Miksis | 25.00 | 12.50 |
| 40 | John Lipon | 25.00 | 12.50 |
| 41 | Enos Slaughter | 90.00 | 45.00 |
| 42 | Gus Zernial | 16.00 | 8.00 |
| 43 | Gil McDougald | 50.00 | 25.00 |
| 44 | Ellis Kinder | 30.00 | 15.00 |
| 45 | Grady Hatton | 16.00 | 8.00 |
| 46 | Johnny Klippstein | 16.00 | 8.00 |
| 47 | Bubba Church | 16.00 | 8.00 |
| 48 | Bob Del Greco | 16.00 | 8.00 |
| 49 | Faye Throneberry | 16.00 | 8.00 |
| 50 | Chuck Dressen | 25.00 | 12.50 |
| 51 | Frank Campos | 16.00 | 8.00 |
| 52 | Ted Gray | 16.00 | 8.00 |
| 53 | Sherman Lollar | 16.00 | 8.00 |
| 54 | Bob Feller | 125.00 | 67.00 |
| 55 | Maurice McDermott | 16.00 | 8.00 |
| 56 | Gerald Staley | 16.00 | 8.00 |

| | | NR MT | EX | | | NR MT | EX |
|---|---|---|---|---|---|---|---|
| 57 | Carl Scheib | 25.00 | 12.50 | 123 | Tommy Byrne | 16.00 | 8.00 |
| 58 | George Metkovich | | | 124 | Sibby Sisti | 16.00 | 8.00 |
| | | 25.00 | 12.50 | 125 | Dick Williams | 25.00 | 12.50 |
| 59 | Karl Drews | 16.00 | 8.00 | 126 | Bill Connelly | 16.00 | 8.00 |
| 60 | Cloyd Boyer | 16.00 | 8.00 | 127 | Clint Courtney | 16.00 | 8.00 |
| 61 | Early Wynn | 80.00 | 40.00 | 128 | Wilmer Mizell | 16.00 | 8.00 |
| 62 | Monte Irvin | 45.00 | 23.00 | 129 | Keith Thomas | 16.00 | 8.00 |
| 63 | Gus Niarhos | 16.00 | 8.00 | 130 | Turk Lown | 16.00 | 8.00 |
| 64 | Dave Philley | 25.00 | 12.50 | 131 | Harry Byrd | 16.00 | 8.00 |
| 65 | Earl Harrist | 25.00 | 12.50 | 132 | Tom Morgan | 25.00 | 12.50 |
| 66 | Orestes Minoso | 30.00 | 15.00 | 133 | Gil Coan | 16.00 | 8.00 |
| 67 | Roy Sievers | 25.00 | 12.50 | 134 | Rube Walker | 25.00 | 12.50 |
| 68 | Del Rice | 25.00 | 12.50 | 135 | Al Rosen | 35.00 | 17.50 |
| 69 | Dick Brodowski | 25.00 | 12.50 | 136 | Ken Heintzelman | 16.00 | 8.00 |
| 70 | Ed Yuhas | 25.00 | 12.50 | 137 | John Rutherford | 25.00 | 12.50 |
| 71 | Tony Bartirome | 25.00 | 12.50 | 138 | George Kell | 65.00 | 32.50 |
| 72 | Fred Hutchinson | 25.00 | 12.50 | 139 | Sammy White | 16.00 | 8.00 |
| 73 | Eddie Robinson | 25.00 | 12.50 | 140 | Tommy Glaviano | 16.00 | 8.00 |
| 74 | Joe Rossi | 25.00 | 12.50 | 141 | Allie Reynolds | 35.00 | 17.50 |
| 75 | Mike Garcia | 25.00 | 12.50 | 142 | Vic Wertz | 25.00 | 12.50 |
| 76 | Pee Wee Reese | 175.00 | 87.00 | 143 | Billy Pierce | 25.00 | 12.50 |
| 77 | John Mize | 60.00 | 30.00 | 144 | Bob Schultz | 16.00 | 8.00 |
| 78 | Al Schoendienst | 65.00 | 33.00 | 145 | Harry Dorish | 16.00 | 8.00 |
| 79 | Johnny Wyrostek | 25.00 | 12.50 | 146 | Granville Hamner | 16.00 | 8.00 |
| 80 | Jim Hegan | 25.00 | 12.50 | 147 | Warren Spahn | 150.00 | 75.00 |
| 82 | Mickey Mantle | 3000.00 | 1500.00 | 148 | Mickey Grasso | 16.00 | 8.00 |
| 83 | Howie Pollet | 25.00 | 12.50 | 149 | Dom DiMaggio | 30.00 | 15.00 |
| 84 | Bob Hooper | 16.00 | 8.00 | 150 | Harry Simpson | 16.00 | 8.00 |
| 85 | Bobby Morgan | 25.00 | 12.50 | 151 | Hoyt Wilhelm | 70.00 | 35.00 |
| 86 | Billy Martin | 125.00 | 67.00 | 152 | Bob Adams | 16.00 | 8.00 |
| 87 | Ed Lopat | 35.00 | 17.50 | 153 | Andy Seminick | 16.00 | 8.00 |
| 88 | Willie Jones | 16.00 | 8.00 | 154 | Dick Groat | 25.00 | 12.50 |
| 89 | Chuck Stobbs | 16.00 | 8.00 | 155 | Dutch Leonard | 16.00 | 8.00 |
| 90 | Hank Edwards | 16.00 | 8.00 | 156 | Jim Rivera | 16.00 | 8.00 |
| 91 | Ebba St. Claire | 16.00 | 8.00 | 157 | Bob Addis | 16.00 | 8.00 |
| 92 | Paul Minner | 16.00 | 8.00 | 158 | *John Logan* | 25.00 | 12.50 |
| 93 | Hal Rice | 16.00 | 8.00 | 159 | Wayne Terwilliger | 16.00 | 8.00 |
| 94 | William Kennedy | 16.00 | 8.00 | 160 | Bob Young | 16.00 | 8.00 |
| 95 | Willard Marshall | 16.00 | 8.00 | 161 | Vern Bickford | 16.00 | 8.00 |
| 96 | Virgil Trucks | 25.00 | 12.50 | 162 | Ted Kluszewski | 50.00 | 25.00 |
| 97 | Don Kolloway | 16.00 | 8.00 | 163 | Fred Hatfield | 16.00 | 8.00 |
| 98 | Cal Abrams | 16.00 | 8.00 | 164 | Frank Shea | 16.00 | 8.00 |
| 99 | Dave Madison | 16.00 | 8.00 | 165 | Billy Hoeft | 16.00 | 8.00 |
| 100 | Bill Miller | 25.00 | 12.50 | 166 | Bill Hunter | 16.00 | 8.00 |
| 101 | Ted Wilks | 16.00 | 8.00 | 167 | Art Schult | 16.00 | 8.00 |
| 102 | Connie Ryan | 16.00 | 8.00 | 168 | Willard Schmidt | 16.00 | 8.00 |
| 103 | Joe Astroth | 16.00 | 8.00 | 169 | Dizzy Trout | 16.00 | 8.00 |
| 104 | Yogi Berra | 250.00 | 125.00 | 170 | Bill Werle | 16.00 | 8.00 |
| 105 | Joe Nuxhall | 25.00 | 12.50 | 171 | Bill Glynn | 16.00 | 8.00 |
| 106 | Johnny Antonelli | 25.00 | 12.50 | 172 | Rip Repulski | 16.00 | 8.00 |
| 107 | Danny O'Connell | 16.00 | 8.00 | 173 | Preston Ward | 16.00 | 8.00 |
| 108 | Bob Porterfield | 16.00 | 8.00 | 174 | Billy Loes | 16.00 | 8.00 |
| 109 | Alvin Dark | 30.00 | 15.00 | 175 | Ron Kline | 16.00 | 8.00 |
| 110 | Herman Wehmeier | | | 176 | *Don Hoak* | 16.00 | 8.00 |
| | | 16.00 | 8.00 | 177 | Jim Dyck | 16.00 | 8.00 |
| 111 | Hank Sauer | 16.00 | 8.00 | 178 | Jim Waugh | 16.00 | 8.00 |
| 112 | Ned Garver | 16.00 | 8.00 | 179 | Gene Hermanski | 16.00 | 8.00 |
| 113 | Jerry Priddy | 16.00 | 8.00 | 180 | Virgil Stallcup | 16.00 | 8.00 |
| 114 | Phil Rizzuto | 125.00 | 62.00 | 181 | Al Zarilla | 16.00 | 8.00 |
| 115 | George Spencer | 16.00 | 8.00 | 182 | Bob Hofman | 16.00 | 8.00 |
| 116 | Frank Smith | 16.00 | 8.00 | 183 | *Stu Miller* | 16.00 | 8.00 |
| 117 | Sid Gordon | 16.00 | 8.00 | 184 | *Hal Brown* | 16.00 | 8.00 |
| 118 | Gus Bell | 16.00 | 8.00 | 185 | Jim Pendleton | 16.00 | 8.00 |
| 119 | John Sain | 40.00 | 20.00 | 186 | Charlie Bishop | 16.00 | 8.00 |
| 120 | Davey Williams | 16.00 | 8.00 | 187 | Jim Fridley | 16.00 | 8.00 |
| 121 | Walt Dropo | 16.00 | 8.00 | 188 | *Andy Carey* | 16.00 | 8.00 |
| 122 | Elmer Valo | 16.00 | 8.00 | 189 | Ray Jablonski | 16.00 | 8.00 |

| | NR MT | EX |
|---|---|---|
| 190 Dixie Walker | 16.00 | 8.00 |
| 191 Ralph Kiner | 70.00 | 35.00 |
| 192 Wally Westlake | 16.00 | 8.00 |
| 193 Mike Clark | 16.00 | 8.00 |
| 194 Eddie Kazak | 16.00 | 8.00 |
| 195 Ed McGhee | 16.00 | 8.00 |
| 196 Bob Keegan | 16.00 | 8.00 |
| 197 Del Crandall | 16.00 | 8.00 |
| 198 Forrest Main | 16.00 | 8.00 |
| 199 Marion Fricano | 16.00 | 8.00 |
| 200 Gordon Goldsberry | 16.00 | 8.00 |
| 201 Paul LaPalme | 16.00 | 8.00 |
| 202 Carl Sawatski | 16.00 | 8.00 |
| 203 Cliff Fannin | 16.00 | 8.00 |
| 204 Dick Bokelmann | 16.00 | 8.00 |
| 205 Vern Benson | 16.00 | 8.00 |
| 206 *Ed Bailey* | 16.00 | 8.00 |
| 207 Whitey Ford | 150.00 | 75.00 |
| 208 Jim Wilson | 16.00 | 8.00 |
| 209 Jim Greengrass | 16.00 | 8.00 |
| 210 *Bob Cerv* | 16.00 | 8.00 |
| 211 J.W. Porter | 16.00 | 8.00 |
| 212 Jack Dittmer | 16.00 | 8.00 |
| 213 Ray Scarborough | 16.00 | 8.00 |
| 214 *Bill Bruton* | 16.00 | 8.00 |
| 215 *Gene Conley* | 16.00 | 8.00 |
| 216 Jim Hughes | 16.00 | 8.00 |
| 217 Murray Wall | 16.00 | 8.00 |
| 218 Les Fusselman | 16.00 | 8.00 |
| 219 Pete Runnels (photo actually Don Johnson) | 16.00 | 8.00 |
| 220 Satchell Paige | 450.00 | 225.00 |
| 221 Bob Milliken | 90.00 | 45.00 |
| 222 Vic Janowicz | 50.00 | 25.00 |
| 223 John O'Brien | 50.00 | 25.00 |
| 224 Lou Sleater | 50.00 | 25.00 |
| 225 Bobby Shantz | 100.00 | 50.00 |
| 226 Ed Erautt | 90.00 | 45.00 |
| 227 Morris Martin | 50.00 | 25.00 |
| 228 Hal Newhouser | 125.00 | 67.00 |
| 229 Rocky Krsnich | 90.00 | 45.00 |
| 230 Johnny Lindell | 50.00 | 25.00 |
| 231 Solly Hemus | 50.00 | 25.00 |
| 232 Dick Kokos | 90.00 | 45.00 |
| 233 Al Aber | 90.00 | 45.00 |
| 234 Ray Murray | 50.00 | 25.00 |
| 235 John Hetki | 50.00 | 25.00 |
| 236 Harry Perkowski | 90.00 | 45.00 |
| 237 Clarence Podbielan | 50.00 | 25.00 |
| 238 Cal Hogue | 50.00 | 25.00 |
| 239 Jim Delsing | 90.00 | 45.00 |
| 240 Freddie Marsh | 50.00 | 25.00 |
| 241 Al Sima | 50.00 | 25.00 |
| 242 Charlie Silvera | 90.00 | 45.00 |
| 243 Carlos Bernier | 50.00 | 25.00 |
| 244 Willie Mays | 2500.00 | 1250.00 |
| 245 Bill Norman | 90.00 | 45.00 |
| 246 *Roy Face* | 80.00 | 40.00 |
| 247 Mike Sandlock | 50.00 | 25.00 |
| 248 Gene Stephens | 50.00 | 25.00 |
| 249 Ed O'Brien | 50.00 | 25.00 |
| 250 Bob Wilson | 90.00 | 45.00 |
| 251 Sid Hudson | 90.00 | 45.00 |
| 252 Henry Foiles | 90.00 | 45.00 |

| | NR MT | EX |
|---|---|---|
| 253 Not Issued | | |
| 254 Preacher Roe | 80.00 | 40.00 |
| 255 Dixie Howell | 90.00 | 45.00 |
| 256 Les Peden | 90.00 | 45.00 |
| 257 Bob Boyd | 90.00 | 45.00 |
| 258 *Jim Gilliam* | 300.00 | 150.00 |
| 259 Roy McMillan | 90.00 | 45.00 |
| 260 Sam Calderone | 90.00 | 45.00 |
| 261 Not Issued | | |
| 262 Bob Oldis | 90.00 | 45.00 |
| 263 *John Podres* | 250.00 | 125.00 |
| 264 Gene Woodling | 70.00 | 35.00 |
| 265 Jackie Jensen | 100.00 | 50.00 |
| 266 Bob Cain | 90.00 | 45.00 |
| 267 Not Issued | | |
| 268 Not Issued | | |
| 269 Duane Pillette | 90.00 | 45.00 |
| 270 Vern Stephens | 90.00 | 45.00 |
| 271 Not Issued | | |
| 272 Bill Antonello | 90.00 | 45.00 |
| 273 *Harvey Haddix* | 125.00 | 62.00 |
| 274 John Riddle | 90.00 | 45.00 |
| 275 Not Issued | | |
| 276 Ken Raffensberger | 50.00 | 25.00 |
| 277 Don Lund | 90.00 | 45.00 |
| 278 Willie Miranda | 90.00 | 45.00 |
| 279 Joe Coleman | 50.00 | 25.00 |
| 280 Milt Bolling | 300.00 | 150.00 |

## 1954 Topps

The first issue to use two player pictures on the front, the 1954 Topps set is very popular today. Solid color backgrounds frame both color head- and-shoulders and black and white action pictures of the player. The player's name, position, team and team logo appear at the top. Backs include an "Inside Baseball" cartoon regarding the player as well as statistics and biography. The 250-card, 2-5/8" by 3-3/4", set includes manager and coaches cards, and the first use of two players together on a modern card; the players were, appropriately, the O'Brien twins.

| | | NR MT | EX |
|---|---|---|---|
| | Complete Set: | 8200.00 | 4100.00 |
| | Common Player: 1-50 | 13.00 | 6.50 |
| | Common Player: 51-75 | 30.00 | 15.00 |
| | Common Player: 76-250 | | |
| | | 13.00 | 6.50 |
| 1 | Ted Williams | 650.00 | 200.00 |
| 2 | Gus Zernial | 13.00 | 6.50 |
| 3 | Monte Irvin | 35.00 | 17.50 |
| 4 | Hank Sauer | 15.00 | 7.50 |
| 5 | Ed Lopat | 20.00 | 10.00 |
| 6 | Pete Runnels | 13.00 | 6.50 |
| 7 | Ted Kluszewski | 30.00 | 15.00 |
| 8 | Bobby Young | 13.00 | 6.50 |
| 9 | Harvey Haddix | 13.00 | 6.50 |
| 10 | Jackie Robinson | 300.00 | 150.00 |
| 11 | Paul Smith | 13.00 | 6.50 |
| 12 | Del Crandall | 13.00 | 6.50 |
| 13 | Billy Martin | 85.00 | 42.00 |
| 14 | Preacher Roe | 40.00 | 20.00 |
| 15 | Al Rosen | 20.00 | 10.00 |
| 16 | Vic Janowicz | 13.00 | 6.50 |
| 17 | Phil Rizzuto | 70.00 | 35.00 |
| 18 | Walt Dropo | 13.00 | 6.50 |
| 19 | Johnny Lipon | 13.00 | 6.50 |
| 20 | Warren Spahn | 110.00 | 55.00 |
| 21 | Bobby Shantz | 13.00 | 6.50 |
| 22 | Jim Greengrass | 13.00 | 6.50 |
| 23 | Luke Easter | 13.00 | 6.50 |
| 24 | Granny Hamner | 13.00 | 6.50 |
| 25 | *Harvey Kuenn* | 50.00 | 25.00 |
| 26 | Ray Jablonski | 13.00 | 6.50 |
| 27 | Ferris Fain | 13.00 | 6.50 |
| 28 | Paul Minner | 13.00 | 6.50 |
| 29 | Jim Hegan | 13.00 | 6.50 |
| 30 | Ed Mathews | 100.00 | 50.00 |
| 31 | Johnny Klippstein | 13.00 | 6.50 |
| 32 | Duke Snider | 150.00 | 75.00 |
| 33 | Johnny Schmitz | 13.00 | 6.50 |
| 34 | Jim Rivera | 13.00 | 6.50 |
| 35 | Junior Gilliam | 30.00 | 15.00 |
| 36 | Hoyt Wilhelm | 50.00 | 25.00 |
| 37 | Whitey Ford | 100.00 | 50.00 |
| 38 | Eddie Stanky | 13.00 | 6.50 |
| 39 | Sherm Lollar | 13.00 | 6.50 |
| 40 | Mel Parnell | 13.00 | 6.50 |
| 41 | Willie Jones | 13.00 | 6.50 |
| 42 | Don Mueller | 13.00 | 6.50 |
| 43 | Dick Groat | 13.00 | 6.50 |
| 44 | Ned Garver | 13.00 | 6.50 |
| 45 | Richie Ashburn | 40.00 | 20.00 |
| 46 | Ken Raffensberger | | |
| | | 13.00 | 6.50 |
| 47 | Ellis Kinder | 13.00 | 6.50 |
| 48 | Billy Hunter | 13.00 | 6.50 |
| 49 | Ray Murray | 13.00 | 6.50 |
| 50 | Yogi Berra | 260.00 | 130.00 |
| 51 | Johnny Lindell | 30.00 | 15.00 |
| 52 | Vic Power | 30.00 | 15.00 |
| 53 | Jack Dittmer | 30.00 | 15.00 |
| 54 | Vern Stephens | 30.00 | 15.00 |
| 55 | Phil Cavarretta | 30.00 | 15.00 |
| 56 | Willie Miranda | 30.00 | 15.00 |
| 57 | Luis Aloma | 30.00 | 15.00 |
| 58 | Bob Wilson | 30.00 | 15.00 |
| 59 | Gene Conley | 30.00 | 15.00 |
| 60 | Frank Baumholtz | 30.00 | 15.00 |
| 61 | Bob Cain | 30.00 | 15.00 |
| 62 | Eddie Robinson | 30.00 | 15.00 |
| 63 | Johnny Pesky | 30.00 | 15.00 |
| 64 | Hank Thompson | 30.00 | 15.00 |
| 65 | Bob Swift | 30.00 | 15.00 |
| 66 | Ted Lepcio | 30.00 | 15.00 |
| 67 | Jim Willis | 30.00 | 15.00 |
| 68 | Sammy Calderone | | |
| | | 30.00 | 15.00 |
| 69 | Bud Podbielan | 30.00 | 15.00 |
| 70 | Larry Doby | 70.00 | 35.00 |
| 71 | Frank Smith | 30.00 | 15.00 |
| 72 | Preston Ward | 30.00 | 15.00 |
| 73 | Wayne Terwilliger | 30.00 | 15.00 |
| 74 | Bill Taylor | 30.00 | 15.00 |
| 75 | Fred Haney | 30.00 | 15.00 |
| 76 | Bob Scheffing | 13.00 | 6.50 |
| 77 | Ray Boone | 13.00 | 6.50 |
| 78 | Ted Kazanski | 13.00 | 6.50 |
| 79 | Andy Pafko | 13.00 | 6.50 |
| 80 | Jackie Jensen | 13.00 | 6.50 |
| 81 | Dave Hoskins | 13.00 | 6.50 |
| 82 | Milt Bolling | 13.00 | 6.50 |
| 83 | Joe Collins | 13.00 | 6.50 |
| 84 | Dick Cole | 13.00 | 6.50 |
| 85 | *Bob Turley* | 30.00 | 15.00 |
| 86 | Billy Herman | 13.00 | 6.50 |
| 87 | Roy Face | 13.00 | 6.50 |
| 88 | Matt Batts | 13.00 | 6.50 |
| 89 | Howie Pollet | 13.00 | 6.50 |
| 90 | Willie Mays | 500.00 | 250.00 |
| 91 | Bob Oldis | 13.00 | 6.50 |
| 92 | Wally Westlake | 13.00 | 6.50 |
| 93 | Sid Hudson | 13.00 | 6.50 |
| 94 | *Ernie Banks* | 800.00 | 400.00 |
| 95 | Hal Rice | 13.00 | 6.50 |
| 96 | Charlie Silvera | 13.00 | 6.50 |
| 97 | Jerry Lane | 13.00 | 6.50 |
| 98 | Joe Black | 13.00 | 6.50 |
| 99 | Bob Hofman | 13.00 | 6.50 |
| 100 | Bob Keegan | 13.00 | 6.50 |
| 101 | Gene Woodling | 20.00 | 10.00 |
| 102 | Gil Hodges | 75.00 | 38.00 |
| 103 | *Jim Lemon* | 13.00 | 6.50 |
| 104 | Mike Sandlock | 13.00 | 6.50 |
| 105 | Andy Carey | 13.00 | 6.50 |
| 106 | Dick Kokos | 13.00 | 6.50 |
| 107 | Duane Pillette | 13.00 | 6.50 |
| 108 | Thornton Kipper | 13.00 | 6.50 |
| 109 | Bill Bruton | 13.00 | 6.50 |
| 110 | Harry Dorish | 13.00 | 6.50 |
| 111 | Jim Delsing | 13.00 | 6.50 |
| 112 | Bill Renna | 13.00 | 6.50 |
| 113 | Bob Boyd | 13.00 | 6.50 |
| 114 | Dean Stone | 13.00 | 6.50 |
| 115 | "Rip" Repulski | 13.00 | 6.50 |
| 116 | Steve Bilko | 13.00 | 6.50 |
| 117 | Solly Hemus | 13.00 | 6.50 |
| 118 | Carl Scheib | 13.00 | 6.50 |
| 119 | Johnny Antonelli | 13.00 | 6.50 |
| 120 | Roy McMillan | 13.00 | 6.50 |
| 121 | Clem Labine | 13.00 | 6.50 |
| 122 | Johnny Logan | 13.00 | 6.50 |
| 123 | Bobby Adams | 13.00 | 6.50 |
| 124 | Marion Fricano | 13.00 | 6.50 |

| | | NR MT | EX | | | | NR MT | EX |
|---|---|---|---|---|---|---|---|---|
| 125 | Harry Perkowski | 13.00 | 6.50 | | 189 | Bob Ross | 13.00 | 6.50 |
| 126 | Ben Wade | 13.00 | 6.50 | | 190 | Ray Herbert | 13.00 | 6.50 |
| 127 | Steve O'Neill | 13.00 | 6.50 | | 191 | Dick Schofield | 13.00 | 6.50 |
| 128 | Henry Aaron | 2000.00 | 1000.00 | | 192 | "Cot" Deal | 13.00 | 6.50 |
| 129 | Forrest Jacobs | 13.00 | 6.50 | | 193 | Johnny Hopp | 13.00 | 6.50 |
| 130 | Hank Bauer | 30.00 | 15.00 | | 194 | Bill Sarni | 13.00 | 6.50 |
| 131 | Reno Bertoia | 13.00 | 6.50 | | 195 | Bill Consolo | 13.00 | 6.50 |
| 132 | Tom Lasorda | 150.00 | 75.00 | | 196 | Stan Jok | 13.00 | 6.50 |
| 133 | Del Baker | 13.00 | 6.50 | | 197 | "Schoolboy" Rowe | | |
| 134 | Cal Hogue | 13.00 | 6.50 | | | | 13.00 | 6.50 |
| 135 | Joe Presko | 13.00 | 6.50 | | 198 | Carl Sawatski | 13.00 | 6.50 |
| 136 | Connie Ryan | 13.00 | 6.50 | | 199 | "Rocky" Nelson | 13.00 | 6.50 |
| 137 | Wally Moon | 13.00 | 6.50 | | 200 | Larry Jansen | 13.00 | 6.50 |
| 138 | Bob Borkowski | 13.00 | 6.50 | | 201 | Al Kaline | 800.00 | 400.00 |
| 139 | Ed & Johnny O'Brien | | | | 202 | Bob Purkey | 13.00 | 6.50 |
| | | 30.00 | 15.00 | | 203 | Harry Brecheen | 13.00 | 6.50 |
| 140 | Tom Wright | 13.00 | 6.50 | | 204 | Angel Scull | 13.00 | 6.50 |
| 141 | Joe Jay | 13.00 | 6.50 | | 205 | Johnny Sain | 35.00 | 17.50 |
| 142 | Tom Poholsky | 13.00 | 6.50 | | 206 | Ray Crone | 13.00 | 6.50 |
| 143 | Rollie Hemsley | 13.00 | 6.50 | | 207 | Tom Oliver | 13.00 | 6.50 |
| 144 | Bill Werle | 13.00 | 6.50 | | 208 | Grady Hatton | 13.00 | 6.50 |
| 145 | Elmer Valo | 13.00 | 6.50 | | 209 | Charlie Thompson | | |
| 146 | Don Johnson | 13.00 | 6.50 | | | | 13.00 | 6.50 |
| 147 | John Riddle | 13.00 | 6.50 | | 210 | Bob Buhl | 13.00 | 6.50 |
| 148 | Bob Trice | 13.00 | 6.50 | | 211 | Don Hoak | 13.00 | 6.50 |
| 149 | Jim Robertson | 13.00 | 6.50 | | 212 | Mickey Micelotta | 13.00 | 6.50 |
| 150 | Dick Kryhoski | 13.00 | 6.50 | | 213 | John Fitzpatrick | 13.00 | 6.50 |
| 151 | Alex Grammas | 13.00 | 6.50 | | 214 | Arnold Portocarrero | | |
| 152 | Mike Blyzka | 13.00 | 6.50 | | | | 13.00 | 6.50 |
| 153 | "Rube" Walker | 13.00 | 6.50 | | 215 | Ed McGhee | 13.00 | 6.50 |
| 154 | Mike Fornieles | 13.00 | 6.50 | | 216 | Al Sima | 13.00 | 6.50 |
| 155 | Bob Kennedy | 13.00 | 6.50 | | 217 | Paul Schreiber | 13.00 | 6.50 |
| 156 | Joe Coleman | 13.00 | 6.50 | | 218 | Fred Marsh | 13.00 | 6.50 |
| 157 | Don Lenhardt | 13.00 | 6.50 | | 219 | Charlie Kress | 13.00 | 6.50 |
| 158 | "Peanuts" Lowrey | | | | 220 | Ruben Gomez | 13.00 | 6.50 |
| | | 13.00 | 6.50 | | 221 | Dick Brodowski | 13.00 | 6.50 |
| 159 | Dave Philley | 13.00 | 6.50 | | 222 | Bill Wilson | 13.00 | 6.50 |
| 160 | "Red" Kress | 13.00 | 6.50 | | 223 | Joe Haynes | 13.00 | 6.50 |
| 161 | John Hetki | 13.00 | 6.50 | | 224 | Dick Weik | 13.00 | 6.50 |
| 162 | Herman Wehmeier | | | | 225 | Don Liddle | 13.00 | 6.50 |
| | | 13.00 | 6.50 | | 226 | Jehosie Heard | 13.00 | 6.50 |
| 163 | Frank House | 13.00 | 6.50 | | 227 | Buster Mills | 13.00 | 6.50 |
| 164 | Stu Miller | 13.00 | 6.50 | | 228 | Gene Hermanski | 13.00 | 6.50 |
| 165 | Jim Pendleton | 13.00 | 6.50 | | 229 | Bob Talbot | 13.00 | 6.50 |
| 166 | Johnny Podres | 30.00 | 15.00 | | 230 | Bob Kuzava | 13.00 | 6.50 |
| 167 | Don Lund | 13.00 | 6.50 | | 231 | Roy Smalley | 13.00 | 6.50 |
| 168 | Morrie Martin | 13.00 | 6.50 | | 232 | Lou Limmer | 13.00 | 6.50 |
| 169 | Jim Hughes | 13.00 | 6.50 | | 233 | Augie Galan | 13.00 | 6.50 |
| 170 | Jim Rhodes | 13.00 | 6.50 | | 234 | Jerry Lynch | 13.00 | 6.50 |
| 171 | Leo Kiely | 13.00 | 6.50 | | 235 | Vern Law | 13.00 | 6.50 |
| 172 | Hal Brown | 13.00 | 6.50 | | 236 | Paul Penson | 13.00 | 6.50 |
| 173 | Jack Harshman | 13.00 | 6.50 | | 237 | Mike Ryba | 13.00 | 6.50 |
| 174 | Tom Qualters | 13.00 | 6.50 | | 238 | Al Aber | 13.00 | 6.50 |
| 175 | Frank Leja | 13.00 | 6.50 | | 239 | Bill Skowron | 90.00 | 45.00 |
| 176 | Bob Keely | 13.00 | 6.50 | | 240 | Sam Mele | 13.00 | 6.50 |
| 177 | Bob Milliken | 13.00 | 6.50 | | 241 | Bob Miller | 13.00 | 6.50 |
| 178 | Bill Gylnn (Glynn) | 13.00 | 6.50 | | 242 | Curt Roberts | 13.00 | 6.50 |
| 179 | Gair Allie | 13.00 | 6.50 | | 243 | Ray Blades | 13.00 | 6.50 |
| 180 | Wes Westrum | 13.00 | 6.50 | | 244 | Leroy Wheat | 13.00 | 6.50 |
| 181 | Mel Roach | 13.00 | 6.50 | | 245 | Roy Sievers | 13.00 | 6.50 |
| 182 | Chuck Harmon | 13.00 | 6.50 | | 246 | Howie Fox | 13.00 | 6.50 |
| 183 | Earle Combs | 35.00 | 17.50 | | 247 | Eddie Mayo | 13.00 | 6.50 |
| 184 | Ed Bailey | 13.00 | 6.50 | | 248 | Al Smith | 13.00 | 6.50 |
| 185 | Chuck Stobbs | 13.00 | 6.50 | | 249 | Wilmer Mizell | 13.00 | 6.50 |
| 186 | Karl Olson | 13.00 | 6.50 | | 250 | Ted Williams | 700.00 | 225.00 |
| 187 | "Heinie" Manush | 35.00 | 17.50 | | | | | |
| 188 | Dave Jolly | 13.00 | 6.50 | | | | | |

# 1955 Topps

ANDY CAREY

The 1955 Topps set is numerically the smallest of the regular issue Topps sets. The 3-3/4" by 2-5/8" cards mark the first time that Topps used a horizontal format. While that format was new, the design was not; they are very similar to the 1954 cards to the point many pictures appeared in both years. Although it was slated for a 210-card set, the 1955 Topps set turned out to be only 206 cards with numbers 175, 186, 203 and 209 never being released. The scarce high numbers in this set begin with #161.

|  | NR MT | EX |
|---|---|---|
| Complete Set: | 7500.00 | 3750.00 |
| Common Player: 1-150 | 8.00 | 4.00 |
| Common Player: 151-160 | | |
| | 17.00 | 8.50 |
| Common Player: 161-210 | | |
| | 25.00 | 12.50 |

| | | NR MT | EX |
|---|---|---|---|
| 1 | "Dusty" Rhodes | 50.00 | 15.00 |
| 2 | Ted Williams | 400.00 | 200.00 |
| 3 | Art Fowler | 8.00 | 4.00 |
| 4 | Al Kaline | 200.00 | 100.00 |
| 5 | Jim Gilliam | 10.00 | 5.00 |
| 6 | Stan Hack | 8.00 | 4.00 |
| 7 | Jim Hegan | 8.00 | 4.00 |
| 8 | Hal Smith | 8.00 | 4.00 |
| 9 | Bob Miller | 8.00 | 4.00 |
| 10 | Bob Keegan | 8.00 | 4.00 |
| 11 | Ferris Fain | 8.00 | 4.00 |

A player's name in italic type indicates a rookie card. An (FC) indicates a player's first card for that particular card company.

| | | NR MT | EX |
|---|---|---|---|
| 12 | "Jake" Thies | 8.00 | 4.00 |
| 13 | Fred Marsh | 8.00 | 4.00 |
| 14 | Jim Finigan | 8.00 | 4.00 |
| 15 | Jim Pendleton | 8.00 | 4.00 |
| 16 | Roy Sievers | 15.00 | 7.50 |
| 17 | Bobby Hofman | 8.00 | 4.00 |
| 18 | Russ Kemmerer | 8.00 | 4.00 |
| 19 | Billy Herman | 12.00 | 6.00 |
| 20 | Andy Carey | 9.00 | 4.50 |
| 21 | Alex Grammas | 8.00 | 4.00 |
| 22 | Bill Skowron | 15.00 | 7.50 |
| 23 | Jack Parks | 8.00 | 4.00 |
| 24 | Hal Newhouser | 8.00 | 4.00 |
| 25 | Johnny Podres | 20.00 | 10.00 |
| 26 | Dick Groat | 15.00 | 7.50 |
| 27 | Billy Gardner | 8.00 | 4.00 |
| 28 | Ernie Banks | 225.00 | 112.00 |
| 29 | Herman Wehmeier | 8.00 | 4.00 |
| 30 | Vic Power | 8.00 | 4.00 |
| 31 | Warren Spahn | 80.00 | 40.00 |
| 32 | Ed McGhee | 8.00 | 4.00 |
| 33 | Tom Qualters | 8.00 | 4.00 |
| 34 | Wayne Terwilliger | 8.00 | 4.00 |
| 35 | Dave Jolly | 8.00 | 4.00 |
| 36 | Leo Kiely | 8.00 | 4.00 |
| 37 | *Joe Cunningham* | 10.00 | 5.00 |
| 38 | Bob Turley | 17.00 | 8.50 |
| 39 | Bill Glynn | 8.00 | 4.00 |
| 40 | Don Hoak | 10.00 | 5.00 |
| 41 | Chuck Stobbs | 8.00 | 4.00 |
| 42 | "Windy" McCall | 8.00 | 4.00 |
| 43 | Harvey Haddix | 8.00 | 4.00 |
| 44 | "Corky" Valentine | 8.00 | 4.00 |
| 45 | Hank Sauer | 8.00 | 4.00 |
| 46 | Ted Kazanski | 8.00 | 4.00 |
| 47 | Hank Aaron | 400.00 | 200.00 |
| 48 | Bob Kennedy | 8.00 | 4.00 |
| 49 | J.W. Porter | 8.00 | 4.00 |
| 50 | Jackie Robinson | 250.00 | 125.00 |
| 51 | Jim Hughes | 8.00 | 4.00 |
| 52 | Bill Tremel | 8.00 | 4.00 |
| 53 | Bill Taylor | 8.00 | 4.00 |
| 54 | Lou Limmer | 8.00 | 4.00 |
| 55 | "Rip" Repulski | 8.00 | 4.00 |
| 56 | Ray Jablonski | 8.00 | 4.00 |
| 57 | *Billy O'Dell* | 8.00 | 4.00 |
| 58 | Jim Rivera | 8.00 | 4.00 |
| 59 | Gair Allie | 8.00 | 4.00 |
| 60 | Dean Stone | 8.00 | 4.00 |
| 61 | "Spook" Jacobs | 8.00 | 4.00 |
| 62 | Thornton Kipper | 8.00 | 4.00 |
| 63 | Joe Collins | 9.00 | 4.50 |
| 64 | *Gus Triandos* | 10.00 | 5.00 |
| 65 | Ray Boone | 8.00 | 4.00 |
| 66 | Ron Jackson | 8.00 | 4.00 |
| 67 | Wally Moon | 8.00 | 4.00 |
| 68 | Jim Davis | 8.00 | 4.00 |
| 69 | Ed Bailey | 8.00 | 4.00 |
| 70 | Al Rosen | 17.00 | 8.50 |
| 71 | Ruben Gomez | 8.00 | 4.00 |
| 72 | Karl Olson | 8.00 | 4.00 |
| 73 | Jack Shepard | 8.00 | 4.00 |
| 74 | Bob Borkowski | 8.00 | 4.00 |
| 75 | Sandy Amoros | 8.00 | 4.00 |
| 76 | Howie Pollet | 8.00 | 4.00 |
| 77 | Arnold Portocarrero | | |
| | | 8.00 | 4.00 |

| | NR MT | EX | | | NR MT | EX |
|---|---|---|---|---|---|---|
| 78 | Gordon Jones | 8.00 | 4.00 | 144 | Joe Amalfitano | 8.00 | 4.00 |
| 79 | Danny Schell | 8.00 | 4.00 | 145 | Elmer Valo | 8.00 | 4.00 |
| 80 | Bob Grim | 9.00 | 4.50 | 146 | *Dick Donovan* | 8.00 | 4.00 |
| 81 | Gene Conley | 8.00 | 4.00 | 147 | Laurin Pepper | 8.00 | 4.00 |
| 82 | Chuck Harmon | 8.00 | 4.00 | 148 | Hal Brown | 8.00 | 4.00 |
| 83 | Tom Brewer | 8.00 | 4.00 | 149 | Ray Crone | 8.00 | 4.00 |
| 84 | *Camilo Pascual* | 8.00 | 4.00 | 150 | Mike Higgins | 8.00 | 4.00 |
| 85 | Don Mossi | 8.00 | 4.00 | 151 | "Red" Kress | 17.00 | 8.50 |
| 86 | Bill Wilson | 8.00 | 4.00 | 152 | *Harry Agganis* | 75.00 | 38.00 |
| 87 | Frank House | 8.00 | 4.00 | 153 | "Bud" Podbielan | 17.00 | 8.50 |
| 88 | *Bob Skinner* | 8.00 | 4.00 | 154 | Willie Miranda | 17.00 | 8.50 |
| 89 | Joe Frazier | 8.00 | 4.00 | 155 | Ed Mathews | 125.00 | 67.00 |
| 90 | Karl Spooner | 9.00 | 4.50 | 156 | Joe Black | 20.00 | 10.00 |
| 91 | Milt Bolling | 8.00 | 4.00 | 157 | Bob Miller | 17.00 | 8.50 |
| 92 | *Don Zimmer* | 40.00 | 20.00 | 158 | Tom Carroll | 20.00 | 10.00 |
| 93 | Steve Bilko | 8.00 | 4.00 | 159 | Johnny Schmitz | 17.00 | 8.50 |
| 94 | Reno Bertoia | 8.00 | 4.00 | 160 | Ray Narleski | 17.00 | 8.50 |
| 95 | Preston Ward | 8.00 | 4.00 | 161 | *Chuck Tanner* | 30.00 | 15.00 |
| 96 | Charlie Bishop | 8.00 | 4.00 | 162 | Joe Coleman | 25.00 | 12.50 |
| 97 | Carlos Paula | 8.00 | 4.00 | 163 | Faye Throneberry | 25.00 | 12.50 |
| 98 | Johnny Riddle | 8.00 | 4.00 | 164 | *Roberto Clemente* | | |
| 99 | Frank Leja | 9.00 | 4.50 | | | 1800.00 | 900.00 |
| 100 | Monte Irvin | 30.00 | 15.00 | 165 | Don Johnson | 25.00 | 12.50 |
| 101 | Johnny Gray | 8.00 | 4.00 | 166 | Hank Bauer | 40.00 | 20.00 |
| 102 | Wally Westlake | 8.00 | 4.00 | 167 | Tom Casagrande | 25.00 | 12.50 |
| 103 | Charlie White | 8.00 | 4.00 | 168 | Duane Pillette | 25.00 | 12.50 |
| 104 | Jack Harshman | 8.00 | 4.00 | 169 | Bob Oldis | 25.00 | 12.50 |
| 105 | Chuck Diering | 8.00 | 4.00 | 170 | Jim Pearce | 25.00 | 12.50 |
| 106 | *Frank Sullivan* | 8.00 | 4.00 | 171 | Dick Brodowski | 25.00 | 12.50 |
| 107 | Curt Roberts | 8.00 | 4.00 | 172 | Frank Baumholtz | 25.00 | 12.50 |
| 108 | "Rube" Walker | 8.00 | 4.00 | 173 | Bob Kline | 25.00 | 12.50 |
| 109 | Ed Lopat | 10.00 | 5.00 | 174 | Rudy Minarcin | 25.00 | 12.50 |
| 110 | Gus Zernial | 8.00 | 4.00 | 175 | Not Issued | | |
| 111 | Bob Milliken | 8.00 | 4.00 | 176 | Norm Zauchin | 25.00 | 12.50 |
| 112 | Nelson King | 8.00 | 4.00 | 177 | Jim Robertson | 25.00 | 12.50 |
| 113 | Harry Brecheen | 8.00 | 4.00 | 178 | Bobby Adams | 25.00 | 12.50 |
| 114 | Lou Ortiz | 8.00 | 4.00 | 179 | Jim Bolger | 25.00 | 12.50 |
| 115 | Ellis Kinder | 8.00 | 4.00 | 180 | Clem Labine | 25.00 | 12.50 |
| 116 | Tom Hurd | 8.00 | 4.00 | 181 | Roy McMillan | 25.00 | 12.50 |
| 117 | Mel Roach | 8.00 | 4.00 | 182 | Humberto Robinson | | |
| 118 | Bob Purkey | 8.00 | 4.00 | | | 25.00 | 12.50 |
| 119 | Bob Lennon | 8.00 | 4.00 | 183 | Tony Jacobs | 25.00 | 12.50 |
| 120 | Ted Kluszewski | 25.00 | 12.50 | 184 | Harry Perkowski | 25.00 | 12.50 |
| 121 | Bill Renna | 8.00 | 4.00 | 185 | Don Ferrarese | 25.00 | 12.50 |
| 122 | Carl Sawatski | 8.00 | 4.00 | 186 | Not Issued | | |
| 123 | *Sandy Koufax* | 1400.00 | 700.00 | 187 | Gil Hodges | 150.00 | 75.00 |
| 124 | *Harmon Killebrew* | | | 188 | Charlie Silvera | 25.00 | 12.50 |
| | | 400.00 | 200.00 | 189 | Phil Rizzuto | 150.00 | 75.00 |
| 125 | *Ken Boyer* | 75.00 | 38.00 | 190 | Gene Woodling | 25.00 | 12.50 |
| 126 | *Dick Hall* | 8.00 | 4.00 | 191 | Ed Stanky | 25.00 | 12.50 |
| 127 | *Dale Long* | 8.00 | 4.00 | 192 | Jim Delsing | 25.00 | 12.50 |
| 128 | Ted Lepcio | 8.00 | 4.00 | 193 | Johnny Sain | 40.00 | 20.00 |
| 129 | Elvin Tappe | 8.00 | 4.00 | 194 | Willie Mays | 550.00 | 275.00 |
| 130 | Mayo Smith | 8.00 | 4.00 | 195 | Ed Roebuck | 25.00 | 12.50 |
| 131 | Grady Hatton | 8.00 | 4.00 | 196 | Gale Wade | 25.00 | 12.50 |
| 132 | Bob Trice | 8.00 | 4.00 | 197 | Al Smith | 25.00 | 12.50 |
| 133 | Dave Hoskins | 8.00 | 4.00 | 198 | Yogi Berra | 250.00 | 125.00 |
| 134 | Joe Jay | 8.00 | 4.00 | 199 | Bert Hamric | 25.00 | 12.50 |
| 135 | Johnny O'Brien | 8.00 | 4.00 | 200 | Jack Jensen | 50.00 | 25.00 |
| 136 | "Bunky" Stewart | 8.00 | 4.00 | 201 | Sherm Lollar | 25.00 | 12.50 |
| 137 | Harry Elliott | 8.00 | 4.00 | 202 | Jim Owens | 25.00 | 12.50 |
| 138 | Ray Herbert | 8.00 | 4.00 | 203 | Not Issued | | |
| 139 | Steve Kraly | 9.00 | 4.50 | 204 | Frank Smith | 25.00 | 12.50 |
| 140 | Mel Parnell | 8.00 | 4.00 | 205 | Gene Freese | 25.00 | 12.50 |
| 141 | Tom Wright | 8.00 | 4.00 | 206 | Pete Daley | 25.00 | 12.50 |
| 142 | Jerry Lynch | 8.00 | 4.00 | 207 | Bill Consolo | 25.00 | 12.50 |
| 143 | Dick Schofield | 8.00 | 4.00 | 208 | Ray Moore | 25.00 | 12.50 |

| | | NR MT | EX |
|---|---|---|---|
| 209 | Not Issued | | |
| 210 | Duke Snider | 500.00 | 200.00 |

## 1956 Topps

This 340-card set is quite similar in design to the 1955 Topps set, again using both a portrait and an "action" picture. Some portraits are the same as those used in 1955 (and even 1954). Innovations found in the 1956 Topps set of 2-5/8" by 3-3/4" cards include team cards introduced as part of a regular set. Additionally, there are two unnumbered checklist cards (the complete set price quoted below does not include the checklist cards). Finally, there are cards of the two league presidents, William Harridge and Warren Giles. On the backs, a three-panel cartoon depicts big moments from the player's career while biographical information appears above the cartoon and the statistics below. Card backs for numbers 1-180 can be found with either white or grey cardboard. Some dealers charge a premium for grey backs (#'s 1-100) and white backs (#'s 101-180).

| | NR MT | EX |
|---|---|---|
| Complete Set: | 7500.00 | 3750.00 |
| Common Player: 1-100 | 7.00 | 3.50 |
| Common Player: 101-180 | | |
| | 9.00 | 4.50 |
| Common Player: 181-260 | | |
| | 15.00 | 7.50 |
| Common Player: 261-340 | | |
| | 9.00 | 4.50 |

| | | NR MT | EX |
|---|---|---|---|
| 1 | William Harridge | 110.00 | 25.00 |
| 2 | Warren Giles | 15.00 | 7.50 |

| | | NR MT | EX |
|---|---|---|---|
| 3 | Elmer Valo | 7.00 | 3.50 |
| 4 | Carlos Paula | 7.00 | 3.50 |
| 5 | Ted Williams | 350.00 | 175.00 |
| 6 | Ray Boone | 9.00 | 4.50 |
| 7 | Ron Negray | 7.00 | 3.50 |
| 8 | Walter Alston | 40.00 | 20.00 |
| 9 | Ruben Gomez | 7.00 | 3.50 |
| 10 | Warren Spahn | 80.00 | 40.00 |
| 11a | Cubs Team (with date) | | |
| | | 50.00 | 25.00 |
| 11b | Cubs Team (no date, name centered) | | |
| | | 15.00 | 7.50 |
| 11c | Cubs Team (no date, name at left) | | |
| | | 15.00 | 7.50 |
| 12 | Andy Carey | 10.00 | 5.00 |
| 13 | Roy Face | 10.00 | 5.00 |
| 14 | Ken Boyer | 15.00 | 7.50 |
| 15 | Ernie Banks | 125.00 | 62.00 |
| 16 | *Hector Lopez* | 10.00 | 5.00 |
| 17 | Gene Conley | 9.00 | 4.50 |
| 18 | Dick Donovan | 7.00 | 3.50 |
| 19 | Chuck Diering | 7.00 | 3.50 |
| 20 | Al Kaline | 100.00 | 50.00 |
| 21 | Joe Collins | 10.00 | 5.00 |
| 22 | Jim Finigan | 7.00 | 3.50 |
| 23 | Freddie Marsh | 7.00 | 3.50 |
| 24 | Dick Groat | 10.00 | 5.00 |
| 25 | Ted Kluszewski | 20.00 | 10.00 |
| 26 | Grady Hatton | 7.00 | 3.50 |
| 27 | Nelson Burbrink | 7.00 | 3.50 |
| 28 | Bobby Hofman | 7.00 | 3.50 |
| 29 | Jack Harshman | 7.00 | 3.50 |
| 30 | Jackie Robinson | 150.00 | 60.00 |
| 31 | Hank Aaron | 200.00 | 100.00 |
| 32 | Frank House | 7.00 | 3.50 |
| 33 | Roberto Clemente | | |
| | | 450.00 | 225.00 |
| 34 | Tom Brewer | 7.00 | 3.50 |
| 35 | Al Rosen | 15.00 | 7.50 |
| 36 | Rudy Minarcin | 7.00 | 3.50 |
| 37 | Alex Grammas | 7.00 | 3.50 |
| 38 | Bob Kennedy | 7.00 | 3.50 |
| 39 | Don Mossi | 9.00 | 4.50 |
| 40 | Bob Turley | 15.00 | 7.50 |
| 41 | Hank Sauer | 7.00 | 3.50 |
| 42 | Sandy Amoros | 9.00 | 4.50 |
| 43 | Ray Moore | 7.00 | 3.50 |
| 44 | "Windy" McCall | 7.00 | 3.50 |
| 45 | Gus Zernial | 9.00 | 4.50 |
| 46 | Gene Freese | 7.00 | 3.50 |
| 47 | Art Fowler | 7.00 | 3.50 |
| 48 | Jim Hegan | 7.00 | 3.50 |
| 49 | *Pedro Ramos* | 9.00 | 4.50 |
| 50 | "Dusty" Rhodes | 9.00 | 4.50 |
| 51 | Ernie Oravetz | 7.00 | 3.50 |
| 52 | Bob Grim | 10.00 | 5.00 |
| 53 | Arnold Portocarrero | | |
| | | 7.00 | 3.50 |
| 54 | Bob Keegan | 7.00 | 3.50 |
| 55 | Wally Moon | 9.00 | 4.50 |
| 56 | Dale Long | 9.00 | 4.50 |
| 57 | "Duke" Maas | 7.00 | 3.50 |
| 58 | Ed Roebuck | 9.00 | 4.50 |
| 59 | Jose Santiago | 7.00 | 3.50 |
| 60 | Mayo Smith | 7.00 | 3.50 |
| 61 | Bill Skowron | 15.00 | 7.50 |
| 62 | Hal Smith | 7.00 | 3.50 |

| | | NR MT | EX |
|---|---|---|---|
| 63 | *Roger Craig* | 30.00 | 15.00 |
| 64 | Luis Arroyo | 7.00 | 3.50 |
| 65 | Johnny O'Brien | 7.00 | 3.50 |
| 66 | Bob Speake | 7.00 | 3.50 |
| 67 | Vic Power | 7.00 | 3.50 |
| 68 | Chuck Stobbs | 7.00 | 3.50 |
| 69 | Chuck Tanner | 10.00 | 5.00 |
| 70 | Jim Rivera | 7.00 | 3.50 |
| 71 | Frank Sullivan | 7.00 | 3.50 |
| 72a | Phillies Team (with date) | | |
| | | 50.00 | 25.00 |
| 72b | Phillies Team (no date, name centered) | 15.00 | 7.50 |
| 72c | Philadelphia Phillies (no date, name at left) | 15.00 | 7.50 |
| 73 | Wayne Terwilliger | 7.00 | 3.50 |
| 74 | Jim King | 7.00 | 3.50 |
| 75 | Roy Sievers | 9.00 | 4.50 |
| 76 | Ray Crone | 7.00 | 3.50 |
| 77 | Harvey Haddix | 9.00 | 4.50 |
| 78 | Herman Wehmeier | 7.00 | 3.50 |
| 79 | Sandy Koufax | 400.00 | 200.00 |
| 80 | Gus Triandos | 9.00 | 4.50 |
| 81 | Wally Westlake | 7.00 | 3.50 |
| 82 | Bill Renna | 7.00 | 3.50 |
| 83 | Karl Spooner | 9.00 | 4.50 |
| 84 | "Babe" Birrer | 7.00 | 3.50 |
| 85a | Indians Team (with date) | | |
| | | 50.00 | 25.00 |
| 85b | Indians Team (no date, name centered) | 15.00 | 7.50 |
| 85c | Indians Team (no date, name at left) | 15.00 | 7.50 |
| 86 | Ray Jablonski | 7.00 | 3.50 |
| 87 | Dean Stone | 7.00 | 3.50 |
| 88 | Johnny Kucks | 10.00 | 5.00 |
| 89 | Norm Zauchin | 7.00 | 3.50 |
| 90a | Redlegs Team (with date) | 50.00 | 25.00 |
| 90b | Redlegs Team (no date, name centered) | 15.00 | 7.50 |
| 90c | Redlegs Team (no date, name at left) | 15.00 | 7.50 |
| 91 | Gail Harris | 7.00 | 3.50 |
| 92 | "Red" Wilson | 7.00 | 3.50 |
| 93 | George Susce, Jr. | 7.00 | 3.50 |
| 94 | Ronnie Kline | 7.00 | 3.50 |
| 95a | Braves Team (with date) | | |
| | | 50.00 | 25.00 |
| 95b | Braves Team (no date, name centered) | 15.00 | 7.50 |
| 95c | Braves Team (no date, name at left) | 15.00 | 7.50 |
| 96 | Bill Tremel | 7.00 | 3.50 |
| 97 | Jerry Lynch | 7.00 | 3.50 |
| 98 | Camilo Pascual | 9.00 | 4.50 |
| 99 | Don Zimmer | 15.00 | 7.50 |
| 100a | Orioles Team (with date) | | |
| | | 40.00 | 20.00 |
| 100b | Orioles Team (no date, name centered) | 15.00 | 7.50 |
| 100c | Orioles Team (no date, name at left) | 15.00 | 7.50 |
| 101 | Roy Campanella | 150.00 | 75.00 |
| 102 | Jim Davis | 9.00 | 4.50 |
| 103 | Willie Miranda | 9.00 | 4.50 |
| 104 | Bob Lennon | 9.00 | 4.50 |
| 105 | Al Smith | 9.00 | 4.50 |
| 106 | Joe Astroth | 9.00 | 4.50 |
| 107 | Ed Mathews | 60.00 | 30.00 |
| 108 | Laurin Pepper | 9.00 | 4.50 |
| 109 | Enos Slaughter | 30.00 | 15.00 |
| 110 | Yogi Berra | 125.00 | 56.00 |
| 111 | Red Sox Team | 9.00 | 4.50 |
| 112 | Dee Fondy | 9.00 | 4.50 |
| 113 | Phil Rizzuto | 50.00 | 25.00 |
| 114 | Jim Owens | 9.00 | 4.50 |
| 115 | Jackie Jensen | 15.00 | 7.50 |
| 116 | Eddie O'Brien | 9.00 | 4.50 |
| 117 | Virgil Trucks | 9.00 | 4.50 |
| 118 | "Nellie" Fox | 30.00 | 15.00 |
| 119 | *Larry Jackson* | 9.00 | 4.50 |
| 120 | Richie Ashburn | 35.00 | 17.50 |
| 121 | Pirates Team | 15.00 | 7.50 |
| 122 | Willard Nixon | 9.00 | 4.50 |
| 123 | Roy McMillan | 9.00 | 4.50 |
| 124 | Don Kaiser | 9.00 | 4.50 |
| 125 | "Minnie" Minoso | 20.00 | 10.00 |
| 126 | Jim Brady | 9.00 | 4.50 |
| 127 | Willie Jones | 9.00 | 4.50 |
| 128 | Eddie Yost | 9.00 | 4.50 |
| 129 | "Jake" Martin | 9.00 | 4.50 |
| 130 | Willie Mays | 350.00 | 175.00 |
| 131 | Bob Roselli | 9.00 | 4.50 |
| 132 | Bobby Avila | 9.00 | 4.50 |
| 133 | Ray Narleski | 9.00 | 4.50 |
| 134 | Cardinals Team | 15.00 | 7.50 |
| 135 | Mickey Mantle | 1000.00 | 500.00 |
| 136 | Johnny Logan | 9.00 | 4.50 |
| 137 | Al Silvera | 9.00 | 4.50 |
| 138 | Johnny Antonelli | 9.00 | 4.50 |
| 139 | Tommy Carroll | 9.00 | 4.50 |
| 140 | *Herb Score* | 35.00 | 17.50 |
| 141 | Joe Frazier | 9.00 | 4.50 |
| 142 | Gene Baker | 9.00 | 4.50 |
| 143 | Jim Piersall | 9.00 | 4.50 |
| 144 | Leroy Powell | 9.00 | 4.50 |
| 145 | Gil Hodges | 45.00 | 23.00 |
| 146 | Senators Team | 15.00 | 7.50 |
| 147 | Earl Torgeson | 9.00 | 4.50 |
| 148 | Alvin Dark | 9.00 | 4.50 |
| 149 | "Dixie" Howell | 9.00 | 4.50 |
| 150 | "Duke" Snider | 100.00 | 45.00 |
| 151 | "Spook" Jacobs | 9.00 | 4.50 |
| 152 | Billy Hoeft | 9.00 | 4.50 |
| 153 | Frank Thomas | 9.00 | 4.50 |
| 154 | Dave Pope | 9.00 | 4.50 |
| 155 | Harvey Kuenn | 15.00 | 7.50 |
| 156 | Wes Westrum | 9.00 | 4.50 |
| 157 | Dick Brodowski | 9.00 | 4.50 |
| 158 | Wally Post | 9.00 | 4.50 |
| 159 | Clint Courtney | 9.00 | 4.50 |
| 160 | Billy Pierce | 15.00 | 7.50 |
| 161 | Joe DeMaestri | 9.00 | 4.50 |
| 162 | "Gus" Bell | 9.00 | 4.50 |
| 163 | Gene Woodling | 9.00 | 4.50 |
| 164 | Harmon Killebrew | 110.00 | 55.00 |
| 165 | "Red" Schoendienst | 30.00 | 15.00 |
| 166 | Dodgers Team | 200.00 | 100.00 |
| 167 | Harry Dorish | 9.00 | 4.50 |
| 168 | Sammy White | 9.00 | 4.50 |
| 169 | Bob Nelson | 9.00 | 4.50 |

| | | NR MT | EX | | | NR MT | EX |
|---|---|---|---|---|---|---|---|
| 170 | Bill Virdon | 15.00 | 7.50 | 232 | "Toby" Atwell | 15.00 | 7.50 |
| 171 | Jim Wilson | 9.00 | 4.50 | 233 | Carl Erskine | 20.00 | 10.00 |
| 172 | *Frank Torre* | 9.00 | 4.50 | 234 | "Pete" Runnels | 15.00 | 7.50 |
| 173 | Johnny Podres | 15.00 | 7.50 | 235 | Don Newcombe | 50.00 | 25.00 |
| 174 | Glen Gorbous | 9.00 | 4.50 | 236 | Athletics Team | 15.00 | 7.50 |
| 175 | Del Crandall | 15.00 | 7.50 | 237 | Jose Valdivielso | 15.00 | 7.50 |
| 176 | Alex Kellner | 9.00 | 4.50 | 238 | Walt Dropo | 15.00 | 7.50 |
| 177 | Hank Bauer | 15.00 | 7.50 | 239 | Harry Simpson | 15.00 | 7.50 |
| 178 | Joe Black | 9.00 | 4.50 | 240 | "Whitey" Ford | 125.00 | 67.00 |
| 179 | Harry Chiti | 9.00 | 4.50 | 241 | Don Mueller | 15.00 | 7.50 |
| 180 | Robin Roberts | 25.00 | 12.50 | 242 | Hershell Freeman | 15.00 | 7.50 |
| 181 | Billy Martin | 110.00 | 55.00 | 243 | Sherm Lollar | 15.00 | 7.50 |
| 182 | Paul Minner | 15.00 | 7.50 | 244 | Bob Buhl | 15.00 | 7.50 |
| 183 | Stan Lopata | 15.00 | 7.50 | 245 | Billy Goodman | 15.00 | 7.50 |
| 184 | Don Bessent | 15.00 | 7.50 | 246 | Tom Gorman | 15.00 | 7.50 |
| 185 | Bill Bruton | 15.00 | 7.50 | 247 | Bill Sarni | 15.00 | 7.50 |
| 186 | Ron Jackson | 15.00 | 7.50 | 248 | Bob Porterfield | 15.00 | 7.50 |
| 187 | Early Wynn | 30.00 | 15.00 | 249 | Johnny Klippstein | 15.00 | 7.50 |
| 188 | White Sox Team | 15.00 | 7.50 | 250 | Larry Doby | 20.00 | 10.00 |
| 189 | Ned Garver | 15.00 | 7.50 | 251 | Yankees Team | 225.00 | 112.00 |
| 190 | Carl Furillo | 20.00 | 10.00 | 252 | Vernon Law | 15.00 | 7.50 |
| 191 | Frank Lary | 15.00 | 7.50 | 253 | Irv Noren | 15.00 | 7.50 |
| 192 | "Smoky" Burgess | 15.00 | 7.50 | 254 | George Crowe | 15.00 | 7.50 |
| 193 | Wilmer Mizell | 15.00 | 7.50 | 255 | Bob Lemon | 25.00 | 12.50 |
| 194 | Monte Irvin | 30.00 | 15.00 | 256 | Tom Hurd | 15.00 | 7.50 |
| 195 | George Kell | 30.00 | 15.00 | 257 | Bobby Thomson | 15.00 | 7.50 |
| 196 | Tom Poholsky | 15.00 | 7.50 | 258 | Art Ditmar | 15.00 | 7.50 |
| 197 | Granny Hamner | 15.00 | 7.50 | 259 | Sam Jones | 15.00 | 7.50 |
| 198 | Ed Fitzgerald (Fitz Gerald) | 15.00 | 7.50 | 260 | "Pee Wee" Reese | 125.00 | 62.00 |
| 199 | Hank Thompson | 15.00 | 7.50 | 261 | Bobby Shantz | 9.00 | 4.50 |
| 200 | Bob Feller | 110.00 | 55.00 | 262 | Howie Pollet | 9.00 | 4.50 |
| 201 | "Rip" Repulski | 15.00 | 7.50 | 263 | Bob Miller | 9.00 | 4.50 |
| 202 | Jim Hearn | 15.00 | 7.50 | 264 | Ray Monzant | 9.00 | 4.50 |
| 203 | Bill Tuttle | 15.00 | 7.50 | 265 | Sandy Consuegra | 9.00 | 4.50 |
| 204 | Art Swanson | 15.00 | 7.50 | 266 | Don Ferrarese | 9.00 | 4.50 |
| 205 | "Whitey" Lockman | 15.00 | 7.50 | 267 | Bob Nieman | 9.00 | 4.50 |
| 206 | Erv Palica | 15.00 | 7.50 | 268 | Dale Mitchell | 9.00 | 4.50 |
| 207 | Jim Small | 15.00 | 7.50 | 269 | Jack Meyer | 9.00 | 4.50 |
| 208 | Elston Howard | 30.00 | 15.00 | 270 | Billy Loes | 9.00 | 4.50 |
| 209 | Max Surkont | 15.00 | 7.50 | 271 | Foster Castleman | 9.00 | 4.50 |
| 210 | Mike Garcia | 15.00 | 7.50 | 272 | Danny O'Connell | 9.00 | 4.50 |
| 211 | Murry Dickson | 15.00 | 7.50 | 273 | Walker Cooper | 9.00 | 4.50 |
| 212 | Johnny Temple | 15.00 | 7.50 | 274 | Frank Baumholtz | 9.00 | 4.50 |
| 213 | Tigers Team | 50.00 | 25.00 | 275 | Jim Greengrass | 9.00 | 4.50 |
| 214 | Bob Rush | 15.00 | 7.50 | 276 | George Zuverink | 9.00 | 4.50 |
| 215 | Tommy Byrne | 15.00 | 7.50 | 277 | Daryl Spencer | 9.00 | 4.50 |
| 216 | Jerry Schoonmaker | 15.00 | 7.50 | 278 | Chet Nichols | 9.00 | 4.50 |
| 217 | Billy Klaus | 15.00 | 7.50 | 279 | Johnny Groth | 9.00 | 4.50 |
| 218 | Joe Nuxall (Nuxhall) | 15.00 | 7.50 | 280 | Jim Gilliam | 15.00 | 7.50 |
| 219 | Lew Burdette | 15.00 | 7.50 | 281 | Art Houtteman | 9.00 | 4.50 |
| 220 | Del Ennis | 15.00 | 7.50 | 282 | Warren Hacker | 9.00 | 4.50 |
| 221 | Bob Friend | 15.00 | 7.50 | 283 | Hal Smith | 9.00 | 4.50 |
| 222 | Dave Philley | 15.00 | 7.50 | 284 | Ike Delock | 9.00 | 4.50 |
| 223 | Randy Jackson | 15.00 | 7.50 | 285 | Eddie Miksis | 9.00 | 4.50 |
| 224 | "Bud" Podbielan | 15.00 | 7.50 | 286 | Bill Wight | 9.00 | 4.50 |
| 225 | Gil McDougald | 25.00 | 12.50 | 287 | Bobby Adams | 9.00 | 4.50 |
| 226 | Giants Team | 60.00 | 30.00 | 288 | Bob Cerv | 25.00 | 12.50 |
| 227 | Russ Meyer | 15.00 | 7.50 | 289 | Hal Jeffcoat | 9.00 | 4.50 |
| 228 | "Mickey" Vernon | 15.00 | 7.50 | 290 | Curt Simmons | 9.00 | 4.50 |
| 229 | Harry Brecheen | 15.00 | 7.50 | 291 | Frank Kellert | 9.00 | 4.50 |
| 230 | "Chico" Carrasquel | 15.00 | 7.50 | 292 | *Luis Aparicio* | 135.00 | 67.00 |
| 231 | Bob Hale | 15.00 | 7.50 | 293 | Stu Miller | 9.00 | 4.50 |
| | | | | 294 | Ernie Johnson | 9.00 | 4.50 |
| | | | | 295 | Clem Labine | 9.00 | 4.50 |
| | | | | 296 | Andy Seminick | 9.00 | 4.50 |
| | | | | 297 | Bob Skinner | 9.00 | 4.50 |

|  |  | NR MT | EX |
|---|---|---|---|
| 298 | Johnny Schmitz | 9.00 | 4.50 |
| 299 | Charley Neal | 25.00 | 12.50 |
| 300 | Vic Wertz | 9.00 | 4.50 |
| 301 | Marv Grissom | 9.00 | 4.50 |
| 302 | Eddie Robinson | 15.00 | 7.50 |
| 303 | Jim Dyck | 9.00 | 4.50 |
| 304 | Frank Malzone | 9.00 | 4.50 |
| 305 | Brooks Lawrence | 9.00 | 4.50 |
| 306 | Curt Roberts | 9.00 | 4.50 |
| 307 | Hoyt Wilhelm | 35.00 | 17.50 |
| 308 | "Chuck" Harmon | 9.00 | 4.50 |
| 309 | *Don Blasingame* | 9.00 | 4.50 |
| 310 | Steve Gromek | 9.00 | 4.50 |
| 311 | Hal Naragon | 9.00 | 4.50 |
| 312 | Andy Pafko | 9.00 | 4.50 |
| 313 | Gene Stephens | 9.00 | 4.50 |
| 314 | Hobie Landrith | 9.00 | 4.50 |
| 315 | Milt Bolling | 9.00 | 4.50 |
| 316 | Jerry Coleman | 9.00 | 4.50 |
| 317 | Al Aber | 9.00 | 4.50 |
| 318 | Fred Hatfield | 9.00 | 4.50 |
| 319 | Jack Crimian | 9.00 | 4.50 |
| 320 | Joe Adcock | 9.00 | 4.50 |
| 321 | Jim Konstanty | 15.00 | 7.50 |
| 322 | Karl Olson | 9.00 | 4.50 |
| 323 | Willard Schmidt | 9.00 | 4.50 |
| 324 | "Rocky" Bridges | 9.00 | 4.50 |
| 325 | Don Liddle | 9.00 | 4.50 |
| 326 | Connie Johnson | 9.00 | 4.50 |
| 327 | Bob Wiesler | 9.00 | 4.50 |
| 328 | Preston Ward | 9.00 | 4.50 |
| 329 | Lou Berberet | 9.00 | 4.50 |
| 330 | Jim Busby | 9.00 | 4.50 |
| 331 | Dick Hall | 9.00 | 4.50 |
| 332 | Don Larsen | 35.00 | 17.50 |
| 333 | Rube Walker | 9.00 | 4.50 |
| 334 | Bob Miller | 9.00 | 4.50 |
| 335 | Don Hoak | 9.00 | 4.50 |
| 336 | Ellis Kinder | 9.00 | 4.50 |
| 337 | Bobby Morgan | 9.00 | 4.50 |
| 338 | Jim Delsing | 9.00 | 4.50 |
| 339 | Rance Pless | 9.00 | 4.50 |
| 340 | Mickey McDermott | | |
| | | 30.00 | 15.00 |
| ----- | Checklist 1/3 | 200.00 | 75.00 |
| ----- | Checklist 2/4 | 200.00 | 75.00 |

## 1957 Topps

For 1957, Topps reduced the size of its cards to the now-standard 2-1/2" by 3-1/2." Set size was increased to 407 cards.

Another change came in the form of the use of real color photographs as opposed to the hand-colored black and whites of previous years. For the first time since 1954, there were cards with more than one player. The two, "Dodger Sluggers" and "Yankees' Power Hitters" began a trend toward the increased use of mulitple-player cards. Another first-time innovation, found on the backs, is complete players statistics. The scarce cards in the set are not the highest numbers, but rather numbers 265-352. Four unnumbered checklist cards were issued along with the set. They are quite expensive and are not included in the complete set prices quoted below.

|  | NR MT | EX |
|---|---|---|
| Complete Set: | 7500.00 | 3750.00 |
| Common Player: 1-264 | 7.00 | 3.50 |
| Common Player: 265-352 | | |
| | 18.00 | 9.00 |
| Common Player: 353-407 | | |
| | 7.00 | 3.50 |

| 1 | Ted Williams | 425.00 | 100.00 |
|---|---|---|---|
| 2 | Yogi Berra | 150.00 | 70.00 |
| 3 | Dale Long | 7.00 | 3.50 |
| 4 | Johnny Logan | 7.00 | 3.50 |
| 5 | Sal Maglie | 8.00 | 4.00 |
| 6 | Hector Lopez | 7.00 | 3.50 |
| 7 | Luis Aparicio | 30.00 | 15.00 |
| 8 | Don Mossi | 7.00 | 3.50 |
| 9 | Johnny Temple | 7.00 | 3.50 |
| 10 | Willie Mays | 250.00 | 125.00 |
| 11 | George Zuverink | 7.00 | 3.50 |
| 12 | Dick Groat | 6.00 | 3.00 |
| 13 | Wally Burnette | 7.00 | 3.50 |
| 14 | Bob Nieman | 7.00 | 3.50 |
| 15 | Robin Roberts | 20.00 | 10.00 |
| 16 | Walt Moryn | 7.00 | 3.50 |
| 17 | Billy Gardner | 7.00 | 3.50 |
| 18 | *Don Drysdale* | 200.00 | 100.00 |
| 19 | Bob Wilson | 7.00 | 3.50 |
| 20 | Hank Aaron (photo reversed) | 225.00 | 112.00 |
| 21 | Frank Sullivan | 7.00 | 3.50 |
| 22 | Jerry Snyder (photo actually Ed Fitz Gerald) | | |
| | | 7.00 | 3.50 |
| 23 | Sherm Lollar | 7.00 | 3.50 |
| 24 | *Bill Mazeroski* | 60.00 | 30.00 |
| 25 | Whitey Ford | 50.00 | 25.00 |
| 26 | Bob Boyd | 7.00 | 3.50 |
| 27 | Ted Kazanski | 7.00 | 3.50 |
| 28 | Gene Conley | 7.00 | 3.50 |
| 29 | *Whitey Herzog* | 30.00 | 15.00 |
| 30 | Pee Wee Reese | 60.00 | 30.00 |
| 31 | Ron Northey | 7.00 | 3.50 |

| | | NR MT | EX | | | NR MT | EX |
|---|---|---|---|---|---|---|---|
| 32 | Hersh Freeman | 7.00 | 3.50 | 99 | Bob Keegan | 7.00 | 3.50 |
| 33 | Jim Small | 7.00 | 3.50 | 100 | League Presidents | | |
| 34 | Tom Sturdivant | 6.00 | 3.00 | | (Warren Giles, William | | |
| 35 | *Frank Robinson* | 300.00 | 150.00 | | Harridge) | 6.00 | 3.00 |
| 36 | Bob Grim | 6.00 | 3.00 | 101 | Chuck Stobbs | 7.00 | 3.50 |
| 37 | Frank Torre | 7.00 | 3.50 | 102 | Ray Boone | 7.00 | 3.50 |
| 38 | Nellie Fox | 20.00 | 10.00 | 103 | Joe Nuxhall | 6.00 | 3.00 |
| 39 | Al Worthington | 7.00 | 3.50 | 104 | Hank Foiles | 7.00 | 3.50 |
| 40 | Early Wynn | 20.00 | 10.00 | 105 | Johnny Antonelli | 7.00 | 3.50 |
| 41 | Hal Smith | 7.00 | 3.50 | 106 | Ray Moore | 7.00 | 3.50 |
| 42 | Dee Fondy | 7.00 | 3.50 | 107 | Jim Rivera | 7.00 | 3.50 |
| 43 | Connie Johnson | 7.00 | 3.50 | 108 | Tommy Byrne | 6.00 | 3.00 |
| 44 | Joe DeMaestri | 7.00 | 3.50 | 109 | Hank Thompson | 7.00 | 3.50 |
| 45 | Carl Furillo | 9.00 | 4.50 | 110 | Bill Virdon | 6.00 | 3.00 |
| 46 | Bob Miller | 7.00 | 3.50 | 111 | Hal Smith | 7.00 | 3.50 |
| 47 | Don Blasingame | 7.00 | 3.50 | 112 | Tom Brewer | 7.00 | 3.50 |
| 48 | Bill Bruton | 7.00 | 3.50 | 113 | Wilmer Mizell | 7.00 | 3.50 |
| 49 | Daryl Spencer | 7.00 | 3.50 | 114 | Braves Team | 10.00 | 5.00 |
| 50 | Herb Score | 6.00 | 3.00 | 115 | Jim Gilliam | 10.00 | 5.00 |
| 51 | Clint Courtney | 7.00 | 3.50 | 116 | Mike Fornieles | 7.00 | 3.50 |
| 52 | Lee Walls | 7.00 | 3.50 | 117 | Joe Adcock | 6.00 | 3.00 |
| 53 | Clem Labine | 6.00 | 3.00 | 118 | Bob Porterfield | 7.00 | 3.50 |
| 54 | Elmer Valo | 7.00 | 3.50 | 119 | Stan Lopata | 7.00 | 3.50 |
| 55 | Ernie Banks | 110.00 | 55.00 | 120 | Bob Lemon | 15.00 | 7.50 |
| 56 | Dave Sisler | 7.00 | 3.50 | 121 | *Cletis Boyer* | 15.00 | 7.50 |
| 57 | Jim Lemon | 7.00 | 3.50 | 122 | Ken Boyer | 8.00 | 4.00 |
| 58 | Ruben Gomez | 7.00 | 3.50 | 123 | Steve Ridzik | 7.00 | 3.50 |
| 59 | Dick Williams | 6.00 | 3.00 | 124 | Dave Philley | 7.00 | 3.50 |
| 60 | Billy Hoeft | 7.00 | 3.50 | 125 | Al Kaline | 80.00 | 40.00 |
| 61 | Dusty Rhodes | 7.00 | 3.50 | 126 | Bob Wiesler | 7.00 | 3.50 |
| 62 | Billy Martin | 50.00 | 25.00 | 127 | Bob Buhl | 7.00 | 3.50 |
| 63 | Ike Delock | 7.00 | 3.50 | 128 | Ed Bailey | 7.00 | 3.50 |
| 64 | Pete Runnels | 6.00 | 3.00 | 129 | Saul Rogovin | 7.00 | 3.50 |
| 65 | Wally Moon | 7.00 | 3.50 | 130 | Don Newcombe | 10.00 | 5.00 |
| 66 | Brooks Lawrence | 7.00 | 3.50 | 131 | Milt Bolling | 7.00 | 3.50 |
| 67 | Chico Carrasquel | 7.00 | 3.50 | 132 | Art Ditmar | 6.00 | 3.00 |
| 68 | Ray Crone | 7.00 | 3.50 | 133 | Del Crandall | 6.00 | 3.00 |
| 69 | Roy McMillan | 7.00 | 3.50 | 134 | Don Kaiser | 7.00 | 3.50 |
| 70 | Richie Ashburn | 25.00 | 12.50 | 135 | Bill Skowron | 12.00 | 6.00 |
| 71 | Murry Dickson | 7.00 | 3.50 | 136 | Jim Hegan | 7.00 | 3.50 |
| 72 | Bill Tuttle | 7.00 | 3.50 | 137 | Bob Rush | 7.00 | 3.50 |
| 73 | George Crowe | 7.00 | 3.50 | 138 | Minnie Minoso | 8.00 | 4.00 |
| 74 | Vito Valentinetti | 7.00 | 3.50 | 139 | Lou Kretlow | 7.00 | 3.50 |
| 75 | Jim Piersall | 6.00 | 3.00 | 140 | Frank Thomas | 7.00 | 3.50 |
| 76 | Bob Clemente | 250.00 | 125.00 | 141 | Al Aber | 7.00 | 3.50 |
| 77 | Paul Foytack | 7.00 | 3.50 | 142 | Charley Thompson | 7.00 | 3.50 |
| 78 | Vic Wertz | 6.00 | 3.00 | 143 | Andy Pafko | 6.00 | 3.00 |
| 79 | *Lindy McDaniel* | 6.00 | 3.00 | 144 | Ray Narleski | 7.00 | 3.50 |
| 80 | Gil Hodges | 50.00 | 30.00 | 145 | Al Smith | 7.00 | 3.50 |
| 81 | Herm Wehmeier | 7.00 | 3.50 | 146 | Don Ferrarese | 6.00 | 3.00 |
| 82 | Elston Howard | 15.00 | 7.50 | 147 | Al Walker | 6.00 | 3.00 |
| 83 | Lou Skizas | 7.00 | 3.50 | 148 | Don Mueller | 7.00 | 3.50 |
| 84 | Moe Drabowsky | 7.00 | 3.50 | 149 | Bob Kennedy | 7.00 | 3.50 |
| 85 | Larry Doby | 10.00 | 5.00 | 150 | Bob Friend | 6.00 | 3.00 |
| 86 | Bill Sarni | 7.00 | 3.50 | 151 | Willie Miranda | 7.00 | 3.50 |
| 87 | Tom Gorman | 7.00 | 3.50 | 152 | Jack Harshman | 7.00 | 3.50 |
| 88 | Harvey Kuenn | 6.00 | 3.00 | 153 | Karl Olson | 7.00 | 3.50 |
| 89 | Roy Sievers | 7.00 | 3.50 | 154 | Red Schoendienst | | |
| 90 | Warren Spahn | 75.00 | 38.00 | | | 20.00 | 10.00 |
| 91 | Mack Burk | 7.00 | 3.50 | 155 | Jim Brosnan | 7.00 | 3.50 |
| 92 | Mickey Vernon | 6.00 | 3.00 | 156 | Gus Triandos | 7.00 | 3.50 |
| 93 | Hal Jeffcoat | 7.00 | 3.50 | 157 | Wally Post | 7.00 | 3.50 |
| 94 | Bobby Del Greco | 7.00 | 3.50 | 158 | Curt Simmons | 6.00 | 3.00 |
| 95 | Mickey Mantle | 1000.00 | 500.00 | 159 | Solly Drake | 7.00 | 3.50 |
| 96 | *Hank Aguirre* | 6.00 | 3.00 | 160 | Billy Pierce | 7.00 | 3.50 |
| 97 | Yankees Team | 40.00 | 20.00 | 161 | Pirates Team | 8.00 | 4.00 |
| 98 | Al Dark | 8.00 | 4.00 | 162 | Jack Meyer | 7.00 | 3.50 |

| | | NR MT | EX | | | NR MT | EX |
|---|---|---|---|---|---|---|---|
| 163 | Sammy White | 7.00 | 3.50 | 230 | George Kell | 18.00 | 9.00 |
| 164 | Tommy Carroll | 6.00 | 3.00 | 231 | Solly Hemus | 7.00 | 3.50 |
| 165 | Ted Kluszewski | 25.00 | 12.50 | 232 | Whitey Lockman | 7.00 | 3.50 |
| 166 | Roy Face | 6.00 | 3.00 | 233 | Art Fowler | 7.00 | 3.50 |
| 167 | Vic Power | 7.00 | 3.50 | 234 | Dick Cole | 7.00 | 3.50 |
| 168 | Frank Lary | 6.00 | 3.00 | 235 | Tom Poholsky | 7.00 | 3.50 |
| 169 | Herb Plews | 7.00 | 3.50 | 236 | Joe Ginsberg | 7.00 | 3.50 |
| 170 | Duke Snider | 100.00 | 50.00 | 237 | Foster Castleman | 7.00 | 3.50 |
| 171 | Red Sox Team | 9.00 | 4.50 | 238 | Eddie Robinson | 7.00 | 3.50 |
| 172 | Gene Woodling | 6.00 | 3.00 | 239 | Tom Morgan | 7.00 | 3.50 |
| 173 | Roger Craig | 8.00 | 4.00 | 240 | Hank Bauer | 10.00 | 5.00 |
| 174 | Willie Jones | 7.00 | 3.50 | 241 | Joe Lonnett | 7.00 | 3.50 |
| 175 | Don Larsen | 8.00 | 4.00 | 242 | Charley Neal | 7.00 | 3.50 |
| 176 | Gene Baker | 7.00 | 3.50 | 243 | Cardinals Team | 8.00 | 4.00 |
| 177 | Eddie Yost | 7.00 | 3.50 | 244 | Billy Loes | 7.00 | 3.50 |
| 178 | Don Bessent | 7.00 | 3.50 | 245 | Rip Repulski | 7.00 | 3.50 |
| 179 | Ernie Oravetz | 7.00 | 3.50 | 246 | Jose Valdivielso | 7.00 | 3.50 |
| 180 | Gus Bell | 7.00 | 3.50 | 247 | Turk Lown | 7.00 | 3.50 |
| 181 | Dick Donovan | 7.00 | 3.50 | 248 | Jim Finigan | 7.00 | 3.50 |
| 182 | Hobie Landrith | 7.00 | 3.50 | 249 | Dave Pope | 7.00 | 3.50 |
| 183 | Cubs Team | 8.00 | 4.00 | 250 | Ed Mathews | 35.00 | 17.50 |
| 184 | *Tito Francona* | 6.00 | 3.00 | 251 | Orioles Team | 8.00 | 4.00 |
| 185 | Johnny Kucks | 6.00 | 3.00 | 252 | Carl Erskine | 10.00 | 5.00 |
| 186 | Jim King | 7.00 | 3.50 | 253 | Gus Zernial | 7.00 | 3.50 |
| 187 | Virgil Trucks | 7.00 | 3.50 | 254 | Ron Negray | 7.00 | 3.50 |
| 188 | Felix Mantilla | 7.00 | 3.50 | 255 | Charlie Silvera | 7.00 | 3.50 |
| 189 | Willard Nixon | 7.00 | 3.50 | 256 | Ronnie Kline | 7.00 | 3.50 |
| 190 | Randy Jackson | 7.00 | 3.50 | 257 | Walt Dropo | 7.00 | 3.50 |
| 191 | Joe Margoneri | 7.00 | 3.50 | 258 | Steve Gromek | 7.00 | 3.50 |
| 192 | Jerry Coleman | 6.00 | 3.00 | 259 | Eddie O'Brien | 7.00 | 3.50 |
| 193 | Del Rice | 7.00 | 3.50 | 260 | Del Ennis | 7.00 | 3.50 |
| 194 | Hal Brown | 7.00 | 3.50 | 261 | Bob Chakales | 7.00 | 3.50 |
| 195 | Bobby Avila | 7.00 | 3.50 | 262 | Bobby Thomson | 6.00 | 3.00 |
| 196 | Larry Jackson | 7.00 | 3.50 | 263 | George Strickland | 7.00 | 3.50 |
| 197 | Hank Sauer | 7.00 | 3.50 | 264 | Bob Turley | 8.00 | 4.00 |
| 198 | Tigers Team | 9.00 | 4.50 | 265 | Harvey Haddix | 20.00 | 10.00 |
| 199 | Vernon Law | 6.00 | 3.00 | 266 | Ken Kuhn | 18.00 | 9.00 |
| 200 | Gil McDougald | 12.00 | 6.00 | 267 | Danny Kravitz | 18.00 | 9.00 |
| 201 | Sandy Amoros | 7.00 | 3.50 | 268 | Jackie Collum | 18.00 | 9.00 |
| 202 | Dick Gernert | 7.00 | 3.50 | 269 | Bob Cerv | 18.00 | 9.00 |
| 203 | Hoyt Wilhelm | 18.00 | 9.00 | 270 | Senators Team | 25.00 | 12.50 |
| 204 | Athletics Team | 8.00 | 4.00 | 271 | Danny O'Connell | 18.00 | 9.00 |
| 205 | Charley Maxwell | 7.00 | 3.50 | 272 | Bobby Shantz | 25.00 | 12.50 |
| 206 | Willard Schmidt | 7.00 | 3.50 | 273 | Jim Davis | 18.00 | 9.00 |
| 207 | Billy Hunter | 7.00 | 3.50 | 274 | Don Hoak | 18.00 | 9.00 |
| 208 | Lew Burdette | 6.00 | 3.00 | 275 | Indians Team | 35.00 | 17.50 |
| 209 | Bob Skinner | 7.00 | 3.50 | 276 | Jim Pyburn | 18.00 | 9.00 |
| 210 | Roy Campanella | 100.00 | 50.00 | 277 | Johnny Podres | 50.00 | 25.00 |
| 211 | Camilo Pascual | 7.00 | 3.50 | 278 | Fred Hatfield | 18.00 | 9.00 |
| 212 | *Rocco Colavito* | 135.00 | 67.00 | 279 | Bob Thurman | 18.00 | 9.00 |
| 213 | Les Moss | 7.00 | 3.50 | 280 | Alex Kellner | 18.00 | 9.00 |
| 214 | Phillies Team | 8.00 | 4.00 | 281 | Gail Harris | 18.00 | 9.00 |
| 215 | Enos Slaughter | 20.00 | 10.00 | 282 | Jack Dittmer | 18.00 | 9.00 |
| 216 | Marv Grissom | 7.00 | 3.50 | 283 | *Wes Covington* | 18.00 | 9.00 |
| 217 | Gene Stephens | 7.00 | 3.50 | 284 | Don Zimmer | 20.00 | 10.00 |
| 218 | Ray Jablonski | 7.00 | 3.50 | 285 | Ned Garver | 18.00 | 9.00 |
| 219 | Tom Acker | 7.00 | 3.50 | 286 | *Bobby Richardson* | | |
| 220 | Jackie Jensen | 6.00 | 3.00 | | | 125.00 | 67.00 |
| 221 | Dixie Howell | 7.00 | 3.50 | 287 | Sam Jones | 18.00 | 9.00 |
| 222 | Alex Grammas | 7.00 | 3.50 | 288 | Ted Lepcio | 18.00 | 9.00 |
| 223 | Frank House | 7.00 | 3.50 | 289 | Jim Bolger | 18.00 | 9.00 |
| 224 | Marv Blaylock | 7.00 | 3.50 | 290 | Andy Carey | 18.00 | 9.00 |
| 225 | Harry Simpson | 7.00 | 3.50 | 291 | Windy McCall | 18.00 | 9.00 |
| 226 | Preston Ward | 7.00 | 3.50 | 292 | Billy Klaus | 18.00 | 9.00 |
| 227 | Jerry Staley | 7.00 | 3.50 | 293 | Ted Abernathy | 18.00 | 9.00 |
| 228 | Smoky Burgess | 6.00 | 3.00 | 294 | Rocky Bridges | 18.00 | 9.00 |
| 229 | George Susce | 7.00 | 3.50 | 295 | Joe Collins | 18.00 | 9.00 |

| | | NR MT | EX |
|---|---|---|---|
| 296 | Johnny Klippstein | 18.00 | 9.00 |
| 297 | Jack Crimian | 18.00 | 9.00 |
| 298 | Irv Noren | 18.00 | 9.00 |
| 299 | Chuck Harmon | 18.00 | 9.00 |
| 300 | Mike Garcia | 18.00 | 9.00 |
| 301 | Sam Esposito | 18.00 | 9.00 |
| 302 | Sandy Koufax | 400.00 | 200.00 |
| 303 | Billy Goodman | 18.00 | 9.00 |
| 304 | Joe Cunningham | 18.00 | 9.00 |
| 305 | Chico Fernandez | 18.00 | 9.00 |
| 306 | Darrell Johnson | 18.00 | 9.00 |
| 307 | Jack Phillips | 18.00 | 9.00 |
| 308 | Dick Hall | 18.00 | 9.00 |
| 309 | Jim Busby | 18.00 | 9.00 |
| 310 | Max Surkont | 18.00 | 9.00 |
| 311 | Al Pilarcik | 18.00 | 9.00 |
| 312 | *Tony Kubek* | 135.00 | 67.00 |
| 313 | Mel Parnell | 18.00 | 9.00 |
| 314 | Ed Bouchee | 18.00 | 9.00 |
| 315 | Lou Berberet | 18.00 | 9.00 |
| 316 | Billy O'Dell | 18.00 | 9.00 |
| 317 | Giants Team | 50.00 | 25.00 |
| 318 | Mickey McDermott | | |
| | | 18.00 | 9.00 |
| 319 | Gino Cimoli | 18.00 | 9.00 |
| 320 | Neil Chrisley | 18.00 | 9.00 |
| 321 | Red Murff | 18.00 | 9.00 |
| 322 | Redlegs Team | 50.00 | 25.00 |
| 323 | Wes Westrum | 18.00 | 9.00 |
| 324 | Dodgers Team | 90.00 | 45.00 |
| 325 | Frank Bolling | 18.00 | 9.00 |
| 326 | Pedro Ramos | 18.00 | 9.00 |
| 327 | Jim Pendleton | 18.00 | 9.00 |
| 328 | *Brooks Robinson* | | |
| | | 400.00 | 200.00 |
| 329 | White Sox Team | 35.00 | 17.50 |
| 330 | Jim Wilson | 18.00 | 9.00 |
| 331 | Ray Katt | 18.00 | 9.00 |
| 332 | Bob Bowman | 18.00 | 9.00 |
| 333 | Ernie Johnson | 18.00 | 9.00 |
| 334 | Jerry Schoonmaker | | |
| | | 18.00 | 9.00 |
| 335 | Granny Hamner | 18.00 | 9.00 |
| 336 | Haywood Sullivan | 18.00 | 9.00 |
| 337 | Rene Valdes | 18.00 | 9.00 |
| 338 | *Jim Bunning* | 125.00 | 62.00 |
| 339 | Bob Speake | 18.00 | 9.00 |
| 340 | Bill Wight | 18.00 | 9.00 |
| 341 | Don Gross | 18.00 | 9.00 |
| 342 | Gene Mauch | 18.00 | 9.00 |
| 343 | Taylor Phillips | 18.00 | 9.00 |
| 344 | Paul LaPalme | 18.00 | 9.00 |
| 345 | Paul Smith | 18.00 | 9.00 |
| 346 | Dick Littlefield | 18.00 | 9.00 |
| 347 | Hal Naragon | 18.00 | 9.00 |
| 348 | Jim Hearn | 18.00 | 9.00 |
| 349 | Nelson King | 18.00 | 9.00 |
| 350 | Eddie Miksis | 18.00 | 9.00 |
| 351 | Dave Hillman | 18.00 | 9.00 |
| 352 | Ellis Kinder | 18.00 | 9.00 |
| 353 | Cal Neeman | 7.00 | 3.50 |
| 354 | Rip Coleman | 7.00 | 3.50 |
| 355 | Frank Malzone | 7.00 | 3.50 |
| 356 | Faye Throneberry | 7.00 | 3.50 |
| 357 | Earl Torgeson | 7.00 | 3.50 |
| 358 | Jerry Lynch | 7.00 | 3.50 |
| 359 | Tom Cheney | 7.00 | 3.50 |

| | | NR MT | EX |
|---|---|---|---|
| 360 | Johnny Groth | 7.00 | 3.50 |
| 361 | Curt Barclay | 7.00 | 3.50 |
| 362 | Roman Mejias | 7.00 | 3.50 |
| 363 | Eddie Kasko | 7.00 | 3.50 |
| 364 | Cal McLish | 7.00 | 3.50 |
| 365 | Ossie Virgil | 7.00 | 3.50 |
| 366 | Ken Lehman | 7.00 | 3.50 |
| 367 | Ed Fitz Gerald | 7.00 | 3.50 |
| 368 | Bob Purkey | 7.00 | 3.50 |
| 369 | Milt Graff | 7.00 | 3.50 |
| 370 | Warren Hacker | 7.00 | 3.50 |
| 371 | Bob Lennon | 7.00 | 3.50 |
| 372 | Norm Zauchin | 7.00 | 3.50 |
| 373 | Pete Whisenant | 7.00 | 3.50 |
| 374 | Don Cardwell | 7.00 | 3.50 |
| 375 | *Jim Landis* | 6.00 | 3.00 |
| 376 | Don Elston | 7.00 | 3.50 |
| 377 | Andre Rodgers | 7.00 | 3.50 |
| 378 | Elmer Singleton | 7.00 | 3.50 |
| 379 | Don Lee | 7.00 | 3.50 |
| 380 | Walker Cooper | 7.00 | 3.50 |
| 381 | Dean Stone | 7.00 | 3.50 |
| 382 | Jim Brideweser | 7.00 | 3.50 |
| 383 | *Juan Pizarro* | 6.00 | 3.00 |
| 384 | Bobby Gene Smith | 7.00 | 3.50 |
| 385 | Art Houtteman | 7.00 | 3.50 |
| 386 | Lyle Luttrell | 7.00 | 3.50 |
| 387 | *Jack Sanford* | 6.00 | 3.00 |
| 388 | Pete Daley | 7.00 | 3.50 |
| 389 | Dave Jolly | 7.00 | 3.50 |
| 390 | Reno Bertoia | 7.00 | 3.50 |
| 391 | *Ralph Terry* | 10.00 | 5.00 |
| 392 | Chuck Tanner | 6.00 | 3.00 |
| 393 | Raul Sanchez | 7.00 | 3.50 |
| 394 | Luis Arroyo | 7.00 | 3.50 |
| 395 | Bubba Phillips | 7.00 | 3.50 |
| 396 | Casey Wise | 7.00 | 3.50 |
| 397 | Roy Smalley | 7.00 | 3.50 |
| 398 | Al Cicotte | 6.00 | 3.00 |
| 399 | Billy Consolo | 7.00 | 3.50 |
| 400 | Dodgers' Sluggers (Roy Campanella, Carl Furillo, Gil Hodges, Duke Snider) | | |
| | | 200.00 | 100.00 |
| 401 | *Earl Battey* | 6.00 | 3.00 |
| 402 | Jim Pisoni | 7.00 | 3.50 |
| 403 | Dick Hyde | 7.00 | 3.50 |
| 404 | Harry Anderson | 7.00 | 3.50 |
| 405 | Duke Maas | 7.00 | 3.50 |
| 406 | Bob Hale | 7.00 | 3.50 |
| 407 | Yankees' Power Hitters (Yogi Berra, Mickey Mantle) | | |
| | | 400.00 | 200.00 |
| ---a | Checklist Series 1-2 (Big Blony ad on back) | 175.00 | 87.00 |
| ---b | Checklist Series 1-2 (Bazooka ad on back) | | |
| | | 175.00 | 87.00 |
| ---a | Checklist Series 2-3 (Big Blony ad on back) | 300.00 | 150.00 |
| ---b | Checklist Series 2-3 (Bazooka ad on back) | | |
| | | 300.00 | 150.00 |
| ---a | Checklist Series 3-4 (Big Blony ad on back) | 500.00 | 250.00 |
| ---b | Checklist Series 3-4 (Bazooka ad on back) | | |

| | NR MT | EX |
|---|---|---|
| | 500.00 | 250.00 |
| ---a Checklist Series 4-5 (Big Blony ad on back) | 750.00 | 325.00 |
| ---b Checklist Series 4-5 (Bazooka ad on back) | 750.00 | 325.00 |
| ------ Contest Card (Saturday, May 4th) | 15.00 | 7.50 |
| ------ Contest Card (Saturday, May 25th) | 15.00 | 7.50 |
| ------ Contest Card (Saturday, June 22nd) | 15.00 | 7.50 |
| ------ Contest Card (Friday, July 19) | 15.00 | 7.50 |
| ------ Lucky Penny Insert Card | 15.00 | 7.50 |

## 1958 Topps

Topps continued to expand its set size in 1958 with the release of a 494-card set. One card (#145) was not issued after Ed Bouchee was suspended from baseball. Cards retained the 2-1/2" by 3-1/2" size. There are a number of variations, including yellow or white lettering on 33 cards between numbers 2-108 (higher priced yellow letter variations checklisted below are not included in the complete set prices). The number of multiple-player cards was increased. A major innovation is the addition of 20 "All-Star" cards. For the first time, checklists were incorporated into the numbered series, as the backs of team cards.

| | NR MT | EX |
|---|---|---|
| Complete Set: | 5000.00 | 2500.00 |
| Common Player: 1-110 | 7.00 | 3.50 |
| Common Player: 111-440 | 5.00 | 2.50 |
| Common Player: 441-495 | 4.00 | 2.00 |
| 1 Ted Williams | 400.00 | 125.00 |
| 2a Bob Lemon (yellow team letters) | 35.00 | 17.50 |
| 2b Bob Lemon (white team letters) | 12.00 | 6.00 |
| 3 Alex Kellner | 7.00 | 3.50 |
| 4 Hank Foiles | 7.00 | 3.50 |
| 5 Willie Mays | 160.00 | 80.00 |
| 6 George Zuverink | 7.00 | 3.50 |
| 7 Dale Long | 7.00 | 3.50 |
| 8a Eddie Kasko (yellow name letters) | 20.00 | 10.00 |
| 8b Eddie Kasko (white name letters) | 7.00 | 3.50 |
| 9 Hank Bauer | 12.00 | 6.00 |
| 10 Lou Burdette | 8.00 | 4.00 |
| 11a Jim Rivera (yellow team letters) | 20.00 | 10.00 |
| 11b Jim Rivera (white team letters) | 7.00 | 3.50 |
| 12 George Crowe | 7.00 | 3.50 |
| 13a Billy Hoeft (yellow name letters) | 20.00 | 10.00 |
| 13b Billy Hoeft (white name, orange triangle by foot) | 7.00 | 3.50 |
| 13c Billy Hoeft (white name, red triangle by foot) | 7.00 | 3.50 |
| 14 Rip Repulski | 7.00 | 3.50 |
| 15 Jim Lemon | 7.00 | 3.50 |
| 16 Charley Neal | 7.00 | 3.50 |
| 17 Felix Mantilla | 7.00 | 3.50 |
| 18 Frank Sullivan | 7.00 | 3.50 |
| 19 Giants Team/Checklist 1-88 | 10.00 | 5.00 |
| 20a Gil McDougald (yellow name letters) | 25.00 | 12.50 |
| 20b Gil McDougald (white name letters) | 9.00 | 4.50 |
| 21 Curt Barclay | 7.00 | 3.50 |
| 22 Hal Naragon | 7.00 | 3.50 |
| 23a Bill Tuttle (yellow name letters) | 20.00 | 10.00 |
| 23b Bill Tuttle (white name letters) | 7.00 | 3.50 |
| 24a Hobie Landrith (yellow name letters) | 20.00 | 10.00 |
| 24b Hobie Landrith (white name letters) | 7.00 | 3.50 |
| 25 Don Drysdale | 60.00 | 30.00 |
| 26 Ron Jackson | 7.00 | 3.50 |
| 27 Bud Freeman | 7.00 | 3.50 |
| 28 Jim Busby | 7.00 | 3.50 |
| 29 Ted Lepcio | 7.00 | 3.50 |
| 30a Hank Aaron (yellow name letters) | 350.00 | 140.00 |
| 30b Hank Aaron (white name letters) | 175.00 | 87.00 |
| 31 Tex Clevenger | 7.00 | 3.50 |
| 32a J.W. Porter (yellow name letters) | 20.00 | 10.00 |
| 32b J.W. Porter (white name letters) | 7.00 | 3.50 |
| 33a Cal Neeman (yellow team letters) | 20.00 | 10.00 |
| 33b Cal Neeman (white team letters) | 7.00 | 3.50 |
| 34 Bob Thurman | 7.00 | 3.50 |
| 35a Don Mossi (yellow team | | |

| | | NR MT | EX |
|---|---|---|---|
| | letters) | 20.00 | 10.00 |
| 35b | Don Mossi (white team letters) | 7.00 | 3.50 |
| 36 | Ted Kazanski | 7.00 | 3.50 |
| 37 | *Mike McCormick* (photo actually Ray Monzant) | 7.00 | 3.50 |
| 38 | Dick Gernert | 7.00 | 3.50 |
| 39 | Bob Martyn | 7.00 | 3.50 |
| 40 | George Kell | 15.00 | 7.50 |
| 41 | Dave Hillman | 7.00 | 3.50 |
| 42 | *John Roseboro* | 7.00 | 3.50 |
| 43 | Sal Maglie | 10.00 | 5.00 |
| 44 | Senators Team Checklist 1-88 | 10.00 | 5.00 |
| 45 | Dick Groat | 7.00 | 3.50 |
| 46a | Lou Sleater (yellow name letters) | 20.00 | 10.00 |
| 46b | Lou Sleater (white name letters) | 7.00 | 3.50 |
| 47 | *Roger Maris* | 450.00 | 225.00 |
| 48 | Chuck Harmon | 7.00 | 3.50 |
| 49 | Smoky Burgess | 7.00 | 3.50 |
| 50a | Billy Pierce (yellow team letters) | 20.00 | 10.00 |
| 50b | Billy Pierce (white team letters) | 7.00 | 3.50 |
| 51 | Del Rice | 7.00 | 3.50 |
| 52a | Bob Clemente (yellow team letters) | 350.00 | 175.00 |
| 52b | Bob Clemente (white team letters) | 225.00 | 112.00 |
| 53a | Morrie Martin (yellow name letters) | 20.00 | 10.00 |
| 53b | Morrie Martin (white name letters) | 7.00 | 3.50 |
| 54 | *Norm Siebern* | 7.00 | 3.50 |
| 55 | Chico Carrasquel | 7.00 | 3.50 |
| 56 | Bill Fischer | 7.00 | 3.50 |
| 57a | Tim Thompson (yellow name letters) | 20.00 | 10.00 |
| 57b | Tim Thompson (white name letters) | 7.00 | 3.50 |
| 58a | Art Schult (yellow team letters) | 20.00 | 10.00 |
| 58b | Art Schult (white team letters) | 7.00 | 3.50 |
| 59 | Dave Sisler | 7.00 | 3.50 |
| 60a | Del Ennis (yellow name letters) | 20.00 | 10.00 |
| 60b | Del Ennis (white name letters) | 7.00 | 3.50 |
| 61a | Darrell Johnson (yellow name letters) | 20.00 | 10.00 |
| 61b | Darrell Johnson (white name letters) | 7.00 | 3.50 |
| 62 | Joe DeMaestri | 7.00 | 3.50 |
| 63 | Joe Nuxhall | 7.00 | 3.50 |
| 64 | Joe Lonnett | 7.00 | 3.50 |
| 65a | Von McDaniel (yellow name letters) | 20.00 | 10.00 |
| 65b | Von McDaniel (white name letters) | 7.00 | 3.50 |
| 66 | Lee Walls | 7.00 | 3.50 |
| 67 | Joe Ginsberg | 7.00 | 3.50 |
| 68 | Daryl Spencer | 7.00 | 3.50 |
| 69 | Wally Burnette | 7.00 | 3.50 |
| 70a | Al Kaline (yellow name letters) | 20.00 | 10.00 |
| 70b | Al Kaline (white name letters) | 75.00 | 38.00 |
| 71 | Dodgers Team Checklist 1-88 | 20.00 | 10.00 |
| 72 | Bud Byerly | 7.00 | 3.50 |
| 73 | Pete Daley | 7.00 | 3.50 |
| 74 | Roy Face | 7.00 | 3.50 |
| 75 | Gus Bell | 7.00 | 3.50 |
| 76a | Dick Farrell (yellow team letters) | 20.00 | 10.00 |
| 76b | Dick Farrell (white team letters) | 7.00 | 3.50 |
| 77a | Don Zimmer (yellow team letters) | 20.00 | 10.00 |
| 77b | Don Zimmer (white team letters) | 7.00 | 3.50 |
| 78a | Ernie Johnson (yellow name letters) | 20.00 | 10.00 |
| 78b | Ernie Johnson (white name letters) | 7.00 | 3.50 |
| 79a | Dick Williams (yellow team letters) | 20.00 | 10.00 |
| 79b | Dick Williams (white team letters) | 7.00 | 3.50 |
| 80 | Dick Drott | 7.00 | 3.50 |
| 81a | *Steve Boros* (yellow team letters) | 20.00 | 10.00 |
| 81b | *Steve Boros* (white team letters) | 7.00 | 3.50 |
| 82 | Ronnie Kline | 7.00 | 3.50 |
| 83 | Bob Hazle | 7.00 | 3.50 |
| 84 | Billy O'Dell | 7.00 | 3.50 |
| 85a | Luis Aparicio (yellow team letters) | 50.00 | 25.00 |
| 85b | Luis Aparicio (white team letters) | 15.00 | 7.50 |
| 86 | Valmy Thomas | 7.00 | 3.50 |
| 87 | Johnny Kucks | 7.00 | 3.50 |
| 88 | Duke Snider | 75.00 | 38.00 |
| 89 | Billy Klaus | 7.00 | 3.50 |
| 90 | Robin Roberts | 20.00 | 10.00 |
| 91 | Chuck Tanner | 7.00 | 3.50 |
| 92a | Clint Courtney (yellow name letters) | 20.00 | 10.00 |
| 92b | Clint Courtney (white name letters) | 7.00 | 3.50 |
| 93 | Sandy Amoros | 7.00 | 3.50 |
| 94 | Bob Skinner | 7.00 | 3.50 |
| 95 | Frank Bolling | 7.00 | 3.50 |
| 96 | Joe Durham | 7.00 | 3.50 |
| 97a | Larry Jackson (yellow name letters) | 20.00 | 10.00 |
| 97b | Larry Jackson (white name letters) | 7.00 | 3.50 |
| 98a | Billy Hunter (yellow name letters) | 20.00 | 10.00 |
| 98b | Billy Hunter (white name letters) | 7.00 | 3.50 |
| 99 | Bobby Adams | 7.00 | 3.50 |
| 100a | Early Wynn (yellow team letters) | 30.00 | 15.00 |
| 100b | Early Wynn (white team letters) | 15.00 | 7.50 |
| 101a | Bobby Richardson (yellow name letters) | 30.00 | 15.00 |
| 101b | Bobby Richardson | | |

| | | NR MT | EX |
|---|---|---|---|
| | (white name letters) | 15.00 | 7.50 |
| 102 | George Strickland | 7.00 | 3.50 |
| 103 | Jerry Lynch | 7.00 | 3.50 |
| 104 | Jim Pendleton | 7.00 | 3.50 |
| 105 | Billy Gardner | 7.00 | 3.50 |
| 106 | Dick Schofield | 7.00 | 3.50 |
| 107 | Ossie Virgil | 7.00 | 3.50 |
| 108a | Jim Landis (yellow team | | |
| | letters) | 20.00 | 10.00 |
| 108b | Jim Landis (white team | | |
| | letters) | 7.00 | 3.50 |
| 109 | Herb Plews | 7.00 | 3.50 |
| 110 | Johnny Logan | 7.00 | 3.50 |
| 111 | Stu Miller | 5.00 | 2.50 |
| 112 | Gus Zernial | 5.50 | 2.75 |
| 113 | Jerry Walker | 5.00 | 2.50 |
| 114 | Irv Noren | 5.00 | 2.50 |
| 115 | Jim Bunning | 18.00 | 9.00 |
| 116 | Dave Philley | 5.50 | 2.75 |
| 117 | Frank Torre | 5.00 | 2.50 |
| 118 | Harvey Haddix | 5.00 | 2.50 |
| 119 | Harry Chiti | 5.00 | 2.50 |
| 120 | Johnny Podres | 7.00 | 3.50 |
| 121 | Eddie Miksis | 5.00 | 2.50 |
| 122 | Walt Moryn | 5.00 | 2.50 |
| 123 | Dick Tomanek | 5.00 | 2.50 |
| 124 | Bobby Usher | 5.00 | 2.50 |
| 125 | Al Dark | 7.00 | 3.50 |
| 126 | Stan Palys | 5.00 | 2.50 |
| 127 | Tom Sturdivant | 7.00 | 3.50 |
| 128 | *Willie Kirkland* | 5.50 | 2.75 |
| 129 | Jim Derrington | 5.00 | 2.50 |
| 130 | Jackie Jensen | 7.00 | 3.50 |
| 131 | Bob Henrich | 5.00 | 2.50 |
| 132 | Vernon Law | 6.00 | 3.00 |
| 133 | Russ Nixon | 5.00 | 2.50 |
| 134 | Phillies Team/Checklist | | |
| | 89-176 | 8.00 | 4.00 |
| 135 | Mike Drabowsky | 5.00 | 2.50 |
| 136 | Jim Finingan | 5.00 | 2.50 |
| 137 | Russ Kemmerer | 5.00 | 2.50 |
| 138 | Earl Torgeson | 5.00 | 2.50 |
| 139 | George Brunet | 5.00 | 2.50 |
| 140 | Wes Covington | 5.50 | 2.75 |
| 141 | Ken Lehman | 5.00 | 2.50 |
| 142 | Enos Slaughter | 20.00 | 10.00 |
| 143 | Billy Muffett | 5.00 | 2.50 |
| 144 | Bobby Morgan | 5.00 | 2.50 |
| 145 | Not Issued | | |
| 146 | Dick Gray | 5.00 | 2.50 |
| 147 | *Don McMahon* | 6.00 | 3.00 |
| 148 | Billy Consolo | 5.00 | 2.50 |
| 149 | Tom Acker | 5.00 | 2.50 |
| 150 | Mickey Mantle | 550.00 | 275.00 |
| 151 | Buddy Pritchard | 5.00 | 2.50 |
| 152 | Johnny Antonelli | 6.00 | 3.00 |
| 153 | Les Moss | 5.00 | 2.50 |
| 154 | Harry Byrd | 5.00 | 2.50 |
| 155 | Hector Lopez | 5.00 | 2.50 |
| 156 | Dick Hyde | 5.00 | 2.50 |
| 157 | Dee Fondy | 5.00 | 2.50 |
| 158 | Indians Team/Checklist | | |
| | 177-264 | 7.00 | 3.50 |
| 159 | Taylor Phillips | 5.00 | 2.50 |
| 160 | Don Hoak | 5.50 | 2.75 |
| 161 | Don Larsen | 7.00 | 3.50 |
| 162 | Gil Hodges | 25.00 | 12.50 |

| | | NR MT | EX |
|---|---|---|---|
| 163 | Jim Wilson | 5.00 | 2.50 |
| 164 | Bob Taylor | 5.00 | 2.50 |
| 165 | Bob Nieman | 5.00 | 2.50 |
| 166 | Danny O'Connell | 5.00 | 2.50 |
| 167 | Frank Baumann | 5.00 | 2.50 |
| 168 | Joe Cunningham | 5.50 | 2.75 |
| 169 | Ralph Terry | 5.50 | 2.75 |
| 170 | Vic Wertz | 6.00 | 3.00 |
| 171 | Harry Anderson | 5.00 | 2.50 |
| 172 | Don Gross | 5.00 | 2.50 |
| 173 | Eddie Yost | 5.50 | 2.75 |
| 174 | A's Team/Checklist 89 | | |
| 176 | | 8.00 | 4.00 |
| 175 | *Marv Throneberry* | | |
| | | 12.00 | 6.00 |
| 176 | Bob Buhl | 5.50 | 2.75 |
| 177 | Al Smith | 5.00 | 2.50 |
| 178 | Ted Kluszewski | 5.00 | 2.50 |
| 179 | Willy Miranda | 5.00 | 2.50 |
| 180 | Lindy McDaniel | 5.00 | 2.50 |
| 181 | Willie Jones | 5.00 | 2.50 |
| 182 | Joe Caffie | 5.00 | 2.50 |
| 183 | Dave Jolly | 5.00 | 2.50 |
| 184 | Elvin Tappe | 5.00 | 2.50 |
| 185 | Ray Boone | 5.50 | 2.75 |
| 186 | Jack Meyer | 5.00 | 2.50 |
| 187 | Sandy Koufax | 135.00 | 67.00 |
| 188 | Milt Bolling (photo | | |
| | actually Lou Berberet) | | 2.50 |
| 189 | George Susce | 5.00 | 2.50 |
| 190 | Red Schoendienst | | |
| | | 15.00 | 7.50 |
| 191 | Art Ceccarelli | 5.00 | 2.50 |
| 192 | Milt Graff | 5.00 | 2.50 |
| 193 | *Jerry Lumpe* | 5.00 | 2.50 |
| 194 | Roger Craig | 6.00 | 3.00 |
| 195 | Whitey Lockman | 5.00 | 2.50 |
| 196 | Mike Garcia | 5.50 | 2.75 |
| 197 | Haywood Sullivan | 5.50 | 2.75 |
| 198 | Bill Virdon | 6.00 | 3.00 |
| 199 | Don Blasingame | 5.00 | 2.50 |
| 200 | Bob Keegan | 5.00 | 2.50 |
| 201 | Jim Bolger | 5.00 | 2.50 |
| 202 | *Woody Held* | 6.00 | 3.00 |
| 203 | Al Walker | 5.00 | 2.50 |
| 204 | Leo Kiely | 5.00 | 2.50 |
| 205 | Johnny Temple | 5.00 | 2.50 |
| 206 | Bob Shaw | 6.00 | 3.00 |
| 207 | Solly Hemus | 5.00 | 2.50 |
| 208 | Cal McLish | 5.00 | 2.50 |
| 209 | Bob Anderson | 5.00 | 2.50 |
| 210 | Wally Moon | 5.50 | 2.75 |
| 211 | Pete Burnside | 5.00 | 2.50 |
| 212 | Bubba Phillips | 5.00 | 2.50 |
| 213 | Red Wilson | 5.00 | 2.50 |
| 214 | Willard Schmidt | 5.00 | 2.50 |
| 215 | Jim Gilliam | 5.00 | 2.50 |
| 216 | Cards Team/Checklist | | |
| | 177-264 | 7.00 | 3.50 |
| 217 | Jack Harshman | 5.00 | 2.50 |
| 218 | Dick Rand | 5.00 | 2.50 |
| 219 | Camilo Pascual | 5.50 | 2.75 |
| 220 | Tom Brewer | 5.00 | 2.50 |
| 221 | Jerry Kindall | 5.00 | 2.50 |
| 222 | Bud Daley | 5.00 | 2.50 |
| 223 | Andy Pafko | 6.00 | 3.00 |
| 224 | Bob Grim | 7.00 | 3.50 |

| | | NR MT | EX |
|---|---|---|---|
| 225 | Billy Goodman | 5.00 | 2.50 |
| 226 | Bob Smith (photo actually Bobby Gene Smith) | 5.00 | 2.50 |
| 227 | Gene Stephens | 5.00 | 2.50 |
| 228 | Duke Maas | 5.00 | 2.50 |
| 229 | Frank Zupo | 5.00 | 2.50 |
| 230 | Richie Ashburn | 8.00 | 4.00 |
| 231 | Lloyd Merritt | 5.00 | 2.50 |
| 232 | Reno Bertoia | 5.00 | 2.50 |
| 233 | Mickey Vernon | 5.50 | 2.75 |
| 234 | Carl Sawatski | 5.00 | 2.50 |
| 235 | Tom Gorman | 5.00 | 2.50 |
| 236 | Ed Fitz Gerald | 5.00 | 2.50 |
| 237 | Bill Wight | 5.00 | 2.50 |
| 238 | Bill Mazeroski | 15.00 | 7.50 |
| 239 | Chuck Stobbs | 5.00 | 2.50 |
| 240 | Moose Skowron | 10.00 | 5.00 |
| 241 | Dick Littlefield | 5.00 | 2.50 |
| 242 | Johnny Klippstein | 5.00 | 2.50 |
| 243 | Larry Raines | 5.00 | 2.50 |
| 244 | *Don Demeter* | 5.50 | 2.75 |
| 245 | *Frank Lary* | 5.50 | 2.75 |
| 246 | Yankees Team Checklist 177-264 | 40.00 | 20.00 |
| 247 | Casey Wise | 5.00 | 2.50 |
| 248 | Herm Wehmeier | 5.00 | 2.50 |
| 249 | Ray Moore | 5.00 | 2.50 |
| 250 | Roy Sievers | 6.00 | 3.00 |
| 251 | Warren Hacker | 5.00 | 2.50 |
| 252 | Bob Trowbridge | 5.00 | 2.50 |
| 253 | Don Mueller | 5.00 | 2.50 |
| 254 | Alex Grammas | 5.00 | 2.50 |
| 255 | Bob Turley | 5.00 | 2.50 |
| 256 | White Sox Team Checklist 265-352 | 8.00 | 4.00 |
| 257 | Hal Smith | 5.00 | 2.50 |
| 258 | Carl Erskine | 5.00 | 2.50 |
| 259 | Al Pilarcik | 5.00 | 2.50 |
| 260 | Frank Malzone | 5.50 | 2.75 |
| 261 | Turk Lown | 5.00 | 2.50 |
| 262 | Johnny Groth | 5.00 | 2.50 |
| 263 | Eddie Bressoud | 5.50 | 2.75 |
| 264 | Jack Sanford | 5.50 | 2.75 |
| 265 | Pete Runnels | 5.50 | 2.75 |
| 266 | Connie Johnson | 5.00 | 2.50 |
| 267 | Sherm Lollar | 5.50 | 2.75 |
| 268 | Granny Hamner | 5.00 | 2.50 |
| 269 | Paul Smith | 5.00 | 2.50 |
| 270 | Warren Spahn | 50.00 | 25.00 |
| 271 | Billy Martin | 15.00 | 7.50 |
| 272 | Ray Crone | 5.00 | 2.50 |
| 273 | Hal Smith | 5.00 | 2.50 |
| 274 | Rocky Bridges | 5.00 | 2.50 |
| 275 | Elston Howard | 8.00 | 4.00 |
| 276 | Bobby Avila | 5.00 | 2.50 |
| 277 | Virgil Trucks | 5.50 | 2.75 |
| 278 | Mack Burk | 5.00 | 2.50 |
| 279 | Bob Boyd | 5.00 | 2.50 |
| 280 | Jim Piersall | 6.00 | 3.00 |
| 281 | Sam Taylor | 5.00 | 2.50 |
| 282 | Paul Foytack | 5.00 | 2.50 |
| 283 | Ray Shearer | 5.00 | 2.50 |
| 284 | Ray Katt | 5.00 | 2.50 |
| 285 | Frank Robinson | 65.00 | 33.00 |
| 286 | Gino Cimoli | 5.00 | 2.50 |
| 287 | Sam Jones | 5.00 | 2.50 |
| 288 | Harmon Killebrew | 50.00 | 30.00 |
| 289 | Series Hurling Rivals (Lou Burdette, Bobby Shantz) | 4.00 | 2.00 |
| 290 | Dick Donovan | 5.00 | 2.50 |
| 291 | Don Landrum | 5.00 | 2.50 |
| 292 | Ned Garver | 5.00 | 2.50 |
| 293 | Gene Freese | 5.00 | 2.50 |
| 294 | Hal Jeffcoat | 5.00 | 2.50 |
| 295 | Minnie Minoso | 4.00 | 2.00 |
| 296 | *Ryne Duren* | 12.00 | 6.00 |
| 297 | Don Buddin | 5.00 | 2.50 |
| 298 | Jim Hearn | 5.00 | 2.50 |
| 299 | Harry Simpson | 7.00 | 3.50 |
| 300 | League Presidents (Warren Giles, William Harridge) | 7.00 | 3.50 |
| 301 | Randy Jackson | 5.00 | 2.50 |
| 302 | Mike Baxes | 5.00 | 2.50 |
| 303 | Neil Chrisley | 5.00 | 2.50 |
| 304 | Tigers' Big Bats (Al Kaline, Harvey Kuenn) | 10.00 | 5.00 |
| 305 | Clem Labine | 5.50 | 2.75 |
| 306 | Whammy Douglas | 5.00 | 2.50 |
| 307 | Brooks Robinson | 90.00 | 45.00 |
| 308 | Paul Giel | 5.00 | 2.50 |
| 309 | Gail Harris | 5.00 | 2.50 |
| 310 | Ernie Banks | 90.00 | 45.00 |
| 311 | Bob Purkey | 5.00 | 2.50 |
| 312 | Red Sox Team Checklist 353-440 | 8.00 | 4.00 |
| 313 | Bob Rush | 5.00 | 2.50 |
| 314 | Dodgers' Boss & Power (Walter Alston, Duke Snider) | 15.00 | 7.50 |
| 315 | Bob Friend | 6.00 | 3.00 |
| 316 | Tito Francona | 5.50 | 2.75 |
| 317 | *Albie Pearson* | 6.00 | 3.00 |
| 318 | Frank House | 5.00 | 2.50 |
| 319 | Lou Skizas | 5.00 | 2.50 |
| 320 | Whitey Ford | 35.00 | 17.50 |
| 321 | Sluggers Supreme (Ted Kluszewski, Ted Williams) | 20.00 | 10.00 |
| 322 | Harding Peterson | 5.00 | 2.50 |
| 323 | Elmer Valo | 5.00 | 2.50 |
| 324 | Hoyt Wilhelm | 15.00 | 7.50 |
| 325 | Joe Adcock | 6.00 | 3.00 |
| 326 | Bob Miller | 5.00 | 2.50 |
| 327 | Cubs Team/Checklist 265-352 | 8.00 | 4.00 |
| 328 | Ike Delock | 5.00 | 2.50 |
| 329 | Bob Cerv | 5.00 | 2.50 |
| 330 | Ed Bailey | 5.00 | 2.50 |
| 331 | Pedro Ramos | 5.00 | 2.50 |
| 332 | Jim King | 5.00 | 2.50 |
| 333 | Andy Carey | 7.00 | 3.50 |
| 334 | Mound Aces (Bob Friend, Billy Pierce) | 6.00 | 3.00 |
| 335 | Ruben Gomez | 5.00 | 2.50 |
| 336 | Bert Hamric | 5.00 | 2.50 |
| 337 | Hank Aguirre | 5.00 | 2.50 |
| 338 | Walt Dropo | 5.50 | 2.75 |
| 339 | Fred Hatfield | 5.00 | 2.50 |
| 340 | Don Newcombe | 7.00 | 3.50 |
| 341 | Pirates Team/Checklist | | |

| | | NR MT | EX |
|---|---|---|---|
| | 265-352 | 8.00 | 4.00 |
| 342 | Jim Brosnan | 5.50 | 2.75 |
| 343 | Orlando Cepeda | 80.00 | 40.00 |
| 344 | Bob Porterfield | 5.00 | 2.50 |
| 345 | Jim Hegan | 5.00 | 2.50 |
| 346 | Steve Bilko | 5.00 | 2.50 |
| 347 | Don Rudolph | 5.00 | 2.50 |
| 348 | Chico Fernandez | 5.00 | 2.50 |
| 349 | Murry Dickson | 5.00 | 2.50 |
| 350 | Ken Boyer | 5.00 | 2.50 |
| 351 | Braves' Fence Busters (Hank Aaron, Joe Adcock, Del Crandall, Ed Mathews) | 20.00 | 10.00 |
| 352 | Herb Score | 7.00 | 3.50 |
| 353 | Stan Lopata | 5.00 | 2.50 |
| 354 | Art Ditmar | 7.00 | 3.50 |
| 355 | Bill Bruton | 5.50 | 2.75 |
| 356 | Bob Malkmus | 5.00 | 2.50 |
| 357 | Danny McDevitt | 5.00 | 2.50 |
| 358 | Gene Baker | 5.00 | 2.50 |
| 359 | Billy Loes | 5.00 | 2.50 |
| 360 | Roy McMillan | 5.00 | 2.50 |
| 361 | Mike Fornieles | 5.00 | 2.50 |
| 362 | Ray Jablonski | 5.00 | 2.50 |
| 363 | Don Elston | 5.00 | 2.50 |
| 364 | Earl Battey | 5.50 | 2.75 |
| 365 | Tom Morgan | 5.00 | 2.50 |
| 366 | Gene Green | 5.00 | 2.50 |
| 367 | Jack Urban | 5.00 | 2.50 |
| 368 | Rocky Colavito | 30.00 | 15.00 |
| 369 | Ralph Lumenti | 5.00 | 2.50 |
| 370 | Yogi Berra | 100.00 | 50.00 |
| 371 | Marty Keough | 5.00 | 2.50 |
| 372 | Don Cardwell | 5.00 | 2.50 |
| 373 | Joe Pignatano | 5.00 | 2.50 |
| 374 | Brooks Lawrence | 5.00 | 2.50 |
| 375 | Pee Wee Reese | 50.00 | 30.00 |
| 376 | Charley Rabe | 5.00 | 2.50 |
| 377a | Braves Team (alphabetical checklist on back) | 9.00 | 4.50 |
| 377b | Braves Team (numerical checklist on back) | 60.00 | 30.00 |
| 378 | Hank Sauer | 5.50 | 2.75 |
| 379 | Ray Herbert | 5.00 | 2.50 |
| 380 | Charley Maxwell | 5.00 | 2.50 |
| 381 | Hal Brown | 5.00 | 2.50 |
| 382 | Al Cicotte | 7.00 | 3.50 |
| 383 | Lou Berberet | 5.00 | 2.50 |
| 384 | John Goryl | 5.00 | 2.50 |
| 385 | Wilmer Mizell | 5.00 | 2.50 |
| 386 | Birdie's Young Sluggers (Ed Bailey, Frank Robinson, Birdie Tebbetts) | 7.00 | 3.50 |
| 387 | Wally Post | 5.00 | 2.50 |
| 388 | Billy Moran | 5.00 | 2.50 |
| 389 | Bill Taylor | 5.00 | 2.50 |
| 390 | Del Crandall | 6.00 | 3.00 |
| 391 | Dave Melton | 5.00 | 2.50 |
| 392 | Bennie Daniels | 5.00 | 2.50 |
| 393 | Tony Kubek | 20.00 | 10.00 |
| 394 | Jim Grant | 6.00 | 3.00 |
| 395 | Willard Nixon | 5.00 | 2.50 |
| 396 | Dutch Dotterer | 5.00 | 2.50 |
| 397a | Tigers Team (alphabetical checklist on back) | 9.00 | 4.50 |
| 397b | Tigers Team (numerical checklist on back) | 60.00 | 30.00 |
| 398 | Gene Woodling | 5.50 | 2.75 |
| 399 | Marv Grissom | 5.00 | 2.50 |
| 400 | Nellie Fox | 15.00 | 7.50 |
| 401 | Don Bessent | 5.00 | 2.50 |
| 402 | Bobby Gene Smith | 5.00 | 2.50 |
| 403 | Steve Korcheck | 5.00 | 2.50 |
| 404 | Curt Simmons | 6.00 | 3.00 |
| 405 | Ken Aspromonte | 5.00 | 2.50 |
| 406 | Vic Power | 5.00 | 2.50 |
| 407 | Carlton Willey | 5.00 | 2.50 |
| 408a | Orioles Team (alphabetical checklist on back) | 8.00 | 4.00 |
| 408b | Orioles Team (numerical checklist on back) | 60.00 | 30.00 |
| 409 | Frank Thomas | 5.00 | 2.50 |
| 410 | Murray Wall | 5.00 | 2.50 |
| 411 | Tony Taylor | 5.50 | 2.75 |
| 412 | Jerry Staley | 5.00 | 2.50 |
| 413 | Jim Davenport | 5.50 | 2.75 |
| 414 | Sammy White | 5.00 | 2.50 |
| 415 | Bob Bowman | 5.00 | 2.50 |
| 416 | Foster Castleman | 5.00 | 2.50 |
| 417 | Carl Furillo | 7.00 | 3.50 |
| 418 | World Series Batting Foes (Hank Aaron, Mickey Mantle) | 150.00 | 75.00 |
| 419 | Bobby Shantz | 7.00 | 3.50 |
| 420 | Vada Pinson | 25.00 | 12.50 |
| 421 | Dixie Howell | 5.00 | 2.50 |
| 422 | Norm Zauchin | 5.00 | 2.50 |
| 423 | Phil Clark | 5.00 | 2.50 |
| 424 | Larry Doby | 5.00 | 2.50 |
| 425 | Sam Esposito | 5.00 | 2.50 |
| 426 | Johnny O'Brien | 5.00 | 2.50 |
| 427 | Al Worthington | 5.00 | 2.50 |
| 428a | Redlegs Team (alphabetical checklist on back) | 8.00 | 4.00 |
| 428b | Redlegs Team (numerical checklist on back) | 50.00 | 25.00 |
| 429 | Gus Triandos | 5.50 | 2.75 |
| 430 | Bobby Thomson | 6.00 | 3.00 |
| 431 | Gene Conley | 5.50 | 2.75 |
| 432 | John Powers | 5.00 | 2.50 |
| 433 | Pancho Herrera | 5.00 | 2.50 |
| 434 | Harvey Kuenn | 6.00 | 3.00 |
| 435 | Ed Roebuck | 5.00 | 2.50 |
| 436 | Rival Fence Busters (Willie Mays, Duke Snider) | 55.00 | 28.00 |
| 437 | Bob Speake | 5.00 | 2.50 |
| 438 | Whitey Herzog | 7.00 | 3.50 |
| 439 | Ray Narleski | 5.00 | 2.50 |
| 440 | Ed Mathews | 30.00 | 15.00 |
| 441 | Jim Marshall | 4.00 | 2.00 |
| 442 | Phil Paine | 4.00 | 2.00 |
| 443 | Billy Harrell | 7.00 | 3.50 |
| 444 | Danny Kravitz | 4.00 | 2.00 |
| 445 | Bob Smith | 4.00 | 2.00 |
| 446 | Carroll Hardy | 7.00 | 3.50 |
| 447 | Ray Monzant | 4.00 | 2.00 |
| 448 | Charlie Lau | 5.50 | 2.75 |

| | | NR MT | EX |
|---|---|---|---|
| 449 | Gene Fodge | 4.00 | 2.00 |
| 450 | Preston Ward | 7.00 | 3.50 |
| 451 | Joe Taylor | 4.00 | 2.00 |
| 452 | Roman Mejias | 4.00 | 2.00 |
| 453 | Tom Qualters | 4.00 | 2.00 |
| 454 | Harry Hanebrink | 4.00 | 2.00 |
| 455 | Hal Griggs | 4.00 | 2.00 |
| 456 | Dick Brown | 4.00 | 2.00 |
| 457 | *Milt Pappas* | 5.50 | 2.75 |
| 458 | Julio Becquer | 4.00 | 2.00 |
| 459 | Ron Blackburn | 4.00 | 2.00 |
| 460 | Chuck Essegian | 4.00 | 2.00 |
| 461 | Ed Mayer | 4.00 | 2.00 |
| 462 | Gary Geiger | 7.00 | 3.50 |
| 463 | Vito Valentinetti | 4.00 | 2.00 |
| 464 | Curt Flood | 25.00 | 12.50 |
| 465 | Arnie Portocarrero | 4.00 | 2.00 |
| 466 | Pete Whisenant | 4.00 | 2.00 |
| 467 | Glen Hobbie | 4.00 | 2.00 |
| 468 | Bob Schmidt | 4.00 | 2.00 |
| 469 | Don Ferrarese | 4.00 | 2.00 |
| 470 | R.C. Stevens | 4.00 | 2.00 |
| 471 | Lenny Green | 4.00 | 2.00 |
| 472 | Joe Jay | 4.00 | 2.00 |
| 473 | Bill Renna | 4.00 | 2.00 |
| 474 | Roman Semproch | 4.00 | 2.00 |
| 475 | All-Star Managers (Fred Haney, Casey Stengel) | 18.00 | 9.00 |
| 476 | Stan Musial AS | 40.00 | 20.00 |
| 477 | Bill Skowron AS | 4.00 | 2.00 |
| 478 | Johnny Temple AS | 5.00 | 2.50 |
| 479 | Nellie Fox AS | 10.00 | 5.00 |
| 480 | Eddie Mathews AS | 10.00 | 5.00 |
| 481 | Frank Malzone AS | 5.00 | 2.50 |
| 482 | Ernie Banks AS | 20.00 | 10.00 |
| 483 | Luis Aparicio AS | 8.00 | 4.00 |
| 484 | Frank Robinson AS | 20.00 | 10.00 |
| 485 | Ted Williams AS | 65.00 | 33.00 |
| 486 | Willie Mays AS | 50.00 | 25.00 |
| 487 | Mickey Mantle AS | 100.00 | 50.00 |
| 488 | Hank Aaron AS | 40.00 | 20.00 |
| 489 | Jackie Jensen AS | 6.00 | 3.00 |
| 490 | Ed Bailey AS | 5.00 | 2.50 |
| 491 | Sherm Lollar AS | 5.00 | 2.50 |
| 492 | Bob Friend AS | 6.00 | 3.00 |
| 493 | Bob Turley AS | 7.00 | 3.50 |
| 494 | Warren Spahn AS | 15.00 | 7.50 |
| 495 | Herb Score AS | 7.00 | 3.50 |
| ---- | Contest Card (All-Star Game, July 8) | 15.00 | 7.50 |
| ---- | Felt Emblems Insert Card | 15.00 | 7.50 |

autograph is found across the photo. The 572-card set marks the largest set issued to that time. Card numbers below 507 have red and green printing with the card number in white in a green box. On high number cards beginning with #507, the printing is black and red and the card number is in a black box. Specialty cards include multiple-player cards, team cards with checklists; "All-Star" cards, highlights from previous season, and 31 "Rookie Stars." There is also a card of the commissioner, Ford Frick, and one of Roy Campanella in a wheelchair. A handful of cards can be found with and without lines added to the biographies on back indicating trades or demotions; those without the added lines are considerably more rare and valuable and are not included in the complete set price. Card numbers 199-286 can be found with either white or grey backs, with the grey stock being the less common.

| | | NR MT | EX |
|---|---|---|---|
| Complete Set: | | 5000.00 | 2500.00 |
| Common Player: 1-110 | | 5.00 | 2.50 |
| Common Player: 111-506 | | 3.00 | 1.50 |
| Common Player: 507-572 | | 15.00 | 7.50 |

| 1 | Ford Frick | 70.00 | 15.00 |
|---|---|---|---|
| 2 | Eddie Yost | 5.00 | 2.00 |
| 3 | Don McMahon | 5.00 | 2.50 |
| 4 | Albie Pearson | 5.00 | 2.50 |
| 5 | Dick Donovan | 5.00 | 2.50 |
| 6 | Alex Grammas | 5.00 | 2.50 |
| 7 | Al Pilarcik | 5.00 | 2.50 |
| 8 | Phillies Team/Checklist 1-88 | 20.00 | 10.00 |
| 9 | Paul Giel | 5.00 | 2.50 |
| 10 | Mickey Mantle | 450.00 | 225.00 |

## 1959 Topps

These 2-1/2" by 3-1/2" cards have a round photograph at the center of the front with a solid-color background and white border. A facsimile

| | | NR MT | EX | | | | NR MT | EX |
|---|---|---|---|---|---|---|---|---|
| 11 | Billy Hunter | 5.00 | 2.50 | 71 | Don Bessent | | 5.00 | 2.50 |
| 12 | Vern Law | 5.00 | 2.50 | 72 | Bill Renna | | 5.00 | 2.50 |
| 13 | Dick Gernert | 5.00 | 2.50 | 73 | Ron Jackson | | 5.00 | 2.50 |
| 14 | Pete Whisenant | 5.00 | 2.50 | 74 | Directing the Power | | | |
| 15 | Dick Drott | 5.00 | 2.50 | | (Cookie Lavagetto, Jim | | | |
| 16 | Joe Pignatano | 5.00 | 2.50 | | Lemon, Roy Sievers) | | 6.00 | 3.00 |
| 17 | Danny's All-Stars (Ted | | | 75 | Sam Jones | | 5.00 | 2.50 |
| | Kluszewski, Danny | | | 76 | Bobby Richardson | | | |
| | Murtaugh, Frank Thomas) | | | | | | 15.00 | 7.50 |
| | | 5.00 | 2.50 | 77 | John Goryl | | 5.00 | 2.50 |
| 18 | Jack Urban | 5.00 | 2.50 | 78 | Pedro Ramos | | 5.00 | 2.50 |
| 19 | Ed Bressoud | 5.00 | 2.50 | 79 | Harry Chiti | | 5.00 | 2.50 |
| 20 | Duke Snider | 60.00 | 30.00 | 80 | Minnie Minoso | | 5.00 | 2.50 |
| 21 | Connie Johnson | 5.00 | 2.50 | 81 | Hal Jeffcoat | | 5.00 | 2.50 |
| 22 | Al Smith | 5.00 | 2.50 | 82 | Bob Boyd | | 5.00 | 2.50 |
| 23 | Murry Dickson | 5.00 | 2.50 | 83 | Bob Smith | | 5.00 | 2.50 |
| 24 | Red Wilson | 5.00 | 2.50 | 84 | Reno Bertoia | | 5.00 | 2.50 |
| 25 | Don Hoak | 6.00 | 3.00 | 85 | Harry Anderson | | 5.00 | 2.50 |
| 26 | Chuck Stobbs | 5.00 | 2.50 | 86 | Bob Keegan | | 5.00 | 2.50 |
| 27 | Andy Pafko | 6.00 | 3.00 | 87 | Danny O'Connell | | 5.00 | 2.50 |
| 28 | Red Worthington | 5.00 | 2.50 | 88 | Herb Score | | 6.00 | 3.00 |
| 29 | Jim Bolger | 5.00 | 2.50 | 89 | Billy Gardner | | 5.00 | 2.50 |
| 30 | Nellie Fox | 20.00 | 10.00 | 90 | Bill Skowron | | 15.00 | 7.50 |
| 31 | Ken Lehman | 5.00 | 2.50 | 91 | Herb Moford | | 5.00 | 2.50 |
| 32 | Don Buddin | 5.00 | 2.50 | 92 | Dave Philley | | 5.00 | 2.50 |
| 33 | Ed Fitz Gerald | 5.00 | 2.50 | 93 | Julio Becquer | | 5.00 | 2.50 |
| 34 | Pitchers Beware (Al | | | 94 | W. Sox Team/Checklist | | | |
| | Kaline, Charlie Maxwell) | | | | 89-176 | | 15.00 | 7.50 |
| | | 9.00 | 4.50 | 95 | Carl Willey | | 5.00 | 2.50 |
| 35 | Ted Kluszewski | 10.00 | 5.00 | 96 | Lou Berberet | | 5.00 | 2.50 |
| 36 | Hank Aguirre | 5.00 | 2.50 | 97 | Jerry Lynch | | 5.00 | 2.50 |
| 37 | Gene Green | 5.00 | 2.50 | 98 | Arnie Portocarrero | 5.00 | 2.50 |
| 38 | Morrie Martin | 5.00 | 2.50 | 99 | Ted Kazanski | | 5.00 | 2.50 |
| 39 | Ed Bouchee | 5.00 | 2.50 | 100 | Bob Cerv | | 5.00 | 2.50 |
| 40 | Warren Spahn | 50.00 | 25.00 | 101 | Alex Kellner | | 5.00 | 2.50 |
| 41 | Bob Martyn | 5.00 | 2.50 | 102 | *Felipe Alou* | | 20.00 | 10.00 |
| 42 | Murray Wall | 5.00 | 2.50 | 103 | Billy Goodman | | 5.00 | 2.50 |
| 43 | Steve Bilko | 5.00 | 2.50 | 104 | Del Rice | | 5.00 | 2.50 |
| 44 | Vito Valentinetti | 5.00 | 2.50 | 105 | Lee Walls | | 5.00 | 2.50 |
| 45 | Andy Carey | 5.00 | 2.50 | 106 | Hal Woodeshick | | 5.00 | 2.50 |
| 46 | Bill Henry | 5.00 | 2.50 | 107 | Norm Larker | | 5.00 | 2.50 |
| 47 | Jim Finigan | 5.00 | 2.50 | 108 | Zack Monroe | | 5.00 | 2.50 |
| 48 | Orioles Team/Checklist | | | 109 | Bob Schmidt | | 5.00 | 2.50 |
| | 1-88 | 15.00 | 7.50 | 110 | George Witt | | 5.00 | 2.50 |
| 49 | Bill Hall | 5.00 | 2.50 | 111 | Redlegs Team/Checklist | | | |
| 50 | Willie Mays | 160.00 | 80.00 | | 89-176 | | 8.00 | 4.00 |
| 51 | Rip Coleman | 5.00 | 2.50 | 112 | Billy Consolo | | 3.00 | 1.50 |
| 52 | Coot Veal | 5.00 | 2.50 | 113 | Taylor Phillips | | 3.00 | 1.50 |
| 53 | Stan Williams | 5.00 | 2.50 | 114 | Earl Battey | | 3.25 | 1.75 |
| 54 | Mel Roach | 5.00 | 2.50 | 115 | Mickey Vernon | | 3.25 | 1.75 |
| 55 | Tom Brewer | 5.00 | 2.50 | 116 | *Bob Allison* | | 7.00 | 3.50 |
| 56 | Carl Sawatski | 5.00 | 2.50 | 117 | *John Blanchard* | | 3.25 | 1.75 |
| 57 | Al Cicotte | 5.00 | 2.50 | 118 | John Buzhardt | | 3.00 | 1.50 |
| 58 | Eddie Miksis | 5.00 | 2.50 | 119 | *John Callison* | | 5.00 | 2.50 |
| 59 | Irv Noren | 5.00 | 2.50 | 120 | Chuck Coles | | 3.00 | 1.50 |
| 60 | Bob Turley | 6.00 | 3.00 | 121 | Bob Conley | | 3.00 | 1.50 |
| 61 | Dick Brown | 5.00 | 2.50 | 122 | Bennie Daniels | | 3.00 | 1.50 |
| 62 | Tony Taylor | 5.00 | 2.50 | 123 | Don Dillard | | 3.00 | 1.50 |
| 63 | Jim Hearn | 5.00 | 2.50 | 124 | Dan Dobbek | | 3.00 | 1.50 |
| 64 | Joe DeMaestri | 5.00 | 2.50 | 125 | *Ron Fairly* | | 3.50 | 1.75 |
| 65 | Frank Torre | 5.00 | 2.50 | 126 | Eddie Haas | | 3.00 | 1.50 |
| 66 | Joe Ginsberg | 5.00 | 2.50 | 127 | Kent Hadley | | 3.00 | 1.50 |
| 67 | Brooks Lawrence | 5.00 | 2.50 | 128 | Bob Hartman | | 3.00 | 1.50 |
| 68 | Dick Schofield | 5.00 | 2.50 | 129 | Frank Herrera | | 3.00 | 1.50 |
| 69 | Giants Team/Checklist | | | 130 | Lou Jackson | | 3.00 | 1.50 |
| | 89-176 | 18.00 | 9.00 | 131 | *Deron Johnson* | | 3.25 | 1.75 |
| 70 | Harvey Kuenn | 5.00 | 2.50 | 132 | Don Lee | | 3.00 | 1.50 |

| | NR MT | EX |
|---|---|---|
| 133 *Bob Lillis* | 3.25 | 1.75 |
| 134 Jim McDaniel | 3.00 | 1.50 |
| 135 Gene Oliver | 3.00 | 1.50 |
| 136 *Jim O'Toole* | 3.25 | 1.75 |
| 137 Dick Ricketts | 3.00 | 1.50 |
| 138 John Romano | 3.00 | 1.50 |
| 139 Ed Sadowski | 3.00 | 1.50 |
| 140 Charlie Secrest | 3.00 | 1.50 |
| 141 Joe Shipley | 3.00 | 1.50 |
| 142 Dick Stigman | 3.00 | 1.50 |
| 143 Willie Tasby | 3.00 | 1.50 |
| 144 Jerry Walker | 3.00 | 1.50 |
| 145 Dom Zanni | 3.00 | 1.50 |
| 146 Jerry Zimmerman | 3.00 | 1.50 |
| 147 Cub's Clubbers (Ernie Banks, Dale Long, Walt Moryn) | 10.00 | 5.00 |
| 148 Mike McCormick | 3.25 | 1.75 |
| 149 Jim Bunning | 15.00 | 7.50 |
| 150 Stan Musial | 150.00 | 75.00 |
| 151 Bob Malkmus | 3.00 | 1.50 |
| 152 Johnny Klippstein | 3.00 | 1.50 |
| 153 Jim Marshall | 3.00 | 1.50 |
| 154 Ray Herbert | 3.00 | 1.50 |
| 155 Enos Slaughter | 18.00 | 9.00 |
| 156 Ace Hurlers (Billy Pierce, Robin Roberts) | 3.50 | 1.75 |
| 157 Felix Mantilla | 3.00 | 1.50 |
| 158 Walt Dropo | 3.25 | 1.75 |
| 159 Bob Shaw | 3.00 | 1.50 |
| 160 Dick Groat | 3.00 | 1.50 |
| 161 Frank Baumann | 3.00 | 1.50 |
| 162 Bobby G. Smith | 3.00 | 1.50 |
| 163 Sandy Koufax | 150.00 | 75.00 |
| 164 Johnny Groth | 3.00 | 1.50 |
| 165 Bill Bruton | 3.25 | 1.75 |
| 166 Destruction Crew (Rocky Colavito, Larry Doby, Minnie Minoso) | 3.25 | 1.75 |
| 167 Duke Maas | 3.00 | 1.50 |
| 168 Carroll Hardy | 3.00 | 1.50 |
| 169 Ted Abernathy | 3.00 | 1.50 |
| 170 Gene Woodling | 3.25 | 1.75 |
| 171 Willard Schmidt | 3.00 | 1.50 |
| 172 A's Team/Checklist 177 242 | 7.00 | 3.50 |
| 173 *Bill Monbouquette* | 3.25 | 1.75 |
| 174 Jim Pendleton | 3.00 | 1.50 |
| 175 Dick Farrell | 3.00 | 1.50 |
| 176 Preston Ward | 3.00 | 1.50 |
| 177 Johnny Briggs | 3.00 | 1.50 |
| 178 Ruben Amaro | 3.00 | 1.50 |
| 179 Don Rudolph | 3.00 | 1.50 |
| 180 Yogi Berra | 90.00 | 45.00 |
| 181 Bob Porterfield | 3.00 | 1.50 |
| 182 Milt Graff | 3.00 | 1.50 |
| 183 Stu Miller | 3.00 | 1.50 |
| 184 Harvey Haddix | 3.25 | 1.75 |
| 185 Jim Busby | 3.00 | 1.50 |
| 186 Mudcat Grant | 3.25 | 1.75 |
| 187 Bubba Phillips | 3.00 | 1.50 |
| 188 Juan Pizarro | 3.00 | 1.50 |
| 189 Neil Chrisley | 3.00 | 1.50 |
| 190 Bill Virdon | 3.25 | 1.75 |
| 191 Russ Kemmerer | 3.00 | 1.50 |
| 192 Charley Beamon | 3.00 | 1.50 |
| 193 Sammy Taylor | 3.00 | 1.50 |

| | NR MT | EX |
|---|---|---|
| 194 Jim Brosnan | 3.25 | 1.75 |
| 195 Rip Repulski | 3.00 | 1.50 |
| 196 Billy Moran | 3.00 | 1.50 |
| 197 Ray Semproch | 3.00 | 1.50 |
| 198 Jim Davenport | 3.00 | 1.50 |
| 199 Leo Kiely | 3.00 | 1.50 |
| 200 Warren Giles | 3.25 | 1.75 |
| 201 Tom Acker | 3.00 | 1.50 |
| 202 Roger Maris | 150.00 | 75.00 |
| 203 Ozzie Virgil | 3.00 | 1.50 |
| 204 Casey Wise | 3.00 | 1.50 |
| 205 Don Larsen | 7.00 | 3.50 |
| 206 Carl Furillo | 5.00 | 2.50 |
| 207 George Strickland | 3.00 | 1.50 |
| 208 Willie Jones | 3.00 | 1.50 |
| 209 Lenny Green | 3.00 | 1.50 |
| 210 Ed Bailey | 3.00 | 1.50 |
| 211 Bob Blaylock | 3.00 | 1.50 |
| 212 Fence Busters (Hank Aaron, Eddie Mathews) | 55.00 | 28.00 |
| 213 Jim Rivera | 3.00 | 1.50 |
| 214 Marcelino Solis | 3.00 | 1.50 |
| 215 Jim Lemon | 3.00 | 1.50 |
| 216 Andre Rodgers | 3.00 | 1.50 |
| 217 Carl Erskine | 5.00 | 2.50 |
| 218 Roman Mejias | 3.00 | 1.50 |
| 219 George Zuverink | 3.00 | 1.50 |
| 220 Frank Malzone | 3.25 | 1.75 |
| 221 Bob Bowman | 3.00 | 1.50 |
| 222 Bobby Shantz | 3.25 | 1.75 |
| 223 Cards Team/Checklist 265-352 | 7.00 | 3.50 |
| 224 *Claude Osteen* | 3.00 | 1.50 |
| 225 Johnny Logan | 3.25 | 1.75 |
| 226 Art Ceccarelli | 3.00 | 1.50 |
| 227 Hal Smith | 3.00 | 1.50 |
| 228 Don Gross | 3.00 | 1.50 |
| 229 Vic Power | 3.00 | 1.50 |
| 230 Bill Fischer | 3.00 | 1.50 |
| 231 Ellis Burton | 3.00 | 1.50 |
| 232 Eddie Kasko | 3.00 | 1.50 |
| 233 Paul Foytack | 3.00 | 1.50 |
| 234 Chuck Tanner | 3.00 | 1.50 |
| 235 Valmy Thomas | 3.00 | 1.50 |
| 236 Ted Bowsfield | 3.00 | 1.50 |
| 237 Run Preventers (Gil McDougald, Bobby Richardson, Bob Turley) | 5.00 | 2.50 |
| 238 Gene Baker | 3.00 | 1.50 |
| 239 Bob Trowbridge | 3.00 | 1.50 |
| 240 Hank Bauer | 7.00 | 3.50 |
| 241 Billy Muffett | 3.00 | 1.50 |
| 242 Ron Samford | 3.00 | 1.50 |
| 243 Marv Grissom | 3.00 | 1.50 |
| 244 Dick Gray | 3.00 | 1.50 |
| 245 Ned Garver | 3.00 | 1.50 |
| 246 J.W. Porter | 3.00 | 1.50 |
| 247 Don Ferrarese | 3.00 | 1.50 |
| 248 Red Sox Team Checklist 177-264 | 8.00 | 4.00 |
| 249 Bobby Adams | 3.00 | 1.50 |
| 250 Billy O'Dell | 3.00 | 1.50 |
| 251 Cletis Boyer | 6.00 | 3.00 |
| 252 Ray Boone | 3.25 | 1.75 |
| 253 Seth Morehead | 3.00 | 1.50 |

| | | NR MT | EX |
|---|---|---|---|
| 254 | Zeke Bella | 3.00 | 1.50 |
| 255 | Del Ennis | 3.25 | 1.75 |
| 256 | Jerry Davie | 3.00 | 1.50 |
| 257 | *Leon Wagner* | 3.00 | 1.50 |
| 258 | Fred Kipp | 3.00 | 1.50 |
| 259 | Jim Pisoni | 3.00 | 1.50 |
| 260 | Early Wynn | 15.00 | 7.50 |
| 261 | Gene Stephens | 3.00 | 1.50 |
| 262 | Hitters' Foes (Don Drysdale, Clem Labine, Johnny Podres) | 8.00 | 4.00 |
| 263 | Buddy Daley | 3.00 | 1.50 |
| 264 | Chico Carrasquel | 3.00 | 1.50 |
| 265 | Ron Kline | 3.00 | 1.50 |
| 266 | Woody Held | 3.25 | 1.75 |
| 267 | John Romonosky | 3.00 | 1.50 |
| 268 | Tito Francona | 3.25 | 1.75 |
| 269 | Jack Meyer | 3.00 | 1.50 |
| 270 | Gil Hodges | 20.00 | 10.00 |
| 271 | *Orlando Pena* | 3.25 | 1.75 |
| 272 | Jerry Lumpe | 3.25 | 1.75 |
| 273 | Joe Jay | 3.00 | 1.50 |
| 274 | Jerry Kindall | 3.00 | 1.50 |
| 275 | Jack Sanford | 3.00 | 1.50 |
| 276 | Pete Daley | 3.00 | 1.50 |
| 277 | Turk Lown | 3.00 | 1.50 |
| 278 | Chuck Essegian | 3.00 | 1.50 |
| 279 | Ernie Johnson | 3.00 | 1.50 |
| 280 | Frank Bolling | 3.00 | 1.50 |
| 281 | Walt Craddock | 3.00 | 1.50 |
| 282 | R.C. Stevens | 3.00 | 1.50 |
| 283 | Russ Heman | 3.00 | 1.50 |
| 284 | Steve Korcheck | 3.00 | 1.50 |
| 285 | Joe Cunningham | 3.25 | 1.75 |
| 286 | Dean Stone | 3.00 | 1.50 |
| 287 | Don Zimmer | 3.25 | 1.75 |
| 288 | Dutch Dotterer | 3.00 | 1.50 |
| 289 | Johnny Kucks | 3.00 | 1.50 |
| 290 | Wes Covington | 3.25 | 1.75 |
| 291 | Pitching Partners (Camilo Pascual, Pedro Ramos) | 3.25 | 1.75 |
| 292 | Dick Williams | 3.25 | 1.75 |
| 293 | Ray Moore | 3.00 | 1.50 |
| 294 | Hank Foiles | 3.00 | 1.50 |
| 295 | Billy Martin | 15.00 | 7.50 |
| 296 | *Ernie Broglio* | 3.25 | 1.75 |
| 297 | *Jackie Brandt* | 3.25 | 1.75 |
| 298 | Tex Clevenger | 3.00 | 1.50 |
| 299 | Billy Klaus | 3.00 | 1.50 |
| 300 | Richie Ashburn | 20.00 | 10.00 |
| 301 | Earl Averill | 3.00 | 1.50 |
| 302 | Don Mossi | 3.25 | 1.75 |
| 303 | Marty Keough | 3.00 | 1.50 |
| 304 | Cubs Team/Checklist 265-352 | 7.00 | 3.50 |
| 305 | Curt Raydon | 3.00 | 1.50 |
| 306 | Jim Gilliam | 5.00 | 2.50 |
| 307 | Curt Barclay | 3.00 | 1.50 |
| 308 | Norm Siebern | 3.50 | 1.75 |
| 309 | Sal Maglie | 3.00 | 1.50 |
| 310 | Luis Aparicio | 15.00 | 7.50 |
| 311 | Norm Zauchin | 3.00 | 1.50 |
| 312 | Don Newcombe | 6.00 | 3.00 |
| 313 | Frank House | 3.00 | 1.50 |
| 314 | Don Cardwell | 3.00 | 1.50 |
| 315 | Joe Adcock | 3.00 | 1.50 |

| | | NR MT | EX |
|---|---|---|---|
| 316a | Ralph Lumenti (without option statement) | 80.00 | 40.00 |
| 316b | Ralph Lumenti (with option statement) | 3.00 | 1.50 |
| 317 | N.L. Hitting Kings (Richie Ashburn, Willie Mays) | 15.00 | 7.50 |
| 318 | Rocky Bridges | 3.00 | 1.50 |
| 319 | Dave Hillman | 3.00 | 1.50 |
| 320 | Bob Skinner | 3.25 | 1.75 |
| 321a | Bob Giallombardo (without option statement) | 80.00 | 40.00 |
| 321b | Bob Giallombardo (with option statement) | 3.00 | 1.50 |
| 322a | Harry Hanebrink (without trade statement) | 65.00 | 33.00 |
| 322b | Harry Hanebrink (with trade statement) | 3.00 | 1.50 |
| 323 | Frank Sullivan | 3.00 | 1.50 |
| 324 | Don Demeter | 3.00 | 1.50 |
| 325 | Ken Boyer | 5.00 | 2.50 |
| 326 | Marv Throneberry | 5.00 | 2.50 |
| 327 | *Gary Bell* | 3.25 | 1.75 |
| 328 | Lou Skizas | 3.00 | 1.50 |
| 329 | Tigers Team/Checklist 353-429 | 8.00 | 4.00 |
| 330 | Gus Triandos | 3.25 | 1.75 |
| 331 | Steve Boros | 3.25 | 1.75 |
| 332 | Ray Monzant | 3.00 | 1.50 |
| 333 | Harry Simpson | 3.00 | 1.50 |
| 334 | Glen Hobbie | 3.00 | 1.50 |
| 335 | Johnny Temple | 3.00 | 1.50 |
| 336a | Billy Loes (without trade statement) | 65.00 | 33.00 |
| 336b | Billy Loes (with trade statement) | 3.00 | 1.50 |
| 337 | George Crowe | 3.00 | 1.50 |
| 338 | *George Anderson* | 45.00 | 23.00 |
| 339 | Roy Face | 3.00 | 1.50 |
| 340 | Roy Sievers | 3.25 | 1.75 |
| 341 | Tom Qualters | 3.00 | 1.50 |
| 342 | Ray Jablonski | 3.00 | 1.50 |
| 343 | Billy Hoeft | 3.00 | 1.50 |
| 344 | Russ Nixon | 3.00 | 1.50 |
| 345 | Gil McDougald | 8.00 | 4.00 |
| 346 | Batter Bafflers (Tom Brewer, Dave Sisler) | 3.25 | 1.75 |
| 347 | Bob Buhl | 3.25 | 1.75 |
| 348 | Ted Lepcio | 3.00 | 1.50 |
| 349 | Hoyt Wilhelm | 15.00 | 7.50 |
| 350 | Ernie Banks | 75.00 | 38.00 |
| 351 | Earl Torgeson | 3.00 | 1.50 |
| 352 | Robin Roberts | 15.00 | 7.50 |
| 353 | Curt Flood | 3.00 | 1.50 |
| 354 | Pete Burnside | 3.00 | 1.50 |
| 355 | Jim Piersall | 3.00 | 1.50 |
| 356 | Bob Mabe | 3.00 | 1.50 |
| 357 | *Dick Stuart* | 6.00 | 3.00 |
| 358 | Ralph Terry | 3.25 | 1.75 |
| 359 | *Bill White* | 20.00 | 10.00 |
| 360 | Al Kaline | 50.00 | 25.00 |
| 361 | Willard Nixon | 3.00 | 1.50 |
| 362a | Dolan Nichols (without option statement) | 80.00 | 40.00 |
| 362b | Dolan Nichols (with option statement) | 3.00 | 1.50 |

| | | NR MT | EX |
|---|---|---|---|
| 363 | Bobby Avila | 3.00 | 1.50 |
| 364 | Danny McDevitt | 3.00 | 1.50 |
| 365 | Gus Bell | 3.25 | 1.75 |
| 366 | Humberto Robinson | 3.00 | 1.50 |
| 367 | Cal Neeman | 3.00 | 1.50 |
| 368 | Don Mueller | 3.00 | 1.50 |
| 369 | Dick Tomanek | 3.00 | 1.50 |
| 370 | Pete Runnels | 3.25 | 1.75 |
| 371 | Dick Brodowski | 3.00 | 1.50 |
| 372 | Jim Hegan | 3.00 | 1.50 |
| 373 | Herb Plews | 3.00 | 1.50 |
| 374 | Art Ditmar | 3.00 | 1.50 |
| 375 | Bob Nieman | 3.00 | 1.50 |
| 376 | Hal Naragon | 3.00 | 1.50 |
| 377 | Johnny Antonelli | 3.25 | 1.75 |
| 378 | Gail Harris | 3.00 | 1.50 |
| 379 | Bob Miller | 3.00 | 1.50 |
| 380 | Hank Aaron | 125.00 | 62.00 |
| 381 | Mike Baxes | 3.00 | 1.50 |
| 382 | Curt Simmons | 3.25 | 1.75 |
| 383 | Words of Wisdom (Don Larsen, Casey Stengel) | 5.00 | 2.50 |
| 384 | Dave Sisler | 3.00 | 1.50 |
| 385 | Sherm Lollar | 3.25 | 1.75 |
| 386 | Jim Delsing | 3.00 | 1.50 |
| 387 | Don Drysdale | 30.00 | 15.00 |
| 388 | Bob Will | 3.00 | 1.50 |
| 389 | Joe Nuxhall | 3.25 | 1.75 |
| 390 | Orlando Cepeda | 18.00 | 9.00 |
| 391 | Milt Pappas | 3.25 | 1.75 |
| 392 | Whitey Herzog | 6.00 | 3.00 |
| 393 | Frank Lary | 3.25 | 1.75 |
| 394 | Randy Jackson | 3.00 | 1.50 |
| 395 | Elston Howard | 7.00 | 3.50 |
| 396 | Bob Rush | 3.00 | 1.50 |
| 397 | Senators Team Checklist 430-495 | 7.00 | 3.50 |
| 398 | Wally Post | 3.00 | 1.50 |
| 399 | Larry Jackson | 3.00 | 1.50 |
| 400 | Jackie Jensen | 5.00 | 2.50 |
| 401 | Ron Blackburn | 3.00 | 1.50 |
| 402 | Hector Lopez | 3.00 | 1.50 |
| 403 | Clem Labine | 3.25 | 1.75 |
| 404 | Hank Sauer | 3.25 | 1.75 |
| 405 | Roy McMillan | 3.00 | 1.50 |
| 406 | Solly Drake | 3.00 | 1.50 |
| 407 | Moe Drabowsky | 3.00 | 1.50 |
| 408 | Keystone Combo (Luis Aparicio, Nellie Fox) | 7.00 | 3.50 |
| 409 | Gus Zernial | 3.25 | 1.75 |
| 410 | Billy Pierce | 3.25 | 1.75 |
| 411 | Whitey Lockman | 3.00 | 1.50 |
| 412 | Stan Lopata | 3.00 | 1.50 |
| 413 | Camillo Pascual (Camilo) | 3.25 | 1.75 |
| 414 | Dale Long | 3.25 | 1.75 |
| 415 | Bill Mazeroski | 3.50 | 1.75 |
| 416 | Haywood Sullivan | 3.00 | 1.50 |
| 417 | Virgil Trucks | 3.00 | 1.50 |
| 418 | Gino Cimoli | 3.00 | 1.50 |
| 419 | Braves Team/Checklist 353-429 | 8.00 | 4.00 |
| 420 | Rocco Colavito | 25.00 | 12.50 |
| 421 | Herm Wehmeier | 3.00 | 1.50 |
| 422 | Hobie Landrith | 3.00 | 1.50 |

| | | NR MT | EX |
|---|---|---|---|
| 423 | Bob Grim | 3.00 | 1.50 |
| 424 | Ken Aspromonte | 3.00 | 1.50 |
| 425 | Del Crandall | 3.25 | 1.75 |
| 426 | Jerry Staley | 3.00 | 1.50 |
| 427 | Charlie Neal | 3.00 | 1.50 |
| 428 | Buc Hill Aces (Roy Face, Bob Friend, Ron Kline, Vern Law) | 3.25 | 1.75 |
| 429 | Bobby Thomson | 3.25 | 1.75 |
| 430 | Whitey Ford | 30.00 | 15.00 |
| 431 | Whammy Douglas | 3.00 | 1.50 |
| 432 | Smoky Burgess | 3.00 | 1.50 |
| 433 | Billy Harrell | 3.00 | 1.50 |
| 434 | Hal Griggs | 3.00 | 1.50 |
| 435 | Frank Robinson | 50.00 | 25.00 |
| 436 | Granny Hamner | 3.00 | 1.50 |
| 437 | Ike Delock | 3.00 | 1.50 |
| 438 | Sam Esposito | 3.00 | 1.50 |
| 439 | Brooks Robinson | 50.00 | 25.00 |
| 440 | Lou Burdette | 8.00 | 4.00 |
| 441 | John Roseboro | 3.25 | 1.75 |
| 442 | Ray Narleski | 3.00 | 1.50 |
| 443 | Daryl Spencer | 3.00 | 1.50 |
| 444 | *Ronnie Hansen* | 3.25 | 1.75 |
| 445 | Cal McLish | 3.00 | 1.50 |
| 446 | Rocky Nelson | 3.00 | 1.50 |
| 447 | Bob Anderson | 3.00 | 1.50 |
| 448 | Vada Pinson | 5.00 | 2.50 |
| 449 | Tom Gorman | 3.00 | 1.50 |
| 450 | Ed Mathews | 30.00 | 15.00 |
| 451 | Jimmy Constable | 3.00 | 1.50 |
| 452 | Chico Fernandez | 3.00 | 1.50 |
| 453 | Les Moss | 3.00 | 1.50 |
| 454 | Phil Clark | 3.00 | 1.50 |
| 455 | Larry Doby | 3.25 | 1.75 |
| 456 | Jerry Casale | 3.00 | 1.50 |
| 457 | Dodgers Team Checklist 430-495 | 15.00 | 7.50 |
| 458 | Gordon Jones | 3.00 | 1.50 |
| 459 | Bill Tuttle | 3.00 | 1.50 |
| 460 | Bob Friend | 3.25 | 1.75 |
| 461 | Mantle Hits 42nd Homer For Crown | 40.00 | 20.00 |
| 462 | Colavito's Great Catch Saves Game | 3.00 | 1.50 |
| 463 | Kaline Becomes Youngest Bat Champ | 8.00 | 4.00 |
| 464 | Mays' Catch Makes Series History | 20.00 | 10.00 |
| 465 | Sievers Sets Homer Mark | 3.25 | 1.75 |
| 466 | Pierce All Star Starter | 3.25 | 1.75 |
| 467 | Aaron Clubs World Series Homer | 15.00 | 7.50 |
| 468 | Snider's Play Brings L.A. Victory | 9.00 | 4.50 |
| 469 | Hustler Banks Wins M.V.P. Award | 8.00 | 4.00 |
| 470 | Musial Raps Out 3,000th Hit | 18.00 | 9.00 |
| 471 | Tom Sturdivant | 3.00 | 1.50 |
| 472 | Gene Freese | 3.00 | 1.50 |
| 473 | Mike Fornieles | 3.00 | 1.50 |
| 474 | Moe Thacker | 3.00 | 1.50 |
| 475 | Jack Harshman | 3.00 | 1.50 |
| 476 | Indians Team/Checklist | | |

| | | NR MT | EX |
|---|---|---|---|
| 496-572 | | 7.00 | 3.50 |
| 477 | Barry Latman | 3.00 | 1.50 |
| 478 | Bob Clemente | 125.00 | 67.00 |
| 479 | Lindy McDaniel | 3.00 | 1.50 |
| 480 | Red Schoendienst | 18.00 | 9.00 |
| 481 | Charley Maxwell | 3.00 | 1.50 |
| 482 | Russ Meyer | 3.00 | 1.50 |
| 483 | Clint Courtney | 3.00 | 1.50 |
| 484 | Willie Kirkland | 3.00 | 1.50 |
| 485 | Ryne Duren | 3.50 | 1.75 |
| 486 | Sammy White | 3.00 | 1.50 |
| 487 | Hal Brown | 3.00 | 1.50 |
| 488 | Walt Moryn | 3.00 | 1.50 |
| 489 | John C. Powers | 3.00 | 1.50 |
| 490 | Frank Thomas | 3.00 | 1.50 |
| 491 | Don Blasingame | 3.00 | 1.50 |
| 492 | Gene Conley | 3.25 | 1.75 |
| 493 | Jim Landis | 3.00 | 1.50 |
| 494 | Don Pavletich | 3.00 | 1.50 |
| 495 | Johnny Podres | 5.00 | 2.50 |
| 496 | Wayne Terwilliger | 3.00 | 1.50 |
| 497 | Hal R. Smith | 3.00 | 1.50 |
| 498 | Dick Hyde | 3.00 | 1.50 |
| 499 | Johnny O'Brien | 3.00 | 1.50 |
| 500 | Vic Wertz | 3.25 | 1.75 |
| 501 | Bobby Tiefenauer | 3.00 | 1.50 |
| 502 | Al Dark | 3.25 | 1.75 |
| 503 | Jim Owens | 3.00 | 1.50 |
| 504 | Ossie Alvarez | 3.00 | 1.50 |
| 505 | Tony Kubek | 8.00 | 4.00 |
| 506 | Bob Purkey | 3.00 | 1.50 |
| 507 | Bob Hale | 15.00 | 7.50 |
| 508 | Art Fowler | 15.00 | 7.50 |
| 509 | *Norm Cash* | 60.00 | 30.00 |
| 510 | Yankees Team Checklist 496-572 | 70.00 | 35.00 |
| 511 | George Susce | 15.00 | 7.50 |
| 512 | George Altman | 15.00 | 7.50 |
| 513 | Tom Carroll | 15.00 | 7.50 |
| 514 | *Bob Gibson* | 420.00 | 210.00 |
| 515 | Harmon Killebrew | 150.00 | 75.00 |
| 516 | Mike Garcia | 16.00 | 8.00 |
| 517 | Joe Koppe | 15.00 | 7.50 |
| 518 | *Mike Cueller (Cuellar)* | 15.00 | 7.50 |
| 519 | Infield Power (Dick Gernert, Frank Malzone, Pete Runnels) | 18.00 | 9.00 |
| 520 | Don Elston | 15.00 | 7.50 |
| 521 | Gary Geiger | 15.00 | 7.50 |
| 522 | Gene Snyder | 15.00 | 7.50 |
| 523 | Harry Bright | 15.00 | 7.50 |
| 524 | Larry Osborne | 15.00 | 7.50 |
| 525 | Jim Coates | 16.00 | 8.00 |
| 526 | Bob Speake | 15.00 | 7.50 |
| 527 | Solly Hemus | 15.00 | 7.50 |
| 528 | Pirates Team/Checklist 496-572 | 35.00 | 17.50 |
| 529 | *George Bamberger* | 16.00 | 8.00 |
| 530 | Wally Moon | 16.00 | 8.00 |
| 531 | Ray Webster | 15.00 | 7.50 |
| 532 | Mark Freeman | 15.00 | 7.50 |
| 533 | Darrell Johnson | 16.00 | 8.00 |
| 534 | Faye Throneberry | 15.00 | 7.50 |

| | | NR MT | EX |
|---|---|---|---|
| 535 | Ruben Gomez | 15.00 | 7.50 |
| 536 | Dan Kravitz | 15.00 | 7.50 |
| 537 | Rodolfo Arias | 15.00 | 7.50 |
| 538 | Chick King | 15.00 | 7.50 |
| 539 | Gary Blaylock | 15.00 | 7.50 |
| 540 | Willy Miranda | 15.00 | 7.50 |
| 541 | Bob Thurman | 15.00 | 7.50 |
| 542 | *Jim Perry* | 20.00 | 10.00 |
| 543 | Corsair Outfield Trio (Bob Clemente, Bob Skinner, Bill Virdon) | 50.00 | 25.00 |
| 544 | Lee Tate | 15.00 | 7.50 |
| 545 | Tom Morgan | 15.00 | 7.50 |
| 546 | Al Schroll | 15.00 | 7.50 |
| 547 | Jim Baxes | 15.00 | 7.50 |
| 548 | Elmer Singleton | 15.00 | 7.50 |
| 549 | Howie Nunn | 15.00 | 7.50 |
| 550 | Roy Campanella | 125.00 | 62.00 |
| 551 | Fred Haney AS | 16.00 | 8.00 |
| 552 | Casey Stengel AS | 30.00 | 15.00 |
| 553 | Orlando Cepeda AS | 18.00 | 9.00 |
| 554 | Bill Skowron AS | 18.00 | 9.00 |
| 555 | Bill Mazeroski AS | 18.00 | 9.00 |
| 556 | Nellie Fox AS | 20.00 | 10.00 |
| 557 | Ken Boyer AS | 18.00 | 9.00 |
| 558 | Frank Malzone AS | 16.00 | 8.00 |
| 559 | Ernie Banks AS | 50.00 | 25.00 |
| 560 | Luis Aparicio AS | 20.00 | 10.00 |
| 561 | Hank Aaron AS | 125.00 | 62.00 |
| 562 | Al Kaline AS | 50.00 | 25.00 |
| 563 | Willie Mays AS | 135.00 | 67.00 |
| 564 | Mickey Mantle AS | 300.00 | 150.00 |
| 565 | Wes Covington AS | 16.00 | 8.00 |
| 566 | Roy Sievers AS | 16.00 | 8.00 |
| 567 | Del Crandall AS | 16.00 | 8.00 |
| 568 | Gus Triandos AS | 16.00 | 8.00 |
| 569 | Bob Friend AS | 16.00 | 8.00 |
| 570 | Bob Turley AS | 16.00 | 8.00 |
| 571 | Warren Spahn AS | 30.00 | 15.00 |
| 572 | Billy Pierce AS | 25.00 | 12.50 |
| ---- | Elect Your Favorite Rookie Insert (paper stock, September 29 date on back) | 15.00 | 7.50 |
| ---- | Felt Pennants Insert (paper stock) | 15.00 | 7.50 |

## 1960 Topps

In 1960, Topps returned to a horizontal format

(3-1/2" by 2-1/2") with a color portrait and a black and white "action" photograph on the front. The backs returned to the use of just the previous year and lifetime statistics along with a cartoon and short career summary or previous season highlights. Specialty cards in the 572-card set are multi-player cards, managers and coaches cards, and highlights of the 1959 World Series. Two groups of rookie cards are included. The first are numbers 117-148, which are the Sport Magazine rookies. The second group is called "Topps All-Star Rookies." Finally, there is a continuation of the All-Star cards to close out the set in the scarcer high numbers. Card #'s 375-440 can be found with backs printed on either white or grey cardboard, with the white stock being the less common.

|  |  | NR MT | EX |
|---|---|---|---|
| Complete Set: | | 4000.00 | 2000.00 |
| Common Player: 1-286 | | 3.00 | 1.50 |
| Common Player: 287-440 | | | |
| | | 3.00 | 1.50 |
| Common Player: 441-506 | | | |
| | | 4.00 | 2.00 |
| Common Player: 507-572 | | | |
| | | 10.00 | 5.00 |
| 1 | Early Wynn | 40.00 | 20.00 |
| 2 | Roman Mejias | 3.25 | 1.75 |
| 3 | Joe Adcock | 3.25 | 1.75 |
| 4 | Bob Purkey | 3.00 | 1.50 |
| 5 | Wally Moon | 3.00 | 1.50 |
| 6 | Lou Berberet | 3.00 | 1.50 |
| 7 | Master & Mentor (Willie Mays, Bill Rigney) | 12.00 | 6.00 |
| 8 | Bud Daley | 3.00 | 1.50 |
| 9 | Faye Throneberry | 3.00 | 1.50 |
| 10 | Ernie Banks | 55.00 | 28.00 |
| 11 | Norm Siebern | 3.00 | 1.50 |
| 12 | Milt Pappas | 3.00 | 1.50 |
| 13 | Wally Post | 3.00 | 1.50 |
| 14 | Jim Grant | 3.00 | 1.50 |
| 15 | Pete Runnels | 3.00 | 1.50 |
| 16 | Ernie Broglio | 3.00 | 1.50 |
| 17 | Johnny Callison | 3.00 | 1.50 |
| 18 | Dodgers Team Checklist 1-88 | 10.00 | 5.00 |
| 19 | Felix Mantilla | 3.00 | 1.50 |
| 20 | Roy Face | 3.00 | 1.50 |
| 21 | Dutch Dotterer | 3.00 | 1.50 |
| 22 | Rocky Bridges | 3.00 | 1.50 |
| 23 | Eddie Fisher | 3.00 | 1.50 |
| 24 | Dick Gray | 3.00 | 1.50 |
| 25 | Roy Sievers | 4.00 | 2.00 |
| 26 | Wayne Terwilliger | 3.00 | 1.50 |
| 27 | Dick Drott | 3.00 | 1.50 |
| 28 | Brooks Robinson | 40.00 | 20.00 |
| 29 | Clem Labine | 3.00 | 1.50 |
| 30 | Tito Francona | 3.00 | 1.50 |
| 31 | Sammy Esposito | 3.00 | 1.50 |
| 32 | Sophomore Stalwarts (Jim O'Toole, Vada Pinson) | 4.00 | 2.00 |
| 33 | Tom Morgan | 3.00 | 1.50 |
| 34 | George Anderson | 2.50 | 1.25 |
| 35 | Whitey Ford | 40.00 | 20.00 |
| 36 | Russ Nixon | 3.00 | 1.50 |
| 37 | Bill Bruton | 3.00 | 1.50 |
| 38 | Jerry Casale | 3.00 | 1.50 |
| 39 | Earl Averill | 3.00 | 1.50 |
| 40 | Joe Cunningham | 3.00 | 1.50 |
| 41 | Barry Latman | 3.00 | 1.50 |
| 42 | Hobie Landrith | 3.00 | 1.50 |
| 43 | Senators Team Checklist 1-88 | 6.00 | 3.00 |
| 44 | Bobby Locke | 3.00 | 1.50 |
| 45 | Roy McMillan | 3.00 | 1.50 |
| 46 | Jack Fisher | 3.00 | 1.50 |
| 47 | Don Zimmer | 3.25 | 1.75 |
| 48 | Hal Smith | 3.00 | 1.50 |
| 49 | Curt Raydon | 3.00 | 1.50 |
| 50 | Al Kaline | 50.00 | 25.00 |
| 51 | Jim Coates | 3.00 | 1.50 |
| 52 | Dave Philley | 3.00 | 1.50 |
| 53 | Jackie Brandt | 3.00 | 1.50 |
| 54 | Mike Fornieles | 3.00 | 1.50 |
| 55 | Bill Mazeroski | 3.00 | 1.50 |
| 56 | Steve Korcheck | 3.00 | 1.50 |
| 57 | Win - Savers (Turk Lown, Gerry Staley) | 3.00 | 1.50 |
| 58 | Gino Cimoli | 3.00 | 1.50 |
| 59 | Juan Pizarro | 3.00 | 1.50 |
| 60 | Gus Triandos | 3.00 | 1.50 |
| 61 | Eddie Kasko | 3.00 | 1.50 |
| 62 | Roger Craig | 3.25 | 1.75 |
| 63 | George Strickland | 3.00 | 1.50 |
| 64 | Jack Meyer | 3.00 | 1.50 |
| 65 | Elston Howard | 6.00 | 3.00 |
| 66 | Bob Trowbridge | 3.00 | 1.50 |
| 67 | *Jose Pagan* | 3.00 | 1.50 |
| 68 | Dave Hillman | 3.00 | 1.50 |
| 69 | Billy Goodman | 3.00 | 1.50 |
| 70 | Lou Burdette | 3.25 | 1.75 |
| 71 | Marty Keough | 3.00 | 1.50 |
| 72 | Tigers Team/Checklist 89-176 | 10.00 | 5.00 |
| 73 | Bob Gibson | 40.00 | 20.00 |
| 74 | Walt Moryn | 3.00 | 1.50 |
| 75 | Vic Power | 3.00 | 1.50 |
| 76 | Bill Fischer | 3.00 | 1.50 |
| 77 | Hank Foiles | 3.00 | 1.50 |
| 78 | Bob Grim | 3.00 | 1.50 |
| 79 | Walt Dropo | 3.00 | 1.50 |
| 80 | Johnny Antonelli | 3.00 | 1.50 |
| 81 | Russ Snyder | 3.00 | 1.50 |
| 82 | Ruben Gomez | 3.00 | 1.50 |
| 83 | Tony Kubek | 4.50 | 2.25 |
| 84 | Hal Smith | 3.00 | 1.50 |
| 85 | Frank Lary | 3.00 | 1.50 |
| 86 | Dick Gernert | 3.00 | 1.50 |

| | | NR MT | EX |
|---|---|---|---|
| 87 | John Romonosky | 3.00 | 1.50 |
| 88 | John Roseboro | 3.00 | 1.50 |
| 89 | Hal Brown | 3.00 | 1.50 |
| 90 | Bobby Avila | 3.00 | 1.50 |
| 91 | Bennie Daniels | 3.00 | 1.50 |
| 92 | Whitey Herzog | 3.25 | 1.75 |
| 93 | Art Schult | 3.00 | 1.50 |
| 94 | Leo Kiely | 3.00 | 1.50 |
| 95 | Frank Thomas | 3.00 | 1.50 |
| 96 | Ralph Terry | 2.50 | 1.25 |
| 97 | Ted Lepcio | 3.00 | 1.50 |
| 98 | Gordon Jones | 3.00 | 1.50 |
| 99 | Lenny Green | 3.00 | 1.50 |
| 100 | Nellie Fox | 7.00 | 3.50 |
| 101 | Bob Miller | 3.00 | 1.50 |
| 102 | Kent Hadley | 3.00 | 1.50 |
| 103 | Dick Farrell | 3.00 | 1.50 |
| 104 | Dick Schofield | 3.00 | 1.50 |
| 105 | Larry Sherry | 3.00 | 1.50 |
| 106 | Billy Gardner | 3.00 | 1.50 |
| 107 | Carl Willey | 3.00 | 1.50 |
| 108 | Pete Daley | 3.00 | 1.50 |
| 109 | Cletis Boyer | 3.00 | 1.50 |
| 110 | Cal McLish | 3.00 | 1.50 |
| 111 | Vic Wertz | 3.00 | 1.50 |
| 112 | Jack Harshman | 3.00 | 1.50 |
| 113 | Bob Skinner | 3.00 | 1.50 |
| 114 | Ken Aspromonte | 3.00 | 1.50 |
| 115 | Fork & Knuckler (Roy Face, Hoyt Wilhelm) | 4.00 | 2.00 |
| 116 | Jim Rivera | 3.00 | 1.50 |
| 117 | Tom Borland | 3.00 | 1.50 |
| 118 | Bob Bruce | 3.00 | 1.50 |
| 119 | *Chico Cardenas* | 3.00 | 1.50 |
| 120 | Duke Carmel | 3.00 | 1.50 |
| 121 | Camilo Carreon | 3.00 | 1.50 |
| 122 | Don Dillard | 3.00 | 1.50 |
| 123 | Dan Dobbek | 3.00 | 1.50 |
| 124 | Jim Donohue | 3.00 | 1.50 |
| 125 | *Dick Ellsworth* | 3.00 | 1.50 |
| 126 | *Chuck Estrada* | 3.00 | 1.50 |
| 127 | Ronnie Hansen | 3.00 | 1.50 |
| 128 | Bill Harris | 3.00 | 1.50 |
| 129 | Bob Hartman | 3.00 | 1.50 |
| 130 | Frank Herrera | 3.00 | 1.50 |
| 131 | Ed Hobaugh | 3.00 | 1.50 |
| 132 | *Frank Howard* | 18.00 | 9.00 |
| 133 | *Manuel Javier* | 3.00 | 1.50 |
| 134 | Deron Johnson | 3.00 | 1.50 |
| 135 | Ken Johnson | 3.00 | 1.50 |
| 136 | *Jim Kaat* | 35.00 | 17.50 |
| 137 | Lou Klimchock | 3.00 | 1.50 |
| 138 | *Art Mahaffey* | 3.00 | 1.50 |
| 139 | Carl Mathias | 3.00 | 1.50 |
| 140 | Julio Navarro | 3.00 | 1.50 |
| 141 | Jim Proctor | 3.00 | 1.50 |
| 142 | Bill Short | 3.00 | 1.50 |
| 143 | Al Spangler | 3.00 | 1.50 |
| 144 | Al Stieglitz | 3.00 | 1.50 |
| 145 | Jim Umbricht | 3.00 | 1.50 |
| 146 | Ted Wieand | 3.00 | 1.50 |
| 147 | Bob Will | 3.00 | 1.50 |
| 148 | *Carl Yastrzemski* | 300.00 | 150.00 |
| 149 | Bob Nieman | 3.00 | 1.50 |
| 150 | Billy Pierce | 3.25 | 1.75 |
| 151 | Giants Team/Checklist 177-264 | 6.00 | 3.00 |
| 152 | Gail Harris | 3.00 | 1.50 |
| 153 | Bobby Thomson | 3.00 | 1.50 |
| 154 | Jim Davenport | 3.00 | 1.50 |
| 155 | Charlie Neal | 3.00 | 1.50 |
| 156 | Art Ceccarelli | 3.00 | 1.50 |
| 157 | Rocky Nelson | 3.00 | 1.50 |
| 158 | Wes Covington | 3.00 | 1.50 |
| 159 | Jim Piersall | 3.00 | 1.50 |
| 160 | Rival All Stars (Ken Boyer, Mickey Mantle) | 50.00 | 25.00 |
| 161 | Ray Narleski | 3.00 | 1.50 |
| 162 | Sammy Taylor | 3.00 | 1.50 |
| 163 | Hector Lopez | 3.00 | 1.50 |
| 164 | Reds Team/Checklist 89-176 | 7.00 | 3.50 |
| 165 | Jack Sanford | 3.00 | 1.50 |
| 166 | Chuck Essegian | 3.00 | 1.50 |
| 167 | Valmy Thomas | 3.00 | 1.50 |
| 168 | Alex Grammas | 3.00 | 1.50 |
| 169 | Jake Striker | 3.00 | 1.50 |
| 170 | Del Crandall | 3.00 | 1.50 |
| 171 | Johnny Groth | 3.00 | 1.50 |
| 172 | Willie Kirkland | 3.00 | 1.50 |
| 173 | Billy Martin | 10.00 | 5.00 |
| 174 | Indians Team/Checklist 89-176 | 6.00 | 3.00 |
| 175 | Pedro Ramos | 3.00 | 1.50 |
| 176 | Vada Pinson | 3.25 | 1.75 |
| 177 | Johnny Kucks | 3.00 | 1.50 |
| 178 | Woody Held | 3.00 | 1.50 |
| 179 | Rip Coleman | 3.00 | 1.50 |
| 180 | Harry Simpson | 3.00 | 1.50 |
| 181 | Billy Loes | 3.00 | 1.50 |
| 182 | Glen Hobbie | 3.00 | 1.50 |
| 183 | Eli Grba | 3.00 | 1.50 |
| 184 | Gary Geiger | 3.00 | 1.50 |
| 185 | Jim Owens | 3.00 | 1.50 |
| 186 | Dave Sisler | 3.00 | 1.50 |
| 187 | Jay Hook | 3.00 | 1.50 |
| 188 | Dick Williams | 3.00 | 1.50 |
| 189 | Don McMahon | 3.00 | 1.50 |
| 190 | Gene Woodling | 3.00 | 1.50 |
| 191 | Johnny Klippstein | 3.00 | 1.50 |
| 192 | Danny O'Connell | 3.00 | 1.50 |
| 193 | Dick Hyde | 3.00 | 1.50 |
| 194 | Bobby Gene Smith | 3.00 | 1.50 |
| 195 | Lindy McDaniel | 3.00 | 1.50 |
| 196 | Andy Carey | 3.00 | 1.50 |
| 197 | Ron Kline | 3.00 | 1.50 |
| 198 | Jerry Lynch | 3.00 | 1.50 |
| 199 | Dick Donovan | 3.00 | 1.50 |
| 200 | Willie Mays | 110.00 | 55.00 |
| 201 | Larry Osborne | 3.00 | 1.50 |
| 202 | Fred Kipp | 3.00 | 1.50 |
| 203 | Sammy White | 3.00 | 1.50 |
| 204 | Ryne Duren | 2.50 | 1.25 |
| 205 | Johnny Logan | 3.00 | 1.50 |
| 206 | Claude Osteen | 3.00 | 1.50 |
| 207 | Bob Boyd | 3.00 | 1.50 |
| 208 | White Sox Team Checklist 177-264 | 6.00 | 3.00 |
| 209 | Ron Blackburn | 3.00 | 1.50 |
| 210 | Harmon Killebrew | 25.00 | 12.50 |
| 211 | Taylor Phillips | 3.00 | 1.50 |
| 212 | Walt Alston | 6.00 | 3.00 |

| | | NR MT | EX |
|---|---|---|---|
| 213 | Chuck Dressen | 3.00 | 1.50 |
| 214 | Jimmie Dykes | 3.00 | 1.50 |
| 215 | Bob Elliott | 3.00 | 1.50 |
| 216 | Joe Gordon | 3.00 | 1.50 |
| 217 | Charley Grimm | 3.00 | 1.50 |
| 218 | Solly Hemus | 3.00 | 1.50 |
| 219 | Fred Hutchinson | 3.00 | 1.50 |
| 220 | Billy Jurges | 3.00 | 1.50 |
| 221 | Cookie Lavagetto | 3.00 | 1.50 |
| 222 | Al Lopez | 5.00 | 2.50 |
| 223 | Danny Murtaugh | 3.00 | 1.50 |
| 224 | Paul Richards | 3.00 | 1.50 |
| 225 | Bill Rigney | 3.00 | 1.50 |
| 226 | Eddie Sawyer | 3.00 | 1.50 |
| 227 | Casey Stengel | 15.00 | 7.50 |
| 228 | Ernie Johnson | 3.00 | 1.50 |
| 229 | Joe Morgan | 3.00 | 1.50 |
| 230 | Mound Magicians (Bob Buhl, Lou Burdette, Warren Spahn) | 6.00 | 3.00 |
| 231 | Hal Naragon | 3.00 | 1.50 |
| 232 | Jim Busby | 3.00 | 1.50 |
| 233 | Don Elston | 3.00 | 1.50 |
| 234 | Don Demeter | 3.00 | 1.50 |
| 235 | Gus Bell | 3.00 | 1.50 |
| 236 | Dick Ricketts | 3.00 | 1.50 |
| 237 | Elmer Valo | 3.00 | 1.50 |
| 238 | Danny Kravitz | 3.00 | 1.50 |
| 239 | Joe Shipley | 3.00 | 1.50 |
| 240 | Luis Aparicio | 10.00 | 5.00 |
| 241 | Albie Pearson | 3.00 | 1.50 |
| 242 | Cards Team/Checklist 265-352 | 6.00 | 3.00 |
| 243 | Bubba Phillips | 3.00 | 1.50 |
| 244 | Hal Griggs | 3.00 | 1.50 |
| 245 | Eddie Yost | 3.00 | 1.50 |
| 246 | Lee Maye | 3.00 | 1.50 |
| 247 | Gil McDougald | 4.50 | 2.25 |
| 248 | Del Rice | 3.00 | 1.50 |
| 249 | *Earl Wilson* | 3.00 | 1.50 |
| 250 | Stan Musial | 110.00 | 55.00 |
| 251 | Bobby Malkmus | 3.00 | 1.50 |
| 252 | Ray Herbert | 3.00 | 1.50 |
| 253 | Eddie Bressoud | 3.00 | 1.50 |
| 254 | Arnie Portocarrero | 3.00 | 1.50 |
| 255 | Jim Gilliam | 3.25 | 1.75 |
| 256 | Dick Brown | 3.00 | 1.50 |
| 257 | Gordy Coleman | 3.00 | 1.50 |
| 258 | Dick Groat | 4.00 | 2.00 |
| 259 | George Altman | 3.00 | 1.50 |
| 260 | Power Plus (Rocky Colavito, Tito Francona) | 3.00 | 1.50 |
| 261 | Pete Burnside | 3.00 | 1.50 |
| 262 | Hank Bauer | 3.00 | 1.50 |
| 263 | Darrell Johnson | 3.00 | 1.50 |
| 264 | Robin Roberts | 12.00 | 6.00 |
| 265 | Rip Repulski | 3.00 | 1.50 |
| 266 | Joe Jay | 3.00 | 1.50 |
| 267 | Jim Marshall | 3.00 | 1.50 |
| 268 | Al Worthington | 3.00 | 1.50 |
| 269 | Gene Green | 3.00 | 1.50 |
| 270 | Bob Turley | 3.25 | 1.75 |
| 271 | Julio Becquer | 3.00 | 1.50 |
| 272 | Fred Green | 3.00 | 1.50 |
| 273 | Neil Chrisley | 3.00 | 1.50 |
| 274 | Tom Acker | 3.00 | 1.50 |

| | | NR MT | EX |
|---|---|---|---|
| 275 | Curt Flood | 3.00 | 1.50 |
| 276 | Ken McBride | 3.00 | 1.50 |
| 277 | Harry Bright | 3.00 | 1.50 |
| 278 | Stan Williams | 3.00 | 1.50 |
| 279 | Chuck Tanner | 2.50 | 1.25 |
| 280 | Frank Sullivan | 3.00 | 1.50 |
| 281 | Ray Boone | 3.00 | 1.50 |
| 282 | Joe Nuxhall | 3.00 | 1.50 |
| 283 | John Blanchard | 2.75 | 1.50 |
| 284 | Don Gross | 3.00 | 1.50 |
| 285 | Harry Anderson | 3.00 | 1.50 |
| 286 | Ray Semproch | 3.00 | 1.50 |
| 287 | Felipe Alou | 2.50 | 1.25 |
| 288 | Bob Mabe | 3.00 | 1.50 |
| 289 | Willie Jones | 3.00 | 1.50 |
| 290 | Jerry Lumpe | 3.00 | 1.50 |
| 291 | Bob Keegan | 3.00 | 1.50 |
| 292 | Dodger Backstops (Joe Pignatano, John Roseboro) | 3.00 | 1.50 |
| 293 | Gene Conley | 3.00 | 1.50 |
| 294 | Tony Taylor | 3.00 | 1.50 |
| 295 | Gil Hodges | 18.00 | 9.00 |
| 296 | Nelson Chittum | 3.00 | 1.50 |
| 297 | Reno Bertoia | 3.00 | 1.50 |
| 298 | George Witt | 3.00 | 1.50 |
| 299 | Earl Torgeson | 3.00 | 1.50 |
| 300 | Hank Aaron | 125.00 | 67.00 |
| 301 | Jerry Davie | 3.00 | 1.50 |
| 302 | Phillies Team/Checklist 353-429 | 7.00 | 3.50 |
| 303 | Billy O'Dell | 3.00 | 1.50 |
| 304 | Joe Ginsberg | 3.00 | 1.50 |
| 305 | Richie Ashburn | 7.00 | 3.50 |
| 306 | Frank Baumann | 3.00 | 1.50 |
| 307 | Gene Oliver | 3.00 | 1.50 |
| 308 | Dick Hall | 3.00 | 1.50 |
| 309 | Bob Hale | 3.00 | 1.50 |
| 310 | Frank Malzone | 3.00 | 1.50 |
| 311 | Raul Sanchez | 3.00 | 1.50 |
| 312 | Charlie Lau | 3.00 | 1.50 |
| 313 | Turk Lown | 3.00 | 1.50 |
| 314 | Chico Fernandez | 3.00 | 1.50 |
| 315 | Bobby Shantz | 3.25 | 1.75 |
| 316 | *Willie McCovey* | 200.00 | 100.00 |
| 317 | Pumpsie Green | 3.00 | 1.50 |
| 318 | Jim Baxes | 3.00 | 1.50 |
| 319 | Joe Koppe | 3.00 | 1.50 |
| 320 | Bob Allison | 3.25 | 1.75 |
| 321 | Ron Fairly | 3.00 | 1.50 |
| 322 | Willie Tasby | 3.00 | 1.50 |
| 323 | Johnny Romano | 3.00 | 1.50 |
| 324 | Jim Perry | 2.50 | 1.25 |
| 325 | Jim O'Toole | 3.00 | 1.50 |
| 326 | Bob Clemente | 110.00 | 55.00 |
| 327 | *Ray Sadecki* | 3.25 | 1.75 |
| 328 | Earl Battey | 3.00 | 1.50 |
| 329 | Zack Monroe | 3.25 | 1.75 |
| 330 | Harvey Kuenn | 3.00 | 1.50 |
| 331 | Henry Mason | 3.00 | 1.50 |
| 332 | Yankees Team Checklist 265-352 | 20.00 | 10.00 |
| 333 | Danny McDevitt | 3.00 | 1.50 |
| 334 | Ted Abernathy | 3.00 | 1.50 |
| 335 | Red Schoendienst | 15.00 | 7.50 |
| 336 | Ike Delock | 3.00 | 1.50 |

| | | NR MT | EX |
|---|---|---|---|
| 337 | Cal Neeman | 3.00 | 1.50 |
| 338 | Ray Monzant | 3.00 | 1.50 |
| 339 | Harry Chiti | 3.00 | 1.50 |
| 340 | Harvey Haddix | 3.25 | 1.75 |
| 341 | Carroll Hardy | 3.00 | 1.50 |
| 342 | Casey Wise | 3.00 | 1.50 |
| 343 | Sandy Koufax | 110.00 | 55.00 |
| 344 | Clint Courtney | 3.00 | 1.50 |
| 345 | Don Newcombe | 2.50 | 1.25 |
| 346 | J.C. Martin (photo actually Gary Peters) | 3.00 | 1.50 |
| 347 | Ed Bouchee | 3.00 | 1.50 |
| 348 | Barry Shetrone | 3.00 | 1.50 |
| 349 | Moe Drabowsky | 3.00 | 1.50 |
| 350 | Mickey Mantle | 375.00 | 175.00 |
| 351 | Don Nottebart | 3.00 | 1.50 |
| 352 | Cincy Clouters (Gus Bell, Jerry Lynch, Frank Robinson) | 5.00 | 2.50 |
| 353 | Don Larsen | 3.25 | 1.75 |
| 354 | Bob Lillis | 3.00 | 1.50 |
| 355 | Bill White | 3.00 | 1.50 |
| 356 | Joe Amalfitano | 3.00 | 1.50 |
| 357 | Al Schroll | 3.00 | 1.50 |
| 358 | Joe DeMaestri | 3.25 | 1.75 |
| 359 | Buddy Gilbert | 3.00 | 1.50 |
| 360 | Herb Score | 2.50 | 1.25 |
| 361 | Bob Oldis | 3.00 | 1.50 |
| 362 | Russ Kemmerer | 3.00 | 1.50 |
| 363 | Gene Stephens | 3.00 | 1.50 |
| 364 | Paul Foytack | 3.00 | 1.50 |
| 365 | Minnie Minoso | 3.00 | 1.50 |
| 366 | *Dallas Green* | 3.25 | 1.75 |
| 367 | Bill Tuttle | 3.00 | 1.50 |
| 368 | Daryl Spencer | 3.00 | 1.50 |
| 369 | Billy Hoeft | 3.00 | 1.50 |
| 370 | Bill Skowron | 6.00 | 3.00 |
| 371 | Bud Byerly | 3.00 | 1.50 |
| 372 | Frank House | 3.00 | 1.50 |
| 373 | Don Hoak | 3.00 | 1.50 |
| 374 | Bob Buhl | 3.00 | 1.50 |
| 375 | Dale Long | 3.00 | 1.50 |
| 376 | Johnny Briggs | 3.00 | 1.50 |
| 377 | Roger Maris | 120.00 | 60.00 |
| 378 | Stu Miller | 3.00 | 1.50 |
| 379 | Red Wilson | 3.00 | 1.50 |
| 380 | Bob Shaw | 3.00 | 1.50 |
| 381 | Braves Team/Checklist 353-429 | 7.00 | 3.50 |
| 382 | Ted Bowsfield | 3.00 | 1.50 |
| 383 | Leon Wagner | 3.00 | 1.50 |
| 384 | Don Cardwell | 3.00 | 1.50 |
| 385 | World Series Game 1 (Neal Steals Second) | 4.00 | 2.00 |
| 386 | World Series Game 2 (Neal Belts 2nd Homer) | 4.00 | 2.00 |
| 387 | World Series Game 3 (Furillo Breaks Up Game) | 4.00 | 2.00 |
| 388 | World Series Game 4 (Hodges' Winning Homer) | 5.00 | 2.50 |
| 389 | World Series Game 5 (Luis Swipes Base) | 5.00 | 2.50 |
| 390 | World Series Game 6 (Scrambling After Ball) | 4.00 | 2.00 |

| | | NR MT | EX |
|---|---|---|---|
| 391 | World Series Summary (The Champs Celebrate) | 4.00 | 2.00 |
| 392 | Tex Clevenger | 3.00 | 1.50 |
| 393 | Smoky Burgess | 2.50 | 1.25 |
| 394 | Norm Larker | 3.00 | 1.50 |
| 395 | Hoyt Wilhelm | 15.00 | 7.50 |
| 396 | Steve Bilko | 3.00 | 1.50 |
| 397 | Don Blasingame | 3.00 | 1.50 |
| 398 | Mike Cuellar | 3.25 | 1.75 |
| 399 | Young Hill Stars (Jack Fisher, Milt Pappas, Jerry Walker) | 3.25 | 1.75 |
| 400 | Rocky Colavito | 15.00 | 7.50 |
| 401 | Bob Duliba | 3.00 | 1.50 |
| 402 | Dick Stuart | 3.00 | 1.50 |
| 403 | Ed Sadowski | 3.00 | 1.50 |
| 404 | Bob Rush | 3.00 | 1.50 |
| 405 | Bobby Richardson | 6.00 | 3.00 |
| 406 | Billy Klaus | 3.00 | 1.50 |
| 407 | *Gary Peters* (photo actually J.C. Martin) | 3.25 | 1.75 |
| 408 | Carl Furillo | 4.00 | 2.00 |
| 409 | Ron Samford | 3.00 | 1.50 |
| 410 | Sam Jones | 3.00 | 1.50 |
| 411 | Ed Bailey | 3.00 | 1.50 |
| 412 | Bob Anderson | 3.00 | 1.50 |
| 413 | A's Team/Checklist 430 495 | 7.00 | 3.50 |
| 414 | Don Williams | 3.00 | 1.50 |
| 415 | Bob Cerv | 3.00 | 1.50 |
| 416 | Humberto Robinson | 3.00 | 1.50 |
| 417 | Chuck Cottier | 3.00 | 1.50 |
| 418 | Don Mossi | 3.00 | 1.50 |
| 419 | George Crowe | 3.00 | 1.50 |
| 420 | Ed Mathews | 35.00 | 17.50 |
| 421 | Duke Maas | 3.25 | 1.75 |
| 422 | Johnny Powers | 3.00 | 1.50 |
| 423 | Ed Fitz Gerald | 3.00 | 1.50 |
| 424 | Pete Whisenant | 3.00 | 1.50 |
| 425 | Johnny Podres | 3.00 | 1.50 |
| 426 | Ron Jackson | 3.00 | 1.50 |
| 427 | Al Grunwald | 3.00 | 1.50 |
| 428 | Al Smith | 3.00 | 1.50 |
| 429 | American League Kings (Nellie Fox, Harvey Kuenn) | 3.25 | 1.75 |
| 430 | Art Ditmar | 3.00 | 1.50 |
| 431 | Andre Rodgers | 3.00 | 1.50 |
| 432 | Chuck Stobbs | 3.00 | 1.50 |
| 433 | Irv Noren | 3.00 | 1.50 |
| 434 | Brooks Lawrence | 3.00 | 1.50 |
| 435 | Gene Freese | 3.00 | 1.50 |
| 436 | Marv Throneberry | 3.25 | 1.75 |
| 437 | Bob Friend | 2.50 | 1.25 |
| 438 | Jim Coker | 3.00 | 1.50 |
| 439 | Tom Brewer | 3.00 | 1.50 |
| 440 | Jim Lemon | 3.00 | 1.50 |
| 441 | Gary Bell | 4.00 | 2.00 |
| 442 | Joe Pignatano | 4.00 | 2.00 |
| 443 | Charlie Maxwell | 4.00 | 2.00 |
| 444 | Jerry Kindall | 4.00 | 2.00 |
| 445 | Warren Spahn | 40.00 | 20.00 |
| 446 | Ellis Burton | 4.00 | 2.00 |
| 447 | Ray Moore | 4.00 | 2.00 |
| 448 | *Jim Gentile* | 4.00 | 2.00 |

| | | NR MT | EX |
|---|---|---|---|
| 449 | Jim Brosnan | 5.00 | 2.50 |
| 450 | Orlando Cepeda | 15.00 | 7.50 |
| 451 | Curt Simmons | 4.00 | 2.00 |
| 452 | Ray Webster | 4.00 | 2.00 |
| 453 | Vern Law | 4.50 | 2.25 |
| 454 | Hal Woodeshick | 4.00 | 2.00 |
| 455 | Orioles Coaches (Harry Brecheen, Lum Harris, Eddie Robinson) | 5.00 | 2.50 |
| 456 | Red Sox Coaches (Del Baker, Billy Herman, Sal Maglie, Rudy York) | 4.00 | 2.00 |
| 457 | Cubs Coaches (Lou Klein, Charlie Root, Elvin Tappe) | 5.00 | 2.50 |
| 458 | White Sox Coaches (Ray Berres, Johnny Cooney, Tony Cuccinello, Don Gutteridge) | 5.00 | 2.50 |
| 459 | Reds Coaches (Cot Deal, Wally Moses, Reggie Otero) | 5.00 | 2.50 |
| 460 | Indians Coaches (Mel Harder, Red Kress, Bob Lemon, Jo-Jo White) | 4.00 | 2.00 |
| 461 | Tigers Coaches (Luke Appling, Tom Ferrick, Billy Hitchcock) | 4.00 | 2.00 |
| 462 | A's Coaches (Walker Cooper, Fred Fitzsimmons, Don Heffner) | 5.00 | 2.50 |
| 463 | Dodgers Coaches (Joe Becker, Bobby Bragan, Greg Mulleavy, Pete Reiser) | 4.00 | 2.00 |
| 464 | Braves Coaches (George Myatt, Andy Pafko, Bob Scheffing, Whitlow Wyatt) | 5.00 | 2.50 |
| 465 | Yankees Coaches (Frank Crosetti, Bill Dickey, Ralph Houk, Ed Lopat) | 11.00 | 5.50 |
| 466 | Phillies Coaches (Dick Carter, Andy Cohen, Ken Silvestri) | 5.00 | 2.50 |
| 467 | Pirates Coaches (Bill Burwell, Sam Narron, Frank Oceak, Mickey Vernon) | 4.00 | 2.00 |
| 468 | Cardinals Coaches (Ray Katt, Johnny Keane, Howie Pollet, Harry Walker) | 5.00 | 2.50 |
| 469 | Giants Coaches (Salty Parker, Bill Posedel, Wes Westrum) | 5.00 | 2.50 |
| 470 | Senators Coaches (Ellis Clary, Sam Mele, Bob Swift) | 5.00 | 2.50 |
| 471 | Ned Garver | 4.00 | 2.00 |
| 472 | Al Dark | 4.50 | 2.25 |
| 473 | Al Cicotte | 4.00 | 2.00 |
| 474 | Haywood Sullivan | 5.00 | 2.50 |
| 475 | Don Drysdale | 30.00 | 15.00 |
| 476 | Lou Johnson | 4.00 | 2.00 |
| 477 | Don Ferrarese | 4.00 | 2.00 |
| 478 | Frank Torre | 4.00 | 2.00 |
| 479 | Georges Maranda | 4.00 | 2.00 |

| | | NR MT | EX |
|---|---|---|---|
| 480 | Yogi Berra | 80.00 | 40.00 |
| 481 | Wes Stock | 4.00 | 2.00 |
| 482 | Frank Bolling | 4.00 | 2.00 |
| 483 | Camilo Pascual | 5.00 | 2.50 |
| 484 | Pirates Team/Checklist 430-495 | 15.00 | 7.50 |
| 485 | Ken Boyer | 4.50 | 2.25 |
| 486 | Bobby Del Greco | 4.00 | 2.00 |
| 487 | Tom Sturdivant | 4.00 | 2.00 |
| 488 | Norm Cash | 5.00 | 2.50 |
| 489 | Steve Ridzik | 4.00 | 2.00 |
| 490 | Frank Robinson | 50.00 | 25.00 |
| 491 | Mel Roach | 4.00 | 2.00 |
| 492 | Larry Jackson | 4.00 | 2.00 |
| 493 | Duke Snider | 50.00 | 25.00 |
| 494 | Orioles Team/Checklist 496-572 | 7.00 | 3.50 |
| 495 | Sherm Lollar | 4.00 | 2.00 |
| 496 | Bill Virdon | 4.00 | 2.00 |
| 497 | John Tsitouris | 4.00 | 2.00 |
| 498 | Al Pilarcik | 4.00 | 2.00 |
| 499 | Johnny James | 4.00 | 2.00 |
| 500 | Johnny Temple | 4.00 | 2.00 |
| 501 | Bob Schmidt | 4.00 | 2.00 |
| 502 | Jim Bunning | 12.00 | 6.00 |
| 503 | Don Lee | 4.00 | 2.00 |
| 504 | Seth Morehead | 4.00 | 2.00 |
| 505 | Ted Kluszewski | 6.00 | 3.00 |
| 506 | Lee Walls | 4.00 | 2.00 |
| 507 | Dick Stigman | 10.00 | 5.00 |
| 508 | Billy Consolo | 10.00 | 5.00 |
| 509 | *Tommy Davis* | 25.00 | 12.50 |
| 510 | Jerry Staley | 10.00 | 5.00 |
| 511 | Ken Walters | 10.00 | 5.00 |
| 512 | Joe Gibbon | 10.00 | 5.00 |
| 513 | Cubs Team/Checklist 496-572 | 25.00 | 12.50 |
| 514 | *Steve Barber* | 11.00 | 5.50 |
| 515 | Stan Lopata | 10.00 | 5.00 |
| 516 | Marty Kutyna | 10.00 | 5.00 |
| 517 | Charley James | 10.00 | 5.00 |
| 518 | *Tony Gonzalez* | 11.00 | 5.50 |
| 519 | Ed Roebuck | 10.00 | 5.00 |
| 520 | Don Buddin | 10.00 | 5.00 |
| 521 | Mike Lee | 10.00 | 5.00 |
| 522 | Ken Hunt | 11.00 | 5.50 |
| 523 | *Clay Dalrymple* | 11.00 | 5.50 |
| 524 | Bill Henry | 10.00 | 5.00 |
| 525 | Marv Breeding | 10.00 | 5.00 |
| 526 | Paul Giel | 10.00 | 5.00 |
| 527 | Jose Valdivielso | 10.00 | 5.00 |
| 528 | Ben Johnson | 10.00 | 5.00 |
| 529 | Norm Sherry | 10.00 | 5.00 |
| 530 | Mike McCormick | 11.00 | 5.50 |
| 531 | Sandy Amoros | 10.00 | 5.00 |
| 532 | Mike Garcia | 10.00 | 5.00 |
| 533 | Lu Clinton | 10.00 | 5.00 |
| 534 | Ken MacKenzie | 10.00 | 5.00 |
| 535 | Whitey Lockman | 10.00 | 5.00 |
| 536 | Wynn Hawkins | 10.00 | 5.00 |
| 537 | Red Sox Team Checklist 496-572 | 25.00 | 12.50 |
| 538 | Frank Barnes | 10.00 | 5.00 |
| 539 | Gene Baker | 10.00 | 5.00 |
| 540 | Jerry Walker | 10.00 | 5.00 |
| 541 | Tony Curry | 10.00 | 5.00 |
| 542 | Ken Hamlin | 10.00 | 5.00 |

| | | NR MT | EX |
|---|---|---|---|
| 543 | Elio Chacon | 10.00 | 5.00 |
| 544 | Bill Monbouquette | | |
| | | 11.00 | 5.50 |
| 545 | Carl Sawatski | 10.00 | 5.00 |
| 546 | Hank Aguirre | 10.00 | 5.00 |
| 547 | Bob Aspromonte | 11.00 | 5.50 |
| 548 | Don Mincher | 11.00 | 5.50 |
| 549 | John Buzhardt | 10.00 | 5.00 |
| 550 | Jim Landis | 10.00 | 5.00 |
| 551 | Ed Rakow | 10.00 | 5.00 |
| 552 | Walt Bond | 10.00 | 5.00 |
| 553 | Bill Skowron AS | 12.00 | 6.00 |
| 554 | Willie McCovey AS | | |
| | | 45.00 | 22.00 |
| 555 | Nellie Fox AS | 18.00 | 9.00 |
| 556 | Charlie Neal AS | 11.00 | 5.50 |
| 557 | Frank Malzone AS | 11.00 | 5.50 |
| 558 | Eddie Mathews AS | | |
| | | 25.00 | 12.50 |
| 559 | Luis Aparicio AS | 18.00 | 9.00 |
| 560 | Ernie Banks AS | 40.00 | 20.00 |
| 561 | Al Kaline AS | 40.00 | 20.00 |
| 562 | Joe Cunningham AS | | |
| | | 11.00 | 5.50 |
| 563 | Mickey Mantle AS | | |
| | | 250.00 | 125.00 |
| 564 | Willie Mays AS | 100.00 | 50.00 |
| 565 | Roger Maris AS | 100.00 | 50.00 |
| 566 | Hank Aaron AS | 100.00 | 50.00 |
| 567 | Sherm Lollar AS | 11.00 | 5.50 |
| 568 | Del Crandall AS | 11.00 | 5.50 |
| 569 | Camilo Pascual AS | | |
| | | 11.00 | 5.50 |
| 570 | Don Drysdale AS | 20.00 | 10.00 |
| 571 | Billy Pierce AS | 11.00 | 5.50 |
| 572 | Johnny Antonelli AS | | |
| | | 20.00 | 7.00 |
| ---- | Elect Your Favorite Rookie Insert (paper stock, no date on back) | 15.00 | 7.50 |
| ---- | Hot Iron Transfer Insert (paper stock) | 15.00 | 7.50 |

# 1961 Topps

Except for some of the specialty cards, Topps returned to a vertical format with their 1961 cards. The set is numbered through 598, however only 587 cards were printed. No numbers 426, 587 and 588 were issued. Two cards numbered 463 exist (one a

Braves team card and one a player card of Jack Fisher). Actually, the Braves team card is checklisted as #426. Designs for 1961 are basically large color portraits; the backs return to extensive statistics. A three-panel cartoon highlighting the player's career appears on the card backs. Innovations include numbered checklists, cards for statistical leaders, and 10 "Baseball Thrills" cards. The scarce high numbers are card numbers 523-589.

| | | NR MT | EX |
|---|---|---|---|
| Complete Set: | | 5500.00 | 2750.00 |
| Common Player: 1-370 | | 2.00 | 1.00 |
| Common Player: 371-522 | | | |
| | | 4.00 | 2.00 |
| Common Player: 523-589 | | | |
| | | 25.00 | 12.50 |

| 1 | Dick Groat | 20.00 | 5.00 |
|---|---|---|---|
| 2 | Roger Maris | 175.00 | 87.00 |
| 3 | John Buzhardt | 2.00 | 1.00 |
| 4 | Lenny Green | 2.00 | 1.00 |
| 5 | Johnny Romano | 2.00 | 1.00 |
| 6 | Ed Roebuck | 2.00 | 1.00 |
| 7 | White Sox Team | 4.00 | 2.00 |
| 8 | Dick Williams | 4.00 | 2.00 |
| 9 | Bob Purkey | 2.00 | 1.00 |
| 10 | Brooks Robinson | 30.00 | 15.00 |
| 11 | Curt Simmons | 2.25 | 1.25 |
| 12 | Moe Thacker | 2.00 | 1.00 |
| 13 | Chuck Cottier | 2.00 | 1.00 |
| 14 | Don Mossi | 2.25 | 1.25 |
| 15 | Willie Kirkland | 2.00 | 1.00 |
| 16 | Billy Muffett | 2.00 | 1.00 |
| 17 | Checklist 1-88 | 5.00 | 2.50 |
| 18 | Jim Grant | 2.00 | 1.00 |
| 19 | Cletis Boyer | 2.25 | 1.25 |
| 20 | Robin Roberts | 10.00 | 5.00 |
| 21 | Zorro Versalles | 4.00 | 2.00 |
| 22 | Clem Labine | 2.25 | 1.25 |
| 23 | Don Demeter | 2.00 | 1.00 |
| 24 | Ken Johnson | 2.00 | 1.00 |
| 25 | Red's Heavy Artillery (Gus Bell, Vada Pinson, Frank Robinson) | 6.00 | 3.00 |
| 26 | Wes Stock | 2.00 | 1.00 |
| 27 | Jerry Kindall | 2.00 | 1.00 |
| 28 | Hector Lopez | 4.00 | 2.00 |
| 29 | Don Nottebart | 2.00 | 1.00 |
| 30 | Nellie Fox | 6.00 | 3.00 |
| 31 | Bob Schmidt | 2.00 | 1.00 |
| 32 | Ray Sadecki | 2.00 | 1.00 |
| 33 | Gary Geiger | 2.00 | 1.00 |
| 34 | Wynn Hawkins | 2.00 | 1.00 |
| 35 | Ron Santo | 50.00 | 25.00 |
| 36 | Jack Kralick | 2.00 | 1.00 |
| 37 | Charlie Maxwell | 2.00 | 1.00 |
| 38 | Bob Lillis | 2.00 | 1.00 |
| 39 | Leo Posada | 2.00 | 1.00 |

|  |  | NR MT | EX |
|---|---|---|---|
| 40 | Bob Turley | 4.00 | 2.00 |
| 41 | N.L. Batting Leaders (Bob Clemente, Dick Groat, Norm Larker, Willie Mays) | 4.00 | 2.00 |
| 42 | A.L. Batting Leaders (Minnie Minoso, Pete Runnels, Bill Skowron, Al Smith) | 4.00 | 2.00 |
| 43 | N.L. Home Run Leaders (Hank Aaron, Ernie Banks, Ken Boyer, Eddie Mathews) | 4.00 | 2.00 |
| 44 | A.L. Home Run Leaders (Rocky Colavito, Jim Lemon, Mickey Mantle, Roger Maris) | 30.00 | 15.00 |
| 45 | N.L. E.R.A. Leaders (Ernie Broglio, Don Drysdale, Bob Friend, Mike McCormick, Stan Williams) | 3.25 | 1.75 |
| 46 | A.L. E.R.A. Leaders (Frank Baumann, Hal Brown, Jim Bunning, Art Ditmar) | 4.00 | 2.00 |
| 47 | N.L. Pitching Leaders (Ernie Broglio, Lou Burdette, Vern Law, Warren Spahn) | 3.25 | 1.75 |
| 48 | A.L. Pitching Leaders (Bud Daley, Art Ditmar, Chuck Estrada, Frank Lary, Milt Pappas, Jim Perry) | 4.00 | 2.00 |
| 49 | N.L. Strikeout Leaders (Ernie Broglio, Don Drysdale, Sam Jones, Sandy Koufax) | 4.00 | 2.00 |
| 50 | A.L. Strikeout Leaders (Jim Bunning, Frank Lary, Pedro Ramos, Early Wynn) | 5.00 | 2.50 |
| 51 | Tigers Team | 5.00 | 2.50 |
| 52 | George Crowe | 2.00 | 1.00 |
| 53 | Russ Nixon | 2.00 | 1.00 |
| 54 | Earl Francis | 2.00 | 1.00 |
| 55 | Jim Davenport | 2.00 | 1.00 |
| 56 | Russ Kemmerer | 2.00 | 1.00 |
| 57 | Marv Throneberry | 4.00 | 2.00 |
| 58 | Joe Schaffernoth | 2.00 | 1.00 |
| 59 | Jim Woods | 2.00 | 1.00 |
| 60 | Woodie Held | 2.00 | 1.00 |
| 61 | Ron Piche | 2.00 | 1.00 |
| 62 | Al Pilarcik | 2.00 | 1.00 |
| 63 | Jim Kaat | 9.00 | 4.50 |
| 64 | Alex Grammas | 2.00 | 1.00 |
| 65 | Ted Kluszewski | 4.00 | 2.00 |
| 66 | Bill Henry | 2.00 | 1.00 |
| 67 | Ossie Virgil | 2.00 | 1.00 |
| 68 | Deron Johnson | 4.00 | 2.00 |
| 69 | Earl Wilson | 2.00 | 1.00 |
| 70 | Bill Virdon | 4.00 | 2.00 |
| 71 | Jerry Adair | 2.25 | 1.25 |
| 72 | Stu Miller | 2.00 | 1.00 |
| 73 | Al Spangler | 2.00 | 1.00 |
| 74 | Joe Pignatano | 2.00 | 1.00 |

|  |  | NR MT | EX |
|---|---|---|---|
| 75 | Lindy Shows Larry (Larry Jackson, Lindy McDaniel) | 4.00 | 2.00 |
| 76 | Harry Anderson | 2.00 | 1.00 |
| 77 | Dick Stigman | 2.00 | 1.00 |
| 78 | Lee Walls | 2.00 | 1.00 |
| 79 | Joe Ginsberg | 2.00 | 1.00 |
| 80 | Harmon Killebrew | 25.00 | 12.50 |
| 81 | Tracy Stallard | 2.00 | 1.00 |
| 82 | Joe Christopher | 2.00 | 1.00 |
| 83 | Bob Bruce | 2.00 | 1.00 |
| 84 | Lee Maye | 2.00 | 1.00 |
| 85 | Jerry Walker | 2.00 | 1.00 |
| 86 | Dodgers Team | 5.00 | 2.50 |
| 87 | Joe Amalfitano | 2.00 | 1.00 |
| 88 | Richie Ashburn | 6.00 | 3.00 |
| 89 | Billy Martin | 8.00 | 4.00 |
| 90 | Jerry Staley | 2.00 | 1.00 |
| 91 | Walt Moryn | 2.00 | 1.00 |
| 92 | Hal Naragon | 2.00 | 1.00 |
| 93 | Tony Gonzalez | 2.00 | 1.00 |
| 94 | Johnny Kucks | 2.00 | 1.00 |
| 95 | Norm Cash | 5.00 | 2.50 |
| 96 | Billy O'Dell | 2.00 | 1.00 |
| 97 | Jerry Lynch | 2.00 | 1.00 |
| 98a | Checklist 89-176 (word "Checklist" in red on front) | 7.00 | 3.50 |
| 98b | Checklist 89-176 ("Checklist" in yellow, 98 on back in black) | 5.00 | 2.50 |
| 98c | Checklist 89-176 ("Checklist" in yellow, 98 on back in white) | 7.00 | 3.50 |
| 99 | Don Buddin | 2.00 | 1.00 |
| 100 | Harvey Haddix | 4.00 | 2.00 |
| 101 | Bubba Phillips | 2.00 | 1.00 |
| 102 | Gene Stephens | 2.00 | 1.00 |
| 103 | Ruben Amaro | 2.00 | 1.00 |
| 104 | John Blanchard | 4.00 | 2.00 |
| 105 | Carl Willey | 2.00 | 1.00 |
| 106 | Whitey Herzog | 2.25 | 1.25 |
| 107 | Seth Morehead | 2.00 | 1.00 |
| 108 | Dan Dobbek | 2.00 | 1.00 |
| 109 | Johnny Podres | 2.25 | 1.25 |
| 110 | Vada Pinson | 5.00 | 2.50 |
| 111 | Jack Meyer | 2.00 | 1.00 |
| 112 | Chico Fernandez | 2.00 | 1.00 |
| 113 | Mike Fornieles | 2.00 | 1.00 |
| 114 | Hobie Landrith | 2.00 | 1.00 |
| 115 | Johnny Antonelli | 2.25 | 1.25 |
| 116 | Joe DeMaestri | 4.00 | 2.00 |
| 117 | Dale Long | 2.25 | 1.25 |
| 118 | Chris Cannizzaro | 2.00 | 1.00 |
| 119 | A's Big Armor (Hank Bauer, Jerry Lumpe, Norm Siebern) | 4.00 | 2.00 |
| 120 | Ed Mathews | 30.00 | 15.00 |
| 121 | Eli Grba | 2.00 | 1.00 |
| 122 | Cubs Team | 4.00 | 2.00 |
| 123 | Billy Gardner | 2.00 | 1.00 |
| 124 | J.C. Martin | 2.00 | 1.00 |
| 125 | Steve Barber | 2.00 | 1.00 |
| 126 | Dick Stuart | 2.25 | 1.25 |
| 127 | Ron Kline | 2.00 | 1.00 |
| 128 | Rip Repulski | 2.00 | 1.00 |
| 129 | Ed Hobaugh | 2.00 | 1.00 |

| | | NR MT | EX |
|---|---|---|---|
| 130 | Norm Larker | 2.00 | 1.00 |
| 131 | Paul Richards | 2.25 | 1.25 |
| 132 | Al Lopez | 5.00 | 2.50 |
| 133 | Ralph Houk | 5.00 | 2.50 |
| 134 | Mickey Vernon | 2.25 | 1.25 |
| 135 | Fred Hutchinson | 2.25 | 1.25 |
| 136 | Walt Alston | 4.00 | 2.00 |
| 137 | Chuck Dressen | 2.25 | 1.25 |
| 138 | Danny Murtaugh | 2.25 | 1.25 |
| 139 | Solly Hemus | 2.00 | 1.00 |
| 140 | Gus Triandos | 2.25 | 1.25 |
| 141 | *Billy Williams* | 125.00 | 62.00 |
| 142 | Luis Arroyo | 4.00 | 2.00 |
| 143 | Russ Snyder | 2.00 | 1.00 |
| 144 | Jim Coker | 2.00 | 1.00 |
| 145 | Bob Buhl | 2.25 | 1.25 |
| 146 | Marty Keough | 2.00 | 1.00 |
| 147 | Ed Rakow | 2.00 | 1.00 |
| 148 | Julian Javier | 2.25 | 1.25 |
| 149 | Bob Oldis | 2.00 | 1.00 |
| 150 | Willie Mays | 120.00 | 60.00 |
| 151 | Jim Donohue | 2.00 | 1.00 |
| 152 | Earl Torgeson | 2.00 | 1.00 |
| 153 | Don Lee | 2.00 | 1.00 |
| 154 | Bobby Del Greco | 2.00 | 1.00 |
| 155 | Johnny Temple | 2.00 | 1.00 |
| 156 | Ken Hunt | 2.00 | 1.00 |
| 157 | Cal McLish | 2.00 | 1.00 |
| 158 | Pete Daley | 2.00 | 1.00 |
| 159 | Orioles Team | 4.00 | 2.00 |
| 160 | Whitey Ford | 35.00 | 17.50 |
| 161 | Sherman Jones (photo actually Eddie Fisher) | 2.00 | 1.00 |
| 162 | Jay Hook | 2.00 | 1.00 |
| 163 | Ed Sadowski | 2.00 | 1.00 |
| 164 | Felix Mantilla | 2.00 | 1.00 |
| 165 | Gino Cimoli | 2.00 | 1.00 |
| 166 | Danny Kravitz | 2.00 | 1.00 |
| 167 | Giants Team | 4.00 | 2.00 |
| 168 | Tommy Davis | 5.00 | 2.50 |
| 169 | Don Elston | 2.00 | 1.00 |
| 170 | Al Smith | 2.00 | 1.00 |
| 171 | Paul Foytack | 2.00 | 1.00 |
| 172 | Don Dillard | 2.00 | 1.00 |
| 173 | Beantown Bombers (Jackie Jensen, Frank Malzone, Vic Wertz) | 4.00 | 2.00 |
| 174 | Ray Semproch | 2.00 | 1.00 |
| 175 | Gene Freese | 2.00 | 1.00 |
| 176 | Ken Aspromonte | 2.00 | 1.00 |
| 177 | Don Larsen | 4.00 | 2.00 |
| 178 | Bob Nieman | 2.00 | 1.00 |
| 179 | Joe Koppe | 2.00 | 1.00 |
| 180 | Bobby Richardson | 6.00 | 3.00 |
| 181 | Fred Green | 2.00 | 1.00 |
| 182 | Dave Nicholson | 2.00 | 1.00 |
| 183 | Andre Rodgers | 2.00 | 1.00 |
| 184 | Steve Bilko | 2.00 | 1.00 |
| 185 | Herb Score | 4.00 | 2.00 |
| 186 | Elmer Valo | 2.00 | 1.00 |
| 187 | Billy Klaus | 2.00 | 1.00 |
| 188 | Jim Marshall | 2.00 | 1.00 |
| 189 | Checklist 177-264 | 5.00 | 2.50 |
| 190 | Stan Williams | 2.00 | 1.00 |
| 191 | Mike de la Hoz | 2.00 | 1.00 |
| 192 | Dick Brown | 2.00 | 1.00 |
| 193 | Gene Conley | 2.25 | 1.25 |

| | | NR MT | EX |
|---|---|---|---|
| 194 | Gordy Coleman | 2.00 | 1.00 |
| 195 | Jerry Casale | 2.00 | 1.00 |
| 196 | Ed Bouchee | 2.00 | 1.00 |
| 197 | Dick Hall | 2.00 | 1.00 |
| 198 | Carl Sawatski | 2.00 | 1.00 |
| 199 | Bob Boyd | 2.00 | 1.00 |
| 200 | Warren Spahn | 30.00 | 15.00 |
| 201 | Pete Whisenant | 2.00 | 1.00 |
| 202 | Al Neiger | 2.00 | 1.00 |
| 203 | Eddie Bressoud | 2.00 | 1.00 |
| 204 | Bob Skinner | 2.25 | 1.25 |
| 205 | Bill Pierce | 4.00 | 2.00 |
| 206 | Gene Green | 2.00 | 1.00 |
| 207 | Dodger Southpaws (Sandy Koufax, Johnny Podres) | 15.00 | 7.50 |
| 208 | Larry Osborne | 2.00 | 1.00 |
| 209 | Ken McBride | 2.00 | 1.00 |
| 210 | Pete Runnels | 2.25 | 1.25 |
| 211 | Bob Gibson | 40.00 | 20.00 |
| 212 | Haywood Sullivan | 2.25 | 1.25 |
| 213 | *Bill Stafford* | 4.00 | 2.00 |
| 214 | Danny Murphy | 2.00 | 1.00 |
| 215 | Gus Bell | 2.25 | 1.25 |
| 216 | Ted Bowsfield | 2.00 | 1.00 |
| 217 | Mel Roach | 2.00 | 1.00 |
| 218 | Hal Brown | 2.00 | 1.00 |
| 219 | Gene Mauch | 4.00 | 2.00 |
| 220 | Al Dark | 2.25 | 1.25 |
| 221 | Mike Higgins | 2.00 | 1.00 |
| 222 | Jimmie Dykes | 2.00 | 1.00 |
| 223 | Bob Scheffing | 2.00 | 1.00 |
| 224 | Joe Gordon | 2.25 | 1.25 |
| 225 | Bill Rigney | 2.00 | 1.00 |
| 226 | Harry Lavagetto | 2.00 | 1.00 |
| 227 | Juan Pizarro | 2.00 | 1.00 |
| 228 | Yankees Team | 18.00 | 9.00 |
| 229 | Rudy Hernandez | 2.00 | 1.00 |
| 230 | Don Hoak | 2.25 | 1.25 |
| 231 | Dick Drott | 2.00 | 1.00 |
| 232 | Bill White | 4.00 | 2.00 |
| 233 | Joe Jay | 2.00 | 1.00 |
| 234 | Ted Lepcio | 2.00 | 1.00 |
| 235 | Camilo Pascual | 2.25 | 1.25 |
| 236 | Don Gile | 2.00 | 1.00 |
| 237 | Billy Loes | 2.00 | 1.00 |
| 238 | Jim Gilliam | 4.00 | 2.00 |
| 239 | Dave Sisler | 2.00 | 1.00 |
| 240 | Ron Hansen | 2.00 | 1.00 |
| 241 | Al Cicotte | 2.00 | 1.00 |
| 242 | Hal W. Smith | 2.00 | 1.00 |
| 243 | Frank Lary | 2.25 | 1.25 |
| 244 | Chico Cardenas | 2.25 | 1.25 |
| 245 | Joe Adcock | 4.00 | 2.00 |
| 246 | Bob Davis | 2.00 | 1.00 |
| 247 | Billy Goodman | 2.00 | 1.00 |
| 248 | Ed Keegan | 2.00 | 1.00 |
| 249 | Reds Team | 4.00 | 2.00 |
| 250 | Buc Hill Aces (Roy Face, Vern Law) | 4.00 | 2.00 |
| 251 | Bill Bruton | 2.00 | 1.00 |
| 252 | Bill Short | 4.00 | 2.00 |
| 253 | Sammy Taylor | 2.00 | 1.00 |
| 254 | Ted Sadowski | 2.00 | 1.00 |
| 255 | Vic Power | 2.00 | 1.00 |
| 256 | Billy Hoeft | 2.00 | 1.00 |
| 257 | Carroll Hardy | 2.00 | 1.00 |

| | | NR MT | EX |
|---|---|---|---|
| 258 | Jack Sanford | 2.00 | 1.00 |
| 259 | John Schaive | 2.00 | 1.00 |
| 260 | Don Drysdale | 25.00 | 12.50 |
| 261 | Charlie Lau | 2.25 | 1.25 |
| 262 | Tony Curry | 2.00 | 1.00 |
| 263 | Ken Hamlin | 2.00 | 1.00 |
| 264 | Glen Hobbie | 2.00 | 1.00 |
| 265 | Tony Kubek | 5.00 | 2.50 |
| 266 | Lindy McDaniel | 2.00 | 1.00 |
| 267 | Norm Siebern | 2.25 | 1.25 |
| 268 | Ike DeLock (Delock) | | |
| | | 2.00 | 1.00 |
| 269 | Harry Chiti | 2.00 | 1.00 |
| 270 | Bob Friend | 4.00 | 2.00 |
| 271 | Jim Landis | 2.00 | 1.00 |
| 272 | Tom Morgan | 2.00 | 1.00 |
| 273 | Checklist 265-352 | 5.00 | 2.50 |
| 274 | Gary Bell | 2.00 | 1.00 |
| 275 | Gene Woodling | 2.25 | 1.25 |
| 276 | Ray Rippelmeyer | 2.00 | 1.00 |
| 277 | Hank Foiles | 2.00 | 1.00 |
| 278 | Don McMahon | 2.00 | 1.00 |
| 279 | Jose Pagan | 2.00 | 1.00 |
| 280 | Frank Howard | 4.00 | 2.00 |
| 281 | Frank Sullivan | 2.00 | 1.00 |
| 282 | Faye Throneberry | 2.00 | 1.00 |
| 283 | Bob Anderson | 2.00 | 1.00 |
| 284 | Dick Gernert | 2.00 | 1.00 |
| 285 | Sherm Lollar | 2.25 | 1.25 |
| 286 | George Witt | 2.00 | 1.00 |
| 287 | Carl Yastrzemski | | |
| | | 150.00 | 75.00 |
| 288 | Albie Pearson | 2.00 | 1.00 |
| 289 | Ray Moore | 2.00 | 1.00 |
| 290 | Stan Musial | 75.00 | 37.00 |
| 291 | Tex Clevenger | 2.00 | 1.00 |
| 292 | Jim Baumer | 2.00 | 1.00 |
| 293 | Tom Sturdivant | 2.00 | 1.00 |
| 294 | Don Blasingame | 2.00 | 1.00 |
| 295 | Milt Pappas | 2.25 | 1.25 |
| 296 | Wes Covington | 2.00 | 1.00 |
| 297 | Athletics Team | 4.00 | 2.00 |
| 298 | Jim Golden | 2.00 | 1.00 |
| 299 | Clay Dalrymple | 2.00 | 1.00 |
| 300 | Mickey Mantle | 400.00 | 200.00 |
| 301 | Chet Nichols | 2.00 | 1.00 |
| 302 | Al Heist | 2.00 | 1.00 |
| 303 | Gary Peters | 2.25 | 1.25 |
| 304 | Rocky Nelson | 2.00 | 1.00 |
| 305 | Mike McCormick | 2.25 | 1.25 |
| 306 | World Series Game 1 (Virdon Saves Game) | 5.00 | 2.50 |
| 307 | World Series Game 2 (Mantle Slams 2 Homers) | | |
| | | 30.00 | 15.00 |
| 308 | World Series Game 3 (Richardson Is Hero) | 4.00 | 2.00 |
| 309 | World Series Game 4 (Cimoli Is Safe In Crucial Play) | 5.00 | 2.50 |
| 310 | World Series Game 5 (Face Saves the Day) | 5.00 | 2.50 |
| 311 | World Series Game 6 (Ford Pitches Second Shutout) | 5.00 | 2.50 |
| 312 | World Series Game 7 (Mazeroski's Homer Wins | | |

| | | NR MT | EX |
|---|---|---|---|
| | It!) | 5.00 | 2.50 |
| 313 | World Series Summary (The Winners Celebrate) | | |
| | | 5.00 | 2.50 |
| 314 | Bob Miller | 2.00 | 1.00 |
| 315 | Earl Battey | 2.00 | 1.25 |
| 316 | Bobby Gene Smith | 2.00 | 1.00 |
| 317 | *Jim Brewer* | 2.25 | 1.25 |
| 318 | Danny O'Connell | 2.00 | 1.00 |
| 319 | Valmy Thomas | 2.00 | 1.00 |
| 320 | Lou Burdette | 4.00 | 2.00 |
| 321 | Marv Breeding | 2.00 | 1.00 |
| 322 | Bill Kunkel | 2.00 | 1.00 |
| 323 | Sammy Esposito | 2.00 | 1.00 |
| 324 | Hank Aguirre | 2.00 | 1.00 |
| 325 | Wally Moon | 2.25 | 1.25 |
| 326 | Dave Hillman | 2.00 | 1.00 |
| 327 | *Matty Alou* | 4.00 | 1.00 |
| 328 | Jim O'Toole | 2.00 | 1.00 |
| 329 | Julio Becquer | 2.00 | 1.00 |
| 330 | Rocky Colavito | 5.00 | 2.50 |
| 331 | Ned Garver | 2.00 | 1.00 |
| 332 | Dutch Dotterer (photo actually Tommy Dotterer) | | |
| | | 2.00 | 1.00 |
| 333 | Fritz Brickell | 4.00 | 2.00 |
| 334 | Walt Bond | 5.00 | 1.00 |
| 335 | Frank Bolling | 2.00 | 1.00 |
| 336 | Don Mincher | 2.25 | 1.25 |
| 337 | Al's Aces (Al Lopez, Herb Score, Early Wynn) | 5.00 | 2.50 |
| 338 | Don Landrum | 2.00 | 1.00 |
| 339 | Gene Baker | 2.00 | 1.00 |
| 340 | Vic Wertz | 2.25 | 1.25 |
| 341 | Jim Owens | 2.00 | 1.00 |
| 342 | Clint Courtney | 2.00 | 1.00 |
| 343 | Earl Robinson | 2.00 | 1.00 |
| 344 | Sandy Koufax | 85.00 | 42.00 |
| 345 | Jim Piersall | 4.00 | 2.00 |
| 346 | Howie Nunn | 2.00 | 1.00 |
| 347 | Cardinals Team | 4.00 | 2.00 |
| 348 | Steve Boros | 2.00 | 1.00 |
| 349 | Danny McDevitt | 4.00 | 2.00 |
| 350 | Ernie Banks | 40.00 | 20.00 |
| 351 | Jim King | 2.00 | 1.00 |
| 352 | Bob Shaw | 2.00 | 1.00 |
| 353 | Howie Bedell | 2.00 | 1.00 |
| 354 | Billy Harrell | 2.00 | 1.00 |
| 355 | Bob Allison | 2.25 | 1.25 |
| 356 | Ryne Duren | 2.25 | 1.25 |
| 357 | Daryl Spencer | 2.00 | 1.00 |
| 358 | Earl Averill | 2.00 | 1.00 |
| 359 | Dallas Green | 2.25 | 1.25 |
| 360 | Frank Robinson | 30.00 | 15.00 |
| 361a | Checklist 353-429 ("Topps Baseball" in black on front) | 5.00 | 2.50 |
| 361b | Checklist 353-429 ("Topps Baseball" in yellow) | 6.00 | 3.00 |
| 362 | Frank Funk | 2.00 | 1.00 |
| 363 | John Roseboro | 2.25 | 1.25 |
| 364 | Moe Drabowsky | 2.00 | 1.00 |
| 365 | Jerry Lumpe | 2.25 | 1.25 |
| 366 | Eddie Fisher | 2.00 | 1.00 |
| 367 | Jim Rivera | 2.00 | 1.00 |
| 368 | Bennie Daniels | 2.00 | 1.00 |

| | | NR MT | EX |
|---|---|---|---|
| 369 | Dave Philley | 2.25 | 1.25 |
| 370 | Roy Face | 4.00 | 2.00 |
| 371 | Bill Skowron | 5.00 | 2.50 |
| 372 | Bob Hendley | 4.00 | 2.00 |
| 373 | Red Sox Team | 5.00 | 2.50 |
| 374 | Paul Giel | 4.00 | 2.00 |
| 375 | Ken Boyer | 4.00 | 2.00 |
| 376 | Mike Roarke | 4.00 | 2.00 |
| 377 | Ruben Gomez | 4.00 | 2.00 |
| 378 | Wally Post | 4.00 | 2.00 |
| 379 | Bobby Shantz | 4.00 | 2.00 |
| 380 | Minnie Minoso | 5.00 | 2.50 |
| 381 | Dave Wickersham | 4.00 | 2.00 |
| 382 | Frank Thomas | 4.00 | 2.00 |
| 383 | Frisco First Liners (Mike McCormick, Billy O'Dell, Jack Sanford) | 4.00 | 2.00 |
| 384 | Chuck Essegian | 4.00 | 2.00 |
| 385 | Jim Perry | 4.00 | 2.00 |
| 386 | Joe Hicks | 4.00 | 2.00 |
| 387 | Duke Maas | 4.00 | 2.00 |
| 388 | Bob Clemente | 110.00 | 55.00 |
| 389 | Ralph Terry | 5.00 | 2.50 |
| 390 | Del Crandall | 4.00 | 2.00 |
| 391 | Winston Brown | 4.00 | 2.00 |
| 392 | Reno Bertoia | 4.00 | 2.00 |
| 393 | Batter Bafflers (Don Cardwell, Glen Hobbie) | 4.00 | 2.00 |
| 394 | Ken Walters | 4.00 | 2.00 |
| 395 | Chuck Estrada | 4.00 | 2.00 |
| 396 | Bob Aspromonte | 4.00 | 2.00 |
| 397 | Hal Woodeshick | 4.00 | 2.00 |
| 398 | Hank Bauer | 4.00 | 2.00 |
| 399 | Cliff Cook | 4.00 | 2.00 |
| 400 | Vern Law | 4.00 | 2.00 |
| 401 | Babe Ruth Hits 60th Homer | 25.00 | 12.50 |
| 402 | Larsen Pitches Perfect Game | 15.00 | 7.50 |
| 403 | Brooklyn-Boston Play 26 Inning Tie | 4.00 | 2.00 |
| 404 | Hornsby Tops N.L. With .424 Average | 5.00 | 2.50 |
| 405 | Gehrig Benched After 2,130 Games | 18.00 | 9.00 |
| 406 | Mantle Blasts 565 ft. Home Run | 40.00 | 20.00 |
| 407 | Jack Chesbro Wins 41st Game | 4.00 | 2.00 |
| 408 | Mathewson Strikes Out 267 Batters | 5.00 | 2.50 |
| 409 | Johnson Hurls 3rd Shutout in 4 Days | 4.00 | 2.00 |
| 410 | Haddix Pitches 12 Perfect Innings | 4.00 | 2.00 |
| 411 | Tony Taylor | 4.00 | 2.00 |
| 412 | Larry Sherry | 4.00 | 2.00 |
| 413 | Eddie Yost | 4.00 | 2.00 |
| 414 | Dick Donovan | 4.00 | 2.00 |
| 415 | Hank Aaron | 125.00 | 67.00 |
| 416 | Dick Howser | 8.00 | 4.00 |
| 417 | Juan Marichal | 150.00 | 75.00 |
| 418 | Ed Bailey | 4.00 | 2.00 |
| 419 | Tom Borland | 4.00 | 2.00 |
| 420 | Ernie Broglio | 4.00 | 2.00 |
| 421 | Ty Cline | 4.00 | 2.00 |

| | | NR MT | EX |
|---|---|---|---|
| 422 | Bud Daley | 4.00 | 2.00 |
| 423 | Charlie Neal | 4.00 | 2.00 |
| 424 | Turk Lown | 4.00 | 2.00 |
| 425 | Yogi Berra | 60.00 | 30.00 |
| 426 | Not Issued | | |
| 427 | Dick Ellsworth | 4.00 | 2.00 |
| 428 | Ray Barker | 4.00 | 2.00 |
| 429 | Al Kaline | 40.00 | 20.00 |
| 430 | Bill Mazeroski | 10.00 | 5.00 |
| 431 | Chuck Stobbs | 4.00 | 2.00 |
| 432 | Coot Veal | 4.00 | 2.00 |
| 433 | Art Mahaffey | 4.00 | 2.00 |
| 434 | Tom Brewer | 4.00 | 2.00 |
| 435 | Orlando Cepeda | 10.00 | 5.00 |
| 436 | Jim Maloney | 4.00 | 2.00 |
| 437a | Checklist 430-506 (#440 is Louis Aparicio) | 6.00 | 3.00 |
| 437b | Checklist 430-506 (#440 is Luis Aparicio) | 6.50 | 3.25 |
| 438 | Curt Flood | 4.00 | 2.00 |
| 439 | Phil Regan | 4.00 | 2.00 |
| 440 | Luis Aparicio | 12.00 | 6.00 |
| 441 | Dick Bertell | 4.00 | 2.00 |
| 442 | Gordon Jones | 4.00 | 2.00 |
| 443 | Duke Snider | 40.00 | 20.00 |
| 444 | Joe Nuxhall | 4.00 | 2.00 |
| 445 | Frank Malzone | 4.00 | 2.00 |
| 446 | Bob "Hawk" Taylor | 4.00 | 2.00 |
| 447 | Harry Bright | 4.00 | 2.00 |
| 448 | Del Rice | 4.00 | 2.00 |
| 449 | Bobby Bolin | 4.00 | 2.00 |
| 450 | Jim Lemon | 4.00 | 2.00 |
| 451 | Power For Ernie (Ernie Broglio, Daryl Spencer, Bill White) | 4.00 | 2.00 |
| 452 | Bob Allen | 4.00 | 2.00 |
| 453 | Dick Schofield | 4.00 | 2.00 |
| 454 | Pumpsie Green | 4.00 | 2.00 |
| 455 | Early Wynn | 15.00 | 7.50 |
| 456 | Hal Bevan | 4.00 | 2.00 |
| 457 | Johnny James | 4.00 | 2.00 |
| 458 | Willie Tasby | 4.00 | 2.00 |
| 459 | Terry Fox | 4.00 | 2.00 |
| 460 | Gil Hodges | 18.00 | 9.00 |
| 461 | Smoky Burgess | 4.00 | 2.00 |
| 462 | Lou Klimchock | 4.00 | 2.00 |
| 463a | Braves Team (should be card #426) | 4.00 | 2.00 |
| 463b | Jack Fisher | 4.00 | 2.00 |
| 464 | Leroy Thomas | 4.00 | 2.00 |
| 465 | Roy McMillan | 4.00 | 2.00 |
| 466 | Ron Moeller | 4.00 | 2.00 |
| 467 | Indians Team | 5.00 | 2.50 |
| 468 | Johnny Callison | 4.00 | 2.00 |
| 469 | Ralph Lumenti | 4.00 | 2.00 |
| 470 | Roy Sievers | 4.00 | 2.00 |
| 471 | Phil Rizzuto MVP | 12.00 | 6.00 |
| 472 | Yogi Berra MVP | 40.00 | 20.00 |
| 473 | Bobby Shantz MVP | 5.00 | 2.50 |
| 474 | Al Rosen MVP | 5.00 | 2.50 |
| 475 | Mickey Mantle MVP | 125.00 | 62.00 |
| 476 | Jackie Jensen MVP | 5.00 | 2.50 |
| 477 | Nellie Fox MVP | 4.00 | 2.00 |
| 478 | Roger Maris MVP | 40.00 | 20.00 |
| 479 | Jim Konstanty MVP | | |

| | | NR MT | EX |
|---|---|---|---|
| | | 4.00 | 2.00 |
| 480 | Roy Campanella MVP | | |
| | | 25.00 | 12.50 |
| 481 | Hank Sauer MVP | 4.00 | 2.00 |
| 482 | Willie Mays MVP | 40.00 | 20.00 |
| 483 | Don Newcombe MVP | | |
| | | 5.00 | 2.50 |
| 484 | Hank Aaron MVP | 40.00 | 20.00 |
| 485 | Ernie Banks MVP | 25.00 | 12.50 |
| 486 | Dick Groat MVP | 5.00 | 2.50 |
| 487 | Gene Oliver | 4.00 | 2.00 |
| 488 | Joe McClain | 4.00 | 2.00 |
| 489 | Walt Dropo | 4.00 | 2.00 |
| 490 | Jim Bunning | 8.00 | 4.00 |
| 491 | Phillies Team | 5.00 | 2.50 |
| 492 | Ron Fairly | 4.00 | 2.00 |
| 493 | Don Zimmer | 4.00 | 2.00 |
| 494 | Tom Cheney | 4.00 | 2.00 |
| 495 | Elston Howard | 6.00 | 3.00 |
| 496 | Ken MacKenzie | 4.00 | 2.00 |
| 497 | Willie Jones | 4.00 | 2.00 |
| 498 | Ray Herbert | 4.00 | 2.00 |
| 499 | Chuck Schilling | 4.00 | 2.00 |
| 500 | Harvey Kuenn | 5.00 | 2.50 |
| 501 | John DeMerit | 4.00 | 2.00 |
| 502 | Clarence Coleman | 4.00 | 2.00 |
| 503 | Tito Francona | 4.00 | 2.00 |
| 504 | Billy Consolo | 4.00 | 2.00 |
| 505 | Red Schoendienst | | |
| | | 12.00 | 6.00 |
| 506 | *Willie Davis* | 10.00 | 5.00 |
| 507 | Pete Burnside | 4.00 | 2.00 |
| 508 | Rocky Bridges | 4.00 | 2.00 |
| 509 | Camilo Carreon | 4.00 | 2.00 |
| 510 | Art Ditmar | 4.00 | 2.00 |
| 511 | Joe Morgan | 4.00 | 2.00 |
| 512 | Bob Will | 4.00 | 2.00 |
| 513 | Jim Brosnan | 4.00 | 2.00 |
| 514 | Jake Wood | 4.00 | 2.00 |
| 515 | Jackie Brandt | 4.00 | 2.00 |
| 516 | Checklist 507-587 | | |
| | | 10.00 | 5.00 |
| 517 | Willie McCovey | 60.00 | 30.00 |
| 518 | Andy Carey | 4.00 | 2.00 |
| 519 | Jim Pagliaroni | 4.00 | 2.00 |
| 520 | Joe Cunningham | 4.00 | 2.00 |
| 521 | Brother Battery (Larry Sherry, Norm Sherry) | 4.00 | 2.00 |
| 522 | Dick Farrell | 4.00 | 2.00 |
| 523 | Joe Gibbon | 25.00 | 12.50 |
| 524 | Johnny Logan | 27.00 | 13.50 |
| 525 | *Ron Perranoski* | 27.00 | 13.50 |
| 526 | R.C. Stevens | 25.00 | 12.50 |
| 527 | Gene Leek | 25.00 | 12.50 |
| 528 | Pedro Ramos | 25.00 | 12.50 |
| 529 | Bob Roselli | 25.00 | 12.50 |
| 530 | Bobby Malkmus | 25.00 | 12.50 |
| 531 | Jim Coates | 27.00 | 13.50 |
| 532 | Bob Hale | 25.00 | 12.50 |
| 533 | Jack Curtis | 25.00 | 12.50 |
| 534 | Eddie Kasko | 25.00 | 12.50 |
| 535 | Larry Jackson | 25.00 | 12.50 |
| 536 | Bill Tuttle | 25.00 | 12.50 |
| 537 | Bobby Locke | 25.00 | 12.50 |
| 538 | Chuck Hiller | 25.00 | 12.50 |
| 539 | Johnny Klippstein | 25.00 | 12.50 |
| 540 | Jackie Jensen | 35.00 | 17.50 |

| | | NR MT | EX |
|---|---|---|---|
| 541 | Roland Sheldon | 27.00 | 13.50 |
| 542 | Twins Team | 60.00 | 30.00 |
| 543 | Roger Craig | 35.00 | 17.50 |
| 544 | George Thomas | 25.00 | 12.50 |
| 545 | Hoyt Wilhelm | 55.00 | 28.00 |
| 546 | Marty Kutyna | 25.00 | 12.50 |
| 547 | Leon Wagner | 27.00 | 13.50 |
| 548 | Ted Wills | 25.00 | 12.50 |
| 549 | Hal R. Smith | 25.00 | 12.50 |
| 550 | Frank Baumann | 25.00 | 12.50 |
| 551 | George Altman | 25.00 | 12.50 |
| 552 | Jim Archer | 25.00 | 12.50 |
| 553 | Bill Fischer | 25.00 | 12.50 |
| 554 | Pirates Team | 50.00 | 25.00 |
| 555 | Sam Jones | 25.00 | 12.50 |
| 556 | Ken R. Hunt | 25.00 | 12.50 |
| 557 | Jose Valdivielso | 25.00 | 12.50 |
| 558 | Don Ferrarese | 25.00 | 12.50 |
| 559 | Jim Gentile | 27.00 | 13.50 |
| 560 | Barry Latman | 25.00 | 12.50 |
| 561 | Charley James | 25.00 | 12.50 |
| 562 | Bill Monbouquette | | |
| | | 27.00 | 13.50 |
| 563 | Bob Cerv | 27.00 | 13.50 |
| 564 | Don Cardwell | 25.00 | 12.50 |
| 565 | Felipe Alou | 25.00 | 12.50 |
| 566 | Paul Richards AS | 25.00 | 12.50 |
| 567 | Danny Murtaugh AS | | |
| | | 25.00 | 12.50 |
| 568 | Bill Skowron AS | 35.00 | 17.50 |
| 569 | Frank Herrera AS | 25.00 | 12.50 |
| 570 | Nellie Fox AS | 40.00 | 20.00 |
| 571 | Bill Mazeroski AS | 35.00 | 17.50 |
| 572 | Brooks Robinson AS | | |
| | | 75.00 | 38.00 |
| 573 | Ken Boyer AS | 35.00 | 17.50 |
| 574 | Luis Aparicio AS | 45.00 | 23.00 |
| 575 | Ernie Banks AS | 80.00 | 40.00 |
| 576 | Roger Maris AS | 100.00 | 50.00 |
| 577 | Hank Aaron AS | 150.00 | 75.00 |
| 578 | Mickey Mantle AS | | |
| | | 400.00 | 200.00 |
| 579 | Willie Mays AS | 150.00 | 75.00 |
| 580 | Al Kaline AS | 90.00 | 45.00 |
| 581 | Frank Robinson AS | | |
| | | 80.00 | 40.00 |
| 582 | Earl Battey AS | 25.00 | 12.50 |
| 583 | Del Crandall AS | 30.00 | 15.00 |
| 584 | Jim Perry AS | 30.00 | 15.00 |
| 585 | Bob Friend AS | 30.00 | 15.00 |
| 586 | Whitey Ford AS | 90.00 | 45.00 |
| 587 | Not Issued | | |
| 588 | Not Issued | | |
| 589 | Warren Spahn AS | | |
| | | 125.00 | 56.00 |

# 1962 Topps

The 1962 Topps set established another plateau for set size with 598 cards. The 2-1/2" by 3-1/2" cards feature a photograph set against a woodgrain background. The lower righthand corner has been

made to look like it is curling away. Many established specialty cards dot the set including statistical leaders, multi-player cards, team cards, checklists, World Series cards and All-Stars. Of note is that 1962 was the first year of the multi-player rookie card. There is a 9-card "In Action" subset and a 10-card run of special Babe Ruth cards. Photo variations of several cards in the 2nd Series (#'s 110-196) exist. All cards in the 2nd Series can be found with two distinct printing variations, an early printing with the cards containing a very noticeable greenish tint, having been corrected to clear photos in subsequent print runs. The complete set price in the checklist that follows does not include the higher-priced variations.

|  | | NR MT | EX |
|---|---|---|---|
| Complete Set: | | 5000.00 | 2250.00 |
| Common Player: 1-370 | | 2.00 | 1.00 |
| Common Player: 371-522 | | | |
| | | 4.00 | 2.00 |
| Common Player: 523-598 | | | |
| | | 12.00 | 5.50 |

| | | NR MT | EX |
|---|---|---|---|
| 1 | Roger Maris | 225.00 | 45.00 |
| 2 | Jim Brosnan | 2.25 | 1.25 |
| 3 | Pete Runnels | 2.00 | 1.00 |
| 4 | John DeMerit | 2.00 | .90 |
| 5 | Sandy Koufax | 110.00 | 55.00 |
| 6 | Marv Breeding | 2.00 | 1.00 |
| 7 | Frank Thomas | 2.00 | .90 |
| 8 | Ray Herbert | 2.00 | 1.00 |
| 9 | Jim Davenport | 2.00 | 1.00 |
| 10 | Bob Clemente | 110.00 | 55.00 |
| 11 | Tom Morgan | 2.00 | 1.00 |
| 12 | Harry Craft | 2.00 | 1.00 |
| 13 | Dick Howser | 2.25 | 1.25 |
| 14 | Bill White | 2.00 | 1.00 |
| 15 | Dick Donovan | 2.00 | 1.00 |
| 16 | Darrell Johnson | 2.00 | 1.00 |
| 17 | Johnny Callison | 2.25 | 1.25 |

| | | NR MT | EX |
|---|---|---|---|
| 18 | Managers' Dream (Mickey Mantle, Willie Mays) | 100.00 | 50.00 |
| 19 | *Ray Washburn* | 2.00 | 1.00 |
| 20 | Rocky Colavito | 8.00 | 4.00 |
| 21 | Jim Kaat | 5.00 | 2.00 |
| 22a | Checklist 1-88 (numbers 121 - 176 on back) | 5.00 | 2.25 |
| 22b | Checklist 1-88 (numbers 33-88 on back) | 4.00 | 1.75 |
| 23 | Norm Larker | 2.00 | 1.00 |
| 24 | Tigers Team | 5.00 | 2.50 |
| 25 | Ernie Banks | 45.00 | 23.00 |
| 26 | Chris Cannizzaro | 2.00 | .90 |
| 27 | Chuck Cottier | 2.00 | 1.00 |
| 28 | Minnie Minoso | 4.00 | 2.00 |
| 29 | Casey Stengel | 18.00 | 9.00 |
| 30 | Ed Mathews | 20.00 | 10.00 |
| 31 | *Tom Tresh* | 10.00 | 5.00 |
| 32 | John Roseboro | 2.25 | 1.25 |
| 33 | Don Larsen | 2.25 | 1.25 |
| 34 | Johnny Temple | 2.00 | 1.00 |
| 35 | *Don Schwall* | 2.25 | 1.25 |
| 36 | Don Leppert | 2.00 | 1.00 |
| 37 | Tribe Hill Trio (Barry Latman, Jim Perry, Dick Stigman) | 2.25 | 1.25 |
| 38 | Gene Stephens | 2.00 | 1.00 |
| 39 | Joe Koppe | 2.00 | 1.00 |
| 40 | Orlando Cepeda | 5.00 | 2.25 |
| 41 | Cliff Cook | 2.00 | 1.00 |
| 42 | Jim King | 2.00 | 1.00 |
| 43 | Dodgers Team | 5.00 | 2.50 |
| 44 | Don Taussig | 2.00 | 1.00 |
| 45 | Brooks Robinson | 40.00 | 15.00 |
| 46 | *Jack Baldschun* | 2.00 | 1.00 |
| 47 | Bob Will | 2.00 | 1.00 |
| 48 | Ralph Terry | 4.00 | 2.00 |
| 49 | Hal Jones | 2.00 | 1.00 |
| 50 | Stan Musial | 110.00 | 55.00 |
| 51 | A.L. Batting Leaders (Norm Cash, Elston Howard, Al Kaline, Jim Piersall) | 5.00 | 2.50 |
| 52 | N.L. Batting Leaders (Ken Boyer, Bob Clemente, Wally Moon, Vada Pinson) | 5.00 | 2.50 |
| 53 | A.L. Home Run Leaders (Jim Gentile, Harmon Killebrew, Mickey Mantle, Roger Maris) | 40.00 | 20.00 |
| 54 | N.L. Home Run Leaders (Orlando Cepeda, Willie Mays, Frank Robinson) | 5.00 | 2.50 |
| 55 | A.L. E.R.A. Leaders (Dick Donovan, Don Mossi, Milt Pappas, Bill Stafford) | 4.00 | 2.00 |
| 56 | N.L. E.R.A. Leaders (Mike McCormick, Jim O'Toole, Curt Simmons, Warren Spahn) | 5.00 | 2.50 |
| 57 | A.L. Win Leaders (Steve Barber, Jim Bunning, Whitey Ford, Frank Lary) | 5.00 | 2.50 |

| | | NR MT | EX |
|---|---|---|---|
| 58 | N.L. Win Leaders (Joe Jay, Jim O'Toole, Warren Spahn) | 5.00 | 2.50 |
| 59 | A.L. Strikeout Leaders (Jim Bunning, Whitey Ford, Camilo Pascual, Juan Pizzaro) | 5.00 | 2.50 |
| 60 | N.L. Strikeout Leaders (Don Drysdale, Sandy Koufax, Jim O'Toole, Stan Williams) | 5.00 | 2.50 |
| 61 | Cardinals Team | 4.00 | 2.00 |
| 62 | Steve Boros | 2.00 | 1.00 |
| 63 | *Tony Cloninger* | 2.00 | .90 |
| 64 | Russ Snyder | 2.00 | 1.00 |
| 65 | Bobby Richardson | 6.00 | 2.75 |
| 66 | Cuno Barragon (Barragan) | 2.00 | 1.00 |
| 67 | Harvey Haddix | 2.25 | 1.25 |
| 68 | Ken L. Hunt | 2.00 | 1.00 |
| 69 | Phil Ortega | 2.00 | 1.00 |
| 70 | Harmon Killebrew | 20.00 | 10.00 |
| 71 | Dick LeMay | 2.00 | 1.00 |
| 72 | Bob's Pupils (Steve Boros, Bob Scheffing, Jake Wood) | 2.25 | 1.25 |
| 73 | Nellie Fox | 8.00 | 4.00 |
| 74 | Bob Lillis | 2.00 | 1.00 |
| 75 | Milt Pappas | 2.25 | 1.25 |
| 76 | Howie Bedell | 2.00 | 1.00 |
| 77 | Tony Taylor | 2.00 | 1.00 |
| 78 | Gene Green | 2.00 | 1.00 |
| 79 | Ed Hobaugh | 2.00 | 1.00 |
| 80 | Vada Pinson | 4.00 | 2.00 |
| 81 | Jim Pagliaroni | 2.00 | 1.00 |
| 82 | Deron Johnson | 2.00 | 1.00 |
| 83 | Larry Jackson | 2.00 | 1.00 |
| 84 | Lenny Green | 2.00 | 1.00 |
| 85 | Gil Hodges | 15.00 | 7.50 |
| 86 | *Donn Clendenon* | 2.25 | 1.25 |
| 87 | Mike Roarke | 2.00 | 1.00 |
| 88 | Ralph Houk | 4.00 | 2.00 |
| 89 | Barney Schultz | 2.00 | 1.00 |
| 90 | Jim Piersall | 2.00 | .90 |
| 91 | J.C. Martin | 2.00 | 1.00 |
| 92 | Sam Jones | 2.00 | 1.00 |
| 93 | John Blanchard | 2.00 | .90 |
| 94 | Jay Hook | 2.00 | .90 |
| 95 | Don Hoak | 2.25 | 1.25 |
| 96 | Eli Grba | 2.00 | 1.00 |
| 97 | Tito Francona | 2.00 | 1.00 |
| 98 | Checklist 89-176 | 4.00 | 1.75 |
| 99 | *John Powell* | 18.00 | 9.00 |
| 100 | Warren Spahn | 30.00 | 12.50 |
| 101 | Carroll Hardy | 2.00 | 1.00 |
| 102 | Al Schroll | 2.00 | 1.00 |
| 103 | Don Blasingame | 2.00 | 1.00 |
| 104 | Ted Savage | 2.00 | 1.00 |
| 105 | Don Mossi | 2.00 | 1.00 |
| 106 | Carl Sawatski | 2.00 | 1.00 |
| 107 | Mike McCormick | 2.00 | 1.00 |
| 108 | Willie Davis | 4.00 | 2.00 |
| 109 | Bob Shaw | 2.00 | 1.00 |
| 110 | Bill Skowron | 5.00 | 2.25 |
| 111 | Dallas Green | 2.25 | 1.25 |
| 112 | Hank Foiles | 2.00 | 1.00 |
| 113 | White Sox Team | 4.00 | 2.00 |
| 114 | Howie Koplitz | 2.00 | 1.00 |
| 115 | Bob Skinner | 2.00 | 1.00 |
| 116 | Herb Score | 2.00 | .90 |
| 117 | Gary Geiger | 2.00 | 1.00 |
| 118 | Julian Javier | 2.00 | 1.00 |
| 119 | Danny Murphy | 2.00 | 1.00 |
| 120 | Bob Purkey | 2.00 | 1.00 |
| 121 | Billy Hitchcock | 2.00 | 1.00 |
| 122 | Norm Bass | 2.00 | 1.00 |
| 123 | Mike de la Hoz | 2.00 | 1.00 |
| 124 | Bill Pleis | 2.00 | 1.00 |
| 125 | Gene Woodling | 2.25 | 1.25 |
| 126 | Al Cicotte | 2.00 | 1.00 |
| 127 | Pride of the A's (Hank Bauer, Jerry Lumpe, Norm Siebern) | 2.25 | 1.25 |
| 128 | Art Fowler | 2.00 | 1.00 |
| 129a | Lee Walls (facing left) | 15.00 | 7.50 |
| 129b | Lee Walls (facing right) | 2.00 | 1.00 |
| 130 | Frank Bolling | 2.00 | 1.00 |
| 131 | *Pete Richert* | 2.25 | 1.25 |
| 132a | Angels Team (with inset photos) | 10.00 | 4.50 |
| 132b | Angels Team (without inset photos) | 5.00 | 2.50 |
| 133 | Felipe Alou | 2.25 | 1.25 |
| 134a | Billy Hoeft (green sky in background) | 15.00 | 7.50 |
| 134b | Billy Hoeft (blue sky in background) | 2.00 | 1.00 |
| 135 | Babe As A Boy | 7.00 | 3.25 |
| 136 | Babe Joins Yanks | 7.00 | 3.25 |
| 137 | Babe and Mgr. Huggins | 7.00 | 3.25 |
| 138 | The Famous Slugger | 7.00 | 3.25 |
| 139a | Hal Reniff (pitching) | 40.00 | 20.00 |
| 139b | Hal Reniff (portrait) | 18.00 | 9.00 |
| 139c | Babe Hits 60 | 10.00 | 4.00 |
| 140 | Gehrig and Ruth | 9.00 | 4.00 |
| 141 | Twilight Years | 7.00 | 3.25 |
| 142 | Coaching for the Dodgers | 7.00 | 3.25 |
| 143 | Greatest Sports Hero | 7.00 | 3.25 |
| 144 | Farewell Speech | 7.00 | 3.25 |
| 145 | Barry Latman | 2.00 | 1.00 |
| 146 | Don Demeter | 2.00 | 1.00 |
| 147a | Bill Kunkel (pitching) | 15.00 | 7.50 |
| 147b | Bill Kunkel (portrait) | 2.00 | 1.00 |
| 148 | Wally Post | 2.00 | 1.00 |
| 149 | Bob Duliba | 2.00 | 1.00 |
| 150 | Al Kaline | 30.00 | 15.00 |
| 151 | Johnny Klippstein | 2.00 | 1.00 |
| 152 | Mickey Vernon | 2.00 | 1.00 |
| 153 | Pumpsie Green | 2.00 | 1.00 |
| 154 | Lee Thomas | 2.00 | 1.00 |
| 155 | Stu Miller | 2.00 | 1.00 |
| 156 | Merritt Ranew | 2.00 | 1.00 |
| 157 | Wes Covington | 2.00 | 1.00 |
| 158 | Braves Team | 5.00 | 2.50 |

| | | NR MT | EX | | | NR MT | EX |
|---|---|---|---|---|---|---|---|
| 159 | Hal Reniff | 2.00 | .90 | 212 | Jim Owens | 2.00 | 1.00 |
| 160 | Dick Stuart | 2.00 | 1.00 | 213 | Richie Ashburn | 6.00 | 2.75 |
| 161 | Frank Baumann | 2.00 | 1.00 | 214 | Dom Zanni | 2.00 | 1.00 |
| 162 | Sammy Drake | 2.00 | .90 | 215 | Woody Held | 2.00 | 1.00 |
| 163 | Hot Corner Guardians | | | 216 | Ron Kline | 2.00 | 1.00 |
| | (Cletis Boyer, Billy Gardner) | | | 217 | Walt Alston | 4.00 | 1.75 |
| | | 5.00 | 2.50 | 218 | *Joe Torre* | 25.00 | 12.50 |
| 164 | Hal Naragon | 2.00 | 1.00 | 219 | *Al Downing* | 4.00 | 1.75 |
| 165 | Jackie Brandt | 2.00 | 1.00 | 220 | Roy Sievers | 2.25 | 1.25 |
| 166 | Don Lee | 2.00 | 1.00 | 221 | Bill Short | 2.00 | 1.00 |
| 167 | *Tim McCarver* | 30.00 | 12.50 | 222 | Jerry Zimmerman | 2.00 | 1.00 |
| 168 | Leo Posada | 2.00 | 1.00 | 223 | Alex Grammas | 2.00 | 1.00 |
| 169 | Bob Cerv | 2.00 | .90 | 224 | Don Rudolph | 2.00 | 1.00 |
| 170 | Ron Santo | 5.00 | 2.50 | 225 | Frank Malzone | 2.00 | 1.00 |
| 171 | Dave Sisler | 2.00 | 1.00 | 226 | Giants Team | 4.00 | 1.75 |
| 172 | Fred Hutchinson | 2.00 | 1.00 | 227 | Bobby Tiefenauer | 2.00 | 1.00 |
| 173 | Chico Fernandez | 2.00 | 1.00 | 228 | Dale Long | 2.00 | 1.00 |
| 174a | Carl Willey (with cap) | | | 229 | Jesus McFarlane | 2.00 | 1.00 |
| | | 15.00 | 7.50 | 230 | Camilo Pascual | 2.25 | 1.25 |
| 174b | Carl Willey (no cap) | 2.00 | 1.00 | 231 | Ernie Bowman | 2.00 | 1.00 |
| 175 | Frank Howard | 5.00 | 2.50 | 232 | World Series Game 1 | | |
| 176a | Eddie Yost (batting) | | | | (Yanks Win Opener) | 5.00 | 2.50 |
| | | 15.00 | 7.50 | 233 | World Series Game 2 | | |
| 176b | Eddie Yost (portrait) | | | | (Jay Ties It Up) | 5.00 | 2.50 |
| | | 2.00 | 1.00 | 234 | World Series Game 3 | | |
| 177 | Bobby Shantz | 2.25 | 1.25 | | (Maris Wins It In The 9th) | | |
| 178 | Camilo Carreon | 2.00 | 1.00 | | | 8.00 | 3.50 |
| 179 | Tom Sturdivant | 2.00 | 1.00 | 235 | World Series Game 4 | | |
| 180 | Bob Allison | 2.25 | 1.25 | | (Ford Sets New Mark) | 7.00 | 3.25 |
| 181 | Paul Brown | 2.00 | 1.00 | 236 | World Series Game 5 | | |
| 182 | Bob Nieman | 2.00 | 1.00 | | (Yanks Crush Reds In | | |
| 183 | Roger Craig | 5.00 | 2.50 | | Finale) | 5.00 | 2.50 |
| 184 | Haywood Sullivan | 2.00 | 1.00 | 237 | World Series Summary | | |
| 185 | Roland Sheldon | 2.00 | .90 | | (The Winners Celebrate) | | |
| 186 | *Mack Jones* | 2.00 | 1.00 | | | 5.00 | 2.50 |
| 187 | Gene Conley | 2.00 | 1.00 | 238 | Norm Sherry | 2.00 | 1.00 |
| 188 | Chuck Hiller | 2.00 | 1.00 | 239 | Cecil Butler | 2.00 | 1.00 |
| 189 | Dick Hall | 2.00 | 1.00 | 240 | George Altman | 2.00 | 1.00 |
| 190a | Wally Moon (with cap) | | | 241 | Johnny Kucks | 2.00 | 1.00 |
| | | 9.00 | 4.00 | 242 | Mel McGaha | 2.00 | 1.00 |
| 190b | Wally Moon (no cap) | | | 243 | Robin Roberts | 12.00 | 5.50 |
| | | 2.25 | 1.25 | 244 | Don Gile | 2.00 | 1.00 |
| 191 | Jim Brewer | 2.00 | 1.00 | 245 | Ron Hansen | 2.00 | 1.00 |
| 192a | Checklist 177-264 (192 | | | 246 | Art Ditmar | 2.00 | 1.00 |
| | is Check List, 3) | 6.00 | 2.75 | 247 | Joe Pignatano | 2.00 | 1.00 |
| 192b | Checklist 177-264 (192 | | | 248 | Bob Aspromonte | 2.00 | 1.00 |
| | is Check List 3) | 4.00 | 1.75 | 249 | Ed Keegan | 2.00 | 1.00 |
| 193 | Eddie Kasko | 2.00 | 1.00 | 250 | Norm Cash | 5.00 | 2.50 |
| 194 | *Dean Chance* | 5.00 | 2.50 | 251 | Yankees Team | 15.00 | 7.50 |
| 195 | Joe Cunningham | 2.00 | 1.00 | 252 | Earl Francis | 2.00 | 1.00 |
| 196 | Terry Fox | 2.00 | 1.00 | 253 | Harry Chiti | 2.00 | 1.00 |
| 197 | Daryl Spencer | 2.00 | 1.00 | 254 | Gordon Windhorn | 2.00 | 1.00 |
| 198 | Johnny Keane | 2.00 | 1.00 | 255 | Juan Pizarro | 2.00 | 1.00 |
| 199 | Gaylord Perry | 200.00 | 100.00 | 256 | Elio Chacon | 2.00 | .90 |
| 200 | Mickey Mantle | 450.00 | 225.00 | 257 | Jack Spring | 2.00 | 1.00 |
| 201 | Ike Delock | 2.00 | 1.00 | 258 | Marty Keough | 2.00 | 1.00 |
| 202 | Carl Warwick | 2.00 | 1.00 | 259 | Lou Klimchock | 2.00 | 1.00 |
| 203 | Jack Fisher | 2.00 | 1.00 | 260 | Bill Pierce | 2.00 | .90 |
| 204 | Johnny Weekly | 2.00 | 1.00 | 261 | George Alusik | 2.00 | 1.00 |
| 205 | Gene Freese | 2.00 | 1.00 | 262 | Bob Schmidt | 2.00 | 1.00 |
| 206 | Senators Team | 4.00 | 2.00 | 263 | The Right Pitch (Joe | | |
| 207 | Pete Burnside | 2.00 | 1.00 | | Jay, Bob Purkey, Jim | | |
| 208 | Billy Martin | 6.00 | 2.75 | | Turner) | 2.25 | 1.25 |
| 209 | *Jim Fregosi* | 6.00 | 2.50 | 264 | Dick Ellsworth | 2.00 | 1.00 |
| 210 | Roy Face | 2.00 | .90 | 265 | Joe Adcock | 2.00 | .90 |
| 211 | Midway Masters (Frank | | | 266 | John Anderson | 2.00 | 1.00 |
| | Bolling, Roy McMillan) | 2.25 | 1.25 | 267 | Dan Dobbek | 2.00 | 1.00 |

| | | NR MT | EX |
|---|---|---|---|
| 268 | Ken McBride | 2.00 | 1.00 |
| 269 | Bob Oldis | 2.00 | 1.00 |
| 270 | Dick Groat | 2.00 | .90 |
| 271 | Ray Rippelmeyer | 2.00 | 1.00 |
| 272 | Earl Robinson | 2.00 | 1.00 |
| 273 | Gary Bell | 2.00 | 1.00 |
| 274 | Sammy Taylor | 2.00 | 1.00 |
| 275 | Norm Siebern | 2.00 | 1.00 |
| 276 | Hal Kostad | 2.00 | 1.00 |
| 277 | Checklist 265-352 | 4.00 | 1.75 |
| 278 | Ken Johnson | 2.00 | 1.00 |
| 279 | Hobie Landrith | 2.00 | .90 |
| 280 | Johnny Podres | 4.00 | 2.00 |
| 281 | *Jake Gibbs* | 2.25 | 1.00 |
| 282 | Dave Hillman | 2.00 | 1.00 |
| 283 | Charlie Smith | 2.00 | 1.00 |
| 284 | Ruben Amaro | 2.00 | 1.00 |
| 285 | Curt Simmons | 2.00 | .90 |
| 286 | Al Lopez | 5.00 | 2.50 |
| 287 | George Witt | 2.00 | 1.00 |
| 288 | Billy Williams | 30.00 | 15.00 |
| 289 | Mike Krsnich | 2.00 | 1.00 |
| 290 | Jim Gentile | 2.00 | 1.00 |
| 291 | Hal Stowe | 2.00 | .90 |
| 292 | Jerry Kindall | 2.00 | 1.00 |
| 293 | Bob Miller | 2.00 | .90 |
| 294 | Phillies Team | 4.00 | 2.00 |
| 295 | Vern Law | 2.00 | .90 |
| 296 | Ken Hamlin | 2.00 | 1.00 |
| 297 | Ron Perranoski | 2.00 | 1.00 |
| 298 | Bill Tuttle | 2.00 | 1.00 |
| 299 | *Don Wert* | 2.00 | 1.00 |
| 300 | Willie Mays | 160.00 | 75.00 |
| 301 | Galen Cisco | 2.00 | 1.00 |
| 302 | *John Edwards* | 2.00 | 1.00 |
| 303 | Frank Torre | 2.00 | 1.00 |
| 304 | Dick Farrell | 2.00 | 1.00 |
| 305 | Jerry Lumpe | 2.00 | 1.00 |
| 306 | Redbird Rippers (Larry Jackson, Lindy McDaniel) | 2.25 | 1.25 |
| 307 | Jim Grant | 2.00 | 1.00 |
| 308 | Neil Chrisley | 2.00 | .90 |
| 309 | Moe Morhardt | 2.00 | 1.00 |
| 310 | Whitey Ford | 25.00 | 12.50 |
| 311 | Kubek Makes The Double Play | 5.00 | 2.50 |
| 312 | Spahn Shows No-Hit Form | 7.00 | 3.50 |
| 313 | Maris Blasts 61st | 20.00 | 10.00 |
| 314 | Colavito's Power | 5.00 | 2.50 |
| 315 | Ford Tosses A Curve | 6.00 | 2.75 |
| 316 | Killebrew Sends One Into Orbit | 5.00 | 2.25 |
| 317 | Musial Plays 21st Season | 18.00 | 9.00 |
| 318 | The Switch Hitter Connects (Mickey Mantle) | 50.00 | 25.00 |
| 319 | McCormick Shows His Stuff | 2.25 | 1.25 |
| 320 | Hank Aaron | 125.00 | 62.00 |
| 321 | Lee Stange | 2.00 | 1.00 |
| 322 | Al Dark | 2.25 | 1.25 |
| 323 | Don Landrum | 2.00 | 1.00 |
| 324 | Joe McClain | 2.00 | 1.00 |
| 325 | Luis Aparicio | 15.00 | 7.50 |
| 326 | Tom Parsons | 2.00 | 1.00 |
| 327 | Ozzie Virgil | 2.00 | 1.00 |
| 328 | Ken Walters | 2.00 | 1.00 |
| 329 | Bob Bolin | 2.00 | 1.00 |
| 330 | Johnny Romano | 2.00 | 1.00 |
| 331 | Moe Drabowsky | 2.00 | 1.00 |
| 332 | Don Buddin | 2.00 | 1.00 |
| 333 | Frank Cipriani | 2.00 | 1.00 |
| 334 | Red Sox Team | 5.00 | 2.50 |
| 335 | Bill Bruton | 2.00 | 1.00 |
| 336 | Billy Muffett | 2.00 | 1.00 |
| 337 | Jim Marshall | 2.00 | .90 |
| 338 | Billy Gardner | 2.25 | 1.00 |
| 339 | Jose Valdivielso | 2.00 | 1.00 |
| 340 | Don Drysdale | 30.00 | 15.00 |
| 341 | Mike Hershberger | 2.00 | 1.00 |
| 342 | Ed Rakow | 2.00 | 1.00 |
| 343 | Albie Pearson | 2.00 | 1.00 |
| 344 | Ed Bauta | 2.00 | 1.00 |
| 345 | Chuck Schilling | 2.00 | 1.00 |
| 346 | Jack Kralick | 2.00 | 1.00 |
| 347 | Chuck Hinton | 2.00 | 1.00 |
| 348 | Larry Burright | 2.00 | 1.00 |
| 349 | Paul Foytack | 2.00 | 1.00 |
| 350 | Frank Robinson | 50.00 | 25.00 |
| 351 | Braves' Backstops (Del Crandall, Joe Torre) | 5.00 | 2.50 |
| 352 | Frank Sullivan | 2.00 | 1.00 |
| 353 | Bill Mazeroski | 5.00 | 2.50 |
| 354 | Roman Mejias | 2.00 | 1.00 |
| 355 | Steve Barber | 2.00 | 1.00 |
| 356 | Tom Haller | 2.25 | 1.25 |
| 357 | Jerry Walker | 2.00 | 1.00 |
| 358 | Tommy Davis | 4.00 | 2.00 |
| 359 | Bobby Locke | 2.00 | 1.00 |
| 360 | Yogi Berra | 70.00 | 35.00 |
| 361 | Bob Hendley | 2.00 | 1.00 |
| 362 | Ty Cline | 2.00 | 1.00 |
| 363 | Bob Roselli | 2.00 | 1.00 |
| 364 | Ken Hunt | 2.00 | 1.00 |
| 365 | Charley Neal | 2.00 | .90 |
| 366 | Phil Regan | 2.00 | 1.00 |
| 367 | Checklist 353-429 | 4.00 | 1.75 |
| 368 | Bob Tillman | 2.00 | 1.00 |
| 369 | Ted Bowsfield | 2.00 | 1.00 |
| 370 | Ken Boyer | 4.00 | 1.75 |
| 371 | Earl Battey | 4.00 | 2.00 |
| 372 | Jack Curtis | 4.00 | 2.00 |
| 373 | Al Heist | 4.00 | 2.00 |
| 374 | Gene Mauch | 4.00 | 2.00 |
| 375 | Ron Fairly | 4.00 | 2.00 |
| 376 | Bud Daley | 5.00 | 2.50 |
| 377 | Johnny Orsino | 4.00 | 2.00 |
| 378 | Bennie Daniels | 4.00 | 2.00 |
| 379 | Chuck Essegian | 4.00 | 2.00 |
| 380 | Lou Burdette | 4.00 | 1.75 |
| 381 | Chico Cardenas | 4.00 | 2.00 |
| 382 | Dick Williams | 5.00 | 2.50 |
| 383 | Ray Sadecki | 4.00 | 2.00 |
| 384 | Athletics Team | 5.00 | 2.50 |
| 385 | Early Wynn | 20.00 | 10.00 |
| 386 | Don Mincher | 4.00 | 2.00 |
| 387 | Lou Brock | 200.00 | 100.00 |
| 388 | Ryne Duren | 4.00 | 2.00 |
| 389 | Smoky Burgess | 5.00 | 2.50 |
| 390 | Orlando Cepeda AS | | |

| | | NR MT | EX |
|---|---|---|---|
| | | 5.00 | 2.25 |
| 391 | Bill Mazeroski AS | 5.00 | 2.50 |
| 392 | Ken Boyer AS | 5.00 | 2.50 |
| 393 | Roy McMillan AS | 4.00 | 2.00 |
| 394 | Hank Aaron AS | 30.00 | 15.00 |
| 395 | Willie Mays AS | 30.00 | 15.00 |
| 396 | Frank Robinson AS | | |
| | | 12.00 | 5.50 |
| 397 | John Roseboro AS | 4.00 | 2.00 |
| 398 | Don Drysdale AS | 10.00 | 4.50 |
| 399 | Warren Spahn AS | 10.00 | 4.50 |
| 400 | Elston Howard | 7.00 | 3.25 |
| 401 | AL & NL Homer Kings | | |
| | (Orlando Cepeda, Roger Maris) | 25.00 | 10.00 |
| 402 | Gino Cimoli | 4.00 | 2.00 |
| 403 | Chet Nichols | 4.00 | 2.00 |
| 404 | Tim Harkness | 4.00 | 2.00 |
| 405 | Jim Perry | 5.00 | 2.50 |
| 406 | Bob Taylor | 4.00 | 2.00 |
| 407 | Hank Aguirre | 4.00 | 2.00 |
| 408 | Gus Bell | 5.00 | 2.50 |
| 409 | Pirates Team | 5.00 | 2.50 |
| 410 | Al Smith | 4.00 | 2.00 |
| 411 | Danny O'Connell | 4.00 | 2.00 |
| 412 | Charlie James | 4.00 | 2.00 |
| 413 | Matty Alou | 5.00 | 2.50 |
| 414 | Joe Gaines | 4.00 | 2.00 |
| 415 | Bill Virdon | 5.00 | 2.50 |
| 416 | Bob Scheffing | 4.00 | 2.00 |
| 417 | Joe Azcue | 4.00 | 2.00 |
| 418 | Andy Carey | 4.00 | 2.00 |
| 419 | Bob Bruce | 4.00 | 2.00 |
| 420 | Gus Triandos | 5.00 | 2.50 |
| 421 | Ken MacKenzie | 5.00 | 2.50 |
| 422 | Steve Bilko | 4.00 | 2.00 |
| 423 | Rival League Relief Aces | | |
| | (Roy Face, Hoyt Wilhelm) | 5.00 | 2.25 |
| 424 | Al McBean | 4.00 | 2.00 |
| 425 | Carl Yastrzemski | | |
| | | 225.00 | 100.00 |
| 426 | Bob Farley | 4.00 | 2.00 |
| 427 | Jake Wood | 4.00 | 2.00 |
| 428 | Joe Hicks | 4.00 | 2.00 |
| 429 | Bill O'Dell | 4.00 | 2.00 |
| 430 | Tony Kubek | 7.00 | 3.25 |
| 431 | *Bob Rodgers* | 9.00 | 4.50 |
| 432 | Jim Pendleton | 4.00 | 2.00 |
| 433 | Jim Archer | 4.00 | 2.00 |
| 434 | Clay Dalrymple | 4.00 | 2.00 |
| 435 | Larry Sherry | 4.00 | 2.00 |
| 436 | Felix Mantilla | 5.00 | 2.50 |
| 437 | Ray Moore | 4.00 | 2.00 |
| 438 | Dick Brown | 4.00 | 2.00 |
| 439 | Jerry Buchek | 4.00 | 2.00 |
| 440 | Joe Jay | 4.00 | 2.00 |
| 441 | Checklist 430-506 | 5.00 | 2.25 |
| 442 | Wes Stock | 4.00 | 2.00 |
| 443 | Del Crandall | 5.00 | 2.50 |
| 444 | Ted Wills | 4.00 | 2.00 |
| 445 | Vic Power | 4.00 | 2.00 |
| 446 | Don Elston | 4.00 | 2.00 |
| 447 | Willie Kirkland | 4.00 | 2.00 |
| 448 | Joe Gibbon | 4.00 | 2.00 |
| 449 | Jerry Adair | 4.00 | 2.00 |
| 450 | Jim O'Toole | 4.00 | 2.00 |

| | | NR MT | EX |
|---|---|---|---|
| 451 | *Jose Tartabull* | 4.00 | 2.00 |
| 452 | Earl Averill | 4.00 | 2.00 |
| 453 | Cal McLish | 4.00 | 2.00 |
| 454 | Floyd Robinson | 4.00 | 2.00 |
| 455 | Luis Arroyo | 5.00 | 2.50 |
| 456 | Joe Amalfitano | 4.00 | 2.00 |
| 457 | Lou Clinton | 4.00 | 2.00 |
| 458a | Bob Buhl ("M" on cap) | | |
| | | 4.00 | 2.00 |
| 458b | Bob Buhl (plain cap) | | |
| | | 60.00 | 30.00 |
| 459 | Ed Bailey | 4.00 | 2.00 |
| 460 | Jim Bunning | 9.00 | 4.00 |
| 461 | *Ken Hubbs* | 15.00 | 7.50 |
| 462a | Willie Tasby ("W" on cap) | | |
| | | 4.00 | 2.00 |
| 462b | Willie Tasby (plain cap) | | |
| | | 60.00 | 30.00 |
| 463 | Hank Bauer | 5.00 | 2.50 |
| 464 | *Al Jackson* | 5.00 | 2.50 |
| 465 | Reds Team | 4.00 | 1.75 |
| 466 | Norm Cash AS | 4.00 | 1.75 |
| 467 | Chuck Schilling AS | 5.00 | 2.50 |
| 468 | Brooks Robinson AS | | |
| | | 12.00 | 5.50 |
| 469 | Luis Aparicio AS | 8.00 | 3.50 |
| 470 | Al Kaline AS | 18.00 | 7.50 |
| 471 | Mickey Mantle AS | | |
| | | 125.00 | 67.00 |
| 472 | Rocky Colavito AS | 5.00 | 2.25 |
| 473 | Elston Howard AS | 5.00 | 2.25 |
| 474 | Frank Lary AS | 5.00 | 2.50 |
| 475 | Whitey Ford AS | 10.00 | 4.50 |
| 476 | Orioles Team | 5.00 | 2.50 |
| 477 | Andre Rodgers | 4.00 | 2.00 |
| 478 | Don Zimmer | 5.00 | 2.50 |
| 479 | *Joel Horlen* | 4.00 | 2.00 |
| 480 | Harvey Kuenn | 5.00 | 2.50 |
| 481 | Vic Wertz | 4.00 | 2.00 |
| 482 | Sam Mele | 4.00 | 2.00 |
| 483 | Don McMahon | 4.00 | 2.00 |
| 484 | Dick Schofield | 4.00 | 2.00 |
| 485 | Pedro Ramos | 4.00 | 2.00 |
| 486 | Jim Gilliam | 4.00 | 1.75 |
| 487 | Jerry Lynch | 4.00 | 2.00 |
| 488 | Hal Brown | 4.00 | 2.00 |
| 489 | Julio Gotay | 4.00 | 2.00 |
| 490 | Clete Boyer | 4.00 | 1.75 |
| 491 | Leon Wagner | 4.00 | 2.00 |
| 492 | Hal Smith | 4.00 | 2.00 |
| 493 | Danny McDevitt | 4.00 | 2.00 |
| 494 | Sammy White | 4.00 | 2.00 |
| 495 | Don Cardwell | 4.00 | 2.00 |
| 496 | Wayne Causey | 4.00 | 2.00 |
| 497 | Ed Bouchee | 5.00 | 2.50 |
| 498 | Jim Donohue | 4.00 | 2.00 |
| 499 | Zoilo Versalles | 4.00 | 2.00 |
| 500 | Duke Snider | 40.00 | 20.00 |
| 501 | Claude Osteen | 4.00 | 2.00 |
| 502 | Hector Lopez | 5.00 | 2.50 |
| 503 | Danny Murtaugh | 4.00 | 2.00 |
| 504 | Eddie Bressoud | 4.00 | 2.00 |
| 505 | Juan Marichal | 35.00 | 17.50 |
| 506 | Charley Maxwell | 4.00 | 2.00 |
| 507 | Ernie Broglio | 4.00 | 2.00 |
| 508 | Gordy Coleman | 4.00 | 2.00 |
| 509 | *Dave Giusti* | 4.00 | 2.00 |

| | | NR MT | EX |
|---|---|---|---|
| 510 | Jim Lemon | 4.00 | 2.00 |
| 511 | Bubba Phillips | 4.00 | 2.00 |
| 512 | Mike Fornieles | 4.00 | 2.00 |
| 513 | Whitey Herzog | 4.00 | 1.75 |
| 514 | Sherm Lollar | 4.00 | 2.00 |
| 515 | Stan Williams | 4.00 | 2.00 |
| 516 | Checklist 507-598 | 8.00 | 3.50 |
| 517 | Dave Wickersham | 4.00 | 2.00 |
| 518 | Lee Maye | 4.00 | 2.00 |
| 519 | Bob Johnson | 4.00 | 2.00 |
| 520 | Bob Friend | 5.00 | 2.50 |
| 521 | Jacke Davis | 4.00 | 2.00 |
| 522 | Lindy McDaniel | 4.00 | 2.00 |
| 523 | Russ Nixon | 12.00 | 5.50 |
| 524 | Howie Nunn | 12.00 | 5.50 |
| 525 | George Thomas | 12.00 | 5.50 |
| 526 | Hal Woodeshick | 12.00 | 5.50 |
| 527 | *Dick McAuliffe* | 15.00 | 5.00 |
| 528 | Turk Lown | 12.00 | 5.50 |
| 529 | John Schaive | 12.00 | 5.50 |
| 530 | Bob Gibson | 175.00 | 87.00 |
| 531 | Bobby G. Smith | 12.00 | 5.50 |
| 532 | Dick Stigman | 12.00 | 5.50 |
| 533 | Charley Lau | 13.00 | 5.75 |
| 534 | Tony Gonzalez | 12.00 | 5.50 |
| 535 | Ed Roebuck | 12.00 | 5.50 |
| 536 | Dick Gernert | 12.00 | 5.50 |
| 537 | Indians Team | 15.00 | 6.75 |
| 538 | Jack Sanford | 12.00 | 5.50 |
| 539 | Billy Moran | 12.00 | 5.50 |
| 540 | Jim Landis | 12.00 | 5.50 |
| 541 | Don Nottebart | 12.00 | 5.50 |
| 542 | Dave Philley | 12.00 | 5.50 |
| 543 | Bob Allen | 12.00 | 5.50 |
| 544 | Willie McCovey | 125.00 | 62.00 |
| 545 | Hoyt Wilhelm | 55.00 | 25.00 |
| 546 | Moe Thacker | 12.00 | 5.50 |
| 547 | Don Ferrarese | 12.00 | 5.50 |
| 548 | Bobby Del Greco | 12.00 | 5.50 |
| 549 | Bill Rigney | 12.00 | 5.50 |
| 550 | Art Mahaffey | 12.00 | 5.50 |
| 551 | Harry Bright | 12.00 | 5.50 |
| 552 | Cubs Team | 15.00 | 6.75 |
| 553 | Jim Coates | 15.00 | 6.75 |
| 554 | Bubba Morton | 12.00 | 5.50 |
| 555 | John Buzhardt | 12.00 | 5.50 |
| 556 | Al Spangler | 12.00 | 5.50 |
| 557 | Bob Anderson | 12.00 | 5.50 |
| 558 | John Goryl | 12.00 | 5.50 |
| 559 | Mike Higgins | 12.00 | 5.50 |
| 560 | Chuck Estrada | 12.00 | 5.50 |
| 561 | Gene Oliver | 12.00 | 5.50 |
| 562 | Bill Henry | 12.00 | 5.50 |
| 563 | Ken Aspromonte | 12.00 | 5.50 |
| 564 | Bob Grim | 12.00 | 5.50 |
| 565 | Jose Pagan | 12.00 | 5.50 |
| 566 | Marty Kutyna | 12.00 | 5.50 |
| 567 | Tracy Stallard | 12.00 | 5.50 |
| 568 | Jim Golden | 12.00 | 5.50 |
| 569 | Ed Sadowski | 12.00 | 5.50 |
| 570 | Bill Stafford | 15.00 | 6.75 |
| 571 | Billy Klaus | 12.00 | 5.50 |
| 572 | Bob Miller | 13.00 | 5.75 |
| 573 | Johnny Logan | 13.00 | 5.75 |
| 574 | Dean Stone | 12.00 | 5.50 |
| 575 | Red Schoendienst | 35.00 | 15.00 |

| | | NR MT | EX |
|---|---|---|---|
| 576 | Russ Kemmerer | 12.00 | 5.50 |
| 577 | Dave Nicholson | 12.00 | 5.50 |
| 578 | Jim Duffalo | 12.00 | 5.50 |
| 579 | Jim Schaffer | 12.00 | 5.50 |
| 580 | Bill Monbouquette | 13.00 | 5.75 |
| 581 | Mel Roach | 12.00 | 5.50 |
| 582 | Ron Piche | 12.00 | 5.50 |
| 583 | Larry Osborne | 12.00 | 5.50 |
| 584 | Twins Team | 15.00 | 6.75 |
| 585 | Glen Hobbie | 12.00 | 5.50 |
| 586 | Sammy Esposito | 12.00 | 5.50 |
| 587 | Frank Funk | 12.00 | 5.50 |
| 588 | Birdie Tebbetts | 12.00 | 5.50 |
| 589 | Bob Turley | 18.00 | 8.00 |
| 590 | Curt Flood | 18.00 | 8.00 |
| 591 | Rookie Parade Pitchers (Sam McDowell, Ron Nischwitz, Art Quirk, *Dick Radatz, Ron Taylor*) | 60.00 | 30.00 |
| 592 | Rookie Parade Pitchers (Bo Belinsky, Joe Bonikowski, *Jim Bouton*, Dan Pfister, Dave Stenhouse) | 45.00 | 20.00 |
| 593 | Rookie Parade Pitchers (Craig Anderson, *Jack Hamilton*, Jack Lamabe, Bob Moorhead, *Bob Veale*) | 25.00 | 11.25 |
| 594 | Rookie Parade Catchers (Doug Camilli, *Doc Edwards*, Don Pavletich, Ken Retzer, *Bob Uecker*) | 150.00 | 75.00 |
| 595 | Rookie Parade Infielders (*Ed Charles*, Marlin Coughtry, Bob Sadowski, Felix Torres) | 25.00 | 11.25 |
| 596 | Rookie Parade Infielders (Bernie Allen, *Phil Linz, Joe Pepitone, Rich Rollins*) | 65.00 | 33.00 |
| 597 | Rookie Parade Infielders (Rod Kanehl, Jim McKnight, *Denis Menke*, Amado Samuel) | 25.00 | 11.25 |
| 598 | Rookie Parade Outfielders (Howie Goss, *Jim Hickman*, Manny Jimenez, Al Luplow, Ed Olivares) | 65.00 | 33.00 |

## 1963 Topps

Although the number of cards dropped to 576, the

1963 Topps set is among the most popular of the 1960s. A color photo dominates the 2-1/2" by 3-1/2" card, but a colored circle at the bottom carries a black and white portrait as well. A colored band gives the player's name, team and position. The backs again feature career statistics and a cartoon, career summary and brief biographical details. The set is somewhat unlike those immediately preceding it in that there are fewer specialty cards. The major groupings are statistical leaders, World Series highlights and rookies. It is one rookie which makes the set special - Pete Rose. As one of most avidly sought cards in history and a high-numbered card at that, the Rose rookie card accounts for much of the value of a complete set.

|  | NR MT | EX |
|---|---|---|
| Complete Set: | 5000.00 | 2500.00 |
| Common Player: 1-283 | 1.50 | .70 |
| Common Player: 284-446 | 3.00 | 1.50 |
| Common Player: 447-506 | 10.00 | 5.00 |
| Common Player: 507-576 | 7.00 | 3.50 |

| | | NR MT | EX |
|---|---|---|---|
| 1 | N.L. Batting Leaders (Hank Aaron, Tommy Davis, Stan Musial, Frank Robinson, Bill White) | 40.00 | 6.00 |
| 2 | A.L. Batting Leaders (Chuck Hinton, Mickey Mantle, Floyd Robinson, Pete Runnels, Norm Siebern) | 25.00 | 12.50 |
| 3 | N.L. Home Run Leaders (Hank Aaron, Ernie Banks, Orlando Cepeda, Willie Mays, Frank Robinson) | 12.00 | 6.00 |
| 4 | A.L. Home Run Leaders (Norm Cash, Rocky Colavito, Jim Gentile, Harmon Killebrew, Roger Maris, Leon Wagner) | 4.00 | 2.00 |
| 5 | N.L. E.R.A. Leaders (Don Drysdale, Bob Gibson, Sandy Koufax, Bob Purkey, Bob Shaw) | 4.00 | 2.00 |
| 6 | A.L. E.R.A. Leaders (Hank Aguirre, Dean Chance, Eddie Fisher, Whitey Ford, Robin Roberts) | 3.50 | 1.75 |
| 7 | N.L. Pitching Leaders (Don Drysdale, Joe Jay, Art Mahaffey, Billy O'Dell, Bob Purkey, Jack Sanford) | 3.50 | 1.75 |
| 8 | A.L. Pitching Leaders (Jim Bunning, Dick Donovan, Ray Herbert, Camilo Pascual, Ralph Terry) | 3.00 | 1.50 |
| 9 | N.L. Strikeout Leaders (Don Drysdale, Dick Farrell, Bob Gibson, Sandy Koufax, Billy O'Dell) | 4.00 | 2.00 |
| 10 | A.L. Strikeout Leaders (Jim Bunning, Jim Kaat, Camilo Pascual, Juan Pizarro, Ralph Terry) | 3.00 | 1.50 |
| 11 | Lee Walls | 1.50 | .70 |
| 12 | Steve Barber | 1.50 | .70 |
| 13 | Phillies Team | 3.25 | 1.75 |
| 14 | Pedro Ramos | 1.50 | .70 |
| 15 | Ken Hubbs | 3.00 | 1.50 |
| 16 | Al Smith | 1.50 | .70 |
| 17 | Ryne Duren | 1.75 | .90 |
| 18 | Buc Blasters (Smoky Burgess, Bob Clemente, Bob Skinner, Dick Stuart) | 10.00 | 5.00 |
| 19 | Pete Burnside | 1.50 | .70 |
| 20 | Tony Kubek | 7.00 | 3.50 |
| 21 | Marty Keough | 1.50 | .70 |
| 22 | Curt Simmons | 1.75 | .90 |
| 23 | Ed Lopat | 2.00 | 1.00 |
| 24 | Bob Bruce | 1.50 | .70 |
| 25 | Al Kaline | 35.00 | 17.50 |
| 26 | Ray Moore | 1.50 | .70 |
| 27 | Choo Choo Coleman | 2.00 | 1.00 |
| 28 | Mike Fornieles | 1.50 | .70 |
| 29a | 1962 Rookie Stars (John Boozer, *Ray Culp, Sammy Ellis*, Jesse Gonder) | 7.00 | 3.50 |
| 29b | 1963 Rookie Stars (John Boozer, *Ray Culp, Sammy Ellis*, Jesse Gonder) | 2.00 | 1.00 |
| 30 | Harvey Kuenn | 1.50 | .70 |
| 31 | Cal Koonce | 1.50 | .70 |
| 32 | Tony Gonzalez | 1.50 | .70 |
| 33 | Bo Belinsky | 3.00 | 1.50 |
| 34 | Dick Schofield | 1.50 | .70 |
| 35 | John Buzhardt | 1.50 | .70 |
| 36 | Jerry Kindall | 1.50 | .70 |
| 37 | Jerry Lynch | 1.50 | .70 |
| 38 | Bud Daley | 2.00 | 1.00 |
| 39 | Angels Team | 3.25 | 1.75 |
| 40 | Vic Power | 1.50 | .70 |
| 41 | Charlie Lau | 1.75 | .90 |
| 42 | Stan Williams | 2.00 | 1.00 |
| 43 | Veteran Masters (Casey Stengel, Gene Woodling) | 4.00 | 2.00 |
| 44 | Terry Fox | 1.50 | .70 |
| 45 | Bob Aspromonte | 1.50 | .70 |
| 46 | *Tommie Aaron* | 2.00 | 1.00 |
| 47 | Don Lock | 1.50 | .70 |
| 48 | Birdie Tebbetts | 1.50 | .70 |
| 49 | *Dal Maxvill* | 2.00 | 1.00 |

| | | NR MT | EX |
|---|---|---|---|
| 50 | Bill Pierce | 2.00 | 1.00 |
| 51 | George Alusik | 1.50 | .70 |
| 52 | Chuck Schilling | 1.50 | .70 |
| 53 | Joe Moeller | 1.50 | .70 |
| 54a | 1962 Rookie Stars (Jack Cullen, *Dave DeBusschere*, Harry Fanok, Nelson Mathews) | 15.00 | 7.50 |
| 54b | 1963 Rookie Stars (Jack Cullen, *Dave DeBusschere*, Harry Fanok, Nelson Mathews) | 4.00 | 2.00 |
| 55 | Bill Virdon | 1.50 | .70 |
| 56 | Dennis Bennett | 1.50 | .70 |
| 57 | Billy Moran | 1.50 | .70 |
| 58 | Bob Will | 1.50 | .70 |
| 59 | Craig Anderson | 1.75 | .90 |
| 60 | Elston Howard | 8.00 | 4.00 |
| 61 | Ernie Bowman | 1.50 | .70 |
| 62 | Bob Hendley | 1.50 | .70 |
| 63 | Reds Team | 2.50 | 1.25 |
| 64 | Dick McAuliffe | 1.75 | .90 |
| 65 | Jackie Brandt | 1.50 | .70 |
| 66 | Mike Joyce | 1.50 | .70 |
| 67 | Ed Charles | 1.50 | .70 |
| 68 | Friendly Foes (Gil Hodges, Duke Snider) | 8.00 | 4.00 |
| 69 | Bud Zipfel | 1.50 | .70 |
| 70 | Jim O'Toole | 1.50 | .70 |
| 71 | *Bobby Wine* | 1.75 | .90 |
| 72 | Johnny Romano | 1.50 | .70 |
| 73 | Bobby Bragan | 1.75 | .90 |
| 74 | *Denver Lemaster* | 1.75 | .90 |
| 75 | Bob Allison | 2.00 | 1.00 |
| 76 | Earl Wilson | 1.50 | .70 |
| 77 | Al Spangler | 1.50 | .70 |
| 78 | Marv Throneberry | 3.50 | 1.75 |
| 79 | Checklist 1-88 | 2.50 | 1.25 |
| 80 | Jim Gilliam | 3.00 | 1.50 |
| 81 | Jimmie Schaffer | 1.50 | .70 |
| 82 | Ed Rakow | 1.50 | .70 |
| 83 | Charley James | 1.50 | .70 |
| 84 | Ron Kline | 1.50 | .70 |
| 85 | Tom Haller | 1.75 | .90 |
| 86 | Charley Maxwell | 1.50 | .70 |
| 87 | Bob Veale | 1.75 | .90 |
| 88 | Ron Hansen | 1.50 | .70 |
| 89 | Dick Stigman | 1.50 | .70 |
| 90 | Gordy Coleman | 1.50 | .70 |
| 91 | Dallas Green | 1.75 | .90 |
| 92 | Hector Lopez | 2.00 | 1.00 |
| 93 | Galen Cisco | 1.75 | .90 |
| 94 | Bob Schmidt | 1.50 | .70 |
| 95 | Larry Jackson | 1.50 | .70 |
| 96 | Lou Clinton | 1.50 | .70 |
| 97 | Bob Duliba | 1.50 | .70 |
| 98 | George Thomas | 1.50 | .70 |
| 99 | Jim Umbricht | 1.50 | .70 |
| 100 | Joe Cunningham | 1.75 | .90 |
| 101 | Joe Gibbon | 1.50 | .70 |
| 102a | Checklist 89-176 ("Checklist" in red on front) | 3.00 | 1.50 |
| 102b | Checklist 89-176 ("Checklist" in white) | 8.00 | 4.00 |
| 103 | Chuck Essegian | 1.50 | .70 |
| 104 | Lew Krausse | 1.50 | .70 |
| 105 | Ron Fairly | 1.75 | .90 |
| 106 | Bob Bolin | 1.50 | .70 |
| 107 | Jim Hickman | 1.75 | .90 |
| 108 | Hoyt Wilhelm | 11.00 | 5.50 |
| 109 | Lee Maye | 1.50 | .70 |
| 110 | Rich Rollins | 1.75 | .90 |
| 111 | Al Jackson | 1.75 | .90 |
| 112 | Dick Brown | 1.50 | .70 |
| 113 | Don Landrum (photo actally Ron Santo) | 1.75 | .90 |
| 114 | Dan Osinski | 1.50 | .70 |
| 115 | Carl Yastrzemski | 100.00 | 50.00 |
| 116 | Jim Brosnan | 1.75 | .90 |
| 117 | Jacke Davis | 1.50 | .70 |
| 118 | Sherm Lollar | 1.75 | .90 |
| 119 | Bob Lillis | 1.50 | .70 |
| 120 | Roger Maris | 65.00 | 32.50 |
| 121 | Jim Hannan | 1.50 | .70 |
| 122 | Julio Gotay | 1.50 | .70 |
| 123 | Frank Howard | 2.50 | 1.25 |
| 124 | Dick Howser | 1.50 | .70 |
| 125 | Robin Roberts | 8.00 | 4.00 |
| 126 | Bob Uecker | 45.00 | 23.00 |
| 127 | Bill Tuttle | 1.50 | .70 |
| 128 | Matty Alou | 1.75 | .90 |
| 129 | Gary Bell | 1.50 | .70 |
| 130 | Dick Groat | 1.50 | .70 |
| 131 | Senators Team | 3.25 | 1.75 |
| 132 | Jack Hamilton | 1.50 | .70 |
| 133 | Gene Freese | 1.50 | .70 |
| 134 | Bob Scheffing | 1.50 | .70 |
| 135 | Richie Ashburn | 8.00 | 4.00 |
| 136 | Ike Delock | 1.50 | .70 |
| 137 | Mack Jones | 1.50 | .70 |
| 138 | Pride of N.L. (Willie Mays, Stan Musial) | 30.00 | 15.00 |
| 139 | Earl Averill | 1.50 | .70 |
| 140 | Frank Lary | 1.75 | .90 |
| 141 | *Manny Mota* | 7.00 | 3.50 |
| 142 | World Series Game 1 (Yanks' Ford Wins Series Opener) | 3.50 | 1.75 |
| 143 | World Series Game 2 (Sanford Flashes Shutout Magic) | 3.25 | 1.75 |
| 144 | World Series Game 3 (Maris Sparks Yankee Rally) | 4.00 | 2.00 |
| 145 | World Series Game 4 (Hiller Blasts Grand Slammer) | 3.25 | 1.75 |
| 146 | World Series Game 5 (Tresh's Homer Defeats Giants) | 3.00 | 1.50 |
| 147 | World Series Game 6 (Pierce Stars In 3-Hit Victory) | 3.00 | 1.50 |
| 148 | World Series Game 7 (Yanks Celebrate As Terry Wins) | 3.00 | 1.50 |
| 149 | Marv Breeding | 1.50 | .70 |
| 150 | Johnny Podres | 3.00 | 1.50 |
| 151 | Pirates Team | 3.25 | 1.75 |
| 152 | Ron Nischwitz | 1.50 | .70 |
| 153 | Hal Smith | 1.50 | .70 |
| 154 | Walt Alston | 3.00 | 1.50 |

| # | Player | NR MT | EX |
|---|--------|-------|-----|
| 155 | Bill Stafford | 2.00 | 1.00 |
| 156 | Roy McMillan | 1.50 | .70 |
| 157 | *Diego Segui* | 1.75 | .90 |
| 158 | 1963 Rookie Stars (Rogelio Alvarez, *Tommy Harper*, Dave Roberts, Bob Saverine) | 1.75 | .90 |
| 159 | Jim Pagliaroni | 1.50 | .70 |
| 160 | Juan Pizarro | 1.50 | .70 |
| 161 | Frank Torre | 1.50 | .70 |
| 162 | Twins Team | 3.25 | 1.75 |
| 163 | Don Larsen | 2.00 | 1.00 |
| 164 | Bubba Morton | 1.50 | .70 |
| 165 | Jim Kaat | 7.00 | 3.50 |
| 166 | Johnny Keane | 1.50 | .70 |
| 167 | Jim Fregosi | 1.50 | .70 |
| 168 | Russ Nixon | 1.50 | .70 |
| 169 | 1963 Rookie Stars (Dick Egan, Julio Navarro, Gaylord Perry, Tommie Sisk) | 30.00 | 15.00 |
| 170 | Joe Adcock | 1.50 | .70 |
| 171 | Steve Hamilton | 1.50 | .70 |
| 172 | Gene Oliver | 1.50 | .70 |
| 173 | Bomber's Best (Mickey Mantle, Bobby Richardson, Tom Tresh) | 65.00 | 33.00 |
| 174 | Larry Burright | 1.75 | .90 |
| 175 | Bob Buhl | 1.75 | .90 |
| 176 | Jim King | 1.50 | .70 |
| 177 | Bubba Phillips | 1.50 | .70 |
| 178 | Johnny Edwards | 1.50 | .70 |
| 179 | Ron Piche | 1.50 | .70 |
| 180 | Bill Skowron | 1.50 | .70 |
| 181 | Sammy Esposito | 1.50 | .70 |
| 182 | Albie Pearson | 1.50 | .70 |
| 183 | Joe Pepitone | 4.00 | 2.00 |
| 184 | Vern Law | 2.00 | 1.00 |
| 185 | Chuck Hiller | 1.50 | .70 |
| 186 | Jerry Zimmerman | 1.50 | .70 |
| 187 | Willie Kirkland | 1.50 | .70 |
| 188 | Eddie Bressoud | 1.50 | .70 |
| 189 | Dave Giusti | 1.50 | .70 |
| 190 | Minnie Minoso | 1.50 | .70 |
| 191 | Checklist 177-264 | 3.00 | 1.50 |
| 192 | Clay Dalrymple | 1.50 | .70 |
| 193 | Andre Rodgers | 1.50 | .70 |
| 194 | Joe Nuxhall | 1.75 | .90 |
| 195 | Manny Jimenez | 1.50 | .70 |
| 196 | Doug Camilli | 1.50 | .70 |
| 197 | Roger Craig | 3.00 | 1.50 |
| 198 | Lenny Green | 1.50 | .70 |
| 199 | Joe Amalfitano | 1.50 | .70 |
| 200 | Mickey Mantle | 400.00 | 200.00 |
| 201 | Cecil Butler | 1.50 | .70 |
| 202 | Red Sox Team | 2.50 | 1.25 |
| 203 | Chico Cardenas | 1.50 | .70 |
| 204 | Don Nottebart | 1.50 | .70 |
| 205 | Luis Aparicio | 10.00 | 5.00 |
| 206 | Ray Washburn | 1.50 | .70 |
| 207 | Ken Hunt | 1.50 | .70 |
| 208 | 1963 Rookie Stars (Ron Herbel, John Miller, Ron Taylor, Wally Wolf) | 1.50 | .70 |
| 209 | Hobie Landrith | 1.50 | .70 |
| 210 | Sandy Koufax | 160.00 | 80.00 |
| 211 | Fred Whitfield | 1.50 | .70 |
| 212 | Glen Hobbie | 1.50 | .70 |
| 213 | Billy Hitchcock | 1.50 | .70 |
| 214 | Orlando Pena | 1.50 | .70 |
| 215 | Bob Skinner | 1.75 | .90 |
| 216 | Gene Conley | 1.75 | .90 |
| 217 | Joe Christopher | 1.75 | .90 |
| 218 | Tiger Twirlers (Jim Bunning, Frank Lary, Don Mossi) | 3.00 | 1.50 |
| 219 | Chuck Cottier | 1.50 | .70 |
| 220 | Camilo Pascual | 1.75 | .90 |
| 221 | *Cookie Rojas* | 1.75 | .90 |
| 222 | Cubs Team | 3.25 | 1.75 |
| 223 | Eddie Fisher | 1.50 | .70 |
| 224 | Mike Roarke | 1.50 | .70 |
| 225 | Joe Jay | 1.50 | .70 |
| 226 | Julian Javier | 1.75 | .90 |
| 227 | Jim Grant | 1.50 | .70 |
| 228 | 1963 Rookie Stars (*Max Alvis, Bob Bailey, Ed Kranepool, Pedro Oliva*) — | 50.00 | 25.00 |
| 229 | Willie Davis | 1.50 | .70 |
| 230 | Pete Runnels | 1.75 | .90 |
| 231 | Eli Grba (photo actually Ryne Duren) | 1.75 | .90 |
| 232 | Frank Malzone | 1.75 | .90 |
| 233 | Casey Stengel | 15.00 | 7.50 |
| 234 | Dave Nicholson | 1.50 | .70 |
| 235 | Billy O'Dell | 1.50 | .70 |
| 236 | Bill Bryan | 1.50 | .70 |
| 237 | Jim Coates | 2.00 | 1.00 |
| 238 | Lou Johnson | 1.50 | .70 |
| 239 | Harvey Haddix | 1.75 | .90 |
| 240 | Rocky Colavito | 10.00 | 5.00 |
| 241 | Billy Smith | 1.50 | .70 |
| 242 | Power Plus (Hank Aaron, Ernie Banks) | 35.00 | 17.50 |
| 243 | Don Leppert | 1.50 | .70 |
| 244 | John Tsitouris | 1.50 | .70 |
| 245 | Gil Hodges | 15.00 | 7.50 |
| 246 | Lee Stange | 1.50 | .70 |
| 247 | Yankees Team | 10.00 | 5.00 |
| 248 | Tito Francona | 1.75 | .90 |
| 249 | Leo Burke | 1.50 | .70 |
| 250 | Stan Musial | 100.00 | 45.00 |
| 251 | Jack Lamabe | 1.50 | .70 |
| 252 | Ron Santo | 3.00 | 1.50 |
| 253 | 1963 Rookie Stars (Len Gabrielson, Pete Jernigan, Deacon Jones, John Wojcik) | 1.50 | .70 |
| 254 | Mike Hershberger | 1.50 | .70 |
| 255 | Bob Shaw | 1.50 | .70 |
| 256 | Jerry Lumpe | 1.75 | .90 |
| 257 | Hank Aguirre | 1.50 | .70 |
| 258 | Alvin Dark | 1.75 | .90 |
| 259 | Johnny Logan | 1.75 | .90 |
| 260 | Jim Gentile | 1.75 | .90 |
| 261 | Bob Miller | 1.50 | .70 |
| 262 | Ellis Burton | 1.50 | .70 |
| 263 | Dave Stenhouse | 1.50 | .70 |
| 264 | Phil Linz | 1.50 | .70 |
| 265 | Vada Pinson | 2.50 | 1.25 |
| 266 | Bob Allen | 1.50 | .70 |
| 267 | Carl Sawatski | 1.50 | .70 |
| 268 | Don Demeter | 1.50 | .70 |

| | | NR MT | EX |
|---|---|---|---|
| 269 | Don Mincher | 1.75 | .90 |
| 270 | Felipe Alou | 1.75 | .90 |
| 271 | Dean Stone | 1.50 | .70 |
| 272 | Danny Murphy | 1.50 | .70 |
| 273 | Sammy Taylor | 1.75 | .90 |
| 274 | Checklist 265-352 | 3.00 | 1.50 |
| 275 | Ed Mathews | 20.00 | 10.00 |
| 276 | Barry Shetrone | 1.50 | .70 |
| 277 | Dick Farrell | 1.50 | .70 |
| 278 | Chico Fernandez | 1.50 | .70 |
| 279 | Wally Moon | 1.75 | .90 |
| 280 | Bob Rodgers | 1.75 | .90 |
| 281 | Tom Sturdivant | 1.50 | .70 |
| 282 | Bob Del Greco | 1.50 | .70 |
| 283 | Roy Sievers | 1.75 | .90 |
| 284 | Dave Sisler | 3.00 | 1.50 |
| 285 | Dick Stuart | 3.25 | 1.75 |
| 286 | Stu Miller | 3.00 | 1.50 |
| 287 | Dick Bertell | 3.00 | 1.50 |
| 288 | White Sox Team | 3.50 | 1.75 |
| 289 | Hal Brown | 3.50 | 1.75 |
| 290 | Bill White | 3.25 | 1.75 |
| 291 | Don Rudolph | 3.00 | 1.50 |
| 292 | Pumpsie Green | 3.25 | 1.75 |
| 293 | Bill Pleis | 3.00 | 1.50 |
| 294 | Bill Rigney | 3.00 | 1.50 |
| 295 | Ed Roebuck | 3.00 | 1.50 |
| 296 | Doc Edwards | 3.25 | 1.75 |
| 297 | Jim Golden | 3.00 | 1.50 |
| 298 | Don Dillard | 3.00 | 1.50 |
| 299 | 1963 Rookie Stars (Tom Butters, Bob Dustal, Dave Morehead, Dan Schneider) | 3.00 | 1.50 |
| 300 | Willie Mays | 160.00 | 80.00 |
| 301 | Bill Fischer | 3.00 | 1.50 |
| 302 | Whitey Herzog | 3.50 | 1.75 |
| 303 | Earl Francis | 3.00 | 1.50 |
| 304 | Harry Bright | 3.00 | 1.50 |
| 305 | Don Hoak | 3.25 | 1.75 |
| 306 | Star Receivers (Earl Battey, Elston Howard) | 3.50 | 1.75 |
| 307 | Chet Nichols | 3.00 | 1.50 |
| 308 | Camilo Carreon | 3.00 | 1.50 |
| 309 | Jim Brewer | 3.00 | 1.50 |
| 310 | Tommy Davis | 3.00 | 1.50 |
| 311 | Joe McClain | 3.00 | 1.50 |
| 312 | Colt .45s Team | 12.00 | 6.00 |
| 313 | Ernie Broglio | 3.00 | 1.50 |
| 314 | John Goryl | 3.00 | 1.50 |
| 315 | Ralph Terry | 3.00 | 1.50 |
| 316 | Norm Sherry | 2.00 | 1.00 |
| 317 | Sam McDowell | 3.00 | 1.50 |
| 318 | Gene Mauch | 3.25 | 1.75 |
| 319 | Joe Gaines | 3.00 | 1.50 |
| 320 | Warren Spahn | 25.00 | 12.50 |
| 321 | Gino Cimoli | 3.00 | 1.50 |
| 322 | Bob Turley | 3.25 | 1.75 |
| 323 | Bill Mazeroski | 3.50 | 1.75 |
| 324 | 1963 Rookie Stars (Vic Davalillo, Phil Roof, Pete Ward, George Williams) | 2.50 | 1.25 |
| 325 | Jack Sanford | 3.00 | 1.50 |
| 326 | Hank Foiles | 3.00 | 1.50 |
| 327 | Paul Foytack | 3.00 | 1.50 |
| 328 | Dick Williams | 3.50 | 1.75 |
| 329 | Lindy McDaniel | 3.00 | 1.50 |
| 330 | Chuck Hinton | 3.00 | 1.50 |
| 331 | Series Foes (Bill Pierce, Bill Stafford) | 3.00 | 1.50 |
| 332 | Joel Horlen | 3.00 | 1.50 |
| 333 | Carl Warwick | 3.00 | 1.50 |
| 334 | Wynn Hawkins | 3.25 | 1.75 |
| 335 | Leon Wagner | 3.25 | 1.75 |
| 336 | Ed Bauta | 3.00 | 1.50 |
| 337 | Dodgers Team | 10.00 | 5.00 |
| 338 | Russ Kemmerer | 3.00 | 1.50 |
| 339 | Ted Bowsfield | 3.00 | 1.50 |
| 340 | Yogi Berra | 60.00 | 30.00 |
| 341 | Jack Baldschun | 3.00 | 1.50 |
| 342 | Gene Woodling | 2.50 | 1.25 |
| 343 | Johnny Pesky | 3.25 | 1.75 |
| 344 | Don Schwall | 3.00 | 1.50 |
| 345 | Brooks Robinson | 30.00 | 15.00 |
| 346 | Billy Hoeft | 3.00 | 1.50 |
| 347 | Joe Torre | 6.00 | 3.00 |
| 348 | Vic Wertz | 3.25 | 1.75 |
| 349 | Zoilo Versalles | 3.25 | 1.75 |
| 350 | Bob Purkey | 3.00 | 1.50 |
| 351 | Al Luplow | 3.00 | 1.50 |
| 352 | Ken Johnson | 3.00 | 1.50 |
| 353 | Billy Williams | 25.00 | 12.50 |
| 354 | Dom Zanni | 3.00 | 1.50 |
| 355 | Dean Chance | 3.25 | 1.75 |
| 356 | John Schaive | 3.00 | 1.50 |
| 357 | George Altman | 3.00 | 1.50 |
| 358 | Milt Pappas | 3.25 | 1.75 |
| 359 | Haywood Sullivan | 3.25 | 1.75 |
| 360 | Don Drysdale | 30.00 | 15.00 |
| 361 | Clete Boyer | 3.50 | 1.75 |
| 362 | Checklist 353-429 | 4.00 | 2.00 |
| 363 | Dick Radatz | 3.25 | 1.75 |
| 364 | Howie Goss | 3.00 | 1.50 |
| 365 | Jim Bunning | 10.00 | 5.00 |
| 366 | Tony Taylor | 3.00 | 1.50 |
| 367 | Tony Cloninger | 3.25 | 1.75 |
| 368 | Ed Bailey | 3.00 | 1.50 |
| 369 | Jim Lemon | 3.00 | 1.50 |
| 370 | Dick Donovan | 3.00 | 1.50 |
| 371 | Rod Kanehl | 3.25 | 1.75 |
| 372 | Don Lee | 3.00 | 1.50 |
| 373 | Jim Campbell | 3.00 | 1.50 |
| 374 | Claude Osteen | 3.25 | 1.75 |
| 375 | Ken Boyer | 4.00 | 2.00 |
| 376 | Johnnie Wyatt | 3.00 | 1.50 |
| 377 | Orioles Team | 3.50 | 1.75 |
| 378 | Bill Henry | 3.00 | 1.50 |
| 379 | Bob Anderson | 3.00 | 1.50 |
| 380 | Ernie Banks | 55.00 | 28.00 |
| 381 | Frank Baumann | 3.00 | 1.50 |
| 382 | Ralph Houk | 3.50 | 1.75 |
| 383 | Pete Richert | 3.00 | 1.50 |
| 384 | Bob Tillman | 3.00 | 1.50 |
| 385 | Art Mahaffey | 3.00 | 1.50 |
| 386 | 1963 Rookie Stars (John Bateman, Larry Bearnarth, Ed Kirkpatrick, Garry Roggenburk) | 3.25 | 1.75 |
| 387 | Al McBean | 3.00 | 1.50 |
| 388 | Jim Davenport | 3.00 | 1.50 |
| 389 | Frank Sullivan | 3.00 | 1.50 |
| 390 | Hank Aaron | 150.00 | 75.00 |

| | | NR MT | EX |
|---|---|---|---|
| 391 | Bill Dailey | 3.00 | 1.50 |
| 392 | Tribe Thumpers (Tito Francona, Johnny Romano) | 3.25 | 1.75 |
| 393 | Ken MacKenzie | 3.25 | 1.75 |
| 394 | Tim McCarver | 4.00 | 2.00 |
| 395 | Don McMahon | 3.00 | 1.50 |
| 396 | Joe Koppe | 3.00 | 1.50 |
| 397 | Athletics Team | 3.50 | 1.75 |
| 398 | Boog Powell | 7.00 | 3.50 |
| 399 | Dick Ellsworth | 3.00 | 1.50 |
| 400 | Frank Robinson | 45.00 | 23.00 |
| 401 | Jim Bouton | 10.00 | 5.00 |
| 402 | Mickey Vernon | 3.25 | 1.75 |
| 403 | Ron Perranoski | 3.25 | 1.75 |
| 404 | Bob Oldis | 3.00 | 1.50 |
| 405 | Floyd Robinson | 3.00 | 1.50 |
| 406 | Howie Koplitz | 3.00 | 1.50 |
| 407 | 1963 Rookie Stars (Larry Elliot, Frank Kostro, Chico Ruiz, Dick Simpson) | 3.00 | 1.50 |
| 408 | Billy Gardner | 3.00 | 1.50 |
| 409 | Roy Face | 3.50 | 1.75 |
| 410 | Earl Battey | 3.25 | 1.75 |
| 411 | Jim Constable | 3.00 | 1.50 |
| 412 | Dodgers' Big Three (Don Drysdale, Sandy Koufax, Johnny Podres) | 30.00 | 15.00 |
| 413 | Jerry Walker | 3.00 | 1.50 |
| 414 | Ty Cline | 3.00 | 1.50 |
| 415 | Bob Gibson | 30.00 | 15.00 |
| 416 | Alex Grammas | 3.00 | 1.50 |
| 417 | Giants Team | 3.50 | 1.75 |
| 418 | Johnny Orsino | 3.00 | 1.50 |
| 419 | Tracy Stallard | 3.25 | 1.75 |
| 420 | Bobby Richardson | 10.00 | 5.00 |
| 421 | Tom Morgan | 3.00 | 1.50 |
| 422 | Fred Hutchinson | 3.25 | 1.75 |
| 423 | Ed Hobaugh | 3.00 | 1.50 |
| 424 | Charley Smith | 3.00 | 1.50 |
| 425 | Smoky Burgess | 2.50 | 1.25 |
| 426 | Barry Latman | 3.00 | 1.50 |
| 427 | Bernie Allen | 3.00 | 1.50 |
| 428 | Carl Boles | 3.00 | 1.50 |
| 429 | Lou Burdette | 3.00 | 1.50 |
| 430 | Norm Siebern | 3.25 | 1.75 |
| 431a | Checklist 430-506 ("Checklist" in black on front) | 4.50 | 2.25 |
| 431b | Checklist 430-506 ("Checklist" in white) | 7.00 | 3.50 |
| 432 | Roman Mejias | 3.00 | 1.50 |
| 433 | Denis Menke | 3.25 | 1.75 |
| 434 | Johnny Callison | 2.50 | 1.25 |
| 435 | Woody Held | 3.00 | 1.50 |
| 436 | Tim Harkness | 3.25 | 1.75 |
| 437 | Bill Bruton | 3.00 | 1.50 |
| 438 | Wes Stock | 3.00 | 1.50 |
| 439 | Don Zimmer | 3.50 | 1.75 |
| 440 | Juan Marichal | 20.00 | 10.00 |
| 441 | Lee Thomas | 3.00 | 1.50 |
| 442 | J.C. Hartman | 3.00 | 1.50 |
| 443 | Jim Piersall | 3.50 | 1.75 |
| 444 | Jim Maloney | 3.25 | 1.75 |
| 445 | Norm Cash | 3.00 | 1.50 |

| | | NR MT | EX |
|---|---|---|---|
| 446 | Whitey Ford | 35.00 | 17.50 |
| 447 | Felix Mantilla | 10.00 | 5.00 |
| 448 | Jack Kralick | 10.00 | 5.00 |
| 449 | Jose Tartabull | 10.00 | 5.00 |
| 450 | Bob Friend | 11.00 | 5.50 |
| 451 | Indians Team | 10.00 | 5.00 |
| 452 | Barney Schultz | 10.00 | 5.00 |
| 453 | Jake Wood | 10.00 | 5.00 |
| 454a | Art Fowler (card # on orange background) | 10.00 | 5.00 |
| 454b | Art Fowler (card # on white background) | 10.00 | 5.00 |
| 455 | Ruben Amaro | 10.00 | 5.00 |
| 456 | Jim Coker | 10.00 | 5.00 |
| 457 | Tex Clevenger | 11.00 | 5.50 |
| 458 | Al Lopez | 15.00 | 7.50 |
| 459 | Dick LeMay | 10.00 | 5.00 |
| 460 | Del Crandall | 11.00 | 5.50 |
| 461 | Norm Bass | 10.00 | 5.00 |
| 462 | Wally Post | 10.00 | 5.00 |
| 463 | Joe Schaffernoth | 10.00 | 5.00 |
| 464 | Ken Aspromonte | 10.00 | 5.00 |
| 465 | Chuck Estrada | 10.00 | 5.00 |
| 466 | 1963 Rookie Stars (*Bill Freehan*, Tony Martinez, Nate Oliver, Jerry Robinson) | 30.00 | 15.00 |
| 467 | Phil Ortega | 10.00 | 5.00 |
| 468 | Carroll Hardy | 10.00 | 5.00 |
| 469 | Jay Hook | 11.00 | 5.50 |
| 470 | Tom Tresh | 20.00 | 10.00 |
| 471 | Ken Retzer | 10.00 | 5.00 |
| 472 | Lou Brock | 125.00 | 62.00 |
| 473 | Mets Team | 100.00 | 50.00 |
| 474 | Jack Fisher | 10.00 | 5.00 |
| 475 | Gus Triandos | 10.00 | 5.00 |
| 476 | Frank Funk | 10.00 | 5.00 |
| 477 | Donn Clendenon | 11.00 | 5.50 |
| 478 | Paul Brown | 10.00 | 5.00 |
| 479 | *Ed Brinkman* | 11.00 | 5.50 |
| 480 | Bill Monbouquette | 11.00 | 5.50 |
| 481 | Bob Taylor | 10.00 | 5.00 |
| 482 | Felix Torres | 10.00 | 5.00 |
| 483 | Jim Owens | 10.00 | 5.00 |
| 484 | Dale Long | 11.00 | 5.50 |
| 485 | Jim Landis | 10.00 | 5.00 |
| 486 | Ray Sadecki | 10.00 | 5.00 |
| 487 | John Roseboro | 11.00 | 5.50 |
| 488 | Jerry Adair | 10.00 | 5.00 |
| 489 | Paul Toth | 10.00 | 5.00 |
| 490 | Willie McCovey | 110.00 | 55.00 |
| 491 | Harry Craft | 10.00 | 5.00 |
| 492 | Dave Wickersham | 10.00 | 5.00 |
| 493 | Walt Bond | 10.00 | 5.00 |
| 494 | Phil Regan | 10.00 | 5.00 |
| 495 | Frank Thomas | 11.00 | 5.50 |
| 496 | 1963 Rookie Stars (Carl Bouldin, *Steve Dalkowski*, *Fred Newman*, Jack Smith) | 11.00 | 5.50 |
| 497 | Bennie Daniels | 10.00 | 5.00 |
| 498 | Eddie Kasko | 10.00 | 5.00 |
| 499 | J.C. Martin | 10.00 | 5.00 |
| 500 | Harmon Killebrew | 125.00 | 62.00 |
| 501 | Joe Azcue | 10.00 | 5.00 |

| | | NR MT | EX |
|---|---|---|---|
| 502 | Daryl Spencer | 10.00 | 5.00 |
| 503 | Braves Team | 10.00 | 5.00 |
| 504 | Bob Johnson | 10.00 | 5.00 |
| 505 | Curt Flood | 12.00 | 6.00 |
| 506 | Gene Green | 11.00 | 5.50 |
| 507 | Roland Sheldon | 8.00 | 4.00 |
| 508 | Ted Savage | 7.00 | 3.50 |
| 509a | Checklist 507-576 (copyright centered) | 15.00 | 7.50 |
| 509b | Checklist 509-576 (copyright to right) | 12.00 | 6.00 |
| 510 | Ken McBride | 7.00 | 3.50 |
| 511 | Charlie Neal | 7.50 | 3.75 |
| 512 | Cal McLish | 7.00 | 3.50 |
| 513 | Gary Geiger | 7.00 | 3.50 |
| 514 | Larry Osborne | 7.00 | 3.50 |
| 515 | Don Elston | 7.00 | 3.50 |
| 516 | Purnal Goldy | 7.00 | 3.50 |
| 517 | Hal Woodeshick | 7.00 | 3.50 |
| 518 | Don Blasingame | 7.00 | 3.50 |
| 519 | Claude Raymond | 7.00 | 3.50 |
| 520 | Orlando Cepeda | 15.00 | 7.50 |
| 521 | Dan Pfister | 7.00 | 3.50 |
| 522 | 1963 Rookie Stars (Mel Nelson, Gary Peters, Art Quirk, Jim Roland) | 7.50 | 3.75 |
| 523 | Bill Kunkel | 8.00 | 4.00 |
| 524 | Cardinals Team | 10.00 | 5.00 |
| 525 | Nellie Fox | 12.00 | 6.00 |
| 526 | Dick Hall | 7.00 | 3.50 |
| 527 | Ed Sadowski | 7.00 | 3.50 |
| 528 | Carl Willey | 7.50 | 3.75 |
| 529 | Wes Covington | 7.00 | 3.50 |
| 530 | Don Mossi | 7.50 | 3.75 |
| 531 | Sam Mele | 7.00 | 3.50 |
| 532 | Steve Boros | 7.00 | 3.50 |
| 533 | Bobby Shantz | 8.00 | 4.00 |
| 534 | Ken Walters | 7.00 | 3.50 |
| 535 | Jim Perry | 8.00 | 4.00 |
| 536 | Norm Larker | 7.00 | 3.50 |
| 537 | 1963 Rookie Stars (Pedro Gonzalez, Ken McMullen, Pete Rose, Al Weis) | 750.00 | 375.00 |
| 538 | George Brunet | 7.00 | 3.50 |
| 539 | Wayne Causey | 7.00 | 3.50 |
| 540 | Bob Clemente | 225.00 | 112.00 |
| 541 | Ron Moeller | 7.00 | 3.50 |
| 542 | Lou Klimchock | 7.00 | 3.50 |
| 543 | Russ Snyder | 7.00 | 3.50 |
| 544 | 1963 Rookie Stars (Duke Carmel, Bill Haas, Dick Phillips, *Rusty Staub*) | 30.00 | 15.00 |
| 545 | Jose Pagan | 7.00 | 3.50 |
| 546 | Hal Reniff | 8.00 | 4.00 |
| 547 | Gus Bell | 7.50 | 3.75 |
| 548 | Tom Satriano | 7.00 | 3.50 |
| 549 | 1963 Rookie Stars (*Marcelino Lopez*, Pete Lovrich, Elmo Plaskett, Paul Ratliff) | 7.50 | 3.75 |
| 550 | Duke Snider | 50.00 | 25.00 |
| 551 | Billy Klaus | 7.00 | 3.50 |
| 552 | Tigers Team | 20.00 | 10.00 |
| 553 | 1963 Rookie Stars (Brock Davis, Jim Gosger, John Herrnstein, *Willie Stargell*) | 200.00 | 100.00 |
| 554 | Hank Fischer | 7.00 | 3.50 |
| 555 | John Blanchard | 8.00 | 4.00 |
| 556 | Al Worthington | 7.00 | 3.50 |
| 557 | Cuno Barragan | 7.00 | 3.50 |
| 558 | 1963 Rookie Stars (Bill Faul, *Ron Hunt*, Bob Lipski, Al Moran) | 8.00 | 4.00 |
| 559 | Danny Murtaugh | 7.50 | 3.75 |
| 560 | Ray Herbert | 7.00 | 3.50 |
| 561 | Mike de la Hoz | 7.00 | 3.50 |
| 562 | 1963 Rookie Stars (Randy Cardinal, *Dave McNally*, Don Rowe, Ken Rowe) | 18.00 | 9.00 |
| 563 | Mike McCormick | 7.50 | 3.75 |
| 564 | George Banks | 7.00 | 3.50 |
| 565 | Larry Sherry | 7.00 | 3.50 |
| 566 | Cliff Cook | 7.50 | 3.75 |
| 567 | Jim Duffalo | 7.00 | 3.50 |
| 568 | Bob Sadowski | 7.00 | 3.50 |
| 569 | Luis Arroyo | 8.00 | 4.00 |
| 570 | Frank Bolling | 7.00 | 3.50 |
| 571 | Johnny Klippstein | 7.00 | 3.50 |
| 572 | Jack Spring | 7.00 | 3.50 |
| 573 | Coot Veal | 7.00 | 3.50 |
| 574 | Hal Kolstad | 7.00 | 3.50 |
| 575 | Don Cardwell | 7.50 | 3.75 |
| 576 | Johnny Temple | 10.00 | 5.00 |

## 1964 Topps

The 1964 Topps set is a 587-card issue of 2-1/2" by 3-1/2" cards which is considered by many as being among the company's best efforts. Card fronts feature a large color photo which blends into a top panel which contains the team name, while a panel below the picture carries the player's name and position. An interesting innovation on the back is a baseball quiz question which required the rubbing of a white panel to reveal the answer. As in 1963, specialty cards remained modest in number with a 12-card set of statistical leaders, a few multi-player cards, rookies and World Series highlights. An interesting card is an "In Memoriam" card for Ken Hubbs who was killed in an airplane crash.

|  | NR MT | EX |
|---|---|---|
| Complete Set: | 3000.00 | 1500.00 |
| Common Player: 1-370 | 2.00 | 1.00 |
| Common Player: 371-522 | | |
|  | 3.00 | 1.50 |
| Common Player: 523-587 | | |
|  | 7.00 | 3.50 |

| | | NR MT | EX |
|---|---|---|---|
| 1 | N.L. E.R.A. Leaders (Dick Ellsworth, Bob Friend, Sandy Koufax) | 10.00 | 3.00 |
| 2 | A.L. E.R.A. Leaders (Camilo Pascual, Gary Peters, Juan Pizarro) | 3.00 | 1.50 |
| 3 | N.L. Pitching Leaders (Sandy Koufax, Jim Maloney, Juan Marichal, Warren Spahn) | 7.00 | 3.50 |
| 4a | A.L. Pitching Leaders (Jim Bouton, Whitey Ford, Camilo Pascual) (apostrophe after "Pitching" on back) | 7.00 | 3.50 |
| 4b | A.L. Pitching Leaders (Jim Bouton, Whitey Ford, Camilo Pascual) (no apostrophe) | 3.50 | 1.75 |
| 5 | N.L. Strikeout Leaders (Don Drysdale, Sandy Koufax, Jim Maloney) | 7.00 | 3.50 |
| 6 | A.L. Strikeout Leaders (Jim Bunning, Camilo Pascual, Dick Stigman) | 3.00 | 1.50 |
| 7 | N.L. Batting Leaders (Hank Aaron, Bob Clemente, Tommy Davis, Dick Groat) | 7.00 | 3.50 |
| 8 | A.L. Batting Leaders (Al Kaline, Rich Rollins, Carl Yastrzemski) | 7.00 | 3.50 |
| 9 | N.L. Home Run Leaders (Hank Aaron, Orlando Cepeda, Willie Mays, Willie McCovey) | 7.00 | 3.50 |
| 10 | A.L. Home Run Leaders (Bob Allison, Harmon Killebrew, Dick Stuart) | 3.50 | 1.75 |
| 11 | N.L. R.B.I. Leaders (Hank Aaron, Ken Boyer, Bill White) | 7.50 | 3.75 |
| 12 | A.L. R.B.I. Leaders (Al Kaline, Harmon Killebrew, Dick Stuart) | 7.50 | 3.75 |
| 13 | Hoyt Wilhelm | 8.00 | 4.00 |
| 14 | Dodgers Rookies (Dick Nen, Nick Willhite) | 2.00 | 1.00 |
| 15 | Zoilo Versalles | 2.00 | 1.00 |
| 16 | John Boozer | 2.00 | 1.00 |
| 17 | Willie Kirkland | 2.00 | 1.00 |
| 18 | Billy O'Dell | 2.00 | 1.00 |
| 19 | Don Wert | 2.00 | 1.00 |
| 20 | Bob Friend | 3.75 | 2.00 |
| 21 | Yogi Berra | 40.00 | 20.00 |
| 22 | Jerry Adair | 2.00 | 1.00 |
| 23 | Chris Zachary | 2.00 | 1.00 |
| 24 | Carl Sawatski | 2.00 | 1.00 |
| 25 | Bill Monbouquette | 2.00 | 1.00 |
| 26 | Gino Cimoli | 2.00 | 1.00 |
| 27 | Mets Team | 3.50 | 1.75 |
| 28 | Claude Osteen | 2.00 | 1.00 |
| 29 | Lou Brock | 35.00 | 17.50 |
| 30 | Ron Perranoski | 2.00 | 1.00 |
| 31 | Dave Nicholson | 2.00 | 1.00 |
| 32 | Dean Chance | 3.75 | 2.00 |
| 33 | Reds Rookies (Sammy Ellis, Mel Queen) | 2.00 | 1.00 |
| 34 | Jim Perry | 3.75 | 2.00 |
| 35 | Ed Mathews | 20.00 | 10.00 |
| 36 | Hal Reniff | 3.00 | 1.50 |
| 37 | Smoky Burgess | 3.75 | 2.00 |
| 38 | *Jim Wynn* | 3.25 | 1.75 |
| 39 | Hank Aguirre | 2.00 | 1.00 |
| 40 | Dick Groat | 3.25 | 1.75 |
| 41 | Friendly Foes (Willie McCovey, Leon Wagner) | 3.00 | 1.50 |
| 42 | Moe Drabowsky | 2.00 | 1.00 |
| 43 | Roy Sievers | 2.25 | 1.25 |
| 44 | Duke Carmel | 2.00 | 1.00 |
| 45 | Milt Pappas | 2.25 | 1.25 |
| 46 | Ed Brinkman | 2.00 | 1.00 |
| 47 | Giants Rookies (*Jesus Alou*, Ron Herbel) | 3.75 | 2.00 |
| 48 | Bob Perry | 2.00 | 1.00 |
| 49 | Bill Henry | 2.00 | 1.00 |
| 50 | Mickey Mantle | 300.00 | 150.00 |
| 51 | Pete Richert | 2.00 | 1.00 |
| 52 | Chuck Hinton | 2.00 | 1.00 |
| 53 | Denis Menke | 2.00 | 1.00 |
| 54 | Sam Mele | 2.00 | 1.00 |
| 55 | Ernie Banks | 35.00 | 17.50 |
| 56 | Hal Brown | 2.00 | 1.00 |
| 57 | Tim Harkness | 2.00 | 1.00 |
| 58 | Don Demeter | 2.00 | 1.00 |
| 59 | Ernie Broglio | 2.00 | 1.00 |
| 60 | Frank Malzone | 2.00 | 1.00 |
| 61 | Angel Backstops (Bob Rodgers, Ed Sadowski) | 2.00 | 1.00 |
| 62 | Ted Savage | 2.00 | 1.00 |
| 63 | Johnny Orsino | 2.00 | 1.00 |
| 64 | Ted Abernathy | 2.00 | 1.00 |
| 65 | Felipe Alou | 3.75 | 2.00 |
| 66 | Eddie Fisher | 2.00 | 1.00 |
| 67 | Tigers Team | 3.50 | 1.75 |
| 68 | Willie Davis | 3.25 | 1.75 |
| 69 | Clete Boyer | 3.25 | 1.75 |
| 70 | Joe Torre | 2.50 | 1.25 |
| 71 | Jack Spring | 2.00 | 1.00 |
| 72 | Chico Cardenas | 2.00 | 1.00 |
| 73 | *Jimmie Hall* | 2.00 | 1.00 |
| 74 | Pirates Rookies (Tom Butters, Bob Priddy) | 2.00 | 1.00 |
| 75 | Wayne Causey | 2.00 | 1.00 |
| 76 | Checklist 1-88 | 3.00 | 1.50 |
| 77 | Jerry Walker | 2.00 | 1.00 |

| | | NR MT | EX |
|---|---|---|---|
| 78 | Merritt Ranew | 2.00 | 1.00 |
| 79 | Bob Heffner | 2.00 | 1.00 |
| 80 | Vada Pinson | 2.50 | 1.25 |
| 81 | All-Star Vets (Nellie Fox, | | |
| | Harmon Killebrew) | 7.00 | 3.50 |
| 82 | Jim Davenport | 2.00 | 1.00 |
| 83 | Gus Triandos | 2.00 | 1.00 |
| 84 | Carl Willey | 2.00 | 1.00 |
| 85 | Pete Ward | 2.00 | 1.00 |
| 86 | Al Downing | 3.25 | 1.75 |
| 87 | Cardinals Team | 7.00 | 3.50 |
| 88 | John Roseboro | 2.00 | 1.00 |
| 89 | Boog Powell | 2.50 | 1.25 |
| 90 | Earl Battey | 2.00 | 1.00 |
| 91 | Bob Bailey | 2.00 | 1.00 |
| 92 | Steve Ridzik | 2.00 | 1.00 |
| 93 | Gary Geiger | 2.00 | 1.00 |
| 94 | Braves Rookies (Jim | | |
| | Britton, Larry Maxie) | 2.00 | 1.00 |
| 95 | George Altman | 2.00 | 1.00 |
| 96 | Bob Buhl | 2.00 | 1.00 |
| 97 | Jim Fregosi | 3.75 | 2.00 |
| 98 | Bill Bruton | 2.00 | 1.00 |
| 99 | Al Stanek | 2.00 | 1.00 |
| 100 | Elston Howard | 7.00 | 3.50 |
| 101 | Walt Alston | 3.00 | 1.50 |
| 102 | Checklist 89-176 | 3.00 | 1.50 |
| 103 | Curt Flood | 3.00 | 1.50 |
| 104 | Art Mahaffey | 2.00 | 1.00 |
| 105 | Woody Held | 2.00 | 1.00 |
| 106 | Joe Nuxhall | 2.00 | 1.00 |
| 107 | White Sox Rookies | | |
| | (Bruce Howard, Frank | | |
| | Kreutzer) | 2.00 | 1.00 |
| 108 | John Wyatt | 2.00 | 1.00 |
| 109 | Rusty Staub | 9.00 | 4.50 |
| 110 | Albie Pearson | 2.00 | 1.00 |
| 111 | Don Elston | 2.00 | 1.00 |
| 112 | Bob Tillman | 2.00 | 1.00 |
| 113 | Grover Powell | 2.00 | 1.00 |
| 114 | Don Lock | 2.00 | 1.00 |
| 115 | Frank Bolling | 2.00 | 1.00 |
| 116 | Twins Rookies (Tony | | |
| | Oliva, Jay Ward) | 8.00 | 4.00 |
| 117 | Earl Francis | 2.00 | 1.00 |
| 118 | John Blanchard | 3.00 | 1.50 |
| 119 | Gary Kolb | 2.00 | 1.00 |
| 120 | Don Drysdale | 18.00 | 9.00 |
| 121 | Pete Runnels | 2.00 | 1.00 |
| 122 | Don McMahon | 2.00 | 1.00 |
| 123 | Jose Pagan | 2.00 | 1.00 |
| 124 | Orlando Pena | 2.00 | 1.00 |
| 125 | Pete Rose | 150.00 | 75.00 |
| 126 | Russ Snyder | 2.00 | 1.00 |
| 127 | Angels Rookies (Aubrey | | |
| | Gatewood, Dick Simpson) | | |
| | | 2.00 | 1.00 |
| 128 | *Mickey Lolich* | 12.00 | 6.00 |
| 129 | Amado Samuel | 2.00 | 1.00 |
| 130 | Gary Peters | 2.00 | 1.00 |
| 131 | Steve Boros | 2.00 | 1.00 |
| 132 | Braves Team | 3.75 | 2.00 |
| 133 | Jim Grant | 2.00 | 1.00 |
| 134 | Don Zimmer | 3.25 | 1.75 |
| 135 | Johnny Callison | 3.25 | 1.75 |
| 136 | World Series Game 1 | | |
| | (Koufax Strikes Out 15) | | |

| | | NR MT | EX |
|---|---|---|---|
| | | 10.00 | 5.00 |
| 137 | World Series Game 2 | | |
| | (Davis Sparks Rally) | 2.50 | 1.25 |
| 138 | World Series Game 3 | | |
| | (L.A. Takes 3rd Straight) | | |
| | | 2.50 | 1.25 |
| 139 | World Series Game 4 | | |
| | (Sealing Yanks' Doom) | 2.50 | 1.25 |
| 140 | World Series Summary | | |
| | (The Dodgers Celebrate) | | |
| | | 2.50 | 1.25 |
| 141 | Danny Murtaugh | 2.00 | 1.00 |
| 142 | John Bateman | 2.00 | 1.00 |
| 143 | Bubba Phillips | 2.00 | 1.00 |
| 144 | Al Worthington | 2.00 | 1.00 |
| 145 | Norm Siebern | 2.00 | 1.00 |
| 146 | Indians Rookies (Bob | | |
| | Chance, *Tommy John*) | | |
| | | 72.00 | 36.00 |
| 147 | Ray Sadecki | 2.00 | 1.00 |
| 148 | J.C. Martin | 2.00 | 1.00 |
| 149 | Paul Foytack | 2.00 | 1.00 |
| 150 | Willie Mays | 90.00 | 45.00 |
| 151 | Athletics Team | 3.75 | 2.00 |
| 152 | Denver Lemaster | 2.00 | 1.00 |
| 153 | Dick Williams | 3.25 | 1.75 |
| 154 | Dick Tracewski | 2.00 | 1.00 |
| 155 | Duke Snider | 25.00 | 12.50 |
| 156 | Bill Dailey | 2.00 | 1.00 |
| 157 | Gene Mauch | 2.25 | 1.25 |
| 158 | Ken Johnson | 2.00 | 1.00 |
| 159 | Charlie Dees | 2.00 | 1.00 |
| 160 | Ken Boyer | 7.00 | 3.50 |
| 161 | Dave McNally | 3.75 | 2.00 |
| 162 | Hitting Area (Vada | | |
| | Pinson, Dick Sisler) | 2.00 | 1.00 |
| 163 | Donn Clendenon | 3.00 | 1.50 |
| 164 | Bud Daley | 3.00 | 1.50 |
| 165 | Jerry Lumpe | 2.00 | 1.00 |
| 166 | Marty Keough | 2.00 | 1.00 |
| 167 | Senators Rookies (Mike | | |
| | Brumley, *Lou Piniella*) | | |
| | | 30.00 | 15.00 |
| 168 | Al Weis | 2.00 | 1.00 |
| 169 | Del Crandall | 3.75 | 2.00 |
| 170 | Dick Radatz | 2.00 | 1.00 |
| 171 | Ty Cline | 2.00 | 1.00 |
| 172 | Indians Team | 3.75 | 2.00 |
| 173 | Ryne Duren | 2.25 | 1.25 |
| 174 | Doc Edwards | 2.00 | 1.00 |
| 175 | Billy Williams | 12.00 | 6.00 |
| 176 | Tracy Stallard | 2.00 | 1.00 |
| 177 | Harmon Killebrew | 20.00 | 10.00 |
| 178 | Hank Bauer | 2.25 | 1.25 |
| 179 | Carl Warwick | 2.00 | 1.00 |
| 180 | Tommy Davis | 3.25 | 1.75 |
| 181 | Dave Wickersham | 2.00 | 1.00 |
| 182 | Sox Sockers (Chuck | | |
| | Schilling, Carl Yastrzemski) | | |
| | | 10.00 | 5.00 |
| 183 | Ron Taylor | 2.00 | 1.00 |
| 184 | Al Luplow | 2.00 | 1.00 |
| 185 | Jim O'Toole | 2.00 | 1.00 |
| 186 | Roman Mejias | 2.00 | 1.00 |
| 187 | Ed Roebuck | 2.00 | 1.00 |
| 188 | Checklist 177-264 | 3.00 | 1.50 |
| 189 | Bob Hendley | 2.00 | 1.00 |

| | | NR MT | EX | | | | NR MT | EX |
|---|---|---|---|---|---|---|---|---|
| 190 | Bobby Richardson | 7.50 | 3.75 | | 249 | Doug Camilli | 2.00 | 1.00 |
| 191 | Clay Dalrymple | 2.00 | 1.00 | | 250 | Al Kaline | 30.00 | 15.00 |
| 192 | Cubs Rookies (John Boccabella, Billy Cowan) | | | | 251 | Choo Choo Coleman | 2.00 | 1.00 |
| | | 2.00 | 1.00 | | 252 | Ken Aspromonte | 2.00 | 1.00 |
| 193 | Jerry Lynch | 2.00 | 1.00 | | 253 | Wally Post | 2.00 | 1.00 |
| 194 | John Goryl | 2.00 | 1.00 | | 254 | Don Hoak | 2.00 | 1.00 |
| 195 | Floyd Robinson | 2.00 | 1.00 | | 255 | Lee Thomas | 2.00 | 1.00 |
| 196 | Jim Gentile | 2.00 | 1.00 | | 256 | Johnny Weekly | 2.00 | 1.00 |
| 197 | Frank Lary | 2.00 | 1.00 | | 257 | Giants Team | 3.75 | 2.00 |
| 198 | Len Gabrielson | 2.00 | 1.00 | | 258 | Garry Roggenburk | 2.00 | 1.00 |
| 199 | Joe Azcue | 2.00 | 1.00 | | 259 | Harry Bright | 3.00 | 1.50 |
| 200 | Sandy Koufax | 100.00 | 50.00 | | 260 | Frank Robinson | 25.00 | 12.50 |
| 201 | Orioles Rookies (Sam Bowens, *Wally Bunker*) | | | | 261 | Jim Hannan | 2.00 | 1.00 |
| | | 2.00 | 1.00 | | 262 | Cardinals Rookie Stars (Harry Fanok, *Mike Shannon*) | | |
| 202 | Galen Cisco | 2.00 | 1.00 | | | | 3.25 | 1.75 |
| 203 | John Kennedy | 2.00 | 1.00 | | 263 | Chuck Estrada | 2.00 | 1.00 |
| 204 | Matty Alou | 2.25 | 1.25 | | 264 | Jim Landis | 2.00 | 1.00 |
| 205 | Nellie Fox | 7.00 | 3.50 | | 265 | Jim Bunning | 7.00 | 3.50 |
| 206 | Steve Hamilton | 3.00 | 1.50 | | 266 | Gene Freese | 2.00 | 1.00 |
| 207 | Fred Hutchinson | 2.00 | 1.00 | | 267 | *Wilbur Wood* | 3.25 | 1.75 |
| 208 | Wes Covington | 2.00 | 1.00 | | 268 | Bill's Got It (Danny Murtaugh, Bill Virdon) | 2.25 | 1.25 |
| 209 | Bob Allen | 2.00 | 1.00 | | 269 | Ellis Burton | 2.00 | 1.00 |
| 210 | Carl Yastrzemski | 80.00 | 40.00 | | 270 | Rich Rollins | 2.00 | 1.00 |
| 211 | Jim Coker | 2.00 | 1.00 | | 271 | Bob Sadowski | 2.00 | 1.00 |
| 212 | Pete Lovrich | 2.00 | 1.00 | | 272 | Jake Wood | 2.00 | 1.00 |
| 213 | Angels Team | 3.75 | 2.00 | | 273 | Mel Nelson | 2.00 | 1.00 |
| 214 | Ken McMullen | 2.00 | 1.00 | | 274 | Checklist 265-352 | 3.00 | 1.50 |
| 215 | Ray Herbert | 2.00 | 1.00 | | 275 | John Tsitouris | 2.00 | 1.00 |
| 216 | Mike de la Hoz | 2.00 | 1.00 | | 276 | Jose Tartabull | 2.00 | 1.00 |
| 217 | Jim King | 2.00 | 1.00 | | 277 | Ken Retzer | 2.00 | 1.00 |
| 218 | Hank Fischer | 2.00 | 1.00 | | 278 | Bobby Shantz | 3.25 | 1.75 |
| 219 | Young Aces (Jim Bouton, Al Downing) | | | | 279 | Joe Koppe | 2.00 | 1.00 |
| | | 3.00 | 1.50 | | 280 | Juan Marichal | 10.00 | 5.00 |
| 220 | Dick Ellsworth | 2.00 | 1.00 | | 281 | Yankees Rookies (Jake Gibbs, Tom Metcalf) | 3.00 | 1.50 |
| 221 | Bob Saverine | 2.00 | 1.00 | | 282 | Bob Bruce | 2.00 | 1.00 |
| 222 | Bill Pierce | 2.25 | 1.25 | | 283 | *Tommy McCraw* | 2.00 | 1.00 |
| 223 | George Banks | 2.00 | 1.00 | | 284 | Dick Schofield | 2.00 | 1.00 |
| 224 | Tommie Sisk | 2.00 | 1.00 | | 285 | Robin Roberts | 10.00 | 5.00 |
| 225 | Roger Maris | 60.00 | 30.00 | | 286 | Don Landrum | 2.00 | 1.00 |
| 226 | Colts Rookies (*Gerald Grote*, Larry Yellen) | | | | 287 | Red Sox Rookies (*Tony Conigliaro*, Bill Spanswick) | | |
| | | 3.75 | 2.00 | | | | 30.00 | 15.00 |
| 227 | Barry Latman | 2.00 | 1.00 | | 288 | Al Moran | 2.00 | 1.00 |
| 228 | Felix Mantilla | 2.00 | 1.00 | | 289 | Frank Funk | 2.00 | 1.00 |
| 229 | Charley Lau | 2.00 | 1.00 | | 290 | Bob Allison | 2.25 | 1.25 |
| 230 | Brooks Robinson | 30.00 | 15.00 | | 291 | Phil Ortega | 2.00 | 1.00 |
| 231 | Dick Calmus | 2.00 | 1.00 | | 292 | Mike Roarke | 2.00 | 1.00 |
| 232 | Al Lopez | 3.00 | 1.50 | | 293 | Phillies Team | 3.75 | 2.00 |
| 233 | Hal Smith | 2.00 | 1.00 | | 294 | Ken Hunt | 2.00 | 1.00 |
| 234 | Gary Bell | 2.00 | 1.00 | | 295 | Roger Craig | 3.25 | 1.75 |
| 235 | Ron Hunt | 2.00 | 1.00 | | 296 | Ed Kirkpatrick | 2.00 | 1.00 |
| 236 | Bill Faul | 2.00 | 1.00 | | 297 | Ken MacKenzie | 2.00 | 1.00 |
| 237 | Cubs Team | 3.75 | 2.00 | | 298 | Harry Craft | 2.00 | 1.00 |
| 238 | Roy McMillan | 2.00 | 1.00 | | 299 | Bill Stafford | 3.00 | 1.50 |
| 239 | Herm Starrette | 2.00 | 1.00 | | 300 | Hank Aaron | 100.00 | 50.00 |
| 240 | Bill White | 3.25 | 1.75 | | 301 | Larry Brown | 2.00 | 1.00 |
| 241 | Jim Owens | 2.00 | 1.00 | | 302 | Dan Pfister | 2.00 | 1.00 |
| 242 | Harvey Kuenn | 3.25 | 1.75 | | 303 | Jim Campbell | 2.00 | 1.00 |
| 243 | Phillies Rookies (*Richie Allen*, John Herrnstein) | | | | 304 | Bob Johnson | 2.00 | 1.00 |
| | | 10.00 | 5.00 | | 305 | Jack Lamabe | 2.00 | 1.00 |
| 244 | *Tony LaRussa* | 20.00 | 10.00 | | 306 | Giant Gunners (Orlando Cepeda, Willie Mays) | 18.00 | 9.00 |
| 245 | Dick Stigman | 2.00 | 1.00 | | 307 | Joe Gibbon | 2.00 | 1.00 |
| 246 | Manny Mota | 3.75 | 2.00 | | | | | |
| 247 | Dave DeBusschere | 3.00 | 1.50 | | | | | |
| 248 | Johnny Pesky | 2.00 | 1.00 | | | | | |

| | | NR MT | EX | | | NR MT | EX |
|---|---|---|---|---|---|---|---|
| 308 | Gene Stephens | 2.00 | 1.00 | 369 | Jerry Zimmerman | 2.00 | 1.00 |
| 309 | Paul Toth | 2.00 | 1.00 | 370 | Hal Woodeshick | 2.00 | 1.00 |
| 310 | Jim Gilliam | 3.00 | 1.50 | 371 | Frank Howard | 3.00 | 1.50 |
| 311 | Tom Brown | 2.00 | 1.00 | 372 | Howie Koplitz | 3.00 | 1.50 |
| 312 | Tigers Rookies (Fritz | | | 373 | Pirates Team | 3.00 | 1.50 |
| | Fisher, Fred Gladding) | 2.00 | 1.00 | 374 | Bobby Bolin | 3.00 | 1.50 |
| 313 | Chuck Hiller | 2.00 | 1.00 | 375 | Ron Santo | 2.50 | 1.25 |
| 314 | Jerry Buchek | 2.00 | 1.00 | 376 | Dave Morehead | 3.00 | 1.50 |
| 315 | Bo Belinsky | 2.25 | 1.25 | 377 | Bob Skinner | 3.00 | 1.50 |
| 316 | Gene Oliver | 2.00 | 1.00 | 378 | Braves Rookies (Jack | | |
| 317 | Al Smith | 2.00 | 1.00 | | Smith, *Woody Woodward*) | | |
| 318 | Twins Team | 3.75 | 2.00 | | | 3.75 | 2.00 |
| 319 | Paul Brown | 2.00 | 1.00 | 379 | Tony Gonzalez | 3.00 | 1.50 |
| 320 | Rocky Colavito | 3.00 | 1.50 | 380 | Whitey Ford | 30.00 | 15.00 |
| 321 | Bob Lillis | 2.00 | 1.00 | 381 | Bob Taylor | 3.75 | 2.00 |
| 322 | George Brunet | 2.00 | 1.00 | 382 | Wes Stock | 3.00 | 1.50 |
| 323 | John Buzhardt | 2.00 | 1.00 | 383 | Bill Rigney | 3.00 | 1.50 |
| 324 | Casey Stengel | 15.00 | 7.50 | 384 | Ron Hansen | 3.00 | 1.50 |
| 325 | Hector Lopez | 3.00 | 1.50 | 385 | Curt Simmons | 3.75 | 2.00 |
| 326 | Ron Brand | 2.00 | 1.00 | 386 | Lenny Green | 3.00 | 1.50 |
| 327 | Don Blasingame | 2.00 | 1.00 | 387 | Terry Fox | 3.00 | 1.50 |
| 328 | Bob Shaw | 2.00 | 1.00 | 388 | Athletics Rookies (John | | |
| 329 | Russ Nixon | 2.00 | 1.00 | | O'Donoghue, George | | |
| 330 | Tommy Harper | 2.00 | 1.00 | | Williams) | 3.00 | 1.50 |
| 331 | A.L. Bombers (Norm | | | 389 | Jim Umbricht | 3.00 | 1.50 |
| | Cash, Al Kaline, Mickey | | | 390 | Orlando Cepeda | 9.00 | 4.50 |
| | Mantle, Roger Maris) | 90.00 | 45.00 | 391 | Sam McDowell | 3.75 | 2.00 |
| 332 | Ray Washburn | 2.00 | 1.00 | 392 | Jim Pagliaroni | 3.00 | 1.50 |
| 333 | Billy Moran | 2.00 | 1.00 | 393 | Casey Teaches (Ed | | |
| 334 | Lew Krausse | 2.00 | 1.00 | | Kranepool, Casey Stengel) | | |
| 335 | Don Mossi | 2.00 | 1.00 | | | 7.00 | 3.50 |
| 336 | Andre Rodgers | 2.00 | 1.00 | 394 | Bob Miller | 3.00 | 1.50 |
| 337 | Dodgers Rookies (*Al* | | | 395 | Tom Tresh | 3.00 | 1.50 |
| | *Ferrara, Jeff Torborg*) | 2.00 | 1.00 | 396 | Dennis Bennett | 3.00 | 1.50 |
| 338 | Jack Kralick | 2.00 | 1.00 | 397 | Chuck Cottier | 3.00 | 1.50 |
| 339 | Walt Bond | 2.00 | 1.00 | 398 | Mets Rookies (Bill Haas, | | |
| 340 | Joe Cunningham | 2.00 | 1.00 | | Dick Smith) | 3.75 | 2.00 |
| 341 | Jim Roland | 2.00 | 1.00 | 399 | Jackie Brandt | 3.00 | 1.50 |
| 342 | Willie Stargell | 40.00 | 20.00 | 400 | Warren Spahn | 25.00 | 12.50 |
| 343 | Senators Team | 3.75 | 2.00 | 401 | Charlie Maxwell | 3.00 | 1.50 |
| 344 | Phil Linz | 3.00 | 1.50 | 402 | Tom Sturdivant | 3.00 | 1.50 |
| 345 | Frank Thomas | 2.00 | 1.00 | 403 | Reds Team | 3.50 | 1.75 |
| 346 | Joe Jay | 2.00 | 1.00 | 404 | Tony Martinez | 3.00 | 1.50 |
| 347 | Bobby Wine | 2.00 | 1.00 | 405 | Ken McBride | 3.00 | 1.50 |
| 348 | Ed Lopat | 2.25 | 1.25 | 406 | Al Spangler | 3.00 | 1.50 |
| 349 | Art Fowler | 2.00 | 1.00 | 407 | Bill Freehan | 3.00 | 1.50 |
| 350 | Willie McCovey | 20.00 | 10.00 | 408 | Cubs Rookies (Fred | | |
| 351 | Dan Schneider | 2.00 | 1.00 | | Burdette, Jim Stewart) | | |
| 352 | Eddie Bressoud | 2.00 | 1.00 | | | 3.00 | 1.50 |
| 353 | Wally Moon | 2.25 | 1.25 | 409 | Bill Fischer | 3.00 | 1.50 |
| 354 | Dave Giusti | 2.00 | 1.00 | 410 | Dick Stuart | 3.75 | 2.00 |
| 355 | Vic Power | 2.00 | 1.00 | 411 | Lee Walls | 3.00 | 1.50 |
| 356 | Reds Rookies (Bill | | | 412 | Ray Culp | 3.00 | 1.50 |
| | McCool, Chico Ruiz) | 2.00 | 1.00 | 413 | Johnny Keane | 3.00 | 1.50 |
| 357 | Charley James | 2.00 | 1.00 | 414 | Jack Sanford | 3.00 | 1.50 |
| 358 | Ron Kline | 2.00 | 1.00 | 415 | Tony Kubek | 7.00 | 3.50 |
| 359 | Jim Schaffer | 2.00 | 1.00 | 416 | Lee Maye | 3.00 | 1.50 |
| 360 | Joe Pepitone | 2.50 | 1.25 | 417 | Don Cardwell | 3.00 | 1.50 |
| 361 | Jay Hook | 2.00 | 1.00 | 418 | Orioles Rookies (*Darold* | | |
| 362 | Checklist 353-429 | 3.00 | 1.50 | | *Knowles, Les Narum*) | 3.75 | 2.00 |
| 363 | Dick McAuliffe | 2.00 | 1.00 | 419 | *Ken Harrelson* | 7.00 | 3.50 |
| 364 | Joe Gaines | 2.00 | 1.00 | 420 | Jim Maloney | 3.75 | 2.00 |
| 365 | Cal McLish | 2.00 | 1.00 | 421 | Camilo Carreon | 3.00 | 1.50 |
| 366 | Nelson Mathews | 2.00 | 1.00 | 422 | Jack Fisher | 3.75 | 2.00 |
| 367 | Fred Whitfield | 2.00 | 1.00 | 423 | Tops In NL (Hank Aaron, | | |
| 368 | White Sox Rookies (Fritz | | | | Willie Mays) | 100.00 | 50.00 |
| | Ackley, *Don Buford*) | 2.25 | 1.25 | 424 | Dick Bertell | 3.00 | 1.50 |

| | | NR MT | EX | | | NR MT | EX |
|---|---|---|---|---|---|---|---|
| 425 | Norm Cash | 2.50 | 1.25 | 480 | Bob Purkey | 3.00 | 1.50 |
| 426 | Bob Rodgers | 3.75 | 2.00 | 481 | Chuck Schilling | 3.00 | 1.50 |
| 427 | Don Rudolph | 3.00 | 1.50 | 482 | Phillies Rookies (John | | |
| 428 | Red Sox Rookies (Archie | | | | Briggs, Danny Cater) | 3.75 | 2.00 |
| | Skeen, Pete Smith) | 3.00 | 1.50 | 483 | Fred Valentine | 3.00 | 1.50 |
| 429 | Tim McCarver | 3.00 | 1.50 | 484 | Bill Pleis | 3.00 | 1.50 |
| 430 | Juan Pizarro | 3.00 | 1.50 | 485 | Tom Haller | 3.75 | 2.00 |
| 431 | George Alusik | 3.00 | 1.50 | 486 | Bob Kennedy | 3.00 | 1.50 |
| 432 | Ruben Amaro | 3.00 | 1.50 | 487 | Mike McCormick | 3.75 | 2.00 |
| 433 | Yankees Team | 10.00 | 5.00 | 488 | Yankees Rookies (Bob | | |
| 434 | Don Nottebart | 3.00 | 1.50 | | Meyer, Pete Mikkelsen) | | |
| 435 | Vic Davalillo | 3.00 | 1.50 | | | 3.25 | 1.75 |
| 436 | Charlie Neal | 3.00 | 1.50 | 489 | Julio Navarro | 3.00 | 1.50 |
| 437 | Ed Bailey | 3.00 | 1.50 | 490 | Ron Fairly | 3.25 | 1.75 |
| 438 | Checklist 430-506 | 7.00 | 3.50 | 491 | Ed Rakow | 3.00 | 1.50 |
| 439 | Harvey Haddix | 3.25 | 1.75 | 492 | Colts Rookies (Jim | | |
| 440 | Bob Clemente | 125.00 | 62.00 | | Beauchamp, Mike White) | | |
| 441 | Bob Duliba | 3.00 | 1.50 | | | 3.00 | 1.50 |
| 442 | Pumpsie Green | 3.75 | 2.00 | 493 | Don Lee | 3.00 | 1.50 |
| 443 | Chuck Dressen | 3.75 | 2.00 | 494 | Al Jackson | 3.75 | 2.00 |
| 444 | Larry Jackson | 3.00 | 1.50 | 495 | Bill Virdon | 3.00 | 1.50 |
| 445 | Bill Skowron | 2.50 | 1.25 | 496 | White Sox Team | 3.00 | 1.50 |
| 446 | Julian Javier | 3.75 | 2.00 | 497 | Jeoff Long | 3.00 | 1.50 |
| 447 | Ted Bowsfield | 3.00 | 1.50 | 498 | Dave Stenhouse | 3.00 | 1.50 |
| 448 | Cookie Rojas | 3.75 | 2.00 | 499 | Indians Rookies (Chico | | |
| 449 | Deron Johnson | 3.00 | 1.50 | | Salmon, Gordon Seyfried) | | |
| 450 | Steve Barber | 3.00 | 1.50 | | | 3.00 | 1.50 |
| 451 | Joe Amalfitano | 3.00 | 1.50 | 500 | Camilo Pascual | 3.75 | 2.00 |
| 452 | Giants Rookies (Gil | | | 501 | Bob Veale | 3.75 | 2.00 |
| | Garrido, *Jim Hart*) | 3.75 | 2.00 | 502 | Angels Rookies (*Bobby* | | |
| 453 | Frank Baumann | 3.00 | 1.50 | | *Knoop*, Bob Lee) | 3.75 | 2.00 |
| 454 | Tommie Aaron | 3.75 | 2.00 | 503 | Earl Wilson | 3.00 | 1.50 |
| 455 | Bernie Allen | 3.00 | 1.50 | 504 | Claude Raymond | 3.00 | 1.50 |
| 456 | Dodgers Rookies (*Wes* | | | 505 | Stan Williams | 3.25 | 1.75 |
| | *Parker*, John Werhas) | 3.00 | 1.50 | 506 | Bobby Bragan | 3.75 | 2.00 |
| 457 | Jesse Gonder | 3.75 | 2.00 | 507 | John Edwards | 3.00 | 1.50 |
| 458 | Ralph Terry | 3.00 | 1.50 | 508 | Diego Segui | 3.00 | 1.50 |
| 459 | Red Sox Rookies (Pete | | | 509 | Pirates Rookies (*Gene* | | |
| | Charton, Dalton Jones) | | | | *Alley*, Orlando McFarlane) | | |
| | | 3.00 | 1.50 | | | 3.75 | 2.00 |
| 460 | Bob Gibson | 25.00 | 12.50 | 510 | Lindy McDaniel | 3.00 | 1.50 |
| 461 | George Thomas | 3.00 | 1.50 | 511 | Lou Jackson | 3.00 | 1.50 |
| 462 | Birdie Tebbetts | 3.00 | 1.50 | 512 | Tigers Rookies (*Willie* | | |
| 463 | Don Leppert | 3.00 | 1.50 | | *Horton*, Joe Sparma) | 7.00 | 3.50 |
| 464 | Dallas Green | 3.75 | 2.00 | 513 | Don Larsen | 3.25 | 1.75 |
| 465 | Mike Hershberger | 3.00 | 1.50 | 514 | Jim Hickman | 3.75 | 2.00 |
| 466 | Athletics Rookies (*Dick* | | | 515 | Johnny Romano | 3.00 | 1.50 |
| | *Green*, Aurelio Monteagudo) | | | 516 | Twins Rookies (Jerry | | |
| | | 3.75 | 2.00 | | Arrigo, Dwight Siebler) | 3.00 | 1.50 |
| 467 | Bob Aspromonte | 3.00 | 1.50 | 517a | Checklist 507-587 | | |
| 468 | Gaylord Perry | 45.00 | 23.00 | | (wrong numbering on back) | | |
| 469 | Cubs Rookies (Fred | | | | | 7.00 | 3.50 |
| | Norman, Sterling Slaughter) | | | 517b | Checklist 507-587 | | |
| | | 3.00 | 1.50 | | (correct numbering on | | |
| 470 | Jim Bouton | 3.00 | 1.50 | | back) | 7.50 | 3.75 |
| 471 | *Gates Brown* | 3.75 | 2.00 | 518 | Carl Bouldin | 3.00 | 1.50 |
| 472 | Vern Law | 3.25 | 1.75 | 519 | Charlie Smith | 3.75 | 2.00 |
| 473 | Orioles Team | 3.00 | 1.50 | 520 | Jack Baldschun | 3.00 | 1.50 |
| 474 | Larry Sherry | 3.00 | 1.50 | 521 | Tom Satriano | 3.00 | 1.50 |
| 475 | Ed Charles | 3.00 | 1.50 | 522 | Bobby Tiefenauer | 3.00 | 1.50 |
| 476 | Braves Rookies (*Rico* | | | 523 | Lou Burdette | 9.00 | 4.50 |
| | *Carty*, Dick Kelley) | 7.00 | 3.50 | 524 | Reds Rookies (Jim | | |
| 477 | Mike Joyce | 2.25 | 1.25 | | Dickson, Bobby Klaus) | 7.00 | 3.50 |
| 478 | Dick Howser | 3.00 | 1.50 | 525 | Al McBean | 7.00 | 3.50 |
| 479 | Cardinals Rookies (Dave | | | 526 | Lou Clinton | 7.00 | 3.50 |
| | Bakenhaster, Johnny Lewis) | | | 527 | Larry Bearnarth | 7.50 | 3.75 |
| | | 3.00 | 1.50 | 528 | Athletics Rookies (*Dave* | | |

|  |  | NR MT | EX |
|---|---|---|---|
|  | *Duncan*, Tom Reynolds) |  |  |
|  |  | 7.50 | 3.75 |
| 529 | Al Dark | 7.50 | 3.75 |
| 530 | Leon Wagner | 7.50 | 3.75 |
| 531 | Dodgers Team | 8.00 | 4.00 |
| 532 | Twins Rookies (Bud Bloomfield, Joe Nossek) |  |  |
|  |  | 7.00 | 3.50 |
| 533 | Johnny Klippstein | 7.00 | 3.50 |
| 534 | Gus Bell | 7.50 | 3.75 |
| 535 | Phil Regan | 7.00 | 3.50 |
| 536 | Mets Rookies (Larry Elliot, John Stephenson) |  |  |
|  |  | 7.50 | 3.75 |
| 537 | Dan Osinski | 7.00 | 3.50 |
| 538 | Minnie Minoso | 8.00 | 4.00 |
| 539 | Roy Face | 7.00 | 3.50 |
| 540 | Luis Aparicio | 15.00 | 7.50 |
| 541 | Braves Rookies (*Phil Niekro*, Phil Roof) | 225.00 | 112.00 |
| 542 | Don Mincher | 7.50 | 3.75 |
| 543 | Bob Uecker | 60.00 | 30.00 |
| 544 | Colts Rookies (Steve Hertz, Joe Hoerner) | 7.00 | 3.50 |
| 545 | Max Alvis | 7.50 | 3.75 |
| 546 | Joe Christopher | 7.50 | 3.75 |
| 547 | Gil Hodges | 12.00 | 6.00 |
| 548 | N.L. Rookies (Wayne Schurr, Paul Speckenbach) |  |  |
|  |  | 7.00 | 3.50 |
| 549 | Joe Moeller | 7.00 | 3.50 |
| 550 | Ken Hubbs | 20.00 | 10.00 |
| 551 | Billy Hoeft | 7.00 | 3.50 |
| 552 | Indians Rookies (Tom Kelley, *Sonny Siebert*) | 7.50 | 3.75 |
| 553 | Jim Brewer | 7.00 | 3.50 |
| 554 | Hank Foiles | 7.00 | 3.50 |
| 555 | Lee Stange | 7.00 | 3.50 |
| 556 | Mets Rookies (Steve Dillon, Ron Locke) | 7.50 | 3.75 |
| 557 | Leo Burke | 7.00 | 3.50 |
| 558 | Don Schwall | 7.00 | 3.50 |
| 559 | Dick Phillips | 7.00 | 3.50 |
| 560 | Dick Farrell | 7.00 | 3.50 |
| 561 | Phillies Rookies (Dave Bennett, *Rick Wise*) | 7.50 | 3.75 |
| 562 | Pedro Ramos | 7.00 | 3.50 |
| 563 | Dal Maxvill | 7.50 | 3.75 |
| 564 | A.L. Rookies (Joe McCabe, Jerry McNertney) |  |  |
|  |  | 7.00 | 3.50 |
| 565 | Stu Miller | 7.00 | 3.50 |
| 566 | Ed Kranepool | 7.00 | 3.50 |
| 567 | Jim Kaat | 12.00 | 6.00 |
| 568 | N.L. Rookies (Phil Gagliano, Cap Peterson) |  |  |
|  |  | 7.00 | 3.50 |
| 569 | Fred Newman | 7.00 | 3.50 |
| 570 | Bill Mazeroski | 8.00 | 4.00 |
| 571 | Gene Conley | 3.50 | 1.75 |
| 572 | A.L. Rookies (Dick Egan, Dave Gray) | 7.00 | 3.50 |
| 573 | Jim Duffalo | 7.00 | 3.50 |
| 574 | Manny Jimenez | 7.00 | 3.50 |
| 575 | Tony Cloninger | 7.50 | 3.75 |
| 576 | Mets Rookies (Jerry Hinsley, Bill Wakefield) | 7.50 | 3.75 |

|  |  | NR MT | EX |
|---|---|---|---|
| 577 | Gordy Coleman | 7.00 | 3.50 |
| 578 | Glen Hobbie | 7.00 | 3.50 |
| 579 | Red Sox Team | 15.00 | 7.50 |
| 580 | Johnny Podres | 9.00 | 4.50 |
| 581 | Yankees Rookies (Pedro Gonzalez, Archie Moore) |  |  |
|  |  | 7.00 | 3.50 |
| 582 | Rod Kanehl | 7.50 | 3.75 |
| 583 | Tito Francona | 7.50 | 3.75 |
| 584 | Joel Horlen | 7.00 | 3.50 |
| 585 | Tony Taylor | 7.00 | 3.50 |
| 586 | Jim Piersall | 9.00 | 4.50 |
| 587 | Bennie Daniels | 8.00 | 2.50 |

## 1965 Topps

The 1965 Topps set features a large color photograph of the player which was surrounded by a colored, round-cornered frame and a white border. The bottom of the 2-1/2" by 3-1/2" cards include a pennant with a color team logo and name over the left side of a rectangle which features the player's name and position. Backs feature statistics and, if space allowed, a cartoon and headline about the player. There are no multi-player cards in the 1965 set other than the usual team cards and World Series highlights. Rookie cards include team, as well as league groupings from two to four players per card. Also present in the 598-card set are statistical leaders.

|  | NR MT | EX |
|---|---|---|
| Complete Set: | 3500.00 | 1750.00 |
| Common Player: 1-198 | 2.00 | 1.00 |
| Common Player: 199-446 |  |  |
|  | 2.00 | 1.00 |
| Common Player: 447-522 |  |  |
|  | 2.00 | 1.00 |
| Common Player: 523-598 |  |  |
|  | 5.00 | 2.50 |

| | | NR MT | EX |
|---|---|---|---|
| 1 | A.L. Batting Leaders (Elston Howard, Tony Oliva, Brooks Robinson) | 10.00 | 4.00 |
| 2 | N.L. Batting Leaders (Hank Aaron, Rico Carty, Bob Clemente) | 5.00 | 2.50 |
| 3 | A.L. Home Run Leaders (Harmon Killebrew, Mickey Mantle, Boog Powell) | 20.00 | 10.00 |
| 4 | N.L. Home Run Leaders (Johnny Callison, Orlando Cepeda, Jim Hart, Willie Mays, Billy Williams) | 6.00 | 3.00 |
| 5 | A.L. RBI Leaders (Harmon Killebrew, Mickey Mantle, Brooks Robinson, Dick Stuart) | 20.00 | 10.00 |
| 6 | N.L. RBI Leaders (Ken Boyer, Willie Mays, Ron Santo) | 6.00 | 3.00 |
| 7 | A.L. ERA Leaders (Dean Chance, Joel Horlen) | 5.00 | 2.50 |
| 8 | N.L. ERA Leaders (Don Drysdale, Sandy Koufax) | 6.00 | 3.00 |
| 9 | A.L. Pitching Leaders (Wally Bunker, Dean Chance, Gary Peters, Juan Pizarro, Dave Wickersham) | 5.00 | 2.50 |
| 10 | N.L. Pitching Leaders (Larry Jackson, Juan Marichal, Ray Sadecki) | 3.50 | 1.75 |
| 11 | A.L. Strikeout Leaders (Dean Chance, Al Downing, Camilo Pascual) | 5.00 | 2.50 |
| 12 | N.L. Strikeout Leaders (Don Drysdale, Bob Gibson, Bob Veale) | 3.50 | 1.75 |
| 13 | Pedro Ramos | 2.00 | 1.00 |
| 14 | Len Gabrielson | 2.00 | 1.00 |
| 15 | Robin Roberts | 8.00 | 4.00 |
| 16 | Astros Rookies (Sonny Jackson, Joe Morgan) | 175.00 | 87.00 |
| 17 | Johnny Romano | 2.00 | 1.00 |
| 18 | Bill McCool | 2.00 | 1.00 |
| 19 | Gates Brown | 2.00 | 1.00 |
| 20 | Jim Bunning | 5.00 | 2.50 |
| 21 | Don Blasingame | 2.00 | 1.00 |
| 22 | Charlie Smith | 2.00 | 1.00 |
| 23 | Bob Tiefenauer | 2.00 | 1.00 |
| 24 | Twins Team | 5.00 | 2.50 |
| 25 | Al McBean | 2.00 | 1.00 |
| 26 | Bobby Knoop | 2.00 | 1.00 |
| 27 | Dick Bertell | 2.00 | 1.00 |
| 28 | Barney Schultz | 2.00 | 1.00 |
| 29 | Felix Mantilla | 2.00 | 1.00 |
| 30 | Jim Bouton | 5.00 | 2.50 |
| 31 | Mike White | 2.00 | 1.00 |
| 32 | Herman Franks | 2.00 | 1.00 |
| 33 | Jackie Brandt | 2.00 | 1.00 |
| 34 | Cal Koonce | 2.00 | 1.00 |
| 35 | Ed Charles | 2.00 | 1.00 |
| 36 | Bobby Wine | 2.00 | 1.00 |
| 37 | Fred Gladding | 2.00 | 1.00 |
| 38 | Jim King | 2.00 | 1.00 |
| 39 | Gerry Arrigo | 2.00 | 1.00 |
| 40 | Frank Howard | 5.00 | 2.50 |
| 41 | White Sox Rookies (Bruce Howard, Marv Staehle) | 2.00 | 1.00 |
| 42 | Earl Wilson | 2.00 | 1.00 |
| 43 | Mike Shannon | 2.00 | 1.00 |
| 44 | Wade Blasingame | 2.00 | 1.00 |
| 45 | Roy McMillan | 2.00 | 1.00 |
| 46 | Bob Lee | 2.00 | 1.00 |
| 47 | Tommy Harper | 2.00 | 1.00 |
| 48 | Claude Raymond | 2.00 | 1.00 |
| 49 | Orioles Rookies (Curt Blefary, John Miller) | 2.00 | 1.00 |
| 50 | Juan Marichal | 10.00 | 5.00 |
| 51 | Billy Bryan | 2.00 | 1.00 |
| 52 | Ed Roebuck | 2.00 | 1.00 |
| 53 | Dick McAuliffe | 2.00 | 1.00 |
| 54 | Joe Gibbon | 2.00 | 1.00 |
| 55 | Tony Conigliaro | 7.00 | 3.50 |
| 56 | Ron Kline | 2.00 | 1.00 |
| 57 | Cardinals Team | 2.25 | 1.25 |
| 58 | Fred Talbot | 2.00 | 1.00 |
| 59 | Nate Oliver | 2.00 | 1.00 |
| 60 | Jim O'Toole | 2.00 | 1.00 |
| 61 | Chris Cannizzaro | 2.00 | 1.00 |
| 62 | Jim Katt (Kaat) | 5.00 | 2.50 |
| 63 | Ty Cline | 2.00 | 1.00 |
| 64 | Lou Burdette | 2.00 | 1.00 |
| 65 | Tony Kubek | 6.00 | 3.00 |
| 66 | Bill Rigney | 2.00 | 1.00 |
| 67 | Harvey Haddix | 2.00 | 1.00 |
| 68 | Del Crandall | 2.00 | 1.00 |
| 69 | Bill Virdon | 2.00 | 1.00 |
| 70 | Bill Skowron | 2.00 | 1.00 |
| 71 | John O'Donoghue | 2.00 | 1.00 |
| 72 | Tony Gonzalez | 2.00 | 1.00 |
| 73 | Dennis Ribant | 2.00 | 1.00 |
| 74 | Red Sox Rookies (Rico Petrocelli, Jerry Stephenson) | 5.00 | 2.50 |
| 75 | Deron Johnson | 2.00 | 1.00 |
| 76 | Sam McDowell | 2.00 | 1.00 |
| 77 | Doug Camilli | 2.00 | 1.00 |
| 78 | Dal Maxvill | 2.00 | 1.00 |
| 79a | Checklist 1-88 (61 is C. Cannizzaro) | 2.00 | 1.00 |
| 79b | Checklist 1-88 (61 is Cannizzaro) | 5.00 | 2.50 |
| 80 | Turk Farrell | 2.00 | 1.00 |
| 81 | Don Buford | 2.00 | 1.00 |
| 82 | Braves Rookies (Santos Alomar, John Braun) | 2.00 | 1.00 |
| 83 | George Thomas | 2.00 | 1.00 |
| 84 | Ron Herbel | 2.00 | 1.00 |
| 85 | Willie Smith | 2.00 | 1.00 |
| 86 | Les Narum | 2.00 | 1.00 |
| 87 | Nelson Mathews | 2.00 | 1.00 |
| 88 | Jack Lamabe | 2.00 | 1.00 |
| 89 | Mike Hershberger | 2.00 | 1.00 |
| 90 | Rich Rollins | 2.00 | 1.00 |
| 91 | Cubs Team | 2.25 | 1.25 |
| 92 | Dick Howser | 2.00 | 1.00 |
| 93 | Jack Fisher | 2.00 | 1.00 |
| 94 | Charlie Lau | 2.00 | 1.00 |
| 95 | Bill Mazeroski | 5.00 | 2.50 |

| | | NR MT | EX | | | | NR MT | EX |
|---|---|---|---|---|---|---|---|---|
| 96 | Sonny Siebert | 2.00 | 1.00 | | 151 | Athletics Team | 2.25 | 1.25 |
| 97 | Pedro Gonzalez | 2.00 | 1.00 | | 152 | Phil Ortega | 2.00 | 1.00 |
| 98 | Bob Miller | 2.00 | 1.00 | | 153 | Norm Cash | 2.00 | 1.00 |
| 99 | Gil Hodges | 6.00 | 3.00 | | 154 | Bob Humphreys | 2.00 | 1.00 |
| 100 | Ken Boyer | 5.00 | 2.50 | | 155 | Roger Maris | 60.00 | 30.00 |
| 101 | Fred Newman | 2.00 | 1.00 | | 156 | Bob Sadowski | 2.00 | 1.00 |
| 102 | Steve Boros | 2.00 | 1.00 | | 157 | Zoilo Versalles | 2.25 | 1.25 |
| 103 | Harvey Kuenn | 2.00 | 1.00 | | 158 | Dick Sisler | 2.00 | 1.00 |
| 104 | Checklist 89-176 | 2.00 | 1.00 | | 159 | Jim Duffalo | 2.00 | 1.00 |
| 105 | Chico Salmon | 2.00 | 1.00 | | 160 | Bob Clemente | 85.00 | 42.00 |
| 106 | Gene Oliver | 2.00 | 1.00 | | 161 | Frank Baumann | 2.00 | 1.00 |
| 107 | Phillies Rookies (Pat | | | | 162 | Russ Nixon | 2.00 | 1.00 |
| | Corrales, Costen Shockley) | | | | 163 | John Briggs | 2.00 | 1.00 |
| | | 2.00 | 1.00 | | 164 | Al Spangler | 2.00 | 1.00 |
| 108 | Don Mincher | 2.00 | 1.00 | | 165 | Dick Ellsworth | 2.00 | 1.00 |
| 109 | Walt Bond | 2.00 | 1.00 | | 166 | Indians Rookies | | |
| 110 | Ron Santo | 2.25 | 1.25 | | | (Tommie Agee, George | | |
| 111 | Lee Thomas | 2.00 | 1.00 | | | Culver) | 2.25 | 1.25 |
| 112 | Derrell Griffith | 2.00 | 1.00 | | 167 | Bill Wakefield | 2.00 | 1.00 |
| 113 | Steve Barber | 2.00 | 1.00 | | 168 | Dick Green | 2.00 | 1.00 |
| 114 | Jim Hickman | 2.00 | 1.00 | | 169 | Dave Vineyard | 2.00 | 1.00 |
| 115 | Bobby Richardson | 6.00 | 3.00 | | 170 | Hank Aaron | 95.00 | 47.50 |
| 116 | Cardinals Rookies (Dave | | | | 171 | Jim Roland | 2.00 | 1.00 |
| | Dowling, Bob Tolan) | | | | 172 | Jim Piersall | 2.25 | 1.25 |
| 117 | Wes Stock | 2.00 | 1.00 | | 173 | Tigers Team | 3.25 | 1.75 |
| 118 | Hal Lanier | 2.25 | 1.25 | | 174 | Joe Jay | 2.00 | 1.00 |
| 119 | John Kennedy | 2.00 | 1.00 | | 175 | Bob Aspromonte | 2.00 | 1.00 |
| 120 | Frank Robinson | 30.00 | 15.00 | | 176 | Willie McCovey | 20.00 | 10.00 |
| 121 | Gene Alley | 2.00 | 1.00 | | 177 | Pete Mikkelsen | 2.00 | 1.00 |
| 122 | Bill Pleis | 2.00 | 1.00 | | 178 | Dalton Jones | 2.00 | 1.00 |
| 123 | Frank Thomas | 2.00 | 1.00 | | 179 | Hal Woodeshick | 2.00 | 1.00 |
| 124 | Tom Satriano | 2.00 | 1.00 | | 180 | Bob Allison | 2.00 | 1.00 |
| 125 | Juan Pizarro | 2.00 | 1.00 | | 181 | Senators Rookies (Don | | |
| 126 | Dodgers Team | 5.00 | 2.50 | | | Loun, Joe McCabe) | | |
| 127 | Frank Lary | 2.00 | 1.00 | | 182 | Mike de la Hoz | 2.00 | 1.00 |
| 128 | Vic Davalillo | 2.00 | 1.00 | | 183 | Dave Nicholson | 2.00 | 1.00 |
| 129 | Bennie Daniels | 2.00 | 1.00 | | 184 | John Boozer | 2.00 | 1.00 |
| 130 | Al Kaline | 25.00 | 12.50 | | 185 | Max Alvis | 2.00 | 1.00 |
| 131 | Johnny Keane | 2.25 | 1.25 | | 186 | Billy Cowan | 2.00 | 1.00 |
| 132 | World Series Game 1 | | | | 187 | Casey Stengel | 18.00 | 9.00 |
| | (Cards Take Opener) | 5.00 | 2.50 | | 188 | Sam Bowens | 2.00 | 1.00 |
| 133 | World Series Game 2 | | | | 189 | Checklist 177-264 | 2.00 | 1.00 |
| | (Stottlemyre Wins) | 2.00 | 1.00 | | 190 | Bill White | 2.00 | 1.00 |
| 134 | World Series Game 3 | | | | 191 | Phil Regan | 2.00 | 1.00 |
| | (Mantle's Clutch HR) | 25.00 | 12.50 | | 192 | Jim Coker | 2.00 | 1.00 |
| 135 | World Series Game 4 | | | | 193 | Gaylord Perry | 20.00 | 10.00 |
| | (Boyer's Grand-Slam) | 5.00 | 2.50 | | 194 | Angels Rookies (Bill | | |
| 136 | World Series Game 5 | | | | | Kelso, Rick Reichardt) | 2.00 | 1.00 |
| | (10th Inning Triumph) | 5.00 | 2.50 | | 195 | Bob Veale | 2.00 | 1.00 |
| 137 | World Series Game 6 | | | | 196 | Ron Fairly | 2.00 | 1.00 |
| | (Bouton Wins Again) | 2.00 | 1.00 | | 197 | Diego Segui | 2.00 | 1.00 |
| 138 | World Series Game 7 | | | | 198 | Smoky Burgess | 2.00 | 1.00 |
| | (Gibson Wins Finale) | 3.50 | 1.75 | | 199 | Bob Heffner | 2.00 | 1.00 |
| 139 | World Series Summary | | | | 200 | Joe Torre | 5.00 | 2.50 |
| | (The Cards Celebrate) | 5.00 | 2.50 | | 201 | Twins Rookies (Cesar | | |
| 140 | Dean Chance | 2.00 | 1.00 | | | Tovar, Sandy Valdespino) | | |
| 141 | Charlie James | 2.00 | 1.00 | | | | 2.00 | 1.00 |
| 142 | Bill Monbouquette | 2.00 | 1.00 | | 202 | Leo Burke | 2.00 | 1.00 |
| 143 | Pirates Rookies (John | | | | 203 | Dallas Green | 2.00 | 1.00 |
| | Gelnar, Jerry May) | | | | 204 | Russ Snyder | 2.00 | 1.00 |
| 144 | Ed Kranepool | 2.00 | 1.00 | | 205 | Warren Spahn | 20.00 | 10.00 |
| 145 | Luis Tiant | 10.00 | 5.00 | | 206 | Willie Horton | 2.00 | 1.00 |
| 146 | Ron Hansen | 2.00 | 1.00 | | 207 | Pete Rose | 135.00 | 67.00 |
| 147 | Dennis Bennett | 2.00 | 1.00 | | 208 | Tommy John | 10.00 | 5.00 |
| 148 | Willie Kirkland | 2.00 | 1.00 | | 209 | Pirates Team | 5.00 | 2.50 |
| 149 | Wayne Schurr | 2.00 | 1.00 | | 210 | Jim Fregosi | 2.25 | 1.25 |
| 150 | Brooks Robinson | 25.00 | 12.50 | | 211 | Steve Ridzik | 2.00 | 1.00 |

| | | NR MT | EX | | | NR MT | EX |
|---|---|---|---|---|---|---|---|
| 212 | Ron Brand | 2.00 | 1.00 | 275 | Dick Groat | 3.25 | 1.75 |
| 213 | Jim Davenport | 2.00 | 1.00 | 276 | Hoyt Wilhelm | 8.00 | 4.00 |
| 214 | Bob Purkey | 2.00 | 1.00 | 277 | Johnny Lewis | 2.00 | 1.00 |
| 215 | Pete Ward | 2.00 | 1.00 | 278 | Ken Retzer | 2.00 | 1.00 |
| 216 | Al Worthington | 2.00 | 1.00 | 279 | Dick Tracewski | 2.00 | 1.00 |
| 217 | Walt Alston | 3.50 | 1.75 | 280 | Dick Stuart | 2.00 | 1.00 |
| 218 | Dick Schofield | 2.00 | 1.00 | 281 | Bill Stafford | 2.25 | 1.25 |
| 219 | Bob Meyer | 2.00 | 1.00 | 282 | Giants Rookies (Dick | | |
| 220 | Billy Williams | 10.00 | 5.00 | | Estelle, *Masanori* | | |
| 221 | John Tsitouris | 2.00 | 1.00 | | *Murakami)* | 2.00 | 1.00 |
| 222 | Bob Tillman | 2.00 | 1.00 | 283 | Fred Whitfield | 2.00 | 1.00 |
| 223 | Dan Osinski | 2.00 | 1.00 | 284 | Nick Willhite | 2.00 | 1.00 |
| 224 | Bob Chance | 2.00 | 1.00 | 285 | Ron Hunt | 2.00 | 1.00 |
| 225 | Bo Belinsky | 2.00 | 1.00 | 286 | Athletics Rookies (Jim | | |
| 226 | Yankees Rookies (Jake | | | | Dickson, Aurelio | | |
| | Gibbs, Elvio Jimenez) | 2.25 | 1.25 | | Monteagudo) | 2.00 | 1.00 |
| 227 | Bobby Klaus | 2.00 | 1.00 | 287 | Gary Kolb | 2.00 | 1.00 |
| 228 | Jack Sanford | 2.00 | 1.00 | 288 | Jack Hamilton | 2.00 | 1.00 |
| 229 | Lou Clinton | 2.00 | 1.00 | 289 | Gordy Coleman | 2.00 | 1.00 |
| 230 | Ray Sadecki | 2.00 | 1.00 | 290 | Wally Bunker | 2.00 | 1.00 |
| 231 | Jerry Adair | 2.00 | 1.00 | 291 | Jerry Lynch | 2.00 | 1.00 |
| 232 | *Steve Blass* | 2.00 | 1.00 | 292 | Larry Yellen | 2.00 | 1.00 |
| 233 | Don Zimmer | 2.25 | 1.25 | 293 | Angels Team | 5.00 | 2.50 |
| 234 | White Sox Team | 5.00 | 2.50 | 294 | Tim McCarver | 2.75 | 1.50 |
| 235 | Chuck Hinton | 2.00 | 1.00 | 295 | Dick Radatz | 2.00 | 1.00 |
| 236 | *Dennis McLain* | 20.00 | 10.00 | 296 | Tony Taylor | 2.00 | 1.00 |
| 237 | Bernie Allen | 2.00 | 1.00 | 297 | Dave DeBusschere | 3.50 | 1.75 |
| 238 | Joe Moeller | 2.00 | 1.00 | 298 | Jim Stewart | 2.00 | 1.00 |
| 239 | Doc Edwards | 2.00 | 1.00 | 299 | Jerry Zimmerman | 2.00 | 1.00 |
| 240 | Bob Bruce | 2.00 | 1.00 | 300 | Sandy Koufax | 130.00 | 65.00 |
| 241 | Mack Jones | 2.00 | 1.00 | 301 | Birdie Tebbetts | 2.00 | 1.00 |
| 242 | George Brunet | 2.00 | 1.00 | 302 | Al Stanek | 2.00 | 1.00 |
| 243 | Reds Rookies (Ted | | | 303 | Johnny Orsino | 2.00 | 1.00 |
| | Davidson, *Tommy Helms)* | | | 304 | Dave Stenhouse | 2.00 | 1.00 |
| | | 2.00 | 1.00 | 305 | Rico Carty | 2.25 | 1.25 |
| 244 | Lindy McDaniel | 2.00 | 1.00 | 306 | Bubba Phillips | 2.00 | 1.00 |
| 245 | Joe Pepitone | 2.00 | 1.00 | 307 | Barry Latman | 2.00 | 1.00 |
| 246 | Tom Butters | 2.00 | 1.00 | 308 | Mets Rookies *(Cleon* | | |
| 247 | Wally Moon | 2.00 | 1.00 | | *Jones,* Tom Parsons) | 2.00 | 1.00 |
| 248 | Gus Triandos | 2.00 | 1.00 | 309 | Steve Hamilton | 2.25 | 1.25 |
| 249 | Dave McNally | 2.00 | 1.00 | 310 | Johnny Callison | 2.00 | 1.00 |
| 250 | Willie Mays | 110.00 | 55.00 | 311 | Orlando Pena | 2.00 | 1.00 |
| 251 | Billy Herman | 2.00 | 1.00 | 312 | Joe Nuxhall | 2.00 | 1.00 |
| 252 | Pete Richert | 2.00 | 1.00 | 313 | Jimmie Schaffer | 2.00 | 1.00 |
| 253 | Danny Cater | 2.00 | 1.00 | 314 | Sterling Slaughter | 2.00 | 1.00 |
| 254 | Roland Sheldon | 2.25 | 1.25 | 315 | Frank Malzone | 2.00 | 1.00 |
| 255 | Camilo Pascual | 2.00 | 1.00 | 316 | Reds Team | 2.75 | 1.50 |
| 256 | Tito Francona | 2.00 | 1.00 | 317 | Don McMahon | 2.00 | 1.00 |
| 257 | Jim Wynn | 2.00 | 1.00 | 318 | Matty Alou | 2.00 | 1.00 |
| 258 | Larry Bearnarth | 2.00 | 1.00 | 319 | Ken McMullen | 2.00 | 1.00 |
| 259 | Tigers Rookies *(Jim* | | | 320 | Bob Gibson | 30.00 | 15.00 |
| | *Northrup,* Ray Oyler) | 2.00 | 1.00 | 321 | Rusty Staub | 5.00 | 2.50 |
| 260 | Don Drysdale | 18.00 | 9.00 | 322 | Rick Wise | 2.00 | 1.00 |
| 261 | Duke Carmel | 2.25 | 1.25 | 323 | Hank Bauer | 2.00 | 1.00 |
| 262 | Bud Daley | 2.00 | 1.00 | 324 | Bobby Locke | 2.00 | 1.00 |
| 263 | Marty Keough | 2.00 | 1.00 | 325 | Donn Clendenon | 2.00 | 1.00 |
| 264 | Bob Buhl | 2.00 | 1.00 | 326 | Dwight Siebler | 2.00 | 1.00 |
| 265 | Jim Pagliaroni | 2.00 | 1.00 | 327 | Denis Menke | 2.00 | 1.00 |
| 266 | *Bert Campaneris* | 5.00 | 2.50 | 328 | Eddie Fisher | 2.00 | 1.00 |
| 267 | Senators Team | 5.00 | 2.50 | 329 | Hawk Taylor | 2.00 | 1.00 |
| 268 | Ken McBride | 2.00 | 1.00 | 330 | Whitey Ford | 20.00 | 10.00 |
| 269 | Frank Bolling | 2.00 | 1.00 | 331 | Dodgers Rookies (Al | | |
| 270 | Milt Pappas | 2.00 | 1.00 | | Ferrara, John Purdin) | 2.00 | 1.00 |
| 271 | Don Wert | 2.00 | 1.00 | 332 | Ted Abernathy | 2.00 | 1.00 |
| 272 | Chuck Schilling | 2.00 | 1.00 | 333 | Tommie Reynolds | 2.00 | 1.00 |
| 273 | Checklist 265-352 | 3.25 | 1.75 | 334 | Vic Roznovsky | 2.00 | 1.00 |
| 274 | Lum Harris | 2.00 | 1.00 | 335 | Mickey Lolich | 3.50 | 1.75 |

| | | NR MT | EX |
|---|---|---|---|
| 336 | Woody Held | 2.00 | 1.00 |
| 337 | Mike Cuellar | 2.25 | 1.25 |
| 338 | Phillies Team | 5.00 | 2.50 |
| 339 | Ryne Duren | 2.00 | 1.00 |
| 340 | Tony Oliva | 3.50 | 1.75 |
| 341 | Bobby Bolin | 2.00 | 1.00 |
| 342 | Bob Rodgers | 2.00 | 1.00 |
| 343 | Mike McCormick | 2.00 | 1.00 |
| 344 | Wes Parker | 2.00 | 1.00 |
| 345 | Floyd Robinson | 2.00 | 1.00 |
| 346 | Bobby Bragan | 2.00 | 1.00 |
| 347 | Roy Face | 2.25 | 1.25 |
| 348 | George Banks | 2.00 | 1.00 |
| 349 | Larry Miller | 2.00 | 1.00 |
| 350 | Mickey Mantle | 450.00 | 225.00 |
| 351 | Jim Perry | 2.00 | 1.00 |
| 352 | *Alex Johnson* | 2.00 | 1.00 |
| 353 | Jerry Lumpe | 2.00 | 1.00 |
| 354 | Cubs Rookies (Billy Ott, Jack Warner) | 2.00 | 1.00 |
| 355 | Vada Pinson | 5.00 | 2.50 |
| 356 | Bill Spanswick | 2.00 | 1.00 |
| 357 | Carl Warwick | 2.00 | 1.00 |
| 358 | Albie Pearson | 2.00 | 1.00 |
| 359 | Ken Johnson | 2.00 | 1.00 |
| 360 | Orlando Cepeda | 6.00 | 3.00 |
| 361 | Checklist 353–429 | 3.25 | 1.75 |
| 362 | Don Schwall | 2.00 | 1.00 |
| 363 | Bob Johnson | 2.00 | 1.00 |
| 364 | Galen Cisco | 2.00 | 1.00 |
| 365 | Jim Gentile | 2.00 | 1.00 |
| 366 | Dan Schneider | 2.00 | 1.00 |
| 367 | Leon Wagner | 2.00 | 1.00 |
| 368 | White Sox Rookies (*Ken Berry*, Joel Gibson) | 2.00 | 1.00 |
| 369 | Phil Linz | 2.25 | 1.25 |
| 370 | Tommy Davis | 2.25 | 1.25 |
| 371 | Frank Kreutzer | 2.00 | 1.00 |
| 372 | Clay Dalrymple | 2.00 | 1.00 |
| 373 | Curt Simmons | 2.00 | 1.00 |
| 374 | Angels Rookies (*Jose Cardenal*, Dick Simpson) | 2.00 | 1.00 |
| 375 | Dave Wickersham | 2.00 | 1.00 |
| 376 | Jim Landis | 2.00 | 1.00 |
| 377 | Willie Stargell | 25.00 | 12.50 |
| 378 | Chuck Estrada | 2.00 | 1.00 |
| 379 | Giants Team | 5.00 | 2.50 |
| 380 | Rocky Colavito | 2.00 | 1.00 |
| 381 | Al Jackson | 2.00 | 1.00 |
| 382 | J.C. Martin | 2.00 | 1.00 |
| 383 | Felipe Alou | 2.00 | 1.00 |
| 384 | Johnny Klippstein | 2.00 | 1.00 |
| 385 | Carl Yastrzemski | 70.00 | 35.00 |
| 386 | Cubs Rookies (Paul Jaeckel, Fred Norman) | 2.00 | 1.00 |
| 387 | Johnny Podres | 2.00 | 1.00 |
| 388 | John Blanchard | 2.25 | 1.25 |
| 389 | Don Larsen | 2.00 | 1.00 |
| 390 | Bill Freehan | 2.00 | 1.00 |
| 391 | Mel McGaha | 2.00 | 1.00 |
| 392 | Bob Friend | 2.25 | 1.25 |
| 393 | Ed Kirkpatrick | 2.00 | 1.00 |
| 394 | Jim Hannan | 2.00 | 1.00 |
| 395 | Jim Hart | 2.00 | 1.00 |
| 396 | Frank Bertaina | 2.00 | 1.00 |
| 397 | Jerry Buchek | 2.00 | 1.00 |
| 398 | Reds Rookies (Dan Neville, *Art Shamsky*) | 2.00 | 1.00 |
| 399 | Ray Herbert | 2.00 | 1.00 |
| 400 | Harmon Killebrew | 25.00 | 12.50 |
| 401 | Carl Willey | 2.00 | 1.00 |
| 402 | Joe Amalfitano | 2.00 | 1.00 |
| 403 | Red Sox Team | 2.00 | 1.00 |
| 404 | Stan Williams | 2.00 | 1.00 |
| 405 | John Roseboro | 2.00 | 1.00 |
| 406 | Ralph Terry | 2.00 | 1.00 |
| 407 | Lee Maye | 2.00 | 1.00 |
| 408 | Larry Sherry | 2.00 | 1.00 |
| 409 | Astros Rookies (Jim Beauchamp, *Larry Dierker*) | 2.00 | 1.00 |
| 410 | Luis Aparicio | 9.00 | 4.50 |
| 411 | Roger Craig | 2.00 | 1.00 |
| 412 | Bob Bailey | 2.00 | 1.00 |
| 413 | Hal Reniff | 2.25 | 1.25 |
| 414 | Al Lopez | 2.00 | 1.00 |
| 415 | Curt Flood | 2.25 | 1.25 |
| 416 | Jim Brewer | 2.00 | 1.00 |
| 417 | Ed Brinkman | 2.00 | 1.00 |
| 418 | Johnny Edwards | 2.00 | 1.00 |
| 419 | Ruben Amaro | 2.00 | 1.00 |
| 420 | Larry Jackson | 2.00 | 1.00 |
| 421 | Twins Rookies (Gary Dotter, Jay Ward) | 2.00 | 1.00 |
| 422 | Aubrey Gatewood | 2.00 | 1.00 |
| 423 | Jesse Gonder | 2.00 | 1.00 |
| 424 | Gary Bell | 2.00 | 1.00 |
| 425 | Wayne Causey | 2.00 | 1.00 |
| 426 | Braves Team | 5.00 | 2.50 |
| 427 | Bob Saverine | 2.00 | 1.00 |
| 428 | Bob Shaw | 2.00 | 1.00 |
| 429 | Don Demeter | 2.00 | 1.00 |
| 430 | Gary Peters | 2.00 | 1.00 |
| 431 | Cardinals Rookies (*Nelson Briles*, Wayne Spiezio) | 2.00 | 1.00 |
| 432 | Jim Grant | 2.00 | 1.00 |
| 433 | John Bateman | 2.00 | 1.00 |
| 434 | Dave Morehead | 2.00 | 1.00 |
| 435 | Willie Davis | 2.25 | 1.25 |
| 436 | Don Elston | 2.00 | 1.00 |
| 437 | Chico Cardenas | 2.00 | 1.00 |
| 438 | Harry Walker | 2.00 | 1.00 |
| 439 | Moe Drabowsky | 2.00 | 1.00 |
| 440 | Tom Tresh | 5.00 | 2.50 |
| 441 | Denver Lemaster | 2.00 | 1.00 |
| 442 | Vic Power | 2.00 | 1.00 |
| 443 | Checklist 430–506 | 3.25 | 1.75 |
| 444 | Bob Hendley | 2.00 | 1.00 |
| 445 | Don Lock | 2.00 | 1.00 |
| 446 | Art Mahaffey | 2.00 | 1.00 |
| 447 | Julian Javier | 2.00 | 1.00 |
| 448 | Lee Stange | 2.00 | 1.00 |
| 449 | Mets Rookies (Jerry Hinsley, Gary Kroll) | 2.25 | 1.25 |
| 450 | Elston Howard | 5.00 | 2.50 |
| 451 | Jim Owens | 2.00 | 1.00 |
| 452 | Gary Geiger | 2.00 | 1.00 |
| 453 | Dodgers Rookies (*Willie Crawford*, John Werhas) | 2.25 | 1.25 |
| 454 | Ed Rakow | 2.00 | 1.00 |

| | | NR MT | EX |
|---|---|---|---|
| 455 | Norm Siebern | 2.25 | 1.25 |
| 456 | Bill Henry | 2.00 | 1.00 |
| 457 | Bob Kennedy | 2.00 | 1.00 |
| 458 | John Buzhardt | 2.00 | 1.00 |
| 459 | Frank Kostro | 2.00 | 1.00 |
| 460 | Richie Allen | 10.00 | 5.00 |
| 461 | Braves Rookies (*Clay Carroll*, Phil Niekro) | 50.00 | 25.00 |
| 462 | Lew Krausse (photo actually Pete Lovrich) | 2.00 | 1.00 |
| 463 | Manny Mota | 2.25 | 1.25 |
| 464 | Ron Piche | 2.00 | 1.00 |
| 465 | Tom Haller | 2.00 | 1.00 |
| 466 | Senators Rookies (Pete Craig, Dick Nen) | 2.00 | 1.00 |
| 467 | Ray Washburn | 2.00 | 1.00 |
| 468 | Larry Brown | 2.00 | 1.00 |
| 469 | Don Nottebart | 2.00 | 1.00 |
| 470 | Yogi Berra | 50.00 | 30.00 |
| 471 | Billy Hoeft | 2.00 | 1.00 |
| 472 | Don Pavletich | 2.00 | 1.00 |
| 473 | Orioles Rookies (*Paul Blair, Dave Johnson*) | 15.00 | 7.50 |
| 474 | Cookie Rojas | 2.00 | 1.00 |
| 475 | Clete Boyer | 2.00 | 1.00 |
| 476 | Billy O'Dell | 2.00 | 1.00 |
| 477 | Cardinals Rookies (Fritz Ackley, *Steve Carlton*) | 525.00 | 260.00 |
| 478 | Wilbur Wood | 2.00 | 1.00 |
| 479 | Ken Harrelson | 5.00 | 2.50 |
| 480 | Joel Horlen | 2.00 | 1.00 |
| 481 | Indians Team | 2.00 | 1.00 |
| 482 | Bob Priddy | 2.00 | 1.00 |
| 483 | George Smith | 2.00 | 1.00 |
| 484 | Ron Perranoski | 2.25 | 1.25 |
| 485 | Nellie Fox | 6.00 | 3.00 |
| 486 | Angels Rookies (Tom Egan, Pat Rogan) | 2.00 | 1.00 |
| 487 | Woody Woodward | 2.25 | 1.25 |
| 488 | Ted Wills | 2.00 | 1.00 |
| 489 | Gene Mauch | 2.25 | 1.25 |
| 490 | Earl Battey | 2.25 | 1.25 |
| 491 | Tracy Stallard | 2.00 | 1.00 |
| 492 | Gene Freese | 2.00 | 1.00 |
| 493 | Tigers Rookies (Bruce Brubaker, Bill Roman) | 2.00 | 1.00 |
| 494 | Jay Ritchie | 2.00 | 1.00 |
| 495 | Joe Christopher | 2.25 | 1.25 |
| 496 | Joe Cunningham | 2.00 | 1.00 |
| 497 | Giants Rookies (*Ken Henderson*, Jack Hiatt) | 2.25 | 1.25 |
| 498 | Gene Stephens | 2.00 | 1.00 |
| 499 | Stu Miller | 2.00 | 1.00 |
| 500 | Ed Mathews | 30.00 | 15.00 |
| 501 | Indians Rookies (Ralph Gagliano, Jim Rittwage) | 2.00 | 1.00 |
| 502 | Don Cardwell | 2.00 | 1.00 |
| 503 | Phil Gagliano | 2.00 | 1.00 |
| 504 | Jerry Grote | 2.25 | 1.25 |
| 505 | Ray Culp | 2.00 | 1.00 |
| 506 | Sam Mele | 2.00 | 1.00 |
| 507 | Sammy Ellis | 2.00 | 1.00 |
| 508a | Checklist 507-598 (large print on front) | 6.00 | 3.00 |

| | | NR MT | EX |
|---|---|---|---|
| 508b | Checklist 507-598 (small print on front) | 5.00 | 2.50 |
| 509 | Red Sox Rookies (Bob Guindon, Gerry Vezendy) | 2.00 | 1.00 |
| 510 | Ernie Banks | 75.00 | 38.00 |
| 511 | Ron Locke | 2.25 | 1.25 |
| 512 | Cap Peterson | 2.00 | 1.00 |
| 513 | Yankees Team | 10.00 | 5.00 |
| 514 | Joe Azcue | 2.00 | 1.00 |
| 515 | Vern Law | 2.00 | 1.00 |
| 516 | Al Weis | 2.00 | 1.00 |
| 517 | Angels Rookies (Paul Schaal, Jack Warner) | 2.00 | 1.00 |
| 518 | Ken Rowe | 2.00 | 1.00 |
| 519 | Bob Uecker | 45.00 | 22.00 |
| 520 | Tony Cloninger | 2.25 | 1.25 |
| 521 | Phillies Rookies (Dave Bennett, Morrie Stevens) | 2.00 | 1.00 |
| 522 | Hank Aguirre | 2.00 | 1.00 |
| 523 | Mike Brumley | 5.00 | 2.50 |
| 524 | Dave Giusti | 5.00 | 2.50 |
| 525 | Eddie Bressoud | 5.00 | 2.50 |
| 526 | Athletics Rookies (*Jim Hunter, Rene Lachemann, Skip Lockwood, Johnny Odom*) | 150.00 | 75.00 |
| 527 | Jeff Torborg | 6.00 | 3.00 |
| 528 | George Altman | 5.00 | 2.50 |
| 529 | Jerry Fosnow | 5.00 | 2.50 |
| 530 | Jim Maloney | 6.00 | 3.00 |
| 531 | Chuck Hiller | 5.00 | 2.50 |
| 532 | Hector Lopez | 5.00 | 2.50 |
| 533 | Mets Rookies (Jim Bethke, *Tug McGraw*, Dan Napolean, *Ron Swoboda*) | 20.00 | 10.00 |
| 534 | John Herrnstein | 5.00 | 2.50 |
| 535 | Jack Kralick | 5.00 | 2.50 |
| 536 | Andre Rodgers | 5.00 | 2.50 |
| 537 | Angels Rookies (Marcelino Lopez, *Rudy May*, Phil Roof) | 5.00 | 2.50 |
| 538 | Chuck Dressen | 6.00 | 3.00 |
| 539 | Herm Starrette | 5.00 | 2.50 |
| 540 | Lou Brock | 50.00 | 25.00 |
| 541 | White Sox Rookies (Greg Bollo, Bob Locker) | 5.00 | 2.50 |
| 542 | Lou Klimchock | 5.00 | 2.50 |
| 543 | Ed Connolly | 5.00 | 2.50 |
| 544 | Howie Reed | 5.00 | 2.50 |
| 545 | Jesus Alou | 6.00 | 3.00 |
| 546 | Indians Rookies (Ray Barker, Bill Davis, Mike Hedlund, Floyd Weaver) | 5.00 | 2.50 |
| 547 | Jake Wood | 5.00 | 2.50 |
| 548 | Dick Stigman | 5.00 | 2.50 |
| 549 | Cubs Rookies (*Glenn Beckert*, Roberto Pena) | 5.00 | 2.50 |
| 550 | *Mel Stottlemyre* | 25.00 | 12.50 |
| 551 | Mets Team | 15.00 | 7.50 |
| 552 | Julio Gotay | 5.00 | 2.50 |
| 553 | Astros Rookies (Dan Coombs, Jack McClure, | | |

|     |     | NR MT | EX |
|-----|-----|-------|-----|
|     | Gene Ratliff) | 5.00 | 2.50 |
| 554 | Chico Ruiz | 5.00 | 2.50 |
| 555 | Jack Baldschun | 5.00 | 2.50 |
| 556 | Red Schoendienst | 10.00 | 5.00 |
| 557 | Jose Santiago | 5.00 | 2.50 |
| 558 | Tommie Sisk | 5.00 | 2.50 |
| 559 | Ed Bailey | 5.00 | 2.50 |
| 560 | Boog Powell | 12.00 | 6.00 |
| 561 | Dodgers Rookies (Dennis Daboll, *Mike Kekich, Jim Lefebvre,* Hector Valle) | 12.00 | 6.00 |
| 562 | Billy Moran | 5.00 | 2.50 |
| 563 | Julio Navarro | 5.00 | 2.50 |
| 564 | Mel Nelson | 5.00 | 2.50 |
| 565 | Ernie Broglio | 5.00 | 2.50 |
| 566 | Yankees Rookies (Gil Blanco, Art Lopez, Ross Moschitto) | 5.00 | 2.50 |
| 567 | Tommie Aaron | 6.00 | 3.00 |
| 568 | Ron Taylor | 5.00 | 2.50 |
| 569 | Gino Cimoli | 5.00 | 2.50 |
| 570 | Claude Osteen | 6.00 | 3.00 |
| 571 | Ossie Virgil | 5.00 | 2.50 |
| 572 | Orioles Team | 10.00 | 5.00 |
| 573 | Red Sox Rookies (*Jim Lonborg,* Gerry Moses, Mike Ryan, Bill Schlesinger) | 10.00 | 5.00 |
| 574 | Roy Sievers | 6.00 | 3.00 |
| 575 | Jose Pagan | 5.00 | 2.50 |
| 576 | Terry Fox | 5.00 | 2.50 |
| 577 | A.L. Rookies (Jim Buschhorn, Darold Knowles, Richie Scheinblum) | 5.00 | 2.50 |
| 578 | Camilo Carreon | 5.00 | 2.50 |
| 579 | Dick Smith | 5.00 | 2.50 |
| 580 | Jimmie Hall | 5.00 | 2.50 |
| 581 | N.L. Rookies (Kevin Collins, *Tony Perez,* Dave Ricketts) | 175.00 | 87.00 |
| 582 | Bob Schmidt | 5.00 | 2.50 |
| 583 | Wes Covington | 5.00 | 2.50 |
| 584 | Harry Bright | 5.00 | 2.50 |
| 585 | Hank Fischer | 5.00 | 2.50 |
| 586 | Tommy McCraw | 5.00 | 2.50 |
| 587 | Joe Sparma | 5.00 | 2.50 |
| 588 | Lenny Green | 5.00 | 2.50 |
| 589 | Giants Rookies (Frank Linzy, Bob Schroder) | 5.00 | 2.50 |
| 590 | Johnnie Wyatt | 5.00 | 2.50 |
| 591 | Bob Skinner | 6.00 | 3.00 |
| 592 | Frank Bork | 5.00 | 2.50 |
| 593 | Tigers Rookies (Jackie Moore, John Sullivan) | 5.00 | 2.50 |
| 594 | Joe Gaines | 5.00 | 2.50 |
| 595 | Don Lee | 5.00 | 2.50 |
| 596 | Don Landrum | 5.00 | 2.50 |
| 597 | Twins Rookies (Joe Nossek, Dick Reese, John Sevcik) | 6.00 | 3.00 |
| 598 | Al Downing | 10.00 | 3.00 |

## 1966 Topps

In 1966, Topps produced another 598-card set. The 2-1/2" by 3-1/2" cards feature the almost traditional color photograph with a diagonal strip in the upper left-hand corner carrying the team name. A band at the bottom carries the player's name and position. Multi-player cards returned in 1966 after having had a year's hiatus. The statistical leader cards feature the categorical leader and two runners-up. Most team managers have cards as well. The 1966 set features a handful of cards found with without a notice of the player's sale or trade to another team. Cards without the notice bring higher prices not included in the complete set prices below.

|     | NR MT | EX |
|-----|-------|-----|
| Complete Set: | 4500.00 | 2250.00 |
| Common Player: 1-110 | 1.00 | .50 |
| Common Player: 111-446 | 1.25 | .60 |
| Common Player: 447-522 | 5.00 | 2.50 |
| Common Player Singleprint: 523-598 | 20.00 | 10.00 |
| Common Player: 523-598 | 15.00 | 7.50 |

A player's name in italic type indicates a rookie card. An (FC) indicates a player's first card for that particular card company.

| | | NR MT | EX |
|---|---|---|---|
| 1 | Willie Mays | 155.00 | 60.00 |
| 2 | Ted Abernathy | 1.25 | .60 |
| 3 | Sam Mele | 1.00 | .50 |
| 4 | Ray Culp | 1.00 | .50 |
| 5 | Jim Fregosi | 1.50 | .70 |
| 6 | Chuck Schilling | 1.00 | .50 |
| 7 | Tracy Stallard | 1.00 | .50 |
| 8 | Floyd Robinson | 1.00 | .50 |
| 9 | Clete Boyer | 5.00 | 2.50 |
| 10 | Tony Cloninger | 1.25 | .60 |
| 11 | Senators Rookies (Brant Alyea, Pete Craig) | 1.00 | .50 |
| 12 | John Tsitouris | 1.00 | .50 |
| 13 | Lou Johnson | 1.00 | .50 |
| 14 | Norm Siebern | 1.25 | .60 |
| 15 | Vern Law | 1.50 | .70 |
| 16 | Larry Brown | 1.25 | .60 |
| 17 | Johnny Stephenson | 1.25 | .60 |
| 18 | Roland Sheldon | 1.00 | .50 |
| 19 | Giants Team | 5.00 | 2.50 |
| 20 | Willie Horton | 1.25 | .60 |
| 21 | Don Nottebart | 1.00 | .50 |
| 22 | Joe Nossek | 1.00 | .50 |
| 23 | Jack Sanford | 1.00 | .50 |
| 24 | Don Kessinger | 1.25 | .60 |
| 25 | Pete Ward | 1.00 | .50 |
| 26 | Ray Sadecki | 1.00 | .50 |
| 27 | Orioles Rookies (Andy Etchebarren, Darold Knowles) | 1.25 | .60 |
| 28 | Phil Niekro | 12.00 | 6.00 |
| 29 | Mike Brumley | 1.00 | .50 |
| 30 | Pete Rose | 60.00 | 30.00 |
| 31 | Jack Cullen | 1.25 | .60 |
| 32 | Adolfo Phillips | 1.00 | .50 |
| 33 | Jim Pagliaroni | 1.00 | .50 |
| 34 | Checklist 1-88 | 5.00 | 2.50 |
| 35 | Ron Swoboda | 1.25 | .60 |
| 36 | Jim Hunter | 30.00 | 15.00 |
| 37 | Billy Herman | 5.00 | 2.50 |
| 38 | Ron Nischwitz | 1.00 | .50 |
| 39 | Ken Henderson | 1.00 | .50 |
| 40 | Jim Grant | 1.00 | .50 |
| 41 | Don LeJohn | 1.00 | .50 |
| 42 | Aubrey Gatewood | 1.00 | .50 |
| 43 | Don Landrum | 1.00 | .50 |
| 44 | Indians Rookies (Bill Davis, Tom Kelley) | 1.00 | .50 |
| 45 | Jim Gentile | 1.25 | .60 |
| 46 | Howie Koplitz | 1.00 | .50 |
| 47 | J.C. Martin | 1.00 | .50 |
| 48 | Paul Blair | 1.25 | .60 |
| 49 | Woody Woodward | 1.25 | .60 |
| 50 | Mickey Mantle | 200.00 | 100.00 |
| 51 | Gordon Richardson | 1.25 | .60 |
| 52 | Power Plus (Johnny Callison, Wes Covington) | 1.50 | .70 |
| 53 | Bob Duliba | 1.00 | .50 |
| 54 | Jose Pagan | 1.00 | .50 |
| 55 | Ken Harrelson | 5.00 | 2.50 |
| 56 | Sandy Valdespino | 1.00 | .50 |
| 57 | Jim Lefebvre | 1.25 | .60 |
| 58 | Dave Wickersham | 1.00 | .50 |
| 59 | Reds Team | 2.25 | 1.25 |
| 60 | Curt Flood | 5.00 | 2.50 |
| 61 | Bob Bolin | 1.00 | .50 |
| 62a | Merritt Ranew (no sold statement) | 15.00 | 7.50 |
| 62b | Merritt Ranew (with sold statement) | | .50 |
| 63 | Jim Stewart | 1.00 | .50 |
| 64 | Bob Bruce | 1.00 | .50 |
| 65 | Leon Wagner | 1.25 | .60 |
| 66 | Al Weis | 1.00 | .50 |
| 67 | Mets Rookies (Cleon Jones, Dick Selma) | 1.25 | .60 |
| 68 | Hal Reniff | 1.25 | .60 |
| 69 | Ken Hamlin | 1.00 | .50 |
| 70 | Carl Yastrzemski | 50.00 | 25.00 |
| 71 | Frank Carpin | 1.00 | .50 |
| 72 | Tony Perez | 35.00 | 17.50 |
| 73 | Jerry Zimmerman | 1.00 | .50 |
| 74 | Don Mossi | 1.25 | .60 |
| 75 | Tommy Davis | 5.00 | 2.50 |
| 76 | Red Schoendienst | 4.00 | 2.00 |
| 77 | Johnny Orsino | 1.00 | .50 |
| 78 | Frank Linzy | 1.00 | .50 |
| 79 | Joe Pepitone | 5.00 | 2.50 |
| 80 | Richie Allen | 2.50 | 1.25 |
| 81 | Ray Oyler | 1.00 | .50 |
| 82 | Bob Hendley | 1.00 | .50 |
| 83 | Albie Pearson | 1.00 | .50 |
| 84 | Braves Rookies (Jim Beauchamp, Dick Kelley) | 1.00 | .50 |
| 85 | Eddie Fisher | 1.00 | .50 |
| 86 | John Bateman | 1.00 | .50 |
| 87 | Dan Napoleon | 1.25 | .60 |
| 88 | Fred Whitfield | 1.00 | .50 |
| 89 | Ted Davidson | 1.00 | .50 |
| 90 | Luis Aparicio | 9.00 | 4.50 |
| 91a | Bob Uecker (no trade statement) | 70.00 | 35.00 |
| 91b | Bob Uecker (with trade statement) | 20.00 | 10.00 |
| 92 | Yankees Team | 5.00 | 2.50 |
| 93 | Jim Lonborg | 1.50 | .70 |
| 94 | Matty Alou | 1.50 | .70 |
| 95 | Pete Richert | 1.00 | .50 |
| 96 | Felipe Alou | 1.50 | .70 |
| 97 | Jim Merritt | 1.00 | .50 |
| 98 | Don Demeter | 1.00 | .50 |
| 99 | Buc Belters (Donn Clendenon, Willie Stargell) | 5.00 | 2.50 |
| 100 | Sandy Koufax | 110.00 | 55.00 |
| 101a | Checklist 89-176 (115 is Spahn) | 7.00 | 3.50 |
| 101b | Checklist 89-176 (115 is Henry) | 3.00 | 1.50 |
| 102 | Ed Kirkpatrick | 1.00 | .50 |
| 103a | Dick Groat (no trade statement) | 20.00 | 10.00 |
| 103b | Dick Groat (with trade statement) | 5.00 | 2.50 |
| 104a | Alex Johnson (no trade statement) | 15.00 | 7.50 |
| 104b | Alex Johnson (with trade statement) | 1.25 | .60 |
| 105 | Milt Pappas | 1.25 | .60 |
| 106 | Rusty Staub | 2.50 | 1.25 |

|  |  | NR MT | EX |
|---|---|---|---|
| 107 | Athletics Rookies (Larry Stahl, Ron Tompkins) | 1.00 | .50 |
| 108 | Bobby Klaus | 1.25 | .60 |
| 109 | Ralph Terry | 1.25 | .60 |
| 110 | Ernie Banks | 30.00 | 15.00 |
| 111 | Gary Peters | 1.25 | .60 |
| 112 | Manny Mota | 1.25 | .60 |
| 113 | Hank Aguirre | 1.25 | .60 |
| 114 | Jim Gosger | 1.25 | .60 |
| 115 | Bill Henry | 1.25 | .60 |
| 116 | Walt Alston | 2.50 | 1.25 |
| 117 | Jake Gibbs | 1.50 | .70 |
| 118 | Mike McCormick | 1.25 | .60 |
| 119 | Art Shamsky | 1.25 | .60 |
| 120 | Harmon Killebrew | 15.00 | 7.50 |
| 121 | Ray Herbert | 1.25 | .60 |
| 122 | Joe Gaines | 1.25 | .60 |
| 123 | Pirates Rookies (Frank Bork, Jerry May) | 1.25 | .60 |
| 124 | Tug McGraw | 3.00 | 1.50 |
| 125 | Lou Brock | 20.00 | 10.00 |
| 126 | *Jim Palmer* | 225.00 | 112.00 |
| 127 | Ken Berry | 1.25 | .60 |
| 128 | Jim Landis | 1.25 | .60 |
| 129 | Jack Kralick | 1.25 | .60 |
| 130 | Joe Torre | 2.25 | 1.25 |
| 131 | Angels Team | 2.25 | 1.25 |
| 132 | Orlando Cepeda | 5.00 | 2.50 |
| 133 | Don McMahon | 1.25 | .60 |
| 134 | Wes Parker | 1.25 | .60 |
| 135 | Dave Morehead | 1.25 | .60 |
| 136 | Woody Held | 1.25 | .60 |
| 137 | Pat Corrales | 1.50 | .70 |
| 138 | Roger Repoz | 1.50 | .70 |
| 139 | Cubs Rookies (Byron Browne, Don Young) | 1.25 | .60 |
| 140 | Jim Maloney | 1.25 | .60 |
| 141 | Tom McCraw | 1.25 | .60 |
| 142 | Don Dennis | 1.25 | .60 |
| 143 | Jose Tartabull | 1.25 | .60 |
| 144 | Don Schwall | 1.25 | .60 |
| 145 | Bill Freehan | 1.25 | .60 |
| 146 | George Altman | 1.25 | .60 |
| 147 | Lum Harris | 1.25 | .60 |
| 148 | Bob Johnson | 1.25 | .60 |
| 149 | Dick Nen | 1.25 | .60 |
| 150 | Rocky Colavito | 2.50 | 1.25 |
| 151 | Gary Wagner | 1.25 | .60 |
| 152 | Frank Malzone | 1.25 | .60 |
| 153 | Rico Carty | 5.00 | 2.50 |
| 154 | Chuck Hiller | 1.25 | .60 |
| 155 | Marcelino Lopez | 1.25 | .60 |
| 156 | DP Combo (Hal Lanier, Dick Schofield) | 1.50 | .70 |
| 157 | Rene Lachemann | 1.25 | .60 |
| 158 | Jim Brewer | 1.25 | .60 |
| 159 | Chico Ruiz | 1.25 | .60 |
| 160 | Whitey Ford | 25.00 | 12.50 |
| 161 | Jerry Lumpe | 1.25 | .60 |
| 162 | Lee Maye | 1.25 | .60 |
| 163 | Tito Francona | 1.25 | .60 |
| 164 | White Sox Rookies (Tommie Agee, Marv Staehle) | 1.25 | .60 |
| 165 | Don Lock | 1.25 | .60 |
| 166 | Chris Krug | 1.25 | .60 |
| 167 | Boog Powell | 2.50 | 1.25 |
| 168 | Dan Osinski | 1.25 | .60 |
| 169 | Duke Sims | 1.25 | .60 |
| 170 | Cookie Rojas | 1.25 | .60 |
| 171 | Nick Willhite | 1.25 | .60 |
| 172 | Mets Team | 3.00 | 1.50 |
| 173 | Al Spangler | 1.25 | .60 |
| 174 | Ron Taylor | 1.25 | .60 |
| 175 | Bert Campaneris | 5.00 | 2.50 |
| 176 | Jim Davenport | 1.25 | .60 |
| 177 | Hector Lopez | 1.50 | .70 |
| 178 | Bob Tillman | 1.25 | .60 |
| 179 | Cardinals Rookies (Dennis Aust, Bob Tolan) | 1.25 | .60 |
| 180 | Vada Pinson | 2.50 | 1.25 |
| 181 | Al Worthington | 1.25 | .60 |
| 182 | Jerry Lynch | 1.25 | .60 |
| 183a | Checklist 177-264 (large print on front) | 2.50 | 1.25 |
| 183b | Checklist 177-264 (small print on front) | 6.00 | 3.00 |
| 184 | Denis Menke | 1.25 | .60 |
| 185 | Bob Buhl | 1.25 | .60 |
| 186 | Ruben Amaro | 1.50 | .70 |
| 187 | Chuck Dressen | 1.25 | .60 |
| 188 | Al Luplow | 1.25 | .60 |
| 189 | John Roseboro | 1.25 | .60 |
| 190 | Jimmie Hall | 1.25 | .60 |
| 191 | Darrell Sutherland | 1.25 | .60 |
| 192 | Vic Power | 1.25 | .60 |
| 193 | Dave McNally | 1.50 | .70 |
| 194 | Senators Team | 2.25 | 1.25 |
| 195 | Joe Morgan | 40.00 | 20.00 |
| 196 | Don Pavletich | 1.25 | .60 |
| 197 | Sonny Siebert | 1.25 | .60 |
| 198 | *Mickey Stanley* | 1.50 | .70 |
| 199 | Chisox Clubbers (Floyd Robinson, Johnny Romano, Bill Skowron) | 1.50 | .70 |
| 200 | Ed Mathews | 15.00 | 7.50 |
| 201 | Jim Dickson | 1.25 | .60 |
| 202 | Clay Dalrymple | 1.25 | .60 |
| 203 | Jose Santiago | 1.25 | .60 |
| 204 | Cubs Team | 2.25 | 1.25 |
| 205 | Tom Tresh | 5.00 | 2.50 |
| 206 | Alvin Jackson | 1.25 | .60 |
| 207 | Frank Quilici | 1.25 | .60 |
| 208 | Bob Miller | 1.25 | .60 |
| 209 | Tigers Rookies (Fritz Fisher, *John Hiller*) | 1.25 | .60 |
| 210 | Bill Mazeroski | 2.50 | 1.25 |
| 211 | Frank Kreutzer | 1.25 | .60 |
| 212 | Ed Kranepool | 1.50 | .70 |
| 213 | Fred Newman | 1.25 | .60 |
| 214 | Tommy Harper | 1.25 | .60 |
| 215 | N.L. Batting Leaders (Hank Aaron, Willie Clemente, Willie Mays) | 10.00 | 5.00 |
| 216 | A.L. Batting Leaders (Vic Davalillo, Tony Oliva, Carl Yastrzemski) | 6.00 | 3.00 |
| 217 | N.L. Home Run Leaders (Willie Mays, Willie McCovey, Billy Williams) | 5.00 | 2.50 |
| 218 | A.L. Home Run Leaders |  |  |

|  | NR MT | EX |
|---|---|---|
| (Norm Cash, Tony Conigliaro, Willie Horton) | 2.50 | 1.25 |
| 219 N.L. RBI Leaders (Deron Johnson, Willie Mays, Frank Robinson) | 6.00 | 3.00 |
| 220 A.L. RBI Leaders (Rocky Colavito, Willie Horton, Tony Oliva) | 2.50 | 1.25 |
| 221 N.L. ERA Leaders (Sandy Koufax, Vern Law, Juan Marichal) | 6.00 | 3.00 |
| 222 A.L. ERA Leaders (Eddie Fisher, Sam McDowell, Sonny Siebert) | 2.50 | 1.25 |
| 223 N.L. Pitching Leaders (Tony Cloninger, Don Drysdale, Sandy Koufax) | 6.00 | 3.00 |
| 224 A.L. Pitching Leaders (Jim Grant, Jim Kaat, Mel Stottlemyre) | 3.00 | 1.50 |
| 225 N.L. Strikeout Leaders (Bob Gibson, Sandy Koufax, Bob Veale) | 6.00 | 3.00 |
| 226 A.L. Strikeout Leaders (Mickey Lolich, Sam McDowell, Denny McLain, Sonny Siebert) | 2.50 | 1.25 |
| 227 Russ Nixon | 1.25 | .60 |
| 228 Larry Dierker | 1.25 | .60 |
| 229 Hank Bauer | 1.25 | .60 |
| 230 Johnny Callison | 1.25 | .60 |
| 231 Floyd Weaver | 1.25 | .60 |
| 232 Glenn Beckert | 1.50 | .70 |
| 233 Dom Zanni | 1.25 | .60 |
| 234 Yankees Rookies (Rich Beck, Roy White) | 5.00 | 2.50 |
| 235 Don Cardwell | 1.25 | .60 |
| 236 Mike Hershberger | 1.25 | .60 |
| 237 Billy O'Dell | 1.25 | .60 |
| 238 Dodgers Team | 5.00 | 2.50 |
| 239 Orlando Pena | 1.25 | .60 |
| 240 Earl Battey | 1.25 | .60 |
| 241 Dennis Ribant | 1.25 | .60 |
| 242 Jesus Alou | 1.25 | .60 |
| 243 Nelson Briles | 1.25 | .60 |
| 244 Astros Rookies (Chuck Harrison, Sonny Jackson) | 1.25 | .60 |
| 245 John Buzhardt | 1.25 | .60 |
| 246 Ed Bailey | 1.25 | .60 |
| 247 Carl Warwick | 1.25 | .60 |
| 248 Pete Mikkelsen | 1.25 | .60 |
| 249 Bill Rigney | 1.25 | .60 |
| 250 Sam Ellis | 1.25 | .60 |
| 251 Ed Brinkman | 1.25 | .60 |
| 252 Denver Lemaster | 1.25 | .60 |
| 253 Don Wert | 1.25 | .60 |
| 254 Phillies Rookies (Ferguson Jenkins, Bill Sorrell) | 150.00 | 75.00 |
| 255 Willie Stargell | 18.00 | 9.00 |
| 256 Lew Krausse | 1.25 | .60 |
| 257 Jeff Torborg | 1.25 | .60 |
| 258 Dave Giusti | 1.25 | .60 |
| 259 Red Sox Team | 2.50 | 1.25 |

|  | NR MT | EX |
|---|---|---|
| 260 Bob Shaw | 1.25 | .60 |
| 261 Ron Hansen | 1.25 | .60 |
| 262 Jack Hamilton | 1.25 | .60 |
| 263 Tom Egan | 1.25 | .60 |
| 264 Twins Rookies (Andy Kosco, Ted Uhlaender) | 1.25 | .60 |
| 265 Stu Miller | 1.25 | .60 |
| 266 Pedro Gonzalez | 1.25 | .60 |
| 267 Joe Sparma | 1.25 | .60 |
| 268 John Blanchard | 1.25 | .60 |
| 269 Don Heffner | 1.25 | .60 |
| 270 Claude Osteen | 1.25 | .60 |
| 271 Hal Lanier | 1.50 | .70 |
| 272 Jack Baldschun | 1.25 | .60 |
| 273 Astro Aces (Bob Aspromonte, Rusty Staub) | 5.00 | 2.50 |
| 274 Buster Narum | 1.25 | .60 |
| 275 Tim McCarver | 2.50 | 1.25 |
| 276 Jim Bouton | 2.50 | 1.25 |
| 277 George Thomas | 1.25 | .60 |
| 278 Calvin Koonce | 1.25 | .60 |
| 279a Checklist 265-352 (player's cap black) | 6.00 | 3.00 |
| 279b Checklist 265-352 (player's cap red) | 3.00 | 1.50 |
| 280 Bobby Knoop | 1.25 | .60 |
| 281 Bruce Howard | 1.25 | .60 |
| 282 Johnny Lewis | 1.25 | .60 |
| 283 Jim Perry | 1.50 | .70 |
| 284 Bobby Wine | 1.25 | .60 |
| 285 Luis Tiant | 2.50 | 1.25 |
| 286 Gary Geiger | 1.25 | .60 |
| 287 Jack Aker | 1.25 | .60 |
| 288 Dodgers Rookies (Bill Singer, Don Sutton) | 125.00 | 56.00 |
| 289 Larry Sherry | 1.25 | .60 |
| 290 Ron Santo | 5.00 | 2.50 |
| 291 Moe Drabowsky | 1.25 | .60 |
| 292 Jim Coker | 1.25 | .60 |
| 293 Mike Shannon | 1.25 | .60 |
| 294 Steve Ridzik | 1.25 | .60 |
| 295 Jim Hart | 1.25 | .60 |
| 296 Johnny Keane | 1.25 | .60 |
| 297 Jim Owens | 1.25 | .60 |
| 298 Rico Petrocelli | 1.25 | .60 |
| 299 Lou Burdette | 5.00 | 2.50 |
| 300 Bob Clemente | 110.00 | 55.00 |
| 301 Greg Bollo | 1.25 | .60 |
| 302 Ernie Bowman | 1.25 | .60 |
| 303 Indians Team | 2.25 | 1.25 |
| 304 John Herrnstein | 1.25 | .60 |
| 305 Camilo Pascual | 1.25 | .60 |
| 306 Ty Cline | 1.25 | .60 |
| 307 Clay Carroll | 1.25 | .60 |
| 308 Tom Haller | 1.25 | .60 |
| 309 Diego Segui | 1.25 | .60 |
| 310 Frank Robinson | 35.00 | 17.50 |
| 311 Reds Rookies (Tommy Helms, Dick Simpson) | 1.25 | .60 |
| 312 Bob Saverine | 1.25 | .60 |
| 313 Chris Zachary | 1.25 | .60 |
| 314 Hector Valle | 1.25 | .60 |
| 315 Norm Cash | 5.00 | 2.50 |
| 316 Jack Fisher | 1.25 | .60 |
| 317 Dalton Jones | 1.25 | .60 |

| | NR MT | EX |
|---|---|---|
| 318 Harry Walker | 1.25 | .60 |
| 319 Gene Freese | 1.25 | .60 |
| 320 Bob Gibson | 20.00 | 10.00 |
| 321 Rick Reichardt | 1.25 | .60 |
| 322 Bill Faul | 1.25 | .60 |
| 323 Ray Barker | 1.50 | .70 |
| 324 John Boozer | 1.25 | .60 |
| 325 Vic Davalillo | 1.25 | .60 |
| 326 Braves Team | 2.25 | 1.25 |
| 327 Bernie Allen | 1.25 | .60 |
| 328 Jerry Grote | 1.25 | .60 |
| 329 Pete Charton | 1.25 | .60 |
| 330 Ron Fairly | 1.25 | .60 |
| 331 Ron Herbel | 1.25 | .60 |
| 332 Billy Bryan | 1.25 | .60 |
| 333 Senators Rookies (Joe Coleman, Jim French) | 1.25 | .60 |
| 334 Marty Keough | 1.25 | .60 |
| 335 Juan Pizarro | 1.25 | .60 |
| 336 Gene Alley | 1.25 | .60 |
| 337 Fred Gladding | 1.25 | .60 |
| 338 Dal Maxvill | 1.25 | .60 |
| 339 Del Crandall | 1.50 | .70 |
| 340 Dean Chance | 1.25 | .60 |
| 341 Wes Westrum | 1.25 | .60 |
| 342 Bob Humphreys | 1.25 | .60 |
| 343 Joe Christopher | 1.25 | .60 |
| 344 Steve Blass | 1.25 | .60 |
| 345 Bob Allison | 1.50 | .70 |
| 346 Mike de la Hoz | 1.25 | .60 |
| 347 Phil Regan | 1.25 | .60 |
| 348 Orioles Team | 5.00 | 2.50 |
| 349 Cap Peterson | 1.25 | .60 |
| 350 Mel Stottlemyre | 3.00 | 1.50 |
| 351 Fred Valentine | 1.25 | .60 |
| 352 Bob Aspromonte | 1.25 | .60 |
| 353 Al McBean | 1.25 | .60 |
| 354 Smoky Burgess | 1.50 | .70 |
| 355 Wade Blasingame | 1.25 | .60 |
| 356 Red Sox Rookies (Owen Johnson, Ken Sanders) | 1.25 | .60 |
| 357 Gerry Arrigo | 1.25 | .60 |
| 358 Charlie Smith | 1.25 | .60 |
| 359 Johnny Briggs | 1.25 | .60 |
| 360 Ron Hunt | 1.25 | .60 |
| 361 Tom Satriano | 1.25 | .60 |
| 362 Gates Brown | 1.25 | .60 |
| 363 Checklist 353-429 | 3.00 | 1.50 |
| 364 Nate Oliver | 1.25 | .60 |
| 365 Roger Maris | 60.00 | 30.00 |
| 366 Wayne Causey | 1.25 | .60 |
| 367 Mel Nelson | 1.25 | .60 |
| 368 Charlie Lau | 1.25 | .60 |
| 369 Jim King | 1.25 | .60 |
| 370 Chico Cardenas | 1.25 | .60 |
| 371 Lee Stange | 1.25 | .60 |
| 372 Harvey Kuenn | 5.00 | 2.50 |
| 373 Giants Rookies (Dick Estelle, Jack Hiatt) | 1.25 | .60 |
| 374 Bob Locker | 1.25 | .60 |
| 375 Donn Clendenon | 1.25 | .60 |
| 376 Paul Schaal | 1.25 | .60 |
| 377 Turk Farrell | 1.25 | .60 |
| 378 Dick Tracewski | 1.25 | .60 |
| 379 Cardinals Team | 2.25 | 1.25 |
| 380 Tony Conigliaro | 5.00 | 2.50 |

| | NR MT | EX |
|---|---|---|
| 381 Hank Fischer | 1.25 | .60 |
| 382 Phil Roof | 1.25 | .60 |
| 383 Jackie Brandt | 1.25 | .60 |
| 384 Al Downing | 5.00 | 2.50 |
| 385 Ken Boyer | 2.50 | 1.25 |
| 386 Gil Hodges | 6.00 | 3.00 |
| 387 Howie Reed | 1.25 | .60 |
| 388 Don Mincher | 1.25 | .60 |
| 389 Jim O'Toole | 1.25 | .60 |
| 390 Brooks Robinson | 30.00 | 15.00 |
| 391 Chuck Hinton | 1.25 | .60 |
| 392 Cubs Rookies (Bill Hands, Randy Hundley) | 1.25 | .60 |
| 393 George Brunet | 1.25 | .60 |
| 394 Ron Brand | 1.25 | .60 |
| 395 Len Gabrielson | 1.25 | .60 |
| 396 Jerry Stephenson | 1.25 | .60 |
| 397 Bill White | 1.50 | .70 |
| 398 Danny Cater | 1.25 | .60 |
| 399 Ray Washburn | 1.25 | .60 |
| 400 Zoilo Versalles | 1.25 | .60 |
| 401 Ken McMullen | 1.25 | .60 |
| 402 Jim Hickman | 1.25 | .60 |
| 403 Fred Talbot | 1.25 | .60 |
| 404 Pirates Team | 2.25 | 1.25 |
| 405 Elston Howard | 6.00 | 3.00 |
| 406 Joe Jay | 1.25 | .60 |
| 407 John Kennedy | 1.25 | .60 |
| 408 Lee Thomas | 1.25 | .60 |
| 409 Billy Hoeft | 1.25 | .60 |
| 410 Al Kaline | 25.00 | 12.50 |
| 411 Gene Mauch | 1.25 | .60 |
| 412 Sam Bowens | 1.25 | .60 |
| 413 John Romano | 1.25 | .60 |
| 414 Dan Coombs | 1.25 | .60 |
| 415 Max Alvis | 1.25 | .60 |
| 416 Phil Ortega | 1.25 | .60 |
| 417 Angels Rookies (Jim McGlothlin, Ed Sukla) | 1.25 | .60 |
| 418 Phil Gagliano | 1.25 | .60 |
| 419 Mike Ryan | 1.25 | .60 |
| 420 Juan Marichal | 8.00 | 4.00 |
| 421 Roy McMillan | 1.25 | .60 |
| 422 Ed Charles | 1.25 | .60 |
| 423 Ernie Broglio | 1.25 | .60 |
| 424 Reds Rookies (Lee May, Darrell Osteen) | 2.25 | 1.25 |
| 425 Bob Veale | 1.25 | .60 |
| 426 White Sox Team | 2.25 | 1.25 |
| 427 John Miller | 1.25 | .60 |
| 428 Sandy Alomar | 1.25 | .60 |
| 429 Bill Monbouquette | 1.25 | .60 |
| 430 Don Drysdale | 15.00 | 7.50 |
| 431 Walt Bond | 1.25 | .60 |
| 432 Bob Heffner | 1.25 | .60 |
| 433 Alvin Dark | 1.25 | .60 |
| 434 Willie Kirkland | 1.25 | .60 |
| 435 Jim Bunning | 6.00 | 3.00 |
| 436 Julian Javier | 1.25 | .60 |
| 437 Al Stanek | 1.25 | .60 |
| 438 Willie Smith | 1.25 | .60 |
| 439 Pedro Ramos | 1.50 | .70 |
| 440 Deron Johnson | 1.25 | .60 |
| 441 Tommie Sisk | 1.25 | .60 |
| 442 Orioles Rookies (Ed Barnowski, Eddie Watt) | | |

| | | NR MT | EX |
|---|---|---|---|
| | | 1.25 | .60 |
| 443 | Bill Wakefield | 1.25 | .60 |
| 444a | Checklist 430-506 (456 is R. Sox Rookies) | 3.00 | 1.50 |
| 444b | Checklist 430-506 (456 is Red Sox Rookies) | 5.00 | 2.50 |
| 445 | Jim Kaat | 6.00 | 3.00 |
| 446 | Mack Jones | 1.25 | .60 |
| 447 | Dick Ellsworth (photo actually Ken Hubbs) | 5.00 | 2.50 |
| 448 | Eddie Stanky | 6.00 | 3.00 |
| 449 | Joe Moeller | 5.00 | 2.50 |
| 450 | Tony Oliva | 7.00 | 3.50 |
| 451 | Barry Latman | 5.00 | 2.50 |
| 452 | Joe Azcue | 5.00 | 2.50 |
| 453 | Ron Kline | 5.00 | 2.50 |
| 454 | Jerry Buchek | 5.00 | 2.50 |
| 455 | Mickey Lolich | 6.00 | 3.00 |
| 456 | Red Sox Rookies (Darrell Brandon, Joe Foy) | 5.00 | 2.50 |
| 457 | Joe Gibbon | 5.00 | 2.50 |
| 458 | Manny Jiminez (Jimenez) | 5.00 | 2.50 |
| 459 | Bill McCool | 5.00 | 2.50 |
| 460 | Curt Blefary | 5.00 | 2.50 |
| 461 | Roy Face | 6.00 | 3.00 |
| 462 | Bob Rodgers | 2.50 | 1.25 |
| 463 | Phillies Team | 6.00 | 3.00 |
| 464 | Larry Bearnarth | 6.00 | 3.00 |
| 465 | Don Buford | 6.00 | 3.00 |
| 466 | Ken Johnson | 5.00 | 2.50 |
| 467 | Vic Roznovsky | 5.00 | 2.50 |
| 468 | Johnny Podres | 6.00 | 3.00 |
| 469 | Yankees Rookies (*Bobby Murcer*, Dooley Womack) | 20.00 | 10.00 |
| 470 | Sam McDowell | 6.00 | 3.00 |
| 471 | Bob Skinner | 5.00 | 2.50 |
| 472 | Terry Fox | 5.00 | 2.50 |
| 473 | Rich Rollins | 5.00 | 2.50 |
| 474 | Dick Schofield | 5.00 | 2.50 |
| 475 | Dick Radatz | 6.00 | 3.00 |
| 476 | Bobby Bragan | 6.00 | 3.00 |
| 477 | Steve Barber | 5.00 | 2.50 |
| 478 | Tony Gonzalez | 5.00 | 2.50 |
| 479 | Jim Hannan | 5.00 | 2.50 |
| 480 | Dick Stuart | 6.00 | 3.00 |
| 481 | Bob Lee | 5.00 | 2.50 |
| 482 | Cubs Rookies (John Boccabella, Dave Dowling) | 5.00 | 2.50 |
| 483 | Joe Nuxhall | 6.00 | 3.00 |
| 484 | Wes Covington | 5.00 | 2.50 |
| 485 | Bob Bailey | 5.00 | 2.50 |
| 486 | Tommy John | 15.00 | 7.50 |
| 487 | Al Ferrara | 5.00 | 2.50 |
| 488 | George Banks | 5.00 | 2.50 |
| 489 | Curt Simmons | 6.00 | 3.00 |
| 490 | Bobby Richardson | 12.00 | 6.00 |
| 491 | Dennis Bennett | 5.00 | 2.50 |
| 492 | Athletics Team | 5.00 | 2.50 |
| 493 | Johnny Klippstein | 5.00 | 2.50 |
| 494 | Gordon Coleman | 5.00 | 2.50 |
| 495 | Dick McAuliffe | 6.00 | 3.00 |
| 496 | Lindy McDaniel | 5.00 | 2.50 |
| 497 | Chris Cannizzaro | 5.00 | 2.50 |
| 498 | Pirates Rookies (*Woody Fryman*, Luke Walker) | 6.00 | 3.00 |
| 499 | Wally Bunker | 5.00 | 2.50 |
| 500 | Hank Aaron | 110.00 | 55.00 |
| 501 | John O'Donoghue | 5.00 | 2.50 |
| 502 | Lenny Green | 5.00 | 2.50 |
| 503 | Steve Hamilton | 6.00 | 3.00 |
| 504 | Grady Hatton | 5.00 | 2.50 |
| 505 | Jose Cardenal | 5.00 | 2.50 |
| 506 | Bo Belinsky | 6.00 | 3.00 |
| 507 | John Edwards | 5.00 | 2.50 |
| 508 | *Steve Hargan* | 6.00 | 3.00 |
| 509 | Jake Wood | 5.00 | 2.50 |
| 510 | Hoyt Wilhelm | 15.00 | 7.50 |
| 511 | Giants Rookies (Bob Barton, *Tito Fuentes*) | 6.00 | 3.00 |
| 512 | Dick Stigman | 5.00 | 2.50 |
| 513 | Camilo Carreon | 5.00 | 2.50 |
| 514 | Hal Woodeshick | 5.00 | 2.50 |
| 515 | Frank Howard | 7.00 | 3.50 |
| 516 | Eddie Bressoud | 5.00 | 2.50 |
| 517a | Checklist 507-598 (529 is W. Sox Rookies) | 9.00 | 4.50 |
| 517b | Checklist 506-598 (529 is White Sox Rookies) | 10.00 | 5.00 |
| 518 | Braves Rookies (Herb Hippauf, Arnie Umbach) | 5.00 | 2.50 |
| 519 | Bob Friend | 6.00 | 3.00 |
| 520 | Jim Wynn | 6.00 | 3.00 |
| 521 | John Wyatt | 5.00 | 2.50 |
| 522 | Phil Linz | 5.00 | 2.50 |
| 523 | Bob Sadowski | 15.00 | 7.50 |
| 524 | Giants Rookies (Ollie Brown, Don Mason) | 20.00 | 10.00 |
| 525 | Gary Bell | 15.00 | 7.50 |
| 526 | Twins Team | 70.00 | 35.00 |
| 527 | Julio Navarro | 15.00 | 7.50 |
| 528 | Jesse Gonder | 20.00 | 10.00 |
| 529 | White Sox Rookies (*Lee Elia*, Dennis Higgins, Bill Voss) | 18.00 | 9.00 |
| 530 | Robin Roberts | 35.00 | 17.50 |
| 531 | Joe Cunningham | 15.00 | 7.50 |
| 532 | Aurelio Monteagudo | 15.00 | 7.50 |
| 533 | Jerry Adair | 15.00 | 7.50 |
| 534 | Mets Rookies (Dave Eilers, Rob Gardner) | 18.00 | 9.00 |
| 535 | Willie Davis | 35.00 | 17.50 |
| 536 | Dick Egan | 15.00 | 7.50 |
| 537 | Herman Franks | 15.00 | 7.50 |
| 538 | Bob Allen | 15.00 | 7.50 |
| 539 | Astros Rookies (Bill Heath, Carroll Sembera) | 15.00 | 7.50 |
| 540 | Denny McLain | 35.00 | 17.50 |
| 541 | Gene Oliver | 15.00 | 7.50 |
| 542 | George Smith | 15.00 | 7.50 |
| 543 | Roger Craig | 35.00 | 17.50 |
| 544 | Cardinals Rookies (Joe Hoerner, George Kernek, Jimmy Williams) | 20.00 | 10.00 |
| 545 | Dick Green | 20.00 | 10.00 |
| 546 | Dwight Siebler | 15.00 | 7.50 |
| 547 | *Horace Clarke* | 20.00 | 10.00 |

|  |  | NR MT | EX |
|---|---|---|---|
| 548 | Gary Kroll | 20.00 | 10.00 |
| 549 | Senators Rookies (Al Closter, Casey Cox) | 15.00 | 7.50 |
| 550 | Willie McCovey | 125.00 | 62.00 |
| 551 | Bob Purkey | 20.00 | 10.00 |
| 552 | Birdie Tebbetts | 15.00 | 7.50 |
| 553 | Major League Rookies (Pat Garrett, Jackie Warner) | 15.00 | 7.50 |
| 554 | Jim Northrup | 18.00 | 9.00 |
| 555 | Ron Perranoski | 18.00 | 9.00 |
| 556 | Mel Queen | 20.00 | 10.00 |
| 557 | Felix Mantilla | 15.00 | 7.50 |
| 558 | Red Sox Rookies (Guido Grilli, Pete Magrini, *George Scott*) | 20.00 | 10.00 |
| 559 | Roberto Pena | 15.00 | 7.50 |
| 560 | Joel Horlen | 15.00 | 7.50 |
| 561 | Choo Choo Coleman | 20.00 | 10.00 |
| 562 | Russ Snyder | 15.00 | 7.50 |
| 563 | Twins Rookies (Pete Cimino, Cesar Tovar) | 18.00 | 9.00 |
| 564 | Bob Chance | 15.00 | 7.50 |
| 565 | Jimmy Piersall | 35.00 | 17.50 |
| 566 | Mike Cuellar | 18.00 | 9.00 |
| 567 | Dick Howser | 20.00 | 10.00 |
| 568 | Athletics Rookies (Paul Lindblad, Ron Stone) | 15.00 | 7.50 |
| 569 | Orlando McFarlane | 15.00 | 7.50 |
| 570 | Art Mahaffey | 20.00 | 10.00 |
| 571 | Dave Roberts | 15.00 | 7.50 |
| 572 | Bob Priddy | 15.00 | 7.50 |
| 573 | Derrell Griffith | 15.00 | 7.50 |
| 574 | Mets Rookies (Bill Hepler, Bill Murphy) | 18.00 | 9.00 |
| 575 | Earl Wilson | 15.00 | 7.50 |
| 576 | Dave Nicholson | 20.00 | 10.00 |
| 577 | Jack Lamabe | 15.00 | 7.50 |
| 578 | Chi Chi Olivo | 15.00 | 7.50 |
| 579 | Orioles Rookies (Frank Bertaina, Gene Brabender, Dave Johnson) | 20.00 | 10.00 |
| 580 | Billy Williams | 100.00 | 50.00 |
| 581 | Tony Martinez | 15.00 | 7.50 |
| 582 | Garry Roggenburk | 15.00 | 7.50 |
| 583 | Tigers Team | 150.00 | 75.00 |
| 584 | Yankees Rookies (Frank Fernandez, *Fritz Peterson*) | 18.00 | 9.00 |
| 585 | Tony Taylor | 15.00 | 7.50 |
| 586 | Claude Raymond | 15.00 | 7.50 |
| 587 | Dick Bertell | 15.00 | 7.50 |
| 588 | Athletics Rookies (Chuck Dobson, Ken Suarez) | 15.00 | 7.50 |
| 589 | Lou Klimchock | 18.00 | 9.00 |
| 590 | Bill Skowron | 35.00 | 17.50 |
| 591 | N.L. Rookies (*Grant Jackson*, Bart Shirley) | 20.00 | 10.00 |
| 592 | Andre Rodgers | 15.00 | 7.50 |
| 593 | Doug Camilli | 20.00 | 10.00 |
| 594 | Chico Salmon | 15.00 | 7.50 |
| 595 | Larry Jackson | 15.00 | 7.50 |

|  |  | NR MT | EX |
|---|---|---|---|
| 596 | Astros Rookies (*Nate Colbert*, Greg Sims) | 18.00 | 9.00 |
| 597 | John Sullivan | 15.00 | 7.50 |
| 598 | Gaylord Perry | 310.00 | 155.00 |

# 1967 Topps

This 609-card set of 2-1/2" by 3-1/2" cards marked the largest set up to that time for Topps. Card fronts feature large color photographs bordered with white. The player's name and position are printed at the top with the team at the bottom. Across the front of the card with the exception of #254 (Milt Pappas) there is a facsimile autograph. The backs were the first to be done vertically, although they continued to carry familiar statistical and biographical information. The only subsets are statistical leaders and World Series highlights. Rookie cards are done by team or league with two players per card. The high numbers (#'s 534-609) in '67 are quite scarce, and while it is known that some are even scarcer, by virtue of having been short-printed in relation to the rest of the series, there is no general agreement on which cards are involved.

|  | NR MT | EX |
|---|---|---|
| Complete Set: | 5000.00 | 2500.00 |
| Common Player: 1-110 | 1.00 | .50 |
| Common Player: 111-370 | 1.50 | .70 |
| Common Player: 371-457 | 1.25 | .60 |
| Common Player: 458-533 | 5.00 | 2.50 |
| Common Player: 534-609 | 12.00 | 6.00 |

| | | NR MT | EX |
|---|---|---|---|
| 1 | The Champs (Hank Bauer, Brooks Robinson, Frank Robinson) | 20.00 | 9.00 |
| 2 | Jack Hamilton | 1.25 | .60 |
| 3 | Duke Sims | 1.00 | .50 |
| 4 | Hal Lanier | 1.25 | .60 |
| 5 | Whitey Ford | 20.00 | 10.00 |
| 6 | Dick Simpson | 1.00 | .50 |
| 7 | Don McMahon | 1.00 | .50 |
| 8 | Chuck Harrison | 1.00 | .50 |
| 9 | Ron Hansen | 1.00 | .50 |
| 10 | Matty Alou | 1.25 | .60 |
| 11 | Barry Moore | 1.00 | .50 |
| 12 | Dodgers Rookies (Jimmy Campanis, Bill Singer) | 1.50 | .70 |
| 13 | Joe Sparma | 1.00 | .50 |
| 14 | Phil Linz | 1.00 | .50 |
| 15 | Earl Battey | 1.50 | .70 |
| 16 | Bill Hands | 1.00 | .50 |
| 17 | Jim Gosger | 1.00 | .50 |
| 18 | Gene Oliver | 1.00 | .50 |
| 19 | Jim McGlothlin | 1.00 | .50 |
| 20 | Orlando Cepeda | 10.00 | 5.00 |
| 21 | Dave Bristol | 1.00 | .50 |
| 22 | Gene Brabender | 1.00 | .50 |
| 23 | Larry Elliot | 1.50 | .70 |
| 24 | Bob Allen | 1.00 | .50 |
| 25 | Elston Howard | 5.00 | 2.50 |
| 26a | Bob Priddy (no trade statement) | 15.00 | 7.50 |
| 26b | Bob Priddy (with trade statement) | 1.00 | .50 |
| 27 | Bob Saverine | 1.00 | .50 |
| 28 | Barry Latman | 1.00 | .50 |
| 29 | Tommy McCraw | 1.00 | .50 |
| 30 | Al Kaline | 20.00 | 10.00 |
| 31 | Jim Brewer | 1.00 | .50 |
| 32 | Bob Bailey | 1.00 | .50 |
| 33 | Athletics Rookies (Sal Bando, Randy Schwartz) | 1.75 | .90 |
| 34 | Pete Cimino | 1.00 | .50 |
| 35 | Rico Carty | 1.25 | .60 |
| 36 | Bob Tillman | 1.00 | .50 |
| 37 | Rick Wise | 1.50 | .70 |
| 38 | Bob Johnson | 1.00 | .50 |
| 39 | Curt Simmons | 1.25 | .60 |
| 40 | Rick Reichardt | 1.00 | .50 |
| 41 | Joe Hoerner | 1.00 | .50 |
| 42 | Mets Team | 5.00 | 2.50 |
| 43 | Chico Salmon | 1.00 | .50 |
| 44 | Joe Nuxhall | 1.25 | .60 |
| 45 | Roger Maris | 50.00 | 25.00 |
| 46 | Lindy McDaniel | 1.00 | .50 |
| 47 | Ken McMullen | 1.00 | .50 |
| 48 | Bill Freehan | 1.25 | .60 |
| 49 | Roy Face | 1.50 | .70 |
| 50 | Tony Oliva | 4.00 | 2.00 |
| 51 | Astros Rookies (Dave Adlesh, Wes Bales) | 1.00 | .50 |
| 52 | Dennis Higgins | 1.00 | .50 |
| 53 | Clay Dalrymple | 1.00 | .50 |
| 54 | Dick Green | 1.00 | .50 |
| 55 | Don Drysdale | 12.00 | 6.00 |
| 56 | Jose Tartabull | 1.00 | .50 |
| 57 | Pat Jarvis | 1.50 | .70 |

| | | NR MT | EX |
|---|---|---|---|
| 58 | Paul Schaal | 1.00 | .50 |
| 59 | Ralph Terry | 1.25 | .60 |
| 60 | Luis Aparicio | 5.00 | 2.50 |
| 61 | Gordy Coleman | 1.00 | .50 |
| 62 | Checklist 1-109 (Frank Robinson) | 5.00 | 2.50 |
| 63 | Cards' Clubbers (Lou Brock, Curt Flood) | 13.00 | 6.50 |
| 64 | Fred Valentine | 1.00 | .50 |
| 65 | Tom Haller | 1.50 | .70 |
| 66 | Manny Mota | 1.25 | .60 |
| 67 | Ken Berry | 1.00 | .50 |
| 68 | Bob Buhl | 1.50 | .70 |
| 69 | Vic Davalillo | 1.50 | .70 |
| 70 | Ron Santo | 1.75 | .90 |
| 71 | Camilo Pascual | 1.50 | .70 |
| 72 | Tigers Rookies (George Korince, John Matchick) | 1.00 | .50 |
| 73 | Rusty Staub | 2.50 | 1.25 |
| 74 | Wes Stock | 1.00 | .50 |
| 75 | George Scott | 1.25 | .60 |
| 76 | Jim Barbieri | 1.00 | .50 |
| 77 | Dooley Womack | 1.25 | .60 |
| 78 | Pat Corrales | 1.25 | .60 |
| 79 | Bubba Morton | 1.00 | .50 |
| 80 | Jim Maloney | 1.50 | .70 |
| 81 | Eddie Stanky | 1.50 | .70 |
| 82 | Steve Barber | 1.00 | .50 |
| 83 | Ollie Brown | 1.00 | .50 |
| 84 | Tommie Sisk | 1.00 | .50 |
| 85 | Johnny Callison | 1.25 | .60 |
| 86a | Mike McCormick (no trade statement) | 15.00 | 7.50 |
| 86b | Mike McCormick (with trade statement) | 1.50 | .70 |
| 87 | George Altman | 1.00 | .50 |
| 88 | Mickey Lolich | 2.25 | 1.25 |
| 89 | Felix Millan | 1.25 | .60 |
| 90 | Jim Nash | 1.00 | .50 |
| 91 | Johnny Lewis | 1.50 | .70 |
| 92 | Ray Washburn | 1.00 | .50 |
| 93 | Yankees Rookies (Stan Bahnsen, Bobby Murcer) | 2.50 | 1.25 |
| 94 | Ron Fairly | 1.25 | .60 |
| 95 | Sonny Siebert | 1.50 | .70 |
| 96 | Art Shamsky | 1.00 | .50 |
| 97 | Mike Cuellar | 1.25 | .60 |
| 98 | Rich Rollins | 1.00 | .50 |
| 99 | Lee Stange | 1.00 | .50 |
| 100 | Frank Robinson | 20.00 | 10.00 |
| 101 | Ken Johnson | 1.00 | .50 |
| 102 | Phillies Team | 2.00 | 1.00 |
| 103a | Checklist 110-196 (Mickey Mantle) (170 is D McAuliffe) | 15.00 | 7.50 |
| 103b | Checklist 110-196 (Mickey Mantle) (170 is D. McAuliffe) | 12.00 | 6.00 |
| 104 | Minnie Rojas | 1.00 | .50 |
| 105 | Ken Boyer | 2.00 | 1.00 |
| 106 | Randy Hundley | 1.50 | .70 |
| 107 | Joel Horlen | 1.00 | .50 |
| 108 | Alex Johnson | 1.00 | .50 |
| 109 | Tribe Thumpers (Rocky Colavito, Leon Wagner) | | |

| | | NR MT | EX | | | | NR MT | EX |
|---|---|---|---|---|---|---|---|---|
| | | 1.50 | .70 | 164 | Dwight Siebler | | 1.50 | .70 |
| 110 | Jack Aker | 1.00 | .50 | 165 | Cleon Jones | | 1.25 | .60 |
| 111 | John Kennedy | 1.50 | .70 | 166 | Ed Mathews | | 12.00 | 6.00 |
| 112 | Dave Wickersham | 1.50 | .70 | 167 | Senators Rookies (Joe | | | |
| 113 | Dave Nicholson | 1.50 | .70 | | Coleman, Tim Cullen) | | 1.25 | .60 |
| 114 | Jack Baldschun | 1.50 | .70 | 168 | Ray Culp | | 1.50 | .70 |
| 115 | Paul Casanova | 1.50 | .70 | 169 | Horace Clarke | | 1.25 | .60 |
| 116 | Herman Franks | 1.50 | .70 | 170 | Dick McAuliffe | | 1.25 | .60 |
| 117 | Darrell Brandon | 1.50 | .70 | 171 | Calvin Koonce | | 1.50 | .70 |
| 118 | Bernie Allen | 1.50 | .70 | 172 | Bill Heath | | 1.50 | .70 |
| 119 | Wade Blasingame | 1.50 | .70 | 173 | Cardinals Team | | 2.00 | 1.00 |
| 120 | Floyd Robinson | 1.50 | .70 | 174 | Dick Radatz | | 1.25 | .60 |
| 121 | Ed Bressoud | 1.25 | .60 | 175 | Bobby Knoop | | 1.50 | .70 |
| 122 | George Brunet | 1.50 | .70 | 176 | Sammy Ellis | | 1.50 | .70 |
| 123 | Pirates Rookies (Jim | | | 177 | Tito Fuentes | | 1.50 | .70 |
| | Price, Luke Walker) | 1.50 | .70 | 178 | John Buzhardt | | 1.50 | .70 |
| 124 | Jim Stewart | 1.50 | .70 | 179 | Braves Rookies (Cecil | | | |
| 125 | Moe Drabowsky | 1.50 | .70 | | Upshaw, Chas. Vaughn) | | | |
| 126 | Tony Taylor | 1.50 | .70 | | | | 1.50 | .70 |
| 127 | John O'Donoghue | 1.50 | .70 | 180 | Curt Blefary | | 1.50 | .70 |
| 128 | Ed Spiezio | 1.50 | .70 | 181 | Terry Fox | | 1.50 | .70 |
| 129 | Phil Roof | 1.50 | .70 | 182 | Ed Charles | | 1.50 | .70 |
| 130 | Phil Regan | 1.50 | .70 | 183 | Jim Pagliaroni | | 1.50 | .70 |
| 131 | Yankees Team | 5.00 | 2.50 | 184 | George Thomas | | 1.50 | .70 |
| 132 | Ozzie Virgil | 1.50 | .70 | 185 | *Ken Holtzman* | | 2.75 | 1.50 |
| 133 | Ron Kline | 1.50 | .70 | 186 | Mets Maulers (Ed | | | |
| 134 | Gates Brown | 1.50 | .70 | | Kranepool, Ron Swoboda) | | | |
| 135 | Deron Johnson | 1.50 | .70 | | | | 1.50 | .70 |
| 136 | Carroll Sembera | 1.50 | .70 | 187 | Pedro Ramos | | 1.50 | .70 |
| 137 | Twins Rookies (Ron | | | 188 | Ken Harrelson | | 1.50 | .70 |
| | Clark, Jim Ollom) | 1.50 | .70 | 189 | Chuck Hinton | | 1.50 | .70 |
| 138 | Dick Kelley | 1.50 | .70 | 190 | Turk Farrell | | 1.50 | .70 |
| 139 | Dalton Jones | 1.50 | .70 | 191a | Checklist 197-283 (Willie | | | |
| 140 | Willie Stargell | 20.00 | 10.00 | | Mays) (214 is Dick Kelley) | | | |
| 141 | John Miller | 1.50 | .70 | | | | 12.00 | 6.00 |
| 142 | Jackie Brandt | 1.50 | .70 | 191b | Checklist 197-283 (Willie | | | |
| 143 | Sox Sockers (Don | | | | Mays) (214 is Tom Kelley) | | | |
| | Buford, Pete Ward) | 1.25 | .60 | | | | 12.00 | 6.00 |
| 144 | Bill Hepler | 1.25 | .60 | 192 | Fred Gladding | | 1.50 | .70 |
| 145 | Larry Brown | 1.50 | .70 | 193 | Jose Cardenal | | 1.25 | .60 |
| 146 | Steve Carlton | 125.00 | 62.00 | 194 | Bob Allison | | 1.50 | .70 |
| 147 | Tom Egan | 1.50 | .70 | 195 | Al Jackson | | 1.50 | .70 |
| 148 | Adolfo Phillips | 1.50 | .70 | 196 | Johnny Romano | | 1.50 | .70 |
| 149 | Joe Moeller | 1.50 | .70 | 197 | Ron Perranoski | | 1.25 | .60 |
| 150 | Mickey Mantle | 200.00 | 80.00 | 198 | Chuck Hiller | | 1.25 | .60 |
| 151 | World Series Game 1 | | | 199 | Billy Hitchcock | | 1.50 | .70 |
| | (Moe Mows Down 11) | 2.00 | 1.00 | 200 | Willie Mays | | 90.00 | 45.00 |
| 152 | World Series Game 2 | | | 201 | Hal Reniff | | 1.25 | .60 |
| | (Palmer Blanks Dodgers) | | | 202 | Johnny Edwards | | 1.50 | .70 |
| | | 3.50 | 1.75 | 203 | Al McBean | | 1.50 | .70 |
| 153 | World Series Game 3 | | | 204 | Orioles Rookies (*Mike | | | |
| | (Blair's Homer Defeats L.A.) | | | | Epstein*, Tom Phoebus) | | | |
| | | 2.00 | 1.00 | | | | 1.50 | .70 |
| 154 | World Series Game 4 | | | 205 | Dick Groat | | 1.50 | .70 |
| | (Orioles Win 4th Straight) | | | 206 | Dennis Bennett | | 1.50 | .70 |
| | | 2.00 | 1.00 | 207 | John Orsino | | 1.50 | .70 |
| 155 | World Series Summary | | | 208 | Jack Lamabe | | 1.50 | .70 |
| | (The Winners Celebrate) | | | 209 | Joe Nossek | | 1.50 | .70 |
| | | 2.00 | 1.00 | 210 | Bob Gibson | | 18.00 | 9.00 |
| 156 | Ron Herbel | 1.50 | .70 | 211 | Twins Team | | 2.00 | 1.00 |
| 157 | Danny Cater | 1.50 | .70 | 212 | Chris Zachary | | 1.50 | .70 |
| 158 | Jimmy Coker | 1.50 | .70 | 213 | *Jay Johnstone* | | 1.75 | .90 |
| 159 | Bruce Howard | 1.50 | .70 | 214 | Tom Kelley | | 1.50 | .70 |
| 160 | Willie Davis | 1.50 | .70 | 215 | Ernie Banks | | 20.00 | 10.00 |
| 161 | Dick Williams | 1.50 | .70 | 216 | Bengal Belters (Norm | | | |
| 162 | Billy O'Dell | 1.50 | .70 | | Cash, Al Kaline) | | 5.00 | 2.50 |
| 163 | Vic Roznovsky | 1.50 | .70 | 217 | Rob Gardner | | 1.25 | .60 |

| | NR MT | EX |
|---|---|---|
| 218 Wes Parker | 1.25 | .60 |
| 219 Clay Carroll | 1.25 | .60 |
| 220 Jim Hart | 1.25 | .60 |
| 221 Woody Fryman | 1.25 | .60 |
| 222 Reds Rookies (Lee May, Darrell Osteen) | 1.25 | .60 |
| 223 Mike Ryan | 1.50 | .70 |
| 224 Walt Bond | 1.50 | .70 |
| 225 Mel Stottlemyre | 2.25 | 1.25 |
| 226 Julian Javier | 1.25 | .60 |
| 227 Paul Lindblad | 1.50 | .70 |
| 228 Gil Hodges | 5.00 | 2.50 |
| 229 Larry Jackson | 1.50 | .70 |
| 230 Boog Powell | 2.50 | 1.25 |
| 231 John Bateman | 1.50 | .70 |
| 232 Don Buford | 1.25 | .60 |
| 233 A.L. ERA Leaders (Steve Hargan, Joel Horlen, Gary Peters) | 2.00 | 1.00 |
| 234 N.L. ERA Leaders (Mike Cuellar, Sandy Koufax, Juan Marichal) | 12.00 | 6.00 |
| 235 A.L. Pitching Leaders (Jim Kaat, Denny McLain, Earl Wilson) | 2.50 | 1.25 |
| 236 N.L. Pitching Leaders (Bob Gibson, Sandy Koufax, Juan Marichal, Gaylord Perry) | 12.00 | 6.00 |
| 237 A.L. Strikeout Leaders (Jim Kaat, Sam McDowell, Earl Wilson) | 2.50 | 1.25 |
| 238 N.L. Strikeout Leaders (Jim Bunning, Sandy Koufax, Bob Veale) | 12.00 | 6.00 |
| 239 AL 1966 Batting Leaders (Al Kaline, Tony Oliva, Frank Robinson) | 12.00 | 6.00 |
| 240 N.L. Batting Leaders (Felipe Alou, Matty Alou, Rico Carty) | 2.00 | 1.00 |
| 241 A.L. RBI Leaders (Harmon Killebrew, Boog Powell, Frank Robinson) | 3.50 | 1.75 |
| 242 N.L. RBI Leaders (Hank Aaron, Richie Allen, Bob Clemente) | 12.00 | 6.00 |
| 243 A.L. Home Run Leaders (Harmon Killebrew, Boog Powell, Frank Robinson) | 3.50 | 1.75 |
| 244 N.L. Home Run Leaders (Hank Aaron, Richie Allen, Willie Mays) | 12.00 | 6.00 |
| 245 Curt Flood | 2.50 | 1.25 |
| 246 Jim Perry | 1.25 | .60 |
| 247 Jerry Lumpe | 1.25 | .60 |
| 248 Gene Mauch | 1.25 | .60 |
| 249 Nick Willhite | 1.50 | .70 |
| 250 Hank Aaron | 100.00 | 50.00 |
| 251 Woody Held | 1.50 | .70 |
| 252 Bob Bolin | 1.50 | .70 |
| 253 Indians Rookies (Bill Davis, Gus Gil) | 1.50 | .70 |
| 254 Milt Pappas | 1.25 | .60 |
| 255 Frank Howard | 2.50 | 1.25 |

| | NR MT | EX |
|---|---|---|
| 256 Bob Hendley | 1.50 | .70 |
| 257 Charley Smith | 1.25 | .60 |
| 258 Lee Maye | 1.50 | .70 |
| 259 Don Dennis | 1.50 | .70 |
| 260 Jim Lefebvre | 1.25 | .60 |
| 261 John Wyatt | 1.50 | .70 |
| 262 Athletics Team | 2.00 | 1.00 |
| 263 Hank Aguirre | 1.50 | .70 |
| 264 Ron Swoboda | 1.25 | .60 |
| 265 Lou Burdette | 2.50 | 1.25 |
| 266 Pitt Power (Donn Clendenon, Willie Stargell) | 3.50 | 1.75 |
| 267 Don Schwall | 1.50 | .70 |
| 268 John Briggs | 1.50 | .70 |
| 269 Don Nottebart | 1.50 | .70 |
| 270 Zoilo Versalles | 1.25 | .60 |
| 271 Eddie Watt | 1.50 | .70 |
| 272 Cubs Rookies (Bill Connors, Dave Dowling) | 1.50 | .70 |
| 273 Dick Lines | 1.50 | .70 |
| 274 Bob Aspromonte | 1.50 | .70 |
| 275 Fred Whitfield | 1.50 | .70 |
| 276 Bruce Brubaker | 1.50 | .70 |
| 277 Steve Whitaker | 1.25 | .60 |
| 278 Checklist 284-370 (Jim Kaat) | 5.00 | 2.50 |
| 279 Frank Linzy | 1.50 | .70 |
| 280 Tony Conigliaro | 2.00 | 1.00 |
| 281 Bob Rodgers | 1.50 | .70 |
| 282 Johnny Odom | 1.25 | .60 |
| 283 Gene Alley | 1.25 | .60 |
| 284 Johnny Podres | 5.00 | 2.50 |
| 285 Lou Brock | 25.00 | 12.50 |
| 286 Wayne Causey | 1.50 | .70 |
| 287 Mets Rookies (Greg Goossen, Bart Shirley) | 1.25 | .60 |
| 288 Denver Lemaster | 1.50 | .70 |
| 289 Tom Tresh | 1.75 | .90 |
| 290 Bill White | 1.25 | .60 |
| 291 Jim Hannan | 1.50 | .70 |
| 292 Don Pavletich | 1.50 | .70 |
| 293 Ed Kirkpatrick | 1.50 | .70 |
| 294 Walt Alston | 3.25 | 1.75 |
| 295 Sam McDowell | 1.25 | .60 |
| 296 Glenn Beckert | 1.25 | .60 |
| 297 Dave Morehead | 1.50 | .70 |
| 298 Ron Davis | 1.50 | .70 |
| 299 Norm Siebern | 1.25 | .60 |
| 300 Jim Kaat | 13.00 | 6.50 |
| 301 Jesse Gonder | 1.50 | .70 |
| 302 Orioles Team | 2.00 | 1.00 |
| 303 Gil Blanco | 1.50 | .70 |
| 304 Phil Gagliano | 1.50 | .70 |
| 305 Earl Wilson | 1.50 | .70 |
| 306 *Bud Harrelson* | 1.75 | .90 |
| 307 Jim Beauchamp | 1.50 | .70 |
| 308 Al Downing | 1.50 | .70 |
| 309 Hurlers Beware (Richie Allen, Johnny Callison) | 2.00 | 1.00 |
| 310 Gary Peters | 1.25 | .60 |
| 311 Ed Brinkman | 1.25 | .60 |
| 312 Don Mincher | 1.25 | .60 |
| 313 Bob Lee | 1.50 | .70 |
| 314 Red Sox Rookies (*Mike Andrews, Reggie Smith*) | | |

| | | NR MT | EX |
|---|---|---|---|
| | | 5.00 | 2.50 |
| 315 | Billy Williams | 12.00 | 6.00 |
| 316 | Jack Kralick | 1.50 | .70 |
| 317 | Cesar Tovar | 1.50 | .70 |
| 318 | Dave Giusti | 1.50 | .70 |
| 319 | Paul Blair | 1.25 | .60 |
| 320 | Gaylord Perry | 15.00 | 7.50 |
| 321 | Mayo Smith | 1.50 | .70 |
| 322 | Jose Pagan | 1.50 | .70 |
| 323 | Mike Hershberger | 1.50 | .70 |
| 324 | Hal Woodeshick | 1.50 | .70 |
| 325 | Chico Cardenas | 1.50 | .70 |
| 326 | Bob Uecker | 20.00 | 10.00 |
| 327 | Angels Team | 2.00 | 1.00 |
| 328 | Clete Boyer | 1.50 | .70 |
| 329 | Charlie Lau | 1.25 | .60 |
| 330 | Claude Osteen | 1.25 | .60 |
| 331 | Joe Foy | 1.50 | .70 |
| 332 | Jesus Alou | 1.50 | .70 |
| 333 | Ferguson Jenkins | 25.00 | 12.50 |
| 334 | Twin Terrors (Bob Allison, Harmon Killebrew) | | |
| | | 3.50 | 1.75 |
| 335 | Bob Veale | 1.25 | .60 |
| 336 | Joe Azcue | 1.50 | .70 |
| 337 | Joe Morgan | 25.00 | 12.50 |
| 338 | Bob Locker | 1.50 | .70 |
| 339 | Chico Ruiz | 1.50 | .70 |
| 340 | Joe Pepitone | 2.00 | 1.00 |
| 341 | Giants Rookies (Dick Dietz, Bill Sorrell) | 1.25 | .60 |
| 342 | Hank Fischer | 1.50 | .70 |
| 343 | Tom Satriano | 1.50 | .70 |
| 344 | Ossie Chavarria | 1.50 | .70 |
| 345 | Stu Miller | 1.50 | .70 |
| 346 | Jim Hickman | 1.25 | .60 |
| 347 | Grady Hatton | 1.50 | .70 |
| 348 | Tug McGraw | 2.25 | 1.25 |
| 349 | Bob Chance | 1.50 | .70 |
| 350 | Joe Torre | 2.00 | 1.00 |
| 351 | Vern Law | 1.50 | .70 |
| 352 | Ray Oyler | 1.50 | .70 |
| 353 | Bill McCool | 1.50 | .70 |
| 354 | Cubs Team | 2.00 | 1.00 |
| 355 | Carl Yastrzemski | 75.00 | 37.50 |
| 356 | Larry Jaster | 1.50 | .70 |
| 357 | Bill Skowron | 1.50 | .70 |
| 358 | Ruben Amaro | 1.25 | .60 |
| 359 | Dick Ellsworth | 1.50 | .70 |
| 360 | Leon Wagner | 1.25 | .60 |
| 361 | Checklist 371-457 (Bob Clemente) | 13.00 | 6.50 |
| 362 | Darold Knowles | 1.50 | .70 |
| 363 | Dave Johnson | 2.00 | 1.00 |
| 364 | Claude Raymond | 1.50 | .70 |
| 365 | John Roseboro | 1.25 | .60 |
| 366 | Andy Kosco | 1.50 | .70 |
| 367 | Angels Rookies (Bill Kelso, Don Wallace) | 1.50 | .70 |
| 368 | Jack Hiatt | 1.50 | .70 |
| 369 | Jim Hunter | 18.00 | 9.00 |
| 370 | Tommy Davis | 1.50 | .70 |
| 371 | Jim Lonborg | 1.50 | .70 |
| 372 | Mike de la Hoz | 1.25 | .60 |
| 373 | White Sox Rookies (Duane Josephson, Fred Klages) | 1.25 | .60 |

| | | NR MT | EX |
|---|---|---|---|
| 374 | Mel Queen | 1.25 | .60 |
| 375 | Jake Gibbs | 1.25 | .60 |
| 376 | Don Lock | 1.25 | .60 |
| 377 | Luis Tiant | 2.25 | 1.25 |
| 378 | Tigers Team | 5.00 | 2.50 |
| 379 | Jerry May | 1.25 | .60 |
| 380 | Dean Chance | 1.50 | .70 |
| 381 | Dick Schofield | 1.25 | .60 |
| 382 | Dave McNally | 1.25 | .60 |
| 383 | Ken Henderson | 1.25 | .60 |
| 384 | Cardinals Rookies (Jim Cosman, Dick Hughes) | | |
| | | 1.25 | .60 |
| 385 | Jim Fregosi | 1.50 | .70 |
| 386 | Dick Selma | 1.50 | .70 |
| 387 | Cap Peterson | 1.25 | .60 |
| 388 | Arnold Earley | 1.25 | .60 |
| 389 | Al Dark | 1.50 | .70 |
| 390 | Jim Wynn | 1.25 | .60 |
| 391 | Wilbur Wood | 1.50 | .70 |
| 392 | Tommy Harper | 1.50 | .70 |
| 393 | Jim Bouton | 2.25 | 1.25 |
| 394 | Jake Wood | 1.25 | .60 |
| 395 | Chris Short | 1.25 | .60 |
| 396 | Atlanta Aces (Tony Cloninger, Denis Menke) | | |
| | | 1.25 | .60 |
| 397 | Willie Smith | 1.25 | .60 |
| 398 | Jeff Torborg | 1.50 | .70 |
| 399 | Al Worthington | 1.25 | .60 |
| 400 | Bob Clemente | 85.00 | 42.00 |
| 401 | Jim Coates | 1.25 | .60 |
| 402 | Phillies Rookies (Grant Jackson, Billy Wilson) | 1.25 | .60 |
| 403 | Dick Nen | 1.25 | .60 |
| 404 | Nelson Briles | 1.50 | .70 |
| 405 | Russ Snyder | 1.25 | .60 |
| 406 | Lee Elia | 1.50 | .70 |
| 407 | Reds Team | 2.50 | 1.25 |
| 408 | Jim Northrup | 1.50 | .70 |
| 409 | Ray Sadecki | 1.25 | .60 |
| 410 | Lou Johnson | 1.25 | .60 |
| 411 | Dick Howser | 1.50 | .70 |
| 412 | Astros Rookies (Norm Miller, Doug Rader) | 1.25 | .60 |
| 413 | Jerry Grote | 1.50 | .70 |
| 414 | Casey Cox | 1.25 | .60 |
| 415 | Sonny Jackson | 1.25 | .60 |
| 416 | Roger Repoz | 1.25 | .60 |
| 417 | Bob Bruce | 1.25 | .60 |
| 418 | Sam Mele | 1.25 | .60 |
| 419 | Don Kessinger | 1.50 | .70 |
| 420 | Denny McLain | 5.00 | 2.50 |
| 421 | Dal Maxvill | 1.50 | .70 |
| 422 | Hoyt Wilhelm | 15.00 | 7.50 |
| 423 | Fence Busters (Willie Mays, Willie McCovey) | | |
| | | 20.00 | 10.00 |
| 424 | Pedro Gonzalez | 1.25 | .60 |
| 425 | Pete Mikkelsen | 1.25 | .60 |
| 426 | Lou Clinton | 1.25 | .60 |
| 427 | Ruben Gomez | 1.25 | .60 |
| 428 | Dodgers Rookies (Tom Hutton, Gene Michael) | 1.25 | .60 |
| 429 | Garry Roggenburk | 1.25 | .60 |
| 430 | Pete Rose | 75.00 | 38.00 |
| 431 | Ted Uhlaender | 1.25 | .60 |

| | NR MT | EX | | | NR MT | EX |
|---|---|---|---|---|---|---|
| 432 | Jimmie Hall | 1.25 | .60 | 485 | Tim McCarver | 13.00 | 6.50 |
| 433 | Al Luplow | 1.50 | .70 | 486 | Twins Rookies (Rich | | |
| 434 | Eddie Fisher | 1.25 | .60 | | Reese, Bill Whitby) | 5.00 | 2.50 |
| 435 | Mack Jones | 1.25 | .60 | 487 | Tom Reynolds | 5.00 | 2.50 |
| 436 | Pete Ward | 1.25 | .60 | 488 | Gerry Arrigo | 5.00 | 2.50 |
| 437 | Senators Team | 2.25 | 1.25 | 489 | Doug Clemens | 5.00 | 2.50 |
| 438 | Chuck Dobson | 1.25 | .60 | 490 | Tony Cloninger | 12.00 | 6.00 |
| 439 | Byron Browne | 1.25 | .60 | 491 | Sam Bowens | 5.00 | 2.50 |
| 440 | Steve Hargan | 1.25 | .60 | 492 | Pirates Team | 5.50 | 2.75 |
| 441 | Jim Davenport | 1.25 | .60 | 493 | Phil Ortega | 5.00 | 2.50 |
| 442 | Yankees Rookies (Bill | | | 494 | Bill Rigney | 5.00 | 2.50 |
| | Robinson, Joe Verbanic) | | | 495 | Fritz Peterson | 12.00 | 6.00 |
| | | 1.50 | .70 | 496 | Orlando McFarlane | 5.00 | 2.50 |
| 443 | Tito Francona | 1.50 | .70 | 497 | Ron Campbell | 5.00 | 2.50 |
| 444 | George Smith | 1.25 | .60 | 498 | Larry Dierker | 12.00 | 6.00 |
| 445 | Don Sutton | 30.00 | 15.00 | 499 | Indians Rookies (George | | |
| 446 | Russ Nixon | 1.25 | .60 | | Culver, Jose Vidal) | 5.00 | 2.50 |
| 447 | Bo Belinsky | 1.25 | .60 | 500 | Juan Marichal | 20.00 | 10.00 |
| 448 | Harry Walker | 1.50 | .70 | 501 | Jerry Zimmerman | 5.00 | 2.50 |
| 449 | Orlando Pena | 1.25 | .60 | 502 | Derrell Griffith | 5.00 | 2.50 |
| 450 | Richie Allen | 5.00 | 2.50 | 503 | Dodgers Team | 13.00 | 6.50 |
| 451 | Fred Newman | 1.25 | .60 | 504 | Orlando Martinez | 5.00 | 2.50 |
| 452 | Ed Kranepool | 1.25 | .60 | 505 | Tommy Helms | 5.00 | 2.50 |
| 453 | Aurelio Monteagudo | | | 506 | Smoky Burgess | 12.00 | 6.00 |
| | | 1.25 | .60 | 507 | Orioles Rookies (Ed | | |
| 454a | Checklist 458-533 (Juan | | | | Barnowski, Larry Haney) | | |
| | Marichal) (left ear shows) | | | | | 5.00 | 2.50 |
| | | 12.00 | 6.00 | 508 | Dick Hall | 5.00 | 2.50 |
| 454b | Checklist 458-533 (Juan | | | 509 | Jim King | 5.00 | 2.50 |
| | Marichal) (no left ear) | | | 510 | Bill Mazeroski | 13.00 | 6.50 |
| | | 12.00 | 6.00 | 511 | Don Wert | 5.00 | 2.50 |
| 455 | Tommie Agee | 1.50 | .70 | 512 | Red Schoendienst | | |
| 456 | Phil Niekro | 12.00 | 6.00 | | | 15.00 | 7.50 |
| 457 | Andy Etchebarren | 1.25 | .60 | 513 | Marcelino Lopez | 5.00 | 2.50 |
| 458 | Lee Thomas | 5.00 | 2.50 | 514 | John Werhas | 5.00 | 2.50 |
| 459 | Senators Rookies (Dick | | | 515 | Bert Campaneris | 12.00 | 6.00 |
| | Bosman, Pete Craig) | 12.00 | 6.00 | 516 | Giants Team | 5.50 | 2.75 |
| 460 | Harmon Killebrew | 50.00 | 25.00 | 517 | Fred Talbot | 12.00 | 6.00 |
| 461 | Bob Miller | 5.00 | 2.50 | 518 | Denis Menke | 5.00 | 2.50 |
| 462 | Bob Barton | 5.00 | 2.50 | 519 | Ted Davidson | 5.00 | 2.50 |
| 463 | Tribe Hill Aces (Sam | | | 520 | Max Alvis | 5.00 | 2.50 |
| | McDowell, Sonny Siebert) | | | 521 | Bird Bombers (Curt | | |
| | | 12.00 | 6.00 | | Blefary, Boog Powell) | | |
| 464 | Dan Coombs | 5.00 | 2.50 | | | 13.00 | 6.50 |
| 465 | Willie Horton | 12.00 | 6.00 | 522 | John Stephenson | 5.00 | 2.50 |
| 466 | Bobby Wine | 5.00 | 2.50 | 523 | Jim Merritt | 5.00 | 2.50 |
| 467 | Jim O'Toole | 5.00 | 2.50 | 524 | Felix Mantilla | 5.00 | 2.50 |
| 468 | Ralph Houk | 13.00 | 6.50 | 525 | Ron Hunt | 12.00 | 6.00 |
| 469 | Len Gabrielson | 5.00 | 2.50 | 526 | Tigers Rookies (Pat | | |
| 470 | Bob Shaw | 5.00 | 2.50 | | Dobson, George Korince) | | |
| 471 | Rene Lachemann | 5.00 | 2.50 | | | 12.00 | 6.00 |
| 472 | Pirates Rookies (John | | | 527 | Dennis Ribant | 5.00 | 2.50 |
| | Gelnar, George Spriggs) | | | 528 | Rico Petrocelli | 12.00 | 6.00 |
| | | 5.00 | 2.50 | 529 | Gary Wagner | 5.00 | 2.50 |
| 473 | Jose Santiago | 5.00 | 2.50 | 530 | Felipe Alou | 12.00 | 6.00 |
| 474 | Bob Tolan | 12.00 | 6.00 | 531 | Checklist 534-609 | | |
| 475 | Jim Palmer | 100.00 | 50.00 | | (Brooks Robinson) | 12.00 | 6.00 |
| 476 | Tony Perez | 70.00 | 35.00 | 532 | Jim Hicks | 5.00 | 2.50 |
| 477 | Braves Team | 5.50 | 2.75 | 533 | Jack Fisher | 5.00 | 2.50 |
| 478 | Bob Humphreys | 5.00 | 2.50 | 534 | Hank Bauer | 15.00 | 7.50 |
| 479 | Gary Bell | 5.00 | 2.50 | 535 | Donn Clendenon | 12.00 | 6.00 |
| 480 | Willie McCovey | 30.00 | 15.00 | 536 | Cubs Rookies (Joe | | |
| 481 | Leo Durocher | 13.00 | 6.50 | | Niekro, Paul Popovich) | | |
| 482 | Bill Monbouquette | | | | | 30.00 | 15.00 |
| | | 12.00 | 6.00 | 537 | Chuck Estrada | 12.00 | 6.00 |
| 483 | Jim Landis | 5.00 | 2.50 | 538 | J.C. Martin | 15.00 | 7.50 |
| 484 | Jerry Adair | 5.00 | 2.50 | 539 | Dick Egan | 12.00 | 6.00 |

| | | NR MT | EX |
|---|---|---|---|
| 540 | Norm Cash | 35.00 | 17.50 |
| 541 | Joe Gibbon | 15.00 | 7.50 |
| 542 | Athletics Rookies (*Rick Monday*, Tony Pierce) | | |
| | | 12.00 | 6.00 |
| 543 | Dan Schneider | 15.00 | 7.50 |
| 544 | Indians Team | 12.00 | 6.00 |
| 545 | Jim Grant | 15.00 | 7.50 |
| 546 | Woody Woodward | 15.00 | 7.50 |
| 547 | Red Sox Rookies (Russ Gibson, Bill Rohr) | 15.00 | 7.50 |
| 548 | Tony Gonzalez | 12.00 | 6.00 |
| 549 | Jack Sanford | 12.00 | 6.00 |
| 550 | Vada Pinson | 12.00 | 6.00 |
| 551 | Doug Camilli | 12.00 | 6.00 |
| 552 | Ted Savage | 12.00 | 6.00 |
| 553 | Yankees Rookies (Mike Hegan, Thad Tillotson) | | |
| | | 18.00 | 9.00 |
| 554 | Andre Rodgers | 12.00 | 6.00 |
| 555 | Don Cardwell | 15.00 | 7.50 |
| 556 | Al Weis | 12.00 | 6.00 |
| 557 | Al Ferrara | 12.00 | 6.00 |
| 558 | Orioles Rookies (*Mark Belanger*, Bill Dillman) | | |
| | | 40.00 | 20.00 |
| 559 | Dick Tracewski | 12.00 | 6.00 |
| 560 | Jim Bunning | 50.00 | 25.00 |
| 561 | Sandy Alomar | 15.00 | 7.50 |
| 562 | Steve Blass | 12.00 | 6.00 |
| 563 | Joe Adcock | 20.00 | 10.00 |
| 564 | Astros Rookies (Alonzo Harris, Aaron Pointer) | | |
| | | 15.00 | 7.50 |
| 565 | Lew Krausse | 15.00 | 7.50 |
| 566 | Gary Geiger | 12.00 | 6.00 |
| 567 | Steve Hamilton | 15.00 | 7.50 |
| 568 | John Sullivan | 15.00 | 7.50 |
| 569 | A.L. Rookies (Hank Allen, *Rod Carew*) | 500.00 | 250.00 |
| 570 | Maury Wills | 80.00 | 40.00 |
| 571 | Larry Sherry | 12.00 | 6.00 |
| 572 | Don Demeter | 12.00 | 6.00 |
| 573 | White Sox Team | 18.00 | 9.00 |
| 574 | Jerry Buchek | 12.00 | 6.00 |
| 575 | Dave Boswell | 12.00 | 6.00 |
| 576 | N.L. Rookies (Norm Gigon, Ramon Hernandez) | | |
| | | 18.00 | 9.00 |
| 577 | Bill Short | 15.00 | 7.50 |
| 578 | John Boccabella | 15.00 | 7.50 |
| 579 | Bill Henry | 15.00 | 7.50 |
| 580 | Rocky Colavito | 75.00 | 38.00 |
| 581 | Mets Rookies (Bill Denehy, *Tom Seaver*) | | |
| | | 1200.00 | 600.00 |
| 582 | Jim Owens | 12.00 | 6.00 |
| 583 | Ray Barker | 15.00 | 7.50 |
| 584 | Jim Piersall | 20.00 | 10.00 |
| 585 | Wally Bunker | 15.00 | 7.50 |
| 586 | Manny Jimenez | 15.00 | 7.50 |
| 587 | N.L. Rookies (Don Shaw, Gary Sutherland) | 18.00 | 9.00 |
| 588 | Johnny Klippstein | 12.00 | 6.00 |
| 589 | Dave Ricketts | 12.00 | 6.00 |
| 590 | Pete Richert | 15.00 | 7.50 |
| 591 | Ty Cline | 12.00 | 6.00 |

| | | NR MT | EX |
|---|---|---|---|
| 592 | N.L. Rookies (Jim Shellenback, Ron Willis) | | |
| | | 13.00 | 6.50 |
| 593 | Wes Westrum | 15.00 | 7.50 |
| 594 | Dan Osinski | 15.00 | 7.50 |
| 595 | Cookie Rojas | 12.00 | 6.00 |
| 596 | Galen Cisco | 12.00 | 6.00 |
| 597 | Ted Abernathy | 12.00 | 6.00 |
| 598 | White Sox Rookies (Ed Stroud, Walt Williams) | | |
| | | 13.00 | 6.50 |
| 599 | Bob Duliba | 12.00 | 6.00 |
| 600 | Brooks Robinson | 225.00 | 112.00 |
| 601 | Bill Bryan | 15.00 | 7.50 |
| 602 | Juan Pizarro | 15.00 | 7.50 |
| 603 | Athletics Rookies (Tim Talton, Ramon Webster) | | |
| | | 15.00 | 7.50 |
| 604 | Red Sox Team | 100.00 | 50.00 |
| 605 | Mike Shannon | 40.00 | 20.00 |
| 606 | Ron Taylor | 15.00 | 7.50 |
| 607 | Mickey Stanley | 12.00 | 6.00 |
| 608 | Cubs Rookies (Rich Nye, John Upham) | 12.00 | 6.00 |
| 609 | Tommy John | 125.00 | 62.00 |

## 1968 Topps

In 1968, Topps returned to a 598-card set of 2-1/2" by 3-1/2" cards. It is not, however, more of the same by way of appearance as the cards feature a color photograph on a background of what appears to be a burlap fabric. The player's name is below the photo but on the unusual background. A colored circle on the lower right carries the team and position. Backs were also changed. While retaining the vertical format introduced the previous year, with stats in the middle and cartoon at the bottom. The set features many of the old favorite subsets, including statistical leaders, World Series highlights, multi-player cards, checklists, rookie cards and the return of All-Star cards.

|  | NR MT | EX |
|---|---|---|
| Complete Set: | 3200.00 | 1600.00 |
| Common Player: 1-533 | 1.00 | .50 |
| Common Player: 534-598 | 2.50 | 1.25 |

|  | NR MT | EX |
|---|---|---|
| 1 N.L. Batting Leaders (Matty Alou, Bob Clemente, Tony Gonzalez) | 15.00 | 7.50 |
| 2 A.L. Batting Leaders (Al Kaline, Frank Robinson, Carl Yastrzemski) | 4.00 | 2.00 |
| 3 N.L. RBI Leaders (Hank Aaron, Orlando Cepeda, Bob Clemente) | 4.00 | 2.00 |
| 4 A.L. RBI Leaders (Harmon Killebrew, Frank Robinson, Carl Yastrzemski) | 4.00 | 2.00 |
| 5 N.L. Home Run Leaders (Hank Aaron, Willie McCovey, Ron Santo, Jim Wynn) | 4.00 | 2.00 |
| 6 A.L. Home Run Leaders (Frank Howard, Harmon Killebrew, Carl Yastrzemski) | 4.00 | 2.00 |
| 7 N.L. ERA Leaders (Jim Bunning, Phil Niekro, Chris Short) | 2.50 | 1.25 |
| 8 A.L. ERA Leaders (Joe Horlen, Gary Peters, Sonny Siebert) | 2.50 | 1.25 |
| 9 N.L. Pitching Leaders (Jim Bunning, Ferguson Jenkins, Mike McCormick, Claude Osteen) | 2.50 | 1.25 |
| 10a A.L. Pitching Leaders (Dean Chance, Jim Lonborg, Earl Wilson) ("Lonberg" on back) | 3.50 | 1.75 |
| 10b A.L. Pitching Leaders (Dean Chance, Jim Lonborg, Earl Wilson) ("Lonberg" on back) | 2.50 | 1.25 |
| 11 N.L. Strikeout Leaders (Jim Bunning, Ferguson Jenkins, Gaylord Perry) | 3.00 | 1.50 |
| 12 A.L. Strikeout Leaders (Dean Chance, Jim Lonborg, Sam McDowell) | 2.50 | 1.25 |
| 13 Chuck Hartenstein | 1.00 | .50 |
| 14 Jerry McNertney | 1.00 | .50 |
| 15 Ron Hunt | 1.00 | .50 |
| 16 Indians Rookies (Lou Piniella, Richie Scheinblum) | 3.50 | 1.75 |
| 17 Dick Hall | 1.00 | .50 |
| 18 Mike Hershberger | 1.00 | .50 |
| 19 Juan Pizarro | 1.00 | .50 |
| 20 Brooks Robinson | 20.00 | 10.00 |
| 21 Ron Davis | 1.00 | .50 |
| 22 Pat Dobson | 1.00 | .50 |
| 23 Chico Cardenas | 1.00 | .50 |
| 24 Bobby Locke | 1.00 | .50 |
| 25 Julian Javier | 1.00 | .50 |
| 26 Darrell Brandon | 1.00 | .50 |
| 27 Gil Hodges | 6.00 | 3.00 |
| 28 Ted Uhlaender | 1.00 | .50 |
| 29 Joe Verbanic | 1.00 | .50 |
| 30 Joe Torre | 3.00 | 1.50 |
| 31 Ed Stroud | 1.00 | .50 |
| 32 Joe Gibbon | 1.00 | .50 |
| 33 Pete Ward | 1.00 | .50 |
| 34 Al Ferrara | 1.00 | .50 |
| 35 Steve Hargan | 1.00 | .50 |
| 36 Pirates Rookies (Bob Moose, *Bob Robertson*) | 1.00 | .50 |
| 37 Billy Williams | 7.00 | 3.50 |
| 38 Tony Pierce | 1.00 | .50 |
| 39 Cookie Rojas | 1.00 | .50 |
| 40 Denny McLain | 3.75 | 2.00 |
| 41 Julio Gotay | 1.00 | .50 |
| 42 Larry Haney | 1.00 | .50 |
| 43 Gary Bell | 1.00 | .50 |
| 44 Frank Kostro | 1.00 | .50 |
| 45 Tom Seaver | 250.00 | 125.00 |
| 46 Dave Ricketts | 1.00 | .50 |
| 47 Ralph Houk | 3.00 | 1.50 |
| 48 Ted Davidson | 1.00 | .50 |
| 49a Ed Brinkman (yellow team letters) | 60.00 | 30.00 |
| 49b Ed Brinkman (white team letters) | 1.00 | .50 |
| 50 Willie Mays | 65.00 | 33.00 |
| 51 Bob Locker | 1.00 | .50 |
| 52 Hawk Taylor | 1.00 | .50 |
| 53 Gene Alley | 1.00 | .50 |
| 54 Stan Williams | 1.00 | .50 |
| 55 Felipe Alou | 2.50 | 1.25 |
| 56 Orioles Rookies (Dave Leonhard, Dave May) | 1.00 | .50 |
| 57 Dan Schneider | 1.00 | .50 |
| 58 Ed Mathews | 10.00 | 5.00 |
| 59 Don Lock | 1.00 | .50 |
| 60 Ken Holtzman | 2.50 | 1.25 |
| 61 Reggie Smith | 2.50 | 1.25 |
| 62 Chuck Dobson | 1.00 | .50 |
| 63 Dick Kenworthy | 1.00 | .50 |
| 64 Jim Merritt | 1.00 | .50 |
| 65 John Roseboro | 1.00 | .50 |
| 66a Casey Cox (yellow team letters) | 60.00 | 30.00 |
| 66b Casey Cox (white team letters) | 1.00 | .50 |
| 67 Checklist 1-109 (Jim Kaat) | 3.00 | 1.50 |
| 68 Ron Willis | 1.00 | .50 |
| 69 Tom Tresh | 3.00 | 1.50 |
| 70 Bob Veale | 1.00 | .50 |
| 71 Vern Fuller | 1.00 | .50 |
| 72 Tommy John | 5.00 | 2.50 |
| 73 Jim Hart | 1.00 | .50 |
| 74 Milt Pappas | 1.00 | .50 |
| 75 Don Mincher | 1.00 | .50 |
| 76 Braves Rookies (Jim Britton, *Ron Reed*) | 2.50 | 1.25 |
| 77 *Don Wilson* | 1.00 | .50 |
| 78 Jim Northrup | 1.00 | .50 |
| 79 Ted Kubiak | 1.00 | .50 |
| 80 Rod Carew | 150.00 | 75.00 |

| | | NR MT | EX |
|---|---|---|---|
| 81 | Larry Jackson | 1.00 | .50 |
| 82 | Sam Bowens | 1.00 | .50 |
| 83 | John Stephenson | 1.00 | .50 |
| 84 | Bob Tolan | 1.00 | .50 |
| 85 | Gaylord Perry | 15.00 | 7.50 |
| 86 | Willie Stargell | 10.00 | 5.00 |
| 87 | Dick Williams | 2.50 | 1.25 |
| 88 | Phil Regan | 1.00 | .50 |
| 89 | Jake Gibbs | 1.00 | .50 |
| 90 | Vada Pinson | 3.00 | 1.50 |
| 91 | Jim Ollom | 1.00 | .50 |
| 92 | Ed Kranepool | 1.00 | .50 |
| 93 | Tony Cloninger | 1.00 | .50 |
| 94 | Lee Maye | 1.00 | .50 |
| 95 | Bob Aspromonte | 1.00 | .50 |
| 96 | Senators Rookies (Frank Coggins, Dick Nold) | 1.00 | .50 |
| 97 | Tom Phoebus | 1.00 | .50 |
| 98 | Gary Sutherland | 1.00 | .50 |
| 99 | Rocky Colavito | 2.25 | 1.25 |
| 100 | Bob Gibson | 20.00 | 10.00 |
| 101 | Glenn Beckert | 1.00 | .50 |
| 102 | Jose Cardenal | 1.00 | .50 |
| 103 | Don Sutton | 8.00 | 4.00 |
| 104 | Dick Dietz | 1.00 | .50 |
| 105 | Al Downing | 2.50 | 1.25 |
| 106 | Dalton Jones | 1.00 | .50 |
| 107 | Checklist 110-196 (Juan Marichal) | 3.50 | 1.75 |
| 108 | Don Pavletich | 1.00 | .50 |
| 109 | Bert Campaneris | 2.50 | 1.25 |
| 110 | Hank Aaron | 80.00 | 40.00 |
| 111 | Rich Reese | 1.00 | .50 |
| 112 | Woody Fryman | 1.00 | .50 |
| 113 | Tigers Rookies (Tom Matchick, Daryl Patterson) | 1.00 | .50 |
| 114 | Ron Swoboda | 1.00 | .50 |
| 115 | Sam McDowell | 1.00 | .50 |
| 116 | Ken McMullen | 1.00 | .50 |
| 117 | Larry Jaster | 1.00 | .50 |
| 118 | Mark Belanger | 2.50 | 1.25 |
| 119 | Ted Savage | 1.00 | .50 |
| 120 | Mel Stottlemyre | 3.00 | 1.50 |
| 121 | Jimmie Hall | 1.00 | .50 |
| 122 | Gene Mauch | 1.00 | .50 |
| 123 | Jose Santiago | 1.00 | .50 |
| 124 | Nate Oliver | 1.00 | .50 |
| 125 | Joe Horlen | 1.00 | .50 |
| 126 | Bobby Etheridge | 1.00 | .50 |
| 127 | Paul Lindblad | 1.00 | .50 |
| 128 | Astros Rookies (Tom Dukes, Alonzo Harris) | 1.00 | .50 |
| 129 | Mickey Stanley | 1.00 | .50 |
| 130 | Tony Perez | 6.00 | 3.00 |
| 131 | Frank Bertaina | 1.00 | .50 |
| 132 | Bud Harrelson | 2.50 | 1.25 |
| 133 | Fred Whitfield | 1.00 | .50 |
| 134 | Pat Jarvis | 1.00 | .50 |
| 135 | Paul Blair | 1.00 | .50 |
| 136 | Randy Hundley | 1.00 | .50 |
| 137 | Twins Team | 3.00 | 1.50 |
| 138 | Ruben Amaro | 1.00 | .50 |
| 139 | Chris Short | 1.00 | .50 |
| 140 | Tony Conigliaro | 2.50 | 1.25 |
| 141 | Dal Maxvill | 1.00 | .50 |
| 142 | White Sox Rookies (Buddy Bradford, Bill Voss) | 1.00 | .50 |
| 143 | Pete Cimino | 1.00 | .50 |
| 144 | Joe Morgan | 15.00 | 7.50 |
| 145 | Don Drysdale | 8.00 | 4.00 |
| 146 | Sal Bando | 2.50 | 1.25 |
| 147 | Frank Linzy | 1.00 | .50 |
| 148 | Dave Bristol | 1.00 | .50 |
| 149 | Bob Saverine | 1.00 | .50 |
| 150 | Bob Clemente | 65.00 | 33.00 |
| 151 | World Series Game 1 (Brock Socks 4-Hits In Opener) | 3.50 | 1.75 |
| 152 | World Series Game 2 (Yaz Smashes Two Homers) | 5.00 | 2.50 |
| 153 | World Series Game 3 (Briles Cools Off Boston) | 3.00 | 1.50 |
| 154 | World Series Game 4 (Gibson Hurls Shutout!) | 3.50 | 1.75 |
| 155 | World Series Game 5 (Lonborg Wins Again!) | 2.50 | 1.25 |
| 156 | World Series Game 6 (Petrocelli Socks Two Homers) | 2.50 | 1.25 |
| 157 | World Series Game 7 (St. Louis Wins It!) | 3.00 | 1.50 |
| 158 | World Series Summary (The Cardinals Celebrate!) | 3.00 | 1.50 |
| 159 | Don Kessinger | 1.00 | .50 |
| 160 | Earl Wilson | 1.00 | .50 |
| 161 | Norm Miller | 1.00 | .50 |
| 162 | Cardinals Rookies (Hal Gilson, Mike Torrez) | 2.50 | 1.25 |
| 163 | Gene Brabender | 1.00 | .50 |
| 164 | Ramon Webster | 1.00 | .50 |
| 165 | Tony Oliva | 2.50 | 1.25 |
| 166 | Claude Raymond | 1.00 | .50 |
| 167 | Elston Howard | 3.00 | 1.50 |
| 168 | Dodgers Team | 2.50 | 1.25 |
| 169 | Bob Bolin | 1.00 | .50 |
| 170 | Jim Fregosi | 2.50 | 1.25 |
| 171 | Don Nottebart | 1.00 | .50 |
| 172 | Walt Williams | 1.00 | .50 |
| 173 | John Boozer | 1.00 | .50 |
| 174 | Bob Tillman | 1.00 | .50 |
| 175 | Maury Wills | 3.50 | 1.75 |
| 176 | Bob Allen | 1.00 | .50 |
| 177 | Mets Rookies (Jerry Koosman, Nolan Ryan) | 1500.00 | 750.00 |
| 178 | Don Wert | 1.00 | .50 |
| 179 | Bill Stoneman | 1.00 | .50 |
| 180 | Curt Flood | 2.50 | 1.25 |
| 181 | Jerry Zimmerman | 1.00 | .50 |
| 182 | Dave Giusti | 1.00 | .50 |
| 183 | Bob Kennedy | 1.00 | .50 |
| 184 | Lou Johnson | 1.00 | .50 |
| 185 | Tom Haller | 1.00 | .50 |
| 186 | Eddie Watt | 1.00 | .50 |
| 187 | Sonny Jackson | 1.00 | .50 |
| 188 | Cap Peterson | 1.00 | .50 |
| 189 | Bill Landis | 1.00 | .50 |
| 190 | Bill White | 2.50 | 1.25 |

| | | NR MT | EX |
|---|---|---|---|
| 191 | Dan Frisella | 1.00 | .50 |
| 192a | Checklist 197-283 (Carl Yastrzemski) ("To increase the..." on back) | 4.50 | 2.25 |
| 192b | Checklist 197-283 (Carl Yastrzemski) ("To increase your..." on back) | 6.00 | 3.00 |
| 193 | Jack Hamilton | 1.00 | .50 |
| 194 | Don Buford | 1.00 | .50 |
| 195 | Joe Pepitone | 3.00 | 1.50 |
| 196 | Gary Nolan | 1.00 | .50 |
| 197 | Larry Brown | 1.00 | .50 |
| 198 | Roy Face | 2.50 | 1.25 |
| 199 | A's Rookies (Darrell Osteen, Roberto Rodriguez) | 1.00 | .50 |
| 200 | Orlando Cepeda | 4.00 | 2.00 |
| 201 | *Mike Marshall* | 3.00 | 1.50 |
| 202 | Adolfo Phillips | 1.00 | .50 |
| 203 | Dick Kelley | 1.00 | .50 |
| 204 | Andy Etchebarren | 1.00 | .50 |
| 205 | Juan Marichal | 8.00 | 4.00 |
| 206 | Cal Ermer | 1.00 | .50 |
| 207 | Carroll Sembera | 1.00 | .50 |
| 208 | Willie Davis | 2.50 | 1.25 |
| 209 | Tim Cullen | 1.00 | .50 |
| 210 | Gary Peters | 1.00 | .50 |
| 211 | J.C. Martin | 1.00 | .50 |
| 212 | Dave Morehead | 1.00 | .50 |
| 213 | Chico Ruiz | 1.00 | .50 |
| 214 | Yankees Rookies (Stan Bahnsen, Frank Fernandez) | 2.50 | 1.25 |
| 215 | Jim Bunning | 4.50 | 2.25 |
| 216 | Bubba Morton | 1.00 | .50 |
| 217 | Turk Farrell | 1.00 | .50 |
| 218 | Ken Suarez | 1.00 | .50 |
| 219 | Rob Gardner | 1.00 | .50 |
| 220 | Harmon Killebrew | 12.00 | 6.00 |
| 221 | Braves Team | 3.00 | 1.50 |
| 222 | Jim Hardin | 1.00 | .50 |
| 223 | Ollie Brown | 1.00 | .50 |
| 224 | Jack Aker | 1.00 | .50 |
| 225 | Richie Allen | 2.25 | 1.25 |
| 226 | Jimmie Price | 1.00 | .50 |
| 227 | Joe Hoerner | 1.00 | .50 |
| 228 | Dodgers Rookies (*Jack Billingham*, Jim Fairey) | .80 | .40 |
| 229 | Fred Klages | 1.00 | .50 |
| 230 | Pete Rose | 40.00 | 20.00 |
| 231 | Dave Baldwin | 1.00 | .50 |
| 232 | Denis Menke | 1.00 | .50 |
| 233 | George Scott | 1.00 | .50 |
| 234 | Bill Monbouquette | 1.00 | .50 |
| 235 | Ron Santo | 2.50 | 1.25 |
| 236 | Tug McGraw | 3.00 | 1.50 |
| 237 | Alvin Dark | 1.00 | .50 |
| 238 | Tom Satriano | 1.00 | .50 |
| 239 | Bill Henry | 1.00 | .50 |
| 240 | Al Kaline | 20.00 | 10.00 |
| 241 | Felix Millan | 1.00 | .50 |
| 242 | Moe Drabowsky | 1.00 | .50 |
| 243 | Rich Rollins | 1.00 | .50 |
| 244 | John Donaldson | 1.00 | .50 |
| 245 | Tony Gonzalez | 1.00 | .50 |
| 246 | Fritz Peterson | 2.50 | 1.25 |
| 247 | Red Rookies (*Johnny Bench*, Ron Tompkins) | 300.00 | 150.00 |
| 248 | Fred Valentine | 1.00 | .50 |
| 249 | Bill Singer | .80 | .40 |
| 250 | Carl Yastrzemski | 30.00 | 15.00 |
| 251 | *Manny Sanguillen* | 2.50 | 1.25 |
| 252 | Angels Team | 3.00 | 1.50 |
| 253 | Dick Hughes | 1.00 | .50 |
| 254 | Cleon Jones | 1.00 | .50 |
| 255 | Dean Chance | 1.00 | .50 |
| 256 | Norm Cash | 3.00 | 1.50 |
| 257 | Phil Niekro | 5.00 | 2.50 |
| 258 | Cubs Rookies (Jose Arcia, Bill Schlesinger) | 1.00 | .50 |
| 259 | Ken Boyer | 3.00 | 1.50 |
| 260 | Jim Wynn | 1.00 | .50 |
| 261 | Dave Duncan | 1.00 | .50 |
| 262 | Rick Wise | 1.00 | .50 |
| 263 | Horace Clarke | 1.00 | .50 |
| 264 | Ted Abernathy | 1.00 | .50 |
| 265 | Tommy Davis | 2.50 | 1.25 |
| 266 | Paul Popovich | 1.00 | .50 |
| 267 | Herman Franks | 1.00 | .50 |
| 268 | Bob Humphreys | 1.00 | .50 |
| 269 | Bob Tiefenauer | 1.00 | .50 |
| 270 | Matty Alou | 2.50 | 1.25 |
| 271 | Bobby Knoop | 1.00 | .50 |
| 272 | Ray Culp | 1.00 | .50 |
| 273 | Dave Johnson | 3.00 | 1.50 |
| 274 | Mike Cuellar | 1.00 | .50 |
| 275 | Tim McCarver | 3.00 | 1.50 |
| 276 | Jim Roland | 1.00 | .50 |
| 277 | Jerry Buchek | 1.00 | .50 |
| 278a | Checklist 284-370 (Orlando Cepeda) (copyright at right) | 3.00 | 1.50 |
| 278b | Checklist 284-370 (Orlando Cepeda) (copyright at left) | 5.00 | 2.50 |
| 279 | Bill Hands | 1.00 | .50 |
| 280 | Mickey Mantle | 200.00 | 100.00 |
| 281 | Jim Campanis | 1.00 | .50 |
| 282 | Rick Monday | 2.50 | 1.25 |
| 283 | Mel Queen | 1.00 | .50 |
| 284 | John Briggs | 1.00 | .50 |
| 285 | Dick McAuliffe | .80 | .40 |
| 286 | Cecil Upshaw | 1.00 | .50 |
| 287 | White Sox Rookies (Mickey Abarbanel, Cisco Carlos) | 1.00 | .50 |
| 288 | Dave Wickersham | 1.00 | .50 |
| 289 | Woody Held | 1.00 | .50 |
| 290 | Willie McCovey | 10.00 | 5.00 |
| 291 | Dick Lines | 1.00 | .50 |
| 292 | Art Shamsky | .80 | .40 |
| 293 | Bruce Howard | 1.00 | .50 |
| 294 | Red Schoendienst | 2.50 | 1.25 |
| 295 | Sonny Siebert | 1.00 | .50 |
| 296 | Byron Browne | 1.00 | .50 |
| 297 | Russ Gibson | 1.00 | .50 |
| 298 | Jim Brewer | 1.00 | .50 |
| 299 | Gene Michael | 2.50 | 1.25 |
| 300 | Rusty Staub | 3.00 | 1.50 |
| 301 | Twins Rookies (George Mitterwald, Rick Renick) | 1.00 | .50 |
| 302 | Gerry Arrigo | 1.00 | .50 |

| | | NR MT | EX |
|---|---|---|---|
| 303 | Dick Green | 1.00 | .50 |
| 304 | Sandy Valdespino | 1.00 | .50 |
| 305 | Minnie Rojas | 1.00 | .50 |
| 306 | Mike Ryan | 1.00 | .50 |
| 307 | John Hiller | 1.00 | .50 |
| 308 | Pirates Team | 3.00 | 1.50 |
| 309 | Ken Henderson | 1.00 | .50 |
| 310 | Luis Aparicio | 5.00 | 2.50 |
| 311 | Jack Lamabe | 1.00 | .50 |
| 312 | Curt Blefary | 1.00 | .50 |
| 313 | Al Weis | 1.00 | .50 |
| 314 | Red Sox Rookies (Bill Rohr, George Spriggs) | 1.00 | .50 |
| 315 | Zoilo Versalles | 1.00 | .50 |
| 316 | Steve Barber | 1.00 | .50 |
| 317 | Ron Brand | 1.00 | .50 |
| 318 | Chico Salmon | 1.00 | .50 |
| 319 | George Culver | 1.00 | .50 |
| 320 | Frank Howard | 3.00 | 1.50 |
| 321 | Leo Durocher | 2.25 | 1.25 |
| 322 | Dave Boswell | 1.00 | .50 |
| 323 | Deron Johnson | 1.00 | .50 |
| 324 | Jim Nash | 1.00 | .50 |
| 325 | Manny Mota | 1.00 | .50 |
| 326 | Dennis Ribant | 1.00 | .50 |
| 327 | Tony Taylor | 1.00 | .50 |
| 328 | Angels Rookies (Chuck Vinson, Jim Weaver) | 1.00 | .50 |
| 329 | Duane Josephson | 1.00 | .50 |
| 330 | Roger Maris | 40.00 | 20.00 |
| 331 | Dan Osinski | 1.00 | .50 |
| 332 | Doug Rader | 1.00 | .50 |
| 333 | Ron Herbel | 1.00 | .50 |
| 334 | Orioles Team | 3.00 | 1.50 |
| 335 | Bob Allison | 2.50 | 1.25 |
| 336 | John Purdin | 1.00 | .50 |
| 337 | Bill Robinson | 1.00 | .50 |
| 338 | Bob Johnson | 1.00 | .50 |
| 339 | Rich Nye | 1.00 | .50 |
| 340 | Max Alvis | 1.00 | .50 |
| 341 | Jim Lemon | 1.00 | .50 |
| 342 | Ken Johnson | 1.00 | .50 |
| 343 | Jim Gosger | 1.00 | .50 |
| 344 | Donn Clendenon | 1.00 | .50 |
| 345 | Bob Hendley | 1.00 | .50 |
| 346 | Jerry Adair | 1.00 | .50 |
| 347 | George Brunet | 1.00 | .50 |
| 348 | Phillies Rookies (Larry Colton, Dick Thoenen) | 1.00 | .50 |
| 349 | Ed Spiezio | 1.00 | .50 |
| 350 | Hoyt Wilhelm | 6.00 | 3.00 |
| 351 | Bob Barton | 1.00 | .50 |
| 352 | Jackie Hernandez | 1.00 | .50 |
| 353 | Mack Jones | 1.00 | .50 |
| 354 | Pete Richert | 1.00 | .50 |
| 355 | Ernie Banks | 25.00 | 12.50 |
| 356 | Checklist 371-457 (Ken Holtzman) | 2.50 | 1.25 |
| 357 | Len Gabrielson | 1.00 | .50 |
| 358 | Mike Epstein | 1.00 | .50 |
| 359 | Joe Moeller | 1.00 | .50 |
| 360 | Willie Horton | 1.00 | .50 |
| 361 | Harmon Killebrew AS | 5.00 | 2.50 |
| 362 | Orlando Cepeda AS | 2.75 | 1.50 |
| 363 | Rod Carew AS | 12.00 | 6.00 |
| 364 | Joe Morgan AS | 3.00 | 1.50 |
| 365 | Brooks Robinson AS | 6.00 | 3.00 |
| 366 | Ron Santo AS | 3.00 | 1.50 |
| 367 | Jim Fregosi AS | 2.50 | 1.25 |
| 368 | Gene Alley AS | 2.50 | 1.25 |
| 369 | Carl Yastrzemski AS | 15.00 | 7.50 |
| 370 | Hank Aaron AS | 15.00 | 7.50 |
| 371 | Tony Oliva AS | 3.00 | 1.50 |
| 372 | Lou Brock AS | 6.00 | 3.00 |
| 373 | Frank Robinson AS | 8.00 | 4.00 |
| 374 | Bob Clemente AS | 15.00 | 7.50 |
| 375 | Bill Freehan AS | 2.50 | 1.25 |
| 376 | Tim McCarver AS | 2.50 | 1.25 |
| 377 | Joe Horlen AS | 2.50 | 1.25 |
| 378 | Bob Gibson AS | 7.00 | 3.50 |
| 379 | Gary Peters AS | 2.50 | 1.25 |
| 380 | Ken Holtzman AS | 2.50 | 1.25 |
| 381 | Boog Powell AS | 2.50 | 1.25 |
| 382 | Ramon Hernandez | 1.00 | .50 |
| 383 | Steve Whitaker | 1.00 | .50 |
| 384 | Reds Rookies (Bill Henry, *Hal McRae*) | 12.00 | 6.00 |
| 385 | Jim Hunter | 10.00 | 5.00 |
| 386 | Greg Goossen | 1.00 | .50 |
| 387 | Joe Foy | 1.00 | .50 |
| 388 | Ray Washburn | 1.00 | .50 |
| 389 | Jay Johnstone | 1.00 | .50 |
| 390 | Bill Mazeroski | 3.00 | 1.50 |
| 391 | Bob Priddy | 1.00 | .50 |
| 392 | Grady Hatton | 1.00 | .50 |
| 393 | Jim Perry | 2.50 | 1.25 |
| 394 | Tommie Aaron | 1.00 | .50 |
| 395 | Camilo Pascual | 1.00 | .50 |
| 396 | Bobby Wine | 1.00 | .50 |
| 397 | Vic Davalillo | 1.00 | .50 |
| 398 | Jim Grant | 1.00 | .50 |
| 399 | Ray Oyler | 1.00 | .50 |
| 400a | Mike McCormick (white team letters) | 40.00 | 20.00 |
| 400b | Mike McCormick (yellow team letters) | 1.00 | .50 |
| 401 | Mets Team | 3.25 | 1.75 |
| 402 | Mike Hegan | 2.50 | 1.25 |
| 403 | John Buzhardt | 1.00 | .50 |
| 404 | Floyd Robinson | 1.00 | .50 |
| 405 | Tommy Helms | 1.00 | .50 |
| 406 | Dick Ellsworth | 1.00 | .50 |
| 407 | Gary Kolb | 1.00 | .50 |
| 408 | Steve Carlton | 50.00 | 25.00 |
| 409 | Orioles Rookies (Frank Peters, Ron Stone) | 1.00 | .50 |
| 410 | Ferguson Jenkins | 18.00 | 9.00 |
| 411 | Ron Hansen | 1.00 | .50 |
| 412 | Clay Carroll | 1.00 | .50 |
| 413 | Tommy McCraw | 1.00 | .50 |
| 414 | Mickey Lolich | 2.75 | 1.50 |
| 415 | Johnny Callison | 2.50 | 1.25 |
| 416 | Bill Rigney | 1.00 | .50 |
| 417 | Willie Crawford | 1.00 | .50 |
| 418 | Eddie Fisher | 1.00 | .50 |
| 419 | Jack Hiatt | 1.00 | .50 |
| 420 | Cesar Tovar | 1.00 | .50 |
| 421 | Ron Taylor | 1.00 | .50 |
| 422 | Rene Lachemann | 1.00 | .50 |
| 423 | Fred Gladding | 1.00 | .50 |

| | | NR MT | EX |
|---|---|---|---|
| 424 | White Sox Team | 3.00 | 1.50 |
| 425 | Jim Maloney | 1.00 | .50 |
| 426 | Hank Allen | 1.00 | .50 |
| 427 | Dick Calmus | 1.00 | .50 |
| 428 | Vic Roznovsky | 1.00 | .50 |
| 429 | Tommie Sisk | 1.00 | .50 |
| 430 | Rico Petrocelli | 1.00 | .50 |
| 431 | Dooley Womack | 1.00 | .50 |
| 432 | Indians Rookies (Bill Davis, Jose Vidal) | 1.00 | .50 |
| 433 | Bob Rodgers | 1.00 | .50 |
| 434 | Ricardo Joseph | 1.00 | .50 |
| 435 | Ron Perranoski | 1.00 | .50 |
| 436 | Hal Lanier | 1.00 | .50 |
| 437 | Don Cardwell | 1.00 | .50 |
| 438 | Lee Thomas | 1.00 | .50 |
| 439 | Luman Harris | 1.00 | .50 |
| 440 | Claude Osteen | 1.00 | .50 |
| 441 | Alex Johnson | 1.00 | .50 |
| 442 | Dick Bosman | 1.00 | .50 |
| 443 | Joe Azcue | 1.00 | .50 |
| 444 | Jack Fisher | 1.00 | .50 |
| 445 | Mike Shannon | 1.00 | .50 |
| 446 | Ron Kline | 1.00 | .50 |
| 447 | Tigers Rookies (George Korince, Fred Lasher) | 1.00 | .50 |
| 448 | Gary Wagner | 1.00 | .50 |
| 449 | Gene Oliver | 1.00 | .50 |
| 450 | Jim Kaat | 6.00 | 3.00 |
| 451 | Al Spangler | 1.00 | .50 |
| 452 | Jesus Alou | 1.00 | .50 |
| 453 | Sammy Ellis | 1.00 | .50 |
| 454 | Checklist 458-533 (Frank Robinson) | 4.00 | 2.00 |
| 455 | Rico Carty | 2.50 | 1.25 |
| 456 | John O'Donoghue | 1.00 | .50 |
| 457 | Jim Lefebvre | 1.00 | .50 |
| 458 | Lew Krausse | 1.00 | .50 |
| 459 | Dick Simpson | 1.00 | .50 |
| 460 | Jim Lonborg | 2.50 | 1.25 |
| 461 | Chuck Hiller | 1.00 | .50 |
| 462 | Barry Moore | 1.00 | .50 |
| 463 | Jimmie Schaffer | 1.00 | .50 |
| 464 | Don McMahon | 1.00 | .50 |
| 465 | Tommie Agee | 1.00 | .50 |
| 466 | Bill Dillman | 1.00 | .50 |
| 467 | Dick Howser | 2.50 | 1.25 |
| 468 | Larry Sherry | 1.00 | .50 |
| 469 | Ty Cline | 1.00 | .50 |
| 470 | Bill Freehan | 2.50 | 1.25 |
| 471 | Orlando Pena | 1.00 | .50 |
| 472 | Walt Alston | 2.50 | 1.25 |
| 473 | Al Worthington | 1.00 | .50 |
| 474 | Paul Schaal | 1.00 | .50 |
| 475 | Joe Niekro | 2.25 | 1.25 |
| 476 | Woody Woodward | 1.00 | .50 |
| 477 | Phillies Team | 3.00 | 1.50 |
| 478 | Dave McNally | 2.50 | 1.25 |
| 479 | Phil Gagliano | 1.00 | .50 |
| 480 | Manager's Dream (Chico Cardenas, Bob Clemente, Tony Oliva) | 25.00 | 12.50 |
| 481 | John Wyatt | 1.00 | .50 |
| 482 | Jose Pagan | 1.00 | .50 |
| 483 | Darold Knowles | 1.00 | .50 |
| 484 | Phil Roof | 1.00 | .50 |
| 485 | Ken Berry | 1.00 | .50 |
| 486 | Cal Koonce | 1.00 | .50 |
| 487 | Lee May | 2.50 | 1.25 |
| 488 | Dick Tracewski | 1.00 | .50 |
| 489 | Wally Bunker | 1.00 | .50 |
| 490 | Super Stars (Harmon Killebrew, Mickey Mantle, Willie Mays) | 100.00 | 50.00 |
| 491 | Denny Lemaster | 1.00 | .50 |
| 492 | Jeff Torborg | 1.00 | .50 |
| 493 | Jim McGlothlin | 1.00 | .50 |
| 494 | Ray Sadecki | 1.00 | .50 |
| 495 | Leon Wagner | 1.00 | .50 |
| 496 | Steve Hamilton | 1.00 | .50 |
| 497 | Cards Team | 3.50 | 1.75 |
| 498 | Bill Bryan | 1.00 | .50 |
| 499 | Steve Blass | 1.00 | .50 |
| 500 | Frank Robinson | 20.00 | 10.00 |
| 501 | John Odom | 1.00 | .50 |
| 502 | Mike Andrews | 1.00 | .50 |
| 503 | Al Jackson | 1.00 | .50 |
| 504 | Russ Snyder | 1.00 | .50 |
| 505 | Joe Sparma | 1.00 | .50 |
| 506 | Clarence Jones | 1.00 | .50 |
| 507 | Wade Blasingame | 1.00 | .50 |
| 508 | Duke Sims | 1.00 | .50 |
| 509 | Dennis Higgins | 1.00 | .50 |
| 510 | Ron Fairly | 1.00 | .50 |
| 511 | Bill Kelso | 1.00 | .50 |
| 512 | Grant Jackson | 1.00 | .50 |
| 513 | Hank Bauer | 1.00 | .50 |
| 514 | Al McBean | 1.00 | .50 |
| 515 | Russ Nixon | 1.00 | .50 |
| 516 | Pete Mikkelsen | 1.00 | .50 |
| 517 | Diego Segui | 1.00 | .50 |
| 518a | Checklist 534-598 (Clete Boyer) (539 is Maj. L. Rookies) | 3.00 | 1.50 |
| 518b | Checklist 534-598 (Clete Boyer) (539 is Amer. L. Rookies) | 5.00 | 2.50 |
| 519 | Jerry Stephenson | 1.00 | .50 |
| 520 | Lou Brock | 20.00 | 10.00 |
| 521 | Don Shaw | 1.00 | .50 |
| 522 | Wayne Causey | 1.00 | .50 |
| 523 | John Tsitouris | 1.00 | .50 |
| 524 | Andy Kosco | 1.00 | .50 |
| 525 | Jim Davenport | 1.00 | .50 |
| 526 | Bill Denehy | 1.00 | .50 |
| 527 | Tito Francona | 1.00 | .50 |
| 528 | Tigers Team | 60.00 | 30.00 |
| 529 | Bruce Von Hoff | 1.00 | .50 |
| 530 | Bird Belters (Brooks Robinson, Frank Robinson) | 10.00 | 5.00 |
| 531 | Chuck Hinton | 1.00 | .50 |
| 532 | Luis Tiant | 3.00 | 1.50 |
| 533 | Wes Parker | 1.00 | .50 |
| 534 | Bob Miller | 2.50 | 1.25 |
| 535 | Danny Cater | 2.50 | 1.25 |
| 536 | Bill Short | 2.50 | 1.25 |
| 537 | Norm Siebern | 2.50 | 1.25 |
| 538 | Manny Jimenez | 2.50 | 1.25 |
| 539 | Major League Rookies (Mike Ferraro, Jim Ray) | 2.50 | 1.25 |
| 540 | Nelson Briles | 2.50 | 1.25 |
| 541 | Sandy Alomar | 2.50 | 1.25 |

| | | NR MT | EX |
|---|---|---|---|
| 542 | John Boccabella | 2.50 | 1.25 |
| 543 | Bob Lee | 2.50 | 1.25 |
| 544 | Mayo Smith | 2.50 | 1.25 |
| 545 | Lindy McDaniel | 2.50 | 1.25 |
| 546 | Roy White | 2.50 | 1.25 |
| 547 | Dan Coombs | 2.50 | 1.25 |
| 548 | Bernie Allen | 2.50 | 1.25 |
| 549 | Orioles Rookies (Curt Motton, Roger Nelson) | 2.50 | 1.25 |
| 550 | Clete Boyer | 2.50 | 1.25 |
| 551 | Darrell Sutherland | 2.50 | 1.25 |
| 552 | Ed Kirkpatrick | 2.50 | 1.25 |
| 553 | Hank Aguirre | 2.50 | 1.25 |
| 554 | A's Team | 3.00 | 1.50 |
| 555 | Jose Tartabull | 2.50 | 1.25 |
| 556 | Dick Selma | 2.50 | 1.25 |
| 557 | Frank Quilici | 2.50 | 1.25 |
| 558 | John Edwards | 2.50 | 1.25 |
| 559 | Pirates Rookies (Carl Taylor, Luke Walker) | 2.50 | 1.25 |
| 560 | Paul Casanova | 2.50 | 1.25 |
| 561 | Lee Elia | 2.50 | 1.25 |
| 562 | Jim Bouton | 2.50 | 1.25 |
| 563 | Ed Charles | 2.50 | 1.25 |
| 564 | Eddie Stanky | 2.50 | 1.25 |
| 565 | Larry Dierker | 2.50 | 1.25 |
| 566 | Ken Harrelson | 3.00 | 1.50 |
| 567 | Clay Dalrymple | 2.50 | 1.25 |
| 568 | Willie Smith | 2.50 | 1.25 |
| 569 | N.L. Rookies (Ivan Murrell, Les Rohr) | 2.50 | 1.25 |
| 570 | Rick Reichardt | 2.50 | 1.25 |
| 571 | Tony LaRussa | 3.00 | 1.50 |
| 572 | Don Bosch | 2.50 | 1.25 |
| 573 | Joe Coleman | 2.50 | 1.25 |
| 574 | Reds Team | 3.00 | 1.50 |
| 575 | Jim Palmer | 60.00 | 30.00 |
| 576 | Dave Adlesh | 2.50 | 1.25 |
| 577 | Fred Talbot | 2.50 | 1.25 |
| 578 | Orlando Martinez | 2.50 | 1.25 |
| 579 | N.L. Rookies (*Larry Hisle, Mike Lum*) | 3.00 | 1.50 |
| 580 | Bob Bailey | 2.50 | 1.25 |
| 581 | Garry Roggenburk | 2.50 | 1.25 |
| 582 | Jerry Grote | 2.50 | 1.25 |
| 583 | Gates Brown | 2.50 | 1.25 |
| 584 | Larry Shepard | 2.50 | 1.25 |
| 585 | Wilbur Wood | 2.50 | 1.25 |
| 586 | Jim Pagliaroni | 2.50 | 1.25 |
| 587 | Roger Repoz | 2.50 | 1.25 |
| 588 | Dick Schofield | 2.50 | 1.25 |
| 589 | Twins Rookies (Ron Clark, Moe Ogier) | 2.50 | 1.25 |
| 590 | Tommy Harper | 2.50 | 1.25 |
| 591 | Dick Nen | 2.50 | 1.25 |
| 592 | John Bateman | 2.50 | 1.25 |
| 593 | Lee Stange | 2.50 | 1.25 |
| 594 | Phil Linz | 2.50 | 1.25 |
| 595 | Phil Ortega | 2.50 | 1.25 |
| 596 | Charlie Smith | 2.50 | 1.25 |
| 597 | Bill McCool | 2.50 | 1.25 |
| 598 | Jerry May | 3.00 | 1.50 |

## 1969 Topps

The 1969 Topps set broke yet another record for quantity as the issue is officially a whopping 664 cards. With substantial numbers of variations, the number of possible cards runs closer to 700. The design of the 2-1/2" by 3-1/2" cards in the set feature a color photo with the team name printed in block letters underneath. A circle contains the player's name and position. Card backs returned to a horizontal format. Despite the size of the set, it contains no teamcards. It does, however, have multi-player cards, All-Stars, statistical leaders, and World Series highlights. Most significant among the varieties are white and yellow letter cards from the run of #'s 440-511. The complete set prices below do not include the scarcer and more expensive "white letter" variations.

| | NR MT | EX |
|---|---|---|
| Complete Set: | 2500.00 | 1250.00 |
| Common Player: 1-218 | 1.00 | .50 |
| Common Player: 219-327 | | |
| | 1.50 | .70 |
| Common Player: 328-512 | | |
| | 1.00 | .50 |
| Common Player: 513-664 | | |
| | 1.00 | .50 |

A player's name in *italic* type indicates a rookie card. An (FC) indicates a player's first card for that particular card company.

| # | Player | NR MT | EX |
|---|--------|-------|----|
| 1 | A.L. Batting Leaders (Danny Cater, Tony Oliva, Carl Yastrzemski) | 10.00 | 5.00 |
| 2 | N.L. Batting Leaders (Felipe Alou, Matty Alou, Pete Rose) | 4.00 | 2.00 |
| 3 | A.L. RBI Leaders (Ken Harrelson, Frank Howard, Jim Northrup) | 2.00 | 1.00 |
| 4 | N.L. RBI Leaders (Willie McCovey, Ron Santo, Billy Williams) | 3.50 | 1.75 |
| 5 | A.L. Home Run Leaders (Ken Harrelson, Willie Horton, Frank Howard) | 2.00 | 1.00 |
| 6 | N.L. Home Run Leaders (Richie Allen, Ernie Banks, Willie McCovey) | 3.50 | 1.75 |
| 7 | A.L. ERA Leaders (Sam McDowell, Dave McNally, Luis Tiant) | 2.00 | 1.00 |
| 8 | N.L. ERA Leaders (Bobby Bolin, Bob Gibson, Bob Veale) | 3.00 | 1.50 |
| 9 | A.L. Pitching Leaders (Denny McLain, Dave McNally, Mel Stottlemyre, Luis Tiant) | 2.00 | 1.00 |
| 10 | N.L. Pitching Leaders (Bob Gibson, Fergie Jenkins, Juan Marichal) | 3.50 | 1.75 |
| 11 | A.L. Strikeout Leaders (Sam McDowell, Denny McLain, Luis Tiant) | 2.00 | 1.00 |
| 12 | N.L. Strikeout Leaders (Bob Gibson, Fergie Jenkins, Bill Singer) | 3.00 | 1.50 |
| 13 | Mickey Stanley | 1.00 | .50 |
| 14 | Al McBean | 1.00 | .50 |
| 15 | Boog Powell | 2.50 | 1.25 |
| 16 | Giants Rookies (Cesar Gutierrez, Rich Robertson) | 1.00 | .50 |
| 17 | Mike Marshall | 1.50 | .70 |
| 18 | Dick Schofield | 1.00 | .50 |
| 19 | Ken Suarez | 1.00 | .50 |
| 20 | Ernie Banks | 20.00 | 10.00 |
| 21 | Jose Santiago | 1.00 | .50 |
| 22 | Jesus Alou | 1.00 | .50 |
| 23 | Lew Krausse | 1.00 | .50 |
| 24 | Walt Alston | 3.00 | 1.50 |
| 25 | Roy White | 1.50 | .70 |
| 26 | Clay Carroll | 1.00 | .50 |
| 27 | Bernie Allen | 1.00 | .50 |
| 28 | Mike Ryan | 1.00 | .50 |
| 29 | Dave Morehead | 1.00 | .50 |
| 30 | Bob Allison | 1.00 | .50 |
| 31 | Mets Rookies (Gary Gentry, Amos Otis) | 1.50 | .70 |
| 32 | Sammy Ellis | 1.00 | .50 |
| 33 | Wayne Causey | 1.00 | .50 |
| 34 | Gary Peters | 1.00 | .50 |
| 35 | Joe Morgan | 12.00 | 6.00 |
| 36 | Luke Walker | 1.00 | .50 |
| 37 | Curt Motton | 1.00 | .50 |
| 38 | Zoilo Versalles | 1.00 | .50 |
| 39 | Dick Hughes | 1.00 | .50 |
| 40 | Mayo Smith | 1.00 | .50 |
| 41 | Bob Barton | 1.00 | .50 |
| 42 | Tommy Harper | 1.00 | .50 |
| 43 | Joe Niekro | 1.50 | .70 |
| 44 | Danny Cater | 1.00 | .50 |
| 45 | Maury Wills | 2.50 | 1.25 |
| 46 | Fritz Peterson | 1.00 | .50 |
| 47a | Paul Popovich (emblem visible thru airbrush) | 4.00 | 2.00 |
| 47b | Paul Popovich (helmet emblem completely airbrushed) | 1.00 | .50 |
| 48 | Brant Alyea | 1.00 | .50 |
| 49a | Royals Rookies (Steve Jones, Eliseo Rodriquez) (Rodriquez on front) | 6.00 | 3.00 |
| 49b | Royals Rookies (Steve Jones, Eliseo Rodriquez) (Rodriguez on front) | 1.00 | .50 |
| 50 | Bob Clemente | 55.00 | 28.00 |
| 51 | Woody Fryman | 1.00 | .50 |
| 52 | Mike Andrews | 1.00 | .50 |
| 53 | Sonny Jackson | 1.00 | .50 |
| 54 | Cisco Carlos | 1.00 | .50 |
| 55 | Jerry Grote | 1.00 | .50 |
| 56 | Rich Reese | 1.00 | .50 |
| 57 | Checklist 1-109 (Denny McLain) | 3.00 | 1.50 |
| 58 | Fred Gladding | 1.00 | .50 |
| 59 | Jay Johnstone | 1.00 | .50 |
| 60 | Nelson Briles | 1.00 | .50 |
| 61 | Jimmie Hall | 1.00 | .50 |
| 62 | Chico Salmon | 1.25 | .60 |
| 63 | Jim Hickman | 1.00 | .50 |
| 64 | Bill Monbouquette | 1.00 | .50 |
| 65 | Willie Davis | 1.00 | .50 |
| 66 | Orioles Rookies (Mike Adamson, Merv Rettenmund) | 1.00 | .50 |
| 67 | Bill Stoneman | 1.00 | .50 |
| 68 | Dave Duncan | 1.00 | .50 |
| 69 | Steve Hamilton | 1.00 | .50 |
| 70 | Tommy Helms | 1.00 | .50 |
| 71 | Steve Whitaker | 1.00 | .50 |
| 72 | Ron Taylor | 1.00 | .50 |
| 73 | Johnny Briggs | 1.00 | .50 |
| 74 | Preston Gomez | 1.00 | .50 |
| 75 | Luis Aparicio | 5.00 | 2.50 |
| 76 | Norm Miller | 1.00 | .50 |
| 77a | Ron Perranoski (LA visible thru airbrush) | 4.50 | 2.25 |
| 77b | Ron Perranoski (cap emblem completely airbrushed) | 1.00 | .50 |
| 78 | Tom Satriano | 1.00 | .50 |
| 79 | Milt Pappas | 1.00 | .50 |
| 80 | Norm Cash | 1.75 | .90 |
| 81 | Mel Queen | 1.00 | .50 |
| 82 | Pirates Rookies (Rich Hebner, Al Oliver) | 12.00 | 6.00 |
| 83 | Mike Ferraro | 1.25 | .60 |
| 84 | Bob Humphreys | 1.00 | .50 |
| 85 | Lou Brock | 18.00 | 9.00 |

| | | NR MT | EX |
|---|---|---|---|
| 86 | Pete Richert | 1.00 | .50 |
| 87 | Horace Clarke | 1.00 | .50 |
| 88 | Rich Nye | 1.00 | .50 |
| 89 | Russ Gibson | 1.00 | .50 |
| 90 | Jerry Koosman | 2.50 | 1.25 |
| 91 | Al Dark | 1.00 | .50 |
| 92 | Jack Billingham | 1.00 | .50 |
| 93 | Joe Foy | 1.00 | .50 |
| 94 | Hank Aguirre | 1.00 | .50 |
| 95 | Johnny Bench | 150.00 | 75.00 |
| 96 | Denver Lemaster | 1.00 | .50 |
| 97 | Buddy Bradford | 1.00 | .50 |
| 98 | Dave Giusti | 1.00 | .50 |
| 99a | Twins Rookies (Danny Morris, *Graig Nettles*) (black loop above "Twins") | 20.00 | 10.00 |
| 99b | Twins Rookies (Danny Morris, *Graig Nettles*) (no black loop) | 12.00 | 6.00 |
| 100 | Hank Aaron | 60.00 | 30.00 |
| 101 | Daryl Patterson | 1.00 | .50 |
| 102 | Jim Davenport | 1.00 | .50 |
| 103 | Roger Repoz | 1.00 | .50 |
| 104 | Steve Blass | 1.00 | .50 |
| 105 | Rick Monday | 1.25 | .60 |
| 106 | Jim Hannan | 1.00 | .50 |
| 107a | Checklist 110-218 (Bob Gibson) (161 is Jim Purdin) | 3.00 | 1.50 |
| 107b | Checklist 110-218 (Bob Gibson) (161 is John Purdin) | 6.00 | 3.00 |
| 108 | Tony Taylor | 1.00 | .50 |
| 109 | Jim Lonborg | 1.25 | .60 |
| 110 | Mike Shannon | 1.00 | .50 |
| 111 | Johnny Morris | 1.25 | .60 |
| 112 | J.C. Martin | 1.00 | .50 |
| 113 | Dave May | 1.00 | .50 |
| 114 | Yankees Rookies (Alan Closter, John Cumberland) | 1.00 | .50 |
| 115 | Bill Hands | 1.00 | .50 |
| 116 | Chuck Harrison | 1.00 | .50 |
| 117 | Jim Fairey | 1.00 | .50 |
| 118 | Stan Williams | 1.00 | .50 |
| 119 | Doug Rader | 1.00 | .50 |
| 120 | Pete Rose | 35.00 | 17.50 |
| 121 | Joe Grzenda | 1.00 | .50 |
| 122 | Ron Fairly | 1.25 | .60 |
| 123 | Wilbur Wood | 1.25 | .60 |
| 124 | Hank Bauer | 1.25 | .60 |
| 125 | Ray Sadecki | 1.00 | .50 |
| 126 | Dick Tracewski | 1.00 | .50 |
| 127 | Kevin Collins | 1.00 | .50 |
| 128 | Tommie Aaron | 1.00 | .50 |
| 129 | Bill McCool | 1.00 | .50 |
| 130 | Carl Yastrzemski | 30.00 | 15.00 |
| 131 | Chris Cannizzaro | 1.00 | .50 |
| 132 | Dave Baldwin | 1.00 | .50 |
| 133 | Johnny Callison | 1.00 | .50 |
| 134 | Jim Weaver | 1.00 | .50 |
| 135 | Tommy Davis | 1.50 | .70 |
| 136 | Cards Rookies (Steve Huntz, Mike Torrez) | 1.00 | .50 |
| 137 | Wally Bunker | 1.00 | .50 |
| 138 | John Bateman | 1.00 | .50 |
| 139 | Andy Kosco | 1.00 | .50 |

| | | NR MT | EX |
|---|---|---|---|
| 140 | Jim Lefebvre | 1.00 | .50 |
| 141 | Bill Dillman | 1.00 | .50 |
| 142 | Woody Woodward | 1.00 | .50 |
| 143 | Joe Nossek | 1.00 | .50 |
| 144 | Bob Hendley | 1.00 | .50 |
| 145 | Max Alvis | 1.00 | .50 |
| 146 | Jim Perry | 1.00 | .50 |
| 147 | Leo Durocher | 2.25 | 1.25 |
| 148 | Lee Stange | 1.00 | .50 |
| 149 | Ollie Brown | 1.00 | .50 |
| 150 | Denny McLain | 3.00 | 1.50 |
| 151a | Clay Dalrymple (Phillies) | 7.00 | 3.50 |
| 151b | Clay Dalrymple (Orioles) | 1.00 | .50 |
| 152 | Tommie Sisk | 1.00 | .50 |
| 153 | Ed Brinkman | 1.00 | .50 |
| 154 | Jim Britton | 1.00 | .50 |
| 155 | Pete Ward | 1.00 | .50 |
| 156 | Astros Rookies (Hal Gilson, Leon McFadden) | 1.00 | .50 |
| 157 | Bob Rodgers | 1.00 | .50 |
| 158 | Joe Gibbon | 1.00 | .50 |
| 159 | Jerry Adair | 1.00 | .50 |
| 160 | Vada Pinson | 2.00 | 1.00 |
| 161 | John Purdin | 1.00 | .50 |
| 162 | World Series Game 1 (Gibson Fans 17; Sets New Record) | 3.50 | 1.75 |
| 163 | World Series Game 2 (Tiger Homers Deck The Cards) | 2.50 | 1.25 |
| 164 | World Series Game 3 (McCarver's Homer Puts St. Louis Ahead) | 2.50 | 1.25 |
| 165 | World Series Game 4 (Brock's Lead-Off Homer Starts Cards' Romp) | 3.50 | 1.75 |
| 166 | World Series Game 5 (Kaline's Key Hit Sparks Tiger Rally) | 3.50 | 1.75 |
| 167 | World Series Game 6 (Tiger 10-Run Inning Ties Mark) | 2.50 | 1.25 |
| 168 | World Series Game 7 (Lolich Series Hero, Outduels Gibson) | 2.75 | 1.50 |
| 169 | World Series Summary (Tigers Celebrate Their Victory) | 2.50 | 1.25 |
| 170 | Frank Howard | 2.00 | 1.00 |
| 171 | Glenn Beckert | 1.25 | .60 |
| 172 | Jerry Stephenson | 1.00 | .50 |
| 173 | White Sox Rookies (Bob Christian, Gerry Nyman) | 1.00 | .50 |
| 174 | Grant Jackson | 1.00 | .50 |
| 175 | Jim Bunning | 4.00 | 2.00 |
| 176 | Joe Azcue | 1.00 | .50 |
| 177 | Ron Reed | 1.00 | .50 |
| 178 | Ray Oyler | 1.25 | .60 |
| 179 | Don Pavletich | 1.00 | .50 |
| 180 | Willie Horton | 1.25 | .60 |
| 181 | Mel Nelson | 1.00 | .50 |
| 182 | Bill Rigney | 1.00 | .50 |
| 183 | Don Shaw | 1.00 | .50 |

| | | NR MT | EX | | | NR MT | EX |
|---|---|---|---|---|---|---|---|
| 184 | Roberto Pena | 1.00 | .50 | 242 | Frank Kostro | 1.50 | .70 |
| 185 | Tom Phoebus | 1.00 | .50 | 243 | Ron Kline | 1.50 | .70 |
| 186 | John Edwards | 1.00 | .50 | 244 | Indians Rookies (Ray | | |
| 187 | Leon Wagner | 1.00 | .50 | | Fosse, George Woodson) | | |
| 188 | Rick Wise | 1.00 | .50 | | | 1.50 | .70 |
| 189 | Red Sox Rookies (Joe | | | 245 | Ed Charles | 1.50 | .70 |
| | Lahoud, John Thibdeau) | | | 246 | Joe Coleman | 1.50 | .70 |
| | | 1.00 | .50 | 247 | Gene Oliver | 1.50 | .70 |
| 190 | Willie Mays | 65.00 | 33.00 | 248 | Bob Priddy | 1.50 | .70 |
| 191 | Lindy McDaniel | 1.00 | .50 | 249 | Ed Spiezio | 1.50 | .70 |
| 192 | Jose Pagan | 1.00 | .50 | 250 | Frank Robinson | 20.00 | 10.00 |
| 193 | Don Cardwell | 1.00 | .50 | 251 | Ron Herbel | 1.50 | .70 |
| 194 | Ted Uhlaender | 1.00 | .50 | 252 | Chuck Cottier | 1.50 | .70 |
| 195 | John Odom | 1.00 | .50 | 253 | Jerry Johnson | 1.50 | .70 |
| 196 | Lum Harris | 1.00 | .50 | 254 | Joe Schultz | 1.50 | .70 |
| 197 | Dick Selma | 1.00 | .50 | 255 | Steve Carlton | 50.00 | 25.00 |
| 198 | Willie Smith | 1.00 | .50 | 256 | Gates Brown | 1.50 | .70 |
| 199 | Jim French | 1.00 | .50 | 257 | Jim Ray | 1.50 | .70 |
| 200 | Bob Gibson | 12.00 | 6.00 | 258 | Jackie Hernandez | 1.50 | .70 |
| 201 | Russ Snyder | 1.00 | .50 | 259 | Bill Short | 1.50 | .70 |
| 202 | Don Wilson | 1.00 | .50 | 260 | Reggie Jackson | 700.00 | 350.00 |
| 203 | Dave Johnson | 1.50 | .70 | 261 | Bob Johnson | 1.50 | .70 |
| 204 | Jack Hiatt | 1.00 | .50 | 262 | Mike Kekich | 1.50 | .70 |
| 205 | Rick Reichardt | 1.00 | .50 | 263 | Jerry May | 1.50 | .70 |
| 206 | Phillies Rookies (Larry | | | 264 | Bill Landis | 1.50 | .70 |
| | Hisle, Barry Lersch) | 1.25 | .60 | 265 | Chico Cardenas | 1.50 | .70 |
| 207 | Roy Face | 1.50 | .70 | 266 | Dodgers Rookies (Alan | | |
| 208a | Donn Clendenon (Expos) | | | | Foster, Tom Hutton) | 1.50 | .70 |
| | | 7.00 | 3.50 | 267 | Vicente Romo | 1.50 | .70 |
| 208b | Donn Clendenon | | | 268 | Al Spangler | 1.50 | .70 |
| | (Houston) | 1.00 | .50 | 269 | Al Weis | 1.50 | .70 |
| 209 | Larry Haney (photo | | | 270 | Mickey Lolich | 3.50 | 1.75 |
| | reversed) | 1.25 | .60 | 271 | Larry Stahl | 1.50 | .70 |
| 210 | Felix Millan | 1.00 | .50 | 272 | Ed Stroud | 1.50 | .70 |
| 211 | Galen Cisco | 1.00 | .50 | 273 | Ron Willis | 1.50 | .70 |
| 212 | Tom Tresh | 1.50 | .70 | 274 | Clyde King | 1.50 | .70 |
| 213 | Gerry Arrigo | 1.00 | .50 | 275 | Vic Davalillo | 1.50 | .70 |
| 214 | Checklist 219-327 | 2.50 | 1.25 | 276 | Gary Wagner | 1.50 | .70 |
| 215 | Rico Petrocelli | 1.25 | .60 | 277 | Rod Hendricks | 1.50 | .70 |
| 216 | Don Sutton | 5.00 | 2.50 | 278 | Gary Geiger | 1.50 | .70 |
| 217 | John Donaldson | 1.00 | .50 | 279 | Roger Nelson | 1.50 | .70 |
| 218 | John Roseboro | 1.00 | .50 | 280 | Alex Johnson | 1.50 | .70 |
| 219 | Freddie Patek | 2.00 | 1.00 | 281 | Ted Kubiak | 1.50 | .70 |
| 220 | Sam McDowell | 1.50 | .70 | 282 | Pat Jarvis | 1.50 | .70 |
| 221 | Art Shamsky | 1.50 | .70 | 283 | Sandy Alomar | 1.50 | .70 |
| 222 | Duane Josephson | 1.50 | .70 | 284 | Expos Rookies (Jerry | | |
| 223 | Tom Dukes | 1.50 | .70 | | Robertson, Mike Wegener) | | |
| 224 | Angels Rookies (Bill | | | | | 1.50 | .70 |
| | Harrelson, Steve Kealey) | | | 285 | Don Mincher | 1.50 | .70 |
| | | 1.50 | .70 | 286 | Dock Ellis | 1.50 | .70 |
| 225 | Don Kessinger | 1.50 | .70 | 287 | Jose Tartabull | 1.50 | .70 |
| 226 | Bruce Howard | 1.50 | .70 | 288 | Ken Holtzman | 1.50 | .70 |
| 227 | Frank Johnson | 1.50 | .70 | 289 | Bart Shirley | 1.50 | .70 |
| 228 | Dave Leonhard | 1.50 | .70 | 290 | Jim Kaat | 4.50 | 2.25 |
| 229 | Don Lock | 1.50 | .70 | 291 | Vern Fuller | 1.50 | .70 |
| 230 | Rusty Staub | 2.50 | 1.25 | 292 | Al Downing | 1.50 | .70 |
| 231 | Pat Dobson | 1.50 | .70 | 293 | Dick Dietz | 1.50 | .70 |
| 232 | Dave Ricketts | 1.50 | .70 | 294 | Jim Lemon | 1.50 | .70 |
| 233 | Steve Barber | 1.50 | .70 | 295 | Tony Perez | 10.00 | 5.00 |
| 234 | Dave Bristol | 1.50 | .70 | 296 | Andy Messersmith | 1.50 | .70 |
| 235 | Jim Hunter | 10.00 | 5.00 | 297 | Deron Johnson | 1.50 | .70 |
| 236 | Manny Mota | 1.50 | .70 | 298 | Dave Nicholson | 1.50 | .70 |
| 237 | Bobby Cox | 1.50 | .70 | 299 | Mark Belanger | 1.50 | .70 |
| 238 | Ken Johnson | 1.50 | .70 | 300 | Felipe Alou | 1.50 | .70 |
| 239 | Bob Taylor | 1.50 | .70 | 301 | Darrell Brandon | 1.50 | .70 |
| 240 | Ken Harrelson | 2.00 | 1.00 | 302 | Jim Pagliaroni | 1.50 | .70 |
| 241 | Jim Brewer | 1.50 | .70 | 303 | Cal Koonce | 1.50 | .70 |

| | NR MT | EX |
|---|---|---|
| 304 Padres Rookies (Bill Davis, *Clarence Gaston*) | 8.00 | 4.00 |
| 305 Dick McAuliffe | 1.50 | .70 |
| 306 Jim Grant | 1.50 | .70 |
| 307 Gary Kolb | 1.50 | .70 |
| 308 Wade Blasingame | 1.50 | .70 |
| 309 Walt Williams | 1.50 | .70 |
| 310 Tom Haller | 1.50 | .70 |
| 311 *Sparky Lyle* | 12.00 | 6.00 |
| 312 Lee Elia | 1.50 | .70 |
| 313 Bill Robinson | 1.50 | .70 |
| 314 Checklist 328-425 (Don Drysdale) | 3.50 | 1.75 |
| 315 Eddie Fisher | 1.50 | .70 |
| 316 Hal Lanier | 1.50 | .70 |
| 317 Bruce Look | 1.50 | .70 |
| 318 Jack Fisher | 1.50 | .70 |
| 319 Ken McMullen | 1.50 | .70 |
| 320 Dal Maxvill | 1.50 | .70 |
| 321 Jim McAndrew | 1.50 | .70 |
| 322 Jose Vidal | 1.50 | .70 |
| 323 Larry Miller | 1.50 | .70 |
| 324 Tigers Rookies (Les Cain, Dave Campbell) | 1.50 | .70 |
| 325 Jose Cardenal | 1.50 | .70 |
| 326 Gary Sutherland | 1.50 | .70 |
| 327 Willie Crawford | 1.50 | .70 |
| 328 Joe Horlen | 1.00 | .50 |
| 329 Rick Joseph | 1.00 | .50 |
| 330 Tony Conigliaro | 1.50 | .70 |
| 331 Braves Rookies (Gil Garrido, *Tom House*) | 1.00 | .50 |
| 332 Fred Talbot | 1.25 | .60 |
| 333 Ivan Murrell | 1.00 | .50 |
| 334 Phil Roof | 1.00 | .50 |
| 335 Bill Mazeroski | 1.75 | .90 |
| 336 Jim Roland | 1.00 | .50 |
| 337 Marty Martinez | 1.00 | .50 |
| 338 *Del Unser* | 1.00 | .50 |
| 339 Reds Rookies (Steve Mingori, Jose Pena) | 1.00 | .50 |
| 340 Dave McNally | 1.25 | .60 |
| 341 Dave Adlesh | 1.00 | .50 |
| 342 Bubba Morton | 1.00 | .50 |
| 343 Dan Frisella | 1.00 | .50 |
| 344 Tom Matchick | 1.00 | .50 |
| 345 Frank Linzy | 1.00 | .50 |
| 346 Wayne Comer | 1.25 | .60 |
| 347 Randy Hundley | 1.00 | .50 |
| 348 Steve Hargan | 1.00 | .50 |
| 349 Dick Williams | 1.25 | .60 |
| 350 Richie Allen | 2.00 | 1.00 |
| 351 Carroll Sembera | 1.00 | .50 |
| 352 Paul Schaal | 1.00 | .50 |
| 353 Jeff Torborg | 1.00 | .50 |
| 354 Nate Oliver | 1.25 | .60 |
| 355 Phil Niekro | 7.00 | 3.50 |
| 356 Frank Quilici | 1.00 | .50 |
| 357 Carl Taylor | 1.00 | .50 |
| 358 Athletics Rookies (George Lauzerique, Roberto Rodriguez) | 1.00 | .50 |
| 359 Dick Kelley | 1.00 | .50 |
| 360 Jim Wynn | 1.25 | .60 |
| 361 Gary Holman | 1.00 | .50 |
| 362 Jim Maloney | 1.00 | .50 |

| | NR MT | EX |
|---|---|---|
| 363 Russ Nixon | 1.00 | .50 |
| 364 Tommie Agee | 1.25 | .60 |
| 365 Jim Fregosi | 1.00 | .50 |
| 366 Bo Belinsky | 1.00 | .50 |
| 367 Lou Johnson | 1.00 | .50 |
| 368 Vic Roznovsky | 1.00 | .50 |
| 369 Bob Skinner | 1.00 | .50 |
| 370 Juan Marichal | 7.00 | 3.50 |
| 371 Sal Bando | 1.25 | .60 |
| 372 Adolfo Phillips | 1.00 | .50 |
| 373 Fred Lasher | 1.00 | .50 |
| 374 Bob Tillman | 1.00 | .50 |
| 375 Harmon Killebrew | 20.00 | 10.00 |
| 376 Royals Rookies (Mike Fiore, *Jim Rooker*) | 1.00 | .50 |
| 377 Gary Bell | 1.25 | .60 |
| 378 Jose Herrera | 1.00 | .50 |
| 379 Ken Boyer | 1.75 | .90 |
| 380 Stan Bahnsen | 1.25 | .60 |
| 381 Ed Kranepool | 1.25 | .60 |
| 382 Pat Corrales | 1.25 | .60 |
| 383 Casey Cox | 1.00 | .50 |
| 384 Larry Shepard | 1.00 | .50 |
| 385 Orlando Cepeda | 3.50 | 1.75 |
| 386 Jim McGlothlin | 1.00 | .50 |
| 387 Bobby Klaus | 1.00 | .50 |
| 388 Tom McCraw | 1.00 | .50 |
| 389 Dan Coombs | 1.00 | .50 |
| 390 Bill Freehan | 1.00 | .50 |
| 391 Ray Culp | 1.00 | .50 |
| 392 Bob Burda | 1.00 | .50 |
| 393 Gene Brabender | 1.00 | .50 |
| 394 Pilots Rookies (Lou Piniella, Marv Staehle) | 3.00 | 1.50 |
| 395 Chris Short | 1.00 | .50 |
| 396 Jim Campanis | 1.00 | .50 |
| 397 Chuck Dobson | 1.00 | .50 |
| 398 Tito Francona | 1.00 | .50 |
| 399 Bob Bailey | 1.00 | .50 |
| 400 Don Drysdale | 8.00 | 4.00 |
| 401 Jake Gibbs | 1.25 | .60 |
| 402 Ken Boswell | 1.00 | .50 |
| 403 Bob Miller | 1.00 | .50 |
| 404 Cubs Rookies (Vic LaRose, Gary Ross) | 1.00 | .50 |
| 405 Lee May | 1.00 | .50 |
| 406 Phil Ortega | 1.00 | .50 |
| 407 Tom Egan | 1.00 | .50 |
| 408 Nate Colbert | 1.00 | .50 |
| 409 Bob Moose | 1.00 | .50 |
| 410 Al Kaline | 15.00 | 7.50 |
| 411 Larry Dierker | 1.00 | .50 |
| 412 Checklist 426-512 (Mickey Mantle) | 7.00 | 3.50 |
| 413 Roland Sheldon | 1.25 | .60 |
| 414 Duke Sims | 1.00 | .50 |
| 415 Ray Washburn | 1.00 | .50 |
| 416 Willie McCovey AS | 3.50 | 1.75 |
| 417 Ken Harrelson AS | 1.00 | .50 |
| 418 Tommy Helms AS | 1.00 | .50 |
| 419 Rod Carew AS | 10.00 | 7.50 |
| 420 Ron Santo AS | 1.00 | .50 |
| 421 Brooks Robinson AS | 4.00 | 2.00 |
| 422 Don Kessinger AS | 1.00 | .50 |
| 423 Bert Campaneris AS | 1.25 | .60 |

| | | NR MT | EX |
|---|---|---|---|
| 424 | Pete Rose AS | 12.00 | 6.00 |
| 425 | Carl Yastrzemski AS | 6.00 | 3.00 |
| 426 | Curt Flood AS | 1.00 | .50 |
| 427 | Tony Oliva AS | 1.50 | .70 |
| 428 | Lou Brock AS | 5.00 | 2.50 |
| 429 | Willie Horton AS | 1.25 | .60 |
| 430 | Johnny Bench AS | 12.00 | 6.00 |
| 431 | Bill Freehan AS | 1.00 | .50 |
| 432 | Bob Gibson AS | 5.00 | 2.50 |
| 433 | Denny McLain AS | 1.50 | .70 |
| 434 | Jerry Koosman AS | 1.00 | .50 |
| 435 | Sam McDowell AS | 1.25 | .60 |
| 436 | Gene Alley | 1.00 | .50 |
| 437 | Luis Alcaraz | 1.00 | .50 |
| 438 | Gary Waslewski | 1.00 | .50 |
| 439 | White Sox Rookies (Ed Herrmann, Dan Lazar) | 1.00 | .50 |
| 440a | Willie McCovey (last name in white) | 90.00 | 45.00 |
| 440b | Willie McCovey (last name in yellow) | 18.00 | 9.00 |
| 441a | Dennis Higgins (last name in white) | 10.00 | 5.00 |
| 441b | Dennis Higgins (last name in yellow) | 1.00 | .50 |
| 442 | Ty Cline | 1.00 | .50 |
| 443 | Don Wert | 1.00 | .50 |
| 444a | Joe Moeller (last name in white) | 10.00 | 5.00 |
| 444b | Joe Moeller (last name in yellow) | 1.00 | .50 |
| 445 | Bobby Knoop | 1.00 | .50 |
| 446 | Claude Raymond | 1.00 | .50 |
| 447a | Ralph Houk (last name in white) | 15.00 | 7.50 |
| 447b | Ralph Houk (last name in yellow) | 1.50 | .70 |
| 448 | Bob Tolan | 1.00 | .50 |
| 449 | Paul Lindblad | 1.00 | .50 |
| 450 | Billy Williams | 6.00 | 3.00 |
| 451a | Rich Rollins (first name in white) | 10.00 | 5.00 |
| 451b | Rich Rollins (first name in yellow) | 1.25 | .60 |
| 452a | Al Ferrara (first name in white) | 10.00 | 5.00 |
| 452b | Al Ferrara (first name in yellow) | 1.00 | .50 |
| 453 | Mike Cuellar | 1.25 | .60 |
| 454a | Phillies Rookies (Larry Colton, Don Money) (names in white) | 10.00 | 5.00 |
| 454b | Phillies Rookies (Larry Colton, Don Money) (names in yellow) | 1.25 | .60 |
| 455 | Sonny Siebert | 1.00 | .50 |
| 456 | Bud Harrelson | 1.00 | .50 |
| 457 | Dalton Jones | 1.00 | .50 |
| 458 | Curt Blefary | 1.00 | .50 |
| 459 | Dave Boswell | 1.00 | .50 |
| 460 | Joe Torre | 1.75 | .90 |
| 461a | Mike Epstein (last name in white) | 10.00 | 5.00 |
| 461b | Mike Epstein (last name in yellow) | 1.00 | .50 |
| 462 | Red Schoendienst | 1.50 | .70 |
| 463 | Dennis Ribant | 1.00 | .50 |
| 464a | Dave Marshall (last name in white) | 10.00 | 5.00 |
| 464b | Dave Marshall (last name in yellow) | 1.00 | .50 |
| 465 | Tommy John | 4.50 | 2.25 |
| 466 | John Boccabella | 1.00 | .50 |
| 467 | Tom Reynolds | 1.00 | .50 |
| 468a | Pirates Rookies (Bruce Dal Canton, Bob Robertson) (names in white) | 10.00 | 5.00 |
| 468b | Pirates Rookies (Bruce Dal Canton, Bob Robertson) (names in yellow) | 1.00 | .50 |
| 469 | Chico Ruiz | 1.00 | .50 |
| 470a | Mel Stottlemyre (last name in white) | 15.00 | 7.50 |
| 470b | Mel Stottlemyre (last name in yellow) | 1.50 | .70 |
| 471a | Ted Savage (last name in white) | 10.00 | 5.00 |
| 471b | Ted Savage (last name in yellow) | 1.00 | .50 |
| 472 | Jim Price | 1.00 | .50 |
| 473a | Jose Arcia (first name in white) | 10.00 | 5.00 |
| 473b | Jose Arcia (first name in yellow) | 1.00 | .50 |
| 474 | Tom Murphy | 1.00 | .50 |
| 475 | Tim McCarver | 1.50 | .70 |
| 476a | Red Sox Rookies (Ken Brett, Gerry Moses) (names in white) | 10.00 | 5.00 |
| 476b | Red Sox Rookies (Ken Brett, Gerry Moses) (names in yellow) | 1.00 | .50 |
| 477 | Jeff James | 1.00 | .50 |
| 478 | Don Buford | 1.00 | .50 |
| 479 | Richie Scheinblum | 1.00 | .50 |
| 480 | Tom Seaver | 160.00 | 80.00 |
| 481 | Bill Melton | 1.25 | .60 |
| 482a | Jim Gosger (first name in white) | 10.00 | 5.00 |
| 482b | Jim Gosger (first name in yellow) | 1.25 | .60 |
| 483 | Ted Abernathy | 1.00 | .50 |
| 484 | Joe Gordon | 1.00 | .50 |
| 485a | Gaylord Perry (last name in white) | 75.00 | 38.00 |
| 485b | Gaylord Perry (last name in yellow) | 10.00 | 5.00 |
| 486a | Paul Casanova (last name in white) | 10.00 | 5.00 |
| 486b | Paul Casanova (last name in yellow) | 1.00 | .50 |
| 487 | Denis Menke | 1.00 | .50 |
| 488 | Joe Sparma | 1.00 | .50 |
| 489 | Clete Boyer | 1.25 | .60 |
| 490 | Matty Alou | 1.00 | .50 |
| 491a | Twins Rookies (Jerry Crider, George Mitterwald) (names in white) | 10.00 | 5.00 |
| 491b | Twins Rookies (Jerry Crider, George Mitterwald) (names in yellow) | 1.00 | .50 |
| 492 | Tony Cloninger | 1.00 | .50 |
| 493a | Wes Parker (last name in | | |

| | | NR MT | EX |
|---|---|---|---|
| | white) | 10.00 | 5.00 |
| 493b | Wes Parker (last name in yellow) | 1.00 | .50 |
| 494 | Ken Berry | 1.00 | .50 |
| 495 | Bert Campaneris | 1.50 | .70 |
| 496 | Larry Jaster | 1.00 | .50 |
| 497 | Julian Javier | 1.00 | .50 |
| 498 | Juan Pizarro | 1.00 | .50 |
| 499 | Astros Rookies (Don Bryant, Steve Shea) | 1.00 | .50 |
| 500a | Mickey Mantle (last name in white) | 475.00 | 190.00 |
| 500b | Mickey Mantle (last name in yellow) | 175.00 | 87.00 |
| 501a | Tony Gonzalez (first name in white) | 10.00 | 5.00 |
| 501b | Tony Gonzalez (first name in yellow) | 1.00 | .50 |
| 502 | Minnie Rojas | 1.00 | .50 |
| 503 | Larry Brown | 1.00 | .50 |
| 504 | Checklist 513-588 (Brooks Robinson) | 4.00 | 2.00 |
| 505a | Bobby Bolin (last name in white) | 10.00 | 5.00 |
| 505b | Bobby Bolin (last name in yellow) | 1.00 | .50 |
| 506 | Paul Blair | 1.00 | .50 |
| 507 | Cookie Rojas | 1.00 | .50 |
| 508 | Moe Drabowsky | 1.00 | .50 |
| 509 | Manny Sanguillen | 1.00 | .50 |
| 510 | Rod Carew | 60.00 | 30.00 |
| 511a | Diego Segui (first name in white) | 10.00 | 5.00 |
| 511b | Diego Segui (first name in yellow) | 1.25 | .60 |
| 512 | Cleon Jones | 1.25 | .60 |
| 513 | Camilo Pascual | 1.00 | .50 |
| 514 | Mike Lum | 1.00 | .50 |
| 515 | Dick Green | 1.00 | .50 |
| 516 | Earl Weaver | 5.00 | 2.50 |
| 517 | Mike McCormick | 1.25 | .60 |
| 518 | Fred Whitfield | 1.00 | .50 |
| 519 | Yankees Rookies (Len Boehmer, Gerry Kenney) | 1.00 | .50 |
| 520 | Bob Veale | 1.25 | .60 |
| 521 | George Thomas | 1.00 | .50 |
| 522 | Joe Hoerner | 1.00 | .50 |
| 523 | Bob Chance | 1.00 | .50 |
| 524 | Expos Rookies (Jose Laboy, Floyd Wicker) | 1.00 | .50 |
| 525 | Earl Wilson | 1.00 | .50 |
| 526 | Hector Torres | 1.00 | .50 |
| 527 | Al Lopez | 3.00 | 1.50 |
| 528 | Claude Osteen | 1.00 | .50 |
| 529 | Ed Kirkpatrick | 1.00 | .50 |
| 530 | Cesar Tovar | 1.00 | .50 |
| 531 | Dick Farrell | 1.00 | .50 |
| 532 | Bird Hill Aces (Mike Cuellar, Jim Hardin, Dave McNally, Tom Phoebus) | 1.50 | .70 |
| 533 | Nolan Ryan | 500.00 | 250.00 |
| 534 | Jerry McNertney | 1.00 | .50 |
| 535 | Phil Regan | 1.00 | .50 |
| 536 | Padres Rookies (Danny Breeden, Dave Roberts) | 1.25 | .60 |
| 537 | Mike Paul | 1.00 | .50 |
| 538 | Charlie Smith | 1.00 | .50 |
| 539 | Ted Shows How (Mike Epstein, Ted Williams) | 3.25 | 1.75 |
| 540 | Curt Flood | 1.50 | .70 |
| 541 | Joe Verbanic | 1.00 | .50 |
| 542 | Bob Aspromonte | 1.00 | .50 |
| 543 | Fred Newman | 1.00 | .50 |
| 544 | Tigers Rookies (Mike Kilkenny, Ron Woods) | 1.00 | .50 |
| 545 | Willie Stargell | 10.00 | 5.00 |
| 546 | Jim Nash | 1.00 | .50 |
| 547 | Billy Martin | 5.00 | 2.50 |
| 548 | Bob Locker | 1.00 | .50 |
| 549 | Ron Brand | 1.00 | .50 |
| 550 | Brooks Robinson | 15.00 | 7.50 |
| 551 | Wayne Granger | 1.00 | .50 |
| 552 | Dodgers Rookies (Ted Sizemore, Bill Sudakis) | 1.25 | .60 |
| 553 | Ron Davis | 1.00 | .50 |
| 554 | Frank Bertaina | 1.00 | .50 |
| 555 | Jim Hart | 1.25 | .60 |
| 556 | A's Stars (Sal Bando, Bert Campaneris, Danny Cater) | 1.50 | .70 |
| 557 | Frank Fernandez | 1.00 | .50 |
| 558 | Tom Burgmeier | 1.25 | .60 |
| 559 | Cards Rookies (Joe Hague, Jim Hicks) | 1.00 | .50 |
| 560 | Luis Tiant | 1.50 | .70 |
| 561 | Ron Clark | 1.00 | .50 |
| 562 | Bob Watson | 1.00 | .50 |
| 563 | Marty Pattin | 1.00 | .50 |
| 564 | Gil Hodges | 6.00 | 3.00 |
| 565 | Hoyt Wilhelm | 6.00 | 3.00 |
| 566 | Ron Hansen | 1.00 | .50 |
| 567 | Pirates Rookies (Elvio Jimenez, Jim Shellenback) | 1.00 | .50 |
| 568 | Cecil Upshaw | 1.00 | .50 |
| 569 | Billy Harris | 1.00 | .50 |
| 570 | Ron Santo | 1.75 | .90 |
| 571 | Cap Peterson | 1.00 | .50 |
| 572 | Giants Heroes (Juan Marichal, Willie McCovey) | 7.00 | 3.50 |
| 573 | Jim Palmer | 40.00 | 20.00 |
| 574 | George Scott | 1.00 | .50 |
| 575 | Bill Singer | 1.25 | .60 |
| 576 | Phillies Rookies (Ron Stone, Bill Wilson) | 1.00 | .50 |
| 577 | Mike Hegan | 1.00 | .50 |
| 578 | Don Bosch | 1.00 | .50 |
| 579 | Dave Nelson | 1.25 | .60 |
| 580 | Jim Northrup | 1.25 | .60 |
| 581 | Gary Nolan | 1.00 | .50 |
| 582a | Checklist 589-664 (Tony Oliva) (red circle on back) | 3.50 | 1.75 |
| 582b | Checklist 589-664 (Tony Oliva) (white circle on back) | 2.50 | 1.25 |
| 583 | Clyde Wright | 1.25 | .60 |
| 584 | Don Mason | 1.00 | .50 |
| 585 | Ron Swoboda | 1.00 | .50 |

| | | NR MT | EX |
|---|---|---|---|
| 586 | Tim Cullen | 1.00 | .50 |
| 587 | *Joe Rudi* | 1.75 | .90 |
| 588 | Bill White | 1.00 | .50 |
| 589 | Joe Pepitone | 2.00 | 1.00 |
| 590 | Rico Carty | 1.00 | .50 |
| 591 | Mike Hedlund | 1.00 | .50 |
| 592 | Padres Rookies (Rafael Robles, Al Santorini) | 1.00 | .50 |
| 593 | Don Nottebart | 1.00 | .50 |
| 594 | Dooley Womack | 1.00 | .50 |
| 595 | Lee Maye | 1.00 | .50 |
| 596 | Chuck Hartenstein | 1.00 | .50 |
| 597 | A.L. Rookies (Larry Burchart, *Rollie Fingers*, Bob Floyd) | 150.00 | 75.00 |
| 598 | Ruben Amaro | 1.00 | .50 |
| 599 | John Boozer | 1.00 | .50 |
| 600 | Tony Oliva | 4.00 | 2.00 |
| 601 | Tug McGraw | 2.00 | 1.00 |
| 602 | Cubs Rookies (Alec Distaso, Jim Qualls, Don Young) | 1.00 | .50 |
| 603 | Joe Keough | 1.00 | .50 |
| 604 | Bobby Etheridge | 1.00 | .50 |
| 605 | Dick Ellsworth | 1.00 | .50 |
| 606 | Gene Mauch | 1.00 | .50 |
| 607 | Dick Bosman | 1.00 | .50 |
| 608 | Dick Simpson | 1.00 | .50 |
| 609 | Phil Gagliano | 1.00 | .50 |
| 610 | Jim Hardin | 1.00 | .50 |
| 611 | Braves Rookies (Bob Didier, Walt Hriniak, Gary Neibauer) | 1.00 | .50 |
| 612 | Jack Aker | 1.00 | .50 |
| 613 | Jim Beauchamp | 1.00 | .50 |
| 614 | Astros Rookies (Tom Griffin, Skip Guinn) | | — |
| 615 | Len Gabrielson | 1.00 | .50 |
| 616 | Don McMahon | 1.00 | .50 |
| 617 | Jesse Gonder | 1.00 | .50 |
| 618 | Ramon Webster | 1.00 | .50 |
| 619 | Royals Rookies (Bill Butler, *Pat Kelly*, Juan Rios) | 1.25 | .60 |
| 620 | Dean Chance | 1.25 | .60 |
| 621 | Bill Voss | 1.00 | .50 |
| 622 | Dan Osinski | 1.00 | .50 |
| 623 | Hank Allen | 1.00 | .50 |
| 624 | N.L. Rookies (Darrel Chaney, Duffy Dyer, Terry Harmon) | 1.25 | .60 |
| 625 | Mack Jones | 1.00 | .50 |
| 626 | Gene Michael | 1.00 | .50 |
| 627 | George Stone | 1.00 | .50 |
| 628 | Red Sox Rookies (*Bill Conigliaro*, Syd O'Brien, Fred Wenz) | 1.00 | .50 |
| 629 | Jack Hamilton | 1.00 | .50 |
| 630 | *Bobby Bonds* | 35.00 | 17.50 |
| 631 | John Kennedy | 1.00 | .50 |
| 632 | Jon Warden | 1.00 | .50 |
| 633 | Harry Walker | 1.25 | .60 |
| 634 | Andy Etchebarren | 1.00 | .50 |
| 635 | George Culver | 1.00 | .50 |
| 636 | Woodie Held | 1.00 | .50 |
| 637 | Padres Rookies (Jerry DaVanon, *Clay Kirby*, Frank Reberger) | 1.25 | .60 |
| 638 | Ed Sprague | 1.00 | .50 |
| 639 | Barry Moore | 1.00 | .50 |
| 640 | Fergie Jenkins | 18.00 | 9.00 |
| 641 | N.L. Rookies (Bobby Darwin, Tommy Dean, John Miller) | 1.00 | .50 |
| 642 | John Hiller | 1.25 | .60 |
| 643 | Billy Cowan | 1.00 | .50 |
| 644 | Chuck Hinton | 1.00 | .50 |
| 645 | George Brunet | 1.00 | .50 |
| 646 | Expos Rookies (Dan McGinn, *Carl Morton*) | 1.00 | .50 |
| 647 | Dave Wickersham | 1.00 | .50 |
| 648 | Bobby Wine | 1.00 | .50 |
| 649 | Al Jackson | 1.00 | .50 |
| 650 | Ted Williams | 10.00 | 5.00 |
| 651 | Gus Gil | 1.00 | .50 |
| 652 | Eddie Watt | 1.00 | .50 |
| 653 | *Aurelio Rodriguez* (photo actually batboy Leonard Garcia) | 1.50 | .70 |
| 654 | White Sox Rookies (*Carlos May*, Rich Morales, Don Secrist) | 1.00 | .50 |
| 655 | Mike Hershberger | 1.00 | .50 |
| 656 | Dan Schneider | 1.00 | .50 |
| 657 | Bobby Murcer | 2.25 | 1.25 |
| 658 | A.L. Rookies (Bill Burbach, Tom Hall, Jim Miles) | 1.00 | .50 |
| 659 | Johnny Podres | 1.75 | .90 |
| 660 | Reggie Smith | 1.75 | .90 |
| 661 | Jim Merritt | 1.00 | .50 |
| 662 | Royals Rookies (Dick Drago, Bob Oliver, George Spriggs) | 1.25 | .60 |
| 663 | Dick Radatz | 1.00 | .50 |
| 664 | Ron Hunt | 2.00 | .50 |

# 1970 Topps

Topps established another set size record by coming out with 720 cards in 1970. The 2-1/2" by 3-1/2" cards have a color photo with a thin white frame. The photo have the player's team overprinted at the top, while the player's name is in script and his position are at the bottom. A gray border surrounds the front. Card backs follows the normal design pattern, although they are more readable than some issues of the past. Team cards returned and were joined with many of the usual specialty cards. The World Series highlights were joined by cards with playoff highlights. Statistical leaders and All-Stars are also included in the set. High-numbered cards provide the most expensive cards in the set.

|  | | NR MT | EX |
|---|---|---|---|
| Complete Set: | | 2000.00 | 1000.00 |
| Common Player: 1-546 | | .80 | .40 |
| Common Player: 547-633 | | 1.50 | .70 |
| Common Player: 634-720 | | 3.00 | 1.50 |

| | | NR MT | EX |
|---|---|---|---|
| 1 | World Champions (Mets Team) | 10.00 | 3.00 |
| 2 | Diego Segui | 1.00 | .50 |
| 3 | Darrel Chaney | .80 | .40 |
| 4 | Tom Egan | .80 | .40 |
| 5 | Wes Parker | .90 | .45 |
| 6 | Grant Jackson | .80 | .40 |
| 7 | Indians Rookies (Gary Boyd, Russ Nagelson) | .80 | .40 |
| 8 | Jose Martinez | .80 | .40 |
| 9 | Checklist 1-132 | 3.50 | 1.75 |
| 10 | Carl Yastrzemski | 30.00 | 15.00 |
| 11 | Nate Colbert | .80 | .40 |
| 12 | John Hiller | .90 | .45 |
| 13 | Jack Hiatt | .80 | .40 |
| 14 | Hank Allen | .80 | .40 |
| 15 | Larry Dierker | .90 | .45 |
| 16 | Charlie Metro | .80 | .40 |
| 17 | Hoyt Wilhelm | 4.00 | 2.00 |
| 18 | Carlos May | .80 | .40 |
| 19 | John Boccabella | .80 | .40 |
| 20 | Dave McNally | 1.00 | .50 |
| 21 | Athletics Rookies (Vida Blue, Gene Tenace) | 6.00 | 3.00 |
| 22 | Ray Washburn | .80 | .40 |
| 23 | Bill Robinson | .80 | .40 |
| 24 | Dick Selma | .80 | .40 |
| 25 | Cesar Tovar | .80 | .40 |
| 26 | Tug McGraw | 1.75 | .90 |
| 27 | Chuck Hinton | .80 | .40 |
| 28 | Billy Wilson | .80 | .40 |
| 29 | Sandy Alomar | .80 | .40 |
| 30 | Matty Alou | 1.50 | .70 |
| 31 | Marty Pattin | .80 | .40 |
| 32 | Harry Walker | .90 | .45 |
| 33 | Don Wert | .80 | .40 |
| 34 | Willie Crawford | .80 | .40 |
| 35 | Joe Horlen | .80 | .40 |
| 36 | Reds Rookies (Danny Breeden, Bernie Carbo) | .80 | .40 |
| 37 | Dick Drago | .80 | .40 |
| 38 | Mack Jones | .80 | .40 |
| 39 | Mike Nagy | .80 | .40 |
| 40 | Rich Allen | 3.00 | 1.50 |
| 41 | George Lauzerique | .80 | .40 |

| | | NR MT | EX |
|---|---|---|---|
| 42 | Tito Fuentes | .80 | .40 |
| 43 | Jack Aker | .80 | .40 |
| 44 | Roberto Pena | .80 | .40 |
| 45 | Dave Johnson | 1.50 | .70 |
| 46 | Ken Rudolph | .80 | .40 |
| 47 | Bob Miller | .80 | .40 |
| 48 | Gill Garrido (Gil) | .80 | .40 |
| 49 | Tim Cullen | .80 | .40 |
| 50 | Tommie Agee | .90 | .45 |
| 51 | Bob Christian | .80 | .40 |
| 52 | Bruce Dal Canton | .80 | .40 |
| 53 | John Kennedy | .80 | .40 |
| 54 | Jeff Torborg | .90 | .45 |
| 55 | John Odom | .90 | .45 |
| 56 | Phillies Rookies (Joe Lis, Scott Reid) | .80 | .40 |
| 57 | Pat Kelly | .80 | .40 |
| 58 | Dave Marshall | .80 | .40 |
| 59 | Dick Ellsworth | .80 | .40 |
| 60 | Jim Wynn | 1.00 | .50 |
| 61 | N.L. Batting Leaders (Bob Clemente, Cleon Jones, Pete Rose) | 5.00 | 2.50 |
| 62 | A.L. Batting Leaders (Rod Carew, Tony Oliva, Reggie Smith) | 3.50 | 1.75 |
| 63 | N.L. RBI Leaders (Willie McCovey, Tony Perez, Ron Santo) | 3.50 | 1.75 |
| 64 | A.L. RBI Leaders (Reggie Jackson, Harmon Killebrew, Boog Powell) | 3.50 | 1.75 |
| 65 | N.L. Home Run Leaders (Hank Aaron, Lee May, Willie McCovey) | 3.00 | 1.50 |
| 66 | A.L. Home Run Leaders (Frank Howard, Reggie Jackson, Harmon Killebrew) | 3.50 | 1.75 |
| 67 | N.L. ERA Leaders (Steve Carlton, Bob Gibson, Juan Marichal) | 3.00 | 1.50 |
| 68 | A.L. ERA Leaders (Dick Bosman, Mike Cuellar, Jim Palmer) | 3.00 | 1.50 |
| 69 | N.L. Pitching Leaders (Fergie Jenkins, Juan Marichal, Phil Niekro, Tom Seaver) | 3.50 | 1.75 |
| 70 | A.L. Pitching Leaders (Dave Boswell, Mike Cuellar, Dennis McLain, Dave McNally, Jim Perry, Mel Stottlemyre) | 3.00 | 1.50 |
| 71 | N.L. Strikeout Leaders (Bob Gibson, Fergie Jenkins, Bill Singer) | 3.50 | 1.75 |
| 72 | A.L. Strikeout Leaders (Mickey Lolich, Sam McDowell, Andy Messersmith) | 3.00 | 1.50 |
| 73 | Wayne Granger | .80 | .40 |
| 74 | Angels Rookies (Greg Washburn, Wally Wolf) | .80 | .40 |
| 75 | Jim Kaat | 3.00 | 1.50 |
| 76 | Carl Taylor | .80 | .40 |
| 77 | Frank Linzy | .80 | .40 |

| | | NR MT | EX |
|---|---|---|---|
| 78 | Joe Lahoud | .80 | .40 |
| 79 | Clay Kirby | .80 | .40 |
| 80 | Don Kessinger | .90 | .45 |
| 81 | Dave May | .80 | .40 |
| 82 | Frank Fernandez | .80 | .40 |
| 83 | Don Cardwell | .80 | .40 |
| 84 | Paul Casanova | .80 | .40 |
| 85 | Max Alvis | .80 | .40 |
| 86 | Lum Harris | .80 | .40 |
| 87 | Steve Renko | .80 | .40 |
| 88 | Pilots Rookies (Dick Baney, Miguel Fuentes) | .80 | .40 |
| 89 | Juan Rios | .80 | .40 |
| 90 | Tim McCarver | 1.50 | .70 |
| 91 | Rich Morales | .80 | .40 |
| 92 | George Culver | .80 | .40 |
| 93 | Rick Renick | .80 | .40 |
| 94 | Fred Patek | .90 | .45 |
| 95 | Earl Wilson | .80 | .40 |
| 96 | Cards Rookies (Leron Lee, *Jerry Reuss*) | 3.00 | 1.50 |
| 97 | Joe Moeller | .80 | .40 |
| 98 | Gates Brown | .80 | .40 |
| 99 | Bobby Pfeil | .80 | .40 |
| 100 | Mel Stottlemyre | 1.50 | .70 |
| 101 | Bobby Floyd | .80 | .40 |
| 102 | Joe Rudi | 1.50 | .70 |
| 103 | Frank Reberger | .80 | .40 |
| 104 | Gerry Moses | .80 | .40 |
| 105 | Tony Gonzalez | .80 | .40 |
| 106 | Darold Knowles | .80 | .40 |
| 107 | Bobby Etheridge | .80 | .40 |
| 108 | Tom Burgmeier | .90 | .45 |
| 109 | Expos Rookies (Garry Jestadt, Carl Morton) | .90 | .45 |
| 110 | Bob Moose | .80 | .40 |
| 111 | Mike Hegan | .80 | .40 |
| 112 | Dave Nelson | .80 | .40 |
| 113 | Jim Ray | .80 | .40 |
| 114 | Gene Michael | 1.00 | .50 |
| 115 | Alex Johnson | .90 | .45 |
| 116 | Sparky Lyle | 1.50 | .70 |
| 117 | Don Young | .80 | .40 |
| 118 | George Mitterwald | .80 | .40 |
| 119 | Chuck Taylor | .80 | .40 |
| 120 | Sal Bando | 1.50 | .70 |
| 121 | Orioles Rookies (Fred Beene, *Terry Crowley*) | .90 | .45 |
| 122 | George Stone | .80 | .40 |
| 123 | Don Gutteridge | .80 | .40 |
| 124 | Larry Jaster | .80 | .40 |
| 125 | Deron Johnson | .80 | .40 |
| 126 | Marty Martinez | .80 | .40 |
| 127 | Joe Coleman | .90 | .45 |
| 128a | Checklist 133-263 (226 is R Perranoski) | 3.00 | 1.50 |
| 128b | Checklist 133-263 (226 is R. Perranoski) | 3.50 | 1.75 |
| 129 | Jimmie Price | .80 | .40 |
| 130 | Ollie Brown | .80 | .40 |
| 131 | Dodgers Rookies (Ray Lamb, Bob Stinson) | .80 | .40 |
| 132 | Jim McGlothlin | .80 | .40 |
| 133 | Clay Carroll | .90 | .45 |
| 134 | Danny Walton | .80 | .40 |
| 135 | Dick Dietz | .80 | .40 |
| 136 | Steve Hargan | .80 | .40 |
| 137 | Art Shamsky | .80 | .40 |
| 138 | Joe Foy | .80 | .40 |
| 139 | Rich Nye | .80 | .40 |
| 140 | Reggie Jackson | 175.00 | 87.00 |
| 141 | Pirates Rookies (*Dave Cash*, Johnny Jeter) | .80 | .40 |
| 142 | Fritz Peterson | .80 | .40 |
| 143 | Phil Gagliano | .80 | .40 |
| 144 | Ray Culp | .80 | .40 |
| 145 | Rico Carty | 1.50 | .70 |
| 146 | Danny Murphy | .80 | .40 |
| 147 | Angel Hermoso | .80 | .40 |
| 148 | Earl Weaver | 1.75 | .90 |
| 149 | Billy Champion | .80 | .40 |
| 150 | Harmon Killebrew | 7.00 | 3.50 |
| 151 | Dave Roberts | .80 | .40 |
| 152 | Ike Brown | .80 | .40 |
| 153 | Gary Gentry | .80 | .40 |
| 154 | Senators Rookies (Jan Dukes, Jim Miles) | .80 | .40 |
| 155 | Denis Menke | .80 | .40 |
| 156 | Eddie Fisher | .80 | .40 |
| 157 | Manny Mota | .80 | .40 |
| 158 | Jerry McNertney | .80 | .40 |
| 159 | Tommy Helms | .90 | .45 |
| 160 | Phil Niekro | 3.50 | 1.75 |
| 161 | Richie Scheinblum | .80 | .40 |
| 162 | Jerry Johnson | .80 | .40 |
| 163 | Syd O'Brien | .80 | .40 |
| 164 | Ty Cline | .80 | .40 |
| 165 | Ed Kirkpatrick | .80 | .40 |
| 166 | Al Oliver | 3.00 | 1.50 |
| 167 | Bill Burbach | .80 | .40 |
| 168 | Dave Watkins | .80 | .40 |
| 169 | Tom Hall | .80 | .40 |
| 170 | Billy Williams | 6.00 | 3.00 |
| 171 | Jim Nash | .80 | .40 |
| 172 | Braves Rookies (*Ralph Garr*, Garry Hill) | 1.50 | .70 |
| 173 | Jim Hicks | .80 | .40 |
| 174 | Ted Sizemore | .80 | .40 |
| 175 | Dick Bosman | .80 | .40 |
| 176 | Jim Hart | .90 | .45 |
| 177 | Jim Northrup | .90 | .45 |
| 178 | Denny Lemaster | .80 | .40 |
| 179 | Ivan Murrell | .80 | .40 |
| 180 | Tommy John | 4.00 | 2.00 |
| 181 | Sparky Anderson | 1.75 | .90 |
| 182 | Dick Hall | .80 | .40 |
| 183 | Jerry Grote | .90 | .45 |
| 184 | Ray Fosse | .90 | .45 |
| 185 | Don Mincher | .80 | .40 |
| 186 | Rick Joseph | .80 | .40 |
| 187 | Mike Hedlund | .80 | .40 |
| 188 | Manny Sanguillen | .90 | .45 |
| 189 | Yankees Rookies (Dave McDonald, *Thurman Munson*) | 90.00 | 45.00 |
| 190 | Joe Torre | 1.75 | .90 |
| 191 | Vicente Romo | .80 | .40 |
| 192 | Jim Qualls | .80 | .40 |
| 193 | Mike Wegener | .80 | .40 |
| 194 | Chuck Manuel | .80 | .40 |
| 195 | N.L. Playoff Game 1 (Seaver Wins Opener!) | 4.00 | 2.00 |
| 196 | N.L. Playoff Game 2 (Mets Show Muscle!) | 3.50 | 1.75 |

| | | NR MT | EX |
|---|---|---|---|
| 197 | N.L. Playoff Game 3 (Ryan Saves The Day!) | 6.00 | 3.00 |
| 198 | N.L. Playoffs Summary (We're Number One!) | 3.50 | 1.75 |
| 199 | A.L. Playoff Game 1 (Orioles Win A Squeaker!) | 3.00 | 1.50 |
| 200 | A.L. Playoff Game 2 (Powell Scores Winning Run!) | 3.50 | 1.75 |
| 201 | A.L. Playoff Game 3 (Birds Wrap It Up!) | 3.00 | 1.50 |
| 202 | A.L. Playoffs Summary (Sweep Twins In Three!) | 3.00 | 1.50 |
| 203 | Rudy May | .90 | .45 |
| 204 | Len Gabrielson | .80 | .40 |
| 205 | Bert Campaneris | 1.50 | .70 |
| 206 | Clete Boyer | .90 | .45 |
| 207 | Tigers Rookies (Norman McRae, Bob Reed) | .80 | .40 |
| 208 | Fred Gladding | .80 | .40 |
| 209 | Ken Suarez | .80 | .40 |
| 210 | Juan Marichal | 8.00 | 4.00 |
| 211 | Ted Williams | 7.00 | 3.50 |
| 212 | Al Santorini | .80 | .40 |
| 213 | Andy Etchebarren | .80 | .40 |
| 214 | Ken Boswell | .80 | .40 |
| 215 | Reggie Smith | 1.00 | .50 |
| 216 | Chuck Hartenstein | .80 | .40 |
| 217 | Ron Hansen | .80 | .40 |
| 218 | Ron Stone | .80 | .40 |
| 219 | Jerry Kenney | .80 | .40 |
| 220 | Steve Carlton | 40.00 | 20.00 |
| 221 | Ron Brand | .80 | .40 |
| 222 | Jim Rooker | .80 | .40 |
| 223 | Nate Oliver | .80 | .40 |
| 224 | Steve Barber | .80 | .40 |
| 225 | Lee May | 1.00 | .50 |
| 226 | Ron Perranoski | .90 | .45 |
| 227 | Astros Rookies (John Mayberry, Bob Watkins) | 1.50 | .70 |
| 228 | Aurelio Rodriguez | .90 | .45 |
| 229 | Rich Robertson | .80 | .40 |
| 230 | Brooks Robinson | 12.00 | 6.00 |
| 231 | Luis Tiant | 1.75 | .90 |
| 232 | Bob Didier | .80 | .40 |
| 233 | Lew Krausse | .80 | .40 |
| 234 | Tommy Dean | .80 | .40 |
| 235 | Mike Epstein | .90 | .45 |
| 236 | Bob Veale | .90 | .45 |
| 237 | Russ Gibson | .80 | .40 |
| 238 | Jose Laboy | .80 | .40 |
| 239 | Ken Berry | .80 | .40 |
| 240 | Fergie Jenkins | 10.00 | 5.00 |
| 241 | Royals Rookies (Al Fitzmorris, Scott Northey) | .80 | .40 |
| 242 | Walter Alston | 3.50 | 1.75 |
| 243 | Joe Sparma | .80 | .40 |
| 244a | Checklist 264-372 (red bat on front) | 3.00 | 1.50 |
| 244b | Checklist 264-372 (brown bat on front) | 3.50 | 1.75 |
| 245 | Leo Cardenas | .80 | .40 |
| 246 | Jim McAndrew | .80 | .40 |
| 247 | Lou Klimchock | .80 | .40 |
| 248 | Jesus Alou | .90 | .45 |
| 249 | Bob Locker | .80 | .40 |
| 250 | Willie McCovey | 8.00 | 4.00 |
| 251 | Dick Schofield | .80 | .40 |
| 252 | Lowell Palmer | .80 | .40 |
| 253 | Ron Woods | .80 | .40 |
| 254 | Camilo Pascual | .80 | .40 |
| 255 | *Jim Spencer* | .80 | .40 |
| 256 | Vic Davalillo | .90 | .45 |
| 257 | Dennis Higgins | .80 | .40 |
| 258 | Paul Popovich | .80 | .40 |
| 259 | Tommie Reynolds | .80 | .40 |
| 260 | Claude Osteen | .80 | .40 |
| 261 | Curt Motton | .80 | .40 |
| 262 | Padres Rookies (Jerry Morales, Jim Williams) | .80 | .40 |
| 263 | Duane Josephson | .80 | .40 |
| 264 | Rich Hebner | .90 | .45 |
| 265 | Randy Hundley | .80 | .40 |
| 266 | Wally Bunker | .80 | .40 |
| 267 | Twins Rookies (Herman Hill, Paul Ratliff) | .80 | .40 |
| 268 | Claude Raymond | .80 | .40 |
| 269 | Cesar Gutierrez | .80 | .40 |
| 270 | Chris Short | .90 | .45 |
| 271 | Greg Goossen | .80 | .40 |
| 272 | Hector Torres | .80 | .40 |
| 273 | Ralph Houk | 1.50 | .70 |
| 274 | Gerry Arrigo | .80 | .40 |
| 275 | Duke Sims | .80 | .40 |
| 276 | Ron Hunt | .90 | .45 |
| 277 | Paul Doyle | .80 | .40 |
| 278 | Tommie Aaron | .80 | .40 |
| 279 | *Bill Lee* | .80 | .40 |
| 280 | Donn Clendenon | .90 | .45 |
| 281 | Casey Cox | .80 | .40 |
| 282 | Steve Huntz | .80 | .40 |
| 283 | Angel Bravo | .80 | .40 |
| 284 | Jack Baldschun | .80 | .40 |
| 285 | Paul Blair | .90 | .45 |
| 286 | Dodgers Rookies (*Bill Buckner*, Jack Jenkins) | 6.00 | 3.00 |
| 287 | Fred Talbot | .80 | .40 |
| 288 | Larry Hisle | .90 | .45 |
| 289 | Gene Brabender | .80 | .40 |
| 290 | Rod Carew | 60.00 | 30.00 |
| 291 | Leo Durocher | 1.75 | .90 |
| 292 | Eddie Leon | .80 | .40 |
| 293 | Bob Bailey | .80 | .40 |
| 294 | Jose Azcue | .80 | .40 |
| 295 | Cecil Upshaw | .80 | .40 |
| 296 | Woody Woodward | .90 | .45 |
| 297 | Curt Blefary | .80 | .40 |
| 298 | Ken Henderson | .80 | .40 |
| 299 | Buddy Bradford | .80 | .40 |
| 300 | Tom Seaver | 110.00 | 55.00 |
| 301 | Chico Salmon | .80 | .40 |
| 302 | Jeff James | .80 | .40 |
| 303 | Brant Alyea | .80 | .40 |
| 304 | *Bill Russell* | 3.00 | 1.50 |
| 305 | World Series Game 1 (Buford Belts Leadoff Homer!) | 3.50 | 1.75 |
| 306 | World Series Game 2 (Clendenon's Homer Breaks | | |

| | NR MT | EX |
|---|---|---|
| Ice!) | 3.50 | 1.75 |
| 307 World Series Game 3 (Agee's Catch Saves The Day!) | 3.50 | 1.75 |
| 308 World Series Game 4 (Martin's Bunt Ends Deadlock!) | 3.50 | 1.75 |
| 309 World Series Game 5 (Koosman Shuts The Door!) | 3.50 | 1.75 |
| 310 World Series Summary (Mets Whoop It Up!) | 3.50 | 1.75 |
| 311 Dick Green | .80 | .40 |
| 312 Mike Torrez | .90 | .45 |
| 313 Mayo Smith | .80 | .40 |
| 314 Bill McCool | .80 | .40 |
| 315 Luis Aparicio | 4.50 | 2.25 |
| 316 Skip Guinn | .80 | .40 |
| 317 Red Sox Rookies (Luis Alvarado, Billy Conigliaro) | .90 | .45 |
| 318 Willie Smith | .80 | .40 |
| 319 Clayton Dalrymple | .80 | .40 |
| 320 Jim Maloney | .90 | .45 |
| 321 Lou Piniella | 3.00 | 1.50 |
| 322 Luke Walker | .80 | .40 |
| 323 Wayne Comer | .80 | .40 |
| 324 Tony Taylor | .80 | .40 |
| 325 Dave Boswell | .80 | .40 |
| 326 Bill Voss | .80 | .40 |
| 327 Hal King | .80 | .40 |
| 328 George Brunet | .80 | .40 |
| 329 Chris Cannizzaro | .80 | .40 |
| 330 Lou Brock | 8.00 | 4.00 |
| 331 Chuck Dobson | .80 | .40 |
| 332 Bobby Wine | .80 | .40 |
| 333 Bobby Murcer | 1.75 | .90 |
| 334 Phil Regan | .80 | .40 |
| 335 Bill Freehan | .90 | .45 |
| 336 Del Unser | .80 | .40 |
| 337 Mike McCormick | .90 | .45 |
| 338 Paul Schaal | .80 | .40 |
| 339 Johnny Edwards | .80 | .40 |
| 340 Tony Conigliaro | 1.75 | .90 |
| 341 Bill Sudakis | .80 | .40 |
| 342 Wilbur Wood | .90 | .45 |
| 343a Checklist 373-459 (red bat on front) | 3.50 | 1.75 |
| 343b Checklist 373-459 (brown bat on front) | 3.00 | 1.50 |
| 344 Marcelino Lopez | .80 | .40 |
| 345 Al Ferrara | .80 | .40 |
| 346 Red Schoendienst | 1.75 | .90 |
| 347 Russ Snyder | .80 | .40 |
| 348 Mets Rookies (Jesse Hudson, Mike Jorgensen) | .90 | .45 |
| 349 Steve Hamilton | .80 | .40 |
| 350 Roberto Clemente | 50.00 | 25.00 |
| 351 Tom Murphy | .80 | .40 |
| 352 Bob Barton | .80 | .40 |
| 353 Stan Williams | .80 | .40 |
| 354 Amos Otis | .80 | .40 |
| 355 Doug Rader | .80 | .40 |
| 356 Fred Lasher | .80 | .40 |
| 357 Bob Burda | .80 | .40 |

| | NR MT | EX |
|---|---|---|
| 358 *Pedro Borbon* | .90 | .45 |
| 359 Phil Roof | .80 | .40 |
| 360 Curt Flood | 1.50 | .70 |
| 361 Ray Jarvis | .80 | .40 |
| 362 Joe Hague | .80 | .40 |
| 363 Tom Shopay | .80 | .40 |
| 364 Dan McGinn | .80 | .40 |
| 365 Zoilo Versalles | .90 | .45 |
| 366 Barry Moore | .80 | .40 |
| 367 Mike Lum | .80 | .40 |
| 368 Ed Herrmann | .80 | .40 |
| 369 Alan Foster | .80 | .40 |
| 370 Tommy Harper | .70 | .35 |
| 371 Rod Gaspar | .80 | .40 |
| 372 Dave Giusti | .80 | .40 |
| 373 Roy White | 1.50 | .70 |
| 374 Tommie Sisk | .80 | .40 |
| 375 Johnny Callison | 1.50 | .70 |
| 376 Lefty Phillips | .80 | .40 |
| 377 Bill Butler | .80 | .40 |
| 378 Jim Davenport | .80 | .40 |
| 379 Tom Tischinski | .80 | .40 |
| 380 Tony Perez | 3.00 | 1.50 |
| 381 Athletics Rookies (Bobby Brooks, Mike Olivo) | .80 | .40 |
| 382 Jack DiLauro | .80 | .40 |
| 383 Mickey Stanley | .90 | .45 |
| 384 Gary Neibauer | .80 | .40 |
| 385 George Scott | .90 | .45 |
| 386 Bill Dillman | .80 | .40 |
| 387 Orioles Team | 3.00 | 1.50 |
| 388 Byron Browne | .80 | .40 |
| 389 Jim Shellenback | .80 | .40 |
| 390 Willie Davis | 1.50 | .70 |
| 391 Larry Brown | .80 | .40 |
| 392 Walt Hriniak | .80 | .40 |
| 393 John Gelnar | .80 | .40 |
| 394 Gil Hodges | 4.00 | 2.00 |
| 395 Walt Williams | .80 | .40 |
| 396 Steve Blass | .90 | .45 |
| 397 Roger Repoz | .80 | .40 |
| 398 Bill Stoneman | .80 | .40 |
| 399 Yankees Team | 3.00 | 1.50 |
| 400 Denny McLain | 3.00 | 1.50 |
| 401 Giants Rookies (John Harrell, Bernie Williams) | .80 | .40 |
| 402 Ellie Rodriguez | .80 | .40 |
| 403 Jim Bunning | 3.25 | 1.75 |
| 404 Rich Reese | .80 | .40 |
| 405 Bill Hands | .80 | .40 |
| 406 Mike Andrews | .80 | .40 |
| 407 Bob Watson | .90 | .45 |
| 408 Paul Lindblad | .80 | .40 |
| 409 Bob Tolan | .90 | .45 |
| 410 Boog Powell | 3.00 | 1.50 |
| 411 Dodgers Team | 3.00 | 1.50 |
| 412 Larry Burchart | .80 | .40 |
| 413 Sonny Jackson | .80 | .40 |
| 414 Paul Edmondson | .80 | .40 |
| 415 Julian Javier | .80 | .40 |
| 416 Joe Verbanic | .80 | .40 |
| 417 John Bateman | .80 | .40 |
| 418 John Donaldson | .80 | .40 |
| 419 Ron Taylor | .80 | .40 |
| 420 Ken McMullen | .80 | .40 |

| | | NR MT | EX |
|---|---|---|---|
| 421 | Pat Dobson | .90 | .45 |
| 422 | Royals Team | 1.75 | .90 |
| 423 | Jerry May | .80 | .40 |
| 424 | Mike Kilkenny | .80 | .40 |
| 425 | Bobby Bonds | 1.75 | .90 |
| 426 | Bill Rigney | .80 | .40 |
| 427 | Fred Norman | .80 | .40 |
| 428 | Don Buford | .90 | .45 |
| 429 | Cubs Rookies (Randy Bobb, Jim Cosman) | .80 | .40 |
| 430 | Andy Messersmith | .80 | .40 |
| 431 | Ron Swoboda | .90 | .45 |
| 432a | Checklist 460-546 ("Baseball" on front in yellow) | 4.00 | 2.00 |
| 432b | Checklist 460-546 ("Baseball" on front in white) | 3.50 | 1.75 |
| 433 | Ron Bryant | .80 | .40 |
| 434 | Felipe Alou | .70 | .35 |
| 435 | Nelson Briles | .80 | .40 |
| 436 | Phillies Team | 1.75 | .90 |
| 437 | Danny Cater | .80 | .40 |
| 438 | Pat Jarvis | .80 | .40 |
| 439 | Lee Maye | .80 | .40 |
| 440 | Bill Mazeroski | 1.50 | .70 |
| 441 | John O'Donoghue | .80 | .40 |
| 442 | Gene Mauch | .70 | .35 |
| 443 | Al Jackson | .80 | .40 |
| 444 | White Sox Rookies (Bill Farmer, John Matias) | .80 | .40 |
| 445 | Vada Pinson | 1.75 | .90 |
| 446 | *Billy Grabarkewitz* | .90 | .45 |
| 447 | Lee Stange | .80 | .40 |
| 448 | Astros Team | 1.75 | .90 |
| 449 | Jim Palmer | 25.00 | 12.50 |
| 450 | Willie McCovey AS | 3.50 | 1.75 |
| 451 | Boog Powell AS | 1.50 | .70 |
| 452 | Felix Millan AS | .80 | .40 |
| 453 | Rod Carew AS | 4.00 | 2.00 |
| 454 | Ron Santo AS | 1.50 | .70 |
| 455 | Brooks Robinson AS | 3.50 | 1.75 |
| 456 | Don Kessinger AS | .80 | .40 |
| 457 | Rico Petrocelli AS | .80 | .40 |
| 458 | Pete Rose AS | 8.00 | 4.00 |
| 459 | Reggie Jackson AS | 20.00 | 10.00 |
| 460 | Matty Alou AS | .70 | .35 |
| 461 | Carl Yastrzemski AS | 8.00 | 4.00 |
| 462 | Hank Aaron AS | 12.00 | 6.00 |
| 463 | Frank Robinson AS | 8.00 | 4.00 |
| 464 | Johnny Bench AS | 10.00 | 5.00 |
| 465 | Bill Freehan AS | .80 | .40 |
| 466 | Juan Marichal AS | 4.00 | 2.00 |
| 467 | Denny McLain AS | 1.50 | .70 |
| 468 | Jerry Koosman AS | 1.00 | .50 |
| 469 | Sam McDowell AS | 1.00 | .50 |
| 470 | Willie Stargell AS | 7.00 | 3.50 |
| 471 | Chris Zachary | .80 | .40 |
| 472 | Braves Team | 1.75 | .90 |
| 473 | Don Bryant | .80 | .40 |
| 474 | Dick Kelley | .80 | .40 |
| 475 | Dick McAuliffe | .90 | .45 |
| 476 | Don Shaw | .80 | .40 |
| 477 | Orioles Rookies (Roger Freed, Al Severinsen) | .80 | .40 |
| 478 | Bob Heise | .80 | .40 |
| 479 | Dick Woodson | .80 | .40 |
| 480 | Glenn Beckert | .90 | .45 |
| 481 | Jose Tartabull | .80 | .40 |
| 482 | Tom Hilgendorf | .80 | .40 |
| 483 | Gail Hopkins | .80 | .40 |
| 484 | Gary Nolan | .80 | .40 |
| 485 | Jay Johnstone | .80 | .40 |
| 486 | Terry Harmon | .80 | .40 |
| 487 | Cisco Carlos | .80 | .40 |
| 488 | J.C. Martin | .80 | .40 |
| 489 | Eddie Kasko | .80 | .40 |
| 490 | Bill Singer | .90 | .45 |
| 491 | Graig Nettles | 4.00 | 2.00 |
| 492 | Astros Rookies (Keith Lampard, Scipio Spinks) | .80 | .40 |
| 493 | Lindy McDaniel | .80 | .40 |
| 494 | Larry Stahl | .80 | .40 |
| 495 | Dave Morehead | .80 | .40 |
| 496 | Steve Whitaker | .80 | .40 |
| 497 | Eddie Watt | .80 | .40 |
| 498 | Al Weis | .80 | .40 |
| 499 | Skip Lockwood | .80 | .40 |
| 500 | Hank Aaron | 55.00 | 28.00 |
| 501 | White Sox Team | 1.75 | .90 |
| 502 | Rollie Fingers | 35.00 | 17.50 |
| 503 | Dal Maxvill | .90 | .45 |
| 504 | Don Pavletich | .80 | .40 |
| 505 | Ken Holtzman | .90 | .45 |
| 506 | Ed Stroud | .80 | .40 |
| 507 | Pat Corrales | .80 | .40 |
| 508 | Joe Niekro | .70 | .35 |
| 509 | Expos Team | 1.75 | .90 |
| 510 | Tony Oliva | 3.50 | 1.75 |
| 511 | Joe Hoerner | .80 | .40 |
| 512 | Billy Harris | .80 | .40 |
| 513 | Preston Gomez | .80 | .40 |
| 514 | Steve Hovley | .80 | .40 |
| 515 | Don Wilson | .80 | .40 |
| 516 | Yankees Rookies (John Ellis, Jim Lyttle) | .80 | .40 |
| 517 | Joe Gibbon | .80 | .40 |
| 518 | Bill Melton | .90 | .45 |
| 519 | Don McMahon | .80 | .40 |
| 520 | Willie Horton | .70 | .35 |
| 521 | Cal Koonce | .80 | .40 |
| 522 | Angels Team | 1.75 | .90 |
| 523 | Jose Pena | .80 | .40 |
| 524 | Alvin Dark | 1.00 | .50 |
| 525 | Jerry Adair | .80 | .40 |
| 526 | Ron Herbel | .80 | .40 |
| 527 | Don Bosch | .80 | .40 |
| 528 | Elrod Hendricks | .80 | .40 |
| 529 | Bob Aspromonte | .80 | .40 |
| 530 | Bob Gibson | 10.00 | 5.00 |
| 531 | Ron Clark | .80 | .40 |
| 532 | Danny Murtaugh | .80 | .40 |
| 533 | Buzz Stephen | .80 | .40 |
| 534 | Twins Team | 3.00 | 1.50 |
| 535 | Andy Kosco | .80 | .40 |
| 536 | Mike Kekich | .80 | .40 |
| 537 | Joe Morgan | 10.00 | 5.00 |
| 538 | Bob Humphreys | .80 | .40 |
| 539 | Phillies Rookies (*Larry Bowa*, Dennis Doyle) | 3.00 | 1.50 |

| | | NR MT | EX |
|---|---|---|---|
| 540 | Gary Peters | .90 | .45 |
| 541 | Bill Heath | .80 | .40 |
| 542a | Checklist 547-633 (grey bat on front) | 3.50 | 1.75 |
| 542b | Checklist 547-633 (brown bat on front) | 3.50 | 1.75 |
| 543 | Clyde Wright | .80 | .40 |
| 544 | Reds Team | 1.75 | .90 |
| 545 | Ken Harrelson | 1.75 | .90 |
| 546 | Ron Reed | .90 | .45 |
| 547 | Rick Monday | 1.50 | .70 |
| 548 | Howie Reed | 1.50 | .70 |
| 549 | Cardinals Team | 3.50 | 1.75 |
| 550 | Frank Howard | 3.50 | 1.75 |
| 551 | Dock Ellis | 1.50 | .70 |
| 552 | Royals Rookies (Don O'Riley, Dennis Paepke, Fred Rico) | 1.50 | .70 |
| 553 | Jim Lefebvre | 1.50 | .70 |
| 554 | Tom Timmermann | 1.50 | .70 |
| 555 | Orlando Cepeda | 3.50 | 1.75 |
| 556 | Dave Bristol | 1.50 | .70 |
| 557 | Ed Kranepool | 1.50 | .70 |
| 558 | Vern Fuller | 1.50 | .70 |
| 559 | Tommy Davis | 1.75 | .90 |
| 560 | Gaylord Perry | 10.00 | 5.00 |
| 561 | Tom McCraw | 1.50 | .70 |
| 562 | Ted Abernathy | 1.50 | .70 |
| 563 | Red Sox Team | 3.00 | 1.50 |
| 564 | Johnny Briggs | 1.50 | .70 |
| 565 | Jim Hunter | 7.00 | 3.50 |
| 566 | Gene Alley | 1.50 | .70 |
| 567 | Bob Oliver | 1.50 | .70 |
| 568 | Stan Bahnsen | 1.50 | .70 |
| 569 | Cookie Rojas | 1.50 | .70 |
| 570 | Jim Fregosi | 1.50 | .70 |
| 571 | Jim Brewer | 1.50 | .70 |
| 572 | Frank Quilici | 1.50 | .70 |
| 573 | Padres Rookies (Mike Corkins, Rafael Robles, Ron Slocum) | 1.50 | .70 |
| 574 | Bobby Bolin | 1.50 | .70 |
| 575 | Cleon Jones | 1.50 | .70 |
| 576 | Milt Pappas | 1.50 | .70 |
| 577 | Bernie Allen | 1.50 | .70 |
| 578 | Tom Griffin | 1.50 | .70 |
| 579 | Tigers Team | 3.50 | 1.75 |
| 580 | Pete Rose | 60.00 | 30.00 |
| 581 | Tom Satriano | 1.50 | .70 |
| 582 | Mike Paul | 1.50 | .70 |
| 583 | Hal Lanier | 1.50 | .70 |
| 584 | Al Downing | 1.50 | .70 |
| 585 | Rusty Staub | 3.00 | 1.50 |
| 586 | Rickey Clark | 1.50 | .70 |
| 587 | Jose Arcia | 1.50 | .70 |
| 588a | Checklist 634-720 (666 is Adolpho Phillips) | 4.50 | 2.25 |
| 588b | Checklist 634-720 (666 is Adolfo Phillips) | 3.00 | 1.50 |
| 589 | Joe Keough | 1.50 | .70 |
| 590 | Mike Cuellar | 1.50 | .70 |
| 591 | Mike Ryan | 1.50 | .70 |
| 592 | Daryl Patterson | 1.50 | .70 |
| 593 | Cubs Team | 3.50 | 1.75 |
| 594 | Jake Gibbs | 1.50 | .70 |
| 595 | Maury Wills | 3.50 | 1.75 |
| 596 | Mike Hershberger | 1.50 | .70 |
| 597 | Sonny Siebert | 1.50 | .70 |
| 598 | Joe Pepitone | 1.75 | .90 |
| 599 | Senators Rookies (Gene Martin, Dick Stelmaszek, Dick Such) | 1.50 | .70 |
| 600 | Willie Mays | 80.00 | 40.00 |
| 601 | Pete Richert | 1.50 | .70 |
| 602 | Ted Savage | 1.50 | .70 |
| 603 | Ray Oyler | 1.50 | .70 |
| 604 | Clarence Gaston | 1.50 | .70 |
| 605 | Rick Wise | 1.50 | .70 |
| 606 | Chico Ruiz | 1.50 | .70 |
| 607 | Gary Waslewski | 1.50 | .70 |
| 608 | Pirates Team | 3.50 | 1.75 |
| 609 | *Buck Martinez* | 1.50 | .70 |
| 610 | Jerry Koosman | 1.75 | .90 |
| 611 | Norm Cash | 3.00 | 1.50 |
| 612 | Jim Hickman | 1.50 | .70 |
| 613 | Dave Baldwin | 1.50 | .70 |
| 614 | Mike Shannon | 1.50 | .70 |
| 615 | Mark Belanger | 1.50 | .70 |
| 616 | Jim Merritt | 1.50 | .70 |
| 617 | Jim French | 1.50 | .70 |
| 618 | Billy Wynne | 1.50 | .70 |
| 619 | Norm Miller | 1.50 | .70 |
| 620 | Jim Perry | 1.50 | .70 |
| 621 | Braves Rookies (*Darrell Evans*, Rick Kester, Mike McQueen) | 20.00 | 10.00 |
| 622 | Don Sutton | 7.00 | 3.50 |
| 623 | Horace Clarke | 1.50 | .70 |
| 624 | Clyde King | 1.50 | .70 |
| 625 | Dean Chance | 1.50 | .70 |
| 626 | Dave Ricketts | 1.50 | .70 |
| 627 | Gary Wagner | 1.50 | .70 |
| 628 | Wayne Garrett | 1.50 | .70 |
| 629 | Merv Rettenmund | 1.50 | .70 |
| 630 | Ernie Banks | 30.00 | 15.00 |
| 631 | Athletics Team | 3.50 | 1.75 |
| 632 | Gary Sutherland | 1.50 | .70 |
| 633 | Roger Nelson | 1.50 | .70 |
| 634 | Bud Harrelson | 3.50 | 1.75 |
| 635 | Bob Allison | 3.50 | 1.75 |
| 636 | Jim Stewart | 3.00 | 1.50 |
| 637 | Indians Team | 3.00 | 1.50 |
| 638 | Frank Bertaina | 3.00 | 1.50 |
| 639 | Dave Campbell | 3.00 | 1.50 |
| 640 | Al Kaline | 50.00 | 25.00 |
| 641 | Al McBean | 3.00 | 1.50 |
| 642 | Angels Rookies (Greg Garrett, Gordon Lund, Jarvis Tatum) | 3.00 | 1.50 |
| 643 | Jose Pagan | 3.00 | 1.50 |
| 644 | Gerry Nyman | 3.00 | 1.50 |
| 645 | Don Money | 3.00 | 1.50 |
| 646 | Jim Britton | 3.00 | 1.50 |
| 647 | Tom Matchick | 3.00 | 1.50 |
| 648 | Larry Haney | 3.00 | 1.50 |
| 649 | Jimmie Hall | 3.00 | 1.50 |
| 650 | Sam McDowell | 3.50 | 1.75 |
| 651 | Jim Gosger | 3.00 | 1.50 |
| 652 | Rich Rollins | 3.50 | 1.75 |
| 653 | Moe Drabowsky | 3.00 | 1.50 |
| 654 | N.L. Rookies (Boots Day, *Oscar Gamble*, Angel Mangual) | 3.50 | 1.75 |
| 655 | John Roseboro | 3.50 | 1.75 |

| | | NR MT | EX |
|---|---|---|---|
| 656 | Jim Hardin | 3.00 | 1.50 |
| 657 | Padres Team | 4.00 | 2.00 |
| 658 | Ken Tatum | 3.00 | 1.50 |
| 659 | Pete Ward | 3.50 | 1.75 |
| 660 | Johnny Bench | 150.00 | 75.00 |
| 661 | Jerry Robertson | 3.00 | 1.50 |
| 662 | Frank Lucchesi | 3.00 | 1.50 |
| 663 | Tito Francona | 3.50 | 1.75 |
| 664 | Bob Robertson | 3.00 | 1.50 |
| 665 | Jim Lonborg | 3.50 | 1.75 |
| 666 | Adolfo Phillips | 3.00 | 1.50 |
| 667 | Bob Meyer | 3.50 | 1.75 |
| 668 | Bob Tillman | 3.00 | 1.50 |
| 669 | White Sox Rookies (Bart Johnson, Dan Lazar, Mickey Scott) | 3.00 | 1.50 |
| 670 | Ron Santo | 3.25 | 1.75 |
| 671 | Jim Campanis | 3.00 | 1.50 |
| 672 | Leon McFadden | 3.00 | 1.50 |
| 673 | Ted Uhlaender | 3.00 | 1.50 |
| 674 | Dave Leonhard | 3.00 | 1.50 |
| 675 | Jose Cardenal | 3.50 | 1.75 |
| 676 | Senators Team | 3.25 | 1.75 |
| 677 | Woodie Fryman | 3.50 | 1.75 |
| 678 | Dave Duncan | 3.00 | 1.50 |
| 679 | Ray Sadecki | 3.00 | 1.50 |
| 680 | Rico Petrocelli | 3.50 | 1.75 |
| 681 | Bob Garibaldi | 3.00 | 1.50 |
| 682 | Dalton Jones | 3.00 | 1.50 |
| 683 | Reds Rookies (Vern Geishert, Hal McRae, Wayne Simpson) | 4.00 | 2.00 |
| 684 | Jack Fisher | 3.00 | 1.50 |
| 685 | Tom Haller | 3.50 | 1.75 |
| 686 | Jackie Hernandez | 3.00 | 1.50 |
| 687 | Bob Priddy | 3.00 | 1.50 |
| 688 | Ted Kubiak | 3.50 | 1.75 |
| 689 | Frank Tepedino | 3.50 | 1.75 |
| 690 | Ron Fairly | 3.50 | 1.75 |
| 691 | Joe Grzenda | 3.00 | 1.50 |
| 692 | Duffy Dyer | 3.00 | 1.50 |
| 693 | Bob Johnson | 3.00 | 1.50 |
| 694 | Gary Ross | 3.00 | 1.50 |
| 695 | Bobby Knoop | 3.00 | 1.50 |
| 696 | Giants Team | 3.25 | 1.75 |
| 697 | Jim Hannan | 3.00 | 1.50 |
| 698 | Tom Tresh | 4.00 | 2.00 |
| 699 | Hank Aguirre | 3.00 | 1.50 |
| 700 | Frank Robinson | 50.00 | 25.00 |
| 701 | Jack Billingham | 3.00 | 1.50 |
| 702 | A.L. Rookies (Bob Johnson, Ron Klimkowski, Bill Zepp) | 3.50 | 1.75 |
| 703 | Lou Marone | 3.00 | 1.50 |
| 704 | Frank Baker | 3.00 | 1.50 |
| 705 | Tony Cloninger | 3.50 | 1.75 |
| 706 | John McNamara | 3.50 | 1.75 |
| 707 | Kevin Collins | 3.00 | 1.50 |
| 708 | Jose Santiago | 3.00 | 1.50 |
| 709 | Mike Fiore | 3.00 | 1.50 |
| 710 | Felix Millan | 3.00 | 1.50 |
| 711 | Ed Brinkman | 3.50 | 1.75 |
| 712 | Nolan Ryan | 500.00 | 250.00 |
| 713 | Pilots Team | 15.00 | 7.50 |
| 714 | Al Spangler | 3.00 | 1.50 |
| 715 | Mickey Lolich | 5.00 | 2.50 |

| | | NR MT | EX |
|---|---|---|---|
| 716 | Cards Rookies (Sal Campisi, *Reggie Cleveland*, Santiago Guzman) | 3.50 | 1.75 |
| 717 | Tom Phoebus | 3.00 | 1.50 |
| 718 | Ed Spiezio | 3.00 | 1.50 |
| 719 | Jim Roland | 3.50 | 1.75 |
| 720 | Rick Reichardt | 4.00 | 1.00 |

# 1971 Topps

In 1971, Topps again increased the size of its set to 752 cards. These well-liked cards, measuring 2-1/2" by 3-1/2," feature a large color photo which has a thin white frame. Above the picture, in the card's overall black border, is the player's name, team and position. A facsimile autograph completes the front. Backs feature a major change as a black and white "snapshot" of the player appears. Abbreviated statistics, a line giving the player's first pro and major league games and a short biography complete the back of these innovative cards. Specialty cards in this issue are limited. There are statistical leaders as well as World Series and playoff highlights. High numbered cards #644-752 are scarce.

| | | NR MT | EX |
|---|---|---|---|
| Complete Set: | | 2200.00 | 1100.00 |
| Common Player: 1-523 | | .70 | .35 |
| Common Player: 524-643 | | 1.75 | .90 |
| Common Player: 644-752 | | 3.00 | 1.50 |
| 1 | World Champions (Orioles Team) | 12.00 | 6.00 |
| 2 | Dock Ellis | .80 | .40 |
| 3 | Dick McAuliffe | .80 | .40 |
| 4 | Vic Davalillo | .80 | .40 |
| 5 | Thurman Munson | 30.00 | 15.00 |
| 6 | Ed Spiezio | .70 | .35 |
| 7 | Jim Holt | .70 | .35 |

| | | NR MT | EX |
|---|---|---|---|
| 8 | Mike McQueen | .70 | .35 |
| 9 | George Scott | .80 | .40 |
| 10 | Claude Osteen | .80 | .40 |
| 11 | Elliott Maddox | .80 | .40 |
| 12 | Johnny Callison | 2.00 | 1.00 |
| 13 | White Sox Rookies (Charlie Brinkman, Dick Moloney) | .70 | .35 |
| 14 | Dave Concepcion | 20.00 | 10.00 |
| 15 | Andy Messersmith | .80 | .40 |
| 16 | Ken Singleton | 2.25 | 1.25 |
| 17 | Billy Sorrell | .70 | .35 |
| 18 | Norm Miller | .70 | .35 |
| 19 | Skip Pitlock | .70 | .35 |
| 20 | Reggie Jackson | 90.00 | 45.00 |
| 21 | Dan McGinn | .70 | .35 |
| 22 | Phil Roof | .70 | .35 |
| 23 | Oscar Gamble | .80 | .40 |
| 24 | Rich Hand | .70 | .35 |
| 25 | Clarence Gaston | .70 | .35 |
| 26 | Bert Blyleven | 50.00 | 25.00 |
| 27 | Pirates Rookies (Fred Cambria, Gene Clines) | .70 | .35 |
| 28 | Ron Klimkowski | .80 | .40 |
| 29 | Don Buford | .80 | .40 |
| 30 | Phil Niekro | 3.25 | 1.75 |
| 31 | Eddie Kasko | .70 | .35 |
| 32 | Jerry DaVanon | .70 | .35 |
| 33 | Del Unser | .70 | .35 |
| 34 | Sandy Vance | .70 | .35 |
| 35 | Lou Piniella | 1.25 | .60 |
| 36 | Dean Chance | .80 | .40 |
| 37 | Rich McKinney | .70 | .35 |
| 38 | Jim Colborn | .80 | .40 |
| 39 | Tigers Rookies (Gene Lamont, Lerrin LaGrow) | .80 | .40 |
| 40 | Lee May | 2.00 | 1.00 |
| 41 | Rick Austin | .70 | .35 |
| 42 | Boots Day | .70 | .35 |
| 43 | Steve Kealey | .70 | .35 |
| 44 | Johnny Edwards | .70 | .35 |
| 45 | Jim Hunter | 5.00 | 2.50 |
| 46 | Dave Campbell | .70 | .35 |
| 47 | Johnny Jeter | .70 | .35 |
| 48 | Dave Baldwin | .70 | .35 |
| 49 | Don Money | .80 | .40 |
| 50 | Willie McCovey | 7.00 | 3.50 |
| 51 | Steve Kline | .80 | .40 |
| 52 | Braves Rookies (Oscar Brown, Earl Williams) | .80 | .40 |
| 53 | Paul Blair | .80 | .40 |
| 54 | Checklist 1-132 | 3.25 | 1.75 |
| 55 | Steve Carlton | 30.00 | 15.00 |
| 56 | Duane Josephson | .70 | .35 |
| 57 | Von Joshua | .70 | .35 |
| 58 | Bill Lee | .80 | .40 |
| 59 | Gene Mauch | 2.00 | 1.00 |
| 60 | Dick Bosman | .70 | .35 |
| 61 | A.L. Batting Leaders (Alex Johnson, Tony Oliva, Carl Yastrzemski) | 3.00 | 1.50 |
| 62 | N.L. Batting Leaders (Rico Carty, Manny Sanguillen, Joe Torre) | 1.25 | .60 |
| 63 | A.L. RBI Leaders (Tony Conigliaro, Frank Howard, Boog Powell) | 1.25 | .60 |
| 64 | N.L. RBI Leaders (Johnny Bench, Tony Perez, Billy Williams) | 3.00 | 1.50 |
| 65 | A.L. Home Run Leaders (Frank Howard, Harmon Killebrew, Carl Yastrzemski) | 3.00 | 1.50 |
| 66 | N.L. Home Run Leaders (Johnny Bench, Tony Perez, Billy Williams) | 3.00 | 1.50 |
| 67 | A.L. ERA Leaders (Jim Palmer, Diego Segui, Clyde Wright) | 1.25 | .60 |
| 68 | N.L. ERA Leaders (Tom Seaver, Wayne Simpson, Luke Walker) | 1.50 | .70 |
| 69 | A.L. Pitching Leaders (Mike Cuellar, Dave McNally, Jim Perry) | 1.25 | .60 |
| 70 | N.L. Pitching Leaders (Bob Gibson, Fergie Jenkins, Gaylord Perry) | 2.00 | 1.00 |
| 71 | A.L. Strikeout Leaders (Bob Johnson, Mickey Lolich, Sam McDowell) | 1.25 | .60 |
| 72 | N.L. Strikeout Leaders (Bob Gibson, Fergie Jenkins, Tom Seaver) | 3.00 | 1.50 |
| 73 | George Brunet | .70 | .35 |
| 74 | Twins Rookies (Pete Hamm, Jim Nettles) | .70 | .35 |
| 75 | Gary Nolan | .70 | .35 |
| 76 | Ted Savage | .70 | .35 |
| 77 | Mike Compton | .70 | .35 |
| 78 | Jim Spencer | .80 | .40 |
| 79 | Wade Blasingame | .70 | .35 |
| 80 | Bill Melton | .80 | .40 |
| 81 | Felix Millan | .70 | .35 |
| 82 | Casey Cox | .70 | .35 |
| 83 | Mets Rookies (Randy Bobb, Tim Foli) | .80 | .40 |
| 84 | Marcel Lachemann | .70 | .35 |
| 85 | Billy Grabarkewitz | .70 | .35 |
| 86 | Mike Kilkenny | .70 | .35 |
| 87 | Jack Heidemann | .70 | .35 |
| 88 | Hal King | .70 | .35 |
| 89 | Ken Brett | .70 | .35 |
| 90 | Joe Pepitone | .70 | .35 |
| 91 | Bob Lemon | 1.25 | .60 |
| 92 | Fred Wenz | .70 | .35 |
| 93 | Senators Rookies (Norm McRae, Denny Riddleberger) | .70 | .35 |
| 94 | Don Hahn | .70 | .35 |
| 95 | Luis Tiant | 1.50 | .70 |
| 96 | Joe Hague | .70 | .35 |
| 97 | Floyd Wicker | .70 | .35 |
| 98 | Joe Decker | .70 | .35 |
| 99 | Mark Belanger | .80 | .40 |
| 100 | Pete Rose | 40.00 | 20.00 |
| 101 | Les Cain | .70 | .35 |
| 102 | Astros Rookies (Ken Forsch, Larry Howard) | .80 | .40 |
| 103 | Rich Severson | .70 | .35 |

| | | NR MT | EX |
|---|---|---|---|
| 104 | Dan Frisella | .70 | .35 |
| 105 | Tony Conigliaro | 1.25 | .60 |
| 106 | Tom Dukes | .70 | .35 |
| 107 | Roy Foster | .70 | .35 |
| 108 | John Cumberland | .70 | .35 |
| 109 | Steve Hovley | .70 | .35 |
| 110 | Bill Mazeroski | 1.25 | .60 |
| 111 | Yankees Rookies (Loyd Colson, Bobby Mitchell) | .80 | .40 |
| 112 | Manny Mota | 2.00 | 1.00 |
| 113 | Jerry Crider | .70 | .35 |
| 114 | Billy Conigliaro | .80 | .40 |
| 115 | Donn Clendenon | .80 | .40 |
| 116 | Ken Sanders | .70 | .35 |
| 117 | *Ted Simmons* | 20.00 | 10.00 |
| 118 | Cookie Rojas | .70 | .35 |
| 119 | Frank Lucchesi | .70 | .35 |
| 120 | Willie Horton | 2.00 | 1.00 |
| 121 | 1971 Rookie Stars (Jim Dunegan, Roe Skidmore) | .70 | .35 |
| 122 | Eddie Watt | .70 | .35 |
| 123a | Checklist 133-263 (card # on right, orange helmet) | 3.25 | 1.75 |
| 123b | Checklist 133-263 (card # on right, red helmet) | 3.25 | 1.75 |
| 123c | Checklist 133-263 (card # centered) | 3.50 | 1.75 |
| 124 | *Don Gullett* | .70 | .35 |
| 125 | Ray Fosse | .70 | .35 |
| 126 | Danny Coombs | .70 | .35 |
| 127 | *Danny Thompson* | .80 | .40 |
| 128 | Frank Johnson | .70 | .35 |
| 129 | Aurelio Monteagudo | .70 | .35 |
| 130 | Denis Menke | .70 | .35 |
| 131 | Curt Blefary | .80 | .40 |
| 132 | Jose Laboy | .70 | .35 |
| 133 | Mickey Lolich | 1.25 | .60 |
| 134 | Jose Arcia | .70 | .35 |
| 135 | Rick Monday | .80 | .40 |
| 136 | Duffy Dyer | .70 | .35 |
| 137 | Marcelino Lopez | .70 | .35 |
| 138 | Phillies Rookies (Joe Lis, *Willie Montanez*) | .80 | .40 |
| 139 | Paul Casanova | .70 | .35 |
| 140 | Gaylord Perry | 8.00 | 4.00 |
| 141 | Frank Quilici | .70 | .35 |
| 142 | Mack Jones | .70 | .35 |
| 143 | Steve Blass | .80 | .40 |
| 144 | Jackie Hernandez | .70 | .35 |
| 145 | Bill Singer | .80 | .40 |
| 146 | Ralph Houk | 1.75 | .90 |
| 147 | Bob Priddy | .70 | .35 |
| 148 | John Mayberry | .80 | .40 |
| 149 | Mike Hershberger | .70 | .35 |
| 150 | Sam McDowell | .70 | .35 |
| 151 | Tommy Davis | .70 | .35 |
| 152 | Angels Rookies (Lloyd Allen, Winston Llenas) | .70 | .35 |
| 153 | Gary Ross | .70 | .35 |
| 154 | Cesar Gutierrez | .70 | .35 |
| 155 | Ken Henderson | .70 | .35 |
| 156 | Bart Johnson | .70 | .35 |
| 157 | Bob Bailey | .70 | .35 |
| 158 | Jerry Reuss | 2.00 | 1.00 |

| | | NR MT | EX |
|---|---|---|---|
| 159 | Jarvis Tatum | .70 | .35 |
| 160 | Tom Seaver | 65.00 | 33.00 |
| 161 | Coins Checklist | 3.25 | 1.75 |
| 162 | Jack Billingham | .70 | .35 |
| 163 | Buck Martinez | .70 | .35 |
| 164 | Reds Rookies (Frank Duffy, *Milt Wilcox*) | 2.00 | 1.00 |
| 165 | Cesar Tovar | .70 | .35 |
| 166 | Joe Hoerner | .70 | .35 |
| 167 | Tom Grieve | .70 | .35 |
| 168 | Bruce Dal Canton | .70 | .35 |
| 169 | Ed Herrmann | .70 | .35 |
| 170 | Mike Cuellar | 2.00 | 1.00 |
| 171 | Bobby Wine | .70 | .35 |
| 172 | Duke Sims | .70 | .35 |
| 173 | Gil Garrido | .70 | .35 |
| 174 | *Dave LaRoche* | .80 | .40 |
| 175 | Jim Hickman | .80 | .40 |
| 176 | Red Sox Rookies (Doug Griffin, Bob Montgomery) | .70 | .35 |
| 177 | Hal McRae | .70 | .35 |
| 178 | Dave Duncan | .70 | .35 |
| 179 | Mike Corkins | .70 | .35 |
| 180 | Al Kaline | 18.00 | 9.00 |
| 181 | Hal Lanier | 2.00 | 1.00 |
| 182 | Al Downing | .80 | .40 |
| 183 | Gil Hodges | 4.00 | 2.00 |
| 184 | Stan Bahnsen | .80 | .40 |
| 185 | Julian Javier | .80 | .40 |
| 186 | Bob Spence | .70 | .35 |
| 187 | Ted Abernathy | .70 | .35 |
| 188 | Dodgers Rookies (Mike Strahler, *Bob Valentine*) | 2.25 | 1.25 |
| 189 | George Mitterwald | .70 | .35 |
| 190 | Bob Tolan | .80 | .40 |
| 191 | Mike Andrews | .70 | .35 |
| 192 | Billy Wilson | .70 | .35 |
| 193 | *Bob Grich* | 2.25 | 1.25 |
| 194 | Mike Lum | .70 | .35 |
| 195 | A.L. Playoff Game 1 (Powell Muscles Twins!) | 1.25 | .60 |
| 196 | A.L. Playoff Game 2 (McNally Makes It Two Straight!) | 1.25 | .60 |
| 197 | A.L. Playoff Game 3 (Palmer Mows 'Em Down!) | 2.25 | 1.25 |
| 198 | A.L. Playoffs Summary (A Team Effort!) | 1.25 | .60 |
| 199 | N.L. Playoff Game 1 (Cline Pinch-Triple Decides It!) | 1.25 | .60 |
| 200 | N.L. Playoff Game 2 (Tolan Scores For Third Time!) | 1.25 | .60 |
| 201 | N.L. Playoff Game 3 (Cline Scores Winning Run!) | 1.25 | .60 |
| 202 | N.L. Playoffs Summary (World Series Bound!) | 1.25 | .60 |
| 203 | *Larry Gura* | .70 | .35 |
| 204 | Brewers Rookies (George Kopacz, Bernie Smith) | .70 | .35 |

| | | NR MT | EX |
|---|---|---|---|
| 205 | Gerry Moses | .70 | .35 |
| 206a | Checklist 264-393 (orange helmet) | 3.25 | 1.75 |
| 206b | Checklist 264-393 (red helmet) | 3.25 | 1.75 |
| 207 | Alan Foster | .70 | .35 |
| 208 | Billy Martin | 2.25 | 1.25 |
| 209 | Steve Renko | .70 | .35 |
| 210 | Rod Carew | 50.00 | 25.00 |
| 211 | Phil Hennigan | .70 | .35 |
| 212 | Rich Hebner | .80 | .40 |
| 213 | Frank Baker | .80 | .40 |
| 214 | Al Ferrara | .70 | .35 |
| 215 | Diego Segui | .70 | .35 |
| 216 | Cards Rookies (Reggie Cleveland, Luis Melendez) | .70 | .35 |
| 217 | Ed Stroud | .70 | .35 |
| 218 | Tony Cloninger | .80 | .40 |
| 219 | Elrod Hendricks | .70 | .35 |
| 220 | Ron Santo | 1.75 | .90 |
| 221 | Dave Morehead | .70 | .35 |
| 222 | Bob Watson | .80 | .40 |
| 223 | Cecil Upshaw | .70 | .35 |
| 224 | Alan Gallagher | .70 | .35 |
| 225 | Gary Peters | .80 | .40 |
| 226 | Bill Russell | 2.00 | 1.00 |
| 227 | Floyd Weaver | .70 | .35 |
| 228 | Wayne Garrett | .70 | .35 |
| 229 | Jim Hannan | .70 | .35 |
| 230 | Willie Stargell | 8.00 | 4.00 |
| 231 | Indians Rookies (Vince Colbert, John Lowenstein) | .80 | .40 |
| 232 | John Strohmayer | .70 | .35 |
| 233 | Larry Bowa | 2.25 | 1.25 |
| 234 | Jim Lyttle | .80 | .40 |
| 235 | Nate Colbert | .70 | .35 |
| 236 | Bob Humphreys | .70 | .35 |
| 237 | Cesar Cedeno | 1.50 | .70 |
| 238 | Chuck Dobson | .70 | .35 |
| 239 | Red Schoendienst | 2.00 | 1.00 |
| 240 | Clyde Wright | .70 | .35 |
| 241 | Dave Nelson | .70 | .35 |
| 242 | Jim Ray | .70 | .35 |
| 243 | Carlos May | .80 | .40 |
| 244 | Bob Tillman | .70 | .35 |
| 245 | Jim Kaat | 3.25 | 1.75 |
| 246 | Tony Taylor | .70 | .35 |
| 247 | Royals Rookies (Jerry Cram, Paul Splittorff) | .70 | .35 |
| 248 | Hoyt Wilhelm | 3.75 | 2.00 |
| 249 | Chico Salmon | .70 | .35 |
| 250 | Johnny Bench | 45.00 | 23.00 |
| 251 | Frank Reberger | .70 | .35 |
| 252 | Eddie Leon | .70 | .35 |
| 253 | Bill Sudakis | .70 | .35 |
| 254 | Cal Koonce | .70 | .35 |
| 255 | Bob Robertson | .70 | .35 |
| 256 | Tony Gonzalez | .70 | .35 |
| 257 | Nelson Briles | .70 | .35 |
| 258 | Dick Green | .70 | .35 |
| 259 | Dave Marshall | .70 | .35 |
| 260 | Tommy Harper | .80 | .40 |
| 261 | Darold Knowles | .70 | .35 |
| 262 | Padres Rookies (Dave Robinson, Jim Williams) | .70 | .35 |

| | | NR MT | EX |
|---|---|---|---|
| 263 | John Ellis | .80 | .40 |
| 264 | Joe Morgan | 10.00 | 5.00 |
| 265 | Jim Northrup | .80 | .40 |
| 266 | Bill Stoneman | .70 | .35 |
| 267 | Rich Morales | .70 | .35 |
| 268 | Phillies Team | 1.25 | .60 |
| 269 | Gail Hopkins | .70 | .35 |
| 270 | Rico Carty | .70 | .35 |
| 271 | Bill Zepp | .70 | .35 |
| 272 | Tommy Helms | .80 | .40 |
| 273 | Pete Richert | .70 | .35 |
| 274 | Ron Slocum | .70 | .35 |
| 275 | Vada Pinson | 1.25 | .60 |
| 276 | Giants Rookies (Mike Davison, George Foster) | 6.00 | 3.00 |
| 277 | Gary Waslewski | .80 | .40 |
| 278 | Jerry Grote | .80 | .40 |
| 279 | Lefty Phillips | .70 | .35 |
| 280 | Fergie Jenkins | 12.00 | 6.00 |
| 281 | Danny Walton | .70 | .35 |
| 282 | Jose Pagan | .70 | .35 |
| 283 | Dick Such | .70 | .35 |
| 284 | Jim Gosger | .70 | .35 |
| 285 | Sal Bando | 2.00 | 1.00 |
| 286 | Jerry McNertney | .70 | .35 |
| 287 | Mike Fiore | .70 | .35 |
| 288 | Joe Moeller | .70 | .35 |
| 289 | White Sox Team | 1.25 | .60 |
| 290 | Tony Oliva | 1.50 | .70 |
| 291 | George Culver | .70 | .35 |
| 292 | Jay Johnstone | 2.00 | 1.00 |
| 293 | Pat Corrales | .80 | .40 |
| 294 | Steve Dunning | .70 | .35 |
| 295 | Bobby Bonds | 1.25 | .60 |
| 296 | Tom Timmermann | .70 | .35 |
| 297 | Johnny Briggs | .70 | .35 |
| 298 | Jim Nelson | .70 | .35 |
| 299 | Ed Kirkpatrick | .70 | .35 |
| 300 | Brooks Robinson | 12.00 | 6.00 |
| 301 | Earl Wilson | .70 | .35 |
| 302 | Phil Gagliano | .70 | .35 |
| 303 | Lindy McDaniel | .80 | .40 |
| 304 | Ron Brand | .70 | .35 |
| 305 | Reggie Smith | 2.00 | 1.00 |
| 306 | Jim Nash | .70 | .35 |
| 307 | Don Wert | .70 | .35 |
| 308 | Cards Team | 1.25 | .60 |
| 309 | Dick Ellsworth | .70 | .35 |
| 310 | Tommie Agee | .80 | .40 |
| 311 | Lee Stange | .70 | .35 |
| 312 | Harry Walker | .80 | .40 |
| 313 | Tom Hall | .70 | .35 |
| 314 | Jeff Torborg | .80 | .40 |
| 315 | Ron Fairly | .80 | .40 |
| 316 | Fred Scherman | .70 | .35 |
| 317 | Athletics Rookies (Jim Driscoll, Angel Mangual) | .70 | .35 |
| 318 | Rudy May | .80 | .40 |
| 319 | Ty Cline | .70 | .35 |
| 320 | Dave McNally | .80 | .40 |
| 321 | Tom Matchick | .70 | .35 |
| 322 | Jim Beauchamp | .70 | .35 |
| 323 | Billy Champion | .70 | .35 |
| 324 | Graig Nettles | 3.25 | 1.75 |
| 325 | Juan Marichal | 5.00 | 2.50 |
| 326 | Richie Scheinblum | .70 | .35 |

| | | NR MT | EX |
|---|---|---|---|
| 327 | World Series Game 1 (Powell Homers To Opposite Field!) | 1.25 | .60 |
| 328 | World Series Game 2 (Buford Goes 2-For-4!) | 1.25 | .60 |
| 329 | World Series Game 3 (F. Robinson Shows Muscle!) | 2.00 | 1.00 |
| 330 | World Series Game 4 (Reds Stay Alive!) | 1.25 | .60 |
| 331 | World Series Game 5 (B. Robinson Commits Robbery!) | 2.00 | 1.00 |
| 332 | World Series Summary (Clinching Performance!) | 1.25 | .60 |
| 333 | Clay Kirby | .70 | .35 |
| 334 | Roberto Pena | .70 | .35 |
| 335 | Jerry Koosman | 2.00 | 1.00 |
| 336 | Tigers Team | 2.25 | 1.25 |
| 337 | Jesus Alou | .80 | .40 |
| 338 | Gene Tenace | .80 | .40 |
| 339 | Wayne Simpson | .70 | .35 |
| 340 | Rico Petrocelli | .80 | .40 |
| 341 | *Steve Garvey* | 70.00 | 35.00 |
| 342 | Frank Tepedino | .80 | .40 |
| 343 | Pirates Rookies (Ed Acosta, *Milt May*) | .80 | .40 |
| 344 | Ellie Rodriguez | .70 | .35 |
| 345 | Joe Horlen | .70 | .35 |
| 346 | Lum Harris | .70 | .35 |
| 347 | Ted Uhlaender | .70 | .35 |
| 348 | Fred Norman | .70 | .35 |
| 349 | Rich Reese | .70 | .35 |
| 350 | Billy Williams | 4.50 | 2.25 |
| 351 | Jim Shellenback | .70 | .35 |
| 352 | Denny Doyle | .70 | .35 |
| 353 | Carl Taylor | .70 | .35 |
| 354 | Don McMahon | .70 | .35 |
| 355 | Bud Harrelson | .80 | .40 |
| 356 | Bob Locker | .70 | .35 |
| 357 | Reds Team | 1.25 | .60 |
| 358 | Danny Cater | .80 | .40 |
| 359 | Ron Reed | .80 | .40 |
| 360 | Jim Fregosi | 1.75 | .90 |
| 361 | Don Sutton | 3.50 | 1.75 |
| 362 | Orioles Rookies (Mike Adamson, Roger Freed) | .70 | .35 |
| 363 | Mike Nagy | .70 | .35 |
| 364 | Tommy Dean | .70 | .35 |
| 365 | Bob Johnson | .70 | .35 |
| 366 | Ron Stone | .70 | .35 |
| 367 | Dalton Jones | .70 | .35 |
| 368 | Bob Veale | .80 | .40 |
| 369a | Checklist 394-523 (orange helmet) | 3.25 | 1.75 |
| 369b | Checklist 394-523 (red helmet, black line above ear) | 3.25 | 1.75 |
| 369c | Checklist 394-523 (red helmet, no line) | 3.25 | 1.75 |
| 370 | Joe Torre | 3.00 | 1.50 |
| 371 | Jack Hiatt | .70 | .35 |
| 372 | Lew Krausse | .70 | .35 |
| 373 | Tom McCraw | .70 | .35 |
| 374 | Clete Boyer | .80 | .40 |
| 375 | Steve Hargan | .70 | .35 |

| | | NR MT | EX |
|---|---|---|---|
| 376 | Expos Rookies (Clyde Mashore, Ernie McAnally) | .70 | .35 |
| 377 | Greg Garrett | .70 | .35 |
| 378 | Tito Fuentes | .70 | .35 |
| 379 | Wayne Granger | .70 | .35 |
| 380 | Ted Williams | 5.00 | 2.50 |
| 381 | Fred Gladding | .70 | .35 |
| 382 | Jake Gibbs | .80 | .40 |
| 383 | Rod Gaspar | .70 | .35 |
| 384 | Rollie Fingers | 10.00 | 5.00 |
| 385 | Maury Wills | 1.25 | .60 |
| 386 | Red Sox Team | 1.50 | .70 |
| 387 | Ron Herbel | .70 | .35 |
| 388 | Al Oliver | 2.25 | 1.25 |
| 389 | Ed Brinkman | .80 | .40 |
| 390 | Glenn Beckert | .80 | .40 |
| 391 | Twins Rookies (Steve Brye, Cotton Nash) | .70 | .35 |
| 392 | Grant Jackson | .70 | .35 |
| 393 | Merv Rettenmund | .80 | .40 |
| 394 | Clay Carroll | .80 | .40 |
| 395 | Roy White | .70 | .35 |
| 396 | Dick Schofield | .70 | .35 |
| 397 | Alvin Dark | .80 | .40 |
| 398 | Howie Reed | .70 | .35 |
| 399 | Jim French | .70 | .35 |
| 400 | Hank Aaron | 40.00 | 20.00 |
| 401 | Tom Murphy | .70 | .35 |
| 402 | Dodgers Team | 1.50 | .70 |
| 403 | Joe Coleman | .80 | .40 |
| 404 | Astros Rookies (Buddy Harris, Roger Metzger) | .70 | .35 |
| 405 | Leo Cardenas | .70 | .35 |
| 406 | Ray Sadecki | .70 | .35 |
| 407 | Joe Rudi | 2.00 | 1.00 |
| 408 | Rafael Robles | .70 | .35 |
| 409 | Don Pavletich | .70 | .35 |
| 410 | Ken Holtzman | .80 | .40 |
| 411 | George Spriggs | .70 | .35 |
| 412 | Jerry Johnson | .70 | .35 |
| 413 | Pat Kelly | .70 | .35 |
| 414 | Woodie Fryman | .80 | .40 |
| 415 | Mike Hegan | .70 | .35 |
| 416 | Gene Alley | .80 | .40 |
| 417 | Dick Hall | .70 | .35 |
| 418 | Adolfo Phillips | .70 | .35 |
| 419 | Ron Hansen | .80 | .40 |
| 420 | Jim Merritt | .70 | .35 |
| 421 | John Stephenson | .70 | .35 |
| 422 | Frank Bertaina | .70 | .35 |
| 423 | Tigers Rookies (Tim Marting, Dennis Saunders) | .70 | .35 |
| 424 | Roberto Rodriquez (Rodriguez) | .70 | .35 |
| 425 | Doug Rader | .70 | .35 |
| 426 | Chris Cannizzaro | .70 | .35 |
| 427 | Bernie Allen | .70 | .35 |
| 428 | Jim McAndrew | .70 | .35 |
| 429 | Chuck Hinton | .70 | .35 |
| 430 | Wes Parker | .80 | .40 |
| 431 | Tom Burgmeier | .70 | .35 |
| 432 | Bob Didier | .70 | .35 |
| 433 | Skip Lockwood | .70 | .35 |
| 434 | Gary Sutherland | .70 | .35 |
| 435 | Jose Cardenal | .80 | .40 |

| | NR MT | EX | | | NR MT | EX |
|---|---|---|---|---|---|---|
| 436 | Wilbur Wood | .80 | .40 | 500 | Jim Perry | 2.00 | 1.00 |
| 437 | Danny Murtaugh | .80 | .40 | 501 | Andy Etchebarren | .70 | .35 |
| 438 | Mike McCormick | .80 | .40 | 502 | Cubs Team | 1.25 | .60 |
| 439 | Phillies Rookies (Greg | | | 503 | Gates Brown | .70 | .35 |
| | Luzinski, Scott Reid) | 2.00 | 1.00 | 504 | Ken Wright | .70 | .35 |
| 440 | Bert Campaneris | .70 | .35 | 505 | Ollie Brown | .70 | .35 |
| 441 | Milt Pappas | .80 | .40 | 506 | Bobby Knoop | .70 | .35 |
| 442 | Angels Team | 1.25 | .60 | 507 | George Stone | .70 | .35 |
| 443 | Rich Robertson | .70 | .35 | 508 | Roger Repoz | .70 | .35 |
| 444 | Jimmie Price | .70 | .35 | 509 | Jim Grant | .70 | .35 |
| 445 | Art Shamsky | .70 | .35 | 510 | Ken Harrelson | 1.25 | .60 |
| 446 | Bobby Bolin | .70 | .35 | 511 | Chris Short | .80 | .40 |
| 447 | Cesar Geronimo | 2.00 | 1.00 | 512 | Red Sox Rookies (Mike | | |
| 448 | Dave Roberts | .70 | .35 | | Garman, Dick Mills) | .70 | .35 |
| 449 | Brant Alyea | .70 | .35 | 513 | Nolan Ryan | 250.00 | 125.00 |
| 450 | Bob Gibson | 10.00 | 5.00 | 514 | Ron Woods | .80 | .40 |
| 451 | Joe Keough | .70 | .35 | 515 | Carl Morton | .70 | .35 |
| 452 | John Boccabella | .70 | .35 | 516 | Ted Kubiak | .70 | .35 |
| 453 | Terry Crowley | .70 | .35 | 517 | Charlie Fox | .70 | .35 |
| 454 | Mike Paul | .70 | .35 | 518 | Joe Grzenda | .70 | .35 |
| 455 | Don Kessinger | .80 | .40 | 519 | Willie Crawford | .70 | .35 |
| 456 | Bob Meyer | .70 | .35 | 520 | Tommy John | 3.00 | 1.50 |
| 457 | Willie Smith | .70 | .35 | 521 | Leron Lee | .70 | .35 |
| 458 | White Sox Rookies (Dave | | | 522 | Twins Team | 1.25 | .60 |
| | Lemonds, Ron Lolich) | .70 | .35 | 523 | John Odom | .80 | .40 |
| 459 | Jim Lefebvre | .80 | .40 | 524 | Mickey Stanley | 2.00 | 1.00 |
| 460 | Fritz Peterson | .80 | .40 | 525 | Ernie Banks | 30.00 | 15.00 |
| 461 | Jim Hart | .80 | .40 | 526 | Ray Jarvis | 1.75 | .90 |
| 462 | Senators Team | 1.50 | .70 | 527 | Cleon Jones | 2.00 | 1.00 |
| 463 | Tom Kelley | .70 | .35 | 528 | Wally Bunker | 1.75 | .90 |
| 464 | Aurelio Rodriguez | .80 | .40 | 529 | N.L. Rookies (Bill | | |
| 465 | Tim McCarver | 1.75 | .90 | | Buckner, Enzo Hernandez, | | |
| 466 | Ken Berry | .70 | .35 | | Marty Perez) | 4.00 | 2.00 |
| 467 | Al Santorini | .70 | .35 | 530 | Carl Yastrzemski | 40.00 | 20.00 |
| 468 | Frank Fernandez | .70 | .35 | 531 | Mike Torrez | 2.00 | 1.00 |
| 469 | Bob Aspromonte | .70 | .35 | 532 | Bill Rigney | 1.75 | .90 |
| 470 | Bob Oliver | .70 | .35 | 533 | Mike Ryan | 1.75 | .90 |
| 471 | Tom Griffin | .70 | .35 | 534 | Luke Walker | 1.75 | .90 |
| 472 | Ken Rudolph | .70 | .35 | 535 | Curt Flood | 2.25 | 1.25 |
| 473 | Gary Wagner | .70 | .35 | 536 | Claude Raymond | 1.75 | .90 |
| 474 | Jim Fairey | .70 | .35 | 537 | Tom Egan | 1.75 | .90 |
| 475 | Ron Perranoski | .80 | .40 | 538 | Angel Bravo | 1.75 | .90 |
| 476 | Dal Maxvill | .80 | .40 | 539 | Larry Brown | 1.75 | .90 |
| 477 | Earl Weaver | 2.00 | 1.00 | 540 | Larry Dierker | 2.00 | 1.00 |
| 478 | Bernie Carbo | .80 | .40 | 541 | Bob Burda | 1.75 | .90 |
| 479 | Dennis Higgins | .70 | .35 | 542 | Bob Miller | 1.75 | .90 |
| 480 | Manny Sanguillen | .80 | .40 | 543 | Yankees Team | 3.50 | 1.75 |
| 481 | Daryl Patterson | .70 | .35 | 544 | Vida Blue | 3.25 | 1.75 |
| 482 | Padres Team | 1.25 | .60 | 545 | Dick Dietz | 1.75 | .90 |
| 483 | Gene Michael | .80 | .40 | 546 | John Matias | 1.75 | .90 |
| 484 | Don Wilson | .70 | .35 | 547 | Pat Dobson | 2.00 | 1.00 |
| 485 | Ken McMullen | .70 | .35 | 548 | Don Mason | 1.75 | .90 |
| 486 | Steve Huntz | .70 | .35 | 549 | Jim Brewer | 1.75 | .90 |
| 487 | Paul Schaal | .70 | .35 | 550 | Harmon Killebrew | 15.00 | 7.50 |
| 488 | Jerry Stephenson | .70 | .35 | 551 | Frank Linzy | 1.75 | .90 |
| 489 | Luis Alvarado | .70 | .35 | 552 | Buddy Bradford | 1.75 | .90 |
| 490 | Deron Johnson | .70 | .35 | 553 | Kevin Collins | 1.75 | .90 |
| 491 | Jim Hardin | .70 | .35 | 554 | Lowell Palmer | 1.75 | .90 |
| 492 | Ken Boswell | .70 | .35 | 555 | Walt Williams | 1.75 | .90 |
| 493 | Dave May | .70 | .35 | 556 | Jim McGlothlin | 1.75 | .90 |
| 494 | Braves Rookies (Ralph | | | 557 | Tom Satriano | 1.75 | .90 |
| | Garr, Rick Kester) | .80 | .40 | 558 | Hector Torres | 1.75 | .90 |
| 495 | Felipe Alou | 2.00 | 1.00 | 559 | A.L. Rookies (Terry Cox, | | |
| 496 | Woody Woodward | .80 | .40 | | Bill Gogolewski, Gary Jones) | | |
| 497 | Horacio Pina | .70 | .35 | | | 2.00 | 1.00 |
| 498 | John Kennedy | .70 | .35 | 560 | Rusty Staub | 3.00 | 1.50 |
| 499 | Checklist 524-643 | 3.25 | 1.75 | 561 | Syd O'Brien | 1.75 | .90 |

| | | NR MT | EX |
|---|---|---|---|
| 562 | Dave Giusti | 1.75 | .90 |
| 563 | Giants Team | 2.00 | 1.00 |
| 564 | Al Fitzmorris | 1.75 | .90 |
| 565 | Jim Wynn | 2.00 | 1.00 |
| 566 | Tim Cullen | 1.75 | .90 |
| 567 | Walt Alston | 3.25 | 1.75 |
| 568 | Sal Campisi | 1.75 | .90 |
| 569 | Ivan Murrell | 1.75 | .90 |
| 570 | Jim Palmer | 30.00 | 15.00 |
| 571 | Ted Sizemore | 1.75 | .90 |
| 572 | Jerry Kenney | 2.00 | 1.00 |
| 573 | Ed Kranepool | 2.00 | 1.00 |
| 574 | Jim Bunning | 4.00 | 2.00 |
| 575 | Bill Freehan | 2.00 | 1.00 |
| 576 | Cubs Rookies (Brock Davis, Adrian Garrett, Garry Jestadt) | 1.75 | .90 |
| 577 | Jim Lonborg | 2.00 | 1.00 |
| 578 | Ron Hunt | 2.00 | 1.00 |
| 579 | Marty Pattin | 1.75 | .90 |
| 580 | Tony Perez | 6.00 | 3.00 |
| 581 | Roger Nelson | 1.75 | .90 |
| 582 | Dave Cash | 1.75 | .90 |
| 583 | Ron Cook | 1.75 | .90 |
| 584 | Indians Team | 2.00 | 1.00 |
| 585 | Willie Davis | 3.00 | 1.50 |
| 586 | Dick Woodson | 1.75 | .90 |
| 587 | Sonny Jackson | 1.75 | .90 |
| 588 | Tom Bradley | 1.75 | .90 |
| 589 | Bob Barton | 1.75 | .90 |
| 590 | Alex Johnson | 1.75 | .90 |
| 591 | Jackie Brown | 1.75 | .90 |
| 592 | Randy Hundley | 1.75 | .90 |
| 593 | Jack Aker | 2.00 | 1.00 |
| 594 | Cards Rookies (Bob Chlupsa, *Al Hrabosky*, Bob Stinson) | 3.00 | 1.50 |
| 595 | Dave Johnson | 2.25 | 1.25 |
| 596 | Mike Jorgensen | 1.75 | .90 |
| 597 | Ken Suarez | 1.75 | .90 |
| 598 | Rick Wise | 2.00 | 1.00 |
| 599 | Norm Cash | 2.00 | 1.00 |
| 600 | Willie Mays | 80.00 | 40.00 |
| 601 | Ken Tatum | 1.75 | .90 |
| 602 | Marty Martinez | 1.75 | .90 |
| 603 | Pirates Team | 3.00 | 1.50 |
| 604 | John Gelnar | 1.75 | .90 |
| 605 | Orlando Cepeda | 3.25 | 1.75 |
| 606 | Chuck Taylor | 1.75 | .90 |
| 607 | Paul Ratliff | 1.75 | .90 |
| 608 | Mike Wegener | 1.75 | .90 |
| 609 | Leo Durocher | 3.00 | 1.50 |
| 610 | Amos Otis | 2.00 | 1.00 |
| 611 | Tom Phoebus | 1.75 | .90 |
| 612 | Indians Rookies (Lou Camilli, Ted Ford, Steve Mingori) | 1.75 | .90 |
| 613 | Pedro Borbon | 2.00 | 1.00 |
| 614 | Billy Cowan | 1.75 | .90 |
| 615 | Mel Stottlemyre | 2.25 | 1.25 |
| 616 | Larry Hisle | 2.00 | 1.00 |
| 617 | Clay Dalrymple | 1.75 | .90 |
| 618 | Tug McGraw | 3.00 | 1.50 |
| 619a | Checklist 644-752 (no copyright on back) | 4.50 | 2.25 |
| 619b | Checklist 644-752 (with copyright, no wavy line on helmet brim) | 3.00 | 1.50 |
| 619c | Checklist 644-752 (with copyright, wavy line on helmet brim) | 3.00 | 1.50 |
| 620 | Frank Howard | 3.00 | 1.50 |
| 621 | Ron Bryant | 1.75 | .90 |
| 622 | Joe Lahoud | 1.75 | .90 |
| 623 | Pat Jarvis | 1.75 | .90 |
| 624 | Athletics Team | 2.00 | 1.00 |
| 625 | Lou Brock | 25.00 | 12.50 |
| 626 | Freddie Patek | 2.00 | 1.00 |
| 627 | Steve Hamilton | 1.75 | .90 |
| 628 | John Bateman | 1.75 | .90 |
| 629 | John Hiller | 2.00 | 1.00 |
| 630 | Roberto Clemente | 65.00 | 33.00 |
| 631 | Eddie Fisher | 1.75 | .90 |
| 632 | Darrel Chaney | 1.75 | .90 |
| 633 | A.L. Rookies (Bobby Brooks, Pete Koegel, Scott Northey) | 1.75 | .90 |
| 634 | Phil Regan | 1.75 | .90 |
| 635 | Bobby Murcer | 2.00 | 1.00 |
| 636 | Denny Lemaster | 1.75 | .90 |
| 637 | Dave Bristol | 1.75 | .90 |
| 638 | Stan Williams | 1.75 | .90 |
| 639 | Tom Haller | 2.00 | 1.00 |
| 640 | Frank Robinson | 35.00 | 17.50 |
| 641 | Mets Team | 8.00 | 4.00 |
| 642 | Jim Roland | 1.75 | .90 |
| 643 | Rick Reichardt | 1.75 | .90 |
| 644 | Jim Stewart | 3.00 | 1.50 |
| 645 | Jim Maloney | 3.25 | 1.75 |
| 646 | Bobby Floyd | 3.00 | 1.50 |
| 647 | Juan Pizarro | 3.00 | 1.50 |
| 648 | Mets Rookies (Rich Folkers, Ted Martinez, *Jon Matlack*) | 3.50 | 1.75 |
| 649 | Sparky Lyle | 3.00 | 1.50 |
| 650 | Rich Allen | 9.00 | 4.50 |
| 651 | Jerry Robertson | 3.00 | 1.50 |
| 652 | Braves Team | 3.25 | 1.75 |
| 653 | Russ Snyder | 3.00 | 1.50 |
| 654 | Don Shaw | 3.00 | 1.50 |
| 655 | Mike Epstein | 3.25 | 1.75 |
| 656 | Gerry Nyman | 3.00 | 1.50 |
| 657 | Jose Azcue | 3.00 | 1.50 |
| 658 | Paul Lindblad | 3.00 | 1.50 |
| 659 | Byron Browne | 3.00 | 1.50 |
| 660 | Ray Culp | 3.00 | 1.50 |
| 661 | Chuck Tanner | 3.00 | 1.50 |
| 662 | Mike Hedlund | 3.00 | 1.50 |
| 663 | Marv Staehle | 3.00 | 1.50 |
| 664 | Major League Rookies (Archie Reynolds, Bob Reynolds, Ken Reynolds) | 3.00 | 1.50 |
| 665 | Ron Swoboda | 3.00 | 1.50 |
| 666 | Gene Brabender | 3.00 | 1.50 |
| 667 | Pete Ward | 3.25 | 1.75 |
| 668 | Gary Neibauer | 3.00 | 1.50 |
| 669 | Ike Brown | 3.00 | 1.50 |
| 670 | Bill Hands | 3.00 | 1.50 |
| 671 | Bill Voss | 3.00 | 1.50 |
| 672 | Ed Crosby | 3.00 | 1.50 |
| 673 | Gerry Janeski | 3.00 | 1.50 |
| 674 | Expos Team | 3.25 | 1.75 |

| | | NR MT | EX |
|---|---|---|---|
| 675 | Dave Boswell | 3.00 | 1.50 |
| 676 | Tommie Reynolds | 3.00 | 1.50 |
| 677 | Jack DiLauro | 3.00 | 1.50 |
| 678 | George Thomas | 3.00 | 1.50 |
| 679 | Don O'Riley | 3.00 | 1.50 |
| 680 | Don Mincher | 3.25 | 1.75 |
| 681 | Bill Butler | 3.00 | 1.50 |
| 682 | Terry Harmon | 3.00 | 1.50 |
| 683 | Bill Burbach | 3.25 | 1.75 |
| 684 | Curt Motton | 3.00 | 1.50 |
| 685 | Moe Drabowsky | 3.00 | 1.50 |
| 686 | Chico Ruiz | 3.00 | 1.50 |
| 687 | Ron Taylor | 3.00 | 1.50 |
| 688 | Sparky Anderson | 3.50 | 1.75 |
| 689 | Frank Baker | 3.00 | 1.50 |
| 690 | Bob Moose | 3.00 | 1.50 |
| 691 | Bob Heise | 3.00 | 1.50 |
| 692 | A.L. Rookies (Hal Haydel, Rogelio Moret, Wayne Twitchell) | 3.00 | 1.50 |
| 693 | Jose Pena | 3.00 | 1.50 |
| 694 | Rick Renick | 3.00 | 1.50 |
| 695 | Joe Niekro | 3.25 | 1.75 |
| 696 | Jerry Morales | 3.00 | 1.50 |
| 697 | Rickey Clark | 3.00 | 1.50 |
| 698 | Brewers Team | 3.50 | 1.75 |
| 699 | Jim Britton | 3.00 | 1.50 |
| 700 | Boog Powell | 4.00 | 2.00 |
| 701 | Bob Garibaldi | 3.00 | 1.50 |
| 702 | Milt Ramirez | 3.00 | 1.50 |
| 703 | Mike Kekich | 3.25 | 1.75 |
| 704 | J.C. Martin | 3.00 | 1.50 |
| 705 | Dick Selma | 3.00 | 1.50 |
| 706 | Joe Foy | 3.00 | 1.50 |
| 707 | Fred Lasher | 3.00 | 1.50 |
| 708 | Russ Nagelson | 3.00 | 1.50 |
| 709 | Major League Rookies (Dusty Baker, Don Baylor, Tom Paciorek) | 50.00 | 25.00 |
| 710 | Sonny Siebert | 3.00 | 1.50 |
| 711 | Larry Stahl | 3.00 | 1.50 |
| 712 | Jose Martinez | 3.00 | 1.50 |
| 713 | Mike Marshall | 3.50 | 1.75 |
| 714 | Dick Williams | 3.50 | 1.75 |
| 715 | Horace Clarke | 3.25 | 1.75 |
| 716 | Dave Leonhard | 3.00 | 1.50 |
| 717 | Tommie Aaron | 3.25 | 1.75 |
| 718 | Billy Wynne | 3.00 | 1.50 |
| 719 | Jerry May | 3.00 | 1.50 |
| 720 | Matty Alou | 3.50 | 1.75 |
| 721 | John Morris | 3.00 | 1.50 |
| 722 | Astros Team | 3.25 | 1.75 |
| 723 | Vicente Romo | 3.00 | 1.50 |
| 724 | Tom Tischinski | 3.00 | 1.50 |
| 725 | Gary Gentry | 3.00 | 1.50 |
| 726 | Paul Popovich | 3.00 | 1.50 |
| 727 | Ray Lamb | 3.00 | 1.50 |
| 728 | N.L. Rookies (Keith Lampard, Wayne Redmond, Bernie Williams) | 3.00 | 1.50 |
| 729 | Dick Billings | 3.00 | 1.50 |
| 730 | Jim Rooker | 3.00 | 1.50 |
| 731 | Jim Qualls | 3.00 | 1.50 |
| 732 | Bob Reed | 3.00 | 1.50 |
| 733 | Lee Maye | 3.00 | 1.50 |
| 734 | Rob Gardner | 3.25 | 1.75 |
| 735 | Mike Shannon | 3.25 | 1.75 |

| | | NR MT | EX |
|---|---|---|---|
| 736 | Mel Queen | 3.00 | 1.50 |
| 737 | Preston Gomez | 3.00 | 1.50 |
| 738 | Russ Gibson | 3.00 | 1.50 |
| 739 | Barry Lersch | 3.00 | 1.50 |
| 740 | Luis Aparicio | 15.00 | 7.50 |
| 741 | Skip Guinn | 3.00 | 1.50 |
| 742 | Royals Team | 3.25 | 1.75 |
| 743 | John O'Donoghue | 3.00 | 1.50 |
| 744 | Chuck Manuel | 3.00 | 1.50 |
| 745 | Sandy Alomar | 3.00 | 1.50 |
| 746 | Andy Kosco | 3.00 | 1.50 |
| 747 | N.L. Rookies (Balor Moore, Al Severinsen, Scipio Spinks) | 3.00 | 1.50 |
| 748 | John Purdin | 3.00 | 1.50 |
| 749 | Ken Szotkiewicz | 3.00 | 1.50 |
| 750 | Denny McLain | 10.00 | 5.00 |
| 751 | Al Weis | 3.25 | 1.75 |
| 752 | Dick Drago | 3.75 | 1.25 |

## 1972 Topps

MIKE CUELLAR

The largest Topps issue of its time appeared in 1972, with the set size reaching the 787 mark. The 2-1/2" by 3-1/2" cards are something special as well. Their fronts have a color photo which is shaped into an arch and surrounded by two different color borders, all of which is inside the overall white border. The player's name is in a white panel below the picture while the team name is above the picture in what might best be described as "superhero" type in a variety of colors. No mention of the player's position appears on the front. Cards backs are tame by comparison, featuring statistics and a trivia question. The set features a record number of specialty cards including more than six dozen "In Action" (shown as "IA" in checklists below) cards featuring action shots of popular players. There are the usual statistical leaders, playoff and World Series highlights. Other innovations are 16 "Boyhood

Photo" cards which depict scrap-book black and white photos of 1972's top players, and a group of cards depicting the trophies which comprise baseball's major awards. Finally, a group of seven "Traded" cards was included which feature a large "Traded" across the front of the card.

| | | NR MT | EX |
|---|---|---|---|
| | Complete Set: | 2000.00 | 1000.00 |
| | Common Player: 1-394 | .40 | .20 |
| | Common Player: 395-525 | .40 | .20 |
| | Common Player: 526-656 | 1.00 | .50 |
| | Common Player: 657-787 | 3.00 | 1.50 |
| 1 | World Champions (Pirates Team) | 6.00 | 3.00 |
| 2 | Ray Culp | .40 | .20 |
| 3 | Bob Tolan | .40 | .20 |
| 4 | Checklist 1-132 | 3.00 | 1.50 |
| 5 | John Bateman | .40 | .20 |
| 6 | Fred Scherman | .40 | .20 |
| 7 | Enzo Hernandez | .40 | .20 |
| 8 | Ron Swoboda | .40 | .20 |
| 9 | Stan Williams | .40 | .20 |
| 10 | Amos Otis | .60 | .30 |
| 11 | Bobby Valentine | .80 | .40 |
| 12 | Jose Cardenal | .40 | .20 |
| 13 | Joe Grzenda | .40 | .20 |
| 14 | Phillies Rookiess (Mike Anderson, Pete Koegel, Wayne Twitchell) | .40 | .20 |
| 15 | Walt Williams | .40 | .20 |
| 16 | Mike Jorgensen | .40 | .20 |
| 17 | Dave Duncan | .40 | .20 |
| 18a | Juan Pizarro (green under "C" and "S") | 3.50 | 1.75 |
| 18b | Juan Pizarro (yellow under "C" and "S") | .40 | .20 |
| 19 | Billy Cowan | .40 | .20 |
| 20 | Don Wilson | .40 | .20 |
| 21 | Braves Team | 1.25 | .60 |
| 22 | Rob Gardner | .40 | .20 |
| 23 | Ted Kubiak | .40 | .20 |
| 24 | Ted Ford | .40 | .20 |
| 25 | Bill Singer | .40 | .20 |
| 26 | Andy Etchebarren | .40 | .20 |
| 27 | Bob Johnson | .40 | .20 |
| 28 | Twins Rookies (Steve Brye, Bob Gebhard, Hal Haydel) | .40 | .20 |
| 29a | Bill Bonham (green under "C" and "S") | 3.50 | 1.75 |
| 29b | Bill Bonham (yellow under "C" and "S") | .40 | .20 |
| 30 | Rico Petrocelli | .70 | .35 |
| 31 | Cleon Jones | .40 | .20 |
| 32 | Cleon Jones IA | .40 | .20 |
| 33 | Billy Martin | 3.00 | 1.50 |
| 34 | Billy Martin IA | 1.00 | .50 |
| 35 | Jerry Johnson | .40 | .20 |

| | | NR MT | EX |
|---|---|---|---|
| 36 | Jerry Johnson IA | .40 | .20 |
| 37 | Carl Yastrzemski | 15.00 | 7.50 |
| 38 | Carl Yastrzemski IA | 8.00 | 4.00 |
| 39 | Bob Barton | .40 | .20 |
| 40 | Bob Barton IA | .40 | .20 |
| 41 | Tommy Davis | .80 | .40 |
| 42 | Tommy Davis IA | .40 | .20 |
| 43 | Rick Wise | .40 | .20 |
| 44 | Rick Wise IA | .40 | .20 |
| 45a | Glenn Beckert (green under "C" and "S") | 3.50 | 1.75 |
| 45b | Glenn Beckert (yellow under "C" and "S") | .60 | .30 |
| 46 | Glenn Beckert IA | .40 | .20 |
| 47 | John Ellis | .40 | .20 |
| 48 | John Ellis IA | .40 | .20 |
| 49 | Willie Mays | 25.00 | 12.50 |
| 50 | Willie Mays IA | 10.00 | 5.00 |
| 51 | Harmon Killebrew | 5.00 | 2.50 |
| 52 | Harmon Killebrew IA | 2.00 | 1.00 |
| 53 | Bud Harrelson | .60 | .30 |
| 54 | Bud Harrelson IA | .40 | .20 |
| 55 | Clyde Wright | .40 | .20 |
| 56 | Rich Chiles | .40 | .20 |
| 57 | Bob Oliver | .40 | .20 |
| 58 | Ernie McAnally | .40 | .20 |
| 59 | *Fred Stanley* | .60 | .30 |
| 60 | Manny Sanguillen | .40 | .20 |
| 61 | Cubs Rookies (Gene Hiser, *Burt Hooton*, Earl Stephenson) | 1.00 | .50 |
| 62 | Angel Mangual | .40 | .20 |
| 63 | Duke Sims | .40 | .20 |
| 64 | Pete Broberg | .40 | .20 |
| 65 | Cesar Cedeno | 1.00 | .50 |
| 66 | Ray Corbin | .40 | .20 |
| 67 | Red Schoendienst | 1.00 | .50 |
| 68 | Jim York | .40 | .20 |
| 69 | Roger Freed | .40 | .20 |
| 70 | Mike Cuellar | .70 | .35 |
| 71 | Angels Team | 1.25 | .60 |
| 72 | *Bruce Kison* | 1.00 | .50 |
| 73 | Steve Huntz | .40 | .20 |
| 74 | Cecil Upshaw | .40 | .20 |
| 75 | Bert Campaneris | .80 | .40 |
| 76 | Don Carrithers | .40 | .20 |
| 77 | Ron Theobald | .40 | .20 |
| 78 | Steve Arlin | .40 | .20 |
| 79 | Red Sox Rookies (*Cecil Cooper, Carlton Fisk*, Mike Garman) | 135.00 | 67.00 |
| 80 | Tony Perez | 3.00 | 1.50 |
| 81 | Mike Hedlund | .40 | .20 |
| 82 | Ron Woods | .40 | .20 |
| 83 | Dalton Jones | .40 | .20 |
| 84 | Vince Colbert | .40 | .20 |
| 85 | N.L. Batting Leaders (Glenn Beckert, Ralph Garr, Joe Torre) | 1.25 | .60 |
| 86 | A.L. Batting Leaders (Bobby Murcer, Tony Oliva, Merv Rettenmund) | 1.25 | .60 |
| 87 | N.L. RBI Leaders (Hank Aaron, Willie Stargell, Joe Torre) | 3.00 | 1.50 |

| | | NR MT | EX | | | NR MT | EX |
|---|---|---|---|---|---|---|---|
| 88 | A.L. RBI Leaders (Harmon Killebrew, Frank Robinson, Reggie Smith) | 3.00 | 1.50 | 127 | Duffy Dyer | .40 | .20 |
| | | | | 128 | Eddie Watt | .40 | .20 |
| | | | | 129 | Charlie Fox | .40 | .20 |
| 89 | N.L. Home Run Leaders (Hank Aaron, Lee May, Willie Stargell) | 3.00 | 1.50 | 130 | Bob Gibson | 5.00 | 2.50 |
| | | | | 131 | Jim Nettles | .40 | .20 |
| | | | | 132 | Joe Morgan | 5.00 | 2.50 |
| 90 | A.L. Home Run Leaders (Norm Cash, Reggie Jackson, Bill Melton) | 1.75 | .90 | 133 | Joe Keough | .40 | .20 |
| | | | | 134 | Carl Morton | .40 | .20 |
| | | | | 135 | Vada Pinson | 1.00 | .50 |
| 91 | N.L. ERA Leaders (Dave Roberts, Tom Seaver, Don Wilson) | 1.75 | .90 | 136 | Darrel Chaney | .40 | .20 |
| | | | | 137 | Dick Williams | .70 | .35 |
| | | | | 138 | Mike Kekich | .40 | .20 |
| 92 | A.L. ERA Leaders (Vida Blue, Jim Palmer, Wilbur Wood) | 1.50 | .70 | 139 | Tim McCarver | 1.00 | .50 |
| | | | | 140 | Pat Dobson | .40 | .20 |
| 93 | N.L. Pitching Leaders (Steve Carlton, Al Downing, Fergie Jenkins, Tom Seaver) | 2.00 | 1.00 | 141 | Mets Rookies (Buzz Capra, Jon Matlack, Leroy Stanton) | .60 | .30 |
| | | | | 142 | *Chris Chambliss* | 1.25 | .60 |
| | | | | 143 | Garry Jestadt | .40 | .20 |
| 94 | A.L. Pitching Leaders (Vida Blue, Mickey Lolich, Wilbur Wood) | 1.25 | .60 | 144 | Marty Pattin | .40 | .20 |
| | | | | 145 | Don Kessinger | .60 | .30 |
| | | | | 146 | Steve Kealey | .40 | .20 |
| 95 | N.L. Strikeout Leaders (Fergie Jenkins, Tom Seaver, Bill Stoneman) | 1.75 | .90 | 147 | *Dave Kingman* | 6.00 | 3.00 |
| | | | | 148 | Dick Billings | .40 | .20 |
| | | | | 149 | Gary Neibauer | .40 | .20 |
| 96 | A.L. Strikeout Leaders (Vida Blue, Joe Coleman, Mickey Lolich) | 1.25 | .60 | 150 | Norm Cash | 1.00 | .50 |
| | | | | 151 | Jim Brewer | .40 | .20 |
| 97 | Tom Kelley | .40 | .20 | 152 | Gene Clines | .40 | .20 |
| 98 | Chuck Tanner | .70 | .35 | 153 | Rick Auerbach | .40 | .20 |
| 99 | *Ross Grimsley* | .80 | .40 | 154 | Ted Simmons | 2.00 | 1.00 |
| 100 | Frank Robinson | 5.00 | 2.50 | 155 | Larry Dierker | .40 | .20 |
| 101 | Astros Rookies (Ray Busse, Bill Grief, *J.R. Richard*) | 1.00 | .50 | 156 | Twins Team | 1.25 | .60 |
| | | | | 157 | Don Gullett | .60 | .30 |
| 102 | Lloyd Allen | .40 | .20 | 158 | Jerry Kenney | .40 | .20 |
| 103 | Checklist 133-263 | 3.00 | 1.50 | 159 | John Boccabella | .40 | .20 |
| 104 | *Toby Harrah* | 1.00 | .50 | 160 | Andy Messersmith | .60 | .30 |
| 105 | Gary Gentry | .40 | .20 | 161 | Brock Davis | .40 | .20 |
| 106 | Brewers Team | 1.25 | .60 | 162 | Brewers Rookies (Jerry Bell, *Darrell Porter*, Bob Reynolds) (Bell & Porter photos transposed) | 1.00 | .50 |
| 107 | *Jose Cruz* | 1.75 | .90 | | | | |
| 108 | Gary Waslewski | .40 | .20 | | | | |
| 109 | Jerry May | .40 | .20 | 163 | Tug McGraw | 1.00 | .50 |
| 110 | Ron Hunt | .40 | .20 | 164 | Tug McGraw IA | .60 | .30 |
| 111 | Jim Grant | .40 | .20 | 165 | *Chris Speier* | 1.00 | .50 |
| 112 | Greg Luzinski | 1.00 | .50 | 166 | Chris Speier IA | .60 | .30 |
| 113 | Rogelio Moret | .40 | .20 | 167 | Deron Johnson | .40 | .20 |
| 114 | Bill Buckner | 1.25 | .60 | 168 | Deron Johnson IA | .40 | .20 |
| 115 | Jim Fregosi | 1.00 | .50 | 169 | Vida Blue | 1.00 | .50 |
| 116 | *Ed Farmer* | .40 | .20 | 170 | Vida Blue IA | .60 | .30 |
| 117a | Cleo James (green under "C" and "S") | 3.50 | 1.75 | 171 | Darrell Evans | 1.50 | .70 |
| | | | | 172 | Darrell Evans IA | 1.00 | .50 |
| 117b | Cleo James (yellow under "C" and "S") | .40 | .20 | 173 | Clay Kirby | .40 | .20 |
| | | | | 174 | Clay Kirby IA | .40 | .20 |
| 118 | Skip Lockwood | .40 | .20 | 175 | Tom Haller | .40 | .20 |
| 119 | Marty Perez | .40 | .20 | 176 | Tom Haller IA | .40 | .20 |
| 120 | Bill Freehan | .80 | .40 | 177 | Paul Schaal | .40 | .20 |
| 121 | Ed Sprague | .40 | .20 | 178 | Paul Schaal IA | .40 | .20 |
| 122 | Larry Biittner | .40 | .20 | 179 | Dock Ellis | .40 | .20 |
| 123 | Ed Acosta | .40 | .20 | 180 | Dock Ellis IA | .40 | .20 |
| 124 | Yankees (Alan Closter, Roger Hambright, Rusty Torres) | .40 | .20 | 181 | Ed Kranepool | .60 | .30 |
| | | | | 182 | Ed Kranepool IA | .40 | .20 |
| | | | | 183 | Bill Melton | .40 | .20 |
| 125 | Dave Cash | .40 | .20 | 184 | Bill Melton IA | .40 | .20 |
| 126 | Bart Johnson | .40 | .20 | 185 | Ron Bryant | .40 | .20 |
| | | | | 186 | Ron Bryant IA | .40 | .20 |
| | | | | 187 | Gates Brown | .40 | .20 |
| | | | | 188 | Frank Lucchesi | .40 | .20 |

| | NR MT | EX |
|---|---|---|
| 189 Gene Tenace | .60 | .30 |
| 190 Dave Giusti | .40 | .20 |
| 191 *Jeff Burroughs* | 1.00 | .50 |
| 192 Cubs Team | 1.25 | .60 |
| 193 *Kurt Bevacqua* | .60 | .30 |
| 194 Fred Norman | .40 | .20 |
| 195 Orlando Cepeda | 2.00 | 1.00 |
| 196 Mel Queen | .40 | .20 |
| 197 Johnny Briggs | .40 | .20 |
| 198 Dodgers Rookies (*Charlie Hough*, Bob O'Brien, Mike Strahler) | 3.00 | 1.50 |
| 199 Mike Fiore | .40 | .20 |
| 200 Lou Brock | 6.00 | 3.00 |
| 201 Phil Roof | .40 | .20 |
| 202 Scipio Spinks | .40 | .20 |
| 203 *Ron Blomberg* | .70 | .35 |
| 204 Tommy Helms | .40 | .20 |
| 205 Dick Drago | .40 | .20 |
| 206 Dal Maxvill | .40 | .20 |
| 207 Tom Egan | .40 | .20 |
| 208 Milt Pappas | .60 | .30 |
| 209 Joe Rudi | .80 | .40 |
| 210 Denny McLain | 1.25 | .60 |
| 211 Gary Sutherland | .40 | .20 |
| 212 Grant Jackson | .40 | .20 |
| 213 Angels Rookies (Art Kusnyer, Billy Parker, Tom Silverio) | .40 | .20 |
| 214 Mike McQueen | .40 | .20 |
| 215 Alex Johnson | .40 | .20 |
| 216 Joe Niekro | .70 | .35 |
| 217 Roger Metzger | .40 | .20 |
| 218 Eddie Kasko | .40 | .20 |
| 219 Rennie Stennett | .60 | .30 |
| 220 Jim Perry | .80 | .40 |
| 221 N.L. Playoffs (Bucs Champs!) | 1.25 | .60 |
| 222 A.L. Playoffs (Orioles Champs!) | 1.25 | .60 |
| 223 World Series Game 1 | 1.25 | .60 |
| 224 World Series Game 2 | 1.25 | .60 |
| 225 World Series Game 3 | 1.25 | .60 |
| 226 World Series Game 4 | 1.50 | .70 |
| 227 World Series Game 5 | 1.25 | .60 |
| 228 World Series Game 6 | 1.25 | .60 |
| 229 World Series Game 7 | 1.25 | .60 |
| 230 World Series Summary (Series Celebration) | 1.25 | .60 |
| 231 Casey Cox | .40 | .20 |
| 232 Giants Rookies (Chris Arnold, Jim Barr, Dave Rader) | .40 | .20 |
| 233 Jay Johnstone | .60 | .30 |
| 234 Ron Taylor | .40 | .20 |
| 235 Merv Rettenmund | .40 | .20 |
| 236 Jim McGlothlin | .40 | .20 |
| 237 Yankees Team | 1.25 | .60 |
| 238 Leron Lee | .40 | .20 |

| | NR MT | EX |
|---|---|---|
| 239 Tom Timmermann | .40 | .20 |
| 240 Rich Allen | 1.75 | .90 |
| 241 Rollie Fingers | 10.00 | 5.00 |
| 242 Don Mincher | .40 | .20 |
| 243 Frank Linzy | .40 | .20 |
| 244 Steve Braun | .40 | .20 |
| 245 Tommie Agee | .40 | .20 |
| 246 Tom Burgmeier | .40 | .20 |
| 247 Milt May | .40 | .20 |
| 248 Tom Bradley | .40 | .20 |
| 249 Harry Walker | .40 | .20 |
| 250 Boog Powell | 1.25 | .60 |
| 251a Checklist 264-394 (small print on front) | 3.00 | 1.50 |
| 251b Checklist 264-394 (large print on front) | 3.00 | 1.50 |
| 252 Ken Reynolds | .40 | .20 |
| 253 Sandy Alomar | .40 | .20 |
| 254 Boots Day | .40 | .20 |
| 255 Jim Lonborg | .60 | .30 |
| 256 George Foster | 1.50 | .70 |
| 257 Tigers Rookies (Jim Foor, Tim Hosley, Paul Jata) | .40 | .20 |
| 258 Randy Hundley | .40 | .20 |
| 259 Sparky Lyle | 1.00 | .50 |
| 260 Ralph Garr | .60 | .30 |
| 261 Steve Mingori | .40 | .20 |
| 262 Padres Team | 1.25 | .60 |
| 263 Felipe Alou | .70 | .35 |
| 264 Tommy John | 2.00 | 1.00 |
| 265 Wes Parker | .40 | .20 |
| 266 Bobby Bolin | .40 | .20 |
| 267 Dave Concepcion | 1.75 | .90 |
| 268 A's Rookies (Dwain Anderson, Chris Floethe) | .40 | .20 |
| 269 Don Hahn | .40 | .20 |
| 270 Jim Palmer | 12.00 | 6.00 |
| 271 Ken Rudolph | .40 | .20 |
| 272 *Mickey Rivers* | 1.00 | .50 |
| 273 Bobby Floyd | .40 | .20 |
| 274 Al Severinsen | .40 | .20 |
| 275 Cesar Tovar | .40 | .20 |
| 276 Gene Mauch | .70 | .35 |
| 277 Elliott Maddox | .40 | .20 |
| 278 Dennis Higgins | .40 | .20 |
| 279 Larry Brown | .40 | .20 |
| 280 Willie McCovey | 4.00 | 2.00 |
| 281 Bill Parsons | .40 | .20 |
| 282 Astros Team | 1.25 | .60 |
| 283 Darrell Brandon | .40 | .20 |
| 284 Ike Brown | .40 | .20 |
| 285 Gaylord Perry | 6.00 | 3.00 |
| 286 Gene Alley | .40 | .20 |
| 287 Jim Hardin | .40 | .20 |
| 288 Johnny Jeter | .40 | .20 |
| 289 Syd O'Brien | .40 | .20 |
| 290 Sonny Siebert | .40 | .20 |
| 291 Hal McRae | .80 | .40 |
| 292 Hal McRae IA | .40 | .20 |
| 293 Danny Frisella | .40 | .20 |
| 294 Danny Frisella IA | .40 | .20 |
| 295 Dick Dietz | .40 | .20 |
| 296 Dick Dietz IA | .40 | .20 |
| 297 Claude Osteen | .60 | .30 |
| 298 Claude Osteen IA | .40 | .20 |

| | | NR MT | EX | | | | NR MT | EX |
|---|---|---|---|---|---|---|---|---|
| 299 | Hank Aaron | 30.00 | 15.00 | 351 | Braves Rookies (Jimmy | | | |
| 300 | Hank Aaron IA | 15.00 | 7.50 | | Britton, Tom House, Rick | | | |
| 301 | George Mitterwald | .40 | .20 | | Kester) | | .40 | .20 |
| 302 | George Mitterwald IA | | | 352 | Dave LaRoche | | .40 | .20 |
| | | .40 | .20 | 353 | Art Shamsky | | .40 | .20 |
| 303 | Joe Pepitone | .70 | .35 | 354 | Tom Murphy | | .40 | .20 |
| 304 | Joe Pepitone IA | .40 | .20 | 355 | Bob Watson | | .40 | .20 |
| 305 | Ken Boswell | .40 | .20 | 356 | Gerry Moses | | .40 | .20 |
| 306 | Ken Boswell IA | .40 | .20 | 357 | Woodie Fryman | | .40 | .20 |
| 307 | Steve Renko | .40 | .20 | 358 | Sparky Anderson | | 1.00 | .50 |
| 308 | Steve Renko IA | .40 | .20 | 359 | Don Pavletich | | .40 | .20 |
| 309 | Roberto Clemente | | | 360 | Dave Roberts | | .40 | .20 |
| | | 35.00 | 17.50 | 361 | Mike Andrews | | .40 | .20 |
| 310 | Roberto Clemente IA | | | 362 | Mets Team | | 1.25 | .60 |
| | | 15.00 | 7.50 | 363 | Ron Klimkowski | | .40 | .20 |
| 311 | Clay Carroll | .40 | .20 | 364 | Johnny Callison | | .70 | .35 |
| 312 | Clay Carroll IA | .40 | .20 | 365 | Dick Bosman | | .40 | .20 |
| 313 | Luis Aparicio | 4.00 | 2.00 | 366 | Jimmy Rosario | | .40 | .20 |
| 314 | Luis Aparicio IA | 2.00 | 1.00 | 367 | Ron Perranoski | | .40 | .20 |
| 315 | Paul Splittorff | .40 | .20 | 368 | Danny Thompson | | .40 | .20 |
| 316 | Cardinals Rookies (*Jim* | | | 369 | Jim Lefebvre | | .40 | .20 |
| | *Bibby*, Santiago Guzman, | | | 370 | Don Buford | | .40 | .20 |
| | Jorge Roque) | .70 | .35 | 371 | Denny Lemaster | | .40 | .20 |
| 317 | Rich Hand | .40 | .20 | 372 | Royals Rookies (Lance | | | |
| 318 | Sonny Jackson | .40 | .20 | | Clemons, Monty | | | |
| 319 | Aurelio Rodriguez | .40 | .20 | | Montgomery) | | .40 | .20 |
| 320 | Steve Blass | .40 | .20 | 373 | John Mayberry | | .60 | .30 |
| 321 | Joe Lahoud | .40 | .20 | 374 | Jack Heidemann | | .40 | .20 |
| 322 | Jose Pena | .40 | .20 | 375 | Reggie Cleveland | | .40 | .20 |
| 323 | Earl Weaver | 1.00 | .50 | 376 | Andy Kosco | | .40 | .20 |
| 324 | Mike Ryan | .40 | .20 | 377 | Terry Harmon | | .40 | .20 |
| 325 | Mel Stottlemyre | 1.00 | .50 | 378 | Checklist 395-525 | | 3.00 | 1.50 |
| 326 | Pat Kelly | .40 | .20 | 379 | Ken Berry | | .40 | .20 |
| 327 | *Steve Stone* | 1.00 | .50 | 380 | Earl Williams | | .40 | .20 |
| 328 | Red Sox Team | 1.00 | .50 | 381 | White Sox Team | | 1.25 | .60 |
| 329 | Roy Foster | .40 | .20 | 382 | Joe Gibbon | | .40 | .20 |
| 330 | Jim Hunter | 3.50 | 1.75 | 383 | Brant Alyea | | .40 | .20 |
| 331 | Stan Swanson | .40 | .20 | 384 | Dave Campbell | | .40 | .20 |
| 332 | Buck Martinez | .40 | .20 | 385 | Mickey Stanley | | .40 | .20 |
| 333 | Steve Barber | .40 | .20 | 386 | Jim Colborn | | .40 | .20 |
| 334 | Rangers Rookies (Bill | | | 387 | Horace Clarke | | .40 | .20 |
| | Fahey, Jim Mason, Tom | | | 388 | Charlie Williams | | .40 | .20 |
| | Ragland) | .40 | .20 | 389 | Bill Rigney | | .40 | .20 |
| 335 | Bill Hands | .40 | .20 | 390 | Willie Davis | | .70 | .35 |
| 336 | Marty Martinez | .40 | .20 | 391 | Ken Sanders | | .40 | .20 |
| 337 | Mike Kilkenny | .40 | .20 | 392 | Pirates Rookies (Fred | | | |
| 338 | Bob Grich | 1.00 | .50 | | Cambria, *Richie Zisk*) | | 1.00 | .50 |
| 339 | Ron Cook | .40 | .20 | 393 | Curt Motton | | .40 | .20 |
| 340 | Roy White | 1.00 | .50 | 394 | Ken Forsch | | .40 | .20 |
| 341 | Boyhood Photo (Joe | | | 395 | Matty Alou | | .80 | .40 |
| | Torre) | .70 | .35 | 396 | Paul Lindblad | | .40 | .20 |
| 342 | Boyhood Photo (Wilbur | | | 397 | Phillies Team | | 1.25 | .60 |
| | Wood) | .60 | .30 | 398 | Larry Hisle | | .60 | .30 |
| 343 | Boyhood Photo (Willie | | | 399 | Milt Wilcox | | .60 | .30 |
| | Stargell) | 1.50 | .70 | 400 | Tony Oliva | | 1.50 | .70 |
| 344 | Boyhood Photo (Dave | | | 401 | Jim Nash | | .40 | .20 |
| | McNally) | .60 | .30 | 402 | Bobby Heise | | .40 | .20 |
| 345 | Boyhood Photo (Rick | | | 403 | John Cumberland | | .40 | .20 |
| | Wise) | .40 | .20 | 404 | Jeff Torborg | | .60 | .30 |
| 346 | Boyhood Photo (Jim | | | 405 | Ron Fairly | | .70 | .35 |
| | Fregosi) | .60 | .30 | 406 | *George Hendrick* | | 1.50 | .70 |
| 347 | Boyhood Photo (Tom | | | 407 | Chuck Taylor | | .40 | .20 |
| | Seaver) | 4.00 | 2.00 | 408 | Jim Northrup | | .60 | .30 |
| 348 | Boyhood Photo (Sal | | | 409 | Frank Baker | | .60 | .30 |
| | Bando) | .60 | .30 | 410 | Fergie Jenkins | | 6.00 | 3.00 |
| 349 | Al Fitzmorris | .40 | .20 | 411 | Bob Montgomery | | .40 | .20 |
| 350 | Frank Howard | 1.25 | .60 | 412 | Dick Kelley | | .40 | .20 |

| | NR MT | EX |
|---|---|---|
| 413 White Sox Rookies (Don Eddy, Dave Lemonds) | .40 | .20 |
| 414 Bob Miller | .40 | .20 |
| 415 Cookie Rojas | .40 | .20 |
| 416 Johnny Edwards | .40 | .20 |
| 417 Tom Hall | .40 | .20 |
| 418 Tom Shopay | .40 | .20 |
| 419 Jim Spencer | .40 | .20 |
| 420 Steve Carlton | 20.00 | 10.00 |
| 421 Ellie Rodriguez | .40 | .20 |
| 422 Ray Lamb | .40 | .20 |
| 423 Oscar Gamble | .60 | .30 |
| 424 Bill Gogolewski | .40 | .20 |
| 425 Ken Singleton | 1.00 | .50 |
| 426 Ken Singleton IA | .60 | .30 |
| 427 Tito Fuentes | .40 | .20 |
| 428 Tito Fuentes IA | .40 | .20 |
| 429 Bob Robertson | .40 | .20 |
| 430 Bob Robertson IA | .40 | .20 |
| 431 Clarence Gaston | .40 | .20 |
| 432 Clarence Gaston IA | .40 | .20 |
| 433 Johnny Bench | 35.00 | 17.50 |
| 434 Johnny Bench IA | 18.00 | 9.00 |
| 435 Reggie Jackson | 38.00 | 19.00 |
| 436 Reggie Jackson IA | 20.00 | 10.00 |
| 437 Maury Wills | 1.50 | .70 |
| 438 Maury Wills IA | 1.00 | .50 |
| 439 Billy Williams | 4.00 | 2.00 |
| 440 Billy Williams IA | 2.00 | 1.00 |
| 441 Thurman Munson | 15.00 | 7.50 |
| 442 Thurman Munson IA | 10.00 | 5.00 |
| 443 Ken Henderson | .40 | .20 |
| 444 Ken Henderson IA | .40 | .20 |
| 445 Tom Seaver | 30.00 | 15.00 |
| 446 Tom Seaver IA | 10.00 | 5.00 |
| 447 Willie Stargell | 4.00 | 2.00 |
| 448 Willie Stargell IA | 2.00 | 1.00 |
| 449 Bob Lemon | 1.50 | .70 |
| 450 Mickey Lolich | 1.25 | .60 |
| 451 Tony LaRussa | .80 | .40 |
| 452 Ed Herrmann | .40 | .20 |
| 453 Barry Lersch | .40 | .20 |
| 454 A's Team | 2.00 | 1.00 |
| 455 Tommy Harper | .60 | .30 |
| 456 Mark Belanger | .60 | .30 |
| 457 Padres Rookies (Darcy Fast, Mike Ivie, *Derrel Thomas*) | .60 | .30 |
| 458 Aurelio Monteagudo | .40 | .20 |
| 459 Rick Renick | .40 | .20 |
| 460 Al Downing | .60 | .30 |
| 461 Tim Cullen | .40 | .20 |
| 462 Rickey Clark | .40 | .20 |
| 463 Bernie Carbo | .40 | .20 |
| 464 Jim Roland | .40 | .20 |
| 465 Gil Hodges | 3.00 | 1.50 |
| 466 Norm Miller | .40 | .20 |
| 467 Steve Kline | .60 | .30 |
| 468 Richie Scheinblum | .40 | .20 |
| 469 Ron Herbel | .40 | .20 |
| 470 Ray Fosse | .40 | .20 |
| 471 Luke Walker | .40 | .20 |
| 472 Phil Gagliano | .40 | .20 |
| 473 Dan McGinn | .40 | .20 |
| 474 Orioles Rookies (Don Baylor, Roric Harrison, Johnny Oates) | 8.00 | 4.00 |
| 475 Gary Nolan | .40 | .20 |
| 476 Lee Richard | .40 | .20 |
| 477 Tom Phoebus | .40 | .20 |
| 478a Checklist 526-656 (small print on front) | 3.00 | 1.50 |
| 478b Checklist 526-656 (large printing on front) | 3.00 | 1.50 |
| 479 Don Shaw | .40 | .20 |
| 480 Lee May | .80 | .40 |
| 481 Billy Conigliaro | .40 | .20 |
| 482 Joe Hoerner | .40 | .20 |
| 483 Ken Suarez | .40 | .20 |
| 484 Lum Harris | .40 | .20 |
| 485 Phil Regan | .40 | .20 |
| 486 John Lowenstein | .40 | .20 |
| 487 Tigers Team | 1.50 | .70 |
| 488 Mike Nagy | .40 | .20 |
| 489 Expos Rookies (Terry Humphrey, Keith Lampard) | .40 | .20 |
| 490 Dave McNally | .70 | .35 |
| 491 Boyhood Photo (Lou Piniella) | .80 | .40 |
| 492 Boyhood Photo (Mel Stottlemyre) | .60 | .30 |
| 493 Boyhood Photo (Bob Bailey) | .40 | .20 |
| 494 Boyhood Photo (Willie Horton) | .60 | .30 |
| 495 Boyhood Photo (Bill Melton) | .40 | .20 |
| 496 Boyhood Photo (Bud Harrelson) | .60 | .30 |
| 497 Boyhood Photo (Jim Perry) | .60 | .30 |
| 498 Boyhood Photo (Brooks Robinson) | 2.00 | 1.00 |
| 499 Vicente Romo | .40 | .20 |
| 500 Joe Torre | 1.25 | .60 |
| 501 Pete Hamm | .40 | .20 |
| 502 Jackie Hernandez | .40 | .20 |
| 503 Gary Peters | .40 | .20 |
| 504 Ed Spiezio | .40 | .20 |
| 505 Mike Marshall | .70 | .35 |
| 506 Indians Rookies (Terry Ley, Jim Moyer, *Dick Tidrow*) | .80 | .40 |
| 507 Fred Gladding | .40 | .20 |
| 508 Ellie Hendricks | .40 | .20 |
| 509 Don McMahon | .40 | .20 |
| 510 Ted Williams | 6.00 | 3.00 |
| 511 Tony Taylor | .40 | .20 |
| 512 Paul Popovich | .40 | .20 |
| 513 Lindy McDaniel | .60 | .30 |
| 514 Ted Sizemore | .40 | .20 |
| 515 Bert Blyleven | 10.00 | 5.00 |
| 516 Oscar Brown | .40 | .20 |
| 517 Ken Brett | .60 | .30 |
| 518 Wayne Garrett | .40 | .20 |
| 519 Ted Abernathy | .40 | .20 |
| 520 Larry Bowa | 1.25 | .60 |
| 521 Alan Foster | .40 | .20 |
| 522 Dodgers Team | 1.25 | .60 |
| 523 Chuck Dobson | .40 | .20 |
| 524 Reds Rookies (Ed | | |

| | | NR MT | EX |
|---|---|---|---|
| | Armbrister, Mel Behney) | | |
| | | .40 | .20 |
| 525 | Carlos May | .60 | .30 |
| 526 | Bob Bailey | 1.00 | .50 |
| 527 | Dave Leonhard | 1.00 | .50 |
| 528 | Ron Stone | 1.00 | .50 |
| 529 | Dave Nelson | 1.00 | .50 |
| 530 | Don Sutton | 4.00 | 2.00 |
| 531 | Freddie Patek | 1.00 | .50 |
| 532 | Fred Kendall | 1.00 | .50 |
| 533 | Ralph Houk | 1.25 | .60 |
| 534 | Jim Hickman | 1.00 | .50 |
| 535 | Ed Brinkman | 1.00 | .50 |
| 536 | Doug Rader | 1.00 | .50 |
| 537 | Bob Locker | 1.00 | .50 |
| 538 | Charlie Sands | 1.00 | .50 |
| 539 | *Terry Forster* | 2.00 | 1.00 |
| 540 | Felix Millan | 1.00 | .50 |
| 541 | Roger Repoz | 1.00 | .50 |
| 542 | Jack Billingham | 1.00 | .50 |
| 543 | Duane Josephson | 1.00 | .50 |
| 544 | Ted Martinez | 1.00 | .50 |
| 545 | Wayne Granger | 1.00 | .50 |
| 546 | Joe Hague | 1.00 | .50 |
| 547 | Indians Team | 1.50 | .70 |
| 548 | Frank Reberger | 1.00 | .50 |
| 549 | Dave May | 1.00 | .50 |
| 550 | Brooks Robinson | 20.00 | 10.00 |
| 551 | Ollie Brown | 1.00 | .50 |
| 552 | Ollie Brown IA | 1.00 | .50 |
| 553 | Wilbur Wood | 1.25 | .60 |
| 554 | Wilbur Wood IA | 1.00 | .50 |
| 555 | Ron Santo | 1.50 | .70 |
| 556 | Ron Santo IA | 1.00 | .50 |
| 557 | John Odom | 1.00 | .50 |
| 558 | John Odom IA | 1.00 | .50 |
| 559 | Pete Rose | 40.00 | 20.00 |
| 560 | Pete Rose IA | 20.00 | 10.00 |
| 561 | Leo Cardenas | 1.00 | .50 |
| 562 | Leo Cardenas IA | 1.00 | .50 |
| 563 | Ray Sadecki | 1.00 | .50 |
| 564 | Ray Sadecki IA | 1.00 | .50 |
| 565 | Reggie Smith | 1.25 | .60 |
| 566 | Reggie Smith IA | 1.00 | .50 |
| 567 | Juan Marichal | 6.00 | 3.00 |
| 568 | Juan Marichal IA | 3.00 | 1.50 |
| 569 | Ed Kirkpatrick | 1.00 | .50 |
| 570 | Ed Kirkpatrick IA | 1.00 | .50 |
| 571 | Nate Colbert | 1.00 | .50 |
| 572 | Nate Colbert IA | 1.00 | .50 |
| 573 | Fritz Peterson | 1.00 | .50 |
| 574 | Fritz Peterson IA | 1.00 | .50 |
| 575 | Al Oliver | 2.00 | 1.00 |
| 576 | Leo Durocher | 1.25 | .60 |
| 577 | Mike Paul | 1.00 | .50 |
| 578 | Billy Grabarkewitz | 1.00 | .50 |
| 579 | *Doyle Alexander* | 3.25 | 1.75 |
| 580 | Lou Piniella | 2.50 | 1.25 |
| 581 | Wade Blasingame | 1.00 | .50 |
| 582 | Expos Team | 3.00 | 1.50 |
| 583 | Darold Knowles | 1.00 | .50 |
| 584 | Jerry McNertney | 1.00 | .50 |
| 585 | George Scott | 1.00 | .50 |
| 586 | Denis Menke | 1.00 | .50 |
| 587 | Billy Wilson | 1.00 | .50 |
| 588 | Jim Holt | 1.00 | .50 |
| 589 | Hal Lanier | 1.00 | .50 |

| | | NR MT | EX |
|---|---|---|---|
| 590 | Graig Nettles | 3.25 | 1.75 |
| 591 | Paul Casanova | 1.00 | .50 |
| 592 | Lew Krausse | 1.00 | .50 |
| 593 | Rich Morales | 1.00 | .50 |
| 594 | Jim Beauchamp | 1.00 | .50 |
| 595 | Nolan Ryan | 225.00 | 112.00 |
| 596 | Manny Mota | 1.25 | .60 |
| 597 | Jim Magnuson | 1.00 | .50 |
| 598 | Hal King | 1.00 | .50 |
| 599 | Billy Champion | 1.00 | .50 |
| 600 | Al Kaline | 12.00 | 6.00 |
| 601 | George Stone | 1.00 | .50 |
| 602 | Dave Bristol | 1.00 | .50 |
| 603 | Jim Ray | 1.00 | .50 |
| 604a | Checklist 657-787 | | |
| | (copyright on right) | 3.50 | 1.75 |
| 604b | Checklist 657-787 | | |
| | (copyright on left) | 5.00 | 2.50 |
| 605 | Nelson Briles | 1.00 | .50 |
| 606 | Luis Melendez | 1.00 | .50 |
| 607 | Frank Duffy | 1.00 | .50 |
| 608 | Mike Corkins | 1.00 | .50 |
| 609 | Tom Grieve | 1.00 | .50 |
| 610 | Bill Stoneman | 1.00 | .50 |
| 611 | Rich Reese | 1.00 | .50 |
| 612 | Joe Decker | 1.00 | .50 |
| 613 | Mike Ferraro | 1.00 | .50 |
| 614 | Ted Uhlaender | 1.00 | .50 |
| 615 | Steve Hargan | 1.00 | .50 |
| 616 | *Joe Ferguson* | 1.00 | .50 |
| 617 | Royals Team | 3.00 | 1.50 |
| 618 | Rich Robertson | 1.00 | .50 |
| 619 | Rich McKinney | 1.00 | .50 |
| 620 | Phil Niekro | 4.50 | 2.25 |
| 621 | Commissioners Award | | |
| | | 1.25 | .60 |
| 622 | MVP Award | 1.25 | .60 |
| 623 | Cy Young Award | 1.25 | .60 |
| 624 | Minor League Player Of | | |
| | The Year Award | 1.25 | .60 |
| 625 | Rookie Of The Year | | |
| | Award | 1.25 | .60 |
| 626 | Babe Ruth Award | 1.00 | .50 |
| 627 | Moe Drabowsky | 1.00 | .50 |
| 628 | Terry Crowley | 1.00 | .50 |
| 629 | Paul Doyle | 1.00 | .50 |
| 630 | Rich Hebner | 1.00 | .50 |
| 631 | John Strohmayer | 1.00 | .50 |
| 632 | Mike Hegan | 1.00 | .50 |
| 633 | Jack Hiatt | 1.00 | .50 |
| 634 | Dick Woodson | 1.00 | .50 |
| 635 | Don Money | 1.00 | .50 |
| 636 | Bill Lee | 1.25 | .60 |
| 637 | Preston Gomez | 1.00 | .50 |
| 638 | Ken Wright | 1.00 | .50 |
| 639 | J.C. Martin | 1.00 | .50 |
| 640 | Joe Coleman | 1.00 | .50 |
| 641 | Mike Lum | 1.00 | .50 |
| 642 | Denny Riddleberger | | |
| | | 1.00 | .50 |
| 643 | Russ Gibson | 1.00 | .50 |
| 644 | Bernie Allen | 1.00 | .50 |
| 645 | Jim Maloney | 1.00 | .50 |
| 646 | Chico Salmon | 1.00 | .50 |
| 647 | Bob Moose | 1.00 | .50 |
| 648 | Jim Lyttle | 1.00 | .50 |
| 649 | Pete Richert | 1.00 | .50 |

| | | NR MT | EX | | | NR MT | EX |
|---|---|---|---|---|---|---|---|
| 650 | Sal Bando | 1.00 | .50 | 716 | Jesus Alou | 3.25 | 1.75 |
| 651 | Reds Team | 2.00 | 1.00 | 717 | Bruce Dal Canton | 3.00 | 1.50 |
| 652 | Marcelino Lopez | 1.00 | .50 | 718 | Del Rice | 3.00 | 1.50 |
| 653 | Jim Fairey | 1.00 | .50 | 719 | Cesar Geronimo | 3.25 | 1.75 |
| 654 | Horacio Pina | 1.00 | .50 | 720 | Sam McDowell | 3.00 | 1.50 |
| 655 | Jerry Grote | 1.00 | .50 | 721 | Eddie Leon | 3.00 | 1.50 |
| 656 | Rudy May | 1.00 | .50 | 722 | Bill Sudakis | 3.00 | 1.50 |
| 657 | Bobby Wine | 3.00 | 1.50 | 723 | Al Santorini | 3.00 | 1.50 |
| 658 | Steve Dunning | 3.00 | 1.50 | 724 | A.L. Rookies (John | | |
| 659 | Bob Aspromonte | 3.00 | 1.50 | | Curtis, Rich Hinton, Mickey | | |
| 660 | Paul Blair | 3.25 | 1.75 | | Scott) | 3.25 | 1.75 |
| 661 | Bill Virdon | 3.25 | 1.75 | 725 | Dick McAuliffe | 3.25 | 1.75 |
| 662 | Stan Bahnsen | 3.25 | 1.75 | 726 | Dick Selma | 3.00 | 1.50 |
| 663 | Fran Healy | 3.00 | 1.50 | 727 | Jose Laboy | 3.00 | 1.50 |
| 664 | Bobby Knoop | 3.00 | 1.50 | 728 | Gail Hopkins | 3.00 | 1.50 |
| 665 | Chris Short | 3.25 | 1.75 | 729 | Bob Veale | 3.25 | 1.75 |
| 666 | Hector Torres | 3.00 | 1.50 | 730 | Rick Monday | 3.50 | 1.75 |
| 667 | Ray Newman | 3.00 | 1.50 | 731 | Orioles Team | 3.25 | 1.75 |
| 668 | Rangers Team | 3.25 | 1.75 | 732 | George Culver | 3.00 | 1.50 |
| 669 | Willie Crawford | 3.00 | 1.50 | 733 | Jim Hart | 3.25 | 1.75 |
| 670 | Ken Holtzman | 3.50 | 1.75 | 734 | Bob Burda | 3.00 | 1.50 |
| 671 | Donn Clendenon | 3.25 | 1.75 | 735 | Diego Segui | 3.00 | 1.50 |
| 672 | Archie Reynolds | 3.00 | 1.50 | 736 | Bill Russell | 3.00 | 1.50 |
| 673 | Dave Marshall | 3.00 | 1.50 | 737 | *Lenny Randle* | 3.25 | 1.75 |
| 674 | John Kennedy | 3.00 | 1.50 | 738 | Jim Merritt | 3.00 | 1.50 |
| 675 | Pat Jarvis | 3.00 | 1.50 | 739 | Don Mason | 3.00 | 1.50 |
| 676 | Danny Cater | 3.00 | 1.50 | 740 | Rico Carty | 3.25 | 1.75 |
| 677 | Ivan Murrell | 3.00 | 1.50 | 741 | Major League Rookies | | |
| 678 | Steve Luebber | 3.00 | 1.50 | | (Tom Hutton, *Rick Miller,* | | |
| 679 | Astros Rookies (Bob | | | | *John Milner*) | 3.25 | 1.75 |
| | Fenwick, Bob Stinson) | 3.00 | 1.50 | 742 | Jim Rooker | 3.00 | 1.50 |
| 680 | Dave Johnson | 3.50 | 1.75 | 743 | Cesar Gutierrez | 3.00 | 1.50 |
| 681 | Bobby Pfeil | 3.00 | 1.50 | 744 | *Jim Slaton* | 3.25 | 1.75 |
| 682 | Mike McCormick | 3.25 | 1.75 | 745 | Julian Javier | 3.00 | 1.50 |
| 683 | Steve Hovley | 3.00 | 1.50 | 746 | Lowell Palmer | 3.00 | 1.50 |
| 684 | Hal Breeden | 3.00 | 1.50 | 747 | Jim Stewart | 3.00 | 1.50 |
| 685 | Joe Horlen | 3.00 | 1.50 | 748 | Phil Hennigan | 3.00 | 1.50 |
| 686 | Steve Garvey | 70.00 | 35.00 | 749 | Walter Alston | 5.00 | 2.50 |
| 687 | Del Unser | 3.00 | 1.50 | 750 | Willie Horton | 3.50 | 1.75 |
| 688 | Cardinals Team | 3.25 | 1.75 | 751 | Steve Carlton Traded | | |
| 689 | Eddie Fisher | 3.00 | 1.50 | | | 50.00 | 25.00 |
| 690 | Willie Montanez | 3.25 | 1.75 | 752 | Joe Morgan Traded | | |
| 691 | Curt Blefary | 3.00 | 1.50 | | | 40.00 | 20.00 |
| 692 | Curt Blefary IA | 3.00 | 1.50 | 753 | Denny McLain Traded | | |
| 693 | Alan Gallagher | 3.00 | 1.50 | | | 8.00 | 4.00 |
| 694 | Alan Gallagher IA | 3.00 | 1.50 | 754 | Frank Robinson Traded | | |
| 695 | Rod Carew | 100.00 | 50.00 | | | 35.00 | 17.50 |
| 696 | Rod Carew IA | 40.00 | 20.00 | 755 | Jim Fregosi Traded | 3.50 | 1.75 |
| 697 | Jerry Koosman | 4.50 | 2.25 | 756 | Rick Wise Traded | 3.25 | 1.75 |
| 698 | Jerry Koosman IA | 3.25 | 1.75 | 757 | Jose Cardenal Traded | | |
| 699 | Bobby Murcer | 4.00 | 2.00 | | | 3.25 | 1.75 |
| 700 | Bobby Murcer IA | 3.25 | 1.75 | 758 | Gil Garrido | 3.00 | 1.50 |
| 701 | Jose Pagan | 3.00 | 1.50 | 759 | Chris Cannizzaro | 3.00 | 1.50 |
| 702 | Jose Pagan IA | 3.00 | 1.50 | 760 | Bill Mazeroski | 6.00 | 3.00 |
| 703 | Doug Griffin | 3.00 | 1.50 | 761 | Major League Rookies | | |
| 704 | Doug Griffin IA | 3.00 | 1.50 | | (Ron Cey, Ben Oglivie, | | |
| 705 | Pat Corrales | 3.25 | 1.75 | | Bernie Williams) | 18.00 | 9.00 |
| 706 | Pat Corrales IA | 3.00 | 1.50 | 762 | Wayne Simpson | 3.00 | 1.50 |
| 707 | Tim Foli | 3.00 | 1.50 | 763 | Ron Hansen | 3.00 | 1.50 |
| 708 | Tim Foli IA | 3.00 | 1.50 | 764 | Dusty Baker | 8.00 | 4.00 |
| 709 | Jim Kaat | 9.00 | 4.50 | 765 | Ken McMullen | 3.00 | 1.50 |
| 710 | Jim Kaat IA | 5.00 | 2.50 | 766 | Steve Hamilton | 3.00 | 1.50 |
| 711 | Bobby Bonds | 12.00 | 6.00 | 767 | Tom McCraw | 3.00 | 1.50 |
| 712 | Bobby Bonds IA | 6.00 | 3.00 | 768 | Denny Doyle | 3.00 | 1.50 |
| 713 | Gene Michael | 3.25 | 1.75 | 769 | Jack Aker | 3.25 | 1.75 |
| 714 | Gene Michael IA | 3.25 | 1.75 | 770 | Jim Wynn | 3.50 | 1.75 |
| 715 | Mike Epstein | 3.25 | 1.75 | 771 | Giants Team | 3.25 | 1.75 |

| | | NR MT | EX |
|---|---|---|---|
| 772 | Ken Tatum | 3.00 | 1.50 |
| 773 | Ron Brand | 3.00 | 1.50 |
| 774 | Luis Alvarado | 3.00 | 1.50 |
| 775 | Jerry Reuss | 3.50 | 1.75 |
| 776 | Bill Voss | 3.00 | 1.50 |
| 777 | Hoyt Wilhelm | 18.00 | 9.00 |
| 778 | Twins Rookies-(Vic Albury, *Rick Dempsey*, Jim Strickland) | 3.25 | 1.75 |
| 779 | Tony Cloninger | 3.25 | 1.75 |
| 780 | Dick Green | 3.00 | 1.50 |
| 781 | Jim McAndrew | 3.00 | 1.50 |
| 782 | Larry Stahl | 3.00 | 1.50 |
| 783 | Les Cain | 3.00 | 1.50 |
| 784 | Ken Aspromonte | 3.00 | 1.50 |
| 785 | Vic Davalillo | 3.00 | 1.50 |
| 786 | Chuck Brinkman | 3.25 | 1.75 |
| 787 | Ron Reed | 4.50 | 1.25 |

## 1973 Topps

CALIFORNIA ANGELS    OUTFIELD

Topps cut back to 660 cards in 1973. The set is interesting for it marks the last time cards were issued by series, a procedure which had produced many a scarce high number card over the years. These 2-1/2" by 3-1/2" cards have a color photo, accented by a silhouette of a player on the front, indicative of his position. Card backs are vertical for the first time since 1968, with the usual statistical and biographical information. Specialty cards begin with card number 1, which depicted Ruth, Mays and Aaron as the all-time home run leaders. It was followed by statistical leaders, although there also were additional all-time leader cards. Also present are playoff and World Series highlights. From the age-and-youth department, the 1973 Topps set has coaches and managers as well as more "Boy-hood Photos."

| | | NR MT | EX |
|---|---|---|---|
| | Complete Set: | 1200.00 | 600.00 |
| | Common Player: 1-396 | .40 | .20 |
| | Common Player: 397-528 | .70 | .35 |
| | Common Player: 529-660 | | |
| | | 2.00 | 1.00 |
| 1 | All Time Home Run Leaders (Hank Aaron, Willie Mays, Babe Ruth) | 30.00 | 22.50 |
| 2 | Rich Hebner | .50 | .25 |
| 3 | Jim Lonborg | .70 | .35 |
| 4 | John Milner | .40 | .20 |
| 5 | Ed Brinkman | .50 | .25 |
| 6 | Mac Scarce | .40 | .20 |
| 7 | Rangers Team | 1.25 | .60 |
| 8 | Tom Hall | .40 | .20 |
| 9 | Johnny Oates | .40 | .20 |
| 10 | Don Sutton | 2.00 | 1.00 |
| 11 | Chris Chambliss | .90 | .45 |
| 12a | Padres Mgr./Coaches (Dave Garcia, Johnny Podres, Bob Skinner, Whitey Wietelmann, Don Zimmer) (Coaches background brown) | .70 | .35 |
| 12b | Padres Mgr./Coaches (Dave Garcia, Johnny Podres, Bob Skinner, Whitey Wietelmann, Don Zimmer) (Coaches background orange) | .70 | .35 |
| 13 | George Hendrick | .90 | .45 |
| 14 | Sonny Siebert | .40 | .20 |
| 15 | Ralph Garr | .50 | .25 |
| 16 | Steve Braun | .40 | .20 |
| 17 | Fred Gladding | .40 | .20 |
| 18 | Leroy Stanton | .40 | .20 |
| 19 | Tim Foli | .40 | .20 |
| 20a | Stan Bahnsen (small gap in left border) | .70 | .35 |
| 20b | Stan Bahnsen (no gap) | .40 | .20 |
| 21 | Randy Hundley | .40 | .20 |
| 22 | Ted Abernathy | .40 | .20 |
| 23 | Dave Kingman | 2.00 | 1.00 |
| 24 | Al Santorini | .40 | .20 |
| 25 | Roy White | .70 | .35 |
| 26 | Pirates Team | 1.25 | .60 |
| 27 | Bill Gogolewski | .40 | .20 |
| 28 | Hal McRae | .70 | .35 |
| 29 | Tony Taylor | .40 | .20 |
| 30 | Tug McGraw | .80 | .40 |
| 31 | *Buddy Bell* | 4.00 | 2.00 |
| 32 | Fred Norman | .40 | .20 |
| 33 | Jim Breazeale | .40 | .20 |
| 34 | Pat Dobson | .50 | .25 |
| 35 | Willie Davis | .70 | .35 |
| 36 | Steve Barber | .40 | .20 |
| 37 | Bill Robinson | .40 | .20 |
| 38 | Mike Epstein | .50 | .25 |
| 39 | Dave Roberts | .40 | .20 |
| 40 | Reggie Smith | .70 | .35 |
| 41 | Tom Walker | .40 | .20 |
| 42 | Mike Andrews | .40 | .20 |
| 43 | *Randy Moffitt* | .50 | .25 |
| 44 | Rick Monday | .70 | .35 |
| 45 | Ellie Rodriguez (photo actually Paul Ratliff) | .40 | .20 |

| | NR MT | EX |
|---|---|---|
| 46 Lindy McDaniel | .50 | .25 |
| 47 Luis Melendez | .40 | .20 |
| 48 Paul Splittorff | .50 | .25 |
| 49a Twins Mgr./Coaches (Vern Morgan, Frank Quilici, Bob Rodgers, Ralph Rowe, Al Worthington) (Coaches background brown) | .70 | .35 |
| 49b Twins Mgr./Coaches (Vern Morgan, Frank Quilici, Bob Rodgers, Ralph Rowe, Al Worthington) (Coaches background orange) | .50 | .25 |
| 50 Roberto Clemente | 30.00 | 15.00 |
| 51 Chuck Seelbach | .40 | .20 |
| 52 Denis Menke | .40 | .20 |
| 53 Steve Dunning | .40 | .20 |
| 54 Checklist 1-132 | 2.00 | 1.00 |
| 55 Jon Matlack | .70 | .35 |
| 56 Merv Rettenmund | .50 | .25 |
| 57 Derrel Thomas | .40 | .20 |
| 58 Mike Paul | .40 | .20 |
| 59 *Steve Yeager* | .80 | .40 |
| 60 Ken Holtzman | .70 | .35 |
| 61 Batting Leaders (Rod Carew, Billy Williams) | 2.25 | 1.25 |
| 62 Home Run Leaders (Dick Allen, Johnny Bench) | 2.25 | 1.25 |
| 63 Runs Batted In Leaders (Dick Allen, Johnny Bench) | 2.25 | 1.25 |
| 64 Stolen Base Leaders (Lou Brock, Bert Campaneris) | 2.00 | 1.00 |
| 65 Earned Run Average Leaders (Steve Carlton, Luis Tiant) | 2.00 | 1.00 |
| 66 Victory Leaders (Steve Carlton, Gaylord Perry, Wilbur Wood) | 2.00 | 1.00 |
| 67 Strikeout Leaders (Steve Carlton, Nolan Ryan) | 8.00 | 4.00 |
| 68 Leading Firemen (Clay Carroll, Sparky Lyle) | 1.00 | .50 |
| 69 Phil Gagliano | .40 | .20 |
| 70 Milt Pappas | .70 | .35 |
| 71 Johnny Briggs | .40 | .20 |
| 72 Ron Reed | .50 | .25 |
| 73 Ed Herrmann | .40 | .20 |
| 74 Billy Champion | .40 | .20 |
| 75 Vada Pinson | 1.00 | .50 |
| 76 Doug Rader | .40 | .20 |
| 77 Mike Torrez | .50 | .25 |
| 78 Richie Scheinblum | .40 | .20 |
| 79 Jim Willoughby | .40 | .20 |
| 80 Tony Oliva | 2.00 | 1.00 |
| 81a Cubs Mgr./Coaches (Hank Aguirre, Ernie Banks, Larry Jansen, Whitey Lockman, Pete Reiser) (trees in Coaches background) | .90 | .45 |
| 81b Cubs Mgr./Coaches (Hank Aguirre, Ernie Banks, Larry Jansen, Whitey Lockman, Pete Reiser) (orange, solid background) | .70 | .35 |
| 82 Fritz Peterson | .50 | .25 |
| 83 Leron Lee | .40 | .20 |
| 84 Rollie Fingers | 7.00 | 3.50 |
| 85 Ted Simmons | 2.00 | 1.00 |
| 86 Tom McCraw | .40 | .20 |
| 87 Ken Boswell | .40 | .20 |
| 88 Mickey Stanley | .50 | .25 |
| 89 Jack Billingham | .40 | .20 |
| 90 Brooks Robinson | 5.00 | 2.50 |
| 91 Dodgers Team | 2.25 | 1.25 |
| 92 Jerry Bell | .40 | .20 |
| 93 Jesus Alou | .50 | .25 |
| 94 Dick Billings | .40 | .20 |
| 95 Steve Blass | .50 | .25 |
| 96 Doug Griffin | .40 | .20 |
| 97 Willie Montanez | .50 | .25 |
| 98 Dick Woodson | .40 | .20 |
| 99 Carl Taylor | .40 | .20 |
| 100 Hank Aaron | 25.00 | 12.50 |
| 101 Ken Henderson | .40 | .20 |
| 102 Rudy May | .50 | .25 |
| 103 Celerino Sanchez | .50 | .25 |
| 104 Reggie Cleveland | .40 | .20 |
| 105 Carlos May | .50 | .25 |
| 106 Terry Humphrey | .40 | .20 |
| 107 Phil Hennigan | .40 | .20 |
| 108 Bill Russell | .70 | .35 |
| 109 Doyle Alexander | 2.25 | 1.25 |
| 110 Bob Watson | .50 | .25 |
| 111 Dave Nelson | .40 | .20 |
| 112 Gary Ross | .40 | .20 |
| 113 Jerry Grote | .50 | .25 |
| 114 Lynn McGlothlen | .40 | .20 |
| 115 Ron Santo | 1.00 | .50 |
| 116a Yankees Mgr./Coaches (Jim Hegan, Ralph Houk, Elston Howard, Dick Howser, Jim Turner) (Coaches background brown) | 2.25 | 1.25 |
| 116b Yankees Mgr./Coaches (Jim Hegan, Ralph Houk, Elston Howard, Dick Howser, Jim Turner) (Coaches background orange) | .90 | .45 |
| 117 Ramon Hernandez | .40 | .20 |
| 118 John Mayberry | .70 | .35 |
| 119 Larry Bowa | 1.00 | .50 |
| 120 Joe Coleman | .50 | .25 |
| 121 Dave Rader | .40 | .20 |
| 122 Jim Strickland | .40 | .20 |
| 123 Sandy Alomar | .40 | .20 |
| 124 Jim Hardin | .40 | .20 |
| 125 Ron Fairly | .70 | .35 |
| 126 Jim Brewer | .40 | .20 |
| 127 Brewers Team | 1.25 | .60 |
| 128 Ted Sizemore | .40 | .20 |
| 129 Terry Forster | .70 | .35 |
| 130 Pete Rose | 20.00 | 10.00 |
| 131a Red Sox Mgr./Coaches (Doug Camilli, Eddie Kasko, Don Lenhardt, Eddie Popowski, Lee Stange) (Coaches background | | |

| | | NR MT | EX |
|---|---|---|---|
| | brown) | .70 | .35 |
| 131b | Red Sox Mgr./Coaches (Doug Camilli, Eddie Kasko, Don Lenhardt, Eddie Popowski, Lee Stange) (Coaches background orange) | .50 | .25 |
| 132 | Matty Alou | .80 | .40 |
| 133 | Dave Roberts | .40 | .20 |
| 134 | Milt Wilcox | .50 | .25 |
| 135 | Lee May | .70 | .35 |
| 136a | Orioles Mgr./Coaches (George Bamberger, Jim Frey, Billy Hunter, George Staller, Earl Weaver) (Coaches background brown) | 2.25 | 1.25 |
| 136b | Orioles Mgr./Coaches (George Bamberger, Jim Frey, Billy Hunter, George Staller, Earl Weaver) (Coaches background orange) | .90 | .45 |
| 137 | Jim Beauchamp | .40 | .20 |
| 138 | Horacio Pina | .40 | .20 |
| 139 | Carmen Fanzone | .40 | .20 |
| 140 | Lou Piniella | 1.00 | .50 |
| 141 | Bruce Kison | .50 | .25 |
| 142 | Thurman Munson | 10.00 | 5.00 |
| 143 | John Curtis | .40 | .20 |
| 144 | Marty Perez | .40 | .20 |
| 145 | Bobby Bonds | .90 | .45 |
| 146 | Woodie Fryman | .50 | .25 |
| 147 | Mike Anderson | .40 | .20 |
| 148 | *Dave Goltz* | .80 | .40 |
| 149 | Ron Hunt | .50 | .25 |
| 150 | Wilbur Wood | .70 | .35 |
| 151 | Wes Parker | .50 | .25 |
| 152 | Dave May | .40 | .20 |
| 153 | Al Hrabosky | .70 | .35 |
| 154 | Jeff Torborg | .50 | .25 |
| 155 | Sal Bando | .90 | .45 |
| 156 | Cesar Geronimo | .50 | .25 |
| 157 | Denny Riddleberger | .40 | .20 |
| 158 | Astros Team | 1.25 | .60 |
| 159 | Clarence Gaston | .40 | .20 |
| 160 | Jim Palmer | 10.00 | 5.00 |
| 161 | Ted Martinez | .40 | .20 |
| 162 | Pete Broberg | .40 | .20 |
| 163 | Vic Davalillo | .50 | .25 |
| 164 | Monty Montgomery | .40 | .20 |
| 165 | Luis Aparicio | 2.75 | 1.50 |
| 166 | Terry Harmon | .40 | .20 |
| 167 | Steve Stone | .70 | .35 |
| 168 | Jim Northrup | .50 | .25 |
| 169 | Ron Schueler | .40 | .20 |
| 170 | Harmon Killebrew | 5.00 | 2.50 |
| 171 | Bernie Carbo | .40 | .20 |
| 172 | Steve Kline | .50 | .25 |
| 173 | Hal Breeden | .40 | .20 |
| 174 | *Rich Gossage* | 18.00 | 9.00 |
| 175 | Frank Robinson | 5.00 | 2.50 |
| 176 | Chuck Taylor | .40 | .20 |
| 177 | Bill Plummer | .40 | .20 |
| 178 | Don Rose | .40 | .20 |
| 179a | A's Mgr./Coaches (Jerry Adair, Vern Hoscheit, | | |

| | | NR MT | EX |
|---|---|---|---|
| | Irv Noren, Wes Stock, Dick Williams) (Coaches background brown) | 1.00 | .50 |
| 179b | A's Mgr./Coaches (Jerry Adair, Vern Hoscheit, Irv Noren, Wes Stock, Dick Williams) (Coaches background orange) | .70 | .35 |
| 180 | Fergie Jenkins | 4.00 | 2.00 |
| 181 | Jack Brohamer | .40 | .20 |
| 182 | *Mike Caldwell* | .70 | .35 |
| 183 | Don Buford | .50 | .25 |
| 184 | Jerry Koosman | .70 | .35 |
| 185 | Jim Wynn | .70 | .35 |
| 186 | Bill Fahey | .40 | .20 |
| 187 | Luke Walker | .40 | .20 |
| 188 | Cookie Rojas | .40 | .20 |
| 189 | Greg Luzinski | .90 | .45 |
| 190 | Bob Gibson | 5.00 | 2.50 |
| 191 | Tigers Team | 2.00 | 1.00 |
| 192 | Pat Jarvis | .40 | .20 |
| 193 | Carlton Fisk | 45.00 | 23.00 |
| 194 | *Jorge Orta* | .70 | .35 |
| 195 | Clay Carroll | .50 | .25 |
| 196 | Ken McMullen | .40 | .20 |
| 197 | Ed Goodson | .40 | .20 |
| 198 | Horace Clarke | .50 | .25 |
| 199 | Bert Blyleven | 4.00 | 3.00 |
| 200 | Billy Williams | 2.75 | 1.50 |
| 201 | A.L. Playoffs (Hendrick Scores Winning Run.) | 2.25 | 1.25 |
| 202 | N.L. Playoffs (Foster's Run Decides It.) | 2.25 | 1.25 |
| 203 | World Series Game 1 (Tenace The Menace.) | 2.25 | 1.25 |
| 204 | World Series Game 2 (A's Make It Two Straight.) | 2.25 | 1.25 |
| 205 | World Series Game 3 (Reds Win Squeeker.) | 2.25 | 1.25 |
| 206 | World Series Game 4 (Tenace Singles In Ninth.) | 2.25 | 1.25 |
| 207 | World Series Game 5 (Odom Out At Plate.) | 2.25 | 1.25 |
| 208 | World Series Game 6 (Reds' Slugging Ties Series.) | 2.25 | 1.25 |
| 209 | World Series Game 7 (Campy Starts Winning Rally.) | 2.25 | 1.25 |
| 210 | World Series Summary (World Champions.) | 2.25 | 1.25 |
| 211 | Balor Moore | .40 | .20 |
| 212 | Joe Lahoud | .40 | .20 |
| 213 | Steve Garvey | 15.00 | 7.50 |
| 214 | Dave Hamilton | .40 | .20 |
| 215 | Dusty Baker | .70 | .35 |
| 216 | Toby Harrah | .70 | .35 |
| 217 | Don Wilson | .40 | .20 |
| 218 | Aurelio Rodriguez | .50 | .25 |
| 219 | Cardinals Team | 1.25 | .60 |
| 220 | Nolan Ryan | 85.00 | 43.00 |
| 221 | Fred Kendall | .40 | .20 |
| 222 | Rob Gardner | .40 | .20 |
| 223 | Bud Harrelson | .50 | .25 |
| 224 | Bill Lee | .50 | .25 |

| | | NR MT | EX |
|---|---|---|---|
| 225 | Al Oliver | 2.00 | 1.00 |
| 226 | Ray Fosse | .40 | .20 |
| 227 | Wayne Twitchell | .40 | .20 |
| 228 | Bobby Darwin | .40 | .20 |
| 229 | Roric Harrison | .40 | .20 |
| 230 | Joe Morgan | 5.00 | 2.50 |
| 231 | Bill Parsons | .40 | .20 |
| 232 | Ken Singleton | .70 | .35 |
| 233 | Ed Kirkpatrick | .40 | .20 |
| 234 | *Bill North* | .70 | .35 |
| 235 | Jim Hunter | 4.00 | 2.00 |
| 236 | Tito Fuentes | .40 | .20 |
| 237a | Braves Mgr./Coaches (Lew Burdette, Jim Busby, Roy Hartsfield, Eddie Mathews, Ken Silvestri) (Coaches background brown) | 2.00 | 1.00 |
| 237b | Braves Mgr./Coaches (Lew Burdette, Jim Busby, Roy Hartsfield, Eddie Mathews, Ken Silvestri) (Coaches background orange) | 2.25 | 1.25 |
| 238 | Tony Muser | .40 | .20 |
| 239 | Pete Richert | .40 | .20 |
| 240 | Bobby Murcer | .80 | .40 |
| 241 | Dwain Anderson | .40 | .20 |
| 242 | George Culver | .40 | .20 |
| 243 | Angels Team | 1.25 | .60 |
| 244 | Ed Acosta | .40 | .20 |
| 245 | Carl Yastrzemski | 15.00 | 7.50 |
| 246 | Ken Sanders | .40 | .20 |
| 247 | Del Unser | .40 | .20 |
| 248 | Jerry Johnson | .40 | .20 |
| 249 | Larry Biittner | .40 | .20 |
| 250 | Manny Sanguillen | .50 | .25 |
| 251 | Roger Nelson | .40 | .20 |
| 252a | Giants Mgr./Coaches (Joe Amalfitano, Charlie Fox, Andy Gilbert, Don McMahon, John McNamara) (Coaches background brown) | .70 | .35 |
| 252b | Giants Mgr./Coaches (Joe Amalfitano, Charlie Fox, Andy Gilbert, Don McMahon, John McNamara) (Coaches background orange) | .50 | .25 |
| 253 | Mark Belanger | .50 | .25 |
| 254 | Bill Stoneman | .40 | .20 |
| 255 | Reggie Jackson | 32.00 | 16.00 |
| 256 | Chris Zachary | .40 | .20 |
| 257a | Mets Mgr./Coaches (Yogi Berra, Roy McMillan, Joe Pignatano, Rube Walker, Eddie Yost) (Coaches background brown) | 2.25 | 1.25 |
| 257b | Mets Mgr./Coaches (Yogi Berra, Roy McMillan, Joe Pignatano, Rube Walker, Eddie Yost) (Coaches background orange) | 2.00 | 1.00 |
| 258 | Tommy John | 2.25 | 1.25 |

| | | NR MT | EX |
|---|---|---|---|
| 259 | Jim Holt | .40 | .20 |
| 260 | Gary Nolan | .40 | .20 |
| 261 | Pat Kelly | .40 | .20 |
| 262 | Jack Aker | .40 | .20 |
| 263 | George Scott | .50 | .25 |
| 264 | Checklist 133-264 | 2.00 | 1.00 |
| 265 | Gene Michael | .70 | .35 |
| 266 | Mike Lum | .40 | .20 |
| 267 | Lloyd Allen | .40 | .20 |
| 268 | Jerry Morales | .40 | .20 |
| 269 | Tim McCarver | .90 | .45 |
| 270 | Luis Tiant | 1.00 | .50 |
| 271 | Tom Hutton | .40 | .20 |
| 272 | Ed Farmer | .40 | .20 |
| 273 | Chris Speier | .50 | .25 |
| 274 | Darold Knowles | .40 | .20 |
| 275 | Tony Perez | 2.00 | 1.00 |
| 276 | Joe Lovitto | .40 | .20 |
| 277 | Bob Miller | .40 | .20 |
| 278 | Orioles Team | 1.25 | .60 |
| 279 | Mike Strahler | .40 | .20 |
| 280 | Al Kaline | 6.00 | 3.00 |
| 281 | Mike Jorgensen | .40 | .20 |
| 282 | Steve Hovley | .40 | .20 |
| 283 | Ray Sadecki | .40 | .20 |
| 284 | Glenn Borgmann | .40 | .20 |
| 285 | Don Kessinger | .50 | .25 |
| 286 | Frank Linzy | .40 | .20 |
| 287 | Eddie Leon | .40 | .20 |
| 288 | Gary Gentry | .40 | .20 |
| 289 | Bob Oliver | .40 | .20 |
| 290 | Cesar Cedeno | .70 | .35 |
| 291 | Rogelio Moret | .40 | .20 |
| 292 | Jose Cruz | 1.00 | .50 |
| 293 | Bernie Allen | .50 | .25 |
| 294 | Steve Arlin | .40 | .20 |
| 295 | Bert Campaneris | .80 | .40 |
| 296 | Reds Mgr./Coaches (Sparky Anderson, Alex Grammas, Ted Kluszewski, George Scherger, Larry Shepard) | .90 | .45 |
| 297 | Walt Williams | .40 | .20 |
| 298 | Ron Bryant | .40 | .20 |
| 299 | Ted Ford | .40 | .20 |
| 300 | Steve Carlton | 15.00 | 7.50 |
| 301 | Billy Grabarkewitz | .40 | .20 |
| 302 | Terry Crowley | .40 | .20 |
| 303 | Nelson Briles | .40 | .20 |
| 304 | Duke Sims | .40 | .20 |
| 305 | Willie Mays | 35.00 | 17.50 |
| 306 | Tom Burgmeier | .40 | .20 |
| 307 | Boots Day | .40 | .20 |
| 308 | Skip Lockwood | .40 | .20 |
| 309 | Paul Popovich | .40 | .20 |
| 310 | Dick Allen | 1.00 | .50 |
| 311 | Joe Decker | .40 | .20 |
| 312 | Oscar Brown | .40 | .20 |
| 313 | Jim Ray | .40 | .20 |
| 314 | Ron Swoboda | .50 | .25 |
| 315 | John Odom | .50 | .25 |
| 316 | Padres Team | 1.25 | .60 |
| 317 | Danny Cater | .40 | .20 |
| 318 | Jim McGlothlin | .40 | .20 |
| 319 | Jim Spencer | .40 | .20 |
| 320 | Lou Brock | 6.00 | 3.00 |
| 321 | Rich Hinton | .40 | .20 |

| | | NR MT | EX |
|---|---|---|---|
| 322 | *Garry Maddox* | 1.00 | .50 |
| 323 | Tigers Mgr./Coaches (Art Fowler, Billy Martin, Joe Schultz, Charlie Silvera, Dick Tracewski) | 2.25 | 1.25 |
| 324 | Al Downing | .50 | .25 |
| 325 | Boog Powell | 2.25 | 1.25 |
| 326 | Darrell Brandon | .40 | .20 |
| 327 | John Lowenstein | .40 | .20 |
| 328 | Bill Bonham | .40 | .20 |
| 329 | Ed Kranepool | .50 | .25 |
| 330 | Rod Carew | 18.00 | 9.00 |
| 331 | Carl Morton | .40 | .20 |
| 332 | *John Felske* | .50 | .25 |
| 333 | Gene Clines | .40 | .20 |
| 334 | Freddie Patek | .40 | .20 |
| 335 | Bob Tolan | .50 | .25 |
| 336 | Tom Bradley | .40 | .20 |
| 337 | Dave Duncan | .40 | .20 |
| 338 | Checklist 265-396 | 2.00 | 1.00 |
| 339 | Dick Tidrow | .50 | .25 |
| 340 | Nate Colbert | .50 | .25 |
| 341 | Boyhood Photo (Jim Palmer) | 2.00 | 1.00 |
| 342 | Boyhood Photo (Sam McDowell) | .70 | .35 |
| 343 | Boyhood Photo (Bobby Murcer) | .70 | .35 |
| 344 | Boyhood Photo (Jim Hunter) | 2.00 | 1.00 |
| 345 | Boyhood Photo (Chris Speier) | .50 | .25 |
| 346 | Boyhood Photo (Gaylord Perry) | 2.00 | 1.00 |
| 347 | Royals Team | 1.25 | .60 |
| 348 | Rennie Stennett | .50 | .25 |
| 349 | Dick McAuliffe | .50 | .25 |
| 350 | Tom Seaver | 28.00 | 14.00 |
| 351 | Jimmy Stewart | .40 | .20 |
| 352 | *Don Stanhouse* | .70 | .35 |
| 353 | Steve Brye | .40 | .20 |
| 354 | Billy Parker | .40 | .20 |
| 355 | Mike Marshall | .70 | .35 |
| 356 | White Sox Mgr. Coaches (Joe Lonnett, Jim Mahoney, Al Monchak, Johnny Sain, Chuck Tanner) | .70 | .35 |
| 357 | Ross Grimsley | .50 | .25 |
| 358 | Jim Nettles | .40 | .20 |
| 359 | Cecil Upshaw | .40 | .20 |
| 360 | Joe Rudi (photo actually Gene Tenace) | .70 | .35 |
| 361 | Fran Healy | .40 | .20 |
| 362 | Eddie Watt | .40 | .20 |
| 363 | Jackie Hernandez | .40 | .20 |
| 364 | Rick Wise | .50 | .25 |
| 365 | Rico Petrocelli | .70 | .35 |
| 366 | Brock Davis | .40 | .20 |
| 367 | Burt Hooton | .70 | .35 |
| 368 | Bill Buckner | .90 | .45 |
| 369 | Lerrin LaGrow | .40 | .20 |
| 370 | Willie Stargell | 5.00 | 2.50 |
| 371 | Mike Kekich | .50 | .25 |
| 372 | Oscar Gamble | .50 | .25 |
| 373 | Clyde Wright | .40 | .20 |
| 374 | Darrell Evans | .90 | .45 |

| | | NR MT | EX |
|---|---|---|---|
| 375 | Larry Dierker | .50 | .25 |
| 376 | Frank Duffy | .40 | .20 |
| 377 | Expos Mgr./Coaches (Dave Bristol, Larry Doby, Gene Mauch, Cal McLish, Jerry Zimmerman) | .70 | .35 |
| 378 | Lenny Randle | .40 | .20 |
| 379 | Cy Acosta | .40 | .20 |
| 380 | Johnny Bench | 25.00 | 12.50 |
| 381 | Vicente Romo | .40 | .20 |
| 382 | Mike Hegan | .40 | .20 |
| 383 | Diego Segui | .40 | .20 |
| 384 | Don Baylor | 2.25 | 1.25 |
| 385 | Jim Perry | .70 | .35 |
| 386 | Don Money | .50 | .25 |
| 387 | Jim Barr | .40 | .20 |
| 388 | Ben Oglivie | .70 | .35 |
| 389 | Mets Team | 2.00 | 1.00 |
| 390 | Mickey Lolich | .90 | .45 |
| 391 | *Lee Lacy* | 1.00 | .50 |
| 392 | Dick Drago | .40 | .20 |
| 393 | Jose Cardenal | .50 | .25 |
| 394 | Sparky Lyle | .90 | .45 |
| 395 | Roger Metzger | .40 | .20 |
| 396 | Grant Jackson | .40 | .20 |
| 397 | Dave Cash | .70 | .35 |
| 398 | Rich Hand | .70 | .35 |
| 399 | George Foster | 2.25 | 1.25 |
| 400 | Gaylord Perry | 6.00 | 3.00 |
| 401 | Clyde Mashore | .70 | .35 |
| 402 | Jack Hiatt | .70 | .35 |
| 403 | Sonny Jackson | .70 | .35 |
| 404 | Chuck Brinkman | .70 | .35 |
| 405 | Cesar Tovar | .70 | .35 |
| 406 | Paul Lindblad | .70 | .35 |
| 407 | Felix Millan | .70 | .35 |
| 408 | Jim Colborn | .70 | .35 |
| 409 | Ivan Murrell | .70 | .35 |
| 410 | Willie McCovey | 5.00 | 2.50 |
| 411 | Ray Corbin | .70 | .35 |
| 412 | Manny Mota | .80 | .40 |
| 413 | Tom Timmermann | .70 | .35 |
| 414 | Ken Rudolph | .70 | .35 |
| 415 | Marty Pattin | .70 | .35 |
| 416 | Paul Schaal | .70 | .35 |
| 417 | Scipio Spinks | .70 | .35 |
| 418 | Bobby Grich | .80 | .40 |
| 419 | Casey Cox | .70 | .35 |
| 420 | Tommie Agee | .70 | .35 |
| 421 | Angels Mgr./Coaches (Tom Morgan, Salty Parker, Jimmie Reese, John Roseboro, Bobby Winkles) | .70 | .35 |
| 422 | Bob Robertson | .70 | .35 |
| 423 | Johnny Jeter | .70 | .35 |
| 424 | Denny Doyle | .70 | .35 |
| 425 | Alex Johnson | .70 | .35 |
| 426 | Dave LaRoche | .70 | .35 |
| 427 | Rick Auerbach | .70 | .35 |
| 428 | Wayne Simpson | .70 | .35 |
| 429 | Jim Fairey | .70 | .35 |
| 430 | Vida Blue | 1.00 | .50 |
| 431 | Gerry Moses | .70 | .35 |
| 432 | Dan Frisella | .70 | .35 |
| 433 | Willie Horton | .80 | .40 |
| 434 | Giants Team | 2.25 | 1.25 |

| | | NR MT | EX |
|---|---|---|---|
| 435 | Rico Carty | .80 | .40 |
| 436 | Jim McAndrew | .70 | .35 |
| 437 | John Kennedy | .70 | .35 |
| 438 | Enzo Hernandez | .70 | .35 |
| 439 | Eddie Fisher | .70 | .35 |
| 440 | Glenn Beckert | .70 | .35 |
| 441 | Gail Hopkins | .70 | .35 |
| 442 | Dick Dietz | .70 | .35 |
| 443 | Danny Thompson | .70 | .35 |
| 444 | Ken Brett | .70 | .35 |
| 445 | Ken Berry | .70 | .35 |
| 446 | Jerry Reuss | .80 | .40 |
| 447 | Joe Hague | .70 | .35 |
| 448 | John Hiller | .70 | .35 |
| 449a | Indians Mgr./Coaches (Ken Aspromonte, Rocky Colavito, Joe Lutz, Warren Spahn) (Spahn's ear pointed) | .70 | .35 |
| 449b | Indians Mgr./Coaches (Ken Aspromonte, Rocky Colavito, Joe Lutz, Warren Spahn) (Spahn's ear round) | 1.00 | .50 |
| 450 | Joe Torre | 2.25 | 1.25 |
| 451 | John Vukovich | .70 | .35 |
| 452 | Paul Casanova | .70 | .35 |
| 453 | Checklist 397-528 | 2.25 | 1.25 |
| 454 | Tom Haller | .70 | .35 |
| 455 | Bill Melton | .70 | .35 |
| 456 | Dick Green | .70 | .35 |
| 457 | John Strohmayer | .70 | .35 |
| 458 | Jim Mason | .70 | .35 |
| 459 | Jimmy Howarth | .70 | .35 |
| 460 | Bill Freehan | .80 | .40 |
| 461 | Mike Corkins | .70 | .35 |
| 462 | Ron Blomberg | .70 | .35 |
| 463 | Ken Tatum | .70 | .35 |
| 464 | Cubs Team | 2.25 | 1.25 |
| 465 | Dave Giusti | .70 | .35 |
| 466 | Jose Arcia | .70 | .35 |
| 467 | Mike Ryan | .70 | .35 |
| 468 | Tom Griffin | .70 | .35 |
| 469 | Dan Monzon | .70 | .35 |
| 470 | Mike Cuellar | .80 | .40 |
| 471 | Hit Leader (Ty Cobb) | 4.00 | 2.00 |
| 472 | Grand Slam Leader (Lou Gehrig) | 4.00 | 2.00 |
| 473 | Total Base Leader (Hank Aaron) | 4.00 | 2.00 |
| 474 | R.B.I. Leader (Babe Ruth) | 8.00 | 4.00 |
| 475 | Batting Leader (Ty Cobb) | 4.00 | 2.00 |
| 476 | Shutout Leader (Walter Johnson) | 2.00 | 1.00 |
| 477 | Victory Leader (Cy Young) | 2.00 | 1.00 |
| 478 | Strikeout Leader (Walter Johnson) | 2.00 | 1.00 |
| 479 | Hal Lanier | .80 | .40 |
| 480 | Juan Marichal | 4.00 | 2.00 |
| 481 | White Sox Team | 2.00 | 1.00 |
| 482 | *Rick Reuschel* | 4.00 | 2.00 |
| 483 | Dal Maxvill | .70 | .35 |
| 484 | Ernie McAnally | .70 | .35 |

| | | NR MT | EX |
|---|---|---|---|
| 485 | Norm Cash | 1.00 | .50 |
| 486a | Phillies Mgr./Coaches (Carroll Berringer, Billy DeMars, Danny Ozark, Ray Rippelmeyer, Bobby Wine) (Coaches background brown-red) | .90 | .45 |
| 486b | Phillies Mgr./Coaches (Carroll Beringer, Billy DeMars, Danny Ozark, Ray Rippelmeyer, Bobby Wine) (Coaches background orange) | .70 | .35 |
| 487 | Bruce Dal Canton | .70 | .35 |
| 488 | Dave Campbell | .70 | .35 |
| 489 | Jeff Burroughs | .80 | .40 |
| 490 | Claude Osteen | .80 | .40 |
| 491 | Bob Montgomery | .70 | .35 |
| 492 | Pedro Borbon | .70 | .35 |
| 493 | Duffy Dyer | .70 | .35 |
| 494 | Rich Morales | .70 | .35 |
| 495 | Tommy Helms | .70 | .35 |
| 496 | Ray Lamb | .70 | .35 |
| 497 | Cardinals Mgr./Coaches (Vern Benson, George Kissell, Red Schoendienst, Barney Schultz) | 1.25 | .60 |
| 498 | Graig Nettles | 2.50 | 1.25 |
| 499 | Bob Moose | .70 | .35 |
| 500 | A's Team | 2.25 | 1.25 |
| 501 | Larry Gura | .70 | .35 |
| 502 | Bobby Valentine | .80 | .40 |
| 503 | Phil Niekro | 5.00 | 2.50 |
| 504 | Earl Williams | .70 | .35 |
| 505 | Bob Bailey | .70 | .35 |
| 506 | Bart Johnson | .70 | .35 |
| 507 | Darrel Chaney | .70 | .35 |
| 508 | Gates Brown | .70 | .35 |
| 509 | Jim Nash | .70 | .35 |
| 510 | Amos Otis | .80 | .40 |
| 511 | Sam McDowell | .80 | .40 |
| 512 | Dalton Jones | .70 | .35 |
| 513 | Dave Marshall | .70 | .35 |
| 514 | Jerry Kenney | .70 | .35 |
| 515 | Andy Messersmith | .70 | .35 |
| 516 | Danny Walton | .70 | .35 |
| 517a | Pirates Mgr./Coaches (Don Leppert, Bill Mazeroski, Dave Ricketts, Bill Virdon, Mel Wright) (Coaches background brown) | 2.25 | 1.25 |
| 517b | Pirates Mgr./Coaches (Don Leppert, Bill Mazeroski, Dave Ricketts, Bill Virdon, Mel Wright) (Coaches background orange) | .70 | .35 |
| 518 | Bob Veale | .70 | .35 |
| 519 | John Edwards | .70 | .35 |
| 520 | Mel Stottlemyre | .80 | .40 |
| 521 | Braves Team | 2.25 | 1.25 |
| 522 | Leo Cardenas | .70 | .35 |
| 523 | Wayne Granger | .70 | .35 |
| 524 | Gene Tenace | .70 | .35 |
| 525 | Jim Fregosi | .90 | .45 |
| 526 | Ollie Brown | .70 | .35 |

| | | NR MT | EX |
|---|---|---|---|
| 527 | Dan McGinn | .70 | .35 |
| 528 | Paul Blair | .70 | .35 |
| 529 | Milt May | 2.00 | 1.00 |
| 530 | Jim Kaat | 4.00 | 2.00 |
| 531 | Ron Woods | 2.00 | 1.00 |
| 532 | Steve Mingori | 2.00 | 1.00 |
| 533 | Larry Stahl | 2.00 | 1.00 |
| 534 | Dave Lemonds | 2.00 | 1.00 |
| 535 | John Callison | 2.25 | 1.25 |
| 536 | Phillies Team | 2.50 | 1.25 |
| 537 | Bill Slayback | 2.00 | 1.00 |
| 538 | Jim Hart | 2.25 | 1.25 |
| 539 | Tom Murphy | 2.00 | 1.00 |
| 540 | Cleon Jones | 2.25 | 1.25 |
| 541 | Bob Bolin | 2.00 | 1.00 |
| 542 | Pat Corrales | 2.25 | 1.25 |
| 543 | Alan Foster | 2.00 | 1.00 |
| 544 | Von Joshua | 2.00 | 1.00 |
| 545 | Orlando Cepeda | 4.00 | 2.00 |
| 546 | Jim York | 2.00 | 1.00 |
| 547 | Bobby Heise | 2.00 | 1.00 |
| 548 | Don Durham | 2.00 | 1.00 |
| 549 | Rangers Mgr./Coaches (Chuck Estrada, Whitey Herzog, Chuck Hiller, Jackie Moore) | 2.00 | 1.00 |
| 550 | Dave Johnson | 2.75 | 1.50 |
| 551 | Mike Kilkenny | 2.00 | 1.00 |
| 552 | J.C. Martin | 2.00 | 1.00 |
| 553 | Mickey Scott | 2.00 | 1.00 |
| 554 | Dave Concepcion | 2.50 | 1.25 |
| 555 | Bill Hands | 2.00 | 1.00 |
| 556 | Yankees Team | 6.00 | 3.00 |
| 557 | Bernie Williams | 2.00 | 1.00 |
| 558 | Jerry May | 2.00 | 1.00 |
| 559 | Barry Lersch | 2.00 | 1.00 |
| 560 | Frank Howard | 2.25 | 1.25 |
| 561 | Jim Geddes | 2.00 | 1.00 |
| 562 | Wayne Garrett | 2.00 | 1.00 |
| 563 | Larry Haney | 2.00 | 1.00 |
| 564 | Mike Thompson | 2.00 | 1.00 |
| 565 | Jim Hickman | 2.25 | 1.25 |
| 566 | Lew Krausse | 2.00 | 1.00 |
| 567 | Bob Fenwick | 2.00 | 1.00 |
| 568 | Ray Newman | 2.00 | 1.00 |
| 569 | Dodgers Mgr./Coaches (Red Adams, Walt Alston, Monty Basgall, Jim Gillam, Tom Lasorda) | 3.00 | 1.50 |
| 570 | Bill Singer | 2.25 | 1.25 |
| 571 | Rusty Torres | 2.00 | 1.00 |
| 572 | Gary Sutherland | 2.00 | 1.00 |
| 573 | Fred Beene | 2.25 | 1.25 |
| 574 | Bob Didier | 2.00 | 1.00 |
| 575 | Dock Ellis | 2.25 | 1.25 |
| 576 | Expos Team | 2.50 | 1.25 |
| 577 | Eric Soderholm | 2.25 | 1.25 |
| 578 | Ken Wright | 2.00 | 1.00 |
| 579 | Tom Grieve | 2.00 | 1.00 |
| 580 | Joe Pepitone | 2.00 | 1.00 |
| 581 | Steve Kealey | 2.00 | 1.00 |
| 582 | Darrell Porter | 2.25 | 1.25 |
| 583 | Bill Greif | 2.00 | 1.00 |
| 584 | Chris Arnold | 2.00 | 1.00 |
| 585 | Joe Niekro | 2.00 | 1.00 |
| 586 | Bill Sudakis | 2.25 | 1.25 |
| 587 | Rich McKinney | 2.00 | 1.00 |

| | | NR MT | EX |
|---|---|---|---|
| 588 | Checklist 529-660 | 20.00 | 10.00 |
| 589 | Ken Forsch | 2.25 | 1.25 |
| 590 | Deron Johnson | 2.00 | 1.00 |
| 591 | Mike Hedlund | 2.00 | 1.00 |
| 592 | John Boccabella | 2.00 | 1.00 |
| 593 | Royals Mgr./Coaches (Galen Cisco, Harry Dunlop, Charlie Lau, Jack McKeon) | 2.25 | 1.25 |
| 594 | Vic Harris | 2.00 | 1.00 |
| 595 | Don Gullett | 2.25 | 1.25 |
| 596 | Red Sox Team | 2.75 | 1.50 |
| 597 | Mickey Rivers | 2.25 | 1.25 |
| 598 | Phil Roof | 2.00 | 1.00 |
| 599 | Ed Crosby | 2.00 | 1.00 |
| 600 | Dave McNally | 2.25 | 1.25 |
| 601 | Rookie Catchers (George Pena, Sergio Robles, Rick Stelmaszek) | 2.00 | 1.00 |
| 602 | Rookie Pitchers (Mel Behney, Ralph Garcia, *Doug Rau*) | 2.25 | 1.25 |
| 603 | Rookie Third Basemen (Terry Hughes, Bill McNulty, *Ken Reitz*) | 2.25 | 1.25 |
| 604 | Rookie Pitchers (Jesse Jefferson, Dennis O'Toole, Bob Strampe) | 2.00 | 1.00 |
| 605 | Rookie First Basemen (Pat Bourque, *Enos Cabell*, Gonzalo Marquez) | 2.25 | 1.25 |
| 606 | Rookie Outfielders (*Gary Matthews*, Tom Paciorek, Jorge Roque) | 2.25 | 1.25 |
| 607 | Rookie Shortstops (Ray Busse, Pepe Frias, Mario Guerrero) | 2.00 | 1.00 |
| 608 | Rookie Pitchers (*Steve Busby*, Dick Colpaert, *George Medich*) | 2.25 | 1.25 |
| 609 | Rookie Second Basemen (Larvell Blanks, Pedro Garcia, *Dave Lopes*) | 4.00 | 2.00 |
| 610 | Rookie Pitchers (Jimmy Freeman, Charlie Hough, Hank Webb) | 2.25 | 1.25 |
| 611 | Rookie Outfielders (Rich Coggins, Jim Wohlford, Richie Zisk) | 2.25 | 1.25 |
| 612 | Rookie Pitchers (Steve Lawson, Bob Reynolds, Brent Strom) | 2.00 | 1.00 |
| 613 | Rookie Catchers (*Bob Boone*, Mike Ivie, Skip Jutze) | 35.00 | 17.50 |
| 614 | Rookie Outfielders (*Alonza Bumbry, Dwight Evans*, Charlie Spikes) | 60.00 | 30.00 |
| 615 | Rookie Third Basemen (Ron Cey, John Hilton, *Mike Schmidt*) | 450.00 | 225.00 |
| 616 | Rookie Pitchers (Norm Angelini, Steve Blateric, Mike Garman) | 2.25 | 1.25 |

| | | NR MT | EX |
|---|---|---|---|
| 617 | Rich Chiles | 2.00 | 1.00 |
| 618 | Andy Etchebarren | 2.00 | 1.00 |
| 619 | Billy Wilson | 2.00 | 1.00 |
| 620 | Tommy Harper | 2.25 | 1.25 |
| 621 | Joe Ferguson | 2.00 | 1.00 |
| 622 | Larry Hisle | 2.25 | 1.25 |
| 623 | Steve Renko | 2.00 | 1.00 |
| 624 | Astros Mgr./Coaches (Leo Durocher, Preston Gomez, Grady Hatton, Hub Kittle, Jim Owens) | 2.25 | 1.25 |
| 625 | Angel Mangual | 2.00 | 1.00 |
| 626 | Bob Barton | 2.00 | 1.00 |
| 627 | Luis Alvarado | 2.00 | 1.00 |
| 628 | Jim Slaton | 2.25 | 1.25 |
| 629 | Indians Team | 2.50 | 1.25 |
| 630 | Denny McLain | 3.00 | 1.50 |
| 631 | Tom Matchick | 2.00 | 1.00 |
| 632 | Dick Selma | 2.00 | 1.00 |
| 633 | Ike Brown | 2.00 | 1.00 |
| 634 | Alan Closter | 2.25 | 1.25 |
| 635 | Gene Alley | 2.25 | 1.25 |
| 636 | Rick Clark | 2.00 | 1.00 |
| 637 | Norm Niller | 2.00 | 1.00 |
| 638 | Ken Reynolds | 2.00 | 1.00 |
| 639 | Willie Crawford | 2.00 | 1.00 |
| 640 | Dick Bosman | 2.00 | 1.00 |
| 641 | Reds Team | 2.75 | 1.50 |
| 642 | Jose Laboy | 2.00 | 1.00 |
| 643 | Al Fitzmorris | 2.00 | 1.00 |
| 644 | Jack Heidemann | 2.00 | 1.00 |
| 645 | Bob Locker | 2.00 | 1.00 |
| 646 | Brewers Mgr./Coaches (Del Crandall, Harvey Kuenn, Joe Nossek, Bob Shaw, Jim Walton) | 2.25 | 1.25 |
| 647 | George Stone | 2.00 | 1.00 |
| 648 | Tom Egan | 2.00 | 1.00 |
| 649 | Rich Folkers | 2.00 | 1.00 |
| 650 | Felipe Alou | 2.25 | 1.25 |
| 651 | Don Carrithers | 2.00 | 1.00 |
| 652 | Ted Kubiak | 2.00 | 1.00 |
| 653 | Joe Hoerner | 2.00 | 1.00 |
| 654 | Twins Team | 2.50 | 1.25 |
| 655 | Clay Kirby | 2.00 | 1.00 |
| 656 | John Ellis | 2.00 | 1.00 |
| 657 | Bob Johnson | 2.00 | 1.00 |
| 658 | Elliott Maddox | 2.25 | 1.25 |
| 659 | Jose Pagan | 2.25 | 1.25 |
| 660 | Fred Scherman | 2.25 | .70 |

## 1974 Topps

Issued all at once at the beginning of the year, rather than by series throughout the baseball season as had been done since 1952, this 660-card '74 Topps set features a famous group of error cards. At the time the cards were printed, it was uncertain whether the San Diego Padres would move to Washington, D.C., and by the time a decision was made some Padres cards had appeared with a "Washington, Nat'l League" designation on the front. A total of 15 cards were affected, and those with the Washington designation bring prices well in excess of regular cards of the same players (the Washington variations are not included in the complete set prices quoted below). The 2-1/2" by 3-1/2" cards feature color photos (frequently game-action shots) along with the player's name, team and position. Specialty cards abound, starting with a Hank Aaron tribute and running through the usual managers, statistical leaders, playoff and World Series highlights, multiplayer rookie cards and All-Stars.

| | | NR MT | EX |
|---|---|---|---|
| Complete Set: | | 650.00 | 325.00 |
| Common Player: | | .30 | .15 |
| 1 | Hank Aaron | 30.00 | 15.00 |
| 2 | Aaron Special 1954-57 | 3.00 | 1.50 |
| 3 | Aaron Special 1958-61 | 3.00 | 1.50 |
| 4 | Aaron Special 1962-65 | 3.00 | 1.50 |
| 5 | Aaron Special 1966-69 | 3.00 | 1.50 |
| 6 | Aaron Special 1970-73 | 3.00 | 1.50 |
| 7 | Jim Hunter | 4.00 | 2.00 |
| 8 | George Theodore | .30 | .15 |
| 9 | Mickey Lolich | .60 | .30 |
| 10 | Johnny Bench | 15.00 | 7.50 |
| 11 | Jim Bibby | .30 | .15 |
| 12 | Dave May | .30 | .15 |
| 13 | Tom Hilgendorf | .30 | .15 |
| 14 | Paul Popovich | .30 | .15 |
| 15 | Joe Torre | .80 | .40 |
| 16 | Orioles Team | .80 | .40 |
| 17 | Doug Bird | .30 | .15 |
| 18 | Gary Thomasson | .30 | .15 |
| 19 | Gerry Moses | .30 | .15 |

| | | NR MT | EX |
|---|---|---|---|
| 20 | Nolan Ryan | 65.00 | 33.00 |
| 21 | Bob Gallagher | .30 | .15 |
| 22 | Cy Acosta | .30 | .15 |
| 23 | Craig Robinson | .30 | .15 |
| 24 | John Hiller | .30 | .15 |
| 25 | Ken Singleton | .30 | .15 |
| 26 | *Bill Campbell* | .40 | .20 |
| 27 | George Scott | .30 | .15 |
| 28 | Manny Sanguillen | .30 | .15 |
| 29 | Phil Niekro | 2.00 | 1.00 |
| 30 | Bobby Bonds | .50 | .25 |
| 31 | Astros Mgr./Coaches (Roger Craig, Preston Gomez, Grady Hatton, Hub Kittle, Bob Lillis) | .30 | .15 |
| 32a | John Grubb (Washington) | 3.50 | 1.75 |
| 32b | John Grubb (San Diego) | .30 | .15 |
| 33 | Don Newhauser | .30 | .15 |
| 34 | Andy Kosco | .30 | .15 |
| 35 | Gaylord Perry | 4.00 | 2.00 |
| 36 | Cardinals Team | .80 | .40 |
| 37 | Dave Sells | .30 | .15 |
| 38 | Don Kessinger | .30 | .15 |
| 39 | Ken Suarez | .30 | .15 |
| 40 | Jim Palmer | 9.00 | 4.50 |
| 41 | Bobby Floyd | .30 | .15 |
| 42 | Claude Osteen | .30 | .15 |
| 43 | Jim Wynn | .30 | .15 |
| 44 | Mel Stottlemyre | .40 | .20 |
| 45 | Dave Johnson | .70 | .35 |
| 46 | Pat Kelly | .30 | .15 |
| 47 | *Dick Ruthven* | .30 | .15 |
| 48 | Dick Sharon | .30 | .15 |
| 49 | Steve Renko | .30 | .15 |
| 50 | Rod Carew | 12.00 | 6.00 |
| 51 | Bobby Heise | .30 | .15 |
| 52 | Al Oliver | 1.00 | .50 |
| 53a | Fred Kendall (Washington) | 3.50 | 1.75 |
| 53b | Fred Kendall (San Diego) | .30 | .15 |
| 54 | *Elias Sosa* | .30 | .15 |
| 55 | Frank Robinson | 5.00 | 2.50 |
| 56 | Mets Team | 1.00 | .50 |
| 57 | Darold Knowles | .30 | .15 |
| 58 | Charlie Spikes | .30 | .15 |
| 59 | Ross Grimsley | .30 | .15 |
| 60 | Lou Brock | 5.00 | 2.50 |
| 61 | Luis Aparicio | 2.50 | 1.25 |
| 62 | Bob Locker | .30 | .15 |
| 63 | Bill Sudakis | .30 | .15 |
| 64 | Doug Rau | .30 | .15 |
| 65 | Amos Otis | .30 | .15 |
| 66 | Sparky Lyle | .50 | .25 |
| 67 | Tommy Helms | .30 | .15 |
| 68 | Grant Jackson | .30 | .15 |
| 69 | Del Unser | .30 | .15 |
| 70 | Dick Allen | .80 | .40 |
| 71 | Danny Frisella | .30 | .15 |
| 72 | Aurleio Rodriguez | .30 | .15 |
| 73 | Mike Marshall | .70 | .35 |
| 74 | Twins Team | .80 | .40 |
| 75 | Jim Colborn | .30 | .15 |
| 76 | Mickey Rivers | .30 | .15 |
| 77a | Rich Troedson (Washington) | 3.50 | 1.75 |
| 77b | Rich Troedson (San Diego) | .30 | .15 |
| 78 | Giants Mgr./Coaches (Joe Amalfitano, Charlie Fox, Andy Gilbert, Don McMahon, John McNamara) | .30 | .15 |
| 79 | Gene Tenace | .30 | .15 |
| 80 | Tom Seaver | 20.00 | 10.00 |
| 81 | Frank Duffy | .30 | .15 |
| 82 | Dave Giusti | .30 | .15 |
| 83 | Orlando Cepeda | 1.00 | .50 |
| 84 | Rick Wise | .30 | .15 |
| 85 | Joe Morgan | 5.00 | 2.50 |
| 86 | Joe Ferguson | .30 | .15 |
| 87 | Fergie Jenkins | 4.00 | 2.00 |
| 88 | Freddie Patek | .30 | .15 |
| 89 | Jackie Brown | .30 | .15 |
| 90 | Bobby Murcer | .40 | .20 |
| 91 | Ken Forsch | .30 | .15 |
| 92 | Paul Blair | .30 | .15 |
| 93 | Rod Gilbreath | .30 | .15 |
| 94 | Tigers Team | .90 | .45 |
| 95 | Steve Carlton | 10.00 | 5.00 |
| 96 | *Jerry Hairston* | .40 | .20 |
| 97 | Bob Bailey | .30 | .15 |
| 98 | Bert Blyleven | 1.00 | .50 |
| 99 | Brewers Mgr./Coaches (Del Crandall, Harvey Kuenn, Joe Nossek, Jim Walton, Al Widmar) | .30 | .15 |
| 100 | Willie Stargell | 4.00 | 2.00 |
| 101 | Bobby Valentine | .30 | .15 |
| 102a | Bill Greif (Washington) | 3.50 | 1.75 |
| 102b | Bill Greif (San Diego) | .30 | .15 |
| 103 | Sal Bando | .40 | .20 |
| 104 | Ron Bryant | .30 | .15 |
| 105 | Carlton Fisk | 22.00 | 11.00 |
| 106 | Harry Parker | .30 | .15 |
| 107 | Alex Johnson | .30 | .15 |
| 108 | Al Hrabosky | .30 | .15 |
| 109 | Bob Grich | .40 | .20 |
| 110 | Billy Williams | 3.00 | 1.50 |
| 111 | Clay Carroll | .30 | .15 |
| 112 | Dave Lopes | .40 | .20 |
| 113 | Dick Drago | .30 | .15 |
| 114 | Angels Team | .80 | .40 |
| 115 | Willie Horton | .30 | .15 |
| 116 | Jerry Reuss | .30 | .15 |
| 117 | Ron Blomberg | .30 | .15 |
| 118 | Bill Lee | .30 | .15 |
| 119 | Phillies Mgr./Coaches (Carroll Beringer, Bill DeMars, Danny Ozark, Ray Ripplemeyer, Bobby Wine) | .30 | .15 |
| 120 | Wilbur Wood | .30 | .15 |
| 121 | Larry Lintz | .30 | .15 |
| 122 | Jim Holt | .30 | .15 |
| 123 | Nelson Briles | .30 | .15 |
| 124 | Bob Coluccio | .30 | .15 |
| 125a | Nate Colbert (Washington) | 3.50 | 1.75 |
| 125b | Nate Colbert (San Diego) | | |

| | NR MT | EX |
|---|---|---|
| Diego) | .30 | .15 |
| 126 Checklist 1-132 | 1.50 | .70 |
| 127 Tom Paciorek | .30 | .15 |
| 128 John Ellis | .30 | .15 |
| 129 Chris Speier | .30 | .15 |
| 130 Reggie Jackson | 25.00 | 12.50 |
| 131 Bob Boone | 2.00 | 1.00 |
| 132 Felix Millan | .30 | .15 |
| 133 David Clyde | .30 | .15 |
| 134 Denis Menke | .30 | .15 |
| 135 Roy White | .40 | .20 |
| 136 Rick Reuschel | .80 | .40 |
| 137 Al Bumbry | .30 | .15 |
| 138 Ed Brinkman | .30 | .15 |
| 139 Aurelio Monteagudo | .30 | .15 |
| 140 Darrell Evans | .60 | .30 |
| 141 Pat Bourque | .30 | .15 |
| 142 Pedro Garcia | .30 | .15 |
| 143 Dick Woodson | .30 | .15 |
| 144 Dodgers Mgr./Coaches (Red Adams, Walter Alston, Monty Basgall, Jim Gilliam, Tom Lasorda) | 1.25 | .60 |
| 145 Dock Ellis | .30 | .15 |
| 146 Ron Fairly | .30 | .15 |
| 147 Bart Johnson | .30 | .15 |
| 148a Dave Hilton (Washington) | 3.50 | 1.75 |
| 148b Dave Hilton (San Diego) | .30 | .15 |
| 149 Mac Scarce | .30 | .15 |
| 150 John Mayberry | .30 | .15 |
| 151 Diego Segui | .30 | .15 |
| 152 Oscar Gamble | .30 | .15 |
| 153 Jon Matlack | .30 | .15 |
| 154 Astros Team | .80 | .40 |
| 155 Bert Campaneris | .40 | .20 |
| 156 Randy Moffitt | .30 | .15 |
| 157 Vic Harris | .30 | .15 |
| 158 Jack Billingham | .30 | .15 |
| 159 Jim Ray Hart | .30 | .15 |
| 160 Brooks Robinson | 3.50 | 1.75 |
| 161 Ray Burris | .40 | .20 |
| 162 Bill Freehan | .40 | .20 |
| 163 Ken Berry | .30 | .15 |
| 164 Tom House | .30 | .15 |
| 165 Willie Davis | .40 | .20 |
| 166 Royals Mgr./Coaches (Galen Cisco, Harry Dunlop, Charlie Lau, Jack McKeon) | .30 | .15 |
| 167 Luis Tiant | .50 | .25 |
| 168 Danny Thompson | .30 | .15 |
| 169 Steve Rogers | .70 | .35 |
| 170 Bill Melton | .30 | .15 |
| 171 Eduardo Rodriguez | .30 | .15 |
| 172 Gene Clines | .30 | .15 |
| 173a Randy Jones (Washington) | 6.00 | 3.00 |
| 173b Randy Jones (San Diego) | .40 | .20 |
| 174 Bill Robinson | .30 | .15 |
| 175 Reggie Cleveland | .30 | .15 |
| 176 John Lowenstein | .30 | .15 |
| 177 Dave Roberts | .30 | .15 |
| 178 Garry Maddox | .40 | .20 |
| 179 Mets Mgr./Coaches | | |

| | NR MT | EX |
|---|---|---|
| (Yogi Berra, Roy McMillan, Joe Pignatano, Rube Walker, Eddie Yost) | 1.25 | .60 |
| 180 Ken Holtzman | .30 | .15 |
| 181 Cesar Geronimo | .30 | .15 |
| 182 Lindy McDaniel | .30 | .15 |
| 183 Johnny Oates | .30 | .15 |
| 184 Rangers Team | .80 | .40 |
| 185 Jose Cardenal | .30 | .15 |
| 186 Fred Scherman | .30 | .15 |
| 187 Don Baylor | .70 | .35 |
| 188 Rudy Meoli | .30 | .15 |
| 189 Jim Brewer | .30 | .15 |
| 190 Tony Oliva | .80 | .40 |
| 191 Al Fitzmorris | .30 | .15 |
| 192 Mario Guerrero | .30 | .15 |
| 193 Tom Walker | .30 | .15 |
| 194 Darrell Porter | .30 | .15 |
| 195 Carlos May | .30 | .15 |
| 196 Jim Fregosi | .40 | .20 |
| 197a Vicente Romo (Washington) | 3.50 | 1.75 |
| 197b Vicente Romo (San Diego) | .30 | .15 |
| 198 Dave Cash | .30 | .15 |
| 199 Mike Kekich | .30 | .15 |
| 200 Cesar Cedeno | .40 | .20 |
| 201 Batting Leaders (Rod Carew, Pete Rose) | 4.00 | 2.00 |
| 202 Home Run Leaders (Reggie Jackson, Willie Stargell) | 2.00 | 1.00 |
| 203 Runs Batted In Leaders (Reggie Jackson, Willie Stargell) | 2.00 | 1.00 |
| 204 Stolen Base Leaders (Lou Brock, Tommy Harper) | 1.25 | .60 |
| 205 Victory Leaders (Ron Bryant, Wilbur Wood) | .50 | .25 |
| 206 Earned Run Average Leaders (Jim Palmer, Tom Seaver) | 2.00 | 1.00 |
| 207 Strikeout Leaders (Nolan Ryan, Tom Seaver) | 7.00 | 3.50 |
| 208 Leading Firemen (John Hiller, Mike Marshall) | .50 | .25 |
| 209 Ted Sizemore | .30 | .15 |
| 210 Bill Singer | .30 | .15 |
| 211 Cubs Team | .80 | .40 |
| 212 Rollie Fingers | 5.00 | 2.50 |
| 213 Dave Rader | .30 | .15 |
| 214 Billy Grabarkewitz | .30 | .15 |
| 215 Al Kaline | 5.00 | 2.50 |
| 216 Ray Sadecki | .30 | .15 |
| 217 Tim Foli | .30 | .15 |
| 218 Johnny Briggs | .30 | .15 |
| 219 Doug Griffin | .30 | .15 |
| 220 Don Sutton | 2.00 | 1.00 |
| 221 White Sox Mgr. Coaches (Joe Lonnett, Jim Mahoney, Alex Monchak, Johnny Sain, Chuck Tanner) | .30 | .15 |
| 222 Ramon Hernandez | .30 | .15 |
| 223 Jeff Burroughs | .50 | .25 |

| | | NR MT | EX |
|---|---|---|---|
| 224 | Roger Metzger | .30 | .15 |
| 225 | Paul Splittorff | .30 | .15 |
| 226a | Washington Nat'l. Team | 6.00 | 3.00 |
| 226b | Padres Team | 1.00 | .50 |
| 227 | Mike Lum | .30 | .15 |
| 228 | Ted Kubiak | .30 | .15 |
| 229 | Fritz Peterson | .30 | .15 |
| 230 | Tony Perez | 1.25 | .60 |
| 231 | Dick Tidrow | .30 | .15 |
| 232 | Steve Brye | .30 | .15 |
| 233 | Jim Barr | .30 | .15 |
| 234 | John Milner | .30 | .15 |
| 235 | Dave McNally | .30 | .15 |
| 236 | Cardinals Mgr./Coaches (Vern Benson, George Kissell, Johnny Lewis, Red Schoendienst, Barney Schultz) | .40 | .20 |
| 237 | Ken Brett | .30 | .15 |
| 238 | Fran Healy | .30 | .15 |
| 239 | Bill Russell | .30 | .15 |
| 240 | Joe Coleman | .30 | .15 |
| 241a | Glenn Beckert (Washington) | 4.00 | 2.00 |
| 241b | Glenn Beckert (San Diego) | .30 | .15 |
| 242 | Bill Gogolewski | .30 | .15 |
| 243 | Bob Oliver | .30 | .15 |
| 244 | Carl Morton | .30 | .15 |
| 245 | Cleon Jones | .30 | .15 |
| 246 | A's Team | 1.25 | .60 |
| 247 | Rick Miller | .30 | .15 |
| 248 | Tom Hall | .30 | .15 |
| 249 | George Mitterwald | .30 | .15 |
| 250a | Willie McCovey (Washington) | 25.00 | 12.50 |
| 250b | Willie McCovey (San Diego) | 5.00 | 2.50 |
| 251 | Graig Nettles | 1.50 | .70 |
| 252 | *Dave Parker* | 30.00 | 15.00 |
| 253 | John Boccabella | .30 | .15 |
| 254 | Stan Bahnsen | .30 | .15 |
| 255 | Larry Bowa | .40 | .20 |
| 256 | Tom Griffin | .30 | .15 |
| 257 | Buddy Bell | 1.25 | .60 |
| 258 | Jerry Morales | .30 | .15 |
| 259 | Bob Reynolds | .30 | .15 |
| 260 | Ted Simmons | .80 | .40 |
| 261 | Jerry Bell | .30 | .15 |
| 262 | Ed Kirkpatrick | .30 | .15 |
| 263 | Checklist 133-264 | 1.50 | .70 |
| 264 | Joe Rudi | .40 | .20 |
| 265 | Tug McGraw | .60 | .30 |
| 266 | Jim Northrup | .30 | .15 |
| 267 | Andy Messersmith | .30 | .15 |
| 268 | Tom Grieve | .30 | .15 |
| 269 | Bob Johnson | .30 | .15 |
| 270 | Ron Santo | .50 | .25 |
| 271 | Bill Hands | .30 | .15 |
| 272 | Paul Casanova | .30 | .15 |
| 273 | Checklist 265-396 | 1.50 | .70 |
| 274 | Fred Beene | .30 | .15 |
| 275 | Ron Hunt | .30 | .15 |
| 276 | Angels Mgr./Coaches (Tom Morgan, Salty Parker, Jimmie Reese, John | | |

| | | NR MT | EX |
|---|---|---|---|
| | Roseboro, Bobby Winkles) | .30 | .15 |
| 277 | Gary Nolan | .30 | .15 |
| 278 | Cookie Rojas | .30 | .15 |
| 279 | Jim Crawford | .30 | .15 |
| 280 | Carl Yastrzemski | 15.00 | 7.50 |
| 281 | Giants Team | .80 | .40 |
| 282 | Doyle Alexander | .40 | .20 |
| 283 | Mike Schmidt | 75.00 | 38.00 |
| 284 | Dave Duncan | .30 | .15 |
| 285 | Reggie Smith | .40 | .20 |
| 286 | Tony Muser | .30 | .15 |
| 287 | Clay Kirby | .30 | .15 |
| 288 | *Gorman Thomas* | 2.00 | 1.00 |
| 289 | Rick Auerbach | .30 | .15 |
| 290 | Vida Blue | .60 | .30 |
| 291 | Don Hahn | .30 | .15 |
| 292 | Chuck Seelbach | .30 | .15 |
| 293 | Milt May | .30 | .15 |
| 294 | Steve Foucault | .30 | .15 |
| 295 | Rick Monday | .30 | .15 |
| 296 | Ray Corbin | .30 | .15 |
| 297 | Hal Breeden | .30 | .15 |
| 298 | Roric Harrison | .30 | .15 |
| 299 | Gene Michael | .30 | .15 |
| 300 | Pete Rose | 15.00 | 7.50 |
| 301 | Bob Montgomery | .30 | .15 |
| 302 | Rudy May | .30 | .15 |
| 303 | George Hendrick | .30 | .15 |
| 304 | Don Wilson | .30 | .15 |
| 305 | Tito Fuentes | .30 | .15 |
| 306 | Orioles Mgr./Coaches (George Bamberger, Jim Frey, Billy Hunter, George Staller, Earl Weaver) | .70 | .35 |
| 307 | Luis Melendez | .30 | .15 |
| 308 | Bruce Dal Canton | .30 | .15 |
| 309a | Dave Roberts (Washington) | 3.50 | 1.75 |
| 309b | Dave Roberts (San Diego) | .30 | .15 |
| 310 | Terry Forster | .30 | .15 |
| 311 | Jerry Grote | .30 | .15 |
| 312 | Deron Johnson | .30 | .15 |
| 313 | Berry Lersch | .30 | .15 |
| 314 | Brewers Team | .80 | .40 |
| 315 | Ron Cey | .60 | .30 |
| 316 | Jim Perry | .40 | .20 |
| 317 | Richie Zisk | .30 | .15 |
| 318 | Jim Merritt | .30 | .15 |
| 319 | Randy Hundley | .30 | .15 |
| 320 | Dusty Baker | .40 | .20 |
| 321 | Steve Braun | .30 | .15 |
| 322 | Ernie McAnally | .30 | .15 |
| 323 | Richie Scheinblum | .30 | .15 |
| 324 | Steve Kline | .30 | .15 |
| 325 | Tommy Harper | .30 | .15 |
| 326 | Reds Mgr./Coaches (Sparky Anderson, Alex Gramms, Ted Kluszewski, George Scherger, Larry Shepard) | .50 | .25 |
| 327 | Tom Timmermann | .30 | .15 |
| 328 | Skip Jutze | .30 | .15 |
| 329 | Mark Belanger | .30 | .15 |
| 330 | Juan Marichal | 2.75 | 1.50 |
| 331 | All Star Catchers | | |

| | | NR MT | EX |
|---|---|---|---|
| | (Johnny Bench, Carlton Fisk) | 2.00 | 1.00 |
| 332 | All Star First Basemen (Hank Aaron, Dick Allen) | 2.00 | 1.00 |
| 333 | All Star Second Basemen (Rod Carew, Joe Morgan) | 2.00 | 1.00 |
| 334 | All Star Third Basemen (Brooks Robinson, Ron Santo) | 1.25 | .60 |
| 335 | All Star Shortstops (Bert Campaneris, Chris Speier) | .40 | .20 |
| 336 | All Star Left Fielders (Bobby Murcer, Pete Rose) | 2.50 | 1.25 |
| 337 | All Star Center Fielders (Cesar Cedeno, Amos Otis) | .40 | .20 |
| 338 | All Star Right Fielders (Reggie Jackson, Billy Williams) | 2.00 | 1.00 |
| 339 | All Star Pitchers (Jim Hunter, Rick Wise) | .80 | .40 |
| 340 | Thurman Munson | 8.00 | 4.00 |
| 341 | Dan Driessen | .80 | .40 |
| 342 | Jim Lonborg | .30 | .15 |
| 343 | Royals Team | .80 | .40 |
| 344 | Mike Caldwell | .30 | .15 |
| 345 | Bill North | .30 | .15 |
| 346 | Ron Reed | .30 | .15 |
| 347 | Sandy Alomar | .30 | .15 |
| 348 | Pete Richert | .30 | .15 |
| 349 | John Vukovich | .30 | .15 |
| 350 | Bob Gibson | 6.00 | 3.00 |
| 351 | Dwight Evans | 15.00 | 7.50 |
| 352 | Bill Stoneman | .30 | .15 |
| 353 | Rich Coggins | .30 | .15 |
| 354 | Cubs Mgr./Coaches (Hank Aguirre, Whitey Lockman, Jim Marshall, J.C. Martin, Al Spangler) | .30 | .15 |
| 355 | Dave Nelson | .30 | .15 |
| 356 | Jerry Koosman | .40 | .20 |
| 357 | Buddy Bradford | .30 | .15 |
| 358 | Dal Maxvill | .30 | .15 |
| 359 | Brent Strom | .30 | .15 |
| 360 | Greg Luzinski | .70 | .35 |
| 361 | Don Carrithers | .30 | .15 |
| 362 | Hal King | .30 | .15 |
| 363 | Yankees Team | 1.25 | .60 |
| 364a | Clarence Gaston (Washington) | 3.50 | 1.75 |
| 364b | Clarence Gaston (San Diego) | .30 | .15 |
| 365 | Steve Busby | .30 | .15 |
| 366 | Larry Hisle | .30 | .15 |
| 367 | Norm Cash | .50 | .25 |
| 368 | Manny Mota | .40 | .20 |
| 369 | Paul Lindblad | .30 | .15 |
| 370 | Bob Watson | .30 | .15 |
| 371 | Jim Slaton | .30 | .15 |
| 372 | Ken Reitz | .30 | .15 |
| 373 | John Curtis | .30 | .15 |
| 374 | Marty Perez | .30 | .15 |
| 375 | Earl Williams | .30 | .15 |

| | | NR MT | EX |
|---|---|---|---|
| 376 | Jorge Orta | .30 | .15 |
| 377 | Ron Woods | .30 | .15 |
| 378 | Burt Hooton | .30 | .15 |
| 379 | Rangers Mgr./Coaches (Art Fowler, Frank Lucchesi, Billy Martin, Jackie Moore, Charlie Silvera) | .80 | .40 |
| 380 | Bud Harrelson | .30 | .15 |
| 381 | Charlie Sands | .30 | .15 |
| 382 | Bob Moose | .30 | .15 |
| 383 | Phillies Team | .80 | .40 |
| 384 | Chris Chambliss | .40 | .20 |
| 385 | Don Gullett | .30 | .15 |
| 386 | Gary Matthews | .60 | .30 |
| 387a | Rich Morales (Washington) | 3.50 | 1.75 |
| 387b | Rich Morales (San Diego) | .30 | .15 |
| 388 | Phil Roof | .30 | .15 |
| 389 | Gates Brown | .30 | .15 |
| 390 | Lou Piniella | .70 | .35 |
| 391 | Billy Champion | .30 | .15 |
| 392 | Dick Green | .30 | .15 |
| 393 | Orlando Pena | .30 | .15 |
| 394 | Ken Henderson | .30 | .15 |
| 395 | Doug Rader | .30 | .15 |
| 396 | Tommy Davis | .40 | .20 |
| 397 | George Stone | .30 | .15 |
| 398 | Duke Sims | .30 | .15 |
| 399 | Mike Paul | .30 | .15 |
| 400 | Harmon Killebrew | 4.00 | 2.00 |
| 401 | Elliott Maddox | .30 | .15 |
| 402 | Jim Rooker | .30 | .15 |
| 403 | Red Sox Mgr./Coaches (Don Bryant, Darrell Johnson, Eddie Popowski, Lee Stange, Don Zimmer) | .30 | .15 |
| 404 | Jim Howarth | .30 | .15 |
| 405 | Ellie Rodriguez | .30 | .15 |
| 406 | Steve Arlin | .30 | .15 |
| 407 | Jim Wohlford | .30 | .15 |
| 408 | Charlie Hough | .40 | .20 |
| 409 | Ike Brown | .30 | .15 |
| 410 | Pedro Borbon | .30 | .15 |
| 411 | Frank Baker | .30 | .15 |
| 412 | Chuck Taylor | .30 | .15 |
| 413 | Don Money | .30 | .15 |
| 414 | Checklist 397-528 | 1.50 | .70 |
| 415 | Gary Gentry | .30 | .15 |
| 416 | White Sox Team | .80 | .40 |
| 417 | Rich Folkers | .30 | .15 |
| 418 | Walt Williams | .30 | .15 |
| 419 | Wayne Twitchell | .30 | .15 |
| 420 | Ray Fosse | .30 | .15 |
| 421 | Dan Fife | .30 | .15 |
| 422 | Gonzalo Marquez | .30 | .15 |
| 423 | Fred Stanley | .30 | .15 |
| 424 | Jim Beauchamp | .30 | .15 |
| 425 | Pete Broberg | .30 | .15 |
| 426 | Rennie Stennett | .30 | .15 |
| 427 | Bobby Bolin | .30 | .15 |
| 428 | Gary Sutherland | .30 | .15 |
| 429 | Dick Lange | .30 | .15 |
| 430 | Matty Alou | .40 | .20 |
| 431 | Gene Garber | .50 | .25 |
| 432 | Chris Arnold | .30 | .15 |

| | | NR MT | EX |
|---|---|---|---|
| 433 | Lerrin LaGrow | .30 | .15 |
| 434 | Ken McMullen | .30 | .15 |
| 435 | Dave Concepcion | .70 | .35 |
| 436 | Don Hood | .30 | .15 |
| 437 | Jim Lyttle | .30 | .15 |
| 438 | Ed Herrmann | .30 | .15 |
| 439 | Norm Miller | .30 | .15 |
| 440 | Jim Kaat | 1.25 | .60 |
| 441 | Tom Ragland | .30 | .15 |
| 442 | Alan Foster | .30 | .15 |
| 443 | Tom Hutton | .30 | .15 |
| 444 | Vic Davalillo | .30 | .15 |
| 445 | George Medich | .30 | .15 |
| 446 | Len Randle | .30 | .15 |
| 447 | Twins Mgr./Coaches (Vern Morgan, Frank Quilici, Bob Rodgers, Ralph Rowe) | .30 | .15 |
| 448 | Ron Hodges | .30 | .15 |
| 449 | Tom McCraw | .30 | .15 |
| 450 | Rich Hebner | .30 | .15 |
| 451 | Tommy John | 1.50 | .70 |
| 452 | Gene Hiser | .30 | .15 |
| 453 | Balor Moore | .30 | .15 |
| 454 | Kurt Bevacqua | .30 | .15 |
| 455 | Tom Bradley | .30 | .15 |
| 456 | *Dave Winfield* | 150.00 | 75.00 |
| 457 | Chuck Goggin | .30 | .15 |
| 458 | Jim Ray | .30 | .15 |
| 459 | Reds Team | .90 | .45 |
| 460 | Boog Powell | .90 | .45 |
| 461 | John Odom | .30 | .15 |
| 462 | Luis Alvarado | .30 | .15 |
| 463 | Pat Dobson | .30 | .15 |
| 464 | Jose Cruz | .80 | .40 |
| 465 | Dick Bosman | .30 | .15 |
| 466 | Dick Billings | .30 | .15 |
| 467 | Winston Llenas | .30 | .15 |
| 468 | Pepe Frias | .30 | .15 |
| 469 | Joe Decker | .30 | .15 |
| 470 | A.L. Playoffs | 4.00 | 2.00 |
| 471 | N.L. Playoffs | .80 | .40 |
| 472 | World Series Game 1 | .80 | .40 |
| 473 | World Series Game 2 | 4.00 | 2.00 |
| 474 | World Series Game 3 | .80 | .40 |
| 475 | World Series Game 4 | .80 | .40 |
| 476 | World Series Game 5 | .80 | .40 |
| 477 | World Series Game 6 | 4.00 | 2.00 |
| 478 | World Series Game 7 | .80 | .40 |
| 479 | World Series Summary | .80 | .40 |
| 480 | Willie Crawford | .30 | .15 |
| 481 | Jerry Terrell | .30 | .15 |
| 482 | Bob Didier | .30 | .15 |
| 483 | Braves Team | .80 | .40 |
| 484 | Carmen Fanzone | .30 | .15 |
| 485 | Felipe Alou | .40 | .20 |
| 486 | Steve Stone | .40 | .20 |
| 487 | Ted Martinez | .30 | .15 |
| 488 | Andy Etchebarren | .30 | .15 |

| | | NR MT | EX |
|---|---|---|---|
| 489 | Pirates Mgr./Coaches (Don Leppert, Bill Mazeroski, Danny Murtaugh, Don Osborn, Bob Skinner) | .30 | .15 |
| 490 | Vada Pinson | .70 | .35 |
| 491 | Roger Nelson | .30 | .15 |
| 492 | Mike Rogodzinski | .30 | .15 |
| 493 | Joe Hoerner | .30 | .15 |
| 494 | Ed Goodson | .30 | .15 |
| 495 | Dick McAuliffe | .30 | .15 |
| 496 | Tom Murphy | .30 | .15 |
| 497 | Bobby Mitchell | .30 | .15 |
| 498 | Pat Corrales | .40 | .20 |
| 499 | Rusty Torres | .30 | .15 |
| 500 | Lee May | .40 | .20 |
| 501 | Eddie Leon | .30 | .15 |
| 502 | Dave LaRoche | .30 | .15 |
| 503 | Eric Soderholm | .30 | .15 |
| 504 | Joe Niekro | .40 | .20 |
| 505 | Bill Buckner | .50 | .25 |
| 506 | Ed Farmer | .30 | .15 |
| 507 | Larry Stahl | .30 | .15 |
| 508 | Expos Team | .80 | .40 |
| 509 | Jesse Jefferson | .30 | .15 |
| 510 | Wayne Garrett | .30 | .15 |
| 511 | Toby Harrah | .30 | .15 |
| 512 | Joe Lahoud | .30 | .15 |
| 513 | Jim Campanis | .30 | .15 |
| 514 | Paul Schaal | .30 | .15 |
| 515 | Willie Montanez | .30 | .15 |
| 516 | Horacio Pina | .30 | .15 |
| 517 | Mike Hegan | .30 | .15 |
| 518 | Derrel Thomas | .30 | .15 |
| 519 | Bill Sharp | .30 | .15 |
| 520 | Tim McCarver | .60 | .30 |
| 521 | Indians Mgr./Coaches (Ken Aspromonte, Clay Bryant, Tony Pacheco) | .30 | .15 |
| 522 | J.R. Richard | .30 | .15 |
| 523 | Cecil Cooper | 1.50 | .70 |
| 524 | Bill Plummer | .30 | .15 |
| 525 | Clyde Wright | .30 | .15 |
| 526 | Frank Tepedino | .30 | .15 |
| 527 | Bobby Darwin | .30 | .15 |
| 528 | Bill Bonham | .30 | .15 |
| 529 | Horace Clarke | .30 | .15 |
| 530 | Mickey Stanley | .30 | .15 |
| 531 | Expos Mgr./Coaches (Dave Bristol, Larry Doby, Gene Mauch, Cal McLish, Jerry Zimmerman) | .40 | .20 |
| 532 | Skip Lockwood | .30 | .15 |
| 533 | Mike Phillips | .30 | .15 |
| 534 | Eddie Watt | .30 | .15 |
| 535 | Bob Tolan | .30 | .15 |
| 536 | Duffy Dyer | .30 | .15 |
| 537 | Steve Mingori | .30 | .15 |
| 538 | Cesar Tovar | .30 | .15 |
| 539 | Lloyd Allen | .30 | .15 |
| 540 | Bob Robertson | .30 | .15 |
| 541 | Indians Team | .80 | .40 |
| 542 | Rich Gossage | 4.00 | 2.00 |
| 543 | Danny Cater | .30 | .15 |
| 544 | Ron Schueler | .30 | .15 |
| 545 | Billy Conigliaro | .30 | .15 |
| 546 | Mike Corkins | .30 | .15 |

| | NR MT | EX |
|---|---|---|
| 547 Glenn Borgmann | .30 | .15 |
| 548 Sonny Siebert | .30 | .15 |
| 549 Mike Jorgensen | .30 | .15 |
| 550 Sam McDowell | .40 | .20 |
| 551 Von Joshua | .30 | .15 |
| 552 Denny Doyle | .30 | .15 |
| 553 Jim Willoughby | .30 | .15 |
| 554 Tim Johnson | .30 | .15 |
| 555 Woodie Fryman | .30 | .15 |
| 556 Dave Campbell | .30 | .15 |
| 557 Jim McGlothlin | .30 | .15 |
| 558 Bill Fahey | .30 | .15 |
| 559 Darrel Chaney | .30 | .15 |
| 560 Mike Cuellar | .40 | .20 |
| 561 Ed Kranepool | .30 | .15 |
| 562 Jack Aker | .30 | .15 |
| 563 Hal McRae | .40 | .20 |
| 564 Mike Ryan | .30 | .15 |
| 565 Milt Wilcox | .30 | .15 |
| 566 Jackie Hernandez | .30 | .15 |
| 567 Red Sox Team | .90 | .45 |
| 568 Mike Torrez | .30 | .15 |
| 569 Rick Dempsey | .40 | .20 |
| 570 Ralph Garr | .30 | .15 |
| 571 Rich Hand | .30 | .15 |
| 572 Enzo Hernandez | .30 | .15 |
| 573 Mike Adams | .30 | .15 |
| 574 Bill Parsons | .30 | .15 |
| 575 Steve Garvey | 12.00 | 6.00 |
| 576 Scipio Spinks | .30 | .15 |
| 577 Mike Sadek | .30 | .15 |
| 578 Ralph Houk | .40 | .20 |
| 579 Cecil Upshaw | .30 | .15 |
| 580 Jim Spencer | .30 | .15 |
| 581 Fred Norman | .30 | .15 |
| 582 *Bucky Dent* | .90 | .45 |
| 583 Marty Pattin | .30 | .15 |
| 584 Ken Rudolph | .30 | .15 |
| 585 Merv Rettenmund | .30 | .15 |
| 586 Jack Brohamer | .30 | .15 |
| 587 *Larry Christenson* | .30 | .15 |
| 588 Hal Lanier | .40 | .20 |
| 589 Boots Day | .30 | .15 |
| 590 Rogelio Moret | .30 | .15 |
| 591 Sonny Jackson | .30 | .15 |
| 592 Ed Bane | .30 | .15 |
| 593 Steve Yeager | .30 | .15 |
| 594 Leroy Stanton | .30 | .15 |
| 595 Steve Blass | .30 | .15 |
| 596 Rookie Pitchers (*Wayne Garland*, Fred Holdsworth, *Mark Littell*, Dick Pole) | .30 | .15 |
| 597 Rookie Shortstops (Dave Chalk, John Gamble, Pete Mackanin, *Manny Trillo*) | .80 | .40 |
| 598 Rookie Outfielders (Dave Augustine, *Ken Griffey*, Steve Ontiveros, Jim Tyrone) | 20.00 | 10.00 |
| 599a Rookie Pitchers (Ron Diorio, Dave Freisleben, Frank Riccelli, Greg Shanahan) (Freisleben— Washington) | .80 | .40 |
| 599b Rookie Pitchers (Ron Diorio, Dave Freisleben, Frank Riccelli, Greg Shanahan) (Freisleben- San Diego large print) | 3.50 | 1.75 |
| 599c Rookie Pitchers (Ron Diorio, Dave Freisleben, Frank Riccelli, Greg Shanahan) (Freisleben- San Diego small print) | 6.00 | 3.00 |
| 600 Rookie Infielders (Ron Cash, Jim Cox, *Bill Madlock*, Reggie Sanders) | 4.00 | 2.00 |
| 601 Rookie Outfielders (Ed Armbrister, Rich Bladt, *Brian Downing, Bake McBride*) | 5.00 | 2.50 |
| 602 Rookie Pitchers (Glenn Abbott, Rick Henninger, Craig Swan, Dan Vossler) | .30 | .15 |
| 603 Rookie Catchers (Barry Foote, Tom Lundstedt, *Charlie Moore*, Sergio Robles) | .30 | .15 |
| 604 Rookie Infielders (Terry Hughes, John Knox, *Andy Thornton, Frank White*) | 5.00 | 2.50 |
| 605 Rookie Pitchers (Vic Albury, Ken Frailing, Kevin Kobel, *Frank Tanana*) | 2.00 | 1.00 |
| 606 Rookie Outfielders (Jim Fuller, Wilbur Howard, Tommy Smith, Otto Velez) | .30 | .15 |
| 607 Rookie Shortstops (Leo Foster, Tom Heintzelman, Dave Rosello, *Frank Taveras*) | .30 | .15 |
| 608a Rookie Pitchers (Bob Apodaca, Dick Baney, John D'Acquisto, Mike Wallace) | 2.00 | 1.00 |
| 608b Rookie Pitchers (Bob Apodaca, Dick Baney, John D'Acquisto, Mike Wallace) | .30 | .15 |
| 609 Rico Petrocelli | .30 | .15 |
| 610 Dave Kingman | .90 | .45 |
| 611 Rick Stelmaszek | .30 | .15 |
| 612 Luke Walker | .30 | .15 |
| 613 Dan Monzon | .30 | .15 |
| 614 Adrian Devine | .30 | .15 |
| 615 Johnny Jeter | .30 | .15 |
| 616 Larry Gura | .30 | .15 |
| 617 Ted Ford | .30 | .15 |
| 618 Jim Mason | .30 | .15 |
| 619 Mike Anderson | .30 | .15 |
| 620 Al Downing | .30 | .15 |
| 621 Bernie Carbo | .30 | .15 |
| 622 Phil Gagliano | .30 | .15 |
| 623 Celerino Sanchez | .30 | .15 |
| 624 Bob Miller | .30 | .15 |
| 625 Ollie Brown | .30 | .15 |
| 626 Pirates Team | .80 | .40 |
| 627 Carl Taylor | .30 | .15 |
| 628 Ivan Murrell | .30 | .15 |

| | | NR MT | EX |
|---|---|---|---|
| 629 | Rusty Staub | .70 | .35 |
| 630 | Tommie Agee | .30 | .15 |
| 631 | Steve Barber | .30 | .15 |
| 632 | George Culver | .30 | .15 |
| 633 | Dave Hamilton | .30 | .15 |
| 634 | Braves Mgr./Coaches (Jim Busby, Eddie Mathews, Connie Ryan, Ken Silvestri, Herm Starrette) | .90 | .45 |
| 635 | John Edwards | .30 | .15 |
| 636 | Dave Goltz | .30 | .15 |
| 637 | Checklist 529-660 | 1.50 | .70 |
| 638 | Ken Sanders | .30 | .15 |
| 639 | Joe Lovitto | .30 | .15 |
| 640 | Milt Pappas | .40 | .20 |
| 641 | Chuck Brinkman | .30 | .15 |
| 642 | Terry Harmon | .30 | .15 |
| 643 | Dodgers Team | .90 | .45 |
| 644 | Wayne Granger | .30 | .15 |
| 645 | Ken Boswell | .30 | .15 |
| 646 | George Foster | 1.25 | .60 |
| 647 | Juan Beniquez | .70 | .35 |
| 648 | Terry Crowley | .30 | .15 |
| 649 | Fernando Gonzalez | .30 | .15 |
| 650 | Mike Epstein | .30 | .15 |
| 651 | Leron Lee | .30 | .15 |
| 652 | Gail Hopkins | .30 | .15 |
| 653 | Bob Stinson | .30 | .15 |
| 654a | Jesus Alou (no position listed) | 5.00 | 2.50 |
| 654b | Jesus Alou (Outfield) | .40 | .20 |
| 655 | Mike Tyson | .30 | .15 |
| 656 | Adrian Garrett | .30 | .15 |
| 657 | Jim Shellenback | .30 | .15 |
| 658 | Lee Lacy | .30 | .15 |
| 659 | Joe Lis | .30 | .15 |
| 660 | Larry Dierker | .50 | .15 |

## 1975 Topps

This year Topps produced another 660-card set, one which collectors either seem to like or despise. The 2-1/2" by 3-1/2" cards have a color photo which is framed by a round-cornered white frame. Around that is an eye-catching two-color border in bright colors. The team name appears at the top in bright letters while the player name is at the bottom and

his position a baseball at the lower right. A facsimile autograph runs across the picture. The card backs are vertical feature normal statistical and biographical information along with a trivia quiz. Specialty cards include a new 24-card series on MVP winners going back to 1951. Other specialty cards include statistical leaders and post-season highlights. The real highlight of the set, however, are the rookie cards which include their numbers such names as George Brett, Gary Carter, Robin Yount, Jim Rice, Keith Hernandez and Fred Lynn. While the set was released at one time, card numbers 1-132 were printed in somewhat shorter supply than the remainder of the issue.

| | | NR MT | EX |
|---|---|---|---|
| Complete Set: | | 900.00 | 450.00 |
| Common Player: 1-132 | | .35 | .20 |
| Common Player: 133-660 | | .30 | .15 |
| Complete Mini Set: | | 1000.00 | 500.00 |
| Common Mini Player: | | .40 | .20 |

| | | NR MT | EX |
|---|---|---|---|
| 1 | '74 Highlights (Hank Aaron) | 30.00 | 15.00 |
| 2 | '74 Highlights (Lou Brock) | 2.00 | 1.00 |
| 3 | '74 Highlights (Bob Gibson) | 1.75 | .90 |
| 4 | '74 Highlights (Al Kaline) | 1.75 | .90 |
| 5 | '74 Highlights (Nolan Ryan) | 12.00 | 6.00 |
| 6 | '74 Highlights (Mike Marshall) | .40 | .20 |
| 7 | '74 Highlights (Dick Bosman, Steve Busby, Nolan Ryan) | 1.00 | .50 |
| 8 | Rogelio Moret | .35 | .20 |
| 9 | Frank Tepedino | .35 | .20 |
| 10 | Willie Davis | .35 | .20 |
| 11 | Bill Melton | .35 | .20 |
| 12 | David Clyde | .35 | .20 |
| 13 | Gene Locklear | .35 | .20 |
| 14 | Milt Wilcox | .35 | .20 |
| 15 | Jose Cardenal | .35 | .20 |
| 16 | Frank Tanana | .40 | .20 |
| 17 | Dave Concepcion | .60 | .30 |
| 18 | Tigers Team (Ralph Houk) | .90 | .45 |
| 19 | Jerry Koosman | .40 | .20 |
| 20 | Thurman Munson | 7.00 | 3.50 |
| 21 | Rollie Fingers | 5.00 | 2.50 |
| 22 | Dave Cash | .35 | .20 |
| 23 | Bill Russell | .35 | .20 |
| 24 | Al Fitzmorris | .35 | .20 |

| | NR MT | EX | | | NR MT | EX |
|---|---|---|---|---|---|---|
| 25 | Lee May | .40 | .20 | 90 | Rusty Staub | .60 | .30 |
| 26 | Dave McNally | .35 | .20 | 91 | Dick Green | .35 | .20 |
| 27 | Ken Reitz | .35 | .20 | 92 | Cecil Upshaw | .35 | .20 |
| 28 | Tom Murphy | .35 | .20 | 93 | Dave Lopes | .40 | .20 |
| 29 | Dave Parker | 8.00 | 4.00 | 94 | Jim Lonborg | .35 | .20 |
| 30 | Bert Blyleven | 1.00 | .50 | 95 | John Mayberry | .35 | .20 |
| 31 | Dave Rader | .35 | .20 | 96 | Mike Cosgrove | .35 | .20 |
| 32 | Reggie Cleveland | .35 | .20 | 97 | Earl Williams | .35 | .20 |
| 33 | Dusty Baker | .40 | .20 | 98 | Rich Folkers | .35 | .20 |
| 34 | Steve Renko | .35 | .20 | 99 | Mike Hegan | .35 | .20 |
| 35 | Ron Santo | .50 | .25 | 100 | Willie Stargell | 2.50 | 1.25 |
| 36 | Joe Lovitto | .35 | .20 | 101 | Expos Team (Gene | | |
| 37 | Dave Freisleben | .35 | .20 | | Mauch) | .80 | .40 |
| 38 | Buddy Bell | .80 | .40 | 102 | Joe Decker | .35 | .20 |
| 39 | Andy Thornton | .70 | .35 | 103 | Rick Miller | .35 | .20 |
| 40 | Bill Singer | .35 | .20 | 104 | Bill Madlock | 1.25 | .60 |
| 41 | Cesar Geronimo | .35 | .20 | 105 | Buzz Capra | .35 | .20 |
| 42 | Joe Coleman | .35 | .20 | 106 | *Mike Hargrove* | .40 | .20 |
| 43 | Cleon Jones | .35 | .20 | 107 | Jim Barr | .35 | .20 |
| 44 | Pat Dobson | .35 | .20 | 108 | Tom Hall | .35 | .20 |
| 45 | Joe Rudi | .40 | .20 | 109 | George Hendrick | .35 | .20 |
| 46 | Phillies Team (Danny | | | 110 | Wilbur Wood | .35 | .20 |
| | Ozark) | .80 | .40 | 111 | Wayne Garrett | .35 | .20 |
| 47 | Tommy John | 1.25 | .60 | 112 | Larry Hardy | .35 | .20 |
| 48 | Freddie Patek | .35 | .20 | 113 | Elliott Maddox | .35 | .20 |
| 49 | Larry Dierker | .35 | .20 | 114 | Dick Lange | .35 | .20 |
| 50 | Brooks Robinson | 5.00 | 2.50 | 115 | Joe Ferguson | .35 | .20 |
| 51 | *Bob Forsch* | .80 | .40 | 116 | Lerrin LaGrow | .35 | .20 |
| 52 | Darrell Porter | .35 | .20 | 117 | Orioles Team (Earl | | |
| 53 | Dave Giusti | .35 | .20 | | Weaver) | .90 | .45 |
| 54 | Eric Soderholm | .35 | .20 | 118 | Mike Anderson | .35 | .20 |
| 55 | Bobby Bonds | .50 | .25 | 119 | Tommy Helms | .35 | .20 |
| 56 | Rick Wise | .35 | .20 | 120 | Steve Busby (photo | | |
| 57 | Dave Johnson | .80 | .40 | | actually Fran Healy) | .35 | .20 |
| 58 | Chuck Taylor | .35 | .20 | 121 | Bill North | .35 | .20 |
| 59 | Ken Henderson | .35 | .20 | 122 | Al Hrabosky | .35 | .20 |
| 60 | Fergie Jenkins | 4.00 | 2.00 | 123 | Johnny Briggs | .35 | .20 |
| 61 | Dave Winfield | 50.00 | 25.00 | 124 | Jerry Reuss | .40 | .20 |
| 62 | Fritz Peterson | .35 | .20 | 125 | Ken Singleton | .40 | .20 |
| 63 | Steve Swisher | .35 | .20 | 126 | Checklist 1-132 | 1.50 | .70 |
| 64 | Dave Chalk | .35 | .20 | 127 | Glen Borgmann | .35 | .20 |
| 65 | Don Gullett | .35 | .20 | 128 | Bill Lee | .35 | .20 |
| 66 | Willie Horton | .35 | .20 | 129 | Rick Monday | .35 | .20 |
| 67 | Tug McGraw | .50 | .25 | 130 | Phil Niekro | 2.00 | 1.00 |
| 68 | Ron Blomberg | .35 | .20 | 131 | Toby Harrah | .35 | .20 |
| 69 | John Odom | .35 | .20 | 132 | Randy Moffitt | .35 | .20 |
| 70 | Mike Schmidt | 70.00 | 35.00 | 133 | Dan Driessen | .35 | .20 |
| 71 | Charlie Hough | .35 | .20 | 134 | Ron Hodges | .30 | .15 |
| 72 | Royals Team (Jack | | | 135 | Charlie Spikes | .30 | .15 |
| | McKeon) | .80 | .40 | 136 | Jim Mason | .30 | .15 |
| 73 | J.R. Richard | .35 | .20 | 137 | Terry Forster | .35 | .20 |
| 74 | Mark Belanger | .35 | .20 | 138 | Del Unser | .30 | .15 |
| 75 | Ted Simmons | .70 | .35 | 139 | Horacio Pina | .30 | .15 |
| 76 | Ed Sprague | .35 | .20 | 140 | Steve Garvey | 7.00 | 3.50 |
| 77 | Richie Zisk | .35 | .20 | 141 | Mickey Stanley | .30 | .15 |
| 78 | Ray Corbin | .35 | .20 | 142 | Bob Reynolds | .30 | .15 |
| 79 | Gary Matthews | .40 | .20 | 143 | *Cliff Johnson* | .40 | .20 |
| 80 | Carlton Fisk | 20.00 | 10.00 | 144 | Jim Wohlford | .30 | .15 |
| 81 | Ron Reed | .35 | .20 | 145 | Ken Holtzman | .35 | .20 |
| 82 | Pat Kelly | .35 | .20 | 146 | Padres Team (John | | |
| 83 | Jim Merritt | .35 | .20 | | McNamara) | .80 | .40 |
| 84 | Enzo Hernandez | .35 | .20 | 147 | Pedro Garcia | .30 | .15 |
| 85 | Bill Bonham | .35 | .20 | 148 | Jim Rooker | .30 | .15 |
| 86 | Joe Lis | .35 | .20 | 149 | Tim Foli | .30 | .15 |
| 87 | George Foster | 1.25 | .60 | 150 | Bob Gibson | 4.00 | 2.00 |
| 88 | Tom Egan | .35 | .20 | 151 | Steve Brye | .30 | .15 |
| 89 | Jim Ray | .35 | .20 | 152 | Mario Guerrero | .30 | .15 |

| | | NR MT | EX |
|---|---|---|---|
| 153 | Rick Reuschel | .40 | .20 |
| 154 | Mike Lum | .30 | .15 |
| 155 | Jim Bibby | .30 | .15 |
| 156 | Dave Kingman | .90 | .45 |
| 157 | Pedro Borbon | .30 | .15 |
| 158 | Jerry Grote | .30 | .15 |
| 159 | Steve Arlin | .30 | .15 |
| 160 | Graig Nettles | 1.50 | .70 |
| 161 | Stan Bahnsen | .30 | .15 |
| 162 | Willie Montanez | .30 | .15 |
| 163 | Jim Brewer | .30 | .15 |
| 164 | Mickey Rivers | .30 | .15 |
| 165 | Doug Rader | .30 | .15 |
| 166 | Woodie Fryman | .30 | .15 |
| 167 | Rich Coggins | .30 | .15 |
| 168 | Bill Greif | .30 | .15 |
| 169 | Cookie Rojas | .30 | .15 |
| 170 | Bert Campaneris | .40 | .20 |
| 171 | Ed Kirkpatrick | .30 | .15 |
| 172 | Red Sox Team (Darrell Johnson) | 1.25 | .60 |
| 173 | Steve Rogers | .35 | .20 |
| 174 | Bake McBride | .30 | .15 |
| 175 | Don Money | .30 | .15 |
| 176 | Burt Hooton | .35 | .20 |
| 177 | Vic Correll | .30 | .15 |
| 178 | Cesar Tovar | .30 | .15 |
| 179 | Tom Bradley | .30 | .15 |
| 180 | Joe Morgan | 6.00 | 3.00 |
| 181 | Fred Beene | .30 | .15 |
| 182 | Don Hahn | .30 | .15 |
| 183 | Mel Stottlemyre | .40 | .20 |
| 184 | Jorge Orta | .30 | .15 |
| 185 | Steve Carlton | 10.00 | 5.00 |
| 186 | Willie Crawford | .30 | .15 |
| 187 | Denny Doyle | .30 | .15 |
| 188 | Tom Griffin | .30 | .15 |
| 189 | 1951 - MVPs (Larry (Yogi) Berra, Roy Campanella) | 1.50 | .70 |
| 190 | 1952 - MVPs (Hank Sauer, Bobby Shantz) | .40 | .20 |
| 191 | 1953 - MVPs (Roy Campanella, Al Rosen) | .90 | .45 |
| 192 | 1954 - MVPs (Yogi Berra, Willie Mays) | 1.50 | .70 |
| 193 | 1955 - MVPs (Yogi Berra, Roy Campanella) | 1.50 | .70 |
| 194 | 1956 - MVPs (Mickey Mantle, Don Newcombe) | 12.00 | 6.00 |
| 195 | 1957 - MVPs (Hank Aaron, Mickey Mantle) | 12.00 | 6.00 |
| 196 | 1958 - MVPs (Ernie Banks, Jackie Jensen) | .90 | .45 |
| 197 | 1959 - MVPs (Ernie Banks, Nellie Fox) | .90 | .45 |
| 198 | 1960 - MVPs (Dick Groat, Roger Maris) | 1.25 | .60 |
| 199 | 1961 - MVPs (Roger Maris, Frank Robinson) | 1.50 | .70 |
| 200 | 1962 - MVPs (Mickey Mantle, Maury Wills) | 12.00 | 6.00 |
| 201 | 1963 - MVPs (Elston Howard, Sandy Koufax) | 1.50 | .70 |
| 202 | 1964 - MVPs (Ken Boyer, Brooks Robinson) | 1.25 | .60 |
| 203 | 1965 - MVPs (Willie Mays, Zoilo Versalles) | 1.25 | .60 |
| 204 | 1966 - MVPs (Bob Clemente, Frank Robinson) | 1.50 | .70 |
| 205 | 1967 - MVPs (Orlando Cepeda, Carl Yastrzemski) | 1.25 | .60 |
| 206 | 1968 - MVPs (Bob Gibson, Denny McLain) | 1.25 | .60 |
| 207 | 1969 - MVPs (Harmon Killebrew, Willie McCovey) | 1.50 | .70 |
| 208 | 1970 - MVPs (Johnny Bench, Boog Powell) | 1.25 | .60 |
| 209 | 1971 - MVPs (Vida Blue, Joe Torre) | .50 | .25 |
| 210 | 1972 - MVPs (Rich Allen, Johnny Bench) | 1.25 | .60 |
| 211 | 1973 - MVPs (Reggie Jackson, Pete Rose) | 4.00 | 2.00 |
| 212 | 1974 - MVPs (Jeff Burroughs, Steve Garvey) | .90 | .45 |
| 213 | Oscar Gamble | .30 | .15 |
| 214 | Harry Parker | .30 | .15 |
| 215 | Bobby Valentine | .35 | .20 |
| 216 | Giants Team (Wes Westrum) | .80 | .40 |
| 217 | Lou Piniella | .70 | .35 |
| 218 | Jerry Johnson | .30 | .15 |
| 219 | Ed Herrmann | .30 | .15 |
| 220 | Don Sutton | 2.00 | 1.00 |
| 221 | Aurelio Rodriquez (Rodriguez) | .30 | .15 |
| 222 | Dan Spillner | .30 | .15 |
| 223 | *Robin Yount* | 250.00 | 125.00 |
| 224 | Ramon Hernandez | .30 | .15 |
| 225 | Bob Grich | .40 | .20 |
| 226 | Bill Campbell | .30 | .15 |
| 227 | Bob Watson | .30 | .15 |
| 228 | *George Brett* | 250.00 | 125.00 |
| 229 | Barry Foote | .30 | .15 |
| 230 | Jim Hunter | 2.00 | 1.00 |
| 231 | Mike Tyson | .30 | .15 |
| 232 | Diego Segui | .30 | .15 |
| 233 | Billy Grabarkewitz | .30 | .15 |
| 234 | Tom Grieve | .30 | .15 |
| 235 | Jack Billingham | .30 | .15 |
| 236 | Angels Team (Dick Williams) | .80 | .40 |
| 237 | Carl Morton | .30 | .15 |
| 238 | Dave Duncan | .30 | .15 |
| 239 | George Stone | .30 | .15 |
| 240 | Garry Maddox | .30 | .15 |
| 241 | Dick Tidrow | .30 | .15 |
| 242 | Jay Johnstone | .30 | .15 |
| 243 | Jim Kaat | 1.25 | .60 |
| 244 | Bill Buckner | .50 | .25 |
| 245 | Mickey Lolich | .50 | .25 |
| 246 | Cardinals Team (Red | | |

| | NR MT | EX |
|---|---|---|
| | Schoendienst) | .80 | .40 |
| 247 | Enos Cabell | .30 | .15 |
| 248 | Randy Jones | .30 | .15 |
| 249 | Danny Thompson | .30 | .15 |
| 250 | Ken Brett | .30 | .15 |
| 251 | Fran Healy | .30 | .15 |
| 252 | Fred Scherman | .30 | .15 |
| 253 | Jesus Alou | .30 | .15 |
| 254 | Mike Torrez | .30 | .15 |
| 255 | Dwight Evans | 6.00 | 3.00 |
| 256 | Billy Champion | .30 | .15 |
| 257 | Checklist 133-264 | 1.50 | .70 |
| 258 | Dave LaRoche | .30 | .15 |
| 259 | Len Randle | .30 | .15 |
| 260 | Johnny Bench | 12.00 | 6.00 |
| 261 | Andy Hassler | .30 | .15 |
| 262 | Rowland Office | .30 | .15 |
| 263 | Jim Perry | .40 | .20 |
| 264 | John Milner | .30 | .15 |
| 265 | Ron Bryant | .30 | .15 |
| 266 | Sandy Alomar | .30 | .15 |
| 267 | Dick Ruthven | .30 | .15 |
| 268 | Hal McRae | .40 | .20 |
| 269 | Doug Rau | .30 | .15 |
| 270 | Ron Fairly | .35 | .20 |
| 271 | Jerry Moses | .30 | .15 |
| 272 | Lynn McGlothen | .30 | .15 |
| 273 | Steve Braun | .30 | .15 |
| 274 | Vicente Romo | .30 | .15 |
| 275 | Paul Blair | .30 | .15 |
| 276 | White Sox Team (Chuck Tanner) | .80 | .40 |
| 277 | Frank Taveras | .30 | .15 |
| 278 | Paul Lindblad | .30 | .15 |
| 279 | Milt May | .30 | .15 |
| 280 | Carl Yastrzemski | 12.00 | 6.00 |
| 281 | Jim Slaton | .30 | .15 |
| 282 | Jerry Morales | .30 | .15 |
| 283 | Steve Foucault | .30 | .15 |
| 284 | Ken Griffey | .70 | .35 |
| 285 | Ellie Rodriguez | .30 | .15 |
| 286 | Mike Jorgensen | .30 | .15 |
| 287 | Roric Harrison | .30 | .15 |
| 288 | Bruce Ellingsen | .30 | .15 |
| 289 | Ken Rudolph | .30 | .15 |
| 290 | Jon Matlack | .30 | .15 |
| 291 | Bill Sudakis | .30 | .15 |
| 292 | Ron Schueler | .30 | .15 |
| 293 | Dick Sharon | .30 | .15 |
| 294 | *Geoff Zahn* | .40 | .20 |
| 295 | Vada Pinson | .60 | .30 |
| 296 | Alan Foster | .30 | .15 |
| 297 | Craig Kusick | .30 | .15 |
| 298 | Johnny Grubb | .30 | .15 |
| 299 | Bucky Dent | .40 | .20 |
| 300 | Reggie Jackson | 25.00 | 12.50 |
| 301 | Dave Roberts | .30 | .15 |
| 302 | *Rick Burleson* | .50 | .25 |
| 303 | Grant Jackson | .30 | .15 |
| 304 | Pirates Team (Danny Murtaugh) | .80 | .40 |
| 305 | Jim Colborn | .30 | .15 |
| 306 | Batting Leaders (Rod Carew, Ralph Garr) | .80 | .40 |
| 307 | Home Run Leaders (Dick Allen, Mike Schmidt) | .90 | .45 |
| 308 | Runs Batted In Leaders | | |

| | NR MT | EX |
|---|---|---|
| | (Johnny Bench, Jeff Burroughs) | .90 | .45 |
| 309 | Stolen Base Leaders (Lou Brock, Bill North) | .80 | .40 |
| 310 | Victory Leaders (Jim Hunter, Fergie Jenkins, Andy Messersmith, Phil Niekro) | .80 | .40 |
| 311 | Earned Run Average Leaders (Buzz Capra, Jim Hunter) | .50 | .25 |
| 312 | Strikeout Leaders (Steve Carlton, Nolan Ryan) | 4.00 | 2.00 |
| 313 | Leading Firemen (Terry Forster, Mike Marshall) | .50 | .25 |
| 314 | Buck Martinez | .30 | .15 |
| 315 | Don Kessinger | .30 | .15 |
| 316 | Jackie Brown | .30 | .15 |
| 317 | Joe Lahoud | .30 | .15 |
| 318 | Ernie McAnally | .30 | .15 |
| 319 | Johnny Oates | .30 | .15 |
| 320 | Pete Rose | 18.00 | 9.00 |
| 321 | Rudy May | .30 | .15 |
| 322 | Ed Goodson | .30 | .15 |
| 323 | Fred Holdsworth | .30 | .15 |
| 324 | Ed Kranepool | .35 | .20 |
| 325 | Tony Oliva | .80 | .40 |
| 326 | Wayne Twitchell | .30 | .15 |
| 327 | Jerry Hairston | .30 | .15 |
| 328 | Sonny Siebert | .30 | .15 |
| 329 | Ted Kubiak | .30 | .15 |
| 330 | Mike Marshall | .35 | .20 |
| 331 | Indians Team (Frank Robinson) | .90 | .45 |
| 332 | Fred Kendall | .30 | .15 |
| 333 | Dick Drago | .30 | .15 |
| 334 | *Greg Gross* | .35 | .20 |
| 335 | Jim Palmer | 10.00 | 5.00 |
| 336 | Rennie Stennett | .30 | .15 |
| 337 | Kevin Kobel | .30 | .15 |
| 338 | Rick Stelmaszek | .30 | .15 |
| 339 | Jim Fregosi | .40 | .20 |
| 340 | Paul Splittorff | .30 | .15 |
| 341 | Hal Breeden | .30 | .15 |
| 342 | Leroy Stanton | .30 | .15 |
| 343 | Danny Frisella | .30 | .15 |
| 344 | Ben Oglivie | .35 | .20 |
| 345 | Clay Carroll | .30 | .15 |
| 346 | Bobby Darwin | .30 | .15 |
| 347 | Mike Caldwell | .30 | .15 |
| 348 | Tony Muser | .30 | .15 |
| 349 | Ray Sadecki | .30 | .15 |
| 350 | Bobby Murcer | .40 | .20 |
| 351 | Bob Boone | .40 | .20 |
| 352 | Darold Knowles | .30 | .15 |
| 353 | Luis Melendez | .30 | .15 |
| 354 | Dick Bosman | .30 | .15 |
| 355 | Chris Cannizzaro | .30 | .15 |
| 356 | Rico Petrocelli | .35 | .20 |
| 357 | Ken Forsch | .30 | .15 |
| 358 | Al Bumbry | .30 | .15 |
| 359 | Paul Popovich | .30 | .15 |
| 360 | George Scott | .35 | .20 |
| 361 | Dodgers Team (Walter Alston) | 1.00 | .50 |
| 362 | Steve Hargan | .30 | .15 |
| 363 | Carmen Fanzone | .30 | .15 |

| | NR MT | EX | | | NR MT | EX |
|---|---|---|---|---|---|---|
| 364 | Doug Bird | .30 | .15 | 428 | Dave Hamilton | .30 | .15 |
| 365 | Bob Bailey | .30 | .15 | 429 | *Jim Dwyer* | .35 | .20 |
| 366 | Ken Sanders | .30 | .15 | 430 | Luis Tiant | .50 | .25 |
| 367 | Craig Robinson | .30 | .15 | 431 | Rod Gilbreath | .30 | .15 |
| 368 | Vic Albury | .30 | .15 | 432 | Ken Berry | .30 | .15 |
| 369 | Merv Rettenmund | .30 | .15 | 433 | Larry Demery | .30 | .15 |
| 370 | Tom Seaver | 20.00 | 10.00 | 434 | Bob Locker | .30 | .15 |
| 371 | Gates Brown | .30 | .15 | 435 | Dave Nelson | .30 | .15 |
| 372 | John D'Acquisto | .30 | .15 | 436 | Ken Frailing | .30 | .15 |
| 373 | Bill Sharp | .30 | .15 | 437 | *Al Cowens* | .40 | .20 |
| 374 | Eddie Watt | .30 | .15 | 438 | Don Carrithers | .30 | .15 |
| 375 | Roy White | .40 | .20 | 439 | Ed Brinkman | .30 | .15 |
| 376 | Steve Yeager | .30 | .15 | 440 | Andy Messersmith | .35 | .20 |
| 377 | Tom Hilgendorf | .30 | .15 | 441 | Bobby Heise | .30 | .15 |
| 378 | Derrel Thomas | .30 | .15 | 442 | Maximino Leon | .30 | .15 |
| 379 | Bernie Carbo | .30 | .15 | 443 | Twins Team (Frank | | |
| 380 | Sal Bando | .40 | .20 | | Quilici) | .80 | .40 |
| 381 | John Curtis | .30 | .15 | 444 | Gene Garber | .30 | .15 |
| 382 | Don Baylor | .60 | .30 | 445 | Felix Millan | .30 | .15 |
| 383 | Jim York | .30 | .15 | 446 | Bart Johnson | .30 | .15 |
| 384 | Brewers Team (Del | | | 447 | Terry Crowley | .30 | .15 |
| | Crandall) | .80 | .40 | 448 | Frank Duffy | .30 | .15 |
| 385 | Dock Ellis | .30 | .15 | 449 | Charlie Williams | .30 | .15 |
| 386 | Checklist 265-396 | 1.50 | .70 | 450 | Willie McCovey | 3.00 | 1.50 |
| 387 | Jim Spencer | .30 | .15 | 451 | Rick Dempsey | .40 | .20 |
| 388 | Steve Stone | .35 | .20 | 452 | Angel Mangual | .30 | .15 |
| 389 | Tony Solaita | .30 | .15 | 453 | Claude Osteen | .35 | .20 |
| 390 | Ron Cey | .40 | .20 | 454 | Doug Griffin | .30 | .15 |
| 391 | Don DeMola | .30 | .15 | 455 | Don Wilson | .30 | .15 |
| 392 | Bruce Bochte | .40 | .20 | 456 | Bob Coluccio | .30 | .15 |
| 393 | Gary Gentry | .30 | .15 | 457 | Mario Mendoza | .30 | .15 |
| 394 | Larvell Blanks | .30 | .15 | 458 | Ross Grimsley | .30 | .15 |
| 395 | Bud Harrelson | .30 | .15 | 459 | A.L. Championships | .80 | .40 |
| 396 | Fred Norman | .30 | .15 | 460 | N.L. Championships | .80 | .40 |
| 397 | Bill Freehan | .40 | .20 | 461 | World Series Game 1 | | |
| 398 | Elias Sosa | .30 | .15 | | | 2.00 | 1.00 |
| 399 | Terry Harmon | .30 | .15 | 462 | World Series Game 2 | | |
| 400 | Dick Allen | .80 | .40 | | | .80 | .40 |
| 401 | Mike Wallace | .30 | .15 | 463 | World Series Game 3 | | |
| 402 | Bob Tolan | .30 | .15 | | | 1.00 | .50 |
| 403 | Tom Buskey | .30 | .15 | 464 | World Series Game 4 | | |
| 404 | Ted Sizemore | .30 | .15 | | | .80 | .40 |
| 405 | John Montague | .30 | .15 | 465 | World Series Game 5 | | |
| 406 | Bob Gallagher | .30 | .15 | | | .80 | .40 |
| 407 | *Herb Washington* | .35 | .20 | 466 | World Series Summary | | |
| 408 | Clyde Wright | .30 | .15 | | | .80 | .40 |
| 409 | Bob Robertson | .30 | .15 | 467 | Ed Halicki | .30 | .15 |
| 410 | Mike Cueller (Cuellar) | | | 468 | Bobby Mitchell | .30 | .15 |
| | | .40 | .20 | 469 | Tom Dettore | .30 | .15 |
| 411 | George Mitterwald | .30 | .15 | 470 | Jeff Burroughs | .35 | .20 |
| 412 | Bill Hands | .30 | .15 | 471 | Bob Stinson | .30 | .15 |
| 413 | Marty Pattin | .30 | .15 | 472 | Bruce Dal Canton | .30 | .15 |
| 414 | Manny Mota | .35 | .20 | 473 | Ken McMullen | .30 | .15 |
| 415 | John Hiller | .30 | .15 | 474 | Luke Walker | .30 | .15 |
| 416 | Larry Lintz | .30 | .15 | 475 | Darrell Evans | .60 | .30 |
| 417 | Skip Lockwood | .30 | .15 | 476 | *Ed Figueroa* | .35 | .20 |
| 418 | Leo Foster | .30 | .15 | 477 | Tom Hutton | .30 | .15 |
| 419 | Dave Goltz | .30 | .15 | 478 | Tom Burgmeier | .30 | .15 |
| 420 | Larry Bowa | .40 | .20 | 479 | Ken Boswell | .30 | .15 |
| 421 | Mets Team (Yogi Berra) | | | 480 | Carlos May | .30 | .15 |
| | | 1.00 | .50 | 481 | *Will McEnaney* | .35 | .20 |
| 422 | Brian Downing | .35 | .20 | 482 | Tom McCraw | .30 | .15 |
| 423 | Clay Kirby | .30 | .15 | 483 | Steve Ontiveros | .30 | .15 |
| 424 | John Lowenstein | .30 | .15 | 484 | Glenn Beckert | .35 | .20 |
| 425 | Tito Fuentes | .30 | .15 | 485 | Sparky Lyle | .40 | .20 |
| 426 | George Medich | .30 | .15 | 486 | Ray Fosse | .30 | .15 |
| 427 | Clarence Gaston | .30 | .15 | 487 | Astros Team (Preston | | |

| | | NR MT | EX |
|---|---|---|---|
| | Gomez) | .80 | .40 |
| 488 | Bill Travers | .30 | .15 |
| 489 | Cecil Cooper | 1.00 | .50 |
| 490 | Reggie Smith | .35 | .20 |
| 491 | Doyle Alexander | .40 | .20 |
| 492 | Rich Hebner | .30 | .15 |
| 493 | Don Stanhouse | .30 | .15 |
| 494 | *Pete LaCock* | .30 | .15 |
| 495 | Nelson Briles | .30 | .15 |
| 496 | Pepe Frias | .30 | .15 |
| 497 | Jim Nettles | .30 | .15 |
| 498 | Al Downing | .30 | .15 |
| 499 | Marty Perez | .30 | .15 |
| 500 | Nolan Ryan | 65.00 | 33.00 |
| 501 | Bill Robinson | .30 | .15 |
| 502 | Pat Bourque | .30 | .15 |
| 503 | Fred Stanley | .30 | .15 |
| 504 | Buddy Bradford | .30 | .15 |
| 505 | Chris Speier | .30 | .15 |
| 506 | Leron Lee | .30 | .15 |
| 507 | Tom Carroll | .30 | .15 |
| 508 | Bob Hansen | .30 | .15 |
| 509 | Dave Hilton | .30 | .15 |
| 510 | Vida Blue | .50 | .25 |
| 511 | Rangers Team (Billy Martin) | .90 | .45 |
| 512 | Larry Milbourne | .30 | .15 |
| 513 | Dick Pole | .30 | .15 |
| 514 | Jose Cruz | .50 | .25 |
| 515 | Manny Sanguillen | .30 | .15 |
| 516 | Don Hood | .30 | .15 |
| 517 | Checklist 397-528 | 1.25 | .60 |
| 518 | Leo Cardenas | .30 | .15 |
| 519 | Jim Todd | .30 | .15 |
| 520 | Amos Otis | .35 | .20 |
| 521 | Dennis Blair | .30 | .15 |
| 522 | Gary Sutherland | .30 | .15 |
| 523 | Tom Paciorek | .30 | .15 |
| 524 | John Doherty | .30 | .15 |
| 525 | Tom House | .30 | .15 |
| 526 | Larry Hisle | .30 | .15 |
| 527 | Mac Scarce | .30 | .15 |
| 528 | Eddie Leon | .30 | .15 |
| 529 | Gary Thomasson | .30 | .15 |
| 530 | Gaylord Perry | 3.00 | 1.50 |
| 531 | Reds Team (Sparky Anderson) | .90 | .45 |
| 532 | Gorman Thomas | .60 | .30 |
| 533 | Rudy Meoli | .30 | .15 |
| 534 | Alex Johnson | .30 | .15 |
| 535 | Gene Tenace | .30 | .15 |
| 536 | Bob Moose | .30 | .15 |
| 537 | Tommy Harper | .30 | .15 |
| 538 | Duffy Dyer | .30 | .15 |
| 539 | Jesse Jefferson | .30 | .15 |
| 540 | Lou Brock | 4.00 | 2.00 |
| 541 | Roger Metzger | .30 | .15 |
| 542 | Pete Broberg | .30 | .15 |
| 543 | Larry Biittner | .30 | .15 |
| 544 | Steve Mingori | .30 | .15 |
| 545 | Billy Williams | 3.00 | 1.50 |
| 546 | John Knox | .30 | .15 |
| 547 | Von Joshua | .30 | .15 |
| 548 | Charlie Sands | .30 | .15 |
| 549 | Bill Butler | .30 | .15 |
| 550 | Ralph Garr | .30 | .15 |
| 551 | Larry Christenson | .30 | .15 |
| 552 | Jack Brohamer | .30 | .15 |
| 553 | John Boccabella | .30 | .15 |
| 554 | Rich Gossage | 1.50 | .70 |
| 555 | Al Oliver | .80 | .40 |
| 556 | Tim Johnson | .30 | .15 |
| 557 | Larry Gura | .30 | .15 |
| 558 | Dave Roberts | .30 | .15 |
| 559 | Bob Montgomery | .30 | .15 |
| 560 | Tony Perez | 3.00 | 1.50 |
| 561 | A's Team (Alvin Dark) | .90 | .45 |
| 562 | Gary Nolan | .30 | .15 |
| 563 | Wilbur Howard | .30 | .15 |
| 564 | Tommy Davis | .40 | .20 |
| 565 | Joe Torre | .70 | .35 |
| 566 | Ray Burris | .30 | .15 |
| 567 | *Jim Sundberg* | .70 | .35 |
| 568 | Dale Murray | .30 | .15 |
| 569 | Frank White | .40 | .20 |
| 570 | Jim Wynn | .35 | .20 |
| 571 | Dave Lemanczyk | .30 | .15 |
| 572 | Roger Nelson | .30 | .15 |
| 573 | Orlando Pena | .30 | .15 |
| 574 | Tony Taylor | .30 | .15 |
| 575 | Gene Clines | .30 | .15 |
| 576 | Phil Roof | .30 | .15 |
| 577 | John Morris | .30 | .15 |
| 578 | Dave Tomlin | .30 | .15 |
| 579 | Skip Pitlock | .30 | .15 |
| 580 | Frank Robinson | 4.00 | 2.00 |
| 581 | Darrel Chaney | .30 | .15 |
| 582 | Eduardo Rodriguez | .30 | .15 |
| 583 | Andy Etchebarren | .30 | .15 |
| 584 | Mike Garman | .30 | .15 |
| 585 | Chris Chambliss | .40 | .20 |
| 586 | Tim McCarver | .60 | .30 |
| 587 | Chris Ward | .30 | .15 |
| 588 | Rick Auerbach | .30 | .15 |
| 589 | Braves Team (Clyde King) | .80 | .40 |
| 590 | Cesar Cedeno | .40 | .20 |
| 591 | Glenn Abbott | .30 | .15 |
| 592 | Balor Moore | .30 | .15 |
| 593 | Gene Lamont | .30 | .15 |
| 594 | Jim Fuller | .30 | .15 |
| 595 | Joe Niekro | .40 | .20 |
| 596 | Ollie Brown | .30 | .15 |
| 597 | Winston Llenas | .30 | .15 |
| 598 | Bruce Kison | .30 | .15 |
| 599 | Nate Colbert | .30 | .15 |
| 600 | Rod Carew | 12.00 | 6.00 |
| 601 | Juan Beniquez | .35 | .20 |
| 602 | John Vukovich | .30 | .15 |
| 603 | Lew Krausse | .30 | .15 |
| 604 | Oscar Zamora | .30 | .15 |
| 605 | John Ellis | .30 | .15 |
| 606 | Bruce Miller | .30 | .15 |
| 607 | Jim Holt | .30 | .15 |
| 608 | Gene Michael | .35 | .20 |
| 609 | Ellie Hendricks | .30 | .15 |
| 610 | Ron Hunt | .30 | .15 |
| 611 | Yankees Team (Bill Virdon) | 1.25 | .60 |
| 612 | Terry Hughes | .30 | .15 |
| 613 | Bill Parsons | .30 | .15 |
| 614 | Rookie Pitchers (Jack Kucek, Dyar Miller, Vern | | |

| | NR MT | EX |
|---|---|---|
| Ruhle, Paul Siebert) | .30 | .15 |
| 615 Rookie Pitchers (Pat Darcy, *Dennis Leonard*, *Tom Underwood*, Hank Webb) | .60 | .30 |
| 616 Rookie Outfielders (Dave Augustine, Pepe Mangual, *Jim Rice*, John Scott) | 25.00 | 12.50 |
| 617 Rookie Infielders (Mike Cubbage, *Doug DeCinces*, Reggie Sanders, Manny Trillo) | 1.25 | .60 |
| 618 Rookie Pitchers (*Jamie Easterly*, Tom Johnson, *Scott McGregor*, Rick Rhoden) | 2.25 | 1.25 |
| 619 Rookie Outfielders (Benny Ayala, Nyls Nyman, Tommy Smith, Jerry Turner) | .30 | .15 |
| 620 Rookie Catchers Outfielders (*Gary Carter*, Marc Hill, Danny Meyer, Leon Roberts) | 50.00 | 25.00 |
| 621 Rookie Pitchers (*John Denny, Rawly Eastwick, Jim Kern*, Juan Veintidos) | .60 | .30 |
| 622 Rookie Outfielders (Ed Armbrister, *Fred Lynn*, Tom Poquette, Terry Whitfield) | 10.00 | 5.00 |
| 623 Rookie Infielders (*Phil Garner, Keith Hernandez*, Bob Sheldon, Tom Veryzer) | 20.00 | 10.00 |
| 624 Rookie Pitchers (Doug Konieczny, *Gary Lavelle*, Jim Otten, Eddie Solomon) | .35 | .20 |
| 625 Boog Powell | .70 | .35 |
| 626 Larry Haney | .30 | .15 |
| 627 Tom Walker | .30 | .15 |
| 628 *Ron LeFlore* | .80 | .40 |
| 629 Joe Hoerner | .30 | .15 |
| 630 Greg Luzinski | .70 | .35 |
| 631 Lee Lacy | .30 | .15 |
| 632 Morris Nettles | .30 | .15 |
| 633 Paul Casanova | .30 | .15 |
| 634 Cy Acosta | .30 | .15 |
| 635 Chuck Dobson | .30 | .15 |
| 636 Charlie Moore | .30 | .15 |
| 637 Ted Martinez | .30 | .15 |
| 638 Cubs Team (Jim Marshall) | .80 | .40 |
| 639 Steve Kline | .30 | .15 |
| 640 Harmon Killebrew | 5.00 | 2.50 |
| 641 Jim Northrup | .30 | .15 |
| 642 Mike Phillips | .30 | .15 |
| 643 Brent Strom | .30 | .15 |
| 644 Bill Fahey | .30 | .15 |
| 645 Danny Cater | .30 | .15 |
| 646 Checklist 529-660 | 1.50 | .70 |
| 647 *Claudell Washington* | 2.50 | 1.25 |
| 648 Dave Pagan | .30 | .15 |
| 649 Jack Heidemann | .30 | .15 |

| | NR MT | EX |
|---|---|---|
| 650 Dave May | .30 | .15 |
| 651 John Morlan | .30 | .15 |
| 652 Lindy McDaniel | .30 | .15 |
| 653 Lee Richards | .30 | .15 |
| 654 Jerry Terrell | .30 | .15 |
| 655 Rico Carty | .40 | .20 |
| 656 Bill Plummer | .30 | .15 |
| 657 Bob Oliver | .30 | .15 |
| 658 Vic Harris | .30 | .15 |
| 659 Bob Apodaca | .30 | .15 |
| 660 Hank Aaron | 25.00 | 12.50 |

# 1976 Topps

These 2-1/2" by 3-1/2" cards begin a design trend for Topps. The focus was more on the photo quality than in past years with a corresponding trend toward simplicity in the borders. The front of the cards has the player's name and team in two strips while his position is in the lower left corner under a drawing of a player representing that position. The backs have a bat and ball with the card number on the left; statistics and personal information and career highlights on the right. The 660-card set features a number of specialty sets including record-setting performances, statistical leaders, playoff and World Series highlights, the Sporting News All-Time All-Stars and father and son combinations.

| | NR MT | EX |
|---|---|---|
| Complete Set: | 450.00 | 225.00 |
| Commmon Player: | .25 | .13 |

| | NR MT | EX |
|---|---|---|
| 1 '75 Record Breaker (Hank Aaron) | 15.00 | 7.50 |
| 2 '75 Record Breaker (Bobby Bonds) | .40 | .20 |
| 3 '75 Record Breaker (Mickey Lolich) | .35 | .20 |
| 4 '75 Record Breaker | | |

| | NR MT | EX |
|---|---|---|
| (Dave Lopes) | .35 | .20 |
| 5 '75 Record Breaker (Tom Seaver) | 3.00 | 1.50 |
| 6 '75 Record Breaker (Rennie Stennett) | .30 | .15 |
| 7 Jim Umbarger | .25 | .13 |
| 8 Tito Fuentes | .25 | .13 |
| 9 Paul Lindblad | .25 | .13 |
| 10 Lou Brock | 4.00 | 2.00 |
| 11 Jim Hughes | .25 | .13 |
| 12 Richie Zisk | .25 | .13 |
| 13 Johnny Wockenfuss | .25 | .13 |
| 14 Gene Garber | .25 | .13 |
| 15 George Scott | .25 | .13 |
| 16 Bob Apodaca | .25 | .13 |
| 17 Yankees Team (Billy Martin) | 1.25 | .60 |
| 18 Dale Murray | .25 | .13 |
| 19 George Brett | 60.00 | 30.00 |
| 20 Bob Watson | .25 | .13 |
| 21 Dave LaRoche | .25 | .13 |
| 22 Bill Russell | .25 | .13 |
| 23 Brian Downing | .25 | .13 |
| 24 Cesar Geronimo | .25 | .13 |
| 25 Mike Torrez | .25 | .13 |
| 26 Andy Thornton | .25 | .13 |
| 27 Ed Figueroa | .25 | .13 |
| 28 Dusty Baker | .25 | .13 |
| 29 Rick Burleson | .30 | .15 |
| 30 *John Montefusco* | .35 | .20 |
| 31 Len Randle | .25 | .13 |
| 32 Danny Frisella | .25 | .13 |
| 33 Bill North | .25 | .13 |
| 34 Mike Garman | .25 | .13 |
| 35 Tony Oliva | .60 | .30 |
| 36 Frank Taveras | .25 | .13 |
| 37 John Hiller | .25 | .13 |
| 38 Garry Maddox | .25 | .13 |
| 39 Pete Broberg | .25 | .13 |
| 40 Dave Kingman | .80 | .40 |
| 41 *Tippy Martinez* | .40 | .20 |
| 42 Barry Foote | .25 | .13 |
| 43 Paul Splittorff | .25 | .13 |
| 44 Doug Rader | .25 | .13 |
| 45 Boog Powell | .60 | .30 |
| 46 Dodgers Team (Walter Alston) | 1.00 | .50 |
| 47 Jesse Jefferson | .25 | .13 |
| 48 Dave Concepcion | .40 | .20 |
| 49 Dave Duncan | .25 | .13 |
| 50 Fred Lynn | 2.00 | 1.00 |
| 51 Ray Burris | .25 | .13 |
| 52 Dave Chalk | .25 | .13 |
| 53 Mike Beard | .25 | .13 |
| 54 Dave Rader | .25 | .13 |
| 55 Gaylord Perry | 3.00 | 1.50 |
| 56 Bob Tolan | .25 | .13 |
| 57 Phil Garner | .30 | .15 |
| 58 Ron Reed | .25 | .13 |
| 59 Larry Hisle | .25 | .13 |
| 60 Jerry Reuss | .30 | .15 |
| 61 Ron LeFlore | .30 | .15 |
| 62 Johnny Oates | .25 | .13 |
| 63 Bobby Darwin | .25 | .13 |
| 64 Jerry Koosman | .30 | .15 |
| 65 Chris Chambliss | .30 | .15 |
| 66 Father & Son (Buddy Bell, Gus Bell) | .50 | .25 |
| 67 Father & Son (Bob Boone, Ray Boone) | .40 | .20 |
| 68 Father & Son (Joe Coleman, Joe Coleman, Jr.) | .25 | .13 |
| 69 Father & Son (Jim Hegan, Mike Hegan) | .25 | .13 |
| 70 Father & Son (Roy Smalley, Roy Smalley, Jr.) | .25 | .13 |
| 71 Steve Rogers | .25 | .13 |
| 72 Hal McRae | .25 | .13 |
| 73 Orioles Team (Earl Weaver) | .80 | .40 |
| 74 Oscar Gamble | .25 | .13 |
| 75 Larry Dierker | .25 | .13 |
| 76 Willie Crawford | .25 | .13 |
| 77 Pedro Borbon | .25 | .13 |
| 78 Cecil Cooper | 1.00 | .50 |
| 79 Jerry Morales | .25 | .13 |
| 80 Jim Kaat | .90 | .45 |
| 81 Darrell Evans | .50 | .25 |
| 82 Von Joshua | .25 | .13 |
| 83 Jim Spencer | .25 | .13 |
| 84 Brent Strom | .25 | .13 |
| 85 Mickey Rivers | .25 | .13 |
| 86 Mike Tyson | .25 | .13 |
| 87 Tom Burgmeier | .25 | .13 |
| 88 Duffy Dyer | .25 | .13 |
| 89 Vern Ruhle | .25 | .13 |
| 90 Sal Bando | .30 | .15 |
| 91 Tom Hutton | .25 | .13 |
| 92 Eduardo Rodriguez | .25 | .13 |
| 93 Mike Phillips | .25 | .13 |
| 94 Jim Dwyer | .30 | .15 |
| 95 Brooks Robinson | 5.00 | 2.50 |
| 96 Doug Bird | .25 | .13 |
| 97 Wilbur Howard | .25 | .13 |
| 98 *Dennis Eckersley* | 65.00 | 33.00 |
| 99 Lee Lacy | .25 | .13 |
| 100 Jim Hunter | 3.00 | 1.50 |
| 101 Pete LaCock | .25 | .13 |
| 102 Jim Willoughby | .25 | .13 |
| 103 Biff Pocoroba | .25 | .13 |
| 104 Reds Team (Sparky Anderson) | .90 | .45 |
| 105 Gary Lavelle | .25 | .13 |
| 106 Tom Grieve | .25 | .13 |
| 107 Dave Roberts | .25 | .13 |
| 108 Don Kirkwood | .25 | .13 |
| 109 Larry Lintz | .25 | .13 |
| 110 Carlos May | .25 | .13 |
| 111 Danny Thompson | .25 | .13 |
| 112 *Kent Tekulve* | .80 | .40 |
| 113 Gary Sutherland | .25 | .13 |
| 114 Jay Johnstone | .25 | .13 |
| 115 Ken Holtzman | .25 | .13 |
| 116 Charlie Moore | .25 | .13 |
| 117 Mike Jorgensen | .25 | .13 |
| 118 Red Sox Team (Darrell Johnson) | .90 | .45 |
| 119 Checklist 1-132 | 1.25 | .60 |
| 120 Rusty Staub | .35 | .20 |
| 121 Tony Solaita | .25 | .13 |
| 122 Mike Cosgrove | .25 | .13 |
| 123 Walt Williams | .25 | .13 |

| | NR MT | EX |
|---|---|---|
| 124 Doug Rau | .25 | .13 |
| 125 Don Baylor | .50 | .25 |
| 126 Tom Dettore | .25 | .13 |
| 127 Larvell Blanks | .25 | .13 |
| 128 Ken Griffey | .35 | .20 |
| 129 Andy Etchebarren | .25 | .13 |
| 130 Luis Tiant | .40 | .20 |
| 131 Bill Stein | .25 | .13 |
| 132 Don Hood | .25 | .13 |
| 133 Gary Matthews | .25 | .13 |
| 134 Mike Ivie | .25 | .13 |
| 135 Bake McBride | .25 | .13 |
| 136 Dave Goltz | .25 | .13 |
| 137 Bill Robinson | .25 | .13 |
| 138 Lerrin LaGrow | .25 | .13 |
| 139 Gorman Thomas | .35 | .20 |
| 140 Vida Blue | .40 | .20 |
| 141 *Larry Parrish* | .80 | .40 |
| 142 Dick Drago | .25 | .13 |
| 143 Jerry Grote | .25 | .13 |
| 144 Al Fitzmorris | .25 | .13 |
| 145 Larry Bowa | .35 | .20 |
| 146 George Medich | .25 | .13 |
| 147 Astros Team (Bill Virdon) | .80 | .40 |
| 148 Stan Thomas | .25 | .13 |
| 149 Tommy Davis | .30 | .15 |
| 150 Steve Garvey | 5.00 | 2.50 |
| 151 Bill Bonham | .25 | .13 |
| 152 Leroy Stanton | .25 | .13 |
| 153 Buzz Capra | .25 | .13 |
| 154 Bucky Dent | .30 | .15 |
| 155 Jack Billingham | .25 | .13 |
| 156 Rico Carty | .25 | .13 |
| 157 Mike Caldwell | .25 | .13 |
| 158 Ken Reitz | .25 | .13 |
| 159 Jerry Terrell | .25 | .13 |
| 160 Dave Winfield | 25.00 | 12.50 |
| 161 Bruce Kison | .25 | .13 |
| 162 Jack Pierce | .25 | .13 |
| 163 Jim Slaton | .25 | .13 |
| 164 Pepe Mangual | .25 | .13 |
| 165 Gene Tenace | .25 | .13 |
| 166 Skip Lockwood | .25 | .13 |
| 167 Freddie Patek | .25 | .13 |
| 168 Tom Hilgendorf | .25 | .13 |
| 169 Graig Nettles | 1.00 | .50 |
| 170 Rick Wise | .25 | .13 |
| 171 Greg Gross | .25 | .13 |
| 172 Rangers Team (Frank Lucchesi) | .80 | .40 |
| 173 Steve Swisher | .25 | .13 |
| 174 Charlie Hough | .25 | .13 |
| 175 Ken Singleton | .30 | .15 |
| 176 Dick Lange | .25 | .13 |
| 177 Marty Perez | .25 | .13 |
| 178 Tom Buskey | .25 | .13 |
| 179 George Foster | 1.00 | .50 |
| 180 Rich Gossage | 1.50 | .70 |
| 181 Willie Montanez | .25 | .13 |
| 182 Harry Rasmussen | .25 | .13 |
| 183 Steve Braun | .25 | .13 |
| 184 Bill Greif | .25 | .13 |
| 185 Dave Parker | 7.00 | 3.50 |
| 186 Tom Walker | .25 | .13 |
| 187 Pedro Garcia | .25 | .13 |
| 188 Fred Scherman | .25 | .13 |

| | NR MT | EX |
|---|---|---|
| 189 Claudell Washington | .40 | .20 |
| 190 Jon Matlack | .25 | .13 |
| 191 N.L. Batting Leaders (Bill Madlock, Manny Sanguillen, Ted Simmons) | .60 | .30 |
| 192 A.L. Batting Leaders (Rod Carew, Fred Lynn, Thurman Munson) | 2.00 | 1.00 |
| 193 N.L. Home Run Leaders (Dave Kingman, Greg Luzinski, Mike Schmidt) | 1.25 | .60 |
| 194 A.L. Home Run Leaders (Reggie Jackson, John Mayberry, George Scott) | 1.25 | .60 |
| 195 N.L. Runs Batted In Ldrs. (Johnny Bench, Greg Luzinski, Tony Perez) | 1.25 | .60 |
| 196 A.L. Runs Batted In Ldrs. (Fred Lynn, John Mayberry, George Scott) | .60 | .30 |
| 197 N.L. Stolen Base Leaders (Lou Brock, Dave Lopes, Joe Morgan) | .90 | .45 |
| 198 A.L. Stolen Base Leaders (Amos Otis, Mickey Rivers, Claudell Washington) | .50 | .25 |
| 199 N.L. Victory Leaders (Randy Jones, Andy Messersmith, Tom Seaver) | .80 | .40 |
| 200 A.L. Victory Leaders (Vida Blue, Jim Hunter, Jim Palmer) | .90 | .45 |
| 201 N.L. Earned Run Avg. Ldrs. (Randy Jones, Andy Messersmith, Tom Seaver) | .80 | .40 |
| 202 A.L. Earned Run Avg. Ldrs. (Dennis Eckersley, Jim Hunter, Jim Palmer) | .90 | .45 |
| 203 N.L. Strikeout Leaders (Andy Messersmith, John Montefusco, Tom Seaver) | .80 | .40 |
| 204 A.L. Strikeout Leaders (Bert Blyleven, Gaylord Perry, Frank Tanana) | .70 | .35 |
| 205 Major League Leading Firemen (Rich Gossage, Al Hrabosky) | .50 | .25 |
| 206 Manny Trillo | .25 | .13 |
| 207 Andy Hassler | .25 | .13 |
| 208 Mike Lum | .25 | .13 |
| 209 Alan Ashby | .35 | .20 |
| 210 Lee May | .25 | .13 |
| 211 Clay Carroll | .25 | .13 |
| 212 Pat Kelly | .25 | .13 |
| 213 Dave Heaverlo | .25 | .13 |
| 214 Eric Soderholm | .25 | .13 |
| 215 Reggie Smith | .25 | .13 |
| 216 Expos Team (Karl Kuehl) | .80 | .40 |
| 217 Dave Freisleben | .25 | .13 |
| 218 John Knox | .25 | .13 |
| 219 Tom Murphy | .25 | .13 |

| | | NR MT | EX |
|---|---|---|---|
| 220 | Manny Sanguillen | .25 | .13 |
| 221 | Jim Todd | .25 | .13 |
| 222 | Wayne Garrett | .25 | .13 |
| 223 | Ollie Brown | .25 | .13 |
| 224 | Jim York | .25 | .13 |
| 225 | Roy White | .25 | .13 |
| 226 | Jim Sundberg | .25 | .13 |
| 227 | Oscar Zamora | .25 | .13 |
| 228 | John Hale | .25 | .13 |
| 229 | *Jerry Remy* | .30 | .15 |
| 230 | Carl Yastrzemski | 8.00 | 4.00 |
| 231 | Tom House | .25 | .13 |
| 232 | Frank Duffy | .25 | .13 |
| 233 | Grant Jackson | .25 | .13 |
| 234 | Mike Sadek | .25 | .13 |
| 235 | Bert Blyleven | 1.00 | .50 |
| 236 | Royals Team (Whitey Herzog) | .80 | .40 |
| 237 | Dave Hamilton | .25 | .13 |
| 238 | Larry Biittner | .25 | .13 |
| 239 | John Curtis | .25 | .13 |
| 240 | Pete Rose | 12.00 | 6.00 |
| 241 | Hector Torres | .25 | .13 |
| 242 | Dan Meyer | .25 | .13 |
| 243 | Jim Rooker | .25 | .13 |
| 244 | Bill Sharp | .25 | .13 |
| 245 | Felix Millan | .25 | .13 |
| 246 | Cesar Tovar | .25 | .13 |
| 247 | Terry Harmon | .25 | .13 |
| 248 | Dick Tidrow | .25 | .13 |
| 249 | Cliff Johnson | .25 | .13 |
| 250 | Fergie Jenkins | 2.00 | 1.00 |
| 251 | Rick Monday | .30 | .15 |
| 252 | Tim Nordbrook | .25 | .13 |
| 253 | Bill Buckner | .50 | .25 |
| 254 | Rudy Meoli | .25 | .13 |
| 255 | Fritz Peterson | .25 | .13 |
| 256 | Rowland Office | .25 | .13 |
| 257 | Ross Grimsley | .25 | .13 |
| 258 | Nyls Nyman | .25 | .13 |
| 259 | Darrel Chaney | .25 | .13 |
| 260 | Steve Busby | .25 | .13 |
| 261 | Gary Thomasson | .25 | .13 |
| 262 | Checklist 133-264 | 1.50 | .70 |
| 263 | *Lyman Bostock* | .80 | .40 |
| 264 | Steve Renko | .25 | .13 |
| 265 | Willie Davis | .30 | .15 |
| 266 | Alan Foster | .25 | .13 |
| 267 | Aurelio Rodriguez | .25 | .13 |
| 268 | Del Unser | .25 | .13 |
| 269 | Rick Austin | .25 | .13 |
| 270 | Willie Stargell | 3.00 | 1.50 |
| 271 | Jim Lonborg | .25 | .13 |
| 272 | Rick Dempsey | .25 | .13 |
| 273 | Joe Niekro | .30 | .15 |
| 274 | Tommy Harper | .25 | .13 |
| 275 | *Rick Manning* | .40 | .20 |
| 276 | Mickey Scott | .25 | .13 |
| 277 | Cubs Team (Jim Marshall) | .80 | .40 |
| 278 | Bernie Carbo | .25 | .13 |
| 279 | Roy Howell | .25 | .13 |
| 280 | Burt Hooton | .25 | .13 |
| 281 | Dave May | .25 | .13 |
| 282 | Dan Osborn | .25 | .13 |
| 283 | Merv Rettenmund | .25 | .13 |
| 284 | Steve Ontiveros | .25 | .13 |

| | | NR MT | EX |
|---|---|---|---|
| 285 | Mike Cuellar | .25 | .13 |
| 286 | Jim Wohlford | .25 | .13 |
| 287 | Pete Mackanin | .25 | .13 |
| 288 | Bill Campbell | .25 | .13 |
| 289 | Enzo Hernandez | .25 | .13 |
| 290 | Ted Simmons | .60 | .30 |
| 291 | Ken Sanders | .25 | .13 |
| 292 | Leon Roberts | .25 | .13 |
| 293 | Bill Castro | .25 | .13 |
| 294 | Ed Kirkpatrick | .25 | .13 |
| 295 | Dave Cash | .25 | .13 |
| 296 | Pat Dobson | .25 | .13 |
| 297 | Roger Metzger | .25 | .13 |
| 298 | Dick Bosman | .25 | .13 |
| 299 | Champ Summers | .25 | .13 |
| 300 | Johnny Bench | 10.00 | 5.00 |
| 301 | Jackie Brown | .25 | .13 |
| 302 | Rick Miller | .25 | .13 |
| 303 | Steve Foucault | .25 | .13 |
| 304 | Angels Team (Dick Williams) | .80 | .40 |
| 305 | Andy Messersmith | .25 | .13 |
| 306 | Rod Gilbreath | .25 | .13 |
| 307 | Al Bumbry | .25 | .13 |
| 308 | Jim Barr | .25 | .13 |
| 309 | Bill Melton | .25 | .13 |
| 310 | Randy Jones | .30 | .15 |
| 311 | Cookie Rojas | .25 | .13 |
| 312 | Don Carrithers | .25 | .13 |
| 313 | *Dan Ford* | .25 | .13 |
| 314 | Ed Kranepool | .25 | .13 |
| 315 | Al Hrabosky | .25 | .13 |
| 316 | Robin Yount | 60.00 | 30.00 |
| 317 | *John Candelaria* | 2.00 | 1.00 |
| 318 | Bob Boone | .30 | .15 |
| 319 | Larry Gura | .25 | .13 |
| 320 | Willie Horton | .25 | .13 |
| 321 | Jose Cruz | .35 | .20 |
| 322 | Glenn Abbott | .25 | .13 |
| 323 | Rob Sperring | .25 | .13 |
| 324 | Jim Bibby | .25 | .13 |
| 325 | Tony Perez | 2.00 | 1.00 |
| 326 | Dick Pole | .25 | .13 |
| 327 | Dave Moates | .25 | .13 |
| 328 | Carl Morton | .25 | .13 |
| 329 | Joe Ferguson | .25 | .13 |
| 330 | Nolan Ryan | 50.00 | 25.00 |
| 331 | Padres Team (John McNamara) | .80 | .40 |
| 332 | Charlie Williams | .25 | .13 |
| 333 | Bob Coluccio | .25 | .13 |
| 334 | Dennis Leonard | .25 | .13 |
| 335 | Bob Grich | .25 | .13 |
| 336 | Vic Albury | .25 | .13 |
| 337 | Bud Harrelson | .25 | .13 |
| 338 | Bob Bailey | .25 | .13 |
| 339 | John Denny | .25 | .13 |
| 340 | Jim Rice | 8.00 | 4.00 |
| 341 | All Time All-Stars (Lou Gehrig) | 5.00 | 2.50 |
| 342 | All Time All-Stars (Rogers Hornsby) | 1.25 | .60 |
| 343 | All Time All-Stars (Pie Traynor) | .80 | .40 |
| 344 | All Time All-Stars (Honus Wagner) | 1.25 | .60 |
| 345 | All Time All-Stars (Babe | | |

| | NR MT | EX |
|---|---|---|
| Ruth) | 8.00 | 4.00 |
| 346 All Time All-Stars (Ty Cobb) | 6.00 | 3.00 |
| 347 All Time All-Stars (Ted Williams) | 6.00 | 3.00 |
| 348 All Time All-Stars (Mickey Cochrane) | .80 | .40 |
| 349 All Time All-Stars (Walter Johnson) | 1.25 | .60 |
| 350 All Time All-Stars (Lefty Grove) | 1.00 | .50 |
| 351 Randy Hundley | .25 | .13 |
| 352 Dave Giusti | .25 | .13 |
| 353 *Sixto Lezcano* | .30 | .15 |
| 354 Ron Blomberg | .25 | .13 |
| 355 Steve Carlton | 7.00 | 3.50 |
| 356 Ted Martinez | .25 | .13 |
| 357 Ken Forsch | .25 | .13 |
| 358 Buddy Bell | .50 | .25 |
| 359 Rick Reuschel | .30 | .15 |
| 360 Jeff Burroughs | .25 | .13 |
| 361 Tigers Team (Ralph Houk) | 1.00 | .50 |
| 362 Will McEnaney | .25 | .13 |
| 363 *Dave Collins* | .40 | .20 |
| 364 Elias Sosa | .25 | .13 |
| 365 Carlton Fisk | 12.00 | 6.00 |
| 366 Bobby Valentine | .30 | .15 |
| 367 Bruce Miller | .25 | .13 |
| 368 Wilbur Wood | .25 | .13 |
| 369 Frank White | .30 | .15 |
| 370 Ron Cey | .40 | .20 |
| 371 Ellie Hendricks | .25 | .13 |
| 372 Rick Baldwin | .25 | .13 |
| 373 Johnny Briggs | .25 | .13 |
| 374 Dan Warthen | .25 | .13 |
| 375 Ron Fairly | .25 | .13 |
| 376 Rich Hebner | .25 | .13 |
| 377 Mike Hegan | .25 | .13 |
| 378 Steve Stone | .25 | .13 |
| 379 Ken Boswell | .25 | .13 |
| 380 Bobby Bonds | .35 | .20 |
| 381 Denny Doyle | .25 | .13 |
| 382 Matt Alexander | .25 | .13 |
| 383 John Ellis | .25 | .13 |
| 384 Phillies Team (Danny Ozark) | .80 | .40 |
| 385 Mickey Lolich | .40 | .20 |
| 386 Ed Goodson | .25 | .13 |
| 387 Mike Miley | .25 | .13 |
| 388 Stan Perzanowski | .25 | .13 |
| 389 Glenn Adams | .25 | .13 |
| 390 Don Gullett | .25 | .13 |
| 391 Jerry Hairston | .25 | .13 |
| 392 Checklist 265-396 | 1.50 | .70 |
| 393 Paul Mitchell | .25 | .13 |
| 394 Fran Healy | .25 | .13 |
| 395 Jim Wynn | .30 | .15 |
| 396 Bill Lee | .25 | .13 |
| 397 Tim Foli | .25 | .13 |
| 398 Dave Tomlin | .25 | .13 |
| 399 Luis Melendez | .25 | .13 |
| 400 Rod Carew | 8.00 | 4.00 |
| 401 Ken Brett | .25 | .13 |
| 402 Don Money | .25 | .13 |
| 403 Geoff Zahn | .25 | .13 |
| 404 Enos Cabell | .25 | .13 |

| | NR MT | EX |
|---|---|---|
| 405 Rollie Fingers | 5.00 | 2.50 |
| 406 Ed Herrmann | .25 | .13 |
| 407 Tom Underwood | .25 | .13 |
| 408 Charlie Spikes | .25 | .13 |
| 409 Dave Lemanczyk | .25 | .13 |
| 410 Ralph Garr | .25 | .13 |
| 411 Bill Singer | .25 | .13 |
| 412 Toby Harrah | .25 | .13 |
| 413 Pete Varney | .25 | .13 |
| 414 Wayne Garland | .25 | .13 |
| 415 Vada Pinson | .50 | .25 |
| 416 Tommy John | 1.25 | .60 |
| 417 Gene Clines | .25 | .13 |
| 418 Jose Morales | .25 | .13 |
| 419 Reggie Cleveland | .25 | .13 |
| 420 Joe Morgan | 5.00 | 2.50 |
| 421 A's Team | .80 | .40 |
| 422 Johnny Grubb | .25 | .13 |
| 423 Ed Halicki | .25 | .13 |
| 424 Phil Roof | .25 | .13 |
| 425 Rennie Stennett | .25 | .13 |
| 426 Bob Forsch | .25 | .13 |
| 427 Kurt Bevacqua | .25 | .13 |
| 428 Jim Crawford | .25 | .13 |
| 429 Fred Stanley | .25 | .13 |
| 430 Jose Cardenal | .25 | .13 |
| 431 Dick Ruthven | .25 | .13 |
| 432 Tom Veryzer | .25 | .13 |
| 433 Rick Waits | .25 | .13 |
| 434 Morris Nettles | .25 | .13 |
| 435 Phil Niekro | 2.00 | 1.00 |
| 436 Bill Fahey | .25 | .13 |
| 437 Terry Forster | .25 | .13 |
| 438 Doug DeCinces | .50 | .25 |
| 439 Rick Rhoden | .60 | .30 |
| 440 John Mayberry | .25 | .13 |
| 441 Gary Carter | 10.00 | 5.00 |
| 442 Hank Webb | .25 | .13 |
| 443 Giants Team | .80 | .40 |
| 444 Gary Nolan | .25 | .13 |
| 445 Rico Petrocelli | .25 | .13 |
| 446 Larry Haney | .25 | .13 |
| 447 Gene Locklear | .25 | .13 |
| 448 Tom Johnson | .25 | .13 |
| 449 Bob Robertson | .25 | .13 |
| 450 Jim Palmer | 6.00 | 3.00 |
| 451 Buddy Bradford | .25 | .13 |
| 452 Tom Hausman | .25 | .13 |
| 453 Lou Piniella | .60 | .30 |
| 454 Tom Griffin | .25 | .13 |
| 455 Dick Allen | .50 | .25 |
| 456 Joe Coleman | .25 | .13 |
| 457 Ed Crosby | .25 | .13 |
| 458 Earl Williams | .25 | .13 |
| 459 Jim Brewer | .25 | .13 |
| 460 Cesar Cedeno | .30 | .15 |
| 461 NL & AL Championships | .80 | .40 |
| 462 1975 World Series | .80 | .40 |
| 463 Steve Hargan | .25 | .13 |
| 464 Ken Henderson | .25 | .13 |
| 465 Mike Marshall | .30 | .15 |
| 466 Bob Stinson | .25 | .13 |
| 467 Woodie Fryman | .25 | .13 |
| 468 Jesus Alou | .25 | .13 |
| 469 Rawly Eastwick | .25 | .13 |
| 470 Bobby Murcer | .35 | .20 |

| | | NR MT | EX |
|---|---|---|---|
| 471 | Jim Burton | .25 | .13 |
| 472 | Bob Davis | .25 | .13 |
| 473 | Paul Blair | .25 | .13 |
| 474 | Ray Corbin | .25 | .13 |
| 475 | Joe Rudi | .30 | .15 |
| 476 | Bob Moose | .25 | .13 |
| 477 | Indians Team (Frank Robinson) | .80 | .40 |
| 478 | Lynn McGlothen | .25 | .13 |
| 479 | Bobby Mitchell | .25 | .13 |
| 480 | Mike Schmidt | 30.00 | 15.00 |
| 481 | Rudy May | .25 | .13 |
| 482 | Tim Hosley | .25 | .13 |
| 483 | Mickey Stanley | .25 | .13 |
| 484 | Eric Raich | .25 | .13 |
| 485 | Mike Hargrove | .25 | .13 |
| 486 | Bruce Dal Canton | .25 | .13 |
| 487 | Leron Lee | .25 | .13 |
| 488 | Claude Osteen | .25 | .13 |
| 489 | Skip Jutze | .25 | .13 |
| 490 | Frank Tanana | .30 | .15 |
| 491 | Terry Crowley | .25 | .13 |
| 492 | Marty Pattin | .25 | .13 |
| 493 | Derrel Thomas | .25 | .13 |
| 494 | Craig Swan | .25 | .13 |
| 495 | Nate Colbert | .25 | .13 |
| 496 | Juan Beniquez | .25 | .13 |
| 497 | Joe McIntosh | .25 | .13 |
| 498 | Glenn Borgmann | .25 | .13 |
| 499 | Mario Guerrero | .25 | .13 |
| 500 | Reggie Jackson | 20.00 | 10.00 |
| 501 | Billy Champion | .25 | .13 |
| 502 | Tim McCarver | .50 | .25 |
| 503 | Elliott Maddox | .25 | .13 |
| 504 | Pirates Team (Danny Murtaugh) | .80 | .40 |
| 505 | Mark Belanger | .25 | .13 |
| 506 | George Mitterwald | .25 | .13 |
| 507 | Ray Bare | .25 | .13 |
| 508 | Duane Kuiper | .25 | .13 |
| 509 | Bill Hands | .25 | .13 |
| 510 | Amos Otis | .25 | .13 |
| 511 | Jamie Easterly | .25 | .13 |
| 512 | Ellie Rodriguez | .25 | .13 |
| 513 | Bart Johnson | .25 | .13 |
| 514 | Dan Driessen | .30 | .15 |
| 515 | Steve Yeager | .25 | .13 |
| 516 | Wayne Granger | .25 | .13 |
| 517 | John Milner | .25 | .13 |
| 518 | Doug Flynn | .25 | .13 |
| 519 | Steve Brye | .25 | .13 |
| 520 | Willie McCovey | 2.50 | 1.25 |
| 521 | Jim Colborn | .25 | .13 |
| 522 | Ted Sizemore | .25 | .13 |
| 523 | Bob Montgomery | .25 | .13 |
| 524 | Pete Falcone | .25 | .13 |
| 525 | Billy Williams | 2.25 | 1.25 |
| 526 | Checklist 397-528 | 1.50 | .70 |
| 527 | Mike Anderson | .25 | .13 |
| 528 | Dock Ellis | .25 | .13 |
| 529 | Deron Johnson | .25 | .13 |
| 530 | Don Sutton | 1.50 | .70 |
| 531 | Mets Team (Joe Frazier) | .90 | .45 |
| 532 | Milt May | .25 | .13 |
| 533 | Lee Richard | .25 | .13 |
| 534 | Stan Bahnsen | .25 | .13 |

| | | NR MT | EX |
|---|---|---|---|
| 535 | Dave Nelson | .25 | .13 |
| 536 | Mike Thompson | .25 | .13 |
| 537 | Tony Muser | .25 | .13 |
| 538 | Pat Darcy | .25 | .13 |
| 539 | John Balaz | .25 | .13 |
| 540 | Bill Freehan | .25 | .13 |
| 541 | Steve Mingori | .25 | .13 |
| 542 | Keith Hernandez | 6.00 | 3.00 |
| 543 | Wayne Twitchell | .25 | .13 |
| 544 | Pepe Frias | .25 | .13 |
| 545 | Sparky Lyle | .35 | .20 |
| 546 | Dave Rosello | .25 | .13 |
| 547 | Roric Harrison | .25 | .13 |
| 548 | Manny Mota | .25 | .13 |
| 549 | Randy Tate | .25 | .13 |
| 550 | Hank Aaron | 20.00 | 10.00 |
| 551 | Jerry DaVanon | .25 | .13 |
| 552 | Terry Humphrey | .25 | .13 |
| 553 | Randy Moffitt | .25 | .13 |
| 554 | Ray Fosse | .25 | .13 |
| 555 | Dyar Miller | .25 | .13 |
| 556 | Twins Team (Gene Mauch) | .80 | .40 |
| 557 | Dan Spillner | .25 | .13 |
| 558 | Clarence Gaston | .25 | .13 |
| 559 | Clyde Wright | .25 | .13 |
| 560 | Jorge Orta | .25 | .13 |
| 561 | Tom Carroll | .25 | .13 |
| 562 | Adrian Garrett | .25 | .13 |
| 563 | Larry Demery | .25 | .13 |
| 564 | Bubble Gum Blowing Champ (Kurt Bevacqua) | .30 | .15 |
| 565 | Tug McGraw | .35 | .20 |
| 566 | Ken McMullen | .25 | .13 |
| 567 | George Stone | .25 | .13 |
| 568 | Rob Andrews | .25 | .13 |
| 569 | Nelson Briles | .25 | .13 |
| 570 | George Hendrick | .25 | .13 |
| 571 | Don DeMola | .25 | .13 |
| 572 | Rich Coggins | .25 | .13 |
| 573 | Bill Travers | .25 | .13 |
| 574 | Don Kessinger | .25 | .13 |
| 575 | Dwight Evans | 4.00 | 2.00 |
| 576 | Maximino Leon | .25 | .13 |
| 577 | Marc Hill | .25 | .13 |
| 578 | Ted Kubiak | .25 | .13 |
| 579 | Clay Kirby | .25 | .13 |
| 580 | Bert Campaneris | .30 | .15 |
| 581 | Cardinals Team (Red Schoendienst) | .80 | .40 |
| 582 | Mike Kekich | .25 | .13 |
| 583 | Tommy Helms | .25 | .13 |
| 584 | Stan Wall | .25 | .13 |
| 585 | Joe Torre | .50 | .25 |
| 586 | Ron Schueler | .25 | .13 |
| 587 | Leo Cardenas | .25 | .13 |
| 588 | Kevin Kobel | .25 | .13 |
| 589 | Rookie Pitchers (Santo Alcala, Mike Flanagan, Joe Pactwa, Pablo Torrealba) | 2.00 | 1.00 |
| 590 | Rookie Outfielders (Henry Cruz, Chet Lemon, Ellis Valentine, Terry Whitfield) | 1.00 | .50 |
| 591 | Rookie Pitchers (Steve | | |

|  |  | NR MT | EX |
|---|---|---|---|
|  | Grilli, Craig Mitchell, Jose Sosa, George Throop) | .25 | .13 |
| 592 | Rookie Infielders (Dave McKay, *Willie Randolph*, *Jerry Royster*, Roy Staiger) | 8.00 | 4.00 |
| 593 | Rookie Pitchers (Larry Anderson, Ken Crosby, Mark Littell, *Butch Metzger*) | .25 | .13 |
| 594 | Rookie Catchers & Outfielders (Andy Merchant, Ed Ott, Royle Stillman, Jerry White) | .25 | .13 |
| 595 | Rookie Pitchers (Steve Barr, Art DeFilippis, Randy Lerch, Sid Monge) | .25 | .13 |
| 596 | Rookie Infielders (Lamar Johnson, *Johnny LeMaster*, Jerry Manuel, *Craig Reynolds*) | .35 | .20 |
| 597 | Rookie Pitchers *(Don Aase*, Jack Kucek, Frank LaCorte, Mike Pazik) | .50 | .25 |
| 598 | Rookie Outfielders (Hector Cruz, *Jamie Quirk*, Jerry Turner, Joe Wallis) | .25 | .13 |
| 599 | Rookie Pitchers (Rob Dressler, *Ron Guidry*, Bob McClure, Pat Zachry) | 8.00 | 4.00 |
| 600 | Tom Seaver | 12.00 | 6.00 |
| 601 | Ken Rudolph | .25 | .13 |
| 602 | Doug Konieczny | .25 | .13 |
| 603 | Jim Holt | .25 | .13 |
| 604 | Joe Lovitto | .25 | .13 |
| 605 | Al Downing | .25 | .13 |
| 606 | Brewers Team (Alex Grammas) | .80 | .40 |
| 607 | Rich Hinton | .25 | .13 |
| 608 | Vic Correll | .25 | .13 |
| 609 | Fred Norman | .25 | .13 |
| 610 | Greg Luzinski | .40 | .20 |
| 611 | Rich Folkers | .25 | .13 |
| 612 | Joe Lahoud | .25 | .13 |
| 613 | Tim Johnson | .25 | .13 |
| 614 | Fernando Arroyo | .25 | .13 |
| 615 | Mike Cubbage | .25 | .13 |
| 616 | Buck Martinez | .25 | .13 |
| 617 | Darold Knowles | .25 | .13 |
| 618 | Jack Brohamer | .25 | .13 |
| 619 | Bill Butler | .25 | .13 |
| 620 | Al Oliver | .70 | .35 |
| 621 | Tom Hall | .25 | .13 |
| 622 | Rick Auerbach | .25 | .13 |
| 623 | Bob Allietta | .25 | .13 |
| 624 | Tony Taylor | .25 | .13 |
| 625 | J.R. Richard | .25 | .13 |
| 626 | Bob Sheldon | .25 | .13 |
| 627 | Bill Plummer | .25 | .13 |
| 628 | John D'Acquisto | .25 | .13 |
| 629 | Sandy Alomar | .25 | .13 |
| 630 | Chris Speier | .25 | .13 |
| 631 | Braves Team (Dave Bristol) | .80 | .40 |
| 632 | Rogelio Moret | .25 | .13 |
| 633 | *John Stearns* | .30 | .15 |

|  |  | NR MT | EX |
|---|---|---|---|
| 634 | Larry Christenson | .25 | .13 |
| 635 | Jim Fregosi | .25 | .13 |
| 636 | Joe Decker | .25 | .13 |
| 637 | Bruce Bochte | .25 | .13 |
| 638 | Doyle Alexander | .30 | .15 |
| 639 | Fred Kendall | .25 | .13 |
| 640 | Bill Madlock | 1.00 | .50 |
| 641 | Tom Paciorek | .25 | .13 |
| 642 | Dennis Blair | .25 | .13 |
| 643 | Checklist 529-660 | 1.50 | .70 |
| 644 | Tom Bradley | .25 | .13 |
| 645 | Darrell Porter | .25 | .13 |
| 646 | John Lowenstein | .25 | .13 |
| 648 | Al Cowens | .25 | .13 |
| 649 | Dave Roberts | .25 | .13 |
| 650 | Thurman Munson | 7.00 | 3.50 |
| 651 | John Odom | .25 | .13 |
| 652 | Ed Armbrister | .25 | .13 |
| 653 | *Mike Norris* | .30 | .15 |
| 654 | Doug Griffin | .25 | .13 |
| 655 | Mike Vail | .25 | .13 |
| 656 | White Sox Team (Chuck Tanner) | .80 | .40 |
| 657 | *Roy Smalley* | .40 | .20 |
| 658 | Jerry Johnson | .25 | .13 |
| 659 | Ben Oglivie | .25 | .13 |
| 660 | Dave Lopes | .60 | .13 |

## 1977 Topps

The 1977 Topps Set is a 660-card effort featuring front designs dominated on a color photograph on which there is a facsimile autograph. Above the picture are the player's name, team and position. The backs of the 2-1/2" by 3-1/2" cards include personal and career statistics along with newspaper-style highlights and a cartoon. Specialty cards include statistical leaders, record performances, a new "Turn Back The Clock" feature which highlighted great past moments and a "Big League Brothers" feature.

|  | NR MT | EX |
|---|---|---|
| Complete Set: | 400.00 | 200.00 |

| | NR MT | EX |
|---|---|---|
| Common Player: | .20 | .10 |
| 1 Batting Leaders (George Brett, Bill Madlock) | 4.00 | 2.00 |
| 2 Home Run Leaders (Graig Nettles, Mike Schmidt) | 1.25 | .60 |
| 3 Runs Batted In Leaders (George Foster, Lee May) | .50 | .25 |
| 4 Stolen Base Leaders (Dave Lopes, Bill North) | .30 | .15 |
| 5 Victory Leaders (Randy Jones, Jim Palmer) | .80 | .40 |
| 6 Strikeout Leaders (Nolan Ryan, Tom Seaver) | 6.00 | 3.00 |
| 7 Earned Run Avg. Ldrs. (John Denny, Mark Fidrych) | .30 | .15 |
| 8 Leading Firemen (Bill Campbell, Rawly Eastwick) | .30 | .15 |
| 9 Doug Rader | .20 | .10 |
| 10 Reggie Jackson | 18.00 | 9.00 |
| 11 Rob Dressler | .20 | .10 |
| 12 Larry Haney | .20 | .10 |
| 13 Luis Gomez | .20 | .10 |
| 14 Tommy Smith | .20 | .10 |
| 15 Don Gullett | .20 | .10 |
| 16 Bob Jones | .20 | .10 |
| 17 Steve Stone | .25 | .13 |
| 18 Indians Team (Frank Robinson) | .80 | .40 |
| 19 John D'Acquisto | .20 | .10 |
| 20 Graig Nettles | .90 | .45 |
| 21 Ken Forsch | .20 | .10 |
| 22 Bill Freehan | .25 | .13 |
| 23 Dan Driessen | .25 | .13 |
| 24 Carl Morton | .20 | .10 |
| 25 Dwight Evans | 3.00 | 1.50 |
| 26 Ray Sadecki | .20 | .10 |
| 27 Bill Buckner | .35 | .20 |
| 28 Woodie Fryman | .20 | .10 |
| 29 Bucky Dent | .25 | .13 |
| 30 Greg Luzinski | .40 | .20 |
| 31 Jim Todd | .20 | .10 |
| 32 Checklist 1-132 | 1.25 | .60 |
| 33 Wayne Garland | .20 | .10 |
| 34 Angels Team (Norm Sherry) | .70 | .35 |
| 35 Rennie Stennett | .20 | .10 |
| 36 John Ellis | .20 | .10 |
| 37 Steve Hargan | .20 | .10 |
| 38 Craig Kusick | .20 | .10 |
| 39 Tom Griffin | .20 | .10 |
| 40 Bobby Murcer | .30 | .15 |
| 41 Jim Kern | .20 | .10 |
| 42 Jose Cruz | .30 | .15 |
| 43 Ray Bare | .20 | .10 |
| 44 Bud Harrelson | .20 | .10 |
| 45 Rawly Eastwick | .20 | .10 |
| 46 Buck Martinez | .20 | .10 |
| 47 Lynn McGlothen | .20 | .10 |
| 48 Tom Paciorek | .20 | .10 |
| 49 Grant Jackson | .20 | .10 |
| 50 Ron Cey | .35 | .20 |

| | NR MT | EX |
|---|---|---|
| 51 Brewers Team (Alex Grammas) | .70 | .35 |
| 52 Ellis Valentine | .20 | .10 |
| 53 Paul Mitchell | .20 | .10 |
| 54 Sandy Alomar | .20 | .10 |
| 55 Jeff Burroughs | .25 | .13 |
| 56 Rudy May | .20 | .10 |
| 57 Marc Hill | .20 | .10 |
| 58 Chet Lemon | .30 | .15 |
| 59 Larry Christenson | .20 | .10 |
| 60 Jim Rice | 4.50 | 2.25 |
| 61 Manny Sanguillen | .20 | .10 |
| 62 Eric Raich | .20 | .10 |
| 63 Tito Fuentes | .20 | .10 |
| 64 Larry Biittner | .20 | .10 |
| 65 Skip Lockwood | .20 | .10 |
| 66 Roy Smalley | .20 | .10 |
| 67 Joaquin Andujar | .60 | .30 |
| 68 Bruce Bochte | .20 | .10 |
| 69 Jim Crawford | .20 | .10 |
| 70 Johnny Bench | 10.00 | 5.00 |
| 71 Dock Ellis | .20 | .10 |
| 72 Mike Anderson | .20 | .10 |
| 73 Charlie Williams | .20 | .10 |
| 74 A's Team (Jack McKeon) | .70 | .35 |
| 75 Dennis Leonard | .20 | .10 |
| 76 Tim Foli | .20 | .10 |
| 77 Dyar Miller | .20 | .10 |
| 78 Bob Davis | .20 | .10 |
| 79 Don Money | .20 | .10 |
| 80 Andy Messersmith | .25 | .13 |
| 81 Juan Beniquez | .20 | .10 |
| 82 Jim Rooker | .20 | .10 |
| 83 Kevin Bell | .20 | .10 |
| 84 Ollie Brown | .20 | .10 |
| 85 Duane Kuiper | .20 | .10 |
| 86 Pat Zachry | .20 | .10 |
| 87 Glenn Borgmann | .20 | .10 |
| 88 Stan Wall | .20 | .10 |
| 89 Butch Hobson | .20 | .10 |
| 90 Cesar Cedeno | .30 | .15 |
| 91 John Verhoeven | .20 | .10 |
| 92 Dave Rosello | .20 | .10 |
| 93 Tom Poquette | .20 | .10 |
| 94 Craig Swan | .20 | .10 |
| 95 Keith Hernandez | 3.00 | 1.50 |
| 96 Lou Piniella | .40 | .20 |
| 97 Dave Heaverlo | .20 | .10 |
| 98 Milt May | .20 | .10 |
| 99 Tom Hausman | .20 | .10 |
| 100 Joe Morgan | 4.00 | 2.00 |
| 101 Dick Bosman | .20 | .10 |
| 102 Jose Morales | .20 | .10 |
| 103 Mike Bacsik | .20 | .10 |
| 104 Omar Moreno | .25 | .13 |
| 105 Steve Yeager | .20 | .10 |
| 106 Mike Flanagan | .35 | .20 |
| 107 Bill Melton | .20 | .10 |
| 108 Alan Foster | .20 | .10 |
| 109 Jorge Orta | .20 | .10 |
| 110 Steve Carlton | 8.00 | 4.00 |
| 111 Rico Petrocelli | .25 | .13 |
| 112 Bill Greif | .20 | .10 |
| 113 Blue Jays Mgr./Coaches (Roy Hartsfield, Don Leppert, Bob Miller, Jackie | | |

| | | NR MT | EX | | | | NR MT | EX |
|---|---|---|---|---|---|---|---|---|
| | Moore, Harry Warner | .25 | .13 | 179 | Paul Hartzell | | .20 | .10 |
| 114 | Bruce Dal Canton | .20 | .10 | 180 | Dave Lopes | | .25 | .13 |
| 115 | Rick Manning | .20 | .10 | 181 | Ken McMullen | | .20 | .10 |
| 116 | Joe Niekro | .30 | .15 | 182 | Dan Spillner | | .20 | .10 |
| 117 | Frank White | .25 | .13 | 183 | Cardinals Team (Vern | | | |
| 118 | Rick Jones | .20 | .10 | | Rapp) | | .70 | .35 |
| 119 | John Stearns | .20 | .10 | 184 | Bo McLaughlin | | .20 | .10 |
| 120 | Rod Carew | 8.00 | 4.00 | 185 | Sixto Lezcano | | .20 | .10 |
| 121 | Gary Nolan | .20 | .10 | 186 | Doug Flynn | | .20 | .10 |
| 122 | Ben Oglivie | .20 | .10 | 187 | Dick Pole | | .20 | .10 |
| 123 | Fred Stanley | .20 | .10 | 188 | Bob Tolan | | .20 | .10 |
| 124 | George Mitterwald | .20 | .10 | 189 | Rick Dempsey | | .20 | .10 |
| 125 | Bill Travers | .20 | .10 | 190 | Ray Burris | | .20 | .10 |
| 126 | Rod Gilbreath | .20 | .10 | 191 | Doug Griffin | | .20 | .10 |
| 127 | Ron Fairly | .25 | .13 | 192 | Clarence Gaston | | .20 | .10 |
| 128 | Tommy John | 1.25 | .60 | 193 | Larry Gura | | .20 | .10 |
| 129 | Mike Sadek | .20 | .10 | 194 | Gary Matthews | | .25 | .13 |
| 130 | Al Oliver | .60 | .30 | 195 | Ed Figueroa | | .20 | .10 |
| 131 | Orlando Ramirez | .20 | .10 | 196 | Len Randle | | .20 | .10 |
| 132 | Chip Lang | .20 | .10 | 197 | Ed Ott | | .20 | .10 |
| 133 | Ralph Garr | .20 | .10 | 198 | Wilbur Wood | | .20 | .10 |
| 134 | Padres Team (John | | | 199 | Pepe Frias | | .20 | .10 |
| | McNamara) | .70 | .35 | 200 | Frank Tanana | | .30 | .15 |
| 135 | Mark Belanger | .20 | .10 | 201 | Ed Kranepool | | .25 | .13 |
| 136 | *Jerry Mumphrey* | .20 | .10 | 202 | Tom Johnson | | .20 | .10 |
| 137 | Jeff Terpko | .20 | .10 | 203 | Ed Armbrister | | .20 | .10 |
| 138 | Bob Stinson | .20 | .10 | 204 | Jeff Newman | | .20 | .10 |
| 139 | Fred Norman | .20 | .10 | 205 | Pete Falcone | | .20 | .10 |
| 140 | Mike Schmidt | 25.00 | 12.50 | 206 | Boog Powell | | .50 | .25 |
| 141 | Mark Littell | .20 | .10 | 207 | Glenn Abbott | | .20 | .10 |
| 142 | Steve Dillard | .20 | .10 | 208 | Checklist 133-264 | 1.25 | .60 |
| 143 | Ed Herrmann | .20 | .10 | 209 | Rob Andrews | | .20 | .10 |
| 144 | *Bruce Sutter* | 3.00 | 1.50 | 210 | Fred Lynn | | 1.50 | .70 |
| 145 | Tom Veryzer | .20 | .10 | 211 | Giants Team (Joe | | | |
| 146 | Dusty Baker | .25 | .13 | | Altobelli) | | .70 | .35 |
| 147 | Jackie Brown | .20 | .10 | 212 | Jim Mason | | .20 | .10 |
| 148 | Fran Healy | .20 | .10 | 213 | Maximino Leon | | .20 | .10 |
| 149 | Mike Cubbage | .20 | .10 | 214 | Darrell Porter | | .20 | .10 |
| 150 | Tom Seaver | 10.00 | 5.00 | 215 | Butch Metzger | | .20 | .10 |
| 151 | Johnnie LeMaster | .20 | .10 | 216 | Doug DeCinces | | .25 | .13 |
| 152 | Gaylord Perry | 2.50 | 1.25 | 217 | Tom Underwood | | .20 | .10 |
| 153 | Ron Jackson | .20 | .10 | 218 | *John Wathan* | | .60 | .30 |
| 154 | Dave Giusti | .20 | .10 | 219 | Joe Coleman | | .20 | .10 |
| 155 | Joe Rudi | .25 | .13 | 220 | Chris Chambliss | | .30 | .15 |
| 156 | Pete Mackanin | .20 | .10 | 221 | Bob Bailey | | .20 | .10 |
| 157 | Ken Brett | .20 | .10 | 222 | Francisco Barrios | | .20 | .10 |
| 158 | Ted Kubiak | .20 | .10 | 223 | Earl Williams | | .20 | .10 |
| 159 | Bernie Carbo | .20 | .10 | 224 | Rusty Torres | | .20 | .10 |
| 160 | Will McEnaney | .20 | .10 | 225 | Bob Apodaca | | .20 | .10 |
| 161 | *Garry Templeton* | 1.50 | .70 | 226 | Leroy Stanton | | .20 | .10 |
| 162 | Mike Cuellar | .25 | .13 | 227 | *Joe Sambito* | | .25 | .13 |
| 163 | Dave Hilton | .20 | .10 | 228 | Twins Team (Gene | | | |
| 164 | Tug McGraw | .35 | .20 | | Mauch) | | .80 | .40 |
| 165 | Jim Wynn | .25 | .13 | 229 | Don Kessinger | | .20 | .10 |
| 166 | Bill Campbell | .20 | .10 | 230 | Vida Blue | | .40 | .20 |
| 167 | Rich Hebner | .20 | .10 | 231 | Record Breaker (George | | | |
| 168 | Charlie Spikes | .20 | .10 | | Brett) | | 6.00 | 3.00 |
| 169 | Darold Knowles | .20 | .10 | 232 | Record Breaker (Minnie | | | |
| 170 | Thurman Munson | 5.00 | 2.50 | | Minoso) | | .35 | .20 |
| 171 | Ken Sanders | .20 | .10 | 233 | Record Breaker (Jose | | | |
| 172 | John Milner | .20 | .10 | | Morales) | | .20 | .10 |
| 173 | Chuck Scrivener | .20 | .10 | 234 | Record Breaker (Nolan | | | |
| 174 | Nelson Briles | .20 | .10 | | Ryan) | | 10.00 | 5.00 |
| 175 | *Butch Wynegar* | .40 | .20 | 235 | Cecil Cooper | | .60 | .30 |
| 176 | Bob Robertson | .20 | .10 | 236 | Tom Buskey | | .20 | .10 |
| 177 | Bart Johnson | .20 | .10 | 237 | Gene Clines | | .20 | .10 |
| 178 | Bombo Rivera | .20 | .10 | 238 | Tippy Martinez | | .20 | .10 |

| | | NR MT | EX |
|---|---|---|---|
| 239 | Bill Plummer | .20 | .10 |
| 240 | Ron LeFlore | .25 | .13 |
| 241 | Dave Tomlin | .20 | .10 |
| 242 | Ken Henderson | .20 | .10 |
| 243 | Ron Reed | .20 | .10 |
| 244 | John Mayberry | .20 | .10 |
| 245 | Rick Rhoden | .30 | .15 |
| 246 | Mike Vail | .20 | .10 |
| 247 | Chris Knapp | .20 | .10 |
| 248 | Wilbur Howard | .20 | .10 |
| 249 | Pete Redfern | .20 | .10 |
| 250 | Bill Madlock | .40 | .20 |
| 251 | Tony Muser | .20 | .10 |
| 252 | Dale Murray | .20 | .10 |
| 253 | John Hale | .20 | .10 |
| 254 | Doyle Alexander | .30 | .15 |
| 255 | George Scott | .20 | .10 |
| 256 | Joe Hoerner | .20 | .10 |
| 257 | Mike Miley | .20 | .10 |
| 258 | Luis Tiant | .35 | .20 |
| 259 | Mets Team (Joe Frazier) | .80 | .40 |
| 260 | J.R. Richard | .25 | .13 |
| 261 | Phil Garner | .20 | .10 |
| 262 | Al Cowens | .20 | .10 |
| 263 | Mike Marshall | .25 | .13 |
| 264 | Tom Hutton | .20 | .10 |
| 265 | *Mark Fidrych* | .70 | .35 |
| 266 | Derrel Thomas | .20 | .10 |
| 267 | Ray Fosse | .20 | .10 |
| 268 | Rick Sawyer | .20 | .10 |
| 269 | Joe Lis | .20 | .10 |
| 270 | Dave Parker | 4.00 | 2.00 |
| 271 | Terry Forster | .20 | .10 |
| 272 | Lee Lacy | .20 | .10 |
| 273 | Eric Soderholm | .20 | .10 |
| 274 | Don Stanhouse | .20 | .10 |
| 275 | Mike Hargrove | .20 | .10 |
| 276 | A.L. Championship (Chambliss' Dramatic Homer Decides It) | .70 | .35 |
| 277 | N.L. Championship (Reds Sweep Phillies 3 In Row) | .70 | .35 |
| 278 | Danny Frisella | .20 | .10 |
| 279 | Joe Wallis | .20 | .10 |
| 280 | Jim Hunter | 2.00 | 1.00 |
| 281 | Roy Staiger | .20 | .10 |
| 282 | Sid Monge | .20 | .10 |
| 283 | Jerry DaVanon | .20 | .10 |
| 284 | Mike Norris | .20 | .10 |
| 285 | Brooks Robinson | 2.50 | 1.25 |
| 286 | Johnny Grubb | .20 | .10 |
| 287 | Reds Team (Sparky Anderson) | .80 | .40 |
| 288 | Bob Montgomery | .20 | .10 |
| 289 | Gene Garber | .20 | .10 |
| 290 | Amos Otis | .20 | .10 |
| 291 | *Jason Thompson* | .35 | .20 |
| 292 | Rogelio Moret | .20 | .10 |
| 293 | Jack Brohamer | .20 | .10 |
| 294 | George Medich | .20 | .10 |
| 295 | Gary Carter | 6.00 | 3.00 |
| 296 | Don Hood | .20 | .10 |
| 297 | Ken Reitz | .20 | .10 |
| 298 | Charlie Hough | .25 | .13 |
| 299 | Otto Velez | .20 | .10 |
| 300 | Jerry Koosman | .30 | .15 |
| 301 | Toby Harrah | .20 | .10 |
| 302 | Mike Garman | .20 | .10 |
| 303 | Gene Tenace | .20 | .10 |
| 304 | Jim Hughes | .20 | .10 |
| 305 | Mickey Rivers | .25 | .13 |
| 306 | Rick Waits | .20 | .10 |
| 307 | Gary Sutherland | .20 | .10 |
| 308 | Gene Pentz | .20 | .10 |
| 309 | Red Sox Team (Don Zimmer) | .80 | .40 |
| 310 | Larry Bowa | .30 | .15 |
| 311 | Vern Ruhle | .20 | .10 |
| 312 | Rob Belloir | .20 | .10 |
| 313 | Paul Blair | .20 | .10 |
| 314 | Steve Mingori | .20 | .10 |
| 315 | Dave Chalk | .20 | .10 |
| 316 | Steve Rogers | .20 | .10 |
| 317 | Kurt Bevacqua | .20 | .10 |
| 318 | Duffy Dyer | .20 | .10 |
| 319 | Rich Gossage | 1.00 | .50 |
| 320 | Ken Griffey | .30 | .15 |
| 321 | Dave Goltz | .20 | .10 |
| 322 | Bill Russell | .20 | .10 |
| 323 | Larry Lintz | .20 | .10 |
| 324 | John Curtis | .20 | .10 |
| 325 | Mike Ivie | .20 | .10 |
| 326 | Jesse Jefferson | .20 | .10 |
| 327 | Astros Team (Bill Virdon) | .70 | .35 |
| 328 | Tommy Boggs | .20 | .10 |
| 329 | Ron Hodges | .20 | .10 |
| 330 | George Hendrick | .20 | .10 |
| 331 | Jim Colborn | .20 | .10 |
| 332 | Elliott Maddox | .20 | .10 |
| 333 | Paul Reuschel | .20 | .10 |
| 334 | Bill Stein | .20 | .10 |
| 335 | Bill Robinson | .20 | .10 |
| 336 | Denny Doyle | .20 | .10 |
| 337 | Ron Schueler | .20 | .10 |
| 338 | Dave Duncan | .20 | .10 |
| 339 | Adrian Devine | .20 | .10 |
| 340 | Hal McRae | .30 | .15 |
| 341 | Joe Kerrigan | .20 | .10 |
| 342 | Jerry Remy | .20 | .10 |
| 343 | Ed Halicki | .20 | .10 |
| 344 | Brian Downing | .25 | .13 |
| 345 | Reggie Smith | .25 | .13 |
| 346 | Bill Singer | .20 | .10 |
| 347 | George Foster | 1.25 | .60 |
| 348 | Brent Strom | .20 | .10 |
| 349 | Jim Holt | .20 | .10 |
| 350 | Larry Dierker | .20 | .10 |
| 351 | Jim Sundberg | .20 | .10 |
| 352 | Mike Phillips | .20 | .10 |
| 353 | Stan Thomas | .20 | .10 |
| 354 | Pirates Team (Chuck Tanner) | .80 | .40 |
| 355 | Lou Brock | 3.00 | 1.50 |
| 356 | Checklist 265-396 | 1.25 | .60 |
| 357 | Tim McCarver | .40 | .20 |
| 358 | Tom House | .20 | .10 |
| 359 | Willie Randolph | 1.00 | .50 |
| 360 | Rick Monday | .25 | .13 |
| 361 | Eduardo Rodriguez | .20 | .10 |
| 362 | Tommy Davis | .30 | .15 |
| 363 | Dave Roberts | .20 | .10 |

| | NR MT | EX |
|---|---|---|
| 364 Vic Correll | .20 | .10 |
| 365 Mike Torrez | .20 | .10 |
| 366 Ted Sizemore | .20 | .10 |
| 367 Dave Hamlton | .20 | .10 |
| 368 Mike Jorgensen | .20 | .10 |
| 369 Terry Humphrey | .20 | .10 |
| 370 John Montefusco | .20 | .10 |
| 371 Royals Team (Whitey Herzog) | .80 | .40 |
| 372 Rich Folkers | .20 | .10 |
| 373 Bert Campaneris | .30 | .15 |
| 374 Kent Tekulve | .30 | .15 |
| 375 Larry Hisle | .20 | .10 |
| 376 Nino Espinosa | .20 | .10 |
| 377 Dave McKay | .20 | .10 |
| 378 Jim Umbarger | .20 | .10 |
| 379 Larry Cox | .20 | .10 |
| 380 Lee May | .25 | .13 |
| 381 Bob Forsch | .20 | .10 |
| 382 Charlie Moore | .20 | .10 |
| 383 Stan Bahnsen | .20 | .10 |
| 384 Darrel Chaney | .20 | .10 |
| 385 Dave LaRoche | .20 | .10 |
| 386 Manny Mota | .25 | .13 |
| 387 Yankees Team (Billy Martin) | 1.25 | .60 |
| 388 Terry Harmon | .20 | .10 |
| 389 Ken Kravec | .20 | .10 |
| 390 Dave Winfield | 15.00 | 7.50 |
| 391 Dan Warthen | .20 | .10 |
| 392 Phil Roof | .20 | .10 |
| 393 John Lowenstein | .20 | .10 |
| 394 Bill Laxton | .20 | .10 |
| 395 Manny Trillo | .20 | .10 |
| 396 Tom Murphy | .20 | .10 |
| 397 *Larry Herndon* | .40 | .20 |
| 398 Tom Burgmeier | .20 | .10 |
| 399 Bruce Boisclair | .20 | .10 |
| 400 Steve Garvey | 5.00 | 2.50 |
| 401 Mickey Scott | .20 | .10 |
| 402 Tommy Helms | .20 | .10 |
| 403 Tom Grieve | .20 | .10 |
| 404 Eric Rasmussen | .20 | .10 |
| 405 Claudell Washington | .25 | .13 |
| 406 Tim Johnson | .20 | .10 |
| 407 Dave Freisleben | .20 | .10 |
| 408 Cesar Tovar | .20 | .10 |
| 409 Pete Broberg | .20 | .10 |
| 410 Willie Montanez | .20 | .10 |
| 411 World Series Games 1 & 2 | .70 | .35 |
| 412 World Series Games 3 & 4 | .70 | .35 |
| 413 World Series Summary | .70 | .35 |
| 414 Tommy Harper | .20 | .10 |
| 415 Jay Johnstone | .20 | .10 |
| 416 Chuck Hartenstein | .20 | .10 |
| 417 Wayne Garrett | .20 | .10 |
| 418 White Sox Team (Bob Lemon) | .80 | .40 |
| 419 Steve Swisher | .20 | .10 |
| 420 Rusty Staub | .35 | .20 |
| 421 Doug Rau | .20 | .10 |
| 422 Freddie Patek | .20 | .10 |
| 423 Gary Lavelle | .20 | .10 |
| 424 Steve Brye | .20 | .10 |

| | NR MT | EX |
|---|---|---|
| 425 Joe Torre | .40 | .20 |
| 426 Dick Drago | .20 | .10 |
| 427 Dave Rader | .20 | .10 |
| 428 Rangers Team (Frank Lucchesi) | .70 | .35 |
| 429 Ken Boswell | .20 | .10 |
| 430 Fergie Jenkins | 1.75 | .90 |
| 431 Dave Collins | .25 | .13 |
| 432 Buzz Capra | .20 | .10 |
| 433 Turn Back The Clock (Nate Colbert) | .20 | .10 |
| 434 Turn Back The Clock (Carl Yastrzemski) | 2.00 | 1.00 |
| 435 Turn Back The Clock (Maury Wills) | .35 | .20 |
| 436 Turn Back The Clock (Bob Keegan) | .20 | .10 |
| 437 Turn Back The Clock (Ralph Kiner) | .50 | .25 |
| 438 Marty Perez | .20 | .10 |
| 439 Gorman Thomas | .30 | .15 |
| 440 Jon Matlack | .20 | .10 |
| 441 Larvell Blanks | .20 | .10 |
| 442 Braves Team (Dave Bristol) | .70 | .35 |
| 443 Lamar Johnson | .20 | .10 |
| 444 Wayne Twitchell | .20 | .10 |
| 445 Ken Singleton | .25 | .13 |
| 446 Bill Bonham | .20 | .10 |
| 447 Jerry Turner | .20 | .10 |
| 448 Ellie Rodriguez | .20 | .10 |
| 449 Al Fitzmorris | .20 | .10 |
| 450 Pete Rose | 9.00 | 4.50 |
| 451 Checklist 397-528 | 1.25 | .60 |
| 452 Mike Caldwell | .20 | .10 |
| 453 Pedro Garcia | .20 | .10 |
| 454 Andy Etchebarren | .20 | .10 |
| 455 Rick Wise | .20 | .10 |
| 456 Leon Roberts | .20 | .10 |
| 457 Steve Luebber | .20 | .10 |
| 458 Leo Foster | .20 | .10 |
| 459 Steve Foucault | .20 | .10 |
| 460 Willie Stargell | 3.00 | 1.50 |
| 461 Dick Tidrow | .20 | .10 |
| 462 Don Baylor | .35 | .20 |
| 463 Jamie Quirk | .20 | .10 |
| 464 Randy Moffitt | .20 | .10 |
| 465 Rico Carty | .25 | .13 |
| 466 Fred Holdsworth | .20 | .10 |
| 467 Phillies Team (Danny Ozark) | .70 | .35 |
| 468 Ramon Hernandez | .20 | .10 |
| 469 Pat Kelly | .20 | .10 |
| 470 Ted Simmons | .60 | .30 |
| 471 Del Unser | .20 | .10 |
| 472 Rookie Pitchers (Don Aase, Bob McClure, Gil Patterson, Dave Wehrmeister) | .25 | .13 |
| 473 Rookie Outfielders (*Andre Dawson*, Gene Richards, John Scott, *Denny Walling*) | 75.00 | 38.00 |
| 474 Rookie Shortstops (Bob Bailor, Kiko Garcia, Craig Reynolds, Alex Taveras) | .20 | .10 |
| 475 Rookie Pitchers (Chris | | |

| | NR MT | EX |
|---|---|---|
| Batton, Rick Camp, Scott McGregor, Manny Sarmiento) | .30 | .15 |
| 476 Rookie Catchers (Gary Alexander, *Rick Cerone*, *Dale Murphy*, Kevin Pasley) | 40.00 | 20.00 |
| 477 Rookie Infielders (Doug Ault, *Rich Dauer*, Orlando Gonzalez, Phil Mankowski) | .25 | .13 |
| 478 Rookie Pitchers (Jim Gideon, Leon Hooten, Dave Johnson, Mark Lemongello) | .20 | .10 |
| 479 Rookie Outfielders (Brian Asselstine, *Wayne Gross*, Sam Mejias, Alvis Woods) | .25 | .13 |
| 480 Carl Yastrzemski | 7.00 | 3.50 |
| 481 Roger Metzger | .20 | .10 |
| 482 Tony Solaita | .20 | .10 |
| 483 Richie Zisk | .20 | .10 |
| 484 Burt Hooton | .20 | .10 |
| 485 Roy White | .30 | .15 |
| 486 Ed Bane | .20 | .10 |
| 487 Rookie Pitchers (Larry Anderson, Ed Glynn, Joe Henderson, Greg Terlecky) | .20 | .10 |
| 488 Rookie Outfielders (*Jack Clark*, Ruppert Jones, Lee Mazzilli, Dan Thomas) | 10.00 | 5.00 |
| 489 Rookie Pitchers (Len Barker, Randy Lerch, *Greg Minton*, Mike Overy) | .40 | .20 |
| 490 Rookie Shortstops (*Billy Almon*, Mickey Klutts, Tommy McMillan, Mark Wagner) | .25 | .13 |
| 491 Rookie Pitchers (Mike Dupree, *Denny Martinez*, Craig Mitchell, Bob Sykes) | 5.00 | 2.50 |
| 492 Rookie Outfielders (*Tony Armas*, Steve Kemp, Carlos Lopez, Gary Woods) | 1.00 | .50 |
| 493 Rookie Pitchers (*Mike Krukow*, Jim Otten, Gary Wheelock, Mike Willis) | .50 | .25 |
| 494 Rookie Infielders (Juan Bernhardt, Mike Champion, *Jim Gantner*, Bump Wills) | .50 | .25 |
| 495 Al Hrabosky | .20 | .10 |
| 496 Gary Thomasson | .20 | .10 |
| 497 Clay Carroll | .20 | .10 |
| 498 Sal Bando | .25 | .13 |
| 499 Pablo Torrealba | .20 | .10 |
| 500 Dave Kingman | .60 | .30 |
| 501 Jim Bibby | .20 | .10 |
| 502 Randy Hundley | .20 | .10 |
| 503 Bill Lee | .20 | .10 |
| 504 Dodgers Team (Tom Lasorda) | 1.00 | .50 |
| 505 Oscar Gamble | .20 | .10 |

| | NR MT | EX |
|---|---|---|
| 506 Steve Grilli | .20 | .10 |
| 507 Mike Hegan | .20 | .10 |
| 508 Dave Pagan | .20 | .10 |
| 509 Cookie Rojas | .20 | .10 |
| 510 John Candelaria | .80 | .40 |
| 511 Bill Fahey | .20 | .10 |
| 512 Jack Billingham | .20 | .10 |
| 513 Jerry Terrell | .20 | .10 |
| 514 Cliff Johnson | .20 | .10 |
| 515 Chris Speier | .20 | .10 |
| 516 Bake McBride | .20 | .10 |
| 517 *Pete Vuckovich* | .50 | .25 |
| 518 Cubs Team (Herman Franks) | .70 | .35 |
| 519 Don Kirkwood | .20 | .10 |
| 520 Garry Maddox | .20 | .10 |
| 521 Bob Grich | .25 | .13 |
| 522 Enzo Hernandez | .20 | .10 |
| 523 Rollie Fingers | 2.50 | 1.25 |
| 524 Rowland Office | .20 | .10 |
| 525 Dennis Eckersley | 15.00 | 7.50 |
| 526 Larry Parrish | .35 | .20 |
| 527 Dan Meyer | .20 | .10 |
| 528 Bill Castro | .20 | .10 |
| 529 Jim Essian | .20 | .10 |
| 530 Rick Reuschel | .30 | .15 |
| 531 Lyman Bostock | .25 | .13 |
| 532 Jim Willoughby | .20 | .10 |
| 533 Mickey Stanley | .20 | .10 |
| 534 Paul Splittorff | .20 | .10 |
| 535 Cesar Geronimo | .20 | .10 |
| 536 Vic Albury | .20 | .10 |
| 537 Dave Roberts | .20 | .10 |
| 538 Frank Taveras | .20 | .10 |
| 539 Mike Wallace | .20 | .10 |
| 540 Bob Watson | .20 | .10 |
| 541 John Denny | .20 | .10 |
| 542 Frank Duffy | .20 | .10 |
| 543 Ron Blomberg | .20 | .10 |
| 544 Gary Ross | .20 | .10 |
| 545 Bob Boone | .25 | .13 |
| 546 Orioles Team (Earl Weaver) | .80 | .40 |
| 547 Willie McCovey | 2.75 | 1.50 |
| 548 *Joel Youngblood* | .30 | .15 |
| 549 Jerry Royster | .20 | .10 |
| 550 Randy Jones | .20 | .10 |
| 551 Bill North | .20 | .10 |
| 552 Pepe Mangual | .20 | .10 |
| 553 Jack Heidemann | .20 | .10 |
| 554 Bruce Kimm | .20 | .10 |
| 555 Dan Ford | .20 | .10 |
| 556 Doug Bird | .20 | .10 |
| 557 Jerry White | .20 | .10 |
| 558 Elias Sosa | .20 | .10 |
| 559 Alan Bannister | .20 | .10 |
| 560 Dave Concepcion | .35 | .20 |
| 561 Pete LaCock | .20 | .10 |
| 562 Checklist 529-660 | 1.25 | .60 |
| 563 Bruce Kison | .20 | .10 |
| 564 Alan Ashby | .20 | .10 |
| 565 Mickey Lolich | .50 | .25 |
| 566 Rick Miller | .20 | .10 |
| 567 Enos Cabell | .20 | .10 |
| 568 Carlos May | .20 | .10 |
| 569 Jim Lonborg | .20 | .10 |
| 570 Bobby Bonds | .35 | .20 |

| | NR MT | EX |
|---|---|---|
| 571 Darrell Evans | .40 | .20 |
| 572 Ross Grimsley | .20 | .10 |
| 573 Joe Ferguson | .20 | .10 |
| 574 Aurelio Rodriguez | .20 | .10 |
| 575 Dick Ruthven | .20 | .10 |
| 576 Fred Kendall | .20 | .10 |
| 577 Jerry Augustine | .20 | .10 |
| 578 Bob Randall | .20 | .10 |
| 579 Don Carrithers | .20 | .10 |
| 580 George Brett | 35.00 | 17.50 |
| 581 Pedro Borbon | .20 | .10 |
| 582 Ed Kirkpatrick | .20 | .10 |
| 583 Paul Lindblad | .20 | .10 |
| 584 Ed Goodson | .20 | .10 |
| 585 Rick Burleson | .20 | .10 |
| 586 Steve Renko | .20 | .10 |
| 587 Rick Baldwin | .20 | .10 |
| 588 Dave Moates | .20 | .10 |
| 589 Mike Cosgrove | .20 | .10 |
| 590 Buddy Bell | .30 | .15 |
| 591 Chris Arnold | .20 | .10 |
| 592 Dan Briggs | .20 | .10 |
| 593 Dennis Blair | .20 | .10 |
| 594 Biff Pocoroba | .20 | .10 |
| 595 John Hiller | .20 | .10 |
| 596 *Jerry Martin* | .25 | .13 |
| 597 Mariners Mgr./Coaches (Don Bryant, Jim Busby, Darrell Johnson, Vada Pinson, Wes Stock) | .25 | .13 |
| 598 Sparky Lyle | .35 | .20 |
| 599 Mike Tyson | .20 | .10 |
| 600 Jim Palmer | 5.00 | 2.50 |
| 601 Mike Lum | .20 | .10 |
| 602 Andy Hassler | .20 | .10 |
| 603 Willie Davis | .25 | .13 |
| 604 Jim Slaton | .20 | .10 |
| 605 Felix Millan | .20 | .10 |
| 606 Steve Braun | .20 | .10 |
| 607 Larry Demery | .20 | .10 |
| 608 Roy Howell | .20 | .10 |
| 609 Jim Barr | .20 | .10 |
| 610 Jose Cardenal | .20 | .10 |
| 611 Dave Lemanczyk | .20 | .10 |
| 612 Barry Foote | .20 | .10 |
| 613 Reggie Cleveland | .20 | .10 |
| 614 Greg Gross | .20 | .10 |
| 615 Phil Niekro | 1.50 | .70 |
| 616 Tommy Sandt | .20 | .10 |
| 617 Bobby Darwin | .20 | .10 |
| 618 Pat Dobson | .20 | .10 |
| 619 Johnny Oates | .20 | .10 |
| 620 Don Sutton | 1.50 | .70 |
| 621 Tigers Team (Ralph Houk) | .80 | .40 |
| 622 Jim Wohlford | .20 | .10 |
| 623 Jack Kucek | .20 | .10 |
| 624 Hector Cruz | .20 | .10 |
| 625 Ken Holtzman | .25 | .13 |
| 626 Al Bumbry | .20 | .10 |
| 627 Bob Myrick | .20 | .10 |
| 628 Mario Guerrero | .20 | .10 |
| 629 Bobby Valentine | .25 | .13 |
| 630 Bert Blyleven | 1.25 | .60 |
| 631 Big League Brothers (George Brett, Ken Brett) | 3.00 | 1.50 |

| | NR MT | EX |
|---|---|---|
| 632 Big League Brothers (Bob Forsch, Ken Forsch) | .30 | .15 |
| 633 Big League Brothers (Carlos May, Lee May) | .30 | .15 |
| 634 Big League Brothers (Paul Reuschel, Rick Reuschel) (names switched) | .30 | .15 |
| 635 Robin Yount | 35.00 | 17.50 |
| 636 Santo Alcala | .20 | .10 |
| 637 Alex Johnson | .20 | .10 |
| 638 Jim Kaat | .80 | .40 |
| 639 Jerry Morales | .20 | .10 |
| 640 Carlton Fisk | 6.00 | 3.00 |
| 641 Dan Larson | .20 | .10 |
| 642 Willie Crawford | .20 | .10 |
| 643 Mike Pazik | .20 | .10 |
| 644 Matt Alexander | .20 | .10 |
| 645 Jerry Reuss | .25 | .13 |
| 646 Andres Mora | .20 | .10 |
| 647 Expos Team (Dick Williams) | .80 | .40 |
| 648 Jim Spencer | .20 | .10 |
| 649 Dave Cash | .20 | .10 |
| 650 Nolan Ryan | 35.00 | 17.50 |
| 651 Von Joshua | .20 | .10 |
| 652 Tom Walker | .20 | .10 |
| 653 Diego Segui | .20 | .10 |
| 654 Ron Pruitt | .20 | .10 |
| 655 Tony Perez | 2.00 | 1.00 |
| 656 Ron Guidry | 2.75 | 1.50 |
| 657 Mick Kelleher | .20 | .10 |
| 658 Marty Pattin | .20 | .10 |
| 659 Merv Rettenmund | .20 | .10 |
| 660 Willie Horton | .40 | .13 |

## 1978 Topps

At 726 cards, this was the largest issue from Topps since 1972. In design, the color player photo is slightly larger than usual, with the player's name and team at the bottom. In the upper right-hand corner of the 2-1/2" by 3-1/2" cards there is a small white baseball with the player's position. Most of the starting All-Stars from the previous year had a red, white and blue shield instead of the baseball. Backs feature statistics and a baseball situation which made a card game of baseball possible. Specialty cards include baseball records, statistical leaders and the World Series and playoffs. As one row of cards per sheet had to be double-printed to accommodate the 726-card set size, some cards are more common, yet that seems to have no serious impact on their prices.

|  | NR MT | EX |
|---|---|---|
| Complete Set: | 350.00 | 175.00 |
| Common Player: | .12 | .06 |

| | | NR MT | EX |
|---|---|---|---|
| 1 | Record Breaker (Lou Brock) | 3.00 | 1.50 |
| 2 | Record Breaker (Sparky Lyle) | .25 | .13 |
| 3 | Record Breaker (Willie McCovey) | .70 | .35 |
| 4 | Record Breaker (Brooks Robinson) | .90 | .45 |
| 5 | Record Breaker (Pete Rose) | 2.00 | 1.00 |
| 6 | Record Breaker (Nolan Ryan) | 7.00 | 3.50 |
| 7 | Record Breaker (Reggie Jackson) | 3.00 | 1.50 |
| 8 | Mike Sadek | .12 | .06 |
| 9 | Doug DeCinces | .25 | .13 |
| 10 | Phil Niekro | 1.25 | .60 |
| 11 | Rick Manning | .12 | .06 |
| 12 | Don Aase | .20 | .10 |
| 13 | Art Howe | .12 | .06 |
| 14 | Lerrin LaGrow | .12 | .06 |
| 15 | Tony Perez | .25 | .13 |
| 16 | Roy White | .25 | .13 |
| 17 | Mike Krukow | .25 | .13 |
| 18 | Bob Grich | .25 | .13 |
| 19 | Darrell Porter | .20 | .10 |
| 20 | Pete Rose | 4.00 | 2.00 |
| 21 | Steve Kemp | .25 | .13 |
| 22 | Charlie Hough | .20 | .10 |
| 23 | Bump Wills | .12 | .06 |
| 24 | Don Money | .12 | .06 |
| 25 | Jon Matlack | .20 | .10 |
| 26 | Rich Hebner | .12 | .06 |
| 27 | Geoff Zahn | .12 | .06 |
| 28 | Ed Ott | .12 | .06 |
| 29 | Bob Lacey | .12 | .06 |
| 30 | George Hendrick | .20 | .10 |
| 31 | Glenn Abbott | .12 | .06 |
| 32 | Garry Templeton | .30 | .15 |
| 33 | Dave Lemanczyk | .12 | .06 |
| 34 | Willie McCovey | 3.00 | 1.50 |
| 35 | Sparky Lyle | .30 | .15 |
| 36 | *Eddie Murray* | 75.00 | 38.00 |
| 37 | Rick Waits | .12 | .06 |
| 38 | Willie Montanez | .12 | .06 |
| 39 | *Floyd Bannister* | .70 | .35 |
| 40 | Carl Yastrzemski | 5.00 | 2.50 |
| 41 | Burt Hooton | .20 | .10 |
| 42 | Jorge Orta | .12 | .06 |
| 43 | Bill Atkinson | .12 | .06 |
| 44 | Toby Harrah | .20 | .10 |
| 45 | Mark Fidrych | .25 | .13 |
| 46 | Al Cowens | .12 | .06 |
| 47 | Jack Billingham | .12 | .06 |
| 48 | Don Baylor | .35 | .20 |
| 49 | Ed Kranepool | .20 | .10 |
| 50 | Rick Reuschel | .40 | .20 |
| 51 | Charlie Moore | .12 | .06 |
| 52 | Jim Lonborg | .20 | .10 |
| 53 | Phil Garner | .12 | .06 |
| 54 | Tom Johnson | .12 | .06 |
| 55 | Mitchell Page | .12 | .06 |
| 56 | Randy Jones | .20 | .10 |
| 57 | Dan Meyer | .12 | .06 |
| 58 | Bob Forsch | .20 | .10 |
| 59 | Otto Velez | .12 | .06 |
| 60 | Thurman Munson | 5.00 | 2.50 |
| 61 | Larvell Blanks | .12 | .06 |
| 62 | Jim Barr | .12 | .06 |
| 63 | Don Zimmer | .20 | .10 |
| 64 | Gene Pentz | .12 | .06 |
| 65 | Ken Singleton | .25 | .13 |
| 66 | White Sox Team | .50 | .25 |
| 67 | Claudell Washington | .25 | .13 |
| 68 | Steve Foucault | .12 | .06 |
| 69 | Mike Vail | .12 | .06 |
| 70 | Rich Gossage | 1.00 | .50 |
| 71 | Terry Humphrey | .12 | .06 |
| 72 | Andre Dawson | 20.00 | 10.00 |
| 73 | Andy Hassler | .12 | .06 |
| 74 | Checklist 1-121 | .90 | .45 |
| 75 | Dick Ruthven | .12 | .06 |
| 76 | Steve Ontiveros | .12 | .06 |
| 77 | Ed Kirkpatrick | .12 | .06 |
| 78 | Pablo Torrealba | .12 | .06 |
| 79 | Darrell Johnson | .12 | .06 |
| 80 | Ken Griffey | .25 | .13 |
| 81 | Pete Redfern | .12 | .06 |
| 82 | Giants Team | .50 | .25 |
| 83 | Bob Montgomery | .12 | .06 |
| 84 | Kent Tekulve | .25 | .13 |
| 85 | Ron Fairly | .20 | .10 |
| 86 | Dave Tomlin | .12 | .06 |
| 87 | John Lowenstein | .12 | .06 |
| 88 | Mike Phillips | .12 | .06 |
| 89 | Ken Clay | .20 | .10 |
| 90 | Larry Bowa | .30 | .15 |
| 91 | Oscar Zamora | .12 | .06 |
| 92 | Adrian Devine | .12 | .06 |
| 93 | Bobby Cox | .12 | .06 |
| 94 | Chuck Scrivener | .12 | .06 |
| 95 | Jamie Quirk | .12 | .06 |
| 96 | Orioles Team | .50 | .25 |
| 97 | Stan Bahnsen | .12 | .06 |
| 98 | Jim Essian | .12 | .06 |
| 99 | *Willie Hernandez* | .70 | .35 |
| 100 | George Brett | 20.00 | 10.00 |
| 101 | Sid Monge | .12 | .06 |
| 102 | Matt Alexander | .12 | .06 |
| 103 | Tom Murphy | .12 | .06 |
| 104 | Lee Lacy | .12 | .06 |
| 105 | Reggie Cleveland | .12 | .06 |
| 106 | Bill Plummer | .12 | .06 |
| 107 | Ed Halicki | .12 | .06 |

| | | NR MT | EX | | | NR MT | EX |
|---|---|---|---|---|---|---|---|
| 108 | Von Joshua | .12 | .06 | 175 | Jerry Morales | .12 | .06 |
| 109 | Joe Torre | .30 | .15 | 176 | Milt May | .12 | .06 |
| 110 | Richie Zisk | .20 | .10 | 177 | Gene Garber | .12 | .06 |
| 111 | Mike Tyson | .12 | .06 | 178 | Dave Chalk | .12 | .06 |
| 112 | Astros Team | .50 | .25 | 179 | Dick Tidrow | .20 | .10 |
| 113 | Don Carrithers | .12 | .06 | 180 | Dave Concepcion | .35 | .20 |
| 114 | Paul Blair | .20 | .10 | 181 | Ken Forsch | .20 | .10 |
| 115 | Gary Nolan | .12 | .06 | 182 | Jim Spencer | .12 | .06 |
| 116 | Tucker Ashford | .12 | .06 | 183 | Doug Bird | .12 | .06 |
| 117 | John Montague | .12 | .06 | 184 | Checklist 122-242 | .90 | .45 |
| 118 | Terry Harmon | .12 | .06 | 185 | Ellis Valentine | .20 | .10 |
| 119 | Denny Martinez | .25 | .13 | 186 | *Bob Stanley* | .25 | .13 |
| 120 | Gary Carter | 4.00 | 2.00 | 187 | Jerry Royster | .12 | .06 |
| 121 | Alvis Woods | .12 | .06 | 188 | Al Bumbry | .20 | .10 |
| 122 | Dennis Eckersley | 8.00 | 4.00 | 189 | Tom Lasorda | .30 | .15 |
| 123 | Manny Trillo | .20 | .10 | 190 | John Candelaria | .25 | .13 |
| 124 | *Dave Rozema* | .25 | .13 | 191 | Rodney Scott | .12 | .06 |
| 125 | George Scott | .20 | .10 | 192 | Padres Team | .50 | .25 |
| 126 | Paul Moskau | .12 | .06 | 193 | Rich Chiles | .12 | .06 |
| 127 | Chet Lemon | .20 | .10 | 194 | Derrel Thomas | .12 | .06 |
| 128 | Bill Russell | .20 | .10 | 195 | Larry Dierker | .20 | .10 |
| 129 | Jim Colborn | .12 | .06 | 196 | Bob Bailor | .12 | .06 |
| 130 | Jeff Burroughs | .20 | .10 | 197 | Nino Espinosa | .12 | .06 |
| 131 | Bert Blyleven | .90 | .45 | 198 | Ron Pruitt | .12 | .06 |
| 132 | Enos Cabell | .20 | .10 | 199 | Craig Reynolds | .12 | .06 |
| 133 | Jerry Augustine | .12 | .06 | 200 | Reggie Jackson | 12.00 | 6.00 |
| 134 | *Steve Henderson* | .25 | .13 | 201 | Batting Leaders (Rod Carew, Dave Parker) | 1.00 | .50 |
| 135 | Ron Guidry | .70 | .35 | 202 | Home Run Leaders (George Foster, Jim Rice) | .25 | .13 |
| 136 | Ted Sizemore | .12 | .06 | | | | |
| 137 | Craig Kusick | .12 | .06 | 203 | Runs Batted In Ldrs. (George Foster, Larry Hisle) | .25 | .13 |
| 138 | Larry Demery | .12 | .06 | | | | |
| 139 | Wayne Gross | .12 | .06 | | | | |
| 140 | Rollie Fingers | 3.00 | 1.50 | 204 | Stolen Base Leaders (Freddie Patek, Frank Taveras) | .12 | .06 |
| 141 | Ruppert Jones | .20 | .10 | | | | |
| 142 | John Montefusco | .20 | .10 | 205 | Victory Leaders (Steve Carlton, Dave Goltz, Dennis Leonard, Jim Palmer) | .60 | .30 |
| 143 | Keith Hernandez | 2.00 | 1.00 | | | | |
| 144 | Jesse Jefferson | .12 | .06 | | | | |
| 145 | Rick Monday | .20 | .10 | 206 | Strikeout Leaders (Phil Niekro, Nolan Ryan) | .35 | .20 |
| 146 | Doyle Alexander | .30 | .15 | | | | |
| 147 | Lee Mazzilli | .25 | .13 | 207 | Earned Run Avg. Ldrs. (John Candelaria, Frank Tanana) | .12 | .06 |
| 148 | Andre Thornton | .25 | .13 | | | | |
| 149 | Dale Murray | .12 | .06 | | | | |
| 150 | Bobby Bonds | .35 | .20 | 208 | Leading Firemen (Bill Campbell, Rollie Fingers) | .35 | .20 |
| 151 | Milt Wilcox | .12 | .06 | | | | |
| 152 | *Ivan DeJesus* | .20 | .10 | | | | |
| 153 | Steve Stone | .25 | .13 | 209 | Dock Ellis | .12 | .06 |
| 154 | Cecil Cooper | .20 | .10 | 210 | Jose Cardenal | .12 | .06 |
| 155 | Butch Hobson | .12 | .06 | 211 | Earl Weaver | .20 | .10 |
| 156 | Andy Messersmith | .20 | .10 | 212 | Mike Caldwell | .12 | .06 |
| 157 | Pete LaCock | .12 | .06 | 213 | Alan Bannister | .12 | .06 |
| 158 | Joaquin Andujar | .25 | .13 | 214 | Angels Team | .50 | .25 |
| 159 | Lou Piniella | .35 | .20 | 215 | Darrell Evans | .35 | .20 |
| 160 | Jim Palmer | 4.00 | 2.00 | 216 | Mike Paxton | .12 | .06 |
| 161 | Bob Boone | .25 | .13 | 217 | Rod Gilbreath | .12 | .06 |
| 162 | Paul Thormodsgard | .12 | .06 | 218 | Marty Pattin | .12 | .06 |
| 163 | Bill North | .12 | .06 | 219 | Mike Cubbage | .12 | .06 |
| 164 | Bob Owchinko | .12 | .06 | 220 | Pedro Borbon | .12 | .06 |
| 165 | Rennie Stennett | .12 | .06 | 221 | Chris Speier | .20 | .10 |
| 166 | Carlos Lopez | .12 | .06 | 222 | Jerry Martin | .12 | .06 |
| 167 | Tim Foli | .12 | .06 | 223 | Bruce Kison | .12 | .06 |
| 168 | Reggie Smith | .25 | .13 | 224 | Jerry Tabb | .12 | .06 |
| 169 | Jerry Johnson | .12 | .06 | 225 | Don Gullett | .12 | .06 |
| 170 | Lou Brock | 3.00 | 1.50 | 226 | Joe Ferguson | .12 | .06 |
| 171 | Pat Zachry | .12 | .06 | 227 | Al Fitzmorris | .12 | .06 |
| 172 | Mike Hargrove | .20 | .10 | | | | |
| 173 | Robin Yount | 20.00 | 10.00 | | | | |
| 174 | Wayne Garland | .12 | .06 | | | | |

| | | NR MT | EX | | | | NR MT | EX |
|---|---|---|---|---|---|---|---|---|
| 228 | Manny Mota | .12 | .06 | | 295 | Bill Lee | .20 | .10 |
| 229 | Leo Foster | .12 | .06 | | 296 | Biff Pocoroba | .12 | .06 |
| 230 | Al Hrabosky | .20 | .10 | | 297 | Warren Brusstar | .12 | .06 |
| 231 | Wayne Nordhagen | .12 | .06 | | 298 | Tony Armas | .25 | .13 |
| 232 | Mickey Stanley | .20 | .10 | | 299 | Whitey Herzog | .30 | .15 |
| 233 | Dick Pole | .12 | .06 | | 300 | Joe Morgan | 3.00 | 1.50 |
| 234 | Herman Franks | .12 | .06 | | 301 | Buddy Schultz | .12 | .06 |
| 235 | Tim McCarver | .35 | .20 | | 302 | Cubs Team | .50 | .25 |
| 236 | Terry Whitfield | .12 | .06 | | 303 | Sam Hinds | .12 | .06 |
| 237 | Rich Dauer | .12 | .06 | | 304 | John Milner | .12 | .06 |
| 238 | Juan Beniquez | .20 | .10 | | 305 | Rico Carty | .20 | .10 |
| 239 | Dyar Miller | .12 | .06 | | 306 | Joe Niekro | .25 | .13 |
| 240 | Gene Tenace | .20 | .10 | | 307 | Glenn Borgmann | .12 | .06 |
| 241 | Pete Vuckovich | .20 | .10 | | 308 | Jim Rooker | .12 | .06 |
| 242 | Barry Bonnell | .12 | .06 | | 309 | Cliff Johnson | .20 | .10 |
| 243 | Bob McClure | .12 | .06 | | 310 | Don Sutton | 2.00 | 1.00 |
| 244 | Expos Team | .20 | .10 | | 311 | Jose Baez | .12 | .06 |
| 245 | Rick Burleson | .20 | .10 | | 312 | Greg Minton | .12 | .06 |
| 246 | Dan Driessen | .20 | .10 | | 313 | Andy Etchebarren | .12 | .06 |
| 247 | Larry Christenson | .12 | .06 | | 314 | Paul Lindblad | .12 | .06 |
| 248 | Frank White | .12 | .06 | | 315 | Mark Belanger | .20 | .10 |
| 249 | Dave Goltz | .12 | .06 | | 316 | Henry Cruz | .12 | .06 |
| 250 | Graig Nettles | .30 | .15 | | 317 | Dave Johnson | .30 | .15 |
| 251 | Don Kirkwood | .12 | .06 | | 318 | Tom Griffin | .12 | .06 |
| 252 | Steve Swisher | .12 | .06 | | 319 | Alan Ashby | .12 | .06 |
| 253 | Jim Kern | .12 | .06 | | 320 | Fred Lynn | .90 | .45 |
| 254 | Dave Collins | .20 | .10 | | 321 | Santo Alcala | .12 | .06 |
| 255 | Jerry Reuss | .20 | .10 | | 322 | Tom Paciorek | .12 | .06 |
| 256 | Joe Altobelli | .12 | .06 | | 323 | Jim Fregosi | .12 | .06 |
| 257 | Hector Cruz | .12 | .06 | | 324 | Vern Rapp | .12 | .06 |
| 258 | John Hiller | .20 | .10 | | 325 | Bruce Sutter | .50 | .25 |
| 259 | Dodgers Team | .80 | .40 | | 326 | Mike Lum | .12 | .06 |
| 260 | Bert Campaneris | .25 | .13 | | 327 | Rick Langford | .12 | .06 |
| 261 | Tim Hosley | .12 | .06 | | 328 | Brewers Team | .50 | .25 |
| 262 | Rudy May | .12 | .06 | | 329 | John Verhoeven | .12 | .06 |
| 263 | Danny Walton | .12 | .06 | | 330 | Bob Watson | .20 | .10 |
| 264 | Jamie Easterly | .12 | .06 | | 331 | Mark Littell | .12 | .06 |
| 265 | Sal Bando | .12 | .06 | | 332 | Duane Kuiper | .12 | .06 |
| 266 | *Bob Shirley* | .20 | .10 | | 333 | Jim Todd | .12 | .06 |
| 267 | Doug Ault | .12 | .06 | | 334 | John Stearns | .12 | .06 |
| 268 | Gil Flores | .12 | .06 | | 335 | Bucky Dent | .30 | .15 |
| 269 | Wayne Twitchell | .12 | .06 | | 336 | Steve Busby | .20 | .10 |
| 270 | Carlton Fisk | 5.00 | 2.50 | | 337 | Tom Grieve | .12 | .06 |
| 271 | Randy Lerch | .12 | .06 | | 338 | Dave Heaverlo | .12 | .06 |
| 272 | Royle Stillman | .12 | .06 | | 339 | Mario Guerrero | .12 | .06 |
| 273 | Fred Norman | .12 | .06 | | 340 | Bake McBride | .12 | .06 |
| 274 | Freddie Patek | .12 | .06 | | 341 | Mike Flanagan | .25 | .13 |
| 275 | Dan Ford | .12 | .06 | | 342 | Aurelio Rodriguez | .20 | .10 |
| 276 | Bill Bonham | .12 | .06 | | 343 | John Wathan | .12 | .06 |
| 277 | Bruce Boisclair | .12 | .06 | | 344 | Sam Ewing | .12 | .06 |
| 278 | Enrique Romo | .12 | .06 | | 345 | Luis Tiant | .35 | .20 |
| 279 | Bill Virdon | .20 | .10 | | 346 | Larry Biittner | .12 | .06 |
| 280 | Buddy Bell | .30 | .15 | | 347 | Terry Forster | .20 | .10 |
| 281 | Eric Rasmussen | .12 | .06 | | 348 | Del Unser | .12 | .06 |
| 282 | Yankees Team | 1.00 | .50 | | 349 | Rick Camp | .12 | .06 |
| 283 | Omar Moreno | .12 | .06 | | 350 | Steve Garvey | 4.00 | 2.00 |
| 284 | Randy Moffitt | .12 | .06 | | 351 | Jeff Torborg | .20 | .10 |
| 285 | Steve Yeager | .12 | .06 | | 352 | Tony Scott | .12 | .06 |
| 286 | Ben Oglivie | .20 | .10 | | 353 | Doug Bair | .12 | .06 |
| 287 | Kiko Garcia | .12 | .06 | | 354 | Cesar Geronimo | .20 | .10 |
| 288 | Dave Hamilton | .12 | .06 | | 355 | Bill Travers | .12 | .06 |
| 289 | Checklist 243-363 | .90 | .45 | | 356 | Mets Team | .70 | .35 |
| 290 | Willie Horton | .20 | .10 | | 357 | Tom Poquette | .12 | .06 |
| 291 | Gary Ross | .12 | .06 | | 358 | Mark Lemongello | .12 | .06 |
| 292 | Gene Richard | .12 | .06 | | 359 | Marc Hill | .12 | .06 |
| 293 | Mike Willis | .12 | .06 | | 360 | Mike Schmidt | 15.00 | 7.50 |
| 294 | Larry Parrish | .25 | .13 | | 361 | Chris Knapp | .12 | .06 |

| | NR MT | EX | | | NR MT | EX |
|---|---|---|---|---|---|---|
| 362 | Dave May | .12 | .06 | 423 | Dave Rosello | .12 | .06 |
| 363 | Bob Randall | .12 | .06 | 424 | Red Sox Team | .70 | .35 |
| 364 | Jerry Turner | .12 | .06 | 425 | Steve Rogers | .12 | .06 |
| 365 | Ed Figueroa | .20 | .10 | 426 | Fred Kendall | .12 | .06 |
| 366 | Larry Milbourne | .12 | .06 | 427 | *Mario Soto* | .40 | .20 |
| 367 | Rick Dempsey | .20 | .10 | 428 | Joel Youngblood | .20 | .10 |
| 368 | Balor Moore | .12 | .06 | 429 | Mike Barlow | .12 | .06 |
| 369 | Tim Nordbrook | .12 | .06 | 430 | Al Oliver | .40 | .20 |
| 370 | Rusty Staub | .30 | .15 | 431 | Butch Metzger | .12 | .06 |
| 371 | Ray Burris | .12 | .06 | 432 | Terry Bulling | .12 | .06 |
| 372 | Brian Asselstine | .12 | .06 | 433 | Fernando Gonzalez | .12 | .06 |
| 373 | Jim Willoughby | .12 | .06 | 434 | Mike Norris | .12 | .06 |
| 374 | Jose Morales | .12 | .06 | 435 | Checklist 364-484 | .90 | .45 |
| 375 | Tommy John | .90 | .45 | 436 | Vic Harris | .12 | .06 |
| 376 | Jim Wohlford | .12 | .06 | 437 | Bo McLaughlin | .12 | .06 |
| 377 | Manny Sarmiento | .12 | .06 | 438 | John Ellis | .12 | .06 |
| 378 | Bobby Winkles | .12 | .06 | 439 | Ken Kravec | .12 | .06 |
| 379 | Skip Lockwood | .12 | .06 | 440 | Dave Lopes | .25 | .13 |
| 380 | Ted Simmons | .40 | .20 | 441 | Larry Gura | .12 | .06 |
| 381 | Phillies Team | .70 | .35 | 442 | Elliott Maddox | .12 | .06 |
| 382 | Joe Lahoud | .12 | .06 | 443 | Darrel Chaney | .12 | .06 |
| 383 | Mario Mendoza | .12 | .06 | 444 | Roy Hartsfield | .12 | .06 |
| 384 | Jack Clark | 4.00 | 2.00 | 445 | Mike Ivie | .12 | .06 |
| 385 | Tito Fuentes | .12 | .06 | 446 | Tug McGraw | .35 | .20 |
| 386 | Bob Gorinski | .12 | .06 | 447 | Leroy Stanton | .12 | .06 |
| 387 | Ken Holtzman | .25 | .13 | 448 | Bill Castro | .12 | .06 |
| 388 | Bill Fahey | .12 | .06 | 449 | Tim Blackwell | .12 | .06 |
| 389 | Julio Gonzalez | .12 | .06 | 450 | Tom Seaver | 7.00 | 3.50 |
| 390 | Oscar Gamble | .20 | .10 | 451 | Twins Team | .50 | .25 |
| 391 | Larry Haney | .12 | .06 | 452 | Jerry Mumphrey | .20 | .10 |
| 392 | Billy Almon | .12 | .06 | 453 | Doug Flynn | .12 | .06 |
| 393 | Tippy Martinez | .12 | .06 | 454 | Dave LaRoche | .12 | .06 |
| 394 | Roy Howell | .12 | .06 | 455 | Bill Robinson | .12 | .06 |
| 395 | Jim Hughes | .12 | .06 | 456 | Vern Ruhle | .12 | .06 |
| 396 | Bob Stinson | .12 | .06 | 457 | Bob Bailey | .12 | .06 |
| 397 | Greg Gross | .12 | .06 | 458 | Jeff Newman | .12 | .06 |
| 398 | Don Hood | .12 | .06 | 459 | Charlie Spikes | .12 | .06 |
| 399 | Pete Mackanin | .12 | .06 | 460 | Jim Hunter | 2.00 | 1.00 |
| 400 | Nolan Ryan | 30.00 | 15.00 | 461 | Rob Andrews | .12 | .06 |
| 401 | Sparky Anderson | .30 | .15 | 462 | Rogelio Moret | .12 | .06 |
| 402 | Dave Campbell | .12 | .06 | 463 | Kevin Bell | .12 | .06 |
| 403 | Bud Harrelson | .20 | .10 | 464 | Jerry Grote | .20 | .10 |
| 404 | Tigers Team | .60 | .30 | 465 | Hal McRae | .30 | .15 |
| 405 | Rawly Eastwick | .12 | .06 | 466 | Dennis Blair | .12 | .06 |
| 406 | Mike Jorgensen | .12 | .06 | 467 | Alvin Dark | .20 | .10 |
| 407 | Odell Jones | .12 | .06 | 468 | *Warren Cromartie* | .20 | .10 |
| 408 | Joe Zdeb | .12 | .06 | 469 | Rick Cerone | .20 | .10 |
| 409 | Ron Schueler | .12 | .06 | 470 | J.R. Richard | .25 | .13 |
| 410 | Bill Madlock | .50 | .25 | 471 | Roy Smalley | .20 | .10 |
| 411 | A.L. Championships (Yankees Rally To Defeat Royals) | .70 | .35 | 472 | Ron Reed | .20 | .10 |
| | | | | 473 | Bill Buckner | .30 | .15 |
| 412 | N.L. Championships (Dodgers Overpower Phillies In Four) | .50 | .25 | 474 | Jim Slaton | .12 | .06 |
| | | | | 475 | Gary Matthews | .20 | .10 |
| | | | | 476 | Bill Stein | .12 | .06 |
| 413 | World Series (Reggie & Yankees Reign Supreme) | 3.00 | 1.50 | 477 | Doug Capilla | .12 | .06 |
| | | | | 478 | Jerry Remy | .12 | .06 |
| | | | | 479 | Cardinals Team | .50 | .25 |
| 414 | Darold Knowles | .12 | .06 | 480 | Ron LeFlore | .25 | .13 |
| 415 | Ray Fosse | .12 | .06 | 481 | Jackson Todd | .12 | .06 |
| 416 | Jack Brohamer | .12 | .06 | 482 | Rick Miller | .12 | .06 |
| 417 | Mike Garman | .12 | .06 | 483 | Ken Macha | .12 | .06 |
| 418 | Tony Muser | .12 | .06 | 484 | Jim Norris | .12 | .06 |
| 419 | Jerry Garvin | .12 | .06 | 485 | Chris Chambliss | .30 | .15 |
| 420 | Greg Luzinski | .35 | .20 | 486 | John Curtis | .12 | .06 |
| 421 | Junior Moore | .12 | .06 | 487 | Jim Tyrone | .12 | .06 |
| 422 | Steve Braun | .12 | .06 | 488 | Dan Spillner | .12 | .06 |
| | | | | 489 | Rudy Meoli | .12 | .06 |

| | NR MT | EX | | | NR MT | EX |
|---|---|---|---|---|---|---|
| 490 Amos Otis | .20 | .10 | 557 Tony Solaita | | .12 | .06 |
| 491 Scott McGregor | .20 | .10 | 558 Paul Mitchell | | .12 | .06 |
| 492 Jim Sundberg | .20 | .10 | 559 Phil Mankowski | | .12 | .06 |
| 493 Steve Renko | .12 | .06 | 560 Dave Parker | | 4.00 | 2.00 |
| 494 Chuck Tanner | .20 | .10 | 561 Charlie Williams | | .12 | .06 |
| 495 Dave Cash | .12 | .06 | 562 Glenn Burke | | .12 | .06 |
| 496 *Jim Clancy* | .30 | .15 | 563 Dave Rader | | .12 | .06 |
| 497 Glenn Adams | .12 | .06 | 564 Mick Kelleher | | .12 | .06 |
| 498 Joe Sambito | .12 | .06 | 565 Jerry Koosman | | .25 | .13 |
| 499 Mariners Team | .50 | .25 | 566 Merv Rettenmund | | .12 | .06 |
| 500 George Foster | .70 | .35 | 567 Dick Drago | | .12 | .06 |
| 501 Dave Roberts | .12 | .06 | 568 Tom Hutton | | .12 | .06 |
| 502 Pat Rockett | .12 | .06 | 569 *Larry Sorensen* | | .20 | .10 |
| 503 Ike Hampton | .12 | .06 | 570 Dave Kingman | | .60 | .30 |
| 504 Roger Freed | .12 | .06 | 571 Buck Martinez | | .12 | .06 |
| 505 Felix Millan | .12 | .06 | 572 Rick Wise | | .20 | .10 |
| 506 Ron Blomberg | .12 | .06 | 573 Luis Gomez | | .12 | .06 |
| 507 Willie Crawford | .12 | .06 | 574 Bob Lemon | | .30 | .15 |
| 508 Johnny Oates | .12 | .06 | 575 Pat Dobson | | .20 | .10 |
| 509 Brent Strom | .12 | .06 | 576 Sam Mejias | | .12 | .06 |
| 510 Willie Stargell | 3.00 | 1.50 | 577 A's Team | | .50 | .25 |
| 511 Frank Duffy | .12 | .06 | 578 Buzz Capra | | .12 | .06 |
| 512 Larry Herndon | .20 | .10 | 579 *Rance Mulliniks* | | .35 | .20 |
| 513 Barry Foote | .12 | .06 | 580 Rod Carew | | 6.00 | 3.00 |
| 514 Rob Sperring | .12 | .06 | 581 Lynn McGlothen | | .12 | .06 |
| 515 Tim Corcoran | .12 | .06 | 582 Fran Healy | | .20 | .10 |
| 516 Gary Beare | .12 | .06 | 583 George Medich | | .12 | .06 |
| 517 Andres Mora | .12 | .06 | 584 John Hale | | .12 | .06 |
| 518 Tommy Boggs | .12 | .06 | 585 Woodie Fryman | | .12 | .06 |
| 519 Brian Downing | .25 | .13 | 586 Ed Goodson | | .12 | .06 |
| 520 Larry Hisle | .20 | .10 | 587 John Urrea | | .12 | .06 |
| 521 Steve Staggs | .12 | .06 | 588 Jim Mason | | .12 | .06 |
| 522 Dick Williams | .20 | .10 | 589 *Bob Knepper* | | .70 | .35 |
| 523 *Donnie Moore* | .25 | .13 | 590 Bobby Murcer | | .30 | .15 |
| 524 Bernie Carbo | .12 | .06 | 591 George Zeber | | .20 | .10 |
| 525 Jerry Terrell | .12 | .06 | 592 Bob Apodaca | | .12 | .06 |
| 526 Reds Team | .60 | .30 | 593 Dave Skaggs | | .12 | .06 |
| 527 Vic Correll | .12 | .06 | 594 Dave Freisleben | | .12 | .06 |
| 528 Rob Picciolo | .12 | .06 | 595 Sixto Lezcano | | .12 | .06 |
| 529 Paul Hartzell | .12 | .06 | 596 Gary Wheelock | | .12 | .06 |
| 530 Dave Winfield | 10.00 | 5.00 | 597 Steve Dillard | | .12 | .06 |
| 531 Tom Underwood | .12 | .06 | 598 Eddie Solomon | | .12 | .06 |
| 532 Skip Jutze | .12 | .06 | 599 Gary Woods | | .12 | .06 |
| 533 Sandy Alomar | .12 | .06 | 600 Frank Tanana | | .25 | .13 |
| 534 Wilbur Howard | .12 | .06 | 601 Gene Mauch | | .25 | .13 |
| 535 Checklist 485-605 | .90 | .45 | 602 Eric Soderholm | | .12 | .06 |
| 536 Roric Harrison | .12 | .06 | 603 Will McEnaney | | .12 | .06 |
| 537 Bruce Bochte | .20 | .10 | 604 Earl Williams | | .12 | .06 |
| 538 Johnnie LeMaster | .12 | .06 | 605 Rick Rhoden | | .25 | .13 |
| 539 Vic Davalillo | .12 | .06 | 606 Pirates Team | | .50 | .25 |
| 540 Steve Carlton | 5.00 | 2.50 | 607 Fernando Arroyo | | .12 | .06 |
| 541 Larry Cox | .12 | .06 | 608 Johnny Grubb | | .12 | .06 |
| 542 Tim Johnson | .12 | .06 | 609 John Denny | | .12 | .06 |
| 543 Larry Harlow | .12 | .06 | 610 Garry Maddox | | .20 | .10 |
| 544 Len Randle | .12 | .06 | 611 Pat Scanlon | | .12 | .06 |
| 545 Bill Campbell | .12 | .06 | 612 Ken Henderson | | .12 | .06 |
| 546 Ted Martinez | .12 | .06 | 613 Marty Perez | | .12 | .06 |
| 547 John Scott | .12 | .06 | 614 Joe Wallis | | .12 | .06 |
| 548 Billy Hunter | .12 | .06 | 615 Clay Carroll | | .20 | .10 |
| 549 Joe Kerrigan | .12 | .06 | 616 Pat Kelly | | .12 | .06 |
| 550 John Mayberry | .20 | .10 | 617 Joe Nolan | | .12 | .06 |
| 551 Braves Team | .50 | .25 | 618 Tommy Helms | | .12 | .06 |
| 552 Francisco Barrios | .12 | .06 | 619 *Thad Bosley* | | .20 | .10 |
| 553 *Terry Puhl* | .35 | .20 | 620 Willie Randolph | | .30 | .15 |
| 554 Joe Coleman | .20 | .10 | 621 Craig Swan | | .12 | .06 |
| 555 Butch Wynegar | .20 | .10 | 622 Champ Summers | | .12 | .06 |
| 556 Ed Armbrister | .12 | .06 | 623 Eduardo Rodriguez | | .12 | .06 |

| | | NR MT | EX |
|---|---|---|---|
| 624 | Gary Alexander | .12 | .06 |
| 625 | Jose Cruz | .25 | .13 |
| 626 | Blue Jays Team | .25 | .13 |
| 627 | Dave Johnson | .12 | .06 |
| 628 | Ralph Garr | .20 | .10 |
| 629 | Don Stanhouse | .12 | .06 |
| 630 | Ron Cey | .25 | .13 |
| 631 | Danny Ozark | .20 | .10 |
| 632 | Rowland Office | .12 | .06 |
| 633 | Tom Veryzer | .12 | .06 |
| 634 | Len Barker | .20 | .10 |
| 635 | Joe Rudi | .25 | .13 |
| 636 | Jim Bibby | .12 | .06 |
| 637 | Duffy Dyer | .12 | .06 |
| 638 | Paul Splittorff | .20 | .10 |
| 639 | Gene Clines | .12 | .06 |
| 640 | Lee May | .12 | .06 |
| 641 | Doug Rau | .12 | .06 |
| 642 | Denny Doyle | .12 | .06 |
| 643 | Tom House | .12 | .06 |
| 644 | Jim Dwyer | .12 | .06 |
| 645 | Mike Torrez | .20 | .10 |
| 646 | Rick Auerbach | .12 | .06 |
| 647 | Steve Dunning | .12 | .06 |
| 648 | Gary Thomasson | .12 | .06 |
| 649 | Moose Haas | .25 | .13 |
| 650 | Cesar Cedeno | .25 | .13 |
| 651 | Doug Rader | .12 | .06 |
| 652 | Checklist 606-726 | .90 | .45 |
| 653 | Ron Hodges | .12 | .06 |
| 654 | Pepe Frias | .12 | .06 |
| 655 | Lyman Bostock | .20 | .10 |
| 656 | Dave Garcia | .12 | .06 |
| 657 | Bombo Rivera | .12 | .06 |
| 658 | Manny Sanguillen | .12 | .06 |
| 659 | Rangers Team | .50 | .25 |
| 660 | Jason Thompson | .20 | .10 |
| 661 | Grant Jackson | .12 | .06 |
| 662 | Paul Dade | .12 | .06 |
| 663 | Paul Reuschel | .12 | .06 |
| 664 | Fred Stanley | .20 | .10 |
| 665 | Dennis Leonard | .20 | .10 |
| 666 | Billy Smith | .12 | .06 |
| 667 | Jeff Byrd | .12 | .06 |
| 668 | Dusty Baker | .25 | .13 |
| 669 | Pete Falcone | .12 | .06 |
| 670 | Jim Rice | 3.50 | 1.75 |
| 671 | Gary Lavelle | .12 | .06 |
| 672 | Don Kessinger | .20 | .10 |
| 673 | Steve Brye | .12 | .06 |
| 674 | *Ray Knight* | 1.50 | .70 |
| 675 | Jay Johnstone | .20 | .10 |
| 676 | Bob Myrick | .12 | .06 |
| 677 | Ed Herrmann | .12 | .06 |
| 678 | Tom Burgmeier | .12 | .06 |
| 679 | Wayne Garrett | .12 | .06 |
| 680 | Vida Blue | .30 | .15 |
| 681 | Rob Belloir | .12 | .06 |
| 682 | Ken Brett | .20 | .10 |
| 683 | Mike Champion | .12 | .06 |
| 684 | Ralph Houk | .20 | .10 |
| 685 | Frank Taveras | .12 | .06 |
| 686 | Gaylord Perry | 2.00 | 1.00 |
| 687 | *Julio Cruz* | .25 | .13 |
| 688 | George Mitterwald | .12 | .06 |
| 689 | Indians Team | .50 | .25 |
| 690 | Mickey Rivers | .25 | .13 |

| | | NR MT | EX |
|---|---|---|---|
| 691 | Ross Grimsley | .20 | .10 |
| 692 | Ken Reitz | .12 | .06 |
| 693 | Lamar Johnson | .12 | .06 |
| 694 | Elias Sosa | .12 | .06 |
| 695 | Dwight Evans | 2.00 | 1.00 |
| 696 | Steve Mingori | .12 | .06 |
| 697 | Roger Metzger | .12 | .06 |
| 698 | Juan Bernhardt | .12 | .06 |
| 699 | Jackie Brown | .12 | .06 |
| 700 | Johnny Bench | 5.00 | 2.50 |
| 701 | Rookie Pitchers (*Tom Hume*, Larry Landreth, *Steve McCatty*, Bruce Taylor) | .25 | .13 |
| 702 | Rookie Catchers (Bill Nahorodny, Kevin Pasley, Rick Sweet, Don Werner) | .12 | .06 |
| 703 | Rookie Pitchers (*Larry Andersen*, Tim Jones, Mickey Mahler, *Jack Morris*) | 18.00 | 9.00 |
| 704 | Rookie 2nd Basemen (*Garth Iorg*, Dave Oliver, Sam Perlozzo, *Lou Whitaker*) | 16.00 | 8.00 |
| 705 | Rookie Outfielders (*Dave Bergman*, Miguel Dilone, *Clint Hurdle*, Willie Norwood) | .25 | .13 |
| 706 | Rookie 1st Basemen (Wayne Cage, Ted Cox, *Pat Putnam*, Dave Revering) | .20 | .10 |
| 707 | Rookie Shortstops (Mickey Klutts, *Paul Molitor*, Alan Trammell, U.L. Washington) | 60.00 | 30.00 |
| 708 | Rookie Catchers (*Bo Diaz*, Dale Murphy, Lance Parrish, Ernie Whitt) | 15.00 | 7.50 |
| 709 | Rookie Pitchers (Steve Burke, *Matt Keough*, Lance Rautzhan, *Dan Schatzeder*) | .20 | .10 |
| 710 | Rookie Outfielders (Dell Alston, Rick Bosetti, *Mike Easler*, Keith Smith) | .50 | .25 |
| 711 | Rookie Pitchers (Cardell Camper, Dennis Lamp, Craig Mitchell, Roy Thomas) | .12 | .06 |
| 712 | Bobby Valentine | .25 | .13 |
| 713 | Bob Davis | .12 | .06 |
| 714 | Mike Anderson | .12 | .06 |
| 715 | Jim Kaat | .60 | .30 |
| 716 | Clarence Gaston | .12 | .06 |
| 717 | Nelson Briles | .12 | .06 |
| 718 | Ron Jackson | .12 | .06 |
| 719 | Randy Elliott | .12 | .06 |
| 720 | Fergie Jenkins | 2.00 | 1.00 |
| 721 | Billy Martin | 1.00 | .50 |
| 722 | Pete Broberg | .12 | .06 |
| 723 | Johnny Wockenfuss | .12 | .06 |
| 724 | Royals Team | .70 | .35 |
| 725 | Kurt Bevacqua | .12 | .06 |
| 726 | Wilbur Wood | .40 | .10 |

# 1979 Topps

The size of this issue remained the same as in 1978 with 726 cards making their appearance. Actually, the 2-1/2" by 3-1/2" cards have a relatively minor design change from the previous year. The large color photo still dominates the front, with the player's name, team and position below it. The baseball with the player's position was moved to the lower left and the position replaced by a Topps logo. On the back, the printing color was changed and the game situation was replaced by a quiz called "Baseball Dates". Specialty cards include statistical leaders, major league records set during the season and eight cards devoted to career records. For the first time, rookies were arranged by teams under the heading of "Prospects."

|  | | NR MT | EX |
|---|---|---|---|
| Complete Set: | | 250.00 | 125.00 |
| Common Player: | | .12 | .06 |
| | | | |
| 1 | Batting Leaders (Rod Carew, Dave Parker) | 3.00 | 1.50 |
| 2 | Home Run Leaders (George Foster, Jim Rice) | .50 | .25 |
| 3 | Runs Batted In Leaders (George Foster, Jim Rice) | .50 | .25 |
| 4 | Stolen Base Leaders (Ron LeFlore, Omar Moreno) | .25 | .13 |
| 5 | Victory Leaders (Ron Guidry, Gaylord Perry) | .50 | .25 |
| 6 | Strikeout Leaders (J.R. Richard, Nolan Ryan) | 3.00 | 1.50 |
| 7 | Earned Run Avg. Leaders (Ron Guidry, Craig Swan) | .25 | .13 |
| 8 | Leading Firemen (Rollie Fingers, Rich Gossage) | .40 | .20 |
| 9 | Dave Campbell | .12 | .06 |
| 10 | Lee May | .20 | .10 |
| 11 | Marc Hill | .12 | .06 |
| 12 | Dick Drago | .12 | .06 |
| 13 | Paul Dade | .12 | .06 |
| 14 | Rafael Landestoy | .12 | .06 |
| 15 | Ross Grimsley | .20 | .10 |
| 16 | Fred Stanley | .20 | .10 |
| 17 | Donnie Moore | .20 | .10 |
| 18 | Tony Solaita | .12 | .06 |
| 19 | Larry Gura | .12 | .06 |
| 20 | Joe Morgan | .40 | .20 |
| 21 | Kevin Kobel | .12 | .06 |
| 22 | Mike Jorgensen | .12 | .06 |
| 23 | Terry Forster | .20 | .10 |
| 24 | Paul Molitor | 10.00 | 5.00 |
| 25 | Steve Carlton | 4.00 | 2.00 |
| 26 | Jamie Quirk | .12 | .06 |
| 27 | Dave Goltz | .20 | .10 |
| 28 | Steve Brye | .12 | .06 |
| 29 | Rick Langford | .12 | .06 |
| 30 | Dave Winfield | 9.00 | 4.50 |
| 31 | Tom House | .12 | .06 |
| 32 | Jerry Mumphrey | .12 | .06 |
| 33 | Dave Rozema | .12 | .06 |
| 34 | Rob Andrews | .12 | .06 |
| 35 | Ed Figueroa | .20 | .10 |
| 36 | Alan Ashby | .12 | .06 |
| 37 | Joe Kerrigan | .12 | .06 |
| 38 | Bernie Carbo | .12 | .06 |
| 39 | Dale Murphy | 6.00 | 3.00 |
| 40 | Dennis Eckersley | 6.00 | 3.00 |
| 41 | Twins Team (Gene Mauch) | .50 | .25 |
| 42 | Ron Blomberg | .12 | .06 |
| 43 | Wayne Twitchell | .12 | .06 |
| 44 | Kurt Bevacqua | .12 | .06 |
| 45 | Al Hrabosky | .20 | .10 |
| 46 | Ron Hodges | .12 | .06 |
| 47 | Fred Norman | .12 | .06 |
| 48 | Merv Rettenmund | .12 | .06 |
| 49 | Vern Ruhle | .12 | .06 |
| 50 | Steve Garvey | 1.25 | .60 |
| 51 | Ray Fosse | .12 | .06 |
| 52 | Randy Lerch | .12 | .06 |
| 53 | Mick Kelleher | .12 | .06 |
| 54 | Dell Alston | .12 | .06 |
| 55 | Willie Stargell | 2.00 | 1.00 |
| 56 | John Hale | .12 | .06 |
| 57 | Eric Rasmussen | .12 | .06 |
| 58 | Bob Randall | .12 | .06 |
| 59 | John Denny | .12 | .06 |
| 60 | Mickey Rivers | .20 | .10 |
| 61 | Bo Diaz | .20 | .10 |
| 62 | Randy Moffitt | .12 | .06 |
| 63 | Jack Brohamer | .12 | .06 |
| 64 | Tom Underwood | .12 | .06 |
| 65 | Mark Belanger | .20 | .10 |
| 66 | Tigers Team (Les Moss) | .60 | .30 |
| 67 | Jim Mason | .12 | .06 |
| 68 | Joe Niekro | .12 | .06 |
| 69 | Elliott Maddox | .12 | .06 |
| 70 | John Candelaria | .25 | .13 |
| 71 | Brian Downing | .20 | .10 |
| 72 | Steve Mingori | .12 | .06 |

| | NR MT | EX | | | NR MT | EX |
|---|---|---|---|---|---|---|
| 73 | Ken Henderson | .12 | .06 | 137 | Larry Wolfe | .12 | .06 |
| 74 | *Shane Rawley* | .30 | .15 | 138 | Mark Lee | .12 | .06 |
| 75 | Steve Yeager | .12 | .06 | 139 | Luis Pujols | .12 | .06 |
| 76 | Warren Cromartie | .12 | .06 | 140 | Don Gullett | .20 | .10 |
| 77 | Dan Briggs | .12 | .06 | 141 | Tom Paciorek | .12 | .06 |
| 78 | Elias Sosa | .12 | .06 | 142 | Charlie Williams | .12 | .06 |
| 79 | Ted Cox | .12 | .06 | 143 | Tony Scott | .12 | .06 |
| 80 | Jason Thompson | .20 | .10 | 144 | Sandy Alomar | .12 | .06 |
| 81 | Roger Erickson | .12 | .06 | 145 | Rick Rhoden | .25 | .13 |
| 82 | Mets Team (Joe Torre) | | | 146 | Duane Kuiper | .12 | .06 |
| | | .60 | .30 | 147 | Dave Hamilton | .12 | .06 |
| 83 | Fred Kendall | .12 | .06 | 148 | Bruce Boisclair | .12 | .06 |
| 84 | Greg Minton | .12 | .06 | 149 | Manny Sarmiento | .12 | .06 |
| 85 | Gary Matthews | .20 | .10 | 150 | Wayne Cage | .12 | .06 |
| 86 | Rodney Scott | .12 | .06 | 151 | John Hiller | .20 | .10 |
| 87 | Pete Falcone | .12 | .06 | 152 | Rick Cerone | .20 | .10 |
| 88 | Bob Molinaro | .12 | .06 | 153 | Dennis Lamp | .12 | .06 |
| 89 | Dick Tidrow | .20 | .10 | 154 | Jim Gantner | .12 | .06 |
| 90 | Bob Boone | .25 | .13 | 155 | Dwight Evans | 1.25 | .60 |
| 91 | Terry Crowley | .12 | .06 | 156 | Buddy Solomon | .12 | .06 |
| 92 | Jim Bibby | .12 | .06 | 157 | U.L. Washington | .12 | .06 |
| 93 | Phil Mankowski | .12 | .06 | 158 | Joe Sambito | .12 | .06 |
| 94 | Len Barker | .12 | .06 | 159 | Roy White | .25 | .13 |
| 95 | Robin Yount | 12.00 | 6.00 | 160 | Mike Flanagan | .30 | .15 |
| 96 | Indians Team (Jeff | | | 161 | Barry Foote | .12 | .06 |
| | Torborg) | .50 | .25 | 162 | Tom Johnson | .12 | .06 |
| 97 | Sam Mejias | .12 | .06 | 163 | Glenn Burke | .12 | .06 |
| 98 | Ray Burris | .12 | .06 | 164 | Mickey Lolich | .40 | .20 |
| 99 | John Wathan | .20 | .10 | 165 | Frank Taveras | .12 | .06 |
| 100 | Tom Seaver | 4.00 | 2.00 | 166 | Leon Roberts | .12 | .06 |
| 101 | Roy Howell | .12 | .06 | 167 | Roger Metzger | .12 | .06 |
| 102 | Mike Anderson | .12 | .06 | 168 | Dave Freisleben | .12 | .06 |
| 103 | Jim Todd | .12 | .06 | 169 | Bill Nahorodny | .12 | .06 |
| 104 | Johnny Oates | .12 | .06 | 170 | Don Sutton | 1.25 | .60 |
| 105 | Rick Camp | .12 | .06 | 171 | Gene Clines | .12 | .06 |
| 106 | Frank Duffy | .12 | .06 | 172 | Mike Bruhert | .12 | .06 |
| 107 | Jesus Alou | .20 | .10 | 173 | John Lowenstein | .12 | .06 |
| 108 | Eduardo Rodriguez | .12 | .06 | 174 | Rick Auerbach | .12 | .06 |
| 109 | Joel Youngblood | .12 | .06 | 175 | George Hendrick | .20 | .10 |
| 110 | Vida Blue | .30 | .15 | 176 | Aurelio Rodriguez | .20 | .10 |
| 111 | Roger Freed | .12 | .06 | 177 | Ron Reed | .20 | .10 |
| 112 | Phillies Team (Danny | | | 178 | Alvis Woods | .12 | .06 |
| | Ozark) | .50 | .25 | 179 | Jim Beattie | .12 | .06 |
| 113 | Pete Redfern | .12 | .06 | 180 | Larry Hisle | .20 | .10 |
| 114 | Cliff Johnson | .20 | .10 | 181 | Mike Garman | .12 | .06 |
| 115 | Nolan Ryan | 20.00 | 10.00 | 182 | Tim Johnson | .12 | .06 |
| 116 | Ozzie Smith | 70.00 | 35.00 | 183 | Paul Splittorff | .20 | .10 |
| 117 | Grant Jackson | .12 | .06 | 184 | Darrel Chaney | .12 | .06 |
| 118 | Bud Harrelson | .20 | .10 | 185 | Mike Torrez | .20 | .10 |
| 119 | Don Stanhouse | .12 | .06 | 186 | Eric Soderholm | .12 | .06 |
| 120 | Jim Sundberg | .20 | .10 | 187 | Mark Lemongello | .12 | .06 |
| 121 | Checklist 1-121 | .25 | .13 | 188 | Pat Kelly | .12 | .06 |
| 122 | Mike Paxton | .12 | .06 | 189 | *Eddie Whitson* | .50 | .25 |
| 123 | Lou Whitaker | 3.00 | 1.50 | 190 | Ron Cey | .25 | .13 |
| 124 | Dan Schatzeder | .12 | .06 | 191 | Mike Norris | .12 | .06 |
| 125 | Rick Burleson | .20 | .10 | 192 | Cardinals Team (Ken | | |
| 126 | Doug Bair | .12 | .06 | | Boyer) | .50 | .25 |
| 127 | Thad Bosley | .12 | .06 | 193 | Glenn Adams | .12 | .06 |
| 128 | Ted Martinez | .12 | .06 | 194 | Randy Jones | .20 | .10 |
| 129 | Marty Pattin | .12 | .06 | 195 | Bill Madlock | .40 | .20 |
| 130 | Bob Watson | .12 | .06 | 196 | Steve Kemp | .12 | .06 |
| 131 | Jim Clancy | .25 | .13 | 197 | Bob Apodaca | .12 | .06 |
| 132 | Rowland Office | .12 | .06 | 198 | Johnny Grubb | .12 | .06 |
| 133 | Bill Castro | .12 | .06 | 199 | Larry Milbourne | .12 | .06 |
| 134 | Alan Bannister | .12 | .06 | 200 | Johnny Bench | 2.00 | 1.00 |
| 135 | Bobby Murcer | .25 | .13 | 201 | Record Breaker (Mike | | |
| 136 | Jim Kaat | .60 | .30 | | Edwards) | .12 | .06 |

| | | NR MT | EX |
|---|---|---|---|
| 202 | Record Breaker (Ron Guidry) | .35 | .20 |
| 203 | Record Breaker (J.R. Richard) | .20 | .10 |
| 204 | Record Breaker (Pete Rose) | 1.50 | .70 |
| 205 | Record Breaker (John Stearns) | .12 | .06 |
| 206 | Record Breaker (Sammy Stewart) | .12 | .06 |
| 207 | Dave Lemanczyk | .12 | .06 |
| 208 | Clarence Gaston | .12 | .06 |
| 209 | Reggie Cleveland | .12 | .06 |
| 210 | Larry Bowa | .30 | .15 |
| 211 | Denny Martinez | .20 | .10 |
| 212 | *Carney Lansford* | 5.00 | 2.50 |
| 213 | Bill Travers | .12 | .06 |
| 214 | Red Sox Team (Don Zimmer) | .60 | .30 |
| 215 | Willie McCovey | 2.00 | 1.00 |
| 216 | Wilbur Wood | .20 | .10 |
| 217 | Steve Dillard | .12 | .06 |
| 218 | Dennis Leonard | .20 | .10 |
| 219 | Roy Smalley | .20 | .10 |
| 220 | Cesar Geronimo | .20 | .10 |
| 221 | Jesse Jefferson | .12 | .06 |
| 222 | Bob Beall | .12 | .06 |
| 223 | Kent Tekulve | .25 | .13 |
| 224 | Dave Revering | .12 | .06 |
| 225 | Rich Gossage | .70 | .35 |
| 226 | Ron Pruitt | .12 | .06 |
| 227 | Steve Stone | .20 | .10 |
| 228 | Vic Davalillo | .12 | .06 |
| 229 | Doug Flynn | .12 | .06 |
| 230 | Bob Forsch | .20 | .10 |
| 231 | Johnny Wockenfuss | .12 | .06 |
| 232 | Jimmy Sexton | .12 | .06 |
| 233 | Paul Mitchell | .12 | .06 |
| 234 | Toby Harrah | .20 | .10 |
| 235 | Steve Rogers | .20 | .10 |
| 236 | Jim Dwyer | .12 | .06 |
| 237 | Billy Smith | .12 | .06 |
| 238 | Balor Moore | .12 | .06 |
| 239 | Willie Horton | .20 | .10 |
| 240 | Rick Reuschel | .25 | .13 |
| 241 | Checklist 122-242 | .25 | .13 |
| 242 | Pablo Torrealba | .12 | .06 |
| 243 | Buck Martinez | .12 | .06 |
| 244 | Pirates Team (Chuck Tanner) | .80 | .40 |
| 245 | Jeff Burroughs | .20 | .10 |
| 246 | Darrell Jackson | .12 | .06 |
| 247 | Tucker Ashford | .12 | .06 |
| 248 | Pete LaCock | .12 | .06 |
| 249 | Paul Thormodsgard | .12 | .06 |
| 250 | Willie Randolph | .30 | .15 |
| 251 | Jack Morris | 6.00 | 3.00 |
| 252 | Bob Stinson | .12 | .06 |
| 253 | Rick Wise | .20 | .10 |
| 254 | Luis Gomez | .12 | .06 |
| 255 | Tommy John | .80 | .40 |
| 256 | Mike Sadek | .12 | .06 |
| 257 | Adrian Devine | .12 | .06 |
| 258 | Mike Phillips | .12 | .06 |
| 259 | Reds Team (Sparky Anderson) | .60 | .30 |
| 260 | Richie Zisk | .20 | .10 |
| 261 | Mario Guerrero | .12 | .06 |
| 262 | Nelson Briles | .12 | .06 |
| 263 | Oscar Gamble | .20 | .10 |
| 264 | *Don Robinson* | .50 | .25 |
| 265 | Don Money | .12 | .06 |
| 266 | Jim Willoughby | .12 | .06 |
| 267 | Joe Rudi | .20 | .10 |
| 268 | Julio Gonzalez | .12 | .06 |
| 269 | Woodie Fryman | .20 | .10 |
| 270 | Butch Hobson | .12 | .06 |
| 271 | Rawly Eastwick | .12 | .06 |
| 272 | Tim Corcoran | .12 | .06 |
| 273 | Jerry Terrell | .12 | .06 |
| 274 | Willie Norwood | .12 | .06 |
| 275 | Junior Moore | .12 | .06 |
| 276 | Jim Colborn | .12 | .06 |
| 277 | Tom Grieve | .12 | .06 |
| 278 | Andy Messersmith | .25 | .13 |
| 279 | Jerry Grote | .12 | .06 |
| 280 | Andre Thornton | .25 | .13 |
| 281 | Vic Correll | .12 | .06 |
| 282 | Blue Jays Team (Roy Hartsfield) | .50 | .25 |
| 283 | Ken Kravec | .12 | .06 |
| 284 | Johnnie LeMaster | .12 | .06 |
| 285 | Bobby Bonds | .30 | .15 |
| 286 | Duffy Dyer | .12 | .06 |
| 287 | Andres Mora | .12 | .06 |
| 288 | Milt Wilcox | .20 | .10 |
| 289 | Jose Cruz | .25 | .13 |
| 290 | Dave Lopes | .25 | .13 |
| 291 | Tom Griffin | .12 | .06 |
| 292 | Don Reynolds | .12 | .06 |
| 293 | Jerry Garvin | .12 | .06 |
| 294 | Pepe Frias | .12 | .06 |
| 295 | Mitchell Page | .12 | .06 |
| 296 | Preston Hanna | .12 | .06 |
| 297 | Ted Sizemore | .12 | .06 |
| 298 | Rich Gale | .12 | .06 |
| 299 | Steve Ontiveros | .12 | .06 |
| 300 | Rod Carew | 4.00 | 2.00 |
| 301 | Tom Hume | .12 | .06 |
| 302 | Braves Team (Bobby Cox) | .50 | .25 |
| 303 | Lary Sorensen | .12 | .06 |
| 304 | Steve Swisher | .12 | .06 |
| 305 | Willie Montanez | .12 | .06 |
| 306 | Floyd Bannister | .30 | .15 |
| 307 | Larvell Blanks | .12 | .06 |
| 308 | Bert Blyleven | .60 | .30 |
| 309 | Ralph Garr | .20 | .10 |
| 310 | Thurman Munson | 5.00 | 2.50 |
| 311 | Gary Lavelle | .12 | .06 |
| 312 | Bob Robertson | .12 | .06 |
| 313 | Dyar Miller | .12 | .06 |
| 314 | Larry Harlow | .12 | .06 |
| 315 | Jon Matlack | .20 | .10 |
| 316 | Milt May | .12 | .06 |
| 317 | Jose Cardenal | .12 | .06 |
| 318 | *Bob Welch* | 5.00 | 2.50 |
| 319 | Wayne Garrett | .12 | .06 |
| 320 | Carl Yastrzemski | 4.00 | 2.00 |
| 321 | Gaylord Perry | 2.00 | 1.00 |
| 322 | Danny Goodwin | .12 | .06 |
| 323 | Lynn McGlothen | .12 | .06 |
| 324 | Mike Tyson | .12 | .06 |
| 325 | Cecil Cooper | .40 | .20 |

| | | NR MT | EX | | | | NR MT | EX |
|---|---|---|---|---|---|---|---|---|
| 326 | Pedro Borbon | .12 | .06 | | 387 | Gary Thomasson | .12 | .06 |
| 327 | Art Howe | .12 | .06 | | 388 | Jack Billingham | .12 | .06 |
| 328 | A's Team (Jack McKeon) | | | | 389 | Joe Zdeb | .12 | .06 |
| | | .50 | .25 | | 390 | Rollie Fingers | 2.50 | 1.25 |
| 329 | Joe Coleman | .20 | .10 | | 391 | Al Oliver | .40 | .20 |
| 330 | George Brett | 12.00 | 6.00 | | 392 | Doug Ault | .12 | .06 |
| 331 | Mickey Mahler | .12 | .06 | | 393 | Scott McGregor | .20 | .10 |
| 332 | Gary Alexander | .12 | .06 | | 394 | Randy Stein | .12 | .06 |
| 333 | Chet Lemon | .20 | .10 | | 395 | Dave Cash | .12 | .06 |
| 334 | Craig Swan | .12 | .06 | | 396 | Bill Plummer | .12 | .06 |
| 335 | Chris Chambliss | .25 | .13 | | 397 | Sergio Ferrer | .12 | .06 |
| 336 | Bobby Thompson . | .12 | .06 | | 398 | Ivan DeJesus | .12 | .06 |
| 337 | John Montague | .12 | .06 | | 399 | David Clyde | .12 | .06 |
| 338 | Vic Harris | .12 | .06 | | 400 | Jim Rice | 2.00 | 1.00 |
| 339 | Ron Jackson | .12 | .06 | | 401 | Ray Knight | .25 | .13 |
| 340 | Jim Palmer | 4.00 | 2.00 | | 402 | Paul Hartzell | .12 | .06 |
| 341 | *Willie Upshaw* | .40 | .20 | | 403 | Tim Foli | .12 | .06 |
| 342 | Dave Roberts | .12 | .06 | | 404 | White Sox Team (Don Kessinger) | | |
| 343 | Ed Glynn | .12 | .06 | | | | .50 | .25 |
| 344 | Jerry Royster | .12 | .06 | | 405 | Butch Wynegar | .20 | .10 |
| 345 | Tug McGraw | .30 | .15 | | 406 | Joe Wallis | .12 | .06 |
| 346 | Bill Buckner | .30 | .15 | | 407 | Pete Vuckovich | .20 | .10 |
| 347 | Doug Rau | .12 | .06 | | 408 | Charlie Moore | .12 | .06 |
| 348 | Andre Dawson | 12.00 | 6.00 | | 409 | *Willie Wilson* | 2.00 | 1.00 |
| 349 | Jim Wright | .12 | .06 | | 410 | Darrell Evans | .30 | .15 |
| 350 | Garry Templeton | .20 | .10 | | 411 | Hits Record Holders (Ty Cobb, George Sisler) | .70 | .35 |
| 351 | Wayne Nordhagen | .12 | .06 | | 412 | Runs Batted In Record Holders (Hank Aaron, Hack Wilson) | .70 | .35 |
| 352 | Steve Renko | .12 | .06 | | | | | |
| 353 | Checklist 243-363 | .60 | .30 | | | | | |
| 354 | Bill Bonham | .12 | .06 | | | | | |
| 355 | Lee Mazzilli | .20 | .10 | | 413 | Home Run Record Holders (Hank Aaron, Roger Maris) | 1.00 | .50 |
| 356 | Giants Team (Joe Altobelli) | | | | 414 | Batting Avg. Record Holders (Ty Cobb, Roger Hornsby) | .70 | .35 |
| | | .50 | .25 | | | | | |
| 357 | Jerry Augustine | .12 | .06 | | | | | |
| 358 | Alan Trammell | 8.00 | 4.00 | | 415 | Stolen Bases Record Holders (Lou Brock) | .70 | .35 |
| 359 | Dan Spillner | .12 | .06 | | | | | |
| 360 | Amos Otis | .20 | .10 | | 416 | Wins Record Holders (Jack Chesbro, Cy Young) | | |
| 361 | Tom Dixon | .12 | .06 | | | | .40 | .20 |
| 362 | Mike Cubbage | .12 | .06 | | 417 | Strikeouts Record Holders (Walter Johnson, Nolan Ryan) | .40 | .20 |
| 363 | Craig Skok | .12 | .06 | | | | | |
| 364 | Gene Richards | .12 | .06 | | | | | |
| 365 | Sparky Lyle | .30 | .15 | | 418 | Earned Run Avg. Record Holders (Walter Johnson, Dutch Leonard) | .20 | .10 |
| 366 | Juan Bernhardt | .12 | .06 | | | | | |
| 367 | Dave Skaggs | .12 | .06 | | | | | |
| 368 | Don Aase | .20 | .10 | | 419 | Dick Ruthven | .12 | .06 |
| 369a | Bump Wills (Blue Jays) | | | | 420 | Ken Griffey | .25 | .13 |
| | | 2.00 | 1.00 | | 421 | Doug DeCinces | .25 | .13 |
| 369b | Bump Wills (Rangers) | | | | 422 | Ruppert Jones | .12 | .06 |
| | | 2.50 | 1.25 | | 423 | Bob Montgomery | .12 | .06 |
| 370 | Dave Kingman | .35 | .20 | | 424 | Angels Team (Jim Fregosi) | | |
| 371 | Jeff Holly | .12 | .06 | | | | .60 | .30 |
| 372 | Lamar Johnson | .12 | .06 | | 425 | Rick Manning | .12 | .06 |
| 373 | Lance Rautzhan | .12 | .06 | | 426 | Chris Speier | .20 | .10 |
| 374 | Ed Herrmann | .12 | .06 | | 427 | Andy Replogle | .12 | .06 |
| 375 | Bill Campbell | .12 | .06 | | 428 | Bobby Valentine | .25 | .13 |
| 376 | Gorman Thomas | .25 | .13 | | 429 | John Urrea | .12 | .06 |
| 377 | Paul Moskau | .12 | .06 | | 430 | Dave Parker | 2.00 | 1.00 |
| 378 | Rob Picciolo | .12 | .06 | | 431 | Glenn Borgmann | .12 | .06 |
| 379 | Dale Murray | .12 | .06 | | 432 | Dave Heaverlo | .12 | .06 |
| 380 | John Mayberry | .20 | .10 | | 433 | Larry Biittner | .12 | .06 |
| 381 | Astros Team (Bill Virdon) | | | | 434 | Ken Clay | .20 | .10 |
| | | .50 | .25 | | 435 | Gene Tenace | .20 | .10 |
| 382 | Jerry Martin | .12 | .06 | | 436 | Hector Cruz | .12 | .06 |
| 383 | Phil Garner | .20 | .10 | | 437 | Rick Williams | .12 | .06 |
| 384 | Tommy Boggs | .12 | .06 | | | | | |
| 385 | Dan Ford | .12 | .06 | | | | | |
| 386 | Francisco Barrios | .12 | .06 | | | | | |

| | | NR MT | EX | | | NR MT | EX |
|---|---|---|---|---|---|---|---|
| 438 | Horace Speed | .12 | .06 | 501 | Junior Kennedy | .12 | .06 |
| 439 | Frank White | .25 | .13 | 502 | Steve Braun | .12 | .06 |
| 440 | Rusty Staub | .30 | .15 | 503 | Terry Humphrey | .12 | .06 |
| 441 | Lee Lacy | .12 | .06 | 504 | *Larry McWilliams* | .20 | .10 |
| 442 | Doyle Alexander | .25 | .13 | 505 | Ed Kranepool | .20 | .10 |
| 443 | Bruce Bochte | .12 | .06 | 506 | John D'Acquisto | .12 | .06 |
| 444 | *Aurelio Lopez* | .20 | .10 | 507 | Tony Armas | .20 | .10 |
| 445 | Steve Henderson | .12 | .06 | 508 | Charlie Hough | .20 | .10 |
| 446 | Jim Lonborg | .20 | .10 | 509 | Mario Mendoza | .12 | .06 |
| 447 | Manny Sanguillen | .12 | .06 | 510 | Ted Simmons | .40 | .20 |
| 448 | Moose Haas | .12 | .06 | 511 | Paul Reuschel | .12 | .06 |
| 449 | Bombo Rivera | .12 | .06 | 512 | Jack Clark | 1.50 | .70 |
| 450 | Dave Concepcion | .30 | .15 | 513 | Dave Johnson | .30 | .15 |
| 451 | Royals Team (Whitey Herzog) | .50 | .25 | 514 | Mike Proly | .12 | .06 |
| | | | | 515 | Enos Cabell | .12 | .06 |
| 452 | Jerry Morales | .12 | .06 | 516 | Champ Summers | .12 | .06 |
| 453 | Chris Knapp | .12 | .06 | 517 | Al Bumbry | .20 | .10 |
| 454 | Len Randle | .12 | .06 | 518 | Jim Umbarger | .12 | .06 |
| 455 | Bill Lee | .12 | .06 | 519 | Ben Oglivie | .20 | .10 |
| 456 | Chuck Baker | .12 | .06 | 520 | Gary Carter | 3.00 | 1.50 |
| 457 | Bruce Sutter | .60 | .30 | 521 | Sam Ewing | .12 | .06 |
| 458 | Jim Essian | .12 | .06 | 522 | Ken Holtzman | .20 | .10 |
| 459 | Sid Monge | .12 | .06 | 523 | John Milner | .12 | .06 |
| 460 | Graig Nettles | .50 | .25 | 524 | Tom Burgmeier | .12 | .06 |
| 461 | Jim Barr | .12 | .06 | 525 | Freddie Patek | .12 | .06 |
| 462 | Otto Velez | .12 | .06 | 526 | Dodgers Team (Tom Lasorda) | .60 | .30 |
| 463 | Steve Comer | .12 | .06 | | | | |
| 464 | Joe Nolan | .12 | .06 | 527 | Lerrin LaGrow | .12 | .06 |
| 465 | Reggie Smith | .25 | .13 | 528 | Wayne Gross | .12 | .06 |
| 466 | Mark Littell | .12 | .06 | 529 | Brian Asselstine | .12 | .06 |
| 467 | Don Kessinger | .12 | .06 | 530 | Frank Tanana | .25 | .13 |
| 468 | Stan Bahnsen | .12 | .06 | 531 | Fernando Gonzalez | .12 | .06 |
| 469 | Lance Parrish | 3.00 | 1.50 | 532 | Buddy Schultz | .12 | .06 |
| 470 | Garry Maddox | .12 | .06 | 533 | Leroy Stanton | .12 | .06 |
| 471 | Joaquin Andujar | .20 | .10 | 534 | Ken Forsch | .12 | .06 |
| 472 | Craig Kusick | .12 | .06 | 535 | Ellis Valentine | .12 | .06 |
| 473 | Dave Roberts | .12 | .06 | 536 | Jerry Reuss | .20 | .10 |
| 474 | Dick Davis | .12 | .06 | 537 | Tom Veryzer | .12 | .06 |
| 475 | Dan Driessen | .20 | .10 | 538 | Mike Ivie | .12 | .06 |
| 476 | Tom Poquette | .12 | .06 | 539 | John Ellis | .12 | .06 |
| 477 | Bob Grich | .25 | .13 | 540 | Greg Luzinski | .30 | .15 |
| 478 | Juan Beniquez | .12 | .06 | 541 | Jim Slaton | .12 | .06 |
| 479 | Padres Team (Roger Craig) | .50 | .25 | 542 | Rick Bosetti | .12 | .06 |
| | | | | 543 | Kiko Garcia | .12 | .06 |
| 480 | Fred Lynn | .70 | .35 | 544 | Fergie Jenkins | 1.50 | .70 |
| 481 | Skip Lockwood | .12 | .06 | 545 | John Stearns | .12 | .06 |
| 482 | Craig Reynolds | .12 | .06 | 546 | Bill Russell | .20 | .10 |
| 483 | Checklist 364-484 | .25 | .13 | 547 | Clint Hurdle | .12 | .06 |
| 484 | Rick Waits | .12 | .06 | 548 | Enrique Romo | .12 | .06 |
| 485 | Bucky Dent | .25 | .13 | 549 | Bob Bailey | .12 | .06 |
| 486 | Bob Knepper | .25 | .13 | 550 | Sal Bando | .20 | .10 |
| 487 | Miguel Dilone | .12 | .06 | 551 | Cubs Team (Herman Franks) | .50 | .25 |
| 488 | Bob Owchinko | .12 | .06 | | | | |
| 489 | Larry Cox (photo actually Dave Rader) | .12 | .06 | 552 | Jose Morales | .12 | .06 |
| | | | | 553 | Denny Walling | .12 | .06 |
| 490 | Al Cowens | .12 | .06 | 554 | Matt Keough | .12 | .06 |
| 491 | Tippy Martinez | .12 | .06 | 555 | Biff Pocoroba | .12 | .06 |
| 492 | Bob Bailor | .12 | .06 | 556 | Mike Lum | .12 | .06 |
| 493 | Larry Christenson | .12 | .06 | 557 | Ken Brett | .20 | .10 |
| 494 | Jerry White | .12 | .06 | 558 | Jay Johnstone | .20 | .10 |
| 495 | Tony Perez | .60 | .30 | 559 | Greg Pryor | .12 | .06 |
| 496 | Barry Bonnell | .12 | .06 | 560 | John Montefusco | .12 | .06 |
| 497 | Glenn Abbott | .12 | .06 | 561 | Ed Ott | .12 | .06 |
| 498 | Rich Chiles | .12 | .06 | 562 | Dusty Baker | .25 | .13 |
| 499 | Rangers Team (Pat Corrales) | .50 | .25 | 563 | Roy Thomas | .12 | .06 |
| | | | | 564 | Jerry Turner | .12 | .06 |
| 500 | Ron Guidry | .90 | .45 | 565 | Rico Carty | .25 | .13 |

| | NR MT | EX | | | NR MT | EX |
|---|---|---|---|---|---|---|
| 566 | Nino Espinosa | .12 | .06 | 630 | Bake McBride | .12 | .06 |
| 567 | Rich Hebner | .12 | .06 | 631 | Jorge Orta | .12 | .06 |
| 568 | Carlos Lopez | .12 | .06 | 632 | Don Kirkwood | .12 | .06 |
| 569 | Bob Sykes | .12 | .06 | 633 | Rob Wilfong | .12 | .06 |
| 570 | Cesar Cedeno | .25 | .13 | 634 | Paul Lindblad | .20 | .10 |
| 571 | Darrell Porter | .20 | .10 | 635 | Don Baylor | .80 | .40 |
| 572 | Rod Gilbreath | .12 | .06 | 636 | Wayne Garland | .12 | .06 |
| 573 | Jim Kern | .12 | .06 | 637 | Bill Robinson | .12 | .06 |
| 574 | Claudell Washington | .20 | .10 | 638 | Al Fitzmorris | .12 | .06 |
| 575 | Luis Tiant | .30 | .15 | 639 | Manny Trillo | .20 | .10 |
| 576 | Mike Parrott | .12 | .06 | 640 | Eddie Murray | 21.00 | 10.50 |
| 577 | Brewers Team (George Bamberger) | .50 | .25 | 641 | *Bobby Castillo* | .12 | .06 |
| | | | | 642 | Wilbur Howard | .12 | .06 |
| 578 | Pete Broberg | .12 | .06 | 643 | Tom Hausman | .12 | .06 |
| 579 | Greg Gross | .12 | .06 | 644 | Manny Mota | .20 | .10 |
| 580 | Ron Fairly | .20 | .10 | 645 | George Scott | .12 | .06 |
| 581 | Darold Knowles | .12 | .06 | 646 | Rick Sweet | .12 | .06 |
| 582 | Paul Blair | .20 | .10 | 647 | Bob Lacey | .12 | .06 |
| 583 | Julio Cruz | .12 | .06 | 648 | Lou Piniella | .35 | .20 |
| 584 | Jim Rooker | .12 | .06 | 649 | John Curtis | .12 | .06 |
| 585 | Hal McRae | .25 | .13 | 650 | Pete Rose | 4.50 | 2.25 |
| 586 | *Bob Horner* | .90 | .45 | 651 | Mike Caldwell | .12 | .06 |
| 587 | Ken Reitz | .12 | .06 | 652 | Stan Papi | .12 | .06 |
| 588 | Tom Murphy | .12 | .06 | 653 | Warren Brusstar | .12 | .06 |
| 589 | Terry Whitfield | .12 | .06 | 654 | Rick Miller | .12 | .06 |
| 590 | J.R. Richard | .20 | .10 | 655 | Jerry Koosman | .30 | .15 |
| 591 | Mike Hargrove | .20 | .10 | 656 | Hosken Powell | .12 | .06 |
| 592 | Mike Krukow | .20 | .10 | 657 | George Medich | .12 | .06 |
| 593 | Rick Dempsey | .20 | .10 | 658 | Taylor Duncan | .12 | .06 |
| 594 | Bob Shirley | .12 | .06 | 659 | Mariners Team (Darrell Johnson) | .50 | .25 |
| 595 | Phil Niekro | 1.25 | .60 | | | | |
| 596 | Jim Wohlford | .12 | .06 | 660 | Ron LeFlore | .12 | .06 |
| 597 | Bob Stanley | .20 | .10 | 661 | Bruce Kison | .12 | .06 |
| 598 | Mark Wagner | .12 | .06 | 662 | Kevin Bell | .12 | .06 |
| 599 | Jim Spencer | .20 | .10 | 663 | Mike Vail | .12 | .06 |
| 600 | George Foster | .60 | .30 | 664 | Doug Bird | .12 | .06 |
| 601 | Dave LaRoche | .12 | .06 | 665 | Lou Brock | 3.00 | 1.50 |
| 602 | Checklist 485-605 | .60 | .30 | 666 | Rich Dauer | .12 | .06 |
| 603 | Rudy May | .12 | .06 | 667 | Don Hood | .12 | .06 |
| 604 | Jeff Newman | .12 | .06 | 668 | Bill North | .12 | .06 |
| 605 | Rick Monday | .12 | .06 | 669 | Checklist 606-726 | .60 | .30 |
| 606 | Expos Team (Dick Williams) | .50 | .25 | 670 | Jim Hunter | 1.25 | .60 |
| | | | | 671 | Joe Ferguson | .12 | .06 |
| 607 | Omar Moreno | .12 | .06 | 672 | Ed Halicki | .12 | .06 |
| 608 | Dave McKay | .12 | .06 | 673 | Tom Hutton | .12 | .06 |
| 609 | Silvio Martinez | .12 | .06 | 674 | Dave Tomlin | .12 | .06 |
| 610 | Mike Schmidt | 12.00 | 6.00 | 675 | Tim McCarver | .30 | .15 |
| 611 | Jim Norris | .12 | .06 | 676 | Johnny Sutton | .12 | .06 |
| 612 | *Rick Honeycutt* | .30 | .15 | 677 | Larry Parrish | .25 | .13 |
| 613 | Mike Edwards | .12 | .06 | 678 | Geoff Zahn | .12 | .06 |
| 614 | Willie Hernandez | .20 | .10 | 679 | Derrel Thomas | .12 | .06 |
| 615 | Ken Singleton | .20 | .10 | 680 | Carlton Fisk | 5.00 | 2.50 |
| 616 | Billy Almon | .12 | .06 | 681 | *John Henry Johnson* | .12 | .06 |
| 617 | Terry Puhl | .12 | .06 | | | | |
| 618 | Jerry Remy | .12 | .06 | 682 | Dave Chalk | .12 | .06 |
| 619 | *Ken Landreaux* | .25 | .13 | 683 | Dan Meyer | .12 | .06 |
| 620 | Bert Campaneris | .25 | .13 | 684 | Jamie Easterly | .12 | .06 |
| 621 | Pat Zachry | .12 | .06 | 685 | Sixto Lezcano | .12 | .06 |
| 622 | Dave Collins | .20 | .10 | 686 | Ron Schueler | .12 | .06 |
| 623 | Bob McClure | .12 | .06 | 687 | Rennie Stennett | .12 | .06 |
| 624 | Larry Herndon | .20 | .10 | 688 | Mike Willis | .12 | .06 |
| 625 | Mark Fidrych | .25 | .13 | 689 | Orioles Team (Earl Weaver) | .70 | .35 |
| 626 | Yankees Team (Bob Lemon) | .80 | .40 | | | | |
| | | | | 690 | Buddy Bell | .12 | .06 |
| 627 | Gary Serum | .12 | .06 | 691 | Dock Ellis | .12 | .06 |
| 628 | Del Unser | .12 | .06 | 692 | Mickey Stanley | .20 | .10 |
| 629 | Gene Garber | .12 | .06 | 693 | Dave Rader | .12 | .06 |

|     |                | NR MT | EX   |
|-----|----------------|-------|------|
| 694 | Burt Hooton    | .20   | .10  |
| 695 | Keith Hernandez | 2.00 | 1.00 |
| 696 | Andy Hassler   | .12   | .06  |
| 697 | Dave Bergman   | .12   | .06  |
| 698 | Bill Stein     | .12   | .06  |
| 699 | Hal Dues       | .12   | .06  |
| 700 | Reggie Jackson | 5.00  | 2.50 |

701 Orioles Prospects (Mark Corey, John Flinn, *Sammy Stewart*) .20 .10

702 Red Sox Prospects (Joel Finch, Garry Hancock, Allen Ripley) .12 .06

703 Angels Prospects (Jim Anderson, Dave Frost, Bob Slater) .12 .06

704 White Sox Prospects (Ross Baumgarten, Mike Colbern, *Mike Squires*) .20 .10

705 Indians Prospects (*Alfredo Griffin*, Tim Norrid, Dave Oliver) .70 .35

706 Tigers Prospects (Dave Stegman, Dave Tobik, Kip Young) .12 .06

707 Royals Prospects (Randy Bass, Jim Gaudet, Randy McGilberry) .12 .06

708 Brewers Prospects (*Kevin Bass, Eddie Romero*, Ned Yost) 1.00 .50

709 Twins Prospects (Sam Perlozzo, Rick Sofield, Kevin Stanfield) .12 .06

710 Yankees Prospects (Brian Doyle, *Mike Heath*, Dave Rajsich) .30 .15

711 A's Prospects (*Dwayne Murphy*, Bruce Robinson, Alan Wirth) .50 .25

712 Mariners Prospects (Bud Anderson, Greg Biercevicz, Byron McLaughlin) .12 .06

713 Rangers Prospects (*Danny Darwin*, Pat Putnam, *Billy Sample*) .70 .35

714 Blue Jays Prospects (Victor Cruz, Pat Kelly, Ernie Whitt) .20 .10

715 Braves Prospects (*Bruce Benedict, Glenn Hubbard*, Larry Whisenton) .40 .20

716 Cubs Prospects (Dave Geisel, Karl Pagel, *Scot Thompson*) .12 .06

717 Reds Prospects (*Mike LaCoss, Ron Oester, Harry Spilman*) .40 .20

718 Astros Prospects (Bruce Bochy, Mike Fischlin, Don Pisker) .12 .06

719 Dodgers Prospects (*Pedro Guerrero, Rudy Law*, Joe Simpson) 7.00 3.50

720 Expos Prospects (Jerry Fry, Jerry Pirtle, *Scott Sanderson*) .90 .45

721 Mets Prospects (*Juan Berenguer*, Dwight Bernard, Dan Norman) .30 .15

722 Phillies Prospects (*Jim Morrison, Lonnie Smith*, Jim Wright) 2.00 1.00

723 Pirates Prospects (*Dale Berra*, Eugenio Cotes, Ben Wiltbank) .20 .10

724 Cardinals Prospects (Tom Bruno, *George Frazier, Terry Kennedy*) .50 .25

725 Padres Prospects (Jim Beswick, Steve Mura, Broderick Perkins) .12 .06

726 Giants Prospects (Greg Johnston, Joe Strain, John Tamargo) .25 .06

## 1980 Topps

Again numbering 726 cards measuring 2-1/2" by 3-1/2", Topps did make some design changes in 1980. Fronts have the usual color picture with a facsimile autograph. The player's name appears above the picture, while his position is on a pennant at the upper left and his team on another pennant in the lower right. Backs no longer feature games, returning instead to statistics, personal information, a few headlines and a cartoon about the player. Specialty cards include statistical leaders, and previous season highlights. Many rookies again appear in team threesomes.

|                 | NR MT  | EX     |
|-----------------|--------|--------|
| Complete Set:   | 300.00 | 150.00 |
| Common Player:  | .12    | .06    |

1 1979 Highlights (Lou Brock, Carl Yastrzemski) 2.00 1.00

2 1979 Highlights (Willie McCovey) .80 .40

| | | NR MT | EX |
|---|---|---|---|
| 3 | 1979 Highlights (Manny Mota) | .20 | .10 |
| 4 | 1979 Highlights (Pete Rose) | 2.00 | 1.00 |
| 5 | 1979 Highlights (Garry Templeton) | .20 | .10 |
| 6 | 1979 Highlights (Del Unser) | .12 | .06 |
| 7 | Mike Lum | .12 | .06 |
| 8 | Craig Swan | .12 | .06 |
| 9 | Steve Braun | .12 | .06 |
| 10 | Denny Martinez | .20 | .10 |
| 11 | Jimmy Sexton | .12 | .06 |
| 12 | John Curtis | .12 | .06 |
| 13 | Ron Pruitt | .12 | .06 |
| 14 | Dave Cash | .12 | .06 |
| 15 | Bill Campbell | .12 | .06 |
| 16 | Jerry Narron | .20 | .10 |
| 17 | Bruce Sutter | .35 | .25 |
| 18 | Ron Jackson | .12 | .06 |
| 19 | Balor Moore | .12 | .06 |
| 20 | Dan Ford | .12 | .06 |
| 21 | Manny Sarmiento | .12 | .06 |
| 22 | Pat Putnam | .12 | .06 |
| 23 | Derrel Thomas | .12 | .06 |
| 24 | Jim Slaton | .12 | .06 |
| 25 | Lee Mazzilli | .20 | .10 |
| 26 | Marty Pattin | .12 | .06 |
| 27 | Del Unser | .12 | .06 |
| 28 | Bruce Kison | .12 | .06 |
| 29 | Mark Wagner | .12 | .06 |
| 30 | Vida Blue | .30 | .15 |
| 31 | Jay Johnstone | .20 | .10 |
| 32 | Julio Cruz | .12 | .06 |
| 33 | Tony Scott | .12 | .06 |
| 34 | Jeff Newman | .12 | .06 |
| 35 | Luis Tiant | .30 | .15 |
| 36 | Rusty Torres | .12 | .06 |
| 37 | Kiko Garcia | .12 | .06 |
| 38 | Dan Spillner | .12 | .06 |
| 39 | Rowland Office | .12 | .06 |
| 40 | Carlton Fisk | 5.00 | 2.50 |
| 41 | Rangers Team (Pat Corrales) | .50 | .25 |
| 42 | Dave Palmer | .20 | .10 |
| 43 | Bombo Rivera | .12 | .06 |
| 44 | Bill Fahey | .12 | .06 |
| 45 | Frank White | .25 | .13 |
| 46 | Rico Carty | .20 | .10 |
| 47 | Bill Bonham | .12 | .06 |
| 48 | Rick Miller | .12 | .06 |
| 49 | Mario Guerrero | .12 | .06 |
| 50 | J.R. Richard | .20 | .10 |
| 51 | Joe Ferguson | .12 | .06 |
| 52 | Warren Brusstar | .12 | .06 |
| 53 | Ben Oglivie | .20 | .10 |
| 54 | Dennis Lamp | .12 | .06 |
| 55 | Bill Madlock | .40 | .20 |
| 56 | Bobby Valentine | .20 | .10 |
| 57 | Pete Vuckovich | .20 | .10 |
| 58 | Doug Flynn | .12 | .06 |
| 59 | Eddy Putnam | .12 | .06 |
| 60 | Bucky Dent | .25 | .13 |
| 61 | Gary Serum | .12 | .06 |
| 62 | Mike Ivie | .12 | .06 |
| 63 | Bob Stanley | .20 | .10 |
| 64 | Joe Nolan | .12 | .06 |
| 65 | Al Bumbry | .20 | .10 |
| 66 | Royals Team (Jim Frey) | .60 | .30 |
| 67 | Doyle Alexander | .25 | .13 |
| 68 | Larry Harlow | .12 | .06 |
| 69 | Rick Williams | .12 | .06 |
| 70 | Gary Carter | 2.25 | 1.25 |
| 71 | John Milner | .12 | .06 |
| 72 | Fred Howard | .12 | .06 |
| 73 | Dave Collins | .20 | .10 |
| 74 | Sid Monge | .12 | .06 |
| 75 | Bill Russell | .20 | .10 |
| 76 | John Stearns | .12 | .06 |
| 77 | *Dave Stieb* | 3.00 | 1.50 |
| 78 | Ruppert Jones | .12 | .06 |
| 79 | Bob Owchinko | .12 | .06 |
| 80 | Ron LeFlore | .20 | .10 |
| 81 | Ted Sizemore | .12 | .06 |
| 82 | Astros Team (Bill Virdon) | .50 | .25 |
| 83 | *Steve Trout* | .30 | .15 |
| 84 | Gary Lavelle | .12 | .06 |
| 85 | Ted Simmons | .40 | .20 |
| 86 | Dave Hamilton | .12 | .06 |
| 87 | Pepe Frias | .12 | .06 |
| 88 | Ken Landreaux | .20 | .10 |
| 89 | Don Hood | .20 | .10 |
| 90 | Manny Trillo | .20 | .10 |
| 91 | Rick Dempsey | .20 | .10 |
| 92 | Rick Rhoden | .25 | .13 |
| 93 | Dave Roberts | .12 | .06 |
| 94 | *Neil Allen* | .30 | .15 |
| 95 | Cecil Cooper | .35 | .20 |
| 96 | A's Team (Jim Marshall) | .50 | .25 |
| 97 | Bill Lee | .20 | .10 |
| 98 | Jerry Terrell | .12 | .06 |
| 99 | Victor Cruz | .12 | .06 |
| 100 | Johnny Bench | 4.00 | 2.00 |
| 101 | Aurelio Lopez | .12 | .06 |
| 102 | Rich Dauer | .12 | .06 |
| 103 | *Bill Caudill* | .20 | .10 |
| 104 | Manny Mota | .20 | .10 |
| 105 | Frank Tanana | .20 | .10 |
| 106 | *Jeff Leonard* | .80 | .40 |
| 107 | Francisco Barrios | .12 | .06 |
| 108 | Bob Horner | .40 | .30 |
| 109 | Bill Travers | .12 | .06 |
| 110 | Fred Lynn | .35 | .20 |
| 111 | Bob Knepper | .20 | .10 |
| 112 | White Sox Team (Tony LaRussa) | .50 | .25 |
| 113 | Geoff Zahn | .12 | .06 |
| 114 | Juan Beniquez | .12 | .06 |
| 115 | Sparky Lyle | .25 | .13 |
| 116 | Larry Cox | .12 | .06 |
| 117 | Dock Ellis | .12 | .06 |
| 118 | Phil Garner | .20 | .10 |
| 119 | Sammy Stewart | .12 | .06 |
| 120 | Greg Luzinski | .30 | .15 |
| 121 | Checklist 1-121 | .50 | .25 |
| 122 | Dave Rosello | .12 | .06 |
| 123 | Lynn Jones | .12 | .06 |
| 124 | Dave Lemanczyk | .12 | .06 |
| 125 | Tony Perez | .60 | .30 |
| 126 | Dave Tomlin | .12 | .06 |

| | | NR MT | EX |
|---|---|---|---|
| 127 | Gary Thomasson | .12 | .06 |
| 128 | Tom Burgmeier | .12 | .06 |
| 129 | Craig Reynolds | .12 | .06 |
| 130 | Amos Otis | .20 | .10 |
| 131 | Paul Mitchell | .12 | .06 |
| 132 | Biff Pocoroba | .12 | .06 |
| 133 | Jerry Turner | .12 | .06 |
| 134 | Matt Keough | .12 | .06 |
| 135 | Bill Buckner | .30 | .15 |
| 136 | Dick Ruthven | .12 | .06 |
| 137 | *John Castino* | .20 | .10 |
| 138 | Ross Baumgarten | .12 | .06 |
| 139 | *Dane Iorg* | .20 | .10 |
| 140 | Rich Gossage | .60 | .30 |
| 141 | Gary Alexander | .12 | .06 |
| 142 | Phil Huffman | .12 | .06 |
| 143 | Bruce Bochte | .12 | .06 |
| 144 | Steve Comer | .12 | .06 |
| 145 | Darrell Evans | .30 | .15 |
| 146 | Bob Welch | 2.00 | 1.00 |
| 147 | Terry Puhl | .12 | .06 |
| 148 | Manny Sanguillen | .12 | .06 |
| 149 | Tom Hume | .12 | .06 |
| 150 | Jason Thompson | .20 | .10 |
| 151 | Tom Hausman | .12 | .06 |
| 152 | John Fulgham | .12 | .06 |
| 153 | Tim Blackwell | .12 | .06 |
| 154 | Lary Sorensen | .12 | .06 |
| 155 | Jerry Remy | .12 | .06 |
| 156 | Tony Brizzolara | .12 | .06 |
| 157 | Willie Wilson | .20 | .10 |
| 158 | Rob Picciolo | .12 | .06 |
| 159 | Ken Clay | .20 | .10 |
| 160 | Eddie Murray | 11.00 | 5.50 |
| 161 | Larry Christenson | .12 | .06 |
| 162 | Bob Randall | .12 | .06 |
| 163 | Steve Swisher | .12 | .06 |
| 164 | Greg Pryor | .12 | .06 |
| 165 | Omar Moreno | .12 | .06 |
| 166 | Glenn Abbott | .12 | .06 |
| 167 | Jack Clark | 1.00 | .50 |
| 168 | Rick Waits | .12 | .06 |
| 169 | Luis Gomez | .12 | .06 |
| 170 | Burt Hooton | .20 | .10 |
| 171 | Fernando Gonzalez | .12 | .06 |
| 172 | Ron Hodges | .12 | .06 |
| 173 | John Henry Johnson | .12 | .06 |
| 174 | Ray Knight | .20 | .10 |
| 175 | Rick Reuschel | .25 | .13 |
| 176 | Champ Summers | .12 | .06 |
| 177 | Dave Heaverlo | .12 | .06 |
| 178 | Tim McCarver | .30 | .15 |
| 179 | *Ron Davis* | .20 | .10 |
| 180 | Warren Cromartie | .12 | .06 |
| 181 | Moose Haas | .12 | .06 |
| 182 | Ken Reitz | .12 | .06 |
| 183 | Jim Anderson | .12 | .06 |
| 184 | Steve Renko | .12 | .06 |
| 185 | Hal McRae | .25 | .13 |
| 186 | Junior Moore | .12 | .06 |
| 187 | Alan Ashby | .12 | .06 |
| 188 | Terry Crowley | .12 | .06 |
| 189 | Kevin Kobel | .12 | .06 |
| 190 | Buddy Bell | .25 | .13 |
| 191 | Ted Martinez | .12 | .06 |
| 192 | Braves Team (Bobby Cox) | .50 | .25 |
| 193 | Dave Goltz | .20 | .10 |
| 194 | Mike Easler | .20 | .10 |
| 195 | John Montefusco | .20 | .10 |
| 196 | Lance Parrish | 1.50 | .70 |
| 197 | Byron McLaughlin | .12 | .06 |
| 198 | Dell Alston | .12 | .06 |
| 199 | Mike LaCoss | .20 | .10 |
| 200 | Jim Rice | 2.00 | 1.00 |
| 201 | Batting Leaders (Keith Hernandez, Fred Lynn) | .50 | .25 |
| 202 | Home Run Leaders (Dave Kingman, Gorman Thomas) | .25 | .13 |
| 203 | Runs Batted In Leaders (Don Baylor, Dave Winfield) | .50 | .25 |
| 204 | Stolen Base Leaders (Omar Moreno, Willie Wilson) | .20 | .10 |
| 205 | Victory Leaders (Mike Flanagan, Joe Niekro, Phil Niekro) | .40 | .20 |
| 206 | Strikeout Leaders (J.R. Richard, Nolan Ryan) | 2.00 | 1.00 |
| 207 | Earned Run Avg. Leaders (Ron Guidry, J.R. Richard) | .25 | .13 |
| 208 | Wayne Cage | .12 | .06 |
| 209 | Von Joshua | .12 | .06 |
| 210 | Steve Carlton | 4.00 | 2.00 |
| 211 | Dave Skaggs | .12 | .06 |
| 212 | Dave Roberts | .12 | .06 |
| 213 | Mike Jorgensen | .12 | .06 |
| 214 | Angels Team (Jim Fregosi) | .50 | .25 |
| 215 | Sixto Lezcano | .12 | .06 |
| 216 | Phil Mankowski | .12 | .06 |
| 217 | Ed Halicki | .12 | .06 |
| 218 | Jose Morales | .12 | .06 |
| 219 | Steve Mingori | .12 | .06 |
| 220 | Dave Concepcion | .30 | .15 |
| 221 | Joe Cannon | .12 | .06 |
| 222 | *Ron Hassey* | .50 | .25 |
| 223 | Bob Sykes | .12 | .06 |
| 224 | Willie Montanez | .12 | .06 |
| 225 | Lou Piniella | .30 | .15 |
| 226 | Bill Stein | .12 | .06 |
| 227 | Len Barker | .12 | .06 |
| 228 | Johnny Oates | .12 | .06 |
| 229 | Jim Bibby | .12 | .06 |
| 230 | Dave Winfield | 8.00 | 4.00 |
| 231 | Steve McCatty | .12 | .06 |
| 232 | Alan Trammell | 4.00 | 2.00 |
| 233 | LaRue Washington | .12 | .06 |
| 234 | Vern Ruhle | .12 | .06 |
| 235 | Andre Dawson | 7.50 | 3.75 |
| 236 | Marc Hill | .12 | .06 |
| 237 | Scott McGregor | .20 | .10 |
| 238 | Rob Wilfong | .12 | .06 |
| 239 | Don Aase | .12 | .06 |
| 240 | Dave Kingman | .40 | .20 |
| 241 | Checklist 122-242 | .50 | .25 |
| 242 | Lamar Johnson | .12 | .06 |
| 243 | Jerry Augustine | .12 | .06 |
| 244 | Cardinals Team (Ken Boyer) | .50 | .25 |

| | | NR MT | EX |
|---|---|---|---|
| 245 | Phil Niekro | 1.00 | .50 |
| 246 | Tim Foli | .12 | .06 |
| 247 | Frank Riccelli | .12 | .06 |
| 248 | Jamie Quirk | .12 | .06 |
| 249 | Jim Clancy | .20 | .10 |
| 250 | Jim Kaat | .50 | .25 |
| 251 | Kip Young | .12 | .06 |
| 252 | Ted Cox | .12 | .06 |
| 253 | John Montague | .12 | .06 |
| 254 | Paul Dade | .12 | .06 |
| 255 | Dusty Baker | .12 | .06 |
| 256 | Roger Erickson | .12 | .06 |
| 257 | Larry Herndon | .20 | .10 |
| 258 | Paul Moskau | .12 | .06 |
| 259 | Mets Team (Joe Torre) | .60 | .30 |
| 260 | Al Oliver | .35 | .20 |
| 261 | Dave Chalk | .12 | .06 |
| 262 | Benny Ayala | .12 | .06 |
| 263 | Dave LaRoche | .12 | .06 |
| 264 | Bill Robinson | .12 | .06 |
| 265 | Robin Yount | 12.00 | 6.00 |
| 266 | Bernie Carbo | .12 | .06 |
| 267 | Dan Schatzeder | .12 | .06 |
| 268 | Rafael Landestoy | .12 | .06 |
| 269 | Dave Tobik | .12 | .06 |
| 270 | Mike Schmidt | 6.00 | 3.00 |
| 271 | Dick Drago | .12 | .06 |
| 272 | Ralph Garr | .20 | .10 |
| 273 | Eduardo Rodriguez | .12 | .06 |
| 274 | Dale Murphy | 4.00 | 2.00 |
| 275 | Jerry Koosman | .25 | .13 |
| 276 | Tom Veryzer | .12 | .06 |
| 277 | Rick Bosetti | .12 | .06 |
| 278 | Jim Spencer | .20 | .10 |
| 279 | Rob Andrews | .12 | .06 |
| 280 | Gaylord Perry | 1.50 | .70 |
| 281 | Paul Blair | .20 | .10 |
| 282 | Mariners Team (Darrell Johnson) | .50 | .25 |
| 283 | John Ellis | .12 | .06 |
| 284 | Larry Murray | .12 | .06 |
| 285 | Don Baylor | .35 | .20 |
| 286 | Darold Knowles | .12 | .06 |
| 287 | John Lowenstein | .12 | .06 |
| 288 | Dave Rozema | .12 | .06 |
| 289 | Bruce Bochy | .12 | .06 |
| 290 | Steve Garvey | 2.00 | 1.00 |
| 291 | Randy Scarbery | .12 | .06 |
| 292 | Dale Berra | .12 | .06 |
| 293 | Elias Sosa | .12 | .06 |
| 294 | Charlie Spikes | .12 | .06 |
| 295 | Larry Gura | .12 | .06 |
| 296 | Dave Rader | .12 | .06 |
| 297 | Tim Johnson | .12 | .06 |
| 298 | Ken Holtzman | .20 | .10 |
| 299 | Steve Henderson | .12 | .06 |
| 300 | Ron Guidry | .70 | .35 |
| 301 | Mike Edwards | .12 | .06 |
| 302 | Dodgers Team (Tom Lasorda) | .60 | .30 |
| 303 | Bill Castro | .12 | .06 |
| 304 | Butch Wynegar | .20 | .10 |
| 305 | Randy Jones | .20 | .10 |
| 306 | Denny Walling | .12 | .06 |
| 307 | Rick Honeycutt | .20 | .10 |
| 308 | Mike Hargrove | .20 | .10 |
| 309 | Larry McWilliams | .12 | .06 |
| 310 | Dave Parker | 2.00 | 1.00 |
| 311 | Roger Metzger | .12 | .06 |
| 312 | Mike Barlow | .12 | .06 |
| 313 | Johnny Grubb | .12 | .06 |
| 314 | Tim Stoddard | .20 | .10 |
| 315 | Steve Kemp | .25 | .13 |
| 316 | Bob Lacey | .12 | .06 |
| 317 | Mike Anderson | .12 | .06 |
| 318 | Jerry Reuss | .20 | .10 |
| 319 | Chris Speier | .12 | .06 |
| 320 | Dennis Eckersley | 3.00 | 1.50 |
| 321 | Keith Hernandez | 1.50 | .70 |
| 322 | Claudell Washington | .20 | .10 |
| 323 | Mick Kelleher | .12 | .06 |
| 324 | Tom Underwood | .12 | .06 |
| 325 | Dan Driessen | .20 | .10 |
| 326 | Bo McLaughlin | .12 | .06 |
| 327 | Ray Fosse | .12 | .06 |
| 328 | Twins Team (Gene Mauch) | .50 | .25 |
| 329 | Bert Roberge | .12 | .06 |
| 330 | Al Cowens | .12 | .06 |
| 331 | Rich Hebner | .12 | .06 |
| 332 | Enrique Romo | .12 | .06 |
| 333 | Jim Norris | .12 | .06 |
| 334 | Jim Beattie | .20 | .10 |
| 335 | Willie McCovey | 1.50 | .70 |
| 336 | George Medich | .12 | .06 |
| 337 | Carney Lansford | .30 | .15 |
| 338 | Johnny Wockenfuss | .12 | .06 |
| 339 | John D'Acquisto | .12 | .06 |
| 340 | Ken Singleton | .20 | .10 |
| 341 | Jim Essian | .12 | .06 |
| 342 | Odell Jones | .12 | .06 |
| 343 | Mike Vail | .12 | .06 |
| 344 | Randy Lerch | .12 | .06 |
| 345 | Larry Parrish | .20 | .10 |
| 346 | Buddy Solomon | .12 | .06 |
| 347 | Harry Chappas | .20 | .10 |
| 348 | Checklist 243-363 | .50 | .25 |
| 349 | Jack Brohamer | .12 | .06 |
| 350 | George Hendrick | .20 | .10 |
| 351 | Bob Davis | .12 | .06 |
| 352 | Dan Briggs | .12 | .06 |
| 353 | Andy Hassler | .12 | .06 |
| 354 | Rick Auerbach | .12 | .06 |
| 355 | Gary Matthews | .20 | .10 |
| 356 | Padres Team (Jerry Coleman) | .50 | .25 |
| 357 | Bob McClure | .12 | .06 |
| 358 | Lou Whitaker | 1.25 | .60 |
| 359 | Randy Moffitt | .12 | .06 |
| 360 | Darrell Porter | .12 | .06 |
| 361 | Wayne Garland | .12 | .06 |
| 362 | Danny Goodwin | .12 | .06 |
| 363 | Wayne Gross | .12 | .06 |
| 364 | Ray Burris | .12 | .06 |
| 365 | Bobby Murcer | .25 | .13 |
| 366 | Rob Dressler | .12 | .06 |
| 367 | Billy Smith | .12 | .06 |
| 368 | Willie Aikens | .20 | .10 |
| 369 | Jim Kern | .12 | .06 |
| 370 | Cesar Cedeno | .25 | .13 |
| 371 | Jack Morris | 3.00 | 1.50 |
| 372 | Joel Youngblood | .12 | .06 |
| 373 | Dan Petry | .30 | .15 |

| | NR MT | EX |
|---|---|---|
| 374 Jim Gantner | .20 | .10 |
| 375 Ross Grimsley | .12 | .06 |
| 376 Gary Allenson | .12 | .06 |
| 377 Junior Kennedy | .12 | .06 |
| 378 Jerry Mumphrey | .12 | .06 |
| 379 Kevin Bell | .12 | .06 |
| 380 Garry Maddox | .20 | .10 |
| 381 Cubs Team (Preston Gomez) | .50 | .25 |
| 382 Dave Freisleben | .12 | .06 |
| 383 Ed Ott | .12 | .06 |
| 384 Joey McLaughlin | .12 | .06 |
| 385 Enos Cabell | .12 | .06 |
| 386 Darrell Jackson | .12 | .06 |
| 387a Fred Stanley (name in red) | .20 | .10 |
| 387b Fred Stanley (name in yellow) | 3.00 | 1.50 |
| 388 Mike Paxton | .12 | .06 |
| 389 Pete LaCock | .12 | .06 |
| 390 Fergie Jenkins | .40 | .20 |
| 391 Tony Armas | .12 | .06 |
| 392 Milt Wilcox | .12 | .06 |
| 393 Ozzie Smith | 15.00 | 7.50 |
| 394 Reggie Cleveland | .12 | .06 |
| 395 Ellis Valentine | .12 | .06 |
| 396 Dan Meyer | .12 | .06 |
| 397 Roy Thomas | .12 | .06 |
| 398 Barry Foote | .12 | .06 |
| 399 Mike Proly | .12 | .06 |
| 400 George Foster | .50 | .25 |
| 401 Pete Falcone | .12 | .06 |
| 402 Merv Rettenmund | .12 | .06 |
| 403 Pete Redfern | .12 | .06 |
| 404 Orioles Team (Earl Weaver) | .60 | .30 |
| 405 Dwight Evans | 1.00 | .50 |
| 406 Paul Molitor | 5.00 | 2.50 |
| 407 Tony Solaita | .12 | .06 |
| 408 Bill North | .12 | .06 |
| 409 Paul Splittorff | .20 | .10 |
| 410 Bobby Bonds | .25 | .13 |
| 411 Frank LaCorte | .12 | .06 |
| 412 Thad Bosley | .12 | .06 |
| 413 Allen Ripley | .12 | .06 |
| 414 George Scott | .20 | .10 |
| 415 Bill Atkinson | .12 | .06 |
| 416 *Tom Brookens* | .35 | .20 |
| 417 Craig Chamberlain | .12 | .06 |
| 418 Roger Freed | .12 | .06 |
| 419 Vic Correll | .12 | .06 |
| 420 Butch Hobson | .12 | .06 |
| 421 Doug Bird | .12 | .06 |
| 422 Larry Milbourne | .12 | .06 |
| 423 Dave Frost | .12 | .06 |
| 424 Yankees Team (Dick Howser) | .70 | .35 |
| 425 Mark Belanger | .20 | .10 |
| 426 Grant Jackson | .12 | .06 |
| 427 Tom Hutton | .12 | .06 |
| 428 Pat Zachry | .12 | .06 |
| 429 Duane Kuiper | .12 | .06 |
| 430 Larry Hisle | .12 | .06 |
| 431 Mike Krukow | .20 | .10 |
| 432 Willie Norwood | .12 | .06 |
| 433 Rich Gale | .12 | .06 |
| 434 Johnnie LeMaster | .12 | .06 |

| | NR MT | EX |
|---|---|---|
| 435 Don Gullett | .20 | .10 |
| 436 Billy Almon | .12 | .06 |
| 437 Joe Niekro | .20 | .10 |
| 438 Dave Revering | .12 | .06 |
| 439 Mike Phillips | .12 | .06 |
| 440 Don Sutton | 1.00 | .50 |
| 441 Eric Soderholm | .12 | .06 |
| 442 Jorge Orta | .12 | .06 |
| 443 Mike Parrott | .12 | .06 |
| 444 Alvis Woods | .12 | .06 |
| 445 Mark Fidrych | .20 | .10 |
| 446 Duffy Dyer | .12 | .06 |
| 447 Nino Espinosa | .12 | .06 |
| 448 Jim Wohlford | .12 | .06 |
| 449 Doug Bair | .12 | .06 |
| 450 George Brett | 11.00 | 5.50 |
| 451 Indians Team (Dave Garcia) | .50 | .25 |
| 452 Steve Dillard | .12 | .06 |
| 453 Mike Bacsik | .12 | .06 |
| 454 Tom Donohue | .12 | .06 |
| 455 Mike Torrez | .20 | .10 |
| 456 Frank Taveras | .12 | .06 |
| 457 Bert Blyleven | .50 | .25 |
| 458 Billy Sample | .12 | .06 |
| 459 Mickey Lolich | .12 | .06 |
| 460 Willie Randolph | .25 | .13 |
| 461 Dwayne Murphy | .20 | .10 |
| 462 Mike Sadek | .12 | .06 |
| 463 Jerry Royster | .12 | .06 |
| 464 John Denny | .12 | .06 |
| 465 Rick Monday | .20 | .10 |
| 466 Mike Squires | .12 | .06 |
| 467 Jesse Jefferson | .12 | .06 |
| 468 Aurelio Rodriguez | .20 | .10 |
| 469 Randy Niemann | .12 | .06 |
| 470 Bob Boone | .20 | .10 |
| 471 Hosken Powell | .12 | .06 |
| 472 Willie Hernandez | .20 | .10 |
| 473 Bump Wills | .12 | .06 |
| 474 Steve Busby | .12 | .06 |
| 475 Cesar Geronimo | .12 | .06 |
| 476 Bob Shirley | .12 | .06 |
| 477 Buck Martinez | .12 | .06 |
| 478 Gil Flores | .12 | .06 |
| 479 Expos Team (Dick Williams) | .50 | .25 |
| 480 Bob Watson | .20 | .10 |
| 481 Tom Paciorek | .12 | .06 |
| 482 *Rickey Henderson* | 100.00 | 50.00 |
| 483 Bo Diaz | .20 | .10 |
| 484 Checklist 364-484 | .50 | .25 |
| 485 Mickey Rivers | .20 | .10 |
| 486 Mike Tyson | .12 | .06 |
| 487 Wayne Nordhagen | .12 | .06 |
| 488 Roy Howell | .12 | .06 |
| 489 Preston Hanna | .12 | .06 |
| 490 Lee May | .20 | .10 |
| 491 Steve Mura | .12 | .06 |
| 492 Todd Cruz | .12 | .06 |
| 493 Jerry Martin | .12 | .06 |
| 494 Craig Minetto | .12 | .06 |
| 495 Bake McBride | .12 | .06 |
| 496 Silvio Martinez | .12 | .06 |
| 497 Jim Mason | .12 | .06 |
| 498 Danny Darwin | .20 | .10 |

| | | NR MT | EX |
|---|---|---|---|
| 499 | Giants Team (Dave Bristol) | .50 | .25 |
| 500 | Tom Seaver | 3.00 | 1.50 |
| 501 | Rennie Stennett | .12 | .06 |
| 502 | Rich Wortham | .12 | .06 |
| 503 | Mike Cubbage | .12 | .06 |
| 504 | Gene Garber | .12 | .06 |
| 505 | Bert Campaneris | .20 | .10 |
| 506 | Tom Buskey | .12 | .06 |
| 507 | Leon Roberts | .12 | .06 |
| 508 | U.L. Washington | .12 | .06 |
| 509 | Ed Glynn | .12 | .06 |
| 510 | Ron Cey | .25 | .13 |
| 511 | Eric Wilkins | .12 | .06 |
| 512 | Jose Cardenal | .12 | .06 |
| 513 | Tom Dixon | .12 | .06 |
| 514 | Steve Ontiveros | .12 | .06 |
| 515 | Mike Caldwell | .12 | .06 |
| 516 | Hector Cruz | .12 | .06 |
| 517 | Don Stanhouse | .12 | .06 |
| 518 | Nelson Norman | .12 | .06 |
| 519 | Steve Nicosia | .12 | .06 |
| 520 | Steve Rogers | .20 | .10 |
| 521 | Ken Brett | .12 | .06 |
| 522 | Jim Morrison | .12 | .06 |
| 523 | Ken Henderson | .12 | .06 |
| 524 | Jim Wright | .12 | .06 |
| 525 | Clint Hurdle | .12 | .06 |
| 526 | Phillies Team (Dallas Green) | .70 | .35 |
| 527 | Doug Rau | .12 | .06 |
| 528 | Adrian Devine | .12 | .06 |
| 529 | Jim Barr | .12 | .06 |
| 530 | Jim Sundberg | .12 | .06 |
| 531 | Eric Rasmussen | .12 | .06 |
| 532 | Willie Horton | .20 | .10 |
| 533 | Checklist 485-605 | .50 | .25 |
| 534 | Andre Thornton | .25 | .13 |
| 535 | Bob Forsch | .20 | .10 |
| 536 | Lee Lacy | .12 | .06 |
| 537 | *Alex Trevino* | .20 | .10 |
| 538 | Joe Strain | .12 | .06 |
| 539 | Rudy May | .12 | .06 |
| 540 | Pete Rose | 4.00 | 2.00 |
| 541 | Miguel Dilone | .12 | .06 |
| 542 | Joe Coleman | .12 | .06 |
| 543 | Pat Kelly | .12 | .06 |
| 544 | *Rick Sutcliffe* | 3.00 | 1.50 |
| 545 | Jeff Burroughs | .20 | .10 |
| 546 | Rick Langford | .12 | .06 |
| 547 | John Wathan | .20 | .10 |
| 548 | Dave Rajsich | .12 | .06 |
| 549 | Larry Wolfe | .12 | .06 |
| 550 | Ken Griffey | .25 | .13 |
| 551 | Pirates Team (Chuck Tanner) | .50 | .25 |
| 552 | Bill Nahorodny | .12 | .06 |
| 553 | Dick Davis | .12 | .06 |
| 554 | Art Howe | .12 | .06 |
| 555 | Ed Figueroa | .20 | .10 |
| 556 | Joe Rudi | .20 | .10 |
| 557 | Mark Lee | .12 | .06 |
| 558 | Alfredo Griffin | .25 | .13 |
| 559 | Dale Murray | .12 | .06 |
| 560 | Dave Lopes | .25 | .13 |
| 561 | Eddie Whitson | .20 | .10 |
| 562 | Joe Wallis | .12 | .06 |

| | | NR MT | EX |
|---|---|---|---|
| 563 | Will McEnaney | .12 | .06 |
| 564 | Rick Manning | .12 | .06 |
| 565 | Dennis Leonard | .20 | .10 |
| 566 | Bud Harrelson | .20 | .10 |
| 567 | Skip Lockwood | .12 | .06 |
| 568 | *Gary Roenicke* | .25 | .13 |
| 569 | Terry Kennedy | .25 | .13 |
| 570 | Roy Smalley | .20 | .10 |
| 571 | Joe Sambito | .12 | .06 |
| 572 | Jerry Morales | .12 | .06 |
| 573 | Kent Tekulve | .20 | .10 |
| 574 | Scot Thompson | .12 | .06 |
| 575 | Ken Kravec | .12 | .06 |
| 576 | Jim Dwyer | .12 | .06 |
| 577 | Blue Jays Team (Bobby Mattick) | .50 | .25 |
| 578 | Scott Sanderson | .20 | .10 |
| 579 | Charlie Moore | .12 | .06 |
| 580 | Nolan Ryan | 20.00 | 10.00 |
| 581 | Bob Bailor | .12 | .06 |
| 582 | Brian Doyle | .20 | .10 |
| 583 | Bob Stinson | .12 | .06 |
| 584 | Kurt Bevacqua | .12 | .06 |
| 585 | Al Hrabosky | .20 | .10 |
| 586 | Mitchell Page | .12 | .06 |
| 587 | Garry Templeton | .20 | .10 |
| 588 | Greg Minton | .12 | .06 |
| 589 | Chet Lemon | .20 | .10 |
| 590 | Jim Palmer | 3.00 | 1.50 |
| 591 | Rick Cerone | .12 | .06 |
| 592 | Jon Matlack | .20 | .10 |
| 593 | Jesus Alou | .12 | .06 |
| 594 | Dick Tidrow | .12 | .06 |
| 595 | Don Money | .12 | .06 |
| 596 | Rick Matula | .12 | .06 |
| 597 | Tom Poquette | .12 | .06 |
| 598 | Fred Kendall | .12 | .06 |
| 599 | Mike Norris | .12 | .06 |
| 600 | Reggie Jackson | 8.00 | 4.00 |
| 601 | Buddy Schultz | .12 | .06 |
| 602 | Brian Downing | .20 | .10 |
| 603 | Jack Billingham | .12 | .06 |
| 604 | Glenn Adams | .12 | .06 |
| 605 | Terry Forster | .20 | .10 |
| 606 | Reds Team (John McNamara) | .50 | .25 |
| 607 | Woodie Fryman | .20 | .10 |
| 608 | Alan Bannister | .12 | .06 |
| 609 | Ron Reed | .20 | .10 |
| 610 | Willie Stargell | 1.50 | .70 |
| 611 | Jerry Garvin | .12 | .06 |
| 612 | Cliff Johnson | .12 | .06 |
| 613 | Randy Stein | .12 | .06 |
| 614 | John Hiller | .20 | .10 |
| 615 | Doug DeCinces | .20 | .10 |
| 616 | Gene Richards | .12 | .06 |
| 617 | Joaquin Andujar | .20 | .10 |
| 618 | Bob Montgomery | .12 | .06 |
| 619 | Sergio Ferrer | .12 | .06 |
| 620 | Richie Zisk | .20 | .10 |
| 621 | Bob Grich | .20 | .10 |
| 622 | Mario Soto | .20 | .10 |
| 623 | Gorman Thomas | .20 | .10 |
| 624 | Lerrin LaGrow | .12 | .06 |
| 625 | Chris Chambliss | .25 | .13 |
| 626 | Tigers Team (Sparky Anderson) | .60 | .30 |

| | | NR MT | EX |
|---|---|---|---|
| 627 | Pedro Borbon | .12 | .06 |
| 628 | Doug Capilla | .12 | .06 |
| 629 | Jim Todd | .12 | .06 |
| 630 | Larry Bowa | .25 | .13 |
| 631 | Mark Littell | .12 | .06 |
| 632 | Barry Bonnell | .12 | .06 |
| 633 | Bob Apodaca | .12 | .06 |
| 634 | Glenn Borgmann | .12 | .06 |
| 635 | John Candelaria | .20 | .10 |
| 636 | Toby Harrah | .20 | .10 |
| 637 | Joe Simpson | .12 | .06 |
| 638 | *Mark Clear* | .20 | .10 |
| 639 | Larry Biittner | .12 | .06 |
| 640 | Mike Flanagan | .25 | .13 |
| 641 | Ed Kranepool | .20 | .10 |
| 642 | Ken Forsch | .12 | .06 |
| 643 | John Mayberry | .20 | .10 |
| 644 | Charlie Hough | .20 | .10 |
| 645 | Rick Burleson | .20 | .10 |
| 646 | Checklist 606-726 | .50 | .25 |
| 647 | Milt May | .12 | .06 |
| 648 | Roy White | .20 | .10 |
| 649 | Tom Griffin | .12 | .06 |
| 650 | Joe Morgan | 3.00 | 1.50 |
| 651 | Rollie Fingers | 1.00 | .50 |
| 652 | Mario Mendoza | .12 | .06 |
| 653 | Stan Bahnsen | .12 | .06 |
| 654 | Bruce Boisclair | .12 | .06 |
| 655 | Tug McGraw | .25 | .13 |
| 656 | Larvell Blanks | .12 | .06 |
| 657 | Dave Edwards | .12 | .06 |
| 658 | Chris Knapp | .12 | .06 |
| 659 | Brewers Team (George Bamberger) | .50 | .25 |
| 660 | Rusty Staub | .30 | .15 |
| 661 | Orioles Future Stars (Mark Corey, Dave Ford, Wayne Krenchicki) | .12 | .06 |
| 662 | Red Sox Future Stars (Joel Finch, Mike O'Berry, Chuck Rainey) | .12 | .06 |
| 663 | Angels Future Stars (Ralph Botting, Bob Clark, *Dickie Thon*) | .30 | .15 |
| 664 | White Sox Future Stars (Mike Colbern, *Guy Hoffman*, Dewey Robinson) | .20 | .10 |
| 665 | Indians Future Stars (Larry Andersen, Bobby Cuellar, Sandy Wihtol) | .12 | .06 |
| 666 | Tigers Future Stars (Mike Chris, Al Greene, Bruce Robbins) | .12 | .06 |
| 667 | Royals Future Stars (Renie Martin, Bill Paschall, *Dan Quisenberry*) | 1.00 | .50 |
| 668 | Brewers Future Stars (Danny Boitano, Willie Mueller, Lenn Sakata) | .12 | .06 |
| 669 | Twins Future Stars (Dan Graham, Rick Sofield, *Gary Ward*) | .35 | .20 |
| 670 | Yankees Future Stars (Bobby Brown, Brad Gulden, Darryl Jones) | .20 | .10 |
| 671 | A's Future Stars (Derek Bryant, Brian Kingman, *Mike Morgan*) | 2.00 | 1.00 |
| 672 | Mariners Future Stars (Charlie Beamon, Rodney Craig, Rafael Vasquez) | .12 | .06 |
| 673 | Rangers Future Stars (Brian Allard, Jerry Don Gleaton, Greg Mahlberg) | .12 | .06 |
| 674 | Blue Jays Future Stars (Butch Edge, Pat Kelly, Ted Wilborn) | .12 | .06 |
| 675 | Braves Future Stars (Bruce Benedict, Larry Bradford, Eddie Miller) | .12 | .06 |
| 676 | Cubs Future Stars (Dave Geisel, Steve Macko, Karl Pagel) | .12 | .06 |
| 677 | Reds Future Stars (Art DeFreites, *Frank Pastore*, Harry Spilman) | .12 | .06 |
| 678 | Astros Future Stars (Reggie Baldwin, Alan Knicely, *Pete Ladd*) | .12 | .06 |
| 679 | Dodgers Future Stars (Joe Beckwith, *Mickey Hatcher*, Dave Patterson) | .50 | .25 |
| 680 | Expos Future Stars (*Tony Bernazard*, Randy Miller, John Tamargo) | .20 | .10 |
| 681 | Mets Future Stars (Dan Norman, *Jesse Orosco*, *Mike Scott*) | 3.00 | 1.50 |
| 682 | Phillies Future Stars (Ramon Aviles, *Dickie Noles*, Kevin Saucier) | .20 | .10 |
| 683 | Pirates Future Stars (Dorian Boyland, Alberto Lois, Harry Saferight) | .12 | .06 |
| 684 | Cardinals Future Stars (George Frazier, *Tom Herr*, Dan O'Brien) | 1.50 | .70 |
| 685 | Padres Future Stars (Tim Flannery, Brian Greer, Jim Wilhelm) | .12 | .06 |
| 686 | Giants Future Stars (Greg Johnston, Dennis Littlejohn, Phil Nastu) | .12 | .06 |
| 687 | Mike Heath | .12 | .06 |
| 688 | Steve Stone | .20 | .10 |
| 689 | Red Sox Team (Don Zimmer) | .60 | .30 |
| 690 | Tommy John | .60 | .30 |
| 691 | Ivan DeJesus | .12 | .06 |
| 692 | Rawly Eastwick | .12 | .06 |
| 693 | Craig Kusick | .12 | .06 |
| 694 | Jim Rooker | .12 | .06 |
| 695 | Reggie Smith | .20 | .10 |
| 696 | Julio Gonzalez | .12 | .06 |
| 697 | David Clyde | .12 | .06 |
| 698 | Oscar Gamble | .20 | .10 |
| 699 | Floyd Bannister | .20 | .10 |
| 700 | Rod Carew | 2.00 | 1.00 |
| 701 | *Ken Oberkfell* | .30 | .15 |
| 702 | Ed Farmer | .12 | .06 |
| 703 | Otto Velez | .12 | .06 |

|     |               | NR MT | EX  |
|-----|---------------|-------|-----|
| 704 | Gene Tenace   | .20   | .10 |
| 705 | Freddie Patek | .12   | .06 |
| 706 | Tippy Martinez | .12  | .06 |
| 707 | Elliott Maddox | .12  | .06 |
| 708 | Bob Tolan     | .12   | .06 |
| 709 | Pat Underwood | .12   | .06 |
| 710 | Graig Nettles | .35   | .20 |
| 711 | Bob Galasso   | .12   | .06 |
| 712 | Rodney Scott  | .12   | .06 |
| 713 | Terry Whitfield | .12 | .06 |
| 714 | Fred Norman   | .12   | .06 |
| 715 | Sal Bando     | .20   | .10 |
| 716 | Lynn McGlothen | .12  | .06 |
| 717 | Mickey Klutts | .12   | .06 |
| 718 | Greg Gross    | .12   | .06 |
| 719 | Don Robinson  | .20   | .10 |
| 720 | Carl Yastrzemski | 1.50 | .70 |
| 721 | Paul Hartzell | .12   | .06 |
| 722 | Jose Cruz     | .20   | .10 |
| 723 | Shane Rawley  | .20   | .10 |
| 724 | Jerry White   | .12   | .06 |
| 725 | Rick Wise     | .20   | .10 |
| 726 | Steve Yeager  | .20   | .06 |

## 1981 Topps

This is another 726-card set of 2-1/2" by 3-1/2" cards from Topps. The cards have the usual color photo with all cards from the same team sharing the same color borders. The player's name appears under the photo with his team and position appearing on a baseball cap at the lower left. The Topps logo returned in a small baseball in the lower right corner. Card backs include the usual stats along with a headline and a cartoon if there was room. Specialty cards include previous season record-breakers, highlights of the playoffs and World Series, along with the final appearance of team cards.

|               | MT     | NR MT |
|---------------|--------|-------|
| Complete Set: | 100.00 | 75.00 |
| Common Player: | .08   | .06   |

|     |                 | MT   | NR MT |
|-----|-----------------|------|-------|
| 1   | Batting Leaders (George Brett, Bill Buckner) | 2.00 | 1.50 |
| 2   | Home Run Leaders (Reggie Jackson, Ben Oglivie, Mike Schmidt) | .40 | .30 |
| 3   | Runs Batted In Leaders (Cecil Cooper, Mike Schmidt) | .30 | .25 |
| 4   | Stolen Base Leaders (Rickey Henderson, Ron LeFlore) | 1.50 | 1.25 |
| 5   | Victory Leaders (Steve Carlton, Steve Stone) | .20 | .15 |
| 6   | Strikeout Leaders (Len Barker, Steve Carlton) | .20 | .15 |
| 7   | Earned Run Avg. Leaders (Rudy May, Don Sutton) | .15 | .11 |
| 8   | Leading Firemen (Rollie Fingers, Tom Hume, Dan Quisenberry) | .10 | .08 |
| 9   | Pete LaCock     | .08  | .06 |
| 10  | Mike Flanagan   | .12  | .09 |
| 11  | Jim Wohlford    | .08  | .06 |
| 12  | Mark Clear      | .08  | .06 |
| 13  | *Joe Charboneau* | .15 | .11 |
| 14  | *John Tudor*    | .40  | .30 |
| 15  | Larry Parrish   | .15  | .11 |
| 16  | Ron Davis       | .10  | .08 |
| 17  | Cliff Johnson   | .08  | .06 |
| 18  | Glenn Adams     | .08  | .06 |
| 19  | Jim Clancy      | .12  | .09 |
| 20  | Jeff Burroughs  | .10  | .08 |
| 21  | Ron Oester      | .08  | .06 |
| 22  | Danny Darwin    | .08  | .06 |
| 23  | Alex Trevino    | .08  | .06 |
| 24  | Don Stanhouse   | .08  | .06 |
| 25  | Sixto Lezcano   | .08  | .06 |
| 26  | U.L. Washington | .08  | .06 |
| 27  | Champ Summers   | .08  | .06 |
| 28  | Enrique Romo    | .08  | .06 |
| 29  | Gene Tenace     | .10  | .08 |
| 30  | Jack Clark      | .50  | .40 |
| 31  | Checklist 1-121 | .08  | .06 |
| 32  | Ken Oberkfell   | .08  | .06 |
| 33  | Rick Honeycutt  | .08  | .06 |
| 34  | Aurelio Rodriguez | .10 | .08 |
| 35  | Mitchell Page   | .08  | .06 |
| 36  | Ed Farmer       | .08  | .06 |
| 37  | Gary Roenicke   | .08  | .06 |
| 38  | Win Remmerswaal | .08  | .06 |
| 39  | Tom Veryzer     | .08  | .06 |
| 40  | Tug McGraw      | .20  | .15 |
| 41  | Rangers Future Stars (Bob Babcock, John Butcher, Jerry Don Gleaton) | .10 | .08 |
| 42  | Jerry White     | .08  | .06 |
| 43  | Jose Morales    | .08  | .06 |
| 44  | Larry McWilliams | .08 | .06 |
| 45  | Enos Cabell     | .08  | .06 |
| 46  | Rick Bosetti    | .08  | .06 |
| 47  | Ken Brett       | .10  | .08 |
| 48  | Dave Skaggs     | .08  | .06 |
| 49  | Bob Shirley     | .08  | .06 |
| 50  | Dave Lopes      | .12  | .09 |
| 51  | Bill Robinson   | .08  | .06 |

| | | MT | NR MT |
|---|---|---|---|
| 52 | Hector Cruz | .08 | .06 |
| 53 | Kevin Saucier | .08 | .06 |
| 54 | Ivan DeJesus | .08 | .06 |
| 55 | Mike Norris | .08 | .06 |
| 56 | Buck Martinez | .08 | .06 |
| 57 | Dave Roberts | .08 | .06 |
| 58 | Joel Youngblood | .08 | .06 |
| 59 | Dan Petry | .12 | .09 |
| 60 | Willie Randolph | .15 | .11 |
| 61 | Butch Wynegar | .08 | .06 |
| 62 | Joe Pettini | .08 | .06 |
| 63 | Steve Renko | .08 | .06 |
| 64 | Brian Asselstine | .08 | .06 |
| 65 | Scott McGregor | .10 | .08 |
| 66 | Royals Future Stars | | |
| | (Manny Castillo, Tim | | |
| | Ireland, Mike Jones) | .08 | .06 |
| 67 | Ken Kravec | .08 | .06 |
| 68 | Matt Alexander | .08 | .06 |
| 69 | Ed Halicki | .08 | .06 |
| 70 | Al Oliver | .15 | .11 |
| 71 | Hal Dues | .08 | .06 |
| 72 | Barry Evans | .08 | .06 |
| 73 | Doug Bair | .08 | .06 |
| 74 | Mike Hargrove | .08 | .06 |
| 75 | Reggie Smith | .15 | .11 |
| 76 | Mario Mendoza | .08 | .06 |
| 77 | Mike Barlow | .08 | .06 |
| 78 | Steve Dillard | .08 | .06 |
| 79 | Bruce Robbins | .08 | .06 |
| 80 | Rusty Staub | .15 | .11 |
| 81 | Dave Stapleton | .08 | .06 |
| 82 | Astros Future Stars | | |
| | (Danny Heep, Alan Knicely, | | |
| | Bobby Sprowl) | .08 | .06 |
| 83 | Mike Proly | .08 | .06 |
| 84 | Johnnie LeMaster | .08 | .06 |
| 85 | Mike Caldwell | .08 | .06 |
| 86 | Wayne Gross | .08 | .06 |
| 87 | Rick Camp | .08 | .06 |
| 88 | Joe Lefebvre | .08 | .06 |
| 89 | Darrell Jackson | .08 | .06 |
| 90 | Bake McBride | .08 | .06 |
| 91 | Tim Stoddard | .08 | .06 |
| 92 | Mike Easler | .10 | .08 |
| 93 | Ed Glynn | .08 | .06 |
| 94 | Harry Spilman | .08 | .06 |
| 95 | Jim Sundberg | .10 | .08 |
| 96 | A's Future Stars (Dave | | |
| | Beard, *Ernie Camacho*, Pat | | |
| | Dempsey) | .12 | .09 |
| 97 | Chris Speier | .08 | .06 |
| 98 | Clint Hurdle | .08 | .06 |
| 99 | Eric Wilkins | .08 | .06 |
| 100 | Rod Carew | 3.00 | 2.25 |
| 101 | Benny Ayala | .08 | .06 |
| 102 | Dave Tobik | .08 | .06 |
| 103 | Jerry Martin | .08 | .06 |
| 104 | Terry Forster | .10 | .08 |
| 105 | Jose Cruz | .15 | .11 |
| 106 | Don Money | .08 | .06 |
| 107 | Rich Wortham | .08 | .06 |
| 108 | Bruce Benedict | .08 | .06 |
| 109 | Mike Scott | .80 | .60 |
| 110 | Carl Yastrzemski | 2.00 | 1.50 |
| 111 | Greg Minton | .08 | .06 |
| 112 | White Sox Future Stars | | |

| | | MT | NR MT |
|---|---|---|---|
| | (Rusty Kuntz, Fran Mullins, | | |
| | Leo Sutherland) | .08 | .06 |
| 113 | Mike Phillips | .08 | .06 |
| 114 | Tom Underwood | .08 | .06 |
| 115 | Roy Smalley | .08 | .06 |
| 116 | Joe Simpson | .08 | .06 |
| 117 | Pete Falcone | .08 | .06 |
| 118 | Kurt Bevacqua | .08 | .06 |
| 119 | Tippy Martinez | .08 | .06 |
| 120 | Larry Bowa | .20 | .15 |
| 121 | Larry Harlow | .08 | .06 |
| 122 | John Denny | .08 | .06 |
| 123 | Al Cowens | .08 | .06 |
| 124 | Jerry Garvin | .08 | .06 |
| 125 | Andre Dawson | 3.00 | 2.25 |
| 126 | *Charlie Leibrandt* | .50 | .40 |
| 127 | Rudy Law | .08 | .06 |
| 128 | Gary Allenson | .08 | .06 |
| 129 | Art Howe | .08 | .06 |
| 130 | Larry Gura | .08 | .06 |
| 131 | *Keith Moreland* | .35 | .25 |
| 132 | Tommy Boggs | .08 | .06 |
| 133 | Jeff Cox | .08 | .06 |
| 134 | Steve Mura | .08 | .06 |
| 135 | Gorman Thomas | .12 | .09 |
| 136 | Doug Capilla | .08 | .06 |
| 137 | Hosken Powell | .08 | .06 |
| 138 | *Rich Dotson* | .20 | .15 |
| 139 | Oscar Gamble | .10 | .08 |
| 140 | Bob Forsch | .10 | .08 |
| 141 | Miguel Dilone | .08 | .06 |
| 142 | Jackson Todd | .08 | .06 |
| 143 | Dan Meyer | .08 | .06 |
| 144 | Allen Ripley | .08 | .06 |
| 145 | Mickey Rivers | .10 | .08 |
| 146 | Bobby Castillo | .08 | .06 |
| 147 | Dale Berra | .08 | .06 |
| 148 | Randy Niemann | .08 | .06 |
| 149 | Joe Nolan | .08 | .06 |
| 150 | Mark Fidrych | .12 | .09 |
| 151 | Claudell Washington | .12 | .09 |
| 152 | John Urrea | .08 | .06 |
| 153 | Tom Poquette | .08 | .06 |
| 154 | Rick Langford | .08 | .06 |
| 155 | Chris Chambliss | .12 | .09 |
| 156 | Bob McClure | .08 | .06 |
| 157 | John Wathan | .12 | .09 |
| 158 | Fergie Jenkins | 1.00 | .70 |
| 159 | Brian Doyle | .08 | .06 |
| 160 | Garry Maddox | .12 | .09 |
| 161 | Dan Graham | .08 | .06 |
| 162 | Doug Corbett | .08 | .06 |
| 163 | Billy Almon | .08 | .06 |
| 164 | *Lamarr Hoyt (LaMarr)* | | |
| | | .20 | .15 |
| 165 | Tony Scott | .08 | .06 |
| 166 | Floyd Bannister | .12 | .09 |
| 167 | Terry Whitfield | .08 | .06 |
| 168 | Don Robinson | .08 | .06 |
| 169 | John Mayberry | .10 | .08 |
| 170 | Ross Grimsley | .08 | .06 |
| 171 | Gene Richards | .08 | .06 |
| 172 | Gary Woods | .08 | .06 |
| 173 | Bump Wills | .08 | .06 |
| 174 | Doug Rau | .08 | .06 |
| 175 | Dave Collins | .10 | .08 |
| 176 | Mike Krukow | .10 | .08 |

| | | MT | NR MT |
|---|---|---|---|
| 177 | Rick Peters | .08 | .06 |
| 178 | Jim Essian | .08 | .06 |
| 179 | Rudy May | .08 | .06 |
| 180 | Pete Rose | 3.00 | 2.25 |
| 181 | Elias Sosa | .08 | .06 |
| 182 | Bob Grich | .15 | .11 |
| 183 | Dick Davis | .08 | .06 |
| 184 | Jim Dwyer | .08 | .06 |
| 185 | Dennis Leonard | .10 | .08 |
| 186 | Wayne Nordhagen | .08 | .06 |
| 187 | Mike Parrott | .08 | .06 |
| 188 | Doug DeCinces | .15 | .11 |
| 189 | Craig Swan | .08 | .06 |
| 190 | Cesar Cedeno | .15 | .11 |
| 191 | Rick Sutcliffe | .40 | .30 |
| 192 | Braves Future Stars (Terry Harper, Ed Miller, Rafael Ramirez) | .25 | .20 |
| 193 | Pete Vuckovich | .10 | .08 |
| 194 | Rod Scurry | .10 | .08 |
| 195 | Rich Murray | .08 | .06 |
| 196 | Duffy Dyer | .08 | .06 |
| 197 | Jim Kern | .08 | .06 |
| 198 | Jerry Dybzinski | .08 | .06 |
| 199 | Chuck Rainey | .08 | .06 |
| 200 | George Foster | .25 | .20 |
| 201 | Record Breaker (Johnny Bench) | .40 | .30 |
| 202 | Record Breaker (Steve Carlton) | .40 | .30 |
| 203 | Record Breaker (Bill Gullickson) | .08 | .06 |
| 204 | Record Breaker (Ron LeFlore, Rodney Scott) | .10 | .08 |
| 205 | Record Breaker (Pete Rose) | .80 | .60 |
| 206 | Record Breaker (Mike Schmidt) | .80 | .60 |
| 207 | Record Breaker (Ozzie Smith) | .20 | .15 |
| 208 | Record Breaker (Willie Wilson) | .20 | .15 |
| 209 | Dickie Thon | .10 | .08 |
| 210 | Jim Palmer | 2.00 | 1.50 |
| 211 | Derrel Thomas | .08 | .06 |
| 212 | Steve Nicosia | .08 | .06 |
| 213 | Al Holland | .10 | .08 |
| 214 | Angels Future Stars (Ralph Botting, Jim Dorsey, John Harris) | .08 | .06 |
| 215 | Larry Hisle | .10 | .08 |
| 216 | John Henry Johnson | .08 | .06 |
| 217 | Rich Hebner | .08 | .06 |
| 218 | Paul Splittorff | .08 | .06 |
| 219 | Ken Landreaux | .08 | .06 |
| 220 | Tom Seaver | 3.00 | 2.25 |
| 221 | Bob Davis | .08 | .06 |
| 222 | Jorge Orta | .08 | .06 |
| 223 | Roy Lee Jackson | .08 | .06 |
| 224 | Pat Zachry | .08 | .06 |
| 225 | Ruppert Jones | .08 | .06 |
| 226 | Manny Sanguillen | .08 | .06 |
| 227 | Fred Martinez | .08 | .06 |
| 228 | Tom Paciorek | .08 | .06 |
| 229 | Rollie Fingers | 1.00 | .70 |
| 230 | George Hendrick | .10 | .08 |

| | | MT | NR MT |
|---|---|---|---|
| 231 | Joe Beckwith | .08 | .06 |
| 232 | Mickey Klutts | .08 | .06 |
| 233 | Skip Lockwood | .08 | .06 |
| 234 | Lou Whitaker | .60 | .45 |
| 235 | Scott Sanderson | .08 | .06 |
| 236 | Mike Ivie | .08 | .06 |
| 237 | Charlie Moore | .08 | .06 |
| 238 | Willie Hernandez | .12 | .09 |
| 239 | Rick Miller | .08 | .06 |
| 240 | Nolan Ryan | 10.00 | 7.50 |
| 241 | Checklist 122-242 | .08 | .06 |
| 242 | Chet Lemon | .10 | .08 |
| 243 | Sal Butera | .08 | .06 |
| 244 | Cardinals Future Stars (Tito Landrum, Al Olmsted, Andy Rincon) | .15 | .11 |
| 245 | Ed Figueroa | .08 | .06 |
| 246 | Ed Ott | .08 | .06 |
| 247 | Glenn Hubbard | .10 | .08 |
| 248 | Joey McLaughlin | .08 | .06 |
| 249 | Larry Cox | .08 | .06 |
| 250 | Ron Guidry | .50 | .40 |
| 251 | Tom Brookens | .10 | .08 |
| 252 | Victor Cruz | .08 | .06 |
| 253 | Dave Bergman | .08 | .06 |
| 254 | Ozzie Smith | 4.00 | 3.00 |
| 255 | Mark Littell | .08 | .06 |
| 256 | Bombo Rivera | .08 | .06 |
| 257 | Rennie Stennett | .08 | .06 |
| 258 | Joe Price | .12 | .09 |
| 259 | Mets Future Stars (Juan Berenguer, Hubie Brooks, Mookie Wilson) | 2.50 | 2.00 |
| 260 | Ron Cey | .15 | .11 |
| 261 | Rickey Henderson | 20.00 | 15.00 |
| 262 | Sammy Stewart | .08 | .06 |
| 263 | Brian Downing | .12 | .09 |
| 264 | Jim Norris | .08 | .06 |
| 265 | John Candelaria | .12 | .09 |
| 266 | Tom Herr | .15 | .11 |
| 267 | Stan Bahnsen | .08 | .06 |
| 268 | Jerry Royster | .08 | .06 |
| 269 | Ken Forsch | .08 | .06 |
| 270 | Greg Luzinski | .20 | .15 |
| 271 | Bill Castro | .08 | .06 |
| 272 | Bruce Kimm | .08 | .06 |
| 273 | Stan Papi | .08 | .06 |
| 274 | Craig Chamberlain | .08 | .06 |
| 275 | Dwight Evans | .25 | .20 |
| 276 | Dan Spillner | .08 | .06 |
| 277 | Alfredo Griffin | .12 | .09 |
| 278 | Rick Sofield | .08 | .06 |
| 279 | Bob Knepper | .12 | .09 |
| 280 | Ken Griffey | .15 | .11 |
| 281 | Fred Stanley | .08 | .06 |
| 282 | Mariners Future Stars (Rick Anderson, Greg Biercevicz, Rodney Craig) | .08 | .06 |
| 283 | Billy Sample | .08 | .06 |
| 284 | Brian Kingman | .08 | .06 |
| 285 | Jerry Turner | .08 | .06 |
| 286 | Dave Frost | .08 | .06 |
| 287 | Lenn Sakata | .08 | .06 |
| 288 | Bob Clark | .08 | .06 |
| 289 | Mickey Hatcher | .10 | .08 |

| | | MT | NR MT |
|---|---|---|---|
| 290 | Bob Boone | .08 | .06 |
| 291 | Aurelio Lopez | .08 | .06 |
| 292 | Mike Squires | .08 | .06 |
| 293 | *Charlie Lea* | .15 | .11 |
| 294 | Mike Tyson | .08 | .06 |
| 295 | Hal McRae | .15 | .11 |
| 296 | Bill Nahorodny | .08 | .06 |
| 297 | Bob Bailor | .08 | .06 |
| 298 | Buddy Solomon | .08 | .06 |
| 299 | Elliott Maddox | .08 | .06 |
| 300 | Paul Molitor | .40 | .30 |
| 301 | Matt Keough | .08 | .06 |
| 302 | Dodgers Future Stars | | |
| | (Jack Perconte, *Mike Scioscia, Fernando Valenzuela*) | 6.00 | 4.50 |
| 303 | Johnny Oates | .08 | .06 |
| 304 | John Castino | .08 | .06 |
| 305 | Ken Clay | .08 | .06 |
| 306 | Juan Beniquez | .08 | .06 |
| 307 | Gene Garber | .08 | .06 |
| 308 | Rick Manning | .08 | .06 |
| 309 | *Luis Salazar* | .20 | .15 |
| 310 | Vida Blue | .08 | .06 |
| 311 | Freddie Patek | .08 | .06 |
| 312 | Rick Rhoden | .12 | .09 |
| 313 | Luis Pujols | .08 | .06 |
| 314 | Rich Dauer | .08 | .06 |
| 315 | *Kirk Gibson* | 3.50 | 2.75 |
| 316 | Craig Minetto | .08 | .06 |
| 317 | Lonnie Smith | .10 | .08 |
| 318 | Steve Yeager | .08 | .06 |
| 319 | Rowland Office | .08 | .06 |
| 320 | Tom Burgmeier | .08 | .06 |
| 321 | *Leon Durham* | .25 | .20 |
| 322 | Neil Allen | .10 | .08 |
| 323 | Jim Morrison | .08 | .06 |
| 324 | Mike Willis | .08 | .06 |
| 325 | Ray Knight | .12 | .09 |
| 326 | Biff Pocoroba | .08 | .06 |
| 327 | Moose Haas | .08 | .06 |
| 328 | Twins Future Stars | | |
| | (*Dave Engle*, Greg Johnston, Gary Ward) | .12 | .09 |
| 329 | Joaquin Andujar | .12 | .09 |
| 330 | Frank White | .12 | .09 |
| 331 | Dennis Lamp | .08 | .06 |
| 332 | Lee Lacy | .08 | .06 |
| 333 | Sid Monge | .08 | .06 |
| 334 | Dane Iorg | .08 | .06 |
| 335 | Rick Cerone | .08 | .06 |
| 336 | Eddie Whitson | .08 | .06 |
| 337 | Lynn Jones | .08 | .06 |
| 338 | Checklist 243-363 | .25 | .20 |
| 339 | John Ellis | .08 | .06 |
| 340 | Bruce Kison | .08 | .06 |
| 341 | Dwayne Murphy | .10 | .08 |
| 342 | Eric Rasmussen | .08 | .06 |
| 343 | Frank Taveras | .08 | .06 |
| 344 | Byron McLaughlin | .08 | .06 |
| 345 | Warren Cromartie | .08 | .06 |
| 346 | Larry Christenson | .08 | .06 |
| 347 | *Harold Baines* | 5.00 | 3.75 |
| 348 | Bob Sykes | .08 | .06 |
| 349 | Glenn Hoffman | .08 | .06 |
| 350 | J.R. Richard | .12 | .09 |
| 351 | Otto Velez | .08 | .06 |

| | | MT | NR MT |
|---|---|---|---|
| 352 | Dick Tidrow | .08 | .06 |
| 353 | Terry Kennedy | .12 | .09 |
| 354 | Mario Soto | .10 | .08 |
| 355 | Bob Horner | .25 | .20 |
| 356 | Padres Future Stars | | |
| | (George Stablein, Craig Stimac, Tom Tellmann) | .08 | .06 |
| 357 | Jim Slaton | .08 | .06 |
| 358 | Mark Wagner | .08 | .06 |
| 359 | Tom Hausman | .08 | .06 |
| 360 | Willie Wilson | .30 | .25 |
| 361 | Joe Strain | .08 | .06 |
| 362 | Bo Diaz | .10 | .08 |
| 363 | Geoff Zahn | .08 | .06 |
| 364 | *Mike Davis* | .25 | .20 |
| 365 | Graig Nettles | .12 | .09 |
| 366 | Mike Ramsey | .08 | .06 |
| 367 | Denny Martinez | .10 | .08 |
| 368 | Leon Roberts | .08 | .06 |
| 369 | Frank Tanana | .12 | .09 |
| 370 | Dave Winfield | 4.00 | 3.00 |
| 371 | Charlie Hough | .15 | .11 |
| 372 | Jay Johnstone | .10 | .08 |
| 373 | Pat Underwood | .08 | .06 |
| 374 | Tom Hutton | .08 | .06 |
| 375 | Dave Concepcion | .20 | .15 |
| 376 | Ron Reed | .08 | .06 |
| 377 | Jerry Morales | .08 | .06 |
| 378 | Dave Rader | .08 | .06 |
| 379 | Lary Sorensen | .08 | .06 |
| 380 | Willie Stargell | 1.00 | .70 |
| 381 | Cubs Future Stars | | |
| | (Carlos Lezcano, Steve Macko, Randy Martz) | .08 | .06 |
| 382 | *Paul Mirabella*(FC) | .12 | .09 |
| 383 | Eric Soderholm | .08 | .06 |
| 384 | Mike Sadek | .08 | .06 |
| 385 | Joe Sambito | .08 | .06 |
| 386 | Dave Edwards | .08 | .06 |
| 387 | Phil Niekro | .80 | .60 |
| 388 | Andre Thornton | .12 | .09 |
| 389 | Marty Pattin | .08 | .06 |
| 390 | Cesar Geronimo | .08 | .06 |
| 391 | Dave Lemanczyk | .08 | .06 |
| 392 | Lance Parrish | .70 | .50 |
| 393 | Broderick Perkins | .08 | .06 |
| 394 | Woodie Fryman | .10 | .08 |
| 395 | Scot Thompson | .08 | .06 |
| 396 | Bill Campbell | .08 | .06 |
| 397 | Julio Cruz | .08 | .06 |
| 398 | Ross Baumgarten | .08 | .06 |
| 399 | Orioles Future Stars | | |
| | (*Mike Boddicker*, Mark Corey, *Floyd Rayford*) | 1.00 | .70 |
| 400 | Reggie Jackson | 3.25 | 2.40 |
| 401 | A.L. Championships | | |
| | (Royals Sweep Yankees) | .50 | .40 |
| 402 | N.L. Championships | | |
| | (Phillies Squeak Past Astros) | .40 | .30 |
| 403 | World Series (Phillies Beat Royals In 6) | .25 | .20 |
| 404 | World Series Summary | | |
| | (Phillies Win First World Series) | .25 | .20 |

| | | MT | NR MT | | | | MT | NR MT |
|---|---|---|---|---|---|---|---|---|
| 405 | Nino Espinosa | .08 | .06 | | 467 | Dave Stieb | .80 | .60 |
| 406 | Dickie Noles | .08 | .06 | | 468 | Johnny Wockenfuss | .08 | .06 |
| 407 | Ernie Whitt | .10 | .08 | | 469 | Jeff Leonard | .20 | .15 |
| 408 | Fernando Arroyo | .08 | .06 | | 470 | Manny Trillo | .10 | .08 |
| 409 | Larry Herndon | .10 | .08 | | 471 | Mike Vail | .08 | .06 |
| 410 | Bert Campaneris | .12 | .09 | | 472 | Dyar Miller | .08 | .06 |
| 411 | Terry Puhl | .08 | .06 | | 473 | Jose Cardenal | .08 | .06 |
| 412 | *Britt Burns* | .12 | .09 | | 474 | Mike LaCoss | .08 | .06 |
| 413 | Tony Bernazard | .08 | .06 | | 475 | Buddy Bell | .15 | .11 |
| 414 | John Pacella | .08 | .06 | | 476 | Jerry Koosman | .15 | .11 |
| 415 | Ben Oglivie | .10 | .08 | | 477 | Luis Gomez | .08 | .06 |
| 416 | Gary Alexander | .08 | .06 | | 478 | Juan Eichelberger | .08 | .06 |
| 417 | Dan Schatzeder | .08 | .06 | | 479 | Expos Future Stars | | |
| 418 | Bobby Brown | .08 | .06 | | | (Bobby Pate, *Tim Raines*, | | |
| 419 | Tom Hume | .08 | .06 | | | Roberto Ramos) | 7.00 | 5.25 |
| 420 | Keith Hernandez | .50 | .40 | | 480 | Carlton Fisk | 3.00 | 2.25 |
| 421 | Bob Stanley | .08 | .06 | | 481 | Bob Lacey | .08 | .06 |
| 422 | Dan Ford | .08 | .06 | | 482 | Jim Gantner | .10 | .08 |
| 423 | Shane Rawley | .15 | .11 | | 483 | Mike Griffin | .08 | .06 |
| 424 | Yankees Future Stars | | | | 484 | Max Venable | .08 | .06 |
| | (Tim Lollar, Bruce | | | | 485 | Garry Templeton | .12 | .09 |
| | Robinson, Dennis Werth) | | | | 486 | Marc Hill | .08 | .06 |
| | | .08 | .06 | | 487 | Dewey Robinson | .08 | .06 |
| 425 | Al Bumbry | .10 | .08 | | 488 | *Damaso Garcia* | .12 | .09 |
| 426 | Warren Brusstar | .08 | .06 | | 489 | John Littlefield (photo | | |
| 427 | John D'Acquisto | .08 | .06 | | | actually Mark Riggins) | .08 | .06 |
| 428 | John Stearns | .08 | .06 | | 490 | Eddie Murray | 4.00 | 3.00 |
| 429 | Mick Kelleher | .08 | .06 | | 491 | Gordy Pladson | .08 | .06 |
| 430 | Jim Bibby | .08 | .06 | | 492 | Barry Foote | .08 | .06 |
| 431 | Dave Roberts | .08 | .06 | | 493 | Dan Quisenberry | .20 | .15 |
| 432 | Len Barker | .10 | .08 | | 494 | *Bob Walk* | .50 | .40 |
| 433 | Rance Mulliniks | .08 | .06 | | 495 | Dusty Baker | .12 | .09 |
| 434 | Roger Erickson | .08 | .06 | | 496 | Paul Dade | .08 | .06 |
| 435 | Jim Spencer | .08 | .06 | | 497 | Fred Norman | .08 | .06 |
| 436 | Gary Lucas | .08 | .06 | | 498 | Pat Putnam | .08 | .06 |
| 437 | Mike Heath | .08 | .06 | | 499 | Frank Pastore | .08 | .06 |
| 438 | John Montefusco | .10 | .08 | | 500 | Jim Rice | 1.00 | .70 |
| 439 | Denny Walling | .08 | .06 | | 501 | Tim Foli | .08 | .06 |
| 440 | Jerry Reuss | .12 | .09 | | 502 | Giants Future Stars | | |
| 441 | Ken Reitz | .08 | .06 | | | (Chris Bourjos, Al | | |
| 442 | Ron Pruitt | .08 | .06 | | | Hargesheimer, Mike | | |
| 443 | Jim Beattie | .08 | .06 | | | Rowland) | .08 | .06 |
| 444 | Garth Iorg | .08 | .06 | | 503 | Steve McCatty | .08 | .06 |
| 445 | Ellis Valentine | .08 | .06 | | 504 | Dale Murphy | 2.50 | 2.00 |
| 446 | Checklist 364-484 | .25 | .20 | | 505 | Jason Thompson | .08 | .06 |
| 447 | Junior Kennedy | .08 | .06 | | 506 | Phil Huffman | .08 | .06 |
| 448 | Tim Corcoran | .08 | .06 | | 507 | Jamie Quirk | .08 | .06 |
| 449 | Paul Mitchell | .08 | .06 | | 508 | Rob Dressler | .08 | .06 |
| 450 | Dave Kingman | .10 | .08 | | 509 | Pete Mackanin | .08 | .06 |
| 451 | Indians Future Stars | | | | 510 | Lee Mazzilli | .10 | .08 |
| | (Chris Bando, Tom | | | | 511 | Wayne Garland | .08 | .06 |
| | Brennan, Sandy Wihtol) | .12 | .09 | | 512 | Gary Thomasson | .08 | .06 |
| 452 | Renie Martin | .08 | .06 | | 513 | Frank LaCorte | .08 | .06 |
| 453 | Rob Wilfong | .08 | .06 | | 514 | George Riley | .08 | .06 |
| 454 | Andy Hassler | .08 | .06 | | 515 | Robin Yount | 6.00 | 4.50 |
| 455 | Rick Burleson | .10 | .08 | | 516 | Doug Bird | .08 | .06 |
| 456 | *Jeff Reardon* | 10.00 | 7.50 | | 517 | Richie Zisk | .10 | .08 |
| 457 | Mike Lum | .08 | .06 | | 518 | Grant Jackson | .08 | .06 |
| 458 | Randy Jones | .10 | .08 | | 519 | John Tamargo | .08 | .06 |
| 459 | Greg Gross | .08 | .06 | | 520 | Steve Stone | .12 | .09 |
| 460 | Rich Gossage | .40 | .30 | | 521 | Sam Mejias | .08 | .06 |
| 461 | Dave McKay | .08 | .06 | | 522 | Mike Colbern | .08 | .06 |
| 462 | Jack Brohamer | .08 | .06 | | 523 | John Fulgham | .08 | .06 |
| 463 | Milt May | .08 | .06 | | 524 | Willie Aikens | .08 | .06 |
| 464 | Adrian Devine | .08 | .06 | | 525 | Mike Torrez | .10 | .08 |
| 465 | Bill Russell | .12 | .09 | | 526 | Phillies Future Stars | | |
| 466 | Bob Molinaro | .08 | .06 | | | (Marty Bystrom, Jay | | |

| | | MT | NR MT |
|---|---|---|---|
| | Loviglio, Jim Wright) | .08 | .06 |
| 527 | Danny Goodwin | .08 | .06 |
| 528 | Gary Matthews | .12 | .09 |
| 529 | Dave LaRoche | .08 | .06 |
| 530 | Steve Garvey | 1.25 | .90 |
| 531 | John Curtis | .08 | .06 |
| 532 | Bill Stein | .08 | .06 |
| 533 | Jesus Figueroa | .08 | .06 |
| 534 | *Dave Smith* | .60 | .45 |
| 535 | Omar Moreno | .08 | .06 |
| 536 | Bob Owchinko | .08 | .06 |
| 537 | Ron Hodges | .08 | .06 |
| 538 | Tom Griffin | .08 | .06 |
| 539 | Rodney Scott | .08 | .06 |
| 540 | Mike Schmidt | 4.00 | 3.00 |
| 541 | Steve Swisher | .08 | .06 |
| 542 | Larry Bradford | .08 | .06 |
| 543 | Terry Crowley | .08 | .06 |
| 544 | Rich Gale | .08 | .06 |
| 545 | Johnny Grubb | .08 | .06 |
| 546 | Paul Moskau | .08 | .06 |
| 547 | Mario Guerrero | .08 | .06 |
| 548 | Dave Goltz | .10 | .08 |
| 549 | Jerry Remy | .08 | .06 |
| 550 | Tommy John | .50 | .40 |
| 551 | Pirates Future Stars | | |
| | *(Vance Law, Tony Pena, Pascual Perez)* | 1.00 | .70 |
| 552 | Steve Trout | .08 | .06 |
| 553 | Tim Blackwell | .08 | .06 |
| 554 | Bert Blyleven | .25 | .20 |
| 555 | Cecil Cooper | .20 | .15 |
| 556 | Jerry Mumphrey | .08 | .06 |
| 557 | Chris Knapp | .08 | .06 |
| 558 | Barry Bonnell | .08 | .06 |
| 559 | Willie Montanez | .08 | .06 |
| 560 | Joe Morgan | .70 | .50 |
| 561 | Dennis Littlejohn | .08 | .06 |
| 562 | Checklist 485-605 | .25 | .20 |
| 563 | Jim Kaat | .30 | .25 |
| 564 | Ron Hassey | .08 | .06 |
| 565 | Burt Hooton | .10 | .08 |
| 566 | Del Unser | .08 | .06 |
| 567 | Mark Bomback | .08 | .06 |
| 568 | Dave Revering | .08 | .06 |
| 569 | Al Williams | .08 | .06 |
| 570 | Ken Singleton | .12 | .09 |
| 571 | Todd Cruz | .08 | .06 |
| 572 | Jack Morris | .60 | .45 |
| 573 | Phil Garner | .10 | .08 |
| 574 | Bill Caudill | .08 | .06 |
| 575 | Tony Perez | .50 | .40 |
| 576 | Reggie Cleveland | .08 | .06 |
| 577 | Blue Jays Future Stars | | |
| | *(Luis Leal, Brian Milner, Ken Schrom)* | .20 | .15 |
| 578 | *Bill Gullickson* | .20 | .15 |
| 579 | Tim Flannery | .08 | .06 |
| 580 | Don Baylor | .15 | .11 |
| 581 | Roy Howell | .08 | .06 |
| 582 | Gaylord Perry | .70 | .50 |
| 583 | Larry Milbourne | .08 | .06 |
| 584 | Randy Lerch | .08 | .06 |
| 585 | Amos Otis | .10 | .08 |
| 586 | Silvio Martinez | .08 | .06 |
| 587 | Jeff Newman | .08 | .06 |
| 588 | Gary Lavelle | .08 | .06 |
| 589 | Lamar Johnson | .08 | .06 |
| 590 | Bruce Sutter | .25 | .20 |
| 591 | John Lowenstein | .08 | .06 |
| 592 | Steve Comer | .08 | .06 |
| 593 | Steve Kemp | .12 | .09 |
| 594 | Preston Hanna | .08 | .06 |
| 595 | Butch Hobson | .08 | .06 |
| 596 | Jerry Augustine | .08 | .06 |
| 597 | Rafael Landestoy | .08 | .06 |
| 598 | George Vukovich | .08 | .06 |
| 599 | Dennis Kinney | .08 | .06 |
| 600 | Johnny Bench | 2.00 | 1.50 |
| 601 | Don Aase | .08 | .06 |
| 602 | Bobby Murcer | .15 | .11 |
| 603 | John Verhoeven | .08 | .06 |
| 604 | Rob Picciolo | .08 | .06 |
| 605 | Don Sutton | .70 | .50 |
| 606 | Reds Future Stars | | |
| | (Bruce Berenyi, Geoff Combe, Paul Householder) | .08 | .06 |
| 607 | Dave Palmer | .08 | .06 |
| 608 | Greg Pryor | .08 | .06 |
| 609 | Lynn McGlothen | .08 | .06 |
| 610 | Darrell Porter | .10 | .08 |
| 611 | Rick Matula | .08 | .06 |
| 612 | Duane Kuiper | .08 | .06 |
| 613 | Jim Anderson | .08 | .06 |
| 614 | Dave Rozema | .08 | .06 |
| 615 | Rick Dempsey | .12 | .09 |
| 616 | Rick Wise | .10 | .08 |
| 617 | Craig Reynolds | .08 | .06 |
| 618 | John Milner | .08 | .06 |
| 619 | Steve Henderson | .08 | .06 |
| 620 | Dennis Eckersley | 2.00 | 1.50 |
| 621 | Tom Donohue | .08 | .06 |
| 622 | Randy Moffitt | .08 | .06 |
| 623 | Sal Bando | .12 | .09 |
| 624 | Bob Welch | .70 | .50 |
| 625 | Bill Buckner | .15 | .11 |
| 626 | Tigers Future Stars | | |
| | (Dave Steffen, Jerry Ujdur, Roger Weaver) | .08 | .06 |
| 627 | Luis Tiant | .20 | .15 |
| 628 | Vic Correll | .08 | .06 |
| 629 | Tony Armas | .12 | .09 |
| 630 | Steve Carlton | 2.00 | 1.50 |
| 631 | Ron Jackson | .08 | .06 |
| 632 | Alan Bannister | .08 | .06 |
| 633 | Bill Lee | .10 | .08 |
| 634 | Doug Flynn | .08 | .06 |
| 635 | Bobby Bonds | .15 | .11 |
| 636 | Al Hrabosky | .10 | .08 |
| 637 | Jerry Narron | .08 | .06 |
| 638 | Checklist 606 | .25 | .20 |
| 639 | Carney Lansford | .15 | .11 |
| 640 | Dave Parker | .60 | .45 |
| 641 | Mark Belanger | .10 | .08 |
| 642 | Vern Ruhle | .08 | .06 |
| 643 | *Lloyd Moseby* | .40 | .30 |
| 644 | Ramon Aviles | .08 | .06 |
| 645 | Rick Reuschel | .15 | .11 |
| 646 | Marvis Foley | .08 | .06 |
| 647 | Dick Drago | .08 | .06 |
| 648 | Darrell Evans | .25 | .20 |
| 649 | Manny Sarmiento | .08 | .06 |
| 650 | Bucky Dent | .12 | .09 |

| | | MT | NR MT |
|---|---|---|---|
| 651 | Pedro Guerrero | 1.25 | .90 |
| 652 | John Montague | .08 | .06 |
| 653 | Bill Fahey | .08 | .06 |
| 654 | Ray Burris | .08 | .06 |
| 655 | Dan Driessen | .12 | .09 |
| 656 | Jon Matlack | .10 | .08 |
| 657 | Mike Cubbage | .08 | .06 |
| 658 | Milt Wilcox | .08 | .06 |
| 659 | Brewers Future Stars (John Flinn, Ed Romero, Ned Yost) | .08 | .06 |
| 660 | Gary Carter | 1.00 | .70 |
| 661 | Orioles Team (Earl Weaver) | .30 | .25 |
| 662 | Red Sox Team (Ralph Houk) | .30 | .25 |
| 663 | Angels Team (Jim Fregosi) | .25 | .20 |
| 664 | White Sox Team (Tony LaRussa) | .25 | .20 |
| 665 | Indians Team (Dave Garcia) | .25 | .20 |
| 666 | Tigers Team (Sparky Anderson) | .30 | .25 |
| 667 | Royals Team (Jim Frey) | .25 | .20 |
| 668 | Brewers Team (Bob Rodgers) | .25 | .20 |
| 669 | Twins Team (John Goryl) | .25 | .20 |
| 670 | Yankees Team (Gene Michael) | .35 | .25 |
| 671 | A's Team (Billy Martin) | .30 | .25 |
| 672 | Mariners Team (Maury Wills) | .25 | .20 |
| 673 | Rangers Team (Don Zimmer) | .25 | .20 |
| 674 | Blue Jays Team (Bobby Mattick) | .25 | .20 |
| 675 | Braves Team (Bobby Cox) | .25 | .20 |
| 676 | Cubs Team (Joe Amalfitano) | .25 | .20 |
| 677 | Reds Team (John McNamara) | .25 | .20 |
| 678 | Astros Team (Bill Virdon) | .25 | .20 |
| 679 | Dodgers Team (Tom Lasorda) | .35 | .25 |
| 680 | Expos Team (Dick Williams) | .25 | .20 |
| 681 | Mets Team (Joe Torre) | .30 | .25 |
| 682 | Phillies Team (Dallas Green) | .25 | .20 |
| 683 | Pirates Team (Chuck Tanner) | .25 | .20 |
| 684 | Cardinals Team (Whitey Herzog) | .30 | .25 |
| 685 | Padres Team (Frank Howard) | .25 | .20 |
| 686 | Giants Team (Dave Bristol) | .25 | .20 |
| 687 | Jeff Jones | .08 | .06 |
| 688 | Kiko Garcia | .08 | .06 |
| 689 | Red Sox Future Stars | | |

| | | MT | NR MT |
|---|---|---|---|
| | (Bruce Hurst, Keith MacWhorter, Reid Nichols) | 2.00 | 1.50 |
| 690 | Bob Watson | .10 | .08 |
| 691 | Dick Ruthven | .08 | .06 |
| 692 | Lenny Randle | .08 | .06 |
| 693 | Steve Howe | .20 | .15 |
| 694 | Bud Harrelson | .08 | .06 |
| 695 | Kent Tekulve | .10 | .08 |
| 696 | Alan Ashby | .08 | .06 |
| 697 | Rick Waits | .08 | .06 |
| 698 | Mike Jorgensen | .08 | .06 |
| 699 | Glenn Abbott | .08 | .06 |
| 700 | George Brett | 6.00 | 4.50 |
| 701 | Joe Rudi | .12 | .09 |
| 702 | George Medich | .08 | .06 |
| 703 | Alvis Woods | .08 | .06 |
| 704 | Bill Travers | .08 | .06 |
| 705 | Ted Simmons | .25 | .20 |
| 706 | Dave Ford | .08 | .06 |
| 707 | Dave Cash | .08 | .06 |
| 708 | Doyle Alexander | .12 | .09 |
| 709 | Alan Trammell | .30 | .25 |
| 710 | Ron LeFlore | .08 | .06 |
| 711 | Joe Ferguson | .08 | .06 |
| 712 | Bill Bonham | .08 | .06 |
| 713 | Bill North | .08 | .06 |
| 714 | Pete Redfern | .08 | .06 |
| 715 | Bill Madlock | .25 | .20 |
| 716 | Glenn Borgmann | .08 | .06 |
| 717 | Jim Barr | .08 | .06 |
| 718 | Larry Biittner | .08 | .06 |
| 719 | Sparky Lyle | .12 | .09 |
| 720 | Fred Lynn | .35 | .25 |
| 721 | Toby Harrah | .10 | .08 |
| 722 | Joe Niekro | .20 | .15 |
| 723 | Bruce Bochte | .08 | .06 |
| 724 | Lou Piniella | .20 | .15 |
| 725 | Steve Rogers | .10 | .08 |
| 726 | Rick Monday | .15 | .11 |

A player's name in italic indicates a rookie card. An (FC) indicates a player's first card for that particular card company.

## 1981 Topps Traded

The 132 cards in this extension set are numbered from 727 to 858, technically making them a high-numbered series of the regular Topps set. The set was not packaged in gum packs, but rather placed in a specially designed red box and sold through baseball card dealers only. While many complained about the method, the fact remains, even at higher prices, the set has done well for its owners as it features not only mid-season trades, but also single-player rookie cards of some of the hottest prospects. The cards measure 2-1/2" by 3-1/2".

| | MT | NR MT |
|---|---|---|
| Complete Set: | 40.00 | 30.00 |
| Common Player: | .10 | .08 |
| | | |
| 727 Danny Ainge(FC) | 4.00 | 3.00 |
| 728 Doyle Alexander | .20 | .15 |
| 729 Gary Alexander | .10 | .08 |
| 730 Billy Almon | .10 | .08 |
| 731 Joaquin Andujar | .15 | .11 |
| 732 Bob Bailor | .10 | .08 |
| 733 Juan Beniquez | .10 | .08 |
| 734 Dave Bergman | .10 | .08 |
| 735 Tony Bernazard | .10 | .08 |
| 736 Larry Biittner | .10 | .08 |
| 737 Doug Bird | .10 | .08 |
| 738 Bert Blyleven | 1.00 | .70 |
| 739 Mark Bomback | .10 | .08 |
| 740 Bobby Bonds | .20 | .15 |
| 741 Rick Bosetti | .10 | .08 |
| 742 Hubie Brooks | 1.75 | 1.25 |
| 743 Rick Burleson | .15 | .11 |
| 744 Ray Burris | .10 | .08 |
| 745 Jeff Burroughs | .15 | .11 |
| 746 Enos Cabell | .10 | .08 |
| 747 Ken Clay | .10 | .08 |
| 748 Mark Clear | .10 | .08 |
| 749 Larry Cox | .10 | .08 |
| 750 Hector Cruz | .10 | .08 |
| 751 Victor Cruz | .10 | .08 |
| 752 Mike Cubbage | .10 | .08 |
| 753 Dick Davis | .10 | .08 |
| 754 Brian Doyle | .10 | .08 |
| 755 Dick Drago | .10 | .08 |
| 756 Leon Durham | .25 | .20 |
| 757 Jim Dwyer | .10 | .08 |
| 758 Dave Edwards | .10 | .08 |
| 759 Jim Essian | .10 | .08 |
| 760 Bill Fahey | .10 | .08 |
| 761 Rollie Fingers | 5.00 | 3.75 |
| 762 Carlton Fisk | 7.00 | 5.25 |
| 763 Barry Foote | .10 | .08 |
| 764 Ken Forsch | .10 | .08 |
| 765 Kiko Garcia | .10 | .08 |
| 766 Cesar Geronimo | .10 | .08 |
| 767 Gary Gray | .10 | .08 |
| 768 Mickey Hatcher | .15 | .11 |
| 769 Steve Henderson | .10 | .08 |
| 770 Marc Hill | .10 | .08 |
| 771 Butch Hobson | .10 | .08 |
| 772 Rick Honeycutt | .10 | .08 |
| 773 Roy Howell | .10 | .08 |
| 774 Mike Ivie | .10 | .08 |
| 775 Roy Lee Jackson | .10 | .08 |
| 776 Cliff Johnson | .10 | .08 |
| 777 Randy Jones | .15 | .11 |
| 778 Ruppert Jones | .10 | .08 |
| 779 Mick Kelleher | .10 | .08 |

| | MT | NR MT |
|---|---|---|
| 780 Terry Kennedy | .20 | .15 |
| 781 Dave Kingman | .40 | .30 |
| 782 Bob Knepper | .15 | .11 |
| 783 Ken Kravec | .10 | .08 |
| 784 Bob Lacey | .10 | .08 |
| 785 Dennis Lamp | .10 | .08 |
| 786 Rafael Landestoy | .10 | .08 |
| 787 Ken Landreaux | .10 | .08 |
| 788 Carney Lansford | .80 | .60 |
| 789 Dave LaRoche | .10 | .08 |
| 790 Joe Lefebvre | .10 | .08 |
| 791 Ron LeFlore | .15 | .11 |
| 792 Randy Lerch | .10 | .08 |
| 793 Sixto Lezcano | .10 | .08 |
| 794 John Littlefield | .10 | .08 |
| 795 Mike Lum | .10 | .08 |
| 796 Greg Luzinski | .25 | .20 |
| 797 Fred Lynn | .50 | .40 |
| 798 Jerry Martin | .10 | .08 |
| 799 Buck Martinez | .10 | .08 |
| 800 Gary Matthews | .20 | .15 |
| 801 Mario Mendoza | .10 | .08 |
| 802 Larry Milbourne | .10 | .08 |
| 803 Rick Miller | .10 | .08 |
| 804 John Montefusco | .10 | .08 |
| 805 Jerry Morales | .10 | .08 |
| 806 Jose Morales | .10 | .08 |
| 807 Joe Morgan | 2.00 | 1.50 |
| 808 Jerry Mumphrey | .10 | .08 |
| 809 Gene Nelson(FC) | .30 | .25 |
| 810 Ed Ott | .10 | .08 |
| 811 Bob Owchinko | .10 | .08 |
| 812 Gaylord Perry | 1.75 | 1.25 |
| 813 Mike Phillips | .10 | .08 |
| 814 Darrell Porter | .15 | .11 |
| 815 Mike Proly | .10 | .08 |
| 816 Tim Raines | 12.00 | 9.00 |
| 817 Lenny Randle | .10 | .08 |
| 818 Doug Rau | .10 | .08 |
| 819 Jeff Reardon | 15.00 | 11.00 |
| 820 Ken Reitz | .10 | .08 |
| 821 Steve Renko | .10 | .08 |
| 822 Rick Reuschel | .25 | .20 |
| 823 Dave Revering | .10 | .08 |
| 824 Dave Roberts | .10 | .08 |
| 825 Leon Roberts | .10 | .08 |
| 826 Joe Rudi | .20 | .15 |
| 827 Kevin Saucier | .10 | .08 |
| 828 Tony Scott | .10 | .08 |
| 829 Bob Shirley | .10 | .08 |
| 830 Ted Simmons | .40 | .30 |
| 831 Lary Sorensen | .10 | .08 |
| 832 Jim Spencer | .10 | .08 |
| 833 Harry Spilman | .10 | .08 |
| 834 Fred Stanley | .10 | .08 |
| 835 Rusty Staub | .30 | .25 |
| 836 Bill Stein | .10 | .08 |
| 837 Joe Strain | .10 | .08 |
| 838 Bruce Sutter | .50 | .40 |
| 839 Don Sutton | 1.50 | 1.25 |
| 840 Steve Swisher | .10 | .08 |
| 841 Frank Tanana | .20 | .15 |
| 842 Gene Tenace | .15 | .11 |
| 843 Jason Thompson | .10 | .08 |
| 844 Dickie Thon | .15 | .11 |
| 845 Bill Travers | .10 | .08 |
| 846 Tom Underwood | .10 | .08 |

| | | MT | NR MT |
|---|---|---|---|
| 847 | John Urrea | .10 | .08 |
| 848 | Mike Vail | .10 | .08 |
| 849 | Ellis Valentine | .10 | .08 |
| 850 | Fernando Valenzuela | | |
| | | 3.50 | 2.75 |
| 851 | Pete Vuckovich | .15 | .11 |
| 852 | Mark Wagner | .10 | .08 |
| 853 | Bob Walk | .50 | .40 |
| 854 | Claudell Washington | .15 | .11 |
| 855 | Dave Winfield | 10.00 | 7.50 |
| 856 | Geoff Zahn | .10 | .08 |
| 857 | Richie Zisk | .15 | .11 |
| 858 | Checklist 727-858 | .10 | .08 |

## 1982 Topps

At 792 cards, this was the largest issue produced up to that time, eliminating the need for double-printed cards. The 2-1/2" by 3-1/2" cards feature a front color photo with a pair of stripes down the left side. Under the player's photo are found his name, team and position. A facsimile autograph runs across the front of the picture. Specialty cards include great performances of the previous season, All-Stars, statistical leaders and "In Action" cards (indicated by "IA" in listings below). Managers and hitting/pitching leaders have cards, while rookies are shown as "Future Stars" on group cards.

| | | MT | NR MT |
|---|---|---|---|
| Complete Set: | | 150.00 | 110.00 |
| Common Player: | | .08 | .06 |
| 1 | 1981 Highlight (Steve Carlton) | .50 | .40 |
| 2 | 1981 Highlight (Ron Davis) | .08 | .06 |
| 3 | 1981 Highlight (Tim Raines) | .30 | .25 |
| 4 | 1981 Highlight (Pete Rose) | .70 | .50 |
| 5 | 1981 Highlight (Nolan Ryan) | 2.00 | 1.50 |
| 6 | 1981 Highlight (Fernando Valenzuela) | .30 | .25 |
| 7 | Scott Sanderson | .08 | .06 |
| 8 | Rich Dauer | .08 | .06 |
| 9 | Ron Guidry | .35 | .25 |
| 10 | Ron Guidry IA | .15 | .11 |
| 11 | Gary Alexander | .08 | .06 |
| 12 | Moose Haas | .08 | .06 |
| 13 | Lamar Johnson | .08 | .06 |
| 14 | Steve Howe | .10 | .08 |
| 15 | Ellis Valentine | .08 | .06 |
| 16 | Steve Comer | .08 | .06 |
| 17 | Darrell Evans | .25 | .20 |
| 18 | Fernando Arroyo | .08 | .06 |
| 19 | Ernie Whitt | .10 | .08 |
| 20 | Garry Maddox | .12 | .09 |
| 21 | Orioles Future Stars (Bob Bonner, *Cal Ripken*, Jeff Schneider) | 70.00 | 52.00 |
| 22 | Jim Beattie | .08 | .06 |
| 23 | Willie Hernandez | .10 | .08 |
| 24 | Dave Frost | .08 | .06 |
| 25 | Jerry Remy | .08 | .06 |
| 26 | Jorge Orta | .08 | .06 |
| 27 | Tom Herr | .12 | .09 |
| 28 | John Urrea | .08 | .06 |
| 29 | Dwayne Murphy | .10 | .08 |
| 30 | Tom Seaver | 2.00 | 1.50 |
| 31 | Tom Seaver IA | 1.00 | .70 |
| 32 | Gene Garber | .08 | .06 |
| 33 | Jerry Morales | .08 | .06 |
| 34 | Joe Sambito | .08 | .06 |
| 35 | Willie Aikens | .08 | .06 |
| 36 | Rangers Batting & Pitching Ldrs. (George Medich, Al Oliver) | .12 | .09 |
| 37 | Dan Graham | .08 | .06 |
| 38 | Charlie Lea | .08 | .06 |
| 39 | Lou Whitaker | .40 | .30 |
| 40 | Dave Parker | .35 | .25 |
| 41 | Dave Parker IA | .15 | .11 |
| 42 | Rick Sofield | .08 | .06 |
| 43 | Mike Cubbage | .08 | .06 |
| 44 | Britt Burns | .08 | .06 |
| 45 | Rick Cerone | .08 | .06 |
| 46 | Jerry Augustine | .08 | .06 |
| 47 | Jeff Leonard | .15 | .11 |
| 48 | Bobby Castillo | .08 | .06 |
| 49 | Alvis Woods | .08 | .06 |
| 50 | Buddy Bell | .15 | .11 |
| 51 | Cubs Future Stars (*Jay Howell*, Carlos Lezcano, Ty Waller) | .40 | .30 |
| 52 | Larry Andersen | .08 | .06 |
| 53 | Greg Gross | .08 | .06 |
| 54 | Ron Hassey | .08 | .06 |
| 55 | Rick Burleson | .10 | .08 |
| 56 | Mark Littell | .08 | .06 |
| 57 | Craig Reynolds | .08 | .06 |
| 58 | John D'Acquisto | .08 | .06 |
| 59 | *Rich Gedman*(FC) | .50 | .40 |
| 60 | Tony Armas | .12 | .09 |
| 61 | Tommy Boggs | .08 | .06 |
| 62 | Mike Tyson | .08 | .06 |
| 63 | Mario Soto | .10 | .08 |

| | MT | NR MT |
|---|---|---|
| 64 Lynn Jones | .08 | .06 |
| 65 Terry Kennedy | .12 | .09 |
| 66 Astros Batting & Pitching Ldrs. (Art Howe, Nolan Ryan) | .25 | .20 |
| 67 Rich Gale | .08 | .06 |
| 68 Roy Howell | .08 | .06 |
| 69 Al Williams | .08 | .06 |
| 70 Tim Raines | 3.00 | 2.25 |
| 71 Roy Lee Jackson | .08 | .06 |
| 72 Rick Auerbach | .08 | .06 |
| 73 Buddy Solomon | .08 | .06 |
| 74 Bob Clark | .08 | .06 |
| 75 Tommy John | .30 | .25 |
| 76 Greg Pryor | .08 | .06 |
| 77 Miguel Dilone | .08 | .06 |
| 78 George Medich | .08 | .06 |
| 79 Bob Bailor | .08 | .06 |
| 80 Jim Palmer | 1.00 | .70 |
| 81 Jim Palmer IA | .30 | .25 |
| 82 Bob Welch | .60 | .45 |
| 83 Yankees Future Stars (Steve Balboni, Andy McGaffigan, Andre Robertson)(FC) | .25 | .20 |
| 84 Rennie Stennett | .08 | .06 |
| 85 Lynn McGlothen | .08 | .06 |
| 86 Dane Iorg | .08 | .06 |
| 87 Matt Keough | .08 | .06 |
| 88 Biff Pocoroba | .08 | .06 |
| 89 Steve Henderson | .08 | .06 |
| 90 Nolan Ryan | 10.00 | 7.50 |
| 91 Carney Lansford | .12 | .09 |
| 92 Brad Havens | .08 | .06 |
| 93 Larry Hisle | .10 | .08 |
| 94 Andy Hassler | .08 | .06 |
| 95 Ozzie Smith | 2.50 | 2.00 |
| 96 Royals Batting & Pitching Ldrs. (George Brett, Larry Gura) | .35 | .25 |
| 97 Paul Moskau | .08 | .06 |
| 98 Terry Bulling | .08 | .06 |
| 99 Barry Bonnell | .08 | .06 |
| 100 Mike Schmidt | 3.00 | 2.25 |
| 101 Mike Schmidt IA | 1.25 | .90 |
| 102 Dan Briggs | .08 | .06 |
| 103 Bob Lacey | .08 | .06 |
| 104 Rance Mulliniks | .08 | .06 |
| 105 Kirk Gibson | 1.00 | .70 |
| 106 Enrique Romo | .08 | .06 |
| 107 Wayne Krenchicki | .08 | .06 |
| 108 Bob Sykes | .08 | .06 |
| 109 Dave Revering | .08 | .06 |
| 110 Carlton Fisk | 2.00 | 1.50 |
| 111 Carlton Fisk IA | 1.25 | .90 |
| 112 Billy Sample | .08 | .06 |
| 113 Steve McCatty | .08 | .06 |
| 114 Ken Landreaux | .08 | .06 |
| 115 Gaylord Perry | .50 | .40 |
| 116 Jim Wohlford | .08 | .06 |
| 117 Rawly Eastwick | .08 | .06 |
| 118 Expos Future Stars (Terry Francona, Brad Mills, Bryn Smith)(FC) | .40 | .30 |
| 119 Joe Pittman | .08 | .06 |
| 120 Gary Lucas | .08 | .06 |
| 121 Ed Lynch | .08 | .06 |

| | MT | NR MT |
|---|---|---|
| 122 Jamie Easterly | .08 | .06 |
| 123 Danny Goodwin | .08 | .06 |
| 124 Reid Nichols | .08 | .06 |
| 125 Danny Ainge | 1.25 | .90 |
| 126 Braves Batting & Pitching Ldrs. (Rick Mahler, Claudell Washington) | .10 | .08 |
| 127 Lonnie Smith | .10 | .08 |
| 128 Frank Pastore | .08 | .06 |
| 129 Checklist 1-132 | .12 | .09 |
| 130 Julio Cruz | .08 | .06 |
| 131 Stan Bahnsen | .08 | .06 |
| 132 Lee May | .10 | .08 |
| 133 Pat Underwood | .08 | .06 |
| 134 Dan Ford | .08 | .06 |
| 135 Andy Rincon | .08 | .06 |
| 136 Lenn Sakata | .08 | .06 |
| 137 George Cappuzzello | .08 | .06 |
| 138 Tony Pena | .20 | .15 |
| 139 Jeff Jones | .08 | .06 |
| 140 Ron LeFlore | .10 | .08 |
| 141 Indians Future Stars (Chris Bando, Tom Brennan, Von Hayes)(FC) | 1.00 | .70 |
| 142 Dave LaRoche | .08 | .06 |
| 143 Mookie Wilson | .12 | .09 |
| 144 Fred Breining | .08 | .06 |
| 145 Bob Horner | .20 | .15 |
| 146 Mike Griffin | .08 | .06 |
| 147 Denny Walling | .08 | .06 |
| 148 Mickey Klutts | .08 | .06 |
| 149 Pat Putnam | .08 | .06 |
| 150 Ted Simmons | .20 | .15 |
| 151 Dave Edwards | .08 | .06 |
| 152 Ramon Aviles | .08 | .06 |
| 153 Roger Erickson | .08 | .06 |
| 154 Dennis Werth | .08 | .06 |
| 155 Otto Velez | .08 | .06 |
| 156 A's Batting & Pitching Ldrs. (Rickey Henderson, Steve McCatty) | .25 | .20 |
| 157 Steve Crawford | .08 | .06 |
| 158 Brian Downing | .12 | .09 |
| 159 Larry Biittner | .08 | .06 |
| 160 Luis Tiant | .15 | .11 |
| 161 Batting Leaders (Carney Lansford, Bill Madlock) | .20 | .15 |
| 162 Home Run Leaders (Tony Armas, Dwight Evans, Bobby Grich, Eddie Murray, Mike Schmidt) | .35 | .25 |
| 163 Runs Batted In Leaders (Eddie Murray, Mike Schmidt) | .40 | .30 |
| 164 Stolen Base Leaders (Rickey Henderson, Tim Raines) | .35 | .25 |
| 165 Victory Leaders (Denny Martinez, Steve McCatty, Jack Morris, Tom Seaver, Pete Vuckovich) | .20 | .15 |
| 166 Strikeout Leaders (Len Barker, Fernando Valenzuela) | .20 | .15 |
| 167 Earned Run Avg. Leaders (Steve McCatty, | | |

| | | MT | NR MT |
|---|---|---|---|
| | Nolan Ryan) | .20 | .15 |
| 168 | Leading Relievers (Rollie Fingers, Bruce Sutter) | .20 | .15 |
| 169 | Charlie Leibrandt | .12 | .09 |
| 170 | Jim Bibby | .08 | .06 |
| 171 | Giants Future Stars (Bob Brenly, Chili Davis, Bob Tufts) | 2.50 | 2.00 |
| 172 | Bill Gullickson | .10 | .08 |
| 173 | Jamie Quirk | .08 | .06 |
| 174 | Dave Ford | .08 | .06 |
| 175 | Jerry Mumphrey | .08 | .06 |
| 176 | Dewey Robinson | .08 | .06 |
| 177 | John Ellis | .08 | .06 |
| 178 | Dyar Miller | .08 | .06 |
| 179 | Steve Garvey | .80 | .60 |
| 180 | Steve Garvey IA | .40 | .30 |
| 181 | Silvio Martinez | .08 | .06 |
| 182 | Larry Herndon | .10 | .08 |
| 183 | Mike Proly | .08 | .06 |
| 184 | Mick Kelleher | .08 | .06 |
| 185 | Phil Niekro | .50 | .40 |
| 186 | Cardinals Batting & Pitching Ldrs. (Bob Forsch, Keith Hernandez) | .25 | .20 |
| 187 | Jeff Newman | .08 | .06 |
| 188 | Randy Martz | .08 | .06 |
| 189 | Glenn Hoffman | .08 | .06 |
| 190 | J.R. Richard | .12 | .09 |
| 191 | Tim Wallach(FC) | 2.00 | 1.50 |
| 192 | Broderick Perkins | .08 | .06 |
| 193 | Darrell Jackson | .08 | .06 |
| 194 | Mike Vail | .08 | .06 |
| 195 | Paul Molitor | .35 | .25 |
| 196 | Willie Upshaw | .12 | .09 |
| 197 | Shane Rawley | .15 | .11 |
| 198 | Chris Speier | .08 | .06 |
| 199 | Don Aase | .08 | .06 |
| 200 | George Brett | 4.00 | 3.00 |
| 201 | George Brett IA | 1.50 | 1.25 |
| 202 | Rick Manning | .08 | .06 |
| 203 | Blue Jays Future Stars (Jesse Barfield, Brian Milner, Boomer Wells) | 1.00 | .70 |
| 204 | Gary Roenicke | .08 | .06 |
| 205 | Neil Allen | .08 | .06 |
| 206 | Tony Bernazard | .08 | .06 |
| 207 | Rod Scurry | .08 | .06 |
| 208 | Bobby Murcer | .15 | .11 |
| 209 | Gary Lavelle | .08 | .06 |
| 210 | Keith Hernandez | .60 | .45 |
| 211 | Dan Petry | .10 | .08 |
| 212 | Mario Mendoza | .08 | .06 |
| 213 | Dave Stewart(FC) | 4.00 | 3.00 |
| 214 | Brian Asselstine | .08 | .06 |
| 215 | Mike Krukow | .10 | .08 |
| 216 | White Sox Batting & Pitching Ldrs. (Dennis Lamp, Chet Lemon) | .10 | .08 |
| 217 | Bo McLaughlin | .08 | .06 |
| 218 | Dave Roberts | .08 | .06 |
| 219 | John Curtis | .08 | .06 |
| 220 | Manny Trillo | .10 | .08 |
| 221 | Jim Slaton | .08 | .06 |
| 222 | Butch Wynegar | .08 | .06 |

| | | MT | NR MT |
|---|---|---|---|
| 223 | Lloyd Moseby | .20 | .15 |
| 224 | Bruce Bochte | .08 | .06 |
| 225 | Mike Torrez | .10 | .08 |
| 226 | Checklist 133-264 | .12 | .09 |
| 227 | Ray Burris | .08 | .06 |
| 228 | Sam Mejias | .08 | .06 |
| 229 | Geoff Zahn | .08 | .06 |
| 230 | Willie Wilson | .20 | .15 |
| 231 | Phillies Future Stars (Mark Davis, Bob Dernier, Ozzie Virgil)(FC) | .60 | .45 |
| 232 | Terry Crowley | .08 | .06 |
| 233 | Duane Kuiper | .08 | .06 |
| 234 | Ron Hodges | .08 | .06 |
| 235 | Mike Easler | .10 | .08 |
| 236 | John Martin | .08 | .06 |
| 237 | Rusty Kuntz | .08 | .06 |
| 238 | Kevin Saucier | .08 | .06 |
| 239 | Jon Matlack | .10 | .08 |
| 240 | Bucky Dent | .12 | .09 |
| 241 | Bucky Dent IA | .10 | .08 |
| 242 | Milt May | .08 | .06 |
| 243 | Bob Owchinko | .08 | .06 |
| 244 | Rufino Linares | .08 | .06 |
| 245 | Ken Reitz | .08 | .06 |
| 246 | Mets Batting & Pitching Ldrs. (Hubie Brooks, Mike Scott) | .20 | .15 |
| 247 | Pedro Guerrero | .90 | .70 |
| 248 | Frank LaCorte | .08 | .06 |
| 249 | Tim Flannery | .08 | .06 |
| 250 | Tug McGraw | .15 | .11 |
| 251 | Fred Lynn | .30 | .25 |
| 252 | Fred Lynn IA | .15 | .11 |
| 253 | Chuck Baker | .08 | .06 |
| 254 | Jorge Bell(FC) | 10.00 | 7.50 |
| 255 | Tony Perez | .30 | .25 |
| 256 | Tony Perez IA | .15 | .11 |
| 257 | Larry Harlow | .08 | .06 |
| 258 | Bo Diaz | .10 | .08 |
| 259 | Rodney Scott | .08 | .06 |
| 260 | Bruce Sutter | .20 | .15 |
| 261 | Tigers Future Stars (Howard Bailey, Marty Castillo, Dave Rucker) | .08 | .06 |
| 262 | Doug Bair | .08 | .06 |
| 263 | Victor Cruz | .08 | .06 |
| 264 | Dan Quisenberry | .20 | .15 |
| 265 | Al Bumbry | .10 | .08 |
| 266 | Rick Leach | .15 | .11 |
| 267 | Kurt Bevacqua | .08 | .06 |
| 268 | Rickey Keeton | .08 | .06 |
| 269 | Jim Essian | .08 | .06 |
| 270 | Rusty Staub | .15 | .11 |
| 271 | Larry Bradford | .08 | .06 |
| 272 | Bump Wills | .08 | .06 |
| 273 | Doug Bird | .08 | .06 |
| 274 | Bob Ojeda(FC) | .70 | .50 |
| 275 | Bob Watson | .10 | .08 |
| 276 | Angels Batting & Pitching Ldrs. (Rod Carew, Ken Forsch) | .25 | .20 |
| 277 | Terry Puhl | .08 | .06 |
| 278 | John Littlefield | .08 | .06 |
| 279 | Bill Russell | .10 | .08 |
| 280 | Ben Oglivie | .10 | .08 |
| 281 | John Verhoeven | .08 | .06 |

| | | MT | NR MT |
|---|---|---|---|
| 282 | Ken Macha | .08 | .06 |
| 283 | Brian Allard | .08 | .06 |
| 284 | Bob Grich | .15 | .11 |
| 285 | Sparky Lyle | .12 | .09 |
| 286 | Bill Fahey | .08 | .06 |
| 287 | Alan Bannister | .08 | .06 |
| 288 | Garry Templeton | .12 | .09 |
| 289 | Bob Stanley | .08 | .06 |
| 290 | Ken Singleton | .12 | .09 |
| 291 | Pirates Future Stars (Vance Law, Bob Long, *Johnny Ray*)(FC) | .60 | .45 |
| 292 | Dave Palmer | .08 | .06 |
| 293 | Rob Picciolo | .08 | .06 |
| 294 | Mike LaCoss | .08 | .06 |
| 295 | Jason Thompson | .08 | .06 |
| 296 | Bob Walk | .12 | .09 |
| 297 | Clint Hurdle | .08 | .06 |
| 298 | Danny Darwin | .08 | .06 |
| 299 | Steve Trout | .08 | .06 |
| 300 | Reggie Jackson | 2.00 | 1.50 |
| 301 | Reggie Jackson IA | 1.25 | .90 |
| 302 | Doug Flynn | .08 | .06 |
| 303 | Bill Caudill | .08 | .06 |
| 304 | Johnnie LeMaster | .08 | .06 |
| 305 | Don Sutton | .50 | .40 |
| 306 | Don Sutton IA | .25 | .20 |
| 307 | Randy Bass | .08 | .06 |
| 308 | Charlie Moore | .08 | .06 |
| 309 | Pete Redfern | .08 | .06 |
| 310 | Mike Hargrove | .08 | .06 |
| 311 | Dodgers Batting & Pitching Leaders (Dusty Baker, Burt Hooton) | .12 | .09 |
| 312 | Lenny Randle | .08 | .06 |
| 313 | John Harris | .08 | .06 |
| 314 | Buck Martinez | .08 | .06 |
| 315 | Burt Hooton | .10 | .08 |
| 316 | Steve Braun | .08 | .06 |
| 317 | Dick Ruthven | .08 | .06 |
| 318 | Mike Heath | .08 | .06 |
| 319 | Dave Rozema | .08 | .06 |
| 320 | Chris Chambliss | .10 | .08 |
| 321 | Chris Chambliss IA | .10 | .08 |
| 322 | Garry Hancock | .08 | .06 |
| 323 | Bill Lee | .10 | .08 |
| 324 | Steve Dillard | .08 | .06 |
| 325 | Jose Cruz | .15 | .11 |
| 326 | Pete Falcone | .08 | .06 |
| 327 | Joe Nolan | .08 | .06 |
| 328 | Ed Farmer | .08 | .06 |
| 329 | U.L. Washington | .08 | .06 |
| 330 | Rick Wise | .10 | .08 |
| 331 | Benny Ayala | .08 | .06 |
| 332 | Don Robinson | .10 | .08 |
| 333 | Brewers Future Stars (*Frank DiPino*, Marshall Edwards, Chuck Porter) | .12 | .09 |
| 334 | Aurelio Rodriguez | .10 | .08 |
| 335 | Jim Sundberg | .10 | .08 |
| 336 | Mariners Batting & Pitching Ldrs. (Glenn Abbott, Tom Paciorek) | .10 | .08 |
| 337 | Pete Rose AS | .80 | .60 |
| 338 | Dave Lopes AS | .12 | .09 |
| 339 | Mike Schmidt AS | .80 | .60 |

| | | MT | NR MT |
|---|---|---|---|
| 340 | Dave Concepcion AS | .12 | .09 |
| 341 | Andre Dawson AS | .25 | .20 |
| 342a | George Foster AS (no autograph) | 2.25 | 1.75 |
| 342b | George Foster AS (autograph on front) | .40 | .30 |
| 343 | Dave Parker AS | .20 | .15 |
| 344 | Gary Carter AS | .35 | .25 |
| 345 | Fernando Valenzuela AS | .35 | .25 |
| 346 | Tom Seaver AS | .35 | .25 |
| 347 | Bruce Sutter AS | .12 | .09 |
| 348 | Derrel Thomas | .08 | .06 |
| 349 | George Frazier | .08 | .06 |
| 350 | Thad Bosley | .08 | .06 |
| 351 | Reds Future Stars (Scott Brown, Geoff Combe, Paul Householder) | .08 | .06 |
| 352 | Dick Davis | .08 | .06 |
| 353 | Jack O'Connor | .08 | .06 |
| 354 | Roberto Ramos | .08 | .06 |
| 355 | Dwight Evans | .25 | .20 |
| 356 | Denny Lewallyn | .08 | .06 |
| 357 | Butch Hobson | .08 | .06 |
| 358 | Mike Parrott | .08 | .06 |
| 359 | Jim Dwyer | .08 | .06 |
| 360 | Len Barker | .10 | .08 |
| 361 | Rafael Landestoy | .08 | .06 |
| 362 | Jim Wright | .08 | .06 |
| 363 | Bob Molinaro | .08 | .06 |
| 364 | Doyle Alexander | .12 | .09 |
| 365 | Bill Madlock | .20 | .15 |
| 366 | Padres Batting & Pitching Ldrs. (Juan Eichelberger, Luis Salazar) | .10 | .08 |
| 367 | Jim Kaat | .25 | .20 |
| 368 | Alex Trevino | .08 | .06 |
| 369 | Champ Summers | .08 | .06 |
| 370 | Mike Norris | .08 | .06 |
| 371 | Jerry Don Gleaton | .08 | .06 |
| 372 | Luis Gomez | .08 | .06 |
| 373 | *Gene Nelson* | .15 | .11 |
| 374 | Tim Blackwell | .08 | .06 |
| 375 | Dusty Baker | .12 | .09 |
| 376 | Chris Welsh | .08 | .06 |
| 377 | Kiko Garcia | .08 | .06 |
| 378 | Mike Caldwell | .08 | .06 |
| 379 | Rob Wilfong | .08 | .06 |
| 380 | Dave Stieb | .25 | .20 |
| 381 | Red Sox Future Stars (Bruce Hurst, Dave Schmidt, Julio Valdez) | .25 | .20 |
| 382 | Joe Simpson | .08 | .06 |
| 383a | Pascual Perez (no position on front) | 18.00 | 13.50 |
| 383b | Pascual Perez (position on front) | .12 | .09 |
| 384 | Keith Moreland | .12 | .09 |
| 385 | Ken Forsch | .08 | .06 |
| 386 | Jerry White | .08 | .06 |
| 387 | Tom Veryzer | .08 | .06 |
| 388 | Joe Rudi | .12 | .09 |
| 389 | George Vukovich | .08 | .06 |
| 390 | Eddie Murray | 1.25 | .90 |
| 391 | Dave Tobik | .08 | .06 |

| | MT | NR MT |
|---|---|---|
| 392 Rick Bosetti | .08 | .06 |
| 393 Al Hrabosky | .10 | .08 |
| 394 Checklist 265-396 | .12 | .09 |
| 395 Omar Moreno | .08 | .06 |
| 396 Twins Batting & Pitching Ldrs. (Fernando Arroyo, John Castino) | .10 | .08 |
| 397 Ken Brett | .10 | .08 |
| 398 Mike Squires | .08 | .06 |
| 399 Pat Zachry | .08 | .06 |
| 400 Johnny Bench | 1.50 | 1.25 |
| 401 Johnny Bench IA | .40 | .30 |
| 402 Bill Stein | .08 | .06 |
| 403 Jim Tracy | .08 | .06 |
| 404 Dickie Thon | .10 | .08 |
| 405 Rick Reuschel | .15 | .11 |
| 406 Al Holland | .08 | .06 |
| 407 Danny Boone | .08 | .06 |
| 408 Ed Romero | .08 | .06 |
| 409 Don Cooper | .08 | .06 |
| 410 Ron Cey | .15 | .11 |
| 411 Ron Cey IA | .10 | .08 |
| 412 Luis Leal | .08 | .06 |
| 413 Dan Meyer | .08 | .06 |
| 414 Elias Sosa | .08 | .06 |
| 415 Don Baylor | .15 | .11 |
| 416 Marty Bystrom | .08 | .06 |
| 417 Pat Kelly | .08 | .06 |
| 418 Rangers Future Stars (John Butcher, Bobby Johnson, *Dave Schmidt*)(FC) | .20 | .15 |
| 419 Steve Stone | .12 | .09 |
| 420 George Hendrick | .10 | .08 |
| 421 Mark Clear | .08 | .06 |
| 422 Cliff Johnson | .08 | .06 |
| 423 Stan Papi | .08 | .06 |
| 424 Bruce Benedict | .08 | .06 |
| 425 John Candelaria | .12 | .09 |
| 426 Orioles Batting & Pitching Ldrs. (Eddie Murray, Sammy Stewart) | .35 | .25 |
| 427 Ron Oester | .08 | .06 |
| 428 Lamarr Hoyt (LaMarr) | .08 | .06 |
| 429 John Wathan | .10 | .08 |
| 430 Vida Blue | .15 | .11 |
| 431 Vida Blue IA | .10 | .08 |
| 432 Mike Scott | .25 | .20 |
| 433 Alan Ashby | .08 | .06 |
| 434 Joe Lefebvre | .08 | .06 |
| 435 Robin Yount | 4.00 | 3.00 |
| 436 Joe Strain | .08 | .06 |
| 437 Juan Berenguer | .08 | .06 |
| 438 Pete Mackanin | .08 | .06 |
| 439 *Dave Righetti*(FC) | 2.50 | 2.00 |
| 440 Jeff Burroughs | .10 | .08 |
| 441 Astros Future Stars (Danny Heep, Billy Smith, Bobby Sprowl) | .08 | .06 |
| 442 Bruce Kison | .08 | .06 |
| 443 Mark Wagner | .08 | .06 |
| 444 Terry Forster | .10 | .08 |
| 445 Larry Parrish | .12 | .09 |
| 446 Wayne Garland | .08 | .06 |

| | MT | NR MT |
|---|---|---|
| 447 Darrell Porter | .10 | .08 |
| 448 Darrell Porter IA | .10 | .08 |
| 449 *Luis Aguayo*(FC) | .12 | .09 |
| 450 Jack Morris | .50 | .40 |
| 451 Ed Miller | .08 | .06 |
| 452 *Lee Smith*(FC) | 12.00 | 9.00 |
| 453 Art Howe | .08 | .06 |
| 454 Rick Langford | .08 | .06 |
| 455 Tom Burgmeier | .08 | .06 |
| 456 Cubs Batting & Pitching Ldrs. (Bill Buckner, Randy Martz) | .15 | .11 |
| 457 Tim Stoddard | .08 | .06 |
| 458 Willie Montanez | .08 | .06 |
| 459 Bruce Berenyi | .08 | .06 |
| 460 Jack Clark | .30 | .25 |
| 461 Rich Dotson | .12 | .09 |
| 462 Dave Chalk | .08 | .06 |
| 463 Jim Kern | .08 | .06 |
| 464 Juan Bonilla | .08 | .06 |
| 465 Lee Mazzilli | .10 | .08 |
| 466 Randy Lerch | .08 | .06 |
| 467 Mickey Hatcher | .10 | .08 |
| 468 Floyd Bannister | .12 | .09 |
| 469 Ed Ott | .08 | .06 |
| 470 John Mayberry | .10 | .08 |
| 471 Royals Future Stars (*Atlee Hammaker*, Mike Jones, Darryl Motley) | .25 | .20 |
| 472 Oscar Gamble | .10 | .08 |
| 473 Mike Stanton | .08 | .06 |
| 474 Ken Oberkfell | .08 | .06 |
| 475 Alan Trammell | .50 | .40 |
| 476 Brian Kingman | .08 | .06 |
| 477 Steve Yeager | .08 | .06 |
| 478 Ray Searage | .08 | .06 |
| 479 Rowland Office | .08 | .06 |
| 480 Steve Carlton | 1.00 | .70 |
| 481 Steve Carlton IA | .40 | .30 |
| 482 Glenn Hubbard | .10 | .08 |
| 483 Gary Woods | .08 | .06 |
| 484 Ivan DeJesus | .08 | .06 |
| 485 Kent Tekulve | .10 | .08 |
| 486 Yankees Batting & Pitching Ldrs. (Tommy John, Jerry Mumphrey) | .20 | .15 |
| 487 Bob McClure | .08 | .06 |
| 488 Ron Jackson | .08 | .06 |
| 489 Rick Dempsey | .10 | .08 |
| 490 Dennis Eckersley | .20 | .15 |
| 491 Checklist 397-528 | .12 | .09 |
| 492 Joe Price | .08 | .06 |
| 493 Chet Lemon | .10 | .08 |
| 494 Hubie Brooks | .20 | .15 |
| 495 Dennis Leonard | .10 | .08 |
| 496 Johnny Grubb | .08 | .06 |
| 497 Jim Anderson | .08 | .06 |
| 498 Dave Bergman | .08 | .06 |
| 499 Paul Mirabella | .08 | .06 |
| 500 Rod Carew | 1.00 | .70 |
| 501 Rod Carew IA | .40 | .30 |
| 502 Braves Future Stars (Steve Bedrosian, *Brett Butler*, Larry Owen) | 3.00 | 2.25 |
| 503 Julio Gonzalez | .08 | .06 |
| 504 Rick Peters | .08 | .06 |

| | MT | NR MT |
|---|---|---|
| 505 Graig Nettles | .25 | .20 |
| 506 Graig Nettles IA | .12 | .09 |
| 507 Terry Harper | .08 | .06 |
| 508 *Jody Davis*(FC) | .25 | .20 |
| 509 Harry Spilman | .08 | .06 |
| 510 Fernando Valenzuela | 1.50 | 1.25 |
| 511 Ruppert Jones | .08 | .06 |
| 512 Jerry Dybzinski | .08 | .06 |
| 513 Rick Rhoden | .12 | .09 |
| 514 Joe Ferguson | .08 | .06 |
| 515 Larry Bowa | .20 | .15 |
| 516 Larry Bowa IA | .12 | .09 |
| 517 Mark Brouhard | .08 | .06 |
| 518 Garth Iorg | .08 | .06 |
| 519 Glenn Adams | .08 | .06 |
| 520 Mike Flanagan | .12 | .09 |
| 521 Billy Almon | .08 | .06 |
| 522 Chuck Rainey | .08 | .06 |
| 523 Gary Gray | .08 | .06 |
| 524 Tom Hausman | .08 | .06 |
| 525 Ray Knight | .12 | .09 |
| 526 Expos Batting & Pitching Ldrs. (Warren Cromartie, Bill Gullickson) | .10 | .08 |
| 527 John Henry Johnson | .08 | .06 |
| 528 Matt Alexander | .08 | .06 |
| 529 Allen Ripley | .08 | .06 |
| 530 Dickie Noles | .08 | .06 |
| 531 A's Future Stars (Rich Bordi, Mark Budaska, Kelvin Moore) | .08 | .06 |
| 532 Toby Harrah | .10 | .08 |
| 533 Joaquin Andujar | .10 | .08 |
| 534 Dave McKay | .08 | .06 |
| 535 Lance Parrish | .50 | .40 |
| 536 Rafael Ramirez | .10 | .08 |
| 537 Doug Capilla | .08 | .06 |
| 538 Lou Piniella | .15 | .11 |
| 539 Vern Ruhle | .08 | .06 |
| 540 Andre Dawson | 2.00 | 1.50 |
| 541 Barry Evans | .08 | .06 |
| 542 Ned Yost | .08 | .06 |
| 543 Bill Robinson | .08 | .06 |
| 544 Larry Christenson | .08 | .06 |
| 545 Reggie Smith | .15 | .11 |
| 546 Reggie Smith IA | .10 | .08 |
| 547 Rod Carew AS | .35 | .25 |
| 548 Willie Randolph AS | .12 | .09 |
| 549 George Brett AS | 1.00 | .70 |
| 550 Bucky Dent AS | .12 | .09 |
| 551 Reggie Jackson AS | 1.00 | .70 |
| 552 Ken Singleton AS | .12 | .09 |
| 553 Dave Winfield AS | 1.00 | .70 |
| 554 Carlton Fisk AS | .20 | .15 |
| 555 Scott McGregor AS | .12 | .09 |
| 556 Jack Morris AS | .20 | .15 |
| 557 Rich Gossage AS | .20 | .15 |
| 558 John Tudor | .30 | .25 |
| 559 Indians Batting & Pitching Ldrs. (Bert Blyleven, Mike Hargrove) | .15 | .11 |
| 560 Doug Corbett | .08 | .06 |
| 561 Cardinals Future Stars (Glenn Brummer, Luis | | |

| | MT | NR MT |
|---|---|---|
| DeLeon, Gene Roof) | .08 | .06 |
| 562 Mike O'Berry | .08 | .06 |
| 563 Ross Baumgarten | .08 | .06 |
| 564 Doug DeCinces | .15 | .11 |
| 565 Jackson Todd | .08 | .06 |
| 566 Mike Jorgensen | .08 | .06 |
| 567 Bob Babcock | .08 | .06 |
| 568 Joe Pettini | .08 | .06 |
| 569 Willie Randolph | .15 | .11 |
| 570 Willie Randolph IA | .10 | .08 |
| 571 Glenn Abbott | .08 | .06 |
| 572 Juan Beniquez | .08 | .06 |
| 573 Rick Waits | .08 | .06 |
| 574 Mike Ramsey | .08 | .06 |
| 575 Al Cowens | .08 | .06 |
| 576 Giants Batting & Pitching Ldrs. (Vida Blue, Milt May) | .15 | .11 |
| 577 Rick Monday | .12 | .09 |
| 578 Shooty Babitt | .08 | .06 |
| 579 *Rick Mahler*(FC) | .30 | .25 |
| 580 Bobby Bonds | .15 | .11 |
| 581 Ron Reed | .08 | .06 |
| 582 Luis Pujols | .08 | .06 |
| 583 Tippy Martinez | .08 | .06 |
| 584 Hosken Powell | .08 | .06 |
| 585 Rollie Fingers | .30 | .25 |
| 586 Rollie Fingers IA | .15 | .11 |
| 587 Tim Lollar | .08 | .06 |
| 588 Dale Berra | .08 | .06 |
| 589 Dave Stapleton | .08 | .06 |
| 590 Al Oliver | .20 | .15 |
| 591 Al Oliver IA | .10 | .08 |
| 592 Craig Swan | .08 | .06 |
| 593 Billy Smith | .08 | .06 |
| 594 Renie Martin | .08 | .06 |
| 595 Dave Collins | .10 | .08 |
| 596 Damaso Garcia | .08 | .06 |
| 597 Wayne Nordhagen | .08 | .06 |
| 598 Bob Galasso | .08 | .06 |
| 599 White Sox Future Stars (Jay Loviglio, Reggie Patterson, Leo Sutherland) | .08 | .06 |
| 600 Dave Winfield | 3.00 | 2.25 |
| 601 Sid Monge | .08 | .06 |
| 602 Freddie Patek | .08 | .06 |
| 603 Rich Hebner | .08 | .06 |
| 604 Orlando Sanchez | .08 | .06 |
| 605 Steve Rogers | .10 | .08 |
| 606 Blue Jays Batting & Pitching Ldrs. (John Mayberry, Dave Stieb) | .15 | .11 |
| 607 Leon Durham | .10 | .08 |
| 608 Jerry Royster | .08 | .06 |
| 609 Rick Sutcliffe | .25 | .20 |
| 610 Rickey Henderson | 8.00 | 6.00 |
| 611 Joe Niekro | .20 | .15 |
| 612 Gary Ward | .10 | .08 |
| 613 Jim Gantner | .10 | .08 |
| 614 Juan Eichelberger | .08 | .06 |
| 615 Bob Boone | .12 | .09 |
| 616 Bob Boone IA | .10 | .08 |
| 617 Scott McGregor | .10 | .08 |
| 618 Tim Foli | .08 | .06 |
| 619 Bill Campbell | .08 | .06 |
| 620 Ken Griffey | .15 | .11 |

| | | MT | NR MT |
|---|---|---|---|
| 621 | Ken Griffey IA | .10 | .08 |
| 622 | Dennis Lamp | .08 | .06 |
| 623 | Mets Future Stars (Ron Gardenhire, *Terry Leach*, *Tim Leary*)(FC) | .50 | .40 |
| 624 | Fergie Jenkins | .60 | .45 |
| 625 | Hal McRae | .15 | .11 |
| 626 | Randy Jones | .10 | .08 |
| 627 | Enos Cabell | .08 | .06 |
| 628 | Bill Travers | .08 | .06 |
| 629 | Johnny Wockenfuss | .08 | .06 |
| 630 | Joe Charboneau | .10 | .08 |
| 631 | Gene Tenace | .10 | .08 |
| 632 | Bryan Clark | .08 | .06 |
| 633 | Mitchell Page | .08 | .06 |
| 634 | Checklist 529-660 | .12 | .09 |
| 635 | Ron Davis | .10 | .08 |
| 636 | Phillies Batting & Pitching Ldrs. (Steve Carlton, Pete Rose) | .50 | .40 |
| 637 | Rick Camp | .08 | .06 |
| 638 | John Milner | .08 | .06 |
| 639 | Ken Kravec | .08 | .06 |
| 640 | Cesar Cedeno | .15 | .11 |
| 641 | Steve Mura | .08 | .06 |
| 642 | Mike Scioscia | .10 | .08 |
| 643 | Pete Vuckovich | .10 | .08 |
| 644 | John Castino | .08 | .06 |
| 645 | Frank White | .12 | .09 |
| 646 | Frank White IA | .10 | .08 |
| 647 | Warren Brusstar | .08 | .06 |
| 648 | Jose Morales | .08 | .06 |
| 649 | Ken Clay | .08 | .06 |
| 650 | Carl Yastrzemski | 1.50 | 1.25 |
| 651 | Carl Yastrzemski IA | .60 | .45 |
| 652 | Steve Nicosia | .08 | .06 |
| 653 | Angels Future Stars (*Tom Brunansky*, Luis Sanchez, Daryl Sconiers) | 1.25 | .90 |
| 654 | Jim Morrison | .08 | .06 |
| 655 | Joel Youngblood | .08 | .06 |
| 656 | Eddie Whitson | .08 | .06 |
| 657 | Tom Poquette | .08 | .06 |
| 658 | Tito Landrum | .08 | .06 |
| 659 | Fred Martinez | .08 | .06 |
| 660 | Dave Concepcion | .15 | .11 |
| 661 | Dave Concepcion IA | .10 | .08 |
| 662 | Luis Salazar | .08 | .06 |
| 663 | Hector Cruz | .08 | .06 |
| 664 | Dan Spillner | .08 | .06 |
| 665 | Jim Clancy | .12 | .09 |
| 666 | Tigers Batting & Pitching Ldrs. (Steve Kemp, Dan Petry) | .15 | .11 |
| 667 | Jeff Reardon | 2.00 | 1.50 |
| 668 | Dale Murphy | 1.50 | 1.25 |
| 669 | Larry Milbourne | .08 | .06 |
| 670 | Steve Kemp | .12 | .09 |
| 671 | Mike Davis | .10 | .08 |
| 672 | Bob Knepper | .12 | .09 |
| 673 | Keith Drumright | .08 | .06 |
| 674 | Dave Goltz | .10 | .08 |
| 675 | Cecil Cooper | .20 | .15 |
| 676 | Sal Butera | .08 | .06 |
| 677 | Alfredo Griffin | .12 | .09 |
| 678 | Tom Paciorek | .08 | .06 |

| | | MT | NR MT |
|---|---|---|---|
| 679 | Sammy Stewart | .08 | .06 |
| 680 | Gary Matthews | .12 | .09 |
| 681 | Dodgers Future Stars (*Mike Marshall*, Ron Roenicke, *Steve Sax*)(FC) | 5.00 | 3.75 |
| 682 | Jesse Jefferson | .08 | .06 |
| 683 | Phil Garner | .10 | .08 |
| 684 | Harold Baines | .70 | .50 |
| 685 | Bert Blyleven | .20 | .15 |
| 686 | Gary Allenson | .08 | .06 |
| 687 | Greg Minton | .08 | .06 |
| 688 | Leon Roberts | .08 | .06 |
| 689 | Lary Sorensen | .08 | .06 |
| 690 | Dave Kingman | .20 | .15 |
| 691 | Dan Schatzeder | .08 | .06 |
| 692 | Wayne Gross | .08 | .06 |
| 693 | Cesar Geronimo | .08 | .06 |
| 694 | Dave Wehrmeister | .08 | .06 |
| 695 | Warren Cromartie | .08 | .06 |
| 696 | Pirates Batting & Pitching Ldrs. (Bill Madlock, Buddy Solomon) | .15 | .11 |
| 697 | John Montefusco | .08 | .06 |
| 698 | Tony Scott | .08 | .06 |
| 699 | Dick Tidrow | .08 | .06 |
| 700 | George Foster | .25 | .20 |
| 701 | George Foster IA | .12 | .09 |
| 702 | Steve Renko | .08 | .06 |
| 703 | Brewers Batting & Pitching Ldrs. (Cecil Cooper, Pete Vuckovich) | .15 | .11 |
| 704 | Mickey Rivers | .10 | .08 |
| 705 | Mickey Rivers IA | .10 | .08 |
| 706 | Barry Foote | .08 | .06 |
| 707 | Mark Bomback | .08 | .06 |
| 708 | Gene Richards | .08 | .06 |
| 709 | Don Money | .08 | .06 |
| 710 | Jerry Reuss | .12 | .09 |
| 711 | Mariners Future Stars (Dave Edler, *Dave Henderson*, Reggie Walton) | 1.25 | .90 |
| 712 | Denny Martinez | .10 | .08 |
| 713 | Del Unser | .08 | .06 |
| 714 | Jerry Koosman | .12 | .09 |
| 715 | Willie Stargell | .80 | .60 |
| 716 | Willie Stargell IA | .30 | .25 |
| 717 | Rick Miller | .08 | .06 |
| 718 | Charlie Hough | .12 | .09 |
| 719 | Jerry Narron | .08 | .06 |
| 720 | Greg Luzinski | .20 | .15 |
| 721 | Greg Luzinski IA | .12 | .09 |
| 722 | Jerry Martin | .08 | .06 |
| 723 | Junior Kennedy | .08 | .06 |
| 724 | Dave Rosello | .08 | .06 |
| 725 | Amos Otis | .10 | .08 |
| 726 | Amos Otis IA | .10 | .08 |
| 727 | Sixto Lezcano | .08 | .06 |
| 728 | Aurelio Lopez | .08 | .06 |
| 729 | Jim Spencer | .08 | .06 |
| 730 | Gary Carter | .80 | .60 |
| 731 | Padres Future Stars (Mike Armstrong, Doug Gwosdz, Fred Kuhaulua) | .08 | .06 |

|  | | MT | NR MT |
|---|---|---|---|
| 732 | Mike Lum | .08 | .06 |
| 733 | Larry McWilliams | .08 | .06 |
| 734 | Mike Ivie | .08 | .06 |
| 735 | Rudy May | .08 | .06 |
| 736 | Jerry Turner | .08 | .06 |
| 737 | Reggie Cleveland | .08 | .06 |
| 738 | Dave Engle | .08 | .06 |
| 739 | Joey McLaughlin | .08 | .06 |
| 740 | Dave Lopes | .12 | .09 |
| 741 | Dave Lopes IA | .10 | .08 |
| 742 | Dick Drago | .08 | .06 |
| 743 | John Stearns | .08 | .06 |
| 744 | *Mike Witt*(FC) | .80 | .60 |
| 745 | Bake McBride | .08 | .06 |
| 746 | Andre Thornton | .12 | .09 |
| 747 | John Lowenstein | .08 | .06 |
| 748 | Marc Hill | .08 | .06 |
| 749 | Bob Shirley | .08 | .06 |
| 750 | Jim Rice | .70 | .50 |
| 751 | Rick Honeycutt | .08 | .06 |
| 752 | Lee Lacy | .08 | .06 |
| 753 | Tom Brookens | .08 | .06 |
| 754 | Joe Morgan | .70 | .50 |
| 755 | Joe Morgan IA | .20 | .15 |
| 756 | Reds Batting & Pitching Ldrs. (Ken Griffey, Tom Seaver) | .30 | .25 |
| 757 | Tom Underwood | .08 | .06 |
| 758 | Claudell Washington | .12 | .09 |
| 759 | Paul Splittorff | .08 | .06 |
| 760 | Bill Buckner | .15 | .11 |
| 761 | Dave Smith | .12 | .09 |
| 762 | Mike Phillips | .08 | .06 |
| 763 | Tom Hume | .08 | .06 |
| 764 | Steve Swisher | .08 | .06 |
| 765 | Gorman Thomas | .12 | .09 |
| 766 | Twins Future Stars (Lenny Faedo, *Kent Hrbek, Tim Laudner*)(FC) | 3.00 | 2.25 |
| 767 | Roy Smalley | .08 | .06 |
| 768 | Jerry Garvin | .08 | .06 |
| 769 | Richie Zisk | .10 | .08 |
| 770 | Rich Gossage | .35 | .25 |
| 771 | Rich Gossage IA | .15 | .11 |
| 772 | Bert Campaneris | .12 | .09 |
| 773 | John Denny | .08 | .06 |
| 774 | Jay Johnstone | .10 | .08 |
| 775 | Bob Forsch | .10 | .08 |
| 776 | Mark Belanger | .10 | .08 |
| 777 | Tom Griffin | .08 | .06 |
| 778 | Kevin Hickey | .08 | .06 |
| 779 | Grant Jackson | .08 | .06 |
| 780 | Pete Rose | 2.25 | 1.75 |
| 781 | Pete Rose IA | 1.00 | .70 |
| 782 | Frank Taveras | .08 | .06 |
| 783 | *Greg Harris*(FC) | .15 | .11 |
| 784 | Milt Wilcox | .08 | .06 |
| 785 | Dan Driessen | .10 | .08 |
| 786 | Red Sox Batting & Pitching Ldrs. (Carney Lansford, Mike Torrez) | .12 | .09 |
| 787 | Fred Stanley | .08 | .06 |
| 788 | Woodie Fryman | .10 | .08 |
| 789 | Checklist 661-792 | .12 | .09 |
| 790 | Larry Gura | .08 | .06 |
| 791 | Bobby Brown | .08 | .06 |
| 792 | Frank Tanana | .12 | .09 |

## 1982 Topps Traded

Topps released its second straight 132-card Traded set in September of 1982. Again, the 2-1/2" by 3-1/2" cards feature not only players who had been traded during the season, but also promising rookies who were given their first individual cards. The cards follow the basic design of the regular issues, but have their backs printed in red rather than the regular-issue green. As in 1981, the cards were not available in normal retail outlets and could only be purchased through regular baseball card dealers. Unlike the previous year, the cards are numbered 1-132 with the letter "T" following the number.

|  |  | MT | NR MT |
|---|---|---|---|
| Complete Set: | | 300.00 | 225.00 |
| Common Player: | | .10 | .08 |
| 1T | Doyle Alexander | .20 | .15 |
| 2T | Jesse Barfield | 1.00 | .70 |
| 3T | Ross Baumgarten | .10 | .08 |
| 4T | Steve Bedrosian | .80 | .60 |
| 5T | Mark Belanger | .15 | .11 |
| 6T | Kurt Bevacqua | .10 | .08 |
| 7T | Tim Blackwell | .10 | .08 |
| 8T | Vida Blue | .25 | .20 |
| 9T | Bob Boone | .20 | .15 |
| 10T | Larry Bowa | .25 | .20 |
| 11T | Dan Briggs | .10 | .08 |
| 12T | Bobby Brown | .10 | .08 |
| 13T | Tom Brunansky | 2.00 | 1.50 |
| 14T | Jeff Burroughs | .15 | .11 |
| 15T | Enos Cabell | .10 | .08 |
| 16T | Bill Campbell | .10 | .08 |
| 17T | Bobby Castillo | .10 | .08 |
| 18T | Bill Caudill | .10 | .08 |
| 19T | Cesar Cedeno | .20 | .15 |
| 20T | Dave Collins | .15 | .11 |
| 21T | Doug Corbett | .10 | .08 |
| 22T | Al Cowens | .10 | .08 |
| 23T | Chili Davis | 3.00 | 2.25 |
| 24T | Dick Davis | .10 | .08 |

| | MT | NR MT |
|---|---|---|
| 25T Ron Davis | .10 | .08 |
| 26T Doug DeCinces | .20 | .15 |
| 27T Ivan DeJesus | .10 | .08 |
| 28T Bob Dernier | .20 | .15 |
| 29T Bo Diaz | .15 | .11 |
| 30T Roger Erickson | .10 | .08 |
| 31T Jim Essian | .10 | .08 |
| 32T Ed Farmer | .10 | .08 |
| 33T Doug Flynn | .10 | .08 |
| 34T Tim Foli | .10 | .08 |
| 35T Dan Ford | .10 | .08 |
| 36T George Foster | .40 | .30 |
| 37T Dave Frost | .10 | .08 |
| 38T Rich Gale | .10 | .08 |
| 39T Ron Gardenhire | .10 | .08 |
| 40T Ken Griffey | .25 | .20 |
| 41T Greg Harris | .15 | .11 |
| 42T Von Hayes | .80 | .60 |
| 43T Larry Herndon | .15 | .11 |
| 44T Kent Hrbek | 5.00 | 3.75 |
| 45T Mike Ivie | .10 | .08 |
| 46T Grant Jackson | .10 | .08 |
| 47T Reggie Jackson | 9.00 | 6.75 |
| 48T Ron Jackson | .10 | .08 |
| 49T Fergie Jenkins | 2.00 | 1.50 |
| 50T Lamar Johnson | .10 | .08 |
| 51T Randy Johnson | .10 | .08 |
| 52T Jay Johnstone | .15 | .11 |
| 53T Mick Kelleher | .10 | .08 |
| 54T Steve Kemp | .15 | .11 |
| 55T Junior Kennedy | .10 | .08 |
| 56T Jim Kern | .10 | .08 |
| 57T Ray Knight | .20 | .15 |
| 58T Wayne Krenchicki | .10 | .08 |
| 59T Mike Krukow | .15 | .11 |
| 60T Duane Kuiper | .10 | .08 |
| 61T Mike LaCoss | .10 | .08 |
| 62T Chet Lemon | .15 | .11 |
| 63T Sixto Lezcano | .10 | .08 |
| 64T Dave Lopes | .15 | .11 |
| 65T Jerry Martin | .10 | .08 |
| 66T Renie Martin | .10 | .08 |
| 67T John Mayberry | .15 | .11 |
| 68T Lee Mazzilli | .15 | .11 |
| 69T Bake McBride | .10 | .08 |
| 70T Dan Meyer | .10 | .08 |
| 71T Larry Milbourne | .10 | .08 |
| 72T Eddie Milner(FC) | .20 | .15 |
| 73T Sid Monge | .10 | .08 |
| 74T Jose Morales | .10 | .08 |
| 75T Keith Moreland | .20 | .15 |
| 76T John Montefusco | .10 | .08 |
| 77T Jim Morrison | .10 | .08 |
| 78T Rance Mulliniks | .10 | .08 |
| 79T Steve Mura | .10 | .08 |
| 80T Gene Nelson | .10 | .08 |
| 81T Joe Nolan | .10 | .08 |
| 82T Dickie Noles | .10 | .08 |
| 83T Al Oliver | .30 | .25 |
| 84T Jorge Orta | .10 | .08 |
| 85T Tom Paciorek | .10 | .08 |
| 86T Larry Parrish | .20 | .15 |
| 87T Jack Perconte | .10 | .08 |
| 88T Gaylord Perry | 2.00 | 1.50 |
| 89T Rob Picciolo | .10 | .08 |
| 90T Joe Pittman | .10 | .08 |
| 91T Hosken Powell | .10 | .08 |

| | MT | NR MT |
|---|---|---|
| 92T Mike Proly | .10 | .08 |
| 93T Greg Pryor | .10 | .08 |
| 94T Charlie Puleo(FC) | .15 | .11 |
| 95T Shane Rawley | .20 | .15 |
| 96T Johnny Ray | .80 | .60 |
| 97T Dave Revering | .10 | .08 |
| 98T Cal Ripken | 260.00 | 187.50 |
| 99T Allen Ripley | .10 | .08 |
| 100T Bill Robinson | .10 | .08 |
| 101T Aurelio Rodriguez | .15 | .11 |
| 102T Joe Rudi | .20 | .15 |
| 103T Steve Sax | 8.00 | 6.00 |
| 104T Dan Schatzeder | .10 | .08 |
| 105T Bob Shirley | .10 | .08 |
| 106T Eric Show(FC) | .50 | .40 |
| 107T Roy Smalley | .15 | .11 |
| 108T Lonnie Smith | .15 | .11 |
| 109T Ozzie Smith | 15.00 | 11.00 |
| 110T Reggie Smith | .20 | .15 |
| 111T Lary Sorensen | .10 | .08 |
| 112T Elias Sosa | .10 | .08 |
| 113T Mike Stanton | .10 | .08 |
| 114T Steve Stroughter | .10 | .08 |
| 115T Champ Summers | .10 | .08 |
| 116T Rick Sutcliffe | .80 | .60 |
| 117T Frank Tanana | .20 | .15 |
| 118T Frank Taveras | .10 | .08 |
| 119T Garry Templeton | .20 | .15 |
| 120T Alex Trevino | .10 | .08 |
| 121T Jerry Turner | .10 | .08 |
| 122T Ed Vande Berg(FC) | .15 | .11 |
| 123T Tom Veryzer | .10 | .08 |
| 124T Ron Washington | .10 | .08 |
| 125T Bob Watson | .15 | .11 |
| 126T Dennis Werth | .10 | .08 |
| 127T Eddie Whitson | .15 | .11 |
| 128T Rob Wilfong | .10 | .08 |
| 129T Bump Wills | .10 | .08 |
| 130T Gary Woods | .10 | .08 |
| 131T Butch Wynegar | .15 | .11 |
| 132T Checklist 1-132 | .10 | .08 |

## 1983 Topps

The 1983 Topps set totals 792 cards. Missing among the regular 2-1/2" by 3-1/2" cards are some form of future stars cards, as Topps was saving them for the now-established late season "Traded" set. The 1983 cards carry a large color photo as well as a smaller color photo on the front, quite similar in design to the 1963 set. Team colors frame the card, which, at the bottom, have the player's name, position and team. At the upper right-hand corner is a Topps Logo. The backs are horizontal and include statistics, personal information and 1982 highlights. Specialty cards include record-breaking perfor- mances, league leaders, All-Stars, numbered check- lists "Team Leaders" and "Super Veteran" cards which are horizontal with a current and first-season picture of the honored player.

|  |  | MT | NR MT |
|---|---|---|---|
| | Complete Set: | 175.00 | 125.00 |
| | Common Player: | .08 | .06 |
| 1 | Record Breaker (Tony Armas) | .12 | .09 |
| 2 | Record Breaker (Rickey Henderson) | 1.50 | 1.25 |
| 3 | Record Breaker (Greg Minton) | .08 | .06 |
| 4 | Record Breaker (Lance Parrish) | .20 | .15 |
| 5 | Record Breaker (Manny Trillo) | .08 | .06 |
| 6 | Record Breaker (John Wathan) | .08 | .06 |
| 7 | Gene Richards | .08 | .06 |
| 8 | Steve Balboni | .10 | .08 |
| 9 | Joey McLaughlin | .08 | .06 |
| 10 | Gorman Thomas | .12 | .09 |
| 11 | Billy Gardner | .08 | .06 |
| 12 | Paul Mirabella | .08 | .06 |
| 13 | Larry Herndon | .10 | .08 |
| 14 | Frank LaCorte | .08 | .06 |
| 15 | Ron Cey | .15 | .11 |
| 16 | George Vukovich | .08 | .06 |
| 17 | Kent Tekulve | .10 | .08 |
| 18 | Super Veteran (Kent Tekulve) | .10 | .08 |
| 19 | Oscar Gamble | .10 | .08 |
| 20 | Carlton Fisk | 2.00 | 1.50 |
| 21 | Orioles Batting & Pitching Ldrs. (Eddie Murray, Jim Palmer) | .35 | .25 |
| 22 | Randy Martz | .08 | .06 |
| 23 | Mike Heath | .08 | .06 |
| 24 | Steve Mura | .08 | .06 |
| 25 | Hal McRae | .15 | .11 |
| 26 | Jerry Royster | .08 | .06 |
| 27 | Doug Corbett | .08 | .06 |
| 28 | Bruce Bochte | .08 | .06 |
| 29 | Randy Jones | .10 | .08 |
| 30 | Jim Rice | .70 | .50 |
| 31 | Bill Gullickson | .08 | .06 |
| 32 | Dave Bergman | .08 | .06 |
| 33 | Jack O'Connor | .08 | .06 |
| 34 | Paul Householder | .08 | .06 |
| 35 | Rollie Fingers | .60 | .45 |
| 36 | Super Veteran (Rollie Fingers) | .15 | .11 |
| 37 | Darrell Johnson | .08 | .06 |
| 38 | Tim Flannery | .08 | .06 |
| 39 | Terry Puhl | .08 | .06 |
| 40 | Fernando Valenzuela | .50 | .40 |
| 41 | Jerry Turner | .08 | .06 |
| 42 | Dale Murray | .08 | .06 |
| 43 | Bob Dernier | .08 | .06 |
| 44 | Don Robinson | .10 | .08 |
| 45 | John Mayberry | .10 | .08 |
| 46 | Richard Dotson | .12 | .09 |
| 47 | Dave McKay | .08 | .06 |
| 48 | Lary Sorensen | .08 | .06 |
| 49 | *Willie McGee*(FC) | 5.00 | 3.75 |
| 50 | Bob Horner | .20 | .15 |
| 51 | Cubs Batting & Pitching Ldrs. (Leon Durham, Fergie Jenkins) | .15 | .11 |
| 52 | *Onix Concepcion*(FC) | .08 | .06 |
| 53 | Mike Witt | .30 | .25 |
| 54 | Jim Maler | .08 | .06 |
| 55 | Mookie Wilson | .12 | .09 |
| 56 | Chuck Rainey | .08 | .06 |
| 57 | Tim Blackwell | .08 | .06 |
| 58 | Al Holland | .08 | .06 |
| 59 | Benny Ayala | .08 | .06 |
| 60 | Johnny Bench | 1.50 | 1.25 |
| 61 | Super Veteran (Johnny Bench) | .30 | .25 |
| 62 | Bob McClure | .08 | .06 |
| 63 | Rick Monday | .12 | .09 |
| 64 | Bill Stein | .08 | .06 |
| 65 | Jack Morris | 1.00 | .70 |
| 66 | Bob Lillis | .08 | .06 |
| 67 | Sal Butera | .08 | .06 |
| 68 | *Eric Show* | .30 | .25 |
| 69 | Lee Lacy | .08 | .06 |
| 70 | Steve Carlton | 1.25 | .90 |
| 71 | Super Veteran (Steve Carlton) | .30 | .25 |
| 72 | Tom Paciorek | .08 | .06 |
| 73 | Allen Ripley | .08 | .06 |
| 74 | Julio Gonzalez | .08 | .06 |
| 75 | Amos Otis | .10 | .08 |
| 76 | Rick Mahler | .12 | .09 |
| 77 | Hosken Powell | .08 | .06 |
| 78 | Bill Caudill | .08 | .06 |
| 79 | Mick Kelleher | .08 | .06 |
| 80 | George Foster | .20 | .15 |
| 81 | Yankees Batting & Pitching Ldrs. (Jerry Mumphrey, Dave Righetti) | .15 | .11 |
| 82 | Bruce Hurst | .15 | .11 |
| 83 | *Ryne Sandberg*(FC) | 50.00 | 37.00 |
| 84 | Milt May | .08 | .06 |
| 85 | Ken Singleton | .12 | .09 |
| 86 | Tom Hume | .08 | .06 |
| 87 | Joe Rudi | .12 | .09 |
| 88 | Jim Gantner | .10 | .08 |
| 89 | Leon Roberts | .08 | .06 |

| | | MT | NR MT |
|---|---|---|---|
| 90 | Jerry Reuss | .12 | .09 |
| 91 | Larry Milbourne | .08 | .06 |
| 92 | Mike LaCoss | .08 | .06 |
| 93 | John Castino | .08 | .06 |
| 94 | Dave Edwards | .08 | .06 |
| 95 | Alan Trammell | .50 | .40 |
| 96 | Dick Howser | .08 | .06 |
| 97 | Ross Baumgarten | .08 | .06 |
| 98 | Vance Law | .10 | .08 |
| 99 | Dickie Noles | .08 | .06 |
| 100 | Pete Rose | 1.75 | 1.25 |
| 101 | Super Veteran (Pete Rose) | .80 | .60 |
| 102 | Dave Beard | .08 | .06 |
| 103 | Darrell Porter | .10 | .08 |
| 104 | Bob Walk | .08 | .06 |
| 105 | Don Baylor | .15 | .11 |
| 106 | Gene Nelson | .08 | .06 |
| 107 | Mike Jorgensen | .08 | .06 |
| 108 | Glenn Hoffman | .08 | .06 |
| 109 | Luis Leal | .08 | .06 |
| 110 | Ken Griffey | .15 | .11 |
| 111 | Expos Batting & Pitching Ldrs. (Al Oliver, Steve Rogers) | .15 | .11 |
| 112 | Bob Shirley | .08 | .06 |
| 113 | Ron Roenicke | .08 | .06 |
| 114 | Jim Slaton | .08 | .06 |
| 115 | Chili Davis | .20 | .15 |
| 116 | Dave Schmidt | .10 | .08 |
| 117 | Alan Knicely | .08 | .06 |
| 118 | Chris Welsh | .08 | .06 |
| 119 | Tom Brookens | .08 | .06 |
| 120 | Len Barker | .10 | .08 |
| 121 | Mickey Hatcher | .10 | .08 |
| 122 | Jimmy Smith | .08 | .06 |
| 123 | George Frazier | .08 | .06 |
| 124 | Marc Hill | .08 | .06 |
| 125 | Leon Durham | .10 | .08 |
| 126 | Joe Torre | .10 | .08 |
| 127 | Preston Hanna | .08 | .06 |
| 128 | Mike Ramsey | .08 | .06 |
| 129 | Checklist 1-132 | .12 | .09 |
| 130 | Dave Stieb | .20 | .15 |
| 131 | Ed Ott | .08 | .06 |
| 132 | Todd Cruz | .08 | .06 |
| 133 | Jim Barr | .08 | .06 |
| 134 | Hubie Brooks | .15 | .11 |
| 135 | Dwight Evans | .25 | .20 |
| 136 | Willie Aikens | .08 | .06 |
| 137 | Woodie Fryman | .10 | .08 |
| 138 | Rick Dempsey | .10 | .08 |
| 139 | Bruce Berenyi | .08 | .06 |
| 140 | Willie Randolph | .12 | .09 |
| 141 | Indians Batting & Pitching Ldrs. (Toby Harrah, Rick Sutcliffe) | .12 | .09 |
| 142 | Mike Caldwell | .08 | .06 |
| 143 | Joe Pettini | .08 | .06 |
| 144 | Mark Wagner | .08 | .06 |
| 145 | Don Sutton | .40 | .30 |
| 146 | Super Veteran (Don Sutton) | .20 | .15 |
| 147 | Rick Leach | .08 | .06 |
| 148 | Dave Roberts | .08 | .06 |
| 149 | Johnny Ray | .15 | .11 |
| 150 | Bruce Sutter | .20 | .15 |

| | | MT | NR MT |
|---|---|---|---|
| 151 | Super Veteran (Bruce Sutter) | .12 | .09 |
| 152 | Jay Johnstone | .10 | .08 |
| 153 | Jerry Koosman | .12 | .09 |
| 154 | Johnnie LeMaster | .08 | .06 |
| 155 | Dan Quisenberry | .20 | .15 |
| 156 | Billy Martin | .12 | .09 |
| 157 | Steve Bedrosian | .25 | .20 |
| 158 | Rob Wilfong | .08 | .06 |
| 159 | Mike Stanton | .08 | .06 |
| 160 | Dave Kingman | .20 | .15 |
| 161 | Super Veteran (Dave Kingman) | .10 | .08 |
| 162 | Mark Clear | .08 | .06 |
| 163 | Cal Ripken | 25.00 | 18.00 |
| 164 | Dave Palmer | .08 | .06 |
| 165 | Dan Driessen | .10 | .08 |
| 166 | John Pacella | .08 | .06 |
| 167 | Mark Brouhard | .08 | .06 |
| 168 | Juan Eichelberger | .08 | .06 |
| 169 | Doug Flynn | .08 | .06 |
| 170 | Steve Howe | .10 | .08 |
| 171 | Giants Batting & Pitching Ldrs. (Bill Laskey, Joe Morgan) | .15 | .11 |
| 172 | Vern Ruhle | .08 | .06 |
| 173 | Jim Morrison | .08 | .06 |
| 174 | Jerry Ujdur | .08 | .06 |
| 175 | Bo Diaz | .10 | .08 |
| 176 | Dave Righetti | .35 | .25 |
| 177 | Harold Baines | .25 | .20 |
| 178 | Luis Tiant | .15 | .11 |
| 179 | Super Veteran (Luis Tiant) | .10 | .08 |
| 180 | Rickey Henderson | 6.00 | 4.50 |
| 181 | Terry Felton | .08 | .06 |
| 182 | Mike Fischlin | .08 | .06 |
| 183 | *Ed Vande Berg* | .12 | .09 |
| 184 | Bob Clark | .08 | .06 |
| 185 | Tim Lollar | .08 | .06 |
| 186 | Whitey Herzog | .10 | .08 |
| 187 | Terry Leach | .12 | .09 |
| 188 | Rick Miller | .08 | .06 |
| 189 | Dan Schatzeder | .08 | .06 |
| 190 | Cecil Cooper | .20 | .15 |
| 191 | Joe Price | .08 | .06 |
| 192 | Floyd Rayford | .08 | .06 |
| 193 | Harry Spilman | .08 | .06 |
| 194 | Cesar Geronimo | .08 | .06 |
| 195 | Bob Stoddard | .08 | .06 |
| 196 | Bill Fahey | .08 | .06 |
| 197 | *Jim Eisenreich*(FC) | .15 | .11 |
| 198 | Kiko Garcia | .08 | .06 |
| 199 | Marty Bystrom | .08 | .06 |
| 200 | Rod Carew | .70 | .50 |
| 201 | Super Veteran (Rod Carew) | .35 | .25 |
| 202 | Blue Jays Batting & Pitching Ldrs. (Damaso Garcia, Dave Stieb) | .12 | .09 |
| 203 | Mike Morgan | .15 | .11 |
| 204 | Junior Kennedy | .08 | .06 |
| 205 | Dave Parker | .40 | .30 |
| 206 | Ken Oberkfell | .08 | .06 |
| 207 | Rick Camp | .08 | .06 |
| 208 | Dan Meyer | .08 | .06 |

| | | MT | NR MT |
|---|---|---|---|
| 209 | *Mike Moore*(FC) | 1.00 | .70 |
| 210 | Jack Clark | .30 | .25 |
| 211 | John Denny | .08 | .06 |
| 212 | John Stearns | .08 | .06 |
| 213 | Tom Burgmeier | .08 | .06 |
| 214 | Jerry White | .08 | .06 |
| 215 | Mario Soto | .10 | .08 |
| 216 | Tony LaRussa | .10 | .08 |
| 217 | Tim Stoddard | .08 | .06 |
| 218 | Roy Howell | .08 | .06 |
| 219 | Mike Armstrong | .08 | .06 |
| 220 | Dusty Baker | .12 | .09 |
| 221 | Joe Niekro | .15 | .11 |
| 222 | Damaso Garcia | .08 | .06 |
| 223 | John Montefusco | .08 | .06 |
| 224 | Mickey Rivers | .10 | .08 |
| 225 | Enos Cabell | .08 | .06 |
| 226 | Enrique Romo | .08 | .06 |
| 227 | Chris Bando | .08 | .06 |
| 228 | Joaquin Andujar | .10 | .08 |
| 229 | Phillies Batting & Pitching Ldrs. (Steve Carlton, Bo Diaz) | .20 | .15 |
| 230 | Fergie Jenkins | .60 | .45 |
| 231 | Super Veteran (Fergie Jenkins) | .12 | .09 |
| 232 | Tom Brunansky | .30 | .25 |
| 233 | Wayne Gross | .08 | .06 |
| 234 | Larry Andersen | .08 | .06 |
| 235 | Claudell Washington | .10 | .08 |
| 236 | Steve Renko | .08 | .06 |
| 237 | Dan Norman | .08 | .06 |
| 238 | *Bud Black*(FC) | .70 | .50 |
| 239 | Dave Stapleton | .08 | .06 |
| 240 | Rich Gossage | .30 | .25 |
| 241 | Super Veteran (Rich Gossage) | .15 | .11 |
| 242 | Joe Nolan | .08 | .06 |
| 243 | Duane Walker | .08 | .06 |
| 244 | Dwight Bernard | .08 | .06 |
| 245 | Steve Sax | .35 | .25 |
| 246 | George Bamberger | .08 | .06 |
| 247 | Dave Smith | .12 | .09 |
| 248 | Bake McBride | .08 | .06 |
| 249 | Checklist 133-264 | .12 | .09 |
| 250 | Bill Buckner | .15 | .11 |
| 251 | *Alan Wiggins*(FC) | .08 | .06 |
| 252 | Luis Aguayo | .08 | .06 |
| 253 | Larry McWilliams | .08 | .06 |
| 254 | Rick Cerone | .08 | .06 |
| 255 | Gene Garber | .08 | .06 |
| 256 | Super Veteran (Gene Garber) | .08 | .06 |
| 257 | Jesse Barfield | .50 | .40 |
| 258 | Manny Castillo | .08 | .06 |
| 259 | Jeff Jones | .08 | .06 |
| 260 | Steve Kemp | .12 | .09 |
| 261 | Tigers Batting & Pitching Ldrs. (Larry Herndon, Dan Petry) | .10 | .08 |
| 262 | Ron Jackson | .08 | .06 |
| 263 | Renie Martin | .08 | .06 |
| 264 | Jamie Quirk | .08 | .06 |
| 265 | Joel Youngblood | .08 | .06 |
| 266 | Paul Boris | .08 | .06 |
| 267 | Terry Francona | .08 | .06 |

| | | MT | NR MT |
|---|---|---|---|
| 268 | *Storm Davis*(FC) | .30 | .25 |
| 269 | Ron Oester | .08 | .06 |
| 270 | Dennis Eckersley | 2.00 | 1.50 |
| 271 | Ed Romero | .08 | .06 |
| 272 | Frank Tanana | .12 | .09 |
| 273 | Mark Belanger | .10 | .08 |
| 274 | Terry Kennedy | .12 | .09 |
| 275 | Ray Knight | .12 | .09 |
| 276 | Gene Mauch | .10 | .08 |
| 277 | Rance Mulliniks | .08 | .06 |
| 278 | Kevin Hickey | .08 | .06 |
| 279 | Greg Gross | .08 | .06 |
| 280 | Bert Blyleven | .20 | .15 |
| 281 | Andre Robertson | .08 | .06 |
| 282 | Reggie Smith | .12 | .09 |
| 283 | Super Veteran (Reggie Smith) | .10 | .08 |
| 284 | Jeff Lahti | .08 | .06 |
| 285 | Lance Parrish | .40 | .30 |
| 286 | Rick Langford | .08 | .06 |
| 287 | Bobby Brown | .08 | .06 |
| 288 | *Joe Cowley*(FC) | .12 | .09 |
| 289 | Jerry Dybzinski | .08 | .06 |
| 290 | Jeff Reardon | 2.00 | 1.50 |
| 291 | Pirates Batting & Pitching Ldrs. (John Candelaria, Bill Madlock) | .15 | .11 |
| 292 | Craig Swan | .08 | .06 |
| 293 | Glenn Gulliver | .08 | .06 |
| 294 | Dave Engle | .08 | .06 |
| 295 | Jerry Remy | .08 | .06 |
| 296 | Greg Harris | .08 | .06 |
| 297 | Ned Yost | .08 | .06 |
| 298 | Floyd Chiffer | .08 | .06 |
| 299 | George Wright | .08 | .06 |
| 300 | Mike Schmidt | 3.00 | 2.25 |
| 301 | Super Veteran (Mike Schmidt) | 1.00 | .70 |
| 302 | Ernie Whitt | .10 | .08 |
| 303 | Miguel Dilone | .08 | .06 |
| 304 | Dave Rucker | .08 | .06 |
| 305 | Larry Bowa | .15 | .11 |
| 306 | Tom Lasorda | .12 | .09 |
| 307 | Lou Piniella | .15 | .11 |
| 308 | Jesus Vega | .08 | .06 |
| 309 | Jeff Leonard | .12 | .09 |
| 310 | Greg Luzinski | .15 | .11 |
| 311 | Glenn Brummer | .08 | .06 |
| 312 | Brian Kingman | .08 | .06 |
| 313 | Gary Gray | .08 | .06 |
| 314 | Ken Dayley(FC) | .15 | .11 |
| 315 | Rick Burleson | .10 | .08 |
| 316 | Paul Splittorff | .08 | .06 |
| 317 | Gary Rajsich | .08 | .06 |
| 318 | John Tudor | .15 | .11 |
| 319 | Lenn Sakata | .08 | .06 |
| 320 | Steve Rogers | .10 | .08 |
| 321 | Brewers Batting & Pitching Ldrs. (Pete Vuckovich, Robin Yount) | .20 | .15 |
| 322 | Dave Van Gorder | .08 | .06 |
| 323 | Luis DeLeon | .08 | .06 |
| 324 | Mike Marshall | .12 | .09 |
| 325 | Von Hayes | .20 | .15 |
| 326 | Garth Iorg | .08 | .06 |

| | | MT | NR MT |
|---|---|---|---|
| 327 | Bobby Castillo | .08 | .06 |
| 328 | Craig Reynolds | .08 | .06 |
| 329 | Randy Niemann | .08 | .06 |
| 330 | Buddy Bell | .15 | .11 |
| 331 | Mike Krukow | .10 | .08 |
| 332 | *Glenn Wilson*(FC) | | |
| | | .12 | .09 |
| 333 | Dave LaRoche | .08 | .06 |
| 334 | Super Veteran (Dave LaRoche) | .08 | .06 |
| 335 | Steve Henderson | .08 | .06 |
| 336 | Rene Lachemann | .08 | .06 |
| 337 | Tito Landrum | .08 | .06 |
| 338 | Bob Owchinko | .08 | .06 |
| 339 | Terry Harper | .08 | .06 |
| 340 | Larry Gura | .08 | .06 |
| 341 | Doug DeCinces | .15 | .11 |
| 342 | Atlee Hammaker | .10 | .08 |
| 343 | Bob Bailor | .08 | .06 |
| 344 | Roger LaFrancois | .08 | .06 |
| 345 | Jim Clancy | .10 | .08 |
| 346 | Joe Pittman | .08 | .06 |
| 347 | Sammy Stewart | .08 | .06 |
| 348 | Alan Bannister | .08 | .06 |
| 349 | Checklist 265-396 | .12 | .09 |
| 350 | Robin Yount | 4.00 | 3.00 |
| 351 | Reds Batting & Pitching Ldrs. (Cesar Cedeno, Mario Soto) | .12 | .09 |
| 352 | Mike Scioscia | .10 | .08 |
| 353 | Steve Comer | .08 | .06 |
| 354 | Randy Johnson | .08 | .06 |
| 355 | Jim Bibby | .08 | .06 |
| 356 | Gary Woods | .08 | .06 |
| 357 | *Len Matuszek*(FC) | | |
| | | .08 | .06 |
| 358 | Jerry Garvin | .08 | .06 |
| 359 | Dave Collins | .10 | .08 |
| 360 | Nolan Ryan | 8.00 | 6.00 |
| 361 | Super Veteran (Nolan Ryan) | .30 | .25 |
| 362 | Bill Almon | .08 | .06 |
| 363 | *John Stuper*(FC) | .08 | .06 |
| 364 | Brett Butler | .20 | .15 |
| 365 | Dave Lopes | .12 | .09 |
| 366 | Dick Williams | .08 | .06 |
| 367 | Bud Anderson | .08 | .06 |
| 368 | Richie Zisk | .10 | .08 |
| 369 | Jesse Orosco | .15 | .11 |
| 370 | Gary Carter | .50 | .40 |
| 371 | Mike Richardt | .08 | .06 |
| 372 | Terry Crowley | .08 | .06 |
| 373 | Kevin Saucier | .08 | .06 |
| 374 | Wayne Krenchicki | .08 | .06 |
| 375 | Pete Vuckovich | .10 | .08 |
| 376 | Ken Landreaux | .08 | .06 |
| 377 | Lee May | .10 | .08 |
| 378 | Super Veteran (Lee May) | .10 | .08 |
| 379 | Guy Sularz | .08 | .06 |
| 380 | Ron Davis | .08 | .06 |
| 381 | Red Sox Batting & Pitching Ldrs. (Jim Rice, Bob Stanley) | .25 | .20 |
| 382 | Bob Knepper | .12 | .09 |
| 383 | Ozzie Virgil | .10 | .08 |
| 384 | *Dave Dravecky*(FC) | | |

| | | MT | NR MT |
|---|---|---|---|
| | | 1.00 | .70 |
| 385 | Mike Easler | .10 | .08 |
| 386 | Rod Carew AS | .50 | .40 |
| 387 | Bob Grich AS | .10 | .08 |
| 388 | George Brett AS | .65 | .50 |
| 389 | Robin Yount AS | .65 | .50 |
| 390 | Reggie Jackson AS | .50 | .40 |
| 391 | Rickey Henderson AS | | |
| | | 1.75 | 1.25 |
| 392 | Fred Lynn AS | .15 | .11 |
| 393 | Carlton Fisk AS | .15 | .11 |
| 394 | Pete Vuckovich AS | .10 | .08 |
| 395 | Larry Gura AS | .08 | .06 |
| 396 | Dan Quisenberry AS | .12 | .09 |
| 397 | Pete Rose AS | .70 | .50 |
| 398 | Manny Trillo AS | .10 | .08 |
| 399 | Mike Schmidt AS | .60 | .45 |
| 400 | Dave Concepcion AS | | |
| | | .12 | .09 |
| 401 | Dale Murphy AS | .70 | .50 |
| 402 | Andre Dawson AS | .40 | .30 |
| 403 | Tim Raines AS | .35 | .25 |
| 404 | Gary Carter AS | .35 | .25 |
| 405 | Steve Rogers AS | .10 | .08 |
| 406 | Steve Carlton AS | .35 | .25 |
| 407 | Bruce Sutter AS | .12 | .09 |
| 408 | Rudy May | .08 | .06 |
| 409 | Marvis Foley | .08 | .06 |
| 410 | Phil Niekro | .40 | .30 |
| 411 | Super Veteran (Phil Niekro) | .20 | .15 |
| 412 | Rangers Batting & Pitching Ldrs. (Buddy Bell, Charlie Hough) | .15 | .11 |
| 413 | Matt Keough | .08 | .06 |
| 414 | Julio Cruz | .08 | .06 |
| 415 | Bob Forsch | .10 | .08 |
| 416 | Joe Ferguson | .08 | .06 |
| 417 | Tom Hausman | .08 | .06 |
| 418 | Greg Pryor | .08 | .06 |
| 419 | Steve Crawford | .08 | .06 |
| 420 | Al Oliver | .20 | .15 |
| 421 | Super Veteran (Al Oliver) | .12 | .09 |
| 422 | George Cappuzzello | .08 | .06 |
| 423 | *Tom Lawless*(FC) | | |
| | | .10 | .08 |
| 424 | Jerry Augustine | .08 | .06 |
| 425 | Pedro Guerrero | .35 | .25 |
| 426 | Earl Weaver | .10 | .08 |
| 427 | Roy Lee Jackson | .08 | .06 |
| 428 | Champ Summers | .08 | .06 |
| 429 | Eddie Whitson | .08 | .06 |
| 430 | Kirk Gibson | .50 | .40 |
| 431 | *Gary Gaetti*(FC) | .70 | .50 |
| 432 | Porfirio Altamirano | .08 | .06 |
| 433 | Dale Berra | .08 | .06 |
| 434 | Dennis Lamp | .08 | .06 |
| 435 | Tony Armas | .12 | .09 |
| 436 | Bill Campbell | .08 | .06 |
| 437 | Rick Sweet | .08 | .06 |
| 438 | *Dave LaPoint*(FC) | | |
| | | .40 | .30 |
| 439 | Rafael Ramirez | .08 | .06 |
| 440 | Ron Guidry | .30 | .25 |
| 441 | Astros Batting & Pitching Ldrs. (Ray Knight, | | |

| | MT | NR MT |
|---|---|---|
| Joe Niekro) | .12 | .09 |
| 442 Brian Downing | .12 | .09 |
| 443 Don Hood | .08 | .06 |
| 444 Wally Backman(FC) | .25 | .20 |
| 445 Mike Flanagan | .12 | .09 |
| 446 Reid Nichols | .08 | .06 |
| 447 Bryn Smith | .10 | .08 |
| 448 Darrell Evans | .20 | .15 |
| 449 *Eddie Milner* | .12 | .09 |
| 450 Ted Simmons | .20 | .15 |
| 451 Super Veteran (Ted Simmons) | .12 | .09 |
| 452 Lloyd Moseby | .15 | .11 |
| 453 Lamar Johnson | .08 | .06 |
| 454 Bob Welch | .15 | .11 |
| 455 Sixto Lezcano | .08 | .06 |
| 456 Lee Elia | .08 | .06 |
| 457 Milt Wilcox | .08 | .06 |
| 458 Ron Washington | .08 | .06 |
| 459 Ed Farmer | .08 | .06 |
| 460 Roy Smalley | .08 | .06 |
| 461 Steve Trout | .08 | .06 |
| 462 Steve Nicosia | .08 | .06 |
| 463 Gaylord Perry | .40 | .30 |
| 464 Super Veteran (Gaylord Perry) | .20 | .15 |
| 465 Lonnie Smith | .10 | .08 |
| 466 Tom Underwood | .08 | .06 |
| 467 Rufino Linares | .08 | .06 |
| 468 Dave Goltz | .10 | .08 |
| 469 Ron Gardenhire | .08 | .06 |
| 470 Greg Minton | .08 | .06 |
| 471 Royals Batting & Pitching Ldrs. (Vida Blue, Willie Wilson) | .15 | .11 |
| 472 Gary Allenson | .08 | .06 |
| 473 John Lowenstein | .08 | .06 |
| 474 Ray Burris | .08 | .06 |
| 475 Cesar Cedeno | .12 | .09 |
| 476 Rob Picciolo | .08 | .06 |
| 477 Tom Niedenfuer(FC) | .15 | .11 |
| 478 Phil Garner | .10 | .08 |
| 479 Charlie Hough | .12 | .09 |
| 480 Toby Harrah | .10 | .08 |
| 481 Scot Thompson | .08 | .06 |
| 482 *Tony Gwynn*(FC) | 40.00 | 30.00 |
| 483 Lynn Jones | .08 | .06 |
| 484 Dick Ruthven | .08 | .06 |
| 485 Omar Moreno | .08 | .06 |
| 486 Clyde King | .08 | .06 |
| 487 Jerry Hairston | .08 | .06 |
| 488 Alfredo Griffin | .10 | .08 |
| 489 Tom Herr | .12 | .09 |
| 490 Jim Palmer | 1.00 | .70 |
| 491 Super Veteran (Jim Palmer) | .20 | .15 |
| 492 Paul Serna | .08 | .06 |
| 493 Steve McCatty | .08 | .06 |
| 494 Bob Brenly | .10 | .08 |
| 495 Warren Cromartie | .08 | .06 |
| 496 Tom Veryzer | .08 | .06 |
| 497 Rick Sutcliffe | .20 | .15 |
| 498 *Wade Boggs*(FC) | 30.00 | 22.00 |
| 499 Jeff Little | .10 | .08 |
| 500 Reggie Jackson | 1.50 | 1.25 |

| | MT | NR MT |
|---|---|---|
| 501 Super Veteran (Reggie Jackson) | .35 | .25 |
| 502 Braves Batting & Pitching Ldrs. (Dale Murphy, Phil Niekro) | .50 | .40 |
| 503 Moose Haas | .08 | .06 |
| 504 Don Werner | .08 | .06 |
| 505 Garry Templeton | .12 | .09 |
| 506 *Jim Gott*(FC) | .25 | .20 |
| 507 Tony Scott | .08 | .06 |
| 508 Tom Filer | .15 | .11 |
| 509 Lou Whitaker | .40 | .30 |
| 510 Tug McGraw | .15 | .11 |
| 511 Super Veteran (Tug McGraw) | .10 | .08 |
| 512 Doyle Alexander | .12 | .09 |
| 513 Fred Stanley | .08 | .06 |
| 514 Rudy Law | .08 | .06 |
| 515 Gene Tenace | .10 | .08 |
| 516 Bill Virdon | .08 | .06 |
| 517 Gary Ward | .10 | .08 |
| 518 Bill Laskey | .08 | .06 |
| 519 Terry Bulling | .08 | .06 |
| 520 Fred Lynn | .25 | .20 |
| 521 Bruce Benedict | .08 | .06 |
| 522 Pat Zachry | .08 | .06 |
| 523 Carney Lansford | .12 | .09 |
| 524 Tom Brennan | .08 | .06 |
| 525 Frank White | .12 | .09 |
| 526 Checklist 397-528 | .12 | .09 |
| 527 Larry Biittner | .08 | .06 |
| 528 Jamie Easterly | .08 | .06 |
| 529 Tim Laudner | .10 | .08 |
| 530 Eddie Murray | .80 | .60 |
| 531 Athletics Batting & Pitching Ldrs. (Rickey Henderson, Rick Langford) | .30 | .25 |
| 532 Dave Stewart | 1.25 | .90 |
| 533 Luis Salazar | .08 | .06 |
| 534 John Butcher | .08 | .06 |
| 535 Manny Trillo | .10 | .08 |
| 536 Johnny Wockenfuss | .08 | .06 |
| 537 Rod Scurry | .08 | .06 |
| 538 Danny Heep | .08 | .06 |
| 539 Roger Erickson | .08 | .06 |
| 540 Ozzie Smith | 2.00 | 1.50 |
| 541 Britt Burns | .08 | .06 |
| 542 Jody Davis | .12 | .09 |
| 543 Alan Fowlkes | .08 | .06 |
| 544 Larry Whisenton | .08 | .06 |
| 545 Floyd Bannister | .12 | .09 |
| 546 Dave Garcia | .08 | .06 |
| 547 Geoff Zahn | .08 | .06 |
| 548 Brian Giles | .08 | .06 |
| 549 *Charlie Puleo* | .15 | .11 |
| 550 Carl Yastrzemski | 1.00 | .70 |
| 551 Super Veteran (Carl Yastrzemski) | .40 | .30 |
| 552 Tim Wallach | .30 | .25 |
| 553 Denny Martinez | .10 | .08 |
| 554 Mike Vail | .08 | .06 |
| 555 Steve Yeager | .08 | .06 |
| 556 Willie Upshaw | .10 | .08 |
| 557 Rick Honeycutt | .08 | .06 |
| 558 Dickie Thon | .10 | .08 |
| 559 Pete Redfern | .08 | .06 |

| | MT | NR MT |
|---|---|---|
| 560 Ron LeFlore | .10 | .08 |
| 561 Cardinals Batting & Pitching Ldrs. (Joaquin Andujar, Lonnie Smith) | .12 | .09 |
| 562 Dave Rozema | .08 | .06 |
| 563 Juan Bonilla | .08 | .06 |
| 564 Sid Monge | .08 | .06 |
| 565 Bucky Dent | .12 | .09 |
| 566 Manny Sarmiento | .08 | .06 |
| 567 Joe Simpson | .08 | .06 |
| 568 Willie Hernandez | .12 | .09 |
| 569 Jack Perconte | .08 | .06 |
| 570 Vida Blue | .15 | .11 |
| 571 Mickey Klutts | .08 | .06 |
| 572 Bob Watson | .10 | .08 |
| 573 Andy Hassler | .08 | .06 |
| 574 Glenn Adams | .08 | .06 |
| 575 Neil Allen | .08 | .06 |
| 576 Frank Robinson | .12 | .09 |
| 577 Luis Aponte | .08 | .06 |
| 578 David Green | .08 | .06 |
| 579 Rich Dauer | .08 | .06 |
| 580 Tom Seaver | 2.00 | 1.50 |
| 581 Super Veteran (Tom Seaver) | .30 | .25 |
| 582 Marshall Edwards | .08 | .06 |
| 583 Terry Forster | .10 | .08 |
| 584 Dave Hostetler | .08 | .06 |
| 585 Jose Cruz | .15 | .11 |
| 586 Frank Viola(FC) | 6.00 | 4.50 |
| 587 Ivan DeJesus | .08 | .06 |
| 588 Pat Underwood | .08 | .06 |
| 589 Alvis Woods | .08 | .06 |
| 590 Tony Pena | .12 | .09 |
| 591 White Sox Batting & Pitching Ldrs. (LaMarr Hoyt, Greg Luzinski) | .15 | .11 |
| 592 Shane Rawley | .12 | .09 |
| 593 Broderick Perkins | .08 | .06 |
| 594 Eric Rasmussen | .08 | .06 |
| 595 Tim Raines | 1.00 | .70 |
| 596 Randy Johnson | .08 | .06 |
| 597 Mike Proly | .08 | .06 |
| 598 Dwayne Murphy | .10 | .08 |
| 599 Don Aase | .08 | .06 |
| 600 George Brett | 4.00 | 3.00 |
| 601 Ed Lynch | .08 | .06 |
| 602 Rich Gedman | .12 | .09 |
| 603 Joe Morgan | .60 | .45 |
| 604 Super Veteran (Joe Morgan) | .15 | .11 |
| 605 Gary Roenicke | .08 | .06 |
| 606 Bobby Cox | .08 | .06 |
| 607 Charlie Leibrandt | .10 | .08 |
| 608 Don Money | .08 | .06 |
| 609 Danny Darwin | .08 | .06 |
| 610 Steve Garvey | .70 | .50 |
| 611 Bert Roberge | .08 | .06 |
| 612 Steve Swisher | .08 | .06 |
| 613 Mike Ivie | .08 | .06 |
| 614 Ed Glynn | .08 | .06 |
| 615 Garry Maddox | .12 | .09 |
| 616 Bill Nahorodny | .08 | .06 |
| 617 Butch Wynegar | .08 | .06 |
| 618 LaMarr Hoyt | .08 | .06 |
| 619 Keith Moreland | .10 | .08 |
| 620 Mike Norris | .08 | .06 |

| | MT | NR MT |
|---|---|---|
| 621 Mets Batting & Pitching Ldrs. (Craig Swan, Mookie Wilson) | .12 | .09 |
| 622 Dave Edler | .08 | .06 |
| 623 Luis Sanchez | .08 | .06 |
| 624 Glenn Hubbard | .10 | .08 |
| 625 Ken Forsch | .08 | .06 |
| 626 Jerry Martin | .08 | .06 |
| 627 Doug Bair | .08 | .06 |
| 628 Julio Valdez | .08 | .06 |
| 629 Charlie Lea | .08 | .06 |
| 630 Paul Molitor | .30 | .25 |
| 631 Tippy Martinez | .08 | .06 |
| 632 Alex Trevino | .08 | .06 |
| 633 Vicente Romo | .08 | .06 |
| 634 Max Venable | .08 | .06 |
| 635 Graig Nettles | .20 | .15 |
| 636 Super Veteran (Graig Nettles) | .12 | .09 |
| 637 Pat Corrales | .08 | .06 |
| 638 Dan Petry | .10 | .08 |
| 639 Art Howe | .08 | .06 |
| 640 Andre Thornton | .12 | .09 |
| 641 Billy Sample | .08 | .06 |
| 642 Checklist 529-660 | .12 | .09 |
| 643 Bump Wills | .08 | .06 |
| 644 Joe Lefebvre | .08 | .06 |
| 645 Bill Madlock | .15 | .11 |
| 646 Jim Essian | .08 | .06 |
| 647 Bobby Mitchell | .08 | .06 |
| 648 Jeff Burroughs | .10 | .08 |
| 649 Tommy Boggs | .08 | .06 |
| 650 George Hendrick | .10 | .08 |
| 651 Angels Batting & Pitching Ldrs. (Rod Carew, Mike Witt) | .30 | .25 |
| 652 Butch Hobson | .08 | .06 |
| 653 Ellis Valentine | .08 | .06 |
| 654 Bob Ojeda | .15 | .11 |
| 655 Al Bumbry | .10 | .08 |
| 656 Dave Frost | .08 | .06 |
| 657 Mike Gates | .08 | .06 |
| 658 Frank Pastore | .08 | .06 |
| 659 Charlie Moore | .08 | .06 |
| 660 Mike Hargrove | .08 | .06 |
| 661 Bill Russell | .10 | .08 |
| 662 Joe Sambito | .08 | .06 |
| 663 Tom O'Malley | .08 | .06 |
| 664 Bob Molinaro | .08 | .06 |
| 665 Jim Sundberg | .10 | .08 |
| 666 Sparky Anderson | .12 | .09 |
| 667 Dick Davis | .08 | .06 |
| 668 Larry Christenson | .08 | .06 |
| 669 Mike Squires | .08 | .06 |
| 670 Jerry Mumphrey | .08 | .06 |
| 671 Lenny Faedo | .08 | .06 |
| 672 Jim Kaat | .20 | .15 |
| 673 Super Veteran (Jim Kaat) | .12 | .09 |
| 674 Kurt Bevacqua | .08 | .06 |
| 675 Jim Beattie | .08 | .06 |
| 676 Biff Pocoroba | .08 | .06 |
| 677 Dave Revering | .08 | .06 |
| 678 Juan Beniquez | .08 | .06 |
| 679 Mike Scott | .20 | .15 |
| 680 Andre Dawson | 2.00 | 1.50 |
| 681 Dodgers Batting & | | |

| | | MT | NR MT |
|---|---|---|---|
| | Pitching Ldrs. (Pedro Guerrero, Fernando Valenzuela) | .25 | .20 |
| 682 | Bob Stanley | .08 | .06 |
| 683 | Dan Ford | .08 | .06 |
| 684 | Rafael Landestoy | .08 | .06 |
| 685 | Lee Mazzilli | .10 | .08 |
| 686 | Randy Lerch | .08 | .06 |
| 687 | U.L. Washington | .08 | .06 |
| 688 | Jim Wohlford | .08 | .06 |
| 689 | Ron Hassey | .08 | .06 |
| 690 | Kent Hrbek | .70 | .50 |
| 691 | Dave Tobik | .08 | .06 |
| 692 | Denny Walling | .08 | .06 |
| 693 | Sparky Lyle | .12 | .09 |
| 694 | Super Veteran (Sparky Lyle) | .10 | .08 |
| 695 | Ruppert Jones | .08 | .06 |
| 696 | Chuck Tanner | .08 | .06 |
| 697 | Barry Foote | .08 | .06 |
| 698 | Tony Bernazard | .08 | .06 |
| 699 | Lee Smith | 2.50 | 2.00 |
| 700 | Keith Hernandez | .50 | .40 |
| 701 | Batting Leaders (Al Oliver, Willie Wilson) | .15 | .11 |
| 702 | Home Run Leaders (Reggie Jackson, Dave Kingman, Gorman Thomas) | .25 | .20 |
| 703 | Runs Batted In Leaders (Hal McRae, Dale Murphy, Al Oliver) | .35 | .25 |
| 704 | Stolen Base Leaders (Rickey Henderson, Tim Raines) | .35 | .25 |
| 705 | Victory Leaders (Steve Carlton, LaMarr Hoyt) | .20 | .15 |
| 706 | Strikeout Leaders (Floyd Bannister, Steve Carlton) | .20 | .15 |
| 707 | Earned Run Average Leaders (Steve Rogers, Rick Sutcliffe) | .12 | .09 |
| 708 | Leading Firemen (Dan Quisenberry, Bruce Sutter) | .15 | .11 |
| 709 | Jimmy Sexton | .08 | .06 |
| 710 | Willie Wilson | .20 | .15 |
| 711 | Mariners Batting & Pitching Ldrs. (Jim Beattie, Bruce Bochte) | .12 | .09 |
| 712 | Bruce Kison | .08 | .06 |
| 713 | Ron Hodges | .08 | .06 |
| 714 | Wayne Nordhagen | .08 | .06 |
| 715 | Tony Perez | .25 | .20 |
| 716 | Super Veteran (Tony Perez) | .12 | .09 |
| 717 | Scott Sanderson | .08 | .06 |
| 718 | Jim Dwyer | .08 | .06 |
| 719 | Rich Gale | .08 | .06 |
| 720 | Dave Concepcion | .15 | .11 |
| 721 | John Martin | .08 | .06 |
| 722 | Jorge Orta | .08 | .06 |
| 723 | Randy Moffitt | .08 | .06 |
| 724 | Johnny Grubb | .08 | .06 |
| 725 | Dan Spillner | .08 | .06 |
| 726 | Harvey Kuenn | .10 | .08 |

| | | MT | NR MT |
|---|---|---|---|
| 727 | Chet Lemon | .10 | .08 |
| 728 | Ron Reed | .08 | .06 |
| 729 | Jerry Morales | .08 | .06 |
| 730 | Jason Thompson | .08 | .06 |
| 731 | Al Williams | .08 | .06 |
| 732 | Dave Henderson | .15 | .11 |
| 733 | Buck Martinez | .08 | .06 |
| 734 | Steve Braun | .08 | .06 |
| 735 | Tommy John | .25 | .20 |
| 736 | Super Veteran (Tommy John) | .12 | .09 |
| 737 | Mitchell Page | .08 | .06 |
| 738 | Tim Foli | .08 | .06 |
| 739 | Rick Ownbey | .08 | .06 |
| 740 | Rusty Staub | .15 | .11 |
| 741 | Super Veteran (Rusty Staub) | .10 | .08 |
| 742 | Padres Batting & Pitching Ldrs. (Terry Kennedy, Tim Lollar) | .12 | .09 |
| 743 | Mike Torrez | .10 | .08 |
| 744 | Brad Mills | .08 | .06 |
| 745 | Scott McGregor | .10 | .08 |
| 746 | John Wathan | .10 | .08 |
| 747 | Fred Breining | .08 | .06 |
| 748 | Derrel Thomas | .08 | .06 |
| 749 | Jon Matlack | .10 | .08 |
| 750 | Ben Oglivie | .10 | .08 |
| 751 | Brad Havens | .08 | .06 |
| 752 | Luis Pujols | .08 | .06 |
| 753 | Elias Sosa | .08 | .06 |
| 754 | Bill Robinson | .08 | .06 |
| 755 | John Candelaria | .12 | .09 |
| 756 | Russ Nixon | .08 | .06 |
| 757 | Rick Manning | .08 | .06 |
| 758 | Aurelio Rodriguez | .10 | .08 |
| 759 | Doug Bird | .08 | .06 |
| 760 | Dale Murphy | 1.25 | .90 |
| 761 | Gary Lucas | .08 | .06 |
| 762 | Cliff Johnson | .08 | .06 |
| 763 | Al Cowens | .08 | .06 |
| 764 | Pete Falcone | .08 | .06 |
| 765 | Bob Boone | .12 | .09 |
| 766 | Barry Bonnell | .08 | .06 |
| 767 | Duane Kuiper | .08 | .06 |
| 768 | Chris Speier | .08 | .06 |
| 769 | Checklist 661-792 | .12 | .09 |
| 770 | Dave Winfield | 3.00 | 2.25 |
| 771 | Twins Batting & Pitching Ldrs. (Bobby Castillo, Kent Hrbek) | .20 | .15 |
| 772 | Jim Kern | .08 | .06 |
| 773 | Larry Hisle | .10 | .08 |
| 774 | Alan Ashby | .08 | .06 |
| 775 | Burt Hooton | .10 | .08 |
| 776 | Larry Parrish | .12 | .09 |
| 777 | John Curtis | .08 | .06 |
| 778 | Rich Hebner | .08 | .06 |
| 779 | Rick Waits | .08 | .06 |
| 780 | Gary Matthews | .12 | .09 |
| 781 | Rick Rhoden | .12 | .09 |
| 782 | Bobby Murcer | .12 | .09 |
| 783 | Super Veteran (Bobby Murcer) | .10 | .08 |
| 784 | Jeff Newman | .08 | .06 |
| 785 | Dennis Leonard | .10 | .08 |
| 786 | Ralph Houk | .10 | .08 |

| | MT | NR MT |
|---|---|---|
| 787 Dick Tidrow | .08 | .06 |
| 788 Dane Iorg | .08 | .06 |
| 789 Bryan Clark | .08 | .06 |
| 790 Bob Grich | .12 | .09 |
| 791 Gary Lavelle | .08 | .06 |
| 792 Chris Chambliss | .10 | .08 |

## 1983 Topps Traded

These 2-1/2" by 3-1/2" cards mark a continuation of the traded set introduced in 1981. The 132 cards retain the basic design of the year's regular issue, with their numbering being 1-132 with the "T" suffix. Cards in the set include traded players, new managers and promising rookies. Sold only through dealers, the set was in heavy demand as it contained the first cards of Darryl Strawberry, Ron Kittle, Julio Franco and Mel Hall. While some of those cards were very hot in 1983, it seems likely that some of the rookies may not live up to their initial promise.

| | MT | NR MT |
|---|---|---|
| Complete Set: | 110.00 | 82.00 |
| Common Player: | .10 | .08 |
| | | |
| 1T Neil Allen | .10 | .08 |
| 2T Bill Almon | .10 | .08 |
| 3T Joe Altobelli | .10 | .08 |
| 4T Tony Armas | .20 | .15 |
| 5T Doug Bair | .10 | .08 |
| 6T Steve Baker | .10 | .08 |
| 7T Floyd Bannister | .20 | .15 |
| 8T Don Baylor | .30 | .25 |
| 9T Tony Bernazard | .10 | .08 |
| 10T Larry Biittner | .10 | .08 |
| 11T Dann Bilardello | .10 | .08 |
| 12T Doug Bird | .10 | .08 |
| 13T Steve Boros | .10 | .08 |
| 14T Greg Brock(FC) | .30 | .25 |
| 15T Mike Brown | .10 | .08 |
| 16T Tom Burgmeier | .10 | .08 |
| 17T Randy Bush(FC) | .20 | .15 |

| | MT | NR MT |
|---|---|---|
| 18T Bert Campaneris | .20 | .15 |
| 19T Ron Cey | .25 | .20 |
| 20T Chris Codiroli(FC) | .15 | .11 |
| 21T Dave Collins | .15 | .11 |
| 22T Terry Crowley | .10 | .08 |
| 23T Julio Cruz | .10 | .08 |
| 24T Mike Davis | .15 | .11 |
| 25T Frank DiPino | .10 | .08 |
| 26T Bill Doran(FC) | 2.00 | 1.50 |
| 27T Jerry Dybzinski | .10 | .08 |
| 28T Jamie Easterly | .10 | .08 |
| 29T Juan Eichelberger | .10 | .08 |
| 30T Jim Essian | .10 | .08 |
| 31T Pete Falcone | .10 | .08 |
| 32T Mike Ferraro | .10 | .08 |
| 33T Terry Forster | .15 | .11 |
| 34T Julio Franco(FC) | 8.00 | 6.00 |
| 35T Rich Gale | .10 | .08 |
| 36T Kiko Garcia | .10 | .08 |
| 37T Steve Garvey | 1.50 | 1.25 |
| 38T Johnny Grubb | .10 | .08 |
| 39T Mel Hall(FC) | 2.50 | 2.00 |
| 40T Von Hayes | 1.00 | .70 |
| 41T Danny Heep | .10 | .08 |
| 42T Steve Henderson | .10 | .08 |
| 43T Keith Hernandez | 1.00 | .70 |
| 44T Leo Hernandez | .10 | .08 |
| 45T Willie Hernandez | .25 | .20 |
| 46T Al Holland | .10 | .08 |
| 47T Frank Howard | .15 | .11 |
| 48T Bobby Johnson | .10 | .08 |
| 49T Cliff Johnson | .10 | .08 |
| 50T Odell Jones | .10 | .08 |
| 51T Mike Jorgensen | .10 | .08 |
| 52T Bob Kearney | .10 | .08 |
| 53T Steve Kemp | .15 | .11 |
| 54T Matt Keough | .10 | .08 |
| 55T Ron Kittle(FC) | .30 | .25 |
| 56T Mickey Klutts | .10 | .08 |
| 57T Alan Knicely | .10 | .08 |
| 58T Mike Krukow | .15 | .11 |
| 59T Rafael Landestoy | .10 | .08 |
| 60T Carney Lansford | .30 | .25 |
| 61T Joe Lefebvre | .10 | .08 |
| 62T Bryan Little | .10 | .08 |
| 63T Aurelio Lopez | .10 | .08 |
| 64T Mike Madden | .10 | .08 |
| 65T Rick Manning | .10 | .08 |
| 66T Billy Martin | .20 | .15 |
| 67T Lee Mazzilli | .15 | .11 |
| 68T Andy McGaffigan | .10 | .08 |
| 69T Craig McMurtry(FC) | .20 | .15 |
| 70T John McNamara | .10 | .08 |
| 71T Orlando Mercado | .10 | .08 |
| 72T Larry Milbourne | .10 | .08 |
| 73T Randy Moffitt | .10 | .08 |
| 74T Sid Monge | .10 | .08 |
| 75T Jose Morales | .10 | .08 |
| 76T Omar Moreno | .10 | .08 |
| 77T Joe Morgan | 3.00 | 2.25 |
| 78T Mike Morgan | .10 | .08 |
| 79T Dale Murray | .10 | .08 |
| 80T Jeff Newman | .10 | .08 |
| 81T Pete O'Brien(FC) | 1.00 | .70 |
| 82T Jorge Orta | .10 | .08 |
| 83T Alejandro Pena(FC) | 1.00 | .70 |

| | | MT | NR MT |
|---|---|---|---|
| 84T | Pascual Perez | .20 | .15 |
| 85T | Tony Perez | 1.00 | .70 |
| 86T | Broderick Perkins | .10 | .08 |
| 87T | Tony Phillips(FC) | 2.50 | 2.00 |
| 88T | Charlie Puleo | .10 | .08 |
| 89T | Pat Putnam | .10 | .08 |
| 90T | Jamie Quirk | .10 | .08 |
| 91T | Doug Rader | .10 | .08 |
| 92T | Chuck Rainey | .10 | .08 |
| 93T | Bobby Ramos | .10 | .08 |
| 94T | Gary Redus(FC) | .30 | .25 |
| 95T | Steve Renko | .10 | .08 |
| 96T | Leon Roberts | .10 | .08 |
| 97T | Aurelio Rodriguez | .15 | .11 |
| 98T | Dick Ruthven | .10 | .08 |
| 99T | Daryl Sconiers | .10 | .08 |
| 100T | Mike Scott | .70 | .50 |
| 101T | Tom Seaver | 8.50 | 6.40 |
| 102T | John Shelby(FC) | .25 | .20 |
| 103T | Bob Shirley | .10 | .08 |
| 104T | Joe Simpson | .10 | .08 |
| 105T | Doug Sisk(FC) | .15 | .11 |
| 106T | Mike Smithson(FC) | .20 | .15 |
| 107T | Elias Sosa | .10 | .08 |
| 108T | Darryl Strawberry(FC) | | |
| | | 70.00 | 50.00 |
| 109T | Tom Tellmann | .10 | .08 |
| 110T | Gene Tenace | .15 | .11 |
| 111T | Gorman Thomas | .25 | .20 |
| 112T | Dick Tidrow | .10 | .08 |
| 113T | Dave Tobik | .10 | .08 |
| 114T | Wayne Tolleson(FC) | .20 | .15 |
| 115T | Mike Torrez | .15 | .11 |
| 116T | Manny Trillo | .15 | .11 |
| 117T | Steve Trout | .10 | .08 |
| 118T | Lee Tunnell(FC) | .15 | .11 |
| 119T | Mike Vail | .10 | .08 |
| 120T | Ellis Valentine | .10 | .08 |
| 121T | Tom Veryzer | .10 | .08 |
| 122T | George Vukovich | .10 | .08 |
| 123T | Rick Waits | .10 | .08 |
| 124T | Greg Walker(FC) | .20 | .15 |
| 125T | Chris Welsh | .10 | .08 |
| 126T | Len Whitehouse | .10 | .08 |
| 127T | Eddie Whitson | .15 | .11 |
| 128T | Jim Wohlford | .10 | .08 |
| 129T | Matt Young(FC) | .20 | .15 |
| 130T | Joel Youngblood | .10 | .08 |
| 131T | Pat Zachry | .10 | .08 |
| 132T | Checklist 1-132 | .10 | .08 |

## 1984 Topps

Another 792-card regular set from Topps. For the second straight year, the 2-1/2" by 3-1/2" cards featured a color action photo on the front along with a small portrait photo in the lower left. The team name runs in big letters down the left side, while the player's name and position runs under the large action photo. In the upper right-hand corner is the Topps logo. Backs have a team logo in the upper right corner, along with statistics, personal information and a few highlights. The backs have an unusual and hard-to-read red and purple coloring. Specialty cards include past season highlights, team leaders, major league statistical leaders, All-Stars, active career leaders and numbered checklists. Again, promising rookies were saved for the traded set. Late in 1984, Topps introduced a specially boxed "Tiffany" edition of the 1984 set, with the cards printed on white cardboard with a glossy finish. A total of 10,000 sets were produced. Prices for Tiffany edition superstars can run from six to eight times the value of the "regular" edition, while common cards sell in the 40¢ range.

| | | MT | NR MT |
|---|---|---|---|
| | Complete Set: | 90.00 | 67.00 |
| | Common Player: | .08 | .06 |
| 1 | 1983 Highlight (Steve Carlton) | .30 | .25 |
| 2 | 1983 Highlight (Rickey Henderson) | 1.00 | .70 |
| 3 | 1983 Highlight (Dan Quisenberry) | .10 | .08 |
| 4 | 1983 Highlight (Steve Carlton, Gaylord Perry, Nolan Ryan) | .30 | .25 |
| 5 | 1983 Highlight (Bob Forsch, Dave Righetti, Mike Warren) | .15 | .11 |
| 6 | 1983 Highlight (Johnny Bench, Gaylord Perry, Carl Yastrzemski) | .40 | .30 |
| 7 | Gary Lucas | .08 | .06 |
| 8 | *Don Mattingly*(FC) | 10.00 | 7.50 |
| 9 | Jim Gott | .10 | .08 |
| 10 | Robin Yount | 2.00 | 1.50 |
| 11 | Twins Batting & Pitching Leaders (Kent Hrbek, Ken Schrom) | .20 | .15 |

| | | MT | NR MT |
|---|---|---|---|
| 12 | Billy Sample | .08 | .06 |
| 13 | Scott Holman | .08 | .06 |
| 14 | Tom Brookens | .08 | .06 |
| 15 | Burt Hooton | .10 | .08 |
| 16 | Omar Moreno | .08 | .06 |
| 17 | John Denny | .08 | .06 |
| 18 | Dale Berra | .08 | .06 |
| 19 | *Ray Fontenot*(FC) | | |
| | | .10 | .08 |
| 20 | Greg Luzinski | .12 | .09 |
| 21 | Joe Altobelli | .08 | .06 |
| 22 | Bryan Clark | .08 | .06 |
| 23 | Keith Moreland | .10 | .08 |
| 24 | John Martin | .08 | .06 |
| 25 | Glenn Hubbard | .10 | .08 |
| 26 | Bud Black | .10 | .08 |
| 27 | Daryl Sconiers | .08 | .06 |
| 28 | Frank Viola | .80 | .60 |
| 29 | Danny Heep | .08 | .06 |
| 30 | Wade Boggs | 5.00 | 3.75 |
| 31 | Andy McGaffigan | .08 | .06 |
| 32 | Bobby Ramos | .08 | .06 |
| 33 | Tom Burgmeier | .08 | .06 |
| 34 | Eddie Milner | .08 | .06 |
| 35 | Don Sutton | .30 | .25 |
| 36 | Denny Walling | .08 | .06 |
| 37 | Rangers Batting & Pitching Leaders (Buddy Bell, Rick Honeycutt) | .12 | .09 |
| 38 | Luis DeLeon | .08 | .06 |
| 39 | Garth Iorg | .08 | .06 |
| 40 | Dusty Baker | .12 | .09 |
| 41 | Tony Bernazard | .08 | .06 |
| 42 | Johnny Grubb | .08 | .06 |
| 43 | Ron Reed | .10 | .08 |
| 44 | Jim Morrison | .08 | .06 |
| 45 | Jerry Mumphrey | .08 | .06 |
| 46 | Ray Smith | .08 | .06 |
| 47 | Rudy Law | .08 | .06 |
| 48 | Julio Franco(FC) | 2.75 | 2.10 |
| 49 | John Stuper | .08 | .06 |
| 50 | Chris Chambliss | .10 | .08 |
| 51 | Jim Frey | .08 | .06 |
| 52 | Paul Splittorff | .08 | .06 |
| 53 | Juan Beniquez | .08 | .06 |
| 54 | Jesse Orosco | .10 | .08 |
| 55 | Dave Concepcion | .15 | .11 |
| 56 | Gary Allenson | .08 | .06 |
| 57 | Dan Schatzeder | .08 | .06 |
| 58 | Max Venable | .08 | .06 |
| 59 | Sammy Stewart | .08 | .06 |
| 60 | Paul Molitor | .20 | .15 |
| 61 | *Chris Codiroli* | .10 | .08 |
| 62 | Dave Hostetler | .08 | .06 |
| 63 | Ed Vande Berg | .08 | .06 |
| 64 | Mike Scioscia | .08 | .06 |
| 65 | Kirk Gibson | .40 | .30 |
| 66 | Astros Batting & Pitching Leaders (Jose Cruz, Nolan Ryan) | .25 | .20 |
| 67 | Gary Ward | .10 | .08 |
| 68 | Luis Salazar | .08 | .06 |
| 69 | Rod Scurry | .08 | .06 |
| 70 | Gary Matthews | .12 | .09 |
| 71 | Leo Hernandez | .08 | .06 |
| 72 | Mike Squires | .08 | .06 |
| 73 | Jody Davis | .10 | .08 |

| | | MT | NR MT |
|---|---|---|---|
| 74 | Jerry Martin | .08 | .06 |
| 75 | Bob Forsch | .10 | .08 |
| 76 | Alfredo Griffin | .10 | .08 |
| 77 | Brett Butler | .10 | .08 |
| 78 | Mike Torrez | .10 | .08 |
| 79 | Rob Wilfong | .08 | .06 |
| 80 | Steve Rogers | .10 | .08 |
| 81 | Billy Martin | .12 | .09 |
| 82 | Doug Bird | .08 | .06 |
| 83 | Richie Zisk | .10 | .08 |
| 84 | Lenny Faedo | .08 | .06 |
| 85 | Atlee Hammaker | .08 | .06 |
| 86 | *John Shelby*(FC) | .25 | .20 |
| 87 | Frank Pastore | .08 | .06 |
| 88 | Rob Picciolo | .08 | .06 |
| 89 | *Mike Smithson*(FC) | | |
| | | .15 | .11 |
| 90 | Pedro Guerrero | .35 | .25 |
| 91 | Dan Spillner | .08 | .06 |
| 92 | Lloyd Moseby | .12 | .09 |
| 93 | Bob Knepper | .10 | .08 |
| 94 | Mario Ramirez | .08 | .06 |
| 95 | Aurelio Lopez | .08 | .06 |
| 96 | Royals Batting & Pitching Leaders (Larry Gura, Hal McRae) | .10 | .08 |
| 97 | LaMarr Hoyt | .08 | .06 |
| 98 | Steve Nicosia | .08 | .06 |
| 99 | *Craig Lefferts*(FC) | .30 | .25 |
| 100 | Reggie Jackson | 1.00 | .70 |
| 101 | Porfirio Altamirano | .08 | .06 |
| 102 | Ken Oberkfell | .08 | .06 |
| 103 | Dwayne Murphy | .10 | .08 |
| 104 | Ken Dayley | .08 | .06 |
| 105 | Tony Armas | .12 | .09 |
| 106 | Tim Stoddard | .08 | .06 |
| 107 | Ned Yost | .08 | .06 |
| 108 | Randy Moffitt | .08 | .06 |
| 109 | Brad Wellman | .08 | .06 |
| 110 | Ron Guidry | .30 | .25 |
| 111 | Bill Virdon | .08 | .06 |
| 112 | Tom Niedenfuer | .10 | .08 |
| 113 | Kelly Paris | .08 | .06 |
| 114 | Checklist 1-132 | .08 | .06 |
| 115 | Andre Thornton | .12 | .09 |
| 116 | George Bjorkman | .08 | .06 |
| 117 | Tom Veryzer | .08 | .06 |
| 118 | Charlie Hough | .12 | .09 |
| 119 | Johnny Wockenfuss | .08 | .06 |
| 120 | Keith Hernandez | .40 | .30 |
| 121 | *Pat Sheridan*(FC) | .15 | .11 |
| 122 | Cecilio Guante(FC) | .10 | .08 |
| 123 | Butch Wynegar | .08 | .06 |
| 124 | Damaso Garcia | .08 | .06 |
| 125 | Britt Burns | .08 | .06 |
| 126 | Braves Batting & Pitching Leaders (Craig McMurtry, Dale Murphy) | .25 | .20 |
| 127 | Mike Madden | .08 | .06 |
| 128 | Rick Manning | .08 | .06 |
| 129 | Bill Laskey | .08 | .06 |
| 130 | Ozzie Smith | .70 | .50 |
| 131 | Batting Leaders (Wade Boggs, Bill Madlock) | .50 | .40 |

| | MT | NR MT |
|---|---|---|
| 132 Home Run Leaders (Jim Rice, Mike Schmidt) | .50 | .40 |
| 133 Runs Batted In Leaders (Cecil Cooper, Dale Murphy, Jim Rice) | .40 | .30 |
| 134 Stolen Base Leaders (Rickey Henderson, Tim Raines) | .30 | .25 |
| 135 Victory Leaders (John Denny, LaMarr Hoyt) | .10 | .08 |
| 136 Strikeout Leaders (Steve Carlton, Jack Morris) | .25 | .20 |
| 137 Earned Run Average Leaders (Atlee Hammaker, Rick Honeycutt) | .10 | .08 |
| 138 Leading Firemen (Al Holland, Dan Quisenberry) | .12 | .09 |
| 139 Bert Campaneris | .12 | .09 |
| 140 Storm Davis | .12 | .09 |
| 141 Pat Corrales | .08 | .06 |
| 142 Rich Gale | .08 | .06 |
| 143 Jose Morales | .08 | .06 |
| 144 Brian Harper | .08 | .06 |
| 145 Gary Lavelle | .08 | .06 |
| 146 Ed Romero | .08 | .06 |
| 147 Dan Petry | .10 | .08 |
| 148 Joe Lefebvre | .08 | .06 |
| 149 Jon Matlack | .10 | .08 |
| 150 Dale Murphy | .70 | .50 |
| 151 Steve Trout | .08 | .06 |
| 152 Glenn Brummer | .08 | .06 |
| 153 Dick Tidrow | .08 | .06 |
| 154 Dave Henderson | .12 | .09 |
| 155 Frank White | .12 | .09 |
| 156 Athletics Batting & Pitching Leaders (Tim Conroy, Rickey Henderson) | .25 | .20 |
| 157 Gary Gaetti | .70 | .50 |
| 158 John Curtis | .08 | .06 |
| 159 Darryl Cias | .08 | .06 |
| 160 Mario Soto | .10 | .08 |
| 161 Junior Ortiz(FC) | .10 | .08 |
| 162 Bob Ojeda | .12 | .09 |
| 163 Lorenzo Gray | .08 | .06 |
| 164 Scott Sanderson | .08 | .06 |
| 165 Ken Singleton | .12 | .09 |
| 166 Jamie Nelson | .08 | .06 |
| 167 Marshall Edwards | .08 | .06 |
| 168 Juan Bonilla | .08 | .06 |
| 169 Larry Parrish | .12 | .09 |
| 170 Jerry Reuss | .12 | .09 |
| 171 Frank Robinson | .12 | .09 |
| 172 Frank DiPino | .08 | .06 |
| 173 Marvell Wynne(FC) | .20 | .15 |
| 174 Juan Berenguer | .08 | .06 |
| 175 Graig Nettles | .20 | .15 |
| 176 Lee Smith | .15 | .11 |
| 177 Jerry Hairston | .08 | .06 |
| 178 Bill Krueger | .08 | .06 |
| 179 Buck Martinez | .08 | .06 |
| 180 Manny Trillo | .10 | .08 |
| 181 Roy Thomas | .08 | .06 |
| 182 Darryl Strawberry | 12.00 | 9.00 |
| 183 Al Williams | .08 | .06 |

| | MT | NR MT |
|---|---|---|
| 184 Mike O'Berry | .08 | .06 |
| 185 Sixto Lezcano | .08 | .06 |
| 186 Cardinals Batting & Pitching Leaders (Lonnie Smith, John Stuper) | .10 | .08 |
| 187 Luis Aponte | .08 | .06 |
| 188 Bryan Little | .08 | .06 |
| 189 Tim Conroy(FC) | .12 | .09 |
| 190 Ben Oglivie | .10 | .08 |
| 191 Mike Boddicker | .12 | .09 |
| 192 Nick Esasky(FC) | .40 | .30 |
| 193 Darrell Brown | .08 | .06 |
| 194 Domingo Ramos | .08 | .06 |
| 195 Jack Morris | .70 | .50 |
| 196 Don Slaught(FC) | .12 | .09 |
| 197 Garry Hancock | .08 | .06 |
| 198 Bill Doran | .80 | .60 |
| 199 Willie Hernandez | .12 | .09 |
| 200 Andre Dawson | 1.00 | .70 |
| 201 Bruce Kison | .08 | .06 |
| 202 Bobby Cox | .08 | .06 |
| 203 Matt Keough | .08 | .06 |
| 204 Bobby Meacham(FC) | .15 | .11 |
| 205 Greg Minton | .08 | .06 |
| 206 Andy Van Slyke(FC) | 3.25 | 2.45 |
| 207 Donnie Moore | .08 | .06 |
| 208 Jose Oquendo(FC) | .15 | .11 |
| 209 Manny Sarmiento | .08 | .06 |
| 210 Joe Morgan | .30 | .25 |
| 211 Rick Sweet | .08 | .06 |
| 212 Broderick Perkins | .08 | .06 |
| 213 Bruce Hurst | .15 | .11 |
| 214 Paul Householder | .08 | .06 |
| 215 Tippy Martinez | .08 | .06 |
| 216 White Sox Batting & Pitching Leaders (Richard Dotson, Carlton Fisk) | .15 | .11 |
| 217 Alan Ashby | .08 | .06 |
| 218 Rick Waits | .08 | .06 |
| 219 Joe Simpson | .08 | .06 |
| 220 Fernando Valenzuela | .40 | .30 |
| 221 Cliff Johnson | .08 | .06 |
| 222 Rick Honeycutt | .08 | .06 |
| 223 Wayne Krenchicki | .08 | .06 |
| 224 Sid Monge | .08 | .06 |
| 225 Lee Mazzilli | .10 | .08 |
| 226 Juan Eichelberger | .08 | .06 |
| 227 Steve Braun | .08 | .06 |
| 228 John Rabb | .08 | .06 |
| 229 Paul Owens | .08 | .06 |
| 230 Rickey Henderson | 5.00 | 3.75 |
| 231 Gary Woods | .08 | .06 |
| 232 Tim Wallach | .15 | .11 |
| 233 Checklist 133-264 | .08 | .06 |
| 234 Rafael Ramirez | .08 | .06 |
| 235 Matt Young | .15 | .11 |
| 236 Ellis Valentine | .08 | .06 |
| 237 John Castino | .08 | .06 |
| 238 Reid Nichols | .08 | .06 |
| 239 Jay Howell | .10 | .08 |
| 240 Eddie Murray | 1.00 | .70 |
| 241 Billy Almon | .08 | .06 |
| 242 Alex Trevino | .08 | .06 |

| | MT | NR MT |
|---|---|---|
| 243 Pete Ladd | .08 | .06 |
| 244 Candy Maldonado(FC) | | |
| | .50 | .40 |
| 245 Rick Sutcliffe | .15 | .11 |
| 246 Mets Batting & Pitching Leaders (Tom Seaver, Mookie Wilson) | .25 | .20 |
| 247 Onix Concepcion | .08 | .06 |
| 248 *Bill Dawley*(FC) | .10 | .08 |
| 249 Jay Johnstone | .10 | .08 |
| 250 Bill Madlock | .12 | .09 |
| 251 Tony Gwynn | 5.00 | 3.75 |
| 252 Larry Christenson | .08 | .06 |
| 253 Jim Wohlford | .08 | .06 |
| 254 Shane Rawley | .12 | .09 |
| 255 Bruce Benedict | .08 | .06 |
| 256 Dave Geisel | .08 | .06 |
| 257 Julio Cruz | .08 | .06 |
| 258 Luis Sanchez | .08 | .06 |
| 259 Sparky Anderson | .12 | .09 |
| 260 Scott McGregor | .10 | .08 |
| 261 Bobby Brown | .08 | .06 |
| 262 *Tom Candiotti*(FC) | | |
| | .25 | .20 |
| 263 Jack Fimple | .08 | .06 |
| 264 Doug Frobel | .08 | .06 |
| 265 *Donnie Hill*(FC) | .15 | .11 |
| 266 Steve Lubratich | .08 | .06 |
| 267 *Carmelo Martinez*(FC) | | |
| | .25 | .20 |
| 268 Jack O'Connor | .08 | .06 |
| 269 Aurelio Rodriguez | .10 | .08 |
| 270 *Jeff Russell*(FC) | .20 | .15 |
| 271 Moose Haas | .08 | .06 |
| 272 Rick Dempsey | .10 | .08 |
| 273 Charlie Puleo | .08 | .06 |
| 274 Rick Monday | .10 | .08 |
| 275 Len Matuszek | .08 | .06 |
| 276 Angels Batting & Pitching Leaders (Rod Carew, Geoff Zahn) | .20 | .15 |
| 277 Eddie Whitson | .08 | .06 |
| 278 Jorge Bell | 1.00 | .70 |
| 279 Ivan DeJesus | .08 | .06 |
| 280 Floyd Bannister | .12 | .09 |
| 281 Larry Milbourne | .08 | .06 |
| 282 Jim Barr | .08 | .06 |
| 283 Larry Biittner | .08 | .06 |
| 284 Howard Bailey | .08 | .06 |
| 285 Darrell Porter | .10 | .08 |
| 286 Lary Sorensen | .08 | .06 |
| 287 Warren Cromartie | .08 | .06 |
| 288 Jim Beattie | .08 | .06 |
| 289 Randy Johnson | .08 | .06 |
| 290 Dave Dravecky | .10 | .08 |
| 291 Chuck Tanner | .08 | .06 |
| 292 Tony Scott | .08 | .06 |
| 293 Ed Lynch | .08 | .06 |
| 294 U.L. Washington | .08 | .06 |
| 295 Mike Flanagan | .12 | .09 |
| 296 Jeff Newman | .08 | .06 |
| 297 Bruce Berenyi | .08 | .06 |
| 298 Jim Gantner | .10 | .08 |
| 299 John Butcher | .08 | .06 |
| 300 Pete Rose | 1.00 | .70 |
| 301 Frank LaCorte | .08 | .06 |
| 302 Barry Bonnell | .08 | .06 |

| | MT | NR MT |
|---|---|---|
| 303 Marty Castillo | .08 | .06 |
| 304 Warren Brusstar | .08 | .06 |
| 305 Roy Smalley | .08 | .06 |
| 306 Dodgers Batting & Pitching Leaders (Pedro Guerrero, Bob Welch) | .15 | .11 |
| 307 Bobby Mitchell | .08 | .06 |
| 308 Ron Hassey | .08 | .06 |
| 309 *Tony Phillips* | .15 | .11 |
| 310 Willie McGee | .35 | .25 |
| 311 Jerry Koosman | .12 | .09 |
| 312 Jorge Orta | .08 | .06 |
| 313 Mike Jorgensen | .08 | .06 |
| 314 Orlando Mercado | .08 | .06 |
| 315 Bob Grich | .12 | .09 |
| 316 Mark Bradley | .08 | .06 |
| 317 Greg Pryor | .08 | .06 |
| 318 Bill Gullickson | .08 | .06 |
| 319 Al Bumbry | .10 | .08 |
| 320 Bob Stanley | .08 | .06 |
| 321 Harvey Kuenn | .10 | .08 |
| 322 Ken Schrom | .08 | .06 |
| 323 Alan Knicely | .08 | .06 |
| 324 *Alejandro Pena* | .30 | .25 |
| 325 Darrell Evans | .15 | .11 |
| 326 Bob Kearney | .08 | .06 |
| 327 Ruppert Jones | .08 | .06 |
| 328 Vern Ruhle | .08 | .06 |
| 329 Pat Tabler(FC) | .20 | .15 |
| 330 John Candelaria | .12 | .09 |
| 331 Bucky Dent | .12 | .09 |
| 332 *Kevin Gross*(FC) | .40 | .30 |
| 333 Larry Herndon | .10 | .08 |
| 334 Chuck Rainey | .08 | .06 |
| 335 Don Baylor | .15 | .11 |
| 336 Mariners Batting & Pitching Leaders (Pat Putnam, Matt Young) | .10 | .08 |
| 337 Kevin Hagen | .08 | .06 |
| 338 Mike Warren | .08 | .06 |
| 339 Roy Lee Jackson | .08 | .06 |
| 340 Hal McRae | .12 | .09 |
| 341 Dave Tobik | .08 | .06 |
| 342 Tim Foli | .08 | .06 |
| 343 Mark Davis | .08 | .06 |
| 344 Rick Miller | .08 | .06 |
| 345 Kent Hrbek | .40 | .30 |
| 346 Kurt Bevacqua | .08 | .06 |
| 347 Allan Ramirez | .08 | .06 |
| 348 Toby Harrah | .10 | .08 |
| 349 Bob Gibson | .08 | .06 |
| 350 George Foster | .20 | .15 |
| 351 Russ Nixon | .08 | .06 |
| 352 Dave Stewart | .70 | .50 |
| 353 Jim Anderson | .08 | .06 |
| 354 Jeff Burroughs | .10 | .08 |
| 355 Jason Thompson | .08 | .06 |
| 356 Glenn Abbott | .08 | .06 |
| 357 Ron Cey | .12 | .09 |
| 358 Bob Dernier | .08 | .06 |
| 359 *Jim Acker*(FC) | .12 | .09 |
| 360 Willie Randolph | .12 | .09 |
| 361 Dave Smith | .10 | .08 |
| 362 David Green | .08 | .06 |
| 363 Tim Laudner | .08 | .06 |
| 364 Scott Fletcher(FC) | .15 | .11 |
| 365 Steve Bedrosian | .12 | .09 |

| | | MT | NR MT |
|---|---|---|---|
| 366 | Padres Batting & Pitching Leaders (Dave Dravecky, Terry Kennedy) | | |
| | | .12 | .09 |
| 367 | Jamie Easterly | .08 | .06 |
| 368 | Hubie Brooks | .15 | .11 |
| 369 | Steve McCatty | .08 | .06 |
| 370 | Tim Raines | .50 | .40 |
| 371 | Dave Gumpert | .08 | .06 |
| 372 | Gary Roenicke | .08 | .06 |
| 373 | Bill Scherrer | .08 | .06 |
| 374 | Don Money | .08 | .06 |
| 375 | Dennis Leonard | .10 | .08 |
| 376 | *Dave Anderson*(FC) | | |
| | | .15 | .11 |
| 377 | Danny Darwin | .08 | .06 |
| 378 | Bob Brenly | .08 | .06 |
| 379 | Checklist 265-396 | .08 | .06 |
| 380 | Steve Garvey | .50 | .40 |
| 381 | Ralph Houk | .10 | .08 |
| 382 | Chris Nyman | .08 | .06 |
| 383 | Terry Puhl | .08 | .06 |
| 384 | *Lee Tunnell* | .10 | .08 |
| 385 | Tony Perez | .20 | .15 |
| 386 | George Hendrick AS | .10 | .08 |
| 387 | Johnny Ray AS | .12 | .09 |
| 388 | Mike Schmidt AS | .50 | .40 |
| 389 | Ozzie Smith AS | .15 | .11 |
| 390 | Tim Raines AS | .25 | .20 |
| 391 | Dale Murphy AS | .40 | .30 |
| 392 | Andre Dawson AS | .20 | .15 |
| 393 | Gary Carter AS | .30 | .25 |
| 394 | Steve Rogers AS | .10 | .08 |
| 395 | Steve Carlton AS | .25 | .20 |
| 396 | Jesse Orosco AS | .10 | .08 |
| 397 | Eddie Murray AS | .35 | .25 |
| 398 | Lou Whitaker AS | .20 | .15 |
| 399 | George Brett AS | .50 | .40 |
| 400 | Cal Ripken AS | 1.25 | .90 |
| 401 | Jim Rice AS | .30 | .25 |
| 402 | Dave Winfield AS | .30 | .25 |
| 403 | Lloyd Moseby AS | .12 | .09 |
| 404 | Ted Simmons AS | .15 | .11 |
| 405 | LaMarr Hoyt AS | .10 | .08 |
| 406 | Ron Guidry AS | .20 | .15 |
| 407 | Dan Quisenberry AS | .12 | .09 |
| 408 | Lou Piniella AS | .15 | .11 |
| 409 | *Juan Agosto*(FC) | .15 | .11 |
| 410 | Claudell Washington | .10 | .08 |
| 411 | Houston Jimenez | .08 | .06 |
| 412 | Doug Rader | .08 | .06 |
| 413 | *Spike Owen*(FC) | .20 | .15 |
| 414 | Mitchell Page | .08 | .06 |
| 415 | Tommy John | .25 | .20 |
| 416 | Dane Iorg | .08 | .06 |
| 417 | Mike Armstrong | .08 | .06 |
| 418 | Ron Hodges | .08 | .06 |
| 419 | John Henry Johnson | | |
| | | .08 | .06 |
| 420 | Cecil Cooper | .15 | .11 |
| 421 | Charlie Lea | .08 | .06 |
| 422 | Jose Cruz | .12 | .09 |
| 423 | Mike Morgan | .08 | .06 |
| 424 | Dann Bilardello | .08 | .06 |
| 425 | Steve Howe | .10 | .08 |
| 426 | Orioles Batting & Pitching Leaders (Mike Boddicker, Cal Ripken) | .25 | .20 |
| 427 | Rick Leach | .08 | .06 |
| 428 | Fred Breining | .08 | .06 |
| 429 | *Randy Bush* | .15 | .11 |
| 430 | Rusty Staub | .12 | .09 |
| 431 | Chris Bando | .08 | .06 |
| 432 | *Charlie Hudson*(FC) | | |
| | | .20 | .15 |
| 433 | Rich Hebner | .08 | .06 |
| 434 | Harold Baines | .25 | .20 |
| 435 | Neil Allen | .08 | .06 |
| 436 | Rick Peters | .08 | .06 |
| 437 | Mike Proly | .08 | .06 |
| 438 | Biff Pocoroba | .08 | .06 |
| 439 | Bob Stoddard | .08 | .06 |
| 440 | Steve Kemp | .10 | .08 |
| 441 | Bob Lillis | .08 | .06 |
| 442 | Byron McLaughlin | .08 | .06 |
| 443 | Benny Ayala | .08 | .06 |
| 444 | Steve Renko | .08 | .06 |
| 445 | Jerry Remy | .08 | .06 |
| 446 | Luis Pujols | .08 | .06 |
| 447 | Tom Brunansky | .20 | .15 |
| 448 | Ben Hayes | .08 | .06 |
| 449 | Joe Pettini | .08 | .06 |
| 450 | Gary Carter | .40 | .30 |
| 451 | Bob Jones | .08 | .06 |
| 452 | Chuck Porter | .08 | .06 |
| 453 | Willie Upshaw | .10 | .08 |
| 454 | Joe Beckwith | .08 | .06 |
| 455 | Terry Kennedy | .10 | |
| 456 | Cubs Batting & Pitching Leaders (Fergie Jenkins, Keith Moreland) | .15 | .11 |
| 457 | Dave Rozema | .08 | .06 |
| 458 | Kiko Garcia | .08 | .06 |
| 459 | Kevin Hickey | .08 | .06 |
| 460 | Dave Winfield | 1.50 | 1.25 |
| 461 | Jim Maler | .08 | .06 |
| 462 | Lee Lacy | .08 | .06 |
| 463 | Dave Engle | .08 | .06 |
| 464 | Jeff Jones | .08 | .06 |
| 465 | Mookie Wilson | .12 | .09 |
| 466 | Gene Garber | .08 | .06 |
| 467 | Mike Ramsey | .08 | .06 |
| 468 | Geoff Zahn | .08 | .06 |
| 469 | Tom O'Malley | .08 | .06 |
| 470 | Nolan Ryan | 6.00 | 4.50 |
| 471 | Dick Howser | .08 | .06 |
| 472 | Mike Brown | .08 | .06 |
| 473 | Jim Dwyer | .08 | .06 |
| 474 | Greg Bargar | .08 | .06 |
| 475 | *Gary Redus* | .25 | .20 |
| 476 | Tom Tellmann | .08 | .06 |
| 477 | Rafael Landestoy | .08 | .06 |
| 478 | Alan Bannister | .08 | .06 |
| 479 | Frank Tanana | .12 | .09 |
| 480 | Ron Kittle(FC) | .20 | .15 |
| 481 | *Mark Thurmond*(FC) | | |
| | | .10 | .08 |
| 482 | Enos Cabell | .08 | .06 |
| 483 | Fergie Jenkins | .20 | .15 |
| 484 | Ozzie Virgil | .08 | .06 |
| 485 | Rick Rhoden | .12 | .09 |
| 486 | Yankees Batting & Pitching Leaders (Don Baylor, Ron Guidry) | .15 | .11 |

| | MT | NR MT | | | MT | NR MT |
|---|---|---|---|---|---|---|
| 487 Ricky Adams | .08 | .06 | 548 Ron Jackson | | .08 | .06 |
| 488 Jesse Barfield | .25 | .20 | 549 *Walt Terrell* | | .50 | .40 |
| 489 Dave Von Ohlen | .08 | .06 | 550 Jim Rice | | .40 | .30 |
| 490 Cal Ripken | 8.00 | 6.00 | 551 Scott Ullger | | .08 | .06 |
| 491 Bobby Castillo | .08 | .06 | 552 Ray Burris | | .08 | .06 |
| 492 Tucker Ashford | .08 | .06 | 553 Joe Nolan | | .08 | .06 |
| 493 Mike Norris | .08 | .06 | 554 Ted Power(FC) | | .12 | .09 |
| 494 Chili Davis | .12 | .09 | 555 Greg Brock | | .15 | .11 |
| 495 Rollie Fingers | .25 | .20 | 556 Joey McLaughlin | | .08 | .06 |
| 496 Terry Francona | .08 | .06 | 557 Wayne Tolleson | | .10 | .08 |
| 497 Bud Anderson | .08 | .06 | 558 Mike Davis | | .10 | .08 |
| 498 Rich Gedman | .10 | .08 | 559 Mike Scott | | .20 | .15 |
| 499 Mike Witt | .15 | .11 | 560 Carlton Fisk | | 1.00 | .70 |
| 500 George Brett | 2.00 | 1.50 | 561 Whitey Herzog | | .10 | .08 |
| 501 Steve Henderson | .08 | .06 | 562 Manny Castillo | | .08 | .06 |
| 502 Joe Torre | .08 | .06 | 563 Glenn Wilson | | .10 | .08 |
| 503 Elias Sosa | .08 | .06 | 564 Al Holland | | .08 | .06 |
| 504 Mickey Rivers | .10 | .08 | 565 Leon Durham | | .10 | .08 |
| 505 Pete Vuckovich | .10 | .08 | 566 Jim Bibby | | .08 | .06 |
| 506 Ernie Whitt | .10 | .08 | 567 Mike Heath | | .08 | .06 |
| 507 Mike LaCoss | .08 | .06 | 568 Pete Filson | | .08 | .06 |
| 508 Mel Hall | .20 | .15 | 569 Bake McBride | | .08 | .06 |
| 509 Brad Havens | .08 | .06 | 570 Dan Quisenberry | | .12 | .09 |
| 510 Alan Trammell | .40 | .30 | 571 Bruce Bochy | | .08 | .06 |
| 511 Marty Bystrom | .08 | .06 | 572 Jerry Royster | | .08 | .06 |
| 512 Oscar Gamble | .10 | .08 | 573 Dave Kingman | | .15 | .11 |
| 513 Dave Beard | .08 | .06 | 574 Brian Downing | | .12 | .09 |
| 514 Floyd Rayford | .08 | .06 | 575 Jim Clancy | | .10 | .08 |
| 515 Gorman Thomas | .10 | .08 | 576 Giants Batting & | | | |
| 516 Expos Batting & Pitching | | | Pitching Leaders (Atlee | | | |
| Leaders (Charlie Lea, Al | | | Hammaker, Jeff Leonard) | | | |
| Oliver) | .12 | .09 | | | .10 | .08 |
| 517 John Moses | .12 | .09 | 577 Mark Clear | | .08 | .06 |
| 518 *Greg Walker* | .25 | .20 | 578 Lenn Sakata | | .08 | .06 |
| 519 Ron Davis | .08 | .06 | 579 Bob James | | .08 | .06 |
| 520 Bob Boone | .10 | .08 | 580 Lonnie Smith | | .10 | .08 |
| 521 Pete Falcone | .08 | .06 | 581 *Jose DeLeon*(FC) | | | |
| 522 Dave Bergman | .08 | .06 | | | .30 | .25 |
| 523 Glenn Hoffman | .08 | .06 | 582 Bob McClure | | .08 | .06 |
| 524 Carlos Diaz | .08 | .06 | 583 Derrel Thomas | | .08 | .06 |
| 525 Willie Wilson | .15 | .11 | 584 Dave Schmidt | | .08 | .06 |
| 526 Ron Oester | .08 | .06 | 585 Dan Driessen | | .10 | .08 |
| 527 Checklist 397-528 | .08 | .06 | 586 Joe Niekro | | .15 | .11 |
| 528 Mark Brouhard | .08 | .06 | 587 Von Hayes | | .15 | .11 |
| 529 *Keith Atherton*(FC) | | | 588 Milt Wilcox | | .08 | .06 |
| | .20 | .15 | 589 Mike Easler | | .10 | .08 |
| 530 Dan Ford | .08 | .06 | 590 Dave Stieb | | .15 | .11 |
| 531 Steve Boros | .08 | .06 | 591 Tony LaRussa | | .10 | .08 |
| 532 Eric Show | .12 | .09 | 592 Andre Robertson | | .08 | .06 |
| 533 Ken Landreaux | .08 | .06 | 593 Jeff Lahti | | .08 | .06 |
| 534 *Pete O'Brien* | .70 | .50 | 594 Gene Richards | | .08 | .06 |
| 535 Bo Diaz | .10 | .08 | 595 Jeff Reardon | | .60 | .45 |
| 536 Doug Bair | .08 | .06 | 596 Ryne Sandberg | | 8.00 | 6.00 |
| 537 Johnny Ray | .12 | .09 | 597 Rick Camp | | .08 | .06 |
| 538 Kevin Bass | .15 | .11 | 598 Rusty Kuntz | | .08 | .06 |
| 539 George Frazier | .08 | .06 | 599 *Doug Sisk* | | .10 | .08 |
| 540 George Hendrick | .10 | .08 | 600 Rod Carew | | .50 | .40 |
| 541 Dennis Lamp | .08 | .06 | 601 John Tudor | | .12 | .09 |
| 542 Duane Kuiper | .08 | .06 | 602 John Wathan | | .10 | .08 |
| 543 *Craig McMurtry* | .12 | .09 | 603 Renie Martin | | .08 | .06 |
| 544 Cesar Geronimo | .08 | .06 | 604 John Lowenstein | | .08 | .06 |
| 545 Bill Buckner | .15 | .11 | 605 Mike Caldwell | | .08 | .06 |
| 546 Indians Batting & | | | 606 Blue Jays Batting & | | | |
| Pitching Leaders (Mike | | | Pitching Leaders (Lloyd | | | |
| Hargrove, Lary Sorensen) | | | Moseby, Dave Stieb) | | .15 | .11 |
| | .10 | .08 | 607 Tom Hume | | .08 | .06 |
| 547 Mike Moore | .10 | .08 | 608 Bobby Johnson | | .08 | .06 |

| | | MT | NR MT |
|---|---|---|---|
| 609 | Dan Meyer | .08 | .06 |
| 610 | Steve Sax | .30 | .25 |
| 611 | Chet Lemon | .10 | .08 |
| 612 | Harry Spilman | .08 | .06 |
| 613 | Greg Gross | .08 | .06 |
| 614 | Len Barker | .10 | .08 |
| 615 | Garry Templeton | .12 | .09 |
| 616 | Don Robinson | .10 | .08 |
| 617 | Rick Cerone | .08 | .06 |
| 618 | Dickie Noles | .08 | .06 |
| 619 | Jerry Dybzinski | .08 | .06 |
| 620 | Al Oliver | .20 | .15 |
| 621 | Frank Howard | .10 | .08 |
| 622 | Al Cowens | .08 | .06 |
| 623 | Ron Washington | .08 | .06 |
| 624 | Terry Harper | .08 | .06 |
| 625 | Larry Gura | .10 | .08 |
| 626 | Bob Clark | .08 | .06 |
| 627 | Dave LaPoint | .10 | .08 |
| 628 | Ed Jurak | .08 | .06 |
| 629 | Rick Langford | .08 | .06 |
| 630 | Ted Simmons | .15 | .11 |
| 631 | Denny Martinez | .10 | .08 |
| 632 | Tom Foley | .08 | .06 |
| 633 | Mike Krukow | .10 | .08 |
| 634 | Mike Marshall | .15 | .11 |
| 635 | Dave Righetti | .25 | .20 |
| 636 | Pat Putnam | .08 | .06 |
| 637 | Phillies Batting & Pitching Leaders (John Denny, Gary Matthews) | .10 | .08 |
| 638 | George Vukovich | .08 | .06 |
| 639 | Rick Lysander | .08 | .06 |
| 640 | Lance Parrish | .35 | .25 |
| 641 | Mike Richardt | .08 | .06 |
| 642 | Tom Underwood | .08 | .06 |
| 643 | Mike Brown | .08 | .06 |
| 644 | Tim Lollar | .08 | .06 |
| 645 | Tony Pena | .12 | .09 |
| 646 | Checklist 529-660 | .08 | .06 |
| 647 | Ron Roenicke | .08 | .06 |
| 648 | Len Whitehouse | .08 | .06 |
| 649 | Tom Herr | .12 | .09 |
| 650 | Phil Niekro | .30 | .25 |
| 651 | John McNamara | .08 | .06 |
| 652 | Rudy May | .08 | .06 |
| 653 | Dave Stapleton | .08 | .06 |
| 654 | Bob Bailor | .08 | .06 |
| 655 | Amos Otis | .10 | .08 |
| 656 | Bryn Smith | .08 | .06 |
| 657 | Thad Bosley | .08 | .06 |
| 658 | Jerry Augustine | .08 | .06 |
| 659 | Duane Walker | .08 | .06 |
| 660 | Ray Knight | .12 | .09 |
| 661 | Steve Yeager | .08 | .06 |
| 662 | Tom Brennan | .08 | .06 |
| 663 | Johnnie LeMaster | .08 | .06 |
| 664 | Dave Stegman | .08 | .06 |
| 665 | Buddy Bell | .15 | .11 |
| 666 | Tigers Batting & Pitching Leaders (Jack Morris, Lou Whitaker) | .15 | .11 |
| 667 | Vance Law | .10 | .08 |
| 668 | Larry McWilliams | .08 | .06 |
| 669 | Dave Lopes | .10 | .08 |
| 670 | Rich Gossage | .25 | .20 |
| 671 | Jamie Quirk | .08 | .06 |

| | | MT | NR MT |
|---|---|---|---|
| 672 | Ricky Nelson | .08 | .06 |
| 673 | Mike Walters | .08 | .06 |
| 674 | Tim Flannery | .08 | .06 |
| 675 | Pascual Perez | .10 | .08 |
| 676 | Brian Giles | .08 | .06 |
| 677 | Doyle Alexander | .12 | .09 |
| 678 | Chris Speier | .08 | .06 |
| 679 | Art Howe | .08 | .06 |
| 680 | Fred Lynn | .25 | .20 |
| 681 | Tom Lasorda | .12 | .09 |
| 682 | Dan Morogiello | .08 | .06 |
| 683 | *Marty Barrett*(FC) | .35 | .25 |
| 684 | Bob Shirley | .08 | .06 |
| 685 | Willie Aikens | .08 | .06 |
| 686 | Joe Price | .08 | .06 |
| 687 | Roy Howell | .08 | .06 |
| 688 | George Wright | .08 | .06 |
| 689 | Mike Fischlin | .08 | .06 |
| 690 | Jack Clark | .25 | .20 |
| 691 | *Steve Lake*(FC) | .10 | .08 |
| 692 | Dickie Thon | .10 | .08 |
| 693 | Alan Wiggins | .08 | .06 |
| 694 | Mike Stanton | .08 | .06 |
| 695 | Lou Whitaker | .40 | .30 |
| 696 | Pirates Batting & Pitching Leaders (Bill Madlock, Rick Rhoden) | .15 | .11 |
| 697 | Dale Murray | .08 | .06 |
| 698 | Marc Hill | .08 | .06 |
| 699 | Dave Rucker | .08 | .06 |
| 700 | Mike Schmidt | 2.50 | 2.00 |
| 701 | NL Active Career Batting Leaders (Bill Madlock, Dave Parker, Pete Rose) | .35 | .25 |
| 702 | NL Active Career Hit Leaders (Tony Perez, Pete Rose, Rusty Staub) | .35 | .25 |
| 703 | NL Active Career Home Run Leaders (Dave Kingman, Tony Perez, Mike Schmidt) | .30 | .25 |
| 704 | NL Active Career RBI Leaders (Al Oliver, Tony Perez, Rusty Staub) | .15 | .11 |
| 705 | NL Active Career Stolen Bases Leaders (Larry Bowa, Cesar Cedeno, Joe Morgan) | .12 | .09 |
| 706 | NL Active Career Victory Leaders (Steve Carlton, Fergie Jenkins, Tom Seaver) | .30 | .25 |
| 707 | NL Active Career Strikeout Leaders (Steve Carlton, Nolan Ryan, Tom Seaver) | .35 | .25 |
| 708 | NL Active Career ERA Leaders (Steve Carlton, Steve Rogers, Tom Seaver) | .25 | .20 |
| 709 | NL Active Career Save Leaders (Gene Garber, Tug McGraw, Bruce Sutter) | .12 | .09 |
| 710 | AL Active Career Batting Leaders (George Brett, Rod Carew, Cecil Cooper) | .30 | .25 |

| | | MT | NR MT |
|---|---|---|---|
| 711 | AL Active Career Hit Leaders (Bert Campaneris, Rod Carew, Reggie Jackson) | .30 | .25 |
| 712 | AL Active Career Home Run Leaders (Reggie Jackson, Greg Luzinski, Graig Nettles) | .20 | .15 |
| 713 | AL Active Career RBI Leaders (Reggie Jackson, Graig Nettles, Ted Simmons) | .20 | .15 |
| 714 | AL Active Career Stolen Bases Leaders (Bert Campaneris, Dave Lopes, Omar Moreno) | .10 | .08 |
| 715 | AL Active Career Victory Leaders (Tommy John, Jim Palmer, Don Sutton) | .25 | .20 |
| 716 | AL Active Career Strikeout Leaders (Bert Blyleven, Jerry Koosman, Don Sutton) | .15 | .11 |
| 717 | AL Active Career ERA Leaders (Rollie Fingers, Ron Guidry, Jim Palmer) | .15 | .11 |
| 718 | AL Active Career Save Leaders (Rollie Fingers, Rich Gossage, Dan Quisenberry) | .15 | .11 |
| 719 | Andy Hassler | .08 | .06 |
| 720 | Dwight Evans | .20 | .15 |
| 721 | Del Crandall | .08 | .06 |
| 722 | Bob Welch | .15 | .11 |
| 723 | Rich Dauer | .08 | .06 |
| 724 | Eric Rasmussen | .08 | .06 |
| 725 | Cesar Cedeno | .12 | .09 |
| 726 | Brewers Batting & Pitching Leaders (Moose Haas, Ted Simmons) | .12 | .09 |
| 727 | Joel Youngblood | .08 | .06 |
| 728 | Tug McGraw | .12 | .09 |
| 729 | Gene Tenace | .10 | .08 |
| 730 | Bruce Sutter | .20 | .15 |
| 731 | Lynn Jones | .08 | .06 |
| 732 | Terry Crowley | .08 | .06 |
| 733 | Dave Collins | .10 | .08 |
| 734 | Odell Jones | .08 | .06 |
| 735 | Rick Burleson | .10 | .08 |
| 736 | Dick Ruthven | .08 | .06 |
| 737 | Jim Essian | .08 | .06 |
| 738 | *Bill Schroeder*(FC) | .20 | .15 |
| 739 | Bob Watson | .10 | .08 |
| 740 | Tom Seaver | 1.75 | 1.25 |
| 741 | Wayne Gross | .08 | .06 |
| 742 | Dick Williams | .08 | .06 |
| 743 | Don Hood | .08 | .06 |
| 744 | Jamie Allen | .08 | .06 |
| 745 | Dennis Eckersley | .15 | .11 |
| 746 | Mickey Hatcher | .10 | .08 |
| 747 | Pat Zachry | .08 | .06 |
| 748 | Jeff Leonard | .12 | .09 |
| 749 | Doug Flynn | .08 | .06 |
| 750 | Jim Palmer | 1.00 | .70 |
| 751 | Charlie Moore | .08 | .06 |
| 752 | Phil Garner | .10 | .08 |

| | | MT | NR MT |
|---|---|---|---|
| 753 | Doug Gwosdz | .08 | .06 |
| 754 | Kent Tekulve | .10 | .08 |
| 755 | Garry Maddox | .10 | .08 |
| 756 | Reds Batting & Pitching Leaders (Ron Oester, Mario Soto) | .10 | .08 |
| 757 | Larry Bowa | .15 | .11 |
| 758 | Bill Stein | .08 | .06 |
| 759 | Richard Dotson | .12 | .09 |
| 760 | Bob Horner | .15 | .11 |
| 761 | John Montefusco | .08 | .06 |
| 762 | Rance Mulliniks | .08 | .06 |
| 763 | Craig Swan | .08 | .06 |
| 764 | Mike Hargrove | .08 | .06 |
| 765 | Ken Forsch | .08 | .06 |
| 766 | Mike Vail | .08 | .06 |
| 767 | Carney Lansford | .12 | .09 |
| 768 | Champ Summers | .08 | .06 |
| 769 | Bill Caudill | .08 | .06 |
| 770 | Ken Griffey | .12 | .09 |
| 771 | Billy Gardner | .08 | .06 |
| 772 | Jim Slaton | .08 | .06 |
| 773 | Todd Cruz | .08 | .06 |
| 774 | Tom Gorman | .08 | .06 |
| 775 | Dave Parker | .30 | .25 |
| 776 | Craig Reynolds | .08 | .06 |
| 777 | Tom Paciorek | .08 | .06 |
| 778 | *Andy Hawkins*(FC) | .25 | .20 |
| 779 | Jim Sundberg | .10 | .08 |
| 780 | Steve Carlton | .80 | .60 |
| 781 | Checklist 661-792 | .08 | .06 |
| 782 | Steve Balboni | .10 | .08 |
| 783 | Luis Leal | .08 | .06 |
| 784 | Leon Roberts | .08 | .06 |
| 785 | Joaquin Andujar | .10 | .08 |
| 786 | Red Sox Batting & Pitching Leaders (Wade Boggs, Bob Ojeda) | .40 | .30 |
| 787 | Bill Campbell | .08 | .06 |
| 788 | Milt May | .08 | .06 |
| 789 | Bert Blyleven | .20 | .15 |
| 790 | Doug DeCinces | .12 | .09 |
| 791 | Terry Forster | .10 | .08 |
| 792 | Bill Russell | .10 | .08 |

## 1984 Topps Traded

The popular Topps Traded set returned for its fourth year in 1984 with another 132-card set. The 2-1/2" by 3-1/2" cards have an identical design to the regular Topps cards except that the back cardboard is white and the card numbers carry a "T" suffix. As before, the set was sold only through hobby dealers. Also as before, players who changed teams, new managers and promising rookies are included in the set. The presence of several promising young rookies in especially high demand from investors and speculators had made this one of the most expensive Topps issues of recent years. A glossy-finish "Tiffany" version of the set was also issued, valued at four to five times the price of the normal Traded cards.

|  | | MT | NR MT |
|---|---|---|---|
| Complete Set: | | 80.00 | 60.00 |
| Common Player: | | .10 | .08 |

| | | MT | NR MT |
|---|---|---|---|
| 1T | Willie Aikens | .10 | .08 |
| 2T | Luis Aponte | .10 | .08 |
| 3T | Mike Armstrong | .10 | .08 |
| 4T | Bob Bailor | .10 | .08 |
| 5T | Dusty Baker | .20 | .15 |
| 6T | Steve Balboni | .20 | .15 |
| 7T | Alan Bannister | .10 | .08 |
| 8T | Dave Beard | .10 | .08 |
| 9T | Joe Beckwith | .10 | .08 |
| 10T | Bruce Berenyi | .10 | .08 |
| 11T | Dave Bergman | .10 | .08 |
| 12T | Tony Bernazard | .10 | .08 |
| 13T | Yogi Berra | .20 | .15 |
| 14T | Barry Bonnell | .10 | .08 |
| 15T | Phil Bradley(FC) | 1.25 | .90 |
| 16T | Fred Breining | .10 | .08 |
| 17T | Bill Buckner | .25 | .20 |
| 18T | Ray Burris | .10 | .08 |
| 19T | John Butcher | .10 | .08 |
| 20T | Brett Butler | .20 | .15 |
| 21T | Enos Cabell | .10 | .08 |
| 22T | Bill Campbell | .10 | .08 |
| 23T | Bill Caudill | .10 | .08 |
| 24T | Bob Clark | .10 | .08 |
| 25T | Bryan Clark | .10 | .08 |
| 26T | Jaime Cocanower | .10 | .08 |
| 27T | Ron Darling(FC) | 3.00 | 2.25 |
| 28T | Alvin Davis(FC) | 3.00 | 2.25 |
| 29T | Ken Dayley | .10 | .08 |
| 30T | Jeff Dedmon(FC) | .15 | .11 |
| 31T | Bob Dernier | .10 | .08 |
| 32T | Carlos Diaz | .10 | .08 |
| 33T | Mike Easler | .15 | .11 |
| 34T | Dennis Eckersley | 6.00 | 4.50 |
| 35T | Jim Essian | .10 | .08 |
| 36T | Darrell Evans | .25 | .20 |
| 37T | Mike Fitzgerald(FC) | .15 | .11 |
| 38T | Tim Foli | .10 | .08 |
| 39T | George Frazier | .10 | .08 |
| 40T | Rich Gale | .10 | .08 |
| 41T | Barbaro Garbey | .15 | .11 |
| 42T | Dwight Gooden(FC) | 30.00 | 22.00 |
| 43T | Rich Gossage | .40 | .30 |
| 44T | Wayne Gross | .10 | .08 |
| 45T | Mark Gubicza(FC) | 2.00 | 1.50 |
| 46T | Jackie Gutierrez | .10 | .08 |
| 47T | Mel Hall | 1.00 | .70 |
| 48T | Toby Harrah | .15 | .11 |
| 49T | Ron Hassey | .10 | .08 |
| 50T | Rich Hebner | .10 | .08 |
| 51T | Willie Hernandez | .30 | .25 |
| 52T | Ricky Horton(FC) | .40 | .30 |
| 53T | Art Howe | .10 | .08 |
| 54T | Dane Iorg | .10 | .08 |
| 55T | Brook Jacoby(FC) | 1.50 | 1.25 |
| 56T | Mike Jeffcoat(FC) | .15 | .11 |
| 57T | Dave Johnson | .15 | .11 |
| 58T | Lynn Jones | .10 | .08 |
| 59T | Ruppert Jones | .10 | .08 |
| 60T | Mike Jorgensen | .10 | .08 |
| 61T | Bob Kearney | .10 | .08 |
| 62T | Jimmy Key(FC) | 5.00 | 3.75 |
| 63T | Dave Kingman | .40 | .30 |
| 64T | Jerry Koosman | .25 | .20 |
| 65T | Wayne Krenchicki | .10 | .08 |
| 66T | Rusty Kuntz | .10 | .08 |
| 67T | Rene Lachemann | .10 | .08 |
| 68T | Frank LaCorte | .10 | .08 |
| 69T | Dennis Lamp | .10 | .08 |
| 70T | Mark Langston(FC) | 10.00 | 7.50 |
| 71T | Rick Leach | .10 | .08 |
| 72T | Craig Lefferts | .15 | .11 |
| 73T | Gary Lucas | .10 | .08 |
| 74T | Jerry Martin | .10 | .08 |
| 75T | Carmelo Martinez | .25 | .20 |
| 76T | Mike Mason(FC) | .15 | .11 |
| 77T | Gary Matthews | .25 | .20 |
| 78T | Andy McGaffigan | .10 | .08 |
| 79T | Larry Milbourne | .10 | .08 |
| 80T | Sid Monge | .10 | .08 |
| 81T | Jackie Moore | .10 | .08 |
| 82T | Joe Morgan | 3.00 | 2.25 |
| 83T | Graig Nettles | .50 | .40 |
| 84T | Phil Niekro | 2.00 | 1.50 |
| 85T | Ken Oberkfell | .10 | .08 |
| 86T | Mike O'Berry | .10 | .08 |
| 87T | Al Oliver | .30 | .25 |
| 88T | Jorge Orta | .10 | .08 |
| 89T | Amos Otis | .15 | .11 |
| 90T | Dave Parker | 2.00 | 1.50 |
| 91T | Tony Perez | .70 | .50 |
| 92T | Gerald Perry(FC) | 1.00 | .70 |
| 93T | Gary Pettis(FC) | .25 | .20 |
| 94T | Rob Picciolo | .10 | .08 |
| 95T | Vern Rapp | .10 | .08 |
| 96T | Floyd Rayford | .10 | .08 |
| 97T | Randy Ready(FC) | .25 | .20 |
| 98T | Ron Reed | .15 | .11 |
| 99T | Gene Richards | .10 | .08 |
| 100T | Jose Rijo(FC) | 7.00 | 5.25 |
| 101T | Jeff Robinson(FC) | .25 | .20 |
| 102T | Ron Romanick(FC) | .20 | .15 |
| 103T | Pete Rose | 8.00 | 6.00 |
| 104T | Bret Saberhagen(FC) | 15.00 | 11.00 |
| 105T | Juan Samuel(FC) | 1.00 | .70 |

| | | MT | NR MT |
|---|---|---|---|
| 106T | Scott Sanderson | .10 | .08 |
| 107T | Dick Schofield(FC) | .35 | .25 |
| 108T | Tom Seaver | 8.00 | 6.00 |
| 109T | Jim Slaton | .10 | .08 |
| 110T | Mike Smithson | .10 | .08 |
| 111T | Lary Sorensen | .10 | .08 |
| 112T | Tim Stoddard | .10 | .08 |
| 113T | Champ Summers | .10 | .08 |
| 114T | Jim Sundberg | .15 | .11 |
| 115T | Rick Sutcliffe | .40 | .30 |
| 116T | Craig Swan | .10 | .08 |
| 117T | Tim Teufel(FC) | .30 | .25 |
| 118T | Derrel Thomas | .10 | .08 |
| 119T | Gorman Thomas | .25 | .20 |
| 120T | Alex Trevino | .10 | .08 |
| 121T | Manny Trillo | .15 | .11 |
| 122T | John Tudor | .25 | .20 |
| 123T | Tom Underwood | .10 | .08 |
| 124T | Mike Vail | .10 | .08 |
| 125T | Tom Waddell | .10 | .08 |
| 126T | Gary Ward | .10 | .08 |
| 127T | Curt Wilkerson | .10 | .08 |
| 128T | Frank Williams(FC) | .25 | .20 |
| 129T | Glenn Wilson | .20 | .15 |
| 130T | Johnny Wockenfuss | .10 | .08 |
| 131T | Ned Yost | .10 | .08 |
| 132T | Checklist 1-132 | .10 | .08 |

# 1985 Topps

Holding the line at 792 cards, Topps did initiate some major design changes in its 2-1/2" by 3-1/2" cards in 1985. The use of two photos on the front was discontinued in favor of one large color photo. The Topps logo appears in the upper left-hand corner. At the bottom runs a diagonal rectangular box with the team name. It joins a team logo, and below that point runs the player's position and name. The backs feature statistics, biographical information and a trivia question. Some interesting specialty sets were introduced in 1985, including the revival of the father/son theme from 1976, a subset of the 1984 U.S. Olympic Baseball Team members and a set featuring #1 draft choices since the inception of the baseball draft in 1965. Again in 1985, a glossy-finish "Tiffany" edition of the regular set was produced, though the number was cut back to 5,000 sets. Values range from four times regular value for common cards to five-six times for high-demand stars and rookie cards.

| | | MT | NR MT |
|---|---|---|---|
| Complete Set: | | 85.00 | 65.00 |
| Common Player: | | .06 | .05 |
| | | | |
| 1 | Record Breaker (Carlton Fisk) | .15 | .11 |
| 2 | Record Breaker (Steve Garvey) | .20 | .15 |
| 3 | Record Breaker (Dwight Gooden) | 1.00 | .70 |
| 4 | Record Breaker (Cliff Johnson) | .08 | .06 |
| 5 | Record Breaker (Joe Morgan) | .15 | .11 |
| 6 | Record Breaker (Pete Rose) | .60 | .45 |
| 7 | Record Breaker (Nolan Ryan) | 1.00 | .70 |
| 8 | Record Breaker (Juan Samuel)(FC) | .20 | .15 |
| 9 | Record Breaker (Bruce Sutter) | .12 | .09 |
| 10 | Record Breaker (Don Sutton) | .20 | .15 |
| 11 | Ralph Houk | .08 | .06 |
| 12 | Dave Lopes | .08 | .06 |
| 13 | Tim Lollar | .06 | .05 |
| 14 | Chris Bando | .06 | .05 |
| 15 | Jerry Koosman | .10 | .08 |
| 16 | Bobby Meacham | .06 | .05 |
| 17 | Mike Scott | .15 | .11 |
| 18 | Mickey Hatcher | .06 | .05 |
| 19 | George Frazier | .06 | .05 |
| 20 | Chet Lemon | .08 | .06 |
| 21 | Lee Tunnell | .06 | .05 |
| 22 | Duane Kuiper | .06 | .05 |
| 23 | *Bret Saberhagen* | 4.00 | 3.00 |
| 24 | Jesse Barfield | .25 | .20 |
| 25 | Steve Bedrosian | .12 | .09 |
| 26 | Roy Smalley | .06 | .05 |
| 27 | Bruce Berenyi | .06 | .05 |
| 28 | Dann Bilardello | .06 | .05 |
| 29 | Odell Jones | .06 | .05 |
| 30 | Cal Ripken | 4.00 | 3.00 |
| 31 | Terry Whitfield | .06 | .05 |
| 32 | Chuck Porter | .06 | .05 |
| 33 | Tito Landrum | .06 | .05 |
| 34 | Ed Nunez(FC) | .08 | .06 |
| 35 | Graig Nettles | .15 | .11 |
| 36 | Fred Breining | .06 | .05 |
| 37 | Reid Nichols | .06 | .05 |
| 38 | Jackie Moore | .06 | .05 |
| 39 | Johnny Wockenfuss | .06 | .05 |

| | | MT | NR MT | | | MT | NR MT |
|---|---|---|---|---|---|---|---|
| 40 | Phil Niekro | .25 | .20 | 106 | Pascual Perez | .08 | .06 |
| 41 | Mike Fischlin | .06 | .05 | 107 | Tom Foley | .06 | .05 |
| 42 | Luis Sanchez | .06 | .05 | 108 | Darnell Coles(FC) | .15 | .11 |
| 43 | Andre David | .06 | .05 | 109 | Gary Roenicke | .06 | .05 |
| 44 | Dickie Thon | .08 | .06 | 110 | Alejandro Pena | .08 | .06 |
| 45 | Greg Minton | .06 | .05 | 111 | Doug DeCinces | .10 | .08 |
| 46 | Gary Woods | .06 | .05 | 112 | Tom Tellmann | .06 | .05 |
| 47 | Dave Rozema | .06 | .05 | 113 | Tom Herr | .10 | .08 |
| 48 | Tony Fernandez(FC) | .80 | .60 | 114 | Bob James | .06 | .05 |
| 49 | Butch Davis | .06 | .05 | 115 | Rickey Henderson | 2.00 | 1.50 |
| 50 | John Candelaria | .10 | .08 | 116 | Dennis Boyd(FC) | .15 | .11 |
| 51 | Bob Watson | .08 | .06 | 117 | Greg Gross | .06 | .05 |
| 52 | Jerry Dybzinski | .06 | .05 | 118 | Eric Show | .08 | .06 |
| 53 | Tom Gorman | .06 | .05 | 119 | Pat Corrales | .06 | .05 |
| 54 | Cesar Cedeno | .10 | .08 | 120 | Steve Kemp | .08 | .06 |
| 55 | Frank Tanana | .10 | .08 | 121 | Checklist 1-132 | .06 | .05 |
| 56 | Jim Dwyer | .06 | .05 | 122 | Tom Brunansky | .12 | .09 |
| 57 | Pat Zachry | .06 | .05 | 123 | Dave Smith | .08 | .06 |
| 58 | Orlando Mercado | .06 | .05 | 124 | Rich Hebner | .06 | .05 |
| 59 | Rick Waits | .06 | .05 | 125 | Kent Tekulve | .08 | .06 |
| 60 | George Hendrick | .08 | .06 | 126 | Ruppert Jones | .06 | .05 |
| 61 | Curt Kaufman | .06 | .05 | 127 | *Mark Gubicza* | .40 | .30 |
| 62 | Mike Ramsey | .06 | .05 | 128 | Ernie Whitt | .08 | .06 |
| 63 | Steve McCatty | .06 | .05 | 129 | Gene Garber | .06 | .05 |
| 64 | *Mark Bailey*(FC) | .10 | .08 | 130 | Al Oliver | .12 | .09 |
| 65 | Bill Buckner | .12 | .09 | 131 | Father - Son (Buddy Bell, Gus Bell) | .12 | .09 |
| 66 | Dick Williams | .06 | .05 | | | | |
| 67 | *Rafael Santana*(FC) | | | 132 | Father - Son (Dale Berra, Yogi Berra) | .20 | .15 |
| | | .20 | .15 | | | | |
| 68 | Von Hayes | .10 | .08 | 133 | Father - Son (Bob Boone, Ray Boone) | .12 | .09 |
| 69 | *Jim Winn*(FC) | .10 | .08 | | | | |
| 70 | Don Baylor | .12 | .09 | 134 | Father - Son (Terry Francona, Tito Francona) | | |
| 71 | Tim Laudner | .06 | .05 | | | | |
| 72 | Rick Sutcliffe | .12 | .09 | | | .08 | .06 |
| 73 | Rusty Kuntz | .06 | .05 | 135 | Father - Son (Bob Kennedy, Terry Kennedy) | | |
| 74 | Mike Krukow | .08 | .06 | | | | |
| 75 | Willie Upshaw | .08 | .06 | | | .08 | .06 |
| 76 | Alan Bannister | .06 | .05 | 136 | Father - Son (Bill Kunkel, Jeff Kunkel)(FC) | .08 | .06 |
| 77 | Joe Beckwith | .06 | .05 | | | | |
| 78 | Scott Fletcher | .08 | .06 | 137 | Father - Son (Vance Law, Vern Law) | .10 | .08 |
| 79 | Rick Mahler | .06 | .05 | | | | |
| 80 | Keith Hernandez | .30 | .25 | 138 | Father - Son (Dick Schofield, Dick Schofield) | | |
| 81 | Lenn Sakata | .06 | .05 | | | | |
| 82 | Joe Price | .06 | .05 | | | .08 | .06 |
| 83 | Charlie Moore | .06 | .05 | 139 | Father - Son (Bob Skinner, Joel Skinner) | .08 | .06 |
| 84 | Spike Owen | .08 | .06 | | | | |
| 85 | Mike Marshall | .15 | .11 | 140 | Father - Son (Roy Smalley, Roy Smalley) | .08 | .06 |
| 86 | Don Aase | .06 | .05 | | | | |
| 87 | David Green | .06 | .05 | 141 | Father - Son (Dave Stenhouse, Mike Stenhouse) | | |
| 88 | Bryn Smith | .06 | .05 | | | | |
| 89 | Jackie Gutierrez | .06 | .05 | | | .08 | .06 |
| 90 | Rich Gossage | .20 | .15 | 142 | Father - Son (Dizzy Trout, Steve Trout) | .08 | .06 |
| 91 | Jeff Burroughs | .08 | .06 | | | | |
| 92 | Paul Owens | .06 | .05 | 143 | Father - Son (Ossie Virgil, Ozzie Virgil) | .08 | .06 |
| 93 | *Don Schulze*(FC) | .10 | .08 | | | | |
| 94 | Toby Harrah | .08 | .06 | 144 | Ron Gardenhire | .06 | .05 |
| 95 | Jose Cruz | .10 | .08 | 145 | *Alvin Davis* | .60 | .45 |
| 96 | Johnny Ray | .12 | .09 | 146 | Gary Redus | .08 | .06 |
| 97 | Pete Filson | .06 | .05 | 147 | Bill Swaggerty | .06 | .05 |
| 98 | Steve Lake | .06 | .05 | 148 | Steve Yeager | .06 | .05 |
| 99 | Milt Wilcox | .06 | .05 | 149 | Dickie Noles | .06 | .05 |
| 100 | George Brett | 1.00 | .70 | 150 | Jim Rice | .35 | .25 |
| 101 | Jim Acker | .06 | .05 | 151 | Moose Haas | .06 | .05 |
| 102 | Tommy Dunbar | .06 | .05 | 152 | Steve Braun | .06 | .05 |
| 103 | Randy Lerch | .06 | .05 | 153 | Frank LaCorte | .06 | .05 |
| 104 | Mike Fitzgerald | .08 | .06 | 154 | Argenis Salazar(FC) | .06 | .05 |
| 105 | Ron Kittle | .10 | .08 | 155 | Yogi Berra | .12 | .09 |

| | | MT | NR MT |
|---|---|---|---|
| 156 | Craig Reynolds | .06 | .05 |
| 157 | Tug McGraw | .10 | .08 |
| 158 | Pat Tabler | .08 | .06 |
| 159 | Carlos Diaz | .06 | .05 |
| 160 | Lance Parrish | .25 | .20 |
| 161 | Ken Schrom | .06 | .05 |
| 162 | Benny Distefano(FC) | | |
| | | .10 | .08 |
| 163 | Dennis Eckersley | .12 | .09 |
| 164 | Jorge Orta | .06 | .05 |
| 165 | Dusty Baker | .08 | .06 |
| 166 | Keith Atherton | .06 | .05 |
| 167 | Rufino Linares | .06 | .05 |
| 168 | Garth Iorg | .06 | .05 |
| 169 | Dan Spillner | .06 | .05 |
| 170 | George Foster | .15 | .11 |
| 171 | Bill Stein | .06 | .05 |
| 172 | Jack Perconte | .06 | .05 |
| 173 | Mike Young(FC) | .12 | .09 |
| 174 | Rick Honeycutt | .06 | .05 |
| 175 | Dave Parker | .25 | .20 |
| 176 | Bill Schroeder | .06 | .05 |
| 177 | Dave Von Ohlen | .06 | .05 |
| 178 | Miguel Dilone | .06 | .05 |
| 179 | Tommy John | .20 | .15 |
| 180 | Dave Winfield | 1.25 | .90 |
| 181 | Roger Clemens(FC) | | |
| | | 20.00 | 15.00 |
| 182 | Tim Flannery | .06 | .05 |
| 183 | Larry McWilliams | .06 | .05 |
| 184 | Carmen Castillo(FC) | .10 | .08 |
| 185 | Al Holland | .06 | .05 |
| 186 | Bob Lillis | .06 | .05 |
| 187 | Mike Walters | .06 | .05 |
| 188 | Greg Pryor | .06 | .05 |
| 189 | Warren Brusstar | .06 | .05 |
| 190 | Rusty Staub | .12 | .09 |
| 191 | Steve Nicosia | .08 | .06 |
| 192 | Howard Johnson(FC) | | |
| | | 4.00 | 3.00 |
| 193 | Jimmy Key | 1.00 | .70 |
| 194 | Dave Stegman | .06 | .05 |
| 195 | Glenn Hubbard | .06 | .05 |
| 196 | Pete O'Brien | .12 | .09 |
| 197 | Mike Warren | .06 | .05 |
| 198 | Eddie Milner | .06 | .05 |
| 199 | Denny Martinez | .08 | .06 |
| 200 | Reggie Jackson | .60 | .45 |
| 201 | Burt Hooton | .08 | .06 |
| 202 | Gorman Thomas | .10 | .08 |
| 203 | Bob McClure | .06 | .05 |
| 204 | Art Howe | .06 | .05 |
| 205 | Steve Rogers | .08 | .06 |
| 206 | Phil Garner | .08 | .06 |
| 207 | Mark Clear | .06 | .05 |
| 208 | Champ Summers | .06 | .05 |
| 209 | Bill Campbell | .06 | .05 |
| 210 | Gary Matthews | .10 | .08 |
| 211 | Clay Christiansen | .06 | .05 |
| 212 | George Vukovich | .06 | .05 |
| 213 | Billy Gardner | .06 | .05 |
| 214 | John Tudor | .10 | .08 |
| 215 | Bob Brenly | .06 | .05 |
| 216 | Jerry Don Gleaton | .06 | .05 |
| 217 | Leon Roberts | .06 | .05 |
| 218 | Doyle Alexander | .10 | .08 |
| 219 | Gerald Perry | .35 | .25 |

| | | MT | NR MT |
|---|---|---|---|
| 220 | Fred Lynn | .20 | .15 |
| 221 | Ron Reed | .06 | .05 |
| 222 | Hubie Brooks | .10 | .08 |
| 223 | Tom Hume | .06 | .05 |
| 224 | Al Cowens | .06 | .05 |
| 225 | Mike Boddicker | .10 | .08 |
| 226 | Juan Beniquez | .06 | .05 |
| 227 | Danny Darwin | .06 | .05 |
| 228 | Dion James(FC) | .20 | .15 |
| 229 | Dave LaPoint | .08 | .06 |
| 230 | Gary Carter | .35 | .25 |
| 231 | Dwayne Murphy | .08 | .06 |
| 232 | Dave Beard | .06 | .05 |
| 233 | Ed Jurak | .06 | .05 |
| 234 | Jerry Narron | .06 | .05 |
| 235 | Garry Maddox | .10 | .08 |
| 236 | Mark Thurmond | .06 | .05 |
| 237 | Julio Franco | .50 | .40 |
| 238 | Jose Rijo | 1.50 | 1.25 |
| 239 | Tim Teufel | .12 | .09 |
| 240 | Dave Stieb | .12 | .09 |
| 241 | Jim Frey | .06 | .05 |
| 242 | Greg Harris | .06 | .05 |
| 243 | Barbaro Garbey | .10 | .08 |
| 244 | Mike Jones | .06 | .05 |
| 245 | Chili Davis | .10 | .08 |
| 246 | Mike Norris | .06 | .05 |
| 247 | Wayne Tolleson | .06 | .05 |
| 248 | Terry Forster | .08 | .06 |
| 249 | Harold Baines | .15 | .11 |
| 250 | Jesse Orosco | .08 | .06 |
| 251 | Brad Gulden | .06 | .05 |
| 252 | Dan Ford | .06 | .05 |
| 253 | Sid Bream(FC) | .50 | .40 |
| 254 | Pete Vuckovich | .08 | .06 |
| 255 | Lonnie Smith | .08 | .06 |
| 256 | Mike Stanton | .06 | .05 |
| 257 | Brian Little (Bryan) | .06 | .05 |
| 258 | Mike Brown | .06 | .05 |
| 259 | Gary Allenson | .06 | .05 |
| 260 | Dave Righetti | .20 | .15 |
| 261 | Checklist 133-264 | .06 | .05 |
| 262 | Greg Booker(FC) | | |
| | | .12 | .09 |
| 263 | Mel Hall | .08 | .06 |
| 264 | Joe Sambito | .06 | .05 |
| 265 | Juan Samuel(FC) | .50 | .40 |
| 266 | Frank Viola | .20 | .15 |
| 267 | Henry Cotto(FC) | .15 | .11 |
| 268 | Chuck Tanner | .06 | .05 |
| 269 | Doug Baker(FC) | .10 | .08 |
| 270 | Dan Quisenberry | .10 | .08 |
| 271 | 1968 #1 Draft Pick (Tim Foli) | .08 | .06 |
| 272 | 1969 #1 Draft Pick (Jeff Burroughs) | .08 | .06 |
| 273 | 1974 #1 Draft Pick (Bill Almon) | .08 | .06 |
| 274 | 1976 #1 Draft Pick (Floyd Bannister) | .10 | .08 |
| 275 | 1977 #1 Draft Pick (Harold Baines) | .15 | .11 |
| 276 | 1978 #1 Draft Pick (Bob Horner) | .15 | .11 |
| 277 | 1979 #1 Draft Pick (Al Chambers) | .08 | .06 |
| 278 | 1980 #1 Draft Pick | | |

| | MT | NR MT |
|---|---|---|
| (Darryl Strawberry) | 2.00 | 1.50 |
| 279 1981 #1 Draft Pick (Mike Moore)(FC) | .20 | .15 |
| 280 1982 #1 Draft Pick (Shawon Dunston)(FC) | 1.00 | .70 |
| 281 1983 #1 Draft Pick (Tim Belcher)(FC) | 1.25 | .90 |
| 282 1984 #1 Draft Pick (Shawn Abner)(FC) | .20 | .15 |
| 283 Fran Mullins | .06 | .05 |
| 284 Marty Bystrom | .06 | .05 |
| 285 Dan Driessen | .08 | .06 |
| 286 Rudy Law | .06 | .05 |
| 287 Walt Terrell | .08 | .06 |
| 288 *Jeff Kunkel*(FC) | .10 | .08 |
| 289 Tom Underwood | .06 | .05 |
| 290 Cecil Cooper | .12 | .09 |
| 291 Bob Welch | .12 | .09 |
| 292 Brad Komminsk(FC) | .08 | .06 |
| 293 *Curt Young*(FC) | .35 | .25 |
| 294 *Tom Nieto*(FC) | .10 | .08 |
| 295 Joe Niekro | .10 | .08 |
| 296 Ricky Nelson | .06 | .05 |
| 297 Gary Lucas | .06 | .05 |
| 298 Marty Barrett | .15 | .11 |
| 299 Andy Hawkins | .08 | .06 |
| 300 Rod Carew | .50 | .40 |
| 301 John Montefusco | .06 | .05 |
| 302 Tim Corcoran | .06 | .05 |
| 303 *Mike Jeffcoat* | .08 | .06 |
| 304 Gary Gaetti | .25 | .20 |
| 305 Dale Berra | .06 | .05 |
| 306 Rick Reuschel | .10 | .08 |
| 307 Sparky Anderson | .08 | .06 |
| 308 John Wathan | .08 | .06 |
| 309 Mike Witt | .12 | .09 |
| 310 Manny Trillo | .08 | .06 |
| 311 Jim Gott | .06 | .05 |
| 312 Marc Hill | .06 | .05 |
| 313 Dave Schmidt | .06 | .05 |
| 314 Ron Oester | .06 | .05 |
| 315 Doug Sisk | .06 | .05 |
| 316 John Lowenstein | .06 | .05 |
| 317 *Jack Lazorko*(FC) | .10 | .08 |
| 318 Ted Simmons | .12 | .09 |
| 319 Jeff Jones | .06 | .05 |
| 320 Dale Murphy | .60 | .45 |
| 321 *Ricky Horton* | .30 | .25 |
| 322 Dave Stapleton | .06 | .05 |
| 323 Andy McGaffigan | .06 | .05 |
| 324 Bruce Bochy | .06 | .05 |
| 325 John Denny | .06 | .05 |
| 326 Kevin Bass | .10 | .08 |
| 327 Brook Jacoby | .30 | .25 |
| 328 Bob Shirley | .06 | .05 |
| 329 Ron Washington | .06 | .05 |
| 330 Leon Durham | .08 | .06 |
| 331 Bill Laskey | .06 | .05 |
| 332 Brian Harper | .06 | .05 |
| 333 Willie Hernandez | .08 | .06 |
| 334 Dick Howser | .06 | .05 |
| 335 Bruce Benedict | .06 | .05 |
| 336 Rance Mulliniks | .06 | .05 |
| 337 Billy Sample | .06 | .05 |
| 338 Britt Burns | .06 | .05 |

| | MT | NR MT |
|---|---|---|
| 339 Danny Heep | .06 | .05 |
| 340 Robin Yount | 1.00 | .70 |
| 341 Floyd Rayford | .06 | .05 |
| 342 Ted Power | .06 | .05 |
| 343 Bill Russell | .08 | .06 |
| 344 Dave Henderson | .10 | .08 |
| 345 Charlie Lea | .06 | .05 |
| 346 *Terry Pendleton*(FC) | 4.00 | 3.00 |
| 347 Rick Langford | .06 | .05 |
| 348 Bob Boone | .08 | .06 |
| 349 Domingo Ramos | .06 | .05 |
| 350 Wade Boggs | 2.00 | 1.50 |
| 351 Juan Agosto | .06 | .05 |
| 352 Joe Morgan | .30 | .25 |
| 353 Julio Solano | .06 | .05 |
| 354 Andre Robertson | .06 | .05 |
| 355 Bert Blyleven | .12 | .09 |
| 356 Dave Meier | .06 | .05 |
| 357 Rich Bordi | .06 | .05 |
| 358 Tony Pena | .10 | .08 |
| 359 Pat Sheridan | .06 | .05 |
| 360 Steve Carlton | .60 | .45 |
| 361 Alfredo Griffin | .08 | .06 |
| 362 Craig McMurtry | .06 | .05 |
| 363 Ron Hodges | .06 | .05 |
| 364 Richard Dotson | .10 | .08 |
| 365 Danny Ozark | .06 | .05 |
| 366 Todd Cruz | .06 | .05 |
| 367 Keefe Cato | .06 | .05 |
| 368 Dave Bergman | .06 | .05 |
| 369 *R.J. Reynolds*(FC) | .25 | .20 |
| 370 Bruce Sutter | .12 | .09 |
| 371 Mickey Rivers | .08 | .06 |
| 372 Roy Howell | .06 | .05 |
| 373 Mike Moore | .06 | .05 |
| 374 Brian Downing | .10 | .08 |
| 375 Jeff Reardon | .12 | .09 |
| 376 Jeff Newman | .06 | .05 |
| 377 Checklist 265-396 | .06 | .05 |
| 378 Alan Wiggins | .06 | .05 |
| 379 Charles Hudson | .08 | .06 |
| 380 Ken Griffey | .10 | .08 |
| 381 Roy Smith | .06 | .05 |
| 382 Denny Walling | .06 | .05 |
| 383 Rick Lysander | .06 | .05 |
| 384 Jody Davis | .10 | .08 |
| 385 Jose DeLeon | .08 | .06 |
| 386 *Dan Gladden*(FC) | .30 | .25 |
| 387 *Buddy Biancalana*(FC) | .12 | .09 |
| 388 Bert Roberge | .06 | .05 |
| 389 1984 United States Baseball Team (Rod Dedeaux) | .06 | .05 |
| 390 1984 United States Baseball Team (Sid Akins)(FC) | .10 | .08 |
| 391 1984 United States Baseball Team (Flavio Alfaro) | .06 | .05 |
| 392 1984 United States Baseball Team (Don August)(FC) | .20 | .15 |
| 393 1984 United States | | |

| | MT | NR MT |
|---|---|---|
| Baseball Team (Scott Bankhead)(FC) | .60 | .45 |
| 394 1984 United States Baseball Team (Bob Caffrey)(FC) | .08 | .06 |
| 395 1984 United States Baseball Team (Mike Dunne)(FC) | .20 | .15 |
| 396 1984 United States Baseball Team (Gary Green)(FC) | .08 | .06 |
| 397 1984 United States Baseball Team (John Hoover)(FC) | .06 | .05 |
| 398 1984 United States Baseball Team (Shane Mack)(FC) | 4.00 | 3.00 |
| 399 1984 United States Baseball Team (John Marzano)(FC) | .25 | .20 |
| 400 1984 United States Baseball Team (Oddibe McDowell)(FC) | .20 | .15 |
| 401 1984 United States Baseball Team (Mark McGwire)(FC) | 30.00 | 22.00 |
| 402 1984 United States Baseball Team (Pat Pacillo)(FC) | .20 | .15 |
| 403 1984 United States Baseball Team (Cory Snyder)(FC) | 1.25 | .90 |
| 404 1984 United States Baseball Team (Billy Swift)(FC) | 1.50 | 1.25 |
| 405 Tom Veryzer | .06 | .05 |
| 406 Len Whitehouse | .06 | .05 |
| 407 Bobby Ramos | .06 | .05 |
| 408 Sid Monge | .06 | .05 |
| 409 Brad Wellman | .06 | .05 |
| 410 Bob Horner | .15 | .11 |
| 411 Bobby Cox | .06 | .05 |
| 412 Bud Black | .06 | .05 |
| 413 Vance Law | .08 | .06 |
| 414 Gary Ward | .08 | .06 |
| 415 Ron Darling | .60 | .45 |
| 416 Wayne Gross | .06 | .05 |
| 417 *John Franco*(FC) | 1.50 | 1.25 |
| 418 Ken Landreaux | .06 | .05 |
| 419 Mike Caldwell | .06 | .05 |
| 420 Andre Dawson | .50 | .40 |
| 421 Dave Rucker | .06 | .05 |
| 422 Carney Lansford | .10 | .08 |
| 423 Barry Bonnell | .06 | .05 |
| 424 *Al Nipper*(FC) | .15 | .11 |
| 425 Mike Hargrove | .06 | .05 |
| 426 Verne Ruhle | .06 | .05 |
| 427 Mario Ramirez | .06 | .05 |
| 428 Larry Andersen | .06 | .05 |
| 429 Rick Cerone | .06 | .05 |
| 430 Ron Davis | .06 | .05 |
| 431 U.L. Washington | .06 | .05 |
| 432 Thad Bosley | .06 | .05 |
| 433 Jim Morrison | .06 | .05 |
| 434 Gene Richards | .06 | .05 |
| 435 Dan Petry | .08 | .06 |

| | MT | NR MT |
|---|---|---|
| 436 Willie Aikens | .06 | .05 |
| 437 Al Jones | .06 | .05 |
| 438 Joe Torre | .08 | .06 |
| 439 Junior Ortiz | .06 | .05 |
| 440 Fernando Valenzuela | .30 | .25 |
| 441 Duane Walker | .06 | .05 |
| 442 Ken Forsch | .06 | .05 |
| 443 George Wright | .06 | .05 |
| 444 Tony Phillips | .06 | .05 |
| 445 Tippy Martinez | .06 | .05 |
| 446 Jim Sundberg | .08 | .06 |
| 447 Jeff Lahti | .06 | .05 |
| 448 Derrel Thomas | .06 | .05 |
| 449 *Phil Bradley* | .20 | .15 |
| 450 Steve Garvey | .40 | .30 |
| 451 Bruce Hurst | .12 | .09 |
| 452 John Castino | .06 | .05 |
| 453 Tom Waddell | .06 | .05 |
| 454 Glenn Wilson | .08 | .06 |
| 455 Bob Knepper | .08 | .06 |
| 456 Tim Foli | .06 | .05 |
| 457 Cecilio Guante | .06 | .05 |
| 458 Randy Johnson | .06 | .05 |
| 459 Charlie Leibrandt | .08 | .06 |
| 460 Ryne Sandberg | 3.00 | 2.25 |
| 461 Marty Castillo | .06 | .05 |
| 462 Gary Lavelle | .06 | .05 |
| 463 Dave Collins | .08 | .06 |
| 464 *Mike Mason*(FC) | .10 | .08 |
| 465 Bob Grich | .10 | .08 |
| 466 Tony LaRussa | .08 | .06 |
| 467 Ed Lynch | .06 | .05 |
| 468 Wayne Krenchicki | .06 | .05 |
| 469 Sammy Stewart | .06 | .05 |
| 470 Steve Sax | .20 | .15 |
| 471 Pete Ladd | .06 | .05 |
| 472 Jim Essian | .06 | .05 |
| 473 Tim Wallach | .12 | .09 |
| 474 Kurt Kepshire | .06 | .05 |
| 475 Andre Thornton | .10 | .08 |
| 476 *Jeff Stone*(FC) | .12 | .09 |
| 477 Bob Ojeda | .10 | .08 |
| 478 Kurt Bevacqua | .06 | .05 |
| 479 Mike Madden | .06 | .05 |
| 480 Lou Whitaker | .30 | .25 |
| 481 Dale Murray | .06 | .05 |
| 482 Harry Spilman | .06 | .05 |
| 483 Mike Smithson | .06 | .05 |
| 484 Larry Bowa | .10 | .08 |
| 485 Matt Young | .06 | .05 |
| 486 Steve Balboni | .08 | .06 |
| 487 *Frank Williams* | .15 | .11 |
| 488 Joel Skinner(FC) | .08 | .06 |
| 489 Bryan Clark | .06 | .05 |
| 490 Jason Thompson | .06 | .05 |
| 491 Rick Camp | .06 | .05 |
| 492 Dave Johnson | .08 | .06 |
| 493 *Orel Hershiser*(FC) | 2.50 | 2.00 |
| 494 Rich Dauer | .06 | .05 |
| 495 Mario Soto | .08 | .06 |
| 496 Donnie Scott | .06 | .05 |
| 497 Gary Pettis | .15 | .11 |
| 498 Ed Romero | .06 | .05 |
| 499 Danny Cox(FC) | .20 | .20 |
| 500 Mike Schmidt | 1.00 | .70 |

| | | MT | NR MT |
|---|---|---|---|
| 501 | Dan Schatzeder | .06 | .05 |
| 502 | Rick Miller | .06 | .05 |
| 503 | Tim Conroy | .06 | .05 |
| 504 | Jerry Willard | .06 | .05 |
| 505 | Jim Beattie | .06 | .05 |
| 506 | *Franklin Stubbs*(FC) | | |
| | | .40 | .30 |
| 507 | Ray Fontenot | .06 | .05 |
| 508 | John Shelby | .08 | .06 |
| 509 | Milt May | .06 | .05 |
| 510 | Kent Hrbek | .25 | .20 |
| 511 | Lee Smith | .10 | .08 |
| 512 | Tom Brookens | .06 | .05 |
| 513 | Lynn Jones | .06 | .05 |
| 514 | Jeff Cornell | .06 | .05 |
| 515 | Dave Concepcion | .12 | .09 |
| 516 | Roy Lee Jackson | .06 | .05 |
| 517 | Jerry Martin | .06 | .05 |
| 518 | Chris Chambliss | .08 | .06 |
| 519 | Doug Rader | .06 | .05 |
| 520 | LaMarr Hoyt | .06 | .05 |
| 521 | Rick Dempsey | .08 | .06 |
| 522 | Paul Molitor | .15 | .11 |
| 523 | Candy Maldonado | .10 | .08 |
| 524 | Rob Wilfong | .06 | .05 |
| 525 | Darrell Porter | .08 | .06 |
| 526 | Dave Palmer | .06 | .05 |
| 527 | Checklist 397-528 | .06 | .05 |
| 528 | Bill Krueger | .06 | .05 |
| 529 | Rich Gedman | .10 | .08 |
| 530 | Dave Dravecky | .08 | .06 |
| 531 | Joe Lefebvre | .06 | .05 |
| 532 | Frank DiPino | .06 | .05 |
| 533 | Tony Bernazard | .06 | .05 |
| 534 | Brian Dayett(FC) | .06 | .05 |
| 535 | Pat Putnam | .06 | .05 |
| 536 | *Kirby Puckett*(FC) | | |
| | | 21.00 | 15.70 |
| 537 | Don Robinson | .08 | .06 |
| 538 | Keith Moreland | .08 | .06 |
| 539 | Aurelio Lopez | .06 | .05 |
| 540 | Claudell Washington | .08 | .06 |
| 541 | Mark Davis | .06 | .05 |
| 542 | Don Slaught | .06 | .05 |
| 543 | Mike Squires | .06 | .05 |
| 544 | Bruce Kison | .06 | .05 |
| 545 | Lloyd Moseby | .10 | .08 |
| 546 | Brent Gaff | .06 | .05 |
| 547 | Pete Rose | .60 | .45 |
| 548 | Larry Parrish | .10 | .08 |
| 549 | Mike Scioscia | .08 | .06 |
| 550 | Scott McGregor | .08 | .06 |
| 551 | Andy Van Slyke | .35 | .25 |
| 552 | Chris Codiroli | .06 | .05 |
| 553 | Bob Clark | .06 | .05 |
| 554 | Doug Flynn | .06 | .05 |
| 555 | Bob Stanley | .06 | .05 |
| 556 | Sixto Lezcano | .06 | .05 |
| 557 | Len Barker | .08 | .06 |
| 558 | Carmelo Martinez | .08 | .06 |
| 559 | Jay Howell | .08 | .06 |
| 560 | Bill Madlock | .12 | .09 |
| 561 | Darryl Motley | .06 | .05 |
| 562 | Houston Jimenez | .06 | .05 |
| 563 | Dick Ruthven | .06 | .05 |
| 564 | Alan Ashby | .06 | .05 |
| 565 | Kirk Gibson | .35 | .25 |

| | | MT | NR MT |
|---|---|---|---|
| 566 | Ed Vande Berg | .06 | .05 |
| 567 | Joel Youngblood | .06 | .05 |
| 568 | Cliff Johnson | .06 | .05 |
| 569 | Ken Oberkfell | .06 | .05 |
| 570 | Darryl Strawberry | 5.00 | 3.75 |
| 571 | Charlie Hough | .08 | .06 |
| 572 | Tom Paciorek | .06 | .05 |
| 573 | *Jay Tibbs*(FC) | .15 | .11 |
| 574 | Joe Altobelli | .06 | .05 |
| 575 | Pedro Guerrero | .25 | .20 |
| 576 | Jaime Cocanower | .06 | .05 |
| 577 | Chris Speier | .06 | .05 |
| 578 | Terry Francona | .06 | .05 |
| 579 | *Ron Romanick* | .10 | .08 |
| 580 | Dwight Evans | .12 | .09 |
| 581 | Mark Wagner | .06 | .05 |
| 582 | Ken Phelps(FC) | .20 | .15 |
| 583 | Bobby Brown | .06 | .05 |
| 584 | Kevin Gross | .10 | .08 |
| 585 | Butch Wynegar | .06 | .05 |
| 586 | Bill Scherrer | .06 | .05 |
| 587 | Doug Frobel | .06 | .05 |
| 588 | Bobby Castillo | .06 | .05 |
| 589 | Bob Dernier | .06 | .05 |
| 590 | Ray Knight | .10 | .08 |
| 591 | Larry Herndon | .08 | .06 |
| 592 | *Jeff Robinson* | .30 | .25 |
| 593 | Rick Leach | .06 | .05 |
| 594 | Curt Wilkerson(FC) | .08 | .06 |
| 595 | Larry Gura | .06 | .05 |
| 596 | Jerry Hairston | .06 | .05 |
| 597 | Brad Lesley | .06 | .05 |
| 598 | Jose Oquendo | .06 | .05 |
| 599 | Storm Davis | .10 | .08 |
| 600 | Pete Rose | 1.00 | .70 |
| 601 | Tom Lasorda | .10 | .08 |
| 602 | *Jeff Dedmon* | .12 | .09 |
| 603 | Rick Manning | .06 | .05 |
| 604 | Daryl Sconiers | .06 | .05 |
| 605 | Ozzie Smith | .15 | .11 |
| 606 | Rich Gale | .06 | .05 |
| 607 | Bill Almon | .06 | .05 |
| 608 | Craig Lefferts | .08 | .06 |
| 609 | Broderick Perkins | .06 | .05 |
| 610 | Jack Morris | .25 | .20 |
| 611 | Ozzie Virgil | .06 | .05 |
| 612 | Mike Armstrong | .06 | .05 |
| 613 | Terry Puhl | .06 | .05 |
| 614 | Al Williams | .06 | .05 |
| 615 | Marvell Wynne | .06 | .05 |
| 616 | Scott Sanderson | .06 | .05 |
| 617 | Willie Wilson | .12 | .09 |
| 618 | Pete Falcone | .06 | .05 |
| 619 | Jeff Leonard | .10 | .08 |
| 620 | *Dwight Gooden* | 3.00 | 2.25 |
| 621 | Marvis Foley | .06 | .05 |
| 622 | Luis Leal | .06 | .05 |
| 623 | Greg Walker | .12 | .09 |
| 624 | Benny Ayala | .06 | .05 |
| 625 | *Mark Langston* | 2.25 | 1.75 |
| 626 | German Rivera | .06 | .05 |
| 627 | *Eric Davis*(FC) | 3.00 | 2.25 |
| 628 | Rene Lachemann | .06 | .05 |
| 629 | Dick Schofield | .12 | .09 |
| 630 | Tim Raines | .35 | .25 |
| 631 | Bob Forsch | .08 | .06 |
| 632 | Bruce Bochte | .06 | .05 |

| | MT | NR MT |
|---|---|---|
| 633 Glenn Hoffman | .06 | .05 |
| 634 Bill Dawley | .06 | .05 |
| 635 Terry Kennedy | .08 | .06 |
| 636 Shane Rawley | .10 | .08 |
| 637 Brett Butler | .08 | .06 |
| 638 Mike Pagliarulo(FC) | | |
| | .80 | .60 |
| 639 Ed Hodge | .06 | .05 |
| 640 Steve Henderson | .06 | .05 |
| 641 Rod Scurry | .06 | .05 |
| 642 Dave Owen | .06 | .05 |
| 643 Johnny Grubb | .06 | .05 |
| 644 Mark Huismann(FC) | .06 | .05 |
| 645 Damaso Garcia | .06 | .05 |
| 646 Scot Thompson | .06 | .05 |
| 647 Rafael Ramirez | .06 | .05 |
| 648 Bob Jones | .06 | .05 |
| 649 Sid Fernandez(FC) | .90 | .70 |
| 650 Greg Luzinski | .10 | .08 |
| 651 Jeff Russell | .08 | .06 |
| 652 Joe Nolan | .06 | .05 |
| 653 Mark Brouhard | .06 | .05 |
| 654 Dave Anderson | .06 | .05 |
| 655 Joaquin Andujar | .08 | .06 |
| 656 Chuck Cottier | .06 | .05 |
| 657 Jim Slaton | .06 | .05 |
| 658 Mike Stenhouse | .06 | .05 |
| 659 Checklist 529-660 | .06 | .05 |
| 660 Tony Gwynn | .80 | .60 |
| 661 Steve Crawford | .06 | .05 |
| 662 Mike Heath | .06 | .05 |
| 663 Luis Aguayo | .06 | .05 |
| 664 Steve Farr(FC) | .30 | .25 |
| 665 Don Mattingly | 3.00 | 2.25 |
| 666 Mike LaCoss | .06 | .05 |
| 667 Dave Engle | .06 | .05 |
| 668 Steve Trout | .06 | .05 |
| 669 Lee Lacy | .06 | .05 |
| 670 Tom Seaver | .30 | .25 |
| 671 Dane Iorg | .06 | .05 |
| 672 Juan Berenguer | .06 | .05 |
| 673 Buck Martinez | .06 | .05 |
| 674 Atlee Hammaker | .06 | .05 |
| 675 Tony Perez | .15 | .11 |
| 676 Albert Hall(FC) | .15 | .11 |
| 677 Wally Backman | .08 | .06 |
| 678 Joey McLaughlin | .06 | .05 |
| 679 Bob Kearney | .06 | .05 |
| 680 Jerry Reuss | .08 | .06 |
| 681 Ben Oglivie | .08 | .06 |
| 682 Doug Corbett | .06 | .05 |
| 683 Whitey Herzog | .08 | .06 |
| 684 Bill Doran | .12 | .09 |
| 685 Bill Caudill | .06 | .05 |
| 686 Mike Easler | .08 | .06 |
| 687 Bill Gullickson | .06 | .05 |
| 688 Len Matuszek | .06 | .05 |
| 689 Luis DeLeon | .06 | .05 |
| 690 Alan Trammell | .35 | .25 |
| 691 Dennis Rasmussen(FC) | | |
| | .30 | .25 |
| 692 Randy Bush | .06 | .05 |
| 693 Tim Stoddard | .06 | .05 |
| 694 Joe Carter(FC) | 5.00 | 3.75 |
| 695 Rick Rhoden | .10 | .08 |
| 696 John Rabb | .06 | .05 |
| 697 Onix Concepcion | .06 | .05 |

| | MT | NR MT |
|---|---|---|
| 698 Jorge Bell | .40 | .30 |
| 699 Donnie Moore | .06 | .05 |
| 700 Eddie Murray | .50 | .40 |
| 701 Eddie Murray AS | .30 | .25 |
| 702 Damaso Garcia AS | .08 | .06 |
| 703 George Brett AS | .35 | .25 |
| 704 Cal Ripken AS | .30 | .25 |
| 705 Dave Winfield AS | .20 | .15 |
| 706 Rickey Henderson AS | | |
| | .30 | .25 |
| 707 Tony Armas AS | .08 | .06 |
| 708 Lance Parrish AS | .15 | .11 |
| 709 Mike Boddicker AS | .08 | .06 |
| 710 Frank Viola AS | .12 | .09 |
| 711 Dan Quisenberry AS | .10 | .08 |
| 712 Keith Hernandez AS | .20 | .15 |
| 713 Ryne Sandberg AS | .60 | .45 |
| 714 Mike Schmidt AS | .30 | .25 |
| 715 Ozzie Smith AS | .12 | .09 |
| 716 Dale Murphy AS | .35 | .25 |
| 717 Tony Gwynn AS | .35 | .25 |
| 718 Jeff Leonard AS | .10 | .08 |
| 719 Gary Carter AS | .20 | .15 |
| 720 Rick Sutcliffe AS | .12 | .09 |
| 721 Bob Knepper AS | .08 | .06 |
| 722 Bruce Sutter AS | .10 | .08 |
| 723 Dave Stewart | .12 | .09 |
| 724 Oscar Gamble | .08 | .06 |
| 725 Floyd Bannister | .10 | .08 |
| 726 Al Bumbry | .08 | .06 |
| 727 Frank Pastore | .06 | .05 |
| 728 Bob Bailor | .06 | .05 |
| 729 Don Sutton | .30 | .25 |
| 730 Dave Kingman | .15 | .11 |
| 731 Neil Allen | .06 | .05 |
| 732 John McNamara | .06 | .05 |
| 733 Tony Scott | .06 | .05 |
| 734 John Henry Johnson | | |
| | .06 | .05 |
| 735 Garry Templeton | .08 | .06 |
| 736 Jerry Mumphrey | .06 | .05 |
| 737 Bo Diaz | .08 | .06 |
| 738 Omar Moreno | .06 | .05 |
| 739 Ernie Camacho | .06 | .05 |
| 740 Jack Clark | .20 | .15 |
| 741 John Butcher | .06 | .05 |
| 742 Ron Hassey | .06 | .05 |
| 743 Frank White | .10 | .08 |
| 744 Doug Bair | .06 | .05 |
| 745 Buddy Bell | .12 | .09 |
| 746 Jim Clancy | .08 | .06 |
| 747 Alex Trevino | .06 | .05 |
| 748 Lee Mazzilli | .08 | .06 |
| 749 Julio Cruz | .06 | .05 |
| 750 Rollie Fingers | .20 | .15 |
| 751 Kelvin Chapman | .06 | .05 |
| 752 Bob Owchinko | .06 | .05 |
| 753 Greg Brock | .08 | .06 |
| 754 Larry Milbourne | .06 | .05 |
| 755 Ken Singleton | .08 | .06 |
| 756 Rob Picciolo | .06 | .05 |
| 757 Willie McGee | .30 | .25 |
| 758 Ray Burris | .06 | .05 |
| 759 Jim Fanning | .06 | .05 |
| 760 Nolan Ryan | 4.00 | 3.00 |
| 761 Jerry Remy | .06 | .05 |
| 762 Eddie Whitson | .06 | .05 |

|  | | MT | NR MT |
|---|---|---|---|
| 763 | Kiko Garcia | .06 | .05 |
| 764 | Jamie Easterly | .06 | .05 |
| 765 | Willie Randolph | .10 | .08 |
| 766 | Paul Mirabella | .06 | .05 |
| 767 | Darrell Brown | .06 | .05 |
| 768 | Ron Cey | .10 | .08 |
| 769 | Joe Cowley | .06 | .05 |
| 770 | Carlton Fisk | .40 | .30 |
| 771 | Geoff Zahn | .06 | .05 |
| 772 | Johnnie LeMaster | .06 | .05 |
| 773 | Hal McRae | .10 | .08 |
| 774 | Dennis Lamp | .06 | .05 |
| 775 | Mookie Wilson | .10 | .08 |
| 776 | Jerry Royster | .06 | .05 |
| 777 | Ned Yost | .06 | .05 |
| 778 | Mike Davis | .08 | .06 |
| 779 | Nick Esasky | .08 | .06 |
| 780 | Mike Flanagan | .10 | .08 |
| 781 | Jim Gantner | .08 | .06 |
| 782 | Tom Niedenfuer | .08 | .06 |
| 783 | Mike Jorgensen | .06 | .05 |
| 784 | Checklist 661-792 | .06 | .05 |
| 785 | Tony Armas | .10 | .08 |
| 786 | Enos Cabell | .06 | .05 |
| 787 | Jim Wohlford | .06 | .05 |
| 788 | Steve Comer | .06 | .05 |
| 789 | Luis Salazar | .06 | .05 |
| 790 | Ron Guidry | .25 | .20 |
| 791 | Ivan DeJesus | .06 | .05 |
| 792 | Darrell Evans | .12 | .09 |

## 1985 Topps Traded

By 1985, the Topps Traded set had become a yearly feature, and Topps continued the tradition with another 132-card set. The 2-1/2" by 3-1/2" cards followed the pattern of being virtually identical in design to the regular cards issued by Topps. Sold only through established hobby dealers, the set features traded veterans and promising rookies. A glossy-finish "Tiffany" edition of the set is valued at four times normal Traded card value for commons, up to five or six times normal value for superstars and hot rookies.

|  | | MT | NR MT |
|---|---|---|---|
| Complete Set: | | 25.00 | 18.00 |
| Common Player: | | .10 | .08 |
| 1T | Don Aase | .10 | .08 |
| 2T | Bill Almon | .10 | .08 |
| 3T | Benny Ayala | .10 | .08 |
| 4T | Dusty Baker | .15 | .11 |
| 5T | George Bamberger | .10 | .08 |
| 6T | Dale Berra | .10 | .08 |
| 7T | Rich Bordi | .10 | .08 |
| 8T | Daryl Boston(FC) | .20 | .15 |
| 9T | Hubie Brooks | .25 | .20 |
| 10T | Chris Brown(FC) | .25 | .20 |
| 11T | Tom Browning(FC) | 1.25 | .90 |
| 12T | Al Bumbry | .10 | .08 |
| 13T | Ray Burris | .10 | .08 |
| 14T | Jeff Burroughs | .15 | .11 |
| 15T | Bill Campbell | .10 | .08 |
| 16T | Don Carman(FC) | .15 | .11 |
| 17T | Gary Carter | 1.00 | .70 |
| 18T | Bobby Castillo | .10 | .08 |
| 19T | Bill Caudill | .10 | .08 |
| 20T | Rick Cerone | .10 | .08 |
| 21T | Bryan Clark | .10 | .08 |
| 22T | Jack Clark | .35 | .25 |
| 23T | Pat Clements(FC) | .20 | .15 |
| 24T | Vince Coleman(FC) | 5.00 | 3.75 |
| 25T | Dave Collins | .15 | .11 |
| 26T | Danny Darwin | .15 | .11 |
| 27T | Jim Davenport | .10 | .08 |
| 28T | Jerry Davis | .10 | .08 |
| 29T | Brian Dayett | .10 | .08 |
| 30T | Ivan DeJesus | .10 | .08 |
| 31T | Ken Dixon | .10 | .08 |
| 32T | Mariano Duncan(FC) | .20 | .15 |
| 33T | John Felske | .10 | .08 |
| 34T | Mike Fitzgerald | .10 | .08 |
| 35T | Ray Fontenot | .10 | .08 |
| 36T | Greg Gagne(FC) | .35 | .25 |
| 37T | Oscar Gamble | .15 | .11 |
| 38T | Scott Garrelts(FC) | .50 | .40 |
| 39T | Bob Gibson | .10 | .08 |
| 40T | Jim Gott | .10 | .08 |
| 41T | David Green | .10 | .08 |
| 42T | Alfredo Griffin | .15 | .11 |
| 43T | Ozzie Guillen(FC) | 1.25 | .90 |
| 44T | Eddie Haas | .10 | .08 |
| 45T | Terry Harper | .10 | .08 |
| 46T | Toby Harrah | .15 | .11 |
| 47T | Greg Harris | .10 | .08 |
| 48T | Ron Hassey | .10 | .08 |
| 49T | Rickey Henderson | 5.00 | 3.75 |
| 50T | Steve Henderson | .10 | .08 |
| 51T | George Hendrick | .15 | .11 |
| 52T | Joe Hesketh(FC) | .20 | .15 |
| 53T | Teddy Higuera(FC) | .70 | .50 |
| 54T | Donnie Hill | .10 | .08 |
| 55T | Al Holland | .10 | .08 |
| 56T | Burt Hooton | .15 | .11 |
| 57T | Jay Howell | .15 | .11 |
| 58T | Ken Howell(FC) | .15 | .11 |
| 59T | LaMarr Hoyt | .10 | .08 |
| 60T | Tim Hulett(FC) | .15 | .11 |

| | | MT | NR MT |
|---|---|---|---|
| 61T | Bob James | .10 | .08 |
| 62T | Steve Jeltz(FC) | .15 | .11 |
| 63T | Cliff Johnson | .10 | .08 |
| 64T | Howard Johnson | 2.50 | 2.00 |
| 65T | Ruppert Jones | .10 | .08 |
| 66T | Steve Kemp | .15 | .11 |
| 67T | Bruce Kison | .10 | .08 |
| 68T | Alan Knicely | .10 | .08 |
| 69T | Mike LaCoss | .10 | .08 |
| 70T | Lee Lacy | .10 | .08 |
| 71T | Dave LaPoint | .20 | .15 |
| 72T | Gary Lavelle | .10 | .08 |
| 73T | Vance Law | .15 | .11 |
| 74T | Johnnie LeMaster | .10 | .08 |
| 75T | Sixto Lezcano | .10 | .08 |
| 76T | Tim Lollar | .10 | .08 |
| 77T | Fred Lynn | .30 | .25 |
| 78T | Billy Martin | .20 | .15 |
| 79T | Ron Mathis | .10 | .08 |
| 80T | Len Matuszek | .10 | .08 |
| 81T | Gene Mauch | .15 | .11 |
| 82T | Oddibe McDowell | .25 | .20 |
| 83T | Roger McDowell(FC) | | |
| | | .50 | .40 |
| 84T | John McNamara | .10 | .08 |
| 85T | Donnie Moore | .10 | .08 |
| 86T | Gene Nelson | .10 | .08 |
| 87T | Steve Nicosia | .10 | .08 |
| 88T | Al Oliver | .30 | .25 |
| 89T | Joe Orsulak(FC) | .20 | .15 |
| 90T | Rob Picciolo | .10 | .08 |
| 91T | Chris Pittaro | .10 | .08 |
| 92T | Jim Presley(FC) | .60 | .45 |
| 93T | Rick Reuschel | .25 | .20 |
| 94T | Bert Roberge | .10 | .08 |
| 95T | Bob Rodgers | .10 | .08 |
| 96T | Jerry Royster | .10 | .08 |
| 97T | Dave Rozema | .10 | .08 |
| 98T | Dave Rucker | .10 | .08 |
| 99T | Vern Ruhle | .10 | .08 |
| 100T | Paul Runge(FC) | .15 | .11 |
| 101T | Mark Salas(FC) | .15 | .11 |
| 102T | Luis Salazar | .10 | .08 |
| 103T | Joe Sambito | .10 | .08 |
| 104T | Rick Schu(FC) | .20 | .15 |
| 105T | Donnie Scott | .10 | .08 |
| 106T | Larry Sheets(FC) | .50 | .40 |
| 107T | Don Slaught | .10 | .08 |
| 108T | Roy Smalley | .15 | .11 |
| 109T | Lonnie Smith | .15 | .11 |
| 110T | Nate Snell | .10 | .08 |
| 111T | Chris Speier | .10 | .08 |
| 112T | Mike Stenhouse | .10 | .08 |
| 113T | Tim Stoddard | .10 | .08 |
| 114T | Jim Sundberg | .15 | .11 |
| 115T | Bruce Sutter | .25 | .20 |
| 116T | Don Sutton | .60 | .45 |
| 117T | Kent Tekulve | .15 | .11 |
| 118T | Tom Tellmann | .10 | .08 |
| 119T | Walt Terrell | .15 | .11 |
| 120T | Mickey Tettleton(FC) | | |
| | | 5.00 | 3.75 |
| 121T | Derrel Thomas | .10 | .08 |
| 122T | Rich Thompson | .10 | .08 |
| 123T | Alex Trevino | .10 | .08 |
| 124T | John Tudor | .25 | .20 |
| 125T | Jose Uribe(FC) | .25 | .20 |

| | | MT | NR MT |
|---|---|---|---|
| 126T | Bobby Valentine | .10 | .08 |
| 127T | Dave Von Ohlen | .10 | .08 |
| 128T | U.L. Washington | .10 | .08 |
| 129T | Earl Weaver | .15 | .11 |
| 130T | Eddie Whitson | .10 | .08 |
| 131T | Herm Winningham(FC) | | |
| | | .20 | .15 |
| 132T | Checklist 1-132 | .10 | .08 |

## 1986 Topps

The 1986 Topps set consists of 792 cards. Fronts of the 2-1/2" by 3-1/2" cards feature color photos with the Topps logo in the upper right-hand corner while the player's position is in the lower left-hand corner. Above the picture is the team name, while below it is the player's name. The borders are a departure from previous practice, as the top 7/8" is black, while the remainder was white. There are no card numbers 51 and 171 in the set; the card that should have been #51, Bobby Wine, shares #57 with Bill Doran, while #171, Bob Rodgers, shares #141 with Chuck Cottier. Once again, a 5,000-set glossy-finish "Tiffany" edition was produced. Values are four to six times higher than the same card in the regular issue.

| | | MT | NR MT |
|---|---|---|---|
| Complete Set: | | 35.00 | 28.00 |
| Common Player: | | .05 | .04 |
| 1 | Pete Rose | .90 | .70 |
| 2 | Rose Special 1963-66 | | |
| | | .30 | .25 |
| 3 | Rose Special 1967-70 | | |
| | | .30 | .25 |
| 4 | Rose Special 1971-74 | | |
| | | .30 | .25 |
| 5 | Rose Special 1975-78 | | |
| | | .30 | .25 |

| | | MT | NR MT |
|---|---|---|---|
| 6 | Rose Special 1979-82 | .30 | .25 |
| 7 | Rose Special 1983-85 | .30 | .25 |
| 8 | Dwayne Murphy | .07 | .05 |
| 9 | Roy Smith | .05 | .04 |
| 10 | Tony Gwynn | 1.00 | .70 |
| 11 | Bob Ojeda | .07 | .05 |
| 12 | Jose Uribe(FC) | .20 | .15 |
| 13 | Bob Kearney | .05 | .04 |
| 14 | Julio Cruz | .05 | .04 |
| 15 | Eddie Whitson | .05 | .04 |
| 16 | Rick Schu(FC) | .07 | .05 |
| 17 | Mike Stenhouse | .05 | .04 |
| 18 | Brent Gaff | .05 | .04 |
| 19 | Rich Hebner | .05 | .04 |
| 20 | Lou Whitaker | .25 | .20 |
| 21 | George Bamberger | .05 | .04 |
| 22 | Duane Walker | .05 | .04 |
| 23 | Manny Lee(FC) | .15 | .11 |
| 24 | Len Barker | .07 | .05 |
| 25 | Willie Wilson | .12 | .09 |
| 26 | Frank DiPino | .05 | .04 |
| 27 | Ray Knight | .07 | .05 |
| 28 | Eric Davis | 1.00 | .70 |
| 29 | Tony Phillips | .05 | .04 |
| 30 | Eddie Murray | .40 | .30 |
| 31 | Jamie Easterly | .05 | .04 |
| 32 | Steve Yeager | .05 | .04 |
| 33 | Jeff Lahti | .05 | .04 |
| 34 | Ken Phelps(FC) | .07 | .05 |
| 35 | Jeff Reardon | .12 | .09 |
| 36 | Tigers Leaders (Lance Parrish) | .12 | .09 |
| 37 | Mark Thurmond | .05 | .04 |
| 38 | Glenn Hoffman | .05 | .04 |
| 39 | Dave Rucker | .05 | .04 |
| 40 | Ken Griffey | .10 | .08 |
| 41 | Brad Wellman | .05 | .04 |
| 42 | Geoff Zahn | .05 | .04 |
| 43 | Dave Engle | .05 | .04 |
| 44 | Lance McCullers(FC) | .25 | .20 |
| 45 | Damaso Garcia | .05 | .04 |
| 46 | Billy Hatcher(FC) | .20 | .15 |
| 47 | Juan Berenguer | .05 | .04 |
| 48 | Bill Almon | .05 | .04 |
| 49 | Rick Manning | .05 | .04 |
| 50 | Dan Quisenberry | .07 | .05 |
| 51 | Not Issued | | |
| 52 | Chris Welsh | .05 | .04 |
| 53 | Len Dykstra(FC) | 1.25 | .90 |
| 54 | John Franco | .12 | .09 |
| 55 | Fred Lynn | .15 | .11 |
| 56 | Tom Niedenfuer | .07 | .05 |
| 57a | Bobby Wine | .05 | .04 |
| 57b | Bill Doran | .10 | .08 |
| 58 | Bill Krueger | .05 | .04 |
| 59 | Andre Thornton | .07 | .05 |
| 60 | Dwight Evans | .12 | .09 |
| 61 | Karl Best | .05 | .04 |
| 62 | Bob Boone | .07 | .05 |
| 63 | Ron Roenicke | .05 | .04 |
| 64 | Floyd Bannister | .10 | .08 |
| 65 | Dan Driessen | .07 | .05 |

| | | MT | NR MT |
|---|---|---|---|
| 66 | Cardinals Leaders (Bob Forsch) | .07 | .05 |
| 67 | Carmelo Martinez | .07 | .05 |
| 68 | Ed Lynch | .05 | .04 |
| 69 | Luis Aguayo | .05 | .04 |
| 70 | Dave Winfield | .60 | .45 |
| 71 | Ken Schrom | .05 | .04 |
| 72 | Shawon Dunston | .20 | .15 |
| 73 | Randy O'Neal(FC) | .07 | .05 |
| 74 | Rance Mulliniks | .05 | .04 |
| 75 | Jose DeLeon | .07 | .05 |
| 76 | Dion James | .07 | .05 |
| 77 | Charlie Leibrandt | .05 | .04 |
| 78 | Bruce Benedict | .05 | .04 |
| 79 | Dave Schmidt | .07 | .05 |
| 80 | Darryl Strawberry | 1.50 | 1.25 |
| 81 | Gene Mauch | .07 | .05 |
| 82 | Tippy Martinez | .05 | .04 |
| 83 | Phil Garner | .07 | .05 |
| 84 | Curt Young | .07 | .05 |
| 85 | Tony Perez | .15 | .11 |
| 86 | Tom Waddell | .05 | .04 |
| 87 | Candy Maldonado | .10 | .08 |
| 88 | Tom Nieto | .05 | .04 |
| 89 | Randy St. Claire(FC) | .07 | .05 |
| 90 | Garry Templeton | .07 | .05 |
| 91 | Steve Crawford | .05 | .04 |
| 92 | Al Cowens | .05 | .04 |
| 93 | Scot Thompson | .05 | .04 |
| 94 | Rick Bordi | .05 | .04 |
| 95 | Ozzie Virgil | .05 | .04 |
| 96 | Blue Jay Leaders (Jim Clancy) | .07 | .05 |
| 97 | Gary Gaetti | .20 | .15 |
| 98 | Dick Ruthven | .05 | .04 |
| 99 | Buddy Biancalana | .05 | .04 |
| 100 | Nolan Ryan | 2.50 | 2.00 |
| 101 | Dave Bergman | .05 | .04 |
| 102 | Joe Orsulak | .15 | .11 |
| 103 | Luis Salazar | .05 | .04 |
| 104 | Sid Fernandez | .12 | .09 |
| 105 | Gary Ward | .07 | .05 |
| 106 | Ray Burris | .05 | .04 |
| 107 | Rafael Ramirez | .05 | .04 |
| 108 | Ted Power | .05 | .04 |
| 109 | Len Matuszek | .05 | .04 |
| 110 | Scott McGregor | .07 | .05 |
| 111 | Roger Craig | .07 | .05 |
| 112 | Bill Campbell | .05 | .04 |
| 113 | U.L. Washington | .05 | .04 |
| 114 | Mike Brown | .05 | .04 |
| 115 | Jay Howell | .07 | .05 |
| 116 | Brook Jacoby | .10 | .08 |
| 117 | Bruce Kison | .05 | .04 |
| 118 | Jerry Royster | .05 | .04 |
| 119 | Barry Bonnell | .05 | .04 |
| 120 | Steve Carlton | .40 | .30 |
| 121 | Nelson Simmons | .05 | .04 |
| 122 | Pete Filson | .05 | .04 |
| 123 | Greg Walker | .10 | .08 |
| 124 | Luis Sanchez | .05 | .04 |
| 125 | Dave Lopes | .07 | .05 |
| 126 | Mets Leaders (Mookie Wilson) | .07 | .05 |
| 127 | Jack Howell(FC) | .20 | .15 |
| 128 | John Wathan | .07 | .05 |
| 129 | Jeff Dedmon(FC) | .05 | .04 |

| | | MT | NR MT |
|---|---|---|---|
| 130 | Alan Trammell | .30 | .25 |
| 131 | Checklist 1-132 | .05 | .04 |
| 132 | Razor Shines | .05 | .04 |
| 133 | Andy McGaffigan | .05 | .04 |
| 134 | Carney Lansford | .10 | .08 |
| 135 | Joe Niekro | .10 | .08 |
| 136 | Mike Hargrove | .05 | .04 |
| 137 | Charlie Moore | .05 | .04 |
| 138 | Mark Davis | .05 | .04 |
| 139 | Daryl Boston | .10 | .08 |
| 140 | John Candelaria | .10 | .08 |
| 141a | Bob Rodgers | .05 | .04 |
| 141b | Chuck Cottier | .05 | .04 |
| 142 | Bob Jones | .05 | .04 |
| 143 | Dave Van Gorder | .05 | .04 |
| 144 | Doug Sisk | .05 | .04 |
| 145 | Pedro Guerrero | .20 | .15 |
| 146 | Jack Perconte | .05 | .04 |
| 147 | Larry Sheets | .20 | .15 |
| 148 | Mike Heath | .05 | .04 |
| 149 | Brett Butler | .07 | .05 |
| 150 | Joaquin Andujar | .07 | .05 |
| 151 | Dave Stapleton | .05 | .04 |
| 152 | Mike Morgan | .05 | .04 |
| 153 | Ricky Adams | .05 | .04 |
| 154 | Bert Roberge | .05 | .04 |
| 155 | Bob Grich | .10 | .08 |
| 156 | White Sox Leaders (Richard Dotson) | .07 | .05 |
| 157 | Ron Hassey | .05 | .04 |
| 158 | Derrel Thomas | .05 | .04 |
| 159 | Orel Hershiser | .50 | .40 |
| 160 | Chet Lemon | .07 | .05 |
| 161 | Lee Tunnell | .05 | .04 |
| 162 | Greg Gagne | .10 | .08 |
| 163 | Pete Ladd | .05 | .04 |
| 164 | Steve Balboni | .07 | .05 |
| 165 | Mike Davis | .07 | .05 |
| 166 | Dickie Thon | .07 | .05 |
| 167 | Zane Smith(FC) | .15 | .11 |
| 168 | Jeff Burroughs | .07 | .05 |
| 169 | George Wright | .05 | .04 |
| 170 | Gary Carter | .25 | .20 |
| 171 | Not Issued | | |
| 172 | Jerry Reed | .05 | .04 |
| 173 | Wayne Gross | .05 | .04 |
| 174 | Brian Snyder | .05 | .04 |
| 175 | Steve Sax | .15 | .11 |
| 176 | Jay Tibbs | .05 | .04 |
| 177 | Joel Youngblood | .05 | .04 |
| 178 | Ivan DeJesus | .05 | .04 |
| 179 | *Stu Cliburn*(FC) | .10 | .08 |
| 180 | Don Mattingly | 1.00 | .70 |
| 181 | Al Nipper | .05 | .04 |
| 182 | Bobby Brown | .05 | .04 |
| 183 | Larry Andersen | .05 | .04 |
| 184 | Tim Laudner | .05 | .04 |
| 185 | Rollie Fingers | .30 | .25 |
| 186 | Astros Leaders (Jose Cruz) | .07 | .05 |
| 187 | Scott Fletcher | .07 | .05 |
| 188 | Bob Dernier | .05 | .04 |
| 189 | Mike Mason | .05 | .04 |
| 190 | George Hendrick | .07 | .05 |
| 191 | Wally Backman | .07 | .05 |
| 192 | Milt Wilcox | .05 | .04 |
| 193 | Daryl Sconiers | .05 | .04 |

| | | MT | NR MT |
|---|---|---|---|
| 194 | Craig McMurtry | .05 | .04 |
| 195 | Dave Concepcion | .12 | .09 |
| 196 | Doyle Alexander | .10 | .08 |
| 197 | Enos Cabell | .05 | .04 |
| 198 | Ken Dixon | .05 | .04 |
| 199 | Dick Howser | .05 | .04 |
| 200 | Mike Schmidt | 1.00 | .70 |
| 201 | Record Breaker (Vince Coleman)(FC) | .30 | .25 |
| 202 | Record Breaker (Dwight Gooden) | .40 | .30 |
| 203 | Record Breaker (Keith Hernandez) | .20 | .15 |
| 204 | Record Breaker (Phil Niekro) | .15 | .11 |
| 205 | Record Breaker (Tony Perez) | .10 | .08 |
| 206 | Record Breaker (Pete Rose) | .50 | .40 |
| 207 | Record Breaker (Fernando Valenzuela) | .20 | .15 |
| 208 | Ramon Romero | .05 | .04 |
| 209 | Randy Ready | .10 | .08 |
| 210 | Calvin Schiraldi(FC) | .10 | .08 |
| 211 | Ed Wojna | .05 | .04 |
| 212 | Chris Speier | .05 | .04 |
| 213 | Bob Shirley | .05 | .04 |
| 214 | Randy Bush | .05 | .04 |
| 215 | Frank White | .10 | .08 |
| 216 | A's Leaders (Dwayne Murphy) | .07 | .05 |
| 217 | Bill Scherrer | .05 | .04 |
| 218 | Randy Hunt | .05 | .04 |
| 219 | Dennis Lamp | .05 | .04 |
| 220 | Bob Horner | .10 | .08 |
| 221 | Dave Henderson | .10 | .08 |
| 222 | Craig Gerber | .05 | .04 |
| 223 | Atlee Hammaker | .05 | .04 |
| 224 | Cesar Cedeno | .10 | .08 |
| 225 | Ron Darling | .15 | .11 |
| 226 | Lee Lacy | .05 | .04 |
| 227 | Al Jones | .05 | .04 |
| 228 | Tom Lawless | .05 | .04 |
| 229 | Bill Gullickson | .05 | .04 |
| 230 | Terry Kennedy | .07 | .05 |
| 231 | Jim Frey | .05 | .04 |
| 232 | Rick Rhoden | .10 | .08 |
| 233 | Steve Lyons(FC) | .07 | .05 |
| 234 | Doug Corbett | .05 | .04 |
| 235 | Butch Wynegar | .05 | .04 |
| 236 | Frank Eufemia | .05 | .04 |
| 237 | Ted Simmons | .12 | .09 |
| 238 | Larry Parrish | .10 | .08 |
| 239 | Joel Skinner | .05 | .04 |
| 240 | Tommy John | .20 | .15 |
| 241 | Tony Fernandez | .20 | .15 |
| 242 | Rich Thompson | .05 | .04 |
| 243 | Johnny Grubb | .05 | .04 |
| 244 | Craig Lefferts | .05 | .04 |
| 245 | Jim Sundberg | .07 | .05 |
| 246 | Phillies Leaders (Steve Carlton) | .15 | .11 |
| 247 | Terry Harper | .05 | .04 |
| 248 | Spike Owen | .05 | .04 |
| 249 | Rob Deer(FC) | .40 | .30 |
| 250 | Dwight Gooden | 1.00 | .70 |
| 251 | Rich Dauer | .05 | .04 |

| | | MT | NR MT |
|---|---|---|---|
| 252 | Bobby Castillo | .05 | .04 |
| 253 | Dann Bilardello | .05 | .04 |
| 254 | *Ozzie Guillen* | .70 | .50 |
| 255 | Tony Armas | .07 | .05 |
| 256 | Kurt Kepshire | .05 | .04 |
| 257 | Doug DeCinces | .10 | .08 |
| 258 | Tim Burke(FC) | .25 | .20 |
| 259 | Dan Pasqua(FC) | .20 | .15 |
| 260 | Tony Pena | .10 | .08 |
| 261 | Bobby Valentine | .05 | .04 |
| 262 | Mario Ramirez | .05 | .04 |
| 263 | Checklist 133-264 | .05 | .04 |
| 264 | *Darren Daulton*(FC) | | |
| | | .12 | .09 |
| 265 | Ron Davis | .05 | .04 |
| 266 | Keith Moreland | .07 | .05 |
| 267 | Paul Molitor | .15 | .11 |
| 268 | Mike Scott | .15 | .11 |
| 269 | Dane Iorg | .05 | .04 |
| 270 | Jack Morris | .20 | .15 |
| 271 | Dave Collins | .07 | .05 |
| 272 | Tim Tolman | .05 | .04 |
| 273 | Jerry Willard | .05 | .04 |
| 274 | Ron Gardenhire | .05 | .04 |
| 275 | Charlie Hough | .08 | .06 |
| 276 | Yankees Leaders (Willie Randolph) | .07 | .05 |
| 277 | Jaime Cocanower | .05 | .04 |
| 278 | Sixto Lezcano | .05 | .04 |
| 279 | Al Pardo | .05 | .04 |
| 280 | Tim Raines | .30 | .25 |
| 281 | Steve Mura | .05 | .04 |
| 282 | Jerry Mumphrey | .05 | .04 |
| 283 | Mike Fischlin | .05 | .04 |
| 284 | Brian Dayett | .05 | .04 |
| 285 | Buddy Bell | .10 | .08 |
| 286 | Luis DeLeon | .05 | .04 |
| 287 | *John Christensen*(FC) | .10 | .08 |
| 288 | Don Aase | .05 | .04 |
| 289 | Johnnie LeMaster | .05 | .04 |
| 290 | Carlton Fisk | .50 | .40 |
| 291 | Tom Lasorda | .07 | .05 |
| 292 | Chuck Porter | .05 | .04 |
| 293 | Chris Chambliss | .07 | .05 |
| 294 | Danny Cox | .10 | .08 |
| 295 | Kirk Gibson | .30 | .25 |
| 296 | Geno Petralli(FC) | .07 | .05 |
| 297 | Tim Lollar | .05 | .04 |
| 298 | Craig Reynolds | .05 | .04 |
| 299 | Bryn Smith | .05 | .04 |
| 300 | George Brett | .50 | .40 |
| 301 | Dennis Rasmussen | .12 | .09 |
| 302 | Greg Gross | .05 | .04 |
| 303 | Curt Wardle | .05 | .04 |
| 304 | *Mike Gallego*(FC) | | |
| | | .12 | .09 |
| 305 | Phil Bradley | .15 | .11 |
| 306 | Padres Leaders (Terry Kennedy) | .07 | .05 |
| 307 | Dave Sax | .05 | .04 |
| 308 | Ray Fontenot | .05 | .04 |
| 309 | John Shelby | .05 | .04 |
| 310 | Greg Minton | .05 | .04 |
| 311 | Dick Schofield | .05 | .04 |
| 312 | Tom Filer | .05 | .04 |
| 313 | Joe DeSa | .05 | .04 |

| | | MT | NR MT |
|---|---|---|---|
| 314 | Frank Pastore | .05 | .04 |
| 315 | Mookie Wilson | .10 | .08 |
| 316 | Sammy Khalifa | .05 | .04 |
| 317 | Ed Romero | .05 | .04 |
| 318 | Terry Whitfield | .05 | .04 |
| 319 | Rick Camp | .05 | .04 |
| 320 | Jim Rice | .30 | .25 |
| 321 | Earl Weaver | .07 | .05 |
| 322 | Bob Forsch | .07 | .05 |
| 323 | Jerry Davis | .05 | .04 |
| 324 | Dan Schatzeder | .05 | .04 |
| 325 | Juan Beniquez | .05 | .04 |
| 326 | Kent Tekulve | .07 | .05 |
| 327 | Mike Pagliarulo | .20 | .15 |
| 328 | Pete O'Brien | .10 | .08 |
| 329 | Kirby Puckett | 4.00 | 3.00 |
| 330 | Rick Sutcliffe | .12 | .09 |
| 331 | Alan Ashby | .05 | .04 |
| 332 | Darryl Motley | .05 | .04 |
| 333 | Tom Henke(FC) | .15 | .11 |
| 334 | Ken Oberkfell | .05 | .04 |
| 335 | Don Sutton | .25 | .20 |
| 336 | Indians Leaders (Andre Thornton) | .07 | .05 |
| 337 | Darnell Coles | .07 | .05 |
| 338 | Jorge Bell | .25 | .20 |
| 339 | Bruce Berenyi | .05 | .04 |
| 340 | Cal Ripken | 2.00 | 1.50 |
| 341 | Frank Williams | .05 | .04 |
| 342 | Gary Redus | .05 | .04 |
| 343 | Carlos Diaz | .05 | .04 |
| 344 | Jim Wohlford | .05 | .04 |
| 345 | Donnie Moore | .05 | .04 |
| 346 | Bryan Little | .05 | .04 |
| 347 | *Teddy Higuera* | .70 | .50 |
| 348 | Cliff Johnson | .05 | .04 |
| 349 | Mark Clear | .05 | .04 |
| 350 | Jack Clark | .20 | .15 |
| 351 | Chuck Tanner | .05 | .04 |
| 352 | Harry Spilman | .05 | .04 |
| 353 | Keith Atherton | .05 | .04 |
| 354 | Tony Bernazard | .05 | .04 |
| 355 | Lee Smith | .10 | .08 |
| 356 | Mickey Hatcher | .05 | .04 |
| 357 | Ed Vande Berg | .05 | .04 |
| 358 | Rick Dempsey | .07 | .05 |
| 359 | Mike LaCoss | .05 | .04 |
| 360 | Lloyd Moseby | .10 | .08 |
| 361 | Shane Rawley | .10 | .08 |
| 362 | Tom Paciorek | .05 | .04 |
| 363 | Terry Forster | .07 | .05 |
| 364 | Reid Nichols | .05 | .04 |
| 365 | Mike Flanagan | .10 | .08 |
| 366 | Reds Leaders (Dave Concepcion) | .07 | .05 |
| 367 | Aurelio Lopez | .05 | .04 |
| 368 | Greg Brock | .07 | .05 |
| 369 | Al Holland | .05 | .04 |
| 370 | *Vince Coleman* | 1.50 | 1.25 |
| 371 | Bill Stein | .05 | .04 |
| 372 | Ben Oglivie | .07 | .05 |
| 373 | *Urbano Lugo*(FC) | | |
| | | .07 | .05 |
| 374 | Terry Francona | .05 | .04 |
| 375 | Rich Gedman | .10 | .08 |
| 376 | Bill Dawley | .05 | .04 |
| 377 | Joe Carter | .70 | .50 |

| | MT | NR MT | | | MT | NR MT |
|---|---|---|---|---|---|---|
| 378 | Bruce Bochte | .05 | .04 | 435 | Bill Caudill | .05 | .04 |
| 379 | Bobby Meacham | .05 | .04 | 436 | Doug Flynn | .05 | .04 |
| 380 | LaMarr Hoyt | .05 | .04 | 437 | Rick Mahler | .05 | .04 |
| 381 | Ray Miller | .05 | .04 | 438 | Clint Hurdle | .05 | .04 |
| 382 | *Ivan Calderon*(FC) | | | 439 | Rick Honeycutt | .05 | .04 |
| | | .50 | .40 | 440 | Alvin Davis | .30 | .25 |
| 383 | *Chris Brown* | .15 | .11 | 441 | Whitey Herzog | .07 | .05 |
| 384 | Steve Trout | .05 | .04 | 442 | Ron Robinson(FC) | .12 | .09 |
| 385 | Cecil Cooper | .10 | .08 | 443 | Bill Buckner | .10 | .08 |
| 386 | *Cecil Fielder*(FC) | | | 444 | Alex Trevino | .05 | .04 |
| | | 8.00 | 6.00 | 445 | Bert Blyleven | .12 | .09 |
| 387 | Steve Kemp | .07 | .05 | 446 | Lenn Sakata | .05 | .04 |
| 388 | Dickie Noles | .05 | .04 | 447 | Jerry Don Gleaton | .05 | .04 |
| 389 | Glenn Davis(FC) | .50 | .40 | 448 | *Herm Winningham* | .15 | .11 |
| 390 | Tom Seaver | .40 | .30 | 449 | Rod Scurry | .05 | .04 |
| 391 | Julio Franco | .10 | .08 | 450 | Graig Nettles | .15 | .11 |
| 392 | John Russell(FC) | .10 | .08 | 451 | Mark Brown | .05 | .04 |
| 393 | Chris Pittaro | .05 | .04 | 452 | Bob Clark | .05 | .04 |
| 394 | Checklist 265-396 | .05 | .04 | 453 | Steve Jeltz | .07 | .05 |
| 395 | Scott Garrelts | .07 | .05 | 454 | Burt Hooton | .07 | .05 |
| 396 | Red Sox Leaders | | | 455 | Willie Randolph | .10 | .08 |
| | (Dwight Evans) | .07 | .05 | 456 | Braves Leaders (Dale | | |
| 397 | *Steve Buechele*(FC) | | | | Murphy) | .25 | .20 |
| | | .20 | .15 | 457 | *Mickey Tettleton* | .90 | .70 |
| 398 | *Earnie Riles*(FC) | .15 | .11 | 458 | Kevin Bass | .10 | .08 |
| 399 | Bill Swift | .12 | .09 | 459 | Luis Leal | .05 | .04 |
| 400 | Rod Carew | .30 | .25 | 460 | Leon Durham | .07 | .05 |
| 401 | Turn Back The Clock | | | 461 | Walt Terrell | .07 | .05 |
| | (Fernando Valenzuela) | .15 | .11 | 462 | Domingo Ramos | .05 | .04 |
| 402 | Turn Back The Clock | | | 463 | Jim Gott | .05 | .04 |
| | (Tom Seaver) | .15 | .11 | 464 | Ruppert Jones | .05 | .04 |
| 403 | Turn Back The Clock | | | 465 | Jesse Orosco | .07 | .05 |
| | (Willie Mays) | .20 | .15 | 466 | Tom Foley | .05 | .04 |
| 404 | Turn Back The Clock | | | 467 | Bob James | .05 | .04 |
| | (Frank Robinson) | .15 | .11 | 468 | Mike Scioscia | .07 | .05 |
| 405 | Turn Back The Clock | | | 469 | Storm Davis | .10 | .08 |
| | (Roger Maris) | .20 | .15 | 470 | Bill Madlock | .12 | .09 |
| 406 | Scott Sanderson | .05 | .04 | 471 | Bobby Cox | .05 | .04 |
| 407 | Sal Butera | .05 | .04 | 472 | Joe Hesketh | .07 | .05 |
| 408 | Dave Smith | .07 | .05 | 473 | Mark Brouhard | .05 | .04 |
| 409 | *Paul Runge* | .07 | .05 | 474 | John Tudor | .10 | .08 |
| 410 | Dave Kingman | .15 | .11 | 475 | Juan Samuel | .12 | .09 |
| 411 | Sparky Anderson | .07 | .05 | 476 | Ron Mathis | .05 | .04 |
| 412 | Jim Clancy | .07 | .05 | 477 | Mike Easler | .07 | .05 |
| 413 | Tim Flannery | .05 | .04 | 478 | Andy Hawkins | .05 | .04 |
| 414 | Tom Gorman | .05 | .04 | 479 | *Bob Melvin*(FC) | .12 | .09 |
| 415 | Hal McRae | .10 | .08 | 480 | *Oddibe McDowell* | .15 | .11 |
| 416 | Denny Martinez | .07 | .05 | 481 | Scott Bradley(FC) | .10 | .08 |
| 417 | R.J. Reynolds | .07 | .05 | 482 | Rick Lysander | .05 | .04 |
| 418 | Alan Knicely | .05 | .04 | 483 | George Vukovich | .05 | .04 |
| 419 | Frank Wills | .05 | .04 | 484 | Donnie Hill | .05 | .04 |
| 420 | Von Hayes | .10 | .08 | 485 | Gary Matthews | .10 | .08 |
| 421 | Dave Palmer | .05 | .04 | 486 | Angels Leaders (Bob | | |
| 422 | Mike Jorgensen | .05 | .04 | | Grich) | .07 | .05 |
| 423 | Dan Spillner | .05 | .04 | 487 | Bret Saberhagen | .70 | .50 |
| 424 | Rick Miller | .05 | .04 | 488 | Lou Thornton | .05 | .04 |
| 425 | Larry McWilliams | .05 | .04 | 489 | Jim Winn | .05 | .04 |
| 426 | Brewers Leaders | | | 490 | Jeff Leonard | .07 | .05 |
| | (Charlie Moore) | .07 | .05 | 491 | Pascual Perez | .07 | .05 |
| 427 | Joe Cowley | .05 | .04 | 492 | Kelvin Chapman | .05 | .04 |
| 428 | Max Venable | .05 | .04 | 493 | Gene Nelson | .05 | .04 |
| 429 | Greg Booker | .05 | .04 | 494 | Gary Roenicke | .05 | .04 |
| 430 | Kent Hrbek | .20 | .15 | 495 | Mark Langston | .20 | .15 |
| 431 | George Frazier | .05 | .04 | 496 | Jay Johnstone | .07 | .05 |
| 432 | Mark Bailey | .05 | .04 | 497 | John Stuper | .05 | .04 |
| 433 | Chris Codiroli | .05 | .04 | 498 | Tito Landrum | .05 | .04 |
| 434 | Curt Wilkerson | .05 | .04 | 499 | Bob Gibson | .05 | .04 |

| | | MT | NR MT | | | | MT | NR MT |
|---|---|---|---|---|---|---|---|---|
| 500 | Rickey Henderson | 1.25 | .90 | | 563 | Alejandro Sanchez | .05 | .04 |
| 501 | Dave Johnson | .07 | .05 | | 564 | Warren Brusstar | .05 | .04 |
| 502 | Glen Cook | .05 | .04 | | 565 | Tom Brunansky | .12 | .09 |
| 503 | Mike Fitzgerald | .05 | .04 | | 566 | Alfredo Griffin | .07 | .05 |
| 504 | Denny Walling | .05 | .04 | | 567 | Jeff Barkley | .05 | .04 |
| 505 | Jerry Koosman | .10 | .08 | | 568 | Donnie Scott | .05 | .04 |
| 506 | Bill Russell | .07 | .05 | | 569 | Jim Acker | .05 | .04 |
| 507 | Steve Ontiveros(FC) | | | | 570 | Rusty Staub | .10 | .08 |
| | | .12 | .09 | | 571 | Mike Jeffcoat | .05 | .04 |
| 508 | Alan Wiggins | .05 | .04 | | 572 | Paul Zuvella | .05 | .04 |
| 509 | Ernie Camacho | .05 | .04 | | 573 | Tom Hume | .05 | .04 |
| 510 | Wade Boggs | 1.25 | .90 | | 574 | Ron Kittle | .10 | .08 |
| 511 | Ed Nunez | .05 | .04 | | 575 | Mike Boddicker | .07 | .05 |
| 512 | Thad Bosley | .05 | .04 | | 576 | Expos Leaders (Andre | | |
| 513 | Ron Washington | .05 | .04 | | | Dawson) | .12 | .09 |
| 514 | Mike Jones | .05 | .04 | | 577 | Jerry Reuss | .07 | .05 |
| 515 | Darrell Evans | .12 | .09 | | 578 | Lee Mazzilli | .07 | .05 |
| 516 | Giants Leaders (Greg | | | | 579 | Jim Slaton | .05 | .04 |
| | Minton) | .07 | .05 | | 580 | Willie McGee | .15 | .11 |
| 517 | Milt Thompson(FC) | | | | 581 | Bruce Hurst | .12 | .09 |
| | | .25 | .20 | | 582 | Jim Gantner | .07 | .05 |
| 518 | Buck Martinez | .05 | .04 | | 583 | Al Bumbry | .05 | .04 |
| 519 | Danny Darwin | .05 | .04 | | 584 | Brian Fisher(FC) | .12 | .09 |
| 520 | Keith Hernandez | .30 | .25 | | 585 | Garry Maddox | .07 | .05 |
| 521 | Nate Snell | .05 | .04 | | 586 | Greg Harris | .05 | .04 |
| 522 | Bob Bailor | .05 | .04 | | 587 | Rafael Santana | .05 | .04 |
| 523 | Joe Price | .05 | .04 | | 588 | Steve Lake | .05 | .04 |
| 524 | Darrell Miller(FC) | .07 | .05 | | 589 | Sid Bream | .10 | .08 |
| 525 | Marvell Wynne | .05 | .04 | | 590 | Bob Knepper | .07 | .05 |
| 526 | Charlie Lea | .05 | .04 | | 591 | Jackie Moore | .05 | .04 |
| 527 | Checklist 397-528 | .05 | .04 | | 592 | Frank Tanana | .10 | .08 |
| 528 | Terry Pendleton | .15 | .11 | | 593 | Jesse Barfield | .20 | .15 |
| 529 | Marc Sullivan | .05 | .04 | | 594 | Chris Bando | .05 | .04 |
| 530 | Rich Gossage | .20 | .15 | | 595 | Dave Parker | .20 | .15 |
| 531 | Tony LaRussa | .07 | .05 | | 596 | Onix Concepcion | .05 | .04 |
| 532 | Don Carman | .25 | .20 | | 597 | Sammy Stewart | .05 | .04 |
| 533 | Billy Sample | .05 | .04 | | 598 | Jim Presley | .25 | .20 |
| 534 | Jeff Calhoun | .05 | .04 | | 599 | Rick Aguilera(FC) | | |
| 535 | Toby Harrah | .07 | .05 | | | | .40 | .30 |
| 536 | Jose Rijo | .10 | .08 | | 600 | Dale Murphy | .50 | .40 |
| 537 | Mark Salas | .07 | .05 | | 601 | Gary Lucas | .05 | .04 |
| 538 | Dennis Eckersley | .40 | .30 | | 602 | Mariano Duncan | .15 | .11 |
| 539 | Glenn Hubbard | .05 | .04 | | 603 | Bill Laskey | .05 | .04 |
| 540 | Dan Petry | .07 | .05 | | 604 | Gary Pettis | .05 | .04 |
| 541 | Jorge Orta | .05 | .04 | | 605 | Dennis Boyd | .07 | .05 |
| 542 | Don Schulze | .05 | .04 | | 606 | Royals Leaders (Hal | | |
| 543 | Jerry Narron | .05 | .04 | | | McRae) | .07 | .05 |
| 544 | Eddie Milner | .05 | .04 | | 607 | Ken Dayley | .05 | .04 |
| 545 | Jimmy Key | .15 | .11 | | 608 | Bruce Bochy | .05 | .04 |
| 546 | Mariners Leaders (Dave | | | | 609 | Barbaro Garbey | .05 | .04 |
| | Henderson) | .07 | .05 | | 610 | Ron Guidry | .15 | .11 |
| 547 | Roger McDowell | .20 | .15 | | 611 | Gary Woods | .05 | .04 |
| 548 | Mike Young | .05 | .04 | | 612 | Richard Dotson | .10 | .08 |
| 549 | Bob Welch | .12 | .09 | | 613 | Roy Smalley | .05 | .04 |
| 550 | Tom Herr | .10 | .08 | | 614 | Rick Waits | .05 | .04 |
| 551 | Dave LaPoint | .07 | .05 | | 615 | Johnny Ray | .10 | .08 |
| 552 | Marc Hill | .05 | .04 | | 616 | Glenn Brummer | .05 | .04 |
| 553 | Jim Morrison | .05 | .04 | | 617 | Lonnie Smith | .07 | .05 |
| 554 | Paul Householder | .05 | .04 | | 618 | Jim Pankovits | .05 | .04 |
| 555 | Hubie Brooks | .10 | .08 | | 619 | Danny Heep | .05 | .04 |
| 556 | John Denny | .05 | .04 | | 620 | Bruce Sutter | .12 | .09 |
| 557 | Gerald Perry | .12 | .09 | | 621 | John Felske | .05 | .04 |
| 558 | Tim Stoddard | .05 | .04 | | 622 | Gary Lavelle | .05 | .04 |
| 559 | Tommy Dunbar | .05 | .04 | | 623 | Floyd Rayford | .05 | .04 |
| 560 | Dave Righetti | .20 | .15 | | 624 | Steve McCatty | .05 | .04 |
| 561 | Bob Lillis | .05 | .04 | | 625 | Bob Brenly | .05 | .04 |
| 562 | Joe Beckwith | .05 | .04 | | 626 | Roy Thomas | .05 | .04 |

| | MT | NR MT | | | MT | NR MT |
|---|---|---|---|---|---|---|
| 627 Ron Oester | .05 | .04 | | 689 Dave Stewart | .12 | .09 |
| 628 *Kirk McCaskill*(FC) | .35 | .25 | | 690 Ryne Sandberg | 2.00 | 1.50 |
| 629 *Mitch Webster*(FC) | .25 | .20 | | 691 Mike Madden | .05 | .04 |
| 630 Fernando Valenzuela | .30 | .25 | | 692 Dale Berra | .05 | .04 |
| 631 Steve Braun | .05 | .04 | | 693 Tom Tellmann | .05 | .04 |
| 632 Dave Von Ohlen | .05 | .04 | | 694 Garth Iorg | .05 | .04 |
| 633 Jackie Gutierrez | .05 | .04 | | 695 Mike Smithson | .05 | .04 |
| 634 Roy Lee Jackson | .05 | .04 | | 696 Dodgers Leaders (Bill Russell) | .07 | .05 |
| 635 Jason Thompson | .05 | .04 | | 697 Bud Black | .05 | .04 |
| 636 Cubs Leaders (Lee Smith) | .07 | .05 | | 698 Brad Komminsk | .05 | .04 |
| 637 Rudy Law | .05 | .04 | | 699 Pat Corrales | .05 | .04 |
| 638 John Butcher | .05 | .04 | | 700 Reggie Jackson | .35 | .25 |
| 639 Bo Diaz | .07 | .05 | | 701 Keith Hernandez AS | .15 | .11 |
| 640 Jose Cruz | .10 | .08 | | 702 Tom Herr AS | .07 | .05 |
| 641 Wayne Tolleson | .05 | .04 | | 703 Tim Wallach AS | .07 | .05 |
| 642 Ray Searage | .05 | .04 | | 704 Ozzie Smith AS | .10 | .08 |
| 643 Tom Brookens | .05 | .04 | | 705 Dale Murphy AS | .30 | .25 |
| 644 Mark Gubicza | .12 | .09 | | 706 Pedro Guerrero AS | .12 | .09 |
| 645 Dusty Baker | .07 | .05 | | 707 Willie McGee AS | .12 | .09 |
| 646 Mike Moore | .05 | .04 | | 708 Gary Carter AS | .20 | .15 |
| 647 Mel Hall | .07 | .05 | | 709 Dwight Gooden AS | .40 | .30 |
| 648 Steve Bedrosian | .10 | .08 | | 710 John Tudor AS | .07 | .05 |
| 649 Ronn Reynolds | .05 | .04 | | 711 Jeff Reardon AS | .07 | .05 |
| 650 Dave Stieb | .12 | .09 | | 712 Don Mattingly AS | .40 | .30 |
| 651 Billy Martin | .12 | .09 | | 713 Damaso Garcia AS | .05 | .04 |
| 652 Tom Browning | .25 | .20 | | 714 George Brett AS | .30 | .25 |
| 653 Jim Dwyer | .05 | .04 | | 715 Cal Ripken AS | .25 | .20 |
| 654 Ken Howell | .07 | .05 | | 716 Rickey Henderson AS | .25 | .20 |
| 655 Manny Trillo | .07 | .05 | | 717 Dave Winfield AS | .20 | .15 |
| 656 Brian Harper | .05 | .04 | | 718 Jorge Bell AS | .20 | .15 |
| 657 Juan Agosto | .05 | .04 | | 719 Carlton Fisk AS | .12 | .09 |
| 658 Rob Wilfong | .05 | .04 | | 720 Bret Saberhagen AS | .15 | .11 |
| 659 Checklist 529-660 | .05 | .04 | | 721 Ron Guidry AS | .10 | .08 |
| 660 Steve Garvey | .30 | .25 | | 722 Dan Quisenberry AS | .07 | .05 |
| 661 Roger Clemens | 5.00 | 3.75 | | 723 Marty Bystrom | .05 | .04 |
| 662 Bill Schroeder | .05 | .04 | | 724 Tim Hulett | .07 | .05 |
| 663 Neil Allen | .05 | .04 | | 725 Mario Soto | .07 | .05 |
| 664 Tim Corcoran | .05 | .04 | | 726 Orioles Leaders (Rick Dempsey) | .07 | .05 |
| 665 Alejandro Pena | .07 | .05 | | 727 David Green | .05 | .04 |
| 666 Rangers Leaders (Charlie Hough) | .07 | .05 | | 728 Mike Marshall | .12 | .09 |
| 667 Tim Teufel | .05 | .04 | | 729 Jim Beattie | .05 | .04 |
| 668 Cecilio Guante | .05 | .04 | | 730 Ozzie Smith | .15 | .11 |
| 669 Ron Cey | .10 | .08 | | 731 Don Robinson | .07 | .05 |
| 670 Willie Hernandez | .07 | .05 | | 732 *Floyd Youmans*(FC) | .12 | .09 |
| 671 Lynn Jones | .05 | .04 | | 733 Ron Romanick | .05 | .04 |
| 672 Rob Picciolo | .05 | .04 | | 734 Marty Barrett | .10 | .08 |
| 673 Ernie Whitt | .07 | .05 | | 735 Dave Dravecky | .07 | .05 |
| 674 Pat Tabler | .07 | .05 | | 736 Glenn Wilson | .07 | .05 |
| 675 Claudell Washington | .07 | .05 | | 737 Pete Vuckovich | .07 | .05 |
| 676 Matt Young | .05 | .04 | | 738 Andre Robertson | .05 | .04 |
| 677 Nick Esasky | .07 | .05 | | 739 Dave Rozema | .05 | .04 |
| 678 Dan Gladden | .07 | .05 | | 740 Lance Parrish | .20 | .15 |
| 679 Britt Burns | .05 | .04 | | 741 Pete Rose | .40 | .30 |
| 680 George Foster | .15 | .11 | | 742 Frank Viola | .15 | .11 |
| 681 Dick Williams | .05 | .04 | | 743 Pat Sheridan | .05 | .04 |
| 682 Junior Ortiz | .05 | .04 | | 744 Lary Sorensen | .05 | .04 |
| 683 Andy Van Slyke | .15 | .11 | | 745 Willie Upshaw | .07 | .05 |
| 684 Bob McClure | .05 | .04 | | 746 Denny Gonzalez | .05 | .04 |
| 685 Tim Wallach | .12 | .09 | | 747 Rick Cerone | .05 | .04 |
| 686 Jeff Stone | .05 | .04 | | 748 Steve Henderson | .05 | .04 |
| 687 Mike Trujillo | .05 | .04 | | 749 Ed Jurak | .05 | .04 |
| 688 Larry Herndon | .07 | .05 | | 750 Gorman Thomas | .10 | .08 |
| | | | | 751 Howard Johnson | .40 | .30 |

| | | MT | NR MT |
|---|---|---|---|
| 752 | Mike Krukow | .07 | .05 |
| 753 | Dan Ford | .05 | .04 |
| 754 | *Pat Clements* | .12 | .09 |
| 755 | Harold Baines | .15 | .11 |
| 756 | Pirates Leaders (Rick Rhoden) | .07 | .05 |
| 757 | Darrell Porter | .07 | .05 |
| 758 | Dave Anderson | .05 | .04 |
| 759 | Moose Haas | .05 | .04 |
| 760 | Andre Dawson | .20 | .15 |
| 761 | Don Slaught | .05 | .04 |
| 762 | Eric Show | .07 | .05 |
| 763 | Terry Puhl | .05 | .04 |
| 764 | Kevin Gross | .07 | .05 |
| 765 | Don Baylor | .12 | .09 |
| 766 | Rick Langford | .05 | .04 |
| 767 | Jody Davis | .10 | .08 |
| 768 | Vern Ruhle | .05 | .04 |
| 769 | *Harold Reynolds*(FC) | .40 | .30 |
| 770 | Vida Blue | .10 | .08 |
| 771 | John McNamara | .05 | .04 |
| 772 | Brian Downing | .07 | .05 |
| 773 | Greg Pryor | .05 | .04 |
| 774 | Terry Leach | .05 | .04 |
| 775 | Al Oliver | .10 | .08 |
| 776 | Gene Garber | .05 | .04 |
| 777 | Wayne Krenchicki | .05 | .04 |
| 778 | Jerry Hairston | .05 | .04 |
| 779 | Rick Reuschel | .10 | .08 |
| 780 | Robin Yount | .50 | .40 |
| 781 | Joe Nolan | .05 | .04 |
| 782 | Ken Landreaux | .05 | .04 |
| 783 | Ricky Horton | .07 | .05 |
| 784 | Alan Bannister | .05 | .04 |
| 785 | Bob Stanley | .05 | .04 |
| 786 | Twins Leaders (Mickey Hatcher) | .07 | .05 |
| 787 | Vance Law | .07 | .05 |
| 788 | Marty Castillo | .05 | .04 |
| 789 | Kurt Bevacqua | .05 | .04 |
| 790 | Phil Niekro | .25 | .20 |
| 791 | Checklist 661-792 | .05 | .04 |
| 792 | Charles Hudson | .06 | .05 |

## 1986 Topps Traded

ANDRES GALARRAGA

This 132-card set of 2-1/2" by 3-1/2" cards is one of the most popular sets of recent times. As always, the set features traded veterans, including such players as Phil Niekro and Tom Seaver.

They are not, however, the reason for the excitement. The demand is there because of a better than usual crop of rookies who also appear in the sets. Among those are Jose Canseco, Wally Joyner, Pete Incaviglia, Todd Worrell and the first card of Bo Jackson. As in the previous two years, a glossy-finish "Tiffany" edition of 5,000 Traded sets was produced. The "Tiffany" cards are worth four to six times the value of the regular Traded cards.

| | | MT | NR MT |
|---|---|---|---|
| Complete Set: | | 20.00 | 15.00 |
| Common Player: | | .08 | .06 |
| 1T | Andy Allanson(FC) | .20 | .15 |
| 2T | Neil Allen | .08 | .06 |
| 3T | Joaquin Andujar | .10 | .08 |
| 4T | Paul Assenmacher(FC) | .20 | .15 |
| 5T | Scott Bailes(FC) | .20 | .15 |
| 6T | Don Baylor | .15 | .11 |
| 7T | Steve Bedrosian | .15 | .11 |
| 8T | Juan Beniquez | .08 | .06 |
| 9T | Juan Berenguer | .08 | .06 |
| 10T | Mike Bielecki(FC) | .20 | .15 |
| 11T | Barry Bonds(FC) | 5.00 | 3.75 |
| 12T | Bobby Bonilla(FC) | 3.00 | 2.25 |
| 13T | Juan Bonilla | .08 | .06 |
| 14T | Rich Bordi | .08 | .06 |
| 15T | Steve Boros | .08 | .06 |
| 16T | Rick Burleson | .10 | .08 |
| 17T | Bill Campbell | .08 | .06 |
| 18T | Tom Candiotti | .08 | .06 |
| 19T | John Cangelosi(FC) | .20 | .15 |
| 20T | Jose Canseco(FC) | 6.00 | 4.50 |
| 21T | Carmen Castillo | .08 | .06 |
| 22T | Rick Cerone | .08 | .06 |
| 23T | John Cerutti(FC) | .20 | .15 |
| 24T | Will Clark(FC) | 6.00 | 4.50 |
| 25T | Mark Clear | .08 | .06 |
| 26T | Darnell Coles | .12 | .09 |
| 27T | Dave Collins | .10 | .08 |
| 28T | Tim Conroy | .08 | .06 |
| 29T | Joe Cowley | .08 | .06 |
| 30T | Joel Davis(FC) | .12 | .09 |
| 31T | Rob Deer | .15 | .11 |
| 32T | John Denny | .08 | .06 |
| 33T | Mike Easler | .10 | .08 |
| 34T | Mark Eichhorn(FC) | .20 | .15 |
| 35T | Steve Farr | .08 | .06 |
| 36T | Scott Fletcher | .15 | .11 |
| 37T | Terry Forster | .10 | .08 |
| 38T | Terry Francona | .08 | .06 |
| 39T | Jim Fregosi | .08 | .06 |
| 40T | Andres Galarraga(FC) | .25 | .20 |
| 41T | Ken Griffey | .12 | .09 |
| 42T | Bill Gullickson | .08 | .06 |
| 43T | Jose Guzman(FC) | .35 | .25 |

| | MT | NR MT |
|---|---|---|
| 44T Moose Haas | .08 | .06 |
| 45T Billy Hatcher | .20 | .15 |
| 46T Mike Heath | .08 | .06 |
| 47T Tom Hume | .08 | .06 |
| 48T Pete Incaviglia(FC) | .40 | .30 |
| 49T Dane Iorg | .08 | .06 |
| 50T Bo Jackson(FC) | 3.00 | 2.25 |
| 51T Wally Joyner(FC) | 1.00 | .70 |
| 52T Charlie Kerfeld(FC) | .15 | .11 |
| 53T Eric King(FC) | .20 | .15 |
| 54T Bob Kipper(FC) | .12 | .09 |
| 55T Wayne Krenchicki | .08 | .06 |
| 56T John Kruk(FC) | .50 | .40 |
| 57T Mike LaCoss | .08 | .06 |
| 58T Pete Ladd | .08 | .06 |
| 59T Mike Laga | .08 | .06 |
| 60T Hal Lanier | .08 | .06 |
| 61T Dave LaPoint | .12 | .09 |
| 62T Rudy Law | .08 | .06 |
| 63T Rick Leach | .08 | .06 |
| 64T Tim Leary | .08 | .06 |
| 65T Dennis Leonard | .10 | .08 |
| 66T Jim Leyland | .08 | .06 |
| 67T Steve Lyons | .12 | .09 |
| 68T Mickey Mahler | .08 | .06 |
| 69T Candy Maldonado | .15 | .11 |
| 70T Roger Mason(FC) | .10 | .08 |
| 71T Bob McClure | .08 | .06 |
| 72T Andy McGaffigan | .08 | .06 |
| 73T Gene Michael | .08 | .06 |
| 74T Kevin Mitchell(FC) | 1.50 | 1.25 |
| 75T Omar Moreno | .08 | .06 |
| 76T Jerry Mumphrey | .08 | .06 |
| 77T Phil Niekro | .40 | .30 |
| 78T Randy Niemann | .08 | .06 |
| 79T Juan Nieves(FC) | .15 | .11 |
| 80T Otis Nixon(FC) | .12 | .09 |
| 81T Bob Ojeda | .12 | .09 |
| 82T Jose Oquendo | .08 | .06 |
| 83T Tom Paciorek | .08 | .06 |
| 84T Dave Palmer | .08 | .06 |
| 85T Frank Pastore | .08 | .06 |
| 86T Lou Piniella | .12 | .09 |
| 87T Dan Plesac(FC) | .20 | .15 |
| 88T Darrell Porter | .10 | .08 |
| 89T Rey Quinones(FC) | .20 | .15 |
| 90T Gary Redus | .10 | .08 |
| 91T Bip Roberts | .60 | .45 |
| 92T Billy Jo Robidoux(FC) | .15 | .11 |
| 93T Jeff Robinson | .12 | .09 |
| 94T Gary Roenicke | .08 | .06 |
| 95T Ed Romero | .08 | .06 |
| 96T Argenis Salazar | .08 | .06 |
| 97T Joe Sambito | .08 | .06 |
| 98T Billy Sample | .08 | .06 |
| 99T Dave Schmidt | .08 | .06 |
| 100T Ken Schrom | .08 | .06 |
| 101T Tom Seaver | .60 | .45 |
| 102T Ted Simmons | .20 | .15 |
| 103T Sammy Stewart | .08 | .06 |
| 104T Kurt Stillwell(FC) | .20 | .15 |
| 105T Franklin Stubbs | .12 | .09 |
| 106T Dale Sveum(FC) | .20 | .15 |
| 107T Chuck Tanner | .08 | .06 |
| 108T Danny Tartabull(FC) | 1.25 | .90 |

| | MT | NR MT |
|---|---|---|
| 109T Tim Teufel | .08 | .06 |
| 110T Bob Tewksbury(FC) | .15 | .11 |
| 111T Andres Thomas(FC) | .12 | .09 |
| 112T Milt Thompson | .12 | .09 |
| 113T Robby Thompson(FC) | .30 | .25 |
| 114T Jay Tibbs | .08 | .06 |
| 115T Wayne Tolleson | .08 | .06 |
| 116T Alex Trevino | .08 | .06 |
| 117T Manny Trillo | .10 | .08 |
| 118T Ed Vande Berg | .08 | .06 |
| 119T Ozzie Virgil | .08 | .06 |
| 120T Bob Walk | .08 | .06 |
| 121T Gene Walter(FC) | .12 | .09 |
| 122T Claudell Washington | .12 | .09 |
| 123T Bill Wegman(FC) | .20 | .15 |
| 124T Dick Williams | .08 | .06 |
| 125T Mitch Williams(FC) | .50 | .40 |
| 126T Bobby Witt(FC) | .35 | .25 |
| 127T Todd Worrell(FC) | .20 | .15 |
| 128T George Wright | .08 | .06 |
| 129T Ricky Wright | .08 | .06 |
| 130T Steve Yeager | .08 | .06 |
| 131T Paul Zuvella | .08 | .06 |
| 132T Checklist | .08 | .06 |

## 1987 Topps

Many collectors feel that Topps' 1987 set of 792 card is a future classic. The 2-1/2" by 3-1/2" design is closely akin to the 1962 set in that the player photo is set against a woodgrain border. Instead of a rolling corner, as in 1962, the player photos in '87 feature a couple of clipped corners at top left and bottom right, where the team logo and player name appear. The player's position is not given on the front of the card. For the first time in several years, the trophy which designates members of Topps All-Star Rookie Team returned to the card design. As in the previous three years, Topps issued a glossy-finish "Tiffany" edition of their 792-card set. However, it was speculated that as many as 50,000 sets were produced as opposed to the 5,000 sets printed in 1985 and 1986. Because of the large print run, the values for the Tiffany cards are only 3-4 times higher than the same card in the regular issue.

|  | | MT | NR MT |
|---|---|---|---|
| | Complete Set: | 25.00 | 18.00 |
| | Common Player: | .05 | .04 |
| 1 | Record Breaker (Roger Clemens) | .35 | .25 |
| 2 | Record Breaker (Jim Deshaies) | .07 | .05 |
| 3 | Record Breaker (Dwight Evans) | .07 | .05 |
| 4 | Record Breaker (Dave Lopes) | .07 | .05 |
| 5 | Record Breaker (Dave Righetti) | .07 | .05 |
| 6 | Record Breaker (Ruben Sierra) | .25 | .20 |
| 7 | Record Breaker (Todd Worrell) | .07 | .05 |
| 8 | Terry Pendleton | .07 | .05 |
| 9 | Jay Tibbs | .05 | .04 |
| 10 | Cecil Cooper | .10 | .08 |
| 11 | Indians Leaders (Jack Aker, Chris Bando, Phil Niekro) | .07 | .05 |
| 12 | Jeff Sellers(FC) | .15 | .11 |
| 13 | Nick Esasky | .07 | .05 |
| 14 | Dave Stewart | .12 | .09 |
| 15 | Claudell Washington | .07 | .05 |
| 16 | Pat Clements | .05 | .04 |
| 17 | Pete O'Brien | .10 | .08 |
| 18 | Dick Howser | .05 | .04 |
| 19 | Matt Young | .05 | .04 |
| 20 | Gary Carter | .20 | .15 |
| 21 | Mark Davis | .05 | .04 |
| 22 | Doug DeCinces | .07 | .05 |
| 23 | Lee Smith | .10 | .08 |
| 24 | Tony Walker | .05 | .04 |
| 25 | Bert Blyleven | .12 | .09 |
| 26 | Greg Brock | .07 | .05 |
| 27 | Joe Cowley | .05 | .04 |
| 28 | Rick Dempsey | .07 | .05 |
| 29 | Jimmy Key | .10 | .08 |
| 30 | Tim Raines | .25 | .20 |
| 31 | Braves Leaders (Glenn Hubbard, Rafael Ramirez) | .07 | .05 |
| 32 | Tim Leary | .07 | .05 |
| 33 | Andy Van Slyke | .12 | .09 |
| 34 | Jose Rijo | .07 | .05 |
| 35 | Sid Bream | .07 | .05 |
| 36 | Eric King | .25 | .20 |
| 37 | Marvell Wynne | .05 | .04 |
| 38 | Dennis Leonard | .07 | .05 |
| 39 | Marty Barrett | .07 | .05 |
| 40 | Dave Righetti | .12 | .09 |
| 41 | Bo Diaz | .07 | .05 |
| 42 | Gary Redus | .05 | .04 |
| 43 | Gene Michael | .05 | .04 |
| 44 | Greg Harris | .05 | .04 |
| 45 | Jim Presley | .10 | .08 |
| 46 | Danny Gladden | .05 | .04 |
| 47 | Dennis Powell | .07 | .05 |
| 48 | Wally Backman | .07 | .05 |
| 49 | Terry Harper | .05 | .04 |
| 50 | Dave Smith | .07 | .05 |
| 51 | Mel Hall | .07 | .05 |
| 52 | Keith Atherton | .05 | .04 |
| 53 | Ruppert Jones | .05 | .04 |
| 54 | Bill Dawley | .05 | .04 |
| 55 | Tim Wallach | .10 | .08 |
| 56 | Brewers Leaders (Jamie Cocanower, Paul Molitor, Charlie Moore, Herm Starrette) | .07 | .05 |
| 57 | Scott Nielsen(FC) | .10 | .08 |
| 58 | Thad Bosley | .05 | .04 |
| 59 | Ken Dayley | .05 | .04 |
| 60 | Tony Pena | .07 | .05 |
| 61 | Bobby Thigpen(FC) | .70 | .50 |
| 62 | Bobby Meacham | .05 | .04 |
| 63 | Fred Toliver(FC) | .07 | .05 |
| 64 | Harry Spilman | .05 | .04 |
| 65 | Tom Browning | .10 | .08 |
| 66 | Marc Sullivan | .05 | .04 |
| 67 | Bill Swift | .05 | .04 |
| 68 | Tony LaRussa | .07 | .05 |
| 69 | Lonnie Smith | .07 | .05 |
| 70 | Charlie Hough | .07 | .05 |
| 71 | Mike Aldrete(FC) | .15 | .11 |
| 72 | Walt Terrell | .07 | .05 |
| 73 | Dave Anderson | .05 | .04 |
| 74 | Dan Pasqua | .10 | .08 |
| 75 | Ron Darling | .12 | .09 |
| 76 | Rafael Ramirez | .05 | .04 |
| 77 | Bryan Oelkers | .05 | .04 |
| 78 | Tom Foley | .05 | .04 |
| 79 | Juan Nieves | .10 | .08 |
| 80 | Wally Joyner | .80 | .60 |
| 81 | Padres Leaders (Andy Hawkins, Terry Kennedy) | .07 | .05 |
| 82 | Rob Murphy(FC) | .15 | .11 |
| 83 | Mike Davis | .07 | .05 |
| 84 | Steve Lake | .05 | .04 |
| 85 | Kevin Bass | .07 | .05 |
| 86 | Nate Snell | .05 | .04 |
| 87 | Mark Salas | .05 | .04 |
| 88 | Ed Wojna | .05 | .04 |
| 89 | Ozzie Guillen | .25 | .20 |
| 90 | Dave Stieb | .10 | .08 |
| 91 | Harold Reynolds | .10 | .08 |
| 92a | Urbano Lugo (no trademark on front) | .30 | .25 |
| 92b | Urbano Lugo (trademark on front) | .07 | .05 |
| 93 | Jim Leyland | .05 | .04 |
| 94 | Calvin Schiraldi | .05 | .04 |
| 95 | Oddibe McDowell | .07 | .05 |
| 96 | Frank Williams | .05 | .04 |
| 97 | Glenn Wilson | .07 | .05 |
| 98 | Bill Scherrer | .05 | .04 |
| 99 | Darryl Motley | .05 | .04 |
| 100 | Steve Garvey | .20 | .15 |
| 101 | Carl Willis(FC) | .10 | .08 |

| | MT | NR MT |
|---|---|---|
| 102  Paul Zuvella | .05 | .04 |
| 103  Rick Aguilera | .06 | .05 |
| 104  Billy Sample | .05 | .04 |
| 105  Floyd Youmans | .07 | .05 |
| 106  Blue Jays Leaders | | |
| (George Bell, Willie Upshaw) | | |
| | .07 | .05 |
| 107  John Butcher | .05 | .04 |
| 108  Jim Gantner (photo reversed) | .07 | .05 |
| 109  R.J. Reynolds | .05 | .04 |
| 110  John Tudor | .10 | .08 |
| 111  Alfredo Griffin | .07 | .05 |
| 112  Alan Ashby | .05 | .04 |
| 113  Neil Allen | .05 | .04 |
| 114  Billy Beane | .05 | .04 |
| 115  Donnie Moore | .05 | .04 |
| 116  Bill Russell | .07 | .05 |
| 117  Jim Beattie | .05 | .04 |
| 118  Bobby Valentine | .05 | .04 |
| 119  Ron Robinson | .05 | .04 |
| 120  Eddie Murray | .30 | .25 |
| 121  *Kevin Romine*(FC) | | |
| | .12 | .09 |
| 122  Jim Clancy | .07 | .05 |
| 123  *John Kruk* | .40 | .30 |
| 124  Ray Fontenot | .05 | .04 |
| 125  Bob Brenly | .05 | .04 |
| 126  *Mike Loynd*(FC) | .15 | .11 |
| 127  Vance Law | .07 | .05 |
| 128  Checklist 1-132 | .05 | .04 |
| 129  Rick Cerone | .05 | .04 |
| 130  Dwight Gooden | .60 | .45 |
| 131  Pirates Leaders (Sid Bream, Tony Pena) | .07 | .05 |
| 132  *Paul Assenmacher* | .15 | .11 |
| 133  Jose Oquendo | .05 | .04 |
| 134  *Rich Yett*(FC) | .12 | .09 |
| 135  Mike Easler | .07 | .05 |
| 136  Ron Romanick | .05 | .04 |
| 137  Jerry Willard | .05 | .04 |
| 138  Roy Lee Jackson | .05 | .04 |
| 139  *Devon White*(FC) | | |
| | .60 | .45 |
| 140  Bret Saberhagen | .15 | .11 |
| 141  Herm Winningham | .05 | .04 |
| 142  Rick Sutcliffe | .10 | .08 |
| 143  Steve Boros | .05 | .04 |
| 144  Mike Scioscia | .07 | .05 |
| 145  Charlie Kerfeld | .07 | .05 |
| 146  *Tracy Jones*(FC) | .25 | .20 |
| 147  Randy Niemann | .05 | .04 |
| 148  Dave Collins | .07 | .05 |
| 149  Ray Searage | .05 | .04 |
| 150  Wade Boggs | .70 | .50 |
| 151  Mike LaCoss | .05 | .04 |
| 152  Toby Harrah | .07 | .05 |
| 153  *Duane Ward*(FC) | .12 | .09 |
| 154  Tom O'Malley | .05 | .04 |
| 155  Eddie Whitson | .05 | .04 |
| 156  Mariners Leaders (Bob Kearney, Phil Regan, Matt Young) | .07 | .05 |
| 157  Danny Darwin | .05 | .04 |
| 158  Tim Teufel | .05 | .04 |
| 159  Ed Olwine | .05 | .04 |
| 160  Julio Franco | .10 | .08 |

| | MT | NR MT |
|---|---|---|
| 161  Steve Ontiveros | .05 | .04 |
| 162  *Mike LaValliere* | .25 | .20 |
| 163  Kevin Gross | .07 | .05 |
| 164  Sammy Khalifa | .05 | .04 |
| 165  Jeff Reardon | .10 | .08 |
| 166  Bob Boone | .07 | .05 |
| 167  *Jim Deshaies* | .25 | .20 |
| 168  Lou Piniella | .07 | .05 |
| 169  Ron Washington | .05 | .04 |
| 170  Future Stars (*Bo Jackson*) | 1.00 | .70 |
| 171  *Chuck Cary*(FC) | .10 | .08 |
| 172  Ron Oester | .05 | .04 |
| 173  Alex Trevino | .05 | .04 |
| 174  Henry Cotto | .05 | .04 |
| 175  Bob Stanley | .05 | .04 |
| 176  Steve Buechele | .07 | .05 |
| 177  Keith Moreland | .07 | .05 |
| 178  Cecil Fielder | 1.75 | 1.25 |
| 179  Bill Wegman | .10 | .08 |
| 180  Chris Brown | .07 | .05 |
| 181  Cardinals Leaders (Mike LaValliere, Ozzie Smith, Ray Soff) | .07 | .05 |
| 182  Lee Lacy | .05 | .04 |
| 183  Andy Hawkins | .05 | .04 |
| 184  *Bobby Bonilla* | 2.00 | 1.50 |
| 185  Roger McDowell | .10 | .08 |
| 186  Bruce Benedict | .05 | .04 |
| 187  Mark Huismann | .05 | .04 |
| 188  Tony Phillips | .05 | .04 |
| 189  Joe Hesketh | .05 | .04 |
| 190  Jim Sundberg | .07 | .05 |
| 191  Charles Hudson | .05 | .04 |
| 192  Cory Snyder(FC) | .40 | .30 |
| 193  Roger Craig | .07 | .05 |
| 194  Kirk McCaskill | .07 | .05 |
| 195  Mike Pagliarulo | .10 | .08 |
| 196  Randy O'Neal | .05 | .04 |
| 197  Mark Bailey | .05 | .04 |
| 198  Lee Mazzilli | .07 | .05 |
| 199  Mariano Duncan | .05 | .04 |
| 200  Pete Rose | .40 | .30 |
| 201  *John Cangelosi* | .12 | .09 |
| 202  Ricky Wright | .05 | .04 |
| 203  *Mike Kingery*(FC) | | |
| | .15 | .11 |
| 204  Sammy Stewart | .05 | .04 |
| 205  Graig Nettles | .10 | .08 |
| 206  Twins Leaders (Tim Laudner, Frank Viola) | .07 | .05 |
| 207  George Frazier | .05 | .04 |
| 208  John Shelby | .05 | .04 |
| 209  Rick Schu | .05 | .04 |
| 210  Lloyd Moseby | .07 | .05 |
| 211  John Morris(FC) | .07 | .05 |
| 212  Mike Fitzgerald | .05 | .04 |
| 213  *Randy Myers*(FC) | | |
| | .30 | .25 |
| 214  Omar Moreno | .05 | .04 |
| 215  Mark Langston | .12 | .09 |
| 216  Future Stars (*B.J. Surhoff*)(FC) | .30 | .25 |
| 217  Chris Codiroli | .05 | .04 |
| 218  Sparky Anderson | .07 | .05 |
| 219  Cecilio Guante | .05 | .04 |
| 220  Joe Carter | .12 | .09 |

| | | MT | NR MT |
|---|---|---|---|
| 221 | Vern Ruhle | .05 | .04 |
| 222 | Denny Walling | .05 | .04 |
| 223 | Charlie Leibrandt | .07 | .05 |
| 224 | Wayne Tolleson | .05 | .04 |
| 225 | Mike Smithson | .05 | .04 |
| 226 | Max Venable | .05 | .04 |
| 227 | *Jamie Moyer*(FC) | | |
| | | .20 | .15 |
| 228 | Curt Wilkerson | .05 | .04 |
| 229 | *Mike Birkbeck*(FC) | | |
| | | .15 | .11 |
| 230 | Don Baylor | .10 | .08 |
| 231 | Giants Leaders (Bob Brenly, Mike Krukow) | .07 | .05 |
| 232 | Reggie Williams | .10 | .08 |
| 233 | *Russ Morman*(FC) | | |
| | | .10 | .08 |
| 234 | Pat Sheridan | .05 | .04 |
| 235 | Alvin Davis | .10 | .08 |
| 236 | Tommy John | .15 | .11 |
| 237 | Jim Morrison | .05 | .04 |
| 238 | Bill Krueger | .05 | .04 |
| 239 | Juan Espino | .05 | .04 |
| 240 | Steve Balboni | .07 | .05 |
| 241 | Danny Heep | .05 | .04 |
| 242 | Rick Mahler | .05 | .04 |
| 243 | Whitey Herzog | .07 | .05 |
| 244 | Dickie Noles | .05 | .04 |
| 245 | Willie Upshaw | .07 | .05 |
| 246 | Jim Dwyer | .05 | .04 |
| 247 | Jeff Reed(FC) | .07 | .05 |
| 248 | Gene Walter | .07 | .05 |
| 249 | Jim Pankovits | .05 | .04 |
| 250 | Teddy Higuera | .15 | .11 |
| 251 | Rob Wilfong | .05 | .04 |
| 252 | Denny Martinez | .05 | .04 |
| 253 | Eddie Milner | .05 | .04 |
| 254 | *Bob Tewksbury* | .12 | .09 |
| 255 | Juan Samuel | .10 | .08 |
| 256 | Royals Leaders (George Brett, Frank White) | .10 | .08 |
| 257 | Bob Forsch | .07 | .05 |
| 258 | Steve Yeager | .05 | .04 |
| 259 | *Mike Greenwell*(FC) | | |
| | | .40 | .30 |
| 260 | Vida Blue | .07 | .05 |
| 261 | *Ruben Sierra*(FC) | | |
| | | 2.75 | 2.00 |
| 262 | Jim Winn | .05 | .04 |
| 263 | Stan Javier(FC) | .07 | .05 |
| 264 | Checklist 133-264 | .05 | .04 |
| 265 | Darrell Evans | .10 | .08 |
| 266 | *Jeff Hamilton*(FC) | | |
| | | .25 | .20 |
| 267 | Howard Johnson | .10 | .08 |
| 268 | Pat Corrales | .05 | .04 |
| 269 | Cliff Speck | .05 | .04 |
| 270 | Jody Davis | .07 | .05 |
| 271 | Mike Brown | .05 | .04 |
| 272 | Andres Galarraga | .35 | .25 |
| 273 | Gene Nelson | .05 | .04 |
| 274 | *Jeff Hearron*(FC) | | |
| | | .05 | .04 |
| 275 | LaMarr Hoyt | .05 | .04 |
| 276 | Jackie Gutierrez | .05 | .04 |
| 277 | Juan Agosto | .05 | .04 |
| 278 | Gary Pettis | .05 | .04 |
| 279 | *Dan Plesac* | .30 | .25 |
| 280 | Jeffrey Leonard | .07 | .05 |
| 281 | Reds Leaders (Bo Diaz, Bill Gullickson, Pete Rose) | .10 | .08 |
| 282 | Jeff Calhoun | .05 | .04 |
| 283 | *Doug Drabek*(FC) | | |
| | | .80 | .60 |
| 284 | John Moses | .05 | .04 |
| 285 | Dennis Boyd | .07 | .05 |
| 286 | Mike Woodard(FC) | .07 | .05 |
| 287 | Dave Von Ohlen | .05 | .04 |
| 288 | Tito Landrum | .05 | .04 |
| 289 | Bob Kipper | .07 | .05 |
| 290 | Leon Durham | .07 | .05 |
| 291 | *Mitch Williams*(FC) | | |
| | | .40 | .30 |
| 292 | Franklin Stubbs | .07 | .05 |
| 293 | Bob Rodgers | .05 | .04 |
| 294 | Steve Jeltz | .05 | .04 |
| 295 | Len Dykstra | .12 | .09 |
| 296 | *Andres Thomas* | .15 | .11 |
| 297 | Don Schulze | .05 | .04 |
| 298 | Larry Herndon | .05 | .04 |
| 299 | Joel Davis | .07 | .05 |
| 300 | Reggie Jackson | .30 | .25 |
| 301 | Luis Aquino(FC) | .10 | .08 |
| 302 | Bill Schroeder | .05 | .04 |
| 303 | Juan Berenguer | .05 | .04 |
| 304 | Phil Garner | .05 | .04 |
| 305 | John Franco | .10 | .08 |
| 306 | Red Sox Leaders (Rich Gedman, John McNamara, Tom Seaver) | .07 | .05 |
| 307 | *Lee Guetterman*(FC) | | |
| | | .15 | .11 |
| 308 | Don Slaught | .05 | .04 |
| 309 | Mike Young | .05 | .04 |
| 310 | Frank Viola | .15 | .11 |
| 311 | Turn Back The Clock (Rickey Henderson) | .10 | .08 |
| 312 | Turn Back The Clock (Reggie Jackson) | .10 | .08 |
| 313 | Turn Back The Clock (Roberto Clemente) | .15 | .11 |
| 314 | Turn Back The Clock (Carl Yastrzemski) | .10 | .08 |
| 315 | Turn Back The Clock (Maury Wills) | .07 | .05 |
| 316 | Brian Fisher | .07 | .05 |
| 317 | Clint Hurdle | .05 | .04 |
| 318 | Jim Fregosi | .05 | .04 |
| 319 | *Greg Swindell*(FC) | | |
| | | .60 | .45 |
| 320 | Barry Bonds | 2.00 | 1.50 |
| 321 | Mike Laga | .05 | .04 |
| 322 | Chris Bando | .05 | .04 |
| 323 | *Al Newman* | .07 | .05 |
| 324 | Dave Palmer | .05 | .04 |
| 325 | Garry Templeton | .07 | .05 |
| 326 | Mark Gubicza | .10 | .08 |
| 327 | *Dale Sveum* | .20 | .15 |
| 328 | Bob Welch | .10 | .08 |
| 329 | Ron Roenicke | .05 | .04 |
| 330 | Mike Scott | .12 | .09 |
| 331 | Mets Leaders (Gary Carter, Keith Hernandez, | | |

| | MT | NR MT |
|---|---|---|
| Dave Johnson, Darryl Strawberry) | .10 | .08 |
| 332 Joe Price | .05 | .04 |
| 333 Ken Phelps | .07 | .05 |
| 334 *Ed Correa* | .15 | .11 |
| 335 Candy Maldonado | .07 | .05 |
| 336 *Allan Anderson*(FC) | .25 | .20 |
| 337 Darrell Miller | .05 | .04 |
| 338 Tim Conroy | .05 | .04 |
| 339 Donnie Hill | .05 | .04 |
| 340 Roger Clemens | 1.00 | .70 |
| 341 Mike Brown | .05 | .04 |
| 342 Bob James | .05 | .04 |
| 343 Hal Lanier | .05 | .04 |
| 344a Joe Niekro (copyright outside yellow on back) | .30 | .25 |
| 344b Joe Niekro (copyright inside yellow on back) | .07 | .05 |
| 345 Andre Dawson | .20 | .15 |
| 346 Shawon Dunston | .07 | .05 |
| 347 Mickey Brantley(FC) | .07 | .05 |
| 348 Carmelo Martinez | .07 | .05 |
| 349 Storm Davis | .10 | .08 |
| 350 Keith Hernandez | .20 | .15 |
| 351 Gene Garber | .05 | .04 |
| 352 Mike Felder(FC) | .07 | .05 |
| 353 Ernie Camacho | .05 | .04 |
| 354 Jamie Quirk | .05 | .04 |
| 355 Don Carman | .07 | .05 |
| 356 White Sox Leaders (Ed Brinkman, Julio Cruz) | .07 | .05 |
| 357 *Steve Fireovid*(FC) | .07 | .05 |
| 358 Sal Butera | .05 | .04 |
| 359 Doug Corbett | .05 | .04 |
| 360 Pedro Guerrero | .15 | .11 |
| 361 Mark Thurmond | .05 | .04 |
| 362 *Luis Quinones*(FC) | .12 | .09 |
| 363 Jose Guzman | .12 | .09 |
| 364 Randy Bush | .05 | .04 |
| 365 Rick Rhoden | .07 | .05 |
| 366 *Mark McGwire* | 2.00 | 1.50 |
| 367 Jeff Lahti | .05 | .04 |
| 368 John McNamara | .05 | .04 |
| 369 Brian Dayett | .05 | .04 |
| 370 Fred Lynn | .15 | .11 |
| 371 *Mark Eichhorn* | .15 | .11 |
| 372 Jerry Mumphrey | .05 | .04 |
| 373 Jeff Dedmon | .05 | .04 |
| 374 Glenn Hoffman | .05 | .04 |
| 375 Ron Guidry | .12 | .09 |
| 376 Scott Bradley | .05 | .04 |
| 377 John Henry Johnson | .05 | .04 |
| 378 Rafael Santana | .05 | .04 |
| 379 John Russell | .05 | .04 |
| 380 Rich Gossage | .15 | .11 |
| 381 Expos Leaders (Mike Fitzgerald, Bob Rodgers) | .07 | .05 |
| 382 Rudy Law | .05 | .04 |
| 383 Ron Davis | .05 | .04 |
| 384 Johnny Grubb | .05 | .04 |
| 385 Orel Hershiser | .30 | .25 |
| 386 Dickie Thon | .07 | .05 |

| | MT | NR MT |
|---|---|---|
| 387 *T.R. Bryden*(FC) | .10 | .08 |
| 388 Geno Petralli | .05 | .04 |
| 389 Jeff Robinson | .07 | .05 |
| 390 Gary Matthews | .07 | .05 |
| 391 Jay Howell | .07 | .05 |
| 392 Checklist 265-396 | .05 | .04 |
| 393 Pete Rose | .40 | .30 |
| 394 Mike Bielecki | .07 | .05 |
| 395 Damaso Garcia | .05 | .04 |
| 396 Tim Lollar | .05 | .04 |
| 397 Greg Walker | .07 | .05 |
| 398 Brad Havens | .05 | .04 |
| 399 Curt Ford(FC) | .07 | .05 |
| 400 George Brett | .35 | .25 |
| 401 Billy Jo Robidoux | .07 | .05 |
| 402 Mike Trujillo | .05 | .04 |
| 403 Jerry Royster | .05 | .04 |
| 404 Doug Sisk | .05 | .04 |
| 405 Brook Jacoby | .10 | .08 |
| 406 Yankees Leaders (Rickey Henderson, Don Mattingly) | .25 | .20 |
| 407 Jim Acker | .05 | .04 |
| 408 John Mizerock | .05 | .04 |
| 409 Milt Thompson | .07 | .05 |
| 410 Fernando Valenzuela | .25 | .20 |
| 411 Darnell Coles | .07 | .05 |
| 412 Eric Davis | .90 | .70 |
| 413 Moose Haas | .05 | .04 |
| 414 Joe Orsulak | .05 | .04 |
| 415 *Bobby Witt* | .50 | .40 |
| 416 Tom Nieto | .05 | .04 |
| 417 Pat Perry(FC) | .07 | .05 |
| 418 Dick Williams | .05 | .04 |
| 419 *Mark Portugal*(FC) | .10 | .08 |
| 420 *Will Clark* | 3.00 | 2.25 |
| 421 Jose DeLeon | .07 | .05 |
| 422 Jack Howell | .07 | .05 |
| 423 Jaime Cocanower | .05 | .04 |
| 424 Chris Speier | .05 | .04 |
| 425 Tom Seaver | .30 | .25 |
| 426 Floyd Rayford | .05 | .04 |
| 427 Ed Nunez | .05 | .04 |
| 428 Bruce Bochy | .05 | .04 |
| 429 Future Stars *(Tim Pyznarski)*(FC) | .10 | .08 |
| 430 Mike Schmidt | .40 | .30 |
| 431 Dodgers Leaders (Tom Niedenfuer, Ron Perranoski, Alex Trevino) | .07 | .05 |
| 432 Jim Slaton | .05 | .04 |
| 433 *Ed Hearn*(FC) | .10 | .08 |
| 434 Mike Fischlin | .05 | .04 |
| 435 Bruce Sutter | .12 | .09 |
| 436 *Andy Allanson* | .15 | .11 |
| 437 Ted Power | .05 | .04 |
| 438 *Kelly Downs*(FC) | .30 | .25 |
| 439 Karl Best | .05 | .04 |
| 440 Willie McGee | .10 | .08 |
| 441 *Dave Leiper*(FC) | .10 | .08 |
| 442 Mitch Webster | .07 | .05 |
| 443 John Felske | .05 | .04 |
| 444 Jeff Russell | .05 | .04 |
| 445 Dave Lopes | .07 | .05 |

| | | MT | NR MT |
|---|---|---|---|
| 446 | *Chuck Finley*(FC) | | |
| | | 1.00 | .70 |
| 447 | Bill Almon | .05 | .04 |
| 448 | *Chris Bosio*(FC) | .25 | .20 |
| 449 | Future Stars *(Pat Dodson)*(FC) | | |
| | | .10 | .08 |
| 450 | Kirby Puckett | 1.00 | .70 |
| 451 | Joe Sambito | .05 | .04 |
| 452 | Dave Henderson | .10 | .08 |
| 453 | *Scott Terry*(FC) | .12 | .09 |
| 454 | Luis Salazar | .05 | .04 |
| 455 | Mike Boddicker | .07 | .05 |
| 456 | A's Leaders (Carney Lansford, Tony LaRussa, Mickey Tettleton, Dave Von Ohlen) | | |
| | | .07 | .05 |
| 457 | Len Matuszek | .05 | .04 |
| 458 | Kelly Gruber(FC) | 1.00 | .70 |
| 459 | Dennis Eckersley | .10 | .08 |
| 460 | Darryl Strawberry | .35 | .25 |
| 461 | Craig McMurtry | .05 | .04 |
| 462 | Scott Fletcher | .07 | .05 |
| 463 | Tom Candiotti | .05 | .04 |
| 464 | Butch Wynegar | .05 | .04 |
| 465 | Todd Worrell | .30 | .25 |
| 466 | Kal Daniels(FC) | .30 | .25 |
| 467 | Randy St. Claire | .05 | .04 |
| 468 | George Bamberger | .05 | .04 |
| 469 | *Mike Diaz*(FC) | .15 | .11 |
| 470 | Dave Dravecky | .07 | .05 |
| 471 | Ronn Reynolds | .05 | .04 |
| 472 | Bill Doran | .07 | .05 |
| 473 | Steve Farr | .05 | .04 |
| 474 | Jerry Narron | .05 | .04 |
| 475 | Scott Garrelts | .05 | .04 |
| 476 | Danny Tartabull | .70 | .50 |
| 477 | Ken Howell | .05 | .04 |
| 478 | Tim Laudner | .05 | .04 |
| 479 | *Bob Sebra*(FC) | .10 | .08 |
| 480 | Jim Rice | .25 | .20 |
| 481 | Phillies Leaders (Von Hayes, Juan Samuel, Glenn Wilson) | | |
| | | .07 | .05 |
| 482 | Daryl Boston | .05 | .04 |
| 483 | Dwight Lowry | .05 | .04 |
| 484 | Jim Traber(FC) | .15 | .11 |
| 485 | Tony Fernandez | .10 | .08 |
| 486 | Otis Nixon | .05 | .04 |
| 487 | Dave Gumpert | .05 | .04 |
| 488 | Ray Knight | .07 | .05 |
| 489 | Bill Gullickson | .05 | .04 |
| 490 | Dale Murphy | .40 | .30 |
| 491 | *Ron Karkovice*(FC) | | |
| | | .10 | .08 |
| 492 | Mike Heath | .05 | .04 |
| 493 | Tom Lasorda | .07 | .05 |
| 494 | *Barry Jones*(FC) | .12 | .09 |
| 495 | Gorman Thomas | .10 | .08 |
| 496 | Bruce Bochte | .05 | .04 |
| 497 | *Dale Mohorcic*(FC) | | |
| | | .15 | .11 |
| 498 | Bob Kearney | .05 | .04 |
| 499 | *Bruce Ruffin*(FC) | .20 | .15 |
| 500 | Don Mattingly | .60 | .45 |
| 501 | Craig Lefferts | .05 | .04 |
| 502 | Dick Schofield | .05 | .04 |
| 503 | Larry Andersen | .05 | .04 |

| | | MT | NR MT |
|---|---|---|---|
| 504 | Mickey Hatcher | .05 | .04 |
| 505 | Bryn Smith | .05 | .04 |
| 506 | Orioles Leaders (Rich Bordi, Rick Dempsey, Earl Weaver) | | |
| | | .07 | .05 |
| 507 | Dave Stapleton | .05 | .04 |
| 508 | *Scott Bankhead* | .25 | .20 |
| 509 | Enos Cabell | .05 | .04 |
| 510 | Tom Henke | .07 | .05 |
| 511 | Steve Lyons | .05 | .04 |
| 512 | *Dave Magadan*(FC) | | |
| | | .30 | .25 |
| 513 | Carmen Castillo | .05 | .04 |
| 514 | Orlando Mercado | .05 | .04 |
| 515 | Willie Hernandez | .07 | .05 |
| 516 | Ted Simmons | .10 | .08 |
| 517 | Mario Soto | .07 | .05 |
| 518 | Gene Mauch | .07 | .05 |
| 519 | Curt Young | .07 | .05 |
| 520 | Jack Clark | .15 | .11 |
| 521 | Rick Reuschel | .10 | .08 |
| 522 | Checklist 397-528 | .05 | .04 |
| 523 | Earnie Riles | .05 | .04 |
| 524 | Bob Shirley | .05 | .04 |
| 525 | Phil Bradley | .10 | .08 |
| 526 | Roger Mason | .05 | .04 |
| 527 | Jim Wohlford | .05 | .04 |
| 528 | Ken Dixon | .05 | .04 |
| 529 | *Alvaro Espinoza*(FC) | | |
| | | .07 | .05 |
| 530 | Tony Gwynn | .50 | .40 |
| 531 | Astros Leaders (Yogi Berra, Hal Lanier, Denis Menke, Gene Tenace) | | |
| | | .07 | .05 |
| 532 | Jeff Stone | .05 | .04 |
| 533 | Argenis Salazar | .05 | .04 |
| 534 | Scott Sanderson | .05 | .04 |
| 535 | Tony Armas | .07 | .05 |
| 536 | *Terry Mulholland*(FC) | | |
| | | .10 | .08 |
| 537 | Rance Mulliniks | .05 | .04 |
| 538 | Tom Niedenfuer | .07 | .05 |
| 539 | Reid Nichols | .05 | .04 |
| 540 | Terry Kennedy | .07 | .05 |
| 541 | *Rafael Belliard*(FC) | | |
| | | .10 | .08 |
| 542 | Ricky Horton | .07 | .05 |
| 543 | Dave Johnson | .07 | .05 |
| 544 | Zane Smith | .07 | .05 |
| 545 | Buddy Bell | .07 | .05 |
| 546 | Mike Morgan | .05 | .04 |
| 547 | Rob Deer | .10 | .08 |
| 548 | *Bill Mooneyham*(FC) | | |
| | | .10 | .08 |
| 549 | Bob Melvin | .05 | .04 |
| 550 | *Pete Incaviglia* | .20 | .15 |
| 551 | Frank Wills | .05 | .04 |
| 552 | Larry Sheets | .07 | .05 |
| 553 | *Mike Maddux*(FC) | | |
| | | .15 | .11 |
| 554 | Buddy Biancalana | .05 | .04 |
| 555 | Dennis Rasmussen | .10 | .08 |
| 556 | Angels Leaders (Bob Boone, Marcel Lachemann, Mike Witt) | | |
| | | .07 | .05 |
| 557 | *John Cerutti* | .15 | .11 |
| 558 | Greg Gagne | .05 | .04 |

| | | MT | NR MT | | | | MT | NR MT |
|---|---|---|---|---|---|---|---|---|
| 559 | Lance McCullers | .07 | .05 | | 615 | Teddy Higuera AS | .10 | .08 |
| 560 | Glenn Davis | .25 | .20 | | 616 | Dave Righetti AS | .10 | .08 |
| 561 | *Rey Quinones* | .15 | .11 | | 617 | Al Nipper | .05 | .04 |
| 562 | *Bryan Clutterbuck*(FC) | .10 | .08 | | 618 | Tom Kelly | .05 | .04 |
| | | | | | 619 | Jerry Reed | .05 | .04 |
| 563 | John Stefero | .05 | .04 | | 620 | Jose Canseco | 3.00 | 2.25 |
| 564 | Larry McWilliams | .05 | .04 | | 621 | Danny Cox | .07 | .05 |
| 565 | Dusty Baker | .07 | .05 | | 622 | *Glenn Braggs*(FC) | | |
| 566 | Tim Hulett | .05 | .04 | | | | .30 | .25 |
| 567 | *Greg Mathews*(FC) | | | | 623 | *Kurt Stillwell*(FC) | .30 | .25 |
| | | .20 | .15 | | 624 | Tim Burke | .05 | .04 |
| 568 | Earl Weaver | .07 | .05 | | 625 | Mookie Wilson | .07 | .05 |
| 569 | Wade Rowdon(FC) | .07 | .05 | | 626 | Joel Skinner | .05 | .04 |
| 570 | Sid Fernandez | .10 | .08 | | 627 | Ken Oberkfell | .05 | .04 |
| 571 | Ozzie Virgil | .05 | .04 | | 628 | Bob Walk | .05 | .04 |
| 572 | Pete Ladd | .05 | .04 | | 629 | Larry Parrish | .07 | .05 |
| 573 | Hal McRae | .07 | .05 | | 630 | John Candelaria | .07 | .05 |
| 574 | Manny Lee | .05 | .04 | | 631 | Tigers Leaders (Sparky | | |
| 575 | Pat Tabler | .07 | .05 | | | Anderson, Mike Heath, | | |
| 576 | Frank Pastore | .05 | .04 | | | Willie Hernandez) | | |
| 577 | Dann Bilardello | .05 | .04 | | | | .07 | .05 |
| 578 | Billy Hatcher | .07 | .05 | | 632 | Rob Woodward(FC) | .07 | .05 |
| 579 | Rick Burleson | .07 | .05 | | 633 | Jose Uribe | .07 | .05 |
| 580 | Mike Krukow | .07 | .05 | | 634 | Future Stars *(Rafael Palmeiro)*(FC) | 1.25 | .90 |
| 581 | Cubs Leaders (Ron Cey, Steve Trout) | .07 | .05 | | 635 | Ken Schrom | .05 | .04 |
| 582 | Bruce Berenyi | .05 | .04 | | 636 | Darren Daulton | .05 | .04 |
| 583 | Junior Ortiz | .05 | .04 | | 637 | *Bip Roberts* | .40 | .30 |
| 584 | Ron Kittle | .07 | .05 | | 638 | Rich Bordi | .05 | .04 |
| 585 | *Scott Bailes* | .15 | .11 | | 639 | Gerald Perry | .10 | .08 |
| 586 | Ben Oglivie | .07 | .05 | | 640 | Mark Clear | .05 | .04 |
| 587 | Eric Plunk(FC) | .10 | .08 | | 641 | Domingo Ramos | .05 | .04 |
| 588 | Wallace Johnson | .05 | .04 | | 642 | Al Pulido | .05 | .04 |
| 589 | Steve Crawford | .05 | .04 | | 643 | Ron Shepherd | .05 | .04 |
| 590 | Vince Coleman | .30 | .25 | | 644 | John Denny | .05 | .04 |
| 591 | Spike Owen | .05 | .04 | | 645 | Dwight Evans | .12 | .09 |
| 592 | Chris Welsh | .05 | .04 | | 646 | Mike Mason | .05 | .04 |
| 593 | Chuck Tanner | .05 | .04 | | 647 | Tom Lawless | .05 | .04 |
| 594 | Rick Anderson | .05 | .04 | | 648 | *Barry Larkin* | 1.75 | 1.25 |
| 595 | Keith Hernandez AS | .12 | .09 | | 649 | Mickey Tettleton | .05 | .04 |
| 596 | Steve Sax AS | .07 | .05 | | 650 | Hubie Brooks | .07 | .05 |
| 597 | Mike Schmidt AS | .20 | .15 | | 651 | Benny Distefano | .05 | .04 |
| 598 | Ozzie Smith AS | .07 | .05 | | 652 | Terry Forster | .07 | .05 |
| 599 | Tony Gwynn AS | .20 | .15 | | 653 | *Kevin Mitchell* | 1.25 | .90 |
| 600 | Dave Parker AS | .10 | .08 | | 654 | Checklist 529-660 | .05 | .04 |
| 601 | Darryl Strawberry AS | | | | 655 | Jesse Barfield | .15 | .11 |
| | | .20 | .15 | | 656 | Rangers Leaders (Bobby | | |
| 602 | Gary Carter AS | .15 | .11 | | | Valentine, Rickey Wright) | | |
| 603a | Dwight Gooden AS (no trademark on front) | .80 | .60 | | | | .07 | .05 |
| 603b | Dwight Gooden AS (trademark on front) | .30 | .25 | | 657 | Tom Waddell | .05 | .04 |
| 604 | Fernando Valenzuela AS | | | | 658 | *Robby Thompson* | .30 | .25 |
| | | .12 | .09 | | 659 | Aurelio Lopez | .05 | .04 |
| 605 | Todd Worrell AS | .10 | .08 | | 660 | Bob Horner | .10 | .08 |
| 606a | Don Mattingly AS (no trademark on front) | 1.25 | .90 | | 661 | Lou Whitaker | .15 | .11 |
| | | | | | 662 | Frank DiPino | .05 | .04 |
| 606b | Don Mattingly AS (trademark on front) | .70 | .50 | | 663 | Cliff Johnson | .05 | .04 |
| | | | | | 664 | Mike Marshall | .10 | .08 |
| 607 | Tony Bernazard AS | .05 | .04 | | 665 | Rod Scurry | .05 | .04 |
| 608 | Wade Boggs AS | .40 | .30 | | 666 | Von Hayes | .07 | .05 |
| 609 | Cal Ripken AS | .20 | .15 | | 667 | Ron Hassey | .05 | .04 |
| 610 | Jim Rice AS | .15 | .11 | | 668 | Juan Bonilla | .05 | .04 |
| 611 | Kirby Puckett AS | .15 | .11 | | 669 | Bud Black | .05 | .04 |
| 612 | George Bell AS | .12 | .09 | | 670 | Jose Cruz | .07 | .05 |
| 613 | Lance Parrish AS | .10 | .08 | | 671a | Ray Soff (no "D*" before copyright line) | .20 | .15 |
| 614 | Roger Clemens AS | .30 | .25 | | 671b | Ray Soff ("D*" before copyright line) | .05 | .04 |
| | | | | | 672 | Chili Davis | .07 | .05 |

| | | MT | NR MT |
|---|---|---|---|
| 673 | Don Sutton | .15 | .11 |
| 674 | Bill Campbell | .05 | .04 |
| 675 | Ed Romero | .05 | .04 |
| 676 | Charlie Moore | .05 | .04 |
| 677 | Bob Grich | .07 | .05 |
| 678 | Carney Lansford | .07 | .05 |
| 679 | Kent Hrbek | .15 | .11 |
| 680 | Ryne Sandberg | 1.00 | .70 |
| 681 | George Bell | .25 | .20 |
| 682 | Jerry Reuss | .07 | .05 |
| 683 | Gary Roenicke | .05 | .04 |
| 684 | Kent Tekulve | .07 | .05 |
| 685 | Jerry Hairston | .05 | .04 |
| 686 | Doyle Alexander | .07 | .05 |
| 687 | Alan Trammell | .25 | .20 |
| 688 | Juan Beniquez | .05 | .04 |
| 689 | Darrell Porter | .07 | .05 |
| 690 | Dane Iorg | .05 | .04 |
| 691 | Dave Parker | .20 | .15 |
| 692 | Frank White | .07 | .05 |
| 693 | Terry Puhl | .05 | .04 |
| 694 | Phil Niekro | .20 | .15 |
| 695 | Chico Walker | .05 | .04 |
| 696 | Gary Lucas | .05 | .04 |
| 697 | Ed Lynch | .05 | .04 |
| 698 | Ernie Whitt | .07 | .05 |
| 699 | Ken Landreaux | .05 | .04 |
| 700 | Dave Bergman | .05 | .04 |
| 701 | Willie Randolph | .07 | .05 |
| 702 | Greg Gross | .05 | .04 |
| 703 | Dave Schmidt | .05 | .04 |
| 704 | Jesse Orosco | .07 | .05 |
| 705 | Bruce Hurst | .10 | .08 |
| 706 | Rick Manning | .05 | .04 |
| 707 | Bob McClure | .05 | .04 |
| 708 | Scott McGregor | .07 | .05 |
| 709 | Dave Kingman | .10 | .08 |
| 710 | Gary Gaetti | .15 | .11 |
| 711 | Ken Griffey | .07 | .05 |
| 712 | Don Robinson | .07 | .05 |
| 713 | Tom Brookens | .05 | .04 |
| 714 | Dan Quisenberry | .07 | .05 |
| 715 | Bob Dernier | .05 | .04 |
| 716 | Rick Leach | .05 | .04 |
| 717 | Ed Vande Berg | .05 | .04 |
| 718 | Steve Carlton | .25 | .20 |
| 719 | Tom Hume | .05 | .04 |
| 720 | Richard Dotson | .07 | .05 |
| 721 | Tom Herr | .07 | .05 |
| 722 | Bob Knepper | .07 | .05 |
| 723 | Brett Butler | .07 | .05 |
| 724 | Greg Minton | .05 | .04 |
| 725 | George Hendrick | .07 | .05 |
| 726 | Frank Tanana | .07 | .05 |
| 727 | Mike Moore | .05 | .04 |
| 728 | Tippy Martinez | .05 | .04 |
| 729 | Tom Paciorek | .05 | .04 |
| 730 | Eric Show | .07 | .05 |
| 731 | Dave Concepcion | .10 | .08 |
| 732 | Manny Trillo | .07 | .05 |
| 733 | Bill Caudill | .05 | .04 |
| 734 | Bill Madlock | .10 | .08 |
| 735 | Rickey Henderson | .70 | .50 |
| 736 | Steve Bedrosian | .10 | .08 |
| 737 | Floyd Bannister | .07 | .05 |
| 738 | Jorge Orta | .05 | .04 |
| 739 | Chet Lemon | .07 | .05 |

| | | MT | NR MT |
|---|---|---|---|
| 740 | Rich Gedman | .07 | .05 |
| 741 | Paul Molitor | .12 | .09 |
| 742 | Andy McGaffigan | .05 | .04 |
| 743 | Dwayne Murphy | .07 | .05 |
| 744 | Roy Smalley | .05 | .04 |
| 745 | Glenn Hubbard | .05 | .04 |
| 746 | Bob Ojeda | .07 | .05 |
| 747 | Johnny Ray | .07 | .05 |
| 748 | Mike Flanagan | .07 | .05 |
| 749 | Ozzie Smith | .35 | .25 |
| 750 | Steve Trout | .07 | .05 |
| 751 | Garth Iorg | .05 | .04 |
| 752 | Dan Petry | .07 | .05 |
| 753 | Rick Honeycutt | .05 | .04 |
| 754 | Dave LaPoint | .07 | .05 |
| 755 | Luis Aguayo | .05 | .04 |
| 756 | Carlton Fisk | .25 | .20 |
| 757 | Nolan Ryan | 1.25 | .90 |
| 758 | Tony Bernazard | .05 | .04 |
| 759 | Joel Youngblood | .05 | .04 |
| 760 | Mike Witt | .07 | .05 |
| 761 | Greg Pryor | .05 | .04 |
| 762 | Gary Ward | .07 | .05 |
| 763 | Tim Flannery | .05 | .04 |
| 764 | Bill Buckner | .07 | .05 |
| 765 | Kirk Gibson | .20 | .15 |
| 766 | Don Aase | .05 | .04 |
| 767 | Ron Cey | .07 | .05 |
| 768 | Dennis Lamp | .05 | .04 |
| 769 | Steve Sax | .15 | .11 |
| 770 | Dave Winfield | .25 | .20 |
| 771 | Shane Rawley | .07 | .05 |
| 772 | Harold Baines | .12 | .09 |
| 773 | Robin Yount | .35 | .25 |
| 774 | Wayne Krenchicki | .05 | .04 |
| 775 | Joaquin Andujar | .07 | .05 |
| 776 | Tom Brunansky | .10 | .08 |
| 777 | Chris Chambliss | .07 | .05 |
| 778 | Jack Morris | .20 | .15 |
| 779 | Craig Reynolds | .05 | .04 |
| 780 | Andre Thornton | .07 | .05 |
| 781 | Atlee Hammaker | .05 | .04 |
| 782 | Brian Downing | .07 | .05 |
| 783 | Willie Wilson | .10 | .08 |
| 784 | Cal Ripken | 1.25 | .90 |
| 785 | Terry Francona | .05 | .04 |
| 786 | Jimy Williams | .05 | .04 |
| 787 | Alejandro Pena | .07 | .05 |
| 788 | Tim Stoddard | .05 | .04 |
| 789 | Dan Schatzeder | .05 | .04 |
| 790 | Julio Cruz | .05 | .04 |
| 791 | Lance Parrish | .15 | .11 |
| 792 | Checklist 661-792 | .05 | .04 |

## 1987 Topps Traded

The Topps Traded set consists of 132 cards as have all Traded sets issued by Topps since 1981. The cards measure the standard 2 1/2" by 3 1/2" and are identical in design to the regular edition set. The purpose of the set is to update player trades and feature rookies not included in the regular

issue. As they had done the previous three years, Topps produced a glossy-coated "Tiffany" edition of the Traded set. The Tiffany edition cards are valued at two to three times greater than the regular Traded cards.

|  | MT | NR MT |
|---|---|---|
| Complete Set: | 10.00 | 7.50 |
| Common Player: | .06 | .05 |
| | | |
| 1T Bill Almon | .06 | .05 |
| 2T Scott Bankhead | .08 | .06 |
| 3T Eric Bell(FC) | .15 | .11 |
| 4T Juan Beniquez | .06 | .05 |
| 5T Juan Berenguer | .06 | .05 |
| 6T Greg Booker | .06 | .05 |
| 7T Thad Bosley | .06 | .05 |
| 8T Larry Bowa | .10 | .08 |
| 9T Greg Brock | .10 | .08 |
| 10T Bob Brower(FC) | .15 | .11 |
| 11T Jerry Browne(FC) | .30 | .25 |
| 12T Ralph Bryant(FC) | .12 | .09 |
| 13T DeWayne Buice(FC) | .15 | .11 |
| 14T Ellis Burks(FC) | .60 | .45 |
| 15T Ivan Calderon | .25 | .20 |
| 16T Jeff Calhoun | .06 | .05 |
| 17T Casey Candaele(FC) | .10 | .08 |
| 18T John Cangelosi | .06 | .05 |
| 19T Steve Carlton | .30 | .25 |
| 20T Juan Castillo(FC) | .06 | .05 |
| 21T Rick Cerone | .06 | .05 |
| 22T Ron Cey | .10 | .08 |
| 23T John Christensen | .06 | .05 |
| 24T Dave Cone(FC) | 2.00 | 1.50 |
| 25T Chuck Crim(FC) | .15 | .11 |
| 26T Storm Davis | .06 | .05 |
| 27T Andre Dawson | .40 | .30 |
| 28T Rick Dempsey | .08 | .06 |
| 29T Doug Drabek | .40 | .30 |
| 30T Mike Dunne | .30 | .25 |
| 31T Dennis Eckersley | .30 | .25 |
| 32T Lee Elia | .06 | .05 |
| 33T Brian Fisher | .10 | .08 |
| 34T Terry Francona | .06 | .05 |
| 35T Willie Fraser(FC) | .15 | .11 |
| 36T Billy Gardner | .06 | .05 |
| 37T Ken Gerhart(FC) | .15 | .11 |
| 38T Danny Gladden | .06 | .05 |
| 39T Jim Gott | .06 | .05 |
| 40T Cecilio Guante | .06 | .05 |
| 41T Albert Hall | .06 | .05 |

|  | MT | NR MT |
|---|---|---|
| 42T Terry Harper | .06 | .05 |
| 43T Mickey Hatcher | .06 | .05 |
| 44T Brad Havens | .06 | .05 |
| 45T Neal Heaton | .06 | .05 |
| 46T Mike Henneman(FC) | .30 | .25 |
| 47T Donnie Hill | .06 | .05 |
| 48T Guy Hoffman | .06 | .05 |
| 49T Brian Holton(FC) | .15 | .11 |
| 50T Charles Hudson | .06 | .05 |
| 51T Danny Jackson(FC) | .30 | .25 |
| 52T Reggie Jackson | .50 | .40 |
| 53T Chris James(FC) | .40 | .30 |
| 54T Dion Leary | .10 | .08 |
| 55T Stan Jefferson(FC) | .20 | .15 |
| 56T Joe Johnson(FC) | .08 | .06 |
| 57T Terry Kennedy | .08 | .06 |
| 58T Mike Kingery | .08 | .06 |
| 59T Ray Knight | .10 | .08 |
| 60T Gene Larkin(FC) | .30 | .25 |
| 61T Mike LaValliere | .10 | .08 |
| 62T Jack Lazorko | .06 | .05 |
| 63T Terry Leach | .06 | .05 |
| 64T Tim Leary | .06 | .05 |
| 65T Jim Lindeman(FC) | .15 | .11 |
| 66T Steve Lombardozzi(FC) | .06 | .05 |
| 67T Bill Long(FC) | .20 | .15 |
| 68T Barry Lyons(FC) | .15 | .11 |
| 69T Shane Mack | .40 | .30 |
| 70T Greg Maddux(FC) | 3.00 | 2.25 |
| 71T Bill Madlock | .15 | .11 |
| 72T Joe Magrane(FC) | .50 | .40 |
| 73T Dave Martinez(FC) | .25 | .20 |
| 74T Fred McGriff(FC) | 3.00 | 2.25 |
| 75T Mark McLemore(FC) | .10 | .08 |
| 76T Kevin McReynolds(FC) | .40 | .30 |
| 77T Dave Meads(FC) | .15 | .11 |
| 78T Eddie Milner | .06 | .05 |
| 79T Greg Minton | .06 | .05 |
| 80T John Mitchell(FC) | .15 | .11 |
| 81T Kevin Mitchell | .40 | .30 |
| 82T Charlie Moore | .06 | .05 |
| 83T Jeff Musselman(FC) | .12 | .09 |
| 84T Gene Nelson | .06 | .05 |
| 85T Graig Nettles | .12 | .09 |
| 86T Al Newman | .06 | .05 |
| 87T Reid Nichols | .06 | .05 |
| 88T Tom Niedenfuer | .08 | .06 |
| 89T Joe Niekro | .10 | .08 |
| 90T Tom Nieto | .06 | .05 |
| 91T Matt Nokes(FC) | .40 | .30 |
| 92T Dickie Noles | .06 | .05 |
| 93T Pat Pacillo | .15 | .11 |
| 94T Lance Parrish | .20 | .15 |
| 95T Tony Pena | .10 | .08 |
| 96T Luis Polonia(FC) | .40 | .30 |
| 97T Randy Ready | .06 | .05 |
| 98T Jeff Reardon | .12 | .09 |
| 99T Gary Redus | .08 | .06 |
| 100T Jeff Reed | .06 | .05 |
| 101T Rick Rhoden | .10 | .08 |
| 102T Cal Ripken, Sr. | .06 | .05 |
| 103T Wally Ritchie(FC) | .15 | .11 |
| 104T Jeff Robinson(FC) | .40 | .30 |
| 105T Gary Roenicke | .06 | .05 |

| | | MT | NR MT |
|---|---|---|---|
| 106T | Jerry Royster | .06 | .05 |
| 107T | Mark Salas | .06 | .05 |
| 108T | Luis Salazar | .06 | .05 |
| 109T | Benny Santiago(FC) | .50 | .40 |
| 110T | Dave Schmidt | .08 | .06 |
| 111T | Kevin Seitzer(FC) | .50 | .40 |
| 112T | John Shelby | .06 | .05 |
| 113T | Steve Shields(FC) | .08 | .06 |
| 114T | John Smiley(FC) | .60 | .45 |
| 115T | Chris Speier | .06 | .05 |
| 116T | Mike Stanley(FC) | .20 | .15 |
| 117T | Terry Steinbach(FC) | .40 | .30 |
| 118T | Les Straker(FC) | .20 | .15 |
| 119T | Jim Sundberg | .08 | .06 |
| 120T | Danny Tartabull | .35 | .25 |
| 121T | Tom Trebelhorn | .08 | .06 |
| 122T | Dave Valle(FC) | .12 | .09 |
| 123T | Ed Vande Berg | .06 | .05 |
| 124T | Andy Van Slyke | .20 | .15 |
| 125T | Gary Ward | .06 | .05 |
| 126T | Alan Wiggins | .06 | .05 |
| 127T | Bill Wilkinson(FC) | .15 | .11 |
| 128T | Frank Williams | .08 | .06 |
| 129T | Matt Williams(FC) | 1.50 | 1.25 |
| 130T | Jim Winn | .06 | .05 |
| 131T | Matt Young | .06 | .05 |
| 132T | Checklist 1T-132T | .06 | .05 |

# 1988 Topps

The 1988 Topps set features a clean, attractive design that should prove to be very popular with collectors for many years to come. The full-color player photo is surrounded by a thin yellow frame which is encompassed by a white border. The player's name appears in the lower right corner in a colored band which appears to wrap around the player photo. The player's team nickname is located in large letters at the top of the card. The Topps logo is placed in the lower left corner of the card. The card backs feature black print on orange and gray stock and includes the usual player personal and career statistics. Many of the cards contain a new feature

entitled "This Way To The Club-house", which explains how the player joined his current team, be it by trade, free agency, etc. The 792-card set includes a number of special subsets including "Future Stars", "Turn Back The Clock", All-Star teams, All-Star rookie selections, and Record Breakers. All cards measure 2-1/2" by 3-1/2". For the fifth consecutive year, Topps issued a glossy "Tiffany" edition of its 792-card regular-issue set. The Tiffany cards have a value of 3-4 times greater than the same card in the regular issue. The Tiffany edition could be purchased by collectors directly from Topps for $99. The company placed ads for the Tiffany set in publications such as USA Today and The Sporting News.

| | | MT | NR MT |
|---|---|---|---|
| Complete Set: | | 18.00 | 13.50 |
| Common Player: | | .04 | .03 |
| 1 | '87 Record Breakers (Vince Coleman) | .08 | .06 |
| 2 | '87 Record Breakers (Don Mattingly) | .40 | .30 |
| 3a | '87 Record Breakers (Mark McGwire) (white triangle by left foot) | .40 | .30 |
| 3b | '87 Record Breakers (Mark McGwire) (no triangle by left foot) | .25 | .20 |
| 4a | '87 Record Breakers (Eddie Murray) (no mention of record on front) | .10 | .08 |
| 4b | '87 Record Breakers (Eddie Murray) (record stated on card front) | .60 | .45 |
| 5 | '87 Record Breakers (Joe Niekro, Phil Niekro) | .10 | .08 |
| 6 | '87 Record Breakers (Nolan Ryan) | .10 | .08 |
| 7 | '87 Record Breakers (Benito Santiago) | .15 | .11 |
| 8 | Kevin Elster(FC) | .25 | .20 |
| 9 | Andy Hawkins | .04 | .03 |
| 10 | Ryne Sandberg | .35 | .25 |
| 11 | Mike Young | .04 | .03 |
| 12 | Bill Schroeder | .04 | .03 |
| 13 | Andres Thomas | .06 | .05 |
| 14 | Sparky Anderson | .06 | .05 |
| 15 | Chili Davis | .06 | .05 |
| 16 | Kirk McCaskill | .06 | .05 |
| 17 | Ron Oester | .04 | .03 |
| 18a | Al Leiter (no "NY" on shirt, photo actually Steve George)(FC) | .40 | .30 |

| | | MT | NR MT |
|---|---|---|---|
| 18b | Al Leiter ("NY" on shirt, correct photo)(FC) | .20 | .15 |
| 19 | Mark Davidson(FC) | | |
| | | .12 | .09 |
| 20 | Kevin Gross | .06 | .05 |
| 21 | Red Sox Leaders (Wade Boggs, Spike Owen) | .15 | .11 |
| 22 | Greg Swindell | .15 | .11 |
| 23 | Ken Landreaux | .04 | .03 |
| 24 | Jim Deshaies | .06 | .05 |
| 25 | Andres Galarraga | .12 | .09 |
| 26 | Mitch Williams | .06 | .05 |
| 27 | R.J. Reynolds | .04 | .03 |
| 28 | Jose Nunez(FC) | .10 | .08 |
| 29 | Argenis Salazar | .04 | .03 |
| 30 | Sid Fernandez | .08 | .06 |
| 31 | Bruce Bochy | .04 | .03 |
| 32 | Mike Morgan | .04 | .03 |
| 33 | Rob Deer | .06 | .05 |
| 34 | Ricky Horton | .06 | .05 |
| 35 | Harold Baines | .10 | .08 |
| 36 | Jamie Moyer | .06 | .05 |
| 37 | Ed Romero | .04 | .03 |
| 38 | Jeff Calhoun | .04 | .03 |
| 39 | Gerald Perry | .08 | .06 |
| 40 | Orel Hershiser | .20 | .15 |
| 41 | Bob Melvin | .04 | .03 |
| 42 | Bill Landrum(FC) | | |
| | | .10 | .08 |
| 43 | Dick Schofield | .04 | .03 |
| 44 | Lou Piniella | .06 | .05 |
| 45 | Kent Hrbek | .12 | .09 |
| 46 | Darnell Coles | .06 | .05 |
| 47 | Joaquin Andujar | .06 | .05 |
| 48 | Alan Ashby | .04 | .03 |
| 49 | Dave Clark(FC) | .10 | .08 |
| 50 | Hubie Brooks | .08 | .06 |
| 51 | Orioles Leaders (Eddie Murray, Cal Ripken) | .12 | .09 |
| 52 | Don Robinson | .06 | .05 |
| 53 | Curt Wilkerson | .04 | .03 |
| 54 | Jim Clancy | .06 | .05 |
| 55 | Phil Bradley | .08 | .06 |
| 56 | Ed Hearn | .04 | .03 |
| 57 | Tim Crews(FC) | .15 | .11 |
| 58 | Dave Magadan | .10 | .08 |
| 59 | Danny Cox | .06 | .05 |
| 60 | Rickey Henderson | .35 | .25 |
| 61 | Mark Knudson(FC) | | |
| | | .10 | .08 |
| 62 | Jeff Hamilton | .08 | .06 |
| 63 | Jimmy Jones(FC) | .10 | .08 |
| 64 | Ken Caminiti(FC) | | |
| | | .30 | .25 |
| 65 | Leon Durham | .06 | .05 |
| 66 | Shane Rawley | .06 | .05 |
| 67 | Ken Oberkfell | .04 | .03 |
| 68 | Dave Dravecky | .06 | .05 |
| 69 | Mike Hart(FC) | .10 | .08 |
| 70 | Roger Clemens | .50 | .40 |
| 71 | Gary Pettis | .04 | .03 |
| 72 | Dennis Eckersley | .10 | .08 |
| 73 | Randy Bush | .04 | .03 |
| 74 | Tom Lasorda | .06 | .05 |
| 75 | Joe Carter | .10 | .08 |
| 76 | Denny Martinez | .04 | .03 |
| 77 | Tom O'Malley | .04 | .03 |

| | | MT | NR MT |
|---|---|---|---|
| 78 | Dan Petry | .06 | .05 |
| 79 | Ernie Whitt | .06 | .05 |
| 80 | Mark Langston | .10 | .08 |
| 81 | Reds Leaders (John Franco, Ron Robinson) | .06 | .05 |
| 82 | Darrel Akerfelds(FC) | | |
| | | .12 | .09 |
| 83 | Jose Oquendo | .04 | .03 |
| 84 | Cecilio Guante | .04 | .03 |
| 85 | Howard Johnson | .08 | .06 |
| 86 | Ron Karkovice | .04 | .03 |
| 87 | Mike Mason | .04 | .03 |
| 88 | Earnie Riles | .04 | .03 |
| 89 | Gary Thurman(FC) | | |
| | | .20 | .15 |
| 90 | Dale Murphy | .30 | .25 |
| 91 | Joey Cora(FC) | .12 | .09 |
| 92 | Len Matuszek | .04 | .03 |
| 93 | Bob Sebra | .04 | .03 |
| 94 | Chuck Jackson(FC) | | |
| | | .15 | .11 |
| 95 | Lance Parrish | .12 | .09 |
| 96 | Todd Benzinger(FC) | | |
| | | .25 | .20 |
| 97 | Scott Garrelts | .04 | .03 |
| 98 | Rene Gonzales(FC) | | |
| | | .15 | .11 |
| 99 | Chuck Finley | .06 | .05 |
| 100 | Jack Clark | .12 | .09 |
| 101 | Allan Anderson | .06 | .05 |
| 102 | Barry Larkin | .35 | .25 |
| 103 | Curt Young | .06 | .05 |
| 104 | Dick Williams | .04 | .03 |
| 105 | Jesse Orosco | .06 | .05 |
| 106 | Jim Walewander(FC) | | |
| | | .12 | .09 |
| 107 | Scott Bailes | .06 | .05 |
| 108 | Steve Lyons | .04 | .03 |
| 109 | Joel Skinner | .04 | .03 |
| 110 | Teddy Higuera | .08 | .06 |
| 111 | Expos Leaders (Hubie Brooks, Vance Law) | .06 | .05 |
| 112 | Les Lancaster(FC) | | |
| | | .15 | .11 |
| 113 | Kelly Gruber | .04 | .03 |
| 114 | Jeff Russell | .04 | .03 |
| 115 | Johnny Ray | .06 | .05 |
| 116 | Jerry Don Gleaton | .04 | .03 |
| 117 | James Steels(FC) | | |
| | | .10 | .08 |
| 118 | Bob Welch | .08 | .06 |
| 119 | Robbie Wine(FC) | .12 | .09 |
| 120 | Kirby Puckett | .40 | .30 |
| 121 | Checklist 1-132 | .04 | .03 |
| 122 | Tony Bernazard | .04 | .03 |
| 123 | Tom Candiotti | .04 | .03 |
| 124 | Ray Knight | .06 | .05 |
| 125 | Bruce Hurst | .08 | .06 |
| 126 | Steve Jeltz | .04 | .03 |
| 127 | Jim Gott | .04 | .03 |
| 128 | Johnny Grubb | .04 | .03 |
| 129 | Greg Minton | .04 | .03 |
| 130 | Buddy Bell | .08 | .06 |
| 131 | Don Schulze | .04 | .03 |
| 132 | Donnie Hill | .04 | .03 |
| 133 | Greg Mathews | .06 | .05 |
| 134 | Chuck Tanner | .04 | .03 |

| | | MT | NR MT |
|---|---|---|---|
| 135 | Dennis Rasmussen | .08 | .06 |
| 136 | Brian Dayett | .04 | .03 |
| 137 | Chris Bosio | .06 | .05 |
| 138 | Mitch Webster | .06 | .05 |
| 139 | Jerry Browne | .06 | .05 |
| 140 | Jesse Barfield | .10 | .08 |
| 141 | Royals Leaders (George Brett, Bret Saberhagen) | | |
| | | .12 | .09 |
| 142 | Andy Van Slyke | .10 | .08 |
| 143 | Mickey Tettleton | .04 | .03 |
| 144 | *Don Gordon*(FC) | .08 | .06 |
| 145 | Bill Madlock | .08 | .06 |
| 146 | *Donell Nixon*(FC) | | |
| | | .15 | .11 |
| 147 | Bill Buckner | .08 | .06 |
| 148 | Carmelo Martinez | .06 | .05 |
| 149 | Ken Howell | .04 | .03 |
| 150 | Eric Davis | .40 | .30 |
| 151 | Bob Knepper | .06 | .05 |
| 152 | *Jody Reed*(FC) | .35 | .25 |
| 153 | John Habyan | .04 | .03 |
| 154 | Jeff Stone | .04 | .03 |
| 155 | Bruce Sutter | .10 | .08 |
| 156 | Gary Matthews | .06 | .05 |
| 157 | Atlee Hammaker | .04 | .03 |
| 158 | Tim Hulett | .04 | .03 |
| 159 | *Brad Arnsberg*(FC) | | |
| | | .12 | .09 |
| 160 | Willie McGee | .10 | .08 |
| 161 | Bryn Smith | .06 | .05 |
| 162 | Mark McLemore | .06 | .05 |
| 163 | Dale Mohorcic | .04 | .03 |
| 164 | Dave Johnson | .06 | .05 |
| 165 | Robin Yount | .20 | .15 |
| 166 | *Rick Rodriguez*(FC) | | |
| | | .10 | .08 |
| 167 | Rance Mulliniks | .04 | .03 |
| 168 | Barry Jones | .04 | .03 |
| 169 | *Ross Jones*(FC) | .12 | .09 |
| 170 | Rich Gossage | .12 | .09 |
| 171 | Cubs Leaders (Shawon Dunston, Manny Trillo) | .06 | .05 |
| 172 | *Lloyd McClendon*(FC) | .10 | .08 |
| 173 | Eric Plunk | .04 | .03 |
| 174 | Phil Garner | .04 | .03 |
| 175 | Kevin Bass | .06 | .05 |
| 176 | Jeff Reed | .04 | .03 |
| 177 | Frank Tanana | .06 | .05 |
| 178 | Dwayne Henry(FC) | .06 | .05 |
| 179 | Charlie Puleo | .04 | .03 |
| 180 | Terry Kennedy | .06 | .05 |
| 181 | Dave Cone | .50 | .40 |
| 182 | Ken Phelps | .06 | .05 |
| 183 | Tom Lawless | .04 | .03 |
| 184 | Ivan Calderon | .08 | .06 |
| 185 | Rick Rhoden | .06 | .05 |
| 186 | Rafael Palmeiro | .35 | .25 |
| 187 | Steve Kiefer(FC) | .06 | .05 |
| 188 | John Russell | .04 | .03 |
| 189 | *Wes Gardner*(FC) | | |
| | | .20 | .15 |
| 190 | Candy Maldonado | .06 | .05 |
| 191 | John Cerutti | .06 | .05 |
| 192 | Devon White | .20 | .15 |
| 193 | Brian Fisher | .06 | .05 |

| | | MT | NR MT |
|---|---|---|---|
| 194 | Tom Kelly | .04 | .03 |
| 195 | Dan Quisenberry | .06 | .05 |
| 196 | Dave Engle | .04 | .03 |
| 197 | Lance McCullers | .06 | .05 |
| 198 | Franklin Stubbs | .06 | .05 |
| 199 | *Dave Meads* | .12 | .09 |
| 200 | Wade Boggs | .30 | .25 |
| 201 | Rangers Leaders (Steve Buechele, Pete Incaviglia, Pete O'Brien, Bobby Valentine) | .06 | .05 |
| 202 | Glenn Hoffman | .04 | .03 |
| 203 | Fred Toliver | .04 | .03 |
| 204 | Paul O'Neill(FC) | .12 | .09 |
| 205 | *Nelson Liriano*(FC) | | |
| | | .12 | .09 |
| 206 | Domingo Ramos | .04 | .03 |
| 207 | John Mitchell, John Mitchell(FC) | .20 | .15 |
| 208 | Steve Lake | .04 | .03 |
| 209 | Richard Dotson | .06 | .05 |
| 210 | Willie Randolph | .06 | .05 |
| 211 | Frank DiPino | .04 | .03 |
| 212 | Greg Brock | .06 | .05 |
| 213 | Albert Hall | .04 | .03 |
| 214 | Dave Schmidt | .04 | .03 |
| 215 | Von Hayes | .06 | .05 |
| 216 | Jerry Reuss | .06 | .05 |
| 217 | Harry Spilman | .04 | .03 |
| 218 | Dan Schatzeder | .04 | .03 |
| 219 | Mike Stanley | .08 | .06 |
| 220 | Tom Henke | .06 | .05 |
| 221 | Rafael Belliard | .04 | .03 |
| 222 | Steve Farr | .04 | .03 |
| 223 | Stan Jefferson | .08 | .06 |
| 224 | Tom Trebelhorn | .04 | .03 |
| 225 | Mike Scioscia | .06 | .05 |
| 226 | Dave Lopes | .06 | .05 |
| 227 | Ed Correa | .04 | .03 |
| 228 | Wallace Johnson | .04 | .03 |
| 229 | Jeff Musselman | .08 | .06 |
| 230 | Pat Tabler | .06 | .05 |
| 231 | Pirates Leaders (Barry Bonds, Bobby Bonilla) | .10 | .08 |
| 232 | Bob James | .04 | .03 |
| 233 | Rafael Santana | .04 | .03 |
| 234 | Ken Dayley | .04 | .03 |
| 235 | Gary Ward | .06 | .05 |
| 236 | Ted Power | .04 | .03 |
| 237 | Mike Heath | .04 | .03 |
| 238 | *Luis Polonia* | .30 | .25 |
| 239 | Roy Smalley | .04 | .03 |
| 240 | Lee Smith | .08 | .06 |
| 241 | Damaso Garcia | .04 | .03 |
| 242 | Tom Niedenfuer | .06 | .05 |
| 243 | Mark Ryal(FC) | .04 | .03 |
| 244 | Jeff Robinson | .04 | .03 |
| 245 | Rich Gedman | .06 | .05 |
| 246 | *Mike Campbell*(FC) | | |
| | | .10 | .08 |
| 247 | Thad Bosley | .04 | .03 |
| 248 | Storm Davis | .08 | .06 |
| 249 | Mike Marshall | .10 | .08 |
| 250 | Nolan Ryan | .60 | .45 |
| 251 | Tom Foley | .04 | .03 |
| 252 | Bob Brower | .06 | .05 |
| 253 | Checklist 133-264 | .04 | .03 |

| | | MT | NR MT |
|---|---|---|---|
| 254 | Lee Elia | .04 | .03 |
| 255 | Mookie Wilson | .06 | .05 |
| 256 | Ken Schrom | .04 | .03 |
| 257 | Jerry Royster | .04 | .03 |
| 258 | Ed Nunez | .04 | .03 |
| 259 | Ron Kittle | .06 | .05 |
| 260 | Vince Coleman | .15 | .11 |
| 261 | Giants Leaders (Will Clark, Candy Maldonado, Kevin Mitchell, Robby Thompson, Jose Uribe) | .10 | .08 |
| 262 | Drew Hall(FC) | .12 | .09 |
| 263 | Glenn Braggs | .08 | .06 |
| 264 | *Les Straker* | .15 | .11 |
| 265 | Bo Diaz | .06 | .05 |
| 266 | Paul Assenmacher | .04 | .03 |
| 267 | *Billy Bean*(FC) | .10 | .08 |
| 268 | Bruce Ruffin | .06 | .05 |
| 269 | *Ellis Burks* | .60 | .45 |
| 270 | Mike Witt | .06 | .05 |
| 271 | Ken Gerhart | .06 | .05 |
| 272 | Steve Ontiveros | .04 | .03 |
| 273 | Garth Iorg | .04 | .03 |
| 274 | Junior Ortiz | .04 | .03 |
| 275 | Kevin Seitzer | .15 | .11 |
| 276 | Luis Salazar | .04 | .03 |
| 277 | Alejandro Pena | .06 | .05 |
| 278 | Jose Cruz | .06 | .05 |
| 279 | Randy St. Claire | .04 | .03 |
| 280 | Pete Incaviglia | .12 | .09 |
| 281 | Jerry Hairston | .04 | .03 |
| 282 | Pat Perry | .04 | .03 |
| 283 | Phil Lombardi(FC) | .06 | .05 |
| 284 | Larry Bowa | .06 | .05 |
| 285 | Jim Presley | .08 | .06 |
| 286 | *Chuck Crim* | .12 | .09 |
| 287 | Manny Trillo | .06 | .05 |
| 288 | *Pat Pacillo* | .15 | .11 |
| 289 | Dave Bergman | .04 | .03 |
| 290 | Tony Fernandez | .10 | .08 |
| 291 | Astros Leaders (Kevin Bass, Billy Hatcher) | .06 | .05 |
| 292 | Carney Lansford | .08 | .06 |
| 293 | *Doug Jones*(FC) | .25 | .20 |
| 294 | *Al Pedrique*(FC) | .12 | .09 |
| 295 | Bert Blyleven | .10 | .08 |
| 296 | Floyd Rayford | .04 | .03 |
| 297 | Zane Smith | .06 | .05 |
| 298 | Milt Thompson | .04 | .03 |
| 299 | Steve Crawford | .04 | .03 |
| 300 | Don Mattingly | .30 | .25 |
| 301 | Bud Black | .04 | .03 |
| 302 | Jose Uribe | .04 | .03 |
| 303 | Eric Show | .06 | .05 |
| 304 | George Hendrick | .06 | .05 |
| 305 | Steve Sax | .12 | .09 |
| 306 | Billy Hatcher | .06 | .05 |
| 307 | Mike Trujillo | .04 | .03 |
| 308 | Lee Mazzilli | .06 | .05 |
| 309 | *Bill Long* | .15 | .11 |
| 310 | Tom Herr | .06 | .05 |
| 311 | Scott Sanderson | .04 | .03 |
| 312 | Joey Meyer(FC) | .20 | .15 |
| 313 | Bob McClure | .04 | .03 |
| 314 | Jimy Williams | .04 | .03 |
| 315 | Dave Parker | .12 | .09 |
| 316 | Jose Rijo | .06 | .05 |

| | | MT | NR MT |
|---|---|---|---|
| 317 | Tom Nieto | .04 | .03 |
| 318 | Mel Hall | .06 | .05 |
| 319 | Mike Loynd | .04 | .03 |
| 320 | Alan Trammell | .15 | .11 |
| 321 | White Sox Leaders (Harold Baines, Carlton Fisk) | .08 | .06 |
| 322 | *Vicente Palacios*(FC) | .15 | .11 |
| 323 | Rick Leach | .04 | .03 |
| 324 | Danny Jackson | .20 | .15 |
| 325 | Glenn Hubbard | .04 | .03 |
| 326 | Al Nipper | .04 | .03 |
| 327 | Larry Sheets | .06 | .05 |
| 328 | *Greg Cadaret*(FC) | .15 | .11 |
| 329 | Chris Speier | .04 | .03 |
| 330 | Eddie Whitson | .04 | .03 |
| 331 | Brian Downing | .06 | .05 |
| 332 | Jerry Reed | .04 | .03 |
| 333 | Wally Backman | .06 | .05 |
| 334 | Dave LaPoint | .06 | .05 |
| 335 | Claudell Washington | .06 | .05 |
| 336 | Ed Lynch | .04 | .03 |
| 337 | Jim Gantner | .04 | .03 |
| 338 | Brian Holton | .08 | .06 |
| 339 | Kurt Stillwell | .08 | .06 |
| 340 | Jack Morris | .15 | .11 |
| 341 | Carmen Castillo | .04 | .03 |
| 342 | Larry Andersen | .04 | .03 |
| 343 | Greg Gagne | .04 | .03 |
| 344 | Tony LaRussa | .04 | .03 |
| 345 | Scott Fletcher | .06 | .05 |
| 346 | Vance Law | .06 | .05 |
| 347 | Joe Johnson | .04 | .03 |
| 348 | Jim Eisenreich | .04 | .03 |
| 349 | Bob Walk | .04 | .03 |
| 350 | Will Clark | .80 | .60 |
| 351 | Cardinals Leaders (Tony Pena, Red Schoendienst) | .06 | .05 |
| 352 | *Billy Ripken*(FC) | .20 | .15 |
| 353 | Ed Olwine | .04 | .03 |
| 354 | Marc Sullivan | .04 | .03 |
| 355 | Roger McDowell | .08 | .06 |
| 356 | Luis Aguayo | .04 | .03 |
| 357 | Floyd Bannister | .06 | .05 |
| 358 | Rey Quinones | .04 | .03 |
| 359 | Tim Stoddard | .04 | .03 |
| 360 | Tony Gwynn | .25 | .20 |
| 361 | Greg Maddux | .35 | .25 |
| 362 | Juan Castillo | .04 | .03 |
| 363 | Willie Fraser | .06 | .05 |
| 364 | Nick Esasky | .06 | .05 |
| 365 | Floyd Youmans | .04 | .03 |
| 366 | Chet Lemon | .06 | .05 |
| 367 | Tim Leary | .06 | .05 |
| 368 | *Gerald Young*(FC) | .15 | .11 |
| 369 | Greg Harris | .04 | .03 |
| 370 | Jose Canseco | .80 | .60 |
| 371 | Joe Hesketh | .04 | .03 |
| 372 | *Matt Williams* | 1.00 | .70 |
| 373 | Checklist 265-396 | .04 | .03 |
| 374 | Doc Edwards | .04 | .03 |
| 375 | Tom Brunansky | .08 | .06 |
| 376 | *Bill Wilkinson* | .12 | .09 |

| | MT | NR MT |
|---|---|---|
| 377 *Sam Horn*(FC) | .20 | .15 |
| 378 *Todd Frohwirth*(FC) | | |
| | .15 | .11 |
| 379 Rafael Ramirez | .04 | .03 |
| 380 *Joe Magrane* | .30 | .25 |
| 381 Angels Leaders (Jack Howell, Wally Joyner) | .12 | .09 |
| 382 *Keith Miller*(FC) | .15 | .11 |
| 383 Eric Bell | .06 | .05 |
| 384 Neil Allen | .04 | .03 |
| 385 Carlton Fisk | .30 | .25 |
| 386 Don Mattingly AS | .40 | .30 |
| 387 Willie Randolph AS | .06 | .05 |
| 388 Wade Boggs AS | .35 | .25 |
| 389 Alan Trammell AS | .08 | .06 |
| 390 George Bell AS | .10 | .08 |
| 391 Kirby Puckett AS | .12 | .09 |
| 392 Dave Winfield AS | .12 | .09 |
| 393 Matt Nokes AS | .15 | .11 |
| 394 Roger Clemens AS | .15 | .11 |
| 395 Jimmy Key AS | .06 | .05 |
| 396 Tom Henke AS | .06 | .05 |
| 397 Jack Clark AS | .06 | .05 |
| 398 Juan Samuel AS | .06 | .05 |
| 399 Tim Wallach AS | .06 | .05 |
| 400 Ozzie Smith AS | .08 | .06 |
| 401 Andre Dawson AS | .10 | .08 |
| 402 Tony Gwynn AS | .15 | .11 |
| 403 Tim Raines AS | .12 | .09 |
| 404 Benny Santiago AS | .10 | .08 |
| 405 Dwight Gooden AS | .15 | .11 |
| 406 Shane Rawley AS | .06 | .05 |
| 407 Steve Bedrosian AS | .08 | .06 |
| 408 Dion James | .06 | .05 |
| 409 Joel McKeon(FC) | .04 | .03 |
| 410 Tony Pena | .06 | .05 |
| 411 Wayne Tolleson | .04 | .03 |
| 412 Randy Myers | .10 | .08 |
| 413 John Christensen | .04 | .03 |
| 414 John McNamara | .04 | .03 |
| 415 Don Carman | .06 | .05 |
| 416 Keith Moreland | .06 | .05 |
| 417 *Mark Ciardi*(FC) | .10 | .08 |
| 418 Joel Youngblood | .04 | .03 |
| 419 Scott McGregor | .06 | .05 |
| 420 Wally Joyner | .25 | .20 |
| 421 Ed Vande Berg | .04 | .03 |
| 422 Dave Concepcion | .06 | .05 |
| 423 *John Smiley* | .50 | .40 |
| 424 Dwayne Murphy | .06 | .05 |
| 425 Jeff Reardon | .08 | .06 |
| 426 Randy Ready | .04 | .03 |
| 427 *Paul Kilgus*(FC) | .20 | .15 |
| 428 John Shelby | .04 | .03 |
| 429 Tigers Leaders (Kirk Gibson, Alan Trammell) | .08 | .06 |
| 430 Glenn Davis | .12 | .09 |
| 431 Casey Candaele | .04 | .03 |
| 432 Mike Moore | .04 | .03 |
| 433 *Bill Pecota*(FC) | .15 | .11 |
| 434 Rick Aguilera | .04 | .03 |
| 435 Mike Pagliarulo | .08 | .06 |
| 436 Mike Bielecki | .04 | .03 |
| 437 *Fred Manrique*(FC) | | |
| | .12 | .09 |
| 438 *Rob Ducey*(FC) | .12 | .09 |
| 439 Dave Martinez | .08 | .06 |

| | MT | NR MT |
|---|---|---|
| 440 Steve Bedrosian | .10 | .08 |
| 441 Rick Manning | .04 | .03 |
| 442 *Tom Bolton*(FC) | .15 | .11 |
| 443 Ken Griffey | .06 | .05 |
| 444 Cal Ripken, Sr. | .04 | .03 |
| 445 Mike Krukow | .06 | .05 |
| 446 Doug DeCinces | .06 | .05 |
| 447 *Jeff Montgomery*(FC) | .30 | .25 |
| 448 Mike Davis | .06 | .05 |
| 449 *Jeff Robinson* | .15 | .11 |
| 450 Barry Bonds | .40 | .30 |
| 451 Keith Atherton | .04 | .03 |
| 452 Willie Wilson | .08 | .06 |
| 453 Dennis Powell | .04 | .03 |
| 454 Marvell Wynne | .04 | .03 |
| 455 *Shawn Hillegas*(FC) | | |
| | .15 | .11 |
| 456 Dave Anderson | .04 | .03 |
| 457 Terry Leach | .04 | .03 |
| 458 Ron Hassey | .04 | .03 |
| 459 Yankees Leaders (Willie Randolph, Dave Winfield) | | |
| | .08 | .06 |
| 460 Ozzie Smith | .12 | .09 |
| 461 Danny Darwin | .04 | .03 |
| 462 Don Slaught | .04 | .03 |
| 463 *Fred McGriff* | .80 | .60 |
| 464 Jay Tibbs | .04 | .03 |
| 465 Paul Molitor | .10 | .08 |
| 466 Jerry Mumphrey | .04 | .03 |
| 467 Don Aase | .04 | .03 |
| 468 Darren Daulton | .04 | .03 |
| 469 Jeff Dedmon | .04 | .03 |
| 470 Dwight Evans | .10 | .08 |
| 471 Donnie Moore | .04 | .03 |
| 472 Robby Thompson | .06 | .05 |
| 473 Joe Niekro | .06 | .05 |
| 474 Tom Brookens | .04 | .03 |
| 475 Pete Rose | .20 | .15 |
| 476 Dave Stewart | .08 | .06 |
| 477 Jamie Quirk | .04 | .03 |
| 478 Sid Bream | .06 | .05 |
| 479 Brett Butler | .06 | .05 |
| 480 Dwight Gooden | .40 | .30 |
| 481 Mariano Duncan | .04 | .03 |
| 482 Mark Davis | .04 | .03 |
| 483 *Rod Booker*(FC) | .12 | .09 |
| 484 Pat Clements | .04 | .03 |
| 485 Harold Reynolds | .06 | .05 |
| 486 *Pat Keedy*(FC) | .10 | .08 |
| 487 Jim Pankovits | .04 | .03 |
| 488 Andy McGaffigan | .04 | .03 |
| 489 Dodgers Leaders (Pedro Guerrero, Fernando Valenzuela) | | |
| | .08 | .06 |
| 490 Larry Parrish | .06 | .05 |
| 491 B.J. Surhoff | .10 | .08 |
| 492 Doyle Alexander | .06 | .05 |
| 493 Mike Greenwell | .25 | .20 |
| 494 *Wally Ritchie* | .12 | .09 |
| 495 Eddie Murray | .25 | .20 |
| 496 Guy Hoffman | .04 | .03 |
| 497 Kevin Mitchell | .30 | .25 |
| 498 Bob Boone | .06 | .05 |
| 499 Eric King | .06 | .05 |
| 500 Andre Dawson | .15 | .11 |

| | MT | NR MT |
|---|---|---|
| 501 Tim Birtsas(FC) | .06 | .05 |
| 502 Danny Gladden | .04 | .03 |
| 503 *Junior Noboa*(FC) | | |
| | .10 | .08 |
| 504 Bob Rodgers | .04 | .03 |
| 505 Willie Upshaw | .06 | .05 |
| 506 John Cangelosi | .04 | .03 |
| 507 Mark Gubicza | .10 | .08 |
| 508 Tim Teufel | .04 | .03 |
| 509 Bill Dawley | .04 | .03 |
| 510 Dave Winfield | .20 | .15 |
| 511 Joel Davis | .04 | .03 |
| 512 Alex Trevino | .04 | .03 |
| 513 Tim Flannery | .04 | .03 |
| 514 Pat Sheridan | .04 | .03 |
| 515 Juan Nieves | .06 | .05 |
| 516 Jim Sundberg | .06 | .05 |
| 517 Ron Robinson | .04 | .03 |
| 518 Greg Gross | .04 | .03 |
| 519 Mariners Leaders (Phil Bradley, Harold Reynolds) | | |
| | .06 | .05 |
| 520 Dave Smith | .06 | .05 |
| 521 Jim Dwyer | .04 | .03 |
| 522 *Bob Patterson*(FC) | | |
| | .12 | .09 |
| 523 Gary Roenicke | .04 | .03 |
| 524 Gary Lucas | .04 | .03 |
| 525 Marty Barrett | .06 | .05 |
| 526 Juan Berenguer | .04 | .03 |
| 527 Steve Henderson | .04 | .03 |
| 528a Checklist 397-528 (#455 is Steve Carlton) | .80 | .60 |
| 528b Checklist 397-528 (#455 is Shawn Hillegas) | | |
| | .06 | .05 |
| 529 Tim Burke | .04 | .03 |
| 530 Gary Carter | .15 | .11 |
| 531 Rich Yett | .04 | .03 |
| 532 Mike Kingery | .04 | .03 |
| 533 *John Farrell*(FC) | .15 | .11 |
| 534 John Wathan | .06 | .05 |
| 535 Ron Guidry | .12 | .09 |
| 536 John Morris | .04 | .03 |
| 537 Steve Buechele | .04 | .03 |
| 538 Bill Wegman | .04 | .03 |
| 539 Mike LaValliere | .06 | .05 |
| 540 Bret Saberhagen | .25 | .20 |
| 541 Juan Beniquez | .04 | .03 |
| 542 *Paul Noce*(FC) | .10 | .08 |
| 543 Kent Tekulve | .06 | .05 |
| 544 Jim Traber | .06 | .05 |
| 545 Don Baylor | .08 | .06 |
| 546 John Candelaria | .06 | .05 |
| 547 *Felix Fermin*(FC) | .12 | .09 |
| 548 *Shane Mack* | .15 | .11 |
| 549 Braves Leaders (Ken Griffey, Dion James, Dale Murphy, Gerald Perry) | .08 | .06 |
| 550 Pedro Guerrero | .15 | .11 |
| 551 Terry Steinbach | .15 | .11 |
| 552 Mark Thurmond | .04 | .03 |
| 553 Tracy Jones | .10 | .08 |
| 554 Mike Smithson | .04 | .03 |
| 555 Brook Jacoby | .08 | .06 |
| 556 *Stan Clarke*(FC) | .12 | .09 |
| 557 Craig Reynolds | .04 | .03 |

| | MT | NR MT |
|---|---|---|
| 558 Bob Ojeda | .06 | .05 |
| 559 *Ken Williams*(FC) | | |
| | .20 | .15 |
| 560 Tim Wallach | .08 | .06 |
| 561 Rick Cerone | .04 | .03 |
| 562 Jim Lindeman | .10 | .08 |
| 563 Jose Guzman | .06 | .05 |
| 564 Frank Lucchesi | .04 | .03 |
| 565 Lloyd Moseby | .06 | .05 |
| 566 *Charlie O'Brien*(FC) | | |
| | .12 | .09 |
| 567 Mike Diaz | .06 | .05 |
| 568 Chris Brown | .06 | .05 |
| 569 Charlie Leibrandt | .06 | .05 |
| 570 Jeffrey Leonard | .06 | .05 |
| 571 *Mark Williamson*(FC) | | |
| | .12 | .09 |
| 572 Chris James | .15 | .11 |
| 573 Bob Stanley | .04 | .03 |
| 574 Graig Nettles | .08 | .06 |
| 575 Don Sutton | .12 | .09 |
| 576 *Tommy Hinzo*(FC) | | |
| | .12 | .09 |
| 577 Tom Browning | .08 | .06 |
| 578 Gary Gaetti | .10 | .08 |
| 579 Mets Leaders (Gary Carter, Kevin McReynolds) | | |
| | .08 | .06 |
| 580 Mark McGwire | .40 | .30 |
| 581 Tito Landrum | .04 | .03 |
| 582 *Mike Henneman* | .25 | .20 |
| 583 Dave Valle | .06 | .05 |
| 584 Steve Trout | .04 | .03 |
| 585 Ozzie Guillen | .06 | .05 |
| 586 Bob Forsch | .06 | .05 |
| 587 Terry Puhl | .04 | .03 |
| 588 *Jeff Parrett*(FC) | .20 | .15 |
| 589 Geno Petralli | .04 | .03 |
| 590 George Bell | .20 | .15 |
| 591 Doug Drabek | .06 | .05 |
| 592 Dale Sveum | .06 | .05 |
| 593 Bob Tewksbury | .04 | .03 |
| 594 Bobby Valentine | .04 | .03 |
| 595 Frank White | .06 | .05 |
| 596 John Kruk | .08 | .06 |
| 597 Gene Garber | .04 | .03 |
| 598 Lee Lacy | .04 | .03 |
| 599 Calvin Schiraldi | .04 | .03 |
| 600 Mike Schmidt | .40 | .30 |
| 601 Jack Lazorko | .04 | .03 |
| 602 Mike Aldrete | .06 | .05 |
| 603 Rob Murphy | .06 | .05 |
| 604 Chris Bando | .04 | .03 |
| 605 Kirk Gibson | .15 | .11 |
| 606 Moose Haas | .04 | .03 |
| 607 Mickey Hatcher | .04 | .03 |
| 608 Charlie Kerfeld | .04 | .03 |
| 609 Twins Leaders (Gary Gaetti, Kent Hrbek) | .08 | .06 |
| 610 Keith Hernandez | .15 | .11 |
| 611 Tommy John | .12 | .09 |
| 612 Curt Ford | .04 | .03 |
| 613 Bobby Thigpen | .08 | .06 |
| 614 Herm Winningham | .04 | .03 |
| 615 Jody Davis | .06 | .05 |
| 616 *Jay Aldrich*(FC) | .10 | .08 |
| 617 Oddibe McDowell | .06 | .05 |

| | MT | NR MT |
|---|---|---|
| 618 Cecil Fielder | .60 | .45 |
| 619 *Mike Dunne* | .15 | .11 |
| 620 Cory Snyder | .15 | .11 |
| 621 Gene Nelson | .04 | .03 |
| 622 Kal Daniels | .15 | .11 |
| 623 Mike Flanagan | .06 | .05 |
| 624 Jim Leyland | .04 | .03 |
| 625 Frank Viola | .12 | .09 |
| 626 Glenn Wilson | .06 | .05 |
| 627 *Joe Boever*(FC) | .12 | .09 |
| 628 Dave Henderson | .08 | .06 |
| 629 Kelly Downs | .08 | .06 |
| 630 Darrell Evans | .08 | .06 |
| 631 Jack Howell | .06 | .05 |
| 632 *Steve Shields* | .12 | .09 |
| 633 Barry Lyons | .12 | .09 |
| 634 Jose DeLeon | .06 | .05 |
| 635 Terry Pendleton | .06 | .05 |
| 636 Charles Hudson | .04 | .03 |
| 637 *Jay Bell*(FC) | .35 | .25 |
| 638 Steve Balboni | .06 | .05 |
| 639 Brewers Leaders (Glenn Braggs, Tony Muser) | .06 | .05 |
| 640 Garry Templeton | .06 | .05 |
| 641 Rick Honeycutt | .04 | .03 |
| 642 Bob Dernier | .04 | .03 |
| 643 *Rocky Childress*(FC) | .12 | .09 |
| 644 Terry McGriff(FC) | .06 | .05 |
| 645 *Matt Nokes* | .30 | .25 |
| 646 Checklist 529-660 | .04 | .03 |
| 647 Pascual Perez | .06 | .05 |
| 648 Al Newman | .04 | .03 |
| 649 *DeWayne Buice* | .15 | .11 |
| 650 Cal Ripken | .40 | .30 |
| 651 *Mike Jackson*(FC) | .15 | .11 |
| 652 Bruce Benedict | .04 | .03 |
| 653 Jeff Sellers | .06 | .05 |
| 654 Roger Craig | .06 | .05 |
| 655 Len Dykstra | .08 | .06 |
| 656 Lee Guetterman | .04 | .03 |
| 657 Gary Redus | .04 | .03 |
| 658 Tim Conroy | .04 | .03 |
| 659 Bobby Meacham | .04 | .03 |
| 660 Rick Reuschel | .08 | .06 |
| 661 Turn Back The Clock (Nolan Ryan) | .08 | .06 |
| 662 Turn Back The Clock (Jim Rice) | .08 | .06 |
| 663 Turn Back The Clock (Ron Blomberg) | .04 | .03 |
| 664 Turn Back The Clock (Bob Gibson) | .08 | .06 |
| 665 Turn Back The Clock (Stan Musial) | .12 | .09 |
| 666 Mario Soto | .06 | .05 |
| 667 Luis Quinones | .04 | .03 |
| 668 Walt Terrell | .06 | .05 |
| 669 Phillies Leaders (Lance Parrish, Mike Ryan) | .06 | .05 |
| 670 Dan Plesac | .08 | .06 |
| 671 Tim Laudner | .04 | .03 |
| 672 *John Davis*(FC) | .15 | .11 |
| 673 Tony Phillips | .04 | .03 |
| 674 Mike Fitzgerald | .04 | .03 |
| 675 Jim Rice | .20 | .15 |

| | MT | NR MT |
|---|---|---|
| 676 Ken Dixon | .04 | .03 |
| 677 Eddie Milner | .04 | .03 |
| 678 Jim Acker | .04 | .03 |
| 679 Darrell Miller | .04 | .03 |
| 680 Charlie Hough | .06 | .05 |
| 681 Bobby Bonilla | .40 | .30 |
| 682 Jimmy Key | .08 | .06 |
| 683 Julio Franco | .08 | .06 |
| 684 Hal Lanier | .04 | .03 |
| 685 Ron Darling | .10 | .08 |
| 686 Terry Francona | .04 | .03 |
| 687 Mickey Brantley | .04 | .03 |
| 688 Jim Winn | .04 | .03 |
| 689 *Tom Pagnozzi*(FC) | .25 | .20 |
| 690 Jay Howell | .06 | .05 |
| 691 Dan Pasqua | .08 | .06 |
| 692 Mike Birkbeck | .06 | .05 |
| 693 Benny Santiago | .30 | .25 |
| 694 *Eric Nolte*(FC) | .12 | .09 |
| 695 Shawon Dunston | .08 | .06 |
| 696 Duane Ward | .04 | .03 |
| 697 Steve Lombardozzi | .08 | .06 |
| 698 Brad Havens | .04 | .03 |
| 699 Padres Leaders (Tony Gwynn, Benny Santiago) | .12 | .09 |
| 700 George Brett | .30 | .25 |
| 701 Sammy Stewart | .04 | .03 |
| 702 Mike Gallego | .04 | .03 |
| 703 Bob Brenly | .04 | .03 |
| 704 Dennis Boyd | .06 | .05 |
| 705 Juan Samuel | .10 | .08 |
| 706 Rick Mahler | .04 | .03 |
| 707 Fred Lynn | .10 | .08 |
| 708 Gus Polidor(FC) | .06 | .05 |
| 709 George Frazier | .04 | .03 |
| 710 Darryl Strawberry | .30 | .25 |
| 711 Bill Gullickson | .04 | .03 |
| 712 John Moses | .04 | .03 |
| 713 Willie Hernandez | .06 | .05 |
| 714 Jim Fregosi | .06 | .05 |
| 715 Todd Worrell | .08 | .06 |
| 716 Lenn Sakata | .04 | .03 |
| 717 Jay Baller(FC) | .06 | .05 |
| 718 Mike Felder | .04 | .03 |
| 719 Denny Walling | .04 | .03 |
| 720 Tim Raines | .20 | .15 |
| 721 Pete O'Brien | .06 | .05 |
| 722 Manny Lee | .04 | .03 |
| 723 Bob Kipper | .04 | .03 |
| 724 Danny Tartabull | .20 | .15 |
| 725 Mike Boddicker | .06 | .05 |
| 726 Alfredo Griffin | .06 | .05 |
| 727 Greg Booker | .04 | .03 |
| 728 Andy Allanson | .06 | .05 |
| 729 Blue Jays Leaders (George Bell, Fred McGriff) | .10 | .08 |
| 730 John Franco | .08 | .06 |
| 731 Rick Schu | .04 | .03 |
| 732 Dave Palmer | .04 | .03 |
| 733 Spike Owen | .04 | .03 |
| 734 Craig Lefferts | .04 | .03 |
| 735 Kevin McReynolds | .20 | .15 |
| 736 Matt Young | .04 | .03 |
| 737 Butch Wynegar | .04 | .03 |

| | | MT | NR MT |
|---|---|---|---|
| 738 | Scott Bankhead | .04 | .03 |
| 739 | Daryl Boston | .04 | .03 |
| 740 | Rick Sutcliffe | .08 | .06 |
| 741 | Mike Easler | .06 | .05 |
| 742 | Mark Clear | .04 | .03 |
| 743 | Larry Herndon | .04 | .03 |
| 744 | Whitey Herzog | .06 | .05 |
| 745 | Bill Doran | .06 | .05 |
| 746 | *Gene Larkin* | .25 | .20 |
| 747 | Bobby Witt | .08 | .06 |
| 748 | Reid Nichols | .04 | .03 |
| 749 | Mark Eichhorn | .06 | .05 |
| 750 | Bo Jackson | .70 | .50 |
| 751 | Jim Morrison | .04 | .03 |
| 752 | Mark Grant | .04 | .03 |
| 753 | Danny Heep | .04 | .03 |
| 754 | Mike LaCoss | .04 | .03 |
| 755 | Ozzie Virgil | .04 | .03 |
| 756 | Mike Maddux | .06 | .05 |
| 757 | *John Marzano* | .15 | .11 |
| 758 | Eddie Williams(FC) | | |
| | | .08 | .06 |
| 759 | A's Leaders (Jose Canseco, Mark McGwire) | | |
| | | .40 | .30 |
| 760 | Mike Scott | .10 | .08 |
| 761 | Tony Armas | .06 | .05 |
| 762 | Scott Bradley | .04 | .03 |
| 763 | Doug Sisk | .04 | .03 |
| 764 | Greg Walker | .06 | .05 |
| 765 | Neal Heaton | .06 | .05 |
| 766 | Henry Cotto | .04 | .03 |
| 767 | *Jose Lind*(FC) | .25 | .20 |
| 768 | Dickie Noles | .04 | .03 |
| 769 | Cecil Cooper | .08 | .06 |
| 770 | Lou Whitaker | .20 | .15 |
| 771 | Ruben Sierra | .50 | .40 |
| 772 | Sal Butera | .04 | .03 |
| 773 | Frank Williams | .04 | .03 |
| 774 | Gene Mauch | .06 | .05 |
| 775 | Dave Stieb | .08 | .06 |
| 776 | Checklist 661-792 | .04 | .03 |
| 777 | Lonnie Smith | .06 | .05 |
| 778a | *Keith Comstock* (white team letters)(FC) | 2.00 | 1.50 |
| 778b | *Keith Comstock* (blue team letters)(FC) | .25 | .20 |
| 779 | *Tom Glavine*(FC) | | |
| | | 2.00 | 1.50 |
| 780 | Fernando Valenzuela | | |
| | | .15 | .11 |
| 781 | *Keith Hughes*(FC) | | |
| | | .15 | .11 |
| 782 | *Jeff Ballard*(FC) | .15 | .11 |
| 783 | Ron Roenicke | .04 | .03 |
| 784 | Joe Sambito | .04 | .03 |
| 785 | Alvin Davis | .10 | .08 |
| 786 | Joe Price | .04 | .03 |
| 787 | Bill Almon | .04 | .03 |
| 788 | Ray Searage | .04 | .03 |
| 789 | Indians Leaders (Joe Carter, Cory Snyder) | .08 | .06 |
| 790 | Dave Righetti | .12 | .09 |
| 791 | Ted Simmons | .08 | .06 |
| 792 | John Tudor | .08 | .06 |

## 1988 Topps Traded

In addition to new players and traded veterans, 21 members of the U.S.A. Olympic Baseball team are showcased in this 132-card set, numbered 1T-132T. The standard-size (2-1/2" by 3-1/2") set follows the same design as the basic Topps issue - white borders, large full-color photos, team name (or U.S.A.) in large bold letters at the top of the card face, player name on a diagonal stripe across the lower right corner. Topps has issued its traded series each year since 1981 in boxed complete sets available through hobby dealers.

| | | MT | NR MT |
|---|---|---|---|
| | Complete Set: | 40.00 | 30.00 |
| | Common Player: | .06 | .05 |
| 1T | Jim Abbott (U.S.A.)(FC) | | |
| | | 7.00 | 5.25 |
| 2T | Juan Agosto | .06 | .05 |
| 3T | Luis Alicea(FC) | .15 | .11 |
| 4T | Roberto Alomar(FC) | | |
| | | 10.00 | 7.50 |
| 5T | Brady Anderson(FC) | | |
| | | 1.50 | 1.25 |
| 6T | Jack Armstrong(FC) | .25 | .20 |
| 7T | Don August | .15 | .11 |
| 8T | Floyd Bannister | .08 | .06 |
| 9T | Bret Barberie (U.S.A.)(FC) | | |
| | | .60 | .45 |

**A player's name in italic type indicates a rookie card. An (FC) indicates a player's first card for that particular card company.**

| | MT | NR MT |
|---|---|---|
| 10T Jose Bautista(FC) | .15 | .11 |
| 11T Don Baylor | .10 | .08 |
| 12T Tim Belcher | .20 | .15 |
| 13T Buddy Bell | .10 | .08 |
| 14T Andy Benes (U.S.A.)(FC) | 3.00 | 2.25 |
| 15T Damon Berryhill(FC) | .25 | .20 |
| 16T Bud Black | .06 | .05 |
| 17T Pat Borders(FC) | .60 | .45 |
| 18T Phil Bradley | .10 | .08 |
| 19T Jeff Branson (U.S.A.)(FC) | .20 | .15 |
| 20T Tom Brunansky | .12 | .09 |
| 21T Jay Buhner(FC) | .40 | .30 |
| 22T Brett Butler | .08 | .06 |
| 23T Jim Campanis (U.S.A.)(FC) | .20 | .15 |
| 24T Sil Campusano(FC) | .20 | .15 |
| 25T John Candelaria | .08 | .06 |
| 26T Jose Cecena(FC) | .15 | .11 |
| 27T Rick Cerone | .06 | .05 |
| 28T Jack Clark | .15 | .11 |
| 29T Kevin Coffman(FC) | .10 | .08 |
| 30T Pat Combs (U.S.A.)(FC) | .30 | .25 |
| 31T Henry Cotto | .06 | .05 |
| 32T Chili Davis | .08 | .06 |
| 33T Mike Davis | .08 | .06 |
| 34T Jose DeLeon | .08 | .06 |
| 35T Richard Dotson | .10 | .08 |
| 36T Cecil Espy(FC) | .08 | .06 |
| 37T Tom Filer | .06 | .05 |
| 38T Mike Fiore (U.S.A.)(FC) | .20 | .15 |
| 39T Ron Gant(FC) | 3.00 | 2.25 |
| 40T Kirk Gibson | .20 | .15 |
| 41T Rich Gossage | .15 | .11 |
| 42T Mark Grace(FC) | 2.00 | 1.50 |
| 43T Alfredo Griffin | .08 | .06 |
| 44T Ty Griffin (U.S.A.)(FC) | .15 | .11 |
| 45T Bryan Harvey(FC) | .40 | .30 |
| 46T Ron Hassey | .06 | .05 |
| 47T Ray Hayward(FC) | .08 | .06 |
| 48T Dave Henderson | .20 | .15 |
| 49T Tom Herr | .10 | .08 |
| 50T Bob Horner | .10 | .08 |
| 51T Ricky Horton | .08 | .06 |
| 52T Jay Howell | .08 | .06 |
| 53T Glenn Hubbard | .06 | .05 |
| 54T Jeff Innis(FC) | .15 | .11 |
| 55T Danny Jackson | .15 | .11 |
| 56T Darrin Jackson(FC) | .10 | .08 |
| 57T Roberto Kelly(FC) | 1.00 | .70 |
| 58T Ron Kittle | .10 | .08 |
| 59T Ray Knight | .08 | .06 |
| 60T Vance Law | .08 | .06 |
| 61T Jeffrey Leonard | .08 | .06 |
| 62T Mike Macfarlane(FC) | .25 | .20 |
| 63T Scotti Madison(FC) | .15 | .11 |
| 64T Kirt Manwaring(FC) | .20 | .15 |
| 65T Mark Marquess (U.S.A.) | .06 | .05 |
| 66T Tino Martinez (U.S.A.)(FC) | 3.00 | 2.25 |
| 67T Billy Masse (U.S.A.)(FC) | | |

| | MT | NR MT |
|---|---|---|
| | | .30 | .25 |
| 68T Jack McDowell(FC) | 3.50 | 2.75 |
| 69T Jack McKeon | .06 | .05 |
| 70T Larry McWilliams | .06 | .05 |
| 71T Mickey Morandini (U.S.A.)(FC) | .50 | .40 |
| 72T Keith Moreland | .08 | .06 |
| 73T Mike Morgan | .06 | .05 |
| 74T Charles Nagy (U.S.A.)(FC) | 2.00 | 1.50 |
| 75T Al Nipper | .06 | .05 |
| 76T Russ Nixon | .06 | .05 |
| 77T Jesse Orosco | .08 | .06 |
| 78T Joe Orsulak | .06 | .05 |
| 79T Dave Palmer | .06 | .05 |
| 80T Mark Parent(FC) | .20 | .15 |
| 81T Dave Parker | .12 | .09 |
| 82T Dan Pasqua | .10 | .08 |
| 83T Melido Perez(FC) | .40 | .30 |
| 84T Steve Peters(FC) | .15 | .11 |
| 85T Dan Petry | .08 | .06 |
| 86T Gary Pettis | .08 | .06 |
| 87T Jeff Pico(FC) | .20 | .15 |
| 88T Jim Poole (U.S.A.)(FC) | .20 | .15 |
| 89T Ted Power | .06 | .05 |
| 90T Rafael Ramirez | .06 | .05 |
| 91T Dennis Rasmussen | .10 | .08 |
| 92T Jose Rijo | .08 | .06 |
| 93T Earnie Riles | .06 | .05 |
| 94T Luis Rivera(FC) | .08 | .06 |
| 95T Doug Robbins (U.S.A.)(FC) | .20 | .15 |
| 96T Frank Robinson | .10 | .08 |
| 97T Cookie Rojas | .06 | .05 |
| 98T Chris Sabo(FC) | 1.00 | .70 |
| 99T Mark Salas | .06 | .05 |
| 100T Luis Salazar | .06 | .05 |
| 101T Rafael Santana | .06 | .05 |
| 102T Nelson Santovenia(FC) | .20 | .15 |
| 103T Mackey Sasser(FC) | .25 | .20 |
| 104T Calvin Schiraldi | .06 | .05 |
| 105T Mike Schooler(FC) | .30 | .25 |
| 106T Scott Servais (U.S.A.)(FC) | .30 | .25 |
| 107T Dave Silvestri (U.S.A.)(FC) | .20 | .15 |
| 108T Don Slaught | .06 | .05 |
| 109T Joe Slusarski (U.S.A.)(FC) | .35 | .25 |
| 110T Lee Smith | .10 | .08 |
| 111T Pete Smith(FC) | .10 | .08 |
| 112T Jim Snyder | .06 | .05 |
| 113T Ed Sprague (U.S.A.)(FC) | .80 | .60 |
| 114T Pete Stanicek(FC) | .15 | .11 |
| 115T Kurt Stillwell | .10 | .08 |
| 116T Todd Stottlemyre(FC) | .90 | .70 |
| 117T Bill Swift | .06 | .05 |
| 118T Pat Tabler | .08 | .06 |
| 119T Scott Terry(FC) | .10 | .08 |
| 120T Mickey Tettleton | .06 | .05 |
| 121T Dickie Thon | .08 | .06 |
| 122T Jeff Treadway(FC) | .20 | .15 |
| 123T Willie Upshaw | .08 | .06 |

| | MT | NR MT |
|---|---|---|
| 124T Robin Ventura(FC) | 12.00 | 9.00 |
| 125T Ron Washington | .06 | .05 |
| 126T Walt Weiss(FC) | .30 | .25 |
| 127T Bob Welch | .10 | .08 |
| 128T David Wells(FC) | .15 | .11 |
| 129T Glenn Wilson | .08 | .06 |
| 130T Ted Wood (U.S.A.)(FC) | .30 | .25 |
| 131T Don Zimmer | .06 | .05 |
| 132T Checklist 1T-132T | .06 | .05 |

# 1989 Topps

Ten top young players who led the June 1988 draft picks are featured on "#1 Draft Pick" cards in this full-color basic set of 792 standard-size baseball cards. An additional five cards salute 1989 Future Stars, 22 cards highlight All-Stars, seven contain Record Breakers, five are designated Turn Back The Clock, and six contain checklists. This set features the familiar white borders, but two inner photo corners (upper left and lower right) have been rounded off and the rectangular player name was replaced by a curved name banner in bright red or blue that leads to the team name in large script in the lower right corner. The card backs are printed in black on a red background and include personal information and complete minor and major league stats. Another new addition in this set is the special Monthly Scoreboard chart that lists monthly stats (April through September) in two of several categories (hits, run, home runs, stolen bases, RBIs, wins, strikeouts, games or saves).

| | MT | NR MT |
|---|---|---|
| Complete Set: | 20.00 | 15.00 |
| Common Player: | .03 | .02 |
| 1 Record Breaker (George Bell) | .08 | .06 |
| 2 Record Breaker (Wade Boggs) | .20 | .15 |
| 3 Record Breaker (Gary Carter) | .10 | .08 |
| 4 Record Breaker (Andre Dawson) | .08 | .06 |
| 5 Record Breaker (Orel Hershiser) | .10 | .08 |
| 6 Record Breaker (Doug Jones) | .06 | .05 |
| 7 Record Breaker (Kevin McReynolds) | .08 | .06 |
| 8 *Dave Eiland*(FC) | .20 | .15 |
| 9 Tim Teufel | .03 | .02 |
| 10 Andre Dawson | .15 | .11 |
| 11 Bruce Sutter | .08 | .06 |
| 12 Dale Sveum | .06 | .05 |
| 13 Doug Sisk | .03 | .02 |
| 14 Tom Kelly | .03 | .02 |
| 15 Robby Thompson | .06 | .05 |
| 16 Ron Robinson | .03 | .02 |
| 17 Brian Downing | .06 | .05 |
| 18 Rick Rhoden | .06 | .05 |
| 19 Greg Gagne | .03 | .02 |
| 20 Steve Bedrosian | .08 | .06 |
| 21 White Sox Leaders (Greg Walker) | .06 | .05 |
| 22 Tim Crews | .06 | .05 |
| 23 Mike Fitzgerald | .03 | .02 |
| 24 Larry Andersen | .03 | .02 |
| 25 Frank White | .06 | .05 |
| 26 Dale Mohorcic | .03 | .02 |
| 27 *Orestes Destrade*(FC) | .12 | .09 |
| 28 Mike Moore | .03 | .02 |
| 29 Kelly Gruber | .03 | .02 |
| 30 Doc Gooden | .20 | .15 |
| 31 Terry Francona | .03 | .02 |
| 32 Dennis Rasmussen | .08 | .06 |
| 33 B.J. Surhoff | .08 | .06 |
| 34 Ken Williams | .06 | .05 |
| 35 John Tudor | .08 | .06 |
| 36 Mitch Webster | .06 | .05 |
| 37 Bob Stanley | .03 | .02 |
| 38 Paul Runge | .03 | .02 |
| 39 Mike Maddux | .03 | .02 |
| 40 Steve Sax | .12 | .09 |
| 41 Terry Mulholland | .03 | .02 |
| 42 Jim Eppard(FC) | .08 | .06 |
| 43 Guillermo Hernandez | .06 | .05 |
| 44 Jim Snyder | .03 | .02 |
| 45 Kal Daniels | .12 | .09 |
| 46 Mark Portugal | .03 | .02 |
| 47 Carney Lansford | .06 | .05 |
| 48 Tim Burke | .03 | .02 |
| 49 *Craig Biggio*(FC) | .35 | .25 |
| 50 George Bell | .20 | .15 |
| 51 Angels Leaders (Mark McLemore) | .06 | .05 |
| 52 Bob Brenly | .03 | .02 |
| 53 Ruben Sierra | .30 | .25 |

| | | MT | NR MT |
|---|---|---|---|
| 54 | Steve Trout | .03 | .02 |
| 55 | Julio Franco | .08 | .06 |
| 56 | Pat Tabler | .06 | .05 |
| 57 | Alejandro Pena | .06 | .05 |
| 58 | Lee Mazzilli | .06 | .05 |
| 59 | Mark Davis | .03 | .02 |
| 60 | Tom Brunansky | .10 | .08 |
| 61 | Neil Allen | .03 | .02 |
| 62 | Alfredo Griffin | .06 | .05 |
| 63 | Mark Clear | .03 | .02 |
| 64 | Alex Trevino | .03 | .02 |
| 65 | Rick Reuschel | .08 | .06 |
| 66 | Manny Trillo | .03 | .02 |
| 67 | Dave Palmer | .03 | .02 |
| 68 | Darrell Miller | .03 | .02 |
| 69 | Jeff Ballard | .06 | .05 |
| 70 | Mark McGwire | .25 | .20 |
| 71 | Mike Boddicker | .06 | .05 |
| 72 | John Moses | .03 | .02 |
| 73 | Pascual Perez | .06 | .05 |
| 74 | Nick Leyva | .03 | .02 |
| 75 | Tom Henke | .06 | .05 |
| 76 | Terry Blocker(FC) | .12 | .09 |
| 77 | Doyle Alexander | .06 | .05 |
| 78 | Jim Sundberg | .06 | .05 |
| 79 | Scott Bankhead | .03 | .02 |
| 80 | Cory Snyder | .15 | .11 |
| 81 | Expos Leaders (Tim Raines) | .08 | .06 |
| 82 | Dave Leiper | .03 | .02 |
| 83 | Jeff Blauser(FC) | .15 | .11 |
| 84 | #1 Draft Pick (Bill Bene)(FC) | .15 | .11 |
| 85 | Kevin McReynolds | .12 | .09 |
| 86 | Al Nipper | .03 | .02 |
| 87 | Larry Owen | .03 | .02 |
| 88 | Darryl Hamilton(FC) | .35 | .25 |
| 89 | Dave LaPoint | .06 | .05 |
| 90 | Vince Coleman | .12 | .09 |
| 91 | Floyd Youmans | .03 | .02 |
| 92 | Jeff Kunkel | .03 | .02 |
| 93 | Ken Howell | .03 | .02 |
| 94 | Chris Speier | .03 | .02 |
| 95 | Gerald Young | .10 | .08 |
| 96 | Rick Cerone | .03 | .02 |
| 97 | Greg Mathews | .06 | .05 |
| 98 | Larry Sheets | .06 | .05 |
| 99 | Sherman Corbett(FC) | .12 | .09 |
| 100 | Mike Schmidt | .35 | .25 |
| 101 | Les Straker | .06 | .05 |
| 102 | Mike Gallego | .03 | .02 |
| 103 | Tim Birtsas | .03 | .02 |
| 104 | Dallas Green | .03 | .02 |
| 105 | Ron Darling | .10 | .08 |
| 106 | Willie Upshaw | .06 | .05 |
| 107 | Jose DeLeon | .06 | .05 |
| 108 | Fred Manrique | .06 | .05 |
| 109 | Hipolito Pena(FC) | .12 | .09 |
| 110 | Paul Molitor | .12 | .09 |
| 111 | Reds Leaders (Eric Davis) | .10 | .08 |
| 112 | Jim Presley | .06 | .05 |
| 113 | Lloyd Moseby | .06 | .05 |

| | | MT | NR MT |
|---|---|---|---|
| 114 | Bob Kipper | .03 | .02 |
| 115 | Jody Davis | .06 | .05 |
| 116 | Jeff Montgomery | .06 | .05 |
| 117 | Dave Anderson | .03 | .02 |
| 118 | Checklist 1-132 | .03 | .02 |
| 119 | Terry Puhl | .03 | .02 |
| 120 | Frank Viola | .12 | .09 |
| 121 | Garry Templeton | .06 | .05 |
| 122 | Lance Johnson(FC) | .10 | .08 |
| 123 | Spike Owen | .03 | .02 |
| 124 | Jim Traber | .06 | .05 |
| 125 | Mike Krukow | .06 | .05 |
| 126 | Sid Bream | .06 | .05 |
| 127 | Walt Terrell | .06 | .05 |
| 128 | Milt Thompson | .03 | .02 |
| 129 | Terry Clark(FC) | .12 | .09 |
| 130 | Gerald Perry | .08 | .06 |
| 131 | Dave Otto(FC) | .08 | .06 |
| 132 | Curt Ford | .03 | .02 |
| 133 | Bill Long | .06 | .05 |
| 134 | Don Zimmer | .03 | .02 |
| 135 | Jose Rijo | .06 | .05 |
| 136 | Joey Meyer | .08 | .06 |
| 137 | Geno Petralli | .03 | .02 |
| 138 | Wallace Johnson | .03 | .02 |
| 139 | Mike Flanagan | .06 | .05 |
| 140 | Shawon Dunston | .08 | .06 |
| 141 | Indians Leaders (Brook Jacoby) | .06 | .05 |
| 142 | Mike Diaz | .06 | .05 |
| 143 | Mike Campbell | .08 | .06 |
| 144 | Jay Bell | .06 | .05 |
| 145 | Dave Stewart | .08 | .06 |
| 146 | Gary Pettis | .03 | .02 |
| 147 | DeWayne Buice | .03 | .02 |
| 148 | Bill Pecota | .06 | .05 |
| 149 | Doug Dascenzo(FC) | .20 | .15 |
| 150 | Fernando Valenzuela | .15 | .11 |
| 151 | Terry McGriff | .03 | .02 |
| 152 | Mark Thurmond | .03 | .02 |
| 153 | Jim Pankovits | .03 | .02 |
| 154 | Don Carman | .06 | .05 |
| 155 | Marty Barrett | .06 | .05 |
| 156 | Dave Gallagher(FC) | .15 | .11 |
| 157 | Tom Glavine | .08 | .06 |
| 158 | Mike Aldrete | .06 | .05 |
| 159 | Pat Clements | .03 | .02 |
| 160 | Jeffrey Leonard | .06 | .05 |
| 161 | #1 Draft Pick (Gregg Olson)(FC) | .40 | .30 |
| 162 | John Davis | .03 | .02 |
| 163 | Bob Forsch | .06 | .05 |
| 164 | Hal Lanier | .03 | .02 |
| 165 | Mike Dunne | .08 | .06 |
| 166 | Doug Jennings(FC) | .12 | .09 |
| 167 | Future Star (Steve Searcy)(FC) | .25 | .20 |
| 168 | Willie Wilson | .08 | .06 |
| 169 | Mike Jackson | .06 | .05 |
| 170 | Tony Fernandez | .10 | .08 |
| 171 | Braves Leaders (Andres Thomas) | .06 | .05 |
| 172 | Frank Williams | .03 | .02 |

| # | Player | MT | NR MT |
|---|--------|----|-------|
| 173 | Mel Hall | .06 | .05 |
| 174 | *Todd Burns*(FC) | .12 | .09 |
| 175 | John Shelby | .03 | .02 |
| 176 | Jeff Parrett | .08 | .06 |
| 177 | #1 Draft Pick *(Monty Fariss)*(FC) | .25 | .20 |
| 178 | Mark Grant | .03 | .02 |
| 179 | Ozzie Virgil | .03 | .02 |
| 180 | Mike Scott | .10 | .08 |
| 181 | *Craig Worthington*(FC) | .12 | .09 |
| 182 | Bob McClure | .03 | .02 |
| 183 | Oddibe McDowell | .06 | .05 |
| 184 | *John Costello* | .20 | .15 |
| 185 | Claudell Washington | .06 | .05 |
| 186 | Pat Perry | .03 | .02 |
| 187 | Darren Daulton | .03 | .02 |
| 188 | Dennis Lamp | .03 | .02 |
| 189 | Kevin Mitchell | .20 | .15 |
| 190 | Mike Witt | .06 | .05 |
| 191 | Sil Campusano | .20 | .15 |
| 192 | Paul Mirabella | .03 | .02 |
| 193 | Sparky Anderson | .06 | .05 |
| 194 | *Greg Harris*(FC) | .25 | .20 |
| 195 | Ozzie Guillen | .06 | .05 |
| 196 | Denny Walling | .03 | .02 |
| 197 | Neal Heaton | .03 | .02 |
| 198 | Danny Heep | .03 | .02 |
| 199 | *Mike Schooler* | .30 | .25 |
| 200 | George Brett | .30 | .25 |
| 201 | Blue Jays Leaders (Kelly Gruber) | .06 | .05 |
| 202 | *Brad Moore*(FC) | .12 | .09 |
| 203 | Rob Ducey | .03 | .02 |
| 204 | Brad Havens | .03 | .02 |
| 205 | Dwight Evans | .10 | .08 |
| 206 | Roberto Alomar | .50 | .40 |
| 207 | Terry Leach | .03 | .02 |
| 208 | Tom Pagnozzi | .06 | .05 |
| 209 | *Jeff Bittiger*(FC) | .12 | .09 |
| 210 | Dale Murphy | .30 | .25 |
| 211 | Mike Pagliarulo | .08 | .06 |
| 212 | Scott Sanderson | .03 | .02 |
| 213 | Rene Gonzales | .06 | .05 |
| 214 | Charlie O'Brien | .03 | .02 |
| 215 | Kevin Gross | .06 | .05 |
| 216 | Jack Howell | .06 | .05 |
| 217 | Joe Price | .03 | .02 |
| 218 | Mike LaValliere | .06 | .05 |
| 219 | Jim Clancy | .06 | .05 |
| 220 | Gary Gaetti | .12 | .09 |
| 221 | Cecil Espy | .08 | .06 |
| 222 | #1 Draft Pick *(Mark Lewis)*(FC) | .40 | .30 |
| 223 | Jay Buhner | .10 | .08 |
| 224 | Tony LaRussa | .06 | .05 |
| 225 | *Ramon Martinez*(FC) | .80 | .60 |
| 226 | Bill Doran | .06 | .05 |
| 227 | John Farrell | .06 | .05 |
| 228 | *Nelson Santovenia* | .15 | .11 |
| 229 | Jimmy Key | .08 | .06 |
| 230 | Ozzie Smith | .12 | .09 |
| 231 | Padres Leaders (Roberto Alomar) | .10 | .08 |
| 232 | Ricky Horton | .06 | .05 |
| 233 | Future Star (Gregg Jefferies)(FC) | .30 | .25 |
| 234 | Tom Browning | .08 | .06 |
| 235 | John Kruk | .06 | .05 |
| 236 | Charles Hudson | .03 | .02 |
| 237 | Glenn Hubbard | .03 | .02 |
| 238 | Eric King | .03 | .02 |
| 239 | Tim Laudner | .03 | .02 |
| 240 | Greg Maddux | .10 | .08 |
| 241 | Brett Butler | .06 | .05 |
| 242 | Ed Vande Berg | .03 | .02 |
| 243 | Bob Boone | .06 | .05 |
| 244 | Jim Acker | .03 | .02 |
| 245 | Jim Rice | .20 | .15 |
| 246 | Rey Quinones | .03 | .02 |
| 247 | Shawn Hillegas | .06 | .05 |
| 248 | Tony Phillips | .03 | .02 |
| 249 | Tim Leary | .06 | .05 |
| 250 | Cal Ripken | .40 | .30 |
| 251 | *John Dopson*(FC) | .20 | .15 |
| 252 | Billy Hatcher | .06 | .05 |
| 253 | *Jose Alvarez*(FC) | .12 | .09 |
| 254 | Tom LaSorda | .06 | .05 |
| 255 | Ron Guidry | .12 | .09 |
| 256 | Benny Santiago | .12 | .09 |
| 257 | Rick Aguilera | .03 | .02 |
| 258 | Checklist 133-264 | .03 | .02 |
| 259 | Larry McWilliams | .03 | .02 |
| 260 | Dave Winfield | .20 | .15 |
| 261 | Cardinals Leaders (Tom Brunansky) | .06 | .05 |
| 262 | *Jeff Pico* | .15 | .11 |
| 263 | Mike Felder | .03 | .02 |
| 264 | *Rob Dibble*(FC) | .40 | .30 |
| 265 | Kent Hrbek | .15 | .11 |
| 266 | Luis Aquino | .03 | .02 |
| 267 | Jeff Robinson | .06 | .05 |
| 268 | Keith Miller | .06 | .05 |
| 269 | Tom Bolton | .06 | .05 |
| 270 | Wally Joyner | .20 | .15 |
| 271 | Jay Tibbs | .03 | .02 |
| 272 | Ron Hassey | .03 | .02 |
| 273 | Jose Lind | .08 | .06 |
| 274 | Mark Eichhorn | .06 | .05 |
| 275 | Danny Tartabull | .15 | .11 |
| 276 | Paul Kilgus | .08 | .06 |
| 277 | Mike Davis | .06 | .05 |
| 278 | Andy McGaffigan | .03 | .02 |
| 279 | Scott Bradley | .03 | .02 |
| 280 | Bob Knepper | .06 | .05 |
| 281 | Gary Redus | .03 | .02 |
| 282 | *Cris Carpenter*(FC) | .15 | .11 |
| 283 | Andy Allanson | .03 | .02 |
| 284 | Jim Leyland | .03 | .02 |
| 285 | John Candelaria | .06 | .05 |
| 286 | Darrin Jackson | .08 | .06 |
| 287 | Juan Nieves | .06 | .05 |
| 288 | Pat Sheridan | .03 | .02 |
| 289 | Ernie Whitt | .06 | .05 |
| 290 | John Franco | .08 | .06 |
| 291 | Mets Leaders (Darryl Strawberry) | .12 | .09 |
| 292 | *Jim Corsi*(FC) | .15 | .11 |
| 293 | Glenn Wilson | .06 | .05 |
| 294 | Juan Berenguer | .03 | .02 |
| 295 | Scott Fletcher | .06 | .05 |

| | | MT | NR MT |
|---|---|---|---|
| 296 | Ron Gant | .40 | .30 |
| 297 | Oswald Peraza(FC) | | |
| | | .15 | .11 |
| 298 | Chris James | .08 | .06 |
| 299 | Steve Ellsworth(FC) | | |
| | | .12 | .09 |
| 300 | Darryl Strawberry | .35 | .25 |
| 301 | Charlie Leibrandt | .06 | .05 |
| 302 | Gary Ward | .06 | .05 |
| 303 | Felix Fermin | .06 | .05 |
| 304 | Joel Youngblood | .03 | .02 |
| 305 | Dave Smith | .06 | .05 |
| 306 | Tracy Woodson(FC) | .10 | .08 |
| 307 | Lance McCullers | .06 | .05 |
| 308 | Ron Karkovice | .03 | .02 |
| 309 | Mario Diaz(FC) | .10 | .08 |
| 310 | Rafael Palmeiro | .20 | .15 |
| 311 | Chris Bosio | .03 | .02 |
| 312 | Tom Lawless | .03 | .02 |
| 313 | Denny Martinez | .06 | .05 |
| 314 | Bobby Valentine | .03 | .02 |
| 315 | Greg Swindell | .10 | .08 |
| 316 | Walt Weiss | .20 | .15 |
| 317 | Jack Armstrong | .35 | .25 |
| 318 | Gene Larkin | .08 | .06 |
| 319 | Greg Booker | .03 | .02 |
| 320 | Lou Whitaker | .15 | .11 |
| 321 | Red Sox Leaders (Jody Reed) | | |
| | | .06 | .05 |
| 322 | John Smiley | .10 | .08 |
| 323 | Gary Thurman | .10 | .08 |
| 324 | Bob Milacki(FC) | .25 | .20 |
| 325 | Jesse Barfield | .08 | .06 |
| 326 | Dennis Boyd | .06 | .05 |
| 327 | Mark Lemke(FC) | .20 | .15 |
| 328 | Rick Honeycutt | .03 | .02 |
| 329 | Bob Melvin | .03 | .02 |
| 330 | Eric Davis | .35 | .25 |
| 331 | Curt Wilkerson | .03 | .02 |
| 332 | Tony Armas | .06 | .05 |
| 333 | Bob Ojeda | .06 | .05 |
| 334 | Steve Lyons | .03 | .02 |
| 335 | Dave Righetti | .10 | .08 |
| 336 | Steve Balboni | .06 | .05 |
| 337 | Calvin Schiraldi | .03 | .02 |
| 338 | Jim Adduci(FC) | .06 | .05 |
| 339 | Scott Bailes | .03 | .02 |
| 340 | Kirk Gibson | .15 | .11 |
| 341 | Jim Deshaies | .03 | .02 |
| 342 | Tom Brookens | .03 | .02 |
| 343 | Future Star (Gary Sheffield)(FC) | 1.50 | 1.25 |
| 344 | Tom Trebelhorn | .03 | .02 |
| 345 | Charlie Hough | .06 | .05 |
| 346 | Rex Hudler(FC) | .06 | .05 |
| 347 | John Cerutti | .06 | .05 |
| 348 | Ed Hearn | .03 | .02 |
| 349 | Ron Jones(FC) | .15 | .11 |
| 350 | Andy Van Slyke | .12 | .09 |
| 351 | Giants Leaders (Bob Melvin) | | |
| | | .06 | .05 |
| 352 | Rick Schu | .03 | .02 |
| 353 | Marvell Wynne | .03 | .02 |
| 354 | Larry Parrish | .06 | .05 |
| 355 | Mark Langston | .08 | .06 |
| 356 | Kevin Elster | .08 | .06 |
| 357 | Jerry Reuss | .06 | .05 |
| 358 | Ricky Jordan(FC) | | |
| | | .40 | .30 |
| 359 | Tommy John | .10 | .08 |
| 360 | Ryne Sandberg | .30 | .25 |
| 361 | Kelly Downs | .08 | .06 |
| 362 | Jack Lazorko | .03 | .02 |
| 363 | Rich Yett | .03 | .02 |
| 364 | Rob Deer | .06 | .05 |
| 365 | Mike Henneman | .08 | .06 |
| 366 | Herm Winningham | .03 | .02 |
| 367 | Johnny Paredes(FC) | | |
| | | .15 | .11 |
| 368 | Brian Holton | .06 | .05 |
| 369 | Ken Caminiti | .06 | .05 |
| 370 | Dennis Eckersley | .10 | .08 |
| 371 | Manny Lee | .03 | .02 |
| 372 | Craig Lefferts | .03 | .02 |
| 373 | Tracy Jones | .08 | .06 |
| 374 | John Wathan | .06 | .05 |
| 375 | Terry Pendleton | .08 | .06 |
| 376 | Steve Lombardozzi | .03 | .02 |
| 377 | Mike Smithson | .03 | .02 |
| 378 | Checklist 265-396 | .03 | .02 |
| 379 | Tim Flannery | .03 | .02 |
| 380 | Rickey Henderson | .30 | .25 |
| 381 | Orioles Leaders (Larry Sheets) | | |
| | | .06 | .05 |
| 382 | John Smoltz(FC) | .70 | .50 |
| 383 | Howard Johnson | .08 | .06 |
| 384 | Mark Salas | .03 | .02 |
| 385 | Von Hayes | .06 | .05 |
| 386 | Andres Galarraga AS | .08 | .06 |
| 387 | Ryne Sandberg AS | .10 | .08 |
| 388 | Bobby Bonilla AS | .08 | .06 |
| 389 | Ozzie Smith AS | .08 | .06 |
| 390 | Darryl Strawberry AS | | |
| | | .15 | .11 |
| 391 | Andre Dawson AS | .10 | .08 |
| 392 | Andy Van Slyke AS | .08 | .06 |
| 393 | Gary Carter AS | .10 | .08 |
| 394 | Orel Hershiser AS | .12 | .09 |
| 395 | Danny Jackson AS | .08 | .06 |
| 396 | Kirk Gibson AS | .08 | .06 |
| 397 | Don Mattingly AS | .30 | .25 |
| 398 | Julio Franco AS | .06 | .05 |
| 399 | Wade Boggs AS | .20 | .15 |
| 400 | Alan Trammell AS | .08 | .06 |
| 401 | Jose Canseco AS | .30 | .25 |
| 402 | Mike Greenwell AS | .15 | .11 |
| 403 | Kirby Puckett AS | .12 | .09 |
| 404 | Bob Boone AS | .06 | .05 |
| 405 | Roger Clemens AS | .15 | .11 |
| 406 | Frank Viola AS | .08 | .06 |
| 407 | Dave Winfield AS | .12 | .09 |
| 408 | Greg Walker | .06 | .05 |
| 409 | Ken Dayley | .03 | .02 |
| 410 | Jack Clark | .12 | .09 |
| 411 | Mitch Williams | .06 | .05 |
| 412 | Barry Lyons | .03 | .02 |
| 413 | Mike Kingery | .03 | .02 |
| 414 | Jim Fregosi | .03 | .02 |
| 415 | Rich Gossage | .10 | .08 |
| 416 | Fred Lynn | .10 | .08 |
| 417 | Mike LaCoss | .03 | .02 |
| 418 | Bob Dernier | .03 | .02 |
| 419 | Tom Filer | .03 | .02 |
| 420 | Joe Carter | .10 | .08 |

| | | MT | NR MT |
|---|---|---|---|
| 421 | Kirk McCaskill | .06 | .05 |
| 422 | Bo Diaz | .06 | .05 |
| 423 | Brian Fisher | .06 | .05 |
| 424 | Luis Polonia | .06 | .05 |
| 425 | Jay Howell | .06 | .05 |
| 426 | Danny Gladden | .03 | .02 |
| 427 | Eric Show | .06 | .05 |
| 428 | Craig Reynolds | .03 | .02 |
| 429 | Twins Leaders (Greg Gagne) | .06 | .05 |
| 430 | Mark Gubicza | .08 | .06 |
| 431 | Luis Rivera | .06 | .05 |
| 432 | Chad Kreuter(FC) | .15 | .11 |
| 433 | Albert Hall | .03 | .02 |
| 434 | Ken Patterson(FC) | .15 | .11 |
| 435 | Len Dykstra | .08 | .06 |
| 436 | Bobby Meacham | .03 | .02 |
| 437 | #1 Draft Pick (Andy Benes) | .50 | .40 |
| 438 | Greg Gross | .03 | .02 |
| 439 | Frank DiPino | .03 | .02 |
| 440 | Bobby Bonilla | .25 | .20 |
| 441 | Jerry Reed | .03 | .02 |
| 442 | Jose Oquendo | .03 | .02 |
| 443 | Rod Nichols(FC) | .15 | .11 |
| 444 | Moose Stubing | .03 | .02 |
| 445 | Matt Nokes | .15 | .11 |
| 446 | Rob Murphy | .03 | .02 |
| 447 | Donell Nixon | .03 | .02 |
| 448 | Eric Plunk | .03 | .02 |
| 449 | Carmelo Martinez | .03 | .02 |
| 450 | Roger Clemens | .40 | .30 |
| 451 | Mark Davidson | .06 | .05 |
| 452 | Israel Sanchez | .12 | .09 |
| 453 | Tom Prince(FC) | .08 | .06 |
| 454 | Paul Assenmacher | .03 | .02 |
| 455 | Johnny Ray | .06 | .05 |
| 456 | Tim Belcher | .08 | .06 |
| 457 | Mackey Sasser | .06 | .05 |
| 458 | Donn Pall(FC) | .12 | .09 |
| 459 | Mariners Leaders (Dave Valle) | .06 | .05 |
| 460 | Dave Stieb | .08 | .06 |
| 461 | Buddy Bell | .06 | .05 |
| 462 | Jose Guzman | .06 | .06 |
| 463 | Steve Lake | .03 | .02 |
| 464 | Bryn Smith | .03 | .02 |
| 465 | Mark Grace | .70 | .50 |
| 466 | Chuck Crim | .03 | .02 |
| 467 | Jim Walewander | .03 | .02 |
| 468 | Henry Cotto | .03 | .02 |
| 469 | Jose Bautista | .20 | .15 |
| 470 | Lance Parrish | .12 | .09 |
| 471 | Steve Curry(FC) | .15 | .11 |
| 472 | Brian Harper | .03 | .02 |
| 473 | Don Robinson | .03 | .02 |
| 474 | Bob Rodgers | .03 | .02 |
| 475 | Dave Parker | .10 | .08 |
| 476 | Jon Perlman(FC) | .06 | .05 |
| 477 | Dick Schofield | .03 | .02 |
| 478 | Doug Drabek | .06 | .05 |
| 479 | Mike Macfarlane | .25 | .20 |
| 480 | Keith Hernandez | .15 | .11 |
| 481 | Chris Brown | .06 | .05 |
| 482 | Steve Peters | .12 | .09 |

| | | MT | NR MT |
|---|---|---|---|
| 483 | Mickey Hatcher | .03 | .02 |
| 484 | Steve Shields | .03 | .02 |
| 485 | Hubie Brooks | .08 | .06 |
| 486 | Jack McDowell | .20 | .15 |
| 487 | Scott Lusader(FC) | .08 | .06 |
| 488 | Kevin Coffman | .06 | .05 |
| 489 | Phillies Leaders (Mike Schmidt) | .12 | .09 |
| 490 | Chris Sabo | .40 | .30 |
| 491 | Mike Birkbeck | .03 | .02 |
| 492 | Alan Ashby | .03 | .02 |
| 493 | Todd Benzinger | .10 | .08 |
| 494 | Shane Rawley | .06 | .05 |
| 495 | Candy Maldonado | .06 | .05 |
| 496 | Dwayne Henry | .03 | .02 |
| 497 | Pete Stanicek | .12 | .09 |
| 498 | Dave Valle | .03 | .02 |
| 499 | Don Heinkel(FC) | .15 | .11 |
| 500 | Jose Canseco | .40 | .30 |
| 501 | Vance Law | .06 | .05 |
| 502 | Duane Ward | .03 | .02 |
| 503 | Al Newman | .03 | .02 |
| 504 | Bob Walk | .03 | .02 |
| 505 | Pete Rose | .20 | .15 |
| 506 | Kirt Manwaring | .10 | .08 |
| 507 | Steve Farr | .03 | .02 |
| 508 | Wally Backman | .06 | .05 |
| 509 | Bud Black | .03 | .02 |
| 510 | Bob Horner | .08 | .06 |
| 511 | Richard Dotson | .06 | .05 |
| 512 | Donnie Hill | .03 | .02 |
| 513 | Jesse Orosco | .06 | .05 |
| 514 | Chet Lemon | .06 | .05 |
| 515 | Barry Larkin | .20 | .15 |
| 516 | Eddie Whitson | .03 | .02 |
| 517 | Greg Brock | .06 | .05 |
| 518 | Bruce Ruffin | .03 | .02 |
| 519 | Yankees Leaders (Willie Randolph) | .03 | .02 |
| 520 | Rick Sutcliffe | .08 | .06 |
| 521 | Mickey Tettleton | .03 | .02 |
| 522 | Randy Kramer(FC) | .12 | .09 |
| 523 | Andres Thomas | .06 | .05 |
| 524 | Checklist 397-528 | .03 | .02 |
| 525 | Chili Davis | .06 | .05 |
| 526 | Wes Gardner | .06 | .05 |
| 527 | Dave Henderson | .08 | .06 |
| 528 | Luis Medina(FC) | .15 | .11 |
| 529 | Tom Foley | .03 | .02 |
| 530 | Nolan Ryan | .50 | .40 |
| 531 | Dave Hengel(FC) | .08 | .06 |
| 532 | Jerry Browne | .03 | .02 |
| 533 | Andy Hawkins | .03 | .02 |
| 534 | Doc Edwards | .03 | .02 |
| 535 | Todd Worrell | .08 | .06 |
| 536 | Joel Skinner | .03 | .02 |
| 537 | Pete Smith | .08 | .06 |
| 538 | Juan Castillo | .03 | .02 |
| 539 | Barry Jones | .03 | .02 |
| 540 | Bo Jackson | .30 | .25 |
| 541 | Cecil Fielder | .30 | .25 |
| 542 | Todd Frohwirth | .06 | .05 |
| 543 | Damon Berryhill | .15 | .11 |
| 544 | Jeff Sellers | .03 | .02 |
| 545 | Mookie Wilson | .06 | .05 |
| 546 | Mark Williamson | .06 | .05 |

| | | MT | NR MT |
|---|---|---|---|
| 547 | Mark McLemore | .03 | .02 |
| 548 | Bobby Witt | .08 | .06 |
| 549 | Cubs Leaders (Jamie Moyer) | .03 | .02 |
| 550 | Orel Hershiser | .20 | .15 |
| 551 | Randy Ready | .03 | .02 |
| 552 | Greg Cadaret | .06 | .05 |
| 553 | Luis Salazar | .03 | .02 |
| 554 | Nick Esasky | .06 | .05 |
| 555 | Bert Blyleven | .10 | .08 |
| 556 | Bruce Fields(FC) | .06 | .05 |
| 557 | *Keith Miller*(FC) | .15 | .11 |
| 558 | Dan Pasqua | .08 | .06 |
| 559 | Juan Agosto | .03 | .02 |
| 560 | Rock Raines | .15 | .11 |
| 561 | Luis Aguayo | .03 | .02 |
| 562 | Danny Cox | .06 | .05 |
| 563 | Bill Schroeder | .03 | .02 |
| 564 | Russ Nixon | .03 | .02 |
| 565 | Jeff Russell | .03 | .02 |
| 566 | Al Pedrique | .03 | .02 |
| 567 | David Wells | .08 | .06 |
| 568 | Mickey Brantley | .03 | .02 |
| 569 | *German Jimenez*(FC) | .08 | .06 |
| 570 | Tony Gwynn | .30 | .25 |
| 571 | Billy Ripken | .06 | .05 |
| 572 | Atlee Hammaker | .03 | .02 |
| 573 | #1 Draft Pick *(Jim Abbott)* | 1.25 | .90 |
| 574 | Dave Clark | .06 | .05 |
| 575 | Juan Samuel | .10 | .08 |
| 576 | Greg Minton | .03 | .02 |
| 577 | Randy Bush | .03 | .02 |
| 578 | John Morris | .03 | .02 |
| 579 | Astros Leaders (Glenn Davis) | .08 | .06 |
| 580 | Harold Reynolds | .06 | .05 |
| 581 | Gene Nelson | .03 | .02 |
| 582 | Mike Marshall | .10 | .08 |
| 583 | *Paul Gibson*(FC) | .15 | .11 |
| 584 | Randy Velarde(FC) | .10 | .08 |
| 585 | Harold Baines | .10 | .08 |
| 586 | Joe Boever | .03 | .02 |
| 587 | Mike Stanley | .03 | .02 |
| 588 | *Luis Alicea* | .15 | .11 |
| 589 | Dave Meads | .03 | .02 |
| 590 | Andres Galarraga | .12 | .09 |
| 591 | Jeff Musselman | .06 | .05 |
| 592 | John Cangelosi | .03 | .02 |
| 593 | Drew Hall | .10 | .08 |
| 594 | Jimy Williams | .03 | .02 |
| 595 | Teddy Higuera | .08 | .06 |
| 596 | Kurt Stillwell | .06 | .05 |
| 597 | *Terry Taylor*(FC) | .12 | .09 |
| 598 | Ken Gerhart | .06 | .05 |
| 599 | Tom Candiotti | .03 | .02 |
| 600 | Wade Boggs | .40 | .30 |
| 601 | Dave Dravecky | .06 | .05 |
| 602 | Devon White | .10 | .08 |
| 603 | Frank Tanana | .06 | .05 |
| 604 | Paul O'Neill | .03 | .02 |
| 605a | Bob Welch (missing Complete Major League Pitching Record line) | 3.00 | 2.25 |
| 605b | Bob Welch (contains Complete Major League Pitching Record line) | .08 | .06 |
| 606 | Rick Dempsey | .06 | .05 |
| 607 | #1 Draft Pick *(Willie Ansley)*(FC) | .15 | .11 |
| 608 | Phil Bradley | .08 | .06 |
| 609 | Tigers Leaders (Frank Tanana) | .06 | .05 |
| 610 | Randy Myers | .08 | .06 |
| 611 | Don Slaught | .03 | .02 |
| 612 | Dan Quisenberry | .06 | .05 |
| 613 | *Gary Varsho*(FC) | .15 | .11 |
| 614 | Joe Hesketh | .03 | .02 |
| 615 | Robin Yount | .25 | .20 |
| 616 | *Steve Rosenberg*(FC) | .15 | .11 |
| 617 | *Mark Parent* | .15 | .11 |
| 618 | Rance Mulliniks | .03 | .02 |
| 619 | Checklist 529-660 | .03 | .02 |
| 620 | Barry Bonds | .20 | .15 |
| 621 | Rick Mahler | .03 | .02 |
| 622 | Stan Javier | .03 | .02 |
| 623 | Fred Toliver | .03 | .02 |
| 624 | Jack McKeon | .03 | .02 |
| 625 | Eddie Murray | .25 | .20 |
| 626 | Jeff Reed | .03 | .02 |
| 627 | Greg Harris | .03 | .02 |
| 628 | Matt Williams | .10 | .08 |
| 629 | Pete O'Brien | .06 | .05 |
| 630 | Mike Greenwell | .30 | .25 |
| 631 | Dave Bergman | .03 | .02 |
| 632 | *Bryan Harvey* | .25 | .20 |
| 633 | Daryl Boston | .03 | .02 |
| 634 | Marvin Freeman(FC) | .08 | .06 |
| 635 | Willie Randolph | .06 | .05 |
| 636 | Bill Wilkinson | .06 | .05 |
| 637 | Carmen Castillo | .03 | .02 |
| 638 | Floyd Bannister | .06 | .05 |
| 639 | Athletics Leaders (Walt Weiss) | .15 | .11 |
| 640 | Willie McGee | .10 | .08 |
| 641 | Curt Young | .06 | .05 |
| 642 | Argenis Salazar | .03 | .02 |
| 643 | *Louie Meadows*(FC) | .12 | .09 |
| 644 | Lloyd McClendon | .03 | .02 |
| 645 | Jack Morris | .12 | .09 |
| 646 | Kevin Bass | .06 | .05 |
| 647 | *Randy Johnson*(FC) | .30 | .25 |
| 648 | Future Star *(Sandy Alomar)*(FC) | .40 | .30 |
| 649 | Stewart Cliburn | .03 | .02 |
| 650 | Kirby Puckett | .25 | .20 |
| 651 | Tom Niedenfuer | .06 | .05 |
| 652 | Rich Gedman | .06 | .05 |
| 653 | *Tommy Barrett*(FC) | .12 | .09 |
| 654 | Whitey Herzog | .06 | .05 |
| 655 | Dave Magadan | .08 | .06 |
| 656 | Ivan Calderon | .06 | .05 |
| 657 | Joe Magrane | .08 | .06 |
| 658 | R.J. Reynolds | .03 | .02 |
| 659 | Al Leiter | .15 | .11 |
| 660 | Will Clark | .50 | .40 |
| 661 | Turn Back The Clock (Dwight Gooden) | .10 | .08 |

Pitching Record line .08 .06

| | | MT | NR MT |
|---|---|---|---|
| 662 | Turn Back The Clock (Lou Brock) | .08 | .06 |
| 663 | Turn Back The Clock (Hank Aaron) | .15 | .11 |
| 664 | Turn Back The Clock (Gil Hodges) | .06 | .05 |
| 665 | Turn Back The Clock (Tony Oliva) | .06 | .05 |
| 666 | Randy St. Claire | .03 | .02 |
| 667 | Dwayne Murphy | .06 | .05 |
| 668 | Mike Bielecki | .03 | .02 |
| 669 | Dodgers Leaders (Orel Hershiser) | .12 | .09 |
| 670 | Kevin Seitzer | .12 | .09 |
| 671 | Jim Gantner | .03 | .02 |
| 672 | Allan Anderson | .06 | .05 |
| 673 | Don Baylor | .08 | .06 |
| 674 | Otis Nixon | .03 | .02 |
| 675 | Bruce Hurst | .08 | .06 |
| 676 | Ernie Riles | .03 | .02 |
| 677 | Dave Schmidt | .03 | .02 |
| 678 | Dion James | .03 | .02 |
| 679 | Willie Fraser | .03 | .02 |
| 680 | Gary Carter | .15 | .11 |
| 681 | Jeff Robinson | .10 | .08 |
| 682 | Rick Leach | .03 | .02 |
| 683 | Jose Cecena | .15 | .11 |
| 684 | Dave Johnson | .06 | .05 |
| 685 | Jeff Treadway | .10 | .08 |
| 686 | Scott Terry | .08 | .06 |
| 687 | Alvin Davis | .10 | .08 |
| 688 | Zane Smith | .06 | .05 |
| 689 | Stan Jefferson | .03 | .02 |
| 690 | Doug Jones | .10 | .08 |
| 691 | Roberto Kelly | .25 | .20 |
| 692 | Steve Ontiveros | .03 | .02 |
| 693 | Pat Borders | .30 | .25 |
| 694 | Les Lancaster | .06 | .05 |
| 695 | Carlton Fisk | .20 | .15 |
| 696 | Don August | .08 | .06 |
| 697 | Franklin Stubbs | .03 | .02 |
| 698 | Keith Atherton | .03 | .02 |
| 699 | Pirates Leaders (Al Pedrique) | .06 | .05 |
| 700 | Don Mattingly | .60 | .45 |
| 701 | Storm Davis | .08 | .06 |
| 702 | Jamie Quirk | .03 | .02 |
| 703 | Scott Garrelts | .03 | .02 |
| 704 | Carlos Quintana(FC) | .20 | .15 |
| 705 | Terry Kennedy | .06 | .05 |
| 706 | Pete Incaviglia | .08 | .06 |
| 707 | Steve Jeltz | .03 | .02 |
| 708 | Chuck Finley | .03 | .02 |
| 709 | Tom Herr | .06 | .05 |
| 710 | Dave Cone | .20 | .15 |
| 711 | Candy Sierra(FC) | .12 | .09 |
| 712 | Bill Swift | .03 | .02 |
| 713 | #1 Draft Pick (Ty Griffin) | .10 | .08 |
| 714 | Joe Morgan | .03 | .02 |
| 715 | Tony Pena | .06 | .05 |
| 716 | Wayne Tolleson | .03 | .02 |
| 717 | Jamie Moyer | .03 | .02 |
| 718 | Glenn Braggs | .06 | .05 |
| 719 | Danny Darwin | .03 | .02 |

| | | MT | NR MT |
|---|---|---|---|
| 720 | Tim Wallach | .08 | .06 |
| 721 | Ron Tingley(FC) | .12 | .09 |
| 722 | Todd Stottlemyre | .15 | .11 |
| 723 | Rafael Belliard | .03 | .02 |
| 724 | Jerry Don Gleaton | .03 | .02 |
| 725 | Terry Steinbach | .08 | .06 |
| 726 | Dickie Thon | .03 | .02 |
| 727 | Joe Orsulak | .03 | .02 |
| 728 | Charlie Puleo | .03 | .02 |
| 729 | Rangers Leaders (Steve Buechele) | .06 | .05 |
| 730 | Danny Jackson | .12 | .09 |
| 731 | Mike Young | .03 | .02 |
| 732 | Steve Buechele | .03 | .02 |
| 733 | Randy Bockus(FC) | .06 | .05 |
| 734 | Jody Reed | .10 | .08 |
| 735 | Roger McDowell | .08 | .06 |
| 736 | Jeff Hamilton | .06 | .05 |
| 737 | Norm Charlton(FC) | .30 | .25 |
| 738 | Darnell Coles | .06 | .05 |
| 739 | Brook Jacoby | .08 | .06 |
| 740 | Dan Plesac | .08 | .06 |
| 741 | Ken Phelps | .06 | .05 |
| 742 | Future Star (Mike Harkey)(FC) | .30 | .25 |
| 743 | Mike Heath | .03 | .02 |
| 744 | Roger Craig | .06 | .05 |
| 745 | Fred McGriff | .30 | .25 |
| 746 | German Gonzalez(FC) | .15 | .11 |
| 747 | Wil Tejada(FC) | .06 | .05 |
| 748 | Jimmy Jones | .03 | .02 |
| 749 | Rafael Ramirez | .03 | .02 |
| 750 | Bret Saberhagen | .12 | .09 |
| 751 | Ken Oberkfell | .03 | .02 |
| 752 | Jim Gott | .03 | .02 |
| 753 | Jose Uribe | .03 | .02 |
| 754 | Bob Brower | .03 | .02 |
| 755 | Mike Scioscia | .06 | .05 |
| 756 | Scott Medvin(FC) | .12 | .09 |
| 757 | Brady Anderson | .60 | .45 |
| 758 | Gene Walter | .03 | .02 |
| 759 | Brewers Leaders (Rob Deer) | .06 | .05 |
| 760 | Lee Smith | .08 | .06 |
| 761 | Dante Bichette(FC) | .25 | .20 |
| 762 | Bobby Thigpen | .08 | .06 |
| 763 | Dave Martinez | .06 | .05 |
| 764 | #1 Draft Pick (Robin Ventura) | 2.50 | 2.00 |
| 765 | Glenn Davis | .15 | .11 |
| 766 | Cecilio Guante | .03 | .02 |
| 767 | Mike Capel(FC) | .15 | .11 |
| 768 | Bill Wegman | .03 | .02 |
| 769 | Junior Ortiz | .03 | .02 |
| 770 | Alan Trammell | .15 | .11 |
| 771 | Ron Kittle | .06 | .05 |
| 772 | Ron Oester | .03 | .02 |
| 773 | Keith Moreland | .06 | .05 |
| 774 | Frank Robinson | .08 | .06 |
| 775 | Jeff Reardon | .06 | .06 |
| 776 | Nelson Liriano | .06 | .05 |
| 777 | Ted Power | .03 | .02 |

| | | MT | NR MT |
|---|---|---|---|
| 778 | Bruce Benedict | .03 | .02 |
| 779 | Craig McMurtry | .03 | .02 |
| 780 | Pedro Guerrero | .12 | .09 |
| 781 | *Greg Briley*(FC) | .30 | .25 |
| 782 | Checklist 661-792 | .03 | .02 |
| 783 | *Trevor Wilson*(FC) | | |
| | | .20 | .15 |
| 784 | #1 Draft Pick *(Steve Avery)*(FC) | 1.00 | .70 |
| 785 | Ellis Burks | .40 | .30 |
| 786 | Melido Perez | .08 | .06 |
| 787 | *Dave West*(FC) | .20 | .15 |
| 788 | Mike Morgan | .03 | .02 |
| 789 | Royals Leaders (Bo Jackson) | .15 | .11 |
| 790 | Sid Fernandez | .08 | .06 |
| 791 | Jim Lindeman | .03 | .02 |
| 792 | Rafael Santana | .03 | .02 |

## 1989 Topps Traded

For the ninth straight year, Topps issued its annual 132-card "Traded" set at the end of the 1989 baseball season. The set, which was packaged in a special box and sold by hobby dealers, includes traded players and rookies who were not in the regular 1989 Topps set.

| | | MT | NR MT |
|---|---|---|---|
| Complete Set: | | 8.00 | 6.00 |
| Common Player: | | .05 | .04 |
| | | | |
| 1T | Don Aase | .05 | .04 |
| 2T | Jim Abbott | 1.00 | .70 |
| 3T | Kent Anderson(FC) | .15 | .11 |
| 4T | Keith Atherton | .05 | .04 |
| 5T | Wally Backman | .05 | .04 |
| 6T | Steve Balboni | .05 | .04 |
| 7T | Jesse Barfield | .05 | .04 |
| 8T | Steve Bedrosian | .05 | .04 |
| 9T | Todd Benzinger | .05 | .04 |
| 10T | Geronimo Berroa(FC) | .10 | .08 |
| 11T | Bert Blyleven | .05 | .04 |
| 12T | Bob Boone | .05 | .04 |
| 13T | Phil Bradley | .08 | .06 |
| 14T | Jeff Brantley(FC) | .25 | .20 |

| | | MT | NR MT |
|---|---|---|---|
| 15T | Kevin Brown(FC) | .20 | .15 |
| 16T | Jerry Browne | .05 | .04 |
| 17T | Chuck Cary | .20 | .15 |
| 18T | Carmen Castillo | .05 | .04 |
| 19T | Jim Clancy | .05 | .04 |
| 20T | Jack Clark | .10 | .08 |
| 21T | Bryan Clutterbuck | .05 | .04 |
| 22T | Jody Davis | .05 | .04 |
| 23T | Mike Devereaux(FC) | .10 | .08 |
| 24T | Frank DiPino | .05 | .04 |
| 25T | Benny Distefano | .05 | .04 |
| 26T | John Dopson | .20 | .15 |
| 27T | Len Dykstra | .10 | .08 |
| 28T | Jim Eisenreich | .05 | .04 |
| 29T | Nick Esasky | .08 | .06 |
| 30T | Alvaro Espinoza | .25 | .20 |
| 31T | Darrell Evans | .08 | .06 |
| 32T | Junior Felix(FC) | .30 | .25 |
| 33T | Felix Fermin | .05 | .04 |
| 34T | Julio Franco | .15 | .11 |
| 35T | Terry Francona | .05 | .04 |
| 36T | Cito Gaston | .05 | .04 |
| 37T | Bob Geren (incorrect photo)(FC) | .30 | .25 |
| 38T | Tom Gordon(FC) | .60 | .45 |
| 39T | Tommy Gregg(FC) | .25 | .20 |
| 40T | Ken Griffey | .15 | .11 |
| 41T | Ken Griffey, Jr.(FC) | 4.00 | 3.00 |
| 42T | Kevin Gross | .05 | .04 |
| 43T | Lee Guetterman | .05 | .04 |
| 44T | Mel Hall | .05 | .04 |
| 45T | Erik Hanson(FC) | .40 | .30 |
| 46T | Gene Harris(FC) | .20 | .15 |
| 47T | Andy Hawkins | .05 | .04 |
| 48T | Rickey Henderson | .50 | .40 |
| 49T | Tom Herr | .05 | .04 |
| 50T | Ken Hill(FC) | .20 | .15 |
| 51T | Brian Holman(FC) | .30 | .25 |
| 52T | Brian Holton | .10 | .08 |
| 53T | Art Howe | .05 | .04 |
| 54T | Ken Howell | .05 | .04 |
| 55T | Bruce Hurst | .05 | .04 |
| 56T | Chris James | .05 | .04 |
| 57T | Randy Johnson | .30 | .25 |
| 58T | Jimmy Jones | .05 | .04 |
| 59T | Terry Kennedy | .05 | .04 |
| 60T | Paul Kilgus | .05 | .04 |
| 61T | Eric King | .08 | .06 |
| 62T | Ron Kittle | .08 | .06 |
| 63T | John Kruk | .08 | .06 |
| 64T | Randy Kutcher(FC) | .08 | .06 |
| 65T | Steve Lake | .05 | .04 |
| 66T | Mark Langston | .25 | .20 |
| 67T | Dave LaPoint | .05 | .04 |
| 68T | Rick Leach | .05 | .04 |
| 69T | Terry Leach | .05 | .04 |
| 70T | Jim Levebvre | .05 | .04 |
| 71T | Al Leiter | .05 | .04 |
| 72T | Jeffrey Leonard | .05 | .04 |
| 73T | Derek Lilliquist(FC) | .15 | .11 |
| 74T | Rick Mahler | .05 | .04 |
| 75T | Tom McCarthy(FC) | .15 | .11 |
| 76T | Lloyd McClendon | .20 | .15 |
| 77T | Lance McCullers | .05 | .04 |
| 78T | Oddibe McDowell | .05 | .04 |
| 79T | Roger McDowell | .05 | .04 |

| | | MT | NR MT |
|---|---|---|---|
| 80T | Larry McWilliams | .05 | .04 |
| 81T | Randy Milligan | .30 | .25 |
| 82T | Mike Moore | .15 | .11 |
| 83T | Keith Moreland | .05 | .04 |
| 84T | Mike Morgan | .05 | .04 |
| 85T | Jamie Moyer | .05 | .04 |
| 86T | Rob Murphy | .05 | .04 |
| 87T | Eddie Murray | .30 | .25 |
| 88T | Pete O'Brien | .05 | .04 |
| 89T | Gregg Olson | .40 | .30 |
| 90T | Steve Ontiveros | .05 | .04 |
| 91T | Jesse Orosco | .05 | .04 |
| 92T | Spike Owen | .05 | .04 |
| 93T | Rafael Palmeiro | .08 | .06 |
| 94T | Clay Parker(FC) | .20 | .15 |
| 95T | Jeff Parrett | .05 | .04 |
| 96T | Lance Parrish | .05 | .04 |
| 97T | Dennis Powell | .05 | .04 |
| 98T | Rey Quinones | .05 | .04 |
| 99T | Doug Rader | .05 | .04 |
| 100T | Willie Randolph | .08 | .06 |
| 101T | Shane Rawley | .05 | .04 |
| 102T | Randy Ready | .05 | .04 |
| 103T | Bip Roberts | .05 | .04 |
| 104T | Kenny Rogers(FC) | .25 | .20 |
| 105T | Ed Romero | .05 | .04 |
| 106T | Nolan Ryan | 1.50 | 1.25 |
| 107T | Luis Salazar | .05 | .04 |
| 108T | Juan Samuel | .08 | .06 |
| 109T | Alex Sanchez(FC) | .20 | .15 |
| 110T | Deion Sanders(FC) | 2.00 | 1.50 |
| 111T | Steve Sax | .15 | .11 |
| 112T | Rick Schu | .05 | .04 |
| 113T | Dwight Smith(FC) | .15 | .11 |
| 114T | Lonnie Smith | .05 | .04 |
| 115T | Billy Spiers(FC) | .30 | .25 |
| 116T | Kent Tekulve | .05 | .04 |
| 117T | Walt Terrell | .05 | .04 |
| 118T | Milt Thompson | .05 | .04 |
| 119T | Dickie Thon | .05 | .04 |
| 120T | Jeff Torborg | .05 | .04 |
| 121T | Jeff Treadway | .05 | .04 |
| 122T | Omar Vizquel(FC) | .15 | .11 |
| 123T | Jerome Walton(FC) | .20 | .15 |
| 124T | Gary Ward | .05 | .04 |
| 125T | Claudell Washington | .05 | .04 |
| 126T | Curt Wilkerson | .05 | .04 |
| 127T | Eddie Williams | .05 | .04 |
| 128T | Frank Williams | .05 | .04 |
| 129T | Ken Williams | .05 | .04 |
| 130T | Mitch Williams | .20 | .15 |
| 131T | Steve Wilson(FC) | .10 | .08 |
| 132T | Checklist | .05 | .04 |

## 1990 Topps

The 1990 Topps set again included 792 cards, and sported a newly-designed front that featured six different color schemes. The set led off with a special four-card salute to Nolan Ryan, and featured various other specials, including All-Stars, Number 1 Draft Picks, Record Breakers, manager cards, rookies, and "Turn Back the Clock" cards. The set also includes a special card commemorating A. Bartlett Giamatti, the late Baseball Commissioner. The backs are printed in black on a chartreuse background with the card number in the upper left corner. The set features 725 different individual player cards, the most ever, including 138 players making their first appearance in a regular Topps set.

| | | MT | NR MT |
|---|---|---|---|
| | Complete Set: | 20.00 | 15.00 |
| | Common Player: | .03 | .02 |
| 1 | Nolan Ryan | .35 | .25 |
| 2 | Nolan Ryan (The Mets Years) | .20 | .15 |
| 3 | Nolan Ryan (The Angels Years) | .20 | .15 |
| 4 | Nolan Ryan (The Astros Years) | .20 | .15 |
| 5 | Nolan Ryan (The Rangers) | .20 | .15 |
| 6 | 1989 Record Breaker (Vince Coleman) | .10 | .08 |
| 7 | 1989 Record Breaker (Rickey Henderson) | .20 | .15 |
| 8 | 1989 Record Breaker (Cal Ripken) | .15 | .11 |
| 9 | Eric Plunk | .03 | .02 |
| 10 | Barry Larkin | .15 | .11 |
| 11 | Paul Gibson | .04 | .03 |
| 12 | Joe Girardi(FC) | .15 | .11 |
| 13 | Mark Williamson | .03 | .02 |
| 14 | *Mike Fetters*(FC) | .20 | .15 |
| 15 | Teddy Higuera | .06 | .05 |
| 16 | *Kent Anderson* | .10 | .08 |
| 17 | Kelly Downs | .05 | .04 |
| 18 | Carlos Quintana | .09 | .07 |
| 19 | Al Newman | .03 | .02 |
| 20 | Mark Gubicza | .12 | .09 |
| 21 | Jeff Torborg | .03 | .02 |
| 22 | Bruce Ruffin | .03 | .02 |
| 23 | Randy Velarde | .07 | .05 |
| 24 | Joe Hesketh | .03 | .02 |
| 25 | Willie Randolph | .08 | .06 |
| 26 | Don Slaught | .03 | .02 |
| 27 | Rick Leach | .03 | .02 |
| 28 | Duane Ward | .04 | .03 |
| 29 | John Cangelosi | .03 | .02 |

| | MT | NR MT |
|---|---|---|
| 30 David Cone | .10 | .08 |
| 31 Henry Cotto | .03 | .02 |
| 32 John Farrell | .05 | .04 |
| 33 Greg Walker | .05 | .04 |
| 34 Tony Fossas(FC) | .07 | .05 |
| 35 Benito Santiago | .12 | .09 |
| 36 John Costello | .04 | .03 |
| 37 Domingo Ramos | .03 | .02 |
| 38 Wes Gardner | .04 | .03 |
| 39 Curt Ford | .04 | .03 |
| 40 Jay Howell | .06 | .05 |
| 41 Matt Williams | .15 | .11 |
| 42 Jeff Robinson | .05 | .04 |
| 43 Dante Bichette | .07 | .05 |
| 44 #1 Draft Pick (Roger Salkeld)(FC) | .50 | .40 |
| 45 Dave Parker | .09 | .07 |
| 46 Rob Dibble | .07 | .05 |
| 47 Brian Harper | .04 | .03 |
| 48 Zane Smith | .03 | .02 |
| 49 Tom Lawless | .03 | .02 |
| 50 Glenn Davis | .08 | .06 |
| 51 Doug Rader | .03 | .02 |
| 52 Jack Daugherty(FC) | .20 | .15 |
| 53 Mike LaCoss | .04 | .03 |
| 54 Joel Skinner | .04 | .03 |
| 55 Darrell Evans | .05 | .04 |
| 56 Franklin Stubbs | .04 | .03 |
| 57 Greg Vaughn(FC) | .60 | .45 |
| 58 Keith Miller | .10 | .08 |
| 59 Ted Power | .03 | .02 |
| 60 George Brett | .15 | .11 |
| 61 Deion Sanders | .30 | .25 |
| 62 Ramon Martinez | .30 | .25 |
| 63 Mike Pagliarulo | .04 | .03 |
| 64 Danny Darwin | .03 | .02 |
| 65 Devon White | .07 | .05 |
| 66 Greg Litton(FC) | .15 | .11 |
| 67 Scott Sanderson | .04 | .03 |
| 68 Dave Henderson | .06 | .05 |
| 69 Todd Frohwirth | .03 | .02 |
| 70 Mike Greenwell | .30 | .25 |
| 71 Allan Anderson | .05 | .04 |
| 72 Jeff Huson(FC) | .25 | .20 |
| 73 Bob Milacki | .05 | .04 |
| 74 #1 Draft Pick (Jeff Jackson)(FC) | .20 | .15 |
| 75 Doug Jones | .05 | .04 |
| 76 Dave Valle | .03 | .02 |
| 77 Dave Bergman | .03 | .02 |
| 78 Mike Flanagan | .04 | .03 |
| 79 Ron Kittle | .05 | .04 |
| 80 Jeff Russell | .05 | .04 |
| 81 Bob Rodgers | .03 | .02 |
| 82 Scott Terry | .04 | .03 |
| 83 Hensley Meulens | .30 | .25 |
| 84 Ray Searage | .03 | .02 |
| 85 Juan Samuel | .05 | .04 |
| 86 Paul Kilgus | .03 | .02 |
| 87 Rick Luecken(FC) | .15 | .11 |
| 88 Glenn Braggs | .05 | .04 |
| 89 Clint Zavaras(FC) | .15 | .11 |
| 90 Jack Clark | .06 | .05 |

| | MT | NR MT |
|---|---|---|
| 91 Steve Frey(FC) | .20 | .15 |
| 92 Mike Stanley | .03 | .02 |
| 93 Shawn Hillegas | .03 | .02 |
| 94 Herm Winningham | .03 | .02 |
| 95 Todd Worrell | .05 | .04 |
| 96 Jody Reed | .04 | .03 |
| 97 Curt Schilling(FC) | .10 | .08 |
| 98 Jose Gonzalez(FC) | .10 | .08 |
| 99 Rich Monteleone(FC) | .15 | .11 |
| 100 Will Clark | .50 | .40 |
| 101 Shane Rawley | .04 | .03 |
| 102 Stan Javier | .04 | .03 |
| 103 Marvin Freeman | .09 | .07 |
| 104 Bob Knepper | .03 | .02 |
| 105 Randy Myers | .05 | .04 |
| 106 Charlie O'Brien | .03 | .02 |
| 107 Fred Lynn | .05 | .04 |
| 108 Rod Nichols | .04 | .03 |
| 109 Roberto Kelly | .08 | .06 |
| 110 Tommy Helms | .03 | .02 |
| 111 Ed Whited | .20 | .15 |
| 112 Glenn Wilson | .03 | .02 |
| 113 Manny Lee | .03 | .02 |
| 114 Mike Bielecki | .05 | .04 |
| 115 Tony Pena | .06 | .05 |
| 116 Floyd Bannister | .04 | .03 |
| 117 Mike Sharperson(FC) | .09 | .07 |
| 118 Erik Hanson | .10 | .08 |
| 119 Billy Hatcher | .04 | .03 |
| 120 John Franco | .05 | .04 |
| 121 Robin Ventura | .60 | .45 |
| 122 Shawn Abner | .03 | .02 |
| 123 Rich Gedman | .04 | .03 |
| 124 Dave Dravecky | .04 | .03 |
| 125 Kent Hrbek | .07 | .05 |
| 126 Randy Kramer | .03 | .02 |
| 127 Mike Devereaux | .06 | .05 |
| 128 Checklist 1-132 | .03 | .02 |
| 129 Ron Jones | .10 | .08 |
| 130 Bert Blyleven | .05 | .04 |
| 131 Matt Nokes | .06 | .05 |
| 132 Lance Blankenship(FC) | .10 | .08 |
| 133 Ricky Horton | .03 | .02 |
| 134 #1 Draft Pick (Earl Cunningham)(FC) | .15 | .11 |
| 135 Dave Magadan | .05 | .04 |
| 136 Kevin Brown | .06 | .05 |
| 137 Marty Pevey(FC) | .15 | .11 |
| 138 Al Leiter | .04 | .03 |
| 139 Greg Brock | .04 | .03 |
| 140 Andre Dawson | .12 | .09 |
| 141 John Hart | .05 | .04 |
| 142 Jeff Wetherby(FC) | .15 | .11 |
| 143 Rafael Belliard | .03 | .02 |
| 144 Bud Black | .03 | .02 |
| 145 Terry Steinbach | .07 | .05 |
| 146 Rob Richie(FC) | .15 | .11 |
| 147 Chuck Finley | .04 | .03 |
| 148 Edgar Martinez(FC) | .09 | .07 |
| 149 Steve Farr | .04 | .03 |
| 150 Kirk Gibson | .09 | .07 |
| 151 Rick Mahler | .03 | .02 |

| | MT | NR MT | | | MT | NR MT |
|---|---|---|---|---|---|---|
| 152 | Lonnie Smith | .05 | .04 | 215 | Kirk McCaskill | .04 | .03 |
| 153 | Randy Milligan | .05 | .04 | 216 | Ricky Jordan | .20 | .15 |
| 154 | Mike Maddux | .05 | .04 | 217 | Don Robinson | .04 | .03 |
| 155 | Ellis Burks | .25 | .20 | 218 | Wally Backman | .04 | .03 |
| 156 | Ken Patterson | .04 | .03 | 219 | Donn Pall | .03 | .02 |
| 157 | Craig Biggio | .15 | .11 | 220 | Barry Bonds | .10 | .08 |
| 158 | Craig Lefferts | .04 | .03 | 221 | *Gary Mielke*(FC) | .15 | .11 |
| 159 | Mike Felder | .03 | .02 | 222 | Kurt Stillwell | .05 | .04 |
| 160 | Dave Righetti | .06 | .05 | 223 | Tommy Gregg | .06 | .05 |
| 161 | Harold Reynolds | .06 | .05 | 224 | *Delino DeShields*(FC) | | |
| 162 | *Todd Zeile*(FC) | .60 | .45 | | | .60 | .45 |
| 163 | Phil Bradley | .05 | .04 | 225 | Jim Deshaies | .05 | .04 |
| 164 | #1 Draft Pick *(Jeff* | | | 226 | Mickey Hatcher | .03 | .02 |
| | *Juden)*(FC) | .30 | .25 | 227 | *Kevin Tapani*(FC) | | |
| 165 | Walt Weiss | .08 | .06 | | | .30 | .25 |
| 166 | Bobby Witt | .04 | .03 | 228 | Dave Martinez | .03 | .02 |
| 167 | *Kevin Appier*(FC) | | | 229 | David Wells | .03 | .02 |
| | | .35 | .25 | 230 | Keith Hernandez | .07 | .05 |
| 168 | Jose Lind | .04 | .03 | 231 | Jack McKeon | .03 | .02 |
| 169 | Richard Dotson | .03 | .02 | 232 | Darnell Coles | .04 | .03 |
| 170 | George Bell | .12 | .09 | 233 | Ken Hill | .10 | .08 |
| 171 | Russ Nixon | .03 | .02 | 234 | Mariano Duncan | .05 | .04 |
| 172 | Tom Lampkin(FC) | .10 | .08 | 235 | Jeff Reardon | .04 | .03 |
| 173 | Tim Belcher | .12 | .09 | 236 | Hal Morris(FC) | .50 | .40 |
| 174 | Jeff Kunkel | .03 | .02 | 237 | *Kevin Ritz*(FC) | .15 | .11 |
| 175 | Mike Moore | .07 | .05 | 238 | Felix Jose(FC) | .10 | .08 |
| 176 | Luis Quinones | .03 | .02 | 239 | Eric Show | .04 | .03 |
| 177 | Mike Henneman | .05 | .04 | 240 | Mark Grace | .40 | .30 |
| 178 | Chris James | .06 | .05 | 241 | Mike Krukow | .04 | .03 |
| 179 | Brian Holton | .04 | .03 | 242 | Fred Manrique | .03 | .02 |
| 180 | Rock Raines | .10 | .08 | 243 | Barry Jones | .03 | .02 |
| 181 | Juan Agosto | .03 | .02 | 244 | Bill Schroeder | .03 | .02 |
| 182 | Mookie Wilson | .05 | .04 | 245 | Roger Clemens | .25 | .20 |
| 183 | Steve Lake | .03 | .02 | 246 | Jim Eisenreich | .03 | .02 |
| 184 | Danny Cox | .04 | .03 | 247 | Jerry Reed | .03 | .02 |
| 185 | Ruben Sierra | .20 | .15 | 248 | Dave Anderson | .03 | .02 |
| 186 | Dave LaPoint | .03 | .02 | 249 | *Mike Smith*(FC) | .12 | .09 |
| 187 | *Rick Wrona*(FC) | .12 | .09 | 250 | Jose Canseco | .70 | .50 |
| 188 | Mike Smithson | .03 | .02 | 251 | Jeff Blauser | .05 | .04 |
| 189 | Dick Schofield | .04 | .03 | 252 | Otis Nixon | .03 | .02 |
| 190 | Rick Reuschel | .06 | .05 | 253 | Mark Portugal | .03 | .02 |
| 191 | Pat Borders | .08 | .06 | 254 | Francisco Cabrera | .25 | .20 |
| 192 | Don August | .04 | .03 | 255 | Bobby Thigpen | .07 | .05 |
| 193 | Andy Benes | .25 | .20 | 256 | Marvell Wynne | .03 | .02 |
| 194 | Glenallen Hill(FC) | .25 | .20 | 257 | Jose DeLeon | .07 | .05 |
| 195 | Tim Burke | .05 | .04 | 258 | Barry Lyons | .03 | .02 |
| 196 | Gerald Young | .04 | .03 | 259 | Lance McCullers | .05 | .04 |
| 197 | Doug Drabek | .07 | .05 | 260 | Eric Davis | .30 | .25 |
| 198 | Mike Marshall | .06 | .05 | 261 | Whitey Herzog | .03 | .02 |
| 199 | *Sergio Valdez*(FC) | | | 262 | Checklist 133-264 | .03 | .02 |
| | | .20 | .15 | 263 | Mel Stottlemyre, | | |
| 200 | Don Mattingly | .40 | .30 | | Jr.(FC) | .12 | .09 |
| 201 | Cito Gaston | .03 | .02 | 264 | Bryan Clutterbuck | .03 | .02 |
| 202 | Mike Macfarlane | .03 | .02 | 265 | Pete O'Brien | .06 | .05 |
| 203 | *Mike Roesler*(FC) | | | 266 | German Gonzalez | .04 | .03 |
| | | .15 | .11 | 267 | Mark Davidson | .03 | .02 |
| 204 | Bob Dernier | .03 | .02 | 268 | Rob Murphy | .03 | .02 |
| 205 | Mark Davis | .09 | .07 | 269 | Dickie Thon | .03 | .02 |
| 206 | Nick Esasky | .07 | .05 | 270 | Dave Stewart | .08 | .06 |
| 207 | Bob Ojeda | .04 | .03 | 271 | Chet Lemon | .05 | .04 |
| 208 | Brook Jacoby | .04 | .03 | 272 | Bryan Harvey | .04 | .03 |
| 209 | Greg Mathews | .04 | .03 | 273 | Bobby Bonilla | .15 | .11 |
| 210 | Ryne Sandberg | .30 | .25 | 274 | *Goose Gozzo*(FC) | | |
| 211 | John Cerutti | .04 | .03 | | | .15 | .11 |
| 212 | Joe Orsulak | .03 | .02 | 275 | Mickey Tettleton | .07 | .05 |
| 213 | Scott Bankhead | .05 | .04 | 276 | Gary Thurman | .03 | .02 |
| 214 | Terry Francona | .03 | .02 | 277 | Lenny Harris(FC) | .12 | .09 |

| | | MT | NR MT |
|---|---|---|---|
| 278 | Pascual Perez | .04 | .03 |
| 279 | Steve Buechele | .04 | .03 |
| 280 | Lou Whitaker | .07 | .05 |
| 281 | Kevin Bass | .05 | .04 |
| 282 | Derek Lilliquist | .10 | .08 |
| 283 | Joey Belle(FC) | .70 | .50 |
| 284 | Mark Gardner(FC) | | |
| | | .30 | .25 |
| 285 | Willie McGee | .06 | .05 |
| 286 | Lee Guetterman | .03 | .02 |
| 287 | Vance Law | .03 | .02 |
| 288 | Greg Briley | .15 | .11 |
| 289 | Norm Charlton | .10 | .08 |
| 290 | Robin Yount | .20 | .15 |
| 291 | Dave Johnson | .03 | .02 |
| 292 | Jim Gott | .04 | .03 |
| 293 | Mike Gallego | .04 | .03 |
| 294 | Craig McMurtry | .03 | .02 |
| 295 | Fred McGriff | .25 | .20 |
| 296 | Jeff Ballard | .07 | .05 |
| 297 | Tom Herr | .06 | .05 |
| 298 | Danny Gladden | .05 | .04 |
| 299 | Adam Peterson(FC) | .09 | .07 |
| 300 | Bo Jackson | .60 | .45 |
| 301 | Don Aase | .03 | .02 |
| 302 | Marcus Lawton(FC) | | |
| | | .08 | .06 |
| 303 | Rick Cerone | .03 | .02 |
| 304 | Marty Clary(FC) | .08 | .06 |
| 305 | Eddie Murray | .15 | .11 |
| 306 | Tom Niedenfuer | .03 | .02 |
| 307 | Bip Roberts | .08 | .06 |
| 308 | Jose Guzman | .05 | .04 |
| 309 | Eric Yelding(FC) | .20 | .15 |
| 310 | Steve Bedrosian | .05 | .04 |
| 311 | Dwight Smith | .25 | .20 |
| 312 | Dan Quisenberry | .05 | .04 |
| 313 | Gus Polidor | .03 | .02 |
| 314 | #1 Draft Pick (Donald Harris)(FC) | .20 | .15 |
| 315 | Bruce Hurst | .06 | .05 |
| 316 | Carney Lansford | .06 | .05 |
| 317 | Mark Guthrie(FC) | | |
| | | .20 | .15 |
| 318 | Wallace Johnson | .03 | .02 |
| 319 | Dion James | .04 | .03 |
| 320 | Dave Steib | .07 | .05 |
| 321 | Joe Morgan | .03 | .02 |
| 322 | Junior Ortiz | .03 | .02 |
| 323 | Willie Wilson | .04 | .03 |
| 324 | Pete Harnisch(FC) | .10 | .08 |
| 325 | Robby Thompson | .06 | .05 |
| 326 | Tom McCarthy | .10 | .08 |
| 327 | Ken Williams | .03 | .02 |
| 328 | Curt Young | .03 | .02 |
| 329 | Oddibe McDowell | .06 | .05 |
| 330 | Ron Darling | .09 | .07 |
| 331 | Juan Gonzalez(FC) | | |
| | | 1.50 | 1.25 |
| 332 | Paul O'Neill | .07 | .05 |
| 333 | Bill Wegman | .03 | .02 |
| 334 | Johnny Ray | .05 | .04 |
| 335 | Andy Hawkins | .05 | .04 |
| 336 | Ken Griffey, Jr. | 1.00 | .70 |
| 337 | Lloyd McClendon | .06 | .05 |
| 338 | Dennis Lamp | .03 | .02 |
| 339 | Dave Clark | .04 | .03 |

| | | MT | NR MT |
|---|---|---|---|
| 340 | Fernando Valenzuela | | |
| | | .06 | .05 |
| 341 | Tom Foley | .03 | .02 |
| 342 | Alex Trevino | .03 | .02 |
| 343 | Frank Tanana | .04 | .03 |
| 344 | George Canale(FC) | | |
| | | .15 | .11 |
| 345 | Harold Baines | .09 | .07 |
| 346 | Jim Presley | .04 | .03 |
| 347 | Junior Felix | .20 | .15 |
| 348 | Gary Wayne(FC) | .12 | .09 |
| 349 | Steve Finley(FC) | .30 | .25 |
| 350 | Bret Saberhagen | .10 | .08 |
| 351 | Roger Craig | .03 | .02 |
| 352 | Bryn Smith | .05 | .04 |
| 353 | Sandy Alomar | .25 | .20 |
| 354 | Stan Belinda(FC) | | |
| | | .20 | .15 |
| 355 | Marty Barrett | .05 | .04 |
| 356 | Randy Ready | .03 | .02 |
| 357 | Dave West | .20 | .15 |
| 358 | Andres Thomas | .04 | .03 |
| 359 | Jimmy Jones | .03 | .02 |
| 360 | Paul Molitor | .09 | .07 |
| 361 | Randy McCament(FC) | | |
| | | .15 | .11 |
| 362 | Damon Berryhill | .06 | .05 |
| 363 | Dan Petry | .03 | .02 |
| 364 | Rolando Roomes(FC) | | |
| | | .15 | .11 |
| 365 | Ozzie Guillen | .05 | .04 |
| 366 | Mike Heath | .03 | .02 |
| 367 | Mike Morgan | .03 | .02 |
| 368 | Bill Doran | .06 | .05 |
| 369 | Todd Burns | .04 | .03 |
| 370 | Tim Wallach | .07 | .05 |
| 371 | Jimmy Key | .08 | .06 |
| 372 | Terry Kennedy | .03 | .02 |
| 373 | Alvin Davis | .08 | .06 |
| 374 | Steve Cummings(FC) | | |
| | | .15 | .11 |
| 375 | Dwight Evans | .08 | .06 |
| 376 | Checklist 265-396 | .03 | .02 |
| 377 | Mickey Weston(FC) | | |
| | | .15 | .11 |
| 378 | Luis Salazar | .03 | .02 |
| 379 | Steve Rosenberg | .03 | .02 |
| 380 | Dave Winfield | .15 | .11 |
| 381 | Frank Robinson | .03 | .02 |
| 382 | Jeff Musselman | .03 | .02 |
| 383 | John Morris | .04 | .03 |
| 384 | Pat Combs | .20 | .15 |
| 385 | Fred McGriff AS | .20 | .15 |
| 386 | Julio Franco AS | .10 | .08 |
| 387 | Wade Boggs AS | .20 | .15 |
| 388 | Cal Ripken AS | .15 | .11 |
| 389 | Robin Yount AS | .20 | .15 |
| 390 | Ruben Sierra AS | .20 | .15 |
| 391 | Kirby Puckett AS | .20 | .15 |
| 392 | Carlton Fisk AS | .08 | .06 |
| 393 | Bret Saberhagen AS | .10 | .08 |
| 394 | Jeff Ballard AS | .08 | .06 |
| 395 | Jeff Russell AS | .08 | .06 |
| 396 | A. Bartlett Giamatti | .30 | .25 |
| 397 | Will Clark AS | .25 | .20 |
| 398 | Ryne Sandberg AS | .15 | .11 |
| 399 | Howard Johnson AS | .15 | .11 |

| | | MT | NR MT |
|---|---|---|---|
| 400 | Ozzie Smith AS | .10 | .08 |
| 401 | Kevin Mitchell AS | .20 | .15 |
| 402 | Eric Davis AS | .20 | .15 |
| 403 | Tony Gwynn AS | .15 | .11 |
| 404 | Craig Biggio AS | .15 | .11 |
| 405 | Mike Scott AS | .08 | .06 |
| 406 | Joe Magrane AS | .08 | .06 |
| 407 | Mark Davis AS | .08 | .06 |
| 408 | Trevor Wilson | .06 | .05 |
| 409 | Tom Brunansky | .09 | .07 |
| 410 | Joe Boever | .06 | .05 |
| 411 | Ken Phelps | .03 | .02 |
| 412 | Jamie Moyer | .04 | .03 |
| 413 | *Brian DuBois*(FC) | | |
| | | .15 | .11 |
| 414 | #1 Draft Pick *(Frank Thomas)*(FC) | 4.00 | 3.00 |
| 415 | Shawon Dunston | .06 | .05 |
| 416 | *Dave Johnson*(FC) | | |
| | | .12 | .09 |
| 417 | Jim Gantner | .06 | .05 |
| 418 | Tom Browning | .08 | .06 |
| 419 | *Beau Allred*(FC) | .20 | .15 |
| 420 | Carlton Fisk | .08 | .06 |
| 421 | Greg Minton | .03 | .02 |
| 422 | Pat Sheridan | .03 | .02 |
| 423 | Fred Toliver | .03 | .02 |
| 424 | Jerry Reuss | .05 | .04 |
| 425 | Bill Landrum | .05 | .04 |
| 426 | Jeff Hamilton | .05 | .04 |
| 427 | Carmem Castillo | .03 | .02 |
| 428 | *Steve Davis*(FC) | .12 | .09 |
| 429 | Tom Kelly | .03 | .02 |
| 430 | Pete Incaviglia | .06 | .05 |
| 431 | Randy Johnson | .10 | .08 |
| 432 | Damaso Garcia | .03 | .02 |
| 433 | *Steve Olin*(FC) | .12 | .08 |
| 434 | Mark Carreon(FC) | .09 | .07 |
| 435 | Kevin Seitzer | .09 | .07 |
| 436 | Mel Hall | .05 | .04 |
| 437 | Les Lancaster | .05 | .04 |
| 438 | Greg Myers(FC) | .10 | .08 |
| 439 | Jeff Parrett | .06 | .05 |
| 440 | Alan Trammell | .09 | .07 |
| 441 | Bob Kipper | .03 | .02 |
| 442 | Jerry Browne | .07 | .05 |
| 443 | Cris Carpenter | .09 | .07 |
| 444 | *Kyle Abbott* (Number 1 Daft Pick)(FC) | .30 | .25 |
| 445 | Danny Jackson | .05 | .04 |
| 446 | Dan Pasqua | .05 | .04 |
| 447 | Atlee Hammaker | .03 | .02 |
| 448 | Greg Gagne | .04 | .03 |
| 449 | Dennis Rasmussen | .04 | .03 |
| 450 | Rickey Henderson | .25 | .20 |
| 451 | Mark Lemke(FC) | .10 | .08 |
| 452 | Luis de los Santos(FC) | | |
| | | .10 | .08 |
| 453 | Jody Davis | .03 | .02 |
| 454 | Jeff King(FC) | .15 | .11 |
| 455 | Jeffrey Leonard | .06 | .05 |
| 456 | Chris Murphy(FC) | .09 | .07 |
| 457 | Gregg Jefferies | .30 | .25 |
| 458 | Bob McClure | .03 | .02 |
| 459 | Jim Lefebvre | .03 | .02 |
| 460 | Mike Scott | .09 | .07 |
| 461 | *Carlos Martinez*(FC) | | |

| | | MT | NR MT |
|---|---|---|---|
| | | .15 | .11 |
| 462 | Denny Walling | .03 | .02 |
| 463 | Drew Hall | .03 | .02 |
| 464 | *Jerome Walton* | .25 | .20 |
| 465 | Kevin Gross | .06 | .05 |
| 466 | Rance Mulliniks | .03 | .02 |
| 467 | Juan Nieves | .04 | .03 |
| 468 | Billy Ripken | .04 | .03 |
| 469 | John Kruk | .07 | .05 |
| 470 | Frank Viola | .09 | .07 |
| 471 | Mike Brumley | .03 | .02 |
| 472 | Jose Uribe | .04 | .03 |
| 473 | Joe Price | .03 | .02 |
| 474 | Rich Thompson | .04 | .03 |
| 475 | Bob Welch | .06 | .05 |
| 476 | Brad Komminsk | .03 | .02 |
| 477 | Willie Fraser | .03 | .02 |
| 478 | Mike LaValliere | .04 | .03 |
| 479 | Frank White | .06 | .05 |
| 480 | Sid Fernandez | .09 | .07 |
| 481 | Garry Templeton | .05 | .04 |
| 482 | *Steve Carter*(FC) | | |
| | | .15 | .11 |
| 483 | Alejandro Pena | .04 | .03 |
| 484 | Mike Fitzgerald | .03 | .02 |
| 485 | John Candelaria | .05 | .04 |
| 486 | Jeff Treadway | .04 | .04 |
| 487 | Steve Searcy | .05 | .04 |
| 488 | Ken Oberkfell | .03 | .02 |
| 489 | Nick Leyva | .03 | .02 |
| 490 | Dan Plesac | .07 | .05 |
| 491 | *Dave Cochrane*(FC) | | |
| | | .15 | .11 |
| 492 | Ron Oester | .04 | .03 |
| 493 | *Jason Grimsley*(FC) | | |
| | | .25 | .20 |
| 494 | Terry Puhl | .03 | .02 |
| 495 | Lee Smith | .06 | .05 |
| 496 | Cecil Espy | .06 | .05 |
| 497 | Dave Schmidt | .03 | .02 |
| 498 | Rick Schu | .03 | .02 |
| 499 | Bill Long | .04 | .03 |
| 500 | Kevin Mitchell | .35 | .25 |
| 501 | Matt Young | .03 | .02 |
| 502 | Mitch Webster | .04 | .03 |
| 503 | Randy St. Claire | .03 | .02 |
| 504 | Tom O'Malley | .03 | .02 |
| 505 | Kelly Gruber | .08 | .06 |
| 506 | Tom Glavine | .20 | .15 |
| 507 | Gary Redus | .04 | .03 |
| 508 | Terry Leach | .03 | .02 |
| 509 | Tom Pagnozzi | .03 | .02 |
| 510 | Doc Gooden | .25 | .20 |
| 511 | Clay Parker | .07 | .05 |
| 512 | Gary Pettis | .03 | .02 |
| 513 | Mark Eichhorn | .03 | .02 |
| 514 | Andy Allanson | .03 | .02 |
| 515 | Len Dykstra | .06 | .05 |
| 516 | Tim Leary | .05 | .04 |
| 517 | Roberto Alomar | .15 | .11 |
| 518 | Bill Krueger | .03 | .02 |
| 519 | Bucky Dent | .03 | .02 |
| 520 | Mitch Williams | .09 | .07 |
| 521 | Craig Worthington | .15 | .11 |
| 522 | Mike Dunne | .04 | .03 |
| 523 | Jay Bell | .03 | .02 |
| 524 | Daryl Boston | .03 | .02 |

| | MT | NR MT | | | MT | NR MT |
|---|---|---|---|---|---|---|
| 525 | Wally Joyner | .20 | .15 | 588 | Rick Rhoden | .03 | .02 |
| 526 | Checklist 397-528 | .03 | .02 | 589 | Mike Aldrete | .03 | .02 |
| 527 | Ron Hassey | .03 | .02 | 590 | Ozzie Smith | .10 | .08 |
| 528 | Kevin Wickander(FC) | | | 591 | Todd Stottlemyre | .08 | .06 |
| | | .20 | .15 | 592 | R.J. Reynolds | .03 | .02 |
| 529 | Greg Harris | .03 | .02 | 593 | Scott Bradley | .03 | .02 |
| 530 | Mark Langston | .10 | .08 | 594 | Luis Sojo(FC) | .20 | .15 |
| 531 | Ken Caminiti | .06 | .05 | 595 | Greg Swindell | .10 | .08 |
| 532 | Cecilio Guante | .03 | .02 | 596 | Jose DeJesus(FC) | .10 | .08 |
| 533 | Tim Jones(FC) | .07 | .05 | 597 | Chris Bosio | .07 | .05 |
| 534 | Louie Meadows | .07 | .05 | 598 | Brady Anderson | .05 | .04 |
| 535 | John Smoltz | .15 | .11 | 599 | Frank Williams | .03 | .02 |
| 536 | Bob Geren | .15 | .11 | 600 | Darryl Strawberry | .30 | .15 |
| 537 | Mark Grant | .03 | .02 | 601 | Luis Rivera | .04 | .03 |
| 538 | Billy Spiers | .20 | .15 | 602 | Scott Garrelts | .07 | .05 |
| 539 | Neal Heaton | .03 | .02 | 603 | Tony Armas | .03 | .02 |
| 540 | Danny Tartabull | .09 | .07 | 604 | Ron Robinson | .03 | .02 |
| 541 | Pat Perry | .03 | .02 | 605 | Mike Scioscia | .07 | .05 |
| 542 | Darren Daulton | .03 | .02 | 606 | Storm Davis | .07 | .05 |
| 543 | Nelson Liriano | .03 | .02 | 607 | Steve Jeltz | .03 | .02 |
| 544 | Dennis Boyd | .05 | .04 | 608 | Eric Anthony(FC) | | |
| 545 | Kevin McReynolds | .09 | .07 | | | .20 | .15 |
| 546 | Kevin Hickey | .05 | .04 | 609 | Sparky Anderson | .03 | .02 |
| 547 | Jack Howell | .05 | .04 | 610 | Pedro Guerrero | .12 | .09 |
| 548 | Pat Clements | .03 | .02 | 611 | Walt Terrell | .05 | .04 |
| 549 | Don Zimmer | .03 | .02 | 612 | Dave Gallagher | .07 | .05 |
| 550 | Julio Franco | .09 | .07 | 613 | Jeff Pico | .04 | .03 |
| 551 | Tim Crews | .03 | .02 | 614 | Nelson Santovenia | .09 | .07 |
| 552 | Mike Smith(FC) | .12 | .09 | 615 | Rob Deer | .07 | .05 |
| 553 | Scott Scudder(FC) | | | 616 | Brian Holman | .10 | .08 |
| | | .20 | .15 | 617 | Geronimo Berroa | .08 | .06 |
| 554 | Jay Buhner | .08 | .06 | 618 | Eddie Whitson | .05 | .04 |
| 555 | Jack Morris | .07 | .05 | 619 | Rob Ducey | .08 | .06 |
| 556 | Gene Larkin | .03 | .02 | 620 | Tony Castillo(FC) | | |
| 557 | Jeff Innis | .15 | .11 | | | .20 | .15 |
| 558 | Rafael Ramirez | .04 | .03 | 621 | Melido Perez | .07 | .05 |
| 559 | Andy McGaffigan | .04 | .03 | 622 | Sid Bream | .05 | .04 |
| 560 | Steve Sax | .08 | .06 | 623 | Jim Corsi | .05 | .04 |
| 561 | Ken Dayley | .03 | .02 | 624 | Darrin Jackson | .04 | .03 |
| 562 | Chad Kreuter | .10 | .08 | 625 | Roger McDowell | .07 | .05 |
| 563 | Alex Sanchez | .10 | .08 | 626 | Bob Melvin | .03 | .02 |
| 564 | #1 Draft Pick (Tyler | | | 627 | Jose Rijo | .07 | .05 |
| | Houston)(FC) | .20 | .15 | 628 | Candy Maldonado | .04 | .03 |
| 565 | Scott Fletcher | .05 | .04 | 629 | Eric Hetzel(FC) | .10 | .08 |
| 566 | Mark Knudson | .06 | .05 | 630 | Gary Gaetti | .10 | .08 |
| 567 | Ron Gant | .10 | .08 | 631 | John Wetteland(FC) | | |
| 568 | John Smiley | .07 | .05 | | | .25 | .20 |
| 569 | Ivan Calderon | .05 | .04 | 632 | Scott Lusader | .06 | .05 |
| 570 | Cal Ripken | .35 | .25 | 633 | Dennis Cook(FC) | .25 | .20 |
| 571 | Brett Butler | .06 | .05 | 634 | Luis Polonia | .06 | .05 |
| 572 | Greg Harris | .09 | .07 | 635 | Brian Downing | .06 | .05 |
| 573 | Danny Heep | .03 | .02 | 636 | Jesse Orosco | .03 | .02 |
| 574 | Bill Swift | .04 | .03 | 637 | Craig Reynolds | .03 | .02 |
| 575 | Lance Parrish | .07 | .05 | 638 | Jeff Montgomery | .07 | .05 |
| 576 | Mike Dyer(FC) | .20 | .15 | 639 | Tony LaRussa | .03 | .02 |
| 577 | Charlie Hayes(FC) | .10 | .08 | 640 | Rick Sutcliffe | .06 | .05 |
| 578 | Joe Magrane | .09 | .07 | 641 | Doug Strange(FC) | | |
| 579 | Art Howe | .03 | .02 | | | .15 | .11 |
| 580 | Joe Carter | .15 | .11 | 642 | Jack Armstrong | .04 | .03 |
| 581 | Ken Griffey | .05 | .04 | 643 | Alfredo Griffin | .04 | .03 |
| 582 | Rick Honeycutt | .03 | .02 | 644 | Paul Assenmacher | .04 | .03 |
| 583 | Bruce Benedict | .03 | .02 | 645 | Jose Oquendo | .05 | .04 |
| 584 | Phil Stephenson(FC) | | | 646 | Checklist 529-660 | .03 | .02 |
| | | .09 | .07 | 647 | Rex Hudler | .03 | .02 |
| 585 | Kal Daniels | .10 | .08 | 648 | Jim Clancy | .03 | .02 |
| 586 | Ed Nunez | .03 | .02 | 649 | Dan Murphy(FC) | .15 | .11 |
| 587 | Lance Johnson | .08 | .06 | 650 | Mike Witt | .06 | .05 |

| | | MT | NR MT |
|---|---|---|---|
| 651 | Rafael Santana | .06 | .05 |
| 652 | Mike Boddicker | .06 | .05 |
| 653 | John Moses | .03 | .02 |
| 654 | #1 Draft Pick *(Paul Coleman)*(FC) | .20 | .15 |
| 655 | Gregg Olson | .30 | .25 |
| 656 | Mackey Sasser | .05 | .04 |
| 657 | Terry Mulholland | .06 | .05 |
| 658 | Donell Nixon | .03 | .02 |
| 659 | Greg Cadaret | .03 | .02 |
| 660 | Vince Coleman | .10 | .08 |
| 661 | Turn Back The Clock — 1985 (Dick Howser) | .07 | .05 |
| 662 | Turn Back The Clock — 1980 (Mike Schmidt) | .07 | .05 |
| 663 | Turn Back The Clock — 1975 (Fred Lynn) | .07 | .05 |
| 664 | Turn Back The Clock — 1970 (Johnny Bench) | .07 | .05 |
| 665 | Turn Back The Clock — 1965 (Sandy Koufax) | .07 | .05 |
| 666 | Brian Fisher | .05 | .04 |
| 667 | Curt Wilkerson | .03 | .02 |
| 668 | *Joe Oliver*(FC) | .30 | .25 |
| 669 | Tom Lasorda | .03 | .02 |
| 670 | Dennis Eckersley | .09 | .07 |
| 671 | Bob Boone | .09 | .07 |
| 672 | Roy Smith | .03 | .02 |
| 673 | Joey Meyer | .03 | .02 |
| 674 | Spike Owen | .05 | .04 |
| 675 | Jim Abbott | .35 | .25 |
| 676 | Randy Kutcher(FC) | .07 | .05 |
| 677 | Jay Tibbs | .03 | .02 |
| 678 | Kirt Manwaring | .10 | .08 |
| 679 | Gary Ward | .04 | .03 |
| 680 | Howard Johnson | .15 | .11 |
| 681 | Mike Schooler | .07 | .05 |
| 682 | Dann Bilardello | .03 | .02 |
| 683 | *Kenny Rogers* | .10 | .08 |
| 684 | *Julio Machado*(FC) | .20 | .15 |
| 685 | Tony Fernandez | .09 | .07 |
| 686 | Carmelo Martinez | .06 | .05 |
| 687 | Tim Birtsas | .03 | .02 |
| 688 | Milt Thompson | .06 | .05 |
| 689 | Rich Yett | .03 | .02 |
| 690 | Mark McGwire | .30 | .25 |
| 691 | Chuck Cary | .03 | .02 |
| 692 | Sammy Sosa | .35 | .25 |
| 693 | Calvin Schiraldi | .03 | .02 |
| 694 | *Mike Stanton*(FC) | .15 | .11 |
| 695 | Tom Henke | .06 | .05 |
| 696 | B.J. Surhoff | .07 | .05 |
| 697 | Mike Davis | .03 | .02 |
| 698 | *Omar Vizquel* | .10 | .08 |
| 699 | Jim Leyland | .03 | .02 |
| 700 | Kirby Puckett | .25 | .20 |
| 701 | *Bernie Williams*(FC) | .30 | .25 |
| 702 | Tony Phillips | .04 | .03 |
| 703 | *Jeff Brantley* | .12 | .09 |
| 704 | *Chip Hale*(FC) | .15 | .11 |
| 705 | Claudell Washington | .07 | .05 |
| 706 | Geno Petralli | .03 | .02 |
| 707 | Luis Aquino | .03 | .02 |
| 708 | Larry Sheets | .03 | .02 |

| | | MT | NR MT |
|---|---|---|---|
| 709 | Juan Berneguer | .03 | .02 |
| 710 | Von Hayes | .09 | .07 |
| 711 | Rick Aguilera | .05 | .04 |
| 712 | Todd Benzinger | .09 | .07 |
| 713 | *Tim Drummond*(FC) | .15 | .11 |
| 714 | *Marquis Grissom*(FC) | .50 | .40 |
| 715 | Greg Maddux | .15 | .11 |
| 716 | Steve Balboni | .03 | .02 |
| 717 | Ron Kakovice | .03 | .02 |
| 718 | Gary Sheffield | .30 | .25 |
| 719 | *Wally Whitehurst*(FC) | .15 | .11 |
| 720 | Andres Galarraga | .15 | .11 |
| 721 | Lee Mazzilli | .03 | .02 |
| 722 | Felix Fermin | .03 | .02 |
| 723 | Jeff Robinson | .05 | .04 |
| 724 | Juan Bell(FC) | .10 | .08 |
| 725 | Terry Pendleton | .07 | .05 |
| 726 | Gene Nelson | .03 | .02 |
| 727 | Pat Tabler | .05 | .04 |
| 728 | Jim Acker | .03 | .02 |
| 729 | Bobby Valentine | .03 | .02 |
| 730 | Tony Gwynn | .20 | .15 |
| 731 | Don Carman | .05 | .04 |
| 732 | Ernie Riles | .03 | .02 |
| 733 | John Dopson | .09 | .07 |
| 734 | Kevin Elster | .06 | .05 |
| 735 | Charlie Hough | .06 | .05 |
| 736 | Rick Dempsey | .03 | .02 |
| 737 | Chris Sabo | .15 | .11 |
| 738 | *Gene Harris* | .10 | .08 |
| 739 | Dale Sveum | .04 | .03 |
| 740 | Jesse Barfield | .08 | .06 |
| 741 | Steve Wilson | .10 | .08 |
| 742 | Ernie Whitt | .05 | .04 |
| 743 | Tom Candiotti | .05 | .04 |
| 744 | *Kelly Mann*(FC) | .20 | .15 |
| 745 | Hubie Brooks | .06 | .05 |
| 746 | Dave Smith | .06 | .05 |
| 747 | Randy Bush | .03 | .02 |
| 748 | Doyle Alexander | .06 | .05 |
| 749 | Mark Parent | .04 | .03 |
| 750 | Dale Murphy | .10 | .08 |
| 751 | Steve Lyons | .04 | .03 |
| 752 | Tom Gordon | .25 | .20 |
| 753 | Chris Speier | .03 | .02 |
| 754 | Bob Walk | .05 | .04 |
| 755 | Rafael Palmeiro | .08 | .06 |
| 756 | Ken Howell | .03 | .02 |
| 757 | *Larry Walker*(FC) | .40 | .30 |
| 758 | Mark Thurmond | .03 | .02 |
| 759 | Tom Trebelhorn | .03 | .02 |
| 760 | Wade Boggs | .25 | .20 |
| 761 | Mike Jackson | .05 | .04 |
| 762 | Doug Dascenzo | .07 | .05 |
| 763 | Denny Martinez | .07 | .05 |
| 764 | Tim Teufel | .05 | .04 |
| 765 | Chili Davis | .07 | .05 |
| 766 | Brian Meyer(FC) | .10 | .08 |
| 767 | Tracy Jones | .06 | .05 |
| 768 | Chuck Crim | .04 | .03 |
| 769 | *Greg Hibbard*(FC) | .30 | .25 |
| 770 | Cory Snyder | .09 | .07 |

| | | MT | NR MT |
|---|---|---|---|
| 771 | Pete Smith | .06 | .05 |
| 772 | Jeff Reed | .03 | .02 |
| 773 | Dave Leiper | .03 | .02 |
| 774 | *Ben McDonald*(FC) | | |
| | | .60 | .45 |
| 775 | Andy Van Slyke | .09 | .07 |
| 776 | Charlie Leibrandt | .04 | .03 |
| 777 | Tim Laudner | .03 | .02 |
| 778 | Mike Jeffcoat | .03 | .02 |
| 779 | Lloyd Moseby | .06 | .05 |
| 780 | Orel Hershiser | .15 | .11 |
| 781 | Mario Diaz | .03 | .02 |
| 782 | Jose Alvarez | .03 | .02 |
| 783 | Checklist 661-792 | .03 | .02 |
| 784 | Scott Bailes | .03 | .02 |
| 785 | Jim Rice | .07 | .05 |
| 786 | Eric King | .04 | .03 |
| 787 | Rene Gonzales | .03 | .02 |
| 788 | Frank DiPino | .03 | .02 |
| 789 | John Wathan | .03 | .02 |
| 790 | Gary Carter | .07 | .05 |
| 791 | Alvaro Espinoza | .15 | .11 |
| 792 | Gerald Perry | .06 | .05 |

## 1990 Topps Traded

For the first time, Topps "Traded" series cards were made available nationwide in retail wax packs. The 132-card set was also sold in complete boxed form as it has been in recent years. The wax pack traded cards feature gray backs, while the boxed set cards feature white backs. The cards are numbered 1T-132T and showcase rookies, players who changed teams and new managers.

| | | MT | NR MT |
|---|---|---|---|
| Complete Set: | | 8.00 | 6.00 |
| Common Player: | | .05 | .04 |
| 1T | Darrel Akerfelds | .05 | .04 |
| 2T | Sandy Alomar, Jr. | .20 | .15 |
| 3T | Brad Arnsberg | .05 | .04 |
| 4T | Steve Avery | .80 | .60 |
| 5T | Wally Backman | .05 | .04 |
| 6T | Carlos Baerga(FC) | 1.00 | .70 |

| | | MT | NR MT |
|---|---|---|---|
| 7T | Kevin Bass | .06 | .05 |
| 8T | Willie Blair(FC) | .10 | .08 |
| 9T | Mike Blowers(FC) | .20 | .15 |
| 10T | Shawn Boskie(FC) | .20 | .15 |
| 11T | Daryl Boston | .05 | .04 |
| 12T | Dennis Boyd | .06 | .05 |
| 13T | Glenn Braggs | .06 | .05 |
| 14T | Hubie Brooks | .08 | .06 |
| 15T | Tom Brunansky | .08 | .06 |
| 16T | John Burkett(FC) | .25 | .20 |
| 17T | Casey Candaele | .05 | .04 |
| 18T | John Candelaria | .06 | .05 |
| 19T | Gary Carter | .10 | .08 |
| 20T | Joe Carter | .10 | .08 |
| 21T | Rick Cerone | .05 | .04 |
| 22T | Scott Coolbaugh(FC) | | |
| | | .15 | .11 |
| 23T | Bobby Cox | .05 | .04 |
| 24T | Mark Davis | .06 | .05 |
| 25T | Storm Davis | .06 | .05 |
| 26T | Edgar Diaz(FC) | .10 | .08 |
| 27T | Wayne Edwards(FC) | .20 | .15 |
| 28T | Mark Eichhorn | .05 | .04 |
| 29T | Scott Erickson(FC) | .70 | .50 |
| 30T | Nick Esasky | .06 | .05 |
| 31T | Cecil Fielder | .50 | .40 |
| 32T | John Franco | .08 | .06 |
| 33T | Travis Fryman(FC) | 1.25 | .90 |
| 34T | Bill Gullickson | .05 | .04 |
| 35T | Darryl Hamilton | .15 | .11 |
| 36T | Mike Harkey | .20 | .15 |
| 37T | Bud Harrelson | .05 | .04 |
| 38T | Billy Hatcher | .06 | .05 |
| 39T | Keith Hernandez | .08 | .06 |
| 40T | Joe Hesketh | .05 | .04 |
| 41T | Dave Hollins(FC) | .25 | .20 |
| 42T | Sam Horn | .08 | .06 |
| 43T | Steve Howard(FC) | .20 | .15 |
| 44T | Todd Hundley(FC) | .25 | .20 |
| 45T | Jeff Huson | .10 | .08 |
| 46T | Chris James | .05 | .04 |
| 47T | Stan Javier | .05 | .04 |
| 48T | Dave Justice(FC) | 1.50 | 1.25 |
| 49T | Jeff Kaiser(FC) | .12 | .09 |
| 50T | Dana Kiecker(FC) | .20 | .15 |
| 51T | Joe Klink(FC) | .10 | .08 |
| 52T | Brent Knackert(FC) | .12 | .09 |
| 53T | Brad Komminsk | .05 | .04 |
| 54T | Mark Langston | .10 | .08 |
| 55T | Tim Layana(FC) | .25 | .20 |
| 56T | Rick Leach | .05 | .04 |
| 57T | Terry Leach | .05 | .04 |
| 58T | Tim Leary | .05 | .04 |
| 59T | Craig Lefferts | .05 | .04 |
| 60T | Charlie Leibrandt | .05 | .04 |
| 61T | Jim Leyritz(FC) | .20 | .15 |
| 62T | Fred Lynn | .06 | .05 |
| 63T | Kevin Maas(FC) | .60 | .45 |
| 64T | Shane Mack | .08 | .06 |
| 65T | Candy Maldonado | .06 | .05 |
| 66T | Fred Manrique | .05 | .04 |
| 67T | Mike Marshall | .05 | .04 |
| 68T | Carmelo Martinez | .05 | .04 |
| 69T | John Marzano | .06 | .05 |
| 70T | Ben McDonald | .60 | .45 |
| 71T | Jack McDowell | .08 | .06 |
| 72T | John McNamara | .05 | .04 |

| | MT | NR MT |
|---|---|---|
| 73T Orlando Mercado | .05 | .04 |
| 74T Stump Merrill | .05 | .04 |
| 75T Alan Mills(FC) | .20 | .15 |
| 76T Hal Morris | .40 | .30 |
| 77T Lloyd Moseby | .06 | .05 |
| 78T Randy Myers | .08 | .06 |
| 79T Tim Naehring(FC) | .35 | .25 |
| 80T Junior Noboa | .06 | .05 |
| 81T Matt Nokes | .06 | .05 |
| 82T Pete O'Brien | .05 | .04 |
| 83T John Olerud(FC) | .40 | .30 |
| 84T Greg Olson(FC) | .15 | .11 |
| 85T Junior Ortiz | .05 | .04 |
| 86T Dave Parker | .15 | .11 |
| 87T Rick Parker(FC) | .15 | .11 |
| 88T Bob Patterson | .05 | .04 |
| 89T Alejandro Pena | .05 | .04 |
| 90T Tony Pena | .08 | .06 |
| 91T Pascual Perez | .05 | .04 |
| 92T Gerald Perry | .05 | .04 |
| 93T Dan Petry | .05 | .04 |
| 94T Gary Pettis | .06 | .05 |
| 95T Tony Phillips | .05 | .04 |
| 96T Lou Piniella | .05 | .04 |
| 97T Luis Polonia | .05 | .04 |
| 98T Jim Presley | .06 | .05 |
| 99T Scott Radinsky(FC) | .25 | .20 |
| 100T Willie Randolph | .08 | .06 |
| 101T Jeff Reardon | .08 | .06 |
| 102T Greg Riddoch | .05 | .04 |
| 103T Jeff Robinson | .05 | .04 |
| 104T Ron Robinson | .05 | .04 |
| 105T Kevin Romine | .05 | .04 |
| 106T Scott Ruskin(FC) | .20 | .15 |
| 107T John Russell | .05 | .04 |
| 108T Bill Sampen(FC) | .20 | .15 |
| 109T Juan Samuel | .08 | .06 |
| 110T Scott Sanderson | .06 | .05 |
| 111T Jack Savage(FC) | .10 | .08 |
| 112T Dave Schmidt | .05 | .04 |
| 113T Red Schoendienst | .05 | .04 |
| 114T Terry Shumpert(FC) | .20 | .15 |
| 115T Matt Sinatro | .05 | .04 |
| 116T Don Slaught | .05 | .04 |
| 117T Bryn Smith | .05 | .04 |
| 118T Lee Smith | .08 | .06 |
| 119T Paul Sorrento(FC) | .20 | .15 |
| 120T Franklin Stubbs | .05 | .04 |
| 121T Russ Swan(FC) | .20 | .15 |
| 122T Bob Tewksbury | .05 | .04 |
| 123T Wayne Tolleson | .05 | .04 |
| 124T John Tudor | .06 | .05 |
| 125T Randy Veres(FC) | .10 | .08 |
| 126T Hector Villanueva(FC) | .20 | .15 |
| 127T Mitch Webster | .05 | .04 |
| 128T Ernie Whitt | .06 | .05 |
| 129T Frank Wills | .06 | .05 |
| 130T Dave Winfield | .15 | .11 |
| 131T Matt Young | .05 | .04 |
| 132T Checklist | .05 | .04 |

**Regional interest may affect
the value of a card.**

## 1991 Topps

Topps celebrated its 40th anniversary in 1991 with the biggest promotional campaign in baseball card history. More than 300,000 vintage Topps cards (or certificates which can be redeemed for valuable older cards) produced from 1952 to present were randomly inserted in packs. Also a grand prize winner will receive one complete set from each year, and others will receive a single set from 1952-present. The 1991 Topps card fronts feature the "Topps 40 Years of Baseball" logo in the upper left corner. Card borders frame the player photos. All players of the same team have cards with the same frame/border colors. Both action and posed shots appear in full-color on the card fronts. The flip sides are printed horizontally and feature complete statistics. Record Breakers and other special cards were once again included in the set. The cards measure 2-1/2" by 3-1/2". Several cards feature horizontal fronts. 6,313 forms of this set were released with gold "Operation Desert Shield" stamps on the fronts of the cards. The cards were released to U.S. troops serving in the Persian Gulf. Due to scarcity, these cards are quite valuable. Complete "Desert Shield" sets list for $4,000.

**A player's name in italic type
indicates a rookie card. An (FC)
indicates a player's first card for
that particular card company.**

| | | MT | NR MT |
|---|---|---|---|
| | Complete Set: | 18.00 | 13.50 |
| | Common Player: | .03 | .02 |
| 1 | Nolan Ryan | .30 | .25 |
| 2 | Record Breaker (George Brett) | .08 | .06 |
| 3 | Record Breaker (Carlton Fisk) | .08 | .06 |
| 4 | Record Breaker (Kevin Maas) | .10 | .08 |
| 5 | Record Breaker (Cal Ripken) | .08 | .04 |
| 6 | Record Breaker (Nolan Ryan) | .20 | .15 |
| 7 | Record Breaker (Ryne Sandberg) | .10 | .08 |
| 8 | Record Breaker (Bobby Thigpen) | .08 | |
| 9 | Darrin Fletcher(FC) | .10 | .08 |
| 10 | Gregg Olson | .08 | .06 |
| 11 | Roberto Kelly | .08 | .06 |
| 12 | Paul Assenmacher | .04 | .03 |
| 13 | Mariano Duncan | .06 | .05 |
| 14 | Dennis Lamp | .03 | .02 |
| 15 | Von Hayes | .08 | .06 |
| 16 | Mike Heath | .04 | .03 |
| 17 | Jeff Brantley | .06 | .05 |
| 18 | Nelson Liriano | .03 | .02 |
| 19 | Jeff Robinson | .04 | .03 |
| 20 | Pedro Guerrero | .08 | .06 |
| 21 | Joe Morgan | .03 | .02 |
| 22 | Storm Davis | .06 | .05 |
| 23 | Jim Gantner | .04 | .03 |
| 24 | Dave Martinez | .05 | .04 |
| 25 | Tim Belcher | .08 | .06 |
| 26 | Luis Sojo | .06 | .05 |
| 27 | Bobby Witt | .08 | .06 |
| 28 | Alvaro Espinoza | .05 | .04 |
| 29 | Bob Walk | .03 | .02 |
| 30 | Gregg Jefferies | .15 | .11 |
| 31 | Colby Ward(FC) | .15 | .11 |
| 32 | Mike Simms(FC) | .20 | .15 |
| 33 | Barry Jones | .05 | .04 |
| 34 | Atlee Hammaker | .03 | .02 |
| 35 | Greg Maddux | .08 | .06 |
| 36 | Donnie Hill | .03 | .02 |
| 37 | Tom Bolton | .05 | .04 |
| 38 | Scott Bradley | .03 | .02 |
| 39 | Jim Neidlinger(FC) | .15 | .11 |
| 40 | Kevin Mitchell | .20 | .15 |
| 41 | Ken Dayley | .04 | .03 |
| 42 | Chris Hoiles(FC) | .20 | .15 |
| 43 | Roger McDowell | .06 | .05 |
| 44 | Mike Felder | .04 | .03 |
| 45 | Chris Sabo | .10 | .08 |
| 46 | Tim Drummond | .06 | .05 |
| 47 | Brook Jacoby | .06 | .05 |
| 48 | Dennis Boyd | .05 | .04 |
| 49a | Pat Borders (40 stolen bases in 1986) | .20 | .15 |
| 49b | Pat Borders (0 stolen bases in 1986) | .15 | .11 |

| | | MT | NR MT |
|---|---|---|---|
| 50 | Bob Welch | .08 | .06 |
| 51 | Art Howe | .03 | .02 |
| 52 | Francisco Oliveras(FC) | .10 | .08 |
| 53 | Mike Sahrperson | .06 | .05 |
| 54 | Gary Mielke | .05 | .04 |
| 55 | Jeffrey Leonard | .05 | .04 |
| 56 | Jeff Parrett | .04 | .03 |
| 57 | Jack Howell | .04 | .03 |
| 58 | Mel Stottlemyre | .08 | .06 |
| 59 | Eric Yelding | .06 | .05 |
| 60 | Frank Viola | .12 | .09 |
| 61 | Stan Javier | .04 | .03 |
| 62 | Lee Guetterman | .03 | .02 |
| 63 | Milt Thompson | .04 | .03 |
| 64 | Tom Herr | .05 | .04 |
| 65 | Bruce Hurst | .06 | .05 |
| 66 | Terry Kennedy | .03 | .02 |
| 67 | Rick Honeycutt | .03 | .02 |
| 68 | Gary Sheffield | .15 | .11 |
| 69 | Steve Wilson | .06 | .05 |
| 70 | Ellis Burks | .15 | .11 |
| 71 | Jim Acker | .03 | .02 |
| 72 | Junior Ortiz | .03 | .02 |
| 73 | Craig Worthington | .06 | .05 |
| 74 | #1 Draft Pick (Shane Andrews)(FC) | .20 | .15 |
| 75 | Jack Morris | .08 | .06 |
| 76 | Jerry Browne | .05 | .04 |
| 77 | Drew Hall | .03 | .02 |
| 78 | Geno Petralli | .03 | .02 |
| 79 | Frank Thomas | 1.00 | .70 |
| 80a | Fernando Valenzuela (italics error) | .25 | .20 |
| 80b | Fernando Valenzuela (correct italics) | .15 | .11 |
| 81 | Cito Gaston | .03 | .02 |
| 82 | Tom Glavine | .05 | .04 |
| 83 | Daryl Boston | .03 | .02 |
| 84 | Bob McClure | .03 | .02 |
| 85 | Jesse Barfield | .08 | .06 |
| 86 | Les Lancaster | .04 | .03 |
| 87 | Tracy Jones | .03 | .02 |
| 88 | Bob Tewksbury | .04 | .03 |
| 89 | Darren Daulton | .06 | .05 |
| 90 | Danny Tartabull | .08 | .06 |
| 91 | Greg Colbrunn(FC) | .15 | .11 |
| 92 | Danny Jackson | .06 | .05 |
| 93 | Ivan Calderon | .08 | .06 |
| 94 | John Dopson | .05 | .04 |
| 95 | Paul Molitor | .10 | .08 |
| 96 | Trevor Wilson | .04 | .03 |
| 97 | Brady Anderson | .04 | .03 |
| 98 | Sergio Valdez | .05 | .04 |
| 99 | Chris Gwynn | .05 | .04 |
| 100a | Don Mattingly (10 hits in 1990) | .60 | .45 |
| 100b | Don Mattingly (101 hits in 1990) | .40 | .30 |
| 101 | Rob Ducey | .04 | .03 |
| 102 | Gene Larkin | .06 | .05 |
| 103 | #1 Draft Pick (Tim Costo)(FC) | .35 | .25 |
| 104 | Don Robinson | .04 | .03 |
| 105 | Kevin McReynolds | .05 | .04 |
| 106 | Ed Nunez | .03 | .02 |

| | | MT | NR MT | | | | MT | NR MT |
|---|---|---|---|---|---|---|---|---|
| 107 | Luis Polonia | .04 | .03 | | 169 | Luis Aquino | .04 | .03 |
| 108 | Matt Young | .04 | .03 | | 170 | Carlton Fisk | .10 | .08 |
| 109 | Greg Riddoch | .03 | .02 | | 171 | Tony LaRussa | .04 | .03 |
| 110 | Tom Henke | .06 | .05 | | 172 | Pete Incaviglia | .06 | .05 |
| 111 | Andres Thomas | .03 | .02 | | 173 | Jason Grimsley | .06 | .05 |
| 112 | Frank DiPino | .03 | .02 | | 174 | Ken Caminiti | .05 | .04 |
| 113 | #1 Draft Pick *(Carl* | | | | 175 | Jack Armstrong | .08 | .06 |
| | *Everett)*(FC) | .35 | .25 | | 176 | John Orton(FC) | .06 | .05 |
| 114 | *Lance Dickson*(FC) | | | | 177 | *Reggie Harris*(FC) | | |
| | | .40 | .30 | | | | .15 | .11 |
| 115 | Hubie Brooks | .08 | .06 | | 178 | Dave Valle | .04 | .03 |
| 116 | Mark Davis | .05 | .04 | | 179 | Pete Harnisch | .06 | .05 |
| 117 | Dion James | .03 | .02 | | 180 | Tony Gwynn | .12 | .09 |
| 118 | *Tom Edens*(FC) | .10 | .08 | | 181 | Duane Ward | .04 | .03 |
| 119 | Carl Nichols(FC) | .05 | .04 | | 182 | Junior Noboa | .04 | .03 |
| 120 | Joe Carter | .08 | .06 | | 183 | Clay Parker | .04 | .03 |
| 121 | Eric King | .05 | .04 | | 184 | Gary Green | .10 | .08 |
| 122 | Paul O'Neill | .06 | .05 | | 185 | Joe Magrane | .06 | .05 |
| 123 | Greg Harris | .05 | .04 | | 186 | Rod Booker | .03 | .02 |
| 124 | Randy Bush | .04 | .03 | | 187 | Greg Cadaret | .03 | .02 |
| 125 | Steve Bedrosian | .06 | .05 | | 188 | Damon Berryhill | .06 | .05 |
| 126 | *Bernard Gilkey*(FC) | | | | 189 | *Daryl Irvine*(FC) | .15 | .11 |
| | | .20 | .15 | | 190 | Matt Williams | .15 | .11 |
| 127 | Joe Price | .03 | .02 | | 191 | *Willie Blair* | .10 | .08 |
| 128 | *Travis Fryman* | .60 | .45 | | 192 | Rob Deer | .06 | .05 |
| 129 | Mark Eichhorn | .03 | .02 | | 193 | Felix Fermin | .03 | .02 |
| 130 | Ozzie Smith | .08 | .06 | | 194 | Xavier Hernandez(FC) | | |
| 131 | Checklist 1 | .03 | .02 | | | | .08 | .06 |
| 132 | Jamie Quirk | .03 | .02 | | 195 | Wally Joyner | .10 | .08 |
| 133 | Greg Briley | .08 | .06 | | 196 | *Jim Vatcher*(FC) | .12 | .09 |
| 134 | Kevin Elster | .04 | .03 | | 197 | *Chris Nabholz*(FC) | | |
| 135 | Jerome Walton | .08 | .06 | | | | .20 | .15 |
| 136 | Dave Schmidt | .03 | .02 | | 198 | R.J. Reynolds | .04 | .03 |
| 137 | Randy Ready | .03 | .02 | | 199 | Mike Hartley(FC) | .15 | .11 |
| 138 | Jamie Moyer | .04 | .03 | | 200 | Darryl Strawberry | .20 | .15 |
| 139 | Jeff Treadway | .05 | .04 | | 201 | Tom Kelly | .03 | .02 |
| 140 | Fred McGriff | .10 | .08 | | 202 | *Jim Leyritz* | .12 | .09 |
| 141 | Nick Leyva | .03 | .02 | | 203 | Gene Harris | .05 | .04 |
| 142 | Curtis Wilkerson | .04 | .03 | | 204 | Herm Winningham | .04 | .03 |
| 143 | John Smiley | .04 | .03 | | 205 | *Mike Perez*(FC) | .15 | .11 |
| 144 | Dave Henderson | .06 | .05 | | 206 | Carlos Quintana | .08 | .06 |
| 145 | Lou Whitaker | .08 | .06 | | 207 | Gary Wayne | .05 | .04 |
| 146 | Dan Plesac | .06 | .05 | | 208 | Willie Wilson | .06 | .05 |
| 147 | *Carlos Baerga* | .20 | .15 | | 209 | Ken Howell | .05 | .04 |
| 148 | Rey Palacios | .04 | .03 | | 210 | Lance Parrish | .08 | .06 |
| 149 | *Al Osuna*(FC) | .15 | .11 | | 211 | *Brian Barnes*(FC) | | |
| 150 | Cal Ripken | .12 | .09 | | | | .20 | .15 |
| 151 | Tom Browning | .06 | .05 | | 212 | Steve Finley | .06 | .05 |
| 152 | Mickey Hatcher | .04 | .03 | | 213 | Frank Wills | .06 | .05 |
| 153 | Bryan Harvey | .06 | .05 | | 214 | Joe Girardi | .06 | .05 |
| 154 | Jay Buhner | .06 | .05 | | 215 | Dave Smith | .06 | .05 |
| 155 | Dwight Evans | .08 | .06 | | 216 | Greg Gagne | .04 | .03 |
| 156 | Carlos Martinez | .06 | .05 | | 217 | Chris Bosio | .05 | .04 |
| 157 | John Smoltz | .08 | .06 | | 218 | *Rick Parker* | .03 | .02 |
| 158 | Jose Uribe | .04 | .03 | | 219 | Jack McDowell | .06 | .05 |
| 159 | Joe Boever | .03 | .02 | | 220 | Tim Wallach | .08 | .06 |
| 160 | Vince Coleman | .08 | .06 | | 221 | Don Slaught | .04 | .03 |
| 161 | Tim Leary | .04 | .03 | | 222 | *Brian McRae*(FC) | | |
| 162 | *Ozzie Canseco*(FC) | | | | | | .40 | .30 |
| | | .15 | .11 | | 223 | Allan Anderson | .04 | .03 |
| 163 | Dave Johnson | .04 | .03 | | 224 | Juan Gonzalez | .35 | .25 |
| 164 | Edgar Diaz | .05 | .04 | | 225 | Randy Johnson | .06 | .05 |
| 165 | Sandy Alomar | .15 | .11 | | 226 | Alfredo Griffin | .04 | .03 |
| 166 | Harold Baines | .08 | .06 | | 227 | Steve Avery | .15 | .11 |
| 167 | *Randy Tomlin*(FC) | | | | 228 | Rex Hudler | .04 | .03 |
| | | .25 | .20 | | 229 | Rance Mulliniks | .03 | .02 |
| 168 | John Olerud | .30 | .25 | | 230 | Sid Fernandez | .08 | .06 |

| | | MT | NR MT | | | | MT | NR MT |
|---|---|---|---|---|---|---|---|---|
| 231 | Doug Rader | .03 | .02 | | 291 | John Wathan | .03 | .02 |
| 232 | Jose DeJesus | .08 | .06 | | 292 | Bud Black | .04 | .03 |
| 233 | Al Leiter | .03 | .02 | | 293 | Jay Bell | .06 | .05 |
| 234 | *Scott Erickson* | .80 | .60 | | 294 | Mike Moore | .06 | .05 |
| 235 | Dave Parker | .10 | .08 | | 295 | Rafael Palmeiro | .08 | .06 |
| 236 | Frank Tanana | .06 | .05 | | 296 | Mark Williamson | .04 | .03 |
| 237 | Rick Cerone | .03 | .02 | | 297 | Manny Lee | .04 | .03 |
| 238 | Mike Dunne | .03 | .02 | | 298 | Omar Vizquel | .04 | .03 |
| 239 | Darren Lewis(FC) | | | | 299 | *Scott Radinsky* | .15 | .11 |
| | | .30 | .25 | | 300 | Kirby Puckett | .15 | .11 |
| 240 | Mike Scott | .08 | .06 | | 301 | Steve Farr | .04 | .03 |
| 241 | Dave Clark | .04 | .03 | | 302 | Tim Teufel | .03 | .02 |
| 242 | Mike LaCoss | .03 | .02 | | 303 | Mike Boddicker | .06 | .05 |
| 243 | Lance Johnson | .06 | .05 | | 304 | Kevin Reimer(FC) | .10 | .08 |
| 244 | Mike Jeffcoat | .03 | .02 | | 305 | Mike Scioscia | .06 | .05 |
| 245 | Kal Daniels | .08 | .06 | | 306 | Lonnie Smith | .06 | .05 |
| 246 | Kevin Wickander | .05 | .04 | | 307 | Andy Benes | .08 | .06 |
| 247 | Jody Reed | .08 | .06 | | 308 | Tom Pagnozzi | .04 | .03 |
| 248 | Tom Gordon | .08 | .06 | | 309 | Norm Charlton | .08 | .06 |
| 249 | Bob Melvin | .03 | .02 | | 310 | Gary Carter | .08 | .06 |
| 250 | Dennis Eckersley | .10 | .08 | | 311 | Jeff Pico | .03 | .02 |
| 251 | Mark Lemke | .05 | .04 | | 312 | Charlie Hayes | .06 | .05 |
| 252 | *Mel Rojas*(FC) | .15 | .11 | | 313 | Ron Robinson | .06 | .05 |
| 253 | Garry Templeton | .04 | .03 | | 314 | Gary Pettis | .04 | .03 |
| 254 | *Shawn Boskie* | .15 | .11 | | 315 | Roberto Alomar | .10 | .08 |
| 255 | Brian Downing | .05 | .04 | | 316 | Gene Nelson | .03 | .02 |
| 256 | Greg Hibbard | .08 | .06 | | 317 | Mike Fitzgerald | .03 | .02 |
| 257 | Tom O'Malley | .03 | .02 | | 318 | Rick Aguilera | .06 | .05 |
| 258 | Chris Hammond(FC) | | | | 319 | Jeff McKnight(FC) | .06 | .05 |
| | | .15 | .11 | | 320 | Tony Fernandez | .08 | .06 |
| 259 | Hensley Meulens | .08 | .06 | | 321 | Bob Rodgers | .03 | .02 |
| 260 | Harold Reynolds | .06 | .05 | | 322 | *Terry Shumpert* | .15 | .11 |
| 261 | Bud Harrelson | .03 | .02 | | 323 | Cory Snyder | .08 | .06 |
| 262 | Tim Jones | .04 | .03 | | 324 | Ron Kittle | .08 | .06 |
| 263 | Checklist 2 | .03 | .02 | | 325 | Brett Butler | .06 | .05 |
| 264 | *Dave Hollins* | .25 | .20 | | 326 | Ken Patterson | .04 | .03 |
| 265 | Mark Gubicza | .06 | .05 | | 327 | Ron Hassey | .03 | .02 |
| 266 | Carmen Castillo | .03 | .02 | | 328 | Walt Terrell | .04 | .03 |
| 267 | Mark Knudson | .03 | .02 | | 329 | Dave Justice | .50 | .40 |
| 268 | Tom Brookens | .04 | .03 | | 330 | Doc Gooden | .20 | .15 |
| 269 | Joe Hesketh | .03 | .02 | | 331 | Eric Anthony | .10 | .08 |
| 270 | Mark McGwire | .25 | .20 | | 332 | Kenny Rogers | .06 | .05 |
| 271 | *Omar Olivares*(FC) | | | | 333 | #1 Draft Pick *(Chipper* | | |
| | | .15 | .11 | | | *Jones)*(FC) | .50 | .40 |
| 272 | Jeff King | .06 | .05 | | 334 | Todd Benzinger | .05 | .04 |
| 273 | Johnny Ray | .05 | .04 | | 335 | Mitch Williams | .08 | .06 |
| 274 | Ken Williams | .03 | .02 | | 336 | Matt Nokes | .06 | .05 |
| 275 | Alan Trammell | .10 | .08 | | 337 | Keith Comstock | .03 | .02 |
| 276 | Bill Swift | .05 | .04 | | 338 | Luis Rivera | .04 | .03 |
| 277 | Scott Coolbaugh | .06 | .05 | | 339 | Larry Walker | .08 | .06 |
| 278 | *Alex Fernandez*(FC) | | | | 340 | Ramon Martinez | .15 | .11 |
| | | .60 | .45 | | 341 | John Moses | .03 | .02 |
| 279a | Jose Gonzalez (photo of | | | | 342 | *Mickey Morandini* | .15 | .11 |
| | Billy Bean) | .20 | .15 | | 343 | Jose Oquendo | .04 | .03 |
| 279b | Jose Gonzalez (correct | | | | 344 | Jeff Russell | .06 | .05 |
| | photo) | .12 | .09 | | 345 | Jose DeJesus | .06 | .05 |
| 280 | Bret Saberhagen | .08 | .06 | | 346 | Jesse Orosco | .04 | .03 |
| 281 | Larry Sheets | .04 | .03 | | 347 | Greg Vaughn | .10 | .08 |
| 282 | Don Carman | .03 | .02 | | 348 | Todd Stottlemyre | .06 | .05 |
| 283 | Marquis Grissom | .10 | .08 | | 349 | Dave Gallagher | .04 | .03 |
| 284 | Bill Spiers | .06 | .05 | | 350 | Glenn Davis | .12 | .09 |
| 285 | Jim Abbott | .10 | .08 | | 351 | Joe Torre | .06 | .05 |
| 286 | Ken Oberkfell | .04 | .03 | | 352 | Frank White | .06 | .05 |
| 287 | Mark Grant | .03 | .02 | | 353 | Tony Castillo | .05 | .04 |
| 288 | Derrick May(FC) | .40 | .30 | | 354 | Sid Bream | .05 | .04 |
| 289 | Tim Birtsas | .03 | .02 | | 355 | Chili Davis | .06 | .05 |
| 290 | Steve Sax | .08 | .06 | | 356 | Mike Marshall | .06 | .05 |

| | | MT | NR MT | | | MT | NR MT |
|---|---|---|---|---|---|---|---|
| 357 | Jack Savage | .10 | .08 | 420 | Bobby Thigpen | .08 | .06 |
| 358 | Mark Parent | .03 | .02 | 421 | Alex Cole(FC) | .20 | .15 |
| 359 | Chuck Cary | .04 | .03 | 422 | Rick Rueschel | .06 | .05 |
| 360 | Rock Raines | .15 | .11 | 423 | Rafael Ramirez | .04 | .03 |
| 361 | Scott Garrelts | .05 | .04 | 424 | Calvin Schiraldi | .03 | .02 |
| 362 | *Hector Villanueva* | .15 | .11 | 425 | Andy Van Slyke | .08 | .06 |
| 363 | Rick Mahler | .04 | .03 | 426 | *Joe Grahe*(FC) | .15 | .11 |
| 364 | Dan Pasqua | .06 | .05 | 427 | Rick Dempsey | .03 | .02 |
| 365 | Mike Schooler | .06 | .05 | 428 | *John Barfield*(FC) | | |
| 366 | Checklist 3 | .03 | .02 | | | .10 | .08 |
| 367 | *Dave Walsh*(FC) | .15 | .11 | 429 | Stump Merrill | .03 | .02 |
| 368 | Felix Jose | .06 | .05 | 430 | Gary Gaetti | .08 | .06 |
| 369 | Steve Searcy | .06 | .05 | 431 | Paul Gibson | .03 | .02 |
| 370 | Kelly Gruber | .12 | .09 | 432 | Delino DeShields | .20 | .15 |
| 371 | Jeff Montgomery | .06 | .05 | 433 | Pat Tabler | .04 | .03 |
| 372 | Spike Owen | .05 | .04 | 434 | Julio Machado(FC) | .10 | .08 |
| 373 | Darrin Jackson | .04 | .03 | 435 | Kevin Maas | .25 | .20 |
| 374 | *Larry Casian*(FC) | | | 436 | Scott Bankhead | .05 | .04 |
| | | .15 | .11 | 437 | Doug Dascenzo | .04 | .03 |
| 375 | Tony Pena | .06 | .05 | 438 | Vicente Palacios | .05 | .04 |
| 376 | Mike Harkey | .08 | .06 | 439 | Dickie Thon | .03 | .02 |
| 377 | Rene Gonzales | .03 | .02 | 440 | George Bell | .08 | .06 |
| 378 | *Wilson Alvarez*(FC) | | | 441 | Zane Smith | .04 | .03 |
| | | .40 | .30 | 442 | Charlie O'Brien | .04 | .03 |
| 379 | Randy Velarde | .04 | .03 | 443 | Jeff Innis | .05 | .04 |
| 380 | Willie McGee | .08 | .06 | 444 | Glenn Braggs | .05 | .04 |
| 381 | Jose Lind | .05 | .04 | 445 | Greg Swindell | .06 | .05 |
| 382 | Mackey Sasser | .05 | .04 | 446 | *Craig Grebeck*(FC) | | |
| 383 | Pete Smith | .06 | .05 | | | .15 | .11 |
| 384 | Gerald Perry | .05 | .04 | 447 | John Burkett | .12 | .09 |
| 385 | Mickey Tettleton | .05 | .04 | 448 | Craig Lefferts | .05 | .04 |
| 386 | Cecil Fielder (AS) | .10 | .08 | 449 | Juan Berenguer | .03 | .02 |
| 387 | Julio Franco (AS) | .08 | .06 | 450 | Wade Boggs | .15 | .11 |
| 388 | Kelly Gruber (AS) | .08 | .06 | 451 | Neal Heaton | .05 | .04 |
| 389 | Alan Trammell (AS) | .06 | .05 | 452 | Bill Schroeder | .03 | .02 |
| 390 | Jose Canseco (AS) | .10 | .08 | 453 | Lenny Harris | .05 | .04 |
| 391 | Rickey Henderson (AS) | | | 454 | Kevin Appier | .08 | .06 |
| | | .10 | .08 | 455 | Walt Weiss | .06 | .05 |
| 392 | Ken Griffey, Jr. (AS) | .30 | .25 | 456 | Charlie Leibrandt | .05 | .04 |
| 393 | Carlton Fisk (AS) | .08 | .06 | 457 | *Todd Hundley* | .20 | .15 |
| 394 | Bob Welch (AS) | .06 | .05 | 458 | Brian Holman | .06 | .05 |
| 395 | Chuck Finley (AS) | .06 | .05 | 459 | Tom Trebelhorn | .03 | .02 |
| 396 | Bobby Thigpen (AS) | .08 | .06 | 460 | Dave Steib | .08 | .06 |
| 397 | Eddie Murray (AS) | .08 | .06 | 461 | Robin Ventura | .08 | .06 |
| 398 | Ryne Sandberg (AS) | .10 | .08 | 462 | Steve Frey | .05 | .04 |
| 399 | Matt Williams (AS) | .08 | .06 | 463 | Dwight Smith | .06 | .05 |
| 400 | Barry Larkin (AS) | .08 | .06 | 464 | Steve Buechele | .04 | .03 |
| 401 | Barry Bonds (AS) | .10 | .08 | 465 | Ken Griffey | .05 | .04 |
| 402 | Darryl Strawberry (AS) | | | 466 | Charles Nagy(FC) | .10 | .08 |
| | | .10 | .08 | 467 | Dennis Cook | .06 | .05 |
| 403 | Bobby Bonilla (AS) | .10 | .08 | 468 | Tim Hulett | .04 | .03 |
| 404 | Mike Scoscia (AS) | .06 | .05 | 469 | Chet Lemon | .05 | .04 |
| 405 | Doug Drabek (AS) | .08 | .06 | 470 | Howard Johnson | .10 | .08 |
| 406 | Frank Viola (AS) | .08 | .06 | 471 | #1 Draft Pick (*Mike | | |
| 407 | John Franco (AS) | .06 | .05 | | Lieberthal*)(FC) | .30 | .25 |
| 408 | Ernie Riles | .04 | .03 | 472 | Kirt Manwaring | .05 | .04 |
| 409 | Mike Stanley | .03 | .02 | 473 | Curt Young | .04 | .03 |
| 410 | Dave Righetti | .08 | .06 | 474 | *Phil Plantier*(FC) | .40 | .30 |
| 411 | Lance Blankenship | .04 | .03 | 475 | Teddy Higuera | .08 | .06 |
| 412 | Dave Bergman | .03 | .02 | 476 | Glenn Wilson | .05 | .04 |
| 413 | Terry Mulholland | .06 | .05 | 477 | Mike Fetters | .06 | .05 |
| 414 | Sammy Sosa | .15 | .11 | 478 | Kurt Stillwell | .05 | .04 |
| 415 | Rick Sutcliffe | .08 | .06 | 479 | Bob Patterson | .03 | .02 |
| 416 | Randy Milligan | .06 | .05 | 480 | Dave Magadan | .10 | .08 |
| 417 | Bill Krueger | .03 | .02 | 481 | Eddie Whitson | .05 | .04 |
| 418 | Nick Esasky | .06 | .05 | 482 | Tino Martinez | .40 | .30 |
| 419 | Jeff Reed | .03 | .02 | 483 | Mike Aldrete | .04 | .03 |

|  |  | MT | NR MT |
|---|---|---|---|
| 484 | Dave LaPoint | .04 | .03 |
| 485 | Terry Pendleton | .06 | .05 |
| 486 | Tommy Greene(FC) | .10 | .08 |
| 487 | Rafael Belliard | .03 | .02 |
| 488 | Jeff Manto(FC) | .15 | .11 |
| 489 | Bobby Valentine | .03 | .02 |
| 490 | Kirk Gibson | .08 | .06 |
| 491 | #1 Draft Pick (Kurt Miller)(FC) | .30 | .25 |
| 492 | Ernie Whitt | .05 | .04 |
| 493 | Jose Rijo | .08 | .06 |
| 494 | Chris James | .06 | .05 |
| 495 | Charlie Hough | .04 | .03 |
| 496 | Marty Barrett | .05 | .04 |
| 497 | Ben McDonald | .30 | .25 |
| 498 | Mark Salas | .03 | .02 |
| 499 | Melido Perez | .06 | .05 |
| 500 | Will Clark | .30 | .25 |
| 501 | Mike Bielecki | .05 | .04 |
| 502 | Carney Lansford | .06 | .05 |
| 503 | Roy Smith | .04 | .03 |
| 504 | Julio Valera(FC) | .15 | .11 |
| 505 | Chuck Finley | .08 | .06 |
| 506 | Darnell Coles | .04 | .03 |
| 507 | Steve Jeltz | .03 | .02 |
| 508 | Mike York(FC) | .15 | .11 |
| 509 | Glenallen Hill | .06 | .05 |
| 510 | John Franco | .08 | .06 |
| 511 | Steve Balboni | .03 | .02 |
| 512 | Jose Mesa(FC) | .05 | .04 |
| 513 | Jerald Clark | .05 | .04 |
| 514 | Mike Stanton | .08 | .06 |
| 515 | Alvin Davis | .08 | .06 |
| 516 | Karl Rhodes(FC) | .20 | .15 |
| 517 | Joe Oliver | .06 | .05 |
| 518 | Cris Carpenter | .05 | .04 |
| 519 | Sparky Anderson | .04 | .03 |
| 520 | Mark Grace | .15 | .11 |
| 521 | Joe Orsulak | .05 | .04 |
| 522 | Stan Belinda | .06 | .05 |
| 523 | Rodney McCray(FC) | .15 | .11 |
| 524 | Darrel Akerfelds | .04 | .03 |
| 525 | Willie Randolph | .06 | .05 |
| 526 | Moises Alou(FC) | .15 | .11 |
| 527 | Checklist 4 | .03 | .02 |
| 528 | Denny Martinez | .06 | .05 |
| 529 | #1 Draft Pick (Mark Newfield)(FC) | .60 | .45 |
| 530 | Roger Clemens | .20 | .15 |
| 531 | Dave Rhode(FC) | .15 | .11 |
| 532 | Kirk McCaskill | .06 | .05 |
| 533 | Oddibe McDowell | .05 | .04 |
| 534 | Mike Jackson | .04 | .03 |
| 535 | Ruben Sierra | .15 | .11 |
| 536 | Mike Witt | .04 | .03 |
| 537 | Mike LaValliere | .05 | .04 |
| 538 | Bip Roberts | .05 | .04 |
| 539 | Scott Terry | .03 | .02 |
| 540 | George Brett | .12 | .09 |
| 541 | Domingo Ramos | .03 | .02 |
| 542 | Rob Murphy | .03 | .02 |
| 543 | Junior Felix | .08 | .06 |
| 544 | Alejandro Pena | .03 | .02 |
| 545 | Dale Murphy | .10 | .08 |
| 546 | Jeff Ballard | .05 | .04 |
| 547 | Mike Pagliarulo | .04 | .03 |
| 548 | Jaime Navarro | .10 | .08 |
| 549 | John McNamara | .03 | .02 |
| 550 | Eric Davis | .15 | .11 |
| 551 | Bob Kipper | .03 | .02 |
| 552 | Jeff Hamilton | .04 | .03 |
| 553 | Joe Klink | .10 | .08 |
| 554 | Brian Harper | .06 | .05 |
| 555 | Turner Ward(FC) | .20 | .15 |
| 556 | Gary Ward | .04 | .03 |
| 557 | Wally Whitehurst | .06 | .05 |
| 558 | Otis Nixon | .03 | .02 |
| 559 | Adam Peterson | .06 | .05 |
| 560 | Greg Smith(FC) | .15 | .11 |
| 561 | Tim McIntosh(FC) | .15 | .11 |
| 562 | Jeff Kunkel | .03 | .02 |
| 563 | Brent Knackert | .10 | .08 |
| 564 | Dante Bichette | .08 | .06 |
| 565 | Craig Biggio | .08 | .06 |
| 566 | Craig Wilson(FC) | .15 | .11 |
| 567 | Dwayne Henry | .03 | .02 |
| 568 | Ron Karkovice | .04 | .03 |
| 569 | Curt Schilling | .05 | .04 |
| 570 | Barry Bonds | .15 | .11 |
| 571 | Pat Combs | .08 | .06 |
| 572 | Dave Anderson | .03 | .02 |
| 573 | Rich Rodriguez(FC) | .15 | .11 |
| 574 | John Marzano | .04 | .03 |
| 575 | Robin Yount | .15 | .11 |
| 576 | Jeff Kaiser(FC) | .10 | .08 |
| 577 | Bill Doran | .06 | .05 |
| 578 | Dave West | .06 | .05 |
| 579 | Roger Craig | .03 | .02 |
| 580 | Dave Stewart | .12 | .09 |
| 581 | Luis Quinones | .03 | .02 |
| 582 | Marty Clary | .03 | .02 |
| 583 | Tony Phillips | .04 | .03 |
| 584 | Kevin Brown | .06 | .05 |
| 585 | Pete O'Brien | .04 | .03 |
| 586 | Fred Lynn | .05 | .04 |
| 587 | Jose Offerman(FC) | .25 | .20 |
| 588 | Mark Whiten(FC) | .35 | .25 |
| 589 | Scott Ruskin | .10 | .08 |
| 590 | Eddie Murray | .12 | .09 |
| 591 | Ken Hill | .05 | .04 |
| 592 | B.J. Surhoff | .06 | .05 |
| 593 | Mike Walker(FC) | .15 | .11 |
| 594 | Rich Garces(FC) | .15 | .11 |
| 595 | Bill Landrum | .05 | .04 |
| 596 | #1 Draft Pick (Ronnie Walden)(FC) | .30 | .25 |
| 597 | Jerry Don Gleaton | .03 | .02 |
| 598 | Sam Horn | .05 | .04 |
| 599 | Greg Myers | .04 | .03 |
| 600 | Bo Jackson | .40 | .30 |
| 601 | Bob Ojeda | .04 | .03 |
| 602 | Casey Candaele | .04 | .03 |
| 603a | Wes Chamberlain (photo of Louie Meadows)(FC) | 1.25 | .90 |
| 603b | Wes Chamberlain (correct photo)(FC) | .40 | .30 |
| 604 | Billy Hatcher | .05 | .04 |
| 605 | Jeff Reardon | .08 | .06 |
| 606 | Jim Gott | .04 | .03 |
| 607 | Edgar Martinez | .06 | .05 |

| | | MT | NR MT | | | MT | NR MT |
|---|---|---|---|---|---|---|---|
| 608 | Todd Burns | .03 | .02 | 671 | Andy McGaffigan | .03 | .02 |
| 609 | Jeff Torborg | .03 | .02 | 672 | Shane Mack | .06 | .05 |
| 610 | Andres Galarraga | .08 | .06 | 673 | *Greg Olson* | .20 | .15 |
| 611 | Dave Eiland | .04 | .03 | 674 | Kevin Gross | .06 | .05 |
| 612 | Steve Lyons | .04 | .03 | 675 | Tom Brunansky | .08 | .06 |
| 613 | Eric Show | .04 | .03 | 676 | *Scott* | | |
| 614 | Luis Salazar | .04 | .03 | | *Chiamparino*(FC) | .20 | .15 |
| 615 | Bert Blyleven | .08 | .06 | 677 | Billy Ripken | .04 | .03 |
| 616 | Todd Zeile | .15 | .11 | 678 | Mark Davidson | .03 | .02 |
| 617 | Bill Wegman | .04 | .03 | 679 | Bill Bathe(FC) | .04 | .03 |
| 618 | Sil Campusano | .04 | .03 | 680 | David Cone | .06 | .05 |
| 619 | David Wells | .04 | .03 | 681 | *Jeff Schaefer*(FC) | | |
| 620 | Ozzie Guillen | .08 | .06 | | | .10 | .08 |
| 621 | Ted Power | .03 | .02 | 682 | *Ray Lankford*(FC) | | |
| 622 | Jack Daugherty | .05 | .04 | | | .70 | .50 |
| 623 | Jeff Blauser | .04 | .03 | 683 | Derek Lilliquist | .05 | .04 |
| 624 | Tom Candiotti | .04 | .03 | 684 | Milt Cuyler(FC) | .25 | .20 |
| 625 | Terry Steinbach | .06 | .05 | 685 | Doug Drabek | .08 | .06 |
| 626 | Gerald Young | .03 | .02 | 686 | Mike Gallego | .03 | .02 |
| 627 | *Tim Layana* | .15 | .11 | 687 | John Cerutti | .03 | .02 |
| 628 | Greg Litton | .05 | .04 | 688 | *Rosario* | | |
| 629 | Wes Gardner | .04 | .03 | | *Rodriguez*(FC) | .15 | .11 |
| 630 | Dave Winfield | .10 | .08 | 689 | John Kruk | .06 | .05 |
| 631 | Mike Morgan | .04 | .03 | 690 | Orel Hershiser | .10 | .08 |
| 632 | Lloyd Moseby | .06 | .05 | 691 | Mike Blowers | .10 | .08 |
| 633 | Kevin Tapani | .10 | .08 | 692 | *Efrain Valdez*(FC) | | |
| 634 | Henry Cotto | .03 | .02 | | | .15 | .11 |
| 635 | Andy Hawkins | .04 | .03 | 693 | Francisco Cabrera | .08 | .06 |
| 636 | *Geronimo Pena*(FC) | | | 694 | Randy Veres | .03 | .02 |
| | | .20 | .15 | 695 | Kevin Seitzer | .08 | .06 |
| 637 | Bruce Ruffin | .04 | .03 | 696 | Steve Olin | .05 | .04 |
| 638 | Mike Macfarlane | .04 | .03 | 697 | Shawn Abner | .04 | .03 |
| 639 | Frank Robinson | .05 | .04 | 698 | Mark Guthrie | .05 | .04 |
| 640 | Andre Dawson | .10 | .08 | 699 | Jim Lefebvre | .03 | .02 |
| 641 | Mike Henneman | .06 | .05 | 700 | Jose Canseco | .40 | .30 |
| 642 | Hal Morris | .15 | .11 | 701 | Pascual Perez | .05 | .04 |
| 643 | Jim Presley | .06 | .05 | 702 | *Tim Naehring* | .20 | .15 |
| 644 | Chuck Crim | .04 | .03 | 703 | Juan Agosto | .03 | .02 |
| 645 | Juan Samuel | .06 | .05 | 704 | Devon White | .06 | .05 |
| 646 | *Andujar Cedeno*(FC) | | | 705 | Robby Thompson | .05 | .04 |
| | | .30 | .25 | 706 | Brad Arnsberg | .04 | .03 |
| 647 | Mark Portugal | .04 | .03 | 707 | Jim Eisenreich | .04 | .03 |
| 648 | Lee Stevens(FC) | .15 | .11 | 708 | John Mitchell(FC) | .12 | .09 |
| 649 | *Bill Sampen* | .15 | .11 | 709 | Matt Sinatro | .03 | .02 |
| 650 | Jack Clark | .08 | .06 | 710 | Kent Hrbek | .08 | .06 |
| 651 | Alan Mills | .12 | .09 | 711 | Gary Redus, Jose | | |
| 652 | Kevin Romine | .03 | .02 | | DeLeon | .05 | .04 |
| 653 | *Anthony Telford*(FC) | | | 712 | Ricky Jordan | .06 | .05 |
| | | .20 | .15 | 713 | Scott Scudder | .08 | .06 |
| 654 | Paul Sorrento(FC) | .15 | .11 | 714 | Marvell Wynne | .04 | .03 |
| 655 | Erik Hanson | .08 | .06 | 715 | Tim Burke | .06 | .05 |
| 656 | Checklist 5 | .03 | .02 | 716 | Bob Geren | .06 | .05 |
| 657 | Mike Kingery | .03 | .02 | 717 | Phil Bradley | .06 | .05 |
| 658 | *Scott Aldred*(FC) | .15 | .11 | 718 | Steve Crawford | .03 | .02 |
| 659 | *Oscar Azocar*(FC) | | | 719 | Keith Miller | .06 | .05 |
| | | .15 | .11 | 720 | Cecil Fielder | .20 | .15 |
| 660 | Lee Smith | .06 | .05 | 721 | *Mark Lee*(FC) | .15 | .11 |
| 661 | Steve Lake | .03 | .02 | 722 | Wally Backman | .04 | .03 |
| 662 | Rob Dibble | .08 | .06 | 723 | Candy Maldonado | .08 | .06 |
| 663 | Greg Brock | .05 | .04 | 724 | *David Segui*(FC) | .25 | .20 |
| 664 | John Farrell | .04 | .03 | 725 | Ron Gant | .15 | .11 |
| 665 | Jim Leyland | .03 | .02 | 726 | Phil Stephenson | .04 | .03 |
| 666 | Danny Darwin | .06 | .05 | 727 | Mookie Wilson | .06 | .05 |
| 667 | Kent Anderson | .04 | .03 | 728 | Scott Sanderson | .04 | .03 |
| 668 | Bill Long | .04 | .03 | 729 | Don Zimmer | .04 | .03 |
| 669 | Lou Pinella | .04 | .03 | 730 | Barry Larkin | .12 | .09 |
| 670 | Rickey Henderson | .35 | .25 | 731 | *Jeff Gray*(FC) | .15 | .11 |

| | | MT | NR MT |
|---|---|---|---|
| 732 | Franklin Stubbs | .05 | .04 |
| 733 | Kelly Downs | .04 | .03 |
| 734 | John Russell | .03 | .02 |
| 735 | Ron Darling | .06 | .05 |
| 736 | Dick Schofield | .04 | .03 |
| 737 | Tim Crews | .03 | .02 |
| 738 | Mel Hall | .04 | .03 |
| 739 | *Russ Swan* | .10 | .08 |
| 740 | Ryne Sandberg | .20 | .15 |
| 741 | Jimmy Key | .06 | .05 |
| 742 | Tommy Gregg | .04 | .03 |
| 743 | Bryn Smith | .04 | .03 |
| 744 | Nelson Santovenia | .05 | .04 |
| 745 | Doug Jones | .08 | .06 |
| 746 | John Shelby | .03 | .02 |
| 747 | Tony Fossas | .03 | .02 |
| 748 | Al Newman | .03 | .02 |
| 749 | Greg Harris | .04 | .03 |
| 750 | Bobby Bonilla | .12 | .09 |
| 751 | *Wayne Edwards* | .10 | .08 |
| 752 | Kevin Bass | .05 | .04 |
| 753 | *Paul Marak*(FC) | .15 | .11 |
| 754 | Bill Pecota | .04 | .03 |
| 755 | Mark Langston | .10 | .08 |
| 756 | Jeff Huson | .05 | .04 |
| 757 | Mark Gardner | .06 | .05 |
| 758 | Mike Devereaux | .06 | .05 |
| 759 | Bobby Cox | .03 | .02 |
| 760 | Benny Santiago | .08 | .06 |
| 761 | Larry Andersen | .04 | .03 |
| 762 | Mitch Webster | .04 | .03 |
| 763 | *Dana Kiecker* | .10 | .08 |
| 764 | Mark Carreon | .05 | .04 |
| 765 | Shawon Dunston | .08 | .06 |
| 766 | Jeff Robinson | .05 | .04 |
| 767 | #1 Draft Pick *(Dan Wilson)*(FC) | .30 | .25 |
| 768 | Donn Pall | .04 | .03 |
| 769 | *Tim Sherrill*(FC) | .15 | .11 |
| 770 | Jay Howell | .06 | .05 |
| 772 | Kent Mercker(FC) | .10 | .08 |
| 773 | Tom Foley | .03 | .02 |
| 774 | Dennis Rasmussen | .04 | .03 |
| 775 | Julio Franco | .08 | .06 |
| 776 | Brent Mayne(FC) | .15 | .11 |
| 777 | John Candelaria | .05 | .04 |
| 778 | Dan Gladden | .05 | .04 |
| 779 | Carmelo Martinez | .04 | .03 |
| 780 | Randy Myers | .08 | .06 |
| 781 | Darryl Hamilton | .05 | .04 |
| 782 | Jim Deshaies | .05 | .04 |
| 783 | Joel Skinner | .03 | .02 |
| 784 | Willie Fraser | .04 | .03 |
| 785 | Scott Fletcher | .04 | .03 |
| 786 | Eric Plunk | .03 | .02 |
| 787 | Checklist 6 | .03 | .02 |
| 788 | Bob Milacki | .06 | .05 |
| 789 | Tom Lasorda | .04 | .03 |
| 790 | Ken Griffey,Jr. | 1.00 | .70 |
| 791 | Mike Benjamin(FC) | .15 | .11 |
| 792 | Mike Greenwell | .15 | .11 |

**The values quoted are intended to reflect the market price.**

## 1991 Topps Traded

"Team USA" is featured in the 1991 Topps Traded set. The cards feature the same style as the regular 1991 issue, including the 40th anniversary logo. The set includes 132 cards and showcases rookies and traded players along with "Team USA." The cards are numbered with a "T" designation in alphabetical order.

| | | MT | NR MT |
|---|---|---|---|
| | Complete Set: | 10.00 | 7.50 |
| | Common Player: | .05 | .04 |
| 1 | Juan Agosto | .05 | .04 |
| 2 | Roberto Alomar | .25 | .20 |
| 3 | Wally Backman | .05 | .04 |
| 4 | Jeff Bagwell(FC) | 2.00 | 1.50 |
| 5 | Skeeter Barnes(FC) | .15 | .11 |
| 6 | Steve Bedrosian | .06 | .05 |
| 7 | Derek Bell(FC) | .35 | .25 |
| 8 | George Bell | .10 | .08 |
| 9 | Rafael Belliard | .05 | .04 |
| 10 | Dante Bichette | .06 | .05 |
| 11 | Bud Black | .05 | .04 |
| 12 | Mike Boddicker | .06 | .05 |
| 13 | Sid Bream | .06 | .05 |
| 14 | Hubie Brooks | .06 | .05 |
| 15 | Brett Butler | .08 | .06 |
| 16 | Ivan Calderon | .08 | .06 |
| 17 | John Candelaria | .05 | .04 |
| 18 | Tom Candiotti | .06 | .05 |
| 19 | Gary Carter | .08 | .06 |
| 20 | Joe Carter | .12 | .09 |
| 21 | Rick Cerone | .05 | .04 |
| 22 | Jack Clark | .08 | .06 |
| 23 | Vince Coleman | .15 | .11 |
| 24 | Scott Coolbaugh | .10 | .08 |
| 25 | Danny Cox | .05 | .04 |
| 26 | Danny Darwin | .05 | .04 |
| 27 | Chili Davis | .08 | .06 |
| 28 | Glenn Davis | .08 | .06 |
| 29 | Steve Decker(FC) | .25 | .20 |
| 30 | Rob Deer | .06 | .05 |
| 31 | Rich DeLucia(FC) | .15 | .11 |
| 32 | John Dettmer (U.S.A.)(FC) | .20 | .15 |
| 33 | Brian Downing | .05 | .04 |
| 34 | Darren Dreifort (U.S.A.)(FC) | .20 | .15 |

| | | MT | NR MT |
|---|---|---|---|
| 35 | Kirk Dressendorfer(FC) | .40 | .30 |
| 36 | Jim Essian | .05 | .04 |
| 37 | Dwight Evans | .08 | .06 |
| 38 | Steve Farr | .06 | .05 |
| 39 | Jeff Fassero(FC) | .20 | .15 |
| 40 | Junior Felix | .08 | .06 |
| 41 | Tony Fernandez | .08 | .06 |
| 42 | Steve Finley | .08 | .06 |
| 43 | Jim Fregosi | .05 | .04 |
| 44 | Gary Gaetti | .06 | .05 |
| 45 | Jason Giambi (U.S.A.)(FC) | .30 | .25 |
| 46 | Kirk Gibson | .08 | .06 |
| 47 | Leo Gomez(FC) | .30 | .25 |
| 48 | Luis Gonzalez(FC) | .30 | .25 |
| 49 | Jeff Granger (U.S.A.)(FC) | .20 | .15 |
| 50 | Todd Greene (U.S.A.)(FC) | .20 | .15 |
| 51 | Jeffrey Hammonds (U.S.A.)(FC) | 1.00 | .70 |
| 52 | Mike Hargrove | .05 | .04 |
| 53 | Pete Harnisch | .08 | .06 |
| 54 | Rick Helling (U.S.A.)(FC) | .20 | .15 |
| 55 | Glenallen Hill | .08 | .06 |
| 56 | Charlie Hough | .06 | .05 |
| 57 | Pete Incaviglia | .08 | .06 |
| 58 | Bo Jackson | .50 | .40 |
| 59 | Danny Jackson | .06 | .05 |
| 60 | Reggie Jefferson(FC) | .30 | .25 |
| 61 | Charles Johnson (U.S.A.)(FC) | 1.25 | .90 |

| | | MT | NR MT |
|---|---|---|---|
| 62 | Jeff Johnson(FC) | .20 | .15 |
| 63 | Todd Johnson (U.S.A.)(FC) | .20 | .15 |
| 64 | Barry Jones | .05 | .04 |
| 65 | Chris Jones(FC) | .20 | .15 |
| 66 | Scott Kamieniecki(FC) | .20 | .15 |
| 67 | Pat Kelly(FC) | .50 | .40 |
| 68 | Darryl Kile(FC) | .20 | .15 |
| 69 | Chuck Knoblauch(FC) | .40 | .30 |
| 70 | Bill Krueger | .05 | .04 |
| 71 | Scott Leius(FC) | .15 | .11 |
| 72 | Donnie Leshnock (U.S.A.)(FC) | .20 | .15 |
| 73 | Mark Lewis | .30 | .25 |
| 74 | Candy Maldonado | .06 | .05 |
| 75 | Jason McDonald (U.S.A.)(FC) | .25 | .20 |
| 76 | Willie McGee | .08 | .06 |
| 77 | Fred McGriff | .10 | .08 |
| 78 | Billy McMillon (U.S.A.)(FC) | .20 | .15 |
| 79 | Hal McRae | .06 | .05 |
| 80 | Dan Melendez (U.S.A.)(FC) | .30 | .25 |
| 81 | Orlando Merced(FC) | .40 | .30 |
| 82 | Jack Morris | .08 | .06 |
| 83 | Phil Nevin (U.S.A.) (FC) | 1.50 | 1.25 |
| 84 | Otis Nixon | .06 | .05 |
| 85 | Johnny Oates | .05 | .04 |
| 86 | Bob Ojeda | .05 | .04 |
| 87 | Mike Pagliarulo | .05 | .04 |
| 88 | Dean Palmer(FC) | .35 | .25 |
| 89 | Dave Parker | .08 | .06 |
| 90 | Terry Pendleton | .08 | .06 |
| 91 | Tony Phillips (U.S.A.)(FC) | .20 | .15 |
| 92 | Doug Piatt(FC) | .20 | .15 |
| 93 | Ron Polk (U.S.A.) | .06 | .05 |
| 94 | Rock Raines | .12 | .09 |
| 95 | Willie Randolph | .06 | .05 |
| 96 | Dave Righetti | .06 | .05 |
| 97 | Ernie Riles | .05 | .04 |
| 98 | Chris Roberts (U.S.A.)(FC) | .30 | .25 |
| 99 | Jeff Robinson (Angels) | .05 | .04 |
| 100 | Jeff Robinson (Orioles) | .05 | .04 |
| 101 | Ivan Rodriguez(FC) | 2.00 | 1.50 |
| 102 | Steve Rodriguez (U.S.A.)(FC) | .20 | .15 |
| 103 | Tom Runnells | .05 | .04 |
| 104 | Scott Sanderson | .06 | .05 |
| 105 | Bob Scanlan(FC) | .15 | .11 |
| 106 | Pete Schourek(FC) | .15 | .11 |
| 107 | Gary Scott(FC) | .35 | .25 |
| 108 | Paul Shuey (U.S.A.)(FC) | .40 | .30 |
| 109 | Doug Simons(FC) | .20 | .15 |
| 110 | Dave Smith | .06 | .05 |
| 111 | Cory Snyder | .05 | .04 |
| 112 | Luis Sojo | .06 | .05 |
| 113 | Kennie Steenstra (U.S.A.)(FC) | .20 | .15 |
| 114 | Darryl Strawberry | .30 | .25 |

## GRADING GUIDE

**Mint (MT):** A perfect card. Well-centered with all corners sharp and square. No creases, stains, edge nicks, surface marks, yellowing or fading.

**Near Mint (NM):** A nearly perfect card. At first glance, a NM card appears to be perfect. May be slightly off-center. No surface marks, creases or loss of gloss.

**Excellent (EX):** Corners are still fairly sharp with only moderate wear. Borders may be off-center. No creases or stains on fronts or backs, but may show slight loss of surface luster.

**Very Good (VG):** Shows obvious handling. May have rounded corners, minor creases, major gum or wax stains. No major creases, tape marks, writing, etc.

**Good (G):** A well-worn card, but exhibits no intentional damage. May have major or multiple creases. Corners may be rounded well beyond card border.

|     |                          | MT   | NR MT |
| --- | ------------------------ | ---- | ----- |
| 115 | Franklin Stubbs          | .05  | .04   |
| 116 | Todd Taylor (U.S.A.)(FC) |      |       |
|     |                          | .20  | .15   |
| 117 | Wade Taylor(FC)          | .20  | .15   |
| 118 | Garry Templeton          | .06  | .05   |
| 119 | Mickey Tettleton         | .06  | .05   |
| 120 | Tim Teufel               | .05  | .04   |
| 121 | Mike Timlin(FC)          | .20  | .15   |
| 122 | David Tuttle (U.S.A.)(FC)|      |       |
|     |                          | .20  | .15   |
| 123 | Mo Vaughn(FC)            | .50  | .40   |
| 124 | Jeff Ware (U.S.A.)(FC)   |      |       |
|     |                          | .20  | .15   |
| 125 | Devon White              | .08  | .06   |
| 126 | Mark Whiten              | .20  | .15   |
| 127 | Mitch Williams           | .08  | .06   |
| 128 | Craig Wilson             |      |       |
|     | (U.S.A.)(FC)             | .20  | .15   |
| 129 | Willie Wilson            | .06  | .05   |
| 130 | Chris Wimmer             |      |       |
|     | (U.S.A.)(FC)             | .30  | .25   |
| 131 | Ivan Zweig (U.S.A.)(FC)  |      |       |
|     |                          | .20  | .15   |
| 132 | Checklist                | .05  | .04   |

**Values for recent cards and sets are listed in Mint (MT), Near Mint (NM) and Excellent (EX), reflecting the fact that many cards from recent years have been preserved in top condition. Recent cards and sets in less than Excellent condition have little collector interest.**

# 1992 Topps

This 792-card set features white stock much like the 1991 issue. The card fronts feature full-color action and posed photos with a gray inner frame and the player name and position on the bottom.

The backs feature biographical information, statistics and stadium photos on player cards where space is available. All-Star cards and #1 Draft Pick cards are once again included. Topps brought back four-player rookie cards in 1992. Nine Top Prospect cards of this nature can be found within the set. Several cards can once again be found with horizontal fronts. "Match the Stats" game cards were inserted into packs of 1992 Topps cards. Special bonus cards were given away to winners of this insert game. Record Breaker cards are also featured in this set.

|     |                                    | MT    | NR MT |
| --- | ---------------------------------- | ----- | ----- |
|     | Complete Set:                      | 20.00 | 15.00 |
|     | Common Player:                     | .03   | .02   |
| 1   | Nolan Ryan                         | .30   | .25   |
| 2   | Record Breaker (Rickey Henderson)  | .10   | .08   |
| 3   | Record Breaker (Jeff Reardon)      | .05   | .04   |
| 4   | Record Breaker (Nolan Ryan)        | .10   | .08   |
| 5   | Record Breaker (Dave Winfield)     | .06   | .05   |
| 6   | #1 Draft Pick *(Brien Taylor)*(FC) | 2.75  | 2.00  |
| 7   | *Jim Olander*(FC)                  | .10   | .08   |
| 8   | *Bryan Hickerson*(FC)              |       |       |
|     |                                    | .10   | .08   |
| 9   | John Farrell                       | .03   | .02   |
| 10  | Wade Boggs                         | .15   | .11   |
| 11  | Jack McDowell                      | .08   | .06   |
| 12  | Luis Gonzalez                      | .15   | .11   |
| 13  | Mike Scioscia                      | .04   | .03   |
| 14  | Wes Chamberlain                    | .20   | .15   |
| 15  | Denny Martinez                     | .04   | .03   |
| 16  | Jeff Montgomery                    | .04   | .03   |
| 17  | Randy Milligan                     | .06   | .05   |
| 18  | Greg Cadaret                       | .03   | .02   |
| 19  | Jamie Quirk                        | .03   | .02   |
| 20  | Bip Roberts                        | .05   | .04   |
| 21  | Buck Rogers                        | .03   | .02   |
| 22  | Bill Wegman                        | .04   | .03   |
| 23  | Chuck Knoblauch                    | .20   | .15   |
| 24  | Randy Myers                        | .05   | .04   |
| 25  | Ron Gant                           | .15   | .11   |
| 26  | Mike Bielecki                      | .03   | .02   |
| 27  | Juan Gonzalez                      | .20   | .15   |
| 28  | Mike Schooler                      | .04   | .03   |
| 29  | Mickey Tettleton                   | .05   | .04   |
| 30  | John Kruk                          | .06   | .05   |
| 31  | Bryn Smith                         | .03   | .02   |
| 32  | Chris Nabholz                      | .06   | .05   |
| 33  | Carlos Baerga                      | .08   | .06   |

|    |                              | MT  | NR MT |
|----|------------------------------|-----|-------|
| 34 | Jeff Juden                   | .15 | .11   |
| 35 | Dave Righetti                | .06 | .05   |
| 36 | #1 Draft Pick (Scott         |     |       |
|    | Ruffcorn)(FC)                | .25 | .20   |
| 37 | Luis Polonia                 | .04 | .03   |
| 38 | Tom Candiotti                | .04 | .03   |
| 39 | Greg Olson                   | .04 | .03   |
| 40 | Cal Ripken                   | .20 | .15   |
| 41 | Craig Lefferts               | .04 | .03   |
| 42 | Mike Macfarlane              | .04 | .03   |
| 43 | Jose Lind                    | .04 | .03   |
| 44 | Rick Aguilera                | .05 | .04   |
| 45 | Gary Carter                  | .08 | .06   |
| 46 | Steve Farr                   | .04 | .03   |
| 47 | Rex Hudler                   | .04 | .03   |
| 48 | Scott Scudder                | .05 | .04   |
| 49 | Damon Berryhill              | .04 | .03   |
| 50 | Ken Griffey, Jr.             | .50 | .40   |
| 51 | Tom Runnells                 | .03 | .02   |
| 52 | Juan Bell                    | .05 | .04   |
| 53 | Tommy Gregg                  | .03 | .02   |
| 54 | David Wells                  | .04 | .03   |
| 55 | Rafael Palmeiro              | .10 | .08   |
| 56 | Charlie O'Brien              | .03 | .02   |
| 57 | Donn Pall                    | .03 | .02   |
| 58 | Top Prospects-Catchers       |     |       |
|    | (Brad Ausmus, Jim            |     |       |
|    | Campanis, Dave Nilsson,      |     |       |
|    | Doug Robbins)(FC)            | .50 | .40   |
| 59 | Mo Vaughn                    | .25 | .20   |
| 60 | Tony Fernandez               | .05 | .04   |
| 61 | Paul O'Neill                 | .06 | .05   |
| 62 | Gene Nelson                  | .03 | .02   |
| 63 | Randy Ready                  | .03 | .02   |
| 64 | Bob Kipper                   | .03 | .02   |
| 65 | Willie McGee                 | .08 | .06   |
| 66 | #1 Draft Pick (Scott         |     |       |
|    | Stahoviak)(FC)               | .30 | .25   |
| 67 | Luis Salazar                 | .03 | .02   |
| 68 | Marvin Freeman               | .03 | .02   |
| 69 | Kenny Lofton(FC)             | .40 | .30   |
| 70 | Gary Gaetti                  | .06 | .05   |
| 71 | Erik Hanson                  | .08 | .06   |
| 72 | Eddie Zosky(FC)              | .10 | .08   |
| 73 | Brian Barnes                 | .10 | .08   |
| 74 | Scott Leius                  | .10 | .08   |
| 75 | Bret Saberhagen              | .08 | .06   |
| 76 | Mike Gallego                 | .03 | .02   |
| 77 | Jack Armstrong               | .05 | .04   |
| 78 | Ivan Rodriguez               | .60 | .45   |
| 79 | Jesse Orosco                 | .03 | .02   |
| 80 | David Justice                | .20 | .15   |
| 81 | Ced Landrum(FC)              | .15 | .11   |
| 82 | Doug Simons                  | .10 | .08   |
| 83 | Tommy Greene                 | .06 | .05   |
| 84 | Leo Gomez                    | .15 | .11   |

**Regional interest may affect
the value of a card.**

|    |                              | MT  | NR MT |
|----|------------------------------|-----|-------|
| 85 | Jose DeLeon                  | .04 | .03   |
| 86 | Steve Finley                 | .06 | .05   |
| 87 | Bob MacDonald(FC)            | .15 | .11   |
| 88 | Darrin Jackson               | .04 | .03   |
| 89 | Neal Heaton                  | .03 | .02   |
| 90 | Robin Yount                  | .12 | .09   |
| 91 | Jeff Reed                    | .03 | .02   |
| 92 | Lenny Harris                 | .04 | .03   |
| 93 | Reggie Jefferson             | .15 | .11   |
| 94 | Sammy Sosa                   | .08 | .06   |
| 95 | Scott Bailes                 | .03 | .02   |
| 96 | #1 Draft Pick (Tom           |     |       |
|    | McKinnon)(FC)                | .15 | .11   |
| 97 | Luis Rivera                  | .03 | .02   |
| 98 | Mike Harkey                  | .06 | .05   |
| 99 | Jeff Treadway                | .04 | .03   |

## NATIONAL LEAGUE

**Atlanta Braves**, P.O. Box 4064, Atlanta, GA 30302.

**Chicago Cubs**, 1060 W. Addison St., Chicago, IL 60613.

**Cincinnati Reds**, 100 Riverfront Stadium, Cincinnati, OH 45202.

**Colorado Rockies**, 1700 Broadway, Suite 2100, Denver, CO 80290.

**Florida Marlins**.100 NE 3rd Avenue, Third Floor, Ft. Lauderdale, FL 33301.

**Houston Astros**, P.O. Box 288, Houston, TX 77001-0288.

**Los Angeles Dodgers**, 100 Elsian Park Ave., Los Angeles, CA 90012.

**Montreal Expos**, P.O. Box 500, Station M, Montreal, Quebec, Canada, HIV 3P2.

**New York Mets**, Shea Stadium, Flushing, NY 11368.

**Philadelphia Pirates**, P.O. Box 7575, Philadelphia, PA 19101.

**Pittsburgh Pirates**, Three Rivers Stadium, Pittsburgh, PA 15212.

**St. Louis Cardinals**, 250 Stadium Plaza, St. Louis, MO 63102.

**San Diego Padres**, P.O. Box 2000, San Diego, CA 92120.

**San Francisco Giants**, Candlestick Park, San Francisco, CA 94124.

| | | MT | NR MT | | | | MT | NR MT |
|---|---|---|---|---|---|---|---|---|
| 100 | Jose Canseco | .20 | .15 | | 159 | Darrin Fletcher | .05 | .04 |
| 101 | Omar Vizquel | .03 | .02 | | 160 | Bobby Bonilla | .12 | .09 |
| 102 | Scott Kamieniecki | .12 | .09 | | 161 | Casey Candaele | .03 | .02 |
| 103 | Ricky Jordan | .06 | .05 | | 162 | Paul Faries(FC) | .10 | .08 |
| 104 | Jeff Ballard | .04 | .03 | | 163 | Dana Kiecker | .03 | .02 |
| 105 | Felix Jose | .10 | .08 | | 164 | Shane Mack | .08 | .06 |
| 106 | Mike Boddicker | .05 | .04 | | 165 | Mark Langston | .10 | .08 |
| 107 | Dan Pasqua | .04 | .03 | | 166 | Geronimo Pena | .06 | .05 |
| 108 | *Mike Timlin* | .12 | .09 | | 167 | Andy Allanson | .03 | .02 |
| 109 | Roger Craig | .04 | .03 | | 168 | Dwight Smith | .04 | .03 |
| 110 | Ryne Sandberg | .20 | .15 | | 169 | Chuck Crim | .03 | .02 |
| 111 | Mark Carreon | .03 | .02 | | 170 | Alex Cole | .05 | .04 |
| 112 | Oscar Azocar | .04 | .03 | | 171 | Bill Plummer | .03 | .02 |
| 113 | Mike Greenwell | .10 | .08 | | 172 | Juan Berenguer | .03 | .02 |
| 114 | Mark Portugal | .03 | .02 | | 173 | Brian Downing | .04 | .03 |
| 115 | Terry Pendleton | .08 | .06 | | 174 | Steve Frey | .03 | .02 |
| 116 | Willie Randolph | .05 | .04 | | 175 | Orel Hershiser | .08 | .06 |
| 117 | Scott Terry | .03 | .02 | | 176 | *Ramon Garcia(FC)* | | |
| 118 | Chili Davis | .08 | .06 | | | | .15 | .11 |
| 119 | Mark Gardner | .05 | .04 | | 177 | Danny Gladden | .04 | .03 |
| 120 | Alan Trammell | .10 | .08 | | 178 | Jim Acker | .03 | .02 |
| 121 | Derek Bell | .25 | .20 | | 179 | Top Prospects-2nd | | |
| 122 | Gary Varsho | .03 | .02 | | | Baseman *(Cesar Bernhardt,* | | |
| 123 | Bob Ojeda | .04 | .03 | | | *Bobby DeJardin,* | | |
| 124 | #1 Draft Pick *(Shawn* | | | | | *Armando Moreno, Andy* | | |
| | *Livsey)(FC)* | .15 | .11 | | | *Stankiewicz)(FC)* | .25 | .20 |
| 125 | Chris Hoiles | .08 | .06 | | 180 | Kevin Mitchell | .10 | .08 |
| 126 | Top Prospects-1st | | | | 181 | Hector Villanueva | .06 | .05 |
| | Baseman *(Rico Brogna,* | | | | 182 | Jeff Reardon | .06 | .05 |
| | *John Jaha, Ryan Klesko,* | | | | 183 | Brent Mayne | .06 | .05 |
| | *Dave Staton)(FC)* | 1.00 | .70 | | 184 | Jimmy Jones | .03 | .02 |
| 127 | Carlos Quintana | .06 | .05 | | 185 | Benny Santiago | .08 | .06 |
| 128 | Kurt Stillwell | .04 | .03 | | 186 | #1 Draft Pick *(Cliff* | | |
| 129 | Melido Perez | .04 | .03 | | | *Floyd)(FC)* | .60 | .45 |
| 130 | Alvin Davis | .06 | .05 | | 187 | Ernie Riles | .03 | .02 |
| 131 | Checklist 1 | .03 | .02 | | 188 | Jose Guzman | .05 | .04 |
| 132 | Eric Show | .03 | .02 | | 189 | Junior Felix | .06 | .05 |
| 133 | Rance Mulliniks | .03 | .02 | | 190 | Glenn Davis | .08 | .06 |
| 134 | Darryl Kile | .08 | .06 | | 191 | Charlie Hough | .04 | .03 |
| 135 | Von Hayes | .05 | .04 | | 192 | *Dave Fleming(FC)* | | |
| 136 | Bill Doran | .05 | .04 | | | | .40 | .30 |
| 137 | Jeff Robinson | .03 | .02 | | 193 | Omar Oliveras(FC) | .08 | .06 |
| 138 | Monty Fariss | .08 | .06 | | 194 | Eric Karros(FC) | .30 | .25 |
| 139 | Jeff Innis | .05 | .04 | | 195 | David Cone | .08 | .06 |
| 140 | Mark Grace | .12 | .09 | | 196 | *Frank Castillo(FC)* | | |
| 141 | Jim Leyland | .03 | .02 | | | | .12 | .09 |
| 142 | Todd Van Poppel(FC) | | | | 197 | Glenn Braggs | .04 | .03 |
| | | .50 | .40 | | 198 | Scott Aldred | .06 | .05 |
| 143 | Paul Gibson | .03 | .02 | | 199 | Jeff Blauser | .03 | .02 |
| 144 | Bill Swift | .04 | .03 | | 200 | Len Dykstra | .08 | .06 |
| 145 | Danny Tartabull | .08 | .06 | | 201 | Buck Showalter | .03 | .02 |
| 146 | Al Newman | .03 | .02 | | 202 | Rick Honeycutt | .03 | .02 |
| 147 | Cris Carpenter | .04 | .03 | | 203 | Greg Myers | .03 | .02 |
| 148 | Anthony Young(FC) | | | | 204 | Trevor Wilson | .05 | .04 |
| | | .25 | .20 | | 205 | Jay Howell | .04 | .03 |
| 149 | *Brian Bohanon(FC)* | | | | 206 | Luis Sojo | .05 | .04 |
| | | .15 | .11 | | 207 | Jack Clark | .08 | .06 |
| 150 | Roger Clemens | .15 | .11 | | 208 | Julio Machado | .03 | .02 |
| 151 | Jeff Hamilton | .03 | .02 | | 209 | Lloyd McClendon | .03 | .02 |
| 152 | Charlie Leibrandt | .04 | .03 | | 210 | Ozzie Guillen | .06 | .05 |
| 153 | Ron Karkovice | .04 | .03 | | 211 | *Jeremy* | | |
| 154 | Hensley Meulens | .08 | .06 | | | *Hernandez(FC)* | .15 | .11 |
| 155 | Scott Bankhead | .04 | .03 | | 212 | Randy Velarde | .03 | .02 |
| 156 | #1 Draft Pick *(Manny* | | | | 213 | Les Lancaster | .03 | .02 |
| | *Ramirez)(FC)* | .70 | .50 | | 214 | *Andy Mota(FC)* | .15 | .11 |
| 157 | Keith Miller | .03 | .02 | | 215 | Rich Gossage | .05 | .04 |
| 158 | Todd Frohwirth | .03 | .02 | | 216 | #1 Draft Pick *(Brent* | | |

| | MT | NR MT |
|---|---|---|
| *Gates*)(FC) | .25 | .20 |
| 217 Brian Harper | .05 | .04 |
| 218 Mike Flanagan | .03 | .02 |
| 219 Jerry Browne | .04 | .03 |
| 220 Jose Rijo | .08 | .06 |
| 221 Skeeter Barnes | .04 | .03 |
| 222 Jaime Navarro | .04 | .03 |
| 223 Mel Hall | .04 | .03 |
| 224 *Brett Barberie* | .20 | .15 |
| 225 Roberto Alomar | .10 | .08 |
| 226 Pete Smith | .03 | .02 |
| 227 Daryl Boston | .03 | .02 |
| 228 Eddie Whitson | .04 | .03 |
| 229 Shawn Boskie | .04 | .03 |
| 230 Dick Schofield | .03 | .02 |
| 231 *Brian Drahman*(FC) | | |
| | .10 | .08 |
| 232 John Smiley | .05 | .04 |
| 233 Mitch Webster | .04 | .03 |
| 234 Terry Steinbach | .05 | .04 |
| 235 Jack Morris | .08 | .06 |
| 236 Bill Pecota | .04 | .03 |
| 237 *Jose Hernandez*(FC) | | |
| | .10 | .08 |
| 238 Greg Litton | .03 | .02 |
| 239 Brian Holman | .05 | .04 |
| 240 Andres Galarraga | .06 | .05 |
| 241 Gerald Young | .03 | .02 |
| 242 Mike Mussina(FC) | .50 | .40 |
| 243 Alvaro Espinoza | .03 | .02 |
| 244 Darren Daulton | .04 | .03 |
| 245 John Smoltz | .08 | .06 |
| 246 #1 Draft Pick *(Jason Pruitt)*(FC) | | |
| | .15 | .11 |
| 247 Chuck Finley | .08 | .06 |
| 248 Jim Gantner | .04 | .03 |
| 249 Tony Fossas | .03 | .02 |
| 250 Ken Griffey | .05 | .04 |
| 251 Kevin Elster | .04 | .03 |
| 252 Dennis Rasmussen | .03 | .02 |
| 253 Terry Kennedy | .03 | .02 |
| 254 Ryan Bowen(FC) | .15 | .11 |
| 255 Robin Ventura | .15 | .11 |
| 256 Mike Aldrete | .03 | .02 |
| 257 Jeff Russell | .04 | .03 |
| 258 Jim Lindeman | .03 | .02 |
| 259 Ron Darling | .05 | .04 |
| 260 Devon White | .06 | .05 |
| 261 Tom Lasorda | .04 | .03 |
| 262 Terry Lee(FC) | .10 | .08 |
| 263 Bob Patterson | .03 | .02 |
| 264 Checklist 2 | .03 | .02 |
| 265 Teddy Higuera | .05 | .04 |
| 266 Roberto Kelly | .08 | .06 |
| 267 Steve Bedrosian | .04 | .03 |
| 268 Brady Anderson | .03 | .02 |
| 269 *Ruben Amaro*(FC) | | |
| | .15 | .11 |
| 270 Tony Gwynn | .12 | .09 |
| 271 Tracy Jones | .03 | .02 |
| 272 Jerry Don Gleaton | .03 | .02 |
| 273 Craig Grebeck | .04 | .03 |
| 274 *Bob Scanlan* | .10 | .08 |
| 275 Todd Zeile | .10 | .08 |
| 276 #1 Draft Pick *(Shawn Green)*(FC) | | |
| | .25 | .20 |
| 277 Scott Chiamparino | .04 | .03 |

| | MT | NR MT |
|---|---|---|
| 278 Darryl Hamilton | .04 | .03 |
| 279 Jim Clancy | .03 | .02 |
| 280 Carlos Martinez | .04 | .03 |
| 281 Kevin Appier | .05 | .04 |
| 282 *John Wehner*(FC) | | |
| | .15 | .11 |
| 283 Reggie Sanders(FC) | .30 | .25 |
| 284 Gene Larkin | .04 | .03 |
| 285 Bob Welch | .06 | .05 |
| 286 Gilberto Reyes(FC) | .05 | .04 |
| 287 Pete Schourek | .15 | .11 |
| 288 Andujar Cedeno | .15 | .11 |
| 289 Mike Morgan | .04 | .03 |
| 290 Bo Jackson | .20 | .15 |
| 291 Phil Garner | .03 | .02 |
| 292 Ray Lankford | .15 | .11 |
| 293 Mike Henneman | .05 | .04 |
| 294 Dave Valle | .03 | .02 |
| 295 Alonzo Powell(FC) | .08 | .06 |
| 296 Tom Brunansky | .05 | .04 |
| 297 Kevin Brown | .05 | .04 |
| 298 Kelly Gruber | .08 | .06 |
| 299 Charles Nagy | .06 | .05 |
| 300 Don Mattingly | .15 | .11 |
| 301 Kirk McCaskill | .04 | .03 |
| 302 Joey Cora | .04 | .03 |
| 303 Dan Plesac | .04 | .03 |
| 304 Joe Oliver | .04 | .03 |
| 305 Tom Glavine | .08 | .06 |
| 306 #1 Draft Pick *(Al Shirley)*(FC) | .25 | .20 |
| 307 Bruce Ruffin | .03 | .02 |
| 308 Craig Shipley(FC) | | |
| | .08 | .06 |
| 309 Dave Martinez | .04 | .03 |
| 310 Jose Mesa | .03 | .02 |
| 311 Henry Cotto | .03 | .02 |
| 312 Mike LaValliere | .04 | .03 |
| 313 Kevin Tapani | .08 | .06 |
| 314 Jeff Huson | .04 | .03 |
| 315 Juan Samuel | .06 | .05 |
| 316 Curt Schilling | .06 | .05 |
| 317 Mike Bordick(FC) | .06 | .05 |
| 318 Steve Howe | .04 | .03 |
| 319 Tony Phillips | .04 | .03 |
| 320 George Bell | .10 | .08 |
| 321 Lou Pinella | .03 | .02 |
| 322 Tim Burke | .04 | .03 |
| 323 Milt Thompson | .04 | .03 |
| 324 Danny Darwin | .04 | .03 |
| 325 Joe Orsulak | .03 | .02 |
| 326 Eric King | .04 | .03 |
| 327 Jay Buhner | .05 | .04 |
| 328 *Joel Johnson*(FC) | | |
| | .15 | .11 |
| 329 Franklin Stubbs | .03 | .02 |
| 330 Will Clark | .20 | .15 |
| 331 Steve Lake | .03 | .02 |
| 332 *Chris Jones* | .10 | .08 |
| 333 Pat Tabler | .03 | .02 |
| 334 Kevin Gross | .03 | .02 |
| 335 Dave Henderson | .08 | .06 |
| 336 #1 Draft Pick *(Greg Anthony)*(FC) | .15 | .11 |
| 337 Alejandro Pena | .04 | .03 |
| 338 Shawn Abner | .03 | .02 |
| 339 Tom Browning | .06 | .05 |

| # | Player | MT | NR MT |
|---|--------|----|----|
| 340 | Otis Nixon | .04 | .03 |
| 341 | Bob Geren | .03 | .02 |
| 342 | *Tim Spehr*(FC) | .10 | .08 |
| 343 | *Jon Vander Wal*(FC) | .20 | .15 |
| 344 | Jack Daugherty | .03 | .02 |
| 345 | Zane Smith | .04 | .03 |
| 346 | *Rheal Cormier*(FC) | .15 | .11 |
| 347 | Kent Hrbek | .06 | .05 |
| 348 | *Rick Wilkins*(FC) | .15 | .11 |
| 349 | Steve Lyons | .03 | .02 |
| 350 | Gregg Olson | .08 | .06 |
| 351 | Greg Riddoch | .03 | .02 |
| 352 | Ed Nunez | .03 | .02 |
| 353 | *Braulio Castillo*(FC) | .08 | .06 |
| 354 | Dave Bergman | .03 | .02 |
| 355 | *Warren Newson*(FC) | .15 | .11 |
| 356 | Luis Quinones | .03 | .02 |
| 357 | Mike Witt | .04 | .03 |
| 358 | *Ted Wood* | .15 | .11 |
| 359 | Mike Moore | .03 | .02 |
| 360 | Lance Parrish | .06 | .05 |
| 361 | Barry Jones | .03 | .02 |
| 362 | *Javier Ortiz*(FC) | .10 | .08 |
| 363 | John Candelaria | .04 | .03 |
| 364 | Glenallen Hill | .06 | .05 |
| 365 | Duane Ward | .04 | .03 |
| 366 | Checklist 3 | .03 | .02 |
| 367 | Rafael Belliard | .03 | .02 |
| 368 | Bill Krueger | .03 | .02 |
| 369 | #1 Draft Pick (*Steve Whitaker*)(FC) | .20 | .15 |
| 370 | Shawon Dunston | .06 | .05 |
| 371 | Dante Bichette | .04 | .03 |
| 372 | *Kip Gross*(FC) | .10 | .08 |
| 373 | Don Robinson | .03 | .02 |
| 374 | Bernie Williams | .03 | .02 |
| 375 | Bert Blyleven | .05 | .04 |
| 376 | *Chris Donnels*(FC) | .15 | .11 |
| 377 | *Bob Zupcic*(FC) | .30 | .25 |
| 378 | Joel Skinner | .03 | .02 |
| 379 | Steve Chitren | .06 | .05 |
| 380 | Barry Bonds | .15 | .11 |
| 381 | Sparky Anderson | .03 | .02 |
| 382 | Sid Fernandez | .05 | .04 |
| 383 | Dave Hollins | .06 | .05 |
| 384 | Mark Lee | .03 | .02 |
| 385 | Tim Wallach | .05 | .04 |
| 386 | Will Clark (AS) | .10 | .08 |
| 387 | Ryne Sandberg (AS) | .10 | .08 |
| 388 | Howard Johnson (AS) | .05 | .04 |
| 389 | Barry Larkin (AS) | .05 | .04 |
| 390 | Barry Bonds (AS) | .10 | .08 |
| 391 | Ron Gant (AS) | .08 | .06 |
| 392 | Bobby Bonilla (AS) | .08 | .06 |
| 393 | Craig Biggio (AS) | .05 | .04 |
| 394 | Denny Martinez (AS) | .04 | .03 |
| 395 | Tom Glavine (AS) | .05 | .04 |
| 396 | Ozzie Smith (AS) | .08 | .06 |
| 397 | Cecil Fielder (AS) | .10 | .08 |
| 398 | Julio Franco (AS) | .08 | .06 |
| 399 | Wade Boggs (AS) | .10 | .08 |

| # | Player | MT | NR MT |
|---|--------|----|----|
| 400 | Cal Ripken (AS) | .15 | .11 |
| 401 | Jose Canseco (AS) | .15 | .11 |
| 402 | Joe Carter (AS) | .08 | .06 |
| 403 | Ruben Sierra (AS) | .10 | .08 |
| 404 | Matt Nokes (AS) | .04 | .03 |
| 405 | Roger Clemens (AS) | .12 | .09 |
| 406 | Jim Abbott (AS) | .08 | .06 |
| 407 | Bryan Harvey (AS) | .05 | .04 |
| 408 | Bob Milacki | .03 | .02 |
| 409 | Geno Petralli | .03 | .02 |
| 410 | Dave Stewart | .08 | .06 |
| 411 | Mike Jackson | .03 | .02 |
| 412 | Luis Aquino | .03 | .02 |
| 413 | Tim Teufel | .03 | .02 |
| 414 | #1 Draft Pick (*Jeff Ware*)(FC) | .15 | .11 |
| 415 | Jim Deshaies | .04 | .03 |
| 416 | Ellis Burks | .10 | .08 |
| 417 | Allan Anderson | .03 | .02 |
| 418 | Alfredo Griffin | .03 | .02 |
| 419 | Wally Whitehurst | .05 | .04 |
| 420 | Sandy Alomar | .08 | .06 |
| 421 | Juan Agosto | .03 | .02 |
| 422 | Sam Horn | .03 | .02 |
| 423 | *Jeff Fassero* | .10 | .08 |
| 424 | *Paul McClellan*(FC) | .10 | .08 |
| 425 | Cecil Fielder | .15 | .11 |
| 426 | Rock Raines | .10 | .08 |
| 427 | *Eddie Taubensee*(FC) | .20 | .15 |
| 428 | Dennis Boyd | .05 | .04 |
| 429 | Tony LaRussa | .03 | .02 |
| 430 | Steve Sax | .06 | .05 |
| 431 | Tom Gordon | .08 | .06 |
| 432 | Billy Hatcher | .04 | .03 |
| 433 | Cal Eldred(FC) | .25 | .20 |
| 434 | Wally Backman | .03 | .02 |
| 435 | Mark Eichhorn | .03 | .02 |
| 436 | Mookie Wilson | .03 | .02 |
| 437 | *Scott Servais*(FC) | .10 | .08 |
| 438 | Mike Maddux | .03 | .02 |
| 439 | *Chico Walker*(FC) | .10 | .08 |
| 440 | Doug Drabek | .08 | .06 |
| 441 | Rob Deer | .04 | .03 |
| 442 | Dave West | .04 | .03 |
| 443 | Spike Owen | .03 | .02 |
| 444 | #1 Draft Pick (*Tyrone Hill*)(FC) | .25 | .20 |
| 445 | Matt Williams | .12 | .09 |
| 446 | Mark Lewis | .12 | .09 |
| 447 | David Segui | .08 | .06 |
| 448 | Tom Pagnozzi | .04 | .03 |
| 449 | *Jeff Johnson* | .12 | .09 |
| 450 | Mark McGwire | .12 | .09 |
| 451 | Tom Henke | .05 | .04 |
| 452 | Wilson Alvarez | .08 | .06 |
| 453 | Gary Redus | .03 | .02 |
| 454 | Darren Holmes | .03 | .02 |
| 455 | Pete O'Brien | .03 | .02 |
| 456 | Pat Combs | .04 | .03 |
| 457 | Hubie Brooks | .04 | .03 |
| 458 | Frank Tanana | .03 | .02 |
| 459 | Tom Kelly | .03 | .02 |
| 460 | Andre Dawson | .12 | .09 |
| 461 | Doug Jones | .04 | .03 |

| | | MT | NR MT |
|---|---|---|---|
| 462 | Rich Rodriguez | .04 | .03 |
| 463 | *Mike Simms* | .10 | .08 |
| 464 | Mike Jeffcoat | .03 | .02 |
| 465 | Barry Larkin | .12 | .09 |
| 466 | Stan Belinda | .04 | .03 |
| 467 | Lonnie Smith | .04 | .03 |
| 468 | Greg Harris | .03 | .02 |
| 469 | Jim Eisenreich | .03 | .02 |
| 470 | Pedro Guerrero | .08 | .06 |
| 471 | Jose DeJesus | .04 | .03 |
| 472 | *Rich Rowland*(FC) | | |
| | | .15 | .11 |
| 473 | Top Prospects-3rd Baseman *(Frank Bolick, Craig Paquette, Tom Redington, Paul Russo)*(FC) | | |
| | | .35 | .25 |
| 474 | #1 Draft Pick *(Mike Rossiter)*(FC) | .25 | .20 |
| 475 | Robby Thompson | .04 | .03 |
| 476 | Randy Bush | .03 | .02 |
| 477 | Greg Hibbard | .04 | .03 |
| 478 | Dale Sveum | .03 | .02 |
| 479 | *Chito Martinez*(FC) | | |
| | | .15 | .11 |
| 480 | Scott Sanderson | .04 | .03 |
| 481 | Tino Martinez | .10 | .08 |
| 482 | Jimmy Key | .05 | .04 |
| 483 | Terry Shumpert | .03 | .02 |
| 484 | Mike Hartley | .03 | .02 |
| 485 | Chris Sabo | .08 | .06 |
| 486 | Bob Walk | .03 | .02 |
| 487 | John Cerutti | .03 | .02 |
| 488 | Scott Cooper(FC) | .10 | .08 |
| 489 | Bobby Cox | .03 | .02 |
| 490 | Julio Franco | .10 | .08 |
| 491 | Jeff Brantley | .04 | .03 |
| 492 | Mike Devereaux | .04 | .03 |
| 493 | Jose Offerman | .10 | .08 |
| 494 | Gary Thurman | .03 | .02 |
| 495 | Carney Lansford | .06 | .05 |
| 496 | Joe Grahe | .04 | .03 |
| 497 | *Andy Ashby*(FC) | .15 | .11 |
| 498 | Gerald Perry | .03 | .02 |
| 499 | Dave Otto | .03 | .02 |
| 500 | Vince Coleman | .08 | .06 |
| 501 | *Rob Mallicoat*(FC) | | |
| | | .15 | .11 |
| 502 | Greg Briley | .03 | .02 |
| 503 | Pascual Perez | .03 | .02 |
| 504 | #1 Draft Pick *(Aaron Sele)*(FC) | .30 | .25 |
| 505 | Bobby Thigpen | .08 | .06 |
| 506 | Todd Benzinger | .04 | .03 |
| 507 | Candy Maldonado | .04 | .03 |
| 508 | Bill Gullickson | .05 | .04 |
| 509 | Doug Dascenzo | .03 | .02 |
| 510 | Frank Viola | .08 | .06 |
| 511 | Kenny Rogers | .04 | .03 |
| 512 | Mike Heath | .03 | .02 |
| 513 | Kevin Bass | .04 | .03 |
| 514 | *Kim Batiste*(FC) | .15 | .11 |
| 515 | Delino DeShields | .08 | .06 |
| 516 | *Ed Sprague* | .10 | .08 |
| 517 | Jim Gott | .03 | .02 |
| 518 | *Jose Melendez*(FC) | | |
| | | .10 | .08 |

| | | MT | NR MT |
|---|---|---|---|
| 519 | Hal McRae | .03 | .02 |
| 520 | *Jeff Bagwell* | .50 | .40 |
| 521 | Joe Hesketh | .03 | .02 |
| 522 | Milt Cuyler | .12 | .09 |
| 523 | Shawn Hillegas | .03 | .02 |
| 524 | Don Slaught | .03 | .02 |
| 525 | Randy Johnson | .06 | .05 |
| 526 | *Doug Piatt* | .10 | .08 |
| 527 | Checklist 4 | .03 | .02 |
| 528 | Steve Foster(FC) | | |
| | | .15 | .11 |
| 529 | Joe Girardi | .04 | .03 |
| 530 | Jim Abbott | .10 | .08 |
| 531 | Larry Walker | .08 | .06 |
| 532 | Mike Huff | .04 | .03 |
| 533 | Mackey Sasser | .03 | .02 |
| 534 | #1 Draft Pick *(Benji Gil)*(FC) | .20 | .15 |
| 535 | Dave Stieb | .06 | .05 |
| 536 | Willie Wilson | .04 | .03 |
| 537 | *Mark Leiter*(FC) | .10 | .08 |
| 538 | Jose Uribe | .03 | .02 |
| 539 | Thomas Howard | .03 | .02 |
| 540 | Ben McDonald | .12 | .09 |
| 541 | *Jose Tolentino*(FC) | | |
| | | .15 | .11 |
| 542 | *Keith Mitchell*(FC) | | |
| | | .20 | .15 |
| 543 | Jerome Walton | .08 | .06 |
| 544 | *Cliff Brantley*(FC) | | |
| | | .15 | .11 |
| 545 | Andy Van Slyke | .08 | .06 |
| 546 | Paul Sorrento | .04 | .03 |
| 547 | Herm Winningham | .03 | .02 |
| 548 | Mark Guthrie | .04 | .03 |
| 549 | Joe Torre | .03 | .02 |
| 550 | Darryl Strawberry | .12 | .09 |
| 551 | Top Prospects Shortstops *(Manny Alexander, Alex Arias, Wil Cordero, Chipper Jones)* | .50 | .40 |
| 552 | Dave Gallagher | .04 | .03 |
| 553 | Edgar Martinez | .06 | .05 |
| 554 | Donald Harris | .15 | .11 |
| 555 | Frank Thomas | .60 | .45 |
| 556 | Storm Davis | .04 | .03 |
| 557 | Dickie Thon | .03 | .02 |
| 558 | Scott Garrelts | .03 | .02 |
| 559 | Steve Olin | .03 | .02 |
| 560 | Rickey Henderson | .15 | .11 |
| 561 | Jose Vizcaino | .04 | .03 |
| 562 | *Wade Taylor* | .10 | .08 |
| 563 | Pat Borders | .04 | .03 |
| 564 | #1 Draft Pick *(Jimmy Gonzalez)*(FC) | .20 | .15 |
| 565 | Lee Smith | .05 | .04 |
| 566 | Bill Sampen | .05 | .04 |
| 567 | Dean Palmer | .12 | .09 |
| 568 | Bryan Harvey | .05 | .04 |
| 569 | Tony Pena | .05 | .04 |
| 570 | Lou Whitaker | .06 | .05 |
| 571 | Randy Tomlin | .06 | .05 |
| 572 | Greg Vaughn | .12 | .09 |
| 573 | Kelly Downs | .03 | .02 |
| 574 | Steve Avery | .20 | .15 |
| 575 | Kirby Puckett | .15 | .11 |

| | MT | NR MT |
|---|---|---|
| 576 *Heathcliff Slocumb*(FC) | .10 | .08 |
| 577 Kevin Seitzer | .04 | .03 |
| 578 Lee Guetterman | .03 | .02 |
| 579 Johnny Oates | .03 | .02 |
| 580 Greg Maddux | .05 | .04 |
| 581 Stan Javier | .03 | .02 |
| 582 Vicente Palacios | .03 | .02 |
| 583 Mel Rojas | .03 | .02 |
| 584 *Wayne Rosenthal*(FC) | .10 | .08 |
| 585 Lenny Webster(FC) | .10 | .08 |
| 586 Rod Nichols | .03 | .02 |
| 587 Mickey Morandini | .08 | .06 |
| 588 Russ Swan | .03 | .02 |
| 589 Mariano Duncan | .04 | .03 |
| 590 Howard Johnson | .10 | .08 |
| 591 Top Prospects Outfielders *(Jacob Brumfield, Jeromy Burnitz, Alan Cockrell, D.J. Dozier)*(FC) | .60 | .45 |
| 592 *Denny Neagle*(FC) | .15 | .11 |
| 593 Steve Decker | .10 | .08 |
| 594 #1 Draft Pick *(Brian Barber)*(FC) | .15 | .11 |
| 595 Bruce Hurst | .04 | .03 |
| 596 Kent Mercker | .04 | .03 |
| 597 *Mike Magnante*(FC) | .10 | .08 |
| 598 Jody Reed | .04 | .03 |
| 599 Steve Searcy | .03 | .02 |
| 600 Paul Molitor | .10 | .08 |
| 601 Dave Smith | .05 | .04 |
| 602 Mike Fetters | .04 | .03 |
| 603 *Luis Mercedes*(FC) | .25 | .20 |
| 604 Chris Gwynn | .03 | .02 |
| 605 Scott Erickson | .20 | .15 |
| 606 Brook Jacoby | .04 | .03 |
| 607 Todd Stottlemyre | .05 | .04 |
| 608 Scott Bradley | .03 | .02 |
| 609 Mike Hargrove | .03 | .02 |
| 610 Eric Davis | .12 | .09 |
| 611 *Brian Hunter*(FC) | .25 | .20 |
| 612 Pat Kelly | .10 | .08 |
| 613 Pedro Munoz(FC) | .15 | .11 |
| 614 Al Osuna | .04 | .03 |
| 615 Matt Merullo | .03 | .02 |
| 616 Larry Andersen | .03 | .02 |
| 617 Junior Ortiz | .03 | .02 |
| 618 Top Prospects Outfielders *(Cesar Hernandez, Steve Hosey, Dan Peltier, Jeff McNeely)*(FC) | .60 | .45 |
| 619 Danny Jackson | .04 | .03 |
| 620 George Brett | .12 | .09 |
| 621 *Dan Gakeler*(FC) | .10 | .08 |
| 622 Steve Buechele | .04 | .03 |
| 623 Bob Tewksbury | .03 | .02 |
| 624 #1 Draft Pick *(Shawn Estes)*(FC) | .15 | .11 |
| 625 Kevin McReynolds | .08 | .06 |
| 626 Chris Haney(FC) | .15 | .11 |

| | MT | NR MT |
|---|---|---|
| 627 Mike Sharperson | .03 | .02 |
| 628 Mark Williamson | .03 | .02 |
| 629 Wally Joyner | .10 | .08 |
| 630 Carlton Fisk | .12 | .09 |
| 631 *Armando Reynoso*(FC) | .10 | .08 |
| 632 Felix Fermin | .03 | .02 |
| 633 Mitch Williams | .05 | .04 |
| 634 Manuel Lee | .04 | .03 |
| 635 Harold Baines | .08 | .06 |
| 636 Greg Harris | .05 | .04 |
| 637 Orlando Merced | .12 | .09 |
| 638 Chris Bosio | .04 | .03 |
| 639 *Wayne Housie*(FC) | .10 | .08 |
| 640 Xavier Hernandez | .04 | .03 |
| 641 *David Howard*(FC) | .10 | .08 |
| 642 Tim Crews | .03 | .02 |
| 643 Rick Cerone | .03 | .02 |
| 644 Terry Leach | .03 | .02 |
| 645 Deion Sanders | .12 | .09 |
| 646 Craig Wilson | .04 | .03 |
| 647 Marquis Grissom | .12 | .09 |
| 648 Scott Fletcher | .03 | .02 |
| 649 Norm Charlton | .04 | .03 |
| 650 Jesse Barfield | .06 | .05 |
| 651 *Joe Slusarski* | .10 | .08 |
| 652 Bobby Rose | .04 | .03 |
| 653 Dennis Lamp | .03 | .02 |
| 654 #1 Draft Pick *(Allen Watson)*(FC) | .15 | .11 |
| 655 Brett Butler | .06 | .05 |
| 656 Top Prospects Outfielders *(Rudy Pemberton, Henry Rodriguez, Lee Tinsley, Gerald Williams)*(FC) | .50 | .40 |
| 657 Dave Johnson | .03 | .02 |
| 658 Checklist 5 | .03 | .02 |
| 659 Brian McRae | .12 | .09 |
| 660 Fred McGriff | .10 | .08 |
| 661 Bill Landrum | .03 | .02 |
| 662 *Juan Guzman*(FC) | .50 | .40 |
| 663 Greg Gagne | .03 | .02 |
| 664 Ken Hill | .04 | .03 |
| 665 *Dave Haas*(FC) | .15 | .11 |
| 666 Tom Foley | .03 | .02 |
| 667 *Roberto Hernandez*(FC) | .10 | .08 |
| 668 Dwayne Henry | .03 | .02 |
| 669 Jim Fregosi | .03 | .02 |
| 670 Harold Reynolds | .05 | .04 |
| 671 Mark Whiten | .10 | .08 |
| 672 Eric Plunk | .03 | .02 |
| 673 Todd Hundley | .10 | .08 |
| 674 *Mo Sanford*(FC) | .25 | .20 |
| 675 Bobby Witt | .04 | .03 |
| 676 Top Prospects-Pitchers *(Pat Mahomes, Sam Militello, Roger Salkeld, Turk Wendell)*(FC) | .70 | .50 |
| 677 John Marzano | .03 | .02 |
| 678 Joe Klink | .03 | .02 |
| 679 Pete Incaviglia | .04 | .03 |

| | MT | NR MT | | | MT | NR MT |
|---|---|---|---|---|---|---|
| 680 | Dale Murphy | .08 | .06 | 741 | Mark Gubicza | .04 | .03 |
| 681 | Rene Gonzales | .03 | .02 | 742 | Billy Spiers | .04 | .03 |
| 682 | Andy Benes | .08 | .06 | 743 | Darren Lewis | .15 | .11 |
| 683 | Jim Poole(FC) | .08 | .06 | 744 | Chris Hammond | .05 | .04 |
| 684 | #1 Draft Pick (Trever | | | 745 | Dave Magadan | .05 | .04 |
| | Miller)(FC) | .15 | .11 | 746 | Bernard Gilkey | .10 | .08 |
| 685 | Scott | | | 747 | Willie Banks(FC) | .15 | .11 |
| | Livingstone(FC) | .12 | .09 | 748 | Matt Nokes | .04 | .03 |
| 686 | Rich DeLucia | .04 | .03 | 749 | Jerald Clark | .04 | .03 |
| 687 | Harvey Pulliam(FC) | | | 750 | Travis Fryman | .15 | .11 |
| | | .15 | .11 | 751 | Steve Wilson | .03 | .02 |
| 688 | Tim Belcher | .04 | .03 | 752 | Billy Ripken | .03 | .02 |
| 689 | Mark Lemke | .05 | .04 | 753 | Paul Assenmacher | .03 | .02 |
| 690 | John Franco | .06 | .05 | 754 | Charlie Hayes | .04 | .03 |
| 691 | Walt Weiss | .06 | .05 | 755 | Alex Fernandez | .15 | .11 |
| 692 | Scott Ruskin | .04 | .03 | 756 | Gary Pettis | .03 | .02 |
| 693 | Jeff King | .04 | .03 | 757 | Rob Dibble | .08 | .06 |
| 694 | Mike Gardiner(FC) | .06 | .05 | 758 | Tim Naehring | .08 | .06 |
| 695 | Gary Sheffield | .12 | .09 | 759 | Jeff Torborg | .03 | .02 |
| 696 | Joe Boever | .03 | .02 | 760 | Ozzie Smith | .10 | .08 |
| 697 | Mike Felder | .03 | .02 | 761 | Mike Fitzgerald | .03 | .02 |
| 698 | John Habyan | .03 | .02 | 762 | John Burkett | .04 | .03 |
| 699 | Cito Gaston | .03 | .02 | 763 | Kyle Abbott | .06 | .05 |
| 700 | Ruben Sierra | .15 | .11 | 764 | #1 Draft Pick (Tyler | | |
| 701 | Scott Radinsky | .03 | .02 | | Green)(FC) | .50 | .40 |
| 702 | Lee Stevens | .06 | .05 | 765 | Pete Harnisch | .06 | .05 |
| 703 | Mark Wohlers(FC) | | | 766 | Mark Davis | .03 | .02 |
| | | .15 | .11 | 767 | Kal Daniels | .06 | .05 |
| 704 | Curt Young | .03 | .02 | 768 | Jim Thome(FC) | .35 | .25 |
| 705 | Dwight Evans | .06 | .05 | 769 | Jack Howell | .03 | .02 |
| 706 | Rob Murphy | .03 | .02 | 770 | Sid Bream | .05 | .04 |
| 707 | Gregg Jefferies | .12 | .09 | 771 | Arthur Rhodes(FC) | .20 | .15 |
| 708 | Tom Bolton | .03 | .02 | 772 | Garry Templeton | .04 | .03 |
| 709 | Chris James | .03 | .02 | 773 | Hal Morris | .12 | .09 |
| 710 | Kevin Maas | .12 | .09 | 774 | Bud Black | .04 | .03 |
| 711 | Ricky Bones(FC) | .10 | .08 | 775 | Ivan Calderon | .06 | .05 |
| 712 | Curt Wilkerson | .03 | .02 | 776 | Doug Henry(FC) | .15 | .11 |
| 713 | Roger McDowell | .04 | .03 | 777 | John Olerud | .12 | .09 |
| 714 | #1 Draft Pick (Calvin | | | 778 | Tim Leary | .04 | .03 |
| | Reese)(FC) | .50 | .40 | 779 | Jay Bell | .05 | .04 |
| 715 | Craig Biggio | .08 | .06 | 780 | Eddie Murray | .10 | .08 |
| 716 | Kirk Dressendorfer | .15 | .11 | 781 | Paul Abbott(FC) | .08 | .06 |
| 717 | Ken Dayley | .03 | .02 | 782 | Phil Plantier | .20 | .15 |
| 718 | B.J. Surhoff | .05 | .04 | 783 | Joe Magrane | .05 | .04 |
| 719 | Terry Mulholland | .05 | .04 | 784 | Ken Patterson | .03 | .02 |
| 720 | Kirk Gibson | .06 | .05 | 785 | Albert Belle | .15 | .11 |
| 721 | Mike Pagliarulo | .04 | .03 | 786 | Royce Clayton(FC) | .25 | .20 |
| 722 | Walt Terrell | .03 | .02 | 787 | Checklist 6 | .03 | .02 |
| 723 | Jose Oquendo | .03 | .02 | 788 | Mike Stanton | .04 | .03 |
| 724 | Kevin McRoy(FC) | .08 | .06 | 789 | Bobby Valentine | .03 | .02 |
| 725 | Doc Gooden | .12 | .09 | 790 | Joe Carter | .10 | .08 |
| 726 | Kirt Manwaring | .04 | .03 | 791 | Danny Cox | .03 | .02 |
| 727 | Chuck McElroy | .03 | .02 | 792 | Dave Winfield | .12 | .09 |
| 728 | Dave Burba(FC) | .06 | .05 | | | | |
| 729 | Art Howe | .03 | .02 | | | | |
| 730 | Ramon Martinez | .15 | .11 | | | | |
| 731 | Donnie Hill | .03 | .02 | | | | |
| 732 | Nelson Santovenia | .03 | .02 | | | | |
| 733 | Bob Melvin | .03 | .02 | | | | |
| 734 | #1 Draft Pick (Scott | | | | | | |
| | Hatteberg)(FC) | .15 | .11 | | | | |
| 735 | Greg Swindell | .05 | .04 | | | | |
| 736 | Lance Johnson | .03 | .02 | | | | |
| 737 | Kevin Reimer | .05 | .04 | | | | |
| 738 | Dennis Eckersley | .08 | .06 | | | | |
| 739 | Rob Ducey | .03 | .02 | | | | |
| 740 | Ken Caminiti | .04 | .03 | | | | |

## 1992 Topps Traded

Members of the United States baseball team are featured in this 132-card boxed set released by Topps. The cards are styled after the regular 1992 Topps cards and are numbered alphabetically. Several United States baseball players featured in this set were also featured in the 1991 Topps Traded set.

| | | MT | NR MT |
|---|---|---|---|
| | Complete Set: | 10.00 | 7.50 |
| | Common Player: | .05 | .04 |
| 1 | Willie Adams (U.S.A.)(FC) | .20 | .15 |
| 2 | Jeff Alkire (U.S.A.)(FC) | .20 | .15 |
| 3 | Felipe Alou | .05 | .04 |
| 4 | Moises Alou | .20 | .15 |
| 5 | Ruben Amaro(FC) | .10 | .08 |
| 6 | Jack Armstrong | .05 | .04 |
| 7 | Scott Bankhead | .05 | .04 |
| 8 | Tim Belcher | .08 | .06 |
| 9 | George Bell | .08 | .06 |
| 10 | Freddie Benavides(FC) | .12 | .09 |
| 11 | Todd Benzinger | .05 | .04 |
| 12 | Joe Boever | .05 | .04 |
| 13 | Ricky Bones | .10 | .08 |
| 15 | Hubie Brooks | .05 | .04 |
| 16 | Jerry Browne | .05 | .04 |
| 17 | Jim Bullinger(FC) | .10 | .08 |
| 18 | Dave Burba | .05 | .04 |
| 19 | Kevin Campbell(FC) | .12 | .09 |
| 20 | Tom Candiotti | .05 | .04 |
| 21 | Mark Carreon | .05 | .04 |
| 23 | Archi Cianfrocco(FC) | .30 | .25 |
| 24 | Phil Clark(FC) | .10 | .08 |
| 25 | Chad Curtis(FC) | .15 | .11 |
| 26 | Eric Davis | .08 | .06 |
| 27 | Tim Davis (U.S.A.)(FC) | .20 | .15 |
| 28 | Gary DiSarcina | .05 | .04 |
| 29 | Darren Dreifort (U.S.A.) | .12 | .09 |
| 30 | Mariano Duncan | .05 | .04 |
| 31 | Mike Fitzgerald | .05 | .04 |
| 32 | John Flaherty(FC) | .12 | .09 |
| 33 | Darrin Fletcher | .05 | .04 |
| 34 | Scott Fletcher | .05 | .04 |
| 35 | Ron Fraser (U.S.A.) | .08 | .06 |
| 36 | Andres Galarraga | .06 | .05 |
| 37 | Dave Gallagher | .05 | .04 |
| 38 | Mike Gallego | .05 | .04 |
| 39 | Nomar Garciaparra (U.S.A.)(FC) | .20 | .15 |
| 40 | Jason Giambi (U.S.A.) | .12 | .09 |
| 41 | Danny Gladden | .05 | .04 |
| 42 | Rene Gonzales | .05 | .04 |
| 43 | Jeff Granger (U.S.A.) | .12 | .09 |
| 44 | Rick Greene (U.S.A.) | .20 | .15 |
| 45 | Jeffrey Hammonds (U.S.A.) | .20 | .15 |
| 46 | Charlie Hayes | .05 | .04 |
| 47 | Von Hayes | .05 | .04 |
| 48 | Rick Helling (U.S.A.) | .15 | .11 |
| 49 | Butch Henry(FC) | .12 | .09 |
| 50 | Carlos Hernandez(FC) | .12 | .09 |
| 51 | Ken Hill | .08 | .06 |
| 52 | Butch Hobson | .05 | .04 |
| 53 | Vince Horsman(FC) | .10 | .08 |
| 54 | Pete Incaviglia | .06 | .05 |
| 55 | Gregg Jefferies | .08 | .06 |
| 56 | Charles Johnson (U.S.A.) | .25 | .20 |
| 57 | Doug Jones | .05 | .04 |
| 58 | Brian Jordan(FC) | .30 | .25 |
| 59 | Wally Joyner | .08 | .06 |
| 60 | Daron Kirkreit (U.S.A.)(FC) | .20 | .15 |
| 61 | Bill Krueger | .06 | .05 |
| 62 | Gene Lamont | .06 | .05 |
| 63 | Jim Lefebvre | .06 | .05 |
| 64 | Danny Leon(FC) | .20 | .15 |
| 65 | Pat Listach(FC) | 1.00 | .70 |
| 66 | Kenny Lofton | .25 | .20 |
| 67 | Dave Martinez | .05 | .04 |
| 68 | Derrick May | .10 | .08 |
| 69 | Kirk McCaskill | .06 | .05 |
| 70 | Chad McConnell (U.S.A.)(FC) | .20 | .15 |
| 71 | Kevin McReynolds | .06 | .05 |
| 72 | Rusty Meacham(FC) | .10 | .08 |
| 73 | Keith Miller | .06 | .05 |
| 74 | Kevin Mitchell | .08 | .06 |
| 75 | Jason Moler (U.S.A.)(FC) | .20 | .15 |
| 76 | Mike Morgan | .06 | .05 |
| 77 | Jack Morris | .08 | .06 |
| 78 | Calvin Murray (U.S.A.)(FC) | .25 | .20 |
| 79 | Eddie Murray | .08 | .06 |
| 80 | Randy Myers | .06 | .05 |
| 81 | Denny Neagle(FC) | .10 | .08 |
| 82 | Phil Nevin (U.S.A.) | .20 | .15 |
| 83 | Dave Nilsson | .20 | .15 |
| 84 | Junior Ortiz | .05 | .04 |
| 85 | Donovan Osborne(FC) | .20 | .15 |
| 86 | Bill Pecota | .05 | .04 |
| 87 | Melido Perez | .05 | .04 |
| 88 | Mike Perez(FC) | .10 | .08 |
| 89 | Hipolito Pena(FC) | .10 | .08 |
| 90 | Willie Randolph | .06 | .05 |
| 91 | Darren Reed(FC) | .12 | .09 |
| 92 | Bip Roberts | .08 | .06 |
| 93 | Chris Roberts (U.S.A.) | .12 | .09 |
| 94 | Steve Rodriguez (U.S.A.) | .12 | .09 |
| 95 | Bruce Ruffin | .05 | .04 |
| 96 | Scott Ruskin | .05 | .04 |
| 97 | Bret Saberhagen | .08 | .06 |
| 98 | Rey Sanchez(FC) | .12 | .09 |
| 99 | Steve Sax | .08 | .06 |
| 100 | Curt Schilling | .06 | .05 |
| 101 | Dick Schofield | .05 | .04 |
| 102 | Gary Scott | .10 | .08 |
| 103 | Kevin Seitzer | .06 | .05 |
| 104 | Frank Seminara(FC) | .12 | .09 |
| 105 | Gary Sheffield | .10 | .08 |
| 106 | John Smiley | .06 | .05 |
| 107 | Cory Snyder | .06 | .05 |
| 108 | Paul Sorrento | .06 | .05 |
| 109 | Sammy Sosa | .06 | .05 |
| 110 | Matt Stairs(FC) | .12 | .09 |

| | | MT | NR MT |
|---|---|---|---|
| 111 | Andy Stankiewicz | .20 | .15 |
| 112 | Kurt Stillwell | .06 | .05 |
| 113 | Rick Sutcliffe | .06 | .05 |
| 114 | Bill Swift | .06 | .05 |
| 115 | Jeff Tackett(FC) | .12 | .09 |
| 116 | Danny Tartabull | .08 | .06 |
| 117 | Eddie Taubensee(FC) | | |
| | | .12 | .09 |
| 118 | Dickie Thon | .05 | .04 |
| 119 | Michael Tucker (U.S.A.)(FC) | .20 | .15 |
| 120 | Scooter Tucker(FC) | .12 | .09 |
| 121 | Marc Valdes (U.S.A.)(FC) | .20 | .15 |
| 122 | Julio Valera(FC) | .10 | .08 |
| 123 | Jason Vilaitek (U.S.A.)(FC) | .20 | .15 |
| 124 | Ron Villone (U.S.A.)(FC) | | |
| | | .20 | .15 |
| 125 | Frank Viola | .08 | .06 |
| 126 | B.J. Wallace (U.S.A.)(FC) | | |
| | | .25 | .20 |
| 127 | Dan Walters(FC) | .12 | .09 |
| 128 | Craig Wilson (U.S.A.) | | |
| | | .12 | .09 |
| 129 | Chris Wimmer (U.S.A.) | | |
| | | .12 | .09 |
| 130 | Dave Winfield | .08 | .06 |
| 131 | Herm Winningham | .05 | .04 |
| 132 | Checklist | .05 | .04 |

# 1992 Topps Stadium Club

This 900-card set was released in three 300-card series. Like the 1991 issue, the cards feature borderless high gloss photos on the front. The flip sides feature the player's first Topps card and a player evaluation. Topps released updated cards in the third series for traded players and free agents. Several players appear on two cards. Special Members Choice cards are included in the set. Series III featured special inserts of the last three number one picks overall, Phil Nevin, Brien Taylor and Chipper Jones.

| | | MT | NR MT |
|---|---|---|---|
| | Complete Set: | 110.00 | 82.00 |
| | Common Player: | .12 | .09 |
| 1 | Cal Ripken | 4.00 | 3.00 |
| 2 | Eric Yelding | .12 | .09 |
| 3 | Geno Petralli | .12 | .09 |
| 4 | Wally Backman | .12 | .09 |
| 5 | Milt Cuyler | .12 | .09 |
| 6 | Kevin Bass | .12 | .09 |
| 7 | Dante Bichette | .12 | .09 |
| 8 | Ray Lankford | .80 | .60 |
| 9 | Mel Hall | .15 | .11 |
| 10 | Joe Carter | .30 | .25 |
| 11 | Juan Samuel | .12 | .09 |
| 12 | Jeff Motngomery | .15 | .11 |
| 13 | Glenn Braggs | .15 | .11 |
| 14 | Henry Cotto | .12 | .09 |
| 15 | Deion Sanders | .30 | .25 |
| 16 | Dick Schofield | .12 | .09 |
| 17 | David Cone | .20 | .15 |
| 18 | Chili Davis | .20 | .15 |
| 19 | Tom Foley | .12 | .09 |
| 20 | Ozzie Guillen | .15 | .11 |
| 21 | Luis Salazar | .12 | .09 |
| 22 | Terry Steinbach | .15 | .11 |
| 23 | Chris James | .12 | .09 |
| 24 | Jeff King | .12 | .09 |
| 25 | Carlos Quintana | .12 | .09 |
| 26 | Mike Maddux | .12 | .09 |
| 27 | Tommy Greene | .15 | .11 |
| 28 | Jeff Russell | .15 | .11 |
| 29 | Steve Finley | .20 | .10 |
| 30 | Mike Flanagan | .12 | .09 |
| 31 | Darren Lewis | .12 | .09 |
| 32 | Kevin Maas, Mark Lee | | |
| | | .12 | .09 |
| 33 | Willie Fraser | .12 | .09 |
| 34 | Mike Henneman | .15 | .11 |
| 35 | Kevin Maas | .15 | .11 |
| 36 | Dave Hansen | .12 | .09 |
| 37 | Erik Hanson | .12 | .09 |
| 38 | Bill Doran | .12 | .09 |
| 39 | Mike Boddicker | .12 | .09 |
| 40 | Vince Coleman | .15 | .11 |
| 41 | Devon White | .15 | .11 |
| 42 | Mark Gardner | .12 | .09 |
| 43 | Scott Lewis | .25 | .20 |
| 44 | Juan Berenguer | .12 | .09 |
| 45 | Carney Lansford | .12 | .09 |
| 46 | Curt Wilkerson | .12 | .09 |
| 47 | Shane Mack | .15 | .11 |
| 48 | Bip Roberts | .15 | .11 |
| 49 | Greg Harris | .12 | .09 |
| 50 | Ryne Sandberg | 2.00 | 1.50 |
| 51 | Mark Whiten | .30 | .25 |
| 52 | Jack McDowell | .20 | .15 |
| 53 | Jimmy Jones | .12 | .09 |
| 54 | Steve Lake | .12 | .09 |
| 55 | Bud Black | .12 | .09 |
| 56 | Dave Valle | .12 | .09 |
| 57 | Kevin Reimer | .12 | .09 |
| 58 | Rich Gedman | .12 | .09 |
| 59 | Travis Fryman | 1.25 | .90 |
| 60 | Steve Avery | 2.00 | 1.50 |

| | MT | NR MT | | | MT | NR MT |
|---|---|---|---|---|---|---|
| 61 | Francisco DeLaRosa | .25 | .20 | 128 | Mike Heath | .12 | .09 |
| 62 | Scott Hemond | .12 | .09 | 129 | Todd Van Poppel | 1.00 | .70 |
| 63 | Hal Morris | .30 | .25 | 130 | Benny Santiago | .15 | .11 |
| 64 | Hensley Meulens | .12 | .09 | 131 | Gary Thurman | .12 | .09 |
| 65 | Frank Castillo | .25 | .20 | 132 | Joe Girardi | .12 | .09 |
| 66 | Gene Larkin | .12 | .09 | 133 | Dave Eiland | .12 | .09 |
| 67 | Jose DeLeon | .12 | .09 | 134 | Orlando Merced | 1.00 | .70 |
| 68 | Al Osuna | .12 | .09 | 135 | Joe Orsulak | .12 | .09 |
| 69 | Dave Cochrane | .12 | .09 | 136 | John Burkett | .12 | .09 |
| 70 | Robin Ventura | 2.00 | 1.50 | 137 | Ken Dayley | .12 | .09 |
| 71 | John Cerutti | .12 | .09 | 138 | Ken Hill | .15 | .11 |
| 72 | Kevin Gross | .12 | .09 | 139 | Walt Terrell | .12 | .09 |
| 73 | Ivan Calderon | .15 | .11 | 140 | Mike Scioscia | .12 | .09 |
| 74 | Mike Macfarlane | .12 | .09 | 141 | Junior Felix | .12 | .09 |
| 75 | Stan Belinda | .12 | .09 | 142 | Ken Caminiti | .12 | .09 |
| 76 | Shawn Hillegas | .12 | .09 | 143 | Carlos Baerga | .35 | .25 |
| 77 | Pat Borders | .12 | .09 | 144 | Tony Fossas | .12 | .09 |
| 78 | Jim Vatcher | .12 | .09 | 145 | Craig Grebeck | .12 | .09 |
| 79 | Bobby Rose | .12 | .09 | 146 | Scott Bradley | .12 | .09 |
| 80 | Roger Clemens | 1.50 | 1.25 | 147 | Kent Mercker | .12 | .09 |
| 81 | Craig Worthington | .12 | .09 | 148 | Derrick May | .20 | .15 |
| 82 | Jeff Treadway | .12 | .09 | 149 | Jerald Clark | .15 | .11 |
| 83 | Jamie Quirk | .12 | .09 | 150 | George Brett | .40 | .30 |
| 84 | Randy Bush | .12 | .09 | 151 | Luis Quinones | .15 | .11 |
| 85 | Anthony Young | .50 | .40 | 152 | Mike Pagliarulo | .15 | .11 |
| 86 | Trevor Wilson | .12 | .09 | 153 | Jose Guzman | .15 | .11 |
| 87 | Jaime Navarro | .15 | .11 | 154 | Charlie O'Brien | .15 | .11 |
| 88 | Les Lancaster | .12 | .09 | 155 | Darren Holmes | .15 | .11 |
| 89 | Pat Kelly | .30 | .25 | 156 | Joe Boever | .15 | .11 |
| 90 | Alvin Davis | .12 | .09 | 157 | Rich Monteleone | .15 | .11 |
| 91 | Larry Andersen | .12 | .09 | 158 | Reggie Harris | .15 | .11 |
| 92 | Rob Deer | .12 | .09 | 159 | Roberto Alomar | 1.00 | .70 |
| 93 | Mike Sharperson | .12 | .09 | 160 | Robby Thompson | .15 | .11 |
| 94 | Lance Parrish | .12 | .09 | 161 | Chris Hoiles | .25 | .20 |
| 95 | Cecil Espy | .12 | .09 | 162 | Tom Pagnozzi | .12 | .09 |
| 96 | Tim Spehr | .15 | .11 | 163 | Omar Vizquel | .12 | .09 |
| 97 | Dave Stieb | .15 | .11 | 164 | John Candelaria | .12 | .09 |
| 98 | Terry Mulholland | .15 | .11 | 165 | Terry Shumpert | .12 | .09 |
| 99 | Dennis Boyd | .12 | .09 | 166 | Andy Mota | .25 | .20 |
| 100 | Barry Larkin | .30 | .25 | 167 | Scott Bailes | .12 | .09 |
| 101 | Ryan Bowen | .40 | .30 | 168 | Jeff Blauser | .12 | .09 |
| 102 | Felix Fermin | .12 | .09 | 169 | Steve Olin | .12 | .09 |
| 103 | Luis Alicea | .12 | .09 | 170 | Doug Drabek | .20 | .15 |
| 104 | Tim Huulett | .12 | .09 | 171 | Dave Bergman | .12 | .09 |
| 105 | Rafael Belliard | .12 | .09 | 172 | Eddie Whitson | .12 | .09 |
| 106 | Mike Gallego | .12 | .09 | 173 | Gilberto Reyes | .12 | .09 |
| 107 | Dave Righetti | .12 | .09 | 174 | Mark Grace | .25 | .20 |
| 108 | Jeff Schaefer | .12 | .09 | 175 | Paul O'Neill | .15 | .11 |
| 109 | Ricky Bones | .40 | .30 | 176 | Greg Cadaret | .12 | .09 |
| 110 | Scott Erickson | .60 | .45 | 177 | Mark Williamson | .12 | .09 |
| 111 | Matt Nokes | .12 | .09 | 178 | Casey Candaele | .12 | .09 |
| 112 | Bob Scanlan | .12 | .09 | 179 | Candy Maldonado | .12 | .09 |
| 113 | Tom Candiotti | .15 | .11 | 180 | Lee Smith | .15 | .11 |
| 114 | Sean Berry | .15 | .11 | 181 | Harold Reynolds | .12 | .09 |
| 115 | Kevin Morton | .30 | .25 | 182 | Dave Justice | 2.00 | 1.50 |
| 116 | Scott Fletcher | .12 | .09 | 183 | Lenny Webster | .12 | .09 |
| 117 | B.J. Surhoff | .12 | .09 | 184 | Donn Pall | .12 | .09 |
| 118 | Dave Magadan | .12 | .09 | 185 | Gerald Alexander | .12 | .09 |
| 119 | Bill Gullickson | .12 | .09 | 186 | Jack Clark | .12 | .09 |
| 120 | Marquis Grissom | .25 | .20 | 187 | Stan Javier | .12 | .09 |
| 121 | Lenny Harris | .12 | .09 | 188 | Ricky Jordan | .15 | .11 |
| 122 | Wally Joyner | .20 | .15 | 189 | Franklin Stubbs | .12 | .09 |
| 123 | Kevin Brown | .15 | .11 | 190 | Dennis Eckersley | .25 | .20 |
| 124 | Braulio Castillo | .60 | .45 | 191 | Danny Tartabull | .20 | .15 |
| 125 | Eric King | .12 | .09 | 192 | Pete O'Brien | .12 | .09 |
| 126 | Mark Portugal | .12 | .09 | 193 | Mark Lewis | .30 | .25 |
| 127 | Calvin Jones | .30 | .25 | 194 | Mike Felder | .12 | .09 |

| # | Player | MT | NR MT |
|---|--------|----|----|
| 195 | Mickey Tettleton | .15 | .11 |
| 196 | Dwight Smith | .12 | .09 |
| 197 | Shawn Abner | .12 | .09 |
| 198 | Jim Leyritz | .12 | .09 |
| 199 | Mike Devereaux | .20 | .15 |
| 200 | Craig Biggio | .15 | .11 |
| 201 | Kevin Elster | .12 | .09 |
| 202 | Rance Mulliniks | .12 | .09 |
| 203 | Tony Fernandez | .15 | .11 |
| 204 | Allan Anderson | .12 | .09 |
| 205 | Herm Winningham | .12 | .09 |
| 206 | Tim Jones | .12 | .09 |
| 207 | Ramon Martinez | .30 | .25 |
| 208 | Teddy Higuera | .12 | .09 |
| 209 | John Kruk | .15 | .11 |
| 210 | Jim Abbott | .30 | .25 |
| 211 | Dean Palmer, Dean Palmer | .20 | .15 |
| 212 | Mark Davis | .12 | .09 |
| 213 | Jay Buhner | .12 | .09 |
| 214 | Jesse Barfield | .12 | .09 |
| 215 | Kevin Mitchell, Kevin Mitchell | .15 | .11 |
| 216 | Mike LaValliere | .15 | .11 |
| 217 | Mark Wohlers, Mark Wohlers | .15 | .11 |
| 218 | Dave Henderson | .15 | .11 |
| 219 | Dave Smith | .12 | .09 |
| 220 | Albert Belle | .60 | .45 |
| 221 | Spike Owen | .12 | .09 |
| 222 | Jeff Gray | .12 | .09 |
| 223 | Paul Gibson | .12 | .09 |
| 224 | Bobby Thigpen | .15 | .11 |
| 225 | Mike Mussina | 4.00 | 3.00 |
| 226 | Darrin Jackson | .12 | .09 |
| 227 | Luis Gonzalez | .70 | .50 |
| 228 | Greg Briley | .12 | .09 |
| 229 | Brent Mayne | .12 | .09 |
| 230 | Paul Molitor | .20 | .15 |
| 231 | Al Leiter | .12 | .09 |
| 232 | Andy Van Slyke | .15 | .11 |
| 233 | Ron Tingley | .12 | .09 |
| 234 | Bernard Gilkey | .15 | .11 |
| 235 | Kent Hrbek | .15 | .11 |
| 236 | Eric Karros | 3.00 | 2.25 |
| 237 | Randy Velarde | .12 | .09 |
| 238 | Andy Allanson | .12 | .09 |
| 239 | Willie McGee | .15 | .11 |
| 240 | Juan Gonzalez | 2.50 | 2.00 |
| 241 | Karl Rhodes | .12 | .09 |
| 242 | Luis Mercedes | .50 | .40 |
| 243 | Billy Swift | .15 | .11 |
| 244 | Tommy Gregg | .12 | .09 |
| 245 | David Howard | .12 | .09 |
| 246 | Dave Hollins | .20 | .15 |
| 247 | Kip Gross | .30 | .25 |
| 248 | Walt Weiss | .12 | .09 |
| 249 | Mackey Sasser | .12 | .09 |
| 250 | Cecil Fielder | 1.00 | .70 |
| 251 | Jerry Browne | .12 | .09 |
| 252 | Doug Dascenzo | .12 | .09 |
| 253 | Darryl Hamilton | .12 | .09 |
| 254 | Dann Bilardello | .12 | .09 |
| 255 | Luis Rivera | .12 | .09 |
| 256 | Larry Walker | .20 | .15 |
| 257 | Ron Karkovice | .12 | .09 |
| 258 | Bob Tewksbury | .15 | .11 |
| 259 | Jimmy Key | .15 | .11 |
| 260 | Bernie Williams | .60 | .45 |
| 261 | Gary Wayne | .12 | .09 |
| 262 | Mike Simms | .12 | .09 |
| 263 | John Orton | .12 | .09 |
| 264 | Marvin Freeman | .12 | .09 |
| 265 | Mike Jeffcoat | .12 | .09 |
| 266 | Roger Mason | .12 | .09 |
| 267 | Edgar Martinez | .20 | .15 |
| 268 | Henry Rodriguez | .35 | .25 |
| 269 | Sam Horn | .12 | .09 |
| 270 | Brian McRae | .60 | .45 |
| 271 | Kirt Manwaring | .12 | .09 |
| 272 | Mike Bordick | .15 | .11 |
| 273 | Chris Sabo | .15 | .11 |
| 274 | Jim Olander | .12 | .09 |
| 275 | Greg Harris | .12 | .09 |
| 276 | Dan Gakeler | .12 | .09 |
| 277 | Bill Sampen | .12 | .09 |
| 278 | Joel Skinner | .12 | .09 |
| 279 | Curt Schilling | .12 | .09 |
| 280 | Dale Murphy | .25 | .20 |
| 281 | Lee Stevens | .12 | .09 |
| 282 | Lonnie Smith | .12 | .09 |
| 283 | Manuel Lee | .12 | .09 |
| 284 | Shawn Boskie | .12 | .09 |
| 285 | Kevin Seitzer | .12 | .09 |
| 286 | Stan Royer | .15 | .11 |
| 287 | John Dopson | .12 | .09 |
| 288 | Scott Bullett | .35 | .25 |
| 289 | Ken Patterson | .12 | .09 |
| 290 | Todd Hundley | .15 | .11 |
| 291 | Tim Leary | .12 | .09 |
| 292 | Brett Butler | .12 | .09 |
| 293 | Gregg Olson | .15 | .11 |
| 294 | Jeff Brantley | .12 | .09 |
| 295 | Brian Holman | .12 | .09 |
| 296 | Brian Harper | .15 | .11 |
| 297 | Brian Bohanon | .15 | .11 |
| 298 | Checklist 1-100 | .15 | .11 |
| 299 | Checklist 101-200 | .15 | .11 |
| 300 | Checklist 201-300 | .15 | .11 |
| 301 | Frank Thomas | 6.00 | 4.50 |
| 302 | Lloyd McClendon | .15 | .11 |
| 303 | Brady Anderson | .30 | .25 |
| 304 | Julio Valera | .15 | .11 |
| 305 | Mike Aldrete | .15 | .11 |
| 306 | Joe Oliver | .15 | .11 |
| 307 | Todd Stottlemyre | .15 | .11 |
| 308 | Rey Sanchez | .15 | .11 |
| 309 | Gary Sheffield | 1.00 | .70 |
| 310 | Andujar Cedeno | .30 | .25 |
| 311 | Kenny Rogers | .12 | .09 |
| 312 | Bruce Hurst | .15 | .11 |
| 313 | Mike Schooler | .12 | .09 |
| 314 | Mike Benjamin | .12 | .09 |
| 315 | Chuck Finley | .15 | .11 |
| 316 | Mark Lemke | .12 | .09 |
| 317 | Scott Livingstone | .15 | .11 |
| 318 | Chris Nabholz | .12 | .09 |
| 319 | Mike Humphreys | .15 | .11 |
| 320 | Pedro Guerrero | .15 | .11 |
| 321 | Willie Banks | .15 | .11 |
| 322 | Tom Goodwin | .15 | .11 |
| 323 | Hector Wagner | .25 | .20 |
| 324 | Wally Ritchie | .12 | .09 |
| 325 | Mo Vaughn | .25 | .20 |

| | | MT | NR MT | | | | MT | NR MT |
|---|---|---|---|---|---|---|---|---|
| 326 | Joe Klink | .12 | .09 | | 390 | Dave Stewart | .15 | .11 |
| 327 | Cal Eldred | 2.00 | 1.50 | | 391 | Pete Harnisch | .15 | .11 |
| 328 | Daryl Boston | .12 | .09 | | 392 | Tim Burke | .12 | .09 |
| 329 | Mike Huff | .12 | .09 | | 393 | Roberto Kelly | .25 | .20 |
| 330 | Jeff Bagwell | 2.50 | 2.00 | | 394 | Freddie Benavides | .12 | .09 |
| 331 | Bob Milacki | .12 | .09 | | 395 | Tom Glavine | .50 | .40 |
| 332 | Tom Prince | .12 | .09 | | 396 | Wes Chamberlain | .40 | .30 |
| 333 | Pat Tabler | .12 | .09 | | 397 | Eric Gunderson | .12 | .09 |
| 334 | Ced Landrum | .12 | .09 | | 398 | Dave West | .12 | .09 |
| 335 | Reggie Jefferson | .30 | .25 | | 399 | Ellis Burks | .20 | .15 |
| 336 | Mo Sanford | .35 | .25 | | 400 | Ken Griffey, Jr. | 4.00 | 3.00 |
| 337 | Kevin Ritz | .12 | .09 | | 401 | Thomas Howard | .12 | .09 |
| 338 | Gerald Perry | .12 | .09 | | 402 | Juan Guzman | 4.00 | 3.00 |
| 339 | Jeff Hamilton | .12 | .09 | | 403 | Mitch Webster | .12 | .09 |
| 340 | Tim Wallach | .15 | .11 | | 404 | Matt Merullo | .12 | .09 |
| 341 | Jeff Huson | .15 | .11 | | 405 | Steve Buechele | .12 | .09 |
| 342 | Jose Melendez | .15 | .11 | | 406 | Danny Jackson | .12 | .09 |
| 343 | Willie Wilson | .15 | .11 | | 407 | Felix Jose | .30 | .25 |
| 344 | Mike Stanton | .12 | .09 | | 408 | Doug Piatt | .20 | .15 |
| 345 | Joel Johnston | .15 | .11 | | 409 | Jim Eisenreich | .12 | .09 |
| 346 | Lee Guetterman | .12 | .09 | | 410 | Bryan Harvey | .15 | .11 |
| 347 | Francisco Olivares | .12 | .09 | | 411 | Jim Austin | .15 | .11 |
| 348 | Dave Burba | .12 | .09 | | 412 | Jim Poole | .12 | .09 |
| 349 | Tim Crews | .12 | .09 | | 413 | Glenallen Hill | .15 | .11 |
| 350 | Scott Leius | .15 | .11 | | 414 | Gene Nelson | .12 | .09 |
| 351 | Danny Cox | .12 | .09 | | 415 | Ivan Rodriguez | 2.50 | 2.00 |
| 352 | Wayne Housie | .35 | .25 | | 416 | Frank Tanana | .12 | .09 |
| 353 | Chris Donnels | .20 | .15 | | 417 | Steve Decker | .12 | .09 |
| 354 | Chris George | .20 | .15 | | 418 | Jason Grimsley | .12 | .09 |
| 355 | Gerald Young | .12 | .09 | | 419 | Tim Layana | .12 | .09 |
| 356 | Roberto Hernandez | .15 | .11 | | 420 | Don Mattingly | .60 | .45 |
| 357 | Neal Heaton | .12 | .09 | | 421 | Jerome Walton | .12 | .09 |
| 358 | Todd Frohwirth | .12 | .09 | | 422 | Rob Ducey | .12 | .09 |
| 359 | Jose Vizcaino | .12 | .09 | | 423 | Andy Benes | .60 | .45 |
| 360 | Jim Thome | 1.00 | .70 | | 424 | John Marzano | .12 | .09 |
| 361 | Craig Wilson | .12 | .09 | | 425 | Gene Harris | .12 | .09 |
| 362 | Dave Haas | .20 | .15 | | 426 | Rock Raines | .20 | .15 |
| 363 | Billy Hatcher | .12 | .09 | | 427 | Bret Barberie | .30 | .25 |
| 364 | John Barfield | .12 | .09 | | 428 | Harvey Pulliam | .30 | .25 |
| 365 | Luis Aquino | .12 | .09 | | 429 | Cris Carpenter | .12 | .09 |
| 366 | Charlie Leibrandt | .12 | .09 | | 430 | Howard Johnson | .30 | .25 |
| 367 | Howard Farmer | .12 | .09 | | 431 | Orel Hershiser | .25 | .20 |
| 368 | Bryn Smith | .12 | .09 | | 432 | Brian Hunter | .40 | .30 |
| 369 | Mickey Morandini | .15 | .11 | | 433 | Kevin Tapani | .15 | .11 |
| 370 | Jose Canseco | 2.00 | 1.50 | | 434 | Rick Reed | .15 | .11 |
| 370b | Jose Canseco (Members Choice - should be numbered 597) | 3.00 | 2.25 | | 435 | Ron Witmeyer | .30 | .25 |
| | | | | | 436 | Gary Gaetti | .15 | .11 |
| 371 | Jose Uribe | .12 | .09 | | 437 | Alex Cole | .15 | .11 |
| 372 | Bob MacDonald | .12 | .09 | | 438 | Chito Martinez | .25 | .20 |
| 373 | Luis Sojo | .12 | .09 | | 439 | Greg Litton | .15 | .11 |
| 374 | Craig Shipley | .12 | .09 | | 440 | Julio Franco | .20 | .15 |
| 375 | Scott Bankhead | .12 | .09 | | 441 | Mike Munoz | .15 | .11 |
| 376 | Greg Gagne | .12 | .09 | | 442 | Erik Pappas | .15 | .11 |
| 377 | Scott Cooper | .12 | .09 | | 443 | Pat Combs | .15 | .11 |
| 378 | Jose Offerman | .12 | .09 | | 444 | Lance Johnson | .15 | .11 |
| 379 | Billy Spiers | .12 | .09 | | 445 | Ed Sprague | .15 | .11 |
| 380 | John Smiley | .15 | .11 | | 446 | Mike Greenwell | .25 | .20 |
| 381 | Jeff Carter | .12 | .09 | | 447 | Milt Thompson | .15 | .11 |
| 382 | Heathcliff Slocumb | .12 | .09 | | 448 | Mike Magnante | .25 | .20 |
| 383 | Jeff Tackett | .20 | .15 | | 449 | Chris Haney | .20 | .15 |
| 384 | John Kiely | .25 | .20 | | 450 | Robin Yount | .50 | .40 |
| 385 | John Vander Wal | .50 | .40 | | 451 | Rafael Ramirez | .15 | .11 |
| 386 | Omar Olivares | .12 | .09 | | 452 | Gino Minutelli | .15 | .11 |
| 387 | Ruben Sierra | .80 | .60 | | 453 | Tom Lampkin | .15 | .11 |
| 388 | Tom Gordon | .12 | .09 | | 454 | Tony Perezchica | .15 | .11 |
| 389 | Charles Nagy | .35 | .25 | | 455 | Doc Gooden | .40 | .30 |
| | | | | | 456 | Mark Guthrie | .15 | .11 |

| | | MT | NR MT | | | | MT | NR MT |
|---|---|---|---|---|---|---|---|---|
| 457 | Jay Howell | .15 | .11 | | 524 | Gary Redus | .12 | .09 |
| 458 | Gary DiSarcina | .15 | .11 | | 525 | George Bell | .20 | .15 |
| 459 | John Smoltz | .25 | .20 | | 526 | Jeff Kaiser | .20 | .15 |
| 460 | Will Clark | 1.50 | 1.25 | | 527 | Alvaro Espinoza | .12 | .09 |
| 461 | Dave Otto | .15 | .11 | | 528 | Luis Polonia | .12 | .09 |
| 462 | Rob Maurer | .80 | .60 | | 529 | Darren Daulton | .25 | .20 |
| 463 | Dwight Evans | .15 | .11 | | 530 | Norm Charlton | .20 | .15 |
| 464 | Tom Brunansky | .12 | .09 | | 531 | John Olerud | .20 | .15 |
| 465 | Shawn Hare | .50 | .40 | | 532 | Dan Plesac | .12 | .09 |
| 466 | Geronimo Pena | .20 | .15 | | 533 | Billy Ripken | .12 | .09 |
| 467 | Alex Fernandez | .20 | .15 | | 534 | Rod Nichols | .12 | .09 |
| 468 | Greg Myers | .12 | .09 | | 535 | Joey Cora | .12 | .09 |
| 469 | Jeff Fassero | .12 | .09 | | 536 | Harold Baines | .20 | .15 |
| 470 | Len Dykstra | .20 | .15 | | 537 | Bob Ojeda | .12 | .09 |
| 471 | Jeff Johnson | .15 | .11 | | 538 | Mark Leonard | .12 | .09 |
| 472 | Russ Swan | .12 | .09 | | 539 | Danny Darwin | .12 | .09 |
| 473 | Archie Corbin | .30 | .25 | | 540 | Shawon Dunston | .15 | .11 |
| 474 | Chuck McElroy | .12 | .09 | | 541 | Pedro Munoz | .60 | .45 |
| 475 | Mark McGwire | 1.00 | .70 | | 542 | Mark Gubicza | .15 | .11 |
| 476 | Wally Whitehurst | .12 | .09 | | 543 | Kevin Baez | .20 | .15 |
| 477 | Tim McIntosh | .12 | .09 | | 544 | Todd Zeile | .20 | .15 |
| 478 | Sid Bream | .12 | .09 | | 545 | Don Slaught | .12 | .09 |
| 479 | Jeff Juden | .50 | .40 | | 546 | Tony Eusebio | .20 | .15 |
| 480 | Carlton Fisk | .50 | .40 | | 547 | Alonzo Powell | .12 | .09 |
| 481 | Jeff Plympton | .30 | .25 | | 548 | Gary Pettis | .12 | .09 |
| 482 | Carlos Martinez | .12 | .09 | | 549 | Brian Barnes | .15 | .11 |
| 483 | Jim Gott | .12 | .09 | | 550 | Lou Whitaker | .15 | .11 |
| 484 | Bob McClure | .12 | .09 | | 551 | Keith Mitchell | .40 | .30 |
| 485 | Tim Teufel | .12 | .09 | | 552 | Oscar Azocar | .12 | .09 |
| 486 | Vicente Palacios | .12 | .09 | | 553 | Stu Cole | .15 | .11 |
| 487 | Jeff Reed | .12 | .09 | | 554 | Steve Wapnick | .20 | .15 |
| 488 | Tony Phillips | .15 | .11 | | 555 | Derek Bell | .50 | .40 |
| 489 | Mel Rojas | .12 | .09 | | 556 | Luis Lopez | .20 | .15 |
| 490 | Ben McDonald | .50 | .40 | | 557 | Anthony Telford | .15 | .11 |
| 491 | Andres Santana | .15 | .11 | | 558 | Tim Mauser | .20 | .15 |
| 492 | Chris Beasley | .20 | .15 | | 559 | Glenn Sutko | .20 | .15 |
| 493 | Mike Timlin | .15 | .11 | | 560 | Darryl Strawberry | .80 | .60 |
| 494 | Brian Downing | .12 | .09 | | 561 | Tom Bolton | .12 | .09 |
| 495 | Kirk Gibson | .12 | .09 | | 562 | Cliff Young | .20 | .15 |
| 496 | Scott Sanderson | .12 | .09 | | 563 | Bruce Walton | .12 | .09 |
| 497 | Nick Esasky | .12 | .09 | | 564 | Chico Walker | .12 | .09 |
| 498 | Johnny Guzman | .30 | .25 | | 565 | John Franco | .15 | .11 |
| 499 | Mitch Williams | .15 | .11 | | 566 | Paul McClellan | .15 | .11 |
| 500 | Kirby Puckett | 1.25 | .90 | | 567 | Paul Abbott | .15 | .11 |
| 501 | Mike Harkey | .12 | .09 | | 568 | Gary Varsho | .12 | .09 |
| 502 | Jim Gantner | .12 | .09 | | 569 | Carlos Maldonado | .20 | .15 |
| 503 | Bruce Egloff | .20 | .15 | | 570 | Kelly Gruber | .20 | .15 |
| 504 | Josias Manzanillo | .20 | .15 | | 571 | Jose Oquendo | .12 | .09 |
| 505 | Delino DeShields | .20 | .15 | | 572 | Steve Frey | .12 | .09 |
| 506 | Rheal Cormier | .30 | .25 | | 573 | Tino Martinez | .20 | .15 |
| 507 | Jay Bell | .15 | .11 | | 574 | Bill Haselman | .12 | .09 |
| 508 | Rich Rowland | .25 | .20 | | 575 | Eric Anthony | .15 | .11 |
| 509 | Scott Servais | .15 | .11 | | 576 | John Habyan | .12 | .09 |
| 510 | Terry Pendleton | .20 | .15 | | 577 | Jeffrey McNeely | .80 | .60 |
| 511 | Rich DeLucia | .12 | .09 | | 578 | Chris Bosio | .15 | .11 |
| 512 | Warren Newson | .12 | .09 | | 579 | Joe Grahe | .15 | .11 |
| 513 | Paul Faries | .12 | .09 | | 580 | Fred McGriff | .35 | .25 |
| 514 | Kal Daniels | .12 | .09 | | 581 | Rick Honeycutt | .12 | .09 |
| 515 | Jarvis Brown | .20 | .15 | | 582 | Matt Williams | .25 | .20 |
| 516 | Rafael Palmeiro | .30 | .25 | | 583 | Cliff Brantley | .20 | .15 |
| 517 | Kelly Downs | .12 | .09 | | 584 | Rob Dibble | .20 | .15 |
| 518 | Steve Chitren | .12 | .09 | | 585 | Skeeter Barnes | .12 | .09 |
| 519 | Moises Alou | .20 | .15 | | 586 | Greg Hibbard | .12 | .09 |
| 520 | Wade Boggs | .80 | .60 | | 587 | Randy Milligan | .12 | .09 |
| 521 | Pete Schourek | .12 | .09 | | 588 | Checklist 301-400 | .12 | .09 |
| 522 | Scott Terry | .12 | .09 | | 589 | Checklist 401-500 | .12 | .09 |
| 523 | Kevin Appier | .20 | .15 | | 590 | Checklist 501-600 | .12 | .09 |

| | MT | NR MT |
|---|---|---|
| 591 Frank Thomas (Members Choice) | 5.00 | 3.75 |
| 592 David Justice (Members Choice) | 1.00 | .70 |
| 593 Roger Clemens (Members Choice) | .80 | .60 |
| 594 Steve Avery (Members Choice) | 1.00 | .70 |
| 595 Cal Ripken (Members Choice) | 1.50 | 1.25 |
| 596 Barry Larkin (Members Choice) | .40 | .30 |
| 598 Will Clark (Members Choice) | 1.00 | .70 |
| 599 Cecil Fielder (Members Choice) | .60 | .45 |
| 600 Ryne Sandberg (Members Choice) | 1.00 | .70 |
| 601 Chuck Knoblauch (Members Choice) | 1.00 | .70 |
| 602 Dwight Gooden (Members Choice) | .50 | .40 |
| 603 Ken Griffey, Jr. (Members Choice) | 3.00 | 2.25 |
| 604 Barry Bonds (Members Choice) | 1.00 | .70 |
| 605 Nolan Ryan (Members Choice) | 3.00 | 2.25 |
| 606 Jeff Bagwell (Members Choice) | 1.25 | .90 |
| 607 Robin Yount (Members Choice) | .60 | .45 |
| 608 Bobby Bonilla (Members Choice) | .30 | .25 |
| 609 George Brett (Members Choice) | .60 | .45 |
| 610 Howard Johnson | .25 | .20 |
| 611 Esteban Beltre | .12 | .09 |
| 612 Mike Christopher | .20 | .15 |
| 613 Troy Afenir | .12 | .09 |
| 614 Mariano Duncan | .12 | .09 |
| 615 Doug Henry | .15 | .11 |
| 616 Doug Jones | .15 | .11 |
| 617 Alvin Davis | .12 | .09 |
| 618 Craig Lefferts | .12 | .09 |
| 619 Kevin McReynolds | .20 | .15 |
| 620 Barry Bonds | .80 | .60 |
| 621 Turner Ward | .20 | .15 |
| 622 Joe Magrane | .15 | .11 |
| 623 Mark Parent | .12 | .09 |
| 624 Tom Browning | .15 | .11 |
| 625 John Smiley | .15 | .11 |
| 626 Steve Wilson | .12 | .09 |
| 627 Mike Gallego | .12 | .09 |
| 628 Sammy Sosa | .15 | .11 |
| 629 Rico Rossy | .15 | .11 |
| 630 Royce Clayton | .60 | .45 |
| 631 Clay Parker | .12 | .09 |
| 632 Pete Smith | .12 | .09 |
| 633 Jeff McKnight | .12 | .09 |
| 634 Jack Daugherty | .12 | .09 |
| 635 Steve Sax | .20 | .15 |
| 636 Joe Hesketh | .12 | .09 |
| 637 Vince Horsman | .20 | .15 |
| 638 Joe Boever | .12 | .09 |
| 640 Jack Morris | .30 | .25 |
| 641 Arthur Rhodes | .50 | .40 |

| | MT | NR MT |
|---|---|---|
| 642 Bob Melvin | .12 | .09 |
| 643 Rick Wilkins | .20 | .15 |
| 644 Scott Scudder | .12 | .09 |
| 645 Bip Roberts | .20 | .15 |
| 646 Julio Valera | .20 | .15 |
| 647 Kevin Campbell | .20 | .15 |
| 648 Steve Searcy | .12 | .09 |
| 649 Scott Kamieniecki | .12 | .09 |
| 650 Kurt Stillwell | .12 | .09 |
| 651 Bob Welch | .15 | .11 |
| 652 Andres Galarraga | .15 | .11 |
| 653 Mike Jackson | .12 | .09 |
| 654 Bo Jackson | .60 | .45 |
| 655 Sid Fernandez | .15 | .11 |
| 656 Mike Bielecki | .12 | .09 |
| 657 Jeff Reardon | .15 | .11 |
| 658 Wayne Rosenthal | .12 | .09 |
| 659 Eric Bullock | .12 | .09 |
| 660 Eric Davis | .25 | .20 |
| 661 Randy Tomlin | .20 | .15 |
| 662 Tom Edens | .12 | .09 |
| 663 Rob Murphy | .12 | .09 |
| 664 Leo Gomez | .30 | .25 |
| 665 Greg Maddux | .25 | .20 |
| 666 Greg Vaughn | .15 | .11 |
| 667 Wade Taylor | .12 | .09 |
| 668 Brad Arnsberg | .12 | .09 |
| 669 Mike Moore | .15 | .11 |
| 670 Mark Langston | .15 | .11 |
| 671 Barry Jones | .12 | .09 |
| 672 Bill Landrum | .12 | .09 |
| 673 Greg Swindell | .20 | .15 |
| 674 Wayne Edwards | .12 | .09 |
| 675 Greg Olson | .12 | .09 |
| 676 Bill Pulsipher | .20 | .15 |
| 677 Bobby Witt | .15 | .11 |
| 678 Mark Carreon | .12 | .09 |
| 679 Patrick Lennon | .30 | .25 |
| 680 Ozzie Smith | .40 | .30 |
| 681 John Briscoe | .20 | .15 |
| 682 Matt Young | .12 | .09 |
| 683 Jeff Conine | .20 | .15 |
| 684 Phil Stephenson | .12 | .09 |
| 685 Ron Darling | .15 | .11 |
| 686 Bryan Hickerson | .15 | .11 |
| 687 Dale Sveum | .12 | .09 |
| 688 Kirk McCaskill | .12 | .09 |
| 689 Rich Amaral | .15 | .11 |
| 690 Danny Tartabull | .40 | .30 |
| 691 Donald Harris | .15 | .11 |
| 692 Doug Davis | .20 | .15 |
| 693 John Farrell | .12 | .09 |
| 694 Paul Gibson | .12 | .09 |
| 695 Kenny Lofton | 2.50 | 2.00 |
| 696 Mike Fetters | .12 | .09 |
| 697 Rosario Rodriguez | .12 | .09 |
| 698 Chris Jones | .15 | .11 |
| 699 Jeff Manto | .12 | .09 |
| 700 Rick Sutcliffe | .15 | .11 |
| 701 Scott Bankhead | .12 | .09 |
| 702 Donnie Hill | .12 | .09 |
| 703 Todd Worrell | .15 | .11 |
| 704 Rene Gonzales | .12 | .09 |
| 705 Rick Cerone | .12 | .09 |
| 706 Tony Pena | .12 | .09 |
| 707 Paul Sorrento | .12 | .09 |
| 708 Gary Scott | .15 | .11 |

| | | MT | NR MT |
|---|---|---|---|
| 709 | Junior Noboa | .12 | .09 |
| 710 | Wally Joyner | .20 | .15 |
| 711 | Charlie Hayes | .15 | .11 |
| 712 | Rich Rodriguez | .12 | .09 |
| 713 | Rudy Seanez | .12 | .09 |
| 714 | Jim Bullinger | .40 | .30 |
| 715 | Jeff Robinson | .12 | .09 |
| 716 | Jeff Branson | .25 | .20 |
| 717 | Andy Ashby | .12 | .09 |
| 718 | Dave Burba | .12 | .09 |
| 719 | Rich Gossage | .20 | .15 |
| 720 | Randy Johnson | .20 | .15 |
| 721 | David Wells | .12 | .09 |
| 722 | Paul Kilgus | .12 | .09 |
| 723 | Dave Martinez | .12 | .09 |
| 724 | Denny Neagle | .15 | .11 |
| 725 | Andy Stankiewicz | .40 | .30 |
| 726 | Rick Aguilera | .15 | .11 |
| 727 | Junior Noboa | .12 | .09 |
| 728 | Storm Davis | .12 | .09 |
| 729 | Don Robinson | .12 | .09 |
| 730 | Ron Gant | .40 | .30 |
| 731 | Paul Assenmacher | .12 | .09 |
| 732 | Mark Gardiner | .12 | .09 |
| 733 | Milt Hill | .12 | .09 |
| 734 | Jeremy Hernandez | .15 | .11 |
| 735 | Ken Hill | .20 | .15 |
| 736 | Xavier Hernandez | .12 | .09 |
| 737 | Gregg Jefferies | .25 | .20 |
| 738 | Dick Schofield | .12 | .09 |
| 739 | Ron Robinson | .12 | .09 |
| 740 | Sandy Alomar | .20 | .15 |
| 741 | Mike Aldrete | .12 | .09 |
| 742 | Butch Henry | .30 | .25 |
| 743 | Floyd Bannister | .12 | .09 |
| 744 | Brian Drahman | .15 | .11 |
| 745 | Dave Winfield | .50 | .40 |
| 746 | Bob Walk | .12 | .09 |
| 747 | Chris James | .12 | .09 |
| 748 | Don Prybylinski | .20 | .15 |
| 749 | Dennis Rasmussen | .12 | .09 |
| 750 | Rickey Henderson | .80 | .60 |
| 751 | Chris Hammond | .15 | .11 |
| 752 | Bob Kipper | .12 | .09 |
| 753 | Dave Rohde | .12 | .09 |
| 754 | Hubie Brooks | .12 | .09 |
| 755 | Bret Saberhagen | .20 | .15 |
| 756 | Jeff Robinson | .12 | .09 |
| 757 | Pat Listach | 4.00 | 3.00 |
| 758 | Bill Wegman | .15 | .11 |
| 759 | John Wetteland | .15 | .11 |
| 760 | Phil Plantier | .80 | .60 |
| 761 | Wilson Alvarez | .12 | .09 |
| 762 | Scott Aldred | .12 | .09 |
| 763 | Armando Reynoso | .30 | .25 |
| 764 | Todd Benzinger | .12 | .09 |
| 765 | Kevin Mitchell | .20 | .15 |
| 766 | Gary Sheffield | 1.25 | .90 |
| 767 | Allan Anderson | .12 | .09 |
| 768 | Rusty Meacham | .15 | .11 |
| 769 | Rick Parker | .12 | .09 |
| 770 | Nolan Ryan | 2.50 | 2.00 |
| 771 | Jeff Ballard | .12 | .09 |
| 772 | Cory Snyder | .12 | .09 |
| 773 | Denis Boucher | .15 | .11 |
| 774 | Jose Gonzales | .12 | .09 |
| 775 | Juan Guerrero | .40 | .30 |
| 776 | Ed Nunez | .12 | .09 |
| 777 | Scott Ruskin | .12 | .09 |
| 778 | Terry Leach | .12 | .09 |
| 779 | Carl Willis | .12 | .09 |
| 780 | Bobby Bonilla | .20 | .15 |
| 781 | Duane Ward | .15 | .11 |
| 782 | Joe Slusarski | .15 | .11 |
| 783 | David Segui | .15 | .11 |
| 784 | Kirk Gibson | .12 | .09 |
| 785 | Frank Viola | .20 | .15 |
| 786 | Keith Miller | .12 | .09 |
| 787 | Mike Morgan | .12 | .09 |
| 788 | Kim Batiste | .15 | .11 |
| 789 | Sergio Valdez | .15 | .09 |
| 790 | Eddie Taubensee | .30 | .25 |
| 791 | Jack Armstrong | .12 | .09 |
| 792 | Scott Fletcher | .12 | .09 |
| 793 | Steve Farr | .12 | .09 |
| 794 | Dan Pasqua | .12 | .09 |
| 795 | Eddie Murray | .20 | .15 |
| 796 | John Morris | .12 | .09 |
| 797 | Francisco Cabrera | .12 | .09 |
| 798 | Mike Perez | .20 | .15 |
| 799 | Ted Wood | .20 | .15 |
| 800 | Jose Rijo | .20 | .15 |
| 801 | Danny Gladden | .12 | .09 |
| 802 | Arci Cianfrocco | .50 | .40 |
| 803 | Monty Fariss | .15 | .11 |
| 804 | Roger McDowell | .12 | .09 |
| 805 | Randy Myers | .15 | .11 |
| 806 | Kirk Dressendorfer | .15 | .11 |
| 807 | Zane Smith | .12 | .09 |
| 808 | Glenn Davis | .15 | .11 |
| 809 | Tory Lovullo | .12 | .09 |
| 810 | Andre Dawson | .40 | .30 |
| 811 | Bill Pecota | .12 | .09 |
| 812 | Ted Power | .12 | .09 |
| 813 | Willie Blair | .12 | .09 |
| 814 | Dave Fleming | 2.00 | 1.50 |
| 815 | Chris Gwynn | .12 | .09 |
| 816 | Jody Reed | .12 | .09 |
| 817 | Mark Dewey | .12 | .09 |
| 818 | Kyle Abbott | .12 | .09 |
| 819 | Tom Henke | .12 | .09 |
| 820 | Kevin Seitzer | .12 | .09 |
| 821 | Al Newman | .12 | .09 |
| 822 | Tim Sherrill | .20 | .15 |
| 823 | Chuck Crim | .12 | .09 |
| 824 | Darren Reed | .15 | .11 |
| 825 | Tony Gwynn | .80 | .60 |
| 826 | Steve Foster | .20 | .15 |
| 827 | Steve Howe | .12 | .09 |
| 828 | Brook Jacoby | .12 | .09 |
| 829 | Rodney McCray | .12 | .09 |
| 830 | Chuck Knoblauch | 1.00 | .70 |
| 831 | John Wehner | .15 | .11 |
| 832 | Scott Garrelts | .12 | .09 |
| 833 | Alejandro Pena | .12 | .09 |
| 834 | Jeff Parrett | .12 | .09 |
| 835 | Juan Bell | .12 | .09 |
| 836 | Lance Dickson | .12 | .09 |
| 837 | Darryl Kile | .15 | .11 |
| 838 | Efrain Valdez | .15 | .11 |
| 839 | Bob Zupcic | .60 | .45 |
| 840 | George Bell | .15 | .11 |
| 841 | Dave Gallagher | .12 | .09 |
| 842 | Tim Belcher | .15 | .11 |

| | | MT | NR MT |
|---|---|---|---|
| 843 | Jeff Shaw | .12 | .09 |
| 844 | Mike Fitgerald | .12 | .09 |
| 845 | Gary Carter | .20 | .15 |
| 846 | John Russell | .12 | .09 |
| 847 | Eric Hillman | .30 | .25 |
| 848 | Mike Witt | .12 | .09 |
| 849 | Curt Wilkerson | .12 | .09 |
| 850 | Alan Trammell | .15 | .11 |
| 851 | Rex Hudler | .12 | .09 |
| 852 | Michael Walkden | .30 | .25 |
| 853 | Kevin Ward | .30 | .25 |
| 854 | Tim Naehring | .15 | .11 |
| 855 | Bill Swift | .15 | .11 |
| 856 | Damon Berryhill | .12 | .09 |
| 857 | Mark Eichhorn | .12 | .09 |
| 858 | Hector Villanueva | .12 | .09 |
| 859 | Jose Lind | .12 | .09 |
| 860 | Denny Martinez | .15 | .11 |
| 861 | Bill Krueger | .12 | .09 |
| 862 | Mike Kingery | .12 | .09 |
| 863 | Jeff Innis | .12 | .09 |
| 864 | Derek Lilliquist | .12 | .09 |
| 865 | Reggie Sanders | 1.75 | 1.25 |
| 866 | Ramon Garcia | .20 | .15 |
| 867 | Bruce Ruffin | .12 | .09 |
| 868 | Dickie Thon | .12 | .09 |
| 869 | Melido Perez | .15 | .11 |
| 870 | Ruben Amaro | .15 | .11 |
| 871 | Alan Mills | .12 | .09 |
| 872 | Matt Sinatro | .12 | .09 |
| 873 | Eddie Zosky | .20 | .15 |
| 874 | Pete Incaviglia | .12 | .09 |
| 875 | Tom Candiotti | .12 | .09 |
| 876 | Bob Patterson | .12 | .09 |
| 877 | Neal Heaton | .12 | .09 |
| 878 | Terrel Hansen | .35 | .25 |
| 879 | Dave Eiland | .12 | .09 |
| 880 | Von Hayes | .12 | .09 |
| 881 | Tim Scott | .20 | .15 |
| 882 | Otis Nixon | .15 | .11 |
| 883 | Herm Winningham | .12 | .09 |
| 884 | Dion James | .12 | .09 |
| 885 | Dave Wainhouse | .15 | .11 |
| 886 | Frank DiPino | .12 | .09 |
| 887 | Dennis Cook | .12 | .09 |
| 888 | Jose Mesa | .12 | .09 |
| 889 | Mark Leiter | .12 | .09 |
| 890 | Willie Randolph | .15 | .11 |
| 891 | Craig Colbert | .15 | .11 |
| 892 | Dwayne Henry | .12 | .09 |
| 893 | Jim Lindeman | .12 | .09 |
| 894 | Charlie Hough | .12 | .09 |
| 895 | Gil Heredia | .12 | .09 |
| 896 | Scott Chiamparino | .12 | .09 |
| 897 | Lance Blankenship | .12 | .09 |
| 898 | Checklist 601-700 | .12 | .09 |
| 899 | Checklist 701-800 | .12 | .09 |
| 900 | Checklist 801-900 | .12 | .09 |
| ----- | Chipper Jones (#1 Draft Pick) | 8.00 | 6.00 |
| ----- | Brien Taylor (#1 Draft Pick) | 15.00 | 11.00 |
| ----- | Phil Nevin (#1 Draft Pick) | 10.00 | 7.50 |

# 1993 Topps Series I

Topps used a two series format in 1993. Series I featured cards 1-396. The card fronts feature full-color photos enclosed by a white border. The player's name and team appear at the bottom. The backs feature an additional player photo and biographical information at the top. The bottom box includes statistics and player information. Like in recent years, several cards are printed horizontally. The cards are numbered in red on the back. The number appears in a yellow flag in the upper left corner of the card.

| | | MT | NR MT |
|---|---|---|---|
| Complete Set: | | 15.00 | 11.00 |
| Common Player: | | .03 | .02 |
| 1 | Robin Yount | .10 | .08 |
| 2 | Barry Bonds | .15 | .11 |
| 3 | Ryne Sandberg | .15 | .11 |
| 4 | Roger Clemens | .15 | .11 |
| 5 | Tony Gwynn | .12 | .09 |
| 6 | *Jeff Tackett* | .12 | .09 |
| 7 | Pete Incaviglia | .05 | .04 |
| 8 | Mark Wohlers | .05 | .04 |
| 9 | Kent Hrbek | .06 | .05 |
| 10 | Will Clark | .15 | .11 |
| 11 | Eric Karros | .15 | .11 |
| 12 | Lee Smith | .06 | .05 |
| 13 | Esteban Beltre | .05 | .04 |
| 14 | Greg Briley | .03 | .02 |
| 15 | Marquis Grissom | .08 | .06 |
| 16 | Dan Plesac | .04 | .03 |
| 17 | Dave Hollins | .08 | .06 |

A player's name in italic indicates a rookie card. An (FC) indicates a player's first card for that particular card company.

| # | Player | MT | NR MT | | # | Player | MT | NR MT |
|---|---|---|---|---|---|---|---|---|
| 18 | Terry Steinbach | .06 | .05 | | 84 | Kurt Stillwell | .04 | .03 |
| 19 | Ed Nunez | .03 | .02 | | 85 | Sandy Alomar | .08 | .06 |
| 20 | *Tim Salmon* | .15 | .11 | | 86 | John Habyan | .03 | .02 |
| 21 | Luis Salazar | .04 | .03 | | 87 | Kevin Reimer | .05 | .04 |
| 22 | Jim Eisenreich | .03 | .02 | | 88 | Mike Stanton | .05 | .04 |
| 23 | Todd Stottlemyre | .05 | .04 | | 89 | Eric Anthony | .06 | .05 |
| 24 | Tim Naehring | .05 | .04 | | 90 | Scott Erickson | .08 | .06 |
| 25 | John Franco | .06 | .05 | | 91 | Craig Colbert | .06 | .05 |
| 26 | Skeeter Barnes | .06 | .05 | | 92 | Tom Pagnozzi | .06 | .05 |
| 27 | *Carlos Garcia* | .15 | .11 | | 93 | *Pedro Astacio*(FC) | .15 | .11 |
| 28 | Joe Orsulak | .04 | .03 | | 94 | Lance Johnson | .04 | .03 |
| 29 | Dwayne Henry | .03 | .02 | | 95 | Larry Walker | .10 | .08 |
| 30 | Fred McGriff | .10 | .08 | | 96 | Russ Swan | .03 | .02 |
| 31 | Derek Lilliquist | .03 | .02 | | 97 | Scott Fletcher | .03 | .02 |
| 32 | Don Mattingly | .12 | .09 | | 98 | *Derek Jeter*(FC) | .15 | .11 |
| 33 | B.J. Wallace | .12 | .09 | | 99 | *Mike Williams*(FC) | .15 | .11 |
| 34 | Juan Gonzalez | .15 | .11 | | 100 | Mark McGwire | .15 | .11 |
| 35 | John Smoltz | .08 | .06 | | 101 | *Jim Bullinger* | .12 | .09 |
| 36 | Scott Servais | .08 | .06 | | 102 | Brian Hunter | .08 | .06 |
| 37 | Lenny Webster | .08 | .06 | | 103 | Jody Reed | .03 | .02 |
| 38 | Chris James | .04 | .03 | | 104 | *Mike Butcher*(FC) | .15 | .11 |
| 39 | Roger McDowell | .04 | .03 | | 105 | Gregg Jefferies | .08 | .06 |
| 40 | Ozzie Smith | .10 | .08 | | 106 | Howard Johnson | .08 | .06 |
| 41 | Alex Fernandez | .08 | .06 | | 107 | *John Kiely* | .12 | .09 |
| 42 | Spike Owen | .03 | .02 | | 108 | Jose Lind | .04 | .03 |
| 43 | Ruben Amaro | .05 | .04 | | 109 | Sam Horn | .03 | .02 |
| 44 | Kevin Seitzer | .05 | .04 | | 110 | Barry Larkin | .08 | .06 |
| 45 | Dave Fleming | .10 | .08 | | 111 | Bruce Hurst | .05 | .04 |
| 46 | *Eric Fox* | .12 | .09 | | 112 | Brian Barnes | .04 | .03 |
| 47 | Bob Scanlan | .03 | .02 | | 113 | Thomas Howard | .04 | .03 |
| 48 | Bert Blyleven | .06 | .05 | | 114 | Mel Hall | .06 | .05 |
| 49 | Brian McRae | .06 | .05 | | 115 | Robby Thompson | .04 | .03 |
| 50 | Roberto Alomar | .12 | .09 | | 116 | Mark Lemke | .04 | .03 |
| 51 | Mo Vaughn | .05 | .04 | | 117 | Eddie Taubensee | .08 | .06 |
| 52 | Bobby Bonilla | .10 | .08 | | 118 | David Justice | .10 | .08 |
| 53 | Frank Tanana | .04 | .03 | | 119 | Pedro Munoz | .10 | .08 |
| 54 | Mike LaValliere | .04 | .03 | | 120 | Ramon Martinez | .08 | .06 |
| 55 | Mark McLemore | .03 | .02 | | 121 | Todd Worrell | .05 | .04 |
| 56 | *Chad Mottola*(FC) | .15 | .11 | | 122 | Joey Cora | .03 | .02 |
| 57 | Norm Charlton | .06 | .05 | | 123 | Moises Alou | .08 | .06 |
| 58 | Jose Melendez | .08 | .06 | | 124 | Franklin Stubbs | .03 | .02 |
| 59 | Carlos Martinez | .03 | .02 | | 125 | Pete O'Brien | .03 | .02 |
| 60 | Roberto Kelly | .08 | .06 | | 126 | *Bob Aryault*(FC) | .12 | .09 |
| 61 | Gene Larkin | .03 | .02 | | 127 | Carney Lansford | .05 | .04 |
| 62 | Rafael Belliard | .03 | .02 | | 128 | Kal Daniels | .05 | .04 |
| 63 | Al Osuna | .03 | .02 | | 129 | Joe Grahe | .05 | .04 |
| 64 | Scott Chiamparino | .03 | .02 | | 130 | Jeff Montgomery | .05 | .04 |
| 65 | Brett Butler | .06 | .05 | | 131 | Dave Winfield | .10 | .08 |
| 66 | John Burkett | .04 | .03 | | 132 | *Preston Wilson*(FC) | .15 | .11 |
| 67 | Felix Jose | .08 | .06 | | 133 | Steve Wilson | .04 | .03 |
| 68 | Omar Vizquel | .03 | .02 | | 134 | Lee Guetterman | .03 | .02 |
| 69 | *John Vander Wal* | .12 | .09 | | 135 | Mickey Tettleton | .08 | .06 |
| 70 | Roberto Hernandez | .08 | .06 | | 136 | Jeff King | .04 | .03 |
| 71 | Ricky Bones | .05 | .04 | | 137 | Alan Mills | .03 | .02 |
| 72 | *Jeff Grotewold* | .12 | .09 | | 138 | Joe Oliver | .04 | .03 |
| 73 | Mike Moore | .05 | .04 | | 139 | Gary Gaetti | .03 | .02 |
| 74 | Steve Buechele | .05 | .04 | | 140 | Gary Sheffield | .10 | .08 |
| 75 | Juan Guzman | .10 | .08 | | 141 | Dennis Cook | .03 | .02 |
| 76 | Kevin Appier | .08 | .06 | | 142 | Charlie Hayes | .04 | .03 |
| 77 | Junior Felix | .05 | .04 | | 143 | Jeff Huson | .04 | .03 |
| 78 | Greg Harris | .04 | .03 | | 144 | Kent Mercker | .04 | .03 |
| 79 | Dick Schofield | .04 | .03 | | 145 | *Eric Young*(FC) | .15 | .11 |
| 80 | Cecil Fielder | .10 | .08 | | 146 | Scott Leius | .04 | .03 |
| 81 | Lloyd McClendon | .04 | .03 | | | | | |
| 82 | David Segui | .05 | .04 | | | | | |
| 83 | Reggie Sanders | .15 | .11 | | | | | |

| | | MT | NR MT | | | | MT | NR MT |
|---|---|---|---|---|---|---|---|---|
| 147 | Bryan Hickerson | .04 | .03 | | 210 | Mark Langston | .08 | .06 |
| 148 | Steve Finley | .06 | .05 | | 211 | Doug Dascenzo | .03 | .02 |
| 149 | Rheal Cormier | .08 | .06 | | 212 | Rick Reed | .03 | .02 |
| 150 | Frank Thomas | .30 | .25 | | 213 | Candy Maldonado | .05 | .04 |
| 151 | *Archi Cianfrocco* | .15 | .11 | | 214 | Danny Darwin | .03 | .02 |
| 152 | Rich DeLucia | .04 | .03 | | 215 | *Pat Howell*(FC) | .12 | .09 |
| 153 | Greg Vaughn | .06 | .05 | | 216 | Mark Leiter | .03 | .02 |
| 154 | Wes Chamberlain | .05 | .04 | | 217 | Kevin Mitchell | .08 | .06 |
| 155 | Dennis Eckersley | .08 | .06 | | 218 | Ben McDonald | .08 | .06 |
| 156 | Sammy Sosa | .04 | .03 | | 219 | Bip Roberts | .08 | .06 |
| 157 | Gary DiSarcina | .06 | .05 | | 220 | Benny Santiago | .08 | .06 |
| 158 | *Kevin Koslofski*(FC) | | | | 221 | Carlos Baerga | .10 | .08 |
| | | .12 | .09 | | 222 | Bernie Williams | .10 | .08 |
| 159 | *Doug Linton*(FC) | .12 | .09 | | 223 | *Roger Pavlik*(FC) | .12 | .09 |
| 160 | Lou Whitaker | .06 | .05 | | 224 | Sid Bream | .04 | .03 |
| 161 | Chad McDonnell | .12 | .09 | | 225 | Matt Williams | .08 | .06 |
| 162 | Joe Hesketh | .03 | .02 | | 226 | Willie Banks | .08 | .06 |
| 163 | *Tim Wakefield* | .15 | .11 | | 227 | Jeff Bagwell | .12 | .09 |
| 164 | Leo Gomez | .05 | .04 | | 228 | Tom Goodwin | .08 | .06 |
| 165 | Jose Rijo | .06 | .05 | | 229 | Mike Perez | .08 | .06 |
| 166 | *Tim Scott*(FC) | .12 | .09 | | 230 | Carlton Fisk | .08 | .06 |
| 167 | Steve Olin | .05 | .04 | | 231 | John Wetteland | .08 | .06 |
| 168 | Kevin Maas | .05 | .04 | | 232 | Tino Martinez | .08 | .06 |
| 169 | Kenny Rogers | .04 | .03 | | 233 | *Rick Greene*(FC) | .12 | .09 |
| 170 | David Justice | .10 | .08 | | 234 | Tim McIntosh | .04 | .03 |
| 171 | Doug Jones | .04 | .03 | | 235 | Mitch Williams | .06 | .05 |
| 172 | *Jeff Reboulet*(FC) | | | | 236 | *Kevin Campbell* | .10 | .08 |
| | | .12 | .09 | | 237 | Jose Vizcaino | .03 | .02 |
| 173 | Andres Galarraga | .05 | .04 | | 238 | Chris Donnels | .05 | .04 |
| 174 | Randy Velarde | .03 | .02 | | 239 | Mike Boddicker | .04 | .03 |
| 175 | Kirk McCaskill | .04 | .03 | | 240 | John Olerud | .12 | .09 |
| 176 | Darren Lewis | .04 | .03 | | 241 | Mike Gardiner | .04 | .03 |
| 177 | Lenny Harris | .04 | .03 | | 242 | Charlie O'Brien | .03 | .02 |
| 178 | Jeff Fassero | .04 | .03 | | 243 | Rob Deer | .04 | .03 |
| 179 | Ken Griffey, Jr. | .30 | .25 | | 244 | Denny Neagle | .08 | .06 |
| 180 | Darren Daulton | .08 | .06 | | 245 | Chris Sabo | .08 | .06 |
| 181 | John Jaha | .12 | .09 | | 246 | Gregg Olson | .08 | .06 |
| 182 | Ron Darling | .05 | .04 | | 247 | Frank Seminara | .08 | .06 |
| 183 | Greg Maddux | .08 | .06 | | 248 | Scott Scudder | .03 | .02 |
| 184 | *Damion Easley*(FC) | | | | 249 | Tim Burke | .03 | .02 |
| | | .15 | .11 | | 250 | Chuck Knoblauch | .10 | .08 |
| 185 | Jack Morris | .08 | .06 | | 251 | Mike Bielecki | .04 | .03 |
| 186 | Mike Magnante | .05 | .04 | | 252 | Xavier Hernandez | .03 | .02 |
| 187 | John Dopson | .05 | .04 | | 253 | Jose Guzman | .04 | .03 |
| 188 | Sid Fernandez | .08 | .06 | | 254 | Cory Snyder | .04 | .03 |
| 189 | Tony Phillips | .08 | .06 | | 255 | Orel Hershiser | .08 | .06 |
| 190 | Doug Drabek | .08 | .06 | | 256 | Wil Cordero | .12 | .09 |
| 191 | Sean Lowe | .15 | .11 | | 257 | Luis Alicea | .04 | .03 |
| 192 | Bob Milacki | .03 | .02 | | 258 | Mike Schooler | .04 | .03 |
| 193 | *Steve Foster*(FC) | | | | 259 | Craig Grebeck | .03 | .02 |
| | | .15 | .11 | | 260 | Duane Ward | .04 | .03 |
| 194 | Jerald Clark | .05 | .04 | | 261 | Bill Wegman | .04 | .03 |
| 195 | Pete Harnisch | .06 | .05 | | 262 | Mickey Morandini | .08 | .06 |
| 196 | Pat Kelly | .06 | .05 | | 263 | *Vince Horsman* | .12 | .09 |
| 197 | *Jeff Frye*(FC) | .12 | .09 | | 264 | Paul Sorrento | .06 | .05 |
| 198 | Alejandro Pena | .04 | .03 | | 265 | Andre Dawson | .10 | .08 |
| 199 | Junior Ortiz | .03 | .02 | | 266 | Rene Gonzales | .03 | .02 |
| 200 | Kirby Puckett | .15 | .11 | | 267 | Keith Miller | .04 | .03 |
| 201 | Jose Uribe | .03 | .02 | | 268 | Derek Bell | .10 | .08 |
| 202 | Mike Scioscia | .04 | .03 | | 269 | *Todd Steverson*(FC) | | |
| 203 | Bernard Gilkey | .06 | .05 | | | | .20 | .15 |
| 204 | Dan Pasqua | .04 | .03 | | 270 | Frank Viola | .08 | .06 |
| 205 | Gary Carter | .08 | .06 | | 271 | Wally Whitehurst | .04 | .03 |
| 206 | Henry Cotto | .03 | .02 | | 272 | *Kurt Knudsen* | .12 | .09 |
| 207 | Paul Molitor | .08 | .06 | | 273 | *Dan Walters* | .12 | .09 |
| 208 | Mike Hartley | .04 | .03 | | 274 | Rick Sutcliffe | .06 | .05 |
| 209 | Jeff Parrett | .03 | .02 | | 275 | Andy Van Slyke | .08 | .06 |

|  | | MT | NR MT |  | | MT | NR MT |
|---|---|---|---|---|---|---|---|
| 276 | Paul O'Neill | .06 | .05 | 341 | Mel Rojas | .04 | .03 |
| 277 | Mark Whiten | .10 | .08 | 342 | Erik Hanson | .06 | .05 |
| 278 | Chris Nabholz | .06 | .05 | 343 | Doug Henry | .06 | .05 |
| 279 | Todd Burns | .03 | .02 | 344 | Jack McDowell | .08 | .06 |
| 280 | Tom Glavine | .10 | .08 | 345 | Harold Baines | .08 | .06 |
| 281 | *Butch Henry*(FC) | | | 346 | Chuck McElroy | .03 | .02 |
|  | | .12 | .09 | 347 | Luis Sojo | .03 | .02 |
| 282 | Shane Mack | .08 | .06 | 348 | Andy Stankiewicz | .10 | .08 |
| 283 | Mike Jackson | .03 | .02 | 349 | *Hipolito Pichardo* | .10 | .08 |
| 284 | Henry Rodriguez | .06 | .05 | 350 | Joe Carter | .08 | .06 |
| 285 | Bob Tewksbury | .06 | .05 | 351 | Ellis Burks | .06 | .05 |
| 286 | Ron Karkovice | .04 | .03 | 352 | Pete Schourek | .06 | .05 |
| 287 | Mike Gallego | .04 | .03 | 353 | Buddy Groom | .20 | .15 |
| 288 | Dave Cochrane | .03 | .02 | 354 | Jay Bell | .06 | .05 |
| 289 | Jesse Orosco | .03 | .02 | 355 | Brady Anderson | .08 | .06 |
| 290 | Dave Stewart | .08 | .06 | 356 | Freddie Benavides | .06 | .05 |
| 291 | Tommy Greene | .08 | .06 | 357 | Phil Stepheson | .03 | .02 |
| 292 | Rey Sanchez | .08 | .06 | 358 | Kevin Wickander | .03 | .02 |
| 293 | Rob Ducey | .03 | .02 | 359 | Mike Stanley | .03 | .02 |
| 294 | Brent Mayne | .04 | .03 | 360 | Ivan Rodriguez | .12 | .09 |
| 295 | Dave Stieb | .05 | .04 | 361 | Scott Bankhead | .04 | .03 |
| 296 | Luis Rivera | .03 | .02 | 362 | Luis Gonzalez | .08 | .06 |
| 297 | Jeff Innis | .04 | .03 | 363 | John Smiley | .06 | .05 |
| 298 | Scott Livingstone | .08 | .06 | 364 | Trevor Wilson | .04 | .03 |
| 299 | Bob Patterson | .03 | .02 | 365 | Tom Candiotti | .04 | .03 |
| 300 | Cal Ripken | .20 | .15 | 366 | Craig Wilson | .04 | .03 |
| 301 | Cesar Hernandez | .10 | .08 | 367 | Steve Sax | .06 | .05 |
| 302 | Randy Myers | .06 | .05 | 368 | Delino Deshields | .06 | .05 |
| 303 | Brook Jacoby | .04 | .03 | 369 | Jaime Navarro | .06 | .05 |
| 304 | Melido Perez | .04 | .03 | 370 | Dave Valle | .03 | .02 |
| 305 | Rafael Palmeiro | .08 | .06 | 371 | Mariano Duncan | .04 | .03 |
| 306 | Damon Berryhill | .03 | .02 | 372 | Rod Nichols | .03 | .02 |
| 307 | *Dan Serafini*(FC) | .20 | .15 | 373 | Mike Morgan | .05 | .04 |
| 308 | Darryl Kile | .06 | .05 | 374 | Julio Valera | .08 | .06 |
| 309 | *J.T. Bruett* | .15 | .11 | 375 | Wally Joyner | .08 | .06 |
| 310 | Dave Righetti | .05 | .04 | 376 | Tom Henke | .08 | .06 |
| 311 | Jay Howell | .05 | .04 | 377 | Herm Winningham | .03 | .02 |
| 312 | Geronimo Pena | .05 | .04 | 378 | Orlando Merced | .06 | .05 |
| 313 | Greg Hibbard | .05 | .04 | 379 | Mike Munoz | .08 | .06 |
| 314 | Mark Gardner | .05 | .04 | 380 | Todd Hundley | .08 | .06 |
| 315 | Edgar Martinez | .08 | .06 | 381 | Mike Flanagan | .03 | .02 |
| 316 | Dave Nilsson | .10 | .08 | 382 | Tim Belcher | .06 | .05 |
| 317 | Kyle Abbott | .08 | .06 | 383 | Jerry Browne | .03 | .02 |
| 318 | Willie Wilson | .06 | .05 | 384 | Mike Benjamin | .03 | .02 |
| 319 | Paul Assenmacher | .04 | .03 | 385 | Jim Leyritz | .03 | .02 |
| 320 | *Tim Fortugno* | .12 | .09 | 386 | Ray Lankford | .12 | .09 |
| 321 | Rusty Meacham | .08 | .06 | 387 | Devon White | .06 | .05 |
| 322 | Pat Borders | .05 | .04 | 388 | Jeremy Hernandez | .08 | .06 |
| 323 | Mike Greenwell | .06 | .05 | 389 | Brian Harper | .06 | .05 |
| 324 | Willie Randolph | .06 | .05 | 390 | Wade Boggs | .12 | .09 |
| 325 | Bill Gullickson | .05 | .04 | 391 | Derrick May | .10 | .08 |
| 326 | Gary Varsho | .03 | .02 | 392 | Travis Fryman | .15 | .11 |
| 327 | Tim Hulett | .03 | .02 | 393 | Ron Gant | .10 | .08 |
| 328 | Scott Ruskin | .03 | .02 | 394 | Checklist 1-132 | .03 | .02 |
| 329 | Mike Maddux | .03 | .02 | 395 | Checklist 133-264 | .03 | .02 |
| 330 | Danny Tartabull | .08 | .06 | 396 | Checklist 265-396 | .03 | .02 |
| 331 | Kenny Lofton | .15 | .11 |  | | | |
| 332 | Geno Petralli | .03 | .02 |  | | | |
| 333 | Otis Nixon | .05 | .04 |  | | | |
| 334 | *Jason Kendall*(FC) | | |  | | | |
|  | | .20 | .15 |  | | | |
| 335 | Mark Portugal | .03 | .02 |  | | | |
| 336 | Mike Pagliarulo | .04 | .03 |  | | | |
| 337 | Kirt Manwaring | .04 | .03 |  | | | |
| 338 | Bob Ojeda | .04 | .03 |  | | | |
| 339 | *Mark Clark*(FC) | .12 | .09 |  | | | |
| 340 | John Kruk | .08 | .06 |  | | | |

A player's name in italic indicates a rookie card. An (FC) indicates a player's first card for that particular card company.

# UPPER DECK

## 1989 Upper Deck

This premiere "Collector's Choice" issue from Upper Deck contains 700 cards (2-1/2" by 3-1/2") with full-color photos on both sides. The first 26 cards feature Star Rookies. The set also includes 26 special portrait cards with team checklist backs and seven numberical checklist cards (one for each 100 numbers). Team Checklist cards feature individual player portraits by artist Vernon Wells. Major 1988 award winners (Cy Young, Rookie of Year, MVP) are honored on 10 cards in the set, in addition to their individual player cards. There are also special cards for the Most Valuable Players in both League Championship series and the World Series. The card fronts feature head-and-shoulder poses framed by a white border. A vertical brown and green artist's rendition of the runner's lane that leads from home plate to first base is found along the right margin. The backs carry full-color action poses that fill the card back, except for a compact (yet complete) stats chart. A high-number series, cards 701-800, featuring rookies and traded players, was released in mid-season in foil packs mixed within the complete

**Regional interest may affect the value of a card.**

set, in boxed complete sets and in high number set boxes.

|  | | MT | NR MT |
|---|---|---|---|
| Complete Set: 1-700 | | 125.00 | 90.00 |
| Common Player: 1-700 | | .08 | .06 |
| Complete Set: 1-800 | | 150.00 | 125.00 |
| Common Player: 701-800 | | .10 | .08 |
| 1 | Star Rookie (Ken Griffey, Jr.) | 50.00 | 37.00 |
| 2 | Star Rookie (Luis Medina) | .30 | .25 |
| 3 | Star Rookie (Tony Chance) | .15 | .11 |
| 4 | Star Rookie (Dave Otto) | .08 | .06 |
| 5 | Star Rookie (Sandy Alomar, Jr.) | 1.00 | .70 |
| 6 | Star Rookie (Rolando Roomes) | .20 | .15 |
| 7 | Star Rookie (David West) | .25 | .20 |
| 8 | Star Rookie (Cris Carpenter) | .30 | .25 |
| 9 | Star Rookie (Gregg Jefferies) | 1.00 | .70 |
| 10 | Star Rookie (Doug Dascenzo) | .25 | .20 |
| 11 | Star Rookie (Ron Jones) | .20 | .15 |
| 12 | Star Rookie (Luis de los Santos) | .25 | .20 |
| 13a | Star Rookie (Gary Sheffield) (SS position on front is upside down) | 8.00 | 6.00 |
| 13b | Star Rookie (Gary Sheffield) (SS position on front is correct) | 12.00 | 9.00 |
| 14 | Star Rookie (Mike Harkey) | .30 | .25 |
| 15 | Star Rookie (Lance Blankenship) | .25 | .20 |
| 16 | Star Rookie (William Brennan) | .15 | .11 |
| 17 | Star Rookie (John Smoltz) | 4.00 | 3.00 |
| 18 | Star Rookie (Ramon Martinez) | 2.00 | 1.50 |
| 19 | Star Rookie (Mark Lemke) | .50 | .40 |
| 20 | Star Rookie (Juan Bell) | .25 | .20 |
| 21 | Star Rookie (Rey Palacios) | .15 | .11 |
| 22 | Star Rookie (Felix Jose) | 3.00 | 2.25 |
| 23 | Star Rookie (Van Snider) | .25 | .20 |
| 24 | Star Rookie (Dante Bichette) | .40 | .30 |
| 25 | Star Rookie (Randy Johnson) | .70 | .50 |
| 26 | Star Rookie (Carlos Quintana) | .40 | .30 |

| | | MT | NR MT |
|---|---|---|---|
| 27 | Star Rookie Checklist 1 – 26 | .08 | .06 |
| 28 | *Mike Schooler* | .40 | .30 |
| 29 | Randy St. Claire | .08 | .06 |
| 30 | *Jerald Clark* | .35 | .25 |
| 31 | Kevin Gross | .08 | .06 |
| 32 | *Dan Firova* | .20 | .15 |
| 33 | Jeff Calhoun | .08 | .06 |
| 34 | Tommy Hinzo | .08 | .06 |
| 35 | *Ricky Jordan* | .60 | .45 |
| 36 | Larry Parrish | .08 | .06 |
| 37 | Bret Saberhagen | .15 | .11 |
| 38 | Mike Smithson | .08 | .06 |
| 39 | Dave Dravecky | .08 | .06 |
| 40 | Ed Romero | .08 | .06 |
| 41 | Jeff Musselman | .08 | .06 |
| 42 | Ed Hearn | .08 | .06 |
| 43 | Rance Mulliniks | .08 | .06 |
| 44 | Jim Eisenreich | .08 | .06 |
| 45 | *Sil Campusano* | .20 | .15 |
| 46 | Mike Krukow | .08 | .06 |
| 47 | *Paul Gibson* | .20 | .15 |
| 48 | Mike LaCoss | .08 | .06 |
| 49 | Larry Herndon | .08 | .06 |
| 50 | Scott Garrelts | .08 | .06 |
| 51 | Dwayne Henry | .08 | .06 |
| 52 | Jim Acker | .08 | .06 |
| 53 | Steve Sax | .15 | .11 |
| 54 | Pete O'Brien | .08 | .06 |
| 55 | Paul Runge | .08 | .06 |
| 56 | Rick Rhoden | .08 | .06 |
| 57 | *John Dopson* | .25 | .20 |
| 58 | Casey Candaele | .08 | .06 |
| 59 | Dave Righetti | .12 | .09 |
| 60 | Joe Hesketh | .08 | .06 |
| 61 | Frank DiPino | .08 | .06 |
| 62 | Tim Laudner | .08 | .06 |
| 63 | Jamie Moyer | .08 | .06 |
| 64 | Fred Toliver | .08 | .06 |
| 65 | Mitch Webster | .08 | .06 |
| 66 | John Tudor | .10 | .08 |
| 67 | John Cangelosi | .08 | .06 |
| 68 | Mike Devereaux | .15 | .11 |
| 69 | Brian Fisher | .08 | .06 |
| 70 | Mike Marshall | .12 | .09 |
| 71 | Zane Smith | .08 | .06 |
| 72a | Brian Holton (ball not visible on card front, photo actually Shawn Hillegas) | 1.50 | 1.25 |
| 72b | Brian Holton (ball visible, correct photo) | .15 | .11 |
| 73 | Jose Guzman | .10 | .08 |
| 74 | Rick Mahler | .08 | .06 |
| 75 | John Shelby | .08 | .06 |
| 76 | Jim Deshaies | .08 | .06 |
| 77 | Bobby Meacham | .08 | .06 |
| 78 | Bryn Smith | .08 | .06 |
| 79 | Joaquin Andujar | .08 | .06 |
| 80 | Richard Dotson | .08 | .06 |
| 81 | Charlie Lea | .08 | .06 |
| 82 | Calvin Schiraldi | .08 | .06 |
| 83 | Les Straker | .08 | .06 |
| 84 | Les Lancaster | .08 | .06 |
| 85 | Allan Anderson | .08 | .06 |
| 86 | Junior Ortiz | .08 | .06 |
| 87 | Jesse Orosco | .08 | .06 |

| | | MT | NR MT |
|---|---|---|---|
| 88 | Felix Fermin | .08 | .06 |
| 89 | Dave Anderson | .08 | .06 |
| 90 | Rafael Belliard | .08 | .06 |
| 91 | Franklin Stubbs | .08 | .06 |
| 92 | Cecil Espy | .08 | .06 |
| 93 | Albert Hall | .08 | .06 |
| 94 | Tim Leary | .08 | .06 |
| 95 | Mitch Williams | .08 | .06 |
| 96 | Tracy Jones | .10 | .08 |
| 97 | Danny Darwin | .08 | .06 |
| 98 | Gary Ward | .08 | .06 |
| 99 | Neal Heaton | .08 | .06 |
| 100 | Jim Pankovits | .08 | .06 |
| 101 | Bill Doran | .08 | .06 |
| 102 | Tim Wallach | .10 | .08 |
| 103 | Joe Magrane | .10 | .08 |
| 104 | Ozzie Virgil | .08 | .06 |
| 105 | Alvin Davis | .12 | .09 |
| 106 | Tom Brookens | .08 | .06 |
| 107 | Shawon Dunston | .10 | .08 |
| 108 | Tracy Woodson | .10 | .08 |
| 109 | Nelson Liriano | .08 | .06 |
| 110 | Devon White | .12 | .09 |
| 111 | Steve Balboni | .08 | .06 |
| 112 | Buddy Bell | .08 | .06 |
| 113 | *German Jimenez* | .08 | .06 |
| 114 | Ken Dayley | .08 | .06 |
| 115 | Andres Galarraga | .15 | .11 |
| 116 | Mike Scioscia | .08 | .06 |
| 117 | Gary Pettis | .08 | .06 |
| 118 | Ernie Whitt | .08 | .06 |
| 119 | Bob Boone | .08 | .06 |
| 120 | Ryne Sandberg | .80 | .60 |
| 121 | Bruce Benedict | .08 | .06 |
| 122 | Hubie Brooks | .10 | .08 |
| 123 | Mike Moore | .08 | .06 |
| 124 | Wallace Johnson | .08 | .06 |
| 125 | Bob Horner | .10 | .08 |
| 126 | Chili Davis | .08 | .06 |
| 127 | Manny Trillo | .08 | .06 |
| 128 | Chet Lemon | .08 | .06 |
| 129 | John Cerutti | .08 | .06 |
| 130 | Orel Hershiser | .25 | .20 |
| 131 | Terry Pendleton | .10 | .08 |
| 132 | Jeff Blauser | .10 | .08 |
| 133 | Mike Fitzgerald | .08 | .06 |
| 134 | Henry Cotto | .08 | .06 |
| 135 | Gerald Young | .12 | .09 |
| 136 | Luis Salazar | .08 | .06 |
| 137 | Alejandro Pena | .08 | .06 |
| 138 | Jack Howell | .08 | .06 |
| 139 | Tony Fernandez | .12 | .09 |
| 140 | Mark Grace | 1.25 | .90 |
| 141 | Ken Caminiti | .08 | .06 |
| 142 | Mike Jackson | .08 | .06 |
| 143 | Larry McWilliams | .08 | .06 |
| 144 | Andres Thomas | .08 | .06 |
| 145 | Nolan Ryan | 4.00 | 3.00 |
| 146 | Mike Davis | .08 | .06 |
| 147 | DeWayne Buice | .08 | .06 |
| 148 | Jody Davis | .08 | .06 |
| 149 | Jesse Barfield | .10 | .08 |
| 150 | Matt Nokes | .15 | .11 |
| 151 | Jerry Reuss | .08 | .06 |
| 152 | Rick Cerone | .08 | .06 |
| 153 | Storm Davis | .10 | .08 |
| 154 | Marvell Wynne | .08 | .06 |

| # | Player | MT | NR MT | # | Player | MT | NR MT |
|---|--------|----|----|---|--------|----|----|
| 155 | Will Clark | 2.00 | 1.50 | 222 | Angel Salazar | .08 | .06 |
| 156 | Luis Aguayo | .08 | .06 | 223 | Kirk McCaskill | .08 | .06 |
| 157 | Willie Upshaw | .08 | .06 | 224 | Steve Lyons | .08 | .06 |
| 158 | Randy Bush | .08 | .06 | 225 | Bert Blyleven | .10 | .08 |
| 159 | Ron Darling | .12 | .09 | 226 | Scott Bradley | .08 | .06 |
| 160 | Kal Daniels | .15 | .11 | 227 | Bob Melvin | .08 | .06 |
| 161 | Spike Owen | .08 | .06 | 228 | Ron Kittle | .08 | .06 |
| 162 | Luis Polonia | .08 | .06 | 229 | Phil Bradley | .10 | .08 |
| 163 | Kevin Mitchell | .50 | .40 | 230 | Tommy John | .12 | .09 |
| 164 | *Dave Gallagher* | .25 | .20 | 231 | Greg Walker | .08 | .06 |
| 165 | Benito Santiago | .15 | .11 | 232 | Juan Berenguer | .08 | .06 |
| 166 | Greg Gagne | .08 | .06 | 233 | Pat Tabler | .08 | .06 |
| 167 | Ken Phelps | .08 | .06 | 234 | *Terry Clark* | .20 | .15 |
| 168 | Sid Fernandez | .10 | .08 | 235 | Rafael.Palmeiro | .25 | .20 |
| 169 | Bo Diaz | .08 | .06 | 236 | Paul Zuvella | .08 | .06 |
| 170 | Cory Snyder | .15 | .11 | 237 | Willie Randolph | .08 | .06 |
| 171 | Eric Show | .08 | .06 | 238 | Bruce Fields | .08 | .06 |
| 172 | Rob Thompson | .08 | .06 | 239 | Mike Aldrete | .08 | .06 |
| 173 | Marty Barrett | .08 | .06 | 240 | Lance Parrish | .15 | .11 |
| 174 | Dave Henderson | .10 | .08 | 241 | Greg Maddux | .12 | .09 |
| 175 | Ozzie Guillen | .08 | .06 | 242 | John Moses | .08 | .06 |
| 176 | Barry Lyons | .08 | .06 | 243 | Melido Perez | .10 | .08 |
| 177 | *Kelvin Torve*(FC) | .20 | .15 | 244 | Willie Wilson | .10 | .08 |
| 178 | Don Slaught | .08 | .06 | 245 | Mark McLemore | .08 | .06 |
| 179 | Steve Lombardozzi | .08 | .06 | 246 | Von Hayes | .10 | .08 |
| 180 | *Chris Sabo* | 1.00 | .70 | 247 | Matt Williams | .12 | .09 |
| 181 | Jose Uribe | .08 | .06 | 248 | John Candelaria | .08 | .06 |
| 182 | Shane Mack | .08 | .06 | 249 | Harold Reynolds | .08 | .06 |
| 183 | Ron Karkovice | .08 | .06 | 250 | Greg Swindell | .12 | .09 |
| 184 | Todd Benzinger | .12 | .09 | 251 | Juan Agosto | .08 | .06 |
| 185 | Dave Stewart | .10 | .08 | 252 | Mike Felder | .08 | .06 |
| 186 | Julio Franco | .10 | .08 | 253 | Vince Coleman | .15 | .11 |
| 187 | Ron Robinson | .08 | .06 | 254 | Larry Sheets | .08 | .06 |
| 188 | Wally Backman | .08 | .06 | 255 | George Bell | .25 | .20 |
| 189 | Randy Velarde | .08 | .06 | 256 | Terry Steinbach | .10 | .08 |
| 190 | Joe Carter | .12 | .09 | 257 | *Jack Armstrong* | .20 | .15 |
| 191 | Bob Welch | .10 | .08 | 258 | Dickie Thon | .08 | .06 |
| 192 | Kelly Paris | .08 | .06 | 259 | Ray Knight | .08 | .06 |
| 193 | Chris Brown | .08 | .06 | 260 | Darryl Strawberry | .40 | .30 |
| 194 | Rick Reuschel | .10 | .08 | 261 | Doug Sisk | .08 | .06 |
| 195 | Roger Clemens | .50 | .40 | 262 | Alex Trevino | .08 | .06 |
| 196 | Dave Concepcion | .10 | .08 | 263 | Jeff Leonard | .08 | .06 |
| 197 | Al Newman | .08 | .06 | 264 | Tom Henke | .08 | .06 |
| 198 | Brook Jacoby | .10 | .08 | 265 | Ozzie Smith | .15 | .11 |
| 199 | Mookie Wilson | .08 | .06 | 266 | Dave Bergman | .08 | .06 |
| 200 | Don Mattingly | 1.00 | .70 | 267 | Tony Phillips | .08 | .06 |
| 201 | Dick Schofield | .08 | .06 | 268 | Mark Davis | .08 | .06 |
| 202 | Mark Gubicza | .10 | .08 | 269 | Kevin Elster | .10 | .08 |
| 203 | Gary Gaetti | .15 | .11 | 270 | Barry Larkin | .20 | .15 |
| 204 | Dan Pasqua | .10 | .08 | 271 | Manny Lee | .08 | .06 |
| 205 | Andre Dawson | .20 | .15 | 272 | Tom Brunansky | .12 | .09 |
| 206 | Chris Speier | .08 | .06 | 273 | *Craig Biggio* | 1.50 | 1.25 |
| 207 | Kent Tekulve | .08 | .06 | 274 | Jim Gantner | .08 | .06 |
| 208 | Rod Scurry | .08 | .06 | 275 | Eddie Murray | .25 | .20 |
| 209 | Scott Bailes | .08 | .06 | 276 | Jeff Reed | .08 | .06 |
| 210 | Rickey Henderson | 1.50 | 1.25 | 277 | Tim Teufel | .08 | .06 |
| 211 | Harold Baines | .12 | .09 | 278 | Rick Honeycutt | .08 | .06 |
| 212 | Tony Armas | .08 | .06 | 279 | Guillermo Hernandez | | |
| 213 | Kent Hrbek | .20 | .15 | | | .08 | .06 |
| 214 | Darrin Jackson | .08 | .06 | 280 | John Kruk | .10 | .08 |
| 215 | George Brett | .35 | .25 | 281 | *Luis Alicea* | .20 | .15 |
| 216 | Rafael Santana | .08 | .06 | 282 | Jim Clancy | .08 | .06 |
| 217 | Andy Allanson | .08 | .06 | 283 | Billy Ripken | .08 | .06 |
| 218 | Brett Butler | .08 | .06 | 284 | Craig Reynolds | .08 | .06 |
| 219 | Steve Jeltz | .08 | .06 | 285 | Robin Yount | .35 | .25 |
| 220 | Jay Buhner | .10 | .08 | 286 | Jimmy Jones | .08 | .06 |
| 221 | Bo Jackson | .70 | .50 | 287 | Ron Oester | .08 | .06 |

| | | MT | NR MT | | | MT | NR MT |
|---|---|---|---|---|---|---|---|
| 288 | Terry Leach | .08 | .06 | 350 | Frank White | .08 | .06 |
| 289 | Dennis Eckersley | .12 | .09 | 351 | Dave Collins | .08 | .06 |
| 290 | Alan Trammell | .20 | .15 | 352 | Jack Morris | .15 | .11 |
| 291 | Jimmy Key | .10 | .08 | 353 | Eric Plunk | .08 | .06 |
| 292 | Chris Bosio | .08 | .06 | 354 | Leon Durham | .08 | .06 |
| 293 | Jose DeLeon | .08 | .06 | 355 | Ivan DeJesus | .08 | .06 |
| 294 | Jim Traber | .08 | .06 | 356 | *Brian Holman* | .40 | .30 |
| 295 | Mike Scott | .12 | .09 | 357a | Dale Murphy (photo on | | |
| 296 | Roger McDowell | .10 | .08 | | card front reversed) | 60.00 | 45.00 |
| 297 | Garry Templeton | .08 | .06 | 357b | Dale Murphy (correct | | |
| 298 | Doyle Alexander | .08 | .06 | | photo) | .35 | .25 |
| 299 | Nick Esasky | .08 | .06 | 358 | Mark Portugal | .08 | .06 |
| 300 | Mark McGwire | .70 | .50 | 359 | Andy McGaffigan | .08 | .06 |
| 301 | *Darryl Hamilton* | .40 | .30 | 360 | Tom Glavine | 2.50 | 2.00 |
| 302 | Dave Smith | .08 | .06 | 361 | Keith Moreland | .08 | .06 |
| 303 | Rick Sutcliffe | .10 | .08 | 362 | Todd Stottlemyre | .15 | .11 |
| 304 | Dave Stapleton | .08 | .06 | 363 | Dave Leiper | .08 | .06 |
| 305 | Alan Ashby | .08 | .06 | 364 | Cecil Fielder | .80 | .60 |
| 306 | Pedro Guerrero | .15 | .11 | 365 | Carmelo Martinez | .08 | .06 |
| 307 | Ron Guidry | .12 | .09 | 366 | Dwight Evans | .10 | .08 |
| 308 | Steve Farr | .08 | .06 | 367 | Kevin McReynolds | .15 | .11 |
| 309 | Curt Ford | .08 | .06 | 368 | Rich Gedman | .08 | .06 |
| 310 | Claudell Washington | .08 | .06 | 369 | Len Dykstra | .10 | .08 |
| 311 | Tom Prince | .08 | .06 | 370 | Jody Reed | .12 | .09 |
| 312 | *Chad Kreuter* | .15 | .11 | 371 | Jose Canseco | 2.00 | 1.50 |
| 313 | Ken Oberkfell | .08 | .06 | 372 | Rob Murphy | .08 | .06 |
| 314 | Jerry Browne | .08 | .06 | 373 | Mike Henneman | .10 | .08 |
| 315 | R.J. Reynolds | .08 | .06 | 374 | Walt Weiss | .40 | .30 |
| 316 | Scott Bankhead | .08 | .06 | 375 | *Rob Dibble* | 1.00 | .70 |
| 317 | Milt Thompson | .08 | .06 | 376 | Kirby Puckett | .30 | .25 |
| 318 | Mario Diaz | .10 | .08 | 377 | Denny Martinez | .08 | .06 |
| 319 | Bruce Ruffin | .08 | .06 | 378 | Ron Gant | 2.00 | 1.50 |
| 320 | Dave Valle | .08 | .06 | 379 | Brian Harper | .08 | .06 |
| 321a | *Gary Varsho* (batting | | | 380 | *Nelson Santovenia* | .20 | .15 |
| | righty on card back, photo | | | 381 | Lloyd Moseby | .08 | .06 |
| | actually Mike Bielecki) | 2.00 | 1.50 | 382 | Lance McCullers | .08 | .06 |
| 321b | *Gary Varsho* (batting | | | 383 | Dave Stieb | .10 | .08 |
| | lefty on card back, correct | | | 384 | Tony Gwynn | .30 | .25 |
| | photo) | .30 | .25 | 385 | Mike Flanagan | .08 | .06 |
| 322 | Paul Mirabella | .08 | .06 | 386 | Bob Ojeda | .08 | .06 |
| 323 | Chuck Jackson | .08 | .06 | 387 | Bruce Hurst | .10 | .08 |
| 324 | Drew Hall | .10 | .08 | 388 | Dave Magadan | .10 | .08 |
| 325 | Don August | .10 | .08 | 389 | Wade Boggs | .60 | .45 |
| 326 | *Israel Sanchez* | .15 | .11 | 390 | Gary Carter | .25 | .20 |
| 327 | Denny Walling | .08 | .06 | 391 | Frank Tanana | .08 | .06 |
| 328 | Joel Skinner | .08 | .06 | 392 | Curt Young | .08 | .06 |
| 329 | Danny Tartabull | .15 | .11 | 393 | Jeff Treadway | .10 | .08 |
| 330 | Tony Pena | .08 | .06 | 394 | Darrell Evans | .10 | .08 |
| 331 | Jim Sundberg | .08 | .06 | 395 | Glenn Hubbard | .08 | .06 |
| 332 | Jeff Robinson | .12 | .09 | 396 | Chuck Cary | .08 | .06 |
| 333 | Odibbe McDowell | .08 | .06 | 397 | Frank Viola | .15 | .11 |
| 334 | Jose Lind | .10 | .08 | 398 | Jeff Parrett | .10 | .08 |
| 335 | Paul Kilgus | .10 | .08 | 399 | *Terry Blocker* | .15 | .11 |
| 336 | Juan Samuel | .12 | .09 | 400 | Dan Gladden | .08 | .06 |
| 337 | Mike Campbell | .10 | .08 | 401 | *Louie Meadows* | .15 | .11 |
| 338 | Mike Maddux | .08 | .06 | 402 | Tim Raines | .25 | .20 |
| 339 | Darnell Coles | .08 | .06 | 403 | Joey Meyer | .10 | .08 |
| 340 | Bob Dernier | .08 | .06 | 404 | Larry Andersen | .08 | .06 |
| 341 | Rafael Ramirez | .08 | .06 | 405 | Rex Hudler | .08 | .06 |
| 342 | Scott Sanderson | .08 | .06 | 406 | Mike Schmidt | 2.00 | 1.50 |
| 343 | B.J. Surhoff | .10 | .08 | 407 | John Franco | .10 | .08 |
| 344 | Billy Hatcher | .08 | .06 | 408 | *Brady Anderson* | 1.50 | 1.25 |
| 345 | Pat Perry | .08 | .06 | 409 | Don Carman | .08 | .06 |
| 346 | Jack Clark | .15 | .11 | 410 | Eric Davis | .40 | .30 |
| 347 | Gary Thurman | .12 | .09 | 411 | Bob Stanley | .08 | .06 |
| 348 | *Timmy Jones* | .20 | .15 | 412 | Pete Smith | .10 | .08 |
| 349 | Dave Winfield | .30 | .25 | 413 | Jim Rice | .25 | .20 |

| | | MT | NR MT | | | | MT | NR MT |
|---|---|---|---|---|---|---|---|---|
| 414 | Bruce Sutter | .10 | .08 | | 481 | Johnny Ray | .08 | .06 |
| 415 | Oil Can Boyd | .08 | .06 | | 482 | Geno Petralli | .08 | .06 |
| 416 | Ruben Sierra | .50 | .40 | | 483 | Stu Cliburn | .08 | .06 |
| 417 | Mike LaValliere | .08 | .06 | | 484 | Pete Incaviglia | .10 | .08 |
| 418 | Steve Buechele | .08 | .06 | | 485 | Brian Downing | .08 | .06 |
| 419 | Gary Redus | .08 | .06 | | 486 | Jeff Stone | .08 | .06 |
| 420 | Scott Fletcher | .08 | .06 | | 487 | Carmen Castillo | .08 | .06 |
| 421 | Dale Sveum | .08 | .06 | | 488 | Tom Niedenfuer | .08 | .06 |
| 422 | Bob Knepper | .08 | .06 | | 489 | Jay Bell | .08 | .06 |
| 423 | Luis Rivera | .08 | .06 | | 490 | Rick Schu | .08 | .06 |
| 424 | Ted Higuera | .10 | .08 | | 491 | *Jeff Pico* | .15 | .11 |
| 425 | Kevin Bass | .08 | .06 | | 492 | *Mark Parent* | .20 | .15 |
| 426 | Ken Gerhart | .08 | .06 | | 493 | Eric King | .08 | .06 |
| 427 | Shane Rawley | .08 | .06 | | 494 | Al Nipper | .08 | .06 |
| 428 | Paul O'Neill | .08 | .06 | | 495 | Andy Hawkins | .08 | .06 |
| 429 | Joe Orsulak | .08 | .06 | | 496 | Daryl Boston | .08 | .06 |
| 430 | Jackie Gutierrez | .08 | .06 | | 497 | Ernie Riles | .08 | .06 |
| 431 | Gerald Perry | .10 | .08 | | 498 | Pascual Perez | .08 | .06 |
| 432 | Mike Greenwell | .60 | .45 | | 499 | Bill Long | .08 | .06 |
| 433 | Jerry Royster | .08 | .06 | | 500 | Kirt Manwaring | .10 | .08 |
| 434 | Ellis Burks | .60 | .45 | | 501 | Chuck Crim | .08 | .06 |
| 435 | Ed Olwine | .08 | .06 | | 502 | Candy Maldonado | .08 | .06 |
| 436 | Dave Rucker | .08 | .06 | | 503 | Dennis Lamp | .08 | .06 |
| 437 | Charlie Hough | .08 | .06 | | 504 | Glenn Braggs | .08 | .06 |
| 438 | Bob Walk | .08 | .06 | | 505 | Joe Price | .08 | .06 |
| 439 | Bob Brower | .08 | .06 | | 506 | Ken Williams | .08 | .06 |
| 440 | Barry Bonds | 1.50 | 1.25 | | 507 | Bill Pecota | .08 | .06 |
| 441 | Tom Foley | .08 | .06 | | 508 | Rey Quinones | .08 | .06 |
| 442 | Rob Deer | .08 | .06 | | 509 | *Jeff Bittiger* | .15 | .11 |
| 443 | Glenn Davis | .15 | .11 | | 510 | Kevin Seitzer | .30 | .25 |
| 444 | Dave Martinez | .08 | .06 | | 511 | Steve Bedrosian | .10 | .08 |
| 445 | Bill Wegman | .08 | .06 | | 512 | Todd Worrell | .10 | .08 |
| 446 | Lloyd McClendon | .08 | .06 | | 513 | Chris James | .10 | .08 |
| 447 | Dave Schmidt | .08 | .06 | | 514 | Jose Oquendo | .08 | .06 |
| 448 | Darren Daulton | .08 | .06 | | 515 | David Palmer | .08 | .06 |
| 449 | Frank Williams | .08 | .06 | | 516 | John Smiley | .12 | .09 |
| 450 | Don Aase | .08 | .06 | | 517 | Dave Clark | .08 | .06 |
| 451 | Lou Whitaker | .15 | .11 | | 518 | Mike Dunne | .10 | .08 |
| 452 | Goose Gossage | .12 | .09 | | 519 | Ron Washington | .08 | .06 |
| 453 | Ed Whitson | .08 | .06 | | 520 | Bob Kipper | .08 | .06 |
| 454 | Jim Walewander | .08 | .06 | | 521 | Lee Smith | .10 | .08 |
| 455 | Damon Berryhill | .12 | .09 | | 522 | Juan Castillo | .08 | .06 |
| 456 | Tim Burke | .08 | .06 | | 523 | Don Robinson | .08 | .06 |
| 457 | Barry Jones | .08 | .06 | | 524 | Kevin Romine | .08 | .06 |
| 458 | Joel Youngblood | .08 | .06 | | 525 | Paul Molitor | .15 | .11 |
| 459 | Floyd Youmans | .08 | .06 | | 526 | Mark Langston | .10 | .08 |
| 460 | Mark Salas | .08 | .06 | | 527 | Donnie Hill | .08 | .06 |
| 461 | Jeff Russell | .08 | .06 | | 528 | Larry Owen | .08 | .06 |
| 462 | Darrell Miller | .08 | .06 | | 529 | Jerry Reed | .08 | .06 |
| 463 | Jeff Kunkel | .08 | .06 | | 530 | Jack McDowell | 1.00 | .70 |
| 464 | *Sherman Corbett* | .20 | .15 | | 531 | Greg Mathews | .08 | .06 |
| 465 | Curtis Wilkerson | .08 | .06 | | 532 | John Russell | .08 | .06 |
| 466 | Bud Black | .08 | .06 | | 533 | Don Quisenberry | .08 | .06 |
| 467 | Cal Ripken, Jr. | 3.00 | 2.25 | | 534 | Greg Gross | .08 | .06 |
| 468 | John Farrell | .10 | .08 | | 535 | Danny Cox | .08 | .06 |
| 469 | Terry Kennedy | .08 | .06 | | 536 | Terry Francona | .08 | .06 |
| 470 | Tom Candiotti | .08 | .06 | | 537 | Andy Van Slyke | .15 | .11 |
| 471 | Roberto Alomar | 5.00 | 3.75 | | 538 | Mel Hall | .08 | .06 |
| 472 | Jeff Robinson | .12 | .09 | | 539 | Jim Gott | .08 | .06 |
| 473 | Vance Law | .08 | .06 | | 540 | Doug Jones | .10 | .08 |
| 474 | Randy Ready | .08 | .06 | | 541 | Criag Lefferts | .08 | .06 |
| 475 | Walt Terrell | .08 | .06 | | 542 | Mike Boddicker | .08 | .06 |
| 476 | Kelly Downs | .10 | .08 | | 543 | Greg Brock | .08 | .06 |
| 477 | *Johnny Paredes* | .15 | .11 | | 544 | Atlee Hammaker | .08 | .06 |
| 478 | Shawn Hillegas | .08 | .06 | | 545 | Tom Bolton | .08 | .06 |
| 479 | Bob Brenly | .08 | .06 | | 546 | *Mike Macfarlane* | .20 | .15 |
| 480 | Otis Nixon | .08 | .06 | | 547 | *Rich Renteria* | .15 | .11 |

| | | MT | NR MT | | | | MT | NR MT |
|---|---|---|---|---|---|---|---|---|
| 548 | John Davis | .08 | .06 | 612 | Keith Hernandez | | .20 | .15 |
| 549 | Floyd Bannister | .08 | .06 | 613 | Willie Fraser | | .08 | .06 |
| 550 | Mickey Brantley | .08 | .06 | 614 | Jim Eppard | | .08 | .06 |
| 551 | Duane Ward | .08 | .06 | 615 | Jeff Hamilton | | .08 | .06 |
| 552 | Dan Petry | .08 | .06 | 616 | Kurt Stillwell | | .08 | .06 |
| 553 | Mickey Tettleton | .08 | .06 | 617 | Tom Browning | | .10 | .08 |
| 554 | Rick Leach | .08 | .06 | 618 | Jeff Montgomery | | .08 | .06 |
| 555 | Mike Witt | .08 | .06 | 619 | Jose Rijo | | .08 | .06 |
| 556 | Sid Bream | .08 | .06 | 620 | Jamie Quirk | | .08 | .06 |
| 557 | Bobby Witt | .10 | .08 | 621 | Willie McGee | | .12 | .09 |
| 558 | Tommy Herr | .08 | .06 | 622 | Mark Grant | | .08 | .06 |
| 559 | Randy Milligan | .08 | .06 | 623 | Bill Swift | | .08 | .06 |
| 560 | *Jose Cecena* | .20 | .15 | 624 | Orlando Mercado | | .08 | .06 |
| 561 | Mackey Sasser | .08 | .06 | 625 | *John Costello* | | .15 | .11 |
| 562 | Carney Lansford | .08 | .06 | 626 | Jose Gonzalez | | .08 | .06 |
| 563 | Rick Aguilera | .08 | .06 | 627a | Bill Schroeder (putting | | | |
| 564 | Ron Hassey | .08 | .06 | | on shin guards on card | | | |
| 565 | Dwight Gooden | .50 | .40 | | back, photo actually Ronn | | | |
| 566 | Paul Assenmacher | .08 | .06 | | Reynolds) | | 1.25 | .90 |
| 567 | Neil Allen | .08 | .06 | 627b | Bill Schroeder (arms | | | |
| 568 | Jim Morrison | .08 | .06 | | crossed on card back, | | | |
| 569 | Mike Pagliarulo | .10 | .08 | | correct photo) | | .15 | .11 |
| 570 | Ted Simmons | .10 | .08 | 628a | Fred Manrique (throwing | | | |
| 571 | Mark Thurmond | .08 | .06 | | on card back, photo | | | |
| 572 | Fred McGriff | .40 | .30 | | actually Ozzie Guillen) | | 1.25 | .90 |
| 573 | Wally Joyner | .25 | .20 | 628b | Fred Manrique (batting | | | |
| 574 | *Jose Bautista* | .20 | .15 | | on card back, correct | | | |
| 575 | Kelly Gruber | .08 | .06 | | photo) | | .15 | .11 |
| 576 | Cecilio Guante | .08 | .06 | 629 | Ricky Horton | | .08 | .06 |
| 577 | Mark Davidson | .08 | .06 | 630 | Dan Plesac | | .10 | .08 |
| 578 | Bobby Bonilla | .12 | .09 | 631 | Alfredo Griffin | | .08 | .06 |
| 579 | Mike Stanley | .08 | .06 | 632 | Chuck Finley | | .08 | .06 |
| 580 | Gene Larkin | .10 | .08 | 633 | Kirk Gibson | | .20 | .15 |
| 581 | Stan Javier | .08 | .06 | 634 | Randy Myers | | .10 | .08 |
| 582 | Howard Johnson | .10 | .08 | 635 | Greg Minton | | .08 | .06 |
| 583a | Mike Gallego (photo on | | | 636 | Herm Winningham | | .08 | .06 |
| | card back reversed) | 1.00 | .70 | 637 | Charlie Leibrandt | | .08 | .06 |
| 583b | Mike Gallego (correct | | | 638 | Tim Birtsas | | .08 | .06 |
| | photo) | .15 | .11 | 639 | Bill Buckner | | .10 | .08 |
| 584 | David Cone | .35 | .25 | 640 | Danny Jackson | | .15 | .11 |
| 585 | *Doug Jennings* | .20 | .15 | 641 | Greg Booker | | .08 | .06 |
| 586 | Charlie Hudson | .08 | .06 | 642 | Jim Presley | | .08 | .06 |
| 587 | Dion James | .08 | .06 | 643 | Gene Nelson | | .08 | .06 |
| 588 | Al Leiter | .15 | .11 | 644 | Rod Booker | | .08 | .06 |
| 589 | Charlie Puleo | .08 | .06 | 645 | Dennis Rasmussen | | .10 | .08 |
| 590 | Roberto Kelly | .25 | .20 | 646 | Juan Nieves | | .08 | .06 |
| 591 | Thad Bosley | .08 | .06 | 647 | Bobby Thigpen | | .10 | .08 |
| 592 | Pete Stanicek | .10 | .08 | 648 | Tim Belcher | | .10 | .08 |
| 593 | *Pat Borders* | .70 | .50 | 649 | Mike Young | | .08 | .06 |
| 594 | *Bryan Harvey* | .60 | .45 | 650 | Ivan Calderon | | .08 | .06 |
| 595 | Jeff Ballard | .10 | .08 | 651 | *Oswaldo Peraza* | | .20 | .15 |
| 596 | Jeff Reardon | .10 | .08 | 652a | Pat Sheridan (no | | | |
| 597 | Doug Drabek | .08 | .06 | | position on front) | | 30.00 | 22.00 |
| 598 | Edwin Correa | .08 | .06 | 652b | Pat Sheridan (position | | | |
| 599 | Keith Atherton | .08 | .06 | | on front) | | .08 | .06 |
| 600 | Dave LaPoint | .08 | .06 | 653 | Mike Morgan | | .08 | .06 |
| 601 | Don Baylor | .10 | .08 | 654 | Mike Heath | | .08 | .06 |
| 602 | Tom Pagnozzi | .08 | .06 | 655 | Jay Tibbs | | .08 | .06 |
| 603 | Tim Flannery | .08 | .06 | 656 | Fernando Valenzuela | | | |
| 604 | Gene Walter | .08 | .06 | | | | .20 | .15 |
| 605 | Dave Parker | .12 | .09 | 657 | Lee Mazzilli | | .08 | .06 |
| 606 | Mike Diaz | .08 | .06 | 658 | Frank Viola | | .08 | .06 |
| 607 | Chris Gwynn | .10 | .08 | 659 | Jose Canseco | | .08 | .06 |
| 608 | Odell Jones | .08 | .06 | 660 | Walt Weiss | | .08 | .06 |
| 609 | Carlton Fisk | .60 | .45 | 661 | Orel Hershiser | | .08 | .06 |
| 610 | Jay Howell | .08 | .06 | 662 | Kirk Gibson | | .08 | .06 |
| 611 | Tim Crews | .08 | .06 | 663 | Chris Sabo | | .08 | .06 |

| | | MT | NR MT |
|---|---|---|---|
| 664 | Dennis Eckersley | .08 | .06 |
| 665 | Orel Hershiser | .08 | .06 |
| 666 | Kirk Gibson | .08 | .06 |
| 667 | Orel Hershiser | .08 | .06 |
| 668 | Angels Checklist (Wally Joyner) | .08 | .06 |
| 669 | Astros Checklist (Nolan Ryan) | .60 | .45 |
| 670 | Athletics Checklist (Jose Canseco) | .08 | .06 |
| 671 | Blue Jays Checklist (Fred McGriff) | .08 | .06 |
| 672 | Braves Checklist (Dale Murphy) | .08 | .06 |
| 673 | Brewers Checklist (Paul Molitor) | .08 | .06 |
| 674 | Cardinals Checklist (Ozzie Smith) | .08 | .06 |
| 675 | Cubs Checklist (Ryne Sandberg) | .08 | .06 |
| 676 | Dodgers Checklist (Kirk Gibson) | .08 | .06 |
| 677 | Expos Checklist (Andres Galarraga) | .08 | .06 |
| 678 | Giants Checklist (Will Clark) | .08 | .06 |
| 679 | Indians Checklist (Cory Snyder) | .08 | .06 |
| 680 | Mariners Checklist (Alvin Davis) | .08 | .06 |
| 681 | Mets Checklist (Darryl Strawberry) | .08 | .06 |
| 682 | Orioles Checklist (Cal Ripken, Jr.) | .08 | .06 |
| 683 | Padres Checklist (Tony Gwynn) | .08 | .06 |
| 684 | Phillies Checklist (Mike Schmidt) | .08 | .06 |
| 685 | Pirates Checklist (Andy Van Slyke) | .08 | .06 |
| 686 | Rangers Checklist (Ruben Sierra) | .08 | .06 |
| 687 | Red Sox Checklist (Wade Boggs) | .08 | .06 |
| 688 | Reds Checklist (Eric Davis) | .08 | .06 |
| 689 | Royals Checklist (George Brett) | .08 | .06 |
| 690 | Tigers Checklist (Alan Trammell) | .08 | .06 |
| 691 | Twins Checklist (Frank Viola) | .08 | .06 |
| 692 | White Sox Checklist (Harold Baines) | .08 | .06 |
| 693 | Yankees Checklist (Don Mattingly) | .08 | .06 |
| 694 | Checklist 1-100 | .08 | .06 |
| 695 | Checklist 101-200 | .08 | .06 |
| 696 | Checklist 201-300 | .08 | .06 |
| 697 | Checklist 301-400 | .08 | .06 |
| 698 | Checklist 401-500 | .08 | .06 |
| 699 | Checklist 501-600 | .08 | .06 |
| 700 | Checklist 601-700 | .08 | .06 |
| 701 | Checklist 701-800 | .20 | .15 |
| 702 | Jessie Barfield | .10 | .08 |
| 703 | Walt Terrell | .10 | .08 |
| 704 | Dickie Thon | .10 | .08 |

| | | MT | NR MT |
|---|---|---|---|
| 705 | Al Leiter | .10 | .08 |
| 706 | Dave LaPoint | .10 | .08 |
| 707 | Charlie Hayes(FC) | .20 | .15 |
| 708 | Andy Hawkins | .10 | .08 |
| 709 | Mickey Hatcher | .10 | .08 |
| 710 | Lance McCullers | .10 | .08 |
| 711 | Ron Kittle | .10 | .08 |
| 712 | Bert Blyleven | .10 | .08 |
| 713 | Rick Dempsey | .10 | .08 |
| 714 | Ken Williams | .10 | .08 |
| 715 | Steve Rosenberg(FC) | .15 | .11 |
| 716 | Joe Skalski(FC) | .20 | .15 |
| 717 | Spike Owen | .10 | .08 |
| 718 | Todd Burns | .10 | .08 |
| 719 | Kevin Gross | .10 | .08 |
| 720 | Tommy Herr | .10 | .08 |
| 721 | Rob Ducey | .10 | .08 |
| 722 | Gary Green(FC) | .15 | .11 |
| 723 | Gregg Olson(FC) | 2.00 | 1.50 |
| 724 | Greg Harris(FC) | .15 | .11 |
| 725 | Craig Worthington(FC) | .50 | .40 |
| 726 | Tom Howard(FC) | .25 | .20 |
| 727 | Dale Mohorcic | .10 | .08 |
| 728 | Rich Yett | .10 | .08 |
| 729 | Mel Hall | .10 | .08 |
| 730 | Floyd Youmans | .10 | .08 |
| 731 | Lonnie Smith | .15 | .11 |
| 732 | Wally Backman | .10 | .08 |
| 733 | Trevor Wilson | .10 | .08 |
| 734 | Jose Alvarez | .10 | .08 |
| 735 | Bob Milacki(FC) | .15 | .11 |
| 736 | Tom Gordon(FC) | .80 | .60 |
| 737 | Wally Whitehurst(FC) | .25 | .20 |
| 738 | Mike Aldrete | .10 | .08 |
| 739 | Keith Miller | .10 | .08 |
| 740 | Randy Milligan | .10 | .08 |
| 741 | Jeff Parrett | .10 | .08 |
| 742 | Steve Finley(FC) | .60 | .45 |
| 743 | Junior Felix(FC) | .80 | .60 |
| 744 | Pete Harnisch(FC) | .50 | .40 |
| 745 | Bill Spiers(FC) | .40 | .30 |
| 746 | Hensley Meulens(FC) | .50 | .40 |
| 747 | Juan Bell | .20 | .15 |
| 748 | Steve Sax | .15 | .11 |
| 749 | Phil Bradley | .10 | .08 |
| 750 | Rey Quinones | .10 | .08 |
| 751 | Tommy Gregg(FC) | .15 | .11 |
| 752 | Kevin Brown(FC) | .10 | .08 |
| 753 | Derek Lilliquist(FC) | .15 | .11 |
| 754 | Todd Zeile(FC) | 3.00 | 2.25 |
| 755 | Jim Abbott(FC) | 4.00 | 3.00 |
| 756 | Ozzie Canseco(FC) | .30 | .25 |
| 757 | Nick Esasky | .10 | .08 |
| 758 | Mike Moore | .15 | .11 |
| 759 | Rob Murphy | .10 | .08 |
| 760 | Rick Mahler | .10 | .08 |
| 761 | Fred Lynn | .10 | .08 |
| 762 | Kevin Blankenship(FC) | .10 | .08 |
| 763 | Eddie Murray | .15 | .11 |
| 764 | Steve Searcy(FC) | .10 | .08 |
| 765 | Jerome Walton(FC) | .30 | .25 |
| 766 | Erik Hanson(FC) | .60 | .45 |

| | | MT | NR MT |
|---|---|---|---|
| 767 | Bob Boone | .15 | .11 |
| 768 | Edgar Martinez(FC) | | |
| | | 2.00 | 1.50 |
| 769 | Jose DeJesus(FC) | .10 | .08 |
| 770 | Greg Briley(FC) | .30 | .25 |
| 771 | Steve Peters(FC) | .10 | .08 |
| 772 | Rafael Palmeiro | .60 | .45 |
| 773 | Jack Clark | .15 | .11 |
| 774 | Nolan Ryan | 4.00 | 3.00 |
| 775 | Lance Parrish | .10 | .08 |
| 776 | Joe Girardi(FC) | .25 | .20 |
| 777 | Willie Randolph | .10 | .08 |
| 778 | Mitch Williams | .30 | .25 |
| 779 | Dennis Cook(FC) | .40 | .30 |
| 780 | Dwight Smith(FC) | .25 | .20 |
| 781 | Lenny Harris(FC) | .40 | .30 |
| 782 | Torey Lovullo(FC) | .15 | .11 |
| 783 | Norm Charlton(FC) | .10 | .08 |
| 784 | Chris Brown | .10 | .08 |
| 785 | Todd Benzinger | .10 | .08 |
| 786 | Shane Rawley | .10 | .08 |
| 787 | Omar Vizquel(FC) | .25 | .20 |
| 788 | LaVel Freeman(FC) | .25 | .20 |
| 789 | Jeffrey Leonard | .10 | .08 |
| 790 | Eddie Williams(FC) | .10 | .08 |
| 791 | Jamie Moyer | .10 | .08 |
| 792 | Bruce Hurst | .10 | .08 |
| 793 | Julio Franco | .30 | .25 |
| 794 | Claudell Washington | .10 | .08 |
| 795 | Jody Davis | .10 | .08 |
| 796 | Odibbe McDowell | .10 | .08 |
| 797 | Paul Kilgus | .10 | .08 |
| 798 | Tracy Jones | .10 | .08 |
| 799 | Steve Wilson(FC) | .20 | .15 |
| 800 | Pete O'Brien, | | |

## 1990 Upper Deck

Tom Candiotti

Following the success of its first issue, Upper Deck released another 800-card set in 1990. The cards contain full-color photos on both sides and are 2-1/2" by 3-1/2" in size. The artwork of Vernon Wells is featured on the front of all team checklist cards. The 1990 set also introduces two new Wells illustrations - a tribute to Mike Schmidt upon his retirement and one commemorating Nolan Ryan's 5,000 career strikeouts. The cards are

similar in design to the 1989 issue. The Wade Boggs card depicts the Red Sox star in four stages of his batting swing via a quad-action photograph, much like the Jim Abbott card of 1989. The high-number series (701-800) was released as a boxed set, in factory sets and in wax packs at mid-season.

| | | MT | NR MT |
|---|---|---|---|
| Complete Set: 1-700 | | 40.00 | 30.00 |
| Common Player: 1-700 | | .06 | .05 |
| Complete Set: 1-800 | | 50.00 | 37.00 |
| Common Player: 701-800 | | .10 | .08 |
| 1 | Star Rookie Checklist | | |
| | | .06 | .05 |
| 2 | Randy Nosek(FC) | .15 | .11 |
| 3 | Tom Dress(FC) | .15 | .11 |
| 4 | Curt Young | .06 | .05 |
| 5 | Angels Checklist | .06 | .05 |
| 6 | Luis Salazar | .06 | .05 |
| 7 | Phillies Checklist | .06 | .05 |
| 8 | Jose Bautista | .08 | .06 |
| 9 | Marquis Grissom(FC) | | |
| | | 2.00 | 1.50 |
| 10 | Dodgers Checklist | .06 | .05 |
| 11 | Rick Aguilera | .08 | .06 |
| 12 | Padres Checklist | .06 | .05 |
| 13 | Deion Sanders(FC) | | |
| | | 2.00 | 1.50 |
| 14 | Marvell Wynne | .06 | .05 |
| 15 | David West | .15 | .11 |
| 16 | Pirates Checklist | .06 | .05 |
| 17 | Sammy Sosa(FC) | .70 | .50 |
| 18 | Yankees Checklist | .06 | .05 |
| 19 | Jack Howell | .06 | .05 |
| 20 | Mike Schmidt (Special Card) | 1.00 | .70 |
| 21 | Robin Ventura(FC) | 3.00 | 2.25 |
| 22 | Brian Meyer(FC) | .20 | .15 |
| 23 | Blaine Beatty(FC) | | |
| | | .20 | .15 |
| 24 | Mariners Checklist | .06 | .05 |
| 25 | Greg Vaughn(FC) | | |
| | | 1.00 | .70 |
| 26 | Xavier Hernandez(FC) | .15 | .11 |
| 27 | Jason Grimsley(FC) | | |
| | | .25 | .20 |
| 28 | Eric Anthony(FC) | .50 | .40 |
| 29 | Expos Checklist | .06 | .05 |
| 30 | David Wells | .06 | .05 |
| 31 | Hal Morris(FC) | 1.25 | .90 |
| 32 | Royals Checklist | .25 | .20 |
| 33 | Kelly Mann(FC) | .15 | .11 |
| 34 | Nolan Ryan (Special Card) | 1.25 | .90 |
| 35 | Scott Service(FC) | | |
| | | .20 | .15 |
| 36 | Athletics Checklist | .06 | .05 |

| | | MT | NR MT |
|---|---|---|---|
| 37 | *Tino Martinez*(FC) | | |
| | | 1.00 | .70 |
| 38 | Chili Davis | .09 | .07 |
| 39 | Scott Sanderson | .06 | .05 |
| 40 | Giants Checklist | .06 | .05 |
| 41 | Tigers Checklist | .06 | .05 |
| 42 | *Scott Coolbaugh*(FC) | | |
| | | .20 | .15 |
| 43 | *Jose Cano*(FC) | .15 | .11 |
| 44 | *Jose Vizcaino*(FC) | | |
| | | .30 | .25 |
| 45 | *Bob Hamelin*(FC) | | |
| | | .20 | .15 |
| 46 | *Jose Offerman*(FC) | | |
| | | .50 | .40 |
| 47 | Kevin Blankenship | .10 | .08 |
| 48 | Twins Checklist | .06 | .05 |
| 49 | *Tommy Greene*(FC) | | |
| | | .50 | .40 |
| 50 | Will Clark (Special Card) | | |
| | | .40 | .30 |
| 51 | Rob Nelson(FC) | .09 | .07 |
| 52 | *Chris Hammond*(FC) | | |
| | | .30 | .25 |
| 53 | Indians Checklist | .06 | .05 |
| 54a | *Ben McDonald* (Orioles Logo)(FC) | 15.00 | 11.00 |
| 54b | *Ben McDonald* (Rookies Logo)(FC) | 2.00 | 1.50 |
| 55 | Andy Benes(FC) | 1.00 | .70 |
| 56 | *John Olerud*(FC) | | |
| | | 1.50 | 1.25 |
| 57 | Red Sox Checklist | .06 | .05 |
| 58 | Tony Armas | .06 | .05 |
| 59 | *George Canale*(FC) | | |
| | | .20 | .15 |
| 60a | Orioles Checklist (Jamie Weston) | 4.00 | 3.00 |
| 60b | Orioles Checklist (Mickey Weston) | .08 | .06 |
| 61 | *Mike Stanton*(FC) | | |
| | | .15 | .11 |
| 62 | Mets Checklist | .06 | .05 |
| 63 | Kent Mercker(FC) | | |
| | | .50 | .40 |
| 64 | *Francisco Cabrera*(FC) | .30 | .25 |
| 65 | Steve Avery(FC) | 3.00 | 2.25 |
| 66 | Jose Canseco | .90 | .70 |
| 67 | *Matt Merullo*(FC) | | |
| | | .15 | .11 |
| 68 | Cardinals Checklist | .06 | .05 |
| 69 | Ron Karkovice | .06 | .05 |
| 70 | *Kevin Maas*(FC) | .80 | .60 |
| 71 | Dennis Cook | .10 | .08 |
| 72 | *Juan Gonzalez*(FC) | | |
| | | 9.00 | 6.75 |
| 73 | Cubs Checklist | .06 | .05 |
| 74 | *Dean Palmer*(FC) | | |
| | | 3.00 | 2.25 |
| 75 | Bo Jackson (Special Card) | .60 | .45 |
| 76 | *Rob Richie*(FC) | .20 | .15 |
| 77 | *Bobby Rose*(FC) | .20 | .15 |
| 78 | *Brian DuBois*(FC) | | |
| | | .15 | .11 |
| 79 | White Sox Checklist | .06 | .05 |

| | | MT | NR MT |
|---|---|---|---|
| 80 | Gene Nelson | .06 | .05 |
| 81 | Bob McClure | .06 | .05 |
| 82 | Rangers Checklist | .06 | .05 |
| 83 | Greg Minton | .06 | .05 |
| 84 | Braves Checklist | .06 | .05 |
| 85 | Willie Fraser | .06 | .05 |
| 86 | Neal Heaton | .06 | .05 |
| 87 | *Kevin Tapani*(FC) | | |
| | | .60 | .45 |
| 88 | Astros Checklist | .06 | .05 |
| 89a | Jim Gott (Incorrect Photo) | 5.00 | 3.75 |
| 89b | Jim Gott (Photo of Gott) | .10 | .08 |
| 90 | Lance Johnson(FC) | .09 | .07 |
| 91 | Brewers Checklist | .06 | .05 |
| 92 | Jeff Parrett | .08 | .06 |
| 93 | *Julio Machado*(FC) | | |
| | | .25 | .20 |
| 94 | Ron Jones | .10 | .08 |
| 95 | Blue Jays Checklist | .06 | .05 |
| 96 | Jerry Reuss | .06 | .05 |
| 97 | Brian Fisher | .06 | .05 |
| 98 | *Kevin Ritz*(FC) | .25 | .20 |
| 99 | Reds Checklist | .06 | .05 |
| 100 | Checklist 1-100 | .06 | .05 |
| 101 | Gerald Perry | .06 | .05 |
| 102 | *Kevin Appier*(FC) | | |
| | | .40 | .30 |
| 103 | Julio Franco | .10 | .08 |
| 104 | Craig Biggio | .20 | .15 |
| 105 | Bo Jackson | 1.00 | .70 |
| 106 | *Junior Felix* | .30 | .25 |
| 107 | Mike Harkey(FC) | .30 | .25 |
| 108 | Fred McGriff | .25 | .20 |
| 109 | Rick Sutcliffe | .08 | .06 |
| 110 | Pete O'Brien | .08 | .06 |
| 111 | Kelly Gruber | .10 | .08 |
| 112 | Pat Borders | .10 | .08 |
| 113 | Dwight Evans | .10 | .08 |
| 114 | Dwight Gooden | .20 | .15 |
| 115 | *Kevin Batiste*(FC) | | |
| | | .15 | .11 |
| 116 | Eric Davis | .25 | .20 |
| 117 | Kevin Mitchell | .40 | .30 |
| 118 | Ron Oester | .06 | .05 |
| 119 | Brett Butler | .09 | .07 |
| 120 | Danny Jackson | .06 | .05 |
| 121 | Tommy Gregg | .06 | .05 |
| 122 | Ken Caminiti | .08 | .06 |
| 123 | Kevin Brown | .10 | .08 |
| 124 | George Brett | .15 | .11 |
| 125 | Mike Scott | .10 | .08 |
| 126 | Cory Snyder | .10 | .08 |
| 127 | George Bell | .15 | .11 |
| 128 | Mark Grace | .50 | .40 |
| 129 | Devon White | .10 | .08 |
| 130 | Tony Fernandez | .15 | .11 |
| 131 | Dan Aase | .06 | .05 |
| 132 | Rance Mulliniks | .06 | .05 |
| 133 | Marty Barrett | .08 | .06 |
| 134 | Nelson Liriano | .07 | .05 |
| 135 | Mark Carreon(FC) | .15 | .11 |
| 136 | Candy Maldonado | .06 | .05 |
| 137 | Tim Birtsas | .06 | .05 |
| 138 | Tom Brookens | .06 | .05 |
| 139 | John Franco | .08 | .06 |

| | | MT | NR MT | | | MT | NR MT |
|---|---|---|---|---|---|---|---|
| 140 | Mike LaCoss | .06 | .05 | 205 | Alex Trevino | .06 | .05 |
| 141 | Jeff Treadway | .07 | .05 | 206 | Dave Henderson | .10 | .08 |
| 142 | Pat Tabler | .07 | .05 | 207 | Henry Cotto | .06 | .05 |
| 143 | Darrell Evans | .06 | .05 | 208 | Rafael Belliard | .06 | .05 |
| 144 | Rafael Ramirez | .06 | .05 | 209 | Stan Javier | .07 | .05 |
| 145 | Oddibe McDowell | .09 | .07 | 210 | Jerry Reed | .06 | .05 |
| 146 | Brian Downing | .09 | .07 | 211 | Doug Dascenzo | .08 | .06 |
| 147 | Curtis Wilkerson | .06 | .05 | 212 | Andres Thomas | .07 | .05 |
| 148 | Ernie Whitt | .07 | .05 | 213 | Greg Maddux | .20 | .15 |
| 149 | Bill Schroeder | .06 | .05 | 214 | Mike Schooler | .09 | .07 |
| 150 | Domingo Ramos | .06 | .05 | 215 | Lonnie Smith | .09 | .07 |
| 151 | Rick Honeycutt | .06 | .05 | 216 | Jose Rijo | .10 | .08 |
| 152 | Don Slaught | .06 | .05 | 217 | Greg Gagne | .08 | .06 |
| 153 | Mitch Webster | .06 | .05 | 218 | Jim Gantner | .08 | .06 |
| 154 | Tony Phillips | .07 | .05 | 219 | Allan Anderson | .09 | .07 |
| 155 | Paul Kilgus | .06 | .05 | 220 | Rick Mahler | .06 | .05 |
| 156 | Ken Griffey, Jr. | 4.00 | 3.00 | 221 | Jim Deshaies | .09 | .07 |
| 157 | Gary Sheffield | .80 | .60 | 222 | Keith Hernandez | .10 | .08 |
| 158 | Wally Backman | .06 | .05 | 223 | Vince Coleman | .12 | .09 |
| 159 | B.J. Surhoff | .08 | .06 | 224 | David Cone | .20 | .15 |
| 160 | Louie Meadows | .08 | .06 | 225 | Ozzie Smith | .20 | .15 |
| 161 | Paul O'Neill | .09 | .07 | 226 | Matt Nokes | .10 | .08 |
| 162 | *Jeff McKnight*(FC) | .15 | .11 | 227 | Barry Bonds | .10 | .08 |
| 163 | Alvaro Espinoza(FC) | .15 | .11 | 228 | Felix Jose | .10 | .08 |
| 164 | *Scott Scudder*(FC) | .20 | .15 | 229 | Dennis Powell | .06 | .05 |
| 165 | Jeff Reed | .06 | .05 | 230 | Mike Gallego | .06 | .05 |
| 166 | Gregg Jefferies | .30 | .25 | 231 | Shawon Dunston | .09 | .07 |
| 167 | Barry Larkin | .15 | .11 | 232 | Ron Gant | .10 | .08 |
| 168 | Gary Carter | .10 | .08 | 233 | *Omar Vizquel* | .10 | .08 |
| 169 | Robby Thompson | .09 | .07 | 234 | Derek Lilliquist | .10 | .08 |
| 170 | Rolando Roomes | .15 | .11 | 235 | Erik Hanson | .10 | .08 |
| 171 | Mark McGwire | .50 | .40 | 236 | Kirby Puckett | .35 | .25 |
| 172 | Steve Sax | .10 | .08 | 237 | *Bill Spiers* | .25 | .20 |
| 173 | Mark Williamson | .06 | .05 | 238 | Dan Gladden | .07 | .05 |
| 174 | Mitch Williams | .15 | .11 | 239 | Bryan Clutterbuck(FC) | .07 | .05 |
| 175 | Brian Holton | .06 | .05 | 240 | John Moses | .06 | .05 |
| 176 | Rob Deer | .08 | .06 | 241 | Ron Darling | .12 | .09 |
| 177 | Tim Raines | .12 | .09 | 242 | Joe Magrane | .12 | .09 |
| 178 | Mike Felder | .06 | .05 | 243 | Dave Magadan | .09 | .07 |
| 179 | Harold Reynolds | .10 | .08 | 244 | Pedro Guerrero | .15 | .11 |
| 180 | Terry Francona | .06 | .05 | 245 | Glenn Davis | .10 | .08 |
| 181 | Chris Sabo | .15 | .11 | 246 | Terry Steinbach | .12 | .09 |
| 182 | Darryl Strawberry | .30 | .25 | 247 | Fred Lynn | .09 | .07 |
| 183 | Willie Randolph | .10 | .08 | 248 | Gary Redus | .06 | .05 |
| 184 | Billy Ripken | .06 | .05 | 249 | Kenny Williams | .06 | .05 |
| 185 | Mackey Sasser | .08 | .06 | 250 | Sid Bream | .06 | .05 |
| 186 | Todd Benzinger | .08 | .06 | 251 | Bob Welch | .08 | .06 |
| 187 | Kevin Elster | .07 | .05 | 252 | Bill Buckner | .07 | .05 |
| 188 | Jose Uribe | .06 | .05 | 253 | Carney Lansford | .09 | .07 |
| 189 | Tom Browning | .10 | .08 | 254 | Paul Molitor | .12 | .09 |
| 190 | Keith Miller | .09 | .07 | 255 | Jose DeJesus | .15 | .11 |
| 191 | Don Mattingly | .60 | .45 | 256 | Orel Hershiser | .25 | .20 |
| 192 | Dave Parker | .12 | .09 | 257 | Tom Brunansky | .10 | .08 |
| 193 | Roberto Kelly | .12 | .09 | 258 | Mike Davis | .06 | .05 |
| 194 | Phil Bradley | .09 | .07 | 259 | Jeff Ballard | .12 | .09 |
| 195 | Ron Hassey | .07 | .05 | 260 | Scott Terry | .09 | .07 |
| 196 | Gerald Young | .06 | .05 | 261 | Sid Fernandez | .10 | .08 |
| 197 | Hubie Brooks | .08 | .06 | 262 | Mike Marshall | .08 | .06 |
| 198 | Bill Doran | .09 | .07 | 263 | Howard Johnson | .20 | .15 |
| 199 | Al Newman | .06 | .05 | 264 | Kirk Gibson | .09 | .07 |
| 200 | Checklist 101-200 | .06 | .05 | 265 | Kevin McReynolds | .15 | .11 |
| 201 | Terry Puhl | .06 | .05 | 266 | Cal Ripken, Jr. | .30 | .25 |
| 202 | Frank DiPino | .06 | .05 | 267 | Ozzie Guillen | .07 | .05 |
| 203 | Jim Clancy | .06 | .05 | 268 | Jim Traber | .06 | .05 |
| 204 | Bob Ojeda | .07 | .05 | 269 | Bobby Thigpen | .09 | .07 |
| | | | | 270 | Joe Orsulak | .06 | .05 |

| # | Player | MT | NR MT |
|---|---|---|---|
| 271 | Bob Boone | .09 | .07 |
| 272 | Dave Stewart | .09 | .07 |
| 273 | Tim Wallach | .09 | .07 |
| 274 | Luis Aquino | .06 | .05 |
| 275 | Mike Moore | .10 | .08 |
| 276 | Tony Pena | .08 | .06 |
| 277 | Eddie Murray | .15 | .11 |
| 278 | Milt Thompson | .07 | .05 |
| 279 | Alejandro Pena | .06 | .05 |
| 280 | Ken Dayley | .06 | .05 |
| 281 | Carmen Castillo | .06 | .05 |
| 282 | Tom Henke | .08 | .06 |
| 283 | Mickey Hatcher | .06 | .05 |
| 284 | Roy Smith(FC) | .06 | .05 |
| 285 | Manny Lee | .06 | .05 |
| 286 | Dan Pasqua | .07 | .05 |
| 287 | Larry Sheets | .06 | .05 |
| 288 | Garry Templeton | .07 | .05 |
| 289 | Eddie Williams | .07 | .05 |
| 290 | Brady Anderson | .07 | .05 |
| 291 | Spike Owen | .07 | .05 |
| 292 | Storm Davis | .09 | .07 |
| 293 | Chris Bosio | .09 | .07 |
| 294 | Jim Eisenreich | .07 | .05 |
| 295 | Don August | .07 | .05 |
| 296 | Jeff Hamilton | .07 | .05 |
| 297 | Mickey Tettleton | .10 | .08 |
| 298 | Mike Scioscia | .09 | .07 |
| 299 | Kevin Hickey(FC) | .06 | .05 |
| 300 | Checklist 201-300 | .06 | .05 |
| 301 | Shawn Abner | .06 | .05 |
| 302 | Kevin Bass | .08 | .06 |
| 303 | Bip Roberts(FC) | .08 | .06 |
| 304 | Joe Girardi | .10 | .08 |
| 305 | Danny Darwin | .06 | .05 |
| 306 | Mike Heath | .06 | .05 |
| 307 | Mike Macfarlane | .06 | .05 |
| 308 | Ed Whitson | .08 | .06 |
| 309 | Tracy Jones | .07 | .05 |
| 310 | Scott Fletcher | .07 | .05 |
| 311 | Darnell Coles | .06 | .05 |
| 312 | Mike Brumley | .06 | .05 |
| 313 | Bill Swift | .06 | .05 |
| 314 | Charlie Hough | .07 | .05 |
| 315 | Jim Presley | .08 | .06 |
| 316 | Luis Polonia | .07 | .05 |
| 317 | Mike Morgan | .06 | .05 |
| 318 | Lee Guetterman | .06 | .05 |
| 319 | Jose Oquendo | .08 | .06 |
| 320 | Wayne Tollenson | .06 | .05 |
| 321 | Jody Reed | .07 | .05 |
| 322 | Damon Berryhill | .09 | .07 |
| 323 | Roger Clemens | .40 | .30 |
| 324 | Ryne Sandberg | .30 | .25 |
| 325 | Benito Santiago | .10 | .08 |
| 326 | Bret Saberhagen | .15 | .11 |
| 327 | Lou Whitaker | .10 | .08 |
| 328 | Dave Gallagher | .10 | .08 |
| 329 | Mike Pagliarulo | .07 | .05 |
| 330 | Doyle Alexander | .07 | .05 |
| 331 | Jeffrey Leonard | .09 | .07 |
| 332 | Torey Lovullo | .20 | .15 |
| 333 | Pete Incaviglia | .09 | .07 |
| 334 | Rickey Henderson | .30 | .25 |
| 335 | Rafael Palmeiro | .10 | .08 |
| 336 | Ken Hill | .10 | .08 |
| 337 | Dave Winfield | .12 | .09 |
| 338 | Alfredo Griffin | .07 | .05 |
| 339 | Andy Hawkins | .07 | .05 |
| 340 | Ted Power | .06 | .05 |
| 341 | Steve Wilson | .10 | .08 |
| 342 | Jack Clark | .10 | .08 |
| 343 | Ellis Burks | .25 | .20 |
| 344 | Tony Gwynn | .20 | .15 |
| 345 | Jerome Walton | .25 | .20 |
| 346 | Roberto Alomar | .10 | .08 |
| 347 | Carlos Martinez(FC) | .15 | .11 |
| 348 | Chet Lemon | .07 | .05 |
| 349 | Willie Wilson | .07 | .05 |
| 350 | Greg Walker | .07 | .05 |
| 351 | Tom Bolton | .06 | .05 |
| 352 | German Gonzalez(FC) | .08 | .06 |
| 353 | Harold Baines | .10 | .08 |
| 354 | Mike Greenwell | .30 | .25 |
| 355 | Ruben Sierra | .20 | .15 |
| 356 | Anres Galarraga | .12 | .09 |
| 357 | Andre Dawson | .15 | .11 |
| 358 | Jeff Brantley(FC) | .10 | .08 |
| 359 | Mike Bielecki | .08 | .06 |
| 360 | Ken Oberkfell | .06 | .05 |
| 361 | Kurt Stillwell | .07 | .05 |
| 362 | Brian Holman | .09 | .07 |
| 363 | Kevin Seitzer | .12 | .09 |
| 364 | Alvin Davis | .15 | .11 |
| 365 | Tom Gordon | .35 | .25 |
| 366 | Bobby Bonilla | .10 | .08 |
| 367 | Carlton Fisk | .10 | .08 |
| 368 | Steve Carter(FC) | .15 | .11 |
| 369 | Joel Skinner | .06 | .05 |
| 370 | John Cangelosi | .06 | .05 |
| 371 | Cecil Espy | .08 | .06 |
| 372 | Gary Wayne(FC) | .15 | .11 |
| 373 | Jim Rice | .08 | .06 |
| 374 | Mike Dyer(FC) | .15 | .11 |
| 375 | Joe Carter | .12 | .09 |
| 376 | Dwight Smith | .20 | .15 |
| 377 | John Wetteland(FC) | .35 | .25 |
| 378 | Ernie Riles | .06 | .05 |
| 379 | Otis Nixon | .06 | .05 |
| 380 | Vance Law | .06 | .05 |
| 381 | Dave Bergman | .06 | .05 |
| 382 | Frank White | .07 | .05 |
| 383 | Scott Bradley | .06 | .05 |
| 384 | Israel Sanchez | .06 | .05 |
| 385 | Gary Pettis | .06 | .05 |
| 386 | Donn Pall(FC) | .06 | .05 |
| 387 | John Smiley | .10 | .08 |
| 388 | Tom Candiotti | .07 | .05 |
| 389 | Junior Ortiz | .06 | .05 |
| 390 | Steve Lyons | .06 | .05 |
| 391 | Brian Harper | .06 | .05 |
| 392 | Fred Manrique | .06 | .05 |
| 393 | Lee Smith | .08 | .06 |
| 394 | Jeff Kunkel | .06 | .05 |
| 395 | Claudell Washington | .08 | .06 |
| 396 | John Tudor | .07 | .05 |
| 397 | Terry Kennedy | .07 | .05 |
| 398 | Lloyd McClendon | .09 | .07 |
| 399 | Craig Lefferts | .06 | .05 |

| | | MT | NR MT |
|---|---|---|---|
| 400 | Checklist 301-400 | .06 | .05 |
| 401 | Keith Moreland | .06 | .05 |
| 402 | Rich Gedman | .07 | .05 |
| 403 | Jeff Robinson | .07 | .05 |
| 404 | Randy Ready | .06 | .05 |
| 405 | Rick Cerone | .06 | .05 |
| 406 | Jeff Blauser | .07 | .05 |
| 407 | Larry Andersen | .06 | .05 |
| 408 | Joe Boever | .08 | .06 |
| 409 | Felix Fermin | .06 | .05 |
| 410 | Glenn Wilson | .06 | .05 |
| 411 | Rex Hudler | .06 | .05 |
| 412 | Mark Grant | .06 | .05 |
| 413 | Dennis Martinez | .08 | .06 |
| 414 | Darrin Jackson | .06 | .05 |
| 415 | Mike Aldrete | .06 | .05 |
| 416 | Roger McDowell | .09 | .07 |
| 417 | Jeff Reardon | .10 | .08 |
| 418 | Darren Daulton | .06 | .05 |
| 419 | Tim Laudner | .08 | .06 |
| 420 | Don Carman | .07 | .05 |
| 421 | Lloyd Moseby | .09 | .07 |
| 422 | Doug Drabek | .10 | .08 |
| 423 | Lenny Harris | .09 | .07 |
| 424 | Jose Lind | .07 | .05 |
| 425 | *Dave Johnson*(FC) | | |
| | | .20 | .15 |
| 426 | Jerry Browne | .09 | .07 |
| 427 | *Eric Yelding*(FC) | .12 | .09 |
| 428 | Brad Komminsk(FC) | .06 | .05 |
| 429 | Jody Davis | .06 | .05 |
| 430 | Mariano Duncan(FC) | | |
| | | .09 | .07 |
| 431 | Mark Davis | .12 | .09 |
| 432 | Nelson Santovenia | .10 | .08 |
| 433 | Bruce Hurst | .10 | .08 |
| 434 | *Jeff Huson*(FC) | .25 | .20 |
| 435 | Chris James | .09 | .07 |
| 436 | *Mark Guthrie*(FC) | | |
| | | .15 | .11 |
| 437 | Charlie Hayes(FC) | .10 | .08 |
| 438 | Shane Rawley | .08 | .06 |
| 439 | Dickie Thon | .06 | .05 |
| 440 | Juan Berenguer | .06 | .05 |
| 441 | Kevin Romine | .06 | .05 |
| 442 | Bill Landrum | .09 | .07 |
| 443 | Todd Frohwirth | .07 | .05 |
| 444 | Craig Worthington | .10 | .08 |
| 445 | Fernando Valenzuela | | |
| | | .09 | .07 |
| 446 | *Joey Belle*(FC) | 2.00 | 1.50 |
| 447 | *Ed Whited*(FC) | .15 | .11 |
| 448 | Dave Smith | .09 | .07 |
| 449 | Dave Clark | .07 | .05 |
| 450 | Juan Agosto | .06 | .05 |
| 451 | Dave Valle | .06 | .05 |
| 452 | Kent Hrbek | .15 | .11 |
| 453 | Von Hayes | .10 | .08 |
| 454 | Gary Gaetti | .15 | .11 |
| 455 | Greg Briley | .20 | .15 |
| 456 | Glenn Braggs | .08 | .06 |
| 457 | Kirt Manwaring | .10 | .08 |
| 458 | Mel Hall | .07 | .05 |
| 459 | Brook Jacoby | .08 | .06 |
| 460 | Pat Sheridan | .06 | .05 |
| 461 | Rob Murphy | .06 | .05 |
| 462 | Jimmy Key | .10 | .08 |

| | | MT | NR MT |
|---|---|---|---|
| 463 | Nick Esasky | .10 | .08 |
| 464 | Rob Ducey | .09 | .07 |
| 465 | Carlos Quintana | .09 | .07 |
| 466 | *Larry Walker*(FC) | | |
| | | 2.00 | 1.50 |
| 467 | Todd Worrell | .10 | .08 |
| 468 | Kevin Gross | .09 | .07 |
| 469 | Terry Pendleton | .09 | .07 |
| 470 | Dave Martinez | .07 | .05 |
| 471 | Gene Larkin | .06 | .05 |
| 472 | Len Dykstra | .09 | .07 |
| 473 | Barry Lyons | .06 | .05 |
| 474 | Terry Mulholland(FC) | | |
| | | .10 | .08 |
| 475 | *Chip Hale*(FC) | .15 | .11 |
| 476 | Jesse Barfield | .08 | .06 |
| 477 | Dan Plesac | .09 | .07 |
| 478a | Scott Garrelts (Photo actually Bill Bathe) | 3.00 | 2.25 |
| 478b | Scott Garrelts (Correct photo) | .10 | .08 |
| 479 | Dave Righetti | .10 | .08 |
| 480 | Gus Polidor(FC) | .06 | .05 |
| 481 | Mookie Wilson | .09 | .07 |
| 482 | Luis Rivera | .06 | .05 |
| 483 | Mike Flanagan | .07 | .05 |
| 484 | Dennis "Oil Can" Boyd | | |
| | | .07 | .05 |
| 485 | John Cerutti | .07 | .05 |
| 486 | John Costello | .07 | .05 |
| 487 | Pascual Perez | .07 | .05 |
| 488 | Tommy Herr | .09 | .07 |
| 489 | Tom Foley | .06 | .05 |
| 490 | Curt Ford | .06 | .05 |
| 491 | Steve Lake | .06 | .05 |
| 492 | Tim Teufel | .06 | .05 |
| 493 | Randy Bush | .06 | .05 |
| 494 | Mike Jackson | .06 | .05 |
| 495 | Steve Jeltz | .06 | .05 |
| 496 | Paul Gibson | .08 | .06 |
| 497 | Steve Balboni | .06 | .05 |
| 498 | Bud Black | .06 | .05 |
| 499 | Dale Sveum | .06 | .05 |
| 500 | Checklist 401-500 | .06 | .05 |
| 501 | Timmy Jones | .06 | .05 |
| 502 | Mark Portugal | .06 | .05 |
| 503 | Ivan Calderon | .07 | .05 |
| 504 | Rick Rhoden | .06 | .05 |
| 505 | Willie McGee | .09 | .07 |
| 506 | Kirk McCaskill | .08 | .06 |
| 507 | Dave LaPoint | .07 | .05 |
| 508 | Jay Howell | .10 | .08 |
| 509 | Johnny Ray | .08 | .06 |
| 510 | Dave Anderson | .06 | .05 |
| 511 | Chuck Crim | .06 | .05 |
| 512 | Joe Hesketh | .06 | .05 |
| 513 | Dennis Eckersley | .10 | .08 |
| 514 | Greg Brock | .08 | .06 |
| 515 | Tim Burke | .08 | .06 |
| 516 | Frank Tanana | .07 | .05 |
| 517 | Jay Bell | .07 | .05 |
| 518 | Guillermo Hernandez | | |
| | | .07 | .05 |
| 519 | Randy Kramer(FC) | .08 | .06 |
| 520 | Charles Hudson | .06 | .05 |
| 521 | Jim Corsi(FC) | .08 | .06 |
| 522 | Steve Rosenberg | .08 | .06 |

| | | MT | NR MT |
|---|---|---|---|
| 523 | Cris Carpenter | .10 | .08 |
| 524 | *Matt Winters*(FC) | .12 | .09 |
| 525 | Melido Perez | .08 | .06 |
| 526 | Chris Gwynn | .08 | .06 |
| 527 | Bert Blyleven | .09 | .07 |
| 528 | Chuck Cary | .07 | .05 |
| 529 | Daryl Boston | .06 | .05 |
| 530 | Dale Mohorcic | .06 | .05 |
| 531 | Geronimo Berroa(FC) | .09 | .07 |
| 532 | Edgar Martinez | .09 | .07 |
| 533 | Dale Murphy | .15 | .11 |
| 534 | Jay Buhner | .09 | .07 |
| 535 | John Smoltz | .15 | .11 |
| 536 | Andy Van Slyke | .15 | .11 |
| 537 | Mike Henneman | .09 | .07 |
| 538 | Miguel Garcia(FC) | .07 | .05 |
| 539 | Frank Williams | .06 | .05 |
| 540 | R.J. Reynolds | .06 | .05 |
| 541 | Shawn Hillegas | .06 | .05 |
| 542 | Walt Weiss | .10 | .08 |
| 543 | *Greg Hibbard*(FC) | .15 | .11 |
| 544 | Nolan Ryan | 1.00 | .70 |
| 545 | *Todd Zeile* | .80 | .60 |
| 546 | Hensley Meulens | .20 | .15 |
| 547 | Tim Belcher | .10 | .08 |
| 548 | Mike Witt | .08 | .06 |
| 549 | Greg Cadaret | .06 | .05 |
| 550 | Franklin Stubbs | .06 | .05 |
| 551 | *Tony Castillo*(FC) | .12 | .09 |
| 552 | Jeff Robinson | .08 | .06 |
| 553 | *Steve Olin*(FC) | .12 | .09 |
| 554 | Alan Trammell | .10 | .08 |
| 555 | Wade Boggs | .50 | .40 |
| 556 | Will Clark | .60 | .45 |
| 557 | Jeff King(FC) | .10 | .08 |
| 558 | Mike Fitzgerald | .06 | .05 |
| 559 | Ken Howell | .06 | .05 |
| 560 | Bob Kipper | .06 | .05 |
| 561 | Scott Bankhead | .09 | .07 |
| 562a | Jeff Innis (Photo actually David West)(FC) | 3.00 | 2.25 |
| 562b | *Jeff Innis* (Corrected)(FC) | .20 | .15 |
| 563 | Randy Johnson | .10 | .08 |
| 564 | *Wally Whithurst* | .10 | .08 |
| 565 | *Gene Harris*(FC) | .10 | .08 |
| 566 | Norm Charlton | .09 | .07 |
| 567 | Robin Yount | .40 | .30 |
| 568 | *Joe Oliver*(FC) | .35 | .25 |
| 569 | Mark Parent | .07 | .05 |
| 570 | John Farrell | .07 | .05 |
| 571 | Tom Glavine | .10 | .08 |
| 572 | Rod Nichols(FC) | .06 | .05 |
| 573 | Jack Morris | .09 | .07 |
| 574 | Greg Swindell | .12 | .09 |
| 575 | Steve Searcy(FC) | .09 | .07 |
| 576 | Ricky Jordan | .20 | .15 |
| 577 | Matt Williams | .35 | .25 |
| 578 | Mike LaValliere | .07 | .05 |
| 579 | Bryn Smith | .08 | .06 |
| 580 | Bruce Ruffin | .06 | .05 |
| 581 | Randy Myers | .08 | .06 |
| 582 | *Rick Wrona*(FC) | .15 | .11 |

| | | MT | NR MT |
|---|---|---|---|
| 583 | Juan Samuel | .09 | .07 |
| 584 | Les Lancaster | .07 | .05 |
| 585 | Jeff Musselman | .07 | .05 |
| 586 | Rob Dibble | .09 | .07 |
| 587 | Eric Show | .07 | .05 |
| 588 | Jesse Orosco | .06 | .05 |
| 589 | Herm Winningham | .06 | .05 |
| 590 | Andy Allanson | .06 | .05 |
| 591 | Dion James | .06 | .05 |
| 592 | Carmelo Martinez | .08 | .06 |
| 593 | Luis Quinones(FC) | .08 | .06 |
| 594 | Dennis Rasmussen | .08 | .06 |
| 595 | Rich Yett | .06 | .05 |
| 596 | Bob Walk | .08 | .06 |
| 597 | Andy McGaffigan | .07 | .05 |
| 598 | Billy Hatcher | .07 | .05 |
| 599 | Bob Knepper | .06 | .05 |
| 600 | Checklist 501-600 | .06 | .05 |
| 601 | Joey Cora(FC) | .10 | .08 |
| 602 | *Steve Finley* | .20 | .15 |
| 603 | Kal Daniels | .10 | .08 |
| 604 | Gregg Olson | .30 | .25 |
| 605 | Dave Steib | .09 | .07 |
| 606 | *Kenny Rogers*(FC) | .15 | .11 |
| 607 | Zane Smith | .06 | .05 |
| 608 | *Bob Geren*(FC) | .15 | .11 |
| 609 | Chad Kreuter | .10 | .08 |
| 610 | Mike Smithson | .06 | .05 |
| 611 | *Jeff Wetherby*(FC) | .15 | .11 |
| 612 | *Gary Mielke*(FC) | .15 | .11 |
| 613 | Pete Smith | .08 | .06 |
| 614 | *Jack Daugherty*(FC) | .15 | .11 |
| 615 | Lance McCullers | .08 | .06 |
| 616 | Don Robinson | .06 | .05 |
| 617 | Jose Guzman | .08 | .06 |
| 618 | Steve Bedrosian | .08 | .06 |
| 619 | Jamie Moyer | .06 | .05 |
| 620 | Atlee Hammaker | .06 | .05 |
| 621 | *Rick Luecken*(FC) | .15 | .11 |
| 622 | Greg W. Harris | .09 | .07 |
| 623 | Pete Harnisch | .10 | .08 |
| 624 | Jerald Clark | .10 | .08 |
| 625 | Jack McDowell | .07 | .05 |
| 626 | Frank Viola | .12 | .09 |
| 627 | Ted Higuera | .09 | .07 |
| 628 | *Marty Pevey*(FC) | .15 | .11 |
| 629 | Bill Wegman | .06 | .05 |
| 630 | Eric Plunk | .06 | .05 |
| 631 | Drew Hall | .06 | .05 |
| 632 | Doug Jones | .08 | .06 |
| 633 | Geno Petralli | .06 | .05 |
| 634 | Jose Alvarez | .06 | .05 |
| 635 | Bob Milacki(FC) | .10 | .08 |
| 636 | Bobby Witt | .07 | .05 |
| 637 | Trevor Wilson | .08 | .06 |
| 638 | Jeff Russell | .08 | .06 |
| 639 | Mike Krukow | .07 | .05 |
| 640 | Rick Leach | .06 | .05 |
| 641 | Dave Schmidt | .06 | .05 |
| 642 | Terry Leach | .06 | .05 |
| 643 | Calvin Schiraldi | .06 | .05 |
| 644 | Bob Melvin | .06 | .05 |

| | | MT | NR MT |
|---|---|---|---|
| 645 | Jim Abbott | .40 | .30 |
| 646 | *Jaime Navarro*(FC) | | |
| | | .30 | .25 |
| 647 | Mark Langston | .10 | .08 |
| 648 | Juan Nieves | .08 | .06 |
| 649 | Damaso Garcia | .06 | .05 |
| 650 | Charlie O'Brien | .06 | .05 |
| 651 | Eric King | .06 | .05 |
| 652 | Mike Boddicker | .08 | .06 |
| 653 | Duan Ward | .07 | .05 |
| 654 | Bob Stanley | .06 | .05 |
| 655 | Sandy Alomar, Jr. | .30 | .25 |
| 656 | Danny Tartabull | .10 | .08 |
| 657 | Randy McCament | .15 | .11 |
| 658 | Charlie Leibrandt | .07 | .05 |
| 659 | Dan Quisenberry | .07 | .05 |
| 660 | Paul Assenmacher | .06 | .05 |
| 661 | Walt Terrell | .07 | .05 |
| 662 | Tim Leary | .07 | .05 |
| 663 | Randy Milligan | .08 | .06 |
| 664 | Bo Diaz | .06 | .05 |
| 665 | Mark Lemke | .07 | .05 |
| 666 | Jose Gonzalez | .08 | .06 |
| 667 | Chuck Finley | .07 | .05 |
| 668 | John Kruk | .08 | .06 |
| 669 | Dick Schofield | .07 | .05 |
| 670 | Tim Crews | .06 | .05 |
| 671 | John Dopson | .09 | .07 |
| 672 | *John Orton*(FC) | .15 | .11 |
| 673 | Eric Hetzel(FC) | .10 | .08 |
| 674 | Lance Parrish | .08 | .06 |
| 675 | Ramon Martinez | .50 | .40 |
| 676 | Mark Gubicza | .10 | .08 |
| 677 | Greg Litton | .20 | .15 |
| 678 | Greg Mathews | .07 | .05 |
| 679 | Dave Dravecky | .07 | .05 |
| 680 | Steve Farr | .07 | .05 |
| 681 | Mike Devereaux | .09 | .07 |
| 682 | Ken Griffey, Sr. | .08 | .06 |
| 683a | *Mickey Weston* (Jamie)(FC) | 4.00 | 3.00 |
| 683b | *Mickey Weston* (corrected)(FC) | .30 | .25 |
| 684 | Jack Armstrong | .07 | .05 |
| 685 | Steve Buechele | .07 | .05 |
| 686 | Bryan Harvey | .07 | .05 |
| 687 | Lance Blankenship | .09 | .07 |
| 688 | Dante Bichette | .09 | .07 |
| 689 | Todd Burns | .09 | .07 |
| 690 | Dan Petry | .06 | .05 |
| 691 | *Kent Anderson*(FC) | | |
| | | .15 | .11 |
| 692 | Todd Stottlemyre | .08 | .06 |
| 693 | Wally Joyner | .15 | .11 |
| 694 | Mike Rochford(FC) | .10 | .08 |
| 695 | Floyd Bannister | .07 | .05 |
| 696 | Rick Reuschel | .09 | .07 |
| 697 | Jose DeLeon | .09 | .07 |
| 698 | Jeff Montgomery | .08 | .06 |
| 699 | Jeff Montgomery | .08 | .06 |
| 700a | Checklist 601-700 (Jamie Weston) | 4.00 | 3.00 |
| 700b | Checklist 601-700 (Mickey Weston) | .10 | .08 |
| 701 | Jim Gott | .10 | .08 |
| 702 | "Rookie Threats" (Delino DeShields, Larry Walker, Marquis Grissom) | .60 | .45 |
| 703 | Alejandro Pena | .10 | .08 |
| 704 | Willie Randolph | .12 | .09 |
| 705 | Tim Leary | .10 | .08 |
| 706 | Chuck McElroy(FC) | .20 | .15 |
| 707 | Gerald Perry | .10 | .08 |
| 708 | Tom Brunansky | .12 | .09 |
| 709 | John Franco | .15 | .11 |
| 710 | Mark Davis | .10 | .08 |
| 711 | Dave Justice(FC) | 6.00 | 4.50 |
| 712 | Storm Davis | .10 | .08 |
| 713 | Scott Ruskin(FC) | .20 | .15 |
| 714 | Glenn Braggs | .10 | .08 |
| 715 | Kevin Bearse(FC) | .20 | .15 |
| 716 | Jose Nunez(FC) | .15 | .11 |
| 717 | Tim Layana(FC) | .20 | .15 |
| 718 | Greg Myers(FC) | .12 | .09 |
| 719 | Pete O'Brien | .10 | .08 |
| 720 | John Candelaria | .10 | .08 |
| 721 | Craig Grebeck(FC) | .25 | .20 |
| 722 | Shawn Boskie(FC) | .30 | .25 |
| 723 | Jim Leyritz(FC) | .20 | .15 |
| 724 | Bill Sampen(FC) | .30 | .25 |
| 725 | Scott Radinsky(FC) | .35 | .25 |
| 726 | Todd Hundley(FC) | .30 | .25 |
| 727 | Scott Hemond(FC) | .20 | .15 |
| 728 | Lenny Webster(FC) | .25 | .20 |
| 729 | Jeff Reardon | .12 | .09 |
| 730 | Mitch Webster | .10 | .08 |
| 731 | Brian Bohanon(FC) | .25 | .20 |
| 732 | Rick Parker(FC) | .20 | .15 |
| 733 | Terry Shumpert(FC) | .25 | .20 |
| 734a | 6th No-Hitter (Nolan Ryan) (with 300 win stripe) | 2.00 | 1.50 |
| 734b | 6th No-Hitter (Nolan Ryan) (without stripe) | 8.00 | 6.00 |
| 735 | John Burkett(FC) | .40 | .30 |
| 736 | Derrick May(FC) | .80 | .60 |
| 737 | Carlos Baerga(FC) | 3.00 | 2.25 |
| 738 | Greg Smith(FC) | .15 | .11 |
| 739 | Joe Kraemer(FC) | .15 | .11 |
| 740 | Scott Sanderson | .10 | .08 |
| 741 | Hector Villanueva(FC) | | |
| | | .30 | .25 |
| 742 | Mike Fetters(FC) | .25 | .20 |
| 743 | Mark Gardner(FC) | .30 | .25 |
| 744 | Matt Nokes | .10 | .08 |
| 745 | Dave Winfield | .20 | .15 |
| 746 | Delino DeShields(FC) | | |
| | | 1.00 | .70 |
| 747 | Dann Howitt(FC) | .20 | .15 |
| 748 | Tony Pena | .12 | .09 |
| 749 | Oil Can Boyd | .12 | .09 |
| 750 | Mike Benjamin(FC) | .25 | .20 |
| 751 | Alex Cole(FC) | .80 | .60 |
| 752 | Eric Gunderson(FC) | .20 | .15 |
| 753 | Howard Farmer(FC) | .25 | .20 |
| 754 | Joe Carter | .15 | .11 |
| 755 | Ray Lankford(FC) | 2.50 | 2.00 |
| 756 | Sandy Alomar,Jr. | .40 | .30 |
| 757 | Alex Sanchez(FC) | .15 | .11 |
| 758 | Nick Esasky | .10 | .08 |
| 759 | Stan Belinda(FC) | .20 | .15 |
| 760 | Jim Presley | .10 | .08 |
| 761 | Gary DiSarcina(FC) | .20 | .15 |
| 762 | Wayne Edwards(FC) | .20 | .15 |

| | | MT | NR MT |
|---|---|---|---|
| 763 | Pat Combs(FC) | .20 | .15 |
| 764 | Mickey Pina(FC) | .20 | .15 |
| 765 | Wilson Alvarez(FC) | .50 | .40 |
| 766 | Dave Parker | .15 | .11 |
| 767 | Mike Blowers(FC) | .20 | .15 |
| 768 | Tony Phillips | .10 | .08 |
| 769 | Pascual Perez | .10 | .08 |
| 770 | Gary Pettis | .10 | .08 |
| 771 | Fred Lynn | .10 | .08 |
| 772 | Mel Rojas(FC) | .20 | .15 |
| 773 | David Segui(FC) | .30 | .25 |
| 774 | Gary Carter | .15 | .11 |
| 775 | Rafael Valdez(FC) | .15 | .11 |
| 776 | Glenallen Hill(FC) | .15 | .11 |
| 777 | Keith Hernandez | .12 | .09 |
| 778 | Billy Hatcher | .12 | .09 |
| 779 | Marty Clary(FC) | .10 | .08 |
| 780 | Candy Maldonado | .12 | .09 |
| 781 | Mike Marshall | .10 | .08 |
| 782 | Billy Jo Robidoux(FC) | | |
| | | .10 | .08 |
| 783 | Mark Langston | .12 | .09 |
| 784 | Paul Sorrento(FC) | .25 | .20 |
| 785 | Dave Hollins(FC) | 1.50 | 1.25 |
| 786 | Cecil Fielder | .50 | .40 |
| 787 | Matt Young | .10 | .08 |
| 788 | Jeff Huson | .15 | .11 |
| 789 | Lloyd Moseby | .12 | .09 |
| 790 | Ron Kittle | .12 | .09 |
| 791 | Hubie Brooks | .12 | .09 |
| 792 | Craig Lefferts | .10 | .08 |
| 793 | Kevin Bass | .10 | .08 |
| 794 | Bryn Smith | .10 | .08 |
| 795 | Juan Samuel | .12 | .09 |
| 796 | Sam Horn(FC) | .15 | .11 |
| 797 | Randy Myers | .12 | .09 |
| 798 | Chris James | .10 | .08 |
| 799 | Bill Gullickson | .10 | .08 |
| 800 | Checklist 701-800 | .10 | .08 |

## 1991 Upper Deck

115 rookies are included among the first 700 cards in the 1991 Upper Deck set. A 100-card high # series was once again planned for release in July or August. The 1991 Upper Deck cards feature high quality white stock and color photos on both the front and backs of the cards. A nine-card "Baseball Heroes" bonus set honoring Nolan Ryan, is among the many insert specials

in the 1991 Upper Deck set. Others include a card of Chicago Bulls superstar Michael Jordan. Along with the Ryan bonus cards, 2,500 limited-edition cards personally autographed and numbered by Ryan will be randomly inserted. Upper Deck cards are packaged in tamper-proof foil packs. Each pack contains 15 cards and a 3-D team logo hologram sticker. The 1991 hologram stickers are full size.

| | | MT | NR MT |
|---|---|---|---|
| Complete Set: 1-700 | | 15.00 | 11.00 |
| Common Player: 1-700 | | .05 | .04 |
| Complete Set: 1-800 | | 40.00 | 30.00 |
| Common Player: 701-800 | | .10 | .08 |
| 1 | Star Rookie Checklist | | |
| | | .05 | .04 |
| 2 | Star Rookie (Phil Plantier)(FC) | 1.00 | .70 |
| 3 | Star Rookie (D.J. Dozier)(FC) | .40 | .30 |
| 4 | Star Rookie (Dave Hansen)(FC) | .25 | .20 |
| 5 | Star Rookie (Maurice Vaughn)(FC) | .70 | .50 |
| 6 | Star Rookie (Leo Gomez)(FC) | .60 | .45 |
| 7 | Star Rookie (Scott Aldred)(FC) | .25 | .20 |
| 8 | Star Rookie (Scott Chiamparino)(FC) | .30 | .25 |
| 9 | Star Rookie (Lance Dickson)(FC) | .30 | .25 |
| 10 | Star Rookie (Sean Berry)(FC) | .20 | .15 |
| 11 | Star Rookie (Bernie Williams)(FC) | .70 | .50 |
| 12 | Star Rookie (Brian Barnes)(FC) | .30 | .25 |
| 13 | Star Rookie (Narciso Elvira)(FC) | .20 | .15 |
| 14 | Star Rookie (Mike Gardiner)(FC) | .30 | .25 |
| 15 | Star Rookie (Greg Colbrunn)(FC) | .20 | .15 |
| 16 | Star Rookie (Bernard Gilkey)(FC) | .50 | .40 |
| 17 | Star Rookie (Mark Lewis)(FC) | .70 | .50 |
| 18 | Star Rookie (Mickey Morandini)(FC) | .15 | .11 |
| 19 | Star Rookie (Charles Nagy)(FC) | .60 | .45 |
| 20 | Star Rookie (Geronimo Pena)(FC) | .25 | .20 |
| 21 | Star Rookie (Henry Rodriguez)(FC) | .50 | .40 |
| 22 | Star Rookie (Scott Cooper)(FC) | .20 | .15 |
| 23 | Star Rookie (Andujar | | |

| | | MT | NR MT |
|---|---|---|---|
| | *Cedeno)*(FC) | .60 | .45 |
| 24 | Star Rookie *(Eric Karros)*(FC) | 2.50 | 2.00 |
| 25 | Star Rookie *(Steve Decker)*(FC) | .25 | .20 |
| 26 | Star Rookie *(Kevin Belcher)*(FC) | .20 | .15 |
| 27 | Star Rookie *(Jeff Conine)*(FC) | .20 | .15 |
| 28 | Oakland Athletics Checklist | .10 | .08 |
| 29 | Chicago White Sox Checklist | .08 | .06 |
| 30 | Texas Rangers Checklist | .08 | .06 |
| 31 | California Angels Checklist | .08 | .06 |
| 32 | Seattle Mariners Checklist | .10 | .08 |
| 33 | Kansas City Royals Checklist | .10 | .08 |
| 34 | Minnesota Twins Checklist | .08 | .06 |
| 35 | Scott Leius(FC) | .10 | .08 |
| 36 | Neal Heaton | .06 | .05 |
| 37 | *Terry Lee*(FC) | .20 | .15 |
| 38 | Gary Redus | .05 | .04 |
| 39 | Barry Jones | .06 | .05 |
| 40 | Chuck Knoblauch(FC) | 1.75 | 1.25 |
| 41 | Larry Andersen | .05 | .04 |
| 43 | Darryl Hamilton | .06 | .05 |
| 44 | Toronto Blue Jays Checklist | .08 | .06 |
| 45 | Detroit Tigers Checklist | .10 | .08 |
| 46 | Cleveland Indians Checklist | .08 | .06 |
| 47 | Baltimore Orioles Checklist | .08 | .06 |
| 48 | Milwaukee Brewers Checklist | .08 | .06 |
| 49 | New York Yankees Checklist | .08 | .06 |
| 50 | Top Prospect Checklist | .05 | .04 |
| 51 | Top Prospect (Kyle Abbott)(FC) | .25 | .20 |
| 52 | Top Prospect (Jeff Juden)(FC) | .25 | .20 |
| 53 | Top Prospect *(Todd Van Poppel)*(FC) | 1.00 | .70 |
| 54 | Top Prospect *(Steve Karsay)*(FC) | .40 | .30 |
| 55 | Top Prospect *(Chipper Jones)*(FC) | 1.25 | .90 |
| 56 | Top Prospect *(Chris Johnson)*(FC) | .25 | .20 |
| 57 | Top Prospect *(John Ericks)*(FC) | .25 | .20 |
| 58 | Top Prospect *(Gary Scott)*(FC) | .50 | .40 |
| 59 | Top Prospect (Kiki Jones)(FC) | .50 | .40 |
| 60 | Top Prospect *(Wilfredo Cordero)*(FC) | .80 | .60 |
| 61 | Top Prospect *(Royce Clayton)*(FC) | .80 | .60 |
| 62 | Top Prospect *(Tim Costo)*(FC) | .30 | .25 |
| 63 | Top Prospect (Roger Salkeld)(FC) | .40 | .30 |
| 64 | Top Prospect *(Brook Fordyce)*(FC) | .25 | .20 |
| 65 | Top Prospect *(Mike Mussina)*(FC) | 2.50 | 2.00 |
| 66 | Top Prospect *(Dave Staton)*(FC) | .40 | .30 |
| 67 | Top Prospect *(Mike Lieberthal)*(FC) | .30 | .25 |
| 68 | Top Prospect *(Kurt Miller)*(FC) | .30 | .25 |
| 69 | Top Prospect *(Dan Peltier)*(FC) | .25 | .20 |
| 70 | Top Prospect (Greg Blosser)(FC) | .40 | .30 |
| 71 | Top Prospect *(Reggie Sanders)*(FC) | 2.50 | 2.00 |
| 72 | Top Prospect (Brent Mayne)(FC) | .15 | .11 |
| 73 | Top Prospect *(Rico Brogna)*(FC) | .35 | .25 |
| 74 | Top Prospect *(Willie Banks)*(FC) | .40 | .30 |
| 75 | Top Prospect *(Len Brutcher)*(FC) | .25 | .20 |
| 76 | Top Prospect *(Pat Kelly)*(FC) | .30 | .25 |
| 77 | Cincinnati Reds Checklist | .08 | .06 |
| 78 | Los Angeles Dodgers Checklist | .08 | .06 |
| 79 | San Francisco Giants Checklist | .08 | .06 |
| 80 | San Diego Padres Checklist | .08 | .06 |
| 81 | Houston Astros Checklist | .08 | .06 |
| 82 | Atlanta Braves Checklist | .10 | .08 |
| 83 | "Fielder's Feat" | .20 | .15 |
| 84 | *Orlando Merced*(FC) | .60 | .45 |
| 85 | Domingo Ramos | .05 | .04 |
| 86 | Tom Bolton | .05 | .04 |
| 87 | *Andres Santana*(FC) | .20 | .15 |
| 88 | John Dopson | .05 | .04 |
| 89 | Kenny Williams | .05 | .04 |
| 90 | Marty Barrett | .06 | .05 |
| 91 | Tom Pagnozzi | .06 | .05 |
| 92 | Carmelo Martinez | .06 | .05 |
| 93 | "Save Master" | .10 | .08 |
| 94 | Pittsburgh Pirates Checklist | .10 | .08 |
| 95 | New York Mets Checklist | .10 | .08 |
| 96 | Montreal Expos Checklist | .08 | .06 |
| 97 | Philadelphia Phillies Checklist | .08 | .06 |
| 98 | St. Louis Cardinals Checklist | .08 | .06 |
| 99 | Chicago Cubs Checklist | | |

| | | MT | NR MT | | | | MT | NR MT |
|---|---|---|---|---|---|---|---|---|
| | | .10 | .08 | | 166 | Kal Daniels | .10 | .08 |
| 100 | Checklist 1-100 | .05 | .04 | | 167 | Kent Hrbek | .12 | .09 |
| 101 | Kevin Elster | .06 | .05 | | 168 | Franklin Stubbs | .06 | .05 |
| 102 | Tom Brookens | .05 | .04 | | 169 | Dick Schofield | .05 | .04 |
| 103 | Mackey Sasser | .08 | .06 | | 170 | Junior Ortiz | .05 | .04 |
| 104 | Felix Fermin | .05 | .04 | | 171 | *Hector Villanueva* | .20 | .15 |
| 105 | Kevin McReynolds | .12 | .09 | | 172 | Dennis Eckersley | .15 | .11 |
| 106 | Dave Steib | .12 | .09 | | 173 | Mitch Williams | .08 | .06 |
| 107 | Jeffrey Leonard | .06 | .05 | | 174 | Mark McGwire | .35 | .25 |
| 108 | Dave Henderson | .08 | .06 | | 175 | Fernando Valenzuela | | |
| 109 | Sid Bream | .06 | .05 | | | | .10 | .08 |
| 110 | Henry Cotto | .05 | .04 | | 176 | Gary Carter | .10 | .08 |
| 111 | Shawon Dunston | .12 | .09 | | 177 | Dave Magadan | .10 | .08 |
| 112 | Mariano Duncan | .08 | .06 | | 178 | Robby Thompson | .08 | .06 |
| 113 | Joe Girardi | .08 | .06 | | 179 | Bob Ojeda | .05 | .04 |
| 114 | Billy Hatcher | .08 | .06 | | 180 | Ken Caminiti | .06 | .05 |
| 115 | Greg Maddux | .12 | .09 | | 181 | Don Slaught | .05 | .04 |
| 116 | Jerry Browne | .08 | .06 | | 182 | Luis Rivera | .05 | .04 |
| 117 | Juan Samuel | .08 | .06 | | 183 | Jay Bell | .06 | .05 |
| 118 | Steve Olin | .06 | .05 | | 184 | Jody Reed | .08 | .06 |
| 119 | Alfredo Griffin | .06 | .05 | | 185 | Wally Backman | .06 | .05 |
| 120 | Mitch Webster | .06 | .05 | | 186 | Dave Martinez | .06 | .05 |
| 121 | Joel Skinner | .05 | .04 | | 187 | Luis Polonia | .05 | .04 |
| 122 | Frank Viola | .15 | .11 | | 188 | Shane Mack | .06 | .05 |
| 123 | Cory Snyder | .10 | .08 | | 189 | Spike Owen | .05 | .04 |
| 124 | Howard Johnson | .12 | .09 | | 190 | Scott Bailes | .05 | .04 |
| 125 | *Carlos Baerga* | .60 | .45 | | 191 | John Russell | .05 | .04 |
| 126 | Tony Fernandez | .12 | .09 | | 192 | Walt Weiss | .08 | .06 |
| 127 | Dave Stewart | .15 | .11 | | 193 | Jose Oquendo | .06 | .05 |
| 128 | Jay Buhner | .08 | .06 | | 194 | Carney Lansford | .08 | .06 |
| 129 | Mike LaValliere | .06 | .05 | | 195 | Jeff Huson | .08 | .06 |
| 130 | Scott Bradley | .05 | .04 | | 196 | Keith Miller | .06 | .05 |
| 131 | Tony Phillips | .06 | .05 | | 197 | Eric Yelding | .10 | .08 |
| 132 | Ryne Sandberg | .20 | .15 | | 198 | Ron Darling | .06 | .05 |
| 133 | Paul O'Neill | .08 | .06 | | 199 | John Kruk | .06 | .05 |
| 134 | Mark Grace | .15 | .11 | | 200 | Checklist 101-200 | .05 | .04 |
| 135 | Chris Sabo | .12 | .09 | | 201 | John Shelby | .05 | .04 |
| 136 | Ramon Martinez | .20 | .15 | | 202 | Bob Geren | .06 | .05 |
| 137 | Brook Jacoby | .08 | .06 | | 203 | Lance McCullers | .05 | .04 |
| 138 | Candy Maldonado | .08 | .06 | | 204 | Alvaro Espinoza | .06 | .05 |
| 139 | Mike Scioscia | .08 | .06 | | 205 | Mark Salas | .05 | .04 |
| 140 | Chris James | .08 | .06 | | 206 | Mike Pagliarulo | .06 | .05 |
| 141 | Craig Worthington | .08 | .06 | | 207 | Jose Uribe | .06 | .05 |
| 142 | Manny Lee | .06 | .05 | | 208 | Jim Deshaies | .06 | .05 |
| 143 | Tim Raines | .15 | .11 | | 209 | Ron Karkovice | .05 | .04 |
| 144 | Sandy Alomar, Jr. | .15 | .11 | | 210 | Rafael Ramirez | .05 | .04 |
| 145 | John Olerud | .40 | .30 | | 211 | Donnie Hill | .05 | .04 |
| 146 | *Ozzie Canseco* | .15 | .11 | | 212 | Brian Harper | .08 | .06 |
| 147 | Pat Borders | .06 | .05 | | 213 | Jack Howell | .05 | .04 |
| 148 | Harold Reynolds | .10 | .08 | | 214 | Wes Gardner | .05 | .04 |
| 149 | Tom Henke | .08 | .06 | | 215 | Tim Burke | .08 | .06 |
| 150 | R.J. Reynolds | .05 | .04 | | 216 | Doug Jones | .08 | .06 |
| 151 | Mike Gallego | .05 | .04 | | 217 | Hubie Brooks | .10 | .08 |
| 152 | Bobby Bonilla | .20 | .15 | | 218 | Tom Candiotti | .06 | .05 |
| 153 | Terry Steinbach | .06 | .05 | | 219 | Gerald Perry | .06 | .05 |
| 154 | Barry Bonds | .20 | .15 | | 220 | Jose DeLeon | .06 | .05 |
| 155 | Jose Canseco | .50 | .40 | | 221 | Wally Whitehurst | .08 | .06 |
| 156 | Gregg Jefferies | .15 | .11 | | 222 | *Alan Mills*(FC) | .15 | .11 |
| 157 | Matt Williams | .20 | .15 | | 223 | Alan Trammell | .12 | .09 |
| 158 | Craig Biggio | .08 | .06 | | 224 | Dwight Gooden | .25 | .20 |
| 159 | Daryl Boston | .05 | .04 | | 225 | *Travis Fryman*(FC) | | |
| 160 | Ricky Jordan | .08 | .06 | | | | 1.50 | 1.25 |
| 161 | Stan Belinda | .20 | .15 | | 226 | Joe Carter | .10 | .08 |
| 162 | Ozzie Smith | .10 | .08 | | 227 | Julio Franco | .10 | .08 |
| 163 | Tom Brunansky | .08 | .06 | | 228 | Craig Lefferts | .06 | .05 |
| 164 | Todd Zeile | .30 | .25 | | 229 | Gary Pettis | .06 | .05 |
| 165 | Mike Greenwell | .15 | .11 | | 230 | Dennis Rasmussen | .06 | .05 |

| | | MT | NR MT | | | | MT | NR MT |
|---|---|---|---|---|---|---|---|---|
| 231 | Brian Downing | .06 | .05 | | 296 | Mickey Tettleton | .06 | .05 |
| 232 | Carlos Quintana | .10 | .08 | | 297 | Luis Sojo(FC) | .15 | .11 |
| 233 | Gary Gaetti | .12 | .09 | | 298 | Jose Rijo | .08 | .06 |
| 234 | Mark Langston | .15 | .11 | | 299 | Dave Johnson | .06 | .05 |
| 235 | Tim Wallach | .10 | .08 | | 300 | Checklist 201-300 | .05 | .04 |
| 236 | Greg Swindell | .10 | .08 | | 301 | Mark Grant | .05 | .04 |
| 237 | Eddie Murray | .15 | .11 | | 302 | Pete Harnisch | .08 | .06 |
| 238 | Jeff Manto(FC) | .20 | .15 | | 303 | Greg Olson(FC) | .10 | .08 |
| 239 | Lenny Harris | .08 | .06 | | 304 | *Anthony Telford*(FC) | | |
| 240 | Jesse Orosco | .05 | .04 | | | | .15 | .11 |
| 241 | Scott Lusader | .05 | .04 | | 305 | Lonnie Smith | .06 | .05 |
| 242 | Sid Fernandez | .08 | .06 | | 306 | *Chris Hoiles*(FC) | .50 | .40 |
| 243 | *Jim Leyritz* | .25 | .20 | | 307 | Bryn Smith | .06 | .05 |
| 244 | Cecil Fielder | .20 | .15 | | 308 | Mike Devereaux | .06 | .05 |
| 245 | Darryl Strawberry | .25 | .20 | | 309 | Milt Thompson | .06 | .05 |
| 246 | Frank Thomas(FC) | 4.00 | 3.00 | | 310 | Bob Melvin | .05 | .04 |
| 247 | Kevin Mitchell | .20 | .15 | | 311 | Luis Salazar | .05 | .04 |
| 248 | Lance Johnson | .06 | .05 | | 312 | Ed Whitson | .06 | .05 |
| 249 | Rick Rueschel | .08 | .06 | | 313 | Charlie Hough | .06 | .05 |
| 250 | Mark Portugal | .05 | .04 | | 314 | Dave Clark | .05 | .04 |
| 251 | Derek Lilliquist | .06 | .05 | | 315 | *Eric Gunderson* | .15 | .11 |
| 252 | Brian Holman | .08 | .06 | | 316 | Dan Petry | .05 | .04 |
| 253 | Rafael Valdez | .08 | .06 | | 317 | Dante Bichette | .08 | .06 |
| 254 | B.J. Surhoff | .06 | .05 | | 318 | Mike Heath | .05 | .04 |
| 255 | Tony Gwynn | .15 | .11 | | 319 | Damon Berryhill | .06 | .05 |
| 256 | Andy Van Slyke | .12 | .09 | | 320 | Walt Terrell | .05 | .04 |
| 257 | Todd Stottlemyre | .08 | .06 | | 321 | Scott Fletcher | .05 | .04 |
| 258 | Jose Lind | .06 | .05 | | 322 | Dan Plesac | .08 | .06 |
| 259 | Greg Myers | .06 | .05 | | 323 | Jack McDowell | .08 | .06 |
| 260 | Jeff Ballard | .06 | .05 | | 324 | Paul Molitor | .12 | .09 |
| 261 | Bobby Thigpen | .10 | .08 | | 325 | Ozzie Guillen | .10 | .08 |
| 262 | *Jimmy Kremers*(FC) | | | | 326 | Gregg Olson | .10 | .08 |
| | | .15 | .11 | | 327 | Pedro Guerrero | .10 | .08 |
| 263 | Robin Ventura | .30 | .25 | | 328 | Bob Milacki | .06 | .05 |
| 264 | John Smoltz | .10 | .08 | | 329 | John Tudor | .08 | .06 |
| 265 | Sammy Sosa | .20 | .15 | | 330 | Steve Finley | .08 | .06 |
| 266 | Gary Sheffield | .15 | .11 | | 331 | Jack Clark | .10 | .08 |
| 267 | Lenny Dykstra | .10 | .08 | | 332 | Jerome Walton | .15 | .11 |
| 268 | Bill Spiers | .06 | .05 | | 333 | Andy Hawkins | .06 | .05 |
| 269 | Charlie Hayes | .08 | .06 | | 334 | Derrick May | .20 | .15 |
| 270 | Brett Butler | .08 | .06 | | 335 | Roberto Alomar | .10 | .08 |
| 271 | Bip Roberts | .08 | .06 | | 336 | Jack Morris | .08 | .06 |
| 272 | Rob Deer | .06 | .05 | | 337 | Dave Winfield | .15 | .11 |
| 273 | Fred Lynn | .08 | .06 | | 338 | Steve Searcy | .08 | .06 |
| 274 | Dave Parker | .15 | .11 | | 339 | Chili Davis | .08 | .06 |
| 275 | Andy Benes | .10 | .08 | | 340 | Larry Sheets | .06 | .05 |
| 276 | Glenallen Hill | .08 | .06 | | 341 | Ted Higuera | .08 | .06 |
| 277 | *Steve Howard*(FC) | | | | 342 | *David Segui* | .30 | .25 |
| | | .12 | .09 | | 343 | Greg Cadaret | .05 | .04 |
| 278 | Doug Drabek | .10 | .08 | | 344 | Robin Yount | .15 | .11 |
| 279 | Joe Oliver | .08 | .06 | | 345 | Nolan Ryan | .30 | .25 |
| 280 | Todd Benzinger | .06 | .05 | | 346 | *Ray Lankford* | .80 | .60 |
| 281 | Eric King | .06 | .05 | | 347 | Cal Ripken, Jr. | .15 | .11 |
| 282 | Jim Presley | .06 | .05 | | 348 | Lee Smith | .08 | .06 |
| 283 | Ken Patterson(FC) | .06 | .05 | | 349 | Brady Anderson | .05 | .04 |
| 284 | Jack Daugherty | .06 | .05 | | 350 | Frank DiPino | .05 | .04 |
| 285 | Ivan Calderon | .10 | .08 | | 351 | Hal Morris | .30 | .25 |
| 286 | *Edgar Diaz*(FC) | .10 | .08 | | 352 | Deion Sanders | .10 | .08 |
| 287 | Kevin Bass | .08 | .06 | | 353 | Barry Larkin | .10 | .08 |
| 288 | Don Carman | .06 | .05 | | 354 | Don Mattingly | .35 | .25 |
| 289 | Greg Brock | .06 | .05 | | 355 | Eric Davis | .20 | .15 |
| 290 | John Franco | .10 | .08 | | 356 | Jose Offerman | .30 | .25 |
| 291 | Joey Cora | .06 | .05 | | 357 | *Mel Rojas* | .12 | .09 |
| 292 | Bill Wegman | .06 | .05 | | 358 | Rudy Seanez(FC) | .10 | .08 |
| 293 | Eric Show | .06 | .05 | | 359 | Oil Can Boyd | .06 | .05 |
| 294 | Scott Bankhead | .08 | .06 | | 360 | Nelson Liriano | .05 | .04 |
| 295 | Garry Templeton | .06 | .05 | | 361 | Ron Gant | .15 | .11 |

| # | Player | MT | NR MT |
|---|---|---|---|
| 362 | *Howard Farmer* | .15 | .11 |
| 363 | David Justice | 1.00 | .70 |
| 364 | Delino DeShields | .30 | .25 |
| 365 | Steve Avery | .25 | .20 |
| 366 | David Cone | .12 | .09 |
| 367 | Lou Whitaker | .10 | .08 |
| 368 | Von Hayes | .10 | .08 |
| 369 | Frank Tanana | .06 | .05 |
| 370 | Tim Teufel | .05 | .04 |
| 371 | Randy Myers | .10 | .08 |
| 372 | Roberto Kelly | .10 | .08 |
| 373 | Jack Armstrong | .08 | .06 |
| 374 | Kelly Gruber | .10 | .08 |
| 375 | Kevin Maas | .50 | .40 |
| 376 | Randy Johnson | .10 | .08 |
| 377 | David West | .06 | .05 |
| 378 | *Brent Knackert*(FC) | .12 | .09 |
| 379 | Rick Honeycutt | .05 | .04 |
| 380 | Kevin Gross | .08 | .06 |
| 381 | Tom Foley | .05 | .04 |
| 382 | Jeff Blauser | .06 | .05 |
| 383 | *Scott Ruskin* | .15 | .11 |
| 384 | Andres Thomas | .05 | .04 |
| 385 | Dennis Martinez | .08 | .06 |
| 386 | Mike Henneman | .08 | .06 |
| 387 | Felix Jose | .15 | .11 |
| 388 | Alejandro Pena | .05 | .04 |
| 389 | Chet Lemon | .06 | .05 |
| 390 | *Craig Wilson*(FC) | .20 | .15 |
| 391 | Chuck Crim | .05 | .04 |
| 392 | Mel Hall | .06 | .05 |
| 393 | Mark Knudson | .05 | .04 |
| 394 | Norm Charlton | .08 | .06 |
| 395 | Mike Felder | .05 | .04 |
| 396 | *Tim Layana* | .15 | .11 |
| 397 | *Steve Frey*(FC) | .06 | .05 |
| 398 | Bill Doran | .08 | .06 |
| 399 | Dion James | .05 | .04 |
| 400 | Checklist 301-400 | .05 | .04 |
| 401 | Ron Hassey | .05 | .04 |
| 402 | Don Robinson | .06 | .05 |
| 403 | Gene Nelson | .05 | .04 |
| 404 | Terry Kennedy | .05 | .04 |
| 405 | Todd Burns | .05 | .04 |
| 406 | Roger McDowell | .08 | .06 |
| 407 | Bob Kipper | .05 | .04 |
| 408 | Darren Daulton | .08 | .06 |
| 409 | Chuck Cary | .06 | .05 |
| 410 | Bruce Ruffin | .05 | .04 |
| 411 | Juan Berenguer | .05 | .04 |
| 412 | Gary Ward | .05 | .04 |
| 413 | Al Newman | .05 | .04 |
| 414 | Danny Jackson | .08 | .06 |
| 415 | Greg Gagne | .06 | .05 |
| 416 | Tom Herr | .06 | .05 |
| 417 | Jeff Parrett | .06 | .05 |
| 418 | Jeff Reardon | .08 | .06 |
| 419 | Mark Lemke | .06 | .05 |
| 420 | Charlie O'Brien | .05 | .04 |
| 421 | Willie Randolph | .08 | .06 |
| 422 | Steve Bedrosian | .08 | .06 |
| 423 | Mike Moore | .08 | .06 |
| 424 | Jeff Brantley | .08 | .06 |
| 425 | Bob Welch | .10 | .08 |
| 426 | Terry Mulholland | .08 | .06 |
| 427 | *Willie Blair*(FC) | .15 | .11 |

| # | Player | MT | NR MT |
|---|---|---|---|
| 428 | Darrin Fletcher(FC) | .10 | .08 |
| 429 | Mike Witt | .06 | .05 |
| 430 | Joe Boever | .05 | .04 |
| 431 | Tom Gordon | .12 | .09 |
| 432 | *Pedro Munoz*(FC) | 1.00 | .70 |
| 433 | Kevin Seitzer | .10 | .08 |
| 434 | Kevin Tapani | .15 | .11 |
| 435 | Bret Saberhagen | .12 | .09 |
| 436 | Ellis Burks | .20 | .15 |
| 437 | Chuck Finley | .10 | .08 |
| 438 | Mike Boddicker | .08 | .06 |
| 439 | Francisco Cabrera | .08 | .06 |
| 440 | *Todd Hundley* | .25 | .20 |
| 441 | Kelly Downs | .06 | .05 |
| 442 | *Dann Howitt*(FC) | .15 | .11 |
| 443 | Scott Garrelts | .08 | .06 |
| 444 | Rickey Henderson | .40 | .30 |
| 445 | Will Clark | .40 | .30 |
| 446 | Ben McDonald | .50 | .40 |
| 447 | Dale Murphy | .12 | .09 |
| 448 | Dave Righetti | .10 | .08 |
| 449 | Dickie Thon | .05 | .04 |
| 450 | Ted Power | .05 | .04 |
| 451 | Scott Coolbaugh | .08 | .06 |
| 452 | Dwight Smith | .08 | .06 |
| 453 | Pete Incaviglia | .08 | .06 |
| 454 | Andre Dawson | .15 | .11 |
| 455 | Ruben Sierra | .20 | .15 |
| 456 | Andres Galarraga | .10 | .08 |
| 457 | Alvin Davis | .10 | .08 |
| 458 | Tony Castillo | .06 | .05 |
| 459 | Pete O'Brien | .06 | .05 |
| 460 | Charlie Leibrandt | .06 | .05 |
| 461 | Vince Coleman | .10 | .08 |
| 462 | Steve Sax | .10 | .08 |
| 463 | *Omar Oliveras*(FC) | .15 | .11 |
| 464 | *Oscar Azocar*(FC) | .20 | .15 |
| 465 | Joe Magrane | .08 | .06 |
| 466 | *Karl Rhodes*(FC) | .30 | .25 |
| 467 | Benito Santiago | .10 | .08 |
| 468 | *Joe Klink*(FC) | .10 | .08 |
| 469 | Sil Campusano | .05 | .04 |
| 470 | Mark Parent | .05 | .04 |
| 471 | *Shawn Boskie* | .20 | .15 |
| 472 | Kevin Brown | .10 | .08 |
| 473 | Rick Sutcliffe | .08 | .06 |
| 474 | Rafael Palmeiro | .12 | .09 |
| 475 | Mike Harkey | .10 | .08 |
| 476 | Jaime Navarro | .15 | .11 |
| 477 | Marquis Grissom | .20 | .15 |
| 478 | Marty Clary | .05 | .04 |
| 479 | Greg Briley | .10 | .08 |
| 480 | Tom Glavine | .08 | .06 |
| 481 | Lee Guetterman | .05 | .04 |
| 482 | Rex Hudler | .06 | .05 |
| 483 | Dave LaPoint | .06 | .05 |
| 484 | Terry Pendleton | .08 | .06 |
| 485 | Jesse Barfield | .08 | .06 |
| 486 | Jose DeJesus | .08 | .06 |
| 487 | *Paul Abbott*(FC) | .15 | .11 |
| 488 | Ken Howell | .06 | .05 |
| 489 | Greg W. Harris | .05 | .05 |
| 490 | Roy Smith | .05 | .04 |
| 491 | Paul Assenmacher | .05 | .04 |

| | | MT | NR MT |
|---|---|---|---|
| 492 | Geno Petralli | .05 | .04 |
| 493 | Steve Wilson | .08 | .06 |
| 494 | Kevin Reimer(FC) | .08 | .06 |
| 495 | Bill Long | .05 | .04 |
| 496 | Mike Jackson | .06 | .05 |
| 497 | Oddibe McDowell | .06 | .05 |
| 498 | Bill Swift | .06 | .05 |
| 499 | Jeff Treadway | .06 | .05 |
| 500 | Checklist 401-500 | .05 | .04 |
| 501 | Gene Larkin | .06 | .05 |
| 502 | Bob Boone | .08 | .06 |
| 503 | Allan Anderson | .06 | .05 |
| 504 | Luis Aquino | .06 | .05 |
| 505 | Mark Guthrie | .06 | .05 |
| 506 | Joe Orsulak | .06 | .05 |
| 507 | *Dana Kiecker*(FC) | | |
| | | .15 | .11 |
| 508 | Dave Gallagher | .05 | .04 |
| 509 | Greg W. Harris | .06 | .05 |
| 510 | Mark Williamson | .05 | .04 |
| 511 | Casey Candaele | .05 | .04 |
| 512 | Mookie Wilson | .06 | .05 |
| 513 | Dave Smith | .08 | .06 |
| 514 | *Chuck Carr*(FC) | .15 | .11 |
| 515 | Glenn Wilson | .06 | .05 |
| 516 | Mike Fitzgerald | .05 | .04 |
| 517 | Devon White | .08 | .06 |
| 518 | *Dave Hollins* | .25 | .20 |
| 519 | Mark Eichhorn | .05 | .04 |
| 520 | Otis Nixon | .05 | .04 |
| 521 | *Terry Shumpert* | .20 | .15 |
| 522 | *Scott Erickson*(FC) | | |
| | | .50 | .40 |
| 523 | Danny Tartabull | .10 | .08 |
| 524 | Orel Hershiser | .15 | .11 |
| 525 | George Brett | .15 | .11 |
| 526 | Greg Vaughn | .20 | .15 |
| 527 | *Tim Naehring*(FC) | | |
| | | .40 | .30 |
| 528 | Curt Schilling(FC) | .06 | .05 |
| 529 | Chris Bosio | .06 | .05 |
| 530 | Sam Horn | .08 | .06 |
| 531 | Mike Scott | .10 | .08 |
| 532 | George Bell | .15 | .11 |
| 533 | Eric Anthony | .20 | .15 |
| 534 | *Julio Valera*(FC) | .15 | .11 |
| 535 | Glenn Davis | .15 | .11 |
| 536 | Larry Walker | .15 | .11 |
| 537 | Pat Combs | .15 | .11 |
| 538 | *Chris Nabholz*(FC) | | |
| | | .20 | .15 |
| 539 | Kirk McCaskill | .08 | .06 |
| 540 | Randy Ready | .05 | .04 |
| 541 | Mark Gubicza | .10 | .08 |
| 542 | Rick Aguilera | .08 | .06 |
| 543 | *Brian McRae*(FC) | | |
| | | .60 | .45 |
| 544 | Kirby Puckett | .20 | .15 |
| 545 | Bo Jackson | .50 | .40 |
| 546 | Wade Boggs | .25 | .20 |
| 547 | Tim McIntosh(FC) | .20 | .15 |
| 548 | Randy Milligan | .08 | .06 |
| 549 | Dwight Evans | .08 | .06 |
| 550 | Billy Ripken | .05 | .04 |
| 551 | Erik Hanson | .15 | .11 |
| 552 | Lance Parrish | .10 | .08 |
| 553 | Tino Martinez | .20 | .15 |

| | | MT | NR MT |
|---|---|---|---|
| 554 | Jim Abbott | .15 | .11 |
| 555 | Ken Griffey, Jr. | 1.50 | 1.25 |
| 556 | Milt Cuyler(FC) | .30 | .25 |
| 557 | *Mark Leonard*(FC) | | |
| | | .25 | .20 |
| 558 | Jay Howell | .08 | .06 |
| 559 | Lloyd Moseby | .08 | .06 |
| 560 | Chris Gwynn | .06 | .05 |
| 561 | *Mark Whiten*(FC) | | |
| | | .70 | .50 |
| 562 | Harold Baines | .10 | .08 |
| 563 | Junior Felix | .15 | .11 |
| 564 | *Darren Lewis*(FC) | | |
| | | .50 | .40 |
| 565 | Fred McGriff | .15 | .11 |
| 566 | Kevin Appier | .15 | .11 |
| 567 | *Luis Gonzalez*(FC) | | |
| | | .40 | .30 |
| 568 | Frank White | .08 | .06 |
| 569 | Juan Agosto | .05 | .04 |
| 570 | Mike Macfarlane | .06 | .05 |
| 571 | Bert Blyleven | .10 | .08 |
| 572 | Ken Griffey, Sr. | .10 | .08 |
| 573 | Lee Stevens(FC) | .20 | .15 |
| 574 | Edgar Martinez | .08 | .06 |
| 575 | Wally Joyner | .10 | .08 |
| 576 | Tim Belcher | .08 | .06 |
| 577 | John Burkett | .10 | .08 |
| 578 | Mike Morgan | .06 | .05 |
| 579 | Paul Gibson | .05 | .04 |
| 580 | Jose Vizcaino | .10 | .08 |
| 581 | Duane Ward | .06 | .05 |
| 582 | Scott Sanderson | .06 | .05 |
| 583 | David Wells | .06 | .05 |
| 584 | Willie McGee | .10 | .08 |
| 585 | John Cerutti | .05 | .04 |
| 586 | Danny Darwin | .08 | .06 |
| 587 | Kurt Stillwell | .08 | .06 |
| 588 | Rich Gedman | .05 | .04 |
| 589 | Mark Davis | .08 | .06 |
| 590 | Bill Gullickson | .06 | .05 |
| 591 | Matt Young | .06 | .05 |
| 592 | Bryan Harvey | .08 | .06 |
| 593 | Omar Vizquel | .06 | .05 |
| 594 | *Scott Lewis*(FC) | .20 | .15 |
| 595 | Dave Valle | .06 | .05 |
| 596 | Tim Crews | .05 | .04 |
| 597 | Mike Bielecki | .06 | .05 |
| 598 | Mike Sharperson | .06 | .05 |
| 599 | Dave Bergman | .05 | .04 |
| 600 | Checklist 501-600 | .05 | .04 |
| 601 | Steve Lyons | .06 | .05 |
| 602 | Bruce Hurst | .08 | .06 |
| 603 | Donn Pall | .05 | .04 |
| 604 | *Jim Vatcher*(FC) | .15 | .11 |
| 605 | Dan Pasqua | .06 | .05 |
| 606 | Kenny Rogers | .08 | .06 |
| 607 | *Jeff Schulz*(FC) | .15 | .11 |
| 608 | Brad Arnsberg(FC) | .10 | .08 |
| 609 | Willie Wilson | .08 | .06 |
| 610 | Jamie Moyer | .06 | .05 |
| 611 | Ron Oester | .05 | .04 |
| 612 | Dennis Cook | .08 | .06 |
| 613 | Rick Mahler | .05 | .04 |
| 614 | Bill Landrum | .06 | .05 |
| 615 | Scott Scudder | .15 | .11 |
| 616 | *Tom Edens*(FC) | .08 | .06 |

| | | MT | NR MT | | | MT | NR MT |
|---|---|---|---|---|---|---|---|
| 617 | "1917 Revisited" | .25 | .20 | 675 | Hensley Meulens | .10 | .08 |
| 618 | Jim Gantner | .06 | .05 | 676 | Jeff M. Robinson | .06 | .05 |
| 619 | Darrel Akerfelds(FC) | .06 | .05 | 677 | "Ground Breaking" | .25 | .20 |
| 620 | Ron Robinson | .06 | .05 | 678 | Johnny Ray | .06 | .05 |
| 621 | *Scott Radinsky* | .20 | .15 | 679 | Greg Hibbard | .10 | .08 |
| 622 | Pete Smith | .06 | .05 | 680 | Paul Sorrento | .20 | .15 |
| 623 | Melido Perez | .08 | .06 | 681 | Mike Marshall | .06 | .05 |
| 624 | Jerald Clark | .06 | .05 | 682 | Jim Clancy | .05 | .04 |
| 625 | Carlos Martinez | .08 | .06 | 683 | Rob Murphy | .05 | .04 |
| 626 | Wes | | | 684 | Dave Schmidt | .05 | .04 |
| | Chamberlain(FC) | 1.00 | .70 | 685 | *Jeff Gray*(FC) | .15 | .11 |
| 627 | Bobby Witt | .08 | .06 | 686 | Mike Hartley(FC) | .20 | .15 |
| 628 | Ken Dayley | .06 | .05 | 687 | Jeff King | .08 | .06 |
| 629 | *John Barfield*(FC) | | | 688 | Stan Javier | .06 | .05 |
| | | .10 | .08 | 689 | Bob Walk | .06 | .05 |
| 630 | Bob Tewksbury | .06 | .05 | 690 | Jim Gott | .06 | .05 |
| 631 | Glenn Braggs | .06 | .05 | 691 | Mike LaCoss | .05 | .04 |
| 632 | *Jim Neidlinger*(FC) | | | 692 | John Farrell | .06 | .05 |
| | | .20 | .15 | 693 | Tim Leary | .06 | .05 |
| 633 | Tom Browning | .08 | .06 | 694 | *Mike Walker*(FC) | .20 | .15 |
| 634 | Kirk Gibson | .12 | .09 | 695 | Eric Plunk | .05 | .04 |
| 635 | Rob Dibble | .12 | .09 | 696 | Mike Fetters(FC) | .15 | .11 |
| 636 | "Stolen Base Leaders" | | | 697 | Wayne Edwards | .10 | .08 |
| | | .30 | .25 | 698 | Tim Drummond(FC) | .15 | .11 |
| 637 | Jeff Montgomery | .08 | .06 | 699 | Willie Fraser | .05 | .04 |
| 638 | Mike Schooler | .08 | .06 | 700 | Checklist 601-700 | .05 | .04 |
| 639 | Storm Davis | .06 | .05 | 701 | Mike Heath | .10 | .08 |
| 640 | *Rich Rodriguez*(FC) | | | 702 | "Rookie Threats" | .60 | .45 |
| | | .15 | .11 | 703 | Jose Mesa | .10 | .08 |
| 641 | Phil Bradley | .08 | .06 | 704 | Dave Smith | .10 | .08 |
| 642 | Kent Mercker | .15 | .11 | 705 | Danny Darwin | .10 | .08 |
| 643 | Carlton Fisk | .12 | .09 | 706 | Rafael Belliard | .10 | .08 |
| 644 | *Mike Bell*(FC) | .15 | .11 | 707 | Rob Murphy | .10 | .08 |
| 645 | *Alex Fernandez*(FC) | | | 708 | Terry Pendleton | .15 | .11 |
| | | .40 | .30 | 709 | Mike Pagliarulo | .10 | .08 |
| 646 | Juan Gonzalez | .50 | .40 | 710 | Sid Bream | .12 | .09 |
| 647 | Ken Hill | .06 | .05 | 711 | Junior Felix | .12 | .09 |
| 648 | Jeff Russell | .08 | .06 | 712 | Dante Bichette | .10 | .08 |
| 649 | *Chuck Malone*(FC) | | | 713 | Kevin Gross | .10 | .08 |
| | | .15 | .11 | 714 | Luis Sojo | .12 | .09 |
| 650 | Steve Buechele | .06 | .05 | 715 | Bob Ojeda | .10 | .08 |
| 651 | Mike Benjamin | .15 | .11 | 716 | Julio Machado | .12 | .09 |
| 652 | Tony Pena | .08 | .06 | 717 | Steve Farr | .10 | .08 |
| 653 | Trevor Wilson | .08 | .06 | 718 | Franklin Stubbs | .10 | .08 |
| 654 | Alex Cole | .30 | .25 | 719 | Mike Boddicker | .12 | .09 |
| 655 | Roger Clemens | .25 | .20 | 720 | Willie Randolph | .12 | .09 |
| 656 | "The Bashing Years" | .25 | .20 | 721 | Willie McGee | .15 | .11 |
| 657 | *Joe Grahe*(FC) | .20 | .15 | 722 | Chili Davis | .15 | .11 |
| 658 | Jim Eisenreich | .06 | .05 | 723 | Danny Jackson | .12 | .09 |
| 659 | Dan Gladden | .06 | .05 | 724 | Cory Snyder | .10 | .08 |
| 660 | Steve Farr | .06 | .05 | 725 | "MVP Lineup" | .25 | .20 |
| 661 | *Bill Sampen* | .20 | .15 | 726 | Rob Deer | .10 | .08 |
| 662 | *Dave Rohde*(FC) | .15 | .11 | 727 | Rich DeLucia(FC) | .15 | .11 |
| 663 | Mark Gardner | .20 | .15 | 728 | Mike Perez(FC) | .15 | .11 |
| 664 | *Mike Simms*(FC) | .25 | .20 | 729 | Mickey Tettleton | .12 | .09 |
| 665 | Moises Alou(FC) | .15 | .11 | 730 | Mike Blowers | .10 | .08 |
| 666 | Mickey Hatcher | .06 | .05 | 731 | Gary Gaetti | .12 | .09 |
| 667 | Jimmy Key | .08 | .06 | 732 | Brett Butler | .12 | .09 |
| 668 | John Wetteland | .10 | .08 | 733 | Dave Parker | .15 | .11 |
| 669 | John Smiley | .06 | .05 | 734 | Eddie Zosky(FC) | .20 | .15 |
| 670 | Jim Acker | .05 | .04 | 735 | Jack Clark | .12 | .09 |
| 671 | Pascual Perez | .06 | .05 | 736 | Jack Morris | .12 | .09 |
| 672 | *Reggie Harris*(FC) | | | 737 | Kirk Gibson | .12 | .09 |
| | | .30 | .25 | 738 | Steve Bedrosian | .10 | .08 |
| 673 | Matt Nokes | .08 | .06 | 739 | Candy Maldonado | .10 | .08 |
| 674 | *Rafael Novoa*(FC) | | | 740 | Matt Young | .10 | .08 |
| | | .15 | .11 | 741 | Rich Garces(FC) | .20 | .15 |

| | | MT | NR MT |
|---|---|---|---|
| 742 | George Bell | .15 | .11 |
| 743 | Deion Sanders | .15 | .11 |
| 744 | Bo Jackson | 1.00 | .70 |
| 745 | Luis Mercedes(FC) | .40 | .30 |
| 746 | Reggie Jefferson(FC) | .80 | .60 |
| 747 | Pete Incaviglia | .10 | .08 |
| 748 | Chris Hammond(FC) | .20 | .15 |
| 749 | Mike Stanton | .12 | .09 |
| 750 | Scott Sanderson | .10 | .08 |
| 751 | Paul Faries(FC) | .20 | .15 |
| 752 | Al Osuna(FC) | .15 | .11 |
| 753 | Steve Chitren(FC) | .15 | .11 |
| 754 | Tony Fernandez | .15 | .11 |
| 755 | Jeff Bagwell(FC) | 3.00 | 2.25 |
| 756 | Kirk Dressendorfer(FC) | .50 | .40 |
| 757 | Glenn Davis | .15 | .11 |
| 758 | Gary Carter | .12 | .09 |
| 759 | Zane Smith | .10 | .08 |
| 760 | Vance Law | .10 | .08 |
| 761 | Denis Boucher(FC) | .20 | .15 |
| 762 | Turner Ward(FC) | .20 | .15 |
| 763 | Roberto Alomar | .15 | .11 |
| 764 | Albert Belle | .25 | .20 |
| 765 | Joe Carter | .15 | .11 |
| 766 | Pete Schourek(FC) | .15 | .11 |
| 767 | Heathcliff Slocumb(FC) | .15 | .11 |
| 768 | Vince Coleman | .15 | .11 |
| 769 | Mitch Williams | .12 | .09 |
| 770 | Brian Downing | .10 | .08 |
| 771 | Dana Allison(FC) | .15 | .11 |
| 772 | Pete Harnisch | .12 | .09 |
| 773 | Tim Raines | .15 | .11 |
| 774 | Darryl Kile(FC) | .25 | .20 |
| 775 | Fred McGriff | .15 | .11 |
| 776 | Dwight Evans | .12 | .09 |
| 777 | Joe Slusarski(FC) | .20 | .15 |
| 778 | Dave Righetti | .12 | .09 |
| 779 | Jeff Hamilton | .10 | .08 |
| 780 | Ernest Riles | .10 | .08 |
| 781 | Ken Dayley | .10 | .08 |
| 782 | Eric King | .10 | .08 |
| 783 | Devon White | .12 | .09 |
| 784 | Beau Allred | .10 | .08 |
| 785 | Mike Timlin(FC) | .25 | .20 |
| 786 | Ivan Calderon | .15 | .11 |
| 787 | Hubie Brooks | .12 | .09 |
| 788 | Juan Agosto | .10 | .08 |
| 789 | Barry Jones | .10 | .08 |
| 790 | Wally Backman | .10 | .08 |
| 791 | Jim Presley | .10 | .08 |
| 792 | Charlie Hough | .10 | .08 |
| 793 | Larry Andersen | .10 | .08 |
| 794 | Steve Finley | .12 | .09 |
| 795 | Shawn Abner | .10 | .08 |
| 796 | Jeff M. Robinson | .10 | .08 |
| 797 | Joe Bitker(FC) | .10 | .08 |
| 798 | Eric Show | .10 | .08 |
| 799 | Bud Black | .10 | .08 |
| 800 | Checklist 701-800 | .10 | .08 |
| ---- | Michael Jordan (Special Insert) | 8.00 | 6.00 |

# 1992 Upper Deck

Upper Deck introduced a new look in 1992. The baseline style was no longer used. The 1992 cards feature full-color action photos on white stock, with the player's name and the Upper Deck logo along the top border. The team name is inserted in the bottom right corner of the photo.. Once again a 100-card high number series was set for release in July or August. 2,500 Ted Williams autographed Baseball Heroes cards were randomly inserted into Upper Deck packs. Several subsets are also featured in the 1992 issue including Star Rookies and Top Prospects. At press time, Upper Deck was considering changes in its 1992 card set. This explains any discrepancies in the price list from what was actually released from Upper Deck.

| | | MT | NR MT |
|---|---|---|---|
| Complete Set: | | 40.00 | 30.00 |
| Common Player: | | .05 | .04 |
| 1 | Star Rookie Checklist | .06 | .05 |
| 2 | Star Rookie (Royce Clayton) | .20 | .15 |
| 3 | Star Rookie (Brian Jordan)(FC) | .60 | .45 |
| 4 | Star Rookie (Dave Fleming)(FC) | .60 | .45 |
| 5 | Star Rookie (Jim Thome) | .25 | .20 |

**The values quoted are intended to reflect the market price.**

| | MT | NR MT |
|---|---|---|
| 6 Star Rookie (Jeff Juden) | .20 | .15 |
| 7 Star Rookie (*Roberto Hernandez*)(FC) | .20 | .15 |
| 8 Star Rookie (Kyle Abbott)(FC) | .10 | .08 |
| 9 Star Rookie (*Chris George*)(FC) | .20 | .15 |
| 10 Star Rookie (*Rob Maurer*)(FC) | .30 | .25 |
| 11 Star Rookie (Donald Harris)(FC) | .20 | .15 |
| 12 Star Rookie (*Ted Wood*)(FC) | .25 | .20 |
| 13 Star Rookie (*Patrick Lennon*) | .20 | .15 |
| 14 Star Rookie (Willie Banks) | .15 | .11 |
| 15 Star Rookie (Roger Salkeld) | .25 | .20 |
| 16 Star Rookie (Wilfredo Cordero) | .20 | .15 |
| 17 Star Rookie (*Arthur Rhodes*) | .40 | .30 |
| 18 Star Rookie (*Pedro Martinez*) | .80 | .60 |
| 19 Star Rookie (*Andy Ashby*) | .10 | .08 |
| 20 Star Rookie (Tom Goodwin) | .15 | .11 |
| 21 Star Rookie (*Braulio Castillo*)(FC) | .20 | .15 |
| 22 Star Rookie (Todd Van Poppel) | .35 | .25 |
| 23 Star Rookie (*Brian Williams*)(FC) | .30 | .25 |
| 24 Star Rookie (Ryan Klesko) | .70 | .50 |
| 25 Star Rookie (*Kenny Lofton*) | .70 | .50 |
| 26 Star Rookie (Derek Bell) | .35 | .25 |
| 27 Star Rookie (Reggie Sanders) | .40 | .30 |
| 28 "Winfield's 400th" | .10 | .08 |
| 29 Atlanta Checklist | .05 | .04 |
| 30 Cincinnati Checklist | .05 | .04 |
| 31 Houston Checklist | .05 | .04 |
| 32 Los Angeles Checklist | .05 | .04 |
| 33 San Diego Checklist | .05 | .04 |
| 34 San Francisco Checklist | .05 | .04 |
| 35 Chicago Checklist | .05 | .04 |
| 36 Montreal Checklist | .05 | .04 |
| 37 New York Checklist | .05 | .04 |
| 38 Philadelphia Checklist | .05 | .04 |
| 39 Pittsburgh Checklist | .05 | .04 |
| 40 St. Louis Checklist | .05 | .04 |
| 41 "Playoff Perfection" | .10 | .08 |
| 42 *Jeremy Hernandez*(FC) | .20 | .15 |
| 43 Doug Henry(FC) | .20 | .15 |
| 44 Chris Donnels | .25 | .20 |
| 45 *Mo Sanford*(FC) | .20 | .15 |
| 46 *Scott Kamieniecki* | .15 | .11 |
| 47 Mark Lemke | .06 | .05 |
| 48 Steve Farr | .05 | .04 |
| 49 Francisco Oliveras | .05 | .04 |
| 50 *Ced Landrum*(FC) | .10 | .08 |
| 51 Top Prospect Checklist | .06 | .05 |
| 52 Top Prospect (*Eduardo Perez*)(FC) | .50 | .40 |
| 53 Top Prospect (*Tom Nevers*)(FC) | .20 | .15 |
| 54 Top Prospect (*David Zancanaro*)(FC) | .20 | .15 |
| 55 Top Prospect (*Shawn Green*)(FC) | .20 | .15 |
| 56 Top Prospect (*Mark Wohlers*) | .20 | .15 |
| 57 Top Prospect (*Dave Nilsson*) | .50 | .40 |
| 58 Top Prospect (*Dmitri Young*) | .50 | .40 |
| 59 Top Prospect (*Ryan Hawblitzel*)(FC) | .30 | .25 |
| 60 Top Prospect (*Raul Mondesi*)(FC) | .30 | .25 |
| 61 Top Prospect (Rondell White)(FC) | .35 | .25 |
| 62 Top Prospect (Steve Hosey)(FC) | .20 | .15 |
| 63 Top Prospect (*Manny Ramirez*)(FC) | 1.25 | .90 |
| 64 Top Prospect (Marc Newfield) | .50 | .40 |
| 65 Top Prospect (Jeromy Burnitz)(FC) | .80 | .60 |
| 66 Top Prospect (*Mark Smith*)(FC) | .30 | .25 |
| 67 Top Prospect (*Joey Hamilton*)(FC) | .40 | .30 |
| 68 Top Prospect (*Tyler Green*)(FC) | .80 | .60 |
| 69 Top Prospect (*John Farrell*)(FC) | .30 | .25 |
| 70 Top Prospect (*Kurt Miller*)(FC) | .20 | .15 |
| 71 Top Prospect (*Jeff Plympton*) | .30 | .25 |
| 72 Top Prospect (Dan Wilson)(FC) | .35 | .25 |
| 73 Top Prospect (*Joe Vitiello*)(FC) | .40 | .30 |
| 74 Top Prospect (Rico Brogna)(FC) | .10 | .08 |
| 75 Top Prospect (*David McCarty*)(FC) | 1.50 | 1.25 |
| 76 Top Prospect (Bob Wickman)(FC) | .60 | .45 |
| 77 Top Prospect (Carlos Rodriguez)(FC) | .30 | .25 |
| 78 "Stay In School" | .10 | .08 |
| 79 Bloodlines (Ramon & Pedro Martinez) | .40 | .30 |
| 80 Bloodlines (Kevin & Keith Mitchell) | .10 | .08 |
| 81 Bloodlines (Sandy Jr. & Roberto Alomar) | .10 | .08 |
| 82 Bloodlines (Cal Jr. & | | |

| | | MT | NR MT | | | | MT | NR MT |
|---|---|---|---|---|---|---|---|---|
| | Billy Ripken) | .15 | .11 | | 144 | Barry Larkin | .15 | .11 |
| 83 | Bloodlines (Tony & Chris | | | | 145 | Ryne Sandberg | .25 | .20 |
| | Gwynn) | .10 | .08 | | 146 | Scott Erickson | .25 | .20 |
| 84 | Bloodlines (Dwight | | | | 147 | Luis Polonia | .06 | .05 |
| | Gooden & Gary Sheffield) | | | | 148 | John Burkett | .06 | .05 |
| | | .10 | .08 | | 149 | Luis Sojo | .06 | .05 |
| 85 | Bloodlines (Ken Sr., Ken | | | | 150 | Dickie Thon | .05 | .04 |
| | Jr. & Craig Griffey) | .80 | .60 | | 151 | Walt Weiss | .06 | .05 |
| 86 | California Checklist | .05 | .04 | | 152 | Mike Scioscia | .06 | .05 |
| 87 | Chicago Checklist | .05 | .04 | | 153 | Mark McGwire | .15 | .11 |
| 88 | Kansas City Checklist | | | | 154 | Matt Williams | .15 | .11 |
| | | .05 | .04 | | 155 | Rickey Henderson | .25 | .20 |
| 89 | Minnesota Checklist | .05 | .04 | | 156 | Sandy Alomar, Jr. | .10 | .08 |
| 90 | Oakland Checklist | .05 | .04 | | 157 | Brian McRae | .25 | .20 |
| 91 | Seattle Checklist | .05 | .04 | | 158 | Harold Baines | .08 | .06 |
| 92 | Texas Checklist | .05 | .04 | | 159 | Kevin Appier | .06 | .05 |
| 93 | Baltimore Checklist | .05 | .04 | | 160 | Felix Fermin | .05 | .04 |
| 94 | Boston Checklist | .05 | .04 | | 161 | Leo Gomez | .15 | .11 |
| 95 | Cleveland Checklist | .05 | .04 | | 162 | Craig Biggio | .10 | .08 |
| 96 | Detroit Checklist | .05 | .04 | | 163 | Ben McDonald | .20 | .15 |
| 97 | Milwaukee Checklist | .05 | .04 | | 164 | Randy Johnson | .08 | .06 |
| 98 | New York Checklist | .05 | .04 | | 165 | Cal Ripken, Jr. | .30 | .25 |
| 99 | Toronto Checklist | .05 | .04 | | 166 | Frank Thomas | 1.00 | .70 |
| 100 | Checklist 1-100 | .05 | .04 | | 167 | Delino DeShields | .08 | .06 |
| 101 | Joe Oliver | .05 | .04 | | 168 | Greg Gagne | .05 | .04 |
| 102 | Hector Villanueva | .06 | .05 | | 169 | Ron Karkovice | .05 | .04 |
| 103 | Ed Whitson | .05 | .04 | | 170 | Charlie Leibrandt | .05 | .04 |
| 104 | Danny Jackson | .05 | .04 | | 171 | Dave Righetti | .08 | .06 |
| 105 | Chris Hammond | .06 | .05 | | 172 | Dave Henderson | .10 | .08 |
| 106 | Ricky Jordan | .06 | .05 | | 173 | Steve Decker | .15 | .11 |
| 107 | Kevin Bass | .05 | .04 | | 174 | Darryl Strawberry | .15 | .11 |
| 108 | Darrin Fletcher | .05 | .04 | | 175 | Will Clark | .25 | .20 |
| 109 | Junior Ortiz | .05 | .04 | | 176 | Ruben Sierra | .15 | .11 |
| 110 | Tom Bolton | .05 | .04 | | 177 | Ozzie Smith | .15 | .11 |
| 111 | Jeff King | .06 | .05 | | 178 | Charles Nagy | .08 | .06 |
| 112 | Dave Magadan | .08 | .06 | | 179 | Gary Pettis | .05 | .04 |
| 113 | Mike LaValliere | .06 | .05 | | 180 | Kirk Gibson | .08 | .06 |
| 114 | Hubie Brooks | .06 | .05 | | 181 | Randy Milligan | .06 | .05 |
| 115 | Jay Bell | .05 | .04 | | 182 | Dave Valle | .05 | .04 |
| 116 | David Wells | .05 | .04 | | 183 | Chris Hoiles | .10 | .08 |
| 117 | Jim Leyritz | .05 | .04 | | 184 | Tony Phillips | .05 | .04 |
| 118 | Manuel Lee | .05 | .04 | | 185 | Brady Anderson | .05 | .04 |
| 119 | Alvaro Espinoza | .05 | .04 | | 186 | Scott Fletcher | .05 | .04 |
| 120 | B.J. Surhoff | .06 | .05 | | 187 | Gene Larkin | .05 | .04 |
| 121 | Hal Morris | .20 | .15 | | 188 | Lance Johnson | .05 | .04 |
| 122 | Shawon Dunston | .08 | .06 | | 189 | Greg Olson | .05 | .04 |
| 123 | Chris Sabo | .10 | .08 | | 190 | Melido Perez | .05 | .04 |
| 124 | Andre Dawson | .15 | .11 | | 191 | Lenny Harris | .05 | .04 |
| 125 | Eric Davis | .15 | .11 | | 192 | Terry Kennedy | .05 | .04 |
| 126 | Chili Davis | .08 | .06 | | 193 | Mike Gallego | .05 | .04 |
| 127 | Dale Murphy | .10 | .08 | | 194 | Willie McGee | .08 | .06 |
| 128 | Kirk McCaskill | .06 | .05 | | 195 | Juan Samuel | .06 | .05 |
| 129 | Terry Mulholland | .06 | .05 | | 196 | Jeff Huson | .05 | .04 |
| 130 | Rick Aguilera | .08 | .06 | | 197 | Alex Cole | .06 | .05 |
| 131 | Vince Coleman | .10 | .08 | | 198 | Ron Robinson | .06 | .05 |
| 132 | Andy Van Slyke | .12 | .09 | | 199 | Joel Skinner | .06 | .05 |
| 133 | Gregg Jefferies | .15 | .11 | | 200 | Checklist 101-200 | .05 | .05 |
| 134 | Barry Bonds | .20 | .15 | | 201 | Kevin Reimer | .06 | .05 |
| 135 | Dwight Gooden | .15 | .11 | | 202 | Stan Belinda | .05 | .04 |
| 136 | Dave Stieb | .08 | .06 | | 203 | Pat Tabler | .05 | .04 |
| 137 | Albert Belle | .25 | .20 | | 204 | Jose Guzman | .05 | .04 |
| 138 | Teddy Higuera | .08 | .06 | | 205 | Jose Lind | .05 | .04 |
| 139 | Jesse Barfield | .08 | .06 | | 206 | Spike Owen | .05 | .04 |
| 140 | Pat Borders | .06 | .05 | | 207 | Joe Orsulak | .05 | .04 |
| 141 | Bip Roberts | .06 | .05 | | 208 | Charlie Hayes | .05 | .04 |
| 142 | Rob Dibble | .10 | .08 | | 209 | Mike Devereaux | .06 | .05 |
| 143 | Mark Grace | .15 | .11 | | 210 | Mike Fitzgerald | .05 | .04 |

| | | MT | NR MT | | | | MT | NR MT |
|---|---|---|---|---|---|---|---|---|
| 211 | Willie Randolph | .05 | .04 | | 277 | Frank Viola | .10 | .08 |
| 212 | Rod Nichols | .05 | .04 | | 278 | Randy Myers | .06 | .05 |
| 213 | Mike Boddicker | .05 | .04 | | 279 | Ken Caminiti | .06 | .05 |
| 214 | Bill Spiers | .05 | .04 | | 280 | Bill Doran | .06 | .05 |
| 215 | Steve Olin | .05 | .04 | | 281 | Dan Pasqua | .05 | .04 |
| 216 | *David Howard*(FC) | | | | 282 | Alfredo Griffin | .05 | .04 |
| | | .15 | .11 | | 283 | Jose Oquendo | .05 | .04 |
| 217 | Gary Varsho | .05 | .04 | | 284 | Kal Daniels | .08 | .06 |
| 218 | Mike Harkey | .06 | .05 | | 285 | Bobby Thigpen | .08 | .06 |
| 219 | Luis Aquino | .05 | .04 | | 286 | Robby Thompson | .05 | .04 |
| 220 | Chuck McElroy | .05 | .04 | | 287 | Mark Eichhorn | .05 | .04 |
| 221 | Doug Drabek | .08 | .06 | | 288 | Mike Felder | .05 | .04 |
| 222 | Dave Winfield | .15 | .11 | | 289 | Dave Gallagher | .05 | .04 |
| 223 | Rafael Palmeiro | .12 | .09 | | 290 | Dave Anderson | .05 | .04 |
| 224 | Joe Carter | .12 | .09 | | 291 | Mel Hall | .06 | .05 |
| 225 | Bobby Bonilla | .12 | .09 | | 292 | Jerald Clark | .06 | .05 |
| 226 | Ivan Calderon | .10 | .08 | | 293 | Al Newman | .05 | .04 |
| 227 | Gregg Olson | .10 | .08 | | 294 | Rob Deer | .05 | .04 |
| 228 | Tim Wallach | .08 | .06 | | 295 | Matt Nokes | .06 | .05 |
| 229 | Terry Pendleton | .10 | .08 | | 296 | Jack Armstrong | .06 | .05 |
| 230 | Gilberto Reyes(FC) | .08 | .06 | | 297 | Jim Deshaies | .05 | .04 |
| 231 | Carlos Baerga | .10 | .08 | | 298 | Jeff Innis | .05 | .04 |
| 232 | Greg Vaughn | .10 | .08 | | 299 | Jeff Reed | .05 | .04 |
| 233 | Bret Saberhagen | .10 | .08 | | 300 | Checklist 201-300 | .05 | .04 |
| 234 | Gary Sheffield | .10 | .08 | | 301 | Lonnie Smith | .05 | .04 |
| 235 | Mark Lewis | .15 | .11 | | 302 | Jimmy Key | .06 | .05 |
| 236 | George Bell | .10 | .08 | | 303 | Junior Felix | .08 | .06 |
| 237 | Danny Tartabull | .10 | .08 | | 304 | Mike Heath | .05 | .04 |
| 238 | Willie Wilson | .06 | .05 | | 305 | Mark Langston | .10 | .08 |
| 239 | Doug Dascenzo | .05 | .04 | | 306 | Greg W. Harris | .06 | .05 |
| 240 | Bill Pecota | .05 | .04 | | 307 | Brett Butler | .08 | .06 |
| 241 | Julio Franco | .12 | .09 | | 308 | Luis Rivera | .05 | .04 |
| 242 | Ed Sprague | .10 | .08 | | 309 | Bruce Ruffin | .05 | .04 |
| 243 | Juan Gonzalez | .35 | .25 | | 310 | Paul Faries | .08 | .06 |
| 244 | Chuck Finley | .10 | .08 | | 311 | Terry Leach | .05 | .04 |
| 245 | *Ivan Rodriguez* | .80 | .60 | | 312 | *Scott Brosius*(FC) | | |
| 246 | Lenny Dykstra | .10 | .08 | | | | .15 | .11 |
| 247 | Deion Sanders | .15 | .11 | | 313 | Scott Leius | .15 | .11 |
| 248 | Dwight Evans | .08 | .06 | | 314 | Harold Reynolds | .08 | .06 |
| 249 | Larry Walker | .10 | .08 | | 315 | Jack Morris | .10 | .08 |
| 250 | Billy Ripken | .05 | .04 | | 316 | David Segui | .10 | .08 |
| 251 | Mickey Tettleton | .06 | .05 | | 317 | Bill Gullickson | .06 | .05 |
| 252 | Tony Pena | .06 | .05 | | 318 | Todd Frohwirth | .05 | .04 |
| 253 | Benito Santiago | .08 | .06 | | 319 | *Mark Leiter*(FC) | .10 | .08 |
| 254 | Kirby Puckett | .20 | .15 | | 320 | Jeff M. Robinson | .05 | .04 |
| 255 | Cecil Fielder | .20 | .15 | | 321 | Gary Gaetti | .08 | .06 |
| 256 | Howard Johnson | .12 | .09 | | 322 | John Smoltz | .10 | .08 |
| 257 | Andujar Cedeno | .20 | .15 | | 323 | Andy Benes | .10 | .08 |
| 258 | Jose Rijo | .08 | .06 | | 324 | Kelly Gruber | .08 | .06 |
| 259 | Al Osuna | .05 | .04 | | 325 | Jim Abbott | .10 | .08 |
| 260 | Todd Hundley | .15 | .11 | | 326 | John Kruk | .06 | .05 |
| 261 | Orel Hershiser | .08 | .06 | | 327 | Kevin Seitzer | .06 | .05 |
| 262 | Ray Lankford | .15 | .11 | | 328 | Darrin Jackson | .05 | .04 |
| 263 | Robin Ventura | .15 | .11 | | 329 | Kurt Stillwell | .05 | .04 |
| 264 | Felix Jose | .10 | .08 | | 330 | Mike Maddux | .05 | .04 |
| 265 | Eddie Murray | .15 | .11 | | 331 | Dennis Eckersley | .10 | .08 |
| 266 | Kevin Mitchell | .15 | .11 | | 332 | Dan Gladden | .05 | .04 |
| 267 | Gary Carter | .10 | .08 | | 333 | Jose Canseco | .25 | .20 |
| 268 | Mike Benjamin | .05 | .04 | | 334 | Kent Hrbek | .06 | .05 |
| 269 | Dick Schofield | .05 | .04 | | 335 | Ken Griffey, Sr. | .06 | .05 |
| 270 | Jose Uribe | .05 | .04 | | 336 | Greg Swindell | .08 | .06 |
| 271 | Pete Incaviglia | .06 | .05 | | 337 | Trevor Wilson | .06 | .05 |
| 272 | Tony Fernandez | .08 | .06 | | 338 | Sam Horn | .05 | .04 |
| 273 | Alan Trammell | .10 | .08 | | 339 | Mike Henneman | .06 | .05 |
| 274 | Tony Gwynn | .15 | .11 | | 340 | Jerry Browne | .05 | .04 |
| 275 | Mike Greenwell | .10 | .08 | | 341 | Glenn Braggs | .05 | .04 |
| 276 | *Jeff Bagwell* | .70 | .50 | | 342 | Tom Glavine | .10 | .08 |

| | | MT | NR MT | | | | MT | NR MT |
|---|---|---|---|---|---|---|---|---|
| 343 | Wally Joyner | .10 | .08 | 409 | *Mike Timlin* | | .15 | .11 |
| 344 | Fred McGriff | .10 | .08 | 410 | Mitch Williams | | .08 | .06 |
| 345 | Ron Gant | .15 | .11 | 411 | Garry Templeton | | .06 | .05 |
| 346 | Ramon Martinez | .15 | .11 | 412 | Greg Cadaret | | .05 | .04 |
| 347 | Wes Chamberlain | .20 | .15 | 413 | Donnie Hill | | .05 | .04 |
| 348 | Terry Shumpert | .05 | .04 | 414 | Wally Whitehurst | | .05 | .04 |
| 349 | Tim Teufel | .05 | .04 | 415 | Scott Sanderson | | .06 | .05 |
| 350 | Wally Backman | .05 | .04 | 416 | Thomas Howard | | .06 | .05 |
| 351 | Joe Girardi | .05 | .04 | 417 | Neal Heaton | | .05 | .04 |
| 352 | Devon White | .08 | .06 | 418 | Charlie Hough | | .05 | .04 |
| 353 | Greg Maddux | .08 | .06 | 419 | Jack Howell | | .05 | .04 |
| 354 | *Ryan Bowen* | .15 | .11 | 420 | Greg Hibbard | | .06 | .05 |
| 355 | Roberto Alomar | .10 | .08 | 421 | Carlos Quintana | | .06 | .05 |
| 356 | Don Mattingly | .25 | .20 | 422 | *Kim Batiste*(FC) | | .10 | .08 |
| 357 | Pedro Guerrero | .10 | .08 | 423 | Paul Molitor | | .10 | .08 |
| 358 | Steve Sax | .10 | .08 | 424 | Ken Griffey, Jr. | | .80 | .60 |
| 359 | Joey Cora | .05 | .04 | 425 | Phil Plantier | | .60 | .45 |
| 360 | Jim Gantner | .05 | .04 | 426 | *Denny Neagle*(FC) | | | |
| 361 | Brian Barnes | .10 | .08 | | | | .20 | .15 |
| 362 | Kevin McReynolds | .10 | .08 | 427 | Von Hayes | | .06 | .05 |
| 363 | *Bret Barberie*(FC) | | | 428 | Shane Mack | | .08 | .06 |
| | | .15 | .11 | 429 | Darren Daulton | | .06 | .05 |
| 364 | David Cone | .08 | .06 | 430 | Dwayne Henry | | .05 | .04 |
| 365 | Dennis Martinez | .08 | .06 | 431 | Lance Parrish | | .06 | .05 |
| 366 | *Brian Hunter* | .25 | .20 | 432 | *Mike* | | | |
| 367 | Edgar Martinez | .08 | .06 | | *Humphreys*(FC) | | .10 | .08 |
| 368 | Steve Finley | .08 | .06 | 433 | Tim Burke | | .05 | .04 |
| 369 | Greg Briley | .05 | .04 | 434 | Bryan Harvey | | .06 | .05 |
| 370 | Jeff Blauser | .05 | .04 | 435 | Pat Kelly | | .15 | .11 |
| 371 | Todd Stottlemyre | .06 | .05 | 436 | Ozzie Guillen | | .08 | .06 |
| 372 | Luis Gonzalez | .20 | .15 | 437 | Bruce Hurst | | .06 | .03 |
| 373 | *Rick Wilkins* | .20 | .15 | 438 | Sammy Sosa | | .08 | .06 |
| 374 | *Darryl Kile* | .15 | .11 | 439 | Dennis Rasmussen | | .05 | .04 |
| 375 | John Olerud | .15 | .11 | 440 | Ken Patterson | | .05 | .04 |
| 376 | Lee Smith | .08 | .06 | 441 | Jay Buhner | | .08 | .06 |
| 377 | Kevin Maas | .20 | .15 | 442 | Pat Combs | | .06 | .05 |
| 378 | Dante Bichette | .06 | .05 | 443 | Wade Boggs | | .15 | .11 |
| 379 | Tom Pagnozzi | .06 | .05 | 444 | George Brett | | .15 | .11 |
| 380 | Mike Flanagan | .05 | .04 | 445 | Mo Vaughn | | .35 | .25 |
| 381 | Charlie O'Brien | .05 | .04 | 446 | Chuck Knoblauch | | .35 | .25 |
| 382 | Dave Martinez | .05 | .04 | 447 | Tom Candiotti | | .06 | .05 |
| 383 | Keith Miller | .05 | .04 | 448 | Mark Portugal | | .05 | .04 |
| 384 | Scott Ruskin | .05 | .04 | 449 | Mickey Morandini | | .10 | .08 |
| 385 | Kevin Elster | .05 | .04 | 450 | Duane Ward | | .05 | .04 |
| 386 | Alvin Davis | .08 | .06 | 451 | Otis Nixon | | .05 | .04 |
| 387 | Casey Candaele | .05 | .04 | 452 | Bob Welch | | .08 | .06 |
| 388 | Pete O'Brien | .05 | .04 | 453 | *Rusty Meacham*(FC) | | | |
| 389 | Jeff Treadway | .05 | .04 | | | | .10 | .08 |
| 390 | Scott Bradley | .05 | .04 | 454 | *Keith Mitchell* | | .20 | .15 |
| 391 | Mookie Wilson | .05 | .04 | 455 | Marquis Grissom | | .10 | .08 |
| 392 | Jimmy Jones | .05 | .04 | 456 | Robin Yount | | .20 | .15 |
| 393 | Candy Maldonado | .05 | .04 | 457 | *Harvey Pulliam*(FC) | | | |
| 394 | Eric Yelding | .05 | .04 | | | | .20 | .15 |
| 395 | Tom Henke | .06 | .05 | 458 | Jose DeLeon | | .05 | .04 |
| 396 | Franklin Stubbs | .05 | .04 | 459 | Mark Gubicza | | .06 | .05 |
| 397 | Milt Thompson | .05 | .04 | 460 | Darryl Hamilton | | .05 | .04 |
| 398 | Mark Carreon | .05 | .04 | 461 | Tom Browning | | .08 | .06 |
| 399 | Randy Velarde | .05 | .04 | 462 | Monty Fariss | | .10 | .08 |
| 400 | Checklist 301-400 | .05 | .04 | 463 | Jerome Walton | | .10 | .08 |
| 401 | Omar Vizquel | .05 | .04 | 464 | Paul O'Neill | | .08 | .06 |
| 402 | Joe Boever | .05 | .04 | 465 | Dean Palmer | | .20 | .15 |
| 403 | Bill Krueger | .05 | .04 | 466 | Travis Fryman | | .20 | .15 |
| 404 | Jody Reed | .06 | .05 | 467 | John Smiley | | .05 | .04 |
| 405 | Mike Schooler | .06 | .05 | 468 | Lloyd Moseby | | .05 | .04 |
| 406 | Jason Grimsley | .05 | .04 | 469 | *John Wehner*(FC) | | | |
| 407 | Greg Myers | .05 | .04 | | | | .15 | .11 |
| 408 | Randy Ready | .05 | .04 | 470 | Skeeter Barnes(FC) | | .06 | .05 |

| # | Player | MT | NR MT | | # | Player | MT | NR MT |
|---|--------|----|-------|---|---|--------|----|-------|
| 471 | Steve Chitren | .06 | .05 | | 538 | *Scott Livingstone* | .20 | .15 |
| 472 | Kent Mercker | .06 | .05 | | 539 | Jim Eisenreich | .05 | .04 |
| 473 | Terry Steinbach | .06 | .05 | | 540 | Don Slaught | .05 | .04 |
| 474 | Andres Galarraga | .08 | .06 | | 541 | Scott Cooper(FC) | .20 | .15 |
| 475 | Steve Avery | .20 | .15 | | 542 | Joe Grahe | .06 | .05 |
| 476 | Tom Gordon | .10 | .08 | | 543 | Tom Brunansky | .06 | .05 |
| 477 | Cal Eldred(FC) | .50 | .40 | | 544 | Eddie Zosky | .10 | .08 |
| 478 | Omar Olivares(FC) | .08 | .06 | | 545 | Roger Clemens | .20 | .15 |
| 479 | Julio Machado | .05 | .04 | | 546 | David Justice | .30 | .25 |
| 480 | Bob Milacki | .05 | .04 | | 547 | Dave Stewart | .10 | .08 |
| 481 | Les Lancaster | .05 | .04 | | 548 | David West | .05 | .04 |
| 482 | John Candelaria | .05 | .04 | | 549 | Dave Smith | .06 | .05 |
| 483 | Brian Downing | .05 | .04 | | 550 | Dan Plesac | .06 | .05 |
| 484 | Roger McDowell | .05 | .04 | | 551 | Alex Fernandez | .20 | .15 |
| 485 | Scott Scudder | .05 | .04 | | 552 | Bernard Gilkey | .10 | .08 |
| 486 | Zane Smith | .06 | .05 | | 553 | Jack McDowell | .10 | .08 |
| 487 | John Cerutti | .05 | .04 | | 554 | Tino Martinez | .10 | .08 |
| 488 | Steve Buechele | .06 | .05 | | 555 | Bo Jackson | .30 | .25 |
| 489 | Paul Gibson | .05 | .04 | | 556 | Bernie Williams | .25 | .20 |
| 490 | Curtis Wilkerson | .05 | .04 | | 557 | Mark Gardner | .06 | .05 |
| 491 | Marvin Freeman | .05 | .04 | | 558 | Glenallen Hill | .08 | .06 |
| 492 | Tom Foley | .05 | .04 | | 559 | Oil Can Boyd | .05 | .04 |
| 493 | Juan Berenguer | .05 | .04 | | 560 | Chris James | .05 | .04 |
| 494 | Ernest Riles | .05 | .04 | | 561 | *Scott Servais* | .15 | .11 |
| 495 | Sid Bream | .06 | .05 | | 562 | *Rey Sanchez*(FC) | .20 | .15 |
| 496 | Chuck Crim | .05 | .04 | | 563 | *Paul McClellan*(FC) | .15 | .11 |
| 497 | Mike Macfarlane | .05 | .04 | | 564 | *Andy Mota* | .15 | .11 |
| 498 | Dale Sveum | .05 | .04 | | 565 | Darren Lewis | .15 | .11 |
| 499 | Storm Davis | .05 | .04 | | 566 | *Jose Melendez*(FC) | .15 | .11 |
| 500 | Checklist 401-500 | .05 | .04 | | 567 | Tommy Greene | .08 | .06 |
| 501 | Jeff Reardon | .08 | .06 | | 568 | Rich Rodriguez | .06 | .05 |
| 502 | Shawn Abner | .05 | .04 | | 569 | *Heathcliff Slocumb* | .10 | .08 |
| 503 | Tony Fossas | .05 | .04 | | 570 | Joe Hesketh | .05 | .04 |
| 504 | Cory Snyder | .05 | .04 | | 571 | Carlton Fisk | .15 | .11 |
| 505 | Matt Young | .05 | .04 | | 572 | Erik Hanson | .10 | .08 |
| 506 | Allan Anderson | .05 | .04 | | 573 | Wilson Alvarez | .10 | .08 |
| 507 | Mark Lee | .05 | .04 | | 574 | *Rheal Cormier*(FC) | .20 | .15 |
| 508 | Gene Nelson | .05 | .04 | | 575 | Tim Raines | .10 | .08 |
| 509 | Mike Pagliarulo | .05 | .04 | | 576 | Bobby Witt | .06 | .05 |
| 510 | Rafael Belliard | .05 | .04 | | 577 | Roberto Kelly | .10 | .08 |
| 511 | Jay Howell | .06 | .05 | | 578 | Kevin Brown | .06 | .05 |
| 512 | Bob Tewksbury | .05 | .04 | | 579 | Chris Nabholz | .06 | .05 |
| 513 | Mike Morgan | .06 | .05 | | 580 | Jesse Orosco | .05 | .04 |
| 514 | John Franco | .06 | .05 | | 581 | Jeff Brantley | .06 | .05 |
| 515 | Kevin Gross | .05 | .04 | | 582 | Rafael Ramirez | .05 | .04 |
| 516 | Lou Whitaker | .08 | .06 | | 583 | Kelly Downs | .05 | .04 |
| 517 | Orlando Merced | .20 | .15 | | 584 | Mike Simms | .10 | .08 |
| 518 | Todd Benzinger | .05 | .04 | | 585 | *Mike Remlinger* | .10 | .08 |
| 519 | Gary Redus | .05 | .04 | | 586 | Dave Hollins | .08 | .06 |
| 520 | Walt Terrell | .05 | .04 | | 587 | Larry Andersen | .05 | .04 |
| 521 | Jack Clark | .08 | .06 | | 588 | Mike Gardiner | .08 | .06 |
| 522 | Dave Parker | .10 | .08 | | 589 | Craig Lefferts | .05 | .04 |
| 523 | Tim Naehring | .15 | .11 | | 590 | Paul Assenmacher | .05 | .04 |
| 524 | Mark Whiten | .15 | .11 | | 591 | Bryn Smith | .05 | .04 |
| 525 | Ellis Burks | .10 | .08 | | 592 | Donn Pall | .05 | .04 |
| 526 | *Frank Castillo* | .20 | .15 | | 593 | Mike Jackson | .05 | .04 |
| 527 | Brian Harper | .06 | .05 | | 594 | Scott Radinsky | .05 | .04 |
| 528 | Brook Jacoby | .06 | .05 | | 595 | Brian Holman | .06 | .05 |
| 529 | Rick Sutcliffe | .06 | .05 | | 596 | Geronimo Pena | .08 | .06 |
| 530 | Joe Klink | .05 | .04 | | 597 | Mike Jeffcoat | .05 | .04 |
| 531 | Terry Bross | .05 | .04 | | 598 | Carlos Martinez | .05 | .04 |
| 532 | Jose Offerman | .15 | .11 | | 599 | Geno Petralli | .05 | .04 |
| 533 | Todd Zeile | .15 | .11 | | 600 | Checklist 501-600 | .05 | .04 |
| 534 | Eric Karros | .30 | .25 | | | | | |
| 535 | *Anthony Young* | .25 | .20 | | | | | |
| 536 | Milt Cuyler | .10 | .08 | | | | | |
| 537 | Randy Tomlin | .08 | .06 | | | | | |

| No. | Player | MT | NR MT | | No. | Player | MT | NR MT |
|---|---|---|---|---|---|---|---|---|
| 601 | Jerry Don Gleaton | .05 | .04 | | 661 | Mike Moore | .06 | .05 |
| 602 | Adam Peterson | .05 | .04 | | 662 | Chris Haney | .20 | .15 |
| 603 | Craig Grebeck | .05 | .04 | | 663 | Joe Slusarski | .20 | .15 |
| 604 | Mark Guthrie | .05 | .04 | | 664 | Wayne Housie(FC) | | |
| 605 | Frank Tanana | .05 | .04 | | | | .20 | .15 |
| 606 | Hensley Meulens | .08 | .06 | | 665 | Carlos Garcia(FC) | .08 | .06 |
| 607 | Mark Davis | .05 | .04 | | 666 | Bob Ojeda | .05 | .04 |
| 608 | Eric Plunk | .05 | .04 | | 667 | Bryan Hickerson(FC) | | |
| 609 | Mark Williamson | .05 | .04 | | | | .20 | .15 |
| 610 | Lee Guetterman | .05 | .04 | | 668 | Tim Belcher | .06 | .05 |
| 611 | Bobby Rose | .05 | .04 | | 669 | Ron Darling | .06 | .05 |
| 612 | Bill Wegman | .06 | .05 | | 670 | Rex Hudler | .05 | .04 |
| 613 | Mike Hartley | .05 | .04 | | 671 | Sid Fernandez | .08 | .06 |
| 614 | Chris Beasley(FC) | | | | 672 | Chito Martinez | .20 | .15 |
| | | .10 | .08 | | 673 | Pete Schourek | .15 | .11 |
| 615 | Chris Bosio | .05 | .04 | | 674 | Armando Reneso | | |
| 616 | Henry Cotto | .05 | .04 | | | | .15 | .11 |
| 617 | Chico Walker(FC) | | | | 675 | Mike Mussina | .50 | .40 |
| | | .10 | .08 | | 676 | Kevin Morton(FC) | .15 | .11 |
| 618 | Russ Swan | .05 | .04 | | 677 | Norm Charlton | .06 | .05 |
| 619 | Bob Walk | .05 | .04 | | 678 | Danny Darwin | .05 | .04 |
| 620 | Billy Swift | .05 | .04 | | 679 | Eric King | .05 | .04 |
| 621 | Warren Newson | .15 | .11 | | 680 | Ted Power | .05 | .04 |
| 622 | Steve Bedrosian | .05 | .04 | | 681 | Barry Jones | .05 | .04 |
| 623 | Ricky Bones(FC) | .15 | .11 | | 682 | Carney Lansford | .08 | .06 |
| 624 | Kevin Tapani | .10 | .08 | | 683 | Mel Rojas | .06 | .05 |
| 625 | Juan Guzman(FC) | | | | 684 | Rick Honeycutt | .05 | .04 |
| | | 1.25 | .90 | | 685 | Jeff Fassero(FC) | .15 | .11 |
| 626 | Jeff Johnson(FC) | | | | 686 | Cris Carpenter | .06 | .05 |
| | | .15 | .11 | | 687 | Tim Crews | .05 | .04 |
| 627 | Jeff Montgomery | .06 | .05 | | 688 | Scott Terry | .05 | .04 |
| 628 | Ken Hill | .06 | .05 | | 689 | Chris Gwynn | .05 | .04 |
| 629 | Gary Thurman | .05 | .04 | | 690 | Gerald Perry | .05 | .04 |
| 630 | Steve Howe | .06 | .05 | | 691 | John Barfield | .05 | .04 |
| 631 | Jose DeJesus | .06 | .05 | | 692 | Bob Melvin | .05 | .04 |
| 632 | Bert Blyleven | .06 | .05 | | 693 | Juan Agosto | .05 | .04 |
| 633 | Jaime Navarro | .06 | .05 | | 694 | Alejandro Pena | .06 | .05 |
| 634 | Lee Stevens | .08 | .06 | | 695 | Jeff Russell | .06 | .05 |
| 635 | Pete Harnisch | .08 | .06 | | 696 | Carmelo Martinez | .05 | .04 |
| 636 | Bill Landrum | .05 | .04 | | 697 | Bud Black | .05 | .04 |
| 637 | Rich DeLucia | .06 | .05 | | 698 | Dave Otto | .05 | .04 |
| 638 | Luis Salazar | .05 | .04 | | 699 | Billy Hatcher | .05 | .04 |
| 639 | Rob Murphy | .05 | .04 | | 700 | Checklist 601-700 | .05 | .04 |
| 640 | Diamond Skills Checklist | | | | 701 | Clemente Nunez(FC) | | |
| | | .05 | .04 | | | | .40 | .30 |
| 641 | Roger Clemens (DS) | .25 | .20 | | 702 | "Rookie Threats" | .25 | .20 |
| 642 | Jim Abbott (DS) | .15 | .11 | | 703 | Mike Morgan | .06 | .05 |
| 643 | Travis Fryman (DS) | .25 | .20 | | 704 | Keith Miller | .06 | .05 |
| 644 | Jesse Barfield (DS) | .10 | .08 | | 705 | Kurt Stillwell | .06 | .05 |
| 645 | Cal Ripken, Jr. (DS) | .25 | .20 | | 706 | Damon Berryhill | .06 | .05 |
| 646 | Wade Boggs (DS) | .20 | .15 | | 707 | Von Hayes | .06 | .05 |
| 647 | Cecil Fielder (DS) | .20 | .15 | | 708 | Rick Sutcliffe | .10 | .08 |
| 648 | Rickey Henderson (DS) | | | | 709 | Hubie Brooks | .06 | .05 |
| | | .25 | .20 | | 710 | Ryan Turner(FC) | .50 | .40 |
| 649 | Jose Canseco (DS) | .25 | .20 | | 711 | Diamond Skills Checklist | | |
| 650 | Ken Griffey, Jr. (DS) | .50 | .40 | | | | .06 | .05 |
| 651 | Kenny Rogers | .05 | .04 | | 712 | Jose Rijo (DS) | .06 | .05 |
| 652 | Luis Mercedes(FC) | | | | 713 | Tom Glavine (DS) | .10 | .08 |
| | | .20 | .15 | | 714 | Shawon Dunston (DS) | | |
| 653 | Mike Stanton | .06 | .05 | | | | .08 | .06 |
| 654 | Glenn Davis | .10 | .08 | | 715 | Andy Van Slyke (DS) | .08 | .06 |
| 655 | Nolan Ryan | .40 | .30 | | 716 | Ozzie Smith (DS) | .15 | .11 |
| 656 | Reggie Jefferson | .20 | .15 | | 717 | Tony Gwynn (DS) | .20 | .15 |
| 657 | Javier Ortiz(FC) | .15 | .11 | | 718 | Will Clark (DS) | .20 | .15 |
| 658 | Greg A. Harris | .05 | .04 | | 719 | Marquis Grissom (DS) | | |
| 659 | Mariano Duncan | .06 | .05 | | | | .08 | .06 |
| 660 | Jeff Shaw | .05 | .04 | | 720 | Howard Johnson (DS) | | |

| | | MT | NR MT |
|---|---|---|---|
| 721 | Barry Bonds (DS) | .20 | .15 |
| 722 | Kirk McCaskill | .06 | .05 |
| 723 | Sammy Sosa | .06 | .05 |
| 724 | George Bell | .08 | .06 |
| 725 | Gregg Jefferies | .12 | .09 |
| 726 | Gary DiSarcina | .06 | .05 |
| 727 | Mike Bordick | .12 | .09 |
| 728 | "400 Homerun Club" | | |
| | | .12 | .09 |
| 729 | Rene Gonzales | .06 | .05 |
| 730 | Mike Bielecki | .06 | .05 |
| 731 | Calvin Jones(FC) | .12 | .09 |
| 732 | Jack Morris | .12 | .09 |
| 733 | Frank Viola | .12 | .09 |
| 734 | Dave Winfield | .15 | .11 |
| 735 | Kevin Mitchell | .12 | .09 |
| 736 | Billy Swift | .08 | .06 |
| 737 | Dan Gladden | .06 | .05 |
| 738 | Mike Jackson | .06 | .05 |
| 739 | Mark Carreon | .06 | .05 |
| 740 | Kirt Manwaring | .06 | .05 |
| 741 | Randy Myers | .06 | .05 |
| 742 | Kevin McReynolds | .08 | .06 |
| 743 | Steve Sax | .08 | .06 |
| 744 | Wally Joyner | .12 | .09 |
| 745 | Gary Sheffield | .30 | .25 |
| 746 | Danny Tartabull | .15 | .11 |
| 747 | Julio Valera | .10 | .08 |
| 748 | Denny Neagle | .10 | .08 |
| 749 | Lance Blankenship | .06 | .05 |
| 750 | Mike Gallego | .06 | .05 |
| 751 | Bret Saberhagen | .12 | .09 |
| 752 | Ruben Amaro(FC) | .15 | .11 |
| 753 | Eddie Murray | .15 | .11 |
| 754 | Kyle Abbott | .15 | .11 |
| 755 | Bobby Bonilla | .15 | .11 |
| 756 | Eric Davis | .15 | .11 |
| 757 | Eddie Taubensee(FC) | | |
| | | .20 | .15 |
| 758 | Andres Galarraga | .08 | .06 |
| 759 | Pete Incaviglia | .08 | .06 |
| 760 | Tom Candiotti | .08 | .06 |
| 761 | Tim Belcher | .08 | .06 |
| 762 | Ricky Bones | .15 | .11 |
| 763 | Bip Roberts | .08 | .06 |
| 764 | Pedro Munoz | .20 | .15 |
| 765 | Greg Swindell | .08 | .06 |
| 766 | Kenny Lofton | .25 | .20 |
| 767 | Gary Carter | .08 | .06 |
| 768 | Charlie Hayes | .06 | .05 |
| 769 | Dickie Thon | .06 | .05 |
| 770 | Diamond Debut Checklist | | |
| | | .06 | .05 |
| 771 | Bret Boone (DD)(FC) | | |
| | | .60 | .45 |
| 772 | Arol Cianfroco (DD)(FC) | | |
| | | .25 | .20 |
| 773 | Mark Clark (DD)(FC) | .25 | .20 |
| 774 | Chad Curtis (DD)(FC) | | |
| | | .25 | .20 |
| 775 | Pat Listach (DD)(FC) | | |
| | | 2.00 | 1.50 |
| 776 | Pat Mahomes (DD)(FC) | | |
| | | .50 | .40 |
| 777 | Donovan Osborne (DD)(FC) | | |
| | | .40 | .30 |

| | | MT | NR MT |
|---|---|---|---|
| 778 | John Patterson (DD)(FC) | .15 | .11 |
| 779 | Andy Stankiewicz (DD)(FC) | .25 | .20 |
| 780 | Turk Wendell (DD)(FC) | | |
| | | .25 | .20 |
| 781 | Bill Krueger | .06 | .05 |
| 782 | "Grand Theft" | .15 | .11 |
| 783 | Kevin Seitzer | .06 | .05 |
| 784 | Dave Martinez | .06 | .05 |
| 785 | John Smiley | .08 | .06 |
| 786 | Matt Stairs(FC) | .08 | .06 |
| 787 | Scott Scudder | .06 | .05 |
| 788 | John Wetteland | .10 | .08 |
| 789 | Jack Armstrong | .06 | .05 |
| 790 | Ken Hill | .08 | .06 |
| 791 | Dick Schofield | .06 | .05 |
| 792 | Mariano Duncan | .06 | .05 |
| 793 | Bill Pecota | .06 | .05 |
| 794 | Mike Kelly(FC) | 1.25 | .90 |
| 795 | Willie Randolph | .06 | .05 |
| 796 | Butch Henry(FC) | .20 | .15 |
| 797 | Carlos Hernandez(FC) | | |
| | | .10 | .08 |
| 798 | Doug Jones | .06 | .05 |
| 799 | Melido Perez | .06 | .05 |
| 800 | Checklist | .06 | .05 |

## 1993 Upper Deck

Upper Deck introduced its 1993 set in a two series format to adjust to expansion. Cards 1-420 make up the first series. Special subsets in series one include rookies, teammates and community heroes. The card fronts feature full-color player photos surrounded by a white border. "Upper Deck" appears at the top of the photo and the player's name, team and position appear at the bottom. The backs feature vertical photos which is a change from the past and more ccmplete statistics than what Upper Deck has had in the past. The hologram appears in the lower left corner on the card back.

| | MT | NR MT |
|---|---|---|
| Complete Set: | 18.00 | 13.50 |

| | | MT | NR MT |
|---|---|---|---|
| Common Player: | | .05 | .04 |
| 1 | Star Rookie Checklist | | |
| | | .05 | .04 |
| 2 | Mike Piazza(FC) | .30 | .25 |
| 3 | Rene Arocha(FC) | .15 | .11 |
| 4 | Willie Greene(FC) | .15 | .11 |
| 5 | Manny Alexander(FC) | .25 | .20 |
| 6 | Dan Wilson | .12 | .09 |
| 7 | Dan Smith(FC) | .20 | .15 |
| 8 | Kevin Rogers(FC) | | |
| | | .20 | .15 |
| 9 | Nigel Wilson(FC) | .35 | .25 |
| 10 | Joe Vitko(FC) | .15 | .11 |
| 11 | Tim Costo | .15 | .11 |
| 12 | Alan Embree(FC) | | |
| | | .15 | .11 |
| 13 | Jim Tatum(FC) | .25 | .20 |
| 14 | Cris Colon(FC) | .15 | .11 |
| 15 | Steve Hosey(FC) | .12 | .09 |
| 16 | Sterling Hitchcock(FC) | .20 | .15 |
| 17 | Dave Mlicki(FC) | .15 | .11 |
| 18 | Jessie Hollins(FC) | | |
| | | .15 | .11 |
| 19 | Bobby Jones(FC) | | |
| | | .15 | .11 |
| 20 | Kurt Miller(FC) | .15 | .11 |
| 21 | Melvin Nieves(FC) | | |
| | | .20 | .15 |
| 22 | Billy Ashley(FC) | .20 | .15 |
| 23 | J.T. Snow(FC) | .25 | .20 |
| 24 | Chipper Jones | .20 | .15 |
| 25 | Tim Simon(FC) | .15 | .11 |
| 26 | Tim Pugh(FC) | .15 | .11 |
| 27 | Dave Nied(FC) | .30 | .25 |
| 28 | Mike Trombley(FC) | | |
| | | .20 | .15 |
| 29 | Javy Lopez(FC) | .30 | .25 |
| 30 | Community Heroes Checklist | .05 | .04 |
| 31 | Jim Abbott | .10 | .08 |
| 32 | Dale Murphy | .10 | .08 |
| 33 | Tony Pena | .10 | .08 |
| 34 | Kirby Puckett | .20 | .15 |
| 35 | Harold Reynolds | .10 | .08 |
| 36 | Cal Ripken Jr | .20 | .15 |
| 37 | Nolan Ryan | .20 | .15 |
| 38 | Ryne Sandberg | .20 | .15 |
| 39 | Dave Stewart | .10 | .08 |
| 40 | Dave Winfield | .15 | .11 |
| 41 | Teammates Checklist | | |
| | | .05 | .04 |
| 42 | Blockbuster Trade | .12 | .09 |
| 43 | Brew Crew | .12 | .09 |
| 44 | Iron and Steal | .12 | .09 |
| 45 | Youthful Tribe | .12 | .09 |
| 46 | Motown Mashers | .12 | .09 |
| 47 | Yankee Pride | .12 | .09 |
| 48 | Boston Cy Sox | .12 | .09 |
| 49 | Bash Brothers | .12 | .09 |
| 50 | Twin Titles | .12 | .09 |
| 51 | Southside Sluggers | .20 | .15 |
| 52 | Latin Stars | .15 | .11 |
| 53 | Lethal Lefties | .12 | .09 |
| 54 | Royal Family | .12 | .09 |

| | | MT | NR MT |
|---|---|---|---|
| 55 | Pacific Sox Exchange | .12 | .09 |
| 56 | George Brett | .15 | .11 |
| 57 | Scott Cooper | .08 | .06 |
| 58 | Mike Maddux | .05 | .04 |
| 59 | Rusty Meacham(FC) | .12 | .09 |
| 60 | Wilfredo Cordero | .15 | .11 |
| 61 | Tim Teufel | .05 | .04 |
| 62 | Jeff Montgomery | .06 | .05 |
| 63 | Scott Livingstone | .08 | .06 |
| 64 | Doug Dascenzo | .05 | .04 |
| 65 | Bret Boone | .20 | .15 |
| 66 | Tim Wakefield(FC) | .20 | .15 |
| 67 | Curt Schilling | .08 | .06 |
| 68 | Frank Tanana | .05 | .04 |
| 69 | Lenny Dykstra | .08 | .06 |
| 70 | Derek Lilliquist | .05 | .04 |
| 71 | Anthony Young | .08 | .06 |
| 72 | Hipolito Pichardo(FC) | .12 | .09 |
| 73 | Rob Beck | .06 | .05 |
| 74 | Kent Hrbek | .08 | .06 |
| 75 | Tom Glavine | .12 | .09 |
| 76 | Kevin Brown | .08 | .06 |
| 77 | Chuck Finley | .08 | .06 |
| 78 | Bob Walk | .05 | .04 |
| 79 | Rheal Cormier | .10 | .08 |
| 80 | Rick Sutcliffe | .08 | .06 |
| 81 | Harold Baines | .08 | .06 |
| 82 | Lee Smith | .08 | .06 |
| 83 | Geno Petralli | .05 | .04 |
| 84 | Jose Oquendo | .05 | .04 |
| 85 | Mark Gubicza | .06 | .05 |
| 86 | Mickey Tettleton | .08 | .06 |
| 87 | Bobby Witt | .06 | .05 |
| 88 | Mark Lewis | .06 | .05 |
| 89 | Kevin Appier | .05 | .04 |
| 90 | Mike Stanton | .05 | .04 |
| 91 | Rafael Belliard | .05 | .04 |
| 92 | Kenny Rogers | .05 | .04 |
| 93 | Randy Velarde | .05 | .04 |
| 94 | Luis Sojo | .05 | .04 |
| 95 | Mark Leiter | .05 | .04 |
| 96 | Jody Reed | .06 | .05 |
| 97 | Pete Harnisch | .06 | .05 |
| 98 | Tom Candiotti | .06 | .05 |
| 99 | Mark Portugal | .05 | .04 |
| 100 | Dave Valle | .05 | .04 |
| 101 | Shawon Dunston | .08 | .06 |
| 102 | B.J. Surhoff | .08 | .06 |
| 103 | Jay Bell | .08 | .06 |
| 104 | Sid Bream | .05 | .04 |
| 105 | Checklist 1-105 | .05 | .04 |
| 106 | Mike Morgan | .05 | .04 |
| 107 | Bill Doran | .05 | .04 |
| 108 | Lance Blankenship | .05 | .04 |
| 109 | Mark Lemke | .05 | .04 |
| 110 | Brian Harper | .06 | .05 |
| 111 | Brady Anderson | .08 | .06 |
| 112 | Bip Roberts | .08 | .06 |
| 113 | Mitch Williams | .08 | .06 |
| 114 | Craig Biggio | .08 | .06 |
| 115 | Eddie Murray | .08 | .06 |
| 116 | Matt Nokes | .06 | .05 |
| 117 | Lance Parrish | .06 | .05 |

| | | MT | NR MT | | | MT | NR MT |
|---|---|---|---|---|---|---|---|
| 118 | Bill Swift | .06 | .05 | 184 | Lenny Harris | .05 | .04 |
| 119 | Jeff Innis | .05 | .04 | 185 | Tony Pena | .06 | .05 |
| 120 | Mike LaValliere | .05 | .04 | 186 | Mike Felder | .05 | .04 |
| 121 | Hal Morris | .08 | .06 | 187 | Greg Olson | .05 | .04 |
| 122 | Walt Weiss | .06 | .05 | 188 | Rene Gonzales | .05 | .04 |
| 123 | Ivan Rodriguez | .15 | .11 | 189 | Mike Bordick | .08 | .06 |
| 124 | Andy Van Slyke | .08 | .06 | 190 | Mel Rojas | .05 | .04 |
| 125 | Roberto Alomar | .15 | .11 | 191 | Todd Frohwirth | .05 | .04 |
| 126 | Robby Thompson | .06 | .05 | 192 | Darryl Hamilton | .08 | .06 |
| 127 | Sammy Sosa | .06 | .05 | 193 | Mike Fetters | .05 | .04 |
| 128 | Mark Langston | .06 | .05 | 194 | Omar Olivares | .05 | .04 |
| 129 | Jerry Browne | .05 | .04 | 195 | Tony Phillips | .08 | .06 |
| 130 | Chuck McElroy | .05 | .04 | 196 | Paul Sorrento | .08 | .06 |
| 131 | Frank Viola | .08 | .06 | 197 | Trevor Wilson | .06 | .05 |
| 132 | Leo Gomez | .08 | .06 | 198 | Kevin Gross | .05 | .04 |
| 133 | Ramon Martinez | .10 | .08 | 199 | Ron Karkovice | .05 | .04 |
| 134 | Don Mattingly | .12 | .09 | 200 | Brook Jacoby | .05 | .04 |
| 135 | Roger Clemens | .15 | .11 | 201 | Mariano Duncan | .05 | .04 |
| 136 | Rickey Henderson | .15 | .11 | 202 | Dennis Cook | .05 | .04 |
| 137 | Darren Daulton | .12 | .09 | 203 | Daryl Boston | .05 | .04 |
| 138 | Ken Hill | .08 | .06 | 204 | Mike Perez | .08 | .06 |
| 139 | Ozzie Guillen | .08 | .06 | 205 | Manuel Lee | .05 | .04 |
| 140 | Jerald Clark | .08 | .06 | 206 | Steve Olin | .05 | .04 |
| 141 | Dave Fleming | .15 | .11 | 207 | Charlie Hough | .05 | .04 |
| 142 | Delino DeShields | .12 | .09 | 208 | Scott Scudder | .05 | .04 |
| 143 | Matt Williams | .08 | .06 | 209 | Charlie O'Brien | .05 | .04 |
| 144 | Larry Walker | .08 | .06 | 210 | Checklist 106-210 | .05 | .04 |
| 145 | Ruben Sierra | .12 | .09 | 211 | Jose Vizcaino | .05 | .04 |
| 146 | Ozzie Smith | .12 | .09 | 212 | Scott Leius | .05 | .04 |
| 147 | Chris Sabo | .08 | .06 | 213 | Kevin Mitchell | .08 | .06 |
| 148 | Carlos Hernandez(FC) | .12 | .09 | 214 | Brian Barnes | .08 | .06 |
| 149 | Pat Borders | .08 | .06 | 215 | Pat Kelly | .08 | .06 |
| 150 | Orlando Merced | .08 | .06 | 216 | Chris Hammond | .08 | .06 |
| 151 | Royce Clayton | .08 | .06 | 217 | Rob Deer | .06 | .05 |
| 152 | Kurt Stillwell | .06 | .05 | 218 | Cory Snyder | .06 | .05 |
| 153 | Dave Hollins | .10 | .08 | 219 | Gary Carter | .10 | .08 |
| 154 | Mike Greenwell | .08 | .06 | 220 | Danny Darwin | .05 | .04 |
| 155 | Nolan Ryan | .20 | .15 | 221 | Tom Gordon | .05 | .04 |
| 156 | Felix Jose | .08 | .06 | 222 | Gary Sheffield | .10 | .08 |
| 157 | Junior Felix | .06 | .05 | 223 | Joe Carter | .10 | .08 |
| 158 | Derek Bell | .10 | .08 | 224 | Jay Buhner | .06 | .05 |
| 159 | Steve Buechele | .06 | .05 | 225 | Jose Offerman | .06 | .05 |
| 160 | John Burkett | .06 | .05 | 226 | Jose Rijo | .06 | .05 |
| 161 | Pat Howell(FC) | .15 | .11 | 227 | Mark Whiten | .08 | .06 |
| 162 | Milt Cuyler | .06 | .05 | 228 | Randy Milligan | .05 | .04 |
| 163 | Terry Pendleton | .10 | .08 | 229 | Bud Black | .05 | .04 |
| 164 | Jack Morris | .10 | .08 | 230 | Gary DiSarcina | .05 | .04 |
| 165 | Tony Gwynn | .15 | .11 | 231 | Steve Finley | .08 | .06 |
| 166 | Deion Sanders | .15 | .11 | 232 | Dennis Martinez | .08 | .06 |
| 167 | Mike Devereaux | .08 | .06 | 233 | Mike Mussina | .20 | .15 |
| 168 | Ron Darling | .08 | .06 | 234 | Joe Oliver | .06 | .05 |
| 169 | Orel Hershiser | .08 | .06 | 235 | Chad Curtis | .15 | .11 |
| 170 | Mike Jackson | .05 | .04 | 236 | Shane Mack | .08 | .06 |
| 171 | Doug Jones | .06 | .05 | 237 | Jaime Navarro | .08 | .06 |
| 172 | Dan Walters(FC) | .12 | .09 | 238 | Brian McRae | .08 | .06 |
| 173 | Darren Lewis | .08 | .06 | 239 | Chili Davis | .06 | .05 |
| 174 | Carlos Baerga | .12 | .09 | 240 | Jeff King | .06 | .05 |
| 175 | Ryne Sandberg | .15 | .11 | 241 | Dean Palmer | .06 | .05 |
| 176 | Gregg Jefferies | .12 | .09 | 242 | Danny Tartabull | .10 | .08 |
| 177 | John Jaha(FC) | .20 | .15 | 243 | Charles Nagy | .10 | .08 |
| 178 | Luis Polonia | .05 | .04 | 244 | Ray Lankford | .15 | .11 |
| 179 | Kirt Manwaring | .05 | .04 | 245 | Barry Larkin | .15 | .11 |
| 180 | Mike Magnante | .08 | .06 | 246 | Steve Avery | .15 | .11 |
| 181 | Billy Ripken | .05 | .04 | 247 | John Kruk | .08 | .06 |
| 182 | Mike Moore | .06 | .05 | 248 | Derrick May | .08 | .06 |
| 183 | Eric Anthony | .06 | .05 | 249 | Stan Javier | .05 | .04 |
| | | | | 250 | Roger McDowell | .05 | .04 |

| # | Player | MT | NR MT |
|---|--------|----|----|
| 251 | Dan Gladden | .05 | .04 |
| 252 | Wally Joyner | .08 | .06 |
| 253 | *Pat Listach* | .25 | .20 |
| 254 | Chuck Knoblauch | .10 | .08 |
| 255 | Sandy Alomar Jr. | .10 | .08 |
| 256 | Jeff Bagwell | .15 | .11 |
| 257 | Andy Stankiewicz | .15 | .11 |
| 258 | Darrin Jackson | .06 | .05 |
| 259 | Brett Butler | .08 | .06 |
| 260 | Joe Orsulak | .06 | .05 |
| 261 | Andy Benes | .10 | .08 |
| 262 | Kenny Lofton | .20 | .15 |
| 263 | Robin Ventura | .15 | .11 |
| 264 | Ron Gant | .15 | .11 |
| 265 | Ellis Burks | .08 | .06 |
| 266 | Juan Guzman | .15 | .11 |
| 267 | Wes Chamberlain | .08 | .06 |
| 268 | John Smiley | .06 | .05 |
| 269 | Franklin Stubs | .05 | .04 |
| 270 | Tom Browning | .06 | .05 |
| 271 | Dennis Eckersley | .12 | .09 |
| 272 | Carlton Fisk | .12 | .09 |
| 273 | Lou Whitaker | .08 | .06 |
| 274 | Phil Plantier | .15 | .11 |
| 275 | Bobby Bonilla | .10 | .08 |
| 276 | Ben McDonald | .10 | .08 |
| 277 | Bob Zupcic | .10 | .08 |
| 278 | Terry Steinbach | .06 | .05 |
| 279 | Terry Mulholland | .06 | .05 |
| 280 | Lance Johnson | .06 | .05 |
| 281 | Willie McGee | .06 | .05 |
| 282 | Bret Saberhagen | .08 | .06 |
| 283 | Randy Myers | .08 | .06 |
| 284 | Randy Tomlin | .08 | .06 |
| 285 | Mickey Morandini | .08 | .06 |
| 286 | Brian Williams | .08 | .06 |
| 287 | Tino Martinez | .08 | .06 |
| 288 | Jose Melendez | .08 | .06 |
| 289 | Jeff Huson | .05 | .04 |
| 290 | Joe Grahe | .05 | .04 |
| 291 | Mel Hall | .06 | .05 |
| 292 | Otis Nixon | .06 | .05 |
| 293 | Todd Hundley | .08 | .06 |
| 294 | Casey Candaele | .05 | .04 |
| 295 | Kevin Seitzer | .06 | .05 |
| 296 | Eddie Taubensee | .10 | .08 |
| 297 | Moises Alou | .10 | .08 |
| 298 | Scott Radinsky | .05 | .04 |
| 299 | Thomas Howard | .05 | .04 |
| 300 | Kyle Abbott | .08 | .06 |
| 301 | Omar Vizquel | .05 | .04 |
| 302 | Keith Miller | .05 | .04 |
| 303 | Rick Aguilera | .08 | .06 |
| 304 | Bruce Hurst | .08 | .06 |
| 305 | Ken Caminiti | .06 | .05 |
| 306 | Mike Pagiarulo | .05 | .04 |
| 307 | Frank Seminara(FC) | .12 | .09 |
| 308 | Andre Dawson | .15 | .11 |
| 309 | Jose Lind | .06 | .05 |
| 310 | Joe Boever | .05 | .04 |
| 311 | Jeff Parrett | .05 | .04 |
| 312 | Alan Mills | .05 | .04 |
| 313 | Kevin Tapani | .08 | .06 |
| 314 | Daryl Kile | .08 | .06 |
| 315 | Checklist 211-315 | .05 | .04 |
| 316 | Mike Sharperson | .05 | .04 |
| 317 | John Orton | .05 | .04 |
| 318 | Bob Tewksbury | .08 | .06 |
| 319 | Xavier Hernandez | .05 | .04 |
| 320 | Paul Assenmacher | .05 | .04 |
| 321 | John Franco | .08 | .06 |
| 322 | Mike Timlin | .06 | .05 |
| 323 | Jose Guzman | .06 | .05 |
| 324 | Pedro Martinez | .15 | .11 |
| 325 | Bill Spiers | .06 | .05 |
| 326 | Melido Perez | .06 | .05 |
| 327 | Mike Macfarlane | .06 | .05 |
| 328 | Ricky Bones | .06 | .05 |
| 329 | Scott Bankhead | .06 | .05 |
| 330 | Rich Rodriguez | .05 | .04 |
| 331 | Geronimo Pena | .06 | .05 |
| 332 | Bernie Williams | .10 | .08 |
| 333 | Paul Molitor | .10 | .08 |
| 334 | Roger Mason | .05 | .04 |
| 335 | David Cone | .10 | .08 |
| 336 | Randy Johnson | .06 | .05 |
| 337 | Pat Mahomes | .15 | .11 |
| 338 | Erik Hanson | .08 | .06 |
| 339 | Duane Ward | .06 | .05 |
| 340 | *Al Martin*(FC) | .15 | .11 |
| 341 | Pedro Munoz | .10 | .08 |
| 342 | Greg Colbrunn | .06 | .05 |
| 343 | Julio Valera | .06 | .05 |
| 344 | John Olerud | .10 | .08 |
| 345 | George Bell | .10 | .08 |
| 346 | Devon White | .08 | .06 |
| 347 | Donovan Osborne | .15 | .11 |
| 348 | Mark Gardner | .06 | .05 |
| 349 | Zane Smith | .06 | .05 |
| 350 | Wilson Alvarez | .06 | .05 |
| 351 | *Kevin Koslofski*(FC) | .15 | .11 |
| 352 | Roberto Hernandez | .10 | .08 |
| 353 | Glenn Davis | .08 | .06 |
| 354 | Reggie Sanders | .15 | .11 |
| 355 | Ken Griffey Jr. | .40 | .30 |
| 356 | Marquis Grissom | .12 | .09 |
| 357 | Jack McDowell | .12 | .09 |
| 358 | Jimmy Key | .06 | .05 |
| 359 | Stan Belinda | .05 | .04 |
| 360 | Gerald Williams | .10 | .08 |
| 361 | Sid Fernandez | .08 | .06 |
| 362 | Alex Fernandez | .08 | .06 |
| 363 | John Smoltz | .10 | .08 |
| 364 | Travis Fryman | .15 | .11 |
| 365 | Jose Canseco | .25 | .20 |
| 366 | David Justice | .15 | .11 |
| 367 | *Pedro Astacio*(FC) | .25 | .20 |
| 368 | Tim Belcher | .08 | .06 |
| 369 | Steve Sax | .08 | .06 |
| 370 | Gary Gaetti | .06 | .05 |
| 371 | *Jeff Frye*(FC) | .12 | .09 |
| 372 | Bob Wickman | .20 | .15 |
| 373 | *Ryan Thompson*(FC) | .20 | .15 |
| 374 | David Hulse | .15 | .11 |
| 375 | Cal Eldred | .20 | .15 |
| 376 | Ryan Klesko | .20 | .15 |
| 377 | *Damion Easley*(FC) | .20 | .15 |
| 378 | *John Kiely*(FC) | .20 | .15 |
| 379 | *Jim Bullinger*(FC) | .12 | .09 |

*Card Companies*

| | | MT | NR MT |
|---|---|---|---|
| 380 | Brian Bohanon | .08 | .06 |
| 381 | Rod Brewer | .08 | .06 |
| 382 | *Fernando Ramsey*(FC) | .15 | .11 |
| 383 | Sam Militello | .15 | .11 |
| 384 | Arthur Rhodes | .15 | .11 |
| 385 | Eric Karros | .25 | .20 |
| 386 | Rico Brogna | .12 | .09 |
| 387 | *John Valentin*(FC) | .12 | .09 |
| 388 | *Kerry Woodson*(FC) | .12 | .09 |
| 389 | *Ben Rivera*(FC) | .12 | .09 |
| 390 | *Matt Whiteside*(FC) | .15 | .11 |
| 391 | Henry Rodriguez | .08 | .06 |
| 392 | John Wetteland | .08 | .06 |
| 393 | Kent Mercker | .06 | .05 |
| 394 | Bernard Gilkey | .08 | .06 |
| 395 | Doug Henry | .08 | .06 |
| 396 | Mo Vaughn | .08 | .06 |
| 397 | Scott Erickson | .08 | .06 |
| 398 | Bill Gullickson | .08 | .06 |
| 399 | Mark Guthrie | .05 | .04 |
| 400 | Dave Martinez | .05 | .04 |
| 401 | *Jeff Kent* | .15 | .11 |
| 402 | Chris Hoiles | .15 | .11 |
| 403 | Mike Henneman | .08 | .06 |
| 404 | Chris Nabholz | .08 | .06 |
| 405 | Tom Pagnozzi | .08 | .06 |
| 406 | Kelly Gruber | .08 | .06 |
| 407 | Bob Welch | .08 | .06 |
| 408 | Frank Castillo | .08 | .06 |
| 409 | John Dopson | .05 | .04 |
| 410 | Steve Farr | .06 | .05 |
| 411 | Henry Cotto | .05 | .04 |
| 412 | Bob Patterson | .05 | .04 |
| 413 | Todd Stottlemyre | .06 | .05 |
| 414 | Greg A. Harris | .05 | .04 |
| 415 | Denny Neagle | .08 | .06 |
| 416 | Bill Wegman | .06 | .05 |
| 417 | Willie Wilson | .06 | .05 |
| 418 | Terry Leach | .05 | .04 |
| 419 | Willie Randolph | .06 | .05 |
| 420 | Checklist 316-420 | .05 | .04 |

**Values for recent cards and sets are listed in Mint (MT), Near Mint (NM) and Excellent (EX), reflecting the fact that many cards from recent years have been preserved in top condition. Recent cards and sets in less than Excellent condition have little collector interest.**

**AW Sports**, 17842 Mitchell North, Suite 200, Irvine, CA 92714.

**Action Packed**, 851 N. Villa, Suite 101, Villa Park, Il 60181.

**Bowman** — See Topps.

**Classic Games Inc.**, 8055 Troon Circle, Suite C, Austell, GA 30001.

**Collector's Edge**, P.O. Box 9010, Denver, CO 80209.

**Courtside**, 1247 Broadway Ave., Burlingame, CA 94010

**Fleer Corporation**, 1120 Rte. 73, Mt. Laurel, NJ 08054.

**Front Row**, 201 W. Main St., Dalton, PA 18414.

**Kayo**, One Meadowlands Plaza, Suite 1020, East Rutherford, NJ 07073.

**Leaf/Donruss**, 2355 Waukegan Road, Bannockburn, Il 60015.

**Megacards, Inc.**, 5650 Wattsburg Rd., Erie, PA 16509

**NBA Hoops**, P.O. Box 14930, Research Triangle Park, NC 27709-4930.

**O-Pee-Chee**, P.O. Box 6306, London, Ontario, Canada, N5W 5S1.

**Pacific Trading Cards**, 18424 Hwy. 99, Lynwood, WA 98039.

**Pro Line Portraits**, P.O. Box 14930, Research Triangle Park, NC 27709-4930.

**Pro Set**, 17250 Dallas Parkway, Dallas, TX 75248.

**Score**, 25 Ford Road, Westport, CT 06880.

**SilverStar Holograms**, P.O. Box 8195, Van Nuys, CA 91406.

**SkyBox Int'l.**, P.O. Box 14930, Research Triangle Park, NC 27709-4930.

**Topps**, 254 36th St., Brooklyn, NY 11232.

**Upper Deck**, 5909 Sea Otter Place, Carlsbad, CA 92008.

**Wild Card**, 2715 Dixie Highway, Hamilton, OH 45015.

# NOTES